WEBSTER'S
NEW WORLD™
CROSSWORD
PUZZLE
DICTIONARY

W^{SECOND EDITION}EBSTER'S NEW WORLD™ CROSSWORD PUZZLE DICTIONARY

Compiled by

Jane Shaw Whitfield

Macmillan • USA

Webster's New World™ Crossword Puzzle Dictionary,
Second Edition

Copyright © 1983, 1975 by Jane Shaw Whitfield

Second Edition copyright © 1997 by Simon & Schuster, Inc.

Macmillan General Reference
A Simon & Schuster Macmillan Company
1633 Broadway
New York, NY 10019-6785

A Webster's New World™ Book

MACMILLAN is a registered trademark of Macmillan, Inc.
WEBSTER'S NEW WORLD DICTIONARY is a
registered trademark of Simon & Schuster, Inc.

Dictionary Editorial Offices:
New World Dictionaries
850 Euclid Avenue
Cleveland, OH 44114-3354

Library of Congress Cataloging-in-Publication Data
Whitfield, Jane Shaw.
    Webster's new world crossword puzzle dictionary /
compiled by Jane Shaw Whitfield. — 2nd ed.
        p.   cm.
    ISBN 0-02-861213-2. — ISBN 0-02-861212-4 (pbk.)
    1. Crossword puzzles—Glossaries, vocabularies, etc.   I. Title.
GV1507.C7W485 1997
793.73'2'0321—dc20
                                                        96-2077
                                                        CIP

Principal typesetting by ÆSTHETEX, LTD, Edinburgh, Scotland

Manufactured in the United States of America
    4 5 6 7 8 9 10   98 99 00 01 02

CONTENTS

STAFF

Editor in Chief
Michael Agnes

Project Editor
James E. Naso

Managing Editor
James J. Heaney

Editor and
Database Administrator
Donald Stewart

Editorial Staff
Jonathan L. Goldman
Katherine Soltis
Andrew N. Sparks
Stephen P. Teresi
Laura Borovac Walker

Administrative, Data Processing,
and Clerical Staff
Alisa Murray Davis
Cynthia M. Sadonick
Betty Dziedzic Thompson

Citation Readers
Batya Jundef
Joan Komic

FOREWORD

This new edition of *Webster's New World Crossword Puzzle Dictionary* represents a thorough revision and updating of the highly successful work originally compiled by Jane Shaw Whitfield. Thousands of new clue words and answer terms have been added from crossword puzzles published since the last revision. Biographical and geographical entries are now completely up to date. Tables have been introduced to provide a particularly effective and convenient way to locate large blocks of related terms in one place. In addition, a user's guide created especially for this edition will assist readers in finding precisely the words they want quickly and easily.

Crossword puzzle dictionaries and crossword puzzle solvers share, predictably, some special characteristics. Both are distinguished by their breadth of vocabulary and by their unique intellectual focus on the relationship between clues and answers. The editors of Webster's New World dictionaries wish to acknowledge the contributions to this edition of one very gifted crossword puzzle enthusiast, Mr. Joe Forest of Sharonville, Ohio, whose insightful suggestions have been invaluable.

This all-new second edition remains in one respect unchanged, namely, it is, as Jane Shaw Whitfield wrote in her foreword to the first edition, dedicated "to all enthusiasts of crossword puzzles and to their creators."

GUIDE TO THE USE OF THIS BOOK

1. ***The Arrangement of Entries***—Each entry block has a clue word set in boldface type as its headword.
   All clue words, including single words, hyphenated and unhyphenated compounds, idioms, phrases, and proper names, are listed in strict alphabetical order:

   > **A** . . .
   > **aa** (Haw) . . .
   > **aal** . . .
   > **Aani** (Egypt) . . .
   > **abdominal limb** (crustacean) . . .
   > **Abel's brother** . . .
   > **aberration** . . .

2. ***Clue Words and Answer Terms***—Answer terms for each clue word are arranged by the count of letters in each word or phrase. Answer terms of varying parts of speech may be gathered together in a single entry block. Words in each group of answers with the same letter count are arranged in alphabetical order:

   > **abandon** . . . **4.** quit **5.** cease, leave, remit, waive, yield **6.** abjure, depart, desert, disuse, give up, maroon, reject, resign, vacate
   > **7.** cast off, discard, forsake, freedom, neglect
   > **8.** abdicate, forswear, renounce
   > **9.** surrender, turpitude **10.** relinquish
   > **11.** abandonment, discontinue, unrestraint
   > **12.** carelessness, heedlessness

3. ***Variant Spellings and Forms***—When variants are some distance apart alphabetically, the full entry appears at the spelling or spellings most frequently used, and the other spellings are cross-referred to this entry:

   > **align, aline** . . . **4.** true **5.** level, match **6.** equate, line up . . .
   >
   > . . .
   >
   > **aline** . . . see *align*

   Variants not alphabetically distant are given together in boldface type:

   > **harbor, harbour** . . . **3.** bay **4.** cave, port
   > **5.** haven **6.** covert, foster, . . .

> **narghile, nargile, nargileh** . . . **4.** pipe
> **6.** hookah

Variant spellings of answer words are given immediately after the answer word in parentheses:

> **monument** . . . **4.** tomb **5.** cairn, stele (stela), tower, vault **6.** . . .

4. ***Labels, Abbreviations, and Explanatory Notes—***
   Additional information for either clue words or answer terms may appear abbreviated in parentheses. A list of abbreviations used in this book appears below, p. x.

   > **Aaru** (Egypt Relig) . . . **12.** fields of Aaru
   > **14.** abode of the dead

   > **monopoly** . . . **5.** grant, right, trust . . .
   > **10.** possession (exclusive)

   > **oomancy** (divination by) . . . **4.** eggs

5. ***Cross-references—***Cross-references to related terms are introduced by "see" or "see also" and given in italics:

   > **absence of** . . . (see also *without*)

6. ***Subcategories—***Answer terms may be divided into informational subcategories related to the clue word. They are introduced by the label "(pert to)":

   > **cardinal** (pert to) . . .
   > *astrology* . . **5.** nadir **6.** zenith
   > *astronomy* . . **10.** solstitial **11.** equinoctial . . .
   > *compass point* . . **4.** east, west **5.** north, south . . .
   > *virtues (Theol)* . . **4.** hope **5.** faith **7.** charity

7. ***Variety Lists—***When the clue word is a general term covering a variety of things, a list of those is supplied, introduced by the label "(types of)":

   > **flower** (types of) . . . **3.** gul (rose) **4.** iris, ixia, lily, pink, rose **5.** aster, calla, canna, . . .

8. ***Tables—***Tables at the end of this book provide lists of persons, things, or events in a particular category along with a letter count for each item.

ABBREVIATIONS USED IN THIS WORK

Abbr   Abbreviation
abdom   abdominal
aborig   aboriginal
Acad   Academy
adj   adjective
adm   admitted
Afr   African
Agric   Agriculture
Alex   Alexander
Am Ind   American Indian
Anat   Anatomy
anc   ancient
Anglo-Ir   Anglo-Irish
Anthrop   Anthropology
Antiq   Antiquity
Arab   Arabian
Arch   Architecture
Archaeol   Archaeology
Astrol   Astrology
Astron   Astronomy
Austral   Australia(n)

Babyl   Babylonia(n)
Belg   Belgium
Bib   Bible, Biblical
Biol   Biology
Bot   Botany
Braz   Brazil(ian)
Brit   Britain, British
Brit Col   British Columbia
Buddh   Buddhism
Bus   Business

Can   Canada, Canadian
Capt   Captain
Caucas   Caucasian
Celt   Celtic
Cent   Central, Century
Cent Am   Central America
Chem   Chemistry
Chin   Chinese
Chr   Christian
coll   colloquialism
comb form
    combining form
Confed   Confederation
Constell   Constellation
contemp   contemporary
Criminol   Criminology

Dan   Danish
Dept   Department
derog   derogatory
dial   dialectal
div   division
Du   Dutch

E   East
East Ch   Eastern Church

Eccl   Ecclesiastical
Educ   Education
Egypt   Egyptian
Elec   Electricity
Eng   England, English
Episcop   Episcopal
equiv   equivalent
Esk   Eskimo
est   established
Eur   Europe(an)
exclam   exclamation
ext   extinct

FDR   Franklin D. Roosevelt
Fem   Feminine
Finan   Finance, Financial
Flem   Flemish
Fr   France, French

Gen   General
Geog   Geography
Geol   Geology
Geom   Geometry
Ger   German
Gov   Governor
Govt   Government
Gr   Greek
Gram   Grammar
Gr Brit   Great Britain

Haw   Hawaiian
Heb   Hebrew
Hem   Hemisphere
Her   Heraldry
Hind   Hinduism
Hindu   Hindustani
Hist   Historical
Holl   Holland
Horol   Horology
Hung   Hungarian

illeg   illegal
Ind   India, Indian
Indo-Chin   Indo-China
Ins   Insurance
Internat   International
Ir   Irish
irreg   irregular
Isl(s)   Island(s)
It   Italian

Jap   Japanese
Jew   Jewish

L   Latin
Legislat   Legislature
Lit   Literature
Log   Logic

Maced   Macedonia
Malay   Malayan
Math   Mathematics
MD   Doctor of Medicine
Med   Medical
Mex   Mexican
Mil   Military
Mohamm   Mohammedan
Mt(s)   Mountain(s)
Mus   Music
Myth   Mythology

Nat'l   National
Naut   Nautical
Nav   Naval, Navy
neg   negative
New Test   New Testament
NZ   New Zealand
No   North
No Am   North American

obs   obsolete
Old Test   Old Testament
opp   opposite
Orient   Oriental
Oxf Univ
    Oxford University

Penol   Penology
Pers   Persian
pert   pertaining
Petrol   Petrology
Pg   Portuguese
Pharm   Pharmaceutical
Philat   Philately
Phil I   Philippine Islands
Philol   Philology
Philos   Philosophy
Phonet   Phonetics
Phys   Physical
pl   plural
PO   Post Office
poet   poetic
Polit   Politics, Political
Polyn   Polynesian
ppty   property
pref   prefix
P Rico   Puerto Rico
Pros   Prosody
pseud   pseudonym

R   Roman
RCCh
    Roman Catholic Church
Rd   Road
ref   referring
Relig   Religion
R Estate   Real Estate
Rev War   Revolutionary War

x

Rhet   Rhetoric
Riv   River
Rom   Roman
rr   railroad
Rum   Rumania
Russ   Russian

S   South
Scot   Scotland, Scottish
Scand   Scandinavian
Shaksp   Shakespeare
sing   singular
sl   slang
Slav   Slavonic
So Afr   South Africa
So Am   South America
Sp   Spanish
Surg   Surgical
sym   symbol

Tag   Tagalog
Tahit   Tahiti
Terat   Teratology
terr   territory
Teut   Teutonic
Theat   Theatrical
Theol   Theology
Theos   Theosophy
triang   triangular
TID   Ter in die
Trop   Tropical
Turk   Turkish
TV   Television

U   Union
Univ   University
USS   United States Ship
USSR   Union of Soviet
      Socialist Republics

Vet   Veterinary

W   West
WAC
   Women's Army Corps
W Indies   West Indies
WWI   World War I
WWII   World War II

Yidd   Yiddish
YMCA   Young Men's
      Christian Association
yr   year

Zool   Zoology

Webster's New World

CROSSWORD PUZZLE DICTIONARY

A

A ... **5.** alpha, first **7.** article
A 1 ... **5.** prime **6.** symbol **8.** superior
10. first-class
aa (Haw) ... **4.** lava
aal ... **8.** morindin (dye), mulberry
aam (Du) ... **7.** measure (liquid) **11.** water
bucket
Aani (Egypt) ... **3.** ape (sacred) **6.** baboon
12. cynocephalus
aardvark ... **3.** pig **6.** farrow **8.** anteater
aardwolf ... **5.** hyena **8.** Proteles
Aaron (pert to) ...
ally (Bib) .. **3.** Hur
brother .. **5.** Moses
burial place .. **3.** Hor
leader (Jew) .. **9.** Levitical **10.** High
Priest
rod .. **4.** wand (magic) **7.** molding,
mullein
sister .. **6.** Miriam
son .. **5.** Abihu, Nadab
Aaru (Egypt Relig) ... **12.** fields of Aaru
14. abode of the dead
aasvogel ... **7.** vulture
abaca ... **4.** hemp **5.** lupis **6.** linaga
abacus ... **4.** slab **8.** cupboard
10. calculator **11.** compartment
Abaddon ... **3.** pit (bottomless) **4.** Hell
5. Sheol **8.** Apollyon (angel)
11. destruction
abaft ... **3.** aft **5.** after **6.** astern, behind
abalone ... **5.** awabi, ormer, uhllo (ullo)
6. sea ear **8.** ear shell
abandon ... **4.** quit **5.** cease, leave, remit,
waive, yield **6.** abjure, depart, desert,
disuse, give up, maroon, reject, resign,
vacate **7.** cast off, discard, forsake,
freedom, neglect **8.** abdicate, forswear,
renounce **9.** surrender, turpitude
10. relinquish **11.** abandonment,
discontinue, unrestraint
12. carelessness, heedlessness
abandoned ... **4.** left, lost **7.** disused,
forlorn, given up **8.** derelict, deserted,
forsaken **9.** desolated, discarded,
neglected **11.** surrendered
12. relinquished, unredeemable,
unrestrained
abase ... **5.** lower, shame **6.** bemean,
depose, humble, reduce **7.** degrade,
mortify **8.** cast down, disgrace
9. humiliate **10.** depreciate
abash ... **5.** shame **6.** appall, dismay
7. astound, confuse, disturb, mortify
8. bewilder, confound **9.** discomfit,
embarrass, humiliate **10.** disconcert,
put to shame
abate ... **3.** ebb **4.** lull, wane **5.** let up,
relax, remit **6.** deduct, lessen, reduce
7. abolish, nullify, qualify, slacken,
subside **8.** decrease, diminish, discount,
moderate
abatement ... **5.** letup **6.** myosis (miosis),
rebate **8.** decrease **9.** lessening,
reduction **10.** diminution, mitigation,

moderation
abb ... **4.** wool, yarn **6.** fleece (pert to)
Abba ... **5.** abbot, title **6.** Father
abbe ... **4.** monk **6.** cleric, curate, priest
abbess ... **4.** amma **15.** spiritual mother
abbreviate ... **7.** abridge, curtail, shorten
8. compress, condense, contract,
simplify **9.** epitomize **11.** make briefer
abbreviation ... **5.** brief, lapse **6.** digest
8. abstract **9.** reduction **10.** abridgment,
compendium, shortening
11. contraction **12.** condensation
abdicate ... **4.** cede, quit **5.** demit, leave
6. depose, disown, resign, retire **7.** lay
down **8.** disclaim, renounce, withdraw
9. surrender **10.** disinherit, relinquish
Abdiel (Heb) ... **5.** angel **12.** servant of
God
abdomen ... **3.** gut, pot (sl) **4.** wame
5. belly, tharm (obs) **6.** paunch, venter
7. stomach **8.** potbelly **12.** pelvic cavity
abdominal ... **7.** coeliac, gastric, ventral
11. ventricular
abdominal limb (crustacean) ...
7. pleopod
Abel's brother ... **4.** Cain, Seth
aberration ... **5.** mania, wrong **6.** lunacy,
oddity **7.** errancy, madness **8.** dementia,
insanity **9.** departure, deviation,
variation, wandering **10.** alienation,
digression, divergence **11.** abnormality,
derangement, distraction, peculiarity
12. eccentricity, irregularity
14. disorientation
abet ... **3.** aid, egg **4.** back, help **5.** egg on
6. assist, foment, incite, second, succor,
uphold **7.** connive, endorse, support,
sustain **8.** advocate **9.** encourage,
instigate **11.** countenance
abeyance ... **4.** rest, stay **5.** lapse, pause
7. waiting **9.** inertness **10.** expectancy,
suspension
abhor ... **2.** ug **4.** hate, shun **6.** detest,
loathe **7.** despise, dislike **8.** execrate
9. abominate
abhorrence ... **5.** odium **6.** hatred,
horror **7.** dislike **8.** aversion, loathing
9. antipathy, disliking, repulsion
10. repugnance
abide ... **4.** bide, live, stay, wait **5.** await,
dwell, pause, tarry **6.** endure, remain,
reside **7.** sojourn **8.** continue, submit
to, tolerate **9.** acquiesce, withstand
abide by ... **3.** own **4.** avow, heed
5. admit, allow, yield **6.** accept, follow,
regard **7.** concede, respect **8.** adhere
to **9.** conform to **11.** acknowledge
abiding ... **7.** durable, lasting **8.** constant,
enduring **9.** permanent, steadfast
10. continuing, indwelling, persisting
Abies ... **4.** firs **5.** pines **8.** conifers
10. evergreens
abigail ... **4.** ayah, maid **5.** bonne
7. servant **9.** soubrette
Abijah's son (Bib) ... **3.** Asa

ability ... **4.** gift **5.** force, might, power, skill **6.** genius, talent **7.** caliber, faculty, fitness, potency **8.** aptitude, capacity, strength **10.** capability, competence, efficiency **11.** proficiency, sufficiency **13.** qualification

abiosis ... **11.** without life

abject ... **3.** low **4.** base, mean, meek, vile **6.** humble, menial, supine **7.** hangdog, ignoble, servile, slavish **8.** beggarly, contrite, cringing, degraded, wretched **9.** groveling, miserable **10.** despicable, obsequious

abjuration ... **6.** denial **8.** palinode (song), yielding **9.** disavowal, rejection, surrender **10.** abjurement, retraction, withdrawal **11.** abandonment, forswearing, recantation, repudiation **12.** disclamation **14.** relinquishment

abjure ... **4.** deny, wave **6.** disown, recant, reject, revoke **7.** abandon, disavow **8.** disclaim, forswear, renounce **9.** disaffirm, repudiate

able ... **3.** can, fit **5.** adept, smart **6.** clever, fitted, suited **7.** adapted, capable, learned, solvent **8.** adjusted, literate, powerful, skillful (skilful), vigorous **9.** competent, effective, efficient, qualified **10.** omnipotent, proficient

able (pert to) ...
suffix .. **7.** capable, fitness
to pay .. **7.** moneyed, solvent **8.** affluent **10.** prosperous
to read and write .. **8.** lettered, literate **10.** book taught

ablepsia ... **9.** blindness

ably ... **7.** capably **11.** competently, effectively, efficiently

abnormal ... **6.** albino **7.** erratic, unusual **8.** aberrant **9.** deviative, eccentric, irregular, unnatural **11.** exceptional **13.** extraordinary

aboard ... **4.** onto **6.** across **7.** athwart **9.** alongside

abode ... **3.** dar, hut **4.** cell, cote, Eden, home **5.** delay, house, lodge **7.** habitat, Olympus, sojourn **8.** dwelling, tenement **9.** apartment, residence **10.** habitation

abode of the dead ... **3.** Dar **4.** Aalu, Aaru, Hell **5.** Aralu, Hades, limbo, Orcus, Sheol **6.** Asgard, heaven, Naraka **7.** Abaddon, Elysium, Nirvana **8.** paradise, Valhalla **9.** perdition, purgatory **11.** Pandemonium

abolish ... **4.** undo **5.** annul, quash **6.** cancel, recall, repeal, revoke, vacate **7.** destroy, nullify, rescind, retract, reverse **8.** abrogate, withdraw **10.** annihilate, invalidate **11.** countermand

abominable ... **4.** base, dire, foul, vile **5.** awful, gross **6.** odious, wicked, woeful **7.** beastly, hateful **8.** dreadful, grievous, infamous, shocking, terrible, wretched **9.** execrable, loathsome, obnoxious **10.** despicable, detestable, outrageous, unpleasant **12.** disagreeable, disreputable

Abominable Snowman ... **4.** Yeti

abominate ... **4.** hate **5.** abhor **6.** detest, loathe **8.** execrate

abomination ... **3.** woe **4.** evil **5.** odium, wrong **6.** hatred, horror, plague **7.** disgust, outrage **8.** aversion, loathing, vexation **9.** grievance **10.** abhorrence, defilement, odiousness, repugnance

aboriginal ... **5.** first, natal **6.** binghi, native **7.** ancient **8.** original **9.** beginning, primitive **10.** autochthon, indigenous

aborigines ... **4.** Ainu (Aino), Toda **5.** lubra, Sakai, Vedda **7.** cave men, Indians, natives, savages **9.** indigenes, old-timers **10.** Dravidians **11.** preadamites

abortion ... **6.** arrest **7.** failure **11.** embryoctomy, miscarriage, miscreation **13.** misconception

abound ... **4.** flow, teem **5.** swarm **8.** overflow **9.** exuberate, plentiful

abounding ... **4.** rife **5.** ample, flush **7.** copious, teeming **8.** abundant **9.** exuberant, luxuriant, plentiful

abounding in ...
blossoms .. **7.** flowery
forests .. **6.** sylvan
grass .. **6.** cressy
snow .. **5.** nival

about ... **2.** of, on, re **3.** amb (pref) **5.** anent, astir, circa **6.** almost, around, nearly **8.** circiter **10.** concerning **13.** approximately

about to happen ... **8.** imminent

above ... **2.** on, up **3.** o'er, sur (pref) **4.** atop, over, upon **5.** aloft, super, supra (pref)

abrade ... **3.** rub **4.** file, fret, gall **5.** chafe, grate **6.** scrape **9.** excoriate

Abraham (pert to) ...
birthplace .. **2.** Ur
concubine .. **5.** Hagar
father .. **5.** Terah
grandfather .. **5.** Nahor
grandson .. **4.** Esau
nephew .. **3.** Lot
son .. **4.** Shua (Shuah) **5.** Isaac, Medan **7.** Ishmael
wife .. **5.** Sarah (Sara, Sarai) **7.** Keturah

abrasion ... **4.** flaw, gall, hurt **5.** scuff **6.** lesion, scrape **8.** limation **9.** attrition

abrasive ... **4.** file, sand **5.** emery **6.** garnet, polish, pumice **7.** erodent **8.** abradant, corundum **9.** attritive, sandpaper

abraxas ... **3.** gem **5.** charm, stone

Abraxas (pert to) ...
god (anc Gnostic) .. **12.** Supreme Deity
source of mind .. **4.** Nous
the Word .. **5.** Logos

abreast ... **4.** even (with) **6.** beside **8.** opposite **9.** alongside

abrege ... **7.** epitome **10.** abridgment

abri ... **4.** shed **6.** cavity, dugout **7.** shelter

abridge ... **5.** brief, razee (rasee) **7.** curtail, shorten **8.** abstract, condense, diminish, retrench **9.** epitomize **10.** abbreviate

abridgment ... **6.** digest **7.** compend, epitome, summary **8.** abstract, syllabus, synopsis **9.** lessening, reduction **10.** compendium, diminution **11.** deprivation

abroad ... **4.** away **5.** forth **6.** astray,

widely 7. at large, broadly, distant
8. away from 9. spread out 11. widely
apart
abrogate ... 5. annul, quash 6. cancel,
repeal, revoke 7. abolish, rescind 8. set
aside 10. put an end to
abrogation ... 8. quashing 9. annulling,
cessation 10. rescinding, rescission
11. dissolution
abrupt ... 4. curt, rude 5. blunt,
hasty, quick, sharp, sheer, steep,
terse 6. broken, craggy, sudden
7. brusque 8. headlong, vertical
9. broken off, impetuous 10. unexpected
11. precipitous 12. disconnected
13. perpendicular, unceremonious
abruptly ... 7. briefly, in brief 8. suddenly
Absalom (pert to) ...
father .. 5. David (King)
host's captain .. 5. Amasa
sister .. 5. Tamar
slayer .. 4. Joab
abscond ... 3. run 4. bolt, flee, hide
5. elope 6. decamp, desert, eloine,
levant 8. steal off
absence ... 4. AWOL, lack, void, want
5. exeat, leave 6. vacuum 7. silence
10. deficiency, withdrawal
13. nonappearance, nonattendance
absence of ... (see also *without)*
animal, plant .. 8. lipotype
hair .. 6. acomia
pain .. 8. anodynia
pigment .. 8. alphosis
self-worth .. 7. modesty
taste .. 7. ageusia
absent ... 3. off, out 4. away, gone, lost
6. dreamy, musing, truant 7. lacking
8. absorbed 9. engrossed 10. abstracted
11. preoccupied 12. nonattendant
absinthe ... 5. green 6. ajenjo, liquor
8. wormwood
absolute ... 4. alod, dead, pure, real, true,
very 5. freed, sheer, total, utter, whole
6. empery, simple 7. certain, elative,
perfect, plenary 8. absolved, complete,
positive 9. arbitrary, downright,
unlimited 10. autocratic, disengaged,
peremptory 11. categorical,
independent 13. unconditional
15. plenipotentiary
absolute (pert to) ...
dominion .. 6. empery
property .. 4. alod 7. alodium
sovereign .. 8. autocrat
superlative .. 7. elative
time .. 9. Greenwich, universal
absolutely ... 3. yea, yes 5. stark
6. wholly 7. utterly 8. entirely
10. altogether, positively, thoroughly
13. unequivocally 15. unconditionally
absolution ... 6. pardon, shrive
7. penance 9. acquittal, remission
11. exculpation, forgiveness
absolve ... 4. free 5. remit 6. acquit,
finish, pardon 9. discharge, exonerate
10. accomplish
absonant ... 8. contrary 10. discordant
12. unreasonable
absorb ... 3. eat 4. soak, suck 5. drink,
eat up, learn, use up 6. corner,

digest, engulf, imbibe, soak up, sponge
7. consume, swallow 10. assimilate,
monopolize, understand 11. incorporate
absorbed ... 4. deep, lost, rapt, sunk
6. buried, intent, lost in 7. bemused,
devoted, engaged 8. occupied
9. engrossed 11. monopolized,
preoccupied
absorbent ... 5. fomes 6. spongy
7. blotter 9. adsorbent 10. imbibitory
absorption ... 10. imbibition
abstain ... 4. deny, fast, hold, shun
5. avoid, cease, forgo, waive 6. eschew
7. forbear, refrain 8. restrain, teetotal,
withhold
abstemious ... 5. sober 7. sparing
8. moderate 9. abstinent, temperate
11. abstentious
abstinence ... 6. disuse 7. encraty
8. sobriety 9. restraint, sacrifice
10. abstention, continence, desistance,
moderation, self-denial, temperance
11. abandonment, forbearance, self-
control 13. self-restraint
14. abstemiousness, discontinuance
abstract ... 4. deed, part, take 5. brief,
steal 6. deduct, noetic (purely), remove
7. abridge, epitome, shorten, summary
8. argument, condense, syllabus,
withdraw 9. capsulize, statement
10. abridgment, compendium
12. nonobjective
abstract being ... 3. ens 6. entity
abstruse ... 4. deep 6. hidden 7. obscure
8. esoteric, profound 9. concealed,
recondite 10. acroamatic (acroatic)
16. incomprehensible
absurd ... 4. wild 5. droll, inept, silly
6. stupid 7. asinine, foolish 8. fabulous,
farcical 9. ludicrous 10. impossible,
irrational, ridiculous 11. incongruous,
nonsensical 12. inconsistent,
unbelievable, unreasonable
absurdity ... 5. farce 7. twaddle
8. nonsense 10. absurdness
11. foolishness 13. contradiction,
impossibility 14. ridiculousness
16. inconceivability
abundance ... 4. mass, much, rife
5. ample 6. galore, plenty, riches,
volume 8. fullness (fulness), opulence,
overflow, quantity 9. affluence
10. exuberance 11. copiousness,
superfluity 12. extravagance,
generousness 13. plenteousness
abundant ... 4. lush, much, rich, rife,
teem 5. ample 6. galore, plenty
7. copious, profuse 9. abounding,
exuberant, luxuriant, plentiful
10. sufficient
abundant, not ... 5. spare 6. lenten,
meager (meagre)
abuse ... 4. gali, harm, hurt, maul, rail,
rape 5. crime, curse, scold, snash
6. berate, ill use, injure, insult, malign,
misuse, ravish, revile 7. calumny,
deceive, obloquy, offense, pervert,
traduce, upbraid 8. dishonor, maltreat,
misapply, reproach 9. contumely,
disparage, invective, violation
10. opprobrium, revilement, scurrility

11. debauchment, malediction, objurgation 12. mistreatment, vituperation
abusive . . . 3. mud (throw) 10. scurrilous 12. catachrestic
abut . . . 4. butt, join 5. touch 6. adjoin, appose, border, rest on 7. conjoin, connect 8. adjacent, neighbor
abutment . . . 4. arch, pier, wall 6. alette 7. abuttal, sea wall 8. buttress, shoulder 13. fortification
abysmal . . . 4. deep 7. yawning 8. profound, unending 9. plumbless 10. bottomless, fathomless
abyss . . . 3. pit 4. Absu, gulf, hell, hole, void, well 5. abysm, chaos, chasm, cleft, shaft 6. cavity, vorago 15. infernal regions
Abyssinia, Ethiopia . . .
capital . . 10. Addis Ababa
city . . 5. Aduwa, Aksum (Axum) 6. Gondar 7. Ankober, Gambela, Magdala
dialect . . 4. Geez
Empire (old) . . 7. Axumite
Hamite . . 4. Afar
King . . 13. Haile Selassie
kingdom (former) . . 4. Shoa 5. Tigre 6. Amhara
river (famed) . . 5. Abdai (Blue Nile)
sea . . 3. Red
title (anc) . . 12. Negusa Nagast
Abyssinian (pert to) . . .
fly . . 4. zimb
gold (artificial) . . 5. talmi
lyre . . 6. kissar
tea leaves . . 3. kat
wolf . . 6. kaberu
academic . . . 4. moot 5. ideal, rigid 6. formal 7. classic, elegant 8. abstract, pedantic, Platonic 9. scholarly 10. Ciceronian, scholastic 11. educational, impractical, speculative, theoretical 12. conventional, hypothetical 13. institutional
academy . . . 5. école , lycée 6. lyceum, manège, school, Schule 7. college, escuela, society 8. academie, seminary 9. accademia, Gymnasium, institute 10. university 11. institution
Academy of Plato . . . 7. Academe
Acadia . . . 6. Acadie 10. Nova Scotia
acarpous . . . 7. sterile 9. fruitless
acaudal . . . 7. anurous 8. tailless
accede . . . 5. agree, enter, grant, yield 6. assent, attain, comply, concur, relent, submit 7. conform, consent 9. acquiesce 11. acknowledge
accelerate . . . 4. rush 6. hasten, step up 7. advance, forward, further, quicken, speed up 8. activate, dispatch, expedite
acceleration . . . 5. haste 7. pickup 8. velocity 9. catalysis, hastening 10. expedition, quickening 11. advancement
accelerator . . . 6. muscle 7. speeder 8. betatron, throttle 9. cyclotron, quickener 11. atom smasher, synchrotron
accent . . . 4. beat, mark, tone 5. breve,

ictus, pitch, twang 6. brogue, stress 7. cadence, dialect 8. emphasis 9. emphasize 10. accentuate, expression, inflection, modulation 12. accentuation
accent (pert to) . . .
Irish . . 4. blas 6. brogue
on last syllable . . 7. oxytone
Scot . . 4. birr
unaccented syllable . . 5. arsis
accept . . . 2. OK 3. buy, own 4. avow, fang, take 5. admit, adopt, agree, allow, grant, trust, yield 6. assent, comply, credit, expect, ratify 7. approve, believe, certify, condone, confess, consent, embrace, receive, swallow (coll) 8. accredit, tolerate, validate 9. undertake 11. countenance
accept (as one's own) . . . 12. nostrificate (of foreign degrees)
acceptable . . . 2. OK 6. worthy 7. welcome 8. eligible, passable, pleasant, pleasing, suitable 9. agreeable, allowable, desirable, expedient, qualified, tolerable 10. admissible 11. comfortable 12. satisfactory
accepted . . . 6. chosen, deemed 7. adopted, assumed, popular, reputed, trusted 8. admitted, approved, believed, credited, embraced, espoused, inferred, orthodox, received, standard, supposed 9. customary, prevalent 10. accredited, understood, undertaken 11. traditional 12. conventional, unquestioned 13. authoritative
access . . . 3. way 4. adit, door, gain 5. entry 6. avenue, entree, ingate, tunnel 7. ingress 8. approach, entrance, entryway, increase 9. accession, accretion, admission 10. admittance 11. entranceway 13. accessibility, attainability 15. approachability
accessible . . . 4. open 5. handy 6. open to, public 7. getable 8. amenable, pervious 9. admissive, available, permeable, reachable, receptive 10. attainable, obtainable, open-minded, penetrable, procurable 11. persuasible 12. approachable 13. communicative
accession . . . 6. access, assent, attack, growth 7. adjunct, consent, joining, uniting 8. addition, increase 9. accretion, agreement, increment 10. acceptance, affixation, annexation, attainment, compliance, concession, coronation 12. acquiescence 13. reinforcement 14. aggrandizement
accessory, accessary . . . 5. extra, party 7. abettor 8. addition, litigant 9. adjective, appendage, assistant, attendant, auxiliary, obbligato 10. accomplish, additional, collateral, subsidiary 11. appurtenant, concomitant, participant 12. accompanying, appurtenance, contributory, nonessential, participator 13. accompaniment, supplementary
accident . . . 3. hap 4. luck 6. chance, hazard, mishap 8. calamity, casualty, disaster 9. adventure, befalling,

mischance 10. misfortune
11. catastrophe
accidental . . . 6. casual, chance
9. unwitting 10. contingent, unforeseen,
unintended
acclaim . . . 4. hail, laud 6. praise
7. applaud 8. applause 11. acclamation,
approbation
acclamation . . . 3. cry, joy 5. shout
7. acclaim, ovation, plaudit 8. applause,
approval 9. unanimity
acclimate . . . 5. adapt, inure 6. adjust,
season 8. accustom 9. condition,
habituate 10. naturalize 11. acclimatize,
familiarize
acclivity . . . 4. bank, brow, hill, rise
5. climb, slope, talus 6. ascent
7. upgrade 9. ascendant (ascendent)
11. inclination
accolade . . . 4. fold, rite 5. award,
brace, clasp, Oscar 6. praise, reward
7. embrace, tribute 8. encomium
9. panegyric 10. enfoldment
accommodate . . . 3. fit 4. help, lend,
meet, suit 5. adapt, favor, lodge, shape,
yield 6. adjust, afford, comply, invest,
oblige, orient, settle, supply 7. conform,
furnish 9. reconcile 10. correspond
accommodation . . . 3. aid 4. loan,
room 5. limit, space, terms 6. giving,
volume 7. advance, lodging, service
8. capacity 9. advantage, provision
10. adaptation, adjustment, attunement,
conformity, settlement 11. convenience,
integration, orientation, subsistence
12. coordination 13. harmonization
14. reconciliation
accompaniment . . . 7. adjunct, descant,
support 8. ornament 9. attendant,
obbligato 11. concurrence
12. concomitance
accompany . . . 4. join 6. attend, convoy,
escort, follow, squire 7. conduct
11. synchronize 12. contemporize
accomplice . . . 3. pal 4. aide, ally, chum
6. stooge 7. abettor 9. accessory,
assistant, associate 11. confederate,
conspirator
accomplish . . . 2. do 3. win 4. make,
work 5. enact, equip 6. attain,
effect 7. achieve, compass, execute,
furnish, operate, perfect, produce,
realize, succeed 8. contrive, engineer
9. negotiate 10. consummate, effectuate
accomplishment . . . 4. deed, feat
5. skill 8. dispatch 9. discharge,
execution 10. attainment, completion
11. achievement, acquirement,
fulfillment, performance, proficiency,
transaction 12. effectuation
accord . . . 5. award, grant, unity 6. accede,
unison 7. comport, concede, concert,
concord, harmony, rapport 8. diapason,
symphony 9. agreement, harmonize,
reconcile, unanimity 10. accordance,
conformity, uniformity 11. concurrence
accordant . . . 7. attuned 8. agreeing,
suitable 9. agreeable, assenting,
consonant 10. concordant, concurrent,
consenting, consilient, consistent
11. conformable, homogeneous

13. corresponding
accordingly . . . 2. so 4. then, thus
9. therefore 12. consequently
according to . . . 3. a la, aux 4. alla, fact,
true 5. datal 7. a la mode 8. pursuant
accost . . . 4. hail, meet 5. greet, speak
6. halloo, salute 7. address 8. approach
accoucheuse . . . 7. midwife
account . . . 3. sum, tab 4. bill, cast, sake,
tale, word 5. debit, honor, score, tally
6. assign, credit, esteem, profit, reckon,
regard, report 7. compute, memoirs,
recital 9. narration, reckoning, rehearsal,
statement, summation 10. numeration,
recitation 11. description, explanation,
information 13. communication
accountable . . . 6. liable 8. amenable,
knowable 9. divinable, traceable
10. answerable, ascribable, assignable,
calculable, explicable, fathomable
11. explainable, predictable, responsible
12. attributable, intelligible
13. apprehensible 14. comprehensible
accountant . . . 5. clerk 7. actuary, auditor
8. reckoner 9. defendant, registrar
10. bookkeeper, calculator
accouter, accoutre . . . 3. fit, rig 4. deck,
gird, suit 5. array, dress, equip, habit
6. attire, fettle, outfit 7. appoint,
costume, furnish, provide
accouterment, accoutrement . . .
5. dress, sword 6. attire 8. trapping
9. equipment, haversack
accoy . . . 4. tame 5. daunt 6. soothe,
subdue
accredit . . . 5. trust 6. accept, affirm,
credit, depute, ratify 7. approve, ascribe,
believe, certify, confirm, empower,
endorse 8. deputize, sanction, validate
9. authorize 10. commission
accrete . . . 3. add 6. attach
accretion . . . 4. gain 6. growth 8. addition,
adhesion, increase 9. coherence,
increment 10. concretion
11. coagulation, enlargement
12. accumulation, augmentation
13. amplification
accrue . . . 4. grow 5. arise, ensue, issue
6. mature, result 7. acquire, collect,
redound 8. accresce 10. accumulate
accumulate . . . 4. grow, heap, mass,
save 5. amass, hoard, store 6. accrue,
garner, gather, muster 7. advance,
collect, store up 8. increase 9. aggregate
accumulation . . . 4. fund, gain, mass
5. hoard, store 7. accrual 8. gleaning,
increase, treasure 9. accession,
accretion, extension, gathering
10. acervation, assemblage, collection
11. acquisition, serendipity
12. augmentation 13. amplification
14. aggrandizement
accuracy . . . 6. nicety 9. exactness,
fussiness, precision, rightness
11. correctness 14. meticulousness,
scrupulousness
accurate . . . 4. just, nice, prim 5. close,
exact, right 6. proper, strict 7. correct,
perfect, precise 8. faithful 9. syntactic
10. meticulous, particular
11. grammatical

accursed ... **6.** cursed, damned, doomed **9.** execrable, execrated **10.** detestable **13.** anathematized

accusation ... **5.** blame **6.** attack, charge, taxing **7.** calumny **8.** reproach **9.** complaint **10.** imputation, indictment **11.** impeachment **12.** denunciation

accuse ... **3.** tax **5.** blame **6.** attack, charge, delate, indict **7.** arraign, censure, impeach **8.** denounce **9.** criminate **11.** incriminate, recriminate

accuser ... **7.** delator **8.** accusant, libelant (libellant) **9.** plaintiff **10.** prosecutor **11.** complainant **12.** incriminator

accustom ... **3.** use **4.** wont **5.** enure, habit, inure, train **6.** addict **7.** educate, toughen **9.** habituate **11.** familiarize

accustomed ... **4.** used, wont **5.** usual **6.** enured, inured **8.** familiar **9.** customary, sedentary (to sit)

ace ... **3.** jot, one, pip, tib **4.** atom, card, dole, dram, unit, whit **5.** monad, pilot, point, shark (sl) **7.** aviator **8.** particle, pittance, superior **10.** crackajack (sl), proficient **11.** crackerjack (sl)

ace (pert to) ...
ace-queen .. **6.** tenace
of clubs .. **5.** basto

acedia (Gr) ... **5.** sloth **6.** torpor

acedia (Sp) ... **8.** flatfish

Aceldama, Akeldama (Bib) ... **12.** Field of Blood, potter's field

acemila ... **8.** pack mule

acephalous ... **8.** headless **10.** leaderless

acephalus ... **15.** headless monster

acerb ... **4.** sour **5.** harsh, sharp **6.** bitter, unripe **7.** acerbic, austere, pungent

acerbity ... **7.** acidity **8.** acridity, acrimony, asperity, mordancy, pungency, severity **9.** harshness **10.** bitterness, causticity **11.** astringency

acetic acid ... **7.** vinegar **8.** vesicant **9.** corrosive

Achaean, Achaian ... **5.** Greek (a) **6.** Greece

ache ... **4.** burn, long, pain, pang **5.** throb, yearn **6.** grieve, sorrow, twinge **7.** agonize, longing **10.** suffer pain

achieve ... **2.** do **3.** get, win **4.** gain, kill **6.** arrive, attain, effect, finish **7.** compass, execute, fulfill, perform, produce, realize, succeed **8.** complete, conclude, contrive **10.** accomplish, consummate, effectuate

achievement ... **3.** act **4.** deed, feat **5.** doing, stunt **6.** action, record **7.** arrival, exploit **8.** dispatch **9.** adventure **10.** attainment, escutcheon (Her) **11.** fulfillment, performance, transaction **12.** effectuation **14.** accomplishment, implementation

Achilles (pert to) ...
advisor .. **6.** Nestor
dipped into .. **9.** River Styx
father .. **6.** Peleus
friend .. **9.** Patroclus
horse .. **7.** Xanthus
mother .. **6.** Thetis
slayer .. **5.** Paris
slayer of .. **6.** Hector

son .. **7.** Pyrrhus **11.** Neoptolemus
vulnerable spot .. **4.** heel

achromatic ... **4.** gray **8.** achromic **9.** achromous, colorless, uncolored **13.** free from color

achropsia ... **14.** color blindness

acid ... **4.** keen, sour, tart **5.** acrid, amino, boric, malic, mucic, pyrol **6.** acetic, arabic, biting, bromic, nitric, oxalic, tannic **7.** acetose, caustic, chloric, racemic, stearic, terebic, vinegar **8.** carbolic, lysergic, sulfuric **9.** corrosive **11.** acrimonious **12.** hydrochloric

acid, removing ... **12.** edulcoration

acidity ... **4.** acor, sour **8.** acrimony, mordancy, sourness, tartness, verjuice **9.** sharpness **10.** bitterness **13.** acidulousness

acknowledge ... **3.** nod, own, pay, say **4.** avow, sign **5.** admit, allow, grant, own up, reply, swear, thank, vouch, yield **6.** accede, accept, answer, assent, attest, redeem **7.** certify, concede, confess, testify **8.** disclose **9.** recognize

acknowledgment ... **5.** favor, reply **6.** answer, avowal, avowry, shrift, thanks **7.** apology, epistle, receipt, voucher, warrant **8.** rescript **9.** admission **10.** acceptance, concession, confession, disclosure, owning up to **11.** recognition **12.** thanksgiving

acme ... **3.** top **4.** apex **5.** limit **6.** apogee, climax, crisis, heyday, summit, tip-top, vertex, zenith **7.** ceiling, maximum **11.** culmination **12.** consummation

acology, science of ... **8.** remedies

acolyte ... **7.** patener **8.** altar boy **9.** assistant

acomia ... **8.** alopecia, baldness **12.** hairlessness

aconite ... **8.** Cammarum, Eranthis **9.** monkshood

acorn ... **3.** nut **4.** duck **6.** camata **10.** meadowlark (color)

acosmic ... **11.** unorganized

acquaint ... **4.** tell **6.** advise, impart, inform **7.** apprise **9.** enlighten, introduce **11.** familiarize

acquaintance ... **3.** ken **5.** amigo **6.** friend **7.** privity **8.** familiar, intimacy, intimate **9.** companion, knowledge **10.** fellowship **11.** familiarity, information, sympathizer **15.** familiarization

acquainted ... **6.** au fait **7.** versant **8.** familiar **9.** cognizant **10.** conversant

acquiesce ... **3.** bow **5.** abide, agree, chime, yield **6.** accede, assent, comply, concur, relent, resign, submit **7.** conform, consent, succumb

acquire ... **3.** buy, get, win **4.** earn, gain, reap **5.** adopt, catch, incur, learn, steal **6.** attain, effect, obtain, secure **7.** procure, receive **8.** contract **9.** cultivate

acquire (pert to) ...
beforehand .. **7.** pre-empt
feathers .. **6.** fledge
immunity .. **14.** serum injection
knowledge .. **5.** clear, study **9.** ascertain

acquit ... **4.** free **5.** clear **6.** excuse,

pardon, pay off **7.** absolve, fulfill,
release, requite **9.** exculpate, exonerate
acquittal . . . **7.** freeing, payment, release
8. clearing, requital **9.** clearance,
discharge **10.** observance
11. exculpation, fulfillment
12. satisfaction
acquittance . . . **7.** payment, quietus,
receipt **9.** discharge, quittance
acre . . . **5.** field **6.** arpent **7.** measure
8. farmhold
acre (pert to) . . .
    half . . **3.** erf (So Afr)
    hundred . . **7.** hectare (metric)
    quarter . . **4.** rood (Brit)
acres . . . **5.** lands **6.** estate, ground
acrid . . . **4.** acid, bask (dial), keen,
sour, tart **5.** harsh, rough, sharp
6. acetic, biting, bitter **7.** acetose,
caustic, mordant, pungent, reeking
8. unsavory, virulent **9.** acidulous,
corrosive **10.** escharotic, irritating
11. acrimonious
acrimonious . . . **4.** acid, keen **5.** acrid,
angry, gruff, harsh, irate, sharp **6.** bitter
7. caustic **8.** stinging **9.** rancorous,
resentful
acrimony . . . **5.** venom **6.** rancor **7.** ill will,
vitriol **8.** acerbity, acridity, asperity,
mordancy, pungency, rudeness,
severity, sourness, tartness
9. animosity, virulence **10.** bitterness,
causticity, resentment **11.** astringency,
crabbedness
acroamatic . . . **4.** oral **5.** parol **6.** arcane,
occult, secret, verbal **8.** abstract,
abstruse, anagogic, esoteric, profound
9. recondite, unwritten **11.** nuncupative
acrobat . . . **7.** gymnast, tumbler
8. balancer **10.** ropedancer, ropewalker
11. funambulist **13.** contortionist,
schoenobatist
acrochordon . . . **4.** wart (small)
Acrocorinth, Acrocorinthus . . .
9. acropolis (Corinth) **12.** Pirene Spring
(site)
acromegaly . . . **7.** disease
11. enlargement (head, hands, feet)
acronical, acronichal (opp of
cosmical) . . . **10.** rising star **11.** setting
star
acronyx . . . **13.** ingrowing nail
acrophobia . . . fear of **7.** heights
acropolis . . . **6.** refuge **7.** citadel
Acropolis (pert to) . . .
    Argos . . **7.** Larissa
    Corinth . . **11.** Acrocorinth
    Thebes . . **6.** Cadmea
across . . . **4.** over, span **5.** cross **6.** thwart
7. athwart **8.** crossway, traverse
9. crossways, crosswise **10.** crisscross,
transverse
across (pref) . . . **3.** dia **4.** tran **5.** trans
acrostic . . . **4.** agla, game, poem **6.** puzzle
7. erratic **8.** wordplay **9.** crosswise,
jeu de mots, telestich
act . . . **2.** do **3.** jus, law, lex **4.** deed, feat,
play, skit, turn, work **5.** actus, emote,
favor, of God, stunt **6.** action, behave,
demean, motion **7.** comport, measure,
perform, pretend, process **8.** function,

kindness, simulate **9.** enactment,
represent **10.** enterprise, exert power,
theatrical **11.** impersonate, legislation,
performance, transaction
act (pert to) . . .
    a part . . **8.** simulate **9.** dissemble
    causing ruin . . **11.** Kiss of Death
    criminal . . **8.** villainy
    detestable . . **11.** abomination
    formal . . **10.** instrument
    game . . **7.** charade
    illegal . . **4.** tort **5.** crime **6.** delict
    nonsense . . **10.** tomfoolery
    planned . . **12.** premeditated
    pompously . . **11.** pontificate
    suffix . . **3.** ure
acting . . . **5.** doing **6.** action, posing
7. playing, serving **8.** pretense
9. dramatics, execution, operating
10. masquerade, performing, simulating
11. make-believe **13.** impersonating,
impersonation
acting with force . . . **8.** vehement
action . . . **2.** re **3.** act, res **4.** deed, feat,
play, stir, suit, work **5.** award, doing,
order, works **6.** battle, decree, motion,
praxis, ruling **7.** conduct, contest,
lawsuit, verdict, working **8.** activity,
behavior, demeanor, exercise,
movement, sentence **9.** mechanism,
operation **10.** automation, enterprise
11. performance **13.** pronouncement
active . . . **4.** spry **5.** acute, agile,
alert, brisk, quick, ready, smart,
yauld **6.** breezy, dapper, lively,
nimble, prompt, strong **7.** dynamic,
intense, kinetic, vibrant **8.** animated,
forceful, spirited, vigorous **9.** assiduous,
effective, effectual, energetic, energized,
operating, pragmatic, sprightly,
vivacious **11.** industrious
active, not . . . **6.** static **7.** dormant
11. inoperative
activity . . . **3.** ado, gog, pep, vir **4.** stir,
work **5.** vigor **6.** action, energy
7. agility, bristle **8.** business, movement
9. athletics, briskness, operation,
quickness **10.** activeness, employment,
nimbleness, occupation
act of . . .
    cutting . . **4.** kerf **8.** shearing
    endearment . . **4.** kiss **6.** caress
    God . . **8.** accident, disaster
    kindness . . **5.** favor
    leaving . . **6.** congee, egress
    respect . . **6.** curtsy, homage
    ruling . . **5.** regle
    self-examination . . **13.** introspection
    sharing . . **13.** participation
    witnessing . . **11.** attestation
    working together . . **13.** collaboration
    worship . . **6.** prayer **8.** devotion
actor . . . **3.** ham **4.** doer, hero, mime,
star, supe **5.** agent **6.** mummer,
player, worker **7.** Roscius, trooper
8. aisteoir, comedian, histrion, Thespian
9. performer, portrayer, pretender,
tragedian **10.** comedienne, dramatizer,
pantomimic, personator
11. barnstormer, entertainer,
pantomimist, protagonist, tragedienne

12. impersonator
actor (personage) ... **4.** Lunt, Ward
  5. Booth **7.** Skinner **8.** Warfield
  9. Faversham
actors' group ... **4.** cast **6.** troupe
actor's hint ... **3.** cue **12.** teleprompter
actress (personage) ... **5.** Adams, Bates,
  Hayes, Terry **6.** Robson, Scheff
  7. Marlowe, Russell **8.** Fontanne,
  Modjeska **9.** Bernhardt
actual ... **4.** real, true **5.** posit **7.** factual,
  genuine, present **8.** absolute, positive,
  tangible **9.** practical, veritable
  11. substantial
actual being ... **4.** esse
actuality ... **4.** fact **6.** verity **7.** reality
  8. realness **9.** existence **10.** factuality
  14. substantiality
actually ... **5.** quite, truly **6.** indeed,
  really, verily **8.** actively **9.** assuredly,
  certainly
actuary ... **5.** clerk **9.** registrar
  10. accountant, bookkeeper, calculator
  13. arithmetician, mathematician
actuate ... **3.** egg **4.** move **5.** force, impel,
  rouse **6.** arouse, induce, prompt, propel
  7. animate **8.** motivate **9.** stimulate
acuate ... **7.** sharpen **12.** needle-shaped,
  sharp-pointed
acumen ... **7.** insight **8.** gumption,
  keenness, sagacity **9.** acuteness,
  sharpness **10.** astuteness, perception,
  shrewdness **11.** discernment
  12. perspicacity **14.** discrimination
acute ... **4.** high, keen, tart, thin
  5. canny, sharp, smart, vivid **6.** accent,
  biting, crafty, fierce, severe, shrewd,
  shrill, subtle **7.** crucial, cutting,
  dynamic, intense, knowing, painful,
  pointed, violent **8.** critical, deep-felt,
  forceful, incisive, piercing, poignant,
  rigorous, stabbing, stinging, vigorous
  9. energetic, ingenious, sensitive
  11. sharp-witted **13.** perspicacious
  14. discriminating
acuteness of ...
  sight .. **7.** oxyopia **10.** oxyblepsia
  taste .. **9.** oxygeusia
  touch .. **8.** oxyaphia
A.D. ... **10.** Anno Domini
Adam (pert to) ...
  grandson .. **4.** Enos
  son .. **4.** Abel, Cain, Seth
  wife .. **3.** Eve **6.** Lilith (legend)
adage ... **3.** saw **5.** maxim **6.** saying
  7. proverb
adamant ... **4.** hard **8.** stubborn
  10. unyielding
Adam's ...
  ale .. **5.** water
  apple .. **6.** larynx **10.** pomum Adami
  herb .. **7.** mullein
  needle .. **5.** yucca
adapt ... **3.** fit, set **4.** suit **6.** adjust,
  attune, comply, modify, orient, season
  7. arrange, conform, prepare, qualify
  8. accustom, regulate **9.** acclimate,
  condition, habituate, harmonize,
  reconcile **11.** accommodate
adaptable ... **7.** elastic, pliable
  9. tractable, versatile **10.** adjustable,

responsive **11.** conformable
  13. accommodative
adaptation ... **7.** fitting **10.** adjustment,
  attunement, conformity, regulation
  11. arrangement, habituation,
  orientation **12.** conditioning,
  coordination, modification
  13. accommodation, harmonization,
  orchestration, qualification
  15. familiarization
add ... **3.** eke, tot **4.** foot, give, join,
  plus, tote **5.** affix, annex, sum up,
  total, unite **6.** append, attach, reckon
  7. accrete, augment, compile, compute,
  put with, subjoin **8.** increase **9.** calculate
  10. supplement
adda ... **5.** skink (scink) **6.** lizard **7.** reptile
addax ... **6.** pygarg (Bib) **8.** antelope
added ... **3.** and **4.** plus **5.** extra
  6. joined, united **7.** affixed, annexed
  8. appended, attached **9.** appendant
  13. supplementary
adder ... **3.** asp **5.** Bitis, krait, snake,
  viper **6.** nedder **7.** machine, serpent
  13. mathematician
addict ... **4.** buff **5.** fiend **7.** adjudge,
  devotee, hophead **9.** habituate **15.** apply
  habitually
addicted ... **4.** wont **5.** prone **8.** attached,
  disposed, inclined **9.** devoted to
  10. accustomed, habituated **11.** given
  over to
addiction ... **5.** habit **9.** surrender
  10. attachment **11.** enslavement
Addison, name for ... **4.** Clio (The
  Spectator) **7.** Atticus (by Pope)
addition ... **3.** and, ell, too **4.** also,
  gain, plus, wing **5.** farse (Relig),
  rider **6.** addend, augend, lean-to
  7. additum, adjunct, joining, uniting
  8. addendum, additory, increase
  9. accession, accretion, amendment,
  appendage, extension, reckoning
  10. annexation **11.** calculation,
  computation, enlargement
  12. augmentation
additional ... **3.** new **4.** else, more
  5. added, extra, fresh, spare **7.** another,
  besides, further **9.** auxiliary, extrinsic
  12. supervenient, supplemental
  13. supplementary
additional (pert to) ...
  explanation .. **10.** epexegesis
    11. elucidation
  grant .. **3.** ann **5.** bonus
  specimen .. **6.** cotype
address ... **3.** air, wit, woo **4.** call, hail,
  mien, pray, tact, talk **5.** abode, court,
  grace, greet, guise, place, skill, speak
  6. accost, direct, eulogy, salute, sermon,
  speech **7.** arrange, conduct, consign,
  declaim, finesse, lecture, manners,
  oration, prepare, prowess, request
  8. behavior, demeanor, greeting,
  harangue, inscribe, perorate, petition,
  presence **9.** dexterity, diplomacy,
  direction, discourse, ingenuity,
  readiness **11.** comportment, destination,
  inscription, savoir-faire
  14. sophistication, superscription
addressee ... **8.** occupant **10.** inhabitant

12. communicator 13. correspondent
adduce . . . 4. cite, name 5. argue, infer, offer, plead, quote 6. allege, assign 7. advance, mention, present, produce
Adelphi . . . 7. theater (Strand, London) 13. London Quarter
adeps . . . 4. lard 9. animal fat
adept . . . 3. ace, apt 4. deft, whiz (coll) 6. adroit, artist, expert, versed 7. capable, dabster, mahatma, skilled 8. skillful (skilful) 9. alchemist (formerly), occultist 10. conversant, proficient 11. crackerjack
adequate . . . 3. due, fit 4. able, full 5. ample, digne, equal 6. enough 7. capable 8. all right, equalize, suitable 9. competent, effective, effectual, sufficing, tolerable 10. sufficient 12. commensurate, satisfactory 13. proportionate
adhere . . . 4. cleg, glue, hold 5. cling, stick 6. cleave, cohere 7. accrete, observe, persist
adherent . . . 4. ally 6. adnate, sticky, votary 7. dangler, sequela 8. adhesive, clinging, disciple, faithful, follower, hanger-on, partisan, sticking, upholder 9. appendage, dependent, supporter
adherent to the Crown . . . 4. Tory
adhesive . . . 3. gum, wax 4. glue 5. paste 6. cement, mastic, sticky 8. adherent, mucilage 9. tenacious
adhesiveness . . . 4. stay 8. tenacity 12. cohesiveness 13. tenaciousness 16. stick-to-itiveness
adhibit . . . 3. use 5. admit, affix, apply 6. attach, devote 7. bring in 10. administer
adieu . . . 4. vale 5. adios, aloha 6. good-by, so long (sl) 7. cheerio, good-bye, good day 8. au revoir, farewell 11. leave-taking
adipose . . . 3. fat 4. oily 5. fatty, plump, pursy, squab 9. sebaceous
adit . . . 3. way 4. duct 5. entry, stulm 6. access, ingate, intake, tunnel 7. channel, conduit, haulage, ingress, passage 8. approach, drainage, entrance 9. admission 11. entranceway, ventilation
adjacent . . . 4. abut, near, nigh 5. close, handy 6. next to 7. meeting, nearest 8. abutting, touching 9. adjoining, bordering 10. contiguous, juxtaposed 11. neighboring 12. conterminous
adject . . . 3. add 4. join 5. annex
adjective . . . 3. the 6. adnoun 7. epithet (significant) 8. modifier 9. accessory, dependent
adjective (pert to) . . .
  demonstrative . . 4. that, this 5. these, those
  suffix . . 2. ic, il 3. ent, ial, ian, ile, ish, ist, ite, ive, ous
  verbal . . 9. gerundive
adjoin . . . 3. add 4. abut, butt, join 5. unite 6. attach, border 7. conjoin 8. neighbor
adjourn . . . 3. end 5. close, defer, delay 6. recess 7. suspend 8. dissolve, postpone, prorogue 11. discontinue

adjudge, adjudicate . . . 3. try 4. deem, doom, find, hold, pass 5. award, judge, order 6. assign, decree, esteem, ordain, reckon, regard, settle 7. condemn 8. consider, sentence 9. determine
adjunct . . . 4. ally, word 5. added 6. device 7. additum, annexed, consort 8. addition, appanage (apanage) 9. appendant, associate, auxiliary, colleague, companion, component, qualifier 11. confederate 12. appurtenance, nonessential
adjuration . . . 4. oath, plea 6. appeal, avowal, charge 8. entreaty, swearing, vouching 10. deposition 11. beseechment, obsecration, obtestation
adjure . . . 3. ask, beg, bid 4. bind, pray 5. plead 6. appeal, charge 7. beseech, command, entreat, implore, swear in
adjust . . . 3. fit, fix, set 4. meet, size, suit, trim, true 5. adapt, align, amend, frame, group, match, right, shape 6. accord, attune, orient, remedy, settle, square 7. arrange, conform, correct, justify, mediate, rectify, redress 8. accustom, organize, regulate 9. condition, habituate, harmonize, reconcile 10. compromise, coordinate, straighten 11. accommodate, systematize
adjuster, adjustor . . . 6. fitter 8. arranger 11. coordinator
adjustment . . . 4. gear 5. means, terms 7. fitting, suiting 8. bearings, disposal 9. bundobust 10. adaptation, attunement, compromise, concession, conclusion, conformity, regulation, settlement 11. arrangement, disposition, habituation, orientation 12. assimilation, coordination, organization 13. harmonization, methodization, rectification 14. naturalization, reconciliation
adjutant . . . 4. aide, ally 6. helper 7. officer 9. assistant, auxiliary
adjutant bird . . . 5. stork 6. argala 7. hurgila, marabou
ad lib, ad libit, ad libitum . . . 6. make up 7. cadenza 9. extempore, impromptu, improvise 10. at pleasure 11. play it by ear 13. accompaniment
administer . . . 4. give 5. apply, issue 6. bestow, direct, govern, manage, supply, tender 7. adhibit, conduct, dispose, execute, fulfill, furnish, give out, husband, perform 8. dispatch, dispense, transact 9. discharge 10. distribute 12. administrate
administer extreme unction . . . 5. anele 6. anoint
administration . . . 3. use 4. rule 6. employ, giving, policy 7. conduct, regimen 8. bestowal, disposal, issuance, ministry 9. direction, execution 10. employment, government, management, regulation 11. application, directorate, disposition 12. dispensation, ministration 13. apportionment
administration of justice . . .

10. judicatory, judicature
administrator . . . **2.** fu **5.** dewan
   7. alcalde, manager, provost, trustee
   8. director, executor **9.** dispenser,
   executive **12.** entrepreneur
admirable . . . **5.** sweet **6.** worthy
   7. likable (likeable), winning, winsome
   8. adorable, laudable **9.** estimable,
   excellent, marvelous, wonderful
   10. creditable **11.** commendable,
   meritorious **12.** praiseworthy
admiration . . . **6.** esteem, liking, regard,
   wonder **7.** respect **8.** surprise
   9. adoration, amazement, reverence
   10. wonderment **11.** astoundment,
   idolization **12.** appreciation,
   confoundment
admire . . . **4.** like, love **5.** adore, honor
   6. esteem, regard, revere **7.** approve,
   idolize, respect **8.** venerate
admissible . . . **3.** fit **4.** just, sane **5.** sound
   6. worthy **7.** apropos, germane, logical
   8. apposite, eligible, rational, relevant,
   suitable **9.** admissory, agreeable,
   allowable, desirable, pertinent,
   qualified, receptive, tolerable
   10. acceptable, applicable, legitimate,
   reasonable **11.** justifiable, permissible,
   warrantable **12.** satisfactory
admission . . . **4.** adit **5.** entry **6.** access,
   assent, avowal, entree, shrift
   8. entrance **9.** agreement, allowance,
   inclusion, letting in, receiving,
   reception, testimony **10.** accordance,
   admittance, allegation, avouchment,
   compliance, concession, confession,
   initiation, permission **11.** affiliation,
   affirmation, declaration
   12. acquiescence, assimilation
   14. acknowledgment, naturalization
   15. enfranchisement
Admission Day holiday . . . **6.** Nevada
   (Oct 31) **7.** Arizona (Feb 14)
   10. California (Sept 9)
admit . . . **3.** own **4.** avow **5.** adopt, allow,
   enter, grant, let in, own up, trust,
   yield **6.** accept, credit, embody, permit
   7. adhibit, believe, concede, confess,
   embrace, include, profess, receive
   8. initiate **9.** affiliate **10.** naturalize
   11. acknowledge, incorporate
admittance . . . **6.** access **8.** entrance,
   sanction **9.** admission, letting in
   10. initiation
admitted . . . **6.** indeed **8.** believed,
   conceded **12.** acknowledged
admixture . . . **5.** alloy, blend **6.** fusion
   7. mixture **8.** compound, infusion
   7. mixture **8.** compound, infusion
   10. minglement **11.** combination,
   composition
admonish . . . **4.** warn **5.** chide, scold
   6. advise, enjoin, exhort, preach,
   rebuke, remind **7.** caution, monitor,
   reprove, upbraid **8.** dissuade
   9. reprimand **11.** expostulate,
   remonstrate, give warning
admonition . . . **6.** advice **7.** caution,
   censure, reproof, warning **8.** reminder
   10. counseling (counselling), dissuasion
   11. exhortation **12.** remonstrance,

reprehension
ado . . . **4.** fuss, stir **5.** doing, hurry
   6. bustle, flurry, hubbub, pother,
   rumpus, tumult **7.** trouble, turmoil
   9. commotion **10.** excitement
   11. disturbance
adobe . . . **4.** clay, silt **5.** brick, house
   (clay)
adolescent . . . **3.** lad **5.** minor, youth
   6. nonage **9.** pubescent, youngster
   10. developing
Adonis (pert to) . . .
   beloved by . . **9.** Aphrodite
   festival . . **6.** Adonia
   modern youth . . **6.** a dandy
   mother . . **5.** Myrrh
   slain by . . **8.** wild boar
adopt . . . **4.** take **5.** admit, usurp
   6. accept, assume, borrow, choose,
   father, mother, select **7.** embrace,
   espouse, receive, welcome **9.** affiliate
   10. assimilate, naturalize **11.** appropriate
adoption . . . **6.** choice **8.** espousal
   9. admission, borrowing, reception
   10. acceptance, assumption, conversion,
   redemption, usurpation
   11. embracement **13.** appropriation
   14. naturalization
adore . . . **4.** love **5.** enjoy, honor **6.** esteem,
   regard, revere **7.** idolize, worship
   8. venerate
adorn . . . **4.** clad, deck, trim **5.** array,
   begem, drape, grace, primp, prink
   6. attire, bedeck, clothe, enrich
   7. bedight, bejewel, dignify, festoon,
   garnish **8.** beautify, decorate
   9. embellish
adorn (with) . . .
   color . . **4.** gild **5.** paint **7.** emblaze
   feathers . . **7.** implume
   needlework . . **9.** embroider
   ornaments . . **6.** tinsel **7.** imagery
adorned . . . **4.** clad **6.** ornate **7.** clothed,
   prinked **9.** decorated
   16. chryselephantine
adornment . . . **5.** decor, frill **6.** frills,
   tinsel **10.** decoration, embroidery
   13. embellishment **14.** beautification
ad patres . . . **4.** dead **12.** to his Fathers
Adriatic (pert to) . . .
   city . . **5.** Fiume **6.** Venice **7.** Lagosta,
   Trieste **8.** Brandisi
   island . . **7.** Lagosta
   peninsula . . **6.** Istria
   wind (cold) . . **4.** bora
adrift . . . **4.** asea, free, lost **5.** at sea,
   loose **6.** afloat, astray, aweigh, undone
   7. aimless, unfixed **8.** aberrant, derelict,
   floating, insecure, straying, unmoored,
   unstable **9.** erroneous **10.** bewildered,
   unanchored, unfastened, without aim
adroit . . . **4.** neat **5.** quick, ready,
   smart **6.** clever, expert, habile,
   nimble **7.** cunning **8.** skillful (skilful)
   9. dexterous, ingenious
adroitness . . . **4.** tact **5.** knack, skill
   7. address **9.** dexterity, ingenuity,
   readiness, smartness
adsorbent, absorbent . . . **6.** spongy
   7. osmotic, soaking **8.** blotting
   12. assimilative

adulation . . . **6.** praise **8.** flattery
9. adoration **10.** compliment
adult . . . **6.** mature, X-rated **7.** grown up
adulterate . . . **3.** mix **5.** alter, taint
6. debase, defile **7.** corrupt **8.** denature
11. contaminate
adulterated . . . **6.** impure **7.** debased
8. spurious **9.** denatured **11.** counterfeit
12. contaminated
adust . . . **3.** tan (color) **4.** burn **5.** burnt,
dried, fiery **6.** singed **7.** parched
8. scorched **9.** blistered
advance . . . **2.** go **3.** aid **4.** gain,
inch, loan, move, near, nose, pass,
push, rise (in price) **5.** ahead, boost,
creep, march, raise **6.** better, stride
7. elevate, process, promote, propose
8. approach, heighten, increase,
progress **9.** aforehand, elevation,
promotion, upgrading **10.** accelerate,
beforehand, preferment
11. advancement, development,
furtherance, improvement, progression
advanced . . . **3.** old **4.** aged **6.** modern
7. elderly, forward **8.** bettered,
enhanced, enriched, foremost,
unproved **9.** venerable **10.** in the front,
precocious, senectuous **11.** enlightened,
progressive
advanced (pert to) . . .
equally . . **7.** abreast
study . . **7.** seminar
time . . **6.** modern **8.** up-to-date
12. contemporary
advantage . . . **3.** use **4.** boot, bote (bot),
edge, gain, good, hold, odds **5.** avail,
favor, start, stead **6.** behalf, behoof,
profit **7.** benefit, further, promote,
service, vantage **8.** facility, interest,
purchase **9.** appliance **10.** expedience
11. convenience, superiority
13. accommodation, vantage ground
advantageous . . . **5.** handy **6.** aidful,
useful **7.** helpful **8.** edifying, salutary
9. expedient, favorable **10.** auspicious,
beneficial, convenient, profitable,
propitious, worthwhile **11.** encouraging
advent . . . **6.** coming **7.** arrival **8.** approach
11. forthcoming
Advent (Eccl) . . . **14.** Coming of Christ
adventitious . . . **4.** rale **6.** casual
8. acquired **9.** extrinsic **10.** accidental,
incidental **12.** nonessential
adventure . . . **3.** act (heroic), hap **4.** bout,
dare, deed, feat, gest, risk **5.** event,
quest, stunt **6.** action, hazard **7.** episode,
exploit, fortune, venture **8.** escapade,
incident (novel), maneuver, occasion
9. happening **10.** enterprise, experience,
occurrence **11.** performance, undertaking
12. happenstance **13.** striking event
14. accomplishment
adventurer . . . **4.** goer **5.** sport **7.** bounder,
gambler, Hessian, parvenu, soldier,
upstart **8.** gamester, hazarder,
merchant, traveler **9.** sportsman
10. speculator **16.** soldier of fortune
adventuress . . . **7.** demirep **10.** gold
digger
adventurous . . . **4.** rash **5.** risky **6.** daring
8. reckless **9.** dangerous, foolhardy,

hazardous, venturous **11.** venturesome
12. enterprising, presumptuous
adversary . . . **3.** foe **5.** enemy, Satan
6. foeman **8.** opponent **9.** archfiend,
assailant **10.** antagonist, competitor,
Philistine
adverse . . . **3.** ill **4.** anti **5.** loath **7.** opposed
8. contrary, converse, opposing,
sinister, untoward **9.** reluctant, unwilling
10. afflictive, calamitous, indisposed
11. conflicting, disinclined, unfavorable
12. antagonistic, unpropitious
adversity . . . **6.** misery **7.** trouble
8. calamity, distress, hardship
9. suffering **10.** affliction, misfortune,
opposition **11.** destitution
advert . . . **5.** recur, refer **6.** allude, return
advertent . . . **7.** heedful **9.** attentive
advertise . . . **4.** plug, warn **5.** boast,
boost **6.** notify **7.** promote, publish
8. announce, ballyhoo, proclaim
9. publicize **10.** promulgate
advertisement . . . **2.** ad **4.** bill, copy,
Neon, plug, sign **6.** notice, poster,
spread **7.** placard **10.** commercial (TV)
advice . . . **4.** rede **5.** aviso **6.** caveat,
wisdom **7.** counsel, opinion, warning
8. prudence, reminder **9.** knowledge
10. admonition, suggestion
11. exhortation, information, instruction
12. consultation, deliberation,
intelligence **13.** consideration
14. recommendation
advice, containing . . . **9.** mentorial
advisable . . . **6.** proper **7.** prudent
9. befitting, desirable, expedient
11. commendable **13.** recommendable
advise . . . **4.** rede, tell, warn **5.** coach
6. exhort, impart, inform, remind
7. apprise, bethink, caution, counsel,
suggest **8.** acquaint, admonish, advocate
9. enlighten, recommend **11.** communicate, familiarize, take counsel
adviser, advisor . . . **5.** guide **6.** Egeria,
nestor **7.** monitor **8.** appriser, kibitzer
(sl) **9.** counselor (counsellor), informant
10. admonisher
advisers, advisors . . . **7.** Cabinet, Council
10. councilors, counselors, informants
advocate . . . **3.** pro **4.** urge **5.** advise,
backer, defend, deputy, lawyer
7. endorse, espouse, pleader, support
8. attorney, champion, defender,
exponent, plead for **9.** barrister,
counselor, justifier, paraclete,
proponent, recommend, solicitor,
supporter **11.** protagonist
advocate of the simple life . . .
14. simplicitarian
adytum . . . **6.** shrine **7.** chamber (inner),
sanctum **9.** sanctuary
Aeetes (pert to) . . .
daughter . . **5.** Medea
keeper of . . **12.** Golden Fleece
king of . . **7.** Colchis
Aegean Islands . . . **5.** Chios, Samos
6. Lesbos **8.** Cyclades **10.** Dodecanese
aegis, egis . . . **4.** care **5.** guard **6.** screen,
shield, symbol (anc) **7.** backing, defense
8. guidance **9.** fosterage, patronage
10. protection

Aello (Gr) ... **5.** Harpy **7.** monster

Aeneid ... **4.** poem (Vergil)

aerage ... **11.** ventilation

aerate ... **6.** aerify **7.** freshen, inflate, refresh **9.** ventilate

aerial ... **3.** ear **4.** aery, airy, mast **5.** aeric, lofty **6.** unreal **7.** airlike, antenna **8.** ethereal, fanciful, vaporous **9.** pneumatic **10.** chimerical **12.** aeronautical **13.** unsubstantial

aerie, eyrie ... **4.** nest **5.** brood (birds) **6.** family **9.** penthouse

aeriform ... **6.** unreal **7.** gaseous

aeroplane ... **8.** airplane

Aesir, Norse Gods ... **3.** Tyr (Tiu), Ull **4.** Odin (Woden), Thor (Donar), Vali **5.** Bragi **6.** Balder, Hoenir **7.** Forseti **8.** Heimdall

Aeson's son ... **5.** Jason (Gr Myth)

Aesop (Gr) ... **5.** fable, moral

affability ... **6.** comity **8.** civility, courtesy, urbanity **9.** geniality **10.** amiability, cordiality, politeness **11.** sociability **12.** conviviality **14.** gregariousness **16.** companionability **17.** communicativeness

affable ... **4.** mild **5.** civil, suave **6.** benign, fluent, social **7.** amiable **8.** gracious, sociable **9.** convivial, courteous **10.** accessible, gregarious **11.** complaisant **13.** communicative

affair ... **4.** duel, love **5.** fight, issue, thing, topic **6.** action, gadget, matter, object, soiree **7.** concern, problem **8.** business, interest, question, sociable **9.** gathering, reception, something **10.** proceeding **11.** get-together, transaction **12.** circumstance

affect ... **4.** melt, move, stir **5.** feign, grate, haunt, touch **6.** assume, excite, regale, relate, soften, thrill **7.** concern, involve, operate, pretend, qualify **8.** frequent, interest, simulate **9.** influence **11.** counterfeit, hypothecate

affectation ... **3.** air **4.** pose, sham **7.** display, foppery, pietism **8.** elegance, pretense **9.** mannerism **12.** affectedness **13.** artificiality **14.** grandiloquence **15.** pretentiousness

affected ... **4.** airy, sham **5.** faked, moved, posey, put-on **6.** fal-lal, formal **7.** assumed, beloved, elegant, feigned, gushing, stilted **8.** disposed, mannered **9.** impressed, pretended, unnatural **10.** artificial, euphuistic **11.** pretentious **12.** ostentatious **13.** counterfeited, grandiloquent

affected by ...

age .. **6.** senile

love .. **4.** smit **7.** smitten

pain .. **4.** pang **6.** twinge

paralysis .. **7.** paretic

wonder .. **6.** marvel **9.** convulsed

affectedly languid ... **13.** lackadaisical

affectedly shy ... **3.** coy, mim **4.** prim **6.** demure **10.** coquettish

affection ... **4.** amor, love **6.** animus, defect, storge (animal) **7.** disease, emotion, feeling, illness, leaning, passion **8.** devotion, fondness, tendency **9.** attribute, infirmity, sentiment **10.** affliction, attachment, disability, proclivity, propensity, tenderness **11.** disposition, inclination, temperament

affectionate ... **4.** fond, soft, warm **6.** ardent, loving, tender **7.** adoring, devoted, earnest, zealous **8.** attached, friendly, parental, romantic **10.** headstrong **13.** demonstrative

afferent ... **6.** esodic (nerves), inward **7.** sensory **11.** centripetal

affiance ... **5.** faith, troth, trust **6.** belief, pledge, plight **7.** betroth, promise **8.** credence, reliance **9.** assurance, betrothal **10.** confidence, engagement

affiche ... **6.** poster **7.** placard

affidavit ... **4.** oath **9.** statement **10.** deposition **11.** affirmation, certificate, declaration

affiliation ... **4.** body, sect **5.** group, union **6.** church, fusion, hookup, league **7.** faction, lineage **8.** adoption, alliance, espousal, relation **9.** admission, alignment, coalition **10.** connection, federation, fellowship, persuasion **11.** association, cooperation **12.** denomination, organization **13.** confederation, consanguinity **14.** naturalization

affinity ... **3.** kin **6.** accord, family, liking **7.** kinship, rapport **8.** relation, soul mate **9.** agreement **10.** attraction, connection, similarity **11.** propinquity, resemblance **12.** congeniality, relationship **13.** compatibility, rapprochement

affirm ... **3.** say **4.** aver, avow **5.** posit, state, swear, vouch **6.** allege, assert, attest, avouch, ratify **7.** asseverate, confirm, declare, endorse, profess, testify, warrant **8.** sanction, validate **9.** predicate, pronounce **10.** asseverate **12.** authenticate, substantiate

affirmation ... **3.** vow **4.** amen, oath, word **5.** basis **6.** ground **7.** premise **8.** averment **9.** admission, assertion, statement, testimony **10.** affirmance, allegation, avouchment, deposition, foundation, profession **11.** declaration, proposition **12.** confirmation, ratification

affirmative ... **3.** aye (ay), nod, yea, yes **8.** dogmatic, positive, thumbs up (coll) **10.** cataphatic (rare) **11.** affirmation, declarative, predicative

affirmatory ... **9.** assertive **11.** affirmative, assertional

affix ... **3.** add, fix, pen, tag **4.** seal **5.** annex, stamp **6.** anchor, append, attach, fasten, impose **7.** connect, subjoin **9.** increment **11.** superimpose

afflict ... **3.** ail, try, vex **4.** hurt, pain **5.** upset, wound **6.** grieve, harass, sicken **7.** agitate, chasten, derange, disturb, oppress, torment, trouble **8.** disorder, distress, lacerate **9.** overthrow, persecute

afflicted ... **3.** sad **6.** ailed **6.** pained **7.** smitten, wounded **8.** troubled **9.** depressed, suffering **10.** distressed

affliction ... **3.** woe **4.** airs, bane, evil, pain, pest **5.** curse, grief **6.** misery, plague **7.** illness, scourge, torment,

trouble **8.** calamity, distress, hardship
9. adversity **10.** misfortune, visitation
12. wretchedness
afflictive . . . **6.** severe **11.** causing pain,
distressing
affluence . . . **4.** ease, flow **6.** afflux, influx,
plenty, riches, wealth **8.** opulence,
richness **9.** abundance, concourse,
plenitude, profusion **10.** prosperity
affluent . . . **4.** rich **5.** flush **6.** fluent
7. copious, moneyed, opulent, wealthy
8. abundant, well-to-do **9.** luxuriant,
pecunious, plenteous **10.** prosperous
afford . . . **4.** bear, cost, give, lend
5. allow, endow, grant, spare, stand,
yield **6.** accord, confer, invest, supply
7. furnish, provide, support, undergo
affray . . . **3.** war **4.** feud, fray, riot **5.** brawl,
fight, melee, scrap (sl), set-to (coll)
6. battle, combat, tumult **7.** assault,
contest, quarrel, scuffle **9.** encounter
11. disturbance
affright . . . **5.** alarm, scare **6.** appall
(appal), dismay **7.** confuse, startle,
terrify **8.** frighten
affront . . . **4.** defy, face, meet, slap
5. abuse **6.** harass, insult, offend,
oppose **7.** offense, outrage, provoke
8. confront, dishonor, envisage, ill-
treat, irritate **9.** encounter, humiliate,
indignity **11.** provocation
afghan (pert to) . . .
fox . . **6.** corsac
language . . **11.** Afghanistan
prince . . **4.** amir (ameer), emir (emeer)
rug . . **5.** Herat **6.** carpet
stitch . . **7.** crochet
wrap . . **7.** blanket (woolen)
Afghanistan . . .
capital . . **5.** Kabul
city . . **5.** Herat **8.** Kandahar
language . . **6.** Pushtu **7.** Persian
mountain . . **9.** Hindu Kush
Pass (famed) . . **6.** Khyber
pony . . **4.** yabu (yaboo)
religion . . **5.** Islam
river . . **5.** Indus
Africa . . . see also *African*
desert . . **6.** Libyan, Sahara **8.** Kalahari
gulf . . **4.** Aden **5.** Gabes, Sidra
island (largest) . . **10.** Madagascar
lake . . **6.** Nyassa **8.** Victoria
10. Tanganyika
Mt. . . **5.** Atlas, Kenya, Natal **7.** Stanley
8. Cameroon **9.** Ruwenzori
11. Kilimanjaro
river . . **4.** Nile **5.** Congo, Niger **7.** Senegal,
Zambezi
size (in world) . . **6.** second
African (pert to) . . .
charm, fetish . . **4.** juju **6.** grigri
drum . . **8.** bamboula
enclosure . . **4.** boma **5.** kraal
garment . . **4.** haik, tobe **6.** kaross
grass . . **7.** esparto
grassland . . **4.** veld (veldt) **8.** bushveld
harp (Nubian) . . **5.** nanga
hemp . . **3.** ife
herb . . **4.** ocra
instrument . . **4.** gora (gorah) **5.** nanga,
rebab **6.** balafo

language . . **3.** Ibo **4.** Zulu **5.** Bantu, Sotho,
Tonga **6.** Somali, Yoruba **7.** Ashanti
(Ashantee)
palm . . **6.** ronier **7.** palmyra
secret society . . **4.** Egbo **6.** Mau Mau
8. Bachichi (cannibal)
soldier . . **5.** spahi **6.** askari
sorcery . . **5.** obeah
spiritual power . . **4.** ngai
thong (rawhide) . . **4.** riem
tree . . **3.** oak **4.** akee, baku, cola
(kola), etua, shea **5.** artar, sassy, siris
6. baobab
African people (pert to) . . .
Islamitic sect . . **9.** Almohades
Natal . . **4.** Zulu **6.** kaffir **7.** Amazulu
people . . **3.** Ibo **4.** Arab, Boer, Copt,
Hutu, Kafa (Kaffa), Zulu **5.** Bantu,
Fulah, Negro, Pygmy, Tutsi **6.** Berber,
Kabyle, Nubian, Semite, Somali, Yoruba
7. Ashanti (Ashantee), Bushman,
Swahili **8.** Bechuana **9.** Hottentot
African wildlife (pert to) . . .
antelope . . **3.** gnu **4.** oryx **5.** addax,
eland, oribi **6.** dik-dik, impala, rhebok
7. blaubok (small), blesbok, gemsbok
10. duikerbuck, hartebeest
bird . . **4.** lory, taha **6.** weaver **8.** umbretti
9. beefeater, hammerkop
fly . . **4.** kivu **6.** tsetse
goat . . **5.** Capra
horse disease . . **5.** surra
mammal . . **8.** anteater, pangolin
monkey . . **4.** mona, waag **6.** baboon,
grivet, guenon **7.** guereza **8.** talapoin
peacock . . **5.** paauw
rhinoceros . . **6.** borele **7.** keitloa
rodent . . **4.** jird **5.** ratel
sheep . . **4.** zenu **5.** oudad (udad)
squirrel . . **5.** xerus
stork . . **6.** simbil **7.** marabou
toad . . **7.** Xenopus
worm . . **3.** loa
aft, after . . . **4.** anon, past, rear **5.** abaft,
later, since **6.** astern, behind **9.** posterior
10. subsequent, succeeding
after (pert to) . . .
all . . **11.** considering **12.** nevertheless
awhile . . **4.** anon **5.** later
breast (Zool) . . **10.** metathorax
date . . **8.** postdate
dinner . . **12.** postprandial
dinner coffee . . **9.** demitasse
prefix . . **4.** meta, post
aftermath . . . **4.** crop **5.** rowen
9. afterglow **12.** consequences
aftermost . . . **4.** last **7.** aftmost
8. hindmost, rearmost
afterpiece . . . **3.** act **4.** heel **5.** epode,
exode **8.** postlude **9.** aftercome,
afterpart, tailpiece
after song . . . **5.** epode
afterthought . . . **6.** regret, sequel
10. reflection **13.** arrière-pensée, second
thought
afterward, afterwards . . . **4.** next **5.** after,
later, since **6.** ensues **7.** by and by
9. afterhand **10.** thereafter **11.** in the
future **12.** subsequently
aga, agha . . . **5.** chief, title **9.** commander
agacant, agacante . . . **8.** exciting

11. provocative
agacella (Her) . . . 8. antelope
again . . . 2. re (pref) 3. yet 4. anew,
anon, back, over, then 5. ditto, newly,
often, recur 6. afresh, de novo, encore,
rather 7. freshly 8. eftsoons (eftsoon),
likewise, moreover, once more 9. twice
over 10. repeatedly, second time
11. furthermore
against . . . 2. on, to, vs 3. con, non
4. agin (dial), anti, upon 6. contra,
versus 7. counter, opposed, towards
8. averse to, converse, opposite
against the . . .
clock . . 4. race, time 7. in haste
current . . 8. upstream
grain . . 6. across 7. oblique 9. backwards
10. contrarily 11. unwillingly
law . . 7. illegal, illicit 8. wrongful
12. illegitimate
sun . . 16. counterclockwise
agal . . . 4. cord (Bedouin head wrap)
agalloch . . . 4. agar 5. aloes 7. linalon
8. calambac 9. eaglewood, lignaloes
agama, agamoid . . . 6. iguana, lizard
Agamemnon (pert to) . . .
brother . . 8. Menelaus
daughter . . 7. Electra 9. Iphigenia
father . . 6. Atreus
king of . . 7. Mycenae
rival . . 9. Aegisthus
son . . 7. Orestes
wife . . 12. Clytemnestra
wife's paramour . . 9. Aegisthus
agape . . . 4. agog, ajar 6. aghast,
gaping 7. curious, yawning 8. open-
eyed 9. expectant, love feast (Chr)
10. astonished, bewildered, breathless
agate . . . 3. taw 4. onyx, ruby, type 5. color
6. achate, marble (game), pebble,
quartz 10. birthstone, chalcedony
agave . . . 4. aloe 5. datil, istle 6. maguey,
mescal, pulque 8. henequen
age . . . 3. eon, era, old 4. aeon, date,
eral, eval, time 5. cycle, epoch, major,
minor, older, ripen 6. junior, mature,
mellow, modern, period, remote, senior
7. century, grow old 8. eternity, lifetime,
maturity 9. antiquate, senectude
10. generation
Age . . . 3. Air, Ice, Jet 4. Iron, Jazz,
Yuga 5. Azoic, Kalpa, Space, Steel,
Stone 6. Atomic, Bronze, Copper,
Eocene, Gilded, Golden, Heroic,
Silver 7. Glacial, Homeric, Miocene
8. Cambrian, Cenozoic, Mesozoic
10. Geological, Supersonic
11. Elizabethan
aged . . . 3. eld, old 5. anile, hoary, olden
6. feeble, infirm, senile 7. ancient,
elderly, Ogygian 8. gerontic
9. Nestorian 10. senectuous
agency . . . 5. means 6. action, medium,
office 8. function 9. operation
10. collection, commission, efficiency,
management 14. intermediation
15. instrumentality
agenda . . . 5. slate 6. docket 7. agendum
(sing), program 9. memoranda
14. memorandum book, things to be
done

agent . . . 3. spy 4. doer, test, tool 5. actor,
buyer, envoy, proxy 6. author, broker,
deputy, factor, medium 7. creator,
proctor, reagent, scalper 8. aumildar,
emissary, operator, salesman
9. canvasser, comprador, consignee,
go-between, operative 10. instrument,
originator 11. facilitator 12. intermediary
14. representative
Age of Reason . . . 7. Diderot 8. Voltaire
9. d'Alembert 10. philosophe
12. Encyclopedia 13. Enlightenment
Ages . . . 4. Dark 6. Middle
aggrandize . . . 5. add to, exalt 6. extend
7. advance, enhance, enlarge, glorify,
magnify, promote 8. increase
10. exaggerate
aggravate . . . 3. irk, nag, vex 4. miff,
rile, twit 5. anger, annoy, chafe, pique,
sting, taunt, tease, worry 6. nettle,
pester, ruffle, worsen 7. bedevil, disturb,
incense, magnify, provoke 8. heighten,
increase, irritate 9. infuriate, intensify
10. exasperate
aggravation . . . 6. bother 7. anguish,
torment, trouble 8. vexation
9. annoyance, worsening 10. affliction,
excitement, irritation, resentment
11. displeasure, provocation
12. exasperation 15. intensification
aggregate . . . 3. all, sum 4. mass 5. total,
whole 6. amount, volume 8. compound,
ensemble 9. accretion 10. collection
11. combination 12. accumulation
aggregate (pert to) . . .
definable member . . 4. unit
fruit . . 7. etaerio
in the . . 7. en masse, totally 8. together
12. collectively
of plants . . 5. flock, flora 7. cluster
aggregation . . . 4. heap 5. group, union
9. congeries 10. assemblage, collection
11. combination 12. accumulation,
amalgamation 13. consolidation
aggression . . . 6. attack, injury 7. assault,
offense 8. invasion 9. hostility,
intrusion, offensive 10. enterprise,
initiative 11. provocation
12. encroachment 13. aggressiveness
aggressive . . . 7. hostile, pushing
9. assertive, attacking, bellicose,
combative, offensive 10. assaulting,
pugnacious 11. belligerent, contentious,
provocative 12. enterprising
aggrieve . . . 4. pain 6. grieve 7. afflict,
oppress, trouble 9. displease, persecute,
tyrannize
aggrieved . . . 6. pained, woeful 7. doleful
8. mournful 9. sorrowful 10. displeased
aghast . . . 4. agog 5. agape 6. afraid
8. appalled, dismayed 9. astounded,
horrified, terrified 10. astonished
agile . . . 4. fast, spry 5. alert, brisk, quick,
ready, swift 6. active, lively, nimble,
prompt, supple 7. lissome, springe
11. expeditious
aging . . . 6. doting, fading 8. maturing,
ripening 9. mellowing, senescent
10. senescence
agio . . . 7. premium 8. discount, exchange
9. brokerage 13. money changing

agitate . . . **3.** fan, jar, wey **4.** fret, move, plot, rile, stir **5.** alarm, churn, rouse, shake, upset **6.** debate, devise, excite, foment, incite, ruffle **7.** canvass, perturb, revolve, trouble **8.** disquiet, distract, distress **10.** discompose
agitated . . . **7.** anxious, excited, ruffled **8.** alarming, troubled **9.** disturbed, perturbed, turbulent **10.** distressed **11.** discomposed, overwrought
agitation . . . **4.** fury, rage, stir **5.** alarm, storm **6.** debate, dither, foment, frenzy, furore, hubbub, tumult, unrest, uproar **7.** anxiety, flutter, shaking, turmoil **8.** disorder, distress, upheaval, vexation **9.** commotion, trepidity **10.** discussion, excitement, incitement, turbulence **11.** disturbance, fomentation, trepidation **12.** deliberation, perturbation, restlessness
agnate . . . **3.** sib **4.** akin **6.** allied **7.** connate, kindred, related (father's side) **10.** equiparent **11.** correlative **14.** consanguineous
agnomen . . . **4.** name **5.** alias, nomen **7.** epithet, surname **8.** nickname
agnus castus (Eccl) . . . **4.** lamb **6.** chaste **14.** tree of chastity
Agnus Dei, Lamb of God . . . **4.** disk **6.** anthem, prayer **7.** the Mass (part)
ago, agone . . . **2.** by **4.** erst, gone, over, past, yore **5.** since **6.** bygone, passed **7.** extinct
agog . . . **4.** avid, keen **5.** agape, astir, eager **6.** lively, wonder **7.** all eyes, curious, excited, zestful **8.** open-eyed, vigilant **9.** expectant, impatient **10.** astonished, breathless
agonize . . . **4.** pain, rack **6.** grieve, harrow, strive **7.** crucify, torture **8.** struggle **10.** excruciate
agony . . . **4.** pain, pang, rack **5.** grief, gripe, panic, throe **7.** anguish, torment, torture **8.** distress **9.** suffering **11.** crucifixion
agrarian . . . **5.** rural **6.** rustic, sylvan (silvan) **7.** bucolic, hoosier **8.** agrestic, Arcadian, frontier, pastoral **10.** campestral, hinterland, provincial **11.** countrified **12.** agricultural
agree . . . **3.** fit **4.** give, jive, make, rime, side **5.** chime, ditto, grant, match, rhyme, tally **6.** accede, accord, assent, commit, comply, concur, engage, submit **7.** bargain, comport, concede, conform, consent, promise **8.** coincide, contract **9.** acquiesce, harmonize, stipulate **10.** coordinate, correspond
agreeable . . . **4.** nice **5.** amene, sapid, suave **6.** comely, dulcet, savory **7.** amiable, likable, welcome, willing **8.** charming, friendly, obliging, pleasant, pleasing **9.** accordant, compliant, desirable, indulgent **10.** acceptable, compatible, concordant, consenting, euphonious, harmonious **11.** conformable, considerate **12.** reconcilable, satisfactory
agreement . . . **4.** mise, pact **5.** terms **6.** accord, assent, cartel, parity, treaty, unison **7.** bargain, compact,

concord, consent, entente, promise, rapport **8.** contract, covenant, identity **9.** accession, consensus **10.** accordment, comparison, compliance, conformity, similarity **11.** coincidence, concurrence, parallelism, stipulation
agrestic . . . **5.** rural **6.** rustic **7.** bucolic **8.** pastoral **10.** provincial
agriculture . . . **7.** culture, farming, tillage **8.** agrology, agronomy **9.** husbandry **10.** agrotechny **11.** cultivation **13.** sharecropping
agriculture (pert to) . . .
goddess of . . **3.** Ops **4.** Gaea (Gaia) **5.** Ceres, Flora **6.** Pomona, Vacuna **7.** Demeter
god of . . **4.** Nabu, Nebo **6.** Faunus **8.** Dionysus
means of . . **3.** hoe **4.** plow (plough) **6.** harrow, header, reaper, seeder **7.** combine, planter, tractor **8.** thrasher **10.** cultivator **11.** caterpillar
ref to . . **7.** georgic
science, crop growing . . **11.** arviculture
terms . . **5.** arado, grove, ranch, thorp **6.** garden, hamlet **7.** cropper, orchard **8.** haymaker, vineyard **9.** homestead
agriculturist . . . **6.** farmer **7.** planter **10.** agricolist, husbandman
Agrippina's son . . . **4.** Nero
agrise . . . **5.** abhor, dread **6.** loathe **7.** shudder, terrify, tremble **8.** affright
agronomy, study of . . . **11.** agriculture
aground . . . **5.** stuck **6.** ashore **7.** swamped, wrecked **8.** grounded, stranded **10.** high and dry
agrypnia . . . **5.** vigil **8.** insomnia **13.** sleeplessness
agua . . . **4.** toad **5.** water
aguacate . . . **7.** avocado
ague . . . **5.** chill, fever **7.** disease, malaria, shaking, shivers **9.** shivering
ague tree . . . **9.** sassafras
agueweed . . . **7.** boneset, gentian
Ahab (pert to) . . .
daughter . . **7.** Athalie
king of . . **6.** Israel
wife . . **7.** Jezebel
ahead . . . **2.** on **3.** pre (pref) **4.** fore **5.** afore, early **6.** before, onward **7.** advance, forward, leading **10.** successful, surpassing
ahoy . . . **4.** hail, yo-ho **5.** hello **8.** ship ahoy **9.** attention
ahu . . . **5.** mound **7.** gazelle **8.** memorial
ai . . . **5.** sloth **11.** exclamation
aid . . . **4.** abet, aide, help, pony **5.** allay, devil (printer's), favor, serve **6.** assist, helper, incite, relief, remedy, succor **7.** benefit, service, stipend, subsidy, support **8.** befriend, ministry **9.** alleviate, allowance, assistant **10.** assistance, benefactor **11.** countenance **13.** accommodation
aim . . . **3.** end, fix, way **4.** bent, goal, plan **5.** point, scope **6.** aspire, direct, intend, intent, object, strive **7.** bearing, current, meaning, purpose **8.** endeavor **9.** direction, intention, objective **11.** destination

aimful ... 8. aspiring 10. purposeful
aimless ... 4. idle 5. blind, loose
6. chance, random 8. drifting
9. desultory, orderless, senseless
10. designless, unarranged, undirected
11. meaningless, purposeless,
unorganized
aine ... 5. elder 6. senior
air ... 3. gas, oam, sky 4. aria, aura,
mien, tune, wind 5. draft, ether, ozone,
vapor 6. aerate, aerial, aspect, breath,
breeze, bubble, manner, melody,
oxygen 7. aerator, bearing, climate,
display, hyaline, posture, publish,
refresh 8. attitude, aviation, behavior,
buoyance, demeanor, hydrogen,
presence 9. lightness, publicize,
ventilate 10. appearance, atmosphere,
deportment, navigation 11. haughtiness
12. stratosphere
air (pert to) ...
disease .. 5. bends 7. caisson
12. aeroembolism
music .. 4. aria, lilt, solo, tune 6. melody
7. arietta, sortita
passage .. 4. duct, flue, vent 7. pharynx
9. ventiduct
pressure unit .. 8. millebar
stone .. 8. aerolite 9. meteorite
term .. 5. aural 6. flight, flying 9. jet
stream, katabatic 11. aeronautics
tight .. 5. close, proof 6. sealed
7. compact 8. hermetic 9. resistant
11. impermeable
travel .. 6. jet lag 7. skyjack
aircraft ... 3. jet 4. kite, link 5. avion,
blimp 6. bomber, glider 7. airship,
aviette, balloon, biplane, chopper
8. airplane, jetliner, triplane, turbojet,
zeppelin 9. amphibian, dirigible, fixed-
wing, monoplane, orthopter, simulator,
spaceship, transport, turboprop
10. helicopter, hydroplane, whirlybird
aircraft (pert to) ...
carrier .. 7. flattop
designer .. 8. Sikorsky
formation .. 5. fleet 7. echelon
inventor .. 6. Wright (Brothers)
motorless .. 6. glider
part .. 3. fin, pod 4. keel, tail, wing
5. rotor 6. cabane 7. aileron, cockpit,
nacelle 8. fusilage 9. empennage (tail)
airily ... 5. gaily 6. thinly 7. lightly, loftily
8. jauntily 10. delicately
13. pretentiously 14. ostentatiously
airiness ... 6. rarity 7. tenuity 8. delicacy
9. gauziness, gustiness, lightness,
loftiness, unreality, windiness
10. breeziness, jauntiness
16. lightheartedness, unsubstantiality
airing ... 4. walk 8. exposure
air mail ... 8. par avion
airport (pert to) ... 4. beam, dock, gate,
shed, taxi 5. apron, pylon, tower
6. hangar, runway, skycap 7. airpost,
fairway, jetport, taxiway 8. airfield,
airstrip, heliport 9. aerodrome
(airdrome), helidrome
airy ... 3. gay 4. aery, cool, rare,
thin 5. foamy, light, lofty, merry,
windy 6. aerial, breezy, drafty, frothy,

jaunty, lively 7. gaseous, haughty,
soaring 8. animated, aspiring, delicate,
ethereal, fanciful, feathery, flippant,
towering, volatile 9. gossamery,
vivacious 10. chimerical, phantasmal
11. atmospheric 12. lighthearted,
ostentatious
aiseweed ... 8. goutweed
aisle ... 4. lane, nave 5. alley 6. artery,
avenue 7. passage 8. corridor
10. passageway
ait, eyot ... 3. oat 4. holm, isle, reef
5. atoll, islet 6. island
aitu ... 3. god 5. demon 6. spirit
Aix ... 4. duck
aizle ... 4. soot 5. ember, spark
Ajax (pert to) ...
called .. 11. Ajax the Less (next swiftest
to Achilles)
father .. 7. Telamen
hero of .. 8. The Iliad (Homer)
ajonjoli ... 6. sesame
a k a ... 5. alias
akimbo ... 4. bent 6. angled, hooked
7. angular, crooked
akin ... 3. sib 4. like, near 5. close
6. agnate, allied 7. cognate, germane,
kindred, related, similar 9. connected
10. correlated 14. consanguineous
ala ... 4. wing 8. winglike
a la ... 2. so 4. thus 11. identically 13. in
the manner of
Alabama ...
capital .. 10. Montgomery
Capitol, Confederate (2 months) ..
10. White House (1st 1861)
carnival .. 11. Azalea Trail
city .. 6. Mobile 7. Gadsden
10. Birmingham
monument .. 11. Russell Cave
museum .. 22. George Washington
Carver
native woman (famed) .. 11. Helen Keller
President Confederate .. 5. Davis
(Jefferson)
State admission .. 12. Twenty-second
State bird .. 12. yellowhammer
State flower .. 8. camellia
State motto .. 21. We Dare Defend Our
Rights
State nickname .. 12. Heart of Dixie
statue (huge) .. 6. Vulcan
alabaster ... 6. gypsum, marble
7. mineral
alacrity ... 4. zest 7. avidity 9. briskness,
eagerness, immediacy, quickness,
readiness, swiftness 10. promptness
11. promptitude, punctuality,
willingness 13. sprightliness
Aladdin (pert to) ...
possessor of (magic) .. 4. lamp, ring
spirit (of Magic) .. 4. jinn
window .. 4. task (impossible)
youth (character) .. 13. Arabian Nights
á la diable ... 7. deviled (devilled)
8. seasoned
alameda ... 4. mall, walk 5. prado
9. esplanade, promenade
Alamo ... 6. poplar (tree) 7. Mission
(San Antonio, Tex)
a la mode ... 4. mode 5. smart 6. modish,

spruce **7.** fashion, stylish, voguish
8. up-to-date **9.** stylishly **11.** fashionably
12. with ice cream
alan . . . **3.** dog (Her)
alar (pert to) . . . **4.** wing **6.** pteric
8. axillary, shoulder
alarm . . . **3.** din **4.** call, fear, flap
5. alert, broil, clock, daunt, panic,
scare **6.** alarum, arouse, dismay, fright,
terror, tocsin **7.** startle, terrify, warning
8. affright, frighten **11.** trepidation
12. apprehension **13.** consternation
alarmist . . . **6.** scarer **9.** pessimist, terrorist
10. frightener **11.** scaremonger
alas . . . **2.** ah, ay, oh **3.** ach, heu, och
4. oime **5.** alack, ohone **6.** dear me
7. woe is me **8.** lackaday
Alaska . . . see also *Alaskan*
capital . . **6.** Juneau
city . . **4.** Nome **5.** Sitka **7.** Skagway
9. Anchorage, Fairbanks, Ketchikan
discoverer . . **11.** Vitus Bering
fish . . **6.** salmon, wachna **7.** inconnu
glacier . . **4.** Muir
highway . . **5.** Alcan **6.** Alaska
island . . **6.** Kodiak, Unimak **7.** Diomede
(Little), Nunivak **9.** Aleutians, Probilofs
mountain . . **3.** Ada **7.** Foraker **8.** McKinley
(highest in N Am), Wrangell
northernmost point . . **11.** Point Barrow
oil region . . **10.** Prudhoe Bay
peninsula . . **5.** Kenai **6.** Seward
port (oil) . . **6.** Valdez
rapids . . **10.** Whitehorse
river . . **5.** Yukon **9.** Kuskokwim
State admission . . **10.** Forty-ninth
State bird . . **9.** (willow) ptarmigan
State flower . . **11.** forget-me-not
State symbol . . **9.** bald eagle
strait . . **6.** Bering
volcano . . **6.** Katmai **8.** Wrangell
Alaskan (pert to) . . .
boat . . **5.** kayak, umiak **7.** bidarka
(bidarkee)
codfish . . **6.** wachna
liquor . . **9.** hoochinoo
people . . **3.** Aht **5.** Aleut, Haida, Tinna
6. Ahtena, Eskimo **7.** Tlingit **8.** Aleutian
9. Tsimpsean **10.** Athapascan
albacore . . . **4.** tuna **5.** tunny **6.** bonito,
germon
Albania . . .
capital . . **6.** Tirana
city . . **5.** Berat **6.** Durres, Valona **7.** Scutari
8. Elbasani
dialect . . **4.** Gheg, Tosk
lake . . **6.** Prespa **7.** Scutari
mountain . . **5.** Koreb **6.** Pindus
river . . **4.** Drin **6.** Bojana
soldier . . **7.** palikar
triba . . **4.** Cham
albatross . . . **5.** nelly (sooty) **6.** burden
7. pelican **9.** mallemuck
albatross around the neck . . . **6.** burden
8. distress (cause of)
albe (anc) . . . **5.** album
albert (pert to) . . .
jewelry . . **10.** watch chain
medal . . **4.** gold (for bravery)
Albion . . . **7.** England (Poet)
albumin . . . **5.** glair **7.** protein

9. endosperm
alcazar . . . **6.** palace **8.** fortress
alchemy . . . **5.** magic **6.** change **7.** sorcery
10. changeover, conversion
alcohol . . . **5.** drink **6.** liquor **7.** ethanol,
spirits, talitol, terpene **8.** beverage
9. aqua vitae, firewater **10.** intoxicant
alcoholic beverage . . . **3.** gin, rum
4. beer, brew, grog, malt, mead,
wine **5.** booze, hooch, negus, punch,
vodka **6.** arrack (arrak), brandy, mao-
tai, whisky (whiskey) **7.** bourbon,
cordial, liqueur, tequila **8.** champers
(Brit sl), cocktail, highball **9.** applejack,
champagne, moonshine
alcoholism . . . **9.** addiction, oenomania
10. dipsomania **11.** drunkenness
12. intoxication
Alcott character . . . **2.** Jo **3.** Amy, Meg
4. Beth
alcove . . . **3.** bay **4.** cove, nook **5.** arbor,
bower, kiosk, niche, oriel **6.** carrel,
recess **7.** cubicle, dinette, pergola
8. alhacena
alder (pert to) . . .
chief . . **5.** ruler **6.** prince
fishing . . **3.** fly (artificial)
tree . . **8.** sagerose (yellow)
ale . . . **3.** mum **4.** beer, flip **5.** stout
6. alegar, liquor (malt) **8.** festival
alee . . . **7.** leeward (opp of windward)
Aleppo (pert to) . . .
city . . **5.** Syria
grass . . **7.** Johnson
stone . . **3.** gem **5.** agate **8.** eye agate
alert . . . **4.** keen, warn, wary **5.** agile,
alarm, alive, aware, brisk, peart (pert),
quick, ready, sharp **6.** active, bright,
lively, nimble, prompt **7.** guarded
8. vigilant, watchful **9.** attentive,
observant, sprightly, wide-awake
11. circumspect
Aleut . . . **4.** Atka **6.** Eskimo **7.** Unungun
8. Unalaska
Aleutians . . .
islands (chain) . . **8.** volcanic
native of . . **5.** Aleut
site . . **6.** Alaska **9.** Bering Sea
alewife . . . **4.** fish **7.** herring, pompano,
walleye **9.** gaspereau
Alexander the Great (pert to) . . .
birthplace . . **5.** Pella (Macedonia)
conqueror of . . **6.** Persia
expedition . . **10.** Hellespont
horse . . **10.** Bucephalus
Alexandria, Egypt . . .
bishop . . **5.** Arius **10.** Athanasius
12. Eratosthenes
island . . **6.** Pharos
obelisks . . **17.** Cleopatra's Needles (now
in NY City & London)
ruler . . **7.** Ptolemy
world wonder . . **10.** Lighthouse (Pharos)
alfa . . . **5.** grass **7.** esparto
alfalfa . . . **3.** hay **5.** medic **6.** clover,
fodder **7.** lucerne (lucern)
alforja . . . **3.** bag **5.** pouch **6.** wallet
9. saddlebag
alfresco . . . **4.** airy **7.** open-air, outside
alga, algae . . . **4.** cell, moss, nori
5. Dasya, fungi **6.** Alaria, diatom, fungus

7. seaweed 8. plankton 9. spirulina, stonewort

Algeria . . .
capital . . 7. Algiers
Mohammedan saint . . 8. Marabout
monastery . . 5. ribat
mountain . . 5. Atlas (Range)
native . . 5. Arabs 7. Berbers, Kabyles
ruler . . 3. bey, dey
ship . . 5. xebec
soldier . . 5. spahi (spahee) 6. Zouave

algid . . . 3. icy 4. cold 5. brisk, crisp, nippy
6. frigid, frosty, wintry 7. ice-cold

algodon . . . 6. cotton

algology, study of . . . 5. algae
8. seaweeds

Algonquian spirit . . . 6. manito (manitou)

Algonquian people . . . 4. Cree, Sauk
5. Miami 6. Ottawa 7. Arapaho,
Ojibway, Shawnee 8. Cheyenne,
Delaware 9. Blackfoot

Alhambra (pert to) . . .
architecture . . 7. Moorish
palace, alcazar of . . 12. Moorish Kings
site . . 7. Granada (Spain)

alias . . . 6. anonym 7. epithet
8. cognomen, nickname 9. otherwise,
pseudonym, sobriquet

Ali Baba (pert to) . . .
adventurer . . 4. cave (Forty Thieves)
password to cave . . 6. Sesame
tale . . 13. Arabian Nights

alien . . . 3. ger 5. fremd 6. exotic,
remote 7. adverse, foreign, hostile,
opposed, strange 8. outsider, stranger
9. foreigner, peregrine, unrelated
10. extraneous, unfriendly
11. incongruous

alienate . . . 4. part, wean 6. demise,
detach, devest, divest, divide
8. disunite, estrange, separate

alienation . . . 4. outs 5. split 6. breach
8. disfavor 10. conveyance, falling-
out, withdrawal 12. amortization,
disaffection, estrangement

alienist . . . 12. psychiatrist

aliform . . . 8. winglike 10. wing-shaped

alight . . . 4. land, rest, stop 5. ditch, lodge,
perch 6. settle 7. burning, descend,
lighted 8. dismount

align, aline . . . 4. true 5. level, match
6. equate, line up 7. arrange, marshal
10. collineate, straighten 11. parallelize

alike . . . 3. iso (comb form) 4. akin,
like, same, twin 7. similar, uniform
8. selfsame 9. duplicate, identical
10. homonymous 17. indistinguishable

aliment . . . 4. food, keep 5. broma,
manna 7. nurture, pabulum, support
9. nutriment, nutrition, refection
10. sustenance 11. nourishment,
refreshment

alimentary canal, part . . . 5. mouth
7. pharynx, stomach 9. esophagus,
intestine

alimony . . . 7. stipend 8. estovers
9. allotment

aline . . . see *align*

alipin . . . 5. slave (Phil)

alipod . . . 3. bat 10. wing-footed

aliquid . . . 8. somewhat 9. something

aliquot . . . 4. part 5. prime 7. decimal,
digital, divisor, partial 10. fractional,
reciprocal 11. submultiple (opp of
aliquant)

alive . . . 3. vif 4. keen 5. alert, awake,
brisk, vital 6. extant, lively, loving, zoetic
7. animate, current, topical 8. animated,
existent 9. breathing, conscious,
sensitive, sprightly 11. clear-witted,
unforgotten

alkali . . . 3. lye 4. salt, soda 8. saltwort

alkaline . . . 3. reh 4. usar 6. alkali
7. antacid, nonacid

alkaline forming . . . 10. kaligenous

alkaloid . . . 6. codein, conine, eserin
7. aricine, caffein, cocaine, codeine
8. atropine, morphine 10. strychnine
13. physostigmine

alkaloid (pert to) . . .
bark . . 7. aricine
bean . . 13. physostigmine
beverage . . 8. caffeine (caffein)
drug . . 7. cocaine, codeine, eucaine
8. morphine 10. strychnine
extract . . 6. curare (curari) 11. arrow
poison
hemlock . . 7. coniine
ipecac . . 7. emetine
lupine . . 8. lupinine
mustard seed . . 7. sinapin

all . . . 3. pan (pref), sum 4. omni (pref),
only, toto 5. alone, every, sum of,
total, tutti, whole 6. entire, wholly
7. perfect 8. ensemble, entirely, totality
9. aggregate, everybody 10. altogether,
completely, everything, thoroughly
11. exclusively

all (pert to) . . .
absorbing . . 4. main 5. chief, prime
6. ruling 7. capital, leading, primary
8. foremost 9. paramount, principal
11. controlling
around . . 5. handy 9. versatile
devouring . . 6. greedy 9. rapacious
10. gluttonous
in all . . 9. generally 10. on the whole
inclusive . . 6. global 7. omneity
8. catholic, ecumenic, pandemic
9. universal 12. cosmopolitan
knowing . . 4. wise 6. divine
10. omniscient
powerful . . 6. divine 7. all-wise, supreme
8. absolute, almighty 9. all-seeing
10. all-knowing, omnipotent,
omniscient, ubiquitous
the same . . 9. identical 10. equivalent
12. nevertheless
together . . 7. en masse

Allah . . . 3. God 5. deity 12. Supreme
Being

allay . . . 4. cool, ease 5. abate, check, slake
6. pacify, soothe, subdue 7. appease,
assuage, compose, relieve, repress,
satisfy 8. moderate 9. alleviate

allée . . . 4. mall, walk 5. aisle 6. avenue
7. passage

allege . . . 4. aver, cite 5. offer, plead,
quote, state 6. adduce, affirm, assert,
assign 7. advance, ascribe, declare,
present, pretend, profess, propose
8. maintain 9. attribute

allegiance . . . **3.** tie **4.** bond **5.** faith, liege **6.** fealty, homage **7.** loyalty **8.** devotion, fidelity, firmness **9.** adherence, constancy **12.** faithfulness **13.** steadfastness

allegory . . . **5.** fable, story **6.** emblem **7.** parable **8.** apologue

alleviate . . . **4.** ease **5.** abate, allay, erase, quiet, salve, slake **6.** lessen, pacify, reduce, soften, solace, soothe **7.** assuage, compose, lighten, relieve **8.** mitigate, moderate, palliate **9.** extenuate **11.** tranquilize

alley . . . **3.** mig (marble), way **4.** lane, mall, path, slum **5.** aisle, byway, tewer **6.** arcade, artery, byroad **8.** cul-de-sac

alliance . . . **4.** pact **5.** union **6.** fusion, league, treaty **7.** compact, entente **8.** affinity, agnation, covenant **9.** coalition **10.** federation **11.** association, combination, confederacy **13.** confederation

allied . . . **4.** akin **6.** agnate, linked, united **7.** cognate, germane, kindred, leagued, related, similar **10.** associated, correlated

alligator . . . **5.** gator, niger **6.** Caiman, cayman, jacare (yacare) **7.** lagarto **9.** crocodile

alligator pear . . . **7.** avocado **8.** aguacate

alliteration . . . **4.** rime **5.** rhyme **6.** jingle **9.** assonance **10.** repetition

allocate . . . **4.** deal, mete **5.** allot **6.** assign, locate, ordain **7.** appoint, arrange, consign, reserve **9.** apportion **10.** distribute

allocation . . . **8.** disposal **9.** billeting **11.** collocation, disposition **12.** distribution

allot . . . **3.** fix **4.** cast, dole, mete **5.** grant **6.** assign, billet, design, intend, ordain, ration, select **7.** appoint, destine, specify **9.** apportion, attribute, prescribe **11.** appropriate

allotment . . . **5.** cavel, share **6.** ration **7.** subsidy **10.** allocation, assignment, ordainment **13.** apportionment

allow . . . **3.** let **4.** bear, give **5.** admit, think **6.** endure, permit, rebate, suffer **7.** approve, concede, suppose **8.** consider, discount, tolerate **9.** authorize **11.** acknowledge

allowance . . . **3.** fee **4.** tare, tret **5.** arras, grant **6.** ration **7.** pension, scalage, stipend **8.** appenage (prince's), discount, granting, sanction **9.** admitting, allotment, conceding, tolerance **10.** permission **11.** scholarship **13.** authorization

allowing for . . . **2.** if **8.** provided

allow to pass . . . **5.** lapse **6.** expire, revert

alloy . . . **3.** mix **4.** asem **5.** blend, mokum **6.** billon, fusion, oroide **7.** amalgam, bullion, corrupt, mixture **8.** compound **9.** composite **10.** adulterate, amalgamate

alloys . . .
copper, aluminum . . **9.** duralumin
copper, sulphur . . **6.** niello
copper, tin . . **6.** bronze

copper, white metal . . **6.** oroide
copper, zinc . . **5.** brass **6.** tombac
copper, zinc, iron . . **4.** Aich (Chin)
copper, zinc, nickel . . **4.** iron **7.** paktong (packtong)
copper, zinc, nickel, iron . . **7.** rheotan
German silver . . **6.** albata
gold, silver . . **4.** asem
iron, carbon . . **5.** steel
iron, nickel . . **6.** Calite (trademark)
lead, tin . . **6.** pewter, solder
nickel, steel . . **5.** Invar

All Saints' Day . . . **4.** Nov 1 **10.** Allhallows

allspice tree . . . **7.** pimento

alltud . . . **5.** alien, slave **9.** foreigner

allude . . . **4.** hint **5.** get at, imply, point, refer **6.** relate **7.** mention, suggest **8.** indicate, intimate **9.** insinuate

allure . . . **3.** win **4.** bait, draw, lead, lure, tice, tole **5.** charm, decoy, snare, tempt **6.** entice, entrap, invite, seduce **7.** attract, prevail **8.** inveigle, persuade **9.** captivate, fascinate, influence

allurement . . . **4.** bait, lure **5.** bride **7.** glamour (glamor) **8.** agacerie, coquetry **10.** attraction, enticement, inducement, temptation **12.** inveiglement

allusion . . . **4.** clue, hint **7.** inkling **8.** innuendo, instance **9.** reference **11.** implication

alluvial deposit . . . **3.** mud **4.** silt **5.** delta, geest **6.** placer

ally . . . **3.** pal **4.** aide, join **5.** union **6.** fellow, friend, league **7.** comrade, consort, kinsman, partner **8.** adherent, relative **9.** associate, attendant, colleague **10.** accomplice **11.** confederate **12.** collaborator

Alma (lt) . . . **4.** soul **6.** spirit **10.** cherishing, nourishing

alma . . . **6.** fabric (silk)

almacen . . . **4.** shop **8.** magazine **9.** warehouse

Alma Mater . . . **6.** school **7.** college **9.** goddesses **10.** university

almanac . . . **5.** fasti **6.** record **7.** calends (kalends) **8.** calendar, register **9.** ephemeris (obs)

almighty . . . **5.** great **6.** divine **10.** omnipotent **11.** all-powerful **12.** irresistible

almond (pert to) . . .
confection . . **8.** marzipan
dish with . . **8.** amandine
liqueur . . **8.** amaretto

almost . . . **4.** most, nigh **5.** anear, close **6.** all but, nearly **8.** well-nigh **9.** nearabout **13.** approximately

alms . . . **4.** dole, mite **6.** aumous, bounty, corban, relief **7.** charity, handout **8.** donation, gratuity, pittance **12.** contribution, philanthropy

alms (pert to) . . .
box . . **4.** arca **5.** chest
giver . . **5.** donor **7.** almoner **11.** contributor **14.** philanthropist
man . . **5.** donee **6.** pauper **7.** feoffee **9.** pensioner

alodium . . . **4.** land **6.** tenure **8.** freehold **10.** real estate

aloe, aloes ... **4.** drug **5.** agave, plant
  6. tambac **7.** incense **8.** agalloch
aloft ... **2.** up **4.** high, over **5.** aloof
  7. skyward **8.** overhead
aloha ... **4.** hail, love **7.** good-bye
  9. affection, greetings **11.** salutations
Aloha State ... **6.** Hawaii
aloin ... **4.** drug **5.** aloes **8.** nataloin
  9. barbaloin (Barbados) **12.** isobarbaloin
alone ... **4.** solo **5.** apart, solus **6.** single,
  singly, solely, unique **8.** desolate,
  homeless, isolated, separate, solitary
  9. exclusive, matchless **10.** unassisted
  12. single-handed **13.** companionless,
  independently, unaccompanied
along ... **2.** on **3.** via **4.** with **6.** beside,
  onward **7.** forward **8.** together
alongside ... **2.** by **4.** near **6.** beside
  7. abreast **8.** parallel
aloof ... **6.** offish, remote **7.** distant,
  haughty **8.** reserved **10.** unsociable
  11. indifferent, standoffish
  15. uncommunicative
aloofness ... **7.** reserve **10.** offishness,
  remoteness **11.** haughtiness
  12. indifference **13.** unsociability
alopecia ... **6.** acomia **8.** baldness
  12. hairlessness
aloud ... **4.** oral **6.** loudly **7.** audibly,
  plainly
alp ... **3.** tor **4.** peak, pico, pike **6.** summit
  8. mountain **9.** bullfinch
alp (Teut Folklore) ... **5.** demon, witch
  9. nightmare
alpaca ... **4.** coat, paco **5.** llama
  7. garment
Alph ... **11.** sacred river (Kubla Khan)
alpha ... **4.** star **5.** prime **6.** letter **7.** initial,
  numeral **9.** beginning
alphabet ... **4.** ABC's **6.** Sarada (Kashmir)
  9. abecedary **10.** Davanagari (Sanskrit)
alphabet characters (Teut) ... **4.** ogam,
  rune
alphabetize ... **4.** file **5.** group, index
  6. codify, letter **8.** classify, tabulate
  9. catalogue (catalog) **10.** categorize
alpha test (Army) ... **12.** intelligence
alpine ... **5.** alpen, hilly **6.** knobby
  10. alpestrine **11.** mountainous
Alpine (pert to) ...
  climber .. **10.** alpestrian
  dance .. **7.** gavotte (gavot)
  dress .. **6.** dirndl
  dwelling .. **6.** chalet
  goat .. **4.** ibex
  herdsman .. **4.** senn
  peak .. **5.** Blanc **9.** Monte Rosa
  10. Matterhorn
  plant ... **9.** edelweiss
  province .. **5.** Tyrol
  shelter .. **7.** hospice
  snowfield .. **4.** firn, neve
  tunnel .. **7.** Simplon **10.** St Gotthard
  wind .. **4.** bise **5.** foehn
Alps ... **5.** Blanc, Tirol (Tyrol) **6.** Julian
  7. Dinaric **8.** Jungfrau **9.** Dolomites,
  Monte Rosa (peak) **10.** Matterhorn
already ... **3.** ere, yet **5.** afore **6.** before
  7. earlier **8.** hitherto **10.** heretofore
  11. theretofore
also ... **2.** as, et, so **3.** and, too, yet

4. more, plus **7.** besides, further
  8. likewise, moreover **9.** similarly
  11. furthermore
altar (pert to) ...
  boy .. **7.** acolyte
  cloth .. **6.** dossal (dossel) **7.** haploma
  9. ependytes
  constellation .. **3.** Ara
  curtain .. **6.** riddel
  end of church .. **4.** apse **7.** chancel
  Greek .. **5.** bomos **6.** hestia **7.** eschara
  Latin .. **7.** scrobis
  ledge .. **7.** retable
  platform .. **8.** predella
  screen .. **7.** reredos
  shelf, table .. **6.** gradin **7.** retable
  8. credence
  step .. **8.** predella
  top slab .. **5.** mensa
alter ... **4.** geld, vary, veer **5.** amend,
  emend, reset, shift **6.** adjust, change,
  immute, modify, mutate, revise **7.** falsify
  8. castrate **9.** transform
alteration ... **6.** change **9.** diversity,
  variation **10.** castration, correction
  12. modification **13.** interpolation
  15. diversification
altercation ... **3.** row **4.** feud, spat,
  tiff **5.** fight, snarl **6.** fracas, strife
  7. dispute, quarrel, wrangle **8.** squabble,
  vendetta **9.** imbroglio **10.** contention
  11. controversy
alter ego ... **4.** mate, self, twin **7.** oneself
  10. complement **11.** counterpart
alternate ... **4.** vary **5.** proxy **6.** change,
  deputy, rotate, seesaw **7.** reverse,
  stand-in **8.** delegate **9.** oscillate
  10. substitute **11.** alternative,
  interchange, reciprocate
alternate writing mode (anc) ...
  13. boustrophedon
alternative ... **2.** or **3.** nor **5.** other
  6. choice, either, option, switch
  7. dilemma **8.** election, loophole
  9. secondary **10.** nip-and-tuck,
  preference, substitute **11.** replacement
although, altho ... **4.** even, when **5.** while
  6. albeit, though **7.** despite, whereas
  15. notwithstanding
altimetry ... **6.** height **10.** hypsometry
  11. measurement
altitude ... **6.** height (highth) **7.** heroics,
  stature **8.** eminence, highness, tallness
  9. elevation, loftiness
altogether ... **5.** fully, quite **6.** bodily,
  wholly **7.** utterly **8.** entirely, outright
  9. generally **10.** completely, thoroughly
  12. collectively
alto horn ... **7.** althorn, saxhorn
  10. mellophone
altruism ... **7.** charity, concern **8.** kindness
  11. beneficence, benevolence
  12. philanthropy
aluminum ore ... **7.** bauxite
alumnus (alumni) ... **4.** grad **5.** pupil
  6. alumna (alumnae) **8.** graduate,
  postgrad **12.** postgraduate
alveary ... **4.** hive **6.** apiary **7.** beehive
alveola ... **3.** dip, pit **4.** pore, sink **6.** crater,
  pocket
alveolar ... **6.** pitted, pocked **7.** notched

8. indented 9. depressed
always . . . 2. ay 3. aye, e'er 4. ever
6. anyway, semper 7. forever
8. evermore 9. eternally, uniformly
10. constantly, invariably
11. continually, everlasting, perpetually,
universally
ama . . . 4. tree 5. amula (Bib) 6. vessel
amabile . . . 6. gentle, tender 9. agreeable
Amadis de Gaul (Arthurian) . . . 4. hero
5. lover
amadou . . . 4. punk 6. tinder 7. styptic
amah . . . 5. nurse 7. servant 9. nursemaid
11. maidservant
amain . . . 5. apace 7. hastily, quickly,
swiftly 9. posthaste
amalgamate . . . 3. mix 4. fuse, join,
weld 5. blend, merge, unite 6. commix
7. combine 8. coalesce, compound,
intermix 11. consolidate
amalgamation . . . 6. fusion, merger
7. mixture 11. combination
Amalkite . . . 4. Agag (King) 5. nomad
7. Bedouin
amant . . . 5. lover 6. amante
amaryllis . . . 4. bulb, lily 5. agave, plant
6. flower 8. mistress 10. sweetheart
11. shepherdess
amass . . . 4. save 5. hoard, stack, store
6. gather 7. collect 8. assemble
10. accumulate
amate . . . 5. daunt 6. subdue
10. dishearten
amateur . . . 3. ham 4. tyro 6. novice
7. dabbler, fancier 8. beginner, virtuoso
10. aficionado, apprentice, dilettante
15. nonprofessional
amateurish . . . 5. inapt 9. unskilled,
untrained, untutored 10. unfinished
15. nonprofessional
Amati . . . 6. family, violin
amatory . . . 4. fond 6. ardent, erotic,
loving, tender 7. amorous, philter
9. loverlike 10. passionate
amaze . . . 3. awe 4. stun 7. astound,
perplex, stagger, startle, stupefy
8. astonish, bewilder, confound,
surprise 9. dumbfound, overwhelm
amazement . . . 3. awe 5. alarm 6. wonder
8. surprise 10. perplexity
12. bewilderment 13. consternation
Amazon . . . 5. Queen (Myth), river
6. virago 9. androgyne 10. warrioress
11. Penthesilea
Amazon river (pert to) . . .
cetacean . . 4. Inia
discoverer . . 6. Pinzon (1500)
mouth . . 4. Para
rain forest . . 5. selva
tributary . . 3. Apa 4. Napo
ambary . . . 2. da 4. hemp 5. fiber 6. Nolita
ambassador . . . 5. envoy 6. legate,
nuncio 8. diplomat, emissary, minister
9. messenger 12. intermediary
14. representative 15. plenipotentiary
amber . . . 6. yellow 8. electrum
ambidextrous . . . 7. capable 8. two-faced
9. two-handed, versatile
11. ambidextral, treacherous 13. double-
dealing
ambiguous . . . 6. double 7. Delphic,

dubious 9. equivocal, uncertain,
unsettled 10. indefinite, indistinct,
mistakable 12. questionable
13. indeterminate
ambit . . . 5. orbit, scope 6. extent, sphere
7. circuit 8. precinct
ambition . . . 4. goal, spur 6. desire
10. aspiration
amble . . . 4. pace, rack, trot 7. piaffer
ambrosia . . . 4. food 5. honey, manna
6. nectar 7. perfume 8. delicacy, libation
ambulate . . . 4. hike, move, walk
ambush . . . 4. trap 5. snare 6. hiding,
waylay 7. mantrap 9. ambuscade
10. subterfuge 11. concealment
ameliorate . . . 4. ease, mend 5. emend
6. better 7. improve 8. progress
9. meliorate
amelioration . . . 10. betterment
11. improvement, restoration
amenable . . . 6. liable, pliant 7. movable
9. receptive 10. answerable, open-
minded, responsive 11. accountable,
persuadable, responsible
amend . . . 4. beat (dial), beet (beete)
5. alter, atone, emend 6. reform, repeal
7. convert, correct, improve, rectify,
redress, restore
amendment . . . 5. rider 8. addition
10. conversion, correction
11. improvement, reformation
amends . . . 7. redress 8. reprisal
9. atonement 10. recompense,
reparation 11. restitution
amenities . . . 5. mores 7. decorum,
manners 9. etiquette 10. civilities,
courtesies 11. formalities, gentilities,
proprieties
ament . . . 6. catkin 7. cattail
American (pert to) . . .
bear . . 7. musquaw (black)
buffalo . . 5. bison
cactus . . 4. bleo 7. saguaro
carnivore . . 4. puma
cataract . . 7. Niagara (Falls)
cedar (red) . . 5. savin
elk . . 6. wapiti
Japanese . . 5. Nisei 6. Kibbei
leopard . . 6. ocelot
marsupial . . 7. opossum
merganser . . 4. duck (fish-eating)
Mexican . . 6. gringo
mink . . 5. vison
moth . . 2. io
nickname . . 6. Yankee (Yank)
ostrich . . 4. rhea
palm . . 5. Sabal 8. palmetto
quail . . 5. colin
rail . . 4. sora
squirrel . . 9. chickaree (red)
vulture . . 5. urubu 6. condor
American, famed . . .
architect . . 3. Pei 6. Wright 7. Johnson,
Venturi 8. Sullivan
artist . . 4. Cole, West 5. Homer, Marsh,
Mount, Peale, Wyeth 6. Benton,
Demuth, Hopper, O'Keefe, Rivers,
Stuart, Warhol 7. Bellows, Bingham,
Gropper, Pollock, Sargent 8. Rockwell
9. Remington 10. Burchfield
chemist . . 6. Carver (G Washington)

composer.. **4.** Ives, Kern **5.** Grofé, Sousa **6.** Barber, Foster **7.** Copland, Rodgers (Richard) **8.** Gershwin **9.** Bernstein, Ellington

crusader (Temperance).. **12.** Carrie Nation

doctor, surgeon.. **4.** Mayo **6.** Schick **7.** Cushing

dramatist.. **4.** Rice **5.** Albee, Odets **6.** Miller, O'Neill, Wilder **8.** Williams (Tennessee)

educator.. **4.** Hume, Mann **5.** Eliot **10.** Washington (Booker T)

explorer.. **4.** Byrd **5.** Boone, Clark, Lewis, Peary **6.** Carson (Kit) **9.** Ellsworth

naturalist.. **4.** Muir **5.** Beebe **7.** Audubon, Burbank

patriot.. **4.** Clay, Hale, Otis **5.** Dawes, Henry (Patrick), Paine (Thomas) **6.** Revere

physicist.. **6.** Teller (H-bomb)

pianist.. **5.** Blake (Eubie), Tatum **6.** Duchin, Levant, Morton (Jelly Roll) **7.** Cliburn (Van) **8.** Horowitz, Liberace **10.** Gottschalk

poet.. **5.** Auden, Eliot, Frost, Pound **6.** Kilmer, Lowell, Millay **7.** Whitman **8.** Cummings, Ginsberg, Sandburg, Teasdale **9.** Dickinson **10.** Longfellow

Red Cross organizer.. **6.** Barton (Clara)

Scouts (Girl) organizer.. **3.** Low (Juliette)

sculptor.. **6.** Calder **7.** Borglum

singer.. **4.** Cole (Nat), Pons **5.** Lanza, Sills, Torme **6.** Callas, Crosby, Jolson **7.** Garland, Holiday (Billie), Merrill, Presley, Robeson, Sinatra **9.** Streisand **10.** Fitzgerald (Ella)

writer.. **3.** Poe **5.** Crane, James (Henry), Lewis (Sinclair), Stowe, Twain (Clemens) **6.** Cather, Cooper, Ferber, Irving, Mailer **7.** Dreiser, Emerson, Thoreau, Wharton **8.** Faulkner, Melville **9.** Hawthorne, Hemingway, Steinbeck **10.** Fitzgerald

American Indian (pert to) ...

chief.. **5.** brave **6.** sachem

child.. **7.** papoose

conference.. **6.** powwow

girl.. **7.** Nokomis (Myth) **9.** Minnehaha, Sacagawea (Sakajawea) **10.** Pocahontas

hero (Myth).. **8.** Hiawatha

magician.. **6.** shaman, wabeno (Ojibway)

shelter.. **4.** tent **5.** hogan, tepee (teepee) **6.** wigwam **7.** wickiup (wikiup)

American Indian people ... see also Indian **3.** Fox, Oto (Otoe), Ree, Sac, Ute **4.** Cree, Crow, Erie, Hopi, Iowa, Pima **5.** Creek, Kansa, Osage, Piute, Sioux **6.** Cayuga, Dakota, Mohawk, Oneida, Pueblo, Seneca **7.** Arapaho, Choctaw, Mohican, Ojibway, Siksika **8.** Cherokee, Chippewa, Iroquois, Onondaga, Seminole **9.** Algonquin, Blackfoot, Chickasaw **10.** Athapascan, Muskhogean

ami ... **5.** lover **6.** friend (law)

amiable ... **6.** kindly **7.** lovable **8.** charming, friendly, pleasant, pleasing **9.** agreeable, indulgent **10.** hospitable

amicable ... **4.** kind **8.** friendly, sociable **9.** congenial, peaceable **10.** harmonious

amicus curiae ... **5.** judge **6.** deputy, lawyer **16.** friend of the court

amid, amidst ... **2.** in **5.** among **7.** amongst, between

amigo ... **6.** friend **8.** neighbor

amiss ... **3.** ill **5.** badly, fault, wrong **6.** astray, sinful **8.** faultily, improper **10.** disorderly **11.** erroneously

amity ... **4.** love **5.** peace **7.** harmony **10.** friendship **11.** sociability **12.** congeniality, friendliness

amma ... **6.** abbess, mother (spiritual)

ammonia ... **9.** hartshorn **10.** fertilizer **11.** refrigerant

ammoniac plant ... **5.** oshac

ammunition (pert to) ...

box.. **9.** bandoleer

chest.. **7.** caisson

type.. **4.** arms, bomb, shot **7.** bullets **8.** grenades, missiles, munition, shrapnel **10.** explosives

wagon.. **7.** caisson

amnesty ... **6.** pardon **8.** oblivion **9.** acquittal **13.** forgetfulness

amoeba, ameba ... **3.** olm **4.** cell **7.** proteus **10.** protoplasm **13.** microorganism

among, amongst ... **2.** in **3.** mid **4.** amid, with **5.** midst **6.** amidst, imelle **7.** between

among nations ... **13.** international

amontillado ... **6.** sherry

Amor ... **4.** Eros **5.** Cupid

AMORC ... **11.** Rosicrucian

amorous ... **4.** fond **6.** ardent, erotic, loving, tender **7.** adoring, devoted **8.** enamored **10.** passionate **12.** affectionate

amorous looks ... **4.** ogle **5.** stare **8.** coquetry **10.** come-hither, flirtation

amorphous ... **8.** abnormal, formless **9.** deviative, shapeless, subnormal **14.** uncrystallized

amorphous mineral ... **4.** opal

amort ... **8.** dejected, lifeless **9.** inanimate **10.** spiritless

amortize ... **5.** clear **6.** convey, payoff, settle **9.** discharge, negotiate

amount ... **3.** lot, sum **4.** cost, rate, rise, unit **5.** chunk, price, ratal, store, total **6.** ascend, degree **7.** quantum, signify **8.** quantity

amount (pert to) ...

due.. **5.** price **6.** arrear **7.** default, deficit

mean.. **7.** average

realized.. **4.** take **6.** intake **8.** proceeds

small.. **6.** morsel **7.** modicum

smallest.. **5.** least

to.. **3.** all **4.** even **5.** equal, match, total **10.** correspond

amour ... **6.** affair **7.** liaison, romance **8.** intrigue, triangle **10.** flirtation

ampere ... **3.** amp **4.** unit **6.** ohmage **7.** current, voltage

ampersand ... **3.** and **4.** also

Amphibia ... **5.** Anura, frogs, toads **7.** Aglossa **8.** tadpoles **9.** Salientia **11.** salamanders

amphibious ... **5.** mixed **9.** adaptable **10.** fifty-fifty **11.** half-and-half, mixed nature (land and water)

amphibole . . . **7.** edenite, mineral, uralite
  8. aluminum, nephrite
amphigory, amphigouri . . . **5.** rhyme
  6. jingle, poetry **8.** doggerel **9.** rigmarole
amphilogism, amphilogy . . .
  9. ambiguity, duplexity (meaning)
  10. equivocacy
Amphion (pert to) . . .
  capturer of. . **6.** Thebes
  husband of. . **5.** Niobe
  son of. . **4.** Zeus
  twin of. . **6.** Zethus
amphitheater . . . **4.** bowl **5.** arena, cavea,
  scene, stage **6.** circus, cirque **7.** stadium
  8. coliseum, platform **10.** hippodrome
amphora . . . **3.** jar, urn **4.** vase **5.** diota,
  prize **7.** measure **8.** ornament
ample . . . **4.** full, rich, wide **5.** broad, large,
  roomy **6.** enough, plenty **7.** liberal
  8. abundant **9.** bountiful, capacious,
  extensive, plenteous, plentiful,
  unstinted **10.** munificent **12.** satisfactory
ampliation . . . **5.** flare **9.** expansion,
  extension **11.** enlargement
  12. postponement **13.** amplification
  14. aggrandizement
amplify . . . **3.** pad **5.** widen **6.** dilate,
  extend **7.** develop, enlarge **8.** increase
  9. aggravate, expatiate **10.** exaggerate,
  overstress
amplitude . . . **4.** size **6.** amount **7.** breadth
  8. fullness **9.** greatness, plenitude
  12. spaciousness
amputate . . . **4.** trim **5.** prune, sever **6.** cut
  off **8.** mutilate, retrench, truncate
amuck, amok . . . **3.** fit **4.** rage **6.** attack,
  frenzy, malady **12.** corybantiasm
amulet . . . **3.** gem **5.** charm **6.** fetish,
  scarab, voodoo **7.** periapt **8.** ornament,
  talisman **10.** protection
amuse . . . **3.** wow **6.** divert, please, regale,
  tickle **7.** beguile, gratify **8.** recreate
  9. entertain, titillate **10.** exhilarate
amusement . . . **3.** fun **4.** play **5.** farce,
  mirth, sport **7.** pastime **9.** avocation,
  diversion **10.** recreation, relaxation
  13. divertisement, entertainment
amusement place . . . **4.** club, park
  6. casino, midway **7.** cabaret, theater
ana . . . **5.** books **6.** events **8.** analecta,
  excerpts **9.** Americana **10.** collection
  11. collectanea, compilation,
  memorabilia
anachronous . . . **8.** misdated, mistimed
  10. beforehand, behindhand
anaglyph . . . **5.** cameo, carve **6.** chisel,
  plaque, relief **10.** embossment
Anak (Eccl) . . . **5.** giant (Canaan) **6.** Anakim
analogous . . . **4.** like **7.** similar **8.** parallel
  10. comparable, equivalent
  11. correlative
analogue . . . **8.** parallel **11.** resemblance
  13. correspondent **14.** correspondence
analogy . . . **8.** likeness, sameness
  9. agreement **10.** accordance,
  comparison, similarity
  14. correspondence
analysis . . . **5.** assay, logic **6.** biopsy,
  theory **9.** breakdown, diagnosis
  10. compendium, discussion, dissection
  11. examination **14.** classification

analyze . . . **5.** assay, parse, study
  7. discuss, dissect, examine **8.** classify,
  describe, diagnose, separate
Ananias (Bib) . . . **4.** liar **8.** disciple
  (Damascus), Shadrack (Sidrack) **10.** high
  priest **12.** prevaricator
anarch, anarchist . . . **3.** red **7.** radical
  8. nihilist **9.** socialist, terrorist
  13. revolutionist
anarchy . . . **4.** riot **5.** chaos **6.** acracy
  7. license, misrule **8.** disorder
  9. confusion, mobocracy, rebellion
  10. ochlocracy
anathema . . . **3.** ban **5.** curse **9.** damnation
  11. abomination, imprecation,
  malediction
Anatolian rug . . . **4.** Kurd **5.** Tuzla
anatomy . . . **4.** body **5.** build, frame
  7. carcass **8.** analysis, skeleton
  9. formation, structure **11.** arrangement
anatomy of animals . . . **7.** zootomy
ancestor . . . **4.** Adam, sire **5.** elder, stock
  6. atavus, family, parent **8.** forebear
  9. patriarch, precursor **10.** antecedent,
  forefather, forerunner, progenitor
  11. grandfather, predecessor
ancestral . . . **4.** aval **6.** avital, lineal
  7. atavism **8.** maternal, paternal
  9. atavistic, primitive **10.** hereditary
  11. patrimonial
ancestral spirits . . . **5.** lares, manes
  7. lemures, penates
ancestry . . . **4.** race, rank **5.** birth, blood
  7. descent, lineage **11.** antecedents
  14. progenitorship
anchor . . . **3.** fix, tie **4.** hook, moor, rest,
  stop **5.** affix, clamp, kedge **6.** attach,
  batten, fasten, secure **7.** grapnel, killick
anchor (pert to) . . . **3.** arm, cat, pee **4.** cast,
  palm, tore (ring) **5.** fluke **7.** capstan
anchorite, anchoret . . . **6.** hermit, shut-
  in **7.** ascetic, eremite, recluse, stylite
  8. homebody
anchor-shaped . . . **8.** ankyroid **10.** hook-
  shaped
anchovy . . . **4.** alec **5.** sauce, sprat
  7. herring
ancienne noblesse . . . **5.** elect, elite
  7. royalty **8.** nobility **11.** aristocracy
ancient . . . **3.** eld, old **4.** aged, auld, wise
  5. adept, early, hoary, olden **7.** antique
  8. historic, obsolete, outdated, primeval,
  pristine **9.** grandeval, primitive,
  venerable **10.** aboriginal, antiquated,
  preadamite **12.** antediluvian
ancient (pert to) . . .
  chariot. . **5.** essed
  city. . **4.** Elis, Tyre **5.** Argos, Sedon
  6. Athens, Sparta, Thebes
  drink. . **5.** morat
  empire. . **4.** Gaul **5.** Roman **6.** Lydian
  7. Persian **8.** Assyrian, Athenian,
  Chaldean, Hellenic **10.** Babylonian,
  Phoenician
  god. . **4.** Esus (Gaulish)
  isles. . **5.** Chios, Crete, Samos **6.** Aegina,
  Ionian, Ithaca, Lemnos, Lesbos, Rhodes
  7. Salamis **8.** Cyclades
  language. . **4.** Pali **5.** Latin **6.** Celtic,
  Gaelic **7.** Cornish, Gaulish
  mariner. . **4.** Rime (of) **5.** rover **6.** roamer,

sailor, seaman **8.** seafarer, wanderer **9.** navigator
soldier . . **7.** peltast
theater . . **5.** odeum
and . . . **2.** et **4.** also, plus **8.** et cetera **9.** ampersand, including **12.** additionally
andante . . . **5.** largo, tempo **6.** slowly
Andean (pert to) . . .
beast . . **5.** llama **6.** alpaca, vicuña **7.** guanaco
deer . . **4.** pudu
region, wind . . **4.** puna
term . . **5.** grand, lofty
andiron . . . **3.** dog **7.** firedog, Hessian
and others . . . **4.** et al
andrenid . . . **3.** bee **10.** Andrenidae
androgyny . . . **9.** sissiness **10.** effeminacy **11.** unmanliness **15.** hermaphroditism
android . . . **5.** robot **9.** automaton
anecdote . . . **4.** tale, yarn **5.** story **7.** account **9.** chronicle, narrative
anecdotes . . . **3.** ana **7.** sayings, stories
anemone . . . **7.** actinia **10.** windflower
anent . . **2.** of, on, re **4.** upon, with **5.** about **8.** opposite **10.** concerning
anesthesia, anaesthesia . . . **8.** deadness, numbness **13.** insensibility
anesthetic . . . **3.** gas **5.** ether **8.** freezing, Novocain, procaine **9.** pentothal **10.** chloroform **13.** refrigeration
anesthetize . . . **4.** dull, numb, stun **6.** benumb, deaden, freeze **7.** stupefy **8.** etherize, paralyze **9.** narcotize **10.** chloroform **11.** desensitize
anew . . . **5.** again, newly **6.** afresh, de novo **8.** recently
angel . . . **6.** cherub, genius, seraph (seraf) **7.** Madonna, prophet
angel (pert to) . . .
Arab (apostate) . . **5.** Eblis
archangel . . **5.** Uriel **7.** Gabriel, Michael, Raphael
Biblical . . **6.** bishop, pastor
Fallen . . **6.** Belial, Mammon
financial . . **6.** backer, patron **7.** sponsor **8.** promoter
fish . . **5.** shark **9.** spadefish
Hebrew . . **6.** Abdiel **8.** cherubim, seraphim
Jewish . . **6.** Azrael (of death) **7.** Zadkiel (of planet Jupiter) **8.** Metatron
Mohammedan (Mus) . . **7.** Israfil (Israfeel)
Moslem . . **5.** Nakir (Repudiating) **6.** Munkar (Unknown)
angelic . . . **5.** godly **7.** lovable, saintly **8.** cherubic, heavenly, seraphic, virtuous **9.** celestial **10.** beneficent
angelica . . . **4.** herb **6.** lovely **7.** liqueur
Angelus . . . **4.** bell, call **6.** prayer **8.** devotion
anger . . . **3.** ire, vex **4.** fume, rage, rile **5.** annoy, chafe, wrath **6.** choler, dander, enrage, nettle, offend, temper **7.** dudgeon, emotion, inflame, madness, passion, trouble **8.** vexation **9.** infuriate **10.** affliction, enragement, irritation, resentment **11.** displeasure, indignation **12.** exasperation
angered . . . **3.** mad **5.** irate, wroth **8.** incensed, wrathful **9.** indignant, irascible

angle . . . **3.** ell, tee, zig **4.** axil, coin, fish, fork, hade, nook **5.** acute, ancon, arris, right, slant, story **6.** akimbo, distal, epaule, obtuse, octant **7.** bastion, outlook, ravelin, salient **8.** attitude **9.** incidence, rectangle, viewpoint
angler . . . **6.** fisher **7.** dibbler, trawler, troller **8.** piscator **9.** fisherman, Waltonian
angler's basket . . . **5.** creel
Anglican . . . **7.** English
Anglo-Celtic . . . **7.** British **10.** Anglo-Saxon
Anglo-Indian (pert to) . . .
Empire founder . . **5.** Clive
measure . . **3.** ser **4.** tola
pageant . . **7.** tamasha
peasant . . **4.** ryot
princess . . **5.** begum
wealthy . . **5.** nabob
Anglo-Saxon (pert to) . . .
armor . . **7.** hauberk
assembly . . **4.** moot **5.** gemot (gemote)
attendant . . **5.** thane
consonant . . **3.** edh, eth
council . . **9.** heptarchy
councilman . . **5.** witan
epic (heroic) . . **7.** Beowulf
native . . **7.** English **11.** Anglo-Celtic
prince (heir apparent) . . **8.** atheling
slave . . **4.** esne
tenant . . **6.** geneat
warrior . . **5.** thane
Angora . . .
capital of . . **6.** Turkey
garment . . **5.** shawl
goat . . **6.** chamal
wool fabric . . **6.** mohair
angry . . . **3.** hot, mad **4.** sore **5.** cross, grame, irate, irked, vexed **6.** ireful, stormy **7.** enraged, painful, steamed **8.** inflamed, wrathful **9.** indignant, irascible, resentful, ticked off, turbulent **10.** passionate
anguish . . . **3.** woe **4.** bale, pain, pang **5.** agony, dolor, grief, throe **6.** misery **7.** remorse, sadness, torment, torture **8.** distress **9.** heartache **10.** desolation **11.** lamentation
angular . . . **4.** bent, bony, edgy **5.** gaunt, sharp **6.** abrupt, akimbo, forked **7.** crooked, pointed, scrawny **8.** cornered, crotched
ani . . . **8.** keelbill (keelbird) **9.** blackbird
animadversion . . . **7.** censure, comment, obloquy **8.** judgment, reproach **9.** aspersion, criticism **10.** imputation, reflection **12.** condemnation
animadvert . . . **4.** note **5.** watch **6.** notice, regard, remark **7.** censure, comment, observe **9.** criticize (criticise)
anima humana . . . **4.** mind, self, soul **5.** heart, human **6.** psyche, spirit
animal (pert to) . . .
anatomy . . **7.** zootomy
back, spine . . **4.** nota **5.** chine
Biblical . . **8.** Behemoth
body . . **4.** soma
castrated . . **3.** seg (segg)
coat . . **6.** pelage
cud . . **5.** rumen

disease .. **8.** enzootic
enclosure .. **3.** pen, sty **4.** cage, coop, cote, reem, yard **5.** hutch, kraal, stall **6.** corral **7.** pasture
fabulous .. **7.** griffin
group .. **3.** gam, pod **4.** herd **5.** drove, flock, pride **9.** menagerie
hairless .. **5.** pelon
hindleg part .. **4.** crus
hornless .. **7.** pollard
hybrid .. **4.** mule **5.** hinny
hypnosis .. **9.** cataplexy
male .. **3.** tom **4.** bull, jack, stag **5.** steer **8.** stallion
many-egged .. **5.** zooid
many-footed .. **7.** polyped
molt .. **8.** exuviate
mother .. **3.** dam
no feet .. **4.** apod
nose .. **5.** snout
oar-footed .. **7.** remiped
one-egged .. **4.** zoon
one-footed .. **6.** uniped
pet .. **4.** cade
reference to .. **4.** wild **6.** carnal **7.** bestial, fleshly, kingdom **8.** domestic **12.** ferae naturae **14.** domitae naturae
regional .. **5.** fauna
small .. **10.** animalcule
symbolic .. **5.** totem
track, trail .. **4.** rack **5.** piste, spoor
web-footed .. **8.** pinniped
wing-footed .. **6.** aliped
worship .. **8.** zoolatry
young .. **3.** cub, kid, pup **4.** calf, colt, fawn, foal, lamb **5.** filly, puppy **6.** kitten
animal family . . .
  bear .. **6.** ursine
  cat .. **6.** feline
  cow .. **6.** bovine
  deer .. **7.** cervine
  dog .. **6.** canine
  fox .. **7.** vulpine
  horse .. **6.** equine
  pig .. **7.** porcine
  sheep .. **5.** ovine
  wolf .. **6.** lupine
animal stomach . . .
  1st .. **5.** rumen **6.** paunch
  2nd .. **5.** tripe **9.** honeycomb, reticulum
  3rd .. **6.** omasum **9.** manyplies
  4th .. **3.** maw **4.** read (reed) **8.** abomasum
animate . . . **3.** act **4.** fire, live, move **5.** alive, cheer, imbue, impel, liven **6.** arouse, ensoul, spirit, vivify **7.** enliven, inspire, organic, refresh **8.** energize, vitalize **9.** stimulate **10.** exhilarate
animated . . . **3.** gay **5.** alive, brisk **6.** active, lively, living, minded **8.** disposed (in mind), prompted **9.** energetic, refreshed
animated spirit . . . **6.** animus
animation . . . **3.** pep **4.** brio, dash, life **5.** ardor **6.** energy, gaiety, spirit **8.** airiness, buoyancy, vivacity **10.** excitement, liveliness, motivation **11.** earnestness, inspiration **12.** invigoration, vivification **13.** sprightliness
animation suspended . . . **6.** apathy,

torpor **8.** dormancy, lethargy
animé . . . **6.** bright **8.** animated
animosity . . . **5.** clash, spite **6.** enmity, hatred, rancor **7.** ill will **8.** conflict **9.** antipathy, hostility **10.** antagonism, opposition, repugnance
animoso . . . **6.** lively **8.** animated **9.** energetic
animous . . . **3.** hot **8.** resolute, vehement
animus . . . **4.** mind, will **6.** desire, hatred, spirit, temper **8.** attitude, volition **9.** intention **10.** discretion **11.** disposition, inclination
anise-flavored liqueur . . . **4.** anis, ouzo **6.** pastis **8.** anisette
ankh (Egypt) . . . **3.** tau **4.** life **5.** cross **6.** emblem, symbol
ankle . . . **4.** tali (pl) **5.** joint, pivot, talus **6.** tarsus **8.** astragal **9.** ginglymus **10.** astragalus **11.** diarthrosis
ankle cover . . . **4.** spat **6.** gaiter
ankylostoma . . . **7.** lockjaw
annalist . . . **6.** writer **8.** recorder **9.** historian **10.** chronicler **11.** memorialist **12.** chronologist
annals . . . **5.** diary **6.** record **7.** history, journal **8.** register **9.** chronicle **11.** publication
Annam . . . **5.** Hanoi **6.** Tonkin (Tongking)
Annamese . . . **7.** Chinese **8.** Buddhist **9.** Mongolian
anneal . . . **4.** fuse, heat **6.** harden, temper **7.** inflame, toughen **8.** indurate
Anne Hathaway's home . . . **8.** Shattery
annelid . . . **3.** lug **4.** lurg, naid, worm **6.** phylum **7.** lugworm
annex . . . **3.** add, ell **4.** join, wing **5.** affix **6.** append, attach, fasten **7.** acquire, subjoin **8.** addition **9.** extension
annexation . . . **7.** adjunct **8.** addition **9.** accession **10.** affixation **13.** appropriation
Annie Oakley . . . **4.** pass **6.** ticket (free)
annihilate . . . **4.** undo, void **5.** erase, wreck **6.** quench, reduce, stifle **7.** abolish, destroy, expunge, nullify, smother **8.** decimate **9.** extirpate **10.** extinguish, obliterate **11.** exterminate
annihilation . . . **5.** death **6.** demise **7.** passing **10.** extinction **11.** destruction, dissolution **13.** extermination **14.** extinguishment
anniversary . . . **5.** cycle **6.** course **7.** jubilee, wedding **8.** birthday **10.** centennial, regularity **13.** commemoration
annotation . . . **4.** note **5.** gloss **7.** apostil, comment **8.** exegesis, notation, rescript, scholium **9.** reference **10.** commentary
annotator . . . **6.** critic **7.** analyst **9.** expositor, expounder, publicist, scholiast **10.** glossarist **11.** commentator
announce . . . **3.** bid **4.** call, tell **5.** bruit **6.** affirm, assert, herald, notify **7.** declare, forerun, gazette, presage **8.** proclaim **9.** advertise, broadcast, pronounce **10.** annunciate, promulgate
announcement . . . **4.** fiat **5.** blurb, edict **6.** decree, notice **8.** bulletin **9.** manifesto **10.** commercial **11.** affirmation,

declaration **12.** notification,
proclamation **13.** advertisement
announcer ... **4.** page **5.** crier, emcee
6. nuncio **9.** harbinger, informant
10. newscaster, proclaimer
11. broadcaster
annoy ... **3.** irk, nag, try, vex **4.** bore,
rile **5.** anger, devil, harry, peeve,
spite, tease **6.** bother, harass, molest,
offend, pester, ruffle **7.** disturb, trouble
8. irritate **9.** displease **13.** inconvenience
annoyance ... **4.** bore, pest **8.** nuisance,
vexation **10.** resentment **11.** molestation
13. inconvenience
annoying ... **4.** sore **7.** galling **9.** vexatious
11. distressing
annual ... **4.** book **5.** plant **6.** yearly
7. etesian **10.** periodical **11.** publication
annuity ... **5.** rente, trust **6.** income (life)
7. pension, subsidy, tontine **9.** allotment
10. investment, life income
annul ... **4.** cass, undo, void **5.** avoid,
blank, quash **6.** cancel, repeal, revoke
7. abolish, nullify, rescind **8.** abrogate,
derogate, overrule, withdraw
9. disaffirm **10.** invalidate, neutralize,
obliterate **11.** countermand
annular ... **6.** banded, cyclic, ringed
8. cingular, circular
annulet ... **4.** ring (Her) **6.** fillet **7.** circlet,
ringlet
annulment ... **6.** repeal **7.** erasure,
vacatur **9.** abolition **10.** abrogation,
defeasance, revocation **12.** invalidation
14. neutralization
annunciate ... **6.** affirm, assert
8. announce, proclaim
annunciation ... **11.** affirmation
12. announcement, proclamation
13. pronouncement
anoa ... **2.** ox (wild) **8.** sapiutan
anode ... **8.** terminal (positive)
9. electrode (opp of cathode)
anodic ... **12.** turned toward
anodyne ... **4.** balm **6.** opiate **7.** soother
8. antalgic, narcotic, pacifier, sedative
9. analgesic **10.** depressant, palliative
anoesia ... **6.** idiocy
anoint ... **3.** oil **4.** balm, cere, nard
5. anele, bribe, smear **6.** chrism,
grease, spread **7.** moisten **8.** medicate
9. embrocate, lubricate **10.** consecrate
Anointing of the Sick ... **9.** last rites,
sacrament **14.** Extreme Unction
anoli, anole ... **6.** lizard
anomalous ... **3.** odd **7.** erratic, strange,
unusual **8.** aberrant, abnormal, peculiar
9. eccentric, irregular **10.** dissimilar
11. exceptional **13.** unconformable
anomaly ... **6.** oddity, rarity
11. abnormality, nondescript
12. irregularity
anomy ... **7.** miracle
anon ... **4.** soon **5.** again, later **6.** mañana,
thence **7.** by-and-by **8.** tomorrow
10. eventually **11.** straightway
anonymous (opp of onomatous) ...
7. unknown **8.** nameless, unavowed
9. undefined
anoöpsia ... **10.** strabismus (upward)
Anopheles ... **10.** mosquitoes

anophthalmia ... **13.** absence of eyes
(congenital)
anopia ... **15.** defective vision
anorak ... **5.** parka **12.** hooded jacket
(Arctic)
anorexia ... **10.** no appetite
anorthopia ... **15.** distorted vision
anosmia ... **11.** loss of smell
another ... **3.** new **4.** more **5.** alias, extra,
other **6.** second **7.** further **10.** additional
another time ... **5.** again **10.** otherwhile
ansa ... **4.** loop **6.** ansate, handle
anserine ... **6.** stupid **9.** gooselike
answer ... **2.** do **3.** say **4.** echo
5. avail, reply, sauce, serve **6.** oracle,
retort **7.** defense, epistle, respond,
riposte **8.** conclude, reaction, repartee,
response, solution **9.** rejoinder
10. correspond, responsory
11. acknowledge **16.** counterstatement
answerable ... **6.** liable **8.** amenable,
solvable **11.** responsible
12. commensurate **13.** proportionate
answer the purpose ... **2.** so **3.** fit **4.** suit
5. avail, serve **6.** become **7.** benefit,
satisfy, suffice
ant (pert to) ...
family .. **10.** Formicidae, Myrmicidae
   11. Formicoidea (super), Hymenoptera
feeding on .. **13.** formicivorous
genus .. **6.** Eciton, Termes **7.** Formica
killer .. **9.** formicide
male .. **8.** macraner (large), micraner
(small)
nest .. **9.** formicary
ref to .. **6.** formic
type .. **5.** emmet **7.** formica, pismire
white .. **4.** anay (anai) **7.** termite
wingless .. **8.** ergatoid
worker .. **6.** ergate **9.** harvester
antacid ... **6.** alkali, remedy **8.** medicine
9. absorbent **11.** neutralizer
12. counteragent **13.** counteractant
Antaeus, Antaios (Gr) ... **5.** giant
6. Libyan **8.** wrestler
antagonism ... **3.** war **5.** clash **8.** conflict
9. antipathy, hostility **10.** opposition,
repugnance **11.** contrariety
12. disagreement **13.** counteraction
antagonist ... **3.** foe **5.** enemy, rival
6. foeman **8.** opponent **9.** adversary
antagonistic ... **7.** hostile, opposed
8. contrary, converse, inimical, opposite
9. repugnant **10.** unfriendly
11. belligerent, disagreeing
13. counteractive
Antarctic ...
Circle .. **4.** Pole **6.** region
Coast .. **6.** Adélie
continent .. **10.** Antarctica
explorer .. **4.** Byrd, Ross
islands .. **11.** Archipelago
rel to .. **8.** subpolar **9.** antipodal, South
Pole
sea .. **4.** Ross **7.** Weddell
seal (brown) discoverer .. **7.** Weddell
volcano .. **6.** Erebus
ante ... **3.** pay, pot **4.** bank, fund, pool
5. kitty, stake **7.** jackpot
anteater ... **5.** Manis **7.** echidna
8. aardvark, edentate, pangolin,

tamandua
antebellum ... **6.** prewar
antecede ... **4.** head **5.** front **6.** prefix
7. outrank, precede, preface
antecedent ... **4.** fore **5.** prior, scout
6. former **7.** pioneer **8.** ancestor,
previous **9.** foregoing, precedent,
preceding, precursor **10.** forerunner,
precedence **11.** voortrekker (Dutch)
12. avant-courier
antecedents ... **7.** fathers **9.** ancestors,
forebears **10.** ascendants (ascendents)
11. forefathers **12.** predecessors
13. prerequisites
antechamber ... **4.** hall **5.** lobby **6.** lounge
7. chamber **8.** anteroom **9.** vestibule
antedate ... **7.** precede, predate
8. datemark, pre-exist **10.** anticipate
antelope ... **3.** gau, gnu, goa, kob, nil
4. guib, koba, oryx, roan **5.** addax,
bovid, eland, goral, oribi, peele, saiga,
serow **6.** cabree, dik-dik, dzeren,
impala, nilgai, pygarg **7.** blaubok,
blesbok, bubalia, chamois, gazella,
gazelle, gemsbok, sassaby **8.** agacella,
bontebok, steinbok **9.** duikerbok,
pronghorn **10.** hartebeest
antenna ... **4.** horn, mast, palp **5.** clava
(Zool), tower **6.** aerial, feeler **7.** scanner
antepast ... **6.** canape, repast **8.** aperitif
9. antipasto, appetizer, foretaste
11. hors d'oeuvre, prelibation
anteroom ... **4.** hall **5.** lobby **6.** lounge
7. chamber **9.** vestibule
11. antechamber
anthem ... **3.** lay **4.** hymn, song **5.** motet,
music, psalm **7.** chorale **8.** doxology
9. antiphony, offertory **10.** responsory
anthill ... **5.** mound **9.** formicary
anthology ... **3.** ana **5.** album **6.** corpus
7. omnibus, prayers **8.** analects
9. potpourri **10.** collection
11. collectanea, compilation
Anthozoa ... **6.** corals, polyps
8. anemones
anthropoid ... **3.** ape, lar, man **6.** gibbon
7. gorilla, primate, siamang
9. orangutan (orangoutang)
10. chimpanzee, troglodyte
12. Anthropoidea (suborder)
anthropophagi ... **9.** cannibals, man-
eaters
anti ... **6.** contra **7.** adverse, counter,
opposed **8.** contrary, converse
13. contradictory
antibiotics ... **5.** drugs **7.** vaccine
10. penicillin **12.** streptomycin
antic ... **4.** dido **5.** caper, prank, stunt
6. frolic, gambol **7.** bizarre, buffoon,
gambado **9.** grotesque **11.** merry-
andrew, monkeyshine
anticipate ... **4.** hope **5.** await, dread
6. expect **7.** foresee, obviate, portend,
prevent **8.** preclude **9.** forestall,
foretaste, forethink **11.** contemplate
anticipation ... **4.** hope **9.** foresight,
foretaste, intuition, prolepsis
10. foreboding **11.** expectation,
forethought **12.** presentiment
13. preoccupation
anticlimax ... **6.** bathos **8.** comedown,

decrease
antidote ... **6.** remedy **10.** corrective,
preventive **11.** neutralizer
12. counteragent, prophylactic
13. counteractant
Antilles ...
Greater .. **4.** Cuba **7.** Jamaica
10. Hispaniola, Puerto Rico
Lesser .. **7.** Leeward (Islands)
8. Windward (Islands)
Antioch ... **7.** capital (Syria)
antipathy ... **6.** hatred, nausea **7.** dislike
8. aversion, loathing **9.** disrelish,
hostility **10.** abhorrence, antagonism,
opposition, reluctance, repugnance
11. contrariety, detestation, inimicality
13. counteraction **14.** disinclination
antipodal ... **5.** polar **7.** counter (global)
8. contrary, opposite **14.** contrapositive
antiquated ... **4.** aged **5.** passé **6.** bygone,
voided **7.** antique, archaic, elderly
8. absolute, medieval **9.** Victorian
10. fossilized **12.** antediluvian, old-
fashioned **13.** superannuated
antique ... **3.** old **5.** hoary, relic
7. ageless, ancient **8.** dateless,
outmoded **9.** venerable **12.** old-
fashioned
antiquities ... **5.** codex, ruins **6.** relics
7. fossils, papyrus, remains, tablets
9. archaisms, artifacts, monuments
11. manuscripts, palimpsests
antiquity ... **3.** ago, eld **4.** past, yore
7. oldness **9.** paleology **11.** ancientness,
elderliness **13.** aboriginality,
primitiveness
antisepsis ... **7.** asepsis **11.** prophylaxis
12. disinfection, immunization
13. sterilization
antiseptic ... **5.** Salol **6.** cresol, iodine
(iodin), phenol **7.** alcohol, aristol,
aseptic **8.** creosote, peroxide
9. germicide **12.** disinfectant,
formaldehyde, prophylactic
antispasmodic ... **7.** anodyne **8.** sedative
9. asadulcis (deadly carrot), asafetida
(asafoetida) **10.** depressant
12. tranquilizer
antithesis (opp of thesis) ... **8.** contrast,
opposite **9.** antipodes **10.** opposition
11. contrariety **14.** contraposition
antitoxin ... **5.** serum **7.** vaccine
8. antibody **9.** antivenin (antivenene)
10. antibiotic **11.** antipyretic,
immunotoxin
antler ... **3.** dag **4.** horn, snag, tine
5. dague, point, prong, spike **6.** bosset,
rights **8.** advancer **10.** caducicorn
Antony & Cleopatra characters ...
4. Eris, Iras **6.** Caesar **7.** Octavia
9. Demetrius
antonym (opp of synonym) ... **7.** reverse
8. contrary, opposite
antrum ... **3.** pit **5.** sinus **6.** cavern,
cavity, hollow **10.** depression
Anu ... **3.** god (sky, heavens)
Anubis ... **3.** god (Necropolis) **6.** Hermes
Anura ... **4.** Rana **5.** frogs, toads
9. Salientia **10.** amphibians
anvil ... **5.** block, incus, teest **6.** stithy
7. bickern, incudes (pl) **8.** beakiron

(horned)
anxiety . . . **4.** care, fear **5.** angst,
dread, worry **7.** concern, trouble
8. disquiet, distress, neurosis, suspense
9. eagerness, misgiving **10.** foreboding,
perplexity, solicitude, uneasiness
12. apprehension, restlessness
anxious . . . **4.** cark **5.** antsy, eager
6. uneasy **7.** fearful, unquiet **8.** watchful
9. concerned, disturbed, expectant,
impatient **10.** disquieted
any . . . **3.** all, ary (dial), one, oni (dial)
4. some, that, this **5.** aught, every
8. quantity **9.** unlimited **10.** unmeasured
12. undetermined
anybody . . . **3.** any, one **5.** aught
6. anyone **7.** someone, whoever
15. no-account person
anything . . . **3.** any **4.** some **5.** at all,
aught **7.** anywise **8.** no choice, whatever
9. something **14.** choicelessness
anything (pert to) . . .
existing . . **6.** entity **8.** quiddity
of value . . **5.** asset
of value, least . . **5.** plack
puzzling . . **4.** crux **11.** mind-boggler
remote . . **6.** forane
small . . **3.** tot **5.** minim
spiral . . **4.** gyre **5.** helix
terrifying . . **5.** ghost **9.** scarecrow
true . . **4.** fact **9.** certitude
worthless . . **4.** mean **7.** useless
9. valueless
aoudad . . . **5.** sheep **7.** chamois
apa . . . **7.** wallaba
Apache (pert to) . . .
French . . **4.** thug **5.** dance **8.** assassin
Indian . . **5.** nomad
Indian Chief (famed) . . **8.** Geronimo
Indian jacket (deerskin) . . **6.** bietle
State . . **7.** Arizona
apart . . . **3.** dis (pref) **4.** away **5.** alone,
aloof, aside, solus, split **6.** singly
7. asunder, distant **8.** secluded,
separate, unjoined **9.** severally,
unrelated **10.** separately
apartheid . . . **4.** bias **5.** twist **7.** bigotry
9. prejudice **11.** segregation
13. provincialism **14.** discrimination
apartment . . . **3.** pad (sl) **4.** flat **5.** condo,
suite **6.** studio **7.** chamber **8.** tenement
11. compartment, condominium
apathetic . . . **4.** dull **5.** inert **6.** torpid
7. passive **8.** listless, sluggish
10. insouciant, phlegmatic
11. indifferent, unconcerned
apathy . . . **6.** acedia (in a monastery),
torpor **7.** languor **8.** neurosis
9. lassitude, unconcern **12.** indifference,
sluggishness **13.** insensibility,
unfeelingness
ape . . . **4.** copy, dupe, fool, mine **5.** mimic
6. alalus, mocker, monkey, parrot
7. barbary, copycat, emulate, imitate,
portray **8.** imitator, mimicker, simulate
10. anthropoid **11.** impersonate
ape (pert to) . . .
anthropoid . . **6.** pongid **10.** chimpanzee,
troglodyte
Egypt Relig . . **4.** Aani
genus . . **5.** Cebus, Simia

India . . **3.** kra
kind . . **6.** simian **7.** macaque
largest . . **6.** baboon **7.** gorilla
Malay . . **3.** lar **5.** orang **6.** gibbon
9. orangutan (orangoutang)
nocturnal . . **5.** lemur
aperitif . . . **5.** drink **6.** canape **8.** antepast
9. antipasto, appetizer **11.** hors d'oeuvre
aperture . . . **3.** gap, vue **4.** hole, leak,
pore, rift, rima, slit, slot, vent **5.** chasm,
chink, cleft, inlet, mouth, stoma
6. hiatus, window **7.** fissure, foramen,
opening, orifice, osteole **8.** fenestra
10. passageway
apex . . . **3.** tip, top **4.** acme, cone, cusp,
noon **5.** point, spire **6.** apogee, height,
macron, summit, tittle, vertex, zenith
7. cacumen **8.** pinnacle **11.** culmination
apex ornament . . . **6.** finial
aphid . . . **5.** Aphis, louse **6.** insect
7. puceron
aphorism . . . **3.** saw **5.** adage, axiom,
gnome, maxim, moral **6.** dictum, saying
7. proverb **8.** apothegm
Aphrodite (pert to) . . .
consort . . **4.** Ares **10.** Hephaestus
father . . **4.** Zeus
goddess of . . **4.** love **6.** beauty
Roman equivalent . . **5.** Venus
sacred birds . . **5.** doves **8.** sparrows
statue . . **17.** Aphrodite of Cnidus (by
Praxiteles)
zoology . . **9.** butterfly
apiarist . . . **9.** beekeeper
apiary . . . **7.** beehive
Apis . . . **4.** bull (sacred)
aplomb . . . **5.** poise **6.** surety **7.** balance
8. fastness, firmness, security, solidity
9. assurance, erectness, plumbness,
restraint, soundness, stability
10. confidence, equanimity
11. equilibrium
apocalypse . . . **8.** prophecy, teaching
9. discovery, scripture **10.** revealment,
revelation
a poco . . . **6.** little, slowly **9.** gradually
apocryphal . . . **4.** mock, sham **5.** bogus,
false **6.** mythic, unreal **8.** doubtful,
mythical, spurious **9.** imitative
10. fictitious, unorthodox **11.** counterfeit
15. unauthoritative
apod . . . **8.** footless
Apodes . . . **4.** eels **6.** morays
apogee (opp of perigee) . . . **4.** acme,
apex, peak **6.** climax, summit, zenith
11. culmination
apograph . . . **4.** copy **5.** tenor **7.** tracing
8. transfer **9.** recording **10.** transcript
13. transcription
Apoidea . . . **4.** Apis, bees **9.** honeybees
11. Hymenoptera
Apollo (pert to) . . .
birthplace . . **5.** Delos
father . . **4.** Zeus
festival . . **5.** Delia
god . . **3.** sun (personified)
mother . . **4.** Leto **6.** Larona
oracle . . **6.** Delphi
sage follower . . **6.** Abaris
sister (twin) . . **5.** Diana (Rom) **7.** Artemis
son . . **3.** Ion **5.** Hymen, Linos

apologetic ... **5.** sorry **7.** apology
8. excusing **10.** excusatory, justifying,
remorseful **11.** vindicative
12. propitiatory **13.** justification
apologue ... **4.** myth **5.** fable, story
6. legend **7.** fantasy, parable **8.** allegory
apology ... **4.** plea **6.** excuse **7.** pretext,
regrets **9.** makeshift **11.** explanation,
vindication **13.** justification
14. acknowledgment
aport ... **8.** larboard, leftward **9.** sinistrad
apostasy ... **5.** lapse **9.** desertion,
recreancy **11.** backsliding
apostate ... **6.** bolter **7.** pervert, runaway,
seceder **8.** deserter, recreant, renegade,
turncoat, turntail **10.** unfaithful
apostle ... **5.** saint **8.** disciple, follower
10. evangelist
Apostle (Bib) ... **4.** John, Jude **5.** James,
Judas (Iscariot), Peter (Simon Peter),
Simon **6.** Andrew, Philip, Thomas
7. Matthew **8.** Matthias
11. Bartholomew (Nathanael)
Apostle of ...
France (Gauls) .. **5.** Denis
Franks .. **4.** Remi
Gentiles .. **4.** Paul
Germany .. **8.** Boniface
Goths .. **7.** Ulfilas
Indies .. **6.** Xavier
Ireland .. **7.** Patrick
Rome .. **4.** Neri
Apostle to the Indians ... **5.** Eliot
apostolic ... **5.** faith, papal **6.** gospel
8. Biblical **9.** evangelic **10.** pontifical,
scriptural
apostrophe ... **8.** squiggle **9.** soliloquy
apothecary ... **8.** druggist, gallipot
9. dispenser **10.** pharmacist, posologist
13. pharmaceutist **14.** pharmacologist
apothecary measure ... **4.** dram, pint
5. minim, ounce
apothecary weight ... **4.** dram **5.** grain,
ounce, pound **7.** scruple
apothegm ... **3.** saw **4.** dict **5.** adage,
axiom, gnome, maxim **6.** dictum,
saying **7.** precept **8.** aphorism
apotheosis ... **5.** ideal **10.** exaltation
11. deification, ennoblement, idolization
12. resurrection **13.** dignification,
glorification, magnification
14. aggrandizement
apotheosize ... **5.** deify, exalt **7.** ennoble,
glorify, idolize **8.** enshrine
11. immortalize
appall, appal ... **3.** awe **5.** shock
6. dismay
appalling ... **4.** grim **5.** awful **7.** awesome,
fearful **8.** dreadful, shocking, terrible,
terrific **9.** frightful **10.** remarkable
appalto ... **8.** monopoly
appanage ... **7.** adjunct, pendant
8. property **9.** appendage, endowment
10. perquisite **11.** prerogative
12. appurtenance
apparatus ... **4.** gear, tool **6.** outfit
7. machine, rigging, trapeze **8.** recorder
9. appliance, equipment, mechanism,
trappings **10.** instrument
13. paraphernalia
apparatus (pert to) ...

distillation .. **7.** alembic
dyeing .. **4.** ager
heating .. **4.** etna **5.** stove **6.** boiler
7. furnace **8.** radiator
hoisting .. **3.** pry **4.** jack **5.** davit, lever,
lewis **7.** capstan, derrick
planetarium .. **6.** orrery
steering .. **4.** helm **5.** wheel **6.** rudder,
tiller
water .. **4.** pump **5.** noria **6.** faucet,
siphon, tremie
apparel ... **3.** alb **4.** deck, duds, garb,
gear, togs, wear **5.** dress, equip, habit
6. attire **7.** clothes, costume, garment,
raiment, toggery, vesture **8.** clothing,
fatigues **10.** garmenture **11.** habiliments
apparent ... **4.** open **5.** clear, overt, plain
6. patent, visual **7.** certain, evident,
obvious, seeable, seeming, visible
8. distinct, illusory, manifest, specious
9. notorious, plausible **10.** ostensible
11. discernible, indubitable, perceivable,
superficial **12.** recognizable
apparently ... **7.** visibly **9.** evidently,
obviously, seemingly **10.** manifestly,
presumably, speciously **11.** perceptibly
apparition ... **4.** bogy, form **5.** ghost,
shade, spook **6.** shadow, spirit, sprite,
vision, wraith **7.** eidolon, fantasy,
phantom, specter (spectre) **8.** illusion,
phantasm, revenant **9.** hobgoblin
10. appearance, phenomenon,
revelation
appassionato ... **9.** emotional
11. impassioned
appeal ... **3.** beg, cry **4.** call, cite,
plea, pray, suit **5.** charm, plead
6. avouch, invoke, prayer **7.** address,
beseech, entreat, implore, request,
solicit **8.** entreaty, petition **9.** importune
10. lovability, loveliness, supplicate
11. winsomeness **12.** supplication
appealing ... **4.** nice **7.** winsome
8. alluring, charming, engaging,
pleasant **9.** agreeable, glamorous,
imploring **10.** attractive, beseeching,
bewitching, delightful, enchanting,
entreating **11.** fascinating, interesting
appear ... **4.** loom, seem **5.** occur
6. arrive, attend, emerge **11.** materialize
appearance ... **3.** air **4.** form, look, mien
5. front, guise, looks, phase **6.** aspect,
format, manner, ostent **7.** arrival,
feature, specter (spectre) **8.** illusion,
presence, pretense **9.** emergence,
semblance **10.** apparition, disclosure,
revelation **11.** resemblance
13. manifestation
appearance (pert to) ...
book .. **6.** format
brief .. **5.** cameo
false .. **8.** disguise
first .. **4.** dawn **5.** debut **8.** premiere
frontal .. **6.** facade
surface .. **6.** patina
truth (appearance of) .. **14.** verisimilitude
white .. **6.** pallid
appease ... **4.** calm **5.** allay, atone,
mease, quiet, salve **6.** pacify, soothe
7. content, placate, relieve, satisfy
8. mitigate **10.** conciliate **11.** tranquilize

appeasement . . . 6. relief 7. salving
8. easement 10. compromise,
mitigation, palliation 12. pacification
appellation . . . 3. tag 4. name 5. label,
style, title 7. calling, epithet
8. cognomen, nickname 9. sobriquet
11. designation 12. denomination,
nomenclature 14. identification
append . . . 3. add 4. hang 5. affix,
annex 6. adjoin, attach 7. subjoin
11. superimpose
appendage . . . 3. arm, awn, cue, tab,
tag 4. barb, flap, lobe, tail 5. cauda,
queue 6. ligule (Bot), palpus 7. adjunct,
pigtail 8. addition, hanger-on, pendicle
9. accessory, tailpiece 10. dependency
12. appurtenance 13. accompaniment
appendix . . . 6. sequel 7. codicil, process
8. addendum, addition 9. accessory,
appendage 10. dependency
12. augmentation
appertain . . . 4. bear 5. apply 6. affect,
belong, regard, relate 7. involve, pertain
appetite . . . 4. zest 5. taste 6. desire,
hunger, orexis, thirst 7. longing, passion
8. cupidity 9. appetency 10. hungriness,
propensity
appetizer . . . 4. fish (sauce) 6. canape
8. antepast, aperitif 9. antipasto,
foretaste 11. hors d'oeuvre
appetizing . . . 6. savory 7. piquant
8. tempting 9. appealing, desirable
10. attractive 11. captivating,
provocative, tantalizing
applaud . . . 4. clap, hail, laud, root,
yell 5. cheer, extol, shout 6. hurrah,
praise 7. acclaim, approve, commend,
endorse 10. compliment
applauders (paid) . . . 6. claque 8. clappers
9. claqueurs
applause . . . 4. clap, hand 5. bravo, éclat,
huzza 6. encore, praise 7. acclaim,
ovation 8. plaudits 11. acclamation
12. commendation
apple . . . 3. May, Spy 4. crab, pome
6. annona, pippin, rennet, russet
7. Baldwin, codling (codlin), costard,
Newtown, Roxbury, winesap
8. Greening, Jonathan, Mandrake,
McIntosh, queening 9. astrachan,
Delicious 10. bellflower, Rome Beauty
11. Granny Smith, Gravenstein,
Northern Spy
apple (pert to) . . .
acid . . 5. malic
brandy . . 8. Calvados
crushed . . 6. pomace
dessert . . 10. brown betty
disease . . 7. stippen
genus . . 5. Malus
juice . . 5. cider 9. applejack
love . . 6. tomato
seed . . 3. pip
shaped . . 8. pomiform
Apple of Discord (Gr Myth) . . . 4. Eris
apple of one's eye . . . 3. pet 4. idol
5. jewel, pupil 7. darling, desired
8. favorite 10. preference
applesauce . . . 4. bunk, pooh 5. tripe
6. phooey 7. baloney, hogwash
8. malarkey, nonsense, tommyrot

12. fiddlesticks 13. horsefeathers
appliance . . . 3. dam (dental) 4. tool
6. device, gadget 7. utensil 8. facility
9. commodity, implement
10. instrument 11. application,
contraption, convenience
applicable . . . 3. apt, fit 6. usable
7. pliable 8. apposite, relative, relevant
9. compliant, pertinent 11. appropriate
application . . . 3. use 6. appeal, effort
7. bearing, concern, request 8. petition,
recourse 9. attention, constancy,
diligence, relevance, relevancy
10. connection, employment, pertinence
11. attribution, disposition,
engrossment, persistence, requisition
12. perseverance 14. administration
application (body) . . . 4. balm 5. salve,
stupe (hot) 7. plaster 8. cosmetic,
poultice
apply . . . 3. use 4. suit 6. appose,
bestow, comply, devote, employ, relate
7. solicit, utilize 9. associate, attribute
10. administer 11. appropriate
appoggiature . . . 9. grace note
13. embellishment
appoint . . . 3. fix 4. name 5. equip
6. assign, decree, depute, detail, ordain
7. destine, prepare 8. delegate, deputize
9. designate, establish, prescribe
10. constitute
appointment . . . 4. date 5. order, tryst
7. command 8. position 9. direction,
equipment, ordinance 10. engagement
11. designation 13. establishment
appointments . . . 6. things 8. fittings,
fixtures 9. equipment, furniture
10. belongings, upholstery
11. acquirement, furnishings
12. accumulation, conveniences
13. accouterments, paraphernalia
apportion . . . 3. fix, lot 4. deal, dele,
mete, part 5. allot, carve, share
6. assign, budget, divide 7. arrange,
dispose 8. allocate 9. collocate, partition
10. distribute
appose . . . 4. abut 5. audit, liken,
place 6. adjoin 7. compare, examine
9. juxtapose
apposite . . . 3. apt 4. like 5. close, match
6. timely 7. fitting, germane 8. position,
relative, relevant 9. pertinent
11. appropriate
appraise . . . 4. mark, rank, rate 5. assay,
gauge, judge, price, value 6. assess,
evalue, praise 7. apprise, commend,
measure 8. consider, estimate, evaluate
10. adjudicate, appreciate
appraiser (tax) . . . 5. rater 6. lister
8. assessor
appreciable . . . 3. any 8. tangible
9. estimable 11. perceptible
appreciate . . . 4. feel, grow, know
5. enjoy, prize, savor, value 6. admire,
esteem 7. advance, amplify, approve,
augment, realize, respect 8. estimate,
increase, treasure
appreciation . . . 7. respect 9. appraisal,
awareness, gratitude 10. estimation
11. realization, recognition, sensibility
12. gratefulness, thankfulness

apprehend . . . **3.** ken, see **4.** know, take
5. dread, grasp, pinch (sl), savvy,
seize, sense **6.** arrest **7.** capture,
imagine, realize **8.** conceive, perceive
10. anticipate, comprehend, understand
apprehensible . . . **8.** knowable
9. scrutable **10.** explicable, fathomable
11. accountable **12.** discoverable,
intelligible **14.** comprehensible,
understandable
apprehension . . . **4.** fear, idea **5.** alarm,
doubt, dread, qualm **6.** arrest **7.** anxiety,
capture, concern, opinion, seizure
8. distress, distrust, suspense
9. misgiving, suspicion **10.** foreboding,
solicitude, uneasiness **11.** fearfulness,
premonition **12.** intelligence
13. understanding
apprehensive . . . **5.** smart **6.** uneasy
7. alarmed, fearful, knowing, nervous,
worried **8.** troubled **9.** cognizant,
concerned, conscious, perturbed
10. perceptive, solicitous
apprentice . . . **4.** tyro **6.** novice
7. amateur, trainee **8.** beginner
apprize, apprise . . . **4.** rate, tell **5.** price,
value **6.** advise, assess, impart, inform,
reckon **8.** acquaint, appraise **9.** enlighten
11. communicate
apprized . . . **5.** aware **8.** informed
9. cognizant
approach . . . **3.** way **4.** adit, come, near,
road **5.** stalk, verge **6.** access, accost,
advent, impend **7.** arrival, nearing, sea
gate **8.** entryway, likeness, nearness,
overture, resemble **11.** approximate,
entranceway
approachable . . . **4.** open **8.** gettable,
passable **9.** reachable **10.** accessible,
attainable **13.** communicative
approbation . . . **5.** favor, proof **6.** praise
7. plaudit **8.** applause, approval,
sanction **10.** acceptance, admiration
12. commendation, confirmation
appropriate . . . **3.** apt, fit **4.** akin,
meet, take **5.** allot, steal, usurp
6. borrow, pirate, proper, timely,
worthy **7.** condign, germane, related,
special **8.** deserved, relevant, suitable
9. befitting, expedient, favorable,
opportune, pertinent **10.** assimilate,
monopolize, plagiarize **11.** conformable
appropriately . . . **4.** duly **5.** aptly **6.** timely
appropriation . . . **5.** theft **6.** corner,
taking **8.** monopoly **9.** allotment
10. assignment, possession, usurpation
approval . . . **6.** assent **7.** consent,
support **8.** sanction **10.** admiration
11. approbation, endorsement
12. ratification
approve . . . **2.** OK **4.** like, okay, pass, sign,
test **6.** attest, ratify **7.** applaud, betoken,
certify, confirm, endorse (indorse),
signify **8.** accredit, sanction, validate
9. authorize, undersign **10.** appreciate
11. countenance **12.** authenticate
approve of . . . **5.** favor **6.** accept
7. endorse (indorse) **8.** sanction
11. countenance
approximate . . . **4.** near **5.** about, circa,
match **8.** approach, draw near, parallel,

resemble **10.** correspond
approximately . . . **4.** or so **5.** about, circa
6. around, nearly **11.** thereabouts
appui . . . **4.** prop, stay **6.** bridle (manège)
7. support
appulse . . . **6.** syzygy **7.** impinge
8. approach **9.** collision **11.** conjunction
(Astron)
appurtenance . . . **4.** gear **7.** adjunct
8. addition **9.** accessory, apparatus,
appendage, belonging, component
appurtenant . . . **7.** annexed **8.** incident,
relevant **9.** appendant, belonging
11. appropriate
après . . . **5.** after **10.** afterwards
apricot (pert to) . . .
  African . . **6.** meebos (dried)
  beverage . . **7.** cordial, liqueur, persico
  color . . **9.** red-yellow
  confection . . **6.** meebos (mebos)
  Japanese . . **3.** ume **4.** ansu
  vine . . **6.** maypop
a priori (opp of posteriori) . . . **9.** deductive
11. conditional, presumptive
12. hypothetical **13.** presumptively
apron . . . **3.** bib **4.** boot, brat, tier **5.** smock
6. barvel (barvell), runway **7.** garment,
tablier **8.** airstrip, lambskin (Masonic),
pinafore **9.** appendage
apropos, a propos . . . **3.** apt, pat
7. germane, purpose **8.** by the
way, relevant, suitably **9.** pertinent
10. applicable, seasonable
11. appurtenant, opportunely
12. incidentally
apt . . . **3.** fit, pat **4.** deft **5.** adept,
prone, ready, smart **6.** clever, expert,
likely, prompt, suited **7.** capable,
elegant, subject **8.** apposite, disposed,
inclined, skillful, suitable **9.** competent,
dexterous, ingenious, masterful,
pertinent, qualified, teachable
10. proficient **11.** appropriate
apteral . . . **8.** apterous, wingless
Apteryx . . . **3.** moa (extinct) **4.** kiwi
aptitude . . . **3.** art **4.** bent, gift, turn **5.** flair,
skill **6.** genius, talent **7.** ability, aptness,
fitness, leaning **8.** penchant, tendency
9. liability **10.** likelihood, proclivity
11. inclination **12.** suitableness
15. appropriateness
aptly . . . **7.** exactly, readily **8.** suitably
11. pertinently
aptness . . . **5.** skill **7.** fitness **8.** tendency
9. smartness **11.** suitability
12. teachability
aqua . . . **3.** eau **4.** agua **5.** water
aquatic . . . **6.** natant, wading, watery
8. natatory, swimming **12.** grallatorial
13. water-dwelling
Aquila . . . **6.** eagles **13.** constellation
(Milky Way)
aquiline . . . **6.** hanate, hooked **7.** curving
8. aduncous, unciform **10.** Roman-
nosed
ara . . . **5.** macaw **7.** goddess (vengeance)
8. aracanga **9.** screw pine
13. constellation
Arab . . . **4.** waif **5.** gamin, horse,
nomad **6.** Semite **7.** Bedouin, Saracen
8. wanderer, Yemenite **9.** Caucasian

araba . . . **3.** cab **5.** coach **6.** monkey (howling)
Arabia . . . see *Saudi-Arabia*
Arabian (pert to) . . .
antelope . . **5.** addax
beverage . . **4.** boza (bosa) **5.** leban (lebban)
bird . . **7.** phoenix
chief . . **5.** sheik
cloth (shoulder) . . **6.** cabaan (caban)
demon . . **5.** Eblis, jinni (jinnee) **6.** afreet
father . . **3.** Abu (Ab, Abou) **4.** Abba
garment . . **3.** aba **4.** haik **8.** burnoose
gazelle . . **4.** cora, oryx **5.** ariel
horse . . **4.** Kohl **8.** kadischi, palomino
jasmine . . **4.** bela
judge . . **4.** cadi
juniper (Bib) . . **5.** retem
nomad . . **7.** Saracen
peasant . . **6.** fellah
people (anc) . . **3.** Aus
physician . . **8.** Avicenna
poet . . **5.** Antar
prince . . **4.** emir (amir) **5.** emeer (ameer), sheik **6.** sherif, sultan
ravine . . **4.** wadi
romance . . **5.** Antar (Antara)
ruler . . **6.** caliph (calif)
Satan . . **5.** Eblis **6.** Azazel
scripture . . **7.** Alcoran
seaport . . **4.** Aden **5.** Mocha
state of bliss . . **3.** kef (kaif)
street urchin . . **5.** gamin
tambourine . . **4.** taar
vessel . . **4.** dhow **6.** boutre, sambuk
winds (hot) . . **6.** simoom (simoon)
Arabic letter . . . **4.** alif
arable land . . . **4.** farm **5.** arada, arado **6.** plowed, tilled **10.** cultivated
arachnid . . . **4.** mite, tick **6.** spider **8.** scorpion **9.** Arachnida
Aralu . . . **5.** Hades
Aram (Bib) . . . **6.** Rimmon (deity) **7.** Aramaic, Semitic **8.** language
araneous . . . **4.** thin **7.** weblike **8.** delicate **10.** cobweblike
arapunga . . . **8.** bellbird **9.** campanero
Arawak . . . **5.** Guana **6.** Indian
arbeit . . . **4.** work **8.** research
arbiter . . . **3.** ump **5.** judge **6.** umpire **7.** arbiter, referee **8.** mediator **9.** moderator **10.** arbitrator
arbitrary . . . **6.** thetic **8.** absolute, despotic, dogmatic **9.** imperious, unlimited **10.** autocratic, capricious, high-handed, peremptory, tyrannical **11.** determinate, dictatorial **13.** discretionary
arbitrate . . . **6.** decide **7.** bargain, mediate **9.** determine, intervene, negotiate **12.** intermediate
arbitrator . . . **5.** judge **6.** umpire **7.** arbiter, referee **8.** mediator **9.** moderator **11.** conciliator
arbor, arbour . . . **5.** bower, kiosk **6.** alcove, garden, pandal **7.** pergola, retreat, trellis **11.** latticework, summerhouse
arboreal . . . **6.** ramous **8.** branched, treelike **10.** arboriform
arboreal mammal . . . **2.** ai **4.** unau **5.** lemur, sloth **6.** aye-aye, monkey

arc . . . **3.** bow **5.** curve **6.** radian **7.** azimuth, rainbow
arca . . . **3.** box **5.** chest, paten **9.** reliquary
arcade . . . **3.** orb **4.** arch, hall **6.** arches, avenue **7.** gallery, portico **8.** arcature, corridor **9.** colonnade, peristyle **10.** passageway
Arcadia . . .
composition . . **4.** poem **5.** prose **7.** romance
district . . **6.** Greece
huntress . . **8.** Atalanta
pert to . . **5.** rural **6.** rustic **8.** pastoral
poetic . . **6.** Arcady
priestess . . **4.** Auge
woodland spirit . . **3.** Pan
arcanum . . . **6.** elixir, enigma, remedy, secret **7.** mystery
arch . . . **3.** arc, sly **4.** ogee **5.** chief, hance (part), ogive, vault **6.** fornix, instep **7.** cunning, eminent, roguish **8.** greatest, memorial, monument **9.** principal **11.** mischievous
arch (pert to) . . .
enemy . . **5.** devil, Satan **9.** adversary
inner curve . . **8.** intrados
memorial . . **6.** pailou (pailoo)
stone . . **8.** keystone
title . . **4.** duke **6.** bishop, deacon **7.** duchess
archaic . . . **3.** old **8.** obsolete, old-world **10.** antiquated **12.** old-fashioned
archangel (celestial) . . . **5.** Uriel **7.** Gabriel, Michael, Raphael
archangel plant . . . **4.** mint **8.** angelica
archbishop . . . **6.** bishop (chief), exarch **9.** patriarch
arched . . . **6.** curved **7.** embowed
Archer (Astron) . . . **11.** Sagittarius
archery . . . **3.** bow **4.** vane **5.** arrow, clout **6.** quiver **8.** fistmele, shooting **10.** ballistics
archetype . . . **4.** idea **5.** model **7.** pattern **8.** standard **9.** prototype
Archie (sl) . . . **3.** gun **12.** antiaircraft
Archipelago (pert to) . . .
Alaska . . **9.** Alexander
Australia . . **8.** Bismarck
Indonesia (largest) . . **5.** Malay
Italy . . **6.** Aegean
architect . . . **6.** artist, author **7.** builder, planner **8.** designer **9.** artificer, draftsman **11.** constructor, enterpriser
architectural (pert to) . . .
arch . . **8.** keystone, voussoir
base . . **5.** socle **6.** plinth
construction . . **8.** tectonic
ornament (part) . . **5.** gutta **6.** bezant, finial, frieze **8.** acanthus, dosseret, fretwork **10.** chambranle
pier . . **4.** anta
space (triang) . . **8.** pediment
style . . **5.** Doric, Greek, Ionic, Tudor **6.** Gothic **7.** Baroque, Cape Cod, Moorish, Spanish **8.** Colonial, Etruscan, Georgian **9.** Byzantine, Palladian **10.** Corinthian, Romanesque **11.** Renaissance **13.** Mediterranean
archives . . . **6.** annals **7.** records **8.** chancery, registry **9.** documents, registers **10.** chronicles

arch traitor . . . **6.** Arnold (Benedict), Brutus **8.** Quisling **13.** Judas Iscariot
archway . . . **6.** pailou (pailoo)
arctic . . . **5.** polar **6.** boreal, frigid, galosh **7.** Alaskan **8.** hibernal, Northern, Siberian **11.** hyperborean
Arctic (pert to) . . .
  base . . **4.** Etah (Greenland)
  bird . . **3.** auk **4.** skua, xema **6.** falcon
  cetacean . . **7.** narwhal
  current . . **8.** Labrador
  dog . . **5.** Husky (Siberian) **8.** Malemute
  food . . **8.** pemmican (pemican)
  jacket (hooded) . . **5.** parka (parkee) **6.** anorak
  native . . **5.** Aleut **6.** Eskimo, Indian
  polar . . **6.** Circle
  sea . . **7.** Barents **8.** Beaufort
arctoid . . . **6.** ursine **8.** bearlike
Arctoidea . . . **4.** bear **6.** weasel **7.** raccoon
ardent . . . **3.** hot **4.** avid, keen, warm **5.** eager, fiery, rethe **6.** fervid, fierce **7.** amorous, cordial, fervent, flaming, glowing, intense, shining, violent, zealous **8.** eloquent, vehement **10.** passionate **12.** affectionate, enthusiastic
ardilla . . . **8.** squirrel
ardor . . . **4.** élan, fire, heat, love, zeal **5.** estro, flame, gusto, verve **6.** fervor, fougue, spirit, warmth **8.** fervency **9.** affection, eagerness, eloquence, intensity **10.** enthusiasm **11.** impetuosity
arduous . . . **4.** hard **5.** steep **6.** trying **7.** onerous **8.** toilsome **9.** difficult, laborious, strenuous, wearisome **10.** burdensome, exhausting
area . . . **4.** belt, loci (pl), size, zone **5.** areal, basin, field, locus, range, scope, space, tract **6.** extent, locale, region, sector, sphere **7.** circuit, compass, environ, expanse **8.** province, vicinity **9.** bailiwick, territory **12.** neighborhood
Areca . . . **4.** palm
arena . . . **4.** bowl, oval, ring, rink **5.** court, field **6.** campus, circus **7.** cockpit, stadium, theater **8.** coliseum, platform **9.** gymnasium **10.** hippodrome **12.** amphitheater
arenose . . . **5.** sandy **6.** grainy, gritty **8.** sabulous
areola . . . **4.** halo, ring **5.** space **6.** armlet, wreath **7.** aureole, garland **10.** interstice
Ares (pert to) . . .
  consort . . **9.** Aphrodite
  father . . **4.** Zeus
  god . . **3.** war
  Roman name . . **4.** Mars
argala . . . **7.** marabou **8.** adjutant (bird)
argent . . . **5.** white **6.** silver **7.** shining, silvery **9.** whiteness
Argentina . . .
  capital . . **11.** Buenos Aires (1535)
  city . . **5.** Lanus **6.** Paraná **7.** Cordoba, Mendoza, Rosario
  Indian . . **4.** Lule
  mountain . . **5.** Andes **9.** Aconcagua (peak) **10.** Cordillera (Range)
  native . . **7.** Mestizo
  Plains . . **6.** Pampas **9.** Gran Chaco
  plateau . . **9.** Patagonia

  poet . . **7.** Andrade **10.** Echeverria
  river . . **5.** Plata **6.** Chubut, Paraná
Argentine (pert to) . . .
  color . . **7.** silvery **8.** art brown
  cowboy . . **6.** gaucho
  dance . . **5.** tango
Argonauts (pert to) . . .
  destination . . **7.** Colchis (anc)
  leader . . **5.** Jason
  objective . . **12.** Golden Fleece
  of '49 . . **6.** miners (gold)
  ship . . **5.** Argos
  sorceress . . **5.** Medea
Argos . . . **3.** dog (of Odysseus)
argosy . . . **4.** ship **5.** fleet **6.** armada, vessel **8.** flotilla
argot . . . **4.** cant, jive **5.** lingo, slang **6.** jargon, patois **7.** dialect **10.** vernacular
argue . . . **3.** rap **4.** moot, spar **5.** plead, prove **6.** bicker, debate, evince, reason **7.** contend, contest, discuss, dispute, wrangle **8.** indicate, maintain, persuade **10.** controvert **11.** expostulate, ratiocinate, remonstrate
argument . . . **4.** case, plea, spar **5.** cavil, lemma, proof, theme **6.** debate, hassle **7.** defense, dispute, fallacy, polemic, premise, sophism **8.** brouhaha, squabble **9.** dialectic, discourse, enthymeme, pro and con **10.** discussion **11.** altercation, disputation **13.** consideration, ratiocination
argumentative . . . **7.** eristic **8.** forensic **10.** indicative, rhetorical **11.** belligerent, contentious, presumptive, quarrelsome **12.** disputatious **13.** controversial
Argus (Gr Myth) . . . **7.** monster (founder of Argos)
Argus-eyed . . . **8.** vigilant **9.** observant **11.** hundred-eyed **12.** sharpsighted
argute . . . **5.** acute, sharp **6.** astute, shrewd, shrill, subtle **9.** sagacious
aria . . . **3.** air, lay **4.** solo, song, tune **5.** canto **6.** cantus, melody, strain **7.** ariette, sortita
arid . . . **3.** dry **4.** dull **6.** barren, jejune, vacant **7.** parched, sterile, thirsty **9.** anhydrous, waterless **13.** unimaginative
Arid Austral zone . . . **7.** Sonoran
Ariel . . . **5.** angel, sylph **6.** spirit **7.** lioness **9.** Jerusalem
ariel . . . **7.** gazelle
Aries (Astron) . . . **3.** ram **4.** sign **6.** meteor **13.** constellation
aries . . . **12.** battering-ram (anc)
aright . . . **4.** fine, well **7.** exactly **8.** directly, straight **11.** straightway
aril . . . **3.** pod **7.** arillus, coating **8.** arillode (false), covering
Arion . . . **4.** poet (of Lesbos) **5.** horse (talking)
arioso . . . **7.** melodic, tuneful **9.** melodious
arise . . . **4.** lift, rise, soar, stem, zoom **5.** begin, issue, mount, occur, rebel, surge, tower, waken **6.** appear, ascend, emerge, revolt, spring **7.** emanate **9.** originate
Aristarch . . . **6.** critic **10.** grammarian
Aristides . . . **7.** The Just **9.** statesman

(Athens)
aristocracy . . . **5.** elite **7.** peerage, royalty
8. nobility **10.** government, patriciate,
upper class
aristocrat . . . **4.** lord, peer **5.** noble
7. aristos, Brahman, Brahmin, grandee,
parvenu **8.** cavalier, eupatrid (Athens),
nobleman **9.** blueblood, patrician
12. silk-stocking
aristology, science of . . . **6.** dining
Aristole (pert to) . . .
birthplace . . **6.** Thrace **7.** Stagira
(Macedonia)
famed as . . **9.** scientist **11.** philosopher
12. The Stagirite
school . . **6.** Athens
teacher . . **5.** Plato
wife . . **7.** Pythias
arithmetic . . . **4.** sums **7.** numbers
11. computation, enumeration,
mathematics
arithmetic terms . . . **5.** prime **6.** result
7. divisor, product **8.** dividend, multiple,
quotient **9.** remainder **10.** multiplier
12. multiplicand
Arizona . . .
capital . . **7.** Phoenix
city . . **4.** Yuma **5.** Tempe **6.** Bisbee,
Tucson
famed site . . **9.** Hoover Dam **11.** Grand
Canyon **13.** Painted Desert **15.** Petrified
Forest
Indian . . **4.** Hano, Hopi, Pima **6.** Apache,
Navaho (Navajo)
river . . **4.** Gila **8.** Colorado
State admission . . **11.** Forty-eighth
State bird . . **10.** cactus wren
State flower . . **6.** cactus **7.** saguaro
State motto . . **9.** Ditat Deus **11.** God
Enriches
State nickname . . **11.** Grand Canyon
ark . . . **3.** vat **4.** boat, ship **5.** chest, haven
6. asylum, refuge, vessel **8.** flatboat
9. broadhorn, sanctuary (Ararat)
Arkansas . . .
capital . . **10.** Little Rock
city . . **8.** El Dorado **9.** Fort Smith
famed for . . **8.** diamonds (found in
Murfreesboro)
famed newspaper . . **7.** Gazette (1819)
mountain . . **6.** Ozarks **9.** Ouachitas
Park (Nat) . . **10.** Hot Springs
river . . **5.** White **11.** Mississippi
State admission . . **11.** Twenty-fifth
State bird . . **11.** mockingbird
State flower . . **12.** apple blossom
State motto . . **13.** Regnat Populus **16.** Let
the People Rule
State nickname . . **17.** Land of
Opportunity
arm . . . **4.** limb **5.** equip, saber, sword
6. branch, member, pistol, tappet,
weapon **7.** forearm, fortify, protect,
quillon (of sword), support **8.** revolver
9. appendage **10.** projection
12. ramification
arm (pert to) . . .
armpit . . **5.** oxter **6.** axilla
bone . . **4.** ulna **6.** radius **7.** humerus
hole . . **4.** scye (of sleeve)
muscle . . **6.** biceps **7.** triceps **8.** pronator

9. supinator
projection . . **6.** tappet
sea . . **4.** gulf, mere **5.** bayou, firth, inlet
7. estuary
sundial . . **6.** gnomon
walk arm in arm . . **5.** oxter
armada . . . **5.** fleet **6.** argosy **8.** armament,
flotilla, squadron, warships
10. escadrille
Armada (famed) . . . **7.** Spanish (1588)
10. Invincible
armadillo . . . **4.** apar, peba (peva) **5.** apara,
poyou, tatou (tatu) **6.** mulita, peludo
(giant) **7.** tatouay **10.** pichiciago,
Tolypeutes **11.** quirquincho (hairy)
Armageddon . . . **3.** war **7.** Megiddo (Bib)
8. conflict, world war
armed . . . **6.** fitted, rigged **7.** clothed,
endowed **8.** equipped, invested,
prepared, provided, supplied
9. furnished, outfitted **10.** laquearian
(with noose)
armed (pert to) . . .
conflict . . **3.** war **6.** combat **7.** warfare
11. hostilities
forces . . **4.** army, host **5.** ranks **6.** troops
8. military **9.** besiegers
vessel . . **3.** HMS, sub, USS **5.** U-boat
9. destroyer, submarine **10.** battleship
11. battlewagon
Armenia . . .
anc name . . **9.** Armenenak
capital . . **6.** Erivan
founder . . **4.** Haik
herb . . **5.** cumin **7.** caraway
highlanders . . **5.** Gomer
mountain . . **6.** Ararat, Taurus
river . . **3.** Kur **5.** Cyrus **6.** Araxes, Tigris
9. Euphrates
worshiper . . **7.** Yesidio (Yesdi)
9. Gregorian
armistice . . . **5.** peace, truce **9.** cessation
12. pacification
armoire . . . **5.** ambry **8.** cupboard,
wardrobe **10.** repository
armor . . . **4.** arms, bard (barde), egis,
jamb, mail, tace **5.** acton, aegis,
plate, seton, tasse **6.** cuisse, gorget,
graith, greave, helmet, lorica, sconce,
shield, tasset, tuille **7.** ailette, cuirass,
hauberk, jambeau, panoply **8.** aventail,
brassort, ordnance, pallette, solleret
9. cubitiere, epauliere, gardebras,
mainferre, rerebrace **10.** cataphract
armor-bearer . . . **6.** squire **7.** armiger,
esquire
armored . . . **6.** mailed **8.** equipped,
ironclad, mailclad **9.** cuirassed,
loricated, panoplied
armpit . . . **5.** oxter **6.** axilla
arms . . . **7.** weapons **8.** armament,
ordnance **9.** munitions
arms depository . . . **5.** depot **6.** armory
7. arsenal
army . . . **3.** mob **4.** host, unit **5.** array,
crowd, horde, posse **6.** forces, galaxy,
legion, rabble, throng, troops
9. multitude, Salvation
army (pert to) . . .
brown . . **7.** rosario
commission (special) . . **6.** brevet

trader.. **6.** sutler
army unit ... **4.** ROTC **5.** corps, guard
(Nat), squad **7.** brigade, cavalry,
company, militia, platoon, Sabaoth
(Bib) **8.** division, infantry, Landwehr,
regiment, reserves **9.** artillery, battalion,
minutemen **10.** volunteers
Arnold's co-conspirator ... **5.** Andre
(Maj)
aroma ... **4.** musk, odor, tang **5.** attar,
balmy, nidor, savor, scent, smell, spice
6. flavor **7.** bouquet, feature, incense,
perfume **9.** fragrance, muskiness,
redolence **11.** peculiarity, singularity
aromatic ... **5.** spicy **6.** savory **7.** odorous,
pungent **8.** fragrant, redolent
11. fluorescent
aromatic (pert to) ...
gum.. **5.** myrrh **12.** frankincense
herb.. **4.** mint **5.** clary, nondo
oil.. **4.** balm **6.** balsam **9.** sassafras
seed.. **4.** anis **6.** nutmeg **7.** aniseed,
caraway
tree.. **5.** aromo **6.** balsam **7.** champac
8. huisache
around ... **4.** near, peri (pref) **5.** about,
circa **9.** bordering, somewhere
11. thereabouts **13.** approximately
arouse ... **4.** fire, stir, wake **5.** alarm,
anger, evoke, pique, raise, rally, roust
6. awaken, elicit, excite, incite, kindle,
summon **7.** animate
arpa ... **4.** harp
arpeggio ... **5.** chord **7.** roulade
8. division, flourish
arraign ... **4.** cite **6.** accuse, charge, indict
7. impeach **8.** denounce, reproach
9. prosecute
arrange ... **3.** fix **4.** cast, cite, file,
plan, plot, sort **5.** adapt, aline, besee,
drape, ettle, frame, grade, preen,
range, stack **6.** adjust, deploy, design,
devise **7.** dispose, mediate, prepare,
provide, seriate **8.** classify, contract,
contrive, laminate, organize, tabulate
9. catalogue (catalog), negotiate
10. distribute, paniculate
11. alphabetize, systematize
arranged ... **5.** fixed, timed **6.** ranked,
sorted **7.** aligned, grouped, ordered,
orderly, planned, settled, uniform
9. regulated **10.** contracted
arranged in ...
fives.. **7.** quinate
fours.. **11.** tetramerous
hours.. **9.** staggered
rays.. **6.** radial
threes.. **7.** ternate
arrangement ... **3.** art, rig (sails)
4. plan, rank **5.** order, setup **6.** series,
syntax, system **7.** echelon (troops),
musical **8.** disposal, neatness, trimness
9. agreement, condition, structure
10. adaptation, engagement, settlement
11. collocation, combination,
permutation, preparation
12. distribution
arrant ... **3.** bad **6.** wicked **8.** rascally
9. confirmed, shameless
11. unmitigated **12.** disreputable
array ... **3.** don **4.** deci, robe **5.** adorn,

align, dress, order **6.** clothe, muster,
series, throng **7.** arrange, dispose,
envelop, marshal **8.** clothing, garments
9. adornment **11.** arrangement
arrears ... **3.** due **4.** debt **5.** short
7. wanting **8.** arrearage, deficient
10. behindhand, defaulting
arrest ... **4.** halt, hold, stop **5.** check,
delay, seize **6.** detain, hinder, impede,
retard **7.** custody, seizure **8.** obstruct,
restrain, stoppage **9.** apprehend,
hindrance, intercept, restraint
11. retardation
arrested ... **6.** behind **7.** checked, delayed,
impeded, stopped **8.** detained, retarded
10. restrained **11.** intercepted
arrested development ... **6.** simple
7. dwarfed, idiotic, moronic
8. backward, retarded **10.** half-witted
13. unintelligent
arrival ... **5.** comer (anc) **6.** advent,
coming **7.** landing **8.** approach,
reaching **10.** attainment, homecoming
11. achievement
arrive ... **4.** come **5.** debus, reach **6.** alight,
debark, happen **7.** detrain **9.** disembark
arrogance ... **5.** pride **7.** conceit,
disdain, hauteur **8.** audacity, rudeness,
snobbery **9.** brashness, insolence,
loftiness **10.** effrontery **11.** haughtiness
12. impertinence
arrogant ... **4.** bold, pert **5.** cocky, lofty,
proud **6.** lordly, uppish **7.** forward
8. impudent, insolent **9.** audacious,
insulting, masterful, presuming
10. disdainful **11.** domineering, highfalutin, impertinent, overbearing
12. contemptuous, contumelious,
presumptuous, supercilious
arrogate ... **5.** seize, usurp, wrest
6. assume **11.** appropriate
arrow ... **4.** barb, dart, reed, vire
(feathered) **5.** guide, shaft **6.** finger
7. missile, pointer **10.** guideboard
arrow (pert to) ...
astronomy.. **7.** Sagitta
bows.. **6.** bowyer (maker, seller)
case.. **6.** quiver
end.. **4.** nock **9.** arrowhead
feather (to).. **6.** fletch
handle.. **5.** stele
head.. **4.** dart
poison.. **4.** inee, upas **5.** urali **6.** curare,
uzarin
poisoned.. **6.** sumpit **8.** sumpitan
propeller.. **3.** bow
shape.. **6.** beloid **9.** cuneiform, sagittate
stone.. **9.** belemnite
variety.. **4.** self **6.** footed **7.** chested
9. bobtailed
arrowroot ... **3.** pia **5.** araru **6.** ararao,
starch **7.** Maranta
arroyo ... **5.** brook, creek **6.** ravine,
stream **11.** watercourse
arroz ... **4.** rice
arse ... **4.** butt, rump (vulgar) **8.** buttocks
9. posterior
arsenal ... **4.** dump **5.** depot, plant
6. armory **7.** factory **8.** magazine
10. depository, storehouse
arsis ... **5.** ictus **6.** accent, stress (opp

of thesis), upbeat
arson . . . **7.** burning, cautery **9.** pyromania
12. incendiarism
art . . . **4.** wile **5.** cameo, craft, knack, skill,
taste, trade **6.** design **7.** calling, cartoon,
cunning, drawing, science **8.** aptitude,
artifice, artistry, business, ceramics,
drafting, intaglio, painting, vocation
9. dexterity, duplicate, engraving,
ingenuity, readiness, sculpture,
sketching **10.** adroitness, decoration,
profession **11.** contrivance,
photography, portraiture
12. architecture
art (pert to) . . .
addict . . **8.** aesthete (esthete)
decoration . . **9.** sgraffito
design . . **7.** graphic
fancier . . **10.** dilettante
gallery . . **5.** salon
grotesque . . **11.** incongruous
mystic . . **6.** cabala
of assaying . . **8.** docimasy
of discourse . . **8.** rhetoric
of embossing . . **9.** toreutics
of government . . **8.** politics
of horsemanship . . **6.** manège
of imitation . . **7.** mimicry
of manual craft . . **5.** sloyd
of memory . . **10.** mneumonics
of metal inlay . . **6.** niello
primitive . . **9.** artifacts
realistic . . **5.** genre
rhyming . . **5.** poesy **6.** poetry
self-defense . . **6.** boxing **7.** fencing,
jujitsu (jiujitsu)
style, movement . . **3.** pop **6.** cubism,
rococo **7.** baroque, Bauhaus, Dadaism,
Fauvism **8.** futurism **9.** modernism
10. surrealism **11.** romanticism
13. expressionism, impressionism
theme . . **5.** motif
tooling . . **10.** diesinking
transmutation . . **7.** alchemy
Artemis (pert to) . . .
brother (twin) . . **6.** Apollo
epithet (Homeric) . . **6.** Phoebe
father . . **4.** Zeus
goddess of . . **4.** moon **6.** nature **7.** the
Hunt **8.** Olympian
Mother . . **4.** Leto
religion . . **4.** Upis
Roman equivalent . . **5.** Diana
artery . . . **4.** tube, vein **6.** avenue, street,
vessel **7.** channel, highway, passage
8. ligament **10.** passageway
artery (Anat) . . . **4.** tube, vein **5.** aorta
6. vessel **7.** anonyma, carotid, trachea
9. capillary, pulmonary **10.** innominate
artery pulsation . . . **4.** beat **5.** ictus
artful . . . **3.** sly **4.** foxy, wily **5.** cagey
6. adroit, clever, crafty, shrewd,
subtle, tricky **7.** crooked, cunning,
knowing, politic **8.** skillful, stealthy
9. deceitful, deceptive, designing,
dexterous, imitative **10.** artificial
Artful Dodger . . . **3.** fox **6.** rascal **7.** slicker
8. deceiver **11.** John Dawkins (Dickens
tale) **12.** crafty person
artfulness . . . **5.** skill **7.** finesse **8.** artifice,
subtlety, wiliness **9.** stratagem

10. cleverness, refinement, shrewdness
arthron . . . **5.** hinge, joint, pivot
12. articulation
Arthurian abode . . . **6.** Avalon
9. Lyonnesse (Leonnoys)
Arthurian character . . . **6.** Arthur (King),
Elaine, Merlin **7.** Geraint **8.** Lancelot
9. Percivale
artichoke . . . **6.** canada, Cynara
7. chorogi, thistle **9.** Jerusalem
article . . . **3.** mat **4.** item, news, term
5. scoop, story, thing **6.** belief,
clause, detail, gadget, object, treaty
7. camelot, feature (news), grammar,
integer **8.** treatise **9.** commodity,
editorial **10.** particular **11.** composition,
stipulation
article (Gram) . . .
English . . **1.** a **2.** an **3.** the
French . . **2.** la, le, un **3.** les, une
Spanish . . **2.** el, un **3.** las, los, una
article (of) . . .
agreement . . **8.** contract
apparel . . **5.** smock, tunic **6.** duster,
gaiter, mantle **8.** pinafore
faith . . **5.** canon, creed, dogma, tenet
6. belief **7.** precept
property . . **7.** chattel
virtu . . **5.** curio, relic **6.** rarity **7.** antique
articulation . . . **4.** tone **5.** hinge, joint,
sound, voice **7.** voicing **8.** locution,
sonation **9.** phonation, utterance
11. enunciation **12.** vocalization
13. pronunciation
artifact . . . **5.** curio, relic, virtu **6.** fossil
7. antique, remains **8.** archaism
artifice . . . **4.** plot, ruse, wile **5.** blind,
chest, craft, dodge, fraud, guile, shift,
trick **6.** deceit **7.** cunning, evasion,
finesse, knavery, sleight **8.** intrigue,
maneuver, trickery **9.** chicanery,
collusion, deception, expedient,
imposture, stratagem **10.** connivance,
imposition, subterfuge **11.** contrivance,
machination, skulduggery
artificer . . . **5.** smith **6.** artist, framer
7. artisan, creator, deviser, workman
8. Daedalus, inventor, mechanic
9. architect, carpenter, craftsman,
goldsmith **11.** coppersmith, silversmith
artificial . . . **4.** fake, faux, mock, sham
5. bogus, dummy, false, phony
6. ersatz, forged, unreal **7.** assumed,
bastard, elegant, feigned **8.** affected,
fabulous, spurious **9.** imaginary,
imitation, pretended, unnatural
11. adulterated, counterfeit, unauthentic
12. suppositious
artificial (pert to) . . .
butter . . **4.** oleo **13.** oleomargarine
channel . . **3.** gat **4.** leat **5.** canal, flume
6. sluice
gum . . **7.** dextrin
language . . **2.** ro **3.** Ido **5.** Arulo
7. Volapuk **9.** Esperanto **10.** Occidental
silk . . **5.** nylon, rayon
surface . . **4.** rink
voice . . **8.** falsetto
artillery . . . **4.** army, guns **5.** bombs
6. cannon, slings **7.** cavalry, gunners,
gunnery, mortars **8.** ordnance

9. arbalests, catapults 10. ballistics
artillery (pert to) . . .
emplacement . . 7. battery
fire . . 5. salvo 6. rafale
man . . 6. gunner 8. rifleman, topechee
9. cannoneer, musketeer 11. artillarist
wagon . . 7. battery
artiodactyl . . . (opp of perissodactyl) 2. ox
3. pig 4. deer, goat 5. camel, sheep
6. artiad 7. giraffe 12. hippopotamus
artisan . . . 6. artist, limner 7. painter,
workman 8. mechanic, virtuoso
9. artificer, craftsman
artist . . . 5. rapin (Fr pupil) 6. etcher,
limner, potter 7. artisan, painter
8. designer, sculptor 9. architect,
decorator 10. cartoonist, ceramacist
11. illustrator 12. photographer
artist (pert to) . . .
equipment . . 5. easel 7. palette
8. maquette
sleight of hand . . 4. mage 5. Magus
8. magician 9. alchemist
artiste . . . 5. actor, adept 6. dancer, singer
7. artisan 8. musician 9. performer
artistic . . . 4. pure 6. ornate 7. classic
8. graceful, skillful, tasteful 9. aesthetic
(esthetic), art-minded, beautiful,
exquisite
artistic (pert to) . . .
ardor . . 5. verve 6. spirit
dance . . 6. ballet
quality . . 6. virtue
symbol of the dead . . 5. orant
temperament . . 7. caprice, emotion
artless . . . 4. naif, open, rude 5. frank,
naive 6. candid, simple 7. natural,
sincere 8. ignorant 9. guileness,
ingenuous, unskilled 10. inartistic,
unaffected, uncultured 11. undesigning
15. unsophisticated
artlessness . . . 6. candor 7. naiveté
9. frankness, innocence 11. naturalness
13. ungenuousness
arts (pert to) . . .
liberal . . 7. trivium 10. quadrivium
quadrivium . . 5. music 8. geometry
9. astronomy 10. arithmetic
trivium . . 5. logic 7. grammar 8. rhetoric
aru . . . 6. indeed, really
arui . . . 5. oudad, sheep 7. chamois (Bib)
arum . . . 4. taro 5. calla (lily) 6. starch
9. arrowroot
arx . . . 7. citadel
Aryan (pert to) . . .
God of Fire . . 4. Agni
invader . . 4. Pict
people . . 4. Mede 5. Hindu 9. Caucasian
11. Indo-Iranian
as . . . 3. qua 4. como, than, thus 5. since,
while 7. because, equally, similar
9. similarly
Asa . . . 11. King of Judah
asafetida . . . 8. medicine
13. antispasmodic
Asa's son . . . 11. Jehoshaphat
ascend . . . 3. fly 4. rise, soar, upgo
5. arise, climb, mount, scale, tower
6. aspire 7. clamber, upsurge
ascendancy . . . 4. sway 7. control,
mastery 8. dominion, prestige, priority

9. authority, influence, supremacy
10. domination 11. sovereignty,
superiority 12. predominance
13. preponderance
ascendant, ascendent . . . 5. elder
6. father 7. supreme 8. ancestor,
forebear, superior 9. governing,
patriarch 10. antecedent, decoration
(Arch)
ascended . . . 4. rose 5. arose, risen
6. uprose
ascending . . . 6. anodic, rising 7. scaling,
sloping 8. mounting, racemose
9. emanating
ascending signs . . . 5. Aries 6. Gemini,
Pisces, Taurus 8. Aquarius 9. Capricorn
ascenseur . . . 8. elevator
Ascension Day . . . 8. Thursday (Holy)
(40 days after Easter)
Ascension lily . . . 7. Madonna
ascertain . . . 4. find 5. learn, prove, solve
6. decide 7. certify 9. determine
ascetic . . . 4. yati, yoga, yogi 5. fakir,
stoic 6. Essene, hermit, strict 7. austere,
eremite, puritan, recluse 8. anchoret,
Diogenes, solitary 9. abstainer,
anchorite, mendicant 10. abstemious
asceticism . . . 4. Yoga 9. austerity,
nephalism 10. abstention, abstinence,
puritanism 11. anchoritism, teetotalism
ascribable . . . 3. due 9. traceable
10. assignable 11. attributive
12. attributable
ascribe . . . 5. count, refer 6. assign,
attach, credit, impute, reckon 7. ascribe
8. accredit 9. attribute
ascus fruit . . . 8. truffles
asepsis . . . 6. purity 7. clarity 9. sterility
13. taintlessness
ash . . . 4. sorb, tree 5. rowan 6. samara
(fruit) 8. Fraxinus
ashes . . . 4. dust, lava, lees, slag 5. dregs,
ruins 6. embers 7. cinders, residue
ash tree symbol (Norse Myth) . . .
10. Yggdrasill (horse of Yggr)
Asia . . . 4. East 6. Orient, region 7. Far
East 8. Old World 9. continent
Asia Minor . . .
city (anc) . . 4. Myra, Teos, Troy
5. Ilium, Issus, Lydia 6. Nicaea, Sardes
7. Ephesus
district . . 4. Aria 5. Ionia, Troad (The
Troad) 6. Aeolis
island . . 6. Lesbos
language (anc) . . 6. Lycian, Lydian
8. Etruscan
mountain . . 3. Ida
old name . . 8. Anatolia
sea . . 5. Black 6. Aegean 7. Marmosa
13. Mediterranean
Asiatic (pert to) . . .
barbarian (anc) . . 3. Hun 6. Vandal
cyclone . . 7. typhoon
desert . . 4. Gobi
gulf . . 4. Aden, Oman, Siam 6. Tonkin
7. Persian
island . . 4. Java 5. Luzon, Malay
7. Celebes, Diomede (Big), Formosa,
Sumatra 8. Japanese, Mindanao,
Sakhalin 11. Philippines
mountain . . 4. Ural 5. Altai, Sayan

7. Everest 8. Caucasus, Himalaya
9. Hindu Kush
native.. 4. Arab, Turk, Yuit 5. Tatar
6. Indian, Innuit (Esk), Syrian 7. Chinese,
Malayan 8. Annamese, Japanese
9. Mongolian
nomad.. 4. Arab
river.. 2. Ob 4. Amur, Lena, Yalu
5. Huang (Hwang), Indus 6. Ganges,
Tigris 7. Yangtze, Yenisei 9. Euphrates,
Irrawaddy 11. Brahmaputra
sea.. 4. Azov (Azof) 5. Black, China,
Japan 6. Bering, Yellow 7. Caspian,
Okhotsk
wind.. 7. monsoon

Asiatic animal ...
antelope.. 5. goral
ass.. 6. onager
camel.. 8. Bactrian 9. dromedary
carnivore.. 5. panda, tiger
cattle.. 4. zobo
deer.. 4. axis 10. chevrotain
elephant.. 7. Elephas
fox.. 6. corsac
gazelle.. 3. ahu
goat.. 5. serow
lemur.. 5. loris 6. macaco
lynx.. 7. caracal
mongoose.. 4. urva
monkey.. 6. langur (long-tailed)
ox.. 3. yak
rodent.. 4. pika
sheep.. 3. sha 5. uriel 6. argali
squirrel.. 8. jelerang 10. polatouche

Asiatic bird ...
finch.. 9. brambling
jay.. 7. sirgang
owl.. 4. utum
partridge.. 6. seesee
plover.. 8. dotterel
songless.. 5. Pitta
talking.. 4. myna (mynah)

Asiatic snake ... 3. asp 5. cobra
8. ringhals

Asiatic storm (pert to) ...
sand.. 6. simoom (simoon) 7. tebbard
snow.. 5. buran
wind.. 5. buran 7. monsoon

aside ... 4. away 5. apart, hence 6. aslant,
astray, beside 7. whisper 8. sidewise
9. alongside, privately, sotto voce
12. interjection

asinine ... 4. dumb 5. inane, inept, silly
6. mulish, stupid 7. doltish, foolish,
idiotic 9. obstinate

ask ... 3. beg 4. quiz 5. claim, exact,
query, speer 6. assess, demand, invite
7. beseech, entreat, implore, inquire,
request, require, solicit 8. petition,
question 9. catechize, obsecrate (Relig)
11. interrogate

askance ... 4. awry 5. askew 7. asquint,
crooked 8. sideways 9. obliquely

askew ... 4. agee, alop, awry 5. agley,
amiss 6. faulty 7. askance, asquint,
crooked 8. deranged 9. distorted,
obliquely 10. catawampus, disorderly

aslant ... 5. atilt 6. tilted, tipped
7. athwart, leaning, listing, pitched,
sloping 8. inclined 9. careening,
obliquely

asleep ... 4. dead, dull, numb 7. dormant,
unaware 8. deadened, sleeping,
unarisen 9. oblivious, senseless,
unruffled 10. motionless 11. inattentive,
insensitive, unconscious

Asoka's Empire (anc Ind) ... 5. Patna

asp ... 5. cobra, snake, viper 6. uraeus
(sacred sym)

aspect ... 3. air 4. look, mien, pose,
side, view 5. angle, decil, facet, guise,
phase, shape, sight, state 6. decile,
facies, status, visage 7. bearing,
posture, scenery 8. attitude 9. astrology,
component, influence, seaminess,
situation 10. appearance
11. countenance

aspen ... 4. tree, wood 6. poplar
7. quaking 9. quivering, shivering,
trembling, tremulous, vibrating

asperge ... 3. wet 4. damp 5. spray,
water 7. baptize 8. humidify, sprinkle

asperge ... 9. asparagus

Asperges ... 4. rite 6. anthem
10. sprinkling (altar)

aspergillum ... 5. brush 7. sprayer
8. baptizer 9. sprinkler

asperity ... 5. rigor 7. raucity 8. acerbity,
acrimony, hardship, severity, tartness
9. bleakness, roughness 10. causticity,
difficulty, inclemency, moroseness,
resentment

asperse ... 4. slur 5. abuse, decry,
libel 6. defame, malign, revile, vilify
7. blacken, slander, traduce 8. besmirch
9. bespatter, discredit 10. calumniate

aspersion ... 4. rite, slur 6. insult
7. affront, baptism, calumny, outrage,
wetting 8. innuendo 9. indignity
10. defamation, sprinkling
12. calumniating, calumniation
13. disparagement

asphalt ... 4. pave 5. pitch 7. bitumen,
mineral 8. blacktop, pavement, uintaite
9. gilsonite 10. macadamize

asphyxia ... 5. apnea (apnoea) 7. choking
11. suffocation 12. smotheration

aspic ... 3. asp (poet) 5. jelly 6. cannon
8. lavender 9. galantine

aspiration ... 3. aim 4. hope, wish
5. ideal 6. breath, desire 7. pumping,
sucking, suction 8. ambition, staccato
9. breathing 10. exhalation
11. inspiration

aspire ... 4. long, plan, rise, soar
5. tower 6. attain, desire, expect, intend
7. breathe, propose

ass ... 3. ono (comb form) 4. dolt, dope,
fool, jack 5. burro, jenny

assail ... 4. pelt 5. beset, stone 6. attack
7. assault 9. implicate 11. incriminate

assailant ... 3. foe 5. enemy 7. invader
8. assailer, attacker, opponent
9. adversary, aggressor 10. antagonist,
challenger

Assam ...
capital.. 8. Shillong
native.. 4. Ahom 8. Assamite 11. Indo-
Chinese
people.. 3. Aka 4. Garo, Naga
province of.. 5. India
river.. 11. Brahmaputra

tribe . . **2.** Ao **3.** Aka **4.** Garo, Naga
assassin . . . **4.** Cain, thug **5.** bravo
  6. apache, cuttle, gunman, killer, slayer
  7. gorilla, ruffian **8.** murderer, sicarian
  9. manslayer **11.** slaughterer
assassination . . . **5.** purge **6.** murder
  7. killing **8.** regicide **11.** liquidation
  12. manslaughter
Assassin Order . . . **8.** Ismalian
  10. Mohammedan
assault . . . **5.** onset, storm **6.** assail, attack,
  charge **7.** descent, seizure **8.** invasion
  9. incursion **13.** incrimination
assay . . . **3.** try **4.** test **5.** prove, trial
  6. accost **7.** attempt **8.** analysis,
  docimasy (art), endeavor
  10. experiment **12.** verification
assay cup . . . **5.** cupel
assemblage . . . **3.** all **4.** herd **6.** throng
  8. assembly, entirety **9.** gathering
  12. congregation
assemblage (pert to) . . .
  cattle . . **5.** drove, rodeo **7.** roundup
  fashionable . . **5.** salon
  mob . . **4.** rout **6.** rabble
  splendid . . **6.** galaxy
  tents . . **4.** camp **10.** encampment
assemble . . . **3.** pod **4.** mass, meet
  5. amass, piece, rally, unite **6.** couple,
  gather, muster **7.** cluster, collect,
  convene, convoke, recruit
  10. congregate
assembly . . . **4.** bevy, diet, moot **5.** agora,
  gemot, group, synod, troop **6.** assize,
  sabbat **7.** company, council, landtag,
  meeting **8.** auditory, conclave (secret),
  folkmoot (Hist) **9.** concourse, gathering
  10. collection, convention
  11. convocation **12.** congregation
assent . . . **3.** aye, nod, yea, yes **4.** amen
  5. admit, agree, grant **6.** accede,
  accord, concur **7.** consent **8.** sanction
  9. acquiesce, agreement **10.** compliance
  12. acquiescence
assert . . . **3.** say **4.** aver, pose **5.** claim,
  plead, posit, state, voice **6.** affirm,
  allege, avouch, relate, uphold
  7. contend, declare, profess, protest,
  support **8.** advocate **9.** pronounce,
  vindicate **10.** asseverate
assertion . . . **5.** claim **6.** remark, thesis
  7. premise **8.** averment **9.** statement
  10. assumption, hypothesis
  11. affirmation, declaration,
  maintenance, proposition, vindication
assertiveness . . . **10.** pragmatism
  14. aggressiveness
assertor . . . **8.** affirmer, defender
  9. supporter **10.** vindicator
assess . . . **3.** ask, tax **4.** cess, levy, mise,
  rate **5.** price, value **6.** charge **7.** measure
  8. appraise, estimate
assessment . . . **3.** fee, tax **4.** levy,
  rate, scot **5.** ratal, stock, value
  6. surtax **7.** pricing, scutage **8.** estimate
  9. appraisal, valuation **10.** evaluation
  11. measurement
assets . . . **5.** funds, means **6.** wealth
  7. capital **8.** accounts, property
  9. resources
asseverate . . . **3.** say, vow **4.** aver

5. state, swear **6.** affirm, allege, assert
  7. contend, declare, profess, protest
  8. maintain **9.** pronounce
asseveration . . . **3.** vow **4.** oath (solemn)
  8. averment **9.** assertion **11.** affirmation,
  declaration **13.** pronouncement
assiduity . . . **8.** industry **9.** diligence
  11. painstaking, persistence
  12. perseverance
assiduous . . . **4.** busy **6.** active **7.** intense,
  zealous **8.** diligent, sedulous
  9. energetic, laborious, unwearied
  11. industrious, perseverant
  13. indefatigable, unintermitted
assign . . . **3.** fix, set **4.** cast, cede, seal
  5. allot, refer **6.** allege, commit, detail
  7. address, adjudge, appoint, ascribe,
  consign, empower **8.** accredit, allocate,
  delegate, nominate, transfer **9.** attribute
  10. commission **11.** appropriate
assignment . . . **3.** job **4.** task **5.** chore,
  stint **6.** lesson **7.** mission **8.** exercise,
  transfer **9.** allotment **10.** allocation,
  commission, commitment
  11. attribution **13.** specification
assimilate . . . **5.** adapt, learn, liken
  6. absorb, digest, imbibe **7.** convert
  10. understand **11.** approximate
assimilation . . . **8.** imbibing, learning
  9. anabolism, digestion, ingestion,
  reduction **10.** absorption, adaptation,
  comparison, conversion
  14. naturalization
assist . . . **3.** aid **4.** abet, back, help **5.** avail,
  boost, favor **6.** attend, prompt, second,
  succor **7.** benefit, relieve, support,
  sustain **8.** befriend **9.** accompany,
  subsidize
assistance . . . **3.** aid **4.** help **5.** grant
  6. relief, succor **7.** service, subsidy,
  support **10.** logrolling (Polit)
  11. furtherance
assistant . . . **4.** aide, ally **5.** tutor
  6. deputy, helper **7.** abettor, famulus,
  servant, teacher **9.** associate, attendant,
  auxiliary **11.** subordinate **12.** right-hand
  man
assize . . . **3.** fix **4.** rate **5.** edict, trial,
  value **6.** assess, decree **9.** ordinance
  10. regulation **11.** instruction,
  measurement
associate . . . **3.** mix, pal **4.** ally, chum,
  mate **5.** buddy, crony **6.** fellow,
  friend, hobnob, mingle **7.** combine,
  comrade, consort, partner **9.** colleague,
  companion **10.** accomplice
  11. concomitant, confederate
associated . . . **6.** allied, banded, joined,
  united **7.** coupled, leagued, related
  9. connected **10.** affiliated, concurrent
associates . . . **4.** crew **5.** force, staff
  7. retinue **9.** personnel **12.** constituency
association . . . **4.** body, club **5.** artel,
  cabal, guild, hanse (Hist), union
  6. league, lyceum, symbol **7.** company,
  society **8.** alliance, relation, sodality,
  sorority **9.** syndicate **10.** fellowship,
  fraternity **11.** affiliation, combination,
  comradeship, concurrence, corporation
  13. communication, interrelation
assonance . . . **3.** pun **4.** rime **5.** rhyme

8. paragram 9. agreement
11. paronomasia, resemblance
12. alliteration
as soon as possible ... 4. ASAP
assort ... 4. sort, suit 5. adapt, class,
grade, group 7. consort (with)
8. classify, separate 9. associate (with)
10. categorize, distribute
assortment ... 3. mix, set 4. hash,
mess, olio 5. class, group 6. jumble,
medley 7. mélange, mixture, sorting
9. potpourri 10. collection, hodgepodge,
miscellany 11. arrangement
14. conglomeration
assuage ... 4. calm, ease 5. allay, slake
6. lessen, mellow, pacify, quench,
soften, solace, soothe 7. appease,
comfort, gratify, qualify, relieve, satisfy
8. mitigate, palliate 9. alleviate
assuasive ... 5. balmy 6. easing
8. remedial, soothing 9. relieving,
softening 10. mitigating, palliative
11. alleviative 13. tranquilizing
assume ... 3. don 4. deem, sham, take
5. adopt, feign, guess, imply, infer,
judge, think, usurp 6. affect, allege,
betake, borrow, deduce 7. believe,
imagine, premise, presume, pretend,
suppose, surmise 8. arrogate, conclude,
simulate 9. undertake 11. appropriate,
counterfeit
assume (pert to) ...
character .. 11. impersonate
different forms .. 7. protean
unduly .. 5. usurp 8. arrogate
without proof .. 11. theoretical
12. hypothetical
assumed ... 6. deemed 7. alleged,
implied, thought 8. affected, inferred,
presumed, supposed 9. fictional,
pretended 10. fictitious, understood,
undertaken 11. conjectured, make-
believe, presumptive, presupposed,
theoretical 12. appropriated,
hypothetical, supposititious
assuming ... 5. lofty 8. arrogant,
superior 9. presuming 10. assumptive
11. overweening, pretentious
12. presumptuous
assumption ... 8. adoption 9. arrogance,
postulate, reception 10. usurpation
11. implication, proposition, supposition
13. appropriation, incorporation
14. presupposition
assurance ... 4. hope, oath 5. poise,
trust 6. aplomb, belief, pledge, surety
7. comfort, courage, promise 8. security,
sureness 9. certainty, guarantee,
impudence, insurance 10. confidence,
steadiness 11. assuredness, intrepidity
12. cocksureness 14. self-confidence
assure ... 4. aver 5. vouch 6. assert,
avouch, depose, ensure, insure, secure
7. confirm, declare, protest, satisfy
8. convince, embolden, persuade,
reassure 9. encourage, guarantee
10. asseverate
Assyria ...
capital .. 7. Nineveh
city .. 5. Calab (Bib) 9. Khorsabad (ruins)
empire (anc) .. 5. Assur (Ashur)

language .. 6. Semite 9. cuneiform
(written)
people .. 6. Semite 7. Amorite (Bib)
Assyrian god ...
atmosphere .. 5. Hadad
fire .. 5. Nusku
hunt .. 7. Ninurta
moon .. 3. Sin
storm .. 2. Zu
sun .. 7. Shamash
war .. 6. Nergal 7. Ninurta
winds .. 4. Adad 5. Hadad
Assyrian goddess ... 5. Nanai 6. Allatu,
Ishtar 9. Sarpanitu (Zirbanit)
Assyriology, science of ... 8. language
11. antiquities
aster ... 4. star 9. asterwort, karyaster
10. Carduaceae
asterisk ... 4. mark (reference), star
6. accent, figure (star) 9. highlight
10. asteriskos (Eccl)
astern ... 3. aft 4. baft, rear 5. abaft,
after 6. behind 8. hindward, rearward,
tailward
asteroid ... 5. Ceres (largest) 6. planet
8. starlike 9. planetoid
Asteroidea ... 8. starfish
astir ... 2. up 5. about, afoot, eager
6. active, moving 8. stirring
11. forthcoming
as to ... 7. apropos, suppose 9. regarding
10. concerning, respecting
astonish ... 4. stun 5. amaze, appal
7. astound, stagger, startle 8. bewilder,
confound, surprise 9. overwhelm
astonishing ... 7. amazing 8. fabulous
9. appalling, marvelous, wonderful
10. incredible, remarkable
astound ... 4. stun 5. abash, amaze,
shock 6. appall (appal), dismay
7. stagger, stupefy 8. astonish, surprise
10. disconcert
astounding ... 8. horrible, shocking
9. appalling, frightful 10. horrendous,
horrifying 11. astonishing
astraddle ... 7. astride 9. horseback,
pickaback (piggyback) 10. straddling
astral ... 6. spirit, starry 7. stellar
8. sidereal, starlike 9. celestial 11. star-
studded
astray ... 4. lost 5. amiss, wrong 6. adrift,
afield, erring 8. aberrate, mistaken
9. erroneous 10. bewildered
astray, to go ... 3. err, sin 4. mang,
rove 5. drift, lapse, stray 6. wander
7. deviate, digress 8. miscarry
9. backslide 10. misbelieve
astriction ... 4. bond 7. binding 8. thirlage
9. fastening 10. litigation
11. confinement, contraction
12. constipation
astride ... 8. straddle 9. astraddle,
horseback, pickaback (piggyback)
astringent ... 4. acid, alum, sloe,
sour 5. acerb, acrid, harsh, sapan,
stern 6. tannin 7. austere, bitters,
caustic, pungent, rhatany (root),
styptic 9. vitriolic 10. antiseptic
11. acrimonious, argentamine
12. constrictive
astrologer ... 8. Chaldean 9. stargazer

11. astrologian, astromancer, Nostradamus
astrology (pert to)... 5. house, signs 6. aspect, zodiac 7. mansion, mundane 8. siderism 9. horoscope, planetary 11. horoscopist
astronaut... 7. Martian 8. spaceman 9. cosmonaut, rocketeer
astronomer... 9. stargazer 11. uranologist 12. uranographer 13. meteorologist, uranographist
astronomer, famed... 6. Kepler 7. Galileo 12. Eratosthenes
astronomical... 4. huge, vast 5. large 6. cosmic, uranic 7. immense, mammoth, Uranian 8. colossal, empyreal, heavenly 9. celestial 10. prodigious, stupendous, tremendous
astronomy (pert to)... 4. coma (the) 5. apsis, saros (Bab) 6. syzygy 7. almanac, apsides, azimuth, gibbous 8. sidereal 9. idiometer, insulated 11. debilissima
astute... 3. sly 4. keen, wily 5. acute, canny, smart 6. artful, clever, crafty, shrewd 7. cunning, skilled 9. insidious, sagacious 10. discerning 14. discriminating
asunder... 5. apart, cleft, rived (riven), split 6. atwain, halved 7. divided 9. disjoined, separated
as yet... 8. hitherto
asylum... 3. ark 4. home, jail, port 5. haven 6. harbor, refuge 7. retreat, shelter 9. hospitium, infirmary, sanctuary 10. stronghold 11. institution
asymmetrical... 6. uneven, warped 7. twisted, unequal 9. contorted, distorted 11. zygomorphic 16. disproportionate
at... 2. by, in 4. near, nigh 5. there 8. location, position 9. direction, situation
at (pert to)...
great length.. 7. on and on 9. tediously
home.. 2. in 4. here 9. en famille
last.. 3. end 7. finally 9. extremely 10. ultimately
once.. 3. now 7. readily
the same..
time.. 6. coeval 10. coetaneous 12. contemporary
atabal... 4. drum 5. tabor 10. kettledrum
atabeg... 5. title 6. vizier
Atalanta (pert to)...
defeated in romantic race by.. 10. Hippomenes 17. three golden apples (Gr Myth)
famed.. 8. huntress
foe.. 9. Aphrodite
husband.. 8. Milanion
legend.. 8. Arcadian, Boeotian
atalaya... 10. watchtower
atap... 4. nipa, palm
atavism... 8. heredity 9. reversion 10. regression
ate... 5. dined, fared 6. dieted, gnawed, supped
Ate... 7. goddess (of infatuation)
atelier... 5. easel 6. studio 8. workshop

a tempo... 4. time
Aten (Egypt)... 9. solar disk
ates... 8. sweetsop
athanasia... 8. athanasy 11. immortality 13. deathlessness 15. imperishability
athanor (Fr)... 7. furnace (alchemist's)
Athapascan Indian... 5. Tinne 6. Apache, Navaho (Navajo)
atheist... 5. pagan 7. heathen, infidel, nastika 8. agnostic 10. unbeliever 11. disbeliever, unchristian 13. antichristian
Athena (pert to)...
attributes.. 3. owl 5. aegis 7. serpent
festival.. 11. Panathenaea
Rom equivalent.. 7. Minerva
shrine.. 9. Parthenon (Athens)
Athena, goddess of...
arts, crafts.. 6. Ergane
health.. 6. Hygeia
horses, tamer of.. 6. Hippia
light.. 4. Alea
maid of Athens.. 12. Pallas Athene
poetry.. 6. Pallas
victory.. 4. Nike
wisdom.. 8. Palladis
Athenian (pert to)...
assembly.. 4. Pnyx
Bee.. 5. Plato
general.. 8. Xenophon
lawgiver.. 5. Draco, Solon
sculptor.. 7. Phidias
statesman.. 8. Pericles 9. Aristides (The Just) 10. Alcibiades
temple.. 11. Nike Apteros
Athens...
capital of.. 6. Attica (anc), Greece
citadel.. 9. Acropolis
magistrate.. 5. Draco, Solon
rival.. 6. Sparta (anc)
senate.. 5. boule
temple.. 9. Parthenon
Athens of...
America.. 6. Boston 9. Nashville (The South)
Ireland.. 4. Cork 7. Belfast
North.. 9. Edinburgh 10. Copenhagen
Switzerland.. 6. Zurich
West.. 7. Cordoba
athlete... 7. acrobat, gymnast, tumbler 11. funambulist, palaestrian, pancratiast 13. contortionist
athlete (pert to)...
foot disease.. 15. dermatophytosis
of Christendom.. 10. Scanderbeg
portico (Gr, Rom).. 6. xystus (xyst)
athletic... 5. lusty, thewy, yauld 6. brawny, robust, sinewy, strong 8. muscular, stalwart, vigorous 9. acrobatic, agonistic, gymnastic 10. palaestral (palestral) 15. broad-shouldered
athwart... 6. across, aslant 8. sideways, sidewise, traverse 9. crosswise, obliquely 10. crisscross, perversely
atimon... 9. muskmelon
Atlantean... 6. strong 7. titanic 8. gigantic 9. Atlaslike 10. Gargantuan
atlantes (opp of caryatids)... 7. columns (carved men) 9. telamones
Atlantic Sisters (Gr)... 8. Pleiades (stars)

Atlas (pert to) . . .
  converted into . . **7**. Mt Atlas
  daughter . . **7**. Calypso **8**. Pleiades
  famed as a . . **5**. giant, Titan
  king of . . **10**. Mauretania
  mother . . **4**. Asia **7**. Clymene
  supporter of . . **5**. earth **10**. the heavens
Atman (Hind) . . . **3**. ego **4**. Self, Soul
  6. Brahma
atmosphere . . . **3**. air **4**. aura, mood
  5. ether, ozone **7**. climate
  10. aerosphere, background
  11. environment, hydrosphere
atmosphere (pert to) . . .
  condition . . **9**. epedaphic
  density . . **8**. isostere, isoteric
  disturbance . . **5**. storm **6**. static
  9. tornadoes, whirlwind
  pressure . . **10**. barometric
  shooting star . . **6**. meteor
  spectrum . . **7**. rainbow
atole . . . **5**. gruel **8**. porridge
atoll . . . **4**. belt, reef (coral) **6**. island
atom . . . **3**. ace, bit, ion, jot **4**. gram,
  iota, mite, whit **5**. monad **8**. particle
  9. corpuscle
atom (pert to) . . .
  central part . . **7**. nucleus
  charged . . **3**. ion
  energy . . **5**. gluon **6**. photon **7**. quantum
  particle . . **4**. muon **5**. boson, meson,
  quark **6**. baryon, lepton **7**. fermion,
  neutron **8**. electron, neutrino
atomic . . . **3**. Age, ray **4**. beam, bomb, tiny
  5. power **6**. energy, minute, number,
  radius, weight **7**. nuclear **8**. atomistic,
  molecular, radiation **10**. intangible
  11. microscopic **13**. infinitesimal
atomize . . . **4**. fume **5**. smash, spray
  6. aerate, gasify **7**. fission, perfume,
  shatter **8**. dissolve, fumigate, nucleize
  9. carbonate, decompose, evaporate,
  micronize, pulverize **11**. disorganize
  12. disintegrate
atom smasher . . . **11**. accelerator
atomy . . . **4**. atom, mote **5**. dwarf,
  pygmy **6**. droich, midget **8**. skeleton
  10. micromorph
atonement . . . **6**. amends **7**. apology,
  penance, redress **8**. requital
  10. recompense, redemption, reparation
  11. reclamation, restitution
  12. propitiation **15**. indemnification
Atreus (pert to) . . .
  brother . . **8**. Thyestes
  father . . **6**. Pelops
  king of . . **7**. Mycenae
  mother . . **10**. Hippodamia
  slayer of . . **12**. Thyestes' sons
  son . . **8**. Menelaus **9**. Agamemnon
  wife . . **6**. Aerope
atrium . . . **4**. hall, room **5**. court (inner)
  6. cavity (Anat) **7**. chamber **9**. peristyle
atrocious . . . **4**. rank, vile **5**. awful,
  cruel, grave **6**. brutal, savage, sinful,
  wicked **7**. heinous, vicious, violent
  8. dreadful, flagrant, horrible, infamous,
  ruthless, shocking, terrible, wretched
  9. monstrous, nefarious **10**. abominable,
  deplorable, detestable, outrageous
atrociousness . . . **8**. baseness, vileness

  12. dreadfulness, shamefulness
  13. nefariousness **15**. Schrecklichkeit
atrocity . . . **4**. evil, harm **5**. abuse, havoc,
  wrong **7**. misdeed, outrage **8**. enormity
  9. indignity **12**. mistreatment
atrophy . . . **5**. tabes **7**. disease
  8. marasmus **10**. emaciation
  11. attenuation
Atropos (Gr) . . . **7**. goddess (Fate)
attach . . . **3**. add, fix, pin, put, tag, tie
  4. bind, glue, join, vest **5**. affix, annex,
  hitch, paste, seize, unite **6**. append,
  assign, fasten **7**. ascribe, connect,
  postfix, subjoin **9**. associate, attribute
  11. superimpose
attached . . . **4**. fond **6**. adnate, welded
  7. annexed, devoted, engaged, sessile
  (Bot), smitten **8**. cemented, enamored
attachment . . . **4**. bond, love **5**. fancy
  6. liking, regard **7**. adjunct, fixture
  8. addition, devotion, fidelity, fondness
  9. accession, adherence, affection,
  fastening, increment **10**. annexation
  11. attribution **12**. augmentation
attack . . . **3**. fit **4**. pang, raid **5**. beset, blitz,
  drive, feint, foray, ictus, onset, sally,
  siege, spasm **6**. affret, assail, charge,
  onrush, oppugn, sortie **7**. aggress,
  assault, bowling, descent, offense,
  seizure **8**. camisado (anc), paroxysm,
  sickness **9**. offensive, onslaught
  10. aggression **11**. enunciation
  13. incrimination
attain . . . **2**. do **3**. get, win **4**. earn, gain
  5. enact, reach **6**. accede, arrive, effect,
  obtain **7**. achieve, acquire, compass,
  fulfill, perform, realize **9**. discharge
  10. accomplish, consummate
attainable . . . **8**. gettable **9**. available
  10. achievable
attainment . . . **5**. skill **7**. arrival **8**. learning
  9. accession **11**. acquirement,
  acquisition, cultivation, edification,
  realization **14**. accomplishment
attar . . . **4**. otto **5**. scent **6**. parfum
  7. essence, perfume, rose oil
attempt . . . **3**. aim, jab (sl), try **4**. dare,
  seek, stab **5**. assay, ensue, essay,
  fling, offer, onset, siege, trial **6**. attack,
  effort, result **7**. venture **8**. endeavor
  9. undertake
attend . . . **4**. hark, heed, help, mind,
  note, tend, wait **5**. ensue, nurse, serve,
  treat, visit **6**. doctor, escort, follow,
  foster, listen, result **7**. conduct, hearken,
  nurture, observe **9**. accompany
attendance . . . **4**. draw **5**. court **7**. service,
  turnout **8**. presence, tendance
  9. following **13**. accompaniment
attendant . . . **4**. maid, page **5**. nurse, staff,
  usher **6**. caddie, escort, gillie, porter,
  waiter **7**. bellboy, orderly **8**. follower
  9. associate, attending, companion
  10. subsequent **11**. concomitant,
  ministering
attendants, train of . . . **5**. suite
  7. cortege, retinue **9**. entourage
attention . . . **3**. ear **4**. care, heed, hist,
  note **6**. notice, regard **7**. concern,
  hearing, respect, thought **8**. courtesy
  11. mindfulness **13**. concentration,

consideration
attentive ... **5.** alert, awake, eared
6. intent **7.** careful, heedful, mindful
8. obedient, vigilant, watchful
9. courteous, listening, observant,
wide-awake **10.** meticulous, respectful
11. circumspect, considerate, surveillant
attenuated ... **3.** cut **4.** fine, rare, slim,
thin **5.** svelte, wasted **7.** diluted,
gracile, reduced, slender, thinned,
watered **8.** lessened, rarefied, weakened
9. decreased, emaciated
attest ... **4.** seal **5.** vouch **6.** adjure,
affirm, avouch, depose **7.** certify,
testify, witness **8.** evidence, indicate,
manifest **9.** testimony **10.** deposition
12. authenticate
attestation ... **4.** oath (solemn) **5.** proof
6. avowal **8.** swearing **9.** assertion
10. allegation **11.** affirmation, certificate,
declaration, testimonial **13.** testification
14. authentication
attic ... **3.** top **4.** dome, head, loft, wall
6. belfry, garret **8.** cockloft
Attic ... **5.** salty, witty **6.** simple **7.** elegant,
refined **8.** academic, Athenian, tasteful
9. classical **10.** Ciceronian
Attic (pert to) ...
  Bee .. **9.** Sophocles (poet)
  bird .. **11.** nightingale (Milton)
  Muse .. **8.** Xenophon
  native .. **8.** Athenian
  school .. **9.** sculpture
Attica (pert to) ...
  capital of .. **6.** Athens
  state of .. **6.** Greece (anc)
  famed as .. **15.** world's first city
Attila ... **3.** Hun (leader) **5.** Etzel (fabled)
12. Scourge of God
attired ... **7.** arrayed, clothed, dressed
attitude ... **3.** air, set **4.** pose, view
5. angle, slant, stand **7.** bearing, feeling,
opinion, outlook, posture, thought
8. position, reaction **9.** arabesque
(dance), sentiment, viewpoint
10. estimation, impression
attitude (reverent) ... **6.** salaam
8. kneeling **9.** obeisance
12. genuflection (genuflexion)
attorney ... **6.** lawyer **7.** counsel, pleader
9. barrister, counselor (counsellor)
11. intercessor
attract ... **4.** bait, draw, lure, pull
5. charm, tempt **6.** appeal, beckon,
enamor, engage, entice, invite
8. interest **9.** captivate, fascinate,
influence, magnetize
attraction ... **4.** lure, pull, star **6.** appeal
7. gravity **8.** affinity, headline, interest,
penchant **9.** magnetism, seduction
10. allurement **11.** fascination
attractive ... **4.** cute **6.** lovely, pretty,
taking **7.** winsome **8.** alluring, engaging,
fetching, graceful, magnetic **9.** allicient,
appealing, beauteous, beautiful,
desirable **10.** attracting, delightful
11. captivating, interesting
attractive and repellent ...
10. ambivalent
attrahent ... **6.** magnet **7.** drawing
8. sinapism (Med) **10.** attracting

attribute ... **3.** owe **5.** refer, trait
6. impute, nature, symbol **7.** ascribe,
feature, quality **8.** property **9.** adjective,
qualifier, specialty
attrition ... **4.** wear **5.** grief (Theol)
7. massage **8.** abrasion, friction,
limation **9.** detrition **10.** contrition
attune ... **4.** tune **5.** chime **6.** accord,
adjust **7.** concord, harmony, syntony
9. melodious **10.** symphonize
11. concordance
atwain ... **7.** asunder
atweel ... **5.** truly **6.** surely
aubade (Fr) ... **3.** lay **4.** poem, song
6. ballad **7.** concert (morning)
8. serenade
auberge ... **3.** inn
aubergiste ... **9.** innkeeper
auction ... **3.** bid **4.** cant, roup, sale
5. block **6.** vendue **7.** bidding
auction (game) ... **4.** pool **5.** pitch
6. bridge, euchre, hearts **8.** pinochle
audacious ... **4.** bold **5.** saucy **6.** brazen,
daring **7.** defiant **8.** impudent, insolent,
intrepid, spirited **9.** barefaced,
foolhardy, insulting **11.** adventurous,
challenging, impertinent, presumptive,
venturesome
audacity ... **5.** cheek, crust, nerve
6. daring **7.** courage **8.** defiance,
temerity **9.** assurance, hardihood,
impudence, insolence, sauciness
10. effrontery, enterprise
11. presumption **12.** impertinence
13. audaciousness, foolhardiness,
shamelessness
audible ... **5.** aloud, clear **8.** distinct,
hearable **10.** articulate
audible respiration ... **4.** sigh
audience ... **3.** ear **5.** house, trial
6. parley, tryout **7.** hearing, theater
8. audition, auditory, congress
9. interview, listeners **10.** conference
12. congregation
audit ... **5.** check **6.** reckon, verify
7. certify, collate **10.** accounting
11. examination
audition ... **6.** try out
auditor ... **5.** clerk **6.** censor, hearer
7. actuary, apposer **8.** examiner,
listener **10.** accountant, bookkeeper
11. comptroller
auditorium ... **4.** hall, nave (anc)
5. house **7.** theater **8.** auditory, building
9. Guildhall
auditory ... **4.** otic **5.** audio, aural
6. phonic **7.** hearers **8.** audience
9. accoustic, auricular **12.** congregation
au fait ... **4.** able **6.** expert **7.** equal
to **8.** informed, skillful **9.** qualified
10. conversant (with)
au fond ... **9.** basically, primarily
11. essentially **13.** fundamentally
auger ... **3.** bit **4.** bore, tool **5.** borer,
drill **6.** gimlet, wimble **10.** perforator
aught ... **3.** any **4.** none, some, zero
5. ought **6.** cipher **7.** nothing **8.** anything
augment ... **3.** add, eke **5.** affix,
annex, exalt, swell **6.** expand, extend
7. amplify, broaden, develop, enhance,
enlarge **8.** increase **9.** reinforce

Augsburg Church ... **8.** Lutheran

augur ... **4.** bode, omen, seer **5.** sibyl, vates (Gauls) **6.** oracle **7.** betoken, presage **8.** forebode, forecast, foretell, forewarn, haruspex (Rom), indicate, prophesy **10.** anticipate, astrologer, conjecture, soothsayer **13.** prognosticate **14.** prognosticator

augury ... **4.** omen, rite **7.** auspice, portent **8.** ceremony

august ... **5.** awful, grand, novel, regal **6.** sedate, solemn **7.** courtly, eminent, stately **8.** imposing, majestic **9.** dignified, honorable, important, venerable **11.** magnificent, ritualistic **12.** aristocratic

August ... **6.** Lammas **8.** Sextilis **10.** First month (Rom year)

August meteor (11th of month) ... **7.** Perseid

auk ... **4.** Alca, Alle, bird (sea), falk **5.** murre, noddy **6.** auklet, rotche (rotch) **7.** Alcidae, dovekie **9.** guillemot, razorbill

Auk ... **6.** Indian **7.** Alaskan, Tlingit **9.** Koluschan

aula ... **4.** hall, room **5.** court **6.** emblic (E Ind tree) **9.** ventricle

aulos ... **5.** flute **8.** woodwind **9.** woodwinds (collectively)

au naturel ... **4.** nude **5.** naked

aura ... **3.** air **4.** glow, halo, ring **6.** astral, circle, fringe (Psychol), nimbus **7.** aureola **9.** effluvium, emanation **10.** atmosphere, exhalation

aureole ... **4.** halo **5.** glory **6.** circle, nimbus

auricle ... **3.** ear **4.** lobe **5.** pinna **6.** atrium (heart) **9.** appendage

auricular ... **4.** otic **5.** aural, eared **6.** phonic **8.** acoustic, auditory

aurifex ... **9.** goldsmith

aurochs ... **3.** tur **4.** goat, urus **5.** bison

aurora ... **3.** eos **4.** dawn **5.** sunup **7.** sunrise **8.** borealis, daybreak, daylight **9.** australis **11.** polar lights

aurora borealis ... **14.** northern lights

auroral ... **4.** dawn, eoan, rosy **7.** eastern, radiant, roseate

auspices ... **3.** aid **4.** care, sign, wing **5.** aegis (egis) **6.** charge **7.** backing, custody **8.** guidance **9.** patronage **10.** management, protection **11.** sponsorship, supervision

auspicious ... **4.** good **6.** timely **9.** favorable, fortunate, opportune **10.** convenient, propitious, prosperous, seasonable **12.** advantageous

Aussie ... **6.** digger **10.** Australian

Auster ... **9.** southland, south wind

austere ... **4.** dour, hard **5.** acrid, harsh, rigid, rough, stern **6.** bitter, severe, strict **7.** ascetic, pungent **8.** exacting **10.** astringent

Australasia ... **7.** Oceania **15.** South Sea Islands

Australasian bird ... **8.** lorikeet **9.** pardalote

Australia ... see also *Australian*
capital .. **8.** Canberra
city .. **5.** Perth **6.** Sidney (largest)
   8. Adelaide, Brisbane **9.** Melbourne
desert .. **10.** Great Sandy **13.** Great Victoria
explorer .. **4.** Cook
First Englishman (1688) .. **14.** William Dampier
holiday .. **13.** Foundation Day (Jan 26)
inlet .. **9.** Botany Bay
island .. **8.** Tasmania
mountain peak .. **9.** Kosciusko
ocean .. **6.** Indian
river .. **6.** Murray
sea .. **5.** Coral **6.** Tasman
state .. **8.** Victoria **10.** Queensland
   13. New South Wales
Tropic (southern) .. **9.** Capricorn

Australian (pert to) ...
bee .. **5.** karbi
bedroll .. **6.** bindle **7.** matilda
candy .. **5.** lolly
feast .. **10.** corroboree
fish .. **4.** mako (shark) **5.** yabby
flag .. **13.** Southern Cross
flower .. **7.** waratah (tulip) **9.** rhodanthe
hut .. **6.** miamia
native .. **5.** myall **6.** Aussie, binghi
   8. kangaroo, warragal **9.** aborigine, Dravidian
reptile .. **6.** elapid, goanna, lizard (barking, frilled)
soldier .. **5.** Anzac **6.** digger

Australian animal ...
dog (wild) .. **5.** dingo
horse (wild) .. **6.** brumby
sheep dog .. **6.** kelpie
mammal .. **7.** daysure **8.** duckbill, platypus **9.** blind mole
marsupial .. **4.** tait **5.** koala **6.** wombat **7.** echidna **8.** anteater, kangaroo **9.** phalanger, teddy bear **10.** kookaburra **14.** Tasmanian Devil

Australian bird ... **3.** emu, owl **4.** lory, titi **5.** arara, ariel, galah **6.** leipoa, petrel **7.** boobook, bustard, corella (parrot), grinder, rosella (parakeet) **8.** ganggang, lorikeet, lyrebird, morepork, nightjar, paradise **9.** bowerbird, cassowary, pardalote **10.** flycatcher, goatsucker **11.** budgereegah (parakeet)

Australian tree ... **4.** teak, toon **5.** belah, penda **6.** jarrah, mallee, marara, she-oak, wattle **7.** gunnung (mahogany) **8.** Alstonia (dogbane), ironbark (eucalypt) **9.** boobyalla (willow)

Austria ...
alpine lake .. **8.** Bodensee (Ger) **9.** Constance
capital .. **4.** Wien (Ger) **6.** Vienna
city .. **4.** Graz, Linz **8.** Salzburg **9.** Innsbruck
forest belt .. **10.** Wiener Wald
monarchy .. **14.** Austria-Hungary
mountain .. **4.** Alps **6.** Otztal **9.** Dolomites
mountain peak .. **10.** Wildspitze **13.** Gross-Glockner
Pass (famed) .. **7.** Brenner
river .. **3.** Inn, Mur **6.** Danube

Austrian (pert to) ...
artist .. **5.** Klimt
author .. **10.** Schnitzler
botanist .. **6.** Mendel

chemist, inventor.. **8.** Welsbach
composer.. **4.** Berg **5.** Haydn **6.** Mozart,
Webern **7.** Strauss (Johann) **8.** Bruckner,
Schubert
physicist.. **7.** Doppler **11.** Schrödinger
psychiatrist.. **5.** Adler, Freud
ruler (former).. **6.** kaiser
soldier.. **5.** jäger
theaterman.. **9.** Reinhardt (Max)
violinist.. **8.** Kreisler
autarch... **6.** despot, tyrant **8.** autocrat
authentic... **4.** pure, real, true **5.** valid
  6. native **7.** certain, correct, genuine,
natural **8.** bona fide, credible, official,
original, orthodox, reliable **9.** firsthand
11. trustworthy **13.** authoritative
authenticate... **6.** affirm, attest, ratify
  7. certify, confirm, warrant **8.** validate
12. substantiate
authenticity... **11.** genuineness,
reliability **13.** dependability
15. trustworthiness
author... **4.** doer, poet **5.** ghost, maker
  6. parent, penman, writer **7.** creator,
inditer **8.** annalist, begetter, compiler,
composer, essayist, inventor, novelist,
producer **9.** dramatist, scribbler
10. originator **13.** encyclopedist
(encyclopaedist)
authoritative... **4.** wise **5.** valid **6.** potent,
ruling, strong **7.** weighty **8.** approved,
forceful, official, oracular, orthodox,
positive, powerful **9.** authentic,
imperious **10.** commanding, peremptory
11. dictatorial, influential
13. determinative
authoritative (pert to)...
command.. **4.** fiat **5.** usage **6.** decree,
dictum **7.** mandate
example.. **9.** precedent **10.** antecedent
letter.. **4.** writ **5.** breve
authority... **5.** judge, power, right
  6. critic, expert, oracle, regent
7. command, warrant, witness
8. dominion, validity **9.** influence,
testimony **10.** commission, competency
11. connoisseur, prerogative **12.** carte
blanche, jurisdiction **13.** authorization
authorize... **6.** accept, permit, ratify
  7. certify, charter, empower, endorse,
entitle, justify, license, warrant
8. accredit, delegate, sanction, validate
10. commission **11.** enfranchise
12. legitimatize
authorless... **8.** nameless **9.** anonymous
autobiography... **7.** journal, letters,
memoirs **11.** memorabilia
autochton... **6.** binghi, native **8.** indigene
  9. primitive **10.** aboriginal
autocracy... **8.** monarchy **9.** despotism
10. absolutism **15.** totalitarianism
autocrat... **4.** czar (tsar) **5.** mogul
  6. despot **7.** arbiter, monarch **8.** dictator
9. sovereign **10.** taskmaster
autodidactic... **8.** self-made **10.** self-
taught **12.** self-educated
autograph... **4.** seal, sign **5.** cross
  9. signature **11.** John Hancock
automatic... **7.** machine **10.** mechanical,
self-acting **11.** instinctive, involuntary,
spontaneous

automatic device... **3.** gun **4.** gear
  5. drill, pilot, rifle, robot **6.** pistol, switch
8. computer, revolver **10.** six-shooter
automaton... **5.** golem, robot **6.** puppet
  7. android, machine
automobile... **3.** cab, car **4.** auto, taxi
  5. coupe **6.** jalopy **7.** autocar, flivver,
machine, taxicab, vehicle **8.** motorcar
autosuggestion... **7.** therapy **8.** hypnosis
  9. hypnology, mesmerism
10. psychology **14.** self-suggestion
autumn... **4.** fall **6.** mature, old
age, season (yearly) **7.** equinox,
harvest, October **8.** maturity, November
9. September
auxiliary... **4.** ally, plus **5.** extra **6.** aiding,
helper **7.** adjunct, helping **9.** accessory,
ancillary, assistant, attendant, coadjutor,
colleague, companion, secondary
10. additional, subsidiary, supporting
11. confederate, cooperating,
subordinate, subservient
12. nonessential, supplemental
13. supplementary
auxiliary army... **6.** relief **7.** support
  8. Landwehr, recruits, reserves
11. contingents **14.** reinforcements
auxiliary verb... **3.** can, had, has, may
  4. hast, have, will **5.** could, shall,
would **6.** should
avail... **3.** use **4.** good, help **5.** value
  6. inform, profit **7.** benefit, service,
utility **9.** advantage, expedient
availability... **7.** utility **9.** usability
  10. usefulness **13.** acquirability,
attainability **14.** serviceability
available... **4.** free, open **5.** handy,
ready, valid **6.** on hand, usable, vacant
8. unfilled **9.** securable **10.** accessible,
attainable, convenient, obtainable,
unoccupied
avalanche... **5.** slide **7.** descent (sudden)
  8. slippage
avant-garde... **3.** van **8.** vanguard
avant-propos... **7.** preface
12. introduction (remarks)
avarice... **4.** lust **5.** greed **7.** avidity
  8. avidness, cupidity, grasping, rapacity,
voracity **10.** greediness
12. covetousness
avarice demon... **6.** Mammon
avaricious... **5.** close **6.** grabby, greedy
  7. miserly **8.** covetous, grasping
9. niggardly, penurious, rapacious,
voracious **12.** parsimonious
avatar... **8.** epiphany **10.** embodiment
  11. incarnation **14.** transmigration
avatars of Vishnu (Hind Relig)...
  11. incarnation (deity to man)
avaunt... **4.** away **5.** allez, boast, scram,
vaunt **6.** begone, depart **7.** advance,
vamoose
ave... **4.** hail, viva, vive **8.** farewell
avec (Fr)... **4.** with
Ave Maria... **4.** bead (rosary), song
  6. prayer **10.** devotional
Avena... **4.** oats **7.** grasses
avenge... **7.** requite **9.** retaliate, vindicate
Avenging Angels... **8.** nickname (Polit
1858) **10.** Danite Band (Mormons)
Avenging Spirit... **4.** Fate, Fury **6.** Erinys

7. Alastor, Atropos

avenue ... **3.** rue **4.** land, pike, road,
vent **5.** alley **6.** arcade, artery, defile,
egress, outlet, street **7.** channel,
freeway, highway, opening **8.** corridor,
turnpike **9.** boulevard, concourse
10. passageway **12.** thoroughfare

aver ... **3.** say **5.** state **6.** affirm, allege,
assert **7.** declare, profess, protect
10. asseverate

average ... **2.** go **3.** par, run **4.** mean, rule
6. common, medial, medium, normal
7. balance **8.** mediocre **10.** generality

averment ... **6.** dictum, remark **7.** witness
9. assertion, statement, testimony,
utterance **10.** allegation **11.** affirmation,
attestation **12.** verification
13. pronouncement

Avernus ... **4.** lake (poison vapors)
5. Hades

averse ... **5.** loath **7.** adverse **9.** reluctant,
unwilling **11.** disinclined

aversion ... **4.** hate **5.** odium **6.** hatred,
horror **7.** disgust, dislike **9.** antipathy,
repulsion **10.** abhorrence, repugnance
11. abomination **12.** estrangement
13. indisposition, unwillingness

aversion to ... see also *fear of*
novelty .. **9.** neophobia
society .. **14.** anthropophobia
strangers .. **10.** xenophobia
wine .. **10.** oenophobia

avert ... **4.** fend, save **5.** check, deter,
evade, repel **6.** forbid, retard, switch,
thwart **7.** deflect, prevent **8.** alienate,
prohibit **9.** forestall, sidetrack

aviary ... **4.** cage **5.** house **7.** dovecot
(dovecote) **8.** ornithon **9.** birdhouse,
columbary **11.** columbarium

aviation ... **6.** flight, flying **7.** winging
9. skyriding **10.** airplaning
11. aeronautics

aviation maneuver ... **9.** Immelmann
(Ger)

aviator ... **3.** Ace **5.** flier (flyer),
pilot **6.** airman, Icarus (fabled first)
7. wingman **8.** aeronaut, aviatrix,
operator **9.** astronaut, birdwoman,
Immelmann

avichi (Buddh) ... **4.** Hell **5.** Hades
9. depravity, perdition **10.** underworld

avid ... **4.** agog, keen **5.** eager **6.** grabby,
greedy **7.** anxious, craving, zestful
8. grasping **9.** rapacious, voracious
10. avaricious

avidity ... **4.** lust **5.** greed **7.** avarice
8. cupidity, grasping **9.** eagerness
10. greediness **12.** covetousness

avion ... **5.** plane **8.** airplane

avis ... see *rara avis*

avisa ... **4.** news **6.** advice, caveat
7. tidings, warning **11.** information

Avis Indica (Astron) ... **4.** Apus
13. constellation

avital ... **9.** ancestral

avoid ... **4.** shun, snub **5.** annul, dodge,
elude, evade **6.** escape, eschew, repeal,
revoke, vacate **7.** abstain, forbear
10. invalidate

avoidance ... **6.** outlet **7.** evasion,
removal **8.** emptying, shunning,

vacating **9.** annulment **10.** withdrawal

avoirdupois ... **4.** beef **6.** weight
7. gravity, tonnage **8.** poundage
9. heaviness

avoirdupois weight ... **3.** ton **4.** dram
5. grain, ounce, pound **13.** hundredweight

avow ... **3.** own, vow **5.** admit, swear,
vouch **6.** allege, assert, pledge
7. confess, declare, profess, promise
10. avouchment **11.** acknowledge

avulsion ... **7.** removal **9.** severance
10. extraction, separation (ppty),
withdrawal

awabi ... **7.** abalone

awaft ... **6.** adrift, afloat, wafted

await ... **4.** bide, come, heed, loom,
pend, wait **5.** abide, tarry, watch
6. ambush, attend, expect, impend,
waylay **8.** approach **9.** forthcome

awake ... **5.** alert, alive, astir, rouse
6. arouse, excite, waking **8.** open-
eyed **9.** attentive, conscious, sleepless,
wide-awake

awaken ... **5.** awake **6.** arouse, excite,
stir up **8.** roust out

award ... **4.** gift, give, meed, mete **5.** allot,
grant, medal, prize **6.** reward, trophy
7. adjudge, present, verdict **8.** accolade
9. medallion

award (pert to) ...
book .. **4.** Hugo **5.** Edgar **6.** Nebula
film .. **5.** Oscar
television .. **4.** Emmy
theater .. **4.** Tony

aware ... **3.** hep **4.** know **5.** sense
7. mindful **8.** apprized, sensible
9. cognizant, conscious **11.** intelligent

awareness ... **5.** sense **6.** feeling
9. sensation **10.** impression, perception
11. mindfulness, sensibility
13. consciousness

away ... **2.** on **3.** awa, far, fro, off, out
4. gone **5.** aside, hence **6.** abroad,
absent, begone, onward, thence
7. escaped **8.** vanished **9.** elsewhere

away from ...
body center .. **5.** ectad **6.** distal
mouth .. **6.** aborad, aboral
wind .. **4.** alee

awe ... **3.** cow **4.** fear **5.** dread
6. regard, terror, wonder **7.** emotion,
respect **8.** astonish, frighten, surprise
9. reverence **10.** admiration, veneration,
wonderment **13.** consideration

aweather (opp of alee) ... **8.** windward
11. weatherward

awe-inspiring ... **5.** eerie (eery)
7. awesome, ghostly **8.** glorious,
imposing, splendid, terrific **9.** wonderful
10. impressive **11.** magnificent

awe-struck ... **4.** awed **9.** terrified
10. astonished, fear-struck, spellbound
12. wonder-struck **13.** thunderstruck

awful ... **4.** awed, ugly **5.** dread,
great, gross **6.** sacred, silent, solemn,
woeful **7.** awesome, fearful, hideous
8. dreadful, infamous, reverent,
shocking, terrible **9.** appalling,
atrocious, deathlike, ludicrous,
venerable, wonderful **10.** deplorable,

impressive, outrageous, unpleasant
11. exceedingly
awkward . . . **5.** gawky, inapt, inept
6. clumsy, gauche **7.** froward, loutish,
unhandy **8.** bungling, clownish,
lubberly, perverse, ungainly, unwieldy
9. graceless, inelegant, lumbering,
maladroit, ponderous **10.** backhanded,
blundering, ungraceful
12. embarrassing, incommodious,
inconvenient
awkward age . . . **4.** teen **5.** teens
awkward fellow . . . **6.** galoot
11. hobbledehoy
awless, aweless . . . **4.** bald **6.** brazen
8. fearless, unafraid **9.** bold-faced,
dauntless **10.** irreverent **11.** unsurprised
12. unastonished
awn . . . **4.** barb **5.** beard (plant) **6.** arista,
papous **7.** bristle
awning . . . **6.** canopy, screen, shield
7. shelter **8.** velarium (anc)
AWOL . . . **5.** hooky **7.** truancy **9.** truantism
11. absenteeism
awry . . . **4.** agee **5.** agley, amiss, askew
6. faulty **7.** askance, asquint, crooked,
oblique **9.** distorted **10.** disorderly
11. disarranged **12.** disorganized
ax, axe . . . **3.** adz (adze), ask (dial) **4.** tool
6. hammer, poleax (poleaxe) **7.** hatchet
(small) **8.** axhammer **9.** discharge,
dismissal
ax (pert to) . . .
ancient . . **4.** celt **6.** chisel
blade . . **3.** bit
execution . . **10.** guillotine
handle . . **4.** haft **5.** helve
axial . . . **7.** central, midmost, pivotal
axilla . . . **3.** ala **4.** axil **5.** oxter **6.** armpit
8. shoulder
axiom . . . **3.** law, saw **4.** rule **5.** adage,
maxim, motto, truth **6.** byword,
dictum, saying, truism **7.** dictate,
precept, proverb, theorem
8. aphorism, apothegm **9.** principle
11. proposition
axiomatic . . . **10.** aphoristic, proverbial
11. self-evident, sententious

12. epigrammatic
axis . . . **3.** hub **4.** axle, bloc, nave,
stem **5.** pivot, stalk **6.** caulis, center,
league **7.** fulcrum **8.** alliance, vertebra
9. coalition
axle . . . **3.** pin **4.** axis **5.** pivot, shaft
6. swivel **7.** spindle **8.** axletree
axle tooth . . . **5.** molar
ayal . . . **4.** amah, maid **5.** mammy
9. governess, nursemaid
11. maidservant
aye . . . **2.** ay **3.** pro, yea, yes **4.** ever, vote
5. voice **6.** always, assent **8.** thumbs
up, viva-voce
aye-aye . . . **5.** lemur (Madagascar)
ayes . . . **10.** all in favor
Azazel . . . **5.** Eblis, Satan **9.** scapegoat
Azerbaijanian . . . **4.** Turk
14. Transcaucasian
azimuth . . . **3.** arc **4.** dial **6.** circle
7. compass, horizon **8.** distance,
magnetic **10.** North point
Azores . . .
capital . . **5.** Angra
city . . **5.** Horta
group (islands) . . **6.** St Mary **8.** St
George **9.** St Michael
locale . . **8.** Atlantic (Ocean)
owner . . **8.** Portugal
Aztec (pert to) . . .
calendar . . **7.** Mexican
capital (anc) . . **12.** Tenochtitlan
emperor . . **9.** Montezuma
god . . **4.** Xipe (sowing) **12.** Quetzalcoatl
(peace)
hero . . **4.** Nata (Myth) **6.** Cortez
language . . **7.** Nahuatl
locale (anc) . . **6.** Aztlan
Noah (Mex) . . **6.** Coxcox
people . . **7.** Nahuatl (Nahuatlan)
stone . . **12.** chalchihuitl
temple . . **8.** teocalli
azure . . . **4.** blue **7.** celeste, sky-blue
8. bice blue, cerulean **9.** blue vault,
cloudless **11.** lapis lazuli
azygous . . . **3.** odd **4.** only, sole **6.** single,
unique **8.** singular **10.** unrepeated
azymous . . . **10.** unleavened

B

B . . . **4.** beta **6.** letter (2nd)
ba (Egypt) . . . **3.** khu **4.** soul
baa . . . **5.** bleet
baahling . . . **4.** lamb
Baal . . . **4.** idol **5.** deity **6.** Baalim (pl)
7. Baalath **8.** false god **9.** fertility
baba (pert to) . . .
India . . **4.** baby **5.** child
Malaya . . **4.** male
Slavic . . **5.** nurse **7.** midwife **8.** old
woman
Turkey . . **5.** title (of respect)
babacoote . . . **5.** lemur (Madagascar)
Babbar . . . **3.** Utu (Utug) **6.** sun god
babbo . . . **5.** daddy **6.** father

babel . . . **5.** clang **6.** jargon, tumult
7. discord **9.** confusion
11. pandemonium
Babel (pert to) . . .
Bible . . **5.** Tower **8.** ziggurat
presently . . **14.** Temple of Marduk
site (ancient) . . **6.** Shinar (land of)
site (present) . . **7.** Babylon
babirusa, babiroussa . . . **9.** quadruped
(hoglike)
Babism (Persia) . . . **4.** sect
baboon . . . **3.** ape **5.** Papio **6.** chacma
7. babuina, monster **8.** mandrill
babushka . . . **11.** grandmother
baby . . . **4.** babe, doll **6.** coward, infant,

puppet, weanie **7.** bambino, chicken
8. juvenile, weakling **9.** miniature,
youngling, youngster **10.** diminutive
baby carriage . . . **4.** pram **5.** wagon
6. go-cart **8.** stroller **12.** perambulator
babyish . . . **6.** simple **7.** dollish, puerile
8. childish **9.** childlike, infantile
Babylon . . . see also *Babylonian*
capital of . . **9.** Babylonia
kingdom . . **4.** Elam **5.** Akkad (Accad)
meaning . . **9.** Gate of God
mountain . . **6.** Ararat
river . . **6.** Tigris **9.** Euphrates
World Wonder . . **14.** Hanging Gardens
Babylonian (pert to) . . .
abode of the dead . . **5.** Aralu
chaos . . **4.** Apsu
deity . . **5.** Alalu (Alala), Siris
earth mother . . **6.** Ishtar
god . . **2.** Ea, Zu **3.** Anu, Bel **4.** Adad,
Apsu, Irra **5.** Dagan, Enlil **6.** Nergal
7. Shamash
goddess . . **3.** Aya **4.** Nina **5.** Belit (Beltis)
hero (Myth) . . **5.** Adapa, Etana
9. Tilgamesh
king . . **6.** Sargon **9.** Habonidus,
Hammurabi **10.** Nabonassar
14. Nebuchadnezzar (Nebuchadrezzar)
temple, tower . . **8.** ziggurat
bacach . . . **6.** beggar **7.** cripple
bacalao . . . **7.** codfish, grouper
bacalao bird . . . **3.** auk **5.** murre
9. guillemot
Bacardi . . . **3.** rum
bacca . . . **5.** berry
baccalaureate . . . **6.** degree (college),
sermon **8.** bachelor
baccate . . . **5.** pulpy **9.** berrylike
bacchanal . . . **7.** reveler **8.** carouser
Bacchanalia . . . **4.** orgy **5.** feast
7. debauch **8.** festival (Bacchus)
bacchante . . . **6.** maenad **7.** bacchae
Bacchus . . . **4.** wine **9.** god of wine
baccivorous . . . **11.** berry-eating
bachelor . . . **4.** male **6.** degree (Acad),
garçon **8.** benedict, celibate
10. misogamist
bacillus . . . **9.** bacterium
Bacis . . . **2.** Ra **4.** bull (sacred)
back . . . **3.** aft, aid, fro **4.** abet, hind,
past, rear **5.** stern **6.** behind, second,
uphold **7.** finance, sponsor, support,
sustain **8.** extrados, intrados, resource
9. encourage, posterior **10.** background
back (Anat) . . . **4.** loin, nape **5.** notum
6. dorsal, dorsum, lumbar, tergal,
tergum **7.** occiput **8.** backbone, notalgia
10. opisthenar (hand)
backbone . . . **4.** grit, guts **5.** nerve, pluck,
spunk **6.** mettle, spirit **7.** courage,
stamina, support **8.** firmness,
gameness, mainstay **10.** dependence
backbone (Anat) . . . **4.** axis **5.** brace,
chine, spine **6.** column, spinal
7. spinule, support **8.** ossicles
9. vertebrae
backer . . . **5.** angel **6.** patron **7.** abettor,
sponsor **8.** financer, promoter, upholder
9. supporter, sustainer **10.** maintainer
background (opp of foreground) . . .
4. rear **5.** stage **6.** offing **7.** horizon,

setting **8.** backdrop, distance, practice,
training **9.** education **10.** experience
11. savoir-faire
backhanded . . . **6.** clumsy **7.** awkward,
devious **9.** insincere, insulting, sarcastic
10. circuitous
backslider . . . **8.** apostate, deserter,
recreant **10.** unfaithful
back-to-back . . . **7.** dos-à-dos
backward . . . **4.** back, dull, late **5.** arear,
loath, tardy **6.** averse, modest,
stupid **7.** bashful, belated, reverse
8. arrested, dilatory, perverse, rearward,
retarded, reticent, retrorse, reversed
9. hindwards, recessive, reluctant,
subnormal, unwilling **10.** behindhand,
hesitating, regressive, retrograde
11. unfavorable **13.** retrogressive,
retrospective
bacon . . . **4.** lard, pork, side **5.** prize
6. flitch, gammon, rasher **8.** Canadian,
sowbelly
Bacon's Rebellion . . . **6.** revolt (Va 1676)
bacteria . . . **5.** cocci, germs **7.** aerobes,
aerobia, bacilli **8.** microbes, spirilla
9. organisms
bacteriologist culture . . . **4.** agar
Bactrian camel . . . **9.** two-humped
bad . . . **3.** ill, mal (pref) **4.** evil, fell,
foul, poor, vile **5.** drole, fetid,
nasty, wrong **6.** arrant, in pain,
putrid, rotten, sinful, wanton, wicked
7. corrupt, hurtful, naughty, noxious,
spoiled, tainted, unlucky, unmoral,
unsound, vicious **8.** annoying, criminal,
improper, inferior, iniquity, sinister
9. dangerous, defective, offensive,
perverted, worthless **10.** iniquitous,
malodorous, unsuitable **11.** inexpedient,
inopportune **12.** disagreeable,
inauspicious
bad (pert to) . . .
blood . . **4.** feud **6.** enmity, rancor **7.** ill
will **10.** bitterness, resentment
custom . . **9.** cacoethes
film . . **4.** bomb
legislation . . **7.** dysnomy
luck . . **5.** deuce **7.** ambsace
man's oatmeal . . **7.** hemlock (poison)
11. wild chervil
writer . . **4.** hack
Baden . . . **3.** spa
badge . . . **3.** pin **4.** mark, sign, star
5. index, token **6.** emblem, ensign,
plaque, shield, symbol **7.** earmark
8. insignia **14.** identification
badger . . . **3.** nag, rag **4.** bait **5.** harry,
tease, worry **6.** bother, extort, harass,
hawker, heckle, hector, pester
8. huckster
badger (animal) . . . **5.** Meles (anc), pahmi,
ratel **6.** bauson, mammal, teledu,
wombat **9.** bandicoot, mistonusk
Badger State . . . **9.** Wisconsin
badinage . . . **4.** fool **5.** joker, sport
6. banter **8.** raillery **9.** badinerie,
simpleton **10.** persiflage, pleasantry
badly . . . **3.** bad, ill **4.** sick **5.** amiss,
wrong **6.** poorly, unwell **8.** faultily,
wickedly **9.** viciously **11.** exceedingly,
imperfectly **12.** disagreeably, unskillfully

13. unfortunately
badly off . . . **3.** sad **7.** hapless, unblest, unhappy, unlucky **8.** luckless **11.** impecunious, unfortunate **12.** unprosperous **14.** unprovidential
baff . . . **4.** beat, blow, thud **6.** strike, stroke (golf)
baffle . . . **4.** balk, foil **5.** cheat, elude, evade, spike **6.** defeat, delude, muffle, puzzle, thwart **7.** mystify, nonplus, perplex **8.** bewilder, confound **9.** bamboozle, frustrate **10.** disconcert
baffling . . . **7.** elusive, evasive **8.** puzzling **9.** bothering, confusing, dismaying **10.** mystifying, perplexing, perturbing **11.** frustrating **13.** disconcerting
baft . . . **3.** aft **4.** baff **5.** abaff, cloth, shaft **6.** astern
bag . . . **3.** net, pac, pot, sac, sag **4.** etui, grip, load, poke, sack, trap **5.** ascus, belly, catch, droop, pouch, purse, seize, snare, steal **6.** entrap, sachet, valise **7.** bladder, capture, distend, handbag, pannier, satchel **8.** reticule, suitcase **9.** Gladstone, haversack, sac de nuit **10.** pocketbook **11.** portmanteau
bag and baggage . . . **10.** completely **11.** impedimenta
bagatelle . . . **3.** toy **4.** game **6.** bauble, geegaw, trifle **7.** trinket **10.** knickknack, triviality **12.** fiddle-faddle
Bagdad, Baghdad . . .
capital of . . **4.** Iraq
character . . **6.** Sinbad (The Sailor)
founder (762) . . **8.** Almanzor
kingdom (anc) . . **11.** Mesopotamia
Oriental term . . **8.** lambskin (raw)
river . . **6.** Tigris
transportation (famed) . . **7.** Railway
bagpipe, bagpipes . . . **5.** drone, pipes **7.** musette **9.** Dudelsack **10.** doodlesack, sordellina
bagpipe (pert to) . . .
music variations . . **7.** pibroch
parts . . **4.** lill, oboe **5.** drone **7.** chanter **9.** chalumeau
player . . **5.** piper
tube . . **6.** drones **7.** chanter
tune . . **4.** port
Bahamas, Bahama Islands . . .
capital . . **6.** Nassau
discoverer . . **8.** Columbus
native . . **5.** conch
naval base (US) . . **9.** Mayaguana
San Salvador (now) . . **14.** Watlings Island (Watling Island)
bahan . . . **6.** poplar, willow (Bib)
bahay . . . **5.** house
bahi . . . **7.** fortune (gypsy)
bail . . . **3.** dip **4.** bond, hoop, lade, lave, ring, rynd **5.** court, ladle, throw **6.** bucket, dipper, handle, pledge, secure, surety **8.** replevin, security **9.** guarantee
bailiff . . . **5.** agent, bobby, reeve, staff **6.** deputy, staves (pl) **7.** marshal, officer, sheriff, shrieve, steward **8.** bluecoat, gendarme, overseer **9.** constable **12.** understeward
bailiwick . . . **6.** canton, county, domain **7.** commune, diocese **8.** precinct,

province **12.** municipality
bain . . . **4.** near **5.** lithe, ready, short **6.** direct, limber, supple **7.** forward, willing
bairn . . . **3.** kid, tot **4.** mite **5.** child **6.** urchin
bait . . . **3.** fly **4.** feed, hook, lure, trap **5.** bribe, decoy, snare **6.** badger, harass, hockle **7.** fulcrum, torment **8.** inveigle **9.** persecute **10.** enticement, exasperate, temptation
bait . . . **3.** dap, dib **4.** fish, hook **6.** dibble
bakal (Orient) . . . **9.** tradesman **10.** shopkeeper
bake . . . **3.** dry **4.** cake, cook, fire, kiln **5.** roast **6.** anneal, harden **8.** clambake **9.** dehydrate
bakehead . . . **4.** rail **5.** guard, shack **6.** stoker **7.** fireman **8.** trainman
baken . . . **4.** buoy **6.** beacon **8.** landmark
baker's dozen . . . **4.** long **6.** devil's **7.** inbread **8.** thirteen
baksheesh . . . **3.** sop, tip **5.** bribe **7.** largess (largesse) **8.** gratuity **12.** compensation
bal . . . **4.** ball, mine, prom
balance . . . **4.** even, rest, rule **5.** poise, ratio, scale, weigh **6.** adjust, aplomb, normal, offset, reason, rhythm, sanity **7.** average, ballast, compare, euphony, measure, remains, surplus **8.** equality, equalize, leftover, residual, saneness, serenity, symmetry **9.** composure, equipoise, remainder, stability **10.** equanimity, neutralize, proportion, symmetrize **11.** equilibrium **12.** counterpoise
balanced . . . **4.** even, just **6.** poised **7.** equable **8.** measured **9.** equitable **10.** euphonious **11.** symmetrical **13.** self-possessed
balancer . . . **7.** acrobat, gymnast **10.** ropedancer **11.** equilibrist
balcony . . . **4.** dais **5.** stage **6.** podium **7.** estrade, gallery, rostrum **8.** brattice, platform
bald . . . **4.** bare, dull, mere, open **5.** crude, naked, plain **6.** simple **7.** epilose **8.** depilous, hairless **9.** bald-pated **11.** unconcealed
baldachin, baldaquin . . . **6.** canopy (St Peter's, Rome), fabric
Balder (pert to) . . .
father . . **4.** Odin
god of . . **5.** light, peace
mother . . **5.** Frigg
slain by . . **9.** mistletoe (dart)
wife . . **5.** Nanna
balderdash . . . **3.** rot **4.** bosh **5.** trash **6.** bunkum, jargon **7.** bombast **8.** buncombe, falderal, nonsense, tommyrot **9.** poppycock
baldness . . . **6.** acomia **8.** alopecia **11.** phalacrosis **12.** hairlessness
baldric . . . **4.** belt (ornament) **6.** zodiac **7.** support (sword)
bale . . . **3.** woe **4.** bind, load, pack **5.** truss **6.** ballot, bundle, burden, misery, packet, seroon **7.** anguish, package **11.** encumbrance
Balearic Islands . . . **5.** Ibiza (Iviza), Palma

(capital) **7.** Majorca (Mallorca), Minorca **10.** Formentera

baleful . . . **3.** bad, sad **4.** dire **6.** woeful **7.** baneful, harmful, malific, noisome, noxious **8.** damaging **9.** ill-omened, malignant **10.** pernicious **12.** inauspicious

balk . . . **4.** foil **5.** check, ridge **6.** baffle, defeat, fallow, rafter, signal (fishing), thwart **7.** blunder, faux pas, stickle **9.** frustrate, hindrance **10.** bafflement, disappoint **14.** disappointment

Balkan Peninsula . . .
native . . **4.** Serb
river . . **3.** Une **4.** Sava **6.** Danube
sea . . **5.** Black **6.** Aegean **7.** Marmosa **8.** Adriatic **13.** Mediterranean
State . . **6.** Bosnia, Greece, Serbia, Turkey (Eur) **7.** Albania, Rumania **8.** Bulgaria **10.** Yugoslavia

balky . . . **7.** restive **9.** faltering, obstinate, shrinking, stickling

ball . . . **3.** bal, fly, hop, lob, orb **4.** bead, clew (yarn), pill, shot **5.** dance, globe, pearl, pinda (rice) **6.** pellet, pelota, sphere **7.** rissole **8.** conglobe, snowball **9.** eight ball **10.** cannonball **12.** medicine ball

ball (of games) . . . **4.** golf, hand, polo, soft **6.** basket, tennis, volley **7.** bowling, cricket, croquet, jai alai **8.** baseball, billiard, ping-pong

ballad . . . **3.** lay **4.** lied, poem, song **5.** derry, rhyme, verse **6.** sonnet **7.** ballade, canzone

ballast . . . **5.** poise **6.** aplomb, steady, weight **7.** balance **9.** kentledge, saburrate, stabilize **10.** equanimity, equivalent **14.** counterbalance

balled up . . . **7.** complex, mixed up, muddled **8.** confused, fouled up **9.** befuddled, entangled, snarled up **10.** disordered **11.** complicated

ballet (pert to) . . .
arrangement . . **12.** choreography
dance . . **6.** adagio **9.** pantomime
dancer . . **8.** coryphee, danseuse **9.** ballerina
jump . . **4.** jeté **5.** coupé
lover . . **11.** balletomane
music . . **5.** opera **6.** comedy **7.** d'action **14.** divertissement
painter of . . **5.** Degas
skirt . . **4.** tutu

balloon . . . **3.** bag **4.** ball, tire **5.** barge (Siam), blimp, swell **6.** aviate, ballon, dilate, expand, gasbag **7.** distend, nacelle **8.** aerostat, aircraft **9.** dirigible

balloon (type) . . . **4.** free, kite **5.** pilot **7.** captive **8.** sounding **11.** montgolfier, observation

ballot . . . **4.** bale, poll, vote **5.** elect, slate, voice **6.** select, ticket **8.** suffrage

ballyhoo . . . **4.** plug **5.** boost, noise **6.** fracas, hoopla, hubbub, ruckus, rumpus **7.** promote **9.** advertise, publicity **10.** hullabaloo

balm . . . **3.** oil **4.** bito, calm **5.** cream, salve **6.** balsam, elixir, lotion, pacify **7.** anodyne, cushion, Melissa, perfume, relieve, unction, unguent **8.** liniment,

mitigate, ointment **9.** calmative, fragrance, mitigator **10.** palliative

balm (pert to) . . . **5.** Vicks **6.** arnica, zachun **7.** camphor, lanolin, menthol **8.** glycerin, ointment, vaseline **10.** petrolatum

Balm of . . . **6.** Gilead

balmy . . . **4.** mild **5.** batty, daffy, dippy, drunk, goofy, moony, spicy, sweet **6.** dreamy, insane, savory **7.** healing **8.** aromatic, fragrant, lenitive, redolent, soothing **9.** ambrosial, assuaging, emollient **10.** palliative, refreshing **11.** odoriferous **12.** sweet-scented

balsam . . . **3.** fir **4.** riga, tolu **5.** resin **6.** embalm, poplar, storax **7.** benzoin, perfume **8.** bdellium (Bib), medicine **9.** oleoresin **12.** Balsam of Peru, Balsam of Tolu

Baltic States . . . **6.** Latvia **7.** Estonia **9.** Lithuania

Baltimore . . .
Belle . . **4.** rose
bird . . **6.** oriole
butterfly . . **7.** phaeton
city of . . **8.** Maryland
hemp . . **4.** flax
history of . . **18.** Star Spangled Banner (1814)

baluster . . . **4.** post **7.** support, upright **8.** banister

bam . . . **4.** fake, hoax, mock, sham **5.** cheat, spoof, trick **6.** deceit **7.** wheedle **8.** flimflam **9.** deception, imitation

bambino . . . **4.** babe, baby, icon **5.** child, Pietà **6.** infant (Christ)

bamboo (pert to) . . .
curtain . . **8.** frontier
English . . **10.** Philippine
genus . . **7.** Bambuss
sacred . . **6.** nandin
sprouts (pickled) . . **5.** achar
stems . . **4.** cane
sugar . . **6.** silica **9.** tabasheer

bamboozle . . . **4.** dupe, hoax **5.** trick **6.** baffle, cajole, humbug **7.** beguile, deceive, mystify, perplex **9.** victimize

ban . . . **4.** coin, tabu, veto **5.** curse, edict, taboo, title (anc) **6.** muslin, outlaw **7.** embargo, exclude, kokumin **8.** anathema **9.** interdict, ostracism, ostracize **10.** injunction, kokumingun **11.** malediction, prohibition **12.** proscription **15.** excommunication

banal . . . **4.** flat **5.** corny, stale, trite **6.** cliché, common, old hat **11.** commonplace, stereotyped **13.** platitudinous

banana . . . **4.** Musa, saba **6.** ensete **8.** Musaceae, plantain

banana (pert to) . . .
Bananaland . . **10.** Queensland
bananalike . . **8.** plantain
bird . . **4.** quit **6.** oriole
boa . . **5.** snake
color . . **7.** sunbeam
fish . . **8.** ladyfish
freckle . . **7.** disease
leaf . . **5.** frond
oil . . **7.** lacquer
Philippine . . **7.** saguing

shrub . . **9.** evergreen
bananas . . . **5.** crazy **7.** excited
band . . . **3.** bar, tie **4.** belt, body, crew, hoop, line, pack, ring, sash, zone **5.** bunch, corps, group, patte, strap, stria, strip, tribe, unite **6.** cohort, collar, fascia, fillet, girdle, ligula, outfit, pledge, radula (Zool), tether **7.** bandage, company **8.** cincture, encircle, ensemble, neckband, striping **9.** frequency (radio), orchestra, striation
bandage . . . **3.** gag **4.** bind, tape **5.** sling, spica, truss **6.** ligate, swathe **7.** wrapper **8.** compress, dressing, ligature **9.** accipiter, blindfold **10.** tourniquet
bandicoot . . . **3.** rat **9.** Perameles
bandit . . . **4.** thug **5.** thief **6.** dacoit, outlaw, robber **7.** bandido, brigand, footpad, ladrone **8.** marauder, picaroon **9.** bandolero **10.** highwayman
bandmaster . . . **5.** Sousa **6.** leader **7.** maestro **8.** choragus, director **9.** conductor **13.** Kapellmeister
bandolero . . . **5.** thief **6.** robber **10.** highwayman
bandy . . . **4.** beat, cart, game **5.** bowed **6.** curved, strive, stroke (tennis) **7.** contend, embowed **8.** carriage (Ind), exchange, to and fro **9.** bowlegged **11.** bandy-legged, reciprocate
bandy words . . . **5.** argue **6.** bicker, parley **7.** contend, wrangle **8.** converse
bane . . . **3.** woe **4.** evil, harm, kill, pest, ruin **5.** curse, venom **6.** injury, plague, poison, slayer **7.** disease (sheep), scourge **8.** murderer, vexation **9.** grievance **10.** affliction, pestilence, visitation
baneful . . . **3.** ill **4.** vile **7.** harmful, noxious **9.** injurious **10.** pernicious **11.** detrimental
bang . . . **3.** hit, rap **4.** beat, blow, dash, drub, kick, lift, shut, slam **5.** crack, knock, pound, punch, smack, thump, verve, whack **6.** energy, report, strike, thrash, thrill **7.** collide **8.** coiffure
bangle . . . **5.** charm **7.** circlet **8.** bracelet
banish . . . **3.** ban **4.** oust **5.** exile, expel **6.** deport, dispel, outlaw, punish **7.** condemn, dismiss, exclude **8.** relegate **9.** ostracize, proscribe **10.** expatriate **13.** excommunicate
banister . . . **4.** post, rail **8.** baluster **10.** balustrade
banjo . . . **7.** samisen
bank . . . **3.** row **4.** brae, edge, heap, quay, ripa **5.** brink, flock, hurst (sandy), marge, shoal, shore, slope, table **6.** aviate, margin, quarry, rivage, series, stakes, strand **7.** anthill, barrier, deposit, incline **8.** buttress, treasury **9.** acclivity, riverside **13.** fortification
bank account . . . **5.** funds, means **6.** assets, moneys **8.** finances **9.** exchequer
banker . . . **4.** game **6.** broker, lender **9.** financier **11.** moneylender **12.** money-changer
bankrupt . . . **4.** bust, ruin **5.** broke, smash **6.** failed, quisby (sl) **7.** failure

9. destiture, insolvent, moneyless, penniless **12.** impoverished
banner . . . **4.** fane, flag **6.** ensign, poster **7.** leading, pennant, placard **8.** foremost, headline, standard, streamer **9.** exemplary **10.** surpassing
banns, marriage . . . **6.** notice **7.** sibrede **12.** proclamation
banquet . . . **4.** fete **5.** diffa, feast, festa **6.** fiesta, junket, regale, repast, spread **8.** festival, jamboree **10.** regalement
Banquo . . . **9.** character (Macbeth)
banshee, banshie . . . **4.** shee **5.** fairy, Geist, sidhe **6.** spirit, sprite
banshee, banshie (pert to) . . . **3.** cry **4.** keen, wail **5.** death
bantam (pert to) . . .
cock . . **3.** fop **5.** dandy, sport **7.** peacock **8.** strutter **9.** swaggerer **12.** swashbuckler
Java . . **4.** duck, fowl **5.** breed **6.** Brahma, Cochin
slang . . **4.** runt **6.** peewee, shrimp
sports . . **6.** weight
bantamweight . . . **5.** boxer (118 lbs) **7.** fighter **8.** pugilist **9.** contender **10.** contestant
banter . . . **4.** jest, josh, mock, twit **5.** borak, chaff, sport, tease, trick **6.** delude, deride, satire **7.** asteism, wheedle **8.** badinage, raillery, ridicule **10.** persiflage, pleasantry
Bantu, South Africa . . .
language . . **3.** Ila **8.** Kongoese
people . . **4.** Vili, Zulu **5.** Duala, Xhosa **6.** Basuto, Damara **7.** Swahili **8.** Bechuana
banzai . . . **4.** hail **5.** hello, hullo **6.** attack, charge **9.** greetings **11.** salutations
baobab tree (pert to) . . .
bark . . **4.** rope **5.** cloth, paper
fruit . . **11.** monkey bread
genus . . **9.** Adansonia
pulp . . **8.** beverage
baptism . . . **4.** rite **6.** naming **7.** wetting **8.** ablution **9.** aspersion, immersion, sacrament **10.** initiation, sprinkling **11.** christening **12.** consecration, purification, regeneration (spiritual)
baptism (pert to) . . .
cloth . . **7.** chrisom
dead (RCCh) . . **5.** Blood **6.** Desire
fire . . **9.** fuertaufe
place . . **4.** font **10.** baptistery (anc)
receptacle . . **5.** basin **7.** piscina
water . . **5.** laver
bar . . . **3.** ban, dam, fid, pry, pub, rod **4.** bolt, deny, fess, joke, line, rack, rail, sess, type **5.** betty (thieves' slang), block, court, deter, easer, estop, ingot, lever, shoal, space, staff **6.** except, forbid, hinder, lounge, ripper, saloon, stitch, stripe, tavern **7.** barrier, barroom, bass-bar, chevron, counter, crowbar, exclude, gin mill, prevent, railing, sandbar, trapeze **8.** blockade, disallow, obstacle, obstruct, preclude, prohibit **9.** barricade, hindrance, roadhouse **10.** impediment, profession, singletree **11.** obstruction, rathskeller, whippletree **12.** underscoring, watering hole

barb . . . **3.** jag **4.** clip, flue, harl, herl, seta
   5. horse, point, ramus, scarf (nun's),
   speed **6.** setula, striga **7.** bristle,
   feather, pinnula **8.** kingfish **9.** arrowhead
   10. projection
Barbados Island . . .
   capital . . **10.** Bridgetown
   drink . . **3.** rum
   government . . **7.** British
   location . . **8.** Antilles (Lesser) **10.** West
   Indies
   native . . **3.** Bim (nickname)
barbarian . . . **3.** hun **4.** Goth, rude
   5. beast, brute **6.** savage, vandal
   8. cannibal, man-eater **9.** untutored,
   vulgarian **10.** extraneous, Philistine,
   unlettered **11.** uncivilized
   15. anthropophagite
barbaric . . . **5.** cruel **6.** brutal, Gothic,
   savage **7.** foreign, inhuman, vicious
   8. non-Greek, non-Latin, ruthless
   9. barbarous, primitive **10.** extraneous
   11. uncivilized **12.** non-Christian
barbarism . . . **6.** ferity **8.** rudeness,
   solecism **9.** barbarity, crudeness,
   Gothicism, ignorance, vulgarism
   10. coarseness, corruption, foreignism
   11. impropriety
Barbarossa . . . **7.** emperor (Rom) **8.** red
   beard
Barbary ape . . . **5.** magot
Barbary State (former) . . . **5.** Tunis
   7. Algiers, Morocco **12.** Tripolitania
barbate . . . **7.** bearded, stubbly
   9. whiskered **11.** barbigerous
barbecue . . . **5.** feast, roast **6.** animal
   (whole), picnic **7.** brazier, hibachi
   9. Dutch oven **10.** shish kebab
   13. entertainment (out-of-doors)
barber . . . **5.** shave **6.** figaro, shaver,
   tonsor **7.** tonsure **10.** haircutter
   12. tonsorialist
Barber of Seville character . . . **6.** Figaro,
   Rosina
Barcelona, Spain . . .
   building (famed) . . **6.** palace (Kings of
   Aragon) **9.** Cathedral (Gothic)
   port . . **13.** Mediterranean
   street (famed) . . **6.** Rambla
bard . . . **4.** muse, poet, scop (Hist) **5.** druid,
   runer, vates **8.** minstrel, musician
   (wandering) **10.** Parnassian
Bard of . . .
   Avon . . **11.** Shakespeare
   Ayrshire . . **5.** Burns
   Rydal Mount . . **10.** Wordsworth
bare . . . **3.** raw **4.** bald, mere, nude,
   open **5.** alone, empty, naked, plain,
   shear, sheer, stark, strip **6.** barren,
   denude, divest, expose, reveal, simple,
   vacant **7.** exposed, unarmed, uncover
   8. desolate, disclose, stripped
   9. destitute, unadorned, uncovered
   10. stark-naked, threadbare
   11. defenseless, unconcealed
barefaced . . . **4.** bare, bold **6.** brassy,
   brazen **8.** impudent **9.** audacious,
   shameless **11.** undisguised
barely . . . **4.** jimp, only **5.** faint **6.** hardly,
   merely, nudely, poorly, simply
   7. nakedly **8.** narrowly, scantily, scarcely

14. insufficiently
bargain . . . **3.** buy **4.** deal, pact, prig, sell
   5. trade **6.** barter, chisel, dicker, haggle
   7. chaffer, compact, mediate **8.** contract,
   covenant, purchase **9.** agreement,
   Bon Marché, cheapness, negotiate
   10. engagement **11.** stipulation,
   transaction
barge . . . **3.** ark, hoy **4.** raft, scow, ship
   5. ferry, float, praam, scold **6.** berate,
   lumber, rebuke, tender **7.** birlinn
   (birling), lighter **9.** transport
barge in . . . **5.** enter **6.** bungle, butt in,
   invade, push in **7.** blunder, intrude
barghest . . . **6.** goblin
bargoose . . . **4.** duck **9.** merganser,
   sheldrake
bark . . . **3.** bay, yap, yip **4.** bang, bast,
   husk, peel, rind, ross, ship, skin, tapa,
   yelp **5.** cough, niepa, shout, strip, youff
   6. bowwow, clamor, cortex, outcry,
   packet, scrape **7.** canella **8.** ballyhoo,
   periderm **9.** sassafras
barker . . . **4.** tout **6.** pistol **7.** spieler
   9. solicitor **10.** ballyhooer, theaterman
barking . . . **7.** latrant **8.** hylactic
Barlaam and Josaphet (Joasaph) . . .
   11. Buddha story (Christian version)
barley . . . **4.** bigg, food, seed **5.** grain
   6. ptisan, tsamba **7.** Hordeum
barley (pert to) . . .
   bird . . **6.** siskin **7.** wagtail (yellow),
   wryneck **11.** nightingale
   bree . . **3.** ale **6.** liquor
   shaped . . **10.** hordeiform
barlow . . . **9.** jackknife (one-bladed)
barm . . . **5.** froth, yeast **6.** leaven
   7. ferment
barn . . . **3.** bay, mow **4.** loft
barnacle . . . **4.** bray (Her) **5.** acorn, goose,
   leech **6.** animal, sucker **8.** adherent,
   parasite **9.** sycophant **10.** Cirripedia,
   crustacean
barnstormer . . . **5.** actor **7.** aviator
   11. entertainer
baron . . . **4.** peer **5.** mogul, noble
   6. daimio, tycoon **7.** freeman
   8. nobleman, somebody **9.** financier,
   personage **10.** capitalist **13.** industrialist
baroque . . . **6.** ornate, quaint, rococo
   7. bizarre **9.** irregular **11.** extravagant
barracks . . . **4.** camp, huts **6.** casern,
   laager **9.** barracoon **10.** encampment
barraclade . . . **7.** blanket (homemade)
barracuda . . . **4.** fish, spet **5.** barry
   (Bahamas) **6.** sennet
barrage . . . **3.** dam **4.** weir **5.** blitz
   6. strafe **7.** barrier, gunfire, milldaw
   9. cannonade, roadblock **11.** obstruction
barrage (military) . . . **3.** box **5.** mines
   6. normal **7.** balloon **8.** creeping,
   standing **9.** emergency **12.** anti-aircraft
barranca . . . **4.** bank **5.** bluff **6.** ravine
barratry . . . **6.** breach, simony **8.** bad faith,
   mala fide **10.** infidelity **11.** dereliction
barred . . . **6.** cooped, fenced, grated,
   ribbed **7.** striped **8.** confined, debarred,
   excluded, streaked
barrel . . . **3.** box, keg, tun **4.** cade, cask,
   drum, knag **5.** quill, speed **6.** runlet,
   tierce **7.** calamus (Zool), rundlet

8. cylinder, hogshead 9. kilderkin
barrel (pert to) . . .
maker . . 6. cooper
miscellaneous . . 3. gun, pen 4. pipe
6. pencil
sling . . 9. parbuckle
stopper . . 4. bung
barren . . . 3. dry 4. arid, bare, dull 5. blank,
empty, heath, inane 6. desert, effete,
jejune, karroo, meager, Sahara, stupid
7. sterile 8. desolate, impotent, unpoetic
9. infertile 10. unfruitful, unprolific
12. unproductive, unprofitable
barricade . . . 3. bar 4. bolt, rail, seal, stop
5. block, close, fence 6. abatis 7. barrier,
padlock 8. blockade, obstacle, obstruct
11. obstruction 13. fortification
barrico . . . 3. keg 4. cask
barrier . . . 3. Alp, bar, dam 4. clog,
door, gate, wall, weir 5. block, fence,
hedge, panel 6. screen 7. parapet,
railing 8. blockade, boundary, fortress,
obstacle, stockade, stoppage
9. partition, restraint 10. impediment,
portcullis 11. obstruction
Barrie's boy . . . 8. Peter Pan
barrikin (Eng sl) . . . 6. jargon 9. gibberish
barrister . . . 6. lawyer 7. adviser, pleader
8. advocate, attorney 9. counselor
(counsellor), solicitor
barroom . . . 3. bar, pub, tap 6. lounge,
saloon, tavern 7. cantina, gin mill,
taproom 8. alehouse 9. roadhouse
11. rathskeller 12. watering hole
barrow . . . 3. hod, hog (male) 4. brae,
fell, hill, knap, moor 5. grave (anc),
mound 7. tumulus 8. mountain
11. wheelbarrow 12. Reihengräber
bartender . . . 5. mixer 6. barman, bistro
7. barkeep, tapster 8. publican
barter . . . 4. deal, sell, swap 5. trade,
truck 7. bargain, permute, traffic
8. commerce, exchange
Bartholomew (pert to) . . . 4. Fair, Play
(Shaksp) 5. Saint 6. martyr 7. Apostle
(one of 12) 8. Massacre
Bartimeus (Bib) . . . 6. beggar (blind)
barton . . . 4. farm 5. abode, manor
6. grange 7. demesne 8. farmyard,
hacienda 9. homestead
baru . . . 4. tree (fiber) 7. majagua
base . . . 3. bed, low 4. dado, evil, foot,
foul, mean, root, seat, site, sole
5. basis, basso, cause, petty, radix,
socle, voice 6. abject, bottom, center,
factor, patten, plinth, podium, singer,
sordid, vulgar, wicked 7. servile, station
8. basement, cosmetic, degraded,
infamous, inferior, pedestal, shameful,
standard 9. principle, worthless
10. despicable, foundation, villainous
12. contemptible, dishonorable,
headquarters
baseball (terms) . . . 3. bag, bat, box,
fan, fly, hit, lob, out, RBI, run 4. ball,
base, bunt, deck, foul, home, nine, pill,
sack, save, walk, wild 5. bench, clout,
coach, count, curve, drive, error, field,
first, force, glove, homer, liner, mound,
pitch, plate, pop-up, score, slide, sport,
swing, third 6. assist, batter, bungle,

double, dugout, fumble, ground, putout,
rubber, runner, screen, second, series,
single, sinker, stance, strike, string,
target, triple, windup 7. battery, bullpen,
diamond, fielder, floater, rhubarb (sl),
squeeze, stretch 8. backstop, grounder,
keystone, knuckler, outfield, pinch-
hit, powdered, spit ball 9. sacrifice,
strikeout 10. ballplayer
baseborn . . . 3. low 4. mean 5. lowly,
plain 6. common, humble 7. bastard,
ignoble, lowborn 8. plebeian, spurious
11. commonplace 12. illegitimate
based on . . .
evidence . . 7. damning 8. decisive
10. conclusive
experience . . 7. empiric 9. empirical
numbers . . 5. hexad 6. nonary, senary
7. tertial
baseness . . . 6. infamy 7. badness
9. servility, vulgarity 10. wickedness
11. inferiority 13. dastardliness,
subordination
bash . . . 3. bat, jab, lam 4. beat, belt, biff,
blow, conk, mash, slug, sock 5. clout,
paste, punch, smack, whack 6. bruise,
strike, wallop 7. clobber
Basham's King . . . 2. Og
bashful . . . 3. coy, shy 5. heloe, mousy,
timid 6. demure, modest 8. blushing,
retiring, sheepish, timorous, verecund
9. diffident 13. self-conscious
basic . . . 4. root 5. basal, basis 7. essence,
primary 8. alkaline, original 9. essential
10. underlying 11. fundamental
Basilian . . . 3. art 4. monk, rule 6. bishop
7. liturgy, St Basil (The Great)
8. precepts 10. Cappadocia
basilica . . . 5. major, minor, title
6. canopy, church, shrine, temple
11. patriarchal
Basilican (pert to) . . .
books . . 5. sixty 6. Digest
century . . 5. Tenth
empire . . 9. Byzantine
laws . . 9. Justinian
basin . . . 3. bed (water), cup, pit, tub
4. bowl, cock, font, hole, sink, tank
5. laver, plain, playa, stoup 6. cavity,
chafer, coulee, ground, lavabo, marine,
valley, vessel 7. lowland, piscina
8. curvette 9. washbasin 10. depression
basis . . . 4. base, fond, root 5. cause,
start 6. bottom, factor, motive, reason,
thesis 7. premise, warrant 9. assertion,
principle 10. foundation, groundwork
13. justification
bask . . . 3. sin, tub 4. warm 5. bathe,
revel 7. suffuse 8. apricate 9. luxuriate
basket . . . 3. bin, box, car (balloon), net,
ped, pod 4. caba, cage, kish, skep,
trug 5. cabas 6. dosser, gabion, vessel,
wisket 7. corbeil, hanaper, pannier,
scuttle, wattage 9. container
basket (pert to) . . .
coal mine . . 3. tub 4. corf
fig . . 5. frail 6. tapnet
fire . . 5. grate 7. cresset
fishing . . 3. pot 4. buck (eel), caul, weel
5. crail, crate, creel 6. hamper
making . . 5. slath 6. slarth

wicker . . **3.** cob **5.** cesta, osier **6.** hamper **7.** hanaper **8.** bassinet
Basque (pert to) . . .
ancestors . . **8.** Iberians
cap . . **5.** beret
home . . **5.** Spain **8.** Pyrenees
bas-relief . . . **7.** carving, relievo **12.** basso-relievo (basso-rilievo)
bass . . . **4.** fish **5.** fiber, voice (low) **6.** singer **8.** weakfish **13.** basso profundo
bassoon . . . **4.** oboe **6.** fagott **7.** fagotto
bast . . . **4.** bass **5.** fiber
Bast (Egypt) . . . **4.** Ptah **7.** goddess **10.** lady of life
bastard . . . **3.** odd **4.** heel (sl), sham **5.** false, louse (sl) **7.** bâtarde (Fr) **8.** abnormal, bantling, spurious **9.** scoundrel **10.** adulterate **12.** illegitimate **13.** nullius filius
baste . . . **3.** hit, sew **4.** cook, lard, lash, tack, whip **6.** stitch, thrash **7.** trounce **8.** lambaste
bastion . . . **5.** redan **8.** fastness **10.** stronghold **13.** fortification
bat . . . **3.** hit, jag, lam, rap **4.** belt, blow, clip, club, slug, sock, swat, wink **5.** binge, clout, paste, smack, spree, stick, whack **6.** bender, cudgel, racket, wallop **7.** clobber
bat (mammal) . . . **6.** aliped, fox bat, kalong **7.** noctule, vampire **8.** serotine **9.** flying fox, pipistrel (pipistrelle), reremouse **10.** Chiroptera
batch . . . **3.** lot **4.** heap, lump, mess, slew **5.** bunch, group, stack **6.** amount, baking **7.** mixture **8.** quantity **10.** collection
bath . . . **3.** dip, tub **4.** sitz **5.** steam, sweat, vapor **6.** plunge, shower, sponge **7.** Finnish, mineral, sulphur
bath (pert to) . . .
Eccl . . **8.** ablution
house . . **6.** bagnic, cabana **8.** balneary **10.** natatorium
photography . . **5.** toner **9.** developer
Roman . . **7.** balneum **11.** Warm Springs
sitz . . **5.** bidet
warm . . **5.** therm
bathe . . . **3.** tub, wet **4.** bask, lave, swim, wash **5.** flush **6.** drench **7.** immerse, moisten, pervade, suffuse **8.** medicate, permeate
baton . . . **3.** rod **4.** mace, wand **5.** staff, stick **6.** baston, cudgel, fasces **7.** scepter, support **9.** truncheon
Batrachia . . . **5.** Anura, frogs, toads **7.** Surinam **8.** Salienta
Battalion of Death (Russ) . . . **13.** legion of women
batten . . . **5.** close, gloat **6.** fasten, fatten, secure, thrive, timber
battered . . . **6.** beaten, pasted **7.** bruised **8.** impaired **9.** shattered, weathered
battery . . . **3.** set **4.** guns, pack **6.** cohort, series **7.** assault, platoon **8.** baseball (term) **9.** artillery
battery (Elec) . . . **4.** cell, grid, pole **5.** anode, plate **6.** Leyden **7.** storage, voltaic **9.** electrode
battle . . . **3.** war **4.** fray, meet, tilt **5.** brush, fight, joust, scrap **6.** action, affray,

barney, combat, tussle **7.** contest, scuffle, warfare **8.** conflict, skirmish, struggle **9.** challenge, encounter **10.** engagement
Battle (pert to) . . .
Bib . . **8.** Aceldama **12.** potter's field
Civil War . . **7.** Bull Run **15.** Lookout Mountain
formation . . **4.** line **5.** herse, order
Great . . **10.** Armageddon
Hundred Years (1346) . . **5.** Crecy
Revolution . . **10.** Bunker Hill
slogan . . **8.** aux-armes **9.** battle cry
World War I . . **6.** Verdun (1916)
World War II . . **11.** Pearl Harbor (1941)
battologize . . . **6.** repeat **7.** iterate, recount, restate **9.** reiterate **12.** recapitulate
bauble . . . **3.** toy **4.** gaud **6.** doodad, geegaw, trifle, trivia **7.** bibelot, trinket **8.** falderal (folderol) **9.** bagatelle, plaything **10.** knickknack
bauxite product . . . **8.** aluminum
Bavaria . . .
capital . . **6.** Munich
city . . **8.** Augsburg, Wurzburg **9.** Nuremburg **12.** Ludwigshafen
freeway . . **8.** autobahn
king (former) . . **10.** Maximilian
prince . . **6.** Rupert
river . . **4.** Eger, Isar
bawdy . . . **4.** lewd **6.** coarse, ribald, risqué
bawl . . . **3.** cry, say, sob **4.** bark, howl, roar, wail, weep, yell **5.** blare, shout **6.** bellow, boohoo, plaint **8.** proclaim **10.** vociferate
bay . . . **3.** ria **4.** cove, howl, roan, wail **5.** bight, horse, inlet, oriel, sinus **6.** recess, window **7.** ululate
bay (pert to) . . .
antler . . **9.** stag's tine (2nd)
bird . . **5.** snipe **6.** curlew, godwit, plover
color . . **4.** roan
tree . . **6.** laurel
Bayard . . . **5.** horse, steed (Rinaldo's)
bayonet . . . **5.** lance, saber, spear, sword **6.** dagger, weapon **7.** poniard
bayou . . . **5.** creek, marsh **6.** slough, stream **7.** channel **11.** watercourse
Bayou State . . . **11.** Mississippi
Bay State . . . **13.** Massachusetts
bazaar . . . **4.** fair, shop **6.** market **7.** canteen (army) **10.** exposition
be . . . **2.** am **3.** are **4.** live **5.** exist **7.** prevail
beach . . . **5.** coast, plage, playa, praya, sands, shore **6.** shilla, strand **9.** waterside
beachcomber . . . **4.** wave **6.** loafer **8.** vagabond
beach shelter . . . **6.** cabana
beacon . . . **4.** beam, flag, sign, vane **5.** fanal, light, radar, radio **6.** marker, pharos, signal **7.** cresset, lantern, seamark **10.** lighthouse, watchtower
bead . . . **4.** ball, drop **5.** bugle, pearl, sight (firearm) **6.** rondel **8.** ornament
beads . . . **5.** grain, sewan **6.** rosary **7.** chaplet, granose (antennae), jewelry, prayers
beak . . . **3.** neb, nib **4.** bill, lora, nose, peck, prow **5.** judge, mouth, spout,

tutel **10.** magistrate **11.** stipendiary
beaker . . . **3.** cup **6.** vessel (Chem)
beakless . . . **9.** erostrate
beam . . . **3.** ray **4.** emit, grin, sile, sill,
stud **5.** caber, gleam, joist, shaft, shine,
smile, tonka, trave **6.** girder, mantel,
rafter, timber **7.** radiate, support,
trimmer **8.** trabeate
bean . . . **4.** buck, faba, gram, lima, mung,
navy, seed, snap, soya **5.** black, coral,
pinto, Sieva **6.** adzuki, castor, frijol
(frijole), kidney, legume, lentil, string
7. calabar **9.** Phaseolus
bean (pert to) . . .
eye of . . **5.** hilum
game . . **7.** beanbag
licorice seed . . **9.** jequirity
lima . . **4.** haba
seed (string bean) . . **7.** haricot
shaped . . **8.** fabiform
slang . . **4.** buck, head **5.** brain **6.** dollar,
noodle, trifle
bear . . . **3.** aim, cub, lug **4.** dubb, tote, turn,
ursa **5.** bring, brown, bruin, carry, clack,
crank, koala, polar, press, short, sloth,
stand, ursus, yield **6.** animal, endure,
grouch, harbor, Kodiak, stress, suffer,
Syrian, uphold **7.** Ephraim (nickname),
furnish, grizzly, incline, musquaw,
produce, support **8.** cinnamon, fructify,
maintain, Melursus, sorehead, tolerate
10. speculator **11.** short seller (Finan)
bear (pert to) . . .
cat . . **5.** panda **9.** binturong
class . . **6.** ursine **7.** Ursidaw
color . . **6.** yellow
constellation . . **9.** Ursa Major, Ursa
Minor
flag . . **10.** California (State)
head . . **4.** hure
The . . **6.** Russia
beard . . . **3.** awn **6.** arista, goatee
7. stubble, Vandyke **8.** whiskers
bearded . . . **5.** awned **7.** barbate, pappose
8. aristate **9.** whiskered
beards, science of . . . **10.** pogonology
bearer . . . **3.** boy **5.** macer, usher **6.** porter,
tender **7.** carrier **8.** cargador, conveyor,
escudero **9.** attendant **10.** khidmatgar,
pallbearer
bearing . . . **3.** air **4.** mien, port **5.** poise
6. bel air, regard **7.** concern, conduct,
dignity, meaning, posture **8.** behavior,
carriage, demeanor, relation, tendency
9. direction, influence, relevance
10. connection, deportment, supporting
12. significance
bearing (Her) . . . **4.** enté, orle **5.** bevel,
pheon **6.** billet
bear witness . . . **6.** attest **7.** testify
beast . . . **4.** bête, game, lion, pard **5.** brute,
camel, demon, fiend, horse, spado,
tiger **6.** animal, cattle, dragon, savage
7. carrier, critter, leopard, monster
8. behemoth, creature **9.** dromedary
beastly . . . **5.** gross **6.** animal, bloody,
carnal, odious **7.** bestial, brutish,
hideous, inhuman, leonine, theroid,
ungodly **8.** dreadful **9.** execrable
10. abominable, disgusting
beat . . . **3.** hit, lam, tan, taw, wap **4.** bang,

bash, best, cane, drub, drum, flog,
lace, lash, maul, pelt, tund **5.** baste,
excel, pound, pulse, route, scoop,
throb, thump **6.** bruise, cudgel, defeat,
larrup, pommel, punish, rhythm,
strike, stroke, swinge, thrash, thresh
7. baffled, belabor, cadence, clobber,
conquer, flutter, musical, pulsate,
routine, surpass, trounce **8.** chastise,
fatigued, lambskin, overcome, vanquish
9. exhausted, pulsation
beat (pert to) . . .
back . . **7.** repulse
black and blue . . **9.** suggilate
down . . **6.** haggle **7.** cheapen
into plate . . **8.** malleate
slang . . **4.** blow **5.** scoot, scram **6.** beat
it, skidoo **7.** vamoose
traverse . . **6.** patrol
beatify . . . **5.** bless, cheer, saint **6.** hallow
7. gladden, glorify **8.** enshrine, sanctify
beatnik . . . **8.** Bohemian, maverick,
sulphite **13.** nonconformist
beau . . . **3.** fop **5.** blade, dandy, flame,
lover, spark, swain **6.** escort, squire
7. admirer, courter **9.** caballero,
inamorato **10.** beau-garçon
Beau Brummell . . . **3.** fop **5.** dandy
beaucoup (Fr) . . . **4.** many, much
Beaumarchais comedy . . . **15.** Barber
of Seville **16.** Marriage of Figaro
beautiful . . . **4.** fair, fine **5.** bonny,
kalon (Gr) **6.** comely, lovely, poetic,
pretty **7.** elegant, Tempean **8.** graceful,
handsome, stunning **9.** aesthetic
(esthetic), exquisite **15.** pulchritudinous
beautify . . . **4.** deck, trim **5.** adorn, grace
6. bedeck, doll up, enrich **8.** decorate,
prettify **9.** embellish, glamorize
beauty . . . **5.** belle, charm, glory, grace
8. elegance **10.** loveliness, prettiness
11. pulchritude
beauty, famed . . .
Egypt . . **9.** Cleopatra
Greek . . **4.** Hebe **6.** Graces **9.** Aphrodite
11. Helen of Troy
Historical . . **4.** Lais
Persian . . **4.** peri **5.** houri
Norse . . **5.** Freya
Roman . . **5.** Venus
Becken . . . **7.** cymbals
beckon . . . **4.** beck **5.** court **6.** invite,
summon **7.** gesture **11.** gesticulate
becloud . . . **5.** bedim, cloud, shade, smoke
6. bemist, darken, opaque **7.** conceal,
encloud, obscure **8.** nubilate, overcast
9. adumbrate
become . . . **2.** go **3.** fit, get, wax **4.** grow,
rise, suit **5.** befit, grace **6.** befall,
beseem, mature, mellow **7.** behoove,
benefit **8.** befuddle **9.** originate
becoming . . . **3.** fit **6.** comely, decent,
fitted, likely, proper, seemly, suited
7. decorum, suiting **8.** decorous,
pleasing, suitable, tasteful **9.** befitting,
expedient **11.** appropriate
Becquerel rays . . . **9.** gamma rays
bec-scie . . . **4.** duck **9.** merganser
becuna . . . **9.** barracuda
bed . . . **3.** cot, kip, tye (feather) **4.** bunk,
crib, doss, lair, nest **5.** basin, berth,

couch, futon **6.** billet, bottom, flower, litter, pallet **7.** channel, feather, stratum **8.** bassinet **9.** stretcher **10.** foundation
bed (pert to) . . .
canopy . . **4.** ceil **6.** tester
coverlet . . **5.** quilt **6.** spread **7.** blanket **9.** comforter **11.** counterpane
famed . . **15.** bed of Procrustes
bedaub . . . **3.** dab **4.** blur, daub, soil **5.** paint, smear, stain **6.** belaud, smudge **7.** bedizen, besmear **8.** besmudge, ornament
bedazzle . . . **4.** daze, stun **5.** blind, shine **6.** dazzle **7.** astound, confuse **8.** astonish, bewilder
bedeck . . . **3.** gem **4.** trim **5.** adorn, array, grace, prink **6.** clothe, rag out **7.** bedrape **8.** ornament
bedevil . . . **3.** hex **4.** foul, ride **5.** abuse, tease **6.** befoul, muddle, needle, pester, plague **7.** bewitch, confuse, torment **8.** demonize **9.** diabolize, tantalize **10.** complicate
bedight . . . **5.** adorn, array, equip
bedikah . . . **6.** ritual
bedim . . . **3.** dim, fog **4.** blur, fade **5.** blear, cloud **6.** bemist, darken **8.** bedarken
bedlam . . . **3.** din **6.** clamor, tumult, uproar **8.** madhouse **9.** charivari **11.** pandemonium
Bedlam (London) . . . **6.** priory (1247) **8.** Hospital (St Mary of Bethlehem)
Bedouin . . . **4.** Arab, Moor **5.** gypsy, nomad **7.** Saracen, vagrant
Bedouin head cord . . . **4.** agal
bedroll . . . **6.** bindle **7.** matilda
bee . . . **3.** dor **4.** apis **5.** drone, karbi, queen **6.** insect, worker **8.** andrenid, angelito, honeybee **9.** bumblebee **12.** carpenter bee
bee (pert to) . . .
fear of . . **9.** apiphobia
glue . . **8.** propolis
hive . . **4.** butt, scap, skep (straw) **6.** apiary **7.** alveary **8.** workshop
keeper . . **8.** apiarist, skeppist
sociable . . **7.** husking, raising **8.** quilting, spelling
study . . **10.** apiculture **11.** melittology
wax . . **7.** beeswax, ceresin, cerotic **9.** cera flava
Beebe, William . . . **13.** ichthyologist
beef . . . **4.** heft, kine, thew **5.** brawn, sinew, steer **6.** buccan (dried), cattle, muscle **8.** poundage **10.** brawniness **11.** muscularity
Beelzebub (pert to) . . .
Bible . . **5.** deity **6.** oracle **14.** prince of demons
literature . . **5.** demon (Prince), devil **11.** fallen angel
zoology . . **6.** monkey
beer . . . **3.** ale **4.** bock, flip, suds **5.** lager, stout, weiss **6.** liquor, porter, swipes **8.** Pilsener (Pilsner)
beer (pert to) . . .
cask . . **4.** butt
inventor . . **9.** Gambrinus (Myth king)
making . . **4.** hops, malt, wort
mug . . **4.** toby **5.** stein **8.** schooner
vessel . . **6.** tanker **9.** blackjack

beet . . . **4.** Beta **5.** chard **6.** mangel **8.** beet root **9.** sugar beet
Beethoven, Ludwig Van (pert to) . . .
birthplace . . **4.** Bonn (Ger)
composed . . **6.** Eroica **7.** Fidelio **10.** symphonies
famed as . . **7.** pianist **8.** composer
beetle . . . **3.** bat, bug, dor, jut, ram **4.** June, rose **5.** Amara, gogga, Hispa, meloe, snout **6.** chafer, elater, golach, goloch, hammer, masher, sawyer, scarab, weevil **7.** ladybug, prionid **8.** circulio, sharnbud, skipjack **9.** cockroach, dorbeetle **10.** cockchafer, Elateridae
beetlehead . . . **5.** stupe **6.** plover (bird), stupid **8.** bonehead **9.** blockhead **10.** loggerhead
befall . . . **3.** hap **4.** come **5.** occur **6.** betide, chance, happen **9.** eventuate, transpire
befit . . . **4.** suit **5.** serve **6.** become, beseem, please
befitting . . . **3.** fit **4.** meet **6.** filial, proper, seemly, timely **7.** ethical, fitting, suiting **8.** becoming, decorous, suitable **9.** expedient **10.** seasonable **11.** appropriate
befog . . . **3.** dim, fog **5.** blind, cloud **6.** bemist **7.** becloud, conceal, confuse, mystify, obscure
before . . . **3.** ere **5.** afore, ahead, avant, early, prior **6.** anteal, facing, openly, sooner **7.** already, earlier, forward, yestern **8.** anterior, foremost, formerly, hitherto **9.** foregoing, preceding **10.** beforehand, face to face, heretofore, previously **11.** theretofore
before (pert to) . . .
birth . . **8.** prenatal
long . . **4.** soon
mentioned . . **4.** said, same, such **5.** named **6.** former **10.** aforenamed
others . . **5.** first
this . . **3.** ere **5.** prior **6.** erenow
before (pref) . . . **3.** pre, pro **4.** ante, prae
befoul . . . **4.** soil **5.** taint **6.** bemire, defile, muddle **7.** bedevil **8.** entangle **10.** complicate **11.** contaminate
befriend . . . **3.** aid **4.** abet, help **5.** favor **6.** assist, foster, succor **7.** benefit, support, sustain **11.** countenance
befuddle . . . **3.** fog **5.** addle, besot **6.** fuddle, muddle **7.** becloud, confuse **9.** inebriate **10.** intoxicate
beg . . . **3.** ask, sue, woo **4.** pray, sorn **5.** cadge, crave, mooch, plead, touch (sl) **6.** appeal **7.** beseech, entreat, implore, solicit **8.** petition **9.** importune **10.** supplicate
beget . . . **3.** ean **4.** sire **5.** breed, hatch, spawn **6.** father **7.** develop **8.** engender, generate **9.** procreate, reproduce
begetter . . . **4.** sire **5.** pater **6.** author, father, mother, parent **7.** creator **10.** procreator, progenitor
beggar . . . **3.** bum **4.** hobo, waif **5.** fakir (Muslim), gamin, lazar, rogue **6.** loafer, pauper, wretch **7.** almsman, dervish, vagrant, wastral **8.** indigent, vagabond **9.** mendicant, suppliant **10.** panhandler, ragamuffin **14.** tatterdemalion

beggarly . . . **3.** low **4.** base, mean,
poor, rank **5.** petty **6.** abject, meanly,
paltry, vulgar **7.** hangdog, ignoble
8. bankrupt, indigent, infamous,
wretched **9.** miserable, niggardly
10. despicably, obsequious
12. contemptible
Beggars, King of (Eng) . . . **5.** Carew
beggary . . . **4.** want **6.** penury
9. indigence, mendicity, pauperism
10. mendicancy **11.** destitution,
panhandling
begin . . . **4.** open **5.** enter, start **6.** attack
8. commence, initiate, take rise
9. institute, introduce, originate
10. inaugurate
begin again . . . **5.** renew **6.** resume
10. recommence
beginner . . . **3.** dub **4.** tyro (tiro) **5.** chela
6. infant, novice **7.** amateur, entrant,
recruit **8.** begetter, freshman, neophyte
9. debutante, fledgling, initiator,
novitiate **10.** catechumen, originator,
tenderfoot **11.** inaugurator
beginning . . . **4.** head, rise, root **5.** alpha,
birth, debut, onset, start **6.** origin,
outset, source **7.** genesis, infancy,
opening **8.** entrance, inchoate,
nascency, outstart, starting **9.** inception,
threshold **10.** derivation, foundation,
incomplete, initiation
12. commencement, introduction
begone . . . **3.** out **4.** away, scat, shoo
5. allez, scram **6.** aroint, avaunt, depart
7. vamoose
begrudge . . . **4.** envy **5.** covey, stint
6. grudge, refuse **7.** grumble
beguile . . . **4.** dupe, lure, vamp **5.** amuse,
charm, cozen, elude, spend, trick
6. delude, divert, regale **7.** bewitch,
deceive, ensnare, mislead **8.** enthrall,
intrigue **9.** bamboozle, captivate,
deception, entertain, fascinate, victimize
11. double-cross **14.** disappointment
begum (Hind) . . . **5.** queen **7.** heiress
8. princess
begunk . . . **4.** jilt **5.** trick
behalf . . . **4.** gain, good, part, sake, side
5. avail, stead **6.** affair, matter, profit
7. benefit, defense, service, support,
welfare **8.** interest **9.** advantage
behalf of . . . **3.** for **6.** lieu of, rather
7. defense (of), instead
Behan Boy . . . **7.** Borstal
behave . . . **2.** do **3.** act **4.** bear **5.** carry
6. demean, deport, manage **7.** conduct
8. regulate, restrain
behavior, behaviour . . . **3.** air **4.** mien
6. action, manner **7.** actions, address,
bearing, conduct, decorum, manners
8. carriage, demeanor, maintien
10. deportment **11.** comportment
behavior (pert to) . . .
good . . **7.** decorum, P's and Q's
riotous . . **7.** rampage
wicked . . **10.** wrongdoing
behead . . . **7.** execute **9.** decollate
10. decapitate, guillotine
Behemoth (Bib) . . . **5.** beast
12. hippopotamus
behest . . . **3.** vow **5.** order **7.** bidding,

command, mandate, promise
10. injunction **11.** commandment
behind . . . **3.** aft **4.** late, past, rear, rump
(vulgar), slow, tail **5.** abaff, abaft, after,
ahind, arear, later, tardy **6.** astern
7. delayed, impeded **8.** arrested,
backward, retarded **9.** in the past,
posterior, remaining
behindhand . . . **4.** late **5.** tardy **7.** arrears,
belated, overdue **8.** backward, dilatory,
misdated, mistimed **10.** defaulting,
delinquent
behind the times . . . **5.** passé
behold . . . **2.** lo **3.** see **4.** ahoy, ecce,
ecco, espy, look, scan, view **5.** voilà
6. descry, regard, retain **7.** discern,
observe, witness **8.** maintain, perceive
beholden . . . **5.** bound **7.** bounden,
obliged **8.** grateful, indebted, thankful
9. obligated
beholder . . . **5.** gazer **7.** watcher, witness
8. looker-on, observer, onlooker
9. spectator
beige . . . **4.** ecru, hopi **5.** grège **6.** dorado
13. reddish-yellow
being . . . **3.** ego, ens, man, one **4.** bion,
body, esse, home, life, self **5.** entia,
gnome, human, thing, wight **6.** actual,
animal, entity, extant, mortal, person
7. Adamite, essence, present, reality
8. creature, existent, existing, organism,
presence **9.** actuality, existence,
personage, something **10.** individual
11. subsistence
being (pert to) . . .
celestial . . **4.** deva **5.** angel **6.** cherub,
seraph
imaginary . . **4.** pixy (pixie) **5.** fairy, sylph
science of . . **8.** ontology
supernatural . . **6.** Garuda (Hind)
Supreme . . **3.** God **7.** Creator
Belarus (pert to) . . .
capital . . **5.** Minsk
name, former . . **10.** Belorussia
11. Byelorussia, White Russia
belaud . . . **4.** laud **5.** extol **6.** praise
7. glorify
belay . . . **4.** halt, quit, stop **5.** beset,
cease, cover, halte **6.** fasten, invest,
waylay **7.** besiege, silence **8.** encircle
belch . . . **4.** burp, emit, vent **5.** eject,
eruct, erupt, spout, vomit **7.** gush out
8. disgorge, eructate **9.** small beer
(vulgar) **10.** eructation
beldam, beldame . . . **3.** cat, hag
4. fury **5.** crone, frump, shrew, vixen,
witch **6.** virago **7.** she-wolf, tigress
8. ancestor (fem), harridan **9.** termagant
11. grandmother
Belgian (pert to) . . . see also *Belgium*
anthem . . **13.** La Brabanconne
artist . . **8.** Magritte
hare . . **8.** leporide
horse . . **9.** Brabancon
marble . . **5.** rance
resort . . **6.** Ostend
sheep dog . . **8.** Malinois **11.** Groenendael
violinist . . **5.** Ysaye
Belgian Congo . . . see *Zaire*
Belgium . . .
capital . . **8.** Brussels

city . . **5.** Ghent, Liege **6.** Bruges
  7. Antwerp, Louvain **9.** Charleroi
commune . . **3.** Ath
forest . . **8.** Ardennes
king . . **6.** Albert **7.** Leopold **8.** Baudouin
native . . **7.** Fleming (of Flanders),
  Flemish, Walloon
nickname . . **15.** cockpit of Europe
World War I Battles of . . **5.** Ypres
World War II Battle of . . **8.** The Bulge
Belgravia (London) . . . **8.** district (fashion)
Belial . . . **5.** devil, Satan (New Test)
  10. wickedness (Old Test) **11.** Fallen
  Angel
belie . . . **4.** deny **6.** belong, defame,
  oppose, oppugn **7.** besiege, falsify,
  gainsay, pertain, slander **8.** disclaim,
  disprove, surround **9.** encompass
  10. calumniate **12.** misrepresent
belief . . . **3.** fay (anc), ism **4.** cult, rule,
  sect, view **5.** credo, creed, dogma,
  faith, maxim, tenet **7.** opinion, precept
  8. credence, doctrine, reliance, religion,
  teaching **9.** assurance, certainty,
  principle **10.** confidence, conviction,
  persuasion **13.** Apostles' Creed
believe . . . **3.** buy **4.** deem, feel, trow,
  ween **5.** think, trust **6.** accept, credit,
  reckon **7.** suppose, swallow **8.** conceive,
  consider
believer (pert to) . . .
all religions . . **6.** omnist
facts . . **7.** realist
religion . . **5.** deist **6.** theist **9.** Adventist,
  Calvinist **13.** particularist
Belit (Bab) . . . **7.** goddess (wife of Bel)
belittle . . . **4.** slur **5.** decry, dwarf,
  scoff, scorn **6.** debase, demean,
  deride, impugn **7.** detract, run down
  8. minimize **9.** discredit, disparage,
  underrate **10.** depreciate
  13. underestimate
bell . . . **4.** gong **5.** codon, knell **6.** curfew,
  tocsin **7.** campana, cowbell **8.** carillon,
  doorbell **9.** ship's bell **10.** dinnerbell,
  schoolbell **12.** glockenspiel
  13. tintinnabulum
bell, bells (pert to) . . .
bird . . **9.** campanero **10.** wood thrush
botany . . **7.** corolla
evening . . **6.** curfew **7.** Angelus
flat . . **4.** gong **6.** tam-tam (Chin), tom-tom
funeral . . **5.** knell
nautical . . **8.** half hour
ringer . . **6.** toller
ringing . . **7.** peeling **14.** tintinnabulism
science of . . **11.** campanology
set of . . **6.** chimes **8.** carillon
shaped . . **11.** campaniform
specialist . . **9.** campanist
  13. campanologist
tongue . . **7.** clapper
tower . . **6.** belfry **9.** campanile
warning . . **6.** tocsin
belle . . . **4.** lady (fine) **5.** toast **6.** beauty
  7. charmer **8.** handsome **10.** grande
  dame
belles-lettres . . . **8.** classics
  10. humanities (The), literature
bellflower . . . **8.** daffodil
belligerent . . . **7.** hostile, scrappy, warlike

  8. choleric, militant **9.** bellicose,
  irascible, litigious, offensive, wrangling
  10. aggressive, pugnacious
  11. contentious, quarrelsome
  12. disputatious
belligerent's right (Internat law) . . .
  6. angary
bellow . . . **3.** cry, low, moo, say **4.** bawl,
  roar, wail, yawp **5.** blare, shout
  6. clamor **7.** thunder **10.** vociferate
bellows . . . **4.** fish **5.** gills, lungs **6.** blower,
  lights (Zool), rotary **8.** ctenidia (Zool)
bellwether . . . **5.** sheep **6.** leader, wether
  (with bell)
belly . . . **3.** bag, pot **4.** crap, wame
  5. bulge, front, tummy **6.** bottom,
  paunch, venter **7.** abdomen, stomach
  8. potbelly, swell out **9.** ingluvies
bellyache . . . **5.** gripe **7.** grumble
  8. complain
belong (to) . . . **6.** answer, inhere **7.** pertain,
  related **8.** appendant, ingrained,
  possessed (by) **10.** correspond
belonging (to) . . .
collector, hobbyist . . **10.** collection
  11. collectible (collectable)
dean . . **7.** decanal
era . . **7.** epochal
Fall . . **8.** autumnal
pencil, a . . **6.** desmic
people . . **7.** endemic
present, the . . **7.** current
Spring . . **6.** vernal
Summer . . **7.** estival
Winter . . **6.** hiemal
belongings . . . **4.** duds, gear **5.** goods,
  traps **6.** family, things **7.** baggage,
  effects, kinsmen **8.** chattels, property
  9. homefolks, relations, trappings
  11. connections, perquisites
  possessions **13.** accouterments,
  appurtenances
beloved . . . **3.** pet **4.** dear **6.** prized
  7. darling **8.** precious, truelove
  9. cherished, inamorata
beloved physician . . . **6.** St Luke
below . . . **4.** alow, here, less **5.** Hades,
  neath, sotto, under **6.** aneath, in hell
  7. beneath, short of **10.** downstairs
  11. belowstairs
Belshazzar (Bib) . . . **11.** crown prince
Bel's wife . . . **5.** Belit (Beltis)
belt . . . **3.** bar, bat, hit **4.** area, band,
  beat, blow, cest, mark, pelt, ring,
  sash, sock, whip, zone **5.** apron,
  Libya, strap, whack, zonar **6.** cestus,
  cingle, cordon, fascia, fasten, fillet,
  girdle, region, strait, streak, stripe
  7. baldric, kurbash, sjambok, stratum,
  terrain **8.** cincture, encircle, surround
  9. encompass **10.** cummerbund
Belteshazzar (Bib) . . . **6.** Daniel
belt of heaven . . . **6.** zodiac **7.** circuit
beluga . . . **5.** whale (white)
Belus (pert to) . . .
father of . . **4.** Dido
king of . . **4.** Tyre **7.** Assyria
son of . . **5.** Libya
sons . . **7.** Cepheus, Phineus **8.** Aegyptus
belvedere . . . **5.** cigar **7.** cypress (mock)
  10. watchtower **11.** summerhouse

bema . . . **8.** platform **9.** sanctuary
bemoan . . . **4.** pity, wail **5.** mourn
6. bewail, grieve, lament, regret, repine
7. deplore **10.** sympathize
bemuse . . . **4.** daze **5.** addle, besot
6. absorb, muddle **7.** stupefy
8. befuddle, distract **10.** intoxicate
ben . . . **2.** in **3.** oil, son **4.** tree (Moringa)
6. within
bench . . . **3.** pew **4.** banc (judge's), seat
5. chair, court, siege, staff, stand, stool,
table **6.** exedra, settee, settle **7.** terrace
8. platform, woolsack **9.** committee
bend . . . **3.** bow, nod, ply, sag, sny
4. bias, flex, genu, kink, knot, sway,
turn, warp **5.** crimp, crook, curve,
drink, kneel, prone, squat, stoop,
twist, yield **6.** buckle, crouch, curtsy,
direct, divert, humble, inflex, kowtow,
pleach, relent, salaam, strain, swerve
7. bendlet (Her), chevron (Her), incline,
refract, retract **9.** genuflect, introvert,
sinuosity **10.** inflection
bend (pert to) . . .
an ear . . **4.** hear, heed **6.** listen
one's will . . **4.** bias, move, sway
the elbow . . **5.** drink
the knee . . **5.** kneel **6.** kowtow, salaam
9. genuflect
the mind . . **5.** think
bends . . . **7.** caisson, disease **8.** blackout
(aeronaut)
beneath . . . **4.** alow **5.** below, lower
(than), neath, under **6.** aneath, nether
7. in Hades **11.** underground
beneath one's dignity . . . **8.** infradig
15. infra dignitatem
benedict . . . **7.** husband **10.** bridegroom,
married man (newly)
benediction . . . **4.** rite **6.** praise, prayer,
thanks **7.** benison **8.** blessing
10. invocation **12.** thanksgiving
benefaction . . . **4.** alms, boon, gift, good
5. favor **7.** benefit, present **8.** courtesy,
donation, gratuity, kindness **9.** beau
geste **11.** beneficence, benevolence
benefactor . . . **5.** angel, donor **6.** backer,
helper, patron **8.** promoter
10. befriender
beneficence . . . **7.** charity **8.** goodness,
kindness **11.** benefaction, benevolence
12. philanthropy
beneficial . . . **4.** good **6.** benign, useful
7. helpful **8.** edifying, salutary
9. favorable, healthful, lucrative,
wholesome **10.** profitable, salubrious
11. serviceable **12.** advantageous,
remunerative
beneficiary . . . **4.** heir **5.** donee **6.** vassal
7. devisee, feoffee, grantee, legatee
8. assignee **9.** annuitant
benefit . . . **3.** aid, use **4.** boon, gift, good,
help, vail **5.** avail, favor, trust **6.** profit,
relief, succor **7.** advance, concert,
improve, service, welfare **8.** blessing,
kindness **9.** advantage **11.** benefaction,
convenience, performance
benevolence . . . **3.** tax **4.** gift, good
6. bounty, giving **7.** charity **8.** altruism,
bestowal, blessing, donation, kindness
10. generosity, liberality **11.** munificence

12. contribution, philanthropy
14. charitableness
benevolent . . . **4.** free, good, king
6. benign **7.** liberal **8.** generous, princely
9. benignant, bountiful **10.** altruistic,
charitable, munificent **11.** magnanimous
13. philanthropic
Bengal, Indian State . . .
capital . . **8.** Calcutta
gentleman . . **5.** baboo (babu)
language . . **7.** Bengali
native . . **3.** Kol (Kohl) **6.** banian **7.** Bengali
river . . **6.** Ganges **11.** Brahmaputra
river boat . . **7.** bauleah
benign . . . **4.** mild **5.** bland **6.** genial,
humane, kindly **7.** benefic (Astrol),
liberal **8.** gracious, salutary
9. benignant, favorable, healthful,
wholesome **10.** propitious, salubrious
benignity . . . **5.** favor **7.** benefit
8. blessing, goodness, mildness
9. salubrity **10.** kindliness
11. benevolence **12.** graciousness
benison . . . **8.** blessing **9.** beatitude
10. invocation **11.** benediction
benjamin . . . **6.** jacket **7.** benzoin
8. overcoat **9.** spicebush
Benjamin (Bib), (pert to) . . .
father . . **5.** Jacob
history . . **5.** tribe
mother . . **6.** Rachel
Benjamin's mess . . . **6.** big end **10.** lion's
share
benjy (Brit sl) . . . **3.** hat (straw) **9.** waistcoat
benne . . . **6.** sesame
bennet . . . **4.** herb **5.** daisy **7.** hemlock
bent . . . **3.** aim, way, wry **4.** bias, turn,
warp **5.** drift, grass, slant, tenor,
trend, twist **6.** course, curved, desire,
minded, nature, swayed **7.** angular,
aptness, crooked, heather, leaning,
stooped **8.** aptitude, penchant, tendency
9. obliquity, prejudice, proneness
10. propensity **11.** disposition,
inclination **12.** idiosyncrasy, predilection
13. prepossession **14.** predisposition
Benthamism . . . **9.** welfarism
14. utilitarianism
benthonic . . . **7.** benthal, deep sea
benthonic plant . . . **6.** enalid
benthos . . . **5.** deeps **6.** depths **8.** ocean
bed **16.** Davy Jones's locker
benumb . . . **3.** nip **4.** drug, numb, stun
5. chill **6.** deaden, freeze **7.** stupefy
8. paralyze **11.** anesthetize, desensitize
Beowulf . . . **4.** epic, poem (oldest in
Teutonic language)
bequeath . . . **4.** give, will **5.** endow, leave
6. bestow, demise, devise, invest, will
to **7.** bequest **8.** transmit
bequest . . . **4.** will **6.** devise, legacy
8. heritage **9.** patrimony, testament
10. birthright **11.** inheritance
berate . . . **3.** jaw, nag **4.** lash, rail **5.** chide,
scold, slate **7.** censure, reprove, upbraid
Berber . . . **4.** Riff **6.** Hamite, Kabyle,
Taureg
berceau . . . **4.** walk (leaf-covered) **5.** arbor,
bower **6.** cradle
berceuse . . . **10.** cradlesong
11. composition

bereave . . . 3. die, rob 5. leave, strip
6. divest, orphan, sadden 7. deprive,
despoil 10. disentitle, dispossess
bereavement . . . 4. loss 5. death
9. privation 10. divestment
bereft . . . 4. lorn 7. denuded, fleeced,
shorn of, witless 8. bereaved, divested,
orphaned, stripped 9. senseless
10. parentless, pauperized
Bereshith (Jew) . . . 7. Genesis
9. Beginning
beret . . . 3. cap, tam 7. biretta
bergamot . . . 4. pear 5. snuff 6. orange
7. essence 9. fragrance
beriberi . . . 5. kakke 7. disease
Berkeleianism (pert to) . . .
founder . . 8. Berkeley (Bishop)
science . . 10. philosophy
system . . 8. idealism 13. immaterialism
Berlin, Germany . . .
avenue . . 14. Unter den Linden
capital . . 7. Germany
garden (Zool) . . 10. Tiergarten
gate . . 11. Brandenburg
government . . 9. Reichstag
berm, berme . . . 4. mall, path 5. prado
6. runway 7. terrace 8. shoulder (road)
Bermuda . . .
capital . . 8. Hamilton
color . . 12. geranium pink
discoverer . . 8. Bermudez
government . . 7. British
grass . . 5. decil
ocean site . . 8. Atlantic
Bernardine Order . . . 11. Cistercians
Berne, Bern (Switz) . . . 7. capital
Bernstein musical . . . 13. West Side
Story
Bernoulli forte . . . 8. calculus
berry . . . 3. haw 4. buck, seed 5. bacca,
cubeb, fruit, grain, money 6. acinus,
kernel
berry, fruit . . . 5. grape, salal 6. banana,
tomato 7. currant 8. bilberry, dewberry,
hagberry, mulberry 9. bearberry,
blueberry, cranberry, raspberry
10. blackberry, elderberry, gooseberry,
loganberry, strawberry 11. boysenberry,
huckleberry 12. checkerberry,
whortleberry
berserk . . . 4. amok, bunk, dock, post,
room 5. house, roost 6. billet, marina,
office, reside 8. quarters 9. situation
11. appointment
bertha . . . 4. cape 6. cannon, collar
7. Perchta (goddess) 9. Big Bertha
(Ger gun)
Besant belief . . . 9. theosophy
beseech . . . 3. beg, sue 4. pray 5. crave,
plead 6. obtest 7. entreat, implore,
solicit 9. obsecrate 10. supplicate
beset . . . 3. dun, ply, vex 4. stud 5. harry,
haunt, hem in, siege, worry 6. attack,
harass, infest, invade, obsess, plague,
ravage 7. besiege 8. blockade, surround
9. beleaguer, importune, infatuate
beset with danger . . . 5. risky 6. chancy
8. perilous 9. dangerous 10. jeopardous
beset with hairs . . . 7. barbate, bearded
beside, besides . . . 2. by 3. too, yet
4. also, else, near, nigh, para (pref)

5. about, along 6. nearby 8. likewise,
moreover 9. other than 11. furthermore
12. over and above
beside oneself . . . 3. mad 4. wild
5. crazy, rabid 6. beserk, raging,
raving 7. frantic, ranting 8. frenzied
9. desperate, overjoyed 10. distracted,
distraught 11. overwrought
besiege . . . 5. beset 6. attack, harass,
obsess, plague 7. torment 8. blockade,
surround 9. beleaguer
besmear . . . 3. dab 4. coat, daub, mark,
soil, spot 5. paint, smear, stain, taint
6. bedaub 7. tarnish 8. besmudge
besmirch . . . 4. blot, soil 5. smear,
sully 6. defile, smirch, smudge, vilify
7. besmear, blacken, tarnish 8. discolor
besom . . . 5. broom, hussy
besotted . . . 4. dull 5. drunk 7. muddled,
sottish 8. obsessed 9. senseless,
stupefied 10. infatuated 11. intoxicated
bespangled . . . 5. aglow 7. lighted,
studded, trimmed 8. spangled
9. decorated, garnished 10. glittering,
ornamented 11. embellished,
illuminated
bespatter . . . 3. wet 4. blot, spot 5. dirty,
slosh, smear, stain, sully 6. splash,
vilify 7. asperse, scatter, spatter,
tarnish 8. besmirch, splatter, sprinkle
9. denigrate 10. stigmatize
bespeak . . . 4. mean, show 5. imply 6. ask
for, attest, engage, evince 7. address,
betoken, connote, exhibit, suggest,
testify 8. foretell, indicate, manifest
11. demonstrate
Bessemer product . . . 5. steel
best . . . 4. aces, beat, most, tops 5. cream,
elite, queen 6. choice, finest 7. largest
8. champion, outstrip 9. nonpareil,
overmatch 11. superlative
bestial . . . 3. low 4. vile 5. cruel 6. brutal,
filthy, savage 7. beastly, brutish,
inhuman, sensual 8. depraved, ruthless
9. barbarous
bestow . . . 4. deal, give 5. allot, apply,
award, grant, spend 6. accord, confer,
convey, demise, devote, donate, impart,
render, tender 7. deposit, present
8. transmit 10. administer
bestow honor upon . . . 5. adorn, exalt,
grace 7. dignify, ennoble, glorify
10. aggrandize 11. distinguish
bestride . . . 4. pass 5. mount 7. climb
on, protect, support 8. straddle
10. bestraddle
bet . . . 3. bas (roulette), pot 4. play
5. stake, wager 6. gamble, hazard,
pledge
beta test (army) . . . 12. intelligence
bête . . . 5. beast, silly 6. stupid 7. foolish
betel (pert to) . . .
leaf . . 3. pan 4. buyo, paun (pan)
palm . . 5. areca
pepper . . 4. itmo (ikmo)
bête noire . . . 4. ogre 7. bugbear 10. black
beast, frightener, mumbo jumbo
bethel . . . 4. kirk 6. chapel, church
8. Bethesda (Jerusalem)
12. meetinghouse
bethink . . . 5. think 6. recall 7. reflect

8. cogitate, remember 9. cerebrate, recollect

betide . . . 3. hap 4. fall 5. occur 6. befall, happen 7. betoken, presage 9. come about, eventuate, transpire

betimes . . . 4. anon, soon 5. early 7. ere long, shortly 8. directly, speedily 9. forthwith, presently 10. beforehand, seasonably 12. occasionally

betise . . . 5. folly 9. asininity, silliness, stupidity 11. foolishness

betoken . . . 4. mark, mean, note 5. augur 6. denote, typify 7. bespeak, connote, express, portend, presage, purport, signify 8. evidence, indicate 9. foretoken, symbolize

betray . . . 4. blab, dupe, hoax, sell 5. bluff, peach, trick 6. reveal, seduce, tattle 7. beguile, deceive, divulge, mislead, sell out 8. disclose, inform on 9. bamboozle, victimize 11. double-cross

betrayal . . . 4. ruse 5. trick 7. sellout, treason 8. giveaway 9. Judas kiss, seduction, treachery 10. disclosure

betrayer . . . 5. Judas 6. Arnold, Brutus 7. seducer, traitor 8. derelict, informer, Quisling, turncoat 10. treasonist 13. double-crosser, Judas Iscariot

betroth . . . 4. affy, earl 5. tryst 6. engage, pledge, plight 7. espouse, promise 8. affiance, contract, espousal 10. engagement

better . . . 3. top 4. more 5. amend, emend, excel, raise (poker), safer, wiser 6. bigger, exceed, outwit, reform 7. advance, choicer, greater, improve, promote, surpass, victory 8. improved, superior 9. advantage, meliorate 10. ameliorate, preferable 11. superiority

betting term . . . 4. ante, odds, tout 6. exacta, parlay 7. pyramid 8. perfecta, quinella, trifecta 10. parimutuel 11. sweepstakes

between . . . 5. among, mesne 6. atween 7. average, betwixt

bevel . . . 4. edge, ream 5. angle, bezel, slant, slope, snape, splay 6. square 7. incline, oblique 9. obliquity

beverage . . . 3. ade, opo (comb form), pop, tea 4. coke, malt, maté, mead, milk, soda 5. cider, cocoa, drink, leban, morat (anc), punch, water 6. coffee, eggnog, frappé, nectar 7. Seltzer 8. Adam's ale, Coca-Cola, lemonade, root beer, sourdook 9. ginger ale, orangeade, phosphate 10. buttermilk, grape juice 12. sarsaparilla

beverage (alcoholic) . . . 3. ale, gin, rum 4. beer, brew, grog, kava, port, raki 5. booze, cider, hooch, julep, lager, negus, punch, smash, vodka 6. arrack, bishop, brandy, cognac, eggnog, kumiss, kummel, likker, porter, posset, sherry, smash, whisky (whiskey), zythum (anc) 7. Bacardi, bootleg, bourbon, cordial, liqueur, martini, tequila 8. absinthe, aleberry, Burgundy, cocktail, highball, muscatel, sauterne, vermouth 9. applejack, aqua vitae,

firewater, Manhattan 10. shandygaff, Tom Collins 11. Benedictine, boilermaker, grasshopper, mountain dew

bevy . . . 4. bund, gang, herd, host 5. covey, flock, group, party, troop 6. galaxy, throng 7. company 8. assembly 10. collection

bewail . . . 3. rue 4. keen, mean 5. mourn 6. bemoan, grieve, lament, regret, repine, sorrow 7. deplore

bewilder . . . 3. fog 4. daze 5. addle, amaze 6. baffle, dazzle, puzzle 7. buffalo, confuse, fluster, mystify, nonplus, perplex 8. astonish, confound, distract 9. bamboozle, embarrass

bewilderment . . . 3. awe, fog 4. maze 6. wonder 9. confusion 10. perplexity 11. distraction 12. perturbation 13. disconcertion, embarrassment

bewitch . . . 3. hex 5. charm, witch 6. enamor, entice, hoodoo, voodoo 7. beguile, delight, enchant 8. enthrall 9. captivate, enrapture, ensorcell, fascinate, infatuate

bewitching . . . 5. siren 6. hexing, lovely 7. magical 8. alluring, charming, enticing 10. enchanting 11. captivating, fascinating

bey (Turk) . . . 5. title 8. governor

Beyle's pseud . . . 8. Stendahl

beyond . . . 2. by 3. too, yet 4. meta (pref), past, plus, well 5. above, extra, ultra 6. yonder 7. besides, farther, further, yonside 8. moreover 9. exceeding, Hereafter (The) 11. furthermore 12. additionally, ultraliminal

beyond hope . . . 9. desperate

bezant (pert to) . . .
architecture . . 4. disc 8. ornament
coin (anc) . . 7. solidus (gold)
heraldry . . 4. disc (gold)
offering (Eng king) . . 4. gold

bezel . . . 4. edge 5. crown (gem), facet 6. chaton, flange 8. pavilion, template (templet) 9. obliquity

bezonian . . . 6. mucker, wretch 7. budmash, caitiff, recruit 8. blighter 9. pilgarlic, scoundrel

bhikshu . . . 6. gelong 7. ascetic 8. sannyasi 9. mendicant

bhut (Dravidian) . . . 5. demon, ghost 6. goblin

bias . . . 3. ply 4. awry, bent, turn, warp 5. amiss, slant, twist 6. desire 7. leaning, oblique 8. diagonal, slanting, tendency 9. obliquity, prejudice 10. favoritism, partiality, prepossess, transverse 11. disposition

biased . . . 4. bent 6. narrow, swayed 7. bigoted, partial 8. diagonal, partisan, slanting 10. prejudiced

bib . . . 3. sip, sup 4. swig 5. apron, drink, quaff 6. guzzle, imbibe, tipple, tucker 7. tablier 8. pinafore

bibacious . . . 6. toping 7. drunken, sottish 8. bibulous, drinking, tippling

Bible . . . 7. The Book, The Word, Vulgate 10. Scriptures, Testaments (Old, New) 11. The Good Book

Bible (pert to) . . .

battle site . . **10.** Armageddon
city . . **2.** Ur **5.** Joppa, Sidon, Sodom
  6. Hebron **9.** Bethlehem, Jerusalem
coin . . **6.** talent
Commandments . . **9.** Decalogue
Holy Land . . **9.** Palestine
interpretation . . **7.** anagoge
introduction . . **9.** Isagogics
kingdom . . **4.** Elam **6.** Basham, Canaan
  7. Chaldea
land of plenty . . **6.** Goshen
language . . **7.** Aramaic
mountain . . **4.** Ebol, Zion **5.** Horeb,
  Sinai **6.** Ararat, Gilead, Moriah, Olives
  (Olivet), Pisgah
pause . . **5.** selah
pool . . **6.** Siloam
precious stone . . **6.** ligure (jacinth)
Promised Land . . **6.** Canaan
sea . . **3.** Red **4.** Dead **7.** Galilee
Sermon on the Mount . . **10.** Beatitudes
sheep . . **7.** chamois
town . . **4.** Edar **5.** Babel
Wells of . . **5.** Hagar, Jacob
Bible character . . .
archangel . . **7.** Raphael
giant . . **4.** Anak **7.** Goliath
High Priest . . **3.** Eli
hunter . . **6.** Nimrod
liar . . **7.** Ananias
patriarch . . **5.** Jacob **6.** Israel
prophet . . **4.** Amos, Joel **5.** Hosea,
  Jonah, Micah, Nahum **6.** Daniel,
  Haggai, Isaiah, Joseph, Joshua,
  Samuel **7.** Ezekiel, Malachi, Obadiah
  8. Habakkuk, Jeremiah **9.** Zachariah,
  Zephaniah
Bible version . . . **5.** Douay, Reims
  6. Geneva **7.** Bishop's, Luther's,
  Revised, Targums, Vulgate
  8. Cranmer's, Matthew's, Peshitta,
  Tyndale's, Wartburg, Wycliffe
  9. Jerusalem, King James, Maccabees
  10. Great Bible, Septuagint
  15. American Revised
bicker . . . **5.** argue, cavil **6.** hassle,
  quiver, strife **7.** dispute, flicker, flutter,
  quarrel, quibble, rhubarb (sl), wrangle
  8. argument, pettifog **9.** scrimmage,
  tremulous **10.** contention **11.** altercation
bicuspid . . . **5.** bifid, tooth, valve
  6. cuspid **8.** premolar **10.** two-pointed
  13. double-pointed
bid . . . **3.** beg **4.** pray **5.** offer, order,
  utter **6.** charge, direct, enjoin, invite,
  reveal, tender **7.** command, declare,
  entreat, offered, summons **8.** overture,
  proclaim **9.** quotation **12.** presentation
biddy . . . **3.** hen **4.** dame **5.** skirt
  6. female **7.** chicken, Partlet **8.** bedmaker
  11. maidservant
bide . . . **4.** bear, stay, wait **5.** abide,
  await, tarry **6.** endure, remain, suffer
  8. continue, tolerate **9.** encounter,
  withstand
bield . . . **3.** den **4.** cozy **7.** comfort,
  courage, hearten, shelter **8.** boldness,
  embolden **9.** sheltered **10.** confidence,
  habitation
bien . . . **4.** fine, good, snug
bienseance . . . **7.** decorum, manners

9. propriety **11.** correctness, proprieties
  (the) **12.** mannerliness
  17. conventionalities
bier . . . **6.** coffin, litter **10.** catafalque
Bier . . . **4.** beer
biff . . . **4.** bash, blow, slug, sock **5.** paste,
  punch
bifold . . . **4.** dual **5.** duple **6.** binary,
  binate, double **7.** twofold
bifurcate . . . **3.** wye (letter) **4.** fork
  7. forking, furcate **8.** biforked, branched,
  forklike **9.** two-forked
big . . . **4.** huge **5.** bulky, grand, great,
  grown, jumbo, large **6.** august,
  famous, mighty **7.** massive, pompous,
  teeming **8.** boastful, powerful, pregnant,
  swelling **9.** momentous **10.** tremendous
  11. magnanimous, pretentious
big (pert to) . . .
shot . . **3.** VIP
stick . . **5.** power (T Roosevelt)
toe . . **6.** hallux
top . . **6.** circus
wig . . **3.** VIP (humorous)
Big (pert to) . . .
Ben . . **5.** clock **13.** Tower of London
Bend State . . **9.** Tennessee
Bertha . . **3.** gun **5.** Krupp (factory)
Blue . . **3.** IBM
Board . . **4.** NYSE **13.** stock exchange
Easy . . **10.** New Orleans
House . . **3.** pen **6.** prison (State)
  12. penitentiary
Push (WWI) . . **5.** Somme
Bigfoot . . . **9.** Sasquatch
bight . . . **3.** bay **4.** bend, gulf, loop
  5. angle, noose, point **6.** corner, hollow
  7. estuary
bigot . . . **3.** bug, nut **6.** zealot **7.** fanatic
  9. dogmatist, hypocrite, illiberal
  10. enthusiast, opinionist, positivist
bigoted . . . **5.** petty **6.** little, narrow
  10. intolerant, prejudiced **12.** narrow-
  minded
bijou . . . **5.** jewel **7.** trinket
bilbi, bilby . . . **8.** kangaroo
bilbo . . . **5.** sword **6.** rapier
bilingual . . . **6.** diglot **12.** linguistical
bilious . . . **3.** ill **8.** choleric, liverish
  9. dyspeptic, jaundiced **11.** ill-tempered
bilk . . . **2.** do **3.** gyp **4.** balk, hoax, sell
  5. cheat, cozen, trick **6.** delude, fleece,
  illude **7.** decaive, defraud, swindle
  8. flimflam **11.** hornswoggle
bill . . . **3.** dun, nab, nib, pee, tab, Vee
  ($5) **4.** beak, deed, list, menu, sign
  5. carte, money **6.** docket, pickax,
  poster, ticket **7.** account, invoice,
  mattock, placard, program, receipt,
  statute, voucher **8.** billhook, schedule
  9. publicize, statement **10.** prospectus
  11. legislative **13.** advertisement
billet . . . **3.** bar, log **4.** note, pass
  5. berth, stick, strap **6.** assign, docket,
  letter, notice, ticket **7.** bearing (Her),
  epistle, missive, molding **8.** dispatch,
  document, insignia, position, quarters
  11. appointment
billiard shot . . . **5.** carom, masse
  6. cannon
Billingsgate . . . **4.** Gate (London) **10.** fish

market **12.** vituperation
billow . . . **3.** sea **4.** roll, toss, wave
  5. eagre, heave, surge, swell **6.** dilate
  7. distend **10.** undulation
billowy . . . **4.** wavy **5.** surgy **7.** surging
  8. swelling **10.** undulating
bin . . . **3.** box **4.** crib, loft, vina **5.** frame,
  kench, pungi (Hind flute) **6.** manger
  8. elevator
binary . . . **4.** dual **6.** bifold, binate, double,
  duplex **9.** duplicate
bind . . . **3.** jam, tie **4.** ally, frap, gird,
  gyve, hold, lace, lash, rope, tape
  5. chain, leash, stick, truss, withe
  6. engage, fasten, fetter, pinion, pledge,
  secure **7.** confine, shackle **8.** obligate
  10. constipate
binding . . . **4.** tape **5.** valid **6.** binder,
  edging **7.** girding, joining, liaison
  8. trimming, trussing, wrapping
  9. bordering, fastening, stringent
  10. astringent, compulsory, obligatory
  11. restraining, restrictive
binding (agreement) . . . **4.** bond, pact
  7. bargain, promise **8.** contract
binding (book) . . . **4.** yapp **5.** cover
  6. jacket **10.** bibliopegy
binge . . . **4.** bout **5.** spree **6.** bender
  8. carousal **11.** celebration
bingo . . . **3.** pop **4.** bang, keno **5.** lotto,
  socko **6.** brandy **7.** tombola
biographer . . . **8.** annalist **9.** historian
  10. chronicler **11.** biographist,
  memorialist
biography . . . **4.** life **6.** memoir **7.** history,
  memoire, recount **8.** memorial
  11. hagiography
biological . . . **4.** gene **5.** class, genus,
  order, vital **6.** biotic, family **7.** animate,
  organic, paracme, species
biology, science of . . . **6.** botany
  7. ecology, zoology **8.** eugenics,
  genetics **9.** bionomics, organisms
  10. embryology, morphology,
  physiology
biopsy (Med) . . . **8.** analysis (tissue)
  9. diagnosis **11.** examination
  (microscopic)
biped . . . **3.** man **9.** two-legged
birch . . . **4.** flog **5.** stick **6.** switch
birch tree (pert to) . . .
  family . . **10.** Betulaceae
  genera . . **5.** alder, birch, hazel
  order . . **7.** Fagales
  product . . **16.** oil of wintergreen
  variety . . **5.** paper, river, sweet, white
  6. cherry, yellow
bird (pert to) . . .
  best swimmer . . **4.** loon **6.** gannet
  cage . . **6.** aviary **7.** paddock **8.** dovecote
  Class . . **4.** Aves
  crested . . **7.** hoatzin **9.** stinkbird
  extinct . . **3.** moa **4.** dodo
  fabled, sacred . . **3.** roc **4.** ibis
  fastest flyer . . **4.** hawk **5.** eagle, swift
  6. falcon
  fastest runner . . **7.** ostrich
  feathers . . **5.** remix (sing) **7.** remiges
  first . . **13.** archaeopteryx
  footless . . **4.** apod
  greatest traveler . . **4.** tern

greatest wingspread . . **9.** albatross
halcyon . . **10.** kingfisher
highest flyer . . **5.** goose
immortal . . **7.** phoenix
killing . . **7.** avicide
largest . . **6.** condor **7.** ostrich
  13. whooping crane
Latin . . **4.** avis
life . . **5.** ornis
longest-lived . . **5.** macaw
lover . . **12.** ornithophile
most dangerous . . **9.** cassowary
naked hatched . . **11.** gymnogenous
of prey (prized) . . **6.** falcon
oldest known . . **13.** archaeopteryx
one year old . . **8.** annotine
Order . . **7.** Rasores **8.** Raptores
smallest . . **14.** bee hummingbird
smartest . . **4.** crow
study . . **6.** oology
young . . **4.** eyas **8.** birdikin, nestling
  9. fledgling
bird, anatomy (pert to) . . .
  beak . . **3.** neb, nib **4.** bill, lora **5.** ceral
  7. rostrum
  eye process . . **6.** pecten
  head . . **4.** lore **6.** pileum
  jaw . . **4.** mala
  leg (featherless) . . **9.** cnemidium
  wing part . . **5.** alula
bird, Arctic . . . **3.** auk **4.** gull, skua **5.** brant
  6. dunlin, fulmar, jaeger **7.** penguin
  9. ptarmigan
bird, colorful . . . **3.** kea **5.** egret, macaw
  6. magpie, parrot, trogon **7.** peacock,
  quetzal (quezal) **8.** lyrebird **10.** kingfisher
  14. bird of paradise
bird, common . . . **3.** ani, daw, owl
  4. chat, dove, lark, pisk, wren **5.** finch,
  pipit, robin, vireo **6.** dunlin, linnet,
  martin, oriole, phoebe, pigeon, shrike,
  siskin, thrush, towhee **7.** blue jay,
  bunting, catbird, cowbird, flicker,
  grackle, kinglet, sparrow, swallow,
  tanager, warbler, waxwing **8.** blackcap,
  bluebird, bobolink, cardinal, grosbeak,
  kingbird, redstart, starling, titmouse
  9. chickadee, goldfinch, nighthawk,
  sandpiper **10.** flycatcher, meadowlark,
  turtledove, woodpecker
  11. hummingbird, mockingbird,
  nightingale, pyrrhuloxia
  12. whippoorwill, yellowhammer
  14. scarlet tanager
bird, crow family . . . **4.** crow, rook
  5. crake, raven **6.** chough, magpie
  7. corvine, jackdaw
bird, duck family . . . **4.** clee, coot, lory,
  smew, teal, wood **5.** eider, goose
  6. scoter **7.** gadwall, mallard, Muscovy,
  pintail, pochard **8.** baldpate, redshank,
  shoveler **9.** merganser **10.** bufflehead,
  canvasback
bird, flightless . . . **3.** emu, moa **4.** dodo
  (ext), kiwi, rhea, weka **7.** apteryx,
  ostrich, peacock, penguin **8.** Notornis
  9. cassowary
bird, foreign . . .
  Africa . . **4.** taha **5.** crane **6.** cuckoo
  7. ostrich **8.** umbrette **10.** weaverbird
  Arctic . . **3.** auk **4.** gull, skua **5.** brant

6. dunlin, falcon, jaeger 7. penguin
8. grayling 9. gyrfalcon, ptarmigan
Asia . . 4. myna 5. pitta 6. bulbul,
linnet 7. boobook, peacock, sirgang
8. dotterel, leaf bird 9. brambling,
muted swan
Australia . . 3. emu 4. kiwi, lory
5. lowan 6. leipoa 7. boobook,
grinder 8. ganggang, lorikeet, lyrebird,
morepork, parakeet, platypus
9. bowerbird, cassowary, pardalote
Central America . . 6. barbet, toucan
7. quetzal (quezal) 8. puffbird
Cuba . . 6. trogon 8. tocororo 14. bee
hummingbird
England . . 4. kite, rook 9. cormorant
11. carrion crow
Europe . . 4. merl 5. pipit, stilt (3-
toed), stork (white), swift, tarin
6. godwit, hoopoe, merlin, roller, siskin
7. bittern, ortolan, skylark, starnel 8. bee
eater, dotterel, garganey, nuthatch,
redstart 9. brambling, chaffinch,
gallinule, sheldrake 10. lammergeir,
turtledove 11. nightingale, wallcreeper
12. capercaillie (grouse)
Hawaii . . 2. io, o-o 3. ava, iwa, poe
4. iiwi, mamo 6. parson 7. frigate
India . . 5. shama 8. amadavat, pheasant
11. red hornbill
Java . . 7. sparrow 8. rice bird 9. fruit
dove
New Guinea . . 9. cassowary 14. bird
of paradise
New Zealand . . 3. ihi, kea, moa, tui
4. kuku, weka
So America . . 4. guan 5. macaw
6. barbet, motmot, toucan 7. jacamar,
tinamou, warrior 8. boatbill, caracara
9. trumpeter 11. scarlet ibis
bird, game . . . 4. teal 5. brant, goose,
quail, snipe 6. grouse, pigeon,
plover, turkey (wild) 7. bustard,
gadwall, mallard 8. bobwhite, pheasant,
woodcock 9. partridge, ptarmigan
10. canvasback 14. prairie chicken
bird, group . . .
partridge . . 5. covey
pheasant . . 3. nye 4. nide
quail . . 4. bevy
bird, long-legged . . . 4. ibis, rail, sora
5. crane, egret, heron, stilt, stork
6. avocet, curlew, jacana 7. seriema
8. flamingo 9. sandpiper 10. demoiselle
Bird of . . .
Freedom . . 9. bald eagle
Jove . . 5. eagle
June . . 7. peacock
Minerva . . 3. owl
Wonder . . 7. phoenix
bird, pet . . . 4. myna (mynah) 6. canary,
parrot 8. cockatoo, lovebird, parakeet
bird, poultry . . . 4. duck 5. goose
6. pigeon, turkey 7. chicken 8. pheasant
bird, shore . . . 4. swan 5. egret, heron,
stork 6. avocet, curlew, plover, willet
7. frigate, pelican 8. dotterel, killdeer
10. demoiselle
bird, sky . . . 4. erne (ern), gier (Bib),
hawk, kite 5. Buteo, eagle, saker
6. condor, falcon, gannet, jaeger,

merlin, osprey 7. buzzard, harrier,
kestral, vulture 8. caracara, ringtail
9. Accipiter 10. lammergeir
bird, water . . . 3. auk 4. coot, gull,
ibis, loon, rail, shag, skua, swan
5. cahow, crane, grebe, heron, stork
6. curlew, cygnet, gannet, jabiru,
jacana, petrel, plover 7. bittern, bustard,
dovekie, pelican, seriema, skimmer
8. dabchick, flamingo, umbrette
9. albatross, cormorant, gallinule,
guillemot, phalarope, spoonbill
10. kingfisher, yellowlegs
biretta . . . 8. skullcap 9. headdress
birl . . . 4. spin 6. rattle 7. resolve
birler . . . 10. lumberjack
Biro . . . 9. ballpoint
birth . . . 3. nee 4. line 5. blood,
breed 6. origin 7. descent, genesis,
lineage 8. heritage, nativity, nobility
9. beginning 10. derivation, extraction,
renascence 11. inheritance, Renaissance
birthday (pert to) . . .
astrology . . 7. casting, lineage (the gods)
nativities . . 9. genethlic 10. genethliac
poems . . 12. genethliacon
birth flower (by months) . . .
Jan . . 9. carnation
Feb . . 8. primrose
Mar . . 6. violet
Apr . . 5. daisy
May . . 15. lily of the valley
June . . 4. rose
July . . 8. sweet pea
Aug . . 9. gladiolus
Sept . . 5. aster
Oct . . 6. dahlia
Nov . . 13. chrysanthemum
Dec . . 5. holly 10. poinsettia
birthmark . . . 4. mole 5. nevus (naevus)
birthright . . . 6. rights 8. heritage
9. privilege 10. possession
11. inheritance
birth seniority . . . 9. first-born
13. primogeniture
birthstone (by days) . . .
Sun . . 5. topaz 7. diamond
Mon . . 5. pearl 7. crystal
Tues . . 4. ruby 7. emerald
Wed . . 8. amethyst 9. loadstone
Thurs . . 8. sapphire 9. carnelian
Fri . . 7. cat's eye, emerald
Sat . . 7. diamond 9. turquoise
birthstone (by months) . . .
Jan . . 6. garnet
Feb . . 8. amethyst
Mar . . 10. aquamarine, bloodstone
Apr . . 7. diamond
May . . 7. emerald
June . . 5. pearl 11. alexandrite
July . . 4. ruby
Aug . . 7. peridot 8. sardonyx
Sept . . 8. sapphire
Oct . . 8. opal 10. tourmaline
Nov . . 5. topaz 7. citrine
Dec . . 6. zircon 9. turquoise
bis . . . 5. again, ditto, twice 6. encore,
repeat 7. replica 8. repetend 9. duplicate
10. repetition
biscuit . . . 3. bun, doe 4. rusk 5. bread,
cooky, scone, wafer 6. pommel

7. cracker **8.** biscotin, zwieback
bise . . . **4.** wind (cold) **6.** winter **7.** Norther
bisect . . . **4.** fork **5.** cross, halve, split
  6. cleave, divide
bishop . . . **4.** Abba **7.** pontiff, prelate
  8. chessman, director, overseer
  9. churchman, clergyman, inspector
  14. superintendent
bishop (pert to) . . .
  Bible . . **10.** Great Bible
  cap . . **4.** hura **5.** miter
  revenue . . **7.** annates
  staff . . **7.** baculus, crosier (crozier)
  throne . . **3.** see **4.** apse
  vestment . . **4.** cope **5.** stole **6.** rochet
    7. gremial, pallium **8.** dalmatic
    10. omophorion
bishopric . . . **3.** see **4.** seat **7.** diocese
  10. episcopacy, episcopate
Bismark . . . **14.** Iron Chancellor
bison . . . **2.** ox **4.** gaur, urus **6.** catalo
  (hybrid) **7.** aurochs, buffalo
  9. quadruped
bisque (pert to) . . .
  ceramics (unglazed) . . **7.** biscuit
  color . . **9.** red-yellow
  food . . **4.** soup **8.** ice cream
  term (sports) . . **4.** turn **5.** point **6.** stroke
bissext (pert to) . . .
  calendar . . **6.** Julian (Rom)
  day . . **5.** sixth (intercalary)
  year . . **8.** Leap Year
bistro . . . **4.** cafe **6.** tavern **7.** barroom
  8. wine shop **10.** restaurant
bit . . . **3.** ace, jot, ort **4.** atom, bite, coin,
  iota, mite, mote, part (acting), role, snip,
  tool, tube, whit **5.** check, crumb, hitch,
  money, piece, scrap, speck **6.** morsel,
  smidge, tittle **7.** portion, smidgen,
  traneen **8.** somewhat **9.** something
bit (harness) . . . **4.** curb **6.** bridle, Pelham
  7. snaffle **9.** Liverpool
bit (money) . . .
  two bits . . **7.** quarter **9.** ninepence
    (Bahamas)
  four bits . . **10.** half dollar
bitch . . . **6.** female (animal) **8.** slattern,
  strumpet **9.** complaint
bite . . . **3.** cut, eat, nip, zip **4.** food, gnaw,
  grip, hold, knap, pang, tang, zest
  5. champ, smart, snack, sting, taste
  6. morsel, nibble, pierce **8.** pungency
biting . . . **4.** acid, tart **5.** acerb, acrid, sharp
  6. bitter, rodent **7.** caustic, cutting,
  mordant, nipping, painful, piquant,
  pungent **8.** piercing, poignant, scathing,
  stinging **9.** sarcastic, trenchant, vitriolic,
  withering **10.** astringent, irritating
  11. acrimonious, penetrating
biting nails . . . **12.** phaneromania
bito (pert to) . . .
  bark . . **10.** fish poison
  seeds . . **6.** zachun (oil)
  tree . . **7.** hajilij
bitter . . . **4.** acid, cold, keen, sore, sour
  5. acerb, acrid, irate, sharp **6.** severe
  7. cutting, hostile, pungent **8.** grievous,
  stinging, virulent **9.** rancorous, resentful
  10. embittered, unpleasant
  11. acrimonious, distressful, reproachful
bitter (pert to) . . .

apple (herb) . . **9.** colocynth
chemical . . **4.** alum
earth . . **8.** magnesia
gentian . . **9.** baldmoney
grass . . **9.** colicroot
herb . . **3.** rue **4.** aloe **5.** aloin **8.** centaury
plant . . **10.** bitterroot **11.** bittersweet
  (poisonous)
prefix . . **5.** picro
salts . . **5.** Epsom
suffix . . **6.** picrin
vetch . . **3.** ers
waters (Bib) . . **5.** Marah
wintergreen . . **10.** pipsissewa
wormwood . . **8.** de Gaulle (said of)
bitterness . . . **3.** rue **5.** venom **6.** rancor
  7. remorse **8.** acerbity, acrimony,
  tartness, wormwood **9.** animosity,
  poignancy, virulence **10.** causticity,
  resentment
bivalve . . . **4.** clam, spat, Unio **5.** pinna
  6. Anomia, mussel, oyster, Teredo
  7. mollusk, pandora, scallop
  10. brachiopod (fossil form)
bivocal . . . **9.** diphthong (dipthong)
bivouac . . . **4.** camp **6.** encamp, laager
  7. camping, leaguer (Hist)
  10. encampment
biwa . . . **6.** loquat
bizarre . . . **3.** odd **5.** dedal, outré, queer
  6. absurd, exotic, quaint, rococo
  7. baroque **8.** fanciful **9.** eccentric,
  fantastic, grotesque, highflown
  11. extravagant, sensational
Bizen . . . **7.** pottery (unglazed)
Bizet opera . . . **6.** Carmen
bizzarro (Mus) . . . **7.** bizarre **9.** whimsical
blab . . . **6.** gossip, reveal, snitch, tattle,
  tell on **7.** blabber, chatter **8.** informer,
  squealer, telltale **10.** tateteller, tattletale
  11. taletelling
blabber . . . **4.** blab **6.** babble, gabber,
  gossip, tattle **7.** chatter, twaddle
  8. informer, nonsense
black . . . **3.** ink, jet **4.** ebon, evil, foul,
  inky, noir **5.** color, cruel, ebony, murky,
  niger (L), raven, sable, tarry **6.** dismal,
  filthy, gloomy, pitchy, somber, sullen,
  wicked **7.** hateful, melanic, nigrine,
  nigrous, ominous, unclean **8.** atrament,
  menacing, mournful, sinister
  9. atrocious, lightless, nigricant
  10. calamitous, disastrous, forbidding
black (pert to) . . . see also *Black*
  African . . **10.** blackamoor
  alloy . . **6.** niello
  and blue . . **5.** livid **7.** bruised
    10. discolored, ecchymosed,
    ecchymosis **11.** bluish-black, lead-
    colored
  art . . **5.** magic **7.** alchemy **8.** wizardry
    10. black magic
  ball . . **7.** exclude **9.** ostracize
  bird . . **2.** Zu (Myth) **3.** ani, daw, pie
    4. crow, merl, rook **5.** amsel, ouzel,
    raven **6.** thrush **7.** grackle, jackdaw
    10. Melanesian, Polynesian
  bottom . . **9.** clog dance
  coffee . . **8.** café noir
  diamond . . **4.** coal
  duck . . **6.** Cayuga

earth.. **4.** mold **9.** chernozem (Russ)
face.. **4.** type **5.** sheep **8.** minstrel
fish.. **6.** tautog
garnet.. **8.** melanite
gibbon.. **7.** siamang
guard.. **5.** drole, gamin, knave, rogue,
scamp **6.** rascal **7.** vagrant, villain
8. criminal, scalawag, scullion,
vagabond **9.** scoundrel **11.** rapscallion
Harry.. **7.** sea bass
jack.. **4.** flag (pirate) **6.** coerce, cudgel,
hijack **9.** strong-arm **10.** Jolly Roger
partridge.. **9.** francolin
rhinoceros.. **7.** borelle
sheep.. **10.** scapegrace
smith.. **5.** smith **6.** forger, smithy
7. farrier
spruce.. **7.** yewpine
strap.. **8.** molasses
widow spider.. **6.** pokomo
Black (pert to) ...
Bess.. **4.** mare (Dick Turpin's)
Current.. **5.** Japan
Death.. **6.** Plague (bubonic)
Foot.. **6.** Indian (Siksika) **10.** Algonquian
Friar.. **4.** monk **9.** Dominican (mendicant
Order)
Friday.. **4.** Fisk **5.** Gould, panic **10.** Good
Friday
Hand.. **7.** anarchy, Camorra, Society
(secret) **9.** blackmail
Hawk.. **3.** War (1831) **11.** Indian Chief
Hole.. **8.** Calcutta
Jack (General).. **5.** Logan (Civil War)
8. Pershing (WWI)
Maria.. **7.** vehicle (prisoner's)
14. explosive shell
Monday.. **12.** Easter Monday (1630)
Monk.. **11.** Benedictine
Plague.. **7.** bubonic
Prince.. **6.** Edward
Republic.. **5.** Haiti
Rood.. **8.** crucifix, Holy Rood (anc)
Sea.. **6.** Euxine (anc), Odessa (port)
8. Bosporus (Bosphorus) (strait)
Shirt.. **7.** Fascist **9.** Mussolini
Watch.. **16.** Royal Highlanders
Water State (nickname).. **8.** Nebraska
blacken ... **5.** sully **6.** defame **9.** denigrate
bladder ... **3.** bag, sac **4.** sack **5.** pouch
6. bubble, pocket **7.** blister, globule
blade ... **3.** arm, bit, fop **4.** beau, dude,
edge, epee, foil, leaf, vane **5.** blood,
dandy, frond, knife, spark, spear, spire,
sport, sword **6.** cutter, rafter (roof),
runner, Toledo (sword) **7.** gallant,
sabreur, scapula, traneen **9.** swordsman
blague ... **6.** humbug **8.** claptrap
blah ... **4.** bunk **8.** contempt, nonsense
blain ... **4.** bleb, sore **5.** bulla **7.** blister,
inflame, pustule **8.** swelling **9.** chilblain
blame ... **5.** chide, curse, shend **6.** accuse,
charge, revile **7.** accusal, censure,
obloquy, reproof, reprove **8.** denounce,
reproach **9.** criticism, damnation,
reprehend **10.** accusation, imputation
11. attribution, reprobation
12. condemnation, denunciation,
reprehension **14.** responsibility
blameless ... **7.** sinless **8.** innocent
9. faultless, guiltless **12.** sans reproche

blame taker ... **4.** goat **9.** scapegoat
blameworthy ... **8.** culpable
10. censurable, reprovable
11. impeachable **13.** reprehensible
blanch ... **4.** fade, pale **5.** gloss, scald
6. whiten **8.** etiolate **9.** whitewash
blanc mange ... **7.** dessert, pudding
bland ... **4.** glib, mild, oily, smug, soft,
tame **5.** suave **6.** gentle, smooth
7. affable **8.** soothing (manner),
unctuous **9.** temperate **10.** flattering
12. hypocritical, ingratiating, mealy-
mouthed, smooth-spoken
blandishment ... **7.** amenity, coaxing,
palaver **8.** cajolery, flattery **9.** wheedling
10. allurement, inducement
blank ... **4.** arid, bare, dash, dull,
form, nude, null, void **5.** empty,
naked, verse **6.** closed, hollow,
jejune, poetry, stupid, vacant, vacuum
8. bull's-eye, document, spotless
(domino) **9.** fruitless, unadorned,
untrimmed **10.** instrument (law), tabula
rasa **11.** empty-headed, thoughtless
13. unembellished, unintelligent
14. expressionless
blank book ... **5.** album **6.** tablet **8.** memo
book, notebook **10.** memorandum,
pocketbook
blanket ... **3.** rug **4.** robe **5.** bluey,
cloak, cotta, cover, manta, quilt, throw
6. afghan, shroud, spread **7.** lap robe
8. covering, coverlet **10.** barraclade
(homespun)
blankness ... **7.** vacancy, vacuity
8. negation **9.** emptiness
blare ... **4.** bawl, blow, bray, honk, peal,
toot **5.** blast, blaze, glare **6.** bellow
7. fanfare, tantara **9.** tantarara
blarney ... **6.** bunkum **7.** wheedle
8. buncombe, cajolery, flattery, soft-
soap **9.** adulation
Blarney Stone site ... **13.** Blarney Castle
(Cork, Ir)
blart ... **4.** blab, roar **5.** bleat **6.** bellow
blasé ... **5.** bored, sated **6.** casual
9. easygoing, sans souci, surfeited
10. hard-boiled, nonchalant
11. indifferent, self-assured,
unconcerned, worldly-wise
12. disenchanted **13.** disillusioned,
disinterested, lackadaisical
blaspheme ... **4.** damn **5.** abuse, curse,
swear **6.** revile, vilify **10.** calumniate
blasphemy ... **7.** cursing, impiety
8. anathema, swearing **9.** profanity,
sacrilege **10.** execration **11.** desecration,
imprecation, irreverence, malediction
blast ... **3.** jet, pop **4.** bang, blow, gust,
ruin, shot, toot **5.** curse, stunt **6.** blight,
flurry, onrush, wither **7.** blowout,
explode **9.** discharge, explosion,
explosive, frustrate **10.** detonation,
propulsion **11.** fulmination
blasted ... **5.** blown **6.** blamed, cursed,
danged (sl), darned, ruined **7.** wrecked
8. blighted **10.** confounded
blatant ... **5.** crude, noisy **6.** garish,
puling, vulgar **7.** flaring, glaring,
howling, ululant, wailing **8.** brawling
9. clamorous, turbulent **10.** blustering,

uproarious, vociferous **12.** obstreperous

blate . . . **4.** blab, dull, slow **5.** bleat, blunt, prate, timid **7.** bashful **8.** sheepish **9.** diffident **10.** spiritless

blaw . . . **4.** blow, brag **5.** boast

blaze . . . **4.** fire, gash, mark (trail), sign **5.** flame, flare **6.** luster **7.** bonfire, flare-up **8.** eruption, outburst, radiance, splendor **9.** explosion, firebrand **10.** effulgence **11.** resplendent

blazer . . . **6.** jacket

blazon . . . **4.** deck, show **5.** adorn, blaze, grace, paint **6.** enrich, shield **7.** display, étalage, exhibit, furbish **8.** proclaim **9.** embellish **10.** coat of arms, exhibition **11.** publication

blazoning arms . . . **8.** bearings, heraldry

bleach . . . **3.** lye, sun **4.** lime **6.** blanch, purify, whiten **7.** decolor, lighten **8.** chemical, chlorine, etiolate, peroxide **9.** whiteness **10.** dealbation, decolorant **11.** decolorizer

bleaching vat . . . **4.** kier **5.** kieve

bleak . . . **3.** dry, raw **4.** arid, bare, cold, pale **5.** gaunt, sharp **6.** bitter, desert, dismal, dreary, frigid, pallid, severe **7.** cutting, exposed **8.** desolate, rigorous **9.** cheerless, wind-blown, wind-swept **10.** depressing

blear . . . **3.** dim, fog **4.** blur, dull, film **6.** bleary **7.** blurred **10.** indistinct

bleat . . . **3.** baa **4.** blat **5.** blate, whine **7.** blather

bleb . . . **5.** bulge, bulla **6.** bubble **7.** bladder, blister, globule, pustule, vesicle

bleed . . . **3.** cup, tap **4.** milk, soak **5.** drain **6.** fleece, grieve, let out, suffer **7.** agonize, despoil, exploit, overtax **8.** let blood, transude **9.** surcharge **10.** hemorrhage, overcharge

bleeding . . . **7.** cupping **9.** hemorrhea **10.** hemorrhage, phlebotomy **11.** venesection **12.** bloodletting

blemish . . . **3.** mar **4.** blot, blue, dent, flaw, mole, mote, pock, rift, scar, spot, wart **5.** crack, fault, nevus, sully, taint **6.** breach, macula, macule, stigma **7.** failing, fissure, freckle, lentigo **8.** cicatrix, pockmark **9.** birthmark, cicatrice, deformity, disfigure **10.** defacement, deficiency **12.** imperfection **13.** disfigurement

blench . . . **4.** duck, pale, wile **5.** blink, dodge, quail, trick, wince **6.** bleach, cringe, flinch, recoil, shrink, whiten **9.** stratagem **10.** disconcert

blend . . . **3.** mix **4.** fuse, melt **5.** merge, shift, unite **6.** fusion, mingle **7.** combine, mixture, scumble **8.** coalesce, compound, tincture **9.** commingle, composite, harmonize **10.** amalgamate **11.** combination, incorporate

blended . . . **5.** fondu, mixed **6.** merged **7.** mingled **9.** confluent

blending . . . **6.** crasis **11.** inheritance

blessing . . . **4.** boon, gift, good, luck, rite **5.** favor, grace **7.** benefit, benison, fortune, godsend, service, welfare **8.** good turn, kindness **9.** advantage **10.** benedicite, good

wishes **11.** benediction, benevolence **12.** felicitation **13.** beatification

Bligh's ship . . . **6.** Bounty

blight . . . **3.** mar, nip **4.** dash (hope), ruin, rust, seer, smut **5.** blast, crush, spoil **6.** freeze, mildew, wither **7.** destroy, shatter **9.** frustrate **10.** disappoint

blighter . . . **4.** chap **6.** beggar (anc), fellow

blimp . . . **6.** ballon **7.** airship, balloon **8.** potbelly, zeppelin **9.** dirigible **10.** bureaucrat **12.** Graf Zeppelin, stuffed shirt

blind . . . **3.** dim **4.** ante (poker), mask, peed, ruse, seel, slat, veil, wile **5.** ciego, guise, trick **6.** ambush, scheme, screen **7.** benight, conceal, dim-eyed, eyeless, gimmick, obscure, pretext, shutter **8.** artifice, hoodwink, jalousie, purblind, unseeing **9.** dead-drunk, senseless, sightless **10.** ableptical, dim-sighted, subterfuge **11.** inattentive **13.** undiscerning **13.** stalking-horse

blind (pert to) . . .
alley . . **7.** impasse **8.** cul-de-sac
fear . . **5.** panic
girl (of Pompeii) . . **5.** Nydia
gut . . **6.** caecum, window **10.** persiennes
one eye . . **4.** peed
printing for . . **7.** braille

blindness . . . **7.** anopsia, meropia (part) **8.** ablepsia **9.** achropsia, amaurosis **10.** bleariness, nyctalopia **11.** gutta serena, hemeralopia **13.** achromatopsia

blink . . . **4.** wink **5.** light, quail, wince **6.** cringe, flinch **7.** flicker, glimmer, glimpse, glitter, nictate, shimmer, twinkle **9.** nictitate **10.** bat the eyes

blink at . . . **6.** accept, ignore **7.** condone **8.** overlook, tolerate **9.** be blind to, disregard

bliss . . . **3.** joy **4.** Eden **6.** heaven **7.** delight, harmony, rapture **8.** felicity, gladness **9.** beatitude, happiness **11.** blessedness **12.** spirituality **14.** blithesomeness

blissful . . . **4.** holy **5.** seely **6.** Edenic **7.** blessed, Elysian, Utopian **8.** ecstatic **9.** beatified, glorified

blister . . . **4.** bleb, blob, burn, flay **5.** blain, bulge, bulla, roast **6.** beat up, bubble, oyster, scorch (with words), thrash **7.** bladder, blemish, pustule, trounce, vesicle **9.** criticize **10.** vesicatory

blistered . . . **6.** seared, singed **7.** parched **8.** scorched **9.** vesicated

blithe . . . **4.** airy, glad **5.** merry **6.** cheery, joyous **7.** jocular **8.** cheerful **10.** blithesome

blitz . . . **5.** shell **6.** strafe **7.** bombard **10.** blitzkrieg

blizzard . . . **4.** blow, wind **5.** purga **7.** tornado **9.** snowstorm **10.** snow squall **11.** white squall

Blizzard State . . . **11.** South Dakota

bloated . . . **5.** cured (herring), proud, tumid **6.** sodden, turgid **7.** dilated, pompous, swollen **8.** inflated, puffed up, tumefied **9.** distended, flatulent, plethoric **10.** incrassate **13.** emphysematous

bloated plutocrat . . . **9.** bourgeois

10. capitalist

blob . . . **3.** wen **4.** bleb, blot, daub, drop, lump, mark **5.** bulge **6.** bubble, pimple **7.** blister, globule, pustule, splotch

bloc (political) . . . **4.** axis **5.** cabal, union **6.** league **7.** faction **8.** alliance **9.** coalition **11.** combination

block . . . **3.** bar, dam, set **4.** cake, clog, cube, mass, peck, plot, stop **5.** check, parry, shape, solid **6.** hamper, hinder, impede, oppose, shares, stymie **7.** auction, barrier, outline **8.** blockage, obstacle, obstruct **9.** barricade **10.** impediment **11.** obstruction

block (pert to) . . .
architecture . . **5.** socle **6.** dentil, mutule, plinth **7.** tessera
blacksmith's . . **5.** anvil
coal (Eng) . . **3.** jud
executioner's . . **10.** guillotine
falconry . . **5.** perch
finance . . **6.** shares
football . . **4.** clip
glacier . . **5.** serac
insulating . . **6.** taplet
land . . **4.** city **5.** tract **7.** section
medicine . . **10.** anesthesia
railroad . . **6.** signal
sandstone (Eng) . . **6.** sarsen

blockade . . . **3.** bar, dam **5.** hem in, siege **6.** shut in **7.** closure, exclude, fortify **8.** obstacle, obstruct **9.** exclusion **11.** obstruction

blockhead . . . **3.** oaf **4.** dolt, fool, mome (anc) **5.** dunce, idiot **7.** half-wit, tomfool **8.** bonehead, lunkhead **11.** knucklehead

blockhouse . . . **4.** fort **7.** shelter **8.** log cabin **10.** stronghold

bloke . . . **3.** man **4.** bird, chap, tuff **6.** fellow **9.** personage

blond, blonde . . . **4.** fair **5.** color, light **6.** flaxen **10.** goldilocks

blood . . . **4.** cell, clot, type, vein **5.** aorta, fluid, group, grume, hemad (haemad), hemal, hemic, ichor (gods'), lymph, serum **6.** artery, factor, fibrin, haemal, plasma, Rhesus (type) **7.** blister, carotid **8.** platelet **9.** corpuscle, hemamoeba, leucocyte **10.** hemachrome, hemoglobin, hemorrhage, phlebotomy **11.** erythrocyte, transfusion **12.** bloodletting

blood (pert to) . . .
classification . . **3.** ABO
clotted . . **4.** gore **5.** cruor **8.** thrombus
color . . **7.** crimson, para red **8.** blood red, sanguine **11.** sanguineous **13.** sanguinaceous
disease . . **6.** anemia **8.** leukemia (leukaemia, leucemia)
feud . . **8.** vendetta
flower . . **5.** hippo **9.** blood lily
horse . . **7.** blooded **12.** thoroughbred
hound . . **4.** lyam (lyme)
money (anc) . . **3.** cro **4.** eric **7.** galanas, wergild **9.** bloodwite
particle (foreign) . . **7.** embolus
poisoning **6.** pyemia (pyaemia)
pressure . . **12.** hypertension
pudding . . **7.** sausage
relationship . . **3.** sib **6.** agnate **7.** cognate,

kinship, kinsman, progeny, sibship
shed . . **6.** murder **7.** killing, slaying **9.** slaughter
stone . . **10.** chalcedony
sucker . . **5.** leech **8.** parasite **10.** sanguisuge
thirsty . . **5.** cruel **8.** sanguine **9.** ferocious, murderous **10.** sanguinary **11.** ensanguined
vessel . . **3.** vas **4.** vein **6.** artery **9.** capillary

blood, kinship . . . **4.** race, ties **5.** birth, breed, stock **6.** strain **7.** descent, kinsman, lineage, royalty, sibship **8.** heredity, nobility, relation **9.** blue blood, lifeblood, life force **10.** extraction **13.** consanguinity

bloodless . . . **4.** pale **5.** ashen, faint **6.** anemic (aenemic) **7.** ghastly, inhuman **8.** lifeless, peaceful **9.** unfeeling **11.** cold of heart

bloody . . . **4.** gory **5.** cruel, wound **6.** cruent (obs), cursed **7.** smeared **8.** infamous **9.** murderous **10.** sanguinary **11.** ensanguined **12.** bloodstained, bloodthirsty

Bloody (pert to) . . .
Angle . . **11.** battlefield (Spotsylvania, 1860)
Mary . . **5.** Queen (Eng) **8.** cocktail

bloom . . . **3.** dew **4.** glow, posy **5.** blush, flush, youth **6.** beauty, flower, health, heyday, thrive **7.** blossom **11.** healthiness

bloomer . . . **5.** boner, error **6.** bobble, boo-boo **7.** blooper, blunder, failure, faux pas, mistake, trouser

blossom . . . **4.** bell, blow, grow, posy **5.** bloom, ripen **6.** floret, flower, mature, thrive **7.** develop, prosper **8.** flourish, floweret, progress **10.** effloresce **13.** efflorescence

blossoming . . . **4.** rise **6.** growth **8.** anthesis, blooming **9.** flowerage, flowering **10.** florescent, unfoldment **11.** development, florescence, flourishing, progressing **13.** efflorescence, inflorescence

blot . . . **3.** dry, mar **4.** blur, soil, spot **5.** erase, error, fleck, smear, speck, stain, sully **6.** absorb, blotch, damage, impair, smutch, soak up, sponge, stigma **7.** blacken, blemish, erasure, expunge **9.** bespatter **10.** obliterate, stigmatize **12.** obliteration

blot out . . . **3.** fix **4.** dele, kill **5.** purge **6.** absorb, cancel, delete, efface, excise, rub out **7.** bump off, destroy, expunge, obscure, wipe out **8.** black out **10.** obliterate

blotch . . . **4.** bleb, mark, soil, spot **5.** patch, stain **6.** macula, mottle, stigma **7.** blemish

blotched . . . **4.** pied **5.** pinto **6.** spotty **7.** mottled **8.** speckled

blouse . . . **4.** blou, sark **5.** bluey, middy, shift, shirt, smock, tunic, waist **6.** basque **7.** casaque **10.** shirtwaist

blow . . . **3.** dab, hit, rap, tap **4.** brag, bump, coup, gust, pant, puff, slap, toot, waft, wind **5.** bloom, devel, feint, impel, knock, shock, sound, utter **6.** expand, puff up **7.** beating, bluster, whiffle **8.** calamity, disaster, disclose, lambskin (obs) **14.** disappointment

blow . . . **4.** flee, over, rant, slog **5.** boast, clout, scram **6.** beat it, betray, buffet, depart, wallop **8.** squander **10.** blow me down

blow (pert to) . . .
  hard . . **6.** blower **7.** windbag **8.** braggart **11.** braggadocio
  hot and cold . . **4.** vary **5.** shift, waver **6.** seesaw **7.** quibble **9.** fluctuate, vacillate **12.** shilly-shally
  out . . **5.** douse, snuff **10.** extinguish

blower . . . **4.** blow, gale, wind **5.** whale **6.** puffer (fish), squall **7.** bellows, bloomer, blowgun, boaster, monsoon, tornado **8.** braggart **9.** hurricane, whirlwind, windstorm **11.** braggadocio

blow up . . . **4.** fail, rage **5.** blast, bloat, burst, fluff **6.** berate, dilate, excite, expand, forget, praise **7.** blow out, enlarge, explode, inflate **8.** demolish, detonate, disprove **9.** fulminate **10.** exaggerate

blowzy . . . **5.** dowdy, ruddy, tacky **6.** coarse, frowzy, sloppy, untidy **7.** unkempt **8.** careless, frumpish, slovenly **10.** disheveled, slatternly

blubber . . . **3.** fat **4.** weep **6.** bubble **7.** whimper **8.** whale fat

blubbery . . . **3.** fat **7.** swollen **9.** quivering **10.** gelatinous

bludgeon . . . **3.** bat, hit **4.** beat, club, mace **5.** billy, bully, stick **6.** coerce, cudgel, menace **8.** browbeat, bulldoze, threaten **9.** truncheon **10.** intimidate, shillelagh (shillalah)

blue . . . **4.** anil, baby, bice, bleu, navy **5.** azure, beryl, Ching, email, king's, merle, perse, royal, smalt **6.** cobalt, cyanic, French, indigo, powder **7.** aniline, azarite, cesious, Dresden, Dumont's, gobelin, lobelia, mesange, peacock, Persian **8.** caesious, calamine, cerulean, Coventry, electric, lavender, midnight, pavonine, sapphire, wisteria **9.** turquoise **10.** aquamarine, cornflower

blue (pert to) . . . see also *Blue*
  baby . . **8.** cyanotic
  bonnet . . **3.** cap **4.** Scot **6.** flower (Texas State) **8.** Scotsman, titmouse
  china . . **7.** Nanking
  circle (archery) . . **6.** target
  day . . **6.** Monday
  emblem of . . **6.** Oxford **9.** Cambridge
  grass . . **3.** poa
  ground . . **10.** kimberlite
  hero . . **9.** Bluebeard
  melancholy . . **3.** sad **6.** gloomy **7.** pensive, wistful **8.** tristful **9.** cheerless, depressed, penseroso **10.** atrabiliar **11.** atrabilious, melancholic **13.** hypochondriac
  nose . . **4.** snob **5.** prude **7.** Puritan **10.** goody-goody **11.** Nova Scotian
  pencil . . **4.** dele, edit **6.** delete, excise, revise
  print . . **4.** plan, plot **5.** graph **6.** layout **7.** diagram, program **8.** schedule

9. cyanotype **10.** master plan, photograph, photoprint
  ribbon . . **5.** award, badge **10.** cordon bleu, decoration
  skin . . **5.** livid
  sky . . **5.** ether, vault **6.** caelum, heaven, welkin **7.** the blue **8.** empyrean **9.** firmament **10.** blue yonder, the heavens
  stocking . . **4.** blue **6.** pedant **7.** bas bleu **8.** Gamaliel (Bib) **9.** formalist, pedagogue **10.** Parliament

Blue (pert to) . . .
  Boy . . **8.** painting (Gainsborough)
  Grass State . . **8.** Kentucky
  Grotto site . . **5.** Capri
  Law State . . **11.** Connecticut

Bluebeard's wife . . . **6.** Fatima

blue-gray . . . **7.** cesious (caesious)

blue-green . . . **8.** calamine

bluff . . . **4.** bank (steep), crag, curt, dupe, fool, rude, wall **5.** brash, cliff, frank, gruff, krans, sheer, short **6.** abrupt, crusty **7.** beguile, blinder, blinker, bluffer, bluster, brusque, deceive, pretend, uncivil **8.** impolite **9.** bamboozle, blusterer, charlatan, falseness, four-flush, precipice **11.** four-flusher **13.** unceremonious

bluffer . . . **5.** quack **9.** blusterer, charlatan **10.** mountebank **11.** four-flusher

bluffness . . . **6.** candor **9.** bluntness **10.** abruptness **11.** brusqueness

blunder . . . **3.** err, mix **4.** bull, goof, slip **5.** boner, botch, error, misdo **6.** boo-boo, bungle, fumble **7.** faux pas, mistake, stumble **8.** flounder, solecism (speech) **9.** mismanage

blunt . . . **4.** curt, dull, open **5.** bluff, frank, gruff, plain **6.** benumb, candid, deaden, obtund, obtuse, snippy, stupid, weaken **7.** artless, brusque, sincere **8.** hebetate **9.** ingenuous **13.** unceremonious

blur . . . **3.** bog, dim, hum **4.** blob, blot, film, mist, soil, spot **5.** blear, cloud, smear, stain **6.** blotch, darken, mackle **7.** blemish, dimness, obscure, splotch **9.** disfigure

blurb . . . **2.** ad **4.** plug **5.** boost, brief **6.** notice **7.** write-up **8.** ballyhoo **9.** publicity **12.** announcement, commendation **13.** advertisement

blurt out . . . **4.** blab, bolt **7.** blunder **9.** ejaculate

blush . . . **4.** glow, look **5.** bloom, color, flush **6.** glance, mantle, redden **7.** modesty, redness **9.** suffusion

blushing . . . **4.** meek **5.** ruddy **6.** modest **7.** roseate **8.** flushing, sheepish **9.** reddening, rubescent **10.** erubescent

bluster . . . **4.** blow, bray, fume, rage, rant, roar **5.** broil, bully, furor, noise **6.** flurry, hoopla, hubbub, squall, tumult **7.** roister, swagger, turmoil **8.** boasting, bullying, threaten **9.** agitation, confusion **10.** swaggering, turbulence **11.** rodomontade

blusterer . . . **5.** bully **7.** boaster **8.** blowhard, braggart **9.** roisterer, swaggerer **11.** braggadocio **12.** swashbuckler

bo ... **4.** hobo **5.** buddy, tramp **9.** sundowner **10.** landlouper **11.** bindle stiff

bo, boh (Burma) ... **5.** chief **6.** leader **7.** captain

boa ... **5.** aboma, scarf (feather), snake **8.** anaconda

boar ... **3.** hog, sus **4.** apex, hure (head) **5.** swine **6.** barrow, hogget (2-year) **9.** hoggaster (3-year)

board ... **4.** deal, doll, feed, lath, side, slat, wood **5.** curia (anc), enter, forum, meals, plank, table **6.** border, lumber, timber **7.** binding (book), council, lodging **8.** approach, exchange (Finan), tribunal **9.** committee, provision **11.** accommodate, bed and board, directorate, refreshment **14.** accommodations

boast ... **4.** brag, crow **5.** extol, exult, glory, pride, vapor, vaunt **6.** menace **7.** bluster, swagger **8.** braggart, flourish **9.** gasconade

boastful ... **4.** vain **8.** bragging **9.** conceited, overproud, presuming **11.** thrasonical **12.** vainglorious **13.** self-important

boat ... **3.** ark, bac, gig, tub, tug **4.** brig, dhow, dory, junk, punt, saic, scow, ship, trow, yawl **5.** aviso, balsa, barge, canoe, craft, dandy, dhoni, dingy, ferry, kayak, ketch, liner, oolak, praam, scull, skiff, U-boat, umiak, xebec, yacht **6.** argosy, baidak, bateau, convoy, cutter, dinghy, dogger, launch, mistic, oomiac, packet, randan, sampan, settee, tanker, vessel, whaler **7.** bidarka, caravel, coracle (anc), cruiser, gondola, masoola, piragua, pirogue, rowboat, scooter, shallop, trawler, tugboat, warship **8.** dahabeah, man-of-war, palander, sailboat, seaplane **9.** catamaran, destroyer, steamship, submarine **10.** brigantine, windjammer **11.** side-wheeler, treckschuyt

boat (pert to) ...
boatswain .. **5.** bosun **6.** serang
captain .. **4.** rais (reis) **6.** master **7.** skipper
deck .. **4.** poop **6.** flight **9.** promenade
man .. **5.** rower **6.** bargee **7.** ferrier, oarsman **9.** gondolier, yachtsman
sail .. **3.** jib **4.** main, reef **6.** lateen, mizzen
shaped .. **9.** navicella, navicular
side .. **7.** gunwale
song .. **7.** chantey **9.** barcarole

bob ... **3.** bow, cut, nod, rap, tap **4.** bend, jeer, jerk, jest **5.** cheat, filch, float, flout, plumb, shake, taunt, trick **6.** bobble, curtsy, delude, hairdo, kowtow, sinker, weight **7.** haircut **8.** coiffure, greeting, shilling **9.** obeisance, oscillate

bobac ... **5.** pahmi **6.** marmot

bobber ... **4.** duck (ruddy) **5.** float **6.** bobfly **7.** dropper **8.** deadhead

bobbin ... **3.** pin **4.** coil, cord, pirn, reel **5.** braid, spool **7.** spindle

bobble ... **3.** bob, dib (angling) **4.** muff **5.** shake **6.** boggle, bungle, fumble **7.** blunder **9.** oscillate

bobby ... **6.** peeler **9.** policeman

Boccaccio's tales ... **9.** Decameron

Boche ... **6.** German (a)

bodach ... **5.** churl, clown **7.** bugaboo

bodacious ... **4.** bold **8.** insolent, reckless **9.** audacious, bumptious, insulting **12.** contumelious

bode ... **5.** augur **6.** divine **7.** portend, presage **8.** forebode, foreshow, foretell **13.** prognosticate

bodhisattva ... **8.** Buddhism **13.** Enlightenment

bodice ... **4.** belt **5.** stays, waist **6.** basque, girdle **7.** corsage, garment

bodily ... **6.** carnal **7.** fleshly, somatic **8.** corporal, material, physical **9.** corporeal **10.** completely

boding ... **7.** ominous **10.** foreboding, portentous, prediction, prognostic **12.** apprehension

bodkin ... **3.** awl **6.** dagger, needle **7.** hairpin, poniard **8.** stiletto **9.** eyeleteer

body ... **3.** man **4.** deha (Theos), homo, soma **5.** being, human, trunk **6.** corpse, entity, licham, mortal, person **7.** carcass **8.** creature, organism **9.** substance **10.** individual **13.** corpus delicti **14.** substantiality

body (pert to) ...
armed .. **5.** corps, posse
business .. **7.** company **11.** cooperation **12.** organization
celestial .. **3.** sun **4.** luna, star **5.** comet **6.** meteor, planet
church .. **4.** nave
dead .. **6.** corpse **7.** cadaver
division (mollusk) .. **7.** prosoma
injury .. **6.** mayhem, trauma
petrified .. **6.** fossil
political .. **4.** weal **6.** senate **7.** cabinet **11.** legislature
small .. **6.** nanoid **8.** dwarfish

body of ...
people .. **3.** mob **4.** band, bevy, gang, host **5.** bunch, crowd, flock, group, horde **6.** rabble, throng **9.** multitude
singers .. **5.** choir **6.** chorus
soldiers .. **4.** file **5.** corps, squad, troop **7.** brigade, company, platoon **8.** division
water .. **3.** bay, sea **4.** lake, pond, pool **5.** fiord (fjord), inlet, ocean **6.** lagoon **9.** reservoir

Boeotian (pert to) ...
city .. **5.** Ionia (Dist) **6.** Thebes
figurine .. **7.** Tanagra
king (Myth) .. **6.** Ogyges

Boer (pert to) ...
General, statesman .. **5.** Botha
language .. **4.** Taal **9.** Afrikaans
War site .. **9.** Ladysmith (So Afr)

bog ... **3.** bug, fen **4.** blei, bold, holm, mire, moor, moss, ooze, quag, sink **5.** jheel, marsh, saucy, swamp **6.** morass, slough **8.** quagmire **9.** everglade

bogey, bogie, bogy ... **3.** par **5.** Devil **6.** goblin **7.** bugaboo, bugbear

boggle ... **3.** shy **4.** foil, quip **5.** botch, cavil, demur, parry, pause, start **6.** bicker, bungle, falter, object, shrink **7.** dispute, quibble, scruple **8.** hesitate,

sidestep **9.** dissemble, objection
10. difficulty, equivocate
bogglebo . . . **5.** bogle **7.** bugaboo, specter
9. hobgoblin, scarecrow
bogus . . . **4.** fake, mock, sham **5.** phony,
queer **8.** spurious **10.** apocryphal,
factitious, fictitious **11.** counterfeit
bohawn . . . **3.** hut **5.** cabin **7.** cottage
Bohemia . . .
capital . . **6.** Prague
city . . **5.** Praha **6.** Aussig, Pilsen
7. Budweis, Teplitz **11.** Reichenberg
dance . . **6.** redowa
measure . . **5.** stopa **6.** merice
mineral . . **6.** egeran
reformer . . **4.** Huss
river . . **4.** Elbe, Iser **6.** Moldau
vagabond . . **5.** gypsy (gipsy)
bohunk . . . **6.** Slovak **7.** laborer
8. Bohemian, Croatian (formerly)
boil . . . **3.** sty (styr) **4.** buck, cook, fume,
stew **5.** churn, steam **6.** bubble, pimple,
seethe **7.** bristle **8.** furuncle
boiling . . . **5.** angry **7.** cooking, flushed,
stewing **8.** seething, sizzling **9.** agitating,
ebullient **10.** smoldering
bois (Fr) . . . **4.** wood
boisterous . . . **4.** loud **5.** noisy, rough,
rowdy **6.** stormy **7.** blatant, excited,
furious, roaring, violent **8.** brawling
9. clamorous, turbulent **10.** blustering,
roisterous, tumultuous, unyielding
12. obstreperous
Bokhara (pert to) . . .
fur . . **9.** astrakhan, broadtail
rug . . **8.** Turkoman
sheep . . **7.** karakul (caracul)
site . . **4.** Asia (Russ)
bola . . . **4.** tree (fiber) **6.** weapon
bold . . . **4.** deep, pert, rash, rude, snug
5. steep, stout **6.** abrupt, brazen, daring,
heroic, raised **7.** dashing, defiant,
eminent, forward, salient, valiant
8. fearless, immodest, impudent, in
relief, intrepid, powerful, repoussé,
stalwart **9.** audacious, confident,
dauntless, shameless, unabashed
10. courageous **11.** lionhearted,
outstanding, precipitous, venturesome
12. presumptuous, stouthearted
boldness . . . **5.** valor **6.** defial, virtue
7. bravery, courage **8.** audacity,
defiance, salience, temerity
9. assurance, gallantry, hardihood,
immodesty, impudence **10.** brazenness,
confidence, effrontery, prominence,
resolution **11.** forwardness, intrepidity,
obviousness **12.** protuberance
13. dauntlessness **14.** courageousness
bolero . . . **5.** dance, music, waist **6.** jacket
boliche . . . **3.** inn **5.** bowls
Bolivia . . .
capital . . **5.** La Paz (Polit), Oruro (anc),
Sucre (law)
hero . . **5.** Sucre **7.** Bolivar, Pizarro
Indian . . **3.** Uro **4.** Iten, Moxo
lake . . **8.** Titicaca (world's highest)
mountain . . **5.** Andes **6.** Sorata **8.** Illimani
product . . **3.** tin **8.** tungsten
river . . **4.** Beni **6.** Blanco
bolo . . . **5.** knife **7.** machete **8.** pacifist

(Bolo Pasha, traitor) **9.** defeatist
Bolshevik, bolshevik . . . **5.** Lenin
7. Marxian, radical (Bolsheviki)
9. Communist (1918), Socialist
13. revolutionist **14.** Social Democrat
18. Third International
bolster . . . **3.** pad **4.** bear, hold **5.** boost
6. pillow **7.** cushion, support, sustain
8. maintain
bolt . . . **3.** bar **4.** dart, flee, lock, roll,
sift **5.** arrow, rivet, scram, screw,
shaft, speed **6.** decamp, devour,
faster, flight, pintle, secede, staple,
toggle **7.** missile, padlock **8.** firebolt,
separate **10.** projectile **11.** eat greedily,
fulguration, thunderbolt
bolus . . . **4.** bite, clay, clod, food (chewed),
mass, pill **6.** tablet, troche **8.** mouthful
bomb . . . **3.** dud, egg **5.** shell **6.** petard
7. grenade, missile **8.** divebomb,
fireball, surprise **9.** bombshell,
pineapple **10.** projectile
bomb (type of) . . . **4.** time **5.** stink **6.** aerial,
atomic, rocket **7.** nuclear, tear gas
8. hydrogen **10.** demolition
bombard . . . **3.** zap **5.** blitz, shell **6.** assail,
attack, strafe **7.** atomize, barrage
9. cannonade
bombardier . . . **5.** jager **6.** bomber,
gunner **9.** cannoneer, musketeer
12. artilleryman
bombast . . . **4.** blow, brag, rage, rant, rave
5. boast **7.** fustian **8.** boasting, inflated,
stuffing (hist) **9.** bombastic, turgidity
11. rodomontade **12.** magniloquent
13. grandiloquent
bombastic . . . **5.** tumid **7.** orotund,
pompous, stilted **8.** boastful, inflated
12. high-sounding **13.** grandiloquent
Bombay . . .
capital of . . **11.** Maharashtra (state)
college . . **11.** Elphinstone
duck . . **10.** lizard fish
hemp . . **4.** sunn **6.** ambary
merchant . . **4.** Arab
seaport of . . **5.** India
bombed . . . **5.** drunk
bomber . . . **5.** stuka **10.** bombardier
Bombyx . . . **4.** eria, moth **8.** silkworm
bona fide . . . **4.** real **7.** genuine
9. authentic **10.** constantly, faithfully,
legitimate
bona mano . . . **3.** tip **8.** gratuity
bon ami . . . **5.** lover **6.** friend **10.** good
friend, sweetheart
bonanza . . . **6.** riches **8.** El Dorado (Myth),
gold mine (US)
Bonanza State . . . **7.** Montana
Bonaparte . . . see *Napoleon I*
bond . . . **3.** tie, vow **4.** duty, gyve, link,
mise, pact, yoke **5.** chain, nexus,
rente **6.** fetter, league **7.** entente,
manacle, shackle **8.** contract, covenant,
relation, security (Finan) **9.** agreement,
captivity **10.** allegiance, connection
11. association, certificate
bondage . . . **4.** yoke **6.** chains **7.** serfdom,
slavery **9.** captivity, restraint, servitude,
thralldom **11.** enslavement, subjugation
bondman, bondsman . . . **4.** esne, serf
5. churl, helot, slave **6.** thrall, vassal

7. servant 8. bailsman 9. guarantor
bone . . . 2. os 4. chip 5. boner 6. dollar,
osteon 7. blunder, counter (game),
ossicle 8. skeleton, wishbone 9. funny
bone (humerus), pygostyle (bird's),
whalebone
bone (Anat) . . . 3. rib 4. ulna 5. femur,
ilium, incus (ear), malar, skull, spine,
talus, tibia 6. carpus, coccyx, fibula,
tarsus 7. humerus, maxilla, patella,
scapula, sternum 8. astragal, clavicle,
mandible, phalange, vertebra
9. calcaneus, occipital 10. metacarpus,
metatarsus
bone (pert to) . . .
bonelike . . 6. osteal 7. osteoid
cell . . 10. osteoblast
china . . 7. English
curvature . . 8. lordosis
divination . . 10. osteomancy
fish . . 9. operculum
marrow . . 7. medulla
process . . 7. mastoid 8. alveolar
9. apophysis
science . . 9. osteology
surgery . . 9. osteotomy 11. osteoclasis
12. osteoplastic
tissue . . 6. ossein
tumor . . 7. osteoma
bones . . . 4. body, dice, form, ossa
5. cubes, frame, money, torso, trunk
6. end man, refuse 7. carcass, ivories
8. skeleton 11. rattlebones
boneyard . . . 4. bank (game) 8. golgotha
9. graveyard 10. necropolis
11. polyandrium
Bonheur subject . . . 6. animal
bonhomie . . . 8. pleasant 9. good humor
10. affability, amiability
Bonhomme Richard . . . 4. ship 8. man-
of-war (1779) (opponent of Serapis)
bonito, bonita . . . 4. nice 6. pretty
8. mackerel, skipjack
bon mot . . . 9. witticism 10. jeu d'esprit
11. smart saying
bonne . . . 5. mammy 9. nursemaid
10. baby sitter 11. maidservant
bonnet . . . 3. cap, hat 4. coif, hood, poke
5. toque 7. chapeau 9. headdress
bonnetman . . . 10. Highlander
bonny, bonnie . . . 3. bon 4. good
5. plump 6. comely, lively, pretty
7. healthy, très bon 8. handsome
9. beautiful
Bontok . . . 7. Malayan (Luzon)
10. Indonesian
bonus . . . 3. tip 4. cash, gift 5. batta, bribe,
extra, share, stock (Finan) 7. cumshaw,
douceur, premium, rake-off, subsidy
8. dividend, gratuity 9. Trinkgeld
10. honorarium
bon vivant . . . 7. epicure, gourmet
8. gourmand, hedonist, sybarite
10. boonfellow, good fellow, voluptuary
12. Heliogabalus (anc)
bony . . . 4. hard, thin 6. osteal, skinny
7. osseous 8. rawboned, skeletal
bonze (Far East) . . . 2. bo 4. monk
boo . . . 4. hoot, jeer, razz 7. catcall, feather
(ostrich) 9. raspberry 10. Bronx cheer
boob . . . 4. dupe, fool, goon, jerk

5. chump, dunce 6. nitwit 7. fathead
9. schlemiel, simpleton
boobook . . . 3. owl 8. morepork
booby hatch . . . 3. can, jug 4. jail
6. asylum, cooler, prison 8. hoosegow,
madhouse 11. institution (mental)
boodle . . . 3. sop 4. loot, swag 5. booty,
bribe, bunch, crowd, graft, money
(hush) 6. spoils 8. caboodle 10. pork
barrel 11. counterfeit
boohoo . . . 3. rob 4. bawl, hoot, weep
5. shout 8. sailfish
book . . . 2. mo (abbr) 3. day 4. hire, opus,
tome 5. album, atlas, Bible, canto,
diary, folio, liber, novel 6. agenda,
engage, ledger, manual, missal, primer,
record, sign up, volume 7. diurnal,
journal, mystery 8. brochure, libretto,
register, schedule, songbook, whodunit
9. paperback, storybook 10. literature,
memorandum 11. publication
book (pert to) . . .
announcement . . 5. blurb
back . . 5. spine
binder . . 12. bibliopegist
binding devise . . 7. trindle
collector . . 10. bibliothec 12. bibliomaniac
14. bibliothecaire
cover . . 5. recto 6. jacket
destroyer . . 11. biblioclast
division . . 7. chapter
lore . . 10. bibliology
lover . . 11. bibliophile
one versed in . . 11. bibliognost
page . . 5. folio
seller . . 10. bibliopole (rare books)
sheath . . 5. forel
size . . 6. quarto
stealer . . 11. biblioklept
style . . 6. Aldine 8. Etruscan 9. Arabesque
treatise . . 8. isagogue
worshiper . . 11. bibliolater
writer . . 13. bibliographer
book (religious) . . . 4. Ordo 5. Bible, Kells,
Tobit 6. Esdras, Mormon 7. Psalter
8. Holy Writ 9. Apocrypha, Catechism,
Testament 10. Pentateuch, Scriptures
Book of . . .
award (Harvard) . . 5. detur
Concord . . 8. Lutheran
Discipline . . 12. Presbyterian
Hours . . 5. Horae
Moses (Laws) . . 10. Pentateuch
Psalms . . 7. Psalter
the Dead . . 12. Pyramid Texts
boom . . . 3. hum 4. gain, peal, raft, roar,
spar, zoom 5. boost, cable, speed, sprit,
withe 6. thrive, upturn 7. pontoon,
resound, thunder 8. bowsprit, flourish,
increase 9. cannonade, Golden Age,
outrigger 10. navigation, prosperity
boomerang . . . 6. resile 7. rebound
8. backfire, ricochet
Boomer State . . . 8. Oklahoma
boon . . . 3. gay 4. bene, gift, good, nice
5. favor, jolly 6. jovial, kindly 7. benefit,
gleeful, godsend, present 8. blessing
9. convivial 11. benefaction
boor . . . 3. cad, oaf 4. hick, lout 5. churl,
clown, yokel 6. rustic 7. bumpkin,
cauboge, peasant, ruffian 9. roughneck,

vulgarian **10.** clodhopper; husbandman
boorish . . . **4.** rude **5.** gawky, surly
6. clumsy, rustic, sullen **7.** awkward,
crabbed, loutish, uncouth **8.** churlish,
inurbane, lubberly, ungainly
9. farmerish, unrefined **11.** countrified
boost . . . **4.** help, hike, lift, plug, push
5. heist, raise, shove **6.** assist,
thrust **7.** commend, hearten, inspire,
promote, upswing **8.** advocate, increase
9. promotion, publicize **10.** assistance
11. advancement **12.** commendation
boot . . . **3.** pac **4.** kick, pack, sack, shoe
5. armor, bonus, jemmy, kamik, wader
6. buskin, fumble, rookie, sheath
7. dismiss, recruit, trainee **8.** balmoral,
enlistee, inductee, napoleon
9. discharge
booth . . . **3.** hut, pew **4.** crib, loge **5.** stall,
stand, store **6.** manger **11.** compartment
booty . . . **4.** gain, loot, pelf, swag **5.** graft,
prize, spoil **6.** spoils **7.** pillage, plunder
booze . . . **4.** bout **5.** drink, spree **6.** liquor
8. potation
boozer . . . **3.** pub, sot **5.** toper **6.** barfly,
bibber, saloon **7.** guzzler, reveler, tippler
8. drunkard **9.** alcoholic, inebriate
11. dipsomaniac
borax . . . **4.** salt **5.** cheap
Bordeaux, France . . .
capital . . **7.** Gironde
entrance gate . . **16.** Porte de Bourgogne
Roman name . . **9.** Burdigala
wine . . **5.** Cotes, Medoc, Palus **6.** claret
(best-known), Graves
border . . . **3.** hem, rim, tip **4.** abut,
brow, dado, edge, line, rand, rund
5. bound, brink, flank, limit, marge,
shore, skirt, touch, verge, wings
6. adjoin, fringe, margin, ruffle
7. bordure, confine, flounce, selvage,
valance **8.** boundary, frontier, neighbor
9. periphery **10.** borderland, sidepieces
border (pert to) . . .
heraldry . . **4.** orle **7.** bordure
lace . . **5.** picot **9.** hemstitch
picture . . **3.** mat **4.** orle
stamps (PO) . . **8.** tressure
wall . . **4.** dado
Border Country (Russ) . . . **6.** Latvia,
Poland **7.** Estonia, Finland, Romania
9. Lithuania
bordering . . . **4.** near **6.** edging **7.** binding
8. abutting, adjacent, marginal, skirting,
trimming **9.** adjoining, immediate
10. contiguous
Border State (Civil War Era) . . .
8. Arkansas, Delaware, Kentucky,
Maryland, Missouri, Virginia
9. Tennessee **13.** North Carolina
bore . . . **3.** irk, tap **4.** drip, hole, pest,
pill, ream **5.** auger, drill, eagre (tidal
wave), weary **6.** bother, cavity, pierce
7. caliber, carried **8.** diameter, nuisance,
ordnance (anc), puncture, terebate
9. penetrate, perforate, tidal wave,
worriment **10.** capability **11.** perforation
boreal . . . **8.** northern
boredom . . . **5.** ennui **6.** tedium
Borglum work . . . **8.** Rushmore
boring . . . **3.** dry **5.** yawny **6.** tiring

7. irksome, tedious **8.** piercing,
tiresome, wearying **11.** penetrating
boring tool . . . **3.** awl, bit **4.** rime (Eng)
5. auger, drill **6.** gimlet, reamer, wimble
born . . . **3.** ean, nee **4.** bred, foal, lamb
5. calve, hatch, issue **7.** hatched,
quicken **9.** originate
born (pert to) . . .
after father's death . . **10.** posthumous
again (Theos) . . **7.** renewed
high . . **8.** imperial **11.** to the purple
14. porphyrogenite
in the country . . **10.** rurigenous
well . . **7.** eugenic
yesterday . . **5.** naive **6.** simple **8.** gullible
borne . . . **4.** held **6.** eolian, upheld
7. aeolian, carried, endured **8.** produced
9. cherished, supported **10.** maintained
borné . . . **6.** narrow **7.** limited **12.** narrow-
minded
Borneo . . .
aborigine . . **4.** Dyak (Dayak), Iban
5. Dusun, Malay
ape . . **9.** orangutan (orangoutang)
island of . . **11.** Archipelago (Malay)
mountain . . **8.** Kinibalu
pirate people (anc) . . **5.** Bajau **9.** Samal
Laut
protectorate . . **6.** Brunei **7.** Sarawak
river . . **6.** Rejang
rubber . . **9.** gutta susu
sea . . **4.** Java, Sulu **10.** South China
tree (antproof) . . **7.** billian
borough . . . **4.** burg, town, ward **5.** burgh,
manor **6.** suffix **8.** precinct, township
10. municipium **11.** corporation
12. municipality
borrow . . . **4.** copy, take **5.** adopt,
steal, touch **8.** simulate **10.** plagiarize,
substitute **11.** appropriate
borscht, borsch . . . **4.** soup (beet juice)
6. ragout
borscht belt . . . **6.** resort **9.** Catskills
borzoi . . . **9.** wolfhound
Bos . . . **2.** ox **3.** cow **4.** beef, calf, neat
6. cattle **8.** ruminant **9.** quadruped
bosh . . . **4.** bull, bunk **5.** trash **6.** humbug,
piffle **7.** baloney **8.** buncombe, falderal,
nonsense **9.** poppycock **10.** balderdash
bosky . . . **5.** braky, bushy, shady, tipsy,
woody **6.** woodsy **7.** fuddled, shadowy
11. intoxicated (Eng)
Bosnia . . .
capital . . **8.** Sarajevo
site . . **10.** Yugoslavia (formerly)
15. Balkan Peninsula
bosom . . . **4.** bust **5.** chest **6.** breast,
dickey, spirit **7.** cherish, embrace
8. inner man, interior **9.** enclosure
(loving), innermost **10.** affections
12. heartstrings
boss . . . **4.** dean **6.** manage, master
7. foreman **8.** director **9.** supervise
14. superintendent
boss (pert to) . . .
architecture . . **4.** knob, stud
12. protuberance
politics . . **4.** whip **6.** leader **7.** cacique
(W Indies) **8.** dictator
sculpture . . **5.** chase, raise **6.** emboss,
relief **7.** relievo **8.** ornament

shield.. **4.** umbo
bosthoon (Anglo-Ir) . . . **4.** boor, dolt
  5. clout
Boston . . .
  building (Hist).. **11.** Faneuil Hall **14.** Old
  North Church
  capital of.. **13.** Massachusetts
  famed names.. **6.** Holmes, Lowell
  7. Emerson **8.** Whittier **9.** Hawthorne
  10. Longfellow
  hero.. **10.** Paul Revere
  history.. **8.** Massacre (1770), Tea Party
  (1773)
  Puritan leader.. **8.** Winthrop (Gov)
  river.. **7.** Charles
botany (pert to) . . .
  development (plant).. **7.** peloria
  10. craticular
  research terms.. **7.** ecology **8.** cytology,
  taxonomy **9.** pathology **10.** morphology
  science.. **7.** biology **9.** plant life
Botany Bay . . .
  colony (original).. **5.** penal
  discoverer.. **4.** Cook (1770)
  settlers.. **8.** convicts (Eng)
  site.. **9.** Australia
botch . . . **3.** fix, mar **4.** hash, mend, mess,
  mull **5.** patch, spoil **6.** boggle, bungle,
  fiasco, goof up, muddle **7.** blunder,
  failure
both . . . **3.** two **4.** duad, pair **5.** twain
  6. as well **7.** equally
bother . . . **3.** ado, ail, nag **4.** fuss,
  to-do **5.** annoy, tease **6.** badger,
  bustle, harass, molest, pester, pother
  7. concern, confuse, fluster, torment,
  trouble **8.** bewilder, distress, irritate,
  nuisance **9.** commotion
  10. discommode, excitement, perplexity
  11. botheration, disturbance
  13. inconvenience
bothersome . . . **6.** trying **7.** galling,
  irksome, onerous **8.** annoying
  9. difficult, worrisome **10.** disturbing
  11. troublesome
both sexes . . . **7.** epicene, sexless
  10. effeminate
bo tree (Buddh) . . . **5.** pipal **6.** sacred
  (at Buddh Gaya)
Botticelli masterpiece . . . **12.** Birth of
  Venus
bottle . . . **3.** pig **4.** lota, vial **5.** cruet,
  flask, gourd, phial **6.** carafe, carboy,
  flagon, lagena, matara, vacuum
  7. ampoule (ampule), ampulla (anc),
  costrel, enclose **8.** borachio, calabash,
  decanter, preserve **9.** aryballus (anc)
bottom . . . **3.** bed (water) **4.** base, glen,
  hulk, less, root, rump, vale, vlei
  5. basin, fanny, floor, marsh, nadir
  6. coulee, hopper (RR) **7.** bedrock,
  channel **9.** underside **10.** nethermost
bottomless . . . **7.** abysmal, abyssal
  8. baseless **9.** plumbless, soundless
  10. fathomless **12.** unfathomable
boudoir . . . **7.** bedroom, cabinet, chamber
  10. bedchamber
bouffant . . . **4.** full **7.** bulging **9.** puffed
  out
bough . . . **4.** fork, limb, spur, twig **5.** shoot,
  spray, sprig **6.** branch **8.** offshoot

bought . . . **8.** boughten (dial) **9.** purchased
  (see also *buy*)
bouillabaisse . . . **7.** chowder (fish)
boulangerie (Fr) . . . **6.** bakery
boulevard . . . **4.** pike **7.** highway
  8. highroad, turnpike **12.** thoroughfare
bounce . . . **3.** hop **4.** bang, brag, bump,
  jump, kick, leap, snap **5.** bound, burst,
  carom, eject, shake, thump, verve
  6. levity, recoil, spring **7.** bluster,
  bravado, rebound **8.** buoyancy,
  outburst, ricochet **9.** discharge,
  lightness **10.** resilience **11.** fanfaronade,
  ostentation, springiness
  16. lightheartedness
bouncer . . . **4.** liar **5.** bully **6.** fibber,
  ouster **7.** boaster, chucker, whopper
  8. braggart, fanfaron **9.** falsehood
bound . . . **3.** hop, run **4.** jump, leap,
  skip, tied **5.** ambit, limit, speed,
  taped, tiled (secrecy), vault, verge
  6. border, bounce, bourne, domain,
  hurdle, spring, sprint **7.** barrier, certain,
  confine, cramped, limited, obliged,
  pledged, rebound, secured, trussed
  8. beholden, boundary, confined,
  enclosed, frontier, precinct, promised,
  resolved, surround **9.** committed,
  duty-bound, encompass (incompass)
  10. borderland, determined, restrained,
  restricted **11.** termination
  12. circumscribe
boundary . . . **3.** end, rim **4.** edge, mere
  (obs), mete, term, wall **5.** ambit,
  bourn, fence, limit, march, verge
  7. barrier **8.** terminus **9.** perimeter
  11. conterminal, termination
  13. circumference
bounder . . . **3.** cad **4.** snob **6.** rotter
  7. epicier, parvenu, upstart
bounding (Mus) . . . **8.** saltando
boundless . . . **4.** vast **7.** endless **8.** infinite,
  termless **9.** limitless, unlimited
  10. unconfined **11.** illimitable
  12. interminable, unfathomable
bounds . . . **4.** pale **6.** frames, limits,
  skirts **7.** borders, margins **8.** confines,
  outlines **9.** outskirts **10.** delineated
  11. limitations
bounteous . . . **5.** ample **6.** freely, lavish
  7. liberal **8.** generous, prodigal
  9. bountiful, plentiful **10.** munificent
  11. extravagant
bountiful . . . **4.** rich **7.** copious, fertile,
  liberal, teeming, uberous **8.** abundant,
  fruitful, generous, prolific **9.** bounteous,
  exuberant, luxuriant, plentiful
bounty . . . **3.** fee **4.** gift **5.** bonus
  6. reward **7.** largess, premium,
  subsidy **8.** gratuity, solatium, sportula
  9. pourboire **10.** generosity, liberality
  11. beneficence **12.** compensation
bouquet . . . **4.** odor, posy **5.** aroma,
  cigar, spray **7.** corsage, flowers,
  incense, nosegay, perfume **9.** fragrance,
  redolence **10.** compliment
Bourbon, bourbon . . .
  ancient.. **7.** Reunion (Isl)
  dynasty.. **5.** Spain **6.** France, Naples
  famed personage.. **4.** Duke **13.** French
  General

famed ruins . . **7.** castles (Dukes')
liquor . . **6.** whisky (whiskey)
rose . . **9.** Le Phoenix
bourd . . . **3.** fun **4.** jest **7.** mockery
bourdon . . . **4.** stop (organ) **5.** baton, music (bagpipe), spear, staff **6.** burden (Fr), cudgel
bourgeois . . . **4.** type (size) **8.** commoner **9.** common man, plutocrat **10.** capitalist **11.** middle-class, proletarian
bourn, bourne . . . **3.** aim **4.** goal, port **5.** bound, brook, limit, realm **6.** arroyo, stream **7.** rivulet **8.** boundary **11.** destination
bourock . . . **3.** hut **4.** heap (stone) **5.** crowd, mound **7.** cluster
Bourse . . . **5.** Board **8.** Exchange **13.** Stock Exchange
bouse . . . **3.** cup **4.** haul (Naut), swig, tope **5.** booze, drink, heave **6.** beaker **7.** carouse
bouser . . . **5.** toper **6.** boozer, bursar **7.** fuddler, swigger
bout . . . **2.** go **3.** act, war **4.** coup, fray, game, spar, turn **5.** cycle, fight, match, revel, round, scrap, set-to, spree, trial **6.** fracas, inning, series, stroke **7.** attempt, circuit, contest, exploit **8.** conflict, maneuver, rotation **9.** encounter **10.** enterprise, prize fight **11.** celebration
boutade . . . **4.** whim **5.** dance, prank **7.** caprice **8.** outbreak **11.** composition (Mus)
boutonniere . . . **6.** flower **7.** bouquet, nosegay **8.** incision **10.** buttonhole
bovine . . . **2.** ox **3.** Bos, cow, yak **4.** bull, dull, goat, kine, zebu **5.** bison, dogie, steer, stirk, zebus **6.** catalo, cattle, oxlike, stolid, stupid **7.** bullock, cattalo, taurine, vaccine **8.** maverick, sluggish **10.** complacent **11.** beef-brained
bow . . . **3.** arc, bob, nod **4.** arch, beak, bend, knot, node, prow **5.** bulge, curve, debut, embow, kneel, stoop, yield **6.** assent, convex, curtsy, encore, kowtow, salaam, submit, weapon **7.** curtain (Theat), incline, rainbow **8.** crossbow, greeting **9.** obeisance **11.** fiddlestick **12.** bow and scrape
bow (out) . . . **4.** exit **6.** depart **7.** concede, dismiss
Bow Bells (pert to) . . .
area . . **10.** cockneydom
bells of . . **9.** Bow Church (St Mary le Bow)
city . . **6.** London
bowels . . . **3.** pit **4.** guts **5.** abyss, chasm, depth **7.** innards, insides, viscera **8.** entrails, interior (earth) **10.** compassion (Shaksp), tenderness
bower . . . **5.** abode, arbor, cards (game), kiosk **6.** alcove, pandal **7.** retreat, shelter **11.** summerhouse
Bowery denizen . . . **4.** wino
bowfin . . . **4.** Amia **7.** mudfish
bowhead (Arctic) . . . **10.** Right whale
Bowie, bowie (pert to) . . .
instrument . . **5.** knife
knife inventor . . **5.** Bowie (James)
Scottish . . **3.** tub **4.** cask **8.** milk pail

State nickname . . **8.** Arkansas
bowkail . . . **4.** kale (kail) **7.** cabbage
bowl . . . **3.** cup, jug **4.** ball, roll, vase **5.** arena, basin, kitty (poker), mazer, rogan **6.** cavity, crater, hollow, patina (anc), vessel **7.** stadium **8.** washbowl **9.** washbasin **10.** hippodrome, receptacle **12.** amphitheater
Bowl (sports) . . .
Abilene . . **5.** Pecan
Atlanta . . **5.** Peach
Dallas . . **6.** Cotton
El Paso . . **3.** Sun
Honolulu . . **4.** Hula
Houston . . **10.** Bluebonnet
Jacksonville . . **5.** Gator
Memphis . . **7.** Liberty
Miami . . **6.** Orange
Mobile . . **6.** Senior
New Orleans . . **5.** Sugar
Orlando . . **9.** Tangerine
Pasadena . . **4.** Rose
Sacramento . . **8.** Camellia
bowlegged . . . **6.** valgus
bowler . . . **3.** hat **5.** derby **6.** kegler **7.** trundle
bowling . . . **4.** ball, rink **5.** alley, green, spare **6.** strike **7.** rolling, tenpins **8.** ninepins **10.** greensward, playground
Bowling Green . . . **4.** Park (Ky, NY)
bowsprit . . . **3.** jib **4.** boom **6.** steeve
box . . . **2.** ro (Jap) **3.** bin, pew, pyx **4.** arca (alms), cage, case, cist (anc), cuff, kist, kite, loge, safe, spar, tray **5.** brace (faro), caddy (tea), cheat, crate, stall, vault **6.** buffet, carton, casket, coffin, encase **7.** confine, enclose **8.** bungalow **9.** fisticuff **11.** compartment
box (pert to) . . .
alms . . **4.** arca
bed . . **7.** springs
cosmetic . . **4.** inro
floating . . **3.** car (for fish)
lifesaving . . **9.** faking box
railroad . . **6.** boxcar **8.** box wagon
resistance . . **8.** rheostat
sewing . . **5.** plait, pleat
sleigh . . **4.** pung
sports . . **5.** score
tea . . **5.** caddy **8.** canister
theater . . **4.** loge, seat
tree . . **8.** Buxaceae
boxer . . . **3.** dog, pug **5.** champ **6.** miller **7.** bruiser, fighter, sparrer **8.** derby hat, pugilist **11.** fisticuffer **12.** prizefighter **13.** militia member (Chin)
boxer weight . . . **3.** fly **5.** heavy, light **6.** bantam, middle, welter **7.** feather **10.** light heavy
boxing . . . **4.** bout **5.** match, set-to **7.** contest, crating **8.** pugilism, sparring **10.** encasement, fisticuffs **12.** shadowboxing
boy . . . **2.** bo **3.** bat, bus, lad, tad, tot **4.** nino, page, puer **5.** child, gamin, knave, rogue, water, youth **6.** garcon, laddie, master, rascal, shaver, urchin, varlet **7.** callant, gossoon **8.** muchacho
boy (pert to) . . .
book author . . **5.** Alger, Henty
errand . . **4.** page **9.** messenger

friend.. **4.** beau **10.** sweetheart
interjection.. **5.** Oh boy
organization.. **6.** Scouts
Scout founder.. **11.** Baden-Powell
street.. **4.** Arab **6.** urchin
boycott... **3.** ban **6.** oppose, strike
 9. blackball, ostracize
Boz (pseud)... **7.** Dickens
brace... **3.** leg, tie, two **4.** bind, cord,
 gird, pair, prop, span, stay, yoke
 5. spale, staff, stave, strut **6.** couple
 7. bandage, bracket, fulcrum, refresh,
 rigging, support **8.** encircle **9.** reinforce,
 stimulate **10.** invigorate, recuperate,
 strengthen
bracelet... **5.** armil, armor, chain
 6. sankha **7.** armilla **8.** handcuff,
 vambrace **10.** calombigas
bracer... **4.** prop **5.** tonic **7.** reviver,
 support **8.** pick-me-up, roborant
 9. stimulant
bracing... **5.** crisp, tonic **10.** salubrious
 11. stimulating **12.** invigorating
bracken... **4.** fern **5.** brake, plaid
bracket... **4.** mark **5.** ancon, angle,
 group, strut **6.** corbel, sconce **7.** fixture
 11. electrolier
brackish... **4.** foul **5.** salty **7.** saltish
 8. nauseous **11.** distasteful
bract... **4.** leaf **5.** glume, palea, palet
 6. spathe **8.** bractlet **9.** bracteole
brad... **3.** pin **4.** nail **5.** sprig
brae... **4.** bank, down, hill, moor **5.** slope
 6. valley **8.** hillside
brag... **4.** crow **5.** bluff, boast, vaunt
 6. flaunt **7.** blow off, bluster, deceive,
 roister, swagger **8.** braggart
 9. gasconade **11.** braggadocio
braggart... **4.** brag **6.** crower **7.** boaster
 8. boastful, fanfaron **9.** blusterer,
 swaggerer **11.** braggadocio
 12. swashbuckler
bragging... **11.** thrasonical
Brahma... **3.** God **4.** fowl **5.** Hindu
Brahman (pert to)...
learned.. **6.** pundit
precept.. **5.** sutra **8.** netineti
sacred book.. **4.** Veda
Sanskrit scholar.. **6.** pundit
Supreme soul.. **6.** Brahma
title.. **3.** Aya
Trinity.. **4.** Siva **6.** Brahma, Vishnu
woman created by.. **6.** Alalya
Brahmin... **4.** prig, snob **7.** egghead
 8. highbrow **10.** high-hatter
 12. intellectual
braid... **3.** cue **4.** cord, gimp, hair, plat,
 trim **5.** lacet, orris, plait, pleat, queue,
 tress, twist, weave **6.** oxreim, sennit
 7. entwine, outline, pigtail, topknot
 8. ornament, soutache **9.** interlace
 10. interweave
brain... **4.** head, mind, nous **6.** psyche,
 reason **9.** intellect, mentality
 10. encephalon, vital organ
brain (pert to)...
canal.. **4.** iter
case.. **3.** pan **5.** skull **7.** cranium
child.. **4.** idea **5.** storm
division.. **8.** cerebrum **10.** cerebellum
 11. pons Varolii **16.** medulla oblongata

matter.. **4.** alba, dura, tela
operation.. **6.** trepan **8.** trephine
term.. **4.** lobe, lura
 6. sulcus **7.** fissure **9.** ventricle
 11. convolution
tumor.. **6.** glioma
X-ray.. **14.** encephalograph
brainless... **4.** dumb **5.** dizzy, giddy,
 silly **6.** unwise **7.** asinine, foolish,
 witless **9.** senseless **10.** unthinking
 11. thoughtless **14.** scatterbrained
brainy... **5.** smart **6.** bright, clever
 9. brilliant
brake... **4.** cage, curb, drag, fern,
 reef, skid, trap **5.** check, delay, snare
 6. bridle, retard **7.** dilemma, thicket
 9. canebrake **10.** decelerate
bramble... **4.** burr **5.** berry, brier, shrub
 (prickly), thorn **6.** nettle **7.** prickle,
 thicket **9.** brierbush **10.** blackberry
 12. brambleberry
branch... **3.** arm, set **4.** axil, fork, limb,
 rame, stem, twig, wing **5.** bough,
 class, frond, ramus, shoot, spray,
 sprig, vimen, withe **6.** divide, member,
 ramify, sprout, stolon, stream, switch
 7. descent, diverge, lineage **8.** category,
 division, offshoot **9.** affiliate, bloodline,
 filiation **10.** department, descendant,
 triskelion (three branches)
Branchiata (Group)... **6.** fishes
 9. Crustacea **10.** Amphibians
brand... **4.** burn, iron, kind, mark, sear,
 smit **5.** label, stamp, sword, torch
 6. smirch, stigma **7.** earmark, feature,
 hot iron, quality **8.** gridiron (Hist),
 hallmark **9.** trademark **10.** stigmatize
brandish... **5.** shake, swing, wield
 6. flaunt **7.** flutter, glitter, flourish
brandy... **4.** marc **6.** cognac, grappa,
 kirsch **8.** Armagnac, eau de vie (Fr)
 9. applejack, slivovitz
brash... **4.** dash, rain, rash **5.** gruff,
 saucy, storm **6.** scurry **7.** brittle (lumber)
 8. impudent, tactless **9.** impetuous
brass... **4.** cash, gall **5.** alloy, braze,
 cheek, money, nerve, plate **6.** latten,
 ormolu, platen **8.** brass hat, officers,
 sisterce (anc coin) **9.** impudence
 10. instrument (wind)
brass (wind instrument)... **5.** bugle
 6. cornet, lituus (anc) **7.** althorn,
 brasses, clarion, saxhorn, trumpet
 8. trombone **9.** saxophone
 10. flügelhorn, French horn
brasserie... **6.** saloon **7.** brewery **8.** beer
 shop
brassy... **4.** bold **6.** aerose, brazen
 8. impudent
brat... **3.** bib, elf, imp **4.** film, minx,
 scum **5.** apron, bairn, child, cloak,
 minor **6.** mantle **7.** garment **8.** clothing
 9. offspring **14.** enfant terrible,
 whippersnapper
brattice... **7.** support **9.** partition (mining)
 10. breastwork
bravado... **6.** bounce, daring, defial
 7. bluster, bombast, bravery, bravura
 8. defiance **11.** braggadocio
brave... **4.** bold, buck, dare, game,
 hero, meet **5.** boast, bravo, bully,

front, manly, showy, stout **6.** daring,
endure, heroic, Indian **7.** Amerind,
gallant, soldier, spartan, valiant,
warrior **8.** confront, fearless, intrepid,
valorous **10.** courageous, untimorous
12. stouthearted
bravery . . . **5.** valor **7.** bravado, bravura,
courage
bravo . . . **3.** mug **4.** good, thug **5.** rough,
tough **6.** bandit **7.** gorilla, ruffian
8. assassin **9.** blusterer, cutthroat,
roisterer, roughneck, swaggerer
11. exclamation
bravura . . . **4.** dash **5.** macho **6.** daring
7. bravado, bravery **10.** brilliance (Mus),
confidence
brawl . . . **3.** row **4.** fray, fury, rage, riot
5. broil, fight, furor, melee, scold
6. affray, clamor, fracas, hubbub,
rumpus, shindy, tumult, uproar
7. dispute, quarrel, rampage, turmoil,
wrangle **10.** hullabaloo, turbulence
11. altercation, embroilment
brawny . . . **5.** beefy, burly, lusty, thewy
6. fleshy, robust, sinewy, strong,
sturdy **7.** callous **8.** muscular, powerful,
stalwart **9.** corpulent
bray . . . **4.** beat **5.** blare, bleat, grind, neigh
6. heehaw, powder, thrash, whinny
9. pulverize, triturate **12.** disintegrate
braze . . . **4.** weld **5.** plate (with metal)
6. solder
brazen . . . **4.** bold, pert **5.** brass, brave,
harsh **6.** brassy, cheeky, harden
7. aweless, callous **8.** immodest,
impudent, indurate, insolent, metallic
9. bold-faced, shameless, unabashed
10. unblushing **13.** bronze-colored,
harsh-sounding
brazier . . . **5.** grill **6.** brazer **7.** hibachi
8. barbecue, gridiron **10.** money chest
(anc)
brazil . . . **3.** red **4.** wood (hard) **8.** dyestuff
Brazil . . . see also *Brazilian*
capital . . **8.** Brasilia **12.** Rio de Janeiro
(old)
city . . **5.** Bahia, Belem **6.** Recife, Santos
8. Sao Paulo **9.** Horizonte **11.** Porto
Alegre, Sao Salvador
discoverer . . **6.** Cabral (1500)
Falls (world wonder) . . **6.** Iguacu
lake . . **12.** Lago dos Patos
product . . **6.** coffee
river . . **5.** Negro **6.** Amazon, Branco,
Paraná **7.** Madeira, Orinoco **8.** Paraguay
9. Tocantins
Brazilian (pert to) . . .
aborigine . . **5.** Carib
ant (powerful) . . **9.** tucandera
bird . . **3.** ani, ara **5.** arara, macaw
6. cuckoo, darter, tiribo **7.** maracan,
sierema
crab (land) . . **8.** horseman
dance . . **5.** samba **6.** maxixe
drink . . **5.** assai
flycatcher . . **6.** yetapa
Indian . . **4.** Anta **5.** Arara, Araua, Guana
6. Tupian **8.** Araquayu, Arawakan
mammal . . **5.** tapir
parrot . . **3.** ara **5.** macaw **6.** tiriba
plant . . **4.** yaje **5.** caroa **7.** ayapana

(Med)
tree . . **3.** apa **4.** anda (oil), jara **5.** assai
(palm) **6.** embuia, satiné **7.** araroba,
gomavel, seringa (rubber), wallaba
8. bakupari **10.** barbatimao
weight . . **4.** onza **5.** libra **6.** arroba
7. quintal
breach . . . **3.** gap **4.** rent, rift **5.** break,
burst, chasm, cleft, split **6.** schism
7. caesura, dispute, quarrel, rupture
8. fracture, solecism **9.** violation
10. disruption, falling-out, infraction,
separation **12.** infringement,
interruption **16.** misunderstanding
bread . . . **3.** rye **4.** naan, pita, rusk
5. matzo, quick **6.** simnel **7.** anadama,
challah, chapati, hoecake **8.** baguette,
hardtack, tortilla, zwieback **9.** sourdough
12. pumpernickel
bread (pert to) . . .
basket . . **7.** stomach
bread and butter . . **5.** plate **6.** letter
(of thanks), pickle, staple **7.** prosaic
8. juvenile
fruit . . **3.** nut **4.** tree **6.** simnel **7.** castana
8. chestnut
winner . . **6.** earner, toiler, worker
7. workman **8.** provider **10.** wage
earner
break . . . **3.** gap **4.** dash, knap, luck,
lull, rent, rift, ruin, rush, slip, snap,
stop **5.** blank, burst, cleft, lapse,
letup, pause, smash, train **6.** breach,
chance, change, depose, escape,
hiatus, injury, lacuna, market (Finan),
recess, subdue, weaken **7.** blunder,
caesura (cesura), disrupt, getaway,
respite, rupture, shatter, violate **8.** bad
break, bankrupt, breakage, breather,
fracture, interval **9.** interlude, jail break,
violation **10.** depreciate, falling-out,
infraction, suspension **11.** fragmentize
12. intermission, interruption
13. discontinuity
break down . . . **3.** cry, sob **4.** bawl,
raze, weep **5.** crush **6.** boohoo,
divide, master, reduce, revolt, subdue
7. analyze, crack up, dissect, resolve,
unnerve **8.** classify, collapse, separate
9. decompose, overwhelm, subdivide
breakdown . . . **7.** debacle, failure
8. analysis **9.** cataclysm **10.** dissection,
impairment, revolution
breakfast . . . **6.** brunch (late) **8.** dejeuner
10. chota hazri
break in . . . **4.** open, tame **5.** enter,
force, train **6.** butt in, subdue **7.** barge
in, intrude, prepare **9.** interrupt
10. housebreak
break up . . . **4.** cure, rift, ruin **5.** decay,
leave, smash, spall, split, upset
7. adjourn, atomize, crumble, disband,
relieve, scatter, shatter **8.** disperse,
dissolve, separate, unsettle
9. decompose **10.** demobilize,
dispersion, disruption **11.** disorganize,
dissolution **12.** disintegrate
breakwater . . . **4.** dike, mole, pier
5. jetty, jutty **6.** refuge, riprap **7.** sea
wall **8.** buttress **10.** embankment
11. obstruction

bream . . . **4.** fish, scup **5.** clean (Naut)
breast . . . **4.** bust, soul, teat **5.** bosom, cheat, gland (mammary), heart **6.** spirit, thorax **8.** inner man **9.** encounter
breast (pert to) . . .
absence of . . **7.** amastia
bone . . **6.** ratite **7.** sternum
breastlike . . **7.** mastoid
plate . . **4.** Urim **5.** armor, ephod **6.** gorget, lorica **7.** poitrel **12.** breastsummer
works . . **7.** defense, parapet, railing (Naut), ravelin **8.** mantelet **9.** banquette
breath . . . **3.** air **4.** fume, life, odor, pant, puff, wind **5.** draft, pause, prana, scent, smell, touch, vapor, whiff **6.** breeze, caress, flatus, pneuma, spirit **7.** halitus, respite, whisper **8.** breather **9.** emanation, ozostomia, utterance **10.** exhalation **11.** respiration
breathe . . . **3.** say, tip **4.** gulp, live, mean, pneo (comb form), rest, sigh, tell **5.** exist, imbue, imply, scent, smell, snuff **6.** evince, exhale, infuse, inhale, let out, reveal **7.** bespeak, divulge, emanate, instill (instil), pervade, respire, suspire, whisper **8.** aspirate, indicate
breathe (pert to) . . .
comb form . . **4.** pnea, pneo
convulsively . . **4.** sigh
hard . . **4.** pant
one's last . . **3.** die **6.** expire, perish **7.** decease, succumb
vengeance . . **9.** retaliate
breather . . . **4.** lull, rest **5.** break, pause, truce **6.** recess **7.** interim, respite **9.** interlude **12.** intermission
breathing . . . **5.** alive, vital **6.** living, zoetic **7.** animate, panting, respite **8.** animated **9.** conscious, phonation, utterance **10.** aspiration **11.** respiration, respiratory, ventilation **12.** articulation
breathing (pert to) . . .
apertures . . **5.** stoma **8.** spiracle
morbid . . **4.** rale **7.** stridor **8.** rhonchus
painful . . **8.** dyspnoea
pause . . **7.** caesura
smooth . . **4.** lene
breathless . . . **4.** awed, dead, gone, keen **5.** eager **6.** ardent, fervid, winded **7.** airless, demised, fervent **8.** deceased, lifeless, windless, wordless **9.** impatient **10.** astonished, speechless, spellbound
bred . . . **6.** hybrid, inbred, reared, tablet (compressed) **7.** lowbred, mongrel **8.** exogamic, purebred **9.** autogamic, crossbred, endogamic, half-caste, interbred **11.** half-blooded, impregnated, inseminated **12.** thoroughbred
bree . . . **4.** brow **5.** broth, scare **6.** liquor **7.** eyebrow **9.** commotion **11.** disturbance
breech . . . **4.** doup, rump, tall **5.** fanny, stern **6.** bottom **8.** buttocks **9.** posterior, underside
breeches . . . **5.** chaps, jeans, pants, trews **8.** britches, jodhpurs, trousers **10.** pantaloons **12.** galligaskins (jocular)
breed . . . **3.** ilk **4.** kind, race, rear, sort **5.** beget, brood, caste, class, mixed, raise, stock, train, tribe **6.** family **7.** descent, educate, lineage, mongrel, produce **8.** engender, generate, instruct **9.** originate, posterity, procreate, propagate **10.** crossbreed
breeding . . . **6.** polish **7.** culture, decorum, exogamy, manners, raising, rearing **8.** autogamy, endogamy, hatching, training **9.** education, fostering, gentility **10.** deportment, upbringing **11.** instruction, procreation, propagation
breeding place . . . **4.** nest **5.** nidus **7.** brooder **8.** hatchery **9.** incubator **10.** birthplace
breeze . . . **3.** air, row **4.** aura, pirr, snap, stir, wind **5.** cinch, rumor **6.** squall, zephyr **7.** ill wind, whisper **8.** duck soup, pushover **9.** commotion **11.** disturbance
breezy . . . **4.** airy, spry **5.** blowy, brisk, gusty, windy **6.** drafty, jaunty, lively **7.** squally **8.** animated, blustery, spirited **9.** vivaceous **12.** lighthearted
Brehon Law . . . **4.** eric (anc) **10.** Senchus Mor **12.** Book of Aicill
breve . . . **4.** note (Mus), writ **5.** brief, order **7.** compose
brevet . . . **4.** fiat **5.** ukase **6.** decree **7.** warrant **10.** commission **11.** certificate (teaching)
breveté . . . **8.** patented
breviary . . . **6.** manual, ritual **7.** compend, epitome
brevity . . . **9.** briefness, shortness, terseness **11.** conciseness, transcience **12.** succinctness
brew . . . **3.** ale, mix **4.** grog, plot **5.** hatch, steep **6.** cook up, foment, gather, menace, scheme **7.** concoct, distill (distil) **8.** contrive, threaten **9.** aqua vitae
brewer's grain . . . **4.** corn, malt **6.** barley
brewer's yeast . . . **4.** barm **6.** leaven
bribe . . . **3.** oil, sop **5.** bonus **6.** boodle, buy off, grease, suborn **9.** hush money
bric-a-brac . . . **6.** curios **7.** artware **8.** antiques, trinkets **9.** artifacts, objet d'art **11.** knickknacks
bric-a-brac cabinet . . . **7.** étagère, whatnot
brick . . . **3.** bat **4.** dobe, tile **5.** adobe, stone **6.** pament (pamment) **7.** clinker **8.** hardness
brick (pert to) . . .
color . . **3.** red **7.** Saravan
kiln . . **5.** clamp
layer . . **3.** cad (helper) **5.** mason
laying . . **8.** toothing
slang . . **3.** pip **4.** lulu **5.** dilly, peach **6.** corker, winner **8.** jim-dandy **10.** sweetheart **11.** crackerjack **12.** lollapaloosa
unburned . . **5.** samel
brickbat . . . **4.** rock **5.** stone **7.** affront, missile, offense **9.** indignity
bridal (pert to) . . .
chest . . **9.** trousseau
flower . . **13.** orange blossom
ode, song . . **9.** Brautlied **11.** Epithalamon (anc)
portion . . **3.** dot **5.** dower, dowry (dowery)

rite . . **7.** wedding **8.** marriage, nuptials

bridge . . . **3.** tie **4.** arch, bond, link, pons, pont, span **5.** unite **7.** connect, passage (Mus), ponteon, viaduct **9.** structure **13.** steppingstone

bridge (pert to) . . . **4.** deck, game, nose **5.** magas, truss **6.** phoebe (bird) **7.** bascule, trestle **9.** dentistry **10.** ponticello (Mus)

bridge, historic . . .
Bridge of Boats . . **10.** Hellespont
Bridge of Sighs . . **6.** Venice (Doge's Palace) **7.** Al Sirat (Muslim, over infernal fire)
Norse Myth . . **7.** Bifrost (rainbow)
Old Bridge . . **12.** Ponte Vecchio (Florence It, 1345)

Bridge game . . . **3.** bid **4.** pass, ruff, slam **5.** Goren (expert) **6.** honors, points, renege, tenace **7.** finesse **9.** part-score

bridle . . . **3.** bit **4.** cord (kite), curb, rein **5.** check, guide, smirk **6.** fetter, govern, halter, master, simper, subdue **7.** harness, manacle, repress, shackle, snaffle **8.** cavesson, headgear, noseband, restrain, suppress **9.** hackamore, headstall, restraint

brief . . . **4.** curt, plan, writ **5.** breve, charm, pithy, short, terse **6.** report **7.** compact, concise, laconic, summary **8.** fleeting, instruct, succinct **9.** condensed, ephemeral, summarize, transient **10.** compendium, short-lived, transitory **11.** compendious **14.** inconsiderable

brier, briar . . . **4.** burr, pipe **5.** heath, shrub, spine, thorn **7.** bramble, bruyère, clotbur, prickle, sticker, thistle **8.** adherent **11.** French brier

brig . . . **4.** boat **6.** vessel **10.** guardhouse

brigade . . . **4.** unit **6.** troops **7.** company **8.** regiment

brigand . . . **5.** rover, thief **6.** bandit, dacoit, pirate, robber **7.** bedouin, cateran, ladrone **8.** picaroon **10.** highwayman

bright . . . **3.** apt, gay **4.** naif, rosy **5.** alert, beamy, fresh, lucid, nitid, palmy, sleek, smart, sunny, vivid, witty **6.** brainy, clever, florid, garish, golden **7.** halcyon, radiant, shining, unfaded **8.** cheerful, colorful, flashing, gleaming, luminous, lustrous, splendid **9.** brilliant, effulgent, refulgent, sparkling **10.** auspicious, epiphanous, glistening, glittering, optimistic **11.** intelligent, resplendent

brightness . . . **5.** sheen **6.** luster **7.** sparkle **8.** radiance, splendor **9.** alertness, clearness, smartness **10.** brilliance **12.** cheerfulness, colorfulness, pleasantness

brilliance, brilliancy . . . **5.** éclat, glory **6.** luster **7.** glitter, oriency, success **8.** radiance, splendor **9.** smartness, vividness **10.** brightness, cleverness

brilliant . . . **5.** smart, vivid, witty **6.** bright **7.** eminent, radiant, shining **8.** gorgeous, meteoric, splendid **9.** refulgent, sparkling **10.** glittering **11.** illustrious

brilliant group . . . **6.** galaxy

brim . . . **3.** hem, lip, rim **4.** edge **5.** brink, marge, verge **6.** border, margin

7. selvage

brine . . . **3.** sea **4.** main, salt **5.** brack, ocean, tears **6.** pickle **7.** the deep **12.** preservative

bring . . . **3.** get **4.** bear, cost, haul, lead **5.** carry, fetch, go get, yield **6.** convey, entail, induce, obtain **7.** contain, involve, require **8.** comprise **9.** transport

bring about . . . **2.** do **4.** make **5.** cause **6.** create, effect **7.** achieve, produce **8.** generate **9.** instigate **10.** accomplish, consummate, effectuate

bring around . . . **4.** cure, heal, ween **5.** renew, sober **6.** revive **7.** convert, restore, win over **8.** persuade **10.** rejuvenate

bring back . . . **5.** fetch **6.** recall, return, revive **7.** restore **8.** rekindle, remember, retrieve **9.** recollect, resurrect

bring forth . . . **3.** ean **4.** bear, rise **5.** beget, breed, cause, educe, hatch, spawn, yield **6.** adduce, elicit, reveal **7.** develop, produce **8.** disclose, fructify, generate, manifest

bring forward . . . **4.** cite **5.** offer **6.** adduce, broach, submit **7.** advance, improve, promote, propose **8.** manifest **9.** introduce

bring into . . .
bondage . . **7.** enslave
court . . **7.** arraign
harmony . . **6.** attune
position . . **5.** align, aline
union . . **9.** correlate

bring together . . . **5.** amass, group **6.** gather **7.** cluster, compile, reunite **8.** assemble **9.** harmonize, reconcile **10.** accumulate

bring to light . . . **4.** find **5.** trace **6.** elicit, expose, reveal **7.** uncover, unearth **8.** disclose, discover

bring to mind . . . **6.** recall, remind **8.** look like, remember, resemble

bring to pass . . . **2.** do **5.** cause **6.** author, father **9.** originate **10.** accomplish, effectuate

bring up . . . **4.** rear, spew **5.** drill, raise, train, vomit **6.** foster, muster **7.** advance, educate, nurture, propose **9.** challenge, condition, cultivate **10.** discipline **11.** regurgitate

bring up to date . . . **4.** post **6.** update **9.** modernize **10.** streamline

brink . . . **3.** lip, rim **4.** bank, brow, edge, near **5.** ditch, marge, skirt, verge **6.** border, margin

briny . . . **3.** sea **4.** salt **5.** salty **6.** saline **8.** brackish

Brisbane, capital of . . . **10.** Queensland (Austral)

Brisbane tree . . . **3.** box **8.** quandong

brisk . . . **3.** gay **4.** cold, fast, keen, racy, spry, yern **5.** agile, alert, alive, crisp, fresh, peart, quick, sharp, tangy, zippy **6.** breezy, lively, nimble, snappy **7.** caustic, pungent **8.** animated, forceful, spirited, vigorous **9.** energetic, sprightly, vivacious **11.** stimulating

bristle . . . **4.** barb, hair, seta **5.** anger, seton **6.** chaeta, palpus, ruffle, rumple, see red, setula, setule **7.** acicula, prickle,

stubble
bristling . . . **5.** angry **6.** horrid (anc)
7. horrent **9.** offensive
bristly . . . **5.** rough, setal **6.** hispid, setose,
thorny **7.** prickly, scopate, unshorn
8. acicular, echinate **9.** setaceous
11. bristlelike
Bristol . . .
church (England's finest) . . **15.** St Mary
Redcliffe
fashion . . **6.** ataunt **9.** shipshape
library . . **6.** oldest (British Isles)
milk . . **6.** sherry
Britain . . .
name, ancient . . **6.** Albion
name, modern . . **12.** British Isles,
Commonwealth, Great Britain
13. United Kingdom
name, Roman . . **9.** Brittania
native . . **5.** Iceni, Jutes, Picts, Scots
6. Angles **7.** Britons, Silures
native (sl) . . **5.** limey (limy), tommy
7. Blighty
sea . . **5.** Irish, North **8.** Atlantic, Hebrides
British (pert to) . . . see also *English*
battle . . **8.** Hastings
boat (anc) . . **7.** coracle
cavalry . . **8.** yeomanry
emblem . . **4.** lion
fish . . **8.** dragonet (gobylike)
oak . . **5.** robur
Order of . . **9.** The Garter
prison . . **4.** gaol
pudding . . **4.** suet **9.** Yorkshire
tavern . . **3.** pub **9.** beerhouse, jerry shop
thief (wharf) . . **6.** tosher
Z (letter) . . **3.** Zed
British people . . .
buccaneer . . **4.** Kidd **5.** Drake **6.** Morgan
explorer . . **4.** Cook, Ross **6.** Baffin
7. Stanley **11.** Livingstone
hero (sea) . . **6.** Nelson
king (legend, Myth) . . **3.** Lud **4.** Beli,
Bran, Brut **7.** Belenus
soldier . . **7.** Redcoat (Hist)
Brittany . . . **7.** Armoric **8.** Bretagne
brittle . . . **4.** weak **5.** brash, candy, crisp,
frail **6.** feeble, infirm, slight **7.** fragile,
friable **8.** delicate, insecure **9.** breakable,
frangible **11.** shatterable
broad . . . **4.** free, girl, lake (Eng), wide
5. ample, large, roomy, thick, wench
7. breadth, diffuse, general, liberal
8. spacious, strumpet, sweeping,
tabulate, tolerant **9.** expansive,
extensive **10.** collective, commodious,
indefinite, voluminous
13. comprehensive
broad (pert to) . . .
arrow . . **5.** pheon (Her) **6.** stigma
8. insignia
footed . . **8.** platypod
hearted . . **8.** generous **11.** magnanimous
minded . . **7.** liberal **8.** tolerant
9. receptive
broaden . . . **5.** swell, widen **6.** dilate,
expand, extend, spread **7.** augment,
enlarge, ennoble **8.** increase
broadly . . . **3.** far **6.** widely **10.** far and
wide **11.** extensively **12.** indefinitely,
right and left

broadside . . . **4.** guns, side **6.** folder
7. gunfire, quarter, surface **8.** enfilade,
sideways **10.** broadsheet, floodlight
11. breadthwise
broadsword . . . **7.** cutlass, Ferrara
8. claymore, scimitar
Brobdingnagian . . . **5.** giant, titan
8. colossal, gigantic **10.** gargantuan
brocade . . . **6.** broché, fabric **8.** baudekin
9. baldachin
brochan . . . **7.** oatmeal **8.** porridge
brochure . . . **5.** tract **6.** folder **7.** booklet,
leaflet **8.** chapbook, pamphlet
brod . . . **3.** awl **4.** goad, pike, urge **5.** thorn
6. sprout **9.** incentive
brode, brodee . . . **11.** embroidered
brodyaga . . . **7.** vagrant **8.** vagabond
brogan, brogue . . . **4.** shoe
brogue . . . **4.** burr **5.** twang **6.** accent
7. dialect
broil . . . **4.** cook, fray, fume **5.** brawl,
grill, melee **6.** affray, braise (braize),
scorch **7.** contest, discord, dispute,
quarrel **8.** conflict, grillade, scramble
10. contention, dissension, turbulence
11. altercation, embroilment
broke . . . **4.** flat **6.** busted, ruined
8. bankrupt, strapped **9.** destitute,
insolvent, penniless
broken . . . **4.** tame **5.** broke, bumpy,
burst, rough, tamed **6.** chined, ruined,
shaken, uneven, zigzag **7.** crushed,
décousu, severed, subdued **8.** bankrupt,
detached, impaired, ruptured, sporadic,
weakened **9.** conquered, dispersed,
irregular, shattered, unsettled
10. incoherent, incomplete
11. fragmentary, housebroken,
interrupted **12.** disconnected,
domesticated, intermittent
13. discontinuous
broken pottery (anc) . . . **5.** shard (sherd)
8. potsherd
broker . . . **5.** agent **6.** dealer, jobber
7. cambist, scalper (ticket) **8.** marriage
9. go-between, insurance, middleman,
schatchen **10.** pawnbroker, real estate
11. internuncio, stockbroker
12. intermediary
brokerage . . . **3.** fee **4.** agio **6.** charge
8. agiotage, business **9.** exactment
10. commission
brolly . . . **5.** chute **8.** umbrella **9.** brollyhop,
parachute
bromide . . . **4.** corn **5.** trite **6.** Babbit,
cliché, halide, old hat **8.** banality,
sedative **9.** conformer, criticism,
platitude **10.** conformist, Philistine
15. conventionalist
bronco, broncho . . . **4.** pony **5.** horse
6. cayuse **7.** mustang **10.** broomstick
bronco, bucking . . . **9.** estrapade
broncobuster, bronchobuster . . .
6. cowboy **7.** trainer, vaquero
Brontë (pert to) . . .
Charlotte . . **7.** Shirley **8.** Jane Eyre,
Villette **10.** Currer Bell (pseud)
Emily . . **16.** Wuthering Heights
Bronx cheer . . . **3.** boo **4.** hiss, razz
9. raspberry
bronze . . . **3.** aes (anc), tan **5.** alloy, color

6. ormolu, patina, suntan **9.** sculpture
Bronze Age . . . **6.** Aegean **9.** Neolithic
  11. Aeneolithic
Bronze Plaques (pert to) . . .
  called . . **14.** Eugubine Tables (Iguvine
  Tables, 1444)
  number . . **5.** Seven
  site . . **6.** Gubbio (It)
brooch . . . **3.** bar, pin **4.** boss, ouch
  5. cameo, clasp **6.** fibula (anc), shield
  8. pectoral **9.** breastpin
brood . . . **3.** fry, nye, set **4.** kind, mope,
  mull, muse, nide, race **5.** breed,
  covey, folks, hatch, pride (lions),
  young **6.** clutch, family, farrow
  (pigs), litter, ménage, people, strain
  7. lineage, progeny, reflect **8.** cogitate,
  incubate, meditate, ruminate, soredium
  9. household, offspring **11.** contemplate
brood over . . . **4.** fret, mope **5.** hover
  6. grieve, ponder **7.** agonize
  8. remember
brook . . . **3.** run **4.** bear, beck, burn,
  rill, sike **5.** abide, bourn, creek,
  crick **6.** arroyo, endure, rillet, runlet,
  suffer **7.** freshet, rivulet **8.** brooklet
  9. arroyuelo, streamlet
broom . . . **5.** besom, shrub, spart, sweep,
  whisk
broth . . . **4.** soup **5.** stock **6.** brewis
  8. bouillon, consommé
brother . . . **3.** fra **4.** mate, monk **5.** friar,
  title **6.** frater, friend, member, oblate
  8. alter ego, relative **9.** associate
  11. counterpart
brotherhood . . . **5.** lodge **7.** kinship,
  society **8.** sodality **10.** fellowship,
  fraternity **11.** association
  12. fraternalism **13.** confraternity
brotherly . . . **4.** kind **6.** tender **8.** friendly
  9. fraternal **11.** sympathetic
  12. affectionate
Brothers . . . **7.** Danites (Mormon)
  9. Christian (RCCh)
brothers and sisters (same family) . . .
  8. siblings
brow . . . **3.** cap, rim, tip, top **4.** brae
  5. brink, crest, crown **6.** border, summit,
  tiptop, visage **7.** eyebrow, feature
  8. boldness, forehead **9.** gangplank
  10. effrontery **11.** countenance
browbeat . . . **3.** cow **5.** bully **6.** hector
  7. buffalo, henpeck **8.** bulldoze,
  domineer **10.** intimidate
brown . . . **4.** dark **5.** cheat, dusky
  6. august, braise, tanned **9.** red-yellow
  (class)
brown . . . **3.** bay, dun, nut, tan **4.** ecru,
  faon, fawn, roan, rust, seal **5.** acorn,
  cocoa, hazel, henna, khaki, mocha,
  olive, otter, sepia, snuff, sumac, tawny,
  tenné, toast, topaz **6.** auburn, bister,
  bronze, burnet, coffee, copper, loutre,
  oriole, russet, sienna, sorrel, titian,
  walnut **7.** asphalt (smoke), gazelle,
  perique, rosario (army) **8.** chestnut,
  cinnamon, mahogany **9.** buckthorn,
  chocolate **10.** café au lait, terra cotta
brown (pert to) . . .
  Bess . . **6.** musket
  betty . . **5.** daisy **7.** pudding

10. coneflower
  earth . . **5.** umber
  ebony . . **6.** wamara **10.** coffeewood
browned in deep fat . . . **7.** rissole
Brownian movement (Bot) . . . **7.** pedesis
brownie . . . **3.** elf **4.** cake **5.** dwarf, gnome,
  nisse, pixie, Scout, urisk **6.** camera,
  goblin **9.** sandpiper
Brownism (Eng) . . .
  17. Congregationalism
browze . . . **4.** brut (obs), read, scan
  5. graze **6.** nibble
bruckle . . . **5.** frail **7.** brittle **9.** breakable
  10. changeable, inconstant
bruin . . . **4.** bear
bruise . . . **4.** bash, beat, hurt, maul
  5. abuse, crush, dinge, pound, wound
  6. batter, buffet, injury **7.** contuse
  8. abrasion, black eye **9.** contusion,
  pulverize, triturate
bruiser . . . **3.** mug, pug **5.** boxer, bravo,
  tough **7.** fighter, ruffian, sparrer
  8. pugilist **11.** fisticuffer
bruit, bruit about . . . **3.** din **4.** fame,
  hawk, tell **5.** bandy, noise, rumor
  6. clamor, report **9.** advertise
brujo . . . **8.** magician, sorcerer **11.** witch
  doctor
brumal . . . **4.** cold **6.** hiemal, wintry
  8. hibernal **10.** winterlike
brune . . . **6.** brunet (brunette)
  11. Melanochroi
Brunhild . . . **5.** Queen (wife of Siegfried)
  8. Valkyrie (Myth)
brunt . . . **3.** rub **4.** crux **5.** pinch, shock
  6. stress **7.** squeeze
brush . . . **3.** art **4.** bush, comb, tail
  (fox), tuft **5.** besom, briar, broom,
  clash, graze, groom, sweep, touch
  6. artist, forest, pappus, stroke, teazel
  7. painter, scuffle, thicket **8.** conflict
  9. brushwood, encounter **10.** paintbrush
  11. undergrowth
brush aside . . . **5.** spurn **6.** reject
  7. dismiss **8.** shrug off **9.** disregard
brush wolf . . . **6.** coyote
brusque . . . **4.** curt **5.** bluff, blunt, brash,
  brusk, frank, gruff, rough, sharp, short
  6. abrupt, candid, snippy
brutal . . . **5.** cruel, gross **6.** animal, carnal,
  coarse, savage **7.** bestial, inhuman
  8. ruthless **9.** barbarous
brutality . . . **7.** cruelty **9.** barbarian,
  carnality **12.** ruthlessness
brute . . . **5.** beast, gross, harsh, rough
  6. animal **7.** beastly, bestial, sensual,
  varment **8.** soulless **9.** barbarian,
  inanimate **10.** unpolished **11.** uncivilized
brutish . . . **4.** rude **5.** cruel, gross
  6. brutal, carnal, fierce, savage, stupid
  7. bestial, inhuman, sensual, vicious
  9. barbarous, ferocious, insensate,
  unfeeling **10.** insensible, irrational
Brutus . . . **3.** wig **6.** hairdo, peruke
  7. traitor (Julius Caesar)
  13. chrysanthemum
Bryan's speech (1896) . . . **11.** Cross of
  Gold **13.** Crown of Thorns
bryology, science of . . . **6.** mosses
  10. bryophytes, liverworts
Brython . . . **4.** Celt **6.** Briton **8.** Welshman

Brythonic god ... **3.** Ler **4.** Bran
Brythonic goddess ... **9.** Arianrhod
bubble ... **4.** bead, bleb, blob, boil, foam
  5. bulge, empty, fancy, tumor **6.** burble,
  gurgle, murmur, ripple, scheme,
  trifle **7.** chimera (chimaera), globule,
  trickle **8.** bubbling, delusive, illusion
  9. ephemeron, intumesce, lightness
  10. effervesce **11.** unsubstantiality
buccal ... **4.** oral **5.** cheek, mouth
buccaneer ... **4.** Kidd (Capt) **5.** rover
  6. Morgan, pirate, rifler, viking
  7. corsair, Lafitte, spoiler **8.** marooner,
  picaroon **9.** privateer **10.** Blackbeard
  (Capt Teach), freebooter
Bucephalus ... **5.** horse, steed **7.** charger
  8. war horse (Alex the Great)
buck ... **3.** man, ram, rat **4.** bunt, butt,
  deer, goat, hare, jump, male, sore (4-yr
  deer) **5.** fight, sasin **6.** animal, combat,
  dollar, Indian, oppose **7.** contest,
  launder, pricket **8.** antelope, sawhorse
  10. fallow deer
buckaroo ... **6.** cowboy **7.** trainer,
  vaquero **8.** horseman **12.** broncobuster
  (bronchobuster)
bucket ... **3.** tub **4.** bail, bowk, pail, ship
  5. chest, cozen, scoop, skeel **6.** bailer,
  bushel, drench, sityla **10.** bucket shop
Buckeye State ... **4.** Ohio
Buckingham Palace ... **9.** residence
  11. St James Park (London)
buckle ... **3.** bow **4.** bend, curl, kink,
  warp **5.** tache **6.** fasten **8.** marriage
  9. fastening
buckthorn ... **4.** tree **5.** brown, shrub
  7. cascara, Rhamnus
buckwheat ... **4.** cake, coal, herb, seed,
  titi **5.** flour
bucolic ... **4.** idyl, poem, poet **5.** idyll,
  local, rural **6.** farmer, poetic, rustic
  7. eclogue, georgic **8.** agrestic, pastoral
  9. bucoliast
bud ... **3.** deb **4.** bulb, cion, germ, grow,
  knop, stem **5.** brier, buddy, gemma,
  graft, plant, shoat, youth **6.** embryo,
  sprout **7.** blossom, brother, burgeon,
  develop **8.** rudiment, soredium
  9. debutante, germinate
Buddha (Gautama) ... **2.** Fo **4.** sage
  (Shakya) **5.** amita, deity **7.** ascetic,
  teacher **8.** Daibutsu **10.** Blessed One
Buddhism (pert to) ...
  church .. **4.** tera
  city (sacred) .. **5.** Lassa (Lhasa)
  evil spirit .. **4.** Mara
  fate .. **5.** Karma
  festival .. **3.** Bon
  friar, monk .. **2.** Bo **5.** arbat, bonze
    6. bhikku, gelong **7.** Mahatma
    8. poonghia **9.** Dalai Lama
  goal .. **13.** Enlightenment
  hell .. **6.** Naraka
  language (sacred) .. **4.** Pali **5.** sutra
    9. Tripitaka
  liberation .. **7.** Nirvana
  monk .. **4.** lama (Tibet)
  mountain (sacred) .. **4.** Omei (Chin)
  paradise .. **4.** Jodo **8.** gokuraku
  sect .. **3.** Zen
  shrine (Ind) .. **4.** tope **5.** stupa **6.** dagoba

  temple .. **4.** rath, Tera **6.** vihara
  temple column .. **3.** lat
  term .. **6.** nidana
buddy ... **3.** pal **4.** chum, mate **5.** crony
  7. brother, comrade **8.** tentmate
  9. bedfellow, companion
budge ... **3.** fur (lambskin) **4.** grog, move,
  stir **5.** booze, brisk, stiff **6.** guzzle,
  jocund, liquor, solemn, tipple **7.** austere,
  pompous **8.** movement **11.** nervousness
budget ... **3.** bag **4.** bulk, plan, sack
  5. funds, pouch, purse, store **6.** agenda,
  assets, bundle, moneys, packet,
  parcel, ration, wallet **7.** program,
  stipend **8.** finances, quantity, schedule
  9. allowance, statement
  12. accumulation
Buenos Aires (pert to) ...
  avenue (famed) .. **13.** Avenida de Mayo
  bourse .. **5.** Bolsa
  capital .. **9.** Argentina
  river .. **7.** La Plata
buff ... **3.** rub **4.** hide (animal) **5.** color,
  scour **6.** polish **7.** burnish, leather
buffalo (animal) ...
  American .. **5.** bison
  Asian, African .. **2.** ox **4.** arna, Cape,
    gaur **8.** seladang
  European .. **7.** aurochs
  hybrid .. **7.** cattalo (catalo)
  Indian .. **4.** arna
  Philippines .. **7.** carabao, timarau
buffalo (pert to) ...
  grass .. **5.** grama **6.** guinea **11.** St
    Augustine
  pea .. **4.** plum **5.** vetch **10.** bluebonnet
  slang .. **3.** cow **5.** bully **7.** perplex
  8. bulldoze, confound
Buffalo Bill ... **11.** William Cody
buffer ... **4.** buff **5.** guard, wheel
  6. bumper **7.** bulwark, cushion
  8. backstop, polisher
buffet ... **3.** bar, box, hit **4.** beat,
  blow, cuff, slap, toss, whip **5.** abuse,
  smite, stool **6.** bruise, oppose, strike
  12. chastisement **14.** disappointment
buffet ... **6.** supper **7.** counter, hassock
  8. cupboard **9.** sideboard
buffo ... **7.** buffoon **10.** bass singer
  (comic opera), buffo-basso
buffoon ... **4.** fool, mima (fem), mime,
  zany **5.** actor, clown, droll, mimer
  6. jester, mummer **8.** humorist,
  ridicule **9.** Hanswurst, harlequin
  12. Eulenspiegel (Tyll) **13.** pickel-herring
  (pickle-herring)
buffoonery ... **6.** japery, pranks **7.** fooling
  8. clownery, drollery, trickery
  9. slapstick **10.** buffoonism
  12. harlequinade
bug (insect) ... **3.** fly, sow **4.** flea,
  gnat, moth, pill, tick **5.** Anasa,
  aphid, Aphis, cimex, louse **6.** beetle,
  cicada, earwig, locust, mantis, needle,
  scarab, slater, spider, weevil **7.** firefly,
  hexapod, katydid, ladybug, Ranatra,
  termite **8.** chilipod, diplopod, mosquito,
  myriapod **9.** arthropod (jointed),
  centipede, cockroach, lightning,
  millipede, tarantula **10.** silverfish
  11. grasshopper

bug (slang) . . . **3.** nut **4.** bogy, flaw, rage
  5. craze, fault, manis **6.** defect, zealot
  7. bugaboo, bugbear, fanatic, passion
  9. energumen
bugaboo . . . **4.** bogy, ogre, trap (golf)
bugan . . . **5.** ghost **6.** spirit (evil)
  9. hobgoblin
bugger . . . **3.** guy, rat **4.** chap, heel
  6. booger, jasper, wretch
buggy . . . **3.** bus **4.** ga-ga, shay **5.** wagon
  6. cuckoo **7.** caboose, foolish, haywire,
  vehicle **8.** carriage, demented, infested,
  stanhope **9.** insectile **10.** insectlike
bug juice . . . **6.** liquor (strong), whisky
  (inferior)
bugle . . . **3.** iva (ragweed) **4.** bead,
  call (mating), honk, horn, nose,
  toot **7.** clarion, trumpet **9.** schnozzle
  10. instrument
bugle call . . . **4.** taps **6.** alerte, sennet
  (Hist) **7.** retreat, tantara **8.** last post,
  reveille
build . . . **4.** form, rear **5.** edify, erect,
  found, frame, raise, shape **6.** create,
  evolve, figure, nidify **7.** fashion, stature
  8. increase, physique **9.** construct,
  establish
building . . . **4.** barn, casa, crib, shed,
  wing **5.** annex, tower **6.** casino, castle,
  lean-to, making, museum **7.** edifice,
  factory, forming, rookery, rotunda,
  theater **8.** creation, dwelling, erecting,
  erection, tenement **9.** apartment,
  structure **10.** fashioning, production,
  skyscraper, storehouse **11.** fabrication
build-up . . . **5.** boost **9.** promotion
  11. advertising **12.** commendation
built . . . **4.** made **6.** formed, shaped
  7. crested, erected **9.** fashioned
  10. fabricated **11.** constructed
bulb . . . **3.** bud **4.** corm, lily, root,
  sego, stem **5.** onion, swell, tuber,
  tulip **6.** bulbil, camass, crocus, dahlia
  7. bulblet, globule, rhizome **8.** earthnut
bulbous . . . **5.** round **7.** bulbose, bulging
  8. swelling, tuberous
Bulgaria . . .
  capital . . **5.** Sofia
  city . . **5.** Varna **6.** Plevna, Sliven
  7. Ruschuk
  native . . **6.** Bulgar
  origin . . **4.** Slav **9.** Mongolian
  river . . **6.** Danube, Marica (Maritsa),
  Struma
bulge . . . **3.** bow **4.** bump, edge, hump,
  jump, knob, odds **5.** bilge, bloat,
  flash, pouch, swell **6.** convex, wallet
  7. vantage **9.** advantage **10.** projection
  12. protuberance
bulk . . . **3.** sum **4.** loom, mass, most, size
  6. extent, staple, volume **7.** bigness,
  quantum **8.** majority, quantity
  9. dimension, largeness, substance,
  thickness **11.** massiveness
  12. accumulation **13.** preponderance
bulky . . . **5.** heavy, hulky, stout, thick
  6. clumsy **7.** awkward, lumpish, massive
  8. unwieldy **9.** corpulent, policemen
  (Eng sl), ponderous **10.** cumbersome,
  unwielding **11.** substantial
bull . . . **4.** fiat, seal **5.** edict, error,

large, ukase **6.** brevet, decree, firman,
  humbug, letter (papal), market (Finan),
  rising, Taurus **7.** blunder **8.** nonsense,
  solecism **9.** Irish bull, policeman
  10. speculator
bull (male animal) . . . **2.** ox **3.** cow **4.** Apis
  (sacred), stot, toro, zebu **5.** moose,
  steer, whale **6.** walrus **7.** bullock
  8. elephant, Minotaur, terrapin
bull (slang) . . . **4.** blah, bosh, bunk
  5. hokum **6.** hot air **7.** baloney
  8. buncombe, flimflam
bulla . . . **4.** bleb, boss, case (leather), knob,
  seal (papal), stud **6.** button **7.** blister,
  globule, pendant, vesicle **8.** ornament
bulldog . . . **3.** ant **4.** pipe **5.** leech
  7. courage, forceps **8.** barnacle,
  stubborn, tenacity **9.** newspaper (early),
  tenacious
bulldoze . . . **3.** cow **5.** bully, grade, level
  6. coerce, harass **7.** buffalo **8.** browbeat
  10. intimidate
bullet . . . **4.** ball (cannon), shot, slug
  6. dumdum, pellet, sinker (angling),
  tracer **9.** missile
bulletin . . . **5.** brief, flash **6.** notice,
  record **7.** account, message **8.** newsbill
  9. statement **10.** newsletter, periodical
  11. publication **12.** announcement
bullfighting (pert to) . . .
  assistant . . **9.** cuadrilla
  bullfighter . . **6.** torero **7.** matador, picador
  8. toreador
  dart . . **10.** banderilla
  final thrust . . **8.** estocada **13.** moment
  of truth
  maneuver . . **4.** pase **5.** faena **8.** veronica
  matador, famed . . **8.** Belmonte, Manolete
  10. El Cordobés
  matador's tool . . **4.** capa **6.** muleta
  music . . **9.** pasodoble
  parade . . **5.** paseo
  program, series . . **7.** corrida
  shout . . **3.** olé
bullfinch . . . **3.** alp **4.** nope **5.** hedge
  11. pyrrhuloxia **12.** gray grosbeak
Bull Moose . . . **16.** Progressive Party
bullpen (pert to) . . .
  camp . . **8.** barracks **9.** enclosure
  ice hockey . . **5.** bench (penalty)
  ring cell . . **5.** toril
  Western US . . **6.** corral
Bull Run (battle) . . . **8.** Manassas
bully . . . **4.** beef **5.** hector, jovial
  7. gleeful, ruffian **8.** browbeat, bulldoze
  9. bulldozer, tormentor **10.** browbeater,
  intimidate
bulwark . . . **4.** bank **6.** buffer, sconce
  7. barrier, parapet, rampart **8.** abutment,
  buttress **10.** protection **13.** fortification
bum . . . **3.** beg **5.** idler, revel, rummy,
  souse, spree **6.** beggar, loafer,
  tipple, wretch **7.** budmash, moocher,
  wastrel **8.** blighter, drunkard, vagabond
  9. lazzarone, schnorrer **10.** panhandler
bump . . . **3.** hit, jog **4.** bang, clop, jolt,
  lump, meet, push, thud **5.** bulge, cahot,
  crash, crump, knock, lower, plunk,
  tumor **6.** demote, impact, reduce, strike
  7. collide **8.** demotion, dilation, swelling
  9. air pocket, collision, downgrade

bumpkin . . . 4. boor, clod, gawk, hick, lout, rube, tike 5. yokel 6. farmer, rustic 7. cauboge, hayseed, hoosier, lumpkin 9. chawbacon 10. clodhopper

bumptious . . . 8. insolent 9. audacious, insulting 12. contumelious

bunch . . . 3. bob, lot, mop, set 4. pack, tuft, wisp 5. batch, clump, covey, crowd, flock, grist, group 6. bundle 7. cluster, company 8. assemble, quantity 9. multitude 10. congregate

bundle . . . 3. lot, wad 4. bale, bolt, hank, pack, send 5. bluey, bunch, fagot, sheaf, shook 6. bindle, fardel, fascis, packet, parcel, seroon 7. fascine, package, rouleau 10. collection

bung . . . 3. tap 4. cork, plug, stop 5. spile 6. bruise 7. contuse, stopper, stopple, tampeon, tampoon 8. bankrupt, bunghole 9. falsehood

bungle . . . 3. err 4. muff 5. botch, fudge 6. bobble, foozle, fumble, tailor (hunting) 7. blunder

bungling . . . 5. fudgy 6. clumsy 7. awkward, unhandy 8. botchery 9. unskilled 10. blundering, unskillful

bunion . . . 12. hallux valgus

bunk . . . 3. bed, kip, rot 4. blah, brag 5. abide, berth, couch, dwell, hokum, hooey, sleep 6. humbug, kibosh 7. baloney, hogwash 8. nonsense, tommyrot 9. cross-beam (logging)

Bunker Hill (Mass) . . . 6. battle (1775)

bunkum . . . see *buncombe*

Bunsen . . . 4. cell, disk 5. flame, valve 6. burner 9. Professor (Ger)

bunt . . . 3. bat, dig, jab, jog, tap 4. blow, bump, butt, pike, push, tail (Scot) 5. knock, shove 7. bunting 10. propulsion

bunting . . . 4. flag, hood 5. flags 6. banner, pennon 7. pennant 8. streamer

bunting (bird) . . . 3. red 4. cirl, corn, crow, lark, pape (Creole) 5. finch 6. indigo, towhee 7. cowbird, ortolan 8. bobolink 12. yellowhammer

Bunyan (John) **work** . . . 16. Pilgrim's Progress

Bunyan (Paul) **ox** . . . 4. Babe, blue

buoy . . . 3. dan 4. bell 5. float 6. marker 7. can buoy, nunbuoy 8. bell buoy, deadhead, life buoy, spar buoy 11. mooring buoy 12. breeches buoy 13. whistling buoy

buoyance, buoyancy . . . 4. hope, snap 5. verve 6. bounce 7. flotage 9. lightness 10. levitation, resilience 12. floatability 16. lightheartedness

buoyant . . . 5. light 7. elastic 8. cheerful, floating, levitate, volatile 11. supernatant 12. lighthearted, recuperative

bur, burr . . . 3. nut 5. thorn 8. adherent (see also *burr*)

burble . . . 6. muddle 7. confuse, trouble 8. disorder

burbot . . . 4. ling, Lota 7. eelpout

burden . . . 3. key, tax 4. birn, care, cark, clog, lade, load, note, onus, task, tone 5. cargo, cross, music, tenor, voice 6. charge, cumber, hamper, saddle, weight 7. bourdon, freight, oppress, payload, refrain 8. capacity, overload, pressure 10. impediment, imposition 11. encumbrance

burdensome . . . 5. heavy 7. arduous, massive, onerous, weighty 8. unwieldy 9. difficult, laborious, ponderous 10. cumbersome, oppressive 11. troublesome 12. impedimental

bureau . . . 4. desk, shop 6. office 7. dresser 8. chambers 10. chiffonier, department

bureaucracy . . . 10. government 11. directorate, officialdom, officialism

burgeon . . . 3. bud 4. grow 5. gemma, shoot, sprit 6. sprout

burglar . . . 4. yegg 5. thief 9. cracksman 11. safecracker 12. housebreaker

burglary . . . 5. theft 6. burgle 7. larceny, robbery 8. stealage 13. housebreaking

burgle . . . 3. rob 8. burglary 10. burglarize

burgomaster . . . 5. mayor 7. alcalde 10. magistrate 11. burghmaster

burgoo, burgout . . . 4. stew 5. gruel 7. pudding (oatmeal) 8. porridge

burial . . . 5. inurn 7. funeral 9. interment, sepulture 10. engulfment, inhumation, submersion 11. concealment, submergence

burial ground . . . 4. pyre 5. grave 6. barrow 7. tumulus 8. bone yard, catacomb, cemetery, golgotha 9. graveyard 10. churchyard, necropolis 11. polyandrium 12. potter's field

burlesque . . . 3. fun 4. jest 5. farce, comic 6. parody, review, satire 7. mimicry, mockery, overact, take-off 8. burletta, doggerel, ridicule, travesty 9. charivari, imitation, travestie 10. caricatura, caricature 13. entertainment

Burlingame Treaty . . . 11. Immigration (Chin 1868)

burly . . . 3. fat 5. bulky, large, noble, obese, stout 6. brawny 7. stately 8. imposing, stalwart 9. corpulent, excellent

Burma, Burmese . . .
alphabet . . 4. Pali
capital (anc) . . 3. Ava 4. Pegu
capital, modern . . 6. Yangon 7. Rangoon
city . . 8. Mandalay
dagger . . 3. dah (dhao)
gibbon . . 3. lar
girl . . 4. mima
monk . . 2. bo
native . . 3. Lai
people . . 3. Mon, Tai 4. Laos, Shan 7. Siamese
relation . . 5. Thais (Tais) 6. Malays 7. Chinese 8. Tibetans 10. Mongolians
religion . . 8. Buddhism
robber . . 6. dacoit
shed (public) . . 5. zayat
viol . . 4. turr (3-stringed)

Burma Road . . . 6. Lashio (to China, 1938--1942, replaced by Ledo Rd)

burn . . . 3. dry, tan 4. char, fire, glow, hurt, pain, sear, sere 5. blaze, brand, brook, cense, flame, scald, singe 6. ignite, injury, scorch 7. cremate, encauma,

flicker, sunburn, swelter, torrefy
9. cauterize, sacrifice **10.** incandesce,
incinerate
burner . . . **3.** jet **4.** lamp **5.** torch
6. Bunsen, candle, censer (incense)
7. cresset **9.** blowtorch **10.** lucubrator
11. incinerator
burning . . . **3.** hot **4.** fire, pain, sore
5. afire, angry, ardor, arson, blaze, fiery,
flame **6.** ablaze, ardent, fervid **7.** blazing,
cautery, excited, fervent, flaming,
glowing, shining, zealous **8.** eloquent,
feverish, inustion **9.** cremating,
cremation, execution **10.** combustion,
ustulation **13.** conflagration
burning place . . . **4.** ghat **9.** crematory
10. cinerarium
burnish . . . **3.** rub **4.** buff **5.** glaze, gloss,
shine **6.** patina, polish
burnt . . . **3.** red **5.** dried **6.** burned,
seared, singed **7.** charred **8.** hardened,
scorched, sunburnt **9.** blistered,
sunburned
burnt (pert to) . . .
art . . **11.** pygrography, pyrogravure
color . . **4.** rose **5.** ocher, topaz **6.** almond,
orange, russet, sienna **8.** amethyst
sugar . . **7.** caramel
burn with anger, excitement . . . **4.** fume
5. smoke **6.** seethe, simmer, sizzle
7. smolder
burp . . . **5.** belch, eruct **8.** eructate
burr . . . **3.** cut, hem **4.** buzz, whir
5. brier, drone, gnarl, knurl, thorn
6. brogue, corona (moon), meatus (ear)
7. bramble, clotbur, prickle, silique,
sticker **8.** excavate, follicle **9.** cocklebur,
whetstone
burro . . . **3.** ass **4.** jack **5.** cuddy, neddy
6. dickey, donkey **7.** jackass
burrow . . . **3.** dig **4.** abri, hide, hole,
lair, mine **5.** couch (otter's), lodge
(beaver's) **6.** search, tunnel **7.** shelter
burrowing . . . **9.** effodient, fossorial
11. lithodomous (in rock)
burrowing animal . . . **4.** mole, peba
5. poyou **6.** peludo **8.** suricate
9. armadillo
burst . . . **3.** pop **4.** bang, rend **5.** blast,
blaze, break, broke, erupt, flare, flash,
shots, spurt **6.** volley **7.** explode,
flare-up, gunfire, implode **8.** outbreak,
outburst, ruptured **9.** discharge,
explosion, fractured **10.** detonation
11. dissiliency
burst (forth) . . . **4.** grow **5.** erupt, sally
6. sprout
burst (pert to) . . .
applause . . **5.** éclat, hands **7.** ovation,
plaudit **8.** clapping
cheers . . **5.** salvo
gunfire . . **6.** rafale
laughter . . **3.** fit **4.** peal, roar
10. convulsion
temper . . **4.** rage **5.** scene, storm
7. passion **9.** explosion
bursting . . . **4.** full **7.** brimful, crammed,
excited, replete **8.** overfull, thrilled,
volcanic **9.** explosive, surfeited
10. detonating **11.** impassioned,
overflowing, overwhelmed

bury . . . **4.** hide, sink **5.** cache, cover, inter,
inurn, plant, stash **6.** engulf, entomb,
inhume **7.** conceal, embosom, repress,
secrete **8.** submerge **9.** overwhelm,
sepulture
bus . . . **6.** jitney **7.** omnibus **10.** motor
coach
bush . . . **3.** tod **4.** shag (hair) **5.** brush,
plain, shrub, wahoo, wilds **6.** branch,
lining **7.** boscage, bushing **8.** bushveld,
woodland **10.** hinterland
bushed . . . **4.** beat **5.** all in **6.** pooped
7. baffled **8.** dog-tired **9.** exhausted,
nonplused, perplexed, played out
10. nonplussed
bushel . . . **3.** foo **4.** full **6.** basket, vessel
7. measure (dry) **8.** imperial, standard
10. Winchester
Bushido (Jap) . . . **11.** code of honor
bushing . . . **4.** bush **6.** lining, sleeve
(mach) **7.** bearing, padding (piano)
Bushman . . . **3.** San **4.** Saan **5.** nomad,
pygmy **6.** Abatua, rustic **8.** woodsman
9. aborigine
bushmaster . . . **5.** snake
bushwhacker . . . **7.** pioneer **8.** guerilla
10. forerunner **11.** bushfighter,
voortrekker **12.** frontiersman
bushy . . . **5.** hairy, thick, woody
6. dumose, shaggy, woodsy **7.** hirsute,
scrubby, shrubby
business . . . **3.** job **4.** firm, game, line,
work **5.** craft, house, trade **6.** affair,
career, matter, racket **7.** calling,
company, concern, pursuit
8. commerce, industry, interest,
practice, vocation **10.** enterprise,
occupation, proceeding, profession
11. transaction **13.** establishment
business (pert to) . . .
agreement . . **6.** cartel
businesslike . . **11.** pragmatical
customer . . **6.** patron
cycle . . **9.** recession **10.** depression,
prosperity **11.** liquidation
deal . . **4.** turn **9.** operation
11. negotiation, transaction
Exchange . . **4.** bank **5.** Bolsa **6.** Bourse
11. stock market
man . . **6.** tycoon **8.** salesman **9.** solicitor
place . . **4.** mart, shop **5.** store **6.** office,
shoppe **8.** Exchange
bust . . . **4.** bang, fail, hand (Bridge), tame
(bronco) **5.** burst, chest, crash, flunk,
spree **6.** breast, figure **7.** degrade,
explode, failure **8.** collapse, demotion,
fracture **9.** sculpture **10.** bankruptcy
bustard . . . **4.** bird (Old World), kori, Otis
5. goose, paauw **6.** curlew **8.** Otididae
busted . . . **4.** flat **5.** broke **6.** broken, failed,
ruined **7.** severed **8.** bankrupt, ruptured,
strapped **9.** insolvent, penniless
10. stone-broke
bustle . . . **3.** ado **4.** fuss, stir, to-do
5. haste, whirl **6.** flurry, hubbub,
hustle, pother, scurry, tumult **7.** bluster,
ferment, fluster, scamper, turmoil
8. activity **9.** agitation, commotion
10. excitement, hurly-burly
11. disturbance
bustling . . . **6.** active **7.** hurried, rushing

8. eventful, stirring
busy . . . **4.** nosy, work **5.** drive **6.** active,
devote, employ, engage, occupy
7. engaged, on the go, operose
8. diligent, employed, meddling,
occupied, on the run, sedulous
9. assiduous, attentive, laborious,
officious **10.** meddlesome
11. industrious, inquisitive, persevering
busy . . . **4.** dick **6.** gossip **7.** gumshoe,
meddler **8.** busybody, flatfoot
9. detective
busybody . . . **6.** gossip **8.** quidnunc
9. pragmatic
but . . . **2.** ma **3.** yet **4.** even, just, mere,
save **5.** hence, outer, still **6.** except
7. however, without **10.** regardless
12. nevertheless **15.** notwithstanding
butcher . . . **3.** fly (angling), mar **4.** kill,
slay **5.** botch, spoil **6.** killer, vendor
7. croaker, meatman **8.** merchant,
train-boy **9.** slaughter **11.** slaughterer
12. bloodshedder
butchery . . . **6.** murder **7.** carnage
8. business, massacre, shambles
9. slaughter **14.** slaughterhouse
butt . . . **3.** aim, end, jut, pit, ram, tun, tup
4. buck, bunt, cart, cask, goat, rump,
stub **5.** cigar, hinge, joint, mound,
piece, stump **6.** target (archery), thrust
(fencing) **7.** buttock, parapet, project
8. flatfish **9.** cigarette laughingstock
butter . . . **3.** pat **4.** coat, ghee (ghi), oleo
5. smear **6.** bedaub, spread **7.** butyric
8. flattery **9.** margarine, suaveness
10. semiliquid **13.** oleomargarine
butter-and-eggs . . . **8.** flaxweed, ranstead,
toadflax
buttercup fruit . . . **6.** achene **7.** crowtoe
butterfingered . . . **6.** clumsy **7.** awkward,
unhandy **8.** bungling, careless **9.** all
thumbs **10.** blundering
butterflies (slang) . . . **6.** nerves **7.** fidgets,
jitters
butterfly (pert to) . . .
American . . **7.** viceroy
family . . **10.** Agapetidae **11.** Rhopalocera
genus . . **7.** Lycaena **11.** Lepidoptera
large . . **7.** monarch
larva . . **11.** caterpillar
lily . . **4.** sego **8.** mariposa
peacock . . **2.** io **7.** buckeye
swallowtail . . **5.** black, tiger, zebra
type . . **4.** moth **5.** satyr **10.** fritillary,
silverspot
buttocks . . . **4.** butt (vulgar), hips, rear,
rump, seat **5.** fanny, podex **6.** bottom
8. haunches, maneuver (wrestling)
9. backsides, posterior
buttress . . . **4.** pier, pile, prop, stay
5. brace, tower **7.** shelter, support
8. abutment **10.** projection,
strengthen **11.** counterfort
13. fortification

buttress (Arch) . . . **4.** pier **6.** flying
7. hanging
buxom . . . **3.** gay **4.** boon, rosy **5.** jolly,
plump **6.** blithe, jocund, jovial **7.** gleeful
buy . . . **5.** bribe **6.** accept, redeem
7. bargain, expiate **8.** purchase
buy back . . . **6.** redeem
Buyer Beware . . . **12.** Caveat Emptor
buzz . . . **3.** hum, saw **5.** rumor, snore
6. bustle, murmur, rumble **7.** ferment,
whisper **9.** fricative, murmuring
10. sibilation
buzzard . . . **4.** aura (turkey), hawk, pern
5. buteo **6.** osprey, stupid **7.** harrier
9. dorbeetle, senseless **10.** cockchafer
buzz bomb . . . **9.** doodlebug
10. bumblebomb **14.** Chase-Me-Charlie
bwana (Afr) . . . **4.** boss **6.** master
by . . . **2.** at, in, on **3.** ago, bei, par, per,
via **4.** away, gone, near, over, pass
(bridge), past, with **5.** after, aside
6. beside, beyond, nearby, toward
7. abreast, close by, through **9.** in
reserve
by-and-by . . . **4.** anon, soon **5.** later,
sweet **6.** mañana **7.** betimes, bientôt,
ere long, shortly **8.** directly **9.** presently
11. tout à l'heure
by birth . . . **3.** nee
bygone . . . **3.** ago **4.** lost, over, past
6. buried, bypast, gone by, passed
7. elapsed, extinct **8.** departed, preterit
(preterite)
byname . . . **6.** eponym **7.** babyism,
epithet, surname **8.** cognomen,
monicker, nickname **9.** sobriquet
10. patronymic **11.** appellation
bypass . . . **4.** go by, miss **5.** byway, elude
6. byroad, detour, escape **7.** deviate,
digress **8.** side path **10.** circumvent,
roundabout
By the Grace of God . . . **9.** Dei Gratia
byword . . . **3.** mot, saw **5.** adage,
maxim **6.** byname, phrase, saying,
slogan **7.** adagium, parable, proverb
8. aphorism, nickname, reproach
9. catchword, sobriquet **10.** shibboleth
by word of mouth . . . **4.** oral **5.** parol
(parole)
Byzantine Empire . . .
architecture . . **7.** St Marks (Venice)
9. elaborate
bookbinding . . **9.** unadorned (earlier)
10. bejewelled (later)
church . . **7.** Eastern
city . . **14.** Constantinople (Istanbul)
creator . . **11.** Constantine (the Great)
historian . . **9.** Procopius **11.** Anna
Comnena
poetry . . **5.** hymns
scepter . . **6.** ferula
writer . . **6.** Prazes **7.** Priscus, Romanus
Byzantium . . . **14.** Constantinople
(Istanbul)

C

C . . . **4.** clef **7.** cedilla, century, hundred, keynote
caama . . . **3.** fox **4.** asse **10.** hartebeest
cab . . . **4.** pony, taxi **7.** measure, purloin, shelter, taxicab, vehicle **8.** carriage (anc) **9.** cabriolet **10.** locomotive (part) **11.** translation
cabal . . . **4.** clan, plot **5.** group, junta, party **7.** chatter, complot, coterie, dispute, faction **8.** intrigue **9.** camarilla, collusion, Committee **10.** complicity, conspiracy
cabala . . . **7.** mystery **9.** mystic art, occultism
cabalessou . . . **9.** armadillo (giant)
cabalistic . . . **6.** occult **7.** cabalic **8.** abstract, anagogic, esoteric, mystical **10.** mysterious
caballeria . . . **7.** measure (land) **8.** chivalry **10.** knighthood
caballero . . . **5.** lover, rider **6.** knight **8.** cavalier, horseman **9.** chevalier, gentleman **10.** equestrian
caballo . . . **5.** horse
cabaret . . . **3.** inn **4.** cafe **6.** hostel, posado, tavern **7.** barroom **9.** night club, roadhouse **11.** café dansant **13.** entertainment
cabbage . . . **3.** kos (cos) **4.** cole, kale, palm **5.** colza, savoy **7.** collard **8.** colewort, kohlrabi **11.** cauliflower **15.** Brussels sprouts
cabbage (pert to) . . .
  curly leaf . . **5.** savoy
  daisy . . **11.** globeflower
  fermented . . **5.** kraut
  headless . . **4.** kale
  salad . . **4.** slaw
  seed . . **5.** colza
  slang . . **4.** crib, fool **6.** pilfer **7.** fathead, purloin **9.** numbskull **11.** cabbagehead, knucklehead
  species . . **8.** Brassica
  tree . . **4.** palm **7.** angelin **8.** palmetto
  white . . **9.** butterfly
  yellows . . **7.** disease (destructive)
caber . . . **4.** apar, beam, pole **6.** rafter, timber
cabin . . . **3.** hut **4.** shed **5.** booth, coach (Naut), house, hovel, lodge, shack **6.** cabana, saloon **7.** caboose **10.** blockhouse
cabinet . . . **3.** box, den **4.** Body, buhl, case **6.** bureau, closet, office **7.** almirah, boudoir, council, étagère, whatnot **8.** cellaret, cupboard, ministry **9.** committee
cable . . . **4.** boom, cord, rope, wire **5.** chain, twine **6.** fasten, hawser **7.** coaxial, measure, molding, ropeway **8.** telegram **9.** cablegram
cable (pert to) . . .
  car . . **7.** telpher
  holder (Naut) . . **7.** wildcat **10.** cable wheel
  post . . **4.** bitt
cabling . . . **9.** rudenture
cabochon . . . **5.** jewel, stone (uncut), style (convex cut) **8.** ornament
caboodle . . . **3.** all, kit, lot **5.** bunch, whole **10.** collection **14.** kit and caboodle
caboose . . . **3.** car (RR) **5.** buggy **6.** galley **7.** kitchen **9.** deckhouse
cabotin . . . **5.** actor (strolling) **9.** charlatan
cachaca . . . **3.** rum (white)
cache . . . **4.** hide, hole **5.** stash, store **7.** conceal, hide-out, retreat **8.** hideaway **10.** storehouse
cachet . . . **4.** seal **5.** sigil, stamp, wafer **6.** signet **7.** capsule
cachilla . . . **8.** white man
cachot . . . **7.** dungeon
cackle . . . **3.** gab **4.** cank, chat, crow, talk **5.** clack, laugh, prate **6.** babble, gabble, giggle, gossip, jabber **7.** chatter, prattle **8.** laughter
cacodemon . . . **4.** deva **5.** devil, fiend, lndra **10.** evil spirit
cacology . . . **10.** bad diction, corruption (speech) **16.** mispronunciation
cacophonous . . . **7.** raucous **8.** jangling, strident **9.** diaphonic, dissonant **10.** discordant **11.** unmelodious
cacophony . . . **5.** clash **6.** jangle **7.** discord **8.** diaphony (Mus) **9.** harshness **10.** dissodence
cactus . . . **4.** bleo **5.** agave **6.** chaute, cholla, mescal **7.** Opuntia, saguaro **8.** fishhook **9.** Turk's-head **11.** prickly pear **12.** Echinocactus
cad . . . **4.** boor, chum, heel, hick **5.** yokel **6.** mucker **7.** bounder, servant **8.** townsman **9.** scoundrel, vulgarian
cadaver . . . **4.** body (dead) **5.** stiff **6.** corpse **7.** carcass **8.** skeleton
cadaverous . . . **4.** pale **5.** gaunt, lurid **6.** sickly, wasted **7.** ghastly, haggard **9.** emaciated **10.** attenuated, corpselike
caddis (pert to) . . .
  bait . . **3.** fly **4.** worm **5.** cadew
  material . . **4.** yarn **5.** twill **6.** crewel **7.** worsted
  worm . . **5.** larva (aquatic)
caddle . . . **4.** fuss **5.** annoy, worry **6.** gossip **7.** confuse, trouble **8.** disarray **9.** confusion
cade . . . **3.** keg, oil (Med), pet **4.** cask, lamb (orphan) **6.** barrel, coddle, petted
cadeau . . . **4.** gift
cadence . . . **4.** beat, liit, tone **5.** meter **6.** rhythm **7.** balance **9.** free verse, vers libre **10.** modulation
cadence . . . **4.** half **5.** trill **6.** plagal **7.** perfect **9.** authentic, deceptive, imperfect, suspended **11.** interrupted
cadency (Her) . . . **4.** rose **5.** label **6.** mullet **7.** annulet, martlet **8.** crescent **10.** fleur-de-lis **11.** cross moline
cadenza . . . **7.** cadence **8.** flourish
cadet . . . **3.** son **4.** pleb **5.** color (blue),

youth **6.** junior **10.** midshipman
cadge ... **3.** beg **4.** hawk **5.** fakir, mooch
6. beggar, hawker, mumper, peddle,
sponge, vendor **7.** carrier, moocher,
sponger **8.** huckster, sannyasi
cadgy ... **6.** wanton **7.** lustful **8.** cheerful,
mirthful
Cadmus (pert to) ...
　daughter .. **3.** Ino **6.** Semele
　father .. **6.** Agenor
　founder of .. **6.** Thebes (Boetia)
　sister .. **6.** Europa
　wife .. **8.** Harmonia
cadre ... **4.** list, unit **5.** frame, panel **6.** line-
up, roster, scheme **8.** cadastre, register,
schedule, skeleton **9.** framework
caduceus (Gr Antiq) ... **4.** wand (Hermes')
5. staff **6.** symbol **8.** insignia (Med
Corps)
Caesar (pert to) ...
　betrayer .. **6.** Brutus
　colleague .. **7.** Bibulus
　death site .. **4.** Nola
　Emperor, Dictator of .. **4.** Rome
　fatal day .. **4.** Ides (of March) **11.** Ides
　of March
　language .. **5.** Latin
　rival .. **6.** Pompey
　river .. **7.** Rubicon
　sister .. **4.** Atia
　uncle .. **11.** Caius Marius
　wife .. **8.** Cornelia
caesura, cesura ... **4.** rest **5.** break,
colon, comma, pause **8.** interval
12. interruption
cafard ... **5.** bigot, blues **6.** humbug
9. hypocrite **10.** depression
café ... **5.** coffe **6.** coffee **10.** restaurant
11. coffeehouse
café (pert to) ...
　au lait .. **5.** brown **6.** alesan **10.** French
　nude
　creme .. **5.** suede (color)
　noir .. **4.** musk (color) **11.** black coffee
　parfait .. **8.** beverage
cafetière ... **9.** coffeepot **10.** percolator
caffeine ... **6.** coffee, theine (in tea)
8. alkaloid **9.** stimulant
cafila ... **7.** caravan (camel)
cage ... **3.** mew, pen **4.** coop **6.** corral
7. confine, goal net, impound **8.** goal
post
cagey ... **3.** sly **4.** foxy, wary, wily
5. canny, leery **6.** artful, crafty, shifty,
shrews **7.** cunning, evasive, knowing
Cain (pert to) ...
　brother .. **4.** Abel
　founder of .. **5.** Enoch (1st city)
　Land of .. **3.** Nod
　slayer of .. **4.** Abel
　son .. **5.** Enoch
cairn ... **4.** heap (stones) **6.** menhir
8. catstone (catstane), landmark,
memorial, monument
Cairo ...
　capital .. **5.** Egypt
　city gate (famed) .. **9.** Bab-el-Nasr
　mosque .. **12.** Sultan Hassan
　resident .. **7.** Cairene
　river .. **4.** Nile
　seaport .. **10.** Alexandria

　tomb .. **10.** Mehemet Ali
　warrior .. **9.** Rameses II
caisson ... **3.** box **4.** case **5.** chest, wagon
7. chamber
caitiff ... **4.** base, mean, vile **6.** coward,
wicked, wretch **7.** budmash, captive
10. despicable
cajole ... **4.** coax, urge **5.** cheat, jolly
6. delude **7.** flatter, palaver, sweeten,
wheedle **8.** blandish **9.** importune
10. honeyfogle
Cajun (pert to) ...
　descent .. **6.** French (Canadian)
　dialect .. **5.** Cajun
　home (present) .. **9.** Louisiana
　native of .. **6.** Acadia (Nova Scotia)
cake ... **3.** bun, wig **4.** bake, food, lump,
mass, wigg **5.** batty, block, crust,
solid, torte, wafer **6.** gateau, harden
7. bannock, congeal, oatcake, pancake
8. corn pone, solidify **9.** charlotte,
simpleton **11.** griddle-cake
cake (pert to) ...
　almond paste .. **7.** ratafia
　corn .. **4.** pone
　flat .. **7.** placent
　fried .. **7.** cruller **8.** doughnut
　Lenten .. **6.** cimbal, simnel
　Scotch .. **4.** farl (farle) **5.** scone
　unleavened .. **8.** tortilla
Cake Day (Scot) ... **8.** hogmanay (New
Year's)
calabar bean ... **6.** myotic, ordeal
7. eserine **8.** alkaloid **13.** physostigmine
calabash ... **5.** gourd **6.** baobab, bronze
(color)
calaboose ... **4.** gaol, jail **5.** choky, clink
6. bagnio, lockup, prison **8.** bastille,
calabozo **9.** Bridewell
calamitous ... **3.** sad **4.** dire, evil **5.** black
6. tragic, woeful **7.** adverse, baleful,
ruinous, unhappy **8.** grievous, tragical,
wretched **10.** afflictive, deplorable,
disastrous **11.** cataclysmic, destructive,
distressful, unfortunate **12.** catastrophic
calamity ... **4.** blow, evil, ruin **5.** wrack
6. mishap **7.** tragedy **8.** casualty,
disaster, distress, fatality **9.** adversity
10. affliction, misfortune
11. catastrophe, direfulness,
unhappiness **12.** wretchedness
calathiform ... **9.** cup-shaped
calcarea ... **5.** coral **7.** sponges
calceiform ... **10.** orchidlike **13.** clipper-
shaped
calcitrant ... **8.** stubborn **12.** recalcitrant
calcitrate ... **4.** boot, kick **6.** oppose
calculate ... **3.** aim **4.** deem, rate, tell
5. allow, count, frame, judge, score,
tally, think **6.** cipher, deduce, figure,
gather, number, reckon **7.** average,
compute, suppose **8.** conclude, estimate
9. determine, enumerate
calculated ... **7.** advised, studied,
weighed **8.** measured **10.** considered,
deliberate **11.** intentional
12. contemplated
calculating ... **8.** plotting, scheming
9. computing, designing, judicious
10. estimating, numerative, reflecting,
thoughtful **11.** circumspect, considerate

14. discriminative
calculator . . . **5.** table **6.** abacus **7.** suan pan (swan pan, Chin) **8.** computer **9.** estimator, tabulator **10.** parimutuel **11.** Comptometer, totalizator
caldron, cauldron . . . **3.** pot, red (color), vat **6.** boiler, kettle, mortar, retort **7.** alembic **8.** crucible
Caleb (pert to) . . .
daughter . . **7.** Achsaph
literally . . **3.** dog
son . . **3.** Hur, Iru
spy of . . **6.** Canaan
calèche . . . **7.** vehicle (Quebec)
Caledonia (anc) . . . **8.** Scotland
Caledonia bird . . . **4.** kagu
Caledonian . . . **5.** brown **6.** Scotch **8.** Scotsman, Scottish
calefacient . . . **4.** warm **6.** remedy **7.** heating **11.** calefactory
calendar . . . **4.** list, Ordo **5.** index, slate **6.** docket, line-up, record **7.** almanac, calends (kalends), program **8.** register, schedule **9.** catalogue, ephemeris **10.** chronology, prospectus
calendar (type) . . . **5.** Roman, Swiss **6.** Jewish, Julian **7.** Chinese **9.** Cotsworth, Gregorian, perpetual **13.** International (fixed)
calenture . . . **4.** glow **5.** ardor, fever **7.** passion, pyrexia **9.** febrility, sunstroke
calepin . . . **4.** book (ref) **7.** lexicon **10.** dictionary
calf . . . **3.** leg (part) **4.** dolt, fool, skin **6.** bovine, island, weaner **7.** iceberg, leather **9.** youngling
calf (pert to) . . .
flesh . . **4.** veal
hide . . **3.** kip
leg (part) . . **5.** sural
motherless . . **5.** dogie **8.** maverick
sweetbread . . **9.** ris de veau
time . . **5.** youth
Caliban (pert to) . . .
character . . **5.** brute, slave (The Tempest)
deity . . **7.** Setebos
mother . . **7.** Sycorax (witch)
caliber, calibre . . . **4.** bore **7.** ability
calico . . . **4.** dame **5.** cloth **6.** salloo **8.** goldfish **12.** multicolored
calico (pert to) . . .
bird . . **9.** turnstone
bush . . **6.** laurel
horse, pony . . **5.** pinto **7.** piebald
printing . . **4.** teer **7.** topical
calid . . . **3.** hot **4.** mild, warm **6.** genial **7.** burning, thermal
California . . .
bay . . **8.** Monterey
capital . . **10.** Sacramento
city . . **6.** Fresno **7.** Oakland **8.** San Diego, Stockton **9.** Long Beach **10.** Los Angeles **12.** San Francisco, Santa Barbara
desert . . **6.** Mojave **8.** Colorado
discoverer . . **6.** Cortez (1535)
fault . . **10.** San Andreas
flower . . **5.** poppy
history . . **8.** Gold Rush (1848), Missions **11.** Sutter's Mill
lake . . **5.** Tahoe **8.** Elsinore **9.** Salton Sea

lowest point . . **11.** Death Valley
missionary . . **5.** Serra
mountain . . **6.** Lassen, Shasta **7.** Whitney
river . . **4.** Kern **7.** Feather, Russian **10.** Sacramento
pageant . . **10.** Rose Parade **17.** Tournament of Roses
State admission . . **11.** thirty-first
State motto . . **6.** Eureka
State nickname . . **6.** Golden
State tree . . **7.** redwood
wine region . . **4.** Napa
caliph, calif . . . **3.** Ali (4th) **4.** Imam (Imaum), Omar **6.** Othman **7.** Abu Bekr **8.** Islamite
Caliph Ali's descendants . . . **5.** Alids (Alides)
caliphate . . . **7.** Omniads, Shiites (Sectaries) **8.** Idrisids **9.** Fatimites
calk, caulk . . . **4.** copy, plug, stop **5.** close, sleep (Naut sl) **6.** calque, catnap, chinse, plug up, stop up **7.** occlude
call . . . **3.** bid, cry, dub, hip, nod **4.** ahoy, beck, dial, name, plea, ring, soho, sook (hog), taps, term, yell **5.** alarm, basis, cause, clepe, rally, rouse, shout, style, visit, waken **6.** appeal, beckon, demand, ground, invoke, motive, muster, option, reason, sennet, signal, slogan, summon **7.** appoint, bidding, collect, convoke, fanfare, summons, trumpet **8.** assemble, nominate, occasion, reveille **9.** battle cry, challenge, designate, induction, telephone, watchword **10.** denominate, invitation **11.** recruitment, requisition **12.** conscription **13.** justification
call (pert to) . . .
attention . . **6.** direct, remind **8.** point out
back . . **6.** recall, recant, repeal, revive, revoke **7.** retract **8.** remember **9.** recollect
down . . **6.** invoke **7.** bawl out, reprove, tell off
evil upon . . **8.** execrate
forth . . **5.** evoke, rouse **6.** elicit, excite, induce, prompt, summon
names . . **4.** cite **5.** abuse, curse **6.** insult, revile, vilify **8.** besmirch **10.** vituperate
together . . **6.** muster, summon **7.** convoke
to mind . . **4.** cite **8.** remember **9.** visualize
callant, callan . . . **3.** boy, lad **4.** chap **5.** youth **6.** fellow, garcon, laddie **8.** customer, muchacho **11.** hobbledehoy
calle . . . **6.** street
called . . . **5.** named **6.** dubbed, y-clept, yermed **7.** y-cleped
calling . . . **3.** art, nod **4.** beck, lure, name, work **5.** trade **6.** career, metier, naming, outcry **7.** bidding, mission, pursuit, styling, summons **8.** biddance, business, labeling (labelling), practice, vocation **9.** condition, evocation **10.** employment, invitation, occupation, profession **13.** circumstances
calling crab . . . **7.** fiddler
calling hare . . . **4.** pika
Calliope . . . **4.** Muse (poet) **5.** organ

8. asteroid
Calliope's son . . . **7.** Orpheus
callous, calloused . . . **4.** horn, sear
5. horny, inure **6.** harden, seared
8. hardened **9.** heartless, indurated,
unfeeling **10.** impervious
11. hardhearted **12.** thick-skinned
14. pachydermatous
callow . . . **5.** crude, green **6.** tender,
unripe, vernal **7.** budding **8.** immature,
unformed **9.** unfledged **10.** unseasoned
11. undeveloped **15.** unsophisticated
callus . . . **6.** tyloma
calm . . . **3.** lay **4.** cool, dill, fair, lull, mild
5. allay, balmy, peace, quiet, sober,
still **6.** becalm, hushed, pacify, placid,
sedate, serene, smooth, soothe, steady
7. appease, compose, halcyon, orderly,
pacific, placate, restful, unmoved
8. peaceful, tranquil **9.** quiescent,
unruffled **10.** phlegmatic **11.** tranquilize,
undisturbed **13.** dispassionate,
imperturbable
calmant, calmative . . . **7.** anodyne,
soother **8.** lenitive, pacifier, sedative,
soothing **10.** depressant, palliative
11. alleviative **12.** tranquilizer
calmato (Mus) . . . **4.** calm **8.** tranquil
calmness . . . **4.** calm, lull **5.** peace, poise,
quiet **6.** repose **8.** quietude, serenity
9. composure, placidity **10.** equanimity,
quiescence **11.** restfulness, self-control
calor . . . **4.** heat **5.** therm **7.** thermal
calorifics . . . **4.** heat **7.** heating
calumet . . . **9.** peace pipe
calumniate . . . **4.** slur **5.** belie, libel
6. accuse, malign, revile **7.** asperse,
slander, traduce **9.** blaspheme
calumnious . . . **7.** abusive **8.** derisive,
insolent, libelous **9.** insulting
10. defamatory, derogatory, slanderous
11. maledictory, opprobrious
calumny . . . **5.** abuse **7.** lampoon, slander
9. contumely **10.** detraction, scurrility
11. malediction **12.** vilification
calvary . . . **8.** crucifix
Calvary (Bib) . . . **8.** Damascus, Golgotha
9. Jerusalem
Calvinism (pert to) . . .
author . . **6.** Calvin
doctrine . . **5.** Grace **9.** Atonement,
Depravity (total) **12.** Perseverance (of
Saints) **14.** Predestination
site . . **6.** Geneva
Calvinistic Methodist . . . **5.** Welsh
10. Whitefield **14.** Lady Huntingdon
Calypso . . . **6.** Ogygia (home) **8.** Cytherea,
sea nymph (The Odyssey)
calyx . . . **3.** cup **4.** husk **5.** galea, sepal
6. corona **7.** corolla **8.** epicalyx, perianth
camarada . . . **7.** comrade, partner
9. companion
camaraderie . . . **8.** good will
11. familiarity **14.** good-fellowship
camarilla . . . **5.** cabal **6.** clique **7.** council
camata . . . **6.** acorns **8.** oak fruit
cambist . . . **6.** banker, broker **9.** financier
11. moneylender **12.** money-changer
Cambodia . . .
capital . . **6.** Angkor **8.** Pnom-Penh
king . . **8.** Sihanouk

language . . **5.** Khmer **9.** Cambodian
name, former . . **9.** Kampuchea
religion . . **8.** Buddhism
Cambria . . . **5.** Wales
Cambridge University (pert to) . . .
English examination . . **6.** tripos
English student . . **5.** sizar **6.** optime
(honor)
Massachusetts . . **3.** MIT **7.** Harvard
camel . . . **4.** oont **5.** llama **6.** deloul,
mammal, vicuna **7.** Camelus **8.** Bactrian
(2-humped) **9.** Camelidae, dromedary
camel hair shawl . . . **8.** cashmere
camelopard . . . **7.** giraffe **13.** constellation
Camelot . . . **6.** legend **10.** King Arthur,
palace site, Round Table
cameo . . . **4.** onyx **7.** relievo **8.** anaglyph
camera type . . . **5.** Kodak **7.** Brownie
10. Rollieflex
Cameroon . . .
capital . . **7.** Yaounde (Afr)
native . . **4.** Sara
people . . **3.** Abo **5.** Bantu
river . . **5.** Shari
seaport . . **6.** Douala
Camino Real (Calif) . . . **9.** Royal Road
12. El Camino Real, King's Highway
Camorra (It) . . . **12.** organization (secret)
camouflage . . . **7.** falsify **8.** disguise
9. dissemble **10.** false front
12. misrepresent
camp . . . **4.** clan, tent **5.** abode, etape,
junto, tabor **6.** campoo, clique, laager
7. bivouac, faction **10.** encampment
campaign . . . **5.** serve **7.** crusade
9. operation
camphorated tincture of opium . . .
9. paregoric
campus . . . **4.** quad **5.** field (academic)
can . . . **3.** jar, may, tin **6.** hopper,
vessel **7.** capable **8.** canister, conserve
9. competent **10.** receptacle
can . . . **5.** skill **7.** ability **9.** competent
10. receptacle
can (sl) . . . **3.** jug, tin **4.** boot, bump,
fire, jail, john, kick **6.** bounce, cooler,
toilet **7.** dismiss **9.** discharge **11.** give
the gate
Canaan . . . **9.** Palestine **12.** Promised
Land
Canada . . . see also *Canadian*
capital (Federal) . . **6.** Ottawa
city . . **7.** Toronto **8.** Hamilton, Montreal,
Winnipeg **9.** Vancouver
discoverer . . **9.** John Cabot (1497)
Hudson's Bay Co . . . **8.** fur trade
native . . **6.** French **7.** English
nickname . . **6.** Canuck
park . . **6.** Jasper
peninsula . . **5.** Gaspé
police . . **8.** Mounties **12.** Royal Mounted
(7,000)
river . . **5.** Peace, Slave **6.** Fraser, Nelson,
Ottawa **8.** Gatineau **9.** Athabasca,
Churchill, Mackenzie **10.** St Lawrence
Canadian (pert to) . . .
flour . . **6.** Shorts (milling) **8.** canaille
jay . . **9.** moose bird **10.** whisky jack
lynx . . **5.** pishu
plum . . **6.** cheney
porcupine . . **5.** urson **7.** cawquaw

squaw .. **6.** mahala
canaille ... **3.** mob **4.** ruck **6.** rabble,
ragtag, Shorts **8.** riffraff **10.** roughscuff
canal ... **4.** duct, iter (brain), pipe, tube
5. drain **6.** meatus **7.** acequia, channel
10. waterspout **11.** watercourse
Canal ... **4.** Erie, Kiel, Suez **6.** Panama
13. Sault Ste Marie (Soo)
Canal Zone Lock ... **5.** Gatun
10. Miraflores
canard ... **4.** duck, hoax **5.** rumor
6. humbug **9.** falsehood
canary ... **6.** yellow **8.** song-bird, songster,
weakling
Canary Islands ...
  capital .. **9.** Santa Cruz (Teneriffe)
  city .. **9.** Las Palmas (Grand Canary)
  commune .. **4.** Icod
  owner .. **5.** Spain
cancel ... **4.** blot, dele, kill, omit, undo
5. annul, erase **6.** delete, excise, recall,
repeal, revoke **7.** abolish, destroy,
nullify, rescind, retract **8.** write off
10. invalidate, neutralize, obliterate
11. countermand
cancellation ... **6.** repeal **7.** erasure
8. deletion, write-off **10.** moratorium
12. obliteration
cancer ... **4.** evil **5.** tumor **6.** canker,
growth **7.** sarcoma **8.** neoplasm
9. carcinoma
Cancer ... **4.** crab **7.** mansion (moon)
10. zodiac sign **13.** constellation
cancion ... **4.** song **5.** lyric
Candia ... **5.** Crete (Isl)
candid ... **4.** fair, just, open, pure **5.** frank
6. direct, honest **7.** sincere **9.** guileless,
impartial, ingenuous **10.** impersonal
13. dispassionate **15.** straightforward
candidate ... **6.** seeker **7.** aspirer,
electee, nominee **8.** aspirant, selectee
9. applicant, appointee, postulant
10. solicitant
candidate list ... **4.** leet **5.** slate **6.** roster
Candide (pert to) ...
  hero, title .. **5.** novel
  novel, author .. **8.** Voltaire
  philosophy .. **8.** optimism
candied ... **5.** sweet **7.** honeyed
9. congealed, incrusted, preserved
10. flattering, granulated **12.** crystallized
candied sea holly ... **6.** eryngo (eringo)
candle ... **3.** dip, wax **5.** light, power,
taper **6.** bougie, cierge, tallow, votive
7. paschal **8.** bayberry **9.** chandelle
candlestick (pert to) ...
  Bib .. **6.** lampad
  branched .. **9.** girandole
  ornamental .. **10.** candelabra
  Scot .. **6.** crusie
  spike .. **7.** pricket
  three-branched .. **9.** tricerion
  torch type .. **8.** flambeau
  wall .. **6.** sconce
candlewood ... **6.** flower **8.** ocotillo
candor ... **8.** fairness, openness
9. frankness, sincerity, unreserve
10. directness **11.** artlessness,
unrestraint **13.** outspokenness
candy ... **5.** sweet **6.** penide (pulled),
sweets **7.** sweeten **8.** crystals

9. granulate, sweetmeat **10.** confection
11. crystallize **13.** confectionary
candy (type) ... **4.** mint **5.** fudge, taffy
6. bonbon, nougat, toffee **7.** brittle,
caramel, fondant, panocha, penuche,
praline **8.** licorice, lollipop **9.** chocolate
11. marshmallow
candytuft ... **6.** iberis
cane ... **3.** rod **4.** beat, club, reed, stem,
whip **5.** crook, sorgo, staff, stick, sugar
6. bamboo, rattan **7.** bagasse, bourdon,
sorghum, sucrose **9.** handstaff,
truncheon **12.** swagger stick
canescent ... **5.** hoary, white **7.** grizzly,
silvery, whitish **9.** snow-white
Canfield ... **9.** solitaire
canine ... **3.** cur, dog, fox, pug, pup
4. lobo, mutt, tike **5.** dingo, pooch,
puppy, whelp **6.** animal, coyote
7. Canidae, doggish, laniary, mastiff,
mongrel, reynard **8.** dogtooth, eyetooth
canis ... **3.** dog
Canis Majoris ... **13.** Constellation (with
Dog Star, Sirius)
cannibalism ... **9.** barbarity, endophagy
10. perversion **11.** blood thirst
13. anthropophagy
cannon ... **3.** gun **5.** crash **6.** mortar
7. firearm, robinet **8.** dog of war,
howitzer, ordnance **9.** artillery, collision
cannon (pert to) ...
  ball .. **6.** pellet **7.** missile
  bore .. **6.** breech
  fire .. **7.** barrage
  handle .. **4.** anse
  nautical .. **5.** chase
  part .. **8.** cascabel
  pivot .. **8.** trunnion
  platform .. **10.** terreplein
  plug .. **7.** tampion
  shot .. **5.** grape
  shoulder part .. **7.** rimbase
cannonade ... **4.** boom, peal, roar **5.** blitz,
shell **6.** rumble, strafe **11.** bombardment
canny ... **3.** sly **4.** foxy, wary, wily **6.** artful,
frugal, shrewd, subtle **7.** cunning,
knowing, prudent, thrifty **8.** cautious
9. sagacious
canoe ... **4.** kiak, pahi, proa, waka
5. bongo, bungo, kayak, umiak, waapa
6. corial, dugout, oomiak, pitpan
7. almadia, buckeye (bugeye), coracle,
piragua, pirogue **12.** pambanmanche
canon ... **3.** law **4.** code, list, rule,
type **5.** model, nodus (Mus) **6.** belief,
clergy, decree, ritual **7.** measure,
precept **8.** decision **9.** catalogue,
criterion **10.** regulation **11.** composition
12. constitution
canonical ... **4.** None (hour), Sext
(hour) **5.** Lauds, Prime **6.** Matins
7. creedal **8.** dogmatic, orthodox
9. doctrinal **10.** scriptural **11.** theological
14. ecclesiastical
canonization ... **8.** sainting
10. ordainment, ordination
12. consecration, enshrinement
canopy ... **3.** sky **4.** ceil, cope, dais,
tent **5.** cover, shade, vault **6.** awning,
tester **7.** blanket, marquee, shelter
8. caponier (caponiere), ciborium,

pavilion **9.** baldachin, firmament
canorous ... **5.** clear **8.** sonorous
9. melodious **10.** euphonious
cant ... **3.** tip **4.** lean, list, sing, song,
sway, tack, tilt **5.** angle, argot, chant,
lingo, pitch, slang, slope, whine
6. careen, intone, jargon, patois,
snivel **7.** auction, incline, mummery
8. pretense **9.** hypocrisy **10.** intonation,
sanctimony **17.** sanctimoniousness
cantabank ... **6.** singer (ballad)
cantador ... **6.** singer (folk songs)
cantankerous ... **8.** perverse **9.** malicious
10. contention, ill-natured **12.** cross-
grained
cantata ... **5.** motet **8.** serenata
9. pastorale
canter ... **4.** gait, lope **6.** gallop
(Canterbury) **8.** vagabond
Canterbury ...
archbishop .. **7.** Cranmer, Primate
13. Thomas à Becket (murdered)
capital (Eng) .. **14.** ecclesiastical
famed building .. **9.** Cathedral
gallop .. **5.** aubin **6.** canter
Tales, author .. **7.** Chaucer
canticle ... **3.** lay, ode **4.** hymn, lied,
song **5.** carol, ditty **6.** Te Deum
Canticle of Canticles (Bib) ... **11.** Song
of Songs **13.** Song of Solomon
cantilena ... **6.** legato, melody **8.** graceful
cantina ... **3.** bag **6.** pocket, saloon
7. canteen
cantle ... **4.** nook, part **5.** crown, slice
6. corner, saddle (part) **7.** segment
11. cornerpiece
canto ... **4.** book, song **5.** poems (div
of), tenor, verse **6.** cantus, melody,
poetry **7.** descort
canton ... **3.** Uri (Switz) **6.** county
7. commune, quarter **8.** district, insignia
(Her), mofussil (Ind) **9.** bailiwick,
partition
cantor ... **6.** leader, singer **7.** soloist
8. melodist, vocalist **9.** precentor
cantoria ... **7.** balcony, gallery (choir)
cantrip ... **5.** charm, magic, spell, trick
canty ... **6.** lively **7.** chipper **8.** cheerful
9. sprightly
Canuck ... **8.** Canadian
canvas ... **4.** sail, tent, tuke (tewke)
5. cloth **6.** circus **7.** picture, tentage
8. covering, likeness, pavilion
9. tarpaulin **14.** representation
canvasback ... **4.** duck
canvass ... **4.** poll **5.** study **6.** survey
7. examine, inquiry, solicit **8.** campaign,
consider **10.** scrutinize **11.** electioneer
12. solicitation **13.** questionnaire
canyon, cañon ... **4.** abra (mouth)
5. chasm, dalle (wall), gorge, gulch
6. arroyo, coulee, ravine, violet
7. couloir
canzone, canzonetta ... **4.** poem, song
6. ballad, melody **8.** canzonet, madrigal
caoba ... **8.** mahogany, muskwood
caoutchouc ... **3.** ule **6.** caucho, rubber
cap ... **3.** fez, hat, lid, taj, tam **4.** atef,
coif, hood, kepi **5.** beret, boina, busby,
shako, toque **6.** barret, biggin, bonnet,
calpac, cloche, pileus, turban **7.** biretta

(beretta), calotte, calpack, chapeau
8. Balmoral, havelock **9.** headdress,
headpiece, shtreimal, sou'wester,
zucchetto **10.** cervelière
11. mortarboard, tam-ó-shanter
cap (outer part) ... **3.** lid, tip, top **4.** dome,
fuze, peak, type **5.** cover, crown, excel,
match, spire, trump **6.** summit, top
off **7.** capital (Arch), overlie, patella
8. complete **9.** copestone, detonator
capa ... **5.** cloak **6.** mantle **7.** tobacco
capability ... **5.** power, skill **6.** genius
7. ability, caliber, faculty, potency
8. ableness, adequacy, capacity
10. competence **13.** qualification
capable ... **3.** apt, can, fit **4.** able **5.** adept
6. expert **7.** equal to, skilled **8.** adequate
9. competent, effective, efficient,
qualified **10.** proficient **12.** accomplished
capable of ...
boring .. **10.** zylotomous
carrying .. **9.** portative
flying .. **6.** volant
growing .. **6.** viable
living in harmony .. **10.** compatible
penetration .. **8.** pervious
suffering .. **8.** passible **9.** sensitive
capable of being ...
ascertained .. **12.** determinable
cultivated .. **6.** arable
cut .. **7.** sectile
defended .. **7.** tenable
done .. **10.** effectible
heard .. **7.** audible
prevented .. **9.** avertible
proved .. **8.** testable **12.** demonstrable
regulated .. **12.** controllable
separated .. **9.** divisible
spread .. **10.** infectious **12.** communicable
thrown .. **7.** missile
uttered .. **7.** effable
capacious ... **4.** full, much, wide **5.** ample,
broad, large, roomy **8.** generous,
spacious **9.** expansive, extensive
10. commodious, voluminous
12. considerable **13.** comprehensive
capacitance unit ... **5.** farad
capacity ... **4.** role, room, size **5.** limit,
power, skill, space **6.** extent, spread,
status, talent, volume **7.** caliber,
content, faculty, fitness, measure
8. adequacy, aptitude, function,
position, relation, strength **9.** character
10. capability, efficiency **11.** capacitance
(Elec) **12.** intelligence
13. accommodation
capacity for knowing ... **9.** intellect
cap and bells ... **6.** bauble, comedy
(symbol), motley **7.** costume, marotti
9. headdress
caparison ... **3.** rig **4.** tack **5.** armor, dress,
get-up **6.** livery **7.** harness, housing,
panoply **10.** horsecloth **12.** horse
blanket
cape ... **3.** ras **4.** hood, mino, naze, ness,
spur **5.** amice, cappa, cloak, fichu, orale,
point, sagum, talma **6.** mantle, sontag,
tippet **8.** pelerine (fur) **9.** Inverness
cape (pert to) ...
gooseberry .. **4.** poha
hen .. **4.** skua **6.** petrel

pigeon . . **7.** pintado
polecat . . **5.** zoril
ruby . . **6.** garnet, pyrope
sheep . . **9.** albatross (Naut term)
Cape Cod turkey . . . **7.** codfish (humor)
Cape Dutch . . . **9.** Afrikaans (language)
Cape of Good Hope discoverer . . .
  4. Diaz (1488)
Capek play . . . **3.** RUR
caper . . . **3.** tea **4.** dido, leap, romp,
  skip **5.** antic, berry, dance, frisk,
  prank **6.** cavort, frolic, gambol, prance
  8. capriole, marigold **9.** privateer (Hist)
capercaille . . . **6.** grouse **13.** cock of the
  wood
caper herb family . . . **6.** Cleome
  8. Capparis **9.** Polanisia
  10. clammyweed **13.** Capparidaceae
capias . . . **4.** writ **6.** caveat **7.** process,
  warrant **8.** mandamus **9.** nisi prius
capillary . . . **4.** fine, tube **6.** minute,
  vessel **7.** slender **8.** hairlike, trichoid
capilliform . . . **7.** thready **8.** hairlike
capillus . . . **4.** hair
capistrate . . . **6.** cowled, hooded
capital . . . **3.** top **4.** city, main, rare,
  seat, type **5.** chief, crest, crown, funds,
  major, means, prime, vital **6.** assets,
  letter, ruling, supply **7.** leading, primary,
  serious, weighty **8.** cardinal, dominant,
  foremost, splendid **9.** excellent,
  financial, important, paramount,
  principal, prominent **10.** commanding,
  preeminent, shoestring
capitalism . . . **8.** politics **10.** government
  11. bourgeoisie **14.** free enterprise
capitalist . . . **5.** baron **6.** tycoon **7.** rich
  man **8.** investor **9.** bourgeois, financier,
  plutocrat
capital letter . . . **6.** uncial **9.** majuscule
capital punishment . . . **5.** noose
  7. gallows, hanging **8.** shooting,
  the chair **9.** beheading, execution,
  fusillade **10.** guillotine **12.** decapitation
  13. electrocution
capitano . . . **3.** don **4.** capo **5.** chief
  7. captain, headman
capitate . . . **7.** globose **8.** enlarged,
  headlike
Capitol (pert to) . . .
Federal . . **10.** Washington (DC)
State . . **10.** Statehouse
capitulate . . . **4.** cede, fall **9.** surrender
capitulation . . . **6.** resumé, review, treaty
  7. recount, summary **9.** agreement,
  reckoning, rehearsal, statement,
  summation, surrender **10.** compendium
  11. enumeration, stipulation
  14. relinquishment
capon . . . **3.** hen **4.** cock, fowl **6.** pullet,
  rabbit (castrated) **7.** chicken, poulard,
  poultry, rooster
caporal . . . **4.** boss **7.** foreman, tobacco
  8. overseer
capote . . . **4.** hood **5.** cloak **6.** bonnet,
  mantle, piquet **8.** overcoat
capped . . . **7.** crested, pileata, pileate
Capri . . .
beverage . . **4.** wine (white)
color . . **4.** blue **9.** blue-green
island site . . **11.** Bay of Naples

ruins (famed) . . **7.** palaces (Tiberius)
  8. grottoes **10.** Blue Grotto
caprice . . . **3.** fad, toy **4.** kink, mood,
  whim **5.** fancy, freak, humor, prank,
  quirk **6.** vagary **7.** whimsey (whimsy)
  8. crotchet, escapade, flimflam
capricious . . . **5.** moody **6.** fickle, fitful
  7. erratic, wayward **8.** fanciful, freakish,
  humorous, notional, sporadic, unsteady
  9. arbitrary, crotchety, eccentric,
  fantastic, whimsical **10.** inconstant
  12. inconsistent **13.** temperamental
Capricorn . . . **4.** goat **7.** mansion (of
  Saturn) **10.** zodiac sign **13.** constellation
capriole . . . **4.** leap **5.** caper **6.** cavort,
  curvet, gambol
capsicum . . . **4.** herb **5.** chili **6.** pepper
capsize . . . **5.** spill, upset **7.** subvert, tip
  over **8.** overturn **9.** overthrow **10.** turn
  turtle
capsule . . . **3.** sac **4.** pill **5.** ascus, brief,
  theca, wafer **6.** précis, sheath **7.** enclose,
  epitome **8.** abstract, envelope, pericarp,
  seedcase, synopsis **10.** compendium
capsulize . . . **5.** brief **7.** abridge, outline
  8. abstract, condense **9.** epitomize,
  summarize
captain . . . **4.** skip **5.** chief, ruler
  6. leader, master, patron, police
  7. headman, officer, skipper **8.** overlord
  9. commander **10.** shipmaster
Captain Kidd . . . **6.** pirate
Captains Courageous (pert to) . . .
author . . **7.** Kipling
setting . . **9.** Grand Bank (Newfoundland)
tale of . . **7.** romance
caption . . . **5.** title **6.** legend, rubric
  7. capture, seizure **8.** headline, subtitle
captious . . . **6.** severe **7.** carping, cynical,
  peevish **8.** caviling, critical **9.** bickering,
  paltering, quibbling **12.** equivocatory,
  faultfinding **13.** hypercritical
captivate . . . **4.** lure, vamp **5.** charm,
  snare **6.** allure, enamor, ravish, seduce
  7. attract, becharm, beguile, bewitch,
  capture, delight, enchant **8.** enthrall
  9. enrapture, fascinate, infatuate,
  transport
captive . . . **4.** bond, serf **5.** helot
  6. détenu, thrall, unfree, vassal
  7. hostage **8.** conquest, enslaved,
  prisoner **10.** subjugated
captivity . . . **6.** duress **7.** bondage,
  durance, serfdom, slavery **9.** detention,
  servitude, thralldom **10.** internment,
  subjection **11.** confinement,
  impoundment **12.** imprisonment
  13. incarceration
captor . . . **5.** taker **7.** catcher **8.** capturer
capture . . . **3.** beg, nab, net, win **4.** gain,
  haul, take **5.** catch, pinch, raven, snare
  6. arrest, collar **7.** caption, seizure
  9. apprehend, detention
  12. apprehension
capuche (Eccl) . . . **4.** cowl, hood
capuchin . . . **3.** sai **5.** Cebus **6.** monkey,
  pigeon
caput . . . **3.** cap, top **4.** head **5.** crest,
  crown **7.** chapter, section **9.** paragraph
car . . . **4.** auto, cart, jeep, tram **5.** coupe,
  motor, sedan, truck, wagon **6.** hot rod,

jalopy, wheels (sl) **7.** caboose, chariot, clunker (sl), compact, flivver, machine, Pullman, vehicle **8.** carriage **9.** dune buggy, hatchback **10.** automobile, subcompact
carabao . . . **5.** mango **7.** buffalo
carabinieri . . . **9.** policeman **10.** carabineer
caracal . . . **3.** fur **4.** lynx, pelt
caracara . . . **4.** hawk **8.** carancha
caracole . . . **5.** caper (manège) **9.** staircase
caract . . . **5.** charm **6.** symbol (magic)
carafe . . . **6.** bottle
carafon . . . **8.** decanter
carapace . . . **5.** plate, shell (turtle) **6.** chitin, lorica, shield **7.** carapax
caravan . . . **3.** van **5.** wagon **6.** cafila (camel) **9.** cavalcade, motorcade **10.** expedition, procession
caravansary . . . **3.** inn **4.** khan (chan) **5.** hotel, serai **6.** hostel, imaret, posado **8.** hostelry **9.** resthouse, roadhouse
carbine . . . **5.** rifle **6.** musket **7.** escopet
carbohydrate . . . **5.** sugar **6.** starch **7.** dextrin, glucose, lactose, maltose, sucrose **8.** dextrose, glycogen, nutrient **9.** cellulose **10.** saccharide, saccharose
carbon . . . **4.** coke, copy, fuel, lead, soot **7.** diamond, residue **8.** graphite
carbonate . . . **3.** ore **5.** trona **6.** aerate, natron **9.** carbonize **11.** chemicalize
carbon dioxide . . . **3.** gas **6.** dry ice **7.** seeding (cloud) **11.** refrigerant
Carborundum . . . **5.** emery **8.** abrasive **14.** silicon carbide
carcass . . . **4.** body **5.** bones, kreng (whale) **6.** corpse **7.** cadaver, remains **8.** skeleton
carcer . . . **5.** stall (Rom circus) **6.** prison
card . . . **3.** map, tum **4.** comb, menu, post, rove **6.** docket, domino, oddity, postal, record, ticket **7.** calling, program **8.** calendar, schedule **9.** character **13.** communication
card game . . . **3.** gin, hoc, loo, pan **4.** bank, faro, keno, skat **5.** cinch, comet, monte, pitch, poker, rummy, stuss, tarot, whist **6.** bridge, casino, écarté, hearts, piquet, rounce **7.** auction, bezique, canasta, cassino, cayenne **8.** baccarat, contract, cribbage, pinochle **9.** solitaire **10.** panguingui
card game term . . . **3.** ace **4.** meld, pass, pone, slam, trey, vole **5.** joker, pedro, tarot **6.** cathop, misère, tenace, tricon **7.** declare **9.** mistigris
cardinal . . . **3.** red **4.** bird, fish, main **5.** chief **6.** bishop, deacon, number, priest, ruling **8.** crowning, dominant, foremost **9.** paramount, principal **10.** preeminent
cardinal (pert to) . . .
  astrology . . **5.** nadir **6.** zenith
  astronomy . . **10.** solstitial **11.** equinoctial
  biology . . **7.** maximum, minimum, optimum
  compass point . . **4.** east, west **5.** north, south
  number . . **7.** primary (one, two, three)
  office . . **6.** datary **7.** dataria
  virtues . . **7.** justice **8.** prudence **9.** fortitude **10.** temperance

virtues (Theol) . . **4.** hope **5.** faith **7.** charity
cardinal's hat . . . **3.** red **4.** rank **6.** office
care . . . **4.** duty, fret, heed, reck, task, tend, wish **5.** aegis, worry **6.** desire, regard **7.** anxiety, caution, cherish, concern, custody, keeping **9.** attention, patronage **10.** affliction, protection, solicitude **11.** carefulness, heedfulness, supervision, thriftiness **12.** jurisdiction **13.** consideration
careen . . . **3.** tip **4.** cant, heel, keel, lean, list, tilt **5.** slant, slope
career . . . **3.** set **4.** flow, flux, line, work **6.** course, stream **7.** calling, mission, passage, pursuit **8.** business, practice, progress, vocation **10.** occupation, profession
care for . . . **4.** help, like, love, mind, reck, tend **5.** fancy, guard, nurse, prize, watch **6.** attend, dote on, foster, mother, relish, wait on **7.** nurture **10.** appreciate
carefree . . . **5.** happy **6.** jaunty **8.** debonair **10.** insouciant **12.** lighthearted
careful . . . **4.** wary **5.** canny, chary, exact **7.** anxious, guarded, heedful, mindful, prudent, thrifty **8.** cautious, discreet, gingerly, vigilant **9.** advertent, attentive **10.** meticulous, scrupulous, solicitous, thoughtful **11.** circumspect, considerate, painstaking, punctilious
careless . . . **3.** lax **5.** loose **6.** rakish, remiss, sloppy **8.** heedless, mindless, reckless, slipshod, slovenly **9.** impulsive, negligent, unheeding, unmindful **10.** nonchalant, regardless, unthinking **11.** inadvertent, thoughtless, unconcerned **13.** inconsiderate
carelessness . . . **8.** bungling, disorder **9.** disregard, unconcern **10.** blundering, negligence **11.** nonchalance **12.** heedlessness, indifference, recklessness **13.** impulsiveness **15.** inconsideration, thoughtlessness
caress . . . **3.** pat, pet **4.** bill, kiss **5.** touch **6.** coddle, cosset, dandle, fondle, pamper, stroke **10.** endearment
caressing . . . **7.** hugging, kissing **8.** fondling **9.** endearing
cargo . . . **4.** load **5.** goods **6.** burden, charge, lading **7.** carload, freight **8.** boatload, shipload **9.** truckload
cargo (pert to) . . .
  afloat . . **7.** flotsam
  cast overboard . . **6.** jetsam
  loader, unloader . . **9.** stevedore
Carib . . . **6.** Indian
caribou . . . **4.** deer **8.** reindeer
caricature . . . **5.** comic **6.** overdo, parody **7.** cartoon, lampoon, picture **8.** satirize, travesty **9.** burlesque **10.** caricatura, distortion **12.** exaggeration
caricaturist . . . **6.** artist **8.** humorist, parodist **10.** burlesquer
caries . . . **5.** decay (Dent) **10.** ulceration
carillon . . . **4.** lyra **5.** bells (fixed) **6.** chimes **12.** glockenspiel
cark . . . **3.** vex **4.** care, heed, load **5.** pains, worry **6.** burden, charge, harass **7.** trouble **8.** distress

carl, carlot ... **4.** boor **5.** churl **6.** rustic
7. peasant, villein **8.** bondsman
10. husbandman, pinchpenny
Carmelite ... **3.** nun **4.** monk **5.** friar
8. White Nun **10.** White Friar
carmen ... **4.** poem, song **11.** incantation
Carmen ... **5.** gypsy, opera (1875)
7. heroine, romance
carmine ... **3.** red **5.** color, stain
7. crimson, scarlet
carnage ... **8.** butchery, massacre
9. bloodshed, slaughter **10.** decimation
carnal ... **4.** lewd **6.** bodily, fleshy
7. earthly, mundane, sensual, worldly
9. corporeal **11.** unspiritual
12. bloodthirsty
carnation ... **3.** red **4.** pink, self **7.** bizarre,
picotee **8.** Dianthus
carnelian ... **4.** sard **9.** copper red
10. chalcedony
carnival ... **4.** fair, show **6.** circus
7. revelry **8.** feasting, festival
9. amusement, Mardi Gras
11. merrymaking **12.** masquerading
carnivore ... **3.** cat, dog **4.** bear, lion,
puma, seal **5.** civet, coati, genet, hyena,
otter, panda, ratel, sable, tiger, ursus
6. badger, mammal, marten, weasel
7. meerkat, raccoon **8.** mongoose
9. ichneumon **10.** cacomistle
carnivorous ... **10.** meat-eating,
predaceous **11.** omophageous
carol ... **3.** lay **4.** lied, lilt, noel, sing,
song **5.** dance (anc) **6.** ballad, warble
7. rejoice
Caroline Islands (coral) ... **3.** Yap
5. Parao **6.** Ponape
carom ... **4.** bump **6.** bounce, cannon,
strike **8.** ricochet
carousal ... **4.** lark, orgy, romp **5.** binge,
feast, fling, revel, spree **6.** frolic
7. banquet, carouse, revelry, wassail
carouse ... **4.** birl **5.** bouse, drink, spree,
toast **9.** dissipate
carpet ... **3.** mat, rug **4.** Agra, Kali,
Kuba **5.** Herat (Herati), namda,
tapis **6.** nammad, Wilton **7.** drugget
8. Brussels, flooring, moquette
9. Axminster, broadloom
11. Baluchistan
carpetbagger ... **8.** swindler **10.** politician
carriage ... **3.** air **4.** mien, pose **7.** bearing,
posture **8.** attitude, demeanor, presence
10. deportment
carriage (pert to) ...
English .. **6.** waggon **7.** growler
8. dormeuse, stanhope
French .. **6.** fiacre **7.** caliche, voiture
general .. **3.** bus, cab, car, gig, rig,
van **4.** baby, hack, pram, shay, trap
5. buggy, coach, wagon **6.** calssh,
chaise, cisium, dennet, go-cart, hansom,
landau, surrey, tandem **7.** cariole,
chariot, omnibus, phaeton, tallyho,
vehicle **8.** carryall, clarence, dearborn,
rockaway, victoria **9.** kittereen, landaulet
10. conveyance, shandrydan
12. perambulator
history .. **7.** tumbrel, vis-à-vis, whiskey
8. curricle
Indian .. **4.** okka **5.** tonga **6.** gharry

7. hackery
Italian .. **7.** vettura
one-horse .. **3.** gig **4.** shay **5.** sulky
Orient .. **4.** sado **10.** jinrikisha
Philippines .. **9.** carromata
Russia .. **5.** araba **6.** troika **7.** droshky
9. tarantass
carried ... **5.** borne, giddy, toted
6. carted, lugged **8.** conveyed, ravished
11. transported
carrier ... **3.** boy **4.** mail, mule, rail,
ship, wave **5.** crate **6.** bearer,
coolie, pigeon, porter, redcap, runner,
vessel **7.** courier, drayman, express
8. cargador, conveyor, teamster
9. messenger, stevedore
carrier (pert to) ...
disease .. **3.** fly, rat **7.** typhoid
8. mosquito
Indian .. **5.** Tinne (Brit)
staff .. **5.** macer
carrion ... **4.** vile **6.** corpse, rotten
7. carcass, corrupt **9.** loathsome
carrion (pert to) ...
bug .. **6.** beetle
buzzard .. **4.** hawk **7.** vulture **8.** caracara
flower .. **5.** morel
fungus .. **9.** stinkhorn
carrot ... **5.** drias (deadly) **6.** Daucus (Old
World) **9.** Ammiaceae **10.** nivernaise
(glazed), umbellifer
carrousel ... **9.** whirligig **10.** roundabout,
tournament **12.** merry-go-round
carry ... **3.** lug **4.** bear, cart, hold, take,
tote, wart **5.** ferry **6.** convey **7.** conduct,
publish **8.** transfer, transmit **9.** transport
carry away, off ... **3.** win **6.** abduct,
eloign, enamor, remove **7.** succeed
9. fascinate **10.** accomplish
carry on ... **4.** rage, wage **6.** endure,
frolic, manage **7.** conduct, operate
8. continue **9.** misbehave, persevere
carry out, through ... **2.** do **5.** apply
6. ravish **7.** execute, perform, sustain
8. complete, continue, transact
10. accomplish
cart ... **4.** dray, wain **5.** carry, sulky,
wagon **6.** convey, reckla, telega
7. morfrey (morphrey), tumbrel (anc),
vehicle (2-wheeled)
carta, Charta ... **4.** deed **5.** Magna (Eng)
7. charter **9.** parchment
cartage ... **7.** drayage, portage **8.** carriage,
teamster, truckage **10.** expressage
14. transportation
carte ... **3.** map **4.** card, list, menu
5. chart **7.** diagram **10.** bill of fare
cartel ... **4.** bloc (Polit), defy, pact,
pool **5.** paper, truce, trust **6.** letter
7. compact, entente **8.** covenant
9. agreement, challenge, syndicate
10. convention **11.** arrangement
Carthage ... see also *Carthaginian*
capital .. **13.** Vandal Kingdom
destroyer .. **6.** Romans
queen .. **4.** Dido
rebuilt by .. **8.** Augustus
Carthaginian (pert to) ...
apple .. **11.** pomegranate
foe .. **4.** Cato
general .. **6.** Xerxes **8.** Hannibal

god.. **6.** Moloch **8.** Melkarth
language.. **5.** Punic
Lion.. **8.** Hannibal
magistrate.. **7.** suffete
name (later).. **15.** Justinianopolis
wars (three).. **5.** Punic
Carthusian Order (pert to)...
　founder.. **7.** St Bruno
　monastery.. **7.** Certosa (It, 1396)
　site.. **8.** Grenoble (Fr)
cartilage... **4.** bone (ossified) **6.** tissue
　7. gristle
cartload... **6.** fother
cartograph... **3.** map **4.** plat **5.** chart
cartoon... **6.** design, sketch **7.** pattern,
　picture **10.** caricature
cartoonist... **4.** Arno, Capp, Ding, Nast
　6. Disney
cartouche... **5.** shell **6.** corbel, design,
　shield (Her), tablet **7.** console
　9. cartridge **10.** cantilever (Arch)
cartwheel... **4.** coin **6.** dollar **8.** somerset
　10. handspring, somersault
carve... **3.** cut, hew **4.** form, make
　5. chase, grave, sever, shape **6.** chisel,
　cleave, furrow, incise **7.** engrave,
　fashion **9.** apportion, fabricate,
　sculpture
carving... **5.** cameo **8.** diaglyph, intaglio
　9. anaglyphy, embossing, sculpture
　11. anaglyptics
caryatid... **6.** column, figure (fem)
　8. pilaster **11.** priestesses (temple)
casa... **5.** adobe, cabin, house **8.** building
cascade... **4.** fall, linn **5.** Falls, Sault
　7. Niagara **8.** cataract **9.** waterfall
case... **3.** box **4.** etui, file **5.** cover,
　crate, crush (sl), event, folio **6.** carton,
　coffer, pillow, sheath, victim **7.** attaché,
　cabinet, example, holster, lawsuit
　8. argument, covering, cupboard,
　instance **9.** condition, portfolio
　10. receptacle **12.** circumstance
case (in any)... **3.** yet **4.** even
　6. anyhow, anyway **7.** anywise,
　however **8.** possibly, provided
　10. regardless **15.** notwithstanding
case (pert to)...
　arrow.. **6.** quiver
　book.. **5.** forel
　bottle (liquor).. **8.** cellaret
　cigar.. **7.** humidor
　conscience (Sci).. **9.** casuistry
　grammar.. **6.** dative **8.** ablative, genitive,
　vocative **10.** nominative
　history (disease).. **6.** record **9.** anamnesis
　image (Bib).. **5.** ephod
　jewel, relics.. **3.** tye **4.** apse
　spore.. **5.** ascus
　surgeon's.. **7.** trousse
cash... **4.** coin, dust (gold) **5.** darby,
　funds, money **6.** silver, specie **7.** capital,
　coinage, mintage **8.** currency
　9. spondulix
cashmere... **4.** goat, wool **5.** shawl
　6. fabric
casino... **6.** tavern **7.** cabaret, cassino
　(game) **8.** ballroom, gambling
　9. roadhouse **11.** summerhouse
cask... **3.** tun **4.** butt, case, drum, pipe
　5. terce **6.** bareca, barrel, casket, firkin,

tierce **8.** puncheon **9.** kilderkin
cask (pert to)...
　amt when not filled.. **6.** ullage
　bulge.. **5.** bilge
　oil.. **4.** rier
　part.. **3.** lag **4.** hoop **5.** stave
　rim.. **5.** chime (chimb)
　support.. **8.** stillage
casket... **3.** box, pyx, tye (jewel)
　4. cist, kist, tomb **5.** chest **8.** cassette
　11. sarcophagus
casserole... **4.** dish, mold **5.** brown
　(color) **6.** vessel **8.** saucepan
cassine... **4.** game (card)
cast... **3.** hue **4.** form, hurl, kind,
　look, mold, role, shed, tone, toss,
　type **5.** eject, fling, heave, model,
　pitch, sling, throw **6.** glance, matrix,
　squint, troupe **7.** pattern **8.** template
　9. facsimile **10.** impression, strabismus
　16. dramatis personae
cast (pert to)...
　aside.. **4.** jilt, junk, shed **5.** scrap **6.** reject
　7. discard
　away.. **5.** eject, wreck **6.** unmoor
　9. shipwreck
　blame.. **6.** accuse **7.** censure **8.** reproach
　9. reprehend
　off.. **4.** doff, knit, molt, shed **5.** untie
　6. unmoor **7.** discard **9.** eliminate
castaway... **6.** pariah **7.** outcast
　8. derelict **9.** reprobate
caste... **4.** race, rank **5.** breed, class,
　stock **6.** status **7.** lineage, society
　8. standing
caste (Ind)... **3.** Dom, Meo **4.** Ahir, Jati,
　Koli, Magi, Mali, Pasi, Teli **5.** Gaddi,
　Sudra, Varna **6.** banian, pariah, Vaisya
　7. Brahman **9.** Kshatriya
caster, castor... **4.** vial **5.** cruet, horse
　(old), wheel **6.** roller, vessel (condiment)
castigate... **5.** emend **6.** punish, revise,
　strafe **7.** chasten, correct, reprove
　8. chastise, penalize **9.** criticize
　10. discipline
Castile... **4.** soap **7.** kingdom
Castilian... **7.** Iberian, Spanish
castle... **4.** fort, keep, rook (chess)
　5. house, tower, villa **6.** donjon
　7. chateau, citadel **8.** fortress
　10. stronghold **13.** fortification
Castor (pert to)...
　brother (twin).. **6.** Pollux
　constellation.. **6.** Gemini
　mother.. **4.** Leda
　stars.. **6.** Castor, Pollux
castrate... **4.** geld, spay **5.** alter, prune
　10. emasculate
castrated (pert to)...
　bull.. **5.** steer
　cat.. **3.** gib
　horse.. **7.** gelding
　man.. **6.** eunoch
　rooster.. **5.** capon
casual... **5.** stray **6.** chance, random
　9. offhanded **10.** contingent, fortuitous,
　incidental, occasional, unforeseen
　11. indifferent **14.** unpremeditated
casual observation... **6.** remark
casualty... **6.** chance, hazard, injury,
　mishap **7.** payment, tragedy **8.** accident,

calamity, disaster, fatality **9.** mischance
10. misfortune **11.** contingency,
contretemps **12.** misadventure
casus (pert to) . . .
   act of God . . **14.** casus fortuitus
   common law . . **12.** casus omissus
   conscience . . **17.** casus conscientiae
   Latin . . **4.** case **5.** event **8.** occasion
   treaty . . **13.** casus foederis
   war . . **10.** casus belli
cat . . . **3.** gib **4.** balu, eyra, lynx, pard,
   puma **5.** alley, civet, Felid, Felis,
   genet, hyena, manul, ounce, tabby,
   tiger **6.** caffre, cougar, feline, jaguar,
   margay, ocelot, pajero, rasset, serval
   7. cheetah, dasyure, leopard, panther,
   wildcat **9.** catamount, grimalkin
cat (pert to) . . .
   cartoon . . **5.** Felix **8.** Krazy Kat
   fear of . . **12.** ailurophobia
   fictional . . **8.** Cheshire **9.** Mehitabel
   fish . . **4.** pout, raad **6.** hassar, tandan
   7. eelpout
   game . . **6.** tipcat
   gut . . **5.** tharm **6.** string (violin)
   slang . . **6.** hepcat
   term . . **3.** tom **5.** kitty, pussy, tabby
   6. feline, kitten, mouser **9.** grimalkin
   wild . . **4.** lion, lynx, puma **5.** tiger
   6. bobcat, cougar, jaguar, ocelot, tiglon
   7. cheetah, leopard, panther, wildcat
cat (breed) . . . **3.** Rex **4.** Manx **5.** korat
   6. Angora, Birman, Bombay **7.** Burmese,
   Maltese, Persian, Siamese, Turkish
   (Van) **8.** Egyptian (Mau) **9.** shorthair
   10. Abyssinian
cataclysm . . . **4.** ruin **6.** deluge **7.** debacle
   8. calamity, disaster, The Flood,
   upheaval **10.** convulsion, inundation,
   revolution **11.** catastrophe
catacomb . . . **4.** tomb **5.** crypt, vault
   6. grotto, locule **8.** cemetery
   (underground) **9.** Appian Way
catalepsy . . . **6.** trance **8.** hypnosis
   9. cataplexy **10.** thanatosis
catalogue . . . **4.** book, file, list **5.** index,
   tally **6.** codify, digest, record
   8. calendar, classify, pamphlet, register,
   schedule, tabulate **11.** enumeration
catamaran . . . **4.** boat, raft **5.** balsa, float
   6. vessel **7.** jangada
catamount . . . **3.** cat **6.** cougar
   12. catamountain
catapult . . . **4.** hurl **5.** shoot, sling
   6. engine, onager **7.** robinet **8.** arbalest,
   ballista, scorpion **9.** slingshot
cataract . . . **4.** fall, linn **5.** Falls, flood,
   sault (soo) **6.** deluge **7.** cascade,
   disease, Niagara, opacity (eye), torrent
   8. downpour, Victoria **9.** cachoeira,
   waterfall
cataria . . . **6.** catnip
catasta . . . **5.** stage (slave traffic) **6.** stocks
   8. scaffold
catastrophe . . . **4.** doom, ruin **6.** finale,
   mishap, payoff **7.** tragedy **8.** calamity,
   disaster **9.** cataclysm **10.** denouement,
   misfortune, revolution **11.** termination
catastrophic . . . **4.** dire **5.** black **7.** ruinous
   10. calamitous, deplorable, disastrous
catawba . . . **4.** wine **5.** color (red), grape

6. Indian
catch . . . **3.** get, nab **4.** draw, hear, hold,
   hook, take, trap **5.** fault, ketch, prize,
   reach, rondo, seize, snare, trick, troll
   6. detent (clock), engage, entrap, ignite
   7. attract, capture, seizure **8.** overtake
   9. intercept
catch (pert to) . . .
   a likeness . . **4.** draw **6.** depict **7.** portray
   a ride . . **4.** hook **5.** hitch, thumb
   9. hitchhike
   sight of . . **3.** see **4.** espy **6.** behold,
   descry **7.** discern, glimpse
catchword . . . **3.** cry, cue **6.** byword,
   phrase, slogan **7.** formula **10.** shibboleth
cate . . . **4.** food **6.** viands **8.** dainties
   10. delicacies, provisions (bought)
catechism . . . **5.** guide **6.** belief, manual
   9. questions (set of) **11.** instruction
   (oral)
catechumen . . . **5.** chela, pupil **6.** layman,
   novice **7.** convert **8.** disciple, neophyte
categoric, categorical . . . **6.** direct
   7. crucial, logical **8.** absolute, explicit,
   positive **9.** arbitrary, pragmatic
   10. convincing **11.** dictatorial,
   unequivocal, unqualified
category . . . **4.** head **5.** class, genre,
   genus, group, order, state **6.** branch,
   family, specie **7.** bracket, species
   8. division **12.** denomination
   14. classification
catena . . . **5.** chain **6.** series **8.** sequence
   10. continuity
catenary . . . **5.** curve (Math) **9.** chainlike
cater, cater to . . . **4.** feed **5.** favor, humor,
   serve, toady **6.** oblige, pander, please,
   purvey **7.** indulge, procure, provide,
   satisfy **10.** minister to **11.** diagonalize
   13. cater-cornered
caterpillar . . . **4.** grub, weri **5.** aweto,
   eruca, larva **9.** tractor
caterwaul . . . **3.** woo (derog) **4.** meow,
   wail **5.** court, miaow **7.** screech
cathedral . . . **3.** dom **4.** fane (anc)
   5. duomo **6.** church **8.** official **10.** ex
   cathedra **13.** authoritative
Cathedral . . .
   England . . **6.** Durham **9.** Salisbury
   10. Canterbury
   France . . **5.** Reims (Rheims) **6.** Amiens
   8. Chartres **9.** Notre Dame
   Istanbul (Constantinople) . . **8.** St Sophia
   Italy . . **7.** Lateran, St Mark's **8.** St Peter's
   Scotland . . **7.** St Giles
cathedral (pert to) . . .
   chair (Bishop's) . . **8.** cathedra
   chapter member . . **10.** capitulary
   part . . **4.** apse, nave **5.** choir **6.** chapel
   7. chancel, narthex **8.** sacristy, transept
   10. baptistery (baptistry)
   style . . **6.** Gothic
catholic . . . **4.** wide **5.** broad **6.** church,
   global **7.** general, liberal **8.** orthodox,
   pandemic **9.** Christian, universal
   10. ecumenical **12.** cosmopolitan
Catholic Church (Roman) . . .
   Bible books . . **16.** deuterocanonical
   calendar . . **4.** ordo
   clergy . . **4.** monk **5.** friar **6.** bishop,
   Jesuit, priest **8.** cardinal **9.** monsignor

head .. **4.** pope **7.** pontiff
papal residence, state .. **7.** Vatican
rite .. **4.** Mass **7.** baptism, penance
   9. Communion, Eucharist, matrimony,
   sacrament **10.** Holy Orders
   12. confirmation
seat of authority .. **7.** Holy See
catkin ... **5.** ament, spike **7.** cattail
catlike ... **5.** catty **6.** feline **8.** stealthy
   9. noiseless
catling ... **3.** cat (little) **6.** kitten, string
   (violin)
Cato (pert to) ...
   author of .. **13.** De Agri Cultura
   famed as .. **7.** General **9.** statesman
   10. ambassador (to Carthage)
   nickname .. **8.** The Elder **11.** Cato of
   Utica
Catoism ... **9.** austerity, harshness
cats ... **8.** Kilkenny
cat's cradle ... **3.** hei **4.** game **7.** ribwort
cat's-paw ... **4.** dupe, gull, loof, pawn,
   tool **5.** cully, hitch (knot) **6.** breeze
   (Naut), puppet, stooge **10.** instrument
cattail ... **4.** musk, reed, tule **5.** ament,
   raupo, teree **6.** catkin, totora **7.** matreed
   9. Typhaceae
cattle ... **3.** Bos **4.** cows, kine, neat,
   oxen, stot, yaks **5.** asses, goats, mules,
   sheep, stock, swine **6.** bovine, camels,
   horses, llamas, niatas, rabble , Taurus
   7. banteng, chattel **8.** bullocks, property
   9. livestock
cattle (breed) ... **4.** Zebu **5.** Angus,
   Devon, Kerry, Niata, Welsh **6.** Brahma,
   Durham, Jersey, Sussex **7.** Dishley
   8. Guernsey, Hereford, Holstein,
   Longhorn **9.** Charolais, Leicester,
   Shorthorn **14.** Santa Gertrudis
cattle (pert to) ...
   collection .. **4.** herd **5.** drove
   disease .. **7.** murrain **10.** rinderpest
   driver .. **6.** drover
   food .. **6.** fodder, forage, silage
   herder .. **6.** cowboy, drover
   hybrid .. **4.** Zobo **7.** cattalo **9.** cattleyak
   motherless .. **6.** dogies
   pen .. **4.** crew **5.** barth, reeve
   shed .. **6.** hemmel
   stealer .. **7.** abactor, abigeus, rustler
   unbranded .. **9.** mavericks
catty ... **6.** feline, weight **7.** catlike, cattish
   8. spiteful, stealthy **11.** treacherous
cauboge ... **4.** boor **7.** bumpkin
Caucasian ... **4.** race, Slav, Svan,
   Turk **5.** gypsy, Latin, Norse, Osset,
   Pshav, white **6.** Hebrew, Semite,
   Teuton, Viking **8.** Armenian, Bohemian,
   Georgian, White Man **10.** Anglo-Saxon
   11. Xanthochroi
Caucasian (pert to) ...
   blond .. **6.** Teuton **8.** Estonian
   11. Xanthochroi
   brunette .. **7.** Iberian **8.** Armenian
   11. Melanochroi
   Chinese .. **4.** Lolo, Nosu
   dialect .. **4.** Andi, Avar, Svan
   European .. **8.** Japhetic
   goat (wild) .. **3.** tur
   liquor .. **5.** kefir
   Moslem .. **3.** Laz (Laze, Lazi) **7.** Sunnite

mountain .. **8.** Caucasus
peak .. **6.** Elbrus (Elbruz), Kazbek
cauchemar ... **9.** nightmare
caucus ... **7.** meeting (Polit), primary
   8. assembly
cauda ... **4.** scut, tail **9.** appendage
caudata ... **5.** newts **8.** Amphibia
   11. salamanders
caught ... see also *catch* **5.** treed
   7. latched **8.** cornered
caught (pert to) ...
   napping .. **7.** unready **8.** unprimed
   10. unprepared
   sight of .. **3.** saw **6.** espied **8.** descried
   up in .. **4.** tied **7.** engaged, tangled
   8. absorbed, intent on, involved
   10. implicated
caul ... **3.** net **6.** basket **7.** netting,
   network, omentum **8.** membrane
cause ... **5.** aetio (comb form), agent,
   basis, drive, greed **6.** create, factor,
   ground, induce, motive, reason,
   source **7.** crusade, produce, provoke
   8. campaign, etiology, movement,
   occasion **9.** originate **10.** mainspring
   13. justification
cause (pert to) ...
   approach .. **7.** attract
   be done .. **4.** writ **11.** fieri facias
   bring about .. **6.** effect
   buy and sell .. **7.** whipsaw
   coagulate .. **4.** curd **6.** curdle **7.** congeal,
   thicken
   contract unevenly .. **6.** pucker
   face East .. **6.** orient
   harm .. **4.** bane
   irritate .. **6.** rankle
   raise in relief .. **6.** emboss
   remember .. **6.** remind
   roll .. **7.** trundle
   speed up .. **10.** accelerate
   take root .. **8.** radicate
causerie ... **4.** chat, talk **6.** parley **7.** article
   8. converse, treatise **9.** paragraph
   10. discussion **12.** conversation
causes, science of ... **8.** etiology
causeuse ... **4.** sofa **9.** tête-à-tête
causeway ... **4.** dike **7.** highway
   10. embankment
causing ...
   destiny .. **5.** fatal
   emotion .. **7.** emotive
   forgetfulness .. **8.** nepenthe
   laughter .. **8.** risorial
   motion .. **6.** motile
caustic ... **4.** acid, tart **5.** acrid, curve
   (optic), sharp **6.** biting, bitter, severe
   7. acerbic, burning, cutting, erodent,
   mordant, pungent, pyrotic **8.** snappish
   stinging, virulent **9.** corrosive, satirical,
   vitriolic **10.** astringent, escharotic
   11. acrimonious, penetrating
caustic agent ... **3.** lye **4.** alum, lime
   7. erodent **9.** quicklime
cautel ... **5.** trick **7.** caution **8.** prudence
   9. direction (Eccl) **10.** precaution
cauterize ... **4.** burn, char, sear **5.** brand,
   singe **7.** torrefy
cautery ... **7.** burning, searing **8.** inustion
   10. instrument **13.** cauterization
caution ... **4.** card (coll), care, heed, warn

5. aviso 6. advice, caveat, notice, oddity
7. anxiety, counsel, precept, proviso,
warning 8. forecast, prudence, wariness
9. chariness, vigilance 10. admonition,
providence, solicitude 11. exhortation,
forethought, mindfulness
12. cautiousness, notification,
watchfulness 14. circumspection
cautious . . . 4. wary 5. canny, chary
6. Fabian 7. careful, guarded, heedful,
mindful, prudent 11. circumspect
cautiously . . . 6. cagily, warily 7. cannily,
charily 8. gingerly 9. carefully,
guardedly, heedfully, mindfully, prud-
ently 10. discreetly 13. circumspectly
cavalcade . . . 4. raid, ride 5. march
6. parade, review 7. caravan, pageant
9. motorcade 10. procession
cavalier . . . 3. gay 4. coin (Fr), curt
5. brave, frank, lover, rider 6. escort,
knight, squire 7. admirer, brusque,
esquire, gallant, haughty, soldier
8. horseman, Royalist 9. caballero,
cavaliere, chevalier, Roundhead
10. disdainful, equestrian 12. high-
spirited, supercilious
cavalry . . . 4. army 6. horses, yellow
(color) 8. horsemen 10. knighthood
cavalry (pert to) . . .
horse . . 6. lancer
man . . 5. spahy, uhlan 6. Hussar, lancer
7. dragoon, trooper
unit . . 5. troop
weapon . . 5. lance, saber 9. demilance
cave . . . 3. den, mew 4. abri, cove,
grot, hole, lair 5. antre, cover, lodge
(beaver), speos 6. antrum, cavern,
cellar, covert, dugout, grotto, subway,
tunnel 7. chamber, shelter, spelunk
10. subterrane
cave (pert to) . . .
fish . . 9. blindfish
man . . 11. Paleolithic
nature of . . 9. speluncar
study of . . 10. speleology
cave canem . . . 11. Beware of Dog
cave dweller . . . 10. troglodyte
Cave of Adullam . . . 9. Seceeders (1866)
caviar, caviare . . . 3. roe 5. garum
6. relish 8. delicacy, fish eggs
cavil . . . 4. cark, carp, marl, quip 5. dodge,
evade, parry, shift 6. bicker, boggle,
haggle, palter 7. quibble, shuffle
9. criticize, pussyfoot 10. equivocate
caviler . . . 5. momus 6. critic, hedger
8. frondeur, quibbler 10. criticizer
11. equivocator, faultfinder
cavity . . . 3. dip, pit, sac, vug (voog)
4. aula, bore (gun), cava, hole, sink,
well 5. abyss, antra, atria, bursa, chasm,
fossa, fosse, geode, lumen, shaft,
sinus 6. antrum, areole, atrium, caries,
coelom, crater, hollow 7. cochlea,
loculus 10. depression 11. compartment
cavort . . . 4. dido, romp, skip 5. antic,
caper, cut up, frisk, prank 6. curvet,
gambol, prance 7. flounce, gambade,
gambado
cavy . . . 3. pig 4. paca 5. stray 6. agouti,
rodent 8. capybara (capibara) 9. guinea
pig

caw . . . 3. cry 5. croak, quark, quawk
11. exclamation
cay . . . 3. kay 5. islet
cease . . . 3. end 4. quit, rest (law), stop
5. avast, pause, stint 6. desist, perish
7. abandon, fade out, refrain 8. intermit,
leave off, shutdown 9. disappear,
pretermit 11. discontinue
ceaseless . . . 7. endless, nonstop
8. constant, unbroken, unending
9. continued, incessant, perennial,
perpetual, unceasing 10. continuous
12. interminable 13. round the clock,
uninterrupted
ceaselessness . . . 9. constancy
10. continuity, incessancy, perpetuity
11. endlessness 14. successiveness
cease to be . . . 3. die 6. expire, perish
8. dissolve 9. disappear
cease to please . . . 4. pall
Cebus . . . 3. sai 6. monkey 8. capuchin
cecils . . . 10. croquettes
cecity . . . 9. blindness
Cecrops (pert to) . . .
daughter . . 5. Herse 8. Aglauros
founder of (tradition) . . 6. Athens
king of . . 6. Attica
symbol . . 7. half man 10. half dragon
cedar (pert to) . . .
bird . . 7. waxwing
class . . 7. conifer
fruit . . 6. cedron
genus . . 5. Thuja, Toona 6. Cedrus
9. Juniperus
green . . 5. cedre
moss . . 8. hornwort
type . . 5. savin 6. deodar, sabine
7. incense, juniper, Lebanon (Bib),
Spanish 10. arborvitae
11. cryptomeria
cede . . . 5. grant, waive, yield 6. assign,
confer 7. abandon 8. renounce
9. surrender 10. capitulate, relinquish
cedula . . . 3. tax 6. permit 8. schedule,
security (Finan) 10. obligation
11. certificate
ceil . . . 4. line 5. cover 7. overlay
8. wainscot
ceiling . . . 4. acme, roof 5. astel, limit,
price, trave 6. apogee, lining, screen,
utmost 7. curtain, lacunar, maximum,
plafond 8. covering 9. lacunaria
10. planchment, visibility
12. consummation
celebrant . . . 6. priest (Eucharist)
9. worshiper (worshipper)
11. communicant
celebrate . . . 4. keep, laud, sing 5. extol,
honor, revel 6. herald, praise 7. glorify,
maffick, observe, roister 8. emblazon,
proclaim 9. solemnize
11. commemorate, memorialize
celebrated . . . 5. famed, noted 6. famous
7. feasted, honored, popular 8. far-
famed, observed, renowned
9. distingué, well-known 11. illustrious
13. distinguished
celebration . . . 4. bout, fete, rite 5. fling,
revel, spree 6. bender 7. fanfare, jubilee
8. ceremony, function 9. epinicion,
festivity, rejoicing 10. observance

13. commemoration
celebrity ... 3. VIP 4. fame 5. éclat,
glory 6. notary 7. notable 8. luminary,
somebody 10. famousness, popularity
11. recognition
celerity ... 5. haste, speed 8. dispatch,
rapidity, velocity 9. swiftness
10. speediness
celery ... 4. ache 8. smallage (wild)
9. Ammiacaea
celestial ... 6. astral, divine, uranic
7. angelic, sky blue 8. ethereal, heavenly
12. paradisaical
Celestial (pert to) ...
being .. 5. angel 6. cherub, seraph
body .. 4. star 5. comet 6. nebula
city .. 6. heaven, utopia 9. Jerusalem
empire .. 7. Chinese, Tien Chu
equator .. 8. meridian
mind elevation .. 7. anagoge
teacher .. 6. Taoist
celibate ... 4. monk 6. single 8. bachelor,
monastic, Platonic, spinster 9. abstinent,
continent, unmarried
cell ... 3. egg, kil 4. cyst, germ,
ovum 5. cnida, crypt 6. cytode,
prison 7. alveola, cellule, dungeon
11. compartment
cell (pert to) ...
animal .. 6. amoeba (ameba) 7. rotifer
8. protozoa
biology .. 7. energid, meiosis, mitosis,
nucleus, spireme
cell-like .. 9. celliform
division .. 5. linin 7. spireme 8. amitosis
eating .. 9. cytophagy
Egyptian (tomb) .. 6. serdab
honeycomb .. 8. alveolus
Irish .. 3. kil (kill)
locomotive .. 5. sperm, zooid
Roman .. 4. alla, naos
study .. 8. cytology
substance .. 5. linin
walls .. 9. cellulose
cellaret ... 4. case 8. tantalus 9. sideboard
Celt ... 4. Erse, Gael, Manx, Scot 5. Welsh
6. Breton 7. Cornish
Celtic (pert to) ...
abbot .. 5. coarb
bard .. 6. Ossian
cattle .. 2. ox
church .. 9. Christian
deity .. 7. Taranis
foot soldier .. 4. kern
horse .. 4. pony (Shetland)
island .. 4. Manx
king .. 4. Bran
language .. 4. Erse
minstrel .. 4. bard
Mother of Gods .. 3. Ana (Anu)
mountain .. 3. ben
Neptune .. 3. Ler
nickname .. 10. Turtleback
Order .. 5. Druid
people .. 5. Gauls, Irish, Scots, Welsh
7. Bretons, Britons
perfume .. 4. nard 9. spikenard
sun god .. 3. Lug (Lugh)
cembalo ... 8. dulcimer 11. harpsichord
12. clavicembalo
cement ... 4. bind, fuse, glue, join,

paar, pave 5. putty, stick, unite
6. cohere, fasten, mastic, mortar,
solder 8. adhesive, concrete, pavement,
solidify
cemetery ... 6. litten 7. Calvary
8. boneyard, catacomb, Golgotha, lich
gate (entrance), mortuary 9. graveyard,
mausoleum 10. churchyard, necropolis
11. polyandrium 12. potter's field
cenobite ... 4. Monk 5. Order (anc)
6. Essene 7. recluse
cenotaph ... 4. tomb (empty) 7. memento
8. memorial, monument
censer bearer ... 7. acolyte 8. altar boy,
thurifer
censor ... 5. judge 6. critic 7. monitor
8. censurer, reviewer, superego
11. faultfinder
censure ... 4. flay 5. blame, chide,
slate, targe 6. accuse 7. chasten,
condemn, impeach, inveigh, reprove,
slating 8. reproach 9. damnation,
expurgate, reprimand 11. reprobation
12. condemnation, denunciation,
reprehension
cent ... 4. coin, game (old) 5. penny
6. copper, trifle 7. hundred, red cent
centaur (Myth) ... 4. race (Thessaly)
6. Nessus 8. Lapithae, man-horse (half
man) 9. bucentaur, Centaurus (Astron)
centennial ... 4. game (dice)
9. hundredth, red-yellow
11. anniversary
Centennial State ... 8. Colorado
center ... 3. cor, hub 4. base, core, nave
5. axial, focus, heart, midst 6. kernel
marrow, middle 7. midmost, nucleus,
pivotal, seaport 8. emporium
center (pert to) ...
away from .. 6. distal
bull's-eye .. 5. clout 6. target
line .. 6. axiate, cesura
center of ...
attention .. 8. cynosure
earth .. 9. epicenter
gravity .. 6. kernel 7. centrum
nervous system .. 5. brain
sail .. 4. bunt
target .. 3. eye 8. bull's-eye
centerpiece ... 4. bowl 7. epergne
centipede ... 4. rope (Naut) 6. earwig,
insect 8. chilipod, myriapod
central ... 3. mid 4. arch, main 5. axial,
basic, chief, focal, prime 6. master,
middle 7. capital, centric, leading,
midmost, pivotal, primary 8. cardinal,
dominant, foremost 9. principal
11. equidistant
Central America ...
bird .. 7. jacamar 8. puffbird
boat .. 6. cayuco, pitpan
country .. 6. Panama 8. Honduras
9. Costa Rica, Guatemala, Nicaragua
10. El Salvador
Indian .. 4. Maya 5. Carib
monkey .. 4. mono
rodent .. 4. paca
snake .. 10. bushmaster
tree .. 3. ebo, ule 5. amate 9. sapodilla
Central Asia (pert to) ...
gazelle .. 3. ahu

wild horse .. **6.** tarpan
wind storm .. **5.** buran
Central State ... **6.** Kansas
centuries (ten) ... **7.** chiliad
century ... **3.** Age **4.** aeon (eon) **7.** centred (anc), hundred **8.** eternity **9.** centenary **10.** centennial
century plant ... **4.** aloe **5.** agave **6.** maguey
ceorl (Eng Hist) ... **5.** churl, thane **7.** freeman, villein
cepa ... **5.** onion
cephalon ... **4.** head (Zool)
cephalopod ... **3.** ink (secretion) **5.** sepia **6.** cuttle **7.** octopus **10.** cuttlefish
ceramics ... **4.** tile **5.** china, delft, spode **6.** mosaic **7.** pottery, Satsuma **8.** crockery, majolica, Wedgwood **9.** porcelain
ceramics term ... **4.** clay, kiln, laun **5.** adobe, stove, wheel **6.** sleeve (silk) **7.** furnace **8.** ceramist **10.** ceramicist **12.** ceramography
ceratoid ... **5.** horny **8.** hornlike **10.** horn-shaped
cere ... **3.** wax **4.** wrap (dead body) **6.** anoint **12.** protuberance (bird's)
cereal ... **4.** bran, mush, rice **5.** grits, gruel, maize, wheat **6.** farina, hominy **7.** granola, oatmeal **8.** porridge **10.** corn flakes
cereal grass ... **3.** oat, rye **4.** ragi **5.** grain, maize, wheat **6.** barley, millet, raggee
cereal spike ... **3.** ear
cerebellum ... **5.** brain (part)
cerebral (pert to) ... **4.** lobe **5.** brain **6.** speech **8.** arteries, peduncle **9.** consonant (Phonet) **11.** crus cerebri, hemispheres
cerebrum ... **5.** brain **10.** encephalon
cere cloth ... **7.** wrapper (corpse) **8.** cerement, chrismal **12.** grave clothes
ceremonial ... **4.** prim **5.** stiff **6.** custom, formal, ritual **7.** precise, service, studied **8.** ceremony, function, liturgic **9.** formality **11.** punctilious **12.** conventional
ceremonial (pert to) ...
chamber .. **4.** kiva
departure .. **6.** congee
splendor .. **9.** pageantry
ceremonious ... **6.** formal, polite **7.** precise **8.** gracious **9.** attentive, courteous **10.** ceremonial, respectful **11.** deferential, ritualistic
ceremony ... **4.** form, pomp, rite, show **6.** parade, review, ritual **8.** function **9.** formality, solemnity **10.** observance **11.** performance
ceremony, without ... **6.** humbly, meekly, simply **7.** quietly **8.** casually, modestly **9.** sans façon **10.** informally **15.** unceremoniously
Ceres, Rom (pert to) ...
astronomy .. **8.** asteroid (1st found)
father .. **6.** Saturn
Feast .. **8.** Cerialia (Apr 19)
Goddess of .. **4.** Corn **5.** Grain **9.** Fertility **11.** Agriculture
Greek name .. **7.** Demeter
mother .. **3.** Ops

Cereus ... **6.** cactus **7.** saguaro **13.** night-blooming
cerise ... **5.** color **7.** blue-red, fuchsia **10.** cherrylike
ceroplastics ... **8.** modeling, waxworks
certain ... **3.** one **4.** sure **5.** clear, exact, fixed, plain **7.** assured, decided, insured, precise **8.** absolute, definite, positive **9.** certified, confident, exclusive, indubious, undoubted, warranted **10.** guaranteed, inevitable, undeniable, undoubting **11.** determinate, trustworthy **14.** unquestionable **16.** incontrovertible
certainly ... **3.** yea, yes **4.** amen **5.** truly **6.** indeed, really, surely, verily **7.** clearly, in truth, utterly **8.** actually, of course **9.** assuredly, precisely **10.** absolutely, by all means, definitely, inevitably, positively
certainty ... **5.** cinch **6.** pledge, shoo-in, surety **8.** sureness **9.** assurance, certitude **13.** inevitability, infallibility
certificate ... **5.** check, money **6.** ticket **7.** diploma, voucher **10.** credential **11.** testimonial
certificate (pert to) ...
financial .. **3.** IOU **5.** draft, scrip **9.** debenture
India .. **5.** hundi
medical (Eng college) .. **8.** aegrotat
certification ... **2.** OK **3.** fix **5.** proof **8.** sanction **10.** validation **11.** affirmation, attestation, certificate, endorsement **12.** confirmation, ratification **13.** ascertainment, authorization **14.** substantiation
certify ... **5.** prove, swear, vouch **6.** assure, attest, avouch, ratify, verify **7.** approve, confirm, endorse, witness **8.** accredit, validate **9.** ascertain, determine, establish, guarantee **11.** acknowledge, corroborate
cerulean ... **4.** blue **5.** azure **7.** sky-blue
cerumen ... **6.** earwax
cervine ... **8.** deerlike
cess ... **3.** bag, tax **4.** cede, duty, levy, toll **5.** yield **6.** assess, impost, tariff **7.** revenue **9.** surrender **10.** assessment
cessation ... **3.** end **4.** lull, stay **5.** letup, truce **7.** respite **8.** abeyance, desition **9.** interlude **10.** suspension **12.** intermission, interruption **14.** discontinuance
cetacea, cetacean ... **3.** orc **4.** apod, orca, susu (blind) **5.** whale **6.** whales **7.** cowfish, finback, grampus, narwhal (narwal), rorqual
Cete ... **5.** whale **10.** The Cetacea
Cetus ... **8.** The Whale **13.** constellation (Equator)
Ceylon ...
capital .. **7.** Colombo
city .. **5.** Galle, Kandy (famed Buddhist Temple) **6.** Jaffna
mountain peak .. **14.** Pidurutalagala
new name .. **8.** Sri Lanka
ocean .. **6.** Indian
old name .. **9.** Taprobane
people .. **5.** Tamil **6.** Malays, Veddas **8.** Malabars **10.** Singhalese

Ceylon (pert to)...
boat.. **5.** dhoni (doni)
canoe.. **5.** balsa
Festival.. **8.** Perahera
garment.. **6.** sarong
hill dweller.. **4.** Toda
monkey.. **4.** maha **6.** langur, rillow
moss.. **4.** alga **6.** Jaffna **7.** gulaman
8. agar-agar
palm.. **7.** talipot
rat.. **9.** bandicoot
sand (sea bottom).. **4.** paar
tree.. **4.** doon
chabouk, chabuk (Ind)... **4.** whip
9. horsewhip
chacma... **6.** baboon
chafe... **3.** cut, irk, rub, vex **4.** fret,
fume, fuss, gall, heat, rage, skin, warm
5. anger, annoy, grate, grind, pique,
scuff, worry, wound **6.** abrade, banter,
excite, harass, injure, nettle, rankle
7. inflame **8.** irritate
chaff... **3.** hay **4.** bran, husk, quiz, twit
5. dregs, fluff, husks, palea, straw,
trash, waste **6.** banter, cobweb, glumes,
refuse, scraps **7.** remains, residue,
tailing **8.** raillery, ridicule, riffraff
chaffer... **5.** trade, wares **6.** buying,
dicker, haggle, higgle, market
7. bargain, chaffer, chatter, selling
9. negotiate **11.** merchandise
chafing dish... **7.** cresset
chagrin... **7.** anxiety, mortify **8.** distress,
troubles, vexation **13.** mortification
chain... **4.** bind, bond, boom, gyve, reef,
torc **5.** cable, range **6.** catena, fasten,
fetter, secure, series, tether, torque
7. creeper, sorites **15.** contravallation
(fort series)
chair... **4.** seat, sill **5.** bench, sedan
6. rocker, throne **7.** enchair, speaker
chair (pert to)...
back.. **5.** splat **7.** upright
collegiate.. **10.** fellowship
13. professorship
cover.. **4.** tidy **12.** antimacassar
India.. **6.** musnud
Japan.. **4.** kago
maker.. **5.** caner **6.** reeder
chair (type of)... **4.** camp, deck, easy,
high, lawn, wing **6.** lounge, Morris,
swivel **7.** contour, folding, steamer,
Windsor **8.** armchair, captain's, electric,
fauteuil, straight **10.** ladder-back
11. overstuffed
chairman... **7.** officer, speaker **8.** director
9. moderator
chalcedony... **4.** onyx, opal, sard
5. agate **6.** jasper, quartz **7.** opaline
9. carnelian **11.** chrysoprase
Chaldean (pert to)... **2.** Ur **4.** seer
6. Semite **10.** astrologer, soothsayer
13. Neo-Babylonian (language)
chalice... **3.** ama, cup **5.** amula (anc),
calix, grail **6.** goblet **8.** daffodil
chalice pall... **4.** veil **8.** animetta
chalk... **4.** draw, mark, pale, tick **5.** score
6. blanch, bleach, crayon, credit,
pastel, whiten **7.** account, drawing
9. limestone, reckoning
chalker... **7.** milkman (Eng sl)

chalklike... **10.** calcareous
chalky... **5.** white **7.** crumbly, friable,
powdery **10.** cretaceous
challenge... **4.** dare, defy, gage **5.** claim,
doubt, query **6.** accost, cartel, defial,
demand, impugn **7.** dispute, protest
8. question, reproach **10.** accusation,
controvert **11.** questioning
chamal... **4.** goat (Angora)
chamber... **4.** cave, hall, kiva, room
5. court **6.** camera, cavity **7.** bedroom,
boudoir, cabinet, chambre, cubicle
10. bedchamber **11.** compartment
chamber (pert to)...
harem.. **3.** oda
heart.. **7.** auricle **9.** ventricle
King's.. **9.** camarilla
music.. **14.** sonata da camera
chambers... **4.** flat **5.** suite **6.** office
9. apartment, bicameral (Legis) **14.** Inns
of Chancery (Eng)
chameleon... **6.** lizard **10.** vacillator
13. changeability, constellation
chamfer (to)... **5.** bevel, carve, flute,
score **6.** chisel, groove
chamois... **5.** Gemse, izard **8.** antelope
champ... **4.** bite, chew, mash **5.** gnash
6. victor **7.** trample **11.** battlefield
champagne... **4.** wine **9.** red-yellow
13. chrysanthemum
champaign... **5.** field, plain **7.** expanse
11. battlefield
champion... **3.** Ace **4.** best, hero
5. champ **6.** defend, expert, victor,
winner **7.** espouse, fighter, titlist
8. advocate, defender **9.** combatant,
conqueror **10.** unexcelled
champion (pert to)...
Christian (anc).. **3.** Cid
constellation.. **7.** Perseus
knight (legend).. **7.** Paladin
Spanish.. **12.** conquistador
chance... **3.** die, hap, lot **4.** fate, luck,
odds, risk, turn **6.** casual, gamble,
happen, mishap, tossup **7.** fortune,
lottery, tychism **8.** fortuity, Lady Luck,
occasion **9.** happening, mischance
10. likelihood **11.** opportunity,
possibility, probability **12.** happenstance
chancel (pert to)...
part.. **4.** bema
screen.. **4.** jube
seats.. **7.** sedilia
change... **4.** flux, move, turn, vary,
veer **5.** alter, amend, break, coins,
money, shift **6.** modify, mutate, switch
7. caprice, convert, deviate, variety
8. transfer **9.** diversity, transform,
transmute, variation **10.** alteration,
fickleness, modulation **11.** inconstancy,
vicissitude **12.** substitution
13. metamorphosis **14.** transformation
15. diversification
change (pert to)...
color.. **3.** dye, wan **4.** fade, pale **5.** blush
6. blanch, redden
medicine.. **11.** heterotopia
mind.. **6.** repent **12.** tergiversate
music.. **4.** muta
order of.. **9.** metabolic, rearrange,
transpose

changeable . . . **6.** fickle, fitful, mobile **7.** erratic, flighty, mutable, protean **8.** freakish, notional, unstable, variable, volatile, weathery **9.** alterable, chameleon, metabolic, uncertain, unsettled, whimsical **10.** capricious, inconstant **15.** interchangeable

changeling . . . **3.** oaf **4.** dolt **5.** idiot **7.** waverer **8.** imbecile, renegade, turncoat **9.** simpleton **10.** substitute (child)

channel . . . **3.** bed, cut, gat, way **4.** dike, duct, gate, gurt, lane, leat, pass, vein **5.** basin, canal, ditch, drain, flume, flute, fosse, radio, river, sinus, stria **6.** alveus, avenue, coulee, groove, gutter, outlet, sluice, trench, trough **7.** conduit, tideway **8.** aqueduct, tailrace **9.** broadcast **10.** passageway

Channel Islands . . . **4.** Sark (Sercq) **6.** Jersey **8.** Alderney

chanson . . . **4.** song **5.** lyric **6.** ballad

chant . . . **3.** say **4.** sing **6.** intone, melody, warble **7.** introit, singing **8.** canticle **10.** intonation **11.** composition

chanter . . . **6.** cantor, singer **7.** bagpipe (part), intoner, sparrow (hedge) **8.** songster, vocalist **9.** chanteuse, chorister

chanticleer . . . **4.** cock **7.** rooster **11.** cock-a-doodle **14.** cock-a-doodle-doo

chaos . . . **2.** Nu (Egypt) **3.** pie (type) **4.** gulf, mess **5.** abyss, babel, chasm **7.** anarchy **8.** disorder **9.** confusion, imbroglio **10.** unruliness **13.** orderlessness

Chaos (pert to) . . .
daughter . . **3.** Nox, Nyx
parent of . . **5.** earth **6.** heaven **8.** Creation
son . . **6.** Erebus

chaotic . . . **6.** muddle **8.** confused, formless **12.** disorganized

chap . . . **3.** boy, buy, guy, lad, man **4.** kibe (sore) **5.** buyer, chink, cleft, crack, scout, split, youth **6.** barter, choose (Scot), fellow, galoot **7.** chapman **8.** customer

chapeau . . . **3.** cap, hat, lid **5.** beret

chapel . . . **4.** cape, cope, cowl, hood **5.** altar, choir **6.** bethel **7.** chantry, galilee, oratory, service, Sistine **8.** sacellum (anc) **9.** reliquary

chaperon . . . **4.** hood **6.** attend, duenna, escort **8.** guardian **9.** attendant **10.** gooseberry

chaplet . . . **4.** band **5.** beads **6.** anadem, wreath **7.** garland, prayers **8.** beadroll, insignia, necklace

chappaul . . . **9.** squawfish

chaps . . . **8.** overalls **10.** chaparajos

chapter . . . **4.** Sura **5.** topic **6.** clause **7.** council, meeting, passage, section, Society **8.** division **9.** capitular **10.** fraternity **12.** organization

chaptrel . . . **6.** impost

char . . . **4.** burn **5.** trout **6.** scorch **8.** charcoal, sandbank

character . . . **4.** hero, kind, mark, role, sign, star **5.** trait **6.** cipher, letter, nature, repute, status, symbol **7.** quality **8.** function **9.** reference **10.** reputation **11.** temperament **14.** characteristic

character (pert to) . . .

giver . . **5.** toner
Hebrew . . **3.** Tav, Taw
Irish . . **5.** Ogham
musical . . **3.** bar **4.** clef, rest **5.** neume
of people . . **5.** ethos
real . . **7.** essence
science of . . **8.** ethology
Teutonic . . **4.** rune

characteristic . . . **4.** mark **5.** habit, trait **7.** feature, impress, quality, typical **8.** peculiar, symbolic **9.** attribute, character, idiopathy, lineament, specialty **11.** distinctive, peculiarity, singularity, symptomatic **13.** individualism

characteristic (pert to) . . .
descent . . **6.** racial
peculiar . . **9.** idiopathy
spirit . . **5.** ethos
tone (Mus) . . **7.** seventh

characterization . . . **4.** role **5.** drama **9.** depiction, portrayal **11.** description, distinction **13.** impersonation **14.** identification, representation

characterize . . . **4.** mark, name **5.** enact **7.** engrave, imprint, portray **8.** describe, inscribe **9.** delineate, designate, epitomize, represent **11.** distinguish

characterized by . . .
abstinence . . **7.** ascetic
bacteria exclusion . . **7.** asepsis
cruelty . . **7.** Neronic
exact thinking . . **13.** ratiocinative
melody . . **6.** ariose
poison (bloodstream) . . **6.** sepsis
pomposity . . **13.** grandiloquent

characterless . . . **5.** inane **9.** colorless, pointless

charcoal . . . **4.** coke, fuel, lave, peat **5.** black, chark **6.** carbon, fusain **7.** drawing, residue **9.** boneblack, briquette

charge . . . **4.** bill, cost, dues, fill, load, onus, rate, task, toll, ward **5.** blame, chore, debit, onset, order, price, trust **6.** accuse, advice, advise, allege, amount, attack, client, commit, credit, demand, dictum, impute, indict **7.** assault, command, concern, custody, expense, impeach, keeping, mandate, precept, primage, protégé **8.** guidance, insignia, instruct, tutelage **9.** dependent, electrify, exactment **10.** accusation, commission, imposition, impregnate, injunction, management **11.** arrangement, attribution, instruction, supervision **13.** incrimination **14.** responsibility

charged atom . . . **3.** ion

charge of affairs . . . **8.** diplomat **15.** chargé d'affaires

charge off . . . **5.** debit **6.** forget **7.** dismiss, forgive **8.** discount

charges (law) . . . **4.** dues, fees **5.** costs **9.** retainers

charge with . . .
crime . . **6.** indict **7.** impeach **11.** incriminate
debt . . **5.** debit
gas . . **6.** aerate
offense . . **6.** accuse

to .. **5.** blame **7.** ascribe **9.** attribute

charily ... **6.** cagily, warily **8.** frugally **9.** carefully, thriftily **10.** cautiously **12.** economically, suspiciously

chariness ... **7.** caution **8.** caginess, distrust, wariness **9.** frugality **11.** heedfulness, thriftiness

chariot ... **3.** car **4.** biga, cart, rath (ratha), wain **5.** essed (anc), wagon **7.** vehicle **8.** quadriga

charioteer ... **6.** Auriga (Astron), Ben Hur

charitable ... **3.** big **4.** kind **6.** kindly **7.** lenient, liberal **8.** generous, tolerant **9.** forgiving, indulgent **10.** altruistic, benevolent, bighearted **11.** beneficient **12.** eleemosynary, humanitarian **13.** compassionate, philanthropic

charity ... **4.** alms, dole **6.** bounty, virtue **7.** handout, largess **8.** lenience, pittance **9.** tolerance **10.** almsgiving, liberality **11.** benevolence **12.** philanthropy

charity dispenser ... **7.** almoner

charivari ... **5.** babel **6.** medley, uproar **8.** serenade (mock) **10.** callithump

charlatan ... **5.** faker, fraud, phony, quack **6.** humbug **7.** empiric **8.** impostor **9.** pretender **10.** medicaster, mountebank

Charlemagne, Emperor (pert to) ...
brother .. **8.** Carloman
emperor of .. **7.** The West
father .. **5.** Pepin (the Short)
name also .. **15.** Charles The Great
nephew .. **7.** Orlando

charm ... **3.** obi **4.** lure, mojo, play, song **5.** grace, magic, oomph, spell **6.** allure, amulet, appeal, beauty, enamor, entice, fetish, glamor, scarab **7.** beguile, bewitch, cantrip, delight, enchant, glamour, periapt **8.** breloque, elegance, entrance, ornament, talisman **9.** captivate, fascinate, sex appeal, sweetness **10.** allurement, attraction, brimborion (brimborium), lovability **11.** captivation, conjuration, incantation, pulchritude, winsomeness **12.** antinganting **14.** attractiveness, delightfulness

charmer ... **5.** siren **6.** beauty **7.** enticer **8.** exorcist, magician, sorcerer **9.** bewitcher

charming ... **7.** winsome **8.** alluring, pleasing **10.** bewitching, delightful **11.** captivating, fascinating

Charon's river ... **4.** Styx

chart ... **3.** map **4.** list, plat, plot **7.** diagram

charter ... **4.** hire **5.** carta, grant **6.** charta, firman, treaty **7.** license **9.** privilege (special), purwannah

chartreuse ... **4.** mold (cookery) **5.** color **7.** liqueur

Chartreuse ... **9.** monastery **18.** La Grande Chartreuse (Grenoble)

chary ... **4.** wary **5.** cagey **6.** frugal, skimpy **7.** thrifty **8.** cautious **10.** suspicious **12.** parsimonious

Charybdis ... **6.** Scylla **8.** Galofaro **9.** whirlpool (Messina)

chase ... **3.** gun (Naut), set (gem) **4.** hunt,

park, race **5.** chevy (chivy), raise, sport, track **6.** emboss, follow, furrow, groove, hasten, pursue, shikar, stroke (tennis) **7.** engrave, pursuit, repulse **8.** ornament **12.** steeplechase

Chase (The)**, goddess of** ... **5.** Diana

chasm ... **3.** gap, pit **4.** gulf, hole, rift, well **5.** abyss, cleft, shaft **6.** breach, canyon, cavity, hiatus **7.** fissure, opening **8.** crevasse

chasma ... **7.** yawning

chasse ... **4.** step (dance) **6.** shrine **9.** reliquary

chaste ... **4.** pure **6.** modest, simple **8.** innocent, virtuous **9.** continent, uncorrupt, undefiled, unmarried **10.** immaculate

chasten ... **4.** rate **5.** smote **6.** punish, refine **7.** correct **8.** chastise, penalize, restrain **9.** castigate **10.** discipline

chastened ... **4.** meek **5.** smote **7.** subdued **8.** punished, purified, tempered **10.** restrained

chastise ... **4.** beat, slap, whip **5.** amend, blame, scold, spank, taunt **6.** punish, rebate, rebuke, swinge **7.** correct, reprove **9.** castigate **10.** discipline

chastity ... **6.** purity, virtue **9.** cleanness **10.** chasteness **12.** virtuousness

chat ... **3.** gab, rap, yak **4.** chin, coze, jist, talk, tove **5.** prate **6.** babble, confab, gabble, gibber, gossip, jabber **7.** chatter, prattle **8.** causerie, chitchat, converse **12.** conversation **14.** chitter-chatter

chatelaine ... **3.** pin **4.** etui, hook **5.** clasp, purse, watch **6.** brooch, torque

chattels ... **4.** naam **5.** goods, money, wares **6.** estate **7.** effects **8.** holdings, property **9.** livestock, principal **11.** possessions

chatter ... **3.** gab, yap **5.** clack, prate **7.** clatter, prattle

chatterer ... **3.** jay, mag **4.** bird, piet **6.** magpie **10.** chatterbox

chatty ... **3.** pot (earthen) **4.** glib **5.** gabby **7.** affable **8.** sociable **9.** garrulous, prattling, talkative **14.** conversational

Chaucer (pert to) ...
author of .. **15.** Canterbury Tales
Inn .. **6.** (The) Tabard
pilgrimage city .. **10.** Canterbury
style of work .. **7.** novella

chauvinist ... **5.** jingo **6.** Rajput **7.** chauvin, patriot **8.** jingoist **9.** warmonger **10.** militarist

cheap ... **5.** small, tacky, tinny, trade, value **6.** cheesy, paltry, plenty, sleazy **7.** abashed, bargain, chintzy, cut-rate, reduced, schlock **9.** niggardly **11.** inexpensive

cheapen ... **3.** cut **4.** trim **5.** lower, slash **6.** debase, reduce **7.** degrade **8.** mark down

cheat ... **2.** do **3.** ban, con, fob, gyp **4.** bilk, fake, flam, hoax, liar, rook, scam, sell, sham **5.** cozen, elude, guile, phony, scalp **6.** deceit, fleece, humbug, hustle, illude, rip-off **7.** deceive, finesse, sharpen, swindle **8.** artifice, impostor **9.** bamboozle, overreach, stratagem, victimize **10.** thimblerig

13. bait-and-switch
check ... **3.** nip, tab **4.** balk, curb, damp,
    mark, rein, stem, stop, test **5.** agree,
    brake, count, delay, limit, money,
    plaid, repel, stunt, tally **6.** bridle,
    cheque, detain, detent, impede, oppose,
    rebuff, retard, ticket, verify **7.** counter,
    examine, inhibit, measure, monitor,
    pattern, repress **9.** hindrance, restraint
    12. verification
check (pert to) ...
   in .. **3.** die **6.** arrive **8.** register
   out .. **3.** die **5.** croak, leave **6.** assess
    8. withdraw
   pattern .. **11.** houndstooth
   game, term .. **5.** chess **8.** gambling
checkered ... **4.** vair **5.** diced, plaid
    6. mosaic, tartan, varied **7.** checked
    10. changeable, tesserated, variegated
    11. diversified
checkers, chequers ... **4.** game
    8. draughts (Brit)
cheek ... **4.** gall, gena, jowl **5.** brass,
    bucca, crust, malar, nerve **8.** audacity,
    chutzpah **9.** impudence **10.** buccinator
cheer ... **3.** rah **4.** yell **5.** bravo,
    elate, huzza, liven, mirth, salvo
    6. gaiety, hurrah, regale, repast, salute,
    solace **7.** animate, applaud, console,
    gladden, hearten, jollity, refresh, rejoice
    8. applause, inspirit, pleasure, vivacity
    9. encourage, merriment **10.** exhilarate
    12. conviviality
cheerful ... **3.** gay **4.** gleg (Scot), rosy
    5. happy, peart, sunny **6.** blithe,
    cheery, genial, hearty, jocund, joyful
    8. gladsome, homelike **9.** contented,
    lightsome **12.** lighthearted
cheerfulness ... **3.** joy **4.** glee **5.** cheer,
    mirth **6.** gaiety **7.** jollity **8.** gladness,
    hilarity **9.** happiness, merriment
    12. exhilaration
cheerio ... **5.** adios, aloha, skoal, toast
    6. hurrah, prosit **8.** au revoir, farewell,
    Godspeed **9.** greetings
cheerless ... **3.** sad **4.** cold, drab
    5. drear **6.** dismal, dreary, gloomy
    7. forlorn, joyless, unhappy **8.** dejected
    9. unsmiling **10.** depressing, melancholy
    11. dispiriting **12.** disconsolate
cheese ... **4.** blue (bleu), brie, Edam,
    feta, jack **5.** cream, Gouda, Swiss
    6. chevre, Romano **7.** Cheddar,
    cottage, fromage (Fr), Gruyère, havarti,
    ricotta, sapsago, Stilton **8.** American,
    Monterey (jack), Muenster, Parmesan
    9. Camembert, Jarlsberg, Limburger,
    Roquefort **10.** Gorgonzola, Neufchâtel
cheese dish ... **6.** fondue, omelet, quiche,
    strata **7.** rarebit, soufflé
cheesy ... **3.** bad **6.** paltry **8.** inferior
    9. worthless **12.** disreputable
cheetah ... **3.** cat **5.** youse (youze)
    7. guepard (gueparde)
cheilos ... **3.** lip
chela ... **4.** claw **6.** novice **8.** disciple
Chelonia ... **7.** reptile, turtles **9.** tortoises
chemical (pert to) ...
   analysis .. **5.** assay
   cleanser .. **6.** kryton
   etching .. **11.** chemigraphy

   strength .. **5.** titer (titre)
   term .. **3.** gas **4.** acid, atom, base, salt
    5. imine **6.** alkali, eluate **7.** hormone,
    nonacid, organic, radical, valence
    8. catalyst, compound **10.** bathoflore
    11. bathochrome
   vessel .. **4.** etna **6.** aludel, retort
    7. alembic **8.** crucible, reductor
chemical suffix ... **2.** ac, el, yl **3.** ane,
    ene, ile, ine, ole, ose **4.** enol, olic,
    osan
chemin de fer ... **7.** railway **8.** baccarat,
    railroad
chemise ... **4.** slip **5.** shift
chemist ... **7.** analyst **8.** druggist
    9. alchemist **10.** apothecary, biochemist
    12. iatrochemist (anc)
cherish ... **3.** aid, hug, pet, woo **4.** love
    5. adore, cheer, nurse, prize **6.** caress,
    faddle, fondle, foster **7.** care for,
    comfort, nourish, nurture, protect,
    support **8.** enshrine, remember,
    treasure **9.** cultivate, encourage,
    entertain
cheroot ... **5.** cigar
cherry ... **3.** pin **4.** Bing, bird, gean,
    ming **5.** black **6.** egriot, Prunus
    7. capulin, marasca, mazzard, Morello,
    oxheart **8.** Napoleon **9.** amarelles,
    bigarreau, Queen Anne **11.** chokecherry,
    Montmorency
cherub ... **5.** angel, child, saint **6.** seraph,
    spirit **7.** darling, eudemon **8.** cherubim,
    seraphim
chess (pert to) ...
   chessman .. **4.** king, pawn, rook **5.** piece,
    queen **6.** bishop, castle, knight
   Italian .. **7.** scacchi
   term .. **4.** dual, move **5.** debut **6.** chassé,
    fidate, gambit **7.** endgame, opening,
    problem **9.** checkmate, en passant,
    roo k's tour, stalemate **10.** fianchetto
chesslike ... **8.** scacchic
chest ... **3.** ark, box **4.** arca, cist, kist
    5. bahut **6.** breast, cajeta, coffer, coffin,
    locker **7.** highboy, wanigan (wangan)
    10. chiffonier **11.** gardeviance
chest (pert to) ...
   ammunition .. **7.** caisson
   animal .. **7.** brisket
   human .. **6.** thorax **7.** midriff
   sound .. **4.** rale
   sepulchral .. **6.** larnax
Chester (Eng), **inhabitant** ... **8.** Cestrian
chesterfield ... **4.** sofa **5.** divan
    8. overcoat **9.** cigarette, davenport
chestnut ... **4.** ling, rata **5.** horse, water
    6. marron **7.** buckeye **8.** Aesculus,
    Castanea **10.** breadfruit, chinquapin
chestnut ... **4.** joke **6.** cliché **7.** bromide
    8. banality
chestnut color ... **4.** roan **5.** brown
    6. sorrel **12.** reddish-brown
chevalier ... **5.** cadet (nobility), noble
    6. knight **7.** gallant **8.** cavalier,
    horseman **10.** greenshank (bird)
chevron ... **4.** beam **5.** glove **6.** rafter,
    stripe, zigzag **8.** insignia
chevrotain ... **4.** napu **7.** deerlet, kenchil,
    meminna **9.** Tragulina
chevy ... **3.** cry (hunting) **4.** game, hunt

5. chase 6. flight, harass, pursue
7. torment
chew . . . 3. cud 4. bite, chaw, gnaw,
quid 5. champ, chomp, grind, munch
6. chavel, ponder 8. meditate, ruminate
9. masticate
chiasma . . . 11. decussation
12. intersection
chiasmus . . . 9. inversion (of words)
chib (Gypsy) . . . 6. tongue 8. language
chic . . . 4. trig, trim 5. natty, smart
6. modish, spruce 7. stylish
Chicago's nickname . . . 9. Windy City
chicanery . . . 4. ruse, wile 5. feint, trick
6. deceit 7. knavery 8. artifice, trickery
9. stratagem 11. skulduggery
chickadee . . . 8. titmouse 10. Pebthestes
chicken . . . 3. hen 4. cock, fowl,
girl 5. biddy, capon, chick, deedy,
fryer, poult, young 6. coward, pullet
7. broiler, rooster 8. cockerel, weakling
9. youngling 11. chanticleer,
milquetoast
chickenhearted . . . 5. timid 8. cowardly
12. fainthearted
chicory . . . 6. endive 7. succory
12. Cichoriaceae
chickpea . . . 8. garbanzo
chide . . . 4. rate 5. blame, scold 6. berate,
rebuke 7. censure, reprove, wrangle
8. admonish, reproach 9. reprimand
chief . . . 3. dux, top 4. arch, head,
main, rais (reis) 5. first, forte, major,
mogul 6. leader, primal, staple, syndic
7. kingpin, supreme 9. directing,
governing, paramount, potentate,
principal, prominent 11. predominant
chief (pert to) . . .
African . . 3. dey 4. kaid 5. negus
6. induna
Am Indian . . 6. sachem 7. Osceola
8. sagamore
Arab . . 5. sheik
Chinook . . 4. tyee
Cossack . . 6. ataman, hetman
Egypt . . 3. Min (Panopolis)
Europe . . 6. syndic
Germany . . 6. Führer (Fuehrer), Kaiser
Iran . . 9. ayatollah
Italy . . 4. doge, duce
Japan . . 6. mikado, shogun
Mexico . . 7. cacique
Nepal . . 4. Rais
Oriental . . 4. kahn 6. sirdar
Persia . . 4. shah
Russia . . 4. czar (tsar)
Spain . . 7. alcalde
Tibet . . 9. Dalai Lama
Turkey . . 3. aga (agha) 6. vizier
chilblain . . . 6. pernio
child . . . 3. imp, kid, tad, tot 4. babe,
baby, bata, brat, teen, tike, waif
5. bairn, cupid, elfin, fetus 6. cherub,
childe (anc), infant, urchin 7. adoptee,
nestler, preteen, progeny 9. offspring,
youngster 10. descendant
childish . . . 4. weak 5. naive, petty,
young 6. senile, simple 7. babyish,
kiddish, puerile, unmanly 8. immature
9. infantile, kittenish
children (pert to) . . .

doctor . . 12. pediatrician
mythology . . 6. Titans
Patron Saint . . 5. Santa
slain by Herod . . 12. The Innocents
study of . . 8. pedology 10. pediatrics
Chile . . . see also *Chilean*
cape . . 4. Horn
capital . . 8. Santiago (1541)
city . . 4. Lota 5. Arica 8. Valdivia
10. Concepcion, Valparaiso (1543)
conqueror . . 7. Pizarro 8. Valdivia
desert . . 7. Atacama
explorer . . 8. Magellan (1520)
mountain . . 5. Andes
poet . . 6. Neruda
river . . 3. Loa 6. Biobio
settlement (southernmost) . . 8. Navarino
(Isl) 14. Puerto Williams
Chilean (pert to) . . .
coconut . . 7. coquito
evergreen . . 6. pepino 10. arborvitae
shrub (poison) . . 5. lithi
wind . . 5. sures 11. sures pardos
workman . . 4. rote
chiliad . . . 8. thousand 9. millenium
13. thousand years
chill . . . 3. ice, raw 4. ague, cold, damp
5. algor, frost, rigor 6. damper, formal,
shiver 7. malaria 8. coldness, coolness,
dispirit 10. depressing 11. refrigerate
chilly . . . 3. raw 4. ague, cold 5. gelid
6. aguish, freeze, frosty 12. refrigerated
chiloplasty . . . 10. lip surgery 12. mouth
surgery
chime . . . 4. bell, peal, ring, suit 5. agreé,
bells, prate, rhyme 6. accord, concur,
cymbal, jingle 7. harmony
chimera . . . 5. dream, fancy, vapor
6. bubble, utopia 7. monster 8. illusion,
paradise (fool's)
chimerical . . . 4. vain 7. utopian
8. delusive, fanciful, romantic
9. fantastic, imaginary, unfounded
chimney . . . 3. lum 4. flue 5. cleft, stack,
tewel 10. smokestack
chimpanzee . . . 6. gibbon, nohega
7. gorilla
chin . . . 4. talk 5. genio (comb form)
6. mentum, weight (Chin) 8. converse
10. chew the rag 11. genioplasty (Surg),
mentoplasty (Surg)
china . . . 7. Dresden, pottery 8. crockery
9. porcelain 11. earthenware
China . . . see also *Chinese*
Buddha . . 2. Fo
capital . . 7. Beijing
capital, old name . . 7. Peiping (Peking)
city . . 4. Amoy, Tsin, Wuhu 6. Canton,
Hankow, Ningpo 7. Foochow, Nanking,
Soochow 8. Hangchow, Shanghai,
Tientsin
Communist leader . . 3. Mao 4. Deng
dynasty . . 3. Han, Kin, Sui 4. Chou,
Hsia (BC), Ming, Tsin, Yuan 5. Ching
6. Manchu, Mongol (Kublai Khan's)
island . . 5. Matsu 6. Quemoy, Taiwan
(Formosa)
magistrate . . 5. tupan 6. tuchun
8. mandarin
Mainland . . 15. People's Republic
Military Academy . . 7. Whompoa

Mongol.. **3.** Hun
mountain.. **7.** Kuen-lun **9.** Himalayas
Nationalist leader.. **13.** Chiang Kai-shek
nickname.. **14.** Flowery Kingdom
philosopher.. **6.** Laotse **9.** Confucius
poet.. **4.** Li Po **7.** Li Tai Po
race.. **9.** Mongoloid
religion.. **6.** Taoism **8.** Buddhism
9. Confucian **12.** Confucianism
revolutionary leader.. **9.** Sun Yat-sen
river.. **5.** Chang (formerly Yangtze)
7. Huang He (formerly Hwang Ho)
sea.. **5.** China **6.** Yellow
treaty port.. **4.** Amoy
Chinese (pert to) ...
antelope.. **6.** dzeren
boat.. **4.** junk **5.** tanka **6.** sampan
cabbage.. **7.** pakchoi
card game.. **6.** fantan
carpet.. **6.** Khotan **7.** Kashgar, Yarkand
9. Samarkand, Turkestan
Catholic Church.. **11.** Tien Chu T'ang
12. Tien Chu Chiao
chestnut.. **4.** ling
confection.. **8.** chowchow
deer.. **8.** elaphure
defense.. **4.** Wall (2,000 mi long)
desert.. **4.** Gobi **5.** Shamo
dragon.. **6.** chi-lin
fabric.. **3.** sha **7.** nankeen
festival (Spring).. **9.** Ch'ing Ming
flute.. **4.** tche (che)
fruit.. **6.** litchi (nut)
game.. **6.** fantan
ginger.. **9.** galingale
God.. **4.** Shen (Chr) **7.** Shangti, Tien
Chu (RCCh)
gong.. **6.** tam-tam, tom-tom
grass.. **5.** ramee
idol.. **4.** joss **6.** pagoda (pagod)
instrument.. **3.** che, kin **4.** tche **5.** sheng
(cheng)
jade.. **2.** yu
jute.. **7.** chingma
laborer.. **6.** coolie
lily.. **9.** narcissus
liquor.. **6.** samshu (rice)
literary degree.. **8.** hsiu tsai
monkey.. **4.** douc
nurse.. **4.** amah
officer.. **4.** kwan
oil.. **4.** tung
ox.. **4.** zebu
pagoda.. **3.** taa
paradise (Buddh).. **4.** Jodo **7.** Ching-tu
8. Gekuraku
philosophy.. **10.** Yang and Yin
religion.. **6.** Taoism **8.** Buddhism
12. Confucianism
residence (official).. **5.** yamen
screen (folding).. **10.** Coromandel
silkworm.. **4.** sina **9.** ailanthus
silver ingot.. **5.** sycee
sky.. **4.** tien
society (secret).. **3.** hui (hoey) **4.** tong
vessel.. **4.** junk **6.** lorcha
chink ... **4.** rent, rift, rima, rime, ring
5. cleft, crack **6.** cranny, furrow
7. bunting (bird), fissure **10.** interstice
chinook ... **4.** herb, wind **6.** salmon
7. quinnat

Chinook (pert to) ...
chief.. **4.** tyee
people.. **8.** Flathead
State (nickname of).. **10.** Washington
chinquapin ... **3.** oak **6.** bonnet (water)
8. chestnut
chip ... **3.** cut, hew **4.** coin **5.** break, carve,
flake, piece, scrap, token **6.** chisel,
gallet (stone) **7.** counter
chipmunk ... **6.** hackee
chipped stone (instrument) ...
9. paleolith
chipper ... **5.** chirp **6.** babble, chisel,
hammer, lively **7.** chirrup, twitter
8. cheerful
chirognomy ... **9.** palmistry
10. chiromancy
chironomy ... **7.** gesture (hands)
9. pantomime
chiropter ... **3.** bat **6.** aliped
chirp ... **3.** pew (pue) **4.** peep **5.** cheep,
chirl, tweet **7.** chirrup, twitter
chisel ... **3.** cut, gad, hew **4.** celt (anc),
form, pare **5.** bruzz, burin, carve, cheat,
drove, gouge, grave **6.** furrow, jagger,
mallet, peeker, pommel **7.** engrave,
swindle **9.** sculpture
chit ... **4.** note, runt, wisp **5.** child,
shoot **6.** sprout **10.** memorandum
14. recommendation
chitarra, chitarrine ... **6.** guitar
chiton ... **7.** garment (anc), mollusk
chivalrous ... **5.** brave **6.** gentle,
heroic **7.** gallant, valiant **8.** knightly
9. courteous **11.** magnanimous
chive ... **4.** stab **5.** onion, plant **6.** garlic
chloride ... **3.** ore **4.** salt **5.** ester
7. calomel
chlorine ... **2.** Cl **7.** bromine, halogen,
radical **8.** cyanogen, fluorine
chloroform ... **4.** dope, kill **6.** poison
7. stupefy **9.** narcotize **11.** anesthetize
chlorophyll ... **5.** ester, green **7.** etiolin
9. deodorant
chocolate ... **5.** brown, cacao, candy,
cocoa, color **6.** pinole **8.** beverage
13. Sterculiaceae
choice ... **4.** beat, rare, will **5.** prime
6. dainty, option, select, tidbit
8. election, free will, uncommon
9. recherché, selection **10.** preference,
well-chosen **11.** alternative
choir ... **6.** chorus **7.** singers
choir leader ... **6.** cantor **9.** precentor
choke ... **3.** gag, jam, ram **4.** clog **5.** burke,
check **6.** hinder, impede, muffle, stifle
7. garrote, repress, smother **8.** obstruct,
strangle, throttle **9.** constrict, suffocate
choler ... **3.** ire **4.** bile, foam, gall, rage
5. anger, wrath **6.** spleen **10.** resentment
11. biliousness **12.** irascibility
choleric ... **5.** angry, testy **7.** bilious,
enraged, iracund **8.** wrathful
9. dyspeptic, irascible **10.** passionate
chololith ... **9.** gallstone
choose ... **3.** opt **4.** cull, like, list, pick,
want **5.** elect **6.** desire, optate, prefer,
select
choosing ... **6.** optant **8.** eclectic, elective
9. selecting
chop ... **3.** axe, cut, hew, jaw, lop

4. dice, fell, hack, jowl, meat, raze, seal **5.** cheek, mince, prune, sever, stamp **7.** griskin **8.** noisette (eye of)

choppy ... **5.** bumpy, rough **6.** uneven **7.** jolting **8.** unstable, variable **9.** irregular **10.** changeable, incoherent **13.** discontinuous

chord ... **4.** rope **6.** radius, secant, string, tendon **7.** concord, harmony **8.** arpeggio, concento, filament

chord (terms) ... **5.** major, minor, tonic, triad **6.** broken, common, tetrad **7.** seventh **8.** dominant, unbroken **10.** enharmonic

chords ... **4.** tune **7.** cadence, cantata

chore ... **3.** job (odd) **4.** task, work **5.** stint **10.** assignment

chorography ... **5.** chart **7.** diagram **10.** topography **11.** cartography, description (region), ichnography

chortle ... **5.** laugh, snort **7.** chuckle, snortle

chorus ... **4.** echo **5.** choir **6.** accord, outcry, unison **7.** refrain, singers **8.** chanters **9.** unanimity

chorus (pert to) ...
girl .. **7.** chorine, chorist
leader .. **8.** choragus **9.** conductor
small .. **7.** octette

Chosen (Jap) ... **5.** Korea

Chosen People ... **10.** Israelites

chrism ... **7.** unction, unguent **10.** anointment **12.** confirmation

christen ... **4.** name **6.** launch **7.** baptize **10.** denominate, inaugurate **12.** Christianize

Christian (pert to) ...
Eastern .. **5.** Uniat
feast .. **5.** agape (anc) **8.** Epiphany **9.** Christmas
martyr (first) .. **7.** Stephen
philosopher (anc) .. **6.** Jesuit **9.** Schoolman **10.** Scholastic
sect .. **7.** Docetae
symbol .. **5.** orant (fem)

Christie detective ... **10.** Jane Marple **13.** Hercule Poirot

Christmas (pert to) ...
bag .. **6.** piñata
carol .. **4.** Noel
decoration .. **6.** crèche
feast .. **4.** Yule
hymn .. **13.** Adeste Fideles
mummer .. **6.** guiser
plant .. **5.** holly **9.** evergreen, mistletoe
term .. **4.** Noel, Xmas **8.** Nativity, Yuletide **11.** Weihnachten
time before .. **6.** Advent

Christ's-thorn ... **4.** nabk

chromosome ... **2.** id **5.** idant **8.** biophore, germ cell

chronic ... **7.** abiding **8.** constant, enduring, habitual **9.** confirmed **10.** continuous, inveterate, persistent **14.** valetudinarian

chronicle ... **4.** sard **5.** annal, diary **6.** record **7.** account, archive, history **8.** register **9.** narrative **10.** chronology

chronicler ... **6.** writer **8.** annalist, compiler, recorder **9.** historian **12.** chronologist

chronology error ... **9.** prolepsis

chronometer ... **5.** clock, timer, watch **6.** ghurry **7.** sundial **9.** hourglass, metronome, timepiece

chrysolite ... **5.** green (color) **7.** olivine, peridot

chthonian ... **4.** gods (underworld) **7.** hellish, worship **9.** diabolist **11.** demonolater

chub ... **4.** bass, dace, dolt, fool, lout **6.** shiner, tautog **8.** fallfish **9.** hornyhead, squawfish

chubby ... **3.** fat **5.** plump, pudgy, round **6.** stocky, stubby **9.** corpulent

chuck ... **4.** beef, cast, food, hurl, jerk, toss **5.** fling, heave, pitch, throw **9.** eliminate

chuckle ... **5.** cluck, laugh **6.** cackle, wabble **7.** chortle

chuff ... **3.** fat **4.** boor **5.** churl, clown, cross, proud, sulky, surly **6.** chubby, elated, rustic **9.** conceited **11.** ill-tempered

chum ... **3.** pal **4.** bait, pard **5.** buddy, crony **6.** fellow, hobnob **7.** company, comrade, consort, partner **8.** playmate, roommate **9.** associate, classmate, colleague, companion

chump ... **3.** ass **4.** dolt, dupe, fool, head **5.** block, booby **8.** endpiece

chunk ... **3.** dab, gob, pat, wad **4.** hunk, junt, lump, slug (metal) **5.** stick, stump, throw **8.** fragment

chunky ... **3.** fat **4.** game (Am Ind), junt **5.** lumpy, stout, tubby **6.** chubby, portly, stocky, stodgy, stubby **8.** thickset

church ... **3.** dom **4.** fane (anc), kirk, sect **5.** abbey **6.** bethel, temple **7.** Lateran, minster, templet **8.** basilica, conclave **9.** cathedral **10.** House of God, worshipers **11.** Christendom **12.** denomination

church (pert to) ...
assistant .. **5.** Elder
attendant .. **5.** usher **6.** sexton, verger
calendar .. **4.** ordo
Court .. **10.** Consistory
dignitary .. **4.** dean **6.** bishop, priest **7.** prelate, primate **8.** benefice, cardinal, minister **9.** monsignor
dissenter .. **7.** sectary **10.** anti-Nicean, anti-Nicene
doctrine (State, church) .. **8.** Erastian
dominion .. **10.** sacerdotum
doorkeeper .. **7.** ostiary
Elder .. **9.** Presbyter
feast .. **4.** utas (octave of) **6.** Easter
governing body .. **7.** classis
law .. **5.** canon, synod **7.** council
part .. **4.** apse, bema, nave **5.** altar, canon **7.** chancel, narthex **8.** transept **10.** clerestory
peace device .. **8.** irenicon
property .. **5.** glebe
receptacle .. **10.** monstrance
Roman .. **7.** Lateran **8.** basilica
screen .. **4.** rood
seats .. **4.** pews **7.** sedilla
service (part) .. **3.** pax **4.** Mass **5.** crede **7.** epistle, introit, sanctus **8.** Agnus Dei, blessing **9.** communion

stipend . . **7.** prebend
traffic (preferments) . . **6.** simony
vessel . . **3.** ama, pyx (pix) **6.** lavabo
   7. chalice **8.** ciborium
vestry . . **8.** sacristy
churl . . . **3.** cad, oaf **4.** boor, carl, hind,
   lout, serf **5.** ceorl, knave **6.** rustic
   7. bondman, freeman, peasant, villain
   9. vulgarian **10.** countryman
churlish . . . **4.** mean **5.** gruff, rough,
   surly **6.** rustic, sordid, sullen, vulgar
   7. boorish, crabbed, knavish
   9. gruffness, niggardly **10.** ill-humored
   11. countrified
churn . . . **4.** beat, kirn, stir, whip **5.** mixer,
   shake **6.** beater, seethe, vessel **7.** agitate
   8. agitator, emulsify
chute . . . **4.** tube **5.** flume, scarp, slide
   6. trough **7.** channel, incline, passage
   9. parachute
cibel . . . **5.** chive, onion **7.** shallot
ciborium . . . **3.** pyx **6.** canopy, coffer,
   vessel
cicada . . . **6.** dog-day, locust **9.** Cicadidae
cicatrix . . . **4.** mark, scar **7.** blemish
Cid . . . **3.** Ruy **4.** hero, poem **5.** Chief
   6. leader (Christian) **7.** Rodrigo
cider (weak) . . . **6.** perkin
Cid's sword . . . **6.** colada
cienaga . . . **5.** marsh, swamp
cigar . . . **4.** rope, toby **5.** claro **6.** corona,
   Havana, maduro, stogie **7.** cheroot
   8. panatela **9.** cigarillo
cigarette . . . **3.** fag **4.** pill **5.** cubeb, smoke
   6. gasper, reefer **9.** cigarillo **10.** coffin
   nail
cilium . . . **4.** hair, lash **7.** eyelash
   8. barbicel, ciliolum, filament
   9. eyewinker
cimarron . . . **6.** marron **7.** bighorn, wild
   dog **8.** district (Okla)
cimex . . . **6.** bedbug
Cimmerian, Homer Myth . . . **4.** dark
   5. Nomad (anc) **6.** gloomy (abode)
   8. Cimmeria
cinch . . . **4.** game (cards), grip, sure
   5. girth **6.** fasten **7.** harness (part)
   9. certainty, sure thing
cinders . . . **3.** ash **4.** lava, slag **5.** ashes,
   dross **6.** embers **7.** residue **8.** clinkers
cinerarium . . . **8.** mortuary
cinerator . . . **7.** furnace **9.** crematory
   11. crematorium, incinerator
cingular . . . **7.** annular **8.** circular
cinnamon . . . **5.** brown, spice **6.** cassia
   8. ishpingo (So Am) **10.** Cinnamomum
cinque . . . **4.** dice
cipher . . . **3.** nil **4.** code, zero **5.** aught
   6. figure, nobody, number, symbol
   7. compute **9.** calculate, character,
   nonentity
circa . . . **5.** about **6.** around
   13. approximately
Circe (pert to) . . .
   brother . . **6.** Aeetes
   father . . **6.** Helios
   Island abode . . **5.** Aeaea
   role, Odyssey . . **5.** siren **7.** charmer
      9. sorceress, temptress
   sister . . **5.** Medea
circle . . . **3.** orb **4.** halo, hoop, loop, ring

   5. ambit, orbit, rhomb, rigol, round,
   wheel **6.** clique, cordon, girdle, rotate,
   sphere **7.** annulus, aureole, circuit,
   compass, enclose, revolve **9.** circulate,
   encompass **13.** circumference
circle (pert to) . . .
   astronomy . . **6.** tropic
   celestial . . **6.** colure **10.** almucantar
   Japan . . **4.** maru
   luminous . . **6.** corona
   of hell (8th) . . **9.** Malebolge
   of monoliths . . **8.** cromlech **9.** cyclolith
   part . . **3.** arc **6.** areola, octant, radius,
      sector **7.** sextant **8.** diameter
circuit . . . **3.** lap, orb **4.** bout, gyre,
   loop, tour, zone **5.** ambit, cycle, orbit,
   relay, round, route **6.** circle, detour
   7. compass **9.** round trip **10.** revolution
circuit court . . . **4.** eyre
circuitous . . . **4.** mazy **6.** curved
   7. crooked, devious, sinuous, twisted,
   vagrant, winding **8.** circular, flexuous,
   indirect, tortuous **9.** deceitful, deviating,
   underhand, wandering **10.** roundabout,
   serpentine **12.** disingenuous,
   labyrinthine **14.** circumlocutory
circular . . . **5.** round **6.** ringed **7.** annular,
   discoid, program **8.** cingular, coronary,
   ringlike **9.** crownlike, orbicular
   10. circuitous, roundabout
   13. advertisement
circular (pert to) . . .
   enclosure . . **3.** lis (liss)
   indicator . . **4.** dial
   letter . . **10.** encyclical
   ornament . . **6.** patera
circulate . . . **4.** pass **5.** issue **6.** circle,
   rotate, spread **7.** diffuse, publish
   8. monetize **9.** propagate
   11. disseminate
circumference . . . **4.** girt **5.** ambit, bound,
   girth **6.** bounds **7.** circuit, compass
   8. encircle, surround **9.** outskirts,
   perimeter, periphery
circumscribe . . . **5.** bound, fence, limit
   6. define **7.** enclose, environ **8.** encircle,
   restrict **9.** encompass
circumscribed . . . **6.** finite, narrow
   9. definable **10.** restricted
circumspect . . . **4.** wary **5.** chary
   7. careful, politic, prudent **8.** cautious,
   discreet **9.** judicious **10.** thoughtful
   11. considerate
circumstance . . . **4.** fact, item, pomp
   5. event, state **7.** proviso **8.** incident,
   occasion, position **9.** condition,
   provision, situation **10.** occurrence,
   particular **11.** arrangement, opportunity,
   stipulation
circumstantial . . . **5.** exact **6.** minute
   7. precise **8.** detailed **10.** evidential,
   incidental, particular **11.** conditional
   12. nonessential
circumvent . . . **5.** cheat, evade **6.** delude,
   entrap, outwit, thwart **7.** capture, circuit,
   deceive **8.** surround **9.** encompass,
   frustrate
circus . . . **4.** hawk, ring, show **5.** arena
   6. big top, circle, cirque **7.** harrier,
   theater **8.** carnival, side show
   12. amphitheater

circus (pert to) . . .
concessionaire . . **7.** grifter
hawk . . **15.** circus assimilis
rider . . **8.** desultor
Roman . . **13.** Circus Maximus
sideshow . . **6.** freaks
superintendent . . **10.** ringmaster
cirque . . . **6.** circle, corrie **7.** circlet
cis (pref) . . . **8.** this side
cist . . . **3.** box, pit **5.** chest **7.** chamber
8. cistvaen (kistvaen)
Cistercian . . . **4.** monk, Rule (Benedictine)
5. Order **8.** Trappist
cistern . . . **3.** bac, sac, tub, vat **4.** back,
tank, well **7.** cuvette, raintub
9. impluvium, reservoir
citadel . . . **3.** arx **4.** fort **5.** Alamo, tower
6. castle **7.** bastion, bulwark **8.** fastness,
fortress **9.** acropolis **10.** stronghold
13. fortification **14.** propungnaculum
citation . . . **5.** honor **6.** eulogy, notice
7. mention, summons **8.** subpoena
9. quotation **11.** enumeration
12. verification
cite . . . **5.** quote **6.** adduce, allege, repeat,
summon **7.** extract **8.** indicate
citizen . . . **3.** cit **6.** native **7.** citoyen,
denizen (of beasts), dweller **8.** civilian,
townsman **10.** inhabitant
citizenship . . . **10.** citizenism
15. enfranchisement
citron . . . **5.** melon **6.** cedrat (cedrate),
citrus, yellow
citrus fruit . . . **4.** lime **5.** lemon **6.** orange
7. kumquat **8.** citrange, shaddock
10. grapefruit
cittern, cithern . . . **4.** lute (anc) **6.** zither
7. cithara, gittern
city . . . **4.** town **8.** township **10.** metropolis
12. municipality
city (parts) . . . **4.** ward **5.** civic, urban
8. district, precinct
City of . . .
Bells . . **10.** Strasbourg
Bridges . . **6.** Bruges
Brotherly Love . . **12.** Philadelphia
Churches . . **8.** Brooklyn
David . . **9.** Jerusalem
Dead (The) . . **8.** cemetery **10.** Necropolis
Elms . . **8.** New Haven
Gods . . **6.** Asgard (Asgarth)
Golden Gate (The) . . **12.** San Francisco
Great King . . **9.** Jerusalem
Hundred Towers . . **5.** Pavia
Kings . . **4.** Lira
Lilies . . **8.** Florence
Magnificent Distances . . **10.** Washington
(DC)
Masts . . **6.** London
Palms (Bib) . . **7.** Jericho
Prophet (The) . . **6.** Medina
Rams . . **6.** Canton
Saints . . **8.** Montreal
Seven Hills . . **4.** Rome
Straits . . **7.** Detroit
Sun (the) . . **7.** Baalbek **10.** Heliopolis
Victory . . **5.** Cairo
Violated Treaty . . **8.** Limerick
Violet Crown . . **6.** Athens
civet . . . **5.** fossa, genet, rasse **6.** foussa,
musang **7.** nandine **10.** paradoxure

civic . . . **5.** civil, urban **6.** public **7.** burghal,
oppidan **9.** municipal **12.** metropolitan
civil . . . **4.** hend (hende) **5.** suave **6.** decent,
polite, public, urbane **7.** affable,
courtly, elegant, secular **8.** discreet,
gracious, obliging, polished, well-bred
9. courteous, political **10.** respectful
11. complaisant **13.** condescending
civil (pert to) . . .
dress . . **5.** mufti **7.** civvies
fraud (Rom) . . **11.** stellionate
process . . **4.** writ
strife . . **6.** stasis
wrong . . **4.** tort
civility . . . **6.** comity **7.** amenity
8. courtesy, urbanity **9.** attention,
etiquette, gentility **10.** affability,
politeness
civilization . . . **6.** kultur, polish **7.** culture
10. refinement **11.** cultivation
civilize . . . **4.** tame **6.** polish **8.** humanize,
urbanize **9.** cultivate **11.** domesticate
clad . . . **5.** robed **6.** decked, garbed
7. arrayed, attired, clothed, dressed
9. appareled, garmented
claim . . . **3.** hak (hakh) **4.** case, lien,
name **5.** right, title **6.** assert, demand
7. preempt, profess, require **8.** arrogate,
maintain, pretense (pretence), proclaim
9. postulate **10.** pretension
claimant . . . **7.** claimer **9.** applicant,
plaintiff, pretender **10.** solicitant
clairvoyance . . . **3.** ESP **7.** insight
8. lucidity, sagacity **9.** intuition
10. divination **11.** penetration
clairvoyant . . . **4.** seer **7.** prophet, seeress
9. sagacious **12.** clearsighted
clam . . . **3.** Mya **5.** Chama, razor, Solen
6. gweduc, Mactra, quahog **7.** mollusk
10. veneriform (shape)
clam destroyer . . . **6.** winkle
10. periwinkle
clammy . . . **4.** cool, damp, dank, soft
5. moist, mucid **6.** sticky, sweaty
clamor . . . **3.** cry, din, hue **4.** roar, wail
5. decry, noise, vocal **6.** hubbub, outcry,
racket, uproar **10.** hullabaloo
clamorous . . . **4.** loud **5.** noisy **7.** blatant,
clamant, excited **8.** brawling
9. demanding, insistent, turbulent
10. blustering, uproarious, vociferous
clamp . . . **4.** vise **6.** fasten **9.** appliance
clan . . . **3.** set **4.** camp, club, cult, gens,
race, sept **5.** group, party, tribe **6.** circle,
clique, family **7.** coterie, society
clan (quarrel) . . . **4.** feud **8.** vendetta
clandestine . . . **3.** sly **5.** privy **6.** covert,
secret **7.** furtive, illicit **8.** stealthy
9. concealed, underhand **10.** frandulent,
undercover **11.** unobtrusive
13. surreptitious
clang . . . **4.** ding, ring **5.** clank, sound
6. jangle **7.** ringing
clang color . . . **6.** timbre **8.** tonality
clangor . . . **3.** din **4.** ring **5.** clang, noise
6. fracas, hubbub, jangle, racket, ruckus,
rumpus, tumult, uproar **7.** discord,
ringing
clank . . . **4.** ring **5.** clang **7.** ringing
clapper . . . **4.** bell, clap **5.** bones (minstrel)
claque . . . **8.** chaqueur, opera hat

9. applauder
clarify ... **5.** clear **6.** filter, purify, refine, render, strain **7.** cleanse, explain, rectify
clash ... **3.** jar **4.** bang, bump **5.** crash **6.** impact, jangle, tussle **7.** collide, scuffle **8.** conflict, disagree, skirmish **9.** collision, encounter, hostility **10.** dissonance
clasp ... **3.** hug **4.** belt, grip, hasp, hold, ouch (anc), tach **5.** grasp, morse (priest's), seize, stick, tache (anc) **6.** buckle, enwrap, fasten, secure **7.** agraffe (agrafe), embrace, tendril **8.** fastener **10.** chatelaine
class ... **3.** ilk **4.** rank, sect **5.** caste, genus (pl genera), grade, order, tribe **6.** brevet (mil), status **7.** station **8.** category, classify, division **9.** catalogue **14.** classification
class (learned) ... **8.** literate, literati **14.** intelligentsia
classical ... **4.** pure **5.** Attic **6.** chaste **7.** classis, elegant **8.** academic, literary, tasteful **10.** Ciceronian
classification ... **4.** rank, sort **5.** genus, grade **6.** rating, system **7.** species **8.** analysis, category, grouping **12.** distribution
classify ... **4.** list, rank, rate, sort, type **5.** grade, label, range **6.** assort, digest, ticket **7.** aggroup, arrange **8.** register **9.** catalogue
clatter ... **3.** din, jar **5.** noise, rumor **6.** babble, gabble, hubbub, racket, rattle, rumpus, tattle, uproar **7.** chatter, prattle **9.** commotion **11.** disturbance
clause ... **5.** rider **6.** phrase **7.** passage, proviso, section
claustral ... **9.** cloistral **10.** cloistered
claw ... **4.** hand, nail, unce **5.** chela, cloof, clufe, talon **6.** nipper, unguis
claw ... **3.** dig **4.** grab, grip, pull, tear **5.** grasp, seize **6.** clutch, scrape, snatch **7.** grapple, scratch
clay ... **3.** mud **4.** marl, mire, soil **5.** argil, earth **6.** corpse, kaolin
clay (pert to) ...
baked .. **4.** tile **5.** brick
box .. **6.** sagger
covered .. **6.** lutose
mix .. **3.** pug
mold .. **3.** dod
molded .. **7.** fictile
nodule .. **10.** eaglestone
pipe .. **2.** TD **10.** meerschaum
plug .. **4.** bott
polish .. **5.** rabat
softening .. **8.** malaxage
variety .. **4.** bole, loam, marl **5.** gault, ocher, tasco **8.** petuntse
clayey ... **4.** soft **5.** adobe, bolar **6.** earthy **12.** argillaceous
clean, cleanse ... **4.** dust, swab, wash, wipe **5.** brush, purge, rinse, scrub **6.** kosher, purify, refine **7.** cleanse, deterge, launder **8.** absterge, depurate, renovate **9.** disinfect, elutriate, expurgate
cleanness ... **6.** purity (of life) **7.** clarity **8.** chastity, elegance, neatness, pureness, tidiness **10.** immaculacy

13. impeccability
clear ... **3.** net, rid **4.** free, gain, over, pure **5.** clean, lucid, plain **6.** acquit, excuse, exempt, hurdle, limpid, pardon, purify **7.** absolve, concise, crystal, evident, explain, graphic, lighten, release **8.** apparent, distinct, incisive, luculent **9.** cloudless, exonerate, extricate, vindicate
clear land ... **7.** thwaite (Eng)
clearsighted ... **4.** keen **10.** discerning **13.** perspicacious
cleat ... **4.** bitt **5.** level, strip, wedge **7.** joinery
cleave ... **3.** cut **4.** part, rend, rive, tear **5.** clave, cling, clove, crack, sever, shear, split **6.** adhere, bisect, cohere, divide, pierce **7.** dispart **8.** separate
cleek ... **5.** marry, pluck, seize **6.** clutch, snatch
clef ... **1.** C, F, G **4.** alto, bass **6.** treble **7.** descant, soprano **9.** character
cleft ... **3.** gap **4.** reft, rent, rift, rima **5.** chasm, chink, crack, notch, riven, split **6.** chappy, cranny, gaping, recess **7.** crevice, fissure **8.** scissure
cleft palate operation ... **13.** staphyloraphy (staphylorrhaphy)
clemency ... **5.** favor, grace, mercy **6.** lenity **7.** quarter **8.** kindness, leniency, mildness **10.** compassion, indulgence **11.** forbearance
Clemens (Samuel) **pen name** ... **9.** Mark Twain
clench ... **4.** fist, grip, grit, hold **5.** grasp **6.** clinch, clutch **8.** purchase **9.** interlock
Cleopatra (pert to) ...
attendant .. **4.** Iras
downfall .. **3.** asp
lover .. **6.** Antony (Marc), Caesar
obelisk (two) .. **6.** Needle
queen of .. **5.** Egypt
river .. **4.** Nile
clepe ... **3.** bid **4.** call, name **6.** invite, invoke **7.** address **8.** christen
clergy ... **5.** cloth **6.** pulpit **9.** clergymen, clericals **10.** priesthood
clergyman ... **4.** abbé, dean **5.** canon, vicar **6.** cleric, curate, divine, parson, pastor, priest, rector **7.** dominie, prelate **8.** minister, preacher, sky pilot **9.** presbyter **12.** ecclesiastic
clergywoman ... **3.** nun **8.** minister **9.** parsoness, priestess **10.** religieuse
cleric, non ... **4.** laic
clerical ... **7.** scribal **11.** ministerial
clerical (pert to) ...
attire .. **3.** alb **5.** amice, cloth, fanon, orale, stole
collar .. **5.** rabat
hat .. **7.** biretta
clerk ... **3.** nun **4.** monk **5.** write **6.** cleric, hermit, layman, scribe **7.** scholar (anc) **8.** salesman **9.** assistant, clergyman **12.** ecclesiastic
cleronomy ... **8.** heritage **11.** inheritancy
clever ... **3.** apt **4.** able, cute, deft **5.** handy, slick, smart, witty **6.** adroit, astute, brainy, bright, expert, habile, nimble **7.** amiable, cunning, parlous **8.** pleasing, skillful, talented **9.** brilliant,

dexterous, ingenious **11.** good-natured

cleverness . . . **4.** tact, wits **5.** skill **6.** esprit **7.** cunning **9.** ingenuity, smartness, wittiness **10.** adroitness, astuteness, shrewdness

clew, clue . . . **3.** key **4.** ball, loop (Naut) rope **5.** globe **6.** cocoon, tackle (see also *clue)*

cliché . . . **4.** joke **5.** banal, trite **6.** old saw **7.** bromide **8.** banality, chestnut **9.** Joe Miller, platitude

click . . . **3.** rap **4.** snap **5.** clack **6.** go over **7.** prosper, succeed

click beatle . . . **3.** dor (dorr) **6.** elater

cliff . . . **3.** gat **4.** crag, klip, rock, wall **5.** bluff, cleve, crest, scarp, slope **6.** rocher **7.** clogwyn **8.** palisade **9.** precipice **10.** escarpment

climax . . . **3.** cap, epi (Arch) **4.** acme, near, peak, shut **5.** tight **6.** apogee, result, summit **7.** heights **11.** culmination **12.** consummation

climb . . . **3.** fly, gad **4.** shin **5.** grimp, scale, speel **6.** ascend, ascent **7.** clamber, upgrade **9.** acclivity

climbing . . . **7.** scaling **8.** scandent **10.** scansorial

climbing plant . . . **3.** hop, ivy **4.** bine, nito, vine **5.** betel, liana **6.** bryony

clime . . . **4.** zone **5.** realm, tract **6.** region **7.** climate

clinch . . . **4.** bind, grip, hold, seal **5.** grasp, prove, seize **6.** clutch, fasten, secure **7.** confirm, grapple **8.** conclude, purchase **9.** establish

cling . . . **4.** hold **5.** stick **6.** adhere, cohere

clingfish . . . **6.** testar

clink . . . **4.** rime, slap **5.** rhyme **6.** jingle, lockup, prison, strike **9.** assonance

clinquant . . . **4.** gold, sham **6.** tinsel **8.** frippery, tinseled **10.** glittering

clip . . . **3.** bob, lop, mow **4.** barb, blow, dock, gaff, snip, trim **5.** clasp, prune, shear **6.** clutch, fasten **7.** curtail, scissor, shorten **8.** ornament **10.** instrument

clique . . . **3.** set **4.** cell, clan, club, ring **5.** group, Junta, junto **6.** circle (people) **7.** coterie

Cloaca Maxima (anc Rome) . . . **5.** sewer **10.** repository

cloak . . . **3.** aba **4.** cape, mask, pall, wrap **5.** cover, grego, jelab, manta, sagum **6.** abolla, capote, dolman, mantle, mantua, screen, serape, shield **7.** chlamys (anc), conceal, galabia, manteau, paenula (anc), paletot, pelisse, pretext, protect **8.** disguise **9.** dissemble, new-market **10.** witzchoura

clobber . . . **3.** hit **4.** beat, conk, poke, swat **5.** clout, punch, whack **6.** defeat, strike, wallop

clock . . . **3.** nef (ship's) **4.** dial, time **5.** knock **6.** record **7.** digital **8.** recorder, sidereal **9.** clepsydra, metronome, timepiece **10.** isochronon **11.** chronometer

clockwise . . . **6.** deasil (dessil) **11.** withershins **14.** dextrorotation, dextrorotatory

clog . . . **4.** stop **5.** choke, dance **6.** daggle, hamper, impede **8.** encumber, obstruct,

restrain

clog shoe . . . **4.** geta **5.** sabot **6.** chopin, cobcab (Orient), patten **7.** chopine

cloister . . . **4.** stoa **5.** abbey **6.** arcade, friary, immure, priory **7.** confine, convent, nunnery, retreat **9.** anchorage, hermitage, monastery, peristyle **10.** passageway

cloistered . . . **7.** recluse **8.** enclosed, monastic **11.** sequestered

clone . . . **4.** copy, twin **7.** replica

close . . . **2.** at, by **3.** end **4.** near, nigh, seal, shut, slam **5.** dense, finis, stivy **6.** finale, finish, period, secret, stingy, sultry **7.** airless, extreme, occlude, related **8.** complete, conclude, familiar, imminent, intimate, stifling **9.** extremity, secretive, terminate **11.** approximate, termination **13.** juxtaposition

close (pert to) . . .
    eyes (the) . . **4.** seel **5.** blink
    fasten . . **6.** batten
    of day . . **8.** eventide **9.** nightfall
    poetic . . **4.** nigh **5.** anear
    tightly . . **3.** bar **4.** bung, seal **6.** clench, enseal **8.** obturate

closely . . . **4.** just **6.** almost, barely, nearly **8.** narrowly

closely allied . . . **6.** chummy **7.** germane **8.** intimate

closeness . . . **7.** density, secrecy **8.** fidelity, intimacy, likeness, nearness, sameness **9.** tightness **10.** chumminess, narrowness, similarity, stinginess, strictness, sultriness **11.** airlessness, compactness, conciseness, familiarity, resemblance **14.** oppressiveness

closet . . . **5.** ambry, cuddy, emery **6.** locker, pantry **7.** cabinet **8.** cupboard, wardrobe **9.** cloakroom, storeroom

closing device . . . **3.** key **4.** lock, snap **5.** clasp, hinge, latch **6.** Velcro (tm), zipper

closing measure (Mus) . . . **4.** coda

clot . . . **4.** lump, mass **5.** grume **7.** thicken **8.** coagulum, concrete **9.** coagulate **12.** crassamentum

cloth . . . **3.** net, tat **4.** brin, crea, drap, felt, lamé, silk, tapa, wool **5.** adati, baize, bezan, bluet, carda, crash, crepe, denim, khaki, linen, manta, nylon, orlon, rayon, satin, scrim, surat, tamis, terry, tulle, twill, voile **6.** alpaca, burlap, calico, canvas, chintz, cotton, damask, dimity, dowlas, duffel, faille, jersey, madras, mohair, muslin, nankin, pongee, poplin, samite (gold), sateen, velour **7.** acetate, baracan, brocade, bunting, cambric, challis, chiffon, drap d'or, flannel, foulard, gingham, nankeen, organdy, organza, percale, sacking, spandex, taffeta, ticking, worsted **8.** cashmere, chambray, corduroy, cretonne, drilling, nainsook, Shantung **9.** crinoline, gabardine, polyester, sailcloth, tarpaulin, tricotine **10.** broadcloth, seersucker **11.** cheesecloth, drap d'argent (silver), marquisette

cloth (pert to) . . .
    checkered . . **5.** plaid

dealer .. **6.** draper
finisher .. **7.** beetler
measure .. **4.** nail
piece .. **4.** bolt **5.** scrap
ridge .. **4.** wale
selvage .. **4.** roon **6.** border **7.** listing
twilled .. **5.** denim, serge
weaving .. **4.** warp, weft, woof
clothe . . . **3.** tog **4.** deck, garb, gird, robe, vest **5.** array, drape, dress, endue, indue **6.** afford, enrobe, invest **7.** empower, provide, sheathe **8.** accouter
clothes . . . **3.** rig **4.** duds, garb, togs **5.** guise, habit, jeans, Levis **6.** attire, bikini, briefs **7.** apparel, costume, raiment, regalia, threads (sl) **8.** clothing, garments, leotards, swimsuit **9.** dungarees **10.** bedclothes, garmenture **11.** habiliments, investiture
cloud . . . **3.** fog, low **4.** dust, film, haze, mist, rack, scud **5.** nepho (comb form), nubia, stain, sully, taint, vapor **6.** cirrus, damage, darken, defame, defect, nebule, nimbus, shadow, stigma **7.** blacken, blemish, cumulus, nubilus, obscure, pea-soup, stratus, tarnish, tornado **8.** cat's-tail, cocktail, overcast **10.** horizontal
clouds (pert to) . . .
astronomy .. **4.** coma **9.** nubeculae
kind .. **6.** cirrus, nimbus **7.** cumulus, fractus, stratus **9.** mare's-tail
luminous .. **5.** nimbi
Magellanic .. **5.** Major, Minor
photography .. **9.** nephogram
science of .. **9.** nephology
seeding .. **10.** nucleation
vapory .. **4.** rack
cloudy . . . **4.** dark, hazy **5.** filmy, foggy, misty, murky, shady, vague **6.** gloomy, lowery, opaque **7.** nebular, obscure **8.** confused, overcast, vaporous **9.** cloudlike **10.** indistinct, lackluster
clout . . . **3.** hit, jab, rag **4.** blow, bump, clod, mend, nail, swat **5.** patch, power, shred, smack **6.** influence **12.** handkerchief
clove . . . see also *cleave* **5.** spice
clover . . . **3.** red **4.** bush **5.** lotus, snail, white **6.** alsike **7.** crimson, melilot, prairie, spotted **9.** Melilotus
clown . . . **3.** oaf **4.** boor, fool, lout, mime, mome, zany **5.** comic, Kelly (Emmet), mimer, yahoo **6.** jester, rustic **7.** buffoon **9.** harlequin **10.** countryman **11.** merry-andrew
clownish . . . **4.** rude **5.** gawky, rough **6.** clumsy, coarse, rustic **7.** awkward, boorish, ill-bred, loutish, uncivil **8.** churlish, ungainly **9.** untutored **10.** buffoonish **11.** countrified
cloy . . . **4.** clog, glut, pall, sate **5.** gorge, stuff **6.** accloy **7.** satiate, satisfy, surfeit
club . . . **3.** bat, hit **4.** beat, join, mace **5.** billy, clout, staff, unite, yokel **6.** cudgel, league, weapon **7.** society **8.** bludgeon, spontoon **9.** boomerang, espantoon **10.** nulla-nulla, pogamoggan **11.** association
club (pert to) . . .
actors .. **6.** Friars

historic .. **5.** Whigs **8.** Jacobins **10.** Cordeliers
Service .. **7.** Kiwanis
Women's (first) .. **7.** Sorosis
clubfoot . . . **7.** talipes **9.** deformity, pes valgus **13.** talipes valgus
club-shaped . . . **7.** clavate
clue, clew . . . **3.** key, tip **4.** data, hint **5.** scent **6.** thread **7.** inkling **8.** evidence **9.** suspicion **11.** fingerprint
clump . . . **3.** tod **4.** heap, lump, thud, tuft **5.** bunch, chunk, group, motte (mott), patch, stamp **6.** growth, trudge **7.** cluster, thicket
clumsy . . . **4.** ugly **5.** bulky, gawky, inapt, inept, unfit **6.** gauche, oafish **7.** awkward, uncouth, unhandy **8.** slipshod, ungainly, unwieldy **9.** inelegant, lumbering, maladroit, misshapen **10.** blundering, cumbersome, left-handed **13.** inappropriate
clumsy person . . . **4.** gawk **5.** jumbo, staup **7.** bungler
clupeoid fish . . . **7.** herring
cluster . . . **4.** crop, cyme, gang, tuft **5.** bunch, clump, group **6.** huddle **8.** fascicle **9.** glomerule
cluster (pert to) . . .
bean .. **4.** guar **6.** legume
fibers .. **3.** nep
flowers .. **6.** raceme **7.** rosette **8.** anthemia, panticle
fruit .. **6.** grapes
spores .. **5.** sorus
stars .. **8.** Globular, Pleiades (The)
clustery . . . **8.** racemose
clutch . . . **3.** nab **4.** claw, grip, hold, nest **5.** brood, catch, clasp, grasp, seize **6.** clench, cletch, crisis
clyster . . . **5.** enema **6.** lavage **9.** injection
Clytemnestra's mother . . . **4.** Leda
cnemis . . . **4.** shin **5.** tibia
coach . . . **3.** car, rig **5.** prime, stage, train, tutor **6.** direct, fiacre, jarvey **7.** adviser, prepare, tallyho, teacher **8.** carriage, equipage, instruct, preparer **9.** charabanc **10.** instructor
coach dog . . . **9.** Dalmatian
coachman . . . **3.** fly (angling) **4.** fish, jehu, whip **6.** driver
coagulate . . . **3.** gel, jel, set **4.** cake, clot, curd, lump **6.** curdle, posset **7.** congeal **8.** solidify
coagulator . . . **6.** enzyme, rennet
coagulum . . . **4.** clot, curd **5.** grume **7.** clabber
coal . . . **4.** fuel **5.** black, ember **6.** carbon, cinder **7.** lignite, residue
coal (pert to) . . .
bin .. **6.** bunker
car .. **3.** dan **4.** corf, tram **6.** hopper
dust .. **4.** coom (coomb), culm, smut
gas .. **7.** Pintsch **9.** acetylene
miner .. **7.** collier
miner's disease .. **11.** anthracosis
oil .. **8.** kerosene
residue .. **4.** coke
tar .. **5.** lysol, pitch **6.** cresol, decane, phenol **7.** toluene
tunnel .. **4.** adit

type.. **3.** egg, nut, pea **4.** dant, hard, peat, soft **6.** broken, cannel **8.** charcoal, chestnut **9.** buckwheat **10.** anthracite, bituminous

coalition ... **4.** bloc **5.** trust, union **6.** fusion, hookup, league, merger **7.** society **8.** alliance **10.** federation **11.** affiliation, combination, confederacy, conjunction

coalition advocate ... **9.** fusionist

coals ... **5.** gleed **6.** embers **7.** cinders

coarse ... **3.** fat, low **4.** dank, lewd, rude, vile **5.** broad, crass, gross, thick **6.** carnal, earthy, impure, ribald, rustic, vulgar **7.** goatish, obscene, sensual **8.** granular, immodest, indecent, inferior, unchaste **9.** inelegant, offensive, unrefined **10.** unfinished, unpolished

coarse (pert to) ...
grain.. **4.** meal
grass.. **4.** reed **5.** sedge **6.** quitch
hominy.. **4.** corn, samp

coast ... **4.** sail **5.** beach, glide, shore, slide **6.** rivage **7.** seaside **8.** seaboard, seashore

coast (pert to) ...
dweller.. **7.** orarian
live oak.. **6.** encina
projection.. **4.** cape, ness

coat ... **4.** jupe **5.** cloak, frock, parka, tunic **6.** blazer, capote, duster, jacket, raglan, reefer, trench, tuxedo, ulster **7.** cassock, cutaway, paletot, slicker **8.** gossamer, Mackinaw, tegument **9.** newmarket, redingote

coat (pert to) ...
fastener.. **4.** frog **6.** zipper
of animal.. **3.** fur **4.** pelt, wool **6.** pelage **8.** feathers
of arms.. **5.** crest **8.** blazonry **10.** escutcheon
of mail.. **6.** byrnia **7.** hauberk
of the eye (inner).. **6.** retina

coati ... **5.** Nasua **6.** narica **7.** raccoon

coating (pert to) ...
cake.. **5.** glacé, icing **8.** frosting
copper, bronze.. **6.** patina
grain.. **4.** bran
medical.. **9.** collodion
metal.. **5.** plate
seed.. **5.** testa **6.** tegmen **10.** endopleura
tin, lead.. **5.** terne
vitreous.. **6.** enamel

coax ... **3.** beg, ply **4.** lure, urge **5.** press, tease **6.** cajole, entice, exhort **7.** beguile, flatter, implore, wheedle **8.** blandish, inveigle, persuade **9.** importune **10.** manipulate

cob ... **4.** axis, blow, gull, loaf, mole, pier, swan **5.** block, chief, horse **6.** basket, leader, muffin, spider **7.** beating, corncob **8.** dumpling **10.** breakwater

cobbler ... **3.** pie **5.** coler, sutor **6.** bungle, repair, souter **7.** botcher, crispin **9.** fortescue (fortesque), shoemaker

cobbra ... **4.** head **5.** skull

cobby ... **5.** stout **6.** hearty, lively, stocky **10.** headstrong

cobra ... **3.** asp **4.** Naga (Myth), Naja **5.** mamba, snake, viper **8.** ringhals

cobweb ... **3.** net **4.** trap **5.** snare, wevet **7.** fiction, network **8.** filament, gossamer **9.** intricacy

cobweblike ... **8.** araneous **9.** arachnoid

cocaine ... **4.** coca, snow (sl) **8.** narcotic **9.** mydriatic **10.** anesthetic

coccus ... **4.** cell **5.** spore **9.** bacterium, cochineal

cochleate ... **6.** spiral **11.** shell-shaped

cock ... **3.** nab, tap **4.** bird, heap, kora, pile, vane (weather) **5.** strut, valve **6.** faucet, grouse, leader, muckna **7.** rooster, swagger

cockade ... **4.** knot **7.** rosette

Cockade State ... **8.** Maryland

cockatoo ... **3.** ara **5.** arara (palm), galah **6.** parrot **8.** ganggang

cockle ... **4.** boat, gith, kiln, oast **5.** shell, stove **6.** pucker **7.** mollusk, wrinkle

cockpit ... **3.** pit **4.** well **5.** arena, cabin (airplane) **7.** gallera

cockscomb (coxcomb) ... **5.** crest, plant

cocktail ... **5.** cloud, drink, horse **6.** beetle **9.** appetizer

cocky ... **4.** pert **5.** saucy **6.** jaunty **7.** stuck-up **9.** conceited

cocoa ... **5.** broma, cacao **8.** beverage **9.** chocolate **11.** theobromine

coconut (pert to) ...
fiber.. **4.** coir, kyar
India.. **6.** nargil (narghile)
meat.. **5.** copra
tree.. **4.** palm

cocoon ... **3.** pod **4.** bave (silk), clew, kell, pupa **9.** chrysalis

cod ... **3.** bib, cor **4.** fish, ling **5.** scrod, sprag **6.** burbot, cultus, gadoid **7.** bacalao

coddle ... **3.** pet **4.** baby, cock **5.** humor, spoil **6.** caress, fondle, pamper **11.** mollycoddle

code ... **3.** law **5.** canon, codex, Morse, salic **6.** digest, equity, signal, symbol **7.** pandect, precept **12.** Commandments

codfish (pert to) ...
Alaska.. **6.** wachna
genus.. **5.** Gadus
ready for cooking.. **5.** scrod
type.. **3.** cod, red **4.** cusk, rock **6.** Murray, tomcod **7.** buffalo

codger ... **5.** crank, miser **6.** oddity

codicil ... **4.** will **5.** rider **6.** sequel **8.** addition, appendix **10.** instrument

Cody (William) ... **11.** Buffalo Bill

coerce ... **4.** curb **5.** force **6.** compel **7.** dragoon, enforce, repress **9.** blackjack, strong-arm, terrorize **10.** intimidate

coercion ... **5.** force **6.** duress **8.** violence **10.** compulsion, constraint

coffee (pert to) ...
bean.. **3.** nib
container.. **8.** canister
cup holder.. **4.** zarf
drink.. **8.** espresso **10.** café au lait, cappuccino
extract.. **8.** caffeine
kind.. **3.** Rio **4.** Java, Kona **5.** Kenya, Milds, Mocha **6.** Bogota, Brazil, Santos **7.** Sumatra, Turkish **8.** Medellin **9.** Maracaibo

mix . . **7.** chicory
pot . . **6.** biggin **10.** percolator
coffin . . . **3.** box, urn **4.** bier, case, kist,
    mold **5.** chest, crust **6.** basket, casing,
    casket **11.** sarcophagus
coffin (pert to) . . .
cloth . . **4.** pall **5.** cloak
litter . . **4.** bier
nail . . **9.** cigarette
prehistoric . . **4.** cist **5.** chest
structure . . **10.** catafalque
cog . . . **3.** cam **4.** boat (fishing), gear
    5. catch, cheat, cozen, tenon, tooth
    7. ratchet, wheedle **8.** sprocket
    9. deception
cogent . . . **5.** valid **6.** potent, strong
    7. telling **8.** powerful **9.** effective
    10. compelling, conclusive, convincing,
    persuasive
cogitate . . . **4.** mull, muse, plan **5.** think
    6. ponder **8.** meditate **9.** cerebrate
cognizance . . . **3.** ken **4.** heed, plea
    5. badge (knight's) **9.** knowledge
    11. recognition **12.** apprehension
cognizant . . . **5.** aware **7.** knowing
    8. sensible **9.** conscious **10.** perceptive
    11. intelligent
cognomen . . . **4.** name **5.** title **6.** y-clept
    7. surname **8.** nickname **10.** patronymic
    11. appellation
coheir . . . **5.** joint **8.** parcener
cohere . . . **5.** agree, cling, serry, stick,
    unite **6.** adhere, cleave **9.** glutinate
coherence . . . **5.** cling **8.** adhesion,
    cohesion, sticking **9.** adherence,
    connected **11.** consistency
coil . . . **4.** ansa, clew, curl, loop, mesh,
    wind **5.** querl, twine, twist **6.** spiral
    7. haycock **8.** encircle **11.** convolution
coiled . . . **7.** tortile, twirled
coin . . . **3.** rin, sou, yen **4.** cash, cent
    5. money, penny, stamp **6.** specie
coin (pert to) . . .
Bib . . **6.** talent
brass . . **13.** Rosa Americana (1722)
gold . . **3.** lev **4.** ryal (rial) **5.** daric, eagle
    6. guinea
minor . . **4.** doit
parts of . . **4.** flan **5.** field, tails, verso
    6. legend **7.** exergue, obverse (front),
    reverse
silver . . **4.** batz, obol, ryal (rial) **5.** crown,
    ducat, sceat **6.** tester
tester . . **6.** shroff (saraf)
coincide . . . **5.** agree, check, chime,
    match, tally **6.** concur **7.** consent
    10. correspond **11.** synchronize
coincident . . . **9.** consonant **10.** concurrent
    12. contemporary
coiner . . . **8.** inventor **9.** neologist (words)
    10. fabricator **13.** counterfeiter
coins (pert to) . . .
roll of . . **7.** rouleau
science of . . **11.** numismatics
specialist . . **11.** numismatist
colander . . . **5.** sieve **6.** filter, sorter
    8. strainer
Colchis King . . . **6.** Aeetes
cold . . . **3.** icy, nip, raw **4.** dank, dead,
    drow, dull, frio, sure **5.** algid, bland,
    bleak, frore (anc), gelid **6.** chilly, frigid,

frosty **7.** chilled, cinched **8.** chilling,
    reserved, unheated **9.** heartless
    10. lackluster **11.** indifferent,
    passionless, unconscious
cold (pert to) . . .
blooded . . **9.** heartless, unfeeling
    13. dispassionate, heterothermal
    14. poikilothermal
feet . . **9.** cowardice
infection . . **4.** post **5.** rheum **6.** coryza
    7. catarrh
sore . . **6.** herpes **7.** simplex, vesicle
    14. herpes labialis
steel . . **5.** sword **7.** bayonet, weapons
term . . **8.** frigoric
wind . . **4.** bise
Coleoptera . . . **7.** beetles, insects
Coleridge (Samuel Taylor) (pert to) . . .
place . . **6.** Xanadu
poem . . **9.** Kubla Khan
Rime of the . . **14.** Ancient Mariner
river . . **4.** Alph
colewort . . . **4.** kale **7.** cabbage
colic . . . **4.** pain **5.** gripe, spasm **7.** tormina
    10. enteralgia **11.** stomachache
coliseum . . . **4.** bowl **5.** arena **6.** circus
    7. stadium, theater **9.** Colosseum
    10. hippodrome **12.** amphitheater
collaborate . . . **3.** aid **6.** co-work
    8. coauthor **9.** cooperate **10.** fraternize
collage . . . **6.** gluing **7.** montage
    8. abstract, adhesive **9.** cyclorama
collapse . . . **4.** cave, fail, fall **5.** crash,
    slump **6.** cave-in, defeat **7.** crack-up,
    debacle, deflate, failure **8.** downfall
    9. breakdown, shrinking **10.** bankruptcy,
    exhaustion **11.** prostration
collar . . . **4.** band, grab, ruff **5.** chain,
    rabat, ruche **6.** arrest, bertha, rabato,
    tackle, torque **7.** barghan, capture,
    harness (part), shackle **8.** carcanet,
    neckband **10.** pickadilly
collard . . . **4.** kale
collate . . . **5.** audit, check **6.** verify
    7. certify, compare, examine
collateral . . . **5.** extra **6.** margin **7.** related
    8. indirect, relation (folks), security
    9. accessory, secondary **10.** contingent,
    obligation, subsidiary **11.** subordinate
    12. nonessential
collation . . . **3.** tea **4.** meal **5.** lunch
    6. repast, sermon **7.** address, reading
    8. luncheon, treatise **10.** collection,
    comparison, conference
    12. consultation, contribution
colleague . . . **6.** fellow **7.** compeer,
    comrade, consort, partner **8.** camarada,
    confrere **9.** associate, companion
    11. confederate
collect . . . **3.** bag, tax **4.** levy, mass
    5. amass, glean, raise, rally **6.** deduce,
    forage, garner, gather, muster, prayer,
    sheave **7.** compile, procure **8.** assemble,
    mobilize **9.** aggregate **10.** accumulate,
    congregate
collection . . . **3.** ana, bag, set **4.** book,
    olio **5.** group, hoard, store **6.** rosary,
    sorite **8.** assembly, donation, offering
    9. aggregate, congeries, gathering,
    repertory **10.** assemblage, repertoire
    11. acquisition

collection (pert to) . . .
anecdotes . . **3.** ana **4.** data **8.** analecta
animals (wild) . . **3.** zoo **9.** menagerie
bubbles . . **4.** foam
curiosities . . **6.** museum
documents . . **4.** Veda **6.** corpus **7.** dossier
fruit . . **7.** syncarp
implements (Surg) . . **7.** trousse
of four . . **6.** tetrad
of twenty-four . . **5.** quire
poems . . **5.** sylva **9.** anthology
proper names . . **11.** onomasticon
type . . **4.** font
writing . . **10.** literature
collector (pert to) . . .
bird eggs . . **8.** oologist
books . . **10.** bibliothec **11.** bibliophile
12. bibliomaniac
coins . . **11.** numismatist
rent . . **8.** landlord
stamps . . **11.** philatelist
colleen . . . **4.** girl, lass, maid **6.** damsel,
maiden **7.** girleen
college . . . **6.** school **7.** academy, society
9. Alma Mater, institute **10.** université,
university **11.** corporation, institution
college (pert to) . . .
campus . . **4.** lawn, quad **7.** grounds
graduate . . **6.** alumna **7.** alumnus
license for absence . . **5.** exeat
official . . **4.** dean **5.** prexy **6.** beadle,
bursar, regent **7.** proctor
collegiate . . . **8.** academic **9.** collegian,
scholarly **11.** college-bred
collide with . . . **3.** hit, ram **5.** clash, crash
6. hurtle, strike **7.** contend **8.** conflict,
disagree
collier . . . **5.** miner **6.** plover
collieshangie . . . **3.** row **7.** quarrel
8. squabble **11.** disturbance (noisy)
collision . . . **4.** bump **5.** clash, crash
6. impact **7.** smashup **8.** accident
9. hostility **11.** composition,
impingement **12.** interference
colloquial . . . **6.** common **8.** everyday,
familiar, informal **9.** unstudied
10. vernacular **11.** undignified
14. conversational
colloquy . . . **4.** chat, talk **6.** parley
9. discourse **10.** conference
12. conversation
Cologne Kings (legend) . . . **4.** Magi
6. Gaspar **8.** Melchior **9.** Balthasar
Colombia . . .
capital . . **6.** Bogota (1538)
city . . **4.** Cali **5.** Pasto **6.** Medellin
9. Cartagena **10.** Santa Marta
Falls . . **10.** Tequendama
Liberator . . **7.** Bolivar (Simon)
mountain . . **5.** Andes **11.** Cordilleras
river . . **9.** Magdalena
colonize . . . **6.** gather, people, settle
8. populate **9.** establish
colonizer . . . **3.** ant **6.** oecist **7.** planter,
settler
colonnade . . . **3.** row (columns) **4.** stoa
6. arcade **7.** columns, pillars, portico
8. cloister **9.** peristyle
colony . . . **4.** body **5.** group, swarm
8. dominion **9.** community
10. dependency, settlement

colophon . . . **4.** logo **6.** emblem
9. bookplate **11.** inscription (book)
color . . . **3.** dun, dye, hue **4.** tint, tone
5. blush, paint, shade, stain, terne,
tinge **6.** flaxen, nuance, pastel, sallow,
timbre **7.** piebald, pigment **8.** tincture
(Her) **10.** complexion
color (pert to) . . .
application (paste) . . **7.** impasto
blending . . **4.** teer **5.** fondu **9.** scumbling
blind . . **13.** achromatopsia
clouded . . **9.** nebulated
colorful . . **9.** chromatic
colorless . . **4.** drab, dull, pale **6.** pallid
7. whitish **8.** blanched **10.** achromatic
irregularity . . **5.** fleck **6.** streak
10. rivulation
material . . **5.** eosin, morin, smalt
7. pigment **11.** chlorophyll
off color . . **6.** risqué **8.** improper
organ . . **8.** clavilux
paint, rouge . . **6.** ruddle **7.** blusher
science of . . **10.** chromatics
11. spectrology
variegated . . **7.** rainbow, The Flag,
vibgyor **8.** spectrum **11.** iridescence
Colorado . . .
canyon . . **5.** Black **10.** Royal Gorge
capital . . **6.** Denver
city . . **5.** Aspen, Lamar **6.** Pueblo
7. Boulder, Manassa, Manitou
Indian . . **7.** Arapaho
lake (highest) . . **10.** Frozen Lake
Mt peak . . **6.** Elbert **9.** Pike's Peak
park . . **5.** Estes **15.** Garden of the Gods
river . . **4.** Gila **6.** Platte **8.** Arkansas
State admission . . **12.** Thirty-eighth
State bird . . **11.** lark bunting
State flower . . **9.** columbine
State motto . . **13.** Nil Sine Numine
(Nothing Without God)
State nickname . . **10.** Centennial
colossal . . . **4.** huge **5.** great, large
6. absurd, superb **7.** mammoth
8. gigantic **9.** monstrous
colossal beast . . . **8.** behemoth (Bib)
colt . . . **3.** gun **4.** foal **5.** filly, horse
8. yearling
Columbus (pert to) . . .
birthplace . . **5.** Genoa (It)
companion . . **5.** Ojeda
discoverer . . **7.** America (1492)
landing site . . **11.** San Salvador
sailing site . . **5.** Palos (Sp)
vessel . . **4.** Nina **5.** Pinta **10.** Santa
Maria
column . . . **3.** lat (Buddh) **4.** anta **5.** pylon,
shaft, stele (stela) **6.** pillar **7.** telamon
8. baluster, caryatid, pilaster
column (pert to) . . .
base . . **5.** socle **6.** plinth **9.** stylobate
military . . **4.** unit **9.** formation
Order (Arch) . . **5.** Doric, Ionic **6.** Tuscan
9. Composite **10.** Corinthian
ref to . . **5.** train **7.** cortege **8.** cylinder,
memorial, monument **10.** procession
shaft . . **4.** fust **5.** scape **8.** apophyge
term . . **5.** bague, galbe, shank **7.** capital,
entasis
coma . . . **4.** daze, tuft **5.** carus, sleep,
sopor **6.** stupor, trance **9.** catalepsy

12. sluggishness 13. insensibility
15. unconsciousness
comatose . . . **6.** drowsy, torpid
9. apathetic, lethargic **10.** cataleptic,
insensible **11.** unconscious
comb . . . **4.** card, wave **5.** cock's, crest,
curry, groom, scour, tease **6.** search
7. rummage **8.** caruncle
combat . . . **3.** war **4.** cope, duel, fray, tilt
5. fight, joust (anc), repel **6.** action,
battle, karate, kung fu, oppose, strife
7. contest, jujitsu, scuffle **8.** argument,
conflict **9.** withstand **10.** antagonize,
contention, engagement
combat (pert to) . . .
challenge . . **6.** cartel **8.** gauntlet
code . . **6.** duello
scene . . **5.** arena **8.** coliseum
combatant . . . **6.** dueler **7.** battler, fighter
8. disputer **9.** contender **10.** competitor,
contestant
combative . . . **8.** militant **9.** agonistic,
bellicose **10.** aggressive, pugnacious
11. belligerent, contentious
combination . . . **4.** gang, pact, pool
5. blend, combo, party, trust, union
6. clique, fusion, hookup, league,
merger **7.** amalgam, combine, faction,
mixture **8.** alliance, coalesce, ensemble,
junction **9.** camarilla, coalition,
synthesis **10.** embodiment
11. aggregation, association,
confederacy, unification
12. undergarment **13.** incorporation
combine . . . **3.** add, mix **4.** join, pool
5. merge, unite **6.** concur, mingle
7. machine **10.** synthesize
combining form . . .
above, beyond . . **3.** sur **5.** ultra
across . . **4.** tran **5.** trans
bad . . **3.** dys, mal
black . . **4.** mela
earth . . **3.** geo **5.** terra
equal . . **3.** iso **4.** homo, pari
far . . **3.** tel **4.** tele
good . . **2.** eu
hundred . . **4.** cent
inner, within . . **4.** ento (ent)
kidney . . **4.** reni
middle . . **4.** medi **5.** medio
mountain . . **3.** oro
needle . . **3.** acu
new . . **3.** neo
not . . **2.** un **3.** non
old, ancient . . **5.** paleo
one . . **3.** uni **4.** mono
outside, without . . **3.** ect, ext **4.** ecto
personal . . **4.** idio
soft . . **4.** leni
stone . . **4.** lith
thought . . **4.** ideo
thrice . . **3.** ter
tooth . . **6.** odonto
touch . . **3.** tac
up, upward . . **3.** ano
watery . . **4.** sero
comblike . . . **7.** ctenoid **8.** pectinal
combustible . . . **5.** fiery, quick **7.** piceous
8. volcanic **9.** flammable, irascible
10. accendible **11.** hot-tempered,
inflammable

combustion . . . **4.** fire **6.** tumult **7.** blazing,
flaming **8.** ignition **9.** agitation,
confusion, cremation **12.** inflammation
13. conflagration
come . . . **3.** hop **4.** near **5.** issue, occur
6. appear, arrive, happen **8.** approach
9. transpire
come (pert to) . . .
across . . **3.** pay **4.** meet **7.** confess
10. contribute
back . . **6.** answer, retort, return
7. rebound, recover **8.** remember,
repartee
before . . **4.** lead **7.** precede, prevene
8. antecede, antedate
between . . **6.** divide **8.** estrange, interlie
9. interpose, intervene
by . . **3.** get **4.** gain **6.** obtain **7.** acquire,
inherit, receive
forth . . **3.** jet **4.** gush, spew **5.** hatch,
issue, occur **6.** appear, emerge, spring
7. emanate **9.** originate
together . . **4.** join, knit, meet **5.** clash,
merge **7.** collide, convene **8.** assemble,
converge
come (to) . . .
light . . **7.** develop
maturity . . **5.** ripen
pass . . **5.** occur **6.** befall, betide, happen
9. eventuate
rest . . **3.** sit **5.** light **6.** settle
comedian, comedienne . . . **3.** wit **4.** buff
5. actor, comic **6.** player **7.** farcist
8. funnyman **9.** dramatist
comedy . . . **5.** drama, farce, revue
7. comedie, stand-up **8.** travesty
9. burlesque, slapstick
comestibles . . . **4.** food **5.** manna
8. eatables, victuals
comet (pert to) . . .
cloud . . **4.** Oort
famous . . **7.** Halley's **8.** Kohoutek
part . . **4.** coma, tail **7.** nucleus
comfort . . . **4.** ease **5.** cheer, quilt **6.** relief,
solace, soothe, succor **7.** confirm,
console, enliven, fortify, refresh, relieve,
support, sustain **8.** inspirit, nepenthe
(drug) **9.** enjoyment **10.** invigorate,
strengthen **11.** consolation
12. satisfaction
comfortable . . . **4.** cozy, easy, snug
5. scarf **8.** adequate, cheerful, homelike,
wristlet **9.** contented, endemonic
10. complacent, prosperous
11. consolatory, encouraging
comforter . . . **5.** quilt **6.** tippet **7.** solacer
8. pacifier **9.** Paraclete
comfortless . . . **7.** forlorn **8.** desolate
9. cheerless, heartsick **10.** despairing
11. distressing **12.** disconsolate,
inconsolable
comic, comical . . . **3.** odd **5.** cutup, droll,
funny, queer, witty **6.** absurd, quaint
7. cartoon, risible **8.** comedian, farcical,
humorous **9.** burlesque, laughable,
ludicrous, quizzical, whimsical
10. capricious, outlandish
coming . . . **3.** due **6.** access, advent, future
7. arrival, forward, looming **8.** eventual,
expected, imminent **9.** imminence
11. approaching, forthcoming

coming into being . . . 7. genesis, nascent

comity . . . 7. amenity, suavity 8. civility, courtesy, urbanity 10. affability

command . . . 3. bid, gee, haw, hup
4. bade, beck, fiat, hest, rule, sway
5. avast, check, edict, exact, grasp, order, power, ukase 6. behest, charge, compel, decree, direct, enjoin, govern
7. control, dictate, mandate, mastery
8. dominion, restrain 9. authority, prescribe 10. domination
11. commandment 12. jurisdiction

commander . . . 3. cid 5. chief, ruler
6. leader 7. admiral, captain, skipper
8. dictator, governor, myriarch, overlord

commander, Eastern . . . 3. ras 4. amir, emir, Imam, khan, rani 5. ameer, begum, dewan, emeer, nawab, Nizam
6. caliph, regent, Sultan

commanding . . . 8. dominant 9. imperious
10. imperative 13. authoritative

commandments . . . 4. laws 6. orders, tables 8. mandates, precepts
9. Decalogue (Ten)

comme il faut . . . 8. properly 9. correctly
10. decorously 12. as it should be

commemoration . . . 7. service
8. Encaenia (Oxford Univ)
10. observance 11. anniversary, celebration, remembrance
13. solemnization

commence . . . 4. open 5. arise, begin, start 6. spring 8. initiate 9. originate

commencement . . . 4. rite 6. source
8. ceremony, nascency 9. beginning, formality, inception, novitiate
10. initiation

commend . . . 4. plug 5. boost, extol, offer
6. assign, commit, praise, remand, resign 7. approve, deliver, entrust
8. advocate, delegate 9. recommend
10. compliment

commendation . . . 4. hype, plug, puff
5. boost, kudos 8. approval
10. assignment, commitment, compliment, delegation
11. approbation, consignment, entrustment

comment . . . 4. note, talk 6. gossip, postil, remark, report 7. descant, discuss, explain, mention 8. annotate, critique
9. criticism, discourse

commentary . . . 5. gloss 6. memoir
7. remarks 8. treatise 9. memoranda
10. annotation 11. explanation

commerce . . . 5. trade 7. traffic 8. dealings
9. communion 11. interchange
13. communication

commis . . . 5. agent, clerk 6. deputy

commiserate . . . 4. pity 7. condole, console 10. sympathize

commiseration . . . 4. pity, ruth 5. mercy
6. sorrow 7. empathy, feeling
8. sympathy 10. compassion, condolence

commission . . . 4. duty, task 5. allot, board, share, trust 6. brevet, depute, office, ordain 7. empower, mandate, mission, payment, rake-off, warrant
8. delegate 9. authority 10. assignment, constitute, delegation, deputation

11. performance 12. perpetration

commissioned . . . 8. allotted, assigned, breveted 9. delegated 10. accredited, authorized

commissioner . . . 5. envoy 6. dubash, legate 7. steward 8. delegate, emissary, official 9. commissar

commissure . . . 4. seam 5. cleft, joint, mitre, raphe 6. stitch, suture 7. closure
8. juncture 10. interstice

commit . . . 2. do 3. con 4. game (cards)
5. refer 6. remand 7. confide, consign, entrust, promise 8. memorize, relegate
10. commission, perpetrate

commode . . . 3. cap 5. chest 8. fontange
9. washstand 10. chiffonier

commodious . . . 3. fit 5. ample, roomy
6. proper 8. suitable 9. capacious, expansive, opportune 10. convenient
11. comfortable, serviceable
13. accommodating

commodity, commodities . . . 5. goods, wares 6. profit 7. staples

common . . . 4. park 5. cheap, plain, stale, trite, usual 6. mutual, paltry, vulgar 7. average 8. familiar, frequent, mediocre, ordinary, plebeian
9. customary, household, universal
11. commonplace

common (pert to) . . .
ancestor . . 4. Adam 10. progenitor
funds . . 4. pool 7. tontine
gender . . 6. unisex 7. epicene
informer . . 7. delator
people . . 3. mob 5. demos, gente
6. vulgus 7. demotic 8. populace

commonly accepted . . . 7. vulgate

commonly thought . . . 8. putative

commonplace . . . 5. banal, daily, stale, theme, trite, usual 6. truism
7. humdrum, prosaic 8. ordinary, workaday 9. platitude

commonwealth . . . 5. group, State
7. society 8. Kentucky, Virginia
9. Australia, community
12. Pennsylvania 13. Massachusetts

commotion . . . 3. ado 4. fray, riot, stir, to-do, whir 5. flare, tizzy 6. flurry, fracas, hubbub, rumpus, tumult, unrest 7. turmoil 8. foofaraw, uprising
9. agitation, confusion 10. concussion
(med), excitement, turbulence
12. perturbation

commune . . . 4. area, soil 5. realm, share
6. confer, impart 7. kibbutz 8. converse
9. communion 10. commonalty
11. intercourse (spiritual)
12. conversation

Commune of Paris (1871) . . .
10. government

communicate . . . 3. say 4. give, join
5. share 6. bestow, impart, inform
7. apprize 8. converse, transmit
9. communion

communication . . . 4. word 5. radio
6. letter, report 7. account, contact, epistle, message 8. buzzword, feedback
9. statement 10. communique, connection 11. computerese, impartation, information, intercourse
12. body language 14. word processing

communion ... **5.** share **6.** church
7. concord, rapport **8.** converse
9. agreement **11.** intercourse
12. denomination **13.** participation
Communion ... **4.** host **9.** Eucharist,
Sacrament **10.** intinction, Last Supper
communion (pert to) ...
bread (blessed) .. **4.** host **5.** wafer
7. eulogia **9.** antidoron
cloth .. **8.** corporal, corporas
plate .. **5.** paten **12.** processional
table .. **5.** altar
vessel .. **3.** ama, pyx
communique ... **4.** word **7.** message
8. dispatch **13.** communication
comose ... **5.** hairy **6.** tufted
compact ... **4.** etui, firm, pact, plot, snug,
trim **5.** brief, close, dense, pithy, press,
solid, terse, tight **6.** treaty, united, vanity
7. concise, crowded, entente, leagued,
serried **8.** alliance, compress, contract,
covenant, succinct **9.** agreement,
condensed **10.** compressed, conspiracy
11. compendious, sententious,
stipulation
companion ... **3.** pal **4.** ally, fare, mate,
twin **5.** amigo, crony **6.** fellow, shadow
7. Achates, compeer, comrade, consort
8. alter ego, co-worker **9.** associate
11. confederate, counterpart
companionship ... **5.** amity **7.** society
10. fellowship, fraternity
11. comradeship, sociability
13. accompaniment
company ... **3.** set **4.** band, bevy, body,
crew, gang, ging, host **5.** crowd, flock,
group, party, troop **6.** circle, cohort,
throng, troupe **9.** concourse, gathering
company (pert to) ...
detachment .. **5.** posse
people, players .. **4.** bevy, crew, gang,
team **5.** troop **6.** galaxy, guests, troupe
9. cavalcade
ships .. **5.** fleet **6.** armada **8.** squadron
soldiers .. **5.** corps, squad **7.** brigade,
phalanx, platoon **9.** battalion
travelers .. **7.** caravan **8.** pilgrims, tourists
9. merchants
comparative ... **5.** equal, rival **8.** relative
10. comparable, relational
compare ... **4.** even **5.** liken **6.** confer,
semble **7.** collate, examine **8.** contrast
comparison ... **6.** simile **7.** analogy,
parable **8.** likening, metaphor
10. accordance, similarity
11. parallelism
compartment ... **3.** bin **4.** cell, part **5.** stall
6. alcove **7.** cellule, chamber, quarter
8. district, division **10.** department
compass ... **3.** arc **4.** area, plot, ring
5. guide, range (Mus), reach, solar,
sweep **6.** attain, bounds, circle, curved,
degree, extent **7.** circuit, divider,
enclose, imagine **8.** circular, distance,
surround
compass (pert to) ...
housing .. **8.** binnacle
part .. **3.** pen **6.** needle
point .. **4.** airt **5.** rhumb **7.** azimuth
sight .. **4.** vane
suspender .. **6.** gimbal

compassion ... **4.** pity, ruth (anc) **5.** mercy
8. humanity, sympathy **10.** condolence
13. commiseration
compassionate ... **6.** gentle, humane
7. clement, pitiful **8.** merciful
11. sympathetic, warmhearted
12. sympathizing
compatible ... **8.** affinity, suitable
9. accordant, agreeable, congruous
10. consistent, harmonious
12. congeniality
compeer ... **4.** mate, peer **5.** equal,
match, rival **7.** comrade **9.** companion
compel ... **4.** urge **5.** drive, force,
impel, press **6.** coerce, incite, oblige,
obsess **7.** actuate, dragoon, require
9. constrain, influence, instigate
compelling ... **6.** urgent **7.** driving
8. pressing **9.** insistent, necessary,
obsessing **10.** compulsory, motivating,
obligatory, persuasive
compelling assent ... **6.** cogent
compelling attention ... **9.** insistent
compendious ... **5.** brief, short, terse
7. compact, concise **8.** abridged,
succinct **9.** condensed **10.** summarized
compendium ... **5.** brief **6.** abrégé,
digest **7.** capsule, epitome, medulla,
pandect, summary **8.** abstract, syllabus,
synopsis **9.** comprisal **10.** abridgment
11. compilation, contraction
12. abbreviation
compensate ... **3.** pay **5.** atone, repay
6. reward **7.** redress, requite
9. indemnity **10.** recompense,
remunerate **14.** counterbalance
compensation ... **3.** pay **4.** hire **5.** bonus,
wages **6.** manbot (manbote), reward,
salary **7.** penalty, stipend **8.** gratuity,
pittance, requital, solatium
9. atonement, indemnity **10.** reparation
12. remuneration, satisfaction
15. indemnification
compete ... **3.** vie **4.** cope **5.** match
6. outvie, strive **7.** contend, contest,
emulate
competence ... **5.** means, skill **7.** ability,
fitness **8.** adequacy, capacity, property
10. capability, efficiency **11.** proficiency,
sufficiency, suitability **13.** effectiveness,
qualification
competent ... **3.** apt, can, fit **4.** able
5. capax, smart **7.** capable **8.** adequate,
suitable **9.** effective, effectual, efficient,
qualified **10.** catechumen, sufficient
12. appertaining (to)
competition ... **5.** match, trial **6.** strife
7. contest, rivalry **8.** ambition, concours
9. emulation **10.** corrivalry
compilation ... **5.** cento **6.** digest
9. Americana **10.** collection
compile ... **3.** add **4.** edit **5.** amass
6. gather **8.** assemble
complacent ... **4.** smug **6.** bovine
7. fatuous **9.** contented, satisfied
11. considerate **13.** self-satisfied
complain ... **4.** beef, carp, fret, kick,
pule, wail **5.** gripe, growl, whine
6. accuse, bewail, grieve, grouse,
lament, murmur, mutter, repine,
squawk, yammer **7.** deplore, grumble,

protest **9.** bellyache

complaint ... **4.** beef **6.** charge, lament, malady **7.** ailment, disease, illness, protest **8.** disorder, repining, reproach **9.** grievance, murmuring **10.** accusation, imputation **11.** declaration, lamentation

complaisance ... **6.** regard **7.** amenity, concern, suavity **8.** civility, courtesy, urbanity **10.** indulgence, solicitude, submission, toleration **13.** consideration

complaisant ... **4.** easy, kind **5.** civil **6.** polite **7.** lenient **8.** gracious, obliging **9.** compliant, courteous

complement ... **4.** crew **7.** adjunct **8.** addition, complete **10.** correspond, supplement **11.** counterpart

complete ... **3.** all, end **4.** dead, fill, full, sole **5.** stark, total, utter, whole **6.** effect, entire, finish, intact, mature **7.** achieve, execute, germane, perfect, plenary, realize **8.** absolute, conclude, detailed, outright **9.** terminate **10.** accomplish, complement, consummate **11.** unqualified

completely ... **3.** all **5.** fully, quite, stark **6.** in toto **7.** solidly, totally, utterly **8.** entirely

completeness ... **9.** entelechy, integrity

complex ... **4.** mazy **5.** mixed **6.** knotty **7.** twisted **8.** involute, involved **9.** entangled, intricate, perplexed **10.** interlaced **11.** complicated

complexion ... **4.** blee, mode, tone **5.** color, guise, tinge **10.** appearance

compliance ... **6.** assent **7.** consent **9.** accession, obedience **10.** concession, conformity, observance, submission **11.** willingness **12.** acquiescence

compliant ... **6.** docile **7.** duteous, dutiful, willing **8.** obedient **10.** submissive **11.** acquiescent, complaisant, conformable

complicated ... **6.** daedal **7.** complex, Gordian, snarled, tangled **8.** involved **9.** difficult, embroiled, intricate **11.** embarrassed **12.** labyrinthine

complication ... **4.** node (drama) **5.** nodus **7.** illness **9.** complexus **10.** complexity **11.** combination

compliment ... **6.** praise **7.** adulate, commend, flatter **8.** encomium, flattery **12.** blandishment, commendation **14.** congratulation

comply ... **4.** obey **5.** agree, yield **6.** accede, accord, assent, submit **7.** conform, observe **9.** acquiesce

compone ... **6.** settle **7.** arrange, compose **8.** compound

component ... **3.** ion **4.** part **5.** basis **6.** factor **7.** element **8.** integral **10.** ingredient **11.** constituent

comport ... **3.** act **6.** accord, behave **7.** conduct **10.** correspond

comfortable ... **8.** suitable **10.** consistent

compose ... **3.** pen **4.** calm, form, make **5.** order, score, write **7.** arrange, fashion, prepare **8.** compound, melodize **9.** reconcile **10.** constitute **11.** orchestrate, tranquilize

composed ... **4.** calm, cool **5.** quiet, sober, wrote **6.** sedate, serene **7.** consist **8.** arranged, tranquil **9.** collected **11.** unflappable

composed of ...
flat plates .. **9.** lamellate
lobes .. **6.** lobate

composer ... **6.** author **7.** idylist (idyllist) **10.** compositor, typesetter

composer of ...
Aida .. **5.** Verdi
Carmen .. **5.** Bizet
Faust .. **6.** Gounod
La Boheme .. **7.** Puccini
Merry widow .. **5.** Lehar
Mikado .. **8.** Sullivan
Naughty Marietta .. **7.** Herbert
Stars and Stripes Forever .. **5.** Sousa

composition ... **4.** opus **5.** piece, theme **6.** make-up **7.** melange **9.** formation, synthesis **12.** constitution, construction

composition (pert to) ...
literature .. **5.** cento, essay, poesy, prose **6.** poetry, satire, thesis **8.** treatise **10.** brainchild

music .. **2.** op **4.** aria, glee, hymn, opus **5.** drama, étude, motet, nonet, opera, rondo, suite **6.** anthem, septet (septuor), sextet (sestet), sonata **7.** duetino, quartet **8.** concerto, oratorio, postlude, symphony

composure ... **6.** repose **8.** calmness, coolness, serenity **9.** placidity **10.** equanimity, quiescence, sedateness **11.** tranquility

compound ... **3.** mix **4.** olio **5.** agree, amide, ester, oxide, pyran, unite **6.** anisil, elixir, iodide, ketone **7.** ammonia, combine, farrago, metamer **8.** tincture **9.** composite

comprehend ... **3.** see **4.** know **5.** grasp, sense **6.** embody, fathom **7.** enclose, imagine, include, involve, realize **8.** comprise, conceive **10.** understand

comprehensible ... **8.** exoteric, included, knowable **9.** comprised **11.** conceivable, discernible, perceptible **12.** intelligible

comprehensive ... **4.** full, wide **5.** large **7.** generic, knowing **8.** thorough **9.** extensive, inclusive, universal **11.** compendious

compress ... **4.** firm **5.** cling, crowd, pinch, press, stupe **7.** compact, densify, embrace, squeeze **8.** astringe, condense, contract, decrease

comprise, comprize ... **5.** imply **6.** number **7.** contain, embrace, enclose, include, involve **8.** perceive **10.** comprehend, constitute

compromise ... **4.** bind **6.** adjust **8.** compound, trade-off **9.** agreement **10.** adjustment, concession, settlement **11.** appeasement, arbitration

compulsion ... **5.** drive, force **6.** duress, urging **7.** impulse **8.** coaction, coercion **9.** necessity, obsession **10.** compelling

compulsory ... **7.** driving **9.** mandatory, necessary **10.** compelling, imperative, obligatory **11.** involuntary

compunction ... **3.** rue **5.** guilt, pangs, qualm **6.** regret **7.** remorse **8.** pricking **9.** penitence **11.** impenitence **13.** regretfulness

compute ... **5.** count, score, tally
6. cipher, figure, number, reckon
8. estimate **9.** calculate, enumerate
computer terms ... **3.** bit, LAN, RAM,
ROM **4.** byte, GIGO **5.** BASIC,
COBOL, coder, e-mail, input, modem
6. access, analog, glitch, laptop,
Pascal, server **7.** digital, FORTRAN,
monitor **8.** database, download,
gigabyte, Internet, megabyte, printout,
software, terminal **9.** mainframe,
videodisc **10.** cyberspace, floppy disc
11. computerese **12.** minicomputer
13. microcomputer, word processor
comrade ... **3.** pal **4.** ally, chum, mate,
peer **5.** buddy, crony **6.** fellow, frater
7. compeer **8.** camarada, sidekick
9. associate, colleague, companion
con ... **2.** no **3.** nay **4.** know, read,
scam **5.** cheat, learn, steer, study
6. peruse **7.** convict, deceive, swindle
8. memorize, negative **10.** understand
13. confidence man
conceal ... **4.** dern, hide, mask, palm,
veil **5.** cloak, cover, derne, eloin, feign
6. eloign, pocket, screen **7.** secrete
8. bescreen, disguise, enshield
concealed ... **5.** doggo **6.** covert, hidden,
latent, perdue, secret, veiled, velate
7. covered, larvate, obscure, unknown,
velated **9.** disguised, incognito,
insidious **11.** clandestine
concede ... **3.** own **5.** admit, agree,
allow, grant, yield **6.** accord **7.** confess,
consent **8.** consider **9.** surrender
11. acknowledge
conceit ... **3.** ego **4.** idea **5.** fancy,
pride **6.** vagary, vanity **7.** caprice,
egotism, foppery, tympany **8.** priggery
12. boastfulness
conceited ... **4.** smug, vain **5.** proud
7. foppish **8.** arrogant, boastful, priggish
9. egotistic, pragmatic **11.** egotistical,
opinionated **12.** stuffed shirt
conceivable ... **7.** tenable **8.** credible
9. plausible **10.** believable, imaginable
12. intelligible
conceive ... **5.** dream, fancy, think
6. create, devise, ideate **7.** imagine,
produce, realize, suppose, suspect
9. originate **10.** understand
concentrate ... **4.** mass **5.** focus
6. center **7.** compact, densify, extract
8. condense, converge **9.** intensify
10. centralize **11.** consolidate
concept ... **4.** idea **5.** image **7.** opinion,
thought **8.** category
conception ... **4.** idea **5.** image, savvy
6. notion **7.** conceit, opinion
9. pregnancy **12.** apprehension
13. comprehension, understanding
concern ... **4.** care, firm, sake **5.** event,
grief **6.** affair, affect, import, matter
7. anxiety, pertain **8.** business, interest,
salience **9.** relevance **10.** importance
11. consequence **12.** significance
13. consideration
concerning ... **3.** for **4.** as to, over,
upon **5.** about, anent **9.** regarding
10. respecting
concert ... **6.** aubade **7.** recital

9. agreement, unanimity **11.** co-
operation, performance
concert hall ... **5.** odeum (odeon)
6. lyceum **7.** theater **9.** music hall,
playhouse
concession ... **5.** grant **6.** market
7. consent **8.** discount **10.** compromise,
confession **13.** qualification
concierge ... **6.** porter, warden **7.** ostiary
8. chokidar **10.** doorkeeper
conciliate ... **4.** ease **6.** pacify **7.** appease,
mollify, placate **9.** reconcile
10. propitiate
conciliatory ... **6.** assent, irenic **8.** irenical
9. appeasing, forgiving **10.** mollifying
concise ... **4.** curt, neat **5.** brief, crisp,
pithy, terse **6.** précis **7.** laconic,
pointed, serried, summary **8.** succinct
11. compendious, sententious
13. comprehensive
conclude ... **3.** end **4.** rest **5.** close,
infer **6.** deduce, endeth, finish, settle
7. arrange, presume, resolve, suppose
8. complete **9.** determine, terminate
conclusion ... **3.** end **4.** last **5.** close,
finis **6.** finale, finish, result **8.** decision,
epilogue **9.** deduction, diagnosis,
inference **10.** completion
13. determination
conclusive ... **5.** final, valid **8.** decisive,
ultimate **9.** mandatory **10.** convincing,
evidential **11.** irrefutable, sockdologer
(answer) **12.** unanswerable
concoct ... **3.** mix **4.** brew, cook, make
6. devise, digest, invent, scheme
7. perfect, prepare **9.** fabricate
concoction ... **4.** dish, plan, plot **6.** device
7. mixture **8.** compound **9.** falsehood,
invention **11.** combination, fabrication,
preparation
concomitant ... **9.** accessory, attendant,
co-operant **10.** coincident, concurrent
11. synchronous **12.** accompanying,
simultaneous
concord ... **4.** tune **5.** chord, peace
6. accord, treaty, unison **7.** concert,
harmony, rapport **8.** symphony
9. agreement, unanimity
Concorde ... **3.** SST
concordant ... **8.** agreeing, harmonic,
unisonal **9.** consonant, unanimous
10. harmonious **11.** conformable
13. correspondent
concrete ... **4.** hard, pave **5.** béton,
solid **6.** cement **7.** congeal, plaster
8. hardness, pavement, solidify
11. substantial
concur ... **5.** agree, chime, unite
6. accede, assent **7.** approve, combine,
consent **9.** acquiesce, co-operate
11. synchronize
concurrence ... **6.** united **7.** joining
9. adherence, concourse, unanimity
11. coincidence, conjunction,
convergence, co-operation, parallelism
concurrent ... **5.** joint **6.** united
7. meeting, uniting **8.** parallel,
syndrome **9.** unanimous **10.** associated,
coincident, synergetic **11.** co-operative,
synchronous **12.** accompanying,
simultaneous

concussion . . . **5.** clash, shock, smash, wound **6.** injury, trauma **9.** collision

condemn . . . **3.** ban **4.** doom **5.** blame, decry **7.** adjudge, censure, convict **8.** penalize, sentence

condense . . . **3.** mix **5.** unite **6.** absorb, decoct, deepen, harden, lessen, narrow, reduce **7.** abridge, combine, compact, densify, enhance, shorten, squeeze, thicken **8.** compress, contract, diminish, heighten, solidify **9.** constrict, intensify **11.** concentrate, consolidate

condensed . . . **7.** compact, concise, cramped, tabloid **9.** shortened **10.** compressed, contracted **12.** concentrated

condenser (anc) . . . **9.** Leyden jar

condescend . . . **5.** deign, stoop **6.** submit, unbend **7.** concede, descend **9.** patronize, vouchsafe

condign . . . **3.** fit **4.** just **6.** severe, worthy **7.** fitting **8.** adequate, deserved, suitable

condiment . . . **3.** soy **4.** dill, mace, mint, sage, salt **5.** chili, clove, curry, sauce, spice **6.** catsup, garlic, ginger, nutmeg, pepper, relish **7.** cayenne, ketchup, mustard, paprika, vinegar **9.** seasoning **10.** peppermint

condition . . . **2.** if **4.** case, haze, rank, term **5.** covin, limit, stage, state **6.** estate, fettle, health, plight, status **7.** posture, proviso, quality, station **8.** capacity, position, standing **9.** requisite, situation **10.** limitation **11.** predicament **12.** circumstance

condition (pert to) . . .
favorable . . **4.** odds
flushed . . **4.** rosy
habitual . . **5.** tenor
hypnotic . . **4.** daze **6.** stupor, trance **7.** narcose
made . . **7.** premise
murk . . **3.** fog **4.** haze, mist **5.** gloom
proper . . **6.** kilter
stipulation . . **7.** proviso

conditionally . . . **2.** if **8.** provided **11.** tentatively **13.** provisionally

condone . . . **5.** remit **6.** accept, excuse, pardon **7.** absolve, forgive **8.** tolerate **11.** countenance

condor . . . **6.** falcon **7.** vulture

conduce . . . **4.** lend, tend **5.** serve **6.** effect **7.** advance, dispose, incline, redound **10.** contribute

conducive . . . **6.** useful **7.** helpful **11.** implemental, serviceable **12.** instrumental

conduct . . . **3.** act, run **4.** lead, mien, rule **5.** guide, usage, usher **6.** action, convey, convoy, direct, escort, govern, manage **7.** bearing, comport, control, manners **8.** behavior, demeanor, regulate **9.** operation, supervise **10.** deportment, management **11.** comportment, superintend

conduct (pert to) . . .
a cause . . **5.** plead
breach . . **6.** guilty
doctrine of . . **6.** morals
one's self . . **6.** behave, demean **7.** comport

conducting inward . . . **9.** afference

conductor . . . **5.** guide **6.** escort, leader **7.** cathode, maestro, manager **8.** cicerone, director, operator, trainman

conduit . . . **3.** way **4.** adit, duct, pain, pipe, tube **5.** canal, sewer **6.** course **7.** channel **8.** aqueduct

cone (pert to) . . .
conelike . . **5.** conic **6.** pineal **7.** conical
pine . . **8.** strobile
silver . . **4.** pina
tree . . **5.** larch **7.** conifer

confab, confabulation . . . **4.** chat, talk **7.** palaver, prattle **8.** chinfest, talkfest **12.** conversation

confection . . . **3.** jam **5.** candy, dulce, icing, jelly **6.** cimbal, comfit, nougat, sweets **7.** caramel, fondant, praline, succade **8.** preserve **9.** sweetmeat **11.** bittersweet, marshmallow

confederacy . . . **5.** cabal, hanse, union **6.** fusion, league **8.** alliance, covenant **9.** coalition **10.** complicity, conspiracy, federation **11.** affiliation, association, combination **13.** consolidation

confederate . . . **3.** pal, reb **4.** ally **5.** stall **7.** abettor **9.** accessory, assistant, associate, auxiliary **10.** accomplice

confer . . . **4.** give **6.** advise, bestow, invest, parley **7.** collate, commune, consign, consult, counsel **8.** ordinate (knighthood) **10.** deliberate

conference . . . **5.** trust **6.** huddle, parley, powwow **7.** council, palaver **9.** interview **10.** discussion **12.** consultation

conferring respect . . . **9.** honorific

conferring title . . . **9.** ennobling

confess . . . **3.** own, rue **4.** avow **5.** admit, own up **6.** regret, repent, reveal, shrive **7.** concede **11.** acknowledge

confession . . . **5.** credo (of faith), creed **6.** avowal, shrift **9.** admission, communion **10.** profession **14.** acknowledgment (acknowledgement)

confetti . . . **5.** paper **6.** ribbon **7.** bonbons **9.** cascarons (in eggshells) **10.** sweetmeats **11.** confections

confidant . . . **6.** friend **8.** intimate

confide . . . **4.** hope, rely **5.** trust **6.** commit, depend, repose

confidence . . . **5.** faith, poise **6.** aplomb, belief, morals, secret **7.** courage **8.** credence, sureness **9.** assurance, impudence **10.** effrontery **12.** impertinence

confident . . . **4.** smug, sure **6.** secure **7.** assured, certain, hopeful, reliant **8.** cocksure, positive, sanguine, unafraid **9.** convinced **10.** determined

confidential . . . **5.** privy **6.** secret **7.** private **8.** esoteric, intimate **9.** auricular **10.** unquotable **11.** trustworthy

confidentially . . . **7.** sub rosa

configuration . . . **4.** form **5.** shape **6.** figure **7.** contour, Gestalt, pattern **8.** asterism **13.** constellation

confine . . . **3.** dam, hem, mew, pen, sty, tie **4.** bind, cage, coop, jail, lock **5.** bound, limit, stint **6.** border, immure,

intern, secure, strain **7.** compass
8. imprison, restrain **9.** enclosure
11. incarcerate, restriction
12. circumscribe
confined . . . **4.** pent **5.** bound, caged
6. shut-in **7.** cribbed, endemic,
limited **8.** esoteric, impended, interned
9. bedridden, impounded, invalided,
parochial
confinement . . . **5.** limbo **7.** durance,
lying-in **9.** detention, isolation, restraint
10. cabin fever, childbirth
12. accouchement, imprisonment
13. incomm unicado **15.** circumscription
confirm . . . **4.** seal **5.** prove **6.** assure,
attest, ratify, settle, verify **7.** approve,
fortify, sustain **8.** convince, sanction,
validate **9.** establish **11.** corroborate
12. substantiate
confirmed . . . **6.** proved **7.** chronic
8. habitual, ratified **10.** encouraged,
inveterate **11.** established
confiscate . . . **5.** seize, usurp **7.** impound
11. appropriate
conflagrant . . . **5.** afire **6.** ablaze, aflame
7. blazing, burning
conflagration . . . **4.** fire **5.** blaze, fever
8. wildfire **9.** holocaust **12.** inflammation
conflict . . . **3.** war **4.** bout, duel, fray
5. clash, fight, run-in **6.** action,
battle, combat, oppose, strife, tussle
7. contend, contest, discord **8.** clashing,
struggle **9.** antipathy, collision,
encounter, hostility **10.** contention,
donnybrook, opposition **11.** competition
confluence . . . **4.** flow **5.** crowd **6.** stream
7. flowing (together), meeting
8. junction **10.** assemblage
11. concurrence, convergence
12. assimilation
conform . . . **2.** go **3.** fit **4.** lean, obey,
suit **5.** adapt, agree **6.** adjust, concur,
settle **7.** compose, consent, observe
8. coincide, fine-tune **9.** reconcile
11. accommodate
conformity . . . **6.** dharma **7.** harmony
8. legality, symmetry **9.** agreement,
congruity **10.** compliance
15. conventionality
confound . . . **3.** mix **5.** abash, amaze
6. baffle, dismay, puzzle, thwart
7. astound, buffalo, mystify, nonplus,
perplex **8.** astonish, bewilder
9. dumbfound, embarrass, frustrate
10. complicate, contradict, disconcert
11. intermingle
confront . . . **4.** face, meet **5.** front
6. oppose **7.** compare **9.** encounter
confrontation . . . **6.** crisis **7.** face-off
8. showdown **9.** encounter
10. opposition
confuse . . . **3.** mix **4.** maze **5.** abash,
addle, upset **6.** baffle, flurry, garble,
jumble, muddle **7.** derange, fluster
8. befuddle, bewilder, disorder, distract,
entangle **9.** embrangle **10.** complicate,
disarrange, discompose, disconcert
confused . . . **4.** asea **6.** addled **7.** chaotic,
jumbled, rattled **8.** deranged
9. chagrined, flustered, perplexed,
uncertain **10.** indistinct

confusion . . . **3.** ado, din **4.** mess, moil
5. babel, chaos **6.** jumble, pother, welter
7. anarchy, clutter, turmoil **8.** disarray,
disorder **9.** abashment, agitation
10. perplexity **11.** derangement
12. bewilderment **13.** embarrassment
confute . . . **4.** deny **5.** rebut **6.** answer,
expose, refute **7.** dismiss **8.** confound,
overcome, redargue **9.** overwhelm (by
argument)
congeal . . . **3.** gel, ice, set **4.** rime **6.** freeze
7. pectize, thicken
congenial . . . **4.** boon **7.** kindred **8.** friendly
9. accordant, agreeable **10.** affinitive,
compatible **11.** sympathetic
congenital . . . **6.** inborn, innate
7. connate, genetic, natural
14. constitutional
conger . . . **3.** eel **8.** cucumber
13. Leptocephalus
congeries . . . **4.** heap **9.** amassment
10. collection **11.** aggregation
congestion . . . **3.** jam **4.** heap **8.** fullness,
stoppage **9.** gathering **11.** obstruction
12. accumulation
Congo . . .
capital . . **11.** Brazzaville
city . . **6.** Makoua **7.** Louboma
port . . **11.** Pointe Noire
river . . **5.** Congo (Zaire) **6.** Sangha
congratulate . . . **4.** laud **5.** bless **6.** salute
7. rejoice **8.** macarize **10.** compliment,
felicitate
congregate . . . **4.** herd, mass, meet
5. group, troop **6.** gather, muster
7. collect **8.** assemble **9.** forgather
congregation . . . **4.** mass **5.** house,
laity **7.** council **8.** assembly, audience
9. gathering **10.** collection
11. churchgoers
congress . . . **4.** diet **5.** synod **6.** durbar,
indaba, soviet **7.** council, meeting
8. assembly, conclave **9.** Sanhedrin
10. convention, parliament
11. convergence, convocation,
legislature **12.** congregation
congruous . . . **3.** fit **4.** meet **6.** proper
7. fitting **8.** agreeing, becoming, suitable
9. consonant
conic, conical . . . **8.** parabola
9. pyramidal **10.** cone-shaped, funnellike
conifers . . . **4.** yews **5.** pines **6.** cedars
7. larches, Pinales, Sabines, spruces,
Torreys **8.** hemlocks, Soledads
9. Coniferae, Corsicans **10.** evergreens
conjecture . . . **3.** aim **5.** ettle, guess,
opine, think **6.** divine **7.** conjoin,
imagine, presume, suppose, surmise,
suspect **8.** supposal **9.** inference
10. assumption, hypothesis
11. supposition
conjoin . . . **4.** join, link, yoke **5.** hitch,
unite **6.** adjoin, concur **7.** combine,
connect **8.** corelate **9.** correlate
conjoined parts . . . **6.** adnexa
conjointly . . . **10.** hand-in-hand
conjugal . . . **7.** marital, nuptial
9. connubial **11.** matrimonial
conjugate . . . **4.** join **5.** yoked **6.** couple,
united **7.** coupled, related **8.** bijugate,
combined **10.** paronymous

12. etymological
conjugation . . . 5. union 6. fusion
7. duality, joining, uniting
10. assemblage 11. combination
13. juxtaposition
conjunct . . . 6. united 8. combined
9. conjoined, corporate
conjunction . . . 2. as, et, if, or 3. and,
but, nor 4. than, that 5. since,
union 6. casual, though 7. whether
10. connection 11. adversative,
association, combination, concurrence,
correlative
conjure . . . 4. pray 5. charm 6. adjure,
enjoin, invoke, juggle, summon (magic)
7. beseech, enchant, entreat, implore
10. supplicate
conjure (up) . . . 5. raise 6. call up
8. exorcise (exorcize), remember
9. visualize
conjurer, conjuror . . . 4. mage 6. voodoo,
wizard 7. juggler 8. exorcist, magician
conk . . . 4. head, nose 5. decay (tree)
conk out . . . 4. fade, fail 5. stall 6. fizzle,
perish, weaken
connate . . . 4. akin 6. allied 7. cognate,
related, similar 9. congenial
10. congenital
connect . . . 3. tie 4. ally, join, link, meet
5. unite 6. adjoin, attach, couple,
enlink, fasten, relate 7. bracket, succeed
9. associate, hyphenate
connected . . . 3. met 5. telic 6. adnate,
joined 7. serried, similar 8. coherent,
inlinked, syndetic 10. continuous,
correlated
Connecticut . . .
capital . . 8. Hartford
city . . 6. Darien, Mystic 7. Meriden
8. Hartford, New Haven 9. Waterbury
10. Bridgeport
college (famed) . . 4. Yale (1701)
historic site . . 10. Charter Oak (1687,
Hartford)
museum . . 6. Barnum (P T)
river . . 6. Thames 9. Naugatuck
10. Hoosatonic 11. Connecticut
State admission . . 5. Fifth
State Motto . . 21. Qui Transtulit Sustinet
(He Who Transplants Sustains)
State nickname . . 6. Nutmeg
12. Constitution
connecting link . . . 3. tie 4. bond
6. connex 7. kiaison 8. ligament,
vinculum 11. intermedium
12. intermediary
connection . . . 4. bond 5. nexus, union
6. clevis, family, series 7. kinship,
passage 8. alliance, commerce,
junction, relation 9. coherence, go-
between, relevance 10. continuity
11. association, intercourse
12. intermediary, relationship
13. communication, juxtaposition
conner . . . 5. pilot 6. balker, tester
7. peruser 8. examiner 9. inspector
connive . . . 4. plot, wink 5. blink 6. scheme
7. collude, complot, finagle 8. conspire,
contrive, maneuver, overlook
conniving . . . 8. scheming 9. collusive,
deceitful 10. conspiring 11. calculating

connoisseur . . . 5. judge, maven 6. expert
7. epicure, gourmet 8. gourmand
11. cognoscente, connaisseur
connotation . . . 5. sense 6. import,
intent 7. meaning, purport 8. overtone
10. denotation 11. implication
12. significance 13. comprehension
connubial . . . 7. martial, nuptial
8. conjugal 11. matrimonial
12. epithalamium (song)
conquer . . . 3. win 4. beat, best 5. crush
6. defeat, humble, master, reduce,
subdue 7. subject 8. overcome,
overturn, surmount, vanquish
9. discomfit, overpower, overthrow,
subjugate
conqueror . . . 4. hero 6. captor, Cortez,
victor, winner 7. subduer 10. subjugator
12. conquistador
conquest . . . 6. Norman (1066) 7. mastery,
triumph, victory
consanguinity . . . 5. nabob 7. kinship,
sibship 8. affinity, relation (blood)
12. relationship
conscience . . . 4. mind, self 6. psyche
8. superego 9. casuistry
conscientious . . . 7. dutiful, servile
8. faithful 10. fastidious, meticulous,
scrupulous 11. punctilious
conscientious objection . . . 7. scruple
conscious . . . 4. keen 5. alive, awake,
aware, vital 7. animate, feeling
8. sensible, sentient 9. breathing,
cognizant 13. self-conscious
consecrate . . . 4. sain 5. bless, exalt
6. anoint, devote, hallow, ordain
7. glorify 8. dedicate, sanctify
consecrated (pert to) . . .
bread . . 4. host 5. wafer
oil . . 6. chrism
thing . . 6. sacrum
consent . . . 4. give 5. agree, grant, yield
6. accede, accord, assent, concur,
permit 8. approval 9. acquiesce
10. compliance, permission
11. concurrence 13. understanding
consequence . . . 3. end 5. event 6. course,
effect, result, weight 7. dignity,
outcome 8. pursuant (in), sequence
9. aftermath, inference, influence,
loftiness, outgrowth 10. importance,
notability 11. distinction
consequential . . . 7. pompous 8. eventual
9. important 13. self-important
consequently . . . 2. do 4. ergo, then
5. hence 9. as a result, therefore,
wherefore 12. subsequently
13. consecutively
conservative . . . 4. Tory 5. staid 7. die-
hard, fogyish, old-line 8. moderate
10. long-haired 11. reactionary
12. preservative 13. unprogressive
conserve . . . 3. jam 4. save 5. guard,
uvate 6. defend, secure, shield,
uphold 7. protect, sustain 8. maintain
9. preserves, sweetmeat
consider . . . 3. ain, see 4. care, deem,
heed, muse, rate 5. judge, think, treat,
weigh 6. esteem, intend, ponder,
regard 7. discuss, examine, reflect,
revolve 8. cogitate, meditate, ruminate

10. deliberate 11. contemplate
considerable . . . 5. great, large 7. notable, several 8. numerous 9. important 10. noteworthy, remarkable 13. authoritative
considerate . . . 4. kind 6. gentle 7. careful, heedful, prudent, serious 8. obliging 9. attentive, judicious 10. deliberate, reflective, solicitous, thoughtful
consideration . . . 4. self 5. study 6. esteem, regard 7. respect, thought 9. attention, deference, incentive, influence 10. cogitation, importance, meditation, reflection, reputation, rumination 11. examination 12. compensation, deliberation
considering . . . 2. if 5. since 8. after all, inasmuch, in view of
consign . . . 5. allot 6. assign, commit, devote, remand, resign 7. deliver, entrust 8. transfer 11. subscribe to
consignee . . . 6. factor 7. awardee 8. assignee 9. committee
consign to . . .
  a place . . 8. allocate
  prison . . 6. commit, send up
  ruin . . 4. doom
  unimportance . . 8. relegate
consistent . . . 5. equal, solid, stiff 7. equable, logical, uniform 8. coherent 9. agreement, consonant, steadfast 10. persisting
consisting of . . .
  cavities . . 9. cellulose
  layers (thin) . . 8. laminate
  names . . 8. onomatic
  one word . . 7. monepic
  pages . . 7. paginal
  three measures . . 8. trimeter
  three spots . . 4. trey
  three styles (Bot) . . 10. tristylous
  two parts . . 6. binary
consist of . . . 5. imply 6. embody 7. contain, embrace, enclose, involve 8. comprise (comprize)
consolation . . . 6. solace 7. comfort 10. condolence
console . . . 4. desk 5. cheer, organ, table 6. solace, soothe 7. bracket, cabinet, comfort, support, sustain 9. alleviate, encourage
consolidate . . . 4. knit, mass 5. merge, unify, unite 7. combine, densify 8. coalesce, compress, organize, solidify 9. intensify 10. strengthen
consonant . . . 4. lene, surd 5. lenis, nasal, velar 6. dental, labial 7. lingual, palatal, spirate 8. gutteral 9. accordant, congruous 10. compatible, concordant, consistent
consonant (pert to) . . .
  hissing . . 8. sibilant
  rustling . . 9. fricative
  voiceless (breathed) . . 6. atonic 7. spirate
consort . . . 4. Devi (of Siva), mate, wife 5. group, Sakti 6. mingle, spouse 7. husband, partner 9. associate, colleague, companion, harmonize 11. combination, confederate, conjunction
conspicuous . . . 6. famous, signal

7. eminent, glaring, obvious, salient, visible 8. distinct, lionized, manifest, striking 9. important, prominent 10. celebrated, noticeable, remarkable 11. illustrious, outstanding 13. distinguished
conspiracy . . . 4. plot 5. cabal, unite 6. scheme 8. intrigue 9. collusion 10. connivance 11. confederacy, machination
conspire . . . 4. plot 5. unite 6. concur, scheme 7. collude, complot, finagle 9. fainaigue 11. confederate
constable . . . 3. cop 5. staff 6. beadle, keeper, warden 7. bailiff 8. tipstaff 9. policeman
constabulary . . . 6. bureau (police) 10. constables
constancy . . . 4. zeal 5. ardor, faith, truth 6. fealty, garnet (symbol) 7. honesty, loyalty 8. devotion, fidelity 9. adherence, continual, eagerness, integrity, stability 10. allegiance, attachment, permanence, perpetuity, uniformity 11. devotedness, earnestness 12. faithfulness
constant . . . 4. firm, true 5. fixed 7. regular, uniform 8. faithful, resolute 9. continual, invariant, parameter (Math), perpetual, steadfast 10. continuous, invariable, persistent 12. unchangeable
constant desire . . . 4. itch 9. hankering
Constantine (pert to) . . .
  birthplace . . 4. Nish (Nis) 7. Naissus (now Yugoslavia)
  known as . . 8. The Great
  title . . 7. Emperor (Rome)
Constantinople . . .
  official name . . 8. Istanbul
  patriarch . . 9. Nestorius
  site . . 6. Turkey (Eur)
constellation . . . 5. stars 6. galaxy 8. asterism 10. luminaries 13. configuration (stars)
Constellations (partial list) . . .
  arrow . . 7. Sagitta
  bears (Dipper) . . 9. Ursa Major, Ursa Minor
  Bird of Paradise (S Pole) . . 4. Apus
  bull . . 6. Taurus
  crab . . 6. Cancer
  crane . . 4. Grus
  crow . . 6. Corvus
  dog . . 5. Canis
  dragon . . 5. Draco
  eagle . . 6. Aquila
  fishes . . 6. Pisces
  goat . . 9. Capricorn
  goldfish . . 6. Dorado
  hunter . . 5. Orion (most conspicuous)
  lion . . 3. Leo
  Noah's Ark . . 4. Argo
  Northern Crown . . 14. Corona Borealis, Northern Lights
  peacock . . 4. Pavo
  scorpion . . 7. Scorpio
  serpent (sea) . . 5. Hydra
  Southern Cross . . 4. Crux
  swan . . 6. Cygnus
  Twins . . 6. Gemini

virgin . . **5.** Virgo
water bearer . . **8.** Aquarius
whale . . **6.** Cestus
winged horse . . **7.** Pegasus
wolf . . **5.** Lupus
Constellations' brightest star . . . **3.** Cor
Constellations of the Zodiac . . . **3.** Leo
  5. Aries, Libra, Virgo **6.** Cancer, Gemini,
  Pisces, Taurus **7.** Scorpio **8.** Aquarius
  11. Capricornus, Sagittarius
constituent . . . **5.** voter **6.** factor,
  matter **7.** elector, element, essence
  8. elective **9.** component **10.** ingredient
  11. determinant (Math)
constituent of . . .
  blood serum . . **7.** opsonin
  coal . . **6.** carbon
  coffee, tea . . **8.** caffeine
  hair, nails . . **7.** keratin
  oil of cloves . . **7.** eugenol
constitute . . . **4.** form **5.** enact, found
  6. create, depute **7.** appoint, compose
  8. legalize **9.** determine, establish
constitution . . . **3.** law **6.** crasis, custom
  7. passage **8.** creation **9.** enactment,
  essential, ordinance, structure
  11. composition, institution
  12. organization
Constitution (ship) . . . **12.** Old Ironsides
constitutional . . . **5.** legal, valid **6.** innate
  9. essential, healthful **12.** governmental
  13. dispositional
constitutional (pert to) . . .
  health . . **4.** walk **6.** stroll **8.** exercise
  right . . **9.** franchise
  temperament . . **6.** crasis
  vigor . . **5.** nerve
Constitution State . . . **11.** Connecticut
constrain . . . **4.** curb, urge **5.** chain, check,
  drive, force, impel, press **6.** compel,
  oblige **7.** confine, repress **8.** restrain
  11. necessitate
constrained . . . **6.** forced, modest
  7. cramped **8.** moderate, reserved
  9. obligated
constraint . . . **4.** bond, urge **5.** force
  6. duress, stress **7.** modesty, reserve
  8. coercion, pressure **9.** restraint,
  stiffness **10.** compulsion, moderation
  11. confinement
constrict . . . **3.** tie **4.** bind **5.** cramp
  6. narrow, shrink **7.** squeeze, tighten
  8. astringe, condense, contract
  10. constringe
constriction . . . **9.** narrowing, stricture,
  tightness **11.** contraction
  13. strangulation
constrictor . . . **3.** boa **5.** snake **7.** serpent,
  styptic **9.** sphincter **10.** compressor
construct . . . **4.** make, rear **5.** build,
  erect, frame **6.** create **7.** compose
  9. establish, fabricate, originate
constructive . . . **7.** virtual **8.** creative,
  implicit **9.** anabolism **10.** suggestive
  14. interpretation, interpretative
construe . . . **5.** parse **6.** deduce, render
  7. explain **9.** interpret, translate
consuetude . . . **5.** habit, usage **6.** custom
consuetudinary . . . **6.** manual (customs),
  ritual **9.** customary
consult (with) . . . **6.** advise, confer, take

up **7.** discuss **10.** deliberate
consultation . . . **7.** counsel **8.** audition,
  congress **9.** interview **10.** conference,
  discussion **12.** deliberation
consume . . . **3.** eat, use **4.** burn **5.** spend,
  waste **6.** absorb, devour, expend
  7. destroy (fire) **8.** squander **9.** dissipate
  12. disintegrate
consumed . . . **3.** pau
consummate . . . **3.** end, top **4.** ripe
  5. ideal **6.** finish, utmost **7.** achieve,
  perfect **8.** complete **10.** accomplish
consumption . . . **3.** use **4.** loss **5.** decay,
  waste **6.** eating **7.** disease, using up
  8. phthisis **9.** decrement **11.** destruction
  12. tuberculosis **13.** deterioration
contact . . . **4.** meet **5.** touch, union
  6. impact, syzygy (Astron) **7.** meeting,
  oscnode (Math) **8.** junction, tangency,
  touching **10.** contiguity
  13. communication
contain . . . **4.** have, hold, keep **5.** cover
  6. embody, number, retain **7.** embrace,
  enclose, include, involve, subsume
  8. comprise, restrain **9.** divisible (by)
  10. comprehend
container . . . **3.** bag, bin, box, can, cup,
  jar, jug, lug, pan, pod, pot, tin, tub,
  urn, vat **4.** case, crib, ewer, pail, sack,
  vase **5.** crate, cruet, pouch **6.** basket,
  bottle, carboy, carton, hamper, hatbox
  7. capsule, hanaper **8.** canister, decanter
containing . . .
  air . . **9.** pneumatic
  antimony . . **8.** stibiate
  boron . . **5.** boric **7.** boracic
  carbon . . **7.** organic **13.** carboniferous
  copper . . **6.** cupric
  fire . . **7.** igneous
  gold . . **4.** doré **5.** auric
  iron . . **6.** ferric
  silver . . **5.** lunar
  slag . . **6.** drossy
  ten . . **6.** denary
  tin . . **7.** stannic
containing maxims . . . **6.** gnomic
contaminate . . . **4.** slur, soil **5.** stain,
  sully, taint **6.** befoul, defile, infect,
  poison **7.** corrupt, debauch, degrade,
  pollute, vitiate **8.** dishonor **9.** desecrate
  10. adulterate
contemn . . . **4.** defy, hate **5.** scorn, spurn
  6. reject **7.** despise, disdain
contemplate . . . **4.** muse, plan, scan,
  view **5.** study **6.** design, expect, intend,
  ponder **7.** examine, foresee, propose
  8. consider, envision, meditate
contemplation . . . **5.** study **6.** musing
  7. theoria, thought **8.** scrutiny
  9. foresight, intuition **10.** expectancy,
  reflection **11.** examination, expectation,
  speculation
contemplative . . . **6.** sedate **7.** pensive
  10. meditative, reflective, ruminative,
  thoughtful **11.** speculative
  13. retrospective
contemporary . . . **6.** coeval **7.** present
  10. coetaneous, coexistent, coincident
  11. concomitant, synchronous
  12. simultaneous **15.** contemporaneous
contempt . . . **4.** fico, geck **5.** scorn, shame,

sneer **7.** despect, disdain **8.** defiance, derision, ridicule **9.** arrogance, contumely **10.** disrespect **12.** disobedience

contemptible ... **3.** low **4.** base **5.** cheap, petty, sorry **6.** abject, paltry, sordid **7.** pitiful **8.** beggarly, inferior, unworthy **9.** groveling, worthless **10.** despicable **13.** insignificant

contemptuous ... **6.** sneery **7.** haughty **8.** insolent, scornful **10.** disdainful **12.** contumelious, supercilious

contemptuous action ... **9.** indignity **10.** incivility

contend ... **3.** vie, war **4.** cope, deal, race **5.** argue, fight **6.** assert, bicker, insist, strive **7.** compete, contest, grapple, quarrel, wrangle **8.** contrive, maintain, militate

content, contents ... **4.** list, room **5.** index, space **6.** amount, please, volume **7.** filling, gratify, makings, satisfy, suffice **8.** capacity **9.** contented, happiness, satisfied **10.** components, dimensions **11.** ingredients

contention ... **3.** war **4.** feud **6.** combat, debate, strife **7.** quarrel, rivalry **8.** argument, conflict, struggle, variance **9.** emulation **10.** dissension, litigation **11.** altercation, competition, controversy **12.** disagreement

contentious ... **7.** peevish **8.** perverse **9.** combative, litigious, wrangling **10.** pugnacious **11.** belligerent, dissentious, quarrelsome **13.** argumentative

contentment ... **4.** ease **5.** bliss **8.** pleasure **11.** peace of mind **12.** satisfaction **13.** contentedness, gratification

conterminous ... **4.** next **8.** abutting, adjacent, proximal **9.** adjoining

contest ... **3.** sue, vie **4.** agon, bout, cope, deny, game, race, tilt **5.** argue, set-to, trial **6.** debate, oppose, strife, strive, tryout **7.** contend, dispute, tourney, wrangle **8.** argument, disclaim, litigate, skirmish, struggle **9.** emulation **10.** engagement **11.** altercation, competition

contest (pert to) ...
art of .. **10.** agonistics
draw .. **9.** stalemate
log hurling .. **5.** roleo
prize .. **5.** stake
undecided .. **4.** draw

contestant ... **5.** rival **6.** player **7.** athlete, entrant **8.** opponent **9.** candidate, combatant, contender **10.** competitor

contiguous ... **4.** near, next **8.** adjacent, touching **9.** adjoining, immediate, proximate **11.** neighboring

continent ... **4.** Asia **6.** Africa, Europe **7.** Eurasia, Lemuria **8.** Atlantis (lost), Cascadia, landmass **9.** Australia, Greenland **10.** Antarctica **12.** North America, South America

contingency ... **4.** case **5.** event **6.** chance **8.** accident, casualty, exigency, juncture **9.** emergency, liability **11.** eventuality, possibility, uncertainty

contingent ... **6.** casual **8.** eventual **9.** dependent (law), provisory **10.** accidental, fortuitous, incidental **11.** conditional, provisional

continual ... **7.** endless, eternal, regular, undying, uniform **8.** constant, enduring, frequent, unbroken **9.** ceaseless, connected, continued, incessant, perennial, permanent, perpetual, unceasing **10.** continuous, invariable **11.** everlasting, intermitted, unremitting **12.** imperishable **13.** uninterrupted

continually ... **3.** aye **4.** ever **5.** often **7.** eternal **9.** eternally **10.** constantly **11.** perpetually, unceasingly **12.** continuously

continuation ... **6.** sequel **8.** addition, sequence **10.** continuity **11.** continuance, propagation, protraction **12.** postponement, prolongation

continue ... **3.** run **4.** go on, last, stay **5.** abide **6.** endure, extend, remain, resume **7.** perdure, persist, proceed, sustain **8.** protract **9.** persevere, steadfast (be)

continuing ... **5.** still **7.** chronic, durable, lasting **9.** permanent **10.** continuous **11.** persevering

continuous ... **7.** chronic, endless, uniform **8.** unbroken **9.** continued, perpetual **13.** uninterrupted

contorted ... **3.** wry **4.** bent **6.** coiled, warped **7.** garbled, gnarled, twisted, wristed **8.** deformed **9.** perverted

contour ... **4.** form, line **5.** curve, graph **6.** figure **7.** isobase, outline, profile **9.** lineament, periphery **13.** configuration

contra ... **6.** offset **7.** against, counter, reverse **8.** contrary, opposite **9.** vice versa **10.** conversely **12.** contrariwise

contraband ... **7.** bootleg, illegal, illicit **8.** unlawful **9.** moonshine **10.** prohibited

contract ... **4.** hale, knit, pact **5.** incur, lease **6.** cartel, engage, pledge, reduce, shrink **7.** bargain, compact, promise, shorten, shrivel **8.** covenant **9.** agreement, constrict, indenture **10.** convention, obligation, straighten **11.** arrangement **13.** understanding

contraction ... **3.** tic **4.** coup, fist **5.** spasm **7.** elision, systole **8.** decrease **9.** reduction, short-hand, stricture **11.** compression

contrada ... **3.** way **4.** ward **6.** street **7.** quarter

contradict ... **4.** deny **5.** belie, rebut **6.** impugn, negate, oppose, refute **7.** gainsay **10.** counteract

contradiction ... **6.** denial **7.** paradox **10.** opposition, refutation **11.** contrariety **13.** counteraction

contradictory ... **7.** denying **8.** contrary, opposite **9.** refutatory **12.** inconsistent

contrary ... **7.** adverse, counter, froward, opposed, reverse **8.** captious, inimical, opposite, perverse, refutive **9.** different, repugnant **10.** discordant, unorthodox **12.** antagonistic

contrast ... **7.** compare **8.** opposite

11. contrariety

contravene . . . 4. defy 6. hinder, oppose, refute, thwart 7. violate 8. infringe 9. disregard

contravention . . . 6. denial 9. violation 10. opposition, refutation

contribute . . . 3. aid 4. give 6. donate 7. benefit, conduce, provide 9. subscribe

contribution . . . 3. tax, tip 4. boon, gift, scot 6. tariff 7. payment, tribute 8. donation 12. subscription 13. participation

contrite . . . 6. abject, humble 8. penitent 9. repentant, sorrowful 10. remorseful 11. penitential

contrition . . . 7. remorse 9. attrition, penitence 11. compunction

contrivance . . . 3. art 5. means, shift 6. design, devise 7. coinage, machine, measure, project 8. artifice, intrigue 9. expedient, invention, makeshift 11. contraption

contrive . . . 4. plan, plot 5. frame, hatch, weave 6. design, devise, invent, manage, scheme 7. fashion, project 9. fabricate

control . . . 4. hold, rein, rule, sway, test 5. check, gripe, guide, leash, power, wield 6. direct, govern, manage, subdue 7. conduct, mastery, preside, regimen 8. dominate, dominion, ironhand, regulate, restrain 9. direction, influence, regulator, restraint 10. management, regulation 11. self-control, superintend

controller, comptroller . . . 7. auditor 8. governor 9. dominator, regulator

controversial . . . 7. eristic, polemic 9. eristical, polemical, pro and con 11. contentious 12. disputatious, questionable 13. argumentative

controversy . . . 6. debate 7. dispute, quarrel, wrangle 8. argument 10. contention 11. altercation 12. disagreement, disputatious

controvert . . . 4. deny, moot 5. argue 6. debate, oppose, refute 7. discuss, dispute 10. contradict

contumacious . . . 6. unruly 7. riotous 8. mutinous, perverse 9. seditious 10. headstrong, rebellious, refractory, unyielding 11. disobedient, intractable 12. ungovernable 13. insubordinate

contumelious . . . 7. haughty 8. insolent 9. insulting 10. derogatory, despiteful, disdainful 12. contemptuous

contumely . . . 5. scorn 8. contempt 9. indignity, insolence 10. revilement 11. humiliation, malediction

contusion . . . 4. blow 6. bruise, injury 8. black eye 13. discoloration

conundrum . . . 5. rebus 6. enigma, puzzle, riddle 7. charade

convalesce . . . 5. rally 7. recover, recruit 10. recuperate

convene . . . 3. sit 4. come, meet 5. unite 6. summon 8. assemble 10. congregate, foregather

convenient . . . 5. handy, ready 6. fitted, nearby, suited, timely 7. adapted 8. suitable 9. agreeable, available, opportune 10. accessible, commodious,

seasonable 11. comfortable

convent . . . 4. meet 6. concur, friary, priory 7. convene, nunnery 8. cloister, lamasery 9. monastery, sanctuary

convention . . . 4. rule 5. usage 6. accord, custom 7. meeting 8. assembly 9. gathering, tradition 10. assemblage, compliance, conformity

conventional . . . 5. fixed, nomic, usual 6. formal, modish 7. correct 8. accepted, orthodox 9. customary 10. ceremonial 11. established, traditional

converge . . . 4. meet 5. focus, unite

conversant (with) . . . 5. adept 6. expert, versed (in) 7. skilled 8. familiar 9. practiced 10. acquainted, proficient

conversation . . . 4. chat, talk 7. trialog 8. causerie, converse, dialogue 9. communion, discourse 10. conference 11. association 13. conversazione, interlocution

conversationalist . . . 6. talker 9. converser 10. discourser 12. confabulator

converse . . . 4. chat, talk 8. contrary, opposite

convey . . . 4. cede, deed, pass, send 5. bring, carry, eloin, grant 6. assign, convoy, demise, devise, impart, import 7. dispone 8. transfer, transmit 9. transport 10. commission 11. communicate

conveyance . . . 3. bus, car, van 4. auto, sled, taxi, tram 5. plane, train 6. demise, litter 7. cession, norimon, trailer, vehicle 8. airplane, carriage 10. automobile

conveyer, conveyor . . . 6. bearer, coolie, pigeon (homing), porter 7. bheesty, carrier 8. cargador 9. stevedore

convict . . . 4. damn 5. felon, lifer 6. refute, termer, trusty 7. condemn, culprit 6. refute 8. criminal, prisoner 10. malefactor

conviction . . . 4. hope 6. belief 7. opinion 9. certainty 10. persuasion 12. condemnation

convince . . . 6. assure, subdue 7. confute, jawbone 8. overcome, persuade 9. overpower

convincing . . . 5. proof 6. cogent, potent 7. telling 8. assuring 10. conclusive, persuasive, satisfying

convivial . . . 3. gay 4. gala 5. jolly, merry 6. festal, jovial, joyful, joyous, social 7. festive, jocular 9. hilarious

convocation . . . 4. diet 5. synod 7. bidding, council, meeting, summons 8. assembly, congress 10. convention 12. congregation

convoke . . . 4. call 6. summon 7. convene 8. assemble

convoy . . . 5. guard, guide 6. attend, escort 7. conduct 8. navigate 9. accompany, conductor

convulse . . . 5. amuse, shake 6. regale 7. agitate, disturb, torture 9. entertain 10. discompose

convulsion . . . 5. cramp, spasm, throe 6. tumult, uproar 8. laughter, paroxysm 9. agitation, commotion 10. revolution 11. disturbance

cony, coney . . . 3. das, fur 4. dupe, hare, pika 5. daman, hyrax 6. burbot, rabbit

cony catcher . . . 5. cheat 7. sharper 8. swindler

coo . . . 4. bill (and), curr 5. chirr 6. murmur, mutter

cook . . . 4. bake, boil, chef, stew 5. broil, roast, sauté, spoil (chess), steam, trill 6. braise, seethe 7. parboil, stir-fry 8. barbecue, magirist 9. charbroil, cuisinier

cookie . . . 5. scone 7. biscuit, brownie 8. macaroon 10. gingersnap, ladyfinger, shortbread

cooking (pert to) . . .
art . . 8. magirics
device . . 3. wok 4. etna, olla 5. grill, plate, stove 6. spider 7. griddle 9. autoclave, microwave (oven)
room . . 6. galley 7. cuisine, kitchen 8. scullery 11. kitchenette
scent . . 4. reek 5. nidor

cool . . . 3. fan, ice 4. calm 5. chill, fresh, nervy, sober, tepid 6. chilly, freeze, sedate, serene, temper 7. unmoved 8. careless, composed, impudent, mitigate, reserved, tranquil 9. apathetic, collected, unruffled 10. nonchalant, unfriendly, unsociable 11. indifferent, levelheaded, unconcerned 13. dispassionate, imperturbable, self-possessed

cooler . . . 4. icer, jail 6. icebox, lockup, prison 7. chiller 10. ventilator 11. refrigerant 12. refrigerator

coolness . . . 4. cold 5. nerve 6. aplomb 7. reserve 12. indifference 14. unfriendliness

coop . . . 3. mew, pen 4. cage, cote, yard 5. court, hutch 7. confine 9. enclosure

cooper . . . 5. drink 7. vessel 8. grogshop (floating) 11. barrel maker 12. wine retailer

Cooper, (James Fenimore) (pert to) . . .
hero . . 10. Deerslayer, Natty Bumpo, Pathfinder
tales . . 15. Leatherstocking

cooperate . . . 4. join, tend 5. agree, coact 6. concur 7. combine, conduce, connive 8. conspire 9. interface, synergize 10. contribute 11. collaborate

coordinate . . . 5. talky 6. adjust 7. syntony (radio) 8. classify, equalize, organize, regulate 9. harmonize, integrate 10. proportion 11. systematize

copious . . . 4. full, rich 5. ample 7. diffuse, profuse 8. abundant, numerous 9. exuberant, plenteous, plentiful 11. overflowing

copper . . . 2. Cu 3. aes 4. cent, coin 5. metal, penny 6. cuprum 9. policeman 12. reddish-brown

copper (pert to) . . .
alloy . . 5. brass 6. bronze, oroide
brass . . 6. chalco
cup . . 3. dop
engraving . . 9. mezzotint
film . . 6. patina
kettle (anc) . . 5. lebes
pewter . . 7. rheotan

Copperfield characters . . . 4. Dora 6. Dartle 8. Micawber 9. Uriah Heep 11. Little Emily

coppice . . . 4. bosk, holt 5. copse, grove 6. growth 7. boscage, thicket 9. brushwood, underwood

Coptic (pert to) . . .
church . . 8. Egyptian
color . . 7. oxblood
title . . 4. anba

copy . . . 3. ape 4. news 5. clone, model, Xerox (tm) 6. ectype, follow 7. edition, estreat, imitate, pattern, replica, purify, tracing 8. protocol, revision 9. duplicate, imitation 10. transcribe, transcript 11. counterfeit 12. reproduction

coquet, coquette . . . 4. vamp 5. flirt 7. amorous 11. hummingbird

coquille . . . 5. shell 7. ruching

Coquille . . . 6. Indian 10. Athapascan

coquin . . . 5. knave, rogue 6. rascal

coral . . . 3. red 6. polyps, porite 8. Anthozoa 9. madrepore, millepore

coral (pert to) . . .
branch . . 7. ramicle
division . . 7. Aporosa
formation . . 5. palus
island . . 3. key 5. atoll
ridge . . 4. reef 5. shoal
snake . . 5. Elaps 6. garter 7. Micurus
worm . . 6. palolo

corbie (Scot) . . . 4. crow. 5. raven

cord . . . 3. guy, rib 4. lace, line, rope, welt, wood 5. sinew, twine 6. lariat, sennet, spinal, string, tendon 7. measure (cubic), skirreh 8. corduroy, shoelace 9. hamstring 11. clothesline

cordage . . . 5. ropes 7. rigging 8. ropework

Corday's victim . . . 5. Marat

cordelle . . . 6. hauler 7. towline, towrope

cordial . . . 4. real, warm 5. ardent, elixir, genial, hearty, liquor 7. fervent, liqueur, sincere, zealous 8. friendly, vigorous 9. unfeigned 10. hospitable

cordial (liqueur) . . . 5. shrub 6. kummel 8. anisette, periscot 9. Cointreau 11. Benedictine, crème de moka 13. crème de menthe

cordiality . . . 4. zeal 5. ardor 6. fervor 7. ardency 8. kindness, warmness 9. geniality 11. hospitality 12. empressement, friendliness

corduroy feature . . . 4. wale

core . . . 3. ame, hub, nub, nut 4. gist, nave, pith 5. heart, nowel 6. center, kernel, matrix 7. nucleus 9. substance

Corinthian (pert to) . . .
Age . . 5. plush 11. extravagant
color . . 3. red 4. pink 6. purple
Epistles (Bib) . . 12. New Testament
General (Rom) . . 9. Flaminius
King . . 8. Polybius
Spring . . 14. Pirene Fountain
Temple . . 5. Doric 7. Minerva

cork . . . 3. ork 4. bark, bung, plug 5. float, shive, suber (oak) 7. blacken, stopgap, stopper, stopple

corm . . . 4. bulb (flower)

cormorant . . . 4. bird, shag 5. norie, scart, urile 8. ravenous 9. snakebird,

voracious 13. Phalacrocorax
corn ... 4. joke 5. grain, grist 6. cliché,
kaffir, kernel, liquor
corn (pert to) ...
bread .. 4. pone 8. dumpling
10. corndodger
goddess .. 5. Ceres
hulled .. 4. samp 6. hominy
Indian .. 3. Zea 5. maize
lily .. 4. Ixia 8. bindweed 10. wandflower
liquor .. 6. whisky (whiskey)
meal .. 4. masa 7. hoecake
porridge .. 5. atole
salad .. 8. fetticus
Corn Belt ... 4. Iowa, Ohio 6. Dakota,
Kansas 7. Indiana 8. Illinois, Missouri,
Nebraska 9. Minnesota
Corncracker State ... 8. Kentucky
corner ... 2. in 4. nook, pose, trap, tree
5. angle, coign (coigne), herne, ingle,
niche, quoin
cornered ... 5. cater (diagonal), sharp,
treed 7. angular, up a tree
10. cornerwise
cornerstone ... 4. coin 5. quoin
8. keystone 10. foundation
Cornhusker State ... 8. Nebraska
cornice ... 4. drip, eave 7. antefix
8. astragal
Cornish ... 3. elm 4. fowl 5. heath
7. dialect, diamond (Cornwall)
Cornwallis surrender site ... 4. York
(Va)
corolla ... 5. galea (Her), petal 8. perianth
corollary ... 6. effect, porism, result
7. adjunct 8. addition 9. deduction
11. proposition
corona ... 4. coin, halo 5. cigar, crown
6. circle 7. aureole, circlet, garland,
scyphus 8. Borealis 11. corona lucis
Corona Australis ... 13. Southern Crown
Corona Borealis ... 13. Northern Crown
coronet ... 5. crown, tiara 6. anadem,
circle, diadem, wreath 8. insignia,
ornament
Corot subject ... 9. landscape
corporate ... 5. joint 6. united 7. leagued
8. conjoint 10. associated
corporeal ... 5. hylic, somal 6. bodily
7. fleshly, somatic 8. corporal, material,
physical, tangible
corpse ... 4. body 7. cadaver, carcass
9. endowment (Eccl)
corpulent ... 3. fat 5. bulky, obese, stout
6. fleshy
corpus ... 4. body, mass 9. principal
10. collection
corpuscle ... 11. poikilocyte, schistocyte
12. erythroblast
corral ... 3. mew, pen, sty 4. coop, herd
5. atajo, pound, tambo 7. impound
8. stockade 9. enclosure, inclosure
correct ... 2. OK 4. edit, okay, true
5. amend, emend, right 6. better,
proper, punish, reform, remedy, revise,
strict 7. chasten, improve, perfect,
rectify, regular, retouch 8. accurate,
definite, orthodox, rigorous 9. faultless
10. particular, scrupulous
11. grammatical, punctilious
12. conventional

correlative ... 2. or 3. nor 6. mutual
7. similar 8. conjoint 10. reciprocal
11. conjunction, counterpart
13. corresponding
correspond ... 3. fit 4. suit 5. agree,
equal, match, tally 6. accord 7. comport
8. assonate (sound), coincide, parallel
9. analogous, harmonize 11. parallelize
correspondence ... 4. mail 8. homology
(Biol), identity, symmetry
10. conformity, epistolary, similarity
11. equivalence, intercourse
corresponding ... 8. balanced
9. analogous, homologic, isometric
10. coinciding 11. paralleling
corrida sound ... 3. olé
corridor ... 4. hall 5. aisle 6. airway,
arcade 7. gallery 10. passageway
corrige (obs) ... 6. punish 7. correct
corrigible ... 8. amenable 10. submissive
11. rectifiable
corroborate ... 5. prove 7. certify,
confirm, support 8. calidate, roborate
9. establish 12. adminiculate,
substantiate
corroborative ... 11. adminicular
corrode ... 3. eat 4. bite, etch, gnaw,
rust 5. erode, waste 11. deteriorate
12. disintegrate
corrosive ... 4. acid 7. caustic, erodent,
erodine, mordant 9. corroding
10. escharotic 14. disintegrative
corrugate ... 5. crimp 6. rugate
7. crumble, wrinkle 8. crumpled,
furrowed, wrinkled
corrupt ... 3. rot 5. bribe, taint, venal
6. Augean, debase, putrid, rotten
7. attaint, crooked, defiled, deprave,
putrefy, vitiate 8. polluted 9. dishonest
11. adulterated 12. contaminated
corruption ... 5. taint 6. pidgin (language)
8. impurity 9. chicanery, pollution
10. debasement, defilement, distortion
11. depravation, putrescence
12. adulteration 13. contamination
corsage ... 5. waist 6. bodice 7. bouquet
(boquet), flowers
corsair ... 5. rover 6. pirate 7. Saracen
8. picaroon, rockfish 9. buccaneer,
privateer 10. freebooter
Corsica ...
capital .. 7. Ajaccio
birthplace of .. 8. Napoleon
feud (blood) .. 8. vendetta
seaport .. 6. Bastia
cortege ... 5. train 6. parade 7. funeral,
retinue 10. procession
Cortes palace site ... 8. Coyoacan
(Mexico)
cortex ... 4. bark, peel, rind
corundum ... 3. gem 5. emery 7. mineral
8. abrasive
corundum colors ...
blue .. 5. white 8. sapphire
brown .. 14. adamantine spar
green .. 7. emerald
purple .. 8. amethyst
red .. 4. ruby
topaz .. 6. yellow
coruscate ... 5. gleam, shine 7. glitter,
radiate, sparkle 11. scintillate

cosmetic ... **5.** cream, henna, paint, rouge **6.** enamel, lotion, make-up **7.** blusher, mascara **8.** lipstick, toiletry **11.** beautifying

cosmic ... **4.** vast **5.** great **7.** orderly **8.** catholic, infinite **9.** grandiose, universal **10.** harmonious

Cosmic Order ... **4.** Rita (Vedic law)

Cossack (pert to) ...
chief .. **6.** ataman, hetman
district .. **6.** Voisko
native .. **5.** Tatar **7.** Russian
squadron .. **6.** sotnia
village .. **8.** stanitsa (stanitza)
whip (knotted) .. **5.** knout

cosset ... **3.** pet **4.** lamb **6.** caress, coddle, cuddle, fondle, pamper

cost ... **4.** loss, rate **5.** price **6.** amount, charge, figure, outlay, rental **7.** expense **9.** detriment, suffering **11.** deprivation, expenditure

costa ... **3.** rib **4.** vein (Bot) **5.** ridge **6.** border, midrib

Costa Rica ...
capital .. **7.** San José
crater (world's greatest) .. **4.** Poas
discovered .. **8.** Columbus (4th visit)
export .. **6.** coffee **7.** bananas
port .. **5.** Limon **10.** Puntarenas

costate ... **6.** ribbed (Bot)

costermonger ... **6.** coster, hawker **7.** peddler **9.** costerman **11.** apple seller

costly ... **4.** dear, rich **8.** gorgeous, splendid **9.** expensive, sumptuous **10.** high-priced **11.** extravagant

costume ... **3.** rig **4.** garb, suit **5.** dress, habit **6.** attire, tights **7.** apparel, raiment **8.** clothing

cot ... **3.** bed, hut, pen, set **4.** boat (Ir), coop, cote **5.** cabin, cover, house **6.** cabana **7.** charpoy, cottage, shelter **8.** bedstead

cote ... **3.** hut, pen **4.** coop **5.** house **7.** cottage, shelter **9.** sheepfold

Côte d'Azur ... **7.** Riviera

coterie ... **3.** set **4.** clan, club, ring **5.** cabal, group, junto **6.** circle, clique **9.** camarilla (secret)

cotillion ... **4.** ball **5.** belle, dance **9.** debutante, petticoat, quadrille

cottage ... **3.** cot, hut **4.** shed **5.** cabin, house, villa **6.** cabana **7.** shelter **8.** bungalow

cottager ... **6.** cottar (cotter) **7.** cottier, laborer, peasant

cotton (pert to) ...
cloth .. **4.** jean, lawn **5.** denim, khaki, scrim, surat, terry **6.** calico, dimity, madras, nettle **7.** batiste, percale
fiber .. **4.** lint **6.** staple **7.** viscose
gin inventor .. **7.** Whitney (Eli)
knot .. **3.** nep
layer .. **7.** batting
medical .. **5.** gauze **6.** sponge
raw .. **5.** bayal
roll .. **4.** slub
seed .. **4.** bole, boll
seed sugar .. **9.** raffinose
staple .. **6.** upland (short) **8.** Egyptian (long) **9.** Sea Island (long)

thread .. **5.** lisle

Cotton State ... **7.** Alabama

couch ... **3.** bed, cot **4.** lair, sofa **5.** divan **6.** canapé, canopy, litter, lounge, pallet, phrase **8.** loveseat **9.** embroider (with gold), stretcher

cougar ... **3.** cat **4.** lion, puma **7.** panther **9.** catamount

cough ... **4.** bark (sl), hack **6.** tussis

council ... **4.** diet, rede **5.** cabal, synod **6.** senate **7.** cabinet **8.** assembly, conclave, tribunal **10.** conference, parliament **12.** consultation **15.** League of Nations

council table cover ... **5.** tapis

counsel ... **4.** rede **6.** advice, advise, confer, lawyer **8.** guidance **9.** recommend **10.** suggestion **11.** instruction **12.** deliberation

counselor, counsellor ... **4.** sage **6.** lawyer, mentor, nestor **7.** adviser, advisor, counsel **8.** attorney **9.** barrister, solicitor

count ... **3.** sum, tot **4.** tale, tell **5.** check, judge, relay, taily **6.** number, reckon, rely on **7.** compute, summary **8.** nobleman, quantify **9.** calculate, enumerate, reckoning, summation **12.** capitulation

Count (pert to) ...
Mayence .. **3.** Gan **7.** Ganelon
Monte Cristo .. **6.** Dantes
Rousillon .. **7.** Bertram

countenance ... **3.** aid **4.** abet, brow, face, mien **6.** aspect, permit, visage **7.** approve, endorse, support **8.** approval, sanction, tolerate **9.** composure, encourage **10.** appearance, permission

counter ... **4.** chip **5.** table, token **7.** adverse **8.** computer, contrary, opposite **9.** retaliate **10.** calculator

counteract ... **6.** offset, oppose, thwart **7.** nullify **8.** antidote **10.** neutralize **11.** countermand

counter current ... **4.** eddy **5.** swirl **6.** vortex **9.** whirlpool **12.** counterforce

counterfeit ... **4.** base, fake, mock, sham **5.** bogus, false, feign, forge, phony, queer **6.** assume, forged, unreal **7.** falsify, forgery, imitate **8.** simulant, spurious **10.** artificial, fictitious **11.** unauthentic

counterirritant ... **4.** moxa **5.** seton **6.** arnica, iodine, pepper **7.** mustard

countermand ... **5.** annul **6.** cancel, forbid, recall, revoke **7.** abolish, reverse **8.** prohibit **9.** frustrate **10.** counteract **12.** counterorder

counterpane ... **5.** quilt **8.** bedcover, coverlet **9.** comforter **10.** counterpin **11.** comfortable

counterpart ... **4.** copy, like, twin **5.** image **6.** double, eponym (name) **8.** parallel **9.** duplicate **10.** complement, equivalent

counterpoise ... **6.** offset **8.** equalize **10.** compensate, counteract **12.** counterforce **14.** counterbalance

countersign ... **4.** sign **6.** signal **7.** tessera **8.** password **9.** signature, watchword

10. mot de passé, open sesame
12. counterstamp
countersink ... **4.** ream **5.** bevel
  6. deepen **7.** chamfer
countertenor ... **4.** alto (male) **8.** falsetto
counterthrust (fencing) ... **7.** riposte
  (ripost) **12.** return thrust
countless ... **8.** infinite **10.** numberless,
  unnumbered **11.** innumerable
  12. incalculable
countrified ... **5.** rural **7.** boorish, hickish,
  uncouth **8.** inurbane **10.** unpolished
country ... **4.** land, pais (law), vale
  5. rural, state, weald **6.** nation,
  region **9.** territory **10.** fatherland
  12. commonwealth
country (pert to) ...
  alien .. **7.** enclave, exclave
  ancient .. **4.** Aram, Elis, Gaul
  bumpkin .. **4.** clod, jake, rube **5.** churl,
    yokel **9.** greenhorn
  gallant .. **5.** swain
  mythical .. **2.** Oz
  native (earliest) .. **9.** aborigine
  Roman .. **8.** campagna
  term .. **5.** rural, urban **6.** rustic **8.** agrestic,
    pastoral, praedial (predial)
countryman ... **4.** rube **5.** yokel **6.** rustic
  7. hayseed, patriot, peasant
  10. compatriot, home towner
county ... **4.** seat **5.** shire **6.** domain,
  parish **8.** district
coup ... **3.** buy **4.** blow, move (games)
  5. scoop, upset **6.** barter, strike,
  stroke (master) **8.** overturn, strategy
  9. overthrow, trump card
coup de grâce ... **9.** deathblow
coup de main ... **6.** attack (sudden)
  8. strategy **9.** stratagem
coup d'état ... **6.** stroke (political)
  8. strategy **9.** overthrow
couple ... **3.** duo, tie, two **4.** bond, dyad,
  join, link, mate, pair, span, team, twin,
  yoke **5.** brace, marry, twain, unite
  6. Gemini **7.** bracket
coupled ... **5.** gemel, mated **6.** braced,
  joined, linked, paired, teamed, united
  7. leagued, married
couplet ... **3.** two **4.** pair **5.** brace, verse
  7. distich, doublet
coupon ... **5.** scrip, stock, token **6.** ticket
  11. certificate (Finan)
courage ... **4.** grit, sand, will **5.** heart,
  metal, moxie, nerve, pluck, spine,
  valor **7.** bravery, heroism, prowess
  8. audacity, backbone, boldness,
  firmness **9.** fortitude, gallantry,
  hardihood **11.** intrepidity
  12. fearlessness **13.** dauntlessness
courageous ... **4.** bold, game **5.** brave,
  hardy, manly, stout **6.** daring, heroic,
  spunky **7.** gallant, spartan, valiant
  8. fearless, intrepid, knightly, resolute,
  stalwart, valorous **11.** adventurous
  12. enterprising, stouthearted
courant ... **4.** romp **5.** caper **6.** letter
  7. gazette, running (Her) **9.** messenger,
  newspaper
courier ... **5.** guide **8.** dragoman,
  horseman **9.** attendant, messenger
course ... **3.** run **4.** flow, line, mode, path,

road, rote, tack **5.** route, study, trend
  6. career, manner, method, policy,
  series, stream **8.** progress **9.** direction,
  procedure **10.** succession
course (pert to) ...
  college .. **7.** seminar
  direct .. **7.** beeline
  golf .. **5.** links
  regular .. **4.** rote **6.** regime **7.** routine
  roundabout .. **6.** detour **11.** indirection
course of ...
  action .. **5.** habit **7.** routine **9.** procedure
  eating .. **4.** diet
  instruction .. **6.** lesson
  procedure .. **4.** rule
  thought .. **5.** tenor
courser ... **5.** horse, steed **6.** hunter,
  plover **7.** charger **8.** war horse
court ... **3.** see (papal), woo **4.** area, eyre,
  fawn (upon), rota **5.** atria, curia, dairi,
  gemot, patio, spark **6.** palace, parvis,
  street **7.** council, tribune **8.** tribunal
  10. attendance, curry favor, quadrangle
court (Eng) ... **3.** soc **4.** eyre, leet
  8. woodmate **10.** court-baron
court (pert to) ...
  assistant .. **5.** staff **6.** elisor
  crier, cry .. **4.** hear, oyez (oyes) **6.** beadle
  criminal .. **6.** assize
  exemption, excuse .. **6.** essoin
  game .. **6.** tennis **9.** badminton
  hearing .. **4.** oyer
  minutes .. **4.** acta
  order .. **4.** writ **5.** arret **6.** capias
    7. summons **8.** subpoena
  public .. **5.** forum **8.** forensic
  sitting .. **7.** session
courteous ... **5.** civil **6.** gentle, polite,
  urbane **7.** affable, gallant **8.** debonair,
  gracious **9.** attentive **10.** respectful
courtly ... **4.** hend (hende) **5.** aulic, civil
  7. elegant, gallant, stately **9.** dignified
  10. obsequious **11.** ceremonious
courtship ... **4.** suit **6.** plight, wooing
  7. romance **8.** courting
covenant ... **4.** bond, pact **6.** engage
  7. bargain, compact, entente, promise
  8. contract **9.** agreement, stipulate,
  testament **11.** undertaking
Covenant of God to Noah ... **7.** rainbow
Coventry equestrienne ... **6.** Godiva
cover ... **3.** cap, lap, lid **4.** coat, cozy,
  hide, mask, pale, pave, roof, span, veil
  5. blind, crust, drape, tapis **6.** canopy,
  mantle, purdah, screen, shield, thatch
  7. elytron, overlay, shelter **8.** chrismal,
  coverlet **9.** tarpaulin **10.** overspread
cover (pert to) ...
  alloy .. **5.** terne
  cork .. **9.** corticate
  crumbs .. **5.** bread
  dots .. **7.** stipple
  figures (Her) .. **4.** seme
  straw .. **6.** thatch
  turf .. **3.** sod
  up .. **4.** bury **5.** inter **7.** conceal
    8. submerge **10.** camouflage
  with wax .. **4.** cere
covering ... **3.** mat, rug **4.** caul, film,
  hull, tile **5.** apron, armor, shell, testa
  6. awning, carpet, cestus, lorica,

pelage, screen, shroud 7. epeiric, shelter, tegumen, wrapper 8. lineolum, pericarp 9. caparison 10. integument, protection 11. smoke screen

covering (head) . . . 3. cap, hat, wig 4. hood 5. beret, scarf, snood 6. bonnet, peruke, toupee 7. chapeau 10. fascinator

coverlet . . . 5. quilt 6. afghan, spread 7. blanket, lap robe 11. counterpane

covert . . . 3. den, lie 4. abri, lair 6. hidden, refuge, secret 7. covered, private, thicket 9. concealed, disguised, insidious, sheltered

covet . . . 4. envy 5. crave, yisse (obs) 6. aspire, desire, grudge, hanker 7. long for 8. begrudge

covetousness . . . 5. greed 7. avarice

covey . . . 4. bevy, pack 5. brood, flock, hatch 6. flight 7. company 9. multitude

cow . . . 3. awe 5. abash, daunt 7. overawe, terrify 8. browbeat, frighten 10. intimidate

cow (animal) . . . 3. Bos 4. calf, kine, moil 5. Angus, bossy, brock (obs), Kerry, vache 6. bovine, heifer 7. pollard 8. Ayrshire, maverick, moulleen

cow (pert to) . . .
barn . . 4. byre, shed 5. reeve, stall 6. stable 7. vaccary, vachery
food (chewed) . . 3. cud 5. rumen
hornless . . 6. mulley 7. pollard 8. moulleen
sea . . 6. dugong, walrus 7. manatee, Sirenia 12. hippopotamus
tether . . 4. rope 6. baikie
unbranded . . 8. maverick
young . . 4. calf 6. heifer

coward, cowardly . . . 3. shy 5. sneak 6. afraid, craven, scared, yellow 7. caitiff, chicken, dastard, milksop 8. poltroon, recreant, weakling 9. dastardly, fraidy-cat, jellyfish 12. uncourageous 13. pusillanimous

cowboy . . . 5. roper, waddy 6. herder 7. llamero, puncher, vaquero 8. jackaroo, neatherd 12. broncobuster (sl)

cowboy garb . . . 5. chaps 7. Stetson 8. jodhpurs

cower . . . 4. fawn 5. crawl, quail, stoop 6. cringe, crouch, grovel

cowfish . . . 3. ray 4. toto 7. dolphin, grampus, manatee 8. porpoise

cowled . . . 9. cucullate

coxcomb . . . 3. fop 4. dude, fool 5. cleat (Naut), dandy 8. popinjay

coy . . . 3. shy 4. arch 5. timid 6. demure, modest 7. bashful 10. coquettish 13. self-conscious

coyote . . . 4. wolf (prairie)

Coyote State . . . 11. South Dakota

coypu . . . 6. nutria, rodent

cozen . . . 5. cheat, trick 7. beguile, deceive, defraud

cozy . . . 4. easy, snug 6. chatty 8. cheerful, familiar, homelike, sociable 9. contented, talkative 11. comfortable

crab . . . 3. Uca 4. king, Maia (genus) 5. ayuyu (Guam) 6. nebula, partan, spider 7. fiddler, limulus, mollusk,

Ocypode 8. Lithodes 9. horseshoe 10. crustacean

crabbed . . . 5. cross 6. bitter, crusty, morose, trying 7. bilious, peevish 8. abstruse, liverish 9. difficult, fractious, irascible, irregular 10. perplexing

crab claw . . . 5. chela 6. metope, nipper

crab walk . . . 5. sidle

crachoir . . . 8. cuspidor, spittoon

crack . . . 4. blow, chap, clap, flaw, kibe, leak, quip, rift, rime, snap 5. brack, break, chink, craze, spang, split 6. breach, cleave, cranny 7. crackle, crevice, fissure, rupture 8. fracture

Cracker State . . . 7. Georgia

crackle . . . 4. snap 5. craze (art), crink 9. crepitate

crackman . . . 4. yegg 7. burglar

cradle . . . 4. slee (ship's) 7. infancy, nursery 8. bassinet, cunabula 10. beginnings, incunabula

cradle book . . . 11. incunabulum

Cradle of Liberty . . . 11. Faneuil Hall (Boston)

cradle song . . . 7. lullaby 8. berceuse 13. Schlummerlied

craft . . . 3. art 4. boat 5. skill, trade 6. device, tender 7. cunning, finesse, know-how, prowess 8. aptitude, vocation 9. dexterity 10. employment, handicraft, occupation, watercraft 12. skillfulness

craftsman . . . 6. artist, writer 7. artisan, workman 9. artificer

crafty . . . 3. sly 4. foxy, slim, wily, wise 6. artful, astute, shifty, shrewd, subtle, tricky 7. cunning 8. skillful (skilful) 9. deceitful, ingenious, underhand 10. fraudulent 13. Machiavellian 15. Mephistophelean

crag . . . 3. tor 4. spur 5. arête, cliff 7. nunatak 9. precipice

craggy . . . 5. rough 6. cliffy, clifty, jagged, knotty, rugged

cram . . . 4. fill 5. choke, crowd, drive, force, gorge, press, study, stuff 9. overstuff 10. gluttonize

cramp . . . 4. pain 5. stunt 6. hamper 7. confine, seizure 8. compress, restrict 9. hindrance, paralysis (muscle) 11. restriction

cranberry . . . 3. red 9. sourberry

cranberry center of trade . . . 10. Barnstable (Mass)

crane . . . 3. gib, jib 5. davit, jenny, titan 7. derrick, machine

crane . . . 4. Grus 5. heron, sarus 7. Gruidae 9. cormorant 10. Gruiformes 13. constellation

cranial nerve . . . 5. radix, vagus

cranium . . . 5. skull 8. cerebrum

crank . . . 3. wit 4. bear, crab 5. crook, winch 6. griper, grouch, handle 7. fanatic, growler, hothead 8. frondeur, grumbler, sorehead 9. eccentric 10. bellyacher, crosspatch, monomaniac

cranny . . . 4. hole, nook 5. chink, cleft, crack 6. corner, furrow 7. crevice, fissure 8. crevasse

crash . . . 4. bank, fail 5. smash 7. debacle, failure, intrude, shatter 8. accident

9. collision 10. bankruptcy

crate . . . 3. box 4. case 6. basket, cradle, encase, hamper 8. airplane 9. container 10. automobile

crater . . . 3. pit 6. cavity 7. caldera 13. constellation (The Cup)

cravat . . . 3. tie 4. teck 5. ascot, stock 7. bandage, bolo tie, necktie 9. neckcloth 10. four-in-hand

crave . . . 3. ask, beg 4. long, seek 5. covet, yearn 6. desire, hanker 7. beseech, entreat, implore, request, solicit 10. supplicate

craven . . . 6. afraid, coward 7. caitiff, dastard 8. cowardly, poltroon, recreant 12. fainthearted 13. pusillanimous

craving . . . 4. pica 6. desire, thirst 7. longing 8. appetite, yearning

craw . . . 3. maw 4. crop 6. gebbie 7. gizzard, stomach 9. ingluvies

crawfish . . . 5. yabby (yabbie) 7. back out, crawdad, lobster, retreat 8. crayfish

crawl . . . 4. fawn, inch, shug 5. creep 6. cringe, grovel, recant

crayon . . . 5. chalk 6. pastel, pencil 8. charcoal

craze . . . 3. fad 4. flaw, maze 5. crack (ceramics), crush, furor, mania, vogue 6. defect, whimsy 7. crackle, fashion 9. infirmity 11. infatuation

craze (for) . . . see also *madness, mania*
foreign customs . . 9. xenomania
freedom . . 14. eleutheromania
love (erotic) . . 10. erotomania
music . . 9. melomania
setting fires . . 9. pyromania
shopping . . 9. oniomania
single subject . . 9. monomania
stamps (postage) . . 11. timbromania
stealing . . 11. kleptomania
wandering . . 10. dromomania
wealth . . 10. plutomania

crazed . . . 4. amok 6. insane, marked (with crazes) 7. severed 8. deranged 10. distraught

crazy . . . 3. mad 4. amok, daft, loco 5. batty, loony, nutty, silly 6. dottle, insane 7. damaged, foolish, unsound 9. deficient

cream . . . 4. best, ream 5. elite 6. lotion 8. sillabub (with wine)

cream of tartar . . . 5. argol

crease . . . 4. fold, ruck 5. crimp, pleat 7. wrinkle 9. plication

create . . . 4. make 5. build, cause, clone, hatch 6. invent 7. fashion, produce 8. generate 9. originate

creation . . . 3. art 5. virtu, world 6. cosmos, making 7. classic, fantasy, forming, product 8. artifact, universe 9. objet d'art 10. providence 11. composition, fabrication, manufacture, masterpiece

creator . . . 5. maker 6. author 8. designer, inventor, producer 10. originator

Creator . . . 3. God 5. Maker 7. Jehovah 8. Almighty, Demiurge 11. King of Kings

creature (pert to) . . .
civetlike . . 3. cat
duplicate . . 5. clone
elflike . . 4. peri 6. hobbit
evil . . 7. helicat 8. hellicat
fire . . 10. salamander
folklore . . 3. elf 4. Yeti 5. dwarf, fairy, pixie 9. sasquatch
ghost . . 11. poltergeist
minute . . 10. animalcule
outer space . . 5. alien
sentient . . 6. animal
timid . . 4. deer 5. sheep
underground . . 5. gnome
water . . 5. sylph 6. undine
winged (Myth) . . 6. wivern 10. cockatrice

crèche figure . . . 4. Magi 6. Infant 8. shepherd

credence . . . 5. trust 6. belief, credit 8. affiance, reliance 10. acceptance, confidence, dependence 15. trustworthiness

credential . . . 7. voucher 11. certificate, testimonial 14. recommendation

credible . . . 6. likely 7. tenable 8. probable 9. plausible 10. believable 11. well-founded

credit . . . 5. faith, honor, trust 6. belief, esteem, impute 7. account, believe 8. accredit, credence 10. estimation, regulation 15. trustworthiness

creditor . . . 5. agent (collection) 6. debtee, dunner, usurer 7. Shylock (greedy)

creed . . . 5. credo, dogma, tenet 6. belief, Nicene 8. Apostles' 9. Catechism 10. Athanasian, confession

creek . . . 3. rio 4. burn, slue, wick 6. arroyo, estero, slough, spruit, stream

creel . . . 4. rack, trap 6. basket (fish)

creep . . . 5. crawl, prowl, skulk, slink, sneak, steal (away) 6. grovel 8. scramble 9. pussyfoot

creeping . . . 4. slow 7. reptant 8. crawling 10. slithering 11. reptatorial

Cremona, famed name . . . 5. Amati 8. Guarneri 10. Stradivari

crena . . . 4. gash, kerf, nick 5. cleft, notch 7. scallop 10. depression 11. indentation

creole . . . 6. French 7. mestizo 9. half-breed, janissary

Creole State . . . 9. Louisiana

crepitate . . . 4. snap 7. crackly

crescent . . . 4. cusp, horn, lune 5. curve 8. meniscus

crescent-shaped . . . 4. horn, lune 6. bicorn, lunate 7. lunular 8. lunulate 9. horseshoe, meniscate, semilunar

crest . . . 3. top 4. comb, peak, tuft 5. arête, crown, ridge 6. copple, crista, height, summit 7. panache, topknot, wave top 8. feathers, insignia, pinnacle 9. cockscomb 11. mountaintop

crested . . . 6. capped, topped, tufted 7. coppled, cristed, crowned, pileate

creta . . . 5. chalk

Crete . . .
capital . . 5. Canea
city . . 6. Candia, Khanis
civilization (anc) . . 6. Aegean, Minoan
king (anc) . . 5. Minos (Gr)
monster . . 8. Minotaur (man, bull)
mountain . . 3. Ida 9. Theodoros
priests . . 7. Curetes

cretin . . . 5. idiot 8. imbecile

crevice . . . **3.** gap **4.** rift **5.** chink,
  cleft **6.** cranny **7.** fissure, opening
  8. peephole **10.** interstice
crew . . . **3.** men **4.** band, body, gang, pack
  5. force, staff **7.** company **9.** employees,
  personnel
crib . . . **3.** bed, bin, den (gambling)
  5. cheat, stall, steal **6.** Cratch (stars),
  manger, pilfer **7.** brothel **8.** Praesepe
cricket . . . **4.** game, grig **6.** acheta,
  cicada, locust **7.** katydid **9.** footstool
  10. Orthoptera **11.** grasshopper
cricket (pert to) . . .
  game term . . **3.** bye, run **6.** yorker
  noise . . **5.** chirp **7.** stridor
  symbol (Myth) . . **4.** tice **5.** ashes
cried . . . **4.** wept **6.** bawled, called, wailed,
  yelled **7.** shouted, uttered **8.** lamented,
  screamed, shrieked **9.** exclaimed
  10. proclaimed
crime . . . **3.** sin **4.** evil **5.** guilt, wrong
  6. delict, felony, mayhem **7.** offense
  8. delictum, iniquity **9.** violation
  10. illegality, wickedness, wrongdoing
  11. malfeasance
crime (pert to) . . .
  benefice (Eccl) . . **6.** simony
  goddess (Myth) . . **3.** Ate
  of 1873 . . **12.** Silver Dollar
  scene . . **5.** venue
Crimea . . .
  city . . **5.** Kerch, Yalta **6.** Odessa
  10. Sevastopol
  isthmus site . . **8.** Black Sea
  Russian . . **4.** Krim
  sea (Russ) . . **4.** Azof
criminal . . . **4.** thug, yegg **5.** crook,
  felon, thief **6.** nocent **7.** convict,
  yeggman **8.** swindler **9.** desperado,
  dishonest, felonious **10.** malefactor,
  recivibist **11.** blameworthy, disgraceful
  13. reprehensible
criminal refuge . . . **7.** Alsatia
  11. Whitefriars (London)
criminology . . . **8.** penology
crimp . . . **4.** curl, fold **5.** frizz, notch, plait
  6. ruffle, thwart **7.** crinkle, wrinkle
  8. Shanghai
cringe . . . **4.** fawn **5.** cower, quail, sneak,
  wince **6.** flinch, grovel, shrink, submit
  7. truckle
crinkle . . . **4.** curl, kink, turn, wind **5.** twist
  6. rustle **7.** wrinkle
crinose . . . **5.** hairy **7.** hirsute
  11. barbigerous
cripple . . . **4.** halt, hock, lame, maim
  6. injure, weaken **7.** amputee, disable
  8. handicap **9.** hamstring
  12. incapacitate
crisis . . . **5.** cycle, peril **8.** exigency,
  juncture **9.** criterion, emergency
  11. climacteric
crisp . . . **4.** cold **5.** curly, flaky, sharp,
  short, spalt **7.** brittle, concise, crackle,
  crinkle, friable **8.** clear-cut **9.** frangible
criterion . . . **4.** norm, rule, test, type
  5. canon, model **7.** measure **8.** standard
  9. yardstick
critic . . . **5.** judge, Momus (Myth)
  6. censor, slater, Zoilus **8.** collator,
  reviewer **9.** literator **11.** connoisseur,

criticaster, faultfinder
critical . . . **4.** edgy **7.** carping, crucial,
  cynical, Zoilean **8.** captious, caviling,
  exacting **10.** censorious, particular
  12. faultfinding **13.** hairsplitting
  14. discriminating
Critical system of philosophy . . .
  10. Kantianism
criticism . . . **3.** rap **5.** cavil, roast **6.** report,
  review **7.** censure, Zoilism **8.** critique,
  judgment **9.** aspersion **10.** commentary
criticize, criticise . . . **3.** pan **4.** carp, flay
  5. cavil, judge, knock, slate **6.** review
  7. censure, comment **9.** castigate
  10. animadvert
Croatian capital . . . **6.** Zagreb
crock . . . **3.** ewe (old), jug, pot, urn
  4. smut, soil, soot **5.** horse (old)
  7. ceramic **8.** potsherd **11.** earthenware
crocodile . . . **3.** goa **5.** nakoo **6.** gavial,
  mugger **7.** reptile, sophism **9.** Niloticus
  10. Crocodilia, Crocodilus
crocus . . . **4.** bulb, herb, iris **6.** flower,
  yellow **7.** saffron
croft . . . **5.** crypt, field, vault **6.** carafe,
  cavern **7.** hillock
cromlech . . . **6.** dolmen **8.** monument
crone . . . **3.** ewe (old), hag **5.** witch
  6. beldam (beldame)
Cronus (pert to) . . .
  god of . . **8.** Harvests
  father . . **6.** Uranus
  son . . **4.** Zeus
  wife . . **4.** Rhea
crony . . . **3.** pal **4.** chum **5.** buddy **6.** friend
  9. companion **10.** playfellow
crook . . . **4.** bend, warp **5.** angle, curve,
  staff, thief **6.** akimbo **7.** crosier
  8. criminal, insignia **10.** camshachle
crooked . . . **3.** wry, zag **4.** agee, awry,
  bent **5.** agley, askew, false **6.** aslant,
  curved, hooked, zigzag **7.** angular,
  askance, asquint, oblique **8.** deformed
  9. dishonest, distorted **10.** circuitous,
  fraudulent **12.** dishonorable
crooked legs . . . **8.** rhebosis (rhaebosis)
  10. tortuosity
croon . . . **3.** hum **4.** boom, sing, wail
  5. whine **6.** bellow, lament, murmur
  8. complain
crop . . . **3.** lop, maw **4.** clip, craw,
  dick, reap, whip **5.** belly, shear,
  yield **6.** gebbie, growth, sheave
  7. harvest, produce, soilage, stomach
  11. cultivation
cross . . . **2.** go **3.** tau **4.** crux, ford,
  rood **5.** bless, corse, croix (Fr),
  irate, staff **6.** oppose, thwart, touchy
  7. athwart, fretful, oblique, peevish,
  pettish **8.** crucifix, insignia, monument,
  obstruct, petulant, snappish, swastika,
  traverse **9.** hybridize, intersect, irritable
  10. disappoint, transverse **11.** crucifixion
cross (pert to) . . .
  archaeology . . **4.** ankh
  astronomy . . **13.** Southern Cross
  barred . . **11.** trabeculate
  beam . . **5.** spale, trave **6.** girder
  bow . . **8.** arbalest
  breed . . **5.** Husky (dog) **6.** hybrid
  British . . **6.** Celtic

Egypt.. **10.** life symbol
eye.. **9.** esotropia **10.** strabismus
heraldry.. **6.** pattée **7.** erminee, patonce
Latin.. **12.** crux commissa
palm.. **5.** bribe (gypsy)
St Anthony's.. **3.** tau
stroke.. **5.** serif
tau-shaped.. **10.** crux ansata
crossing ... **6.** voyage **7.** chiasma,
fording, passage **8.** cheating, opposing
9. hybridism **10.** traversing
13. crossbreeding
crossing (famed) ...
Alps.. **8.** Hannibal, Napoleon
Hellespont.. **6.** Xerxes
Pyrenees.. **8.** Hannibal
Rubicon.. **6.** Caesar
crouch ... **4.** bend, fawn **5.** cower, squat,
stoop **6.** cringe, grovel, hunker
crow ... **3.** daw **4.** brag, rook **5.** aylet,
boast, crake, raven, vaunt **6.** chough,
Corvus, Indian (Sioux) **7.** corvine,
jackdaw **8.** laughter **13.** constellation
crowbar ... **5.** jimmy, lever **7.** gablock
crowberry ... **5.** shrub **8.** bilberry
9. cranberry
crowd ... **3.** jam, mob **4.** bike (Scot), cram,
host, pack, push, ruck, urge **5.** crush,
drive, drove, horde, press, serry,
swarm, three, wedge **6.** galaxy, hasten,
legion, masses, throng **7.** squeeze
8. compress **9.** multitude
10. assemblage
crowded ... **6.** packed **7.** compact,
crammed, serried, teeming
8. numerous, populous **9.** congested,
jampacked
crown ... **3.** cap, top **4.** atef, coin, pate,
peak, poll, tiar **5.** crest, miter (mitre),
tiara **6.** anadem, circle, corona, diadem,
fillet, reward, summit, trophy, wreath
7. chaplet, coronet, garland, glorify,
install **8.** coronate, enthrone, ornament,
pinnacle, surmount
crowning glory ... **8.** last word
crucial ... **5.** final **6.** severe, trying,
urgent **7.** crossed **8.** critical, decisive
9. cruciform **13.** demonstrative
crucible ... **3.** pot **4.** etna, test **6.** retort,
vessel **10.** conversion
crucifix ... **3.** pax **4.** rood **5.** cross
6. emblem
crucifixion ... **5.** death (on a cross)
7. torture **9.** execution, suffering
11. persecution
crude ... **3.** raw **4.** rude **5.** crass, green,
rough **6.** callow, coarse, common,
garish, savage, vulgar **8.** unseemly
9. inelegant, rough-hewn, tasteless,
uncourtly, unrefined **10.** outlandish,
unpolished **13.** inexperienced
crudity ... **7.** rawness **9.** crassness,
harshness, roughness, vulgarity
10. immaturity
cruel ... **4.** fell, hard **5.** harsh **6.** brutal,
savage, severe, unkind **7.** inhuman,
painful, unhuman **8.** dreadful, fiendish,
pitiless, ruthless, sadistic, tyrannic
9. ferocious, heartless, merciless,
murderous, truculent **11.** remorseless
cruelty ... **9.** brutality **10.** inclemency,

inhumanity **12.** ruthlessness
13. heartlessness **15.** remorselessness
cruelty, lover of ... **6.** sadist **9.** masochist
cruet ... **3.** ama **4.** vial **6.** bottle, caster
(castor), vessel **7.** ampulla, urceole
crulier ... **7.** olycook (olykoek)
8. doughnut **9.** friedcake
crumb ... **3.** bit **5.** break, piece **6.** little
8. fragment
crumble ... **5.** decay **6.** molder, powder
7. friable **9.** pulverize **12.** disintegrate
crumple ... **4.** ruck **6.** crease, raffle,
rumple **7.** wrinkle **9.** corrugate
cruor ... **4.** gore **5.** blood, ichor
crusade ... **5.** cause, drive, issue,
jihad (jehad) **7.** crusado **8.** campaign
10. expedition
Crusades ... **8.** Holy Land **9.** Children's
(1212)
crush ... **3.** jam **4.** bray, mash, sink
5. crash, crowd, grind, press, smash
6. bruise, crunch **7.** conquer, mortify,
oppress, shatter, squeeze **8.** compress,
suppress **9.** humiliate, pulverize
11. infatuation
crushed sugar cane ... **7.** bagasse
Crusoe's creator ... **5.** Defoe
crust ... **4.** rind **5.** shell **8.** dumpling,
exterior **9.** impudence **11.** lithosphere
14. aggressiveness
crustacean ... **4.** crab **5.** prawn **6.** huitre,
isopod, limpet, mussel, oyster, shrimp
7. limulus, lobster, scallop **8.** barnacle,
crawfish, starfish **9.** shellfish, trunkfish
10. coquillage, periwinkle
crustacean (pert to) ...
extinct.. **5.** Eryon
footless.. **4.** apod, apus
fossil.. **9.** trilobite
genus.. **5.** Hippa **6.** Triops **7.** Caridea
(Carida) **8.** Copepoda, Decapoda
10. Notostraca
larva.. **5.** alima
limb.. **6.** endite, podite
crutch ... **5.** brace, staff, stave **6.** crotch
7. support
cry ... **3.** baa, caw, cri, hue, mew, olé,
sob **4.** alas, barr, call, evoe, home,
hoot, mewl, pish, pule, wail, weep,
yell, yelp **5.** alack, avast, bleat, crook,
miaou, yoick **6.** bellow, boohoo, clamor,
outcry, scream, shriek, slogan, snivel,
squawk **7.** tantivy (hunting), trumpet,
weeping **8.** entreaty, jeremiad, lackaday,
proclaim **10.** shibboleth **11.** lamentation
cry (out) ... **5.** crake, decry, shout
6. accuse, clamor, object, scream,
suffer **7.** censure, exclaim **8.** complain,
denounce **10.** vociferate
crying ... **6.** puling, urgent **7.** clamant,
heinous, howling, sobbing, weeping
9. insistent, notorious
crying bird ... **6.** Aramus **7.** courlan,
limpkin **8.** raillike
crypt ... **4.** tomb **5.** vault **6.** cavity, recess
7. chamber
cryptic ... **4.** Rite (Freemasonry)
6. hidden, occult, secret **8.** puzzling
9. concealed, enigmatic **10.** mysterious
11. problematic **12.** hieroglyphic
cryptogram ... **4.** code **5.** agama

7. writing (secret) **8.** symbolic
crystal . . . **4.** dial **5.** clear, glass, lucid
6. argent (Her), quartz **7.** diamond
8. pellucid **9.** glassware, snowflake
11. crystalline, transparent
crystal (pert to) . . .
diamond . . **7.** glassie
gazer . . **4.** seer **7.** diviner **8.** presager
10. soothsayer **13.** fortuneteller
gazing . . **4.** scry
twin . . **5.** macle
crystalline . . . **4.** pure **8.** pellucid
11. transparent **12.** crystal-clear
crystalline (pert to) . . .
colorless . . **7.** orcinol
compound . . **5.** oscin **6.** anisil, dulcin
mineral . . **4.** spar **7.** apatite **8.** elaterin,
feldspar
rock . . **7.** diorite, greisen
salt . . **5.** borax **8.** analgene (analgen)
cub . . . **3.** bin, boy, fox, pen, pup **4.** bear,
coop, crib, lion, shed **5.** shark, stall,
tiger, whale, whelp **8.** boy scout,
cupboard **9.** youngling
Cuba . . .
capital . . **6.** Havana
castle . . **5.** Morro
city . . **8.** Santiago **10.** Bahia Honda,
Guantánamo
discoverer . . **8.** Columbus (1492)
island . . **11.** Isle of Pines (Isla de Pinos)
mountain . . **8.** Camaguey **9.** Las Villas
12. Pico Turquino
nickname . . **18.** Pearl of the Antilles
province . . **7.** Oriente
Cuban (pert to) . . .
asphalt . . **9.** chapapote
bird . . **6.** trogan **8.** tocororo
dance . . **5.** rumba
fish . . **4.** bobo
rodent . . **5.** hutia (jutia) **6.** pilori
rum . . **7.** Bacardi
cube . . . **3.** die **4.** dice **5.** solid **6.** triple
7. tessera (marble) **10.** third power
cubic (pert to) . . .
body . . **3.** die **4.** dice
decimeter . . **5.** litre
math . . **9.** isometric
measure . . **4.** cord
meter . . **5.** stere
shape . . **6.** cuboid **8.** cubiform
cubicle . . . **4.** cell, room, tomb
7. bedroom, chamber, roomlet
9. cubiculum
cuckoo . . . **5.** mimic **8.** imitator, songbird
cuckoo (pert to) . . .
ally . . **3.** ani
American . . **8.** Coccyzus
bees . . **9.** Nomadidae
bird (Orient) . . **4.** coel (koel)
cap . . **9.** monkshood
family . . **9.** Cuculidae
fool . . **7.** wryneck
pint . . **4.** arum **10.** cuckoo spit
cucullate (Bot) . . . **6.** cowled, hooded
cucumber . . . **4.** cuke, pepo **6.** pedata
(sea), pepino
cucurbit . . . **5.** flask, gourd **7.** matrass
cud . . . **4.** bite, quid **5.** rumen **8.** merycism
cuddle . . . **3.** hug, pet **6.** fondle, nestle
7. snuggle

cudgel . . . **3.** bat, hit **4.** beat, club, drub
5. baste, staff, stave, stick **6.** alpeen
7. belabor **8.** fustigate, shillalah
(shillelagh)
cue . . . **3.** nod, rod, tip **4.** ball, clue,
hint, role, tail **5.** braid, queue, twist
6. prompt **8.** billiard (term), function
9. catchword **10.** intimation
cuerpo . . . **4.** body, hulk **5.** naked, torso
10. dishabille (in)
cuff . . . **3.** hit **4.** band, blow, slap **5.** clout
6. strike **8.** chastise, gauntlet, handcuff
12. chastisement
cuirass . . . **4.** mail **5.** armor **6.** lorica
11. breastplate
cul-de-sac . . . **5.** alley (blind) **7.** impasse
14. pouch of Douglas
cull . . . **4.** pick **6.** assort, choose, gather,
select **8.** separate
culmination . . . **3.** end **4.** acme, apex,
auge, noon **6.** ascent, climax, result,
vertex, zenith **10.** perfection
12. consummation
culpability . . . **5.** blame, fault, guilt
11. criminality **15.** blameworthiness
culpable . . . **6.** faulty, guilty **7.** immoral
8. criminal **9.** accusable, imputable
10. censurable, indictable
11. blameworthy **12.** reproachable
13. reprehensible
cult . . . **4.** sect **9.** following
cultivate . . . **3.** ear (dial), hoe **4.** farm,
grow, plow, teel, till **5.** court, train
6. excite, foster, harrow, plough, refine
7. educate, improve **8.** approach, civilize
cultivated . . . **4.** grew, hoed **6.** seeded,
tilled, urbane **7.** genteel, refined
8. cultured, polished, well-bred
cultivation . . . **5.** tilth **7.** culture, farming,
tillage **9.** husbandry **10.** refinement
12. civilization
culver . . . **4.** dove **6.** pigeon **10.** wood
pigeon
cumbersome . . . **5.** bulky **6.** clumsy
8. cumbrous, unwieldy **10.** burdensome
cummer . . . **4.** lass **5.** witch **6.** friend (girl)
7. midwife **9.** companion, godmother
cummerbund . . . **4.** band, belt, sash
6. cestus, girdle
cumshaw . . . **3.** tip **5.** bonus **6.** thanks
7. present **8.** gratuity
cunning . . . **3.** sly **4.** cute, foxy, wile,
wily **5.** sharp, skill **6.** artful, clever,
crafty, dainty, shrewd, subtle, tricky
7. politic, shyness **8.** dextrous,
foxiness, skillful, stealthy, trickery
9. designing, dexterity, ingenious,
ingenuity, insidious **13.** Machiavellian
cunningly formed . . . **6.** daedal (dedal)
cup . . . **3.** ama, can, dop, mug, tyg
4. tass, teet, Toby **5.** calyx, chark,
cruse, cupel, cylix, grail, jorum, ladle,
stein **6.** beaker, goblet, noggin, trophy
7. chalice, tumbler
cupbearer . . . **4.** Hebe, saki **8.** Ganymede
cupboard . . . **3.** kas **5.** ambry (anc)
6. buffet, closet, larder, pantry
7. armoire, dresser **8.** aparador
9. sideboard
Cupid . . . **3.** boy, Dan **4.** amor, Eros, Kama,
love **5.** Freya **7.** Amorino, cupidon

Cupid (pert to) . . .
  mother . . **5.** Venus
  sweetheart . . **6.** Psyche
  title . . **3.** Dan
cupidity . . . **4.** lust **5.** greed **6.** desire
  7. avarice, avidity, longing **8.** appetite,
  avidness, rapacity
cuplike (pert to) . . .
  calyx . . **9.** calicular
  stone . . **5.** geode
  vessel . . **4.** zarf
cupola . . . **4.** dome, kiln **5.** tower **6.** concha
  (Arch) **7.** ceiling, furnace (foundry)
cur . . . **3.** dog **4.** mutt **7.** gurnard (fish),
  mongrel **9.** goldeneye
curare, curari . . . **5.** urali **7.** extract
  9. Strychnos **11.** arrow poison
curate . . . **4.** abbé **6.** cleric, parson, pastor,
  priest **7.** dominie **9.** clergyman
curator . . . **6.** keeper **7.** manager, steward
  8. guardian **9.** custodian, librarian,
  treasurer
curb . . . **3.** bit **4.** rein **5.** check, limit
  6. arrest, border, bridle, market (Finan)
  7. control, inhibit, repress **8.** restrict
  9. hindrance, restraint
curd . . . **4.** crud **6.** casein
curds and whey . . . **7.** clabber
cure . . . **4.** balm, heal, salt **5.** smoke
  6. elixir, remedy, rizzor **7.** nostrum,
  panacea, restore, therapy **8.** preserve
  10. corrective
curio . . . **8.** artifact **9.** bric-a-brac, curiosity
curiosity . . . **5.** curio **6.** gabion (rare),
  oddity, prying, wonder **8.** interest
  9. exception, spectacle
  14. meddlesomeness **15.** inquisitiveness
curious . . . **3.** odd **4.** rare **5.** nosey (nosy),
  outre, queer **6.** prying, quaint **7.** careful,
  strange, unusual **8.** cautious, meddling,
  singular **9.** inquiring, intrusive
  10. meticulous **11.** inquisitive
curl . . . **4.** coil, kink, lock, roll **5.** crimp,
  crisp, frizz, tress, twirl, twist **6.** marcel,
  spiral **7.** crinkle, frizzle, ringlet
  8. curlicue **9.** corkscrew **11.** convolution
curled . . . **5.** curly, spiry **6.** coiled
  7. crimped, savoyed, twisted **8.** wrinkled
  (Bot)
curlew . . . **4.** bird, fute **5.** kioea, snipe,
  whaup **6.** marlin **7.** bustard **8.** whimbrel
curlewlike . . . **6.** godwit **9.** sandpiper
curly . . . **4.** wavy **5.** kinky, oundy (obs)
  6. crispy, frizzy, kinked **8.** crinkled
curmudgeon . . . **4.** crab **5.** churl, miser
  7. niggard **8.** tightwad **9.** skinflint
currant . . . **3.** red **5.** berry, Ribes **6.** raisin,
  rizzar (rizzart)
currency . . . **5.** money, scrip **6.** dinero
  9. publicity **10.** greenbacks, popularity,
  prevalence **15.** fashionableness
current . . . **4.** eddy, flow, race (water),
  rife, tide **5.** draft, going, rapid, trend,
  usual **6.** course, stream **7.** present,
  topical **8.** existent **9.** direction, prevalent
  11. fashionable
current regulator . . .
  electric . . **9.** rheometer **12.** galvanometer
  physiology . . **11.** hematometer
curriculum . . . **7.** courses, studies, Three
  R's **8.** curricle

curry . . . **4.** comb, cook, drub **5.** dress,
  groom **6.** cajole **9.** condiment
curry favor . . . **6.** cajole **7.** flatter,
  smoodge (smooge), wheedle
curse . . . **3.** ban **4.** bane, damn, oath
  5. swear **7.** bewitch, malison
  8. anathema, execrate **9.** blaspheme
  10. affliction **11.** imprecation,
  malediction **13.** excommunicate
cursed . . . **6.** damned, odious, wicked
  7. hateful **8.** damnable, shrewish
  9. execrable **12.** cantankerous
Cursores . . . **5.** birds (long-legged)
  7. spiders (wolf)
Cursoria . . . **6.** mantes (mantis)
  10. Orthoptera **11.** cockroaches
cursory . . . **5.** hasty **6.** fitful, roving,
  slight **7.** passing **8.** careless, rambling
  9. desultory, irregular **10.** evanescent
  12. disconnected, unmethodical
curt . . . **4.** buff **5.** bluff, brief, brusk,
  gruff, short, terse **6.** abrupt **7.** brusque,
  concise, curtate, laconic **9.** condensed
curtail . . . **3.** lop **4.** crop, dock, pare,
  slip **5.** short **6.** lessen, reduce
  7. abridge, shorten **8.** compress,
  decrease, diminish, retrench
curtain . . . **4.** mask, veil **5.** drape, shade
  6. coster (altar), encore, purdah, riddel,
  screen, shadow, shield **7.** drapery,
  secrecy, shelter, vitrage **8.** portiere
curtsy, curtsey . . . **3.** bow, nod **4.** bend
  6. kowtow, salaam **12.** genuflection
curvature . . . **3.** arc, bow **4.** arch,
  bend **5.** plane, sinus **6.** camber
  7. arching, curving, evolute **8.** aduncity,
  cyrtosis, lordosis, vaulting **9.** curvation
  11. convolution
curve . . . **3.** arc, bow, ess **4.** arch,
  bend, ogee, turn **5.** crook, polar
  6. spiral, toroid **7.** cissoid, evolute,
  flexure **8.** extrados, parabola, sinusoid
  9. curvature, sinuosity
curved (pert to) . . .
  arch . . **8.** arciform, arcuated
  glass . . **4.** lens
  inward . . **5.** adunc **8.** aduncous
  molding . . **4.** ogee
  planking (ship's) . . **3.** sny
  process . . **5.** hamus (Zool)
  roundabout . . **10.** circuitous
  staircase . . **8.** caracole
  wedge . . **3.** cam
curvet . . . **4.** leap **5.** bound, caper, frisk,
  prank **6.** frolic, gambol
cush . . . **3.** cow **5.** money **7.** cookery,
  sorghum
Cush (pert to) . . .
  father . . **3.** Ham
  land of . . **8.** Ethiopia **10.** land of Cush
  son . . **4.** Seba **6.** Nimrod
cushion . . . **3.** pad **4.** mute, seat **6.** ignore,
  pillow, sachet **7.** brioche, conceal,
  dashpot, muffler **8.** plantula, pulvinus,
  suppress, swelling (Queen Mary's)
  9. pulvillus **10.** pincushion
cusk . . . **4.** fish (codlike), tusk **5.** torsk
  6. burbot
cusp . . . **3.** end, tip **4.** apex, peak **5.** crown,
  point **6.** cantle, corner **8.** paracone
custard . . . **4.** flan **7.** charlet, pudding

custard apple . . . **4.** tree **5.** papaw **8.** sweetsop
custodian . . . **5.** guard **6.** bailee, jailer, keeper, warden, warder **7.** curator, janitor **8.** curatrix, guardian
custody . . . **4.** care, keep **5.** trust **6.** charge **8.** guidance **10.** protection **12.** guardianship, jurisdiction
custom . . . **3.** fad, law, mos, use **4.** mode, wont **5.** habit, mores, usage, vogue **7.** fashion **8.** practice **9.** patronage, tradition **10.** consuetude, consuetudo
customary . . . **5.** usual **6.** wonted **7.** general, usitate **8.** habitual, orthodox **11.** traditional **12.** conventional
customs . . . **4.** duty **5.** mores, taxes
cut . . . **3.** bob, lob, lop, mow, nip, rip **4.** blow, chop, crop, dock, edit, fell, gash, hack, make, mode, nick, open, pain, pare, reap, slit, snee, snip, snub, trim **5.** canal, carve, cleft, lance, notch, piece, plate, scarp, sever, share, shear, shorn, slash, slice, slish (Shaksp), snick, split, vogue **6.** dilute, furrow, injury, mangle, reduce, trench **7.** affront, curtail, engrave, offense, sectile, serrate, truancy, whittle **8.** discount, excision, incision **9.** engraving, indignity, reduction **10.** adulterate
cut (pert to) . . .
and furrow . . **7.** chamfer
and polish . . **8.** lapidate
and weave . . **5.** plash
back . . **6.** polled **7.** shorten
capable of being . . **7.** sectile
down . . **5.** razee
fine . . **5.** mince
in . . **7.** intrude **9.** interpose, interrupt, introduce
in half . . **9.** dimidiate
in squares . . **4.** dice
into . . **6.** incise
jaggedly . . **4.** snag
out . . **6.** excide, excise
up . . **6.** frolic, grieve **9.** apportion, misbehave
vertically . . **5.** scarp, slice
with shears . . **4.** snip **5.** shirl
cutaneous . . . **4.** skin **6.** dermal, dermic
cute . . . **4.** keen **5.** peart, sharp **6.** brainy, clever, dainty, pretty, shrewd **7.** cunning **10.** attractive **11.** picturesque
cuticle . . . **4.** skin **5.** cutin, cutis **8.** membrane, pellicle **9.** epidermis, scarfskin **10.** integument
cut of beef . . . **4.** loin, ribs, rump **5.** chine, roast, steak **6.** corned, cutlet, rosbif, saddle **7.** brisket, icebone **8.** shoulder **9.** aitchbone, roundbone
cut off . . . **3.** bob **4.** crop, dock, drib, snip **5.** elide, pared, roach (Naut) **6.** bereft, bobbed, divest, lopped, screen **7.** abscind, abscise, clipped, deprive, severed **8.** amputate **9.** amputated, apocopate, intercept **10.** disinherit
cut off (pert to) . . .
by bits . . **4.** drib
edges (coins) . . **3.** nig
on slant . . **4.** bias **5.** bevel, miter
short . . **3.** bob **4.** crop

syllable . . **5.** elide
with die . . **4.** dink
wool . . **3.** dod (dodd)
cut short . . . **3.** bob, lop **4.** crop, dock, halt, stop **5.** check **6.** arrest **7.** clipped, cropped, curtail, shorten **9.** terminate
cutter . . . **4.** boat **5.** knife, sloop, tooth **6.** sleigh, vessel **7.** incisor
cutting . . . **4.** cold, slip, tart **5.** piece, scion, sharp **6.** biting, secant, severe **7.** caustic, incisal, satiric, sectile **8.** chilling, piercing **9.** sarcastic, severance, trenchant **10.** separating **11.** penetrating **12.** adulteration
cutting (pert to) . . .
diamonds (imperfect) . . **4.** bort
edge . . **5.** blade
in two . . **6.** secant
last letter of word . . **7.** apocope
off . . **7.** apocope **10.** abscission, amputation
tool . . **3.** axe (ax), bit **4.** adze **5.** razor **6.** chisel
wit . . **6.** satire
cuttle . . . **4.** thug **5.** knife **7.** ruffian **8.** assassin **9.** swaggerer
cuttlebone . . . **7.** osselet
cuttlefish . . . **5.** Sepia, squid **7.** mollusk, octopus
cuttlefish secretion . . . **3.** ink (black)
cuttyhunk . . . **11.** fishing line
Cuzco native . . . **4.** Inca
Cyclades Islands (Gr) . . . (200 in all) **3.** Ios **5.** Delos (smallest), Melos, Naros, Paros, Tenos, Thera **6.** Andros **7.** Amorgos, Myconus
cycle . . . **3.** Age, eon, era **4.** aeon **5.** orbit, recur, saros (Astron), wheel **6.** course, period, series **7.** bicycle, circuit **8.** electric, tricycle **9.** Arthurian **10.** revolution **12.** Carlovingian (Charlemagne)
cyclone . . . **5.** storm **6.** baguio **7.** tornado, twister, typhoon **9.** hurricane
cyclopean . . . **4.** huge, vast **7.** massive, one-eyed **8.** gigantic
Cyclops (pert to) . . .
assistant to . . **6.** Vulcan (Fire God)
father . . **6.** Uranus
forger of . . **12.** thunderbolts
home . . **6.** Sicily (Mt Etna)
oddity . . **7.** one-eyed
race (Myth) . . **6.** giants
cygneous . . . **8.** swanlike
cygnet . . . **4.** swan
cylinder . . . **4.** drum, pipe, roll, tube **5.** inker, stele **6.** barrel, gabion, platen, record, roller, rounce, terete **10.** cylindroid
cylindrical . . . **5.** conic **6.** terete **7.** tubular
cymbal, cymbals . . . **3.** tal, zel **6.** Becken, piatti **7.** potlids **8.** doughnut
Cymric . . . **5.** Welsh **9.** Brythonic
Cymric (pert to) . . .
bard . . **6.** Merlin **7.** Aneurin
god of the dead . . **5.** Pwyll
god of the sky . . **7.** Gwydion
god of the sun . . **4.** Lleu
god of the waves . . **5.** Dylan
cynic . . . **5.** Timon **7.** ascetic, doglike, egotist, snarler **9.** pessimist

11. misanthrope
Cynic (pert to) . . .
pupil . . **8.** Socrates
school . . **10.** Philosophy
teacher . . **8.** Diogenes
teaching . . **6.** virtue
cynical . . . **7.** currish **8.** captious,
snarling **9.** sarcastic **11.** pessimistic
12. misanthropic
cynosure . . . **5.** guide **8.** lodestar
(loadstar), polestar **9.** celebrity, North
Star **13.** constellation
cyprinoid (fish) . . . **2.** id **3.** ide, orf
(orfe) **4.** bass (black), carp, chub,
dace **6.** chevin, shiner **7.** herring
(lake) **8.** fallfish **9.** hornyhead,
squawfish
Cyprus . . .
capital . . **7.** Nicosia (Sicily)
colonizer (anc) . . **11.** Phoenicians
history . . **11.** New Stone Age
mountain . . **7.** Troodos
port . . **7.** Lorcana **8.** Limassol
9. Famagusto
Cyrenaic (pert to) . . .
city . . **6.** Cyrene
country . . **9.** Cyrenaica (Afr)
division of . . **5.** Libya

harbor . . **6.** Tobruk **7.** Bengazi
philosophy . . **8.** hedonism, pleasure
Cyrene . . . **4.** city (anc) **5.** nymph
7. goddess
cyrus . . . **5.** crane, sarus
Cyrus the Elder (pert to) . . .
conqueror of . . **7.** Babylon
founder of . . **6.** Persia (Empire)
king of . . **5.** Lydia, Media
subduer of . . **9.** Palestine
cyst . . . **3.** box, sac, wen **5.** chest, pouch
7. vesicle
Czar . . . **4.** Ivan, tsar, tzar **5.** Peter
8. Nicholas
Czechoslovakia . . .
capital . . **6.** Prague (Praha)
city . . **6.** Pilsen **7.** Ostrava **10.** Bratislava
divided (1993) . . **8.** Slovakia **13.** Czech
Republic
empire (anc) . . **7.** Bohemia, Moravia
8. Slovakia
forest . . **12.** Great Bohemia
mountain, peak . . **3.** Ore **6.** Tatras
11. Carpathians
people . . **6.** Czechs **7.** Slovaks
river . . **4.** Elbe (Labe), Iser, Oder **6.** Vltava
statesman . . **7.** Masaryk
czigany . . . **5.** gypsy

D

D . . . **3.** 500 **6.** letter (4th)
dab . . . **3.** hit, tap **4.** blow **5.** paint, smear
6. expert, lizard, smooth **7.** dabster
8. flatfish
dabble . . . **4.** mass **5.** dally **6.** befoul,
meddle, paddle, potter, splash, tamper,
trifle **7.** spatter **8.** sprinkle
dabbler . . . **7.** trifler **8.** sciolist
10. dilettante
dabchick . . . **5.** grebe **9.** gallinule
dab hand . . . **6.** expert
dacha (Russ) . . . **5.** villa **12.** country house
dacoit . . . **6.** bandit, robber
dacry, dacryo (comb form) . . . **5.** tears
dactyl . . . **3.** toe **4.** foot **6.** finger
8. dactylus
dactyliomancy . . . **17.** divination by rings
(finger)
dactylogram . . . **11.** fingerprint
dactylology . . . **12.** sign language
Dadaism . . . **4.** cult **8.** negation
daddy longlegs . . . **5.** stilt **6.** curlew,
spider, Tipula **7.** spinner **10.** harvestman
daedal, dedal . . . **4.** rich **6.** varied
8. artistic, skillful (skilful) **9.** ingenious,
intricate **10.** variegated
Daedalus (Gr Myth) . . . **9.** artificer
daemon (Gr Myth) . . . **6.** spirit **8.** guardian
daffodil . . . **6.** yellow **9.** narcissus
10. bellflower
daffy, daft . . . **3.** gay, mad **4.** wild **5.** batty,
crazy, giddy, goofy, loony **6.** insane
7. foolish, idiotic
Dagda (pert to) . . .
children . . **6.** Aengus (Angus), Brigit

famed as . . **7.** harpist
Gaelic name . . **7.** Jupiter
god of . . **10.** pagan Irish
dagger . . . **4.** dirk, kris, snee **5.** kalar
6. anlace, bodkin, creese **7.** bayonet,
poniard **10.** misericord
Dahomey . . . **5.** Benin
Daibutsu (pert to) . . .
famed image . . **6.** Buddha
Japanese Bronze . . **11.** Great Buddha
site . . **8.** Kamakura (near Tokyo)
daikon . . . **6.** radish
daily . . . **4.** a day **7.** diurnal, journal
9. hodiurnal, newspaper, quotidian
11. day in day out
daily food . . . **4.** fare **5.** bread
10. livelihood **11.** subsistence,
substenance
dainties . . . **5.** cates, estes **7.** titbits
(tidbits)
dainty . . . **4.** fair, fine, rare **5.** frail, small
6. choice, pretty, select **8.** elegance
9. exquisite, toothsome **10.** fastidious
dairy . . . **4.** farm **8.** creamery **9.** lactarium
dairymen caste (Ind) . . . **4.** Ahir
dais . . . **5.** stage, table **6.** podium
7. estrade **8.** platform
daisy . . . **5.** gowan, oxeye **6.** morgan,
Shasta **7.** Gerbera **9.** Whiteweed
dale . . . **4.** dell, dene, vale **5.** spout
6. dingle, ravine, trough, valley
dalles . . . **5.** dells **11.** canyon walls
dalliance . . . **4.** chat **5.** delay **6.** gossip,
trifle **8.** fondling, trifling **10.** flirtation
dally . . . **3.** toy **5.** tarry **6.** dawdle, linger

13. procrastinate
Dalmatia . . .
  capital . . **7.** Spalato (Yugoslavia)
  cherry . . **7.** marasca
  coast . . **8.** Adriatic
  dog . . **5.** coach **8.** carriage
  home of . . **10.** Diocletian
  people . . **5.** Serbs **8.** Adriatic **9.** Yugoslavs
  product . . **4.** lace
dam . . . **4.** stay, stem, stop, weir **5.** Aswan,
  block, check, choke, Gatun (CZ)
  6. Hoover (Boulder), mother, Norris,
  parent **7.** barrier **8.** millpond, obstruct,
  Oroville, restrain **9.** Roosevelt **10.** Bull
  Shoals, Glen Canyon **11.** Grand Coulee
damage . . . **3.** mar **4.** harm, hurt, loss,
  maim, noxa **6.** impair, injury, mayhem,
  scathe, strafe **8.** disserve, sabotage
  9. detriment, vandalism **10.** impairment
daman . . . **4.** cony (Bib) **5.** Hyrax
  6. mammal **8.** Procavia
Damascus, Syria (pert to) . . .
  Bib scene . . **20.** Street Called Straight
  division . . **6.** Jewish, Moslem **9.** Christian
  history . . **16.** world's oldest city
    (inhabited)
  mosque (renowned) . . **7.** Ommiade
  river . . **5.** Abana **6.** Barada
damask . . . **3.** red (color) **5.** cloth, steel
  (Damascus) **8.** to deface (the Great
  Seal, Eng)
dame . . . **4.** lady, Miss **5.** Madam, title
  6. matron, Nature, parent
damn . . . **4.** cuss, ruin **5.** abuse, curse
  6. revile, shucks **7.** accurse, condemn,
  swear at
damp . . . **3.** wet **5.** moist
dampen . . . **3.** wet **6.** dismay **7.** depress,
  moisten
damsel . . . **4.** girl, lass **5.** Rhoda (Bib),
  wench **7.** colleen **10.** damoiselle
dance . . . **4.** jazz, prom, skip, trip **5.** frisk,
  glide **6.** cavort, frolic, gambol **7.** flicker,
  flutter, rejoice, saltate **10.** tripudiate
dance (pert to) . . .
  art . . **12.** choreography
  clumsily . . **6.** balter
  mimetic (Rom) . . **5.** Salii **7.** Luperci
  8. Curetics
  movement . . **6.** chassé, gestic **7.** saltant
  9. pirouette
  step . . **3.** pas **5.** coupe **6.** chassé
  7. gambado (gambade), shuffle
  8. glissade **9.** arabesque, grapevine
  10. pigeonwing
dance (type) . . . **3.** bal, hop, jig, tap,
  toe **4.** ball, clog, haka, kolo, polo,
  reel, shag **5.** gavot (gavotte), gigue,
  pavan, polka, tango, twist, waltz
  6. althea, apache, ballet, bolero,
  cancan, cha-cha, corant, maxixe,
  minuet, morris, redowa, rhumba
  (rumba), shimmy, square, watusi
  7. beguine, coranto (old), courant,
  foxtrot, gavotte, hoedown, mazurka,
  one-step, ridotto, tempete, two-step
  8. bunny hug, cakewalk, courante,
  fandango, flamenco, halliard (anc),
  hornpipe, lanciers, rigadoon, saraband
  9. allemande (anc), butterfly, farandole,
  polonaise, quadrille **10.** Charleston,

tarantella **11.** schottische (schottish)
dancer . . . **6.** hoofer **7.** danseur
  8. coryphee, danseuse, stripper
  9. ballerina, ecdysiast, jitterbug
  11. terpsichore **13.** choreographer
dancer (pert to) . . .
  Bib . . **6.** Salome
  Egyptian . . **4.** alme (almeh) **7.** ghawazi
  8. Baramika
  Japanese . . **6.** geisha (girl)
  Oriental . . **4.** hula **6.** nautch **8.** bayadere
dancing (pert to) . . .
  arrangement . . **12.** choreography
  Muse of . . **11.** Terpsichore
  term . . **6.** ballet, chassé, gestic **7.** hoofing,
  saltant
dandelion . . . **4.** herb **5.** plant **6.** yellow
  9. Taraxacum
dander . . . **3.** ire **5.** anger **6.** temper
dandified . . . **7.** foppish
dandify . . . **6.** spruce **7.** adonize, smarten
  8. titivate (tittivate)
dandy . . . **3.** fop **4.** beau, dude, good,
  toff **5.** daisy **6.** Adonis **7.** coxcomb
  9. exquisite **11.** Beau Brummel
dangerous . . . **3.** bad **4.** dire **5.** feral,
  risky **6.** chancy **7.** ominous, parlous
  8. alarming, critical, insecure, menacing,
  perilous **9.** hazardous **10.** jeopardous,
  precarious
dangle . . . **3.** lop **4.** hang, loll, yawl
  5. droop, swing **6.** flaunt, mizzen
Daniel (pert to) . . .
  Bib . . **4.** Book (Old Test) **7.** prophet
  (Heb)
  form of verse . . **7.** lyrical, sestina
  verse adopted by . . **5.** Dante **8.** Petrarch
Danish . . . see also *Denmark*
  capital . . **10.** Copenhagen
  council (anc) . . **8.** Rigsraad
  country . . **7.** Denmark
  doctor . . **6.** Finsen
  export . . **8.** cryolite
  fiord . . **3.** Ise
  flag . . **9.** Dannebrog
  island . . **3.** Als (Alsen) **5.** Faroe
  9. Greenland
  King (anc) . . **6.** Canute
  native . . **4.** Dane **12.** Scandinavian
  parliament . . **7.** Rigsdag
  prince (legend) . . **6.** Hamlet
  settlers in Ireland . . **6.** Ostmen
  storyteller . . **8.** Andersen (Hans Christian)
dank . . . **3.** wet **4.** damp **5.** humid, moist,
  muggy
Dan McGrew . . . **11.** Hound of Hell
danseuse . . . **7.** danseur **8.** coryphee
  9. ballerina
Dante (pert to) . . .
  birthplace . . **8.** Florence
  famed as . . **4.** poet **6.** lyrist
  famed poem . . **12.** Divine Comedy
  poem's companion . . **6.** Vergil (Virgil)
  poem's division . . **4.** Hell **6.** Heaven
  9. Purgatory
  poem's love . . **8.** Beatrice
Danube River (pert to) . . .
  end . . **8.** Black Sea
  source . . **11.** Black Forest
  tributary . . **4.** Isar, Raab **5.** Drava
  6. Morava

D

Danubian (pert to) . . .
  color . . **5.** green
  fish . . **6.** huchen (huch)
  goose . . **10.** Sevastopol
Danzig . . .
  Polish name . . **6.** Gdansk
  river site . . **7.** Vistula
  Sea . . **6.** Baltic
  territory of (now) . . **6.** Poland
dap . . . **3.** bob, dab, dib, dip **6.** bounce,
  dibble, guddle **7.** rebound
Daphne (pert to) . . .
  Bib . . **4.** Park (Antioch, Syria)
  father . . **5.** Ladon **6.** Peneus
  lover . . **6.** Apollo
  transformation . . **10.** laurel tree
dapper . . . **4.** braw, neat, pert, trim
  5. natty, sleek **6.** jaunty, little, lively,
  spruce **7.** dashing, finical
dappled . . . **6.** dotted **7.** flecked, piebald,
  spotted
dare . . . **4.** daze, defy, face, osse,
  risk **5.** brave **6.** assume, dazzle
  7. venture **8.** confront, defiance,
  paralyze **9.** challenge, undertake
daring . . . **4.** bold, rash **5.** brave, manly
  8. boldness, defiance **9.** audacious,
  foolhardy **11.** adventurous,
  venturesome **12.** enterprising
dark . . . **3.** dim, mum, sad **4.** ebon
  5. black, blind, dense, faint, mirky,
  murky, night, unlit, vague **6.** closed,
  gloomy, occult, opaque, secret, wicked
  7. joyless, melanic, obscure, stygian
  8. abstruse, darkling (poet), ignorant,
  moonless **9.** ambiguous, atrocious,
  Cimmerian (realm), lightless, nightfall,
  tenebrous, uncertain **10.** foreboding,
  indistinct
dark (pert to) . . .
  Ages . . **6.** Middle **8.** Medieval **9.** Neolithic
  Continent . . **6.** Africa (formerly)
  10. unexplored
  horse . . **7.** unknown **9.** candidate
  hue . . **5.** dusky, swart **6.** somber
  7. swarthy
  moon area . . **4.** mare
darken . . . **3.** dim **4.** dull **5.** blind, umber
  6. darkle, sadden, shadow **7.** becloud,
  blacken, confuse, eclipse, enshade
  8. bewilder **9.** obfuscate
darkness . . . **4.** dark, dusk, mirk, murk
  5. shade **6.** Erebus, shadow **7.** dimness,
  tenebra **9.** blackness, blindness,
  ignorance, obscurity **10.** opaqueness
darling . . . **2.** jo **3.** pet **4.** dear, idol, lief
  5. cheri, sweet **6.** minion **7.** acushla,
  beloved **8.** favorite **9.** mavournin
  10. mavourneen, sweetheart
  13. cushlamochree (cushlamachree)
darnel . . . **4.** tare, weed **5.** grass **6.** Lolium
dart . . . **4.** barb, bolt, flit, leap, vire
  5. arrow, bound, lance, scoot, shoot,
  start, throw **6.** dartle, elance, glance,
  spring, weapon **7.** javelin, missile,
  stinger **8.** jaculate
Darwinism . . . **9.** Evolution (theory, 1858)
  12. Evolutionism
das, dasse . . . **6.** badger
dash . . . **4.** code, élan, gift, race, ruin,
  rush, slam **5.** ardor, crash, haste, onset,

plash, smash, speed, swash **6.** energy,
obelus (anc), spirit, sprint, strike, stroke
7. bravura, spatter, splurge **8.** confound,
gratuity **9.** animation **11.** punctuation
dashing . . . **3.** gay **4.** fast **5.** showy
  6. dapper, jaunty, sporty **7.** stylish
dastardly . . . **4.** base, foul **6.** craven
  8. cowardly
data . . . **5.** facts, logic **7.** grounds (for
  facts) **11.** information
date . . . **3.** age **4.** line (newspaper), time
  5. fruit, tryst **6.** person **10.** engagement
  11. appointment
date (pert to) . . .
  birth . . **5.** natal
  coin line . . **7.** exergue
  error . . **11.** anachronism
  fruit of . . **4.** palm
  plum . . **6.** sapote
dated . . . **8.** outmoded **10.** antiquated
  12. old-fashioned
daub . . . **3.** dab **4.** blob, gaum, soil, teer
  5. paint, smear, stain, sully **6.** bedaub
  7. besmear, picture (art), plaster
  8. scribble
daughter . . . **5.** child **7.** cadette **9.** offspring
  10. descendant
daughter of . . .
  Inachus (river god) . . **2.** Io
  Night . . **7.** Nemesis
  the moon . . **7.** Nokomis
  the Spanish king . . **7.** infanta
daunt . . . **3.** awe, cow **4.** faze **5.** amate
  (anc) **6.** dismay, subdue **7.** overawe,
  repress **10.** discourage, dishearten,
  intimidate
dauntless . . . **4.** bold **7.** aweless (awless)
  8. fearless, intrepid, resolute
  9. dreadless **11.** unfaltering
davenport . . . **3.** bed **4.** desk, sofa **5.** divan
  12. Chesterfield
David (Bib) . . .
  daughter . . **5.** Tamar
  father . . **5.** Jesse
  helpers . . **4.** Igal **5.** Abner **7.** Shammah
  king of . . **6.** Israel (40 years)
  slayer of . . **7.** Goliath
  son . . **7.** Solomon
  wife . . **7.** Abigail
davit . . . **4.** spar **5.** crane
dawdle . . . **3.** lag **4.** idle, poke, toit **5.** dally
  6. linger, loiter, potter, trifle **9.** vacillate
  10. dillydally **13.** procrastinate
dawn . . . **2.** eo (comb form) **3.** Eos
  (goddess), red **4.** morn **5.** sunup
  6. appear, aurora, sink in **7.** sunrise
  8. daybreak **9.** beginning, penetrate
day (pert to) . . .
  Athenians, Jews . . **6.** sunset
  Babylonians . . **7.** sunrise
  blindness . . **10.** nyctalopia
  11. hemeralopia
  divisions . . **5.** lunar, solar **8.** sidereal
  dream . . **4.** muse **5.** fancy **7.** fantasy,
  reverie **8.** phantasy
  Egyptians, Romans . . **8.** midnight
  god . . **5.** Horus
  nursery . . **6.** crèche
  scholar . . **7.** externe
Day of . . .
  Atonement . . **9.** Yom Kippur

Brahma . . **9.** Maha Yugas
doom . . **8.** Judgment
day's march . . . **5.** étape
day's work . . . **4.** darg (dargue)
daze . . . **3.** fog **4.** asea, maze, stun
5. sopor, swoon **6.** benumb, dazzle,
stupid, trance **7.** confuse, stupefy
8. bewilder **9.** dumbfound **12.** razzle-
dazzle
dazzling . . . **6.** bright, garish **7.** glaring
8. blinding, gorgeous **9.** beautiful,
brilliant **11.** bewildering
dead . . . **3.** fey **4.** flat, numb, obit
5. amort, blind, inert, napoo, passé
6. active, barren, lapsed **7.** defunct,
expired, insipid, tedious **8.** ad patres,
complete, deceased, inactive, lifeless,
obsolete **9.** apathetic, inanimate
10. lusterless, motionless, spiritless,
unexciting **11.** nonexistent
dead (pert to) . . .
Dead Sea apple . . **12.** Apple of Sodom
Dead Sea country . . **4.** Moab **5.** Sodom
8. Gomorrah
language . . **5.** Latin
rise from the . . **7.** resurge **9.** reanimate,
resurrect
set (slang) . . **8.** full tilt, hell-bent
tree . . **7.** rampike (rampick)
deaden . . . **4.** damp, dull, mute, numb
6. muffle, obtund, opiate, weaken
7. relieve, repress **8.** enfeeble
10. devitalize
deadly . . . **4.** dire, mort **5.** fatal **6.** lethal,
mortal **7.** deathly **8.** venomous
10. implacable, lifelessly **11.** destructive,
internecine
dead ringer . . . **9.** look-alike
deaf . . . **4.** surd **7.** earless **10.** intolerant
11. inattentive, preoccupied
deaf alphabet . . . **11.** dactylology **12.** sign
language
deaf and dumb . . . **9.** surdomute
10. deaf-mutism **11.** surdimutism
deafness . . . **6.** amusia (tone) **7.** surdity
13. insensibility
deafness operation . . . **8.** fenestra
deal . . . **3.** lot **4.** dole, give, mede,
mete, sale, sell **5.** allot, share, trade,
treat **6.** parcel **7.** dispose, portion,
wrestle **8.** business, dispense, quantity
9. apportion, entertain **10.** administer,
distribute
dealer (pert to) . . .
cattle . . **6.** drover, herder
cloth . . **6.** draper, mercer
drug . . **8.** druggist **10.** apothecary,
pharmacist **14.** pharmacopolist
retail . . **6.** grocer, monger **8.** merchant
9. tradesman
stock exchange . . **6.** broker, jobber,
trader **11.** stockbroker
dean, dene . . . **4.** dell **6.** valley
dean . . . **4.** head, Inge **5.** decan, doyen
6. fellow (Educ), master, senior, verger
7. officer **9.** churchman, principal
dear . . . **5.** chere, cheri, deary, lover, sugar,
sweet **7.** beloved, darling **8.** precious
9. expensive **10.** sweetheart
dearth . . . **4.** want **6.** famine, rarity
7. paucity, poverty **8.** rareness, scarcity,

sparsity
death . . . **4.** doom, mort, obit **5.** sleep
(eternal) **6.** demise **7.** decease, passing,
quietus, release **10.** euthanasia (mercy),
expiration **11.** evanishment
death (pert to) . . .
after . . **10.** posthumous
eternal . . **9.** perdition
foreboding . . **6.** funest **7.** doleful
lawless . . **8.** lynching
notice . . **4.** obit **5.** orbit **8.** obituary
of a deity . . **4.** Mors
rattle . . **4.** rale
stoning (by) . . **8.** lapidate
deathlessness . . . **9.** athanasis
11. immortality **15.** everlastingness
debacle . . . **4.** rout **5.** crash, flood
7. washout **8.** collapse, stampede
9. breakdown, cataclysm
11. catastrophe, destruction
debar . . . **3.** bar **4.** deny **5.** estop **6.** forbid,
hinder, refuse **7.** exclude **8.** obstruct,
preclude, prohibit
debark . . . **4.** land **8.** go ashore
9. disembark
debase . . . **5.** abase, alloy, lower
6. demean, demote, reduce **7.** corrupt,
degrade, deprave **8.** disgrace
10. adulterate, depreciate **11.** deteriorate
debasement . . . **8.** demotion
9. abasement, abjection, reduction,
vitiation **11.** degradation
13. deterioration
debatable . . . **4.** moot **9.** refutable
10. disputable **11.** contestable
13. controversial
debate . . . **4.** agon (anc), moot **5.** argue,
forum, plead, weigh **6.** reason
7. analyze, closure, cloture, dispute,
wrangle **8.** argument, consider, forensic,
militate **9.** quodlibet **10.** deliberate,
discussion **11.** controversy
12. deliberation, dissertation
13. argumentation
debauch . . . **4.** bout, orgy **5.** broil, spree,
taint **6.** defile, seduce, splore **7.** mislead
8. carousal, escapade **9.** disaffect,
dissipate **11.** contaminate
debauchee . . . **4.** rake, roué **5.** satyr
7. rounder **9.** libertine **10.** profligate
debenture (Finan) . . . **4.** bond **5.** claim
6. pledge **7.** voucher **10.** instrument
11. certificate
debilitated . . . **4.** weak **5.** seedy **6.** feeble,
infirm, sapped, sickly **7.** languid
8. asthenic, impaired, weakened
9. enfeebled, langorous **11.** devitalized
debility . . . **5.** atony **7.** languor
8. adynamia, asthenia, cachexia,
weakness **9.** infirmity, lassitude
10. feebleness, sickliness
debit . . . **4.** debt **5.** entry **6.** charge
debonair, debonaire . . . **4.** airy **5.** suave
6. breezy, jaunty, urbane **7.** affable,
buoyant **8.** carefree
debris . . . **4.** junk **5.** attle, ruins, scrap,
talus, trash **6.** litter, refuse, rubble
7. deposit, remains, rubbish **8.** detritus
10. clamjamfry
debt . . . **3.** due, IOU, sin (Bib) **7.** arrears,
default **8.** trespass **9.** arrearage, liability

10. obligation
debut . . . 3. bow 8. entrance (formal)
9. coming out 12. introduction,
presentation
debutante . . . 3. bud, deb 6. subdeb
9. socialite
decade . . . 3. ten 9. decennium
decadence . . . 5. decay 7. decline
13. deterioration, retrogression
Decalogue . . . 15. Ten Commandments
Decameron author . . . 9. Boccaccio
decamp . . . 4. flee 6. depart 7. abscond,
vamoose 12. absquatulate
decanter . . . 4. ewer 5. croft 6. bottle,
carafe, vessel (liquors)
decapitate . . . 6. behead 10. guillotine
decapod . . . 4. crab 5. prawn 6. shrimp
7. Homarus, lobster 8. Decapoda
10. crustacean
decay . . . 3. rot 4. blet, doty 5. spoil, waste
6. caries, wither 7. crumble, mortify,
putrefy 8. spoilage 9. decadence,
decompose 11. deteriorate, dissolution
13. decomposition, deterioration
deceased . . . 4. dead, gone, late 6. at
rest 7. defunct, demised 8. decedent,
departed
deceit . . . 5. covin, craft, fraud, guile,
guise 7. cunning 8. artifice, cozenage,
intrigue, subtlety, trickery, wiliness
9. chicanery, deception, duplicity,
imposture, mendacity, sophistry,
treachery 10. craftiness, sneakiness
13. deceitfulness, dissimulation
14. tergiversation 15. treacherousness
deceitful . . . 4. wily 5. false 6. artful,
crafty, sneaky, tricky 8. guileful,
scheming, trickish 9. deceptive,
gnathonic, insincere 10. fraudulent
11. treacherous 13. Machiavellian
deceive . . . 3. cog, lie 4. bilk, dupe, flam,
fool, gull, hoax, sile 5. cheat, cozen,
elude, hocus, trick, troil 6. baffle,
delude, illude, seduce 7. beguile,
mislead 8. hoodwink
deceiver . . . 3. gay 5. cheat 6. hoaxer,
trepan (trapan) 8. betrayer, impostor
9. trickster
decency . . . 7. decorum, fitness, modesty
8. chastity, niceness 9. propriety
10. seemliness 12. tastefulness
decent . . . 4. kind 6. comely, kindly,
proper, seemly 7. clothed 8. adequate,
gracious, suitable, tasteful 9. tolerable
deception . . . 3. lie 4. hoax, wile 5. cheat,
fraud, guile 6. deceit, misled 7. fallacy
8. artifice, deceived, flimflam, illusion
9. duplicity, imposture
deceptive . . . 5. vague 8. illusive,
illusory 9. deceiving, sirenical (sirenic)
10. fallacious
decide (upon) . . . 3. opt 4. vote 5. adapt,
elect, judge 6. choose, settle 7. referee,
resolve 9. arbitrate, ascertain,
determine, influence
decided . . . 8. clear-cut, definite
10. determined
decima . . . 4. stop (organ) 5. tenth, tithe
8. interval
decimal . . . 3. ten 5. tenth 7. tenfold
8. repetend

decimate . . . 3. few 4. kill, slay 5. burke,
tenth 6. divide 7. destroy 8. subtract
9. devastate, slaughter
decipher . . . 4. read 5. crack 6. decode,
detect 7. unravel 8. discover 9. translate
decision . . . 4. grit 5. arret, nerve, pluck
6. mettle, report 7. verdict 8. firmness
10. conclusion, resolution, settlement
12. announcement 13. determination
decisive . . . 3. end 5. final 7. certain,
crucial 8. critical, resolute 9. mandatory
10. conclusive, convincing
decisive moment . . . 6. crisis
deck (ship's) . . . 3. gun 4. main,
poop 5. orlop, upper 6. bridge
7. scupper (gutter) 8. hatchway,
platform 9. promenade 10. forecastle
deck . . . 4. gild 5. adorn, array, cards
(playing), equip, floor 6. blazon, clothe,
enrich 7. bedizen, dress up 8. emblazon
9. knock down
declaim . . . 4. rant, rave 5. orate, spiel,
spout 6. herald, recite 8. denounce,
harangue, perorate 9. discourse
11. declamation
declamation . . . 7. lecture 9. elocution
10. recitation
declaration . . . 3. vow 4. oath 6. avowal,
decree, oracle 8. pleading (law)
9. assertion, manifesto, testimony
10. confession (of faith) 11. affirmation
12. proclamation 13. pronouncement
declare . . . 3. say 4. aver, avow, meld
5. bruit, state 6. affirm, allege, assert,
blazon, herald, spread 7. publish
8. announce, indicate, maintain
9. advertise
declare (pert to) . . .
against . . 6. indict
as fact . . 5. posit
innocent . . 6. acquit
declension . . . 4. drop, fall 5. slope
7. decline, descent, refusal 10. inflection
13. deterioration
decline . . . 3. dip, ebb, set 4. fade, fail, fall,
flag, sink, wane 5. droop, repel, slope,
slump, stoop 6. refuse, reject, weaken
7. dwindle 8. decrease, downhill
9. decadence, declivity, repudiate
10. retrograde 12. depreciation
declivity . . . 3. dip 4. drop, hill 5. scarp,
slope 7. descent 8. downgate
9. downgrade
decoction . . . 4. sapa (sape) 6. apozem,
cremor, tisane 7. boiling 10. extraction
11. preparation
décolleté . . . 6. low-cut 8. plunging
9. revealing
decompose . . . 3. rot 4. frit 5. decay
7. resolve 10. photolysis 12. disintegrate
decorate . . . 4. deck, trim 5. adorn, honor
6. emboss 7. bedizen, brocade, miniate
8. beautify, ornament 9. scrimshaw
decorated . . . 5. fancy 6. ornate
7. adorned 8. nielloed 9. sigillate
(pottery) 11. embellished
decoration . . . 4. buhl 5. gutta (anc),
medal 6. plaque, purfle, ribbon
7. epergne, festoon, garnish 8. gold
star, ornament, trimming 9. adornment,
garniture, sgraffito 10. cordon bleu,

emblazonry, embroidery
decorous ... **4.** calm, prim **5.** grave,
quiet, staid **6.** decent, demure,
modest, proper, sedate, seemly, serene
7. fitting, regular, settled **8.** becoming,
composed, suitable, tasteful **9.** unruffled
12. conventional
decorticate ... **4.** bark, flay, husk, pare,
peel, skin **5.** strip **9.** excoriate
decoy ... **4.** bait, lure, tole **6.** capper,
entrap **8.** by-bidder **9.** come-on man
11. stool pigeon
decrease ... **3.** ebb **4.** drop, sink,
wane **5.** abate, waste **6.** decess,
lessen, reduce, shrink **7.** decline,
dwindle, shorten, slacken, subside
8. compress, diminish, moderate
9. abatement, deduction, deflation,
lessening **10.** diminution **11.** contraction
12. depreciation
decree ... **3.** act, law **4.** bull, fiat, rede
(anc), will **5.** arret, canon, edict,
enact, irade, order, ukase **6.** dictum,
ordain **7.** command, mandate, verdict
8. decision, rescript **9.** ordinance
decree beforehand ... **7.** destine
decree nisi ... **7.** divorce
decrepit ... **3.** old **4.** aged, lame, weak
6. infirm, senile, wasted (with age)
7. worn out **8.** unstable, unsturdy
decry ... **3.** boo **4.** slur **5.** lower
7. condemn, degrade, detract **8.** belittle,
denounce, derogate **9.** discredit,
disparage, underrate **10.** depreciate,
undervalue
dedal ... see *daedal*
dedicate ... **6.** devote, hallow **7.** address
8. inscribe **10.** consecrate
deduce ... **5.** infer **6.** deduct, derive,
elicit, evolve **7.** suppose
deduct ... **4.** bate, faik, take **6.** remove
8. discount, retrench, separate, subtract
deduction ... **6.** rebate **7.** reprise
8. discount, illation **9.** allowance,
corollary, induction, inference,
reasoning, syllogism
deed ... **3.** act, ado **4.** feat, fiat,
gest (geste) **5.** actum, actus, stunt,
title **6.** action, doings **7.** exploit
8. contract, tenendum **11.** achievement,
malefaction, performance
deem ... **5.** judge, opine, think **6.** esteem,
regard **7.** believe, presume, suppose
8. conclude, consider **10.** adjudicate
deemed ... **7.** assumed, reputed
8. adjudged, inferred, presumed,
supposed **10.** considered
deep ... **3.** low, pit **4.** rich, wide,
wise **5.** great **6.** hidden, remote,
solemn **7.** learned, obscure, serious
8. immersed, involved, powerful,
profound **9.** engrossed, entangled,
sagacious **10.** deep-seated, mysterious
deep (pert to) ...
dish pie .. **7.** cobbler
sea .. **6.** depths
seated .. **8.** habitual **9.** ingrained
11. established
sleep .. **5.** sopor
sound .. **4.** bell, gong
deepen ... **5.** lower **6.** dredge **7.** broaden,

enhance **9.** aggravate, intensify
10. strengthen
deer ... **3.** elk, red, roe **4.** buck, fawn, hart,
hind, maha, stag **5.** eland, moose, ratwa
6. fallow, sambar, wapiti **7.** caribou,
deerlet, roebuck **8.** reindeer, ruminant
deer (pert to) ...
antler .. **3.** dag **4.** snag **8.** tres-tine
(royal)
Asiatic .. **6.** sambar
barking .. **7.** muntjac (muntjak)
deerlike .. **10.** chevrotain
female .. **3.** doe, roe **4.** hind
genus .. **4.** Dama **6.** Cervus **8.** Cervidae
Japanese .. **4.** sika
Java .. **4.** napu **7.** muntjac (muntjak)
Lapland .. **8.** reindeer
male .. **4.** buck, hart, stag **6.** havier
7. brocket (brok), pricket
meat .. **7.** venison
mouse .. **7.** plandok
Oriental .. **4.** axis, Rusa **5.** kakar **6.** chital,
rativa, sambar **7.** kanchil, muntjac
(muntjak)
Russian .. **4.** olen
S American .. **4.** pita **6.** guemal (guemul)
7. brocket, spitter
Tibet .. **4.** shou
tiger .. **6.** cougar
tracks .. **3.** run **4.** slot **5.** spoor
type .. **3.** red, roe **4.** mule **6.** fallow
11. black-tailed, white-tailed
deface ... **3.** mar **4.** ruin, scar **5.** spoil
6. damage, injure **7.** blemish, distort
9. discredit, disfigure
defalcate ... **8.** embezzle
defamation ... **5.** libel **7.** calumny,
slander, spatter **8.** disgrace, dishonor
9. aspersion **10.** defilement, detraction
defame ... **5.** libel **6.** accuse, charge,
infamy, malign, vilify **7.** asperse,
blacken, detract, slander, traduce
8. dishonor **10.** calumniate
default ... **4.** fail, lack, loss, mora
7. deficit, failure, neglect **9.** deficient,
denigrate, oversight **10.** nonpayment
11. delinquency **14.** nonfulfillment
defeat ... **4.** beat, best, lose, rout
5. worst **6.** baffle, derout, master,
refute **7.** beating, clobber, confute,
conquer, failure, mastery, repulse,
triumph (over), undoing **8.** Waterloo
9. frustrate, overthrow **10.** disappoint
11. subjugation **12.** discomfiture
14. disappointment
defeating ... **7.** beating, routing
10. anatreptic, conquering
11. vanquishing
defeatism ... **6.** malism **7.** Boloism
10. retreatism
defect ... **4.** flaw, lisp, lock, quit, want
5. fault **7.** blemish, forsake **8.** withdraw
9. discredit **10.** deficiency, inadequacy
12. imperfection, irregularity
defection ... **4.** loss **7.** failing, failure
9. desertion **10.** abjurement
11. abandonment
defective ... **3.** bad **4.** lame **5.** idiot
6. cretin, faulty **7.** half-wit, lacking
8. crippled **9.** deficient, imperfect,
subnormal **10.** incomplete

defective vision . . . 6. anopia, myopia

defend . . . 4. save, ward 5. guard, plead, shend, watch 6. screen, secure, shield, uphold 7. contest, justify, protect, shelter, support, sustain 8. enshield, preserve 10. controvert

defendant . . . 4. reus 7. accused, libelee, suspect 8. appellee 10. respondent

defender . . . 8. advocate, champion 9. justifier, protector 10. vindicator

defense . . . 4. boma, fort, plea 5. alibi, guard 6. abatis (abattis), glacis (slope) 7. bastion, bulwark, rampart, ravelin 8. estacade (dike), sepiment, stockade 10. protection 12. counterscarp 13. justification, machicolation

defenseless . . . 7. aidless, forlorn, unarmed 8. helpless 9. unarmored, unguarded 10. undefended, unshielded 11. unfortified, unprotected

defer . . . 3. bow 4. wait 5. delay 6. retard 7. adjourn, suspend 8. postpone, protract, stave off 13. procrastinate

defer (to) . . . 5. yield 6. admire, regard, submit 7. concede, respect 9. recognize 11. acknowledge

deference . . . 5. honor 6. esteem, fealty, homage, regard 7. respect 8. courtesy 9. reverence 10. politeness, submission 12. complaisance 13. consideration

deferential . . . 8. obeisant 9. attentive, courteous 10. respectful, submissive 11. ceremonious

defiance . . . 6. defial 8. audacity, boldness 9. challenge, disregard, insolence

deficiency . . . 4. lack, want 6. dearth, ullage 7. aneuria, deficit 8. scarcity, shortage 10. inadequacy 13. insufficiency 14. incompleteness

deficient . . . 5. minus, short 6. faulty, meager (meagre), scarce 7. lacking, missing, wanting 8. inferior 9. defective, imperfect 10. inadequate, incomplete 12. insufficient

defile . . . 4. file, pass (Mt), soil 5. dirty, gorge, notch, sully, taint 6. befoul, debase, ravine, vilify 7. corrupt, debauch, deprave, pollute, tarnish 8. dishonor 10. passageway

define . . . 3. fix 4. name 5. bound, limit 6. decide 7. delimit, explain, outline 8. boundary 9. delineate, determine, stipulate 11. distinguish 12. characterize, circumscribe

defined (sharply) . . . 8. clear-cut 9. trenchant

defined track . . . 3. rut 4. slot

definite . . . 4. sure 7. certain, limited, precise 8. absolute, distinct, explicit, manifest, positive 10. undeniable 11. determining, unqualified 12. unmistakable 14. unquestionable

definitely . . . 10. explicitly, positively 12. conclusively, unmistakably

definition . . . 6. naming 7. clarity, meaning 9. sharpness 11. description, explanation 12. delimitation, distinctness 14. interpretation

deflation . . . 7. decline 8. collapse 9. reduction 10. cheapening 11. devaluation, humiliation

12. depreciation

deflect . . . 4. bend, warp 5. avert 6. divert 7. deviate

Defoe character . . . 6. Crusoe, Friday, Roxana 12. Moll Flanders

deformed . . . 5. varus 7. taliped 8. formless 9. amorphous, distorted, grotesque, loathsome, malformed, misshapen, monstrous 10. clubfooted

defraud . . . 3. gyp, rob 4. bilk, gull 5. cheat, cozen 6. fleece 7. swindle

deft . . . 3. apt, fit, pat 4. meet, trim 5. adept, handy, quick 6. adroit, clever, expert 8. skillful (skilful) 9. dexterous, masterful

defunct . . . 3. die 4. dead, gone 6. depart, finish 7. extinct 8. deceased 11. nonexistent

defy . . . 4. dare 5. beard, brave, stump 6. cartel 7. disdain, disobey 9. challenge

degenerate . . . 6. debase, wicked, worsen 7. atrophy, corrupt, degrade, deprave 8. decadent 10. retrogress 11. deteriorate

degeneration . . . 7. decline 9. decadence, turpitude 10. degeneracy 11. degradation 13. deterioration, retrogression

degradation . . . 5. shame 7. censure, decline 8. demotion, disgrace, ignominy 9. reduction, turpitude 10. debasement, punishment 11. humiliation 13. deterioration

degrade . . . 5. abase, lower 6. debase, demean, demote, depose, humble 7. corrupt 8. disgrace, dishonor 9. humiliate 10. depreciate

degrade (socially) . . . 8. déclassé

degree . . . 4. rank, step, tate 5. class, grade, order, point, scope, shade, stage, stair 6. extent 7. station 8. capacity, relation 9. intensity

degree (pert to) . . .
academic . . 8. bachelor 9. doctorate, masterate 11. engineering 13. baccalaureate
slight . . 5. shade 9. gradation
to what . . 9. howsoever 10. howsomever
with honors . . 8. cum laude

dehydrate . . . 3. dry 5. dry up 6. wither 8. preserve 9. anhydrate, dessicate, evaporate, exsiccate

deify . . . 5. exalt 7. ennoble, glorify, idolize 8. enshrine 11. apotheosize, immortalize

deign . . . 7. consent 9. vouchsafe 10. condescend

deity . . . 2. El 3. Dea, God 4. Deus, deva 5. numen 6. Elohim 7. goddess, godhead, godhood 8. Almighty, Divinity, Immortal 12. Supreme Being

deity (aboriginal) . . . 4. mana, Zemi 5. huaca, wakan 6. manito (manitou), nagual, orenda, pokunt 8. tamanoas

deity (pert to) . . .
avenging . . 6. Erinys 7. Alastor, Anteros
destroying . . 4. Siva (Shiva)
evil . . 5. Sebek (crocodile-headed)
hearth . . 5. Vesta
household . . 3. Lar 7. Penates
human sacrifice . . 6. Moloch

judge of the dead . . **4.** Yama
love . . **4.** Amor, Eros **5.** Cupid
mockery . . **5.** Momus
music . . **6.** Apollo
solar . . **5.** Mentu (Ment, falcon-headed)
sun . . **2.** Ra
supreme . . **6.** Ormazd
two-faced . . **5.** Janus
underworld . . **3.** Dis **4.** Gwyn **5.** Pluto
   6. Osiris
war . . **4.** Ares
woodland . . **3.** Pan **4.** faun **5.** satyr
   7. silenus
dejected . . . **3.** sad **5.** amort **6.** abased,
   droopy **7.** à la mort, lowered
   8. downcast **9.** depressed, prostrate
   10. despondent **11.** downhearted,
   low-spirited
dejection . . . **7.** lowness, sadness
   10. depression, melancholy
   11. despondency
déjeuner . . . **5.** lunch
Delaware . . .
   beach . . **8.** Rehoboth
   capital . . **5.** Dover
   church (oldest Prot) . . **9.** Old Swedes
   city . . **5.** Lewes **9.** New Castle
      10. Wilmington (Fort Christina, 1638)
   corporation . . **6.** DuPont
   product . . **9.** chemicals **13.** Blue Hen
      chicks
   river . . **8.** Delaware **10.** Brandywine
   State admission . . **5.** first
   State motto . . **22.** Liberty and
      Independence
   State nickname . . **5.** First **7.** Diamond
delay . . . **3.** lag **4.** halt, mora, stay, wait
   5. block, check, daily, defer, demur,
   pause, tarry **6.** arrest, detain, hinder,
   impede, loiter, retard **7.** confine,
   setback **8.** lateness, obstruct, postpone,
   reprieve, slow-down **9.** detention,
   hindrance **10.** cunctation, moratorium
   13. procrastinate **15.** procrastination
delayed . . . **4.** late, slow **5.** tardy
   7. belayed, overdue **10.** behindhand
delectable . . . **6.** savory **8.** luscious,
   pleasing **9.** ambrosial, delicious
   10. delightful **11.** scrumptious
delegate . . . **4.** name, send **6.** assign,
   commit, depute, deputy, legate
   7. appoint, consign, entrust **8.** deputize
   9. authorize **10.** commission
   12. commissioner **14.** representative
delete . . . **4.** dele **5.** erase **6.** cut out,
   excise, remove **7.** edit out, expunge
   9. eradicate **10.** obliterate
deleterious . . . **7.** harmful, hurtful,
   noxious **9.** injurious **10.** pernicious,
   prejudiced **11.** destructive, detrimental,
   prejudicial
deletion . . . **4.** stet **7.** apocope **8.** excision
   9. expunging
delf, delft . . . **3.** pit **4.** mine **6.** quarry
Delhi . . . **7.** capital (Ind)
deliberate . . . **4.** cool, muse, pore, slow
   5. study, think, weigh **6.** ponder
   7. discuss, reflect, studied **8.** consider,
   measured, prepense **9.** calculate,
   leisurely, speculate, unhurried,
   voluntary **11.** contemplate, intentional,

premeditate **12.** premeditated
   13. dispassionate
deliberately . . . **6.** slowly **7.** tardily **8.** by
   design **9.** expressly, purposely, willfully
   13. intentionally
delicacy . . . **4.** cate, tact **5.** snack, taste
   6. caviar, luxury, nicety, tidbit **7.** finesse,
   frailty, tenuity **8.** fineness, niceness,
   softness, subtlety **9.** exactness, fragility,
   precision **10.** daintiness, refinement,
   slightness **11.** sensitivity
delicate . . . **3.** sly **4.** fine, lacy, nice, soft
   5. frail, light **6.** dainty, mignon, petite,
   pretty, queasy, subtle, tender **7.** elegant,
   fragile, minikin, refined, tenuous
   8. araneous, graceful, luscious, tasteful
   9. exquisite, sensitive **10.** fastidious,
   meticulous, scrupulous **11.** considerate
delicious . . . **5.** tasty **8.** luscious
   9. ambrosial, nectarean **10.** delightful,
   nectareous
delight . . . **3.** joy **4.** glee **5.** amuse,
   bliss, charm, exult, mirth **6.** divert,
   please, ravish, regale, relish **7.** enchant,
   gratify, overjoy **8.** pleasure **9.** delectate,
   enrapture, happiness **13.** gratification
delightful . . . **6.** lovely, savory **7.** amusing,
   winsome **8.** charming, engaging,
   pleasant **9.** appealing, delicious,
   enjoyable **10.** enchanting **11.** fascinating
delineate . . . **3.** map **4.** draw, limn, line
   5. trace **6.** define, depict **7.** outline,
   picture, portray **8.** describe **9.** represent
delinquency . . . **7.** default, failure
   8. omission **9.** violation **10.** nonpayment
   11. malfeasance, misdemeanor,
   misfeasance **13.** nonobservance
deliquesce . . . **4.** give, melt **6.** ramify
   7. liquefy **8.** diminish, dissolve
delirious . . . **6.** insane, raving **8.** frenzied
   9. wandering (mental) **14.** disorientation
delirium . . . **4.** fury, rage **6.** frenzy,
   lunacy **7.** madness, passion **8.** insanity
   9. phrenitis **10.** aberration, excitement,
   unsaneness **11.** derangement
   13. hallucination
deliver . . . **4.** free, give, save **5.** speak
   6. commit, impart, ransom, redeem,
   render, resign **7.** consign, release,
   relieve **8.** transfer **9.** discharge,
   enunciate, extradite, surrender
deliver of evil spirits . . . **8.** exorcise
deliver oration . . . **7.** declaim
dell . . . **4.** dale, dene, vale **5.** slade **6.** dalles
   (pl), dingle, ravine, valley
Delos . . .
   famed for . . **5.** ruins **10.** Stone Lions
   island group . . **8.** Cyclades
   sea . . **6.** Aegean
Delphi, Delphoi (Gr) . . .
   god . . **6.** Apollo
   modern name . . **6.** Kastri
   mount . . **9.** Parnassus
   oracle . . **7.** Delphic **8.** Delphian
   priestess . . **6.** Pythia
delude . . . **3.** jig **4.** dupe, flam, fool, hoax
   5. elude, trick **6.** befool **7.** beguile,
   deceive, mislead **9.** bamboozle,
   frustrate, victimize **11.** double-cross
deluge . . . **5.** flood **6.** drench **7.** freshet,
   Niagara, torrent **8.** cataract, flooding,

inundate, overflow, submerge, The
Flood **9.** cataclysm, overwhelm
10. oversupply **14.** superabundance
delusion . . . **4.** ruse **6.** mirage **7.** fallacy,
fantasm **8.** illusion, phantasm
9. deception **10.** misleading
13. hallucination
delve . . . **3.** dig **4.** mine, till **5.** gouge,
scoop, spade **6.** exhume **8.** excavate
demand . . . **3.** ask, COD, cry, dun, fee
4. call, need **5.** claim, query **6.** elicit
7. require **8.** exaction, question
9. requisite, ultimatum **11.** requirement,
requisition
demandant . . . **9.** plaintiff
demeanor, demeanour . . . **4.** mien
7. bearing, conduct, posture **8.** behavior,
carriage **11.** comportment
demented . . . **3.** mad **4.** daft, loco,
luny **5.** crazy, loony **6.** crazed, insane
7. cracked **8.** deranged **10.** unbalanced
11. disoriented
demesne . . . **4.** land **6.** estate
10. possession
Demeter . . . **7.** goddess (Agric)
demigod . . . **4.** hero **5.** satyr (sylvan)
6. Triton **7.** godling, half-god
10. semidivine
demise . . . **5.** death, lease **6.** convey
7. decease **8.** bequeath **10.** alienation,
conveyance
demit . . . **4.** quit **5.** leave **6.** resign,
vacate **8.** abdicate **10.** relinquish
11. resignation
demiurgic . . . **8.** creative **9.** formative
demivolt . . . **4.** jump **5.** vault (half)
6. curvet **8.** capriole
Democrat (Polit slang) . . . **6.** Hunker
demoded . . . **5.** passe **6.** passed **10.** out
of style
demolish . . . **4.** rase, raze, ruin, undo
5. level, wreck **7.** destroy, shatter
9. devastate, dismantle, overthrow
11. disassemble
demon, daemon . . . **3.** hag, imp, nat
4. atua, jinn, Mara, ogre, Rahu **5.** asura,
devil, Eolis, fiend, genie, jinni (jinnee),
lamia, Satan **6.** afreet **7.** Amaimon,
villain **8.** Asmodeus **9.** cacodemon
(cacodaemon)
demoniac . . . **8.** devilish, fiendish
demons (pert to) . . .
adjurers . . **9.** exorcists
assembly of . . **6.** sabbat
charm against . . **10.** demonifuge
possessed of . . **8.** demoniac
theory of . . **10.** demonology
worship of . . **11.** demonolatry
demonstrate . . . **4.** show **5.** prove
6. evince, typify **7.** display, explain,
portray **8.** manifest **9.** exemplify
demonstrative . . . **7.** gushing **8.** effusive
9. emotional **10.** indicative
11. explanatory **12.** affectionate,
illustrative
Demosthenes (Gr) . . . **6.** orator (greatest)
demotic . . . **6.** common **7.** popular
8. everyday **10.** vernacular
demur . . . **4.** stay **5.** delay, pause,
tarry **6.** linger, object (to) **7.** scruple
8. demurrer, hesitate **9.** objection

12. irresolution
demure . . . **3.** coy, mim, shy **4.** prim,
smug **5.** grave, staid, timid **6.** sedate,
solemn, stuffy **7.** bashful, prudish,
serious **8.** decorous
den . . . **4.** cave, dell, lair, nest, room
5. cavea (anc), group (scouts), haunt,
study **6.** cavern, grotto, hollow, ravine
7. retreat **8.** hideaway
denial . . . **5.** cross **7.** refusal **8.** demurrer,
negation **9.** disavowal, disowning,
rejection **10.** refutation **11.** deprivation
12. disallowance **13.** disaffirmance
denizen . . . **3.** cit **6.** native **7.** citizen,
dweller, hellion (of hell) **9.** indweller
10. inhabitant **11.** cosmopolite
Denmark . . . see also *Danish*
anc name . . **5.** Thule
capital . . **10.** Copenhagen
city . . **6.** Nyborg (Fyn Isl), Odense
7. Aalborg **8.** Elsinore
founder . . **7.** Absalon (Axel)
Hamlet's grave . . **8.** Elsinore
island possession . . **6.** Faroes
9. Greenland
peninsula . . **7.** Jutland
river . . **5.** Guden
ruler (anc) . . **6.** Canute (Kanute)
denomination . . . **3.** ism **4.** cult, name,
sect **5.** class, party, value **6.** church,
number, school **7.** society **8.** category
10. persuasion **11.** appellation,
designation, stipulation
denote . . . **4.** mark, mean, note, show
5. imply **6.** convey **7.** bespeak, betoken,
connote, express, purport, signify
8. indicate **10.** denominate
denoting (pert to) . . .
equal pressure . . **8.** isobaric
final end (Gram) . . **5.** telic
usual action . . **9.** usitative
denouement . . . **3.** end **5.** issue **6.** result
7. outcome (plot) **8.** solution
10. revelation
denounce . . . **4.** damn, rail (at, against)
6. accuse, assail, scathe **7.** arraign,
censure, condemn, upbraid **9.** reprobate
10. denunciate, stigmatize
de novo . . . **3.** new **4.** anew **5.** fresh,
newly **6.** afresh
dense . . . **4.** dewy, firm **5.** close,
crass, gross, heavy, solid, thick
6. opaque, stupid **7.** compact, crowded
8. populous, thickset **11.** thickheaded
density . . . **4.** dord (Chem) **8.** dumbness
9. stupidity **11.** compactness
dent . . . **3.** pit **4.** dint **5.** dinge, notch, tooth
6. batter, hollow, indent **7.** imprint
10. depression, impression
11. indentation
dentagra . . . **7.** forceps **9.** dentalgia,
toothache
dental (pert to) . . .
appliance . . **3.** dam **6.** scaler **7.** forceps
drill . . **8.** cavitron
filling . . **5.** inlay
measure . . **10.** dentimeter
toothache . . **8.** dentagra **9.** dentalgia
dentate . . . **7.** serried, toothed
dentine . . . **5.** ivory
dentist . . . **10.** exodontist **12.** orthodontist

14. prosthodontist
denude . . . **4.** bate **5.** scalp, strip **6.** divest, expose, unrobe **7.** uncover
denunciation . . . **6.** menace, threat **7.** inveigh **8.** reproach **10.** accusation **11.** arraignment
deny . . . **4.** nego **5.** debar **6.** abjure, impugn, negate, recant, refuse, renege **7.** confute, disavow, dispute, gainsay **8.** disclaim, forswear, traverse **9.** repudiate **10.** contradict, contravene, controvert
deodar (species) . . . **5.** cedar
depart . . . **2.** go **3.** die **4.** exit, quit **5.** leave, mosey **6.** decamp, demise, egress, perish **7.** abscond, vamoose **8.** separate (Chem), withdraw
depend . . . **4.** rely **5.** hinge
depraved . . . **4.** evil, vile **6.** shrewd, wicked **7.** corrupt, immoral, vicious **8.** vitiated **9.** debauched, dissolute, perverted **10.** degenerate
depravity . . . **8.** depraved **9.** turpitude **10.** corruption, wickedness **15.** incorrigibility
depreciate . . . **4.** fall **5.** lower, slump **6.** debase, lessen, reduce, shrink **7.** cheapen, deflate **8.** belittle, discount, pejorate, vilipend **9.** disparage **10.** undervalue
depreciation . . . **8.** decrease, discount **9.** deflation **10.** cheapening, pejoration **12.** belittlement **13.** disparagement **14.** undervaluation
depredator . . . **5.** thief **6.** looter, robber **7.** spoiler **8.** marauder, ravisher **9.** despoiler, plunderer
depress . . . **4.** dent, sink **5.** lower **6.** dampen, deepen, deject, indent, reduce, sadden **7.** flatten, imprint, oppress **8.** dispirit, enfeeble **10.** discourage
depressed . . . **3.** low, sad **4.** dire, sunk **6.** dismal, oblate **8.** dejected, downcast **9.** debruised (Her), flattened (vertically) **10.** dispirited **11.** downhearted **12.** disheartened
depressing . . . **5.** chill **6.** dismal, dreary, gloomy, somber **7.** joyless **9.** saddening **10.** melancholy
depression . . . **3.** col, dip, pit **4.** dent, fall **5.** blues, fossa (Anat), gloom, gully **6.** cavity, crater, ravine, trough, vapors **10.** melancholy **11.** despondency, humiliation
deprivation . . . **4.** loss, want **7.** deposal, ousting, removal **9.** privation, unseating **10.** divestment **11.** bereavement
deprive . . . **3.** rob **4.** take **5.** debar, mulct, strip **6.** divest, remove **7.** bereave, despoil **10.** dispossess
deprived of . . .
authority . . **9.** dethroned
life . . **5.** slain **6.** killed **12.** exterminated
limb . . **6.** maimed
natural qualities . . **9.** denatured
possessions . . **12.** expropriated
professional standing . . **8.** laicized
rank . . **7.** deposed
reason . . **8.** demented
vigor . . **6.** sapped **8.** deadened, unnerved

9. enervated, enfeebled
depth . . . **5.** abyss, midst **6.** extent **9.** intensity **10.** profundity
depths . . . **3.** sea **5.** adyta (spiritual), ocean **16.** Davy Jones's locker
depute . . . **6.** assign, devote **7.** appoint **8.** delegate, deputize
deputy . . . **5.** agent, envoy, proxy, vicar **6.** legate **8.** alter ego **9.** alternate **10.** substitute
deracinate . . . **6.** evulse, unroot, uproot **7.** extract (forcibly)
deride . . . **3.** pan **4.** dupe, geck, gibe, jeer, mock, razz **5.** cheat, fleer, flout, scoff, scorn, trick **6.** insult **8.** ridicule
derision . . . **5.** fleer, scorn **7.** asteism, mockery **8.** contempt, ridicule
derivation . . . **6.** effect, origin, source **7.** descent, lineage **9.** deduction, education, evolution **10.** derivative **12.** transmission
derivation of . . .
descent . . **7.** lineage **8.** pedigree **9.** genealogy
name (race, tribe) . . **7.** eponymy
word . . **9.** etymology
derivative of . . .
bauxite . . **8.** aluminum
benzine . . **6.** phenol
coal tar . . **8.** creosote
flax . . **5.** linen
mercury . . **11.** quicksilver
milk . . **6.** lactic
morphine . . **6.** heroin
pitchblende . . **6.** radium **7.** uranium
sorrel . . **10.** oxalic acid
derogate . . . **5.** annul, decry **6.** repeal **7.** detract **8.** restrict, withdraw **9.** disparage
derogatory . . . **10.** detracting, detractory, pejorative **11.** deprecatory, disparaging **12.** depreciatory
derrick . . . **3.** rig **4.** spar **5.** crave, hoist, tower **6.** lifter, steeve, tackle **7.** hangman, staging
dervish . . . **4.** monk **5.** fakir, friar **6.** beggar, fakeer **7.** ascetic **11.** religionist
dervish cap . . . **3.** taj **4.** atef
dervishes . . .
howling . . **8.** Rufaiyah
wandering . . **12.** Kalandariyah
whirling, dancing . . **10.** Maulawiyah
Descartes (pert to) . . .
geometry . . **8.** analytic **10.** coordinate
system . . **9.** Cartesian
tenet . . **13.** cogito ergo sum
descend . . . **4.** fall, sink **5.** deign, stoop **6.** alight, unbend **7.** decline **9.** gravitate **10.** condescend
descendant . . . **3.** son **5.** child, scion **8.** daughter, offshoot **9.** offspring
descendants . . . **5.** breed **7.** progeny **9.** posterity
descent . . . **4.** drop, fall, root **5.** birth, issue, scarp, slope, stock **7.** assault, decline, lineage **8.** ancestry, downfall, invasion (sea), pedigree **9.** declivity, incursion, posterity **10.** extraction **11.** degradation
describe . . . **4.** name **5.** paint, parse, state **6.** define, depict, relate **7.** explain,

express, narrate, outline **9.** delineate, designate, represent **12.** characterize

description... **4.** idyl, kind, sort **5.** idyll **7.** account, version **8.** features, relation **9.** discourse, narration, narrative, portrayal **10.** definition **11.** delineation, explanation **14.** representation **18.** descriptio personae

descry... **3.** see **4.** espy, view **6.** behold, detect, reveal **7.** discern, observe, witness **8.** discover **9.** determine **11.** distinguish

Desdemona's husband... **7.** Othello

desecrate... **5.** abuse **6.** misuse **7.** profane, violate **8.** misapply

Deseret... **4.** Utah (1849)

desert... **3.** due **4.** bolt, fail **5.** merit, oasis **6.** defect, renege, reward **7.** abandon, forsake **8.** desolate **10.** apostatize, relinquish, wilderness

desert (pert to)...
Africa.. **5.** El Erg **6.** Karroo, Sahara **8.** Kalahari
Algeria.. **3.** Erg
Australia.. **10.** Great Sandy **13.** Great Victoria
beast.. **5.** camel
dweller.. **4.** Arab
Mongolia (Asia).. **4.** Gobi
phenomenon.. **6.** mirage
prospector.. **3.** rat
ship.. **5.** camel
shrub.. **5.** ratem **6.** Alhagi **7.** juniper (Bib)
train, travelers.. **7.** caravan
US.. **6.** Mojave (Mohave) **7.** Painted **11.** Death Valley
wind (hot).. **6.** simoom (simoon) **7.** sirocco

deserter... **3.** rat **6.** bolter **8.** apostate, recreant, renegade, turncoat, turntail

deserved... **3.** due **4.** fair, just **5.** rated **6.** earned, worthy **7.** condign, merited **8.** rightful **9.** justified, warranted **11.** appropriate

deserving... **6.** worthy **8.** laudable **10.** creditable, entitled to **11.** commendable, meritorious **12.** praiseworthy

desiccated... **3.** dry **4.** arid, sere **5.** dried **6.** seared **7.** parched **9.** preserved **10.** dehydrated, exsiccated

design... **3.** aim, art, end **4.** draw, form, idea, mean, plan, plot **5.** ettle **6.** intent, layout, motive, object, scheme, sketch **7.** destine, drawing, meaning, outline, pattern, propose **8.** artifice, artistry, contrive **11.** arrangement

design (pert to)...
carved.. **4.** seme **5.** cameo **8.** intaglio
metal glass.. **4.** etch **6.** niello
ornamental.. **9.** medallion **10.** needlework
pattern.. **5.** batik **6.** mosaic
skin.. **6.** tattoo

designate... **3.** fix, set **4.** call, mark, name, show **5.** state, style, title **6.** select **7.** appoint, entitle, specify **8.** describe, indicate, nominate **9.** determine, stipulate **10.** denominate **11.** distinguish **12.** characterize

designation... **4.** name **7.** meaning **9.** selection **10.** indication **12.** denomination **13.** signification

desire... **3.** yen **4.** care, urge, want, wish **5.** covet, crave, yearn **6.** aspire, hunger, prefer, thirst **7.** craving, longing, passion, request **8.** appetite **9.** appetency, eagerness **10.** desiderium **11.** inclination

desire (pert to)...
expectant.. **4.** hope
greatly.. **6.** aspire
liquid.. **6.** thirst
ungovernable.. **5.** mania

desirous... **4.** avid **5.** eager **6.** ardent **7.** envious, lustful, willing **8.** covetous, spirited **9.** ambitious **10.** solicitous

desist... **2.** ho **3.** end **4.** don't, halt, quit, stay, stop **5.** cease **6.** lay off **7.** forbear, refrain **8.** cut it out **11.** discontinue

desk... **4.** ambo, dais **5.** board, table **6.** pulpit **7.** lectern, rostrum **8.** kneehole **9.** monocleid (monocleide), secretary **10.** escritoire

desolate... **3.** sad **4.** arid, lorn, ruin **5.** alone, bleak, drear, gaunt **6.** barren, dismal, gloomy, lonely, ravage **7.** forlorn **8.** deserted, forsaken, solitary, wretched **9.** destitute **10.** depopulate **11.** comfortless, uninhabited

desolation... **3.** woe **4.** ruin **5.** gloom, grief, havoc, waste **6.** ravage **7.** sadness **10.** gloominess, loneliness, melancholy **11.** destitution, destruction, devastation, forlornness **12.** depopulation, solitariness, wretchedness

despair... **11.** desperation, despondency, forlornness **12.** hopelessness

desperado... **5.** brave **6.** outlaw **7.** ruffian **8.** criminal **10.** lawbreaker

desperate... **3.** mad **4.** rash, wild **7.** frantic, furious **8.** headlong, heedless, hopeless, reckless **10.** despairing, desponding, distraught, infuriated **11.** extravagant, precipitate **13.** irretrievable

despicable... **4.** base, vile **6.** odious, shabby **8.** terrible, unworthy, wretched **9.** miserable **12.** contemptible, contemptuous, disreputable, vilipendious

despise... **4.** defy, hate **5.** scorn, scout, spurn **6.** detest, slight **7.** contemn, disdain **8.** vilipend **9.** disregard

despised being... **6.** pariah **7.** outcast

despoil... **3.** rip, rob **4.** riot **5.** reave, rifle, strip **6.** divest, fleece, injure, ravage, ravish **7.** bereave, debauch, deprive, disrobe, pillage, plunder **9.** depredate

despondency... **7.** despair **10.** depression **11.** desperation **13.** heartlessness

despot... **4.** czar (tsar), lord **6.** master, satrap, tyrant **8.** autocrat, dictator **9.** patriarch

despotic... **8.** arrogant **9.** arbitrary, tyrannous **10.** autocratic, tyrannical **11.** dictatorial, patriarchal **12.** governmental

dessert... **3.** ice, pie **4.** cake **5.** fruit,

glacé, sweet **6.** mousse, pastry, sweets **7.** parfait, pudding, sherbet, strudel **8.** ice cream **10.** shoofly pie

destination . . . **3.** end **4.** goal, port **5.** bourn (bourne) **7.** address, destiny **9.** objective

destine . . . **4.** doom, fate **5.** allot **6.** design, devote, intend, ordain **7.** appoint **8.** set apart **9.** designate **10.** foreordain, predestine **12.** predetermine

destiny . . . **3.** end, lot, ure (anc) **4.** bahi, doom, eure, fate, goal **5.** karma, stars **6.** Kismet **7.** fortune **11.** destination

destitute . . . **4.** void **5.** needy **6.** bereft, devoid **7.** forlorn, lacking **8.** bankrupt, forsaken, homeless **9.** abandoned, penniless **10.** down-and-out

destitution . . . **6.** penury **7.** poverty **11.** deprivation **12.** helplessness

destroy . . . **3.** end **4.** kill, rase, raze, root, ruin, sack, slay, undo **5.** abash, annul, erase **6.** ravage **7.** abolish, consume, nullify, unbuild **8.** decimate, demolish, overturn **9.** dismantle, eradicate **10.** annihilate, neutralize **11.** exterminate

destroyer . . . **3.** hun **6.** ruiner, vandal **7.** marplot, wrecker **8.** nihilist, saboteur **9.** iconclast (of images) **11.** torpedo boat

destroying angel . . . **6.** Danite **7.** Abaddon, Amanita (fungus) **8.** Apollyon

destruction . . . **4.** loss, ruin **5.** havoc, waste **7.** killing **8.** downfall, genocide, ravaging, sabotage, shambles **9.** holocaust, overthrow, perdition, ruination **10.** decimation, demolition, desolation, extinction, subversion **11.** devastation, dissolution, extirpation **13.** extermination

destructive . . . **5.** fatal **6.** deadly, mortal **7.** baleful, fateful, ruinous **8.** aneretic (anaeretic), ravaging **10.** calamitous, catawampus, pernicious, subversive

desuetude . . . **6.** disuse, nonuse **9.** cessation **12.** obsolescence **13.** nonemployment **14.** discontinuance

desultory . . . **4.** idle **5.** hasty **6.** roving, wanton **7.** aimless, cursory, wayward **8.** rambling, unsteady, wavering **9.** deviative, orderless, unsettled **10.** discursive, inconstant

detach . . . **4.** part, wean **5.** sever **7.** disjoin, isolate **8.** disunite, separate, withdraw **9.** disengage

detached . . . **4.** free **5.** alone, aloof, scarp **7.** detaché, retired, severed **8.** isolated, secluded, separate, solitary **9.** unrelated, withdrawn **11.** unconnected **12.** disconnected

detachment . . . **8.** disunion **9.** aloneness, aloofness, isolation, seclusion, unconcern **10.** separation **11.** disjunction **14.** demobilization

detail . . . **4.** item, unit **6.** assign **7.** appoint, itemize, minutia, narrate, specify **9.** enumerate, narrative **10.** particular **12.** technicality

details . . . **6.** trivia **8.** minutiae **10.** ins and outs **11.** particulars

detain . . . **4.** hold, keep, stop **5.** check, delay **6.** arrest, hinder, intern, retard **8.** imprison, restrain, withhold

detect . . . **3.** see, spy **4.** show, spot, tail **6.** accuse, descry, reveal **7.** discern, find out, uncover **8.** discover, perceive **9.** recognize

detective . . . **4.** dick **6.** beagle, sleuth, tailer, tracer **7.** gumshoe, spotter **8.** exposing, flatfoot, Hawkshaw, mouchard **9.** operative **12.** investigator

detent . . . **3.** dog **4.** pawl **5.** catch, click, fence **6.** tongue **7.** ratchet

detention . . . **5.** delay, duress **7.** detinue **9.** captivity, hindrance **10.** detainment, internment **11.** restraining, retardation, withholding **12.** imprisonment

deter . . . **5.** daunt, delay, repel **6.** divert, hinder **7.** prevent **8.** restrain **10.** discourage, disincline

deterge . . . **5.** purge **6.** purify **7.** cleanse **8.** depurate **9.** elutriate

detergent . . . **4.** soap **7.** cleaner, purging, saponin (saponine), smectic, solvent **8.** cleanser, medicine, purifier **9.** cleansing **10.** abstergent, lixiviator

deteriorate . . . **4.** wear **6.** impair, weaken, worsen **10.** degenerate, retrogress

deterioration . . . **5.** decay **7.** decline **9.** decadence **10.** debasement, declension, impairment, perversion **11.** degradation **12.** degeneration **13.** retrogression

determinate . . . **5.** fixed **6.** cymose **7.** certain, special **8.** definite, resolute, resolved, specific **9.** arbitrary **10.** definitive, invariable **11.** established, unqualified

determination . . . **4.** will **5.** limit, proof **6.** choice **7.** purpose, resolve, verdict **8.** decision, firmness, judgment **9.** impulsion **10.** conclusion, definition, discussion, resolution, settlement **11.** disputation, measurement, termination **12.** decisiveness, dijudication, resoluteness **13.** specification

determine . . . **3.** end **5.** impel, learn, prove, state **6.** assess, choose, decide, define, direct, ordain, settle **7.** delimit, resolve, specify **8.** conclude, discover **9.** arbitrate, ascertain, stipulate, terminate, variously **10.** dijudicate, foreordain

determined . . . **3.** set **4.** sure **5.** fixed **6.** mulish **7.** assured, cinched, decided, settled **8.** foregone, perverse, resolute, stubborn **9.** obstinate, pigheaded

detest . . . **4.** hate **5.** abhor **6.** loathe **8.** execrate **9.** abominate

detestable . . . **6.** odious **7.** hateful **8.** accursed, terrible **9.** abhorrent, execrable, loathsome, obnoxious **10.** abominable **12.** contemptible

dethrone . . . **6.** depose, disbar, divest **7.** uncrown **8.** disbench

detonation . . . **4.** bang, boom **5.** blast **7.** blowout **8.** backfire **9.** discharge, explosion **10.** combustion

detract . . . **6.** deduce, deduct, vilify **7.** asperse, traduce **8.** belittle, derogate,

distract, subtract, withdraw 9. disparage
10. depreciate
detraction . . . 5. delay 7. calumny,
slander 9. aspersion 10. belittling
11. distraction, subtraction
detriment . . . 4. hurt, loss 6. damage,
injury 8. mischief, weakness
10. impairment, impediment
12. disadvantage
detrimental . . . 7. baleful, baneful,
harmful, hurtful, noxious 9. injurious
10. pernicious 11. deleterious,
mischievous, prejudicial
15. disadvantageous
Deus Fidius . . . 7. Jupiter
Deus vobiscum . . . 12. God be with you
Deus vult . . . 8. God wills (anc cry)
deuterogamy . . . 6. digamy
Deuteronomy (pert to) . . .
comprising . . 10. law of Moses
Fifth Book of . . 10. Pentateuch
meaning . . 11. repeated law (of Moses)
devastate . . . 4. rape, ruin, sack 5. havoc,
strip, waste 6. ravage 7. destroy,
pillage, plunder, scourge 8. demolish,
desolate 10. depopulate
devastation . . . 4. ruin 5. havoc, waste
6. ravage 7. scourge
develop . . . 4. grow 5. arise, ripen, train
6. appear, detect, evolve, expand,
mature, reveal 7. advance, convert,
enlarge, expound, further, improve,
perfect, promote 8. discover, generate
9. elaborate (details)
developed . . . 4. ripe, zoon 5. adult
6. mature, mellow 7. grownup
8. improved 9. perfected 10. precocious
development . . . 6. growth 7. changes,
endysis 8. increase, maturity
9. evolution, expansion, formation,
unfolding 10. maturation
11. elaboration, improvement,
ontogenesis 12. phylogenesis
devest . . . 5. strip 6. denude, divest
7. deprive, undress 8. alienate
Devi (Hind) . . . 3. Uma 4. Kali 5. Durga,
Gauri 6. Chandi, Shakti 7. heroine,
Parvati 8. divinity 9. Haimavati
deviate . . . 3. err, yaw 4. hade, miss, slew,
vary, veer 5. sheer, stray 6. change,
depart, swerve, wander 7. deflect,
digress, diverge
deviation . . . 3. yaw 5. lapse 6. change
7. circuit, synesis 8. aberrant
9. aberrance, deformity, departure,
diverging, obliquity, variation
10. deflection, difference, digressing,
digression, distortion, divergence
11. abnormality 12. eccentricity
device . . . 4. plan, tool 5. motto,
shift, trick 6. design, desire, dingus,
gadget, scheme 7. adjunct, compass,
project, purpose 8. artifice, insignia
9. appliance, expedient, implement,
invention, stratagem 10. instrument
11. contrivance
device (pert to) . . .
bark peeling . . 8. stripper
clamping . . 4. vise 7. pincers
distilling . . 7. alembic
fabric stretching . . 7. stenter

heating . . 4. etna 5. stove
hoisting . . 5. crane, davit, lewis 6. garnet
7. derrick 8. elevator 9. parbuckle
leveling . . 6. gimbal
measuring . . 4. gage, tape 5. chain,
gauge, meter, ruler 9. ergometer,
yardstick 10. micrometer
nautical . . 4. bitt 5. cleat, otter 6. becket
8. paravane
regulating . . 5. valve 9. remontoir
spraying . . 8. atomizer 9. sprinkler
steering . . 4. helm 5. wheel 6. rudder,
tiller
stopping . . 5. brake, sprag
devil . . . 3. imp 4. deil, deva, evil, haze
5. annoy, demon, error, fiend, grill,
ruler (of Hell), Satan, tease 7. hellion,
serpent, tempter, torment 8. printer's
9. archenemy, daredevil, dust devil
devil (pert to) . . .
dog . . 6. marine
bird . . 3. owl 5. swift 10. goatsucker
fish . . 3. ray 5. manta, whale (gray)
7. octopus
grass . . 7. Bermuda
lore . . 10. demonology
tree . . 4. dita
Devil, the . . . 5. Deuce, Eblis, Satan
6. Azazel, Belial, Diablo, Teufel
7. Ahriman, Amaimon (Amammion),
diavolo, Evil One, Lucifer, Old Nick,
Sammael, Shaitan (Sheitan)
8. Apollyon, Asmodeus, Diabolos
9. Archenemy, Archfiend, Beelzebub
11. Auld Clootie 14. Mephistopheles
devilish . . . 5. cruel 6. daring, rakish,
wicked 7. extreme, hellish, satanic
8. fiendish, infernal 9. chthonian
10. demoniacal 11. mischievous
deviltry . . . 6. malice 7. cruelty, devilry
8. mischief 9. diablerie, diabolism
10. black magic, wickedness
12. fiendishness
devious . . . 6. errant, erring, roving,
sinful 7. oblique, vagrant, winding
8. rambling, tortuous 9. deviative,
eccentric 10. circuitous 11. out-of-the-
way 14. unconventional
devise . . . 3. aim 4. form, plan 5. array,
build, frame 6. create, divide, evolve,
invent, scheme, will to 7. appoint,
arrange, bequest, concoct, fashion
8. bequeath, contrive 9. fabricate
10. distribute, excogitate 11. distinguish
deviser of IQ test . . . 5. Binet
devitalize . . . 3. sap 6. weaken
devoid . . . 4. free, void 5. empty
6. faulty, vacant 7. without 9. destitute
11. nonexistent
devoid of . . .
feeling . . 9. apathetic, insensate
interest . . 6. jejune
devote . . . 3. use, vow 5. apply 6. employ,
hallow, resign 7. address, consign,
destine 8. dedicate, set apart
10. consecrate 11. appropriate
devoted . . . 5. loyal, pious, vowed
6. doomed, loving 7. betaken, zealous
8. addicted, constant, faithful, friendly,
obedient 9. dedicated, engrossed,
patriotic

devotee . . . **3.** fan, ist, nun **4.** monk
6. votary **7.** epicure, fanatic, Pietist
8. aesthete (esthete), partisan
devotion . . . **4.** love, zeal **5.** ardor, piety
6. novena, prayer **7.** pietism, worship
8. idolatry **9.** addiction, adoration,
constancy **10.** attachment, dedication,
devoutness, friendship **11.** devotedness,
earnestness, engrossment
12. consecration **13.** appropriation,
religiousness
devour . . . **3.** eat **4.** bolt, gulp, wolf
5. gorge, use up, waste **6.** absorb,
engulf **7.** consume, engorge, swallow
(up) **8.** prey upon **9.** devastate
10. annihilate
devout . . . **4.** holy, warm **5.** godly, pious
6. hearty, solemn **7.** cordial, devoted,
saintly, sincere, zealous **8.** reverent
9. religious, righteous **10.** worshipful
dew . . . **4.** rime **5.** bedew, bloom, roris
dewy . . . **5.** roral, roric
dexterity . . . **3.** art **5.** knack, magic,
skill **7.** ability, address, aptness,
finesse, sleight **8.** aptitude, deftness,
facility **9.** smartness **10.** adroitness
15. right-handedness
dexterous . . . **3.** apt **4.** deft, yare **5.** adept,
handy, quick, ready **6.** adroit, artful,
clever **7.** skilful **8.** skillful **11.** right-
handed
dextral . . . **5.** right (to the) **9.** favorable
diabolical . . . **5.** cruel **6.** wicked **7.** beastly,
demonic, hellish, satanic, ungodly
8. damnable, demoniac, devilish,
fiendish, infernal
diacritic . . . **4.** mark **5.** point **7.** symptom
10. diagnostic **14.** distinguishing
diacritical mark . . . **5.** breve, tilde **6.** tittle
9. diaeresis (dieresis)
diadem . . . **5.** crown, tiara **6.** anadem,
circle, emblem, empire, fillet **7.** coronet
8. headband, insignia, ornament
11. sovereignty
diaeresis, dieresis . . . **4.** mark **5.** break
8. division **10.** resolution
diagnose . . . **7.** analyze **8.** construe
9. interpret
diagnosis . . . **8.** analysis, decision,
nosology **9.** prognosis **14.** interpretation
diagonal . . . **4.** bias **7.** oblique **8.** bendwise
(Her) **10.** transverse **11.** cater-corner
13. cater-cornered
diagram . . . **4.** draw, icon, plan, plot,
tree **5.** chart, epure, gamut, graph
6. design **7.** drawing **9.** blueprint
dial . . . **4.** disk **5.** plate **8.** horologe
9. indicator, timepiece **11.** chronometer
dialect . . . **5.** idiom, lingo **6.** patois,
speech **7.** diction **8.** language, locution,
parlance **10.** vernacular
dialect (pert to) . . .
Afrikaans . . **4.** Taal
Aramaic . . **6.** Syriac
Aryan . . **4.** Pali
provincial . . **6.** patois
Semitic . . **4.** Geez
diameter . . . **2.** pi (3.1416) **4.** bore **5.** width
6. module, radius **7.** breadth, caliber
(calibre) **9.** thickness
diametric, diametrical . . . **6.** averse

7. adverse **8.** antipode, opposite
9. antipodal, diametral
diamond . . . **3.** gem, ice **5.** cards, field
(baseball), jager, jewel, plane **6.** carbon
7. adamant, infield, lozenge, rhombus
8. treasure
diamond (pert to) . . .
base . . **5.** culet
crystal . . **7.** glassie
cutting . . **4.** bort
cutting cups . . **3.** dop
famed . . **4.** pitt **5.** Sancy **6.** Orloff
7. Lesotho (601 carat) **8.** Cullinan, Koh-
i-noor **9.** Excelsior **10.** Great Mogul
14. Star of the South
surface . . **5.** facet
weight . . **5.** carat (karat)
Diamond State . . . **8.** Delaware
diaphanous . . . **4.** fine, thin **5.** filmy,
gauzy, lucid, sheer **6.** flimsy
9. gossamery **11.** translucent,
transparent
diaphragm . . . **4.** wall **6.** middle, septum
7. midriff **9.** partition
diary . . . **3.** log **6.** record **7.** journal
8. register **9.** chronicle
13. autobiography
diaskeuast . . . **6.** editor **7.** reviser
diatribe . . . **6.** screed, tirade **7.** lecture
8. berating, harangue **9.** invective,
philippic **10.** discussion (prolonged)
dice . . . **3.** cog, die (sing) **4.** cube, game,
sice (6's) **5.** bones, craps, cubes
7. ivories, tessera
Dickens characters . . . **3.** Tim **4.** Dora,
Nell **5.** Fagin, Miggs, Sikes **6.** Cuttle
7. Barnaby, Scrooge **9.** Pecksniff
10. Chuzzlewit **11.** Oliver Twist
Dickens pseudonym . . . **3.** Boz
dictate . . . **3.** law **4.** rule **5.** maxim,
order, utter **6.** advise, dictum, enjoin,
impose **7.** command, deliver, require,
suggest **9.** prescribe **10.** injunction
dictatorial . . . **5.** bossy **6.** lordly
7. pompous **8.** absolute, arrogant,
despotic, dogmatic, oracular, positive
9. imperious, masterful, pragmatic
10. autocratic, dogmatical, imperative,
peremptory **11.** categorical,
domineering, magisterial, opinionated,
overbearing **13.** authoritative
diction . . . **5.** style **6.** language, parlance
phrasing **9.** elocution **10.** vocabulary
11. enunciation, phraseology
14. expressiveness
dictionary . . . **5.** words **7.** calepin, lexicon
8. wordbook **9.** reference **10.** vocabulary
11. terminology
dictionary compiler . . . **7.** Webster
(Noah) **13.** lexicographer
dictum . . . **3.** saw **5.** adage, maxim
6. saying **7.** opinion, precept, proverb
8. aphorism, apothegm **11.** declaration
didactic . . . **8.** teaching **9.** mentorial
10. preceptive **11.** instructive
dido . . . **5.** antic, caper, prank, trick **6.** frolic
Dido (also Elissa) . . . **5.** Queen (of
Carthage) **8.** Princess (Tyrian)
die . . . see also *dice* **4.** fade, mold, pass,
seal, wane **5.** stamp **6.** expire, perish,
recede, vanish, wither **7.** decease,

succumb **8.** languish **12.** extinguished (to be)
die-hard . . . **4.** Tory **11.** British Army **12.** Conservative
dies . . . **3.** day
dies atri . . . **9.** black days
dies faustus . . . **13.** favorable omen (day of)
diet . . . **4.** fare **5.** board **6.** Hoftag, ration, viands **7.** Council, Landtag, regimen **8.** assembly, Kreistag **9.** allowance, nutrition, Reichstag **10.** Parliament
Diet (of) . . . **5.** Worms (1521) **6.** Speyer (1529), Spires **8.** Augsburg (1530)
dietetics . . . **8.** sitology **9.** nutrition **12.** biochemistry, dietotherapy
differ . . . **4.** vary **5.** clash **7.** dispute, dissent, quarrel **8.** disagree
difference . . . **3.** sum **5.** shade **6.** nuance **8.** variance **10.** inequality, unlikeness **11.** contrariety, distinction, distinguish **12.** disagreement, discriminate **13.** differentiate, dissimilarity
different . . . **4.** many **5.** novel, other **6.** divers, sundry, unlike **7.** diverse, several, unequal, unusual, variant **8.** assorted, contrary, distinct, manifold, opposite, separate, variform **9.** divergent, otherwise **10.** dissimilar, variegated **11.** diversified **13.** heterogeneous
different place . . . **9.** elsewhere **10.** otherwhere
difficulty . . . **3.** bar, rub **4.** clog, crux, knot, snag **5.** cavil, check, demur, nodus **6.** plight, scrape, strait **7.** barrier, problem, trouble **8.** obstacle **9.** hindrance **10.** impediment, ruggedness **11.** obstruction **12.** disagreement
difficulty in swallowing . . . **9.** dysphagia
diffidence . . . **5.** doubt, qualm **7.** anxiety, modesty **8.** distrust, humility, timidity **10.** hesitation **11.** bashfulness **12.** apprehension
diffident . . . **3.** coy, shy **5.** timid **6.** modest **7.** anxious **8.** doubtful, reserved, retiring **9.** shrinking, unwilling **11.** distrustful **12.** apprehensive
diffuse . . . **4.** full, shed **5.** strew **6.** expand, extend, prolix **7.** copious, perplex, pervade, publish, radiate, refract, verbose **8.** disperse **9.** redundant **10.** widespread
diffused . . . **5.** loose **6.** sparse **7.** flowing **9.** dispersed
diffusion . . . **7.** osmosis **9.** pervasion, radiation **10.** dispersion, refraction
dig . . . **3.** jab **4.** find, grub, mine, open, pion, prod, root **5.** delve, dwell, spade **6.** exhume, loosen, pierce, plunge, search, thrust **7.** extract, unearth **8.** excavate **10.** understand
digamy . . . **11.** deuterogamy **12.** twice married (legally)
digest . . . **4.** code **5.** brief **6.** abrégé, codify **7.** epitome, Pandect **8.** abstract, classify, synopsis **10.** assimilate, compendium
digestion . . . **6.** pepsis **8.** eupepsia **9.** dyspepsia, ingestion **10.** absorption **12.** alimentation, assimilation

digestive secretions . . . **4.** bile, gall **6.** pepsin, rennin **7.** chalone, gastric, glucase, hormone, maltase **8.** salivary, thyroxin **9.** endocrine **10.** intestinal, pancreatic
digestive tract . . . **7.** enteron **15.** alimentary canal
digger . . . **3.** loy, pal **4.** plow, wasp **5.** spade **6.** Indian, sapper **7.** comrade, soldier **8.** Levelers **9.** excavator **12.** New Zealander
digit . . . **3.** toe **4.** unit **5.** thumb **6.** finger, number (under 10) **7.** dewclaw, integer, measure
digits repeated . . . **8.** repetend
digitus . . . **6.** finger, tarsus **8.** dactylus
dignified . . . **5.** grand, lofty, manly, sober, staid **6.** august, graced, sedate **7.** courtly, pompous, togated **8.** decorous, ennobled, imposing, majestic **9.** venerable **11.** ceremonious **12.** aristocratic
dignify . . . **5.** exalt, grace, honor **7.** elevate, ennoble **9.** solemnize **11.** distinguish
dignitary . . . **3.** don **4.** rank **5.** mogul **6.** priest, sachem **7.** magnate, notable, prelate **9.** clergyman
dignity . . . **4.** rank **5.** grace, honor **6.** status **7.** decorum, majesty **8.** nobility, prestige, standing **9.** loftiness, nobleness **10.** excellence, sedateness
diagraph . . . **8.** ligature **9.** diphthong
digress . . . **4.** veer **5.** shift **6.** swerve, wander **7.** deviate **9.** turn aside **10.** transgress
digression . . . **4.** loop **6.** ecbole **7.** circuit, episode **8.** excursus **9.** deviation, excursion, obliquity **10.** discussion
digressive . . . **8.** rambling **9.** deviative, excursive, wandaring **10.** circuitous, discursive
dike, dyke . . . **3.** bar, dig, gap **4.** bank, gulf, ha-ha, mole, pond, pool **5.** ditch, levee, mound **7.** barrier, channel **8.** causeway, estacade **9.** earthwork **10.** embankment **11.** watercourse **13.** fortification
diked land . . . **6.** polder
dike rock . . . **7.** odinite
dik-dik . . . **8.** antelope
dilapidation . . . **4.** ruin **5.** decay, waste **7.** breakup **9.** disrepair **10.** impairment **11.** dissolution **13.** decomposition **14.** disintegration
dilate . . . **5.** bulge, swell, widen **6.** expand **7.** distend, enlarge, inflate **9.** expatiate
dilation . . . **7.** ectasia, ectasis **8.** swelling **9.** expansion **10.** dilatation, distension
dilatory . . . **3.** lax **4.** slow **5.** slack, tardy **6.** fabian, remiss **8.** backward, delaying, inactive, sluggish **10.** behindhand **13.** lackadaisical **15.** procrastinating
dilemma . . . **4.** trap **5.** brike (obs), snare **8.** argument, quandary **10.** perplexity **11.** alternative, predicament
dilettante . . . **7.** amateur, dabbler, devotee, esthete (aesthete)
diligence . . . **4.** care, heed **6.** effort **7.** caution **8.** industry, sedulity **9.** assiduity, attention, constancy

10. stagecoach **11.** application, earnestness, painstaking
12. heedlessness, perseverance, sedulousness **15.** industriousness
diligent . . . **4.** busy **6.** active **7.** operose **8.** sedulous **9.** assiduous, attentive, laborious **11.** industrious, persevering
dill, dill seed . . . **4.** anet, herb **5.** anise (Bib) **6.** fennel
dillydally . . . **3.** lag **6.** linger, loiter, trifle **9.** vacillate **12.** shilly-shally **13.** procrastinate
dilute . . . **3.** cut **4.** thin **6.** debase, rarefy, reduce, weaken **8.** lengthen **9.** attenuate **10.** adulterate **12.** denaturalize
diluted . . . **4.** thin, weak **7.** reduced, thinned, watered **10.** attenuated
dim . . . **4.** dull, fade, pale **5.** bleak, blear, faint **6.** darken **7.** darkish, dimness, eclipse, obscure **8.** overcast **10.** caliginous, indistinct, mysterious
dimension . . . **4.** size **6.** extent, height, length **7.** breadth **9.** magnitude, thickness **11.** measurement **13.** circumference
diminish . . . **3.** ebb **4.** bate, fade, pare, ploy, wane **5.** abase, abate, lower, peter, taper **6.** lessen, recede, reduce, weaken **7.** curtail, dwindle **8.** decrease, subtract **9.** disparage
diminution . . . **5.** abate, taper **7.** litotes **8.** decrease, lowering **9.** decrement, lessening, reduction **10.** moderation
diminutive . . . **3.** wee **4.** runt, slip **5.** minny, small **6.** bantam, little, peewee, petite **7.** bendlet
diminutive suffix . . . **2.** el, ie **3.** ole, ule **4.** ette
dimmer . . . **8.** rheostat
din . . . **4.** ding **5.** clang, noise **6.** clamor, hubbub, racket, rattle, tumult, uproar **7.** clatter, turmoil **9.** commotion
diner . . . **5.** eater
dingle . . . **4.** dale, dell, glen, ring, vale **6.** jingle, tingle, tinkle, valley **7.** tremble **9.** storm door
dining room . . . **4.** hall **5.** salon **6.** spence **7.** cenacle **8.** mess hall **9.** refectory **12.** salle à manger
dining science . . . **10.** aristology
dinosaur . . . **7.** reptile **8.** sauropod **9.** Sauropoda **10.** Diplodocus, Morosaurus **11.** Ornithopoda, Stegosaurus **12.** Brontosaurus, Ceratosaurus, Megalosaurus, Palaeosaurus **13.** Atlantosaurus, Tyrannosaurus
diocese . . . **3.** see **6.** parish **8.** district, province **9.** bishopric **12.** jurisdiction
Diocletian martyr (Rome) . . . **5.** Agnes
Dionysian . . . **4.** wild **8.** frenzied, sensuous **9.** orgiastic
Dionysus (pert to) . . .
  birthplace . . **6.** Thebes
  father . . **4.** Zeus
  festival . . **8.** Dionysia
  god of (Gr) . . **4.** wine (Bacchus, later) **10.** vegetation
  lover . . **6.** Selene
  mother . . **6.** Semele
Dioscuri, The (Gr Myth) . . . **4.** cult

5. twins (Castor and Pollux) **8.** Castores **10.** Polydeuces
dip . . . **3.** dap, dib, sop **4.** bail, dunk, lade **5.** merge, merse, pitch, rinse, scoop, slope, souse **6.** candle, plunge **7.** baptize, immerse **9.** declivity **10.** pickpocket **11.** hors d'oeuvre
diphthong, dipthong . . . **5.** sound **7.** digraph **8.** ligature
diploma . . . **8.** testamur **9.** sheepskin **10.** credential **11.** certificate, testimonial
diplomacy . . . **4.** tact **7.** address, cunning **9.** dexterity **10.** artfulness, discretion **11.** arbitration, diplomatism, negotiation, savoir-faire
diplomat . . . **5.** doyen (head), envoy **6.** consul **7.** attaché **8.** emissary, minister **10.** ambassador, politician **15.** chargé d'affaires, plenipotentiary
diplomatic . . . **6.** crafty **7.** cunning **8.** consular **11.** mediatorial
diplomatic corps, staff . . . **7.** embassy **8.** legation **17.** corps diplomatique
dipsomania . . . **9.** addiction, oenomania, potomania **10.** alcoholism **15.** delirium tremens
dipthong . . . see *diphthong*
dire . . . **3.** bad **4.** base, evil, rank, want **5.** awful, fatal, needy **6.** deadly, dismal, funest, odious **7.** baneful, doleful, fearful, ghastly **8.** dreadful, horrible, terrible, ultimate **10.** oppressive **12.** inauspicious, overpowering
direct . . . **3.** ain, bid, con **4.** bend, boss, head, lead, turn **5.** order, pilot, refer, steer, teach **6.** govern, manage **7.** avigate, command, conduct, marshal **8.** instruct, straight **9.** influence
direction . . . **3.** way **4.** airt, bent, care, east, west **5.** avast, belay, north, route, south, trend **6.** advice, course **7.** address, command, pointer **8.** guidance **10.** management **11.** instruction **15.** superintendence
directly . . . **4.** soon **6.** pronto **7.** shortly **8.** as soon as, promptly **9.** forthwith, instantly, presently **11.** immediately
directly opposite . . . **9.** antipodal, diametric **10.** antipodean
director . . . **4.** boss **5.** aimer (gunner) **6.** conner, leader **7.** manager, teacher **8.** governor, producer **14.** superintendent
director's cry . . . **3.** Cut!
direful . . . **4.** dire **6.** woeful **8.** dreadful, terrible **10.** calamitous
dirge . . . **4.** keen, Mass, song **5.** psalm, rites **6.** lament **7.** requiem **8.** coronach
dirigible . . . **4.** Roma **5.** blimp **7.** balloon **10.** Shenandoah **12.** Graf Zeppelin
Dirigo . . . **5.** I Lead **7.** I Direct (Maine motto)
dirk . . . **4.** snee, stab **5.** knife, sword **6.** dagger
dirt . . . **3.** mud **4.** dust, foul, land, muck, soil **5.** earth, filth, grime, stain **6.** gossip, refuse **7.** scandal, slander **9.** obscenity
dirty . . . **4.** foul, mean **5.** dingy, foggy, gusty, mucky, nasty **6.** bemire, filthy, soiled, stormy, untidy **7.** clouded, muddied, squalid, sullied

dis (pert to) . . .
Greek . . **5.** Pluto
Norse . . **5.** Freya **7.** spirits **9.** Valkyries
11. superhumans
prefix . . **5.** twice **6.** double
Roman . . **3.** Dis **8.** Dis pater **12.** realm
of Pluto

disable . . . **4.** maim **5.** unfit **6.** impair,
weaken **7.** cripple **9.** disparage,
hamstring **10.** disqualify **12.** incapacitate

disadvantage . . . **3.** out **4.** harm, hurt
6. damage, injury **7.** penalty, trouble
8. drawback, handicap **9.** detriment,
liability, prejudice **12.** inexpedience
13. inconvenience

disagreeable . . . **4.** edgy **5.** cross, nasty
7. fulsome **8.** unsavory **9.** dissonant,
invidious, irritable, offensive, repugnant
10. ill-humored, unpleasant
11. displeasing, ill-tempered,
incongruous **13.** uncomfortable

disagreement . . . **5.** clash **7.** detente,
discord, dispute, dissent, wrangle
8. variance **9.** diversity **10.** contention,
difference, dissension, unlikeness
11. contrariety, controversy,
discrepancy, incongruity
13. nonconformity
16. misunderstanding

disappear . . . **3.** die **4.** face, pass **5.** cease
6. be lost, perish, vanish **7.** dwindle
8. evanesce **9.** evaporate

disappoint . . . **4.** balk, bilk, fail, fall, foil
6. baffle, thwart **7.** let down **9.** frustrate
10. disenchant, dissatisfy **11.** disillusion

disappointment . . . **3.** rue **6.** defeat
7. failure **10.** bafflement **11.** frustration
15. dissatisfaction

disapprobation . . . **5.** odium
11. disapproval **12.** condemnation
13. disparagement

disapproval . . . **3.** boo **4.** hiss, veto
7. censure, protest **9.** objection,
rejection **12.** condemnation
14. disapprobation

disarrange . . . **4.** muss **5.** upset **6.** foul up,
jumble **7.** disturb **8.** disorder, unsettle
10. discompose **11.** disorganize

disarray . . . **5.** strip **6.** unrobe **7.** despoil,
undress, unkempt **8.** disorder
9. confusion, ungarment **10.** disarrange,
dishabille **12.** discomposure,
dishevelment

disaster . . . **4.** evil, ruin **6.** mishap
8. accident, calamity, casualty, fatality
9. cataclysm, mischance **10.** misfortune
11. catastrophe **12.** misadventure

disastrous . . . **4.** dire **7.** unlucky **8.** ill-
fated **9.** ill-boding **10.** calamitous
11. destructive, unfortunate
12. unpropitious

disavow . . . **4.** deny **6.** abjure, disown,
recant, refuse **7.** decline, retract
8. disclaim, renounce **9.** disaffirm,
repudiate

disbeliever . . . **5.** pagan **7.** atheist,
heathen, heretic, infidel **8.** agnostic

disburse . . . **5.** spend **6.** defray, expend,
pay out

disbursement . . . **5.** outgo **6.** outlay
7. payment **8.** spending **11.** expenditure

disc . . . see also *disk* **3.** man **4.** dial,
puck **5.** medal, plate, quoit, wheel
6. circle, record **7.** discoid **8.** artifact
9. gyroscope, medallion

discard . . . **4.** drip, shed **5.** scrap, sluff
6. disuse, reject, remove **7.** abandon,
cast off, dismiss, forsake **9.** eliminate,
eradicate, throw away

discern . . . **3.** see, spy **4.** espy, know,
read, view **5.** sight **6.** behold,
descry, detect **7.** witness **8.** discover,
perceive **10.** understand **11.** distinguish
12. discriminate **13.** differentiate

discernible . . . **7.** evident, obvious,
visible **8.** apparent, distinct, knowable,
manifest **11.** conspicuous, perceptible
15. distinguishable

discerning . . . **4.** sage **5.** acute, sharp
6. astute, shrewd **9.** sagacious
14. discriminating, discriminative

discernment . . . **4.** tact **5.** taste **6.** acumen
7. insight **8.** sagacity **9.** sharpness
10. astuteness, perception, shrewdness
12. perspicacity **14.** discrimination

discharge . . . **2.** do **4.** bang, cass, fire,
sack, shot **5.** blast, egest, eject, erupt,
expel, exude, flash, salvo, shoot,
speed **6.** acquit, bounce, defray,
exempt, pay off, report, unload, volley
7. dismiss, execute, explode, payment,
quietus, release **8.** emission, eruption
9. acquittal, dismissal, excretion,
execution, explosion, fusillade
10. accomplish, detonation, observance
11. performance

disciple . . . **5.** chela, Judas, pupil
7. apostle, convert, learner, scholar,
student **8.** adherent, believer, follower

disciples (Bib) . . . **6.** twelve (72, Vulgate)
10. Christians

disciplinarian . . . **7.** Puritan, teacher,
trainer **8.** martinet

discipline . . . **4.** rule, whip **6.** govern,
punish **7.** chasten, control, culture,
educate, penance, scourge **8.** training
9. education, restraint **10.** correction,
punishment **11.** castigation, instruction,
self-control **12.** chastisement
13. regimentation

disclaim . . . **4.** deny **6.** abjure, cry
out, disown, recant, refuse, reject
7. disavow **8.** abnegate, disallow,
renounce **9.** repudiate

disclose . . . **4.** bare, open, show, tell
5. utter **6.** expose, impart, reveal,
unmask, unveil **7.** divulge, uncloak,
unclose **8.** discover, indicate

disclosure . . . **6.** exposé **8.** exposure
9. discovery, revealing, unmasking,
unveiling **10.** appearance, revealment,
revelation

discolor . . . **4.** spot **5.** stain **6.** bruise
7. distain (anc), tarnish **9.** ecchymose
(by blood)

discolored . . . **4.** doty (by decay) **5.** faded
7. altered **8.** ustulate **10.** variegated

discomfit . . . **4.** balk, rout **5.** upset
6. baffle, defeat, dismay **7.** confuse
9. embarrass, frustrate, overthrow
10. disconcert

discomfiture . . . **4.** rout **6.** defeat, flurry

7. letdown **9.** confusion, overthrow
10. bafflement **11.** frustration
13. embarrassment, inconvenience
14. disappointment
discomfort . . . **4.** pain **6.** sorrow
   7. misease **8.** distress **9.** annoyance
   10. uneasiness **11.** displeasure
   13. embarrassment, inconvenience
discommode . . . **6.** bother, molest,
   put out **7.** trouble **9.** incommode
   13. inconvenience
discompose . . . **4.** fret **5.** upset **6.** excite,
   flurry, rubble **7.** agitate, confuse,
   derange, disturb, fluster **8.** unsettle
   9. embarrass **10.** disarrange, disconcert
disconcert . . . **5.** abash, alarm **6.** rattle,
   thwart **7.** confuse, disturb, fluster,
   nonplus **8.** bewilder **9.** discomfit
   embarrass **10.** disarrange
disconnect . . . **5.** sever **6.** detach, unyoke
   7. disjoin **8.** disunite, separate, uncouple
disconnected . . . **6.** broken **8.** detached,
   rambling **9.** desultory, scattered
   10. disjointed, incoherent
   11. unconnected
disconsolate . . . **3.** sad **6.** gloomy,
   woeful **7.** forlorn **8.** desolate, hopeless
   9. sorrowful **10.** despairing, despondent,
   melancholy **12.** inconsolable
discontent . . . **6.** misery, unrest
   8. disquiet **10.** unquietude, uneasiness
   11. displeasure, unhappiness
   14. discontentment **15.** dissatisfaction
discontinue . . . **3.** end **4.** drop, quit, stop
   5. cease **6.** desist, give up **7.** abandon,
   refrain **8.** intermit **9.** terminate
discord . . . **3.** din **5.** noise **6.** strife
   7. dissent **8.** disunity, variance
   9. cacophony, Discordia, harshness
   10. antagonism, contention, difference,
   discordant, disharmony, dissension,
   dissonance **11.** altercation
   12. disagreement
discord (goddess of) . . . **3.** Ate **4.** Eris
discordant . . . **5.** harsh **7.** grating, jarring
   8. contrary, jangling **11.** cacophonous,
   disagreeing, incongruous, quarrelsome,
   unmelodious **12.** inconsistent,
   inharmonious **14.** irreconcilable
discordant (pert to) . . .
   music . . **8.** scordato
   serenade . . **9.** charivari **10.** callithump
   sound . . **6.** jangle
discount . . . **3.** cut **4.** agio **6.** rebate,
   reduce **8.** mark down **9.** abatement,
   allowance, reduction **10.** concession,
   percentage
discourage . . . **4.** damp **5.** check, daunt,
   deter **6.** deject, dismay, oppose
   7. depress **8.** dispirit, dissuade
   10. dishearten
discourse . . . **4.** talk, tell **5.** essay,
   paper (written), prose, speak, spiel
   6. homily, lesson, screed, sermon
   7. account, address, article, declaim,
   discant, dissert, expound, lecture,
   narrate, oration **8.** converse, treatise
   9. expatiate, narrative **10.** exposition,
   recitation **12.** conversation, dissertation
discourteous . . . **4.** rude **7.** uncivil
   8. impolite, insolent **9.** ungallant

10. ungracious **13.** disrespectful
discover . . . **3.** see **4.** espy, find **5.** learn
   6. descry, detect, expose **7.** exhibit, find
   out, uncover, unearth **9.** apprehend,
   ascertain
discoverer . . . **3.** spy **5.** scout
discoverer of . . .
   America . . **4.** Eric (the Red) **7.** Vikings
   8. Columbus (1492)
   blood circulation . . **6.** Harvey
   electric light . . **6.** Edison
   North Pole . . **5.** Peary (1909)
   radium . . **5.** Curie (Madame)
   South Pole . . **8.** Amundsen (1911)
   telegraph . . **5.** Morse (Samuel)
   telephone . . **4.** Bell (Alexander)
   vaccination . . **6.** Jenner
discovery, logic of . . . **8.** heuretic
discredit . . . **5.** doubt **7.** asperse, falsify,
   scandal **8.** disgrace, dishonor, disprove,
   distrust **9.** disbelief, disparage,
   disrepute, misgiving, suspicion
   10. invalidate **11.** discredence
discreet . . . **4.** wary **5.** civil **6.** polite
   7. careful, mindful, politic, prudent
   8. cautious **9.** judicious, selective
   11. circumspect **12.** noncommittal
   13. discretionary
discrepancy . . . **8.** variance **9.** disaccord,
   disparity, diversity **10.** difference
   11. contrariety **12.** disagreement
   13. inconsistency **15.** incompatibility
discretion . . . **4.** tact, will **6.** option
   7. caution, reserve **8.** judgment,
   prudence, wariness **11.** disjunction
   12. cautiousness, discreetness
   13. discontinuity, judiciousness,
   secretiveness **14.** circumspection,
   discrimination
discretionary . . . **7.** politic, prudent
   8. discreet **9.** arbitrary, judicious,
   voluntary **10.** prudential **11.** considerate
   14. discriminating
discriminate . . . **6.** divide, screen, secern
   8. separate, set apart **11.** distinguish
   13. differentiate
discrimination . . . **5.** taste **6.** acumen,
   option **9.** prejudice **10.** discretion
   11. discernment, distinction,
   penetration, segregation
discursive . . . **6.** roving **7.** cursory
   9. desultory, diffusive, wandering
   10. circuitous, digressive
discus . . . **4.** disk **5.** plate, quoit
discuss . . . **3.** air, rap **4.** moot **5.** argue,
   treat **6.** confer, debate, parley
   7. bargain, canvass, dispute, dissert,
   mention **8.** talk over **9.** discourse,
   thrash out
discus thrower . . . **10.** discobolus
disdain . . . **5.** pride, scorn **7.** askance,
   contemn, despise **8.** contempt
   9. arrogance **11.** haughtiness
   16. contemptuousness
disease . . . **6.** malady **7.** ailment, illness,
   trouble **8.** disorder, sickness **9.** affection,
   infirmity **10.** affliction, disability
   11. derangement
disease (of) . . .
   animals (Afr) . . **5.** nenta
   apoplexy . . **4.** esca

apples.. **7.** stippen **9.** bitter pit
blood.. **6.** anemia **8.** leukemia
(leukaemia, leucemia)
cattle.. **5.** hoose (hooze) **6.** nagana,
wheeze **7.** anthrax
chickens.. **3.** pip **4.** roup
diet.. **7.** rickets **8.** pellagra, rachitis
divers.. **5.** bends **7.** caisson
dog.. **5.** lyssa **6.** rabies **11.** hydrophobia
eye.. **6.** caligo **7.** pinkeye **8.** cataract,
glaucoma, trachoma **9.** amaurosis
14. conjunctivitis
fungus.. **6.** mildew **9.** elm blight
Oriental.. **8.** beriberi
painful.. **7.** lumbago **9.** arthritis
plant.. **4.** rust, smut **5.** ergot, scald
6. Panama (banana) **7.** erinose (grape)
potato, tomato.. **8.** dartrose
skin.. **5.** hives, psora **6.** eczema, herpes,
tetter **7.** scabies **8.** impetigo, shingles
9. psoriasis, urticaria **10.** erysipelas
stonecutter's.. **9.** silicosis
sugar cane.. **5.** sereh
disease (pert to)...
classification.. **8.** nosology
10. nosography
decline.. **9.** catabasis
determination of.. **9.** diagnosis
germ transfer.. **7.** vection
native to.. **7.** endemic
outlook.. **9.** prognosis
science of.. **8.** etiology, medicine
spread of.. **8.** epidemic
suffix.. **4.** itis, osis
treatment.. **7.** therapy **12.** kinesiatrics
disembark... **4.** land **6.** alight, debark
7. deplane, detrain, pile out (sl)
disembowel... **3.** gut **10.** eviscerate
disengage... **5.** clear **6.** detach, loosen
7. release **8.** liberate, unfasten
9. extricate **11.** disencumber,
disentangle **12.** disembarrass
disentangle... **4.** card, comb **5.** clear,
loose, ravel, solve **6.** evolve, sleave,
sleeve **7.** unravel, unsnare, untwine,
untwist **9.** simplify **9.** disengage,
extricate **10.** disinvolve, unscramble
disfavor... **7.** dislike **8.** distaste
9. detriment, disrepute **10.** alienation
11. disapproval, displeasure
14. discountenance
disfigure... **3.** mar **4.** scar **6.** deface,
deform, injure, mangle, uglify
7. blemish **8.** mutilate
disgorge... **4.** barf (sl), spew, vent
5. eject, eruct, erupt, expel, heave,
vomit **7.** exhaust **9.** discharge
10. relinquish **11.** regurgitate
disgrace... **5.** abase, odium, shame,
shend, sully **7.** attaint, degrade, distain,
obloquy, upbraid **8.** dishonor, ignominy,
reproach **9.** discredit, disesteem,
disrepute, humiliate **10.** opprobrium
11. abomination, humiliation
13. disparagement
disguise... **3.** mum (mumm) **4.** mask,
veil **5.** cloak, feign **6.** covert, masque
7. conceal, costume, falsify, pretend
9. dissemble, incognito, inebriate
10. camouflage, masquerade
11. dissimulate **12.** misrepresent

disgust... **6.** nausea **7.** offense, quarrel
8. aversion, loathing, nauseate
9. animosity, annoyance, antipathy,
revulsion **10.** abhorrence, repugnance
11. abomination
disgusting... **5.** gross, nasty **6.** filthy,
odious **9.** loathsome, obnoxious,
offensive, repellent, repulsive, revolting,
sickening
dish... **3.** jar, pot **4.** boat (gravy) **5.** cruse,
nappy, paten, plate **6.** patera, saucer,
tureen **7.** charger (anc), platter, ramekin
9. casserole
dish (food)... **5.** kibbe (kibbeh), pilaf,
pilau, salmi **6.** hachis, haslet, omelet,
potage, ragout **7.** bok choy, chowder,
falafel (felafel), pudding, soufflé **10.** egg
foo yong, shish kabob **11.** ratatouille
dishabille... **6.** kimono **7.** négligé,
undress **8.** bathrobe, negligee, peignoir
9. housecoat, nightgown
dishearten... **5.** amate (anc), appal,
daunt, deter, unman **6.** deject, dismay
7. depress, unnerve **8.** dispirit
10. disconcert, discourage
disheveled... **5.** tousy **6.** frowzy,
mussed, shaggy, untidy **7.** ruffled,
tousled, tumbled, unkempt **8.** deranged,
uncombed **10.** disarrayed, disordered
11. disarranged
dishonest... **4.** base **5.** false, lying
6. crafty, unjust **7.** corrupt, crooked,
knavish **8.** rascally, scheming
9. deceitful, truthless **10.** fraudulent,
mendacious, perfidious, untruthful
12. dishonorable
dishonor... **5.** shame **6.** defame,
infamy **7.** debauch, degrade, obloquy
8. disgrace, ignominy, reproach
9. desecrate, disrepute, improbity
10. disrespect, opprobrium
13. disparagement
dishonorable... **7.** ignoble **8.** infamous,
shameful **9.** dishonest **10.** inglorious
11. disesteemed, disgraceful
12. disreputable
disillusion... **10.** disquixote
disillusioned... **8.** thwarted
12. disappointed, disenchanted
disinclination... **7.** dislike **8.** aversion,
distaste **10.** reluctance, repugnance
12. disaffection **13.** indisposition
disinclined... **6.** averse **8.** indolent
9. reluctant, unwilling **10.** indisposed
disinfectant... **5.** Lysol **6.** cresol,
iodine, phenol **7.** alcohol **9.** germicide
10. antiseptic **12.** formaldehyde
disintegrate... **5.** decay, erode **7.** break
up, corrode, crumble, disband, resolve
8. dissolve **9.** decompose
11. disorganize
disinter... **5.** dig up **6.** exhume, reveal
disjoin... **4.** part, undo **5.** sever,
untie **6.** detach, sunder, unhook
7. unhitch **8.** disunite, separate,
unbutton **9.** disengage **10.** disconnect,
dissociate
disk, disc... **4.** puck **5.** medal, paten,
plate, quoit, wafer, wheel **6.** harrow,
record, sequin **7.** discoid, medalet
9. faceplate, gyroscope, medallion

dislike . . . **4.** mind **5.** odium **6.** detest
8. aversion, distaste **9.** antipathy,
disrelish **12.** disaffection
dislike of children . . . **9.** misopedia
dislike of home . . . **9.** ecophobia
disloyal . . . **5.** false **6.** fickle, untrue
9. faithless **10.** inconstant, perfidious,
unfaithful **11.** treacherous
dismal . . . **3.** sad, wan **4.** dark **5.** black,
bleak, drear, lurid **6.** dreary, gloomy,
somber **7.** doleful, joyless, Stygian,
unhappy, unlucky **8.** dolorous, dreadful,
funereal, lonesome, mournful, overcast,
sinister **9.** ill-omened, sorrowful
10. calamitous, depressing, lugubrious
11. pessimistic, unfortunate
dismantle . . . **4.** raze, undo **5.** strip
6. divest **7.** deprive, destroy, disrobe,
uncloak **8.** demolish **11.** disassemble
dismay . . . **4.** fear **5.** alarm, daunt
6. appall, fright, terror **8.** affright,
bewilder **9.** dejection **10.** depression,
disconcert **12.** apprehension
13. consternation **14.** discouragement
dismiss . . . **4.** drip, fire **5.** amand, amove,
eject, exile, remue **6.** acquit, bounce,
depose, recall, refute, shelve **7.** forgive,
release **8.** relegate **9.** discharge,
disregard **10.** relinquish
dismount . . . **6.** alight **7.** descend,
unhorse, unmount **11.** disassemble
disobedient . . . **7.** forward, froward,
wayward **8.** mutinous **10.** rebellious,
refractory **11.** intractable
12. contumacious
disorder . . . **3.** tic **4.** mess, riot **5.** chaos,
deray, snarl **6.** malady, tumult
7. ailment, anarchy, derange, illness,
misdeed **8.** disarray, paranoia, sickness
9. confusion, craziness, distemper,
paranomia **10.** discompose, revolution
11. lawlessness, misdemeanor
12. irregularity **13.** indisposition
14. disarrangement **15.** disorganization
disorderly . . . **3.** bad **5.** mussy, rowdy
6. unruly **7.** chaotic, naughty, violent
8. confused, rowdyish, slipshod
9. irregular, offensive, turbulent
12. ungovernable, unmanageable
disorganization . . . **5.** decay **7.** anarchy,
breakup, split-up **8.** disorder
10. separation **11.** destruction,
dissolution **13.** disbandment
14. disarrangement, disintegration
disown . . . **4.** deny **5.** expel **6.** recant,
reject **7.** disavow **8.** disclaim, renounce
9. disaffirm, repudiate **10.** disinherit
disparage . . . **3.** dis **4.** slam, slur **5.** decry,
lower **6.** lessen, slight **7.** degrade,
detract, run down **8.** bad-mouth,
belittle, dishonor, minimize **9.** discredit
10. depreciate, disapprove, disrespect,
undervalue
disparagement . . . **7.** diasyrm **8.** disgrace
9. indignity **10.** detraction
12. depreciation
disparaging . . . **8.** decaying
10. defamatory, pejorative
11. unfavorable
disparity . . . **3.** gap **7.** deficit **8.** shortage
10. deficiency, difference, inequality

dispart . . . **4.** open, rend, rive **5.** break,
sever, split **6.** cleave, divide
dispassionate . . . **4.** cool, fair **6.** serene
8. composed, moderate **9.** collected,
impartial, temperate, unruffled
11. unemotional **12.** unprejudiced
dispatch . . . **4.** kill, mail, post, send,
slay **5.** haste, speed **6.** hasten
7. message **8.** celerity, conclude,
expedite **9.** diligence **10.** accelerate,
accomplish, promptness
dispatch boat . . . **5.** aviso **6.** packet
Dis pater (Rom) . . . **3.** god (underworld)
5. Pluto (Gr) **12.** realm of Pluto
dispel . . . **6.** vanish **7.** scatter **8.** disperse
9. dissipate
dispensation . . . **6.** scheme **7.** economy
9. exemption, remission **10.** dispersion,
management, misericord (misericorde)
11. arrangement **12.** distribution
13. apportionment **14.** administration
dispense . . . **4.** deal, dole, give, vend
6. effuse, excuse, exempt **7.** absolve
8. disperse **9.** apportion **10.** administer
dispenser of alms . . . **7.** almoner
disperse . . . **3.** sow **4.** rout **5.** strew
6. branch, spread, vanish **7.** diffuse,
refract, scatter **9.** apportion, dissipate
10. distribute **11.** disseminate
dispirit . . . **3.** cow **4.** damp **5.** daunt
6. deject **7.** depress **10.** discourage,
dishearten, intimidate
displace . . . **6.** depose, mislay, remove
8. misplace **9.** discharge, dislocate,
supersede **10.** substitute
display . . . **3.** air **4.** pomp, show,
wear **5.** array **6.** evince, flaunt,
parade, set out **7.** exhibit, pageant,
splurge **8.** emblazon **9.** advertise
10. appearance **11.** demonstrate,
ostentation **13.** manifestation
display (pert to) . . .
case . . **10.** show window
in public . . **5.** stage
of emotion . . **10.** enthusiasm
of force (distant) . . **9.** telenergy
of temper . . **5.** scene **9.** spectacle
displease . . . **3.** vex **4.** miff, roil **5.** anger,
annoy, pique **6.** offend **7.** provoke
8. irritate **10.** dissatisfy
displeasure . . . **5.** anger **7.** disgust,
dislike, offense, trouble **8.** disfavor,
distaste **10.** resentment, uneasiness
11. indignation, unhappiness
14. disapprobation **15.** dissatisfaction
dispose (of) . . . **3.** set **4.** give, mind, sell,
tend **5.** order, place **6.** adjust, assign,
bestow, settle **7.** arrange, destroy,
discard, testate **8.** give away, regulate
9. eliminate **10.** distribute, relinquish
disposed . . . **5.** prone **7.** settled, willing
8. arranged, assigned, inclined
11. distributed
disposed (pert to) . . .
favorably . . **7.** propend
to cling together . . **8.** clannish
to doubt . . **9.** skeptical
to please . . **11.** complaisant
disposition . . . **3.** use **4.** bent, bias,
mood, turn **6.** animus, giving, morale,
nature, temper **7.** control **8.** tendency

9. character 10. management, settlement 11. arrangement, elimination, temperament 12. organization 13. apportionment

dispossess ... 5. eject, evict 6. divest, refute 8. disseize

dispossessed ... 6. bereft, ousted 7. ejected, evicted 8. deprived, divested

disproof ... 6. answer, denial 8. negation, rebuttal 10. refutation 11. confutation 12. invalidation

disprove ... 5. belie, rebut 6. refute 7. confute 9. discredit 10. invalidate

disputation ... 6. debate 7. polemic 8. argument 10. contention 11. controversy 12. conversation

disputatious ... 7. eristic, polemic 11. contentious, quarrelsome 13. argumentative, controversial

dispute ... 4. deny, feud, moot, spar 5. brawl, broil 6. bicker, debate, haggle, higgle, naggle 7. contest, dissent, protest, quarrel, wrangle 8. argument, squabble 11. altercation, controversy

disqualify ... 5. debar 9. indispose 10. invalidate 12. incapacitate

disquiet ... 3. vix 4. fret 5. alarm 6. excite 7. agitate, concern, disturb 8. distress, frighten 12. apprehension

disquisition ... 5. essay 10. discussion 12. dissertation

disregard ... 4. snub 6. ignore, slight 7. neglect 8. defiance 9. unconcern 11. inattention

disreputable ... 3. low 4. base 5. seamy 7. raffish 8. shameful, unworthy 13. discreditable 15. persona non grata

disrespect ... 7. affront 9. disesteem, insolence 10. incivility 11. discourtesy

disrespectful ... 7. uncivil 8. impudent, insolent 10. irreverent 12. discourteous

disrupt ... 4. part (forcibly), rend, tear 5. upset 6. thwart 11. disorganize

dissatisfaction ... 8. vexation 10. discontent 11. displeasure, unsatisfied

dissect ... 3. cut 6. divide 7. analyze 8. separate 9. anatomize

disseize (law) ... 4. oust 5. evict 6. depose 10. dispossess 11. expropriate

dissemble ... 4. hide 5. cloak, feign 7. conceal 8. disguise 9. disregard 11. counterfeit

disseminate ... 3. sow 6. effuse, spread 7. publish, scatter 8. disperse 9. circulate, propagate

dissension ... 7. discord 8. brouille, friction 10. dissidence 12. disagreement

dissent ... 3. nay 8. apostasy, disagree 10. separation 12. disagreement, nonagreement 13. nonconformity 14. nonconcurrence

dissenter ... 7. heretic, Sectary 8. apostate, recusant 9. protester 10. Protestant 13. nonconformist

dissertation ... 5. essay, tract 6. debate, thesis 7. article, lecture 8. treatise 9. discourse 10. discussion, exposition 12. disquisition

dissidence ... 7. dissent 8. variance 9. cacophony 10. difference, dissension

12. disagreement

dissimilarity ... 7. variety 9. disparity, diversity 10. difference, unlikeness, unsameness 13. dissimilation, heterogeneity 17. heterogeneousness

dissipate ... 5. spend, waste 6. dispel, expend 7. consume, scatter, shatter 8. dispense, dissolve, squander 9. disappear

dissipation ... 4. loss 9. decrement, diffusion 10. dispersion, profligacy 11. consumption, prodigality 12. intemperance 13. disappearance, dissoluteness 14. disintegration

dissolute ... 3. lax 4. lewd, wild 5. loose 6. loosed, rakish, wanton, wicked 7. lawless, vicious 8. reckless, uncurbed 9. abandoned, debauched, unbridled 10. dissipated, licentious, profligate 11. demoralized 12. unrestrained

dissolve ... 4. fuse, melt 5. solve 7. adjourn, liquefy 9. decompose, disappear 11. disorganize 12. disintegrate

dissolved ... 6. solute 7. soluble

dissonant ... 5. harsh 7. grating, jarring 8. jangling 9. deviative, different, differing 10. discordant, discrepant 11. disagreeing, unmelodious 12. inconsistent, inharmonious 13. contradictory

dissuade ... 5. deter 6. advise, dehort, divert 8. admonish 10. discourage, disincline 11. expostulate

distaff side ... 5. women 6. female

distain ... 5. stain, tinge 6. define 7. tarnish 8. discolor

distance ... 4. step, yond 5. depth, range, space 6. offing 7. mileage, reserve, yardage 8. coldness, outstrip 9. aloofness, antiquity, dimension 10. remoteness

distant ... 3. far, tel, yon 4. afar, cold, tele (pref) 5. aloof 6. remote, utmost, yonder 7. foreign 8. ulterior

distaste ... 7. disgust 8. aversion 9. disrelish 10. repugnance 11. displeasure 14. disinclination 15. dissatisfaction

distasteful ... 7. hateful 8. nauseous, unsavory 9. loathsome, offensive 10. disgusting, unpleasant 11. displeasing, unpalatable 12. disagreeable

distemper ... 3. vex 4. soak 5. anger, color, steep 6. dilute, malady, ruffle 7. ailment, disease, disturb 8. painting (process), sickness 13. indisposition

distend ... 4. grow 5. bulge, swell 6. dilate, expand, spread 7. enlarge, inflate, stretch 8. lengthen

distended ... 5. tumid 7. bloated, swollen 8. inflated, patulous, puffed up

distich ... 7. couplet 8. two lines

distill, distil ... 4. leak 6. decoct, infuse 7. extract, squeeze, trickle 8. vaporize

distilling device ... 5. flask 6. retort 7. alembic 10. distillery

distinct ... 4. fair 5. clear 7. audible, obvious, precise, several 8. explicit, manifest 9. different 10. individual

13. distinguished

distinction . . . **4.** rank **5.** honor **6.** repute **8.** nobility **9.** clearness, greatness, variation **10.** difference **14.** discrimination **15.** differentiation

distinctive . . . **7.** typical **8.** peculiar **9.** prominent **14.** characteristic, discriminative

distinctive mark . . . **4.** sign **5.** badge **6.** cachet, emblem, symbol

distinctive quality . . . **6.** genius, talent **9.** specialty

distinguish . . . **6.** secern **7.** discern **8.** perceive, separate **9.** recognize **12.** discriminate **13.** differentiate

distinguished . . . **5.** great, noted **6.** famous, marked **7.** defined, eminent, honored, special **8.** laureate, renowned, superior **9.** different, egregious, prominent **10.** celebrated **11.** conspicuous, illustrious **13.** extraordinary **14.** characteristic

distort . . . **4.** skew, warp **5.** screw, twist, wrest **6.** deform **7.** contort, falsify, pervert **10.** camshackle **12.** misrepresent

distorted . . . **4.** awry **6.** rubato **7.** twisted

distortion . . . **5.** loxia **10.** perversion **12.** malformation

distract . . . **5.** craze **6.** divert, harass, madden, puzzle **7.** confuse, perplex **10.** distraught

distracted . . . **3.** mad **7.** frantic **8.** distrait, diverted, rambling **9.** disturbed **10.** distraught **11.** overwrought

distraction . . . **6.** frenzy, tumult **7.** despair, madness **8.** disorder **9.** agitation, confusion, diversion **10.** dissension, perplexity **11.** derangement, disturbance, inattention **12.** perturbation

distrain . . . **5.** seize

distress . . . **3.** ail **4.** pain **5.** agony, annoy, grief, worry **6.** danger, grieve, harrow, misery **7.** anguish, anxiety, perplex, poverty, trouble **8.** distrain, vexation **9.** necessity **10.** affliction, discomfort

distress call . . . **3.** SOS

distribute . . . **3.** dot, sow **4.** deal, dole, mete **5.** allot, share **6.** assign, assort, divide, spread **7.** deal out, prorate, scatter **8.** allocate, classify, dispense, disperse **9.** apportion, broadcast **10.** administer

distribution . . . **8.** disposal **9.** allotment **10.** dispersion **11.** arrangement, disposition **12.** dispensation **13.** apportionment **14.** classification

distribution of favors . . . **9.** patronage **11.** benefaction

distributor . . . **5.** agent **6.** agency **8.** merchant **11.** broadcaster

district . . . **4.** pale, slum, ward **5.** realm **6.** canton, domain, ghetto, region **7.** circuit, demesne, quarter **8.** province **9.** bailiwick, territory

District of Columbia . . . see *Washington, DC*

distrust . . . **5.** doubt, qualm **8.** jealousy, mistrust, wariness **9.** misgiving, suspicion, treachery

disturb . . . **3.** vex **4.** riot, roil **5.** alarm, annoy, rouse, roust, upset **6.** excite, molest, ruffle **7.** agitate, derange, fluster, perturb, trouble **8.** disorder, distract **9.** interrupt **10.** discompose, disconcert

disturbance . . . **5.** alarm, brawl **6.** hubbub, rumpus, static, tumult, uproar **7.** anxiety, clatter **8.** stramash **9.** agitation, annoyance, commotion, confusion **10.** excitement, turbulence **11.** derangement **12.** perturbation

disturbed . . . **6.** uneasy **7.** annoyed, excited, inquiet, unquiet **8.** agitated **10.** bewildered **12.** disconcerted

disunion . . . **9.** severance **10.** alienation, detachment, dissension, separation **11.** disjunction **13.** disconnection

disunite . . . **3.** rip **4.** part **5.** sever, untie **6.** divide, sunder, unteam, unyoke **7.** discerp, disjoin, unravel **8.** alienate, separate **9.** dismember

disuse . . . **6.** misuse, nonuse **7.** abandon, discard **8.** disusage **9.** desuetude **11.** antiquation, discontinue **12.** obsolescence

ditch . . . **3.** sap **4.** dike, hole, moat, rine **5.** canal, evade, fossa, fosse, rhine **6.** escarp, furrow, relais, trench **7.** abandon, acequia, channel

dithyramb . . . **3.** ode **4.** hymn **6.** poetry **7.** epithet (of Dionysus)

ditty . . . **3.** lay **4.** poem, sing, song **5.** carol **6.** saying **7.** canzone **8.** canticle

diurnal . . . **5.** daily **8.** everyday **9.** quotidian

divan . . . **4.** sofa **5.** couch **6.** leewan, settee **9.** davenport **12.** Chesterfield

diva's forte . . . **4.** aria

dive . . . **4.** swim **6.** plunge, resort, saloon **7.** brothel, descend, descent, explore **8.** submerge

divergence . . . **7.** theorem **9.** deviation, obliquity **10.** difference, separation **12.** disagreement, divarication

divers . . . **5.** cruel **6.** sundry **7.** several, various **8.** perverse **9.** different

diver's disease . . . **5.** bends **7.** caisson

diverse . . . **6.** sundry, unlike **7.** several, various **8.** distinct, separate **9.** different, multiform

diver's gear . . . **8.** flippers **12.** respirometer

diversify . . . **4.** vary **6.** change **7.** variate **9.** variegate **10.** distribute **13.** differentiate

diversion . . . **4.** game, play **5.** hobby, sport **6.** change **7.** pastime **8.** apostasy **9.** amusement **10.** deflection, recreation **11.** distraction **13.** entertainment

diversity . . . **7.** variety **10.** difference **11.** variegation **12.** multiformity

divert . . . **5.** amuse, avert, parry **7.** deflect, delight **8.** dissuade, distract, recreate **9.** entertain **10.** disincline

divest . . . **4.** doff, reft, tirl **5.** strip **6.** debunk, depose **8.** unclothe **10.** dispossess

divide . . . **3.** lot **4.** fork, part **5.** cleft, halve, sever, share, slice, space, split **6.** bisect, cleave, septum, sunder **7.** prorate **8.** alienate, classify, separate **9.** apportion, bifurcate, calculate,

dismember, partition, segregate,
watershed **11.** distinguish
divide (pert to) . . .
areas (small) . . **8.** areolate
feet . . **4.** scan
four parts . . **4.** paly (Her) **7.** quarter
many parts . . **8.** fraction **9.** multisect
seven parts . . **9.** septimole
steps . . **8.** graduate
transversely . . **12.** cross-section
two parts . . **6.** bisect
divided . . . **4.** enté (Her), reft **5.** bifid,
split, zoned **6.** halved, parted **7.** partial,
partite, septate **8.** aerolate, bifidate,
unjoined **9.** alienated, disunited
11. distributed
dividend . . . **5.** bonus, share **6.** number
7. payment
divination . . . **3.** art (magic) **4.** omen,
sors **6.** augury, sortes **7.** presage
9. intuition
divination by . . .
ashes (sacrificial) . . **11.** tephromancy
cards . . **10.** cartomancy
dead spirits . . **10.** necromancy
dreams . . **11.** oneiromancy
eggs . . **7.** oomancy
fig leaf . . **9.** sycomancy
figures . . **8.** geomancy
fire . . **9.** pyromancy
footprints . . **10.** ichnomancy
forehead . . **11.** metapomancy
fountains . . **9.** pegomancy
letters of a name . . **7.** nomancy
8. onomancy
mice . . **8.** myomancy
moon . . **10.** seleomancy
neighing horse . . **10.** hippomancy
oracles . . **9.** theomancy
palmistry . . **10.** chiromancy
pebbles . . **9.** thrioboly
romantic medium . . **5.** daisy
salt . . **9.** halomancy
serpents . . **10.** ophiomancy
smoke (sacrificial) . . **10.** capromancy
stars . . **11.** sideromancy
straws (burning) . . **11.** sideromancy
sword . . **13.** machairomancy
verses . . **13.** rhapsodomancy
wands, rods . . **11.** rhabdomancy
water . . **10.** hydromancy
weather . . **9.** aeromancy
wild animals . . **11.** theriomancy
wine . . **9.** oenomancy
divine . . . **5.** divus, guess, pious **6.** priest,
sacred, superb **7.** foresee, godlike,
predict **8.** forebode, foretell, heavenly,
minister, prophecy **8.** beautiful,
celestial, clergyman, religious
10. anticipate, superhuman, theologian
12. supernatural
divine (pert to) . . .
being . . **4.** deva
breath . . **4.** soul
force . . **5.** deity, numen **6.** spirit
gift . . **8.** blessing
inspiration . . **8.** afflatus
messenger . . **7.** apostle
opinion . . **14.** theologoumenon
power . . **7.** entheos (obs)
utterance . . **8.** prophecy

wisdom . . **8.** theogamy
word . . **5.** grace, logos
work . . **7.** theurgy
divining rod . . . **4.** wand **6.** dowser
9. doodlebug
divinity . . . **3.** God, Ler **4.** Deus,
Lord **5.** Allah, deity, Khuda, Mazda
6. Brahma, Christ **7.** Jehovah, Saviour,
Taranis, Trinity **8.** Almighty
division . . . **4.** part, sect, unit **5.** share
6. schism, sector **7.** faction, section
8. cleavage, disunion, variance
9. allotment, bisection, partition
10. alienation, department, separation
11. compartment, disjunction
12. distribution **13.** apportionment,
disconnection, dismemberment
14. classification
division (pert to) . . .
center (Biol) . . **9.** centriole
city . . **4.** ward **5.** block **8.** precinct
French . . **6.** canton **7.** Commune
10. department **14.** arrondissement
mankind . . **4.** race
poem . . **5.** canto, verse **6.** stanza
time . . **3.** Age, Eon (Aeon), Era **6.** Eogaea
(Zool)
zone (earth) . . **6.** frigid, torrid, tropic
9. temperate
divorce, Mohammedan law . . . **5.** talak
divot . . . **3.** sod **4.** clod, turf
divulge . . . **4.** tell **6.** expose, impart, reveal
7. confide, publish, uncover **8.** disclose,
discover, proclaim **11.** communicate
Dixie, Dixieland . . . **4.** song **6.** utopia
7. Sunbelt **8.** The South (US)
dizziness . . . **5.** whirl **7.** vertigo
9. giddiness **10.** fickleness
dizzy . . . **5.** crazy, giddy, tipsy **6.** fickle,
stupid **7.** foolish **8.** confused,
swimming, unsteady **9.** delirious
10. capricious **11.** vertiginous
Djibouti, east Africa . . .
city . . **5.** Obock **6.** Dikkil
gulf . . **4.** Aden
do . . . **2.** ut (Mus) **3.** act, pay **4.** dost, fare,
make, suit, work **5.** avoid, cause, cheat,
exert, serve, solve **6.** answer, effect,
finish **7.** achieve, deceive, execute,
perform, produce, prosper, suffice
8. transact **9.** discharge **10.** administer
docile . . . **4.** calm, tame **6.** gentle
7. duteous **9.** compliant, teachable,
tractable
dock . . . **4.** clip, pier, slip **5.** basin,
jetty, plant, wharf **6.** cut off, deduct,
hangar **7.** curtail, shorten **8.** waterway
9. anchorage **12.** witness stand
docket . . . **4.** list, mark **6.** record, ticket
8. calendar, schedule **11.** certificate
docking post . . . **7.** bollard
dock worker . . . **6.** loader **7.** laborer
9. stevedore **12.** longshoreman
doctor . . . **3.** cut, fly (angling) **4.** dose
5. spike, title, treat **6.** degree, dilute,
healer, intern (interne) **7.** surgeon,
teacher **9.** physician **10.** adulterate,
veterinary **12.** psychiatrist
doctrine . . . **3.** ism, ist **4.** rule **5.** credo,
creed, dogma, logic, maxim, tenet
6. gospel **7.** article, opinion, precept

8. position 9. principle
doctrine (pert to) . . .
existence (Philos) . . 6. henism
finality (Theol) . . 11. eschatology
good . . 8. agathism
inevitability . . 8. fatalism
philosophy . . 10. pragmatism
secrecy . . 6. cabala 8. esoteric
selfishness . . 6. egoism
doctus . . . 7. learned
document . . . 4. deed, writ 5. paper,
proof, scrip 6. escrow 7. archive
11. corroborate
document (pert to) . . .
copy (true) . . 5. Xerox 7. estreat
8. syngraph 9. duplicate, photostat
depository . . 8. archives
file, report . . 7. dossier
hamper . . 7. hanaper
dodecade . . . 5. dozen 6. twelve (series)
dodge . . . 4. duck, jouk, snub 5. avoid,
cheat, elude, evade, parry, trick
6. escape, palter 7. deceive 8. artifice
9. expedient
dodger . . . 7. biscuit, shirker 8. deceiver,
handbill
dodo . . . 3. moa 4. bird (extinct)
doe . . . 3. tag, teg 4. deer, hind
doer . . . 5. actor, agent, maker 6. author,
factor, worker 7. manager 8. attorney,
executor, producer 9. performer
doff . . . 4. shed, vail 5. strip 6. divest,
remove 7. take off, undress
dog . . . 3. cur, pug 4. foot, lyam
(lyme) 5. canis, hound, pooch,
whelp 6. canine, fallow, shadow,
wretch, yelper 7. mongrel 9. carnivore
13. constellation
dog (breed) . . . 3. pom 4. chow, Dane
5. boxer, husky 6. basset, beagle, collie,
lucern, nootka, poodle, Saluki, setter,
Sussex 7. bulldog, griffon, mastiff,
pointer, Samoyed, Shih Tzu, spaniel,
terrier, whippet 8. Airedale, Doberman,
Keeshong,Labrador,Malemute,Pekinese,
Sealyham, shepherd 9. Chihuahua,
dachshund, Dalmatian, greyhound,
Pekingese, retriever, schnauzer, St
Bernard, wolfhound 10. bloodhound,
Pomeranian, schipperke 11. Skye terrier
12. gazelle hound 13. Boston terrier
dog (pert to) . . .
Buster Brown . . 4. Tige
Cape (hunting) . . 8. cynhyena
days . . 8. canicule
F D R's . . 4. Fala (Falla)
ferocious . . 7. agouara
fictional . . 4. Asta, Toby 6. Lassie 9. Rin
Tin Tin
heroic . . 5. Balto
house . . 6. kennel
howl . . 9. ululation
like . . 6. cynoid
mythical . . 7. Cerebus
part . . 5. flews 7. dewclaw
short-eared (Her) . . 4. alan (aland)
star . . 6. Sirius 8. Canicula
Victor records . . 6. Nipper (His Master's
Voice)
wild . . 5. dhole, dingo 6. bandog, kolsun
8. cimarron

Doge's barge . . . 9. Bucentaur
dogfish . . . 5. shark 6. burbot 9. blackfish
10. nursehound
dogma . . . 4. code 5. tenet 6. belief,
dictum (pl dicta), ritual 7. precept
8. doctrine 9. Levitical, principle
dogmatic . . . 7. certain 8. absolute,
positive 9. assertive, canonical,
doctrinal, pragmatic 11. dictatorial,
doctrinaire, magisterial, opinionated
dogmatism . . . 10. pragmatism
11. intolerance
dogwood . . . 5. osier 6. cornel 7. boxwood
do it again . . . 5. itero
dole . . . 4. alms, mete 5. grief 6. sorrow
8. pittance 9. allotment 10. distribute,
misfortune 12. distribution
doleful . . . 3. sad 4. dree 5. drear
6. dismal, dreary, rueful, woeful
8. doloroso, dolorous, grievous,
jeremiad, mournful 10. lugubrious,
melancholy
doll . . . 3. toy 4. baby (toy), girl 6. moppet,
puppet 9. miniature, plaything
dolmen . . . 8. cromlech
dolphin . . . 4. fish, inia 5. bouto 6. dorado,
dugong, sea pig 8. Cetacean, porpoise
9. goosebeak 10. bottlenose
dolt . . . 3. ass, oaf 4. clod, dope,
loon, lout, moke 5. dunce, idiot
7. dullard, half-wit 8. clodpate,
dumbbell, numskull 9. blockhead, dumb
bunny 10. ignoramous
domain . . . 5. realm 6. empery, empire,
sphere 7. country, demesne 8. dominion
dome . . . 4. arch, head, roof (Astron)
5. spire, tower 6. cupola, turret
Domesday, doomsday . . . 4. Book (Eng
Hist) 11. Judgment Day 13. Great
Domesday 14. Little Domesday
17. Domesday of St Paul's
domestic . . . 4. tame 5. domal 7. servant
9. enchorial, home-grown, intestine
(not foreign)
domestic establishment . . . 6. ménage
9. household
domicile . . . 5. abode, house 7. habitat
8. dwelling 9. residence 10. habitation
dominant . . . 5. chief, chord 6. ruling
7. regnant, supreme 8. superior
9. ascendant, governing, imperious,
paramount, principal 10. pre-eminent,
prevailing 11. influential, outweighing,
overtopping 12. preponderant
13. authoritative, overbalancing
dominate . . . 4. boss, rule, sway 5. reign
6. govern 7. command, control, overtop,
possess 11. predominate
domineering . . . 6. lordly 7. haughty
8. arrogant, blustery 9. imperious,
masterful 10. oppressive
11. overbearing
Dominican Republic . . .
capital . . 12. Santo Domingo
city . . 14. Ciudad Trujillo
discoverer . . 8. Columbus
island site . . 10. Hispaniola
oldest city (W Hem) . . 12. Santo Domingo
(1496)
dominion . . . 4. rule, sway 5. realm
6. empery, empire, sphere 7. control

9. authority, hierarchy (celestial)
12. jurisdiction
domino . . . 3. pip (spot) 4. game (in pl), hood, mask 5. amice, cloak, ivory 7. costume
dominoes, galloping . . . 7. ivories
donate . . . 3. tip 4. give 6. bestow 7. present
done . . . 4. fini 5. baked, ended, finis 6. agreed, cooked 7. through 8. finished, tired out 9. completed, concluded, exhausted
done (pert to) . . .
by stealth . . 13. surreptitious
by word of mouth . . 5. parol
for pay . . 9. mercenary
with effort . . 5. labor
Don Juan's lover . . . 6. Haidee
donkey . . . 3. ass 4. moke 5. burro, neddy 6. onager
donna . . . 4. Dona, lady, wife 5. madam, woman 8. mistress
Don Quixote's steed . . . 9. Rosinante
doom . . . 3. fey, lot 4. fate, ruin 5. death 7. condemn, destine, destiny 8. sentence 11. destruction
doomed . . . 3. fey 5. death, fated, goner 9. sentenced
doomsayer . . . 9. Cassandra
doomsday . . . 8. Ragnarok 11. Judgment Day (see *Domesday)*
door . . . 4. gate 6. portal 7. doorway, opening, passage, postern 11. entranceway 12. porte-cochere
doorframe . . . 3. dar 4. jamb, rail, sash, sill 5. janua, panel, stile 6. lintel 9. threshold
doorkeeper . . . 4. hasp 5. tiler 6. porter 7. durwaum, ostiary 8. chokidar 9. concierge
dope . . . 3. hop, LSD 4. hemp 6. mescal, opiate, peyoti (peyote) 7. fathead 8. narcotic 9. marijuana
Dorian Festival (Sparta) . . . 6. carnea (carneia)
Dorian magistrates . . . 6. ephors
Doric Order (Gr Arch) . . .
capital . . 6. abacus
frieze fillet . . 6. taenia
frieze space . . 6. metope
history . . 6. oldest 8. simplest
dormant . . . 5. inert 6. asleep, latent, torpid 7. resting 8. inactive, sleeping 9. quiescent
dormer window . . . 5. oriel 6. gablet 7. dormant (obs), lucarne
dormeuse . . . 5. couch 8. carriage (sleeping), nightcap
dormouse . . . 4. Glis, loir 5. lerot 6. rodent
dorsal (pert to) . . .
back . . 5. notal, notum 6. dorsum, lumbar, neural, tergal, tergum
column . . 6. spinal
dose . . . 5. bolus, draft, treat 6. potion 7. portion
Dos Passos trilogy . . . 3. USA
dot . . . 3. jot 4. clot, code, lump 5. dowry, fleck, point, speck, telia (fungus) 6. period 7. stipple
dote . . . 3. rot 5. decay, dowry 6. babble, dotage, dotard, drivel, stupor 7. portion

(marriage) 8. imbecile
dotted . . . 5. pinto 7. piebald, specked, studded 8. stippled 9. sprinkled 11. diversified
dotty . . . 5. crazy 6. feeble, senile
Douay Bible . . . 4. Aree
double . . . 2. di (pref) 4. dual, fold, twin 5. duple, plait, twice 6. binary, binate, duplex, folded 7. twofold 8. artifice, two-faced 9. deceitful, duplicate, insincere, intensify 11. counterpart
double (pert to) . . .
bars (Her) . . 5. gemel
cross . . 7. deceive, two-time
dagger . . 6. diesis
edged . . 9. ancipital
ghost (live person) . . 11. counterpart 12. Doppelgänger, doubleganger
meaning . . 9. equivocal
doubt . . . 5. demur, waver 8. hesitate, mistrust, question 9. misgiving, suspicion 10. Pyrrhonism, skepticism 11. uncertainty
doubter . . . 5. cynic 6. Humist 7. skeptic 10. Pyrrhonist
doubtful . . . 7. dubious 8. wavering 9. ambiguous, equivocal, uncertain, undecided 10. hesitating, improbable, precarious 11. distrustful, vacillating 12. questionable, unbelievable, undetermined 13. problematical
doubtful authority . . . 6. mythic, unreal 10. apocryphal
dough . . . 4. cash, mash 5. money, paste 6. leaven, noodle
doughnut . . . 6. sinker 7. cruller, simball 9. friedcake
dour . . . 5. harsh, stern 6. gloomy, severe 9. obstinate 10. inflexible
dove . . . 3. nun 4. blue (color), Inca 5. color 6. culver, pigeon 7. Columba, tumbler 8. pacifist, peacenik
Dove, the . . . 6. symbol (Relig) 10. Holy Spirit
dovefoot . . . 8. geranium (wild)
dovekey, dovekie . . . 3. auk 4. Alle 6. rotche 9. guillemot
dowdy . . . 3. pie (deep-dish) 6. pastry, shabby, untidy 7. pudding 8. slovenly 10. slatternly
dowel . . . 3. pin 4. coak 5. tenon 6. fasten, pintle
dower . . . 3. dos 5. dowry, endow, grant 6. dotate 7. bequest 8. dotation, jointure
down . . . 2. de (pref) 3. nap 4. fuzz, hair 5. adown, below, floor 7. descent 8. softness
downcast . . . 3. low, sad 7. lowered 8. dejected 9. bowed down, depressed 10. despondent, dispirited 11. discouraged, downhearted
downright . . . 4. flat 5. blunt, plain, sheer, stark, utter 6. arrant, candid 8. positive, thorough 10. absolutely, forthright 11. unqualified 13. unceremonious
down source . . . 5. eider
downy . . . 4. soft, wary 5. nappy, pilar, quiet 6. placid 7. villous 8. feathery 10. flocculent, lanuginose, lanuginous
dowry . . . 3. dos, dot 4. gift 5. dower, sulka 6. talent 9. endowment

dowser's tool . . . **4.** wand **6.** willow
Doxology . . . **4.** hymn **6.** praise **7.** Kaddish
doze . . . **3.** nap, nod **5.** sleep **6.** catnap,
   drowse, snooze **7.** stupefy (obs)
Dracula (pert to) . . .
   actor . . **6.** Lugosi (Bela)
   author . . **6.** Stoker (Bram)
   film (Murnau) . . **9.** Nosferatu
   homeland . . **12.** Transylvania
   inspiration for . . **4.** Vlad (Tepes) **14.** Vlad
      the Impaler
draft, draught . . . **3.** map, nip **4.** dose,
   dram, draw, plan, pull, swig **5.** drink,
   epure **7.** current, diagram, drawing,
   outline **8.** protocol, recruits, traction
   9. conscript **10.** money order
drag . . . **3.** lag, lug, tow, tug **4.** clog, draw,
   hale, haul, pull, sing, tump **5.** drawl,
   scent (hunt), smoke, trail **6.** drogue,
   harrow **7.** grapnel **8.** dragrope, linger
   on, obstacle **10.** conveyance
dragoman . . . **11.** interpreter (official)
dragon . . . **4.** lung **5.** drake, Rahab (Bib)
   6. animal, duenna, lizard, musket (anc),
   pigeon **7.** dragoon, monster (Her),
   serpent **10.** earthdrake **14.** Dragon of
   Komodo
drain . . . **3.** gaw, sap **4.** lade, loss, sink,
   sump **5.** ditch, dreen, empty, rhine,
   sewer, siver **6.** filter, trench **7.** acequia,
   alberca, channel, consume, exhaust,
   outflow **11.** watercourse
dram . . . **3.** nip **4.** mite, slug **5.** draft, drink
   6. drachm **8.** potation **11.** indifferent
drama (pert to) . . .
   beginning . . **8.** Dyonysia (anc)
   form . . **4.** play **5.** opera **6.** comedy
      7. tragedy **10.** peripeteia
      11. composition
   parts . . **8.** epitasis, protasis
      12. introduction
   scenery . . **7.** diorama
dramatic . . . **4.** wild **5.** stagy, vivid,
   vocal **6.** poetic, scenic **8.** thespian
   10. histrionic, theatrical **11.** pretentious,
   spectacular **12.** melodramatic
dramatic piece . . . **4.** skit
drastic . . . **5.** stern **6.** fierce, severe
   7. intense, radical **8.** rigorous
draught . . . see *draft*
Dravidian (pert to) . . .
   country (anc) . . **5.** India
   ghost . . **4.** bhut
   language . . **5.** Tamil **8.** Kanarese
      12. Dravido-Munda
   native . . **5.** Croat **8.** Croatian
   people . . **4.** Nair **6.** Slavic
   soldier . . **8.** Croatian
draw . . . **3.** lug, tie, tow, tug **4.** drag, etch,
   haul, limn, lure, plot, pull, tole **5.** draft,
   smoke **6.** allure, arroyo, convey, entice
   7. attract, conduct, extract, lottery
   9. delineate **10.** attraction
draw (pert to) . . .
   away . . **6.** abduce, divert **7.** detract
   close . . **4.** loom, near **5.** hover
      8. approach
   forth . . **5.** educe **6.** elicit, ferret **7.** extract
   off . . **6.** siphon **7.** extract **8.** abstract,
      withdraw
   through an eye . . **4.** rove

together . . **4.** coul, frap, lace, rake
   8. assemble
drawback . . . **5.** fault, wince **6.** defect,
   resile, retire **8.** obstacle **9.** objection
   12. disadvantage
drawing . . . **3.** art **5.** draft **7.** diagram,
   hauling, picture, pulling **8.** doodling
   9. animation **10.** attracting, extracting
drawing back . . . **9.** retrahent
drawing room . . . **6.** parlor, saloon
drayage . . . **6.** charge **7.** cartage, haulage
   8. truckage **14.** transportation
dread . . . **3.** awe **4.** fear **5.** timor **6.** dismay,
   horror, terror **7.** anxiety **8.** affright,
   disquiet **9.** reverence **12.** apprehension
dreadful . . . **4.** dire **6.** horrid **7.** awesome,
   fearful, hideous **8.** horrible, terrible,
   terrific **9.** frightful **10.** formidable,
   outrageous
dreadnaught, dreadnought . . . **5.** cloth
   7. garment **8.** fearless **10.** battleship,
   fearnought
dream . . . **4.** muse, rêve **5.** fancy
   6. bubble, vision **7.** imagine, reverie,
   romance, suppose **8.** illusion, stargaze
   11. contemplate
dream (pert to) . . .
   interpretation . . **10.** oneirology
   interpreter . . **12.** oneirocritic
   tranquility . . **3.** kef (keef) **7.** reverie
dreamer . . . **4.** seer **7.** fantast **8.** idealist,
   puffbird **9.** visionary **11.** romanticist
   13. castle-builder
dreamy . . . **3.** kef (keef) **6.** poetic **7.** languid
   8. soothing **9.** visionary **11.** imaginative
dreary . . . **3.** sad **4.** dull, gray **5.** bleak,
   ourie **6.** dismal, elenge, gloomy,
   remote **7.** doleful, tedious **9.** cheerless
   10. depressing, foreboding, melancholy,
   monotonous **11.** comfortless
dredge . . . **4.** tong (for oysters) **5.** scoop
   6. burrow, deepen, grains, tunnel
   8. excavate
dregs . . . **4.** faex, lees, marc, silt **5.** draff,
   dross, magma **6.** refuse, scoria, sludge
   7. grounds, hogwash, residue **8.** riffraff,
   sediment **9.** settlings **10.** faex populi
drench . . . **4.** hose, soak **5.** douse, draft,
   imbue, purge, scour, souse **6.** potion
   7. immerse **8.** inundate, permeate,
   saturate, submerge
drenched . . . **4.** asop **5.** asoak **6.** doused,
   soaked **9.** saturated
dress . . . **3.** rig, tog **4.** deck, garb, gown,
   suit, trim **5.** getup, mufti, preen **6.** attire,
   clothe, enrobe, livery, toilet **7.** apparel,
   threads (sl) **8.** clothing, decorate,
   negligee **10.** habiliment **13.** mother
   hubbard
dress (pert to) . . .
   flax . . **3.** ted
   gaudily . . **5.** prank **7.** bedizen, spangle
   leather . . **3.** taw, tew **5.** curry
   of Mecca pilgrims . . **5.** ihram
   riding . . **5.** chaps, habit **7.** hacking
      (jacket) **8.** jodhpurs **10.** chaparajos
   stone . . **3.** dab, nig **5.** nidge
   surgically . . **5.** dight, panse **7.** bandage
      8. ligature
   up . . **4.** dude **5.** preen, primp **6.** spruce
      8. titivate

dressed loosely . . . **8.** discinct, ungirded
dressing . . . **4.** lint **5.** sauce **7.** bandage, pledget, raiment, reproof **8.** attiring, scolding **9.** condiment, neatsfoot (leather) **11.** castigation
drew . . . see *draw*
Dreyfus defender . . . **4.** Zola
dried . . . **4.** sere **5.** wiped **6.** seared, wasted **7.** drained, parched, wizened **9.** shriveled **10.** dehydrated, desiccated, exsiccated
dried meat . . . **7.** biltong (biltongue), charqui **8.** pemmican **10.** jerked beef
dried tubers (orchids) . . . **5.** salep
drift . . . **3.** aim, sag **4.** idle, pile, sail, soar, tide, tool **5.** float, stray, tenor, trend **6.** course, intent **7.** deposit, impetus, meaning **8.** crescent (sidewise), movement, seaweeds, tendency **9.** deviation
drill . . . **3.** gad, row (seeds), tap **4.** bore **5.** auger, borer, train **6.** baboon, pierce **7.** machine **8.** excavate, exercise, practice, rehearse **9.** perforate
drilling . . . **5.** denim **7.** nurture **8.** training **11.** inculcation
drink . . . **3.** ade, ale, bib, lap, nip, pop, rum, sip, tea, tot **4.** flip, fram, grog, shot, slug, soda, soma, swig, tope **5.** bouse, draft, julep, negus, posca, punch, quaff, skink, toast, toddy, water **6.** caudle, coffee, imbibe, liquor, mai tai, mao-tai, posset, potion, ptisan, tipple **8.** beverage, cocktail, highball, sillabub **9.** decoction **10.** intoxicant, mixed drink
drink (pert to) . . .
ancient . . **5.** morat
Arabian . . **4.** boza
English . . **7.** wassail **8.** champers
fond of . . **8.** bibulous
frozen . . **6.** frappé
gods (of the) . . **6.** nectar
honey . . **4.** mead **5.** morat
hot . . **5.** salep, toddy **6.** posset, saloop
Irish . . **10.** shandygaff
Japanese . . **4.** sake
mix . . **5.** setup **8.** vermouth **9.** grenadine
rum . . **5.** bumbo
Russian . . **5.** vodka **6.** kumiss (koumiss)
Spanish . . **7.** tequila
together . . **9.** symposium
tropical . . **7.** sangria **8.** sangaree
Turkish . . **4.** raki **5.** airan, arrak
drinking salutation . . . **5.** skoal, toast **6.** prosit **7.** propine, slainte
drinking vessel . . . **3.** mug **4.** bowl, tass **5.** cylix (anc), glass, gourd, jorum, mazer, stein **6.** goblet, rhyton **7.** tankard **8.** schooner **10.** Vaphio cups (gold)
drip . . . **4.** bore, drop, leak **5.** droop **7.** dribble, falling, trickle
drive . . . **3.** caa **4.** herd, ride, slog, urge **5.** force, guide, impel, pilot, press, rouse **6.** attack, compel, energy, propel, thrust **7.** crusade, operate **8.** campaign **10.** compulsion
drive (pert to) . . .
away . . **4.** rout **5.** chase, exile, expel, repel **6.** banish, dispel, rebuff **7.** repulse

8. disperse
down . . **4.** tamp
frantic . . **4.** loco **6.** madden **7.** bedevil
obliquely . . **3.** toe **5.** slice
stakes . . **4.** camp, park **6.** locate, settle
drivel . . . **4.** dote **5.** drool **6.** slaver **7.** slobber, twaddle **8.** nonsense
driveler . . . **4.** fool **5.** doter, idiot **6.** dotard, prater **8.** jabberer **9.** blatherer, chatterer
driver . . . **4.** club (golf), jehu **6.** drover, hammer, mahout, sarwan **7.** speeder **8.** coachman, engineer, motorist, operator, overseer, reinsman **9.** propeller **10.** charioteer, taskmaster
drizzle . . . **4.** mist, rain, smur **6.** mizzle (misle)
droll . . . **3.** odd **4.** zany **5.** comic, merry, queer, witty **6.** jester **7.** amusing, buffoon, waggish **8.** farcical, humorous **9.** diverting, laughable, whimsical **10.** ridiculous **11.** merry-andrew
drollery . . . **3.** wit **4.** jest **5.** farce, humor **6.** puppet **9.** absurdity **10.** buffoonery
dromedary . . . **4.** oont **5.** camel (one-hump) **6.** hageen **7.** Camelus **8.** Bactrian (two-hump)
drone . . . **3.** bee, dor, hum **4.** male (bee) **5.** idler, snail **6.** loafer **7.** bagpipe, humming, slacker **8.** sluggard **9.** non-worker, slow mover
drool . . . **6.** drivel, slaver **7.** dribble, slabber, slobber
droop . . . **3.** lop, sag **4.** flag, hang, loll, pine, sink, tire, wilt **6.** nutate, slouch **7.** decline **8.** languish
drooping . . . **4.** alop, weak **5.** loose **7.** hanging, nodding, sinking **8.** dejected, fatigued **11.** languishing
drooping eyelids . . . **6.** ptosis
drop . . . **4.** bead, blob, dose, dram, drib, drip, fall, omit, shed, sink, slot, stop, tear **5.** candy, dreep, droop, gutta, lower, minim, remit **6.** letter, plunge **7.** abandon, descent, distill (distil), earring, globule, pendant, trickle **8.** ornament, trapdoor **9.** declivity **10.** relinquish
drop (pert to) . . .
anchor . . **4.** moor
by drop . . **7.** guttate **9.** guttation
measure . . **7.** pipette **11.** stactometer
nautical . . **5.** hance
serene . . **9.** amaurosis (Med)
vowel . . **5.** elide
dropsy . . . **5.** edema **8.** hydropsy, swelling
dross . . . **4.** lees, scum, slag **5.** chaff, dregs, scobs, sprue, waste **6.** refuse, scoria, sinter (iron)
drove . . . **4.** herd **5.** crowd, drive, flock
drover . . . **4.** boat **6.** dealer (cattle), driver **8.** herdsman
drowse . . . **3.** nid, nod **4.** doze **5.** dover (Eng), sleep **6.** snooze
drowsiness . . . **7.** languor **8.** dullness, lethargy **9.** lassitude, oscitance **10.** narcolepsy, sleepiness **12.** listlessness, sluggishness
drowsy . . . **4.** logy **6.** sleepy **8.** oscitant, soothing **9.** somnolent, soporific
drudge . . . **3.** fag **4.** grub, hack, mail,

plod, toil **5.** labor, slave **6.** toiler
   7. plodder
drug . . . **4.** alum, dope, dull, numb
   6. opiate **7.** stupefy **8.** narcotic, sedative
   10. medication **11.** anesthetize
drug (pert to) . . .
   action . . **7.** synergy
   addict . . **6.** junkie
   analgesic . . **6.** Anacin **7.** aspirin
   10. acetanilid, phenacetin
   anesthesia . . **3.** gas **5.** ether **8.** Novocain
   10. chloroform
   dangerous . . **11.** thalidomide
   emetic . . **6.** ipecac **11.** ipecacuanha
   eye . . **8.** atropine **10.** belladonna
   forgetfulness . . **8.** nepenthe
   narcotic . . **3.** hop, kif **4.** hemp **5.** bhang,
   daggo, opium **6.** codein **7.** cocaine
   9. marijuana
   sedative . . **7.** bromide, Seconal, Veronal
   8. barbital, Nembutal **11.** scopolamine
   13. phenobarbital
drugget . . . **3.** mat, rug **5.** cloth
druggist . . . **8.** gallipot **10.** apothecary,
   pharmacist
Druids (anc) . . . **5.** Order (Relig)
   9. conjurers **12.** philosophers
drum . . . **4.** beat **5.** naker, snare, tabor,
   tombe **6.** atabal, barrel, tambor
   (tambour), tom-tom, tympan **7.** taboret,
   timbrel, timpany **8.** cylinder, tympanum
   (ear)
drum (pert to) . . .
   call . . **4.** dian (diana) **6.** rappel, tattoo
   8. rataplan
   Indian . . **6.** nagara
   nautical term . . **7.** capstan
   Oriental . . **6.** tom-tom **7.** anacara
drumming fingers . . . **12.** devil's tattoo
drunkard . . . **3.** sot **4.** soak, wino
   5. souse, toper **6.** addict, barfly, boozer
   7. guzzler, tippler **9.** alcoholic, inebriate
   11. dipsomaniac
dry . . . **3.** sec, ted **4.** arid, blot, brut,
   dull, keen, seco, sere, wipe **5.** drain,
   parch, vapid **6.** aerify, barren, jejune,
   shrewd **7.** insipid, sterile, thirsty, xerotic
   8. solidify, tiresome **9.** dehydrate,
   fruitless, pointless **12.** unprofitable
   13. uninteresting
dryad . . . **5.** deity, Napea, nymph, oread
duck . . . **3.** dip **4.** flee, fowl **5.** dodge,
   douse **6.** plunge **7.** bob down
duck (breed) . . . **4.** Anas, coot, pato,
   skua, smee, smew, teal **5.** Anser, eider,
   scaup **6.** Aythya, Nyroca, Peking, scoter
   7. mallard, Muscovy, pintail, pochard,
   Spatula, widgeon **8.** Anatinae, bluebill,
   shoveler (shoveller) **9.** harlequin,
   merganser, sheldrake **10.** bufflehead,
   canvasback, ring-necked
duck (pert to) . . .
   baby . . **8.** duckling
   class . . **3.** sea **5.** river **7.** Muscovy
   crested . . **4.** smew
   disabled . . **4.** lame
   ducklike . . **5.** decoy **8.** duckbill
   fabric . . **5.** cloth
   flock (mallards) . . **4.** sord
   flower . . **12.** lady's slipper
   game . . **6.** tenter

hawk . . **6.** falcon **7.** harrier
litter . . **4.** team
male . . **5.** drake
ruddy . . **5.** noddy
duct . . . **3.** vas **4.** main, pipe, race, tube
   5. canal **7.** channel, passage, trachea
   8. aqueduct
ductile . . . **6.** docile, facile, pliant **7.** elastic,
   plastic, tensile **8.** flexible, tractile,
   yielding **9.** compliant, complying,
   malleable, tractable **10.** manageable
dude . . . **3.** fop **5.** dandy **7.** coxcomb,
   Johnnie **10.** tenderfoot
dudeen . . . **4.** pipe (tobacco)
due . . . **4.** debt, duty, just, meed, owed
   5. owing **6.** charge, lawful **7.** exactly
   8. adequate, directly, expected, rightful
   9. appointed **10.** ascribable, sufficient
duel . . . **4.** tilt **5.** fence **6.** combat
   7. contest **8.** conflict **9.** monomachy
   12. satisfaction
duelist's aide . . . **6.** second
duet . . . **3.** duo **8.** duettino
dug . . . see *dig*
dugong . . . **7.** manatee, Sirenia **8.** Halicore
dugout . . . **4.** abri, cave, shed **5.** canoe
   6. cavity **7.** pirogue, shelter
dulcet . . . **5.** sweet **6.** ariose **7.** tuneful
   8. pleasant, soothing **9.** agreeable,
   melodious **10.** harmonious
dulcimer . . . **6.** citole **7.** bagpipe, cembalo
   8. psaltery **10.** instrument
dull . . . **3.** dim, dry, dun **4.** dead, drab,
   gray, logy, poky **6.** barren, cloudy,
   deaden, dismal, dreary, drowsy,
   jejune, leaden, muffle, obtund, obtuse,
   sleepy, somber, stupid **7.** doltish,
   irksome, prosaic, tedious **8.** lifeless,
   listless, overcast, sluggish, stagnant,
   tiresome **9.** apathetic, inanimate,
   saturnine, unfeeling **10.** insensible,
   lackluster, melancholy, slow-witted
   13. unimaginative
dull (pert to) . . .
   finish . . **3.** mat (matte)
   heavy . . **4.** logy **5.** leady **6.** stodgy
   of cloth . . **6.** starry (Eng)
   statement . . **9.** platitude
dullard . . . **3.** oaf **4.** dope, mope **5.** dunce
   8. dumbbell, numskull **9.** dumb
   bunny
dumb . . . **4.** mute **6.** aphony, silent,
   stupid **7.** aphonia **8.** ignorant, taciturn
   9. inanimate, irregular **10.** speechless
   12. inarticulate
dumbfounded . . . **6.** amazed **7.** crabbed
   9. staggered, surprised **10.** astonished,
   bewildered **11.** overwhelmed
   13. flabbergasted
dummy . . . **3.** pel **4.** copy, dolt, mort
   (cards), sham **5.** model **6.** pontic, silent
   9. imitation, mannequin, nonentity
   10. figurehead, substitute **11.** counterfeit
dump . . . **3.** tip **4.** bump, game (Eng),
   jail, sell, thud, tune **5.** empty,
   hovel **6.** plunge, unload **7.** discard
   10. rendezvous
dumpling . . . **7.** biscuit, gnocchi
   10. appleberry
dupe . . . **3.** fox **4.** bilk, cull, tool
   5. cheat, fraud, trick **6.** delude, sucker

7. cat's-paw, deceive, mislead

duplicate . . . **4.** copy, game (cards),
twin **6.** double, duplex **7.** estreat,
mislead, replica, twofold **8.** likeness
9. analogous, facsimile, identical,
replicate **10.** transcript **11.** counterpart
12. reproduction

duplicated . . . **7.** dittoed **8.** repeated
10. repetitive

duplicity . . . **5.** fraud, guile **6.** deceit
7. duality **9.** deception, duplexity,
falsehood, treachery **13.** dissimulation,
double-dealing

durable . . . **4.** firm **5.** stout, tough
6. staple **7.** lasting **8.** constant, enduring
9. permanent **10.** continuing, persistent
11. everlasting, substantial

duration . . . **3.** age **4.** date, span,
term, time **6.** period **8.** eternity,
lifetime **10.** durability, permanence
11. continuance

during . . . **4.** time **5.** while **6.** whilst
7. pending, through **10.** throughout

dusk . . . **4.** dark **5.** dusky, gloom, slate
(color) **8.** gloaming, twilight

dusky . . . **3.** dim, sad **4.** dark, dusk
5. murky, tawny, umbra **6.** gloomy,
somber **7.** swarthy **8.** blackish
10. melancholy

dust . . . **4.** cash, coom (coomb), dirt,
gold, pilm, soil **5.** briss, brush, chaff,
clean, color, earth, money, stive, stour
(dial), trash **6.** corpse, pollen, powder
7. dryness, turmoil **9.** commotion,
confusion, sweepings

dust (pert to) . . .
flax . . **5.** pouce
flour . . **5.** stive
glacier . . **10.** kryokonite
reduce to . . **4.** mull
speck . . **4.** mote

Dutch (pert to) . . . see also *Netherlands*
cheese . . **4.** Edam **7.** cottage
country . . **7.** Germany, Holland
11. Netherlands
man . . **10.** Hogen-Mogen
news agency . . **5.** Aneta
painter . . **3.** Dou **4.** Hals **7.** van Gogh,
van Eyck, Vermeer **8.** Mondrian,
Ruisdael (Ruysdael) **9.** Rembrandt (van
Rijn)
poet . . **7.** Da Costa
pottery . . **4.** delf (delft) **9.** delftware
river . . **3.** Eem **4.** Maas **5.** Meuse
scholar . . **7.** Erasmus (Humanist)
woman, wife . . **4.** frow
uncle . . **3.** eme (dial), oom

Dutch East Indies (Indonesia) . . .
capital . . **7.** Batavia (former), Jakarta
(Djakarta)
islands (3,000), largest . . **4.** Bali, Java
6. Borneo (part) **7.** Celebes, Sumatra
8. Malaysia (part) **9.** New Guinea
(part)
renamed . . **9.** Indonesia

Dutch Guiana (Netherlands Antilles) . . .
capital . . **10.** Paramaribo
mountain . . **10.** Tumuc Humac
renamed . . **7.** Surinam

dutiful . . . **6.** devout, docile **7.** duteous
8. obedient, reverent **9.** compliant

10. respectful, submissive
11. deferential, reverential

duty . . . **3.** job, tax **4.** care, onus, rite,
task, toll **5.** chore, stint, trick **6.** devoir,
dharma, excise, heriot (anc), impost,
tariff **7.** payment, respect **9.** reverence
10. imposition, obligation

duvet . . . **9.** comforter

dwale . . . **5.** sable (Her) **6.** opiate,
potion **9.** soporific **10.** belladonna,
nightshade

dwarf . . . **3.** elf, urf **4.** grig, puny, runt
5. crile, gnome, midge, pygmy (pigmy),
small, stunt, troll **6.** droich, durgan,
midget **7.** manikin, Pacolet, stunted
9. dandiprat, micrander **10.** diminished,
homunculus

dwarfish . . . **6.** nanoid

dwarfishness . . . **6.** nanism

Dwarfs, The Seven . . . **3.** Doc **5.** Dopey,
Happy **6.** Grumpy, Sleepy, Sneezy
7. Bashful

dweeb . . . **4.** nerd

dwell . . . **4.** bide, harp, live, stay **5.** abide,
delay, lodge, pause, tarry **6.** linger,
remain, reside

dwelling . . . **3.** hut **4.** flat **5.** abode,
hotel, house, hovel **6.** duplex, shanty
7. trailer **8.** abidance, domicile,
tenement **9.** apartment, residence
10. habitation

dwelling (pert to) . . .
house (law) . . **8.** messuage
in field . . **10.** arvicoline
in groves . . **10.** nemoricole
of dead (Bab) . . **5.** Aralu
of souls (Polyn) . . **2.** Po
Oriental . . **3.** dar

dwindle . . . **4.** melt, wane **5.** taper, waste
6. lessen, shrink, sicken **8.** decrease,
diminish **10.** degenerate

dyad . . . **3.** two **4.** duad, pair **6.** couple,
dyadic

Dyak, Dayak . . . **6.** Borneo **7.** blowgun
8. sumpiter **9.** aborigine

dye . . . **4.** anil **5.** color, imbue, stain,
tinge **7.** pigment **8.** colorant

dyeing method . . . **5.** batik

dye stuff (pert to) . . .
blue . . **4.** woad (wad, wade)
brown . . **5.** erika, sumac
indigo . . **4.** anil
mulberry . . **3.** aal
red . . **4.** chay **5.** aurin, eosin, henna
6. isatin, madder, relbun **7.** annatto,
magenta **8.** morindin **9.** rhodamine
10. orseilline
violet . . **5.** murex **6.** archil
yellow . . **7.** xanthic **8.** luteolin, orpiment
10. quercitron

dyke . . . see *dike*

dynamic . . . **4.** keen **5.** acute, vivid
6. potent **7.** intense, kinetic **8.** forceful,
forcible **9.** energetic, strenuous

dynamite inventor . . . **5.** Nobel (1866)

dynamo (pert to) . . .
attachment . . **10.** commutator
inventor . . **7.** Faraday
machine . . **9.** generator
part . . **5.** rotor **8.** armature

dynast . . . **5.** ruler **6.** prince **8.** governor

dynasty . . . **4.** race **8.** dominion,
  lordship **10.** succession
  11. sovereignty
dynasty (pert to) . . .
  Chinese . . **2.** Fo **3.** Han, Yin **4.** Isin,
  Ming, Sung, Tang
  Spanish . . **6.** Ommiad
dysphoria . . . **7.** illness **8.** debility
dyvour . . . **6.** beggar **8.** bankrupt
dzeren . . . **8.** antelope

E

E . . . **7.** Epsilon (Gr)
Ea (Bab) . . . **3.** God **5.** deity
each . . . **3.** all, per **5.** alike, every **6.** apiece,
  singly **10.** separately **12.** individually
  14. distributively
eager . . . **3.** apt **4.** agog, avid, keen, yare
  5. agasp, sharp **6.** ardent, greedy, intent
  7. anxious, burning, excited, thirsty,
  willing, zealous **8.** desirous, spirited
  9. strenuous
eager beaver . . . **7.** hustler **8.** go-getter
  10. enthusiast
eagerness . . . **4.** élan, zeal **5.** ardor
  6. fervor **7.** avidity **8.** alacrity, cupidity,
  fervency **9.** alertness, readiness
  10. enthusiasm, impatience
  13. impetuousness
eagle . . . **4.** erne (ern), gier (Bib), seal
  6. bergut, eaglet, emblem **8.** standard
  (Rom) **13.** constellation (Milky Way)
eagle (pert to) . . .
  American . . **4.** bald
  brood . . **5.** aerie, eyrie
  coin . . **4.** gold
  European . . **3.** sea **5.** harpy **6.** golden
    8. imperial
  genus . . **6.** Aquila
  heraldry . . **8.** allerion
  male . . **6.** tercil
  sacred to Jupiter . . **9.** Jove's bird
  S America . . **9.** eagle hawk
  scout badge . . **5.** merit
Eagles . . . **14.** Fraternal Order
eagre (acker) . . . **4.** bore, flow, wave
  5. flood (tidal)
ear . . . **4.** head **5.** auris **7.** auricle, hearing
  8. orillion **9.** appendage, attention,
  orecchion (obs)
ear (pert to) . . .
  anvil . . **5.** incus
  bone . . **6.** stapes, tegman **7.** stirrup
  canal . . **7.** cochlea **9.** labyrinth
    10. Eustachian, scala media
  drum . . **8.** tympanum
  external . . **6.** concha
  grain . . **3.** epi **5.** spica **6.** mealie, rizzom
    (ressum)
  hammer . . **7.** malleus
  inflammation . . **6.** otitis
  part . . **5.** helix, pinna **6.** tragus
  science . . **7.** otology
  shell . . **5.** ormer **7.** abalone
  specialist . . **6.** aurist **9.** otologist
  stone . . **7.** otolith
  term . . **4.** otic **5.** aural **9.** auricular
  wax . . **7.** cerumen
earache . . . **6.** otalgy **7.** otalgia

early . . . **4.** soon **7.** ancient, betimes,
  matinal **9.** premature, primitive
  10. beforehand, beforetime
earn . . . **3.** get, win **4.** gain **5.** ettle, merit
  7. acquire, deserve
earnest . . . **5.** arles (pledge), grave,
  sober, staid **6.** ardent, hearty, pledge,
  sedate, solemn **7.** handsel (money),
  serious, sincere, zealous **8.** resolute
  9. heartfelt, important **10.** thoughtful
  12. wholehearted
earnestly . . . **8.** solemnly **9.** intensely,
  zealously **10.** resolutely
earphone . . . **7.** trumpet (double)
  8. otoscope **9.** auriphone, topophone
  (double) **11.** stethescope
earring . . . **4.** hoop **6.** earbob, pendle
  7. earstud, pendant **9.** girandole
  (girandola)
earth . . . **3.** erd **4.** clay, clod, dirt, land,
  marl, muck, sand, soil, vale **5.** geest,
  loess, sloam, terra **6.** ground, planet,
  rideau **7.** topsoil **8.** alluvium
earth (pert to) . . .
  center . . **10.** geocentric **12.** centrosphere
  comb form . . **3.** geo
  deformation . . **10.** epeirogeny
  formed beneath . . **8.** hypogene, plutonic
  formed by ores . . **9.** supergene
  formed on surface . . **7.** epigene
  god (Egypt) . . **3.** Geb (Keb)
  goddess . . **4.** Erda, Gaea (Gaia), Tari
    6. Semele **7.** Demeter
  produced by . . **6.** mortal **11.** terrigenous
  satellite . . see *satellite*
  volcanic . . **5.** trass
earthdrake . . . **6.** dragon
earthly . . . **7.** mundane, secular, terrene,
  worldly **8.** temporal **11.** terrestrial,
  universally, unspiritual **13.** materialistic
earthmover . . . **6.** digger **7.** backhoe,
  leveler **9.** bulldozer, excavator **11.** steam
  shovel
earth pig . . . **8.** aardvark
earthquake . . . **5.** quake, seism **7.** temblor
  12. diastrophism
earthstar . . . **6.** fungus **7.** Geaster
earthworm . . . **7.** annalid, dew worm,
  ipokoea **9.** Lumbricus
earthy . . . **3.** low **5.** gross, marly **6.** coarse
  7. worldly **8.** material **9.** unrefined
ease . . . **4.** calm, rest **5.** abate, allay,
  peace, quiet, relax **6.** pacify, relief,
  repose, soothe **7.** assuage, comfort,
  content, leisure, relieve, slacken
  8. facility, mitigate **9.** alleviate,
  disburden, enjoyment **10.** prosperity,

relaxation, solicitude **11.** informality,
tranquilize **12.** tranquillity (tranquility)
easily . . . **4.** eath (eith) **6.** gently,
slowly, softly **7.** readily **8.** smoothly
11. comfortably, dexterously
12. effortlessly
easily (pert to) . . .
broken . . **6.** shelly **7.** fragile, friable
frightened . . **8.** skittish
managed . . **6.** docile
moved . . **6.** mobile
offended . . **9.** sensitive
split . . **8.** schistic
understood . . **5.** lucid
east . . . **4.** Asia, dawn **6.** Levant, Orient
7. sunrise **8.** eastward
East Africa . . .
hartebeest . . **4.** tora
house (mud) . . **5.** tembe
republic . . **5.** Kenya **7.** Somalia
island . . **8.** Zanzibar
people . . **3.** Luo **4.** Embu, Teso **5.** Bantu,
Masai **6.** Kikuyu, Mau Mau **7.** Nilotes
vessel . . **4.** dhow
East India . . . see also *East Indian*
drink . . **4.** nipa
fan . . **6.** punkah (punka)
gateway (temple) . . **5.** toran (torana)
hat, helmet . . **5.** topee (topi)
money of account . . **4.** anna
mountain pass . . **4.** ghat (ghaut)
musical instrument . . **4.** vina **5.** ruana,
saron
police station . . **5.** thana (tanna)
sailing vessel . . **5.** dhoni (doni)
7. patamar
sugar, molasses . . **3.** gur **10.** massecuite
water vessel (brass) . . **4.** lota (lotah)
East Indian animal . . .
antelope . . **5.** bongo, takin **6.** impala,
nilgai **8.** axis deer
cattle . . **4.** gaur, zebu **5.** gayal, tsine
7. banteng
civet . . **6.** musang **10.** paradoxure
goat (wild) . . **4.** tahr **7.** markhor
lemurlike . . **7.** tarsier
raccoonlike . . **3.** wah **5.** panda
rat . . **9.** bandicoot
swine . . **8.** babirusa (babiroussa)
East Indian bird . . .
broadbill . . **4.** raya
bulbul . . **4.** kala
falcon . . **5.** besra
fruit pigeon . . **6.** treron
thrush . . **5.** shama
weaverbird . . **4.** baya
East Indian people . . .
boatswain . . **6.** serang
chief . . **6.** sirdar
groom . . **4.** syce
harem . . **6.** zenana
native sailor, soldier . . **5.** sepoy **6.** lascar
nurse . . **4.** amah, ayah
peasant . . **4.** ryot
poet . . **6.** Tagore
princess . . **4.** rani (ranee)
robber . . **6.** dacoit
title . . **4.** raja **5.** rajah, sahib
warrior . . **5.** singh
East Indian tree, plant . . .
bark . . **4.** lodh **5.** niepa

cedar . . **6.** deodar
cotton . . **5.** simal
fiber . . **4.** jute
fruit . . **3.** bel **6.** lanseh (lansa)
gum . . **4.** kino
herb . . **5.** tikor **6.** sesame **7.** roselle
mahogany . . **4.** toon
mulberry . . **4.** tapa
palm . . **3.** tal (fiber) **4.** nipa (thatch)
5. sural (juice), toddy **7.** palmyra
pea . . **4.** dhak **5.** Butea
rubber . . **3.** saj
shade . . **6.** banyan
timber . . **3.** saj, sal (saul) **4.** poon, teak
5. siris **6.** sissoo
walnut . . **6.** lebbek
east wind . . . **5.** Eurus
easy . . . **4.** calm, slow **5.** loose, suave
6. cinchy, facile, gentle, simple
7. natural **8.** gullible, informal,
moderate, tranquil, unforced
9. leisurely, unhurried **10.** manageable,
nonchalant, unaffected **11.** comfortable,
complaisant, unconcerned
easy-going . . . **4.** calm **11.** unflappable
easy job . . . **8.** sinecure
easy mark . . . **4.** dupe, gull **6.** sucker,
victim **7.** cat's-paw
eat . . . **3.** sup **4.** dine, etch, feed, gnaw
5. board, erode **6.** devour, ravage
7. consume, corrode, destroy
eat (pert to) . . .
between meals . . **4.** nosh **5.** bever,
snack
by rule . . **4.** diet
earth, clay . . **8.** geophagy
12. chthonophagy
greedily . . **3.** lab **4.** glut **5.** gorge, scarf
(down) **6.** gobble, pig out (sl) **7.** edacity
8. voracity
eatable . . . **6.** edible **8.** esculent, gustable
10. comestible
eater . . . **5.** diner **7.** epicure, glutton,
gourmet **8.** gourmand
eating (pert to) . . .
alone . . **9.** monophagy
comb form . . **7.** phagous
decay . . **12.** saprophagous
fish . . **11.** piscivorous **13.** icthyophagous
flesh, raw . . **9.** omophagia
flesh-eating . . **9.** creophagy
10. zoophagous **11.** carnivorous
man-eating . . **12.** androphagous
13. anthropophagy
nuts . . **10.** nucivorous **11.** nuciphagous
plants, herbs . . **11.** herbivorous
12. phytophagous
roots . . **12.** rhizophagous
eavesdrop . . . **3.** bug **4.** drip **6.** harken,
listen **7.** wiretap **10.** stillicide **14.** listen
secretly
ebb . . . **3.** low **4.** neap, sink, tide, wane
5. abate, decay **6.** recede, reflux, retire
7. decline, dwindle, shallow, subside
8. decrease
ebb and flow . . . **5.** surge **6.** aestus
(estus) **11.** alternation
ebb tide . . . **8.** low water
ebullition . . . **7.** boiling, ferment
8. bubbling **9.** agitation, commotion
12. fermentation **13.** effervescence

eccentric . . . **3.** cam (shaft), odd **5.** flaky, kinky **6.** weirdo **7.** erratic, strange **8.** abnormal **9.** erratical, irregular **13.** nonconformist **15.** idiosyncratical

eccentricity . . . **6.** oddity **9.** queerness **10.** aberration, erraticism **11.** abnormality, peculiarity, strangeness **12.** idiosyncrasy, irregularity **13.** nonconformity **17.** unconventionality

Ecclesiastes . . . **8.** Koheleth (Gr)

echidna . . . **7.** monster (Gr Myth) **8.** anteater

echinoderm . . . **8.** starfish **9.** sea urchin

echo . . . **4.** mute, stop (organ) **5.** nymph (Myth), reply **6.** repeat **7.** imitate, resound, respond **8.** resemble, response **9.** duplicate **10.** repetition **13.** reverberation

echoism . . . **12.** onomatopoeia

Eciton . . . **4.** ants (legionary)

eclipse . . . **5.** cloud, sully **6.** darken **7.** obscure, surpass **10.** extinguish

ecliptic term . . . **5.** lagna, orbit **6.** circle **9.** penumbral

ecology, oecology . . . **4.** sere **6.** botany **7.** biology **8.** bionomics, sociology **10.** bioecology

economical . . . **5.** canny, chary **6.** frugal, saving **7.** careful, thrifty **8.** domestic **9.** provident **12.** parsimonious

economics terms . . . **5.** T-bill **7.** bailout **8.** bankable, cash flow, rollover **9.** plutology **10.** monetarism, production (wealth)

economize . . . **4.** save **5.** skimp, stint **6.** scrimp **7.** husband, utilize **8.** retrench

economy . . . **4.** care **6.** saving, thrift **7.** cutback **8.** prudence **9.** canniness, husbandry **10.** providence

ecru . . . **3.** tan **5.** beige

ecstasy . . . **5.** bliss **6.** trance **7.** emotion, rapture

ecstatic . . . **4.** rapt **7.** rapture **9.** rapturous, rhapsodic

ectad . . . **7.** outward

ecto (comb form) . . . **7.** outside, without **8.** external

Ecuador (pert to) . . .
capital . . **5.** Quito
export . . **7.** bananas
hat . . **6.** Panama **8.** 'Jipijapa'
island . . **9.** Galapagos
mountain . . **5.** Andes
reptile . . **6.** iguana **8.** tortoise
volcano . . **10.** Chimborazo

ecumenical . . . **7.** general, liberal **8.** catholic, tolerant **9.** universal, world-wide **12.** cosmopolitan

eczema . . . **6.** herpes, tetter **8.** eruption **9.** salt rheum

edacity . . . **5.** greed **7.** avarice **8.** appetite, gulosity, voracity **10.** greediness

eddy . . . **4.** bore, gulf **5.** gurge, surge, swirl, whirl **6.** vortex **7.** current, wreathe **9.** whirlpool

Edentate (Zool) . . . **6.** sloths **7.** mammals **9.** aardvarks, anteaters **10.** armadillos

edge . . . **3.** hem, jag, lip, rim **4.** brim, brow, side **5.** arris, brink, crest, marge, sharp, sidle (to), splay, verge **6.** border, flange,

labrum, margin **7.** ambitus, selvage **8.** acrimony, pungency, selvedge **9.** advantage, sharpness **10.** escarpment

edged . . . **5.** erose **7.** crenate **8.** bordered, invected (Her)

edging . . . **3.** hem **4.** lace, welt **5.** frill, ruche **6.** border, fringe, ruffle **7.** binding, bordure (Her), flounce, tatting

edgy . . . **5.** sharp **7.** angular, nervous **8.** critical, snappish **9.** excitable, impatient **13.** sharp-cornered

edict . . . **3.** act, ban **4.** Bull (Pope's), fiat **5.** arret, dicta (pl), irade, order, ukase **6.** assize, decree, dictum, firman **7.** command, mandate **8.** decretal **9.** ordinance **12.** proclamation

edification . . . **8.** learning **9.** knowledge **11.** improvement, instruction

edifice . . . **5.** house **6.** church, palace, temple **7.** Capitol **8.** building **9.** structure **10.** tabernacle

edify . . . **5.** build, teach **7.** educate, improve **8.** instruct, organize **9.** construct, enlighten, establish

Edinburgh . . .
burgh . . **5.** Leith
capital of . . **8.** Scotland
county . . **10.** Midlothian
famed street . . **9.** Royal Mile
Gaelic name . . **7.** Dun Edin (Dunedin)
nickname . . **16.** Athens of the North
site . . **12.** Firth of Forth

Edison's workplace . . . **9.** Menlo Park

edit . . . **5.** emend **6.** direct, excise, redact, revise, reword **7.** arrange, correct, prepare

edition . . . **4.** copy **5.** issue **6.** number **7.** version

editions (Bib) . . .
eight texts . . **7.** octapla
four texts . . **8.** tetrapla
six texts . . **7.** hexapla
style and type . . **7.** Elzevir (1583)

editor . . . **7.** analyst, newsman, reviser **8.** arranger, redactor **9.** annotator, gazetteer **10.** journalist, supervisor **11.** commentator **12.** newspaperman

editor's word . . . **4.** dele, stet

Edom . . . **5.** Teman (Bib) **7.** Idumaea

Edomite . . . **4.** Esau **5.** Isaac, Jacob **8.** Idumaean

educate . . . **4.** rear **5.** teach, train **6.** inform **7.** develop **8.** instruct **9.** cultivate, enlighten **10.** discipline **12.** indoctrinate

educated . . . **6.** taught **7.** erudite, learned, trained **8.** cultured, informed, lettered, literate **11.** enlightened

education . . . **8.** breeding, literacy, training **9.** opsimathy (late in life), schooling **10.** discipline

educe . . . **4.** draw **6.** deduce, elicit, evolve, obtain, secure

eel (pert to) . . .
colorful . . **5.** moray **7.** Muraena
genus . . **8.** Anguilla **13.** Leptocephalus
marine . . **5.** elver **6.** conger
mud . . **5.** siren
sand . . **4.** grig
young . . **5.** elver

eellike . . . **4.** lant, ling **7.** eelpout, lamprey **8.** Ophidion **10.** anguilloid

11. Lepidosiren
eels, fishing for . . . 7. sniggle
eels, migration of . . . 7. eelfare
eelworm . . . 4. nema 8. Nematoda
  9. roundworm 10. vinegar eel
eerie, eery . . . 5. scary, timid, weird
  6. gloomy, spooky 7. awesome,
  fearful, uncanny 9. deathlike, unearthly
  10. frightened
efface . . . 5. erase 6. cancel, delete 7. blot
  out, expunge 10. obliterate
effect . . . 4. does 5. close, éclat,
  force, mneme 6. mirage, obtain,
  result 7. achieve, compass, conjure,
  execute, fulfill, meaning, operate,
  outcome, perform, reality, realize
  8. complete 9. discharge, execution,
  influence 10. accomplish, appearance,
  consummate, impression
  11. consequence, performance
effective . . . 4. able 6. active, actual,
  cogent 7. capable, telling 8. adequate,
  eloquent, equipped, striking 9. brilliant,
  competent, effectual, efficient,
  operative, trenchant 11. efficacious,
  influential
effects . . . 5. goods, wares 8. movables,
  property
effeminate . . . 3. sop 5. sissy 6. female,
  tender 7. cockney, epicene, womanly
  8. feminine, womanish 9. Sybaritic
  11. mollycoddle 12. overdelicate
  13. overemotional
effervescent . . . 5. fizzy 6. bubbly,
  lively 7. boiling, hissing 8. bubbling,
  mousseux 9. ebullient, sparkling
  10. boisterous
effete ∴ . . 4. aged, idle 5. spent 6. barren
  7. worn out 9. exhausted, fruitless
  11. ineffectual
efficacious . . . 4. able 5. valid 6. potent
  9. effective, effectual, operative
  11. influential
efficacy . . . 4. dint 5. force, power
  6. virtue 7. ability, potency 10. efficiency
efficiency . . . 5. power, skill 7. ability,
  utility 8. efficacy 10. capability,
  competence 11. proficiency
  12. productivity 13. effectiveness
  15. efficaciousness
efficient . . . 4. able 7. capable, operant
  9. competent, effective, effectual,
  operative 10. productive
  12. businesslike
effigy . . . 4. copy, icon 5. image 8. likeness
  9. facsimile, jackstraw, semblance
  11. resemblance
effluvium . . . 4. aura, fume, odor
  9. ectoplasm, emanation
efflux . . . 3. end 6. expiry, runoff
  7. outflow 8. effusion 9. effluence,
  emanation
effodient . . . 9. burrowing, fossorial
effort . . . 3. try, tug 4. dint, jump, toil,
  will, work 5. assay, burst, labor, nisus,
  pains, trial 6. strain 7. attempt, conatus,
  trouble 8. endeavor, exertion, struggle
  11. application
effrontery . . . 5. brass 8. audacity,
  boldness 9. arrogance, impudence,
  sauciness 11. presumption

effulgence . . . 5. aglow, glory 6. luster
  8. radiance, rutilant, splendor
  10. brightness, brilliance
effusive . . . 7. gushing 9. exuberant,
  rhapsodic 13. demonstrative
eft . . . 4. evet, newt 6. lizard, triton
  7. urodele 10. salamander
egest . . . 4. emit, void 7. excrete
  9. discharge, ejaculate, eliminate
egg . . . 3. nit, ova (pl), ove 4. goad,
  ovum, prod, urge 5. ovule 6. incite
  9. instigate
egg (pert to) . . .
  bird's . . 7. chalaza (white of), treadle
  (embryo)
  case . . 6. ovisac
  comb form . . 2. oo 3. ovi
  part . . 7. latebra
  shaped . . 4. ooid, oval 5. ovate, ovoid
  6. ooidal 9. ovaliform
  shell . . 5. shard 6. ovisac
  undeveloped . . 5. addle
  white . . 5. glair 7. albumen
  yolk, yelk . . 7. liaison 8. lecithin
eggplant . . . 9. melongena
eggs (pert to) . . .
  feeding on . . 9. ovivorous
  fish . . 3. roe 5. berry, spawn
  preserved . . 5. pidan
  tester of . . 7. candler
  two at a time . . 8. ditokous
egis, aegis . . . 4. care 5. guard 6. shield,
  symbol (anc) 7. backing, defense
  8. advocacy, auspices, guidance,
  tutelage 9. fosterage, patronage
  10. protection 11. sponsorship
ego . . . 3. man 4. self 5. atman (Hind)
  6. psyche, spirit 7. conceit, jivatma
  (Hind) 11. selfishness
egress . . . 4. exit 5. issue 6. outlet
  8. issuance 9. departure
egret . . . 5. heron, plume 8. aigrette
Egypt, UAR . . . see also *Egyptian*
  capital . . 5. Cairo
  Christian . . 4. Copt
  city (ruined) . . 5. Luxor, Tanis 6. Karnak,
  Thebes
  dam . . 5. Aswan
  desert . . 5. Dakla
  gulf . . 4. Suez 5. Aqaba
  king . . 6. Farouk (Faruk)
  language (anc) . . 6. Coptic
  lighthouse (anc) . . 6. Pharos
  mother . . 3. Mut
  peninsula . . 5. Sinai
  philosopher . . 8. Plotinus
  port . . 4. Said, Suez 10. Alexandria
  president . . 5. Sadat 6. Nasser
  queen . . 9. Cleopatra
  river . . 4. Nile
  ruler . . 5. pasha 6. caliph 7. khedive
  ruler . . 7. Busiris (Myth), Pharaoh,
  Ptolemy, Rameses
  sea . . 3. Red 13. Mediterranean
Egyptian (pert to) . . .
  abode of dead . . 4. Aaru (fields of)
  6. Amenti
  antelope . . 7. bubalis
  ape (sacred) . . 4. Aani
  beetle . . 6. scarab
  bird (crocodile) . . 6. sicsac

bird (sacred) .. **4.** Benu, ibis **7.** phoenix
bull .. **4.** apis
cobra .. **4.** haje
cross .. **3.** tau **4.** ankh (emblem of life)
   10. crux ansata
crown .. **4.** atef
dancing girl .. **4.** alma (alme, Almeh)
   7. ghawazi **8.** Baramika
dog .. **6.** saluki (gazelle hound)
headdress of ruler .. **6.** Uraeus
heaven .. **4.** Aaru
lizard .. **4.** adda **5.** skink
lute .. **5.** nable
paper .. **7.** papyrus
solar disk .. **4.** aten
soul .. **2.** Ba **4.** khet, sahu
stone (famed) .. **7.** Rosetta
symbol .. **3.** asp **6.** scarab (beetle)
tomb .. **6.** serdab (cell) **7.** mastaba
watchman .. **6.** ghafir (ghaffir)
writing .. **13.** hieroglyphics
Egyptian god of ...
day .. **5.** Horus
earth .. **3.** Geb, Keb
life .. **4.** Ptah
pleasure .. **3.** Bes
primeval fluid .. **2.** Nu
sea .. **5.** Aegir
sun .. **2.** Ra **3.** Tem (Tum) **4.** Atmu
   5. Mentu (Ment) **7.** Khepera
   11. Harpocrates
supreme .. **4.** Amon (Amun) **6.** Amon-Re
underworld .. **6.** Osiris **7.** Hershef
unknown .. **2.** Ka
wisdom .. **5.** Thoth **6.** Dhouti
Egyptian goddess of ...
arms .. **4.** Anta
fertility .. **4.** Isis
gods .. **4.** Sati
motherhood .. **4.** Apet
sea .. **3.** Ran
truth .. **4.** Maat
eidolon ... **5.** image **7.** phantom **8.** illusion
   10. apparition
eight, eighth (pert to) ...
day (every) .. **5.** octan
feast day .. **4.** utas
group .. **5.** octad, octet **6.** octave
   7. octette
heaven .. **5.** stars (fixed)
number .. **4.** ocho **6.** ogdoad
philosophy .. **8.** Diagrams
sided .. **9.** octagonal
tone, note .. **4.** unca **6.** quaver (8th)
   8. diatonic
eighteen inches ... **5.** cubit
Eire ... **4.** Erin **7.** Ireland
ejaculate ... **4.** emit, oust, void **5.** blurt,
   eject, evict, expel **7.** exclaim **8.** dislodge
eject ... **4.** emit, oust, spew, void **5.** evict,
   expel, spout, spurt **6.** banish **7.** extrude
   9. discharge, eliminate
ejection ... **6.** ouster **8.** eviction
   9. expulsion **11.** elimination
eke (out) ... **3.** add, imp, tab **4.** also, etch
   8. addition, appendix (dial), increase,
   piece out **10.** postscript
El ... **3.** God **5.** deity
elaborate ... **6.** ornate, refine **7.** develop,
   improve, perfect, studied **9.** embellish,
   perfected, superfine **11.** complicated,

high-wrought
Elam capital ... **4.** Susa (anc)
élan ... **4.** dash **5.** ardor **6.** spirit
   9. eagerness **10.** enthusiasm
elapse ... **2.** go **3.** die, fly, run **4.** flit,
   pass, slip **5.** lapse **6.** expire
elastic ... **6.** pliant, rubber **7.** buoyant,
   ductile, springy **8.** flexible, stretchy
   9. expansive, resilient **12.** recuperative
elasticity ... **4.** give **6.** elater, spring
   7. pliancy, rebound **9.** ductility
   10. resilience
elated ... **6.** jovial **7.** gleeful **8.** exultant,
   jubilant **9.** overjoyed
Elbe tributary ... **4.** Eger, Iser
elbow ... **5.** ancon, joint, nudge **6.** jostle
   8. chelidon (hollow of)
El Camino Real ... **9.** Royal Road
   12. King's Highway (Pac Hwy)
elder ... **3.** iva **4.** ainé, blue (color)
   5. berry, judge, ruler **6.** Mormon, senior
   7. ancient **8.** ancestor **10.** forefather
eldest ... **5.** eigne **6.** oldest **8.** earliest
   9. firstborn
eldritch ... **4.** wild **5.** eerie (eery), weird
   9. frightful
Eleatic philosopher ... **4.** Zeno
   10. Parmenides
elect ... **3.** ort **4.** name **5.** elite **6.** choose,
   select **9.** designate
election ... **6.** choice **11.** alternative
   13. determination **14.** discrimination
Electra (pert to) ...
brother .. **7.** Orestes
father .. **9.** Agamemnon
mother .. **12.** Clytemnestra
electric (pert to) ...
atom .. **8.** electron
condenser (anc) .. **9.** Leyden jar
conductor .. **6.** ohmage
current .. **2.** AC, DC **7.** circuit
force .. **4.** elod
generator .. **6.** dynamo
light .. **3.** arc **4.** neon **12.** incandescent
meter .. **7.** ammeter **9.** voltmeter,
   wattmeter
particle .. **3.** ion **6.** cation (kation)
power .. **7.** wattage
safety device .. **4.** fuse
unit .. **3.** ohm, rel **4.** volt, watt
   5. farad, henry, joule **6.** ampere, proton
   7. coulomb, oersted **8.** kilowatt
electricity ... **5.** juice, power
   10. illuminant
eleemosynary ... **4.** alms, free **7.** charity
   10. almsgiving
elegance ... **5.** charm, grace, taste
   6. beauty, polish **9.** propriety
   10. ornateness, politeness, refinement
   13. sumptuousness
elegant ... **4.** rich **6.** dressy, ornate
   soigné, urbane **7.** courtly, genteel,
   refined **8.** graceful, handsome, polished,
   tasteful **9.** admirable, beautiful,
   excellent **10.** fastidious **11.** fashionable
   13. grandiloquent
element ... **3.** air **4.** fire **5.** earth, water
elementary ... **5.** basic **6.** simple
   7. primary **8.** inchoate, original
   9. beginning **11.** fundamental
elephant ... **3.** cow **4.** bull, calf **5.** hathi,

rogue 6. tusker 8. behemoth
9. pachyderm
elephant (pert to) . . .
apple . . 7. Feronia
boy . . 4. Sabu
call, cry . . 4. barr 7. trumpet
enclosure, trap . . 6. keddah
extinct . . 7. mammoth
goad . . 5. ankus
keeper . . 6. mahout
seat . . 6. howdah
tusk . . 5. ivory 9. scrivello
young . . 4. calf
elevate . . . 4. lift, rear 5. elate, exalt, raise
6. refine, uplift 7. advance, dignify,
ennoble, glorify, inspire, promote
10. exhilarate
elevated . . . 2. el 5. lofty, risen 6. elated
7. exalted, sublime 8. eminence
elevation . . . 4. hill 6. height (highth)
9. promotion 10. exaltation
11. composition (Eccl), distinction
13. glorification
elevation of the mind . . . 7. anagoge
elevator . . . 3. bin 4. cage, lift, silo
9. ascenseur
elevator name . . . 4. Otis
eleven . . . 7. hendeca (comb form)
elf . . . 3. fay, hob, imp, nix 4. peri 5. fairy,
gnome, ouphe, pixie 6. goblin, sprite
7. brownie
elfish . . . 5. elfin 6. elvish, impish 7. elflike,
tricksy 8. eldritch 11. mischievous
Elgin Marbles . . . 10. sculptures (by
Phidias)
Elia . . . 4. Lamb (Charles)
Eli alma mater . . . 4. Yale
elicit . . . 3. get 4. draw, pump 5. claim,
educe, evoke, exact, wrest, wring
6. deduce, demand, entice, extort,
induce, obtain 7. extract
elide . . . 4. dele, omit 5. annul 6. ignore
7. destroy, nullify, shorten 8. demolish,
suppress 9. eliminate
eligible . . . 3. apt, fit 4. meet 6. worthy
8. entitled, suitable 9. competent,
desirable, qualified 10. acceptable,
admissible
Elijah . . . 7. prophet 8. oratorio 14. John
the Baptist (Bib)
eliminate . . . 3. rid 4. kill 5. erase, expel
6. detach, remove 7. discard, divulge,
exclude, excrete, release 8. evacuate,
separate 9. segregate 11. exterminate
Eliot, George (pseud) . . . 12. Mary Ann
Evans
Elisha . . . 7. prophet 8. disciple (of Elijah)
elision . . . 7. syncope 9. severance
10. abridgment, shortening
11. suppression (vowel)
elite . . . 5. stars 6. flower, galaxy
7. fashion, society 9. beau monde
10. upper crust
elixir . . . 6. remedy 7. cure-all, essence,
extract, heal-all, panacea 8. medicine,
tincture 10. catholicon 12. quintessence
elixir of life . . . 11. elixir vitae
Elixir of Love . . . 13. L'Elisir d'Amore
elk . . . 4. deer 5. Alces, eland, moose
6. sambar, wapiti
ellipse . . . 5. curve, focus (foci), ovoid

ellipsis . . . 4. dots 6. points 8. omission
elliptical . . . 5. ovoid, vague 7. obscure
10. incomplete
elm (pert to) . . .
borer . . 6. beetle, lamiid
fruit . . 6. samara
genus . . 5. Ulmus
rock, wing (kinds) . . 5. wahoo
Elm City . . . 8. New Haven
Elmo . . . 11. patron saint (sailors)
elocution . . . 7. oratory 8. rhetoric
9. eloquence 10. expression
elocutionist . . . 6. reader 7. reciter
11. elocutioner 13. recitationist
eloge . . . 6. eulogy 7. address, oration
8. encomium, eulogium
eloign . . . 6. convey, remove 7. conceal
elongate . . . 6. extend, remove 7. stretch
8. continue, lengthen, protract
elongated . . . 4. lank, long 6. linear,
oblong 7. prolate, slender 8. extended
9. stretched 10. attenuated
elope . . . 6. decamp 7. abscond, skip out
8. slip away
eloquence . . . 7. fluency, oratory
9. discourse, elocution
14. expressiveness
eloquence, teacher of . . . 6. rhetor
eloquent . . . 5. vivid 10. Ciceronian,
expressive, meaningful, oratorical
11. significant
else . . . 2. or 4. ense (ens) 5. if not,
other 9. otherwise 10. additional
12. accompanying
elsewhere . . . 4. away 5. alibi (law)
elucidate . . . 5. clear, lucid 7. clarify, clear
up 8. simplify 9. interpret 10. illustrate
elude . . . 4. flee, foil, mock, shun 5. avoid,
dodge, evade 6. baffle, befool, escape
10. circumvent
elusive . . . 4. eely 6. subtle 7. elusory,
evasive 8. baffling 9. equivocal
10. impalpable
elves . . . see *elf*
Elysium (Myth) . . . 8. paradise
em . . . 2. en (half) 4. unit (Elec)
emaciated . . . 4. lean 5. gaunt 6. peaked,
wasted 7. pinched 10. attenuated,
cadaverous
emanation . . . 4. aura, odor 5. light,
niton (radium), vapor 7. outcome
8. creation, effluvia 9. ectoplasm,
radiation 10. exhalation, generation
11. consequence
emancipation . . . 6. rescue 7. freedom,
release 10. liberation 11. manumission
15. enfranchisement
emancipator, famous . . . 7. Lincoln
emasculate . . . 4. geld, spay 5. unman
6. soften 8. castrate 9. expurgate,
sterilize 10. effeminize
embalmer . . . 5. cerer 9. mortician,
preserver 10. undertaker
embankment . . . 3. dam 4. bund, dike
5. levee, revet, shore 7. barrier, pilapil
(rice field) 8. buttress 10. breakwater
13. fortification
embargo . . . 5. edict, order 7. exclude
8. blockade, prohibit, stoppage
9. exclusion 10. impediment
11. prohibition, requisition

embark . . . **4.** sail, ship **5.** begin **6.** depart, invest, set off (out), unmoor **7.** cast off, entrain

embarrass . . . **5.** abash, shame **6.** hamper, hinder, impede **7.** confuse, fluster, involve, mortify, nonplus **8.** bewilder, confound, encumber, handicap **9.** discomfit, dumbfound **10.** complicate, disconcert

embarrassed . . . **8.** red-faced

embarrassment . . . **5.** shame **9.** abashment, confusion **11.** involvement, predicament **12.** discomfiture, entanglement **13.** inconvenience, mortification

embellish . . . **3.** gem **4.** deck, gild **5.** adorn, array, dress, gouge, grace **6.** bedeck, enrich **7.** bedrape, enhance, garnish **8.** beautify, emblazon, furbelow, ornament **9.** embroider **10.** exaggerate

embellishment . . . **9.** garniture **10.** decoration, furbishing **12.** exaggeration **13.** ornamentation

ember . . . **3.** ash **4.** coal (live), izle **5.** gleed **6.** cinder **7.** residue

embers . . . **5.** ashes **8.** emotions (past), memories

embezzle . . . **5.** steal, swipe **6.** lessen, thieve, weaken (obs) **7.** purloin **8.** peculate, squander **9.** dissipate **11.** appropriate

embitter . . . **4.** sour **5.** anger **7.** envenom **8.** acerbate **10.** antagonize, exacerbate

emblazon . . . **4.** laud **5.** color, extol **6.** praise **7.** display, exhibit, glorify **9.** celebrate, embellish

emblem . . . **3.** rue **4.** mace, sign, type **5.** badge, crown, image, token, totem **6.** device, figure, symbol **7.** balance (justice), coronet, sceptor **9.** prototype

emblematic . . . **5.** typal **7.** typical **8.** symbolic **10.** figurative **14.** characteristic

embodiment . . . **4.** Apis **6.** avatar, matter **7.** epitome **9.** inclusion **10.** enfoldment **11.** combination, composition, incarnation **12.** organization **13.** incorporation **14.** representative **15.** personification

embolden . . . **5.** nerve **6.** assure **7.** hearten **8.** reassure **9.** encourage

embosom . . . **6.** foster **7.** cherish, embrace, enclose **8.** surround

embrace . . . **3.** hug **4.** fold, gain, hold, love, wrap **5.** adopt, clasp, cling, grasp, inarm, seize **6.** accoll (obs), caress, enfold **7.** cherish, contain, enclose, espouse, include, involve, welcome **8.** comprise, encircle, greeting, surround **9.** encompass

embroider . . . **7.** falsify **8.** decorate, ornament **9.** embellish **10.** exaggerate

embroidery . . . **8.** appliqué **9.** hardanger

embroidery frame . . . **7.** taboret (tabouret)

embroil . . . **5.** upset **6.** jumble **7.** agitate, disturb, perplex, trouble **8.** convulse, disorder, distract **9.** commingle, implicate **10.** complicate, discompose

emcee . . . **4.** host

eme . . . **5.** uncle **6.** friend, gossip

emend . . . **4.** edit, mend **5.** amend, right **6.** better, remedy, revise **7.** correct, improve, rectify

emerald . . . **5.** beryl, color, green **7.** smaragd

Emerald Isle . . . **4.** Erin **7.** Ireland

emerge . . . **3.** dip **4.** pend, rise **5.** hatch, issue **6.** appear **7.** debouch, emanate **10.** disembogue

emergency . . . **5.** pinch **6.** clutch, crisis, strait **8.** exigency, juncture **9.** extremity, necessity **10.** substitute

emery . . . **6.** pumice **8.** abradant, abrasive, corundum **9.** sandpaper

emesis . . . **6.** puking **7.** spewing **8.** vomiting **12.** disgorgement **13.** regurgitation

emeute . . . **4.** riot **6.** Putsch **8.** outbreak **10.** insurgence **12.** insurrection

emigrant . . . **6.** emigré **7.** migrant, outgoer, settler **8.** colonist, stranger **9.** immigrant, migratory (of birds)

eminence . . . **4.** hill **5.** title **6.** height, rideau **7.** dignity **9.** authority, elevation, greatness, loftiness **10.** famousness, importance, projection **11.** superiority **13.** transcendency

eminent . . . **4.** arch, high **5.** great, lofty, noted **6.** famous, marked, signal **8.** renowned, superior, towering **9.** important **10.** celebrated, protruding **11.** illustrious **13.** distinguished

emissary . . . **3.** spy **5.** agent, scout **8.** delegate, diplomat

emit . . . **4.** glow, reek, shed **5.** eject, eruct, exude, issue, pluff, voice **6.** exhale **7.** distill (distil), emanate, publish, radiate **8.** opalesce (colors), transmit **9.** discharge, irradiate

emmet . . . **3.** ant **7.** pismire **8.** formicid

emollient . . . **4.** balm **8.** ointment, soothing **9.** lubricant, softening

emolument . . . **4.** fees, gain **5.** wages **6.** profit, salary **7.** stipend, tribute **9.** allowance **12.** compensation

emotion . . . **5.** agony, stoic **6.** pathos **7.** feeling, passion **9.** agitation, gratitude, sensation, sentiment **10.** excitement **11.** disturbance, sensibility

emotional seat . . . **5.** bosom

emotionless . . . **9.** apathetic, impassive, unfeeling **10.** spiritless **11.** unemotional **12.** unresponsive

emperor . . . **4.** czar, tsar **5.** Mogul **7.** monarch **9.** commander, imperator, sovereign

emphasis . . . **6.** accent, stress **7.** cadence **8.** salience **10.** insistence **14.** impressiveness

emphasize . . . **6.** accent, insist, stress **7.** point up **9.** punctuate **10.** accentuate

emphatic . . . **7.** earnest **8.** forcible, positive, striking **9.** energetic, insistent **10.** expressive **11.** significant

empire . . . **4.** rule, sway **5.** green (color), reign, state **6.** domain **7.** control, country

Empire (pert to) . . .
of the Rising Sun . . **5.** Japan
State . . **7.** New York

State of the South .. **7.** Georgia

empiric ... **4.** fake **5.** cheat, quack
8. impostor **9.** charlatan **10.** mountebank

employ ... **3.** use **4.** busy, coax,
hire **5.** apply, exert **6.** devote,
occupy **7.** concern, entrust, service
10. occupation

employees ... **4.** crew, gang, help **5.** force,
hands, staff **9.** personnel **10.** associates

employer ... **4.** user **5.** hirer **6.** master
8. consumer **12.** entrepreneur

employment ... **3.** use **4.** work **5.** trade
7. calling, purpose, service **8.** business,
vocation **10.** occupation, profession

emporium ... **4.** fair, mart **5.** store
6. bazaar, market **10.** exposition

empower ... **6.** enable **7.** entitle
8. delegate, deputize **9.** authorize
10. commission

empty ... **4.** idle, toom, vain, void **5.** blank,
clear, drain, inane **6.** hollow, hungry,
jejune, vacant, vacate **7.** deplete,
foolish, vacuous **8.** evacuate, unfilled
9. insincere **10.** unburdened,
unoccupied

empusa (Gr Myth) ... **5.** fungi **7.** specter
9. hobgoblin

empyrean ... **3.** sky **5.** ether **6.** Caelus,
welkin **7.** heavens, the blue

emulate ... **5.** equal, outdo, rival
7. compete, imitate, vie with
11. competition

emulsion ... **9.** demulcent **10.** semiliquid,
suspension

enable ... **5.** equip **6.** clothe **7.** empower,
qualify **9.** authorize **10.** capacitate

enact ... **4.** pass, play **6.** decree,
enjoin, ordain, record **7.** actuate,
appoint, perform **9.** legislate, represent
10. constitute **11.** impersonate

enactment ... **3.** law **4.** veto **5.** canon,
edict, usage **6.** decree **7.** statute
9. ordinance **11.** legislation

encamp, encampment ... **4.** camp, tent
5. siege **7.** bivouac, camping

enchant ... **5.** charm **6.** delude **7.** bewitch,
delight **8.** ensorcel **9.** captivate,
enrapture, fascinate

enchantment ... **5.** charm, magic, spell
7. sorcery **8.** witchery **10.** allurement,
necromancy, witchcraft
11. bewitchment, fascination,
incantation

enchantress ... **5.** Circe, Medea
7. charmer **9.** bewitcher, sorceress,
temptress

encina ... **7.** live oak

encircle ... **3.** orb **4.** gird, ring, zone
5. belay, inorb, twist **6.** enfold
7. besiege, circuit, enclose, environ,
include, wreathe **8.** surround
12. circumscribe

encircled ... **4.** girt **5.** orbed, paled,
zoned **6.** belted, forded, hooped, ringed
7. enlaced **8.** enclosed, enfolded,
wreathed **10.** surrounded

enclose ... **3.** hem, mew **5.** bound, fence
6. corral, encase, engulf **7.** enclave,
envelop, harness, include **8.** imprison,
surround **9.** encompass
12. circumscribe

enclosed ... **4.** pent, sept (area)
7. encased **8.** confined **10.** surrounded

enclosure ... **3.** pen **4.** bawn, cage, yair
(yare), yard **5.** carol (cloister), kraal
(craal), sekos **6.** corral **8.** contents,
poundage, stockade

encomium ... **4.** hymn **5.** eloge **6.** eulogy,
praise **7.** tribute **8.** accolade **9.** panegyric

encompass ... **4.** ring **5.** hem in **6.** begird,
effect **7.** besiege, circuit, compass,
contain, enclose, environ, include
8. encircle, surround **10.** accomplish
12. circumscribe

encompassing ... **7.** ambient
13. circumambient

encore ... **3.** bis **4.** echo, over **5.** again
8. applause, once more

encounter ... **4.** bout, meet **5.** brave,
brush, fight, incur, onset **6.** attack,
breast, oppose **7.** collide, meeting
8. conflict **10.** engagement, experience

encourage ... **4.** abet, urge **5.** boost,
cheer, impel, nerve, rally **6.** assure,
exhort, foster, incite **7.** advance,
comfort, console, hearten, inspire,
promote **8.** embolden, inspirit
9. instigate, stimulate **11.** countenance

encouragement ... **3.** aid **7.** comfort
9. fosterage, incentive **10.** inducement
11. emboldening

encroach upon ... **5.** poach **6.** invade,
trench **7.** impinge, intrude **8.** infringe,
overstep, trespass

encumber ... **4.** clog, load **5.** check
6. burden, hamper, hinder, retard,
saddle **7.** involve, oppress **8.** entangle,
handicap, obstruct, overload
9. embarrass **10.** overburden

encumbrance ... **5.** alien (law), claim
6. burden **9.** dependent **10.** impediment
11. impedimenta

encyclic ... **6.** letter **7.** pandect **8.** circular,
treatise **10.** encircling
13. comprehensive

encyclopedic learning, person of ...
10. polyhistor **13.** encyclopedist

end ... **3.** aim, neb, tip, toe **4.** fate,
kill, ruin, tail **5.** amend, close, death,
finis, limit, omega, point, telos, upend
6. expire, finale, finish, result, thirty
7. destroy, purpose **8.** complete,
conclude, dissolve **9.** cessation,
determine, extremity, intention,
objective, terminate **10.** completion
11. termination

end (pert to) ...
arrow .. **4.** nock
boundary .. **5.** bourn **7.** abuttal
cloth .. **7.** remnant
game .. **4.** goal
man .. **8.** minstrel
news .. **6.** bulletin
timber .. **5.** tenon

endanger ... **4.** risk **6.** expose, hazard
7. imperil **10.** compromise, jeopardize

endeavor ... **3.** aim, try, vie **4.** seek
5. essay, ettle, nisus, tempt **6.** effort,
strive **7.** attempt **8.** struggle

endemic ... **6.** native **10.** indigenous
14. characteristic

ending ... **5.** death **6.** result **9.** cessation,
desinence **10.** completion, conclusion

11. destruction, termination

endless . . . **4.** many **6.** eterne **7.** eternal, undying **8.** eternity, infinite, numerous, unending **9.** boundless, continual, incessant, perpetual, unceasing, unstinted **10.** continuous **11.** everlasting **12.** interminable **13.** uninterrupted

endorse, indorse . . . **4.** sign **6.** attest, second **7.** approve, support **8.** sanction **9.** authorize, guarantee

endorsement . . . **4.** fiat, visa (vise) **8.** approval, sanction **9.** provision, signature **10.** acceptance, validation **12.** ratification **14.** authentication

endow . . . **3.** dow, due **4.** dote, vest **5.** dower, endue, indue **6.** bestow, clothe, enrich, give to, invest **7.** empower, furnish, provide

endowment . . . **4.** gift **5.** dower, grant **7.** talents **8.** appanage (apanage) **9.** insurance, provision **11.** empowerment, instruction (Mormon)

endue . . . **5.** endow, teach **6.** clothe, digest, invest, supply **7.** empower

endurable . . . **8.** bearable **9.** tolerable **10.** sufferable **11.** supportable

endurance . . . **7.** stamina **8.** patience, strength **9.** fortitude, suffering **10.** durability, permanence, sufferance **11.** continuance, resignation **12.** perseverance

endure . . . **4.** bear, bide, dree, last, live, tide, wear **5.** abide, allow, brook, stand **6.** afford, remain, suffer **7.** condone, persist, sustain, undergo **8.** continue, tolerate **9.** persevere, withstand

enduring . . . **7.** durable, lasting, patient **9.** permanent **11.** persevering, substantial, unforgotten **13.** long-suffering

enemy . . . **3.** foe **5.** devil, force, fremd (frenne), hater, rival, Satan **6.** foeman **8.** opponent **9.** adversary **10.** antagonist

energetic . . . **5.** fresh **6.** active **8.** forceful, forcible, vigorous **9.** strenuous **11.** industrious

energy . . . **2.** go **3.** erg, pep, vim **4.** bent **5.** force, nerve, power, vigor **6.** spirit **7.** potency, sthenia **8.** strength **9.** animation

energy (pert to) . . .
lack of . . **5.** atony **6.** anergy **7.** aneuria, inertia **8.** asthenia
mental . . **9.** psychurgy
personified . . **6.** Shakti
potential . . **5.** ergal
unit . . **3.** erg **5.** ergon

enervate . . . **3.** sap **5.** drain, unman **6.** weaken **7.** exhaust, unnerve **8.** enfeeble **10.** debilitate

enfeeble . . . **4.** numb **6.** sicken, soften, weaken **7.** depress **8.** enervate **9.** attenuate **10.** debilitate

enfilade . . . **4.** rake **5.** vista **7.** barrage **9.** broadside **11.** arrangement (in rows)

enfold, infold . . . **4.** fold, wrap **5.** clasp, cover **6.** infold **7.** embrace, envelop **8.** surround

enforce . . . **5.** drive **6.** assail, compel **7.** execute, inspire **9.** constrain,

encourage, intensify, reinforce **10.** invigorate

enfranchise . . . **4.** free **5.** admit **7.** deliver, set free **8.** liberate **10.** emancipate

engage . . . **4.** bind, draw, hire, rent **5.** lease **6.** absorb, embark, employ, enlist, induce, occupy, pledge **7.** attract, betroth, engross, involve, promise **8.** contract, entangle **9.** interlock, intermesh

engaged . . . **4.** busy **5.** hired **6.** bonded, meshed **7.** earnest, entered, pledged, versant **8.** embedded, employed, involved, occupied, promised **9.** affianced, betrothed, engrossed **10.** contracted

engaged in controversy . . . **9.** disputant

engagement . . . **4.** date **6.** battle **7.** promise **9.** betrothal, encounter **10.** attachment **11.** appointment, involvement

engaging . . . **5.** sapid **6.** taking **8.** alluring, duelling **10.** attractive, delightful **11.** interesting

engender . . . **3.** sow (seeds) **5.** beget, breed, cause **6.** excite **7.** develop, produce **8.** generate, occasion **9.** call forth, procreate, propagate

engine . . . **3.** gin, ram **5.** mogul, motor **6.** onager **7.** machine, robinet, turbine **10.** locomotive

engine (type) . . . **3.** gas **5.** motor, solar, steam **6.** Diesel, rocket **8.** gasoline **10.** combustion

engineer . . . **4.** plan **7.** manager **8.** computer, contrive, designer, inventor, maneuver, operator, therblig **9.** construct **11.** constructor, superintend

engineer (type) . . . **5.** civil, corps, sales **6.** driver, mining **7.** planner **8.** chemical, geodetic, military, railroad, research, sanitary **9.** hydraulic **10.** electrical, industrial, mechanical, structural **11.** electronics **12.** aeronautical, construction **14.** administrative

engird . . . **6.** begird, circle, girdle **7.** envelop **8.** encircle, ensphere

England . . . see also *English*
called . . **6.** Albion (anc) **7.** Britain **9.** Britannia
capital . . **6.** London
city . . **3.** Ely **4.** Hull, York **5.** Derby, Leeds **6.** Exeter **7.** Bristol, Croydon **8.** Brighton, Coventry, Hastings, Plymouth **9.** Liverpool, Sheffield **10.** Birmingham, Epsom Downs, Manchester, Nottingham, Portsmouth **11.** Southampton
college (famed) . . **6.** Oxford **9.** Cambridge, Sandhurst (military)
conqueror . . **5.** Danes **6.** Angles, Saxons **7.** Normans
constitution . . **10.** Magna Carta (1215) **12.** Bill of Rights (1688)
county . . **4.** Kent **5.** Devon, Essex **6.** Dorset, Sussex **9.** Yorkshire
emblem . . **4.** lion, rose
House of . . **4.** York **5.** Blois, Tudor **6.** Stuart **7.** Hanover, Windsor **8.** Normandy **9.** Lancaster **11.** Plantagenet

island.. **5.** Wight **6.** Scilly, Virgin
  7. Bahamas, Bermuda, Channel,
  Solomon **8.** Falkland, Windward **9.** Isle
  of Man
king (anc).. **6.** Arthur (legend), Egbert
  8. Ethelred **9.** Ethelwulf
native (anc).. **4.** Celt, Dane, Jute
  5. Saxon **8.** Anglican **9.** Sassenach
  10. Anglo-Saxon
river.. **3.** Exe **4.** Avon, Ouse **5.** Trent
  6. Thames
royal residence.. **7.** Windsor
school.. **4.** Eton **5.** Rugby **6.** Harrow
street (London).. **10.** Piccadilly
  12. Threadneedle
English (pert to)...
bride's gift.. **3.** dos
court.. **4.** eyre (circuit), leet (anc)
dislike of.. **11.** Anglophobia
district.. **4.** Soho
estate (feudal).. **4.** fief
excuse (legal).. **6.** essoin
festival (country).. **3.** ale
field.. **5.** croft
forest.. **5.** Arden **8.** Sherwood
freeman.. **5.** ceorl, thane, thegn
hamlet.. **4.** dorp
heather.. **4.** ling
lawyer.. **9.** barrister, solicitor
leave of absence (school).. **5.** exeat
lover of.. **10.** Anglophile
Marbles.. **6.** Oxford **7.** Arundel
money of account.. **3.** ora
news agency.. **6.** Reuter
Parliament process.. **7.** Hansard
political party.. **4.** Tory, Whig **8.** Laborite
  12. Conservative
porcelain.. **5.** Spode **8.** Wedgwood
prehistóric site.. **8.** Piltdown
race course.. **5.** Ascot **9.** Newmarket
  10. Epsom Downs
races (famed).. **5.** Derby **7.** The Oaks
sheep (blackface).. **4.** Lonk
song (mock).. **12.** lillibullero
stolen article (on thief).. **7.** mainour
subway.. **4.** tube **11.** underground
symbol.. **4.** bull, lion, rose
thicket.. **5.** copse **7.** spinney
tract (sandy).. **4.** dean (dene)
trolley.. **4.** tram
uplands.. **5.** downs
wren.. **6.** tomtit
English Channel... **8.** La Manche
English, famed...
architect.. **4.** Wren
composer.. **4.** Arne, Byrd **5.** Elgar
  6. Handel, Tallis **7.** Dowland, Stainer
  15. Vaughan Williams
diarist.. **5.** Pepys
dramatist.. **6.** Jonson, Pinter **7.** Marlowe
  8. Sheridan
engraver.. **3.** Pye **7.** Hogarth
essayist.. **4.** Elia (Charles Lamb), Lang
  6. Arnold, Steele **7.** Addison
explorer.. **4.** Ross **5.** Cabot **6.** Baffin,
  Beatty, Hudson **7.** Raleigh
  10. Shackleton
financier.. **7.** Gresham
historian.. **4.** Bede **7.** Spelman, Toynbee
  8. Macaulay
humorist.. **4.** Lear (Edward)

navigator.. **4.** Cook **5.** Drake **6.** Nelson
painter.. **6.** Turner **7.** Millais **8.** Reynolds,
  Rossetti **9.** Constable **12.** Gainsborough
philosopher.. **7.** Russell, Spencer
poet.. **4.** Pope **5.** Byron, Keats
  6. Dryden **7.** Bridges, Chaucer, Shelley,
  Skelton, Southey, Spenser **8.** Browning,
  Tennyson **10.** Wordsworth
printer.. **6.** Caxton
reformer.. **4.** Owen **6.** Spence
saint.. **6.** George (patron saint)
  7. Alphege, Swithin
satirist.. **5.** Swift
scientist.. **4.** Davy **5.** Boyle **6.** Dalton,
  Darwin, Halley, Harvey, Huxley, Jenner,
  Kelvin, Lister, Newton **7.** Faraday,
  Fleming **9.** Cavendish, Priestley
  10. Rutherford
spy (in Am Rev).. **5.** André
statesman.. **4.** Peel, Pitt **7.** Baldwin,
  Balfour, Walpole **8.** Cromwell, Disraeli,
  Thatcher **9.** Churchill **11.** Chamberlain,
  Lloyd George
theologian.. **5.** Booth **6.** Becket **7.** Tyndall
  8. Wycliffe **10.** Whitefield
thesaurus compiler.. **5.** Roget
writer.. **5.** Hardy, Woolf **6.** Austen,
  Barrie **7.** Boswell, Dickens, Johnson
  8. Fielding, Lawrence, Trollope
  9. Thackeray
engrave... **3.** cut **4.** etch, rist **5.** carve,
  chase, hatch, infix **6.** chisel, incise
  7. enchase, impress, imprint, stipple
  9. sculpture
engraver's tool... **5.** burin
engraving... **3.** cut **5.** print **7.** etching,
  chasing, tooling **8.** celature, incising,
  intaglio **9.** stippling **10.** xylography
  (wood) **11.** lithography **12.** glyptography
engross... **6.** absorb, engage
  10. monopolize **11.** concentrate
engrossed... **4.** busy, rapt **6.** intent
  8. absorbed, employed **10.** interested
engulf... **4.** gulf, gulp **5.** swamp **6.** absorb
  7. swallow **8.** inundate, submerge
  9. overwhelm
enhance... **4.** lift **5.** exalt, extol, raise
  7. advance, augment, elevate, enlarge,
  magnify **8.** increase **9.** aggravate
  10. exaggerate
enigma... **3.** why **5.** rebus **6.** puzzle,
  riddle **7.** charade, mystery
  9. conundrum **11.** mind-boggler
enigmatic... **6.** arcane, mystic **8.** puzzling
  12. inexplicable
enjoin... **3.** bid **5.** order **6.** advise, charge,
  decree, direct, forbid **7.** command
  8. admonish, prohibit
enjoy... **4.** bask, have **5.** savor **6.** relish
  10. appreciate
enjoyment... **4.** ease, zest **6.** relish
  7. delight **8.** felicity, fruition, pleasure
  9. amusement, happiness
enlarge... **3.** eke **4.** ream **5.** swell **6.** dilate,
  expand, extend, spread **7.** amplify,
  augment, develop, distend **8.** increase
  9. expatiate **10.** exaggerate
enlargement... **8.** increase **9.** expansion,
  extension **12.** augmentation
  13. amplification
enlighten... **5.** teach **6.** inform **7.** educate,

explain **8.** enkindle, instruct
10. illuminate **11.** disillusion
enlightened person . . . **10.** illuminate
enlist . . . **4.** join, list **6.** engage, enroll, induce, muster
enliven . . . **5.** amuse, cheer, rouse
7. animate, comfort, inspire, refresh
8. brighten, energize, inspirit
9. encourage, stimulate **10.** exhilarate, invigorate
enmity . . . **3.** war **4.** feud **6.** hatred, malice, rancor **7.** discord **8.** aversion
9. antipathy, disaccord, hostility
10. antagonism, repugnance
11. malevolence **14.** unfriendliness
ennead . . . **4.** gods (nine), nine **18.** Ennead of Heliopolis (famed)
ennoble . . . **5.** exalt, honor, raise **6.** uplift
7. elevate, glorify, promote
ennui . . . **4.** bore **5.** bored **6.** tedium
7. boredom, fatigue, languor
9. weariness **15.** dissatisfaction
enormous . . . **4.** huge, vast **5.** great
6. wicked **7.** immense, massive, titanic **8.** abnormal, colossal, gigantic, infamous **9.** atrocious, excessive, monstrous **10.** inordinate, prodigious, stupendous
Enos' father . . . **4.** Seth
enough . . . **4.** enow **5.** ample, basta, fully, quite **6.** plenty **8.** adequate **9.** amplitude
10. sufficient **12.** satisfactory
enounce . . . **5.** state, utter **8.** proclaim
9. enunciate, pronounce
enow . . . **9.** presently
enrage . . . **5.** anger **6.** madden **7.** incense, inflame **9.** infuriate
enraged . . . **5.** irate **7.** angered
8. maddened **10.** infuriated
enraptured . . . **6.** enrapt **8.** ecstatic
9. delighted, entranced **10.** enravished
enravished . . . **4.** rapt **9.** enchanted, entranced, rapturous **10.** enraptured
enrich . . . **4.** lard **5.** adorn, endow **6.** fatten
7. improve **8.** increase, ornament
9. embellish, fertilize
enroll . . . **4.** coil, join, list, roll **5.** enter
6. enlist, induct, unfurl, wrap up
7. engross, impanel **8.** initiate, register
11. matriculate
ens . . . **5.** being **6.** entity **7.** essence
ensconce . . . **4.** hide **5.** cover **6.** settle
7. conceal, protect, shelter **9.** establish
ensemble . . . **3.** all **5.** decor, group, whole
7. costume
enshroud . . . **4.** wrap **6.** clothe, swathe
7. conceal, enclose **8.** enshrine
ensiform . . . **12.** xiphisternum
ensign . . . **4.** flag **6.** banner **7.** officer
8. gonfalon, standard **9.** oriflamme (oriflamb, anc)
ensign of Othello . . . **4.** Iago
enslave . . . **8.** enthrall
ensnare . . . **3.** web **4.** trap **5.** benet, catch, innet, noose **6.** allure, enmesh, entrap, seduce **7.** involve
ensorcell, ensorcel . . . **7.** bewitch, enchant
ensue . . . **6.** follow, pursue, result
7. imitate, succeed **8.** come next
ensuing . . . **4.** next **9.** resultant

10. subsequent, succeeding
ensure . . . **6.** assure, insure, secure
7. protect, warrant **9.** guarantee
entad . . . **6.** inward (opp of ectad)
ental . . . **5.** inner (opp of ectal)
entangle . . . **3.** mat, web **4.** mesh, mire
5. afoul, ravel, snarl, twist **6.** enlace, enmesh, puzzle, raffle **7.** confuse, ensnare, involve, perplex **8.** bewilder
9. embarrass **10.** interweave
entanglement . . . **4.** knot **5.** snare, snarl
6. abatis **8.** obstacle **9.** barricade, imbroglio **10.** barbed wire, complexity
11. involvement
enter . . . **4.** join, list **5.** begin, start, train
6. come in, engage, enlist, enroll, insert, record **8.** initiate, inscribe, register
9. introduce, penetrate **11.** participate
enter (pert to) . . .
career . . **6.** incept
legal objection . . **5.** demur
with hostility . . **6.** invade
without permission . . **7.** intrude
8. encroach, infringe
enterprise . . . **4.** firm **5.** essay **6.** daring
7. attempt, crusade, exploit, venture
10. initiative **11.** undertaking
enterprising . . . **4.** bold **6.** daring
9. energetic **11.** up-and-coming
entertain . . . **4.** fete **5.** amuse, treat
6. divert, regale **7.** beguile, cherish
8. interest
entertainer . . . **5.** actor **6.** dancer, singer **7.** actress, speaker **8.** magician
9. performer **11.** pantomimist
12. impersonator
entertainment . . . **4.** play **5.** party, revue, sport **6.** kermis (kermess), repast
7. pastime, ridotto, theater **8.** entr'acte, musicale **9.** amusement, diversion, reception, wayzgoose **10.** recreation
12. Roman holiday
enthralled . . . **10.** captivated, fascinated, spellbound
enthusiasm . . . **4.** élan, fire, zeal, zest
5. ardor, craze, estro, furor (furore), mania, verve **6.** fervor **7.** ecstasy
8. interest **9.** animation, eagerness, transport **10.** exaltation
enthusiast . . . **3.** fan **5.** bigot **6.** rooter, zealot **7.** devotee, fanatic
enthusiastic . . . **5.** eager, nutty, rabid
6. active, ardent **7.** zealous
10. interested
entice . . . **4.** bait, coax, lure, tole **5.** decoy, tempt **6.** allure, cajole, incite, seduce
7. attract, wheedle **8.** inveigle, persuade
enticement . . . **9.** seduction
10. allurement, attraction, incitement, inducement, persuasion, temptation
12. inveiglement
entire . . . **3.** all **5.** cover (Philat), sound, total, utter, whole **6.** intact
7. perfect, sincere, upright **8.** complete, faithful, stallion **9.** integrate, undivided
10. unimpaired **11.** unqualified
12. undiminished
entirely . . . **3.** all **5.** clean, fully, stark
6. solely, wholly **7.** totally **9.** every inch, perfectly, sincerely **10.** completely
entitle . . . **3.** dub **4.** call, name, term

5. style 6. assign, enable, impute
7. empower, qualify 9. authorize,
designate 10. denominate

entity . . . 3. ens 4. soul, unit 5. being,
entia, thing 7. integer 8. infinity (Math)
9. existence

entomb . . . 4. bury 5. inter, inurn
6. hearse, inhume 7. confine
9. sepulture

entourage . . . 5. suite, train 7. retinue
10. associates, attendants
12. surroundings

entr'acte . . . 3. act 5. dance, music
7. interim 9. interlude

entrails . . . 4. guts 6. bowels 7. insides,
viscera 8. interior 10. intestines

entrance . . . 3. way 4. adit, door,
gate 5. entry, inlet 6. access, portal
7. gateway, ingress, postern
9. admission, insertion, threshold,
vestibule 10. admittance

entrance (pert to) . . .
church (Eastern) . . 5. Great 6. Little
formal . . 5. debut 12. introduction
hostile . . 9. incursion
temple (Buddh) . . 5. toran (torana)

entranced . . . 4. rapt 7. charmed
8. dreaming 9. delighted, overjoyed
10. fascinated, hypnotized, spellbound
11. overpowered

entrap . . . 3. net 4. trap 5. catch, decoy,
noose, snare 6. tangle 7. beguile,
ensnare 8. entangle, inveigle

entreat . . . 3. ask, beg, woo 4. pray
5. crave, halse (obs), plead 6. adjure,
appeal 7. beseech, implore, solicit
8. petition 9. importune 10. supplicate

entreaty . . . 4. plea, suit 6. appeal, prayer
7. request 8. petition 10. invitation
11. importunity 12. solicitation,
supplication

entree, entrée . . . 4. dish 6. access
7. ingress, opening 9. admission
10. permission (to enter)

entrench . . . 6. invade 7. enter on,
fortify, intrude 8. encroach, trespass
9. establish

entrenchment . . . 7. defense, parapet
9. intrusion 10. protection
12. encroachment, infringement
13. establishment

entrepot . . . 5. depot, store 9. warehouse
10. depository

entrepreneur . . . 7. provost 9. executive
10. impresario 13. administrator

entrust . . . 6. commit 7. confide, consign
8. delegate 10. commission

entry . . . 4. hall, item, lane, post 7. ingress
8. entrance, register 9. admission,
vestibule 10. contestant, memorandum
12. introduction

entwine . . . 4. lace 5. clasp, twine, twist,
weave 6. enlace 7. wreathe 9. interknit

enumerate . . . 4. list, tell 5. count 6. detail,
number, reckon, relate 7. compute
8. estimate, name over, rehearse
9. calculate, catalogue (catalog)
12. recapitulate 13. particularize

enumeration . . . 4. list 5. count 6. census
10. numeration 14. recapitulation

enunciate . . . 3. say 5. utter 6. affirm

7. declare 8. announce, proclaim
9. postulate, pronounce 10. articulate

enunciation . . . 9. statement, utterance
11. affirmation, attestation, declaration
12. announcement 13. pronouncement,
pronunciation

envelop . . . 4. case, wrap 5. cover
6. clothe, encase, enwrap, infold,
invest, sheath, shroud 7. conceal,
enclose, sheathe 8. encircle, surround
9. encompass, enwreathe
10. integument

envelope . . . 3. bur (burr) 5. cover, curve
6. jacket 7. conceal, rampart, vesicle,
wrapper 8. membrane 10. integument

enveloped . . . 6. amidst 7. covered
10. surrounded

envenom . . . 5. taint 6. poison 8. embitter

envious . . . 7. jealous 8. covetous,
grudging, spiteful 9. green-eyed
10. begrudging

environ . . . 3. hem 6. suburb 7. compass,
envelop, hedge in, involve, purlieu
8. encircle, outskirt, surround
9. encompass

environment . . . 4. area 6. medium,
milieu 7. setting, suburbs, terrain
8. environs 10. background
12. neighborhood, surroundings
13. encompassment

environmental . . . 10. ecological

envisage . . . 4. face 8. confront 9. visualize
11. contemplate 12. meet squarely

envision . . . 5. dream 7. picture
9. visualize 11. contemplate 12. meet
squarely

envoy . . . 5. agent 6. legate, l'envoi,
stanza 7. refrain 8. ablegate, delegate,
diplomat 9. messenger 10. ambassador,
postscript 12. commissioner

envy . . . 5. covet 6. grudge 8. jealousy
12. covetousness

enwrap, inwrap . . . 4. roll, wrap 6. clothe,
enfold, infold 7. engross 8. surround

enzyme . . . 3. ase (suff) 5. bread (Eccl)
6. lotase, olease, pepsin, rennin,
urease 7. amylase, ferment, laccase,
ptyalin, trypsin 8. diastase, protease
9. digestant

enzyme activator . . . 11. biocatalyst

eoan . . . 7. auroral 8. daybreak, easterly

eon, aeon . . . 3. age, era 4. time 5. cycle
8. eternity 10. generation

ephemeral . . . 7. diurnal 9. chickweed,
deciduous, transient 10. short-lived

ephemeris . . . 5. diary 7. almanac, journal
8. calendar 10. periodical 11. publication

Ephesus (pert to) . . .
city of . . 6. Greece (anc)
famed for . . 5. ruins 12. Christianity
site . . 9. Aegean Sea
temple . . 7. Artemis
visitor (early) . . 6. St Paul

Ephraim . . . 4. bear (grizzly) 5. tribe
8. fruitful

epi . . . 6. finial

epic . . . 3. cid 4. epos, poem, saga
5. epode 6. Aeneid (by Vergil), epopee,
heroic 9. narrative

epicene . . . 7. neutral, sexless
10. effeminate

epicure . . . **6.** friand (obs) **7.** glutton, gourmet **8.** gourmand, Sybarite **9.** bon vivant **10.** gastronome, voluptuary **11.** connoisseur

epidemic . . . **4.** pest **6.** plague **8.** pandemic **9.** prevalent, spreading **10.** contagious, pestilence

epidermis . . . **4.** skin **7.** cuticle **8.** ectoderm **9.** scarfskin

epigram . . . **3.** mot, saw **4.** poem, quip **5.** adage, maxim **6.** dictum, saying **7.** distich **11.** inscription (obs)

epigraph . . . **5.** motto, title **9.** quotation **11.** inscription

Epiphany (Eccl) . . . **5.** Feast (Jan 6)

Epirus, oracle of . . . **6.** Dodona (Mt Tomarus, Gr)

episode . . . **5.** event, story **8.** incident **10.** digression (Mus), occurrence

epistle . . . **4.** note, post **6.** billet, lesson, letter **7.** message, missive, writing **8.** dispatch, rescript **13.** communication

epitaph . . . **7.** writing (monument) **8.** hic jacet **11.** inscription

epithet . . . **4.** name, term **5.** label **6.** byname **7.** agnomen **9.** sobriquet **11.** appellation (significant)

epitome . . . **6.** digest **7.** summary **8.** abstract **9.** comprisal **10.** abridgment, compendium

epitomize . . . **7.** abridge, curtail **8.** abstract, compress, condense, contract, diminish **9.** capsulize

epoch . . . **3.** age, day, eon, era **4.** date, time **5.** event **6.** period

epopee . . . **4.** epic, epos, poem **5.** genre (epic) **6.** poetry (epic)

epoptic . . . **6.** mystic, secret

Epstein-Barr . . . **4.** mono **5.** virus

equable . . . **4.** even **6.** steady **7.** uniform

equal . . . **3.** iso (pref), par, tie **4.** both, even, fere (obs), just, pari (pref), peer, same **5.** match, rival **7.** compeer, emulate, equable, uniform **8.** adequate, parallel **9.** equitable, identical **10.** coordinate, equivalent, substitute **11.** counterpart **12.** commensurate **13.** proportionate

equal day and night . . . **11.** equidiurnal, equinoctial

equal density (atmospheric) . . . **8.** isoteric

equality . . . **3.** par, tie **6.** equity, owelty (payment), parity **7.** egalite, isonomy (law) **8.** adequacy, evenness, fairness, identity, sameness **10.** uniformity **12.** impartiality

Equality State . . . **7.** Wyoming (first with Woman Suffrage)

equalize . . . **4.** even **5.** equal, level, match **6.** equate, smooth **7.** balance **10.** symmetrize

equally . . . **2.** as **4.** equi (pref) **5.** alike **6.** evenly, justly **11.** identically **15.** correspondingly

equanimity . . . **5.** poise **6.** aplomb **7.** balance **8.** calmness, evenness, serenity **9.** assurance, composure **10.** confidence, equability **11.** tranquility **12.** tranquillity

equilibrium . . . **5.** poise **6.** stasis **7.** balance **8.** equality **9.** stability

10. equanimity

equine . . . **3.** ass **4.** colt, foal, mare **5.** filly, horse, steed, zebra **6.** donkey

equine cry . . . **5.** neigh **6.** whinny

equip . . . **3.** arm, fit, imp, rig **4.** deck, gear, gird **5.** dress, endow **7.** costume, furnish, qualify **8.** accouter

equipment . . . **4.** gear **5.** armor **6.** outfit, tackle, traits (personal) **7.** ability, panoply (warriors) **8.** equipage **9.** apparatus **11.** preparation **12.** accouterment, accoutrement

equitable . . . **4.** fair, just **5.** right **6.** honest **7.** upright **9.** impartial **10.** bonitarian (Rom law), reasonable

equity . . . **4.** laws **6.** rights **7.** honesty, justice **8.** fairness **9.** rectitude **11.** uprightness

equivalence . . . **3.** par **7.** valence **8.** equality, sameness **10.** relativity **11.** correlation

equivalent . . . **5.** alike, equal **9.** identical **10.** tantamount

equivocal . . . **7.** dubious, obscure **8.** doubtful, puzzling **9.** ambiguous, enigmatic, uncertain **10.** amphibolic, mysterious, perplexing **11.** problematic **13.** indeterminate

equivocate . . . **3.** lie **5.** dodge, evade, fence, shift **6.** palter, trifle **7.** quibble, shuffle **11.** prevaricate **12.** tergiversate

era . . . **2.** AD, BC **3.** age, eon **4.** date, time **5.** cycle, epoch **6.** period **10.** Anno Domini **12.** Before Christ

eradicate . . . **4.** dele, root, weed **5.** annul, erase **6.** remove, uproot **7.** abolish, destroy, epilate, extract, root out **9.** eliminate, extirpate **10.** annihilate **11.** exterminate

erase . . . **4.** dele, kill **5.** arase (obs) **6.** cancel, delete, efface, excise **7.** expunge, relieve **10.** obliterate

Erasmus satire . . . **16.** The Praise of Folly

Erastus (Swiss) . . . **9.** physician **10.** theologian

ere . . . **4.** also, soon **5.** early, prior **6.** before, erenow, sooner **7.** earlier, ere long **8.** erewhile, formerly **10.** before long, previously, sooner than

Erebus (pert to) . . .
    brother . . **3.** Nox
    father of . . **3.** Day **6.** Aether
    Greek myth . . **8.** darkness (nether)
    native of . . **5.** Hades
    son . . **5.** Chaos

erect . . . **4.** lift, rear, stay **5.** build, found, raise, stand, upend **6.** raised **7.** elevate, upright **8.** uplifted, vertical **9.** construct, establish, institute **13.** perpendicular

eremite . . . **6.** hermit **7.** recluse **8.** anchoret, solitary **9.** anchorite

erenow . . . **5.** prior **8.** erewhile, formerly **10.** heretofore

ergo . . . **5.** hence **9.** therefore

Erin . . . **4.** Eire **7.** Ireland

Eritrea, Africa . . .
    capital . . **6.** Asmara
    formerly part of . . **8.** Ethiopia
    site . . **6.** Red Sea

ermine . . . **3.** fur **4.** robe (emblem)

5. stoat (stot) 6. clothe, lasset, weasel
7. ermelin
erode . . . 3. eat 4. gnaw, wear 7. corrode,
decline, destroy 11. deteriorate
12. disintegrate
erotic . . . 6. loving, sexual 7. amative,
amatory, amorous, sensual
err . . . 3. sin 4. miss, slip 5. stray 6. bungle
7. blunder, deviate 10. transgress
12. miscalculate, misinterpret
Er Rai . . . 5. stars 6. shepherd
errand . . . 4. task, trip 7. journey, mission
8. business (special) 10. commission
errand boy . . . 4. page 7. bellboy, bellhop,
courier 9. messenger
errant . . . 6. erring, roving 7. peccant
8. fallible 9. deviating, erroneous,
itinerant, wandering 10. journeying
erratic . . . 5. queer, rogue 6. whacky
7. nomadic, strange 8. abnormal
9. eccentric, irregular, planetary,
wandering 10. capricious, changeable
erroneous . . . 5. false, wrong 6. untrue
7. peccant 8. illusory, mistaken
9. wandering
error . . . 3. sin 4. flub, muff, slip 5. boner,
lapse 6. errata (pl), miscue 7. blunder,
falsity, misstep, mistake 8. iniquity
11. anachronism, misjudgment
14. miscalculation
ersatz . . . 5. proxy, token 9. vicarious
10. equivalent, substitute 11. alternative,
replacement 12. substitution
Erse . . . 5. Irish 6. Celtic, Gaelic
erst, erstwhile . . . 4. also, once 5. first
6. former, sooner 8. earliest, formerly
10. heretofore, previously
erudite . . . 4. wise 7. learned 8. cultured,
educated, literate 9. scholarly
erudition . . . 4. lore 6. finish, wisdom
7. letters 8. learning, pedantry
9. knowledge
eruption . . . 4. rash 6. geyser 7. volcano
8. ejection, outbreak, outburst
9. commotion, exanthema 10. nettlerash
13. efflorescence
Esau (pert to) . . .
  Bible ref . . 7. Genesis
  brother . . 5. Jacob
  father . . 5. Isaac
  home . . 4. Seir
  mother . . 7. Rebekah
  name (later) . . 4. Edom
escape . . . 4. flee 5. dodge, elope, elude,
evade, spill 7. evasion 9. avolation
13. circumvention
escargot . . . 5. snail
escarpment . . . 5. cliff, slope 9. precipice
13. fortification
eschar . . . 4. scab, sore 5. crust 6. slough
escharotic . . . 7. caustic, mordant
8. stinging 9. corrosive
escheat . . . 4. fall 5. lapse 6. revert (land)
7. forfeit 9. reversion 10. forfeiture
eschew . . . 4. shun 5. avoid 7. abstain,
refrain
escolar . . . 4. fish 8. mackerel (like)
escort . . . 3. see 4. beau 5. guard
(honor), usher 6. attend, convoy, gigolo,
squire 7. conduct, retinue 8. chaperon
9. accompany 13. accompaniment

escritoire . . . 4. desk 6. bureau 7. dresser
9. secretary 10. secretaire
escrow . . . 4. bond, deed (deposit)
9. muniments
esculent . . . 6. edible 7. eatable
8. gustable 10. comestible
escutcheon . . . 4. fess (band), orle
(voided) 5. crest 6. shield
esker, eskar . . . 2. os 4. osar (pl) 5. drift,
hills, mound, ridge
Eskimo . . . 3. Ita 4. Yuit 5. Aleut 6. Innuit
10. skraelling 11. Yikirgaulit (Diomede
Isles)
Eskimo (pert to) . . .
  boat, canoe . . 5. kayak, umiak (oomiac)
  boot (sealskin) . . 5. kamik
  coat (bird skin) . . 5. parka 6. temiak
  color . . 5. brown (rustic)
  dog . . 5. Husky 8. Malemute
  family . . 9. Eskimauan
  fish . . 4. Atka 8. mackerel
  hut, house . . 5. igloo, tupek (tupik)
  jacket . . 6. temiak
  knife (woman's) . . 3. ulu
  memorial post . . 3. xat
  settlement . . 4. Etah
  totem . . 4. pole, post 6. symbol
esne . . . 4. serf 5. slave 8. hireling
esophagus, oesophagus . . . 4. crop,
gula 6. gullet, throat 7. pharynx
esoteric . . . 5. inner 6. occult, secret
7. private 8. abstruse, initiate, personal
9. recondite 12. confidential
esoteric doctrine . . . 6. cabala
esoteric wisdom . . . 6. gnosis
espalier . . . 7. epaulet, railing, trellis
Español . . . 7. Spanish
especial . . . 5. chief 7. special 8. peculiar,
uncommon
Esperanto . . . 3. Ido 8. language (Internat)
espionage . . . 4. espy 6. spying
11. observation (secret)
14. reconnaissance
esplanade . . . 4. walk 5. drive, level,
Prado, praya 6. strand 7. walkway
espousal . . . 7. wedding 8. adoption,
ceremony 10. acceptance
11. embracement
espouse . . . 3. wed 4. bind, mate 5. adopt,
marry 6. defend, pledge 7. betroth,
embrace, support 8. maintain, plead
for
esprit de corps . . . 3. wit 6. spirit
8. devotion 10. enthusiasm, fellowship
11. partisanism
esprit fort (Relig) . . . 11. freethinker
espy . . . 3. see 5. watch 6. behold, descry,
detect 7. discern 8. discover 9. look
about
esquire . . . 5. title 6. escort, gentry
7. armiger 8. escudero, nobleman
11. armor-bearer 12. shield-bearer
essay . . . 3. try 4. test 5. assay, chris
(Rhet), paper, theme, tract, trial 6. effort,
thesis 7. attempt 8. endeavor, treatise
11. composition 12. disquisition,
dissertation
esse . . . 5. being (real) 9. existence
essence . . . 3. ens 4. core, gist, odor,
pith 5. attar, being, scent 6. kernel,
nature 7. element, extract, perfume

9. principle, substance 12. quintessence
essential . . . 5. vital 6. mortal 7. needful
8. existent, inherent 9. necessary,
necessity 13. indispensable
essential oil . . . 8. volatile 12. attar of
roses
essential part . . . 4. core, crux, gist, pith
7. element 8. inherent 10. inwardness
establish . . . 3. fix 4. base, seat 5. build,
enact, erect, found, plant, prove, set
up 6. create, ground, locate, ordain,
settle 7. confirm, pre-empt 8. ensconce,
legalize, radicate (rare) 9. ascertain,
originate
established . . . 5. fixed 6. proved, rested,
stable 11. naturalized, traditional
12. conventional
established (pert to) . . .
  church . . 9. Episcopal (Eng)
  rule . . 8. standard
  thing . . 4. fact
  truth . . 8. verified
establishment . . . 4. mill 5. plant
6. custom, menage 7. factory
9. structure 12. organization
establishment of cordial relations . . .
13. rapprochement
establishment of new plant home . . .
6. ecesis
estate . . . 4. alod, fief (feudal), rank
(social) 5. manor, title 6. assets,
equity 7. alodium, demesne, fortune
8. freehold, interest, property
9. situation
esteem . . . 4. dear 5. adore, honor, judge,
pride, value 6. admire, regard, repute,
revere 7. respect 8. appraise, venerate
10. appreciate 13. consideration
ester of . . .
  silicic acid . . 8. silicate
  stearic acid . . 7. stearin 8. stearate
  tropic acid . . 7. tropate
  vinegar . . 7. acetate
esthetic, aesthetic . . . 6. essene
8. artistic, tasteful 9. beautiful
estimable . . . 6. worthy 8. valuable
9. admirable, honorable, reputable,
venerable 10. measurable
12. praiseworthy
estimate . . . 3. aim, set 4. gage, rank,
rate 5. audit, gauge, guess, prize, think
6. assess, repute 7. adjudge, compute,
measure, opinion 8. appraise, judgment
9. calculate, statement, valuation
Estonia . . .
  capital . . 5. Revel 7. Tallinn
  industry . . 3. oil
  island . . 5. Oesel
estop . . . 3. bar 4. fill, halt, plug, stay
6. impede, stop up 7. prevent 8. prohibit
estrange . . . 4. part, wean 6. divert,
divide 8. alienate, disunite, separate
estreat . . . 4. copy 6. amerce, sconce
7. extract 9. duplicate, penalties (law)
estuary . . . 3. bay 4. Pará 5. firth, frith,
Plata
etch . . . 3. cut 4. bite 5. infix 7. corrode,
engrave, impress (upon)
eternal . . . 6. eonian 7. aeonian, ageless,
endless, lasting 8. enduring, immortal,
timeless 9. boundless, ceaseless,

immutable, incessant, unceasing
10. unchanging 11. everlasting
12. imperishable, interminable,
unchangeable
Eternal City . . . 4. Rome
eternal death . . . 9. perdition
eternal home . . . 6. heaven 12. The
Hereafter
eternity . . . 3. eon 4. aeon, ages, olam
8. Olam haba
etesian . . . 4. wind (Aegean Sea) 6. annual
8. seasonal 10. periodical
Ethan Frome author . . . 7. Wharton
ether . . . 3. air, sky 5. ester, space
6. anisol, heaven (anc) 8. empyrean
10. anesthetic
ethereal . . . 4. rare 5. aerie (aery), light
7. fragile, slender, tenuous 8. delicate,
heavenly, vaporous 9. celestial
10. atmosphere (earth's), spiritlike
11. phantomlike 13. unsubstantial
ethereal (pert to) . . .
  being . . 5. sylph
  color . . 7. sky blue
  fluid . . 5. ichor (icor)
  poetic . . 4. aery
  salt . . 5. ester
ethical . . . 5. moral, right 7. upright
8. virtuous
ethics . . . 6. morals 8. hedonics
10. principles (moral) 11. highest good,
summum bonum 12. Magna Moralia
(Aristotle)
Ethiopia (Abyssinia) . . .
  capital . . 10. Addis Ababa
  city . . 5. Adowa
  empress . . 7. Zauditu
  king (Myth) . . 5. Negus 6. Memnon
  people . . 6. Hamite 10. Abyssinian
  people (anc) . . 5. Bejas, Galla 6. Hamite,
  Semite
  river . . 3. Omo 4. Juba 5. Abbai (Blue
  Nile)
  ruler . . 7. Menelik 13. Haile Selassie
  tribes (anc) . . 5. Bejas, Galla 7. Hamites,
  Semites
Ethiopian (pert to) . . .
  ape . . 6. gelada
  banana . . 6. ensete
  dialect . . 4. Geez
  lily . . 5. calla
  Torah . . 5. tetel
ethnic . . . 5. pagan 6. racial 7. gentile,
heathen
ethnology . . . 5. races (Man)
ethology . . . 7. manners 9. bionomics,
character
ethos (opp of pathos) . . . 9. attitudes
(moral), esthetics
etiquette . . . 4. form 5. label, mores
6. ticket 7. decorum, manners
9. amenities, propriety 10. civilities
etiquette, breach of . . . 8. solecism
Etruria, Italy . . . see *Etruscan*
Etruscan (pert to) . . .
  bookbinding (anc) . . 9. classical
  deity . . 3. Lar, Uni
  pottery . . 8. bucchero (black)
  race . . 7. Rasenna 8. Tursenoi, Tyrrheni
  soothsayer . . 8. haruspex (a)
  soothsayer's function . . 8. extispex

ettle ... 3. try 4. plan 6. aspire, design,
   intent 8. consider, endeavor
etui, etwee ... 4. case 7. trousse
etymology ... 10. word origin
eucalyptus ... 4. lerp (laap, juice) 7. gum
   tree 8. eucalypt
eucalyptus eater ... 5. koala
Eucharist (pert to) ...
   administer to .. 6. housel 8. viaticum
      (dying)
   plate .. 5. paten
   rite .. 9. Communion (Holy) 11. Lord's
      Supper
   wafer .. 4. host
   wafer vessel .. 8. ciborium
   wine .. 5. krama
   wine vessel .. 3. ama 5. amula
Euclid (Gr) ... 8. geometer (BC)
eulogist ... 9. encomiast 10. panegyrist
eulogize ... 4. laud 5. boost, extol
   6. praise 7. commend, glorify
   9. celebrate 10. panegyrize
eulogy ... 5. eloge 6. hesped (Heb),
   praise 7. oration 8. citation, encomium
   9. laudation, panegyric
euphony ... 5. meter 6. melody, rhythm,
   speech (ease of) 7. harmony
Eurafrica ... 5. Egypt 6. Europe 7. Algeria
   9. Abyssinia (anc)
Eurasia ... 4. Asia 6. Europe 7. Scythia
   (anc)
Eurasian (pert to) ...
   herb .. 6. yarrow 7. gosmore
   mint .. 6. Nepeta
   people .. 5. Finns 7. Ugrians
      9. Armenians, Turanians
eureka ... 3. aha 11. exclamation 12. I
   Have Found It (Calif motto)
Euripedes (Gr) ... 4. poet (BC)
Europe ... see also *European*
   basin (coal) .. 4. Saar
   battlefield .. 5. Marne 6. Verdun
      8. Normandy, Waterloo 11. Belleau
      Wood
   capitals .. 4. Bonn, Oslo, Riga, Rome
      5. Berne, Paris, Sofia 6. Athens,
      Berlin, Dublin, Lisbon, London, Madrid,
      Moscow, Prague, Warsaw 8. Belgrade,
      Brussels, Budapest, Helsinki
      9. Amsterdam, Bucharest, Stockholm
      10. Bratislava, Copenhagen, Monte
      Carlo
   country (anc) .. 4. Elis (Gr) 7. Etruria
      (It)
   country (modern) .. 5. Italy, Spain
      6. France, Greece, Latvia, Monaco,
      Norway, Poland, Russia, Sweden
      7. Belgium, Denmark, England, Finland,
      Germany, Hungary, Ireland, Rumania
      8. Bulgaria, Portugal, Slovakia
      10. Yugoslavia 11. Netherlands,
      Switzerland 13. Czech Republic
      14. Czechoslovakia
   economic union .. 7. Benelux
   gulf .. 4. Riga 7. Bothnia
   invaders .. 4. Huns 5. Arabs, Turks
      7. Mongols
   kingdom (anc) .. 5. Arles 6. Aragon
      8. Burgundy
   lancer .. 5. uhlan 6. hussar
   mountain region .. 4. Alps 5. Tirol (Tyrol)

8. Pyrenees 9. Apennines
   race (anc) .. 5. Goths 7. Teutons
      9. Visigoths 10. Ostrogoths
   river .. 4. Elbe, Isar 5. Loire, Meuse,
      Rhine, Rhone, Seine, Volga 6. Danube
      7. Dneiper, Moselle
   sea .. 4. Azov 5. North 6. Baltic
   strait .. 8. Bosporus
   valley .. 4. Ruhr
   volcano .. 4. Etna 8. Vesuvius
      9. Stromboli
European (pert to) ...
   antelope .. 7. chamois
   bat .. 8. serotine
   bird .. 3. ani, daw, mew (gull) 4. kite,
      stag 5. glede, mavis, ousel, serin
      6. godwit, linnet, marten, merlin (falcon)
      7. bittern, jackdaw, ortolan, starnel
      8. dotterel, garganey 9. brambling,
      gallinule 10. turtledove 11. lammergeier
      12. capercaillie
   bison .. 7. aurochs
   clover .. 6. alsike
   dog .. 7. griffin
   fish .. 3. gar 4. dace, rudd, spet, tope
      (shark) 5. sprat 6. allice, barbel, brasse,
      morgay, turbot
   grape .. 6. muscat
   linden .. 4. teil
   mint .. 6. hyssop 9. horehound
   mouse .. 4. loir, vole
   polecat .. 7. fitchew
   rodent .. 3. erd 4. loir 6. leriot 7. hamster
   sandpiper .. 4. ruff 5. terek
   squirrel .. 5. sisel 10. polatouche
   tree .. 4. cade (juniper), sorb (apple)
      5. carob 9. terebinth
   weasel .. 5. stoat
   wheat .. 5. emmer (speltz) 7. einkorn
evacuant ... 6. emetic 8. diuretic
   9. cathartic, purgative
evacuate ... 4. void 5. empty, expel
   6. depart, vacate 7. deprive, exhaust
   8. withdraw 9. discharge
evade ... 3. gee 4. duck, foil, shun
   5. avoid, dodge, elude, parry, shirk,
   shunt 6. baffle, escape, illude 7. beguile,
   quibble 8. sidestep, slip away
   10. circumvent
evaluate ... 5. judge, weigh 6. assess
   8. appraise
evanescent ... 8. fleeting 9. ephemeral,
   transient, vanishing 11. impermanent
   12. disappearing 13. infinitesimal
evangelical ... 7. Gospels 8. orthodox
   10. Protestant, scriptural
Evangeline (pert to) ...
   home .. 6. Acadia
   lover .. 7. Gabriel
   poem by .. 10. Longfellow (1847)
evangelist ... 6. Graham, Sunday (Billy)
   7. apostle, Roberts 9. McPherson
evaporate ... 3. dry 5. steam 6. escape,
   exhale 7. avolate 8. vaporize 9. cease
   to be, dehydrate, disappear
evasion ... 5. dodge, shift 6. escape
   8. avoiding 9. avoidance, quibbling,
   shuffling 12. equivocation
   13. circumvention, secretiveness
evasive ... 3. sly 4. eely 6. shifty
   7. elusive, elusory 9. deceitful,

quibbling, secretive
eve . . . **3.** iva (herb), wet **4.** dusk, thaw **6.** sunset **12.** on the brink of, on the verge of
even . . . **3.** e'en, tie **4.** just, tied **5.** equal, exact, level, match, plane **6.** placid, smooth, square, steady **7.** abreast, balance, equable, neutral, regular, uniform **8.** directly, parallel **9.** impartial, precisely **11.** symmetrical
even (if) . . . **8.** although **12.** nevertheless **15.** notwithstanding
even (so) . . . **3.** yes **12.** nevertheless
evener . . . **9.** equalizer **10.** doubletree
evenglow . . . **3.** red (color) **8.** twilight
evening . . . **5.** Abend **6.** sunset
evening dress . . . **4.** gown **6.** jewels, tuxedo **8.** slippers (high heel) **9.** full dress, headdress **10.** dinner coat **11.** tie and tails **17.** swallow-tailed coat
event . . . **4.** fate (obs), game **5.** drama, issue **6.** result **7.** contest, episode, scandal **8.** incident **9.** adventure, happening, milestone **10.** conclusion, occurrence **11.** consequence, termination **12.** circumstance
event (pert to) . . .
extraordinary . . **10.** phenomenon
supernatural . . **7.** miracle
theater . . **6.** opener **8.** premiere
turning point . . **6.** crisis **8.** decision, landmark
eventide . . . **4.** dusk **6.** sunset, vesper **7.** evening, sundown **8.** twilight **9.** nightfall
eventually . . . **3.** yet **6.** lastly **7.** finally **10.** ultimately
ever . . . **3.** e'er **4.** anon **5.** at all **6.** always **7.** forever **10.** constantly **11.** perpetually
Everest peak . . . **6.** Lhotse (28,100 ft)
evergreen shrub . . . **4.** Ilex, moss, Olax, titi **5.** heath, holly, savin, toyon **6.** laurel **7.** baretta, jasmine **9.** perennial **12.** rhododendron
evergreen tree . . . **3.** fir, yew **4.** pine **5.** carob, cedar, larch, olive, Taxus **6.** balsam, deodar, spruce, tarata **7.** conifer, hemlock, madrona, redwood
everlasting . . . **6.** eterne **7.** aeonian, agelong, durable, endless, eternal, forever, lasting, tedious **8.** enduring, evermore, immortal, infinite **9.** continual, incessant, perpetual, unceasing, wearisome **10.** immortelle, indefinite **11.** never-ending, strawflower **12.** Eternal Being, imperishable **13.** unintermitted, uninterrupted
every . . . **3.** all, any, ilk **4.** each, ilka **6.** entire **8.** complete
every one, everyone . . . **3.** all **4.** each **9.** everybody **10.** individual
everything . . . **3.** all, sum **5.** total
evict . . . **4.** oust **5.** eject, expel, prove **6.** remove **7.** confute **8.** force out
eviction . . . **6.** ouster **9.** ejectment **11.** dislodgment **13.** dispossession
evidence . . . **4.** clue, sign **5.** proof, token **6.** attest, evince **7.** constat (law), probate, support **8.** argument, manifest, rebuttal **9.** testimony **10.** indication **15.** circumstantiate

evident . . . **5.** clear, plain **6.** patent **7.** obvious, visible **8.** apparent, manifest, palpable **9.** notorious **11.** indubitable
eviscerate . . . **3.** gut **10.** disembowel
evil . . . **3.** bad, ill, mal (pref) **4.** bane, vile **6.** injury, sinful, wicked **7.** adverse, baleful, corrupt, hurtful, immoral, malefic, misdeed, satanic, unsound, vicious **8.** depraved, iniquity, sinister **9.** injurious, malignant, offensive **10.** calamitous, malevolent, pernicious, wrongdoing **12.** unpropitious
evil (pert to) . . .
child . . **3.** imp
deed . . **3.** sin **4.** harm
devil (little) . . **9.** deevilick (Scot)
doer . . **5.** cheat **9.** miscreant, wrongdoer **10.** malefactor
omen . . **5.** knell
spirit . . **5.** bugan, demon, devil, ghoul, Satan **6.** Belial **7.** Ahriman, Amaimon **8.** Asmodeus **9.** cacodemon, demonkind, lost souls
evils . . . **4.** ills, mala
evince . . . **4.** show **7.** display, exhibit, express, provoke **8.** convince, evidence, indicate, manifest
evoke . . . **4.** call (out) **5.** educe, voice **6.** elicit, prompt, summon **7.** conjure
evolution . . . **7.** biogeny, cosmism **8.** heredity, maneuver, movement **9.** Darwinism, phylogeny, unfolding, unrolling **10.** evolvement **11.** development **13.** manifestation, Spencerianism
evolve . . . **4.** emit **5.** educe **6.** create, deduce, derive, unfold, unroll **7.** develop, grow out **9.** disengage, expatiate, extricate **11.** disentangle
ewe . . . **3.** keb **4.** lamb **5.** crone (old), sheep **6.** theave
ewer . . . **3.** jug **5.** crock **7.** pitcher
exacerbate . . . **5.** anger **6.** incite **8.** embitter, irritate **9.** aggravate
exact . . . **4.** just, levy, nice **5.** assess, demand, elicit, extort, formal, minute, oblige, strict **7.** careful, correct, literal, precise, regular, require **8.** accurate **10.** methodical, meticulous
exact (pert to) . . .
opposite of . . **8.** antipode **9.** antipodal
penalty . . **4.** fine **7.** estreat
thinking . . **13.** ratiocination
vengeance . . **6.** avenge
exacting . . . **6.** severe, strict **7.** arduous **8.** critical **9.** demanding, elicitory **10.** fastidious **12.** extortionate
exacting devotion (exclusive) . . . **7.** jealous
exactly . . . **3.** due **5.** spand **6.** nicely **7.** quite so **8.** as you say **9.** precisely **10.** accurately
exaggerated . . . **5.** outré **8.** enhanced, enlarged, overdone, romanced **9.** excessive, increased, magnified **10.** overstated **11.** exceptional **13.** overestimated **14.** misrepresented
exaggerated comedy . . . **5.** farce
exalt . . . **5.** elate, extol, raise **6.** praise **7.** elevate, ennoble, glorify, inspire,

promote, worship 8. enthrone, increase, sanctify 10. aggrandize

exalted ... 5. grand, noble, sheen 6. elated 7. refined, sublime 8. elevated, extolled 9. dignified 11. illustrious

examination ... 4. test 5. audit, trial 7. inquiry 8. research, scrutiny, specimen 10. discussion, inspection 11. inquisition 13. investigation

examine ... 3. pry, spy, try (law) 4. pore, scan, sift, test 5. audit, probe, quest 6. censor, debate, ponder 7. analyze, collate, discuss, explore, inspect 8. consider 10. scrutinize 11. interrogate

examiner ... 6. censor, conner, tester 7. auditor, officer (court) 9. inspector

example ... 4. case, norm, type 5. bysen (obs), model 6. sample 7. pattern, warning 8. instance, paradigm, specimen 9. exemplify, precedent 12. illustration 15. exemplification

ex animo ... 9. sincerely 12. from the heart

Excalibur ... 5. sword

excavate ... 3. dig 4. cave, mine 5. dig up, scoop, stope 6. dredge, exhume, quarry 9. hollow out

excavation ... 3. pit 4. hole, mine 5. stope 6. cavity, dugout 7. digging 8. opencast

exceed ... 3. top 4. pass 5. excel, outdo 6. outvie, overdo 7. eclipse, outrank, surpass 8. outstrip, overstep 9. overshoot, transcend 11. predominate

exceedingly ... 4. many, very 9. extremely 13. extraordinary

excel ... 3. cap, top 4. beat, best 5. outdo, outgo, rival 6. better, exceed, precel 7. surpass 8. dominate, outshine 9. transcend

excellence ... 4. meed 5. merit 6. desert, virtue 7. classic, probity 9. supremacy 13. inimitability

excellent ... 4. A-one, best, fine, good 5. bravo, prime, super 6. choice, select, tiptop, worthy 7. capital, corking, stellar 8. skillful (skilful), stunning, valuable 9. admirable, exquisite, first-rate 12. transcendent

except ... 3. bar, but 4. omit, save 6. exempt, reject, unless 7. besides 9. eliminate, other than

exception ... 4. plea 5. cavil, doubt 6. oddity 7. dissent 8. demurrer 9. condition, exclusion, exemption, objection, rejection 11. restriction

exceptional ... 4. rare 7. notable, unusual 8. superior, uncommon 9. exclusive, wonderful 10. remarkable 11. outstanding 13. extraordinary

excerpt ... 4. cite 5. quote, scrap 6. choice 7. extract, passage (selected) 9. selection

excess ... 3. too 4. over, plus 5. luxus 7. nimiety, overage, profuse, surplus 10. indulgence (undue), redundancy 11. superfluity 12. intemperance 14. immoderateness, superabundance

excess (solar over lunar month) ... 5. epact

excessive ... 3. too 5. undue 6. overly 7. extreme, profuse 8. overmuch 9. fanatical, plethoric 10. exorbitant, immoderate, inordinate, redundancy 11. exaggerated, extravagant 12. unreasonable

excessive (pert to) ...
development .. 11. hypertrophy
fear .. 5. panic 6. phobia
gushing .. 8. effusion
waste .. 12. extravagance

excessively ... 3. too 5. enorm 6. unduly 12. exorbitantly, inordinately 13. intemperately

exchange ... 4. swap 5. bandy, trade 6. barter, resale, rialto 7. dealing, traffic 9. transpose 10. substitute 11. interchange, reciprocate

exchange (pert to) ...
discount .. 4. agio
for money .. 4. cash, sell
letters .. 10. correspond
place .. 4. mart 5. store 6. bourse, market, shoppe
premium .. 4. agio
visits .. 3. gam

exchequer ... 4. fisc (fisk) 5. funds, purse 8. finances, treasury 11. possessions (money)

excise ... 3. tax 4. toll 6. impost

exciseman ... 5. gager 7. officer 8. revenuer

excision ... 7. erasure, removal 10. cutting off, cutting out, mutilation 11. destruction, extirpation

excite ... 4. fire, roil, spur, stir, urge 5. elate, impel, rouse 6. arouse, awaken, bestir, incite, kindle, prompt, stir up 7. agitate, animate, inflame, provoke, psych up 8. energize, interest 9. electrify, impassion, instigate, stimulate

excited ... 4. agog 6. hoopla 7. aroused, fevered, keyed up 8. agitated, startled 10. interested 11. impassioned

excited, not easily ... 6. stolid 7. stoical 9. impassive

excitement ... 3. ado 4. stir 5. fever 6. furore 7. emotion, ferment 9. agitation, commotion 10. incitement, irritation 11. disturbance, stimulation

exciting ... 5. kicky 6. gung-ho, hectic 7. parlous 8. alluring 9. desirable, thrilling 10. delightful 11. interesting, provocative

exciting compassion ... 7. piteous

exclamation ... 2. ah, lo, oh, so 3. aha, bah, boo, fic, hep, oho, tut, ugh, yah 4. ahem, alas, drat, egad, evoe, phew, pish, rats, yech 5. bravo, humph, pshaw 6. indeed, shezam 7. kerwham 9. alackaday 11. ejaculation 12. interjection

exclude ... 3. bar 4. omit 5. debar, eject, expel 6. banish 7. shut out 8. disallow, preclude, prohibit 9. eliminate 13. excommunicate

exclusive ... 5. aloof, ritzy 6. select 7. special 8. limiting, snobbish 9. seclusive 10. definitive, unsociable 11. prohibitive, restrictive

exclusive right . . . **6.** patent
10. concession **11.** restriction
excoriate . . . **4.** flay, gall, peel **5.** strip
6. abrade **9.** criticize
excrescence . . . **4.** boss (Arch), lump
6. growth, nodule **9.** appendage,
outgrowth **10.** protrusion
excrete . . . **5.** egest **9.** discharge, eliminate
excruciating . . . **7.** painful, racking
9. agonizing, torturing **11.** distressing
excursion . . . **3.** row **4.** ride, sail, tour,
trek, trip **5.** jaunt, sally **6.** junket, outing,
ramble **7.** circuit, journey, outlope
8. circuity **10.** expedition
excusable . . . **6.** venial **9.** allowable,
justified **10.** defensible, exemptible,
pardonable, remissible **11.** justifiable
excuse . . . **4.** plea **5.** alibi, remit **6.** acquit,
essoin, pardon **7.** absolve, apology,
condone, forgive, pretext **8.** overlook
9. exonerate, extenuate
execrate . . . **4.** hate **5.** abhor, curse
6. detest, loathe **8.** denounce
execute . . . **2.** do **3.** act **4.** hang, kill,
vest **6.** direct, effect, finish, manage
7. conduct, enforce, perform **8.** carry
out, complete, transact **10.** accomplish,
administer
execution . . . **4.** writ **7.** hanging
10. production, punishment
11. achievement, performance,
transaction **14.** accomplishment
exegate . . . **6.** leader **7.** adviser
8. dragoman **11.** interpreter
exegesis . . . **7.** explain **9.** interpret
10. exposition, expounding
exemplar . . . **5.** ideal, model **7.** example,
paragon, pattern **8.** specimen
9. archetype
exemplary . . . **8.** laudable, monitory
11. commendable **12.** exemplifying,
praiseworthy **14.** representative
exemplify . . . **4.** copy **6.** typify **7.** explain
10. illustrate, transcribe
exempt . . . **4.** exon **5.** clear **6.** immune
7. absolve, release **8.** dispense,
excepted, excluded, released, set apart
10. privileged
exemption . . . **6.** essoin **7.** freedom
8. immunity, impunity, navicert
12. dispensation
exercise . . . **3.** ply, ure (anc), use
4. task, yoga **5.** drill, étude, exert,
train **6.** action, employ, lesson, praxis,
school, tai chi **7.** display, jogging,
problem, workout **8.** activity, aerobics,
ceremony, practice, training **9.** athletics
10. exhibition, gymnastics, isometrics
exertion . . . **5.** essay, trial **6.** effort
7. attempt **8.** endeavor
exhalation . . . **4.** aura, fume **5.** steam
6. breath **7.** halitus **9.** effluvium,
emanation **10.** expiration
11. evaporation **12.** vaporization
exhale . . . **4.** emit **6.** vanish **7.** exhaust,
respite **9.** transpire **10.** breathe out
exhaust . . . **3.** fag, sap **4.** emit, jade, tire
5. drain, empty, spend, waste, weary
6. exhale, overdo, weaken **7.** consume,
deplete, fatigue **9.** discharge
10. impoverish

exhausted . . . **4.** done, worn **5.** spent,
tired **6.** used up **7.** emptied, petered
(out) **8.** dog-tired, forspent
exhaustion . . . **6.** effete **7.** burnout, fatigue
9. depletion, lassitude **11.** prostration
14. impoverishment
exhibit . . . **3.** air **4.** fair, shew (anc),
show, wear **5.** stage, state **6.** evince,
expose, flaunt, parade, reveal **7.** display
8. disclose, evidence, manifest
9. spectacle **11.** demonstrate
15. circumstantiate
exhibit (pert to) . . .
colors (change of) . . **8.** iridesce, opalesce
pleasure . . **5.** gloat, revel (in)
taste (refined) . . **6.** ostent **7.** elegant
exhibition . . . **4.** fair, show **9.** spectacle
10. exposition **11.** ostentation
13. manifestation
exhibition room . . . **10.** panopticon
exhilaration . . . **6.** gaiety **7.** jollity
8. gladness, hilarity **9.** animation,
merriment **10.** excitement, joyousness
11. gleefulness, refreshment
12. cheerfulness, invigoration
exhort . . . **4.** urge, warn **6.** advise, dehort,
incite, preach **7.** caution **9.** encourage,
stimulate
exhume . . . **3.** dig **5.** delve **7.** unearth
8. disinter, exhumate
exigeant . . . **8.** exacting **11.** importunate
exigency . . . **4.** need, urge **6.** crisis
7. demands, urgency **8.** juncture,
pressure **9.** emergency, extremity,
necessity **12.** requirements
exigent . . . **4.** writ **6.** strict, urgent
8. critical, exacting, pressing
9. demanding, necessary **10.** compelling
13. indispensable
exile . . . **6.** banish, deport **7.** outcast
8. outlawry, relegate **9.** expulsion
10. banishment, expatriate
12. expatriation, proscription
exist . . . **2.** am, be, is **3.** are **4.** live
5. alive **6.** abound **9.** be present
existence . . . **3.** ens **4.** esse, life **5.** actus,
being, entia **6.** extant **7.** essence, reality
8. presence **9.** actuality
13. manifestation
existing (pert to) . . .
fancifully . . **9.** imaginary **10.** transitory
name only (in) . . **7.** nominal, titular
now . . **6.** extant **7.** current, present
9. immediate
same time . . **15.** contemporaneous
way of . . **9.** lifestyle
exit . . . **3.** die **4.** door, gate, vent **5.** going,
go out, issue **6.** egress, outlet **7.** leaving,
passage (out), walkout **9.** departure
exitus . . . **5.** death, issue **6.** exodus, outlet
7. outcome
exlex . . . **6.** outlaw
ex libris . . . **8.** colophon **9.** bookplate
exodus . . . **4.** Book (Bib), exit **5.** going
6. flight, hegira **9.** departure
Exodus author . . . **4.** Uris
exonerate . . . **4.** free **5.** clear **6.** acquit
7. absolve, release, relieve **9.** disburden
(obs), exculpate
exorbitant . . . **5.** undue **9.** excessive
10. high-priced

exorbitant interest . . . 5. usury
exorcism . . . 5. spell 7. formula
9. expulsion (of evil spirits)
11. conjuration, incantation
exordium . . . 5. proem 7. preface, prelude
8. overture 9. beginning 12. introduction
exoteric . . . 8. exterior, external, outsider
14. comprehensible
exotic . . . 5. alien 7. foreign, strange
8. colorful, ulterior 9. not native,
peregrine, unrelated 10. extraneous,
outlandish
expand . . . 4. grow, open 5. sheet, splay,
tract 6. dilate, spread 7. broaden,
develop, distend, enlarge 9. expatiate,
intumesce
expanse . . . 3. sea 4. main (broad)
5. ocean, plain, reach, tract 6. desert,
extent, spread 7. stretch 8. eternity
(time) 9. expansion
expansion . . . 4. size 6. extent, growth,
spread 8. dilation, increase
10. distention 11. development,
enlargement, expatiation
expansive . . . 4. wide 5. broad, large
7. elastic, liberal 8. effusive, spacious
9. bombastic, grandiose 11. extensional,
sympathetic 12. unrestrained
13. comprehensive
expatiate . . . 5. dwell 6. dilate 7. descant,
enlarge 10. widespread
expatriate . . . 5. exile, expel 6. banish,
outlaw 7. exclude, outcast 9. ostracize
13. excommunicate
expect . . . 4. deem, hope, wait 5. await,
think 6. intend 7. suppose 10. anticipate
expectation . . . 4. hope 9. imminence,
intention 12. anticipation
expedience . . . 6. wisdom 7. fitness
10. adaptation, timeliness 11. suitability
expedient . . . 4. wise 5. shift 6. timely
7. fitting, politic, ressort, stopgap
8. artifice, resource 9. advisable
10. profitable 12. advantageous
expedite . . . 3. hie 4. easy, free 5. hurry,
light, speed 6. hasten 7. further, quicken
8. dispatch 10. accelerate, facilitate
expedition . . . 5. drave, foray, haste,
speed 6. safari 7. Crusade, entrada,
journey 8. Crusades 9. excursion,
hastening
expel . . . 4. oust, void 5. eject, evict,
exile 6. banish, exhale 7. extrude
9. discharge, eliminate 10. dispossess
expend . . . 3. pay, use 5. spend, waste
7. consume 8. disburse 10. distribute
expenditure . . . 5. outgo, price 6. outlay
7. expense, payment 11. consumption
12. disbursement
expense . . . 4. cost 5. price 6. outlay
9. allowance 11. consumption
12. disbursement
expensive . . . 4. dear, high 5. fancy, steep
6. costly, lavish 7. liberal 10. high-priced
11. extravagant
experience . . . 3. see, try 4. feel, have,
know, test 5. maxim, sense, skill
6. ordeal, suffer, wisdom 7. emotion,
undergo 8. facility 9. knowledge,
sensation 10. occurrence
experience (pert to) . . .

pleasure . . 5. enjoy
regret . . 6. repent
suffering . . 7. calvary
worldly . . 14. sophistication
experiment . . . 3. try 4. test 5. essay,
proof, prove, trial 6. verify
11. observation
expert . . . 3. ace 4. deft, whiz (whizz)
5. adept 6. adroit, clever, habile,
master 7. casuist (in conscience), dab
hand 8. artistic, skillful 10. proficient
11. connoisseur, experienced
12. professional
expiate . . . 5. atone, purge 6. purify,
shrive (anc)
expiation . . . 4. rite 6. amends 7. redress
8. piacular 9. atonement 10. redemption
12. compensation, propitiation
expire . . . 3. die, end 4. pass 5. cease,
lapse 6. elapse, perish 7. breathe (out)
9. terminate
explain . . . 5. clear, solve 6. define
7. expound, premise 8. describe
9. elucidate, interpret 10. demonstrate
explanation . . . 6. theory 7. meaning
8. exegesis, scholium, solution
10. exposition 11. description,
explication 13. clarification
14. interpretation 15. exemplification
expletive . . . 3. gee 4. egad, gosh,
oath 5. curse, there, voilà 6. behold
8. addition 9. added word
11. exclamation
explicit . . . 4. open 5. exact, fixed
6. candid 7. express, precise 8. absolute,
distinct, implicit, manifest, positive
9. outspoken 11. unambiguous,
unequivocal, unqualified
13. unconditional 14. discriminating
explode . . . 3. pop 4. fail 5. blast, burst
6. blow up 7. implode 8. backfire,
detonate
exploit . . . 3. act (heroic) 4. dare,
deed, feat, gest, milk 5. bleed
7. heroism 9. advantage 10. overcharge
11. achievement
explore . . . 4. look, view 5. probe 6. search
7. examine 8. discover 9. penetrate
11. investigate
explorer . . . 5. diver 7. pioneer
10. discoverer
explorer . . . 4. Byrd, Cook, Dias, Polo
(Marco), Ross 5. Cabot, Drake, Peary,
Scott 6. Balboa, Cortes (Cortez), De
Soto, Hudson, Pinzón 7. Cartier,
Pizarro, Raleigh (Ralegh) 8. Columbus,
Coronado, Magellan 9. Champlain
10. Shackleton 11. Ponce de León
explosion . . . 3. pop 4. bank 5. blast,
noise 6. report 7. failure 8. outburst
10. detonation
explosive . . . 3. cap, TNT 4. mine
5. niter, shell 6. amatol, petard,
powder, tittle, tonite 7. cordite, grenade,
lyddite 8. dynamite 9. cartridge,
cellulose, fulgurite, guncotton, pyroxylin
11. firecracker 13. nitroglycerin
15. trinitrotoluene
exponent . . . 4. note 5. index 7. symptom
9. explainer, expounder 10. explaining
11. interpreter

expose . . . 3. air 4. bare, open 6. divest, reveal, unmask 7. exhibit, unearth 8. disclose, discover, endanger 9. ventilate 10. exposition

expose to danger . . . 11. periclitate

expose to scorn . . . 6. satire 7. pillory

exposition . . . 4. fair 6. bazaar, expose, lesson 7. display 8. exposure, treatise 9. discourse, spectacle 10. disclosure, exhibition 11. abandonment, explanation 12. dissertation 14. interpretation

expostulate . . . 5. orate 6. advise, demand 7. call for, discuss, protest 8. complain, dissuade 11. remonstrate

exposure . . . 8. disproof, jeopardy, openness, snapshot 9. liability 10. appearance, disclosure, exposition, visibility

express . . . 3. say 4. mean, show 5. exude, speak, state, train, utter, voice 6. depict, evince, extort, phrase 7. betoken, carrier, declare, exhibit, expound, extract, signify, testify 8. describe, dispatch, indicate, intimate, manifest 9. delineate, messenger, posthaste, utterance 11. declaration

express (pert to) . . .
censure . . 10. animadvert
disapproval . . 9. deprecate
fervor . . 7. enthuse
gratitude . . 5. thank
indirectly . . 5. imply
in words . . 6. phrase
numerically . . 8. evaluate
regard . . 6. praise 10. compliment
regret . . 9. apologize
sympathy . . 7. condole, console 10. grieve with 11. commiserate

expressing . . .
doubt . . 10. dubitative
extra phrase (Gram) . . 12. periphrastic
feeling . . 7. emotive
past tense . . 11. preteritive
pique . . 5. pouty
praise . . 9. laudatory

expression . . . 4. grin, show, term 5. scowl, smile 6. aspect, oracle, phrase 7. diction, meaning 8. locution 9. statement, utterance 10. extraction, indication 11. delineation 13. manifestation 14. representation

expression (pert to) . . .
mathematics . . 8. equation
of approval . . 4. clap 7. ovation 8. applause
of contempt . . 3. fie 5. pshaw, sneer
of disapproval . . 6. rebuke
of ideas . . 4. mode 5. style 7. fashion
of politics . . 4. vote
of weariness . . 4. sigh
peculiar . . 5. idiom
without . . 7. deadpan

expressive motion . . . 7. gesture 13. gesticulation

expulsion . . . 5. exile 10. banishment, expiration 11. elimination

expunction . . . 4. blot 7. erasure 10. effacement 12. obliteration

expunge . . . 4. dele 5. erase 6. cancel, delete, efface, excise, rub out 7. blot

out, destroy 9. strike out 10. annihilate, obliterate

expurgate . . . 5. bathe, purge 6. censor, excise, purify 7. cleanse

exquisite . . . 4. fine, rare 6. dainty, superb 7. perfect, refined 8. delicate 9. beautiful, delicious, matchless 10. delightful, fastidious

exsanguine . . . 6. anemic 9. bloodless

exsiccate . . . 3. dry 4. arid, sear 5. dry up, parch 7. exhaust 9. evaporate

extant . . . 5. being 7. in vogue, present, visible 8. existent, existing

extempore . . . 7. offhand 8. ad-libbed 9. impromptu 10. improvised 14. unpremeditated

extend . . . 2. go 3. eke, jut, lie, run 4. give, span 5. bulge, reach, renew, steal, widen 6. deepen, deploy, expand, spread 7. amplify, broaden, draw out, proffer, prolong, radiate, stretch 8. continue, increase, lengthen, postpone, protract, protrude 10. exaggerate, straighten

extended . . . 4. open 5. broad 6. valued 7. assured, diffuse 8. expanded, spacious 10. lengthened 12. outstretched

extended view . . . 8. panorama

extension . . . 4. area 5. range, scope 6. extent 8. addition, duration, increase, sequence 9. expansion 10. denotation 11. continuance, enlargement, lengthening 12. augmentation 13. extensiveness

extension of time . . . 4. stay 7. respite

extensive . . . 4. vast, wide 5. broad, large 7. immense, titanic 8. expanded, spacious 9. expansive, wholesale 10. widespread 11. far-reaching

extent . . . 4. area, bulk, room, side, writ 5. areal, range, reach, scope 6. amount, degree, length 7. breadth, compass, expanse, measure 8. distance, frontage 9. dimension 10. assessment (Hist), denotation, proportion

extenuate . . . 4. thin 6. excuse, lessen, reduce, sicken, weaken 7. justify 8. diminish, palliate 9. attenuate

extenuating . . . 10. justifying, qualifying

exterior . . . 5. ectad (toward), ectal, outer 7. outside 8. external 10. extraneous

exterminate . . . 4. kill 5. expel 7. abolish, destroy 8. get rid of 9. eradicate, extirpate 10. annihilate

extermination . . . 9. expulsion 11. destruction, eradication

extern . . . 7. outward 8. exterior, external 9. extrinsic

external . . . 4. ecto 5. outer, outre 6. nonego 7. outside 8. cortical 10. extraneous

external appearance . . . 5. guise, image, looks 6. aspect 8. features 9. semblance

extinct . . . 4. dead, past 5. passé 7. defunct, died out, expired 8. quenched 11. nonexistent 12. extinguished

extinct bird . . . 3. moa 4. dodo

extinction . . . 5. death 9. quenching

11. destruction **12.** annihilation
extinct reptile ... **11.** pterodactyl
extinguish ... **5.** annul, choke, douse,
quell **6.** put out, quench, stifle **7.** destroy
8. suppress
extirpate ... **4.** dele, root, stub **5.** erase,
expel **6.** excise, uproot **7.** destroy
9. eradicate **11.** exterminate
extol ... **4.** laud **5.** exalt, kudos **6.** praise
7. applaud, commend, elevate, glorify
8. emblazon **9.** celebrate
extort ... **5.** bleed, exact, steal, wrest,
wring **6.** compel, elicit, wrench
7. extract **10.** overcharge
extortion ... **7.** robbery, seizure
8. exaction, rapacity **10.** extraction,
oppression, overcharge
extortionist ... **5.** harpy **7.** vampire,
vulture **9.** profiteer **11.** blackmailer
extra ... **3.** bye **4.** over **5.** added, spare,
super **7.** surplus **8.** superior **9.** accessory
10. additional
extra cache ... **5.** stock, store **7.** reserve
9. reservoir
extract ... **4.** cite, pull **6.** deduce, elicit,
select **7.** essence, estreat, excerpt
8. withdraw
extract (pert to) ...
balsam .. **7.** toluene
Bible .. **7.** passage **8.** pericope
forcibly .. **6.** evulse
newspaper .. **8.** clipping
orchid (climbing) .. **7.** vanilla
extraction ... **5.** birth, stock **6.** origin
7. essence, excerpt **8.** tincture
9. parentage **10.** withdrawal
extraneous ... **5.** outer **6.** exotic **7.** foreign
9. extrinsic, separated, unrelated
11. unessential
extraordinary ... **3.** odd **4.** rare, unco
5. great **7.** notable, special, unusual
8. singular **9.** irregular, marvelous,
wonderful **10.** noteworthy, remarkable
11. exceptional **13.** distinguished
extravagance ... **5.** waste **6.** excess
8. wildness **9.** abundance **10.** fanaticism,
lavishness **11.** exorbitance, prodigality
12. exaggeration, intemperance,
recklessness
extravagant ... **3.** E la **4.** ee la (Mus), high
(priced) **5.** outré **6.** absurd **7.** baroque,
bizarre, diffuse, fanatic **8.** boastful,
prodigal, wasteful **9.** excessive,
fanatical, fantastic, luxurious, plentiful
10. digressive **11.** intemperate
12. unrestrained
extreme ... **3.** end **4.** last, sore **5.** final,
great, ultra **6.** excess, severe, utmost
7. drastic, intense, outward, radical
8. farthest, greatest, ultimate
9. excessive, extremity, fanatical,
outermost **10.** conclusive, immoderate
extreme degree ... **3.** nth
extreme fear ... **5.** panic **6.** horror
extreme unction ... **5.** anele **9.** last
rites, sacrament

extremist ... **7.** radical **8.** ultraist
extremity ... **3.** end, tip **4.** foot, limb
(body), pole **5.** verge **6.** border,
crisis, summit **8.** terminal **9.** necessity
11. termination
extricate ... **4.** free **5.** loose **6.** evolve,
rescue, wangle **7.** extract **8.** liberate
9. disengage **10.** disembroil
11. disentangle **12.** disembarrass
extrinsic ... **7.** foreign, outward
8. external **9.** objective **10.** accidental
(Log), contingent, extraneous, incidental
12. adventitious, nonessential
extrovert ... **11.** personality (opp of
introvert)
exuberance ... **6.** excess, plenty
8. overflow, rankness, vivacity
9. abundance, animation, profusion
10. friskiness, liveliness, luxuriance
11. copiousness **14.** superabundance
exuberant ... **6.** frisky, lavish **7.** fertile,
profuse **8.** effusive, fruitful, thriving
9. luxuriant, plentiful **11.** overflowing
13. superabundant
exudation ... **3.** gum, lac, tar **5.** pitch,
resin **6.** oozing **8.** emission, sweating
9. discharge, excretion
exude ... **4.** emit, ooze, reek **5.** sweat
7. excrete, give out **9.** discharge
exult ... **3.** joy **4.** crow, leap (obs), rave
5. boast, elate, ovare, pride **7.** rejoice
8. jubilate
exultant ... **5.** ovant **6.** elated
exultation ... **3.** joy **7.** delight **8.** boasting
9. jubilance, rejoicing **10.** jubilation
exults ... **5.** leaps **7.** glories, springs
9. jubilates
eye ... **2.** ee **3.** orb, see **4.** auge, glim, hole,
ogle **5.** optic, organ (human), sight,
watch **6.** look at, peeper **7.** observe,
witness **10.** scrutinize
eye (pert to) ...
absence of pupil .. **6.** acorea
black .. **5.** mouse **6.** shiner
brow .. **4.** arch **6.** eebree **11.** supercilium
cavity .. **5.** orbit **6.** hippus, socket
disease .. **8.** cataract, glaucoma,
hypopyon, trachoma **9.** amblyopia
14. conjunctivitis
disorder .. **6.** squint **7.** walleye
9. exotropia **10.** strabismus
dropper .. **7.** pipette
glass .. **4.** lens **7.** lorgnon, monocle
8. pince-nez **10.** spectacles
inflammation .. **6.** ititis **7.** uveitis
lash, lashes .. **5.** cilia (pl) **6.** cilium
lid .. **8.** palpebra
part .. **4.** iris, uvea **5.** pupil **6.** cornea,
retina
to blind (falconry) .. **4.** seel
eyelet ... **7.** cringle, grommet, ocellus
8. loophole, peephole
eyetooth ... **6.** cuspid **8.** dogtooth
eyot ... **3.** ait **4.** holm **5.** islet
eyra ... **7.** wildcat
eyrie, eyry ... **4.** nest **5.** aerie, nidus

F

F . . . **6.** letter (6th)
fabes . . . **10.** gooseberry
fabian . . . **7.** caution **8.** dilatory, inaction
   15. procrastination
Fabian . . . **7.** General (Rom), Society
fable . . . **3.** lie **4.** myth **5.** story **6.** legend
   7. fabliau, fantasy, fiction, Marchen,
   parable **8.** allegory, apologue, folk tale
   9. falsehood
fable (pert to) . . .
   being . . **5.** troll
   king . . **3.** Log
   monster . . **4.** ogre **7.** centaur
   narrator . . **10.** parabolist
   writer . . **5.** Aesop
fabric . . . **5.** build, cloth **6.** tissue **7.** texture
   8. erection, material **9.** framework
   11. workmanship **12.** construction
fabric (types of) . . . **3.** rep **4.** alma, duck,
   felt, gros, jean, lamé, lawn, leno, silk
   5. baize, batik, beige, crash, crepe,
   denim, linen, nylon, pekin, rumal,
   satin, scrim, serge, suede, toile, tulle,
   tweed, twill, voile, wigan **6.** agaric,
   alpaca, burlap, calico, canvas, chintz,
   cotton, damask, dimity, étoile, madras,
   mohair, moreen, muslin, penang,
   pongee, poplin, ratiné, sateen, tricot
   7. batiste, brocade, bunting, challis,
   chiffon, delaine, elastic, etamine,
   flannel, galatea, gingham, hernani,
   paisley, percale, satinet, ticking,
   worsted **8.** cashmere, chambray,
   chenille, corduroy, cretonne, drilling,
   prunella, sarcenet, Shantung, sheeting,
   whipcord **9.** bombazine, crinoline,
   gabardine, grenadine, lansdowne,
   matelassé, paramatta **10.** broadcloth,
   seersucker, terry cloth
fabric (pert to) . . .
   dealer . . **6.** mercer
   ornamental . . **4.** lace **8.** fagoting
   silk, watered . . **5.** moiré
   silk and gold . . **4.** acca (anc) **7.** brocade
   twill . . **6.** caddis (cadis)
   velvet . . **5.** panne, terry **6.** velure
   7. velours
   waste . . **5.** mungo
   window shade . . **7.** Holland
   woven . . **6.** tricot
fabricate . . . **4.** coin, form, make, mint
   5. build, frame, weave **6.** create,
   devise, invent, scheme **7.** falsify,
   fashion, produce, trump up **9.** construct
   11. manufacture
fabrication . . . **3.** lie, web **5.** guile
   6. cogger, deceit, making **7.** fiction,
   forging, untruth **9.** falsehood, invention
   12. construction
fabulist . . . **4.** liar **5.** Aesop **11.** storyteller
fabulous . . . **6.** absurd **7.** feigned
   8. mythical **9.** fictional, imaginary,
   legendary **10.** fictitious, remarkable
   11. astonishing **12.** mythological
fabulous (pert to) . . .

animal . . **7.** unicorn **9.** rosmarine (walrus)
beast . . **4.** lung **6.** dragon, wivern
   7. griffon, serpent **10.** earthdrake
being . . **6.** Lapith, Nessus **7.** centaur
bird . . **3.** moa, roc **4.** rukh
facade . . . **4.** face **5.** facia, front **7.** frontal
face . . . **3.** mug **4.** dare, defy, dial, line,
   meet, moue, phiz **5.** brave, cover, front
   6. answer, obvert, oppose, phizog,
   visage **7.** grimace **8.** boldness, confront,
   envisage, exterior, features, pretense
   9. encounter, impudence **10.** effrontery
   11. countenance, physiognomy, self-
   respect
face (pert to) . . .
   bone . . **6.** zygoma (cheek) **7.** maxilla
   (jaw)
   card . . **4.** jack, king **5.** queen
   east . . **9.** orientate
   gem . . **5.** facet
   lifting . . **13.** rhytidoplasty
   masonry . . **5.** revet
   nose . . **11.** rhinoplasty
   pains . . **4.** ague **13.** tic douloureux
   surgery . . **14.** blepharoplasty (eyelid)
   to face . . **6.** afront **7.** vis-à-vis **8.** opposite
   value . . **3.** par
faces (twelve) . . . **12.** dodecahedron
facet . . . **4.** face **5.** bezel, culet **6.** aspect,
   collet **8.** exterior
facetious . . . **5.** droll, funny, witty
   6. facete, jocose **7.** comical, jesting
   8. laughter **9.** whimsical
facia . . . **5.** plate **6.** tablet
facial pain . . . **3.** tic **4.** ague **9.** neuralgia
   13. tic douloureux
facient . . . **4.** doer **5.** agent **10.** multiplier
facile . . . **4.** easy **5.** quick, ready **6.** expert,
   fluent, gentle, pliant **7.** affable, lenient,
   pliable **9.** compliant, teachable
facilitate . . . **3.** aid **4.** ease, help **6.** assist
facility . . . **3.** art **4.** ease, help **5.** éclat,
   means, skill **7.** address, pliancy
   8. easiness **9.** readiness **10.** adroitness,
   expertness, pliability **11.** convenience,
   furtherance **13.** accommodation
facing . . . **6.** lining, veneer **7.** coating,
   surface **8.** opposite
facing (pert to) . . .
   glacier direction . . **5.** stoss
   inward . . **8.** introrse
   outward . . **8.** extrorse
facsimile . . . **4.** copy **5.** match **7.** replica
   9. duplicate **11.** counterpart
fact, facts . . . **4.** data, deed, feat,
   fiat **5.** datum, event, posit, truth
   6. really **7.** keynote, lowdown, paradox
   9. actuality
fact collector . . . **7.** statist **12.** statistician
faction . . . **4.** bloc, camp, sect, side
   5. cabal, junto, party **6.** clique
   7. machine (Polit) **11.** combination,
   partisanism
factious . . . **9.** demagogic, seditious,
   turbulent

F

factitious... **4.** made (by art), mock, sham **5.** phony **9.** unnatural **10.** artificial **11.** make-believe

factor... **4.** ager, gene **5.** agent, cause **6.** detail **9.** component **11.** constituent

factotum... **4.** maid **5.** do-all **7.** servant **8.** busybody

faculties... **4.** wits **6.** senses **7.** talents **9.** abilities, aptitudes **12.** capabilities

faculty... **3.** art **4.** body, ease, gift **6.** talent **7.** ability, know-how **8.** aptitude, teachers **9.** endowment (mental) **12.** professorate

fad... **4.** rage, whim **5.** craze, fancy, hobby, mania **6.** custom **7.** caprice, fashion

faddist... **10.** monomaniac

fade, fade out... **3.** age, dim, dow, wan **4.** flat, pale, wilt **5.** daver, decay, peter **6.** perish, vanish, weaken, wither **7.** decline, insipid **8.** discolor, dissolve, languish **9.** disappear **11.** deteriorate

faded... **3.** dim **4.** dull, pale **5.** faint, passé **8.** impaired

Faerie Queene (pert to)...
author.. **7.** Spenser
character.. **3.** Ate, Una **5.** Guyon, Truth **7.** Acrasia **8.** Gloriana
theme.. **8.** chivalry **10.** knighthood
type work.. **4.** poem **8.** allegory

fag... **4.** flag, hack, jade, tire, toil, work **5.** droop, slave, weary **6.** drudge, menial **7.** exhaust, fatigue, untwist (rope end) **8.** drudgery **9.** cigarette

fag end... **3.** end **4.** tail **6.** scraps, tag end **7.** remnant **8.** last part, leavings

Fagin... **3.** Jew (Oliver Twist)

Fagin's pupil... **12.** Artful Dodger (John Dawkins)

fagot, faggot... **4.** bind **5.** bunch **6.** bundle, emblem (Her) **8.** firewood, slattern

fail... **3.** ebb, err **4.** flop, lack, miss, sink **5.** decay, flunk, lapse **6.** defect, desert, weaken **7.** decline, exhaust **8.** unbetide **9.** fall short **10.** disappoint, go bankrupt **11.** deteriorate

failed admission... **11.** blackballed

failed to follow suit... **7.** reneged

failure... **3.** dud **4.** flop, foil, lack, lose, miss **5.** decay, fault, lapse **6.** defeat, fiasco **7.** default **10.** bankruptcy, deficiency, insolvency, nonsuccess, suspension **11.** delinquency

faint... **3.** dim, ill **4.** pale, soft, weak **5.** swelt, swoon, timid **6.** feeble, sickly **7.** languid **8.** cowardly, fatigued, listless, timorous **10.** indistinct, oppressive

faintness... **5.** qualm (sudden) **7.** dimness, syncope **8.** paleness, weakness **10.** feebleness

fair... **4.** just, mart **6.** bazaar, blonde, comely, honest, kermis **8.** festival, mediocre, rainless, unbiased **9.** impartial **10.** auspicious, reasonable **12.** unprejudiced **13.** dispassionate

fairy, faery... **3.** elf, fay **4.** peri, pixy **5.** genie, magic, nymph, ouphe, pixie **6.** elfkin, sprite **7.** brownie, gremlin **8.** illusion

fairy (pert to)...

abode (Scot).. **4.** shee (sidhe)
death spirit.. **7.** banshee
evil.. **4.** ogre, puck **9.** hobgoblin
fort.. **3.** lis (liss)
German.. **6.** kobold
Irish.. **10.** cluricaune, leprechaun
king.. **6.** Oberon
Persian.. **4.** peri
queen.. **3.** Mab, Una **7.** Titania
Scandinavian.. **5.** nisse
tale.. **3.** fib **7.** Marchen **8.** allegory **9.** narrative

faith... **4.** hope **5.** creed, piety, troth, trust **6.** belief, credit, verily, virtue **7.** loyalty **8.** credence, fidelity **9.** assurance, authority, orthodoxy **10.** confidence **11.** credibility

faithful... **4.** fast, feal, leal, true **5.** liege, loyal, pious **6.** devout, steady, trusty **7.** devoted, sincere, staunch **8.** constant, obedient, reliable **9.** believers, steadfast, veracious

faithful friend... **7.** Achates (Vergil's Aeneid)

faithless... **5.** false, punic **6.** fickle, untrue **8.** apostate, disloyal, shifting **9.** deceptive, mercurial, skeptical **10.** perfidious, unfaithful **11.** incredulous, irreligious, treacherous, unbelieving **12.** falsehearted

fake... **3.** rob **4.** faux, sham **5.** cheat, fraud, trick **6.** ersatz **7.** trump up **8.** doctor up **9.** deception, fabricate, imitation **10.** artificial **11.** counterfeit

faker... **5.** cheat, fraud **7.** bluffer **8.** impostor **9.** hypocrite, pretender

fakir... **4.** sect (Muslim, Islam), yogi **7.** dervish **9.** mendicant

falcon... **4.** hawk **5.** besra, saker **6.** laggar, lanner, luggar, merlin, shahin (shaheen), sorage, tercel **7.** kestrel, sakeret **8.** lanneret, Raptores **9.** gyrfalcon (gerfalcon), peregrine

falcon, military... **8.** ordnance

falconry term... **4.** hood, jess, lure, seel **6.** rebate **7.** hawking

fall... **3.** ebb **4.** bang, drop, plop, ruin, sink, slip **5.** crash, spill **6.** autumn, defeat, perish, plunge, tumble **7.** descend, descent, devolve, failure, plummet, relapse **8.** collapse, commence, downfall, rainfall **9.** abatement, overthrow, surrender, waterfall **10.** depreciate, subversion **11.** degradation, precipitate

fall (pert to)...

asleep.. **6.** nod off
back.. **6.** recede, recoil **7.** relapse, retreat **10.** retrogress
behind.. **3.** lag **4.** lose **7.** regress
guy.. **5.** patsy
in.. **4.** cave **5.** agree, lapse **6.** concur, line up **8.** collapse **9.** terminate
rhythmical.. **6.** cadent
short.. **4.** lack, want **10.** disappoint

fallacious... **4.** wily **5.** false **6.** crafty, untrue **8.** delusive, guileful **9.** deceitful, deceptive, erroneous, illogical, insidious **10.** fraudulent, misleading **13.** disappointing

fallacy... **5.** error **6.** idolum **7.** sophism

9. deception, falseness, sophistry
13. deceitfulness

false ... **4.** sham, tale **5.** bogus, paste
6. betray, impugn, pseudo, untrue
7. mislead **8.** apostate, spurious
9. deceitful, deceptive, erroneous,
faithless, incorrect, insincere,
pretended, unfounded **10.** fictitious,
mendacious, traitorous, unfaithful,
unreliable, untruthful **11.** counterfeit
12. illegitimate

false (pert to) ...
friend .. **5.** Judas **7.** traitor
front .. **8.** disguise **11.** affectation
fruit .. **10.** pseudocarp
god .. **4.** idol
hearted .. **9.** deceitful **10.** perfidious
11. treacherous
items .. **6.** spuria
jewelry .. **5.** paste **6.** strass
reasoning .. **10.** paralogism
report .. **5.** rumor **6.** canard **7.** slander
show .. **6.** tinsel
wing (bird's) .. **5.** alula

falsehood ... **3.** lie **4.** tale **7.** falsity,
fiction, perjury, untruth **9.** imposture,
mendacity **11.** counterfeit, fabrication
12. exaggeration

falseness ... **5.** error **8.** illusion
9. deception, falsehood **10.** infidelity

falsetto ... **5.** voice (false) **10.** artificial
11. high-pitched

falsify ... **3.** lie **5.** belie, forge **7.** distort,
pervert **8.** disprove **10.** adulterate
11. counterfeit **12.** misrepresent

Falstaff ... **5.** opera (Verdi) **9.** character
(Shaksp)

falter ... **3.** lag **4.** fail **5.** demur,
pause, waver **7.** flinch, quaver, totter
7. stagger, stammer, stumble, tremble
8. hesitate, lose hope

fame ... **4.** note **5.** éclat, glory, kudos
6. renown, repute **9.** celebrity

famed ... **7.** eminent, honored, popular
8. renowned **9.** notorious **10.** celebrated

familiar ... **4.** easy **5.** usual **6.** common,
versed **7.** affable **8.** domestic, frequent,
friendly, habitual, informal
9. companion, customary, well-known
10. accustomed, colloquial, conversant
12. domesticated, presumptuous
13. unconstrained

familiarity ... **8.** intimacy **9.** awareness,
knowledge, liberties **10.** affability
12. acquaintance (close), friendliness

familiarize ... **6.** inform **8.** accustom
9. habituate

family ... **3.** ilk, kin **4.** clan, line, race
5. class, group, house, tribe **6.** stirps
7. kindred, lineage **9.** community,
household, posterity **10.** kith and kin

family (pert to) ...
bees .. **5.** apina **7.** Apoidea
favoritism .. **8.** nepotism
herbs .. **7.** Ranales
Italians (famed) .. **4.** Este
kings .. **7.** dynasty
name .. **7.** surname

famous ... **5.** named, noted **7.** eminent,
namable, notable **8.** renowned
9. excellent, notorious **10.** celebrated,

remarkable **13.** distinguished
famous murderer ... **4.** Aram, Cain
9. Bluebeard
famous pirate ... **4.** Kidd (Capt)
fan ... **4.** blow, cool, vane, whip
5. punka (punkah) **6.** blower, foment,
incite, rooter, spread, thresh, winnow
7. admirer, devotee, refresh
9. stimulate, strike out (baseball),
ventilate **10.** enthusiast

fanatic, fanatical ... **3.** mad **5.** bigot,
crank, crazy, rabid **6.** maniac, zealot
7. devotee, frantic, lunatic **8.** frenzied
9. energumen, phrenetic **10.** enthusiast,
unbalanced **11.** extravagant,
overzealous **12.** enthusiastic
13. nonconformist, overreligious

fanatical partisan ... **6.** zealot
fancied ... **6.** unreal **7.** dreamed, ideated
8. favorite, imagined **9.** well-liked
10. ornamental

fanciful ... **3.** odd **5.** queer **7.** bizarre,
strange **8.** romantic **9.** fantastic,
grotesque, visionary, whimsical
10. capricious, chimerical
11. imaginative **13.** grandiloquent

fancy ... **3.** fad **4.** idea, like, love, ween,
whim **5.** dream, freak **6.** design, desire,
devise, humour, ideate, megrim, notion,
ornate, vagary **7.** caprice, conceit,
fantasy, imagine, impulse, suppose,
thought **8.** illusion, phantasy, superior
9. expensive **10.** conception, impression
11. extravagant, imagination, inclination
12. ostentatious

fandango ... **3.** hop **4.** ball, prom **5.** dance
7. cantico

fandango bird ... **7.** manakin
Faneuil Hall (1742) ... **4.** hall **6.** market
(Boston) **15.** Cradle of Liberty

fanion ... **4.** flag **6.** guidon, marker
fanon ... **4.** cape (Pope's) **5.** orale
6. banner **7.** maniple

fan-shaped ... **10.** flabellate
fan sticks (radiating) ... **4.** brin
7. panache

fantastic ... **3.** odd **5.** outré, queer
6. absurd, rococo, unreal **7.** baroque,
bizarre, caprice, foppish, unusual
8. fanciful, freakish, illusory **9.** eccentric,
grotesque, visionary **10.** capricious,
chimerical, irrational **11.** extravagant,
imaginative **12.** phantastical

fantastic imitation ... **6.** parody
8. travesty

fantasy ... **5.** dream, fancy, story **6.** vision
7. caprice, phantom, romance **8.** illusion
10. apparition **13.** hallucination

far ... **3.** tel (pref) **4.** afar, long, tele
(pref) **6.** marked, remote **9.** separated
10. abstracted

farce ... **4.** mime, play **5.** drama
(humorous), exode, humor, stuff
6. comedy **7.** mockery **8.** stuffing
9. burlesque, forcemeat

farceur ... **5.** joker **8.** comedian
9. dramatist

fare ... **3.** eat **4.** diet, food, rate **5.** crowd,
going, swarm, table **7.** conduct, journey,
passage, prosper, succeed **9.** passenger
10. expedition

farewell ... **3.** ave **4.** vale **5.** adieu, adios, aloha, congé (formal) **7.** good-bye, leaving, parting **8.** au revoir, Godspeed **9.** bon voyage **11.** leave-taking

farinaceous drink ... **6.** ptisan

farinaceous food ... **4.** sago **5.** flour, grain, salep, wheat **7.** cereals

farm ... **4.** plot, till, torp **5.** croft, ranch **6.** grange, rancho **7.** acreage, cotland **9.** cultivate

farm (pert to) ...
English .. **6.** barton
laborer .. **4.** hind **6.** farmer, tiller
prefix .. **4.** agro
repairer .. **10.** plowwright
Spanish .. **8.** hacienda
steward .. **7.** granger
tenant .. **6.** cotter

farmer ... **4.** ryot **5.** kulak **6.** grower, tiller **7.** cropper, metaver, peasant, planter, rancher **10.** agronomist, cultivator **13.** agriculturist

faro term ... **4.** bank **5.** monte, stuss **6.** cathop, layout

Faroe (Faeroe) **Islands** ...
called also .. **12.** Sheep Islands
capital .. **9.** Thorshavn
magistrate .. **4.** foud
rule .. **5.** Norse (anc) **7.** Denmark
whirlwind .. **2.** oe

far-reaching ... **4.** deep, long **5.** scope **7.** intense **9.** extensive

farrow ... **3.** pig **6.** litter

farsighted ... **6.** shrewd **9.** provident, sagacious **10.** presbyopic **11.** foresighted **12.** clearsighted

farther, further ... **4.** also **7.** thither **8.** moreover **10.** additional

farthest ... **5.** final **6.** inmost, utmost **7.** endmost, extreme, longest

farthest point ... **6.** apogee

fascia ... **4.** band, sash **6.** fillet, ribbon **7.** bandage

fascinate ... **5.** charm **6.** allure, enamor, thrill **7.** bewitch, delight, enchant **8.** entrance, interest **9.** captivate, enrapture

fascinating ... **5.** siren **8.** alluring, charming **10.** attractive, bewitching, delightful **11.** interesting

Fascist (1919) ... **6.** Pareto **9.** Mussolini **10.** Black Shirt

fashion ... **3.** fad, fit, ton, way **4.** make, mode, mold, rage **5.** adapt, carve, craze, feign, forge, frame, guise, model, shape, style, vogue **6.** create, custom, invent **7.** compose **8.** contrive **9.** construct, fabricate, smartness **10.** appearance

fashionable ... **5.** smart **6.** formal, modish **7.** a la mode, in vogue, stylish **8.** up-to-date **10.** conforming **13.** well-appearing

fast ... **5.** agile, fixed, fleet, hasty, quick, rapid, sound, space, stuck, swift **6.** lively, speedy, staple **7.** abiding, soundly **8.** enduring, securely **10.** profligate, stationary, unyielding **11.** expeditious

fasten ... **3.** bar, pin, tie **4.** bind, clip, lace, lash, moor, nail, rope, seal, tack,

wire **5.** affix, belay, chain, clamp, clasp, latch, paste, rivet **6.** attach, secure, solder, staple, tether, toggle **7.** padlock

fastening ... **5.** desmo (comb form)

fastest (pert to) ...
animals .. **6.** coyote **7.** cheetah **8.** antelope
birds .. **5.** eagle, goose **7.** ostrich

fast horse ... **6.** pelter

fastidious ... **4.** nice **6.** dainty **7.** elegant, finical, precise **8.** critical, delicate, exacting, overnice **9.** squeamish **10.** meticulous, particular, scrupulous

fastness ... **4.** fort **6.** fixity **7.** citadel **8.** celerity, firmness, velocity **9.** stability **10.** profligacy, stronghold

fat ... **4.** lard, oily, suet **5.** adeps, fatty, lipin, obese, olein, stout **6.** axunge (goose), grease, portly, steato (pref), stocky, tallow **7.** adipose, lanolin, opulent, paunchy, stearin, wealthy **9.** corpulent, plentiful **10.** profitable

fatal ... **5.** fated **6.** deadly, doomed, lethal, mortal **7.** fateful, ominous **8.** destined **9.** condemned, prophetic **10.** calamitous, disastrous **11.** destructive

fatality ... **4.** fate **5.** death **8.** disaster **10.** deadliness

fatally ... **8.** mortally **9.** ruinously

fate ... **3.** end, lot **4.** doom, luck, ruin **5.** karma **6.** chance, kismet **7.** destiny, fortune **8.** disaster, downfall **13.** inevitability

fateful ... **5.** fated **6.** deadly **9.** momentous **10.** inevitable, portentous **11.** destructive, predestined

Fates (Gr) ... **6.** Clotho, Moirae (group of Three) **7.** Atropos **8.** Lachesis

Fates (Norse) ... **4.** Urth **5.** Norns (group of three), Skuld **9.** Verthandi

Fates (Rom) ... **4.** Fata, Mona **5.** Morta **6.** Decuma, Parcae (group of three)

father ... **2.** pa **3.** Abu, dad **4.** abba, papa, père, sire **5.** adopt, friar, padre, pater, vater **6.** priest, senior **7.** creator **8.** generate **9.** confessor, procreate **11.** acknowledge

Father (of) ...
Ajax .. **7.** Telamon
Christmas .. **10.** Santa Claus
English learning .. **4.** Bede
engraving .. **3.** Pye
Evil .. **5.** Satan
his country .. **6.** Cicero (Rom), Medici (It) **10.** Washington (US)
history .. **9.** Herodotus
Mankind (Myth) .. **7.** Iapetus
New York .. **13.** Knickerbocker
Ocean .. **7.** Neptune
the Gods .. **6.** Amen-Ra
Time .. **10.** Methuselah
Waters .. **11.** Mississippi

father (pert to) ...
land .. **6.** native
land, love of .. **10.** philopater
term .. **6.** agnate **8.** paternal
wise .. **6.** mentor

fatherless ... **6.** orbate **7.** forlorn **8.** helpless, orphaned

fathom ... **3.** try **4.** test **5.** delve, plumb,

solve, sound 7. measure, plummet
8. encircle 9. penetrate 10. understand
13. take soundings

fatigued . . . **5.** bored, faint, jaded, spent,
tired, weary **6.** fagged **7.** languid,
wearied **9.** exhausted

Fatima (pert to) . . .
character in . . **13.** Arabian Nights
father . . **8.** Mohammed
husband . . **9.** Bluebeard

fatten . . . **4.** feed **6.** batten, enrich
7. improve, prosper **8.** pinguefy

fatty . . . **5.** suety **6.** greasy **7.** adipose
9. aliphatic

fatty (pert to) . . .
acid . . **6.** adipic **7.** valeric
degeneration . . **8.** adiposis
substance, sheep . . **5.** suint
tumor . . **6.** lipoma

fatuous . . . **4.** vain **5.** inane, silly **6.** vacant
7. foolish, idiotic, witless **8.** demented,
illusory, imbecile **9.** insensate
11. thoughtless

faucet . . . **3.** peg, tap **4.** cock **6.** spigot
7. fixture, hydrant, petcock

fault . . . **4.** hade, lode, slip, vice
5. cavil, cleft, culpa (law), error,
lapse, tache (anc) **6.** defect, foible
7. blemish, blunder, demerit, failing,
frailty, misdeed, offense **8.** fracture
10. peccadillo **11.** delinquency
12. imperfection

faultfinder . . . **6.** carper, nagger **7.** caviler
10. complainer, criticizer

faultfinding . . . **7.** carping, nagging
8. captious, caviling, critical **9.** censorial

faultless . . . **4.** pure **5.** right **7.** correct,
paragon, perfect **8.** flawless, innocent
9. blameless **10.** impeccable
13. unimpeachable **14.** irreproachable

faultlessness . . . **8.** accuracy **9.** innocence
10. perfection **11.** preciseness

faulty . . . **3.** ill **5.** amiss, unfit **6.** guilty
8. culpable **9.** blemished, defective,
deficient, erroneous, imperfect
11. blameworthy

faun . . . **3.** Pan **5.** deity, satyr **6.** Faunus
10. Praxiteles

Faust . . . **4.** hero **5.** drama (Goethe),
opera

faux pas . . . **4.** slip **5.** error, gaffe
6. booboo, slip-up **7.** blunder, misstep,
mistake

favor, favour . . . **3.** aid **4.** boon,
gift, help **5.** bless, grace, token
6. esteem, letter, regard **8.** good
will, kindness, leniency, resemble
9. patronage, patronize, privilege
10. assistance, concession, favoritism,
partiality, permission **11.** approbation

favorable . . . **4.** good, kind, rosy **6.** benign,
timely **7.** helpful, hopeful, popular
8. friendly, gracious, pleasing
9. approving, opportune **10.** auspicious,
beneficial, propitious **11.** complaisant
12. advantageous

favorite . . . **3.** pet **4.** lamb (pet) **6.** minion
7. darling **10.** preference

favoritism . . . **4.** bias **5.** leaning
8. nepotism **10.** partiality
12. predilection

fawn . . . **3.** doe **4.** buck, coax, deer,
faon (color) **5.** color, cower, crawl,
creep, toady **6.** cringe, grovel, shrink
7. truckle **10.** ingratiate

fawning . . . **7.** servile **8.** toadyish
9. truckling **10.** obsequious
11. bootlicking, sycophantic

fawnskin (classic art) . . . **6.** nebris

fay . . . **3.** elf **5.** fairy **6.** sprite

fealty . . . **4.** duty **6.** homage **7.** loyalty,
respect **8.** fidelity **9.** constancy
10. allegiance, obligation

fear . . . **3.** awe **5.** alarm, dread, panic
6. dismay, fright, horror, phobia, terror
7. anxiety **8.** venerate **9.** apprehend,
cowardice, reverence **11.** nervousness
13. consternation

fear (of) . . .
animals . . **9.** zoophobia
bees . . **9.** apiphobia
being alone . . **10.** autophobia,
monophobia
blood . . **10.** hemophobia
cats . . **12.** aelurophobia
crossing streets . . **11.** dromophobia
crowds . . **11.** ochlophobia
darkness . . **11.** nyctophobia, scotophobia
death . . **11.** necrophobia
disease . . **10.** nosophobia
enclosures . . **14.** claustrophobia
fire . . **10.** pyrophobia
food . . **10.** cibophobia
heights . . **10.** acrophobia
11. hypsophobia
holy things . . **11.** hagiophobia
men . . **11.** androphobia
new things . . **9.** neophobia
open spaces . . **11.** agoraphobia
pain . . **10.** algophobia
places (certain) . . **10.** topophobia
poison . . **10.** toxiphobia
reptiles . . **13.** herpetophobia
sea . . **14.** thalassophobia
strangers . . **10.** xenophobia
sunlight . . **11.** heliophobia
thirteen . . **13.** tridecaphobia
weeds . . **11.** runcophobia

fear (pert to) . . .
for fear that . . **4.** lest

fearful . . . **4.** dino (pref), dire **5.** awful,
pavid, timid **6.** afraid, craven **7.** anxious,
nervous **8.** dreadful, horrible, timorous
9. appealing, frightful **11.** distressing,
frightening **12.** apprehensive

fearless . . . **4.** bold **5.** brave **6.** daring
7. impavid **8.** harmless, intrepid
9. audacious, confident, dauntless,
undaunted **10.** courageous

feast . . . **4.** fete, meal **5.** agape, epulo,
revel **6.** junket, picnic, regale, repast
7. banquet, gratify **8.** carousal, festival
9. carrousel

Feast (of) . . .
Lanterns (Jap) . . **3.** Bon
Lots . . **5.** Purim
Nativity . . **9.** Christmas
Pentecost (weeks) . . **8.** Shabuoth
Tabernacles . . **7.** Succoth

feasting . . . **6.** dining **9.** epulation

feat . . . **3.** act **4.** deed **5.** stunt **7.** exploit
11. achievement, performance

14. accomplishment
feather . . . **4.** deck, flaw (jewel), tuft
   5. adorn, penna, plume, quill **6.** clothe,
   fletch, hackle, trifle **7.** plumage
   9. lightness
feather (pert to) . . .
an arrow . . **6.** fledge, fletch
barb . . **7.** pinnula **8.** barbicel
bird (area) . . **7.** pteryle
featherlike . . **7.** pinnate
filament . . **4.** dowl
key (machine) . . **6.** spline
molt . . **3.** mew
repair (falconry) . . **3.** imp
shaft . . **5.** scape
feathered . . . **5.** swift **6.** plumed, winged
   7. fledged **8.** pennated, plumaged
   10. ornamented
feature . . . **4.** face **5.** motif, trait
   6. aspect **7.** special **8.** headline,
   resemble **9.** component, lineament
   10. appearance, comeliness
   11. countenance **14.** characteristic
features . . . **3.** mug **4.** face **5.** looks
   6. visage **7.** outline **9.** geography
February birthstone . . . **8.** amethyst
federal agent . . . **4.** G-man, T-man
Federalist Papers . . . **3.** Jay **7.** Madison
   8. Hamilton
federation . . . **5.** union **6.** league
   8. alliance **10.** government **11.** affiliation
   13. confederation
fed up . . . **5.** bored, jaded **7.** wearied
   8. satiated **9.** surfeited
fee . . . **3.** feu, tip **4.** fief, rate, wage
   5. bribe **6.** charge, estate (law)
   8. gratuity, retainer **9.** emolument
   10. honorarium
feeble . . . **4.** aged, lame, puny, weak
   5. dotty **6.** infirm **10.** indistinct
   11. debilitated
feeble-minded . . . **5.** anile **9.** infirmity
   10. irresolute, weak-willed
   11. vacillating
feed . . . **4.** dine, meal, sate **5.** stoke
   6. fodder, gavage **7.** engorge, foldage,
   furnish, indulge, nourish, nurture,
   pannage (swine) **9.** encourage,
   provision
feel . . . **3.** ail, air **4.** palp **5.** grope, sense,
   touch **6.** handle, suffer **7.** examine,
   explore, quality, texture **8.** perceive
   10. atmosphere, experience
feel (pert to) . . .
compunction . . **6.** repent
dejection . . **6.** repine
fear . . **2.** ug
melancholy . . **6.** grieve
worth of . . **10.** appreciate
feeler . . . **4.** palp, test **6.** barbal, palpus
   7. antenna **9.** question, tentacle
feeling . . . **4.** feel, tact, view **5.** hunch,
   touch **7.** emotion, opinion, passion
   8. attitude **9.** sensation, sentiment
   10. atmosphere, experience,
   perception **11.** sensibility
   13. consciousness
feeling (pert to) . . .
capable of . . **5.** emote **8.** sentient
   9. sensitive
displeasure . . **9.** resentful

hostility . . **6.** animus **9.** animosity
ill . . **7.** malaise **10.** discomfort
impassive . . **8.** stoicism
joyful . . **6.** jocund
offense . . **5.** pique
superiority . . **9.** arrogance
without . . **6.** apathy, steely **7.** callous
   8. numbness **9.** unfeeling
   13. insensibility
feet . . . see also *foot*
designating . . **5.** podal
having . . **6.** pedate
number . . **7.** footage
two (Pros) . . **6.** dipody **7.** dimeter
   9. ditrochee
without . . **4.** apod **6.** apodal **8.** footless
feign . . . **3.** act **4.** sham **5.** fable **6.** affect,
   assume, gammon, garble, invent
   7. connive, imagine, pretend **8.** malinger
   (illness), simulate **9.** dissemble
   11. counterfeit, make-believe
feint . . . **5.** appel (fencing), blind, shift,
   trick **6.** attack (mock), thrust **7.** mislead,
   pretext **8.** artifice, pretense
Felicia . . . **7.** thistle **9.** happiness
felicitate . . . **4.** laud **5.** bless **8.** macarize
   10. compliment **12.** congratulate
felicity . . . **5.** bliss, grace **7.** aptness,
   success **8.** aptitude **9.** happiness,
   well-being **11.** achievement (happy),
   blessedness **12.** blissfulness
Felidae . . . **4.** cats, lion, lynx, pard, puma
   5. tiger **6.** jaguar **7.** cheetah, leopard,
   wildcat
feline . . . **3.** sly **5.** Felis **6.** animal **7.** catlike,
   furtive **8.** stealthy **11.** treacherous
Felis . . . **3.** cat
fell . . . **3.** cut, hem, hew **4.** beat, hill,
   kill, pelt, ruin, skin **5.** cruel, level
   6. fierce, fleece, lay low, mighty,
   savage **7.** brutish, tumbled
   9. barbarous, ferocious, overthrow,
   prostrate
fellow . . . **3.** lad, man **4.** beau, chap,
   peer **5.** equal **6.** member, person
   7. comrade **8.** neighbor **9.** associate,
   companion **10.** sweetheart
   11. confederate
fellow (pert to) . . .
accomplice . . **7.** abettor **9.** accessory
   11. confederate
awkward . . **4.** boor, gawk
clumsy . . **3.** oaf **4.** lout, pleb **5.** yahoo
   7. bumpkin
coward . . **3.** cad, fop **4.** drip **7.** bounder
   8. spalpeen
droll . . **3.** wag **4.** card
old . . **6.** geezer **7.** callant
small . . **6.** shaver
smart . . **5.** aleck
young . . **4.** chap **5.** blade, youth
   7. younker **9.** stripling
fellowman . . . **7.** brother **11.** fellow being
fellowship . . . **4.** sect **5.** guild, union
   7. company **8.** alliance, sodality
   9. communion **10.** membership
   11. affiliation, comradeship, partnership,
   scholarship **12.** friendliness
   13. companionship
felon . . . **3.** bum **4.** wild **5.** cruel **6.** wicked
   7. convict, culprit, outcast, villain,

whitlow 8. criminal, disloyal 9. infection, malignant, murderous 10. malefactor, paronychia, traitorous

felony . . . 3. sin 5. crime, wrath 6. daring, deceit 8. baseness, burglary, outlawry 9. treachery 10. illegality, wickedness 11. misdemeanor

female . . . 4. bibi, dame, doña, girl, gyne, lady, miss 5. donna, femme, rhyme, squaw, woman 6. maiden, matron 7. distaff, dowager, fair sex, Sahibah 8. mistress 9. weaker sex

female (pert to) . . .
architecture . . 8. Caryatid
comb form . . 5. gyneo, thely
erudite . . 10. pedantress
fox . . 5. vixen
government . . 8. gynarchy
hormone . . 8. estrogen
monster . . 6. gorgon
prayerful . . 5. orant
spirit . . 7. banshee 8. succubus
suffix . . 4. ette
term . . 7. distaff 8. gynecoid
warrior . . 6. Amazon

feminine . . . 4. soft, weak 6. female, gender, tender 7. womanly 8. maidenly 10. effeminate

femme fatale . . . 4. vamp 5. siren 7. Lorelei, vampire

femur . . . 3. hip (bone) 4. bone (thigh), coxa

fen . . . 3. bog 4. moor, pool 5. marsh, swale 7. The Fens

fence . . . 3. aha 4. bank, duel, ha-ha, pale, rail, wall 5. close, ditch, fight, hedge, stile 6. paling, picket, secure 7. barrier, confine, enclose, fortify, protect, railing 8. palisade, prohibit 9. enclosure, swordplay 11. self-defense

fencing (pert to) . . .
breastplate . . 8. plastron
defense . . 5. carte, parry, prime, sixte 6. octave, quinte, tierce 7. seconds, septime
master . . 7. lanista
position . . 9. pronation 10. supination
sword . . 4. epee, foil, tuck 5. extoc 6. rapier
term . . 4. volt 7. corrida 8. estocado
thrust . . 6. remise 7. riposte

fend . . . 4. ward 5. avert, parry, shift 6. defend, resist 7. prevent, repulse, ward off

fender . . . 5. guard 6. buffer, bumper, shield, sluice 7. cushion 9. fireguard 10. firescreen 11. splashboard

fenestra . . . 6. window 7. foramen, opening, orifice

Fenian (Ir) . . . 4. hero 11. nationalist

fennel . . . 4. herb 6. Seseli 7. Azorian, Nigella

feral . . . 4. wild 6. deadly, ferine, savage 7. bestial, untamed 8. funereal, unbroken 9. malignant 12. uncultivated

feretory . . . 4. bier 6. chapel, shrine (saint's) 8. feretrum

ferment . . . 4. barm, brew, fret, sour, stum, zyme 5. anger, fever, yeast 6. enzyme, foment, leaven, rennin, seethe, uproar 7. glucase, maltase

8. diastase, disorder 9. agitation 10. effervesce, turbulence

fermentation . . . 6. unrest 9. agitation, chemistry, leavening 10. ebullition 13. effervescence

fermented drink . . . 3. ale 4. beer, mead 6. kumiss (koumiss) 9. hard cider 10. malt liquor

fermenting vat . . . 4. gyle

fern . . . 4. tara 5. brake, heath, holly 6. osmund, spider 7. bracken 8. polypody 10. maidenhair 11. elephant-ear

fern (pert to) . . .
family . . 12. pteridophyte
genus . . 6. Anemia
leaf . . 5. frond
scale . . 8. ramentum
seedlike part . . 5. spore

ferocious . . . 4. grim, wild 5. cruel, feral 6. bloody, brutal, fierce, savage 7. acharne, inhuman 8. pitiless, ravenous, ruthless 9. barbarous, malignant, merciless, murderous, rapacious, truculent 10. implacable, malevolent, relentless, sanguinary 11. remorseless 12. bloodthirsty

ferret . . . 3. hob 4. hunt, jill, tape 5. worry 6. badger, harass, search, weasel 7. polecat

ferrotype . . . 7. tintype 10. photograph

ferrum . . . 2. Fe (sym) 4. iron

ferry . . . 7. traject 9. transport 10. sail across

ferryboat . . . 3. bac 4. pont 6. wherry

ferryman . . . 6. Charon (River Styx) 7. ferrier

fertile . . . 4. rank, rich 7. teeming 8. abundant, fruitful, prolific 9. exuberant, inventive, plenteous, plentiful 10. productive

fertilizer . . . 4. marl 5. guano 6. pollen 7. compost, nitrate 8. bone meal, dressing 9. phosphate

ferule . . . 3. rod 5. ruler 6. fennel 10. punishment

fervency . . . 4. heat, keen, zeal 5. ardor, eager, fiery, gusto, verve 6. fervor, warmth 7. ardency, passion 9. eloquence, vehemence 12. empressement 15. impassionedness

fervent . . . 3. hot 4. keen, warm 5. eager, fiery 6. ardent, fervid 7. excited, intense, zealous 8. eloquent, vehement 10. passionate 11. impassioned

fervid . . . 3. hot 5. fiery 6. ardent, tropic 7. boiling, fervent, zealous 8. vehement 11. impassioned

fervor . . . 4. rage, zeal, zest 5. ardor 7. ecstasy, passion 11. earnestness

fester . . . 6. rankle 7. abscess, pustule, putrefy 9. suppurate

festival . . . 3. ale, bal 4. fete, gala 5. Delia (Apollo), feast, revel, Seder 6. Easter, Kermis 7. holiday, uphelya 8. apodosis (Church) 9. Christmas, Mardi gras 10. Parentalia, Saturnalia

festive . . . 3. gay 4. gala 5. merry 6. joyous 8. mirthful, sportive 9. convivial

festivity . . . 3. joy 4. fete, gala 5. mirth, revel 6. gaiety 7. jollity, whoopee

8. festival, jamboree 10. joyfulness
11. celebration, merrymaking
12. conviviality

festoon ... 4. loop 5. adorn 6. wreath
7. garland

fetch ... 3. get 5. bring, reach 6. attain,
deduce, revive 7. achieve 8. go and
get, retrieve

fetching ... 8. alluring, charming,
pleasing 10. attractive, delightful
11. fascinating

fete ... 4. gala 5. feast, party 6. fiesta
8. carnival, festival 10. Saturnalia
13. entertainment

fetid ... 4. olid, rank 5. fusty 7. noisome
10. maladorous 11. ill-smelling

fetish ... 3. obi 4. idol, joss, juju 5. charm,
image, totem 6. amulet, avatar, mascot
7. Dahoman 8. talisman

fetter ... 4. band, bond, gyve, iron
5. chain 6. hamper, hobble, hopple,
thrall 7. enchain, manacle, shackle

feud ... 4. fief, fray 5. broil 6. affray,
estate, strife 7. contest, dispute, quarrel
8. vendetta 9. hostility

feudal (pert to) ...
estate .. 3. fee 4. fief, soke
French .. 4. feod
lord .. 6. tenure 8. overlaid, suzerain
payment .. 6. socage
service .. 5. banal
tenant .. 4. leud 6. vassal
tribute .. 6. heriot

fever ... 4. ague 5. ardor 6. frenzy
8. delirium, sickness 9. calenture
10. excitement

fever (pert to) ...
heat .. 9. sunstroke
intermittent .. 5. octan 7. quartan
malarial .. 4. ague
marsh .. 6. elodes 7. helodes
subsidence .. 12. defervescent
term .. 7. febrile, pyretic
tropical .. 6. dengue 9. calenture

feverish ... 5. hasty 7. excited, febrile,
fervent, fevered 8. restless 9. delirious,
overeager 10. disordered

fey ... 4. dead 5. dying, elfin, fatal, spell
9. enfeebled, visionary 12. otherworldly

fez ... 3. cap 5. busby, shako 8. tarboosh
9. headdress

fiat ... 3. act 5. edict, order 6. decree
7. command 8. decision, sanction

fiber ... 3. nap, nep, tal 4. bast, eruc,
hemp, imbe, jute, lint, pile, pita, silk,
yarn 5. datil, istle, kapok, linen, nerve,
rayon, sisal 6. fibril, raffia, staple,
thread 7. filasse, texture 8. fibrilla,
filament

fiber plant ... 4. hemp, imbe, palm
5. abaca, agave 6. ambary, cotton,
linaga

fibers ... 5. hairs 7. strands 9. filaments

fibula ... 4. bone (arm) 5. class 6. brooch
(anc), buckle 9. safety pin

fickle ... 5. false 6. mobile 7. mutable
8. unstable, unsteady, variable,
wavering 9. changeful, deceitful,
faithless, unsettled 10. capricious,
changeable, inconstant, irresolute,
unfaithful 11. vacillating

fiction ... 4. tale 5. false, fancy,
novel, story 6. legend 7. coinage,
figment, forgery, romance 9. falsehood,
invention 11. fabrication

fictitious ... 5. false 6. poetic, pseudo
(pref) 7. assumed, feigned 8. chimeric
9. imaginary, imitative, pretended
10. artificial

fictitious name ... 5. alias 6. anonym
7. pen name 8. nickname
9. pseudonym, stage name 10. nom
de plume 11. nom de guerre

Fidel (eg) ... 8. caudillo

Fidelio (eg) ... 5. opera

fidelity ... 5. topaz, troth, truth 6. fealty
7. honesty 8. accuracy, devotion,
veracity 9. adherence, constancy,
exactness 10. allegiance 12. faithfulness

fidget ... 4. fuss 5. worry 6. twitch
9. dysphoria 10. uneasiness
12. restlessness

fidgety ... 5. jerky 6. uneasy 7. nervous,
restive, twitchy 8. bustling, restless
9. excitable, impatient

fiducial ... 4. firm 5. solid, sound
6. secure, stable 7. trusted 8. trustful
9. confident 11. trustworthy

fiduciary ... 4. held (in trust) 5. trust
7. founded, holding, in trust, trustee
12. confidential

fief ... 3. fee 4. feud 6. estate

field ... 3. lea, lot 4. acre, ager, land,
mead, rand 5. croft, glebe, range,
tract 6. campus, ground, meadow,
sphere 7. compass, diamond, expanse,
pasture, savanna (savannah), terrain
8. clearing, gridiron 11. battlefield

field (pert to) ...
athletic .. 4. oval 5. arena, court, track
6. course, sphere 7. diamond, stadium
8. gridiron
bloodshed .. 8. Aceldama (Akeldama)
13. Ager Sanguinis
duck .. 7. bustard
god of .. 4. Faun
mouse .. 4. vole
snow .. 4. neve
stubble .. 5. rowen
term .. 3. agral 8. agrarian 10. campestral

fiend ... 3. foe 5. demon, devil, enemy,
Satan 6. addict, wizard 7. Amaimon
(Amamon) 9. archfiend 10. evil spirit

fiendish ... 5. cruel 6. wicked 7. Avernal,
demonic 8. demoniac, devilish, diabolic

fierce ... 4. grim 5. cruel, eager 6. raging,
savage 7. furious, racking, violent
9. ferocious, impetuous, truculent
10. catawampus, forbidding, passionate
11. belligerent, overwrought
12. overpowering

fierceness ... 7. cruelty 8. violence
10. truculence

fiery ... 3. hot, red 4. sore 5. angry
6. ardent 7. burning, excited, fervent,
flaming, glowing, igneous, parched,
violent 8. choleric, feverish, inflamed,
spirited, vehement 9. impetuous,
irascible 10. mettlesome, passionate
11. hot-tempered, inflammable

fiery cross ... 5. alarm 6. emblem, signal,
symbol 8. crantara 10. call to arms

fiesta . . . 5. color 7. holiday 8. festival
9. festivity
fifish . . . 6. cranky 9. half crazy
fig . . . 4. fico 5. eleme, gruit 6. Carica,
Fiscus, Smyrna, trifle
fig basket . . . 5. cabas, seron
fight . . . 3. row, war 4. bout, duel, fray,
mell, tilt 5. brawl, melee, scrap, set-to
6. affray, attack, barney, battle, combat,
oppose, strife, strike, strive 7. contest,
quarrel, warfare 8. conflict, struggle
9. pugnacity 13. combativeness
fighter . . . 7. battler, duelist, soldier,
warrior 8. champion, pugilist, scrapper
9. combatant
fighting . . . 3. war 4. game 6. plucky
7. warlike 8. militant 10. contention,
pugnacious 11. belligerent
fig leaf . . . 6. symbol (modesty) 8. clothing
(Bib), covering
figment . . . 5. fancy 7. fiction 9. falsehood,
invention
figurative . . . 6. florid 7. flowery,
typical 8. allusive 9. numerical
12. emblematical, metaphorical
figure . . . 4. body, dash, dope, form,
nude, rank, type 5. digit, image, judge,
price, shape, solve 6. aspect, emblem,
entail, number, symbol 7. diagram,
numeral, outline, pattern 8. ornament,
phantasm 9. calculate, celebrity,
character, personage 10. appearance,
impression, similitude 11. distinction
figure (pert to) . . .
column . . 6. elamon 7. telamon
8. Atlantes, Caryatid, pilaster
geometric . . 4. cone, lune 5. prism,
rhomb 6. isagon, isogen, isogon
(rare) 7. ellipse, rhombus 8. pentagon,
triangle 13. parallelogram, quadrilateral
16. parallelepipedon
praying . . 5. orant
repeated digits . . 8. repetend
speech . . 5. trope 6. aporia, simile
8. metaphor
star-shaped . . 8. pentacle
figured . . . 4. rich 6. ornate 7. façonné
10. ornamented
figurine . . . 4. doll 7. carving, tanagra
9. sculpture, statuette
Fiji Island, Viti Levu . . .
capital . . 4. Suva
export . . 5. sugar
mountain . . 8. Victoria
people . . 11. Melanesians
ruler . . 7. British
filament . . . 4. barb, dowl (dowle), hair
5. fiber (fibre), harle 6. strand, thread
filament lamp . . . 12. incandescent
filbert . . . 3. nut 5. brown, hazel 7. Corylus
8. hazelnut
filch . . . 3. nim, rob 4. beat 5. steal, theft
6. pilfer 7. purloin
file . . . 3. row 4. list, rasp, rate 5. enter,
march, store 6. abrade, smooth
7. sharpen 8. classify 9. catalogue
10. pickpocket 11. triggerfish (filefish)
file (combmaking) . . . 5. grail (graille)
6. carlet 7. quannet
filibeg . . . 4. kilt 5. skirt
filibuster . . . 6. pirate 7. impeder

8. thwarter 9. legislate 10. freebooter,
obstructer 14. obstructionist
filicide . . . 6. murder (child by parent)
filigree . . . 4. lace 5. adorn (with)
7. pattern 8. fanciful 10. decorative
13. unsubstantial
Filipino, Filipina (pert to) . . .
homeland (mostly) . . 5. Luzon
people . . 5. Bikol (Bicol) 7. Malayan
(Christian), Tagalog (Tagal), Visayan
(see also *Philippine*)
fill . . . 3. pad 4. calk, feed, glut, hold, plug
5. block, close, gorge, stuff 6. occupy,
stop up 7. execute, fulfill, pervade,
satiate, satisfy, suffuse 8. complete,
compound, permeate 10. accomplish
11. superabound
fille . . . 4. girl 8. daughter
filled . . . 5. dated, laden 7. replete
8. suffused 9. saturated
filled with crevices . . . 7. areolar
fillet . . . 4. band, orle, ring, tape 5. snood,
tiara 6. anadem, border, ribbon, taenia
7. bandage 8. headband, insignia
9. lemniscus, scantling 10. tenderloin
fillet (Arch) . . . 5. stria 6. cimbia, listel,
reglet, regula, taenia 7. chaplet, molding
(part)
filly . . . 4. colt, foal, girl, mare
film . . . 4. brat, haze, scum, skin, veil
5. cover, layer 6. lamina, patina
7. coating 8. pellicle 10. photograph
film fan . . . 8. cinéaste
filmy . . . 3. dim 4. fine 5. gauzy,
misty 6. cloudy, opaque 7. clouded
9. laminated 10. indistinct
fils . . . 3. son
filter . . . 4. ooze 5. clean, drain 6. purify,
strain 7. trickle 8. colature 9. percolate
filth . . . 4. dirt, muck, slut 5. lucre
6. vermin 7. squalor 9. excrement,
obscenity, scoundrel
filthiness . . . 8. cenosity 9. fetidness,
obscenity 10. odiousness
filthy . . . 3. low 4. foul, vile 5. dirty,
fetid, gross 6. impure, odious, putrid
7. obscene, squalid, unclean 9. polluting
10. licentious
filthy lucre . . . 4. gain (shameful)
5. money
fimbriated . . . 5. edged 7. fringed
8. bordered (Her), margined
fin . . . 3. arm 4. five, keel
fin (pert to fish) . . .
median . . 4. anal 6. caudal, dorsal
paired . . 6. pelvic 7. ventral 8. pectoral
final . . . 3. end 4. last 5. be-all, telic
7. dernier 8. decisive, definite, eventual,
ultimate 9. mandatory, ultimatum
10. conclusive, definitive 11. unqualified
13. determinating
final argument . . . 11. ultima ratio
finale . . . 3. end 4. coda 5. close
6. result 8. swan song 10. completion,
conclusion 11. termination
finality . . . 5. finis 6. finale, finish,
windup 10. conclusion 11. termination
12. decisiveness 14. conclusiveness
finally . . . 10. eventually, ultimately
12. conclusively
final notice . . . 4. obit

final outcome ... 5. issue 6. upshot
10. denouement
financial ... 6. fiscal 8. monetary
9. pecuniary
finch ... 4. moro 5. Junco, serin, spink,
tarin 6. burion, linnet, siskin, towhee
7. chewink, redpoll 9. brambling,
chaffinch, Fringilla
find ... 3. get 4. gain 5. learn 6. detect,
locate, summon, supply 7. procure,
provide 8. discover, meet with, perceive
9. determine, discovery, good thing
10. experience 11. acquisition
find fault ... 4. beef, carp 5. cavil
8. complain 9. criticize
finding ... 7. verdict 8. solution
9. discovery 11. serendipity
find out ... 5. learn, solve 6. detect
8. discover 9. ascertain
fine ... 3. fit 4. good, lacy, pure, rare, thin
5. dandy, filmy, frail, gaudy, noble,
sharp, sheer 6. ornate, slight, smooth
7. elegant, fragile, healthy, perfect,
powdery, precise, slender 8. absolute,
ethereal, handsome, polished, skillful,
superior 9. beautiful, excellent, sensitive
10. fastidious, pulverized, surpassing
finery ... 6. beauty 7. clothes, gaudery,
gewgaws 8. elegance, fineness,
frippery, ornament 10. decoration,
lavishness 11. refinements
finesse ... 5. skill 6. purity, serene
7. cunning 8. artifice, card play,
subtlety, thinness 9. clearness, good
taste, stratagem 10. refinement
14. discrimination (subtle)
finger ... 3. toy (with) 4. hook 5. digit,
touch 6. dactyl, handle, pilfer
7. measure, purloin 8. identify
finger (pert to) ...
alphabet .. 11. dactylology
cymbal .. 8. castanet
fish .. 8. starfish
flower .. 8. foxglove
foods .. 12. hors d'oeuvres
fore .. 5. index 7. pointer
little .. 6. pinkie 7. minimus 9. auricular
middle .. 6. medius
ring .. 7. annular
stall .. 3. cot
term .. 7. digital
Finger Lakes ... 6. Cayuga, Seneca
fingernail moon ... 6. lunule
fingernail overgrowth ... 10. onychauxis
fingerprint (term) ... 4. arch, loop
5. whorl 9. composite 11. dactylogram
12. dactyloscopy
finial ... 3. epi, tee
finical ... 4. nice 5. fussy 6. dainty,
dapper, jaunty, spruce 7. finicky,
foppish, mincing, prudish 8. delicate
9. finicking, squeamish 10. fastidious,
meticulous 11. overprecise
14. overscrupulous
finis ... 3. end 4. goal 6. finale 8. finality
10. conclusion 11. culmination
finish ... 3. end 4. kill 5. chare, close,
matte (mat), style 6. enamel, polish
7. destroy, perfect, surface, texture
8. complete, conclude 9. terminate
10. completion, consummate, perfection

finished ... 3. o'er 4. done, fine, over, ripe
5. ended 6. closed 7. refined, stopped
8. climaxed, complete, lustered,
polished 9. completed, concluded,
perfected 10. terminated
finite ... 7. fleshly, limited 9. definable
10. restricted, terminable 11. conditional
fink ... 3. spy 4. scab 5. finch 8. informer
13. strikebreaker
Finland ... see also *Finnish*
capital .. 8. Helsinki (Helsingfors)
Finnish for Finland .. 5. Suomi
government .. 8. republic
island .. 5. Aland
language .. 6. Magyar 7. Swedish
8. Estonian
legislature .. 9. Eduskunta
port .. 3. Abo 5. Turku 9. Mariehamn
Finnish (pert to) ...
bath .. 5. sauna
dramatist .. 4. Kivi 7. Waltari
people .. 5. Finns, Suomi 9. Karelians
10. Tavastians
fire ... 4. heat, zeal 5. blaze, fever,
flame 6. excite, fervor, igneus,
ignite, incite, kindle 7. barrage,
explode, inspire 8. detonate, illumine
9. discharge, eloquence 11. inspiration
12. inflammation 13. conflagration
fire (pert to) ...
basket .. 5. grate 7. cresset
comb form .. 4. igni
cracker .. 6. petard
dog .. 7. andiron
fear of .. 10. pyrophobia
god .. 6. Vulcan
opal .. 7. girasol (girasole)
power over .. 10. ignipotent
worshiper .. 5. Parsi 9. pyrolater
10. ignicolist
firearm ... 3. BAR, gat, gun, rod,
Uzi 4. heat 5. luger, piece, rifle
6. musket, pistol 7. handgun, shotgun,
sidearm 8. ordnance, petronel, repeater,
revolver, tommy gun 9. flintlock,
harquebus (arquebus) 10. six-shooter
11. Springfield (rifle)
firearms discharge ... 9. fusillade
firearms maker ... 4. Colt 7. Beretta
8. Browning 9. Remington
10. Winchester 14. Smith and Wesson
fired ... 3. lit 4. shot 5. baked 6. on
fire (Her) 7. excited 8. inspired
10. discharged
fireman ... 4. vamp 6. fueler, stoker
8. trainman 9. fire-eater 11. firefighter
fireplace ... 5. fogon, forge, ingle
6. hearth 9. inglenook 13. Franklin
stove
fireside (home) ... 11. hearthstone
firewood ... 6. billet
fireworks ... 4. caps, gerb 6. flares
7. fizgigs, gunfire, rip-raps, rockets
8. serpents 9. pinwheels, sparklers,
torpedoes 10. girandoles
12. firecrackers, Roman candles
firm ... 4. fast, hard, safe, sure, trig
5. dense, fixed, rigid, solid, sound,
stout, tight 6. secure, stable, stanch,
steady, strict, strong 7. compact,
company, decided, devoted, staunch

8. faithful 9. immovable, steadfast
10. determined, unslipping, unyielding
11. substantial
firmament ... 3. sky 5. vault 6. Caelus,
welkin 7. heavens 8. empyrean
firmly set ... 5. fixed, solid 6. rooted
10. inveterate
firmness ... 8. fidelity, rigidity, solidity,
strength, tenacity 9. constancy, stability
10. immobility, steadiness 11. reliability
15. indissolubility
firmness, want of ... 5. loose 6. laxity
8. weakness 11. instability, vacillation
firn ... 3. ice 4. neve, snow
firs ... 5. Abies, pines
first ... 5. chief, front, prime 6. maiden,
primal, primus 7. highest, initial,
leading, primary 8. earliest, foremost,
original 9. beginning, elemental,
principal 10. primordial
first (pert to) ...
appearance .. 5. debut 8. premiere
born .. 5. eigne 6. eldest
Christian martyr .. 7. Stephen
coin (silver) .. 8. sesterce
days of Rom month .. 7. calends
(kalends)
fruits (Eccl) .. 7. annates
letter .. 4. Alif 5. Aleph
stages .. 8. inchoate 9. rudiments
world navigator .. 8. Magellan
fish ... 3. dib 4. food 5. angle, drail,
seine, troll 6. Pisces 13. constellation
fish (types of) ... 2. id 3. cat, cod, gar, ray
4. bass, carp, char, chub, cusk, dace,
goby, hake, ling, opah, parr, peto, pike,
ruff, scup, shad, sisi, sole, tuna, ulua
5. bream, cisco, fluke, guppy, perch,
porgy, shark, skate, smelt, snook, sprat,
trout, tunny, wahoo 6. barbel, bonito,
bowfin, burbot, conger, darter, marlin,
minnow, puffer, redfin, salmon, shiner,
sucker, tarpon, tautog, turbot 7. alewife,
anchovy, catfish, crappie, croaker,
dogfish, garfish, grouper, haddock,
halibut, herring, hogfish, jewfish,
lamprey, mudfish, oquassa, pollack,
pompano, redfish, sardine, sawfish,
sunfish, torpedo, walleye 8. albacore,
blue fish, bluegill, bonefish, bullhead,
chimaera, filefish, flatfish, flounder,
goldfish, grayling, kingfish, lumpfish,
mackerel, menhaden, pickerel, pilchard,
sailfish, sergeant, sting ray, sturgeon,
toadfish, weakfish 9. barracuda,
cigarfish, devilfish, jellyfish, namaycush,
sheatfish, whitefish 10. barramunda,
butterfish, candlefish, hammerhead,
yellowtail 11. muskellunge (see also
mammal)
fish (pert to) ...
adhering .. 4. pega 6. remora
ascending rivers .. 7. anadrom
10. anadromous
bait .. 4. chum 5. chack 6. minnow
9. killifish (killy)
basket .. 4. caul 5. creel, slath (slarth)
bivalve, mollusk .. 4. clam, slug 5. snail,
whelk 6. limpet, mussel, oyster
7. abalone, Ocypode (crab), scallop
caviar-yielding .. 7. sterlet

climbing, jumping .. 5. saury 6. anabas
7. skipper
club .. 6. muckle
codfish .. 4. cusk 5. torsk 7. bacalao,
buffalo
comb form .. 7. ichthyo
crustacean .. 3. Uca 4. crab 6. shrimp
7. lobster 8. Decapoda
devil .. 3. ray 5. manta
eaters .. 12. ichthyophagi
eating .. 11. piscivorous
14. ichthyophagous
fabled (Pers) .. 4. Mahi (Mah)
gaff (through ice) .. 5. ching
game .. 4. tuna 5. chiro, sword, trout
6. marlin, salmon, tarpon 8. grayling
11. muskellunge
genus .. 4. Amia (bowfin), Mola
(sunfish) 5. Elops (tarpon), Perca
(perch) 8. Haliotis (abalone), Octopoda
(octopus)
hook .. 5. Kirby, snell (part) 8. Aberdeen,
barbless, Carlisle, Limerick
largest (freshwater) .. 8. arapaima
like .. 8. ichthyic
line .. 6. nossel (norsel) 7. spillet
living by .. 9. piscatory
living on .. 12. ichthyophagy
man-eating .. 6. caribe 7. piranha
mollusk .. see *bivalve*
nest building .. 5. acara
net .. 4. fyke 5. seine, snell, trawl
7. boulter, spiller
pond .. 7. piscina 8. aquarium
roe .. 6. caviar
salmon .. 3. fog 4. masu, parr 5. sprod
6. alevin 7. gilling
sauce .. 4. alec
spear .. 3. gig
taboo .. 13. ichthyophobia
treatise .. 11. ichthyology
worship .. 12. ichthyolatry
young brood .. 3. fry
fisherman ... 6. angler 8. piscator
fishery ... 7. piscary
fishing ... 4. chug (through ice) 8. snelling
9. halieutic, piscation
fishing vessel ... 5. smack 6. seiner
7. trawler
fishy ... 4. dull 6. vacant 8. fishlike
9. deceptive, dishonest 10. improbable,
lusterless, suspicious, unreliable
11. extravagant 14. expressionless
fissure ... 3. gap 4. leak, lode, open,
rent, rift, rima, seam, slit, vein 5. break,
chasm, chine, chink, cleft, crack, sever,
split 7. crevice
fissured ... 5. cleft 6. rimate, rimose
fist ... 4. duke, hand (closed) 5. nieve
6. clench 8. tightwad 11. handwriting
fit ... 3. due, fay, pat 4. able, gear,
meet, mesh, ripe, suit, whim 5. adapt,
equip, fancy, ready, spasm, train
6. attack, enmesh, frenzy, proper,
stroke, suited 7. adapted, caprice,
conform, healthy, prepare, tantrum
8. disposed, dovetail, eligible, outbreak,
suitable 9. competent, qualified
11. accommodate, appropriate
fit (pert to) ...
an arrow (archery) .. 4. nock

fury . . **4.** rage
groove (Arch) . . **4.** dado
resentment . . **4.** huff, mood **5.** pique
   7. tantrum
to eat . . **6.** edible
to till . . **6.** arable
fitchew . . . **5.** skink, zoril **7.** foumart,
   polecat
fitful . . . **8.** restless, unstable, variable
   9. impulsive, irregular, orderless,
   spasmodic **10.** capricious, convulsive
   12. intermittent
fitly . . . **4.** duly **5.** right **6.** timely
   8. properly, suitably **10.** decorously
fitness . . . **7.** decorum **9.** congruity
   10. expedience, timeliness **11.** eligibility,
   suitability **12.** preparedness
fitting . . . **3.** apt, pat **4.** just, meet
   6. proper, seemly, timely **8.** adapting,
   suitable **9.** expedient **11.** appropriate
five (pert to) . . .
   Books of Moses . . **10.** Pentateuch
   children (born at once) . . **11.** quintuplets
   Civilized Tribes (Ind) . . **5.** Creek
   7. Choctaw **8.** Cherokee, Seminole
   9. Chickasaw
   comb form . . **5.** penta
   cornered . . **11.** pentagonous
   divided by . . **11.** quinquesect
   dollar bill . . **1.** V **3.** fin **5.** fiver
   feet . . **10.** pentameter
   five-year period . . **6.** pentad **7.** lustrum
   (census) **12.** quinquennial
   fold . . **9.** quintuple
   group . . **6.** pentad **8.** fivesome
   lines (nonsense) . . **8.** limerick
   Nations (Ind Confed) . . **7.** Cayugas,
   Mohawks, Oneidas, Senecas
   9. Onondagas
   trump card (auction pitch) . . **5.** pedro
fix . . . **3.** peg, pin, set **4.** mend, moor,
   nail **5.** amend, brace, bribe, imbed,
   limit, stamp **6.** adjust, anchor, cement,
   define, fasten, ossify, punish, repair,
   settle **7.** arrange, confirm, delimit,
   dilemma, prepare, rectify **8.** organize,
   solidify **9.** condition, establish, stabilize,
   stipulate **10.** prearrange
fixed . . . **3.** set **4.** firm **5.** rigid **6.** formal,
   intent, nailed, static **7.** assured, limited,
   settled, special **8.** arranged, habitual
   9. immovable, permanent, unwinking
   11. established, prearranged, traditional
fixed (pert to) . . .
   allowance . . **4.** diet **6.** ration **7.** stipend
   10. remittance
   beforehand . . **13.** predetermined
   by choice . . **8.** elective
   idea . . **8.** idée fixe **9.** obsession
   manner . . **9.** immovably
   routine . . **4.** rote
   star . . **4.** Veda
   time . . **3.** era **4.** date, fast
fizgig . . . **9.** fireworks, whirligig
flabellate . . . **9.** fan-shaped
flabrum . . . **3.** fan **9.** flabellum
flaccid . . . **4.** limp, weak **6.** flabby
   8. yielding
flag . . . **3.** sag **4.** fail, fane, iris, pave,
   pine, sign, weak, wilt **5.** Roger
   (pirate) **6.** banner, burgee, colors,

cornet, ensign, fanion, flower, guidon,
pennon, signal **7.** bunting, calamus,
decline, pennant **8.** gonfalon, masthead,
standard, streamer, vexillum
9. banderole **16.** Quincunx of Heaven
flagging . . . **4.** weak **7.** languid
   8. pavement **10.** flagstones, spiritless
   11. languishing
flagging in energy . . . **9.** lassitude
flagitious . . . **6.** wicked **7.** corrupt, heinous
   8. criminal, flagrant **10.** scandalous,
   villainous
flag maker . . . **9.** Betsy Ross
flagon . . . **3.** jug **4.** ewer **5.** stoup **6.** bottle,
   carafe **7.** canteen **8.** demijohn
flagpole standard . . . **7.** bracket
   9. bracciale
flagrant . . . **4.** rank **5.** great **6.** absurd,
   wanton, wicked **7.** glaring, hateful,
   heinous, obvious, scarlet, violent
   8. infamous, terrible **9.** abandoned,
   atrocious, monstrous, nefarious
   10. profligate, villainous
flail . . . **4.** beat, flag, whip **6.** thrash,
   weapon (anc) **7.** swingle
flam . . . **4.** hoax **5.** cheat, spoof, trick
   6. cajole **7.** pretext **8.** drumbeat,
   flimflam **9.** deception, falsehood
flambeau . . . **5.** torch (flaming) **7.** cresset
   11. candlestick
flamboyant . . . **4.** wavy (Arch) **6.** florid,
   ornate **9.** brilliant, flamelike
   11. resplendent
flame . . . **3.** arc **4.** beam, burn, fire,
   glow, leye (obs), love, zeal **5.** ardor,
   blaze, flare, flash, glare, ingle, light,
   lover **6.** redden **7.** scarlet **8.** flammule
   (small) **10.** brightness, sweetheart
flamen . . . **6.** priest (anc)
flamenco . . . **5.** dance (gypsy)
Flaminian Way . . . **4.** Rome
Flanders, Belgium . . .
   brick . . **4.** Bath
   capital . . **5.** Ghent (East) **6.** Bruges
   (West)
   city . . **5.** Alost **6.** Ostend **7.** Dixmude
   (Dixmuide)
   people (anc) . . **5.** Celts **6.** Franks
   11. Burgundians
   poppy . . **9.** corn poppy
flâneur . . . **5.** idler
flap . . . **3.** tab **4.** blow, slap, sway,
   wave **5.** skirt **6.** dangle, lappet, stroke
   7. flapper, flutter **9.** appendage
flare . . . **5.** blaze, flame, flash, fusee,
   glare, light **6.** signal, spread **7.** display,
   flicker **8.** outburst **10.** illuminate
flaring . . . **5.** gaudy **6.** spread **7.** burning,
   glaring **8.** dazzling, flashing
flash . . . **4.** show **5.** blaze, burst, gleam,
   glint, shine, spark **6.** glance, signal
   7. display, glimmer, glisten, glitter,
   instant, shimmer, sparkle **8.** dispatch
   9. telegraph
flashing . . . **5.** showy **6.** flashy **8.** meteoric,
   snapping **9.** transient
flashy . . . **3.** gay **5.** fiery, gaudy, showy
   6. frothy, garish, sporty **7.** raffish
   8. vehement **9.** flaunting, impetuous
   13. grandiloquent
flask . . . **4.** ewer, olpe **5.** betty **6.** flagon

7. ampulla, canteen 9. aryballus (aryballas, anc)
flask-shaped . . . 10. lageniform
flat . . . 3. low 4. palm 5. banal, blunt, level, molle, plain, plane, prone, stale, suite, tract, vapid 6. boring, dreary, wholly 7. insipid, uniform 8. tenement, unbroken 10. horizontal
flat (pert to) . . .
boat . . 3. ark 4. punt, scow 5. barge
breastbone . . 6. ratite
canopy . . 6. tester
flatfoot . . 9. pes planus 13. talipes planus
iron . . 7. sadiron
nosed . . 6. simous
piece . . 4. slab
surface . . 4. area 6. pagina 7. tabular
worm . . 9. planarian, trematode
flatfish . . . 3. dab 4. sole 5. brill, fluke 6. acedia, turbot 7. halibut 8. flounder
flatten . . . 4. even 5. level 6. deject, smooth 7. depress 8. dispirit 9. prostrate 10. discourage, dishearten
flattened . . . 6. evened, oblate 7. leveled 8. smoothed 9. applanate
flatter . . . 3. oil 4. coax, palp 5. charm, float 6. cajole, caress, please, praise, smooge, soothe 7. adulate, beguile, blarney, flutter 8. blandish 9. encourage 10. compliment, ingratiate
flatterer . . . 6. flunky, glozer 7. Jenkins 8. adulator, courtier, parasite 9. sycophant
flattering . . . 9. adulatory, gnathonic, insincere 10. obsequious 13. complimentary
flattery . . . 5. gloze, taffy 6. praise 7. blarney, eyewash, fawning, palaver 8. cajolery 9. adulation 10. compliment, sycophancy 14. obsequiousness
flaunt . . . 4. wave 5. boast, vaunt 6. parade 7. display, flutter 8. brandish
Flavian, House of Flavius, Emperors . . . 5. Titus 8. Domitian 9. Vespasian
Flavian Amphitheater . . . 9. Colosseum (Rome)
flavor . . . 4. gust, odor, tang, zest 5. aroma, imbue, sapid, sapor, sauce, savor, scent, taste 6. season 7. perfume 8. piquancy 9. flavoring 14. characteristic
flaw . . . 3. gap, mar 4. rase, rift 5. cleft, fault 6. breach, defect 7. blemish, fissure, sophism 8. fracture 12. imperfection
flawless . . . 5. ideal 7. perfect 8. unmarked 11. unblemished
flax . . . 3. lin, tow 5. linen
flax (pert to) . . .
capsule . . 4. boll
dust . . 5. pouce
filaments . . 4. harl
process plant . . 7. rettery
refuse . . 3. pob, tow 5. hurds
seed . . 7. linseed
soak . . 3. ret
weed . . 8. toadflax
flaxweed . . . 8. toadflax
flay . . . 4. peel, skin 6. fleece 7. censure, reprove, scarify 9. criticize, excoriate
flea . . . 4. puce 5. pulex 6. beetle,

chigoe 7. chigger, cyclops 8. reminder 13. Ctenocephalus
fleam . . . 6. lancet, stream 10. millstream
fleck . . . 4. flea, mark, spot 5. flake 6. blotch, dapple, streak, stripe 7. freckle, speckle, stipple 8. particle 9. variegate
flection, flexion . . . 7. bending, turning
flee . . . 3. fly, run 4. shun 5. avoid, elope, evade, speed 6. vanish 7. abandon, forsake 9. disappear
fleece . . . 3. abb, nap 4. flay, pile, skin, wool 5. fleck, mulct, sheer, strip 6. divest 7. despoil, swindle 10. overcharge
fleer . . . 4. gibe, jeer, mock 5. flout, scoff, sheer, taunt
fleet . . . 4. fast, flit, flow, navy, sail, swim 5. drift, group, quick, rapid, swift 6. armada, hasten, nimble, speedy 9. transient 10. evanescent, transitory
fleeting . . . 7. passing 9. transient 10. evanescent, transitory
Fleet Street . . . 5. Fleta (book written in prison) 6. prison (London) 11. London press
Flemish painter . . . 5. David 6. Rubens 7. Van Dyke
flesh . . . 3. kin 4. body, meat, pink, pulp, race (human) 6. family, fatten, muscle 7. kindred, kinsmen, mankind 8. humanity 9. mortality 10. sensuality
flesh (pert to) . . .
eating . . 8. omophagy (raw) 9. omophagia 10. omophagous, zoophagous 11. carnivorous, creophagous
fond of . . 12. sarcophilous
like . . 7. carnose
lust for . . 9. carnality
resembling . . 7. sarcoid
slain animals . . 7. carnage
fleshpots . . . 6. plenty, wealth 10. high living, prosperity 12. fat of the land
fleshy . . . 3. fat 5. beefy, human, obese, plump, pulpy, stout 6. carnal 7. adipose, carnose 9. corpulent
fleshy fruit . . . 4. pear, pome 5. bacca, berry, drupe
fleur-de-lis . . . 3. lis (Her) 4. iris, lily, luce 6. emblem
flew . . . see *fly*
flexible . . . 4. limp 5. lithe 6. limber, pliant, supple 7. elastic, lissome
flexion, flection . . . 9. anaclasis
flexure . . . 4. genu 5. crook 7. bending
flick (sl) . . . 4. film 5. movie
flicker . . . 4. burn, flit 5. blaze, glare, waver 7. flutter, high-hoe 10. woodpecker
flickering . . . 7. burning, lambent 8. flickery 9. irregular
flier, flyer . . . 3. ace 4. bird 5. pilot, train 6. airman, gamble, insect 7. aviator, speeder, sunfish, venture 11. speculation
flight . . . 3. hop 4. rout 5. arrow (volley), flock, skein (wild fowl), speed 6. exodus, fletch (arrows), flying, hegira, perron, stairs, throng 7. soaring 8. escapism, mounting, stampede,

swarming **9.** excursion, formation, migration **10.** volitation

flightless bird ... see *bird, flightless*

flighty ... **5.** barmy, swift **6.** fickle, fitful **7.** foolish **8.** fanciful, freakish, volatile **9.** frivolous **10.** capricious

flimflam ... **5.** freak, hocus, trick **6.** humbug **7.** caprice, swindle **8.** nonsense, trifling **9.** deception, deceptive **11.** nonsensical

flimmer ... **7.** flicker, glimmer

flimsy ... **4.** limp, rare, thin, vain, weak **5.** frail **6.** feeble, paltry, sleazy, slimsy **7.** flaccid, shallow, trivial **9.** illogical **11.** superficial **13.** unsubstantial

flinch ... **4.** game **5.** quail, start, wince, wonde **6.** blench, cringe, falter, flense, recoil, shrink, swerve

fling ... **3.** shy **4.** dart, dash, gibe, hurl, toss **5.** cheat, dance, flock (sandpipers), revel, sling, sneer, throw **6.** baffle, spirit **7.** cast off, sarcasm **9.** prostrate

flint ... **5.** chert, clint, silex **6.** quartz **7.** lighter **8.** hardness **9.** firestone, skinflint

flip ... **3.** hop, tap **4.** flap, glib, snap, toss **5.** drink (spiced), flick, flirt, throw **6.** fillip **8.** flippant, turn over **10.** somersault **11.** impertinent

flippant ... **4.** flip, glib, pert **5.** cocky **6.** chatty, fluent **8.** impudent **10.** persiflate **11.** impertinent

flipper ... **3.** arm, fin, paw **4.** hand **5.** panel **8.** flapjack

flirt ... **3.** toy **4.** dart, fike, flip, jerk, jilt, mash, play, toss **5.** dally **6.** coquet, fillip, masher, trifle **7.** trifler **8.** coquette **11.** philanderer

flirtation ... **5.** dance **8.** coquetry, trifling **10.** love affair

flit ... **3.** fly **4.** dart **5.** glide, hover **6.** nimble **7.** flicker, flutter, migrate

flitter ... **3.** rag **5.** hover, piece **6.** tatter **7.** flicker, flutter, fritter **8.** fragment

flittermouse ... **3.** bat

float ... **4.** buoy, cork, hove, lure, raft, ride, sail, soar, swim, waft **5.** balsa, drift, hover, ladle **6.** launch **7.** support **8.** navigate, undulate **9.** transport **10.** inaugurate

floating ... **4.** free **5.** awash, loose **6.** adrift, natant **7.** buoyant, movable, rumored **8.** changing, drifting, shifting **9.** launching, wandering

floating herb ... **7.** frogbit **16.** Hydrocharitaceae

flock ... **4.** bevy, fold, herd, pack, raft **6.** flight, hirsel **7.** company **9.** multitude **10.** assemblage, collection **11.** aggregation

flock (pert to) ...
bees .. **4.** hive **5.** swarm **6.** colony
cattle .. **4.** herd
fish .. **5.** shoal
geese .. **5.** skein **6.** gaggle
herons .. **5.** sedge
insects .. **5.** swarm
like .. **6.** gregal
lions .. **5.** pride
partridge .. **5.** covey
pheasants .. **4.** nide (nid)

sandpipers .. **5.** fling
walrus .. **3.** pod

flocks, god of ... **3.** Pan

floe ... **3.** ice **4.** berg

flog ... **3.** cat, tan **4.** beat, cane, goad, lash, wale, welt, whip **6.** larrup, punish, strike, thrash **8.** chastise

flogging ... **4.** toco (toko) **7.** beating **8.** whipping **9.** thrashing **10.** punishment **12.** chastisement

flood ... **3.** sea **5.** eagre, spate **6.** deluge, drench, excess **7.** freshet, torrent **8.** cataract, inundate, overflow **9.** cataclysm **10.** oversupply **14.** superabundance

flood (pert to) ...
disaster .. **9.** Galveston (1900), Johnstown (1889)
gate .. **4.** gool, lock, slow **6.** sluice **8.** penstock
lights .. **5.** klieg
tidal .. **5.** eagre

floor ... **4.** base, pave, sill **5.** chess (pontoon), story **6.** baffle, bottom, defeat **7.** coaming, silence **9.** overthrow **10.** substratum

floor leader ... **4.** whip

flora ... **6.** plants **11.** florilegium

flora and fauna ... **5.** biota

Florence gallery ... **5.** Pitti **6.** Uffizi

Florentine (pert to) ...
color .. **7.** scarlet
family (famed) .. **6.** Medici
lily .. **6.** giglio
school .. **6.** Tuscan
sculptor .. **8.** Ammanati, Ghiberti

florid ... **3.** red **5.** ruddy **6.** ornate, rococo **7.** flowery, flushed **8.** enriched, rubicund **10.** figurative, melismatic, rhetorical **11.** embellished **13.** grandiloquent

Florida ...
cape .. **9.** Canaveral
capital .. **11.** Tallahassee
city .. **5.** Miami, Tampa **7.** Daytona, Key West, Orlando **8.** Sarasota **9.** Pensacola **11.** St Augustine (1565) **12.** Jacksonville, St Petersburg **14.** Fort Lauderdale
discoverer .. **11.** Ponce de Leon (1513)
fish .. **6.** mullet, shrimp, tarpon, testar, tetard **8.** blue crab
flower .. **13.** orange blossom
Indian .. **8.** Seminole
lake .. **10.** Okeechobee
museum .. **10.** Circus Hall (Ringling)
plant .. **7.** coontie
river .. **8.** Suwannee
State motto .. **22.** Liberty and Independence
State nickname .. **8.** Sunshine
swamp, park .. **10.** Everglades
trail .. **7.** Tamiami

flounce ... **4.** flap, fold, jerk, trim **5.** caper, frill, twist **6.** edging, frolic **8.** flounder, struggle

flounder ... **4.** roll **6.** bungle, muddle, welter **7.** stumble **8.** struggle **9.** fluctuate

flounder (fish) ... **3.** dab **5.** fluke **6.** plaice, turbot **8.** flatfish

flour ... **4.** bran, meal **6.** farina, pinole, powder **9.** middlings, pulverize

flour (pert to) ...

diabetic . . **9.** aleuronat
gravy . . **4.** roux
maker . . **6.** miller
pudding . . **4.** duff
flourish . . . **4.** grow, show, wave **5.** vaunt
  6. flaunt, paraph (signature), thrive
  7. display, fanfare, prosper, roulade
  8. arpeggio, brandish, ornament
  9. embellish, luxuriate **11.** ostentation
flout . . . **4.** defy, gibe, jeer, mock **5.** fleer,
  scoff, scout, sneer, taunt **6.** insult
  8. ridicule
flow . . . **3.** jet, run **4.** bore, flow, flux,
  gush, ooze, pour, roll, teem **5.** glide,
  issue, river, spout **6.** abound, afflux,
  course, stream **7.** current, fluency,
  flutter **9.** streaming **10.** outpouring
flow (pert to) . . .
along . . **4.** lave
back . . **7.** redound
jet . . **4.** gush **5.** spurt
out . . **5.** exude, issue, spill
over . . **5.** slosh, spill **6.** deluge, engulf
  8. inundate **9.** overwhelm
tide . . **3.** ebb **4.** flow, neap
flower . . . **3.** bud **4.** best, blow **5.** bloom
  6. unfold **7.** blossom, develop, essence,
  produce **8.** choicest, ornament **11.** Four
  Hundred (Society)
flower (types of) . . . **3.** gul (rose) **4.** iris,
  ixia, lily, pink, rose **5.** aster, calla,
  canna, daisy, pansy, peony, phlox,
  poppy, stock, tulip **6.** azalea, cosmos,
  crocus, dahlia, lupine, maypop, orchid,
  oxalis, violet, zinnia **7.** arbutus,
  begonia, fuchsia, gentian, passion,
  petunia, rhodora, verbena **8.** amaranth,
  arethusa, camomile, cyclamen, daffodil,
  geranium, hepatica, hyacinth, larkspur,
  magnolia, marigold, Mariposa (lily),
  primrose, sweet pea **9.** amaryllis,
  calendula, carnation, edelweiss,
  gladiolus, hollyhock, mayflower,
  narcissus, water lily **10.** cornflower,
  delphinium, fleur-de-lis, marguerite,
  mignonette, nasturtium, periwinkle,
  poinsettia, snapdragon **11.** forget-me-
  not, strawflower **13.** chrysanthemum
  15. lily of the valley
flower (pert to) . . .
arranging . . **7.** ikebana
bed, garden . . **8.** floretum, parterre
bloom (full) . . **8.** anthesis
bud (sauce) . . **5.** caper
bunch . . **4.** posy **7.** bouquet, corsage,
  nosegay
bursting into . . **12.** efflorescent
cluster, clustered . . **4.** cyme **5.** umbel
  8. racemose **9.** glomerule **10.** paniculate
largest . . **9.** rafflesia (3-ft diameter)
like . . **7.** anthoid
meadow-grown . . **6.** pratal
part . . **4.** stem **5.** bract, calyx, petal,
  sepal, spike, torus **6.** carpel, pistil,
  stamen **7.** corolla, petiole **8.** epicalyx,
  peduncle, perianth
poet's . . **8.** asphodel **9.** narcissus
sacred . . **5.** lotus
seed . . **5.** ovule
shaped . . **7.** fleuron
small . . **7.** fleuret

stand . . **7.** epergne
flower, shrub . . . **5.** lilac **6.** azalea,
  laurel **7.** dogwood, heather, jasmine,
  spiraea, syringa **8.** bayberry, hawthorn
  9. jessamine, mistletoe, sagebrush
  10. bitterroot **12.** rhododendron
flower, vine . . . **8.** clematis, wisteria
  11. honeysuckle **12.** morning glory
flower, wild . . . **5.** bluet, daisy **6.** cactus,
  clover, myrtle, pasque **7.** anemone,
  cowslip **8.** bluebell, camellia
  9. buttercup, goldenrod, mayflower,
  sunflower **10.** bluebonnet **12.** lady's-
  slipper
flowering again . . . **9.** remontant
flowers . . . **9.** flowerage
flowers, goddess of . . . **5.** Flora (Rom)
Flowery Kingdom . . . **5.** China
flowing . . . **5.** fluid **6.** afflux, fluent
  7. copious, cursive, emanant, fluxing
  8. coursing, eloquent **9.** streaming
  10. transitive
flowing (pert to) . . .
from source . . **6.** rising **9.** emanating
together . . **9.** confluent
veil . . **5.** colet (anc)
well . . **6.** gusher
fluctuate . . . **4.** roll, vary, veer **5.** waver
  7. vibrate **8.** intermit, undulate,
  unsteady **9.** oscillate, vacillate
  10. irresolute **12.** undetermined
flue . . . **4.** barb **5.** fluke **6.** funnel, tunnel
  7. chimney
fluent . . . **4.** glib **5.** fluid, ready **6.** facile,
  smooth, solute **7.** copious, elegant,
  flowing, gliding, verbose, voluble
  8. eloquent **9.** talkative **10.** loquacious
fluff . . . **4.** down, girl, lint, yarn **5.** floss
  6. bungle **8.** softness **9.** lightness
fluffy . . . **4.** soft **5.** downy, drunk,
  fuzzy, linty **8.** feathery **9.** forgetful
  12. undependable
fluid . . . **3.** gas, ink, oil **4.** bile, milk
  5. ichor, serum, water **6.** fluent, liquid,
  plasma, watery **7.** flowing **8.** floating,
  nonsolid
fluke . . . **4.** fish, worm **5.** blade (whale)
  8. accident, flatfish, flounder
flume . . . **5.** shoot **6.** raving, sluice
  7. channel, conduit
flummox . . . **7.** confuse, perplex
flunk . . . **4.** fail, miss, slip **5.** shirk **6.** flinch
  7. back out
flunky, flunkey . . . **4.** snob **5.** toady
  6. cookee, lackey **7.** footman, servant
  8. henchman **9.** stagehand
flurry . . . **3.** ado **4.** fret, gust **5.** haste,
  hurry **6.** bustle, squall **7.** bluster,
  fluster, flutter **8.** snowfall **9.** agitation,
  commotion, confusion **10.** excitement
flush . . . **3.** hot, jet **4.** full, glow, gush,
  rush **5.** blush, cards, color, drunk, fever,
  rinse, ruddy **6.** drench, lavish, redden,
  thrill **7.** healthy, wealthy **8.** abundant,
  affluent, prodigal, rosiness, squarely,
  unbroken **10.** prosperous
flushed . . . **3.** hot, red **4.** ruby **5.** aglow,
  drunk, elated, florid **7.** excited,
  fervent **8.** blushing, exultant, feverish,
  reddened
fluster . . . **4.** move **5.** shake **6.** bustle,

excite, flurry, pother 8. distract
10. excitement 11. distraction
flute ... 5. crimp, twill 6. furrow, groove
7. magadis 9. organ stop, wineglass
10. instrument
flute (pert to) ...
bagpipe part .. 7. chanter
nose .. 3. bin 5. pungi
player .. 6. aulete 7. tootler
shrill .. 7. piccolo
stop .. 7. ventage
transverse .. 4. fife
fluting ... 5. strix 7. gadroon, shading
10. decoration
flutter ... 4. flap, flit, wave 5. float, haste,
hover, waver 6. bustle, ruffle 7. agitate,
pitapat 8. disorder 9. agitation,
confusion, palpitate
flux ... 4. flow, fuse, melt 5. flood, purge,
resin, rosin, smalt, smear 6. course
7. flowing, liquefy, outflow, solvent
fly ... 3. hop 4. flee, flit, leap, melt,
soar, wave, whir, wing 5. alate, float,
glide, speed 6. aviate, elapse, escape,
insect, spring, vanish 7. avigate, avolate
8. fishhook 9. cease to be, disappear
fly (types of) ... 3. bot 4. gnat 5. cadew,
horse, house, midge 6. Asilus, caddis,
gadfly, punkie, tsetse 7. Diptera, nosee-
um 8. dipteron, lacewing, mosquito
11. caterpillar
fly (pert to) ...
African .. 4. zimb (zebub) 6. tsetse
agaric .. 8. mushroom (poisonous)
artificial .. 4. harl 5. alder, sedge 6. Cahill,
claret 7. grannom
blow .. 4. eggs 5. larva
catcher .. 4. tody 6. peewee (pewit),
phoebe 8. kingbird
flying ... 5. a-wing, brief, hasty, yarak
(falcon) 6. volant, waving 7. fleeing
8. fleeting, floating 9. temporary,
transient 12. aeronautical
flying (pert to) ...
adder .. 9. dragonfly
boat .. 8. airplane, seaplane 9. amphibian
cat .. 5. lemur 6. marmot
Dutchman .. 5. opera 7. mariner (fabled)
8. wanderer
fox .. 3. bat 6. kalong
island .. 6. Laputa (Gulliver's Travels)
machine .. 9. gyroplane, orthopter
foal ... 4. colt 5. filly 8. Equuleus (Astron)
9. youngling
foam ... 4. barm, boil, fume, rage, scum,
suds 5. froth, spume, yeast 6. trivia
7. bubbles
foaming ... 7. spumous 8. bubbling
10. fermenting, infuriated
11. overwrought
fob ... 4. sham 5. cheat, trick 6. impose,
pocket 7. palm off 8. ornament
focal point ... 8. omphalos
focus ... 6. center 8. converge, omphalos
10. adjustment 11. concentrate
fodder ... 3. hay 4. corn, feed 5. straw,
vetch 6. forage, silage, stover 7. stubble
8. ensilage 9. pasturage, provender
fodder (pert to) ...
pit .. 4. silo
storage .. 6. haymow

store .. 6. ensile
stored .. 6. silage
foe ... 4. army 5. enemy, rival 8. opponent
9. ill-wisher
fog ... 4. blur, daze, haar, haze, mist,
roke, smog 5. brume, cloud, vapor
6. nebula, opaque, stupor 7. aerosol,
confuse, pogonip (Sierras) 9. confusion
fogdog ... 5. stubb 8. fogeater
foggy ... 3. dim 4. dull, hazy, roky
5. dense, misty, vague 6. cloudy,
opaque 7. muddled, obscure
8. confused, nubilous 9. beclouded,
uncertain 10. indistinct
12. muddleheaded
foghorn ... 5. siren, voice (hoarse)
6. signal
fogle ... 12. handkerchief (thieves')
fogy ... 4. dull, slow 6. dotard, fogram,
Hunker 8. mossback 10. Barnburner
12. conservative, old-fashioned
16. overconservative
foible ... 5. blade (part), fault 7. failing,
frailty 8. weakness 9. infirmity
12. imperfection
foil ... 4. balk 5. actor, metal, sheet,
stump, sword 6. defeat, offset, outwit,
stooge, thwart, weapon 7. failure,
repulse 9. frustrate 10. disappoint
11. frustration
Foism ... 8. Buddhism
foist ... 4. palm 5. cheat 7. intrude
9. interpose 11. interpolate
fold ... 3. end, lap, pen, ply 4. coil
(serpent), fail, furl, loop, pile, reef, ruga,
sile, tuck, wrap 5. clasp, close, crimp,
drape, laity, plait, pleat, plica 6. crease,
dewlap, double, infold, lamina, lappet,
rimple, suffix 7. entwine, envelop,
plicate (fanlike) 8. collapse 9. plicature
10. go bankrupt
folded, not ... 8. eplicate
folder ... 7. booklet, leaflet 8. pamphlet
13. advertisement
foliage ... 5. spray 6. leaves, ramage
7. bouquet, leafage, umbrage
8. ornament (Arch)
folio ... 4. case, leaf 5. paper (folded)
6. folder, number (serial)
folk ... 4. race 5. tribe 6. nation, people
8. servants 9. followers, relatives,
retainers 11. aggregation
folk (pert to) ...
learned .. 7. pedants
lore .. 6. legend 9. mythology, tradition
12. superstition
song .. 4. fado, lied 7. art song, lullaby
9. Kunstlied, Volkslied
tale .. 4. myth, saga 5. fable, Nancy
6. legend, mythos, mythus 7. fantasy,
parable
follow ... 3. dog, tag 4. heed, heel, next,
nose, obey, seek, tail 5. after, ensue,
trace, trail 6. pursue, result, shadow
7. conform, draggle, emulate, imitate,
observe, replace, succeed 8. come
next, practice, supplant 9. persevere,
supervene 10. understand
follower ... 3. fan, ist (suff), ite (suff), son
4. aper 5. lover (of) 6. copier, ensuer,
votary, zealot 7. devotee, pursuer,

sequent **8.** adherent, believer, disciple, henchman, partisan **9.** Christian, dependent, satellite **10.** enthusiast **11.** cuadrillero

follower of . . .
Arius . . **5.** Arian
Buddha . . **8.** Buddhist
Confucius . . **9.** Confucian
Falstaff . . **3.** Nym
Mohammed . . **6.** Moslem **8.** Islamite

following . . . **4.** next, sect **5.** suant **7.** ensuing, pursuit, sequent **8.** trailing **9.** resultant **10.** subsequent, succeeding, successive **13.** accompaniment

following (pert to) . . .
exact words . . **7.** literal
one's death . . **10.** posthumous
stories . . **6.** sequel, series

folly . . . **3.** sin **5.** crime **6.** levity, lunacy **7.** blunder, foolery, madness **8.** lewdness, unwisdom **9.** silliness **10.** desipience, imprudence, wantonness **11.** foolishness **12.** indiscretion

foment . . . **3.** egg **4.** abet, brew, spur **5.** bathe, rouse **6.** arouse, excite, incite **7.** agitate, cherish **9.** encourage, instigate

fomentation . . . **6.** lotion, stupes **10.** excitement **11.** instigation **13.** encouragement

Fomoriana (Celt Myth) . . . **10.** sea robbers (race of)

fonda . . . **3.** inn **5.** hotel **6.** fonduk

fondle . . . **3.** pet **4.** neck **5.** ingle **6.** caress, coddle, cosset, foster, pamper **7.** cherish **8.** blandish

fondling . . . **3.** pet **4.** fool **5.** ninny **9.** caressing, simpleton **10.** love-making

fondly . . . **6.** dearly **8.** tenderly **14.** affectionately

fondness . . . **3.** gra **4.** love **6.** desire, doting, liking, relish **8.** appetite **9.** affection **10.** attachment, propensity

fond of . . .
hunting . . **7.** venatic
sea . . **15.** thalassophilous
wife (overly) . . **8.** uxorious

font . . . **3.** jet **4.** fons, lava **5.** stoup **6.** source, spring **7.** piscina **8.** fountain **9.** reservoir

food . . . **3.** cud, pap **4.** cate, chow, diet, eats, fare, grub, junk (food), meat, tofu **5.** bread, manna, scran **6.** bulgur (wheat), cereal, gluten, quiche, snacks, Tex-Mex, viands **7.** aliment, cuisine, edibles, tapioca **8.** chili dog, fast-food, kreplach, munchies, victuals **9.** nutriment, nutrition, provender **10.** sustenance **11.** charcuterie, comestibles, nourishment

food (pert to) . . .
animal . . **6.** forage **9.** provender
bit . . **4.** bite **6.** morsel **7.** munchie
devotee . . **7.** epicure, gourmet
digestant . . **5.** chyle
digested (partly) . . **5.** chyme
dislike of . . **9.** sitomania **10.** cibophobia
element . . **7.** protein, vitamin
fasting (Lenten) . . **9.** xerophagy
gods, the . . **6.** amrita **8.** ambrosia

heavenly . . **5.** manna
impure . . **4.** tref
provide . . **5.** cater, scaff **6.** tucker
room . . **5.** ambry **6.** pantry, spence **7.** butlery, pantler

fool . . . **3.** ass, toy **4.** butt, dolt, dupe, jerk, nerd, nizy, raca (Bib), simp **5.** clown, idiot, moron, ninny **6.** dotard, jester, noodle, trifle, turkey **7.** buffoon, deceive, dingbat, fathead **9.** ignoramus, simpleton

foolhardy . . . **4.** rash **7.** Icarian **8.** reckless **11.** adventurous

fool hen . . . **6.** grouse

foolish . . . **3.** mad **4.** daft, raca, rash, zany **5.** inane, inept, silly **6.** absurd, harish **5.** palty **6.** simple, stupid, unwise **7.** asinine, fatuous, idiotic, puerile, witless **9.** brainless, desipient, imprudent, ludicrous, senseless **10.** illadvised, irrational, ridiculous **12.** preposterous **13.** insignificant

foolish fancy . . . **7.** chimera (chimaera)

foolishness . . . **5.** folly **6.** levity **9.** absurdity, stupidity **10.** triviality

fool's bauble . . . **7.** marotte

fool's gold . . . **6.** pyrite

foot . . . **3.** pad **6.** paw pes (pref) **4.** base, hoof, inch (part), sole, step, walk **5.** sum up, tread **6.** reckon **7.** residue **9.** calculate, extremity

foot (pert to) . . .
bone . . **6.** tarsus **10.** metatarsus
care of . . **8.** pedicure, podiatry **9.** chiropody **11.** chiropodist
combining form . . **4.** pede, pedi
lever . . **5.** pedal **7.** treadle
like . . **8.** pediform
measure . . **4.** inch
part . . **3.** toe **4.** arch, heel, sole
prefix . . **4.** pedi
race course (anc) . . **7.** diaulos
reference to . . **5.** pedal, podal
rest . . **4.** rail **7.** cricket, hassock, ottoman, support **8.** footrail **9.** footstool
sole . . **7.** plantar
unstressed part (Pros) . . **5.** arsis

foot, feet (metric) . . . **4.** iamb, mora, unit **6.** dactyl, dipody, iambus **7.** anapest, dimeter, pyrrhic, spondee, tripody **8.** trimeter **9.** hexameter **10.** heptameter, pentameter

footed . . . **5.** biped **7.** bipedal, megapod (large), metered

footing . . . **4.** lace, rank **5.** basis, dance, tread **6.** status **7.** support **8.** foothold, progress, standing **9.** condition **11.** calculation

footlike part . . . **3.** pes

footman . . . **6.** varlet, walker **7.** servant **9.** attendant **10.** pedestrian

footprint mold . . . **7.** moulage

footway . . . **7.** catwalk (Naut)

fop . . . **3.** nob **4.** Adon, buck, dude **5.** dandy, puppy, sport, swell **6.** Adonis, masher **7.** coxcomb, gallant **9.** exquisite, pretender **12.** boulevardier

foppish . . . **6.** dapper, spruce **7.** finical, foplike **8.** dandyish **9.** conceited, dandified

for . . . **2.** to **3.** pro **5.** spite **7.** because,

instead **8.** behalf of **9.** intending
10. indicating **11.** preparation
for (pert to) . . .
  each . . **3.** per
  example . . **2.** as, eg **4.** vide **13.** exempli
  gratia
  fear . . **4.** lest
  most part . . **6.** mostly **7.** chiefly, usually
  9. generally
  nothing . . **6.** gratis, naught **9.** lagniappe
  (lagnappe)
  this reason . . **4.** ergo **5.** hence
forage . . . **4.** food, mast, raid **5.** spoil
  6. browse, ravage **7.** plunder
  9. pasturage
foramen . . . **4.** pore **7.** opening, orifice,
  passage **8.** fenestra
foray . . . **4.** raid **6.** ravage, sortie **7.** pillage
  9. incursion
forbear . . . **4.** lose, shun **5.** avoid **6.** desist,
  endure **7.** abstain, decline, refrain
  8. part with **9.** be patient
forbearance . . . **5.** mercy **6.** disuse,
  lenity **8.** leniency, mildness, patience
  9. tolerance **10.** abstinence, temperance
  11. forgiveness, placability
forbid . . . **3.** ban **4.** deny, tabu, veto
  5. debar, taboo **6.** disbar, hinder,
  impede, oppose **7.** exclude, inhibit,
  prevent **8.** disallow, preclude, prohibit
  9. interdict, proscribe **11.** countermand
forbiddance . . . **3.** ban **4.** veto
  11. unallowable **12.** illiberality,
  interdiction, proscription
forbidden city . . . **5.** Lhasa (Tibet), Pekin
  (walled)
forbidden food (Bib) . . . **4.** tref
  8. terephah
forbidding . . . **4.** grim, ugly **5.** plain,
  stern **6.** fierce, odious **9.** offensive,
  revolting **10.** prevention, unpleasant
  11. displeasing, prohibitive
force . . . **3.** vim, vis **4.** dint, make, urge
  5. drive, impel, power, press, repel,
  staff, vigor **6.** coerce, compel, effect,
  energy, extort, hasten, strain **7.** impetus,
  meaning **8.** eloquent, momentum,
  pressure, validity, violence **9.** constrain,
  influence, puissance **10.** compulsion,
  constraint **11.** necessitate
force (pert to) . . .
  alleged . . **2.** od
  armed . . **4.** army **5.** posse
  by seizure . . **5.** usurp
  down . . **7.** detrude
  full . . **5.** amain
  substance . . **8.** catalyst
  unit . . **4.** dyne **5.** staff, tonal **7.** poundal
forced . . . **7.** labored **9.** reluctant, unwilling
  10. artificial, compulsory, farfetched
  11. constrained
forced feeding . . . **6.** gavage
forceful . . . **5.** valid **6.** mighty, potent,
  strong **7.** dynamic **8.** eloquent,
  emphatic, vigorous **9.** effective,
  energetic **10.** compulsory
forces . . . **4.** army **5.** armed **6.** troops
forcible . . . **6.** cogent, mighty, potent
  7. violent, weighty **8.** eloquent,
  emphatic, positive, puissant **9.** energetic
  10. compulsory, impressive

11. influential
forcible entry . . . **10.** effraction
forciform . . . **6.** forked **7.** furcate
  11. forficulate **14.** scissors-shaped
ford . . . **4.** wade **5.** cross **6.** stream
fore . . . **3.** way **5.** front, prior, track
  6. former **7.** journey
forebear . . . **4.** sire **5.** elder **6.** parent
  8. ancestor **10.** antecedent, forefather,
  progenitor
forebode . . . **5.** augur **7.** betoken,
  portend, predict, presage **8.** foretell
  15. prognostication
foreboding . . . **6.** augury **8.** croaking,
  sinister **11.** pessimistic, presagement
  12. apprehension, presentiment
forecast . . . **4.** bode, plan **6.** scheme
  7. foresee, fortune, predict **8.** foretell,
  prophecy **9.** calculate, foresight,
  foretoken **10.** foreordain, prediction
  12. predetermine
forecaster . . . **4.** seer **5.** vates **6.** oracle
  7. diviner, palmist, prophet **8.** dopester,
  presager **10.** astrologer, soothsayer
  11. Nostradamus **13.** meteorologist
  14. prognosticator
foreclose . . . **5.** debar **6.** hinder **7.** prevent,
  shut out **8.** preclude **10.** dispossess
foredoom . . . **4.** doom **7.** predict
  12. predestinate
foredoomed . . . **3.** fey **5.** fatal **8.** accursed
forefather . . . **4.** sire **5.** elder **6.** parent
  8. ancestor, forebear **10.** progenitor
forefinger . . . **5.** index
foregather . . . **4.** meet **7.** convene
  8. assemble **9.** encounter
forego, forgo . . . **6.** pass by **7.** neglect,
  precede **8.** renounce
foregoing . . . **4.** past **5.** above **6.** former,
  prefix **7.** leading **10.** antecedent
foregone . . . **4.** past **8.** previous
  11. predestined, preordained,
  preresolved **13.** predetermined
foregone conclusion . . . **9.** certainty
forehead . . . **4.** brow **8.** calvaria, glabella,
  sinciput **9.** assurance **10.** effrontery
forehead, divination by . . .
  11. metopomancy
forehead, frontal . . . **7.** metopic
foreign . . . **4.** xeno (comb form) **5.** alien,
  fremd **6.** exotic, remote **7.** distant,
  outside (of country), strange **8.** excluded
  9. extrinsic, peregrine, unrelated
  10. extraneous, outlandish
  11. incongruous **12.** adventitious
foreign (pert to) . . .
  accent . . **4.** burr **6.** brogue, patois
  7. dialect
  crystals (Geol) . . **7.** epigene
  disease . . **7.** ecdemic
  insertion . . **13.** interpolation
  place . . **6.** forane
  quarter . . **4.** Para **5.** Latin **6.** French
  7. enclave
  service residence . . **9.** consulate
foreigner . . . **5.** alien **6.** gringo **8.** outsider,
  stranger **9.** outlander, uitlander
  10. tramontane **12.** ultramontane
foreland . . . **8.** headland **10.** promontory
forelock . . . **4.** bang **7.** cowlick, fetlock
  8. linchpin **9.** cotter pin, fastening

(armor)

foreman ... **4.** boss **5.** chief **6.** leader **7.** juryman, overman **10.** supervisor **14.** superintendent

foremost ... **5.** chief, first, front **7.** leading, supreme **8.** headmost **13.** most important

forensic ... **10.** rhetorical **13.** argumentative

foreordain ... **7.** destine **9.** predicate, preordain **12.** foreordinate, predestinate, predetermine

forerun ... **6.** herald **7.** advance, prelude, presage **8.** announce, antecede **9.** forestall, introduce, prefigure **10.** anticipate, foreshadow

forerunner ... **4.** omen, sign **6.** augury, herald **8.** ancestor **9.** harbinger, messenger, precursor **10.** forefather, foreganger, progenitor, prognostic **11.** predecessor

foreshadow ... **6.** shadow (beforehand) **7.** presage **9.** adumbrate, prefigure

foresight ... **8.** sagacity **9.** prevision **10.** precaution, prediction, prescience, prevoyance, providence **11.** omniscience **13.** foreknowledge

forest ... **4.** wold, wood **5.** grove, woods **6.** jungle, timber **8.** woodland **9.** greenwood **10.** timberland, wilderness

forest (pert to) ...
deity .. **3.** Pan **7.** Aegipan
fire .. **5.** crown, stand **6.** ground **7.** surface
fire-finding instrument .. **7.** alidade
glade .. **6.** camass (camas, cammas)
love of, lover of .. **9.** nemophile, nemophily
regarding .. **6.** sylvan **7.** nemoral
tilled .. **7.** thwaite
warden .. **6.** ranger

forestall ... **6.** hinder **7.** exclude, head off, prevent **9.** intercept **10.** anticipate, monopolize

foretell ... **4.** bode, spae **5.** augur, insee **7.** portend, predict, presage **8.** forebode, forecast, prophesy **10.** vaticinate **13.** prognosticate

foretelling ... **6.** augury **7.** fatidic **9.** fatidical, prophetic **10.** vaticinant

forethought ... **8.** prepense, prudence **9.** foresight, provident **10.** deliberate, precaution **12.** aforethought, anticipation **13.** premeditation

foretoken ... **4.** omen **7.** presage **8.** foreshow, indicant **10.** presignify **13.** preindication, prognosticate

foretooth ... **5.** biter **6.** cutter **7.** incisor **9.** milk tooth

forever ... **3.** ake (Maori), aye (ay) **4.** olam, ever **6.** always, eterne **7.** endless **8.** infinity **9.** continual, perpetual **10.** constantly, invariably **11.** ceaselessly, continually, incessantly, perpetually, unceasingly **12.** interminably, unchangeably **13.** everlastingly

forewarning ... **4.** omen **7.** caution, portent **9.** informing **10.** admonition, foreboding

foreword ... **5.** proem **7.** preface, prelude **8.** exordium, preamble, prologue **12.** introduction

forfeit ... **4.** fine, lose, loss **5.** forgo, mulct **6.** forego, pledge **7.** deodand, penalty

forfeiture ... **4.** fine, loss **5.** dédit, mulct **7.** penalty **10.** amercement

forfend ... **5.** avert **6.** forbid **7.** prevent, protect **8.** preserve, prohibit

forfex ... **6.** shears

forgather ... **4.** meet **7.** consort, convene **8.** assemble **9.** encounter **10.** fraternize

forge ... **4.** coin, form, mint **5.** feign **6.** create, smithy, stithy, swinge **7.** falsify, imitate **8.** bloomery, smithery **11.** counterfeit

forgery ... **4.** sham **7.** fiction **9.** falsehood, invention **11.** counterfeit, fabrication **13.** falsification

forget ... **4.** omit **5.** lapse, remit **6.** slight **7.** neglect **9.** disregard **11.** disremember

forgetfulness ... **5.** Lethe (Myth), lotus (legend) **7.** amnesia, amnesty **8.** Manassah, oblivion **12.** carelessness, heedlessness **13.** obliviousness

forgive ... **5.** remit, spare **6.** acquit, excuse, pardon **7.** condone

forgiveness ... **6.** pardon **9.** remission **10.** absolution **11.** condonation, exoneration, magnanimity

forgiving ... **6.** humane **8.** merciful, placable **9.** remissive **11.** magnanimous

forgo ... **4.** quit **5.** leave, waive **6.** give up, resign **7.** abstain, forbear, forfeit, forsake, neglect, refrain **8.** overlook, renounce **9.** do without **10.** relinquish

forhoo ... **7.** abandon, despise

fork ... **6.** expend, pay out **7.** dilemma, diverge **10.** divaricate, divergence, headstream **11.** bifurcation

fork (pert to) ...
feature .. **4.** tine **5.** prong
garden .. **5.** graip
pickle .. **13.** runcible spoon
table .. **5.** salad **6.** dinner, oyster **7.** dessert **8.** ice-cream

forked ... **5.** bifid **6.** horned, ramous **7.** divided, furcate **8.** branched, crotched **9.** ambiguous, equivocal **10.** bifurcated, branchlike

forlorn ... **4.** reft **5.** alone **6.** abject, bereft **8.** deserted, desolate, forsaken, helpless, pitiable **9.** abandoned, destitute, miserable **10.** friendless **12.** disconsolate

form ... **4.** body, cast, idea, mold, rite **5.** build, guise, model, shape **6.** beauty, create, figure, invent, ritual **7.** compose, contour, formula, outline, pattern, profile, species, variety **8.** ceremony, conceive, document **9.** establish, formality **10.** appearance **11.** arrangement **12.** conformation **13.** configuration, questionnaire **15.** conventionality

form (pert to) ...
bust .. **6.** taille
chainlike .. **8.** catenate
deceptive .. **5.** ghost **7.** specter **8.** phantasm

display . . **4.** rack
good . . **4.** chic **6.** fettle
government . . **6.** polity
hollow . . **5.** shell
into fabric . . **4.** knit, spin **5.** weave
primitive . . **9.** prototype
spiral . . **5.** helix
suffix . . **5.** shape **10.** resembling
formal . . . **4.** prim **5.** exact, stiff **6.** solemn
  7. orderly, outward, precise, regular,
  stilted **8.** affected, apparent, starched
  9. formative **10.** ceremonial, methodical
  11. pharisaical, ritualistic, superficial
  12. conventional
formal introduction . . . **5.** debut
  12. presentation
formalities . . . **5.** rites **9.** etiquette
  10. ceremonies
formal warning . . . **5.** alarm **6.** caveat
  12. caveat emptor
format . . . **4.** size **5.** shape, style
formation . . . **4.** form **5.** order **9.** structure
  11. arrangement, composition
  12. construction
formation (pert to) . . .
  chain (twisted) . . **9.** torquated
  geologic . . **7.** terrain, terrane
  military . . **4.** line **5.** herse **7.** echelon
  sand . . **4.** dene, dune
formed . . . **4.** made **5.** built **7.** created,
  decided, matured, settled **8.** arranged
  9. fashioned, organized **11.** constructed
formed (pert to) . . .
  by law . . **9.** corporate
  by lips . . **6.** labial
  mountain foot . . **8.** piedmont
  on earth's surface . . **7.** epigene
  plates (two) . . **11.** bilamellate
formed into . . .
  chain . . **8.** catenate **9.** torquated
  fabric . . **4.** spun **5.** woven **7.** knitted
  mass (hard) . . **4.** iced **5.** caked **6.** frozen
  9. congealed
  mosaic . . **9.** tessellar **11.** tessellated
former . . . **2.** ex **3.** old **4.** erst, late,
  once, past **5.** front, prior **6.** passed,
  whilom **7.** ancient, earlier **8.** previous
  9. erstwhile, foregoing, preceding
  10. antecedent
former days . . . **3.** eld, old **4.** yore
formerly . . . **3.** nee **4.** erst, once,
  then **6.** before, whilom **7.** one-time
  8. sometime **9.** aforetime, erstwhile
  10. heretofore, previously
formicary . . . **7.** anthill **8.** ant's nest
formicid . . . **3.** ant **5.** emmet **7.** Formica
formidable . . . **7.** fearful **8.** alarming,
  dreadful, menacing, terrible **9.** difficult
  11. redoubtable, threatening
formless . . . **5.** arupa **7.** anidian, chaotic
  9. amorphous, shapeless
  13. indeterminate
Formosa, Taiwan . . .
  capital . . **6.** Taipei
  city . . **6.** Tainan **7.** Hualien, Keelung
  9. Kaohsiung
  group . . **6.** Penghu (64 Isls)
  island . . **5.** Matsu **6.** Quemoy
formula . . . **3.** law **4.** form, rule **5.** axiom,
  creed, lurry, maxim, model **6.** method,
  recipe, ritual **12.** prescription

forsake . . . **4.** deny, quit, shun **5.** avoid,
  leave **6.** depart, desert, refuse, reject
  7. abandon **8.** renounce, withdraw
  9. surrender
forsaken . . . **4.** lorn **6.** vacant **7.** forlorn
  8. deserted, lovelorn, rejected
  9. abandoned
forspeak . . . **5.** curse **6.** forbid **7.** asperse,
  bewitch **8.** renounce **10.** relinquish
fort . . . **5.** redan, tower **6.** abatis, castle,
  escarp, glacis (bank of) **7.** bastion,
  bulwark, castlet **8.** bastille, fastness,
  fortress **10.** stronghold **13.** fortification,
  propugnaculum
Fort (Fr Ind War) . . . **9.** Necessity
forte . . . **4.** loud **5.** skill **8.** strength
  10. strong suit
forth . . . **3.** out **4.** away **6.** abroad, onward
  7. forward, outward
forthright . . . **5.** ahead **7.** frankly
  8. forwards **9.** downright
  11. immediately, straightway
  13. straightforth
forthwith . . . **3.** now **6.** pronto **8.** promptly
  9. summarily **11.** immediately,
  straightway
fortification . . . **4.** wall **5.** redan **6.** abatis
  7. bastion, citadel, defense, parados,
  ravelin, redoubt **8.** barbette (part),
  fortress **10.** stronghold
  13. corroboration, strengthening
fortify . . . **3.** arm, man **4.** gird **5.** add
  to, spike, stank **6.** defend, secure
  7. confirm, refresh **8.** embattle
  10. adulterate (drink), invigorate
  strengthen, vitaminize **11.** corroborate
fortitude . . . **6.** virtue **7.** bravery, courage
  8. strength **9.** endurance **10.** resolution
  12. resoluteness **14.** impregnability
fortress . . . see **fort**
fortuitous . . . **3.** hap **6.** chance
  10. accidental **12.** unexpectedly
fortunate . . . **5.** happy, lucky **6.** timely
  7. favored **10.** auspicious, prosperous,
  successful **12.** providential
fortune . . . **3.** hap, lot **4.** doom, fate,
  luck **6.** chance, estate, riches, wealth
  7. destiny, success **8.** accident
  10. prosperity **13.** circumstances
fortune (pert to) . . .
  gypsy . . **4.** bahi
  ill . . **9.** mischance
  place . . **6.** cookie
  planet (Astrol) . . **5.** Venus **7.** Jupiter
  teller . . **4.** seer **5.** sibyl, Tyche **6.** oracle
  7. spaeman
fortuneteller's deck . . . **5.** tarot (cards)
forum fashion . . . **4.** toga
forward . . . **2.** on, to **3.** aid **4.** abet,
  bold, fore, help, pert, send, ship,
  vain **5.** ahead, along, eager, front,
  impel, ready, relay, saucy, ultra
  6. active, bright, hasten, onward
  7. deliver, earnest, extreme, further,
  radical, willing **8.** advanced, immodest,
  impudent, transmit **9.** audacious,
  encourage **10.** precocious
  11. progressive **12.** presumptuous
forward moving (Zool) . . . **5.** proal
  (digestion) **11.** mastication
fosse, foss . . . **3.** pit **4.** moat **5.** canal,

ditch, fossa, grave **6.** cavity, trench
10. depression
fossil, fossils . . . **5.** relic, stone **7.** antique,
remains
fossil (pert to) . . .
egg . . **7.** ovulite
footprint . . **7.** ichnite
resin . . **5.** amber
shell . . **6.** dolite **8.** ammonite
site . . **8.** Badlands
study of . . **12.** paleontology
toothlike . . **8.** conodont
worm track . . **7.** nereite
foster . . . **4.** rear **5.** breed, nurse **7.** cherish,
gratify, indulge, promote **9.** cultivate
fosterage . . . **7.** nurture **11.** development
foster child . . . **4.** dalt **5.** norry (nurry)
7. stepson **8.** nursling **12.** stepdaughter
fought . . . see *fight*
foul . . . **3.** bad **4.** olid, ugly **5.** dirty,
fetid, grimy, nasty, reeky, spoil,
sully **6.** defame, filthy, malign,
odious, putrid, rotten, thwart, unfair
7. abusive, confuse, noisome, obscene,
profane, unclean **8.** entangle, indecent,
infamous, shameful, stagnant, stinking
9. dishonest, obnoxious **10.** complicate,
malodorous, scurrilous **11.** contaminate,
ill-smelling, unfavorable
12. inauspicious, unpropitious
foul play . . . **6.** murder, unfair (play)
7. perfidy **8.** violence **9.** deception,
treachery **10.** unfairness
found . . . **3.** fix **4.** base, cast **5.** endow,
set up **6.** attach, create **9.** establish,
institute, originate
foundation . . . **3.** bed **4.** base, plot,
sill **5.** basal, basis **6.** legacy, riprap
7. bedding, charity, premise, support
8. cosmetic, creation, donation, pedestal
9. placement **11.** corporation
13. justification
found by chance (thing) . . .
11. serendipity
founded on . . .
base . . **10.** predicated
evidence . . **10.** evidential
experience . . **7.** empiric **9.** empirical
imagination . . **7.** Utopian
founder . . . **4.** fail, fall, sink **6.** author
7. capsize, creator, stumble **8.** miscarry
9. break down, organizer **10.** originator
foundling . . . **3.** oaf **4.** waif **5.** child
(unclaimed) **6.** orphan **8.** derelict,
nursling
fountain . . . **3.** jet, spa **4.** font, head, well
6. spring **9.** reservoir **11.** scuttlebutt
(ship's) **12.** fountainhead
fountain (pert to) . . .
god of . . **4.** Fons
Muse (Gr) . . **8.** Aganippe
nymph . . **5.** naiad **6.** Egeria
of Lions . . **8.** Alhambra (Spain)
four (pert to) . . .
bits . . **7.** quarter (silver)
Books . . **8.** Classics (Chin)
footed . . **8.** tetrapod
genii, of Amenti . . **13.** Horus' children
group . . **6.** tetrad
Hundred . . **5.** elect, elite **7.** society
letters, word of . . **9.** tetragram

seas . . **13.** Great Britain's
senses (Bib) . . **15.** interpretations
four-flusher . . . **5.** cheat, fraud **7.** bluffer
8. impostor **9.** pretender
four-in-hand . . . **3.** tie **4.** team (horses)
6. cravat **7.** necktie
fourth (pert to) . . .
Caliph . . **3.** Ali
century martyr . . **8.** St Blaise
estate . . **5.** press **10.** newspapers
part . . **6.** fardel **7.** quarter
stomach (cow) . . **8.** abomasum
fowl . . . **3.** hen **6.** bantam, Gallus **7.** Blue
Hen, broiler, chicken, Dorking, leghorn,
Minorca, poultry, rooster, seafowl
8. pheasant **9.** guinea hen, waterfowl
11. chanticleer
fox . . . **3.** cub, tod **4.** stag **5.** vixen
fox (pert to) . . .
African . . **4.** asse
Asian . . **5.** adive **6.** corsac
fabled . . **7.** Reynard
female . . **5.** vixen
genus . . **6.** Vulpes
hedge (hunter's) . . **4.** oxer
foot . . **3.** pad
Indian . . **10.** Algonquian
Russian . . **6.** corsac **7.** karagan
foxglove . . . **9.** digitalis
foxy . . . **3.** sly **4.** sexy, wily **6.** artful,
crafty **7.** cunning, vulpine
foyer . . . **5.** lobby **8.** anteroom, entrance
9. greenroom
fracas . . . **3.** row **5.** brawl, melee, set-
to **6.** uproar **7.** quarrel **9.** commotion
11. disturbance
fraction . . . **3.** bit **4.** part **5.** piece, scrap
6. sector **7.** element, ruction **8.** division,
fragment **9.** commotion
fractious . . . **4.** ugly **5.** cross **6.** unruly
7. peevish, waspish **8.** perverse,
snappish **9.** irritable **10.** ill-humored
11. disobedient
fracture . . . **4.** rend **5.** break, cleft, crack
6. breach, injury **7.** rupture
fragile . . . **4.** weak **5.** brash, frail **6.** frough
(obs), infirm, slight **7.** brittle **8.** delicate,
slattery **9.** frangible
fragment . . . **3.** bit, ort **4.** chip, grot, part,
snip **5.** groat, piece, relic, scrap, shard,
sherd, shred, torso (art) **6.** morsel,
sippet **7.** flinder **8.** fraction
fragments . . . **3.** ana **6.** fardel, groats,
rubble **8.** buttings, excerpts, flinders
10. miscellany **11.** smithereens
fragrance . . . **4.** odor **5.** aroma, elemi,
smell **7.** incense, perfume **9.** redolence
fragrant . . . **4.** nard **5.** balmy, olent,
spicy, sweet **7.** odorous **8.** aromatic,
redolent **9.** ambrosial **11.** odoriferous
12. sweet-scented **13.** sweet-smelling
frail . . . **4.** girl, thin, weak **5.** woman
6. basket (fig), feeble, sickly, slimsy
7. brittle, fragile **8.** strumpet, unchaste
10. weak-willed **12.** destructible
frailty . . . **5.** fault **6.** defect **7.** failing
8. thinness, weakness **9.** fragility,
infirmity **12.** imperfection
frame . . . **4.** body, make, plan, rack, sess,
sill **5.** build, easel, grate, herse, knape
6. abacus, border, charge (falsely),

direct, tenter 7. carcass, chassis,
cresset (torch), fashion, prepare,
setting, taboret 8. conceive, skeleton
9. construct 10. prearrange
framework ... 4. rack, sill 5. cadre,
shell 6. cradle 7. trestle 8. skeleton
11. scaffolding
France ... see also *French*
anc name .. 4. Gaul 6. Gallia
Bay .. 6. Biscay
Botanical Gardens .. 16. Jardin des
Plantes
capital .. 5. Paris
city .. 4. Nice 5. Lyons 7. LeHavre
8. Bordeaux, Toulouse 9. Marseille
10. Strasbourg
dread of .. 11. Gallophobia
12. Francophobia
island .. 6. Comoro (Afr), Tahiti
7. Corsica, Réunion 10. Guadeloupe
(Leeward), Martinique (Windward)
12. New Caledonia
lover of .. 10. Gallophile 11. Francophile
mountain .. 4. Alps, Jura 5. Pelat
8. Pyrenees 9. Mont Blanc 11. Pic
Montcalm
port .. 4. Caen 5. Brest 6. Calais, Toulon
7. Dunkirk (Dunkerque), Le Havre
8. Bordeaux
resort .. 3. Pau 5. Vichy 6. Cannes,
Menton (Mentone) 7. Riviera 9. Côte
d'Azur 11. Aix-les-Bains (anc)
river .. 3. Lys 4. Yser 5. Aisne, Eiser,
Loire, Meuse, Rhône, Seine
Southern .. 4. Midi
Verdun battle site .. 4. Vaux
wine region .. 8. Bordeaux, Burgundy
franchise ... 4. vote 5. right 6. patent
7. freedom, license 8. immunity,
suffrage 9. exemption
frank ... 4. free, mail, open 5. blunt,
naive, plain 6. candid, direct, honest
7. artless, liberal, sincere 8. generous
9. ingenuous, outspoken 10. unreserved
11. frankfurter 15. straightforward,
unsophisticated
frankincense ... 4. thus 8. gum resin,
olibanum 9. fragrance
Frankish (pert to) ...
dynasty .. 11. Carolingian, Merovingian
king .. 5. Pepin 6. Clovis
law .. 5. Salic
people (anc) .. 6. Salian
site .. 4. Gaul
Franklin, Benjamin ... 11. Poor Richard
frantic ... 3. mad 4. mang 5. moved,
rabid 7. furious 8. frenetic, frenzied
9. delirious, desperate, turbulent
10. distracted, distraught
11. overwrought
frappé ... 3. ice 5. chill 6. freeze 7. dessert,
mixture (sweet) 8. beverage
fraternal ... 4. kind 5. order, twins
7. society 8. friendly 9. brotherly
fraud ... 4. fake, sham, wile 5. cheat,
covin, craft, guile 6. deceit, ringer
7. defraud, roguery 8. artifice, cozenage,
impostor, subtlety, swindler, trickery
9. deception, imposture, stratagem
10. imposition 13. circumvention
fraudulence ... 9. improbity

10. subreption
fraudulent ... 4. fake, wily 5. snide
6. crafty, quacky 7. cunning, knavish
8. cheating, guileful, spurious
9. deceitful, deceiving, deceptive,
designing, dishonest, insidious
10. fallacious 11. counterfeit,
treacherous
fraught ... 4. lade, load 5. cargo, equip,
laden 6. burden, filled 7. freight
9. freighted, transport
fray ... 4. fret (cloth), wear 5. broil,
dread, melee, panic, ravel 6. affray,
combat, fright, hassle, terror, tumult
7. contest, frazzle, ruction 9. commotion
12. apprehension
freak ... 4. flam, lune, whim 5. fancy,
prank, sport 6. streak, vagary 7. caprice,
checker, crochet, monster 9. eccentric,
variegate 11. monstrosity
12. whimsicality
freakish ... 7. curious 9. eccentric,
fantastic, whimsical 10. capricious,
changeable
freck ... 4. bold, hale 5. eager, frack,
lusty, ready, stout 6. strong 7. forward
8. desirous
freckle ... 4. mark, spot 7. blemish,
ephelis, lentigo, speckle 10. ferntickle
free ... 3. rid 4. easy, open 5. clear,
frank, loose 6. acquit, candid, exempt,
gratis, immune, vacant 7. absolve,
inexact, manumit, not busy, release,
relieve, unbound 8. liberate 9. extricate,
footloose, voluntary 10. autonomous,
gratuitous, unconfined, unhampered
11. emancipated 12. uncontrolled,
unrestrained, unrestricted
free (pert to) ...
bacteria .. 7. aseptic, sterile
difficulty .. 9. extricate
doubt .. 7. resolve
flesh (dietary) .. 6. maigre
knots .. 7. enodate, unravel
reproach .. 9. blameless
slavery .. 7. manumit 10. emancipate
suspicion .. 5. clear, purge 6. acquit
7. absolve 9. exculpate, exonerate
sweetness .. 3. sec
freebooter ... 5. rover 6. pirate 8. pillager
9. plunderer 10. filibuster
freed ... 3. rid 6. loosed, spared, untied
8. released 9. delivered, liberated
10. manumitted 11. emancipated
freedom ... 6. candor 7. leisure, liberty,
license 8. latitude 9. exemption,
privilege 11. manumission
12. emancipation, independence
freedom (pert to) ...
abused .. 7. liberty (excess), license
from doubt .. 9. assurance, certitude
from sepsis .. 7. asepsis
Freedom Our Rock (motto) ...
7. Tammany (1789)
free enterprise ... 6. policy 8. commerce
10. capitalism 15. noninterference
freely ... 6. gratis 7. largely, readily
9. bountiful, copiously, liberally,
willingly 10. abundantly, generously
11. bounteously, plenteously,
plentifully, voluntarily 12. gratuitously

freeze ... **3.** ice **5.** be-ice, chill **6.** steeve
  7. congeal, terrify **8.** preserve, solidify
  9. stabilize **11.** anesthetize, refrigerate
freezing, science of ... **10.** cyrogenics
freight ... **4.** load, ship **5.** cargo,
  laden, train **6.** burden, charge, lading
  7. fraught, rattler **8.** shipment
  9. transport **14.** transportation
freight boat ... **5.** barge **9.** freighter
freit, freet ... **4.** omen **5.** charm
fremd (obs) ... **5.** alien **7.** foreign, hostile
  9. unrelated
French (people) ...
  artist .. **4.** Dore **5.** Corot, David, Degas,
    Leger, Manet, Monet, Rodin **6.** Braque,
    Gerome, Greuze, Renoir, Seurat
    7. Courbet, Gauguin, Matisse, Watteau
    8. Daubigny, Pissarro, Rousseau
    9. Delacroix, Fragonard
  author .. **4.** Hugo, Loti, Zola **5.** Camus,
    Dumas, Verne **6.** Balzac, Proust
    8. Flaubert, Rabelais
  cardinal, famed .. **7.** Mazarin **9.** Richelieu
  caricaturist .. **7.** Daumier, Gavarni
  chemist .. **7.** Gautier, Holbach, Pasteur
  composer .. **4.** Lalo **5.** Bizet, D'Indy,
    Ravel, Satie **6.** Gounod **7.** Berlioz,
    Debussy, Delibes, Poulenc **8.** Couperin
  conqueror (anc) .. **6.** Clovis
  crusader .. **7.** Godfrey (of Bouillon)
  dramatist .. **6.** Favart, Racine **7.** Molière
    8. Quinault **12.** Beaumarchais
  dynasty .. **5.** Caput **6.** Valois **7.** Bourbon
  emperor .. **8.** Napoleon (Bonaparte)
  encyclopedist .. **7.** Diderot **9.** D'Alembert
  film director .. **6.** Renoir **8.** Truffaut
  film star .. **6.** Bardot **7.** Deneuve
    9. Depardieu
  Foreign Legion creator, 1831 .. **8.** Philippe
    (Louis)
  historian .. **5.** Renan, Taine **7.** Braudel
    8. Michelet **9.** Froissart
  marshal .. **3.** Ney **4.** Foch, Niel, Saxe
    5. Murat
  naturalist .. **8.** Audebert
  navigator .. **9.** Freycinet
  officer, famed .. **7.** Dreyfus
  pantomimist .. **7.** Pierrot
  patron saint .. **5.** Denis **6.** Martin
  philosopher .. **5.** Bayle **6.** Pascal,
    Sartre **7.** Abelard **8.** Rousseau,
    Voltaire **9.** Descartes, Montaigne
    11. Montesquieu
  physician .. **7.** Laveran
  physicist .. **5.** Binet **6.** Ampere
  poet .. **6.** Villon **7.** Mistral, Rimbaud
    10. Baudelaire
  radical .. **7.** Jacobin
  revolutionary ... **5.** Marat **6.** Danton
    11. Robespierre
  scientist .. **5.** Curie **7.** Pasteur
  statesman .. **4.** Coty **5.** Laine, Laval,
    Morny **6.** Carnot **7.** Briande, Herriot
    8. DeGaulle **9.** Lafayette
French (pert to) ...
  academic rank .. **6.** agrégé
  Academy .. **12.** The Institute
  and .. **2.** et
  annuity .. **5.** rente
  anthem .. **12.** Marseillaise
  article .. **2.** la, le, un **3.** les, une

beast .. **4.** bête
bread .. **4.** pain
calender (Rev) .. **6.** Nivose **7.** Ventose
cathedral .. **8.** Chartres **9.** Notre Dame
champagne .. **2.** Ay
cheese .. **4.** Brie **6.** Chevre **9.** Camembert
chorus (male) .. **7.** orpheon
coach .. **6.** fiacre
coat-of-arms .. **10.** fleur-de-lis
coffee (black) .. **8.** café noir
company (Bus) .. **3.** cie
crown (gold coin) .. **3.** ecu
cult (art) .. **7.** Dadaism
daisy .. **10.** marguerite
dance .. **3.** bal **5.** gavot **6.** cancan
decree, edict .. **5.** arrêt
dialect .. **6.** patois
dugout .. **4.** abri
father .. **4.** père
fortification .. **7.** parados
friend .. **3.** ami **4.** amie
fugitive .. **6.** émigré
God .. **4.** Dieu
hairdresser .. **7.** friseur
hat .. **5.** beret **7.** chapeau
here .. **3.** ici
inn .. **6.** hostel
king .. **3.** roi
lace .. **5.** Cluny
language (Provence) .. **9.** Provençal
laugh .. **3.** ris
legal code .. **10.** Napoleonic
liquor .. **8.** absinthe (banned 1915)
love .. **5.** amour
lover .. **5.** amant
mask .. **4.** loup
morning .. **5.** matin
mountain peak .. **3.** pic
museum .. **6.** Louvre
narcissus .. **10.** polyanthus
native .. **8.** Gallican
nursemaid .. **5.** bonne
ornaments (set of) .. **6.** parure
outcast .. **5.** Agote, Cagot **6.** pariah
pancake .. **5.** crepe
parliament .. **5.** Sénat
pastry .. **7.** dariole, galette
plane .. **5.** avion
poem, poetry .. **3.** dit **6.** aubade, rondel
police .. **6.** Sûreté **8.** gendarme
political club .. **7.** Jacobin
porcelain .. **6.** Sèvres **7.** Limoges
priest .. **4.** abbe, père
prison, famed .. **8.** Bastille
racecourse .. **7.** Auteuil
restaurant .. **4.** café **6.** bistro
revolutionary government .. **7.** Commune
sauce .. **8.** ravigote **9.** allemande
school .. **5.** école, lycée
school of painting .. **8.** Barbizon
securities .. **6.** rentes
smoking room .. **9.** estaminet
soldier .. **5.** poilu **6.** Zouave
stable .. **6.** écurie
state .. **4.** état
stock exchange .. **6.** Bourse
storm .. **5.** orage
street .. **3.** rue
summer .. **3.** été
theater .. **16.** Comédie Française
university .. **8.** Sorbonne

uprising . . **6.** Fronde
verse . . **3.** lai **4.** alba **6.** rondel **7.** ballade,
virelay
wall . . **3.** mur
water . . **3.** eau
wind . . **7.** mistral
wine . . **5.** Medoc **6.** Barsac, brandy,
claret, Cognac, masdeu **8.** Bordeaux,
Burgundy, sauterne **10.** Beaujolais
world . . **5.** monde
Frenchy . . . **6.** Gallic
frenzied . . . **4.** amok **5.** rabid **7.** enraged,
frantic, madding **8.** maddened
9. turbulent **11.** overwrought
frenzy . . . **3.** mad **5.** furor, mania **7.** frantic,
madness **8.** delirium **9.** agitation
10. excitement, turbulence
frequent . . . **3.** oft **5.** haunt, often, usual
6. common **7.** current **8.** familiar,
habitual, intimate (with) **9.** recurrent
10. persistent
frequenter . . . **7.** habitué, visitor
8. attender
frère . . . **5.** friar **7.** brother
fresh . . . **3.** new **4.** good, lush **5.** relay,
ruddy, sound, sweet **6.** florid, lively,
strong, unused **7.** healthy, unfaded,
untried **8.** impudent, original
10. additional, refreshing, unimpaired
13. inexperienced
freshen . . . **4.** cool **5.** renew **6.** revive
7. refresh, sweeten
freshet . . . **4.** gush **5.** flood, spate
6. stream **7.** outflow, torrent
10. inundation (sudden)
freshman . . . **5.** frosh **6.** novice **7.** student
freshness . . . **7.** newness, novelty
8. verdancy **9.** impudence **11.** originality
freshwater fish . . . **2.** id (ide) **4.** chub,
dace, inid (porpoise) **6.** anabas
7. herring **8.** drumfish
fret . . . **3.** eat, nag, orp, rub, vex **4.** fray,
fume, gall, gnaw, stew **5.** adorn, annoy,
chafe, grate, tease, worry **6.** abrade,
grieve, harass, plague, strait **7.** agitate,
consume, disturb, network, roughen
8. diminish, irritate, ornament
fretful . . . **5.** angry **6.** repine **7.** peevish,
pettish **8.** captious, petulant
9. impatient, irascible, irritable,
plaintive, querulous **10.** ill-humored,
ill-natured
Freud (pert to) . . .
birthplace . . **6.** Vienna
complex . . **7.** Electra, Oedipus
concept . . **2.** id **3.** ego **8.** superego
topic . . **3.** sex **7.** anxiety
8. hysteria, neurosis **9.** sexuality
10. repression **11.** unconscious
12. subconscious **14.** psychoanalysis
friable . . . **5.** crisp, frail, mealy, short
7. brittle **8.** fragible
friar . . . **3.** fra **4.** fish (small), monk
5. abbot, Minor **6.** lister (obs) **7.** brother
8. cenobite, Minorite, Teresian (anc)
9. Carmelite, Dominican **10.** Franciscan
11. Augustinian
friction . . . **7.** erasure, rubbing **8.** clashing
9. attrition, disaccord **10.** resistance
12. disagreement **13.** counteraction
friend . . . **3.** ami, pal **4.** ally, amie, chum,

kith, sect **5.** amigo, crony **7.** comrade
8. promoter **9.** associate, attendant,
companion, supporter **10.** benefactor,
sweetheart, well-wisher
Friend . . . **6.** Quaker
friendless . . . **5.** alone **7.** forlorn
8. helpless **9.** destitute (friends)
friendly . . . **3.** sib **4.** kind **7.** affable
8. amicable, homelike, sociable
9. favorable **10.** harmonious, hospitable
11. comfortable
Friendly Islands . . . **5.** Tonga
friendship . . . **4.** kelt **5.** amity **7.** harmony
8. good will, relation **9.** affection, right
hand **10.** attachment **12.** friendliness
frieze . . . **4.** band (sculptured) **5.** adorn,
chase **6.** taenia (Doric) **8.** ornament,
trimming **10.** decoration, embroidery
Frigga, Norse Myth (pert to) . . .
goddess . . **3.** sky
maid . . **5.** Fulla
named for . . **6.** Friday
wife of . . **4.** Odin
fright . . . **3.** awe **4.** fear, ogre **5.** alarm,
panic, scare, shock **6.** terror **7.** eyesore
13. consternation
frighten . . . **3.** cow **5.** alarm, appal, scare
7. startle, terrify **10.** intimidate
frightened . . . **3.** rad **5.** eerie, timid
6. afraid **8.** skittish
frightful . . . **5.** awful, great **6.** horrid
7. hideous **8.** alarming, dreadful,
horrible, shocking, terrible, terrific
11. frightening
frightfulness . . . **13.** atrociousness
15. Schrecklichkeit
frigid . . . **3.** icy **4.** cold **5.** stiff **6.** formal
8. freezing, impotent, reserved
frijol, frijole . . . **4.** bean
frill . . . **4.** purl **5.** jabot, ruche (rouche)
6. border, edging, ruffle **8.** furbelow
9. frillback (pigeon) **11.** superfluity
fringe . . . **4.** lace, loma, tuft **5.** thrum
6. border, edging, margin **8.** ciliella,
trimming
frisk . . . **4.** skip **5.** brisk, caper **6.** frolic,
gambol, lively, search **7.** disport, rejoice
frisky . . . **3.** gay **6.** lively **7.** playful
8. sportive **10.** frolicsome
frisson . . . **5.** chill **6.** quiver, shiver, thrill
7. shudder **10.** excitement
frivolous . . . **5.** giddy, petty **6.** fickle,
slight **7.** fatuous, trivial **9.** worthless
13. shallow-witted
frock . . . **4.** gown, wrap **5.** dress, tunic
6. jersey, kirtle (anc), mantle **7.** garment,
soutane
frog . . . **3.** pad (horse's) **4.** Rana,
toad **5.** Anura **6.** peeper **7.** croaker,
paddock, tadpole **8.** Amphibia, pollywog
9. Batrachia, Frenchman, Salientia
10. hoarseness
froglike . . . **6.** ranine
frogman . . . **5.** diver **6.** seaman
7. swimmer **9.** Frenchman
frog pond . . . **8.** ranarium
frolic . . . **3.** fun **4.** lark, ogle, play, ramp,
romp **5.** binge, caper, frisk, prank,
spree, trick **6.** gambol, shindy **7.** disport,
marlock, shindig, wassail **8.** carousal
frolicsome . . . **3.** gay **5.** merry **6.** frisky

7. playful, waggish **8.** sportive
from ... **2.** at, de (pref), of **3.** apo (pref)
4. away **5.** above, out of **6.** source
8. away from, downward
from (pert to) ...
beginning to end .. **4.** over **7.** through
egg to apple .. **16.** ab ovo usque ad
mala
head to foot .. **7.** cap-a-pie
slang .. **10.** soup to nuts **11.** stem to
stern
front ... **3.** bow, van **4.** face, fore **5.** aface,
afore, blind (false), forne (obs) **6.** before,
facade **7.** obverse **8.** confront, mediator
9. forefront **10.** appearance, figurehead
11. affectation **12.** intermediary
frontier defense ... **11.** arcifinious
frontiersman ... **5.** Boone **6.** Carson
(Kit)
frost ... **3.** ice, mat **4.** cold, foam, hoar,
rime **5.** chill **6.** freeze, whiten **7.** failure
8. severity (manner) **14.** unfriendliness
frosty ... **3.** icy **4.** cold, gray, rimy **5.** chill,
hoary, white **6.** frigid **8.** freezing,
inimical **10.** unfriendly
froth ... **4.** foam, scum, suds **5.** spume,
yeast **6.** lather **7.** bubbles
frothy ... **5.** foamy, light, sudsy
7. spumous **8.** sillabub
frow ... **4.** froe (tool), wife **5.** woman
6. maenad **8.** slattern
froward ... **5.** cross **7.** peevish, wayward
8. perverse, petulant, scolding,
shrewish, untoward **9.** obstinate
10. refractory, unyielding
11. disobedient **12.** ungovernable
frowl ... **9.** guillemot
frown ... **5.** gloom, lower, scowl **6.** glower
frowsey, frowzy ... **5.** musty **7.** unkempt
8. slovenly **9.** offensive **10.** discordant,
disordered
frozen ... **4.** cold **5.** frore (anc), froze,
gelid, glacé **6.** chilly, mousse **7.** chilled
9. congealed, terrified, unfeeling,
unmovable **10.** unyielding
11. coldhearted **12.** refrigerated
frugal ... **5.** chary **6.** meager, saving
7. careful, sparing, thrifty **9.** provident
10. economical, unwasteful
11. inexpensive **12.** parsimonious
frugality ... **6.** thrift **7.** economy
9. parsimony
fruit (types of) ... **3.** fig **4.** lime, pear,
plum, pome **5.** apple, berry, drupe,
grape, guava, lemon, mango, melon,
olive, peach, pomum **6.** banana,
cherry, orange, papaya, pawpaw,
pomelo **7.** apricot, azarole, genipap,
tangelo **8.** shaddock **9.** persimmon,
tangerine **10.** grapefruit, watermelon
11. pomegranate
fruit ... **4.** diet, food **5.** yield, young
7. benefit, product **9.** offspring,
outgrowth, posterity **11.** consequence
fruit (pert to) ...
aggregate .. **7.** etaerio
astringent .. **4.** sloe
basket .. **6.** pottle
buttercup .. **6.** achene **8.** achenium
class .. **6.** simple **9.** aggregate
10. collective

cordial .. **7.** ratafia (ratafee)
decay .. **4.** blet
dried .. **6.** raisin **7.** apricot
drink .. **3.** ade **6.** nectar
Goddess .. **6.** Pomona
gourd .. **4.** pepo **7.** chayote
grapefruit .. **6.** pomelo
imperfect .. **6.** nubbin
jelly substance .. **6.** pectin
Jove's .. **9.** persimmon
part .. **7.** epicarp **8.** mesocarp, pericarp
9. sarcocarp
preserve .. **7.** compote **9.** marmalade
pulpy .. **3.** uva
rose .. **3.** hip
study of .. **9.** carpology
tree .. **4.** date, nuts **5.** regma **6.** camato,
samara (winged)
tropical .. **3.** fig **4.** date **5.** guava, mango,
papaw (pawpaw) **6.** papaya
fruitful ... **7.** fertile, uberous **8.** abundant,
prolific **9.** plenteous
fruitfulness, goddess of ... **7.** Demeter
fruitless ... **4.** vain **6.** barren **7.** sterile,
useless **10.** profitless **11.** ineffectual
12. unprofitable, unsuccessful
frump ... **3.** vex **4.** mock, snub **5.** crone,
flout, shrew **6.** gossip, insult **7.** provoke
8. irritate
frustrate ... **4.** balk, bilk, foil **5.** block,
cross, elude **6.** baffle, blight, defeat,
outwit, thwart **7.** nullify **8.** confound
9. checkmate **10.** circumvent,
disappoint, disconcert
frustrater ... **7.** marplot **8.** thwarter
frustration ... **4.** balk **6.** defeat, fiasco
13. circumvention **14.** disappointment
15. disillusionment
fry ... **4.** cook **5.** brood (fish), group,
saute, young **7.** stir-fry **9.** offspring
frying pan ... **6.** spider **7.** skillet
fubsy ... **5.** plump, short **6.** chubby
fuddle ... **4.** bout (drinking) **5.** drink
(strong), spree **6.** muddle, tipple
7. confuse **9.** confusion, inebriate
fudge ... **4.** fake **5.** candy, cheat
6. bungle, humbug **7.** trump up
8. nonsense **9.** makeshift **10.** substitute
11. counterfeit
Fuegian ... **3.** Ona **6.** Indian, Yakgan
8. Alikuluf **14.** Tierra del Fuego (pert
to)
fuel ... **3.** gas, log, oil **4.** coal, coke, peat
6. butane, diesel, elding **7.** gasohol,
nuclear, synfuel **8.** gasoline, kerosene
9. petroleum **11.** combustible
fugie ... **4.** cock (nonfighter) **6.** coward
fugient ... **7.** fleeing **8.** retiring
fugitive ... **5.** exile **6.** outlaw, roving
7. fleeing, refugee, roaming, runaway
8. fleeting, unstable, vagabond, volatile
9. fugacious, strolling, uncertain
10. evanescent
fugue ... **5.** theme, tonal **7.** amnesia,
stretto (stretta) **9.** psychosis, ricercare
fulcrum ... **4.** axis, bait, prop **5.** pivot,
scale (fish), thole **7.** support
fulfill ... **4.** meet **6.** finish, redeem
7. execute, satisfy **8.** complete
10. accomplish, effectuate
fulfillment ... **8.** fruition **9.** execution,

flowering **10.** completion
11. performance **14.** accomplishment
full . . . **3.** fat **4.** fill **5.** drunk, sated **6.** entire,
filled, rotund **7.** perfect, plenary,
replete, satiety **8.** abundant, adequate,
complete, occupied, resonant, satiated,
thorough **9.** satisfied
full (pert to) . . .
 authority . . **12.** carte blanche
 blooded . . **4.** pure, rich **5.** lusty **6.** virile
 7. genuine **8.** purebred, vigorous
 9. authentic
 bloom . . **8.** anthesis, blooming, maturity
 bodied . . **4.** rich **5.** large **6.** robust
 control . . **7.** mastery **10.** domination
 force . . **5.** amain
 house . . **3.** SRO
full of . . .
 cracks . . **6.** rimose
 hollows . . **8.** lacunose
 love . . **7.** amative, amatory
 meaning . . **5.** pithy **10.** meaningful
 openings (tiny) . . **6.** porous
 sand . . **7.** arenose **8.** sabulous
 substance . . **5.** meaty
 suffix . . **3.** ose
 thorns . . **6.** briary
 vigor . . **5.** lusty
fulness, fullness . . . **4.** much **7.** orotund,
pleroma, satiety, surfeit **9.** abundance,
greatness, plenitude, repletion,
resonance **10.** perfection
12. completeness
fulsome . . . **3.** bad, fat **4.** base, foul, full
5. nasty, plump, suave **7.** copious,
overfed **8.** abundant **9.** offensive,
overgrown, repulsive **10.** disgusting
Fulton's Folly . . . **8.** Clermont
fumble . . . **5.** grope **6.** bungle, huddle,
mumble **7.** confuse
fume . . . **4.** odor, rage, rant, reek **5.** anger,
smoke, steam, vapor **8.** outburst
10. excitement, exhalation
fun . . . **4.** gell, jest, joke, play **5.** chaff,
sport•**9.** amusement, merriment
function . . . **3.** act, use **4.** duty, rite,
role, work **5.** party **6.** office **7.** calling,
operate, purpose, service **8.** ceremony,
province **10.** providence
function (pert to) . . .
 math . . **4.** sine **6.** cosine
 mind . . **8.** ideation
 social . . **3.** tea
functional . . . **8.** official **9.** operative
11. ceremonious, utilitarian
fund . . . **5.** basis, money **6.** bottom,
supply **7.** capital, provide, revenue
10. foundation, groundwork
fundamental . . . **4.** tone **5.** basal, basic,
vital **7.** basilar, organic, primary, radical
8. original, rudiment **9.** elemental,
essential, principle **10.** elementary
Fundamental Orders (US Hist) . . .
8. document (1639) **12.** Constitution
(first, 1639 Conn)
funds . . . **5.** means **6.** assets, moneys
8. finances
funeral . . . **5.** rites **6.** burial **8.** exequies
9. obsequies **10.** procession
funeral (pert to) . . .
 bell . . **5.** knell

ceremony . . **6.** exequy
hymn, song . . **5.** dirge, éloge, elogy
 7. requiem **8.** threnody
oration, poem . . **5.** elegy
pile . . **4.** pyre
procession . . **6.** exequy **7.** cortege
vase . . **3.** urn
funereal . . . **3.** sad **4.** dark **6.** dismal,
solemn **8.** exequial, mournful
9. dirgelike
fungi . . . **5.** rusts, Uredo **6.** mildew
7. Boletus
fungoid . . . **6.** fungal, fungus
fungus . . . **4.** bunt, mold, rust, smut
5. ergot, morel, uredo **6.** agaric, lichen,
mildew **7.** aminita, blewits, boletus,
geaster, truffle **8.** mushroom, puffball
9. toadstool
fungus, edible . . . **5.** morel **7.** truffle
8. mushroom
funguslike . . . **6.** agaric
funk . . . **4.** kick, odor, rage **5.** panic, smell
(bad), smoke, spark **6.** flinch, fright,
shrink, terror **8.** frighten **9.** cowardice,
touchwood
funnel . . . **4.** cone, flue, pipe, tube
6. hopper **7.** channel
funnel-shaped . . . **8.** choanoid
funny . . . **3.** odd **5.** comic, droll, queer,
witty **7.** comical, rowboat (Eng), strange
8. humorous **9.** eccentric, laughable
fur . . . **3.** fox **4.** mink, pelt, seal, vair
5. coypu, fitch, genet, otter, sable,
skunk **6.** badger, ermine, martin, nutria
7. miniver (anc) **8.** squirrel **10.** chinchilla
fur (pert to) . . .
 collective . . **6.** peltry
 cover . . **4.** pelt **6.** pelage
 garment . . **4.** robe **5.** stole **6.** tippet
 7. pelisse
 tippet . . **8.** palatine
furbish . . . **3.** rub **4.** vamp **5.** clean,
scour **6.** polish **7.** burnish, touch up
8. renovate **9.** embellish
Furies . . . **5.** Dirae **6.** Alecto, ghosts,
Semnae **7.** Erinyes (Erinys), Magaera,
spirits (avenging) **9.** Eumenides,
Tisiphone
Furies, The Three . . . **6.** Alecto
7. Magaera **9.** Tisiphone
furious . . . **5.** angry, hasty **6.** fierce
7. frantic, violent **8.** frenzied, vehement
9. impetuous, turbulent **10.** boisterous,
passionate, tumultuous
11. overwrought
furl . . . **4.** roll, wrap **6.** bundle, inroll
furlough . . . **5.** leave **14.** leave of absence
furnace . . . **4.** etna, kiln, oven **5.** forge,
stove **6.** boiler **7.** caldron, reactor,
rotator, smelter
furnish . . . **3.** fit **4.** bear, give, lend
5. adorn, cater, endow, equip, indue
6. afford, fit out, render, supply
7. appoint, provide
furnishing . . . **7.** fitting **8.** fixtures,
ornament **9.** adornment, apparatus,
furniture, provision **10.** enrichment
furnish with . . .
 funds . . **5.** endow
 meals . . **5.** board, cater
 Mil equipment . . **8.** accoutre

tapestry . . **5.** arras
wings . . **3.** imp
furniture . . . **4.** Adam **5.** Eames, Louis,
Phyfe, suite (matched set) **6.** Empire,
graith (obs) **7.** mission **8.** Sheraton,
Stickley **9.** Queen Anne **10.** Directoire
11. Chippendale, Hepplewhite
13. Mediterranean **16.** French
Provincial
furor . . . **4.** fury, rage **5.** anger, craze
6. fervor, flurry, frenzy, furore, tumult
7. madness **10.** excitement, turbulence
furrow . . . **3.** rut **4.** plow **6.** groove,
gutter, trench **7.** channel, wrinkle
furrowed . . . **5.** rutty **6.** rivose **7.** grooved
further . . . **3.** aid, and, new, yet **4.** abet,
more **7.** advance, develop, improve,
promote, remoter, thither **10.** additional
furtherance . . . **3.** aid **4.** help **6.** relief,
succor **8.** progress **9.** promotion
11. advancement, development
furtherer . . . **7.** abettor **8.** promoter
furthermore . . . **3.** and, yet **4.** then
5. again **7.** au reste, besides
8. moreover **10.** in addition
12. additionally
furtive . . . **3.** sly **4.** wary **6.** covert, secret,
sneaky, stolen **8.** skulking, stealthy
9. deceitful **11.** clandestine
fury . . . **3.** ire **4.** rage **5.** anger, wrath
6. frenzy **7.** madness **8.** violence
10. excitement, turbulence
13. desperateness

Fury . . . **6.** Erinys, Spirit (avenging)
7. Atropos
furze . . . **4.** Ulex, whin **5.** gorse, shrub
fuse . . . **4.** flux, frit (partly), melt
5. blend, smelt, unite **6.** anneal, mingle,
solder **7.** combine, liquefy **8.** dissolve
9. detonator
fusee . . . **5.** flair, torch **6.** signal
fusion . . . **5.** alloy, blend, union **7.** melting,
mixture, nuclear **8.** fluidity **9.** coalition
fuss . . . **3.** ado **4.** spat, to-do **5.** busle
6. bother, bustle, pother, tumult
7. bombast, dispute, quarrel, trouble
8. brouhaha **9.** confusion
fussy . . . **7.** finical **8.** overnice
10. fastidious, meticulous
fustian . . . **4.** rant **5.** cloth, tumid
7. bombast, pompous **8.** claptrap,
inflated **9.** bombastic, worthless
fustic . . . **3.** dye **5.** amber, morin
7. dyewood
futile . . . **4.** idle, vain **6.** otiose **7.** trivial
8. hopeless **11.** ineffectual
futility . . . **8.** nugacity **10.** invalidity
11. uselessness **12.** bootlessness
future . . . **3.** yet **4.** to be **5.** later, still,
tense **6.** fiancé **8.** expected, intended
9. hereafter **11.** prospective
fuzzy . . . **5.** downy, hairy **6.** fluffy
7. blurred, frizzly **9.** imperfect
10. indistinct
fyke . . . **3.** net **6.** bag net
fylfot . . . **8.** swastika **9.** gammadion

G

G . . . **4.** tone (scale) **6.** letter (7th)
gab . . . **3.** lie **4.** mock, talk **5.** boast,
mouth, prate, scoff, taste **6.** tongue
7. chatter, deceive **9.** utterance
gabardine . . . **6.** cotton, woolen
gabble . . . **4.** chat **6.** babble, jabber,
mumble **7.** chatter **8.** nonsense
gabelle . . . **3.** tax **5.** likin (imports)
6. excise, impost
gaberdine . . . **4.** gown **5.** frock **6.** mantle
7. garment (loose) **8.** covering, pinafore
9. gabardine
gable . . . **4.** roof (part) **7.** aileron (half)
8. pediment
gablock . . . **4.** gaff, spur **5.** spear **6.** gaffle
7. crowbar **8.** gavelock
Gabon, Africa . . .
capital . . **10.** Libreville
Gabriel (pert to) . . .
astrology . . **10.** moon spirit
New Test . . **6.** herald **11.** good tidings
Old Test . . **5.** angel
tradition . . **9.** archangel (one of seven),
messenger
gaby . . . **4.** fool **9.** simpleton
gad . . . **3.** bar, God (oath), rod **4.** goad,
roam, rove, whip **5.** ingot, spear, staff
6. billet, chisel, wander **7.** on the go,
run wild, traipse (trapes) **8.** gadabout

9. gallivant
Gad (pert to) . . .
Bib . . **7.** prophet
deity (Bib) . . **7.** Fortune
father . . **5.** Jacob
tribe . . **6.** Gadite, Israel (one of seven)
gadabout . . . **3.** gad **6.** roving **7.** dogcart,
gadding, on the go
Gaddang, Gaddan . . . **7.** Malayan
8. language (Indonesia)
gadfly . . . **6.** botfly, insect **8.** horsefly
gadget . . . **6.** device, jigger **7.** gimmick
8. gimcrack **11.** contrivance,
thingumajig
Gadsden Purchase (1853) . . . **5.** tract
7. Arizona **9.** New Mexico
gadwall . . . **4.** duck
Gaea, Gaia . . . **12.** Earth Goddess
Gael . . . **4.** Celt, Kelt, Manx, Scot
10. Highlander
Gaelic (pert to) . . .
for John . . **3.** Ian
hero . . **6.** Ossian
language . . **4.** Erse
native . . **4.** Erse **5.** Irish **6.** Celtic, Keltic,
Scotch
pagan god . . **5.** Dagda (harpist)
sea god . . **3.** Ler
spirit . . **7.** banshee

warriors .. **7.** Fenians
gaff ... **4.** hoax, hook, scam, spar, spur,
talk **5.** fraud, spear, trick **6.** deceit,
fleece, gamble **7.** chatter, prating
8. trickery **9.** spearhead
gaffer ... **4.** hick, rube **6.** old man
11. electrician (TV)
gag ... **4.** hoax, joke **5.** choke, retch
7. closure, prevent, shackle **8.** obstruct,
one-liner, restrain, silencer **9.** imposture
10. instrument **13.** interpolation
gage, gauge ... **4.** rule, test **5.** scale
6. device, pledge **7.** measure **8.** capacity,
defiance, diameter (firearm), mortgage,
security **9.** challenge **11.** measurement
gaggle ... **5.** flock (geese), group (women)
6. cackle
gaiety, gayety ... **4.**, **glee, show 5.** mirth
6. finery **7.** jollity **8.** vivacity **9.** festivity,
merriment, showiness **10.** liveliness
12. colorfulness, conviviality
gain ... **3.** get, net, win **4.** earn, pelf,
reap **5.** booty, clear, lucre, reach
6. attain, come by, obtain, profit,
secure, trover **7.** acquire, benefit,
procure, realize **8.** addition, arrive at,
increase **9.** advantage **11.** acquisition
12. accumulation **13.** amplification
gainsay ... **4.** deny **6.** forbid, impugn,
oppose, refute **7.** dispute **10.** contradict,
controvert
gait ... **3.** run, way **4.** lope, pace, trip,
trot, walk **5.** amble, order, strut, tread
6. canter, gallop **8.** slowness, velocity
gaiter ... **4.** boot, spat **5.** strad **6.** puttee
7. legging **8.** overshoe **11.** galligaskin
gala ... **4.** fete, pomp **6.** festal, fiesta,
gaiety **8.** festival **9.** festivity
11. celebration
Galago ... **5.** lemur
Galahad's quest ... **9.** Holy Grail
Galatea ... **7.** heroine **8.** sea nymph
9. Pygmalion (sculptor) **11.** shepherdess
galaxy ... **6.** throng **8.** Milky Way
10. assemblage **11.** celebrities
gale ... **4.** gust, wind **5.** storm **8.** outburst
9. hurricane
galea ... **6.** helmet
galeate ... **12.** helmet-shaped
Galen (Gr) ... **9.** physician
Galilean (pert to) ...
province .. **9.** Palestine
religion .. **9.** Christian
town .. **4.** Cana **8.** Tiberias
gall ... **3.** vex **4.** bile, fret **5.** annoy, chafe,
grate, spite **6.** bitter, harass, rancor
8. irritate **9.** impudence, secretion,
virulence
gallant ... **4.** hero **5.** dandy, lover, noble,
spark, swain **6.** escort, suitor **7.** stately
8. cavalier, cicisbeo **9.** attentive,
courteous **10.** chivalrous, courageous
gallantry ... **7.** bravery, courage, display
8. courtesy **9.** courtship **11.** intrepidity
galleon ... **6.** vessel (sailing)
gallery ... **3.** poy **4.** hall **5.** salon
6. dedans, loggia, museum **7.** passage,
veranda **8.** audience, corridor, platform
9. promenade **10.** ambulatory
11. observatory
galley ... **4.** boat, tray **6.** vessel

7. caboose, caravel (caravelle),
dromond, kitchen **8.** cookroom
galley, Roman ...
one-bank oared .. **7.** unireme
two-bank oared .. **6.** bireme
three-bank oared .. **7.** trireme
six-bank oared .. **7.** hexeris
slave .. **5.** rower **6.** drudge
Gallic ... **4.** Gaul **6.** French
Gallic chariot ... **5.** essed
gallimaufry ... **4.** hash, olio, stew
6. jumble, medley, ragout **9.** potpourri
10. hodgepodge
gallipot ... **6.** vessel (Medit) **8.** druggist
gallo ... **7.** rooster **12.** fighting cock
gallop ... **3.** run **4.** lope, ride **6.** canter
7. tantivy
gallopade ... **5.** dance, galop **6.** curvet
gallows humor, like ... **6.** morbid
gam ... **3.** leg **4.** herd **5.** visit **6.** school
Gambia, Africa ...
capital .. **6.** Banjul
gambit ... **4.** move **7.** comment, opening
(chess) **8.** maneuver **9.** launching
10. concession
gamble ... **3.** bet **4.** dice, game, risk
5. stake, wager **6.** chance, exacta,
hazard, plunge **8.** perfecta **9.** speculate,
totalizer **10.** parimutuel, superfecta
11. daily double, uncertainty
gambler ... **5.** shill **7.** sharper
gambol ... **3.** hop **5.** bound, caper, prank
6. cavort, curvet, frolic
Gambrinus (King) ... **6.** brewer (1st)
game ... **4.** lark, play, prey **5.** brave,
dodge, prank, sport **6.** frolic, gamble,
gritty, plucky, quarry **7.** contest, pastime
8. resolute **9.** amusement, diversion
10. courageous
game, ball ... **4.** golf, polo, pool **5.** rugby
6. hockey, pelota, soccer, squash,
tennis **7.** cricket, croquet **8.** baseball,
football **11.** racquetball
game, beans ... **6.** fan-tan **8.** beanbags
game, board ... **4.** keno **5.** bingo, chess,
lotto **7.** pachisi (parchesi) **8.** checkers,
cribbage, Monopoly **10.** backgammon
game, card ... **3.** gin, pam **4.** bank,
faro, skat **5.** pitch, poker, rummy,
whist **6.** bridge, écarté, flinch, hearts
7. bezique, canasta, cassino, old maid,
seven-up
game, club ... **4.** golf **6.** hockey **7.** cricket
game, court ... **6.** pelota, squash, tennis
7. jai alai **9.** badminton
game, parlor ... **5.** jacks **6.** marbles
8. charades, dominoes **11.** tiddlywinks
game plan ... **6.** scheme **8.** strategy
game, ring ... **6.** quoits
gamin ... **3.** tad **4.** serf **6.** urchin
7. mudlark **10.** street Arab
gamut ... **5.** orbit, range **6.** extent
7. compass
gamy ... **4.** game **7.** lustful **8.** sporting
12. high-flavored
gander ... **5.** goose **6.** stroll **9.** simpleton
Gandhi (Hind) ... **6.** Indira, leader
7. Mahatma (Mohandus)
gang ... **3.** mob, set **4.** band, crew, pack,
team, walk (cattle) **5.** group, horde,
sheet (Print), shift **6.** clique **7.** company

9. pasturage
gangling . . . **5.** lanky **9.** spindling
gangrene . . . **5.** decay **6.** slough
  8. necrosis **9.** sphacelus
  13. mortification
gangster . . . **4.** thug **5.** thief **6.** bandit
  7. mobster **8.** criminal, hireling
  9. racketeer
gannet . . . **4.** ibis, Sula **5.** booby, goose,
  solan **6.** gander
gap . . . **3.** col **4.** hole, pass **5.** break,
  chasm, cleft, fault, meuse, shard, space,
  split **6.** breach, hiatus, lacuna, lacune,
  ravine **7.** opening
gaping . . . **5.** agape **6.** chappy **7.** ringent,
  yawning **9.** expectant
garb . . . **5.** array, dress, habit, mufti
  (civilian), style **6.** attire, clothe
  7. apparel, costume, fashion, raiment,
  uniform **8.** clothing **10.** appearance,
  habiliment
garbage . . . **5.** trash, waste **6.** refuse
garbanzo . . . **8.** chickpea
garbed . . . **4.** clad **7.** attired, dressed,
  habited
garble . . . **5.** alloy **6.** mangle **7.** distort,
  falsify, pervert **8.** mutilate
  12. misinterpret, misrepresent,
  sophisticate
garden . . . **3.** bed **4.** yard **5.** hardy, patch
  6. jardin, verger **7.** topiary **8.** outfield
  9. arboretum, cultivate, enclosure,
  herbarium
garden (pert to) . . .
  Berlin . . **10.** Tiergarten
  Bible . . **4.** Eden
  city . . **4.** Kent **6.** Sicily **7.** Chicago
    8. Touraine
  colony . . **5.** Natal
  Colorado . . **9.** of the Gods
  Kansas . . **9.** of the West
  kind of . . **5.** truck **8.** kaleyard **9.** botanical
    10. zoological
  State . . **9.** New Jersey
garden implement . . . **3.** hoe **4.** fork,
  rake **5.** graip, mower **6.** scythe, sickle,
  trowel, weeder
Garfield's assassin . . . **7.** Guiteau
Gargantua (pert to) . . .
  character . . **4.** King (Rabelais romance)
  son . . **10.** Pantagruel (giant)
gargantuan . . . **4.** huge **7.** titanic
garish . . . **5.** gaudy, showy **7.** flighty,
  glaring **8.** dazzling
garland . . . **3.** lei **6.** anadem, circle,
  corona, fillet, rosary, trophy, wreath
  7. chaplet, coronal, festoon **8.** headband
  9. anthology **11.** compilation
garlic . . . **4.** herb, moly **5.** clove **6.** ramson
garment . . . **4.** cape, coat, gown, robe,
  suit, vest, wrap **5.** cloak, dress,
  frock, shift, simar, smock, stole, tunic
  6. coatee, duster **7.** pelisse, raiment,
  surcoat, topcoat **8.** overcoat, vestment
garment (pert to) . . .
  African . . **6.** kaross
  ancient . . **5.** burel
  Arab . . **3.** aba
  clerical . . **3.** alb **5.** amice **6.** chimer
    7. cassock, zimarra **8.** surplice
  cover . . **5.** apron **8.** overalls, pinafore

9. coveralls
  Eskimo . . **5.** parka
  Jewish . . **5.** ephod
  knight's . . **6.** tabard
  patchwork . . **5.** cento
  thin . . **8.** gossamer
garner . . . **4.** reap **5.** amass, store **6.** gather
  7. collect **10.** accumulate
garnet . . . **3.** gem, red **5.** color **6.** aplome,
  pyrope **7.** olivine (green) **8.** cinnamon
  (stone), essonite (yellow), melanite
  (black) **9.** almandine (almandite, dark
  red), uvarovite (green)
garnish . . . **4.** trim **5.** adorn **6.** attach,
  bedeck **7.** fetters **8.** decorate, ornament
garnishment . . . **4.** lien **7.** summons
  8. ornament **10.** attachment, decoration
garret . . . **4.** loft **5.** attic **6.** turret **8.** cockloft
  10. watchtower
garrot . . . **9.** goldeneye (duck)
  10. tourniquet
garrote, garrotte . . . **8.** strangle
  9. execution **10.** throttling
  13. strangulation
garrulous . . . **5.** gabby, wordy **6.** chatty
  7. diffuse **9.** talkative **10.** loquacious
gas . . . **4.** brag, talk **5.** vapor **6.** poison
  7. chatter **8.** gasoline, nonsense
  10. anesthesia, asphyxiate, illuminant
  11. anesthetize
gas . . . **3.** air **4.** neon **5.** argon,
  ether, ozone, radon, xenon **6.** arsine,
  butane, ethane, helium, ketene, nebula
  (luminous), oxygen **7.** methane
  8. chlorine, cyanogen, etherion,
  hydrogen, nitrogen **9.** butadiene
gascon . . . **7.** boaster **8.** braggart
  11. braggadocio **12.** swashbuckler
gasconade . . . **4.** brag **5.** boast **7.** bluster,
  bravado **11.** fanfaronade, rodomontade
gaseous . . . **4.** smog, thin **5.** smoke
  7. tenuous **8.** vaporous
  13. unsubstantial
gash . . . **3.** cut **5.** cleft, notch, sever,
  slash **6.** furrow, gossip, injury, tattle
  8. incision
gasp . . . **3.** say **4.** pant, yawn **5.** utter
  7. breathe
gasping . . . **5.** agasp **7.** panting
gastropod . . . **4.** slug **5.** Harpa, Murex,
  Oliva, snail, whelk **6.** Nerita, volute
  7. abalone, mollusk **8.** sea snail
gat . . . **3.** gun, rod **7.** channel, passage
  8. revolver
gate . . . **3.** dar **4.** door, hole, pass **5.** start
  (racing), toran, valve **6.** defile, portal
  7. barrier, opening, postern **8.** Lion-
  Gate **9.** floodgate, turnstile **10.** Needle's
  Eye (Jerusalem), portcullis
gateau . . . **4.** cake
gather . . . **4.** bale, brew, fold, meet, reap
  5. amass, glean, pleat, rally, shirr
  6. bundle, deduce, garner, muster,
  pucker **7.** acquire, collect, compile,
  convene, convoke, harvest, procure,
  suppose **8.** assemble **10.** accumulate
gatherer, collector of . . .
  coins . . **11.** numismatist
  money . . **5.** miser
  news . . **8.** reporter **10.** journalist
  stamps . . **11.** philatelist

gathering . . . **3.** sum **4.** stag **5.** crowd, party, troop **6.** galaxy, smoker **7.** abscess, meeting **8.** swelling **10.** assemblage, harvesting **11.** contraction **12.** accumulation, congregation **14.** conglomeration

gaucho . . . **6.** cowboy (pampas) **8.** herdsman, horseman

gaucho weapon . . . **4.** bola

gaud . . . **4.** jest, joke **5.** adorn, fraud, paint, sport, trick **6.** finery, flashy, gewgaw **7.** trinket **8.** artifice, ornament

gaudy . . . **4.** fine, loud **5.** cheap, feast, showy **6.** flashy, flimsy, garish, tawdry, tinsel **7.** glaring, trinket **9.** flaunting **11.** pretentious **12.** meretricious, ostentatious **13.** overdeveloped

gaufre . . . **4.** iron (waffle) **6.** waffle

gauge, gage . . . **4.** norm, rate, rule, size **5.** judge, scale, value **6.** assess **7.** measure **8.** estimate

gauge (pert to) . . .
airplane . . **10.** tachometer
distance . . **10.** micrometer
miles . . **8.** odometer
pointer . . **3.** arm
rain . . **8.** udometer
velocity . . **11.** speedometer
wind . . **10.** anemometer

Gaul . . . **5.** Aedui **6.** France, Gallia **9.** Frenchman

Gauls . . . **4.** Remi **5.** Celts, Cymry

gaunt . . . **4.** bony, lank, lean, thin, ugly **5.** spare **7.** haggard **8.** desolate

gauntlet . . . **4.** cuff **5.** armor (part), glove **7.** bandage

gaur . . . **2.** ox **5.** gayal **7.** buffalo

gauss . . . **4.** unit (Elec)

Gauss . . . **13.** mathematician

Gaussian curve, like a . . . **10.** bell-shaped

gauze . . . **4.** haze, leno **5.** crape, lisse, marli (marly) **6.** barege, filter, tissue **8.** dressing

gauze film on wine . . . **8.** beeswing

gavage . . . **7.** feeding

gave . . . see *give*

Gavia . . . **4.** loon

gavial . . . **11.** crocodilian

gaw . . . **4.** gape **5.** drain **6.** trench

gawk . . . **4.** dolt, gowk, left, lout **5.** booby, stare **9.** simpleton

gawky . . . **6.** clumsy, cuckoo, stupid **7.** awkward, foolish **8.** clownish

gay . . . **4.** airy, glad **5.** drunk, gaudy, jolly, merry, riant, showy **6.** blithe, cheery, jovial, joyful, joyous, lively **7.** dashing, festive, gleeful **8.** cheerful, colorful, rory-tory, sportive **9.** convivial, sprightly, vivacious **10.** frolicsome, profligate **12.** lighthearted

gay time . . . **4.** lark **5.** spree **8.** jamboree

gazabo, gazebo . . . **4.** cony **6.** rabbit, turret **7.** balcony, blunder, whopper **11.** summerhouse

gaze . . . **3.** con, eye **4.** gape, look, moon, peer, pore, scan **5.** glare, gloat, stare **6.** glower, regard

gazelle . . . **3.** ahu, goa **4.** admi, cora, dama, kudu, mohr, oryx **5.** ariel, brown, korin **7.** chikara (4-horn), corinne, dibatag **8.** antelope **9.** springbok

gazette . . . **7.** journal, publish **8.** announce **9.** newspaper **15.** Arkansas Gazette (1819)

gazetteer . . . **7.** newsman **9.** newspaper **10.** dictionary

gear . . . **3.** cam, rig **5.** equip, goods, tools, wheel **6.** things **7.** baggage, conform, harness, rigging **8.** adjust to, clothing, cogwheel, garments **9.** equipment, mechanism, trappings, vestments **10.** appliances, implements

gecko . . . **6.** lizard **7.** tarente

geese . . . **5.** brant, quink, solan

geese (pert to) . . .
fat . . **6.** axunge
flock . . **4.** raft **6.** gaggle
formation . . **3.** vee
genus . . **4.** Chen **5.** Anser **6.** Branta

gecko . . . **6.** lizard

Geisel . . . **7.** Dr Seuss (pseud)

gelatin, gelatine . . . **4.** agar, food, jell **5.** jelly **6.** collin **7.** protein **8.** agar-agar

gelid . . . **3.** icy **4.** cold **6.** frozen

gem . . . **4.** jade, onyx, opal, ruby, sard, type **5.** agate, beryl, bijou, jewel, pearl, stone, topaz **6.** garnet, ligure, spinel, zircon **7.** cat's-eye, diamond, emerald, jacinth **8.** amethyst, hawk's-eye, sapphire **9.** carnelian, moonstone **10.** aquamarine **11.** alexandrite, lapis lazuli **12.** star sapphire

gem (pert to) . . .
artificial . . **5.** paste
base . . **5.** culet
carver . . **8.** lapidary
Egyptian . . **6.** scarab
flaw . . **8.** gendarme
food . . **6.** muffin
imperfect . . **5.** loupe
semiprecious . . **5.** cameo **8.** intaglio
six rays . . **7.** asteria
surface . . **5.** bezel, facet
weight . . **5.** carat
with many facets . . **9.** brilliant

gemel . . . **4.** bars (Her), twin **6.** paired **7.** coupled, doubled

gemsbok . . . **4.** goat, oryx **7.** chamois

Gem State . . . **5.** Idaho

gendarme . . . **4.** blue, flaw (gem) **5.** guard **6.** police **7.** officer, soldier, trooper **9.** policeman **10.** cavalryman

gender . . . **3.** sex **5.** breed, genus **7.** grammar (term) **8.** engender

genealogy . . . **4.** tree **5.** order (of descent) **6.** family **7.** account, history, lineage, peerage, progeny **8.** pedigree, register **9.** offspring

genealogy of the gods . . . **8.** theogony

gener . . . **8.** son-in-law

general . . . **5.** gross, usual, vague, whole **6.** common, public **7.** officer **8.** catholic, communal **9.** extensive, prevalent, universal, well-known **10.** encyclical, indefinite **11.** approximate

general (pert to) . . .
agreement . . **5.** chief, court
aspect . . **6.** facies
chief . . **6.** Führer, Il Duce **9.** president **10.** Grand Mogul **13.** Generalissimo
court . . **5.** Synod
direction . . **5.** tenor, trend **6.** course

favor.. **7.** popular **10.** popularity
feature.. **5.** motif
group.. **8.** ensemble
orders.. **7.** routine
rule.. **5.** canon
summary.. **8.** synopsis
type.. **7.** average
generalize ... **5.** widen **6.** extend, reason, spread **7.** broaden **12.** universalize
General Sherman (pert to) ...
Civil War march.. **15.** Atlanta to the Sea
giant trees.. **8.** sequoias
tree.. **10.** eucalyptus
generate ... **5.** beget, breed, cause **6.** create **7.** develop, produce **8.** engender **9.** originate, procreate, propagate
generation ... **3.** age **7.** descent **8.** lifetime **9.** epigonous (later), formation, genealogy **10.** production **11.** abiogenesis, procreation
generosity ... **10.** liberality **11.** hospitality, magnanimity, munificence
generous ... **4.** free **5.** large **7.** liberal **8.** tolerant **9.** indulgent, plentiful, unstinted **10.** hospitable **11.** magnanimous
genesis ... **4.** Book **5.** birth **6.** origin (of races) **8.** nascency **9.** beginning, ethnology, etymology, inception **10.** generation
genet ... **3.** fur **5.** civet
genethliac ... **5.** stars (influence) **9.** birthdays
genetics term ... **3.** DNA, RNA **4.** gene **8.** dominant, heredity **9.** recessive **10.** chromosome, hereditary **11.** recombinant
Geneva Cross ... **8.** Red Cross
genial ... **4.** warm **5.** bland **6.** jovial, kindly **7.** amiable, festive, nuptial **8.** cheerful, friendly, pleasant **9.** expansive **10.** enlivening
geniculate ... **5.** kneel
genie ... **4.** jinn **6.** genius
genius ... **5.** deity, jinni **6.** talent **7.** ability, prodigy **9.** endowment (supreme) **11.** inspiration **12.** intelligence
Genoa lace ... **4.** tape **6.** bobbin **7.** macramé **13.** gold and silver
genos ... **4.** clan, gens, race
genre ... **3.** art (style) **4.** kind, sort **5.** genus **6.** gender **7.** species **8.** category
genteel ... **6.** polite **7.** refined **8.** wellborn, well-bred
Gentiles ... **6.** goyims **10.** Christians, non-Moslems **14.** non-Mohammedans
gentle ... **4.** calm, easy, meek, mild, soft, tame **5.** bland, quiet **6.** docile, humane, kindly, tender **7.** amabile (Mus), clement, genteel, refined, subdued **8.** moderate, peaceful, soothing, tranquil, wellborn **9.** courteous, honorable, temperate, tractable **10.** chivalrous **11.** considerate **13.** compassionate
gentleman ... **3.** sir **6.** knight **7.** esquire, shoneen (would-be), younker **8.** nobleman
gentleness ... **6.** lenity **8.** elegance,

leniency, meekness, softness **9.** lightness **10.** kindliness, moderation **11.** genteelness
genuflect ... **5.** kneel **6.** curtsy
genuine ... **4.** pure, real, true **5.** frank, pucka (pukka) **7.** germane, sincere **8.** existent **9.** authentic, simon-pure, unalloyed, veritable **10.** unaffected **13.** unadulterated
genus ... **4.** kind, sort **5.** class, order
genus, animal life ...
animals (one-celled).. **6.** Amoeba **8.** Protozoa **9.** Rhizopoda
ants.. **6.** Eciton
apes.. **5.** Simia
armadillos.. **9.** Glyptodon
auks.. **4.** Alle
bears.. **5.** Ursus
bees (honey).. **4.** Apis
beetles.. **10.** Coleoptera
birds.. **7.** Ratitae
bivalve mollusks.. **6.** Anomia **8.** Estheria
bugs (long-legged).. **5.** Emesa
cats.. **5.** Felis
cattle.. **3.** Bos
crabs.. **4.** Maia
dogs.. **5.** Canis
ducks.. **3.** Aix **4.** Anas **7.** Harelda **8.** Clangula
elks.. **5.** Alces
fish.. **6.** Cybium, Remora **7.** Girella, Muraena
flies.. **6.** Asilus **8.** Glossina (tsetse)
frogs.. **4.** Rana **5.** Anura **8.** Amphibia **9.** Batrachia
geese.. **4.** Chen **5.** Anser
goats.. **5.** Capra
gulls.. **4.** Xema
herons.. **7.** Egretta
hogs.. **3.** Sus
horses.. **5.** Equus
insects.. **10.** Coleoptera
lemurs.. **6.** Galago
lizards.. **3.** Uta **5.** Agama
mammals.. **4.** Homo
Man.. **11.** Homo sapiens
marten.. **7.** Mustela
mice.. **3.** Mus
monkeys (spider).. **6.** Ateles
moose.. **5.** Alces
moths.. **5.** Tinea
oysters.. **6.** Ostrea
peacocks.. **4.** Pavo
pigeons (crowned).. **5.** Goura
porcupines.. **7.** Hystrix
porpoise.. **4.** Inia
rats.. **6.** Spalax
roadrunners.. **9.** Geococcyx
scorpions.. **4.** Nepa
seabirds.. **4.** Sula
sloths.. **11.** Megatherium
slugs.. **5.** Arion
snails.. **5.** Mitra **6.** Nerita, Triton **8.** Geophila
snakes.. **4.** Eryx (sand) **7.** Ophidia
spiders.. **7.** Agalena
squirrels.. **7.** Sciurus
swans.. **4.** Olar **6.** Cygnus
ticks.. **6.** Ixodes
tortoises.. **4.** Emys
turkeys.. **9.** Meleagris

wasps . . **5.** Vespa
whales . . **4.** Orca **5.** Areta **9.** Sibbaldus (blue)
genus, plant life . . .
algae (blue-green) . . **10.** Gloeocapsa
apple trees . . **5.** Malus
cabbage . . **3.** Cos
currant . . **5.** Ribes
elms . . **5.** Ulmus
evergreen, heaths . . **5.** Erica
fern . . **6.** Anemia
fungi . . **7.** Boletus **10.** geoglossum
grasses . . **3.** Poa (blue) **5.** Avena **6.** Elymus **7.** Setaria
herbs . . **4.** Arum **6.** Asarum, Asitis (mustard), Cassia, Seseli **7.** Hedeoma, Linaria **8.** Solidago
holly . . **4.** Ilex
ipecac . . **4.** Evea
ivy . . **11.** Hedera helix
lily . . **7.** Bessera
maples . . **4.** Acer
olives . . **4.** Olea
orchids . . **5.** Vanda **7.** Listera
palms . . **5.** Areca, Assai **6.** Bacaba
poplar . . **5.** Alamo
rhubarb . . **5.** Rheum
vines (woody) . . **6.** Hedera
geode . . . **3.** vug (vugg, vugh, voog) **5.** druse **6.** nodule
geological (pert to) . . .
division . . **3.** eon, era
era . . **6.** Eocene **7.** Miocene **8.** Cenozoic, Mesozoic **9.** Paleozoic **11.** Archaeozoic
period . . **4.** Dyas, Lias **5.** Trias
prelife . . **5.** Azoic
zone (fossil) . . **6.** assise
geologist . . . **6.** Strabo (anc Gr) **8.** geognost **12.** mineralogist
geometric (pert to) . . .
angle . . **9.** incidence
axis . . **8.** abscissa
contact . . **10.** osculation
curve . . **6.** spiral **7.** evolute
pottery . . **7.** Dipylon (anc)
geometric figure . . . **4.** cone, cube, lune **5.** prism **6.** gnomon, oblong, square **7.** hexagon, octagon, polygon, rhombus **8.** heptagon, pentagon, triangle **9.** rectangle, trapezoid **10.** quadrangle **13.** parallelogram
geometric proposition (pert to) . . .
ratio . . **2.** pi (3.1416)
surface . . **4.** tore **5.** nappe
term . . **4.** sine **5.** locus **6.** secant **7.** tangent **11.** asses' bridge
geometry (pert to) . . .
figure . . **6.** conoid **9.** ellipsoid **10.** paraboloid
mathematician . . **6.** Euclid, Pascal
proposition . . **6.** porism
geoponic . . . **5.** rural **6.** rustic
Georgia . . .
capital . . **7.** Atlanta
city . . **5.** Macon **7.** Augusta **8.** Columbus, Marietta, Savannah **9.** Brunswick
holiday . . **10.** Georgia Day (Feb 12)
memorial . . **11.** Warm Springs **16.** Little White House (FDR)
mountain . . **7.** Lookout **9.** Blue Ridge **11.** Alleghenies

peak . . **9.** High Point **13.** Brasstown Bald
river . . **8.** Savannah, Suwannee
settler (1st) . . **10.** Oglethorpe
State admission . . **6.** Fourth
State nickname . . **5.** Peach **7.** Cracker **16.** Empire of the South
swamp . . **10.** Okefenokee
Georgian of the Caucasus . . . **4.** Svan
georgic . . . **4.** poem (rural)
geosphere . . . **5.** earth
Geraint, Sir . . . **6.** Knight (Round Table)
germ . . . **3.** bud **4.** ovum, seed **5.** spore **6.** embryo, origin **7.** microbe **8.** bacteria (pl) **9.** bacterium **13.** microorganism
germ (free) . . . **7.** aseptic **10.** antiseptic
German (pert to) . . . *see also Germany*
air force . . **9.** Luftwaffe
art . . **5.** kunst
art movement . . **13.** Sturm und Drang
article . . **3.** das, der, ein
battleship . . **8.** Graf Spee
beverage . . **5.** lager
book . . **4.** buch, heft
cake . . **5.** torte
castle . . **7.** schloss
Christmas . . **11.** Weihnachten
dance . . **9.** allemande
deity . . **5.** Donar (thunder)
drinking salute . . **6.** prosit
folklore . . **5.** gnome **6.** kobold
guild member . . **13.** Meistersinger
gun . . **9.** Big Bertha
hail . . **4.** heil
highway . . **8.** autobahn
language . . **7.** Deutsch
league . . **4.** Bund **6.** Verein **9.** Hanseatic **10.** Turnverein
letter . . **4.** rune
lyric poems . . **6.** lieder
mister . . **4.** Herr
ox (wild) . . **4.** urus
parliament . . **9.** Bundestag, Reichstag (formerly)
people . . **5.** Goths, Quadi **6.** Franks, Saxons **7.** Teutons, Vandals **8.** Lombards **9.** Prussians **10.** Herminones
police . . **7.** Gestapo
prison camp . . **6.** stalag
ruler . . **6.** kaiser
society . . see *league (above)*
song . . **4.** lied
teacher . . **6.** docent **12.** privatdocent
title . . **3.** Von **4.** Graf, Herr **6.** Ritter
tribal group . . **3.** gau
vowel change . . **6.** umlaut
wheat . . **5.** spelt
wine . . **4.** hock, wein **5.** Rhine **7.** Moselle (Mosel) **8.** Riesling **11.** Niersteiner
woman . . **4.** frau **8.** fraulein
yes . . **2.** ja
germane . . . **4.** akin **6.** allied **7.** kindred **8.** relevant **11.** appropriate
Germanic language . . . **5.** Dutch **6.** Danish, German, Gothic **7.** English, Frisian, Swedish, Yiddish **8.** Old Norse **9.** Icelandic, Norwegian
German people (famed) . . .
actor . . **8.** Jannings (Emil)
archaeologist . . **10.** Schliemann
artist . . **5.** Dürer, Ernst, Grosz **8.** Kollwitz

9. Friedrich
astrologer . . **5.** Faust
astronomer . . **5.** Galle **6.** Kepler
author . . **4.** Böll, Mann **5.** Grass,
  Grimm, Hesse, Kafka, Zweig **6.** Goethe
  7. Fontane, Wieland **8.** Brentano
auto engineer . . **4.** Benz **5.** Bosch
  6. Diesel **7.** Daimler, Porsche
bacteriologist . . **4.** Koch (Nobel Prize,
  1905)
chemist . . **5.** Haber **6.** Bunsen, Liebig
composer . . **4.** Bach **5.** Gluck, Weber
  (Carl Maria) **6.** Handel, Schütz,
  Wagner **8.** Schumann **9.** Beethoven
  11. Stockhausen
dramatist . . **6.** Brecht, Kleist **7.** Lessing
  8. Schiller **9.** Hauptmann, Sudermann
Egyptologist . . **5.** Ebers
general . . **6.** Moltke, Rommel **7.** Steuben
  (Rev War) **10.** Hindenburg, Ludendorff
geographer . . **6.** Ritter
Gestapo chief . . **7.** Himmler
goldsmith (anc) . . **5.** Faust
hero . . **8.** Arminius
historian . . **4.** Dahn **5.** Ranke **7.** Meineke,
  Mommsen **8.** Spengler
industrialist . . **5.** Krupp
leader . . **7.** Bismark, Wilhelm (William)
  9. Frederick (the Great) **10.** Hindenburg
mathematician . . **5.** Gauss
military expert . . **10.** Clausewitz
mystic . . **5.** Bohme **7.** Eckhart (Meister)
naturalist . . **8.** Humboldt **9.** Ehrenberg
neurologist . . **11.** Krafft-Ebing
pathologist . . **6.** Eberth
philologist . . **5.** Grimm, Heyne
philosopher . . **4.** Kant, Marx **5.** Hegel
  6. Engels, Fichte, Herder **7.** Liebniz
  8. Schlegel **9.** Feuerbach
  12. Schopenhauer
physicist . . **3.** Ohm **5.** Weber (Wilhelm)
  6. Planck **10.** Fahrenheit
poet . . **5.** Heine, Rilke **6.** Goethe
  9. Holderlin
president (first) . . **5.** Ebert
socialist . . **10.** Liebknecht
sociologist . . **5.** Weber (Max)
teller of tall tales . . **10.** Munchausen
  (Baron)
theologian . . **6.** Luther
Germany . . .
capital . . **6.** Berlin
capital, former . . **4.** Bonn (W Ger)
  6. Berlin (E Ger)
city . . **5.** Essen, Halle, Mainz **6.** Bremen
  7. Cologne, Dresden, Hamburg, Leipzig,
  Munster **9.** Frankfurt, Nuremberg,
  Stuttgart
coal region . . **4.** Ruhr, Saar
lake . . **8.** Konstanz (Constance)
mountain range . . **4.** Harz
mountain region . . **11.** Black Forest
  (Schwarzwald)
Nazi state . . **10.** Third Reich
region, annexed . . **7.** Sudeten
  (Sudetenland)
region, state . . **6.** Anhalt, Saxony
  7. Bavaria, Hanover, Prussia **8.** Saarland
  9. Rhineland, Thuringia **10.** Palatinate,
  Westphalia
republic . . **6.** Weimar

river . . **4.** Elbe, Main, Oder **5.** Rhine,
  Weser **6.** Danube, Neisse **7.** Moselle
  (Mosel)
secondary school . . **9.** gymnasium
germicide . . . **6.** iodine (iodin), phenol
  10. antiseptic **12.** disinfectant
germinate . . . **3.** bud **4.** grow **5.** beget
  6. sprout **7.** develop **8.** vegetate
  10. effloresce
Geronimo . . . **6.** Apache (Chief)
gerrymander (Polit) . . . **6.** divide (unfairly)
  10. manipulate
gesticulation . . . **6.** motion **7.** gesture
gesture . . . **3.** act **4.** gest (geste), sign
  5. sanna **6.** beckon, behave, motion
  7. perform, pretext **8.** carriage (body)
  11. gesticulate **13.** gesticulation
get . . . **3.** pen, win **4.** earn, hear, pain,
  take, trap **5.** beget, fetch, incur, learn
  6. attain, become, derive, induce,
  obtain, profit, secure **7.** achieve,
  acquire, capture, prepare, procure,
  receive **8.** contract, contrive, discover
  9. ascertain, determine **10.** understand
get along . . . **3.** age **4.** fare **5.** hurry
  6. begone, depart, manage, move on
  7. advance, prosper
get around . . . **5.** evade **6.** cajole,
  outwit, spread **7.** deceive **9.** circulate
  10. circumvent
get off . . . **5.** start, utter **6.** alight, depart,
  escape, go free **8.** dismount
get out . . . **4.** exit **5.** scram **6.** elicit,
  escape, reveal **7.** draw out, leak out,
  publish **8.** evacuate **9.** extricate
get over . . . **4.** move **5.** cover **6.** bridge,
  finish **7.** recover **8.** surmount **9.** make
  clear
Ghana, capital of . . . **5.** Accra (Gold
  Coast)
ghastly . . . **3.** wan **4.** grim, pale
  5. lurid **6.** dismal, grisly, pallid
  7. deathly, hideous **8.** gruesome,
  horrible, shocking, terrible **9.** deathlike,
  frightful **10.** cadaverous
ghost . . . **3.** Ker **5.** larva (Rom Relig),
  lemur, shade, spook **6.** daemon,
  spirit, wraith **7.** banshee (banshie),
  eidolon, phantom, specter **8.** phantasm,
  revenant **10.** apparition, glimmering,
  substitute **11.** ghostwriter, poltergeist
ghostly . . . **5.** eerie (eery) **8.** spectral
  9. spiritual
giant . . . **4.** huge, ogre **5.** Titan **6.** afreet,
  nozzle, thurse **7.** monster **8.** colossus
  9. monstrous **10.** gargantuan,
  prodigious, tremendous
giant (pert to) . . .
Biblical . . **7.** Goliath, Rephaim
crafty . . **5.** Cacus
Greek . . **5.** Atlas, Mimas, Titan
  7. Antaeus, cyclops
hundred-armed . . **9.** Enceladus
land, country . . **9.** Utgarthar
  10. Jotunnheim **11.** Brobdingnag
Norse . . **4.** Ymir (Ymer) **5.** Mimir
  6. Jotunn (Jotun) **10.** Utgartha-Loki
one-eyed . . **5.** Arges **7.** Brontes, Cyclops
  10. Polyphemus
primeval . . **4.** Ymir **12.** Utgartha-Loki
Rabelais' . . **9.** Gargantua **10.** Pantagruel

sea god . . **5.** Aegir
seer . . **5.** Mimir
strong . . **6.** Samson, Targan **7.** Antaeus
8. Hercules
Teutonic . . **4.** Wade **5.** Aegir
thousand-armed . . **4.** Bana
three-hundred handed, many-handed . .
8. Briareus
giantess (Teut Myth) . . . **4.** Norn
gibbed . . . **9.** castrated (cat)
gibber . . . **4.** chat, hump, talk (rapid)
5. stone (loose) **6.** mumble **7.** boulder,
chatter **8.** swelling
gibberish . . . **4.** talk **5.** lingo **6.** jargon,
patois, patter **8.** nonsense
gibbet . . . **3.** jib **4.** hang **7.** gallows
9. execution
gibbon . . . **3.** ape, lar **6.** wou-wou
7. hoolock, siamang **10.** anthropoid
gibe . . . **4.** jape, jeer, jibe, quip **5.** fleer,
flirt, flout, scoff, sneer, taunt **6.** heckle
Gibraltar . . .
named for (legend) . . **5.** Gobir
ruled by . . **12.** Great Britain
site . . **5.** Spain (coast)
giddy . . . **4.** reel **5.** dizzy, tipsy, whirl
6. fickle **7.** flighty **8.** gyratory, heedless
9. delirious **14.** scatterbrained
gift . . . **4.** alms, bent, boon, dole, free
5. bribe, grant, knack, token **6.** legacy,
talent **7.** aptness, faculty, largess
(largesse), present **8.** aptitude, blessing,
donation, gratuity **9.** endowment,
lagniappe (lagnappe), readiness
11. serendipity **12.** contribution
gifted . . . **7.** endowed **8.** talented
gigantic . . . **4.** huge **5.** giant, large, titan
7. immense, mammoth **8.** colossal,
enormous **9.** colossean, monstrous
10. prodigious
giggle . . . **5.** laugh (silly), te-hee **6.** tee-hee,
titter **7.** chuckle, snicker, snigger
Gila monster . . . **4.** Gila **6.** lizard
gild . . . **4.** coat, lure **5.** adorn, paint,
tempt **7.** aureate, falsify **8.** brighten
9. embellish
gilding . . . **4.** gilt, gold **6.** ormolu
7. coating **8.** ornament, painting
gill . . . **5.** brook, leach, organ, penny
6. tipple, valley, wattle **7.** measure
10. sweetheart
gimcrackle . . . **3.** fob, toy **5.** showy
6. bauble, gewgaw, paltry, trifle
7. trinket **8.** trumpery, whimwham
15. Jack-of-all-trades
gimlet . . . **3.** awl **4.** tool **5.** drink (mixed)
6. wimble
gimp . . . **5.** orris (upholstery) **6.** fabric,
thread **7.** galloon **8.** fishline, trimming
gin . . . **4.** game, sloe, tool, trap, whim
5. snare, trick **6.** device, liquor, scheme,
thresh **7.** machine **8.** artifice, schnapps
11. contrivance
ginger . . . **3.** pep **5.** color **6.** Asarum,
energy, lively, mettle, spirit
8. pungency, Zingiber **9.** rootstalk
gingerbread . . . **4.** cake **5.** money
6. flimsy, frills, wealth **8.** ornament
(tawdry) **11.** superfluity
gingerly . . . **6.** warily **7.** charily **9.** carefully,
finically, guardedly **10.** cautiously

12. fastidiously
gingham . . . **5.** cloth **8.** umbrella (cheap)
gipsy . . . see *gypsy*
giraffe . . . **5.** okapi **6.** mammal, spinet
10. cameleopard **13.** constellation
girasol, girasole . . . **4.** opal **9.** artichoke,
sunflower
gird . . . **4.** belt, bind, gibe, girt, sill **5.** brace,
equip, scoff, sneer **6.** fasten, girdle,
secure **7.** enclose, environ **8.** surround
10. strengthen
girder . . . **4.** beam **5.** truss **6.** timber
7. support
girdle . . . **3.** obi **4.** band, belt, cest, ring,
sash **6.** cestus, cingle, circle, corset
8. cincture, encircle **10.** cummerbund
girdle bone . . . **12.** sphenethmoid
Girdle of Venus (pert to) . . .
bridal . . **11.** power of love
palmistry line . . **8.** hysteria
11. nervousness
girl . . . **3.** sis **4.** bint, chit, dame, lass,
minx, miss **5.** filly, sissy, skirt **6.** damsel,
female, giglet, hoyden (hoiden), lassie,
maiden, shiver, thrill, tomboy **7.** colleen,
damosel, fillock, ingénue, roebuck
10. sweetheart **11.** maidservant
girlish . . . **4.** pert **5.** sissy **7.** artless
8. immature, maidenly **10.** flapperish
girt . . . **4.** band **6.** fasten, saddle **7.** besiege
9. encircled
girth . . . **4.** band, hoop, size **5.** brace,
strap **6.** girdle, saddle **7.** measure
8. encircle **13.** circumference
gist . . . **3.** nub **4.** core, crux, meat, pith
5. heart, point (main) **7.** essence,
meaning
give . . . **3.** gie **4.** hand **5.** endow, grant,
yield **6.** accord, afford, bestow, confer,
devote, donate, impart, remise, render,
supply **7.** present, proffer, provide
9. attribute, vouchsafe **10.** administer,
elasticity
give (pert to) . . .
and take . . **11.** reciprocity
authority . . **7.** empower
away . . **5.** break, grant, marry, yield
6. bestow, betray **7.** discard, divulge,
succumb **8.** disclose **9.** sacrifice
10. relinquish
back . . **4.** echo **5.** remit **6.** recede,
remand, remise, retire, return
7. replace, restore, retreat
birth to . . **4.** foal **5.** calve **6.** farrow,
mother **9.** originate
expectation . . **7.** promise
forth . . **4.** emit **5.** blaze **6.** afford, exhale
7. publish
information . . **4.** tell **6.** inform, report
7. divulge, publish **8.** disclose
9. advertise
out . . **4.** deal, emit **5.** exude, issue,
print, utter (publicly) **6.** report, weaken
7. declare, publish, release **8.** allocate,
announce **9.** apportion, circulate
10. distribute
prominence . . **4.** star **7.** feature
8. headline
up . . **4.** cede, emit, fail, quit **5.** demit,
waive, yield **6.** betray, disuse, resign,
vacate **7.** abandon, despair, succumb

8. abdicate, part with, renounce, swear off **9.** sacrifice, surrender **10.** capitulate, relinquish

given . . . **5.** dated, datum, fixed **6.** stated **7.** assumed, granted **8.** accorded, addicted, bestowed, inclined, set forth **10.** determined, disposed to

given (pert to) . . .
by word of mouth . . **4.** oral **5.** parol
name . . **7.** surname
particularly . . **9.** specified

given (to) . . .
experiment . . **7.** empiric
expression . . **13.** demonstrative
meditation . . **13.** contemplative
suspicion . . **9.** querulent

giving . . . **6.** ceding **7.** largess (largesse) **9.** bestowing **10.** conferring, liberality **12.** philanthropy, presentation **13.** administering

giving up . . . **8.** yielding **10.** abandoning, despairing **11.** sacrificing **12.** surrendering **13.** relinquishing

glacial (pert to) . . .
deposit . . **6.** placer **7.** moraine
direction . . **5.** stoss (opp to lee)
drift . . **8.** diluvium
dust . . **10.** kryokonite
erosion wall . . **6.** cirque
mill . . **6.** moulin
ridge . . **2.** os (pl osar) **4.** kame (Scot) **5.** esker (eskar)
snow . . **4.** neve

glaciarium . . . **4.** rink (skating)
glacis . . . **5.** slope **7.** incline **13.** fortification
glack . . . **4.** fork (road) **6.** defile, ravine, valley
glad . . . **3.** gay **4.** fain **5.** merry **6.** elated, joyful, joyous **8.** animated, cheering, pleasing **9.** animating, beautiful, delighted, gratified **11.** exhilarated, well-pleased **12.** exhilarating
gladden . . . **5.** cheer, elate **6.** please **7.** gratify
gladdy . . . **12.** yellowhammer
glade . . . **4.** dell, nemo (comb form), vale **5.** laund **6.** valley **8.** clearing **9.** everglade, open space
gladiator . . . **6.** fencer **7.** lanista
gladiator's arena . . . **4.** ludi
gladly . . . **4.** fain, lief **5.** fitly **6.** freely **7.** eagerly, readily **8.** joyfully, properly **9.** willingly **10.** cheerfully, preferably
gladsome . . . **4.** glad **6.** blithe, joyful **7.** festive, jocular, pleased **8.** cheerful
Gladstone . . . **3.** bag (travel) **4.** wine **7.** Liberal (Party) **8.** carriage, Irishman **11.** portmanteau
glad tidings . . . **3.** joy **6.** gospel **7.** evangel
glamorous . . . **8.** alluring, charming **10.** bewitching **11.** fascinating
glance . . . **3.** eye **4.** hint, leer, look, ogle, scry, skew **5.** flash, gleam, glint, touch **6.** allude, signal **7.** glimpse
gland . . . **5.** gonad, liver, lymph, ovary **6.** spleen, thymus **7.** adrenal, carotid, parotid, thyroid **8.** pancreas, salivary **9.** pituitary **10.** suprarenal
gland (pert to) . . .
enlargement . . **6.** ademia
full of . . **7.** adenose

glandlike . . **7.** adenoid **9.** glandular
inflammation . . **8.** adenitis
secretion . . **7.** hormone
tumor . . **7.** adenoma

glaring . . . **5.** clear, plain **6.** bright, garish **7.** evident, flaring, obvious, staring, visible, vividly **8.** apparent, distinct, flagrant, manifest **9.** barefaced **11.** conspicuous

glass . . . **4.** lens, pony **5.** glaze, purex **6.** goblet, liquor, mirror, seidel **7.** binocle, crystal, reflect, tumbler **9.** barometer, binocular, hourglass, telescope **10.** microscope, opera glass **11.** stactometer, thermometer

glass (pert to) . . .
blue . . **5.** smalt
cabinet . . **7.** vitrine
component . . **6.** silica
French for . . **5.** verre
furnace, oven . . **4.** lehr (leer) **5.** bocca, siege, tisar **7.** drosser (part)
jeweler's . . **5.** paste **6.** strass
like . . **6.** vitric **7.** hyaline, hyaloid **8.** vitreous
material . . **4.** frit (fritt)
mineral . . **7.** hyalite **8.** feldspar
molten . . **7.** parison
mosaic . . **7.** tessera
red . . **7.** schmelz (schmelze)
scrap . . **6.** cullet
sheet . . **4.** pane **5.** slide **7.** platten
showcase . . **7.** vitrine
volcanic . . **6.** pumice **8.** obsidian
worker . . **7.** glazier

glass (type of) . . . **3.** cut **4.** milk, spun **5.** crown, plate, Pyrex **6.** ground, safety **7.** Corning, frosted, Lalique, stained, Steuben, Tiffany **8.** Sandwich, Venetian **9.** Waterford **10.** Depression

glass blowing (pert to) . . .
annealing term . . **4.** fuse, heat
glass content . . **4.** sand, zinc **6.** potash, temper **7.** soda ash
oven . . **4.** lehr (leer)
rod . . **5.** punty (pontil)

glass container . . . **3.** jar **4.** vial (phial) **5.** ampul (ampoule, ampule), flask **6.** beaker, bottle, carboy **7.** matrass **8.** test tube

glazier's diamond . . . **5.** emery (emeril)
glazing machine . . . **8.** calender
gleam . . . **3.** ray **4.** glow **5.** flash, glint, gloze, light **7.** glimmer, shimmer **8.** radiance **9.** coruscate **10.** brightness
glean . . . **4.** reap **5.** sheaf (of hemp) **6.** bundle, deduce, gather **7.** collect, harvest, procure
glee . . . **3.** joy **4.** club, song **5.** mirth **7.** delight **8.** pleasure **9.** merriment **12.** cheerfulness
glen . . . **4.** dale, dell, vale **6.** dingle, ravine, valley **10.** depression
glib . . . **4.** easy, oily **5.** suave **6.** facile, fluent, smooth **8.** castrate, flippant, slippery **9.** talkative **10.** loquacious
glide . . . **4.** sail, skid, slip, soar **5.** coast, slide
gliding over . . . **7.** lambent **10.** slithering
glimmer . . . **3.** bit **4.** hint, leam **5.** blink, flash, gleam, glint **7.** glimpse, glitter

10. perception (slight)

glimpse . . . 4. view (quick) 5. flash, tinge, trace 6. glance, luster 7. glimmer, inkling

glisten . . . 5. flash, shine 7. glister, sparkle 9. coruscate

glitter . . . 5. glare, gleam, shine 7. glimmer, glisten, sparkle 9. coruscate, showiness 14. attractiveness

gloaming . . . 4. dusk 8. twilight 9. darkening 11. candlelight

globe . . . 3. map, orb 4. ball, moon 5. earth 6. sphere 10. hemisphere (half)

Globe, The . . . 7. Theater (London, first to play Shakespeare)

globular . . . 5. beady 7. globose 9. orbicular, spherical 10. orbiculate 11. globe-shaped

globule . . . 4. bead, blob, drop, pill, tear 5. minim 6. bubble 8. spherule

glochis . . . 4. hair (barbed) 7. bristle

glockenspiel . . . 4. lyra, stop (organ) 8. carillon 10. instrument

gloom . . . 5. cloud, frown, scowl 7. dimness, sadness 8. darkness 9. dejection, heaviness, obscurity 10. cloudiness, depression, melancholy, sullen look

gloomy . . . 3. dim, sad, wan 4. dark, dour, glum 5. drear, eerie, lurid, moody, murky 6. cloudy, droopy, lowery, morose 7. obscure 8. darkling, dejected, dolesome, downcast 9. darkening, depressed, tenebrous 10. depressing, foreboding, tenebrific 11. pessimistic 12. disheartened

Gloomy Dean . . . 4. Inge

gloomy person . . . 7. killjoy

Gloria . . . 4. rite 8. doxology

glorification . . . 6. praise 7. worship 8. doxology, honoring 9. festivity 10. apotheosis 13. jollification 14. sanctification

glorify . . . 4. laud 5. adore, bless, exalt, extol, honor 6. praise 7. elevate, worship 8. beautify, sanctify 9. celebrate

glorious . . . 3. sri 5. grand, noble 6. elated, superb 7. eminent, radiant 8. ecstatic, renowned, splendid 9. beautiful, hilarious 10. celebrated, delightful 11. illustrious, magnificent, resplendent 12. praiseworthy

glory . . . 4. fame, halo 5. bliss (celestial), boast, éclat, honor 6. heaven, nimbus (cloud of), praise, renown 8. grandeur 10. admiration, brilliancy, effulgence 11. distinction 13. glorification

gloss . . . 4. glow, note 5. color, sheen, shine 6. enamel, luster, polish, remark 7. burnish, comment, pretext 8. glossary, palliate 9. extenuate 10. annotation, brightness, commentary 14. interpretation

gloss over . . . 4. fard (obs), wink 5. blink, color 6. excuse 8. palliate

glossy . . . 5. glacé, nitid, shiny, sleek 6. luster, sheeny, smooth 7. radiant, shining 8. lustrous, polished 10. reflecting

glove . . . 3. mit 4. mitt 5. trank (shaped) 6. boxing, ceatus, mitten 7. gantlet

8. gauntlet 12. mousquetaire

glow . . . 4. burn 5. ardor, flame, flush, glean, shine 6. beauty, redden 7. redness 9. eloquence 10. luminosity 13. incandescence

glower . . . 4. gaze 5. glare, scowl, stare

glowing . . . 3. red 4. warm 5. drunk 6. ardent, cadent 7. burning, excited, fervent, flushed 8. eloquent, luminous 9. beautiful 12. enthusiastic

glucose . . . 5. rutin, sugar 8. dextrose

glue . . . 3. fix 4. join 5. paste, stick 6. adhere, cement, fasten, sizing 7. gelatin 8. adhesive, fastener 9. viscosity

glum . . . 3. sad 5. moody 6. dismal, gloomy, sullen 8. frowning

glut . . . 4. cloy, fill, sate 5. gorge, stuff 6. pamper 7. engorge, satiate, satisfy, surfeit 8. overfill, overload, plethora, saturate

gluten . . . 3. gum 4. glue 6. fibrin 7. gliadin 8. adhesive

glutinous . . . 4. sizy 5. gluey 6. viscid 8. adhesive

glutton . . . 6. rascal, wretch 7. epicure 8. gourmand 9. cormorant, scoundrel, wolverine 11. gormandizer, greedy eater

gluttony . . . 5. greed 7. edacity 8. voracity 12. intemperance 13. voraciousness

glycerine machine man . . . 8. effetman

gnar, gnarr (of dogs) . . . 5. growl, snarl

gnarl . . . 4. knot 5. growl, snarl, twist 6. tangle 7. contort, distort, roughen 10. contortion 12. protuberance (tree)

gnarled . . . 5. rough 6. knotty, rugged 7. complex, knotted, twisted 12. cross-grained

gnash . . . 4. bite 5. grate, grind (teeth)

gnat . . . 3. fly 5. nidge 6. insect 8. mosquito

gnaw . . . 3. eat 4. bite, chew 5. grind, waste 6. rankle 7. corrode 8. wear away

gnede . . . 6. scanty 7. lacking, miserly, sparing

gnib . . . 5. ready, sharp 6. clever

gnome . . . 3. elf, imp, saw 5. bodie, bogey, dwarf, maxim, nisse 6. goblin, kobold, sprite 8. aphorism

gnomic . . . 8. didactic 10. aphoristic

gnomic poets (Gr) . . . 5. Solon 8. Theognis (of Megara) 10. Phocylides (of Miletus)

gnostic . . . 4. wise 6. shrewd 7. knowing 9. sagacious

Gnostic . . . 6. Ophite 7. Abraxas (Abrasax), Sethite

gnu . . . 6. kokoon 8. antelope

go . . . 3. act, die, gae, run 4. fail, fare, game, move, pass, turn, walk, wane, wend, work 5. leave, sally 6. betake, decamp, depart, elapse, embark, energy, extend, result, retire, travel, weaken 7. advance, entrain, journey, proceed 8. continue, diminish, withdraw 9. eventuate, harmonize

go (pert to) . . .
around . . 6. detour 7. circuit 8. surround
ashore . . 4. land 9. disembark

astray . . **3.** err
at . . **6.** attack **9.** undertake
away . . **4.** exit, scat, shoo **5.** scoot,
　scram **6.** begone, depart **9.** disappear
back . . **3.** ebb **6.** recede, repass, retire,
　return, revert
　7. regress, retrace
before . . **7.** precede **8.** antecede
　11. participate
down, under . . **4.** fail, sink **7.** capsize,
　descend, founder, succumb, undergo
　8. submerge **11.** deteriorate
easily . . **4.** lope **5.** amble
furtively . . **5.** steal **6.** tiptoe
over . . **5.** renew **6.** revise **7.** retrace
　8. rehearse, traverse **9.** backtrack,
　re-examine
through . . **4.** pass **5.** spend **6.** suffer
　7. exhaust (fortune), persist, undergo
　9. persevere **10.** experience
up . . **4.** fail, rise **5.** arise, raise **6.** ascend
with . . **4.** suit **5.** agree, court **6.** accord
　8. coincide **9.** accompany
　10. understand
goa . . . **8.** antelope (Tibet)
goad . . . **3.** egg **4.** poke, prod, prog, spur,
　urge **5.** ankus (elephant), decoy, impel,
　prick, sting, thorn, valet (manège)
　6. incite **7.** inflame **8.** irritate, stimulus
　9. incentive
goal . . . **3.** aim, end **4.** base, fate, home,
　mark **5.** bourn (bourne), Mecca, reach,
　score, Thule (Myth) **6.** object **7.** purpose
　9. objective **11.** destination
goanna . . . **6.** iguana, lizard **7.** monitor
goat . . . **4.** buck, dupe **5.** brown **6.** engine,
　lecher **9.** scapegoat **13.** laughingstock
goat (pert to) . . .
　astronomy . . **9.** Capricorn
　fig . . **8.** caprifig
　fish . . **6.** mullet
　get one's . . **3.** irk, vex **4.** rile **5.** pique
　　6. nettle
　god . . **3.** Pan
　haircloth . . **5.** Tibet (Thibet) **6.** camlet
　hair cord (Bedouin) . . **4.** agal
goat (type of) . . . **3.** kid, ram, tur, zac
　4. ibex, tahr, urus **5.** Capra, goral,
　pasan (pasang), serow, takin **6.** Alpine,
　Angora, chamal, Jemlah, mammal
　7. aurochs, markhor **8.** Cashmere,
　ruminant
goatsucker . . . **4.** bird **7.** dorhawk, grinder
　9. nighthawk **12.** whippoorwill
gob . . . **4.** lump, mass **5.** choke, mouth
　6. sailor **8.** mouthful, quantity
goby . . . **4.** fish, mapo
go-by . . . **4.** snub **7.** evasion, passing
　13. circumvention
god (Myth, Relig) . . .
　Babylonian . . **2.** Zu **3.** Anu, Sin **4.** Adad,
　　Enzu, Nama, Nebo (Nebu) **5.** Aruru,
　　Cirru, Dagan, Nintu **8.** Ningirsu
　　10. Ninkhursag **11.** Ningishzida
　Celtic . . **6.** Aengus
　Cymric . . **4.** Lleu (Llew)
　Egyptian . . **2.** Ra **3.** Bes, Dis, Geb
　　(Keb), Min, Seb **4.** Amen, Amon, Ptah
　　5. Horus, Thoth **6.** Dhouti, Osiris
　false . . **4.** Baal, idol **6.** Mammon
　Greek . . **4.** Ares, Zeus **5.** Comus, Hymen,

Momus, Pluto **6.** Hermes, Somnus
　7. Bacchus **8.** Dionysus
　Hebrew . . **6.** Yahweh (Jahveh, Jahweh,
　　Yahveh)
　Hindu . . **4.** Agni, Deva, Kama, Siva
　　(Shiva) **6.** Varuna
　household . . **3.** Lar **5.** Lares **6.** Penate
　Irish . . **5.** Dagda (pagan)
　love of, for . . **5.** piety **6.** bhakti
　　9. theophile
　Muslim . . **5.** Allah
　Norse . . **2.** Er, Ve **3.** Tyr, Ull, Van
　　4. Loki, Odin, Thor, Ymir **5.** Aesir,
　　Donar, Vanir, Wodin
　Roman . . **4.** Jove **5.** Comus, Janus, Orcus
　　7. Bacchus, Mercury **8.** Dis pater
　Semitic . . **5.** Hadad **6.** Nergal
　Supreme . . **3.** Dei, Deo, Dio **4.** Deus,
　　Soul, Zeus **6.** Elohim, Spirit **12.** Infinite
　　Mind, Supreme Being
　Teutonic . . **3.** Tiu **4.** Hoth
god (of) . . .
　agriculture . . **4.** Nebo **6.** Faunus
　beauty . . **6.** Aengus (Oengus)
　beginnings, creation . . **4.** Ptah, Zeus
　　5. Janus **6.** Varuna
　commerce . . **5.** Vanir **7.** Mercury
　darkness, evil . . **3.** Set, Sin **6.** Nergal
　day . . **5.** Horus
　dead . . **5.** Orcus **6.** Osiris
　discord . . **4.** Loki
　earth . . **3.** Geb (Keb), Seb **5.** Dagan
　east wind . . **5.** Eurus
　evil . . **2.** Zu **3.** Set, Sin **6.** Nergal
　fate . . **5.** Moira (Moera)
　fire . . **4.** Agni **5.** Girru **6.** Vulcan
　flocks . . **3.** Pan
　January . . **5.** Janus
　joy . . **5.** Comus
　justice . . **7.** Forseti (Forsete)
　law . . **4.** Zeus
　lightning . . **4.** Agni
　love . . **4.** Amor, Ares, Eros, Kama
　　5. Bhaga, Cupid **6.** Aengus (Oengus)
　March . . **4.** Mars
　marriage . . **5.** Hymen
　medicine . . **11.** Ningishzida
　mountains . . **5.** Atlas **7.** Olympus
　music . . **6.** Apollo
　Northmen . . **5.** Aesir
　oceans . . **7.** Oceanus
　poetry . . **5.** Bragi
　ridicule . . **5.** Momus
　sea . . **7.** Neptune, Proteus
　sky . . **3.** Anu
　sleep, dreams . . **6.** Somnus **8.** Morpheus
　storm . . **2.** Zu **6.** Teshup
　sun . . **2.** Ra (Re) **6.** Apollo, Nergal
　thunder . . **4.** Thor **7.** Jupiter
　Thursday . . **4.** Thor
　Tuesday . . **3.** Tiu, Tyr
　underworld . . **3.** Dis **5.** Pluto **6.** Osiris
　　7. Serapis **8.** Dis pater **11.** Ningishzida
　war . . **3.** Ira, Tyr **4.** Mars **5.** Woden
　　8. Ningirau
　wealth . . **5.** Bhaga **6.** Plutus
　Wednesday . . **5.** Woden
　wind . . **4.** Adad **5.** Eolus, Eurus, Hadad
　　6. Aeolus, zephyr **8.** Favonius
　wine . . **7.** Bacchus **8.** Dionysus
　wisdom . . **4.** Nebo **5.** Thoth **6.** Dhouti

woods.. **7**. Silenus
youth.. **6**. Apollo
goddess... **3**. Ate, Dea, Eir, Eos, Nox,
Nyx, Ops, Pax, Uni **4**. Apet, Eris, Fury,
Gaea, Hera, Isis, Leda, Maat, Nike, Nina,
Sati **5**. Aruru, Damia, Diana, Doris,
Epona, Freya, Hygea, Irene, Pakht,
Salus, Venus, Vesta **6**. Allatu, Athena,
Aurora, Cybele, Hecate, Hestia, Ningal,
Pietho, Selene, Semele, Tellus, Vacuna
7. Artemis, Demeter, Minerva, Parvati
9. Aphrodite, Eumenides, Mnemosyne
10. Persephone, Proserpina
goddess of...
agriculture.. **3**. Ops **7**. Demeter
arts.. **6**. Athena, Pallas
beauty.. **3**. Sri **5**. Freya, Venus
7. Lakshmi
dawn.. **3**. Eos **5**. Ushas **6**. Aurora,
Matuta
destiny.. **4**. Fate **5**. Moira, Parca
discord.. **3**. Ate **4**. Eris
earth.. **4**. Gaea **5**. Aruru **6**. Ishtar, Tellus
Eskimos.. **5**. Sedna
fertility.. **4**. Isis **7**. Demeter
fire.. **6**. Hestia
fortune.. **5**. Tyche
freedom.. **7**. Feronia
fruit.. **6**. Pomona
grain, harvest.. **3**. Ops **5**. Ceres
Hawaiians.. **4**. Pele
healing.. **3**. Eir **4**. Gula
health.. **5**. Damia, Hygea, Salus
hearth.. **5**. Vesta
history.. **4**. Saga
horses.. **5**. Epona
hunt.. **5**. Diana **6**. Vacuna
infatuation.. **3**. Ate
justice.. **7**. Nemesis
light.. **6**. Lucina
love.. **5**. Venus **6**. Ishtar **9**. Aphrodite
magic, witchcraft.. **6**. Hecate
marriage.. **4**. Hera
maternity.. **4**. Apet
mischief.. **3**. Ate **4**. Eris
moon.. **4**. Luna **5**. Diana **6**. Phoebe,
Selene (Selena)
mother of the gods.. **4**. Rhea
nature.. **4**. Rhea **5**. Nymph **6**. Cybele
night.. **3**. Nox, Nyx
peace.. **3**. Pax **5**. Irene **6**. Athena
poetry.. **5**. Erato
rainbows.. **5**. Iris
sea.. **5**. Doris
seasons.. **5**. Horae
summer.. **6**. Aestus
sun.. **5**. Pakht (Pacht)
trees.. **6**. Pomona
truth.. **4**. Maat
underworld.. **4**. Fury **6**. Allatu
10. Persephone, Proserpina
vengeance.. **3**. Ara, Ate **7**. Nemesis
victory.. **4**. Nike
virtue.. **5**. Fides
war.. **5**. Anath, Bella
wealth.. **3**. Sri **7**. Lakshmi
wisdom.. **6**. Athena **7**. Minerva
youth.. **4**. Hebe
Godforsaken... **6**. vacant **7**. forlorn
8. desolate, wretched **9**. neglected
godly... **5**. pious **6**. devout, divine

7. saintly **9**. religious, righteous
godmother... **6**. cummer (kimmer)
7. sponsor
God's...
abode.. **7**. Olympus
acre.. **10**. churchyard
board.. **14**. communion table
country.. **4**. home **8**. homeland
9. Vaterland **10**. fatherland
cupbearer.. **8**. Ganymede
fluid (vein).. **5**. ichor (icor)
food.. **8**. ambrosia
gods, The (pert to)...
death of.. **9**. theoktony
marriage of.. **8**. theogamy
messenger of.. **6**. Hermes
mother of.. **4**. Rhea
Twilight of.. **8**. Ragnarok
worship of.. **9**. theolatry
Goetae... **7**. wizards (anc) **9**. sorcerers
14. thaumaturgists
Goethe (pert to)...
home.. **6**. Weimar (Ger)
masterpiece.. **5**. Faust
talent.. **4**. poet **8**. novelist **9**. dramatist
goffer, gauffer... **5**. crimp, flute, plait
(lace, paper)
gog... **3**. bog **4**. stir **9**. agitation
Gog (Bib)... **5**. Ruler (of Magog)
goggle... **3**. eye **4**. roll **5**. state **6**. squint
11. roll the eyes
goggler... **4**. fish (oceanic)
goggles... **6**. screen **7**. glasses **8**. blinkers,
eyeshade **10**. spectacles
going... **6**. moving, travel **7**. current,
working **9**. departure **10**. obtainable
11. in operation
gola... **7**. granary **9**. storeroom **11**. Indian
caste
golach, goloch... **6**. beetle, earwig
9. centipede
Golconda... **6**. wealth **8**. rich mine
gold... **2**. Au **3**. oro **4**. gelt, gilt **5**. aurum,
color, lucre, metal, money **6**. riches,
wealth **7**. bullion
gold (pert to)...
alloy.. **4**. asem **6**. oroide
artificial.. **8**. Mannheim
assayer cup.. **5**. cupel
bar.. **5**. ingot
braid, lace.. **5**. orris
brick.. **7**. swindle
coin.. **5**. eagle **10**. Krugerrand (So Afr)
compound.. **6**. auride
containing.. **4**. doré
discoverer (US).. **6**. Sutter (1849)
field (Bib).. **5**. Ophir
fish.. **9**. shubunkin
fool's.. **6**. pyrite
gilding.. **6**. ormolu **9**. imitation
Heraldry.. **2**. or
King (Myth).. **5**. Midas
land of (Bib).. **5**. Ophir
like.. **5**. auric **7**. aureate
measure.. **5**. carat
Rush.. **8**. Klondike (1897) **10**. California
(1849)
seekers (Calif).. **9**. Argonauts (1849)
11. Forty-Niners
symbol.. **2**. Au
vein.. **4**. lode

washing pan . . **5.** cupel
gold and silver . . . **11.** noble metals
golden . . . **4.** gilt **5.** auric, blest **6.** blonde, yellow **7.** aureate, aureous, halcyon **8.** metallic, precious, valuable **9.** Pactolian **10.** auspicious **11.** flourishing
golden (pert to) . . .
Age . . **9.** Saturnian, siècle d'or
apple . . **3.** bel **4.** Eris (goddess) **5.** Paris (giver) **6.** tomato
bird . . **6.** oriole
bough . . **9.** mistletoe
Fleece seeker . . **5.** Jason **8.** Argonaut
Fleece ship . . **5.** Argos
rod . . **8.** solidago
goldenrod (pert to) . . .
genus . . **8.** Solidago
State Flower of . . **7.** Alabama
8. Kentucky, Nebraska
goldfish . . . **4.** carp **9.** shubunkin
Goldfish (Astron) . . . **6.** Dorado
golf (pert to) . . .
club . . **4.** iron, wood **5.** baffy, spoon, wedge **6.** driver, mashie, putter **7.** brassie, midiron, niblick
hazard . . **4.** trap **5.** stymy **6.** bunker **11.** restriction
score . . **3.** par **4.** bogy (bogie) **5.** eagle **6.** birdie
stroke . . **4.** baff, chip, fade, hook, loft, putt **5.** drive, slice **8.** approach, mulligan
term . . **3.** ace, par, tee **4.** baff, fore **5.** bogey, divot, eagle, green, links, rough, slice **6.** birdie, dormie, sclaff, stymie (stimy) **7.** fairway, gallery
Golgotha . . . **7.** Calvary **8.** cemetery
goliath . . . **4.** frog **5.** crane, giant, heron
Goliath (pert to) . . .
Bib . . **5.** giant (Philistine)
death site . . **4.** Elah
home . . **4.** Gath
slayer . . **5.** David
Gomorrah (Bib) . . . **5.** Sodom **13.** wicked country
Gomuti palm . . . **5.** areng
gondola race (Venice) . . . **7.** regatta
gone . . . **3.** ago, off **4.** dead, left, lost, past, yore **5.** since **6.** absent, passed, ruined **8.** departed, past hope, vanished **9.** forgotten **10.** infatuated
goober . . . **6.** peanut
good . . . **2.** eu (pref) **3.** bon, fit **4.** able, full, gain, just, kind **5.** ample, godly, moral, nifty, pious, sound, valid **6.** benign, devout, expert, profit, savory **7.** genuine, helpful, liberal, trained, upright **8.** decorous, interest, pleasing, salutary, suitable, virtuous **9.** admirable, competent, enjoyable, estimable, excellent, favorable, honorable, indulgent, reputable **10.** auspicious, beneficial, courageous, gratifying, profitable, sufficient **11.** commendable, well-behaved **12.** considerable, satisfactory, stouthearted
good (pert to) . . .
bye . . **4.** ta-ta **5.** adieu, adios, ciaou **6.** so long **7.** cheerio **8.** farewell
for nothing . . **4.** mean **5.** idler **6.** wretch **7.** useless **8.** indolent **9.** worthless

11. rapscallion
health . . **5.** skoal **6.** prosit
management . . **6.** eutaxy
mighty . . **7.** skookum
ordinarily . . **8.** mediocre
spirit . . **6.** daemon **8.** Eudaemon **12.** agathodaemon
tidings . . **6.** gospel **7.** evangel
will . . **5.** favor **9.** affection, readiness **11.** benevolence **12.** friendliness
Good Book . . . **5.** Bible
goodness . . . **5.** piety **6.** virtue **8.** kindness, validity **9.** godliness, propriety **10.** excellence, generosity, savoriness
goods . . . **5.** wares **7.** ability **8.** chattels, property **11.** information, merchandise
goods cast overboard, sunk . . . **5.** lagan (lagend) **6.** jetsam **7.** flotsam **10.** contraband
goose . . . **4.** bean, dupe, fool, gull, iron, snow, tule **5.** Anser, brant, solan **6.** Canada, gander, gannet, goslet **7.** gosling, graylag (greylag) **8.** barnacle **12.** white-fringed
goose (pert to) . . .
egg . . **4.** zero
grease . . **6.** axunge
group . . **6.** gaggle
pygmy . . **6.** goslet
relating to . . **8.** anserine
story character . . **5.** ganza
gooseberry . . . **5.** fabes (color) **6.** escort, groser (groset), thapes **8.** chaperon, feaberry
gopher . . . **5.** snake **6.** rodent **7.** burglar **8.** squirrel, tortoise **10.** salamander
Gopher State . . . **9.** Minnesota
gore . . . **3.** mud **4.** dirt, dung, stab **5.** blood, cloth (triang), filth, slime **6.** pierce **8.** heraldry **9.** bloodshed, penetrate
gorge . . . **3.** eat **4.** bolt, glut, sate **5.** chasm, gully **6.** canyon, coulee, defile, nullah, ravine, valley **7.** choke up, overeat, pitcher, satiate **8.** overfill
gorgeous . . . **5.** grand, showy **8.** colorful, dazzling **9.** beautiful **10.** delightful **11.** magnificent, resplendent
gorgon . . . **4.** ogre, ugly **7.** Jezebel (Bib), monster
Gorgons (Gr Myth) . . . **6.** Medusa, Stheno **7.** Euryale **9.** sentinels
gorilla . . . **3.** ape **4.** thug **5.** brute **6.** monkey **8.** assassin
gorilla man . . . **9.** Du Chaillu (brought ape from Africa)
gormandizer . . . **9.** chowhound **11.** trencherman
gorse . . . **5.** furze **7.** juniper
goshawk . . . **5.** Astur **6.** tercel
gospel . . . **5.** faith, truth **6.** belief **7.** epistle, evangel **8.** doctrine **9.** orthodoxy, selection (Bib) **11.** revelation **11.** glad tidings **12.** proclamation
Gospels (Four) . . . **11.** diatessaron
gossip . . . **3.** cat, eme, gup **4.** chat, news, talk **5.** on-dit **6.** claver, gabble, norate, report, tattle **7.** clatter **8.** idle talk, quidnunc **9.** chatterer **10.** newsmonger, talebearer
gossoon . . . **3.** boy, lad (serving) **5.** youth **6.** garçon

got . . . see *get*
Gotham . . . **9.** Newcastle (Eng) **11.** New York City
Gothamite . . . **9.** New Yorker
Gothic (pert to) . . .
  alphabet . . **11.** Moeso-Gothic
  architecture . . **6.** French
  design . . **7.** writing **12.** architecture
  era . . **10.** Middle Ages
  people . . **4.** rude **5.** Goths **6.** fierce **7.** Teutons
  printing type . . **5.** Doric **9.** square-cut
gouge . . . **4.** tool **5.** cheat **6.** chisel, groove **7.** defraud, swindle **8.** impostor **10.** imposition
Gounod's opera . . . **5.** Faust
gourd . . . **4.** pepo **5.** color, flask, melon **6.** squash **8.** calabash, cucurbit **9.** Cucurbita **11.** calabazella
gourmand . . . **5.** eater (luxurious) **6.** taster **7.** epicure, glutton, gourmet **10.** fastidious, gluttonous, voluptuary **11.** connoisseur
gourmet . . . **7.** epicure **8.** gourmand **11.** connoisseur
gout . . . **4.** clot, drop **6.** blotch **7.** disease **9.** arthritis
govern . . . **3.** run **4.** curb, lead, rein, rule **5.** reign **6.** bridle, direct, manage **7.** conduct, control, preside **8.** dominate, regulate, restrain **9.** influence, supervise
governess . . . **4.** ayah **5.** nurse **6.** abbess, duenna **8.** guardian **12.** instructress
government . . . **4.** rule, sway **6.** polity **7.** control, regimen **10.** management **12.** jurisdiction **14.** administration
government (pert to) . . .
  absence of . . **6.** acracy **7.** anarchy
  centralized . . **12.** totalitarian
  church . . **9.** hierarchy **10.** heirocracy
  science of . . **8.** politics
  system . . **6.** regime
government by . . .
  church, clergy . . **9.** theocracy **10.** hierocracy
  few . . **9.** oligarchy
  God . . **8.** theonomy
  holy body . . **9.** hagiarchy **10.** hagiocracy
  law . . **9.** nomocracy
  men . . **9.** andocracy
  mob . . **10.** ochlocracy
  no one . . **6.** acracy
  rich . . **10.** plutocracy
  seven . . **9.** heptarchy
  six . . **12.** sextumvirate
  slaves . . **10.** doulocracy
  ten . . **8.** decarchy (dekarchy)
  three . . **8.** triarchy **11.** triumvirate
  women . . **8.** gynarchy **11.** gynecocracy
  worst men . . **12.** kakistocracy
governor . . . **4.** woon **5.** chief, nabob, ruler **6.** dynast, regent **7.** alcalde, decarch (of 10 men), viceroy **8.** decurion, director **9.** mechanism **10.** magistrate
gown . . . **4.** robe, toga **5.** cloak, dress, frock **6.** chiton, clothe, cyclas, invest, kimono, mantle **7.** cassock, college, garment, matinee, soutane (Eccl), sultane **8.** negligee, peignoir **9.** nightgown
gozell, gozill . . . **10.** gooseberry

gozzard . . . **9.** gooseherd
gra . . . **4.** love **5.** agrah **6.** liking **8.** fondness **10.** sweetheart
grab . . . **3.** nab **4.** game (cards), take **5.** grasp, seize **6.** arrest, clutch, snatch, vessel
grabble . . . **4.** feel **5.** grope **6.** grovel, sprawl **7.** harvest **11.** appropriate
grace . . . **4.** fate, luck, note, tact **5.** adorn, charm, favor, honor, mercy, title **6.** beauty, become, bedeck, polish, prayer, virtue **7.** dignify, enhance **8.** clemency, easiness, elegance, kindness, reprieve **10.** comeliness, refinement, seemliness **12.** graciousness, thanksgiving
graceful . . . **4.** airy, easy, feat **6.** comely, seemly **7.** elegant, fitting, tactful **8.** charming, debonair **9.** beautiful, courteous, sylphlike **11.** appropriate
Graces, The Three (Gr Myth) . . . **5.** Aegle (Mother) **6.** Aglaia (Brilliance), Thalia (Bloom) **10.** Euphrosyne (Joy)
gracile . . . **4.** slim, thin **6.** slight **7.** slender
gracious . . . **4.** kind **5.** suave **6.** benign, urbane **7.** affable **8.** generous **9.** courteous, favorable
grackle . . . **3.** daw **4.** bird, myna **7.** jackdaw **9.** blackbird
gradation . . . **4.** step **5.** scale, steps **6.** ablaut, nuance, series, stages **7.** degrees **10.** graduation, succession
grade . . . **4.** even, rank, rate, size, sort, step **5.** level, order **6.** assort, degree, school, smooth **7.** arrange, incline **8.** classify, gradient, graduate
gradual . . . **4.** easy, slow **6.** gentle **9.** leisurely
graduate . . . **4.** pass, size **5.** grade, taper **6.** alumna **7.** alumnus, promote, student **8.** shade off
graffito (scratched crudely) . . . **7.** drawing **10.** scratching **11.** inscription
Graf Spee blown up . . . **7.** Uruguay (1939)
graft . . . **3.** dig **4.** cion (scion), join, toil, work **5.** ditch, fraud, labor, spade, unite **6.** boodle, fasten, inarch, trench **7.** bribery, implant, joining
grafted (Her) . . . **4.** enté
Grail . . . see *Holy Grail*
grain . . . **3.** jot, rye **4.** atom, bran, corn, dram, food, grit, iota, malt, meal, mite, oats, rice, whit **5.** fiber, maize, scrap, spark, trace, wheat **6.** barley, millet, sesame **8.** particle
grain (pert to) . . .
  Bible . . **4.** ador
  bundle . . **5.** sheaf **7.** sheaves
  chaff . . **4.** bran, grit
  cracked . . **6.** groats
  ear of . . **5.** spike **6.** ressum (rizzom)
  exchange (Finan) . . **3.** pit
  feeding on . . **11.** granivorous
  fungus, disease . . **4.** rust, smut **5.** ergot **6.** mildew
  goddess of . . **5.** Ceres
  ground . . **4.** meal **5.** flour, grist
  husks . . **4.** bran **5.** straw
  measure . . **6.** thrave
  mill . . **5.** quern

mixture .. **6.** fodder **7.** farrage
   9. bullimong
small .. **7.** granule
spike .. **3.** ear **6.** rizzom
stack .. **4.** rick
storage, warehouse .. **3.** mow **4.** silo
   5. hutch **8.** elevator
grammar (pert to) ... **5.** parse **6.** gender,
   simile, syntax **7.** diction, parsing,
   prosody, synesis, wordage **8.** enallage,
   language, metaphor, paradigm
   9. accidence, etymology, phonology
   10. conformity, declension, inflection
   11. conjugation
grammatical case ... **6.** dative
   8. ablative, genitive, vocative
   9. objective **10.** accusative, nominative
grampus ... **3.** arc **4.** orca **5.** whale
   6. killer **7.** dolphin **8.** cetacean
granada ... **11.** pomegranate
Granada Moorish Castle site ...
   8. Alhambra (Sp)
granary ... **3.** bin **6.** grange **8.** cornloft
   10. repository, storehouse (grain)
grand ... **4.** epic **5.** great, large, lofty,
   money, noble, piano **6.** august, epical,
   famous, superb, swanky **7.** eminent,
   sublime **8.** gorgeous, majestic, splendid,
   thousand **9.** dignified, grandiose,
   important, sumptuous **11.** illustrious,
   magnificent
Grand Canyon State ... **7.** Arizona
grandchild ... **2.** oe, oy
grandchild, great ... **5.** ieroe
grandee ... **7.** magnate **8.** nobleman
   10. clarissimo
grandeur ... **5.** glory **7.** dignity, majesty
   8. elegance, eminence, vastness
   9. greatness, immensity, sublimity
   10. augustness **11.** stateliness
grandeval ... **4.** aged **7.** ancient
grandfather ... **4.** aiel (obs), avus
   6. atavus **8.** gudesire
grandiloquent ... **5.** grand, lofty **6.** turgid
   7. pompous **9.** bombastic
   12. magniloquent
grandiose ... **4.** epic **5.** grand **6.** turgid
   8. imposing **9.** bombastic, flaunting
   12. ostentatious
Grandma Moses ... **17.** Anna Mary
   Robertson
grandmother ... **6.** beldam (beldame),
   granny, gudame **7.** grandam
   (grandame), grandma **8.** babushka
grandparent (pert to) ... **4.** aval
grandson ... **6.** nepote
Grand Teton peak ... **7.** Wyoming
grange ... **4.** farm **7.** granary **9.** farmhouse
   11. association (1867) **18.** Patrons of
   Husbandry
granite ... **4.** rock **5.** stone **6.** aplite,
   marble, quartz **8.** feldspar **9.** pegmatite
Gran Quivira ... **5.** ruins (mission)
   16. National Monument (N M)
grant ... **4.** cede, deed, enam, gift,
   give, lend, loan, mise **5.** admit, allow,
   bonus, jagir (jaghar), spare **6.** accord,
   bestow, confer, demise, permit,
   remise **7.** appease, concede, confess,
   subsidy **8.** appanage, sanction, transfer
   10. conveyance **11.** acknowledge

granulated ... **5.** rough **6.** coarse
   7. grained **8.** granular, hardened
   12. crystallized
grape ... **3.** fox, uva **5.** Tokay **6.** Malaga,
   Muscat **7.** Catawba, Concord, Hamburg,
   Mission, Niagara **8.** Delaware, grenache,
   Isabella, Thompson **9.** Chasselas,
   muscadine **10.** sweetwater
   11. scuppernong
grape (pert to) ...
cluster .. **6.** raceme
color .. **7.** blue-red **9.** cathedral
conserve .. **5.** uvate
cultivation .. **11.** viticulture
dried .. **4.** pasa **6.** raisin
family, genus .. **5.** Vitus **8.** Vitaceae
juice .. **4.** dibs, must, sapa, stum
military .. **4.** shot
pomace .. **4.** marc, rape
preserve .. **7.** raisine
residue .. **4.** marc, rape **6.** pomace
seed .. **6.** acinus
sugar .. **7.** maltose **8.** dextrose
grapefruit ... **6.** pomelo **8.** shaddock
   12. Citrus Maxima
grapevine ... **4.** caro **5.** rumor **6.** canard,
   report **8.** maneuver (wrestling), pipeline
   9. dance step **11.** information,
   underground
graph ... **5.** chart **7.** contour, diagram,
   drawing
graphic ... **5.** clear, drawn, vivid **7.** written
   8. engraved **9.** pictorial **11.** descriptive,
   picturesque, significant
   12. diagrammatic
grasp ... **4.** grip, hent (obs), hold,
   take **5.** catch, clasp, gripe, seize
   6. clinch, clutch, gowpen (gowpin)
   7. control **8.** handgrip **9.** apprehend
   10. comprehend, understand
grasping ... **4.** avid **5.** close **6.** greedy
   7. holding, miserly **8.** covetous
   9. rapacious **10.** avaricious, prehensive
   11. acquisitive **13.** comprehending,
   understanding
grass ... **3.** eel, hay, Poa, rye **4.** cane, Coix,
   crab, gama, herb, oats, reed, rice, rush,
   tare, wire **5.** ankee, Avena, Briza, brome,
   chess, goose, grain, grama, hedge,
   otate, spart, spear **6.** bamboo, barley,
   darnel, fescue, marram, millet, redtop,
   sesame, switch **7.** alfalfa, Bermuda,
   buffalo, esparto, Hordeum, Poeceae,
   timothy **8.** mesquite **9.** blue-grass,
   Boutelous
grasshopper ... **4.** grig **6.** cicada, locust
   7. katydid
grassland ... **3.** lea, sod **4.** mead, veld
   (veldt) **5.** llano, range, sward **7.** pasture,
   prairie, savanna (savannah)
grasslike plant ... **5.** sedge
grate ... **3.** rub **4.** fret, grid, grit, rasp
   5. annoy, chafe, grind **6.** abrade, scrape
   7. network **8.** irritate
grateful ... **7.** cumshaw (beggar's
   phrase), welcome **8.** pleasing, thankful
   10. gratifying **12.** appreciative
gratification ... **6.** relish, reward
   8. gratuity, pleasure **10.** indulgence,
   recompense
gratified ... **4.** glad **7.** pleased

gratify . . . 5. favor, grace, humor 6. arride, foster, pamper, please 7. appease, delight, flatter, indulge, requite, satisfy 10. remunerate

grating . . . 4. grid 5. grate, grill, harsh, raspy 6. grille 7. lattice, network 8. strident 9. partition 10. irritating 11. latticework 12. nerve-racking

gratis . . . 4. free 6. freely 9. on the cuff 10. for nothing, gratuitous, on the house 12. gratuitously

gratitude . . . 5. grace 6. praise, thanks 12. appreciation, gratefulness, thankfulness

gratuitous . . . 4. free 5. given 6. gratis, wanton 7. assumed 8. baseless, needless 9. voluntary 10. groundless 11. superfluous, unwarranted

gratuity . . . 3. fee, tip 4. dole, gift, give, vail 5. bonus, bribe 6. bounty 7. cumshaw, pension, present 9. baksheesh (bakshish), buonamano, lagniappe (lagnappe), pourboire

grave . . . 3. pit, urn 4. bier, tomb 5. fosse (foss), sober, staid 6. sedate, solemn, trench 7. earnest, engrave, serious 8. sermonic 9. important, momentous, ponderous, sculpture, sepulcher

grave (pert to) . . .
cloth . . 6. shroud 8. cerement 9. cerecloth
coffin . . 4. pall
comb form . . 5. serio
mound (anc) . . 6. barrow 7. hillock, tumulus
person . . 10. sobersides
robber . . 5. ghoul

gravel . . . 5. geest, grain, stone 6. baffle, defeat, refute 7. calculi, erratic (boulder), pebbles 10. meerschaum (color)

graven . . . 6. etched 7. infixed 8. engraved 10. sculptured

gravestone . . . 5. stele (stela) 6. cippus, marker, pillar 8. monument 9. tombstone 11. sarcophagus

gravitation . . . 7. descent, gravity 10. attraction

gravity . . . 6. weight 7. dignity, sadness 8. enormity, grimness, sobriety 9. formality, solemnity 10. attraction, importance 11. earnestness, seriousness, weightiness 12. significance 13. momentousness

gravity law, discoverer . . . 6. Newton

gray, grey . . . 3. dim, old, sad 4. aged, dark, dull, gris, obex 5. dingy, hoary, polio (comb form), sober 6. animal (gray), dismal, somber 7. hueless, neutral, silvery 9. cheerless 10. achromatic

gray, grey (color) . . . 3. ash, bat, dun 4. ashy, dove, iron, lead, mole, zinc 5. acier, ashen, dusty, mouse, pearl, slate, smoke, steel, taupe 6. French, Oxford, Quaker, reseda, silver 7. cesious, dappled, grizzle 8. charcoal, cinereal, gunmetal 10. battleship, dapple-gray 13. pepper-and-salt

graze . . . 3. eat, rub 4. drab, rase, skim 5. brush, shave 6. browse, feed on, scrape 7. scratch

grease . . . 3. fat, oil, tip 4. daub, lard, mort, saim, soil 5. bribe, smear, suint 6. axunge 7. fatness, fawning, lanolin 8. flattery 9. lubricate

greasy . . . 4. oily 5. dirty, gross, thick 6. smooth 8. slippery, unctuous 10. indelicate

great . . . 3. big 4. good, huge, vast 5. ample, chief, large, major, stout, whole 6. famous, grande 7. drastic, eminent, extreme 8. intimate, numerous 9. elaborate, important 11. magnanimous 12. considerable 13. distinguished

great (comb form) . . . 5. macro, megal

Great (pert to) . . .
Barrier (NZ) . . 4. Otea (Isl) 9. coral reef
Beyond . . 5. grave 9. afterlife, hereafter 10. after world, The Unknown 11. eternal home 14. beyond the grave
Cham of Literature . . 13. Samuel Johnson (Dr)
Circle sailing . . 10. orthodromy
Commoner . . 4. Clay, Pitt 7. Stevens (Thaddeus) 9. Gladstone
Divide . . 7. Rockies 8. Rocky Mts 9. watershed (US) 14. Rocky Mountains 17. Continental Divide
Fire . . 6. London (1666) 7. Chicago (1871)
Lakes . . 4. Erie 5. Huron 7. Ontario 8. Michigan, Superior
Mogul . . 5. Akbar (Hind) 7. diamond
Names . . 6. Hector 8. Hercules, Lysander 9. Alexander
Pyramid . . 6. Cheops
Spirit (Ind) . . 4. Mana, Zemi 5. Wakan 6. Manito (orenda), Pokunt
White Way . . 8. Broadway (NY)

Great Britain . . . 5. Wales 7. England 8. Scotland 12. Commonwealth 13. United Kingdom 15. Northern Ireland

greatest . . . 6. utmost 7. extreme, noblest

greatness . . . 9. largeness 10. importance 11. magnanimity

Greco, Graeco (comb form) . . . 5. Greek 7. Grecian

Greece . . . see also *Greek*
ancient . . 4. Elis 5. Argos, Doris, Ionia 6. Attica, Epirus, Hellas 7. Argolis, Boeotia 8. Thessaly
cape . . 5. Melea 7. Matapan
capital . . 4. Elis (anc) 6. Athens
citadel . . 9. Acropolis
city . . 6. Patras, Sparta 7. Corinth, Piraeus 8. Salonika
island . . 5. Chios, Corfu, Crete, Samos 6. Ithaca, Lesbos, Patmos, Rhodes 10. Dodecanese (group), Samothrace
mountain . . 3. Ida 5. Athos 6. Peleon, Pindus 7. Olympus 9. Parnassus
peninsula . . 6. Balkan
river . . 4. Arta 7. Hellada 9. Archelous
sea . . 6. Aegean, Ionian
seaport . . 4. Enor, Volo 5. Corpu, Pylos 8. Salonika

Greek, Grecian (pert to) . . .
abbess . . 4. amma
alphabet . . see *Greek alphabet*
altar . . 7. eschara

architecture . . **5.** Doric, Ionic **6.** xystus
(part) **10.** Corinthian
assembly . . **4.** pynx **5.** agora
avenging spirit . . **3.** Ate, Ker **6.** Erinys
boat . . **6.** caique
bowl (golden) . . **5.** depas
breath . . **6.** pneuma
chariot . . **4.** biga
church section . . **6.** andron, bemata
citadel . . **9.** Acropolis
city (Greek for) . . **5.** polis
commander (anc) . . **7.** navarch
commune . . **4.** deme, nome
contest . . **4.** agon (anc) **6.** Delian
7. Pythian, Olympic **8.** marathon
courtesan (Athen) . . **5.** Thais
culture, literature . . **7.** classic **9.** classical
cup, bowl . . **5.** depas **6.** cotula
cupid . . **4.** Eros
dance (anc) . . **6.** hormos **7.** pyrrhic,
strophe **9.** dithyramb
department . . **8.** nomarchy
dessert . . **7.** baklava
dish . . **8.** moussaka **9.** souvlakia
early . . **5.** Arius **6.** oecist
epic . . **5.** Iliad **7.** Odyssey
female worshipper . . **5.** orant
garment . . **5.** tunic **6.** chiton, peplos
gravestone . . **5.** stele
horse (talking) . . **5.** Arion
hospitality . . **5.** zenia
judge . . **6.** dicast
language . . **6.** Romaic
lawgiver . . **5.** Minos, Solon
magistrate . . **6.** archon, eparch
7. nomarch
mistress . . **7.** hetaera (hetaira)
monster . . **8.** Minotaur, Typhoeus
(100-headed)
note . . **4.** nete **5.** neume **6.** pneuma
9. hexachord **10.** tetrachord
Old Testament . . **10.** Septuagint
platform . . **4.** bema **7.** logeion
poem . . **5.** Iliad **7.** Odyssey
portico . . **4.** stoa, xyst
sacred enclosure . . **5.** sekos
sacred object . . **6.** sacrum
sacrificial offering . . **5.** hiera **8.** sphagion
sandwich . . **4.** gyro
school . . **7.** Eleatic
serpent . . **4.** seps **6.** Python
slave . . **5.** Baubo, helot, iambe **6.** penest
soldier . . **7.** hoplite
song . . **5.** melos
sorceress . . **5.** Circe
spirit . . **5.** Momus (evil)
temple . . **4.** naos **5.** cella (part)
theater . . **5.** odeon
war cry . . **5.** alala
youth (would-be citizen) . . **7.** ephebus
Greek alphabet . . . **2.** Mu, Nu, Pi, Xi
3. Chi, Eta, Phi, Psi, Rho, Tau **4.** Beta,
Iota, Zeta **5.** Alpha, Delta, Gamma,
Kappa, Omega, Sigma, Theta **6.** Lambda
7. Digamma (obs), Epsilon, Omicron,
Upsilon
Greek Furies . . . **6.** Alecto, Erinys
7. Magaero **9.** Tisiphone
Greek god of . . .
atmosphere . . **5.** Hadad
chief . . **4.** Zeus

dreams . . **8.** Morpheus
fire . . **6.** Vulcan
flocks . . **3.** Pan
heavens . . **6.** Uranus
love . . **4.** Eros
lower world . . **5.** Hades
ridicule . . **5.** Momus
river . . **8.** Eridanus
sea . . **6.** Nereus
storm . . **6.** Teshup **7.** Hittite
sun . . **6.** Apollo, Helios **7.** Phoebus
vegetation . . **8.** Dionysus
war . . **4.** Ares **8.** Enyalius
winds . . **5.** Eurus **6.** Aeolus
youth . . **6.** Apollo, Pothos (winged)
Greek goddess of . . .
agriculture . . **7.** Artemis, Demeter
beauty . . **9.** Aphrodite
chase . . **7.** Artemis
clouds . . **5.** Niobe
dawn . . **3.** Eos **7.** Alcmene, Ariadne
discord . . **4.** Eris
earth . . **2.** Ge **4.** Gaea
fate . . **5.** Moira
fortune . . **5.** Tyche
heaven . . **4.** Hera
infatuation . . **3.** Ate
magic . . **6.** Hecate (3-headed)
memory . . **9.** Mnemosyne
moon . . **2.** Io **5.** Diana **6.** Selene
nature . . **7.** Artemis
night . . **3.** Nyx **4.** Leto **6.** Hecate
peace . . **5.** Irene
phallus . . **5.** Baubo
retribution . . **7.** Nemesis
underworld . . **6.** Hecate (Hekate)
vengeance . . **3.** Ara **7.** Nemesis
victory . . **4.** Nike
wisdom . . **6.** Pallas **7.** Minerva
youth . . **4.** Hebe
Greek Myth . . .
character . . **5.** Niobe, Sinon **6.** Adonis,
Gorgon, Rhesus **7.** Calchus, Icarius,
Pandora, Phrixos **8.** Atalanta,
Endymion, Meleager, Tantalus
12. Erichthonius
deity . . **5.** Satyr, Titan **6.** Cronus
enchantress . . **5.** Circe, Medea
giant . . **7.** Antaeus **9.** Enceladus
(100-armed)
huntress . . **8.** Atalanta
monster . . **8.** Typhoeus (100-headed)
nymph . . **5.** Oread **6.** Nereid
serpent . . **6.** Python
spirit (evil) . . **5.** Momus
Greek personalities . . .
astronomer . . **12.** Eratosthenes
biographer . . **8.** Plutarch
counselor . . **6.** Nestor
dramatist . . **9.** Aeschylus, Euripides,
Sophocles **12.** Aristophanes
fabulist . . **5.** Aesop
geographer . . **6.** Strabo
hero . . **4.** Ajax **5.** Talos **6.** Nestor
7. Cecrops, Theseus **8.** Achilles,
Odysseus **10.** Hippolytus
historian . . **8.** Xenophon **9.** Dionysius,
Herodotus **10.** Thucydides
mathematician . . **6.** Euclid
10. Archimedes
painter . . **7.** Apelles

patriarch . . **5.** Arius
philosopher . . **4.** Zeno **5.** Galen,
Plato, Timon **6.** Nestor **8.** Diogenes,
Epicurus **9.** Aristotle **10.** Heraclitus,
Parmenides, Pythagoras, Xenophanes
11. Anaximander
physician . . **5.** Galen
poet . . **5.** Arion, Homer **6.** Hesiod, Pindar
7. Thespis **8.** Anacreon **9.** Aeschylus
poetess . . **6.** Erinna, Sappho **7.** Corinna
sage . . **6.** Thales
satirist . . **6.** Lucian
sculptor . . **5.** Myron **7.** Phidias
statesman . . **8.** Pericles **9.** Aristides
green . . . **3.** raw **4.** vert **5.** fresh, mossy
6. callow, praseo (comb form), unripe
7. emerald, verdant **9.** malachite,
unskilled, untrained **11.** flourishing
13. inexperienced **15.** unsophisticated
green (pert to) . . .
back . . **4.** frog **11.** legal tender (US)
blue . . **4.** cyan, saxe **7.** sistine
comb form . . **6.** praseo
eyed . . **7.** jealous
famous . . **6.** Gretna (Scot)
film . . **6.** patina
gray . . **5.** olive **6.** reseda
pale . . **7.** celadon
pigment . . **10.** terre-verte
quartz . . **5.** prase
sickness . . **9.** chlorosis
tea . . **5.** Hyson
green-back herring . . . **5.** cisco
Greenland . . .
Bay . . **6.** Baffin
capital . . **8.** Godthaab
Danish word . . **8.** Crönland
explorer . . **9.** Frobisher (1576) **10.** Eric
the Red
natives . . **6.** Eskimo (mostly)
settlement . . **4.** Etah
strait . . **5.** Davis
whale . . **5.** right
Green Mt Boys' leader . . . **10.** Ethan
Allen (1775)
Green Mt State . . . **7.** Vermont
greenness . . . **5.** color **8.** sourness
9. ignorance **10.** immaturity
11. gullibility **12.** inexperience
Greenwich time (London) . . . **8.** absolute,
standard **16.** Royal Observatory
Greenwich Village . . . **9.** Manhattan
11. New York City
greeting . . . **3.** ave, how **4.** hail **5.** hallo
6. accoil, halloa, salute **7.** address,
welcome **8.** saluting **9.** reception
10. compliment, salutation
14. correspondence
gregarious . . . **6.** common, social
7. affable **8.** sociable **12.** social-minded
13. communicative
grego . . . **5.** cloak **6.** jacket **9.** greatcoat
Gregory . . . **4.** Code (Rom law), Pope,
year **5.** chant, staff (Mus) **6.** church
8. calendar
grenier . . . **5.** attic
grey . . . see *gray*
grid . . . **5.** grill **7.** grating, griddle, network
8. gridiron **13.** football field
grief . . . **3.** rue, woe **4.** care, pain,
ruth **5.** abuse, dolor, trial **6.** mishap,

sorrow **7.** anguish, offense, remorse,
sadness **8.** disaster, distress, document
9. grievance, suffering **10.** affliction
11. bereavement, lamentation
grieve . . . **3.** cry, rue **4.** erme, pain
5. mourn, wound **6.** lament, sorrow
7. afflict **8.** complain, distress
10. discomfort
grievous . . . **4.** sore **6.** bitter, severe
7. doleful, heinous, intense **8.** terrible
9. sorrowful **10.** disastrous, oppressive
11. distressing, gravaminous
griff . . . **4.** claw, glen **6.** griffe, ravine
griffe . . . **4.** spur (Arch) **7.** mulatto
griffin, griffon . . . **6.** charge (Her)
7. monster **10.** decoration
grig . . . **3.** eel **5.** annoy, dwarf **7.** cricket,
heather **8.** irritate **9.** tantalize
11. grasshopper
grill . . . **4.** cook **5.** broil **7.** griddle, network,
torture **8.** gridiron **10.** restaurant
11. interrogate **12.** cross-examine
grille . . . **6.** window (ticket) **7.** grating,
network
grilse . . . **6.** salmon **7.** botcher
grim . . . **4.** dour, sour **5.** gaunt, harsh,
stern **6.** grisly, horrid, savage, sullen
7. ghastly, hideous **8.** horrible, pitiless,
ruthless, sinister **9.** ferocious, frightful,
merciless, repellent **10.** forbidding,
inexorable, relentless, unyielding
grimace . . . **3.** mop, mow, mug **4.** face,
mock, moue, pout, sham **8.** pretense
10. distortion **11.** affectation
grimalkin . . . **3.** cat **5.** vixen **6.** feline
8. old woman
grime . . . **4.** dirt, smut, soot **5.** sully
9. blackness
grin . . . **5.** fleer, smile, smirk
grind . . . **3.** dig, rub, vex **4.** bray, grit,
mull, whet **5.** crush, gnash, grate,
study **6.** abrade, drudge, harass,
polish, powder, satire, school, squash
7. operate, routine, sharpen **8.** drudgery
9. comminute, masticate, pulverize,
triturate
grinder . . . **5.** molar, tooth, tutor
8. sideshow **9.** announcer **10.** flycatcher,
goatsucker
grinding . . . **6.** boning **7.** grating
9. attrition **10.** burdensome, irritating,
tyrannical **12.** excruciating
grinding (pert to) . . .
mental . . **6.** boning **8.** cramming,
studying
stone . . **4.** mano **6.** metate, muller
9. millstone
substance . . **5.** emery **8.** abrasive
gringo . . . **5.** alien **8.** American **9.** foreigner
10. Englishman
grip . . . **3.** bag **4.** hold **5.** clasp, cleat,
ditch, drain, grasp, seize, spasm
6. clench, clutch, furrow, grippe, handle,
obsess, trench, valise **7.** control, illness
8. gripsack, handfast
gripe . . . **4.** grip, hold, pain **5.** annoy,
brake, colic, grasp, pinch, spasm
6. clutch, harass **7.** afflict, control,
mastery, vulture **8.** complain, distress
9. complaint **10.** affliction, oppression
griskin . . . **4.** chop, loin **5.** steak

grisly ... **4.** grim **5.** harsh **7.** ghastly, hideous **8.** gruesome, terrible **9.** deathlike **10.** forbidding

grist ... **3.** lot **4.** malt **5.** grain, grind **8.** quantity (bees)

grit ... **4.** sand **5.** nerve, pluck **6.** gravel **7.** bravery, courage, Liberal **9.** sandstone **11.** persistence **12.** perseverance

grivet ... **4.** tota, waag **6.** monkey

grizzly bear ... **7.** Ephraim (hunter's) **15.** Ursus horribilis

groats ... **5.** grain, wheat (cracked) **6.** cereal

grog ... **3.** rum **5.** rumbo **8.** beverage **9.** firewater

groggy ... **5.** dazed, drunk, shaky, tipsy **8.** unsteady, wavering **9.** tottering

groin ... **4.** lisk **6.** inguen

groom ... **4.** syce, tidy **5.** brush, curry, dress, preen, train **7.** hostler, servant, shopboy **9.** assistant, stableman **10.** bridegroom, manservant

groove ... **3.** rut **4.** dado **5.** chase, croze, flute, scarf, stria, track **6.** furrow, rabbet, raggle, scrobe, sulcus **7.** channel, rifling, routine **8.** philtrum **10.** excavation **11.** canaliculus

grooved ... **6.** fluted **7.** striate, sulcate **11.** canalicular **12.** canaliculate

grope ... **4.** feel **6.** fumble, search **7.** grabble, grubble

groper ... **4.** fish **7.** grouper

grosbeak ... **5.** finch **8.** hawfinch

gros point ... **4.** lace (Venetian) **6.** stitch (Aubusson) **8.** tapestry (Gobelin) **11.** cross-stitch

gross ... **3.** fat **5.** obese **6.** brutal, coarse, earthy, greasy, impure, vulgar **7.** brutish, massive, obscene, sensual, witless **8.** flagrant, indecent, receipts **9.** aggregate, unrefined **10.** indefinite, indelicate, scurrilous

grotesque ... **3.** odd **5.** antic, clown, freak **6.** unique **7.** awkward, baroque, bizarre **8.** deformed, fanciful **9.** fantastic **11.** incongruous

grotesque figure (Chin) ... **5.** magot

grotto ... **3.** den **4.** blue, cave, grot **5.** crypt, speos, vault **6.** cavern, recess **8.** catacomb

ground ... **3.** bog **4.** acre, area, base, clay, clod, farm, land, moor, park, plot, root, soil **5.** basis, cause, earth, field, hurst, marsh, ridge, solum, swale, train **6.** belief, bottom, milled, region **7.** country, gritted, opinion, premise, terrain (terrane) **8.** initiate, instruct **9.** establish, territory, viewpoint **10.** background, foundation, substratum

ground (pert to) ...
beetles .. **5.** Amara
berry .. **9.** cranberry **12.** checkerberry
grain .. **4.** bran, meal **5.** flour, grist
nut .. **5.** chufa, gobbe **6.** goober, peanut
squirrel .. **5.** Xerus **6.** gopher, hackee, rodent **8.** chipmunk **11.** spermophile

groundhog (pert to) ...
American .. **6.** marmot
day .. **9.** Candlemas (Feb 2)
home .. **8.** Puxatori

termed .. **6.** marmot, rodent **8.** aardvark, whistler **9.** woodchuck **10.** whistlepig

groundless ... **4.** idle **5.** false **8.** baseless **9.** unfounded **11.** unwarranted **13.** unsubstantial

grounds ... **4.** lees, park **5.** basis, dregs **7.** residue **8.** scruples

group ... **3.** set **4.** band, bevy, clan, crew, gang, herd, pack, sect, sept, team, unit **5.** batch, bunch, class, clump, corps, flock, genus, order, panel, shift, tribe **6.** legion, troupe **7.** arrange, bracket, cluster, company, species **8.** assemble, category, classify, division **10.** assemblage **11.** aggregation

group (pert to) ...
actors .. **6.** troupe
animal .. **3.** gam (whales), pod (seals, whales) **4.** herd, pack **5.** drove, flock, pride (lions)
beautiful women .. **4.** bevy
birds .. **4.** bevy, nest, nide (pheasants) **5.** covey (quail), flock **6.** clutch (eggs), flight, gaggle (geese)
celebrities .. **6.** galaxy
church .. **5.** laity **6.** clergy, parish **12.** congregation
fish .. **6.** school
followers .. **4.** cult, sect
insects .. **4.** hive **5.** swarm **6.** colony
musicians .. **3.** duo **4.** band, trio **5.** combo, nonet (nonette), octet (octette) **6.** septet (septette), sextet (sextette) **7.** quartet (quartette), quintet (quintette) **9.** orchestra
offspring .. **5.** brood **6.** clutch, litter
political .. **4.** bloc, ring **5.** junta, party **7.** machine
secret .. **5.** cabal
singers .. **3.** duo **4.** trio **5.** choir **6.** chorus **7.** quartet (quartette)
trees .. **4.** tope **5.** copse, grove, woods **7.** alameda, orchard, pinetum (pines)
witches .. **5.** coven

group (quota of) ...
eight .. **5.** octad, octet (octette)
five .. **6.** pentad **7.** quintet (quintette)
four .. **6.** tetrad **7.** quartet (quartette)
nine .. **6.** ennead
seven .. **6.** heptad, septet (septette)
six .. **6.** sextet (sextette)
ten .. **5.** decad **6.** decade
three .. **4.** trio **5.** triad, trine **7.** Trinity
two vowels .. **6.** digram **7.** digraph **9.** diphthong

grouped ... **7.** classed **8.** agminate, arranged, gathered **9.** assembled, collected, organized **10.** classified

grouper ... **4.** fish **5.** guasa **6.** groper **8.** rock hind

grouse ... **4.** bird **6.** repine **7.** grumble **8.** complain **9.** ptarmigan **12.** capercaillie

grouse (pert to) ...
courtship .. **3.** lak
red .. **7.** Lagopus
ruffed .. **6.** Bonasa

grouty ... **5.** cross, sulky **6.** crabby, grumpy **7.** grouchy

grove (pert to) ...
living in .. **7.** nemoral

mango . . **4.** tope
pine . . **7.** pinetum
poplar . . **7.** alameda
sacred . . **5.** Altis (Gr), Nemus (to Diana)
small trees . . **5.** copse
grovel . . . **4.** fawn, roll **5.** crawl, creep
   6. cringe, crouch, shrink, tumble,
   wallow, welter **7.** debauch, truckle
   8. flounder
groveling, grovelling . . . **6.** abject
   7. fawning **9.** prostrate, truckling
   11. bootlicking
grow . . . **3.** bud, wax **4.** come **5.** raise
   6. accrue, expand, mature, thrive
   7. augment, develop, enlarge, improve,
   produce **8.** increase, vegetate
   9. cultivate
grow (pert to) . . .
   dark . . **6.** darkle
   dim . . **5.** blear
   intense, profound . . **6.** deepen
   thin . . **8.** emaciate
   tiresome . . **4.** bore, pall
   together . . **7.** accrete
   worse . . **11.** deteriorate
growing (pert to) . . .
   angry . . **8.** irascent
   from without . . **9.** ectogenic
      10. ectogenous
   in . . **6.** linose
   on trees . . **10.** epidendral, epidendric
      11. xylophilous (fungus)
   out from . . **3.** bud **4.** stem **5.** enate
      6. sprout
   spontaneously . . **9.** adventive
   together . . **7.** accrete, joining **8.** adhering
growing in . . .
   clusters . . **8.** racemose
   fields . . **8.** agrestal **9.** agrestial
      10. campestral
   ground . . **9.** geogenous
   mud . . **9.** uliginose
   pairs . . **6.** binate
   rubbish . . **7.** ruderal
   snow . . **5.** nival
   water . . **7.** aquatic
growl . . . **4.** girn, gnar, rome **5.** snarl
   6. mutter **7.** grumble **8.** complain
growler . . . **3.** cab, can **4.** bass (black)
   7. iceberg, pitcher **8.** clarence
growth . . . **3.** bud, wen **4.** rise **5.** felon,
   shoot, tumor **6.** effect, result **8.** increase,
   swelling **9.** expansion **10.** vegetation
   11. consequence, development,
   enlargement **12.** augmentation
growth (pert to) . . .
   from within . . **8.** endogeny
   from without . . **9.** ectogenic
      10. ectogenous
   fungus . . **4.** mold, moss **6.** mildew
   marine . . **7.** seaweed
   of wood . . **5.** copse **7.** coppice
      9. brushwood
   premature . . **9.** precocity
   process of . . **8.** nascency
   retarding . . **9.** paratonic
grub . . . **3.** dig **4.** food, plod, root, spud
   5. larva, mathe, slave, stump **6.** assart,
   drudge, maggot, search **7.** plodder
   8. victuals
grubby . . . **5.** dirty, grimy, small

8. dwarfish, infested, slovenly, toadfish
grudge . . . **4.** envy **5.** covet, spite **6.** hatred
   7. grumble **8.** begrudge **10.** resentment
grudging spender . . . **8.** tightwad
gruel . . . **4.** diet **6.** cereal, liquid **7.** disable
   8. porridge
grueling, gruelling . . . **6.** trying
   9. demanding, punishing, weakening
   10. exhausting
gruesome . . . **4.** ugly **6.** grisly, horrid,
   sordid **7.** ghastly, hideous, macabre
   9. deathlike
gruff . . . **4.** deep, rude, sour **5.** bluff,
   harsh, surly **6.** clumsy, hoarse, morose,
   severe **7.** austere, bearish, brusque
grum . . . **4.** glum, sour **6.** sullen **8.** gutteral
   13. harsh-sounding
grumble . . . **4.** fret, hone, kick **5.** growl,
   snarl **6.** grouse, mumble, mutter, repine,
   rumble **7.** maunder **8.** complain
guacharo . . . **6.** owlish **7.** oilbird
   10. goatsucker
Guam . . .
   capital . . **5.** Agana
   discoverer . . **8.** Magellan (1521)
   idol, fetish . . **5.** anito
   island . . **7.** Mariana
   mountain peak . . **6.** Lamlam
   port . . **4.** Apra
guanaco . . . **5.** llama (like) **6.** alpaca
guarantee . . . **6.** avouch, ensure, insure,
   surety **7.** endorse, promise, warrant
   8. guaranty, security, warranty
   9. agreement
guaranty . . . **4.** bond **6.** pledge **8.** security,
   warranty **9.** agreement, assurance,
   guarantee
guarapucu . . . **5.** wahoo
guard . . . **3.** van **4.** care, curb, keep, tend,
   tile **5.** tiler, watch **6.** bantay, bridle,
   convoy, defend, escort, fender, gaoler,
   jailer, keeper, patrol, picket, police,
   sentry, shield, warden **7.** defense,
   protect **8.** restrain, sentinel, watchman
   9. attention, protector **10.** cowcatcher,
   precaution, protection
guarded . . . **4.** wary **7.** careful **8.** cautious,
   defended, discreet, vigilant, watchful
   9. protected **10.** restrained
   11. circumspect, sentinelled
guardhouse . . . **4.** brig
guardian . . . **5.** angel, tutor **6.** helper,
   keeper, patron, warden **7.** trustee
   8. defender, tutelary **9.** custodian,
   protector **10.** mystagogue (Church
   relics)
guardian (Gr) . . . **5.** Argus (100-eyed)
   8. Cerberus (3-headed)
guardianship . . . **4.** care **6.** charge
   7. custody, tuition **8.** guidance, tutelage
   13. protectorship
Guatemala . . .
   ant . . **5.** kelep
   bird (sacred) . . **7.** quetzal (quezal)
   capital . . **13.** Guatemala City
   coin (gold) . . **7.** quetzal
   fruit (avocadolike) . . **4.** anay
   Indian people . . **4.** Inca
   port . . **7.** San José **10.** Champerico
      13. Puerto Barrios
   ruins . . **5.** Mayan

volcano .. **4.** Agua **5.** Fuego
gudgeon . . . **4.** bait, dupe, goby **9.** killifish
10. allurement
gue . . . **5.** rogue **7.** sharper
guenon . . . **6.** monkey (long-tailed)
guerdon . . . **5.** crown, prize **6.** reward
8. requital **10.** recompense
guereza . . . **6.** monkey
Guernsey . . . **6.** brandy, cattle, Island
(Channel) **7.** garment
guess . . . **5.** fancy, think **6.** divine
7. imagine, presume, surmise, suspect
8. estimate **10.** conjecture
guest . . . **6.** caller, inmate, lodger, patron
7. visitor **9.** inquiline (insect)
Guiana . . .
British capital .. **10.** Georgetown
Dutch (Surinam) capital .. **10.** Paramaribo
French capital .. **7.** Cayenne
guide . . . **3.** con, key **4.** clew, clue,
lead, rein, sign, sley **5.** order, pilot,
steer, teach, tutor, usher **6.** advise,
beacon, direct, dirigo, govern, guidon
7. adviser, conduct, courier, marshal
8. Baedeker (book), cicerone, director,
polestar, regulate **9.** regulator
Guido (scale) . . . **2.** ut **3.** alt, A re, B
mi, E la (highest) **5.** E la mi, gamut
7. alamire
guild . . . **5.** hanse **7.** society **10.** fellowship
11. association, brotherhood
Guildhall statue (London) . . . **3.** Gog
5. Magog (1708)
guile . . . **5.** craft **6.** deceit **9.** duplicity,
falseness, treachery **11.** furtiveness
guileless . . . **5.** naive **6.** simple **7.** artless,
natural, sincere **8.** innocent
guillemot . . . **3.** auk **4.** coot **5.** murre
guilt . . . **3.** sin **4.** sake **5.** culpa
8. iniquity, peccancy **10.** guiltiness,
wickedness **11.** criminality, culpability
14. impeachability
guilty . . . **6.** nocent **8.** culpable
Guinea, W Afr . . .
capital .. **7.** Conakry (Konakri)
city .. **4.** Boke, Labe
export .. **7.** bananas **10.** pineapples
government .. **8.** republic
mineral .. **4.** gold **7.** bauxite **8.** diamonds
people .. **6.** Fullah **7.** Malinke, Soussou
tree .. **4.** akee
guinea fowl . . . **3.** hen **4.** keet **6.** turkey
7. pintado **8.** pheasant
guinea pig . . . **4.** boar, cavy **5.** Cavia
8. capybara
guise . . . **3.** way **4.** form, garb, mask,
mien, mode **5.** cloak, cover **6.** aspect,
custom **7.** fashion, pretext **8.** behavior
9. semblance **10.** appearance
guitar (pert to) . . .
Hindu .. **4.** vina
like .. **4.** lute **7.** bandore
octaves .. **5.** three
Oriental .. **5.** sitar
pitch (term) .. **5.** dital
ridge .. **7.** samisen
small .. **7.** ukulele
gula . . . **4.** cyma, neck, ogee **6.** gullet
7. cavetto, molding
gulch . . . **5.** cleft, gorge **6.** arroyo, coulee,
ravine

gulf . . . **3.** bay, pit, sea (landlocked)
4. eddy **5.** abyss, basin, chasm, cleft,
inlet **6.** vorago **7.** opening **9.** whirlpool
10. separation (wide)
gull . . . **4.** dupe, fool, gray **5.** brick,
cheat, cully, fraud **7.** cheater, deceive,
defraud, mislead **8.** impostor
gull (bird) . . . **3.** cob (cobb), mew
4. Lari, pirr, skua, tern, Xema **5.** pewit
(laughing) **7.** Larinae **8.** seedbird
9. kittiwake
gullet . . . **3.** maw **4.** tube **5.** gully **6.** throat
7. channel, harness (part) **9.** esophagus
gullible one . . . **4.** dupe, fool **8.** easy
mark
Gulliver, Lemuel (pert to) . . .
brutes .. **6.** Yahoos (race of)
character, story by .. **5.** Swift
voyage .. **6.** Laputa **8.** Lilliput
9. Houyhnhnm **11.** Brobdingnag
gully . . . **3.** gut **4.** wadi (wady) **5.** drain,
gorge, gulch **6.** arroyo, gutter, ravine
7. couloir **11.** watercourse
gum . . . **3.** ase **4.** chew, lerp (larp, laarp)
5. elemi, myrrh, xylan **6.** acacia,
arabic, chicle, conima, thwart, tupelo
7. camphor, deceive, elastic, gingiva
8. bdellium (Bib), mucilage
12. frankincense
gum (pert to) . . .
Africa .. **4.** kino **7.** catechy
Asia .. **6.** Storax **7.** galbabum
Australia .. **5.** tuart
Central America .. **6.** chicle
Egypt .. **5.** kikar
India .. **5.** amrad
Philippines .. **8.** galagala
United States .. **5.** Nyssa **6.** tupelo
gumbo . . . **3.** mud **4.** okra (ocra), sail,
soup **6.** patois
gumboil . . . **7.** abscess, parulia
gummy . . . **5.** lumpy **6.** viscid **7.** viscous
8. adhesive, resinous
gumption . . . **8.** sagacity **10.** enterprise,
initiative, shrewdness
gums . . . **3.** ula **6.** resins **8.** gingivae
gun . . . **3.** gat, rod **4.** iron, pump, roer
5. Maxim, rifle, thief, tommy **6.** ack-ack,
Archie, barker, Bertha, cannon, mortar,
pistol, Rodman **7.** bazooka, carbine,
firearm, Gatling, machine, shotgun
8. amusette, ordnance, revolver
gun (pert to) . . .
blow .. **8.** sumpitan
caliber .. **4.** bore
case (leather) .. **7.** holster
chamber .. **5.** gomer
cleaner .. **6.** ramrod
cotton .. **5.** nitro **9.** explosive, pyroxylin
mount .. **6.** turret
platform .. **11.** emplacement
gunfire . . . **5.** salvo **6.** strafe **8.** enfilade
gunner . . . **10.** bombardier **12.** artilleryman
guppy . . . **6.** minnow **8.** Lebistes **9.** killifish
gurnard . . . **4.** fish **6.** rochet, Trigla
8. dragonet, sea robin
guru (Ind) . . . **7.** teacher
gush . . . **3.** jet **4.** flow, pour, spew
5. emote, spurt **7.** chatter **10.** outpouring
14. sentimentalize
gushing . . . **7.** flowing **8.** diffused, effusive,

spurting **9.** exuberant **11.** sentimental **13.** demonstrative

gusset . . . **4.** gore **7.** bracket **9.** abatement (Her)

gust . . . **4.** blow, gale, scud, wind **5.** berry, blast, storm **6.** flurry, squall **8.** outburst **10.** excitement

gusto . . . **4.** élan, zest **5.** savor, taste **6.** fervor, liking, relish **9.** eagerness **12.** appreciation

gut . . . **3.** sac (silkworm) **5.** gully **6.** bowels, catgut, defile, strait **7.** destroy, plunder **8.** entrails **9.** intestine **10.** disembowel, eviscerate

guts . . . **5.** belly, force, pluck **6.** vitals **7.** courage, insides, stamina, stomach **8.** backbone, gluttony **10.** intestines

gutta . . . **4.** drop, spot **5.** latex **7.** campana, marking **8.** ornament

guttate . . . **7.** spotted **8.** droplike

gutter . . . **4.** rone **5.** brook, ditch, drain, eaves, gully, siver **6.** cullis, groove **7.** channel, conduit, scupper **11.** watercourse

gutteral . . . **3.** dry **4.** burr **5.** husky, velar **6.** hoarse **7.** rasping, throaty

guttersnipe . . . **4.** Arab **5.** gamin **6.** poster **9.** ragpicker, sandpiper, vulgarian

guy . . . **3.** rod **4.** flee, rope, stay, vang **5.** chaff, chain, guide **6.** banter,

decamp, effigy (Guy Fawkes), fellow, person

Guy Fawkes Day . . . **13.** Gunpowder Plot (Eng, Nov 5, 1605)

guzzle . . . **3.** tun **4.** tope **5.** drain, drink, spree **6.** gutter, liquor, throat, tipple **7.** debauch, swallow

gymnast . . . **7.** acrobat, athlete, teacher

gymnastics . . . **9.** exercises **10.** acrobatics **12.** calisthenics

gypsy (pert to) . . .
book . . **3.** lil
devil . . **5.** theng
Dutch . . **8.** Heidenen
horse . . **3.** gri (gry)
Hungarian . . **7.** Czigany
husband . . **3.** rom
India . . **7.** Bazigar
language . . **6.** Romany
man . . **4.** chal
sea . . **6.** Selung
Spanish . . **6.** gitano **7.** Zincalo
Syrian . . **5.** Aptal
term . . **4.** calo **5.** nomad
woman . . **4.** chai (chi)

gyrate . . . **4.** spin **5.** twirl, whirl **6.** rotate **7.** revolve

gyre . . . **5.** demon, whirl **10.** revolution

gyves . . . **5.** irons **6.** chains **7.** fetters **8.** shackles

H

H . . . **5.** aitch, zygal (shaped) **6.** letter (8th), symbol **8.** aspirate

haab . . . **8.** calendar (Mayan)

haar . . . **3.** fog

haba . . . **4.** bean **8.** lima bean

Habakkuk . . . **4.** Book (Old Test) **7.** prophet

habble . . . **5.** brawl **6.** gabble, hobble, uproar **9.** confusion **10.** difficulty

habeas corpus . . . **4.** writ **7.** summons (you have the body)

habile . . . **3.** apt, fit **4.** able **6.** adroit, clever, expert **8.** skillful (skilful), suitable **9.** dexterous

habiliment . . . **4.** garb **5.** dress, habit **6.** attire **7.** apparel, costume, raiment **8.** clothing, vestment **11.** furnishings

habilitate . . . **5.** dress, equip **6.** clothe, fit out **7.** entitle, quality (for teaching)

habit . . . **3.** rut, use **4.** garb, suit, vice, wont **5.** array, dress, haunt, usage **6.** attire, clothe, custom, joseph (riding), nature **7.** costume **8.** clothing, habitude, practice **9.** mannerism **10.** deportment, habiliment

habitat . . . **4.** home **5.** abode, house, hovel **6.** harbor, reside **7.** exhibit (museum), lodging, station

habitation . . . **4.** ecad, home **5.** hovel **6.** ghetto, warren (rabbit) **7.** lodging **8.** domicile, dwelling, tenement **9.** occupancy, residence

habitual . . . **5.** usual **6.** common, wonted

7. orderly, regular **9.** customary **10.** accustomed, inveterate

habituate . . . **5.** enure, inure **6.** addict, inborn, season, settle **8.** accustom, frequent, inherent **9.** acclimate **11.** acclimatize, familiarize

habitué . . . **8.** attender **10.** frequenter

hacendero . . . **6.** farmer **10.** proprietor

hache . . . **2.** ax **7.** hatchet

hacienda . . . **4.** farm **5.** abode, croft **6.** estate **7.** revenue **13.** establishment

hack . . . **3.** cut, hew **4.** chop, jade, rent **5.** coach, cough, devil, horse (rented), sever **6.** drudge, mangle, writer **8.** carriage, mutilate **9.** mercenary **11.** chronometer

hackberry . . . **6.** Celtis **8.** hapberry, oneberry **10.** sugarberry

hackee . . . **8.** chipmunk

hackle . . . **3.** fly (angling) **4.** comb, hack **6.** shiner, temper **7.** feather, hatchel, plumage **11.** stickleback

hackneyed . . . **3.** saw **5.** banal, corny, stale, trite **6.** cliché **8.** timeworn **10.** threadbare **11.** commonplace, stereotyped **13.** platitudinous

Hades . . . **3.** pit **4.** hell **5.** abyss, limbo **7.** inferno **9.** perdition **10.** lower world, underworld **11.** netherworld

Hades (pert to) . . .
Babylonian . . **5.** Aralu
capital . . **11.** Pandemonium
ferryman . . **6.** Charon

god . . **5.** Pluto
guide . . **6.** Hermes
Hebrew . . **5.** Sheol **7.** Abaddon, Gehenna
  8. Apollyon
Hindu . . **6.** Naraka
mother . . **4.** Rhea
region, lowest . . **8.** Tartarus
river . . **4.** Styx **5.** Lethe **7.** Acheron
Roman . . **3.** Dis **5.** Orcus
hadj, hajj . . . **10.** pilgrimage (Mecca)
haft . . **4.** ansa, grip, hold **6.** handle
  8. dwelling
hag . . . **4.** Fury, goad **5.** crone, ghost,
  Harpy, vixen, witch **6.** beldam
  (beldame), goblin **8.** harridan, old
  woman **9.** hobgoblin
hageen, hagein . . . **9.** dromedary
hagfish . . . **5.** borer **6.** Mysine **7.** lamprey
  (lowest existing craniate vertebrate)
haggard . . . **4.** bony, lank, lean, pale,
  thin, wild **5.** gaunt, spare **6.** wanton
  7. anxious, untamed **8.** harrowed,
  unchaste, wild-eyed **9.** deathlike,
  suffering, untrained **10.** cadaverous
  11. intractable, overwrought
haggle . . . **3.** cut, hew **4.** hack, prig
  5. cavil **6.** chisel, dicker, higgle, palter
  7. bargain, chaffer, stickle, wrangle
Hague, The . . . **7.** capital (Neth)
Haida (pert to) . . .
famed for . . **6.** totems **7.** carving
  10. seamanship
people . . **11.** Skittagetan
hail . . . **3.** ave, ice **4.** ahoy, call **5.** avast,
  greet, skoal **6.** accost, health, signal
  7. acclaim, address, graupel, pellets
hair . . . **3.** cue, fur, mop **4.** lock,
  mane, seta, shag **5.** pilus, plume,
  tress **6.** thread **7.** bristle **8.** filament
  10. narrowness
hair (pert to) . . .
accessory . . **3.** net, pin **8.** barrette
Angora . . **6.** mohair
band . . **5.** snood **6.** fillet
braid . . **3.** cue **4.** fall **5.** queue **7.** pigtail
cell . . **12.** Organ of Corti
cloth . . **3.** aba **5.** shirt **6.** cilice
comb form . . **4.** pilo
curly . . **10.** cymotrichy
disease . . **8.** dandruff, psilosis
dresser . . **7.** friseur (Fr), stylist
dryness . . **7.** xerasia
excessive growth . . **7.** pilosis
flaxen . . **5.** linus
horse's foot . . **7.** fetlock
intestinal . . **6.** villus
liquid for . . **3.** set **5.** spray **6.** lotion
  7. relaxer
lock . . **5.** tress **7.** earlock, ringlet
  8. lovelock **9.** dreadlock
loss of . . **8.** alopecia, baldness
of the . . **6.** crinal
remover . . **9.** decalvant, epilatory
  10. depilatory
straight . . **10.** leiotrichy
style . . **3.** set **4.** Afro, tete, updo **6.** hairdo
  7. chignon, cornrow **8.** coiffure
tuft . . **4.** coma **5.** beard **6.** goatee
  7. cirrose, Galways, Vandyke
  8. whiskers **9.** sideburns
wave . . **4.** perm **5.** marcel

wig . . **6.** peruke **7.** periwig
wooly . . **9.** ulotrichy
hairiness . . . **7.** villous **9.** villosity
hairless . . . **4.** bald **5.** acoma **7.** acomous,
  epilose **8.** depilous, glabrous
hairpin . . . **6.** bodkin **8.** bobby pin
hairsplitting . . . **9.** quibbling
  11. distinction **13.** hypercritical
  14. hypercriticism, overparticular
hairy . . . **4.** noil **5.** pilar **6.** comate,
  comoid, comose, crinal, pilose, shaggy
  7. bristly, crinose, hirsute **8.** trichoid
Haiti, Haitian . . .
bandit . . **4.** caco
capital . . **12.** Port-au-Prince
dance . . **5.** mambo
dictator . . **7.** Papa Doc **8.** Duvalier
discoverer . . **8.** Columbus (1492)
evil spirit . . **4.** baka (boko)
island . . **10.** Hispaniola **15.** Greater
  Antilles
language . . **6.** Creole, French, patois
liberator . . **9.** Toussaint
product . . **6.** coffee
sweet potato . . **6.** batata
hake . . . **4.** fish **5.** idler, tramp **6.** loiter
  7. handgun **8.** kingfish
halberd . . . **4.** bill **5.** frame (flogging)
  6. glaive, weapon (Mil)
halcyon . . . **4.** bird, calm **8.** peaceful,
  tranquil **10.** auspicious, kingfisher
Halcyone (pert to) . . .
changed to . . **10.** kingfisher
daughter of . . **6.** Aeolus
wife of . . **4.** Ceyx (Gr)
hale . . . **3.** tug **4.** drag, draw, haul, pull,
  well **6.** hearty, robust, strong **7.** healthy
  8. vigorous **9.** strapping
half . . . **4.** demi, hemi, part, semi, term
  5. share **6.** moiety **7.** divided, partial
  8. division, semester **9.** equal part,
  bisection **11.** imperfectly
half (pert to) . . .
and half . . **5.** equal, mixed **6.** halved
  7. neutral
boot . . **3.** pac (pack) **6.** buskin
man, half bull . . **8.** minotaur
man, half horse . . **7.** centaur
mask . . **6.** domino
moon-shaped . . **9.** semilunar
nelson (wrestling) . . **4.** hold
stem to stem . . **8.** midships
turn (manège) . . **8.** caracole (caracol)
wit . . **4.** dolt **5.** dunce **9.** blockhead
Half Moon ship (pert to) . . .
captain . . **11.** Henry Hudson
country . . **11.** Netherlands
first to sail . . **11.** Hudson River (1609)
Halicarnassus, famed for . . .
Historians (Gr) . . **9.** Dionysius, Herodotus
monument . . **9.** Mausoleum (Tomb of
  Mausolus, 325 BC)
hall . . . **4.** aula, room, sala **5.** entry, foyer,
  odeum (odeon) **6.** atrium, lyceum
  7. hallway, passage, theater **8.** corridor
  9. vestibule **10.** auditorium, passageway
hallow . . . **5.** bless **8.** dedicate, sanctify,
  venerate **9.** celebrate **10.** consecrate
hallowed place . . . **4.** fane, holy **5.** altar
  6. bethel, church, shrine, temple
  9. cathedral, synagogue

hallucination ... **4.** trip **6.** mirage **7.** chimera, fantasy **8.** delusion **9.** nightmare

hallucinogen ... **3.** LSD **4.** acid **6.** mescal, peyote **9.** mescaline **10.** psilocybin **12.** lysergic acid

hallux ... **3.** toe **5.** digit

halo ... **3.** arc **4.** aura, glow, nimb, ring **5.** glory, light **6.** areola, brough, circle, corona, nimbus **7.** aureole (aureola) **8.** encircle, halation

halt ... **3.** end **4.** camp, lame, limp, stop **5.** cease, check, pause, stand **6.** arrest, desist, hold up, maimed **7.** limping **8.** blockage, crippled, lameness **9.** mutilated **10.** standstill

halter ... **4.** hang, rope **5.** noose, strap **6.** hamper **7.** shackle **8.** cavesson, restrain **9.** hackamore

halting ... **4.** lame **6.** maimed **7.** limping **8.** spavined **10.** hesitating, stammering

halting place ... **4.** camp **5.** étape **7.** bivouac **10.** encampment

halved ... **9.** dimidiate

Hamburg, Germany ...
color .. **5.** white **6.** yellow **7.** carmine **11.** carmine lake
fowl .. **11.** Leghornlike
fruit .. **5.** grape
lace .. **6.** edging
root (edible) .. **7.** parsley
steak .. **4.** beef

hamiform ... **6.** curved, hooked **7.** hamulus **8.** aquiline **10.** hook-shaped

Hamilton (pert to) ...
killed by .. **4.** Burr
party .. **10.** Federalist
secretary (lst) .. **8.** Treasury

Hamite (No Afr) ... **5.** Fulah **6.** Berber, Somali (Somal)

hamlet ... **4.** dorp, vill **5.** aldea (aldee), casal (casale), thorp (thorpe) **7.** grouper (fish), village

Hamlet (pert to) ...
author .. **11.** Shakespeare
country .. **7.** Denmark
friend .. **7.** Horatio
site .. **8.** Elsinore

hammer ... **4.** beat, claw, jack, maul, peen, tack, tamp **5.** gavel, kevel, madge, pound **6.** beetle, martel, oliver, sledge, strike, swinge **7.** belabor **8.** malleate

hammer (pert to) ...
bird .. **8.** umbrette
blacksmith's .. **6.** fuller, oliver
bricklayer's .. **6.** scutch
end .. **4.** poll
face .. **4.** trip
head .. **4.** peen **5.** shark
medical .. **6.** plexor **7.** plessor
out .. **5.** anvil, forge
smite .. **5.** skite
stone .. **5.** kevel, spall

hamper ... **3.** ped **4.** clog, curb, load, slow **5.** cramp, crate, maund **6.** basket, burden, fetter, hinder, hopple, impede, seroon **7.** confine, hanaper, manacle, shackle, trammel **8.** encumber, restrain, restrict **9.** container, embarrass **10.** impediment

Ham's son ... **4.** Cush

hamster ... **6.** rodent **8.** Cricetus

hamus ... **4.** hook **7.** process (Zool)

hanaper ... **6.** basket, hamper

hand ... **3.** paw **4.** fist, give, mano, palm, part, pass, side, till **5.** claut, grasp, index, manus, power, share, skill **6.** agency, worker **7.** ability, pointer, workman **8.** applause, tendency, transmit **9.** craftsman, handiwork, signature **10.** metacarpus **11.** handwriting, performance **15.** instrumentality

hand (pert to) ...
back of .. **10.** opisthenar
bag .. **4.** etui, grip **5.** cabas, purse **8.** reticule
book .. **4.** tome **5.** codex **6.** manual **9.** vade mecum
cuffs .. **7.** darbies **8.** manacles **9.** bracelets
handful .. **4.** kirn **6.** gowpen **7.** maniple **8.** quantity
measure .. **8.** fistmele
me-down .. **4.** used, worn **5.** cheap **9.** ready-made **10.** secondhand
of the .. **6.** chiral, manual
palm .. **4.** loof **6.** thenar
picked .. **5.** eleme **6.** choice **8.** selected
script .. **6.** Neskhi (Neski)
stone (grinding) .. **4.** mano
without .. **7.** amanous
writing .. **11.** chirography
writing on walls .. **4.** doom, mene (Bib), omen **8.** graffito

handicap ... **4.** lisp, race **6.** burden, hamper, hinder, impede **8.** encumber, equalize, penalize **9.** advantage **10.** impediment, stuttering **11.** encumbrance **12.** disadvantage

handicraftsman ... **7.** artisan

handkerchief ... **7.** malabar **8.** mouchoir **9.** neckcloth **11.** neckerchief

handle ... **3.** ear, paw, ply, use **4.** ansa, bail, deal, feel, haft, hilt, knob, maul, name, toat, tote **5.** helve, pilot, snath, swipe, title, touch, treat, wield **6.** deal in, direct, manage, rounce, second, sneath, tiller **7.** control, operate

handle (pert to) ...
awkwardly .. **6.** fumble, mumble
carelessly .. **6.** cajole **7.** tweedle
roughly .. **4.** maul **6.** bruise, injure, mangle
shaped .. **6.** ansate
skillfully .. **6.** manage **7.** control **10.** manipulate

hands (pert to) ...
nautical .. **4.** crew, gang
off .. **4.** don't, quit, stop **5.** taboo **6.** desist **9.** interdict
on hips .. **6.** akimbo
without .. **7.** amanous

handsome ... **5.** ample **6.** comely, heppen (dial) **7.** elegant, gallant, liberal **8.** generous, gracious, pleasing, suitable **9.** agreeable, beautiful **10.** jimpricute **11.** appropriate, magnanimous **12.** considerable

handwriting on the wall ... **4.** mene (Bib) **8.** graffito, upharsin

handy ... **4.** deft **5.** adept, ready

6. adroit, heppen, nearby, wieldy
8. skillful (skilful) 9. dexterous, versatile
10. accessible, convenient

hang ... 3. sag 4. pend, rest, sway 5. cling, drape, droop, hover, knack 6. cleave, dangle, depend 7. execute, meaning, suspend

hang (pert to) ...
around.. 4. loaf, wait 6. loiter 8. frequent
back.. 3. lag 5. demur, loath 6. falter
9. reluctant
down.. 3. lop 4. lave 5. droop 6. depend
loosely.. 3. lop 4. flag, loll 6. bangle, dangle
on, onto.. 5. cling 6. adhere, depend
9. persevere
over.. 6. impend
together.. 4. loin 6. cohere 9. co-operate

hanger-on ... 3. bur 5. toady 6. heeler
8. follower, loiterer, parasite
9. appendage, dependent, sycophant, toadeater (menial) 10. blackguard

hanging ... 5. arras, drape, loose
7. curtain, pendant (pendent), pensile, valance 8. downcast, pendency
9. execution, suspended

hanging (pert to) ...
Eccl.. 6. dorsal, dossal (dossel)
Gardens of Babylon, builder..
14. Nebuchadnezzar (Nebuchadrezzar)
ornament.. 6. bangle 7. pendant
stage.. 7. scenery

hangman ... 8. carnifex 9. Jack Ketch
11. executioner

hangman's noose ... 4. rope 6. hempen

hangnail ... 6. agnail 7. whitlow

hangout ... 5. joint 10. rendezvous

hank ... 3. ran (twine) 4. coil 5. skein

hanker after ... 5. crave, yearn 6. aspire, desire, hunger 7. long for

Hannibal (pert to) ...
accomplishment.. 8. Punic War (2nd)
father.. 13. Hamilcar Barca
native of.. 8. Carthage
rank.. 7. General (genius)
victory at.. 6. Cannae

Hanover, House of ... 8. Victoria

Hanukkah, Hanukka ... 7. holiday (Jew)
16. Festival of Lights (Bib) 17. Feast of Dedication (Jew)

haphazard ... 6. chance, random
8. accident, careless 9. orderless

haply ... 9. perchance

happen ... 4. come, fall, fare 5. evene (obs), occur 6. arrive, befall, betide, chance, mayhap 9. eventuate, transpire

happening ... 4. fact 5. event (chance)
6. tiding 7. episode 8. incident, periodic, sporadic 10. occurrence

happily ... 5. fitly, haply 6. gladly
9. tactfully, willingly 10. blissfully, cheerfully, gracefully 11. contentedly, opportunely 12. auspiciously, felicitously, prosperously, successfully
13. appropriately

happiness, science of ...
11. eudaemonics

happy ... 3. apt 4. cosh, glad 5. blest, faust, lucky, ready, seely, sunny
6. joyful, timely 7. blessed, content, fitting 8. cheerful 9. contented,

fortunate, pertinent 10. auspicious, felicitous, propitious, prosperous

Happy Valley ... 8. paradise (of Rasselas, Andrew Jackson)

hara-kiri (Jap) ... 7. seppuku, suicide

harangue ... 3. nag 4. rant 5. orate, spiel, spout 6. screed, speech, tirade
7. address, declaim, expound, lecture, oration

harass ... 3. din, fag, nag, try, vex
4. bait, fret, gall, haze, jade, raid, tire
5. annoy, beset, bully, chafe, grind, harry, tease, weary, worry 6. badger, bother, heckle, hector, molest, pester, plague 7. agitate, disturb, hagride, perplex, provoke, torment, trouble
8. distress, irritate 9. persecute, tantalize

harbinger ... 4. host, omen 5. usher
6. herald 7. presage, shelter 8. fourrier, harborer 9. informant, messenger, precursor 10. forerunner

harbinger of Spring ... 5. robin, tulip
6. crocus

harbor, harbour ... 3. bay 4. cave, port 5. haven 6. covert, foster, refuge
7. lodging, outport, retreat, shelter

hard ... 3. fit 4. cold, dour, firm, iron, mean 5. close, harsh, rigid, stern, stony
6. knotty, robust, steely, stingy, strict, strong 7. callous, onerous 8. diligent, rigorous, toilsome 9. difficult, heartless, intricate, strenuous, stringent, wearisome 10. inflexible, relentless, unyielding 12. impenetrable, incorrigible 13. unsympathetic

hard (pert to) ...
boiled.. 4. hard 5. tough 6. strict
7. callous 8. hardened 10. solidified
13. sophisticated
coal.. 10. anthracite
money.. 6. silver 8. metallic
prefix.. 3. dys
question.. 5. poser
rubber.. 7. ebonite 9. vulcanite
shell.. 6. lorica
stone.. 7. adamant (diamond)
wood.. 4. mabi, teak 5. maple 6. walnut
8. mahogany

harden ... 3. gel, set 4. cake, kern
5. enure, inure, steel 6. freeze, ossify, temper 7. toughen 8. indurate, solidify
9. habituate 10. strengthen

hardened ... 4. hard 5. caked 6. frozen, wicked 7. callous, steeled 8. indurate, obdurate, ossified 9. heartless, reprobate, unfeeling 10. impenitent, impervious, inveterate, solidified
12. impenetrable

hardening of the arteries ...
16. arteriosclerosis

hardening of the eyeball ... 8. glaucoma

hardheaded ... 6. shrewd, strict
9. obstinate, sagacious

hardhearted ... 4. mean 5. cruel
7. callous 8. pitiless 9. unfeeling
13. unsympathetic

hardship ... 5. rigor 6. injury 7. trouble
8. hardness 9. adversity, privation

hardtack ... 5. bread 7. galette 10. sea biscuit

hardwood ... 3. ash, oak 4. ipil, mabi,

teak **5.** maple **6.** walnut **8.** mahogany
hardy . . . **4.** bold, hale, rash **5.** brave,
lusty, stout **6.** daring, strong **7.** healthy,
spartan **8.** intrepid, resolute
9. audacious, confident **10.** courageous
Hardy heroine . . . **4.** Tess
hare . . . **3.** doe, wat (watt) **4.** buck, cony,
pika (tailless) **5.** lapin, Lepus **6.** rabbit,
rodent, tapeti **7.** leveret
hare (pert to) . . .
  constellation . . **5.** Lepus
  harelike . . **6.** agouti **8.** leporine
  tail . . **4.** scut
  track . . **4.** slot
  type . . **10.** cottontail, jack rabbit
harem . . . **5.** serai **6.** purdah, zenana
8. seraglio **9.** gynaeceum
harem room . . . **3.** oda (odah)
harem slave . . . **9.** odalisque (odalisk)
hark . . . **4.** heed, hist **6.** listen **7.** hearken,
whisper **9.** attention
harkened . . . **5.** heard **6.** heeded
8. listened **9.** hearkened
harlequin . . . **4.** duck (sea) **5.** clown,
color **7.** buffoon **9.** fantastic, trickster
11. masquerader **12.** multi-colored,
parti-colored
Harlequin (comedy) . . . **11.** pantomimist
harm . . . **3.** mar **4.** bane, dere, evil,
hurt, pain **5.** grief, wrong **6.** damage,
impair, injure, injury, scathe (scath),
sorrow **10.** misfortune, wickedness
12. disadvantage
harmful . . . **3.** bad **4.** evil, upas **6.** nocent
7. baneful, hurtful, malefic, noisome,
noxious **8.** damaging, sinister
9. injurious **10.** pernicious
11. deleterious, detrimental
12. insalubrious
harmless . . . **5.** seely **6.** unhurt
8. dehorned, unharmed **9.** innocuous,
undamaged, uninjured **11.** unoffending
harmonious . . . **6.** syntax **7.** harmony,
musical, orderly, spheral, tuneful
9. accordant, agreeable, congruous,
consonant, eurythmic (eurhythmic),
melodious **10.** compatible, concordant,
euphonious **11.** conformable,
symmetrical
harmonize . . . **2.** go **3.** gee **4.** tone
5. agree, blend, chime **6.** attune
7. conform, consist **9.** reconcile
10. correspond, symmetrize, sympathize
harmony . . . **4.** tone, tune **5.** music,
order, triad, unity **6.** accord, cosmos,
melody, unison **7.** concord, euphony
8. symmetry **9.** agreement, harmonics
10. conformity, consonance
harness . . . **4.** gear **5.** armor, equip
6. graith, tackle **7.** uniform **8.** accouter,
ornament **9.** caparison, parachute
harness part . . . **3.** tug **4.** hame,
rein **5.** trace **6.** collar, halter, terret
7. apparel **9.** hackamore **10.** breastband,
martingale
harp . . . **4.** arpa, koto, lyre, Lyra (Astron)
5. nanga **8.** Irishman **11.** clairschach
harp (pert to) . . .
  key . . **5.** C Flat
  octaves (number) . . **11.** six and a half
  pedals . . **5.** seven

  star . . **12.** Harp of Arthur
  strings . . **8.** forty-six
harping . . . **7.** humdrum, tedious
9. iterating, repeating **11.** repetitious
harpoon . . . **5.** spear **7.** javelin **8.** lily
iron
harpsichord . . . **6.** spinet **8.** clavecin
9. lyrichord **12.** clavicembalo
harpy . . . **3.** bat **5.** eagle, fiend **9.** plunderer
12. extortionist
Harpy (Myth) . . . **5.** Aello, ghoul
7. Celaeno, monster (part bird, woman),
Ocypete, Podarge (The Iliad)
harridan . . . **3.** hag **5.** vixen, witch
6. virago **7.** Jezebel **8.** strumpet
9. termagant
harrier . . . **3.** dog **4.** hawk **5.** bully, hound
7. heckler **8.** badgerer **9.** tormentor
harrow . . . **4.** dish, pain **5.** harry, herse
(Hist), wound **7.** oppress, torment,
torture **8.** distress, lacerate **9.** cultivate,
formation (geese), implement
harrowing . . . **7.** painful, racking, tilling
9. agonizing, torturous **11.** cultivating,
distressing **12.** heart-rending
harry . . . **3.** vex **4.** sack **5.** annoy, hound,
worry **6.** harass, hector, plague,
ravage, ravish **7.** agitate, besiege,
pillage, plunder, violate **8.** lay waste
9. persecute
Harry . . . **5.** Devil (Shaksp)
harsh . . . **3.** raw **4.** dure, grim **5.** acerb,
acrid, asper, crude, gruff, raspy, stern,
stiff **6.** bitter, coarse, severe, unkind
7. drastic, painful, pungent, rasping
8. clashing, gutteral, jangling, rigorous,
strident **9.** inclement, offensive,
repellent **10.** discordant, relentless
11. acrimonious, disagreeing
harshness . . . **5.** rigor **7.** raucity
8. acrimony, pungency, severity
9. gruffness **11.** raucousness
hart . . . **4.** deer, stag **5.** spade
hartebeast . . . **4.** asse, tora **5.** caama
(kaama) **6.** lecama **7.** bubalis **8.** antelope
10. Alcelaphus
Harvard College honor . . . **4.** book
5. detur **12.** let it be given
harvest . . . **4.** crop, gain, rabi, reap
5. fruit, yield **6.** autumn, gather, reward
7. acquire, produce
harvest (pert to) . . .
  god . . **6.** Cronus, Saturn
  goddess . . **3.** Ops **5.** Ceres
  home . . **4.** kirn, mell **6.** hockey
  moon . . **4.** full **15.** autumnal equinox
  second . . **2.** aftermath
  tick . . **6.** acarid
hash . . . **4.** food **5.** mince **6.** jumble,
medley, ragout **7.** mixture
10. hodgepodge **11.** gallimaufry, olla
podrida
hashish . . . **4.** hemp **5.** bhang (bang)
8. cannabis, narcotic
hassle . . . **4.** fray **5.** brawl, melee
hasten . . . **3.** hie **4.** scud, urge **5.** amain,
apace, hurry, scamp, speed **7.** further
8. expedite **10.** accelerate **11.** precipitate
hastened . . . **3.** ran **4.** hied, sped
5. raced **6.** rushed **7.** hurried, scooted
8. galloped **9.** expedited **11.** accelerated

12. precipitated

hasty . . . **4.** fast, rash **5.** brash, eager, fleet, quick, swift **6.** speedy, sudden, urgent **7.** cursory, hurried **8.** reckless **9.** impetuous, impulsive, premature **11.** expeditious, precipitate

hasty pudding . . . **4.** mush **9.** stirabout

hat . . . **3.** fez, tam, top **4.** felt, hood, silk **5.** beret, derby, gibus, opera, straw, terai, toque **6.** bonnet, cloche, cocked, fedora, Panama, sailor, topper, turban **7.** chapeau, picture, pillbox, porkpie, tricorn **8.** sombrero, headdress, sou'wester, stovepipe, ten-gallon **11.** mortarboard **13.** three-cornered

hat (pert to) . . .
antique . . **7.** bycoket (bycocket), petasos (petasus)
covering . . **8.** havelock
crown . . **4.** poll
defensive . . **4.** coif
Eccl . . **7.** biretta **9.** Cardinal's
military . . **5.** shako
opera . . **4.** tile **5.** gibus **6.** topper
pass (the hat) . . **10.** collection
slang . . **4.** plug **5.** dicer
stovepipe . . **8.** caroline
under one's . . **6.** secret **9.** to oneself

hatch . . . **4.** door, gate, line (art), plot **5.** breed **6.** invent **7.** concoct, produce **8.** contrive, hatchway, incubate **9.** floodgate, originate **10.** bring forth, sluice gate

hatchet . . . **2.** ax (axe) **3.** adz (adze) **4.** mogo **8.** tomahawk

hate . . . **4.** miso (comb form) **5.** abhor, odium **6.** detest, hatred, loathe, rancor **7.** despise, dislike **9.** abominate, antipathy

hateful . . . **6.** odious **7.** heinous **8.** terrible **9.** abhorrent, execrable, invidious, loathsome, malicious, obnoxious, offensive, revolting **10.** abominable, detestable, disgusting **11.** distasteful **12.** disagreeable

hater of . . .
children . . **10.** misopedist
mankind . . **11.** misanthrope
marriage . . **10.** misogynist
mathematics . . **8.** misomath
newness . . **9.** misoneist
sights . . **11.** misoscopist
strangers . . **8.** misoxene
work . . **11.** ergophobiac

hatred . . . **5.** odium **6.** animus, enmity, rancor **8.** aversion, loathing **9.** animosity, malignity **10.** abhorrence, repugnance **11.** detestation, malevolence

hatred of . . .
argument . . **8.** misology
change . . **9.** misoneism
children . . **9.** misopedia
God, gods . . **10.** misotheism
mankind . . **11.** misanthropy
marriage . . **8.** misogamy
strangers . . **8.** misoxeny **10.** xenophobia
war . . **9.** polemical **11.** misopolemic
wisdom . . **9.** misosophy
women . . **8.** misogyny

hauberk . . . **5.** armor **9.** habergeon

haughty . . . **4.** airy, bold, high **5.** lofty, noble, proud **6.** snooty **7.** fatuous, stately **8.** arrogant, cavalier, orgulous, scornful **10.** disdainful, hoity-toity **11.** domineering, highfalutin **12.** contemptuous, supercilious

haul . . . **3.** lug, tow, tug **4.** cart, drag, draw, pull **5.** booty, bouse, catch, check, shift **9.** reprimand, transport

haul down a flag . . . **6.** strike

haunch . . . **3.** hip **4.** huck **10.** leg and loin **12.** hindquarters

haunch bone . . . **10.** innominate

haunt . . . **3.** den **4.** dive, nest **5.** ghost, habit **6.** infect, obsess, resort **7.** torment **8.** frequent, practice

hautboy . . . **4.** oboe

have . . . **3.** get, hae, own **4.** hold, keep, know **5.** beget, trick **6.** accept, effect, retain **7.** cherish, perform, possess, swindle **10.** experience, understand, suffer from

have (pert to) . . .
ambition . . **6.** aspire
charge . . **4.** tend
on . . **4.** wear
thoughts of . . **6.** ideate
to do with . . **4.** deal
weight . . **8.** militate

haven . . . **3.** bay **4.** port **5.** hithe (small), inlet **6.** asylum, harbor, recess, refuge **7.** shelter **9.** sanctuary

havier . . . **4.** deer

having (pert to) . . .
blind end . . **6.** caecal
branches . . **6.** ramose
clamp, pincers . . **7.** chelate
dignity . . **8.** majestic
equal sides . . **9.** isosceles
eyes . . **7.** oculate
faith . . **8.** trusting
featherlike petals . . **7.** pinnate
feelers . . **9.** antennate
fingers . . **8.** digitate
foreknowledge . . **9.** prescient
four feet . . **11.** quadrupedal
harmful quality . . **9.** innocuous
leaves . . **6.** foliar **7.** foliate
limits . . **6.** finite
local designation . . **7.** topical
lumps . . **7.** noduled
more than one mate . . **9.** polyandry
no angles . . **6.** agonic
no interest . . **6.** supine
no teeth . . **7.** edental **8.** edentate
nothing to do . . **6.** otiose
one foot . . **6.** uniped
pits, depressions . . **7.** foveate **9.** foveolate
plane surfaces . . **7.** faceted
pointed end . . **6.** peaked **7.** cuspate **8.** aristate
power over fire . . **10.** ignipotent
power to believe . . **9.** creditive
reflecting surface . . **8.** specular
same ending . . **11.** conterminal
same parents . . **7.** germane
sawlike edge . . **7.** serrate
scales . . **8.** perulate
scalloped edge . . **7.** crenate
taste . . **5.** sapid
thorns . . **7.** spinate

three broods yearly.. **11.** trigoneutic
two feet.. **5.** biped **7.** bipedal
two horns.. **6.** bicorn
two meanings.. **9.** ambiguous
unequal sides.. **7.** scalene
web feet.. **8.** pinniped
wings.. **4.** alar
having a...
backbone.. **10.** vertebrate
beak.. **8.** rostrate
beard.. **8.** aristate
handle.. **6.** ansate
large nose.. **6.** nasute
shield.. **9.** clypeated
stem.. **9.** petiolate
tail.. **7.** caudate
tuft.. **6.** comose
veil.. **6.** velate
will.. **7.** testate
havoc... **4.** harm **5.** botch, waste
7. destroy **11.** destruction, devastation
12. annihilation
haw... **4.** sloe **5.** fence, hedge **6.** eyelid
(3rd) **7.** stammer **8.** hawthorn,
messuage, turn left **9.** enclosure
11. exclamation
Hawaii... see also *Hawaiian*
capital.. **8.** Honolulu
city.. **4.** Hilo **7.** Wailuku
district.. **7.** Lahaina
explorer.. **4.** Cook (Capt)
harbor.. **5.** Pearl (bombed 12/7/41)
islands (major).. **4.** Maui, Oahu **5.** Kauai,
Lanai **6.** Hawaii, Niihau **7.** Molokai
9. Kahoolawe
lake.. **5.** Waiau
native.. **10.** Polynesian
old name.. **15.** Sandwich Islands
peak.. **8.** Mauna Kea, Mauna Loa
9. Waialeale
resort.. **7.** Waikiki
Southernmost point (US).. **5.** Ka Lae
State admission.. **8.** Fiftieth
State bird.. **13.** Hawaiian goose
State flower.. **8.** hibiscus
State nickname.. **5.** Aloha **20.** Paradise
of the Pacific
volcano.. **7.** Kilauea **8.** Mauna Loa
(largest active)
Hawaiian... **6.** Kanaka **10.** Melanesian,
Polynesian **16.** South Sea islander
Hawaiian (pert to)...
banquet, feast.. **7.** ahaaina
basket.. **2.** ie
beverage.. **4.** kava **8.** kavakava
bird.. **2.** io, o-o **3.** iwa **4.** iiwi, mamo
(ext), noio, o-o-a-a **6.** olomao (thrush)
8. drepanis
canoe.. **5.** waapa
chant.. **4.** mele
cloth, clothes.. **4.** kapa, tapa
coffee.. **4.** kona
dance.. **4.** hula
fern.. **4.** pulu
fibre (pine).. **2.** ie
fish.. **3.** awa **4.** ulua **5.** akule, lania
flower wreath, garland.. **3.** lei
food.. **3.** poi **4.** kalo, taro
garment.. **6.** holoku, muumuu
god.. **5.** Wakea **7.** Kanaloa (Pantheon)
goddess.. **4.** Pele (volcanoes, fire)

gooseberry.. **4.** poha
grass.. **6.** emoloa
greeting.. **5.** aloha
herb.. **3.** pia (starch root)
king (first).. **10.** Kamehameha
lava.. **2.** aa **8.** pahoehoe
loincloth, girdle.. **4.** malo
musical instrument.. **7.** ukulele
newcomer.. **8.** malihini
pepper.. **3.** ava **4.** kava **8.** kavakava
precipice.. **4.** pali
Queen.. **8.** Kamamalu
royalty.. **4.** alii
seaweed (edible).. **4.** limu
shampoo, massage.. **8.** lomi-lomi
shrub.. **3.** pia **4.** akia, pulu **5.** olona
temple.. **5.** heiau
tern.. **4.** noio
tree.. **3.** koa
veranda.. **5.** lanai
windstorm.. **4.** kona
woman.. **5.** haole **6.** wahine
yam.. **3.** hoi
hawfinch... **8.** grosbeak
hawk... **3.** cry **4.** hunt, sell, vend
6. peddle **7.** canvass **9.** plunderer,
warmonger
hawk (bird)... **2.** io **3.** hen **4.** eyas,
kahu, kite, nyas, seel (blind) **5.** Astur,
Buteo **6.** falcon, osprey, tercel (tiercel)
7. buzzard, Cooper's, goshawk, harrier,
kestrel, puttock, sparrow, vulture
8. caracara **9.** Accipiter, red-tailed
hawker of fruit (Eng)... **6.** coster
12. costermonger
hawk-eyed deity... **2.** Ra
Hawkeye State... **4.** Iowa
hawking... **7.** hunting, vending
8. falconry
hawk's cage... **3.** mew
hawk moth... **6.** sphinx **8.** sphingid
hawksbill... **4.** pawl **6.** turtle **8.** tortoise
hawkshaw... **6.** sleuth **9.** detective
11. sleuthhound
hawk's nest... **5.** aerie (aery)
hawk's opposite... **4.** dove
hawser... **4.** line, rope
hawser post... **4.** bitt **7.** bollard
hawthorn... **3.** may **5.** hazel (fruit) **6.** red
haw **7.** haw tree **9.** mayflower
Hawthorne's...
adultress.. **6.** Hester (Prynne)
House of.. **11.** Seven Gables
Letter.. **7.** Scarlet
reverend.. **10.** Dimmesdale
hay... **6.** fodder **7.** timothy
hay (pert to)...
bird.. **7.** hay jack **8.** black cap
9. sandpiper (pectoral)
bundle.. **3.** mow **4.** bale, cock, rick
5. stack
fork.. **5.** pikel (pikle), pitch
herb.. **8.** sainfoin
mown.. **5.** swath
second cutting.. **5.** rowen
spreader.. **6.** tedder
stack.. **4.** rick **7.** hayrick
storage site.. **3.** mow **4.** barn, loft, silo
haywire... **4.** awry **5.** crazy
hazard... **3.** fog **4.** dare, game, jump,
risk **5.** peril **6.** gamble, sanger, stroke

7. imperil, jeopard, presume, venture
8. cabstand, casualty, endanger, jeopardy 11. restriction
hazardous . . . 5. hairy (sl), jumpy, risky 6. chancy, queasy, unsafe
7. unsound 8. perilous 9. uncertain, venturous 10. fortuitous 11. speculative, venturesome
haze . . . 3. fog 4. beat, film, glin (at sea), mist, smog 5. scold, smoke, vapor
7. dimness, drizzle 8. frighten
hazy . . . 3. dim 5. filmy, foggy, misty, smoky, thick, vague 6. cloudy, opaque, stupid 7. muddled, nebular, obscure
8. overcast 9. invisible, uncertain
10. indistinct
he . . . 2. il 3. man 4. ipsi, male 6. any one, letter 7. pronoun
head . . . 3. aim, nob 4. lead, pate, poll, tête (Fr) 5. caput, chief, skull 6. noggin, noodle (sl), source 7. cranium
head (pert to) . . .
abbey . . 5. abbot 6. abbess
back of . . 7. occiput
bald . . 6. acomia 9. pilgarlic
bone . . 8. parietal 9. occipital
Gorgon . . 6. Medusa (Myth)
hard . . 5. boche
of hair . . 5. crine
pert to . . 8. cephalic
proportion . . 14. mesitacephalic
shaven . . 7. tonsure
shrunken . . 7. tsentsa
headache . . . 6. megrim 8. migraine
11. cephalalgia
head covering . . . 3. cap, hat, tam, wig
4. hair, hood, veil 5. beret, miter, scalp
6. bonnet, peruke, toupee, wimple
7. biretta 8. sombrero 10. fascinator
headdress . . . 3. wig 4. pouf, tête
5. busby, miter, shako, tiara 6. coiffe, diadem, hennin, peruke, pinner
7. bandore, buzz wig, coronet, periwig
8. coiffure, headtire
headdress (Egypt) . . . 6. uraeus (with sacred asp)
headhunters (Luzon) . . . 7. Igorots
heading . . . 3. top 5. front, title, topic
6. pillow 7. bolster, caption 8. headline
9. direction 12. decapitation
headland . . . 4. cape, mull, ness 5. morro, ridge 10. promontory
headless . . . 6. stupid 7. acephal, topless
9. acephalus (monster) 10. acephalous
headline . . . 6. banner 7. caption, display, heading 8. streamer
headliner . . . 4. star 7. feature 8. composer
headlong . . . 4. rash 5. hasty, steep
6. head-on, sudden 8. reckless
9. headfirst, impetuous, impulsive
10. recklessly 11. impulsively, precipitate, precipitous
headpiece . . . 3. cap, hat, top 4. atef
5. crown 6. halter, helmet, lintel
7. fitting 8. covering, ornament, skull cap 9. headboard, headdress, headstall
head-shaped . . . 8. capitate
headstrong . . . 4. rash 6. entêté, unruly
7. violent, wayward 9. obstinate
11. intractable, opinionated
12. contumacious, ungovernable

heal . . . 4. cure, knit, mend 6. doctor, pacify, remedy, repair 7. correct, restore
9. cicatrize
healing (pert to) . . .
agent . . 6. balsam
compound . . 4. balm
goddess . . 3. Eir
magic . . 6. powwow
plant . . 4. aloe (vera)
process . . 4. scar 8. cicatrix
remedy . . 8. curative, sanative
science . . 3. spa 9. iatrology
suffix . . 7. iatrics
health (pert to) . . .
care . . 7. welfare
comb form . . 4. sani
conditions . . 8. sanitary
goddess . . 5. Salus 6. Hygeia 7. Minerva
Latin . . 5. salus
neurotic . . 13. hypochondriac
resort . . 3. spa 7. springs
symbol . . 5. pansy
healthful . . . 7. healthy 8. curative, salutary, sanatory 9. medicinal
10. salubrious
healthy . . . 4. hale, sane, well 6. hearty, robust 8. salutary, vigorous 9. healthful, wholesome 10. salubrious
heap . . . 3. cop 4. dess, load, lump, pile, pyre, raff, raft 5. amass, cairn, crowd, stack 6. plenty, sorite, throng
7. cumulus 9. multitude 10. accumulate
heaped . . . 5. piled 7. stacked 8. acervate
9. collected
hear . . . 3. see 4. feel, heed, oyez (oyes)
5. favor, judge, learn 6. attend, listen
7. hearken (harken) 8. listen to, perceive
9. attention 10. adjudicate
hearer . . . 7. audient, auditor 8. disciple, listener 9. hearkener (harkener)
12. eavesdropper
hearing (pert to) . . . 3. act, aid, ear
4. otic, oyer 5. aural, sense (special), sound, trial 6. otosis, tryout 7. earshot
8. audience, audition, auditory
9. attention, auricular, interview, knowledge
hearken, harken . . . 4. hear, heed
6. attend, listen 7. give ear, inquire
hearsay . . . 4. talk 5. bruit, rumor
6. gossip, report 8. evidence
heart . . . 3. cor 4. card, core, gist, life, love, mood, soul 5. cheer, organ 6. center, depths, kardia, middle, spirit, vitals
7. courage, emotion, essence, feeling
9. affection, substance 10. conscience
11. temperament
heart (pert to) . . .
ache . . 5. grief 6. sorrow 7. anguish
active . . 7. sthenic
artery . . 5. aorta
beat . . 5. pulse, throb 7. systole
8. diastole 9. pulsation 10. palmoscopy
bleeding (flower) . . 8. dicentra
burn . . 4. envy 6. enmity 7. burning, pyrosia 8. jealousy 10. cardialgia, discontent, heartscald (heart-scaud)
cavity . . 6. atrium
chamber . . 6. atrium 7. auricle 9. ventricle
11. ventriculum
contraction . . 7. systole

disease.. **14.** angina pectoris
Egypt.. **2.** Ab **4.** hati
expansion.. **8.** diastole
felt.. **4.** dear, deep, real, true **7.** genuine, sincere
shaped.. **7.** cordate
valve.. **6.** mitral **8.** bicuspid **9.** tricuspid
hearten... **5.** cheer **7.** comfort
  8. embolden, inspirit, reassure
  9. encourage
hearth... **4.** home **5.** ingle **6.** astrer (pert to) **8.** fireside **9.** fireplace
hearth goddess... **5.** Vesta **6.** Hestia
hearty... **4.** hale, real, rich, warm
  5. heavy, lusty **6.** active, robust, stanch **7.** cordial, earnest, fervent
  8. friendly, vigorous **9.** convivial, energetic, unfeigned **10.** nourishing
  11. substantial
heat... **4.** fire, race, warm, zeal
  5. ardor, calor, cauma, fever, tepor
  6. degree, warmth **7.** inflame, passion
  10. excitement **11.** temperature
heat (pert to)...
heating.. **9.** calorific
measure.. **5.** therm (therme) **7.** calorie (calory), Celsius **10.** centigrade, Fahrenheit
pert to.. **7.** thermic
plaster.. **4.** mull **7.** steatin
principle.. **7.** caloric
white.. **13.** incandescence
heater... **4.** etna, kiln, oven **5.** forge, stove, tisar **6.** boiler, retort **7.** brazier, furnace **8.** annealer, register **12.** electron tube
heath... **4.** moor **5.** Erica, plain, savin, waste **8.** tamarisk **10.** underbrush
heathen... **5.** pagan **6.** ethnic, paynim
  7. gentile, godless, infidel **10.** unbeliever
  11. irreligious **13.** unenlightened
heathen deity... **4.** idol **5.** image
  6. symbol
heather... **5.** color, Erica, plant
  9. crowberry **12.** poverty plant
heaume... **6.** helmet (armor)
heave... **4.** cast, draw, hurl, lift, toss
  5. fling, hoist, pitch, raise, retch, scena, throw **11.** rise and fall
heaven... **3.** sky **4.** ciel, Eden **5.** ether
  6. utopia, welkin **7.** arcadia, Elysium, Nirvana **8.** empyrean, Paradise, Valhalla (Valhall) **9.** firmament
heavenly... **5.** godly **6.** divine, sacred
  7. angelic, blessed, uranian **8.** supernal
  9. beautiful, celestial **10.** delightful
heavenly (pert to)...
being.. **5.** angel, saint **6.** cherub, seraph **7.** Madonna **8.** cherubim, Dei Mater, seraphim
belt.. **6.** galaxy, zodiac
body.. **3.** sun **4.** luna, moon, star **5.** comet **6.** planet **8.** luminary
city.. **4.** Zion **12.** New Jerusalem
food.. **5.** manna
path.. **5.** orbit
solar apparatus.. **6.** orrery
sphere.. **8.** empyrean
twins (Gemini).. **6.** Castor, Pollux
heavens... see *heaven*
heaves... **9.** emphysema

heavy... **3.** sad **4.** deep, dull, hard, role **5.** actor, dense, grave, great, inert, massy **6.** coarse, gloomy, leaden, sleepy, strong, viscid **7.** doleful, onerous, serious, villain, violent, weighty **8.** burdened, grievous, overcast, pregnant, profound **9.** difficult, ponderous **10.** afflictive, burdensome, encumbered, oppressive **11.** substantial **13.** consequential
heavy (pert to)...
handed.. **6.** clumsy **7.** awkward, unhandy **8.** bungling **9.** maladroit **10.** oppressive
headed.. **4.** dull, logy **6.** drowsy, stupid
hearted.. **3.** sad **10.** despondent, melancholy
laden.. **6.** loaded **8.** careworm **9.** oppressed **12.** weighted down
with moisture.. **6.** sodden
Hebrew... **3.** Jew **4.** Zion **6.** Habiri, Habiru, Semite **7.** Semitic
Hebrew (pert to)...
abode of the dead.. **5.** Sheol
acrostic.. **4.** agla
amulet.. **4.** agla
demon.. **8.** Asmodeus
eternity.. **4.** Olam **8.** Olam haba
excommunication form.. **5.** herem
festival.. **5.** Purim, Seder **8.** Passover
flute (Bib).. **8.** nehiloth
forbidden.. **4.** tref
God.. **2.** El **5.** Eloah **6.** Adonai, Elohim, Yahweh (Yahveh) **7.** Jehovah
grammar.. **7.** stative
greeting.. **6.** Shalom
instrument (lyrelike).. **4.** asor
kinsman.. **4.** goel
law book.. **5.** Torah (Tora) **6.** Talmud **7.** Mishnah (Mishna) **8.** Tosephta **10.** Pentateuch
lesson (Nebiim).. **9.** haphtarah
marriage custom.. **8.** levirate
month (Spring).. **4.** Abib **5.** Nisan
Order (Cenobite).. **6.** Essene
plural ending.. **2.** im
prayer shawl.. **7.** tallith
proselyte.. **3.** ger
psalm of praise.. **6.** hallel
quarters.. **6.** ghetto
rabbis, teachers.. **6.** sabora **7.** amoraim, tannaim **8.** saboraim
sacred objects.. **4.** Urim **7.** Thummin
school.. **5.** heder (cheder)
spice (anc).. **6.** stacte
town.. **6.** Mizpah (Mizpeh)
trumpet.. **7.** shophar (shofar)
underworld.. **5.** Sheol
Hebrew alphabet... **2.** he, pe **3.** mem, nun, sin, tav, vau **4.** ayin, beth, caph, koph, resh, shin, yodh **5.** aleph, cheth, gimel, sadhe, zayin **6.** daleth, lamedh, samekh
Hebrides, New...
administrators.. **6.** French **7.** British
church.. **6.** Celtic (early)
islands.. **4.** Iona, Skye **5.** Banks **6.** Torres
people.. **10.** Melanesian
type rule.. **11.** Condominium
hecatomb... **9.** sacrifice **11.** hundred oxen
hecco... **8.** hickwall **10.** woodpecker

heckle . . . 4. gibe 6. badger, hackle, harass
hectic . . . 5. fever, flush 7. excited 8. feverish, restless 9. reddening 11. consumptive
hector . . . 5. bully, worry 6. harass 7. bluster, swagger 8. browbeat 9. roisterer 10. intimidate
Hector (pert to) . . .
character in . . 5. (The) Iliad
companion . . 8. Diomedes
father . . 5. Priam
mother . . 6. Hecuba
slain by . . 8. Achilles
wife . . 10. Andromache
heddle . . . 4. loom 5. blade (with eyelet) 7. weaving
hedge . . . 3. bar, haw, hem, pen 4. boma 5. fence 6. hinder, raddle 7. barrier, enclose, quibble 8. boundary, obstruct, sidestep, surround
hedgehog . . . 6. animal, tenrec, urchin 7. dredger, echidna, echinus, pudding (fruit) 8. herisson, hurcheon 9. porcupine 11. transformer
hedge trimmer . . . 7. plasher, topiary
hedonism (pert to) . . .
advocate . . 8. Cyrenaic 9. Epicurean
doctrine of . . 8. pleasure
heed . . . 3. ear 4. care, hear, mind, note, obey 6. attend, listen, notice, regard 7. caution, observe 8. consider 9. attention, be careful, diligence 10. cognizance, solicitude 11. observation
heedful . . . 4. wary 5. alert 6. attent 7. careful, mindful 8. cautious, vigilant 9. advertent, attentive 11. considerate
heedless . . . 6. remiss 8. careless 9. desperate, impulsive, negligent 10. insouciant, regardless 11. improvident, inadvertent, inattentive, thoughtless, unobservant, without heed 13. inconsiderate
heehaw . . . 4. bray
heel . . . 3. cad, tip 4. cant, foot (part), knob, tilt 5. stern 6. careen, follow 7. bounder, deviate, incline 9. scoundrel 12. protuberance
Heidi author . . . 12. Johanna Spyri
heifer . . . 3. cow 4. quey 5. stirk, woman 6. bovine 8. terrapin (fem) 10. colpindach
height . . . 3. alt, top 4. apex 5. crest, pitch 6. summit 7. stature 8. altitude, eminence, highness 9. elevation 10. The Heavens
heighten . . . 5. raise 7. augment, elevate 8. increase 9. aggravate, intensify 10. exaggerate
height of action, drama . . . 10. catastasis
heimlich . . . 10. reticently 12. mysteriously
Heimweh . . . 9. nostalgia 12. homesickness
heinous . . . 3. bad 6. odious, wicked 7. beastly (Brit), hateful 8. flagrant, infamous, terrible 9. atrocious, malicious 10. outrageous
heir . . . 5. scion 7. heritor, legatee 8. atheling (apparent), parcener (joint) 9. firstborn, inheritor, successor

11. beneficiary
Hejaz . . .
city . . 5. Islam, Mecca 6. Medina
monument . . 14. Tomb of Mohammed (Mosque of the Prophet)
district of . . 11. Saudi Arabia
shrine . . 5. Kaaba
helcos . . . 5. ulcer
helcos (pert to) . . .
repair . . 11. helcoplasty
science . . 9. helcology
ulceration . . 8. helcosis
held . . . see *hold*
Helen of Troy (pert to) . . .
abductor, lover . . 5. Paris
brother-in-law . . 9. Agamemnon
famed for . . 6. beauty
husband . . 8. Menelaus (King)
mother . . 4. Leda
sister of . . 11. The Dioscuri
helical . . . 5. helix (formed) 6. spiral
helical year . . . 6. Sothic
helicoid . . . 6. curved, ear rim (like) 10. snail shell (like)
helicon . . . 4. tuba
helicopter (pert to) . . . 5. rotor 7. chopper 8. autogiro (autogyro), heliport 9. eggbeater 10. whirlybird
helicopter developer . . . 8. Sikorsky
heliophobia . . . 14. fear of sunlight 16. sensitivity to sun
Heliopolis . . . 12. City of the Sun (Egypt)
Helios . . . 3. Sol 6. sun god 16. Colossus of Rhodes
helix . . . 4. coil 5. snail 6. spiral
hell . . . 7. dungeon, inferno 9. perdition, purgatory 10. underworld 11. nether world
hell (pert to) . . .
bottomless pit . . 9. barathrum
capital of . . 11. Pandemonium
Greek . . 5. Hades 8. Tartarus
Hebrew . . 5. Sheol
Hindu . . 6. Naraka
Jewish . . 6. Tophet 7. Gehenna
Norse . . 7. Niflhel (Neflheim)
Queen . . 3. Hel
Roman . . 3. Dis 5. Orcus
hellbent . . . 7. dead set, like mad 8. full tilt, reckless 10. determined, recklessly 12. determinedly
Hellene . . . 5. Greek
Hellenistic school (Sculp) . . . 9. Pergamene
Hellespont . . .
city . . 6. Abydos (legend), Sestos
legend . . 4. Hero 7. Leander (swimmer)
modern name . . 11. Dardanelles (The)
peninsula . . 9. Gallipoli
port . . 8. Gelibola (Gallipoli)
sea . . 6. Aegean 7. Marmara
helm . . . 5. wheel 6. helmet, rudder, summit, tiller 7. control 10. management 12. steering gear
helmet . . . 5. armet, armor, galea, topee (topi) 6. casque, heaume, morion, sallet, sconce 7. basinet, hard hat
helmet (pert to) . . .
flap . . 8. aventail
lower part . . 6. beaver
nose guard . . 5. nasal

opening . . **3.** vue
part . . **4.** bell **5.** crest, visor (vizor)
  7. ventail **8.** aventail
shaped . . **7.** galeate
helminth . . . **4.** worm
helmsman . . . **5.** pilot **6.** conner, guider
  8. coxswain **9.** steersman
helot . . . **4.** esne, serf **5.** slave **6.** thrall,
  vassal **7.** servant
help . . . **3.** aid **4.** abet, back, cure **5.** avail,
  boost, serve, stead **6.** assist, relief,
  remedy, succor **7.** benefit, forward,
  further, improve, prevent, relieve,
  servant, serving, subsidy, support,
  sustain
helper . . . **3.** aid (aide) **8.** teammate
  9. assistant, paramedic **10.** apprentice,
  benefactor
helpful . . . **6.** useful **7.** helping **8.** salutary
  10. beneficial, tiding over
  12. contributory, instrumental
helpless . . . **4.** limp, weak **7.** forlorn
  8. impotent, unaiding **9.** destitute,
  powerless, spineless **10.** bewildered,
  unsupplied **11.** defenseless, unprotected
  12. irremediable
helpmate . . . **4.** wife **6.** helper, spouse
  7. husband **8.** helpmeet **9.** assistant,
  companion
Helsinki, Finland . . . **7.** capital
helter-skelter . . . **5.** haste, hurry **7.** hastily
  8. disorder **9.** confusion **10.** carelessly,
  recklessly
helve . . . **5.** lever **6.** handle
hem, hem in . . . **3.** pen **4.** edge **5.** beset
  6. border, margin **7.** environ, stammer
  8. hesitate, surround **9.** hem and haw
  11. exclamation **12.** circumscribe
hemal, haemal (pert to) . . . **5.** blood
  12. blood vessels
hemeralopia . . . **12.** day blindness (opp
  of nyctalopia)
hemi . . . **4.** half, semi (pref)
hemiplegia . . . **9.** paralysis (body half)
hemlock . . . **3.** kex **5.** Tsuga **6.** conium
  (fruit) **9.** evergreen, poisoning
hemophilia . . . **8.** bleeding
  10. hemorrhage (uncontrollable)
hemp . . . **3.** ife, kef **4.** flax, keef, kief,
  rine, sunn **5.** abaca, bhang, istle, sisal
  (sizal) **6.** fennel, Manila **7.** hashish,
  Ihiamba (liamba) **8.** cannabis
hemp (pert to) . . .
  bagasse . . **6.** linaga
  cannabis . . **5.** ganja (smoking)
  fabric . . **6.** burlap
  filament . . **4.** harl
  leaves . . **5.** sabzi
  like . . **9.** cannabine
  loose . . **5.** oakum
  resin (narcotic) . . **6.** charas
  seed . . **5.** rogue, scamp
  short . . **3.** tow
hen . . . **4.** fowl, wife **6.** pullet
hen (pert to) . . .
  clam . . **4.** surf **5.** pismo
  hawk . . **7.** buzzard, harrier
  heath . . **4.** gray **6.** grouse (black)
  of Reynard the Fox . . **7.** Partlet
  poison . . **7.** hebenon, henbane
  water . . **9.** gallinule

hence . . . **2.** so **4.** away, ergo, thus
  8. away from **9.** therefore
henchman . . . **4.** page **5.** groom **6.** gillie,
  squire **7.** mafioso **8.** follower, hanger-on
  9. attendant, supporter **12.** right-hand
  man
hend, hende . . . **4.** fair, kind, near
  5. civil **6.** clever, comely, gentle, kindly
  8. gracious, pleasant, skillful (skilful)
  9. dexterous **10.** convenient
Henley event . . . **7.** Regatta
henpeck . . . **3.** nag
heortology, science of . . . **14.** liturgical
  year
hepar . . . **5.** liver **8.** compound (Chem)
hepatitis . . . **12.** liver disease
Hephaestus (Gr Relig) . . . **9.** god of Fire
Hepplewhite . . . **9.** furniture
heptad . . . **5.** seven (group of)
Hera (pert to) . . .
  husband . . **4.** Zeus
  mother of . . **4.** Ares, Rhea
  rival . . **2.** Io **4.** Leto
herald . . . **5.** crier **6.** tabard **7.** presage,
  usher in **8.** announce, point man,
  proclaim **9.** harbinger, messenger
  10. forerunner
heraldic (pert to) . . .
  balls . . **5.** palle (6 balls of Medici)
  band . . **3.** bar **4.** fess, fill
  barnacle . . **4.** brey
  bearing . . **4.** ente, gore, orle **5.** pheon
    6. charge **8.** tressure
  boss . . **5.** rumbo
  charge . . **5.** fusil, gyron **7.** bearing,
    humetty (humettee)
  circle (gold) . . **6.** bezant
  cross . . **4.** nowy, paty, urde **6.** cleche,
    pattée (patté), raguly **7.** patonce, saltier
    (saltire)
  decoration . . **4.** seme **5.** crest
  design (fur) . . **4.** pean, vair
  division . . **4.** ente, paly **5.** barry **6.** canton
    7. compone **11.** counterpaly
  embattled . . **8.** bretessé
  end (metal) . . **7.** boterol (boteroll)
  large . . **5.** pavis
  lozenge (voided) . . **6.** mascle
  opening . . **6.** rustre
  panel . . **7.** hatchment (death)
  sardonyx . . **8.** sanguine
  scalloped, edged . . **8.** invected
  segment . . **6.** flanch
  ship . . **7.** lymphad
  star . . **6.** mullet **7.** estoile
  stripe . . **4.** pale
  swallow . . **10.** hirondelle
  winged . . **4.** aile
  wreath . . **5.** torse **7.** chaplet, garland
heraldic (pert to animals) . . .
  head . . **8.** caboshed (caboched)
  bear . . **5.** grise
  beast, running . . **7.** courant
  beast, sitting . . **5.** assis **6.** sejant
  beasts . . **6.** enurny
  beast's leg . . **4.** gamb (gambe)
  bird . . **7.** issuant (half visible), martlet
    9. half eagle
  duck (footless) . . **6.** cannet (cannette)
  fish, swimming . . **6.** naiant
  headless . . **5.** etète

heraldic (pert to color) . . .
black . . **5.** sable
blue . . **5.** azure
brown . . **5.** tenne
gold, yellow . . **2.** or
green . . **4.** vert
purple . . **7.** purpure
red . . **5.** gules
heraldic shield (pert to) . . .
back . . **8.** aversant
back to back . . **8.** addorsed
bent . . **9.** debruised
broken . . **5.** rompu
Danes . . **5.** raven
England . . **14.** lilies of France
facing each other . . **8.** affronté
savages . . **6.** tattoo
toward spectator . . **4.** gaze **7.** gardant
tribe of Judah . . **4.** lion
herb . . . **3.** pia, rue **4.** aloe, anet,
balm, dill, hemp, mint, moly, sage,
woad, yamp **5.** anise, basil, nondo,
sedge, senna, tansy, thyme **6.** arnica,
borage, catnip, cicely, clover, endive,
fennel, hyssop, jacoby, madder,
yarrow **7.** boneset, caraway, chervil,
chicory, figwort, gentian, ginseng,
henbane, parsley, ragwort **8.** abelmosk,
licorice, marjoram, rosemary, samphire,
tarragon **9.** coriander, digitalis,
spikenard **10.** elecampane, pennyroyal,
turtlehead
herb (pert to) . . .
bitter . . **3.** rue **4.** aloe **5.** tansy **7.** boneset
8. centaury **9.** snakehead **10.** turtlehead
dill . . **4.** anet
genus . . **3.** Iva **4.** Arum, Ruta **5.** Galax,
Inula, Lemna, Rubia **6.** Cassia, Mentha,
Oxalis, Sagina **7.** Alpenia, Anemone,
Freesia, Hedeoma, Tellima, Tovaria
8. Hepatica, Psorales **9.** Grundelia
living on . . **11.** herbivorous
12. phytophagous
mythical . . **4.** moly
narcotic . . **4.** hemp
onionlike . . **5.** chive
poisonous . . **4.** loco **6.** conium
7. hemlock, henbane **9.** helebore
salad . . **6.** endive **7.** chicory
10. watercress
Hercules (pert to) . . .
captured . . **8.** Cerberus
father . . **4.** Zeus
hero of . . **8.** strength **12.** twelve labors
killed . . **5.** Hydra
mother . . **7.** Alcmene
stables . . **6.** Augean
statue . . **7.** Farnese
stone . . **9.** loadstone
sweetheart . . **4.** Iole
wife . . **4.** Hebe
herd . . . **3.** mob **5.** crowd, drive, drove,
flock, guard **6.** gregis, rabble **7.** shelter
11. aggregation
herd's grass . . . **7.** timothy
herdsman . . . **4.** senn **6.** drover **7.** vaquero
(vaciero) **8.** Damoetas, ranchero,
wrangler
herdsman's god . . . **5.** Pales
here . . . **3.** ici, now **6.** hereat, hither
7. present **8.** vicinity **9.** this place

11. in this place
here and now . . . **8.** thisness **9.** haecceity
11. specificity
here and there . . . **5.** about **6.** passim
10. everywhere
hereditary . . . **6.** inborn, innate, lineal
8. heirship **9.** ancestral, descended,
lineality **11.** inheritable, inheritance,
patrimonial
heredity . . . **4.** gene **5.** birth **7.** atavism
8. heritage **10.** Mendel's law
11. inheritance
heretic . . . **9.** dissenter, sectarian
10. schismatic **13.** nonconformist
heretofore . . . **6.** erenow **7.** prior to
8. formerly, hitherto, previous
heritage . . . **3.** lot **9.** cleronomy
10. birthright **11.** inheritance
heritrix, heretrix . . . **7.** heiress
herl, harl . . . **3.** fly (angling) **4.** barb
hermeneutics . . . **14.** interpretation
(Scriptures)
Hermes (pert to) . . .
birthplace . . **7.** Cyllene
character . . **6.** herald **9.** messenger
father . . **4.** Zeus
god of . . **5.** youth **7.** science **9.** eloquence,
invention
mother . . **4.** Maia
Roman equivalent . . **7.** Mercury
shoes (winged) . . **7.** talaria
hermetic . . . **6.** closed, sealed **7.** magical
8. airtight **10.** alchemical
hermetic art . . . **7.** alchemy
hermit . . . **4.** monk **5.** cooky **7.** ascetic,
eremite, recluse, stylite (Hist)
8. headsman **9.** anchorite, pillarist
11. hummingbird
hermitary . . . **3.** hut **4.** cell
hern, herne . . . **4.** hers, hook **5.** heron
6. corner
hero . . . **4.** idol, star **5.** model **7.** demigod,
warrior **8.** champion **9.** celebrity,
conqueror **11.** protagonist
hero (pert to) . . .
American . . **5.** Allen (Ethan), Bowie
6. Bonham, Travis **8.** Crockett
Babylonian . . **5.** Etana
deified . . **7.** demigod
genealogy . . **9.** heroogony
Greek . . **3.** Ion **4.** Ajax
legendary . . **6.** Amadis, Roland
7. Paladin, Tancred
lore . . **9.** heroology
Persian . . **6.** Rustam (Rustum)
romantic . . **4.** Erec **6.** Amadis **7.** Leander
Russian . . **4.** Igor
heroic . . . **4.** bold, epic, huge **5.** brave,
great, noble **6.** epical, poetic, viking
7. extreme, gallant, valiant **8.** fearless,
intrepid, powerful **10.** courageous
11. magnanimous, venturesome
heroic poem, story . . . **4.** epic, epos
6. epopee
heroine . . . **4.** Tess **5.** actor **6.** Esther,
Europa **8.** Atalanta **9.** celebrity
11. demigoddess
heroism . . . **5.** valor **7.** bravery, courage
9. fortitude **11.** magnanimity
13. unselfishness
heron . . . **5.** Ardea, crane, egret, herle

7. Bittern 8. Ardeidae, heronsew
9. Great Blue 10. Great White, Little
Blue
heron flock ... 5. sedge
herpes ... 6. eczema 8. cold sore, shingles
herring ... 3. cob 4. alec, brit, raun (fem),
sile 5. cisco, matie, sprat 7. alewife,
anchovy, shadine 8. scuddawn
herring (pert to) ...
barrel .. 4. cade, cran
bone .. 7. pattern 11. arrangement
fry .. 4. sile
herringlike .. 5. cisco 7. anchovy
young .. 4. brit 5. sprat (sprot)
Herse (Gr) ... 7. goddess (dew)
Hersey setting ... 5. Adano 9. Hiroshima
Hershef (Egypt) ... 5. deity (tutelary)
hesitate ... 3. haw, hem 4. wait 5. delay,
demur, pause, stall 6. falter, loiter
7. stammer 13. procrastinate
hesitation ... 5. doubt, pause, waltz
9. faltering, hesitancy 10. reluctance,
stammering 11. uncertainty, vacillation
15. procrastination
hesped (Heb) ... 6. eulogy 7. funeral
Hesperides (pert to) ...
group name .. 10. Atlantides
guards of .. 12. golden apples (Hera)
nymph .. 5. Aegle 6. Hestia 7. Hespera
8. Arethusa, Erytheia
Hesperus ... 4. poem (Wreck of the
Hesperus) 5. Venus 6. Hesper
11. evening star
Hessian ... 3. fly 5. boots, Hesse
6. German 9. mercenary 10. adventurer
hest ... 6. behest 7. command, precept,
promise 10. injunction
Hestia (pert to) ...
goddess of .. 6. hearth
guard of .. 12. golden apples
mother .. 4. Rhea
hetaera, hetaira (Gr) ... 4. Lais 6. Phryne
8. mistress, paramour
hetaerocracy, governed by ...
8. hetaerae 10. college men
Heterodontus ... 5. shark
heterodox ... 9. heretical 10. unorthodox
11. nonorthodox
heterogeneous (opposed to
homogeneous) ... 5. mixed 6. unlike
7. diverse 9. different 10. dissimilar
11. diversified 13. miscellaneous
hew ... 3. cut 4. chop, fell, hack 5. carve,
sever
hex ... 3. hag, six 4. jinx 5. lamia, spell
7. bewitch 9. sorceress, witchwife
hexad ... 3. six 6. sestet
hexameter verse ...
meter .. 7. six feet
terms .. 4. iams 8. dipodies, trochees
9. anapaests
hexapod ... 7. six feet 9. six-footed
hexarchy ... 9. six States (group)
hexastich, poem or stanza ... 8. six
lines 9. six verses
heyday ... 3. joy 4. acme 8. wildness
11. high spirits 12. highest vigor
14. frolicsomeness
heyrat ... 8. kinkajou (obs)
Hezekiah (pert to) ...
Biblical .. 4. King (12th)

kingdom .. 5. Judah
mother .. 3. Abi
hiatus ... 3. col, gap 5. break, chasm,
pause, space 6. lacuna 7. fissure,
opening 8. interval 12. interruption
Hiawatha (pert to) ...
character, poem by .. 10. Longfellow
grandmother .. 7. Nokomis
mother .. 7. Wenonah
people .. 8. Iroquois
hibernate ... 6. hole up (summer in
torpor), winter 8. estivate 10. latibulize
Hibernia ... 4. Erin 7. Ireland
Hibernian (pert to) ...
color .. 5. green
native .. 8. Irishman
secret society (US 1832) .. 24. Ancient
Order of Hibernians
hickory ... 4. cane 5. Carya, pecan
6. switch 8. kiskatom 9. shellbark
hidalgo ... 5. title 8. nobleman (lower
class)
hidden ... 4. dern, lurk 5. inner, perdu
6. arcane, buried, cached, closed,
covert, latent, masked, occult, secret
7. covered, cryptic, obscure, unknown
8. abstruse, screened, secluded,
secreted 9. concealed, latescent
10. mysterious 11. clandestine
hide ... 3. kip 4. bury, cyst, dern
(derne), lurk, mask, pelt, skin, veil
5. cache, cloak, cover, skulk 6. screen,
shroud 7. conceal, eelskin, rawhide,
secrete 8. carucate, disguise, ensconce,
suppress 9. dissemble 10. camouflage
hidebound ... 5. bound, petty 6. little,
narrow 7. bigoted 9. barkbound
10. restrained (opinion) 11. strait-
laced 12. conventional, narrow-minded
13. hyperorthodox
hideous ... 4. grim, ugly 6. grisly, horrid,
odious 7. ghastly 8. scabrous, terrible
9. frightful, revolting 10. detestable,
terrifying
hiding place ... 3. mew 4. lair 5. cache
9. latibulum
hi-fi devotee ... 10. audiophile
high ... 3. alt, dry, ela (note) 4. tall
5. aloft, drunk, great, noble, steep
6. costly, shrill 7. eminent, haughty
8. elevated, foremost, stranded,
towering 9. excessive, expensive
high (pert to) ...
and mighty .. 8. arrogant 9. imperious
brow .. 4. snob 7. Brahmin, egghead,
high-hat, learned 12. intellectual
14. intelligentsia
flown diction .. 8. euphuism
flying .. 7. Icarian 9. visionary
11. extravagant, pretentious
12. ostentatious 13. grandiloquent
handed .. 9. arbitrary 10. autocratic,
imperative 11. domineering,
overbearing
hat .. 8. snobbish 12. aristocratic
priest .. 3. Eli (Israel) 11. Melchezedek
(Mormon)
sounding .. 4. loud 7. fustian 9. high-
toned 13. grandiloquent
spirited .. 4. edgy 5. fiery 6. lively
9. excitable 10. mettlesome 11. high-

mettled
strung.. **4.** taut **5.** tense **7.** nervous
9. excitable
time.. **3.** fun **5.** binge, spree **8.** carousal
11. opportunity
toned.. **5.** tense **7.** stylish **8.** elevated
9. dignified **11.** fashionable
highest... **3.** top **4.** best **6.** utmost
7. maximum, supreme, topmost
8. bunemost, dominant **9.** nth degree,
uppermost
highest (pert to)...
comb form.. **4.** acro
dice number.. **3.** six **4.** sise (sice)
point.. **3.** top **4.** acme, apex **5.** crest
6. apogee, climax, summit, vertex,
zenith **7.** ceiling, noonday **8.** meridian,
noontide, pinnacle **11.** ne plus ultra
Highlands, the (pert to)
heavy pole.. **5.** caber
inhabitant.. **4.** Scot
sword.. **8.** claymore
highway... **3.** via, way **4.** bahn, iter, path,
pike, road, toby **6.** artery, course, street
7. beltway, freeway, parkway, thruway
(throughway) **8.** arterial, autobahn,
turnpike **9.** boulevard, concourse
10. expressway **12.** thoroughfare
highwayman... **5.** thief **6.** bandit, robber
7. brigand, footpad, ladrone **8.** hijacker
9. bandolero **10.** bushranger, highjacker
hike... **4.** jerk, toss, walk **5.** hitch,
march, raise, throw, tramp **8.** backpack,
increase
hilarious... **3.** mad **5.** merry, noisy
7. festive **8.** mirthful **9.** ludicrous
hilarity... **4.** glee **5.** mirth **6.** gaiety,
levity **7.** jollity, whoopee **8.** laughter
9. joviality **10.** jocularity, joyousness
12. cheerfulness, exhilaration
hill... **3.** kop, tor **4.** dene, dune, heap,
holt, kame, knob, loma, mesa, paha,
rath **5.** bargh, butte, esker, morra,
mound **6.** barrow, summit **9.** acclivity,
elevation, monadnock
hill myna... **8.** starling
hillside... **4.** bank, brae, hill, knop, ramp
5. cleve (cleeve), cliff, knoll, scarp,
slope **6.** glacia
hilt... **4.** haft **6.** handle
hilum... **3.** eye (bean) **5.** hilar, notch
7. opening (kidney)
Himalaya (pert to)...
antelope.. **5.** goral, serow
bear.. **5.** bhalu
bearcat.. **5.** panda
bird.. **5.** monal (pheasant) **6.** chough
(crow)
cat.. **5.** ounce
country.. **5.** Nepal
dweller.. **8.** Nepalese
formations.. **7.** Siwalik
goat.. **4.** ibex, kail, tahe
kingdom.. **5.** Hunza
mountain peak.. **3.** Api **7.** Everest, The
Hump
pass.. **7.** Nathula
plant.. **4.** nard (Med)
sheep (wild).. **6.** bharal, nahoor
swamp.. **5.** Terai
tree.. **3.** fir (silver) **5.** Neoza (pine)

6. Bhutan, deodar (cedar)
himself... **4.** ipse
hind... **3.** doe **4.** back, deer, rear, stag
6. caudal, haunch, rustic **7.** peasant,
servant **8.** domestic **9.** posterior
11. hindquarter
hind (red fish)... **7.** grouper **8.** cabrilla
hinder... **3.** bar **5.** block, check, cramp,
debar, delay, deter, embar **6.** cumber,
hamper, impede, retard **7.** prevent
8. restrain **9.** posterior
hindrance... **3.** bar, rub **4.** clog, snag,
stop **5.** check, delay **8.** obstacle
9. deterrent, restraint, stricture
10. impediment **11.** obstruction
12. interruption
Hindu, Hindoo... **4.** Koli, Sikh **5.** Tamil
6. Indian **9.** Hindustan
Hindu (pert to)...
alphabet.. **6.** Sarada
apartment.. **5.** mahal
ascetic.. **4.** yati, yogi **5.** fakir, sadhu
atheist.. **7.** nastika
author of law.. **4.** Manu (Code)
bird.. **5.** Munia **6.** garuda
Buddha's mother.. **4.** Maya
caravansary.. **8.** choultry
carriage.. **6.** gharry (gharri)
caste.. **4.** Bhil **5.** Palli, Sudra, Tamil
7. Brahman
ceremony.. **7.** sraddha
city (sacred).. **5.** Mecca **7.** Benares
9. Allahabad
coin.. **4.** anna
cymbals.. **3.** tal
dancing girl.. **8.** bayadere
darkness (spiritual).. **5.** tamas
deity.. **4.** Devi, Rama, Siva (Shiva),
Yama **5.** Ahura, Asura **6.** Brahma,
Vishnu **7.** Krishna **8.** Trimurti
deity consort.. **5.** sakti
dialect.. **5.** Tamil
division.. **5.** Patti, Taraf **6.** zillah
7. Pargana
Dravidian.. **5.** Tamil
drink (sacrificial).. **4.** soma
evil spirit.. **4.** Mara **5.** asura **6.** yaksha
festival.. **4.** Holi, tali **6.** Dewali, Pongal
9. Dashahara
first mortal to die.. **4.** Yama
flute.. **3.** bin **5.** pungi
garment.. **4.** sari (saree)
Gautama's wife.. **6.** Ahalya
gentleman (Mr).. **5.** baboo (babu), sahib
giant.. **4.** Bana (thousand-armed)
government.. **6.** sircar
guitar.. **4.** vina **5.** sitar
hero.. **4.** Nala
incarnation.. **4.** Rama **5.** asura **6.** yaksha
jackal.. **4.** kola
king.. **5.** Rajah
language (oldest).. **5.** Tamil
language (sacred).. **4.** Pali
loincloth.. **5.** dhoti
magic.. **4.** jadu (jadoo), maya
magician.. **4.** yogi **5.** fakir
meal (wheat).. **4.** atta (ata)
mendicant.. **4.** naga **8.** sannyasi
merchant.. **6.** banian (banya) **7.** goladar
mind.. **5.** manas
monkey god.. **7.** Hanuman

mountain.. **4.** Meru
mystic.. **4.** yogi
nursemaid.. **4.** ayah
paradise.. **7.** Nirvana
patriarch.. **5.** Pitri
peasant.. **4.** ryot
philosophy.. **4.** yoga, Yuga **5.** tamas
physicist.. **5.** Raman (Nobel 1930)
pillar.. **3.** lat
poet.. **5.** rishi **6.** Tagore (Nobel 1913)
prince.. **4.** raja
reign.. **3.** raj
sacred river.. **6.** Ganges
sage.. **5.** rishi **6.** Dharma **7.** Gautama, Mahatma
savant.. **5.** swami
scarf.. **4.** sari (saree)
serpent (semi-human).. **4.** Naga
servant.. **5.** hamal
slave.. **4.** dasi (fem)
soldier.. **4.** sikh **5.** sepoy
supernatural being.. **6.** Garuda
swan.. **5.** hansa
syllable of assent.. **2.** om
Taraf ruler.. **8.** tarafdar
title.. **3.** Sri **4.** Raja, Rana, Rani **5.** Rajah, Ranee **6.** sirdar **8.** maharaja (maharajah)
tree (sacred).. **5.** pipal **6.** bo tree
tunic.. **4.** jama (jamah)
underworld (series).. **6.** Patala
village.. **5.** abadi
virtue.. **6.** sharma
widow (cremation).. **6.** suttee
woman (first).. **6.** Ahalya
Hindu Ages, Yoga...
1st.. **5.** Krita
2nd.. **5.** Treta
3rd.. **7.** Dvapara
4th.. **4.** Kali
end.. **7.** Pralaya
total.. **4.** Maha **10.** Manvantara
Hindu goddess... **3.** Sri, Uma **4.** Devi, Kali **5.** Durga, Gauri **6.** Chandi, Shakti **7.** Lakshmi, Parvati **9.** Haimavati (Durga)
Hindu god of...
ancestors.. **5.** Pitri
dead.. **4.** Yama
fire.. **4.** Agni
love.. **4.** Kama
spirit.. **5.** Asura
unknown.. **2.** Ka
wisdom (elephant-headed).. **6.** Ganesa (Ganesha)
Hindu religion...
abode of gods.. **4.** Meru
call to prayer.. **4.** azan (adan)
ceremony, rite.. **7.** araddha
congregation.. **5.** samaj
convert (to Islam).. **6.** shaikh
creator.. **6.** Brahma
cremation.. **4.** sati **6.** suttee
doctrine, destiny.. **5.** karma
first human to die (deified).. **4.** Yama
hell.. **6.** Naraka
Hinduism.. **5.** Agama **6.** Tantra **7.** Jainism **8.** Buddhism **10.** Brahmanism
holy man.. **5.** Sadhu (Sadh)
image worship.. **5.** arati
incarnation.. **4.** Rama **6.** avatar **11.** Ramachandra
literature (sacred).. **4.** Veda **7.** Shastra

lord of the world.. **9.** Jagannath (Jagannatha)
monastery.. **4.** math
philosophy (life).. **5.** artha, atman, prana **6.** tattva
prayer, call to.. **4.** azan (adan)
prayer rug.. **5.** asana, Melas
religion.. **5.** Agama **6.** Tantra **7.** Jainism **8.** Buddhism **10.** Brahmanism
scripture.. **4.** Veda **5.** Agama **6.** Tantra **7.** Shastra
sect.. **4.** Jain (Jaina), Sikh **6.** tantra
Shastra (4 parts).. **5.** aruti **6.** purana, smriti, tantra
Siva worshiper.. **5.** Saiva
Supreme Spirit.. **5.** atman **7.** jivatma
teacher.. **4.** guru **5.** swami
Trimurti (Triad).. **4.** Siva **6.** Brahma, Vishnu
trinity, triad.. **8.** Trimurti (Siva, Brahma, Vishnu)
unorthodox.. **7.** Jainism
widow (cremation).. **6.** suttee
Hindustan (pert to)...
dialect.. **4.** Urdu **10.** Hindustani
people.. **9.** Dravidian
poet.. **5.** Siraj (Beng)
rice.. **7.** aghanee
hinge... **3.** pan (part) **4.** axis, axle, hang, knee, turn **5.** joint, pivot, stand **6.** depend, fasten, lamina, pintle
hint... **3.** cue **5.** imply, refer, tinge, trace **6.** allude, glance **7.** eyewink, inkling, suggest **8.** allusion, innuendo, intimate, reminder **9.** insinuate **10.** intimation, suggestion **11.** insinuation, supposition
hip... **3.** hop, pod **4.** coxa, limp, miss, skip **6.** haunch **8.** greeting
hip, hips (pert to)...
bone.. **4.** coxa **5.** ilium **7.** os coxae **10.** innominate
muscle.. **9.** iliopsoas
nerve.. **7.** sciatic (largest)
rose fruit.. **10.** pseudocarp
Hippocrates (pert to)...
drug.. **5.** mecon (possibly opium)
famed as.. **9.** physician (Gr)
oath.. **11.** Hippocratic
hippopotamus... **3.** hippo **6.** seacow, zeekoe **8.** behemoth (Bib)
hippopotamus, thong of hide... **7.** chicote
Hiram... **9.** most noble **10.** King of Tyre (Bib)
hire... **3.** let, use **4.** hack, rent **5.** bribe, lease, price, wages **6.** employ, engage, reward, salary **7.** charter, stipend **9.** allowance **12.** compensation
hireling... **4.** esne, serf **5.** slave, venal **8.** employee **9.** mercenary
hirmos... **4.** hymn **8.** canticle **9.** troparion
hirondelle (Her)... **7.** swallow
hirsel... **4.** herd **5.** flock **7.** pasture
hirsute... **5.** hairy, rough **6.** coarse, shaggy **7.** boorish, bristly, uncouth
Hispania (anc)... **16.** Spain and Portugal
Hispanic... **6.** Latino **7.** Spanish **13.** Latin American **15.** Spanish American
hispid... **5.** rough **7.** grooved **8.** strigose
hiss... **3.** boo, tst **4.** fizz **7.** condemn **8.** derision, sibilate **10.** effervesce,

sibilation
historian . . . **5.** actor **6.** writer **8.** annalist
  10. chronicler
history . . . **5.** drama **6.** annals, events,
  memoir **7.** account **8.** relation, treatise
  9. chronicle, narrative
history (pert to) . . .
  Father of . . **9.** Herodotus
  muse of (Gr Myth) . . **4.** Clio
  period . . **3.** era
  personal . . **7.** memoirs **9.** biography,
  genealogy **13.** autobiography
histrio . . . **5.** actor
histrion . . . **5.** actor
histrionics . . . **6.** acting, actors **9.** theatrics
  11. theatricals
hit . . . **3.** bop, lob, rap, tap **4.** blow, bunt,
  slam, slap, slog, suit, swat **5.** flick,
  knock, shoot, smite **6.** buffet, larrup,
  please, strike **7.** succeed, success
  9. collision
hitch . . . **3.** hop, tie, tug **4.** halt, jerk, knot,
  limp, pull, yoke **5.** catch, cling, crick,
  marry, unite **6.** enlist, fasten, hobble
  8. obstacle **9.** hindrance **10.** enlistment
hitherto . . . **3.** ago, yet **5.** as yet **7.** prior
  to **8.** formerly, until now
hit or miss . . . **6.** casual **8.** at random,
  by chance, careless **9.** haphazard
Hittite (pert to) . . .
  ancestor (Bib) . . **4.** Heth
  city . . **6.** Hamath, Pteria (ruins)
  country . . **6.** Khatti (Asia Minor)
  people (anc) . . **8.** Hittites **10.** aborigines
  storm god . . **6.** Teshup (Teshub)
hoagie, hoagy . . . **3.** sub **4.** hero
hoar . . . **4.** aged, gray, rime **5.** hoary,
  white **7.** ancient **9.** hoarfrost, venerable
hoard . . . **5.** amass, lay up, store **6.** garner,
  supply **7.** husband **8.** treasure, treasury
  10. accumulate, collection
hoarder . . . **5.** miser **6.** storer **9.** treasurer
hoarfrost . . . **3.** rag **4.** hoar, rime
  7. needles (ice) **9.** Jack Frost
hoarse . . . **3.** old **4.** aged, gray **6.** remote
  (in time) **7.** ancient **9.** canescent
hoatzin, hoactzin . . . **4.** anna **5.** hanna
  8. pheasant **9.** stinkbird **11.** Opisthocomi
  (group)
hoax . . . **3.** bam **4.** bilk, ruse, sham
  5. bluff, cheat, spoof, trick **6.** canard
  7. deceive **8.** artifice **9.** deception
hob . . . **3.** elf, hub, peg, pin **4.** game,
  mark **5.** clown, fairy, havoc **6.** ferret,
  rustic, sprite **7.** hobnail **8.** mischief
  9. fireplace, hobgoblin
hobble . . . **4.** clog, gait (unequal), halt,
  limp **5.** dance **6.** fetter, tether,
  wabble **7.** dilemma, pastern, shackle
  11. predicament
hobbledehoy . . . **4.** gawk **5.** youth
hobbler . . . **5.** pilot **7.** boatman, hoveler,
  laborer, soldier **8.** retainer
hobby . . . **3.** fad, nag **5.** dolly, horse
  6. falcon **7.** bicycle, pastime
  9. avocation, plaything **10.** hobbyhorse
  12. rocking horse
hobgoblin . . . **3.** elf, imp **4.** bogy, pixy,
  Puck **5.** scrat **6.** sprite **7.** bugaboo
  9. coltpixie **10.** apparition **15.** Robin
  Goodfellow

hobnob . . . **9.** associate (with), drink with,
  hit or miss
hobo . . . **3.** bum **5.** tramp **6.** beggar
  7. vagrant **8.** vagabond
hock . . . **3.** ham **4.** pawn, wine **5.** ankle,
  joint, thigh (man) **6.** pledge **7.** disable
  9. hamstring
hockey (pert to) . . .
  ball, disk . . **3.** nur **4.** knur, puck
  cup . . **7.** Stanley (prize)
  goal . . **4.** cage
  stick . . **6.** shinny **7.** cammock
  team number . . **5.** seven
hocus . . . **4.** drug **5.** cheat **6.** liquor
  (drugged) **7.** deceive, falsify **8.** cheating,
  trickery **10.** adulterate
hocus-pocus . . . **5.** cheat, trick **6.** bunkum,
  humbug **7.** juggler **8.** flimflam,
  nonsense, quackery **9.** deception,
  trickster **11.** incantation **12.** charlatanism
  13. sleight of hand **15.** juggler's formula
hod . . . **3.** tub **4.** hide **6.** barrow, trough
  7. scuttle
hodgepodge . . . **4.** hash, mess, olio, stew
  5. cento **6.** jumble, medley **7.** mélange,
  mixture **10.** miscellany **11.** gallimaufry,
  olla-podrida
hog . . . **3.** pig, sow, Sus **4.** bene, boar, galt,
  gilt **5.** sheep (unshorn), shoat, swine
  6. barrow **8.** babirusa (babiroussa),
  javelina **9.** boschvark, razorback
hog . . . **6.** corner (the market) **7.** glutton
  8. slattern **9.** take it all **10.** locomotive,
  monopolist
hog (pert to) . . .
  breed . . **5.** Essex **9.** Hampshire
  food . . **4.** mast
  ground . . **6.** marmot
  hoglike . . **7.** porcine
  salted side . . **5.** bacon **6.** flitch
  shears (snout) . . **7.** snouter
  thigh (cured) . . **3.** ham
hogfish . . . **7.** capitan, pigfish **8.** scorpene
hoggerel . . . **5.** sheep **6.** hogger
hoggery . . . **4.** hogs **5.** greed
  11. beastliness **14.** hoggish manners
hoggish . . . **6.** filthy, greedy **7.** porcine,
  selfish, swinish **10.** gluttonous
hogshead . . . **4.** cask **6.** barrel **7.** measure
hogwash . . . **5.** swill, waste
hoi polloi . . . **3.** mob **5.** herde **6.** masses,
  rabble **7.** the many **8.** populace
  9. multitude
hoist . . . **4.** lift, sail **5.** boost, heave,
  hoise, raise **7.** elevate **8.** elevator
hoisting device . . . **3.** gin **4.** jack
  5. crane, davit, lewis **7.** capstan, derrick
  8. elevator, windlass **9.** parbuckle
hoity-toity . . . **5.** giddy, proud **6.** snooty
  7. flighty, haughty **8.** arrogant
  11. exclamation, harum-scarum,
  patronizing, thoughtless
  13. irresponsible
hold . . . **3.** own **4.** bind, have, keep,
  lien, seat, stow **5.** avast, cling,
  delay, grasp, judge **6.** adhere, arrest,
  cleave, clench, defend, detain, endure,
  harbor, regard, retain **7.** contain,
  control, custody **8.** consider, foothold,
  maintain, thurrock (ship's), treasury
  9. anchorage, constrain, entertain,

prosecute **11.** compartment
hold (pert to) . . .
back . . **3.** dam **4.** last, stem **5.** delay,
  deter, stint **6.** detain, hinder, refuse,
  retard **7.** abstain, inhibit, repress
  8. restrain
belief . . **7.** suppose
dear . . **7.** cherish
fast . . **5.** cling **6.** adhere **9.** persevere
forth . . **5.** offer, speak **7.** declaim,
  descant, exhibit, expound **8.** continue,
  maintain, propound
off . . **5.** avert, delay **7.** repulse, ward
  off **9.** stay aloof, temporize
on . . **4.** stop, wait **6.** endure, retain
  7. forbear **8.** continue
opinion . . **4.** deem
out . . **4.** last **6.** endure, refuse, resist
  7. exclude **8.** continue
session . . **3.** sit **7.** convene **4.** assemble
together . . **6.** adhere, cohere **8.** be joined
  9. co-operate
up . . **3.** rob **4.** buoy, halt, lift, rein
  5. check, delay, raise **6.** hinder, resist,
  retard **7.** display, exhibit, pillory (to
  scorn), robbery, support, sustain
water . . **5.** sound **10.** consistent
holder . . . **3.** cop (yarn) **4.** file **5.** owner,
  payee **6.** bearer, binder, lienor, tenant
  7. trustee **8.** endorsee **9.** mortgagor,
  possessor, recipient **10.** receptacle
hold in . . .
check . . **4.** curb, rein **6.** arrest, bridle
  7. control **8.** restrain
custody . . **4.** jail **6.** detain, intern
hand . . **6.** assure **7.** control, promise,
  toy with
mind . . **6.** harbor **7.** cherish **9.** entertain
holding . . . **5.** asset, claim, stake, tenet,
  title, trust **6.** belief, equity, estate,
  tenure **8.** interest, property **9.** retention
  10. possessing, possession, supporting
holding fast . . . **9.** tenacious **10.** persistent
holding sway . . . **7.** regnant **8.** dominant,
  reigning
hole . . . **3.** den, pit **4.** bore, cave, cove,
  dive, flaw, gulf, lair, nook, slot,
  vent **5.** abyss, chasm, fault, hovel,
  place, shaft **6.** burrow, cavern, cavity,
  cellar, hollow, prison **7.** impasse,
  opening, orifice, ostiole **10.** excavation
  11. predicament
hole (pert to) . . .
bowling ball . . **4.** grip
cable (ship's) . . **5.** hawse
enlarger . . **6.** reamer
implement . . **3.** awl, eye **4.** bore **5.** drill
  8. stiletto
metal mold . . **5.** sprue
mud . . **6.** wallow
wall . . **5.** niche
water . . **5.** oasis
whirlpool . . **5.** gourd (obs)
Holi (or Hoolee) . . . **8.** festival (Hind)
holia . . . **6.** salmon (humpback)
holiday . . . **4.** fete **5.** feria, merry **6.** fiesta,
  jovial, outing **7.** festive, playday
  8. festival, vacation **9.** convivial, festivity
  10. recreation
holiness . . . **5.** piety, title (Pope) **8.** sanctity
  9. godliness **10.** sacredness

11. saintliness **13.** righteousness
Holland . . . **11.** Netherlands (which see)
Holland . . .
capital . . **8.** The Hague (Court)
  9. Amsterdam
city . . **3.** Ede **5.** Doorn **6.** Leyden
  9. Amsterdam, Rotterdam
government . . **8.** monarchy
liquor . . **3.** gin **8.** schnapps
oddity . . **5.** dikes **6.** canals, tulips
painter . . **6.** Rubens **7.** Van Eyck
people . . **5.** Dutch
port . . **4.** Edam
pottery . . **5.** delft (delf)
province . . **4.** Edam **7.** Drenthe, Zeeland
river . . **3.** Ems, Lek **5.** Meuse, Rhine
  7. Scheldt (Schelde)
sea . . **5.** North
village . . **3.** Ede
hollow . . . **3.** den, pit **4.** thin, void
  5. bight, empty, false, gaunt, sinus
  6. cavern, cavity, cirque, corrie,
  groove, hungry, socket, sunken, vacant
  7. concave, unsound **8.** capsular,
  specious **9.** cavernous, depressed,
  faithless, insincere, worthless
  10. sepulchral **12.** unsatisfying
hollowed . . . **6.** cavate **7.** concave, glenoid
holly . . . **4.** holm, hull, Ilex **5.** yapon
  6. hulver, laurel **8.** Eryngium
  9. blackjack, Ilicaceae **10.** Sapindales
hollyhock . . . **5.** color **7.** Althaea, blue-red
  9. perennial
holm . . . **3.** oak **5.** holly, islet, marsh
  7. bottoms, low land
holobaptist . . . **12.** immersionist
holocaust . . . **9.** sacrifice (by fire)
  11. destruction **13.** burnt offering
holy . . . **5.** godly, pious **6.** chaste, devout,
  sacred **7.** epithet (Relig), sainted
  8. hallowed **9.** venerated
Holy, holy (pert to) . . .
Alliance name . . **10.** Metternich
Bottle (Rabelais) . . . **6.** Bacbuc
carpet . . **5.** kiswa (kiswah)
comb form . . **5.** hagio
Communion . . **9.** Eucharist
cow (smoke, Toledo, etc.) . . **3.** wow
Father . . **4.** Pope
Island . . **11.** Lindisfarne
Joe . . **8.** sky pilot **9.** clergyman
Land . . **9.** Palestine
oil . . **6.** chrism **7.** unction
Ones . . **9.** Innocents (slain by Herod)
orders . . **10.** ordination
Roman Empire name . . **4.** Otto **7.** Francis
  9. Frederick (Barbarossa)
  11. Charlemagne
Scripture(s), Writ . . **5.** Bible
water, et al . . **11.** sacramental
water sprinkler . . **11.** aspergillum
war . . **5.** jihad
Willie's Prayer . . **4.** poem **5.** Burns
Holy Grail (pert to) . . .
castle . . **9.** Monsalvat (Mt)
guardian . . **8.** Amfortas
knight . . **7.** Galahad
legend . . **8.** Sangraal (Sangreal)
quest by . . **4.** Bors **7.** Galahad **9.** Percivale
terms . . **7.** platter, wine cup
homage . . . **5.** dulia, honor, liege **6.** fealty,

latria **7.** loyalty, ovation, respect, worship **9.** deference, obeisance, reverence **10.** allegiance **12.** commendation

homard ... **7.** Homarus, lobster

hombre ... **3.** man **4.** homo, male **6.** fellow

home ... **4.** care, goal (games), kern (kirn), nest **5.** abode, astre, grave, heart **6.** asylum, estate, hearth **7.** habitat, village **8.** domicile, dwelling **9.** residence **10.** fatherland, habitation

home (pert to) ...
base .. **3.** den **5.** plate
dislike .. **9.** ecophobia
Home Sweet Home author .. **5.** Payne (John Howard 1823)
Irish King's .. **4.** Tara
of the gods .. **7.** Olympus
of the Golden Fleece .. **7.** Colchis

homely ... **4.** ugly **5.** plain **6.** humble, kindly, simple **7.** plainly **8.** domestic, homelike, informal, plebeian, uncomely **9.** unsightly **10.** intimately **11.** comfortable **13.** unpretentious

homemade ... **5.** plain **6.** simple **8.** domestic, handmade, homespun

Homer (pert to) ...
birthplace .. **5.** Chios (claimed)
book .. **5.** Iliad **7.** Odyssey
burial place .. **3.** Ios (Isl)
hero .. **6.** Aeneas

Homer's poems (pert to) ...
rhapsodists .. **9.** Homeridae
student, reciter of .. **7.** Homerid **8.** Homerist
study of .. **10.** Homerology
style .. **7.** Homeric

homesickness ... **7.** Heimweh **9.** mal du pays, nostalgia

homespun ... **5.** cloth, plain, rough **6.** coarse, russet **8.** domestic, homemade **10.** not elegant, unpolished (person)

homicide ... **5.** morth **6.** murder **7.** killing **12.** manslaughter

homily ... **5.** adage **6.** sermon **8.** assembly, converse **9.** communion, discourse

homing pigeon ... **13.** carrier pigeon

hominy ... **4.** samp **5.** maize **10.** hulled corn

Homo sapiens ... **3.** man **4.** homo **9.** anthropos

Honduras ...
capital .. **11.** Tegucigalpa
city .. **4.** Tela **6.** Roatan **8.** Trujillo **12.** Puerto Cortes
discoverer .. **8.** Columbus
gulf .. **7.** Fonseca
Indian people .. **5.** Lenca
language .. **7.** Spanish
river .. **4.** Ulua **5.** Negro **6.** Patuca

hone ... **4.** long, pine **5.** delay, dress, stone (sharpening), strop, yearn **6.** lament **7.** grumble, sharpen **8.** oilstone **9.** whetstone

honest ... **4.** open **5.** frank **6.** candid, chaste **7.** genuine, up and up, upright **8.** faithful, suitable, virtuous **9.** guileless, honorable, ingenuous, integrity **10.** creditable **13.** unadulterated

15. straightforward

honesty ... **5.** honor **6.** equity **7.** justice **8.** fairness **9.** integrity, rectitude **11.** genuineness, uprightness **12.** truthfulness **15.** trustworthiness

honey ... **3.** mel **5.** melli (comb form), sweet **6.** nectar **7.** sweeten **10.** endearment

honey (pert to) ...
bear (sloth) .. **8.** Melursus
bearing .. **11.** melliferous
bee .. **4.** Apis **6.** dingar **7.** deseret **9.** mellifera
bird .. **3.** iao **6.** manuao **10.** honey eater
brew .. **4.** mead
buzzard .. **4.** kite, pern
comb .. **4.** raat **5.** favus **8.** alveolus
drink .. **4.** mead **5.** morat
flowing .. **11.** mellifluent, mellifluous
pert to .. **8.** melissic
sucking .. **11.** mellisugent, mellivorous
yellow .. **6.** dorado **10.** melichrous

Hong Kong ...
capital .. **8.** Victoria
government .. **11.** Crown Colony
island .. **12.** Stonecutters
peninsula .. **7.** Kowloon

Honolulu ...
capital of .. **6.** Hawaii
island site .. **4.** Oahu
port .. **11.** Pearl Harbor
suburb .. **3.** Ewa

honorable, honourable ... **5.** moral, title **7.** upright **8.** honorary **9.** estimable, reputable, venerable **10.** creditable **11.** commendable, illustrious, meritorious, respectable

honorably ... **5.** nobly **6.** fairly, justly **8.** worthily **9.** equitably, reputably, uprightly

honorarium ... **7.** douceur

honored ... **5.** famed, feted **6.** graced **7.** awarded, revered **8.** knighted **9.** accoladed

hood ... **4.** corf, cowl, hide, mail (armor) **5.** amice, blind, cloak **6.** bonnet, camail, capote **7.** capuche (capouch) **8.** babushka, burnoose (burnous), capsheaf, covering, liripipe, mozzetta, tapadera **12.** strong-arm man

hood (suff) ... **9.** condition

hooded ... **9.** cucullate

hooded seal ... **11.** bladdernose

hoodwink ... **4.** dupe, fool, hide, wile **5.** blear, blind, cheat, cover, cozen **6.** befool, delude **7.** deceive, mislead **9.** blindfold

hooey ... **4.** blah, bunk **5.** tripe **7.** baloney, hogwash **8.** buncombe, malarkey, nonsense **13.** horsefeathers

hoof ... **4.** clee, frog, walk **5.** cloof (clufe, cluve) **6.** ungula **7.** pastern (part) **8.** periople (part), pododerm

hoof-paring tool ... **8.** butteris

hoof-shaped ... **8.** ungulate

hoof track ... **5.** piste

hook ... **4.** gaff, lure **5.** catch, chape, cleek, crome, curve, hamus, snare, steal **6.** anchor, clevis, fasten, hangle, tenter **7.** hamulus

hookah, hooka ... **4.** pipe **8.** narghile

hooked / horse 256

hooked ... **6.** curved, hamate **7.** angular,
cleeked **8.** aduncous (adunc), anchoral,
aquiline, uncinate
Hooker (Thomas) ... **9.** clergyman
18. Luther of New England
hooks (group) ... **5.** Party (Neth)
9. pulldevil, scrodgill **10.** Kabbeljaws
(Nobles)
hookworm ... **7.** Necator **9.** Uncinaria
hooligan ... **6.** loafer **7.** gorilla, hoodlum,
ruffian **8.** larrikin
hoop ... **4.** bail, band, ring **5.** clasp
6. circle, wicket **7.** circlet **8.** surround
hoop skirt ... **9.** crinoline **11.** farthingale
Hoosier poet ... **5.** Riley (J Whitcomb)
Hoosier State ... **7.** Indiana
hop ... **3.** fly **4.** drug, halt, jump, leap,
limp, trip, vine **5.** bound, caper, dance,
frisk, opium **6.** flight, gambol, spring
8. narcotic
hope ... **3.** bay **4.** opal, spes, Spes
(Goddess) **5.** haven, inlet, trust **6.** aspire,
desire, expect **7.** cherish, promise
8. optimism, reliance **11.** expectation
12. anticipation
hoped for ... **7.** sperate
hopeful ... **8.** probable, sanguine
9. confident, expectant **10.** propitious
hopeless ... **4.** vain **6.** futile **7.** forlorn,
useless **8.** downcast **9.** desperate,
incurable **10.** despairing, despondent
11. ineffectual **12.** disconsolate,
irremediable **13.** irrecoverable,
irretrievable
hopelessness ... **7.** despair **8.** futility
13. impossibility
hop kiln ... **4.** oast (ost)
hoplite ... **7.** soldier
hopper ... **3.** box **5.** chute **6.** dancer,
jumper, leaper **7.** penguin (rock)
10. receptacle **11.** grasshopper
hopscotch ... **6.** pebble, peever **7.** pallall
Horace ... **4.** poet **10.** Ars Poetica
Horae (Gr Relig) ... **4.** dike (justice)
6. Eirene (peace) **7.** Eunomia (wisdom)
9. goddesses **11.** Book of Hours
horal ... **6.** hourly
horde ... **4.** army, camp, clan, pack
5. crowd, swarm, tribe, troop
Horde, Golden ... **6.** Tatars (Mongol)
Horde, Great (Anthrop) ... **5.** Kazak
7. Kirghiz
horizon ... **4.** blue **5.** limit, range **6.** circle,
sea rim **7.** azimuth, sea line, sky line
8. junction (earth and sky), boundary
horizon glass ... **7.** sextant
horizontal ... **4.** flat **5.** level **8.** parallel
(to horizon)
hormone ... **8.** estrogen **9.** cortisone
horn ... **4.** Cape, cusp, gore, peak,
tuba **5.** alarm, bugle, cornu, keras,
siren **6.** antler, beaker, cornet, vessel
7. buccina, process (animal), trumpet
8. tentacle **9.** appendage
horn (pert to) ...
  blare .. **4.** toot **7.** fanfare, tantara
    9. tantarara
  comb form .. **5.** kerat **6.** kerato
  crescent moon .. **4.** cusp
  drinking (anc) .. **6.** rhyton
  insect's .. **7.** antenna

Jewish .. **7.** shophar (shofar)
player .. **6.** bugler **9.** cornetist, trumpeter
producing .. **11.** keratogenic
trumpet .. **6.** kerana (kerrana)
unbranched (antler) .. **3.** dag **7.** pricket
hornbeam ... **8.** ironwood
hornbill ... **4.** bird, tock **6.** homrai, toucan
7. Buceros
horned animal (Myth) ... **7.** Unicorn
9. Monoceros
horned rattlesnake ... **3.** asp **5.** viper
8. cerastes **10.** sidewinder
horned toad ... **6.** lizard **9.** Iguanidae
hornet ... **4.** wasp **5.** Vespa **6.** crabro
horny tissue ... **7.** keratin **8.** keratoid
(ceratoid), keratose (ceratose)
horologe ... **4.** dial **5.** clock, watch
horoscope ... **3.** map **5.** chart **6.** scheme
7. diagram
horrendous ... **7.** fearful **8.** horrible
horrible ... **4.** dire, grim **6.** grisly, horrid,
odious **7.** ghastly, hideous **8.** dreadful,
shocking, terrible **9.** atrocious, frightful,
revolting **10.** detestable, horrendous
horror ... **3.** awe **4.** fear **5.** dread
6. aghast, terror **8.** aversion, distress
10. abhorrence **11.** abomination,
detestation **13.** consternation
hors d'oeuvre ... **6.** canapé, relish
8. aperitif **9.** antipasto, appetizer
horse ... **3.** cob, nag **4.** colt, foal, mare,
mule, plug, pony, prad, race, stud
5. beast, burro, draft, filly, genet
(jennet), hobby, mount, pacer, steed
6. bronco (broncho), cheval, dobbin,
donkey, equine, garran, hippos, maiden,
pelter, rouncy **7.** caballo, cavalry,
charger, courser, Equidae, gelding,
hackney, harness, mustang, prancer,
quarter, stepper, trotter **8.** roadster,
stallion, trotting **9.** broomtail
horse (pert to) ...
  ankle .. **4.** hock
  arena .. **10.** hippodrome
  Australian .. **5.** dingo, myall **8.** warragal,
    yarraman
  blanket .. **5.** manta
  breastplate .. **7.** poitrel (peytrel)
  broken-down .. **6.** garran, gleyde
  buyer (of nags) .. **5.** coper **7.** knacker
  calico .. **5.** pinto
  collar .. **7.** bargham
  comb form .. **5.** hipp **5.** hippo **6.** hippus
  command .. **3.** gee, haw, hup **4.** whoa
    6. giddap
  covering .. **9.** caparison
  cry .. **5.** neigh **6.** whinny
  dealer .. **7.** chanter, scorser
  disease .. **5.** surra (surrah) **6.** heaves,
    lampas, spavin **7.** founder, lampers
  draft .. **9.** Percheron
  family .. **7.** Equidae **9.** Miohippus,
    Orohippus
  fast .. **6.** pelter
  feed box .. **6.** manger
  female .. **4.** mare, yaud **5.** filly
  fly .. **4.** cleg (clegg) **6.** botfly
  foot .. **4.** frog, hoof **7.** fetlock, pastern
  forehead .. **8.** chanfrin
  gait .. **3.** run **4.** lope, pace, trot, walk
    6. canter, gallop

genus . . **5.** Equus
giant (Norse) . . **7.** Goldfax
goddess . . **5.** Epona
gray . . **8.** schimmel
hide . . **8.** cordovan
hired . . **4.** hack
hoof (part) . . **7.** caltrop **8.** periople
laugh . . **5.** snort **6.** guffaw, heehaw
leap . . **6.** curvet, hurdle **9.** ballotade
lover . . **10.** hippophile
mackerel . . **5.** atule, tunny **6.** bonita
male . . **4.** stud **7.** gelding **8.** stallion
manège term . . **5.** longe, mount
  6. pesade **7.** piaffer, saccade **8.** caracole
  9. estrapage
measure . . **4.** hand
miracle (Myth) . . **5.** Arion
monster (fabled) . . **11.** Hippocampus
old . . **4.** jade, yaud **5.** skate **8.** harridan,
  old paint
opera . . **7.** Western
pace . . **4.** lope, trot **5.** amble **6.** canter
pack . . **7.** sumpter
pair . . **4.** span, team
pasturage right . . **9.** horsegate
piebald . . **5.** pinto
pole . . **5.** poler, wheel
prehistoric . . **8.** Eohippus
  10. Mesohippus, Pliohippus
  13. Protorohippus
racer . . **4.** pony **6.** mudder, plater, staker
ref to . . **6.** equine, equoid, hippic
  9. caballine
relay (remounts) . . **6.** remuda
riding . . **3.** cob
rope . . **5.** longe **6.** halter
roundup . . **5.** rodeo
saddle . . **3.** cob **5.** mount **7.** palfrey
shoer . . **7.** farrier **10.** blacksmith
slang . . **3.** nag **4.** hack, plug **6.** dobbin
  8. bangtail
small . . **3.** cob, tit **4.** pony **5.** bidet,
  genet (jennet) **8.** Galloway, Shetland
sorrel . . **4.** roan **8.** chestnut
spirited . . **4.** Arab **5.** steed **6.** rearer
  7. courser
stable of . . **6.** string
study of . . **9.** hippology
swift . . **6.** pelter **7.** Pacolet
talking (Myth) . . **5.** Arion
three (harnessed) . . **6.** tandem **7.** unicorn
track, arena . . **10.** hippodrome
trappings . . **5.** manta **6.** tackle **7.** harness
  9. caparison
trotting . . **6.** Morgan
turn . . **7.** passade
war . . **5.** steed **7.** charger **8.** destrier
  (anc)
white-streaked face . . **4.** shim
wild . . **6.** bronco, tarpan **7.** mustang
  8. warragal (warrigal)
winged . . **7.** Pegasus
horse, breed . . . **4.** Arab, Barb **5.** Shire,
  Waler **6.** Cayuse, Morgan **7.** Arabian,
  Belgian, Hackney, Mustang, Suffolk
  8. Galloway, Normandy, Palomino,
  Shetland **9.** Appaloosa, Miohippus,
  Percheron **10.** Clydesdale
horse, color . . . **3.** bay, tan **4.** pied,
  roan **5.** cream, pinto **6.** calico, sorrel
  7. brindle, dappled, piebald **8.** chestnut,

palomino, schimmel, skewbald **10.** flea-
bitten
horse, famed (and rider) . . . **4.** Tony
  (Tom Mix) **5.** Grani (Sigurd) **6.** Bayard
  (Rinaldo), Rienzi (Gen Sherman),
  Silver (Lone Ranger), Trojan (legend),
  Whitey (Zachary Taylor) **7.** Alborak
  (Mohammed), Morengo (Napoleon),
  Pegasus (Gr Myth), Trigger (Roy
  Rogers), Xanthus (Achilles)
  8. Comanche (Gen Custer), Sleipnir
  (Odin), Soapsuds (Will Rogers) **9.** Black
  Bess (Dick Turpin), Houyhnhnm
  (Gulliver's Travels), Incitatus (Caligula),
  Rosinante (Don Quixote), Traveller
  (Gen Robt E Lee) **10.** Bootlegger
  (Will Rogers), Bucephalus (Alexander
  the Great), Cincinnati (Gen Grant),
  Copenhagen (Wellington at Waterloo),
  King Philip (Gen Forrest) **11.** Black
  Beauty (legend), Vegliantino (Orlando)
  12. Little Sorrel (Stonewall Jackson)
horseman . . . **5.** rider **6.** cowboy
  7. centaur, vaquero **8.** buckaroo
  10. cavalryman, equestrian
  12. broncobuster
horsemanship . . . **6.** manège
horseradish tree . . . **3.** ben (oil) **5.** behen
  (behn) **7.** Moringa
Horus (pert to) . . .
bird . . **6.** falcon
father . . **6.** Osiris
hawk-headed god of . . **3.** day
mother . . **4.** Isis
slayer of . . **4.** Seth
hospice . . . **3.** inn **6.** asylum, imaret
  9. hospitium, infirmary
hospitable . . . **6.** kindly **7.** cordial
  8. friendly, gracious **9.** receptive,
  welcoming **10.** neighborly
hospital . . . **6.** crèche, refuge
  9. ambulance (mobile), infirmary
  10. nosocomium, sanatorium,
  sanitarium **11.** institution, xenodochium
  12. ambulatorium
hospitality . . . **7.** accueil, welcome **8.** open
  door **9.** open house, xenodochy
  10. cordiality **13.** receptiveness
host . . . **3.** sum (obs) **4.** army **5.** swarm
  6. legion, throng **8.** assemble, landlord
  9. multitude, sacrifice **11.** entertainer
hostel . . . **3.** inn **5.** hotel, motel **6.** tavern
  8. lodgings **9.** residence (student)
hostelry . . . **3.** inn **5.** hotel **6.** hostel,
  tavern **11.** caravansary
hostile . . . **5.** enemy **7.** adverse (law),
  opposed **8.** contrary, inimical
  10. malevolent, unfriendly
  11. belligerent **12.** antagonistic
  13. unsympathetic
hostilities . . . **3.** war **5.** feuds, raids
hostility . . . **5.** anger **6.** animus, enmity,
  hatred, rancor **7.** ill will, warfare
  8. opponent **9.** animosity, antipathy
  10. antagonism, bitterness, opposition,
  resentment **11.** contrariety
  13. antisocialism **14.** unfriendliness,
  vindictiveness
hostler . . . **5.** groom **7.** equerry
  9. innkeeper, stableboy, stableman
Host vessel . . . **3.** pyx **5.** paten

10. monstrance
hot . . . 3. red 5. calid, eager, fiery
6. fervid, raging, recent, torrid, urgent
7. burning, calidus, excited, fervent,
glowing, peppery, violent 8. feverish,
sizzling, vehement 10. hot-blooded,
passionate
hot cakes . . . 8. kneepads (army sl)
hotel . . . 3. inn 5. lodge 6. hostel, tavern
7. albergo 11. caravansary
hot-tempered . . . 5. angry, breth, fiery
7. enraged, iracund 8. choleric, wrathful
10. hot-blooded
Hottentot, S Africa (pert to) . . .
cloak . . 6. kaross
hut . . 5. kraal
language . . 7. Khoisan
mixed native . . 6. Griqua
musical instrument . . 4. gora (gorah)
nickname . . 9. Khoi-Khoin (Koi-Koin)
(men of men)
people . . 5. Bantu 7. Bushman
hound . . . 4. hunt 5. chase, track 6. follow,
pursue 7. devotee 9. scoundrel
hound (animal) . . . 4. alan 6. Afghan,
basset, beagle, setter 7. harrier, skirter
8. Cerberus (Myth), elkhound, foxhound
9. boarhound, dachshund, deerhound,
greyhound, staghound, wolfhound
10. bloodhound, otterhound
hounds, relay of . . . 8. avantlay
hour (pert to) . . .
astrology . . 7. inequal 9. planetary
by the . . 5. horal 6. horary
Eccl . . 4. sext 9. canonical
Latin . . 4. hora 5. Horae (Book of Hours)
measure . . 9. hourglass
term . . 4. time 6. period 7. measure
8. interval
houri . . . 5. nymph (Muslim)
Hours, Book of . . . 5. Horae
house . . . 3. eco (comb form) 4. casa,
firm, home 5. abode, cover, lodge,
tribe 6. billet, family 7. cottage,
enclose, lineage, mansion, quarter,
shelter, theater 8. audience, bungalow,
Congress, domicile, dwelling
9. playhouse, residence, workhouse
10. habitation, Parliament
house (pert to) . . .
astrology . . 7. mansion, mundane
9. planetary
boarding . . 3. inn 5. hotel 6. tavern
9. dormitory
comb form . . 3. eco 4. oeco, oiko
correction . . 9. Bridewell (Eng)
11. reformatory
dog . . 6. kennel
government . . 5. Lords 7. Commons
15. Representatives
ranch . . 4. casa 6. casita 8. hacienda
roof . . 9. penthouse
small . . 3. hut 4. nest 5. cabin, shack
stately . . 5. villa 6. palace 7. mansion
summer . . 6. casino, gazebo 9. belvedere
warming . . 6. infare
household (pert to) . . .
deity . . 5. Lares 7. Penates
domestic . . 6. family, menage
fairy . . 4. Puck
linen . . 6. napery

housekeeping . . . 8. oikology
10. management 11. hospitality
House of . . . 4. Keys (Isle of Man) 5. David,
Lords, Peers 7. Bishops, Commons,
Windsor 11. Seven Gables
housewarming . . . 6. infare
11. merrymaking
Houston, Texas . . .
capital . . 8. Republic (Texas, 1837)
college . . 4. Rice
named for . . 10. Sam Houston (Gen)
nickname . . 12. Space City USA
site . . 11. Ship Channel
site of . . 4. NASA
hovel . . . 3. den, hut 4. shed 5. cabin,
hutch, shack 6. dugout 7. shelter
hover . . . 4. flit, soar 5. brood, drift,
float 6. linger 7. shelter 9. hang about
12. be irresolute
however . . . 3. but, how, tho, yet
6. anyhow, though 7. at least
8. although 11. at all events
12. nevertheless 15. notwithstanding
howl . . . 3. bay, cry 4. wail, yell, yowl
6. lament 7. ululate
howling monkey . . . 5. araba
hoyden, hoiden . . . 4. rude 5. a romp
6. tomboy 7. ill-bred
Hoyle's forte . . . 5. cards, games
hub . . . 3. hut 4. axle, nave 6. center
(centre) 7. hummock 12. protuberance
(rough)
Hub (The) . . . 6. Boston
hubbub . . . 3. ado, din 4. game (US Ind),
stir 6. bustle, clamor, outcry, racket,
rumpus, tumult, uproar 8. rowdy-dow
9. agitation, commotion, confusion
10. turbulence
hubristic . . . 8. arrogant, insolent
12. contemptuous
huck . . . 3. hip 4. hook, howk 6. haunch,
higgle, hollow 7. bargain
Huck Finn (pert to) . . .
con man . . 4. Duke 7. Dauphin
creator . . 5. Twain 7. Clemens
friend . . 9. Tom Sawyer
feud family . . 7. Granger
11. Shepherdson
raft mate . . 3. Jim
huckleberry . . . 5. bacca 9. blueberry
12. Vacciniaceae
huckleberry endocarp . . . 6. pyrene
huckster . . . 6. broker, hawker, vendor
7. peddler 8. pitchman, retailer
9. middleman
huddle . . . 3. hug 5. crowd 6. bustle,
confer, jumble, mingle 7. confuse
8. assemble, disorder, grouping
(football) 9. confusion, skinflint
10. conference 14. conglomeration
Hudson (pert to) . . .
boat . . 8. Half Moon (Henry Hudson's)
explorer . . 11. Henry Hudson
River School . . 8. Painters (19th Cent)
River seal . . 7. muskrat
hue . . . 4. form, tint, tone 5. color, guise,
shade, shout, swart, tinge 6. outcry
7. swarthy 8. shouting 10. complexion
huff . . . 4. puff 5. anger, bully, swell
6. offend 7. inflate
hug . . . 4. hold 5. clasp, seize 6. adhere

7. embrace, welcome **8.** greeting
huge . . . **3.** big **4.** vast **5.** giant, great,
large **7.** immense, mammoth, massive,
monster, titanic **8.** colossal, enormous,
gigantic **9.** monstrous **10.** gargantuan
Huguenot . . . **10.** Protestant
Huguenot leader . . . **6.** Adrets (Baron)
hui (Chin) . . . **4.** firm **5.** guild **7.** society
(secret) **11.** partnership
huisache . . . **4.** wabe (wabi) **5.** shrub
7. popinac
huissier . . . **5.** usher **7.** bailiff, sheriff
10. doorkeeper
huitre . . . **6.** oyster
hulky . . . **5.** bulky, large **6.** clumsy
7. hulking, loutish
hull . . . **3.** pod **4.** free, husk **5.** calyx, frame
(ship), shell, shoot, strip **8.** covering
hullabaloo . . . **3.** din **6.** clamor (clamour),
hubbub, outcry, racket, tumult, uproar
9. confusion
hulled corn . . . **4.** samp **5.** maize
6. hominy
hulver . . . **5.** holly
hum . . . **4.** buzz, sing (with closed lips)
5. croon, drone **6.** murmur **7.** deceive
human . . . **3.** man **4.** homo, kind
6. humane, mortal **7.** Adamite
8. merciful
human (pert to) . . .
being . . **3.** man **6.** mortal, person
7. Adamite **8.** creature
bondage . . **7.** slavery
race . . **3.** man **7.** mankind
skull . . **10.** death's-head
structure . . **7.** anatomy
trunk . . **5.** torso
humble . . . **3.** low **4.** mean, meek, mild,
poor **5.** abase, abash, demit, lower,
lowly, plain **6.** modest, simple, subdue
7. degrade, mortify **8.** chastise, deferent,
disgrace, plebeian, reverent **9.** humiliate
10. unassuming **12.** unpretending
humbug . . . **4.** bosh, fake, flam, guff,
hoax, sham **5.** cheat, fraud, guile,
trick **7.** deceive, mislead **8.** pretense
9. deception, imposture, stratagem
humid . . . **4.** damp, dank **5.** moist **6.** sultry
8. vaporous
humiliate . . . **5.** abase, abash, shame
6. humble, nither **7.** affront, degrade,
mortify **8.** disgrace
humiliation . . . **7.** subdual **9.** abasement
11. disgraceful **13.** mortification
humility . . . **6.** humble (spirit) **7.** modesty
8. meekness, mildness **9.** lowliness
(mind) **10.** humbleness
hummingbird . . . **3.** ava **4.** star **5.** sylph,
topaz **6.** rufous, Sappho **7.** colibri,
Lucifer **8.** calliope **9.** sheartail, thornbill,
thorntail **10.** rackettail **11.** Trochilidae
humor, humour . . . **3.** fun, wit **4.** baby,
mood, whim **5.** blood, cater, fancy,
fluid, freak, quirk **6.** comedy, levity,
nature, please **7.** caprice, gratify,
indulge **8.** drollery **10.** comicality
11. inclination, temperament
humorist . . . **3.** wag **5.** comic, droll
8. comedian **11.** entertainer
humorist (famed) . . . **3.** Ade, Nye **4.** Cobb,
Ward (Artemus) **5.** Dunne (Peter

Finley), Twain (Clemens) **6.** Rogers
(Will) **7.** Lardner, Leacock, Thurber
8. Benchley, Perelman **9.** Wodehouse
humorous . . . **5.** funny, humid, moist,
witty **6.** jocose **7.** amusing, jocular
9. facetious, laughable, whimsical
10. capricious
hump . . . **4.** arch, hunk, lump **5.** bulge,
exert, hurry, mound, sulks **7.** hummock
8. shoulder **12.** protuberance
humpbacked . . . **6.** humped, kyphos
8. deformed, kyphosis **9.** camel back
11. hunchbacked
humpbacked fish . . . **5.** whale **6.** salmon,
sucker **9.** whitefish
humus . . . **4.** mold, soil **5.** humin, mulch
Hun . . . **6.** Attila, vandal **7.** soldier
9. barbarian **10.** Ephthalite
hunch . . . **4.** bend, hump, lump **5.** crook,
fudge, shove **6.** chilly, crouch, frosty,
thrust **9.** intuition **12.** protuberance
Hunchback of Notre Dame (pert to) . . .
actor . . . **6.** Chaney **8.** Laughton
author . . **4.** Hugo
character . . **9.** Esmeralda (gypsy),
Quasimodo (The Hunchback)
French name . . **16.** Notre Dame de Paris
hunched . . . **7.** gibbous
hundred (pert to) . . .
comb form . . **5.** centi, hecto **7.** hecaton
eyed being . . **5.** Argus
fold . . **8.** centuple **12.** centuplicate
historian (of centuries) . . **11.** centuriator
Latin . . **6.** centum
men, soldiers . . **7.** century
12. centumvirate
number . . **7.** ten tens **9.** five score
symbol . . **1.** C
victim sacrifice . . **8.** hecatomb
weight . . **6.** cental **7.** centner
years . . **7.** century **9.** centenary, centurial
Hundred Days (pert to) . . . **8.** Napoleon,
Waterloo (Battle 1815)
hundred percent . . . **5.** quite **8.** entirely
10. altogether **14.** unquestionable
hundredth of a right angle . . . **4.** grad
Hundred Years War . . . **5.** Crécy (Cressy)
hung . . . see *hang*
Hungarian (pert to) . . . see also *Hungary*
army . . **6.** Honvéd **9.** Honvédség
cavalryman . . **6.** hussar
Communist leader . . **4.** Nagy **5.** Kádár
composer . . **5.** Lehár, Liszt **6.** Bartók,
Kodály
dance . . **7.** czardas
ethnic group . . **6.** Magyar
gypsy . . **7.** tzigane
hash . . **7.** goulash
hero . . **5.** Arpad **7.** Kossuth
Hungarian name . . **12.** Magyarország
language . . **6.** Magyar, Uralic **10.** Finno-
Ugric
legislature . . **8.** Felsohaz
measure . . **5.** antal, itcze
partridge . . **6.** Perdix
Pretender to the throne . . **4.** Otto
turnip . . **8.** kohlrabi
wine . . **5.** Tokay
writer . . **6.** Molnár
Hungary . . .
capital . . **8.** Budapest

city .. **6.** Szeged **8.** Debrecen
lake .. **7.** Balaton
plain .. **6.** Alfold
river .. **6.** Danube

hunger ... **4.** long, want **6.** acoria, desire, famine, thirst **7.** craving **8.** appetite, coveting, voracity **9.** esurience

hungry ... **4.** avid, poor **5.** eager **6.** barren, hollow, jejune **7.** starved **8.** esurient, famished, indigent **10.** avaricious

Hung Society (secret) ... **5.** Triad (Man, Earth, Heaven) **6.** Deluge

hunt ... **3.** dig **4.** seek **5.** chase, delve, hound, probe, quest, track, trail **6.** ferret, follow, pursue, search, shikar

hunter ... **3.** dog **5.** green, horse, jager, Jason, Orion **6.** cuckoo, Nimrod **7.** shikari (shikaree), stalker, trapper, venerer **8.** huntsman

hunting (pert to) ...
act of .. **6.** venery **7.** pursuit **10.** cynegetics
coyotes .. **7.** wolfing
dog .. **5.** dhole **6.** basset, beagle, setter **7.** pointer
Dogs (Astron) .. **13.** Canes Venatici
expedition .. **6.** safari
fond of .. **7.** venatic
horn .. **5.** bugle
leopard .. **7.** cheetah

hurdy-gurdy ... **4.** lire, rota **5.** organ (street) **7.** sambuke **10.** instrument (lutelike), waterwheel

hurl ... **4.** cast, pelt, rush, toss **5.** fling, pitch, sling, throw **6.** elance (dart), hurtle **9.** overthrow

hurlbarrow ... **11.** wheelbarrow

hurled ... **4.** cast, sent **5.** flung, slung, threw **6.** pelted, tossed **7.** hurtled, twisted **8.** betossed

hurly-burly ... **5.** storm **6.** tumult, uproar **9.** agitation, confusion **10.** excitement

huron ... **6.** grison (animal) **9.** black bass

Huron ... **4.** lake **6.** Indian **9.** Iroquoian

hurrah ... **3.** joy **4.** viva **5.** cheer, huzza, shout **7.** triumph **8.** applause **10.** hallelujah **11.** exclamation **13.** encouragement

hurricane ... **5.** storm **6.** baguio **7.** cyclone, Hurakan (god), tornado, typhoon (in China Sea)

hurry ... **3.** hie **4.** rush, scud **5.** chase, haste, impel, sessa, speed **6.** hasten, scurry, tumult, urge on **7.** quicken **8.** dispatch, expedite **9.** agitation, commotion **10.** expedition **11.** disturbance, precipitate

hurst ... **4.** hill, wood **5.** copse, grove, knoll **7.** hillock (wooded)

hurt ... **4.** harm, maim, pain **5.** lesed, parry **6.** damage, grieve, impair, injure, injury, offend **8.** distress, mischief **9.** detriment **10.** impairment

hurtful ... **6.** malign, nocent **7.** baneful, harmful, malefic, nocuous, noisome, noxious, painful **9.** injurious **10.** pernicious **11.** destructive, detrimental, prejudicial **15.** disadvantageous

hurtle ... **4.** dash, push **5.** clash, fling **6.** assail, jostle **7.** collide, resound

8. brandish

husband ... **3.** eke **4.** mate, save **5.** marry, store **6.** direct (frugally), farmer, spouse, tiller **7.** espouse, granger, manager, steward **8.** conserve **9.** cultivate, economize **10.** husbandman

husbandry ... **6.** thrift **7.** economy, farming, tillage **10.** management (domestic) **11.** agriculture, cultivation

husband's brother ... **5.** levir

hush ... **3.** tut **4.** calm, hist, lull **5.** allay, quiet, still **6.** soothe **7.** appease, silence **10.** keep secret

husk ... **4.** bran, leam, rind **5.** shood, shuck, straw

husky ... **3.** dry **5.** burly, harsh **6.** hoarse, strong **7.** raucous **8.** powerful

Husky ... **3.** dog **6.** Eskimo **8.** Malemute

huss ... **7.** dogfish

hussar ... **4.** fish (banded) **6.** dolman (jacket) **10.** cavalryman, skirmisher

hussy ... **4.** girl, jade **8.** strumpet **9.** housewife

hustings ... **5.** court **8.** platform (Guildhall)

hut ... **3.** cot **4.** cote, isba, shed, skeo (fisherman's) **5.** cabin, hogan, hovel, igloo, jacal, scale **6.** lean-to, shanty, wigwam

hutch ... **3.** bin, box, car, hut, pen **4.** coop **5.** chest, hoard, hovel **6.** coffer, humped, shanty, warren

hyacinth (pert to) ...
color .. **5.** tenne **7.** blue-red
genus .. **10.** Hyacinthus
mineral .. **6.** zircon
myth .. **4.** iris, lily (Turk's cap)
of Peru .. **9.** Cuban lily
precious stone .. **8.** sapphire (legend)
wild .. **6.** camass

hybrid ... **7.** mongrel **9.** half-breed

hybrid (pert to) ...
buffalo .. **7.** cattalo
dog .. **5.** Husky **7.** mongrel
fruit .. **7.** plumcot, tangelo **8.** citrange
horse .. **4.** mule **5.** hinny, jenny
vegetable .. **6.** pomato
zebra .. **7.** zebrass, zebrula **8.** zebrinny

hydra ... **4.** evil **6.** polyps **11.** thermometer

Hydra (Gr) ... **6.** island **7.** serpent **13.** constellation

hydraulic (pert to) ...
brake .. **8.** cataract
element .. **5.** water
engine .. **3.** ram **6.** tremie
product .. **5.** power

hydria ... **3.** jar **6.** kalpis

hydrocarbon ... **5.** tolan (tolane) **6.** ethane, octane, pinene, pyrene, tolane, toluol **7.** benzene, methane, terpene **9.** acetylene

hydrocarbon radical ... **4.** amyl **6.** pentyl

hydrocyanic acid ... **7.** cyanide, prussic **8.** fumigant

hydrogen ... **1.** H **3.** gas **7.** element (univalent)

hydroid ... **9.** polyplike

hydrophobia ... **5.** lyssa **6.** rabies

Hydrus ... **12.** water serpent (fabled) **13.** constellation

hyena ... **6.** mammal **8.** aardwolf

9. earthwolf **13.** Tasmanian wolf
hygienic . . . **7.** sterile **8.** sanitary
   9. healthful **10.** uninfected
   12. prophylactic
hylophagous . . . **10.** wood-eating
hymenopter, hymenopteron . . . **3.** ant,
   bee, fly **4.** wasp **9.** ichneumon
hymn . . . **3.** ode **4.** song (of praise)
   5. dirge, music, paean (pean) **6.** anthem,
   hirmos, Te Deum **7.** chorale **8.** doxology
   9. Trisagion **11.** recessional
hymn (pert to) . . .
   book . . **6.** hymnal
   composer . . **7.** hymnist
      12. hymnographer
   science of . . **9.** hymnology
   singing of . . **7.** hymnody
   victory . . **9.** epinicion
hypnotic . . . **6.** opiate, sleepy **8.** mesmeric,
   narcotic, sedative **9.** soporific
   12. somnifacient **13.** sleep-inducing
hypnotist . . . **6.** Mesmer **9.** mesmerist
   10. hypnotizer
hypnotize . . . **5.** charm **6.** dazzle
   8. entrance **9.** fascinate, mesmerize,
   spellbind
hypochondriac . . . **4.** hypo **6.** insane
   7. invalid (imaginary) **8.** dejected,
   neurotic **9.** depressed, psychotic
   10. nosomaniac

hypocrisy . . . **4.** cant **6.** deceit **8.** feigning
   9. falseness **10.** sanctimony, simulation
   11. outward show
hypocrite . . . **4.** fake **5.** cheat **7.** tartufe
   (tartuffe) **8.** deceiver **10.** dissembler
hypocritical . . . **5.** false **8.** specious,
   two-faced **9.** insincere **10.** Janus-faced
   11. pharisaical **13.** sanctimonious,
   self-righteous
hypodermic glass vessel . . . **7.** ampoule
   (ampule)
hypodermic injection . . . **4.** shot
   11. inoculation
hypothesis . . . **3.** ism **6.** theory **7.** premise,
   theorem **8.** proposal **9.** condition,
   postulate **10.** assumption
   11. proposition, supposition
hypothetical . . . **8.** academic
   11. conditional, conjectural, speculative,
   theoretical
hypothetical (pert to) . . .
   being . . **3.** ens **5.** entia (pl) **6.** entity
   biological unit . . **2.** id
   force . . **2.** od
   medium . . **5.** ether
hyrax . . . **8.** procavia
hyssop . . . **4.** mint **11.** aspergillum
hysteria . . . **7.** anxiety **12.** emotionalism
hysterical . . . **7.** frantic **8.** frenzied,
   wild-eyed **9.** emotional **12.** uncontrolled

I

I . . . **2.** me **3.** eye **4.** iota (Gr), self **6.** letter
   (9th), myself **7.** pronoun
I (pert to) . . .
   big . . **3.** ego
   excessive . . **8.** iotacism
   love . . **3.** amo
Iago . . . **7.** villain (Othello)
iambus . . . **4.** foot, iamb
iatrics (comb form) . . . **11.** treatment of
iatrology . . . **7.** healing **8.** treatise
Iberia . . . **5.** Spain **7.** Georgia (anc)
ibex . . . **3.** sac, tur, zac **4.** kail (kyl)
   6. sakeen **8.** antelope
ibid . . . **6.** lizard **7.** monitor
ibidem . . . **4.** ibid **9.** same place
ibis . . . **5.** guara, stork **9.** gourdhead
Ibsen drama . . . **6.** Ghosts **8.** Peer Gynt
   11. A Doll's House, Hedda Gabler
ice . . . **4.** rime **5.** frost, glacé, glaze
   6. freeze **7.** congeal, diamond, jewelry
   11. refrigerant, refrigerate
ice (pert to) . . .
   bartender's . . **5.** rocks (sl)
   cream dish . . **4.** cone, soda **6.** frappé,
      mousse, sundae **7.** parfait
   dessert . . **5.** glacé **6.** frappé **7.** sherbet
   fine, slushy . . **4.** grue, hail, sish, snow
      5. flake, frost, sleet
   fishing . . **4.** chug
   glacier . . **4.** neve **5.** serac
   mass . . **4.** berg, calf, floe **5.** serac
      6. icecap **7.** glacier, growler
   pendent . . **6.** icicle

sea . . **6.** sludge
Iceland . . .
   airport . . **9.** Kopavogur
   assembly . . **7.** Althing
   bird . . **4.** gull **6.** falcon **10.** gyrofalcon
   capital . . **9.** Reykjavik
   city . . **3.** Hof **8.** Akureyri
   dramatist . . **12.** Siguryonsson
   epic . . **4.** Edda
   first discoverer . . **8.** Norseman (about
      870)
   giant . . **4.** Atli
   glacier . . **6.** Jökull **11.** Orafajökull
   god . . see *Norse god(s), goddess*
   government . . **8.** republic (1944)
   legends . . **5.** Eddas, Sagas **12.** Volsunga
      Saga
   Parliament . . **7.** Althing (world's oldest)
   product . . **7.** herring
   sculptor . . **9.** Sveinsson
   volcano . . **5.** Askja, Hekla, Katla
ichneumon . . . **3.** fly **8.** mongoose
   9. Herpestes **12.** hymenopteron
ichor . . . **5.** fluid (of the gods)
ichthus . . . **4.** fish **6.** amulet, symbol
   8. talisman
ichthyophagy . . . **10.** fish eating
icicle . . . **7.** shoggle **10.** stalactite,
   stalagmite
icing . . . **8.** frosting, meringue
icterus . . . **6.** oriole **7.** disease **8.** jaundice
   10. yellowness
ictus . . . **4.** beat (rhythm), blow **6.** accent,

stress, stroke

icy ... **4.** cold **5.** algid, gelid **6.** frigid, frosty, frozen **7.** glacial **8.** chilling

id ... **4.** idem, unit **5.** idant **6.** libido, psyche, suffix **7.** the same

Idaean (pert to) ...
dweller of .. **5.** Mt Ida
goddess .. **4.** Rhea (Crete) **6.** Cybele (Asia Minor)
nature goddess .. **6.** Cybele **11.** Great Mother

Idaho ...
capital .. **5.** Boise
city .. **7.** Orofino **9.** Pocatello
crop (famed) .. **8.** potatoes
dam .. **5.** Oxbow **8.** Brownlee
famed citizen .. **5.** Borah (Sen)
monument .. **16.** Craters of the Moon
mountain .. **8.** Sawtooth **11.** Bitterroots
river .. **5.** Snake
salmon (landlocked) .. **7.** kokanee
State admission .. **10.** Forty-third
State bird .. **8.** bluebird
State flower .. **7.** syringa
State motto .. **11.** Live Forever **12.** Esto Perpetua
State nickname .. **8.** Gem State

ide (id) ... **3.** orf (orfe) **4.** fish **7.** the same

idea ... **4.** clue, idée, ideo (comb form) **5.** ethic, motif **6.** belief, notion **7.** concept, meaning, opinion, wrinkle **10.** impression **11.** supposition

ideal ... **4.** type **5.** dream, model, Thule (Myth) **6.** unreal **7.** paragon, pattern, perfect, typical, Utopian **8.** complete, exemplar, fanciful **9.** faultless, imaginary, visionary **10.** conceptual, consummate, idealistic **11.** mental image, theoretical **12.** intellectual

idealist ... **7.** dreamer **8.** romancer **9.** visionary **11.** illusionist

idealistic ... **9.** fictional, visionary **10.** starry-eyed **13.** philosophical

ideate ... **5.** think **6.** invent **7.** imagine **8.** conceive **9.** prefigure

identical ... **4.** same, self, twin **5.** alike, equal **10.** equivalent, tantamount

identification ... **3.** tag **4.** disk, sign **5.** badge, brand **6.** naming **7.** earmark **11.** recognition, unification

identify ... **4.** name **5.** place, prove **8.** coalesce **9.** designate, establish **13.** associate with

identity ... **5.** unity **7.** oneness **8.** equality, sameness **9.** exactness **11.** homogeneity **13.** individuality

ideologist ... **7.** dreamer **8.** theorist **9.** visionary

idiocy ... **7.** amentia, anoesia, fatuity, idiotry **10.** deficiency (mental) **11.** foolishness

idiograph ... **9.** trademark

idiom ... **6.** phrase **7.** diction **8.** language **11.** peculiarity

idiosyncrasy ... **9.** mannerism **11.** peculiarity **12.** eccentricity **14.** characteristic

idiot ... **3.** oaf **4.** dolt, fool **5.** booby, dunce, moron **6.** cretin, nitwit **7.** dullard, half-wit **8.** imbecile **9.** blockhead, simpleton

idiotic ... **4.** daft **5.** crazy **7.** foolish **9.** senseless **12.** feeble-minded

idle ... **4.** laze, lazy, loaf, sorn, vain **5.** drone, empty, inert **6.** loiter, otiose, tiffle, truant, unused, vacant **7.** leisure, loafing, trivial, useless **8.** baseless, inactive, indolent, slothful, trifling **9.** unfounded, worthless **10.** groundless, unemployed, unoccupied **11.** ineffectual, unwarranted

idleness ... **5.** folly, sloth **6.** vanity **7.** inertia **8.** delirium, faniente, laziness **9.** silliness **10.** inactivity, triviality **15.** lightheadedness

idler ... **4.** hobo **5.** drone **6.** loafer **7.** dawdler, lounger **8.** loiterer

idol ... **3.** god (sacred) **4.** Baal, icon, zemi **5.** afgod, deity (heathen), eikon, satyr **6.** effigy, fetish, idolum, statue **7.** darling, fallacy, phantom, picture **8.** impostor **9.** pretender

idolater ... **5.** pagan **6.** adorer **7.** admirer, Baalist, Baalite, heathen **8.** idolizer **9.** worshiper

idolize ... **5.** adore **6.** esteem, revere **7.** worship **10.** idolatrize

idyl, idyll ... **4.** poem **5.** image **7.** bucolic, eclogue, picture **8.** pastoral

i.e. ... **5.** id est **6.** that is

if ... **2.** si **3.** gif **8.** granting, provided **9.** supposing

if ever ... **4.** once

if not ... **4.** else, nisi (law) **6.** unless

igneous rock ... **4.** boss, dike, trap **5.** magma **6.** basalt **7.** peridot **10.** granophyre **11.** molten magma

ignis ... **4.** fire

ignite ... **4.** burn, fire, heat **5.** light **6.** kindle **7.** blaze up, flare up **9.** set fire to

ignoble ... **3.** low **4.** base, mean, vile **6.** menial **8.** plebeian, shameful **11.** disgraceful **12.** dishonorable, disreputable

ignoramus ... **4.** dolt, fool **5.** dunce **6.** nitwit, no bill (law) **11.** know-nothing

ignorance ... **5.** tamas (Hind) **9.** nescience **12.** inexperience

ignorant ... **7.** unaware **8.** nescient **9.** unknowing, untutored **10.** illiterate, unlettered **13.** inexperienced, unintelligent

ignore ... **3.** cut **4.** omit, snub **7.** condone, disobey, neglect **8.** overlook **9.** disregard, eliminate

Igorot ... **6.** Bontok **7.** Nabaloi **8.** Kankanai **10.** Indonesian

iguana ... **6.** goanna (goana), lizard **7.** monitor, tuatara **9.** Iguanidae **10.** lace lizard

I Have Found It ... **6.** Eureka (Calif motto)

ihi (Maori) ... **7.** skipper **8.** halfbeak **10.** stitchbird

IHS ... **5.** Jesus **6.** symbol **10.** in hoc signo

iiwi ... **4.** bird

ikbal ... **7.** arrival **8.** prestige **10.** prosperity

Iknaton ... **9.** Amenhotep, Amenophis (IV)

ikona . . . **9.** greenhorn, simpleton
ileum . . . **9.** intestine (small)
ilex . . . **5.** holly **7.** holm oak **11.** Paraguay
  tea
Iliad (pert to) . . .
  founder (anc) . . **4.** Troy **5.** Ilium
  poem author . . **5.** Homer
  poem character . . **4.** Ajax **6.** Hector
    7. Stentor **8.** Achilles, Briseis
    9. Agamemnon, Cassandra
ilium . . . **4.** bone (pelvic)
ilium . . . **4.** Troy (anc)
ilk . . . **4.** kind, sort, type **6.** nature
  9. character
ill . . . **3.** bad, mal (comb form) **4.** evil,
  hard, poor, rude, sick **5.** badly, wrong
  6. ailing, malice, poorly, savage,
  unkind **7.** noxious, painful, unlucky
  9. dangerous, difficult **10.** disastrous,
  indisposed, iniquitous, malevolent,
  unpolished, unskillful **11.** unfavorable,
  unfortunate, unwholesome
  12. disagreeable, inauspicious
ill (pert to) . . .
  at ease . . **7.** awkward **9.** graceless,
  maladroit
  bred . . **4.** rude **7.** uncivil **8.** impolite
  9. bourgeois
  hap . . **10.** misfortune
  humored . . **5.** cross, moody
  natured . . **4.** dour **5.** cross, moody,
  surly **6.** morose, sullen **7.** crabbed
  10. crosspatch
  tempered . . **7.** bilious **8.** choleric
  timed . . **5.** inapt **8.** untimely **9.** premature
  10. malapropos **11.** inexpedient,
  inopportune
  will . . **6.** enmity, malice
  11. malevolence
illegal . . . **4.** foul **7.** illicit **8.** outlawry,
  unlawful, wrongful **10.** contraband,
  unofficial **12.** illegitimate, unauthorized
illegal entry . . . **6.** ringer
illimitable . . . **4.** vast **8.** infinite
  9. boundless **11.** measureless
  12. immeasurable, unrestricted
Illinois . . .
  airport . . **5.** O'Hare
  capital . . **8.** Vandalia (first) **11.** Springfield
  city . . **5.** Elgin **6.** Peoria **7.** Chicago,
  Decatur **8.** Evanston, Waukegan
  9. Centralia
  lake . . **8.** Michigan
  slogan . . **13.** Land of Lincoln
  State admission . . **11.** Twenty-first
  State nickname . . **7.** Prairie
illiterate . . . **6.** unread **8.** ignorant,
  untaught **9.** inerudite, unlearned,
  unrefined, untutored, unwritten
ill-mannered . . . **4.** rude **7.** boorish
illness . . . **6.** malady **8.** cachexia, sickness
  9. complaint, distemper **10.** affliction
  13. indisposition
illuminant . . . **3.** gas **4.** lamp **9.** petroleum
  10. Kleig light
illuminate . . . **5.** adorn, color, light
  6. illume **7.** explain, lighten, miniate
  8. emblazen, illumine **9.** elucidate,
  enlighten, irradiate, rubricate
  10. illustrate
illumination, unit of . . . **3.** lux **4.** phot

illusion . . . **5.** fancy **6.** mirage **7.** chimera,
  fallacy, mockery, phantom **8.** delusion,
  phantasy **9.** deception, false show
  10. apparition **13.** hallucination,
  misconception
illusive . . . **5.** false **6.** unreal **8.** spectral
  9. deceitful, deceptive, imaginary
  10. phantasmal, transitory
illusory . . . **5.** false **8.** delusory, illusive
  9. deceptive, erroneous, imaginary,
  unfounded **10.** fallacious
illustrate . . . **4.** cite, draw **5.** adorn
  7. explain, picture **8.** beautify
  9. elucidate, exemplify, represent
  10. illuminate
illustrious . . . **5.** noble, noted **6.** famous,
  heroic **7.** eminent, exalted, radiant
  8. glorious, luminous, renowned,
  splendid **9.** brilliant, honorable
  10. celebrated
image . . . **3.** god **4.** copy, icon, idea,
  idol, ikon, type **6.** alraun, aspect,
  effigy, idolon, mirror, recept, sphinx,
  statue, typify **7.** eidolon, phantom,
  picture, portray **8.** illusion, likeness,
  phantasm **9.** semblance **10.** apparition,
  conception, simulacrum **11.** counterpart
  12. reproduction
imaginary . . . **5.** ideal **7.** fancied **8.** fanciful,
  illusory, mythical **10.** fictitious
imaginary disease . . . **9.** nosomania
imagination . . . **5.** dream, fancy
  8. phantasy, poetical
imagine . . . **5.** dream, fancy, opine, think
  6. ideate **7.** suppose **8.** conceive
  10. conjecture
imam . . . **6.** caliph, priest (Muslim)
imbecile . . . **4.** dolt, weak **5.** anile,
  idiot, inane, moron **6.** cretin, dotard,
  feeble, stupid, witlet **7.** fatuous, idiotic,
  witling **9.** driveling **10.** half-witted
  12. feeble-minded
imbed . . . **5.** embed, inset **6.** cement
  9. establish
imberbe . . . **9.** beardless
imbibe . . . **4.** soak **5.** drink, imbue,
  learn **6.** absorb, inhale **8.** saturate
  10. assimilate
imbroglio . . . **5.** brawl **11.** embroilment,
  predicament **16.** misunderstanding
imbrue . . . **3.** fig, wet **4.** soak **5.** color,
  stain (with blood), steep **6.** defile,
  drench **7.** moisten **8.** saturate
imbue . . . **3.** dye **5.** steep, teach,
  tinge **6.** infuse, leaven **7.** ingrain,
  inspire **8.** permeate, saturate, tincture
  9. inculcate **10.** impregnate
imitant . . . **9.** imitation **11.** counterfeit
imitate . . . **3.** ape **4.** copy, mime,
  mock **5.** mimic **6.** borrow **7.** emulate
  8. pastiche, resemble, simulate
  9. dissemble, reproduce
imitation . . . **4.** copy, echo, sham **5.** apery,
  apism, paste **6.** ectype, olivet (pearl),
  parody **7.** mimesis, mimicry **8.** travesty
  9. burlesque **10.** caricature, simulation
  12. onomatopoeia
imitative . . . **5.** apish **8.** apatetic
  9. emulative, imitation **10.** simulative
  11. counterfeit
immaculate . . . **4.** pure **5.** clean **6.** chaste

8. spotless, unsoiled 9. faultless, undefiled, unstained, unsullied

immanence . . . 7. inbeing 9. inherence 10. indwelling, innateness

immanent . . . 5. inner 6. inward 8. internal 9. intrinsic 10. indwelling

immaterial . . . 6. slight 8. trifling 9. spiritual 10. impalpable, intangible 11. disembodied, incorporeal, unimportant 12. supernatural 13. insignificant, unsubstantial

immature . . . 5. crude, green 6. callow, unripe 7. untried 8. untimely, youthful 9. premature 10. unfinished 11. undeveloped

immeasurable . . . 7. endless 8. infinite 9. boundless, unlimited 10. indefinite 11. illimitable, innumerable 12. immeasurable, incalculable, unfathomable 13. indeterminate 16. incomprehensible

immediacy . . . 9. awareness, closeness 10. directness 11. punctuality

immediate . . . 4. next, stat 6. direct, prompt 7. instant, nearest, present 10. continuous, succeeding

immediately . . . 3. now 4. anon 7. closely 8. directly, promptly 9. instantly, therewith 11. straightway 12. without delay

immemorial . . . 3. old 7. ageless, ancient 8. dateless 9. out of mind 11. prehistoric, traditional

immense . . . 4. huge, vast 5. grand, great 6. superb 7. mammoth, titanic 8. enormous, infinite 9. monstrous 10. prodigious, unmeasured

immerge . . . 3. dip 4. sink 5. merge 6. engulf, plunge 7. immerse 8. inundate, submerge

immerse . . . 3. dip 4. bury, dunk, sink 5. douse, souse 6. absorb, plunge 7. baptize, engross 9. overwhelm

imminent . . . 7. nearing 8. menacing, upcoming 9. impending 10. near at hand 11. approaching, forthcoming, overhanging, threatening

immobile . . . 3. set 5. fixed, inert 6. stable 8. moveless 9. immovable, obstinate, unfeeling 10. inflexible, motionless, stationary

immoderate . . . 5. ultra, undue 7. extreme 9. excessive 10. exorbitant, inordinate 11. extravagant, intemperate 12. unreasonable

immolation . . . 8. oblation, offering 9. sacrifice

immoral . . . 3. bad 6. wicked 7. corrupt, vicious 8. depraved, indecent 9. dissolute 10. licentious, misconduct

immortal . . . 6. divine 7. abiding, endless, eternal, godlike, undying 8. enduring 9. ambrosial, ceaseless, celebrity, perpetual 10. superhuman 11. amaranthine, everlasting 12. imperishable 13. incorruptible

Immortal (Taoism) . . . 8. Chang Kuo

immortality . . . 4. fame 6. amrita (conferring) 9. anathasia 11. lasting fame 13. deathlessness 15. everlastingness

immovable . . . 3. pat 4. fast, firm 5. fixed, rigid 6. stable 7. adamant 8. immobile, obdurate 9. obstinate, unfeeling 10. inflexible, stationary

immunity . . . 7. freedom 8. impunity 9. exemption 10. resistance (power of) 11. unrestraint

immure . . . 4. wall 6. entomb 7. confine 8. imprison, surround 9. encompass 11. incarcerate

immutable . . . 4. firm 6. stable 7. eternal 8. constant 9. obstinate 10. inflexible, invariable 12. unchangeable 13. unadulterated

imp . . . 3. bud, elf, fay 4. brat, cion, pixy, slip 5. child, demon, devil, fairy, graft, rogue, scion, shoot, youth 6. repair (falconry), spirit, sprite 7. progeny 9. offspring

impact . . . 4. pack, slam 5. brunt, force, shock, wedge 6. effect, stroke 7. contact, impulse, meaning 8. striking 9. collision, fix firmly, impinging

impair . . . 3. mar 4. harm, hurt, ruin, rust, wear 5. break, spoil 6. damage, debase, injure, lessen, reduce, weaken 7. vitiate 8. decrease, enfeeble 11. deteriorate

impale . . . 4. edge, gore, join (Her), spit, stab 5. hem in, spike 6. border, pierce, punish 7. confine, torture 8. encircle, surround

impalement . . . 5. calyx 8. stabbing 10. punishment 11. coats of arms (united)

impalpable . . . 4. fine 10. immaterial, intangible 13. infinitesimal

impart . . . 3. say 4. give, lend, tell 5. grant, share, yield 6. confer, convey, inform, reveal 7. divulge 8. disclose, discover 9. partake of 10. distribute 11. communicate

impartial . . . 4. even, fair, just 7. neutral 8. unbiased 9. equitable 12. unprejudiced 13. disinterested, dispassionate

impartiality . . . 7. justice 8. fairness 10. neutrality 11. unprejudice 17. disinterestedness

impassable . . . 6. stolid 9. impassive 10. impervious, unpassable 11. impermeable, unnavigable 12. impenetrable

impasse . . . 8. cul-de-sac 9. stalemate 10. blind alley

impassible . . . 9. impassive, unfeeling

impassioned . . . 6. ardent 7. amorous, zealous 8. eloquent, vehement 10. passionate

impassive . . . 4. calm 5. stoic 6. serene 7. passive 9. apathetic 10. impassable 12. invulnerable 13. insusceptible

impatient . . . 5. eager, testy 6. uneasy 7. anxious, fretful, itching, peevish, restive 8. choleric, petulant, restless 9. impetuous, irascible, irritable 10. intolerant

impavid . . . 8. fearless

impeach . . . 4. harm 6. accuse, charge, hinder, impair, impede, indict 7. arraign, censure, prevent 9. challenge, criminate, discredit, disparage

impeccable ... **8.** flawless, innocent **9.** faultless **10.** immaculate
impede ... **3.** bar, let **4.** clog **5.** block, debar, estop **6.** hamper, hinder, retard, stymie (stimy) **8.** encumber, obstruct, restrict
impediment ... **3.** bar, rub **4.** snag **5.** hitch **6.** defect, malady **7.** baggage, barrier **8.** obstacle **9.** hindrance **10.** difficulty **11.** encumbrance, obstruction
impel ... **3.** put **4.** move, urge **5.** drive, force, forge **6.** compel, incite, induce, obsess, prompt, propel **7.** actuate **9.** constrain, influence
impel a boat ... **3.** oar, row **4.** pole **5.** scull
impelling force ... **7.** impetus **8.** momentum
impending ... **7.** nearing **8.** awaiting, imminent, menacing **9.** hindering **11.** overhanging, threatening
impenetrable ... **5.** dense **10.** impervious **11.** impregnable, inscrutable **12.** inaccessible, unfathomable **13.** unimpressible **14.** unintelligible
impenitent ... **8.** obdurate **10.** uncontrite **11.** unrepentant, unrepenting
imperative ... **4.** mood (Gram) **6.** needed, urgent **7.** binding **8.** pressing **9.** directive, imperious, mandatory, necessary **10.** compulsory, obligatory, peremptory **13.** authoritative
imperceptible ... **6.** subtle **9.** invisible **10.** insensible **13.** inappreciable, indiscernible, infinitesimal **14.** unintelligible
imperfect ... **3.** mal (pref) **4.** cull **5.** frail **6.** faulty, second **7.** errable **8.** fallible, immature, impaired **9.** blemished, defective **10.** inadequate, incomplete
imperfection ... **4.** flaw, vice **5.** fault **6.** defect **7.** blemish, failing **8.** fraility, weakness **10.** deficiency **11.** shortcoming **14.** incompleteness
imperfectly ... **8.** slightly **12.** inadequately
imperial ... **5.** regal, royal **6.** kingly, lordly, purple **8.** majestic **9.** imperious, masterful, monarchal, sovereign
imperial (pert to) ...
Academy .. **6.** Han-lin (Chin)
blue .. **5.** smalt
cap .. **5.** crown
city (anc) .. **4.** Rome
domain .. **6.** empire
legislature .. **4.** Diet (Jap)
officer .. **8.** palatine
imperil ... **4.** risk **6.** expose **8.** endanger **10.** jeopardize
imperious ... **6.** lordly **7.** haughty **8.** arrogant, despotic, dominant, pressing **10.** commanding, compelling, tyrannical **11.** dictatorial, domineering, overbearing
imperishable ... **7.** eternal, undying **8.** enduring, immortal **11.** everlasting **14.** indestructible
impermanent ... **8.** fleeting, temporal, unstable **9.** ephemeral, momentary, temporary, transient **10.** evanescent, short-lived
impersonate ... **3.** ape **4.** pose **6.** pose

as, typify **7.** portray **9.** exemplify, personate (law), personify, represent, symbolize
impertinence ... **4.** sass **9.** impudence, insolence, unfitness **10.** incivility **11.** impropriety, irrelevance
impertinent ... **4.** rude **5.** saucy **7.** ill-bred **8.** impudent, insolent **9.** frivolous, officious **10.** inapposite, irrelevant **12.** inapplicable, inconsequent **13.** disrespectful
imperturbability ... **8.** ataraxia (ataraxy), serenity
imperturbable ... **4.** calm, cool **6.** placid, serene, steady **8.** tranquil **9.** impassive **10.** phlegmatic **13.** dispassionate
impervious ... **5.** tight **6.** opaque **7.** callous **10.** impassable **12.** impenetrable, inaccessible
impetuosity ... **5.** ardor **6.** fougue **8.** rashness
impetuous ... **3.** hot **4.** rash **5.** eager, hasty, heady, sharp **6.** ardent, bensel (motion), fervid, sudden **7.** furious, violent **8.** forcible, headlong, reckless, vehement **9.** impulsive **10.** passionate **11.** precipitate
impetus ... **4.** birr **7.** impulse **8.** momentum, stimulus **9.** incentive
impi (Zulu) ... **8.** armed men, warriors
impignorate ... **4.** pawn **6.** pledge **8.** mortgage
impious ... **7.** godless, profane **9.** nefandous, undutiful **10.** irreverent **11.** irreligious
impish ... **5.** elvan **6.** elfish **7.** puckish **9.** malignant **11.** mischievous
implacable ... **6.** enmity **11.** immitigable **12.** unappeasable **14.** uncompromising
implant ... **4.** root **5.** infix, inset, plant **6.** enroot, infuse, insert **7.** enforce, engraft, impress, inspire, instill **9.** establish, inculcate, inoculate, insinuate, introduce
implement ... **3.** kit **4.** peel, tool **5.** dolly, knife, means, scoop, tongs **6.** pestle, petard **7.** fulfill, utensil **8.** carry out, complete, material, scissors **9.** equipment **10.** accomplish, instrument
implement (pert to) ...
ancient .. **4.** celt **6.** eolith **9.** paleolith (stone)
cleaning .. **3.** mop **5.** broom, brush **6.** vacuum **7.** sweeper
hide flesher .. **6.** slater
holding .. **5.** tongs **6.** pliers **8.** tweezers
lifting .. **3.** pry **5.** crane, lever, tongs
lumbering .. **4.** tode **6.** peavey (peavy)
nap .. **6.** teasel
printing .. **5.** biron, press **6.** brayer
reaping .. **5.** mower **6.** reaper, scythe, shears, sickle
surgical .. **7.** scalpel **9.** tenaculum
threshing .. **5.** flail
implicate ... **5.** imply **7.** embroil, entwine, involve **8.** entangle **10.** interweave **11.** incriminate
implicit ... **5.** tacit **7.** implied, virtual **8.** complete, inherent **9.** entangled, potential **11.** unqualified

12. constructive 13. unquestioning
implied ... 5. tacit 11. inferential 12. not expressed
implore ... 3. ask, beg 4. pray 5. crave 7. beseech, entreat, solicit 8. petition 10. supplicate
imply ... 4. hint, mean 5. argue 6. infold 7. connote, involve, suggest, suppose 9. predicate
impolite ... 4. rude 5. crude, rough 7. uncivil 10. ill-behaved, mannerless, ungracious, unmannerly, unpolished 12. discourteous 13. disrespectful
impolitic ... 6. unwise 9. untactful 10. indiscreet 11. inexpedient 12. undiplomatic
import ... 5. drift, sense, value 6. denote, weight 7. betoken, meaning, signify 8. commerce, indicate 9. introduce, of concern 10. importance 11. consequence, implication, importation, merchandise
importance ... 6. moment, stress, weight 8. prestige 9. influence 10. famousness 11. consequence, importunity 12. solicitation
important ... 3. key 5. grave 6. famous, urgent 7. pompous, weighty 8. material 9. momentous 11. considerate, influential, significant, substantial 12. considerable, ostentatious 13. consequential
import tax ... 4. duty 6. tariff
importune ... 3. beg, ply, tax, woo 4. coax, push, urge 5. beset, impel, plead, press 6. appeal, cajole 7. entreat, press on
importunity ... 11. importunate, pertinacity 12. solicitation
impose ... 3. tax 4. duty, levy 6. burden, entail 7. command, confirm (Eccl), exploit, inflict, intrude, obtrude, penalty, presume 10. discommode
imposing ... 5. noble, regal 6. august 7. stately 9. dignified, grandiose 10. commanding, impressive 11. ceremonious 13. grandiloquent
impossible ... 6. absurd 8. hopeless, terrible 9. insoluble 10. outlandish 11. unthinkable 12. unimaginable 13. contradictory, impracticable
impost ... 3. tax 4. levy, task, toll 5. abwab 6. custom, excise, surtax, tariff, weight 7. tribute 8. handicap
impostor ... 4. fake 5. fraud, phony, quack 6. humbug 7. empiric 9. charlatan, pretender 10. mountebank
imposture ... 5. fraud, trick 8. delusion, quackery 9. deception 10. imposition
impotent ... 4. weak 6. barren 7. cripple, sterile 9. deficient, incapable, powerless 13. uninfluential
impound ... 5. pen in, seize, store 6. freeze 7. collect 8. imprison 9. reservoir 10. confiscate 11. appropriate
impoverish ... 4. ruin 6. beggar 7. despoil, exhaust 8. bankrupt, make poor 11. make sterile
imprecation ... 4. oath 5. curse 8. anathema 10. execration

11. malediction
impregnable ... 4. hard 10. inviolable 12. inexpugnable, invulnerable 13. unconquerable
impregnate ... 5. imbue 6. infuse 8. fructify 9. fertilize, inculcate
impresa ... 5. maxim, motto 6. device, emblem
impresario ... 7. manager 9. conductor, projector (opera) 12. entrepreneur
impress ... 3. awe, fix 4. bite, dent, levy, mark, seal 5. press, print, stamp 6. affect, effect, enlist, indent 7. engrave, imprint 8. printing, shanghai 9. conscript, engraving, inculcate 10. commandeer, impression 11. indentation 14. characteristic
impressed ... 4. awed 7. infixed, stamped 8. affected, engraved 9. imprinted
impression ... 4. form, idea, mark 5. hunch, print, stamp 6. macule, signet 7. emotion, opinion 8. printing 9. engraving, sensation 10. appearance 11. inculcation, indentation, supposition
impressionable ... 6. pliant 7. plastic 9. sensitive, teachable 10. responsive 11. suggestible, susceptible
impressive ... 6. solemn 8. dramatic, eloquent 9. arresting, grandiose 10. convincing
imprint ... 3. fix 4. dint 5. infix, press, stamp 6. indent 7. edition, engrave 8. printing 9. engraving
imprison ... 4. bond, cage, gaol, jail 5. limit 6. arrest, detain, immure, intern, lock up 7. confine, impound 8. restrain 11. incarcerate
imprisonment ... 4. band 6. duress 8. coercion 9. restraint 10. constraint, immurement, internment 11. confinement, impoundment 13. incarceration
impromptu ... 6. extemp 7. offhand 11. extemporary 13. improvisation 14. extemporaneous 15. autoschediastic
improper ... 3. ill, pah 4. evil 5. amiss, wrong 6. vulgar 7. illegal, naughty 8. indecent, unseemly, unsuited, untoward 9. incorrect, inelegant 10. inaccurate, indecorous, indelicate, unbecoming, unsuitable
impropriety ... 5. wrong 8. solecism 9. indecency, vulgarity 11. malapropism, misbehavior
improve ... 4. mend 5. amend, edify, emend, moise, train 6. better, employ, uplift 7. advance, augment, correct, enhance, perfect, promote, recover, rectify, upgrade 9. cultivate, get better, intensify, meliorate 10. ameliorate, recuperate
improvident ... 4. rash 8. prodigal, wasteful 9. negligent 10. thriftless 11. thoughtless
improvise ... 5. ad lib 6. invent 7. ad libit 9. ad libitum 11. extemporize 13. autoschediaze
imprudence ... 5. brass 8. rashness 9. hardihood 12. indiscretion, recklessness
impudence ... 5. cheek 8. rudeness

9. flippancy, indecency, insolence
10. brazenness, disrespect
12. impertinence 13. shamelessness
impudent . . . 4. bold, pert, rude 5. brash,
saucy 6. brazen 8. flippant, insolent,
malapert 9. audacious, shameless
11. impertinent 13. disrespectful
impugn . . . 4. deny 5. blame 6. assail
(by words), oppose, refute 7. asperse,
censure, gainsay
impulse . . . 3. ate 4. rush, urge 5. force
6. motive 7. impetus 8. instinct
9. incentive 11. instigation
impulsive . . . 5. hasty, quick 6. moving
9. impellent, impetuous 10. motivating
11. instinctive 13. ill-considered
impure . . . 4. foul, lewd 5. dirty,
mixed 6. filthy, unholy 7. bastard,
defiled, obscene, unclean 8. unchaste
10. inaccurate, unhallowed
11. adulterated, unwholesome
impure metal . . . 5. alloy, matte 6. speiss
impure rock . . . 5. chert 9. flintlike
imputation . . . 7. censure 8. charging
9. aspersion, criticism 10. accusation,
ascription 11. attribution, insinuation
impute . . . 6. accuse, charge, credit,
impart, reckon, regard 7. arraign,
ascribe 8. consider 9. attribute
impy . . . 11. mischievous
in . . . 2. at 4. amid, into 5. among 6. at
home, inside, within
in (pert to) . . .
  abundance . . 5. store 6. galore
  accordance . . 8. pursuant
  addition . . 3. too, yet 4. also, more,
  plus 11. furthermore
  all directions . . 8. everyway
  12. everywhither
  an undertone . . 9. sotto voce
  as much as . . 3. for 5. since 6. seeing
  7. because, insofar
  back . . 3. aft 5. arear 6. astern 7. postern
  behalf of . . 3. for, pro 7. favor of
  camera . . 9. in private 10. in chambers
  common . . 4. same 5. alike
  concert . . 8. together
  contact . . 8. touching 9. attingent
  current style . . 3. a la 7. alamode,
  popular
  existence . . 6. extant
  fact . . 5. truly 6. indeed 7. de facto
  favor of . . 3. aye, pro, yea
  good health . . 3. fit 4. hale 7. healthy
  love . . 7. smitten 9. enamoured
  name only . . 7. nominal, titular
  need . . 7. straits 8. distress
  open air . . 7. outdoor 8. al fresco
  passing . . 9. en passant
  place of . . 3. for 5. stead 7. instead
  possession . . 5. title 6. seizin
  private . . 8. in camera
  regard to . . 5. anent
  rows . . 4. arow 6. serial 7. aligned
  (alined)
  so far as . . 3. qua
  spite of . . 6. mauger 7. despite, however
  11. nonetheless
  standing position . . 7. statant
  store . . 5. ready 7. waiting 8. awaiting
  straight lines . . 8. e regione

succession . . 6. series 8. serially, seriatim
the future . . 5. hence, later 6. mañana
  12. subsequently
the know . . 3. hep
the same place . . 4. ibid 6. ibidem
the year of . . 4. anno
truth . . 6. certes, indeed, verily
  8. forsooth
what way . . 3. how 7. quo modo
inability . . . 9. impotence 10. inadequacy,
incapacity 12. incapability,
incompetence
inability to . . .
  articulate . . 7. inaudia
  chew . . 8. amasesis
  comprehend . . 11. acatalepsia
  move . . 7. apraxia
  name objects . . 9. paranomia
  read . . 6. alexia
  stand erect . . 7. astasia
  swallow . . 7. aphagia
inaccessible . . . 8. reserved
10. unsociable 11. out-of-the-way
12. unattainable 14. unapproachable
inaccurate . . . 5. loose 6. faulty 7. inexact
9. defective, erroneous, imperfect,
incorrect 13. ungrammatical
inaction . . . 6. torpor 7. inertia
8. abeyance, idleness 9. inertness
10. suspension
inactive . . . 4. idle 5. inert 7. abeyant,
neutral, not busy 8. sluggish
9. sedentary 10. indisposed
inadequacy . . . 9. inability 10. deficiency,
inequality 11. inferiority
12. incompetence 13. insufficiency
14. incompleteness
inadvertence . . . 5. error 7. neglect
11. inattention 12. carelessness,
heedlessness 15. thoughtlessness
inadvertent . . . 9. negligent, unwitting
11. inattentive
inadvertently . . . 10. heedlessly
11. unwittingly 12. neglectfully
inane . . . 4. vain, void 5. empty,
inept, silly 6. famous 7. fatuous,
foolish, puerile, trivial 8. trifling
9. frivolous 11. ineffectual, thoughtless
13. characterless
inappropriate . . . 5. inept, undue
8. untimely 10. irrelevant, unsuitable
11. inexpedient
inapt . . . 5. inept 10. unsuitable
inattentive . . . 3. lax 6. absent, remiss
8. careless, heedless 9. negligent,
unheeding, unmindful 10. distracted,
regardless 11. inadvertent
inaugurate . . . 5. admit, begin, start
6. induct 7. install, instate, usher
in 8. initiate 9. auspicate, institute,
introduce 10. consecrate
inauspicious . . . 7. adverse, ominous,
unlucky 8. sinister, untimely 9. ill-
omened 12. unpropitious
inborn . . . 6. allied, inbred, innate,
native 7. cognate, natural 8. inherent
10. connatural
inbred . . . 6. inborn, innate 9. endogamic
10. bred within 15. to the manner
born
Inca (pert to) . . .

descent . . **6.** the sun
empire . . **4.** Peru (11th cent)
government . . **11.** communistic
king . . **9.** Atahualpa (15th cent)
prince . . **7.** Huascar (16th cent)
incalculable . . . **8.** infinite **9.** boundless, uncertain, very great **11.** illimitable **12.** immeasurable **13.** unforeseeable
incandescent . . . **5.** clear, light, white **7.** glowing, shining
incantation . . . **5.** magic, spell **6.** powwow **7.** sorcery **8.** exorcism **10.** hocus-pocus, mumbo jumbo
incapable . . . **6.** unable **8.** impotent **11.** incompetent, inefficient, unqualified **12.** disqualified
incapacitate . . . **7.** cripple, disable, invalid **10.** disqualify **11.** render unfit
incapacitated . . . **8.** crippled, disabled **9.** hamstrung, paralyzed **11.** invalidated **12.** disqualified **13.** superannuated (retired)
incarcerate . . . **5.** hem in **6.** immure, intern, lock up, retire **7.** confine, impound **8.** imprison **10.** disqualify
incarnate . . . **4.** rosy **6.** embody **9.** enshrined **11.** incorporate, personified **12.** impersonated
incarnation . . . **6.** avatar, Christ **10.** embodiment
Incarnation of Vishnu (eight) . . . **4.** Apis, Rama **7.** Krishna (8th)
incase . . . **3.** box, can **4.** pack **5.** box up, cover, crate **6.** carton **7.** enclose, package **8.** surround
incaution . . . **4.** rash **6.** unwary **8.** careless, heedless, reckless **9.** impolitic, imprudent **10.** indiscreet
incendiarism . . . **5.** arson **9.** pyromania
incendiary . . . **5.** firer **7.** exciter **8.** agitator, arsonist, incitive **9.** seditious **10.** instigator **12.** inflammatory
incense . . . **3.** ire **5.** anger **6.** arouse, enrage, incite **7.** inflame, provoke **8.** irritate **9.** instigate
incense (pert to) . . .
burner . . **6.** censer **8.** thurible **9.** incensory
carrier . . **8.** thurifer
Hebrew for . . **7.** keturah
pert to . . **5.** aroma, spice **7.** perfume **9.** fragrance, redolence
product . . **5.** matti, myrrh **6.** storax **7.** linaloa **8.** gum resin, olibanum, pastille, thurible **9.** lignaloes, tacamahac **12.** frankincense
sacrifice . . **8.** oblation
spice . . **6.** balsam, stacte
tree bearing . . **7.** linaloa **8.** agalloch, calambac **9.** Boswellia
vessel . . **6.** censer **7.** navette
incensed . . . **3.** mad **5.** angry, irate, vexed, wroth **6.** peeved, piqued **7.** angered, enraged, nettled **8.** wrathful **11.** exasperated
incentive . . . **4.** brod, call, goad, spur, urge, whet **5.** spark **6.** motive **7.** impulse, rousing **8.** inciting, stimulus **9.** influence **10.** incitement, inducement **11.** provocation, stimulative **13.** encouragement

inception . . . **6.** origin, source **9.** reception **10.** inchoation, initiation **12.** commencement **15.** intussusception
inceptive . . . **9.** beginning **10.** inchoative
incessant . . . **7.** endless **8.** constant **9.** ceaseless, continual, perpetual **10.** continuous **11.** unremitting **13.** unintermitted
inch (pert to) . . .
barometric . . **6.** degree
forward . . **4.** edge **7.** crowhop
inch by inch . . **9.** gradually, piecemeal
meal . . **9.** gradually
three parts . . **11.** barleycorns (anc)
twelve parts . . **5.** lines
twelve seconds . . **6.** a prime (anc)
verb . . **5.** creep **7.** measure
inches . . . **4.** hand (4), nail (2 1/4), span (9)
inchoate . . . **6.** partly **8.** initiate, recently **9.** beginning, incipient **10.** incomplete
inchpin . . . **10.** sweetbread
incident . . . **5.** event **7.** episode, subject **8.** accident, casualty **9.** befalling, happening **10.** incidental, occurrence **11.** contingency **12.** circumstance, slight matter
incidental . . . **3.** bye **6.** casual, chance, liable **8.** episodic **9.** accessory, extrinsic **10.** accidental, contingent, fortuitous, occasional **11.** subordinate **12.** nonessential **13.** parenthetical
incidentally . . . **6.** obiter **8.** by chance, by the way **9.** en passant, in passing
incinerate . . . **4.** burn **7.** consume, cremate
incipient . . . **4.** seat **6.** induct **7.** initial **8.** inchoate **9.** beginning, embryonic **10.** commencing, inaugurate **11.** rudimentary
incise . . . **3.** cut **4.** open **5.** carve, lance, sever **6.** furrow **7.** engrave
incised . . . **6.** carved **7.** notched **8.** engraved, furrowed **9.** laciniate **10.** laciniated
incision . . . **3.** cut **4.** gash, slit **5.** cleft **6.** furrow, injury **7.** cutting **9.** engraving **10.** laceration, separation **11.** penetration
incisor . . . **5.** tooth
incite . . . **3.** egg, tew **4.** abet, fire, goad, prod, spur, urge **5.** impel, sting **6.** arouse, foment, stir up, suborn **7.** agitate, animate, inflame, provoke **9.** encourage, stimulate
inclement . . . **4.** foul **5.** harsh, rough **6.** severe, stormy **9.** merciless
inclination . . . **3.** dip, nod **4.** bent, bias, love, urge **5.** fancy, grade, slant, slope, taste, trend **6.** animus, bowing, desire, liking, nature **8.** aptitude, penchant, tendency **9.** affection, attention, deviation, direction, intention, obeisance, proneness **10.** attachment, proclivity, propensity **11.** disposition **12.** predilection **13.** prepossession
incline . . . **3.** dip, tip **4.** bend, cant, heel, lean, tend, tilt **5.** alist, bevel, grade, slant, slide, slope, trend **9.** be willing, gravitate
inclined . . . **3.** apt, dip **4.** wont **5.** prone

6. sloped 7. leaning, pronate, willing
8. disposed 11. predisposed
inclined (pert to) . . .
  plane . . **4.** ramp **7.** oblique
  to believe . . **9.** credulous
  to droop . . **3.** sag
  to sin . . **13.** transgressive
inclose . . . see also *enclose* **3.** hem, pen,
  pin **4.** case, mure **5.** embar **6.** encase,
  encave, incase **7.** enclose, environ
inclosure . . . **3.** pen, ree, sty **4.** cage, cote,
  sept **5.** hutch, kraal **6.** corral **8.** sepiment
  9. enclosure **10.** impalement
include . . . **6.** shut up **7.** confine, contain,
  embrace, enclose, inclose, involve
  8. comprise **9.** encompass
including . . . **8.** covering **10.** comprising,
  containing **12.** encompassing
  13. comprehensive
incognito . . . **6.** veiled **7.** feigned
  8. disguise, not known **10.** camouflage
incoherent . . . **5.** loose **6.** broken
  8. detached, inchoate **9.** delirious,
  illogical **11.** incongruous
  12. disconnected, inconsequent,
  inconsistent
income . . . **4.** gain **5.** rente, wages
  6. profit, return, usance **7.** annuity,
  pension, produce, revenue, tontine
  8. interest, proceeds, receipts
  9. emolument
incommensurate . . . **7.** unequal
  12. insufficient **14.** unsatisfactory
  16. disproportionate
incommode . . . **3.** vex **5.** annoy **6.** molest,
  plague, put out **7.** disturb, trouble
  8. disquiet **13.** inconvenience
incomparable . . . **7.** eminent, unalike
  8. peerless **9.** matchless, unrivaled
  10. surpassing **11.** superlative
  12. transcendent, without equal
incompatible . . . **9.** differing **10.** intolerant
  11. disagreeing **12.** inconsistent,
  inharmonious **13.** contradictory,
  unsympathetic **14.** irreconcilable
incompetence . . . **9.** inability, unfitness
  10. disability, inadequacy
  13. insufficiency **15.** unqualification
incompetent . . . **5.** inept, unfit **7.** wanting
  8. impotent **9.** incapable **10.** unskillful
  11. inefficient **12.** disqualified,
  insufficient **14.** incommensurate
incomplete . . . **5.** crude **6.** undone
  7. lacking **8.** immature, inchoate
  9. defective, deficient, imperfect,
  partially **10.** unfinished
incomprehensible . . . **8.** infinite
  9. wonderful **10.** miraculous,
  mysterious, unreadable **11.** unthinkable
  12. unfathomable, unimaginable
  13. inconceivable, unconceivable
  14. unintelligible
incongruity . . . **9.** inharmony
  10. dissonance **11.** incoherence
  12. disagreement, inexpedience
  13. inconsistency **14.** unsuitableness
incongruous . . . **5.** alien **6.** absurd,
  motley **8.** off-color **9.** differing,
  illogical **10.** solecistic, unsuitable
  12. disagreeable, inconsistent,
  inharmonious **13.** inappropriate

inconsequent . . . **7.** invalid **8.** unproved
  9. illogical **10.** irrelevant **11.** impertinent,
  unimportant **12.** inconsistent
  13. inconsecutive
inconsiderate . . . **4.** rash **5.** hasty
  6. unkind **8.** careless, heedless
  9. imprudent, impulsive **10.** ill-advised,
  incautious, indiscreet, neglectful
  11. improvident, injudicious,
  thoughtless
inconsistent . . . **9.** differing, dissonant,
  fanatical, illogical **10.** discordant,
  discrepant, incoherent, inconstant
  11. incongruous **12.** incompatible,
  inharmonious **13.** contradictory
  14. irreconcilable
inconspicuous . . . **9.** unseeable **10.** out
  of sight, unapparent **12.** not prominent
  13. imperceptible, indiscernible
incontestable . . . **7.** certain
  10. undeniable **11.** indubitable,
  irrefutable **13.** unimpeachable
  14. unquestionable
inconvenience . . . **6.** bother **8.** disquiet
  9. incommode **10.** uneasiness
  11. awkwardness, disturbance
  12. disadvantage, untimeliness,
  unwieldiness
inconvenient . . . **5.** unfit **7.** unhandy
  8. annoying, improper, unwieldy
  10. unsuitable **11.** inexpedient,
  inopportune, troublesome
  12. unreasonable **15.** disadvantageous
incorporate . . . **3.** mix **4.** fuse **5.** blend,
  merge, unite **6.** embody **7.** combine,
  include **8.** embodied **10.** assimilate
incorporation . . . **5.** union **9.** inclusion
  10. embodiment **11.** affiliation,
  association, combination, composition,
  incarnation **12.** assimilation
incorporeal . . . **7.** phantom **8.** bodiless
  9. spiritual **10.** immaterial
  13. unsubstantial
incorrect . . . **5.** wrong **6.** faulty
  8. improper **9.** erroneous, inelegant
  10. inaccurate, solecistic, unbecoming
  13. ungrammatical
incorrect naming of objects . . .
  9. paranomia
incorruptible . . . **4.** just **7.** upright
  8. immortal **11.** trustworthy
  14. indestructible
increase . . . **3.** add, eke, wax **4.** gain,
  grow, rise **5.** add to, amass, raise, swell
  6. accrue, dilate, enrich, expand, extend
  7. accrete, advance, augment, enhance
  (inhance), inflate, promote, upswing
  8. heighten, multiply **9.** accession,
  aggravate, crescendo, expansion,
  extension, increment, intensify
  10. accelerate **11.** aggravation,
  enlargement **13.** amplification
  15. intensification
incredible . . . **8.** fabulous, unlikely
  9. fantastic, marvelous, wonderful
  10. improbable, remarkable
  12. unbelievable
increment . . . **6.** growth **8.** addition,
  increase **11.** enlargement
  12. augmentation
incriminate . . . **6.** accuse **7.** involve

9. implicate, inculpate
incubator . . . **8.** couveuse, isolette
incubus . . . **4.** ogre **5.** demon, dream
  6. burden **9.** nightmare **10.** evil spirit
  13. hallucination
inculcate . . . **5.** imbue, infix **7.** implant,
  impress, instill (instil) **12.** indoctrinate
incumbent . . . **5.** vicar **6.** rector **8.** resident
  9. clergyman, impending, overlying
  10. burdensome, obligatory (upon)
  11. threatening **12.** superimposed
incumbents . . . **3.** ins
incunabula . . . **7.** infancy **10.** beginnings
incur . . . **5.** bring **6.** accrue, entail **7.** bring
  on **8.** be liable, contract, fall into **10.** be
  involved
incurable . . . **8.** hopeless **9.** apathetic
  11. inattentive, indifferent, unconcerned,
  uninquiring **12.** uninterested
  13. uninquisitive
incur hostility . . . **10.** antagonize
  11. contend with
incursion . . . **4.** raid **5.** foray **6.** attack,
  influx, inroad **8.** invasion **9.** intrusion
incus . . . **4.** bone (ear) **5.** anvil **6.** hammer
indecency . . . **8.** impurity **9.** immodesty,
  indecorum, obscenity, vulgarity
  10. indelicacy, unchastity
indecent . . . **5.** gross **6.** impure, vulgar
  7. obscene **8.** immodest, improper,
  uncomely **9.** offensive **10.** ill-looking,
  indecorous, indelicate **11.** inexpedient
indecision . . . **5.** doubt **10.** hesitation
  11. uncertainty, vacillation
  12. irresolution
indecisive . . . **7.** dubious **8.** formless
  9. uncertain **10.** hesitating, indefinite,
  indistinct, irresolute **11.** unsupported,
  vacillating **12.** inconclusive
indecorous . . . **4.** rude **5.** wrong **6.** coarse,
  vulgar **7.** uncivil **8.** impolite, improper,
  indecent, unseemly **9.** inelegant **10.** out
  of place, unbecoming **11.** inexpedient
indefatigable . . . **6.** active **8.** sedulous,
  tireless, untiring **9.** unwearied, weariless
  10. unwearying **11.** persevering
indefinite . . . **5.** loose, vague **7.** general,
  inexact, neutral **8.** formless
  9. ambiguous, equivocal, uncertain
  10. inexplicit, unmeasured
  12. undetermined **13.** indeterminate
indefinite amount . . . **3.** any **4.** some
  5. about **10.** more or less
indehiscent (pert to) . . .
  fruit . . **3.** uva **4.** pepo (gourd) **5.** apple,
  grape **6.** orange, samara **9.** sunflower
  legume . . **3.** pea **4.** bean **6.** loment
  vegetable . . **5.** melon **6.** squash, tomato
  7. pumpkin **8.** cucumber
indelible . . . **4.** fast **5.** fixed **8.** deepfelt
  9. permanent **10.** inerasable
  12. ineffaceable, ineradicable,
  inexpungible **13.** unforgettable
indelicate . . . **5.** gross **6.** coarse, vulgar
  7. fulsome **8.** impolite, improper,
  indecent, unseemly **9.** offensive,
  unrefined **10.** indecorous, unbecoming
indemnification . . . **9.** atonement
  10. recompense **11.** restitution
  12. compensation **13.** reimbursement
indemnify . . . **3.** pay **6.** recoup, secure

8. make good **9.** reimburse
  10. compensate, recompense
indent . . . **3.** cut, jag **4.** dent **5.** inlay,
  notch, press, stamp, tooth **6.** emboss,
  furrow, recess, zigzag **7.** impress,
  imprint, press in **8.** contract, covenant,
  draw upon **9.** indenture **11.** requisition
indentation . . . **3.** jab **4.** dint, nick **5.** choil,
  notch **6.** crenel, furrow, hollow, recess
  7. imprint **8.** crenelet **10.** depression,
  impression
indented . . . **6.** dented, jagged, milled
  7. notched, sinuous **8.** serrated (Her)
  9. impressed **10.** undulating
indenture . . . **4.** dent **5.** notch **8.** contract,
  document **9.** agreement **10.** depression
  11. indentation
independence . . . **7.** freedom
  9. exemption **10.** competency,
  neutralism, Urania blue
  13. unrelatedness **14.** nonpartisanism
  15. self-subsistence
independent . . . **4.** free **5.** Party (Polit)
  7. neutral, wealthy **8.** separate
  9. competent, exclusive, free-lance,
  isolative, sovereign, uncoerced,
  unrelated **12.** irrespective, uncontrolled,
  unrestricted **13.** self-governing
independent land . . . **7.** alodium (law)
indescribably . . . **9.** ineffably
  11. wonderfully
indeterminate . . . **5.** vague **7.** apeiron,
  general, neutral, obscure **8.** formless,
  infinite
index . . . **4.** face, file, fist, list **5.** guide,
  ratio, table **6.** gnomon **7.** pointer
  8. exponent **9.** indicator **10.** forefinger,
  indication
India . . . see also *Indian*
  anc . . **9.** Hindustan
  Bay . . **6.** Bengal
  Cape . . **7.** Comorin
  capital . . **4.** Agra (anc) **5.** Simla (summer)
    8. New Delhi
  city . . **4.** Agra, Gaya **5.** Delhi, Poona,
    Surat **6.** Bombay, Jaipur, Madras,
    Madura, Mysore, Nagpur **8.** Calcutta,
    Kolhapur, Mandalay, Mirzapur,
    Shahpura **9.** Bangalore **10.** Darjeeling
  city, sacred . . **5.** Nasik **7.** Benares
  Coast . . **7.** Malabar
  kingdom . . **5.** Asoka, Nepal
  mountain . . **5.** Ghats **8.** Sulaiman (Throne
    of Solomon) **9.** Himalayas, Hindu Kush
    12. Vindhya Hills
  Persian name (anc) . . **9.** Hindustan
  region . . **3.** Goa **5.** Assam, Surat
    6. Baroda, Bengal **7.** Benares, Kashmir
  relics (famed) . . **8.** Taj Mahal (Agra)
    10. Kutab Minar **11.** Ajanta Caves
  river . . **6.** Ganges **7.** Krishna (Kristna)
  State . . **4.** Rewa **5.** Delhi **6.** Baroda,
    Indore, Jaipur, Madras, Marwar, Punjab,
    Rampur, Sakkim **7.** Manipur
Indian (pert to) . . .
  aeon . . **5.** kalpa
  animal . . **4.** gaur, zebu **5.** sasin **6.** nilgai
  apartment . . **6.** zenana
  army officer . . **4.** naik (naig) **7.** jemadar
  attorney . . **6.** muktar
  bandit . . **6.** dacoit

bard . . **4.** bhat
bird . . **4.** baya, kala, koel, kyak **5.** sarus, shama **6.** seesee, shahin **8.** amadavat
boat . . **5.** dhoni (doni)
book (sacred) . . **6.** Avesta
bracelet . . **6.** sankha
bread (unleavened) . . **4.** naan **7.** chapati
breakfast . . **5.** hazri
buffalo . . **4.** arna (arnee)
carpet . . **4.** Agra
carriage . . **4.** ekka **5.** tonga **6.** gharry (gharri)
caste . . **3.** Jat, Meo **4.** Ahir **5.** Sudra, Varna **6.** Lohana, Rajput, Vaisya **7.** Brahman (Brahmin) **9.** Kahatriya
cavalryman . . **5.** sowar **7.** ressala
charm . . **6.** mantra
chief . . **4.** Raja **5.** Rajah **6.** sirdar **7.** Gaekwar
cigarette (cheap) . . **4.** biri
claim (legal) . . **3.** hak (hakh)
college (Sanskrit) . . **3.** tol
Court, Supreme . . **6.** Sudder
crocodile . . **6.** gavial, mugger (muggar, muggur)
cymbal . . **3.** tal
dagger . . **5.** katar
dam . . **6.** anicut (annicut)
dancer (fem) . . **8.** bayadere
dancing girls . . **6.** nautch
deer . . **4.** axis **5.** kakar **6.** sambur
deity . . **4.** Deva
demon . . **4.** bhut **5.** asura **6.** daitya
devil's tree . . **4.** dita
dialect . . **4.** Urdu **5.** Hindi, Tamil **7.** Prakrit
disciple . . **5.** chela
dog . . **5.** dhole **6.** pariah
drama . . **6.** nataka
drink . . **4.** soma **5.** bhang (bang) **6.** arrack
dust storm . . **7.** peesash, shaitan (sheitan)
elephant . . **5.** hathi
elephant driver . . **6.** mahout
elephant trappings . . **5.** jhool
epic . . **8.** Ramayana **11.** Mahabharata
falcon . . **6.** shahin (shaheen)
father . . **4.** babu
festival . . **4.** Holi, Mela **6.** Dewali **10.** Rathayatra
fig tree (sacred) . . **5.** pipal **6.** banian, banyan
garment . . **4.** sari **7.** luhinga
gateway . . **5.** toran
ghost . . **4.** bhut
god . . **4.** Deva, Yama **5.** Shiva
goddess . . **4.** Amma
governor . . **5.** nazim
grove . . **5.** Sarna
guard . . **7.** daloyet
hall . . **6.** durbar
handkerchief . . **7.** malabar
harem . . **5.** serai **6.** zenana **8.** seraglio
heiress . . **5.** Begum
herb . . **6.** sesame **7.** curcuma, tumeric, zeodary
holy . . **3.** sri (shri)
holy powder . . **4.** abir (perfumed)
hunt . . **6.** shikar
intoxicant . . **4.** soma
jungle . . **5.** shola
king . . **4.** Shah

king of serpents (Myth) . . **6.** Shesha (Sesha)
king's son . . **8.** shahzada
knife . . **3.** dah **5.** kukri
lady . . **7.** sahibah
language . . **4.** Urdu **5.** Hindu, Tamil **8.** Sanskrit (anc)
leader . . **13.** Mahatma Gandhi
legal claim . . **3.** hak (hakh)
leopard . . **7.** cheetah
licorice . . **9.** jequirity (bean)
loincloth . . **5.** dhoti
lover of . . **9.** Indophile
mahogany . . **4.** toon
mail . . **3.** dak (dawk)
medicine man . . **6.** Shaman
mendicant . . **5.** fakir
merchant . . **8.** soudagar
midwife . . **4.** dhai
Minister of Finance . . **5.** Dewan
mountain pass . . **4.** ghat
musical instrument . . **5.** ruana
narcotic . . **4.** bang **5.** bhang **7.** hashish
native . . **5.** Hindu, Sepoy, Tamil **8.** Assamese **10.** Hindustani
ox . . **4.** gaur
palanquin (conveyance) . . **6.** palkee (palhi)
palm . . **7.** Calamus, malacca
peasant . . **4.** ryot
pheasant . . **5.** monal (monaul)
philosopher . . **4.** Yogi
pillar . . **3.** lat
pipe . . **6.** hookah
police . . **4.** peon **5.** sepoy
police station . . **5.** thana
priest . . **5.** mobed **6.** shaman
prince . . **4.** rana
princess . . **4.** rani (ranee) **5.** Begum
queen . . **4.** rani (ranee) **8.** maharani
religious body . . **5.** samaj **7.** ajivika (anc)
resort . . **3.** Abu **5.** Mt Abu
rope dancer . . **3.** nat
rubber . . **10.** caoutchouc
ruler . . **4.** rana **5.** nabob, nawab, nizam
sage . . **6.** pundit
sailor . . **6.** lascar
sarsaparilla root . . **7.** nunnari
servant . . **3.** par **4.** amah, maty
sheep . . **5.** urial **6.** nahoor
shrine . . **6.** dagoba
silkworm . . **3.** eri
snake . . **5.** krait **6.** bongar, katuka
soldier . . **4.** peon **5.** sepoy, singh
split pea . . **3.** dal
steps (to a river) . . **4.** ghat
study of . . **8.** Indology
sugar (crude) . . **3.** gur **9.** tabasheer (bamboo)
Supreme Court . . **6.** Sudder
sword (short) . . **5.** kukri
syllable of assent . . **2.** om
tapir . . **8.** saladang
tariff . . **6.** zabeta
teacher . . **6.** mullah (mulla)
temple . . **4.** rath **12.** Seven Pagodas (of Madras)
title of respect . . **3.** sri (shri) **4.** mian
tower . . **5.** minar, sikar **7.** sikhara
tree . . **3.** saj **4.** dita, teak **5.** dhava **6.** banyan, sissoo

umbrella .. **6.** chatta
water carrier .. **7.** bheesty (bheestie)
wheat .. **4.** suji
wine .. **5.** shrab
yellow (color) .. **5.** piuri **7.** majagua
Indian, American (pert to) ...
chief .. **5.** Logan **6.** Joseph, Philip,
sachem **7.** Cochise, Pontiac
8. Geronimo, Red Cloud, Tecumseh
9. Massasoit **10.** Crazy Horse **11.** Sitting
Bull, Spotted Tail
dance .. **7.** cantico
festival .. **8.** potlatch
hatchet .. **8.** tomahawk
hero .. **4.** Rama (So Am)
lodge .. **5.** hogan, igloo, tepee **6.** wigwam
7. wickiup
married .. **5.** squaw (fem) **6.** sannup
(male)
Mexico .. **4.** Maya **5.** Aztec **7.** Tehueco
money .. **5.** sewan (beads) **6.** wampum
Newfoundland .. **6.** Micmac
pipe (peace) .. **7.** calumet
pony .. **6.** cayuse
richest tribe .. **5.** Osage
S America .. **3.** Ona **4.** Cara (anc), Inca,
Peru, Tupi **5.** Carib **6.** Arawak, Aymara
7. Quechua
Spirit, Great .. **6.** Manito **7.** Manitou
12. Gitchi Manito
squaw .. **6.** mahala
symbol .. **5.** totem
tax, impost .. **5.** abwab
village .. **6.** pueblo
water lily .. **5.** wokas (wocas)
Indiana ...
capital .. **12.** Indianapolis
city .. **4.** Gary **6.** Muncie **7.** Hammond
9. Vincennes **10.** Terre Haute
industrial region .. **7.** Calumet
monument (Hist) .. **7.** Lincoln **12.** Indian
Mounds **13.** Wyandotte Cave
post office (famed) .. **10.** Santa Claus
river .. **6.** Maumee, Wabash
10. Tippecanoe
State admission .. **10.** Nineteenth
State bird .. **8.** cardinal
State flower .. **5.** peony
State motto .. **19.** Crossroads of America
State nickname .. **7.** Hoosier
Indian people ... **3.** Aht, Fox, Oto (Otoe),
Ree, Sac, Ute **4.** Cree, Crow, Erie, Hano,
Hopi, Iowa, Maya, Mono, Sauk, Yuma,
Zuni **5.** Aleut, Cadoo, Carib, Coree,
Creek, Haida, Huron, Miami, Moqui,
Omaha, Osage, Piute, Ponca, Sioux,
Sooke, Teton, Yazoo **6.** Ahtena (Alaska),
Apache, Biloxi, Cayuga, Dakota,
Eskimo, Isleta, Lenape, Mohawk,
Mojave, Navaho, Nootka, Oneida,
Paiute (Piute), Pawnee, Santee, Seneca,
Siwash **7.** Amerind, Bannock, Catawba,
Chinook, Ojibway, Tlingit, Yavanai
8. Arapahoe, Cherokee, Chippewa,
Comanche, Iroquois, Kickapoo, Nez
Percé, Onondaga, Sagamore, Seminole,
Shoshone **9.** Algonquin, Athabasca,
Blackfoot, Chickasaw, Winnebago
10. Muskhogean **12.** Narragansett
indicate ... **4.** cite, hint, mark, mean,
show **5.** point **6.** denote, evince,

reveal, sketch **7.** bespeak, betoken,
connote, declare, display, signify,
specify **8.** disclose, evidence, intimate,
manifest, point out, register
9. designate, foretoken
indicated ... **6.** marked, signed
7. denoted, implied **8.** presumed
9. betokened, portended, suggested
indicating succession ... **7.** ordinal
indication ... **4.** clue, hint, mark, note,
omen, sign **5.** proof, token, trace
6. signal **7.** reading (a) **8.** evidence
10. suggestion **13.** manifestation
indicative ... **7.** ominous **10.** evidential,
indication, meaningful, suggestive
11. connotative **13.** significative
indicator ... **4.** dial, hand, sign, vane
5. arrow, gauge, index, level **6.** gnomon
7. indices (pl), pointer **9.** grape fern
(belief) **10.** instrument **11.** annunciator,
thermometer **15.** telethermometer
indicia (sing indicium) ... **5.** marks,
signs **6.** tokens **8.** markings (PO)
11. appearances, indications, metered
mail
indict ... **6.** accuse, charge, decree
7. arraign, impeach **8.** proclaim
indictive ... **8.** declared **9.** appointed
10. proclaimed
indictment ... **6.** charge **10.** accusation,
imputation **11.** arraignment
indifference ... **5.** shrug **6.** apathy
7. inertia **8.** coldness **9.** unconcern
10. mediocrity, negligence, neutrality
12. carelessness, heedlessness,
unimportance **13.** insensibility
14. insignificance
indifferent ... **3.** ill **4.** cold, cool,
sick **5.** blasé **6.** casual, poorly
7. neutral, stoical, uneager **8.** careless,
heedless, listless, mediocre **9.** apathetic
10. nonchalant, regardless
11. adiaphorous, unimportant
12. nonessential, uninterested
indigence ... **4.** lack, need, want **6.** penury
7. poverty **10.** deficiency
indigene ... **6.** native **8.** habitant
9. primitive **10.** autochthon
indigenous ... **6.** inborn, innate, native,
rooted **7.** edaphic, endemic, natural
8. endemism, inherent
13. autochthonous
indigent ... **4.** free, poor, void **5.** needy
6. bereft **7.** lacking, wanting **8.** beggarly
9. destitute, penniless **10.** pauperized
11. impecunious, necessitous
15. poverty-stricken
indigestion ... **8.** disorder, phthisis
9. dyspepsia **10.** immaturity
indignant ... **3.** hot **5.** angry, irate,
wroth **7.** annoyed **8.** incensed, wrathful
9. resentful **11.** exasperated
indignation ... **3.** ire **4.** base, fury
5. anger, wrath **7.** disdain **8.** contempt
indignity ... **7.** affront, dudgeon
10. uncivility
indigo ... **3.** dye **4.** anil, blue
indigo (pert to) ...
bale of .. **6.** seroon
compound .. **6.** isatin
plant .. **4.** anil

source . . **7.** indican **9.** indigotin
wild . . **8.** Baptisia
indirect . . . **7.** devious, oblique
  9. deceitful, dishonest **10.** circuitous,
  contingent, misleading, roundabout
indirect expense . . . **8.** overhead
indiscreet . . . **4.** rash **5.** hasty, silly
  6. unwise **7.** foolish, witless **8.** careless,
  heedless **9.** imprudent **10.** incautious
  11. injudicious **12.** undiscerning
  13. inconsiderate
indiscriminate . . . **5.** mixed **7.** mingled
  9. extensive, haphazard, orderless,
  wholesale **13.** heterogeneous
indispensable . . . **5.** basic, vital **6.** needed
  7. exigent **8.** integral **9.** essential,
  requisite, right-hand **10.** imperative
  13. irreplaceable
indisposed . . . **3.** ill **4.** sick **6.** averse
  9. unwilling **10.** disordered, unfriendly
  11. disinclined
indisposition . . . **7.** ailment, illness,
  malaise **10.** averseness, reluctance
  13. unwillingness
indisputable . . . **4.** sure **7.** certain,
  evident **8.** positive **10.** undeniable
  11. indubitable **12.** irrefragable
  13. incontestable
indistinct . . . **3.** dim **4.** hazy **5.** vague
  7. blurred, obscure, unclear **8.** confused
  9. ambiguous, undefined **10.** indefinite
  16. undiscriminating
  17. indistinguishable
indite . . . **3.** pen **5.** write **6.** phrase
  7. compose **8.** describe, inscribe
individual . . . **3.** man, one **4.** bion, idio
  (comb form), self, sole, unit, zoon
  6. egoist, person, single **7.** special
  8. organism, selfsame **9.** identical
  11. inseparable, personality
individuality . . . **5.** being, seity **6.** nature
  7. oneness **8.** ethology, identity,
  selfness
individually . . . **9.** severally **10.** personally
  12. each by itself **14.** distributively
Indo-Aryan (pert to) . . .
  deity . . **5.** Indra
  native of . . **5.** India
  speech . . **5.** Aryan
  type . . **4.** Jats **7.** khatris, Rajputs
Indochina . . . **4.** Laos **5.** Burma **6.** Malaya
  7. Myanmar (formerly Burma), Vietnam
  8. Cambodia, Thailand
indoctrinate . . . **5.** coach, edify, imbue,
  teach **8.** instruct **12.** rehabilitate
indolence . . . **5.** scorn, sloth **7.** inertia,
  languor **8.** inaction, laziness
  10. ergophobia **11.** lotus-eating, spring
  fever **13.** indisposition
indolent . . . **4.** idle, lazy **5.** inert
  6. otiose **8.** inactive, slothful, sluggish
  10. unemployed
indomitable . . . **10.** invincible
  11. intractable, "never say die"
  13. unconquerable
Indonesia . . .
  capital . . **7.** Jakarta (Djakarta)
  formation . . **11.** archipelago (once
    world's largest)
  former name . . **7.** Batavia **15.** Dutch
    East Indies

government . . **8.** Republic (1950)
islands (3,000 in all) . . **4.** Bali, Java
  7. Sumatra **8.** Sulawesi (Celebes)
  9. New Guinea (W half) **10.** Kalimantan
  (W Borneo)
president . . **7.** Sukarno
race . . **5.** Dyaks (Dayaks) **7.** Battaks
  (Bataks), Igorots **8.** Balinese, Javanese
religion . . **6.** Moslem
shrine . . **6.** dagoba
indorse, endorse . . . see *endorse*
indorsement, endorsement . . . **4.** visa,
  visé (passport)
Indra (Hindu) . . . **3.** God **5.** Deity, Sakra
  (Sakka)
indubitable . . . **4.** fact, sure **7.** evident
  10. infallible, undeniable **11.** irrefutable
  12. irrefragable, unanswerable
  13. incontestable **14.** unquestionable
  16. incontrovertible
induce . . . **4.** lead, move, urge **5.** cause,
  impel, infer **6.** allure, elicit, entice, incite
  8. persuade **9.** influence, instigate,
  prevail on
inducement . . . **6.** motive, reason
  8. stimulus **9.** incentive, influence
  10. persuasion **13.** consideration
induct . . . **6.** enroll **7.** bring in, install
  8. initiate **9.** conscript, introduce
inductance unit . . . **5.** henry
inductile . . . **10.** inflexible, unyielding
induction . . . **5.** logic **7.** causing
  8. entrance **9.** accession, beginning,
  deduction **10.** conclusion, initiation,
  production **12.** commencement,
  conscription, installation, introduction
indue . . . **5.** endow **6.** assume, clothe,
  draw on, invest, supply (spiritual)
  7. furnish
indulge . . . **3.** pet **5.** grant, humor, yield
  6. pamper **7.** cherish, gratify
indulgences . . . **8.** excesses **10.** tolerances
indulgent . . . **4.** easy **7.** lenient, patient
  8. tolerant, yielding **9.** compliant
  10. permissive **11.** considerate,
  intemperate
indurate . . . **6.** harden **7.** callous
  10. solidified
indurated . . . **3.** set **5.** fixed **9.** calloused
  10. solidified
industrial magnate . . . **6.** shogun, tycoon
industrious . . . **4.** busy **6.** active **7.** zealous
  8. diligent, sedulous **9.** assiduous
  11. intentional, painstaking
  13. indefatigable
industry . . . **4.** toil, work **5.** labor, trade
  7. concern **8.** commerce **9.** diligence
  12. perseverance, sedulousness
indweller . . . **6.** native **7.** denizen
  8. indigene
indwelling . . . **7.** inbeing **8.** immanent,
  inherent **9.** immanence, inherence
  10. inhabiting
inearth . . . **5.** inter **6.** inhume
inebriacy . . . **11.** drunkenness
  12. intemperance
inebriate . . . **3.** sot **5.** addle, drunk,
  toper **7.** stupefy, tippler **8.** drunkard
  10. exhilarate (by liquor), intoxicate
ineffable . . . **4.** surd **6.** sacred **9.** wonderful
  11. unspeakable, unutterable

13. indescribable, inexpressible
15. unpronounceable
ineffaceable . . . 9. indelible 10. inerasable
12. ineradicable
ineffectual . . . 4. vain, weak 6. futile
7. useless 9. fruitless 10. unavailing
11. inefficient 12. unsuccessful
13. inefficacious, uninfluential
inefficient . . . 6. unable 10. indisposed
11. incompetent 12. unproficient
inelegant . . . 6. clumsy, vulgar 8. indecent
9. deficient (in beauty) 11. unbeautiful
inept . . . 4. null, void 5. silly, unfit
6. absurd, clumsy 7. foolish 8. unsuited
10. out of place, unbecoming, unskillful,
unsuitable 11. inexpedient
inequality . . . 9. disparity, diversity
10. inadequacy, unevenness
12. disagreement, variableness
13. disproportion
ineradicable . . . 7. lasting 9. indelible,
permanent 12. ineffaceable
inerrant . . . 8. unerring 10. infallible
inert . . . 4. dead, lazy 6. latent, stupid,
supine, torpid 7. passive 8. inactive,
lifeless, listless, slothful, sluggish
9. apathetic, inanimate, lethargic
10. motionless, phlegmatic
inertia . . . 9. indolence, inertness
10. immobility
inesculant (rare) . . . 9. indelible
inestimable . . . 9. priceless 10. invaluable
12. incalculable
inevitable . . . 3. due 5. fated 7. nemesis
9. necessary 11. unavoidable
inexorability . . . 5. rigor 9. obstinacy
10. strictness
inexorable . . . 6. strict 9. obstinate
10. inflexible, relentless, unyielding
inexpedience, inexpedient . . . 6. unwise
8. untimely 9. ignorance, impolitic,
imprudent, unfitting 10. indiscreet,
unwiseness 11. inadvisable
15. disadvantageous
inexperience . . . 6. unwise 9. ignorance,
imprudent 10. immaturity, indiscreet
11. inadvisable 12. unprofitable
14. unskillfulness 15. disadvantageous
inexperienced . . . 3. raw 4. naif 5. green,
naive 6. callow 8. ignorant, immature,
prentice 9. unskilled 10. amateurish
11. unpracticed
inexplicable . . . 11. undefinable
12. supernatural 13. preternatural,
unaccountable, unexplainable
inextricable . . . 4. mazy 5. stuck
8. involved 9. intricate 10. insolvable
infallible . . . 4. sure, true 6. gospel
7. certain 8. inerrant, unerring
9. inerrable 11. indubitable
infamous . . . 4. base 6. odious, wicked
8. shameful, terrible 9. negarious
10. detestable 11. ignominious
12. contemptible, disreputable
infamy . . . 5. shame 8. disgrace, dishonor,
ignominy, reproach 9. disrepute
10. opprobrium 11. abomination
infancy . . . 8. babyhood, minority
9. beginning
infant . . . 4. babe, baby 5. child, minor
6. novice 8. bantling 9. foundling

infantryman . . . 6. Zouave 7. dog-face
8. chasseur 9. musketeer
11. footslogger, foot soldier 14. gravel
agitator
infatuated . . . 7. foolish, smitten
8. enamored, obsessed 9. bewitched
10. captivated, enraptured
12. enthusiastic
infatuation . . . 3. ate, mad 4. love 5. craze,
folly 10. enthusiasm 11. foolishness
infeasible . . . 8. unlikely 10. improbable,
unsuitable 13. impracticable
infect . . . 5. taint 6. defile, excite,
poison 7. corrupt, deprave, pollute
11. contaminate
infection . . . 7. disease 8. epidemic
9. pollution 11. implication (law),
inspiration 13. contamination
infelicity . . . 6. misery 9. inaptness
10. misfortune 11. unhappiness
12. inexpedience, untimeliness,
wretchedness
infer . . . 4. hint 5. drive, guess, imply
6. deduce 7. presume, suppose, surmise
8. conclude, construe
inference . . . 5. truth 8. illation
9. corollary, deduction 10. assumption,
conclusion 11. implication, proposition
inferential . . . 8. illative 9. deductive,
inducible 10. deductible, suggestive
15. inconsequential
inferior . . . 3. bad 4. less, poor 5. baser,
lower, minor, petit, petty 6. lesser,
menial, nether 7. humbler, unequal
8. anterior, mediocre 10. inadequate,
low-blooded 11. subordinate
inferior lawyer . . . 9. leguleian
11. pettifogger
infernal . . . 6. cursed, plaguy, wicked
7. hellish, satanic 8. damnable, devilish
9. chthonian, execrable, malignant,
Tartarean 10. demoniacal, detestable,
outrageous
inferno (pert to) . . .
Bib . . 4. Hell 5. abyss, limbo
Buddah . . 6. Naraka
Egypt . . 6. Amenti
ferry to . . 4. Styx
Hebrew . . 5. Sheol 7. Abaddon, Gehenna
myth . . 5. Aralu, Hades, Orcus
7. Acheron, Niflhel 8. Tartarus
infest . . . 3. vex 5. annoy, beset 6. assail,
molest, plague 7. overrun, torment
8. frequent
infidel . . . 5. deist, pagan 7. atheist,
Saracen, skeptic 8. agnostic
10. unbeliever 11. freethinker 12. non-
Christian 13. non-Mohammedan
infidelity . . . 6. deceit 7. perfidy 8. unbelief
9. misbelief, treachery 10. disloyalty
11. incredulity 13. faithlessness
infinite . . . 4. vast 5. vague 6. divine
7. endless, eternal, immense, perfect
9. boundless, limitless, unlimited
10. indefinite 11. illimitable, interminate,
omnipresent, The Absolute 12. all-
embracing, interminable, undetermined
13. inexhaustible, The Omnipotent
16. all-comprehensive
Infinite Being . . . 3. God
Infinite knowledge . . . 11. omniscience

infinitesimal . . . **5.** small **7.** minimum
9. invisible **10.** evanescent
11. microscopic

infirm . . . **4.** weak **5.** anile, frail **6.** senile
7. fragile **8.** decrepit **9.** doddering
10. irresolute **11.** vacillating

infirmity . . . **6.** defect, foible, malady, old
age **7.** disease, failing, frailty, illness
8. debility, weakness **10.** feebleness

inflame . . . **4.** burn, fire **5.** anger **6.** arouse,
enrage, excite, ignite, kindle, madden,
rankle, redden **7.** incense **8.** irritate
10. exasperate

inflammable . . . **5.** fiery **6.** tinder
7. piceous **8.** burnable **9.** excitable,
irascible, irritable **10.** accendible
11. combustible

inflammable substance . . . **6.** ethane,
tinder **7.** acetone, bitumen

inflammation . . . **8.** ignition, soreness
10. congestion, excitement, incitement

inflammation (pert to) . . .
bladder . . **8.** cystitis
bone . . **7.** rickets **8.** osteitis
13. osteomyelitis
ear . . **6.** otitis
eye . . **6.** iritis **7.** uveitis
joints . . **4.** gout **9.** arthritis
10. rheumatism
spinal cord . . **13.** poliomyelitis
stomach . . **9.** gastritis
suffix . . **4.** itis
vein . . **9.** phlebitis

inflect . . . **3.** bow **4.** bend **5.** curve
7. decline, deflect **8.** modulate

inflection, inflexion . . . **4.** tone **5.** angle,
curve **7.** bending **8.** paradigm
9. accidence **10.** modulation

inflexible . . . **4.** iron **5.** rigid, stiff **6.** strict
8. obdurate, rigorous **9.** immovable,
immutable, obstinate, unbending
10. implacable, inexorable, relentless,
unyielding **11.** unalterable
14. uncompromising

inflict . . . **3.** add **4.** deal **5.** wreak
6. impose, punish

inflorescence . . . **4.** cyme **5.** whorl
6. cymose **7.** budding, flowers
8. racemose **9.** flowerage, flowering
10. unfoldment **13.** efflorescence

inflow . . . **6.** influx **9.** inpouring
11. inspiration

influence . . . **3.** win **4.** lead, move, pull,
sway **5.** aegis (egis), bribe, force,
impel, lobby **6.** affect, effect, induce,
influx, leaven, obsess **7.** control,
inspire, mastery **8.** dominate, effusion,
persuade, prestige **9.** authority,
determine

influence (world-wide) . . . **8.** ecumenic

influenced . . . **6.** biased **7.** induced,
pliable (easily) **8.** affected **10.** prejudiced

influential . . . **6.** potent, strong **7.** weighty
8. momentus, powerful **9.** effective
13. authoritative

influx . . . **4.** tide **5.** firth, mouth (river)
6. import, inflow **7.** estuary, illapse
9. influence, inpouring
11. debouchment

infold . . . see *enfold*

inform . . . **4.** tell **5.** teach, train **6.** advise,

notify, report **7.** animate, apprise,
inspire **8.** instruct **9.** enlighten

informal . . . **7.** offhand **9.** irregular

information . . . **3.** air, tip **4.** data, lore,
news **5.** aviso, datum, facts **6.** digest
7. advices, tidings **9.** knowledge
10. annotation **11.** instruction
12. intelligence

informed . . . **2.** up **3.** hep **4.** up on,
wise **5.** aware **6.** posted **8.** apprised,
educated, versed in, well-read
10. instructed **11.** enlightened

informer . . . **3.** spy **4.** tout **6.** gossip,
snitch, teller **7.** delator **8.** affirmer,
betrayer, mouchard, reporter, telltale
9. informant, spokesman **10.** talebearer,
tattletale

informer (sl) . . . **4.** fink, nark **6.** canary,
snitch **7.** stoolie **8.** snitcher, squealer
9. blabberer **11.** stool pigeon
12. blabbermouth

infraction . . . **6.** breach **8.** fracture,
trespass **9.** intrusion, violation
12. encroachment, infringement,
overstepping **13.** transgression

infrequency . . . **6.** rarity **7.** fewness
8. rareness, solitude **9.** isolation
12. uncommonness

infrequent . . . **4.** rare **6.** scarce, seldom,
sparse **8.** uncommon **9.** spasmodic
10. occasional

infrequently . . . **6.** rarely, seldom **8.** not
often, sparsely

infringe . . . **6.** defeat, refute **7.** confute,
destroy, violate **8.** encroach, overstep,
trespass **9.** frustrate

infringement . . . **6.** breach, piracy
(copyright) **9.** intrusion, violation
10. infraction **12.** overstepping
14. nonfulfillment

infundibulum . . . **4.** cone, lura **10.** gray
matter (brain)

infuriate . . . **5.** anger **6.** enrage, incite,
madden **8.** irritate **10.** antagonize

infuscate . . . **6.** darken **7.** obscure

infuse . . . **4.** fill, shed **5.** steep **6.** drench
7. implant, instill **9.** insinuate, introduce

infusion . . . **3.** tea **4.** wort **8.** affusion,
tincture **9.** admixture, decoction,
inpouring **12.** instillation

ingang . . . **5.** porch **8.** entrance
10. intestines

ingenious . . . **5.** sharp, smart, witty
6. adroit, clever, daedal, gifted, shrewd,
subtle **8.** skillful, talented **9.** Daedalian,
deviceful **11.** intelligent, resourceful

ingenuity . . . **5.** skill **6.** candor, genius
10. adroitness **11.** originality
13. inventiveness

ingenuous . . . **4.** naif, open **5.** frank, naive,
noble, plain **6.** candid, innate **7.** artless,
sincere **8.** freeborn, innocent **9.** guileless
10. unreserved **15.** unsophisticated

ingest . . . **3.** eat **5.** learn **6.** take in
7. consume, swallow

ingot . . . **3.** gad, pig **4.** mold **5.** metal,
sycee **7.** bullion

ingratiate . . . **4.** fawn **7.** commend, flatter
9. insinuate, introduce

ingredient . . . **6.** factor **7.** element
9. component **11.** constituent

ingress ... **4.** go in **5.** entry **6.** access, portal **8.** entrance **9.** reception **11.** entranceway

ingrowing nail ... **7.** acronyx

inhabitant ... **3.** cit **6.** inmate, people, tenant **7.** citizen, denizen **8.** resident

inhabitant (pert to) ...
Alaska .. **9.** sourdough
desert .. **4.** Arab **5.** nomad
earliest .. **9.** aborigine
foreign .. **5.** alien
Maine .. **10.** down-easter
moon .. **8.** selenite
northern .. **6.** Yankee **11.** Septentrion (Lowell)

inhabitants, equator's other side ... **8.** antiscii **10.** antiscians

inhabited ... **5.** lived **7.** dwelled, peopled **8.** occupied, tenanted **9.** populated

inhabiting (pert to) ...
caves .. **8.** spelaean (spelean) **10.** troglodyte
ground .. **9.** terricole **11.** terricolous
groves .. **7.** nemoral **10.** nemoricole
islands .. **7.** nesiote
lakes .. **9.** lacustral
sea .. **7.** pelagic **15.** thalassophilous
seashore .. **8.** littoral

inhale ... **4.** suck **5.** smell, smoke, sniff **7.** breathe, inspire, respire

inharmonious ... **7.** jarring **9.** differing, dissonant, unmusical **10.** discordant **11.** conflicting, disagreeing

inherent ... **6.** inborn, innate **7.** infixed **8.** immanent **9.** immanence, intrinsic **10.** indwelling, subsistent **11.** instinctive **13.** indispensable

inheritance ... **6.** legacy **7.** bequest, legitim **8.** heirship, heredity, heritage, Salic law **9.** cleronomy **10.** birthright

inheritance diminisher ... **6.** abator

inheritor ... **4.** heir **6.** coheir **7.** heiress, legatee **10.** coparcener **11.** beneficiary

inhibit ... **5.** check **6.** forbid, hinder **8.** prohibit, restrain **9.** interdict

inhibition ... **3.** ban, bar **4.** writ **7.** embargo **8.** checking **9.** hindrance, restraint **10.** impediment **11.** prohibition **12.** interdiction

inhuman ... **4.** fell **5.** cruel **6.** brutal, savage **7.** bestial, brutish **8.** devilish, nonhuman **9.** barbarous, ferocious **10.** demoniacal, diabolical

inhumation ... **6.** burial **9.** arenation, interment

inhume ... **4.** bury **5.** inter, inurn **7.** deposit, inearth

inimical ... **7.** adverse, hostile, opposed **8.** contrary **10.** unfriendly **11.** belligerent, unfavorable

iniquity ... **3.** sin **4.** evil, vice **5.** crime **7.** misdeed **9.** injustice **10.** immorality, wickedness

initial ... **6.** paraph **9.** incipient **11.** large letter **12.** commencement

initiate ... **4.** open **5.** admit, begin, epopt (anc) **6.** induct **7.** install, instate **8.** inchoate **10.** inaugurate **11.** preinstruct

initiation ... **8.** ceremony **9.** admission **10.** admittance **12.** inauguration,

introduction

injection ... **4.** hypo **5.** enema **7.** clyster **9.** immission

injudicious ... **4.** rash **6.** unwise **9.** impolitic, imprudent **11.** inexpedient

injunction ... **3.** ado **4.** writ **5.** order, union **6.** behest **7.** mandate, precept **9.** direction **11.** prohibition

injure ... **3.** mar **4.** harm, hurt, lame, maim **5.** wound, wrong **6.** assail, damage, grieve, impair, scathe **7.** affront, slander, tarnish

injurious ... **3.** bad **4.** evil **7.** abusive, harmful, hurtful, noxious **10.** defamatory, slanderous **11.** detrimental, mischievous

injury ... **3.** ill, mar **4.** dere (obs), evil, harm, hurt, loss, pain, tort **5.** wound, wrong **6.** damage, lesion, mayhem, trauma **7.** slander **9.** detriment, indignity, injustice **10.** impairment

injustice ... **5.** wrong **6.** injury **7.** umbrage **8.** hardship, inequity, iniquity **10.** imposition, unfairness

ink ... **3.** jet **5.** black **7.** blacken **8.** atrament, blacking

ink (pert to) ...
bag .. **3.** sac (fish)
berry .. **5.** holly **6.** indigo
black .. **10.** atramental **11.** atramentous
cap .. **8.** mushroom
fish .. **5.** squid **6.** cuttle
pad .. **7.** tompion (tampion)
ref to .. **10.** atramental
source .. **7.** inkweed, oak gall **8.** inkstone, pokeweed **9.** gallberry
spreader .. **6.** brayer

inkle ... **4.** hint, tape, yarn **5.** braid, twist **6.** thread **8.** intimate

inkling ... **4.** hint **5.** rumor **6.** desire, report **10.** intimation **11.** supposition

inlaid ... **6.** mosaic **7.** adorned, set into **9.** champleve, decorated

inlay ... **4.** buhl, line **5.** inset **6.** insert, mosaic, niello, tarsia **7.** filling, implant **8.** buhlwork, intarsia **9.** champleve

inlet ... **3.** bay, ria, voe **4.** cove, slew, sump **5.** admit, bayou, bight, creek, fiord (fjord), firth , inlay **6.** estero, recess, strait **7.** estuary, orifice **8.** entrance, waterway

inn ... **3.** pub **4.** khan **5.** abode, fonda, hotel, motel, serai **6.** hostel, imaret, posada, tavern **7.** albergo, cabaret, hospice, locanda, osteria, pension, shelter **8.** alehouse, hostelry **9.** roadhouse **11.** caravansary

innate ... **4.** born **6.** inborn, inbred, native **7.** natural **9.** ingrained, inherited, intrinsic **10.** congenital, hereditary, inveterate **11.** instinctive **14.** constitutional

innate ability ... **6.** genius, talent

innate idea (Philos) ... **11.** immortality

inn courts ... **11.** Inner Temple

inner ... **4.** ento (comb form) **5.** ental **6.** inside, inward, secret **7.** obscure **8.** esoteric, interior, internal **9.** intestine **10.** indistinct **14.** intramolecular

inner circle ... **3.** set **4.** clan, club, ring **5.** group, junta, junto **6.** clique

inner man . . . **4.** mind, self, soul **6.** psyche
7. stomach
innermost coating . . . **6.** intima
Inner Temple . . . **11.** Inns of Court
Innisfail . . . **4.** Eire, Erin **7.** Ireland
15. Island of Destiny
innocence . . . **6.** purity **7.** diamond
11. sinlessness **12.** harmlessness
13. guiltlessness, innocuousness
innocent . . . **4.** Holy, pure **5.** idiot, naive,
seely **6.** benign, lawful **7.** artless,
sinless, upright **8.** spotless **9.** destitute,
guiltless, ingenuous, permitted,
simpleton, stainless, unsullied
10. unblamable **12.** simple-minded
13. free from guilt
innocuous . . . **8.** harmless, hurtless,
innocent **9.** innoxious **11.** inoffensive,
unoffending
innovation . . . **3.** new **6.** change **7.** novelty
13. prolification
Inns of Court name . . . **4.** Gray **7.** Lincoln
innuendo . . . **4.** hint, slur **6.** change
7. meaning **9.** aspersion **10.** intimation
11. implication, indirection, insinuation
Innuit . . . **4.** Yuit (Eskimo)
innumerable . . . **6.** legion, myriad
7. umpteen **8.** infinite, numerous
9. countless **10.** numberless
inodorous . . . **8.** odorless **9.** scentless
inopportune . . . **8.** ill-timed, untimely
10. malapropos, unsuitable
11. contretemps, inexpedient
12. embarrassing, unseasonable
inordinate . . . **5.** undue **9.** excessive,
fanatical **10.** disordered, disorderly,
exorbitant, immoderate **11.** unregulated
12. unrestrained
inorganic . . . **7.** mineral **9.** inanimate
13. nonbiological
inquest . . . **4.** jury **5.** quest, trial **6.** assize,
search **7.** inquiry **11.** examination
13. investigation
inquire . . . **3.** ask **4.** seek **5.** query
7. examine **8.** question **11.** interrogate,
investigate
inquirer . . . **6.** seeker **7.** querier, student,
zetetic **8.** searcher
inquiry . . . **5.** query **6.** examen, tracer
7. examine, seeking **8.** question,
research **11.** examination
13. investigation
inquisition . . . **5.** trial **6.** search **7.** inquiry
8. tribunal **11.** examination
13. investigation
Inquisition figure . . . **10.** Torquemada
inquisitive . . . **4.** nosy **5.** peery **6.** prying
7. curious **8.** meddling **10.** meddlesome
inquisitor . . . **6.** tracer **7.** coroner, sheriff
8. examiner
in re . . . **10.** concerning **13.** in the matter of
inroad . . . **4.** raid **5.** foray **8.** invasion,
trespass **9.** incursion, intrusion,
irruption **12.** overstepping
13. transgression
insane . . . **3.** mad **4.** daft, loco, luny
5. batty, crazy, loony **6.** crazed
7. cracked, foolish, frantic, rammish,
touched, witless **8.** demented, deranged
9. non compos **15.** non compos mentis
insane urge to steal . . . **11.** kleptomania

insanity . . . **5.** mania **6.** frenzy, lunacy,
trance **7.** madness **8.** delirium, dementia
10. alienation **11.** derangement
16. mental deficiency
inscribe . . . **4.** draw, etch **5.** infix, stamp,
write **6.** blazon, enroll **7.** address,
engrave, impress **8.** dedicate, depencil
inscribed . . . **5.** runed **7.** written
8. engraved, recorded **10.** registered,
rupestrian (on rocks)
inscription . . . **4.** text **5.** motto, title
6. legend **7.** epitaph, writing
8. colophon, epigraph, graffito
9. lettering, sgraffito **10.** dedication
14. superscription
inscrutable . . . **6.** secret **8.** abstruse
10. mysterious **12.** impenetrable,
inexplorable, unfathomable
16. incomprehensible
insect . . . **3.** ant, bee, bug, dor, fly
4. flea, gnat, lerp, lice, mite, moth, tick,
wasp **5.** aphid, borer, cadew, emmet,
leech, louse, roach, Vespa **6.** acarid,
beetle, cicada, earwig, hornet, locust,
mantis, sawfly, scarab, spider **7.** ant
lion, chigger, firefly, gallfly, katydid,
ladybug, pismire, termite **8.** bullhead,
glowworm, mosquito, stinkbug, turicata
9. bumblebee, butterfly, caddis fly,
centipede, cockroach, dragonfly,
ichneumon, tsetse fly, tumblebug
10. silverfish **11.** caterpillar,
grasshopper **12.** yellow jacket
insect (pert to) . . .
adult . . **5.** imago
aquatic . . **7.** Ranatra
arboreal . . **7.** katydid
back . . **5.** notum
Bible . . **7.** ant lion
butterfly . . **11.** Lepidoptera
egg . . **3.** nit
eyes . . **6.** ocelli **7.** stemmas
feelers . . **5.** palps **8.** antennas **9.** tentacles
fly . . **4.** zimb **7.** Diptera
hymenopterous . . **3.** ant, bee **4.** wasp
6. sawfly **7.** gallfly
immature . . **4.** grub, pupa **5.** larva
6. maggot **9.** chrysalis
immature covering . . **6.** cocoon
leg . . **6.** proleg
like . . **8.** entomoid
long-legged . . **5.** emesa **10.** harvestman
13. daddy-longlegs
mature . . **5.** imago
molting . . **6.** instar **7.** ecdysis
parasitic . . **4.** lice **5.** louse
plant . . **5.** aphid, aphis , borer, thrip
plate . . **6.** scutum
praying . . **6.** mantis
reference to . . **11.** entomologic
relationship to host . . **7.** metochy
10. parasitism
science . . **10.** entomology
sound . . **5.** chirr **7.** stridor
stage . . **4.** pupa **5.** imago, larva **6.** instar
9. chrysalis
stinging . . **3.** ant, bee **4.** wasp **6.** hornet
7. sciniph (Bib) **12.** yellow jacket
wingless . . **4.** flea **6.** aptera
wing vein . . **5.** media
Insectivora (mammals) . . . **5.** moles

6. shrews 7. desmans, tenrecs
9. hedgehogs

insecure . . . 5. risky, shaky 6. infirm,
unsafe, unsure 7. dubious, rickety,
unsound 8. unstable 9. dangerous,
hazardous 10. precarious

insensate . . . 5. blind, harsh 6. brutal,
unwise 7. fatuous, foolish 8. lifeless
9. inanimate, unfeeling, untouched
10. insensible, insentient 11. insensitive
13. unintelligent

insensibility . . . 4. coma 8. neurosis
9. analgesia 13. lack of feeling

insensible . . . 4. numb, slow 7. gradual,
unaware 9. apathetic, inanimate,
insensate, senseless 11. indifferent,
unconscious 13. inappreciable

insert . . . 4. gore 5. foist, graft, immit,
inset, panel, wedge 7. ingraft 8. interact,
ornament 9. interface, interpose,
introduce 11. intercalate, interpolate

insertion . . . 5. inset 9. injection
10. embroidery, needlework

insertion (pert to) . . .
cords in cloth . . 5. shirr
day in calendar . . 13. intercalation
newspaper . . 2. ad 13. advertisement
phrases, words . . 11. parenthesis
sound in a word . . 9. anaptyxis
10. epenthesis

inset . . . 5. panel 6. inflow, influx
10. phenocryst

inside out, turning . . . 5. evert 8. aversion
9. evertible

insidious . . . 4. deep, wily 7. cunning
8. guileful 9. deceitful, dishonest 11. full
of plots, treacherous

insight . . . 3. ken 6. acumen, aperçu
9. intuition 11. discernment, penetration
12. clairvoyance 13. understanding

insignia . . . 3. bar 4. ankh, flag 5. badge,
cross, crown 6. banner, emblem,
symbol 7. chevron, regalia, scepter
8. caduceus, swastika 15. hammer and
sickle

insignificance . . . 6. trifle 9. smallness
10. slightness 12. unimportance

insignificant . . . 4. puny 5. minor, petit,
petty, small, zilch 6. paltry 7. trivial
8. inferior 9. senseless 11. meaningless,
unimportant 12. contemptible
13. inconsiderate

insignificant object . . . 8. molehill

insincere . . . 5. false 8. affected
9. deceptive 12. hypocritical

insinuate . . . 4. hint 5. enter, imply
6. allude, infuse 8. intimate 9. penetrate
10. ingratiate

insinuation . . . 4. hint 5. sneer
8. innuendo 9. aspersion, insertion,
intrusion 10. intimation 12. ingratiation,
interjection

insipid . . . 3. dry 4. dead, dull, flat, tame
5. heavy, prosy, stale, vapid, wimpy (sl)
6. jejune 7. prosaic 8. lifeless, mediocre
9. tasteless 10. monotonous, namby-
pamby, spiritless, unanimated, wishy-
washy 11. indifferent 13. uninteresting

insisted . . . 5. urged 6. held to 7. pressed
8. demanded 9. persisted
10. maintained, stipulated

insnare . . . see ensare

insolence . . . 5. serve 6. insult 8. defiance
9. arrogance, contumely, impudence
11. haughtiness

insolent . . . 4. pert, rude 7. abusive,
defiant 8. arrogant, impudent
9. insulting 10. disdainful
11. extravagant, impertinent,
overbearing 12. contemptuous,
contumelious 13. disrespectful

insolvent . . . 8. bankrupt

insouciant . . . 8. carefree 11. indifferent,
unconcerned

inspect . . . 3. pry, spy 4. view 5. grade
7. examine 10. scrutinize

inspector . . . 4. ager 6. conner, grader,
police, sealer, tester 8. examiner,
overseer

inspiration . . . 6. sprite 8. afflatus,
hiccough 9. influence, intuition
10. exhalation, inhalation, motivation

inspire . . . 4. fire 5. cheer, exalt 6. infuse,
inhale 7. animate, breathe, enliven
8. motivate 9. encourage, infatuate
11. communicate (to the spirit)

inspired power . . . 7. entheos

inspiring . . . 8. cheering, eloquent
11. provocative

inspiring (pert to) . . .
awe . . 4. fear 5. awful, eerie
confidence . . 11. encouraging
favor . . 13. prepossessing
horror . . 6. grisly

inspirit . . . 5. cheer, elate, rouse
7. animate, enliven, hearten, inspire,
quicken 9. encourage 10. ingratiate,
invigorate

instability . . . 8. weakness 10. changeable,
insecurity, mutability, unsafeness
11. inconstancy 12. irresolution,
unsteadiness 13. changeability,
unreliability

install . . . 4. seat 6. induct, ordain
7. instate 8. initiate 9. establish
10. inaugurate

instance . . . 4. case, suit 6. motive
7. example, request, urgency
8. occasion 10. suggestion
11. instigation

instant . . . 3. pop 4. time, urge 5. flash,
trice 6. direct, minute, moment,
second, urgent 7. current, solicit
8. pressing 9. immediate, importune
11. importunate

instantly . . . 3. now 8. directly, in a flash,
in a trice

instate . . . 5. admit, endow 6. invest
7. install 9. establish

instead of . . . 4. else 5. stead 6. in lieu,
rather 10. equivalent, substitute

instigate . . . 3. egg 4. abet, goad, move,
prod, spur, urge 5. impel 6. foment,
incite, suborn 7. provoke 8. motivate
9. stimulate

instigator . . . 5. urger 7. abettor, exciter,
inciter 8. agitator, fomenter, inflamer,
provoker 10. ringleader

instill, instil . . . 5. imbue 6. impart,
infuse, pour in 7. pervade 9. inculcate,
insinuate

instinct . . . 5. knack 6. libido, talent

7. impulse 8. aptitude 11. instigation, orientation
instinctive . . . 6. innate 7. natural
8. inherent, original 9. automatic, intuitive 11. involuntary, spontaneous
institute . . . 5. erect, found 6. create, ordain, school 7. academy, college, precept, society 8. initiate, organize, seminary 9. originate, principle
10. inaugurate 12. organization
Institute (The) . . . 5. Gaius 6. France
8. Politics 10. Technology
institute a suit . . . 3. sue 7. go to law
8. litigate 9. prosecute
Institution, International (maritime) . . .
7. Veritas 13. Bureau Veritas
instruct . . . 4. show 5. coach, edify, order, teach, train 6. advise, direct, inform 7. command, confirm, educate, nurture 9. enlighten 10. discipline
12. indoctrinate
instruction . . . 3. act 4. lore, news
6. lesson, report 7. precept, tuition
8. pedagogy, teaching, tutorage
9. paideutic 11. information
13. propaedeutics
instructive . . . 8. didactic, sermonic
10. commanding, preceptive
11. educational, informative
12. propaedeutic
instructor . . . 5. tutor 6. mentor 7. adviser, teacher, trainer 8. lecturer 9. preceptor, professor
instrument . . . 4. barb, bill, deed, tool, writ 5. agent, means 6. medium
7. utensil, writing 8. document
9. implement 11. contrivance
instrument, musical (pert to) . . .
ancient . . 4. asor, lyre 5. rebab, rocta, shawn 7. bandore, cithern, theorbo
8. penorcon, psaltery
brass . . 4. horn 6. cornet 7. helicon
keyboard . . 5. organ, piano 6. spinet
7. celesta (celeste), cembalo 8. virginal
10. clavichord 11. harpsichord
percussion . . 4. drum, gong 5. bells, conga 6. bongos, chimes, claves
7. cymbals, marimba 8. carillon
9. castanets, xylophone 10. vibraphone
12. glockenspiel
sacred (Mormon) . . 4. Urim 7. Thummim
stringed . . 4. asor, harp, lute, lyre, rota 5. banjo, cello, dobro, ribec (ribeck), sitar, viola 6. fiddle, guitar, violin 7. ukulele 8. dulcimer, mandolin
10. hurdy-gurdy
wind . . 3. sax 4. horn, oboe, reed, tuba
5. flute, organ 6. cornet 7. althorn, bassoon, ocarina, piccolo, trumpet
8. clarinet, trombone 9. accordion, flageolet, harmonica, saxophone
10. concertina
instrument, others (pert to) . . .
astronomical . . 5. armil
Biblical . . 4. Urim
butcher's . . 5. steel 7. cleaver
communication . . 9. telegraph, telephone
10. hydrophone
cooking (eggs) . . 7. oometer
cutting . . 5. knife, razor 6. scythe, shears, sickle 7. cutlery 8. scissors, strickle

drawing . . 10. pantograph
gripping . . 4. vise 5. clamp, tongs
7. pincers 8. tweezers
legal . . 4. deed, writ 6. escrow
mathematics . . 6. abacus 8. mesolabe
measure . . 7. ammeter 8. odometer, otoscope, rheostat 9. barometer, koniscope, rheometer 11. pyronometer
medical . . 6. trocar (trochar) 7. dilator, levator, ligator, scalpel 8. trephine
mining . . 6. jumper
music . . 4. bell 9. ergograph, metronome
navigating . . 7. pelorus, sextant
optical . . 7. alidade (alidad) 9. periscope, telescope
pointed . . 3. awl 6. stylet, stylus 8. stiletto
time . . 11. chronometer, chronoscope
two-pronged . . 6. bident
instrumental . . . 6. useful 7. helpful
9. conducive, promoting, symphonic
10. orchestral 11. implemental, serviceable
instrumental (pert to) . . .
composition . . 5. fugue, rondo 6. sonata
7. cantata 8. symphony
grammar . . 4. case
introduction . . 7. intrada
instrumentality . . . 5. means 6. agency, medium 7. organon 9. mechanism
insubordinate . . . 8. mutinous
10. unresigned 11. disobedient
12. contumacious, unsubmissive
insubstantial . . . 5. frail 6. flimsy
9. illogical 10. unreliable
12. apparitional
insufficient . . . 5. short 6. scanty, scarce
7. unequal, wanting 9. deficient
10. inadequate 14. incommensurate, unsatisfactory
insular . . . 5. alone 6. narrow 7. nesiote
8. detached, islander, isolated, secluded
9. illiberal, insulated, sclerosis, separated, unrelated 10. contracted
12. Island of Reil (Anat)
insulated . . . 5. isled, taped 8. isolated
9. separated 10. segregated
insulating material . . . 4. tape 5. kapok
6. balata, Kerite 7. okonite 10. fiber glass 12. friction tape
insult . . . 3. cag 4. mock, slur 5. flout
6. offend, revile 7. affront, assault, offense, outrage 8. contempt
9. contumely, indignity
insulting . . . 8. arrogant, insolent
9. offensive 10. affrontive
13. disrespectful
insurance . . . 4. risk 7. annuity, promise
8. guaranty, security, warranty
9. assurance 10. protection
insurance group . . . 7. tontine
insurance personnel . . . 5. agent
6. broker 7. actuary 8. adjuster
insurgent . . . 5. rebel 8. agitator, mutineer, revolter 10. rebellious
13. insubordinate
insurmountable . . . 10. impassable, invincible 11. insuperable 13. beyond control
insurrection . . . 4. riot 6. mutiny, revolt
8. sedition, uprising 9. rebellion
10. insurgence, revolution

intact . . . 5. sound, whole 9. unchanged, undefiled, undivided, uninjured, untouched 10. unimpaired

intaglio . . . 3. die, gem 6. relief 7. carving 9. engraving

intangible . . . 5. vague 7. phantom 10. immaterial, impalpable 13. imperceptible, insubstantial, unsubstantial

integer . . . 3. one 5. whole 6. entity, number 8. integral

integral . . . 3. all 5. inner, whole 8. totality 9. component, essential

integration . . . 5. whole 10. adjustment 11. unification 12. coordination, equalization 13. accommodation

integrity . . . 5. unity 6. purity, virtue 7. honesty, probity 9. innocence, soundness 12. completeness

integument . . . 4. aril, coat, derm, skin 5. testa 8. covering, envelope 10. investment

intellect . . . 3. wit 4. mind, nous 5. inwit, mahat 6. genius, noesis, reason 7. noetics, wise man 9. mentality 12. intelligence 13. understanding

intellectual . . . 6. brainy, mental, noetic, sophic 7. egghead, learned 8. highbrow 11. intelligent

intelligence . . . 4. mind, news 5. sense, spies 6. acumen, spirit 8. capacity 9. intellect, knowledge 11. information 13. understanding

intelligent . . . 3. apt 4. sane 5. acute, aware, smart 6. astute, bright, versed 7. knowing, skilled 8. rational, sensible 9. cognizant 13. understanding

intelligentsia . . . 8. literati 10. illuminati 11. the educated 13. intellectuals

intelligible . . . 5. clear, plain 8. knowable 10. cognizable, conceptual, explicable, fathomable 11. perspicuous 13. suprasensuous 14. comprehensible, understandable

intelligibly . . . 6. simply 7. clearly, lucidly, plainly 13. unequivocally 14. comprehensibly, understandably

intemerate . . . 4. pure 9. inviolate, undefiled

intemperance . . . 6. excess 8. bibacity, gluttony, severity, tippling 10. debauchery, inclemency 11. drunkenness 12. inabstinence, incontinence

intemperate . . . 6. Frigid (Zone), severe, Torrid (Zone) 7. extreme 8. addicted, bibulous 9. excessive, inclement, indulgent 10. gluttonous, immoderate, inordinate 12. ungovernable, unrestrained

intend . . . 3. aim 4. mean, plan 5. serve 6. design, direct, expect, regard, set out, strive 7. proceed, propose 8. aspire to, attend to, consider

intended . . . 5. meant 8. designed, purposed, remedial 9. affianced, betrothed, meditated 10. calculated, considered 11. deliberated, intentional 12. contemplated

intense . . . 4. deep 5. great, vivid 6. strong 7. violent 8. powerful 9. energetic

10. high degree

intensely . . . 4. very 5. quite 7. acutely

intensify . . . 6. deepen 7. enhance 8. condense, heighten, increase 9. aggravate

intensity . . . 5. ardor, depth 6. deepen, degree, energy 7. density 8. loudness, softness, strength 9. greatness, vehemence 12. colorfulness

intent . . . 4. rapt 5. eager, tense 6. design 7. earnest, meaning, purpose 9. intention

intention . . . 3. aim, end 4. will 6. animus, design, motive, object 7. concept, healing, meaning, purpose 8. intentio 13. determination

intentional . . . 5. aimed, meant 7. knowing 8. designed, intended 9. voluntary 10. calculated, deliberate 12. contemplated

intently . . . 7. eagerly, fixedly 9. earnestly, zealously 10. diligently, sedulously 11. attentively, steadfastly

inter (pref) . . . 5. among, intra 6. mutual, within 7. between 10. reciprocal

inter (verb) . . . 4. bury 5. inurn 6. entomb, inhume 7. inearth

intercalary month . . . 6. Veadar 8. leap year 10. bissextile

intercalate . . . 6. insert 11. interpolate

intercede . . . 6. umpire 7. bargain, mediate, referee 9. arbitrate, go between, interpose, intervene

intercessor . . . 5. agent, front 6. bishop, Christ 8. mediator 9. middleman 10. interceder 11. internuncio

interchange . . . 5. trade 6. barter 7. permute 8. commerce, exchange 9. alternate 10. transposal 11. alternation, reciprocate, retaliation

intercourse . . . 7. dealing 8. commerce 10. connection, fellowship 12. conversation 13. communication

interdependence . . . 9. mutuality 13. interrelation 16. interaffiliation

interdict . . . 3. ban 4. veto 5. debar, taboo (tabu) 6. forbid 7. inhibit 8. prohibit 9. proscribe

interest . . . 4. hold, weal 5. savor, share, usury 6. behalf, engage 7. attract, concern 9. entertain

interested . . . 4. rapt 7. partial 8. a party to, involved, partisan 9. attentive 10. prejudiced

interesting . . . 8. exciting 10. attractive 11. provocative

interfere . . . 5. clash 6. hinder, meddle, molest, tamper 7. intrude 9. interpose, intervene 11. intermeddle

interim . . . 7. respite 8. interval, meantime 9. interlude, meanwhile 12. intermission

interior . . . 5. inner 6. center, inland, inside, secret 8. internal 9. enclosure

interjection . . . 2. eh, lo 3. bah 4. ahem, alas, egad, haha, whew 7. heavens 11. ejaculation, exclamation

interlace . . . 3. mix 5. braid, unite 9. alternate, interlink 10. intertwine, interweave 11. interpolate, intersperse

interlock . . . 4. knit, mesh 5. unite, weave 6. device, engage 7. connect

9. interjoin, interlace 11. interrelate
interlope . . . 6. insert 7. intrude, obtrude
9. interfere, intervene 11. intermeddle,
interpolate
interloper . . . 8. intruder 10. trespasser
11. gate crasher
interlude . . . 5. farce, pause, truce
6. verset 7. interim, respite 8. entr'acte,
overture, versicle 10. intermezzo
11. performance 13. entertainment
intermediary . . . 5. agent 6. medium,
middle 8. mediator 9. go-between
10. interagent 11. intervening,
mediatorial
intermediate . . . 5. mesne 6. grades,
medial, medium, middle 7. aniline
(dye), mediate 8. mediator 9. naphthols
11. interjacent, intervening
12. intermediary
interminable . . . 4. aeon, long 7. endless,
eternal 8. infinite, unending
9. boundless, limitless, perpetual,
unlimited 10. continuous, protracted
intermission . . . 4. rest 5. pause 6. recess
7. respite 8. entr'acte, interval
9. cessation 10. suspension
12. interruption
intermit . . . 4. stop 5. cease, recur
7. suspend 9. interpose, interrupt
11. discontinue
intermittent . . . 6. broken, fitful
8. periodic 9. irregular, recurrent,
spasmodic 11. alternating
internal . . . 5. inner 6. inside, inward,
mental, within 7. revenue 8. domestic,
esoteric, interior 9. intrinsic, spiritual
internal organs . . . 6. vitals 7. viscera
international (pert to) . . .
  agreement . . 4. pact 6. accord, treaty
  7. entente 8. suzerain
  business combine . . 6. cartel
  fixed calendar . . 9. Cotsworth
  language . . 2. Ro 3. Ido 5. Arulo
  7. Volapük 9. Esperanto 10. Occidental
  11. Interlingua
interpolate . . . 5. alter 6. insert 7. corrupt,
implant 11. intercalate
interpose . . . 7. intrude, mediate
9. intercede, interfere, interject,
intervene, introduce
interpret . . . 4. read, rede, scan 6. define
7. explain, expound 8. construe,
diagnose, exegesis 9. elucidate,
translate
interpretation . . . 5. sense 8. solution
9. rendering 10. definition
11. explanation, translation
interpretation, science of . . . 7. anagoge
(Bib) 8. exegesis 9. dittology
12. hermeneutics
interpreter . . . 5. ulema 6. gnomon
7. exegete, latiner 8. dragoman,
exponent 9. catechist, exegetist,
explainer, go-between, hermeneut
12. oneirocritic (dreams)
interrogate . . . 3. ask 4. pump, quiz,
test 5. grill, query 7. examine, inquire
8. question 9. catechize
interrogation . . . 7. eroteme (question
mark) 8. erotisis, question, quizzing
11. examination, questioning

interrupt . . . 4. stop 5. break, check
6. arrest, hinder, thwart 7. break
in, intrude 8. obstruct 9. intercept
11. interpolate
interrupter (electric) . . . 8. rheotome
interruption . . . 3. gap 5. pause 6. hiatus
7. interim 8. interval 9. cessation,
hindrance 10. suspension
11. obstruction 12. intermission,
intervention 13. interposition
intersect . . . 3. cut 4. meet 5. cross
6. divide, pierce 9. decussate
10. intercross
intersperse . . . 6. insert, thread 7. scatter
9. diversify
interstice . . . 4. mesh, pore 5. chink, crack,
space 6. areola 7. crevice 8. interval
10. interspace
intertwine . . . 5. unite, weave 8. entangle
9. interknit, interlace 10. intertwist
interval . . . 3. gap 4. rest 5. break, lapse,
pitch, space 6. degree, period, recess
7. diastem, interim, respite 8. diastema,
distance, half step 10. interspace
12. intermission, interruption
intervals, at . . . 8. brokenly, fitfully
11. haphazardly, irregularly
12. occasionally 14. intermittently
15. longo intervallo
intervene . . . 6. step in 7. intrude, mediate
9. interlude, interpose 10. lie between
11. come between
intervening (pert to) . . .
  between, among . . 11. interjacent
  law . . 5. mesne
  space . . 8. distance
  time . . 7. interim 9. interlude
interweave . . . 3. mat 4. plat 5. braid,
plait, plash 6. enlace, raddle, splice,
wattle 8. intermix 9. interlace 13. twist
together
intestinal . . . 7. enteric 8. visceral
intestine (pert to) . . .
  coating . . 4. caul
  comb form . . 6. entero
  part . . 5. colon, ilium, large, small
  6. caecum, rectum 7. jejunum
  8. appendix, duodenum 15. alimentary
  canal
intestines . . . 4. guts 6. bowels 8. entrails
intimacy . . . 9. closeness 10. connection,
friendship 11. association, familiarity,
sociability
intimate . . . 3. sib 4. hint, near 6. friend,
united 8. familiar, friendly, informal,
personal, sociable 9. confidant,
innermost 12. confidential
intimation . . . 3. cue 4. clue, hint 5. trace
7. inkling 9. reference 10. foreboding,
indication, suggestion 11. supposition
12. announcement, notification
intimidate . . . 3. awe, cow 5. abash,
bully, daunt, deter 7. overawe, terrify
8. browbeat, frighten, threaten
intolerance . . . 7. bigotry 9. dogmatism,
prejudice 10. impatience, narrowness
12. illiberality
intolerant . . . 6. narrow 7. bigoted
8. dogmatic 9. impatient 10. prejudiced
11. not enduring
intolerant person . . . 5. bigot 7. fanatic

intone ... **4.** sing **5.** chant, croon, sound
7. introit

intoxicated ... **3.** lit, sot **4.** tosy **5.** drunk,
heady, tipsy **6.** boiled **7.** fervent,
fuddled, maudlin **8.** besotted, temulent
9. befuddled **10.** inebriated

intractable ... **5.** tough **6.** sullen, unruly
7. restive, willful (wilful) **8.** indocile,
perverse, stubborn **9.** obstinate,
unbending, unpliable **10.** headstrong,
inflexible, refractory **11.** unteachable
12. ungovernable

intransitive ... **6.** neuter, verbal
8. confined **10.** in transitu

intrenchment ... **2.** pa (pah) **4.** fort
7. defense, parapet **8.** stockade
12. encroachment, infringement

intrepid ... **4.** bold **5.** brave **6.** heroic
7. doughty, valiant **8.** fearless, resolute
9. dauntless, undaunted **10.** courageous

intrepidity ... **5.** nerve, valor **7.** courage,
prowess **8.** boldness, valiancy
9. gallantry

intricacy ... **9.** sinuosity **10.** complexity,
involution, perplexity **11.** complexness
12. complication, entanglement

intrigue ... **4.** plot **5.** amour, cabal
6. brigue, scheme **8.** artifice, cheating
9. fascinate **10.** conspiracy
11. machination

intrinsic ... **4.** real, true **5.** inner **6.** inborn,
inbred, inward, native **7.** genuine,
natural **8.** immanent, implicit, inherent
9. essential, necessary **11.** inseparable
13. indispensable

intrinsically ... **5.** truly **6.** really
10. internally **11.** essentially

intrinsic being ... **7.** essence

introduce ... **5.** immit, start, usher
6. broach, herald, infuse, insert, submit
7. bring in, preface, present, sponsor
8. acquaint, approach, initiate, innovate
10. inaugurate **11.** preinstruct

introduced from foreign country ...
6. exotic **10.** extraneous

introduced serum ... **10.** inoculated

introduction ... **5.** debut, guide, proem
7. introit, isagoge, preface **8.** exordium,
foreword, preamble **9.** insertion
10. innovation **11.** instruction,
preparation **12.** inauguration,
presentation

introduction (pert to) ...
Biblical .. **9.** isagogics
drama (anc) .. **8.** protasis
new words .. **7.** neology
spurious matter .. **13.** interpolation

introductory ... **9.** prefatory, prelusive
11. preliminary

introit ... **4.** hymn, rite **5.** psalm
8. entrance **12.** introduction

introrse ... (opp of extrorse) **12.** facing
inward

introversion ... (opp of extroversion)
9. inversion, reticence

intrude ... **5.** enter **6.** invade, meddle
8. encroach, infringe, overstep, trespass
9. interfere, interlope

intruder ... **7.** invader **8.** outsider
9. buttinsky **10.** interloper, trespasser

intrust, entrust ... **6.** commit **7.** confide,

consign **8.** delegate **10.** commission

intuition ... **5.** hunch **6.** noesis, regard
7. insight **9.** knowledge, reference
13. contemplation

intuitive ... **6.** noetic, seeing **7.** sensing
10. perceiving **11.** instinctive

inulase ... **6.** enzyme

inunction ... **7.** unguent **8.** inunctum,
ointment

inundate ... **3.** dip **4.** dunk **5.** douse,
drunk, flood **6.** deluge, engulf **7.** baptize,
immerse **8.** overflow, submerge
9. overwhelm **10.** oversupply

inure ... **6.** harden, season **7.** benefit,
callous, toughen **8.** accustom
9. habituate

inurn ... **4.** bury **5.** inter **6.** entomb

invade ... **4.** raid **5.** enter (foeman), usurp
6. attack, infest **7.** intrude, overrun,
violate **8.** encroach, trespass

invader ... **4.** Pict **8.** attacker, intruder
9. aggressor, assailant **10.** trespasser

invalid ... **4.** null, sick, void, weak **5.** frail
6. feeble, infirm, sickly **8.** nugatory
11. ineffectual **14.** valetudinarian

invalidate ... **4.** undo **5.** annul, quash
7. abolish, nullify, vitiate **8.** disprove
10. disqualify, neutralize

invalidism ... **13.** indisposition
17. valetudinarianism

invaluable ... **6.** useful **8.** precious
9. priceless, worthless **11.** inestimable

invariable ... **7.** uniform **8.** constant
10. unchanging **12.** unchangeable

invasion ... **4.** raid **5.** foray **6.** attack,
breach, inroad **8.** entrance (hostile)
9. incursion, intrusion, irruption
10. infraction **11.** infestation

invective ... **5.** abuse, curse **6.** tirade
7. inveigh, railing **8.** diatribe
10. revilement **11.** malediction
12. vituperation

inveigle ... **4.** lure, rope **5.** snare **6.** allure,
entice, entrap, seduce **7.** deceive,
wheedle **10.** lead astray

invent ... **4.** coin **5.** frame **6.** create,
design, devise **7.** concoct **8.** discover
9. fabricate (mentally), originate

inventive ... **6.** adroit **7.** fertile **8.** creative,
original **9.** ingenious

inventor ... **7.** creator **8.** imaginer
10. discoverer, originator

inventor, discoverer of ...
adding machine .. **9.** Burroughs
air brake .. **12.** Westinghouse
airplane .. **6.** Wright (Bros)
automobile (gasoline) .. **7.** Daimler
ballpoint pen .. **4.** Biro
baseball (reputed) .. **9.** Doubleday
bifocal lens .. **8.** Franklin
brake (safety) .. **4.** Otis
calculating machine .. **7.** Babbage
camera .. **4.** Land **7.** Eastman
cotton gin .. **7.** Whitney
dynamite .. **5.** Nobel
electric light .. **6.** Edison
elevator .. **4.** Otis
frozen food .. **8.** Birdseye
gun .. **4.** Colt **5.** Maxim **7.** Gatling
8. Browning **9.** Remington
harp (Bib) .. **5.** Jubal

helicopter . . **8.** Sikorsky
lamp (safety) . . **4.** Davy
lightning rod . . **8.** Franklin
lock, cylinder . . **4.** Yale
locomotive . . **6.** Cooper **10.** Stephenson
phonograph . . **6.** Edison
printing . . **9.** Gutenberg
radio . . **8.** De Forest
reaper . . **9.** McCormick
safety razor . . **8.** Gillette
sewing machine . . **4.** Howe
sleeping car . . **7.** Pullman
steamboat . . **5.** Fitch **6.** Fulton
steam engine . . **4.** Watt **8.** Newcomen
telegraph . . **5.** Morse
vulcanized rubber . . **8.** Goodyear
wireless . . **7.** Marconi
X-ray . . **8.** Roentgen
inventory . . . **4.** list **5.** index, stock
   6. supply **7.** account , catalog
   (catalogue) **8.** register **10.** tally sheet
inverse . . . **8.** inverted, opposite, reversed
inversely club-shaped . . . **9.** obclavate
inversely oval . . . **7.** obovate
inversion . . . **8.** overturn, reversal
   9. overthrow, reversion **10.** conversion
   12. introversion
invert . . . **7.** capsize, convert, pervert
   (obs), reverse, tip over **8.** overturn
   9. transpose **10.** turn turtle
invertebrate . . . **5.** polyp **6.** insect, sponge
   7. mollusk **9.** spineless **10.** weak-willed
invest . . . **3.** don **4.** vest, wrap **5.** array,
   dress, endow, indue, spend **6.** clothe
   7. empower, envelop, instate
   8. surround
invest (pert to) . . .
   authority . . **8.** accredit, sanction
   ministry . . **6.** ordain
   sovereignty . . **8.** enthrone
investigate . . . **3.** pry **4.** sift **5.** probe,
   study, track **6.** excuse, search **7.** discuss,
   explore **8.** indagate **10.** scrutinize
investigation . . . **6.** examen **7.** inquiry,
   zetetic **8.** research **9.** discovery, heuristic
   10. discussion **11.** examination
investitute . . . **7.** clothes, vesture
   8. clothing, covering **9.** induction
   10. holy orders, investment (money),
   ordination **11.** instatement
   12. installation **15.** enfranchisement
investment . . . **5.** siege **7.** finance,
   garment **8.** blockade, clothing, covering,
   purchase, vestment **9.** endowment
   11. empowerment
investment list . . . **9.** portfolio
inveterate . . . **3.** old **6.** rooted **7.** chronic
   8. habitual, hardened **9.** confirmed,
   ingrained **10.** deep-rooted
   11. established, traditional **15.** long-
   established
invidious . . . **6.** odious, ornery **7.** envious,
   hateful **9.** malignant **14.** discriminating
   (unjustly)
invigorate . . . **3.** pep **5.** brace, cheer,
   nerve, renew **6.** vivify **7.** animate,
   enliven, fortify, refresh **8.** energize
   9. stimulate **10.** exhilarate, strengthen
invigorating . . . **4.** cool **5.** tonic
   8. cheering **10.** energizing, life-giving,
   refreshing **11.** stimulating

invincible . . . **10.** unbeatable
   11. indomitable **13.** unconquerable
inviolate . . . **6.** sacred, secret **8.** faithful,
   unbroken **9.** unchanged, undefiled,
   unstained **10.** inviolable, unimpaired,
   unprofound **13.** incorruptible
invisible . . . **3.** hid **6.** hidden **10.** indistinct,
   unapparent **13.** infinitesimal,
   undiscernible, unperceivable
Invisible, The . . . **3.** God **11.** Rosicrucian
   16. German Protestant
invisible emanation . . . **4.** aura
invitation . . . **3.** bid **4.** call **7.** bidding,
   summons **10.** allurement, inducement
   12. solicitation
invite . . . **3.** ask, beg, bid, try **4.** bade
   5. court, order, tempt **6.** allure, entice,
   induce **7.** request, solicit **9.** encourage
invocation . . . **4.** call, plea, rite **6.** appeal,
   prayer, sermon **7.** summons **8.** entreaty
   11. conjuration, incantation
   12. supplication
invoice . . . **4.** bill **7.** account (written)
   8. manifest **9.** reckoning **12.** bill of
   lading
invoke . . . **3.** beg **4.** pray **6.** appeal
   7. address, conjure, entreat, implore,
   solicit **8.** draw down **10.** supplicate
involuntary . . . **9.** not willed, reluctant,
   unwilling, unwitting **11.** instinctive,
   spontaneous **13.** unintentional
involve . . . **3.** lap **4.** coil, wind, wrap
   5. imply **6.** employ, entail, evince, infold
   7. concern, ensnare, entwine, envelop,
   include **8.** interest **9.** embarrass,
   implicate **10.** complicate **11.** incriminate
involved . . . **7.** complex, implied
   8. involute, tortuous **9.** engrossed
   10. implicated
involving punishment . . . **8.** punitive
invulnerable . . . **10.** invincible
   11. impregnable, insuperable
   12. impenetrable, unassailable
inward . . . **4.** into **5.** entad, inner **6.** inside
   7. ingoing, muffled **8.** interior, internal
   9. spiritual **10.** internally
inwards . . . **8.** entrails **10.** intestines
Io . . . **7.** goddess (Gr) **9.** butterfly, satellite
   (of Jupiter)
iodine, iodin (pert to) . . .
   comb form . . **3.** iod **4.** iodo
   compound . . **6.** iodide
   containing . . **5.** iodic **6.** iodous
   poisoning . . **6.** iodism **9.** iododerma
   source . . **4.** kelp **8.** sea water **9.** salt
   peter **12.** thryoid gland
   standard . . **9.** idiometry
   substitute . . **7.** Aristol
ion . . . **5.** anion **6.** cation (kation)
   8. electron, particle (Elec)
Ionian (pert to) . . .
   city . . **4.** Teos (birthplace of Anacreon)
   islands . . **5.** Greek **9.** Asia Minor
   mode (Mus) . . **6.** Lydian
Ionic (pert to) . . .
   architecture . . **5.** Order
   dialect . . **5.** Greek
   poetry . . **4.** foot **5.** meter
   printing . . **4.** type
iota . . . **3.** ace, jot **4.** atom, mite, star
   (9th brightest), whit **6.** letter (Gr), tittle

8. particle
Iowa . . .
  capital . . **9.** Des Moines
  city . . **4.** Ames **8.** Waterloo **9.** Davenport,
    Fort Dodge, Marquette, Sioux City
    10. West Branch **11.** Cedar Rapids
  famed attractions . . **10.** Hoover home
    12. Effigy Mounds **17.** Little Brown
    Church
  famed first . . **12.** apple orchard (1799)
  famed names . . **6.** Joliet **7.** Dubuque
    9. Marquette
  flower . . **8.** wild rose
  locale . . **8.** farm belt (Midwest)
  river . . **8.** Missouri **11.** Mississippi
  State admission . . **11.** twenty-ninth (1846)
  State nickname . . **7.** Hawkeye
ipecac . . . **4.** evea **6.** emetic **7.** emetive
    9. purgative
irade . . . **6.** decree (Turk)
Iran . . . see also *Iranian, Persia*
  capital . . **6.** Tehran (Teheran)
  city . . **6.** Abadan, Shiraz **7.** Isfahan
  conqueror . . **6.** Darius **9.** Alexander
  lake . . **7.** Rezaieh
  mountain . . **6.** Elburz, Zagros
    8. Damavand (peak)
  old name . . **6.** Persia
  parliament . . **6.** Majlis (Mejlis)
  people (anc) . . **5.** Medes **6.** Aryans
    8. Persians
  ruins . . **10.** Persepolis (Shiraz)
Iranian (pert to) . . .
  almond . . **5.** badam
  Ayatollah . . **8.** Khomeini
  books . . **5.** Koran, Yasma **6.** Avesta
  country . . **4.** Elam **5.** Media
  demigod . . **4.** Yima
  demon . . **7.** Ahriman
  diadem . . **3.** taj
  dynasty . . **6.** Safavi, Seljuk **8.** Sassanid
  fire worshiper . . **5.** Parsi (Parsee)
  god . . **6.** Ormazd (Supreme) **7.** Mithras
  Koran student . . **5.** hafiz
  language . . **5.** Farsi **7.** Avestan, Pehlevi
    (Pahlavi), Persian
  poet . . **4.** Omar **5.** Saadi
  Relig founder . . **9.** Zoroaster
  Shah . . **7.** Pahlavi
  tapestry . . **7.** susanee
  tentmaker . . **4.** Omar
Iraq, Mesopotamia . . .
  capital . . **6.** Bagdad (Baghdad)
  culture (anc) . . **8.** Sumerian
  historic city . . **2.** Ur **5.** Eridu **7.** Babylon,
    Nineveh
  historic Valley . . **15.** Tigris-Euphrates
  port . . **5.** Basra (Busrah)
  product . . **3.** oil **4.** date **5.** sheep
  river . . **6.** Tigris **9.** Euphrates **11.** Shatt-
    al-Arab
irascibility . . . **3.** ire **6.** choler **9.** crossness,
    testiness **10.** perversity **11.** waspishness
    12. churlishness, irritability
irate . . . **3.** hot **5.** angry, wroth **7.** enraged
    8. incensed **9.** irascible
ire . . . **5.** anger, wrath **7.** madness
    8. vexation **9.** vehemence
    10. enragement, resentment
    12. exasperation
ireful . . . **5.** angry, wroth **7.** iracund

9. irascible **10.** passionate
Ireland . . . **4.** Eire, Erin **5.** Irena **6.** Old
    Sod, Ulster **8.** Hibernia **9.** Innisfail
    11. Emerald Isle, Erin go brath
    14. Ireland Forever
Ireland (pert to) . . . see also *Irish*
  Bay . . **6.** Bantry, Dingle, Galway
    7. Donegal
  capital . . **4.** Tara (old) **6.** Dublin
  channel . . **5.** North **9.** St George's
  city . . **4.** Cork, Tara **6.** Galway, Tralee,
    Ulster **7.** Belfast, Donegal, Kildare,
    Wexford **8.** Kilkenny, Limerick
    9. Tipperary
  county . . **4.** Cork, Mayo **5.** Kerry,
    Sligo **6.** Dublin, Galway **7.** Wicklow
    8. Kilkenny, Limerick
  islands . . **4.** Aran
  legislature . . **4.** Dail
  mountain . . **7.** Errigal **13.** Carrantuohill
  northern province . . **6.** Ulster
  river . . **3.** Lee **4.** Erne, Suir **6.** Liffey
    7. Shannon
  sea . . **5.** Irish
  seat of archbishops . . **6.** Armagh
irenic . . . **7.** henotic **8.** peaceful
    11. harmonizing **12.** conciliatory
iridescent . . . **7.** opaline **9.** prismatic
    10. opalescent
iris . . . **4.** flag **6.** flower **7.** rainbow
iris (pert to) . . .
  astronomy . . **8.** asteroid (7th)
  color . . **11.** reddish-blue
  eye part . . **4.** uvea **5.** irian
  Florentine . . **5.** orris (orrice)
  inflammation . . **6.** iritis
  mineral . . **6.** quartz (iridescent)
Iris, goddess . . . **7.** rainbow
Irish (pert to) . . .
  alphabet (early) . . **4.** ogam (ogham)
  battle cry . . **3.** abu (aboo) **9.** To Victory
    11. Erin go brath
  cattle . . **5.** Kerry
  Celtic, chief's heir . . **6.** tanist
  churchman . . **7.** erenach (herenach)
  club, cudgel . . **10.** shillalagh (shillalah)
  convention (anc) . . **4.** Feis **10.** Feis of
    Tara
  cordial . . **10.** usquebaugh
  dagger (anc) . . **5.** skean
  dance . . **3.** jig **4.** rink **10.** rinkafadda
  emblem . . **8.** shamrock
  exclamation . . **3.** aru **5.** arrah
  fairy, spirit . . **4.** shee (sidhe) **7.** banshee
    (banshie) **10.** leprechaun
  festival . . **4.** feis
  goblin . . **5.** pooka
  god . . **3.** Ler (sea)
  goddess . . **4.** Dana
  hero, warrior . . **9.** Cuchulain (Cuchullin)
  king's home . . **4.** Tara
  landholding . . **7.** rundale
  legislature . . **10.** Oireachtas (House)
    11. Dail Eireann (Chamber) **13.** Seanad
    Eireann (Senate)
  liquor house (illegal) . . **7.** shebeen
  love, sweetheart . . **3.** gra
  moss . . **9.** carrageen
  peasant . . **4.** kern (lerne)
  pig . . **5.** bonav
  policeman . . **8.** spalpeen

potato city .. **7.** Youghal
queen (folklore) .. **4.** Medb
Society (secret) .. **6.** Fenian
soldier .. **4.** kern (kerne) **10.** galloglass
tenant .. **4.** saer
theatre, famed .. **5.** Abbey
verse .. **4.** rann
whisky, whiskey (illegal) .. **6.** poteen
(potheen)
Irish (people) . . .
ancestor (fabled) .. **3.** Mil **6.** Miledh
author .. **5.** Behan, Joyce, Synge, Yeats
6. O'Casey **7.** Beckett
chemist .. **5.** Boyle
clan subdivision .. **4.** sept
composer .. **7.** Herbert
family .. **5.** cinel
Irishman .. **4.** Aire, Celt, Gael **6.** Teague
8. Milesian **9.** Hibernian, Orangeman
10. Eireannach
lawyer .. **6.** brehon
Nuns (Order) .. **15.** Ladies of Loretto
patriot .. **5.** Emmet, Tandy **6.** Oakboy
refugee .. **7.** fuidhir
saint .. **7.** Columba, Patrick
Saxon .. **8.** Sasanach
sea robbers (Myth) .. **9.** Fomorians
surgeon .. **6.** Colles
irk . . . **3.** vex **4.** bore, tire **5.** annoy,
weary **6.** nettle **7.** disgust, trouble
10. exasperate
irksome . . . **5.** vexed, weary **7.** operose,
painful, tedious **8.** annoying **9.** fatiguing,
vexatious, wearisome **10.** burdensome,
exhausting, monotonous
12. disagreeable
iron . . . **2.** Fe (symbol) **5.** harsh, metal,
power, press **6.** ferrum, fetter, mangle,
pistol, severe **7.** firearm, manacle,
shackle, sideros **8.** firmness, handcuff,
hardness, strength **10.** inflexible,
unyielding **11.** unrelenting
iron (pert to) . . .
casting .. **5.** mitis
comb form .. **5.** ferro **6.** sidero
compound .. **5.** steel
containing .. **6.** ferric
dog .. **7.** firedog
dross .. **6.** sinter
herb .. **8.** Vernonia **9.** ironweeds
lump .. **3.** pig
magnet .. **8.** armature
meteoric .. **8.** siderite
ore .. **7.** turgite **8.** hematite, siderite
11. sesquioxide
ref to .. **6.** ferric **7.** ferrous **8.** siderous
rod .. **5.** punty (puntee)
salts of .. **10.** chalybeate
sand .. **7.** iserine
science of .. **10.** siderology
symbol .. **2.** Fe
tailor's .. **5.** goose
tool .. **6.** lifter
vessel, basket .. **7.** cresset
ironclad . . . **6.** severe **7.** armored, Monitor
(ship) **8.** exacting, rigorous **9.** stringent
ironic, ironical . . . **3.** dry **7.** cynical,
satiric **9.** sarcastic **10.** figurative
11. Rabelaisian
irons . . . **5.** gyves **6.** chains **7.** fetters
8. manacles, shackles **9.** handcuffs

Ironsides . . . **7.** cavalry (Cromwell's)
8. Cromwell
ironwood . . . **4.** acle **5.** olive **6.** colima
7. breakax **8.** hornbeam **9.** stavewood
irony . . . **6.** banter, satire **7.** lampoon,
sarcasm **8.** ridicule
Iroquoian Indian . . . **4.** Erie **5.** Huron
6. Cayuga, Mohawk, Oneida, Seneca
7. Wyandot **8.** Cherokee, Onondaga
9. Conestoga, Tuscarora
Iroquois (pert to) . . .
Five Nations .. **6.** Cayuga, Mohawk,
Oneida, Seneca **8.** Onondaga
native of .. **7.** New York **9.** Wisconsin
irrational . . . **6.** stupid **9.** fanatical,
illogical, senseless **10.** ridiculous
11. impractical **12.** preposterous,
unreasonable **13.** unintelligent
irregular . . . **4.** wild **5.** erose, rough
6. fitful, rugged, uneven **7.** atactic,
crooked, devious, erratic, mutable,
styptic, unequal **8.** aberrent, abnormal,
atypical, informal, variable
9. anomalous, desultory, distorted,
eccentric, haphazard, orderless,
unsettled **10.** changeable, immoderate,
inconstant **11.** intemperate
12. unsystematic
irregularity . . . **6.** ataxia (muscular)
7. anomaly **8.** disorder **9.** deviation
10. distortion **11.** abnormality,
informality **12.** eccentricity
irrelevant . . . **7.** foreign **9.** unrelated
10. extraneous **11.** impertinent,
unessential **12.** inconsequent
13. insignificant
irreligious . . . **5.** pagan **7.** godless,
impious, profane **11.** unreligious
irreparable . . . **4.** gone, lost **6.** ruined
11. irrevocable **12.** incorrigible,
irremediable **13.** irrecoverable,
irretrievable
irrepressible . . . **7.** Homeric (laughter)
12. ungovernable, unrestrained
irrepressible conflict . . . **8.** civil war
irreproachable . . . **7.** perfect **9.** blameless
10. impeccable, inculpable
irresolute . . . **6.** fickle, unsure **8.** doubtful,
unstable **9.** uncertain, undecided
10. capricious, changeable, inconstant
12. undetermined
irresolution . . . **10.** fickleness, indecision
11. fluctuation, uncertainty, vacillation
14. capriciousness
irresponsible . . . **6.** fickle **7.** lawless
8. carefree **9.** insolvent
12. independable **13.** unaccountable,
untrustworthy
irretrievable . . . **8.** hopeless **9.** incurable
11. irreparable **12.** irremediable,
unchangeable **13.** irrecoverable
irreverence . . . **7.** impiety **8.** dishonor
9. profanity **10.** disrespect
irrevocable . . . **3.** end **4.** past **5.** final
10. inevitable, past recall **11.** unalterable
12. beyond recall, unchangeable
irrigate . . . **3.** wet **5.** water **6.** dilute,
sluice **7.** moisten, refresh
irritable . . . **4.** edgy **5.** cross, techy, testy
6. cranky, ornery, touchy **7.** fretful,
iracund, peevish, tempery, twitchy

8. snappish
irritate . . . 3. irk, nag, vex 4. fret, gall,
rasp, rile 5. anger, annoy, chafe, cross,
grate, peeve, pique, rouse, sting, tease
6. excite, incite, madden, needle,
nettle, rankle 7. incense, provoke
10. exacerbate, exasperate 14. rub the
wrong way
irritated . . . 4. sore 5. afret, testy
6. peeved 7. annoyed, nettled, rankled
8. provoked
irritation . . . 4. itch 5. pique 6. temper
9. annoyance 10. resentment
12. exasperation
irruption . . . 5. foray 6. inroad 8. invasion
9. incursion
Irving pseudonym . . . 13. Knickerbocker
(Diedrich)
is . . . 6. exists 10. represents
11. personifies
Isaac (pert to) . . .
Bib . . **9.** patriarch (Heb)
father of . . **4.** Esau 5. Jacob
grandfather of . . **4.** Edom
husband of . . **7.** Rebekah
son of . . **5.** Sarah 7. Abraham
Ishmael (pert to) . . .
ancestor . . **11.** Ishmaelites
Bib . . **6.** pariah 7. outcast
father of . . **8.** Nebaioth
son of . . **5.** Hagar 7. Abraham
isinglass . . . 4. huso, mica 7. gelatin
8. agar-agar
Isis (pert to) . . .
daughter of . . **3.** Geb, Nut
goddess of . . **9.** fertility 10. motherhood
identified with . . **7.** Dog Star
mother of . . **4.** Sept (Horus)
represented (at times) . . **9.** cow-headed
shrine of . . **5.** Iseum (Iseium)
wife of . . **6.** Osiris
Islam, Islamic (pert to) . . .
adherent . . **6.** Muslim (Moslem)
10. Mohammedan
convert . . **5.** ansar
founder, prophet . . **8.** Mohammed
(Mahomet)
God . . **5.** Allah
holy city . . **5.** Mecca 6. Medina
holy war . . **5.** jihad (jehad)
leader . . **9.** ayatollah
mosque . . **6.** masjid
praying position . . **6.** kiblah
rules for living . . **5.** Sunna
sacred place . . **5.** Kaaba (Caaba) 10. Black
Stone
sacred text . . **5.** Koran
scholary group . . **5.** ulema
teacher . . **4.** alim 6. mullah (mulla)
Islamic (pert to) . . .
convert . . **5.** ansar
holy city . . **5.** Mecca 6. Medina
mosque . . **6.** masjid
pilgrimage . . **5.** Kaaba (Caaba) 10. Black
Stone
Supreme Being . . **5.** Allah
teacher . . **4.** alim 5. ulema 6. mullah
(mulla)
island . . . 3. ait, cay, ile, key 4. calf,
cayo, eyot, holm, isle, reef 5. atoll,
islet 7. isolate 8. insulate

island (pert to) . . .
city . . **8.** Montreal
coral . . **5.** atoll 8. Zanzibar
enchanted . . **4.** Bali
fabled . . **4.** Meru 6. Avalon, Bimini
8. Atlantis
fabulous . . **7.** Zangbar
group . . **8.** Antilles, Marshall
11. archipelago
inhabitant, native . . **7.** nesiote 8. islander
universe (Astron) . . **6.** galaxy
Island of . . .
Langerhans . . **8.** pancreas
Odysseus . . **6.** Ithaca
Reil . . **5.** brain
Saints . . **4.** Erin
Isle of Man . . .
Celtic name . . **4.** Manx
city . . **4.** Peel 6. Ramsey 7. Douglas
division . . **5.** Treen
judge . . **8.** deemster (dempster)
legislature . . **7.** Tynwald
mountain peak . . **8.** Snaefell
Northern point . . **4.** Ayre
site . . **8.** Irish sea
Isle of Wight . . .
Queen's summer home . . **12.** Osborne
House
site . . **10.** English Sea
sport (famed) . . **9.** yacht race
town . . **7.** Newport
watering place . . **4.** Ryde
Isles of Galway Bay . . . 4. Aran
ism . . . 4. cult 5. dogma, ideal, tenet
6. belief, school, system 8. doctrine,
practice 11. abnormality
isochromatic . . . 9. same color
isochronal . . . 9. equal time 11. uniform
time
isocracy . . . 9. equal rule 10. equal power
isodont (Zool) . . . 10. alike teeth
isogonal . . . 11. equal angles
isolate . . . 4. isle 6. enisle 7. seclude
8. insulate, separate 9. segregate,
sequester 10. quarantine
isolation . . . 8. escapism, solitude
9. seclusion 10. insulation, loneliness,
separation 11. segregation
isomer . . . 7. metamer 8. compound
(Chem)
isonomy . . . 11. equal rights
isonym . . . 7. paronym 8. same name
isosceles . . . 10. equal sides (triangle)
Israel (Bib) . . . 4. Jews 5. Jacob, Zions
13. Hebrew Kingdom
Israel (pert to) . . . see also *Israelite*
appellation . . **8.** Jeshurun
capital . . **9.** Jerusalem
city . . **4.** Acre 5. Elath, Haifa, Jaffa
7. Galilee, Jericho, Tel Aviv
desert . . **5.** Negev
dust storm . . **7.** khamsin
lawgiver . . **5.** Moses
Plain of . . **6.** Sharon
priest . . **3.** Eli
river . . **6.** Jordan
sea . . **4.** Dead 7. Galilee
song (Zionist) . . **8.** Hatikvah
statesman . . **4.** Meir 5. Begin
Israelite (pert to) . . .
hero . . **6.** Gideon

judge . . **4.** Elon **8.** Jephthah
king . . **4.** Ahab, Jehu, Saul (1st) **5.** David
(2nd) **7.** Solomon
lawgiver . . **5.** Moses
priest . . **3.** Eli
tribe . . **3.** Dan **5.** Asher **6.** Reuben
tribe, priestly . . **4.** Levi
issue . . . **3.** son **4.** come, emit, flow, gush
5. arise, child, sally, spout, stock, topic,
utter **6.** effect, emerge, escape, sortie,
source, upshot **7.** edition, emanate,
proceed, product, progeny **8.** question
9. emergence, offspring, posterity
11. consequence, publication
Istanbul (Constantinople) . . .
ancient name . . **9.** Byzantium
capital of . . **6.** Turkey (to 1923)
foreign quarter . . **4.** Pera
Greek quarter . . **5.** Fanar
site . . **8.** Bosporus **10.** Golden Horn
isthmus (pert to) . . .
American . . **6.** Panama
anatomy . . **6.** fauces
Greek (anc) . . **7.** Corinth
Siam . . **3.** Kra
it . . . **5.** charm, thing **6.** itself, person
7. egotist, pronoun
Ita . . . **4.** Acta **7.** Negrito
Italian (pert to) . . . see also Italy
card game . . **5.** tarot
carriage . . **7.** vettura
cathedral . . **5.** duomo
cheese . . **6.** Romano **8.** Parmesan
10. mozzarella
condiment . . **6.** tamara (tamarind)
deity . . **4.** faun
dish . . **5.** pizza **7.** calzone **8.** braciola
11. saltimbocca
dome, peak . . **4.** cima
entertainment . . **5.** festa **7.** ridotto
food . . see pasta
grape . . **6.** verdea
hamlet . . **5.** casal
house . . **4.** casa **6.** casino (summer)
inlay . . **6.** tarsia
inn . . **7.** locanda
innkeeper . . **7.** padrone
lady . . **5.** donna **7.** signora
lake . . **4.** lago
law . . **6.** Latium **8.** Jus Latii
lover . . **7.** amoroso
magistrate (anc) . . **8.** podestra
marble . . **4.** Neri **7.** carrara, cipolin
marsh . . **7.** maremma
opera house . . **7.** La Scala (1778)
peasant . . **7.** paesano **9.** contadino
photographers . . **9.** paparazzi (press)
porridge . . **7.** polenta
pottery . . **8.** majolica
secret society . . **5.** Mafia (Maffia)
7. Camorra
sheep . . **6.** merino
unification . . **12.** Risorgimento
vessel . . **9.** trabacolo
wind (hot) . . **7.** sirocco
wine . . **4.** Asti **5.** Capri, Soave **6.** Barolo
7. Chianti, Orvieto **9.** Bardolino **12.** Asti
Spumante, Valpolicella
Italian (pert to people) . . .
anti-Fascist . . **6.** Sforza
architect . . **7.** Bernini **8.** Bramante

artist . . **6.** Titian **7.** Cellini, da Vinci,
Raphael **9.** Donatello **10.** Botticelli,
Caravaggio, Tintoretto, Modigliani
12. Michelangelo
astronomer . . **6.** Secchi **7.** Galileo
author . . **5.** Dante **9.** Boccaccio
11. Machiavelli
biographer (artists) . . **6.** Vasari
composer . . **5.** Verdi **7.** Puccini, Rossini,
Vivaldi **9.** Scarlatti **10.** Palestrina
deity . . **6.** Faunus
dictator . . **9.** Mussolini
educator . . **10.** Montessori
explorer . . **8.** Columbus, Vespucci
9. Marco Polo
family (princely) . . **4.** Este **5.** Doria
6. Medici
family (violin) . . **5.** Amati
friend (outside) . . **10.** Italophile
geographer . . **8.** Amoretti
goddess . . **3.** Ops **4.** Juno **5.** Diana
hero . . **7.** Orlando
historian . . **4.** Dion **5.** Cantu
king . . **7.** Umberto
naturalist . . **4.** Poli
noblewoman . . **8.** Marchesa
11. Marchioness
people . . **5.** Aequi (anc) **7.** Italici
8. Umbrians **9.** Etruscans, Ligurians
philosopher . . **4.** Vico **5.** Croce **7.** Aquinas
physician . . **5.** Abano **9.** Eustachio
physicist . . **5.** Volta **7.** Galvani, Marconi
poet . . **4.** Redi **5.** Dante, Tasso **7.** Manzoni
8. Annunzio, Casanova, Petrarch
9. Boccaccio
saint . . **4.** Neri **7.** Aquinas (Thomas)
sculptor . . **5.** Dupre, Leoni **8.** Ammanati
12. Michelangelo
singer . . **5.** Patti **6.** Caruso
statesman . . **5.** Rossi **8.** Gioberti
11. Machiavelli
theologian . . **7.** Peronne
violinist . . **8.** Paganini
Italy . . .
Alps . . **5.** Cozie **6.** Carnac, Julian
7. Atesine, Letiche, Pennine **8.** Maritime
9. Lepontine
capital . . **4.** Rome
city . . **4.** Lodi, Pisa **5.** Anona, Fiume,
Genoa, Milan, Padua, Pavia, Trent,
Turin **6.** Mantua, Modena, Naples,
Spezia, Venice, Verona **7.** Messina,
Palermo, Pompeii, Ravenna,
Trieste **8.** Brindisi, Florence,
Sorrento
commune . . **6.** Rivoli (Hist) **7.** Trieste
country (anc) . . **7.** Etruria, Lucania,
Tuscany
gulf . . **7.** Salerno
historical site . . **10.** Blue Grotto
18. Leaning Tower of Pisa
island . . **4.** Elba **5.** Capri, Leros **6.** Eschia,
Sicily **8.** Sardinia
lake . . **4.** Como **6.** Albano, Lugano
8. Maggiore
mountain . . **4.** Alps, Rosa **5.** Blanc
12. Gran Paradiso
port (fishing) . . **6.** Amalfi
resort . . **4.** Lido **5.** Capri **6.** Agnone
7. Riviera
river . . **2.** Po **4.** Arno **5.** Tiber

sea . . **6.** Ionian **8.** Apennine
  10. Tyrrhenian
strait . . **7.** Messina, Obranto
volcano . . **4.** Etna **8.** Vesuvius
  9. Stromboli
itch . . . **4.** reef, riff **5.** mange, psora
  6. desire, eczema **7.** scabies, sycosis
  9. cacoethes, hankering, psoriasis,
  sensation **10.** irritation
ite . . . **8.** adherent, disciple, follower
item . . . **3.** bit **4.** news **5.** asset, entry,
  scrap, topic **6.** detail **7.** article, integer
  9. commodity **10.** memorandum
  11. information
iter . . . **4.** eyre, road (Rom) **7.** circuit
iterate . . . **6.** recite, repeat, retell, review
  7. recount **8.** rehearse
iteration . . . **5.** recap **10.** repetition
  11. restatement
ithand . . . **8.** constant, diligent
  14. unintermittent
itinerant . . . **5.** mover, nomad **6.** roamer
  7. nomadic **8.** gadabout **9.** traveling,
  unsettled, wandering, wayfaring
itinerary . . . **4.** gest (royal), plan **5.** route
  6. prayer, record **8.** register, roadbook
  9. directory, guidebook

Ivanhoe (pert to) . . .
  author . . **5.** Scott
  character . . **5.** Boeuf **6.** Cedric, Rowena,
  Ulrica
  hero . . **7.** Ivanhoe
ivories (pert to) . . .
  anatomy . . **5.** teeth
  game . . **4.** dice
  piano . . **4.** keys
ivory (pert to) . . .
  anatomy . . **5.** tooth **7.** dentine
  block . . **4.** dice **7.** tessera
  carving . . **9.** toreutics
  color . . **5.** white (off)
  Latin . . **4.** ebur
  mixture (dust, cement) . . **7.** eburine
  plum . . **11.** wintergreen
  tower . . **7.** retreat
ivy . . . **5.** Rheus, sumac **11.** Hedera helix
iwa . . . **11.** frigate bird
IWW . . . **6.** wobbly
izar (Hind) . . . **4.** star **7.** garment **9.** loin
  cloth
izle . . . **4.** root **5.** ember, spark
Izmir . . . **6.** Smyrna
izzat . . . **5.** honor **6.** credit **8.** prestige
  10. reputation

J

J . . . **3.** Jay **6.** letter (10th)
ja (Ger) . . . **3.** yes
jaal goat . . . **4.** ibex **5.** beden
jab . . . **3.** dig, hit, jag **4.** poke, prod, stab
  5. punch **6.** strike, thrust
jabber . . . **4.** chat **5.** prate **6.** babble,
  gabble, jargon **7.** chatter, twaddle
  8. nonsense **9.** gibberish
Jabberwock . . . **6.** Jubjub **7.** monster
  (Through the Looking Glass)
Jabberwocky . . . **4.** poem **6.** prolix
  8. nonsense **10.** double talk
jabble . . . **6.** splash **7.** dashing **8.** rippling
  9. agitation, confusion, splashing
jabiru . . . **5.** stork
jack . . . **3.** can, jug, man **4.** card, coat, flag,
  male, pump **5.** hoist, knave, money
  6. lifter, sailor **7.** mariner **8.** nickname
jackal . . . **3.** dog (wild) **4.** dieb, kola,
  Thos **7.** cat's-paw **8.** henchman
jackass . . . **3.** ass **4.** deer (mule), dolt,
  fool, hare, nerd **6.** clover, donkey,
  rabbit **7.** morwong, penguin, witling
  9. blockhead
jackdaw . . . **3.** daw, kae **4.** crow **7.** grackle
jacket . . . **4.** coat, Eton, pelt **5.** cover
  (book) **6.** blazer, blouse, bolero, casing,
  jerkin, jumper, reefer **7.** garment, Mae
  West, wrapper
jacket (pert to) . . .
  Arctic . . **6.** anorak
  armor . . **5.** acton
  Eskimo . . **6.** temiak
  horseback riding . . **7.** hacking (jacket)
  knitted . . **6.** jersey, sontag **7.** sweater

  8. cardigan
  Levant . . **5.** grego
  Scottish . . **4.** jupe
  Spanish . . **8.** chaqueta
jack-in-the-pulpit . . . **4.** arum
Jack Ketch . . . **7.** hangman (Eng)
  11. executioner (public)
jackknife . . . **6.** barlow **8.** penknife
  11. toadstabber, toadsticker
jack-of-all-trades . . . **8.** handyman
jackstones . . . **4.** dibs, game **7.** pebbles
Jacob . . . **6.** Israel **9.** patriarch
Jacob (pert to) . . .
  brother . . **4.** Edom, Esau
  daughter . . **5.** Dinah
  father-in-law . . **5.** Laban
  parents . . **5.** Isaac **7.** Rebekah
  retreat . . **5.** Haran
  son . . **3.** Gad, Dan **4.** Levi **5.** Asher,
  Judah **6.** Reuben (oldest)
  wife . . **4.** Leah **6.** Rachel
Jacobin . . . **4.** Club **5.** Friar (Dominican)
  7. plotter, radical, Society **8.** Democrat
  (Fr 1789)
Jacob's ladder . . . **4.** herb **8.** hyacinth
  10. belladonna **11.** bittersweet
  12. Solomon's seal
jade . . . **4.** bore, tire **5.** green, horse,
  stone, wench **7.** fatigue **8.** strumpet
jaded . . . **8.** fatigued, shopworn
  9. dissolute **10.** bedraggled
jaeger (jager) . . . **4.** gull (like), skua
  6. teaser
jager . . . **6.** hunter **7.** diamond
  8. huntsman, rifleman

jagged . . . **5.** erose, rough, sharp
  6. barbed, pinked, ragged, rugged
  7. cutting, notched, pointed, slashed
  8. serrated **10.** saw-toothed
jagua . . . **4.** palm **7.** genipap
jaguar . . . **3.** cat **4.** puma **5.** ounce
  6. cougar **7.** panther **11.** snow leopard
Jah (Heb) . . . **3.** God **7.** Jehovah
jai alai . . . **4.** game **5.** cesta **6.** pelota
  7. fronton
jail . . . **3.** jug **4.** brig, gaol **5.** clink
  6. cooler, lockup **7.** slammer (sl)
  8. hoosegow **9.** Bridewell (London),
  calaboose **11.** incarcerate
jailer, jailor . . . **5.** guard **6.** gaoler, keeper,
  warden **7.** alcaide, turnkey
jail sentence . . . **3.** rap
jalousie . . . **5.** blind **7.** shutter
Jamaica . . .
  beverage . . **3.** rum **4.** jake
  capital . . **8.** Kingston
  cucumber . . **7.** gherkin
  ebony . . **10.** crocuswood
  island . . **10.** West Indies
  pepper . . **8.** allspice
  tree (drug) . . **7.** quassia
jangle . . . **5.** brawl, chide, noise, prate
  6. babble, gossip **7.** chatter, grate on,
  quarrel, ringing, whimper
Janizary (anc) . . . **5.** slave **7.** soldier
Janus (Rom) . . . **3.** god (two-faced)
Japan . . . **5.** Jipun (Chin), Nihon, Nisei
  6. Nippon **7.** Cipango (of Marco Polo)
Japan . . . see also *Japanese*
  capital . . **4.** Nara (anc) **5.** Kyoto (anc),
  Tokyo
  city . . **4.** Kobe **7.** Sapporo **8.** Kawasaki,
  Kumamoto, Nagasaki, Yokohama,
  Yokosuka **9.** Hiroshima **10.** Kitakyushu
  current . . **8.** Kuroshio
  islands . . **6.** Honshu, Kyushu **7.** Shikoku
  9. Haikkaido (Yezo)
  mountain . . **8.** Fujiyama
  naval base . . **8.** Yokosuka
  port . . **4.** Kobe **5.** Osaka **6.** Nagoya
  8. Yokohama
  protectorate . . **9.** Manchukuo
  river . . **4.** Yalu (Annock)
  shrine . . **7.** Toshogu (at Nikko)
  spring (hot) . . **6.** Hakone
  volcano . . **9.** Asamayama
Japanese (pert to) . . .
  airplane . . **4.** Zero
  annals, chronicles . . **7.** Nihongi
  apricot . . **3.** ume
  army (conscription) . . **6.** geneki
  army officer . . **7.** samurai
  art of self-defense . . **4.** judo **7.** jujitsu
  (jujutsu, jiujutsu)
  badge (family) . . **3.** mon
  banjo . . **7.** samisen
  battle cry . . **6.** banzai
  brazier . . **7.** hibachi
  button (carved) . . **7.** netsuke
  cape . . **4.** mino
  cedar . . **4.** sugi
  chess . . **5.** shogi
  church (Buddhist) . . **4.** tera
  circle, ship (suffix) . . **4.** maru
  deer . . **4.** sika
  dog . . **6.** tanate

drama . . **2.** no **6.** no-gaku
drink . . **4.** sake (saki)
entertainer . . **6.** geisha
festival . . **3.** Bon **15.** Feast of Lanterns
fish . . **3.** ayu, tai **4.** fugu
flower arranging . . **7.** ikebano
flower design . . **10.** Shin, Soe, Tai
  (Heaven, Man, Earth)
game (forfeits) . . **3.** ken
gateway . . **5.** torii
girdle . . **3.** obi
girdle box . . **4.** inro
greeting . . **6.** banzai
herb (edible) . . **3.** udo
legislature . . **4.** Diet
litter (covered) . . **7.** norimon
monster (film) . . **8.** Godzilla
news agency . . **5.** domei
newspaper (Tokyo) . . **12.** Asahi Shimbun
outlaw . . **5.** ronin
pagoda . . **3.** taa
painting school . . **4.** Kano
palanquin, litter . . **4.** pago **7.** norimon
paper-folding art . . **7.** origami
partition . . **5.** shoji
persimmon . . **4.** kaki
plant . . **3.** udo (edible) **6.** sugamo
porgy . . **3.** tai (fish)
pottery . . **7.** Satsuma
prefecture . . **2.** fu
radish . . **6.** daikon
religion . . **6.** Shinto **8.** Buddhism
  9. Shintoism
robe . . **6.** kimono
sash . . **3.** obi
salmon . . **4.** masu
screen (partition) . . **5.** shoji
seaweed . . **4.** nori
self-defense, art of . . **4.** judo **7.** jujitsu
  (jujutsu, jiujutsu)
ship suffix . . **4.** maru
shout (greeting) . . **6.** banzai
shrine . . **7.** Toshogu (at Nikko)
silk . . **7.** habutai **8.** chirimen (crepe)
silkworm . . **4.** eria **7.** yamamai
sock (separate big toe) . . **4.** tabi
song . . **3.** uta
suicide . . **7.** seppuku **8.** hara-kiri
  (hari-kari)
tree . . **5.** akeki, kiaki **7.** camphor, hinooki
verse . . **5.** hokku, tanka **6.** haikai
wrestling . . **4.** sumo
Japanese people . . .
  aborigine . . **4.** Ainu (Aino)
  admiral . . **3.** Ito **4.** Togo
  admirer . . **11.** Japanophile
  American-born . . **5.** Issei, Nisei
  army officer . . **7.** samurai
  baron . . **6.** daimio
  Buddha, Great . . **8.** Daibutsu
  caste (nobility) . . **7.** kwazoku
  clan . . **7.** Satsuma **8.** Fujiwara, Minamoto
  deity . . **5.** Amita (Amida) **8.** Amitabba
  Emperor . . **8.** Hirohito
  Emperor, founder . . **5.** Jimmu (660 BC)
  Emperor, title . . **5.** Tenno **6.** Mikado
  God of Happiness . . **7.** Jurojin **10.** Fuku-
  roku ju
  governor . . **6.** shogun
  nobility (caste) . . **7.** kwazoku
  outlaw . . **5.** ronin

J

paradise (of Amita).. **4.** Jodo
race.. **4.** Ainu
jape ... **4.** fool, jeer, jest, jipe, mock
   5. fraud, trick **6.** banter, deride
japery ... **4.** jest, joke **7.** jesting **8.** trickery
   10. buffoonery
jar ... **4.** jolt **5.** grate, shake **6.** incase,
   rattle **7.** startle, vibrate **8.** preserve
   9. vibration
jar ... **3.** jug, urn **4.** ewer, lute (rubber),
   olla **5.** cadus (anc), crock, cruse
   6. dolium, goglet, hydria **7.** amphora,
   terrine **10.** jardiniere
jararaca ... **7.** serpent **10.** fer-de-lance
   11. jararacussu
jardiniere ... **3.** jar, jug, urn **4.** vase
   5. stand (plant) **9.** flowerpot
jargon ... **4.** cant **5.** argot, idiom, lingo,
   slang **6.** drivel, patois, patter, zircon
   7. Chinook, Yiddish **8.** nonsense
   9. gibberish **10.** vocabulary (secret)
jasmine, jasmin ... **4.** bela **5.** color,
   papaw **7.** jessamy **9.** jessamine
Jason (pert to) ...
   friend, sweetheart.. **5.** Medea
   heroes.. **9.** Argonauts
   quest.. **12.** Golden Fleece
   ship.. **4.** Argo
   son.. **5.** Aeson
   uncle.. **6.** Pelias
jaundice ... **7.** disease, icterus **8.** jealousy
   9. prejudice **10.** yellowness
jaunt ... **4.** ride, trip **6.** ramble **7.** journey
   9. excursion
jaunty ... **4.** airy **5.** perky, showy, smart
   6. dapper, rakish **7.** finical, stylish
   12. lighthearted
Java ... see also *Javanese*
   city.. **7.** Batavia, Jakarta (Djakarta)
   8. Samarang, Surabaya **9.** Surakarta
   island group.. **10.** East Indies
   Java Man (anc).. **15.** Pithecanthropus
   (erectus)
   location.. **7.** equator **16.** Malay
   Archipelago
Javanese (pert to) ...
   arrow poison.. **4.** upas
   badger.. **5.** ratel **6.** teledu
   carriage.. **4.** sado (sadoo)
   cotton.. **5.** kapok
   dancers.. **6.** bedoyo
   dog (wild).. **5.** adjag
   ox (wild).. **7.** banteng
   pantomime.. **6.** topeng
   plum.. **5.** jambo (jambul) **6.** lomboy
   puppet show.. **6.** wajang (wayang)
   rice field.. **5.** sawah
   squirrel.. **8.** jelerang
   temple.. **6.** chandi (candi)
   tree.. **4.** upas **5.** ligas **7.** gondang
javelin ... **3.** bat **4.** dart, pike **5.** lance,
   spear **6.** jereed (jirid) **7.** assagai
   (assegai)
javelina ... **4.** boar **7.** peccary
jaw ... **3.** maw **4.** chop **5.** scold **6.** berate,
   splash **7.** chatter, orifice **8.** scolding
jaw (pert to) ...
   angle of.. **6.** gonion
   bone.. **7.** maxilla **8.** mandible
   comb form.. **6.** gnatho
   disease.. **7.** lump jaw **13.** actinomycosis

formation.. **8.** gnathism
Greek for.. **7.** gnathos
muscle.. **8.** masseter
ref to.. **5.** malar **7.** gnathic
without.. **8.** agnathic
jawab ... **5.** reply **6.** answer, mosque
   (false Arch)
jay ... **3.** gae **4.** bird, blue, dupe
   9. chatterer
jayhawker ... **6.** Kansan, spider **7.** soldier
   8. guerilla
Jayhawker State ... **6.** Kansas
jazz ... **4.** jive **5.** dance, music, swing
   9. syncopate **11.** syncopation
jealous ... **7.** envious, zealous **8.** doubtful,
   grudging, vigilant, watchful **9.** jaundiced
   10. solicitous **11.** distrustful
   12. apprehensive
jealousy ... **4.** envy **5.** doubt **7.** rivalry
   8. distrust, jaundice, mistrust
   12. covetousness
jeans ... **8.** overalls, trousers
jeer ... **4.** gibe, hoot, jape, mock **5.** flout,
   scoff, sneer, taunt **6.** deride **8.** ridicule
Jehovah ... **3.** God, Jah **4.** Lord **6.** Yahweh
   (Yahwe) **8.** Almighty (The) **12.** Supreme
   Being
Jehovah's comfort ... **8.** Nehemiah
jehu (humorous) ... **8.** coachman **10.** fast
   driver
Jehu's father (Bib) ... **11.** Jehoshaphat
jejune ... **3.** dry **4.** arid **5.** banal, empty,
   stale, trite **6.** barren, hungry, meager
   7. insipid **8.** foodless **12.** unproductive
jelly ... **3.** jam, rob (rhob) **4.** food, sapa
   5. aspic **6.** pectin **7.** gelatin **8.** gelatine,
   Kei Apple **10.** semiliquid
jellyfish ... **5.** quarl **6.** coward, medusa
   7. acaleph **8.** weakling **9.** Acalephae
jellyfish (pert to) ...
   class.. **9.** Acalephae
   group.. **10.** discophora
   part.. **6.** pileus **8.** umbrella
   10. exumbrella
   stinging.. **9.** sea nettle
   swim organ.. **5.** stene
jemmy ... **4.** boot (riding) **5.** jimmy, lever
   7. crowbar **9.** greatcoat
Jena (Ger) ... **5.** glass **6.** battle (1806)
jenna ... **8.** Paradise (Muslim)
jennet ... **3.** ass **5.** horse **6.** donkey
jenny ... **3.** ass **5.** crane (moving)
   6. female **8.** airplane **13.** spinning
   wheel
jenny (pert to) ...
   billiards.. **6.** hazard
   folklore.. **4.** wren
   howlet.. **3.** owl **5.** owlet
   machine.. **13.** spinning wheel
   spinner.. **3.** fly (angling)
jeopardize ... **4.** risk **6.** expose, hazard
   7. imperil **8.** endanger
jeopardy ... **4.** risk **5.** peril **6.** hazard,
   menace
jeremiad ... **3.** woe **6.** lament, plaint,
   tirade **7.** complaint
jerk ... **3.** tic **4.** flip, jolt, push, yank
   5. shake, tweak **6.** chorea, thrust, twitch
   7. charqui
jerkin ... **4.** coat **6.** jacket, salmon
   9. gyrfalcon, waistcoat

jeroboam . . . **4.** bowl **6.** battle, goblet
Jeroboam . . . **4.** King (of Israel)
jerry . . . **5.** aware **6.** flimsy, Geremy,
German **7.** knowing **9.** beer house,
conscious
jersey . . . **5.** cloth **6.** cattle, jacket
Jersey Red . . . **5.** swine **11.** Duroc-Jersey
Jersey tea . . . **11.** wintergreen
12. checkerberry
Jerusalem . . . **5.** Ariel, Salem **8.** Holy
City **11.** City of David
Jerusalem (pert to) . . .
artichoke . . **7.** girasol **10.** topinambou
capital of . . **6.** Israel
corn . . **5.** durra
Garden . . **10.** Gethsemane
haddock . . **4.** opah
hill . . **6.** Olivet **13.** Mount of Olives
historic site . . **11.** Wailing Wall
12. Mosque of Omar **13.** Mount
of Olives (Olivet) **18.** Garden of
Gethsemane
mosque . . **4.** Omar
pool . . **6.** Siloam **8.** Bethesda
region . . **5.** Perea **6.** Gilead
Relig . . **7.** Judaism **12.** Christianity
13. Mohammedanism
spring . . **5.** Gihon **6.** Siloam
star . . **7.** salsify
Sunday . . **11.** Refreshment
thorn . . **7.** catechu **12.** Christ's-thorn
willow . . **8.** oleaster
jess . . . **5.** strap (hawk's leg) **6.** ribbon
jessamy . . . **3.** fop **5.** dandy **7.** jasmine
jessant (Her) . . . **7.** issuing **9.** lying over
jessur . . . **5.** viper (Russell's)
jest . . . **3.** fun, mot, wit **4.** fool, jape, jeer,
joke, quip **5.** droll, prank, sport, taunt,
trick **6.** banter, rail at, trifle **8.** ridicule
jester . . . **4.** fool, mime **5.** clown
7. buffoon, goliard **8.** humorist
11. merry-andrew
jester's cap . . . **7.** coxcomb
Jesuit . . . **5.** Order **7.** casuist, sectary
8. explorer **9.** intriguer **10.** missionary
14. Society of Jesus (S J)
jet . . . **3.** jut **4.** gush, spew **5.** black,
ebony, ladle, raven, spout, spray, spurt
6. burner, nozzle, stream **7.** mineral,
outpour **8.** spouting **9.** black onyx
jet coal . . . **6.** cannel
jetty . . . **4.** mole, pier **5.** wharf **8.** buttress
Jew . . . **6.** Essene, Hebrew, Semite
9. Israelite
jewel . . . **3.** gem **4.** naif, opal, ruby **5.** beryl,
stone **6.** garnet **7.** bearing, diamond,
emerald **8.** ornament **9.** bespangle,
brilliant **8.** rhinestone **13.** precious
stone, precious thing
jewel cutter . . . **10.** lapidarist
jeweled headdress . . . **5.** tiara **7.** coronet
jeweler's glass . . . **5.** loupe
jeweler's weight . . . **4.** tola **5.** carat
(karat, kerat)
jewelry . . . **3.** ice **4.** ring **5.** paste **6.** parure,
strass **7.** costume **10.** bijouterie
Jewish . . . **6.** Hebrew **7.** Yiddish **9.** Israelite
Jewish (pert to) . . .
academy (Talmudic) . . **8.** Yeshinah
adherent . . **7.** Zionist
benediction . . **5.** Shema

Bible . . **5.** Torah (Tora) **6.** Gemara,
Talmud **7.** Haggada, Halakah
10. Pentateuch
calendar . . **4.** Adar, Ahab, Elul, Iyar
5. Nisan, Sivan, Tebet **6.** Kislev, Shebat,
Tammuz, Tishri, Veadar (leap year)
7. Heshvan
Day of Atonement . . **9.** Yom Kippur
Dispersion . . **8.** Diaspora
divorce . . **3.** get (gett)
doctrine . . **7.** Mishnah (Mishna)
enemy (Bib) . . **5.** Haman
faction . . **7.** Zealots
father, patriarch . . **7.** Abraham
festival . . **5.** Purim, Seder (Sedar)
7. Sukkoth
greeting, peace . . **6.** Shalom
high priest . . **3.** Eli **4.** Ezra **5.** Aaron,
Annas **8.** Caiaphas
high priest costume . . **4.** urim **5.** abnet
7. petalon, tallith, yamilke
historian . . **8.** Josephus
holiday . . **7.** Sukkoth **8.** Hanukkah
(Hannukka), Tishabov **11.** Rosh Hashana
(Rosh Hashonoh)
horn . . **7.** shophar (shofar)
lawgiver . . **5.** Moses
leader . . **8.** Nehemiah
liturgy . . **6.** minhah (PM) **9.** shaharith
(AM)
loaves (unleavened) . . **9.** shewbread
(showbread)
mystical writing . . **6.** atbash
patriots . . **9.** Maccabees
prayer book . . **6.** siddur
prophet . . **6.** Elijah
psalms of praise . . **6.** hallel
quarter (living) . . **6.** ghetto
ram's horn . . **7.** shophar (shofar)
slaughter (Relig) . . **8.** shehitah
song (Zionist anthem) . . **8.** Hatikvah
(Hattikvah)
jew's harp . . . **8.** guimbard **9.** crembalum
Jezebel (pert to) . . .
epithet . . **5.** vixen **6.** virago **8.** strumpet
father . . **7.** Ethbaal
husband . . **4.** Ahab (King)
murdered (caused to be) . . **6.** Naboth
jib . . . **3.** gib, jaw **4.** balk, boom, sail,
spar, tack **5.** crane, shift **6.** fleece
8. underlip
jibe . . . **3.** fit **4.** gibe **5.** agree, shift
9. harmonize
jiff, jiffy . . . **5.** trice **6.** moment **7.** instant,
quickly **9.** instantly, twinkling
jig . . . **4.** jerk, jolt **5.** dance **6.** ballad,
twitch **8.** fishhook
jigger . . . **4.** club, dram
jiggle . . . **5.** sauce, shake
jimmy . . . **3.** pry **5.** handy, smart
6. spruce **7.** coal car, crowbar, pry
open **10.** sheep's head
jimson weed . . . **6.** dature
10. stramonium, thorn apple **11.** apple
of Peru
jingle . . . **4.** poem, rime **5.** clink, rhyme
6. tinkle **13.** two-wheeled car
jinn, jinnee . . . **5.** demon, Eblis, genie
6. afreet **8.** jenniyeh
jinx . . . **3.** hex **5.** Jonah **6.** hoodoo,
whammy

jitters . . . **6.** nerves **7.** dithers, fidgets **8.** trembles

jittery . . . **4.** edgy **5.** jumpy **7.** nervous

jivatma (Hind) . . . **4.** soul **9.** life force **10.** life energy **11.** human spirit

Joan of Arc's appellation . . . **7.** pucelle **13.** Maid of Orleans

job . . . **3.** act **4.** hire, task **5.** chare, chore, stint **8.** position, sinecure

Job (pert to) . . .
Book . . **9.** patriarch **12.** Old Testament
friend . . **6.** Zophar
home . . **2.** Uz
literally . . **9.** afflicted **10.** persecuted

jockey . . . **3.** pad **5.** cheat, racer, rider **6.** outwit **7.** cushion **8.** cavalier, horseman, minstrel, vagabond **9.** Earl Sande (famed)

jocose . . . **3.** dry **5.** droll, lepid, merry **7.** jocular **8.** humorous **9.** facetious

jocular . . . **3.** gay **4.** airy, loco **5.** droll, funny, merry, witty **6.** elated, jocund, lively, ribald **7.** comical, festive, gleeful, jesting, playful, waggish **8.** animated, mirthful **9.** convivial, facetious, hilarious, laughable, vivacious **10.** frolicsome

jocund . . . **3.** gay **4.** airy **5.** merry **6.** lively **7.** jocular **8.** cheerful, sportive

jog . . . **4.** gait, jolt, lope, plod, push, trot, walk **6.** canter, notify, remind, trudge **8.** slow pace **9.** suggest to

John . . . **3.** Ian **4.** Ivan, Jack, Juan **8.** Chinaman, Johannes **9.** policeman

John (pert to) . . .
Bull . . **10.** Englishman
Company . . **9.** East India
Crow . . **7.** buzzard (turkey)
Doe (law) . . **7.** unknown **9.** false name
Hancock . . **9.** autograph, signature
Q Public . . **6.** people **8.** populace

johnnycake . . . **4.** pone **7.** hoecake **9.** corn bread

join . . . **3.** add, mix, pin, tie, wed **4.** ally, fuse, link, lock, meet, pair, seam, team, weld, yoke **5.** annex, blend, enter, graft, group, hitch, marry, merge, unite **6.** adjoin, attach, cement, concur, couple, engage, enlist, fasten, mingle, solder, splice, suture, syzygy **7.** combine, conjoin, connect **8.** assemble, coalesce, compound **9.** associate **11.** incorporate

joint . . . **3.** ell, hip **4.** dive (sl), knee, node, seam **5.** alula, elbow, hinge, miter, nexus, tenon, wrist **6.** rabbet, resort **7.** hangout, pastern **8.** coupling, dovetail **12.** articulation

joint (pert to) . . .
cavity . . **5.** bursa
firs . . **7.** ephedra
fluid . . **7.** synovia **8.** synovial
grass stem . . **4.** culm
pert to . . **5.** nodal **9.** articular
put out of . . **6.** lucate **9.** dislocate
without . . **10.** acondylous

joke . . . **3.** fun, gag, pun **4.** fool, hoax, jape, jest, quip **5.** prank, rally, sport **6.** banter, humbug **7.** bromide **8.** chestnut, one-liner

joker . . . **3.** dor, wag, wit **4.** card

7. buffoon, farceur, gagster **8.** humorist **9.** mistigris

jollity . . . **4.** jest **5.** mirth **6.** gaiety **8.** hilarity **9.** enjoyment, festivity, joviality, merriment **12.** conviviality

jolly . . . **6.** banter, jovial, joyful, mellow **7.** flatter, jocular **9.** make merry

Jolly Roger . . . **5.** Roger **10.** pirate flag

jolt . . . **3.** jar, jig, jut **4.** blow, butt, stun **5.** shake, shock **6.** jostle, jounce **7.** startle **8.** astonish, jail term (thieves)

Jonah (pert to) . . .
Bib . . **7.** prophet (Heb)
Book . . **12.** Old Testament
slang . . **4.** jinx
swallowed by . . **5.** whale

Jordan . . .
capital . . **5.** Amman
city . . **7.** Jericho, Samaria **9.** Bethlehem
historic trove . . **14.** Dead Sea Scrolls
official name . . **9.** Hashemite (The)
people (anc) . . **7.** Essenes
region . . **5.** Perea **6.** Basham
river . . **6.** Jordan

Jorth (pert to) . . .
goddess . . **5.** Earth
husband . . **4.** Odin
named also . . **6.** Forgyn
son . . **4.** Thor

Joseph (pert to) . . .
Bib . . **9.** patriarch
buyer of . . **8.** Potiphar
coat of . . **10.** many colors
father . . **5.** Jacob
mother . . **6.** Rachel
son . . **5.** Jesus **7.** Ephraim

josh . . . **3.** guy, kid **5.** chaff, spoof, tease **6.** banter

Joshi (Ind) . . . **10.** astrologer, astronomer

Joshua (pert to) . . .
associate . . **5.** Caleb
Book . . **12.** Old Testament
burial place . . **5.** Gaash
successor to . . **5.** Moses
tree . . **5.** yucca

jostle . . . **4.** jolt, push, rush **5.** crowd, elbow, joust, shake, shove **6.** hustle, joggle, jounce, thrust

jot . . . **3.** ace, bit **4.** atom, iota, item, mite, whit **5.** minim, point, speck **6.** tittle **7.** smidgen **8.** particle

jouk . . . **4.** dart, duck, fawn, hide **5.** cheat, dodge, evade, perch, roost, skulk **6.** cringe **9.** obeisance

Joule, James P . . . **9.** physicist

journal . . . **3.** log **5.** diary, paper **6.** record **7.** daybook, diurnal, logbook, support **8.** magazine, register **9.** chronicle **10.** periodical **11.** account book

journalist . . . **6.** editor, legman **7.** newsman **8.** reporter **9.** columnist, gazetteer **11.** interviewer **13.** correspondent

journey . . . **3.** run **4.** fare, iter, ride, tour, trek, trip, wend **5.** jaunt **6.** travel, voyage **7.** odyssey **8.** traverse **9.** excursion **10.** expedition, pilgrimage **13.** peregrination

journey (pert to) . . . **4.** eyre (circuit) **6.** viatic **8.** anabasis (upward) **9.** itineracy, itinerary, traveling

10. travelling
joust . . . **4.** bout, spar, tilt **6.** combat
10. tournament
Jove . . . **7.** Jupiter
jovial . . . **5.** jolly, merry **6.** elated,
joyous **7.** festive, jocular **8.** Jovelike
9. convivial, hilarious **14.** mirth-inspiring
jowl . . . **3.** jaw **4.** chop **5.** cheek **6.** dewlap,
wattle **7.** jawbone
joy . . . **4.** glee **5.** bliss, exult, gelid **6.** gaiety
7. delight, ecstasy, rapture, rejoice
8. felicity, gladness, hilarity, pleasure
9. beatitude, happiness, merriment,
transport **10.** exultation **12.** exhilaration
joyous . . . **3.** gay **4.** glad **5.** happy, merry
6. blithe, elated, festal, joyful **7.** festive,
gleeful, jocular **8.** cheerful, mirthful
jubilant . . . **6.** elated **8.** exultant, exulting
9. overjoyed, rejoicing **10.** triumphant
Judah (pert to) . . .
ancestry . . **12.** tribe of Judah
brother . . **4.** Levi **6.** Reuben, Simeon
father . . **5.** Jacob
kingdom . . **9.** Palestine
son . . **2.** Er **6.** Shelah
translation (Heb) . . **10.** celebrated
Judas (pert to) . . .
Bible . . **7.** apostle, traitor **8.** betrayer,
deceiver, disciple
called . . **8.** Iscariot
historic . . **13.** Paschal candle
kiss . . **8.** betrayal **11.** double-cross,
treacherous
priest . . **4.** oath
suicide site . . **8.** Aceldama
Judea (pert to) . . .
governor . . **6.** Pilate
king . . **3.** Asa **6.** Herod **7.** Jehoram
11. Jehoshaphat
location . . **5.** Berea
people . . **4.** Jews
province of . . **9.** Palestine
judge . . . **3.** try **4.** deem, rate **5.** opine,
think **6.** critic, puisne **7.** arbiter,
referee, suppose **8.** deemster, estimate,
mediator, sentence **9.** arbitrate, criticize
10. adjudicate, magistrate
11. connoisseur
judge (pert to) . . .
bench . . **4.** banc (bancus)
chamber . . **6.** camera
circuit . . **4.** iter
gavel . . **4.** mace
group . . **5.** bench **9.** judiciary
of the dead . . **6.** Osiris
opinion . . **12.** obiter dictum
sittings . . **7.** assizes
summary . . **6.** postea
judgment . . . **4.** doom **5.** arrêt, award,
sense, taste **7.** censure, opinion
8. decision, judicium, sentence
9. criticism **10.** conclusion, discretion,
persuasion (Relig), punishment
11. arbitration, sensibility
judgment (pert to) . . .
creditor . . **13.** quasi contract
day . . **7.** last day **8.** Dies Irae, doomsday
left to one's . . **13.** discretionary
note . . **10.** promissory
seat . . **3.** bar **5.** mercy **8.** tribunal,
woolsack

judicial . . . **5.** legal **8.** critical **9.** judicious
10. judicatory
judicial (pert to) . . .
council . . **5.** cabal, junta, junto **7.** coterie
hearing . . **5.** trial
order . . **4.** writ **6.** elegit, venire **7.** precept
security . . **7.** custody
judicious . . . **4.** wise **7.** politic, prudent
8. cautious, discreet **9.** sagacious
10. discerning **11.** circumspect, well-
advised
jug . . . **4.** ewer, jail, olpe, toby **5.** askos,
buire, cruse, gotch **6.** flagon, gomlah,
lockup, prison, tinaja, urceus **7.** pitcher
13. Schnabelkanne
Juggernaut . . . **6.** Vishnu (Hind)
juggler . . . **5.** cheat, trick **7.** buffoon
8. deceiver **13.** sleight of hand
14. legerdemainist
Jugoslavia, Yugoslavia . . .
area . . **6.** Kosovo **8.** Dalmatia
brandy . . **5.** rakia **9.** slivovitz
capital . . **8.** Belgrade
language . . **7.** Slovene **10.** Macedonian,
Serbo-Croat
leader . . **4.** Tito
monarch . . **5.** Peter
money . . **5.** dinar
organization . . **5.** Comitadji
people . . **4.** Serb **5.** Croat **7.** Slovene
juice . . . **3.** rob, sap **4.** milk (plant),
must, stum **5.** fluid, latex, syrup
(sirup) **7.** essence, hebenon, moisten
10. succulence **11.** electricity
jujitsu, jiujitsu . . . **11.** self-defense
juju . . . **5.** charm, magic **6.** amulet, belief,
fetish, voodoo
jujube . . . **3.** ber **5.** fruit, jelly **7.** lozenge
8. Zizyphus
Jules Verne's captain . . . **4.** Nemo (the
Nautilus)
Julian Emperors (first Five) . . . **4.** Nero
8. Augustus, Caligula, Claudius, Tiberius
jumble . . . **2.** pi **3.** mix **4.** cake, hash, heap,
mess, raff, stir **5.** blend, botch, chaos,
shake **6.** medley, muddle **7.** agitate,
confuse, mixture **8.** disorder, riffraff
jumble type . . . **3.** pie (pi)
jump . . . **3.** hop, lep **4.** leap, move
(checkers) **5.** bound, caper, halma, salto,
scold, start, vault **6.** chorea, escape,
hurdle, spring, twitch **7.** saltary, saltate
8. increase **9.** advantage **10.** transition
jumping (pert to) . . .
adjective . . **7.** saltant
Frog, tale by . . **9.** Mark Twain
music . . **7.** saltato
rodent . . **5.** mouse **6.** jerboa **11.** kangaroo
rat
stick . . **4.** pogo, pole
junction . . . **4.** axil, seam **5.** union
6. suture **7.** joining, meeting
11. combination, concurrence
juncture . . . **4.** pass **5.** joint, pinch **6.** crisis,
strait **8.** exigency, quandary
9. emergency **10.** connection
11. conjuncture, predicament
12. articulation
June bug . . . **3.** dor **6.** beetle, May bug
8. figeater
jungle . . . **4.** camp **7.** thicket **8.** woodland

11. dense growth 12. complication
jungle (pert to) . . .
  dweller . . **5.** beast **6.** savage
  fever . . **7.** malaria
  grass . . **3.** poa
  ox . . **4.** gaur **5.** gayal **7.** timarau
  sheep . . **7.** muntjac
junior . . . **5.** cadet, petty **6.** puisne,
  recent **7.** student, younger **8.** inferior
  9. unskilled
juniper . . . **4.** cade, puny **5.** cedar, gorse,
  retem (raetem), savin
junket . . . **4.** dish (milk), food, meal
  5. feast **7.** banquet **8.** festival
  9. excursion, sweetmeat
Juno (pert to) . . .
  consort . . **7.** Jupiter
  goddess (Rom) . . **3.** sky **5.** light
  identified with . . **4.** Hera
  messenger . . **4.** Iris
junta, junto . . . **5.** cabal **6.** circle, clique
  7. coterie, council, faction **8.** intrigue
  11. combination
jupe . . . **4.** coat **5.** jupon, shirt, skirt, tunic
  6. bodice, jacket
Jupiter (pert to) . . .
  angel . . **7.** Zadkiel
  astronomy . . **6.** planet (largest)
  daughter . . **4.** Bura
  deity . . **4.** Jove **9.** Father Sky
  festival . . **14.** Vinalis sustica
  god of . . **7.** Heavens
  heraldry . . **5.** azure
  lover . . **2.** Io
  son . . **6.** Castor, Pollux
  triad . . **4.** Juno **7.** Minerva
  wife . . **4.** Juno
Jupiter, god of . . .
  law . . **6.** Fidius **10.** Dius Fidius
  lightning . . **6.** Fulgur
  rain . . **7.** Pluvius
  thunder . . **6.** Tonans
jurat . . . **5.** juror **8.** recorder **10.** magistrate
  (Channel Isis)
jure . . . **3.** jus (ius), law **5.** right
  13. jurisprudence
jurisprudence . . . **3.** law, soc **4.** soke

5. power (legal) **6.** charge, sphere
7. control, custody, emirate **9.** authority,
consulate **10.** government, judicature,
patriarchy
juror . . . **6.** dicast **7.** assizer, juryman
  9. venireman
jury . . . **5.** panel, tales (additions) **6.** venire
jus . . . **3.** law **5.** gravy, juice **10.** legal
  power, legal right
just . . . **4.** fair, tilt **5.** equal, exact, valid
  7. logical, upright **8.** provided, unbiased
  9. equitable, righteous **10.** legitimate
just begun . . . **8.** inchoate
justice . . . **4.** doom **5.** right **6.** equity,
  virtue **8.** fairness, fair play, justness
  9. rectitude **10.** judicature **11.** give and
  take **12.** rightfulness
justice of the peace . . . **6.** squire
  10. magistrate
justification . . . **7.** apology, defense
  11. vindication
justify . . . **5.** clear **6.** defend, excuse
  7. absolve, support, warrant **8.** maintain,
  sanction, underpin **9.** authorize,
  exculpate, vindicate **12.** substantiate
justly . . . **5.** truly **6.** fairly **7.** equally
  8. honestly **9.** equitably **10.** deservedly
justness . . . **7.** fitness, justice **8.** accuracy,
  validity **9.** exactness **11.** correctness
Justus . . . **4.** just
jute . . . **5.** fiber, gunny **6.** burlap **7.** sacking
Jute . . . **4.** Dane **9.** Jutlander
jutty . . . **4.** mole, pier **5.** jetty **7.** project
  8. buttress, protrude
juvenile . . . **5.** actor, young, youth
  8. immature, youthful **9.** youngling,
  youthlike **11.** undeveloped
juvia . . . **9.** Brazil nut
juxta . . . **4.** near **6.** nearby
juxtaposition . . . **5.** touch **7.** contact
  8. nearness **9.** proximity **10.** contiguity,
  side by side
jynx . . . **5.** charm, spell **7.** wryneck
  10. woodpecker
Jynx . . . **11.** woodpeckers
J'y suis, j'y reste . . . **18.** I am here;
  here I remain

K

K . . . **5.** kappa (Gr) **6.** letter (11th)
Ka . . . **3.** God (Hind)
Kaaba, Caaba (pert to) . . .
  content . . **10.** Black Stone (of Mecca)
  location . . **11.** Great Mosque (Mecca)
  pilgrimage . . **7.** Islamic
  praying direction . . **6.** Kiblah
  shape . . **7.** cubical
kaama . . . **10.** hartebeest
kachina worshipper . . . **4.** Hopi, Zuni
  6. Pueblo
Kaddish . . . **8.** Doxology
Kadiak, Kodiak, bear . . . **5.** brown

  7. Alaskan
Kaiser brown . . . **6.** ginger
Kaiser's residence . . . **5.** Doorn
kaka . . . **6.** parrot
kakapo . . . **6.** parrot **9.** owl parrot
kakar . . . **7.** muntjac
kakariki . . . **6.** lizard
kaki . . . **5.** stilt (bird) **9.** persimmon
kakkak . . . **5.** heron **7.** bittern
kakke . . . **8.** beriberi
kala . . . **6.** bulbul (bird)
kale . . . **4.** cole **5.** money **7.** cabbage,
  collard **8.** colewort, corecole

kaleidoscopic . . . **7.** varying
   10. changeable, variegated
Kali (pert to) . . .
  Hindu . . **10.** evil genius
  Persian . . **6.** carpet
  Vedic Myth . . **12.** tongue of Agni
   (fire-god)
kallah . . . **5.** bride (Jew)
kamavachara . . . **6.** heaven (Buddh)
Kamchatka . . .
  capital . . **13.** Petropavlovsk
  peninsula . . **7.** Siberia
  people . . **7.** Russian **9.** Mongolian
  sea . . **6.** Bering **7.** Okhotsk
Kamehameha Day . . . **7.** holiday (Haw)
Kamerad . . . **7.** comrade **9.** surrender
kamik . . . **12.** sealskin boot
Kammerspiel . . . **5.** drama **7.** theater
Kanaka . . . **3.** man **8.** Hawaiian
  10. Melanesian, Polynesian **16.** South
   Sea islander
Kanaloa . . . **3.** God (Pantheon)
kangaroo (pert to) . . .
  class . . **9.** marsupial
  family . . **12.** Macropodidae
  female . . **3.** doe, gin, 'roo
  giant . . **8.** forester
  leaping . . **6.** jeroba **7.** bettong (bettonga)
  male . . **5.** bilby (bilbi)
  rat . . **7.** pototoo
  reference to . . **7.** wallaby
   11. macropodine
  small . . **7.** wallaby
  young . . **4.** joey
kangaroo court . . . **9.** mock court, moot
  court **14.** irregular court
Kansas . . .
  capital . . **6.** Topeka
  city . . **5.** Dodge **7.** Abilene, Wichita
   10. Hutchinson, Kansas City
   11. Leavenworth
  Eisenhower home . . **7.** Abilene
  military post . . **9.** Fort Riley
  penitentiary . . **11.** Leavenworth
  State admission . . **12.** Thirty-fourth
  State motto . . **16.** Ad Astra per Aspera
   (To the Stars Through Difficulties)
  State nickname . . **9.** Sunflower
kapok tree . . . **7.** God tree **9.** Ceiba tree
  10. silk-cotton
kappa . . . **1.** K (Gr) **4.** star **6.** letter (10th)
karakul, karakule . . . **5.** sheep
  9. astrakhan, broadtail
karma . . . **4.** fate **7.** destiny **8.** casualty
Kartvelian people . . . **4.** Svan (Svane)
  9. Georgians **10.** Imeritians, Svanetians
kasha . . . **4.** mush (Russ)
Kashmir, India . . .
  alphabet . . **6.** Sarada
  capital . . **8.** Srinagar
  deer . . **6.** hangul
  official . . **6.** pundit
Kashyapa (Vedic Myth) . . . **8.** tortoise
Kaskaskia . . . **5.** epoch **6.** Indian
  10. Algonquian
kat . . . **5.** shrub **8.** narcotic
katar . . . **6.** dagger
katchung . . . **6.** peanut
katogle . . . **8.** eagle owl
kava, kavakava . . . **6.** Kawaka, pepper
kayak . . . **5.** canoe

kea . . . **6.** parrot
Keat's poem . . . **8.** Endymion, Hyperion
keek . . . **3.** spy (of rival fashions) **6.** peeper
keel . . . **4.** cool, seel, ship, skeg, tilt
  6. careen, ruddle, timber (ship's)
  7. capsize **8.** overturn, red ocher, turn
  over **10.** guinea fowl
keelbill, keelbird . . . **3.** ani
keeling . . . **7.** codfish
keel-shaped . . . **6.** carina **7.** carinal
keen . . . **4.** avid, cute, gare, good, nice,
  tart **5.** acute, alert, eager, sharp, smart,
  snell, vivid, witty **6.** astute, bitter,
  clever, shrewd, shrill **7.** caustic, fervent
  9. sensitive, trenchant **11.** acrimonious,
  penetrating
keenness . . . **4.** edge **5.** acies (of sight),
  nifty **6.** acuity, acumen **8.** acrimony,
  pungency **9.** acuteness, eagerness,
  sharpness, smartness, wittiness
keep . . . **4.** save **6.** detain, retain
  7. confine, custody, fulfill, husband,
  reserve **8.** conserve, maintain, preserve,
  restrain, withhold **14.** accommodations
keep (pert to) . . .
  account . . **5.** score
  afloat . . **4.** buoy
  apart . . **7.** seclude **8.** separate
  back, out . . **3.** bar, dam **4.** save **5.** debar,
   delay **6.** detain, except, hinder, retard
   7. exclude, reserve **8.** restrain, withhold
  from . . **5.** avoid, delay **7.** abstain, boycott,
   prevent
  hidden . . **7.** secrete
  in . . **6.** retain
  off . . **4.** fend **7.** prevent, repulse, ward
   off
  on . . **6.** endure **9.** persevere
keeper . . . **5.** guard **6.** warden **9.** constable,
  custodian, possessor **10.** maintainer
keeper of . . .
  birds . . **8.** aviarist
  borders . . **8.** margrave
  door . . **5.** tiler
  elephant . . **6.** mahout
  golden apples (Myth) . . **6.** Ithunn (Ithun)
  parks . . **6.** ranger
  prison . . **6.** gaoler, jailer, jailor, warden
   7. turnkey
keeping . . . **4.** care **5.** board, guard, trust
  7. custody **8.** tutelage **9.** retention
  10. caretaking, conformity, possession,
  preserving, protection **11.** maintenance
  12. guardianship
keeve . . . **3.** tub **4.** tuft **5.** knoll, plume
  8. haystack
kef . . . **6.** dreamy **7.** languor **12.** tranquillity
  (tranquility)
keg . . . **3.** tun, vat **4.** cade, cask **6.** firkin
kelly . . . **5.** derby, killy (fish)
kelp . . . **4.** game **5.** sight, wrack **7.** insight,
  seaweed **9.** water lily
ken . . . **4.** lore **9.** recognize **10.** cognizance,
  prescience **13.** understanding
Kentish freedman . . . **4.** laet
Kentucky . . .
  bluegrass . . **3.** poa
  capital . . **9.** Frankfort
  city . . **7.** Paducah **9.** Lexington
   10. Louisville **12.** Bowling Green
  famed road . . **15.** Wilderness Trail

K

famed sights . . **7.** Obelisk (J Davis)
  8. Fort Knox, Log Cabin (Lincoln)
  11. Federal Hill (My Old Ky Home),
  Mammoth Cave
famed sport . . **13.** Kentucky Derby
  (Churchill Downs)
mountain . . **4.** Pine **10.** Cumberland
pioneer . . **11.** Daniel Boone
river . . **4.** Ohio **10.** Cumberland
State admission . . **9.** Fifteenth
State name meaning (Indian) . .
  8. tomorrow
State nickname . . **9.** Bluegrass
Kenya . . .
  capital . . **7.** Nairobi
  leader . . **3.** Moi **8.** Kenyatta
  mountain, volcano . . **5.** Kenya
  people . . **5.** Masai **6.** Kikuyu
  secret society . . **6.** Mau Mau
kept . . . see keep
ker (Gr) . . . **4.** doom, fate **5.** ghost **6.** spirit
kermis, kermess . . . **4.** fair **8.** festival
kernel . . . **3.** nut **4.** core, gist, meat, pith,
  seed **5.** grain, heart **6.** acinus, nutmeg
  7. nucleus
ketch . . . **4.** Jack, saic, ship **6.** vessel
ketone . . . **5.** irone **6.** carone **7.** acetone,
  camphor **8.** deguelin
kettle . . . **3.** pot **4.** drum, pail **6.** kibble
  7. caldron **8.** cauldron **9.** teakettle
  10. kettledrum
kettledrum . . . **4.** drum **5.** naker, tabor
  6. atabal **7.** anacara **8.** tympanon
key . . . **4.** clue, crib, isle, quay, reef,
  tone **5.** islet, pitch, tasto **6.** clavis,
  cotter, fasten, island, opener, switch,
  tapper **7.** digital **8.** mainstay, solution
  11. explanation, fundamental,
  translation
keyed up . . . **4.** agog **5.** eager, fired
  7. aroused, stirred **8.** hopped up,
  worked up **10.** stimulated
Keys, House of . . . **9.** Isle of Man, officials
Keystone State . . . **12.** Pennsylvania
khan . . . **3.** inn **4.** lord **6.** prince
  9. resthouse **11.** caravansary
kiang . . . **5.** diver **6.** onager **7.** wild ass
kick . . . **4.** blow, boot, funk, punt
  6. energy, object, thrill **7.** grumble,
  protest **8.** complain, pungency, sixpence
  9. complaint **10.** calcitrate, enthusiasm
Kickapoo . . . **6.** Indian **10.** Algonquian
kickshaw . . . **3.** toy **6.** trifle **7.** trinket
  8. delicacy
kid . . . **3.** guy **4.** fool, goat, hoax, joke,
  josh, twit **5.** child, jolly, suede **6.** banter,
  humbug **8.** antelope (young), yeanling
  9. youngling
kidang . . . **4.** deer **7.** muntjac
kidney . . . **4.** neer **5.** gland, reins
  7. nephros
kidney (pert to) . . .
  comb form . . **6.** nephro
  disease . . **7.** nephria **9.** nephritis
  pyramid . . **9.** reniculus
  reference to . . **4.** reni **5.** renal **6.** vitals
  7. nephric
  shaped . . **8.** reniform
  stone . . **6.** pebble **8.** nephrite
kiki . . . **14.** castor oil plant
kill . . . **4.** slay, veto **5.** blast, creek **6.** defeat,

murder **7.** channel, destroy, execute,
  silence **8.** dispatch, immolate, lapidate,
  massacre, overbeat **9.** slaughter
  11. assassinate, exterminate
killer . . . **4.** Cain **6.** gunman, slayer
  7. butcher **8.** cannibal, man-eater,
  mongoose, murderer **9.** cutthroat
  12. assassinator
killer whale . . . **3.** orc **4.** orca **7.** grampus
killing . . . **5.** fatal **6.** deadly, murder
  7. amusing, carnage, cleanup
  (speculation), garrote **8.** homicide
  9. execution **10.** euthanasia
  11. captivating **12.** overpowering
killing of . . .
  brother . . **10.** fratricide
  cats . . **8.** felicide
  father . . **9.** patricide
  man . . **8.** homicide
  mother . . **9.** matricide
  old men (tribal) . . **8.** senicide
  self . . **7.** suicide **9.** martyrdom
  sister . . **10.** sororicide
  wolf . . **8.** lupicide
kiln . . . **4.** oast, oven **5.** clamp, stove,
  tiler **7.** furnace
kilo (pref) . . . **8.** thousand
kind . . . **3.** ilk **4.** good, race, sort, type
  5. class, genre, genus, order, seely,
  style **6.** benign, gender, humane,
  loving, strain **7.** kindred, lenient, species
  8. gracious **9.** benignant **10.** benevolent
  11. sympathetic **12.** well-disposed
kindle . . . **4.** burn, fire **5.** brood, light,
  rouse, young **6.** excite, ignite, incite,
  litter **7.** animate, inflame, provoke
kindly . . . **4.** mild **6.** benign, blithe, genial,
  humane **7.** natural **8.** benignly, heartily
  9. agreeably, benignant, indulgent
  10. beneficent, legitimate, pleasantly
  11. sympathetic
kindness . . . **5.** favor **8.** clemency,
  goodness, humanity, mildness
  9. benignity **10.** compassion, generosity,
  gentleness, indulgency, tenderness
kindred . . . **3.** sib, tie **4.** akin, clan, kith
  5. blood **6.** allied, family **7.** cognate,
  descent, kinship, kinsmen, related
  8. kinsfolk **9.** relations **12.** relationship
  14. consanguineous
kine . . . **4.** cows **5.** cattle
kinetic . . . **6.** active, moving
king . . . **3.** rex, rey, roi **4.** rank **5.** chief,
  ruler **6.** master **7.** regulus **8.** chessman
  9. potentate, sovereign
king (pert to) . . .
  beasts . . **4.** lion
  birds . . **5.** eagle
  chamber . . **9.** camarilla
  cheeses . . **4.** Brie
  child . . **6.** prince **8.** princess
  dwarfs . . **8.** Alberich (Ger)
  fairies . . **6.** Oberon
  family . . **7.** dynasty
  gods . . **7.** Jupiter
  heaven . . **3.** God **6.** Christ
  herrings . . **4.** opah **7.** oarfish **8.** chimaera
  mackerel . . **4.** cero
  March (The) . . **5.** Sousa
  metals . . **4.** gold
  monkeys . . **7.** gureza

murder of.. **8.** regicide
myth.. **4.** Atli **5.** Midas
myth (classical).. **4.** Zeus **7.** Jupiter
rivers.. **6.** Amazon
serpents (race of).. **6.** Shesha (Sesha)
symbol.. **7.** scepter (sceptre)
vultures.. **4.** papa
waters.. **7.** Neptune, Pacific
Woods (The).. **13.** Rex Nemorensis
King Arthur (pert to)...
abode.. **6.** Avalon **7.** Camelot
battleground (fatal).. **6.** Camlan
father.. **8.** Uther (Pendragon)
home.. **8.** Caerleon (on the Usk)
Knights of the Round Table.. **3.** Kay
  6. Gawain **7.** Galahad **8.** Lancelot,
  Tristram (Tristan) **9.** Percivale
Lady of the Lake.. **6.** Vivian
magician.. **6.** Merlin
Queen.. **9.** Guinevere
quest of.. **9.** Holy Grail (The)
shield.. **7.** Pridwin
sister.. **11.** Morgan le Fay
son.. **7.** Mordred (Modred)
sword.. **9.** Excalibur
kingdom ... **5.** realm **6.** empire, estate
  8. dominion, kingship, monarchy
kingdom (pert to)...
ancient.. **4.** Elam, Moab
Asia.. **5.** Nepal
between Spain, France.. **7.** Navarra
  (Navarre)
confusion.. **5.** Babel
divisions.. **6.** animal **7.** mineral
  9. vegetable
Indo-China.. **5.** Annam (Anam)
kingfish ... **4.** cero, haku, opah **7.** kingpin,
  pintado **8.** big wheel **9.** threadfin
kingly ... **5.** grand, noble, regal, royal
  6. august **7.** leonine **8.** imperial,
  majestic, princely **9.** dignified, sovereign
  11. monarchical
King of ...
Albania.. **3.** Zog
Bashan.. **2.** Og
Bulgaria.. **5.** Boris
Greece (anc).. **9.** Agamemnon
Israel.. **4.** Ahab, Jehy, Saul **5.** David
  7. Solomon **8.** Jeroboam
Judea.. **3.** Asa
Kings.. **3.** God **6.** Christ
Men.. **4.** Odin, Zeus **7.** Jupiter
Oriental.. **11.** King of Kings
Persia (Iran).. **5.** Cyrus **6.** Xerxes
Troy.. **5.** Priam
Tyre.. **5.** Hiram
Visigoths.. **6.** Alaric
Kipling, Rudyard (pert to)...
award.. **10.** Nobel Prize (1907)
birthplace.. **6.** Bombay
book.. **3.** Kim **10.** Jungle Book
poem (for Queen Victoria)..
  11. Recessional
kissing, science ... **13.** philematology
knee (pert to)...
bend.. **9.** genuflect
bent.. **10.** geniculate
bone.. **6.** rotula **7.** kneepan, patella
britches.. **6.** smalls **8.** knickers
on bended.. **7.** humbled **8.** obeisant
  10. submissive, worshipful

12. supplicatory
kneeling desk ... **8.** prie-dieu
knew ... see know
Knickerbocker, Father ... **9.** New Yorker
  (Hist)
knickknack ... **3.** toy **6.** bauble, gewgaw,
  trifle **7.** trinket **8.** gimcrack
knife ... **4.** bolo, snee, stab **5.** corer,
  prune **6.** cutter, weapon
knife (pert to)...
Burmese.. **3.** dah
Hindu.. **5.** kukri
Irish.. **5.** skean **8.** skean dhu
Malay.. **4.** kris **6.** barong, creese
New Zealand.. **4.** patu
one-bladed.. **6.** barlow
Scottish.. **4.** dirk
Spanish.. **7.** machete
surgical.. **7.** scalpel **10.** greffotome
Turkish.. **8.** yataghan (yatagan)
US Navy.. **7.** cutlass
knife maker ... **6.** cutler
knife-throwing game ...
  11. mumbletypeg **12.** mumble-the-peg
knight (pert to)...
adventure.. **8.** errantry
adventurer.. **8.** cavalier **9.** caballero,
  chevalier
cloak.. **6.** tabard
combat.. **5.** joust
ensign.. **8.** gonfalon, gonfanon
errant.. **7.** Paladin
hero.. **7.** Paladin
servant.. **4.** page **6.** varlet
title.. **3.** Sir **8.** banneret
wife.. **4.** Dame, Lady
wreath (with crest).. **4.** orle
Knight of the Round Table ... **3.** Kay
  6. Gawain **7.** Galahad **8.** Lancelot,
  Tristram (Tristan) **9.** Percivale
Knight of the Rueful Countenance ...
  10. Don Quixote
knit ... **4.** bind, heal, join, seam **5.** plait,
  unite, woven **6.** cement, couple, fasten
  7. conjoin, connect, wrinkle **8.** contract
  9. interlace **11.** consolidate
knitting machine guide ... **4.** sley
knitting stitch ... **4.** knit, purl
knob ... **3.** nub **4.** boss, head, hill, lump,
  node, stud, umbo **5.** bulge, knurl
  6. croche (antler), pommel **8.** tubercle
  12. protuberance
knobkerrie ... **4.** club, kiri **5.** stick
knock ... **3.** hit, rap, tap **4.** bang, bash,
  beat, bump, dash, glow, hill, pass,
  slay, snop **5.** pound, thump **6.** hammer,
  jostle, strike **7.** collide **9.** criticism,
  criticize, disparage **12.** faultfinding
knock (pert to)...
about.. **6.** travel, wander
down.. **4.** fell, raze **6.** deject, strike
  8. vanquish
off.. **3.** die **6.** deduct, recess **9.** improvise
out.. **2.** KO **4.** kayo
knocking ... **6.** rat-tat **7.** rapping, tapping
  9. rat-tat-tat
knock-knee ... **6.** in-knee
knoll ... **4.** bank, clod, hill, knap, knob,
  lump **5.** bunch, hurst, knell, mound
  7. hillock
knot ... **3.** bow, nep, tie **4.** burl, knar,

knob, knur, lump, node, noil, snag
5. gnarl, noose **6.** clique, nodule,
tangle **7.** dilemma, lanyard, problem,
rosette **9.** sandpiper **10.** sheepshank
12. complication, protuberance
knotted ... **3.** nep **5.** noded, nowed (Her)
6. knotty **7.** clotted, complex, gnarled,
knitted, nodated **8.** abstruse, puzzling
9. difficult, entangled
knotty ... **5.** nodal, rough **7.** gnarled,
knarred, knobbed, knurled, nodular
9. difficult, entangled, intricate
10. perplexing
know ... **3.** ken, wis, wot **5.** sense
6. regard, reveal **8.** perceive
9. apprehend, be certain, recognize
11. be cognizant, distinguish
knowing ... **3.** hep **6.** artful, crafty,
scient, shrewd **7.** cunning **8.** informed
9. cognitive, conscious, wide-awake
10. perceptive **11.** intelligent,
intentional **12.** familiar with
13. comprehension
know-it-all ... **6.** gossip **8.** quidnunc,
wiseacre
knowledge ... **3.** ken **4.** kith, lore
5. ology **6.** wisdom **7.** science
8. learning, scientia **9.** erudition
11. familiarity, information, instruction
12. acquaintance
knowledge (pert to) ...
acquisition of .. **7.** organon
ancestral .. **9.** tradition
epithet of Muses .. **7.** Pierian
exhibition of .. **6.** pedant
instrument .. **7.** organon
lack of .. **9.** ignorance, nescience
object of .. **7.** scibile
pert to .. **7.** gnostic **8.** instinct
9. epistemic, intuition, sciential
12. epistemology
pretender to .. **7.** aeolist (eolist) **8.** sciolist
seeker of .. **10.** philonoist
slight .. **7.** inkling, smatter **10.** smattering
summarized .. **12.** encyclopedia
(encyclopaedia)
superficial .. **9.** sociology
system .. **7.** science
universal .. **9.** pantology
without .. **8.** atechnic
know-nothing ... **5.** dunce **8.** agnostic
9. ignoramus

kobird ... **6.** cuckoo
kobold ... **3.** elf, imp **5.** gnome **8.** folklore
9. hobgoblin
Kodiak, Kadiak bear ... **7.** Alaskan
Kohinoor ... **7.** diamond (700 carats)
kohl ... **5.** horse **8.** antimony, cosmetic
kola ... **3.** nut **6.** jackal
kooky ... **7.** offbeat
kopje ... **5.** mound **7.** hillock
Koran, Alcoran (pert to) ...
author .. **8.** Mohammed
division .. **4.** Sura (chapter)
learned man .. **5.** ulema
recording angel .. **6.** sijill (sijil)
scriptures .. **10.** Mohammedan
teacher .. **5.** ulema **7.** alfaqui (alfaquin)
Korea ...
capital .. **5.** Seoul (South) **9.** Pyongyang
(North)
city .. **6.** Gensan
dynasty .. **2.** Yi
leader .. **9.** Kim Il-Sung (North)
11. Syngman Rhee (South)
mountain peak .. **6.** Paekdu
old name .. **6.** Chosen **13.** Hermit
Kingdom
peninsula .. **6.** Ongjin
province .. **5.** Fusan (Fuzan)
river .. **4.** Yalu **5.** Tuman **7.** Naktong
Korean dish ... **6.** kimchi
Krakatoa, et al ... **7.** volcano
kosher ... **5.** clean **8.** kashruth
10. sanctioned
kra ... **3.** ape (long-tailed)
krimmer ... **8.** lambskin
Krishna (Hind) ... **5.** deity (of Vishnu)
6. avatar (8th), Goloka
Krupp steel works, site ... **5.** Essen
(Ger)
kudu ... **8.** antelope **9.** gray-brown
kusimansel ... **6.** mangue **8.** mongoose
kvetch ... **3.** nag
Kwantung capital ... **6.** Dairen
kwazoku (Jap) ... **8.** nobility (modern)
kyah ... **9.** partridge
kyaung ... **9.** monastery
kymatology, science of ... **5.** waves
10. wave motion
kyphosis ... **8.** humpback **9.** hunchback
15. spinal curvature
kyte ... **5.** belly **7.** stomach
Kyushu (Jap) ... **6.** Island (southernmost)

L

L ... **5.** fifty (Rom num) **6.** lambda, letter
(12th) **7.** lammedh
laager, lager ... **4.** camp
laagte ... **6.** bottom, valley **8.** riverbed
Laban (pert to) ...
daughter .. **4.** Leah **6.** Rachel
father .. **7.** Bethuel
son-in-law .. **5.** Jacob
label ... **3.** tab, tag **4.** band, name
6. fillet, lappet, tassel, ticket **8.** insignia
9. designate

labellum ... **3.** lip **6.** labium, labrum
labia ... **4.** lips
labial stop ... **9.** organ stop
labial teeth ... **6.** canine **7.** incisor
labile ... **8.** shifting, unstable
labium ... **3.** lip
La Boheme ... **4.** Mimi **7.** Puccini
labor, labour ... **4.** moil, task, toil, work
5. sweat **6.** strive **7.** travail, work
for **8.** drudgery, endeavor, exertion,
industry

labored . . . **5.** heavy **6.** forced, strove
  7. not easy, operose **8.** strained
  9. difficult, elaborate, laborious
  11. painstaking
laborer . . . **4.** hind, peon, toty **5.** navvy
  6. coolie, toiler, worker **7.** bracero,
  wetback, workman
laborious . . . **4.** hard **7.** arduous, operose
  8. toilsome **9.** difficult **11.** hard working,
  industrious, painstaking
labor leader . . . **5.** Hoffa, Lewis, Meany
  7. Gompers (1st), Reuther **8.** Petrillo
labor letters . . . **3.** AFL, CIO, ILO, UAW
Labrador (pert to) . . .
  Arctic flow . . **7.** Current
  dog . . **9.** retriever **12.** Newfoundland
  missionary . . **8.** Grenfell (Dr)
  part . . **12.** Newfoundland
  tea . . **5.** Ledum **8.** gowiddie
labyrinth . . . **4.** maze **7.** circuit, cochlea
  10. perplexity **12.** complication
labyrinths . . . **7.** complex **8.** involved
  9. intricate **10.** circuitous
  11. complicated
lac . . . **4.** milk **5.** resin **7.** lacquer, shellac
lace . . . **3.** net, tat, tie, web **4.** band, beat,
  cord, flog, lash, line, trim **5.** braid, filet,
  lacis, snare **6.** fasten, string, tissue
  7. network **9.** embroider **10.** intertwine,
  shoestring **13.** dash of spirits
lace (pert to) . . .
  Antwerp . . **7.** pot lace
  bobbin . . **3.** val **12.** Valenciennes
  cape, scarf . . **8.** mantilla
  edge . . **5.** picot
  Flemish . . **7.** malines, Mechlin
  French . . **5.** filet **7.** guipure
  frill . . **5.** ruche
  front . . **5.** jabot
  gold, silver . . **5.** orris
  make . . **3.** tat **5.** weave **7.** crochet,
    entwine
  needlepoint . . **7.** Alencon
  opening . . **6.** eyelet
  patterned . . **7.** guipure
lacerate . . . **3.** cut, rip **4.** pain, rend, tear
  6. harrow, injure, mangle **7.** afflict,
  torture
lachryma . . . **4.** tear **5.** fluid **8.** teardrop
lachrymal, lachrymose . . . **5.** teary,
  weepy **7.** tearful **8.** tearlike
lack . . . **4.** need, want **6.** dearth **7.** absence,
  lacking, missing, require **8.** have
  need, scarcity **9.** fall short, neediness
  10. deficiency
lack (pert to) . . .
  blood cells (red) . . **6.** anemia
  correspondence . . **13.** nonconformity
  energy . . **5.** atony, tepid **6.** energy
    7. aimless, sapless
  feeling . . **10.** insensible **13.** insensibility
  firmness . . **4.** limp **8.** boneless
    9. spineless
  interest . . **6.** apathy **9.** apathetic
  knowledge . . **9.** ignorance, nescience
  melody . . **6.** atonic **9.** atonality
  preparation . . **8.** unfitted
  reasoning . . **7.** idiotic
  refinement . . **5.** gross **9.** grossness,
    inelegant **10.** inelegance
  vigilance . . **6.** unwary

lackadaisical . . . **7.** languid **8.** listless
  10. spiritless
Laconia (anc) . . .
  capital . . **6.** Sparta
  clan . . **3.** obe
  inhabitant . . **5.** Lacon
  location . . **12.** Peloponnesus
  race . . **6.** Dorian
laconic . . . **5.** brief, pithy, short, terse
  7. concise, pointed, summary
  8. succinct, taciturn
lacquer . . . **3.** lac, red (color) **5.** japan,
  resin **6.** enamel **7.** shellac, varnish
lacrimando . . . **9.** lamenting, plaintive
lactarium . . . **5.** dairy
lacteal . . . **5.** milky
lacune, lacuna . . . **3.** gap, pit **5.** break
  6. hiatus **7.** opening (small)
  10. depression
ladder . . . **3.** run, sty **5.** scale **7.** scalade
  8. escalade **10.** stepladder
lade . . . **3.** dip **4.** bail, draw, fill, load,
  ship **5.** drain, ladle **6.** burden
laden . . . **6.** loaded **8.** burdened
  9. freighted
lading . . . **4.** load **5.** cargo **6.** burden
  7. freight
ladle . . . **3.** dip **4.** bowl **5.** scoop, spoon
  6. dipper
lady . . . **4.** burd (anc), dame **5.** donna
  6. domina, female, senora **7.** signora
  8. ladylove **13.** harlequin duck
lady (pert to) . . .
  bird . . **6.** beetle **7.** Vedalia
  fish . . **6.** wrasse
  killer . . **4.** wolf **5.** shiek **7.** Don Juan
    8. Casanova
  like . . **6.** female, polite **7.** genteel
    8. feminine
Lady Godiva's town . . . **8.** Coventry
Lady of the Lake character (legend) . . .
  6. Merlin, Vivian
Lady's Book author . . . **5.** Godey
lady's-slipper . . . **6.** balsam, orchid
  8. Noah's ark **9.** nerveroot
lady's-thumb . . . **9.** peachwort, persicary
lag . . . **4.** slow **5.** delay, tardy **6.** dawdle,
  linger, loiter **7.** belated **10.** dillydally,
  fall behind
lagarto . . . **9.** alligator **10.** lizard fish
laggard . . . **4.** slow **5.** idler **7.** lagging
  8. backward, dilatory, indolent, loiterer,
  sluggish **9.** loitering, straggler
La Gioconda . . . **8.** Mona Lisa
lagniappe, lagnappe . . . **5.** pilon
  7. largess (largesse), present (trifling)
  8. gratuity
lagoon . . . **4.** lake, pond, pool **5.** atoll
laic . . . **3.** lay **5.** civil **6.** layman **7.** secular
  8. temporal
Lais (Gr) . . . **7.** hetaera (of Corinth)
  8. mistress **14.** beautiful woman
laissez faire, laisser faire . . . **5.** let
  go **7.** let pass **8.** inaction, inactive
  9. do-nothing, passivism, unconcern
  12. indifference **15.** noninterference
Laius' son . . . **7.** Oedipus (of Thebes)
lake . . . **4.** loch, mere, pond, pool, tarn
  5. lacus **6.** lagoon **7.** carmine (color)

L

lake (pert to) . . .
bass . . **4.** rock **6.** calico
deposit . . **5.** trona
duck . . **5.** scaup **7.** mallard
dweller . . **10.** lacustrian
dwelling . . **7.** crannog
growing in . . **10.** lacustrine
Hades (of) . . **7.** Avernus
highest . . **8.** Titicaca
pert to . . **9.** lacustral
poet (Eng) . . **6.** lakist **7.** Southey
   9. Coleridge **10.** Wordsworth
State . . **8.** Michigan
lama . . . **4.** monk **5.** Dalai
Lamaism . . . **8.** Buddhism
Lamaism, Buddhism (pert to) . . .
convent . . **8.** lamasery
dignitary . . **8.** hutukhtu
palace site . . **5.** Lhasa
priest, monk . . **4.** lama **6.** Getsul **9.** Dalai
   Lama, Grand Lama
reliquary, stupa . . **7.** chorten
lamb . . . **3.** ean, ewe **4.** cade, yean **5.** gigot,
   sheep **6.** cosset **7.** eanling, lambkin
   8. yearling **9.** youngling **10.** endearment
Lamb, Charles . . . **4.** Elia (pen name)
lambaste . . . **4.** beat, whip **6.** thrash
   7. reprove
lambent . . . **7.** glowing, radiant
   8. wavering **10.** flickering **11.** gliding
   over
Lambeth (London) . . . **6.** palace (of
   Archbishops) **15.** religious center
Lamb of God . . . **7.** paschal **8.** Agnus
   Dei
lame . . . **4.** halt **7.** halting, limping
   8. crippled, disabled, hobbling
   9. defective **11.** inefficient
lame (pert to) . . .
brains . . **9.** balminess, daffiness,
   goofiness, wackiness
duck . . **7.** session **9.** insolvent
   10. politician, speculator
Lamech (pert to) . . .
descendant of . . **4.** Cain
father of . . **5.** Jabal, Jubal **9.** Tubal-cain
lament . . . **3.** rue **4.** keen, moan, sigh,
   wail, weep **5.** mourn **6.** bemoan, bewail,
   grieve, plaint, regret, repine, yammer
   7. condole, deplore, elegize, weeping
   8. jeremiad
lamentation . . . **3.** cry, woe **5.** dolor, grief,
   tears **6.** sorrow **7.** anguish, wailing
Lamentations . . . **4.** Book (Old Test)
lamia . . . **5.** witch **7.** monster, vampire
   (Myth) **8.** cub shark **9.** sorceress
lamina . . . **4.** obex (brain) **5.** blade, flake,
   hinge, layer
lamp . . . **4.** davy, etna **5.** light, torch
   6. crusie **7.** lantern, lucigen **9.** veilleuse
lamp (pert to) . . .
black . . **4.** soot
holder . . **11.** candelabrum
lighter . . **5.** spill
safety . . **4.** davy **7.** Geordie
slang . . **6.** look at
waving of . . **5.** arati
lampadedromy (Gr) . . . **8.** foot race (with
   torch)
lampoon . . . **4.** skit **5.** squib **6.** iambic
   8. ridicule, satirize **10.** pasquinade

lampoon writer . . . **8.** satirist
lamprey . . . **3.** eel **6.** ramper
Lamps of the Lord . . . **5.** yucca (blooms)
Lancashire (Eng) . . . **6.** Eccles
lance . . . **3.** cut **4.** dart, hurl, stab **5.** blade,
   spear **6.** incise, launch, pierce, weapon
   7. javelin
lance (pert to) . . .
battle . . **5.** joust
head . . **5.** morne
knight . . **10.** lansquenet (Hist)
officer . . **4.** Jack
surgical . . **6.** lancet
Lancelot . . . **6.** Knight **13.** Lancelot du
   Lac
Lancelot's beloved . . . **6.** Elaine
lancer . . . **5.** uhlan **6.** Hussar **7.** cossack,
   soldier, spearer
land . . . **3.** lot **4.** acre, farm **5.** arada,
   downs, field, range, tilth **6.** alight,
   debark, ground, region **7.** country,
   pasture **9.** disembark
land (pert to) . . .
absolute ppty . . **4.** alod **7.** alodium
alluvial . . **5.** delta
ancestral . . **5.** ethel
assessor . . **8.** cadastre (cadaster)
church . . **5.** glebe
heritable . . **4.** odal, udal
holding . . **6.** tenure **9.** leasehold
leasehold . . **5.** feoff
locked in . . **13.** mediterranean
mythical . . **4.** Eden **6.** Utopia **9.** Shangri-
   La
northernmost . . **5.** Thule (Greenland)
open . . **4.** moor, wold **5.** heath
pile . . **5.** cairn
prefix . . **4.** agro
reversion . . **7.** escheat
sandy . . **4.** dene
surveyor . . **9.** arpenteur
Sussex tract (Eng) . . **5.** laine
treeless . . **5.** llano **6.** steppe **7.** prairie
verb . . **3.** win **4.** gain **5.** catch **6.** secure
   7. capture
waste . . **5.** heath
landed estate . . . **5.** manor **7.** demesne
landing place . . . **4.** deck, dock, pier, quay
   5. field, levee, strip, wharf **7.** airport
   8. platform **9.** staircase
landmark . . . **4.** copa, tree **5.** senal
Land of (the) . . .
bondage . . **5.** Egypt
Cush . . **8.** Ethiopia
Eden (East of) . . **3.** Nod
Enchantment . . **9.** New Mexico
Leal . . **6.** Heaven
Little Sticks (Canada) . . **19.** Barren Islands
   border
Midnight Sun . . **6.** Alaska, Norway
O'Cakes . . **8.** Scotland
Opportunity . . **8.** Arkansas
Plenty . . **6.** Goshen
Promise . . **6.** Canaan
Regrets . . **5.** India
Rising Sun . . **5.** Japan
Rose . . **7.** England
Shamrock . . **4.** Eire **7.** Ireland
sleep . . **3.** Nod
Steady Habits . . **11.** Connecticut
Thistle . . **8.** Scotland

Thousand Lakes . . **7.** Finland
White Elephant . . **4.** Siam
landscape . . . **7.** paysage, scenery, topiary
landslide . . . **9.** avalanche **10.** éboulement
Landsmaal, Landsmal . . . **8.** language
(Norway)
Landstag . . . **4.** Diet **8.** assembly
11. legislature
lane . . . **4.** path, road **5.** alley, route,
track **6.** airway, course, gullet, throat
7. channel, red land **8.** footpath
10. passageway
language . . . **6.** langue, speech, tongue
7. dialect, diction **8.** parlance
9. utterance **11.** linguistics
language (pert to) . . .
acquiring . . **12.** chrestomathy
ancient . . **4.** Pali **5.** Aryan, Greek, Latin
6. Hebrew **7.** Chinese **8.** Sanskrit
artificial . . **2.** Od, Ro **3.** Ido **7.** Volapük
9. Esperanto
classical . . **5.** Greek, Latin
conversant in . . **9.** pantoglot
dead . . **4.** Pali
deaf-mute . . **11.** dactylology
expression, peculiar . . **5.** idiom, lingo
6. jargon **7.** dialect **13.** colloquialism
international . . **2.** Od, Ro **3.** Ido
7. Volapük **9.** Esperanto
pert to . . **8.** semantic
pretentious . . **7.** bombast **11.** highfalutin
Romance . . **5.** Latin **6.** French **7.** Catalan,
Italian, Spanish **9.** Provencal
10. Portuguese
sacred . . **4.** Pali
sign . . **11.** dactylology
thieves . . **5.** argot
languid . . . **4.** slow, weak **5.** faint, inert,
weary **6.** dreamy, feeble, sickly, supine,
torpid **7.** passive **8.** careless, drooping,
flagging, heedless, indolent, sluggish
9. apathetic **10.** spiritless
languish . . . **3.** die **4.** fade, fail, flag, pine,
wilt **5.** droop, faint **6.** repine, sicken,
weaken, wither **7.** decline
languor . . . **3.** kef (kief) **7.** fatigue
8. dullness, weakness **9.** indolence,
lassitude **10.** dreaminess, drowsiness,
stagnation **12.** listlessness, sluggishness
lanky . . . **4.** lean, tall, thin **5.** gaunt, spare
12. loose-jointed
lanner . . . **6.** falcon
Lanterns, Feast of (Jap) . . . **3.** Bon
Laodicean . . . **8.** lukewarm **9.** apathetic
11. indifferent
Laos . . .
aborigine . . **3.** Kah
capital . . **9.** Vientiane **12.** Luang Prabang
native . . **7.** Chinese **14.** Thai-Indonesian
religion . . **8.** Buddhism
river . . **6.** Mekong
lap . . . **3.** sip **4.** fold, lick, wrap **5.** drink
6. ripple, tipple **7.** circuit
lapel . . . **4.** fold **5.** rever **6.** facing, lappet
lapicide . . . **11.** stonecutter
lapidary's forte . . . **4.** gems
lapin . . . **6.** rabbit
lapis lazuli . . . **4.** blue **5.** stone **8.** lazurite,
sapphire **10.** azure stone
Lapland . . .
people . . **5.** Lapps **10.** Laplanders

11. Ural-Altaics **12.** tent-dwellers
sledge (traveling) . . **5.** pulka (pukk)
sledge puller . . **8.** reindeer
town . . **6.** Kiruna
waterfalls . . **11.** Harspranget
lappet . . . **4.** flap, fold, lobe **5.** lapel
6. wattle **9.** appendage
lapse . . . **3.** err **4.** fall, slip **5.** error, fault,
pause **6.** expiry **7.** decline, misstep,
relapse **8.** apostasy **9.** reversion
lapsus . . . **4.** slip **5.** error **12.** inadvertence
lapsus calami . . . **10.** lipography **12.** slip
of the pen
lapsus linguae . . . **15.** slip of the tongue
lapwing . . . **4.** gull **5.** pewee, pewit
6. plover
larceny . . . **5.** theft **7.** robbery **8.** burglary,
stealage **10.** scrounging
larch . . . **5.** Larix **8.** tamarack
lard . . . **3.** fat **4.** line, pork **5.** adeps, bacon,
baste, enarm **6.** axunge, cerate, enrich,
fatten, grease **7.** garnish **8.** saindoux
9. lubricate
larder . . . **6.** pantry **7.** buttery **8.** cupboard
12. commissariat
lares (Rom) . . . **4.** gods (household)
7. spirits
large . . . **3.** big, nth **4.** bold, huge, much,
vast **5.** ample, bulky, burly, giant, great,
loose, scads **7.** copious, immense,
leonine, liberal, massive, titanic,
weighty **8.** colossal, enormous, gigantic,
spacious **9.** excessive, extensive,
plentiful **11.** exaggerated
12. considerable **13.** comprehensive
large (pert to) . . .
artery . . **5.** aorta
comb form . . **5.** macro
fish . . **4.** opah, tuna **9.** swordfish
intestine . . **5.** colon **6.** caecum, rectum
knife . . **4.** bolo, snee
lettered . . **6.** uncial
number . . **4.** slew **6.** myriad
pulpit . . **4.** ambo
volume . . **4.** tome
largess, largesse . . . **4.** gift **6.** bounty
7. charity, present **10.** generosity,
liberality **11.** beneficence
largest bird . . . **6.** condor **7.** ostrich
13. whooping crane
largest fish (freshwater) . . . **8.** arapaima
larghetto . . . **9.** slow tempo
larghissimo . . . **8.** very slow
lariat . . . **4.** rope **5.** honda (part), lasso,
noose, reata, riata
lark . . . **5.** ghost (anc), prank, revel
6. frolic **7.** skylark, titlark **8.** songbird
9. adventure, Alaudidae, parchment
(color)
larrigan . . . **8.** moccasin
larrikin . . . **5.** rough, rowdy **6.** loafer
10. street Arab
larrup . . . **3.** hit **4.** beat, blow, flog, whip
larva . . . **3.** bot (bott) **4.** grub, pupa
5. redia **6.** embryo, maggot **7.** atrocha
8. cercaria, chrysalis, doodlebug
11. caterpillar
lascivious . . . **4.** lewd **5.** bawdy **6.** erotic,
wanton **7.** lustful, sensual **9.** lecherous,
salacious **10.** libidinous, licentious
laser . . . **9.** light beam

lash . . . **3.** tie **4.** beat, bind, flag,
  whip **5.** scold, smite **6.** splice, strike
  7. scourge
lass . . . **4.** girl **6.** lassie, maiden **7.** colleen
  11. maidservant
lassitude . . . **7.** languor **8.** debility,
  lethargy, weakness **9.** weariness
lasso . . . **4.** lash, rope **5.** noose, reata
  (riata), snare **6.** lariat **8.** cabestro
last . . . **3.** final, omega **6.** endure,
  latest, lowest, newest, penult, ultima,
  utmost **7.** extreme, supreme **8.** eventual,
  rearmost, terminal, ultimate
  9. penultima **10.** antepenult, conclusive,
  most recent
last (pert to) . . .
  at last . . **6.** Eureka
  but one . . **6.** penult
  cry . . **10.** dernier cri
  evening . . **9.** yesterday
  long . . **7.** outwear, perdure **9.** perendure
  month . . **3.** ult **6.** ultimo
  offer . . **9.** ultimatum
  person in contest . . **4.** mell
  shoe . . **5.** block
  syllable but one . . **6.** penult
  syllable but two . . **10.** antepenult
Last (pert to) . . .
  Assize . . **11.** Last Inquest **12.** Last
  Judgment
  Days of Pompeii character . . **4.** Ione
  5. Nydia **7.** Glaucus
  Gospel . . **4.** Mass
  of the Gothic Kings . . **8.** Roderick
  of the Mohicans . . **5.** Uncas (Chief)
  Supper . . **6.** Christ **9.** disciples
lasting . . . **4.** long **6.** stable **7.** abiding,
  durable, eternal **8.** constant **9.** continual,
  lingering, permanent, steadfast
  11. substantial, unforgotten
lasting briefly . . . **9.** ephemeral,
  temporary
lat . . . **6.** column, pillar
latchet . . . **3.** tap **4.** lace (leather) **5.** strap,
  thong **9.** fastening
late . . . **3.** neo (comb form), new **4.** sero
  5. tardy **6.** former, recent **7.** belated,
  overdue **8.** neoteric **10.** behindhand
latent . . . **5.** inert **6.** hidden **7.** dormant
  9. disguised, potential, quiescent,
  suspended **10.** underlying
later . . . **4.** anon, soon **5.** after **6.** future,
  mañana, puisne **9.** posterior, presently
  12. subsequently
lateral . . . **5.** flank, raphe **8.** indirect,
  sideward
lath . . . **4.** slat **9.** wood strip
lathe . . . **4.** tool **7.** mandrel
lather . . . **4.** foam, suds **5.** froth
Latin (pert to) . . .
  alphabet letters . . **9.** twenty-one
  and . . **2.** et
  bath . . **7.** balneum
  behold . . **4.** ecce
  booth . . **7.** taberna
  bowl . . **6.** patina
  bronze . . **3.** aes
  church . . **8.** Catholic
  couch . . **3.** accibutum
  country . . **6.** French **7.** Italian, Spanish
  dish . . **4.** lanx **6.** patina

foot . . **3.** pes
God . . **3.** Dei, Deo **4.** Deus **7.** Mercury
goddess . . **3.** Dea
grammar (case) . . **6.** dative **8.** ablative,
  genitive, vocative **10.** accusative,
  nominative
historian . . **6.** Justin
holidays . . **5.** feria
hymn . . **13.** Adesti Fideles
javelin . . **5.** aclys, pilum
land . . **4.** ager
law . . **3.** lex **6.** Latium
life . . **4.** vita
people . . **6.** Romans
poet . . **4.** Ovid **6.** Horace
pronoun . . **2.** tu **3.** ego, hic **4.** ille, ipse,
  iste
quarter (section) . . **5.** Paris **10.** New
  Orleans
ram . . **5.** aries
rite . . **4.** orgy **5.** sacra
seat . . **5.** sella
trumpet . . **4.** tuba **7.** buccina
Way . . **9.** Via Latina
latite . . . **4.** lava
latitude . . . **4.** zone **5.** scope, width
  6. extent **7.** breadth, freedom **8.** distance
  10. liberality
latrant . . . **7.** barking
latter . . . **4.** last **5.** final **6.** latest
  9. foregoing **10.** more recent
Latter-day Saint . . . **6.** Mormon
lattice . . . **6.** grille **7.** trellis **8.** cancelli
  9. crossbars, framework **12.** crossed
  slats
latticelike . . . **7.** grating **8.** espalier
  9. clathrate **10.** cancellate
Latvia . . .
  capital . . **4.** Riga
  city . . **6.** Dvinsk, Libava (Libau)
  money unit . . **3.** lat (gold)
  people . . **4.** Lett **7.** Lettish
  river . . **2.** Aa
laud . . . **4.** sing **5.** extol **6.** praise
  7. applaud, commend, glorify, magnify
  8. eulogize
laudable . . . **9.** admirable, estimable
  11. commendable, meritorious
  12. praiseworthy
laudatory . . . **9.** panegyric **10.** flattering
  11. approbatory, encomiastic
  12. commendatory
laugh . . . **4.** roar **5.** fleer, smile, snort
  6. cackle, deride, giggle, guffaw,
  hawhaw, tee-hee **7.** chortle, chuckle
  8. ridicule **10.** cachinnate
laughable . . . **3.** odd **5.** droll, funny,
  merry, queer, witty **7.** amusing, comical,
  jocular, risible, strange, waggish
  8. humorous, sportive **9.** burlesque,
  diverting, facetious, ludicrous
  10. ridiculous
laughing . . . **3.** gay **5.** merry, riant **6.** rident
laughing (pert to) . . .
  bird . . **4.** loon **10.** woodpecker
  falcon . . **4.** hawk
  gas . . **12.** nitrous oxide
  jackass . . **10.** kingfisher, kookaburra
  pert to . . **8.** gelastic
laughter . . . **4.** gelo (comb form) **5.** gelos,
  mirth, risus **6.** guffaw **12.** cachinnation

launch ... **4.** hurl **5.** begin, float, lance, shove, start, throw **6.** plunge **7.** descant **9.** undertake **10.** inaugurate

laureate ... **4.** poet **6.** decked (with laurel) **7.** drowned, honored **13.** distinguished

laurel ... **3.** bay, ivy, oak, oil **6.** daphne, Kalmia, salmon **8.** magnolia **9.** sassafras, spoonwood

laurel wreath ... **7.** Iresine

lava ... **2.** aa, oo **3.** ash **5.** ashes **6.** coulee, latite, scoria **8.** lapillus, pahoehoe

lava field ... **8.** pedregal

lavaliere, lavalier ... **7.** pendant **8.** ornament

lavatory ... **5.** basin **7.** piscina **8.** washroom **9.** washbasin

lave ... **4.** lade, pour, wash **5.** bathe, rinse **6.** drench **8.** absterge

lavender ... **4.** mint **6.** purple **7.** blue-red, perfume **9.** fragrance

laver ... **4.** bowl **5.** basin **6.** trough, vessel **7.** cistern, seaweed

Lavinia (pert to) ...
father .. **7.** Latinus
husband .. **6.** Aeneas
mother .. **5.** Amata
myth .. **5.** Roman

lavish ... **4.** free, lush, rank, wild **5.** spend **7.** profuse **8.** abundant, generous, prodigal, reckless, squander **9.** bountiful, exuberant, impetuous, luxuriant, plentiful, unstinted **10.** immoderate **11.** extravagant **12.** unrestrained **13.** superabundant

law ... **3.** act, jus, lex **4.** bill, code, jure, nisi, rule **5.** axiom, canon, droit, edict, mercy, mesne **6.** decree, equity, Latium, police **7.** justice, precept, statute **9.** enactment **12.** constitution **13.** jurisprudence

law (pert to) ...
action .. **3.** res **4.** suit **5.** actus **6.** trover **7.** impeach, implead **8.** gravamen, replevin **9.** ademption
Bible .. **6.** Mosaic **12.** Old Testament
claim .. **4.** lien
code .. **8.** Napoléon **9.** Hammurabi **10.** codex juris **16.** Codex Justinianus
decree .. **4.** nisi **5.** edict
degree .. **3.** LLD
divine .. **11.** commandment
document .. **4.** deed, writ **6.** capias, elegit
drafting .. **10.** nomography
evidence .. **7.** constat
expert (US) .. **5.** Moore (John B)
for fourth offender (NY) .. **6.** Baumes
German Franks .. **5.** Salic
goddess .. **4.** Maat (Egypt)
heredity .. **8.** Gresham's
Manu .. **5.** sutra
mathematics .. **7.** formula
morals .. **7.** conduct
Moses .. **5.** Torah (Tora) **10.** Pentateuch
offender .. **5.** felon **6.** sinner **8.** criminal **9.** wrongdoer
offense .. **4.** tort **5.** crime, malum **6.** delict
pert to .. **3.** res **9.** judiciary
philology .. **6.** Grimm's
science .. **8.** nomology **13.** jurisprudence
student .. **8.** stagiary

thought .. **7.** noetics
warning .. **6.** caveat
within the .. **5.** licit **8.** judicial
wrong .. **4.** tort

lawful ... **3.** due **5.** legal, licit, valid **9.** permitted **10.** legitimate **11.** permissible

lawgiver ... **5.** Moses

lawless ... **4.** lewd **6.** unruly **7.** illegal **10.** anarchical, disorderly

lawlessness ... **4.** riot **6.** mutiny **7.** anarchy, license **12.** disobedience

lawmaker ... **5.** solon **7.** senator **10.** legislator **11.** congressman

lawn ... **5.** green **7.** batiste **9.** grassplot **12.** village green

lawyer ... **5.** agent **6.** jurist, legist **7.** abogado, shyster **8.** advocate, attorney, lawgiver **9.** barrister, counselor (counsellor), leguleian, solicitor **11.** intercessor, pettifogger

lawyer group ... **3.** ABA

lax ... **4.** dull, free, limp, open, slow **5.** loose, slack, tardy **6.** remiss **7.** lenient **8.** backward, dilatory, inactive, indolent, not tense **9.** dissolute, scattered **10.** licentious, unconfined **12.** unrestrained

lay ... **3.** bet, put **4.** lair, pave, poem, song **5.** allay, ditty, place, quiet, stake, still **6.** ballad, hazard, impose, impute, pacify **7.** appease, ascribe, deposit, relieve, store up **9.** direction **10.** profession

lay (pert to) ...
aside .. **5.** table **6.** remove, shelve **7.** dismiss, reserve **8.** postpone **9.** segregate
away .. **4.** heap, hive **5.** amass, cache, hoard, store **7.** husband **8.** treasure **10.** accumulate
bare .. **5.** strip **6.** denude, expose, reveal **7.** uncover
down .. **3.** bet, set **5.** level **6.** give up **7.** declare, deposit **9.** postulate, prescribe, stipulate, surrender
off .. **4.** don't, stop **5.** cease **6.** recess **7.** dismiss, measure
out .. **4.** plan **5.** set up **6.** design **7.** pattern
waste .. **6.** ravage **7.** destroy **8.** desolate **9.** depredate, devastate

layer ... **3.** bed **4.** coat, derm, tier, uvea **5.** sloam (earth) **6.** lamina **7.** stratum (strata, pl) **10.** substratum

lazar ... **5.** leper **9.** loathsome

lazaretto, lazaret ... **3.** hospital **9.** pest house **10.** lazar house

laziness ... **5.** sloth **7.** inertia **8.** oisivity, vagrancy **9.** indolence **10.** ergophobia, remissness **12.** slothfulness **13.** shiftlessness

lazy ... **3.** lax **4.** idle, slow **5.** slack **6.** otiose, remiss **7.** dronish, laggard **8.** dilatory, inactive, indolent, slothful, sluggish **9.** shiftless **13.** lackadaisical

lazy man ... **3.** bum **4.** lusk **5.** drone, idler **6.** rotter **9.** lazybones **11.** Weary Willie

lea ... **4.** mead **5.** haugh **6.** meadow **7.** pasture **9.** grassland

leach ... **3.** wet **7.** moisten **9.** lixiviate,

percolate

lead ... **3.** cue, key, van **4.** cart, clue, head, lode **5.** begin, guide, pilot, plumb, usher **6.** direct, entice, escort, govern, induce **7.** conduct, pioneer, precede **8.** antecede, guidance **9.** direction, influence, precedent **10.** precedence

lead (mineral) ... **4.** came (rod), gray, shot **6.** ceruse, fother, galena, leaden, strass (glass) **7.** bullets, plummet **8.** graphite, litharge, plumbago

lead astray ... **4.** lure, mang **6.** allure, delude, entice, induce **7.** deceive, pervert **8.** inveigle

leader ... **4.** head **5.** chief, guide, sinew **6.** cantor, tendon **7.** special **8.** choragus, director **9.** chieftain, conductor **10.** forerunner

leader (Eccl) ... **3.** fra **4.** pope **5.** rabbi **6.** bishop, priest **8.** cardinal, minister, preacher **10.** evangelist

leading ... **5.** chief, first **6.** ruling **7.** guiding **8.** foremost, in the van **9.** directing, governing **11.** controlling

leaf ... **3.** ola **4.** gear, page **5.** blade, frond, petal, sepal **6.** areola, ligula, spathe **7.** tendril

leaf (pert to) ...
book . . **5.** folio
bud . . **5.** gemma
curvature . . **8.** epinasty (down) **9.** hyponasty (upward)
floating . . **3.** pad
green . . **11.** chlorophyll
heart-shaped . . **9.** obcordate
mold . . **5.** humus
network . . **6.** areola
part . . **5.** bract, costa, stoma **6.** pagina, stipel **7.** petiole **9.** petiolule
point, pointed . . **5.** mucro **9.** mucronate **13.** mucroniferous
pore . . **8.** lenticel
secretion . . **4.** lerp
stalk . . **7.** petiole **8.** petiolus
vein . . **3.** rib **5.** costa

leafless ... **9.** aphyllous

leaflet ... **5.** pinna, tract **6.** folder **7.** booklet **8.** pamphlet **13.** advertisement

league ... **4.** band, Bund **5.** Hanse, union **7.** combine **8.** alliance **9.** coalition **10.** federation **11.** affiliation, combination **13.** confederation

League of Nations site ... **5.** Paris (1920) **6.** Geneva (Secretariat)

League of the Iroquois ... **11.** Five Nations

Leah (pert to) ...
Bible book . . **7.** Genesis
sister . . **6.** Rachel
son . . **4.** Levi
wife of . . **5.** Jacob

leak ... **4.** drip, hole, seep **5.** crack **6.** escape, run out **7.** crevice, fissure **10.** be revealed

leal ... **4.** just, real, true **5.** legal, loyal **6.** lawful **7.** correct, genuine **8.** accurate, faithful

lean ... **4.** bare, cant, lank, poor, rely, slim, tend **5.** gaunt, slope, spare **6.** barren, meager **7.** scraggy, slender

8. not plump **9.** deficient, gravitate

lean (pert to) ...
animal, person . . **4.** ribe (Scot)
emaciated . . **6.** marcid
make . . **8.** macerate
towards . . **6.** prefer

Leander's love ... **4.** Hero

leaning ... **5.** slope **6.** desire **7.** pronate, tending **8.** aptitude, enclitic, penchant, tendency **9.** prejudice **10.** partiality

Leaning Tower ... **4.** Pisa **6.** Venice **7.** Bologna **8.** Zaragoza

lean-to ... **4.** roof, shed, wing **5.** shack **9.** extension (bldg)

leap ... **4.** dive, jump, ramp, skip **5.** bound, caper, lunge, salto, spang, vault **6.** spring **7.** saltary **8.** capriole

leaping ... **7.** jumping, salient, saltant **8.** bounding, salience **9.** saltation

learn ... **4.** lere (anc) **6.** master **8.** memorize **9.** ascertain, determine

learned ... **3.** wot **4.** read, sage **6.** legist **7.** erudite **8.** lettered, literate, schooled **9.** scholarly **12.** well-informed

learned person ... **6.** master, pundit **7.** scholar, teacher **9.** professor

learning ... **3.** art, ken, wit **4.** lore **7.** culture **8.** pedantry **9.** education, erudition, knowledge, philology (love of), philomath **11.** scholarship

lease ... **3.** let **4.** hire, rent **5.** weave **6.** demise, remise, tenure **8.** contract

leasehold ... **6.** rental, tenure

leash ... **4.** bind, cord, lash, lune (hawking) **5.** reins, three **6.** fasten, string, tierce **9.** restraint **11.** subjugation

leash hound ... **5.** limer

least ... **5.** grain **6.** little, lowest, merest **7.** minimum **8.** minority, shortest, simplest, smallest **9.** slightest

leather ... **4.** hide, skin **5.** aluta, leder (old spelling) **6.** vellum **7.** canepin **8.** cheveril (cheverel) **9.** toughness

leather (kinds) ... **3.** kid, kip **4.** calf, napa, vici **5.** Mocha, suede **6.** patent, saddle, skiver **7.** chamois, Morocco **8.** cordovan **9.** sheepskin

leather (pert to) ...
artificial . . **7.** keratol
bookbinding . . **4.** roan **6.** levant
bottle . . **4.** olpe **6.** matara
cuirass . . **6.** lorica
glove . . **5.** suede, trank **8.** capeskin
pare . . **5.** skive
patch . . **5.** clout
piece of . . **5.** strap, thong **6.** latigo
pouch (Highlander's) . . **7.** sporran
process . . **3.** tan, taw
strap . . **5.** thong **6.** latigo
term . . **8.** efflower
tool . . **6.** skiver
worker . . **6.** chamar, tanner **8.** chuckler

leatherneck ... **6.** marine

leave ... **2.** go **4.** quit **6.** depart, retire, vacate **7.** liberty **9.** allowance **10.** permission

leave (pert to) ...
desolate . . **7.** bereave
empty . . **6.** vacate
isolated . . **6.** desert, maroon
of absence . . **5.** exeat **8.** furlough

off.. **4.** don't, stay **5.** cease **6.** desist
out.. **4.** omit, skip **5.** elide **8.** pass over
taking.. **5.** adieu **6.** congee **7.** vamoose
   9. departure
leaven ... **4.** barm **5.** imbue, yeast
   6. enzyme **7.** corrupt (implied), ferment,
   pervade **10.** impregnate
leaves ... **5.** pages, shaws **6.** sepals
   7. foliage
leaves, feeding on ... **13.** phyllophagous
leavings ... **4.** left, orts, rest **5.** culls,
   dregs, dross, waste **6.** refuse **7.** remains,
   residue **8.** remnants
leban, lebban ... **5.** drink **8.** beverage,
   sour milk
Lebanon city ... **5.** Sidon **6.** Beirut
   (capital) **7.** Tripoli
lech (anc) ... **4.** slab **8.** capstone,
   monument
lecher ... **7.** glutton **8.** gourmand, parasite
   9. debauchee, libertine
lectern ... **4.** ambo, desk **6.** pulpit
   10. escritoire
lecture ... **4.** jobe, rate **5.** scold
   6. lesson **7.** declaim, expound, lection,
   reproof, reprove **8.** instruct, scolding
   9. discourse **10.** admonition
lecturer ... **6.** docent, reader **7.** teacher
   9. prelector
Leda (pert to) ...
   geology.. **4.** clay (marine)
   husband.. **9.** Tyndareus
   lover.. **4.** Zeus (swan)
   mother of.. **6.** Castor, Pollux **11.** Helen
   of Troy **12.** Clytemnestra
   zoology.. **7.** mollusk
ledge ... **4.** berm, edge, lode, reef, sill
   5. shelf **7.** retable, stratum
leechlike ... **8.** bdelloid
lees ... **5.** draff, dregs **8.** sediment
leeward ... (opp of windward)
   9. protected, sheltered
Leeward Islands ... **5.** Nevis **7.** Antigua,
   Barbuda, Redonda **8.** Anguilla,
   Sombrero **10.** Montserrat **13.** St
   Christopher
Leeward Islands group ... **6.** Virgin
   7. Society
leeway ... **4.** room **5.** drift
left ... see also *leave* **3.** haw, kay
   8. departed, larboard **9.** abandoned,
   remaining
left (pert to) ...
   aground.. **6.** neaped **8.** beneaped
   animal (motherless).. **4.** cade **5.** dogie
   comb form.. **8.** sinistro
   hand (Mus).. **8.** sinistra
   hand page.. **5.** verso
   hand pitcher.. **8.** southpaw
   out.. **7.** omitted **8.** excluded
   10. eliminated
   spirally.. **11.** sinistrally
   to one's judgment.. **13.** discretionary
   toward the.. **5.** aport **9.** sinistrad,
   sinistral **12.** levorotatory (Chem)
left-handed ... **6.** clumsy, gauche
   7. oblique **8.** southpaw **9.** insincere,
   insulting **14.** sinistromanual
   16. counterclockwise
left-handed marriage ... **10.** morganatic
leftist ... **7.** liberal, radical **10.** left-winger,

liberalist **11.** progressive
leg (pert to) ...
   armor.. **4.** jamb **6.** greave **7.** jambeau
   bone.. **4.** shin **5.** tibia **6.** fibula
   calf.. **5.** sural
   insect.. **4.** coxa
   joint.. **4.** hock, knee **5.** thigh
   longest bone.. **5.** femur
   of lamb (cooked).. **5.** gigot
   term.. **4.** crus **5.** jambe **6.** crural
legacy ... **4.** gift, will **6.** devise **7.** bequest,
   codicil **9.** testament **10.** bequeathal
legal ... **4.** leal **5.** licit, valid **6.** lawful
   10. authorized, legitimate
legal (pert to) ...
   abstract.. **6.** précis
   act, thing.. **5.** actus
   action.. **3.** res **4.** case **7.** detinet, lawsuit,
   summons
   case, postponed.. **7.** remanet
   claim.. **4.** lien
   confirmation.. **10.** validation
   contestant.. **6.** suitor **8.** litigant
   9. plaintiff
   critic.. **6.** censor
   decree, divorce.. **10.** decree nisi
   defense.. **5.** alibi
   delay.. **4.** mora
   denial, stoppage.. **8.** estoppel
   extract.. **7.** estreat
   matter.. **3.** res
   order.. **4.** writ
   paper.. **4.** deed, writ **5.** lease **6.** escrow
   possession.. **6.** seizin (seisin)
   power (to take).. **7.** prender (prendre)
   process.. **6.** caveat **7.** detinet
   right, by.. **6.** ex jure
   security.. **4.** bond
   surrender.. **4.** remise
legally competent ... **5.** capax
legate ... **5.** envoy **8.** bequeath, delegate
   10. ambassador, diplomatic
legend ... **4.** Edda, myth, saga, tale
   5. fable **7.** history **9.** narrative, tradition
   11. inscription
legendary ... **8.** fabulous **9.** imaginary,
   narrative **11.** traditional
   12. mythological
legendary (pert to) ...
   goddess (slave).. **5.** Baube, lambe
   primate.. **6.** Dubric
   water sprite.. **6.** undine
legendry ... **7.** legends (collectively)
leggings ... **5.** chaps, spats **6.** strads
   7. gaiters, greaves, puttees
   8. gamashes, gambados **12.** galligaskins
legislate ... **3.** act **5.** elect, enact **8.** pass
   laws **10.** put through
legislative (pert to) ...
   agent.. **8.** lobbyist
   assembly.. **4.** diet **6.** assize, senate
   8. congress **10.** parliament
   group.. **4.** bloc
legislator ... **5.** solon **7.** senator
   8. lawgiver, lawmaker **9.** statesman
   11. congressman **14.** representative
legislature ... **4.** Diet **5.** House **6.** Senate
   8. Congress **9.** bicameral (2 branches)
legitimate ... **4.** real, true **5.** legal, licit,
   valid **6.** cogent, lawful **7.** genuine
   9. permitted **11.** efficacious, justifiable

legman . . . **8.** newshawk
legume . . . **3.** pea, pod, uva **4.** bean, soya **6.** clover, lentil, loment **7.** alfalfa
leisure . . . **4.** ease, time, toom **5.** otium **6.** otiose **7.** freedom **9.** spare time **11.** convenience, opportunity
lemming . . . **4.** maki, vari **5.** mouse **6.** rodent
lemur . . . **5.** indri, loris, makis, potto **6.** anguid, aye-aye, colugo, galago, macaco, monkey **7.** tarsier **8.** Anguidae, mongoose **10.** angwantibo
Lenape . . . **6.** Indian (Del)
lend . . . **4.** loan **5.** grant **6.** devote (to) **7.** advance
length (pert to) . . .
measure . . **4.** area **5.** gauge **6.** linear, volume
ten meters . . **9.** decameter
three-quarters inch . . **5.** digit
time . . **3.** age, eon, era **6.** moment, period
two and one-quarter inches . . **4.** nail
unit . . **6.** micron, parsec (Astron)
lengthen out . . . **7.** prolong, stretch **8.** continue, elongate, protract
lengthwise . . . **5.** along **12.** horizontally **14.** longitudinally
lenient . . . **3.** lax **4.** easy, mild **7.** clement, patient **8.** merciful, relaxing, tolerant **9.** assuasive, emollient, softening
Lenin (pert to) . . .
leader of . . **10.** Bolsheviks
real name . . **7.** Ulyanov (Ulianov)
Revolution . . **7.** October, Russian
Leningrad (Russ) . . . **9.** Petrograd **12.** St Petersburg **15.** Window on the West
lenis . . . **4.** soft **6.** gentle, smooth
lenitive . . . **4.** mild **6.** gentle **8.** mitigant, ointment, remedial **9.** assuasive, emollient, mitigator, relieving, softening **10.** palliative, qualifying
lens . . . **5.** toric **7.** bifocal, lentoid **8.** meniscus, sunglass **9.** lenticula **10.** anastigmat **13.** apochromatism
Lent . . . **6.** carême **9.** Forty days, Great Fast **12.** Quadragesima
lentamento . . . **6.** slowly
lentando . . . **9.** retarding **14.** becoming slower
lenticula . . . **7.** freckle, lentigo (freckly)
lento . . . **4.** slow
Leo constellation star . . . **7.** Regulus, the Lion
leopard . . . **4.** pard **5.** ounce **6.** jaguar, ocelot **7.** cheetah, panther
leper . . . **5.** lazar, mesel **6.** Naaman (Bib)
lepidopteran . . . **4.** moth **9.** butterfly
Lepontine Alps . . . **10.** Monte Leone (peak)
lepra . . . **7.** leprosy **14.** Hansen's disease
Lesbos . . . **5.** Assos (Aristotle's) **6.** Island (Sappho's) **8.** Mytilene
Les Miserables author . . . **4.** Hugo (Victor)
lessen . . . **4.** bate, wane **5.** abate, lower, peter, relax **6.** impair, minify, narrow, reduce, shrink, weaken **7.** cut down, relieve **8.** decrease, diminish, mitigate, moderate, palliate **11.** deteriorate
lesser . . . **4.** less **5.** minor (Mus) **7.** smaller

8. inferior
Lesser Bear (Astron) . . . **9.** Ursa Minor
Lesser Dog (Astron) . . . **10.** Canis Minor
Lesser Lion (Astron) . . . **8.** Leo Minor
let . . . **4.** hire, rent **5.** allow, lease, leave **6.** hinder, impede, permit **7.** prevent
let (pert to) . . .
down . . **5.** lower **8.** comedown, drawback, relaxing **10.** slackening **14.** disappointment
fall . . **4.** drop, slip **5.** spill **7.** mention
in . . **5.** admit, enter **6.** insert
it be given . . **5.** detur
it stand . . **3.** sta (Mus) **4.** stet
up . . **4.** rest **5.** cease, pause, relax **6.** slow up **7.** slacken **8.** decrease
lethal . . . **5.** fatal, feral **6.** deadly, mortal **7.** deathly, killing **11.** destructive **12.** death-dealing
lethargic . . . **4.** dull **5.** heavy, inert **6.** drowsy, sleepy, torpid **8.** comatose, listless **9.** apathetic
lethargy . . . **4.** coma **5.** sleep, sopor **6.** apathy, stupor, torpor **7.** languor **8.** hebetude, neurosis **9.** lassitude **10.** drowsiness (morbid)
Lethe . . . **5.** abyss, Hades, river **8.** oblivion **13.** forgetfulness
lethiferous . . . **6.** deadly **11.** destructive
Leto (pert to) . . .
mother of . . **6.** Apollo **7.** Artemis
Roman name . . **6.** Latona
wife of . . **4.** Zeus
letter . . . **4.** note, type **7.** epistle, message **9.** character **13.** communication
letter (pert to) . . .
bright star . . **4.** Beta
carrier . . **6.** correo **7.** mailman, postman
cross stroke . . **5.** serif
first . . **7.** initial
letter for letter . . **9.** literatim
marks . . **5.** breve
of advice . . **11.** lettre d'avis
of challenge . . **6.** cartel
representation . . **10.** literation
short . . **4.** line, note **6.** billet
sloping . . **6.** italic
sound loss (last) . . **7.** apocope
two letters (one sound) . . **7.** digraph **9.** diphthong
writer . . **13.** correspondent
letters (pert to) . . .
decorate with . . **7.** miniate **10.** illuminate
man of . . **9.** literatus
ref to . . **8.** literary
lettuce . . . **3.** cos **4.** head **7.** Lactuca, romaine
leukocyte . . . **9.** corpuscle (white)
Levant . . . **4.** East **6.** Orient **7.** leather (Morocco) **8.** East wind
Levantine (pert to) . . .
country . . **13.** Mediterranean
garment . . **6.** caftan
herb . . **6.** madder
ketch . . **3.** bum **4.** jerm, saic **5.** xebec **6.** settee **8.** levanter
valley . . **4.** wadi (wady)
wind . . **7.** Morocco
levee . . . **4.** bank, dike, pier, quay **5.** ridge **6.** durbar, trench **8.** assembly **9.** reception **10.** embankment

level ... **4.** even, fell, flat, just, raze
5. equal, grade, plane, plani (comb
form), point **6.** peavey (peavy), smooth,
steady, topple **7.** flatten, terrace,
uniform **8.** demolish, equalize, parterre
12. well-balanced
lever ... **3.** bar, lam, pry **5.** crank, jimmy,
pedal, prise **6.** peavey (peavy), tappet,
tiller **7.** crowbar, treadle
leveret ... **4.** hare
leviathan (pert to) ...
animal (Bib) .. **5.** whale **6.** dragon
9. crocodile
embroidery .. **6.** canvas **11.** cross-stitch
political .. **12.** (the) commonwealth
size .. **4.** huge **7.** titanic **10.** formidable
Levi's father (Bib) ... **5.** Jacob
levitate ... **4.** rise **5.** float
Levite ... **5.** tribe **10.** descendant
Levitical ... **7.** Aaronic **9.** Aaronical
10. priesthood (Mormon)
Leviticus ... **10.** Pentateuch
levity ... **6.** gaiety **8.** buoyancy **9.** frivolity,
lightness **10.** triviality, volatility
levy ... **3.** tax **4.** fine, wage (war) **5.** rally,
stent **6.** assess, impose **7.** collect,
estreat **9.** recruital
lex ... **3.** law **7.** statute
lexicon ... **4.** book (of words)
10. dictionary, vocabulary
lex loci ... **13.** law of the place
lex non scripta ... **12.** unwritten law
liability ... **4.** debt **5.** debit **8.** cessavit
9. proneness **10.** likelihood, obligation
11. possibility **14.** responsibility
liable ... **3.** apt **5.** bound **6.** likely
7. exposed, subject **10.** answerable,
chargeable **11.** responsible
liable (pert to) ...
likely to .. **3.** apt **5.** prone **11.** predisposed
not liable .. **6.** exempt
to objection .. **13.** exceptionable
to penalty .. **6.** guilty
Lia Fail ... **12.** Stone of Scone
15. Coronation Stone (Ir)
liaison ... **4.** link **7.** joining **8.** intimacy,
intrigue **11.** co-operation
18. intercommunication
liana ... **4.** cipo **5.** vines (woody) **9.** wild
grape
liar ... **5.** cheat **6.** fibber **7.** Ananias,
wernard (obs) **8.** deceiver, fabulist,
perjurer **12.** prevaricator
Lias system ... **8.** Jurassic
libation ... **5.** drink **8.** oblation, offering,
potation
libel ... **4.** bill **6.** defame **7.** lampoon,
request, slander **8.** circular (obs),
handbill, roorback **10.** defamation
11. certificate, declaration
12. supplication
liberal ... **4.** free, Whig **5.** ample,
frank **7.** copious, profuse **8.** eclectic,
generous **9.** bountiful, extensive,
plentiful **10.** hospitable, munificent
11. broad-minded, magnanimous
12. uncontrolled
liberate ... **4.** flee, free **5.** loose **6.** redeem
7. deliver, manumit, release **8.** separate,
unfetter **9.** disengage **10.** emancipate
Liberia ...

capital .. **8.** Monrovia
city .. **8.** Buchanan **10.** Greenville
gulf .. **5.** Sidra
language .. **3.** Kru **7.** English
people .. **3.** Vai (Vei)
libertine ... **4.** rake, roué
liberty ... **4.** ease, free **5.** leave
7. freedom, license **9.** exemption,
privilege **10.** permission **11.** opportunity
librarian ... **7.** bookman **10.** bibliosoph,
bibliothec **13.** bibliothecary
Libya, Africa ...
astronomy .. **4.** Mars (portion)
capital .. **7.** Tripoli **8.** Benghazi
district .. **6.** Fezzan **9.** Cyrenaica
12. Tripolitania
language .. **7.** Hamitic
oasis (saline) .. **6.** Sebkha (Sebka)
people .. **5.** Arabs
sea .. **13.** Mediterranean
Libya, Gr (pert to) ...
children .. **5.** Belus **6.** Agenor
heroine of .. **5.** Libya
husband .. **8.** Poseidon
license ... **5.** right **6.** bandon, permit
7. dismiss, freedom, liberty **8.** sanction
9. approbate, authority, authorize,
privilege **10.** permission **11.** lawlessness
13. authorization
licentious ... **3.** lax **4.** lewd **5.** loose
7. immoral, lawless **9.** debauched,
dissolute **10.** lascivious, profligate
12. uncontrolled, unrestrained
licet ... **6.** lawful **7.** granted **12.** it is
conceded
lichens (pert to) ...
abounding in .. **9.** lichenose
derivative .. **4.** moss **5.** usnic **6.** litmus
genus .. **5.** Usnea **7.** Evernia
study of .. **11.** lichenology
licit ... **3.** sue **4.** just **5.** legal **6.** lawful
9. permitted
lick ... **3.** lap, win **4.** flog, whip **5.** lap
up, taste **6.** baffle, defeat, thrash
7. conquer **8.** overcome, vanquish
licorice ... **5.** abrin **9.** jequirity
licorice-flavored liqueur ... **7.** sambuca
lid ... **3.** cap, hat **4.** bred, case,
roof **5.** cover **6.** eyelid **7.** stopper
9. operculum
lid, put on the ... **3.** end **6.** hush up
7. license **8.** complete, suppress
lie ... **3.** fib **4.** rest **7.** falsify, falsity,
recline, untruth **9.** deception, falsehood,
mendacity **10.** equivocate
13. prevarication
lie (pert to) ...
at ease .. **4.** loll **5.** droop **6.** dangle
face down .. **7.** pronate
hidden, in ambush .. **4.** lurk, plot **6.** in
wait **9.** insidiate **11.** concealment
in warmth .. **4.** bask **9.** luxuriate
low .. **6.** abased **9.** prostrate
prostrate .. **4.** flat **5.** creep **6.** grovel
Liebestraum composer ... **5.** Liszt
Liechtenstein, Europe ...
capital .. **5.** Vaduz
government .. **12.** principality
language .. **6.** German
religion .. **8.** Catholic
lief (anc) ... **4.** dear, fain, glad **7.** willing

8. disposed **9.** agreeably, favorably
lieutenant . . . **6.** deputy **10.** substitute
11. locum tenens
life . . . **3.** vie **4.** bios **5.** being **6.** always,
energy, spirit **8.** vitality, vivacity
9. animation, existence
life (pert to) . . .
after death . . **8.** Olam-haba
animal . . **4.** bios **5.** biota (flora, fauna)
biology . . **4.** bios
comb form . . **3.** bio
giving . . **9.** animative **11.** procreative
god of . . **6.** Faunus
insurance . . **7.** tontine
jacket (sl) . . **7.** Mae West
later, older . . **8.** autumnal
lifelike . . **5.** alike, vital **6.** biotic **9.** realistic
plant . . **4.** bios **5.** biota
principle . . **5.** atman, prana, tenet **6.** spirit
prolonger . . **6.** elixir
science of . . **7.** anatomy, biology, zoology
12. paleontology
sea . . **5.** coral **8.** plankton
staff of . . **5.** bread
without . . **4.** dead **5.** azoic **8.** lifeless
9. inanimate
lifeless . . . **4.** abio (comb form), dead, dull,
flat **5.** amort, azoic, heavy, inert, vapid
6. jejune, torpid **8.** inactive, listless
9. bloodless, exanimate, inanimate,
powerless, tasteless **10.** lackluster,
spiritless, unanimated
lifetime . . . **3.** age, day, eon (aeon)
6. always **8.** duration **10.** generation
lift . . . **3.** aid, pry **4.** jack, perk **5.** boost,
exalt, heave, hoist, raise, steal,
theft **6.** puff up, thrill **7.** derrick,
elevate, improve, inspire **8.** elevator
11. inspiration
lifting device . . . **4.** jack, pump **5.** crane,
davit, lever, tongs **7.** capstan, derrick,
erector **8.** elevator, heighten, windlass
lifting muscle . . . **7.** erector, levator
ligament . . . **4.** bond, cord **6.** tendon
7. bandage
ligan, lagan . . . **6.** debris, jetsam
7. flotsam
ligature . . . **3.** tie **4.** band, bond, cord, note
6. amulet, binder, taenia **7.** bandage
light . . . **3.** arc, gay, sun **4.** dawn,
easy, glim, lamp, lume, mild, pale,
soft **5.** flare, flood, klieg, laser, taper
6. alight, aspect, blonde, bright,
candle, gentle, ignite, illume, medium,
window **7.** cresset, fragile, glimmer,
glowing, trivial **8.** buoyancy, daylight,
delicate, illumine, lambency, radiance,
trifling **9.** effulgent **10.** brightness,
luminosity, weightless **11.** information
12. incandescent
light (pert to) . . .
apparatus . . **9.** holophote
circle . . **4.** halo, nimb **6.** corona, nimbus
7. aureola, aureole
cloud . . **6.** nimbus
coating . . **4.** film
footed . . **4.** fast **5.** agile
globe . . **4.** bulb
god . . **6.** Balder (Baldr)
handed . . **4.** deft
headed . . **5.** dizzy **6.** fickle **9.** beeheaded

image . . **8.** spectrum
leading . . **8.** luminary
reflector . . **4.** lens **6.** mirror
refractor . . **5.** prism
science . . **6.** optics
source . . **3.** sun
touch . . **3.** dab
unit . . **3.** lux, pyr **4.** phot, watt **5.** lumen
6. carcel, Hefner
without . . **4.** dark **7.** aphotic, obscure
8. starless **9.** pitch-dark **10.** caliginous
yellow . . **5.** amber
light and airy . . . **7.** tenuous **8.** delicate,
ethereal
light and quick . . . **6.** nimble, volent
light dress fabric . . . **6.** merino
8. cashmere **9.** bombazine, paramatta
(parramatta)
lighten . . . **4.** ease **5.** allay, cheer, clear
6. reduce **7.** gladden, relieve **8.** brighten,
illumine, jettison **9.** alleviate, disburden
10. illuminate
lighter . . . see also *light* **4.** scow **5.** barge
7. gabbard, igniter, pontoon **8.** chopboat
(Chin)
lighthearted . . . **3.** gay **6.** upbeat
7. buoyant **8.** carefree, cheerful, jubilant
9. vivacious
Light Horse Harry . . . **3.** Lee (Gen Henry
Lee)
lighthouse . . . **5.** tower **6.** beacon, pharos
7. seamark **10.** watchtower
lightness . . . **6.** gaiety, levity **8.** airiness,
buoyancy, sobriety **9.** flippancy,
frivolity, giddiness **10.** fickleness,
triviality, volatility, wantonness
11. flightiness, inconstancy, instability
12. unsteadiness **14.** weightlessness
15. thoughtlessness
lightning . . . **4.** lait **5.** flash, levin **6.** stroke
8. flashing **9.** discharge
lightning (pert to) . . .
bug . . **6.** beetle **7.** firefly
discharge . . **4.** bolt **11.** thunderbolt
form . . **4.** fork **5.** chain, sheet
reference to . . **8.** fulgural
rod . . **8.** arrester
stone . . **9.** fulgurite
war . . **10.** blitzkrieg
lightsome . . . **3.** gay **4.** airy **5.** agile, clear,
light, lucid, merry **6.** fickle, nimble
7. lighted **8.** cheerful, cheering, graceful,
luminous, unsteady **9.** frivolous
12. lighthearted
lights out . . . **4.** taps
ligneous . . . **5.** woody **6.** wooden, xyloid
8. firewood
lignite . . . **4.** coal
like . . . **2.** as **4.** copy, love **5.** enjoy, equal,
liken, savor **6.** admire, desire **7.** similar
10. comparable **11.** counterpart,
homogeneous
like (pert to) . . .
bone . . **6.** osteal
fern . . **8.** frondose, frondous
gland . . **7.** adenose
gold . . **7.** aureate
house, dome . . **5.** domal
kneecap . . **7.** rotular **10.** rotuliform
sea lion . . **7.** otarian, otarine
suffix . . **2.** ar, ic **3.** ine, oid, ose

likeable, likable ... **6.** genial **8.** charming, pleasant
likelihood ... **8.** prospect **10.** good chance **11.** possibility, probability **14.** apparently true
likely ... **3.** apt, fit **5.** prone **6.** comely **8.** credible, feasible, probable, suitable **9.** promising **11.** verisimilar
likeness ... **4.** copy, icon, twin **5.** clone, guise, image **6.** effigy, statue **7.** parable, picture, replica **8.** parallel, portrait **9.** imitation, semblance **10.** comparison, photograph, similarity **11.** counterfeit **12.** reproduction **14.** representation
likewise ... **3.** too **4.** also **5.** ditto **8.** moreover **11.** furthermore
liking ... **4.** like, love, lust **5.** fancy **6.** comely **7.** delight **8.** pleasing **10.** preference **12.** predilection
lilac ... **5.** lilas, mauve **6.** purple **7.** syringa
lilac throat ... **11.** hummingbird
Lilliputian ... **4.** tiny **5.** dwarf, minim **6.** midget **7.** dwarfed **10.** diminutive
lilt ... **3.** air **4.** song, tune **5.** swing **6.** poetic, rhythm **7.** rejoice
lily ... **2.** ti **3.** lis **4.** aloe, ixia, sego **5.** calla, lotus, onion, water, wokas (wocas), yucca **6.** Allium, Nuphar **8.** daffodil, mariposa, martagon, soaproot **9.** narcissus
lily (pert to) ...
family, genus .. **4.** aloe **6.** Tulipa **7.** Bessera **9.** Liliaceae **10.** Hyacinthus
grass .. **10.** cuckoopint
iron .. **7.** harpoon
of France .. **10.** fleur-de-lis
shaped .. **7.** crinoid **9.** crinoidal
water .. **8.** Castalia, Nymphaea
lily of the valley (pert to) ...
bud .. **3.** pip
Cape Cod .. **13.** barney-clapper
English .. **6.** mugget
family .. **15.** Convallariaceae
liliaceous plant .. **5.** yucca
shrub .. **10.** fetterbush
tree .. **6.** sorrel
lima bean disease ... **6.** mildew **9.** yeast spot
liman ... **5.** marsh **6.** lagoon
limb ... **3.** arm, fin, imp, leg **4.** wing **5.** bough, scamp **6.** branch, member **7.** flipper **9.** anaclasis
limber ... **4.** limp, weak **5.** agile, lithe, loose **6.** flabby, pliant, supple **7.** flaccid, lissome **8.** flexible, yielding
limbo ... **4.** hell, jail **6.** prison **9.** purgatory
limbs, absence of ... **6.** amelia **7.** acolous
lime ... **4.** calx **5.** color, fruit **8.** chlorine, fumigant **9.** deodorant, quicklime **11.** green-yellow **12.** linden yellow
limen ... **9.** threshold
limestone ... **4.** calp, malm **5.** chalk **6.** marble, oolite **8.** pisolite
lime tree ... **6.** linden, tupelo
limey ... **6.** sailor **7.** soldier
limit ... **3.** end, fix, ori (comb form) **4.** term **5.** allot, bourn **6.** summit **7.** confine **8.** boundary, capacity, restrain, restrict, terminal **11.** restriction, termination **12.** consummation
limited ... **3.** few **5.** local, scant **6.** finite,

narrow, scanty **7.** bounded, topical **8.** confined, reserved **9.** astricted, parochial **10.** restricted **11.** conditional, topopolitan **13.** circumscribed
limiting ... **7.** hedging **10.** qualifying, relational **11.** restraining, restricting, restrictive
limn ... **4.** draw **5.** paint **6.** depict **7.** portray **8.** decorate **9.** delineate **10.** illuminate
limp ... **3.** hop, lax **4.** halt, soft, thin, weak **5.** loose **6.** flabby, limber **7.** flaccid **8.** drooping, flexible **9.** inelastic **13.** unsubstantial
limpid ... **4.** pure **5.** lucid **6.** bright **7.** crystal **8.** pellucid **11.** translucent, transparent **12.** intelligible
Lincoln, Abraham (pert to) ...
assassin .. **15.** John Wilkes Booth
birthplace .. **8.** Kentucky (1809)
debater .. **7.** Douglas (Stephen A)
dog .. **4.** Fido
mother .. **10.** Nancy Hanks
Secy of State .. **6.** Seward
Secy of War .. **7.** Stanton
son .. **10.** Robert Todd
wife .. **8.** Mary Todd
Lincoln (pert to) ...
color .. **9.** Carthamus **11.** yellow-green
sheep (breed) .. **7.** English
Lindbergh, Charles A (pert to) ...
birthplace .. **7.** Detroit (1902)
flight field .. **9.** Roosevelt (LI)
flight to (1927) .. **5.** Paris (1st)
retreat .. **10.** Illiec Isle (Fr)
wife .. **10.** Anne Morrow
linden ... **3.** lin **4.** lime, teil **5.** Tilia
line ... **3.** row **4.** arow, axis, cant, ceil, clew, cord, face, mark, race, rail, rein, rule, seam, side **5.** agone, align, raphe, ridge, route, stria, track **6.** crease, isobar, policy, series, streak, stripe **7.** engrave, outline **8.** boundary, vocation, wainscot **9.** delineate
line (pert to) ...
adjusting .. **9.** alinement
central .. **4.** axis
comb form .. **4.** lino
conceptual, geological .. **6.** agonic, isotac, tropic **7.** equator **8.** isothere, isotherm, latitude, meridian **9.** longitude
equidistant .. **8.** parallel
fine (type) .. **5.** leger, serif
fishing .. **5.** snell **7.** ratline (ratlin)
imaginary .. **7.** equator, Maginot
mathematics .. **4.** sine **5.** agone **6.** secant **7.** tangent
measure .. **3.** gry **4.** rule
meteoric .. **6.** isobar
nautical .. **6.** earing **7.** halyard, hawsing
poetic .. **5.** stich, verse
racing .. **4.** wire
raised .. **4.** weal, welt **5.** ridge
selling .. **11.** merchandise
soldiers .. **4.** file, rank **6.** cordon
transport .. **5.** stage **7.** carrier **8.** carriage
type .. **5.** agate, serif
up, lineup .. **4.** plan **5.** align **6.** muster **7.** arrange **8.** schedule **9.** formation **11.** arrangement, parallelize
lineage ... **3.** kin **4.** race **5.** birth, blood,

stock, tribe 6. family, strain 7. descent
8. pedigree 9. offspring 10. extraction,
progenitor
lineal . . . 6. racial 10. continuous,
delineated 12. genealogical
lineman . . . 3. end 5. guard 6. center,
tackle 7. wireman 11. electrician
linen . . . 4. crea, duck, lawn, lint 5. crash,
gulix, inkle (tape), toile 6. barras,
damask, dowlas, napery, sheets
7. cambric, Holland, lockram
ling . . . 4. fish, hake 5. heath 6. burbot
7. eelpout, Gidadae, heather 8. chestnut
linger . . . 3. lag 4. drag, idle, wait
5. dally, defer, delay, dwell, hover,
tarry 6. dawdle, go slow, loiter, remain
8. continue, hesitate 13. procrastinate
lingerie . . . 9. underwear 11. underthings
14. unmentionables
lingering . . . 5. delay 7. chronic 8. dilatory,
slowness 10. protracted
lingo . . . 4. cant 6. jargon, lingua, patois,
patter, tongue 8. language
lingua . . . 5. lingo 6. jargon, tongue
11. hypopharynx
lingual . . . 7. glossal 9. lingulate
10. linguiform, tonguelike
linguistics . . . 6. syntax 7. grammar
8. language 9. phonology, semantics
10. lexicology
link . . . 3. tie 4. bond, join, loop, yoke
5. annex, nexus, torch, unite 6. couple,
member, relate 7. connect, liaison,
passage 8. catenate 12. intermediary
linkage . . . 5. tie-up, union 6. hookup
7. joinder, joining 8. junction
11. conjunction
linking . . . 7. liaison 9. annectent
links in a chain . . . 7. hundred
linseed . . . 8. flaxseed
lion . . . 3. cat, cub, leo 4. puma 5. simba
6. cougar, Lionel, lionet 8. Felis leo
9. celebrity 12. King of Beasts
Lion (pert to) . . .
England . . 8. heraldry
God . . 3. Ali
Lucerne . . 11. Switzerland (Sculpture)
St Mark . . 6. Venice (winged)
the North . . 6. Sweden (King Adolphus)
lionlike . . . 6. feline 7. catlike, leonine
lip . . . 3. jib, rim 4. edge, kiss, talk 5. cheil,
words 6. flange, labium, labrum, speech
7. cheilos 8. labellum 10. mouthpiece
12. impertinence
lip (pert to) . . .
comb form . . 5. chilo, labio
formed . . 6. labial
inflammation . . 9. cheilitis
ornament . . 6. labret
service . . 9. hypocrisy 10. sanctimony
12. unctuousness
surgery . . 9. chilotomy 11. chiloplasty
tumor . . 7. chiloma
lipped . . . 6. labial 7. labiate
liquefy . . . 4. fuse, melt, thaw 6. reduce
8. dissolve, fluidify 10. deliquesce
liqueur . . . 4. anis, ouzo 5. crème,
noyau, sirup 6. cognac, genepi,
kummel, Pernod 7. cordial, curaçao,
ratafia 8. absinthe, anisette, Drambuie
9. Cointreau 11. Benedictine

liquid . . . 5. clear, fluid 6. watery 7. flowing
8. beverage, manifest, not solid
liquid (pert to) . . .
assets . . 4. cash 5. money 9. resources
chemical . . 7. acetone 8. furfural
inflammable . . 3. gas 5. ether 7. alcohol
8. gasoline
oily . . 5. olein 7. aniline, picamar
soap . . 6. napalm
thick . . 3. tar 4. dope 5. syrup (sirup)
weak . . 5. blash
liquidate . . . 4. kill 6. depose, pay
off, settle 8. amortize 9. discharge
11. exterminate
liquor . . . 3. ale, dew, gin, rum, rye 4. beer,
brew, grog, lush, sake, wine 5. hooch,
kefir, punch, stout, vodka 6. arrack
(arak), arrope, elixir, whisky (whiskey)
8. cocktail, highball 9. applejack,
moonshine 10. chasse-café
liquor container . . . 3. keg 5. flask
6. barrel, bottle 8. cellaret, decanter
liquor maker . . . 6. abkari (Ind), brewer
7. vintner 9. distiller
liquor server . . . 6. barman 7. barmaid,
skinker (anc), tapster
liquor shop . . . 3. bar 6. saloon, tavern
7. barroom, cabaret, shebeen (Scot),
taproom 8. alehouse 9. groghouse,
honky-tonk 11. rathskeller (ratskeller)
liripipe, liripoop (Hist) . . . 4. hood 5. scarf
6. dotard, tippet
lissom . . . 5. layer 7. stratum 8. platform
12. strand of rope
lissome . . . 5. agile, lithe 6. limber,
nimble, supple 7. willowy 8. flexible
list . . . 3. tip 4. edge, file, roll, rota, rote
5. index, limit, panel, table 6. careen,
edging, enlist, record, roster, stripe
7. catalog, incline 8. calendar, classify,
manifest, register, schedule, tabulate
9. catalogue, enclosure, inventory,
repertory 10. repertoire 11. enumeration
list (pert to) . . .
actors . . 4. cast
competitors . . 5. entry, slate
foods . . 4. menu 5. carte
investments . . 9. portfolio
memoranda . . 5. scrip
officers . . 6. roster
references . . 5. index
listen . . . 3. ear 4. hear, heed 6. attend
7. give ear, hearken (harken) 8. overhear
9. eavesdrop
listening . . . 7. audient 9. attentive
listing . . . 4. list 6. strips 7. selvage
10. enlistment, enrollment
listless . . . 4. dull 6. abject, drowsy,
moping, supine 7. languid 8. careless,
heedless, sluggish 9. apathetic
10. spiritless 11. unconcerned
13. uninteresting
litchi nut . . . 8. rambutan
literary . . . 6. versed 8. lettered 9. classical
11. book-learned
literary (pert to) . . .
composition . . 5. cento, essay, opera
8. rhetoric
criticism . . 9. epicrisis
drudge . . 4. grub, hack
extracts . . 9. anthology

fragments . . **3.** ana **5.** notes **8.** analecta, analects
laws . . **9.** copyright
piracy . . **10.** plagiarism
selection . . **7.** excerpt
style . . **5.** prose **6.** purism **8.** pedantic
literature . . . **4.** book, epic, Veda **5.** drama, lyric, novel **6.** ballad, poetry **7.** fiction, writing **10.** nonfiction **13.** belles-lettres
lithe . . . **4.** slim **6.** limber, supple, svelte **7.** lissome, slender **8.** flexible
Lithuania . . .
capital . . **5.** Vilna (Vilnius) **6.** Kaunas (Kovno)
Jew . . **6.** Litvak
people . . **5.** Balts, Letts **6.** Aestii
port . . **8.** Klaipeda (Memel)
river . . **6.** Niemen
litigant . . . **6.** suitor **9.** defendant, disputant, litigator, plaintiff
litigation . . . **4.** suit **7.** contest, dispute, lawsuit **10.** contention, discussion
litigious . . . **10.** disputable **11.** belligerent, contentious
litten . . . **7.** lighted **8.** cemetery **10.** churchyard
litter . . . **3.** bed, hay **4.** bier, mess **5.** couch, dooly (doolie), mulch, straw, young **6.** coffin, jumble **7.** clutter, rubbish **9.** palanquin, stretcher
litter of pigs . . . **6.** farrow
little . . . **3.** sma, wee **4.** puny, tiny, weak **5.** brief, petit, petty, scant, short, small **6.** dapper, petite, slight **7.** not much **8.** trifling **9.** niggardly **11.** unimportant **12.** narrow-minded **14.** inconsiderable
little (pert to) . . .
bethel . . **6.** chapel (seaman's), church
by little . . **6.** slowly **7.** peu à peu **9.** piecemeal, poco a poco
comb form . . **5.** steno
devil . . **3.** imp **4.** minx **5.** rogue **7.** ruffian **13.** mischief-maker
fellow . . **6.** shaver
finger, toe . . **7.** minimus
flag . . **9.** banderole
music term . . **4.** poco
ring . . **7.** annulet
Little Rhody . . . **11.** Rhode Island
Little Women, author . . . **6.** Alcott (Louisa)
littoral . . . **4.** zone (marine) **5.** shore **7.** coastal **9.** bordering
liturgical . . . **10.** ceremonial **11.** ritualistic
liturgy . . . **4.** rite **5.** ritual **8.** ceremony **14.** consuetudinary
live . . . **5.** dwell, exist **6.** reside **7.** breathe **8.** continue, have life
live (pert to) . . .
by sponging . . **5.** cadge
by stratagems . . **5.** shark
by wits . . **5.** cheat **7.** deceive, falsify **13.** Machiavellize
earlier . . **8.** pre-exist
in . . **7.** inhabit
in tents . . **5.** nomad **7.** scenite
in the country . . **9.** rusticate
live . . . **5.** alert, alive, vital, vivid **6.** bright, lively, living, virgin (mineral) **7.** charged, not dead **8.** vigorous **9.** energetic **11.** electrified

lively . . . **3.** gay, vif **4.** airy, grig, keen, pert, spry, yare **6.** active, blithe, bright, snappy **7.** animate, buoyant, pungent, tittupy (tittuppy) **8.** spirited **9.** energetic, sprightly, vivacious **10.** enlivening, rebounding **11.** interesting **12.** effervescent
liver (pert to) . . .
comb form . . **6.** hepato
disease . . **9.** cirrhosis, hepatitis
duct . . **4.** bile
pert to . . **5.** hepar **7.** hepatic
resembling . . **8.** hepatoid
Liverpool native . . . **12.** Liverpudlian
liverwort . . . **6.** Riccia **8.** agrimony, hepatica **9.** bryophyte
living . . . **4.** life **5.** alive, being, quick **6.** extant **7.** animate, organic, topical **8.** benefice, existent, lifelike **10.** livelihood **11.** subsistence
living (in, on, near) . . .
currents . . **5.** lotic
ground . . **7.** epigeal
holes . . **11.** latebricole
leaves . . **13.** phyllophagous
oxygen . . **7.** aerobic
plane (same) . . **8.** coplanar
poverty . . **11.** necessitous
river bank . . **9.** riparious
rivers, streams . . **9.** rheophile
seas (deep) . . **8.** bathybic
shores . . **8.** littoral
solitude, seclusion . . **10.** eremitical **11.** eremiticism
tents . . **7.** scenite
together . . **11.** contubernal
living (pert to) . . .
again . . **6.** Buddha **7.** revived **8.** Hutukhtu **9.** redivivus
being . . **5.** wight **6.** animal **8.** organism
capable of . . **6.** viable
dull . . **10.** vegetation
individual . . **4.** bion
near the ground . . **7.** epigeal
together . . **8.** intimate **11.** contubernal (contubernial)
lixivium . . . **3.** lye **6.** bleach **8.** cleanser
lizard . . . **3.** dab, eft **4.** adda, gila, newt, seps, uran **5.** agama, anoli, gecko, skink, varan **6.** dragon, hardim, iguana, moloch **7.** monitor, saurian, tuatera **8.** basilisk **9.** chameleon **10.** chuckwalla, salamander
llama . . . **6.** alpaca, vicuna **7.** guanaco
load . . . **3.** jag **4.** fill, lade, onus **5.** cargo **6.** burden, charge, weight **7.** fraught, freight, oppress, prepare **8.** contents, encumber **10.** imposition **11.** encumbrance
loaded . . . **5.** drunk, flush, laden, ready **7.** charged, fraught **8.** burdened, weighted **10.** in the chips
loader of vessels . . . **9.** stevedore
loadstone, lodestone . . . **6.** magnet **8.** terrella **9.** magnetite
loaf . . . **4.** idle, lump **5.** bread **6.** loiter, lounge **9.** Eucharist
loafer . . . **5.** idler **6.** beggar **7.** lounger **8.** vagabond
loam . . . **3.** rab **4.** clay, lime, malm, silt, soil **5.** chalk, loess, regur

loan ... **4.** lend **6.** borrow **7.** advance
10. provisions **13.** accommodation
loath ... **6.** averse **7.** hostile **9.** disliking,
reluctant, unwilling
loathe ... **4.** hate **5.** abhor **6.** detest
7. despise, dislike **9.** abominate
loathsome ... **4.** foul, vile **5.** nasty
6. odious **7.** cloying, hateful
9. abhorrent, offensive, repellant
10. abominable, disgusting
lob ... **3.** box, cop **4.** step, till, toss, vein
5. stair, throw **7.** lugworm, pollack
9. chandelle
lobby ... **4.** hall, room **5.** foyer
8. anteroom, corridor, coulisse
9. enclosure, vestibule **10.** wirepuller
13. pressure group
lobe ... **5.** alula **6.** earlap, lappet, lobule
7. pendant
lobster (pert to) ...
claw . . **5.** chela **6.** nipper, pincer
eggs . . **3.** roe **5.** coral
French . . **6.** homard
genus . . **7.** Homarus, Macrura
8. Nephrops
part . . **6.** thorax
tail . . **6.** telson
trap . . **3.** pot **4.** corf **5.** creel **6.** bow
net
local ... **7.** edaphic, topical **8.** regional
9. parochial **10.** epichorial (epichoric)
13. autochthonous
local court ... **5.** gemot (gemote)
locale ... **4.** site **5.** place, scene, venue
locality ... **4.** area, spot **5.** place, situs
7. endemic, habitat **8.** position
locate ... **4.** find, spot **6.** settle **7.** situate
9. establish
locatio ... **7.** leasing, letting
location ... **4.** seat, site, spot **5.** locus,
place, situs **6.** ubiety **7.** habitat **8.** district
9. situation **12.** neighborhood
locator of forest fires ... **7.** alidade
loch ... **3.** bay **4.** lake, pond **5.** inlet,
lough
lock ... **4.** bolt, hasp, hold **5.** Gatun,
latch **6.** cotter, detent, fasten, fetter
8. fastener **9.** floodgate
lockjaw ... **7.** tetanus, trismus
11. ankylostoma
lockman ... **8.** summoner (Isle of Man)
11. executioner
lock of hair ... **4.** curl **5.** tress **6.** berger
7. daglock, ringlet **8.** lovelock, spit
curl
lockup ... **3.** jug **4.** jail **5.** clink **6.** cooler
8. hoosegow (hoosgow) **9.** calaboose
loco ... **3.** mad **4.** daft **5.** craze, crazy
6. crazed **7.** disease **10.** moonstruck
15. non compos mentis
locomotion ... **6.** lation (Astrol), moving,
travel **7.** transit **8.** progress
locomotive ... **3.** hog **5.** dolly, mogul
6. diesel, dinkey, engine, mikado **9.** iron
horse
locomotive cowcatcher ... **5.** pilot
locus . . **4.** area, drug, site **5.** place
8. locality
locus (pert to) ...
in quo . . **5.** where **12.** place in which
sigilli . . **14.** place of the seal

locust ... **4.** weta **6.** beetle, cicada,
cicala, kowhai **7.** Locusta **9.** wetapunga
11. grasshopper
locust (pert to) ...
berry . . **5.** drupe **9.** glamberry
bird . . **4.** dial **7.** grackle **8.** starling
10. white stork
like . . **5.** mantis
plant . . **5.** senna
sound . . **7.** stridor **10.** stridulate
tree . . **5.** carob, honey **6.** acacia
lode ... **3.** vug (vugg) **4.** path, road,
vein **5.** canal, drain, ledge **6.** course
7. deposit **8.** waterway
lodestar ... **8.** cynosure, polestar
11. guiding star
lodestone, loadstone ... **6.** magnet
8. terrella **9.** magnetite
lodge ... **3.** hut, lie **4.** camp, tent
5. cabin, hovel **6.** billet, encamp, reside
7. deposit, quarter **11.** brotherhood
lodge doorkeeper ... **5.** tiler
lodging ... **3.** inn **4.** gite, room **5.** abode,
hotel, roost **6.** billet, harbor (harbour),
tavern **8.** barracks, dwelling, hostelry,
quarters **9.** dormitory, harborage
(harbourage) **10.** habitation
loess ... **4.** loam, silt, soil
lof ... **6.** praise **7.** measure
loft ... **3.** bin **4.** balk **5.** attic
loftiness ... **6.** height **7.** dignity
8. eminence **9.** eloquence
11. distinction, magnanimity
Lofting's doctor ... **8.** Dolittle
lofty ... **4.** high, tall **5.** proud **6.** aerial,
Alpine, Andean **7.** eminent, exalted,
haughty, stately, sublime **8.** arrogant,
elevated, eloquent, majestic, towering
9. dignified **11.** magisterial,
magnanimous **13.** distinguished
lofty place ... **4.** peak **5.** aerie, eyrie
(eyry) **6.** summit **8.** eminence, pinnacle
log ... **4.** birl, slab **5.** diary **6.** record
8. firewood, mountain, puncheon,
register **11.** speedometer
log (pert to) ...
cock . . **10.** woodpecker
gin . . **6.** jammer
hauler (sled) . . **4.** tode
implement . . **6.** nigger, peavey (peavy),
rosser
measure . . **7.** scalage
noser . . **6.** sniper
rolling . . **7.** birling
section . . **5.** spalt
support . . **3.** nog
logarithmic terms ... **3.** bel **4.** base
5. power **8.** mantissa **14.** characteristic
logarithm inventor ... **6.** Napier
loge ... **3.** box **5.** booth, stall
loggerhead ... **4.** tool **6.** turtle **7.** fathead
8. bonehead, numskull **9.** blockhead
10. thickskull
loggerheads, be at ... **8.** disagree
loggia ... **7.** gallery
logging (pert to) ...
boots . . **4.** pacs
rock . . **6.** loggan
sled . . **4.** tode **7.** travois (travoise)
wheels . . **7.** katydid
logic ... **9.** reasoning **13.** argumentation

logic (pert to)...
fallacy.. **6.** idolum
induction.. **7.** epagoge
proposition.. **5.** lemma **7.** ferison
   9. enthymeme, obvertend
specious.. **7.** sophism
term.. **5.** Darii, Ferio **8.** Celarent
logical... **4.** sane **5.** sound, valid
   8. coherent, credible, rational
   9. plausible **10.** consistent, reasonable
logician... **8.** reasoner
logogriph... **5.** rebus **6.** riddle **7.** anagram
   8. logogram
logy... **4.** dull **6.** drowsy **8.** sluggish
Lohengrin (pert to)...
character.. **4.** Elsa **8.** Parsifal
composer.. **6.** Wagner (1850)
Knight.. **15.** Knight of the Swan
loin (pert to)...
beef.. **10.** tenderloin
mutton.. **4.** rack **5.** chump
pork.. **7.** griskin
loincloth... **5.** dhoti, pagne **7.** G-string
   11. breechcloth
loir... **8.** dormouse
Loire, France...
Dept capital.. **12.** Saint Etienne
river's old name.. **5.** Liger
town.. **6.** Nantes
tributary.. **5.** Indre
loiter... **3.** lag **5.** dally, delay, tarry
   6. dawdle, linger **7.** saunter
loiterer... **4.** slug **5.** drone, idler **6.** lagger
   7. dawdler, laggard **8.** sluggard
Loki (pert to)...
god.. **7.** Discord **8.** Mischief
wife.. **5.** Sigyn
loll... **4.** hang **5.** droop **6.** dangle,
   frowst (froust), lounge, repose, sprawl
   7. recline
loma, lomita... **4.** hill
Lombard (pert to)...
ancient.. **6.** cannon
historic.. **4.** bank, loan
King.. **6.** Alboin (legend)
school.. **11.** Renaissance
street.. **6.** London
Lombardy province... **4.** Como
lomboy... **8.** Java plum
lomilomi (Haw)... **3.** rub **7.** massage,
   shampoo
London, England...
art gallery.. **4.** Tate
bank.. **27.** Old Lady of Threadneedle
   Street
borough.. **6.** Ealing **11.** Westminster
bridge.. **5.** Tower **6.** London **7.** Chelsea
   8. Waterloo
bridle path.. **9.** Rotten Row
brown.. **9.** carbuncle
cathedral.. **7.** St Paul's
clock.. **6.** Big Ben
club (Whigs).. **6.** Kit-Kat
concert hall.. **11.** Royal Albert
district.. **3.** Kew **7.** Chelsea, Mayfair
   8. Vauxhall **9.** Southwark
   10. Bloomsbury, Kensington,
   Marylebone
hawker.. **6.** coster
monument (Guildhall).. **3.** Gog **5.** Magog
Opera Company.. **12.** Sadler's Wells

palace.. **10.** Buckingham
park.. **4.** Hyde **7.** Regent's
   10. Kensington
porter.. **6.** George
press.. **11.** Fleet Street
prison.. **7.** Newgate **9.** Bridewell
quarter.. **8.** Vauxhall
roisterer (Hist).. **3.** mum
Roman name.. **6.** Agusta
square.. **9.** Trafalgar
stables.. **4.** mews
stock exchange.. **17.** Throgmorton Street
street.. **5.** Fleet **6.** Strand **8.** Pall Mall
   9. Cheapside, Whitehall **10.** Piccadilly
   11. Throgmorton **12.** Threadneedle
subway.. **4.** tube **11.** underground
train station.. **6.** Euston **8.** Victoria,
   Waterloo **9.** St Pancras **10.** King's
   Cross, Paddington
Londoner... **7.** Cockney
Londres... **5.** cigar
lone... **3.** one **5.** alone **6.** lonely, single
   7. forlorn **8.** solitary **9.** unmarried
   12. unfrequented
loneliness... **8.** loneness, solitude
   9. aloneness, dejection, isolation
   10. depression, desolation
   12. lonesomeness
lonely... **4.** lorn **6.** dreary **8.** desolate,
   lonesome, secluded, solitary
   10. friendless **11.** sequestered
   12. unfrequented
Lone Star State... **5.** Texas
long... **3.** yen **4.** pine **5.** crave, wordy,
   yearn **6.** aspire, prolix, thirst **7.** lengthy,
   tedious **8.** tiresome **9.** prolonged,
   wearisome **10.** protracted
long (pert to)...
ago, since.. **3.** eld **4.** yore
beard.. **9.** graybeard **10.** bellarmine
   (jug)
discourse, speech.. **6.** screed, tirade
   7. descant **9.** philippic, rigmarole
dog.. **9.** dachshund, greyhound
dozen.. **8.** thirteen
established.. **8.** habitual **10.** inveterate
   11. traditional
for.. **4.** hope, pine **5.** covet, crave
horn.. **6.** cattle (Tex)
inlet.. **3.** ria
journey.. **4.** trek **7.** odyssey
jump.. **5.** halmo
letters.. **7.** screeds
life.. **9.** longevity
limbed.. **5.** rangy
lived.. **9.** macrobian
periods.. **4.** ages, eons
scarf.. **4.** sari
suffering.. **7.** patient **10.** forbearing
Tom.. **3.** gun **8.** titmouse
windedness.. **9.** garrulity, prolixity
   13. longiloquence
longing... **3.** yen **6.** desire, pining
   7. craving, wistful **8.** yearning
   9. hankering, nostalgia
longitudinal... **10.** euthytatic (stress),
   lengthwise
longshoreman... **6.** docker, loader,
   lumper, stower **9.** stevedore
   10. roustabout
loo... **3.** pam **4.** game

look... 3. con, ken, pry, see 4. haze, heed, leer, peep, scry, seek, seem 5. point, stare, watch 6. appear, expect 7. examine, inspect, observe 8. indicate, perceive 9. search for

look (pert to)...
after.. 4. tend 5. serve 6. follow 7. care for 9. keep vigil, supervise
at.. 3. eye 4. face, scan, upon 6. regard 7. examine
back.. 6. recall 7. retrace 8. remember 9. recollect 10. call to mind
down upon.. 4. leer, snub 5. fleer, gloat 7. askance, despise
forward to.. 5. await 6. expect 7. foresee 10. anticipate
like.. 8. resemble
obliquely.. 4. skew
slyly.. 4. leer, ogle, peer
sullen.. 5. frown, lower 6. glower
toward.. 4. face
upon.. 2. at 4. deem 6. behold 11. contemplate

lookout... 4. view 5. guard, watch 6. conner 7. outlook 9. vigilance

looks... 4. cons, face, kens, sees 5. peers, pores, pries, seeks, seems 6. visage 8. features 9. resembles 10. appearance 11. countenance

loom... 3. auk 4. loon, tool 6. appear, puffin, vessel, weaver 7. machine 9. guillemot, implement 10. receptacle

loom part... 3. lam 4. caam, leaf, sley 5. easer, lathe, lever 6. heddle

loon... 5. diver (great Northern), Gavia, grebe, wabby 10. Gavia immer

loon... 4. dolt 6. menial (anc), rascal 7. lunatic

loony... 3. mad 4. daft 5. crazy, silly 8. demented

loop... 3. eye, tab 4. ansa, clew, kink 5. bight, bride, honda, noose, picot, sling, wootz (iron) 6. becket 7. folding 8. doubling

loophole... 4. hole, plea 5. mense, oilet 6. escape, eyelet, outlet 7. opening, pretext 8. aperture

loop-shaped... 9. fundiform 11. sling-shaped

loose... 3. lax 4. free, limp 5. slack 6. detach, remiss, unlash, wanton, wobbly 7. escaped, immoral, movable, relaxed, slacken, unbound, unleash 8. insecure, unstable 9. discharge (gun, arrow) 10. unconfined 11. improvident 12. loose-moraled 14. unconventional

loose (pert to)...
ends.. 4. dags 5. slack 7. tagrags 8. restless
garment.. 5. simar 6. banion, chimar, kimono 7. zimarra 8. peignoir
jointed.. 5. lanky, rangy 6. wobbly 7. rickety 10. ramshackle

loosely dressed... 8. discinct

loosen... 4. ease, free, undo 5. pried, relax 6. soften 7. slacken

looseness... 7. laxness 8. limpness 9. slackness, vagueness 10. remissness, wantonness

loot... 3. rob 4. gelt, haul, sack, swag 5. booty 6. spoils 7. pillage, plunder,

seizure 10. contraband

looter... 6. rifler, sacker 7. ravager, spoiler 8. marauder, pillager

lop (off)... 3. bob, cut 4. oche, sned, trim 5. droop, prune 6. cut off, snathe 8. truncate

lopsided... 4. alop 7. leaning 8. top-heavy 10. unbalanced 13. unsymmetrical

loquacious... 4. glib 6. chatty 7. voluble 9. garrulous, talkative 10. chattering

loquacity... 7. fluency, leresis 8. glibness 9. gabbiness, garrulity 12. effusiveness

lord... 3. aga (agha), bey, God 4. earl, peer, rule, tsar 5. liege, ruler, title 6. master, prince 7. Jehovah, marquis, Saviour 8. governor, nobleman, seignior, suzerain, viscount 10. proprietor 11. Jesus Christ

Lord (pert to)...
Buddhism.. 6. Buddha
Jacobite.. 3. Mar
of Heaven.. 7. Tien Chu (Chin)
of Lords.. 8. Demiurge (Plato) 11. King of Kings 13. Prince of Peace
of Wisdom.. 5. Mazda 6. Ormazd

Lord have mercy upon us... 12. Kyrie eleison 14. Christe eleison

lordly... 6. uppish 8. arrogant, despotic 9. dignified, masterful 10. tyrannical 11. domineering, overbearing

Lord's Prayer... 11. Pater Noster

lore... 4. lear 6. advice, wisdom 7. counsel 8. learning 9. erudition, mythology, tradition 12. superstition

lorgnette... 7. lorgnon 8. eyeglass 10. opera glass

lorica... 5. shell 7. cuirass 11. Breastplate (St Patrick's)

lorikeet... 6. lories, parrot

loris... 5. lemur

lorn... 6. bereft 7. forlorn 8. deserted, desolate, forsaken 9. abandoned 11. Godforsaken

loro... 10. monk parrot, parrot fish

lose... 4. fail, miss, omit 5. leese (obs), spill, waste 6. forget, mislay, perish 7. forfeit, let slip 8. estrange, squander 9. incur loss 10. wander from

lose (pert to)...
balance.. 4. trip 7. stumble
courage.. 7. despair, despond
flesh.. 8. emaciate
freshness.. 4. fade, wilt 6. wither
ground.. 7. regress 8. slow down 9. fall short 10. fall behind
luster.. 7. tarnish
vigor.. 3. fag, sag 4. fail, flag, pine 6. weaken 7. decline

loser... 6. victim 7. also ran 8. defeatee, underdog

loss... 4. ruin, weak 6. damage, injury 9. decrement, detriment, privation 10. forfeiture 11. bereavement, destruction

loss of...
commodities.. 6. ullage
eyebrows, lashes.. 9. madarosis
feeling.. 7. agnosia 10. anesthesia (anaesthesia)
hair.. 8. alopecia
loved one.. 11. bereavement

memory . . **7.** amnesia
reason . . **7.** amentia
smell . . **7.** anosmia
speech . . **4.** mute **6.** alalia **7.** aphasia
   10. laloplegia
voice . . **7.** aphonia
willpower . . **6.** abulia
lost . . . **4.** asea, gone, lorn **5.** unwon
   6. hidden, ruined, sinful, wasted
   7. mislaid **8.** absorbed, confused,
   defeated, obscured, vanished
   9. abandoned, forfeited, forgotten,
   perplexed, reprobate, subverted
   10. abstracted, bewildered, dissipated,
   overthrown, parted with
   11. preoccupied **13.** irreclaimable,
   irretrievable
lost (pert to) . . .
cause . . **8.** Civil War
color . . **5.** faded, paled
consciousness . . **7.** fainted, swooned
life fluid . . **4.** bled
to view . . **5.** perdu
tribes (ten) . . **10.** Israelites
lot . . . **3.** tax **4.** doom, fate, luck, much,
   plat **5.** share **6.** chance, hazard, studio
   7. destiny, fortune, portion **9.** allotment,
   great deal **13.** apportionment
Lot (pert to) . . .
father . . **5.** Haran
penalty . . **12.** pillar of salt
sister . . **6.** Milcah
son . . **4.** Moab
uncle . . **7.** Abraham
lots, divination by . . . **9.** sortilege
lottery . . . **4.** game **5.** bingo, lotto
   6. chance, raffle **7.** Genoese, grab bag
   11. sweepstakes
lottery prize . . . **4.** tern (from three
   numbers)
lotus . . . **7.** nelumbo **10.** chinquapin
lotus (pert to) . . .
bird . . **6.** jacana
eaters . . **9.** indolents, Lotophagi
   11. daydreamers
tree . . **4.** sadr **6.** jujube, nettle
   9. persimmon
loud . . . **5.** crass, gaudy, noisy, showy
   6. coarse, flashy, garish, vulgar
   7. blatant, booming **8.** vehement
   9. clamorous, turbulent, unrefined
   10. blustering, boisterous, tumultuous,
   vociferous **11.** stentorious
   12. obstreperous
loudmouthed . . . **10.** scurrilous, stentorian
   11. thersitical
Louise de la Ramée (novelist) . . . **5.** Ouida
   (pen name)
Louisiana . . .
bird . . **7.** pelican
capital . . **10.** Baton Rouge
city . . **10.** New Orleans, Shreveport
county . . **6.** parish
dialect . . **6.** Creole
dish (cooked) . . **9.** jumbalaya
flower . . **8.** magnolia
hero . . **6.** De Soto, de Vaca, Pineda
   7. La Salle
native . . **5.** Cajun **6.** Creole, French
   7. Acadian, Spanish
purchased from . . **8.** Napoleon (1803)

river . . **5.** Pearl **6.** Sabine **11.** Mississippi
State admission . . **10.** Eighteenth
State motto . . **22.** Union, Justice,
   Confidence
State nickname . . **7.** Pelican
tradition . . **10.** pirate lore
Louis Viaud (author) . . . **10.** Pierre Loti
   (pen name)
lounge . . . **4.** loaf, loll, sofa **5.** divan
   6. frowst, repose **7.** recline
louse . . . **5.** aphis **6.** cootie, insect, slater
   8. Anoplura, arachnid **9.** Hemiptera,
   scoundrel
lout . . . **3.** oaf **4.** boor, clod, dolt **6.** lubber,
   rustic **7.** bumpkin
loutish . . . **4.** rude **7.** awkward, boorish,
   ill-bred **8.** clownish **11.** countrified
lovable . . . **7.** amiable **8.** adorable,
   charming **9.** desirable, endearing
love . . . **3.** amo, gra, woo **4.** like **5.** adore,
   amore, fancy **6.** liking **7.** charity
   8. fondness, good will **9.** affection
   10. endearment, sweetheart
love (pert to) . . .
affair . . **7.** liaison, romance **10.** flirtation
apple . . **6.** tomato
bird . . **6.** parrot
call . . **3.** coo
feast . . **5.** agape
flower . . **4.** lily
full of . . **4.** dote **6.** doting, erotic
   7. amative **9.** idolizing
god of . . **4.** Amor, Ares, Eros, Kama
   5. Bhaga, Cupid
goddess of . . **5.** Athor, Freya (Freyja),
   Venus **6.** Ishtar **9.** Aphrodite
intrigue . . **5.** amour
knot, token of . . **6.** amoret
meeting . . **5.** tryst **10.** rendezvous
of . . **5.** phile (comb form)
parental . . **6.** storge
potion . . **7.** philter
science . . **9.** erotology
song . . **6.** serena (evening) **8.** madrigal
lover . . . **4.** beau **5.** amant, Romeo
   6. minion **7.** amorist, Don Juan
   8. paramour **9.** enamorato
   10. sweetheart
lover of . . . see also *craze for*
animals . . **10.** zoophilist
beauty . . **8.** aesthete (esthete)
wealth . . **9.** plutocrat
work . . **9.** ergophile
Lover's Leap . . . **10.** Cape Ducato
Lovers' Quarrels . . . **12.** amantium Irae
loving . . . **4.** fond **5.** phile (comb
   form) **6.** ardent, erotic **7.** adoring,
   amative, amatory, amorous, devoted
   8. charming, enamored, romantic
   11. sentimental **12.** affectionate
loving cup . . . **3.** tyg (tig)
low . . . **3.** bas, moo **4.** base, deep,
   neap, orra **5.** faint **6.** humble, menial,
   sneaky, vulgar, wicked **8.** dejected,
   indecent, infamous, inferior, plebeian
   9. inelegant **11.** unfavorable
low (pert to) . . .
born . . **4.** rude **5.** lowly **6.** common
   7. lowbred **8.** plebeian
bred . . **5.** crude **6.** coarse, vulgar
brow . . **9.** ignoramus

church.. **11.** evangelical
comedy.. **8.** travesty
country.. **7.** Belgium, Holland
 9. Luxemburg **11.** Netherlands
German.. **5.** Saxon **8.** Frankish
 12. Plattdeutsch
in spirits.. **4.** blue **6.** megrim **8.** dejected,
 downcast **10.** dispirited, melancholy
 11. crestfallen
Roman wall.. **5.** spina
shrubs, plants.. **4.** moss **5.** Erica
syllable (Mus).. **2.** ut
tide.. **3.** ebb **4.** neap **8.** low water
wall.. **7.** parapet
lower... **3.** dip **4.** vail, vase **5.** abase,
 demit, frown, neath **6.** bemean,
 debase, deepen, demean, demote,
 humble, lessen, meaner, nether, reduce
 7. cheapen, degrade, depress, descent
 8. diminish, inferior **10.** depreciate
lower (pert to)...
case letter.. **5.** small
Empire.. **9.** Byzantine
geology.. **5.** Chalk (Eng) **6.** strata
 7. stratum
most.. **6.** bottom, lowest **7.** bedrock
 10. nethermost
world.. **4.** hell **5.** earth, Hades, limbo,
 orcus, Sheol **7.** Abaddon, Gehenna
 8. Cerberus **9.** perdition, purgatory
lowering... **4.** dark **6.** gloomy, sullen
 7. ominous **8.** frowning **9.** deepening
 10. cheapening **11.** threatening
lowery... **6.** cloudy, gloomy **8.** lowering
lowest (pert to)...
animal life.. **6.** amoeba (ameba)
deck.. **5.** orlop
least.. **5.** minim **6.** bottom **7.** minimum
pedestal member (Arch).. **6.** plinth,
 quadra
peer (ranking).. **5.** baron
point.. **5.** depth, nadir **6.** bottom
 10. nethermost
point, planet.. **7.** perigee
lowing... **6.** mooing **7.** mugient
 9. bellowing
lowland... **4.** flat, holm, spit **5.** plain,
 terai **6.** bottom **8.** molehill
lowly... **4.** mean, meek **6.** humble,
 humbly, meekly, menial, modest
 8. inferior, modestly, plebeian
 12. unpretending
loxia... **7.** wryneck **9.** crossbill
loy... **5.** slick (tool), spade
loyal... **4.** feal, leal, true **5.** liege **6.** stanch
 7. staunch **8.** constant, faithful, obedient
loyalty... **5.** faith **6.** fealty, homage
 8. devotion, fidelity **9.** constancy
 10. allegiance, stanchness (staunchness)
 12. faithfulness **13.** steadfastness
Loyolite... **6.** Jesuit
lozenge... **5.** candy, facet **6.** jujube,
 tablet, troche **7.** diamond, molding
 8. pastille (pastil, pastile) **11.** perforation
lubber... **4.** boor, dolt, gawk, lout
 5. churl, drone, idler, thick **6.** sailor
 8. landsman **11.** grasshopper
lubricity... **8.** lewdness **10.** smoothness
 12. slipperiness
lubricous... **4.** lewd **6.** tricky, wanton
 7. elusive **8.** unstable **10.** lascivious

lucban... **8.** shaddock
luce... **4.** pike **10.** fleur-de-lis
lucent... **5.** clear **6.** bright **7.** shining
 11. translucent, transparent
lucern... **3.** dog **4.** lynx
lucerne... **4.** herb **6.** fodder **7.** alfalfa
 11. purple medic
lucet, luce... **4.** pike (fish)
Lucia's home... **10.** Lammermoor
lucid... **4.** sane **5.** clear, vivid **6.** bright,
 lucent **7.** shining **8.** luminous, pellucid
 11. translucent **12.** intelligible
Lucifer... **5.** Satan
luck... **3.** hap **4.** cess **5.** deuce **6.** chance
 7. ambsace **8.** fortuity **11.** good fortune
lucky... **5.** canny, happy **6.** timely
 9. fortunate **10.** auspicious **11.** good
 fortune
lucky animal... **6.** mascot
lucky token... **4.** mojo **5.** charm
 6. amulet **7.** periapt **8.** talisman
 9. alectoria **10.** rabbit foot
 12. antinganting
lucrative... **3.** fat **6.** paying **7.** gainful
 10. productive, profitable, worthwhile
 12. remunerative
lucre... **4.** gain, pelf **6.** profit, riches
 9. emolument **11.** acquisition
lucubrate... **18.** burn the midnight oil
ludicrous... **5.** antic, comic, droll,
 funny **6.** absurd **7.** amusing, comical,
 jesting, risible **9.** burlesque, laughable
 10. ridiculous
Ludolphian... **2.** pi (3.14159)
 14. Ludolph's number
Luftpost... **7.** airmail, air post
lug... **3.** box, ear, hug **4.** drag, hale,
 haul, loop, pull, tote **5.** carry **6.** basket
 9. container
luge... **4.** sled
lugs... **4.** airs **7.** clothes (showy), tobacco
 10. affections
lugubrious... **3.** sad **6.** woeful **7.** doleful
 8. grievous, mournful **9.** plaintive
 10. lamentable
lugworm... **3.** lob **7.** annelid **9.** Arenicola
luhinga... **9.** petticoat
lukewarm... **4.** cool **5.** tepid **6.** tepefy
 8. tepidity **9.** not ardent **10.** irresolute
 11. indifferent
lumber... **4.** wood **6.** bungle, litter, refuse,
 rumble, timber, trudge **7.** lombard
 9. rough wood **10.** pawnbroker
 11. impedimenta
lumberman... **6.** logger, sawyer, scorer
 9. timberman **10.** lumberjack,
 woodcutter
lumberman's half boot... **3.** pac
lumberman's sled... **4.** tode **7.** go-devil,
 travois (travoise)
luminary... **3.** sun **4.** fire, star **5.** light
 7. wise man **9.** celebrity **12.** illumination,
 leading light
luminescence... **7.** foxfire
 12. fluorescence **15.** phosphorescence
luminous... **5.** clear, lucid **6.** bright
 7. shining **9.** brilliant **11.** enlightened,
 illuminated, intelligent, transparent
 14. phosphorescent
luminous circle... **4.** halo
luminous impression... **9.** phosphene

10. afterimage
lummox . . . **3.** oaf **4.** boor, dolt,
  lout **5.** yahoo **7.** bumpkin, bungler
  12. clumsy fellow
lump . . . **3.** gob, lob, wad **4.** beat, blob,
  clot, hunk, loaf, mass **5.** bulge **6.** nodule,
  nubble, nugget, thresh **7.** cluster
  8. swelling **12.** protuberance
lump (pert to) . . .
  butter . . **3.** pat
  clay . . **4.** clag, clod
  metal . . **3.** pig **5.** ingot
lumpish . . . **4.** dull **5.** bulky, inert
  6. clumsy, stolid, stupid **7.** boorish
  8. sluggish **9.** heaviness, inertness,
  ponderous **11.** countrified
  13. shapelessness
lumpy . . . **5.** drunk, rough **6.** choppy
  7. gnarled, nodular
lumpy jaw . . . **6.** big jaw
  13. actinomycosis
luna . . . **6.** silver **11.** moon goddess
lunacy . . . **4.** moon **5.** mania **7.** madness
  8. insanity **9.** craziness
  11. derangement, foolishness
lunar . . . **5.** orbed **6.** lunate **8.** crescent,
  moonlike **9.** celestial, satellite **10.** moon-
  shaped
lunar (pert to) . . .
  appulse . . **7.** eclipse
  bone . . **7.** lunatum
  cycle . . **7.** Metonic **9.** Callippic
  deity . . **6.** Selene (Selena)
  halo . . **6.** corona, nimbus **7.** aureola
  surface feature . . **6.** crater
lunatic . . . **3.** mad **5.** crazy, idiot, loony
  6. insane, madman **8.** demoniac
  10. moonstruck
lunatic asylum . . . **9.** Bethlehem (London)
lunch . . . **5.** snack **6.** brunch, repast, tiffin
  8. brown-bag, luncheon, nuncheon
  9. collation **11.** refreshment
lunchroom . . . **6.** eatery **10.** coffee shop,
  restaurant **12.** luncheonette
lundyfoot . . . **5.** snuff (by Lundy Foot)
lunge . . . **3.** cut, jab **4.** grab, pass, stab
  5. feint, swing **6.** thrust
lungs (pert to) . . .
  ailment . . **9.** emphysema **10.** chalicosis
  12. tuberculosis
  having . . **9.** pulmonate
  part . . **5.** lobes **6.** lights **7.** bronchi,
  trachea
  sound . . **4.** rale **6.** rattle
lunula . . . **8.** crescent, half moon
lurch . . . **4.** joll, roll, sway **5.** lunge
  6. careen, topple **7.** deceive **8.** flounder
  10. disappoint
lure . . . **4.** bait, trap **5.** decoy, snare,
  tempt **6.** allure, entice, invite **7.** attract,
  beguile, trumpet, tweedle
  10. enticement
lurid . . . **3.** wan **4.** dark, pale **5.** color,
  vivid **6.** dismal, gloomy **7.** ghastly,
  obscene **9.** deathlike **11.** sensational
lurk . . . **4.** hide, lote (obs) **5.** creep,
  prowl, skulk, slink, sneak **9.** lie in wait,
  pussyfoot
luscious . . . **4.** rich **5.** sweet **6.** creamy,
  wanton **7.** cloying, honeyed **8.** sensuous
  9. delicious **10.** lascivious, voluptuous

lush . . . **4.** soft **5.** drink, drunk, juicy
  6. lavish, limber, liquor, mellow
  7. verdant **8.** flexible **9.** luxuriant,
  succulent **11.** intoxicated
lusory . . . **7.** playful **8.** sportive
lust . . . **5.** greed **6.** desire, libido
  7. craving, longing, passion **8.** virility
  14. lasciviousness
luster, lustre . . . **4.** naif **5.** glory,
  gloss, sheen, shine **6.** beauty, polish
  7. glitter, lustrum **8.** radiance, schiller,
  splendor **10.** brightness **11.** distinction,
  iridescence
lusterless . . . **3.** dim, mat **4.** dead, dull,
  flat **14.** expressionless
lustful . . . **4.** lewd **5.** randy **9.** lecherous
  10. lascivious
lustrous . . . **4.** naif **5.** nitid **6.** agleam,
  bright **7.** radiant, shining **11.** illustrious,
  transparent
lustrous mineral . . . **4.** spar
lustrum (Roman) . . . **6.** census, luster
  12. purification (5 yrs), quinquennium
lusty . . . **6.** active, robust, strong, sturdy
  7. healthy **8.** vigorous **9.** corpulent
lute . . . **4.** clay, ring (rubber), seal
  6. cement
lute, lutelike . . . **4.** asor **6.** guitar
  7. bandore, pandore, theorbo, ukulele
  8. archlute (archilute)
lute tablature . . . **7.** lyraway
lutjanoid fish . . . **4.** sesi **7.** snapper
Luxembourg . . .
  capital . . **10.** Luxembourg
  government . . **10.** Grand Duchy
  language . . **6.** French, German
  13. Letzeburgesch
  river . . **7.** Moselle
luxuriant . . . **4.** lush, rank, rich **6.** ornate,
  uberty **7.** fertile, opulent, profuse,
  teeming **8.** abundant, prolific
  9. bounteous, Sybaritic
luxuriate . . . **4.** bask **5.** revel **8.** flourish
luxurious . . . **5.** plush, ritzy **6.** ornate,
  superb **8.** imposing **9.** expensive,
  grandiose, sumptuous **10.** impressive
  11. extravagant
luxury . . . **4.** lust **7.** lechery **8.** elegance,
  pleasure, richness **10.** prosperity,
  sensuality **11.** superfluity
  12. extravagance **13.** gratification,
  sumptuousness **14.** voluptuousness
luxury lover . . . **7.** reveler **8.** Sybarite
Luzon . . .
  dialect . . **6.** Itaves
  mountain . . **3.** Iba **6.** Pagsan (Sicapoo)
  people . . **5.** Malay **6.** Igorot (Igorrote)
  7. Tagalog **8.** Tinggian (Tinguian)
  seaport . . **5.** Vigan **6.** Aparri, Cavite
  volcano . . **5.** Mayon
lyam . . . **5.** leash (Her) **10.** bloodhound
lycanthrope . . . **8.** werewolf **9.** loup-garou
Lycia (pert to) . . .
  citizen . . **6.** Lycian
  city . . **4.** Myra
  district of . . **9.** Asia Minor
  language . . **5.** Greek **6.** Lycian
Lydia . . .
  capital . . **6.** Sardis
  dynasty of . . **5.** Gyges **7.** Croesus
  13. Cyrus the Great

name, later . . **6.** Persia
name, old . . **5.** Ionia
queen . . **7.** Omphale
river . . **8.** Pactolus
ruins . . **6.** temple
lye . . . **4.** buck **6.** bleach, potash
8. lixivium
lying . . . **5.** false **6.** deceit **7.** fudging
9. decumbent, mendacity, reclining,
recumbent **10.** untruthful
lying (pert to) . . .
across . . **10.** transverse
at mountain base . . **8.** piedmont
hidden . . **6.** latent **11.** delitescent
in . . **12.** accouchement
near earth's axis . . **5.** polar
on the back . . **5.** prone **6.** supine
7. passive
lymph . . . **3.** sap **5.** chyle, fluid, serum,
water **6.** plasma **7.** cassein
lynch . . . **4.** hang **6.** murder, punish
(lawlessly) **7.** execute
lynx . . . **6.** bobcat, lucern **7.** caracal,

wildcat **8.** carcajou **13.** constellation
lynx-eyed . . . **7.** oxyopia
lyre . . . **4.** asor, harp **6.** kissar, sabeca,
trigon, zither **7.** cithara, cittern, testudo
8. phorminx
lyre (pert to) . . .
bird . . **6.** Menura **8.** lyretail, pheasant
shaped . . **6.** lyrate
tree . . **5.** tulip
turtle . . **11.** leatherback
lyric (pert to) . . .
Arabic . . **5.** gazel
Muse . . **5.** Erato **10.** Polyhymnia
music, poetry . . **3.** lay, ode **4.** epic, poem
5. epode, melic, rhyme (rime), verse,
vocal **6.** epopee, poetic **7.** canzone,
musical, rondeau **8.** operatic, palinode
9. dithyramb
poet . . **5.** odist
lyrical . . . **6.** epodic
lyrichord . . . **11.** harpsichord
lyssa . . . **6.** rabies **11.** hydrophobia
lyssophobia . . . **17.** fear of hydrophobia

M

M . . . **2.** Mu (Gr) **6.** letter (13th) **8.** thousand
Ma (Ma Bellona) . . . **7.** goddess (fertility)
maarib (Jew) . . . **7.** liturgy
Maat (Egypt) . . . **7.** goddess (justice)
Mab (Queen Mab) . . . **4.** poem **10.** fairy
queen
mabolo . . . **4.** plum **7.** camagon
macabre . . . **4.** grim **5.** lurid, weird
6. grisly **7.** ghastly **8.** gruesome
12. Dance of Death
macaco . . . **5.** lemur **6.** Macaca
7. macaque **10.** Barbary ape
macan . . . **4.** rice
macao . . . **4.** game (gambling)
Macao . . . **6.** Island **7.** seaport
macaque . . . **6.** machin, monkey
Macassar . . . **7.** seaport (Celebes)
macaw . . . **3.** ara **5.** arara **6.** parrot
7. maracan **8.** aracanga (blue and red),
ararauna (blue and yellow)
Macbeth (pert to) . . .
author . . **11.** Shakespeare (1605)
character . . **4.** Duff, Ross **5.** Angus
6. Banquo, Hecate, Lennox **7.** Macduff
murder victim . . **6.** Duncan
play type . . **7.** tragedy
rival . . **7.** Macduff
McBurney's Point (Med) . . .
13. abdominal wall
Maccabees . . . **11.** Hasmonaeans
14. fraternal order, Jewish patriots
maccaboy . . . **5.** snuff
mace . . . **4.** maul **5.** baton, gavel, spice
(nutmeg), staff **6.** ensign, mallet
7. scepter (sceptre)
mace bearer . . . **5.** macer **6.** beadle
Macedonia, Balkans . . .
capital (anc) . . **5.** Pella
city . . **5.** Berea **6.** Edessa **8.** Salonika

people . . **6.** Greeks **8.** Serbians
9. Albanians **10.** Bulgarians
ruler . . **6.** Philip **9.** Alexander (the Great)
site . . **15.** Balkan Peninsula
macerate . . . **3.** ret, vex **5.** soak **5.** steep
6. soften **7.** mortify, oppress, torture
8. emaciate **9.** waste away
machete . . . **4.** bolo, fish **5.** knife **6.** guitar
11. cutlass fish
Machiavellian, Machiavelian . . . **4.** wily
6. crafty **7.** cunning **8.** guileful,
scheming **9.** deceitful **12.** falsehearted
machila . . . **7.** hammock
machin . . . **6.** monkey **7.** macaque
machinate . . . **4.** plan, plot **6.** scheme
8. contrive, maneuver
machination . . . **6.** design, device, scheme
7. machine **8.** intrigue **9.** stratagem
10. conspiracy
machine . . . **3.** car **4.** auto **6.** device,
engine **7.** vehicle **9.** apparatus,
automaton **10.** automobile
11. association, standardize
machine (pert to) . . .
cloth maturing . . **4.** ager
cloth stretching . . **6.** tenter
cotton . . **3.** gin **4.** mule **5.** baler
glazing . . **8.** calender
hay . . **5.** baler **6.** tedder
hoisting . . **3.** gin, pry **4.** pump **5.** crane,
davit, lever, tongs **7.** derrick
hummeling . . **5.** awner
hydraulic . . **9.** telemotor
imitating . . **9.** automaton
military . . **3.** ram **6.** onager
mixing . . **9.** malaxator
ore . . **6.** vanner
planing . . **8.** surfacer
planting . . **6.** seeder

political . . **5.** party **6.** system **7.** faction
reckoning . . **6.** abacus **9.** tabulator
  10. calculator
rubber shaping . . **8.** extruder
stage effect . . **13.** deus ex machina
tool . . **5.** drill, lathe
machine gun . . . **4.** nest (hidden place)
  5. Maxim **6.** cannon **7.** Gatling
  9. Hotchkiss **10.** chatterbox
machine-made . . . **11.** stereotyped
machine power, energy . . . **5.** input
  6. output
machinist . . . **7.** artisan **8.** mechanic
mackerel . . . **5.** atule, spike, tunny
  6. sierra, tinker
mackerel (pert to) . . .
bait . . **9.** jellyfish
bird . . **7.** wryneck **9.** kittiwake
genus . . **7.** Scomber
goose . . **9.** phalarope
like . . **4.** cero **6.** bonito **7.** escolar
net . . **7.** spiller
shark . . **9.** porbeagle
sky . . **6.** clouds **9.** striation
small (allowable size) . . **5.** spike **6.** tinker
  7. blinker
mackle . . . **4.** blur, spot **6.** blotch, macule
macrobiotic . . . **9.** long-lived
mad . . . **4.** vain, wild **5.** angry, crazy,
  irate, rabid, vexed **6.** insane, maniac
  7. enraged, foolish, frantic, furious
  8. demented, frenetic, maniacal,
  reckless **9.** hilarious, turbulent
  10. distraught, infatuated, infuriated
  12. arreptitious
Madagascar, Malagasy . . .
animal . . **5.** indri, lemur **6.** aye-aye,
  tenrec (tendrac) **9.** babacoote
capital . . **10.** Tananarive
cattle . . **4.** zebu (humped)
city . . **7.** Majanga **8.** Tamatave
civet . . **7.** fossane
government . . **8.** Republic (1960)
language . . **16.** Malayo-Polynesian
native . . **4.** Hova **8.** Sakalava
palm . . **6.** raffia
religion . . **7.** Animist **9.** Christian
Madam . . . **3.** Mrs **4.** Frau, lady, Ma'am
  5. donna, hussy **6.** Madame, Señora
  8. goodwife, mistress **9.** courtesan
madcap . . . **3.** wag **4.** rash, wild
  5. blood **6.** madman **7.** hotspur, violent
  8. reckless **9.** daredevil, foolhardy
madden . . . **3.** vex **5.** craze **6.** enrage, incite
  7. incense **9.** infuriate **10.** antagonize
madder . . . **2.** al **3.** aal, red **4.** herb, rose
  (color) **5.** brown, Rubia **6.** orange,
  violet, yellow **7.** crimson, xanthin
  9. turkey-red
made . . . **5.** built **7.** created, trained
  8. invented, prepared, produced,
  rendered **10.** artificial, successful
  11. constructed **12.** enfranchised,
  manufactured
made (pert to) . . .
accurate . . **5.** trued
believe . . **7.** feigned **9.** pretended,
  simulated
blind . . **6.** seeled
clear . . **9.** explained **10.** elucidated
destitute . . **6.** bereft

fun of . . **6.** jeered, mocked **7.** derided
  9. ridiculed
hard, obdurate . . **7.** steeled
light of . . **7.** dwarfed **9.** belittled
  10. disparaged
over . . **8.** reformed, revamped
  9. remodeled
plain . . **9.** evidenced, exhibited
  10. manifested
public . . **5.** aired **7.** accused, delated
  8. reported
scalloped edges . . **6.** pinked
sound . . **7.** bleated, rumbled, swished
tart . . **7.** euchred
up . . **9.** composite **10.** artificial, fabricated
  12. manufactured
up mind . . **7.** decided
valid . . **6.** proved **9.** confirmed
  13. authenticated
whole again . . **7.** renewed **10.** reconciled
  13. redintegrated, re-established
Madeira Islands . . .
capital . . **7.** Funchal
embroidery . . **6.** eyelet
nut . . **6.** walnut
owner of Islands . . **8.** Portugal
wind . . **5.** leste
wine . . **4.** bual **5.** tinta (red) **7.** malmsey,
  sercial **8.** verdelho
wood . . **8.** ironwood (white), mahogany
madhouse . . . **5.** chaos **6.** asylum, bedlam
  8. nuthouse
madman . . . **3.** nut **4.** coot, loon **6.** maniac
  7. lunatic **9.** phrenetic
madness . . . **3.** ire **4.** fury, rage **5.** anger,
  mania **6.** frenzy, lunacy **8.** insanity
  9. agitation, theomania (Relig)
  11. foolishness, inspiration
Mad Parliament (1258) . . . **18.** Provisions
  of Oxford
Madras, India . . .
capital . . **6.** Madras
city . . **5.** Adoni, Arcot **7.** Calicut
export . . **4.** lace **7.** fabrics **9.** kerchiefs
  (for turbans)
government . . **10.** presidency
madrepore . . . **5.** coral **6.** fossil, marble
  8. Acropora **12.** Madreporaria
Madrid, Spain . . .
architecture . . **7.** Moorish
boulevard . . **5.** Prado **12.** Salon de Prado
noted buildings . . **7.** Armeria **11.** Prado
  Museum, Royal Palace
madrigal . . . **3.** ode **4.** glee, poem **5.** lyric,
  music **6.** verses
maduro . . . **5.** cigar **6.** mature **11.** dark-
  colored
maelstrom . . . **5.** churn **6.** foment
  7. turmoil **9.** whirlpool (Norway)
maestro . . . **6.** master **7.** teacher
  8. composer, musician **9.** conductor
  13. Kapellmeister
maestro-di-cappela . . . **11.** choirmaster
Mae West . . . **8.** life belt
Mafia . . . **9.** syndicate **10.** Cosa Nostra,
  underworld **12.** organization (Sicilian)
maffle . . . **6.** muddle, mumble **7.** confuse,
  stammer **8.** squander
mafoo, mafu (Chin) . . . **5.** groom **9.** stable
  boy
mag . . . **6.** magpie **7.** chatter **8.** titmouse

M

9. halfpenny
magadis ... 5. flute 9. monochord
magazine ... 4. shop 5. depot, store
  6. review 7. arsenal, chamber (gun),
  tabloid 9. ephemeris, reservoir,
  warehouse 10. periodical, repository,
  storehouse
magazine rifle ... 6. Mauser 8. repeater
mage ... 5. Magus 6. Merlin 7. Houdini
  8. conjurer, magician
magenta ... 3. dye 7. fuchsia
maggot ... 4. grub, mawk 5. larva,
  mathe 6. notion 7. caprice, Diptera
  12. eccentricity
Magi (Three Wise Men) ... 6. Gaspar
  8. Melchior 9. Balthasar
magic ... 3. art 4. juju, mana, maya, rune,
  show 5. charm, fairy, spell 6. voodoo
  10. necromancy 11. conjuration,
  enchantment, legerdemain
magic (pert to) ...
  art (black) .. 7. demonry 9. diablerie,
    diabolism
  art (white) .. 5. turgy 7. theurgy
  ejaculation .. 2. om (um) 6. sesame
  goddess .. 5. Circe 6. Hecate
  image .. 5. sigil 8. sigillum
  lantern .. 11. epidiascope
    12. stereopticon
  lantern slide .. 6. tinter
  staff, wand .. 6. rhabdo 8. caduceus
  symbol .. 5. charm 6. caract, fetish
    8. pentacle 9. pentalpha
  word .. 2. om (um) 5. voilà 6. presto,
    sesame 10. abacadabra
magical ... 6. goetic (goety) 8. charming
magician ... 4. mage 5. magus 6. Merlin,
  wizard 7. Houdini, juggler 8. conjurer,
  mandrake, sorcerer 9. archimage,
  charlatan, enchanter 11. entertainer,
  necromancer, thaumaturge
  13. thaumaturgist 15. prestidigitator
magician (pert to) ...
  attendant .. 7. famulus
  command .. 6. presto 11. abracadabra
  manual .. 8. grimoire
magirics ... 7. cookery
magirist ... 4. cook
magisterial ... 5. lofty, proud 6. august,
  lordly 7. haughty, stately 8. arrogant,
  dogmatic, judicial, official 9. dignified,
  imperious, masterful 10. commanding
  11. dictatorial, domineering,
  overbearing 13. authoritative
magistrate ... 4. cadi, doge 5. ephor,
  judge 6. aedile (edile), archon, bailli,
  puisne, syndic 7. alcaide (alcaid),
  alcalde, bailiff
magistrate's orders ... 4. acta
magma ... 5. dregs 8. sediment
  10. molten rock, suspension (Pharm)
magna cum laude ... 14. with great
  honor
magnanimous ... 4. free 5. lofty,
  noble 7. exalted, liberal 8. generous
  9. honorable, unselfish, unstinted
  10. high-minded 11. great of mind
  13. disinterested
magnate ... 4. lord 5. baron, mogul, noble
  6. bashaw, bigwig, tycoon 7. grandee,
  richman 9. personage 11. millionaire

magnesium (pert to) ...
  limestone .. 8. dolomite
  nitrate .. 9. saltpeter
  silicate .. 4. talc
  sulphate .. 10. Epsom salts
magnet ... 7. terella 8. solenoid
  9. loadstone, lodestone
magnet (type) ... 3. bar 9. horseshoe
  10. artificial
magnetic ... 10. attractive, electrical
  14. attractiveness
magnetism ... 5. oomph 8. polarity
magnificence ... 4. pomp 5. glory
  8. grandeur, splendor
  15. superexcellence
magnificent ... 5. grand, regal 6. lavish,
  superb 7. exalted, pompous, sublime
  8. imposing, palatial, splendid, striking
  9. brilliant, grandiose, sumptuous
  10. munificent
magnify ... 4. laud 5. exalt, extol
  6. expand, praise 7. enlarge, glorify,
  worship 8. increase 9. intensify,
  overstate 10. exaggerate
magnitude ... 4. size 6. extent 7. bigness
  8. grandeur, nobility 9. extension,
  greatness
Magnolia State ... 11. Mississippi
magnum ... 4. bone (wrist) 6. bottle
  9. capitatum
magnum opus ... 9. great work
  11. achievement
magpie ... 3. daw, mag, pie 4. Pica,
  piet (pyet) 5. madge, scold 6. pigeon,
  talker 9. chatterer 10. chattermag
magpie type ...
  diver .. 4. smew
  shrike .. 7. tanager
maguari ... 5. stork
magus ... 8. magician 9. one of Magi
Magyar ... 3. Hun 9. Hungarian
Mah (Persian) ... 9. moon angel
maha ... 10. sambar deer
Mahabharata (blind king, Hind) ...
  13. Dhritarashtra
mahajan, mahajun (Ind) ... 8. great man
  11. moneylender
mahal ... 8. Taj Mahal 9. residence
  (summer) 10. apartments, Natal brown
mahala ... 5. squaw
maharaja, maharajah ... 5. ruler
  6. prince
maharani, maharanee ... 5. queen
mahatma ... 4. sage 7. wise man
  9. great soul, occultist 21. Great White
  Brotherhood (member)
mahi-mahi ... 7. dolphin
mah-jongg piece ... 4. tile
mahogany ... 3. roe (burl) 4. toon, wood
  5. brown 6. totara 7. ratteen
maholi ... 5. lemur
Mahomet ... see *Mohammedan*
Mahound ... 5. Devil 8. Mohammed
mahout ... 6. driver (elephant), keeper
Mah to Mahi ... 10. Fish to Moon
Maia (pert to) ...
  mountain nymph .. 7. Arcadia
  son .. 6. Hermes
  star .. 8. Pleiades
maid ... 4. girl, lass 5. bonne, woman
  6. damsel, maiden, virgin 7. abigail,

servant **8.** spinster **9.** tirewoman
Maid (of) . . .
  Astolat . . **6.** Elaine
  Athens . . **12.** Theresa Macri
  Lydia . . **7.** Arachne (changed to a spider)
  Orléans . . **9.** Joan of Arc
  Zeus . . **2.** Io (changed to heifer)
maidenhair . . . **4.** fern **8.** Adiantum
  10. Venus's hair
maidenhair tree . . . **6.** gingko
maidenly . . . **6.** gentle, modest **7.** girlish
  9. unmarried
maigre . . . **4.** diet, fish
mail . . . **3.** dak (dawk) **4.** post **5.** armor
  7. consign, letters, plumage **8.** dispatch
mail, coat of . . . **5.** armor **6.** byrnie
  (brinie) **7.** broigne, cuirass (part),
  hauberk, panoply
mail boat . . . **6.** packet
maim . . . **6.** injure, mangle, mayhem
  7. disable **8.** mutilate **9.** tear apart
main . . . **3.** sea **4.** duct **5.** chief, first, great,
  prime, sheer, utter **6.** mighty, potent
  7. chiefly, conduit, leading **8.** foremost
  9. conductor, essential, principal **10.** on
  the whole **11.** essentially **13.** most
  important
main (pert to) . . .
  act (drama) . . **8.** epitasis
  beam . . **6.** girder **7.** walking
  part . . **4.** body
  point . . **3.** jet, nub **4.** crux, gist, pith
  post . . **9.** sternpost
  sea (poet) . . **11.** Spanish Main (Caribbean
  Sea)
Maine . . .
  bay . . **5.** Casco **13.** Passamaquoddy
  capital . . **7.** Augusta
  city . . **4.** Saco **5.** Hiram, Orono **6.** Bangor
  8. Lewiston, Portland **11.** Millinocket
  college . . **5.** Bates, Colby **7.** Bowdoin
  Easternmost city . . **8.** Eastport
  Easternmost point . . **19.** West Quoddy
  Head Light
  Easternmost town . . **5.** Lubec
  lake . . **6.** Sebago **9.** Moosehead
  mountain . . **5.** Kineo **8.** Cadillac, Katahdin
  resort . . **9.** Bar Harbor
  resort island . . **8.** Mt Desert
  river . . **8.** Kennebec **9.** Penobscot
  State admission . . **11.** Twenty-third
  State motto . . **6.** Dirigo **7.** I Direct
  State nickname . . **8.** Pine Tree
  trout . . **7.** oquassa
Maine, The . . . **10.** battleship (Sp-Am
  War)
maintain . . . **4.** aver, hold, keep **5.** claim
  6. affirm, allege, assert, avouch, defend,
  endure, insist, retain **7.** justify, support,
  sustain **8.** continue, preserve
maintainable . . . **7.** tenable
maintenance . . . **3.** aid **6.** upkeep
  7. alimony, defense, support
  9. retention **10.** livelihood, sustenance
  11. continuance **12.** conservation,
  preservation, sustentation
maison . . . **5.** house
Maison Carrée . . . **12.** Norman Temple
  (Nimes)
maison de santé . . . **6.** asylum **8.** hospital
  10. sanatorium

maître d'hôtel (famed) . . . **5.** Oscar
maize . . . **3.** Zea **4.** corn **7.** mealies
maja, majo . . . **5.** belle, dandy
majestic . . . **5.** grand, great, lofty,
  noble, regal, royal **6.** august, kingly
  7. stately, sublime **8.** elevated,
  eloquent, imperial, splendid **9.** dignified,
  grandiose **11.** ceremonious, magnificent
majesty . . . **5.** title **7.** crowned (Her),
  dignity **8.** grandeur **9.** eloquence,
  greatness, loftiness, sceptered (Her)
major . . . **3.** dur (Mus) **6.** course (study),
  ditone **7.** greater, officer **8.** legal age,
  majority
major-domo . . . **6.** butler **7.** bailiff, steward
  9. seneschal
majority . . . **3.** age **4.** most **6.** quorum
  7. greater **8.** maturity **9.** majorship,
  plurality, seniority **12.** more than half
make . . . **2.** do **4.** earn, form, gain, kind
  5. shape **6.** compel, create, induce,
  render **7.** compose, execute, produce
  8. contrive, generate **9.** structure
  10. accomplish **11.** composition,
  manufacture
make (pert to) . . .
  affidavit . . **4.** affy
  allowance . . **5.** abate, admit **7.** concede
  allusion to . . **7.** mention
  amends . . **5.** atone **7.** redress
  as if . . **7.** pretend **8.** as though
  bare . . **5.** strip **6.** balden, denude
  believe . . **4.** sham, feign **7.** pretend
  8. pretense
  better . . **5.** widen **6.** soften **7.** broaden,
  improve **9.** meliorate **10.** ameliorate
  book . . **10.** record bets
  buoyant . . **8.** levitate
  calm . . **5.** allay, quiet **6.** serene
  7. appease, compose
  certain . . **6.** assure, ensure
  cheerful . . **6.** solace **7.** comfort, console
  choice . . **3.** opt **4.** cull **6.** choose, select
  7. pick out
  clean breast of . . **7.** confess **8.** disclose
  clear . . **7.** explain **9.** elucidate
  coins . . **4.** mint
  counterchange . . **11.** recriminate
  crisp . . **9.** embrittle
  deduction . . **6.** rebate
  desolate . . **5.** strip **7.** bereave
  diminutive . . **9.** bantamize
  do . . **3.** eke **5.** get by **6.** manage **8.** piece
  out **9.** improvise
  eccentric . . **8.** decenter
  edging . . **3.** tat **7.** crochet
  effective . . **6.** compel **7.** enforce
  enduring . . **6.** anneal, temper
  equal . . **6.** equate
  evident . . **6.** evince
  familiar . . **8.** accustom
  famous . . **8.** eternize **11.** immortalize
  fast . . **4.** snub **5.** belay **6.** batten, secure
  faulty . . **6.** impair **7.** vitiate
  11. contaminate
  firm . . **3.** fix **5.** brace **6.** cement
  fit . . **4.** suit **5.** adapt **6.** adjust **7.** conform
  foolish, stupid . . **4.** daff **8.** stultify
  10. ridiculous
  fun of . . **3.** rib **5.** scoff **8.** ridicule
  glass . . **7.** platten

good.. **7.** absolve, justify, succeed **9.** indemnify, vindicate
happy.. **5.** elate **7.** beatify **8.** felicify (obs)
hard, harsh.. **5.** steel **6.** freeze **7.** roughen
harmonious.. **6.** attune
headway.. **4.** gain **7.** advance **8.** progress
holy.. **5.** bless **6.** hallow **10.** consecrate
honorable.. **5.** exalt **6.** uplift **7.** ennoble
ineffective.. **4.** void **5.** annul
insensible to pain.. **11.** anesthetize (anaesthetize)
into law.. **5.** enact **9.** legislate
known.. **6.** impart, reveal **7.** divulge, publish, uncover **8.** disclose, discover, proclaim
lace.. **3.** tat **7.** crochet
less dense.. **4.** thin **6.** rarefy
less smooth.. **7.** roughen
level.. **4.** true
light.. **6.** jetsam **8.** illumine, jettison
like.. **7.** imitate **11.** impersonate
lively.. **8.** energize
love.. **3.** coo, woo **5.** court
merry.. **5.** laugh **6.** banter **7.** disport
mild.. **8.** mitigate, modulate
moral.. **8.** ethicize
much of.. **6.** praise **7.** enthuse, lionize **10.** exaggerate
muddy.. **4.** roil
notes.. **8.** annotate
off with.. **5.** steal
out.. **4.** know **5.** solve **6.** decode, draw up **7.** analyze, discern **8.** contrive, decipher **10.** understand
over.. **4.** redo **6.** revamp **7.** convert **8.** renovate, transfer **9.** refashion, reproduce
pale, sickly.. **8.** etiolate
possible.. **6.** enable
pottery.. **7.** spattle
precious.. **6.** endear
pretentious.. **7.** buckram
public.. **3.** air **5.** bruit, noise **6.** delate **7.** publish **9.** divulgate **11.** acknowledge
ready.. **4.** gear **5.** coach, prime **7.** prepare
reparation.. **5.** atone
resistance.. **5.** rebel **6.** mutiny, revolt
secure.. **3.** fix, pin **4.** nail, snub **5.** belay **6.** batten, fasten
shift.. **9.** temporary
short work of.. **6.** hasten **7.** destroy **10.** accomplish
shrill noise.. **10.** stridulate
smooth.. **4.** buff, iron **5.** sleek, slick **6.** scrape
spruce.. **4.** perk **7.** smarten
strong.. **7.** stouten
thin.. **9.** attenuate
three-cornered.. **11.** triangulate
unhappy.. **8.** embitter **10.** exacerbate
up.. **5.** atone, build **6.** invent, settle **7.** compose, concoct, prepare **8.** assemble, cosmetic **9.** construct, improvise, reconcile **10.** compensate
use of.. **5.** apply **6.** borrow, employ **7.** utilize **11.** appropriate
waste (law).. **7.** estrepe
watertight.. **4.** calk, seal
white.. **6.** blanch, bleach

worse.. **9.** aggravate
zealous.. **7.** enthuse
maker of...
arrows.. **8.** fletcher
barrels.. **6.** cooper
bundles.. **5.** baler
infusion.. **7.** steeper
knives.. **6.** cutler
pottery.. **6.** potter **8.** ceramist
makeshift... **7.** stopgap
maki... **5.** lemur
mal (comb form)... **3.** bad, ill **5.** badly **7.** disease **8.** sickness
Malabar (pert to)...
bark.. **5.** ochna
nutmeg.. **10.** Bombay mace
palm.. **7.** talipot
rat.. **9.** bandicoot
Malacca... **7.** seaport (Malaya)
Malachi... **4.** Book (Old Test) **7.** prophet
malachite... **4.** bice **5.** green **6.** copper **7.** pigment
maladroit... **6.** clumsy **7.** awkward, unhandy **8.** bungling **9.** all thumbs, graceless **10.** blundering, left-handed, ungraceful
maladventure... **6.** mishap **8.** escapade **12.** ill adventure
malady... **4.** amok **7.** ailment, disease, illness **8.** disorder, sickness **9.** complaint, distemper **13.** indisposition
mala fide... **10.** in bad faith
Malaga... **4.** city (Sp), wine **10.** oxblood red
Malagasy lemur... **6.** aye-aye
Malagasy region... **10.** Madagascar
malaise... **4.** pain **10.** discomfort, uneasiness
malapert... **4.** bold, pert **5.** saucy **8.** impudent
malaria... **5.** miasm **6.** miasma **10.** strophulus
malaxation... **7.** massage **9.** softening
Malay Archipelago...
animal.. **4.** mias **5.** tapir, tsine **6.** gibbon, taguan **7.** banteng
apparel.. **4.** baju **5.** banju **6.** sarong
buffalo.. **4.** gaur **7.** carabao, seldang
canoe.. **4.** proa **5.** prahu
chief (tribal).. **4.** dato (datto)
crane.. **5.** sarus
dagger, knife.. **6.** creese (kris), parong
disease (jumping).. **4.** Lata (Latah)
gentleman.. **3.** sir **4.** tuan
island.. **4.** Bali, Java **5.** Timor **7.** Celebes, Sumatra **9.** New Guinea **11.** Philippines
isthmus.. **3.** Kra
language.. **7.** Tagalog
native.. **5.** Bajau **6.** Ifugao **8.** Filipino **9.** Samal Laut **10.** sea gypsies
palm.. **6.** Arenga, gomuti (gomuto) **8.** Saguerus
pygmy.. **4.** Aeta
rice field.. **5.** sawah
seaport.. **7.** Malacca
state.. **5.** Kedah, Perak **6.** Jahore
tree.. **4.** upas **5.** kapur, niepa, terap **6.** durian (fruit)
vessel.. **4.** toup **6.** lugger
Malaysia...

capital . . **11.** Kuala Lumpur
malcontent . . . **5.** rebel **6.** Fenian,
uneasy **7.** repiner **8.** agitator, grumbler
10. rebellious **12.** discontented
male . . . **2.** he **3.** cob, him, tom **4.** bull,
dude, galt, jack, stud **5.** andro (comb
form), macho, manly **6.** tercel, virile
7. rooster **8.** stallion **9.** masculine
male (pert to) . . .
column (Arch) . . **7.** Telamon **8.** Atlantes
One Hundred eyes . . **5.** Argus
malediction . . . **5.** curse **6.** threat
7. malison, slander **8.** anathema
11. imprecation **12.** denunciation
malefaction . . . **5.** crime **7.** offense
9. malum in se
malefactor . . . **5.** felon **7.** culprit
8. criminal, evildoer **9.** wrongdoer
malevolence . . . **4.** hate **5.** pique, spite
6. grudge, malice, rancor **7.** ill will
8. inimical **9.** animosity, malignity
10. bitterness
malevolent . . . **4.** evil **6.** hating **7.** envious,
hateful **8.** spiteful **9.** malicious,
rancorous **11.** ill-disposed
malfeasance . . . **7.** misrule **8.** impolicy
10. wrongdoing **11.** evil conduct, illegal
deed
malfeasant . . . **8.** criminal, evildoer
malgré . . . **9.** in spite of
15. notwithstanding
malheur . . . **10.** misfortune
Mali, Africa . . .
capital . . **6.** Bamako
malice . . . **4.** envy, evil **5.** malum,
pique, spite, wrong **6.** rancor **7.** ill
will **9.** animosity, malignity, malintent
10. bitterness **11.** malevolence
malicious . . . **4.** evil, mean **6.** bitter,
malign, ornery **7.** hateful **8.** sinister,
spiteful **9.** rancorous, resentful, vitriolic
11. ill-disposed **12.** cantankerous,
unpropitious
malicious (pert to) . . .
destruction . . **5.** arson **8.** sabotage
9. vandalism
gossip . . **4.** dirt **7.** scandal, slander
intention . . **6.** animus
maliform . . . **11.** apple-shaped
malign . . . **4.** evil **5.** abuse, libel **6.** deadly,
defame, revile, vilify **7.** asperse, baleful,
harmful, slander, traduce **8.** badmouth,
virulent **10.** calumniate **12.** unpropitious
malignancy . . . **6.** malice **9.** virulence
10. deadliness **11.** harmfulness,
noxiousness
malignant . . . **3.** ill **4.** evil **5.** felon
6. deadly, wicked **7.** harmful, heinous,
vicious **8.** spiteful, virulent **9.** felonious,
invidious, malicious, poisonous,
rancorous **10.** rebellious **11.** deleterious
maligner . . . **8.** libelist **9.** slanderer
malignity . . . **4.** evil, hate **5.** spite, venom
11. harmfulness, heinousness
maline(s) . . . **3.** net **11.** Mechlin lace
malingerer . . . **6.** truant **7.** quitter, shirker,
slacker, welsher
malison . . . **5.** curse **11.** malediction
malkin . . . **3.** cat, mop **4.** drab, hare
6. sponge **8.** slattern **9.** scarecrow
mall . . . **4.** gull, walk **5.** alley, plaza,

prado **6.** arcade, mallet **7.** alameda
8. assembly **9.** esplanade, promenade
14. shopping center
mallangong . . . **8.** duckbill
mallard . . . **4.** Anas, duck **5.** drake
malleable . . . **4.** soft **6.** pliant **7.** ductile,
plastic **9.** teachable
mallemuck . . . **6.** fulmar, petrel
9. albatross
mallet . . . **3.** tup **4.** club, mace, maul
5. gavel, madge **6.** beater, beetle,
driver, hammer
malm . . . **4.** marl **5.** chalk
malmsey . . . **4.** wine
malodorous . . . **4.** foul, rank **5.** fetid
6. rotten, smelly **7.** noisome, odorous
11. ill-smelling, odoriferous
malt (pert to) . . .
froth . . **4.** barm
ground . . **5.** grist
infusion . . **4.** wort **9.** sweetwort
kiln . . **4.** oast
liquor . . **4.** beer, suds **6.** Scotch (whisky)
mixture . . **6.** zythum **7.** maltate
source . . **5.** grain **6.** barley
vinegar . . **4.** wort **6.** alegar
Malta, Mediterranean Isle . . .
capital . . **8.** Valletta
fever . . **8.** undulent
group island . . **4.** Gozo **6.** Comino
Maltese . . . **3.** cat **5.** cross **6.** Knight,
native (of Malta)
maltreat . . . **5.** abuse **6.** misuse **8.** ill
treat **9.** do wrong by
malty . . . **5.** drunk
malum . . . **4.** evil **5.** wrong **7.** offense
malversation . . . **9.** extortion (in office)
10. corruption **11.** evil conduct,
fraudulence, misbehavior
mammal . . . **3.** ape, man **4.** homo **5.** whale
10. vertebrate
mammal . . . **2.** ai, ox **3.** ape, bat, cat,
cow, dog, hog, orc, pig, rat, yak
4. bear, bull, deer, lion, mink, mole,
paca, seal, tait, zebu **5.** camel, coati,
daman, koala, lemur, llama, moose,
mouse, okapi, otter, ounce, panda,
ratel, rhino, sable, shark, sheep, swine,
tapir, tayra, whale **6.** alpaca, badger,
desman, dugong, marten, monkey,
ocelot, rytina (ext), tenrec (tendrac),
walrus, weasel **7.** dolphin, manatee,
opossum, peccary, raccoon **8.** aardvark,
anteater, antelope, elephant, kangaroo,
mongoose, reindeer **10.** chevrotain,
rhinoceros **12.** hippopotamus
mammal (pert to) . . .
coat . . **4.** hide, skin **6.** pelage
cud-chewing . . **8.** ruminant
edentate . . **8.** anteater, pangolin,
tamandua (anteater)
extinct . . **6.** rytina **8.** mastodon
9. Glyptodon
flying . . **3.** bat
largest . . **5.** whale
man . . **6.** Bimana (group)
meat-eating . . **9.** carnivore
nipple . . **4.** teat **8.** mammilla
omnivorous . . **3.** hog, pig **5.** swine
Order . . **7.** Cetacea **8.** Edentata, Rodentia
Order, highest . . **7.** Primata **8.** Mammalia

Order, lowest . . **9.** Marsupial
plantigrade . . **7.** raccoon
primate (except Man) . . **10.** Quadrumana
scaled . . **8.** pangolin
shelled . . **9.** armadillo
smallest . . **5.** shrew
snake-eating . . **8.** mongoose
toothless . . **8.** edentate
web-footed . . **6.** aliped
wing-footed . . **6.** aliped
zebralike . . **6.** quagga
mammock . . . **4.** tear **5.** break, scrap
  8. fragment
mammon . . . **5.** money **6.** riches, wealth
  11. fallen angel (Bib) **15.** demon of
  cupidity
mammoth . . . **5.** giant, large (very)
  7. titanic **8.** behemoth, elephant,
  gigantic, mastodon **9.** pachyderm
  11. Dinotherium **12.** hippopotamus
man . . . **3.** arm, fit, rig **4.** homo, male
  5. adult, equip, fit up, human, staff
  6. outfit, person **7.** fortify, furnish,
  mankind, prepare, someone **9.** human
  race **10.** human being
man (of) . . .
all work . . **4.** mozo **6.** Friday **8.** factotum
  9. assistant
Blood and Iron . . **8.** Bismarck
Destiny . . **9.** Bonaparte (Napoleon)
Galilee . . **11.** Jesus Christ
God . . **5.** saint **6.** priest **9.** clergyman
  12. ecclesiastic
law . . **6.** lawyer **7.** counsel **8.** attorney
  9. counselor (counsellor)
learning . . **6.** pundit, savant **7.** scholar
  9. literatus **11.** litterateur
quackery . . **7.** buffoon **9.** trickster
  10. mountebank
the sea . . **3.** tar **6.** merman, sailor
the signs . . **12.** homo signorum
the woods . . **6.** rustic **8.** silvanus,
  woodsman **9.** orangutan
the world . . **6.** layman **11.** cosmopolite
  12. sophisticate
war . . **7.** frigate, soldier, warrior
man (pert to) . . .
aged . . **3.** vet **9.** patriarch
  12. octogenarian
bachelor . . **4.** stag **8.** celibate
bald . . **9.** pilgarlic
conceited . . **7.** coxcomb
cunning . . **5.** rogue **6.** rascal **7.** shyster
  10. mountebank
dissolute . . **4.** roué
eccentric, elderly . . **4.** sire **5.** uncle
  6. codger, gaffer **11.** grandfather
effeminate . . **9.** androgyne
entire (soul and body) . . **3.** ego
fashionable . . **3.** fop **4.** dude **5.** dandy
  11. Beau Brummel **12.** boulevardier
fungus . . **9.** earthstar (the)
handsome . . **6.** Adonis
hardheaded . . **5.** Boche
hard-pressed . . **3.** Job
important . . **4.** hero, lion **5.** chief, nabob
  6. tycoon **7.** mugwump
isle of, capital . . **7.** Douglas
lady's . . **4.** beau **6.** fiancé
lawless . . **7.** ruffian
learned . . **6.** pundit, savant **7.** erudite,

scholar **9.** literatus **11.** philologist
like . . **7.** android **10.** anthropoid
little . . **6.** mankin, shrimp, squirt
  10. homunculus
loud-voiced . . **7.** stentor
lowbred . . **4.** serf **5.** churl **6.** rustic
  7. peasant **8.** plebeian
medicine, magic . . **6.** shaman
millionaire . . **7.** Croesus **10.** capitalist,
  Corinthian
newspaper . . **6.** editor **8.** reporter
  10. journalist
old . . **5.** elder **7.** veteran **12.** octogenarian
prehistoric . . **4.** cave **6.** Ice Age **8.** eolithic,
  Grimaldi, Piltdown **9.** neolithic
  11. paleolithic
red . . **6.** Indian
strong . . **6.** Samson **8.** ironside
wise . . **4.** sage, seer **5.** solon **6.** nestor
  7. Solomon
without a country . . **5.** Nolan (Philip)
manacle . . . **4.** gyve, iron **5.** chain **6.** fetter
  7. shackle **8.** handcuff **9.** restraint
manada . . . **4.** herd **5.** drove, flock
manage . . . **3.** man, run **4.** boss, head,
  lead, tend **5.** cater, dight, guide, pilot,
  wield **6.** direct, govern **7.** control,
  husband, operate **9.** contrive, engineer
  10. administer, manipulate
manageable . . . **4.** easy, tame, yare
  6. docile, wieldy **7.** ductile **9.** compliant,
  tractable **10.** governable **12.** controllable
management . . . **4.** care **6.** charge,
  menage **7.** conduct, control, gestion
  9. direction **10.** government
  11. negotiation
manager . . . **4.** boss **6.** gerent **7.** steward
  8. director, governor, operator, overseer
  9. economist **12.** entrepreneur
  13. administrator
managery . . . **7.** cunning **8.** artifice
  9. frugality, husbandry **10.** management
  12. manipulation **14.** administration
mañana . . . **8.** tomorrow **10.** before long
manas (Hind) . . . **3.** ego **4.** mind
Manasseh . . . **5.** tribe (Israel) **11.** King
  of Judah
Manchuria . . .
capital . . **6.** Mukden (old) **9.** Changchun
government . . **5.** China
Japanese name . . **9.** Manchukuo
native . . **9.** Mongolian
river . . **4.** Amur, Liao, Yalu
manciple . . . **5.** slave **7.** servant, steward
  8. purveyor
mandarin (pert to) . . .
bird . . **4.** duck
city . . **9.** Chungking
color . . **3.** red
dialect . . **7.** Chinese
figure in Chinese dress, seated . .
  9. grotesque
fruit . . **6.** orange **9.** tangerine
official . . **8.** governor **10.** bureaucrat
residence . . **5.** yamen
ware . . **9.** porcelain
mandate . . . **5.** edict, order **6.** behest,
  charge, decree, mandat **7.** bidding,
  command, precept **9.** direction
  10. injunction, referendum
mandatory . . . **10.** imperative, obligatory,

preceptive
mandible . . . **3.** jaw **4.** beak **5.** chops, molar (part) **9.** chelicera
mandrel, mandril . . . **3.** hob **4.** axle, pick (miner's) **5.** arbor **7.** spindle
mandriarch . . . **9.** monk ruler
mandrill . . . **6.** baboon
mane . . . **4.** hair, juba, shag **6.** thatch
manege . . . **6.** school (riding) **7.** academy (riding) **8.** cavesson (halter)
manes (Rom) . . . **4.** gods (lower world) **7.** spirits
maneuver, manoeuvre . . . **4.** ruse **5.** trick **6.** device, jockey, scheme, tactic **7.** operate **8.** artifice, intrigue, strategy **9.** stratagem **10.** manipulate **13.** Immelmann turn
mangabey . . . **6.** monkey
manger . . . **3.** bin **4.** crib, meal, rack **6.** bunker, trough **7.** banquet
mangle . . . **3.** cut, mar **4.** hack, maim **5.** press **6.** bruise, injure, ironer **8.** calender, demolish, lacerate, mutilate **9.** dismember
mango (pert to) . . .
  bird . . **6.** oriole **11.** hummingbird
  fish . . **9.** threadfin
  fruit . . **5.** amini, bauno, drupe, melon **9.** muskmelon
  grove . . **4.** tope
mangy . . . **4.** mean **5.** itchy, seedy **6.** ronyon, scurvy, shabby **7.** squalid **12.** contemptible
manhandle . . . **4.** maul **5.** abuse **7.** rough up **8.** maltreat, mistreat
mania . . . **4.** rage **5.** craze, furor **6.** frenzy, furore, lunacy **7.** madness, passion **8.** delirium **10.** alienation **11.** fascination, infatuation
mania (for) . . .
  buying . . **9.** oniomania
  drink . . **9.** potomania **10.** dipsomania
  foreign customs . . **9.** xenomania
  narcotics . . **10.** narcomania
  religion . . **9.** theomania
  stealing . . **10.** erotomania **11.** kleptomania
  wandering . . **10.** dromomania
  work . . **9.** ergomania
manifest . . . **4.** list, open, show **5.** clear, index, overt **6.** evince, liquet, patent **7.** declare, evident, express, obvious, visible **8.** apparent, disclose **11.** indubitable **12.** indisputable, unmistakable
manifestation . . . **4.** aura **5.** phase **7.** display **8.** evidence **10.** appearance, disclosure, exhibition, indication, revelation **13.** demonstration
manifestation of . . .
  deity . . **4.** Apis **7.** serapis
  divinity . . **6.** Christ **8.** Epiphany
  Vishnu . . **6.** avatar
manifesto . . . **5.** edict **6.** decree **8.** evidence, rescript **11.** declaration (public) **12.** announcement **13.** demonstration
manikin . . . **5.** dwarf, model, pygmy **6.** figure **7.** phantom **9.** mannequin
Manila . . .
  boat . . **6.** bilalo

capital of . . **11.** Philippines
hemp . . **5.** abaca
hero . . **5.** Dewey (Adm)
island site . . **5.** Luzon
native . . **7.** Chinese, Tagalog **9.** Filipinos
manioc . . . **7.** cassava
maniple . . . **5.** fanon, orale **7.** handful, phalanx, platoon
manipulate . . . **3.** rig, use **4.** work **5.** pilot, treat, wield **6.** handle, manage **7.** operate
manipulation . . . **5.** using **8.** handling, intrigue **9.** operation, stratagem **10.** management, use of hands
Manitoba, Canada . . .
  capital . . **8.** Winnipeg
  Indian . . **4.** Cree
  lake . . **8.** Manitoba
  river . . **3.** Red
mankind . . . **3.** man **4.** Adam, folk **7.** menfolk **8.** humanity **9.** human race
mankind (pert to) . . .
  division . . **4.** race **5.** tribe
  group (kindred) . . **6.** ethnos, socius
  hater . . **11.** misanthrope
  science . . **9.** ethnogeny, ethnology **12.** anthropology
manly . . . **4.** bold **5.** adult, brave, hardy, noble **6.** daring **8.** resolute **9.** honorable, masculine, undaunted **10.** courageous
manna . . . **4.** food (miracle), lerp (laap, laarp) **7.** godsend **10.** gazangabin
manner . . . **3.** air, way **4.** kind, mien, mode, sort **5.** guise, style **6.** aspect, custom, method **7.** fashion **8.** behavior **10.** appearance, deportment
manner (pert to) . . .
  frenzied . . **4.** amok **5.** amuck, huffy **7.** haughty
  law . . **5.** modus
  like . . **4.** thus **6.** in kind **8.** parallel
  meddlesome . . **9.** officious
  meditative . . **13.** contemplative
  rough . . **7.** brusque **10.** irreverent
mannerism . . . **4.** mode **8.** elegance **11.** affectation
mannerly . . . **4.** nice **5.** moral, suave **6.** seemly **8.** decorous, politely **9.** courteous **10.** well-spoken **12.** ingratiating
manner of . . .
  making something . . **7.** facture
  pronouncing . . **6.** accent, brogue
  speaking . . **7.** grammar
manners . . . **5.** mores **8.** behavior **9.** amenities, etiquette
Mannheim gold . . . **5.** brass
mano (comb form) . . . **4.** hand
manoc . . . **4.** fowl (jungle) **7.** chicken, rooster
manor . . . **4.** hall **5.** abode **6.** estate **7.** demesne, mansion
manred . . . **6.** homage **9.** vassalage **10.** leadership (in war)
mansion . . . **4.** seat **5.** house, manor, manse **8.** dwelling **9.** astrology
manta . . . **3.** ray (fish) **4.** wrap **5.** cloak, cloth **7.** blanket **8.** mantelet (mantlet) **9.** devilfish
mantilla . . . **4.** cape, veil **5.** cloak
mantis . . . **4.** Cagn (deity) **6.** insect

7. mantoid **9.** rearhorse
mantis crab . . . **7.** squilla
mantle . . . **4.** cape, cope, robe **5.** cloak,
cover **6.** capote, kittel **7.** garment
8. filament, insignia, mantelet, mantling
(Her), vestment **10.** witzchoura
11. mantelletta
manto . . . **3.** ore **4.** gown **5.** cloak
6. mantle, mantua
mantoid . . . **6.** mantis
Mantua (pert to) . . .
  birthplace of . . **6.** Vergil (Virgil)
  capital . . **7.** Mantova
  walled by . . **11.** Charlemagne
Manu (Myth) . . .
  laws . . **8.** creation, religion
  progenitors of . . **3.** Man
  Seventh Age, author of . . **10.** Code of
  Manu (Hind laws)
manual . . . **4.** book **7.** clavier (Mus),
didache **8.** exercise, handbook
14. consuetudinary
manual (pert to) . . .
  alphabet (deaf) . . **11.** dactylology
  arts . . **6.** crafts
  crafts . . **5.** sloyd (sloid, slojd)
  10. handicraft
  digit . . **3.** toe **5.** thumb **6.** finger
  8. dactylar
  ritual . . **7.** rituale **8.** breviary **9.** formulary
manufacture . . . **4.** make **6.** invent
7. produce, trump up **9.** fabricate
manufacturer of drugs, liquors . . .
6. abkari (abkary)
manumission . . . **7.** freeing **10.** liberation
(slave) **12.** emancipation
manumit . . . **4.** free **5.** let go **6.** unhand
7. dismiss, release **8.** liberate
manuscript (Ms, Mss) . . . **4.** copy
(author's), opus **5.** codex, folio
7. writing **8.** document **11.** composition,
handwriting **13.** written by hand
manuscript (pert to) . . .
  back . . **5.** dorso
  blank space . . **6.** lacuna
  copier . . **6.** scribe
  mark (old) . . **6.** obelus
many . . . **6.** divers **7.** diverse, several,
various **8.** frequent, manifold, numerous
9. different, multitude **10.** multiplied
many (pert to) . . .
  footed . . **8.** multiped
  prefix . . **4.** poly, vari **5.** multi
  sided . . **9.** versatile **12.** multilateral
  times . . **5.** often **10.** frequently
manyplies . . . **12.** third stomach
(ruminant)
Manx cat characteristic . . . **6.** no tail
8. tailless
mao . . . **7.** peacock
Maori (pert to) . . .
  Adam, ancestor . . **4.** Tiki
  bird . . **3.** tui **4.** weka (flightless)
  canoe, raft . . **4.** moki, waka
  charm (grotesque) . . **7.** heitiki
  compensation . . **3.** utu
  fish . . **4.** hiku **7.** rainbow **9.** trumpeter
  hero . . **4.** Maui
  people . . **3.** Ati **4.** Hapu
  priest . . **7.** tuhunga
  sect . . **7.** Ringatu

  tatooing . . **4.** moko
  tree . . **5.** mapau
  village . . **4.** kaik (kaika)
  weapon . . **4.** mere, patu, rata **6.** marree
Maoriland . . . **10.** New Zealand
map . . . **4.** plat **5.** chart, image **6.** charte,
design, isobar (weather line), sketch,
survey **7.** diagram, epitome, explore,
picture **9.** delineate **10.** embodiment
14. representation
maple (pert to) . . .
  bowl . . **5.** mazer, rogan (sap)
  flowering . . **8.** abutilon
  genus . . **4.** Acer **9.** Aceraceae
  insect scale . . **10.** pulvinaria
  seed . . **6.** samara
  sugar tube . . **5.** stile
  tree . . **8.** box elder **9.** moosewood
map maker . . . **4.** Eric (Father) **7.** charter
8. Mercator **12.** cartographer
mapo . . . **4.** goby (fish)
mar . . . **4.** ruin, scar **5.** botch, spoil
6. damage, deface, impair, mangle
7. blemish **8.** mutilate **9.** disfigure
Mar . . . **4.** Lord (Jacobite)
marabou, marabout . . . **5.** stork **6.** argala,
covert **8.** adjutant
maracan . . . **5.** macaw
maranon . . . **6.** cashew
marasca, maraschino . . . **6.** cherry
marasma . . . **5.** waste **7.** disease
10. emaciation **12.** malnutrition
maraud . . . **3.** rob **4.** loot, raid, rove, sack
6. forage **7.** brigand, cateran, pillage,
plunder **10.** plundering
marble . . . **3.** mib, mig, taw **4.** cold,
hard **5.** agate, white **6.** basalt, marmor
7. pattern (mottled) **8.** dolomite
9. limestone, sculpture, unfeeling
marble (pert to) . . .
  Belgian . . **5.** rance
  Catalonia . . **8.** brocatel (brocatelle)
  cork (tree) . . **9.** tambookie
  famous . . **6.** Parian **7.** Carrara **8.** Pentelec
  game . . **3.** taw **5.** alley
  group (famed) . . **5.** Elgin (Marbles)
  made of . . **9.** marmoreal
  mosaic . . **7.** tessera
  Roman . . **7.** cipolin
  slab . . **5.** dalle, stele
marbled . . . **9.** marmorate
Marbles . . . **5.** Elgin **7.** Arundel
marc . . . **6.** refuse, spirit **7.** residue **14.** eau
de vie de marc
marcato (Mus) . . . **6.** marked **8.** accented,
emphatic
march . . . **4.** fill, hike, step, trek **5.** troop
6. border, parade **7.** advance, proceed
8. boundary, drumbeat, frontier,
lockstep, movement, progress, smallage
9. cavalcade, quickstep
March King . . . **5.** Sousa (John Philip)
marcid . . . **4.** weak **7.** decayed, tabetic
8. withered **9.** exhausted **10.** emaciating
Marcobrunner . . . **4.** wine (White Rhine)
Mardi Gras . . . **8.** carnival **10.** fat Tuesday
(literal) **13.** Shrove Tuesday
Mardi Gras King . . . **3.** Rex
mare . . . **4.** yaud **5.** filly, horse **6.** goblin,
grasni (gypsy) **7.** incubus, specter,
trestle **8.** the blues **9.** nightmare **10.** blue

devils, melancholy
marge, margent . . . **3.** rim **4.** brim, edge,
    side **5.** brink, shore **6.** border, fringe,
    margin **8.** marginal
margin . . . **3.** rim **4.** brim, edge, rand,
    room, side **5.** brink, limit **6.** amount,
    border, reward **10.** collateral
margin (pert to) . . .
    business . . **5.** gross
    notched . . **5.** erose
    note . . **7.** apostil **8.** scholium
        10. annotation
    scalloped . . **7.** crenate
    set in . . **6.** indent
    straighten (to) . . **5.** align
marginal note . . . **4.** kere (kri, keri)
    7. apostil **8.** scholium **10.** annotation
marigold . . . **5.** aster, boots, caper,
    finch **6.** orange (cadmium) **7.** cowslip,
    Tagetes
marijuana . . . **3.** hay **4.** hemp **6.** reefer
    7. tobacco (wild) **8.** locoweed
    9. cigarette
marikina . . . **7.** tamarin **8.** marmoset
marimba . . . **9.** xylophone
marina . . . **4.** dock **5.** basin **9.** esplanade,
    promenade (seaside)
marinal . . . **6.** marine, sailor, saline
marine . . . **3.** tar **5.** jolly, naval **7.** mariner,
    oceanic, pelagic **8.** maritime, nautical
    11. leatherneck
marine (pert to) . . .
    animal . . **3.** orc **4.** brit, seal **5.** coral,
        polyp **6.** dugong, Otaria, teredo, walrus
        7. manatee, mollusk, octopus
    clam . . **8.** shipworm
    crustacean . . **4.** brit **8.** barnacle
    fauna, flora . . **7.** benthos
    fish . . **5.** shark **8.** menhaden
    gastropod . . **5.** conus (snail), murex
        7. terebra
    growth . . **4.** kelp **5.** algae **6.** enalid
        7. seaweed **10.** ditch grass
    individual . . **6.** merman **7.** mermaid
    skeleton . . **5.** coral
    slogan . . **6.** gung-ho
mariner . . . **3.** gob, tar **4.** salt **5.** Jacky
    6. sailor, seaman **8.** waterman
mariner's card . . . **5.** chart
mariner's compass points . . . **6.** rhumba
marionette . . . **4.** doll, duck **6.** figure,
    puppet
maritime . . . **5.** naval **6.** marine **7.** oceanic
    8. nautical
marjoram . . . **3.** dot **4.** mint **6.** origin
    8. origanum **9.** flavoring
mark . . . **3.** aim, tee **4.** heed, line, note, rist,
    seal, sign **5.** brand, label, notch, score,
    stain, stamp, trait **6.** denote, symbol,
    target **7.** betoken, blemish, earmark,
    engrave, impress, imprint, insigne
    8. evidence, identify, insignia, landmark
    9. emphasize, objective, punctuate,
    signature, trademark **10.** indication
    11. distinction, distinguish
    14. characteristic
mark (pert to) . . .
    bad . . **7.** demerit
    bounds . . **7.** delimit **9.** demarcate
    contest (in a) . . **5.** bogey (bogie)
    critical . . **6.** obelus

diacritical . . **5.** hacek, tilde **6.** tittle,
    umlaut **7.** cedilla
disgrace . . **6.** stigma
fingerprint . . **5.** whorl
logic . . **11.** differentia
misconduct . . **7.** demerit
off . . **4.** plot **6.** assign **7.** measure
    12. characterize, circumscribe
of homage . . **7.** ovation
of whip . . **4.** wale, welt
on a seed . . **5.** hilum (pl hila)
out . . **6.** cancel **10.** obliterate
possessive . . **10.** apostrophe
printing . . **4.** dele, stet **5.** caret **6.** dagger,
    diesis, obelus **7.** obelisk **10.** apostrophe
pronunciation . . **5.** breve **6.** macron
proofreading . . **4.** dele **5.** caret
prosody . . **7.** caesura, triseme
    9. diaeresis, tetraseme
punctuation . . **4.** dash **5.** colon, comma
    6. period **9.** diaeresis (dieresis),
    semicolon **10.** apostrophe
question . . **7.** eroteme (erotema)
reference . . **4.** star **6.** dagger, diesis
    8. asterisk
with bars . . **5.** grill
with dots, spots . . **6.** dapple **7.** stipple
with pointed instrument . . **6.** scrive
with ridges . . **3.** rib
marked by . . .
    dispute . . **13.** controversial
    maneuvering . . **8.** tactical
    nicety . . **7.** elegant
    small areas . . **9.** areolated
    time . . **5.** dated
marked with . . .
    colors . . **7.** mottled **10.** variegated
        11. psychedelic
    depressions . . **7.** dimpled
    furrows . . **6.** rivose
    grooves . . **6.** lirate
    lines . . **5.** ruled **6.** linear, notate
    sables (Her) . . **8.** pelleted
    spots . . **6.** notate **7.** mottled
    stripes . . **7.** lineate
    zones . . **6.** zonate
marker . . . **4.** buoy **5.** pylon **6.** scorer,
    signal **7.** brander, counter, monitor
    8. bookmark, marksman, monument,
    recorder **9.** indicator
market . . . **4.** mart, sale, sell, shop
    5. forum, trade **6.** rialto, square
    9. clientele
market (pert to) . . .
    bonds . . **5.** float
    day (Rom) . . **7.** nundine
    French . . **8.** débouché
    place . . **4.** sook **5.** agora, plaza, store
        6. bazaar, rialto **8.** emporium, exchange
marketable . . . **6.** staple **7.** salable **8.** in
    demand, vendible **12.** merchantable
markhor . . . **4.** goat
marking (crescent) . . . **6.** lunula, lunule
    7. lunulet **9.** engraving
markings . . . **7.** rasceta
marksman . . . **4.** shot **6.** gunner, sniper
    7. shooter **9.** Orangeman
Mark Twain (pert to) . . .
    character . . **9.** Tom Sawyer
        15. Huckleberry Finn
    pseud of . . **13.** Samuel (Langhorne)

Clemens
tale.. **9.** Gilded Age **10.** Roughing It
15. Innocents Abroad
marl... **4.** malm **5.** earth, fiber **6.** manure
7. deposit (earthy), marlite **9.** greensand
10. fertilizer, overspread
marli... **4.** lace **5.** gauze, tulle **6.** border
(raised on dish)
marlin... **6.** curlew, godwit **8.** sailfish
9. spearfish
marlinspike... **3.** fid **4.** bird, tool **6.** jaeger
8. skua gull
marmalade... **3.** jam **6.** Achras, sapote
8. plum tree, preserve **12.** mammee
sapota
marmit... **6.** kettle **7.** soup pot
marmite (Mil)... **4.** bomb (soup kettle)
5. shell
marmor... **6.** marble
marmoset... **4.** mico (black-tailed)
6. monkey, sagoin **7.** tamarin
marmot... **5.** bobac **6.** rodent **7.** Marmota
8. Arctomys, whistler **9.** ground hog,
woodchuck
maroon... **5.** slave **7.** abandon, cast off,
forsake, isolate **8.** chestnut **13.** leave
helpless
marquee... **4.** tent **6.** canopy
Marquis, infamous... **4.** Sade
marriage... **5.** union **7.** wedding,
wedlock **9.** matrimony **10.** nuptiality
11. espousement
marriage (pert to)...
absence of.. **5.** agamy
age.. **6.** mature, nubile
broker.. **9.** schatchen **10.** matchmaker
forswearer.. **8.** celibate
god.. **5.** Hymen
goddess.. **4.** Hera
hater.. **10.** misogamist
late in life.. **8.** opsigamy
more than one.. **6.** bigamy, digamy
8. polygamy **9.** polyandry, tetragamy
(4th) **11.** deuterogamy
notice.. **5.** banns
of the gods.. **8.** theogamy
outside the tribe.. **7.** exogamy
pert to.. **7.** marital, spousal **8.** hymeneal
9. connubial, endogamic
portion.. **3.** dot **5.** dotal, dowry
promise.. **7.** betroth **8.** affiance
secret.. **9.** elopement
married... **5.** wived **6.** wedded
8. espoused **9.** connubial
married (pert to)...
more than once at a time.. **9.** polyandry
(woman)
once at a time.. **8.** monandry
person.. **4.** wife **6.** spouse **7.** husband
8. benedict
twice.. **6.** bigamy, digamy
11. deuterogamy
marrow... **4.** pith **6.** center **7.** essence,
medulla **9.** substance
Mars... **3.** god (of War) **4.** Ares **6.** planet,
war-god
Mars (pert to)...
altar.. **13.** Campus Martius (field of
Mars)
constellation.. **3.** Ara
festival.. **5.** March **7.** October

pert to.. **5.** Arean **7.** Martian
priests.. **5.** Salii
red.. **5.** totem
satellites.. **6.** Deimos, Phobos
ship.. **8.** moon ship **9.** spaceship
sons (twin).. **5.** Remus **7.** Romulus
spot.. **5.** oasis
Marseillaise... **4.** song (1792)
Marseille, France...
capital of Dept.. **14.** Bouches du Rhone
church.. **9.** Notre Dame
fort.. **11.** Rue Noailles **13.** Rue
Cannebière
old name.. **8.** Massilia
seaport site.. **13.** Mediterranean
marsh... **3.** bog, fen **4.** meer, mire, moor,
slue **5.** bayou, liman, swale, swamp
6. morass, saline, slough **7.** maremma
marsh (pert to)...
bird.. **4.** rail, sora **5.** crane, snipe, stilt
7. bittern
crocodile.. **3.** goa
elder.. **3.** Iva
fever.. **7.** helodes
gas.. **7.** methane **8.** firedamp
grass.. **5.** sedge, spart
hawk.. **5.** harpy **7.** harrier
hen.. **4.** rail
inhabiting.. **12.** limnophilous
mallow.. **5.** altea
marigold.. **5.** boots, calla **7.** cowslip
pert to.. **8.** paludine
shrub.. **4.** reed **5.** sedge **7.** bulrush,
cattail **8.** moorwort **12.** pickerelweed
marshal... **3.** Ney (Fr) **4.** lead **5.** align,
aline, array, groom, guide, range,
usher **6.** direct, parade **7.** farrier, officer
8. official
Marshall Islands...
chains (two).. **6.** Ralick (eleven isls)
7. Rattack (13 isls)
government.. **11.** trusteeship
WWII scene.. **6.** Bikini **8.** Eniwetok
9. Kwajalein
marshberry, marshwort... **9.** cranberry
marshy... **3.** wet **5.** boggy, fenny, liman
7. moorish **8.** morassey, paludine
marsupial... **4.** frog, tait **5.** kaola
6. wombat **7.** opossum, wallaby
8. kangaroo **9.** bandicoot, phalanger,
tapoatafa **10.** Diprotodon
11. Marsupialia
marsupium... **5.** pouch
martel (Hist)... **6.** hammer
martel-de-fer... **6.** weapon **12.** hammer
of iron
marten... **3.** fur **4.** pelt **5.** sable
6. mammal **7.** Mustela
martial... **4.** Mars (pert to) **5.** brave
7. warlike **8.** fighting, militant, military
Martinique...
capital.. **8.** St Pierre (former) **12.** Fort
de France
formation.. **8.** volcanic
mountain peak.. **9.** Mont Pelée
martyr... **4.** kill **5.** title **7.** Stephen
(Christian), torture **8.** sufferer
marvel... **4.** gape **6.** wonder **7.** miracle,
portent, prodigy **8.** astonish
marvelous... **6.** superb **7.** strange
9. wonderful **10.** improbable, incredible,

remarkable **11.** astonishing
13. extraordinary
Maryland . . .
bay . . **10.** Chesapeake
capital . . **9.** Annapolis
city . . **9.** Baltimore
Hist site . . **8.** Antietam **10.** State House
   (nation's oldest) **11.** Fort Mc Henry
mountain . . **8.** Backbone, Piedmont
   11. Appalachian
race (famed) . . **9.** Preakness
   12. Steeplechase
race track . . **5.** Bowie **6.** Butler, Laurel
   7. Pimlico
school . . **9.** Annapolis (Acad) **12.** Johns
   Hopkins
settler . . **7.** Calvert (Leonard)
State admission . . **7.** Seventh
State motto . . **22.** Manly Deeds,
   Womanly Words
State nickname . . **4.** Free **7.** Old Line
mash . . . **4.** feed, ogle, pulp **5.** crush, flirt,
   press, smash, steep **6.** jumble, soften
   7. mixture **9.** pulverize **11.** infatuation
mashal . . . **7.** parable, proverb
masher . . . **5.** dandy, flirt, ricer **7.** utensil
   10. pulverizer **11.** philanderer
masjid . . . **6.** mosque
mask . . . **4.** ball, loup, veil **5.** cloak,
   cover, dance, drama, onkos **6.** domino,
   screen **7.** conceal, pretext **8.** disguise
   10. subterfuge
masked . . . **6.** comedy, cowled, hidden,
   veiled **7.** larvate, obscure **8.** shrouded
   9. concealed, disguised
masker . . . **5.** mimer **6.** mummer
   11. masquerader
maslin . . . **5.** brass **6.** kettle **7.** mixture
   (grain) **9.** potpourri
Masonic doorkeeper . . . **5.** tiler
Mason, Perry (pert to) . . .
actor . . **4.** Burr (Raymond, TV) **6.** Larkin
   (John, radio) **7.** William (Warren, film)
author . . **18.** Erle Stanley Gardner
detective . . . **5.** Drake (Paul)
secretary . . **6.** Street (Della)
title words . . **9.** The Case of
masonry . . . **6.** ashlar **9.** revetment
mass . . . **3.** cob, dab, gob, mop, pat, wad
   4. blob, body, bulk, load, loaf, lump,
   roll, size **5.** solid **8.** quantity **9.** large
   part, magnitude **11.** large amount
   12. accumulation, congregation
mass (pert to) . . .
book . . **6.** missal
collection . . **9.** aggregate
directory (RCCh) . . **4.** ordo
for dead . . **7.** requiem
matter . . **5.** molar
molten glass . . **7.** parison
nerve tissue . . **8.** ganglion
tangled . . **3.** mop **4.** shag
vestment (Eccl) . . **5.** amice
Massachusetts . . .
capital . . **6.** Boston (1630)
city . . **5.** Salem **7.** Concord **8.** Plymouth
   9. Cambridge, Lexington **10.** Gloucester,
   New Bedford **12.** Provincetown
college (oldest, US) . . **7.** Harvard
explorer . . **5.** Cabot **7.** Gosnold **9.** Capt
   Smith (John)

hero . . **10.** Paul Revere
island . . **9.** Nantucket **15.** Martha's
   Vineyard
mountain . . **3.** Tom **8.** Greylock
   10. Berkshires
river . . **10.** Housatonic **11.** Connecticut
school (first free) . . **6.** Dedham (1649)
settlers . . **8.** Pilgrims, Puritans
State admission . . **5.** Sixth
State nickname . . **8.** Bay State **9.** Old
   Colony
massacre . . . **5.** havoc **6.** pogrom
   7. carnage **8.** butchery, decimate,
   genocide **9.** slaughter
massage . . . **3.** rub **5.** knead **6.** stroke
   7. therapy
masses, the . . . **4.** folk **6.** rabble **9.** hoi
   polloi, multitude **11.** proletariat, rank
   and file **12.** common people **13.** great
   unwashed
massive . . . **3.** big **4.** bold **5.** bulky,
   large, massy **7.** weighty **8.** imposing
   9. ponderous **10.** impressive
   11. substantial
mast . . . **3.** cue, fid **4.** pole, spar **5.** stick,
   stuff (oneself)
master . . . **3.** man, rab **4.** lord, mian, rule
   5. chief, judge, rabbi, tutor **6.** expert,
   humble, subdue **7.** captain, conquer,
   maestro, padrone, subject, teacher
   8. dominate, overcome, regulate,
   surmount, vanquish **9.** commander,
   conqueror, craftsman, preceptor,
   subjugate
master (pert to) . . .
African . . **5.** bwana
Eton . . **4.** beak
fencing . . **7.** lanista
hard . . **6.** despot
Indian . . **5.** sahib
music . . **7.** maestro
of a house . . **13.** paterfamilias
of ceremonies . . **2.** M C **5.** emcee
of Heaven . . **16.** Celestial Teacher
of the horse . . **7.** equerry
stroke . . **4.** coup
masterful . . . **6.** lordly **7.** haughty
   8. arrogant, skillful **9.** arbitrary,
   imperious **10.** commanding
   11. dictatorial, domineering, magisterial,
   overbearing **13.** authoritative
masterpiece . . . **10.** magnum opus
   11. chef d'oeuvre **17.** pièce de
   rèsistance
mastery . . . **4.** gree **5.** power, skill
   7. control, victory **8.** dominion
   10. ascendancy **11.** proficiency
   12. vanquishment
mastic . . . **3.** asa, gum **5.** resin **6.** liquor
   8. adhesive **9.** red-yellow
masticate . . . **4.** chew **5.** crush, grind
   8. macerate
mastiff . . . **3.** dog **5.** burly, matin
   7. massive
mastodon . . . **5.** giant **6.** animal, Mammut
   7. mammoth **8.** behemoth **9.** dinothere
   10. Dinotheres, Mammutidae
   11. Dinotherium
mat . . . **3.** rug **4.** dull (finish) **5.** doily,
   platt, twist **7.** webbing **8.** entangle,
   material **10.** interweave, lusterless

matador . . . see *bullfighting*
matagasse . . . **11.** butcherbird
match . . . **3.** pit **4.** copy, game, mate,
pair, peer, sort **5.** equal, fusee, marry,
tally, vesta **7.** compare, contest, lighter,
lucifer **8.** coincide, marriage, parallel
10. correspond **11.** counterpart
matched . . . **5.** mated **6.** paired, pitted,
teamed **7.** equaled (equalled)
matchless . . . **5.** alone **6.** unlike **7.** unequal
8. peerless **9.** unequaled **10.** inimitable
12. incomparable
matchlock . . . **3.** gun **7.** gunlock
mate . . . **4.** pair, wife **5.** equal, marry,
match **6.** seaman, spouse **7.** comrade,
husband, mariner, partner
9. companion **11.** confederate,
counterpart
matelassé . . . **6.** fabric **8.** quilting
(imitation) **13.** ornamentation
material, materiel . . . **4.** data **5.** goods,
stuff **6.** fabric, matter, plasma, staple,
swatch **7.** weighty **8.** relevant, supplies,
tangible **9.** apparatus, corporeal,
equipment, essential **11.** substantial
12. nonspiritual **13.** materialistic
material (pert to) . . .
building . . **4.** frit, lime, tile, wood
5. adobe, brick, rabat, tapia **6.** cement,
thatch **7.** plywood **8.** asbestos, Masonite
9. wallboard
discard . . **4.** slag **5.** scrap **6.** refuse
7. rubbish
dress . . **4.** silk, wool **5.** crepe, linen,
satin, surah, tulle, tweed **6.** baleen,
faille, sennit, tricot, velvet **8.** corduroy
household . . **5.** scrim **6.** carpet, damask,
lampas, mohair, napery **7.** drapery
8. tapestry
needlework . . **4.** lace, yarn **6.** thread
8. arrasene, chenille
paper . . **3.** wax **4.** bond, news, note,
rice **6.** letter, tissue, vellum **7.** drawing,
writing **8.** wrapping **9.** cardboard,
onionskin, parchment **11.** papier-mâché
polishing . . **11.** rottenstone
materia medica . . . **7.** acology
10. leechcraft
maternal . . . **7.** enation **8.** motherly
10. motherlike
math . . . **6.** mowing **9.** aftermath,
monastery
mathematician . . . **6.** Euclid **7.** actuary
9. physicist, Whitehead
mathematics (pert to) . . .
abbreviation . . **3.** QED
arbitrary . . **5.** radix **9.** parameter
deduction . . **8.** analysis
diagram . . **5.** graph
element . . **4.** cube, root **6.** factor
7. decimal, divisor, formula, minuend
8. dividend, fraction, quotient, repetend
10. multiplier, subtrahend
12. multiplicand
equation . . **2.** pi **4.** cosh, sine, surd
6. cosine
factor . . **10.** quaternion
instrument . . **6.** sector **7.** compass
8. arbalest
number . . **5.** digit
operation, operator . . **5.** nabla **6.** scalar

7. operand **10.** quaternion
proposition . . **7.** theorem
quantity . . **6.** addend, augend, scalar
sheets of . . **4.** cone **5.** nappe
symbol . . **5.** digit **7.** facient, operand
12. multiplicand
type . . **4.** pure **6.** higher **7.** algebra,
physics **8.** abstract, calculus, geometry
10. arithmetic, elementary, quadratics
12. trigonometry
mathemeg . . . **7.** catfish
matie . . . **7.** herring
matin . . . **6.** aubade (song) **7.** morning,
service **8.** watchdog **11.** morning song
13. morning prayer
matinee . . . **5.** levee, party, salon
6. soiree **8.** negligee **9.** reception
13. conversazione, entertainment
matipo . . . **4.** wood (fuel) **5.** napau
matka, matkab . . . **4.** seal
matlow . . . **6.** sailor
matrass . . . **4.** tube **5.** flask **6.** bottle,
carafe **8.** bolthead
matriculate . . . **4.** list **5.** admit, adopt,
enter **6.** enroll **8.** register **10.** naturalize
matrimonial . . . **7.** marital, nuptial,
spousal **8.** conjugal, hymeneal
9. connubial
matrimony . . . **7.** wedlock **8.** marriage
matrix . . . **3.** bed **4.** cast, form, mold,
womb **5.** cutis **6.** gangue **10.** foundation,
impression
matron . . . **4.** dame, wife **5.** widow
11. housekeeper
matter . . . **3.** gas, pus **4.** body, gear,
malm, pith **5.** atoms, fluid, vapor
6. affair, amount, solids **7.** problem,
trouble **8.** business, elements, material
10. importance **11.** constituent
12. circumstance
matter (pert to) . . .
alluvial . . **5.** geest
celestial . . **6.** nebula
coloring . . **5.** eosin **10.** endochrome
fatty . . **5.** sebum
noxious . . **6.** miasma
of doubt . . **7.** dubiety
of fact . . **7.** literal, prosaic **9.** practical,
pragmatic
of law . . **3.** res
of note . . **8.** notandum
particle . . **4.** atom
perfume . . **7.** essence
spinal cord . . **4.** alba
uniform (physics) . . **7.** inertia
volcanic . . **2.** aa, oo **4.** lava
mattress . . . **3.** bed, pad **5.** futon
7. cushion
mature . . . **3.** age, due, old **4.** ripe **5.** adult,
grown, ripen **6.** digest, mellow, season
7. develop, fall due, grow old, perfect
8. complete **9.** full-grown, perfected,
ratheripe
maturity . . . **8.** ripeness **9.** adulthood,
readiness **10.** falling due
11. development
matutinal . . . **5.** early, matin **7.** morning
12. antemeridian
maty . . . **7.** servant
maud . . . **3.** rug **5.** plaid, shawl
maudlin . . . **5.** beery, drunk, silly, tipsy

7. tearful, weeping **10.** lachrymose
11. sentimental (overly)
maul, mall ... **4.** beat, bung, club, mace, mall, moth **5.** abuse, gavel, staff **6.** beetle, bruise, mallet
maumet ... **3.** god (false), guy **4.** doll, idol **5.** image **6.** puppet **9.** scarecrow
maund, maun ... **3.** beg **6.** basket, hamper **7.** begging, measure
Maundy ... **4.** alms **8.** ceremony **10.** Last Supper
Maundy Thursday (Bib) ... **8.** Holy Week **13.** washing of feet
Mauritius, Ile de France ...
    capital .. **9.** Port Louis
    government .. **7.** British
    product .. **5.** coral, sugar
    site .. **11.** Indian Ocean
Mauser ... **5.** rifle **7.** firearm
mauve ... **5.** lilac **6.** mallow, purple, violet **10.** atmosphere (color)
maven ... **6.** expert **11.** connoisseur
maverick ... **4.** calf (unbranded) **5.** dogie (dogy), stray **11.** independent **13.** nonconformist
mavis, mavie ... **6.** thrush
maw ... **4.** craw, crop **6.** gullet, mallow **7.** gizzard, stomach
mawk ... **6.** maggot
mawkish ... **5.** vapid **6.** sickly **8.** nauseous **9.** squeamish **10.** disgusting **11.** sentimental
maxilla ... **7.** jawbone
maxim ... **3.** saw **4.** dict, rule **5.** adage, axiom, gnome, motto, tenet, truth **6.** saying **7.** precept, proverb **8.** aphorism, apothegm **10.** apophthegm
maxims ... **5.** logia **9.** moralisms
maximum ... **4.** most **5.** limit **7.** highest, supreme **8.** greatest **12.** consummation
maximus ... **7.** largest
may ... **3.** can **6.** be able **9.** be allowed **11.** in one's power, opportunity
May (pert to) ...
    apple .. **8.** mandrake
    bird .. **6.** thrush
    cock .. **5.** melon **6.** plover
    curlew .. **8.** whimbrel
    Duke .. **6.** cherry
    festival .. **7.** Beltane (anc)
    First .. **7.** Beltane **14.** May-day festival
    fish .. **9.** killifish
    flower .. **7.** arbutus **8.** hawthorn, marigold **9.** calla lily **10.** stitchwort **12.** cuckooflower
    fly .. **3.** dun **7.** shad fly **9.** ephemerid
    goddess .. **4.** Maia
    gowan .. **5.** daisy
Maya ... **3.** Mam (people) **6.** Indian **8.** Pokonchi
Mayan calendar ...
    five added days .. **5.** uayeb
    no leap year .. **5.** solar
    twenty-day month .. **5.** uinal
    year .. **4.** haab
Mayan underworld ... **7.** xibalba
maybe ... **2.** if **7.** perhaps **8.** possibly **9.** perchance **11.** conceivably, possibility, uncertainty
Mayday ... **3.** SOS **4.** help **8.** distress
Mayfair ... **6.** London (fashionable)

Mayflower (pert to) ...
    boat of .. **8.** Pilgrims (1620)
    Compact .. **9.** agreement (1620)
    sister ship .. **9.** Speedwell
mayhap ... **7.** perhaps **12.** peradventure
mayor ... **5.** maire **7.** alcalde **10.** magistrate **11.** burgomaster
mazarine ... **4.** blue (color from Cardinal Mazarin)
maze ... **5.** fancy **7.** stupefy **8.** confound, delirium, delusion **9.** confusion, deception, labyrinth **12.** bewilderment, complication
mazed ... **4.** lost **7.** in a maze **9.** stupefied **10.** bewildered
mazuma ... **5.** money
mead ... **5.** drink **6.** meadow **8.** hydromel **9.** metheglin
meadow ... **3.** lea **4.** mead **5.** field, haugh, pampa, swale **7.** pasture, savanna (savannah) **9.** grassland **10.** agostadero
meadow (pert to) ...
    chicken .. **8.** sora rail
    crocus .. **7.** saffron
    crowfoot .. **9.** buttercup
    hen .. **4.** coot, rail **7.** bittern
    mouse .. **4.** vole **8.** arvicole
    part .. **5.** swale
    sage .. **6.** salvia
    saxifrage .. **6.** seseli
    sweet .. **7.** Spiraea
meager, meagre ... **4.** arid, bare, lank, poor, slim **5.** gaunt, scant, spare **6.** barren, jejune, lenten, narrow, sparse **7.** starved, sterile, trivial **9.** emaciated **10.** inadequate
meal ... **3.** tub **4.** bran, dune, mess **5.** feast, grout, salep, snack **6.** bucket, fodder, powder, ration, repast, tiffin **7.** banquet **8.** sandbank **9.** collation, pulverize
mealy ... **4.** pale **7.** friable, powdery **10.** soft-spoken **11.** farinaceous **12.** mealymouthed
mealy (pert to) ...
    Amazon .. **6.** parrot
    back .. **6.** cicada
    bird, duck .. **5.** squaw
    bug .. **4.** pest **5.** scale **10.** pear blight
    mouth .. **7.** warbler
    tree .. **9.** arrowwood, wayfaring
mealy-mouthed ... **5.** suave **10.** flattering **12.** hypocritical **13.** sanctimonious
mean ... **3.** low **4.** base **5.** petty, small, snide, solar (time), sorry **6.** common, denote, design, humble, intend, medium, menial, middle, midway, paltry, shabby, sordid, stingy **7.** average, ignoble, purport, purpose, servile, squalid **8.** beggarly, ordinary, plebeian, shameful, wretched **9.** difficult, malicious, niggardly, penurious **10.** despicable, ill-humored, spiritless **11.** closefisted, disgraceful **12.** contemptible, dishonorable, narrow-minded, parsimonious
mean clef (Mus) ... **5.** C clef
meander ... **4.** wind **6.** ramble, wander
meaning ... **4.** null (without) **5.** sense **6.** import, intent, spirit **7.** purport **8.** semantic **9.** intending, intention,

knowledge **10.** understand
12. significance **13.** signification
14. interpretation
meaningless ... **4.** rote **5.** banal, derry
7. aimless **9.** senseless **10.** designless
11. purposeless **13.** insignificant
meanness ... **6.** infamy, malice
8. baseness, ill-humor **9.** servility
10. humbleness, paltriness, sordidness,
stinginess **11.** inferiority
means ... **5.** funds **7.** capital **8.** averages
9. resources **11.** wherewithal
means of ...
access .. **4.** adit **5.** inlet **7.** ingress
8. aperture
communication .. **4.** note **5.** flags, phone,
radio, smoke **6.** letter, postal, tom-tom
8. telegram **9.** telegraph, telephone
livelihood .. **4.** work **5.** labor, trade
8. vocation **10.** profession
outlet .. **4.** door, exit **6.** egress **8.** aperture
support .. **5.** funds **6.** assets **7.** aliment
11. maintenance
meantime ... **5.** while **7.** interim
8. interval, same time **9.** meanwhile
measles ... **7.** rubella, rubeola **8.** morbilli
measure (pert to) ...
area .. **2.** ar **3.** are, rod **4.** acre, area, mile,
rood **6.** square **7.** geodesy, hectare,
section **8.** township
Bible .. **3.** cab (kab), kor, log **4.** epha
5. cubit, homer
gauge .. **3.** erg, lea (yarn) **5.** ergon,
level, plumb, scale, stone **6.** denier,
square **7.** calorie (calory), compass,
sextant **8.** calipers, quadrant
length .. **3.** ell, mil, rod **4.** foot, hand,
inch, knot, mile, nail, pace, rule, tape,
yard **5.** chain, cubit, meter **6.** league
7. furlong **9.** kilometer, yardstick
10. centimeter, micrometer, millimeter
nautical .. **4.** knot **5.** fathom, league
paper .. **4.** page, ream **5.** quire, sheet
poetry .. **6.** dipody, iambic, rhythm,
sestet **7.** anapest, couplet, distich,
tripody **8.** quatrain **9.** hexameter
10. ottava rima, pentastich, tetrameter,
tetrastich **11.** Alexandrine
printer .. **2.** em, en **4.** pica **5.** agate
volume, weight .. **3.** ton, tun (wine)
4. bale, butt, cord **5.** carat, liter,
minim, ounce, pound, quart **6.** barrel,
bushel, finger, gallon, magnum, pottle
8. hogshead, teaspoon **9.** kiloliter
10. tablespoon
measurement ... **4.** size **6.** amount,
alnage, extent, metage **7.** azimuth
8. abscissa, capacity, quantity
9. substance **11.** calculation,
mensuration
measuring instrument ... **6.** stadia
7. alidade, caliper **8.** odometer
12. perambulator (surveyor)
meat ... **4.** beef, fish, food, lamb, pork
5. flesh **6.** fillet, kernel, mutton, quarry
7. brisket **9.** aitchbone (icebone),
spareribs
meat (pert to) ...
ball .. **7.** rissole **9.** croquette, hamburger
cured, dried .. **3.** ham **5.** bacon
6. flitch, jerked **7.** biltong (biltongue)

8. pemmican
jellied .. **5.** aspic
minced, roll .. **7.** rissole
roasted .. **5.** cabob (kabob) **9.** barbecued
slaughterhouse .. **8.** abattoir
smoking place .. **6.** buccan (bucan)
stew .. **8.** mulligan **9.** lobscouse
meatus ... **4.** burr (ear) **5.** canal
7. opening, passage
meaty ... **5.** pithy, solid **11.** substantial
Mecca, Arabia ... **8.** Holy City **16.** City
of the Prophet
Mecca (pert to) ...
birthplace of .. **8.** Mohammed
capital .. **5.** Hejaz
color .. **11.** Tuscan brown
famed for .. **5.** Kaaba (Caaba, Kaabeth)
10. Black Stone **11.** Great Mosque
governor .. **6.** sherif (shereef)
pilgrimage .. **4.** hadj
pilgrim's dress .. **5.** ihram
rug .. **6.** Shiraz
mechanic ... **7.** artisan, workman
8. operator **9.** artificer, craftsman,
machinist, operative
mechanical ... **8.** machinal **9.** automatic,
practical, technical **11.** involuntary,
stereotyped
mechanical (pert to) ...
adjustment .. **9.** tentation
drawing .. **8.** drafting
law, motion .. **8.** dynamics, kinetics
lever .. **6.** tappet
part .. **5.** rotor **6.** stator
mechanics ... **9.** technique
11. mechanology
mechanism ... **4.** gear, tool **5.** means
6. tackle **7.** control, rigging **9.** apparatus,
machinery, technique
medal ... **4.** coin, disk (disc) **5.** badge
6. plaque **9.** medallion **10.** decoration
medallion ... **4.** coin **5.** cameo, medal,
panel **6.** tablet **8.** ornament
meddle ... **3.** pry **4.** nose **6.** dabble,
tamper **7.** obtrude **9.** interfere
meddler ... **8.** busybody **9.** pragmatic
meddlesome ... **7.** Paul Fry **8.** meddling
9. officious **11.** inquisitive, pragmatical
Mede ... **6.** Median **7.** Persian
medial, median ... **4.** mean **5.** mesne,
raphe (valve) **6.** medium, middle
7. average **11.** intervening
12. intermediate
Median ... **4.** Magi, Mede **5.** Medic
mediate ... **5.** opine **9.** intercede,
interpose, reconcile
mediator ... **5.** muser **7.** arbiter **9.** go-
between **10.** interagent **11.** intercessor
medic ... **3.** doc **6.** clover, doctor, median,
medico **9.** physician
medical (pert to) ...
comb form .. **3.** oma **4.** itis **6.** iatric
7. iatrics
compound .. **5.** hepar
fluid .. **5.** blood, lymph, serum
man .. **5.** medic **6.** shaman, voodoo
monster .. **5.** teras
officer .. **7.** coroner
practitioner .. **2.** MD **6.** doctor, intern
(interne) **7.** surgeon **8.** sawbones
system .. **7.** therapy **9.** allopathy

10. homeopathy, psychiatry
term.. **8.** curative **9.** medicinal
medical terms...
chicken pox.. **9.** varicella
flat feet.. **9.** pes planus
headache.. **11.** cephalalgia
heartburn.. **7.** pyrosis
hives.. **9.** urticaria
measles.. **7.** rubella, rubeola
mumps.. **9.** parotitis
whooping cough.. **9.** pertussis
medicinal (pert to)...
agent.. **3.** tea **6.** tisane **9.** decoction
bark.. **6.** cartex
dropper.. **7.** pipette
equal parts.. **3.** ana
herb, plant.. **3.** rue **4.** aloe **5.** ergot,
  jalap, orris, senna, tansy **6.** arnica,
  cohosh, ipecac **7.** boneset, chirata,
  comfrey **8.** licorice, valerian
pain allaying.. **7.** anodyne **8.** sedative
  9. goofballs, paregoric **11.** barbiturate
patent.. **7.** nostrum
remedy.. **5.** drops, salve **6.** elixir, iodine
  7. panacea **8.** antidote, ointment
science.. **7.** biology **10.** physiology,
  psychology
tablet.. **4.** pill **6.** troche **7.** lozenge
term.. **4.** drug **11.** therapeutic
mediety... **6.** loiety **10.** moderation,
  temperance
medieval, mediaeval... **7.** archaic
  10. Middle Ages
medieval (pert to)...
contest.. **4.** tilt **5.** joust **10.** tournament
empire.. **9.** Holy Roman **11.** Carolingian
emperor.. **4.** Otto **11.** Charlemagne
estate.. **4.** fief **5.** manor
freeholder.. **8.** franklin
galley (ship's).. **3.** nef **5.** xebec **6.** bireme,
  galiot (galliot) **7.** dromone (dromon),
  trireme, unireme
garment.. **6.** tabard
headdress.. **6.** abacot, wimple
helmet.. **5.** armet
holy wars.. **8.** Crusades
instrument (stringed).. **5.** rebec (rebeck)
knights' system.. **8.** chivalry
land system.. **9.** feudalism
  11. manorialism
legend.. **9.** Holy Grail **12.** Wandering
  Jew
merchant guild.. **5.** hanse
money of account.. **3.** ora
musical form.. **7.** organum **9.** plainsong
  (plainchant), polyphony **14.** Gregorian
  chant
musical instrument.. **4.** rote **5.** rebec
  (rebeck), shawm **7.** clarion, sackbut
papal seat (temporary).. **7.** Avignon
peasants' overseer.. **5.** reeve
philosopher.. **9.** alchemist, Schoolman
  (Scholastic)
pilgrim.. **6.** palmer
plague.. **10.** Black Death (1347)
poem.. **3.** lay **7.** fabliau (pl fabliaux)
  14. chanson de geste (epic)
poet, singer.. **7.** gleeman **8.** jongleur,
  minstrel, trouvère **9.** troubador
preacher.. **8.** pardoner
secular movement.. **8.** Humanism

shield.. **3.** ecu **5.** pavis (pavise) **6.** scutum
tax.. **8.** Danegeld
title, teacher.. **8.** magister
wandering student.. **7.** goliard
weapon.. **4.** mace **5.** oncin **8.** falchion
Medina, Saudi Arabia (pert to)...
anc name.. **9.** Lathrippa
Mohammed supporters.. **6.** ansars
sacred city of.. **5.** Islam
tombs.. **4.** Omar **6.** Fatima
  8. Mohammed
mediocre... **4.** mean, so-so **6.** medium
  7. average **8.** middling, ordinary,
  passable **9.** tolerable **11.** indifferent
meditate... **4.** muse, plan, pore **5.** brood,
  study, watch, weigh **6.** ponder
  7. purpose, reflect, revolve **8.** cogitate,
  consider **11.** contemplate
meditation... **4.** yoga **7.** thought
  8. devotion **10.** rumination
  11. thanatopsis **13.** contemplation
  14. omphaloskepsis
mediterranean... **6.** inland **7.** midland
  10. landlocked
Mediterranean (pert to)...
boat.. **3.** nef **4.** saic **5.** xebec (zebec)
  6. galiot (galliot), mistic (mistico),
  settee (setee) **7.** felucca, hexeris
cat.. **5.** genet
coast.. **7.** Riviera
falcon.. **6.** lanner
fish.. **6.** remora
fowl.. **7.** leghorn
fruit.. **5.** olive **7.** azarole
gulf.. **5.** Tunis
herb.. **4.** Ammi
inland.. **3.** sea
island.. **4.** Elba, Gozo **5.** Crete, Malta
  6. Candia, Cyprus, Ebusis, Sicily
  7. Majorca **8.** Belearic (group), Sardinia
island, volcanic.. **6.** Lipari, Salina
  7. Vulcano **9.** Stromboli
port.. **5.** Tunis **7.** Tunisia
region.. **6.** Levant
storm.. **7.** borasca (borasco, borasque)
tree.. **5.** carob **7.** azarole
wind.. **6.** solano **7.** etesian, gregale,
  mistral, sirocco **8.** levanter
  10. euroclyden
medium... **4.** agar (cultured), doer, mean
  5. color, organ **6.** degree, medial,
  oracle **7.** average, psychic **8.** mediator,
  mediocre **10.** instrument, interagent
  11. environment **12.** intermediary,
  spiritualist
medium's meeting... **6.** séance
medley... **4.** olio **5.** relay **6.** jumble
  7. ferrago, mélange, mixture **8.** fantasia,
  mingling **9.** potpourri **10.** hodgepodge,
  salmagundi
medrick... **4.** gull (Bonaparte's), tern
  (Wilson's)
medulla... **4.** pith **6.** marrow **7.** summary
  9. oblongata **10.** compendium
Medusa (Myth)... **6.** Gorgon, Stheno
  (sister) **9.** gorgoneum
Medusa's head (pert to)...
constellation (cluster).. **7.** Perseus
star.. **5.** Algol
vegetable.. **8.** mushroom
Zool.. **10.** basket fish

meed ... **5.** bribe, merit, repay, share **6.** desert, reward **7.** bribery **10.** recompense

meek ... **4.** mild **6.** docile, gentle, humble, modest **7.** pacific, patient **8.** moderate, yielding **10.** spiritless, submissive

meerkat ... **6.** monkey

meerschaum ... **4.** pipe **6.** gravel (color) **7.** seafoam **9.** sepiolite

meet ... **3.** fit **4.** face, game, join **5.** equal, match, touch **6.** battle, combat, concur **7.** collide, conform, contact, contest, convene, fulfill, satisfy **8.** assemble, confront **9.** encounter **10.** congregate, experience, rendezvous

meet halfway ... **7.** mediate **10.** compromise

meeting ... **4.** mall, race **5.** court, gemot (gemote), joint, synod, tryst, union **6.** caucus, powwow, séance **7.** contact, joining **8.** assembly, conclave, junction **9.** encounter, gathering, in contact **10.** conference, convention, converging, rendezvous **11.** convergence **12.** congregation, intersection

mega, meg (comb form) ... **5.** great **6.** mighty

megalith ... **5.** stone (huge) **6.** dolman **7.** boulder **8.** monument (Prehist)

megapode, megapod ... **6.** leipoa **9.** mound bird **10.** jungle fowl **11.** brush turkey

megascope ... **12.** magic lantern

megaseism ... **10.** earthquake

megrim, megrims ... **4.** whim **5.** fancy, freak, humor **8.** headache **9.** dizziness **12.** hypochondria

Mehitabel, Mehetabel ... **3.** cat

Mekong River people ... **3.** Moi (Asian)

mel ... **5.** honey

melancholia ... **7.** sadness **8.** neurosis **9.** nostalgia, psychosis **10.** depression

melancholy ... **3.** sad **4.** blue, dark, glum **5.** drear, gloom **6.** sombre, sorrow **7.** doleful, sadness **8.** atrabile, liverish, tristful **9.** dejection **10.** depressing, depression, dispirited, lamentable **11.** despondency, downhearted, pensiveness **12.** hypochondria, mournfulness

Melanesia ... **14.** Pacific Islands

Melanesian (pert to) ...
island .. **4.** Fiji **7.** Solomon **11.** New Hebrides
native .. **4.** Fiji **6.** Papuan **10.** Polynesian
superbeing .. **5.** adaro

mélange ... **4.** olio **6.** jumble, medley **7.** mixture **9.** pasticcio **10.** miscellany **14.** conglomeration

melee ... **3.** row **4.** fray **5.** fight **6.** affray **7.** contest, diamond (small cut) **8.** skirmish **9.** commotion

melicocca ... **5.** genip **9.** soapberry

melicratum ... **4.** mead **8.** beverage, hydromel

melilotus ... **6.** clover

meliorate ... **6.** soften **7.** improve **10.** ameliorate

melisma ... **6.** melody **7.** cadenza

Melissa ... **4.** balm **12.** Old World mint

mell ... **3.** mix **4.** maul **5.** grain (last cut), honey **6.** beetle, hammer, mallet, meddle, mingle

mellow ... **4.** rich, ripe, soft **5.** drunk **6.** genial, jovial, mature, tender **7.** amiable, matured **9.** melodious

melodic ... **6.** ariose **7.** cadenza, melisma **9.** melodious

melodious ... **6.** ariose, arioso, dulcet **7.** musical, tunable, tuneful **10.** harmonious

melodist ... **6.** singer **8.** composer, musician **9.** harmonist

melodramatic ... **8.** dramatic, romantic **11.** sensational

melody ... **3.** air **4.** aria, tune **5.** canto, charm, dirge, melos, music **6.** rhythm, strain **7.** harmony, melisma, rosalia **9.** cantilena, cantilene **11.** tunefulness

melon ... **4.** musk, pepo **6.** casaba **7.** Persian **8.** honeydew **9.** muskmelon, red-yellow **10.** cantaloupe, paddymelon, watermelon

melon (pert to) ...
financial .. **4.** plum **8.** dividend
like .. **5.** gourd
pear .. **6.** pepino
political .. **5.** graft **6.** spoils

melongena ... **7.** brinjal (brinjaul) **8.** eggplant

melos ... **4.** song **6.** melody

melt ... **3.** run **4.** frit, fuse, thaw **5.** smelt, swale **6.** render, soften **7.** liquefy **8.** diminish, dissolve **9.** disappear **12.** disintegrate

Melville (pert to) ...
character .. **4.** Ahab, Babo **5.** Billy (Budd) **6.** Cereno (Benito), Delano **7.** Ishmael **8.** Bartleby, Queequeg, Starbuck
work .. **4.** Omoo **5.** Typee **6.** Pierre **8.** Moby Dick

member ... **4.** limb, part **5.** organ **6.** branch, fellow, joiner **7.** section **8.** belonger, district, enlistee, enroller **9.** associate

member (pert to) ...
boy's club .. **3.** cub **5.** scout
Caliph dynasty .. **6.** Omniad
chapter (Eccl) .. **9.** capitular
crew .. **4.** hand
diplomatic staff .. **6.** consul **7.** attaché **8.** minister **10.** ambassador
Jewish brotherhood .. **6.** Essene
laity .. **6.** layman
literary club .. **9.** academist **11.** academician
oldest .. **4.** dean
regiment .. **8.** legioner **9.** grenadier, legionary **11.** legionnaire
religious sect .. **5.** Amish **6.** Quaker, Shaker
Roman Catholic society .. **6.** Jesuit
State .. **7.** citizen
swing band .. **6.** hepcat **7.** swinger

membrane ... **4.** caul, skin, tela **5.** lemma **6.** lamina **8.** ectoderm, striffin

membrane (pert to) ...
brain .. **13.** meninges mater
diffusion .. **7.** osmosis
ear .. **7.** eardrum
fold .. **5.** plica

optical . . **6.** retina
weblike . . **4.** tela
memento . . . **5.** relic, token **6.** trophy
  8. keepsake, memorial, souvenir
  11. remembrance
Memnon (pert to) . . .
  famed statue . . **11.** vocal Memnon
  father . . **8.** Tithonus
  Greek name . . **9.** Amenhotep
  king of . . **8.** Ethiopia
  mother . . **3.** Eos (Aurora)
  war hero . . **6.** Trojan
memoir . . . **4.** hint, note **5.** éloge, essay
  6. record, report **7.** account, history
  9. biography, narrative, reminding
  10. memorandum **12.** dissertation
  13. autobiography
memorabilia . . . **3.** ana **5.** notes **6.** record
  7. memoirs **8.** memories
memorable . . . **7.** namable, notable
  9. reminding **11.** reminiscent
memorandum . . . **4.** chit, note **5.** diary
  6. minute, record **7.** tickler **8.** protocol,
  reminder
memoria . . . **4.** tomb **6.** chapel, church,
  shrine **8.** monument **9.** reliquary
memorial . . . **6.** memoir, memory, record,
  trophy **8.** mnemonic, monument
  10. memorandum **11.** celebrative,
  remembrance **12.** recollection
  13. commemorative
memorial mound . . . **5.** cairn (stone),
  totem (carved)
memory . . . **4.** mind **6.** recall **9.** retention
  11. remembrance **12.** recollection,
  reminiscence **13.** commemoration
memory (pert to) . . .
  aid . . **8.** mnemonic **10.** anamnestic
  book . . **5.** diary **9.** scrapbook
  jog . . **6.** remind
  loss of . . **5.** lethe **7.** amnesia, aphasia
  (partial) **13.** forgetfulness
  term . . **6.** mnesic **8.** mnemonic
Memphis, Egypt (pert to) . . .
  deity . . **2.** Ra (Re) **3.** Shu, Tem
  dynasty . . **8.** Memphite
  god, chief . . **4.** Ptah
men (pert to) . . .
  armed body . . **5.** posse
  gymnasts . . **8.** acrobats
  learned . . **8.** erudites, literati
  mechanical . . **6.** robots
  of same tongue . . **6.** langue
  old . . **7.** gaffers **10.** patriarchs
  party of . . **4.** stag **6.** smoker
  section, Gr Church . . **6.** andron
  single . . **5.** stags **9.** bachelors, celibates
  slang . . **6.** blokes
  Three Wise . . **4.** Magi (Gaspar, Melchior,
  Balthazar)
  wild . . **7.** savages **9.** cannibals
menace . . . **6.** threat **8.** forebode, threaten
  10. intimidate **11.** fulmination
menacing . . . **7.** ominous **8.** imminent
  11. threatening
menage . . . **4.** club **7.** society
  9. homestead, household, husbandry
  10. management **12.** housekeeping
menagerie . . . **3.** zoo **10.** collection,
  Tiergarten
menald (said of horses) . . . **8.** speckled

10. variegated
Menaspis . . . **5.** shark (crescent-shaped)
mend . . . **3.** fix, sew **4.** cure, darn, heal,
  knit **5.** alter, amend, botch, emend,
  moise, patch **6.** better, cobble, reform,
  repair **7.** correct, improve **9.** reconcile
  10. ameliorate
mendacious . . . **5.** false, lying **6.** untrue
  7. in error **9.** truthless **10.** fallacious
mendacity . . . **3.** lie **5.** lying **6.** deceit
  7. falsity, fibbery, untruth
mendicant . . . **5.** fakir **6.** beggar
  7. begging
mendicant order . . . **10.** Carmelites,
  Dominicans **11.** Franciscans
  12. Augustinians
mendole . . . **4.** fish **8.** cackerel
Menelaus' wife . . . **11.** Helen of Troy
menhaden . . . **4.** pogy **7.** sardine
  8. bonyfish **10.** mossbunker
menhir . . . **5.** stone (standing) **8.** monolith
menial . . . **6.** flunky, varlet **7.** servant,
  servile, serving, slavish
meninges membrane . . . **8.** pia mater
  9. arachnoid, dura mater
meniscus . . . **4.** lens **8.** crescent
  12. crescent moon
Mennonite leader . . . **11.** Menno Simons
Mennonite sect . . . **5.** Amish
meno . . . **4.** less **5.** month (comb form)
menology (Eccl) . . . **8.** calendar, register
Menominee, Menomini . . . **5.** Falls (Wis),
  river **6.** Indian **9.** whitefish
Menorah . . . **11.** candelabrum (Jew)
  12. organization
mensk . . . **5.** adorn, favor, grace, honor
  6. credit **8.** ornament **9.** reverence
  12. graciousness
mental . . . **7.** phrenic **9.** of the mind,
  psychotic **11.** intelligent **12.** intellectual
mental (pert to) . . .
  alienation . . **8.** insanity
  deficiency, deficient . . **5.** ament, idiot,
  moron **6.** idiocy **8.** imbecile
  discipline . . **8.** mathesis
  disorder . . **7.** aphasia **8.** insanity,
  neurosis, paranoia **9.** psychosis
  11. megalomania **12.** hypochondria
  13. forgetfulness, schizophrenia
  faculties . . **4.** mind, wits
  feeling . . **7.** emotion
  image, picture . . **4.** idea **6.** idolus
  8. phantasm **10.** conception
  peculiarity . . **12.** idiosyncracy
  science, study . . **10.** New Thought,
  psychiatry
  state . . **6.** morale **7.** doldrum (doldrums)
  8. euphoria
  strain . . **7.** tension
mentality . . . **4.** mind **5.** sense **6.** acumen,
  sanity **9.** endowment, intellect
  11. mental power **12.** intelligence
mention . . . **4.** cite, mind, name **5.** refer,
  speak, trace **6.** denote, notice, record,
  remark **7.** specify, vestige **8.** citation,
  indicate **9.** make known, statement
  10. indication
mentor . . . **7.** adviser, teacher, wise man
  10. instructor
mentum . . . **4.** chin
menu . . . **4.** card, list **5.** carte **8.** schedule

10. bill of fare
Mephistopheles ... **5.** devil, Faust, Satan
mephitis ... **4.** odor **5.** skunk, smell
  6. stench **7.** polecat **10.** exhilation
  (earth)
mercantile ... **5.** trade **7.** trading
  10. commercial, industrial
mercenary ... **4.** hack **5.** hired, venal
  6. sordid **7.** Hessian **8.** hireling, salaried,
  vendible
merchandise ... **4.** ware **5.** goods, wares
  7. effects **9.** vendibles **10.** emporeutic
  (pert to) **11.** commodities **12.** stock in
  trade
merchant ... **5.** buyer **6.** trader **7.** vintner
  10. shopkeeper, trafficker
  11. storekeeper
merchant (pert to) ...
  group .. **5.** guild, hanse **6.** cartel
  Indian .. **4.** seth
  League .. **9.** Hanseatic
  ship .. **6.** argosy **8.** Indiaman
  wine .. **7.** vintner
Merchant of Bagdad ... **7.** Sindbad
Merchant of Venice character ...
  6. Portia **7.** Antonio, Shylock
merci ... **6.** thanks
merciful ... **4.** kind, mild **6.** humane,
  tender **7.** clement, lenient **9.** benignant
  10. charitable **13.** compassionate
merciless ... **5.** cruel **8.** pitiless
  9. unsparing **10.** relentless
  13. unsympathetic
mercurial (pert to God Mercury) ...
  4. fast **5.** swift **6.** active, clever, fickle
  8. metallic **9.** saturnine **11.** money-
  making
mercurous chloride ... **7.** calomel
mercury ... **5.** azoth, guide, metal
  7. chibrit, element **9.** barometer
  11. quicksilver, temperature,
  thermometer
Mercury (pert to) ...
  astronomy .. **6.** planet (smallest)
  god of .. **8.** commerce
  Greek name .. **6.** Hermes
  staff .. **8.** caduceus
  statue, image .. **5.** herma
  winged cap .. **7.** petasos (petasus)
  winged shoes .. **7.** talaria
mercy ... **4.** pity, ruth **5.** grace **6.** blithe,
  lenity **7.** charity **8.** clemency, lenience,
  leniency **9.** tolerance **10.** compassion,
  indulgence **11.** forbearance
mercy killing ... **10.** euthanasia
mercy seat ... **5.** bench **11.** golden
  plate (on the Ark), Throne of God
  12. judgment seat **13.** seat of justice
mere ... **3.** sea **4.** bare, lake, only, pool,
  sole, such, wisp **5.** bound, limit, sheer,
  small **6.** divide, simple **8.** absolute,
  boundary, landmark, only this
mère ... **6.** mother
merely ... **4.** also, just, only **5.** quite
  6. barely, purely, simply, singly,
  solely **7.** utterly **8.** entirely, scarcely
  9. unmixedly **10.** absolutely
mere show ... **4.** airs **5.** front **8.** pretense
  9. formality **10.** pretension
  11. affectation
mere taste ... **3.** nip, sip **4.** gulp

7. draught
merganser ... **3.** nun **4.** duck, smee,
  smew **6.** Mergus **7.** bec-scie **8.** Merginae
  9. goosander
merge ... **4.** sink **5.** blend, unite **6.** mingle
  7. combine, immerse **8.** coalesce
  11. consolidate
merger ... **4.** pool **5.** union **6.** cartel,
  fusion **8.** monopoly **10.** absorption
  12. amalgamation
meridian ... **3.** top **4.** apex, noon **5.** plane
  6. midday, summit, zenith **8.** latitude,
  southern **9.** celestial **11.** culmination
  12. highest point
meringue ... **5.** icing **8.** egg white, frosting
Merino ... **4.** wool, yarn **5.** sheep
merit ... **4.** earn, meed **5.** worth **6.** desert,
  reward **7.** deserve **10.** excellence
merited ... **3.** fit **4.** just **6.** worthy
  8. adequate, deserved, suitable
  9. warranted
meritorious ... **5.** valid **6.** worthy
  7. merited **9.** deserving, honorable
  12. praiseworthy
merlin ... **6.** falcon
Merlin ... **7.** prophet, romance **8.** magician
mermaid ... **5.** siren **6.** merrow
  7. Oceanid, swimmer **8.** sea nymph
  9. sea spirit **14.** marine creature
mermaid's hair ... **4.** alga
mero ... **4.** fish **5.** guasa **7.** grouper
  8. rock hind
merogenesis ... **12.** segmentation
meropia ... **9.** blindness (partial)
meros ... **5.** thigh **10.** meropodite
merriment ... **3.** fun **4.** glee **5.** mirth
  6. gaiety (gayety) **8.** laughter
  9. amusement, diversion
  11. merrymaking
merrow ... **7.** mermaid
merry ... **3.** gai, gay **4.** glad **5.** funny,
  happy **6.** blithe, bonnie, jocose, jovial,
  joyous **7.** comical, festive, gleeful,
  jocular **8.** cheerful, mirthful, sportive
  9. favorable, hilarious, sprightly
  13. sweet-sounding
merry-andrew ... **4.** mime, zany **5.** antic,
  clown, joker **6.** jester **7.** buffoon
  8. merryman
merry-go-round ... **8.** carousel (carrousel)
  17. revolving platform
merrymaking ... **4.** reel **5.** momus,
  revel **7.** festive, wassail **9.** festivity,
  merriment **12.** conviviality
merrythought ... **8.** wishbone
merrytrotter ... **5.** swing **6.** seesaw
merrywing ... **4.** duck **9.** goldeneye
  10. bufflehead
merse ... **3.** dip **5.** marsh **6.** plunge
  7. immerse
merycism ... **7.** chewing **10.** rumination
mesa ... **5.** butte **7.** mesilla, oakwood
  (color), plateau, terrace **9.** tableland
  14. flat-topped hill
mescal ... **6.** cactus, liquor, peyote
mesel ... **5.** leper
mesh ... **3.** net, web **5.** catch **6.** areola
  7. complex, ensnare, netting, network
  10. crisscross **11.** interaction
mesial plane ... **5.** meson (Zool)
  6. median, middle

mesmeric . . . **11.** fascinating, hypnotizing **12.** irresistible, spellbinding
mesmeric force . . . **2.** od
Mesopotamia . . .
ancient city . . **2.** Ur **5.** Eridu **7.** Babylon, Ninevah
city . . **5.** Basra, Mosul **6.** Edessa
colloquialism . . **6.** Mespot
culture . . **8.** Sumerian
export . . **3.** oil
language . . **6.** Arabic
people (anc) . . **8.** Aramaean (Aramean)
river . . **6.** Tigris **9.** Euphrates
wind . . **6.** shamal
Mesopotamian . . . **5.** Iraqi
Mesozoic era . . . **7.** reptile **8.** dinosaur **10.** evergreens, ganoid fish
mesquin . . . **4.** mean **6.** shabby, sordid
mesquita . . . **6.** mosque
mesquite . . . **5.** pacay **7.** thicket **8.** Prosopis **9.** algaroba
mesquite bean flour . . . **6.** pinole
mess . . . **4.** meal **5.** batch, share, spoil **6.** bungle, jumble, litter **7.** eyesore, failure, mixture **8.** disorder **9.** confusion **11.** predicament **12.** kettle of fish
mess (up) . . . **5.** botch, spoil **6.** muss up **7.** clutter, derange, shuffle **10.** disarrange
message . . . **4.** news, note, wire, word **5.** cable **6.** brevet, letter, notice **7.** epistle, evangel, tidings **8.** dispatch, telegram **10.** communiqué **13.** communication
message medium . . . **5.** Ouija
messenger . . . **4.** Iris, page, sand, toty **5.** angel, envoy **6.** herald, nuncio, Revere (Paul) **7.** apostle, carrier, courier, prophet, totyman **8.** delegate, minister **9.** estafette (estafet) **10.** forerunner
messenger bird . . . **9.** secretary
Messenger of the Gods . . . **6.** Hermes (Gr) **7.** Mercury (Rom)
Messiah . . . **6.** Christ **7.** Saviour (Savior) **8.** Oratorio (Handel) **9.** deliverer
Messina Rock . . . **6.** Scylla
messy . . . **5.** dirty **6.** untidy **7.** jumbled **8.** slovenly **10.** disordered
mestive . . . **8.** mournful
mesto . . . **3.** sad **7.** pensive
met . . . **3.** sat **7.** equaled, measure **11.** measurement (see also meet)
metabolism . . . **9.** anabolism **10.** catabolism **12.** assimilation **13.** dissimilation, metamorphosis **14.** transformation
metacarpus . . . **4.** bone
metad . . . **3.** rat
metagnomy . . . **10.** divination
metagnostic . . . **10.** unknowable
metal . . . **3.** tin **4.** gold, iron, lead, zinc **5.** steel **6.** cobalt, copper, erbium, nickel, radium, silver, sodium **7.** cadmium, calcium, element, gallium, iridium, lithium, mercury, terbium **8.** cast iron **9.** potassium **11.** quicksilver
metal . . . **6.** mettle, spirit **8.** material **9.** substance
metal (pert to) . . .
bar . . **3.** gad **5.** ingot
cake . . **4.** slag

casting . . **3.** pig
cement . . **6.** solder
clippings . . **7.** scissil
coarse . . **5.** matte
coat . . **6.** patina
color . . **9.** pearl blue
content . . **3.** ory
crude . . **5.** matte
deposit . . **4.** lode
disc . . **5.** paten
dross . . **4.** slag
electric . . **6.** magnet
filings . . **5.** lemel
forging term . . **5.** sprue
goldlike . . **6.** oroide
impurity . . **7.** regulus
layer . . **4.** seam, vein **5.** stope
lightest . . **7.** lithium
lump . . **3.** pig **4.** slug **6.** nugget
patch . . **6.** solder
plate . . **4.** foil, shim
rare . . **6.** erbium **7.** iridium, terbium, yttrium **8.** platinum
refuse . . **4.** slag **5.** dross **6.** scoria
rock . . **3.** ore
science of . . **10.** metallurgy
tag . . **5.** aglet (aiglet)
test . . **5.** assay
tool . . **5.** swage **7.** stemmer
ware . . **4.** tole **6.** Revere
worker . . **6.** welder **7.** riveter **9.** goldsmith **11.** silversmith
metamerism . . . **12.** segmentation (Zool)
metamorphosis . . . **6.** change **9.** oxidation **10.** hydrolysis **12.** degeneration, ossification **14.** transformation
metaphor . . . **5.** trope **6.** simile **10.** comparison **11.** tralalition
metaphysics . . . **5.** being **6.** nature **8.** ontology, theology **9.** cosmology **10.** psychology
mete . . . **4.** dole, give, goal **5.** allot, award **7.** measure **8.** boundary **9.** apportion **10.** distribute
meteor . . . **5.** bolis **6.** Bielid, bolide, Leonid, Lyraid **7.** Arietid, Perseid **8.** fireball **9.** Andromede
meteorite (pert to) . . .
iron . . **10.** siderolite
shower . . **6.** Leonid **9.** Andromede (Andromedid)
stony . . **8.** aerolite
meteor mark . . . **6.** crater
meteorology . . . **9.** astronomy **10.** atmosphere **11.** climatology
meter, metre . . . **5.** gauge **6.** rhythm **7.** cadence, measure **8.** measurer
meter (pert to) . . .
cubic . . **5.** stere
measure . . **5.** litre
millionth . . **6.** micron
prosody . . **4.** mora
square . . **7.** centare
ton . . **5.** tonne
unit term . . **3.** are **6.** decare **9.** decameter, decastere
weight . . **4.** gram
methane . . . **8.** paraffin
metheglin . . . **4.** mead **8.** beverage
mether . . . **3.** cup
method . . . **3.** way **4.** mode, plan, rule

5. means, order, usage 6. course, manner, system 7. fashion, process 9. procedure 11. arrangement 14. classification
methodic, methodical . . . 6. formal 7. orderly, regular 10. systematic
Methuselah (pert to) . . .
  Bib . . 7. aged man 9. Patriarch
  father . . 5. Enoch
metic . . . 5. alien 7. settler 9. immigrant
meticulous . . . 4. nice, prim 5. fussy 7. careful, fearful, precise 8. exacting 9. selective 10. fastidious, scrupulous 14. discriminating
métier . . . 4. line 7. calling 8. business 10. occupation, profession
metis, metisse . . . 7. mulatto 8. octoroon 9. half-breed
Metis . . . 8. asteroid 9. Zeus's wife
metrical . . . 8. measured, poetical, rhythmic
metrical composition . . . 4. poem 5. poesy 6. poetry
metrical foot . . . 4. iamb 6. iambus 7. anapest, spondee, trochee 8. choriamb
metrical stress . . . 4. scan 5. arsis, ictus 6. thesis
metronome (Maelzel's) . . . 5. timer
metropolis . . . 4. city, seat, town 6. center 8. district 9. metropole
metropolitan . . . 5. chief, urban 6. bishop, center 7. leading 9. principal
mettle . . . 5. ardor, honor, nerve, pluck, spunk 6. spirit 7. courage 9. fortitude 11. temperament
meuse, muse . . . 3. gap 4. hole 7. opening 8. loophole
Meuse River . . . 4. Maas
mew . . . 3. cob, den 4. cage, cast, coop, gull, molt, shed 5. miaow, miaul 6. change 7. seagull, stables 8. spicknel 11. concealment, confinement
mewl . . . 3. cry, mew 6. squall 7. whimper
Mexican (pert to) . . . see also Mexico
  agave . . 5. datil 6. zapupe 8. henequen
  almond . . 7. malabar
  American . . 6. gringo
  ancient . . 4. Maya 5. Aztec, Nahua 6. Mixtec, Toltec 7. Zapotec
  antelope . . 9. pronghorn
  asphalt . . 9. chapapote
  bean . . 6. frijol 7. frijole
  bedbug . . 8. conenose
  beverage (alcoholic) . . 6. mescal, pulque 7. tepache, tequila
  bird . . 6. jacana, towhee 7. jacamar, tinamou 8. zopilote
  blanket . . 6. serape
  brigand . . 7. ladrone
  bull . . 4. toro
  cactus . . 6. chaute, mescal
  cape . . 6. serape
  cat . . 6. margay
  cherry tree . . 7. capulin
  cheif . . 4. jefe 12. jefe politico
  cloak . . 5. manta
  cockroach . . 9. cucaracha
  common land (law) . . 6. ejidos
  coral drops (lily) . . 7. Bessera
  cottonwood . . 5. alamo

dance (solo) . . 8. guaracha
  dish . . 4. taco 5. atole, chili (chile) 6. tamale 7. burrito 8. frijoles, tortilla 9. enchilada 13. chili con carne
  dog . . 9. Chihuahua
  dollar . . 4. peso 5. adobe
  dove . . 4. Inca
  drug . . 7. damiana
  elm . . 6. mezcal 8. Ulmaceae
  estate, farm . . 8. hacienda
  fever . . 10. tabardillo
  fish (food) . . 6. salema 7. totuava
  game (card) . . 4. frog
  grass . . 3. mat 5. otate 6. petate 8. henequen
  herdsman . . 8. ranchero
  hog . . 7. peccary
  hut, house . . 5. jacal
  insect . . 8. turicata
  labor system . . 7. peonage
  landmark . . 5. senal
  masonry . . 5. adobe
  moon god (Aztec) . . 6. Meztli
  mullet . . 4. bobo
  musical instrument . . 6. clarin (anc) 7. maracas
  Noah . . 6. Coxcox
  onyx . . 6. tecali
  orange . . 7. Choisya
  peasant . . 4. peon
  persimmon . . 7. chapote
  phlox . . 6. cobaea
  plant, shrub . . 4. pita 5. agave, amole, datil, istle, sisal, sotol, yucca 6. maguey 8. ocotillo 10. candlewood, Dasylirion
  rose . . 9. portulaca
  saloon . . 7. cantina
  sandal . . 8. huaracho (huarache)
  sauce . . 7. Tabasco
  scarf . . 6. tapalo
  shawl . . 6. serape
  stirrup . . 7. estribo
  stirrup hood . . 8. tapadera (tapadero)
  sugar . . 7. panocha
  tea . . 6. basote 7. apasote
  thong . . 5. romal
  throwing stick . . 6. atlatl
  tree . . 3. ule 5. alamo, ocote 6. colima, poplar 7. capulin 10. cottonwood
  war god . . 7. Mexitli
  yucca . . 5. izote (isote)
Mexican people . . .
  artist . . 6. Orozco, Posada, Rivera
  composer . . Chavez
  conqueror . . 6. Cortés (Cortez)
  dictator . . 4. Díaz 9. Santa Anna
  emperor . . 10. Maximilian
  president . . 6. Huerta, Juárez, Madero 7. Obregón 8. Cárdenas, Carranza
  revolutionary . . 6. Madero, Zapata 11. Pancho Villa
  writer . . 3. Paz 6. Azuela 7. Fuentes
Mexican War (1846) . . .
  battle site . . 11. Chapultepec
  general . . 5. Scott (Winfield) 6. Taylor (Zachary) 9. Santa Anna (Mex)
  president . . 4. Polk
Mexico . . .
  battleground . . 6. Puebla
  capital . . 10. Mexico City
  city . . 6. Merida, Puebla 7. Durango,

Tampico **8.** Mazatlan, Monterey, Vera Cruz **11.** Guadalajara
conqueror . . **6.** Cortes (Cortez)
hero . . **6.** Juarez **11.** Poncho Villa
lake . . **7.** Chapala
mountain . . **12.** Popocatepetl
peninsula . . **4.** Baja **7.** Yucatan
people . . **5.** Mayas **6.** Aztecs **7.** Toltecs **10.** Cuitlateco
river . . **9.** Rio Grande
volcano . . **6.** Colima **7.** Jorullo, Orizaba **12.** Ixtaccihuatl, Popocatepetl
mezzanine . . . **8.** entresol, low story
miaow, miaou . . . **3.** mew
mias . . . **9.** orangutan
miasma . . . **4.** fume **6.** poison **7.** malaria, malodor **9.** contagion
mib . . . **7.** a marble
mica . . . **4.** talc **5.** glist **7.** biotite **8.** chlorite, silicate **9.** damourite, hydromica, isinglass, muscovite **10.** lepidolite
Micah . . . **4.** Book (Old Test) **7.** prophet
mice . . . **3.** Mus **5.** voles **7.** rodents
miche . . . **5.** skulk, sneak **6.** lie hid **7.** conceal
micher . . . **5.** sneak, thief **6.** truant
Michigan . . .
capital . . **7.** Lansing
city . . **5.** Flint **7.** Detroit, Lansing **8.** Ann Arbor **9.** Marquette
explorer . . **7.** Jolliet, Nicolet **9.** Marquette **13.** Sault Ste Marie
river . . **4.** Cass **5.** Huron
State admission . . **11.** Twenty-sixth
State motto . . **6.** Tuebor **11.** I Will Defend
State nickname . . **9.** Wolverine
mickey finn . . . **5.** drink **8.** narcotic
mico . . . **6.** monkey **8.** marmoset
micraner . . . **3.** ant (small)
micro (comb form) . . . **4.** moth **5.** petty, small
microbe . . . **4.** germ **5.** virus **8.** organism **9.** bacterium **13.** microorganism
microcosm . . . **4.** body (humerous) **5.** world (small) **8.** universe
microscopic (pert to) . . .
algae . . **6.** amoeba, diatom
anatomy . . **9.** histology
size . . **5.** small **6.** minute **9.** very small **13.** infinitesimal
microspores . . . **6.** pollen
microwave (sl) . . . **4.** nuke
Midas (Gr) . . . **13.** King of Phrygia
midday . . . **4.** noon **7.** noonday **8.** meridian, noontide
midday nap . . . **6.** siesta
middle . . . **5.** mesne, midst **6.** center, centry, median, medium, mesial **7.** central **8.** interior **11.** intervening **13.** intermediator
middle (pert to) . . .
Age . . **8.** Medieval
class . . **9.** bourgeois **11.** proletarian
comb form . . **3.** mes **4.** medi, meso
finger . . **6.** medius **10.** third digit
ground . . **4.** mean **7.** average **9.** mid-course
man . . **5.** agent **6.** broker, medium **8.** mediator **9.** go-between **11.** intercessor **12.** intermediary

middling . . . **4.** fair **6.** medium, middle **7.** average, between, midland **8.** mediocre, moderate, ordinary **10.** middle-aged
midge . . . **3.** fly **4.** gnat **6.** midget, punkie **7.** minutia
Midi . . . **8.** The South (France)
Midian king . . . **3.** Evi **4.** Reba
Midian priest . . . **6.** Jethro
midriff . . . **9.** diaphragm
midshipman . . . **5.** cadet **6.** reefer **8.** toadfish
Midsummer Night's Dream (play) . . . **4.** Puck, Snug **6.** Bottom, Oberon **7.** Titania
midwife . . . **4.** baba, dhai **6.** cummer (kimmer) **11.** accoucheuse
mien . . . **3.** air, eye **4.** look **5.** guise **6.** aspect, manner, ostent **7.** bearing, posture **8.** behavior, carriage, demeanor **10.** appearance, deportment
miff . . . **3.** vix **4.** tiff **5.** anger **6.** offend **7.** dudgeon, quarrel **9.** displease, sulkiness **10.** sullenness
mig . . . **4.** duck **7.** a marble
might . . . **3.** arm **5.** force, power **7.** ability **8.** efficacy, strength **9.** greatness
mighty . . . **4.** huge, vast, very **6.** potent, strong **7.** eminent, violent **8.** enormous, forcible, powerful, puissant **9.** extremely **10.** omnipotent **11.** efficacious **13.** authoritative
migniard . . . **6.** dainty, minion **7.** mincing **8.** delicate, mistress
mignon . . . **5.** small **6.** dainty, petite **7.** blue-red **8.** delicate, graceful
mignonette (pert to) . . .
color . . **5.** green **6.** reseda
emblem of . . **6.** Saxony
herb . . **6.** reseda
tree . . **5.** henna
vine . . **7.** Madeira, tarweed
migraine . . . **6.** megrim **8.** headache **10.** hemicrania
migrate . . . **4.** move, trek **8.** resettle, transfer **12.** transmigrate
migration . . . **4.** trek **5.** exode **6.** exodus **7.** passage **8.** shifting (Chem) **10.** relocation
migratory . . . **6.** moving, roving **7.** nomadic **9.** peregrine, wandering
migratory (pert to) . . .
ant . . **6.** driver
cell . . **9.** leucocyte
thrush . . **5.** robin
mihrab . . . **4.** slab **5.** niche **7.** chamber (mosque)
Mikado . . . **5.** dairi, opera, title **9.** red-yellow, sovereign
Mikado character . . . **4.** Ko-Ko **6.** Yum-Yum **7.** Pooh-Bah
Mikania . . . **7.** dogbane, thistle **11.** Willugbaeya (Willugheia) **12.** Ancylocladus
mike . . . **4.** loaf **6.** loiter **10.** microphone
mil . . . **5.** mille **8.** thousand
milady . . . **5.** woman **6.** madame **10.** noblewoman **11.** gentlewoman
Milan (pert to) . . .
hat . . **5.** straw
opera house . . **7.** La Scala

point. . **10.** bobbin lace **12.** point de Milan

mild . . . **4.** calm, kind, meek, soft, warm **5.** balmy, bland **6.** benign, gentle **7.** clement, insipid, lenient **8.** benedict, favonian, gracious, lenitive, moderate, soothing, tranquil **9.** assuasive, indulgent, temperate **10.** mollifying **11.** considerate

mild (pert to) . . .
attack. . **5.** touch (flu)
burn. . **11.** first-degree
cheese. . **10.** mozzarella
cigar. . **5.** claro
illness. . **7.** ailment
nausea. . **11.** butterflies
oath. . **4.** darn, drat, heck **5.** shoot **6.** shucks
reproof. . **10.** admonition
mildew . . . **4.** mold, must, rust, smut **6.** blight, fungus **8.** honeydew
mild expression . . . **9.** euphemism
mild offense . . . **6.** delict
mile (term) . . . **3.** sea **7.** statute **8.** nautical **9.** Admiralty **12.** geographical
Miledh . . . **8.** ancestor (fabled)
Milesian . . . **4.** Celt **8.** Irishman **10.** Miledh's son
milestone . . . **5.** stele **7.** waymark **8.** landmark, milepost
milfoil . . . **4.** herb **6.** yarrow
milieu . . . **7.** ecology **8.** ambience **11.** environment **12.** surroundings
militant . . . **7.** hawkish, warlike **8.** battling, fighting **9.** combating, combative **11.** contentious
military . . . **7.** martial **8.** soldiers
military (pert to) . . .
advance. . **8.** anabasis
aide. . **7.** attaché
base. . **4.** camp **5.** depot, field **7.** billets **8.** barracks, firebase, quarters **10.** encampment
call. . **6.** tattoo **8.** reveille
cap. . **4.** kepi **5.** busby, shako
cap, hat cover. . **8.** havelock
cloak. . **5.** sagum (anc)
commission. . **6.** brevet
defense. . **4.** fort **6.** abatis
depot. . **4.** base
division. . **4.** unit **5.** corps, squad **7.** company, platoon **8.** regiment
engine. . **6.** onager **7.** robinet
expedition to Holy Land. . **7.** Crusade
force. . **4.** army **5.** ranks, troop **6.** legion **7.** reserve **8.** soldiery
guard. . **6.** patrol
horsemen. . **7.** cavalry, hussars
infraction. . **4.** AWOL
inspection. . **5.** drill **6.** parade, review
instrument. . **5.** bugle **7.** althorn
landing point. . **9.** beachhead
maneuver. . **6.** tactic
messenger. . **7.** estafet
night attack. . **8.** camisade
obstruction. . **6.** abatis
officer. . **5.** major **7.** captain, colonel, general **8.** corporal, sergeant **9.** brigadier, subaltern **10.** lieutenant
operations. . **8.** campaign, strategy
order. . **7.** command

organization. . **5.** cadre
pit. . **10.** trou-de-loup
police. . **2.** MP **9.** gendarmes **12.** constabulary
punishment. . **4.** brig **9.** strappado
quarters. . **4.** camp **7.** billets **8.** barracks **10.** cantonment
salute (artillery). . **5.** salvo
science. . **3.** war **7.** war game **8.** warcraft **9.** logistics
service stripes. . **9.** hashmarks
signal. . **7.** chamade (anc)
staff. . **5.** cadre
storehouse. . **5.** étape **7.** arsenal
supplies. . **8.** materiel, ordnance
survey. . **11.** reconnoiter
testament, will. . **11.** nuncupative
tool (hook-shaped). . **4.** croc (anc)
truck (cannon). . **6.** camion
vehicle. . **4.** jeep, tank **6.** camion **7.** caisson
militate . . . **5.** fight **6.** debate, rebuff **7.** contend **8.** conflict
milk . . . **3.** lac **5.** cream, drain, fluid **6.** elicit, suckle **7.** despoil, draw out, exploit, extract **8.** beverage
milk (pert to) . . .
beverage. . **4.** whig **10.** buttermilk
coagulator. . **4.** ruen **6.** rennet
curd. . **5.** zeiga **6.** casein
curdled. . **6.** yogurt **7.** clabber
fermented. . **5.** kefir **6.** kumiss (koumiss) **7.** matzoon
fish. . **3.** awa **6.** Chanos, sabalo
food (fasting). . **10.** lacticinia
glass. . **7.** opaline **8.** cryolite
mouse. . **6.** spurge
pail. . **5.** bowie, eshin
pert to. . **6.** lactic **7.** lactary, lacteal
product. . **6.** cheese, yogurt
sap. . **5.** latex
sop. . **5.** sissy **11.** mollycoddle
sour. . **4.** curd, whey, whig **6.** blinky
store. . **5.** dairy **9.** lactarium
strainer. . **6.** milsey (milsie)
sugar. . **7.** lactose
watery part. . **4.** whey
with (milk). . **6.** au lait
milkweed . . . **6.** spurge **7.** dogbane **10.** sow thistle **14.** Asclepiadaceae
milkwood . . . **8.** Moraceae **9.** paperbark
milky . . . **4.** mild, tame, weak **5.** timid, white **6.** gentle, liquid **7.** lacteal **8.** emulsion, emulsive, lactesce (to become), timorous **10.** effeminate
Milky Way . . . **6.** Galaxy **9.** Via Lactea **14.** galactic circle
Milky Way black spaces . . . **9.** Coalsacks
mill . . . **3.** box **4.** beat, coin (to) **5.** crush, dress, fight, grind, knurl, quern, shape **6.** finish, powder, thrash **7.** factory, machine, serrate **8.** arrastra, snuffbox, vanquish, workshop **9.** comminute, pulverize, transform **10.** move around **12.** housebreaker
mill (pert to) . . .
beetle. . **9.** cockroach
bill. . **3.** adz
clapper. . **10.** chatterbox
course. . **4.** lade **8.** millrace, tailrace
end. . **7.** remnant

grain.. **5.** grist
run of.. **7.** average **8.** millrace, ordinary
millefleurs... **7.** perfume
millenarian... **8.** chiliast
millennium... **6.** period, utopia
   9. millenary **13.** thousand years
millepede... **6.** insect **8.** myriapod
millepore... **5.** coral **9.** madrepore
miller... **3.** ray **4.** moth **5.** boxer **7.** harrier
   8. pugilist **10.** flycatcher
miller's thumb... **4.** bird, fish **7.** warbler
   8. titmouse (long-tailed) **9.** goldcrest
millesimal... **10.** thousandth
millet... **4.** moha **5.** bajra, grass, hirse,
   milly **8.** cenchrus **9.** broomcorn **10.** hirse
   grass **14.** non-Moslem group
millimeter... **6.** micron **14.** thousandth
   part
millions, one thousand... **7.** billion
millions of millions... **9.** trillions
Mills grenade... **4.** bomb
Milne character... **6.** Eeyore (donkey),
   Piglet, Winnie (the Pooh)
   16. Christopher Robin
milo... **5.** durra **12.** grain sorghum
Milvus... **4.** kite
mime... **3.** ape **4.** aper, copy **5.** actor,
   clown, mimic **6.** jester, mummer
   7. buffoon, imitate
mimesis... **7.** mimicry **9.** imitation
mimic... **3.** ape **4.** aper, copy, mime,
   mimo, mock **5.** actor **6.** mummer, parrot
   7. buffoon, copying, imitate, mimetic
   8. imitator **9.** imitative **11.** counterfeit
mimicry... **5.** apery, apism **7.** mimesis,
   mockery **8.** parrotry
mimic thrush... **11.** mockingbird
Mimidae, Miminae... **7.** catbird
   8. thrasher **11.** mockingbird
Mimir... **5.** giant
mimsey... **4.** prim **7.** prudish
min... **5.** ruler **6.** memory, prince, remind
   8. remember **11.** remembrance
Min (Egypt)... **3.** god (procreation)
   5. deity
Minar... **4.** myna **5.** Kutab (Delhi), tower
minaret... **4.** lamp **5.** tower **10.** lighthouse
minaway... **6.** minuet
mince... **3.** cut **4.** chop, dice, hash
   5. slash **8.** diminish, prim step
   9. subdivide **10.** short steps
minced meat... **7.** rissole
minced oath... **4.** drat, egad
minchen... **3.** nun
minchery... **7.** nunnery
minchiate... **5.** tarot
mind... **4.** care, heed, mens, obey,
   reck, tend, will **6.** desire, memory,
   psyche **7.** opinion **9.** intellect, intention
   11. remembrance **12.** intelligence
mind (pert to)...
   development.. **13.** psychogenesis
   peace of.. **8.** ataraxia, calmness
      16. imperturbability
   picture.. **4.** idea **5.** image
   reader.. **8.** telepath
   set.. **8.** attitude
   split.. **13.** schizophrenic
Mindanao...
   language.. **3.** Ata
   people.. **3.** Ata **4.** Moro **5.** Lutao

6. Bagobo, Illano
   site.. **11.** Philippines
   town.. **4.** Dapa **5.** Davao **9.** Zamboanga
   volcano.. **3.** Apo **9.** Malindany
mindful... **8.** disposed **9.** observant,
   regardful **11.** remembering
mine... **2.** my **3.** bal, dig, mio, pit, sap
   4. meum **5.** stope **6.** cavity, quarry
   7. gallery, passage **10.** excavation
   12. entrenchment
mine (pert to)...
   basket, tub.. **4.** corf
   ceiling.. **5.** astel
   coal.. **3.** rob
   deviation (lode).. **4.** hade
   device (sweeper).. **3.** gad **8.** paravane
   entrance, passage.. **4.** adit **5.** stulm
   excavation.. **5.** stope
   floor.. **4.** sill
   guardian (Myth).. **5.** gnome
   holes.. **7.** gophers
   prop.. **5.** sprag, stull
   reservoir.. **4.** sump **8.** standage
   shack.. **3.** doe
   shaft.. **4.** sump **6.** upcast
   signalman.. **5.** cager **7.** cageman
   step.. **7.** stemple (stempel)
   surface.. **6.** placer
   thrower.. **6.** minnie **11.** minenwerfer
   tunnel.. **5.** stulm
   vein.. **4.** lode
   waste.. **3.** gob **4.** goaf
   worker.. **5.** cager, miner **8.** onsetter
miner (pert to)...
   disease.. **8.** phthisis
   instrument.. **4.** dial
   lamp.. **4.** davy
   pick.. **3.** gad **7.** mandrel
   sieve.. **6.** dillue
   worm.. **8.** hookworm
mineral... **3.** ore, tin **4.** alum, iron
   5. pitch **6.** barite, egeran, gangue,
   iolite, pinite, quartz **7.** apatite, asphalt,
   ataxite, bullion, epidote, felsite, felspar
   8. danalite, edentite, misenite
   9. uraninite
mineral (ore)...
   black.. **3.** jet **6.** cerine, yenite (Elba)
      7. niobite **8.** graphite **10.** minguetite
   blue-green.. **5.** beryl
   brittle.. **7.** euclase
   brown.. **6.** cerine, egeran, rutile
      9. elaterite
   calcium, plus.. **7.** calcite **8.** calespar,
      diopside
   crosslike.. **10.** staurolite
   dark.. **7.** minette
   fibrous.. **8.** asbestos (abeston)
   flaky.. **4.** mica
   gray white.. **5.** trona
   green.. **7.** alalite, erinite **9.** malachite
   gunpowder.. **5.** niter **7.** thorite
   hard.. **4.** ruby **6.** spinel (spinelle)
      7. adamant
   jelly.. **8.** vaseline
   jewelry.. **8.** diopside
   lustrous.. **4.** spar **7.** blendes
   magnetic.. **9.** lodestone (loadstone)
   nonmetallic.. **5.** boron **6.** iodine
   plaster of Paris.. **6.** gypsum
   rare, brittle.. **7.** euclase, thorite

red . . **4.** ruby **6.** garnet
soft . . **4.** talc
waxlike . . **9.** ozocerite **11.** hatchettine
white, colorless . . **6.** barite, gypsum
yellow . . **5.** topaz **6.** pyrite **7.** epidote
mineral (pert to) . . .
  cavity . . **3.** vug (vugg, vugh, voog)
  dark spot . . **5.** macle
  deposit . . **4.** lode **6.** placer
  greasy . . **7.** atopite
  oil . . **5.** colza
  pitch . . **7.** asphalt
  pocket . . **4.** nest
  salt . . **4.** alum
  spring . . **3.** spa **4.** well
  tallow, wax . . **9.** ozocerite **11.** hatchettine
  tar . . **6.** maltha
  water . . **6.** lithia **7.** Seltzer **8.** alkaline
Minerva (pert to) . . .
  feast . . **11.** Quinquatrus
  flower, plant . . **6.** azalea
  goddess of . . **5.** civic **6.** health
    11. handicrafts
  shield . . **5.** aegis (egis)
  temple site . . **8.** Aventine (Rome)
ming . . . **6.** remind **7.** mention, recount
  8. remember
Ming (Chin) . . . **7.** dynasty
mingle . . . **3.** mix **4.** fuse, meld **5.** admix,
  blend, merge, unite **7.** combine, concoct
  8. coalesce, intermix **9.** associate
  10. amalgamate **11.** consolidate
mingle-mangle . . . **6.** jumble, medley
  7. mixture **9.** potpourri **10.** hodgepodge,
  miscellany
minhag (Jew) . . . **6.** custom, manner
  7. liturgy
miniate . . . **5.** paint **8.** decorate, luminate
  9. rubricate
minikin . . . **4.** type **5.** baize **6.** dainty
  7. elegant, mincing **8.** affected, delicate
  10. diminutive
minim . . . **3.** jot **4.** drop **5.** Order (RCCh)
  6. minute **8.** smallest **11.** small amount
minimize . . . **6.** reduce **7.** detract
  8. belittle **9.** disparage **10.** depreciate
  13. underestimate
minimum . . . **3.** jot **5.** least **6.** lowest
minion, minionette . . . **4.** idol, neat
  5. lover **6.** dainty, pretty **7.** darling,
  elegant **8.** delicate, favorite, ladylove,
  mistress, paramour
minister . . . **4.** tend **5.** angel, cater, serve
  6. afford, attend, curate, parson, pastor,
  priest, supply **7.** furnish **8.** diplomat,
  executor, preacher **9.** clergyman,
  officiate
ministerial . . . **7.** serving **9.** executive
  12. instrumental **14.** administrative,
  ecclesiastical
minister's home . . . **5.** manse
  9. parsonage
Minnesota . . .
  capital . . **6.** St Paul
  city . . **6.** Duluth **11.** Minneapolis
  hero . . **14.** Father Hennepin
  lake . . **3.** Red **10.** Minnewaska
  land of . . **16.** Ten Thousand Lakes
  mountain . . **6.** Cayuna, Mesabe
    9. Vermilion
  river . . **3.** Red **10.** St Lawrence

  11. Mississippi
  State admission . . **12.** Thirty-second
  State motto . . **13.** L'Etoile du Nord
    14. Star of the North
  State nickname . . **6.** Gopher **9.** North
    Star
Minoan . . . **6.** Cretan **7.** culture (Prehist)
  8. language
minor . . . **3.** key **4.** less, mode **5.** friar
  (Franciscan), petit, petty, scale, youth
  6. course, infant, league, lesser
  7. smaller **8.** inferior, interval, underage
  9. youngling
minority . . . **3.** few **6.** nonage **7.** smaller
  8. underage **10.** immaturity
  11. inferiority
Minos (pert to) . . .
  daughter . . **7.** Ariadne
  father . . **4.** Zeus
  king of . . **5.** Crete
  mother . . **6.** Europa
Minotaur (Gr) . . . **7.** monster (half man,
  half bull)
minster . . . **6.** church **9.** monastery
minstrel . . . **3.** lay **4.** bard, poet, show
  6. end man, troupe **7.** gleeman, goliard
  8. jongleur, musician **9.** troubador
  11. entertainer
minstrel show (pert to) . . .
  end man . . **5.** bones
  middleman . . **12.** interlocutor
  part . . **4.** olio
mint . . . **3.** aim **4.** blow, coin, sage **5.** basil,
  feint, money **6.** hyssop, intend, invent,
  mentha, ramona **7.** attempt, purpose,
  venture **8.** endeavor **9.** fabricate
mint (pert to) . . .
  charge, levy . . **8.** brassage
    11. seigniorage
  drink . . **5.** julep
  family . . **5.** basil **6.** catnip **8.** calamint
    9. Lamiaceae
  genus . . **6.** Ramona **7.** Melissa
  geranium . . **8.** costmary
  hog . . **8.** shilling
  sauce . . **5.** money
minuet . . . **3.** dance **7.** scherzo
minus . . . **4.** lack, less **6.** absent, bereft,
  defect **7.** short of, without **8.** subtract
  10. deficiency
minuscule . . . **4.** type **5.** petty, small
  6. letter (lower case) **10.** diminutive
minute . . . **3.** jot, wee **4.** mite, note,
  tiny **5.** draft, petty, small **6.** atomic,
  little, moment, period, record, slight,
  tittle **7.** instant **8.** atomical, trifling
  10. memorandum **11.** unimportant
  12. sixty seconds **14.** circumstantial
minute (pert to) . . .
  animal . . **10.** animalcule
  details . . **11.** particulars
  difference . . **5.** shade
  glass . . **9.** hourglass
  Jack . . **10.** timeserver
  opening . . **4.** pore **5.** stoma
  organism . . **5.** monad, spore **8.** zoospore
  part . . **6.** tittle
  particle . . **4.** atom, iota, mote
  record . . **8.** protocol
minutely . . . **9.** continual, unceasing
  11. every minute

minutes . . . **4.** acta **6.** record
minutia . . . **6.** detail, minute **11.** minor
 detail, petty matter
minx . . . **4.** brat, doll, miss **6.** pet dog
 7. colleen **8.** pert girl **9.** saucy girl,
 saucy jade **13.** mischief-maker
minyan . . . **6.** quorum **7.** pottery
Miohippus . . . **5.** horse
miqra . . . **9.** Bible text (Heb)
mir (Pers) . . . **4.** head **5.** chief, title
 9. president
miracle . . . **4.** feat, play **5.** anomy
 6. marvel, wonder **10.** occurrence,
 phenomenon **17.** supernatural event
miracle drug . . . **6.** elixir **7.** cure-all,
 panacea
miracle scene . . . **4.** Cana
miracle wheat . . . **7.** poulard
miracle worker . . . **8.** magician
 11. thermaturge
miraculous . . . **9.** marvelous, wonderful
 12. supernatural **13.** wonder-working
mirador . . . **5.** brown, oriel **6.** loggia,
 turret **7.** balcony **9.** bay window
 10. watchtower
mirage . . . **5.** serab **7.** chimera, reflect
 8. illusion **10.** phenomenon
mire . . . **3.** bog, mud, wet **4.** glar, moil,
 ooze, slud **5.** addle, dirty, marsh, slush,
 stall **7.** sludder
mirror . . . **5.** glass **7.** crystal, paragon,
 pattern, reflect **8.** exemplar, speculum
 9. reflector **11.** image worker **12.** looking
 glass
mirror iron . . . **12.** spiegeleisen
mirth . . . **3.** fun, joy **4.** glee **6.** gaiety
 (gayety), levity, spleen **7.** delight, jollity
 8. gladness, hilarity **9.** happiness,
 merriment, rejoicing **10.** joyousness
 12. cheerfulness
mirthful . . . **3.** gay **5.** happy, jolly
miry . . . **4.** oozy **5.** boggy, muddy, slimy
 6. filthy, lutose
mis (comb form) . . . **5.** amiss, wrong
misadventure . . . **6.** mishap **8.** accident,
 calamity, casualty, disaster
 9. mischance **10.** misfortune
misandry (opp of misogyny) . . . **12.** dislike
 of man (by woman)
misanthrope . . . **5.** cynic, Timon (Shaksp)
 8. man hater **9.** pessimist **12.** mankind
 hater
misapply . . . **5.** misdo **6.** misuse
 12. misinterpret
misapprehend . . . **7.** mistake **8.** misapply
 11. misconceive **13.** misunderstand
misbegotten . . . **8.** deformed
 12. illegitimate
miscalculate . . . **3.** err **8.** misjudge
 9. misreckon, overshoot
miscall . . . **5.** abuse **6.** revile **7.** misname
 9. read amiss **12.** mispronounce
miscarriage . . . **5.** lapse **6.** mishap
 7. failure, misdeed, mistake **8.** abortion
 9. mischance **11.** misdemeanor
 13. mismanagement **14.** premature
 birth
miscellaneous . . . **5.** mixed **6.** medley,
 varied **7.** blended, diverse, mingled
 8. combined **12.** conglomerate
 13. heterogeneous **14.** indiscriminate

miscellany . . . **6.** medley **7.** mixture
 8. excerpts **9.** anthology **10.** collection
 11. odds and ends
mischance . . . **6.** mishap **8.** calamity,
 disaster **10.** misfortune
 12. misadventure
mischief . . . **3.** ill **4.** evil, harm **5.** wrack
 6. damage **7.** trouble **9.** devilment
mischief (pert to) . . .
 god . . **4.** Loki
 goddess . . **3.** Ate **4.** Eris
 maker . . **8.** agitator **12.** troublemaker
mischievous . . . **4.** arch **6.** elfish (elvish),
 impish **7.** harmful, mocking, naughty,
 parlous, roguish, waggish **8.** sportive
misconduct . . . **7.** offense **10.** wrongdoing
 11. delinquency, misbehavior,
 misdemeanor **13.** mismanagement
miscreant . . . **6.** rascal, wretch **7.** heretic,
 villain **8.** polisson **9.** reprobate
 10. unbeliever, villainous **11.** fallen
 angel, misbeliever **12.** unscrupulous
miscue . . . **3.** err **4.** miss, slip **5.** error
 6. bungle **7.** mistake
misdeed . . . **5.** crime, wrong **7.** offense
 8. wrongful **11.** misdemeanor
misdemeanor . . . **3.** sin **4.** tort **5.** crime
 7. misdeed, offense **10.** illegality,
 wrongdoing **11.** misbehavior
mise . . . **4.** levy **5.** grant **6.** layout, treaty
 8. expenses (law), immunity **9.** privilege
miser . . . **5.** hunks, Nabal (Bib) **6.** nipper,
 wretch **7.** boarder, niggard
miserable . . . **3.** sad **6.** abject, paltry
 7. forlorn, pitiful, unhappy
 12. disconsolate, disreputable
misericord, misericorde . . . **4.** hall,
 pity **5.** mercy **6.** dagger **9.** refectory
 10. compassion **12.** dispensation
miserly . . . **4.** mean **5.** close, tight **6.** stingy
 7. chintzy (sl) **8.** churlish, covetous
 9. niggardly, penurious **10.** avaricious
 12. parsimonious
misery . . . **3.** woe **5.** grief **7.** anguish,
 avarice, poverty, sadness **8.** calamity,
 distress **9.** heartache, privation
 10. affliction, misfortune
 11. despondency, Pandora's box,
 unhappiness **12.** covetousness,
 wretchedness **13.** niggardliness
misfeasance . . . **5.** wrong **8.** trespass
 10. wrongdoing
misfortune . . . **3.** ill **4.** evil, harm
 6. mishap **7.** bad luck, reverse, setback
 8. calamity, disaster **9.** adversity,
 holocaust, mischance **11.** catastrophe
 12. misadventure
misgiving . . . **5.** doubt, qualm **7.** anxiety
 10. foreboding **12.** apprehension
mishap . . . **4.** slip **8.** accident, casualty
 10. misfortune **11.** contretemps,
 miscarriage **12.** misadventure
Mishnah, Mishna . . . **4.** Moed **5.** tenet
 6. Nashim **7.** Nezikim **8.** doctrine,
 Halakoth, Kodashim, Tohoroth
 9. tradition
misinterpret . . . **3.** err **4.** warp **7.** distort,
 misread **8.** misjudge
misjudge . . . **3.** err **11.** misconstrue
 12. miscalculate
misky . . . **5.** foggy, misty

mislay . . . **4.** lose **8.** displace, misplace
misle . . . **4.** mist, rain **6.** mizzle **7.** drizzle
mislead . . . **4.** fool **5.** blear **6.** delude, seduce **7.** deceive **8.** misguide **9.** deception, misbehave, misinform
misleading . . . **5.** false **7.** crooked **8.** illusory **9.** deceptive **10.** fallacious, fraudulent **12.** misinforming **14.** misinformation
mislippen . . . **6.** delude **7.** neglect, suspect **10.** disappoint
mismanage . . . **5.** blunk, misdo **6.** bungle, misuse **9.** mishandle
misogynist . . . **8.** celibate **10.** woman hater
misplace . . . **4.** lose **6.** mislay, misset **8.** displace **9.** dislocate, mislocate **11.** anachronism
misplay . . . **3.** err **5.** error **6.** renege **7.** mismove **9.** wrong play
misprise, misprize . . . **5.** scorn **6.** slight **7.** despise, disdain, mistake **8.** contempt **9.** underrate **10.** misprision, undervalue **13.** underestimate
misprision . . . **5.** scorn **7.** mistake **8.** contempt, misprize **10.** misconduct **11.** misdemeanor **12.** depreciation **16.** misunderstanding
mispronunciation . . . **8.** cacology **10.** bad diction
misrepresent . . . **5.** belie **7.** deceive, distort, falsify **8.** disserve
miss . . . **2.** Ms. **3.** err **4.** chit, fail, girl, lack, lose, omit, skip **5.** evade, lapse, title **7.** failure, mistake **8.** mistress **9.** fall short **10.** prostitute **12.** mademoiselle
missal . . . **4.** book (Eccl) **8.** breviary
missel . . . **9.** mistletoe
misshapen . . . **4.** ugly **8.** deformed **9.** distorted, monstrous, unshapely
missile . . . **2.** MX **4.** ICBM, Nike, Thor **5.** Atlas, Snark, Titan **6.** rocket **7.** grenade, matador **8.** Redstone **9.** Minuteman
missing . . . **3.** out **4.** gone, lost **6.** absent **7.** lacking, wanting **8.** vanished **11.** nonexistent
missing part . . . **3.** gap **4.** void **5.** space **6.** hiatus, lacuna **8.** omission
mission . . . **3.** job **4.** body, duty, task **5.** Alamo **6.** charge, church, errand **7.** calling, embassy **8.** legation, outreach **10.** assignment, commission, delegation, deputation, missionary
missionary . . . **7.** apostle **8.** emissary, preacher **10.** evangelist
Missionary Ridge . . . **11.** Chattanooga (Tenn)
Mississippi . . .
capital . . **7.** Jackson
city . . **6.** Biloxi **7.** Natchez **8.** Gulfport **9.** Vicksburg **13.** Pass Christian
explorer, colonizer . . **6.** De Soto **9.** Iberville
festival . . **9.** Mardi gras (Biloxi)
king crop . . **6.** cotton
kite (bird) . . **9.** everglade
mountain . . **6.** Woodal
river . . **5.** Yazoo **11.** Mississippi
State admission . . **9.** Twentieth
State bird . . **11.** mockingbird

State flower . . **8.** magnolia
State motto . . **14.** Virtute et Armis (By Valor and Arms)
State nickname . . **5.** Bayou
Mississippian (Geol) . . . **15.** Eocarboniferous (system)
Mississippi River head . . . **10.** Lake Itasca (Minn)
Mississippi River nickname . . . **10.** Great River **14.** Father of Waters
missive . . . **4.** note **6.** billet, letter **7.** message, missile **8.** document
Missouri . . .
capital . . **13.** Jefferson City
city . . **7.** Sedalia, St Louis **8.** Hannibal, St Joseph
famed native . . **6.** Carver (G W), Truman (Pres) **9.** Mark Twain **10.** Jesse James
gourd . . **11.** calabazilla
mountains . . **6.** Ozarks
river . . **8.** Big Muddy, Missouri **11.** Mississippi
skylark . . **13.** Sprague's pipit
State admission . . **12.** Twenty-fourth
State bird . . **8.** bluebird
State flower . . **8.** hawthorn
State nickname . . **6.** Show Me
sucker (fish) . . **10.** black horse
misspelling . . . **10.** cacography
misspend . . . **4.** lose **5.** waste **8.** squander **10.** spend amiss
misstep . . . **4.** slip, trip **7.** faux pas
mist . . . **3.** dim, fog **4.** blur, film, gray, haze, rain, smur **5.** bedim, brume, cloud **7.** droplet **9.** obscurity **11.** uncertainty
mistake . . . **3.** err **4.** bull, goof, slip **5.** boner, botch, error, fault, folly **7.** blooper, blunder, erratum, violate **8.** miscount, solecism **11.** anachronism **12.** inadvertence **13.** misconception **15.** misapprehension
mistaken . . . **5.** wrong **9.** erroneous **12.** misconceived **13.** misunderstood **14.** judging wrongly
mistletoe . . . **6.** emblem (Okla), missel, Viscum **9.** Loranthus
mistonusk . . . **6.** badger
mistreat . . . **5.** abuse, wrong **6.** ill-use
mistress . . . **4.** bibi (beebee) **5.** title, woman **6.** matron **7.** control, teacher **8.** Dulcinia, ladylove **9.** concubine, governess, patroness **10.** proprietor, sweetheart
Mistress of . . .
Adriatic . . **6.** Venice
Charles II . . **4.** Nell
Seas . . **12.** Great Britain
World . . **4.** Rome (anc)
misty . . . **3.** dim **4.** hazy, roky **5.** foggy, rouky, vague **6.** blurry, cloudy, hoarse **7.** obscure, shadowy **10.** indistinct **13.** unenlightened, unilluminated
misuse . . . **5.** abuse **6.** revile **7.** pervert **8.** maltreat, misapply, wrong use **9.** misemploy **12.** misrepresent
misuse of words in speech . . . **11.** heterophemy, malapropism
mite . . . **3.** bit, jot **4.** atom, coin, mote **5.** child, speck **6.** acarus, insect **7.** bdellid, chigger, smidgen (smidge) **8.** acaridan, particle

miter, mitre . . . **4.** belt **5.** frank, joint, tiara **6.** fillet, girdle, gusset, tavern **7.** petalon (Eccl) **8.** dovetail, headband, insignia **9.** headdress

mithridate . . . **8.** antidote **9.** electuary **12.** alexipharmic

mitigate . . . **4.** ease, tone **5.** abate, allay, mease, relax, remit, slake **6.** lessen, reduce, soften, temper **7.** appease, mollify, qualify, relieve **8.** diminish, lenitive, moderate, palliate **9.** alleviate, extenuate, meliorate

mitigation . . . **6.** relief **9.** abatement **10.** diminution, moderation **11.** extenuation **13.** mollification

mix . . . **3.** pug (clay) **4.** ease, join, meng, stir **5.** addle, blend, cross, knead, unite **6.** jumble, mingle, muddle **7.** combine, fluster **8.** coalesce **9.** associate **10.** complicate

mixable . . . **8.** miscible

mixed (pert to) . . .
bag . . **6.** medley **10.** assortment, hodgepodge, miscellany
breed . . **7.** mongrel
type . . **2.** pi
with water . . **6.** slaked
with yeast . . **6.** barmed, frothy

mixer . . . **5.** whisk **6.** beater **7.** mingler **9.** eggbeater, (food) processor

mixture . . . **4.** hash, mash, olio **5.** blend, chaos, mixed **6.** batter, medley, miscue **7.** amalgam, mélange **8.** compound, solution **9.** admixture, potpourri **10.** hodgepodge **11.** combination, preparation

mixture (pert to) . . .
beverage . . **5.** clary **10.** shandygaff
cement . . **5.** putty
medicinal . . **5.** hepar **6.** potion **12.** prescription
metallic . . **6.** speiss
sand and clay . . **4.** loam

mix-up . . . **5.** melee, snafu **6.** muddle, tangle **8.** conflict **9.** confusion

Mizar . . . **4.** Zeta (Great Dipper)

mizmaze . . . **9.** confusion **12.** bewilderment

mizzenmast . . . **9.** aftermast, third mast

mizzle . . . **4.** mist, rain **5.** misle **6.** decamp **9.** slink away

mizzy . . . **3.** bog **8.** quagmire

Mnenosyne (pert to) . . .
ancestor . . **5.** Titan
goddess . . **6.** memory
mother of . . **8.** The Muses

moa . . . **6.** ratite (flightless) **8.** Dinornis

moab . . . **3.** hat (anc)

Moabite (pert to) . . .
dwelling (Bib) . . **7.** Dead Sea
language . . **7.** Semitic
mountain . . **4.** Nebo
people . . **4.** Emim
stone (Bib) . . **11.** black basalt

moan . . . **3.** cry **4.** suum, wail **5.** groan, sough **6.** bemoan, bewail, grieve, lament, suffer **9.** complaint **11.** lamentation

moat . . . **4.** foss (fosse) **5.** ditch **6.** trench **13.** fortification

mob . . . **3.** set **4.** gang, herd, mass

5. crowd, drove, flock, group, Mafia, taunt **6.** clique, rabble, throng **7.** company **8.** canaille, populace

mobile . . . **7.** movable **8.** not fixed **9.** versatile **10.** changeable

Mobile Bay hero . . . **8.** Farragut (Adm)

mobile home . . . **3.** van **6.** camper **7.** caravan (Brit), trailer

mob member . . . **6.** rioter **7.** Mafioso **8.** criminal, mobocrat **9.** roisterer

mobocracy . . . **7.** mob rule

Moby Dick (pert to) . . .
author . . **8.** Melville (Herman)
character . . **4.** Ahab **7.** Ishmael **8.** Queequeg, Starbuck
ship . . **6.** Pequod

moccasin . . . **3.** pac **4.** shoe **5.** snake **6.** Flower (Minn State), orchid **8.** larrigan **10.** argus brown **11.** cottonmouth

moch . . . **4.** moth

mocha . . . **4.** bark, town (Arab) **6.** coffee, dollar **7.** leather **9.** moss agate

mock . . . **3.** ape **4.** defy, gibe, jape, jibe, sham **5.** feign, fleer, flout, mimic, scoff, sneer, taunt **6.** delude, deride **7.** imitate, mockery, pretend **8.** ridicule **10.** disappoint **11.** counterfeit

mock (pert to) . . .
brawn . . **10.** headcheese
cucumber . . **11.** balsam apple
duck . . **4.** meat **8.** pork chop
hero . . **5.** comic
jewelry . . **5.** logie, paste **9.** imitation
lead, ore . . **10.** sphalerite
moon . . **10.** paraselene
nightingale . . **7.** warbler **8.** blackcap
olive . . **9.** axbreaker **12.** cherry laurel
orange . . **7.** syringa (seringa)
plane . . **8.** sycamore
sun . . **9.** parhelion
turtle . . **9.** calf's head

mockage . . . **7.** mimicry, mockery **9.** imitation

mocker . . . **5.** mimic **7.** scoffer **8.** deceiver **11.** mockingbird

mockernut . . . **7.** hickory

mockery . . . **5.** farce **6.** satire **7.** mimicry, sarcasm **8.** derision **9.** imitation **11.** counterfeit

mockingbird . . . **5.** Mimus

mode . . . **3.** fad, way **4.** form **5.** flair, style, vogue **6.** manner, method **7.** fashion, variety

mode (pert to) . . .
expression . . **10.** vernacular
government . . **6.** regime, system
logic . . **7.** Ferison (3rd figure)
procedure . . **5.** order **6.** system
speech . . **8.** parlance **11.** phraseology
standing . . **4.** pose **6.** stance **7.** posture **8.** position

model . . . **3.** act **4.** form, idea, mold, norm, plan, plat, pose **5.** ideal, image, shape **7.** example, manikin, measure, paragon, pattern, templet **8.** ensample, paradigm, standard, template **9.** archetype, mannequin, precedent **11.** meritorious **12.** reproduction

model (of) . . .
a word . . **8.** paradigm

a work . . **9.** archetype
excellence . . **7.** paragon **8.** exemplar
solar system . . **6.** orrery **11.** planetarium
moderate . . . **4.** bate, ease, slow, some
5. abate, lower, slake **6.** frugal,
lessen, soften, temper **7.** control,
lenient, mediate, modesto **8.** mediocre,
modulate, slow down **9.** temperate
10. reasonable **11.** inexpensive
12. conservative **14.** inconsiderable
moderation . . . **7.** control **9.** abatement,
restraint **10.** diminution, governance,
limitation, mitigation **11.** restriction
13. temperateness
moderator . . . **5.** judge **6.** umpire **7.** arbiter
8. mediator **10.** arbitrator, controller
modern . . . **3.** neo (pref), new **4.** late
6. latter **7.** present **8.** neoteric
modernize . . . **6.** update **10.** streamline
Modern School of Art . . . **4.** Dada
7. Dadaism (1920)
modern Syriac script . . . **5.** serta
8. peshitta
modest . . . **3.** coy, mim, shy **6.** chaste,
demure, humble, seemly **8.** reserved,
retiring, virtuous **9.** diffident **11.** well-
behaved **13.** unpretentious
14. inconsiderable
modesty . . . **7.** decency, reserve, shyness
8. chastity, humility, pudicity
10. diffidence, humbleness **11.** self-
control
modicum . . . **3.** bit **4.** drop **5.** minim, share
6. little **11.** small amount **12.** small
portion
modification . . . **4.** tone **6.** change,
umlaut **9.** variation **10.** adaptation,
alteration, limitation **13.** qualification
15. differentiation
modify . . . **4.** vary **5.** alter, limit **6.** change,
master, temper **7.** assuage, qualify
8. attemper, mitigate, moderate,
quantify **9.** influence **13.** differentiate
modish . . . **4.** chic, trim **5.** smart **7.** in
vogue, stylish **8.** vogueish (voguish)
11. fashionable
modiste . . . **8.** milliner **9.** couturier
10. couturière, dressmaker
modulated . . . **5.** toned **6.** merged
7. adapted, attuned, changed, intoned
8. softened, tempered **9.** inflected,
regulated
modulation . . . **4.** tone **6.** change
8. shifting **9.** tempering **10.** alteration,
inflection, moderation
moggan . . . **5.** stocking **10.** knit sleeve
moggy . . . **3.** cat, cow **4.** calf **7.** pet name
8. slattern **9.** scarecrow
mogo . . . **7.** hatchet
mogul . . . **4.** lord **5.** nabob **6.** tycoon
7. magnate **8.** autocrat **9.** dignitary
10. locomotive, panjandrum **14.** great
personage
Mogul . . . **6.** Empire, Mongol **7.** dynasty
9. Mongolian
Mohammed (pert to) . . .
birthplace . . **5.** Mecca
daughter . . **6.** Fatima
flight to Mecca . . **6.** hegira
horse . . **5.** Fadda (white mule) **7.** Alborak
names . . **7.** Mahomet, Mahound

son-in-law . . **3.** Ali
Mohammedan (pert to) . . .
angel of death . . **6.** Azrael
ascetic . . **4.** Sufi **5.** fakir (fakeer)
8. Marabout
caliph . . **3.** Ali **4.** Omar **6.** Othman **7.** Abu
Bekr
chief . . **3.** aga (agha) **4.** dato (datto)
5. sayid **6.** Caliph
crier (for prayer) . . **7.** muezzin
crusader's enemy (Muslim) . . **7.** Saracen
deity . . **5.** Allah **9.** Termagant
demon . . **5.** afrit, eblis, jinni (jinnee)
7. Shaitan (Sheitan)
Malay (Javanese) . . **6.** Sassak
Moslem . . **5.** hanif **9.** Mussulman
noble . . **4.** amir (ameer), emir
nymph . . **5.** houri
officer . . **3.** aga **5.** diwan **6.** vizier (vizir)
princess, queen . . **5.** begum
saint . . **3.** pir **6.** santon
scholars, body of . . **5.** ulema
sect . . **6.** Wahabi (Wahabee, Wahhabi)
student (Theol) . . **5.** softa
successor . . **6.** Caliph (Calif)
teacher . . **5.** mufti **6.** mullah (mollah)
Mohammedanism (pert to) . . .
Bible, book . . **5.** Koran **7.** Alcoran
bier, tomb . . **5.** tabut
cap . . **3.** taj
caravansary . . **6.** imaret
crusade . . **5.** jihad (jehad)
custom, tradition . . **6.** sunnah
divorce . . **5.** talak **7.** mubarat
dome, over tomb . . **6.** turbeh
Easter . . **3.** Eed
Fast (annual) . . **7.** Ramadan
festival . . **6.** Bairam
garment . . **4.** izar **6.** jubbah
house (men's part) . . **8.** selamlik
instrument . . **5.** rebab
marriage custom . . **5.** iddat
marriage settlement . . **4.** mahr
Messiah, priest . . **4.** Imam (Imaum)
5. Mahdi
monastery . . **5.** ribat
platform, porch . . **7.** mastaba
prayer . . **4.** azan (adan) **5.** namaz
property (law) . . **6.** mushaa
religion . . **6.** Moslem **8.** Islamism
saber . . **8.** yataghan (yatagan)
salutation . . **6.** salaam (salam)
shrine (Mecca) . . **5.** Kaaba (Caaba,
Kaabeh) **10.** Black Stone
veil . . **7.** yashmak (yashmac)
war (Relig) . . **5.** jihad (jehad)
moho . . . **4.** rail **9.** gallinule **10.** honey
eater
mohr . . . **7.** gazelle
moider . . . **4.** toil **5.** crowd, worry
6. wander **7.** smother **8.** bewilder,
encumber
moiety . . . **4.** half, part (small) **7.** portion
moil . . . **4.** spot, tire, toil **5.** labor, taint
6. seethe **7.** torment, trouble, turmoil
8. drudgery **9.** confusion **10.** defilement
moiré . . . **7.** clouded, watered
moist . . . **3.** wet **4.** damp, dank, dewy,
uvid **5.** humid, rainy **7.** tearful
moisten . . . **3.** wet **4.** hose, moil **5.** bedew,
spray **6.** anoint, dampen, sparge

8. humidify, sprinkle
moisture ... 3. dew, fog 5. vapor, water
6. liquid 8. dampness, dankness,
dewdrops, humidity
moisture (pert to) ...
body .. 6. humors 9. exudation
condensed .. 4. drip, drop
excess, swelling .. 5. edema
expose to .. 3. ret
remove .. 4. wipe 5. wring
mojo ... 4. Moxo 5. charm (voodoo)
6. amulet 7. majagua
moke ... 4. dolt, mesh 5. horse 6. donkey
7. network 8. minstrel 9. performer
moki ... 4. raft
moko ... 9. tattooing
moky ... 5. foggy, misty
molar ... 5. tooth 6. molary 7. chopper,
grinder 8. grinding
molarimeter ... 11. thermometer
molasses ... 5. sirup 7. treacle 8. theriaca
mold, mould ... 3. die 4. cast, form,
must 5. humus, knead, nowel, plasm,
sprue 6. blight, growth (fungus),
matrix, mildew 7. moulage 9. sculpture
12. reproduction
Moldavia, Rumania ...
balm .. 4. mint
capital .. 5. Balta 8. Tiraspol
govt .. 9. Socialist
molding ... 3. ess 4. bead, beak, cyma,
ogee, reed, tori 5. conge, gulla,
ovolo, splay, torus 6. fascia, fillet,
listel, reglet, scotia 7. cavetto, cornice,
reeding, shaping 8. astragal, bezantee
12. reproduction
molding (pert to) ...
convex .. 5. torus
decoration .. 4. dado
egg and dart .. 9. arrowhead
series .. 7. surbase
suit of .. 8. ledgment (ledgement)
moldy, mouldy ... 5. fusty, mucid, musty,
stale 8. mildewed
mole (rat) ... 4. gray 5. fault, nevus
(naevus), shrew, snake, Talpa, taupe
6. rodent 7. blemish, Nesokia
9. birthmark 12. imperfection
molecule ... 3. ion 4. atom, unit 6. steric
8. particle
molest ... 4. harm 5. annoy, tease
6. bother, harass, pester 7. disturb
8. mistreat 9. incommode 13. interfere
with
Molière (pert to) ...
author of .. 5. drama, Miser, plays
6. comedy, satire 8. Tartuffe
11. Misanthrope
character (story) .. 5. Damis 6. Eraste,
Scapin 7. Dorante
mollify ... 4. calm 5. allay, relax,
sleek 6. pacify, relent, soften, temper
7. appease, lighten, qualify, relieve
9. alleviate 10. conciliate
mollitious ... 8. sensuous 9. luxurious,
softening
mollusk ... 3. asi 4. clam, pipi, slug,
spat 5. chama, snail, squid, whelk
6. cockle, limpet, mussel, oyster
7. abalone, bivalve, octopus, scallop,
veliger 8. univalve 10. cuttlefish

mollusk ... 5. Anoma, Chama, Murex
6. Chiton 7. Astarte, Etheria
8. Buccinum, Mollusca, Nautilus
mollusk (pert to) ...
bait .. 6. limpet
eight-armed .. 7. octopus
freshwater .. 7. etheria
marine .. 7. abalone, scallop 8. nautilus
shell .. 4. test 5. testa 6. cockle, cowrie
(cowry)
shell, without .. 4. slug
shell concretion .. 5. pearl
teeth .. 6. radula
ten-armed .. 5. squid
young .. 4. spat
mollycoddle ... 6. coddle, pamper
8. weakling 12. spoiled child
13. effeminate boy
Moloch (pert to) ...
Bible .. 5. deity
doctrine .. 4. evil
zoology .. 6. agamid, lizard
Molotov cocktail ... 4. bomb
molt, moult ... 3. mew 4. cast, mute,
shed 7. ecdysis 8. exuviate
molten rock ... 2. aa
Moluccas, Spice Islands ...
capital .. 7. Amboina
island .. 5. Banda
product .. 5. spice
site .. 9. Indonesia
moly ... 4. herb (fabled) 6. garlic
momble ... 6. jumble, tangle
mome (anc) ... 4. fool 7. buffoon
9. blockhead
moment ... 4. time 5. avail, flash, nonce,
point, trice, value 6. crisis, minute,
second, weight 7. impetus, instant
9. influence, twinkling 10. importance
11. consequence 13. consideration,
signification
momentary ... 9. ephemeral, transient
10. transitory 13. instantaneous
momentous ... 7. weighty 8. eventful
9. important 11. influential
13. authoritative
momo ... 3. owl
Momus (Gr) ... 3. god (of ridicule) 6. critic
11. faultfinder
mon ... 5. badge (imperial) 7. kikumon
13. chrysanthemum
monachal ... 8. celibate, monastic
9. claustral
monad ... 3. one 4. atom, unit 5. deity,
monas 8. particle 10. individual
12. Supreme Being
monadnock ... 4. hill 8. mountain (NH)
Mona Lisa (pert to) ...
famed for .. 5. smile (subtle)
named also .. 10. La Gioconda
painter .. 7. da Vinci
site (of picture) .. 6. Louvre
monandry ... 10. one husband (at a
time)
monarch ... 4. czar, king, shah 5. chief,
queen, ruler 6. dynast, kaiser, sultan
7. czarina, emperor 9. potentate,
sovereign 13. royal highness
monarch ... 9. butterfly 13. constellation
monastery ... 5. abbey 6. friary, priory
7. convent, hospice, nunnery 8. cloister

monastery (pert to) . . .
head . . **3.** dom **5.** abbot
Pavia . . **10.** Carthusian
room . . **4.** cell
Tibet . . **8.** lamasery
monastic . . . **4.** monk **5.** friar **7.** monkish
8. celibate **9.** claustral
monde . . . **5.** globe, world (fashion)
6. circle (fashion) **7.** coterie, société,
society **9.** beau monde
monetary . . . **7.** coinage **8.** currency
9. financial, pecuniary
monetary unit (sl) . . . **3.** bob (Brit), fin
4. buck **7.** sawbuck, smacker, ten spot
8. simoleon
money . . . **3.** wad **4.** cash, coin, grig, mina,
pelf **5.** frank, funds, lucre, maneh, uhllo
(ullo) **6.** mazuma, talent, wampum,
wealth **8.** currency **10.** spondulics
(spondulix) **11.** legal tender
money (pert to) . . .
ancient . . **3.** aes
bank (Eur) . . **5.** banco
box, chest . . **4.** arca, safe, till, tray
5. chest **6.** drawer **7.** brazier **8.** register
changer . . **6.** banker, broker, shroff
(saraf), usurer **7.** cambist
coinage . . **4.** mint
English slang . . **7.** ooftish (oof)
found . . **5.** trove
gamblers' . . **6.** barato
gift . . **4.** alms **7.** bequest **9.** endowment
lender . . **6.** banker, usurer **7.** Shylock
10. pawnbroker
luck . . **6.** barato **7.** handsel
maker . . **6.** coiner, minter
13. counterfeiter
manual . . **7.** cambist
matters . . **6.** fiscal **9.** economics
of account . . **3.** ora
paper . . **4.** bill, kale **7.** lettuce
pledge . . **5.** arles
premium . . **4.** agio
roll (coins) . . **7.** rouleau
shell . . **5.** uhllo (ullo) **6.** cowrie (cowry)
slang . . **4.** gilt, jack, lour **5.** rhino
6. boodle, wampum
spinner . . **6.** usurer **10.** speculator
substitute . . **5.** scrip
to coin . . **4.** mint
wildcat . . **9.** yellow dog
worthless . . **4.** pelf **11.** shinplaster
moneyed . . . **4.** rich **5.** flush **7.** opulent,
wealthy **8.** affluent, well-to-do
10. prosperous, well-heeled
monger . . . **6.** dealer, mercer, trader,
vendor **7.** peddler **8.** merchant
9. tradesman
mongler . . . **9.** sandpiper
Mongol . . . see also Mongolian **5.** Asian,
Tatar **9.** yellow man
Mongolian (pert to) . . .
ass (wild) . . **8.** chigetai
capital . . **4.** Urga
conjurer . . **6.** shaman
conqueror . . **9.** Tamerlane
desert . . **4.** Gobi
dynasty . . **4.** Yuan
monk, priest . . **4.** lama
people . . **3.** Lai **4.** Lapp **5.** Ordos
7. Khalkas, Tsaktar **9.** Ouryantai

religion . . **9.** Shamanism, Shintoism
12. Confucianism
river . . **3.** Pei **4.** Onon
mongoose . . . **4.** urva **5.** lemur
9. ichneumon
mongrel . . . **3.** cur **5.** mixed **6.** hybrid
10. crossbreed **14.** stilt sandpiper
mongrel fish . . . **5.** skate (angelfish)
8. tullibee (whitefish)
monial . . . **3.** nun
moniker . . . **4.** name **8.** nickname
monition . . . **6.** advice, notice
7. summons, warning **10.** admonition,
dissuasion, intimation **11.** forewarning
monitor . . . **4.** ship (Civil War), uran
5. varan **6.** lizard, manual, mentor,
nozzle **7.** adviser, student, warning
8. conenose (bug), director, recorder,
reminder **9.** informant
monk . . . **3.** fra **4.** bede, lama, saki **5.** fakir,
friar, padre **6.** ferret, monkey **7.** ascetic,
caloyer, dervish **8.** anchoret, capuchin,
celibate, cenobite **9.** anchorite, bullfinch,
touchwood
monkey (pert to) . . .
African . . **4.** waag **5.** potto **6.** grivet,
vernet
American . . **4.** saki **5.** acari **7.** ouakari
8. marmoset **9.** beelzebub
bearded . . **8.** entellus
bonnet . . **4.** zati **5.** toque
bread . . **6.** baobab
chimpanzee . . **6.** nchega
crying . . **4.** kaha
cups . . **9.** nepenthes **12.** pitcher plant
family . . **10.** Catarrhina
flower . . **7.** mimulus (herb)
genus . . **5.** Cebus **6.** Ateles **7.** Colobus,
Saimiri, Tarsius **8.** Alouatta
handsome . . **4.** mona
house . . **5.** apery
howling . . **4.** mono **5.** araba **7.** stentor
8. alouatte
large . . **5.** sajou
Madagascar . . **8.** mangabey (mangaby)
organ grinder . . **5.** Cebus **8.** capuchin
Oriental . . **7.** macaque
puzzle . . **5.** piñon
small . . **8.** marmoset
South American . . **4.** titi **6.** grison
9. beelzebub
spider . . **7.** sapajou
squirrel . . **7.** saimiri
tailless . . **3.** ape
wrench . . **7.** spanner
monk's hood . . . **4.** cowl
monkshood . . . **4.** atis **7.** aconite
9. dandelion
monoceros . . . **4.** fish (one-horned)
7. sawfish, Unicorn **9.** swordfish
13. Constellation
monochord . . . **7.** concord, harmony
9. sonometer **10.** clavichord, instrument
monocle . . . **8.** eyeglass
monocleid, monocleide . . . **4.** desk (one
key) **7.** cabinet
monocracy . . . **9.** autocracy **13.** undivided
rule
Monodelphia . . . **7.** mammals **8.** Eutheria
monody . . . **3.** ode **4.** poem (lament),
song **5.** dirge **6.** melody **9.** homophony

monogamy . . . **11.** one marriage
monogram . . . **6.** cipher, sketch **7.** outline
  8. initials **9.** character
monolith . . . **5.** stone **6.** menhir, pillar,
  statue **8.** monument
monologue . . . **6.** speech **9.** soliloquy
monomachy . . . **4.** duel **6.** combat
monopoly . . . **5.** grant, right, trust
  6. corner **7.** charter, control **9.** privilege,
  syndicate **10.** possession (exclusive)
monotonous . . . **4.** dead, drab, dull
  5. drone, thrum **6.** dreary, samely
  7. humdrum, tedious **8.** singsong
  9. wearisome **11.** repetitious
monotony . . . **6.** tedium **8.** sameness
  9. wearisome **10.** sameliness, uniformity
  15. repetitiousness
monoxylon, monoxyle . . . **4.** boat
  5. canoe
monseigneur . . . **5.** title **6.** My Lord
monster . . . **4.** ogre **5.** fiend, harpy,
  teras **6.** dragon, ellops, geryon,
  gorgon, sphinx **8.** behemoth, Cerberus
  11. monstrosity
monster (pert to) . . .
  abode (Scot) . . **8.** Loch Ness
  actor . . **6.** Chaney **7.** Karloff
  classic . . **8.** minotaur
  comb form . . **6.** terato
  desert . . **4.** Gila
  eight-headed . . **6.** Scylla
  fabled . . **5.** harpy **6.** kraken, sphinx
    7. centaur **9.** bucentaur
  flame-breathing . . **7.** chimera (chimaera)
  half man, half bull . . **8.** minotaur
  headless . . **9.** acephalus
  like . . **8.** teratoid
  man-eating . . **4.** ogre **5.** lamia
  medical . . **5.** teras
  Shelley's . . **12.** Frankenstein
  three-bodied . . **6.** Geryon (slain by
    Hercules)
  Tokyo's . . **8.** Godzilla
  twin . . **10.** xiphopagus
  two-bodied . . **7.** disomus
  two-headed . . **10.** dicephalus,
    opodidymus
  winged . . **5.** harpy
monstrous . . . **4.** huge, ugly, vast
  5. enorm (anc) **6.** absurd, wicked
  7. strange, titanic **8.** deformed, gigantic,
  infamous **9.** fantastic, monstrous,
  unnatural **10.** prodigious, stupendous
  12. overpowering, overwhelming
  13. extraordinary
Montaigne (pert to) . . .
  translator . . **6.** Florio
  writer of . . **6.** essays
Montana . . .
  capital . . **6.** Helena
  city . . **5.** Butte **8.** Anaconda, Billings
    10. Great Falls
  Historic site . . **14.** Custer Cemetery
  lake . . **8.** Flathead
  mountain . . **7.** Rockies **17.** Continental
    Divide
  park . . **7.** Glacier **11.** Yellowstone
  peak . . **7.** Granite
  reservation (Ind) . . **4.** Cree, Crow **5.** Sioux
    8. Cheyenne, Chippewa **9.** Blackfeet
  State admission . . **10.** Forty-first

  State motto . . **13.** Gold and Silver
  State nickname . . **8.** Treasure
montanto . . . **6.** rising **10.** broadsword
Monte Cristo, Count of (pert to) . . .
  author . . **5.** Dumas (Alexandre)
  hero . . **6.** Dantès
Montenegro . . . **10.** Yugoslavia
montero . . . **3.** cap (hunter's) **6.** ranger
  8. forester, huntsman, mountain
Montezuma (pert to) . . .
  Chief of . . **6.** Aztecs
  cypress . . **9.** ahuehuete
  hero of . . **6.** Mexico
  prisoner of . . **6.** Cortez
  ruins, site of . . **6.** Pueblo
month (pert to) . . .
  astronomy . . **5.** lunar, solar
  half . . **9.** fortnight
  revolution . . **8.** sidereal **9.** synodical
  term . . **5.** epact **6.** ultimo **7.** proximo
  twelfth part . . **8.** calendar
monticule . . . **4.** cone (volcano) **5.** mount
  7. hillock **10.** prominence (small)
montilla . . . **6.** sherry
Montmorency . . . **6.** cherry
monture . . . **5.** frame, horse (saddle),
  mount
monument . . . **4.** tomb **5.** cairn, stele
  (stela), tower, vault **6.** bilith, dolmen
  7. obelisk **8.** cenotaph, cromlech,
  monolith **9.** sepulcher **10.** gravestone
  11. commemorate, remembrance
monumental . . . **4.** high **5.** great
  7. mammoth, massive, notable
  8. colossal **10.** impressive, sculptural,
  stupendous
Monumental City . . . **9.** Baltimore
moo . . . **3.** low (of a cow) **6.** lowing
mooch . . . **4.** loaf **5.** skulk, sneak, steal
  6. loiter, pilfer **7.** vagrant
moocha . . . **6.** girdle **9.** loincloth
mood . . . **3.** tid **4.** tone, vein, whim
  5. freak, humor **6.** nature **7.** caprice
  11. disposition
moody . . . **3.** sad **4.** glum **5.** sulky
  6. gloomy, sullen **7.** pensive
  9. whimsical **10.** capricious
mool . . . **4.** bury, mold, soil **5.** earth,
  grave **6.** mingle **7.** crumble
mools . . . **10.** chilblains
moon . . . **4.** idle, Luna **5.** Diana **6.** Phoebe,
  wander **7.** Cynthia **8.** crescent **9.** satellite
  13. celestial body
moon (pert to) . . .
  age (first of year) . . **5.** epact
  area . . **4.** mare
  Astrol . . **6.** Cancer (mansion), planet
  autumn . . **7.** harvest
  beam . . **3.** ray **9.** pearl blue
  bird . . **11.** goldencrest
  blindness . . **10.** nyctalopia
  calf . . **4.** dolt **7.** monster **8.** born fool,
    imbecile
  comb form . . **5.** selen
  fern . . **8.** moonwort
  festival . . **8.** neomenia
  fish . . **4.** opah **6.** minnow **7.** sunfish
    9. spadefish
  flower . . **10.** oxeye daisy
  gazing . . **16.** absent-mindedness
  geographer . . **13.** selenographer

god.. **3.** Sin **6.** Nannar
heraldry.. **6.** argent
inhabitant.. **8.** Selenite
instrument.. **11.** selenoscope
lighter.. **9.** serenader **10.** moonshiner
  11. night worker
lily.. **10.** moonflower
mad.. **7.** lunatic
mock.. **10.** paraselene
month.. **5.** lunar
new.. **6.** phasis
phase.. **7.** gibbous, horning
picture of.. **11.** selenograph
point.. **4.** cusp, horn **5.** apsis **6.** apogee
  7. perigee
position.. **6.** octant
raker.. **10.** stupid lout **12.** woolgatherer
stone.. **3.** gem **8.** feldspar **10.** hecatolite
struck.. **7.** lunatic **8.** obsessed
Uranus's.. **5.** Ariel
valley.. **4.** rill (rille) **5.** cleft
moon goddess . . .
  Greek.. **6.** Hecate, Phoebe **7.** Artemis,
    Cynthia
  Italian.. **5.** Diana
  Phoenician.. **6.** Tanith (Tanit) **7.** Astarte
  Roman.. **3.** Dea **5.** Virgo **9.** Caelestis
moonish . . . **7.** flighty **10.** capricious
moonshine . . . **5.** empty **6.** liquor, poteen,
  whisky (whiskey) **7.** bootleg **8.** egg
  sauce, nonsense **10.** balsamweed
moony . . . **5.** round **6.** dreamy
  9. moonlight **10.** abstracted
  14. crescent-shaped
moor . . . **3.** bog, fen **4.** hill, root **5.** heath,
  marsh, swale **6.** anchor, fasten, secure
  9. fix firmly
Moor . . . **6.** Berber, Moslem **7.** Moorman,
  Othello (Shaksp), Saracen **8.** goldfish
  (black), Moroccan
moor (pert to) . . .
  berry.. **9.** cranberry
  bird.. **6.** grouse
  blackbird.. **5.** ouzel
  buzzard.. **5.** harpy **7.** harrier
  cock.. **9.** blackcock
  dance.. **7.** morisco
  grass.. **5.** heath **6.** sundew
  hen.. **4.** coot **9.** gallinule
  monkey.. **7.** macaque
  stone.. **7.** granite
Moorish . . . **6.** Moslem **8.** Moresque
Moorish (pert to) . . .
  garment.. **5.** jupon
  horse.. **4.** barb (Barbary)
  judge.. **4.** cadi
  kettledrum.. **5.** tabor **6.** atabal
  Order.. **7.** Alcazar **8.** Alhambra
    9. horseshoe, Saracenic
  palace.. **7.** Alcazar
moose . . . **3.** elk **4.** alce **5.** eland **7.** society
  (Loyal Order)
moose bird . . . **9.** Canada jay
moot . . . **4.** pose **5.** argue, plead, speak
  6. debate **7.** discuss, propose
mop . . . **4.** swab, wipe **5.** scrub **6.** merkin
  7. drink up, grimace **9.** blindfold,
  implement
mope . . . **4.** sulk **5.** dumps, idler **6.** grieve
moppet . . . **3.** tot **4.** baby, doll, tike
  7. darling, toddler **9.** youngster

mora . . . **4.** tree (Trinidad) **5.** delay,
  stool **7.** default **8.** syllable **9.** footstool
  11. Spartan army **12.** postponement
moral . . . **4.** good, pure **5.** maxim **6.** lesson
  7. epimyth, ethical, upright, virtual
  8. likeness, virtuous **9.** righteous
moral (pert to) . . .
  excellence.. **6.** virtue
  fault.. **4.** vice
  law.. **9.** Decalogue
  obligation.. **4.** duty
  poem.. **3.** dit
  principle.. **7.** precept
  story.. **5.** fable **7.** parable **8.** apologue
morale . . . **4.** hope, zeal **6.** morals, spirit
  8. morality **10.** confidence
moralist . . . **4.** prig **7.** teacher **9.** moralizer
  10. sermonizer
morality . . . **6.** amoral, ethics, virtue
  13. righteousness
morals . . . **8.** morality **10.** ethography
morass . . . **3.** bog, fen **4.** moor **5.** marsh,
  swamp **6.** slough **8.** quagmire
  9. everglade
moratorium . . . **5.** delay **10.** suspension
Moravia, capital . . . **5.** Brünn (Brno)
Moravian . . . **9.** Christian **10.** Herrnhuter
  13. Unitas Fratrum **19.** Church of the
  Brethren
moray . . . **3.** eel **6.** hamlet **7.** Muraena
  8. food fish **10.** Muraenidae
morbid . . . **4.** sick **6.** gloomy **7.** ghastly,
  unsound **8.** diseased **9.** unhealthy
  11. unwholesome
morbid (pert to) . . .
  appetite.. **10.** adephagous
  complex.. **11.** inferiority
  condition.. **8.** ochlesis
  desire for music.. **9.** melomania
  displacement.. **7.** ectopia
morbus . . . **7.** disease, illness
morceau . . . **3.** bit (Mus) **6.** morsel
mordant . . . **4.** acid, keen **6.** biting
  7. burning, caustic, pungent **8.** scathing
  9. corrosive, sarcastic **11.** acrimonious
more . . . **3.** yea **4.** also, mair, plus, some
  5. again, extra **6.** plural **7.** greater
  10. additional **13.** approximately
more (pert to) . . .
  cunning.. **5.** slyer **6.** tricky
  difficult.. **6.** harder
  distant.. **8.** ulterior
  mature.. **5.** older, riper
  miserly.. **6.** closer, meaner, nearer
  not any.. **4.** dead, past **8.** vanished
    11. nonexistent
  or less.. **4.** some **8.** somewhat
    13. approximately
  over.. **3.** and **4.** also, else **7.** besides,
    further, thereto
  precious.. **6.** dearer
  relative.. **11.** comparative
  severe.. **7.** sterner
  so.. **3.** yea
  than.. **4.** over **5.** above **6.** beyond
    9. exceeding **10.** in excess of
  than enough.. **3.** too
  than one.. **4.** many **6.** plural **7.** several
  than this.. **3.** yes
  unusual.. **5.** rarer
  vapid.. **6.** staler

morel ... **6.** fungus **8.** mushroom
morello ... **4.** ruru **6.** cherry **7.** boobook
   8. morepork, mulberry (color)
morena ... **8.** brunette
mores ... **7.** customs, manners **9.** etiquette
   11. conventions
Moreton Bay ... **9.** Australia
Morgan ... **5.** horse **10.** sea dweller
morganatic marriage ... **10.** left-handed
   (royal)
morgay ... **7.** dogfish
morglay ... **5.** sword
morgue ... **8.** mortuary **9.** deadhouse,
   stolidity **11.** haughtiness, impassivity
Morgue (The) ... **17.** Library of Congress
moribund ... **4.** sick **5.** dying **9.** near
   death
moriform ... **14.** mulberry-shaped
morindin dye ... **2.** al
morion ... **6.** helmet, quartz **8.** cabasset
Mormon Church (pert to) ...
   Band (Polit) .. **6.** Danite (1837)
   cricket .. **11.** grasshopper
   emblem .. **3.** bee
   Indian .. **8.** Lamanite
   instrument .. **4.** Urim **7.** Thummin
   officer .. **5.** Elder
   official name .. **36.** Church of Jesus
      Christ of Latter Day Saints
   patriarch .. **11.** Joseph Smith **12.** Brigham
      Young
   prophet .. **6.** Moroni
   State .. **4.** Utah
   tea plant .. **7.** Brigham
   tree .. **11.** black poplar
morning (pert to) ...
   clouds .. **4.** velo
   coat .. **7.** cutaway
   concert .. **6.** aubade
   glory .. **3.** nil **7.** ipomoea
      14. Convolvulaceae
   goddess .. **3.** Eos
   performance .. **7.** matinee
   prayer .. **5.** matin
   reception .. **5.** levee
   star .. **4.** Mars **5.** Venus **6.** Saturn
      7. Daystar, Jupiter, Lucifer, Mercury
      8. Phosphor
   term .. **2.** AM **4.** dawn **5.** matin, wight
      6. Aurora **7.** sunrise **9.** matutinal
moro ... **5.** finch
moro (comb form) ... **6.** stupid
Moro ... **6.** Muslim
Morocco ...
   capital .. **5.** Rabat
   city .. **3.** Fez **7.** Tangier **9.** Marrakech
      (Marrakesh) **10.** Casablanca
   color .. **3.** red
   enclave .. **4.** Ifni
   famed site .. **5.** Casba
   hat .. **3.** fez
   island .. **7.** Madeira
   Jewish quarter .. **8.** El Millah
   language .. **6.** Arabic
   leather imitation .. **4.** roan
   military expedition .. **5.** harka
   millet .. **12.** Johnson grass
   mountains .. **5.** Atlas
   people .. **4.** Arab, Moor **6.** Berber
   plateau .. **6.** mesata
   ruler .. **4.** king **5.** malek **6.** sultan

   soldier .. **5.** askar
morology ... **5.** folly **8.** nonsense
moron ... **4.** dull **5.** ament, idiot, zombi
   6. nitwit, stupid **8.** imbecile, sluggish
   12. stupid person
morose ... **4.** blue, dour, glum, grum,
   sour **5.** moody, surly **6.** crusty, gloomy,
   sullen **7.** crabbed, unhappy **9.** splenetic
   10. embittered
Morpheus (Gr) ... **10.** god of Sleep
   11. god of Dreams
morphine ... **6.** heroin **8.** hypnotic
   9. analgesic, calmative
morphology ... **7.** anatomy **8.** cytology
   9. histology **10.** embryology
   12. organography
morris ... **4.** game **5.** chair, dance
morro ... **4.** hill **6.** Castle (Havana)
   7. hillock **11.** point of land
Mors (Rom) ... **5.** Death, deity
Morse ... **4.** code, lamp **8.** alphabet
morsel ... **3.** ort **4.** bite, chip **5.** piece,
   scran (sl), scrap, snack **6.** tidbit, titbit
   7. morceau **8.** delicacy, fragment
   11. small amount
mort ... **4.** dead, lard **5.** death, fatal
   6. deadly, grease, salmon **9.** abundance
mortacious ... **4.** very **9.** extremely
mortal ... **5.** fatal, human **6.** deadly,
   lethal **10.** perishable
mortally ... **5.** amort **6.** deadly **7.** à
   la mort, deathly, fatally **9.** extremely
   10. grievously
mortar ... **3.** rab **4.** bowl **5.** putty
   6. cannon **7.** mortier **10.** night light
   (Hist)
mortarboard ... **3.** cap (Acad)
mortgage ... **4.** bond, pawn **6.** pledge
mortician ... **8.** embalmer **10.** undertaker
   15. funeral director
mortification ... **5.** decay, shame
   7. chagrin **8.** gangrene, vexation
   11. humiliation
mortify ... **5.** abase, abash, abuse, shame,
   spite **6.** ashame, deaden, humble
   7. chagrin **9.** embarrass, humiliate
mortis causa ... **15.** by reason of death
mortise, mortice ... **6.** cavity, insert
   8. amortize **10.** foundation
mortuary ... **4.** gift (burial) **6.** morgue
   7. funeral **8.** funereal **9.** deadhouse,
   sepulcher **10.** cinerarium
   12. corsepresent (offering, Hist)
mosaic ... **5.** virus **6.** design **7.** ceramic,
   picture **10.** decoration, variegated
   11. tessellated
mosaic (pert to) ...
   apply .. **7.** incrust
   gold .. **6.** ormolu
   law .. **5.** Torah (Moses)
   piece .. **7.** tessera
Moscow ...
   capital of .. **6.** Russia
   citadel .. **7.** Kremlin
   river .. **6.** Moskva
   shrine .. **9.** Lenin Tomb, Red Square
   Third Internat .. **9.** Comintern
Moselle ... **4.** Saar, wine **5.** river, Ruwer
   9. Rhine wine
Moses (pert to) ...
   Bible .. **7.** prophet **8.** lawgiver

brother .. **5.** Aaron
emissary .. **5.** Caleb
father .. **5.** Amram
father-in-law .. **6.** Jethro
law .. **5.** Torah (Tora) **10.** Pentateuch
mother .. **8.** Jochebed
mountain .. **4.** Nebo
sister .. **6.** Miriam
successor .. **6.** Joshua
wife .. **8.** Zipporah
mosey ... **6.** depart, stroll **7.** shuffle
Moslem ... see *Muslim*
mosque ... **4.** Omar **5.** Kaaba (Caaba)
  6. masjid **11.** Great Mosque
mosque tower ... **7.** minaret
mosque warden ... **5.** nazir
mosquito (pert to) ...
bite preventive .. **10.** culicifuge
coast .. **8.** Honduras **9.** Nicaragua
comb form .. **6.** culici
destroyer .. **8.** culicide
disease .. **7.** malaria **11.** yellow fever
family .. **9.** Culicidae
fish .. **8.** gambusia
genus .. **5.** Aedes, Culex **7.** Diptera
  8. Mansonia **9.** Anopheles, Culicidae
  10. Psorophora
hawk .. **9.** dragonfly, nighthawk
Indian drink .. **6.** mushla
larvae .. **8.** wigglers
plant .. **4.** mint **10.** pennyroyal
shaped .. **10.** culiciform
term .. **7.** culicid **11.** gallinipper
moss ... **3.** bog, rag **4.** agar **5.** Maium,
  money, Musci, swamp **6.** lichen, morass
  7. skeeter **8.** agar-agar **9.** treebeard
moss (pert to) ...
back .. **4.** dodo, fogy (fogey) **9.** old turtle
  10. fuddy-duddy, Southerner (1861)
  12. conservative
berry .. **9.** cranberry
capsule .. **9.** operculum
color .. **5.** green
coral .. **8.** bryozoan
duck .. **7.** mallard **8.** moss-head
  9. merganser
fish .. **8.** menhaden **10.** mossbunker
grown .. **10.** antiquated
kind .. **4.** peat **7.** Spanish
like .. **6.** mnioid
mossy ... **4.** dull **5.** boggy, downy
  6. marshy, stupid **9.** crumbling
most ... **7.** highest, maximum **8.** greatest,
  main part, majority **9.** nearly all
most favorable ... **7.** optimum
Most High ... **3.** God **12.** Supreme Being
most northerly land ... **5.** Thule
mot ... **5.** adage, maxim, motto **7.** opinion
  9. witticism
mote ... **4.** atom, hill, iota **5.** match,
  speck, squib **6.** barrow, height, trifle
  7. tumulus **8.** eminence, particle
mote nut ... **5.** carap
motet ... **4.** hymn **6.** anthem, choral
moth ... **2.** io **5.** egger, tinea **6.** lappet,
  miller **7.** noctuid, Tineina **8.** forester
  (8-spotted), Tineidae **9.** Tineoidea
  11. Lepidoptera
moth (pert to) ...
hawk .. **10.** goatsucker
kind .. **5.** gypsy **6.** carpet **9.** browntail

spot (Med) .. **8.** chloasma
spot (wing) .. **8.** fenestra
mother ... **2.** ma **3.** dam **4.** amma
  5. adopt, mamma, mater **6.** abbess,
  parent **7.** care for, creator **8.** ancestor,
  begetter, genetrix, producer
  10. procreator
mother (pert to) ...
church .. **9.** cathedral **16.** Christian
  Science
goddess .. **6.** matris **7.** Shaktis **10.** sapta-
  matri (7 mothers)
goddess of motherhood (Egypt) .. **4.** Isis
godmother .. **4.** Rhea **6.** cummer
  (kimmer) **9.** Brigantia
Goose character .. **5.** Simon, Sprat
  6. Bo-peep
Govt .. **10.** matriarchy, metrocracy
house .. **7.** convent **9.** monastery
Hubbard .. **4.** gown **5.** dress
lode .. **3.** ore
Maid .. **10.** Virgin Mary
Mother Carey's chickens .. **7.** petrels
  (stormy)
Myth (Gr) .. **5.** Niobe
related .. **6.** enatic
spiritual .. **4.** amma
Tagalog .. **3.** Ina
motherly ... **8.** maternal
mother of ...
Castor .. **4.** Leda
gods .. **4.** Rhea **9.** Brigantia
Graces .. **5.** Aegle
Nature .. **6.** Cybele
Night .. **3.** Nox, Nyx
pearl .. **5.** nacre **7.** abalone
presidents .. **8.** Virginia
States .. **8.** Virginia
the month .. **4.** Moon
motif ... **5.** theme, topic **6.** edging
  7. subject
motion ... **3.** bob **4.** lipe, move **5.** impel,
  trend **6.** seesaw, travel, tremor, unrest
  7. gesture, propose, request, suggest
  8. kinetics, mobility, movement, petition
motionless ... **5.** inert, rigid, still **6.** static
  8. immobile, stagnant **10.** stationary,
  stock-still
motion picture terms ... **4.** film,
  show **5.** flick, klieg (light), movie,
  rerun **6.** cinema **7.** cartoon, feature
  9. filmstrip, videotape **11.** golden oldie
  12. silver screen
motivate ... **4.** move **5.** force, impel
  6. compel, incite, induce, propel
  7. actuate, animate, promote, trigger
  9. stimulate
motive ... **4.** sake, spur **5.** cause,
  motif, topic **6.** reason **7.** pretext
  8. stimulus **9.** incentive, influence,
  intention **10.** incitement, inducement
  11. instigation **13.** consideration
motley ... **5.** mixed **6.** fabric **7.** diverse,
  mixture, mottled **9.** checkered, diversity
  10. variegated **12.** parti-colored
  13. heterogeneous
motor ... **5.** mover, rotor **6.** Diesel,
  dynamo, engine **7.** turbine **8.** motor
  car **9.** locomotor **10.** automobile
motor speed control ... **8.** governor,
  rheocrat

mottled ... **3.** roe **4.** pied **5.** pinto **6.** calico **7.** dappled, marbled, piebald, spotted **13.** pepper-and-salt
mottled soap ... **7.** castile
motto ... **3.** mot **5.** adage, axiom, gnome, maxim **6.** advice **7.** empresa (impresa), precept **8.** aphorism **9.** principle **11.** inscription
motto of ...
Boy Scouts .. **10.** Be Prepared
Coast Guard .. **11.** Always Ready **13.** Semper paratus
Order of the Garter .. **20.** Honi soit qui mal y pense
Queen Elizabeth .. **11.** Semper Eadem **13.** Always the Same
mouche ... **5.** patch (black)
mouchoir ... **12.** handkerchief
mouflon, moufflon ... **5.** sheep
mould, mold ... **5.** knead **6.** matrix
moulrush ... **7.** pollack (food fish)
mound ... **3.** dam, dun, tee **4.** bank, dene, doon, dune, heap, hill, terp, tomb, tump **5.** knoll **6.** bounds **7.** barrier, bulwark, rampart, tumulus **8.** boundary **9.** elevation **10.** embankment **13.** fortification
mound (pert to) ...
bird .. **8.** megapode
City .. **7.** St Louis
lily .. **5.** yucca
memorial .. **5.** cairn
of light .. **8.** Kohinoor (diamond)
Polynesian .. **3.** ahu
prehistoric .. **5.** matte
Scottish .. **5.** toman
mount ... **3.** fly, set (jewel) **4.** glue, hill, lift, pony (polo), rise **5.** arise, climb, horse, paste, steed **6.** ascent **7.** elevate **8.** increase, mountain **10.** promontory
Mount (pert to) ...
Etna city .. **7.** Catania
Everest peak .. **6.** Lhotse
Parnassus fountain, spring .. **8.** Castalia
S Dakota .. **8.** Rushmore
mountain ...
Africa .. **11.** Kilimanjaro
Alaska .. **8.** McKinley
Asia .. **7.** Everest **9.** Himalayas
Babylonia .. **6.** Ararat
California .. **6.** Shasta **7.** Whitney
Crete .. **3.** Ida
Europe .. **4.** Ural **8.** Pyrenees
fabled .. **4.** Meru
Greek (Myth) .. **7.** Helicon
Japan .. **8.** Fujiyama
legendary .. **3.** Kaf, Qaf (Muslim) **4.** Meru
Mexico .. **12.** Popocatepetl
Montana .. **6.** Tetons
South America .. **5.** Andes
Switzerland .. **4.** Alps **10.** Matterhorn
Thessaly .. **4.** Ossa **6.** Pelion
U S Chain .. **5.** Rocky **7.** Sawback, Sierras **9.** Blue Ridge **11.** Appalachian
Yukon .. **5.** Logan
mountain (pert to) ...
ash .. **5.** rowan
badger .. **6.** marmot
balsam .. **3.** fit
banana .. **3.** fei
barometer .. **8.** orometer

beaver .. **8.** sewellel
blackbird .. **5.** ouzel
cat .. **4.** lynx **6.** bobcat, cougar **10.** cacomistle
comb form .. **3.** oro
cowslip .. **8.** auricula
crest, spur .. **5.** arête
curassow (pheasant) .. **10.** oreophasis
defile .. **3.** gap **4.** gate, ghat (ghaut), pass **5.** gorge
depression .. **3.** col
dew .. **6.** whisky
eagle .. **6.** golden
goat .. **4.** ibex
highest .. **7.** Everest
ice .. **4.** berg **7.** glacier
ivy .. **6.** laurel
lake .. **4.** tarn
lion .. **4.** puma **6.** cougar
lodge .. **4.** gite
low .. **5.** butte
nymph .. **5.** oread
oak .. **8.** chestnut
peak .. **3.** tor
raspberry .. **10.** cloudberry
rose .. **6.** laurel
sheep .. **7.** bighorn **13.** Rocky Mountain
shrub .. **10.** fetterbush
sickness .. **7.** soroche
State .. **7.** Montana
sunset .. **9.** alpenglow
Tatars .. **5.** Tauli
witch .. **9.** quail dove
mountaineer ... **7.** climber **11.** backsettler
mountains, science of ... **7.** orology **9.** orography
mountant ... **6.** raised, rising **8.** mounting **9.** ascendant
mountebank ... **4.** gull **5.** cheat, quack **7.** buffoon, empiric **8.** impostor **9.** charlatan, pretender **11.** quack doctor
mounted men ... **7.** knights
mounting ... **6.** ascent **7.** rimbase, seating, setting **9.** adjusting, equipment **13.** embellishment
mourn ... **3.** rue **4.** erme, long, sigh, wail, weep **6.** bemoan, bewail, grieve, lament, murmur, repine, sorrow **7.** deplore
mourner ... **6.** keener, wailer **7.** griever **8.** lamenter
mournful ... **3.** sad **6.** repine **7.** elegiac **8.** grievous **9.** elegiacal, plaintive, saddening, sorrowful, threnodic, woebegone
mournful poem ... **5.** elegy
mourning ... **3.** sad **4.** garb **5.** crape, weeds (dress) **6.** lament, sorrow **7.** drapery **9.** sorrowing **10.** black badge **11.** lamentation
mourning dress ... **5.** weeds **6.** sables
mouse ... **3.** erd, Mus **4.** buck, vole **5.** prowl, shrew **6.** jerboa, migale **7.** harvest, toy with
mouse (pert to) ...
bird .. **4.** coly **6.** shrike
color .. **4.** gray
deer .. **7.** plandok **10.** chevrotain
ear .. **8.** hawkweed **9.** bloodwort, chickweed **11.** forget-me-not
fish .. **9.** sargassum

hare.. **4.** pika
hound.. **6.** weasel
kind.. **6.** pocket **7.** harvest, jumping
leaping.. **6.** jerboa
milk.. **6.** spurge
mouselike.. **6.** murine
web.. **6.** cobweb, phlegm **8.** gossamer
mousse ... **7.** dessert **9.** moss green
   12. gelatine dish
moutan ... **5.** peony
mouth ... **2.** os **3.** mow, mun **4.** boca,
   dupe, lade, lick **5.** inlet, stoma **6.** cavity,
   rictus **7.** declaim, opening, orifice
   8. aperture, lorriker **9.** impudence
mouth (pert to) ...
   away from.. **6.** aboral
   deformity.. **7.** harelip
   disease.. **6.** canker **10.** stomatitis
   furnace.. **5.** bocca
   glands.. **8.** salivary
   muscle.. **7.** caninus
   organ.. **4.** harp **7.** Pandean **8.** jew's-harp
   9. crembalum, harmonica
   part.. **3.** lip **5.** uvula **6.** palate **7.** pharynx
   pert to.. **4.** oral **6.** rictal, stomal
   8. stomatic
   piece (Mus).. **10.** embouchure
   through the.. **7.** peroral
   tissue.. **3.** gum
   toward.. **4.** orad
   wide, gaping.. **6.** rictus
mouthed, loud ... **11.** thersitical
mouton ... **5.** sheep **9.** prison spy
movable ... **6.** mobile **10.** changeable
   12. transferable
movable property ... **8.** chattels
move ... **3.** act, gee, mog, say **4.** goad,
   sell, spur, stir **5.** budge, cause,
   impel, rouse, shift **6.** excite, incite,
   induce, kindle, motion, prompt, travel
   7. actuate, advance, animate, propose,
   provoke **9.** instigate, recommend,
   stimulate
move (pert to) ...
   about.. **5.** locomote
   along.. **5.** mosey, scram **7.** maunder
   back.. **3.** ebb **6.** recede, retire, revert
   7. retreat **10.** retrogress
   back and forth.. **6.** teeter, wigwag
   7. shuttle **9.** oscillate
   clumsily.. **4.** joll
   false.. **4.** balk **5.** feint
   forward.. **4.** edge, scud **5.** drive
   7. advance **8.** progress
   furtively.. **5.** slink, sneak
   heavily.. **3.** lug **6.** fidget, lumber, trudge
   in circles.. **4.** purl
   place to place.. **7.** migrate **8.** emigrate
   quickly.. **3.** ply **4.** dart, dash, scud,
   shot **5.** scoot, spank **6.** bustle, gallop,
   hurtle
   restlessly.. **6.** kelter
   rhythmically.. **5.** dance
   sideways, sidewise.. **4.** slue **5.** sidle
   slowly.. **3.** jog, lag **4.** edge, inch, pant
   smoothly.. **4.** slip **5.** glide, skate, slide
   spasmodically.. **5.** twitch
   to and fro.. **3.** wag **4.** flap, sway
   together.. **5.** unite **8.** converge
   towards each other.. **8.** converge
   towards the east.. **9.** orientate

unsteadily.. **4.** reel **6.** wabble **7.** stagger
up and down.. **3.** bob **6.** teeter
with exertion.. **5.** heave
with measured tread.. **5.** march
moved by entreaty ... **8.** exorable
moved easily ... **5.** loped **6.** mobile
   8. affected **9.** emotional
movement ... **5.** cause, trend **6.** action,
   motion, rhythm, travel **7.** emotion,
   gesture, impulse **8.** activity, maneuver,
   progress
movement (pert to) ...
   backwards.. **13.** retrogression
   dance step.. **4.** lilt **6.** chassé **9.** pirouette
   music.. **4.** moto **7.** con moto
   of ships.. **5.** heave, pitch, scend
   of waves.. **4.** roll, toss **5.** surge
   6. tumble, welter
   vibratory.. **6.** tremor
moving ... **6.** active, motile **7.** nomadic
   8. eloquent, exciting, pathetic
   9. affecting, impelling, traveling
   10. motivating
moving stairway ... **9.** escalator
mow ... **3.** cut, lay, mew **4.** dess, fell,
   heap, mass, math, mock, raze, stow
   5. mouth, stack **6.** garner, smooth
   7. cut down, grimace, harvest, shorten
   9. cornfield
mowana ... **6.** baobab
mowing ... **7.** cutting, mockery **8.** derision
   9. grimacing **10.** harvesting,
   meadowland
mowing machine ... **5.** mower **6.** scythe,
   sickle
moxieberry ... **9.** snowberry
moy ... **4.** mild **6.** demure, gentle
   8. affected
moyen ... **3.** way **5.** means **6.** agency,
   course **8.** property **9.** influence
Mozambique ...
   Bay.. **8.** Mossuril
   capital.. **15.** Lourenco Marques
   native.. **3.** Yao
   port.. **10.** Mozambique
mozo ... **10.** manservant
Mrs ... **5.** madam **8.** goodwife, Mistress
mucaro ... **3.** owl
much ... **3.** lot **4.** high, many **5.** great
   7. greatly **8.** abundant, uncommon
   9. great deal **10.** indefinite
   12. considerable
muchacha ... **4.** girl, lass
muchacho ... **3.** boy, lad **7.** servant
mucid ... **5.** musty, slimy **6.** clammy,
   mucous **8.** muculent
mucilage ... **3.** gum **5.** paste **6.** mucago
   8. adhesive **9.** lubricant
mucilaginous ... **5.** moist **6.** sticky, viscid
muckender ... **12.** handkerchief
mucker ... **4.** fall (from a horse),
   mess **6.** muddle, wretch **8.** disorder
   9. confusion, vulgarian
muckle ... **4.** club, fret **6.** bother, putter
muckraker ... **7.** defamer **8.** vilifier
   9. slanderer
mud ... **4.** mire, muck, silt, slop **5.** abuse,
   gumbo, limus, shine **6.** gobbet, sludge
   12. offscourings **14.** abusive charges
mud (pert to) ...
   bath.. **10.** illutation

dab . . **8.** flounder
dauber . . **4.** wasp
devil . . **10.** hellbender
eel . . **5.** siren
hole . . **6.** puddle **8.** quagmire
lark . . **5.** gamin, horse **6.** magpie, urchin
like . . **7.** luteous
living in . . **10.** limicolous
peep . . **9.** sandpiper **11.** meadow pipit
pike . . **5.** saury
puppy . . **10.** hellbender, salamander
rake . . **5.** claut
shoveler . . **13.** spoonbill duck
snipe . . **8.** woodcock
sunfish . . **4.** bass **8.** warmouth
teal . . **9.** greenwing
volcano . . **5.** salse
Mudcat State . . . **11.** Mississippi
muddle . . . **3.** mix **4.** daze, mess, soss,
    stir **5.** addle, botch, snafu **6.** bemuse,
    bollix, jumble **7.** confuse, perplex,
    stupefy **8.** befuddle, bewilder, confound,
    disorder, squander **10.** intoxicate
    11. predicament
muddled . . . **3.** ree **5.** drunk, muzzy,
    tipsy **7.** burbled, fuddled **8.** confused
    9. befuddled, entangled
muddlehead . . . **4.** dolt **9.** blockhead
muddy . . . **4.** base, miry **5.** dingy, dirty,
    roily, slaky **6.** lutose, opaque, slushy,
    turbid **7.** clouded, obscure **8.** confused
    9. besmeared
muddy places . . . **7.** wallows
muezzin . . . **4.** azan (adan) **5.** crier
    (Muslim)
muff . . . **5.** beard, cover **6.** bungle
    7. bungler, failure **8.** feathers
    11. mollycoddle, whitethroat
muffed . . . **5.** vexed **7.** crested **9.** irritated
muffet . . . **11.** whitethroat
muffetee . . . **7.** muffler **8.** wristlet
muffin . . . **3.** cob, gem **5.** bread, hazel,
    plate, scone **7.** biscuit, crumpet, English,
    popover
muffle . . . **3.** gag **4.** damp, dull, mute,
    wrap **6.** deaden, mumble, shroud,
    stifle **7.** conceal **8.** decorate, envelope
    9. blindfold, soft-pedal
muffler . . . **3.** gag **4.** mute **5.** scarf
    6. muzzle, tippet **8.** silencer
    10. suppressor
mufflin . . . **8.** titmouse
mufti . . . **5.** dress (civilian)
mufti (Muslim) . . . **4.** alim **5.** judge
    6. priest **8.** assessor, official
mug . . . **3.** cup **4.** cram, dupe, face, fool,
    Toby **5.** mungo, pulse, sheep, study
    6. noggin **7.** drizzle, grimace **8.** quantity
    10. photograph
muga . . . **4.** moth, silk **11.** caterpillar
mugger . . . **3.** goa **6.** robber, tinker
    7. peddler **9.** crocodile
mugget . . . **8.** woodruff **15.** lily of the
    valley
muggins (game) . . . **5.** cards **7.** penalty
    8. dominoes
muggy . . . **4.** damp, warm **5.** humid,
    moist, moldy **6.** sticky, stuffy, sultry
    10. sweltering **11.** whitethroat
mug house . . . **6.** tavern **7.** barroom
    8. alehouse, pothouse

mugient . . . **6.** lowing **9.** bellowing
mugwump . . . **5.** chief **8.** apostate,
    objector **11.** independent, nonpartisan
    16. Republican bolter
Muhammed . . . see *Mohammed*
muir . . . **4.** wall
muirfowl . . . **9.** red grouse
muishond . . . **5.** zoril **6.** weasel
mujer . . . **4.** wife **5.** woman
mulberry . . . **2.** al **5.** Morus **6.** murrey
    10. blackberry **12.** thimbleberry
mulberry (pert to) . . .
    bark (paper) . . **4.** tapa (tappa)
    beverage . . **5.** morat
    bird . . **8.** starling
    dye . . **3.** aal **8.** morindin
    fig . . **8.** sycamore
    purple . . **7.** blue-red **8.** camerier
    tree . . **5.** Morus
    wild . . **7.** yawweed
mulch . . . **5.** straw **6.** ground, leaves
    7. sawdust
mulct . . . **4.** fine, scot **6.** amerce, defect,
    punish **7.** blemish, deceive, penalty,
    swindle **10.** amercement
mulcter . . . **7.** amercer
mule . . . **4.** mewl, mool, mute **5.** coble,
    hinny, jenny **6.** acemia, hybrid
    7. slipper, tractor **9.** chilblain
    10. crossbreed, locomotive **15.** obstinate
    person
mule (pert to) . . .
    chair . . **7.** cacolet
    driver . . **7.** skinner **8.** muleteer
    drove . . **5.** atajo
    killer . . **6.** mantis
    leading . . **8.** cencerro
    skinner . . **6.** driver
    untrained . . **9.** shavetail
muleteer . . . **4.** peon **6.** driver
mulga . . . **6.** acacia, shield
muliebria . . . **8.** feminine
muliebriety . . . **9.** womanhood
    10. femininity **11.** womanliness
mulier . . . **4.** wife **5.** woman **6.** mother
mulish . . . **6.** hybrid, sullen **7.** asinine,
    sterile **8.** stubborn **9.** obstinate
mull . . . **3.** cow **4.** crag, dust, heat,
    mess, mold **5.** crush, grind, snout,
    spice **6.** fumble, muddle, muslin,
    muzzle, ponder **7.** failure, rubbish,
    squeeze, steatin, sweeten **8.** cogitate,
    consider, ointment, ruminate, snuffbox
    9. pulverize **10.** promontory
    11. contemplate
mullah . . . **6.** priest **7.** teacher (Muslim)
mullet . . . **4.** bobo, fish, star **6.** puffin
mullet hawk . . . **6.** osprey
mulligan . . . **4.** stew
mulligatawny . . . **4.** soup
mulligrubs . . . **5.** blues, colic, sulks
mullock . . . **5.** spoil, waste **6.** refuse
    (mine) **7.** rubbish
mulloway . . . **7.** jewfish
multi (comb form) . . . **4.** many
multifarious . . . **8.** manifold **9.** multifold,
    multiplex **10.** multiphase
multifold . . . **7.** diverse **8.** manifold,
    multiple, numerous
multilingual . . . **8.** polyglot
multiped . . . **10.** many-footed

multiplier ... **6.** bulbil **7.** facient
  8. operator
multiply ... **5.** breed **6.** spread **7.** amplify,
  magnify **8.** increase **9.** calculate,
  pluralize, procreate
multitude ... **3.** mob **4.** host, many,
  mass, much **5.** crowd, horde, shoal,
  swarm **6.** legion, throng **7.** myriads
  8. populace **9.** profusion **11.** bourgeoisie
  12. numerousness
multitudinous ... **6.** myriad
mum ... **3.** ale **4.** mute **6.** silent **8.** taciturn
  11. not speaking
mumble ... **4.** chew, mump **6.** chavel,
  fumble, mutter, patter
mumbo jumbo ... **6.** genius **7.** bugaboo
  12. superstition **13.** awesome person
mummer ... **5.** actor **6.** guiser **7.** buffoon
  9. performer
mummy ... **5.** brown, Congo (color), relic
  6. corpse, mother **7.** cadaver, carcass
mummy apple ... **6.** papaya
mump ... **3.** beg **5.** cheat, sulks
  6. mumble, sponge **7.** deceive, grimace
  10. impose upon
mumpish ... **4.** dull, glum **5.** sulky
  6. sullen
mumruffin ... **8.** titmouse
mundane ... **6.** cosmic **7.** earthly, horizon,
  secular, terrene, worldly **8.** temporal
  11. unspiritual
mundatory ... **9.** cleansing **11.** purificator
mundil ... **6.** turban (embroidered)
mungo ... **4.** herb, wool (reclaimed)
  8. mongoose, mung bean
  13. mongoose plant
municipal ... **5.** civic, urban **7.** oppidan
  9. political **10.** municipium
munificence ... **6.** bounty **7.** largess
  (largesse) **10.** generosity, liberality
  13. bounteousness, unselfishness
muniment ... **6.** record **7.** defense
  8. evidence, writings **9.** valuables
  10. furnishing **13.** fortification
munity ... see *immunity* **9.** privilege
munshi (Hind) ... **6.** writer **7.** teacher
  9. secretary **11.** interpreter
muntjac, muntjak ... **5.** kakar, ratwa
  6. kidang
mura (Jap) ... **7.** village **9.** community
Mura ... **6.** Indian
mural ... **4.** wall (pert to) **5.** crown
  8. painting
murder ... **4.** kill, slay **7.** carnage
  8. homicide **9.** slaughter **11.** assassinate
  12. manslaughter
murder of ...
  brother .. **10.** fratricide
  father .. **9.** patricide
  king .. **8.** regicide
  mother .. **9.** matricide
  own child .. **9.** prolicide
  parent .. **9.** parricide
  prophet .. **8.** vaticide
  sister .. **10.** sororicide
  spouse (by the other) .. **10.** mariticide
  wife .. **9.** uxoricide
  woman .. **8.** femicide
murderous ... **4.** gory **5.** cruel **6.** bloody,
  deadly, savage **7.** killing **10.** sanguinary
  12. bloodthirsty

mure ... **4.** meek, soft, wall **6.** gentle,
  immure, modest **8.** imprison
murk, mirk ... **3.** fog **4.** dark, mist
  5. gloom **6.** opaque **7.** blacken
  8. darkness **9.** dark color **11.** dark-
  colored
murky, mirky ... **4.** dark **5.** dense,
  foggy, thick **6.** gloomy, opaque
  7. obscure, stained **11.** dark-colored
  12. impenetrable
murmur ... **3.** coo, hum **4.** blow, curr,
  fret, purl **6.** babble, mutter, repine
  7. trickle, whisper **8.** complain
muscle ... **4.** beef, thew **5.** brawn, sinew,
  teres **6.** flexor, lacert, tensor **8.** lacertus,
  retentor
muscle (pert to) ...
  affection .. **5.** crick **6.** ataxia
  bending .. **6.** flexor
  chemistry .. **6.** inosic **8.** inosinic
  chest .. **8.** pectoral
  column .. **10.** sarcostyle
  contracting .. **7.** agonist
  expander .. **7.** dilator
  extending .. **8.** extensor
  eyeball .. **6.** rectus
  lifting .. **7.** levator
  loin, tenderloin .. **5.** psoas
  lower .. **9.** depressor
  raising .. **7.** deltoid, erector, levator
  recording .. **8.** ergogram **9.** ergograph
  round .. **5.** teres
  segment .. **8.** myocomma
  sense .. **11.** kinesthesia
  separating .. **11.** divaricator
  spasm .. **5.** cramp, tonus **12.** charley
  horse
  stretching .. **6.** tensor
  sugar .. **8.** inositol
  thigh .. **10.** quadriceps
  trapezius .. **10.** cucullaris
  triangular .. **7.** deltoid
  turning .. **7.** evertor, rotator
  two-headed .. **6.** biceps
muscovite ... **4.** mica **11.** yellow-green
Muscovite ... **7.** Russian
muscular ... **4.** wiry **5.** beefy, thewy
  6. brawny, mighty, sinewy, strong,
  torose **8.** athletic, stalwart, vigorous
muscular (pert to) ...
  contraction (involuntary) .. **3.** tic **5.** spasm
  co-ordination .. **7.** synergy
  in-co-ordination .. **6.** ataxia **15.** locomotor
  ataxia
  non-co-ordination in walking .. **6.** abasia
  spasm .. **5.** tonus
  stomach .. **7.** gizzard
muse ... **4.** mull, poet, rune **5.** dream
  6. ponder **7.** bagpipe, reverie **8.** cogitate,
  consider, meditate, ruminate
Muse of ...
  astronomy .. **6.** Urania
  choral song .. **11.** Terpsichore
  comedy .. **6.** Thalia
  dancing .. **11.** Terpsichore
  eloquence .. **8.** Calliope
  history .. **4.** Clio
  joy .. **4.** Tara
  music .. **7.** Euterpe
  poetry .. **5.** Erato (lyric) **6.** Thalia (bucolic)
  8. Calliope (heroic)

tragedy . . **9.** Melpomene
Muses . . . **4.** Clio **5.** Erato **6.** Thalia,
   Urania **7.** Euterpe **8.** Calliope, Polymnia
   (Polyhymnia) **9.** Melpomene
   11. Terpsichore
Muses (pert to) . . .
   epithet . . **7.** Pierian
   fountain . . **8.** Aganippe (near Thebes)
   mother of . . **9.** Mnemosyne
   mountain . . **6.** Pierus **7.** Helicon
      9. Parnassus
   number . . **4.** nine
   sacred place . . **5.** Aonia (Boeotia)
   spring . . **7.** Pierian
   The Muses (Gr) . . **8.** Pierides
musette . . . **3.** air, bag **4.** oboe **7.** bagpipe,
   gavotte
museum, famed . . .
   Florence . . **6.** Uffizi
   London . . **4.** Tate **14.** Madame Tussaud's
   Madrid . . **5.** Prado
   New York . . **4.** MOMA **10.** Guggenheim
      12. Metropolitan
   Oxford . . **9.** Ashmolean
   Paris . . **6.** Louvre
   St Petersburg (Russia) . . **9.** Hermitage
   Washington, DC . . **9.** Hirshhorn
      11. Smithsonian
museum keeper . . . **7.** curator
   9. custodian
mush . . . **3.** cut **4.** call, face, pulp **5.** atole,
   march (over snow), notch **6.** cereal,
   indent, sepawn **8.** flattery, umbrella
   12. hasty pudding **14.** sentimentality
mushroom . . . **5.** morel, plant **6.** agaric,
   anchor, fungus **7.** parvenu, upstart
   8. umbrella **11.** beaver brown
mushroom (pert to) . . .
   circle . . **9.** fairy ring
   disease . . **5.** flock
   edible . . **5.** morel **11.** chanterelle
   poisoning . . **8.** mycetism
   poisonous . . **7.** amanita **9.** toadstool
   stem . . **5.** stipe
   umbrella top . . **6.** pileus
music (pert to) . . .
   abridgment . . **7.** ridotto
   accompaniment . . **9.** obbligato
   aftersong . . **5.** epode
   all voices . . **5.** tutti
   as written . . **3.** sta
   chapel . . **9.** a cappella
   character . . **3.** bar, key **4.** clef, rest, slur
      5. cleft, neume, segno
   chord . . **8.** arpeggio
   clear-cut . . **8.** staccato
   closing measure . . **4.** coda
   comic . . **6.** bouffe
   do . . **2.** ut
   drama . . **5.** opera
   duet . . **3.** duo
   encore . . **3.** bis
   flourish . . **7.** cadenza
   half note . . **5.** minim
   half tone . . **8.** semitone
   impassioned, emotional . .
      12. appassionato
   interlude . . **6.** verset
   interval . . **6.** octave **7.** tritone
   introduction . . **7.** prelude
   it proceeds . . **2.** va

knowledge . . **10.** musicology
lead cue . . **5.** presa
left-handed . . **8.** sinistra
light notes . . **6.** ottava
low pitch . . **5.** grave
lutelike . . **10.** hurdy-gurdy
major . . **3.** dur
major third . . **6.** ditone
melodious . . **6.** arioso
melody . . **5.** melos
nine-piece composition . . **5.** nonet
one performer (choral) . . **4.** soli
opera (comic) . . **6.** bouffe
organization . . **4.** band **5.** Ascap, choir
   6. chorus **8.** symphony **9.** orchestra
organ stop . . **6.** dulcet, tromba **7.** celesta
pause . . **4.** rest
performance . . **7.** recital
phrase . . **9.** leitmotiv (leitmotif)
pick . . **8.** plectrum
pitch C . . **2.** du
pompous . . **7.** orotund
refrain . . **5.** epode **8.** repetend
repetition . . **5.** rondo
scale . . **5.** gamut
sestet . . **7.** sestuor
sextuplet . . **7.** sestole (sestolet)
soprano part . . **5.** canto
speaking part . . **8.** parlando
study . . **5.** étude
tenor part . . **5.** canto (original)
theme . . **4.** tema
third . . **6.** tierce
three-chord note . . **5.** triad
thrice . . **3.** ter
time . . **4.** temp **6.** giusto
timing device . . **9.** metronome
twice . . **3.** bis
variations, set of . . **7.** partita
whimsical . . **8.** bizzarro **9.** capriccio
musical direction (pert to) . . .
   accented . . **8.** sforzato **9.** sforzando
   bold . . **6.** audace
   brisk . . **5.** tanto **7.** animato
   detached . . **8.** spiccato, staccato
   dying away . . **7.** calendo
   emphatic . . **7.** marcato
   evenly . . **10.** egualmente
   fantastic . . **11.** carpiccioso
   fast . . **4.** vivo **5.** tosto **6.** presto, vivace
      10. tostamente
   faster . . **7.** stretto
   fluctuating . . **6.** rubato
   gay . . **7.** giocoso **10.** brilliante
   gentle . . **5.** dolce
   half . . **5.** mezzo
   held firmly . . **6.** tenuto
   high . . **3.** alt
   hurried . . **7.** agitato
   less . . **4.** meno
   let it stand . . **3.** sta
   lightly . . **10.** con agilita
   little by little . . **9.** poco a poco
   lively . . **6.** vivace **7.** allegro, animato
   loud . . **5.** forte **10.** fortissimo
   louder . . **9.** crescendo
   lutelike . . **10.** hurdy-gurdy
   more rapid . . **7.** stretto (stretta)
   movement (with) . . **7.** con moto
   muted . . **5.** sorda, sordo
   narrating . . **8.** narrante

one by one . . **7.** uno a uno
quick . . **6.** presto
quickening . . **11.** affrettando
quicker than . . **7.** andante **9.** andantino
repeat . . **3.** bis **6.** da capo **7.** ripresa
sadly . . **7.** dolente **8.** doloroso
shake . . **5.** trill
silent . . **5.** tacet
sliding . . **9.** glissando
slow . . **5.** largo, lento, molto, tardo
  6. adagio **7.** andante
slow (very) . . **5.** molto
slowing . . **9.** allentato **10.** ritardando
  11. rallentando
smooth . . **6.** legato
soft . . **5.** dolce, piano
softer . . **10.** diminuendo
spirited . . **7.** con moto
strict tempo . . **6.** giusto
sustained . . **6.** tenuto **9.** sustenuto
tenderly . . **10.** affettuoso, con affetto
turn . . **5.** verte **9.** gruppetto
vivacious . . **7.** con brio
musical form . . . **3.** jig, ode, pop, rap
  4. aria, folk, jazz, jive, olio, opus, punk
  (rock), scat, song, soul **5.** derry, dirge,
  disco, elegy, fugue, melos, motet,
  opera, salsa **6.** arioso, ballad, fusion,
  hip-hop, medley, melody, minuet,
  New Age, reggae, sonata **7.** ragtime,
  toccata **8.** carillon (bells), hornpipe,
  operetta, oratorio, serenade, symphony
  9. barcarole, bluegrass, interlude,
  polonaise **10.** heavy metal, rockabilly
  11. rock and roll **12.** boogie woogie
musical instruments . . . **3.** sax **4.** asor,
  drum, fife, harp, horn, lute, lyre,
  oboe, pipe, reed, tuba, viol **5.** banjo,
  bugle, cello, Dobro, flute, organ, piano,
  rebec (rebeck), rocta, tabor, vibes,
  viola **6.** atabal, cither, citole, cornet,
  fiddle, guitar, spinet, tabret, violin,
  zither **7.** althorn, bagpipe, bandore,
  bassoon, celesta, clarion, clavier,
  gittern, helicon, marimba, musette,
  ocarina, pandora, piccolo, theorbo,
  timpani (tympani), trumpet, ukulele
  8. castanet, clarinet, dulcimer, keyboard,
  mandolin, trombone **9.** flageolet,
  saxophone **10.** concertina, pianoforte,
  sousaphone (tuba), tambourine
  11. harpsichord, synthesizer, violoncello
musical instruments (foreign) . . .
  Africa . . **5.** nanga **7.** kalimba (thumb
    piano), sistrum
  China . . **3.** kin
  E Indies . . **4.** bina
  Egypt . . **7.** sistrum
  Greece . . **7.** cithara (anc)
  Hindu . . **4.** vina (anc)
  India . . **5.** ruana
  Italy . . **6.** tromba
  Japan . . **7.** samisen (shamisen)
    10. shakuhachi
  Java . . **8.** gamelang (gamelan)
  Mexico . . **6.** clarin **7.** maracas
  Spain . . **6.** atabal **9.** castanets
musician . . . **4.** bard **5.** piper **6.** hepcat,
  lyrist, singer **7.** chorist, crooner,
  drummer, fiddler, flutist, harpist,
  pianist, reedman, yodeler **8.** bandsman,

composer, minstrel, organist
  9. conductor, serenader, troubador,
  violinist **10.** prima donna, trombonist
  11. clarinetist, keyboardist, minnesinger,
  saxophonist **12.** interlocutor
  13. Kapellmeister, percussionist
musicians' group . . . **4.** band, duet, trio
  5. nonet **6.** septet, sextet **7.** nonetto,
  quartet **8.** ensemble, septette, sextette,
  symphony **9.** orchestra, quartette
musicians' patron saint . . . **7.** Cecilia
musk . . . **4.** deer **7.** perfume
musk (pert to) . . .
  beaver . . **7.** muskrat
  cat . . **5.** civet
  cattle . . **4.** oxen
  cucumber . . **11.** cassabanana
  deer . . **10.** chevrotain
  duck . . **7.** Muscovy
  hog . . **7.** peccary
  melon . . **10.** cantaloupe
  okra . . **8.** abelmosk
  shrew . . **6.** desman
  weasel . . **5.** civet
muskellunge . . . **4.** fish, pike
musket . . . **4.** hawk **5.** rifle **7.** firearm
  9. flintlock
Musketeers, Three . . . **5.** Athos **6.** Aramis
  7. Porthos **9.** D'Artagnon
muskmelon . . . **6.** atimon, casaba
  10. cantaloupe
muskrat . . . **5.** shrew **6.** desman **7.** ondatra
Muslim . . . **5.** Hanif, Islam, Salar
  7. Saracen **9.** Mussulman
  10. Mohammedan
Muslim (pert to) . . .
  ablution . . **4.** wudu (widu, wuzu)
  cap . . **3.** fez, taj
  capturer of Jerusalem . . **4.** Omar
  caste . . **5.** mopla (moplah)
  chief . . **4.** dato (datto), rais
  city (holy) . . **5.** Mecca
  college, school . . **8.** madrasah (madrasa,
    madrasseh)
  dagger . . **7.** khanjar
  deity . . **5.** Allah, Eblis
  devil . . **5.** Eblis
  devotee . . **6.** santon **7.** dervish
  Easter . . **3.** Eed
  guide (spiritual) . . **3.** pir
  interpreter . . **4.** ulema
  invocation . . **9.** bismillah
  javelin . . **6.** jereed
  judge . . **4.** cadi
  lawyer . . **5.** mufti
  market, booth . . **4.** sook
  monastery . . **5.** ribat **7.** khankah
  mosque . . **6.** masjid
  noble . . **4.** amir (ameer), emir
  officer . . **5.** dewan (diwan)
  people . . **4.** Moro
  pilgrimage to Mecca . . **4.** hadj
  prayer . . **4.** azan (adan)
  priest . . **4.** imam (imaum)
  saint . . **3.** pir **6.** santon **8.** Marabout
  sect . . **6.** Senusi (Senousi, Senussite)
  shrine, Mecca . . **5.** Kaaba (Caaba,
    Kaabeh)
  teacher . . **4.** Alim **8.** mujtahid
  title . . **3.** Sid **5.** Sayid (Said)
  tradition . . **7.** Al Sirat (Bridge to Paradise)

Turkish . . **5.** Salar
university . . **8.** madrasah (madrasa)
viceroy . . **7.** Saracen
muslin . . . **3.** ban, cap **4.** mull **5.** doria,
   shela **6.** canvas, gurrah **7.** organdy
   8. nainsook, sheeting, tarlatan
muss . . . **4.** mess, soil **5.** chaos, dirty
   6. bitter, muddle, rumple, tousle
   7. confuse, wrinkle **8.** dishevel,
   scramble, squabble **10.** disarrange
mussel . . . **4.** food, naid, unio **5.** horse,
   moule, naiad **6.** byssus, mucket, nerita
   7. mollusk, Mytilus
Musselman . . . **6.** Moslem **7.** Saracen
   10. Mohammedan
must . . . **4.** mold, musk, sapa, stum
   5. juice, ought, shall **6.** blight,
   mildew, refuse **7.** malodor **9.** necessity
   10. obligation
mustang . . . **5.** horse, pinto **6.** bronco,
   sphinx
mustard . . . **5.** nigra, senvy **7.** sinapis
   8. charlock
mustard (pert to) . . .
   chemistry . . **8.** sinapine
   gas . . **7.** yperite
   genus . . **7.** Sinapis **8.** Brassica
   plaster . . **8.** sinapism
Mustelidae . . . **5.** minks **7.** badgers,
   martens, weasels
muster . . . **4.** levy **5.** erect **6.** gather,
   summon **7.** collect, marshal
   8. assemble, comprise **10.** assemblage
muster out . . . **7.** disband
musty . . . **3.** bad, old **4.** damp, hoar,
   rank **5.** fetid, fusty, moist, moldy, rafty,
   stale, trite **6.** rancid **7.** pungent
mutable . . . **6.** fickle **7.** erratic **8.** variable
   9. alterable, changeful
mute . . . **3.** mum **4.** dumb, lene, surd
   6. muffle, silent **8.** deadener, silencer,
   taciturn **9.** voiceless **10.** speechless
mutilate . . . **3.** mar **4.** geld, hack, maim
   6. deface, deform, garble, injure,
   mangle **7.** cripple, destroy **8.** castrate
   9. dismember, tear apart
mutinous . . . **6.** unruly **9.** seditious,
   turbulent **10.** rebellious, refractory
   11. intractable
mutiny . . . **6.** Putsch (Swiss), revolt,
   strife, tumult **9.** commotion, rebellion
   12. insurrection **15.** insubordination
mutter . . . **5.** growl **6.** murmur, patter,
   plaint **7.** grumble, maunder **8.** complain
   9. mussitate
mutton . . . **4.** meat **5.** cabob (kabob),
   gigot, sheep **6.** candle
muttonfish . . . **4.** sama **5.** pargo
   7. abalone, eelpout, mojarra, snapper
mutual . . . **4.** plan **5.** joint **6.** common
   8. intimate **9.** symbiotic **10.** reciprocal,
   responsive **15.** interchangeable
mutual understanding . . . **9.** agreement,
   unanimity **12.** consentience, coordination **13.** interrelation
   17. interrelationship
mux . . . **4.** mess **5.** batch
muy . . . **4.** very **7.** greatly
muzhik, muzjik . . . **7.** peasant
muzzle . . . **3.** gag **4.** cope, maul, nose
   5. mouth, snout **6.** clevis, thrash

7. shackle, sheathe, silence **8.** restrain
   10. respirator
my . . . **3.** mes, mon **4.** mine **7.** due to
   me **11.** exclamation
myall . . . **4.** wild, wood (fragrant) **6.** acacia
   11. uncivilized
Myanmar . . . see *Burma, Burmese*
mycoderma . . . **5.** fungi **6.** mother (formed
   on wine) **8.** membrane (ferment)
mycophagy . . . **11.** eating fungi **15.** eating
   mushrooms
myna, mynah . . . **4.** bird **7.** grackle
   8. starling
Mynheer . . . **8.** Dutchman
myo (comb form) . . . **6.** muscle
myomancy, divination by . . . **14.** muscle
   movement
myopic . . . **11.** nearsighted
myriad . . . **11.** innumerable, ten thousand
   13. multitudinous
myriapod . . . **9.** centipede
myrmicid . . . **3.** ant
myrtle . . . **8.** ramarama **10.** periwinkle
   11. candleberry
mysterious . . . **4.** dark **6.** arcane,
   mystic, occult, secret **7.** cryptic
   8. abstruse, esoteric **9.** recondite,
   sphinxian **10.** cabalistic **12.** inexplicable,
   unfathomable
mystery . . . **4.** cult, rune **6.** arcane, cabala,
   enigma, puzzle, secret **7.** arcanum,
   esotery, miracle **8.** whodunit
   9. sacrament **13.** inexplainable
   19. incomprehensibility
mystery writer's award . . . **5.** Edgar
mystic . . . **4.** seer, yogi **5.** magic, runic
   6. occult, orphic, secret **7.** cryptic,
   Mahatma **8.** cabalist, esoteric, symbolic
   9. enigmatic, recondite **10.** cabalistic,
   mysterious
mystic (pert to) . . .
   cry . . **4.** evoe
   doctrine . . **5.** cabal **7.** esotery **8.** esoteric
   initiate . . **5.** epopt (Gr Antiq)
   ocean isle . . **6.** Avalon
   theosophy . . **6.** cabala
   word . . **2.** om **7.** abraxas **11.** abracadabra
mystical . . . **6.** muddle, puzzle **7.** confuse,
   cryptic, furtive, obscure **9.** enigmatic,
   obfuscate
mystical (pert to) . . .
   character (Teut Myth) . . **8.** Eckehart
   meaning . . **7.** anagoge
   word . . **11.** abracadabra
mystify . . . **5.** befog **6.** muddle, puzzle
   7. becloud, confuse, perplex
   8. befuddle, bewilder **9.** bamboozle,
   obfuscate
myth . . . **4.** tale **5.** fable, fancy, story
   6. legend **7.** figment, parable
   9. apocrypha, falsehood
mythical . . . **7.** fancied **8.** fabulous
   9. fictional, imaginary, legendary
   10. fictitious **12.** mythological
mythical (pert to) . . .
   being . . **6.** Garuda, Icarus **7.** centaur,
   griffin
   bird . . **3.** roc
   deity . . **6.** Moloch (tyrant)
   demon . . **4.** Rahu (tail called Kehu)
   hero . . **4.** Ajax **8.** Achilles

heroine . . **4.** Leda **6.** Europa
8. Atalanta
hunter . . **5.** Orion
island . . **8.** Atlantis
king (Hind) . . **4.** Nala
monster . . **4.** ogre **7.** chimera
mother . . **5.** Niobe

river . . **4.** Styx
serpent . . **5.** Apepi
winged creature . . **7.** Alborak
woman . . **6.** Gorgon, Medusa, Stheno
7. Euryale
mythogony, science of . . . **5.** myths
mythologist . . . **9.** mythmaker

N

N . . . **2.** en, Nu **8.** nitrogen (symbol)
nab . . . **4.** grab **5.** catch, seize **6.** arrest,
nibble, snatch **7.** capture **9.** apprehend
Nabal's wife (Bib) . . . **7.** Abigail
nabob . . . **5.** nawab **6.** bigwig, tycoon
7. viceroy **8.** governor **9.** plutocrat
10. viceregent
Nabokov nymphet . . . **6.** Lolita
nacelle . . . **4.** boat **7.** shelter
nacket . . . **3.** boy **4.** cake **5.** lunch **6.** caddie
8. saucy boy
nacre . . . **9.** shellfish **10.** conchiolin
13. mother-of-pearl
Nadab (Bib) . . . **12.** King of Israel
nadir . . . **4.** pole **11.** lowest point (opp
zenith)
nag . . . **4.** pony, twit **5.** annoy, cobra,
horse, scold, snake, tease **6.** heckle,
hector, peck on, pester, plague
7. henpeck **8.** harangue
nagor . . . **8.** antelope, reedbuck
nahoor . . . **5.** sheep **6.** bharal
naiad . . . **5.** nymph **6.** mussel, Nereid
7. limniad, Oceanid
nail . . . **3.** cut, hob **4.** brad, claw,
spad, stud, tack, wire **5.** clout, spike,
sprig, talon **6.** fasten, secure, unguis,
ungula **7.** capture, measure **8.** sparable
9. finishing, intercept **12.** upholstering
nail (pert to) . . .
headless . . **5.** sprig
ingrowing . . **7.** acronyx
marking, fingernail . . **6.** lunule
size . . **8.** tenpenny
slanted . . **4.** toed
naissance . . . **5.** birth **6.** origin
naive . . . **5.** frank **6.** simple **7.** artless,
ingenue **8.** childish, gullible, untaught
9. guileless, ingenuous, unworldly
10. simplicity **13.** unphilosophic
15. unsophisticated
naked . . . **4.** bald, bare, mere, nude,
open **5.** clear, plain **6.** barren,
meager **7.** exposed, literal, obvious
8. manifest, stripped **9.** unadorned,
uncovered **11.** defenseless, unprotected,
unsupported
nakoo . . . **6.** gavial **9.** crocodile
namaycush . . . **5.** togue, trout
namby-pamby . . . **5.** inane, silly, vapid
7. insipid **10.** wishy-washy
11. sentimental
name . . . **3.** dub, nom **4.** call, cite, term
5. clepe, nomen, style, title **6.** y-
clepe **7.** appoint, entitle, mention

8. cognomen, identify **9.** celebrity,
enumerate, personage **10.** denominate,
reputation **11.** appellation, designation
12. denomination
name (pert to) . . .
added . . **7.** agnomen
assumed . . **3.** pen **5.** alias **7.** John Doe
9. incognito, pseudonym, sobriquet
10. nom de plume
bad . . **7.** caconym
binomial . . **8.** teutonym
by location . . **7.** toponym
derivation . . **7.** eponymy
family (father's) . . **7.** eponymy
9. patronymy
fictitious . . **9.** pseudonym
first . . **9.** baptismal, Christian, praenomen
Japanese . . **4.** maru
known . . **9.** onomatous
nickname . . **7.** moniker (monicker)
8. cognomen
nominate . . **9.** designate
secret . . **9.** cryptonym
spelled backwards (real name) . .
6. ananym
surname . . **7.** eponymy
technical . . **4.** onym
unknown . . **9.** anonymous
wrong . . **8.** misnomer
name as agent . . . **6.** depute
named . . . **5.** cited **6.** called, y-clept
(y-cleped)
named for a god . . . **11.** theophorous
nameless . . . **7.** bastard, obscure **8.** not
known **9.** aforesaid, anonymous,
unnamable **10.** unrenowned
12. illegitimate **13.** indescribable,
inexpressible **15.** undistinguished
namelessness . . . **9.** anonymity
namely . . . **5.** to wit **9.** expressly,
nominally, videlicet (viz)
names, divination by . . . **8.** onomancy
names, science of . . . **11.** onomatology
namesake . . . **6.** eponym **7.** homonym
nanga . . . **4.** harp
nanism . . . **12.** dwarfishness (opp of
gigantism)
Nanking . . .
capital . . **5.** China (1932--1937)
color . . **12.** Naples yellow
province . . **7.** Kiangsu
river site . . **7.** Yangtze
nanoid . . . **8.** dwarfish
nanpie . . . **6.** magpie
naos . . . **5.** cella **6.** shrine, temple

Naos . . . **4.** star
nap . . . **3.** nod **4.** doze, pile, shag, wink
   5. fluff, grasp, seize, sleep, steal
   6. duffel, siesta, snooze
nape . . . **5.** nucha, nuque, scrag **6.** scruff,
   turnip **7.** niddick **9.** auchenium
napellus . . . **9.** monkshood
napery . . . **5.** linen (table)
napiform . . . **12.** turnip-shaped
napkin . . . **5.** doily, towel **6.** diaper
   8. kerchief **9.** serviette **11.** neckerchief
Naples . . .
   biscuit . . **10.** ladyfinger
   famed building . . **9.** Cathedral (Gothic,
   1272)
   red . . **5.** ochre **6.** Indian
   site . . **11.** Bay of Naples
napoleon . . . **4.** game **6.** pastry **7.** top
   boot **11.** reddish-blue, sweet cherry
   13. crimson clover
Napoleon I (pert to) . . .
   birthplace . . **7.** Ajaccio (Corsica)
   brother-in-law . . **5.** Murat
   death site . . **8.** St Helena
   exiled to . . **4.** Elba
   father . . **7.** Charles
   island . . **5.** Capri
   marshal . . **3.** Ney (executed)
   title . . **7.** Emperor (of France)
   warfare site . . **5.** Ligny, Malta **7.** Marengo
   8. Waterloo **10.** Alexandria, Austerlitz
napped (short) . . . **3.** ras
nappy . . . **3.** ale **4.** dish **5.** downy,
   heady, wooly **6.** liquor, shaggy, sleepy
   7. foaming **10.** inebriated
napu . . . **10.** chevrotain
Naraka (Hind) . . . **4.** hell
Narcissus (Gr) . . . **6.** egoist **14.** beautiful
   youth
narcosis . . . **5.** sleep **10.** drowsiness
narcotic . . . **4.** dope, drug, hemp,
   junk **5.** bhang (bang), ether, opium
   6. heroin **7.** anodyne, cocaine, hashish
   8. hypnotic, mandrake, morphine
   9. soporific **10.** belladonna,
   hyoscyamus, stramonium
narcotic (pert to) . . .
   dose . . **3.** fix **5.** locus
   package . . **6.** bindle
   seller . . **6.** pusher **7.** peddler
   user (group) . . **6.** love-in **9.** snow party
nard . . . **6.** anoint **8.** matgrass, ointment,
   rhizomes
nardoo, nardu . . . **6.** clover
nares . . . **8.** nostrils
narghile, nargile, nargileh . . . **4.** pipe
   6. hookah
nargil . . . **7.** coconut
nark . . . **3.** spy **5.** annoy **8.** informer
   11. stool pigeon
Narragansett . . . **3.** Bay **5.** horse **6.** Indian,
   turkey
narrate . . . **4.** tell **6.** detail, recite, relate
   7. recount **8.** describe
narration . . . **4.** tale **5.** drama (acted), story
   6. detail **7.** account, recital **8.** relation
   9. discourse, narrative, rehearsal
narrative . . . **4.** epic, epos, myth, poem,
   saga, tale **5.** conte, drama, fable,
   story **6.** legend **7.** account, episode,
   history, parable **8.** allegory, anecdote

   9. narration, statement
narrator . . . **9.** raconteur **11.** storyteller
narrow . . . **4.** mean, poor **5.** inlet,
   scant, taper **6.** linear, strait **7.** closely,
   slender **8.** strictly **9.** confining, illiberal,
   niggardly **10.** restricted, straighten
   11. reactionary **12.** parsimonious
   13. circumscribed
narrow (pert to) . . .
   comb form . . **4.** sten **5.** steno
   leather strip . . **5.** thong
   minded . . **5.** petty **6.** biased **7.** bigoted
   10. intolerant, prejudiced
   opening . . **4.** rima, slot **9.** stenopaic
   souled . . **10.** ungenerous
narrowly incised . . . **9.** laciniate
narrows . . . **5.** sound **6.** strait
narthex . . . **7.** portico **9.** asafetida
   (asafoetida)
narwhal, narwal . . . **5.** whale **8.** cetacean
nasab (Muslim Law) . . . **7.** kinship
   13. consanguinity
nasal . . . **4.** nose **5.** sound **6.** narine,
   rhinal, twangy **11.** inspiratory
nascency . . . **5.** birth **6.** origin **7.** genesis
   9. beginning
naseberry . . . **9.** sapodilla
Nasi . . . **6.** prince **8.** Gamaliel **9.** patriarch
Nasicornia . . . **10.** rhinoceros
Naso, famed . . . **4.** Ovid
nasology . . . **9.** nose study
Nassau . . .
   capital . . **7.** Bahamas
   hamlet . . **7.** grouper
   sports . . **4.** golf
nastika . . . **7.** atheist
nasty . . . **4.** foul, mean **5.** dirty **6.** filthy,
   odious **7.** obscene **8.** indecent,
   unsavory **9.** offensive **12.** disagreeable,
   dishonorable
Nasua . . . **5.** coati **6.** coatis
nasute . . . **10.** large-nosed
nasutiform . . . **8.** noselike
natal . . . **6.** inborn, native **7.** gluteal,
   nascent **9.** from birth
Natal . . . **7.** seaport (Braz) **8.** Province
   (So Afr)
natator . . . **7.** swimmer
natatorium . . . **4.** pool **6.** plunge
   12. swimming hole
natchbone . . . **9.** aitchbone
Natchez . . . **4.** city (La) **6.** Indian
nation . . . **4.** host, race **5.** caste, class,
   state **6.** people, polity **7.** country
   9. community, multitude
national . . . **4.** blue **6.** racial **7.** citizen,
   federal
nationality . . . **4.** race **6.** nation **8.** nativity
   9. statehood **11.** nationalism
national salute . . . **13.** Twenty-one guns
native . . . **3.** ite, son **4.** natal **5.** innate,
   normal, simple **7.** genuine, natural,
   primary **8.** inherent, original, primeval
   9. unbranded **10.** aboriginal,
   indigenous, unaffected **11.** not acquired
native (pert to) . . .
   agent . . **9.** comprador (compradore)
   bear . . **5.** koala
   cat . . **7.** dasyure
   dog . . **5.** dingo
   Indian . . **4.** Arab

juniper.. **9.** blueberry
Madagascan.. **4.** Hova
naturalized person.. **7.** denizen
plant, animal.. **8.** indigene
salt.. **6.** halite
nativity ... **5.** birth **9.** beginning, horoscope, sculpture
Nativity, The ... **8.** festival **9.** Christmas **13.** birth of Christ
natterjack ... **4.** toad
natty ... **4.** chic, neat, tidy, trim **6.** spruce **10.** fastidious
Natty Bumppo's alias ... **7.** Hawkeye **10.** Deerslayer, Pathfinder **15.** Leatherstocking
natural ... **3.** raw **4.** born **5.** flesh, usual **6.** common, cretin, expert, inborn, inbred, innate, normal **7.** genuine, regular, typical **8.** informal, inherent, lifelike, ordinary **9.** character (Mus), dice throw, unassumed, unfeigned **10.** unaffected
natural (pert to) ...
capacity.. **9.** endowment
condition.. **4.** norm
group.. **4.** race **6.** ethnic, family
location, position.. **4.** site **5.** situs
not (natural).. **5.** alien **8.** acquired **10.** artificial
philosophy.. **7.** physics
science.. **10.** physiology
voice (Mus).. **7.** dipetto
naturalist ... **4.** Muir (John) **7.** Burbank (Luther)
naturalize ... **5.** adapt **8.** accustom **9.** acclimate **11.** domesticate, familiarize
nature ... **4.** kind, self, sort, soul, type **6.** cosmos **7.** essence **8.** tendency, universe **11.** naturalness, temperament **14.** characteristic
nature (pert to) ...
concealed.. **7.** latency
divinity of.. **5.** dryad, naiad, nymph
god.. **3.** Pan
goddess.. **6.** Cybele **7.** Artemis
in the raw.. **6.** nudity
of the case.. **9.** ipso facto
worship.. **11.** physiolatry
natus ... **4.** born
nausea ... **4.** pall **5.** qualm **8.** loathing, mal de mer **10.** queasiness **11.** seasickness
nauseous ... **7.** fulsome, mawkish **9.** loathsome, offensive, sickening, squeamish **10.** disgusting
nautical ... **5.** naval **6.** marine **7.** oceanic **8.** maritime
nautical (pert to) ...
almanac.. **9.** ephemeris
direction.. **5.** avast, belay
hail.. **4.** ahoy
instrument.. **3.** aba **7.** compass, pelorus, sextant
measure.. **3.** ton **4.** knot **6.** fathom **7.** sea mile
nautilus ... **7.** mollusk **8.** argonaut **9.** submarine **10.** diving bell
Navaho, Navajo ... **5.** hogan **6.** Indian **7.** blanket **9.** red-yellow
naval ... **6.** marine **8.** nautical
naval (pert to) ...
brigade.. **7.** militia

commander.. **7.** navarch
depot.. **4.** base
device.. **6.** dolter
officer.. **5.** bosun **6.** ensign, yeoman **7.** admiral, captain **9.** boatswain (bosun), commander **10.** lieutenant
nave ... **3.** hob, hub, nef **4.** apse, fist **5.** nieve **7.** apsidal
navel ... **6.** middle, orange **8.** omphalos **9.** umbilicus **10.** depression
navigate ... **4.** keel, sail **7.** avigate **11.** ship science
navigator ... **5.** navvy **12.** third command (or 4th)
navy (fleet) ... **7.** tankers **8.** cruisers, flattops, gunboats **10.** destroyers, submarines **11.** battleships **12.** mine sweepers **13.** hospital ships **16.** aircraft carriers
navy (pert to) ...
bean.. **6.** kidney
coffee.. **3.** mud
color.. **4.** blue **10.** marine blue
drinking fountain.. **11.** scuttlebutt
fleet.. **6.** armada **13.** combat vessels
plug.. **7.** tobacco
ships, collectively.. **5.** fleet **6.** armada
song.. **13.** Anchors Aweigh
training camp.. **8.** boot camp
underwear.. **8.** skivvies
nawab, nabob ... **5.** ruler, title **7.** viceroy
nay ... **2.** no **4.** deny **5.** flute, never **6.** denial, naysay, refuse **7.** refusal **8.** negative **11.** prohibition
nayaur ... **5.** sheep
nayword ... **6.** byword **7.** proverb (of reproach) **9.** watchword
Nazarene (pert to) ...
artist.. **8.** Overbeck (of Rome)
disciple.. **9.** Christian
native.. **11.** Jesus Christ
native of.. **8.** Nazareth
Nazi ... **9.** Hitlerite
Nazi emblem ... **6.** fylfot **8.** swastika
nchega ... **6.** monkey **10.** chimpanzee
neanic ... **8.** immature, youthful
neap ... **4.** tide **6.** tongue (vehicle) **7.** low tide **8.** low water
Neapolitan (pert to) ...
dance.. **10.** tarantella
fever.. **8.** undulent
Italian.. **6.** Naples
medlar.. **5.** fruit **7.** azarole
music.. **5.** chord (6th)
ointment.. **9.** mercurial
yellow.. **6.** Naples
near ... **2.** at **4.** nigh **5.** about, close, handy **6.** around, within **7.** closely, related **8.** adjacent, approach, imminent, intimate **11.** approximate **13.** propinquitous
nearby, near-by ... **3.** gin **4.** nigh **5.** anent, handy **6.** beside, nearly **7.** close by, close to, vicinal **8.** adjacent **9.** adjoining **10.** convenient
Nearctic ... **9.** Greenland, Holarctic **11.** Palaearctic **13.** Arctic America
Near East ... **7.** Balkans **12.** Balkan States
Near East valley ... **4.** wadi (wady) **5.** oasis **6.** ravine
nearest ... **4.** next **7.** closest **9.** proximate

nearly . . . 5. about 6. almost 7. closely
8. narrowly 10. similarity
13. approximately
nearness . . . 8. affinity, intimacy, likeness,
relation 9. closeness 11. propinquity
near of kin . . . 7. germane
nearsighted . . . 6. myopic 8. purblind
12. narrow-minded, shortsighted,
undiscerning
neat . . . 3. pat 4. prim, smug, snod, tidy,
trig, trim 5. natty 6. adroit, dapper,
spruce 7. orderly, perjink, precise
9. shipshape 10. meticulous, perjinkety
12. spick-and-span
neatherd . . . 7. cowherd 8. herdsman
neathmost . . . 6. lowest
neb . . . 3. tip 4. beak, bill, face, kiss,
nose 5. point, snout
Nebo, Nebu . . . 8. mountain (Bib) 11. god
of wisdom
Nebraska . . .
capital . . 7. Lincoln
city . . 5. Omaha 8. Hastings
11. Scottsbluff
Indian . . 4. Otoe 5. Omaha 6. Pawnee
meaning . . 11. water valley
railroad (1865) . . 12. Union Pacific
river . . 6. Nemaha, Platte 8. Missouri
State admission . . 13. Thirty-seventh
State motto . . 20. Equality Before the
Law
State nickname . . 4. Beef 10. Cornhusker
nebula . . . 3. sky 4. mist 5. cloud, vapor
10. atmosphere
Nebula of . . . 4. Lyra 5. Orion
9. Andromeda
nebulous . . . 4. hazy 5. misty, vague
6. cloudy 7. clouded, nebular
8. nebulose
nebulous envelope . . . 4. coma
9. chevelure
necessarily . . . 8. perforce
11. unavoidably 12. consequently
13. indispensably
necessary . . . 5. vital 7. needful
9. essential, mandatory, requisite
11. requirement, unavoidable
13. indispensable
necessitate . . . 5. force, impel 6. compel,
entail, oblige 7. require 9. constrain
necessity . . . 4. food, need, want
5. drink 7. aliment, poverty, urgency
9. neediness 10. constraint
14. inevitableness
neck . . . 4. hals (halse) 5. crane, scrag,
swire 6. cervix, fondle, strait 7. channel,
embrace, isthmus
neck (pert to) . . .
armor . . 6. gorget 8. gorgerin
artery . . 7. carotid
back of . . 4. nape 5. nucha, nuque
6. scruff
frill . . 5. jabot, ruche 6. wimple
land . . 6. strake 9. peninsula
muscle . . 8. scalenus
pendant . . 6. locket 9. lavaliere
piece . . 3. boa 5. amice, rabat, scarf,
stole 6. collar
water . . 6. strait
zoology . . 4. gula 6. wattle 7. withers
neckcloth . . . 6. cravat 7. muffler

9. barcelona 11. neckerchief
neckerchief . . . 7. belcher 8. kerchief
12. handkerchief
necklace . . . 5. beads 6. torque 7. baldric,
chaplet, rivière 11. shark's-teeth
neckpiece . . . 3. boa 5. ascot, rabat,
scarf, stole 6. collar 8. kerchief
necktie . . . 3. tie 4. band 5. ascot, scarf
6. cravat 10. four-in-hand
necrology . . . 9. death roll 13. death
register 14. obituary notice
necromancy . . . 5. goety, magic 7. sorcery
9. sortilege 11. conjuration,
enchantment
necropolis . . . 8. cemetery
necropsy . . . 7. autopsy 10. post-mortem
nectar . . . 3. red 5. drink, honey
8. beverage
nectar of the gods . . . 8. ambrosia
neddy . . . 6. donkey 13. life preserver
need . . . 4. lack, poor, thar, want
7. poverty, require, urgency 8. exigency
9. extremity, necessity 10. compulsion,
deficiency 11. requirement
needle . . . 3. sew 4. acus, goad,
sail 5. tease, thorn 6. bodkin,
pierce 7. darning, obelisk 9. astatizer
10. upholstery
needle (pert to) . . .
bath . . 3. jet 9. sprinkler
bird . . 9. phalarope 10. needlebill
bug . . 4. Nepa 7. Ranatra
case . . 4. etui (etwee)
fish . . 3. gar 8. pipefish
gun . . 11. Dreyse rifle
kind . . 5. blunt, sharp 7. between,
crochet, darning 8. knitting
long-eyed . . 10. embroidery
medical . . 10. hypodermic
needlelike body . . 7. spicule
needlework . . 7. crochet, sampler
8. knitting 10. embroidery
record . . 10. phonograph
shaped . . 6. acuate 7. acerose 8. acicular
under the skin . . 5. seton
needy . . . 4. poor 7. almoner 8. indigent
9. necessary, penniless, requisite
10. distressed
neel-bhunder . . . 8. wanderoo 10. blue
monkey
neep . . . 6. turnip
ne'er-do-well . . . 5. idler 6. wretch
8. poltroon 9. schlemiel 14. good-for-
nothing
nef . . . 4. nave 5. clock (ship-shaped)
nefarious . . . 6. wicked 7. heinous,
impious 8. horrible, infamous, terrible
9. atrocious 10. detestable, iniquitous,
villainous
nefas . . . 6. sinful
negate . . . 4. deny 6. refuse, refute
7. nullify 8. disprove 10. counteract
negative . . . 2. ir, ne, no 3. nay, non,
nor, not 4. deny, film, veto 5. minus
6. refuse 7. neutral 8. disprove, negation
9. privative 13. contradiction
negative (pert to) . . .
electrode, pole . . 7. cathode (kathode)
eyepiece . . 8. Campani's 9. Huygenian
ion . . 5. anion
sign . . 5. minus

neglect ... **4.** fail, omit, slip, snub **5.** shirk **6.** slight **7.** failure **8.** omission **9.** disregard, negligent, pretermit **11.** inattention

negligee ... **4.** gown, robe **6.** attire **8.** peignoir

negligence ... **7.** laxness **9.** oversight, unconcern **10.** remissness **11.** inattention **12.** carelessness, inadvertence

negligent ... **3.** lax **4.** lash **6.** remiss, supine **8.** careless, heedless **10.** neglectful **11.** unconcerned

negotiate ... **4.** deal, pass **5.** treat **6.** manage, treaty **7.** bargain, mediate **8.** transact

Negrito (pert to) ...
African .. **4.** Akka **5.** Batwa, Pygmy **7.** Bambute, Bushman
Dutch New Guinea .. **6.** Tapiro
Indonesian .. **3.** Ata **4.** Aeta (Ita)
Malay .. **6.** Semang

neigh ... **4.** akin **6.** whinny **7.** whicker

neighborhood ... **7.** purlieu **8.** environs, vicinity **9.** proximity **10.** thereabout

neither right nor wrong ... **11.** adiaphorous, indifferent

Nemesis ... **7.** avenger, goddess, penalty

nemoral ... **6.** sylvan **14.** living in a grove

neology ... **8.** new words **9.** neologism **11.** new doctrine **14.** new expressions

neonate ... **7.** new baby, newborn

neophobia (fear of) ... **6.** the new

neophyte ... **4.** tyro **6.** novice **7.** convert **8.** beginner **9.** proselyte **10.** catechumen

neoplasm ... **5.** tumor

neosology (study of) ... **10.** young birds

neoteric ... **3.** new **4.** late **6.** modern, recent

nep ... **6.** catnip

Nepal ...
aborigines .. **10.** Mongolians
capital .. **8.** Katmandu
district .. **7.** Mustang
mountain .. **7.** Everest **9.** Himalayas
ruler .. **9.** Maharajah

nepesh ... **4.** soul **10.** animal soul **12.** divine breath

nephew ... **4.** neve **6.** nepote

nephrite ... **4.** jade **7.** mineral **11.** kidney stone

nephroid ... **8.** reniform **12.** kidney-shaped

nephros ... **6.** kidney

nepote ... **6.** nephew **8.** grandson

nepotism ... **9.** patronage **10.** favoritism, preference

Neptune ... **3.** sea **5.** ocean **6.** sea god

Neptune (pert to) ...
Astron .. **6.** planet (3rd largest)
Celtic .. **3.** Ler
consort .. **7.** Salacia
emblem .. **7.** trident
Greek .. **8.** Poseidon
Roman .. **6.** sea god
son .. **6.** Triton
wife .. **6.** Medusa

Nereid (Gr) ... **8.** sea nymph

Nero (pert to) ...
excesses .. **7.** cruelty **13.** burning of Rome (64 AD)
mother .. **9.** Agrippina
Roman title .. **7.** Emperor
wife .. **6.** Sabina **7.** Octavia

nerve ... **4.** pulp **5.** cheek, fiber, pluck, sinew **6.** aplomb, energy, tendon, tissue **7.** courage, nervure **8.** audacity, coolness, strength **10.** resolution

nerve (pert to) ...
action .. **9.** neurergic
cell .. **4.** axon **6.** neuron
center .. **8.** ganglion
comb form .. **5.** neuro
fiber .. **5.** motor **7.** sensory **8.** afferent, efferent
force .. **7.** neurism
gray matter .. **7.** cinerea
inflammation, medical .. **8.** neuritis, neurosis **9.** neurotomy **10.** neurectasy, neurolysis, neuropathy **11.** neurologist **13.** tic douloureux
network .. **6.** rete **6.** plexus
of Wrisberg .. **6.** facial
operation .. **10.** neurolysis
passage .. **4.** rete **5.** hilum **8.** ganglion
ref to .. **6.** neural, neuric **7.** neuroid **8.** neurotic
root .. **5.** radix
science .. **9.** neurology
sheath .. **9.** medullary
tissue .. **7.** cinerea, neurine **9.** neuroglia
tumor .. **6.** glioma **7.** neuroma

nerveless ... **4.** dead **5.** inert **9.** foolhardy, powerless **10.** courageous

nervous ... **5.** tense, timid **6.** neural, touchy **7.** fearful, jittery **8.** eloquent, neurotic, timorous **9.** excitable, sensitive **10.** high-strung **12.** apprehensive

nervous (pert to) ...
affliction .. **3.** tic **6.** ataxia, chorea **7.** aphasia **8.** neurosis
energy deficiency .. **7.** aneuria
seizure .. **4.** amok (amuck)
system, center .. **5.** brain, spine
system, description .. **11.** neurography
system, name .. **9.** neuronymy
system, science .. **9.** neurology
system, specialist .. **12.** neuropathist, psychiatrist
tissue tumor .. **11.** neurocytoma

ness ... **4.** cape **8.** headland **10.** promontory

nest ... **3.** bed, den, nye, web **4.** inro **5.** abode, aerie, eyrie, group, haunt, nidus **6.** cuddle, series (graduated) **7.** lodging, retreat **9.** residence **10.** nidificate **13.** breeding place

nest (pert to) ...
boxes .. **4.** inro
eagle's .. **5.** aerie, eyrie (eyry)
pheasant's .. **4.** nide
spider's .. **3.** web
squirrel's .. **4.** dray (drey)
swallow's .. **9.** nidus avis
to build .. **6.** nidify

nestle ... **3.** pet **4.** nest **6.** cuddle, pettle, settle **7.** protect, shelter, snuggle

nestling ... **4.** bird **5.** child **9.** fledgling, youngling

Nestor (pert to) ...
famed for .. **6.** wisdom

King of . . **5.** Pylos
known as . . **4.** sage **7.** adviser **8.** The
   Elder **9.** Patriarch
net . . . **3.** gin, web **4.** mesh, toil, trap,
   weir **5.** clear, lacis, score, seine, snare,
   weave **6.** profit **7.** enclose, network,
   trammel **8.** receipts **9.** reticulum
net (pert to) . . .
fishing . . **4.** fyke **5.** seine, trawl
   7. trammel
hair . . **5.** snood
lacemaking . . **5.** lacis
silk . . **5.** tulle **6.** maline
winged (lacy) . . **12.** neuropteroid
Netherlands . . . see also *Dutch, Holland*
capital . . **9.** Amsterdam
cheese . . **4.** Edam
city . . **5.** Delft **7.** Utrecht **9.** Eindhoven,
   Rotterdam
gin . . **8.** schnapps
government . . **8.** monarchy
government seat . . **8.** The Hague
inhabitant . . **5.** Dutch **7.** Flemish
lake . . **7.** Haarlem
legislative body . . **4.** Raad
low land . . **6.** polder
port . . **9.** Rotterdam
possession . . **7.** Surinam (Dutch Guiana)
   8. Antilles (W Ind)
river . . **3.** Eem **5.** Meuse, Rhine **6.** Ijssel
   (Yssel), Kromme
sea (inland) . . **9.** Wadden Sea, Zuider
   Zee **10.** Ijssel Lake, Ijsselmeer
nettle . . . **3.** vex **4.** fret, herb, line,
   whip **5.** anger, annoy, pique, rouse
   6. incite, Urtica **7.** provoke **8.** irritate
   10. Parietaria, Urticaceae
nettle (pert to) . . .
bird . . **11.** whitethroat
geranium . . **6.** coleus
rash . . **5.** hives, uredo **9.** urticaria
sea . . **5.** cnida
network . . . **3.** web **4.** caul, fret, kell, lace,
   mesh, moke, rete **5.** chain **6.** cobweb,
   plexus, reseau, sagene **7.** webwork
neume . . . **5.** neuma **6.** pneuma
neurad . . . **12.** to neural side
neural . . . **6.** dorsal, nerval **7.** ventral
   9. posterial
neuralgia . . . **3.** tic **4.** pain **8.** face ague
   13. tic douloureux
neuter . . . **6.** gender **7.** neither, neutral,
   sexless **9.** impartial
neutral . . . **7.** antacid **8.** mediocre,
   middling, negative, unbiased
   10. achromatic **11.** indifferent,
   nonpartisan **12.** noncombatant,
   noncommittal
neutral equilibrium . . . **7.** astatic
neutralize . . . **5.** annul **6.** offset **7.** nullify,
   vitiate **9.** frustrate **10.** counteract
   11. countervail **14.** counterbalance
Nevada . . .
capital . . **10.** Carson City
city . . **3.** Ely **4.** Elko **6.** Sparks **7.** Boulder
   8. Las Vegas
lake . . **4.** Mead **6.** Mohave **7.** Pyramid
mine (famed) . . **12.** Comstock Lode
   (1859)
mountain . . **7.** Rockies, Wasatch
   13. Sierra Nevadas

native Indian . . **6.** Digger
resort . . **4.** Reno **8.** Las Vegas (The
   Meadows) **9.** Lake Tahoe
State admission . . **11.** Thirty-sixth
State motto . . **16.** All For Our Country
State nickname . . **6.** Silver **9.** Sagebrush
neve . . . **4.** firn, snow **6.** nephew **7.** glacier
nevel, nevell . . . **9.** fisticuff
never . . . **4.** nary **6.** nowise **7.** not ever
   8. at no time, not at all **9.** by no
   means, nevermore
nevertheless . . . **3.** but, yet **5.** still
   6. anyhow **7.** however
   15. notwithstanding
nevus . . . **4.** mark, mole **5.** tumor
   7. blemish **9.** birthmark
new . . . **3.** neo (pref) **4.** anew, late,
   nova (star) **5.** fresh, novel **6.** growth,
   modern, recent **8.** neoteric, original,
   untested **9.** recreated, renovated
   12. unaccustomed **13.** inexperienced
New Brunswick . . .
capital . . **11.** Fredericton
city . . **6.** St John
gulf . . **10.** St Lawrence
new but yet old . . . **10.** novantique
Newfoundland . . .
city . . **7.** St John's **9.** Grand Bank
discoverer . . **9.** John Cabot (1497)
gulf . . **10.** St Lawrence
New Guinea, Papua Island . . .
capital . . **6.** Rabaul
hog (wild) . . **4.** bene
island size (world) . . **5.** third
native . . **6.** Papuan
parrot . . **4.** lory
port . . **4.** Daru **7.** Moresby
region . . **10.** Melanesian
river . . **3.** Fly
New Hampshire . . .
capital . . **7.** Concord
city . . **6.** Durham **7.** Hanover **8.** Merrimac
   10. Manchester, Portsmouth
cog rail (first) . . **12.** Mt Washington
lake . . **13.** Winnipesaukee
mountains . . **5.** White
Our Town . . **13.** Grover's Corner
park . . **13.** Crawford Notch, Dixville
   Notch
range . . **12.** Presidential
river . . **8.** Merrimac **11.** Connecticut
sculpture . . **14.** Great Stone Face (Profile
   Peak)
State admission . . **5.** Ninth
State motto . . **13.** Live Free or Die
State nickname . . **7.** Granite
New Jersey . . .
capital . . **7.** Trenton
city . . **6.** Camden, Newark **7.** Raritan
   9. Montclair **12.** Fort Monmouth, New
   Brunswick
college . . **9.** Princeton (1746)
inventor . . **6.** Edison
naval air station . . **9.** Lakehurst
poet . . **11.** Walt Whitman
resort . . **7.** Cape May **8.** Wildwood
   9. Ocean City **10.** Asbury Park
   12. Atlantic City
river . . **7.** Raritan
State admission . . **5.** Third
State motto . . **20.** Liberty and Prosperity

State nickname . . **6.** Garden
New Mexico . . .
 capital . . **7.** Santa Fe
 city . . **4.** Taos **7.** Roswell **11.** Albuquerque
 Fort . . **5.** Tejon
 Indian Reservation . . **5.** Acoma (Sky
  City) **11.** Chaco Canyon
 peak . . **7.** Wheeler
 river . . **4.** Gila **5.** Pecos **8.** Canadian
 space center . . **6.** Sandia **8.** Holloman,
  Kirtland **9.** Los Alamos **10.** White Sands
 State admission . . **12.** Forty-seventh
 State bird . . **10.** road runner
 State flower . . **5.** yucca
 State motto . . **12.** Crescit Eundo **15.** It
  Grows as it Goes
 State nickname . . **17.** Land of
  Enchantment
 State wonder . . **15.** Carlsbad Caverns
new moon festival . . . **8.** neomenia
news . . . **5.** flash, scoop **6.** report
 7. courier, evangel, tidings
news agency . . . **2.** AP **3.** DNB, UPI
 4. Tass **5.** Aneta, Domei **7.** Reuters
 9. syndicate
newspaper (pert to) . . .
 editor . . **7.** reviser **8.** redactor
 file . . **6.** morgue
 popular name . . **7.** gazette
 writer . . **8.** reporter **9.** columnist
  10. newscaster **13.** correspondent
newsstand . . . **5.** booth, kiosk, stall
new star . . . **4.** nova
newt . . . **3.** eft **6.** lizard, triton
 10. salamander
New Testament . . . **6.** Gospel **8.** Epistles
 15. Pauline Epistles
new wine . . . **4.** must
new word, usage . . . **7.** neology
 9. neologism, neoterism
New York . . .
 borough . . **5.** Bronx **6.** Queens
  8. Brooklyn, Richmond (formerly)
  9. Manhattan **12.** Staten Island
 buyer (for $24) . . **11.** Peter Minuit
 capital . . **6.** Albany
 city . . **5.** Utica **7.** Buffalo, New York
  8. Saratoga **9.** Rochester
  11. Schenectady **12.** Poughkeepsie
 college . . **7.** Colgate, Cornell **8.** Columbia
  9. West Point
 Falls . . **7.** Niagara
 Indian . . **6.** Oneida, Seneca **8.** Iroquois
 Irving's home . . **9.** Tarrytown
 island . . **6.** Staten **9.** Manhattan
 monument . . **7.** Obelisk **10.** Grant's
  Tomb **15.** Statue of Liberty
 mountains . . **9.** Catskills
 name, old . . **12.** New Amsterdam
 nickname . . **6.** Gotham **8.** Big Apple
 river . . **4.** East **6.** Harlem, Hudson
 river channel . . **8.** Hell Gate
 section (famed) . . **4.** SoHo **16.** Greenwich
  Village
 State admission . . **8.** Eleventh
 State bird . . **8.** bluebird
 State flower . . **4.** rose
 State motto . . **9.** Excelsior **10.** Ever
  Upward
 State nickname . . **6.** Empire
New Yorker . . . **8.** Dutchman **9.** Gothamite

 13. Knickerbocker
New Zealand . . .
 capital . . **10.** Wellington
 city . . **7.** Dunedin **8.** Auckland, Hamilton
  12. Christchurch
 discoverer . . **6.** Tasman
 explorer . . **4.** Cook (Captain James)
 location . . **12.** South Pacific
 native . . **3.** Ati **5.** Maori **10.** Polynesian
 peak . . **6.** Mt Cook
 sect . . **7.** Ringatu
 soldier . . **5.** Anzac
 volcano . . **7.** Ruapehu
New Zealand (pert to) . . .
 bird . . **3.** kea, moa, poe **4.** titi, weka, kiwi
  7. apteryx, boobook, wrybill, Xenicus
 caterpillar . . **5.** aweto
 club, weapon . . **4.** mere
 mahogany . . **6.** totara
 mollusk . . **4.** pipi
 myrtle . . **8.** ramarama
 morepork . . **4.** peho, ruru
 palm . . **5.** nikau
 parrot . . **6.** kakapo **9.** owl parrot
 pigeon . . **4.** kuku
 reptile . . **7.** tuatara
 white pine . . **5.** kauri (kaury)
next . . . **4.** then **5.** aware, neist **7.** closest,
  nearest, proximo **9.** adjoining,
  immediate **10.** contiguous, succeeding
next to . . . **6.** almost, beside, nearly
 8. adjacent
next to last syllable . . . **6.** penult
 11. penultimate
nexus . . . **3.** tie **4.** bond, link **5.** group
 6. series **10.** connection
 15. interconnection
Nez Percé . . . **6.** Indian **11.** pierced nose
Niagara . . . **5.** flood, grape (green)
Niagara Falls (pert to) . . .
 cataract . . **8.** American, Canadian
  9. Horseshoe
 division between . . **10.** Bridal Veil, Goat
  Island
 point of interest . . **14.** Cave of the Winds
nib . . . **3.** end **4.** beak, bill **5.** point (pen),
  prong **6.** tongue
nibble . . . **3.** eat, nab, nip **4.** gnaw, peck
 5. champ, munch **6.** browse
Nicaragua . . .
 capital . . **7.** Managua
 city . . **7.** Granada
 lake . . **7.** Managua
 mountain range . . **10.** Cordillera
 river . . **4.** Coco, Tuma **7.** San Juan
nice . . . **4.** fine, good, kind, neat
 6. dainty, proper, queasy, subtle, tickle
 7. elegant, finical, genteel, prudish,
  refined **8.** exacting, pleasant, pleasing,
  suitable **9.** agreeable, squeamish
 10. appetizing, delightful, fastidious,
  particular, scrupulous **11.** considerate,
  punctilious, well-behaved
 13. hypercritical **14.** discriminating,
  discriminative
Nicene Creed . . . **10.** Confession
nicety . . . **7.** finesse, modesty **8.** accuracy,
  delicacy **9.** precision **11.** preciseness
 13. squeamishness
niche . . . **4.** apse, nook **5.** space (recessed)
 6. alcove, covert, recess **7.** retreat,

secrete 10. tabernacle
nick ... 3. gap 4. dent, dint, slit 5. notch, steal 7. swindle
Nick Charles ... see *Thin Man*
nickel (pert to) ...
alloy .. 5. Invar
bronze .. 11. cupranickel
coin .. 13. five-cent piece
color .. 4. gray 6. nimbus
compound .. 8. argenton 11. maillechort
silver .. 6. German
symbol .. 2. Ni
nickelodeon ... 4. juke 7. jukebox, theater (5-cent)
nickname ... 3. pun 6. monica 7. agnomen, epithet, misname, moniker (monicker), pet name 8. cognomen, misapply 10. soubriquet
nicknaming pun ... 12. prosonomasia
nictate ... 4. wink 5. blink 7. twinkle 9. nictitate
nid ... 3. nod 10. bend and bob
nide ... 4. nest 5. brood
nidge ... 3. nig 5. shake 6. quiver
nidificant ... 12. nestbuilding
nidology, science ... 10. birds' nests
nidor ... 5. aroma, scent
nidus ... 4. nest 5. abode 7. nucleus 13. breeding place
Nietzsche ... 11. philosopher
nieve ... 4. fist, hand
niffer ... 7. bargain 8. exchange
niffy-naffy ... 7. finical 8. trifling
Niflheim, Nifelheim (Norse Myth) ... 8. Universe (division of) 10. Nine Worlds
nifty ... 5. smart 7. stylish 8. very good
Nigeria ...
capital .. 5. Abuja, Lagos (formerly)
city .. 3. Ede 6. Ibadan
people .. 3. Ibo 6. Yoruba
plains .. 5. Bornu
niggardly ... 5. scant 6. paltry, sordid, stingy 9. penurious, scrimping 10. avaricious 12. parsimonious
nigh ... 2. at 3. nei 4. left, near 5. about, anear, close 6. almost, direct, nearly 8. adjacent 10. contiguous 11. neighboring
night ... 4. nuit 5. death 7. evening 8. darkness, wee hours 9. adversity, nightfall 11. concealment
night (pert to) ...
bird .. 5. potoo 8. nightjar 9. nighthawk 10. goatsucker, nightchurr, owl swallow, shearwater 11. nightingale
blindness .. 10. nyctalopia
cap .. 6. biggin
club .. 4. café 5. disco 6. bistro 7. cabaret 11. discotheque
goddess .. 3. Nox, Nyx
jasmine .. 10. hursinghar
Norse .. 4. Nott
sight (only) .. 11. hemeralopia
wandering .. 11. noctivagant
nightfall, at ... 6. sunset 9. acronical (achronical) (opp of cosmical)
nightingale ... 6. thrush 8. philomel 9. bed jacket
night jar ... 5. potoo 10. goatsucker
nightmare ... 3. alp 4. Mara, ogre

5. dream 7. incubus 9. cauchemar 13. hallucination
nightshade ... 5. morel (moril) 7. henbane 10. belladonna 11. bittersweet
nigrescent ... 8. blackish
nihil ... 7. nothing, no value
nihil debet ... 13. he owes nothing
nihil ex nihilo ... 7. nothing (comes) 11. from nothing
Nihilist ... 9. anarchist, Socialist
Nile (pert to) ...
bird .. 4. ibis 7. wryneck
boat .. 5. baris 6. nuggar 8. dahabeah
branch .. 4. Blue 5. White
city .. 7. Rosetta
color .. 3. boa 5. green
dam .. 5. Aswan
Falls .. 5. Ripon
fish .. 5. bagre 8. mormyrid (sacred)
god .. 4. Hapi
headstream .. 6. Kagera
houseboat .. 8. dahabeah
island .. 4. Roda (Rhoda)
waste .. 4. sudd
nilgai ... 8. antelope
nimble ... 4. deft, fast, flit, gleg, lish, spry 5. agile, alert, brisk, fleet, quick, smart, swift 6. active, adroit, clever, lively, prompt, volant
nimbose ... 6. cloudy, stormy 7. clouded 8. nebulous, nubilous, overcast
nimbus ... 4. disk, halo 5. cloud, vapor 6. fabric, gloria, nickel 7. aureole 10. atmosphere
nimiety ... 6. excess 10. redundancy
niminy-piminy ... 7. mincing, refined 10. effeminate
nimmer ... 5. thief
Nimrod (Bib) ... 5. ruler 6. hunter 8. Cush's son
nimshi ... 4. fool 7. half-wit 11. silly person
Nimshi's son (Bib) ... 11. Jehoshaphat
nine (pert to) ...
angles .. 7. nonagon
banded armadillo .. 4. peba
based on .. 8. novenary
Books of nine chapters .. 7. Enneads
comb form .. 6. ennead
composition for nine .. 5. nonet
days' devotion .. 6. novena
eyes .. 7. lamprey
gems .. 7. Vikrama
gods .. 9. Etruscans
group .. 6. ennead, nonary 18. Ennead of Heliopolis
headed monster .. 5. Hydra
inches .. 4. span
number .. 5. ennea, nueve
pert to .. 8. enneadic
players .. 8. baseball
poetic .. 8. ninefold
Nineteenth amendment ... 14. Woman's Suffrage
Nineveh (Bib) ...
capital .. 7. Assyria
famed for .. 11. excavations (1814)
Nine Worlds (Norse) ... 3. Hel 6. Asgard 7. Alfheim, Midgard 8. Niflheim, Vanaheim 10. Jotunnheim

12. Muspellsheim **13.** Svartalfaheim
Nine Worthies ... **5.** David, Judas
  6. Arthur, Caesar, Hector, Joshua
  7. Godfrey **9.** Alexander
  11. Charlemagne
ninny ... **4.** clod, dolt, fool, nerd
  9. blockhead, simpleton
ninth ... **5.** nones (day before Ides)
  8. enneatic, ninefold **11.** ennea-eteric
  (year)
Ninth of Ab (Jew) ... **7.** fast day
ninut ... **6.** magpie
Niobe (pert to) ...
  changed by Zeus to .. **5.** stone
  father .. **8.** Tantalus
  husband .. **12.** King of Thebes
nip ... **3.** bit, cut, sip **4.** bite, clip, dram,
  peck **5.** blast, cheat, check, chill, clamp,
  draft, drink, hurry, pinch, seize, sever,
  steal, thief **6.** benumb, blight, catnip,
  cut off, freeze, snatch, tipple **7.** shorten,
  squeeze **8.** compress **10.** pickpocket
nipa (pert to) ...
  drink .. **9.** alcoholic
  mat .. **6.** thatch
  palm .. **4.** atap
  palm sap .. **5.** sugar **7.** alcohol
nipcheese ... **5.** miser **6.** purser
nipper ... **3.** boy, lad **4.** claw, grab **5.** biter,
  drink, miser, thief **6.** cunner, mitten,
  urchin **7.** gripper, incisor, pincers
  12. costermonger
nippers ... **6.** pliers **7.** pincers **8.** leg
  irons, pince-nez **9.** handcuffs
nipple ... **3.** pap **4.** teat **7.** mamelon,
  papilla **8.** mammilla **10.** projection
  12. protuberance
nippy ... **4.** cold **5.** brisk **6.** active,
  biting **7.** nipping, pungent **8.** grasping,
  vigorous
Nirvana ... **4.** rags **6.** heaven **8.** oblivion
  12. emancipation
Nisan (Jew calendar) ... **10.** first month
  (Mar-Apr)
nisi ... **5.** if not **6.** unless
nissen ... **6.** goblin, kobold **7.** brownie
nisus ... **7.** impulse **8.** endeavor, striving
nit ... **3.** egg **4.** mite **8.** parasite
nitency ... **6.** luster **10.** brightness
niter, nitre ... **6.** natron **9.** saltpeter
  13. sodium nitrate **16.** potassium nitrate
nither ... **5.** blast **6.** debase, shiver
  7. oppress, tremble **9.** humiliate
nithing (anc) ... **6.** coward **7.** niggard
nitid ... **3.** gay **6.** bright **8.** lustrous
nitric acid ... **10.** aqua fortis
nitrogen ... **3.** azo (comb form), gas
  5. azote **7.** element **10.** atmosphere
nitrogen compound ... **7.** ammonia
nitroglycerin, nitroglycerine ...
  8. dynamite (1846) **9.** explosive,
  guncotton
nitrous oxide ... **3.** gas **10.** anesthetic
  11. laughing gas
nitty-gritty ... **4.** base, crux, gist
  7. essence
Niue, Pacific island ...
  territory of .. **10.** New Zealand
niveau ... **5.** level
niveous ... **5.** snowy, white (shining)
nix ... **2.** no **5.** no one **6.** forbid, nobody,

sprite **7.** nothing
Njorth, Njord (Norse) ... **3.** god (fertility)
  5. Vanir
Njorth's daughter ... **5.** Freya (Freyja)
  7. goddess (love and beauty)
Njorth's son ... **3.** god **4.** Frey
no ... **3.** naw, nay, nit **4.** baal, dead, gone,
  none **5.** not so **6.** denial, no-gaki, not
  any **8.** not at all
Noah, Bib (pert to) ...
  boat .. **3.** Ark
  dove .. **7.** Columba
  father .. **6.** Lamech
  flood .. **6.** Deluge
  Genesis .. **9.** patriarch
  grandson .. **4.** Aram
  landing, the Ark .. **6.** Ararat
  raven .. **6.** Corvus
  son .. **3.** Ham **4.** Shem **7.** Japheth
nob ... **4.** head, nave **6.** hobnob
  8. nobleman **9.** personage
nobby ... **4.** boat **5.** smart **7.** stylish
Nobel powder ... **10.** Ballistite
noble ... **4.** epic, fine, peer **5.** ducal,
  grand, lofty, manly **6.** epical **7.** eminent,
  grandee, liberal, stately, sublime
  8. elevated, generous, imposing,
  renowned, splendid **9.** dignified,
  high birth, honorable **10.** impressive
  11. illustrious, magnanimous,
  magnificent **12.** aristocratic
nobleman ... **3.** sir **4.** duke, earl, lord,
  peer **5.** baron **6.** barony, flaith,
  thakur **7.** baronet, grandee, marquis
  8. margrave, optimate, viscount
  9. blueblood, patrician **10.** aristocrat,
  chess piece
nobleness of birth ... **6.** eugeny
noblewoman ... **4.** lady **5.** begum
  7. duchess, peeress **8.** baroness,
  contessa, countess, marquise
  11. marchioness
nobody ... **4.** none **5.** no one **7.** nebbish
  8. no person **9.** jackstraw, nonentity
  10. not anybody
nocent ... **6.** guilty **7.** harmful, hurtful
  8. criminal (opp of innocent)
nocturnal ... **5.** night **7.** nightly
  8. darkness, nocturne
nocturnal (pert to) ...
  animal .. **3.** bat **4.** coon **5.** lemur, ratel
  6. possum **7.** opossum
  astronomy .. **9.** astrolabe
  bird .. **3.** owl
  signs .. **8.** zodiacal
nocturne ... **7.** lullaby **8.** serenade
  10. night scene (art)
nocuous ... **7.** hurtful, noxious
nod ... **3.** bow **4.** bend, bock, doze,
  tend, wink **6.** beckon, signal **7.** bidding
  8. greeting
Nod (Bib) ... **9.** Land of Nod **10.** East
  of Eden
nodding ... **6.** nutant **7.** annuent, weeping
  (as a willow) **8.** cernuous, drooping
noddy ... **3.** auk **4.** fool **6.** drowsy, fulmar,
  noodle, sleepy **7.** foolish, hackney
  9. simpleton
node ... **4.** knob, knot, knur, plot
  5. joint, nodus **7.** dilemma **8.** swelling
  10. difficulty **12.** complication,

protuberance
nodule ... **4.** auge, bump, knot, lump,
mass **5.** geode **7.** granule, nablock
8. tubercle **12.** complication
nodus ... **4.** knot, node **10.** difficulty
12. complication
noel ... **5.** carol (Xmas), shout **9.** sign
of joy
Noel ... **6.** Natale **9.** Christmas
noeud ... **3.** bow **4.** knot
nog ... **3.** peg, pin **5.** block **6.** eggnog,
noggin **8.** treenail **9.** brickwork
nogada ... **10.** pecan candy
nogal ... **5.** pecan
noggin ... **3.** cup, mug **4.** head, pate
noise ... **3.** din, pop, rap **4.** bang, boom,
klop, roar, rout **5.** blare, blast, bruit,
chang, clang, click, rumor, sound
6. clamor, outcry, racket, report, strife,
uproar **7.** brattle, chortle, discord,
quarrel, rapping **9.** shoutings
noise (pert to) ...
ghost .. **11.** poltergeist
harsh .. **4.** bray **7.** stridor **9.** caterwaul
respiration .. **4.** rale
rustling .. **5.** swish
Scotch .. **5.** chang
water .. **5.** plash **6.** ripple, splash
whirring .. **4.** burr
noised ... **6.** dinned **7.** rumored
8. reported
noisemaker ... **4.** horn **5.** siren **6.** rattle
7. clacker, whistle **8.** whiz-bang
noisome ... **3.** bad **4.** foul **5.** fetid,
nasty **7.** harmful, noxious **8.** stinking
9. offensive **10.** malodorous, pernicious
11. destructive, unwholesome
12. insalubrious
noisy ... **4.** loud **7.** blatant **8.** brawling,
clattery **9.** clamorous, turbulent
10. blustering, boisterous, vociferous
12. obstreperous, rattley-bang
nom ... **4.** name
nomad ... **4.** arab **5.** gypsy **6.** roamer,
Romany **7.** Bedouin, Saracen, scenite,
zingaro **8.** wanderer
nomadic ... **9.** itinerant
nomarchy (Gr) ... **4.** nome **8.** province
10. department
nom de plume ... **7.** pen name
9. pseudonym
nomen ... **4.** gens, name **7.** agnomen
8. cognomen **9.** praenomen
nomenclature ... **4.** name **5.** onymy
8. glossary, onymatic, register
10. dictionary, Latin names, vocabulary
11. designation, terminology
nominal ... **3.** par **6.** unreal **7.** not real,
titular, topical **8.** so-called
nominal recognizance (law) ... **3.** Doe
nonage ... **6.** neanic **8.** immature,
minority, pupilage, youthful
nonary ... **9.** nine group **10.** base of
nine **11.** group of nine
nonbeliever ... **5.** pagan **7.** atheist,
heathen, infidel **8.** agnostic
11. disbeliever **12.** non-Christian
nonce ... **3.** now **8.** meantime
11. temporarily
nonchalant ... **4.** cool **6.** casual **8.** careless
10. insouciant **11.** indifferent,

unconcerned **13.** imperturbable
noncompliance ... **7.** refusal
12. disobedience **13.** recalcitrance
non compos mentis ... **7.** unsound
8. demented, deranged **11.** disoriented
nonconformist ... **7.** heretic, sectary
8. objector, recusant **9.** dissenter,
protester
nondescript ... **11.** exceptional
13. indescribable **14.** indeterminable
none ... **2.** no **4.** nary **5.** nones, no one
6. nobody, not any, not one **10.** nobody
else
nonentity ... **7.** a nobody, nullity
8. nihility, nonbeing **9.** res nihili
11. nothingness **12.** nonexistence
nonessential ... **8.** needless **9.** extrinsic
10. adiaphoron, incidental, irrelevant
11. superfluous **12.** adventitious
non licit ... **8.** unlawful
nonmetallic ... **4.** spar **5.** argon, boron
6. carbon, helium, iodine, oxygen
7. bromine **8.** chlorine, nitrogen
nonpareil ... **4.** type **7.** paragon
8. nonesuch, peerless **9.** unrivaled
11. unsurpassed **14.** painted bunting
nonplus ... **4.** stop **5.** blank, stump
6. baffle, puzzle, thwart **7.** mystify,
perplex **8.** quandary
nonproductive ... **6.** barren **7.** sterile
9. fruitless
nonprofessional ... **3.** ham, lay **4.** laic
5. laity **7.** amateur **10.** apprentice
nonsense ... **3.** bah **4.** bosh, bunk,
tosh **5.** folly, stite **6.** drivel, humbug,
jargon **7.** blarney, foolery, rubbish,
trifles, twaddle **8.** falderal, flimflam,
tommyrot, trumpery **9.** absurdity,
frivolity, poppycock, silliness
10. balderdash, tomfoolery, triviality
nonsense verse ... **9.** amphigory
(amphigouri), rigmarole
non tanto (Mus) ... **9.** non troppo, not
as much
noodle ... **4.** fool, head **5.** brain, ninny
9. blockhead, simpleton **12.** stupid
person
nook ... **4.** cant, cove **5.** angle, herne,
niche **6.** corner, cranny, recess
7. crevice **10.** promontory
noon ... **6.** midday, summit **8.** meridian,
noontide **9.** ninth hour **11.** noon of
night (poet)
noonday rest ... **6.** siesta
noose ... **3.** tie **4.** bond, hang, loop
5. snare **6.** circle, halter **7.** laniard
(lanyard) **12.** hangman's rope
Nootka ... **3.** Aht, dog **6.** Indian
norati ... **5.** noise **6.** gossip
Norbertine ... **12.** Premonstrant
Nordic ... **8.** Germanic **12.** Scandinavian
norie ... **9.** cormorant
norm ... **4.** rule, type **5.** model, norma
7. average, measure, pattern
8. standard, template
norma ... **4.** rule **5.** gauge, model
6. square **7.** pattern **8.** standard,
template **9.** constellation
normal ... **3.** par **4.** just, mean, sane
5. usual **6.** common **7.** average,
logical, natural, orderly, regular, typical

8. everyday, ordinary 9. customary
Norman ... 6. French 7. crimson
  8. Northman 10. Romanesque
  17. conquest of England (1066)
Normandy ...
beach .. 5. Omaha
capital .. 4. Caen 5. Rouen (old)
city .. 5. Havre 6. Dieppe 7. Alençon
  9. Cherbourg
conqueror .. 5. Rollo 8. William I
governed by .. 6. France (1940)
Viking duke (anc) .. 5. Rollo
Norn (Teut Myth) ... 4. Urth, Wyrd
  5. Skuld 9. Verthandi
Norse ... 9. Norwegian 12. Scandinavian
Norse (pert to) ...
abode of gods .. 6. Asgard 8. Valhalla
alphabet .. 6. runics
ash tree, universe .. 10. Yddgrasill
bard .. 5. scald (skald) 7. sagaman
collected songs, myths .. 4. Edda
demon (Fire) .. 4. Surt (Surtr)
earth .. 7. Midgard
epic .. 4. saga
explorer .. 11. Leif Ericson
first man .. 4. Askr
giant .. 4. Loki, Ymir (Ymer) 5. Jotun
  6. Fafnir
horse .. 8. Brimfaxi 9. Skinfaksi
horse (Odin's) .. 10. Yggdrasill
king .. 4. Atli
language (old) .. 9. Icelandic
maidens (Odin's) .. 8. Valkyrie
man .. 8. Northman
monster .. 6. kraken 7. Midgard
patron saint .. 4. Olaf
poem .. 4. rune
toast .. 5. skoal
warrior .. 9. berserker
watchdog (Hel's) .. 4. Garm (Garmr)
wolf .. 6. Fenrir
Norse goddess of ...
death, underworld .. 3. Hel, Ran
fate .. 4. Norn, Urth, Wyrd
flowers .. 5. Nanna
giantess .. 4. Nott
love, beauty .. 5. Freya
peace, healing .. 3. Eir
sky .. 5. Frigg (Frigga)
Norse God of ...
day .. 3. Dag
evil .. 4. Loki
fertility .. 4. Frey (Freyr) 6. Njorth (Njord)
giants .. 4. Ymir
justice .. 4. Frey 7. Forseti
light .. 6. Balder
night .. 4. Nott
poetry .. 4. Odin 5. Bragi
primeval (the world) .. 4. Ymir (Ymer)
sea .. 5. Aegir
thunder .. 4. Thor
war, wisdom .. 4. Odin (Wodin)
watchfulness .. 8. Heimdall
Norse gods, chief ... 3. Tyr (Tiu) 4. Frey,
  Jarl, Loki, Odin (Othin, Wodin), Thor
  (Donar), Vali, Ymir 5. Aesir (group)
  6. Balder, Njorth 7. Asynjur (group),
  Forseti 8. Heimdall
North (far) ... 6. Arctic
North Africa ... see also *Africa*
country .. 7. Algeria, Tunisia

fruit .. 3. fig 4. date
people .. 4. Moor 6. Berber, Hamite,
  Libyan
port .. 4. Sfax
North America ... see also *America*
Indian blanket .. 6. stroud
mountain, highest .. 8. McKinley
orchid .. 8. arethusa
owl .. 7. wapacut
rail .. 4. sora
reindeer .. 7. caribou
river, longest .. 5. Yukon 8. Missouri
  11. Mississippi
snake .. 5. adder
North Atlantic (pert to) ...
cape .. 5. Sable
island .. 7. Britain, Iceland, Ireland
  9. Greenland, Manhattan
sea gull .. 4. skua
North Carolina ...
cape .. 4. Fear 7. Lookout 8. Hatteras
capital .. 7. Raleigh
city .. 6. Durham 9. Asheville, Charlotte
  12. Winston-Salem
explorer .. 6. De Soto 9. Verrazano
famed person .. 12. Virginia Dare 16. Sir
  Walter Raleigh
first flight .. 9. Kitty Hawk
mountain .. 10. Mt Mitchell
pine .. 8. loblolly
river .. 3. Tar 5. Neuse 6. Peedee (Yadkin)
State admission .. 7. Twelfth
State bird .. 8. cardinal
State flower .. 7. dogwood
State motto .. 14. Esse Quam Videri
  20. To Be Rather Than To Seem
State nickname .. 7. Tarheel 8. Old
  North
North Dakota ...
capital .. 8. Bismarck
city .. 5. Fargo, Minot
fort .. 6. Mandan 7. Lincoln
  11. Abercrombie
historic site .. 24. International Peace
  Garden
mountain .. 10. White Butte
reservoir .. 8. Garrison
State admission .. 8. Fortieth (or
  Thirty-ninth)
State bird .. 10. meadowlark
State flower .. 11. prairie rose
State nickname .. 5. Sioux 11. Flickertail
northeaster ... 4. gale, wind 5. storm
Northern ... 6. boreal 11. hyperborean
  13. septentrional
Northern constellation ... 3. Cor 4. Lyra
  9. Andromeda
northernmost world (inhabitable) ...
  5. Thule 9. Trondheim
North Pole ... 10. boreal pole
North Sea ... 6. Baltic, German
North Sea arm ... 8. Kattegat
  9. Skagerrak (Skager-Rak)
North Sea canal ... 4. Kiel
North Star ... 7. Polaris 8. Cynosure,
  lodestar (loadstar), polestar
north wind ... 6. Boreas 10. tramontane
Norway ... see also *Norwegian*
capital .. 4. Oslo 11. Christiania (old)
city .. 6. Bergen 7. Drammen
  9. Trondheim

county.. **5.** fylke
inlet.. **5.** fiord (fjord)
mountain.. **6.** Kjolen
parliament.. **8.** Storting (Storthing)
patron saint.. **4.** Olaf (Olaus)
phenomenon.. **11.** midnight sun
   14. Northern Lights
plateau.. **5.** fjeld
river.. **2.** Oi **4.** Tana **7.** Glommen
Norwegian (pert to)...
bird.. **4.** rype **9.** ptarmigan
cart.. **11.** stolkjaerre
dance.. **7.** halling
duck.. **7.** widgeon
embroidery.. **9.** hardanger
goblin.. **5.** Nisse **6.** kobold
guardian spirit.. **6.** fylgia **8.** hamingja
haddock.. **8.** rosefish
language.. **5.** Norse **8.** Rigsmaal
   9. Landsmaal
liquor.. **7.** akevitt
sea monster.. **6.** kraken
tales.. **4.** Edda
Norwegian people...
author.. **6.** Hamsun, Undset
composer.. **5.** Grieg
dramatist.. **5.** Ibsen
explorer.. **6.** Nansen (Nobel Prize)
   8. Sverdrup
king.. **6.** Harold (The Fairhaired)
   15. Harold Hardraade
philologist.. **5.** Assen
raiders.. **7.** Vikings
saint.. **4.** Olaf (Olaus)
violinist.. **7.** Ole Bull
zoologist.. **4.** Sars
nose... **3.** neb, pry **4.** conk, prow
   5. nasus, scent, smell, snout **6.** meddle,
   muzzle, nuzzle **8.** olfactor **9.** detective,
   proboscis **11.** investigate
nose (pert to)...
ailment.. **6.** coryza **8.** rhinitis
bees, birds.. **4.** lore **5.** lorum
bleeding.. **9.** epistaxis
cartilage.. **6.** septum
glasses.. **8.** pince-nez
large.. **6.** nasute
muscle.. **7.** nasalis
opening.. **5.** naris (nares, pl) **7.** nostril
partition.. **5.** vomer
plug.. **12.** rhineurynter
relating to.. **5.** nasal **6.** narial, rhinal
snub.. **6.** simous
surgery.. **11.** rhinoplasty
noseband (bridle)... **6.** misrol
nosegay... **4.** posy **7.** bouquet, perfume
   9. fragrance **10.** frangipani (tree)
nosh... **3.** eat
nosocomium... **8.** hospital
nosography, nosology (science of)...
   7. disease
nostalgia... **8.** yearning **11.** wistfulness
   12. homesickness **14.** sentimentality
nostology (study of)... **8.** senility
   10. geriatrics **11.** gerontology
Nostradamus... **4.** seer **7.** prophet
   10. astrologer
nostril... **5.** naris (nares, pl) **6.** narial
   9. olfactory
nostril-shaped... **8.** nariform
nosy... **5.** nasal **6.** prying **7.** curious

   8. fragrant **10.** malodorous
   11. inquisitive
Nosy, Old (nickname)... **16.** Duke of
   Wellington
not (pert to)...
any.. **2.** no **4.** nane, nary, none **7.** no
   trace
at all.. **5.** nohow **6.** nowise
easy.. **7.** labored
either.. **7.** neither
feral.. **4.** tame
harmed.. **9.** unscathed
having a will.. **9.** intestate
hollow.. **5.** solid
in motion.. **5.** fixed **6.** stable, static
   7. stabile **10.** stationary
in the least.. **6.** nowhit
moral.. **6.** amoral **7.** immoral
open (fruit).. **11.** indehiscent
prefix.. **2.** il, im, in, ir, un **3.** non
professional.. **4.** laic **7.** amateur
qualified.. **5.** unfit
running (stream).. **8.** stagnant
separable.. **11.** indivisible
settled.. **4.** moot
subjugated.. **7.** unbowed
suitable.. **5.** inept
the same.. **5.** other **9.** different
to know.. **5.** unken **10.** unfamiliar
notable... **6.** famous **8.** historic
   9. celebrity, important, memorable,
   notorious **10.** noteworthy, remarkable
   13. distinguished, extraordinary
notandum... **4.** note **5.** entry
   10. memorandum
notary... **5.** notar **8.** attestor, notebook,
   official **9.** scrivener **12.** notary public,
   stenographer
notation... **4.** memo, note **5.** entry
   7. comment, marking **9.** etymology
   10. annotation
notator... **5.** noter **8.** recorder
   9. annotator
notch... **3.** gap, jap **4.** dent, dint,
   kerf, nick, nock **5.** cleft, crena, score
   6. defile, dentil (Her), indent **7.** passage
   8. undercut **9.** indenture **11.** indentation
notched bar (door)... **4.** risp
notched opening (Anat)... **5.** hilum
note... **2.** ut **3.** jot **4.** chit, heed,
   mark, memo, sign, sole, song, tone,
   tune **5.** breve, gloss, sound, token
   6. billet, notice, postil, record, remark,
   report **7.** apostil (apostille), comment,
   epistle **8.** dispatch, eminence, indicate,
   marginal, scholium **9.** character
   10. annotation, importance, indication,
   memorandum, reputation **11.** certificate,
   observation
note (pert to)...
death sound.. **4.** mort
explanatory.. **5.** gloss **8.** scholium
half.. **5.** minim
high.. **3.** alt, E la
marginal.. **6.** postil **7.** apostil (apostille)
musical.. **5.** breve **6.** ecbole **7.** punctus
stem of.. **5.** filum
notebook... **6.** street **7.** estreat
   8. ratebook **10.** adversaria,
   memorandum
noted... **4.** seen **5.** famed **6.** famous,

marked 7. eminent, notable 8. far-
famed, renowned 9. distingué,
prominent, well-known 10. celebrated
notes ... 5. duole 6. strain 7. tiralee
11. solmization
nothing ... 3. nil, nox 4. luke, rien,
void, zero 5. nihil 6. naught, nichil,
nought, trifle 7. a nobody 9. nonentity
11. empty-handed 12. nonexistence
nothing doing ... 4. calm 6. hushed, no
dice, no soap, placid 7. I refuse 9. by
no means, God forbid, quiescent
notice ... 2. ad 3. see 4. heed, idea, mark,
mind, news, note, sign 5. blurb, edict,
quote 6. advice, espial, notion, regard,
remark 7. affiche, mention, observe,
warning 8. bulletin, citation 9. attention
10. commentary 11. information,
observation 12. announcement,
intelligence 13. advertisement
notice (pert to) ...
advance .. 8. ballyhoo
death .. 4. obit 8. obituary
marriage .. 4. bans 5. banns
notify ... 4. cite, page, tell, warn 6. inform,
remind 7. apprise, declare, publish
8. announce
notion ... 4. idea, view, whim 5. freit
6. belief, theory, vagary 7. caprice,
impulse, opinion 9. intention
10. conception, denotation, knickknack
11. supposition
notionable ... 8. fanciful 9. whimsical
notional ... 6. unreal 9. imaginary,
visionary, whimsical
notions ... 5. goods, wares
11. commodities, merchandise
notoriety ... 4. fame, plug 5. éclat
8. ballyhoo 9. limelight, publicity,
spotlight
notorious ... 5. known, noted 6. arrant,
famous, notour 8. flagrant, infamous,
talked of 10. recognized 11. conspicuous
notorious character ... 5. James (Jesse)
7. Cochise, Younger 8. Geronimo,
Jennings, Murietta 9. Jack Ketch, Wyatt
Earp 11. Billy the Kid, Poncho Villa,
Sitting Bull 12. Calamity Jane 13. John
Dillinger 14. Wild Bill Hickok
notum ... 4. back
notus ... 4. back (comb form)
notwithstanding ... 3. but, yet 5. still
6. mauger (maugre), though 7. despite,
however 8. although 9. in spite of
12. nevertheless
nought, naught ... 3. bad, nil 4. zero
5. wrong 7. nothing, useless
9. worthless
noughty ... 3. bad 9. worthless
noumenal ... 4. real 5. ontal (opp of
phenomenal)
noun ... 7. subject
noun (pert to) ...
gender, common .. 7. epicene
indeclinable .. 6. aptote
irregular .. 5. pecus 11. heteroclite
suffix .. 2. et, ia 3. ent, ery, ier, ion,
ior, ist, ite 4. ence
verbal .. 6. gerund
nourish ... 4. feed, grow 5. nurse 6. foster,
suckle, supply 7. support, sustain

9. cultivate 13. promote growth
nourishing ... 6. alible 8. nutrient
9. nutritive 10. alimentary
nourishment ... 3. aid 4. food 5. manna,
meats 7. aliment, pabulum 9. nutriment,
nutrition 10. sustenance
13. nutritiveness 14. nutritiousness
nous ... 4. mind 8. ready wit 9. intellect
11. world spirit
Nova ... 4. star
Nova Scotia ...
bay .. 5. Fundy 10. Chedabucto
cape .. 5. Canso
capital .. 7. Halifax
greens .. 11. sea plantain
island .. 10. Cape Breton
lake, salt .. 7. Bras d'Or
native .. 7. Acadian 8. Bluenose
poetic name .. 6. Acadia (Acadie)
settlement, first .. 9. Port Royal
novel ... 3. new 4. book, rare 5. fresh,
story 7. fiction, romance, strange,
unusual 8. original
novelty ... 3. fad 7. newness 9. freshness
10. innovation, recentness
11. originality
novice ... 3. nun 4. tyro (tiro) 5. chela
6. rookie, tyrone 7. amateur, learner
8. beginner, freshman, initiate,
neophyte, newcomer 9. fledgling,
greenhorn, postulant 10. apprentice,
catechumen 11. abecedarian
novitiate ... 6. novice 9. probation
14. apprenticeship
now ... 3. noo 4. here 6. at once
7. present 9. at present, forthwith,
instantly 10. very lately 12. at this
moment
nowhere ... 5. limbo 6. absent 7. no place
8. oblivion 9. nowhither 11. nonexistent,
not anywhere, nullibicity
nowhere else ... 5. there
nowise ... 8. not at all
Nox (pert to) ...
brother .. 6. Erebus
daughter .. 10. Hesperides
goddess (Rom) .. 5. Night
husband .. 5. Chaos
noxious ... 4. evil 5. nasty, yucky
(sl) 6. nocent, odious 7. baneful,
harmful, hurtful, noisome 9. injurious,
miasmatic 10. corruptive, pernicious
11. destructive, unwholesome
12. insalubrious
nozzle ... 3. tew 4. nose, vent 5. giant,
snout 6. nuzzle, outlet, tuyère 7. conduit
9. sprinkler
nuance ... 5. shade 9. gradation, variation
10. refinement
nub ... 4. gist, knob, knot, knub,
lump, neck, snag 9. main point
12. protuberance
Nubia (pert to) ...
afterglow .. 14. second twilight
animal .. 4. goat 5. horse
autonym .. 6. Berber 7. Barabra
harp .. 5. nanga
people .. 4. Nuba
nubia ... 4. wrap 5. cloud
nucha ... 4. nape, neck
nuclear complex ... 7. Oedipus

nuclear energy (terms) . . . **4.** mass
  6. fusion, ionize **7.** fission, neutron,
  reactor, tokamak **8.** hydrogen,
  meltdown
nuclear network fiber . . . **5.** linin
nucleus . . . **4.** core **5.** cadre, focus, umbra
  6. center, kernel **8.** rudiment
nude . . . **4.** bare **5.** color, naked **6.** Season
  (color) **7.** denuded **8.** stripped, undraped
  9. unadorned, unclothed, undressed
nudge . . . **3.** jog, nog **4.** knub, lump, poke,
  prod, push **5.** block, elbow **6.** jostle,
  remind, signal
nudibranch . . . **7.** mollusk
nugatory . . . **4.** vain **7.** invalid, trivial
  8. trifling **9.** worthless **11.** ineffectual
nuisance . . . **4.** bane, bore, harm, hurt,
  pest **6.** injury **9.** annoyance
nuit . . . **5.** night
null . . . **4.** void **6.** vacant **7.** invalid
  8. nugatory **11.** nonexistent
  13. inefficacious, insignificant
nullifidian . . . **7.** skeptic **9.** nullibist,
  skeptical **10.** unbeliever **11.** disbeliever
nullify . . . **4.** undo, void **5.** annul **6.** cancel,
  negate **7.** abolish, destroy **8.** abrogate
  10. counteract, neutralize
numb . . . **6.** clumsy, freeze, stupid, torpid
  8. benumbed, deadened, helpless
  9. apathetic, incapable, rigescent
  10. insensible **12.** anesthetized
number . . . **3.** sum **5.** count, digit,
  limit **7.** integer, numeral **8.** quantity
  9. aggregate, enumerate
  10. complement **11.** information
number (pert to) . . .
  added . . **6.** encore
  again . . **10.** renumerate
  by tens . . **7.** decimal
  cardinal . . **7.** primary (one, two)
  consecutively . . **5.** folio
  copies (printed) . . **7.** edition
  describable . . **6.** scalar
  irrational . . **4.** surd
  least whole . . **4.** unit
  lucky . . **5.** seven
  many . . **4.** herd **6.** myriad **7.** several
    9. multitude **12.** considerable
  ordinal . . **5.** first **6.** second (etc)
  third power . . **4.** cube
  votes . . **4.** poll
  whole . . **7.** integer
numbles, nombles . . . **6.** umbles
  7. inwards **8.** entrails
numbness . . . **6.** torpor **10.** rigescence
numeral . . . **5.** Roman **6.** Arabic, figure
  9. character
numerous . . . **4.** lots, many **7.** copious,
  crowded **8.** abundant, measured,
  thronged **9.** plentiful
Numidia (pert to) . . .
  city . . **5.** Hippo
  crane . . **10.** demoiselle
  language (written) . . **5.** Punic **6.** Tuareg
    7. Hamitic
  modern kingdom . . **7.** Algeria
numskull . . . **4.** dolt, nerd **5.** dunce
nun . . . **4.** moth, smew **5.** Clare
  (Franciscan), Vesta **6.** monial, pigeon,
  sister **8.** titmouse, votaress **9.** priestess
  13. Lady of Loretto

nun bird . . . **6.** Monasa **8.** puffbird
nunciate . . . **9.** announcer, messenger
nuncio . . . **6.** legate **8.** delegate
  9. messenger **11.** internuncio
nuncupate . . . **7.** declare **8.** dedicate,
  inscribe, proclaim **9.** designate
nuncupative . . . **4.** oral **9.** unwritten (will)
  11. designative
nun headdress . . . **6.** wimple
nunnari root . . . **12.** sarsaparilla
nunnery . . . **5.** abbey **7.** convent **8.** cloister
nunnery head . . . **6.** abbess
nunni . . . **7.** blesbok (blesbuck) **8.** antelope
Nuphar . . . **11.** spatterdock
nuptial . . . **6.** bridal **7.** marital **9.** connubial
  11. matrimonial
nurse . . . **4.** amah, ayah, feed, rear, tend
  5. bonne, mammy **6.** caress, suckle
  7. care for, cherish, nourish, nurture,
  nutrice **9.** nursemaid
nursed . . . **3.** fed **6.** tended **7.** cradled,
  suckled **8.** nurtured **9.** nourished
nursery . . . **6.** crèche, school **7.** day care
  (center)
nurse shark . . . **4.** gata
nurture . . . **3.** aid **4.** feed, rear **5.** nurse
  6. foster **7.** care for, cherish **8.** breeding,
  training **9.** education, encourage,
  nutriment
nut . . . **4.** anta, kola (cola) **5.** acorn,
  betel, pecan, piñon **6.** almond, Brazil,
  cashew, litchi, peanut, walnut **7.** filbert,
  hickory, maranon **8.** beechnut, chestnut
  9. butternut
nut (pert to) . . .
  bearing . . **10.** nuciferous
  brown . . **5.** hazel **6.** walnut **8.** chestnut
  coal . . **10.** anthracite
  collectively . . **4.** food **5.** shack
    9. beechnuts
  confection . . **8.** marzipan
  cracker . . **4.** crow
  eating . . **10.** nucivorous **11.** nuciphagous
  edible part . . **6.** kernel
  grass . . **5.** sedge
  Med . . **4.** kola **5.** bichy **9.** gourounut
  odd . . **9.** eccentric
  palm . . **5.** betel, lichi **7.** coconut
  ref to . . **5.** nucal
  shell . . **4.** case, hull **6.** trifle
Nut (pert to) . . .
  consort of . . **3.** Geb
  daughter . . **4.** Isis **8.** Nephthys
  goddess of . . **5.** earth
  son . . **2.** Ra
nutation . . . **3.** nod **7.** nodding
nuthatch . . . **4.** bird **5.** sitta **6.** xenops
  8. titmouse **9.** nutpecker
nutmeg . . . **4.** mace **5.** drupe **6.** beaver
  (color)
nutmeg (pert to) . . .
  bird, finch . . **5.** cowry **10.** weaverbird
  family . . **13.** Myristicaceae
  tree . . **6.** camara
Nutmeg State . . . **11.** Connecticut
nutpecker . . . **8.** nuthatch
nut quad . . . **6.** en quad
nutria . . . **3.** fur **5.** grège **10.** beaverlike
nutria fur bearer . . . **5.** coypu
nutrice . . . **5.** nurse
nutriment . . . **4.** food **7.** aliment, pabulum

9. nutrition 11. nourishment
nutritious... 9. alimental 10. alimentary, nourishing
nuts... 4. food, mast 5. shack 9. beechnuts
nut's partner... 4. bolt
nutty... 4. gaga, zest 5. queer, smart, spicy 7. amorous, piquant 10. unbalanced 11. fascinating 14. cracker-brained
nuzzle... 5. nurse 6. burrow, cuddle, foster, nestle 7. cherish 8. make snug
nyctalopia... 14. night blindness
nye... 4. eyas, nest, nide 5. brood
nymph... 4. nais 5. deity, dryad, naiad, oread, siren, sylph 6. Nereid 7. Oceanid 9. hamadryad
nymph (pert to)...
 Arcadian.. 6. Syrinx
 beloved of Narcissus.. 4. Echo
 color.. 4. pink
 Cretan.. 8. Cynosura
 fountain, river.. 4. nais 5. naiad 6. Egeria
 German legend.. 7. Lorelei
 Greek.. 4. Echo 6. Daphne 8. Arethusa
 Hesperides (one of).. 5. Aegle 7. Hespera
 hills, mountain.. 5. oread
 laurel tree.. 6. Daphne
 Messina Strait.. 6. Scylla
 monster.. 6. Scylla
 Mt Ida.. 6. Oenone
 Muslim paradise.. 5. houri
 ocean.. 5. siren 6. Nereid 7. Galatea, Oceanid 10. Callirrhoe
 pursued by Apollo.. 6. Daphne, Syrinx 8. Arethusa
 Queen.. 3. Mab
 sea bird.. 6. Scylla
 tree.. 5. Dryad 9. Hamadryad
 water.. 5. Naiad 6. Undine 7. Hydriad
 woods.. 5. Dryad 8. Arethusa 9. Hamadryad
 young.. 7. nymphet
Nymphaea... 8. Castalia 11. water lilies
nymphs... 10. Atlantides, Hesperides
nystagmus... 14. eyeball disease
Nyx, Nox (pert to)...
 daughter.. 4. Eris
 father.. 5. Chaos
 goddess of.. 5. Night
 mother of.. 11. Day and Night
Nzambi... 7. goddess (Afr) 11. earth mother

O

O (pert to)...
 interjection.. 11. exclamation
 letter.. 5. tenth
 mathematics.. 4. zero 6. cipher
 pref (family).. 5. Irish
oaf... 4. boor, dolt, lout 5. idiot, ouphe, yokel 9. blockhead, simpleton 10. changeling
oafish... 6. simple, stupid
oak... 4. club 5. brave, color, oaken, stout 6. strong 7. Quercus 8. hardness, strength 13. artificial fly
oak (pert to)...
 apple.. 4. gall 10. she-oak cone
 beauty.. 4. moth
 California.. 5. roble 6. encina
 comb form.. 6. querci
 evergreen.. 4. holm, ilex 5. holly
 family.. 8. Fagaceae
 fern.. 8. polypody
 fruit.. 5. acorn 6. camata
 fungus.. 10. armillaria
 gall.. 8. oak apple
 Jerusalem.. 7. ambrose
 kinds.. 3. bur, red 5. black, white 6. ground, poison, willow 8. chestnut 10. canyon live
 plantation.. 9. quercetum
 resembling.. 9. roboreous
 tannin.. 7. quercic 9. quercinic
 thicket.. 9. chaparral
 Turkey.. 6. cerris
 web.. 10. cockchafer
 young.. 8. flittern
oam... 5. steam 7. warm air
Oannes (Bab)... 5. deity (part man, part fish)
oar... 3. row 5. blade, remus, rower, scull 6. paddle, propel 7. oarsman
oar (pert to)...
 blade.. 4. palm, peel
 feather.. 5. remex
 fulcrum, lock.. 5. pivot, thole
 lop.. 6. rabbit
 shaft.. 4. loom
 shaped.. 7. remiped 8. remiform
oars (pert to)...
 collective.. 6. oarage, sculls
 one bank.. 7. unireme
 reverse.. 6. sheave
 three banks.. 7. trireme
 two banks.. 6. bireme
oasis... 3. ojo 4. wadi (wady) 5. Gafsa 6. Dakhla 11. fertile spot
oast... 4. kiln, oven
oat (pert to)...
 cake.. 5. caper
 ear (Old World).. 4. bird 7. wagtail
 fowl.. 11. snow bunting
 genus.. 5. Avena 6. oathay
 grass.. 4. ulla 9. chaparral
 husks.. 5. shood (shude)
 like.. 10. avenaceous
 rent (paid as).. 7. avenage
oath... 3. God 4. aith, drat, egad 5. bedad, curse 6. pledge 7. serment 9. affidavit, holy smoke, profanity 10. deposition 11. affirmation
Obadiah (Bib)... 6. Quaker 7. prophet
obbligato... 8. required

13. accompaniment, indispensable
obduction . . . **7.** autopsy **8.** covering
obdurate . . . **4.** firm, hard **5.** rough, stony
6. mulish, rugged **7.** adamant, callous
8. stubborn **9.** heartless, obstinate,
unbending, unfeeling **10.** impenitent,
inflexible, insensible, unyielding
11. hardhearted, intractable
obedient . . . **6.** docile **7.** duteous,
dutiful, orderly **8.** amenable, yielding
9. attentive, compliant **10.** submissive
11. conformable
obeisance . . . **3.** bow **5.** binge, congé
6. curtsy, fealty, homage **9.** deference
10. respectful **14.** obsequiousness
obeisance, to make . . . **3.** bow **6.** congee,
curtsy, salaam
obelisk . . . **5.** pylon **6.** guglia (guglio),
needle, obelus, pillar **16.** Cleopatra's
Needle
Oberon (pert to) . . .
  Astron . . **9.** satellite
  character of . . **11.** Shakespeare
  classic . . **4.** poem **5.** opera
  husband of . . **7.** Titania
  Myth . . **13.** King of Fairies
obese . . . **3.** fat **5.** puffy, pursy, squab,
stout **6.** fleshy, turgid **8.** liparous
9. corpulent
obey . . . **3.** ear **4.** hear, mind **5.** yield
6. comply, submit
obfuscate . . . **3.** dim **6.** darken, opaque
7. confuse, perplex **8.** bewilder
obi . . . **4.** sash **6.** girdle
obit . . . **4.** rest **5.** death **6.** notice
7. decease, release **8.** obituary
9. obsequies **10.** necrologue
11. Requiem Mass **12.** mortuary roll
obiter . . . **9.** in passing **12.** incidentally
obiter dictum . . . **7.** opinion (of judge)
object . . . **3.** aim, end **4.** goal, hulk **5.** cavil,
demur, scoff, thing **6.** appose, expose,
motive, oppose **7.** article, grammar,
protest, purpose **9.** intention
object (pert to) . . .
  bulky . . **4.** hulk
  circular . . **7.** trundle
  cloudlike . . **6.** nebula
  illustrative . . **6.** realia (pl)
  rare . . **5.** curio **7.** antique
  rational . . **8.** noumenon
  sacred . . **4.** Urim **7.** Thummim
  small . . **4.** mite
object for . . .
  devotion, worship . . **4.** icon, idol **5.** totem
  6. fetish
  dread . . **5.** bogey (bogie) **6.** goblin **8.** the
  Devil
  going and coming . . **6.** errand
  greed . . **5.** lucre, money **6.** wealth
  knowledge . . **7.** scibile
objection . . . **3.** bar **5.** cavil **7.** protest,
quarrel **8.** demurrer, obstacle
9. exception **11.** disapproval
objectionable . . . **9.** offensive
11. exceptional, inexpedient
13. uncommendable
objective . . . **3.** aim, end **4.** goal **6.** motive,
target **7.** purpose
objector, conscientious . . . **6.** conchy
objects (Bib) . . . **4.** Urim **7.** Thummim

objects (floating) . . . **7.** flotsam
objurgate . . . **5.** abuse, chide, scold
6. rebuke **7.** reprove, upbraid
9. reprimand
oblate . . . **5.** oblat **7.** devoted **9.** dedicated,
flattened (opp of prolate)
obligated . . . **5.** bound **6.** in debt
7. obliged **8.** beholden **9.** obstringe
obligation . . . **3.** tie, vow **4.** bond, debt,
duty, oath, onus **7.** promise **8.** civility,
contract **9.** agreement, necessity
10. compulsion **11.** obstriction
obligatory . . . **7.** binding **8.** imposing,
required **9.** mandatory, necessary
10. compulsory
oblige . . . **4.** bind, pawn **5.** favor
6. compel, engage **7.** gratify **8.** obligate
9. constrain, obstringe
11. accommodate
obliged . . . **7.** favored **8.** beholden,
grateful **9.** duty bound
obliging . . . **4.** kind **7.** helpful **9.** agreeable,
courteous, indulgent **11.** complaisant,
considerate **13.** accommodating
oblique . . . **4.** cant, skew **5.** bevel, slant,
slope **7.** obscure, scalene **8.** inclined,
perverse, sidelong, sidewise, sinister,
slanting **9.** underhand **10.** circuitous,
collateral, transverse **12.** disingenuous
oblique angle . . . **5.** acute **6.** obtuse
obliquely . . . **4.** skew **6.** aslant **7.** askance
8. sideways, sidewise **9.** on the bias
10. slantingly
obliterate . . . **4.** blot, dele **5.** erase
6. cancel, delete, efface, sponge
7. expunge
obliteration . . . **6.** rasure **7.** erasure
8. deletion **10.** extinction
oblivion . . . **7.** nirvana, silence **9.** unfeeling
13. forgetfulness **15.** unconsciousness
oblivion, producing . . . **8.** nepenthe
oblivion, river of . . . **5.** Lethe
oblivious . . . **6.** asleep **8.** heedless
9. forgetful, unfeeling **10.** abstracted
11. unconscious
oblong . . . **8.** elliptic **9.** elongated
11. rectangular **12.** quadrangular
obloquy . . . **5.** abuse **6.** infamy **7.** calumny
9. criticism **11.** malediction
12. reprehension
obnoxious . . . **4.** vile **5.** nasty **6.** odious,
rancid **7.** hateful **8.** amenable, infamous,
terrible **9.** offensive **13.** objectionable
oboe . . . **4.** reed **5.** shawm (anc)
7. hautboy, musette **8.** schalmei
(schalmey) **9.** chalumeau
obscene . . . **4.** lewd **6.** vulgar **8.** indecent,
prurient **9.** offensive, repulsive
10. disgusting **12.** pornographic
obscuration . . . **7.** eclipse **9.** darkening,
vagueness
obscure . . . **3.** dim, fog **4.** dark, hazy, slur
5. bedim, blind, mirky, misty, murky
6. cloudy, darken, delude, mystic,
opaque, remote **7.** becloud, conceal,
eclipse, shadowy, unknown **8.** darkling,
formless, nameless, nubilous, obstruse,
oversile (obs) **9.** enigmatic, undefined
10. indistinct, unrenowned
obscurity . . . **3.** fog **5.** gloom **7.** dimness,
opacity, unknown **8.** darkness

9. nonentity, vagueness
12. formlessness 13. imperspicuous
14. insignificancy, uncomprehended
obsecrate ... **7.** beseech, entreat
10. supplicate
obsequies ... **5.** wakes **8.** funerals **9.** last
rites
obsequious ... **5.** slick **6.** abject
7. devoted, dutiful, fawning, servile,
slavish **8.** cringing, funereal, obedient,
toadying **9.** attentive, compliant
11. subservient
observance ... **3.** act **4.** form, rite
6. custom **8.** behavior, ceremony,
practice **9.** attention, deference,
sacrament, vigilance **10.** conformity
11. celebration
observant ... **7.** careful, heedful, mindful
8. faithful, vigilant, watchful **9.** attentive,
regardant, regardful
observation ... **4.** idea **6.** espial, remark
7. opinion **9.** attention
observatory ... **4.** Lick **6.** Yerkes
7. lookout, Palomar **8.** Mt Wilson
11. planetarium
observe ... **2.** lo! **3.** eye, see, spy **4.** espy,
heed, keep, nark, note, obey, tout
6. behold, notice, remark **7.** conform,
examine, witness **8.** preserve
9. celebrate, solemnize
observed, to be ... **8.** notandum
10. memorandum
observer ... **4.** eyer, nark **7.** aviator,
student, witness **8.** beholder, informer,
looker-on, onlooker **9.** spectator
11. stool pigeon
obsess ... **5.** beset, haunt **6.** harass
7. bewitch, possess **8.** demonize
9. influence, preoccupy
obsession ... **5.** mania **8.** impelled
11. bewitchment **13.** spirit control
obsignate ... **4.** seal **5.** stamp **6.** ratify
obsolete ... **3.** old **5.** passé **6.** effete
7. archaic, disused, effaced, outworn,
worn out **9.** out of date **10.** antiquated
12. old-fashioned
obstacle ... **3.** dam **4.** snag **6.** hurdle
9. hindrance **10.** difficulty, impediment
11. obstruction
obstetrician ... **6.** doctor **10.** accoucheur
obstetrix ... **7.** midwife
obstinate ... **3.** set **5.** balky, tough
6. dogged, mulish, sullen **7.** willful
8. perverse, stubborn **9.** pigheaded
10. determined, headstrong, self-willed
11. opinionated
obstreperous ... **5.** noisy **6.** unruly
7. blatant **9.** clamorous, turbulent
10. vociferous **11.** disobedient
12. ungovernable
obstruct ... **3.** bar, dam, dit **4.** clog, ditt,
stop **5.** beset, block, check, choke,
delay **6.** arrest, hamper, oppose, stop
up **7.** occlude **9.** barricade, embarrass,
interfere, interrupt
obstruction ... **3.** ban, dam **4.** clog, reef,
snag **7.** barrier **8.** obstacle **9.** hindrance
10. difficulty, filibuster, impediment
11. retardation
obtain ... **3.** buy, eke, get, win **4.** earn,
fang, gain **5.** fetch, reach **6.** attain,

derive, elicit, secure **7.** achieve, acquire,
capture, prevail, procure, receive
obtain (pert to) ...
by intimidation .. **9.** blackmail
by threats .. **6.** extort
control of .. **6.** corner **8.** overcome
equivalent .. **6.** recoup
obtest ... **6.** beg for **7.** beseech
10. supplicate
obtrude ... **5.** eject, expel **6.** impose
7. intrude
obtrusive ... **7.** forward, pushing
9. intrusive, officious
obtund ... **4.** dull **5.** blunt, quell **6.** deaden
8. moderate
obtuse ... **4.** dull, slow **5.** blunt,
crass, dense **6.** stupid **9.** unfeeling
11. insensitive
obvelation ... **7.** veiling **10.** concealing
obverse ... **5.** front **8.** converse
10. complement **11.** counterpart
obviate ... **7.** head off, rule out
8. preclude **9.** forestall **10.** anticipate
obvious ... **5.** clear, gross, plain
7. evident, patient **8.** apparent, distinct,
manifest, palpable **11.** conspicuous,
open and shut
obvolute ... **7.** twisted **9.** contorted,
convolute **11.** overlapping
occasion ... **4.** sele, time **5.** cause, event,
nonce **6.** excuse, motive **7.** pretext
8. ceremony, exigency, function,
incident **9.** condition, happening
11. opportunity **12.** circumstance
occasional ... **3.** odd **4.** orra **5.** stray
6. casual **10.** incidental, infrequent
occasionally ... **7.** at times **9.** sometimes
10. now and then **11.** at intervals
12. sporadically
occasive ... **8.** westward **10.** setting sun
Occident ... **4.** West **6.** sunset **17.** Western
Hemisphere (opp of Orient)
Occidental ... **6.** ponent **7.** The West,
Western **9.** Hesperian
occiput ... **10.** back of head **11.** back
of skull
occlude ... **3.** dam **4.** shut **5.** close **6.** shut
up **8.** obstruct
occult ... **5.** magic **6.** hidden, mystic
7. alchemy, cryptic **8.** esoteric
9. concealed, recondite **10.** mysterious,
necromancy **11.** supernormal
12. supernatural
occultation ... **4.** gone, lost **7.** eclipse
11. concealment
occultism ... **6.** cabala **7.** mystery
occult science ... **9.** esoterics
occupant ... **6.** inmate, tenant
10. inhabitant
occupation ... **3.** job **4.** call, note,
work **5.** hobby, trade **6.** career,
tenure **7.** calling, pursuit **8.** business,
vocation **9.** avocation **10.** employment,
habitation, possession, profession
11. engrossment
occupied ... **3.** sat **4.** busy, held **6.** filled
7. engaged **8.** employed, pervaded
9. engrossed, inhabited
occupy ... **3.** use **4.** fill, hold **6.** employ,
engage, expend, invest **7.** engross,
inhabit, oversit, pervade, possess

8. interest
occur . . . **4.** come, fall, meet **5.** clash
  6. appear, befall, betide, happen
occurrence . . . **3.** hap **5.** event **8.** incident,
  presence, scenario **9.** existence,
  happening **10.** appearance
  11. eventuality **12.** circumstance
occurring (pert to) . . .
  after death . . **10.** posthumous
  at nightfall . . **9.** acronical
  often . . **8.** frequent **10.** frequently
ocean . . . **3.** sea **4.** brim, deep, main
  5. brine **6.** depths, pelago **8.** great sea
ocean (pert to) . . .
  approach . . **7.** sea gate
  bottom . . **3.** bed
  crop cultivation . . **11.** mariculture
  deep . . **7.** bathyal
  deepest, lowest . . **5.** hadal **8.** bathybic
    12. bathypelagic
  division . . **6.** Arctic, Indian **7.** Pacific
    8. Atlantic **9.** Antarctic
  floating matter . . **5.** algae **7.** flotsam
  geography . . **12.** oceanography
  mammal . . **4.** seal **9.** whale
  on (the ocean) . . **4.** asea
  periodic motion . . **4.** tide
  person . . **8.** aquanaut, oceanaut **9.** skin
    diver **10.** scuba diver
  ref to . . **7.** pelagic **9.** Neptunian
  route . . **4.** lane
  sealing . . **7.** pelagic
  vessel . . **6.** Sealab **9.** submarine
    10. bathyscaph **11.** bathysphere
Oceania, Oceanica . . . **9.** Melanesia,
  Polynesia **10.** Micronesia **12.** Pacific
  lands
Oceanids (Gr Myth, pert to) . . .
  father . . **7.** Oceanus
  mother . . **6.** Tethys
  nymphs . . **13.** three thousand
Oceanus (Gr Myth, pert to) . . .
  children . . **5.** Doris **8.** Eurynome
    (goddess), Oceanids
  god of . . **6.** rivers
  wife . . **6.** Tethys
ocellus . . . **3.** eye **6.** stemma **7.** eyespot
ocelot . . . **3.** cat **7.** leopard
ocher, ochre (pert to) . . .
  red . . **5.** tiver **7.** almagra **8.** hematite
    9. faded rose
  yellow . . **3.** sil **7.** Chinese **8.** limonite
    9. ochrolite
ochlocracy . . . **7.** mob rule
ochlophobia (fear of) . . . **6.** crowds
ocotillo . . . **5.** shrub **10.** candlewood
ocracy . . . **9.** group rule
octad . . . **5.** eight (group)
octaemeron . . . **12.** eight-day fast
octagon . . . **8.** octangle **11.** eight angles
octahedron . . . **10.** eight faces
octameter . . . **8.** octapody **9.** eight feet
octarchy . . . **11.** rule by eight
octastich . . . **6.** octave **10.** eight lines
  11. eight verses
Octateuch (Old Test) . . . **10.** Eight Books
  (1st)
octave . . . **4.** utas **5.** eight **6.** eighth
  8. wine cask **10.** eight notes
Octavia (pert to) . . .
  sister of . . **8.** Augustus

wife of . . **10.** Mark Antony
Octavian . . . **7.** Library (Rome's 1st)
  16. committee of eight (one of)
octet, octette . . . **7.** huitain **12.** group
  of eight
October (pert to) . . .
  bird . . **8.** bobolink
  birthstone . . **4.** opal **5.** beryl
  Club . . **9.** political
  drink . . **3.** ale
  month . . **5.** tenth
octogenarian . . . **13.** eighty-year-old
octopod . . . **9.** eight arms, eight legs
Octopoda (Roder) . . . **8.** mollusks (8-
  armed) **9.** argonauts, octopuses
octopus . . . **5.** poulp (poulpe)
octroi, octroy . . . **3.** tax **9.** privilege
  10. concession
ocular . . . **3.** eye (pert to) **5.** optic, sight
  6. visual **10.** ophthalmic
oculus . . . **3.** eye **14.** Corona Borealis
odd . . . **4.** orra, rare **5.** droll, extra, outré,
  queer **6.** uneven, unique **7.** azygous,
  bizarre, strange, unequal, unusual
  8. unpaired **9.** eccentric, remaining,
  unmatched **10.** occasional
oddity . . . **9.** queerness **11.** peculiarity,
  singularity **12.** eccentricity, idiosyncrasy
odds . . . **6.** gamble **7.** dispute, quarrel
  8. gambling, variance **9.** advantage
  10. difference, dissension, inequality
  11. probability **12.** disagreement
  13. probabilities
odds and ends . . . **4.** orts **6.** refuse,
  scraps **7.** mixture, remains **8.** remnants
  10. miscellany
ode . . . **4.** like (suff), poem **5.** psalm
  8. canticle, serenata
ode (type) . . . **7.** Lesbian, regular
  8. Horatian, Pindaric **9.** irregular
odeon . . . **4.** hall **7.** gallery, theater
Odin (pert to) . . .
  attendants . . **9.** Valkyries
  god of . . **3.** war **6.** poetry, wisdom
  hall . . **8.** Valhalla
  horse . . **8.** Sleipner
  son . . **3.** Tyr **4.** Thor **6.** Balder
  Teutonic name . . **5.** Woden (Wotan)
  wife . . **5.** Frigg (Frigga)
odious . . . **4.** foul, vile **5.** nasty **7.** hateful
  8. infamous, terrible
odium . . . **6.** hatred, infamy **9.** antipathy
  10. abhorrence, opprobrium
  11. detestation
odontist . . . **7.** dentist
odontology (science of) . . . **5.** teeth
  9. dentistry
odor, odour . . . **4.** fume, funk, nose
  5. aroma, fetor, nidor, scent, smell
  6. flavor **7.** essence, malodor, perfume
  9. fragrance, redolence
odor, meat cooking . . . **5.** fumet
  (fumette)
odorous . . . **8.** aromatic, fragrant, redolent,
  smelling
Odysseus (pert to) . . .
  chieftain . . **9.** Trojan War
  dog . . **5.** Argos
  father . . **7.** Laertes
  hero of . . **10.** The Odyssey (Homer)
  king of . . **6.** Ithaca (Gr)

magic herb.. **4.** moly
modern name.. **7.** Ulysses
wife.. **8.** Penelope
oecist... **9.** colonizer
oecodomic... **13.** architectural
Oedipus (pert to)...
  daughter.. **8.** Antigone
  father.. **5.** Laius (King of Thebes)
  mother.. **7.** Jocasta
oeno (comb form)... **4.** wine
oenomancy... **12.** wine prophecy
oenophilist... **9.** wine lover
oenopoetic... **10.** wine making
oestrus... **4.** fury **5.** sting **6.** desire,
  frenzy **7.** impulse **8.** stimulus
of... **2.** in, on **4.** over, upon, with **5.** about,
  avent **10.** indication
of (pert to)...
  a chamber.. **7.** cameral
  a class (related).. **7.** generic
  a father.. **6.** agnate
  a flock.. **6.** gregal
  a forefather.. **9.** ancestral
  a grandfather.. **4.** aval
  all.. **3.** ava
  a mother.. **7.** cognate
  an epoch.. **4.** eral
  an order.. **7.** ordinal
  a wife.. **7.** uxorial
  common gender.. **7.** epicene
  each.. **3.** ana
  earth.. **4.** geal
  equal value.. **10.** comparable
  French.. **2.** du **3.** des
  great importance.. **7.** capital
    9. momentous
  high standing.. **8.** sterling
  little importance.. **5.** petty **7.** trivial
  morning.. **5.** matin **7.** matinal
  New Stone Age.. **9.** Neolithic
  no avail.. **6.** futile
  nostrils.. **6.** narine
  old age.. **8.** gerontal
  planet's path.. **7.** orbital
  recent times.. **6.** lately **9.** latter-day
  reign.. **6.** regnal
  river banks.. **8.** riparian
  same family.. **7.** cognate, germane
  sound.. **5.** tonal
  summer.. **7.** estival
  tears.. **8.** lacrimal
  the country.. **5.** rural
  the ear.. **4.** otic
  the eye.. **6.** ocular
  the mouth.. **4.** oral
  the skin.. **6.** dermal
  the third degree.. **7.** cubical
  the throat.. **5.** gular
  the tongue.. **7.** glossal
  the wrist.. **6.** carpal
  this day.. **9.** hodiernal
  thread color.. **7.** ficelle
  winter.. **6.** hiemal
  yore.. **5.** olden
off... **3.** ill **4.** agee, away, doff **5.** aside
  6. begone, insane, remote **7.** distant,
  tainted **9.** dissonant, erroneous,
  imperfect, right-hand **10.** unemployed
offal... **5.** filth **6.** ordure, refuse **7.** carrion,
  garbage, rubbish
offbeat... **14.** unconventional

off-color... **6.** risqué **7.** dubious
  8. inferior
offend... **3.** cag, sin, vex **4.** miff **5.** anger,
  annoy, pique, wound **6.** assail, insult,
  revolt **7.** affront, do wrong, mortify
  9. displease
offender... **6.** sinner **8.** criminal
  9. wrongdoer **10.** malefactor
  12. transgressor
offense... **3.** sin **5.** crime, delit, fault,
  grief, malum **6.** delict, felony, insult
  7. outrage, umbrage **8.** trespass
  9. indignity **10.** resentment
  11. delinquency, misdemeanor,
  stellionate
offensive... **4.** foul, ugly **6.** attack,
  odious, ribald, vulgar **7.** abusive,
  eyesore, fulsome, harmful, obscene
  8. invading, shocking **9.** assailant,
  attacking, insulting, obnoxious,
  repugnant, revolting **10.** aggressive,
  malodorous, scurrilous **11.** approbrious,
  displeasing, distasteful **12.** disagreeable
  13. transgressive
offer... **3.** bid **6.** adduce, tender **7.** proffer,
  propine, propose **8.** immolate, overture
  9. ultimatum
offering... **4.** gift **6.** corban **7.** deodate,
  present **8.** oblation **9.** sacrifice
offering resistance... **8.** renitent
offhand... **8.** careless, informal, slapdash
  9. extempore, impromptu **10.** carelessly,
  nonchalant **11.** extemporary
  12. nonchalantly **15.** autoschediastic
office... **4.** duty, post, rite, wike (obs)
  5. place, trust **7.** station **8.** ceremony,
  function, position **9.** situation
  11. appointment
office (pert to)...
  chief.. **7.** manager
  divine.. **9.** akoluthia
  for the dead.. **7.** trental
  holder.. **8.** placeman
  of a datary (Roman Curia).. **7.** dataria
  of a ruler.. **7.** regency
  relinquish (to).. **5.** demit
  third hour.. **6.** tierce
officer... **6.** tindal **7.** bailiff, command,
  conduct, general, manager, marshal,
  sheriff **8.** adjutant, avigator, director
  9. constable, policeman, president
officer (pert to)...
  assistant.. **4.** aide
  Brit Royal Guard.. **4.** exon
  chief executive.. **3.** dey **4.** czar
    5. mayor **7.** emperor, monarch, premier
    8. governor **9.** president **10.** chancellor
  church.. **5.** elder **6.** sexton
  civil law.. **6.** notary, police **7.** bailiff,
    marshal, sheriff **9.** constable, policeman
    10. magistrate
  club.. **7.** steward
  corrupt.. **7.** grafter
  despotic.. **6.** satrap
  diplomatic.. **7.** attaché
  Jewish Relig.. **6.** parnas
  King's stables.. **6.** avener
  monastic.. **5.** prior
  naval.. **6.** ensign, yeoman
  parish.. **6.** beadle, bedral
  ship's.. **9.** boatswain (boson)

weights, measures . . **6.** sealer
official . . . **6.** formal **9.** authentic
   10. functional **13.** authoritative
official (pert to) . . .
   command . . **5.** edict
   despotic . . **6.** satrap
   game . . **5.** judge **6.** umpire **7.** referee
   government . . **10.** bureaucrat
   insurance . . **7.** actuary **8.** adjuster
   intinerant (Hist) . . **6.** missus
   mark . . **5.** stamp
   order (RCCh) . . **8.** rescript
   proclamation . . **5.** ukase **6.** decree
   record . . **5.** actum
   state . . **8.** governor **9.** secretary
officious . . . **4.** cool, pert **5.** saucy
   6. formal **8.** arrogant, impudent,
   official **9.** pragmatic **10.** meddlesome
   11. efficacious, impertinent, pragmatical
   12. contemptuous
officiousness . . . **10.** pragmatism
offing . . . **10.** background
offshoot . . . **3.** rod **5.** scion **6.** branch,
   member **8.** addition **9.** by-product
   10. descendant **12.** organization
offspring . . . **3.** son **4.** brat, seed **5.** child,
   fruit, issue, sprig **6.** origin, result
   7. produce, product, progeny **8.** fountain
   9. posterity **10.** descendant
oficina . . . **5.** works **6.** office **7.** factory
   10. laboratory
often . . . **3.** oft **9.** many times
   10. frequently, repeatedly **11.** over and
   over **13.** time after time
ogdoad . . . **5.** eight **10.** eight group
ogee . . . **4.** gula **5.** talon **7.** molding
   9. cyma recta **11.** cyma reversa
ogle . . . **3.** eye **4.** gaze, leer **5.** stare
   7. examine
Ogpu . . . **8.** Gay-Pay-Oo (Russ secret
   service)
O Henry . . . **6.** Porter (Wm Sydney)
Ohio . . .
   capital . . **8.** Columbus
   city . . **5.** Akron **6.** Dayton, Toledo
   9. Cleveland **10.** Cincinnati
   first settlement . . **8.** Marietta
   hero . . **12.** Anthony Wayne (Gen)
   lake . . **4.** Erie
   name meaning (Indian) . . **14.** Beautiful
   River
   State admission . . **11.** Seventeenth
   State motto . . **27.** With God All Things
   are Possible
   State nickname . . **7.** Buckeye
oil . . . **3.** ben, fat **4.** balm, ghee **5.** bribe,
   oleum **6.** aceite, anoint, asarum, grease,
   olanin **8.** flattery, medicate, painting
   9. lubricant, lubricate, petroleum
   10. illuminant
oil (pert to) . . .
   beetle . . **5.** meloe
   berry . . **5.** olive
   bird . . **8.** guachare
   cartel . . **4.** OPEC
   cask . . **4.** rier
   class . . **5.** fatty, fixed **6.** animal **7.** mineral
   8. volatile **9.** essential, vegetable
   cloth . . **8.** linoleum
   coal . . **8.** photogen
   comb form . . **2.** ol **3.** ole

fish . . **7.** escolar
flask . . **4.** olpe
gauge . . **9.** oleometer
glands (birds) . . **9.** uropygial
   11. elaeodochon
lamp . . **7.** lucigen
mineral . . **7.** naphtha
plant . . **6.** sesame **9.** castor-oil
prefix . . **2.** ol
rock . . **5.** shale **9.** limestone
seed . . **3.** til (teel) **6.** sesame **7.** linseed
   8. rapeseed **10.** castor bean, cottonseed
skin . . **5.** sebum
stone . . **4.** hone **9.** whetstone
term . . **5.** oleic
tree . . **4.** eboe (ebo), tung **5.** mahua
   6. illupi **7.** oil palm **9.** candlenut,
   castor-oil
tube . . **5.** vitta
whale . . **5.** sperm
oil of . . .
   cloves . . **7.** eugenol
   myrcia . . **6.** bay oil
   orange blossoms . . **6.** neroil
   roses . . **4.** otto **5.** attar (atar)
   salt . . **7.** bittern
oils . . . **10.** elaeoptene (elaeopten) (opp
   of stearoptene)
oily . . . **3.** fat **4.** glib **5.** bland, oleic, suave
   6. olease, supple **7.** pinguid **8.** unctuous
   9. compliant, plausible **10.** flattering,
   oleaginous **11.** insinuating, subservient
   12. hypocritical
oily liquids . . . **3.** tar **6.** cresol, octane
   7. aniline, picamar **8.** creosote
oily tissue . . . **3.** fat
ointment . . . **4.** balm, cere, lard, nard
   5. salve **6.** balsam, carron, cerate,
   ceroma, grease **7.** pomatum, unguent
   8. liniment **9.** spikenard, xeromyron
   10. petrolatum **11.** embrocation
Oise (France) . . . **5.** Aisne (tributary), river
   10. department
Ojibway secret order . . . **4.** mide (meda)
   9. midewiwin
ojo . . . **5.** oasis
OK . . . **6.** righto **7.** correct
Okinawa . . .
   capital . . **4.** Naha
   island group (64) . . **6.** Ryukyu
   prefecture of . . **5.** Japan
Oklahoma . . .
   capital . . **12.** Oklahoma City
   city . . **3.** Ada **4.** Enid **5.** Tulsa **6.** Lawton
   8. Muskogee **9.** Claremore
   12. Bartlesville
   Five Civilized Tribes . . **5.** Creek
   7. Choctaw **8.** Cherokee, Seminole
   9. Chickasaw
   lake . . **6.** Texoma
   migrant from . . **4.** Okie
   mountain . . **5.** Ozark **8.** Ouachita
   museum . . **6.** Indian **8.** Woolaroc
   native son (famed) . . **10.** Will Rogers
   old name . . **15.** Indian Territory
   State admission . . **11.** Thirty-third
   State bird . . **10.** flycatcher
   State flower . . **9.** mistletoe
   State motto . . **16.** Labor Omnia Vincit
   (Labor Conquers All)
   State nickname . . **6.** Sooner

okra . . . **5.** bendy, gumbo **6.** mallow
old . . . **3.** ald, eld **4.** aged **5.** anile **6.** infirm, senile **7.** ancient, antique, archaic **8.** obsolete **9.** doddering, senescent, venerable **10.** antiquated
old (pert to) . . .
age . . **6.** senile **7.** geratic **8.** gerontic, senility **10.** geriatrics (Med), senescence **11.** gerontology
ancient (very) . . **7.** Ogygian
billy, granny . . **5.** squaw
fashioned . . **4.** fogy **7.** antique **9.** primitive **12.** conservative
hat . . **5.** trite **9.** out-of-date
maid . . **5.** prude **10.** fussbudget
man . . **5.** elder **6.** codger, gaffer, geezer, Nestor **7.** oldster **8.** old-timer **10.** fuddy-duddy
sailor . . **3.** tar **4.** salt
saying . . **3.** saw **5.** adage, maxim
time . . **3.** eld **4.** syne
woman . . **3.** hag **5.** crone **6.** dotard, gammer
womanish . . **5.** anile
Old (pert to) . . .
Bailey . . **12.** English court
Bay State . . **13.** Massachusetts
Dominion . . **8.** Virginia
Empire . . **4.** Maya
English alphabet . . **10.** Anglo-Saxon
Faithful . . **6.** geyser
Franklin State . . **9.** Tennessee
Gentleman Harry . . **5.** Devil
Gooseberry . . **5.** Devil, Satan
Glory . . **15.** Stars and Stripes
Guard (Waterloo) . . **9.** Napoleon's
Hickory . . **13.** Andrew Jackson
Ironsides . . **15.** USS Constitution
Kingdom . . **7.** Memphis (Egypt)
Lady of Threadneedle Street . . **13.** Bank of England
Line State . . **8.** Maryland
Man of the Mountain . . **7.** Profile (The)
Noll . . **14.** Oliver Cromwell
North Church . . **12.** Christ Church
North State . . **13.** North Carolina
Rough and Ready . . **13.** (Gen) Zachary Taylor
Serpent . . **5.** Satan
Sod . . **4.** Erin **7.** Ireland
Sol . . **3.** sun
Stone Age . . **11.** Paleolithic
Three Stars . . **5.** (Gen) Grant
World . . **7.** Eastern
olden . . . **6.** bygone
older . . . **5.** elder **6.** senior **8.** ancestor
oldest . . . **4.** dean **6.** eldest **7.** stalest
Old Testament (pert to) . . .
Books (number) . . **10.** Thirty-nine
Elohim . . **3.** God (The Hexateuch)
Hexateuch . . **13.** first Six Books
Land of riches . . **5.** Ophir
objects (sacred) . . **4.** Urim **7.** Thummim
Pentateuch . . **10.** Law of Moses **14.** first Five Books
writer . . **7.** Elohist (The Hexateuch)
Old World (pert to) . . .
ape . . **7.** Primate **10.** Catarrhina
carnivore . . **5.** genet
falcon . . **5.** saker
herb . . **5.** tansy

lizard . . **5.** Agama
shrub . . **4.** Olax
oleaginous . . . **4.** oily **5.** oleic **8.** unctuous
oleander . . . **6.** Nerium **11.** rhododaphne **12.** rhododendron
oleoresin . . . **5.** anime, elemi **6.** balsam **7.** copaiba
oleum . . . **3.** oil
olfaction . . . **7.** osmesis **8.** smelling **12.** sense of smell
olfactory organ . . . **4.** nose **8.** olfactor
olid . . . **4.** foul **5.** fetid **6.** rancid, smelly **10.** malodorous **11.** strong smell
oligarchy . . . **10.** rule by a few
olinda bug . . . **6.** weevil
olio . . . **4.** olla, stem **6.** medley **7.** mixture **8.** chowchow **9.** burlesque, potpourri **10.** collection, hodgepodge **11.** olla-podrida
oliphant . . . **8.** elephant **9.** ivory horn
oliprance . . . **4.** romp, show **7.** jollity **11.** merrymaking, ostentation
olive (pert to) . . .
branch . . **5.** child, peace **6.** symbol (peace)
color . . **11.** yellow-green
dun . . **3.** fly (fishing)
enzyme . . **6.** olease
family . . **8.** Oleaceae
fly . . **3.** dun **4.** gnat **5.** quill
gray . . **10.** Scotch gray
gum . . **6.** olivil
overripe . . **5.** drupe
stuffed . . **6.** pimola
true . . **4.** Olea
wild . . **8.** oleaster
yard . . **6.** olivet
yellow . . **9.** moss green **10.** chartreuse
olla . . . **3.** jug, pot **4.** olio **8.** palm leaf (palmyra) **11.** olla-podrida
olla-podrida . . . **4.** hash, olio **6.** medley **10.** hodgepodge
oloroso . . . **6.** sherry
olpe . . . **5.** flask **8.** oenochoë **11.** wine pitcher
olycook, olykoek . . . **7.** cruller **8.** doughnut
Olympia . . . **4.** ship **7.** capital (Wash) **8.** heavenly **9.** sanctuary (anc)
Olympiad . . . **14.** four-year period
Olympian god . . . **4.** Ares, Zeus **6.** Apollo, Hermes **8.** Dionysus, Hercules, Poseidon **10.** Hephaestus
Olympian goddess . . . **4.** Hera **6.** Athena, Hestia **7.** Artemis, Demeter **9.** Aphrodite
Olympic cupbearer . . . **8.** Ganymede
Olympic Games (pert to) . . .
honor of . . **4.** Zeus
period . . **14.** four years apart
revival site . . **6.** Athens (1896)
site (first) . . **4.** Elis **7.** Olympia
time of games . . **8.** four days
Olympieion, Olympium . . . **6.** temple (Athens)
Olympus (Gr) . . . **3.** sky **5.** Mount **6.** heaven **8.** mountain
Olympus (Hind) . . . **4.** Meru
Omaha . . . **4.** city (Neb) **5.** Sioux **6.** Indian
Omar Khayyam (pert to) . . .
country . . **4.** Iran **6.** Persia
fish (fabled) . . **3.** mah

poem . . **8.** Rubaiyat
omasum . . . **9.** manyplies **10.** psalterium
   12. third stomach
ombro (comb form) . . . **4.** rain
ombrometer . . . **9.** rain gauge
omega . . . **3.** end **4.** last **5.** final **6.** letter
   (Gr)
omen . . . **4.** bode, sign **5.** abode,
   knell, token **6.** augury **7.** auspice,
   portent, presage **8.** forebode, foreshow
   9. abodement **10.** divination
   15. prognostication
omer . . . **5.** ephah, sheaf **9.** fifty days
   (Passover to Pentecost)
ominous . . . **4.** dour, trim **8.** sinister
   9. ferocious **10.** inexorable, portentous
   12. inauspicious
omission . . . **4.** want **5.** caret, error
   7. neglect **9.** oversight **11.** deficiency,
   leaving out **13.** nonobservance
omission of end syllables . . . **7.** apocope
omission of words . . . **8.** ellipsis
omit . . . **4.** dele, pass, skip **5.** elide
   6. delete, ignore **7.** exclude **11.** leave
   undone
omitting . . . **7.** elision **9.** excepting,
   excluding **10.** precluding
omneity . . . **7.** allness **16.** all-
   comprehensive
omnipotent . . . **6.** divine **8.** almighty
   9. unequaled, unlimited **11.** all-powerful
omniscient . . . **4.** wise **6.** divine **7.** learned
   10. all-knowing
omnitude . . . **7.** allness **8.** totality
   12. universality
omnivorous . . . **6.** greedy **9.** all-eating
   10. gluttonous
omoplate . . . **7.** scapula
omphalos . . . **3.** hut **4.** knob **5.** altar,
   navel **6.** center **9.** umbilicus
on . . . **2.** at **4.** atop, upon **5.** above, ahead,
   along **6.** toward **7.** against, forward
   10. concerning **13.** juxtaposition
On (Bib) . . . **7.** Baalbek **8.** holy city
   10. Heliopolis (Egypt) **12.** City of the
   Sun
on (pert to) . . .
   account of . . **3.** for
   all sides . . **5.** about **6.** around
   and on . . **7.** forever, tedious **9.** tediously
   behalf of . . **3.** for
   dit . . **5.** rumor **6.** report
   going . . **7.** forward **10.** proceeding
   grand scale . . **4.** epic
   hand . . **4.** here **7.** present **9.** available
   high . . **5.** aloft
   other side . . **4.** over **6.** across
   sheltered side . . **4.** alee
   this side . . **3.** cis (pref) **9.** cisalpine
      10. cismontane, cispontine
   windward side . . **8.** aweather
onager . . . **3.** ass **5.** kiang **8.** catapult
once in a while . . . **9.** erstwhile **10.** now
   and then **12.** occasionally
once upon a time . . . **6.** one day **7.** the
   past, time was **8.** formerly **10.** the
   long ago
Oncorhynchus . . . **6.** salmon
ondoyant . . . **4.** wavy (art)
one . . . **2.** an, un **3.** ace, ain, ein **4.** unit
   5. alone, unity, whole **6.** person, single

   9. unmarried **10.** individual
one (pert to) . . .
   after the other . . **8.** serially, seriatim
      12. successfully
   bearing heraldic arms . . **7.** armiger
   behind the other . . **6.** tandem
   born in serfdom . . **4.** neif
   bringing good luck . . **6.** mascot
   by one . . **6.** apiece, singly **10.** one at
      a time **12.** individually
   comb form . . **3.** uni **4.** mono
   curious . . **6.** gossip **8.** quidnunc
   despondent in views . . **9.** pessimist
   fond of women . . **11.** philogynist
   footed . . **6.** uniped
   frantic for freedom . .
      15. eleutheromaniac
   gigantic in size . . **5.** giant, titan
   happy in views . . **8.** optimist
   horse . . **5.** petty **6.** little **8.** inferior
      10. second-rate **13.** insignificant
   in a thousand . . **6.** oddity **7.** paragon,
      prodigy
   in second childhood . . **6.** dotard
   instructed in secret system . . **5.** epopt
      8. initiate
   living on another . . **8.** parasite
   moving stealthily . . **7.** prowler
   sided . . **5.** askew **7.** partial **10.** prejudiced,
      unilateral
   thousand . . **3.** mil
   time . . **7.** quondam **8.** formerly
   undergoing change . . **6.** mutant
oneberry . . . **9.** hackberry
   14. partridgeberry
one devoted to . . .
   deviltry . . **7.** hellion
   fast driving . . **4.** jehu **7.** speeder
   indolence . . **10.** daydreamer, lotus-eater
   own opinion . . **6.** bigot
   physical feats . . **7.** athlete
   pursuit . . **3.** ist (suff)
   table delicacies . . **7.** epicure
onefold . . . **6.** simple, single **7.** sincere
   9. guileless
onegite . . . **8.** amethyst
Oneida . . . **6.** Indian **8.** Iroquois
   9. Community (NY)
oneiros . . . **5.** dream
oneirotic . . . **6.** dreams (pert to)
oneism . . . **6.** egoism, monism
oneness . . . **5.** union, unity **7.** concord
   8. identity, sameness **9.** agreement,
   aloneness, constancy **10.** loneliness,
   singleness, uniformity, uniqueness
   11. singularity **13.** undividedness
one of . . .
   ancient race . . **4.** Mede **7.** Iberian
   Buddhist precepts . . **6.** nidana
   Persian dynasty . . **8.** Sassanid
   religious sect . . **10.** Anabaptist
   the Bears . . **4.** Ursa
   the Greek Wise Men . . **6.** Thales
   the initiated . . **5.** epopt
   twins . . **5.** gemel (Her)
onerous . . . **4.** load **5.** heavy **6.** burden
   7. onerose **9.** difficult, laborious,
   ponderous **10.** burdensome, oppressive
   12. impedimental
one versed in . . .
   children's diseases . . **12.** pediatrician

law .. **6.** legist
literature .. **6.** savant **9.** literatus
memory .. **9.** mnemonist
politics .. **9.** statesman
religious law .. **8.** canonist
resources, wealth .. **9.** economist
one who ...
  absconds .. **6.** eloper **8.** decamper, deserter
  appropriates .. **9.** pre-emptor
  attacks .. **9.** aggressor
  believes in all religions .. **6.** omnist
  believes in personal God .. **5.** deist
  believes in self .. **9.** solipsist
  beseeches .. **7.** pleader
  brings meat to royal table .. **7.** dapifer, steward
  cherishes .. **8.** fosterer
  collects voluntary taxes .. **6.** tither
  conveys property .. **7.** alienor
  dies for a cause .. **6.** martyr
  differs .. **4.** anti **9.** dissenter, dissident
  disowns .. **10.** repudiator
  displays learning .. **6.** pedant
  disposes by will .. **7.** devisor
  edits .. **7.** reviser
  feigns illness .. **10.** malingerer
  fights for cause .. **8.** crusader
  forsakes faith principles .. **8.** apostate
  frustrates a plan .. **7.** marplot
  gives up .. **9.** abnegator
  grants by deed .. **7.** remiser
  hates argument .. **10.** misologist
  hates people .. **11.** misanthrope
  holds office .. **2.** in **9.** incumbent
  inculcates .. **7.** infuser **9.** instiller
  inflicts retribution .. **7.** nemesis
  misuses authority .. **6.** satrap
  plunders .. **6.** sacker **8.** pillager
  practises palmistry .. **11.** chiromancer
  prevents entrance .. **5.** hajib
  quarrels .. **5.** rowdy
  removes nuisance .. **6.** abator
  rules, manages .. **6.** gerent
  sells provisions to troops .. **6.** sutler
  shoots from ambush .. **6.** sniper
  sponges .. **6.** cadger **8.** parasite
  stays .. **5.** bider
  summons spirits .. **8.** evocator
  testifies .. **8.** deponent
  transfers property .. **7.** alienor
ongall ... **5.** onset **8.** attack
onion ... **3.** set (bulbs) **4.** boll, bulb, cepa, leek **5.** chive, cibol, pearl, reeve **6.** Allium **7.** Bermuda, onionet, shallot **8.** eschalot, rareripe, scallion
onkos (Gr) ... **7.** topknot
only ... **4.** just, lone, mere, sole **5.** chief **6.** lonely, merely, simple, simply, single, singly, solely **8.** uniquely **11.** exclusively **13.** companionless **14.** above all others
onocentaur ... **3.** ape **5.** demon (fabled)
onomasticon ... **7.** lexicon **10.** dictionary, vocabulary (Gr)
onomatology (science of) ... **5.** names **11.** terminology
onomatopoeic ... **6.** echoic **9.** imitative (of natural sound)
onset, onslaught ... **6.** attack **7.** assault **11.** rushing upon, setting upon
Ontario ...
  Bay .. **6.** Hudson
  capital .. **7.** Toronto
  city .. **6.** Ottawa **7.** Timmins **8.** Hamilton
  lake .. **9.** Great Lake (one of five)
  province .. **6.** Canada
  river .. **6.** Ottawa, Thames **7.** Niagara **10.** St Lawrence
ontogeny ... **9.** evolution
ontology (science of) ... **5.** being **7.** reality
onus ... **4.** duty, load **6.** burden, charge **10.** impediment, imposition, obligation
onus probandi ... **13.** burden of proof
onward, onwards ... **5.** ahead, forth **6.** future, moving **7.** forward **8.** forwards, progress **9.** in advance
onychauxis ... **14.** nail overgrowth
onyx ... **6.** nicolo (niccolo), tecali
ooid ... **9.** egg-shaped
oology (science of) ... **8.** bird eggs
oomancy (divination by) ... **4.** eggs
oont ... **5.** camel **13.** beast of burden
oop ... **4.** join **5.** unite
oopak, oopack ... **3.** tea (black)
oorial ... **3.** sha **5.** sheep, urial
ooze ... **3.** bog **4.** drip, leak, seep, sipe, soak **5.** exude, marsh **6.** be damp **7.** leather **8.** transude **9.** percolate
oozy ... **4.** miry **5.** muddy, slimy
opah ... **4.** fish, soko **8.** kingfish **9.** Lampridae
opal ... **3.** gem **4.** blue **5.** stone **7.** hyalite **10.** pearliness
opal, variety of ... **4.** wood **5.** black, noble, pitch, resin **6.** common **7.** girasol, hyalite **8.** menilite, precious **9.** cacholong, geyserite, harlequin **10.** chalcedony
opalescent ... **6.** pearly **7.** opaline **8.** irisated **10.** iridescent
opaque ... **4.** dark **6.** obtuse, stupid **7.** obscure **8.** eyeshade **10.** not shining **13.** unilluminated **14.** not transparent
open ... **3.** ope **4.** ajar, bare, free, undo **5.** agape, begin, clear, frank, overt, plain, start, untie **6.** candid, honest, patent, public, reveal, unbolt, unfold, unfurl, unlock, unseal, unstop, vacant **7.** artless, evident, exposed, natural, obvious, sincere, unbosom, unclose **8.** apparent, commence, disclose, expanded, initiate, patulous, revealed, unclosed, unfasten **9.** spreading, uncertain, uncovered, unfeigned **10.** accessible, unreserved **11.** unprotected **12.** questionable
open (pert to) ...
  acknowledgment .. **6.** avowal
  air .. **8.** alfresco
  and shut .. **7.** assured, obvious **11.** prearranged
  bursting .. **10.** dehiscence
  cabinet .. **7.** étagère
  country .. **5.** veldt, weald
  court .. **4.** area **5.** patio
  door .. **6.** policy **11.** hospitality
  eyed .. **7.** curious **8.** vigilant **9.** attentive, expectant
  for discussion .. **4.** moot
  fully .. **4.** wide **9.** dehiscent, full-blown
  land .. **4.** moor **5.** heath **6.** desert, plains
  out .. **6.** deploy (Mil)

partly . . **3.** mid **4.** ajar
passage in forests . . **5.** glade
to scorn . . **9.** derisible
to view . . **5.** overt
opening . . . **2.** os **3.** bay, gap **4.** door,
gate, hole, loop, pore, rift, slot,
vent **5.** cleft, mouth, sinus, start
6. breach, eyelet, hiatus, outlet,
portal **7.** display, foramen, initial,
orifice, vacancy **8.** aperture, fenestra,
position **9.** admission, beginning
10. passageway, unfoldment
11. entranceway, opportunity
opening (pert to) . . .
chess . . **6.** gambit
ear . . **4.** burr
enlarge . . **4.** ream
from third ventricle (Anat) . . **4.** pila
having . . **10.** fenestrate
in a mold . . **6.** ingate
minute . . **5.** stoma
narrow . . **4.** rima, slot **7.** crevice
9. stenopaic
nasal . . **4.** nare
small . . **4.** pore **5.** chink **6.** cranny, eyelet,
lacuna **7.** foramen, orifice, pinhole
wide (Bot) . . **9.** dehiscent
openings . . . **3.** ora **7.** stomata
openwork . . . **6.** eyelet **7.** Madeira, tracery
10. decoration
opera (pert to) . . .
comic (singer) . . **5.** buffa, buffo
7. buffoon
glass . . **7.** binocle **9.** binocular, lorgnette
hat . . **5.** crush, gibus **6.** topper
kind . . **4.** soap **5.** horse **8.** burletta
singer . . **4.** bass, diva **5.** buffa, buffo,
tenor **7.** buffoon, soprano **10.** basso
buffo, coloratura
solo . . **4.** aria **5.** scena
star . . **4.** diva **10.** prima donna
text . . **8.** libretto
opera, composer . . . **5.** Bizet, Gluck,
Haydn, Verdi **6.** Glinka, Gounod,
Handel, Mozart, Wagner **7.** Puccini,
Rossini **9.** Donizetti, Meyerbeer
11. Deems Taylor **14.** Rimski-Korsakov
(Korsakoff)
opera, drama . . . **4.** Aida **5.** Boris,
Faust, Orfeo, Thais, Tosca **6.** Bohême,
Carmen, Coq d'or, Daphne, Isolde
7. Alceste, Fidelio **9.** Lohengrin,
Pagliacci, Rigoletto **10.** Magic Flute,
Prince Igor, Tannhäuser **11.** Don
Giovanni, Il Travatore **13.** Peter Ibbetson
14. Tales of Hoffman **15.** Hansel and
Gretel, Madame Butterfly **16.** Marriage
of Figaro
operation . . . **6.** action, agency **7.** surgery
8. creation **9.** influence **11.** functioning,
transaction
Operation Overlord . . . **4.** D-Day
16. Normandy invasion
operation, surgical . . . **6.** trepan
8. excision **9.** resection **10.** amputation,
castration **11.** exploratory
12. appendectomy, hysterectomy
13. tonsillectomy
operative . . . **6.** worker **7.** artisan, working
8. mechanic **9.** detective
operative, become . . . **5.** inure (enure)

operator . . . **5.** agent, quack **6.** dealer,
worker **7.** creator, handler, surgeon
10. mountebank, speculator
operculum (Bot) . . . **3.** cap, lid **7.** stopper
8. covering
operose . . . **4.** busy **8.** diligent **9.** difficult,
laborious **11.** painstaking
Ophidia . . . **6.** snakes **8.** reptiles, serpents
9. Serpentes
ophidian . . . **5.** snake, viper **7.** serpent
ophiolatry . . . **12.** snake worship
ophthalmic . . . **6.** ocular **7.** optical **9.** eye
region
ophthalmology, science . . . **6.** the eye
opiate . . . **4.** drug, hemp, snow **5.** opium
6. heroin **7.** anodyne, cocaine, hashish
(hasheesh), soother **8.** narcotic
9. analgesic, paregoric **11.** somniferous
12. somnifacient
opine . . . **4.** deem **5.** judge, think **6.** remark
7. opinion, suppose **10.** conjecture
opinion . . . **4.** idea, view **6.** belief, esteem,
notion, report **7.** feeling **8.** judgment,
two cents **9.** sentiment **10.** estimation,
impression, ober dictum, reputation
opinion (pert to) . . .
expert . . **9.** expertise
expression, common . . **5.** theme
expression, formal . . **4.** vote
religious, unorthodox . . **6.** heresy
opinions (pert to) . . .
collection . . **9.** anthology, symposium
professed . . **5.** credo
opium . . . **4.** drug **8.** narcotic **10.** intoxicant
opium (pert to) . . .
concentrate . . **6.** heroin
derivative (Chem) . . **7.** meconic
Egyptian . . **8.** thebaine
extract . . **7.** chandoo (chandu), codeine
8. morphine **9.** narcotine **10.** papaverine
overuse . . **8.** opiumism
poppy seed . . **3.** maw
source . . **5.** poppy
tincture . . **9.** paregoric
variety . . **6.** Indian, Smyrna, Turkey
7. Chinese, Persian
opodeldoc . . . **7.** plaster **8.** liniment
opodidymus . . . **7.** monster (two-headed)
opossum . . . **7.** Marmosa **9.** didelphid,
marsupial, phalanger
opossum (pert to) . . .
S America . . **5.** quica **7.** sarigue
variety . . **5.** mouse, water, wooly
water . . **5.** yapok (yapock)
wood . . **10.** silver bell
opponent . . . **3.** foe **4.** anti **5.** enemy, rival
7. adverse **8.** opposite **9.** adversary,
combatant **10.** antagonist
opportune . . . **3.** fit, pat **5.** ready
6. timely **7.** apropos **8.** suitable
9. expedient, well-timed **10.** convenient
11. appropriate
opportunist . . . **10.** politician, vacillator
opportunity . . . **4.** turn **6.** chance
7. opening **8.** occasion **12.** circumstance
16. suitable occasion
oppose . . . **3.** pit **4.** deny, face **5.** fight,
rebel **6.** expose, oppugn, refute, resist
7. contest, exhibit, gainsay **8.** confront
10. antagonize, contradict, contravene,
counteract

opposed . . . 3. met 4. anti, vied
   5. coped 6. averse, pitted 7. adverse,
   fronted 8. contrary, renitent, resisted
   9. contested, withstood 12. oppositional
opposed (pert to) . . .
   against . . 6. pitted
   lee . . 5. stoss
   to change . . 7. die-hard 11. reactionary
      12. conservative
   to entad (inward) . . 5. ectad
   zenith . . 5. nadir
opposite . . . 5. polar 6. facing 7. adverse,
   antonym, hostile, opposed, reverse
   8. contrary, converse 9. different,
   repugnant 10. opposition
   12. antagonistic 13. contradictory
   14. contrapositive
opposite (pert to) . . .
   directly . . 10. antipodean
   exact . . 8. antipode
   in action, in nature . . 5. polar 7. inverse
   prefix . . 6. contra
   science . . 3. art
   to spring tide . . 4. neap
opposition . . . 9. hostility, opponency
   10. antagonism, antithesis, refutation,
   resistance 11. contrariety, disapproval
   13. contradiction
oppress . . . 4. rape 5. crush 6. burden,
   harass, nither (Scot), ravish 7. depress,
   swelter 8. distress, macerate, suppress
   9. overpower, overwhelm, persecute,
   tyrannize 10. extinguish
oppressive . . . 5. harsh 6. severe,
   stuffy, sultry 7. onerous 8. rigorous
   9. ponderous 10. burdensome,
   depressing, tyrannical
oppressor . . . 4. czar (tsar), Nero
   6. despot, tyrant 8. autocrat, burdener
   11. Simon Legree
opprobrious . . . 7. abusive 8. despised,
   infamous 9. insulting, offensive
   10. scurrilous 11. disgraceful
   12. contumelious
opprobrium . . . 5. odium 6. infamy
   8. disgrace 11. malediction
oppugn . . . 6. assail, oppose
   10. controvert, counteract
oppugnant . . . 7. hostile, opposed
   8. contrary 12. antagonistic
   13. counteractive
Ops (pert to) . . .
   called also . . 10. Ops Consiva
   consort of . . 6. Consus, Saturn
   Festival . . 6. Opalia
   Greek counterpart . . 4. Rhea
   Roman goddess of . . 7. Harvest
opsigamy . . . 14. old-age marriage
opt . . . 4. pick 5. elect 6. choose 11. make
   a choice
optic . . . 6. ocular, visual 11. optological
optical (pert to) . . .
   device . . 9. stenopaic
   glass . . 4. lens
   illusion . . 6. mirage
   instrument . . 5. prism 7. alidade, reticle
      9. eriometer, optometer 10. microscope
   membrane . . 6. retina
   organ . . 3. eye
optic defect . . . 6. myopia
optimistic . . . 4. rosy 7. hopeful, roseate

8. cheerful, sanguine 9. expectant
   10. auspicious
optimum . . . 4. best 7. maximum 13. most
   favorable
option . . . 6. choice, future (Finan)
   7. refusal 8. free will 11. alternative
   13. right to choose
optional . . . 8. elective 9. voluntary
   10. permissive 13. not compulsory
opulence . . . 6. plenty, riches, wealth
   9. abundance, affluence, amplitude,
   profusion
opulent . . . 4. rich 6. lavish 7. profuse,
   wealthy 8. abundant, affluent
   9. luxuriant
opulus . . . 11. guelder-rose 13. cranberry
   tree
opus . . . 4. work 5. étude 10. embroidery,
   needlework 11. composition
oquassa . . . 5. trout
oracle . . . 4. seer 5. sibyl 6. Dodona,
   medium, mentor 7. prophet, wise man
   8. Delphian (Delphic) 10. revelation
oracular . . . 4. wise 5. vatic (vatical)
   9. prophetic 10. predictive
   11. forecasting
orage . . . 5. storm 7. tempest
oral . . . 5. parol, vocal 6. spoken, verbal
   10. not written 11. nuncupative
orang . . . 9. orangutan (orangutang)
orange (pert to) . . .
   Bowl site . . 5. Miami
   bird . . 7. tanager
   color . . 5. ocher, peach 6. carrot 7. apricot
      8. mandarin
   covering . . 4. rind
   flower oil . . 6. meroli
   genus . . 6. Citrus
   heraldry . . 5. tenné
   kind . . 4. mock 5. hedge, navel, Osage
      8. bergamot, mandarin, Valencia
      9. tangerine
   leaf . . 6. karamu
   marigold . . 9. tangerine
   membrane . . 4. zest
   mock . . 7. seringa
   seed . . 3. pip
Orangeman . . . 14. North Irelander
orangutan . . . 4. mias 5. orang, Pongo,
   satyr, Simia
orate . . . 5. plead, speak, spiel 8. harangue
oration . . . 5. éloge 6. eulogy, prayer,
   sermon, speech 7. lecture 8. encomium,
   petition 9. discourse
orator . . . 6. rhetor 7. speaker 9. perorator
   10. petitioner 11. rhetorician,
   spellbinder
orator, famed . . . 5. Bryan (Wm Jennings)
   6. Cicero 9. Churchill 11. Demosthenes
oratory . . . 6. chapel 7. chantry
   9. elocution, eloquence
orb . . . 3. eye, sun 4. ball, moon, star
   5. earth, globe, world 6. bereft, circle,
   planet, sphere 7. enclose 8. encircle,
   insignia, surround
orbed . . . 5. lunar, round
orbit . . . 4. path 5. globe, route 6. sphere
   7. circuit 10. trajectory
orbit (pert to) . . .
   cavity . . 9. eye socket
   curve . . 10. trajectory

of a planet.. **7.** ellipse
point.. **5.** apsis **6.** apogee (farthest)
  7. perigee (nearest)
orc, Orca ... **5.** whale **7.** grampus
orchestra (pert to) ...
  bells.. **12.** glockenspiel
  circle.. **7.** parquet **8.** parterre
  small.. **11.** symphonette
orchestra instrument group ...
  brass.. **4.** horn, tuba **6.** cornet **7.** trumpet
  8. trombone
  percussion.. **4.** drum **7.** cymbals, timpani
  (tympani) **8.** triangle
  strings.. **5.** cello, viola **6.** violin
  10. contrabass **11.** violoncello
  wind.. **4.** oboe **5.** flute **7.** bassoon
  8. clarinet
orchid ... **4.** Disa **5.** vanda **6.** Ophrys
  7. Listera, lycaste, pogonia **8.** arethusa,
  Cattleya, Oncidium **9.** cymbidium,
  puttyroot **10.** letterleaf
orchid (pert to) ...
  appendage.. **8.** caudicle
  handsomest.. **4.** Disa
  largest.. **10.** letterleaf
  meal.. **5.** salep
  petal.. **8.** labellum
  tuber, root.. **5.** salep **7.** cullion
Orcus ... **3.** God (Rom) **5.** Hades, Pluto
  (Gr) **10.** lower world
ordain ... **4.** plan **5.** allot, enact,
  equip **6.** decree **7.** appoint, arrange,
  command, destine, install **8.** canonize
  9. institute **10.** predestine
ordeal ... **4.** gaff, test **5.** trial **7.** sorcery
  8. judgment **10.** experience (painful)
order ... **3.** bid **4.** fiat, ordo, rank,
  rule, sect, will **5.** array, class, edict,
  genus, money **6.** cosmos, decree,
  direct, enjoin, genera (pl), manage,
  system **7.** arrange, command, dispose,
  mandate, prepare, verdict **8.** regulate,
  sequence **9.** condition, procedure
  10. injunction **11.** arrangement
order (pert to) ...
  back.. **6.** remand
  connecting.. **6.** in turn **8.** seriatim
  cosmic.. **3.** tao **4.** rita
  for writ.. **7.** precipe
  good.. **6.** eutaxy
  grammar.. **5.** taxis
  judicial.. **4.** fiat, writ **7.** summons
  proper.. **6.** kilter
  written.. **6.** billet
Order, architecture ... **5.** Doric, Ionic
  6. Tuscan **8.** Etruscan **10.** Corinthian
Order, association ... **4.** Club **5.** Guild
  7. DeMolay, Society, St Clare
  8. Sodality, Sorority **9.** The Garter,
  Trappists **10.** Fellowship, Fraternity,
  Sisterhood **11.** Brotherhood, Eastern
  Star, Purple Heart **12.** The Rising Sun
ordered ... **4.** bade, trim **7.** regular
  8. arranged, measured, ordained
  9. regulated
orderly ... **4.** neat, tidy, trim **7.** regular,
  uniform **8.** obedient, peaceful
  9. attendant, regularly, shipshape
  10. methodical, systematic
order of ...
  amphibians.. **5.** Anura

aquatic animals.. **7.** Cetacea
holy beings.. **9.** hierarchy
insects.. **7.** Diptera
mammals.. **8.** Edentata, Primates
mites.. **6.** acarid
the day.. **8.** schedule **12.** instructions
whales.. **4.** Cete
ordinal ... **6.** number, ritual, serial
  10. succession **11.** Book of Rules (Eccl),
  categorical
ordinance ... **3.** law **4.** rite **5.** bylaw, edict
  6. assize, decree **7.** control, statute
  8. decretum **9.** allotment, direction,
  enactment, sacrament **10.** management,
  regulation
ordinarily ... **7.** plainly, usually
  8. commonly **9.** generally, naturally
  11. customarily
ordinary ... **4.** ruck, so-so **5.** judge,
  nomic, plain, prosy, usual **6.** common,
  normal, tavern **7.** average, natural,
  prosaic, vulgate **8.** everyday, habitual,
  mediocre, plebeian, workaday **9.** of
  the Mass **10.** table d'hôte
ordinate ... **6.** ordain **7.** appoint, orderly,
  regular **8.** moderate **9.** harmonize
  10. co-ordinate
ordination ... **5.** order **11.** appointment,
  arrangement, disposition
  12. organization
ordnance ... **4.** guns **5.** armor, orgue
  7. petards, rabinet, weapons
  8. armament, firearms, supplies
  9. artillery, torpedoes **10.** ammunition
  14. apparatus belli
ordo ... **5.** order **11.** publication
ore ... **3.** tin **4.** gold, iron, lead, paco
  5. brass, metal, ochre **6.** copper,
  silver, speiss **7.** mercury, mineral,
  seaweed, uranium **8.** cinnabar, tungsten
  9. loadstone (lodestone) **11.** quicksilver
ore (pert to) ...
  box.. **6.** sluice
  deposit.. **4.** lode, mine **7.** bonanza
  fuser.. **7.** smelter
  horizontal layer.. **5.** stope
  impure.. **6.** speiss
  iron.. **5.** ocher **8.** hematite **9.** magnetite
  lead.. **6.** galena
  loading platform.. **4.** plat
  machine separator.. **6.** vanner
  refuse.. **6.** scoria **8.** tailings
  roller.. **9.** edgestone
  silver.. **5.** noble (metal)
  sluice.. **5.** trunk
  stirrer.. **5.** dolly
  tin.. **5.** scove
  trough.. **6.** strake
  vein.. **4.** lode **5.** scrin, stope
  worthless.. **5.** matte
oread ... **5.** nymph **7.** seamaid
Oregon ...
  capital.. **5.** Salem
  caves.. **11.** Marble Halls
  city.. **6.** Eugene **7.** Astoria, Medford
  8. Portland **12.** Klamath Falls
  crab apple.. **7.** powitch
  emigrant route.. **11.** Oregon Trail
  famed persons.. **4.** Gray (Capt) **5.** Astor,
  Clark, Lewis
  Indian.. **5.** Modoc **7.** Chinook, Klamath

8. Nez Percé
mountain.. **4.** Hood **5.** Coast **8.** Cascades
native nickname.. **7.** webfoot
river.. **5.** Rogue **7.** Klamath **8.** Columbia
  10. Willamette
State admission.. **11.** Thirty-third
State motto.. **8.** The Union
State nickname.. **6.** Beaver **13.** Sawdust
  Empire
wind.. **7.** chinook
oremus... **9.** let us pray
Oreortyx... **5.** quail
Orestes (pert to)...
father.. **9.** Agamemnon
friend.. **7.** Pylades
mother.. **12.** Clytemnestra
sister.. **7.** Electra
wife.. **8.** Hermione
orf, orfe... **3.** ide **4.** fish
orfevrerie... **7.** jewelry **9.** gold plate
organ (pert to)...
anatomy.. **3.** ear, eye **4.** lung, nose
  5. brain, heart, liver **6.** kidney, syrinx,
  tongue, tonsil **7.** viscera (pl)
bristlelike.. **4.** seta
desk.. **7.** console
fish.. **8.** drumfish
honey-secreting.. **7.** nectary
plant.. **5.** stoma **7.** tendril
motion.. **6.** muscle
respiratory.. **4.** lung
secretion.. **5.** gland
spider's spinner.. **9.** spinneret
stop (music).. **8.** register
tactile.. **6.** feeler **8.** tentacle
organic... **5.** state, vital **6.** innate
  8. inherent **9.** organized **10.** structural
  11. fundamental **14.** constitutional
organic (pert to)...
compound.. **5.** amine, ester **6.** enzyme,
  ketone
disease.. **11.** organopathy
memory.. **5.** mneme
radical.. **5.** ethyl
remains.. **5.** azoic
soil.. **5.** humus
organism (pert to)...
bacterial.. **4.** germ **7.** microbe
body of.. **4.** soma
elementary.. **5.** monad
minute.. **5.** spore **6.** amoeba
pelagic.. **6.** nekton
plant.. **5.** spore
potential.. **7.** idorgan
sea.. **6.** nekton **7.** benthos **8.** plankton
type.. **5.** plant **6.** animal **9.** vegetable
vegetable.. **4.** tree **5.** plant
organization... **4.** bloc, sect, unit
  5. cadre, guild, party, setup **6.** empire
  11. association, corporation
  12. constitution **13.** establishment
  14. classification
organized body... **5.** corps, posse
organized matter... **5.** fauna, flora
  6. living, nekton **7.** animate, benthos
  8. plankton
organology, science... **10.** phrenology
  13. splanchnology
organoscopy... **10.** phrenology
orgueil... **5.** pride **11.** haughtiness
orgy... **4.** lark, romp **5.** binge, revel,

rites (anc), spree **6.** frolic, ritual,
  shindy **7.** debauch, revelry, shindig,
  wassail **8.** carousal **11.** celebration,
  merrymaking
oribi... **7.** bleebok, Ourebia **8.** antelope
oriel... **3.** bay **6.** recess, window
  7. balcony, gallery, portion **8.** corridor
  10. moucharaby **11.** meshrabiyeh
  (Muslim)
orient... **4.** dawn **7.** eastern, shining,
  sunrise **8.** oriental, pellucid
  11. resplendent
Orient... **4.** Asia, East **6.** Levant
oriental (pert to)...
abode, gateway.. **3.** dar
animal.. **4.** zebu
archangel.. **5.** Uriel
beverage.. **6.** arrack
building.. **6.** pagoda
burden bearer.. **5.** hamal
cap (sheepskin).. **6.** calpac (calpack)
caravansary.. **4.** khan **5.** serai **6.** imaret
carpet.. **4.** kali
carriage.. **10.** jinrikisha (jinricksha)
cart, wagon.. **5.** araba
chief.. **4.** Khan **6.** Mikado
Christian.. **5.** Uniat
corn.. **4.** para
cosmetic.. **4.** kohl
council.. **5.** Divan
cymbals.. **4.** zels
deity.. **3.** Bel
destiny.. **6.** Kismet
disease.. **8.** beriberi
dish.. **4.** rice **5.** pilau (pilaw) **6.** pilaff
  8. chop suey, chow mein
drug.. **5.** opium **6.** heroin **7.** hashish
  (hasheesh)
drum.. **6.** tom-tom
dulcimer.. **6.** santir
fan.. **3.** ogi
food.. **4.** rice **5.** salep
garment.. **3.** aba **6.** sarong
guitar.. **5.** sitar
head cover.. **6.** turban
hospice.. **6.** imaret
inn.. **5.** serai
instrument (Mus).. **7.** samisen
laborer.. **6.** coolie (cooly)
leader.. **4.** amir (ameer)
liquor.. **4.** sake, saki
litter.. **5.** dooly (doolie) **9.** palanquín
lute.. **3.** tar
maid.. **4.** amah, ayah, eyah
manservant.. **5.** hamal **6.** coolie
marketplace.. **6.** bazaar
monkey.. **7.** macaque
nurse.. **4.** amah, ayah (governess)
obeisance.. **6.** salaam (salam)
pagoda.. **3.** taa
people.. **4.** Sere (anc) **5.** Asian, Malay
  6. Indian **7.** Chinese, Eastern, Tartars
  (Tatars) **8.** Japanese **10.** Mohammedan
pipe.. **8.** narghile
rice paste.. **3.** ame
rug.. **8.** sedjadeh **11.** Baluchistan
ruler.. **4.** Khan, Shah **5.** sahib (saheb)
  6. caliph (calif), sultan
sabre.. **8.** scimitar
sailor.. **6.** lascar
sash.. **3.** obi

tambourine . . **5.** daira
taxi . . **7.** ricksha (rickshaw) **10.** jinrikisha
trousers (women) . . **9.** shaksheer
vessel (sailing) . . **4.** dhow, saic
wagon . . **5.** araba
warehouse . . **6.** godown
wind . . **7.** monsoon
worker . . **6.** coolie (cooly)
orifice . . . **4.** hole, lura, pore, vent **5.** inlet,
   mouth, porus, stoma **6.** outlet, porule
   7. chimney, opening, ostiole **8.** aperture,
   bunghole, spiracle
origin . . . **3.** nee **4.** germ, rise, root,
   seed **5.** alpha, birth, cause, start
   6. nature, parent, source **7.** genesis
   9. beginning, etymology, inception,
   parentage **10.** inconabula, provenance
   11. provenience **12.** commencement,
   fountainhead
original . . . **3.** new **5.** basic, first, novel
   6. fontal, native, primal, primer,
   unused **7.** genuine, pattern, primary
   8. pristine **9.** aborigine, beginning,
   inventive, primitive **10.** inimitable
   11. fundamental, origination
   12. commencement
original copy . . . **6.** ectype
originate . . . **4.** coin, open, rise, stem
   5. arise, begin, breed, start **6.** author,
   create, derive, invent **7.** emanate,
   produce **8.** generate, initiate
   11. etymologize
originator . . . **5.** cause, maker **7.** creator
   8. inventor, producer **9.** contriver
   10. discoverer
oriole . . . **5.** pirol **6.** golden, hooded,
   loriot, Mimeta **7.** orchard **8.** Bullock's
   9. Baltimore, Icteridae
Orion (pert to) . . .
   Astron . . **7.** Dog Star **10.** Canis Major
   11. Orion's Hound **13.** constellation
   color . . **11.** Holland blue
   Gr Myth . . **6.** hunter
   Jacob's Staff . . **10.** Yard and Ell
   13. Golden Yardarm
   slain by . . **7.** Artemis
   star . . **5.** Rigel
orison . . . **6.** prayer
Orkney Islands, Scotland . . .
   capital . . **8.** Kirkwall
   Firth . . **8.** Pentland
   fishing grounds . . **4.** haaf
   island, largest . . **6.** Pomona
   President, Supreme Court . . **4.** foud
   stone tower (Prehist) . . **5.** broch
orle (Her) . . . **6.** border, fillet, wreath
   7. bearing, chaplet **10.** escutcheon
   (voided)
Orloff . . . **5.** horse **7.** diamond (Russ,
   194 3/4 carats)
orlop . . . **4.** deck (lowest)
Ormazd (Pers) . . . **5.** deity (supreme)
ormer . . . **7.** abalone **8.** ear shell
ornament . . . **4.** ouch, semé **5.** adorn,
   decor, gutta, honor **6.** amulet, brooch,
   emboss, finery, sequin **7.** antefix
   8. appliqué, decorate **9.** embellish
   10. decoration **13.** embellishment
ornament (pert to) . . .
   apex . . **6.** finial
   ball . . **6.** pompon

bell-shaped . . **9.** clochette
Bible . . **4.** Urim
boat-shaped . . **3.** nef
brilliant . . **4.** gaud **5.** spang **6.** sequin,
   tinsel **7.** spangle
circular . . **7.** rosette
delicate . . **7.** tracery
diamond-shaped . . **11.** epigonation
dress . . **5.** jabot **9.** stomacher
   10. embroidery
egg-shaped . . **3.** ove
hair, head . . **4.** comb **5.** tiara **8.** barrette
indented . . **5.** chase
Japanese girdle . . **4.** inro
leaves and grapes . . **6.** pampre
magical . . **6.** amulet
mantel . . **7.** bibelot, trinket
pendant . . **6.** bangle, tassel **7.** earring
   9. lavaliere (lavalier)
pretentious . . **6.** rococo
protuberant . . **4.** boss
raised design . . **7.** brocade
scroll-like . . **6.** volute
set of . . **6.** parure
setting in . . **5.** inlay **7.** emblema
silverware . . **7.** gadroon
spiral . . **5.** helix
terminal . . **6.** finial
wall . . **6.** plaque, sconce
ornamental (pert to) . . .
   bottle . . **8.** decanter
   button . . **4.** stud
   description . . **5.** fancy **10.** decorative
   lace edge . . **5.** picot **7.** tatting
   metal . . **6.** niello
   raised . . **7.** brocade
   stand . . **7.** étagère
   vase . . **3.** urn
ornamented . . . **6.** chased, etched, tooled
   8. engraved
ornate . . . **3.** gay **5.** fancy **6.** florid, tawdry
   7. adorned **9.** decorated
ornery . . . **8.** perverse, stubborn
   9. malicious **11.** ill-tempered
ornithoid . . . **8.** birdlike
ornithology (study of) . . . **5.** birds
ornithon . . . **6.** aviary
oro . . . **4.** gold **5.** money
Oro . . . **3.** God (Tahiti)
oro (comb form) . . . **5.** month, serum
   8. mountain
orology (science of) . . . **9.** mountains
orotund . . . **7.** pompous **9.** bombastic
orp . . . **4.** fret, weep
Orpheus (pert to) . . .
   astronomy . . **6.** Cygnus
   eighteenth century . . **6.** Handel
   father . . **6.** Apollo
   mother . . **8.** Calliope
   poet . . **8.** Thracian
   reference . . **6.** Orphic
   river . . **6.** Hebrus
   wife . . **8.** Eurydice
Orphic . . . **3.** egg (Creation's) **5.** hymns
   7. tablets (gold) **13.** Book of the Dead
   (rites)
orphrey . . . **10.** embroidery (gold)
orpit (Scot) . . . **7.** fretful
orra . . . **3.** odd **5.** oddly **10.** not
   matched, occasional, unemployed
   13. miscellaneous

ort . . . 3. end 4. bits 5. scrap 6. refuse,
scraps 7. remnant 8. leavings, leftover
orthodox . . . 7. Trinity 8. accepted,
approved, believer, standard
9. canonical, customary
12. conventional
Orthodox Moslem . . . 5. hanif
orthography . . . 8. spelling
ortolan . . . 7. bunting 8. bobolink, sora
rail, wheatear
Oryx . . . 5. beisa 7. gazelle, gemsbok
8. antelope, leucoryx
os . . . 4. bone 5. mouth, osker (Geol)
7. opening
Osage . . . 5. river 6. Indian (Sioux)
10. orange tree
Osaka, Japan . . . 7. capital 10. prefecture
oscillate . . . 3. wag 4. rock, sway, vary
5. swing, waver, weave 7. vibrate
9. fluctuate
Oscines . . . 12. singing birds
oscitancy . . . 6. gaping 7. yawning
8. dullness, lethargy 10. drowsiness
oscitant . . . 4. dull 6. drowsy, gaping,
sleepy 7. yawning 8. careless, sluggish
9. apathetic
osculate . . . 4. buss, kiss
osier . . . 3. rod 4. wand 6. sallow, willow
7. dogwood
Osiris, Egypt (pert to) . . .
brother . . 3. Set (Seth)
crown . . 4. atef
enemy . . 3. Set 7. brother
father . . 3. Geb
god . . 9. fertility 10. underworld
god (Gr) . . 8. Dionysus
husband of . . 4. Isis
king of . . 5. Egypt
mother . . 3. Nut
seat . . 6. Abydos
son . . 5. Horus 6. Anubis
Osmanli . . . 4. Turk 8. language
osmesis . . . 8. smelling 9. olfaction
osmosis . . . 10. absorption 12. infiltration
osprey . . . 4. hawk 7. feather (hat) 8. fish
hawk 9. ossifrage 10. breakbones
ossature . . . 8. skeleton 9. framework
(Arch)
osse . . . 4. dare 7. attempt, presage,
promise 8. prophecy
osseous . . . 4. bony, hard 10. ossiferous
ossifrage . . . 5. eagle 6. osprey
11. lammergeier
ossuary . . . 3. urn 4. tomb 10. depository
12. charnel house 13. burial chamber
ostend . . . 6. reveal 7. exhibit 8. manifest
11. demonstrate
ostensible . . . 5. shown 6. avowed
7. alleged, seeming 8. apparent,
declared, specious 9. exhibited,
plausible, professed
ostent . . . 3. air 4. mien 5. token 7. portent
10. appearance
ostentatious . . . 4. arty, vain 5. dashy
6. sporty 7. pompous 11. conspicuous,
pretentious
ostiole . . . 4. pore 5. stoma 7. orifice
8. aperture
ostler . . . 7. hostler 9. stableman
ostracize . . . 5. exile, expel 6. banish,
deport 7. cast out, exclude 9. extradite
10. expatriate
ostrich . . . 3. emu 4. Rhea 5. nandu
8. Struthio 9. cassowary
ostrichlike . . . 11. struthiform
ostrich tail feather . . . 3. boo
Otaheite . . . 6. Tahiti
otalgia . . . 7. earache
Othello (pert to) . . .
opera by . . 5. Verdi
tragedy by . . 11. Shakespeare
villain . . 4. Iago
wife . . 9. Desdemona
other . . . 2. or 5. alter, ither 6. either,
second 8. one of two 9. different
10. additional
others . . . 7. the rest 9. remaining
otherwise . . . 2. or 5. alias, ossia, other
6. or else 9. different 10. contrarily
11. differently
Othman . . . 4. Turk 5. Osman 6. sultan
7. Osmanli, Ottoman, Turkish
Othman's successor . . . 3. Ali
otiant . . . 4. idle 8. in repose
10. unemployed
otiose . . . 4. idle 6. at ease, futile 7. sterile,
useless 8. indolent 12. functionless
otium . . . 7. leisure
otkon . . . 4. okee (oki) 5. demon (Iroquois)
otologist . . . 6. aurist 9. ear doctor
ottava . . . 6. eighth, octave
ottava rima . . . 15. eight-line stanza
ottavino . . . 7. piccolo
ottoman . . . 4. seat 5. couch, stool
7. cricket 9. footstool
Ottoman (pert to) . . . see also Othman
color . . 9. vermilion
court . . 5. Porte 12. Sublime Porte
Empire . . 7. Turkish
fabric . . 6. ribbed 10. corded silk
governor . . 3. bey, dey 5. pasha
leader . . 5. Osman
native . . 4. Turk
poetry (couplet) . . 4. beyt
province . . 6. eyalet (former) 7. vilayet
Turkish . . 7. Osmanli
oubliette . . . 7. dungeon (top opening)
ouch . . . 5. bezel, clasp, jewel 6. brooch
8. ornament 11. exclamation
ought . . . 4. duty, must, zero 5. at
all, aught, owned 6. cipher, should
7. behoove, nothing 8. anything, in
need of 9. possessed 10. obligation
Ouija board . . . 10. planchette
ouk . . . 4. week
ouphe . . . 3. elf 6. goblin
Our (pert to) . . .
Father . . 11. Lord's Prayer
French . . 5. notre
Lady . . 10. Virgin Mary
Lady's-mint . . 9. spearmint
Lady's Wand (Astron) . . 10. Orion's Belt
Lady's Way . . 6. Zodiac
ourie . . . 4. cold 5. dingy 6. dreary
ousia . . . 6. nature 7. essence 9. substance,
true being
oust . . . 3. bar 5. eject, evict 6. depose,
remove, unseat 7. turn out
out . . . 3. odd 4. away 5. drunk
6. absent, beyond, excuse, issued,
outlet 9. published 10. dislocated,
extinguish 11. unconscious

12. extinguished, not available
out and out ... **6.** arrant **8.** absolute,
complete, outright, thorough
9. downright **13.** thoroughgoing
outbreak ... **4.** rash, riot **5.** burst,
spurt **6.** emeute, tumult **7.** outcrop,
ruction **8.** eruption, hysteria, outburst
12. insurrection **13.** recrudescence
outburst ... **4.** gale **5.** blast, flare, flash
8. ejection, eruption **9.** explosion
10. ebullition
outcast ... **5.** exile, leper, ronin **6.** pariah
7. quarrel **8.** castaway, derelict,
vagabond **10.** expatriate
outclass ... **5.** excel, outdo **6.** outvie
7. outrank, surpass **8.** outshine
10. outperform
outcome ... **5.** issue **6.** effect, outlet,
result, sequel, upshot **7.** emanate,
product **8.** solution **10.** denouement
11. consequence
outcry ... **4.** wail, yell **5.** alarm, shout
6. clamor, plaint **7.** suction **8.** proclaim
11. exclamation
outdated ... **7.** archaic **8.** obsolete
10. antiquated **12.** old-fashioned
outdo ... **5.** excel **6.** defeat, exceed,
outwit
outdoor game ... **4.** polo **6.** hockey,
tennis **7.** cricket, croquet
outer ... **5.** ectad, ectal **7.** outside, outward
8. exterior, external **9.** objective
10. extraneous
outer (pert to) ...
boundary .. **9.** perimeter
coat .. **4.** coat, hull **5.** testa **6.** extine,
jacket **8.** tegument
garment .. **4.** suit, wrap **5.** cloak, dress
7. paletot, sweater **8.** mackinaw,
mantilla, overcoat, raincoat
layer of roots .. **7.** exoderm
opposed to .. **5.** ental
shell .. **4.** test
skin .. **9.** epidermis
Outer Mongolia ...
capital .. **4.** Urga **14.** Ulan Bator Khoto
desert .. **4.** Gobi
outermost ... **6.** utmost **7.** extreme,
outmost **8.** far-flung, farthest
outfit ... **3.** kit, rig **4.** gear, suit,
unit **5.** equip, group **7.** company,
costume **8.** wardrobe **12.** organization
13. paraphernalia
outflow ... **4.** gush, teem **6.** deluge, efflux
7. freshet, outflux, outpour **8.** effusion
10. ebullience
outgate ... **4.** exit, vent **6.** egress, outlet
7. outcome
outknee ... **6.** bowleg
outlander ... see *outsider*
outlandish ... **3.** odd **6.** remote **7.** bizarre,
foreign, strange, uncouth **8.** freakish
9. barbarous, inelegant, unrelated
10. extraneous, impossible, tramontane
outlaw ... **5.** horse, ronin **6.** bandit,
banish **7.** brigand, outcast **8.** criminal,
fugitive **9.** ostracize, proscribe
outlet ... **4.** exit, vent **5.** bayou **6.** stream
7. culvert, opening, outcast, passage
outline ... **3.** map **5.** chart, draft, frame,
shape **6.** sketch **7.** contour, drawing,

summary **8.** scenario **9.** adumbrate,
delineate, lineament, perimeter,
summarize **10.** compendium
11. delineation **13.** configuration
outlook ... **5.** scope, vista, watch
7. purview **8.** frontage, prospect
9. viewpoint **10.** perception
11. probability **12.** watchfulness
outmoded ... **5.** passé **7.** offbeat
8. outdated **10.** superseded
outmost ... **5.** final, utter **6.** remote,
utmost **8.** farthest **9.** extremest,
outermost, uttermost **15.** farthest
outward
out of ...
agreement .. **6.** dehors
danger .. **4.** safe
date, style .. **3.** old **5.** passé
10. antiquated
place .. **5.** inept
sorts .. **5.** nohow **7.** peevish
the ordinary .. **7.** unusual
the question .. **10.** impossible
the way .. **5.** aside **6.** afield
outpeer ... **5.** excel **7.** surpass
output ... **3.** cut **5.** expel, power,
yield **6.** amount, energy **7.** turnout
10. production
outraged ... **6.** abused, harmed
8. insulted, offended **9.** affronted
10. infuriated, mistreated
outrageous ... **6.** absurd **7.** furious,
heinous, obscene **8.** flagrant
9. atrocious, excessive, monstrous
10. exorbitant, scandalous
11. disgraceful, unwarranted
outré ... **3.** odd **6.** absurd **7.** bizarre
10. immoderate **11.** extravagant
Outre-Mer ... **13.** Book of Travels
(Longfellow, 1835)
outremer ... **12.** beyond the sea, foreign
parts
outrigger ... **4.** proa, spar **5.** canoe
outright ... **8.** thorough **10.** completely
11. unqualified **12.** unreservedly
outrival ... **5.** excel **6.** outvie **7.** eclipse,
outrank **8.** outclass, outshine, outsmart,
outstrip
outside ... **3.** exo (pref) **4.** ecto (comb
form) **8.** exterior, external, outdoors
10. extraneous **11.** superficial
outsider ... **5.** alien **8.** stranger
9. auslander, foreigner, Uitlander
outspoken ... **4.** free **5.** blunt, frank
6. candid, direct **10.** unreserved
13. communicative
outstanding ... **3.** due **5.** famed,
noted **6.** famous, unpaid **7.** eminent,
obvious **8.** exterior **9.** important,
principal, prominent **10.** projecting
11. conspicuous, uncollected
outstrip ... **4.** best, lead **5.** excel, outdo
7. surpass **8.** outrival
outward ... **5.** ectad, evert, outer,
overt **6.** formal, spiral **8.** apparent,
exterior, external, manifest **9.** extrinsic
11. superficial
outwit ... **4.** balk, best, foil **5.** block, check,
cross **6.** baffle, thwart **9.** checkmate,
frustrate **10.** circumvent, disappoint
outwork (Fort) ... **7.** ravelin **8.** tenaille

(tenail)
ouvrage . . . 4. work
ouzel, ousel . . . 4. piet 6. thrush
  8. whistler 9. blackbird
oval . . . 5. ovate, ovoid 6. circle 7. ellipse
  10. elliptical 11. ellipsoidal
ovale . . . 3. egg
ovate . . . 4. bard, oval 7. obovate
  (inversely)
oven . . . 3. umu 4. kiln, oast (oste)
  7. furnace 8. hot place 9. microwave
  12. brick chamber
oven (pert to) . . .
  glass annealing . . 4. lehr (leer)
  hop drying . . 4. oast
  mop . . 6. scovel
over . . . 3. o'er, too 4. also, anew, atop
  5. above, again, ended, super, supra
  8. finished
overact . . . 3. haw 5. emote, spout
overalls . . . 5. chaps 8. trousers
  10. chaparajos
overbearing . . . 7. haughty 8. arrogant,
  cavalier, snobbish, subduing
  9. imperious 10. highhanded
  11. domineering 12. overpowering
overcast . . . 3. dim 4. dark 6. cloudy,
  darken, gloomy 10. overturned (Geol)
overcoat . . . 5. benny, parka 6. capote,
  raglan, slip-on, ulster 7. paletot,
  surtout, topcoat 9. greatcoat, inverness
  (sleeveless)
overcome . . . 3. awe, win 4. beat
  5. crush 6. beaten, defeat, exceed
  7. conquer 8. outstrip, overbear,
  overturn, persuade, surmount,
  unnerved, vanquish 9. overpower,
  overthrow, overwhelm, prostrate
overcrowded . . . 9. congested
overdue . . . 4. late 5. tardy 7. belated
  8. mistimed
overfeed . . . 4. glut 6. agrote, pamper
  7. satiate, surfeit 8. overfill 9. crapulate,
  overstuff
overflow . . . 4. teem 5. spate 6. abound,
  deluge, outlet 7. copious, overrun
  8. inundate, opulence, overload,
  plethora, teem with 9. abundance,
  pour forth 10. ebullience
overfond of . . . 4. dote 5. silly
overfull . . . 8. inflated, satiated 9. plethoric
  10. overloaded
overhang . . . 3. jut 6. beetle 7. project,
  suspend 9. advantage 11. over and
  over
overlapping . . . 8. obvolute 9. imbricate,
  syphering
overloaded . . . 6. turgic 8. inflated, overfill
  9. bombastic, plethoric
overlook . . . 4. face, miss, scan, skip,
  snub 6. acquit, excuse, ignore, slight,
  survey 7. absolve, condone, forgive,
  neglect, overtop 9. disregard, oversight,
  rise above, supervise
overlord . . . 6. master 8. domineer,
  governor 9. tyrannize
overly . . . 3. too 8. careless 9. negligent
  11. overbearing, superficial
  12. supercilious
overmodest . . . 7. prudish 8. priggish
  11. puritanical, strait-laced

overnice . . . 5. fussy 6. purist 7. elegant,
  finicky 8. affected 10. fastidious
overpower . . . 3. awe 4. rout, stun
  5. crush 6. dazzle, defeat, master,
  subdue 7. conquer 8. overbear,
  overcome, vanquish 9. overthrow,
  overwhelm
overpowering . . . 6. fierce 8. exciting
  12. overwhelming
overreach . . . 4. dupe 5. cheat 6. exceed,
  nobble, outwit, overgo, strain 7. deceive
  10. circumvent
overrun . . . 5. crush, swarm 6. abound,
  desert, exceed, infest, outrun, ravage,
  spread 7. destroy, pervade, run over,
  trample 8. overflow 9. overwhelm
  11. superabound
overscrupulous . . . 7. prudish
  9. overexact 10. overstrict
  14. overfastidious
overshadow . . . 5. excel 6. darken
  7. eclipse, obscure, shelter 8. dominate
  9. overcloud
overshoe . . . 3. gum 6. arctic, galosh
  (galoshe)
oversight . . . 4. care 5. error, lapse,
  watch 6. charge 7. control, neglect
  8. omission 9. direction 10. inspection
  11. supervision 12. guardianship,
  surveillance 13. nonobservance
overskirt . . . 7. pannier (anc) 10. upper
  skirt
oversleeve . . . 6. armlet
overspread . . . 5. cover 6. infest
  7. overrun, pervade 8. disperse,
  suffused
overt . . . 4. open 6. patent, public
  7. obvious 8. apparent, manifest
  10. open to view
overtake . . . 5. catch, reach, seize
  6. detect, rejoin 7. ensnare
  9. apprehend, captivate
overthrow . . . 4. down, rout, ruin
  5. worst 6. defeat, depose, refute,
  unseat 7. conquer, deposal, destroy,
  ruinate, unhorse 8. demolish, disprove,
  overcome, overturn, vanquish
  9. prostrate 10. revolution
overthrown . . . 6. fallen, ruined
  8. defeated 9. disproved
overtones . . . 5. tones 8. partials
  9. harmonics
overtop . . . 5. dwarf, excel 7. obscure,
  surpass 8. go beyond, overhead,
  override 9. transcend 10. tower above
overture . . . 5. offer, proem 7. opening,
  prelude 8. aperture, proposal
  11. composition, proposition 13. peace
  offering
overturn . . . 3. tip 4. tilt 5. throw, upset
  6. topple 7. capsize, conquer, destroy,
  overset, reverse, subvert 9. overthrow,
  overwhelm
overweight . . . 7. obesity 11. overbalance
  13. preponderance
overwhelm . . . 4. bury, rout 5. crush
  6. defeat, deluge, engulf 7. confute,
  conquer, engross, immerse, oppress
  8. overturn, submerge 9. overpower,
  overthrow
Ovidae, Ovinae . . . 5. goats, sheep

oviparous . . . **11.** ovoviparous **12.** egg
   producing (opp of viviparous)
ovoid, ovoidal . . . **7.** egglike **9.** egg-
   shaped
ovule . . . **3.** egg **4.** seed **6.** embryo,
   ovulum
ovum . . . **3.** egg **4.** seed **5.** spore **6.** gamete
   8. germ cell
owe . . . **3.** due, own **7.** possess **9.** be
   obliged **10.** be indebted
ower . . . **6.** debtor
owl (pert to) . . .
   barn . . **4.** lulu **5.** padge
   breed . . **6.** pigeon
   eagle . . **7.** katogle **14.** Tiger of the
      Wood
   eye . . **4.** disc
   family . . **9.** Strigidae
   female . . **3.** hen
   genus . . **4.** Bubo **5.** Ninox, Strix
      7. Syrnium
   horned . . **4.** Bubo **6.** aziola (small)
      8. Hush-wing
   light . . **4.** dusk
   like . . **4.** owly **8.** strigine
   parrot . . **6.** kakapo
   Puerto Rican . . **6.** mucaro
   short-eared . . **8.** marsh owl
   tawny . . **8.** billywix
   term . . **4.** hoot **11.** bird of night **13.** bird
      of Minerva
   white . . **7.** wapacut
   young . . **4.** utum **5.** owlet
own . . . **4.** have **5.** admit **7.** confess,
   possess **11.** acknowledge
owner . . . **6.** master **7.** planter (plantation)
   8. landlady, landlord **10.** proprietor
ownership . . . **4.** oadl (anc law) **5.** claim
   7. tenancy **8.** dominium, interest,
   property **10.** possession
   11. seigniorage **12.** seignioralty
   14. proprietorship
ox . . . **5.** beeve, steer **6.** bovine **8.** strength
   13. beast of burden
ox (pert to) . . .
   Celebes . . **4.** anoa

   genus . . **3.** Bos
   harness . . **4.** yoke
   horned . . **4.** reem
   India . . **4.** gaur
   like . . **5.** bison **6.** bovine **7.** taurine
   stall . . **5.** boose
   Tibetan . . **3.** yak
   type . . **4.** zebu
   wild . . **4.** urus **7.** banteng
   working . . **4.** aver
   yoke . . **4.** span
oxeye . . . **4.** boce (fish) **5.** daisy **6.** dunlin,
   plover
oxford . . . **4.** gray, shoe **5.** cloth
Oxford (pert to) . . .
   college accts . . **6.** battel
   color . . **4.** blue, gray
   Marbles . . **7.** Arundel
   Museum . . **9.** Ashmolean (1683)
   officer . . **6.** beadle (bedel at Oxford)
      (bedell at Cambridge)
   scholarship . . **6.** Rhodes
   school . . **10.** University (1570)
   sheep (hornless) . . **4.** Down
oxide of iron . . . **4.** rust
oxide of sodium . . . **4.** soda
oxidize . . . **4.** rust **5.** erode **9.** sulphuret
   (Philat)
oxter . . . **3.** arm **6.** armpit **7.** embrace
oxtongue . . . **5.** plant **7.** biltong, bugloss
oxwort . . . **9.** butterbur
oxygen . . . **3.** gas **5.** oxide, ozone
   7. element
oxyopia . . . **10.** extra sight
oyez, oyes . . . **6.** hear ye
oyster . . . **6.** huitre **7.** bivalve, mollusk
oyster (pert to) . . .
   gatherer . . **7.** tongman
   rake . . **5.** tongs
   shell . . **4.** husk, test **5.** shuck
   spawn . . **6.** cultch
   type . . **9.** bluepoint
   young . . **4.** spat
Ozark State . . . **8.** Missouri
Oz author . . . **4.** Baum (L Frank)
ozone . . . **3.** air **6.** oxygen

P

P . . . **2.** Pi **6.** letter (16th)
pa . . . **4.** Papa **6.** father
pa, pah . . . **4.** fort **7.** village **10.** settlement
   (fortified)
paauw . . . **7.** bustard
pabulum . . . **4.** food, fuel **7.** aliment,
   support **9.** nutriment **10.** sustenance
   11. nourishment
pac, pack . . . **8.** half boot, moccasin
paca . . . **6.** rodent **9.** Cuniculus
pace . . . **3.** run **4.** gait, lope, rate, step, trot,
   walk **5.** speed **7.** measure **8.** movement,
   velocity
pace (L) . . . **5.** peace
Pace . . . **5.** Pasch **6.** Easter
pachyderm . . . **8.** elephant **10.** rhinoceros
   12. hippopotamus, Pachydermata

pachydermous . . . **11.** thick-walled
   12. thick-skinned
pacific . . . **4.** calm **6.** irenic, serene
   8. irenical, peaceful, tranquil
   9. peaceable, quiescent **12.** conciliatory
Pacific (pert to) . . .
   Coast tree . . **7.** madrona **8.** knob pine
   Highway . . **10.** Camino Real
   island bird . . **4.** kagu
   island shark . . **4.** mako **11.** blue pointer
   island tree . . **4.** ipil
   islands . . **4.** Guam, Wake **5.** Samos
      7. Oceania **8.** Caroline, Tasmania
      9. Melanesia, Polynesia **10.** Micronesia
   shrub . . **5.** salal
   States . . **6.** Oregon **10.** California,
      Washington

stepping stones . . **9.** Aleutians (Russia to America)
Pacific Ocean discoverer . . . **6.** Balboa
pacifier . . . **3.** sop **4.** ring (baby's) **6.** nipple **7.** soother **8.** sedative **10.** peacemaker
pacify . . . **4.** calm, ease, lull **5.** abate, allay **6.** soften, soothe **7.** appease, assuage, mollify, placate **8.** mitigate, palliate **9.** alleviate **10.** conciliate, propitiate **11.** tranquilize (tranquillize)
pack . . . **3.** ram, set, wad **4.** cram, fill, load, stow, tamp **5.** carry, flock, horde, steve, truss **6.** bundle, embale **8.** assemble, encumber, quantity, send away
pack (pert to) . . .
  animal . . **3.** ass **5.** burro, camel, llama **6.** donkey
  back . . **8.** knapsack
  horse . . **7.** sumpter
  horse bag . . **5.** kyack **7.** pannier
  of hounds . . **6.** kennel
package . . . **3.** pad **4.** bale **5.** fadge **6.** bundle, packet, parcel, robbin (peppers), seroon **11.** combination
packing . . . **4.** lute, seal **7.** stowage **9.** packaging **10.** rubber ring
paco . . . **3.** ore **6.** alpaca
Pacolet . . . **10.** swift horse
pact . . . **6.** pactum **7.** bargain **8.** contract **9.** agreement
Pactolian . . . **6.** golden
Pactolus, Myth (pert to) . . .
  famed for . . **5.** Midas **11.** gold-bearing
  river (Asia Minor) . . **5.** Lydia
pad . . . **3.** mat, paw **4.** fill, foot, frog, line, path, walk **5.** quilt, stuff, track, tramp **6.** tablet, trudge **7.** bedding, bolster, cushion, footpad **8.** notebook, protract, saturate **9.** footprint, pulvillus **10.** highwayman
pad (pert to) . . .
  cloth . . **7.** housing **11.** saddlecloth
  hair . . **3.** rat
  harness, part . . **5.** panel **6.** terret **7.** housing **10.** horsecloth
  perfume . . **6.** sachet
padding . . . **6.** lining **7.** wadding **8.** softness, stuffing **11.** superfluity
paddle . . . **3.** oar, row **4.** beat, stir, wade, whip **5.** blade, board, scull, spank, spoon **6.** dabble, propel **7.** flipper **8.** lumpfish
paddle (pert to) . . .
  English . . **7.** trample **8.** lumpfish **9.** tread upon **10.** paddlecock
  Scotch . . **3.** hoe **4.** spud
paddock (pert to) . . .
  paddockstool . . **9.** toadstool
  piper . . **9.** horsetail
  stone . . **10.** greenstone
paddy . . . **4.** rice, soft **7.** padlike **8.** cushiony **9.** rice field **10.** hod carrier
Paddy . . . **7.** Patrick **8.** Irishman
paddymelon . . . **7.** wallaby
Paddy's hurricane (Naut) . . . **4.** calm
paddywhack . . . **4.** beat, blow **6.** temper **9.** ruddy duck, thrashing
padge . . . **7.** barn owl
padmasana . . . **11.** cross-legged (Buddha style), lotus-shaped
padre . . . **5.** monk **6.** Father, priest

8. chaplain, minister
padrona . . . **8.** landlady, mistress
padrone . . . **6.** master, patron **8.** landlord **9.** innkeeper
paedarchy . . . **14.** rule by children
pagan . . . **6.** ethnic, paynim **7.** heathen **10.** heathenism, idolatrous, unbeliever **11.** irreligious
Paganalia . . . **8.** festival (Rom)
pagan god . . . **4.** idol
page . . . **3.** boy **4.** leaf **5.** child, folio **6.** summon **9.** attendant, messenger
page (pert to) . . .
  beginning . . **7.** flyleaf
  book . . **5.** folio **6.** cahier, sheets
  lady's . . **7.** esquire **8.** escudero
  left-hand . . **5.** verso
  number . . **5.** folio
  right-hand . . **5.** recto
  title . . **5.** unwan **6.** rubric **12.** frontispiece
pageant . . . **4.** pomp, show **5.** drama **6.** parade **7.** tableau **8.** aquacade **9.** spectacle **10.** exhibition **11.** ostentation
pages . . . **7.** paginal **8.** paginate
Pagliacci . . . **5.** opera **9.** character
pagne . . . **9.** loincloth, petticoat
pagoda . . . **2.** ta **3.** taa **4.** idol **5.** booth **6.** temple **11.** summerhouse
pagoda (pert to) . . .
  finial . . **3.** tee
  sleeve . . **12.** funnel-shaped
  stone . . **12.** Agalmatolite
  tree . . **6.** banyan **10.** frangipani
paha . . . **4.** hill **5.** ridge (glacial)
pahi . . . **4.** ship **5.** canoe (seagoing)
pahmi . . . **5.** bobac **6.** marmot
paho . . . **7.** pahutan **11.** prayer stick
pahutan . . . **5.** mango
paid . . . **5.** hired **6.** cashed **7.** content, settled, yielded **9.** satisfied **10.** discharged
paideutics . . . **8.** pedagogy, teaching
paid office (without work) . . . **8.** sinecure
paid out . . . **5.** spent **8.** expended **9.** disbursed
paigle . . . **7.** cowslip **8.** crowfoot **10.** stitchwort **12.** cuckooflower
pail . . . **3.** can, pan **4.** beat **6.** bucket, harass, situla, thrash, vessel **8.** cannikin
paillasse, palliasse . . . **3.** bed (masonry) **8.** mattress (straw)
pailles . . . **5.** straws (cookery)
paillou, pailoo . . . **7.** archway (memorial)
pain . . . **3.** ail **4.** ache, agra, pang **5.** agony, labor, thraw, throb, wound **6.** grieve, stitch **7.** afflict, ailment, gnawing, torture, trouble **8.** disquiet, distress **9.** suffering **10.** affliction, punishment
painful . . . **4.** sore **7.** careful **8.** diligent **9.** difficult, laborious **10.** afflictive, unpleasant **11.** industrious, painstaking
painkiller . . . **7.** anodyne **8.** medicine, sedative **9.** analgesic, calmative **10.** depressant
painstaking . . . **5.** fussy **7.** careful, labored **8.** diligent, thorough **9.** assiduity, assiduous, laborious
paint . . . **4.** coat, draw, limn **5.** adorn, color, rouge, stain **6.** depict, parget, sketch **7.** picture, pigment, portray

8. cosmetic, describe 9. delineate, embellish 11. application (Med)
paint (pert to) . . .
blue, green . . **4.** bice
comb form . . **5.** picto
face . . **4.** fard
glossy . . **6.** enamel
Latin . . **6.** pinxit
spreader . . **7.** spatula
through pattern . . **7.** stencil
with vermilion . . **7.** miniate
paintbrush . . . **8.** hawkweed **10.** painted cup **11.** St John's wort
painted . . . **6.** coated **7.** colored, feigned **9.** disguised, portrayed **10.** artificial, variegated
painted (pert to) . . .
bat . . **11.** Vespertilio
beauty . . **9.** butterfly
bunting . . **5.** finch
duck . . **8.** mandarin **9.** harlequin
enamel . . **7.** Limoges
hyena . . **14.** Cape hunting dog
lady . . **7.** thistle **8.** sweet pea **9.** butterfly
process . . **7.** scumble
trillium . . **9.** wake-robin
turtle . . **8.** carapace
painter . . . **4.** puma **6.** cougar **7.** panther
painter . . . **4.** Dali **5.** Monet **6.** Millet, Rubens **7.** da Vinci, El Greco, Picasso, van Gogh **8.** Reynolds, Whistler **9.** Rembrandt **12.** Gainsborough, Grandma Moses, Michelangelo
Painter's Easel . . . **6.** Pictor (constellation)
painting . . . **3.** oil **5.** genre, mural, Pietà (sacred), secco **6.** fresco, marine **7.** impasto, tempera **9.** encaustic, grisaille, landscape **10.** cerography **11.** portraiture **12.** illustration
pair . . . **3.** duo, two **4.** dyad, mate, span, team, yoke **5.** brace, unite **6.** couple
paired . . . **5.** gemel (Her) **7.** coupled, leagued
pairs, growing in . . . **6.** binate, double
paisano . . . **7.** peasant **10.** countryman, road runner
pal . . . **4.** chum, pard **5.** buddy, crony **6.** cobber **7.** partner **9.** companion **10.** accomplice
palace . . . **5.** court, Doges, house (Astrol) **6.** palais **7.** palazzo **10.** praetorium (pretorium)
paladin . . . **4.** hero **6.** knight (Round Table)
Paladins of France . . . **9.** The Twelve
palais . . . **6.** palace **10.** courthouse
Palamedes . . . **4.** hero (Trojan War)
palampore . . . **7.** hanging (cotton) **8.** bedcover
palanquin, palankeen . . . **4.** kago **5.** dooly (doolie), palki **6.** litter, palkee **10.** conveyance
palanquin bearer . . . **5.** hamal **6.** sirdar
palas . . . **4.** dhak, tree (yellow dye)
palatable . . . **5.** sapid, tasty **6.** savory **8.** pleading, seasoned **10.** acceptable
palate . . . **4.** cion **5.** taste, uvula, velum **6.** relish **10.** epipharynx
palatine . . . **4.** bone **6.** artery, county **8.** palatial
Palatine Confession . . . **10.** Heidelberg

palaver . . . **4.** talk **6.** confer **7.** chatter **8.** converse, flattery **10.** conference **12.** conversation
pale . . . **3.** dim, wan **4.** ashy, fade, lily **5.** ashen, fence, lurid, pasty, stake, white **6.** blanch, bounds, paling, pallid, pallor, sallow, sickly, sphere **7.** haggard, obscure, whitish **8.** palisade **9.** deathlike **10.** indistinct
palea, palet . . . **4.** fold **5.** bract, scale **6.** dewlap **8.** ramentum
paleo (comb form) . . . **3.** old **7.** ancient
paleolithic culture . . . **8.** Stone Age
Paleozoic . . . **10.** Appalachia
Palestine (pert to) . . .
ancient name . . **6.** Canaan
animal . . **4.** cony (Bib) **5.** daman
conqueror . . **5.** David, Turks **11.** Constantine
country (anc) . . **4.** Edom **5.** Endor (Indur) **8.** Nazareth **9.** Philistia
lake . . **7.** Dead Sea, Galilee
language . . **7.** Aramaic
mountain (Bib) . . **4.** Zion **6.** Carmel, Gilead, Hermon **13.** Mount of Olives
plain, steppe . . **5.** Negeb **6.** Sharon
river . . **6.** Jordan
town, district . . **4.** Gaza **5.** Haifa **7.** Samaria **9.** Jerusalem
paletot . . . **4.** coat **8.** overcoat
pali . . . **9.** precipice **10.** steep slope
pali (comb form) . . . **5.** again **8.** backward
Pali . . . **7.** dialect (anc) **12.** dead language
palimpsest . . . **9.** parchment, rewritten **10.** re-engraved **15.** codex rescriptus
palindrome (same backward, forward) . . . **8.** wordplay **9.** inversion
paling . . . **5.** fence, limit, palis, stake **6.** fading, picket **7.** fencing **9.** enclosure
palisade . . . **5.** cliff, fence, stake **6.** picket **7.** defense, enclose, fortify **8.** espalier, palisado, surround **9.** precipice **10.** impalement **13.** fortification
pall . . . **4.** pale **5.** cloak, cover, faint, qualm **6.** coffin, mantle, nausea **7.** secrecy **12.** graveclothes
pallall . . . **9.** hopscotch
palle . . . **5.** balls **8.** six balls (Medici)
pallet . . . **3.** bed **4.** pate **5.** quilt **7.** blanket **8.** mattress **9.** headpiece, paillasse
palliard . . . **6.** beggar, lecher, rascal **8.** vagabond
palliate . . . **4.** hide **5.** abate, cloak, cover, gloss **6.** excuse, lessen, soften **7.** conceal, qualify, relieve, shelter **8.** disguise, mitigate, moderate **9.** alleviate, extenuate
pallid . . . **3.** wan **4.** gray, pale **5.** pasty, white **6.** anemic, sallow
Pallu . . . **10.** Reuben's son (Bib)
palm . . . **4.** hand (part) **5.** areca, bribe, steal **6.** bacaba, handle, rattan, stroke, trophy
palm (pert to) . . .
civet . . **9.** musang
cockatoo . . **5.** arara
down . . **7.** pronate
drink . . **5.** assai
drink (alcoholic) . . **4.** beno, nipa
hand . . **6.** palmus, thenar
handlike . . **7.** palmate

house.. **8.** palmetum
lily.. **2.** ti
mat.. **6.** petate
off.. **5.** foist
ref to.. **10.** palmaceous
sap (fermented).. **5.** toddy
starch.. **4.** sago
sugar.. **7.** jaggery
thatch.. **4.** nipa
palm (tree)...
  African.. **7.** palmyra (sugar, wine)
  Arab.. **4.** doum (doom)
  Asiatic.. **4.** atap, nipa
  betel.. **5.** areca, bonga **6.** pinang
  book.. **4.** tara **7.** taliera
  Brazil.. **7.** urucuri (urucury)
  bussu, thatching.. **7.** troolie (trooly)
  cabbage.. **5.** Sabal **8.** palmetto
  Ceylon.. **4.** tala **7.** talipot (fanleaf)
  climbing, flexible.. **6.** rattan
  dwarf.. **5.** Sabal
  E Indies.. **4.** atap, nipa **7.** jaggery
    (sugar), tokopat (hat)
  fan.. **7.** talipot **8.** palmetto
  fiber.. **3.** tal **6.** raffia **8.** piassava
    (piassaba)
  Florida.. **5.** royal
  gingerbread tasting.. **4.** doum (doom)
  leaf.. **3.** tal **4.** olla (ola) **12.** chiquichiqui
  Malayan, feather.. **4.** irok **6.** gomuti
  palmyra.. **4.** brab, olla **6.** ronier
  Philippine (coconut).. **4.** niog
  pinnate.. **5.** assai, nikau **7.** calamus,
    feather
  S America.. **5.** bussu, datil **6.** tooroo
    12. chiquichiqui
  spiny.. **6.** grugru
palmate... **6.** antler, webbed **10.** hand-
  shaped
palmer... **6.** ferule **7.** pilgrim (Holy Land)
  8. date palm **15.** prestidigitator
Palmetto State... **13.** South Carolina
palmistry... **10.** chirognomy, chiromancy
palmodic (Med)... **5.** jerky
palp... **6.** feeler, palpus **8.** tentacle
palpable... **5.** plain **6.** patent **8.** manifest,
  tangible **9.** touchable **10.** noticeable,
  ponderable
palpebra... **6.** eyelid
palpebrate... **4.** wink
palpitate... **4.** beat, drum **5.** throb
  7. flutter, pulsate
palpitation... **7.** flutter, tremble
  9. pulsation, quivering, throbbing
  10. excitement
palsied... **5.** shaky **9.** paralyzed, tottering
palter... **5.** shift **6.** babble, haggle,
  mumble, parley **7.** bargain, chatter,
  quibble **9.** vacillate **10.** equivocate
  11. prevaricate
paltry... **4.** mean, vile **5.** petty, trash
  6. trashy **7.** pitiful, rubbish **8.** picayune,
  trifling **9.** worthless **10.** despicable
  12. contemptible
pampass... **5.** Pampa **6.** plains (treeless)
pamper... **3.** pet **4.** cram, glut **5.** humor,
  spoil **6.** caress, coddle, cosset, cuddle,
  dandle, posset **7.** gratify, indulge
  11. mollycoddle
pamphagous... **10.** omnivorous
pamphlet... **5.** tract **6.** folder **7.** booklet,

leaflet **8.** brochure
pan... **3.** tab **4.** part, tina (mining),
  wash **5.** basin, roast, title (nobility)
  6. frying, lappet, spider, vessel
  7. cranium, hardpan, portion, skillet,
  subsoil **8.** ridicule, saucepan **9.** criticize
  10. acetabulum
pan (comb form)... **3.** all **5.** every
Pan (pert to)...
  animal.. **3.** ape **10.** chimpanzee
  god (Gr).. **6.** flocks
  instrument.. **4.** pipe, reed
  music.. **9.** Pan's pipes
  Pipes of.. **6.** syrinx **8.** Panpipes
  Roman identity.. **6.** Faunus
  seat of worship.. **7.** Arcadia
  son.. **7.** Silenus
panacea... **4.** cure **6.** elixir, remedy
  7. allheal (plant), cure-all **8.** nepenthe
  10. catholicon **11.** panchreston
panache... **4.** tuft (feathered) **5.** plume
  7. swagger
Panama...
  bay.. **5.** Limon
  capital.. **10.** Panama City
  city.. **5.** Colon **6.** Balboa **9.** Cristobal
  engineer.. **8.** Goethals
  gulf.. **6.** Darien
  Indian.. **4.** Cuna
  isthmus of.. **6.** Darien (old name),
    Panama **7.** San Blas
  redwood.. **5.** quira
  river.. **7.** Chagres
Panama Canal Lock... **5.** Gatun
  10. Miraflores
panarchy... **13.** universal rule
panaris... **5.** felon **7.** whitlow
  10. paronychia
panary... **5.** bread **11.** breadmaking
panatela... **5.** cigar
pancake... **6.** froise (fraise) **7.** fritter
  8. flapjack **11.** griddlecake
Pancake Day... **13.** Shrove Tuesday
pancreas... **5.** gland **10.** sweetbread
  16. Isle of Langerhans
panda... **7.** bearcat
pandemonium... **4.** hell **5.** noise
  6. tumult, uproar
Pandemonium (pert to)...
  abode of.. **6.** demons
  capital of.. **4.** Hell
  palace of.. **5.** Satan
  pert to.. **15.** infernal regions
pander... **4.** bawd, pimp **5.** cater, serve
  7. toady to **12.** administer to
pandle... **7.** a shrimp
Pandora's Box... **6.** plague **9.** human
  ills
Pandora's husband... **10.** Epimetheus
panegyric... **5.** éloge, elogy **6.** eulogy
  7. oration, writing **8.** encomium
  9. discourse, laudation
pang... **3.** fit **4.** pain **5.** throe **6.** twinge
  8. paroxysm
pangolin... **5.** Manis **8.** anteater
  9. Pholidota
panhandle... **3.** beg
Panhellenic... **5.** games (Isthmian)
  6. Greece **10.** fraternity (Greek-letter)
panic... **4.** fear, fray **5.** alarm, chaos,
  scare **6.** fright **8.** stampede

pannier . . . **6.** basket, dosser (dorser)
   7. corbeit **9.** overskirt
panoply . . . **7.** defense **11.** suit of armor
panorama . . . **4.** view **5.** scene **7.** picture,
   scenery **9.** cyclorama
pant . . . **4.** beat, gasp **5.** heave, throb
   7. breathe, pulsate **11.** palpitation
Pantagruel (pert to) . . .
   character (romantic) . . **5.** giant
   companion . . **7.** Panurge
   father . . **9.** Gargantua
pantaloon, pantaloons . . . **5.** pants
   6. dotard, old man **8.** breeches, trousers
   11. Patron Saint (Venice)
Pantheon (pert to) . . .
   aggregate . . **4.** gods **7.** deities
   builder . . **7.** Hadrian (120 AD)
   building . . **6.** shrine, temple **10.** le
   Pantheon (Paris) **16.** Westminster Abbey
   Rome . . **15.** Temple of the Gods
panther, painter . . . **4.** pard, puma
   6. cougar, jaguar, ocelot **7.** leopard
pantler . . . **6.** butler **7.** servant
pantry . . . **5.** ambry **6.** larder **7.** buttery,
   pannier, pantler **8.** cupboard
pants . . . **5.** chaps **7.** drawers **8.** trousers
   10. chaparajos (chaparejos), pantaloons
panuelo . . . **6.** collar **8.** kerchief
   9. neckcloth
pap . . . **4.** teat **6.** nipple **8.** mammilla,
   soft diet
papa . . . **3.** dad **4.** clay, Pope **6.** baboon,
   father, potato, priest **7.** vulture
papal . . . **9.** apostolic **10.** pontifical
papal (pert to) . . .
   book of decrees . . **8.** decretal
   chancery . . **6.** datary
   Court . . **3.** See **5.** Curia
   envoy . . **8.** ablegate
   legate . . **6.** nuncio
   letter . . **4.** bull
   reformer . . **7.** Gregory
   residence . . **7.** Vatican
   seal . . **5.** bulla
   vestment . . **5.** fanon, orale
paper (pert to) . . .
   absorbent . . **7.** blotter
   broken . . **5.** casse
   brown . . **6.** manila
   coated . . **6.** charta
   collection . . **7.** dossier
   copy . . **6.** carbon
   crinkled . . **5.** crepe
   crisp . . **6.** pelure
   currency . . **5.** scrip
   cutlet wrap . . **8.** papilote
   damaged . . **5.** casse, salle **6.** retree
   design . . **9.** watermark
   fine . . **5.** linen **6.** vellum **9.** parchment
   flower . . **11.** strawflower
   folded . . **5.** folio
   for pounding gold sheets . . **7.** cutches
   gummed . . **5.** label, stamp **7.** plaster,
   sticker
   legal . . **4.** writ **5.** title
   measure . . **4.** page, ream **5.** quire, sheet
   nautilus . . **8.** argonaut
   official . . **5.** targe **8.** document
   pad . . **6.** tablet
   postage stamp . . **6.** pelure
   size . . **3.** cap **4.** copy, demy, pott, quad

   5. atlas, crown, folio, legal **6.** octavo
   8. foolscap, imperial **9.** colombier
   small piece . . **5.** scrip
   thin . . **4.** rice **6.** pelure, tissue **9.** onionskin
   transfer . . **12.** decalcomania
   untrimmed . . **6.** deckle (deckel) **10.** deckle
   edge **11.** deckle-edged
   writing size . . **3.** cap
paper chase . . . **13.** hare and hounds
papilla . . . **6.** nipple **10.** projection
papule . . . **6.** papula, pimple
papyra (comb form) . . . **5.** paper
papyrus . . . **4.** pith, reed **5.** paper, sedge
   6. scroll
par . . . **2.** by **5.** value **7.** average, by
   way of, strokes, through **8.** equality,
   superior
parable . . . **4.** myth, tale **5.** fable, story
   8. allegory, apologue **10.** comparison,
   similitude
parabola . . . **5.** curve
parade . . . **4.** pomp, show **5.** march
   6. flaunt **8.** flourish, grandeur, splendor
   9. pageantry, promenade, spectacle
   10. pretension, procession
   11. ostentation **12.** magnificence
   13. formal display
paradigm . . . **5.** model **7.** example, pattern
paradisaic . . . **6.** Edenic
Paradise . . . **4.** Eden **5.** Jenna **6.** Aidenn,
   heaven, Utopia **7.** Elysium
Paradise (pert to) . . .
   apple . . **5.** dwarf
   Arabic form . . **6.** Aidenn
   Buddhist, Western . . **4.** Jodo
   fool's . . **5.** limbo
   grosbeak . . **9.** cutthroat (bird)
   Mohammedan . . **5.** Jenna
   plumage . . **14.** bird of paradise
   poem (Milton) . . **12.** Paradise Lost
   16. Paradise Regained
   river . . **5.** Gihon (Bib)
   tree . . **9.** China tree
paragon . . . **4.** type **5.** ideal, match,
   model **7.** diamond (100 carats), paladin,
   pattern **8.** parallel **9.** nonpareil
paragram . . . **3.** pun
Paraguay . . .
   capital . . **8.** Asunción
   city . . **9.** Paraguari **10.** Concepcion,
   Villarrica
   language . . **7.** Guarani, Spanish
   river . . **6.** Paraná **8.** Paraguay
   tea . . **4.** maté **5.** yerba **11.** yerba de
   maté
parakeet . . . **5.** green **6.** parrot, puffin
   11. budgereegah (budgerygah)
paralysis . . . **5.** palsy **7.** paresis
   10. hemiplegia, paraplegia **11.** loss of
   power
paralyze . . . **5.** scram **6.** benumb, deaden
   7. astound, terrify, unnerve
paramount . . . **3.** top **5.** chief, liege
   6. ruling **7.** supreme **8.** dominant,
   superior **9.** principal **10.** preeminent
   13. most important
paramour . . . **5.** amour, leman, lover,
   wooer **8.** mistress **9.** gallantry
   10. sweetheart
paranoia . . . **9.** catatonia, monomania,
   nosomania

parapet . . . **5.** redan **7.** barrier, bulwark, rampart
parasite . . . **3.** bur, sug **5.** drone, toady **6.** Gnatho, insect, sponge **7.** entozoa **8.** hanger-on **9.** entophyte, sycophant
parasite (pert to) . . .
　animal . . **6.** cuckoo **7.** cowbird, entozoa
　external . . **12.** ectoparasite
　internal . . **7.** entozoa
　marine . . **6.** remora, sponge
　plant . . **9.** entophyte
　slang . . **6.** flunky
　trout . . **3.** sug
parasitic (pert to) . . .
　fish . . **6.** remora
　fungus . . **4.** rust **6.** lichen
　worm . . **8.** trichina (larva)
parcel . . . **3.** lot **4.** mete, part **5.** piece, solum (law) **6.** bundle, packet **7.** package, portion **8.** fragment
parch . . . **3.** dry **4.** burn **5.** dry up, roast, toast **6.** scorch **7.** shrivel, torrefy
parched . . . **4.** sere **5.** burnt, dried **7.** thirsty **8.** withered
parchment (pert to) . . .
　bookcover . . **5.** forel (forrel)
　fine . . **6.** vellum
　manuscript . . **10.** palimpsest
　roll . . **4.** pell **6.** scroll
　school . . **7.** diploma
pard . . . **4.** chum **5.** tiger **7.** comrade, leopard, panther, partner **10.** camelopard **11.** confederate
pardesi (Hind) . . . **9.** foreigner, outlander
pardie, parde, pardi (anc) . . . **4.** oath **6.** indeed, surely, verily **9.** certainly
pardon . . . **5.** mercy, remit, spare **6.** acquit, excuse **7.** absolve, amnesty, condone, forgive **8.** tolerate **9.** acquittal, remission **10.** absolution, indulgence (Eccl) **11.** forgiveness
pardonable . . . **6.** venial **8.** expiable **9.** excusable **10.** forgivable
pardon chair, stall . . . **12.** confessional
pare . . . **3.** cut **4.** peel, skin **5.** shave **6.** cut off, remove, resect
parent . . . **3.** dad **4.** sire **5.** pater **6.** father, mother, source **7.** genitor **8.** begetter **10.** progenitor
parental affection (animal) . . . **6.** storge
parget . . . **4.** coat **5.** paint **7.** plaster **8.** decorate, ornament **9.** whitewash
parhelion . . . **3.** sun (mock)
pariah . . . **3.** dog (half-wild) **7.** outcast **8.** commoner, low caste
parian . . . **6.** marble, market
Parian . . . **5.** Paros **6.** marble (sculptural) **9.** porcelain
parimutuel machine . . . **9.** totalizer **11.** totalizator
Paris (pert to) . . .
　blue . . **6.** cobalt **8.** Prussian
　daisy . . **10.** marguerite
　Garden (London) . . **10.** bear garden
　green . . **11.** insecticide
Paris, France . . .
　anc name . . **7.** Lutetia (Lutice)
　airport . . **4.** Orly
　capital of . . **6.** France
　criminal . . **6.** apache
　famed sites . . **6.** Louvre **8.** Pantheon

9. Notre Dame **10.** Montmartre **11.** Eiffel Tower **13.** Champs Elysées, Napoleon's Tomb
　native . . **8.** Parisian
　patron saint . . **5.** Denis (Denys)
　racecourse . . **7.** Auteuil
　river . . **5.** Seine
　subway . . **5.** Metro
Paris, Gr legend . . .
　brought about . . **9.** Trojan War **10.** Fall of Troy
　father . . **5.** Priam (King of Troy)
　killer of . . **8.** Achilles
　mother . . **6.** Hecuba
　wife . . **6.** Oenone
parish . . . **5.** laity **7.** diocese **8.** district **9.** parochial
paristhmion . . . **6.** tonsil
park . . . **4.** area (enclosed) **5.** place, tract **6.** claire, common, settle **7.** pasture (Eng) **8.** woodland **9.** grassland, pleasance **10.** playground **11.** reservation, set and leave
Park, Highway . . .
　Avenue . . **9.** Manhattan
　Lane . . **6.** London
　Row . . **9.** Manhattan
Park, Historical . . . **6.** Shiloh **8.** Pea Ridge, Saratoga **9.** Minute Man **10.** Gettysburg, Morristown **12.** Harper's Ferry, Independence
Park, US . . . **4.** Zion **7.** Glacier, Olympic (rain forests) **8.** Sequoyah (Sequoja), Yosemite **9.** Haleakala, Mesa Verde **10.** Everglades, Mt McKinley, Shenandoah **11.** Grand Canyon, Kings Canyon, Yellowstone **12.** Harper's Ferry **15.** Petrified Forest
parlay, parley . . . **4.** chat **5.** parle, treat **6.** confer **7.** discuss **8.** converse **10.** conference, discussion **11.** arbitration
parliament . . . **4.** Diet **8.** Congress **11.** legislature
parlous . . . **4.** keen **5.** risky **6.** shrewd **7.** cunning **8.** shocking **9.** dangerous
Parnassian . . . **4.** muse, poet **9.** butterfly **10.** Parnassius
Parnassus, Greece . . .
　mountain . . **6.** Phocis
　site of . . **6.** Delphi **8.** Castalia (fountain) **13.** Delphic Apollo
　symbol of . . **6.** poetry
parody . . . **5.** farce **6.** satire **7.** mockery, take-off **9.** burlesque, imitation **10.** caricature
paroemia . . . **7.** proverb
parol, parole . . . **4.** oral, word **6.** speech **7.** freedom, promise, release **8.** pleading **11.** word of mouth
paronomasia . . . **3.** pun **7.** punning **8.** wordplay **9.** assonance **12.** agnomination
paroxysm . . . **3.** fit **4.** pang **5.** throe **6.** access, attack, frenzy **7.** illness **9.** agitation **10.** fit of anger **12.** exacerbation
paroxysm of grief . . . **5.** agony
parricide (murder of) . . . **7.** kinsman
parrot . . . **3.** ara, hia, kea **4.** jako, kaka, loro, lory **5.** arara, cagit, macaw,

polly **6.** kakapo, tiriba **7.** corella,
lorilet **8.** cockatoo, lorikeet, lovebird,
parakeet **9.** Psittacus (Old World)
14. Psittaciformes
parrot (pert to) . . .
disease . . **11.** psittacosis
genus . . **6.** Nestor **9.** Psittacus
gray . . **4.** jako
green . . **5.** cagit
hawk . . **3.** hia
long-tailed . . **5.** macaw
monk . . **4.** loro
New Zealand . . **4.** kaka
owl . . **6.** kakapo
parrot fish . . **4.** loro, scar **5.** lauia **6.** scarid
7. labroid **8.** Labridae, Scaridae
parrotlike (tongued) . . **12.** anthropoglot
sheep-killing . . **3.** kea
short-tailed . . **7.** lorilet
parry . . . **4.** fend, ward **5.** avert, avoid,
elude, evade, shift **6.** refute, thwart
pars . . . **4.** part
Parsee Bible . . . **10.** Zend Avesta
Parsei, Parsi . . . **6.** Gheber (Ghebre)
11. Zoroastrian **13.** fire worshiper
Parsifal (pert to) . . .
character . . **6.** Knight
healer of . . **8.** Amfortas
son . . **9.** Lohengrin
parsimonious . . . **4.** near **5.** close
6. frugal, meager, skimpy, sordid,
stingy **7.** miserly, sparing **8.** covetous,
grasping **9.** illiberal, mercenary,
penurious **10.** avaricious
parsley . . . **4.** herb **5.** cumin **7.** garnish
9. Ammiaceae, flavoring
parsley camphor . . . **6.** apiole
parson . . . **6.** rector **8.** minister, preacher,
reverend **9.** clergyman
parsonage . . . **5.** gleve, manse, tithe
7. rectory **8.** benefice, vicarage
9. pastorate **10.** presbytery
parson bird . . . **3.** tui
part . . . **3.** cut, die **4.** open, role, twin
5. allot, break, piece, sever, share
6. depart, divide, member, sunder
7. analyze, disband, disjoin, divorce,
portion, section, segment **8.** dissever,
disunite, division, fragment, function,
separate **9.** component
part (pert to) . . .
basic . . **4.** core, pith **7.** essence, nucleus
choice . . **5.** cream, elite **6.** marrow
coarse . . **5.** dregs
composite . . **7.** section
corresponding . . **7.** isomere
essential . . **4.** core, gist, pith **5.** heart
extra . . **5.** spare
greater . . **4.** bulk
hardest . . **5.** brunt
infinitesimal . . **4.** atom, mite
insignificant . . **3.** bit **4.** iota **6.** trifle
kept . . **6.** retent
main . . **4.** body **5.** trunk
narrow . . **4.** neck
proportional . . **5.** quota
rootlike . . **7.** radicle
sawlike . . **5.** serra
segment . . **5.** tmema
small . . **3.** bit, jot **4.** iota **6.** detail
7. snippet

smallest . . **4.** whit **5.** minim
solo accompaniment . . **9.** obbligato
tenth . . **5.** tithe
unpaid . . **6.** arrear **9.** arrearage
uppermost . . **3.** top **4.** peak **6.** upside
7. topside
winglike . . **3.** ala
with . . **7.** discard **10.** relinquish
partage . . . **4.** part **5.** share **7.** portion
8. division
partake . . . **3.** eat **5.** share **7.** receive
11. participate
partan . . . **4.** crab
parted . . . **5.** cleft **6.** cloven **7.** divided,
severed **9.** separated **11.** apportioned
parterre . . . **10.** level space **12.** theater
boxes, theater space **17.** ornamental
gardens
parthogenesis . . . **7.** apogamy
10. thelyotoky **12.** reproduction
partial . . . **6.** biased, unfair, unjust
7. limited **8.** not total, one-sided,
partisan **9.** imperfect **10.** fractional,
incomplete, prejudiced **11.** predisposed
13. foolishly fond
partiality . . . **4.** bias **6.** desire **9.** injustice,
prejudice **10.** preference **11.** inclination,
partisanism **12.** partisanship,
predilection
participant . . . **6.** sharer **7.** entrant
8. partaker **9.** accessory, colleague
12. participator
particle . . . **3.** ace, bit, ion, jot **4.** atom,
drop, iota, mite, mote, whit **5.** grain,
piece, shred, spark **6.** tittle **7.** globule,
granule, smidgen
particle (pert to) . . .
electric . . **3.** ion **5.** anion **6.** proton
least possible . . **5.** minim
minute . . **3.** jot, ray **4.** atom, iota **5.** grain,
speck **7.** granule
negative . . **3.** nor, not
nuclear . . **5.** gluon, meson, quark
6. baryon, hadron
parti-colored . . . **4.** pied, roan **5.** pinto
6. motley **7.** piebald **9.** harlequin
10. variegated **11.** polychromic
particular . . . **4.** item, nice, part, sole
5. event, fussy **6.** detail **7.** precise,
special, topical **8.** detailed, especial,
peculiar, separate, specific **9.** attentive
10. fastidious, individual, overminute
11. persnickety **12.** circumstance,
technicality
partisan, partizan . . . **4.** pike **5.** staff
6. zealot **7.** partial **8.** adherent, advocate,
follower **9.** supporter **10.** fractional,
prejudiced
partition . . . **4.** wall **5.** allot **6.** divide,
screen, septum **7.** scantle **8.** set apart
9. apportion, severance **10.** distribute,
separation **13.** apportionment
partitioned . . . **7.** septate
partly . . . **6.** in part **9.** partially
partly illuminated . . . **6.** shaded
8. adumbral **9.** penumbral
partly open . . . **4.** ajar
partner . . . **3.** pal **4.** ally, mate, wife
6. sharer, spouse **7.** comrade, husband
9. associate, coadjutor, colleague
10. accomplice **11.** confederate,

participant
partnership . . . **4.** firm **7.** cahoots, co-
   mated **8.** business, contract
   10. fellowship **11.** affiliation
   13. participation
part of . . .
   anchor . . **4.** palm
   bird wing . . **5.** alula
   cannon . . **5.** chase
   church . . **4.** apse, nave **5.** altar **7.** chancel
      8. transept
   circle . . **3.** arc **6.** degree **7.** segment
   compass . . **6.** needle
   ear . . **4.** lobe **5.** pinna **6.** tragus
      8. tympanum **9.** labyrinth
   eye . . **4.** iris, uvea **5.** pupil **6.** cornea,
      retina
   flower . . **4.** stem **5.** calyx, petal, sepal
   foot lever . . **5.** pedal **7.** treadle
   fort . . **5.** redan **7.** bastion
   head . . **4.** pate **5.** scalp, skull **7.** cranium
   minstrel show . . **4.** olio **5.** bones **6.** end
      man **12.** interlocutor
   newspaper . . **3.** ear **4.** item, page
      6. by-line **9.** editorial
   optical measure . . **7.** alidade
   printing press . . **6.** platen
   rifle (anc) . . **4.** tige
   ship . . **3.** bow **4.** brig, deck, helm, keel,
      mast **5.** stern, wheel **6.** anchor, bridge,
      rudder **8.** steerage
   step . . **5.** riser, tread **6.** nosing
   theater . . **3.** box **4.** loge **5.** foyer, stage
      7. balcony, curtain, gallery, parquet
      8. parterre **9.** orchestra
   turtle . . **7.** calipee **8.** calipash
partridge . . . **4.** hill, snow, yutu **5.** covey
   (flock) **6.** bamboo, chukar (chukor),
   Perdix, seesee **7.** cinerea, tinamou
   8. raw umber **9.** francolin
   11. Francolinus **12.** ruffed grouse
party . . . **3.** tea **4.** ball, drum, sect, side
   6. clique, fiesta, person **7.** company,
   faction **8.** sociable **9.** reception
   10. detachment **11.** association,
   combination **12.** participator
party (pert to) . . .
   deserter . . **6.** bolter
   evening . . **6.** soiree
   lawn . . **4.** fete
   man . . **8.** partisan
   member . . **8.** Democrat, Federate
      9. Communist, Dixiecrat, Greenback
      (Hist), Socialist **10.** Republican
      11. Independent
   men's . . **4.** stag **6.** smoker
Parvati (pert to) . . .
   consort . . **4.** Siva
   father . . **7.** Himavat
   goddess . . **8.** mountain
parvenu . . . **4.** snob **7.** upstart **12.** nouveau
   riche
Pasch, pasch . . . **4.** lamb, moon **6.** candle,
   Easter, supper **8.** Passover **10.** Good
   Friday **11.** candlestick, celebration
pascual . . . **8.** pascuage, pastures
pasear . . . **4.** walk **6.** parade, stroll
   9. promenade **11.** perambulate
pasha, pacha . . . **3.** dey **4.** emir
   5. title **6.** bashaw (early) **8.** nobleman
   10. magistrate

pashalik (pashalic) . . . **9.** territory
   (pasha's) **12.** jurisdiction
pashm . . . **6.** fleece (Tibetan goat)
pasigraphy . . . **6.** system (Universal)
   7. symbols **8.** language
Pasiphae (pert to) . . .
   mother of . . **7.** Ariadne
   son . . **8.** minotaur (monster)
   wife of . . **5.** Minos
pasquinade . . . **5.** squib **6.** satire
   7. lampoon, pasquil
pass . . . **2.** go **3.** die, end, gap **4.** ghat,
   hand, lane, pace, step **5.** canto, enact,
   gorge, lapse, occur, relay, spend, throw
   6. convey, crisis, defile, elapse, exceed,
   happen, passus, perish, permit, ratify,
   ticket **7.** excrete, passage **8.** hand
   over, passport, surmount, transfer
   10. permission **11.** Annie Oakley
   13. complimentary
pass (pert to) . . .
   Alpine . . **3.** col
   around . . **5.** skirt **6.** detour
   as genuine . . **5.** cheat, foist
      11. interpolate
   away . . **3.** die, end **6.** perish, vanish
      9. cease to be, disappear, obsolesce
   by . . **4.** cote, omit, skip, snub **6.** elapse,
      forego, ignore **7.** proceed **8.** overlook
      9. disregard
   hurriedly . . **7.** scamper, skitter **9.** skim
      along
   into . . **5.** glide, merge **6.** become **7.** get
      to be **9.** penetrate
   judgment . . **4.** rule **6.** decree, ordain
      8. sentence
   on . . **3.** die **6.** confer, ratify **7.** advance
      8. bequeath, continue
   out . . **3.** die **4.** exit **5.** faint **7.** be dazed
      9. disappear **11.** be dead drunk **13.** be
      unconscious
   over . . **4.** omit, skip **5.** cross **6.** elapse,
      excuse, exempt, ignore, slight
      7. condone, exclude, neglect
      8. overlook, transfer, traverse
   sudden . . **5.** lunge
   through . . **5.** cross, reeve (cringle)
      6. pierce **7.** pervade, undergo **8.** traverse
      9. penetrate **10.** comprehend,
      experience
   up . . **4.** snub **5.** evade **6.** reject **7.** decline
      9. disregard
   without touching . . **5.** clear
passable . . . **4.** so-so **7.** current
   8. mediocre, moderate, traveled
   9. navigable, tolerable, traversed
   10. acceptable, accessible, admissible
   12. satisfactory
passado (fencing) . . . **6.** thrust
passage . . . **4.** adit, exit, flue, ford,
   gang, hall, iter **5.** aisle, allay, allée,
   canal, death **6.** atrium, avenue, egress,
   travel, voyage **7.** channel, excerpt,
   journey, transit **8.** corridor, incident,
   progress, sanction **9.** enactment,
   migration **10.** transition **11.** altercation,
   negotiation, preterition **12.** thoroughfare
passage (pert to) . . .
   book . . **7.** excerpt
   brain . . **4.** iter
   closed end . . **7.** impasse **8.** cul-de-sac

covered.. **4.** pawn
history.. **5.** alure
mine.. **4.** sill **5.** stope
narrow.. **3.** gut **5.** aisle, alley, gully,
slype **6.** defile, strait
river.. **7.** estuary
passageway . . . **4.** hall, lane, ramp, slip
5. aisle, alley, lumen **6.** access, arcade,
avenue, defile, outlet, strait, tunnel
7. gangway **8.** corridor
passant . . . **7.** cursory, walking (Her)
8. passer-by **9.** ephemeral, excelling
10. surpassing, transitory
passé . . . **4.** aged, past, worn **5.** faded
6. gone by **8.** obsolete **10.** antiquated
13. superannuated
passed (pert to) . . .
by.. **6.** bygone, former **8.** preterit
(preterite)
over.. **7.** fleeted **11.** preterition
through pores.. **7.** osmosed **8.** dialyzed
9. permeated, transuded
passenger . . . **4.** fare **6.** pigeon, trekku
7. pilgrim, tourist **8.** commuter, traveler,
wayfarer **9.** sightseer, transient
passerine bird . . . **5.** finch **7.** sparrow
8. songbird
passing . . . **7.** cursory **8.** elapsing,
fleeting **9.** departing, enactment,
ephemeral, exceeding, happening,
transient, vanishing **10.** surpassing,
transitory **11.** preterition
passion . . . **3.** ire, yen **4.** love, lust, rage,
zeal **5.** anger, craze, wrath **6.** desire
7. emotion, feeling **9.** eloquence,
martyrdom **10.** enthusiasm, excitement
passion (pert to) . . .
flower.. **6.** maypop **11.** passionwort
flower family.. **10.** Passiflora
for doing great things.. **11.** megalomania
music.. **8.** oratorio
Play.. **14.** Christ's Passion
(Oberammergau)
Week.. **8.** Holy Week
passionate . . . **3.** sad **5.** angry **6.** ardent
7. amorous, excited, fervent, pitiful,
violent **8.** agitated, eloquent, vehement
9. emotional, irascible **10.** passionato
11. hot-tempered, impassioned
passionless . . . **4.** calm **8.** painless
9. heartless, unfeeling **10.** spiritless
11. unemotional **13.** dispassionate
passive . . . **5.** inert, quiet, stoic **6.** stolíd
7. languid, patient **8.** inactive
9. apathetic **10.** submissive
11. acquiescent, indifferent, unresisting
Passover (pert to) . . .
festival.. **5.** Seder **6.** Jewish
lamb.. **7.** paschal
psalm.. **6.** hallel **14.** Egyptian Hallel
sacrifice.. **11.** paschal lamb
The (Passover).. **5.** Pasch
passport . . . **4.** pass, visa (vise) **5.** congé
6. congee, permit **8.** document **11.** safe
conduct
passus . . . **5.** canto
password . . . **9.** watchword **10.** mot de
passé, open sesame **11.** countersign
past . . . **2.** by **3.** ago **4.** date, dead, gone,
over, yore **5.** after, since **6.** beyond,
ultimo **7.** elapsed, outworn **9.** foregoing,

yesterday
pasta . . . **7.** gnocchi, lasagna, ravioli
8. linguini, macaroni **9.** fettucini,
manicotti, spaghetti **10.** vermicelli
paste . . . **3.** pap, poi **4.** glue, sham
5. dough, stick **6.** mastic, strass
8. adhesive, frippery, mucilage
10. confection **13.** stick together
pastel . . . **5.** light **6.** crayon, sketch **9.** pale
color
pastille . . . **6.** troche **7.** lozenge
pastime . . . **4.** game **5.** hobby, sport
9. amusement, diversion **10.** recreation
13. entertainment
pastor . . . **5.** rabbi **6.** curate, divine,
keeper, parson, priest, rector
8. chaplain, guardian, minister,
Reverend, shepherd
pastoral . . . **4.** poem **5.** drama, rural
6. poetic **9.** romance **14.** ecclesiastical
pastoral (pert to) . . .
cantata.. **8.** serenata
crook, staff.. **5.** pedum **7.** crosier
god.. **3.** Pan
oboe.. **7.** musette
pert to.. **6.** rustic **8.** agrestic, herdsman,
shepherd
pipe.. **3.** oat **4.** reed
poem.. **5.** idyll (idyl) **7.** bucolic, eclogue
pastry . . . **3.** pie **4.** tart **6.** Danish,
éclair **7.** dariole, strudel **8.** napoleon,
pandowdy, turnover **9.** cream puff,
shortcake **10.** pâtisserie
past tense . . . **8.** preterit (preterite)
pasturage, right of . . . **9.** horsegate
pasture . . . **3.** ham, lea **4.** feed, food
5. agist, grama, grass, graze **6.** meadow
9. grassland **10.** agostadero
pasture bird . . . **6.** plover **7.** sparrow
pat . . . **3.** dab, fit, paw, tap **4.** blow,
lump **5.** fixed, impel, known, throw
6. caress, smooth, stroke **7.** flatten
9. immovable **10.** seasonable
Patagonia (So Am) . . .
city.. **11.** Punta Arenas
deity.. **7.** Setebos
Indian people.. **9.** Tehuelche
nearby island.. **14.** Tierra del Fuego
race (said of).. **6.** giants **7.** Big Feet,
tallest **9.** Patagones
rodent.. **4.** cavy **8.** capybara, Caviidae
strait.. **8.** Magellan (Magallanes)
patamar (pattamar) . . . **6.** vessel (Naut)
7. courier **9.** messenger
patata . . . **6.** potato **11.** sweet potato
patch . . . **4.** mend, vamp **5.** bodge, botch,
clump, cover, field **6.** blotch, cobble,
parcel **8.** addition, appliqué **9.** reconcile
patch (pert to) . . .
cloth.. **5.** clout
imprinting.. **5.** friar
metal.. **6.** solder
of trees.. **4.** mott
patcher (humorous) . . . **6.** sartor
patchwork . . . **5.** quilt **6.** jumble, pillow,
scraps **7.** mixture **9.** checkered,
fancywork, fragments **10.** hodgepodge
pate . . . **3.** pie, top **4.** head **5.** brain,
crown, pasty, patty **6.** badger
patella . . . **3.** pan **4.** bone, dish, vase
7. kneecap, kneepan

paten ... **4.** disc, dish, disk **5.** plate
 7. patener (bearer of)
patent ... **4.** open **5.** berat (Turk), right
 7. license, warrant **8.** document,
 manifest **9.** available, copyright,
 privilege, trademark **10.** accessible,
 protection, university **12.** unobstructed
pater ... **6.** father, priest
Pater Noster ... **11.** Lord's Prayer
Paternoster Row ... **6.** street (London)
Pater Patriae ... **18.** Father of his country
 (Cicero, Marius, Trajan, Washington,
 etc)
path ... **3.** way **4.** lane, line **5.** piste,
 route, swath, track, trail **6.** course
 7. footway
path (pert to) ...
 along a slope .. **4.** berm (berme)
 animal .. **5.** piste, spoor **6.** roddin
 7. rodding
 of energy .. **7.** ergodic
 of moving parts .. **5.** locus
 of planets .. **5.** orbit
 Spanish .. **6.** camino, comino
pathetic ... **3.** sad **5.** teary **8.** dolorous,
 grievous, stirring **9.** affecting
 10. lamentable
pathological ... **6.** morbid **9.** unhealthy
pathological reaction ... **7.** allergy
patience ... **9.** endurance, fortitude,
 solitaire, tolerance **10.** submission,
 sufferance **11.** forbearance, resignation
 12. acquiescence, perseverance
patient ... **4.** calm, meek **6.** client
 8. tolerant **9.** unsettled **11.** persevering
 13. long-suffering
patio ... **5.** court **9.** courtyard
patriarch ... **4.** Noah, sire **5.** elder,
 pater **6.** bishop, father **7.** aged man,
 veteran **9.** churchman **10.** Methuselah
 13. paterfamilias
patrimonial ... **9.** inherited **10.** hereditary
patrimony ... **8.** heritage **10.** birthright
 11. ancient rite, inheritance
patriot ... **4.** Cato (Rom), Otis (Am)
 5. jingo **7.** chauvin **9.** flag-waver
 10. chauvinist, countryman
patriotism ... **10.** chauvinism
 11. nationalism **13.** love of country
patrol ... **5.** guard **7.** protect **8.** traverse
 9. keep guard **13.** perambulation
patron ... **5.** buyer, guest **6.** backer,
 seller, trader **8.** customer, guardian
 9. financier, protector, supporter
 10. benefactor
patronage ... **5.** aegis (egis), favor
 6. defend **7.** support **8.** auspices
 9. clientele, fosterage **10.** assistance
 13. condescension, encouragement
patronizing ... **8.** deigning **9.** financing,
 revealing **10.** sponsoring
 13. condescending
patrons (group) ... **7.** backers, masters
 9. clientele, customers
Patron Saint of ...
 beggars .. **5.** Giles
 boys .. **8.** Nicholas
 England .. **4.** Anne **6.** George
 fishermen .. **5.** Peter
 France .. **5.** Denis
 Ireland .. **7.** Patrick

 lawyers .. **4.** Ives
 motherhood .. **6.** Gerard
 musicians .. **7.** Cecilia
 Pueblo Indians .. **7.** Stephen
 sailors .. **4.** Elmo
 Scotland .. **6.** Andrew
 shoemakers .. **7.** Crispin
 swineherds .. **7.** Anthony
 Venice .. **4.** Mark **9.** Pantalone
 Wales .. **5.** David
patten ... **4.** clog **5.** skate **8.** footgear,
 overshoe, snowshoe
pattern ... **4.** norm, seme **5.** habit, model
 6. design, format **7.** diagram, paragon
 8. paradigm, parterre, template
pavilion ... **4.** tent **5.** cover, kiosk
 6. canopy **8.** covering **9.** gloriette
 10. tabernacle
pavis ... **5.** cover **6.** screen, shield
 7. protect
paw ... **3.** pad, pud **4.** foot, hand **5.** patté,
 pedal **6.** handle, stroke **7.** foreleg (Her)
 8. forefoot **10.** manipulate
pawl ... **4.** bolt, sear, trip **5.** click **6.** detent,
 pallet, tongue **7.** ratchet **9.** mechanism
pawn ... **4.** gage, hock, tool **6.** pledge
 7. counter, peacock **8.** chessman,
 guaranty, hockshop **9.** put in pawn
 10. pawnbroker
Pawnee ... **6.** Indian
pawnie ... **7.** peacock
pay ... **3.** aby (abye), fee, tip **4.** ante,
 meet, wage **5.** remit, repay **6.** defray,
 reward, salary, suffer **7.** requite, satisfy
 9. indemnify, reimburse, retaliate
 10. compensate, punishment,
 recompense, remunerate **11.** retribution
 12. compensation
pay (pert to) ...
 attention .. **4.** heed **6.** listen
 back .. **6.** rebate, refund **9.** reimburse,
 retaliate
 dirt .. **3.** ore
 envelope .. **5.** wages **6.** salary **7.** stipend
 extra .. **5.** bonus **8.** kickback
 for .. **3.** aby (abye) **5.** atone **6.** suffer
 off .. **6.** punish **7.** requite **9.** pay in full,
 retribute **10.** compensate
 out .. **5.** spend **6.** expend, settle
 7. hand out **8.** disburse **10.** distribute
 12. exorbitantly **14.** through the nose
 up .. **4.** ante **6.** settle **9.** liquidate
paymaster ... **6.** burser, purser **7.** cashier
payment ... **3.** cro, fee **4.** dues,
 mail **6.** return **8.** defrayal, requital
 10. punishment, recompense
 12. chastisement, compensation
payment (pert to) ...
 for homicide, murder .. **3.** cro **4.** eric
 (Brehon Law) **7.** galanas (Welsh),
 wergild (weregild)
 immediate .. **4.** cash
 upon delivery .. **3.** COD **14.** cash on
 delivery
paynim ... **5.** pagan **7.** heathen, infidel
 8. Pagandom **10.** Mohammedan
payong ... **8.** umbrella (golden)
paysage ... **7.** picture (landscape)
 9. landscape
pea (pert to) ...
 bird .. **6.** oriole

chick .. **4.** gram **5.** Cicer
everlasting (Bib) .. **9.** vetchling
family .. **8.** Fabaceae
flour (seasoned) .. **9.** Erbswurst
heath .. **7.** carmele
pigeon .. **3.** dal **5.** arhar
sausage .. **9.** Erbswurst
shaped .. **8.** pisiform
soup .. **3.** fog (dull yellow)
split .. **3.** dal
tree .. **8.** laburnum
tropical .. **4.** dove **7.** Zenaida
  12. mourning dove
vine .. **8.** earthpea
peace ... **3.** pax **5.** amity, quiet, truce
  6. accord, repose **7.** harmony, Nirvana,
  silence **8.** ataraxia (ataraxy), serenity
  9. stillness **10.** quiescence **11.** tranquility
peaceable ... **5.** quiet, still **6.** irenic,
  silent **7.** henotic, pacific **8.** amicable,
  tranquil **9.** quiescent **10.** concordant,
  harmonious **11.** undisturbed
peaceful ... **4.** calm **5.** irene **6.** irenic,
  placid, serene **7.** halcyon, pacific
  8. tranquil **11.** comfortable
peace pipe ... **7.** calumet
peach ... **5.** fruit **6.** accuse, betray, brandy,
  indict, inform **7.** impeach **8.** quandong
  9. red-yellow
peach (pert to) ...
  cordial .. **7.** persico **8.** persicot
  family .. **12.** Amygdalaceae
  French .. **8.** persicot
  grafted (quince) .. **9.** melocoton
  like .. **6.** almond
  origin .. **5.** China
  stone .. **7.** putamen
  variety .. **7.** Elberta **8.** Crawford
  9. freestone, nectarine **10.** clingstone
peacock ... **3.** mao **4.** Pavo (Astron),
  pawn, pose **5.** strut **9.** swaggerer
peacock (pert to) ...
  blue (color) .. **4.** paon
  butterfly .. **2.** io
  fan .. **9.** flabellum
  feather part .. **4.** marl
  female .. **6.** peahen
  fish .. **6.** wrasse
  flower .. **9.** poinciana
  heron .. **7.** bittern
  ref to .. **7.** peafowl **8.** pavonine
  tail spot .. **3.** eye
peak ... **3.** alp, epi, pic, top, tor **4.** acme,
  apex, cone, crag, cusp, dent, dolt
  5. crown, piton, slink, sneak, steal
  6. finial, shrink, summit **8.** headland,
  mountain **9.** simpleton **10.** promontory
Peak ... **5.** Borah, Logan **7.** Everest,
  St Elias **8.** McKinley **9.** Mont Blanc
  10. Matterhorn **11.** Kilimanjaro
  12. Popocatepetl
peal ... **4.** boom, clap, echo, ring, toll
  6. appeal, shovel **7.** resound, summons,
  thunder **8.** carillon
peanut ... **5.** pinda (pindal, pindar)
  6. goober, trifle **8.** earthnut, earthpea,
  katchung
pear (pert to) ...
  alligator .. **7.** avocado
  cider .. **5.** perry
  Latin .. **5.** pirum

prickly .. **4.** tuna **5.** nopal **7.** Opuntia
shaped .. **8.** pyriform
shaped vessel .. **6.** aludel
squash .. **7.** chayote
type .. **4.** Bosc **8.** Bartlett
pearl ... **3.** gem **4.** drop **5.** nacre, tooth,
  white **9.** margarite
pearl (pert to) ...
  bird .. **10.** guinea fowl
  color .. **4.** blue **13.** mother-of-pearl
  eye .. **8.** cataract
  imitation .. **6.** olivet
  of great luster .. **6.** orient
  opal .. **9.** cacholong (opaque)
  oyster .. **7.** Avicula
  seed .. **7.** aliofar (obs)
  vegetable .. **5.** onion
pearly ... **5.** milky, quick, smart **7.** opaline,
  whitish **8.** pellucid **10.** opalescent
  11. flourishing
Pearly Gates (Bib) ... **6.** heaven, twelve
peasant ... **4.** boor, hind, peon, serf
  5. clown, knave, swain **6.** carlot,
  cotman, cottar, rascal, rustic
  10. countryman
peasant (pert to) ...
  Arab, Syria .. **6.** fellah
  cropsharer .. **7.** metayer
  English .. **4.** hind **5.** churl
  Indian .. **4.** ryot
  Irish .. **4.** kern (kerne) **7.** cottier
  like .. **4.** base, rude **8.** clownish
  Russian .. **5.** kulak (rich)
  Scottish .. **4.** tyke (tike) **6.** cotter (cottar)
pease ... **5.** quiet **6.** pacify **7.** appease
  9. reconcile
peasecrow ... **4.** tern
peat ... **3.** bog, pet **4.** coal, fuel, moor,
  moss, turf **6.** minion **7.** darling
  8. favorite **11.** combustible
peat (pert to) ...
  cutter .. **5.** piner
  moss .. **8.** sphagnum
  turf spade .. **5.** slave
  wood .. **11.** loosestrife
peau ... **4.** skin (silks) **6.** fabric
peba ... **9.** armadillo
pebble ... **5.** scree, stone, talus **6.** quartz
  7. chuckie (chucky), crystal, psephos
  11. gravelstone, pebblestone
peccadillo ... **4.** slip **5.** error, fault, lapse
  12. indiscretion
peccant ... **3.** bad **5.** wrong **6.** guilty,
  morbid, wicked **7.** corrupt, sinning,
  spoiled **9.** incorrect, unhealthy
  12. insalubrious
peccary ... **6.** mammal (piglike)
  7. Tagassu, Tayassu **8.** javelina
pech ... **4.** pant **11.** breathe hard
pecht (Scot) ... **5.** fairy, gnome, pygmy
peck ... **3.** dab, dot, eat, nag **4.** food,
  hole, jerk, kiss **5.** pitch, prick, throw
  6. peggle, stroke **7.** measure **8.** quantity
  11. large amount
peck at ... **3.** nag **4.** carp, twit **5.** tease
  6. attack, harass
pectase ... **6.** enzyme
peculiar ... **3.** odd **4.** idio (comb form)
  5. queer **6.** oddish, unique **7.** curious,
  special, strange, typical **8.** distinct,
  separate, singular **9.** different, eccentric

10. particular 14. characteristic
peculiar expression . . . 5. idiom
peculiarity . . . 4. kink 5. quirk, trait
6. oddity 7. oddness 9. mannerism
10. partiality 11. singularity
12. eccentricity 14. characteristic
peculiar to a district . . . 7. endemic
pecuniary . . . 6. fiscal 8. monetary
9. financial
pedagogue . . . 5. tutor 6. pedant
7. teacher 12. schoolmaster
pedal . . . 4. foot 5. lever 6. driver 7. treadle
9. propeller
pedant . . . 4. prig 5. tutor 6. dorbel, purist
9. formalist, pedagogue 10. conformist
12. bluestocking, precisionist,
schoolmaster
peddle . . . 4. hawk, sell, vend 6. piddle,
retail 11. disseminate
peddler, pedlar . . . 6. cadger, coster,
hawker, mugger, sutler 7. chapman
8. huckster 9. vivandier
12. costermonger
peddler's French . . . 6. jargon (thieves')
9. gibberish
pedestal . . . 7. support 10. foundation
pedestal part . . . 3. die 4. base, dado
5. socle 6. plinth, quadra
pedestrian . . . 3. ped 4. dull, slow 5. hiker
6. hoofer, walker 11. commonplace
12. foot traveler 13. unimaginative
pedicel . . . 3. ray (of an umbel) 4. stem
5. stalk 8. peduncle
pediculosis . . . 9. lousiness
Pediculus . . . 4. lice
pedigree . . . 6. stemma 7. descent, lineage
8. ancestry, register 9. genealogy
10. family tree
pedio (comb form) . . . 4. sole 6. instep
pedology . . . 9. soil study 10. child study
pedometer . . . 5. watch 8. odograph
10. instrument, passometer
pedregal . . . 9. lava field
pedum . . . 5. crook, staff (pastoral)
peduncle . . . 4. stem 5. scape, stalk
7. pedicel, pedicle, sessile
peek . . . 3. pry 4. peep 5. chirp, flash
6. glance 7. glimpse 9. look slyly
peekaboo . . . 4. game 6. bopeep
peel . . . 4. bark, pare, rind, skin 5. slipe,
stake, strip 6. cut off, lamina, shovel
8. car blade, palisade, stockade
peel (off) . . . 4. harl, pare, tear 7. come
off 8. get loose 11. decorticate
peeler . . . 4. crab (shedding), yarn 5. corer
7. hustler 8. pillager 9. policeman
peep . . . 3. pry 4. peek, peer, pule, skeg
5. cheep, chirp, pipit, sight (firearms)
6. glance, squeak 7. crevice 8. peephole
9. sandpiper
peephole . . . 4. hole 6. eyelet 8. aperture
9. sighthole
peer . . . 4. duke, earl, fere, gaze, mate
5. baron, equal, match, noble, stare,
stime (styme) 7. marquis 8. nobleman,
superior, viscount
Peer Gynt (pert to) . . .
drama, poem by . . 5. Ibsen
mother . . 3. Ase
music suite by . . 5. Grieg
peerless . . . 9. matchless, nonpareil,

paper size, unequaled, unmatched
10. unexcelled 11. ne plus ultra,
superlative
peesweep, peeseweep . . . 7. lapwing
10. greenfinch
peetweep . . . 9. sandpiper (spotted)
peeved . . . 4. sore 7. annoyed, nettled
9. irritated
peevish . . . 3. coy 4. sour 5. cross, sulky,
techy, testy 6. crusty, morose, touchy
7. fretful, pettish, spleeny, waspish
8. captious, choleric, contrary, perverse,
petulant, snappish 9. irascible, irritable,
querulous, splenetic
peg . . . 3. hob, leg, nob, nog, pin 4. dram,
skeg 5. drink, stake, tooth 6. drudge,
fasten, reason 7. pretext, support
9. persevere, recognize
peg (pert to) . . .
cribbage . . 4. game
iron . . 5. piton
out . . 7. croquet
shoe . . 5. cleat
wood . . 5. spill, thole 8. treenail
pega . . . 5. shark 6. remora
Pegasus . . . 5. horse (winged), steed
13. constellation
Pegasus's rider . . . 11. Bellerophon
pegomancy, divination by . . . 7. springs
9. fountains
peho . . . 8. morepork
peignoir . . . 8. negligee 12. dressing
gown, dressing sack
pejorative . . . 11. disparaging
12. depreciatory
Peking, Pekin . . . 4. blue, city, duck
7. spaniel
pelagic . . . 6. marine 7. oceanic
9. underseas
pelagic organism . . . 6. nekton 7. benthos
8. plankton
Pele . . . 7. goddess (volcanoes)
pêle-mêle . . . 8. pellmell
Peleus (pert to) . . .
father . . 6. Aeacus
King of . . 9. Myrmidons
son . . 8. Achilles
wife . . 6. Thetis
pelf . . . 3. fur, rob 4. gain 5. booty,
lucre, money, spoil, trash 6. pilfer,
profit, refuse, riches, wealth 7. rubbish
10. ne'er-do-well
Pelias (pert to) . . .
daughter . . 5. Medes
King of . . 6. Iolcus
nephew . . 5. Jason
son . . 7. Acastus
pelican (pert to) . . .
heraldry . . 10. in her piety
symbolic of . . 6. Christ 7. charity
Pelican State . . . 9. Louisiana
pell . . . 3. fur 4. hide, pelt, skin 5. hurry
6. hasten 13. parchment roll
pellagra . . . 5. zeism
pellar, peller . . . 6. wizard 8. conjurer
pellet . . . 4. ball, pill 6. bullet 7. granule,
missile, pallion
pellicle . . . 4. film, scum 6. lamina
7. coating 8. membrane
pell-mell, pellmell . . . 10. vehemently
12. furious haste 13. helter-skelter

pellock ... **8.** porpoise
pellucid ... **5.** clear **6.** bright, limpid
　8. luminous **11.** translucent, transparent
　12. intelligible
pelmet ... **7.** valance (short)
Peloponnesus ...
　capital .. **7.** Corinth
　city .. **7.** Argolis
　League .. **11.** Confederacy
　peninsula (Gr) .. **5.** Morea
　12. Peloponnesos (old), Peloponnesus
　(modern)
　race (anc) .. **6.** Dorian **7.** Spartan
　School .. **6.** Dorian **9.** Sculpture
　War .. **12.** Athens-Sparta (BC)
Pelops (pert to) ...
　father .. **8.** Tantalus
　son .. **6.** Atreus **8.** Thyestes
　wife .. **10.** Hippodamia
pelota ... **4.** ball, game **5.** cesta **7.** fronton,
　jai alai
pelt ... **3.** fur **4.** blow, fell, hide, push,
　skin **5.** stone **6.** hurl at, pelage, refuse,
　strike, thrust **7.** apparel (of skins),
　rubbish **8.** woolfell
peltry ... **4.** furs, pelt **5.** skins
peludo ... **9.** armadillo (six-banded)
pelvic bone ... **5.** ilium **7.** ischium **8.** seat
　bone
pelvic-shaped ... **11.** basin-shaped
pemmican ... **4.** meat (dried) **7.** buffalo,
　venison
pen ... **3.** cot, sty **4.** bolt, coop,
　gaol **5.** abode, hutch, quill, write
　6. fasten, indite **7.** confine **9.** enclosure
　12. penitentiary
pen (pert to) ...
　like .. **7.** styloid
　name .. **6.** anonym **9.** pseudonym
　10. nom de plume
　point .. **3.** neb, nib **4.** stub
　text .. **5.** ronde
penalize ... **4.** fine **5.** mulct **6.** punish
　8. handicap
penalty ... **4.** fine, loss **7.** forfeit
　8. handicap, hardship **10.** punishment,
　repentance
Penang Islands capital ...
　10. Georgetown
penchant ... **4.** bent **6.** desire, liking
　7. leaning **8.** tendency **10.** attraction
　11. inclination **12.** decided taste
pendant ... **3.** bob, tag **4.** tail **5.** aglet
　(aiglet), queue **6.** tassel **7.** eardrop,
　earring, hanging **8.** appendix, pendulum
　9. lavaliere **10.** chandelier
pendent ... **3.** lop **4.** pend **7.** hanging
　8. appended **9.** impending, pendulous
　11. jutting over, overhanging
pendent cone (limestone) ... **10.** stalactite
pendulous fold, skin ... **6.** dewlap
Penelope (pert to) ...
　father .. **7.** Icarius
　husband .. **7.** Ulysses **8.** Odysseus
　island .. **6.** Ithaca
　suitor .. **7.** Agelaus
penetrate ... **4.** bore, gore, stab **5.** delve,
　elbow, enter **6.** pierce **7.** pervade
　8. permeate **9.** perforate **10.** move
　deeply
penetrating ... **4.** cold, deep **5.** acute,

sharp **6.** shrill, subtle **7.** caustic, odorous
　8. incisive **9.** pervading, sagacious,
　searching
penetration ... **6.** acumen **7.** ingress,
　insight **9.** acuteness, sharpness
　11. discernment, perforation
　14. discrimination
Peneus (pert to) ...
　father of .. **6.** Daphne
　genus of .. **6.** prawns
　god of .. **11.** Peneus River (Thessalia)
penguin ... **3.** auk **6.** Johnny **10.** rock
　hopper
penguin (pert to) ...
　aviation .. **13.** training plane
　duck .. **12.** Indian Runner (duck)
　genus .. **8.** Eudyptes
　nest .. **7.** rookery **10.** penguinery
　type .. **4.** king **6.** Adelie **7.** emperor,
　jackass
peninsula ... **4.** neck **6.** penile
　10. chersonese
Peninsula ...
　Asia .. **5.** Malay
　Cimbrian, Cimbric .. **7.** Jutland
　Iberia .. **5.** Spain
　Seward .. **6.** Alaska
　Tauric .. **6.** Crimea
　Thracian .. **9.** Gallipoli
penitent ... **5.** sorry **8.** contrite
　9. repentant
penitential discipline ... **7.** penance
penitential period ... **4.** Lent
pennant ... **4.** fane, flag, whip **6.** banner,
　burgee (yacht), ensign, pennon, pinion
　9. banderole
pennant fish ... **11.** cobblerfish
pennate ... **6.** winged **7.** pinnate
　9. feathered, penniform
pennon ... **4.** flag, wing **6.** banner, pinion
　8. streamer
Pennsylvania ...
　capital .. **10.** Harrisburg
　city .. **4.** Erie **7.** Reading **8.** Scranton
　10. Pittsburgh **12.** Philadelphia
　famed site .. **10.** Gettysburg **11.** Liberty
　Bell, Valley Forge **16.** Independence
　Hall
　founder .. **11.** William Penn
　mountain .. **5.** Davis **11.** Alleghenies
　named, first .. **10.** Penn's Woods
　river .. **4.** Ohio **8.** Delaware **10.** Schuylkill
　11. Susquehanna
　State admission .. **6.** second
　State motto .. **28.** Virtue, Liberty, and
　Independence
　State nickname .. **8.** Keystone
penny ... **4.** cent, coin **5.** pence **6.** copper,
　stiver **8.** denarius (Bib)
penologist, famed ... **5.** Lawes
penology, study of ... **11.** criminology
　18. punishment for crime
pensive ... **3.** sad **5.** mesto, sober
　6. dreamy, musing **7.** wistful
　10. meditative, melancholy, reflective,
　thoughtful **13.** contemplative
pentastich ... **4.** poem **6.** stanza
　7. strophe **10.** five verses
Pentateuch ... **5.** Torah (Tora) **10.** Law
　of Moses **14.** First Five Books (Old
　Test) **16.** Five Books of Moses

Pentecost ... **8.** festival **10.** Whitsunday
Pentheus (pert to) ...
  grandson of .. **6.** Cadmus
  King of .. **6.** Thebes
  mother .. **5.** Agave
penthouse ... **6.** lean-to **7.** leaning,
  pentice **9.** apartment (roof)
  11. overhanging
penury ... **4.** want **7.** poverty **9.** indigence,
  privation **10.** scantiness **11.** destitution,
  miserliness
peon ... **4.** pawn (chess), serf **7.** laborer,
  peasant, soldier **9.** attendant, constable,
  messenger, policeman
peony ... **4.** piny **6.** moutan **7.** Paeonia
  11. Burmese ruby
people ... **3.** kin, men **4.** folk, ones, race,
  Rais **5.** demos, laity **6.** family, nation,
  public **7.** kinsmen, persons **8.** populace,
  subjects **9.** citizenry **10.** population
people (pert to) ...
  Am Indian, Eskimo .. **7.** Amerind
  ancient .. **5.** Medes **6.** Greeks, Romans
  7. Sabines **9.** Egyptians, Etruscans
  class, lowest .. **8.** canaille
  common .. **6.** vulgar **7.** tilikum (tilicum)
  headless (Myth) .. **8.** Acephali
  old-fashioned .. **6.** prudes **7.** squares
  13. antediluvians
  ref to .. **4.** laic **6.** ethnic **7.** demotic
  Spanish .. **5.** gente
  wild young .. **10.** rantipoles
people (of) ...
  culture (earliest) .. **8.** Grecians
  gentle birth .. **6.** gentry
  one government .. **6.** nation
  rank .. **11.** aristocracy, aristocrats
  the people .. **6.** ethnic
peopled ... **5.** abadi (Ind village)
  8. occupied, populous **9.** populated
pep ... **2.** go **3.** vim **4.** dash **6.** energy
  7. quicken **9.** stimulate **10.** initiative,
  liveliness
pepper ... **4.** pelt **5.** shoot **6.** energy
  7. bombard **8.** sprinkle **9.** condiment
pepper (pert to) ...
  betel .. **4.** siri (sirih)
  black .. **11.** Piper nigrum
  box .. **5.** tower **8.** spitfire
  Capsicum, source of .. **7.** cayenne, chilies
  (chili), paprika
  climbing .. **5.** betel **6.** nigrum
  condiment .. **7.** cayenne, paprika
  dulse .. **7.** seaweed (red)
  genus .. **8.** Capsicum
  grass .. **5.** crass **8.** pillwort
  sauce .. **7.** Tabasco
  turnip .. **15.** jack-in-the-pulpit
pepper (pert to country) ...
  Australia .. **4.** kava (cava) **8.** kavakava
  Borneo .. **4.** kava (cava)
  Guinea .. **5.** chili **8.** Capsicum
  Malay .. **4.** siri (sirih)
  Spain .. **7.** paprika, pimento **8.** allspice,
  pimiento
pepper-and-salt ... **4.** gray **17.** harbinger-
  of-spring
peppermint ... **3.** oil **4.** herb **6.** spirit
  7. essence, gum tree, lozenge, menthol
  (camphor)
peppery ... **5.** fiery **7.** piquant, pungent

8. choleric, spirited, stinging
  10. passionate **11.** hot-tempered
per ... **2.** by **7.** for each, through **9.** by
  means of **11.** according to
peradventure ... **3.** hap **5.** doubt **7.** it
  may be **8.** possibly **11.** uncertainty
perambulate ... **4.** walk **6.** ramble, stroll
  8. traverse **9.** promenade, walk about
perceive ... **3.** see **4.** hear, know, note
  5. sense **6.** behold, descry, detect,
  divine, notice, remark **7.** discern,
  observe, sensate **9.** apprehend
  10. comprehend, understand
  11. distinguish **12.** discriminate
perceptible ... **5.** faint **7.** tactile, visible
  8. knowable, manifest, tangible
  10. cognizable **11.** appreciable,
  discernible, perceivable
perception ... **3.** ear **4.** tact **5.** sense,
  taste **6.** acumen, seeing **8.** sagacity
  9. awareness, sensation **10.** cognizance
  11. discernment **13.** consciousness
  14. discrimination
perceptive ... **7.** knowing **8.** sensible
  9. sagacious **14.** discriminative
perch ... **3.** bar, peg, rod, sit **4.** fish,
  pole **5.** aerie, barse, roost, sit on,
  staff **6.** alight, aviary, sauger, settle,
  weapon **7.** measure **9.** trumpeter
Percheron ... **5.** horse **15.** Percheron
  Norman
perchers ... **5.** birds **7.** candles **8.** Passeres
  10. Insessores
percolate ... **4.** ooze, seep, sift, silt, sipe
  5. exude, leach, steep **6.** filter, strain
  7. trickle **8.** permeate, transude
percussion ... **9.** collision **10.** concussion,
  detonation
percussion instrument ... **4.** drum, gong
  5. bells, bones, conga, snare, traps
  6. Becken, bongos, chimes, tom-tom
  7. celesta, cymbals, marimba, potlids,
  timpani (tympani) **8.** carillon, clappers,
  triangle **9.** castanets, xylophone
  10. kettledrum, tambourine, vibraphone
  12. glockenspiel
perdition ... **4.** hell, loss (soul), ruin
  5. wreck **9.** damnation **11.** destruction
peregrinate ... **6.** travel, wander **7.** go
  about, migrate, sojourn
peregrine ... **5.** alien **6.** exotic, falcon
  7. foreign, pilgrim, strange **9.** foreigner
perempt ... **5.** quash **6.** defeat **7.** destroy
peremptory ... **5.** final **7.** express
  8. absolute, arrogant, decisive,
  dogmatic, positive, resolute **9.** arbitrary,
  mandatory **10.** compulsory, conclusive,
  imperative, obligatory **11.** dictatorial
  13. authoritative **16.** incontrovertible
perennial ... **7.** lasting **8.** constant,
  enduring **9.** continual, evergreen,
  permanent, perpetual, unceasing
  10. continuous **12.** never-failing
perennial (pert to) ...
  climbing .. **5.** liana (liane)
  grass .. **4.** lyme **6.** Elymus (genus) **7.** wild
  rye
  herb .. **4.** Geum **5.** avens
  weed .. **8.** toadflax
perfect ... **4.** holy, pure, sole **5.** ideal,
  model, teleo (comb form), whole

6. entire 7. correct, develop, improve
8. finished 9. blameless, faultless,
inviolate, righteous 10. consummate,
satisfying 11. unqualified
perfection ... 4. acme 5. ideal 7. paragon
8. accuracy, maturity 10. completion,
excellence 13. faultlessness
perfectly ... 5. quite 7. ideally, rightly,
utterly 9. correctly 10. absolutely,
accurately, altogether, completely,
flawlessly, thoroughly
perfecto ... 5. cigar (tapering)
perficient ... 6. actual 9. effective,
effectual
perfidious ... 6. shifty 8. disloyal
9. faithless 11. disaffected, treacherous
12. falsehearted
perfidy ... 7. treason 8. apostasy
9. duplicity, treachery 10. disloyalty
13. faithlessness
perforate ... 4. bore, dock 5. drill, punch
6. pierce, pounce, riddle 9. penetrate
10. umbilicate
perforated ...
block .. 3. nut
initials (Philat) .. 10. stamp marks
nozzle .. 4. rose
space .. 5. brain
sphere .. 4. bead
perforation ... 4. bore, hole 6. eyelet
8. aperture, piercing, punching
perform ... 2. do 3. act 4. play 5. enact,
exert 6. effect 7. execute, fulfill, produce
8. complete, transact 9. officiate
10. accomplish, bring about, perpetrate
performance ... 3. act 4. test, work
6. action 7. exploit 8. ceremony
9. operation 10. completion, exhibition,
observance, production
12. consummation 14. accomplishment
performance (pert to) ...
clumsy .. 6. bungle
daytime .. 7. matinee
for one .. 4. solo
notable .. 4. feat
of duty .. 8. feasance
performer ... 4. doer 5. actor 6. dancer,
worker 8. magician, musician, thespian
9. pretender 15. prestidigitator
perfume ... 4. balm, odor 5. aroma, attar,
orris, savor, scent, smell 7. bouquet,
cologne, essence, rose oil 9. fragrance,
redolence 10. frangipani
perfume (pert to) ...
base .. 4. musk 9. ambergris
cherry .. 7. mahaleb
essence .. 5. attar 8. bergamot
medicated .. 8. pastille (pastil)
musky .. 5. civet
oriental .. 5. myrrh 7. incense
12. frankincense
scent .. 7. jasmine 8. lavender
10. heliotrope
toilet .. 6. bay rum 12. eau de Cologne
unguent .. 6. pomade
violet .. 5. irone
pergola ... 5. arbor, bower, kiosk
6. pandal 7. balcony, trellis 9. colonnade
11. summerhouse
perhaps ... 5. maybe 6. ablins (Scot),
belike, mayhap 8. doubtful, possibly,

probably 9. perchance 10. contingent
peri ... 3. elf 5. about (pref), fairy 6. beauty
periapt ... 5. charm 6. amulet
pericarp ... 3. pod 5. berry, shell
8. seedcase
Pericles (Gr) ... 9. statesman
periculum (Rom law) ... 4. risk 5. peril
6. danger
perigee (Astron) ... 12. nearest earth
(opp of apogee)
peril ... 4. risk 6. danger, hazard, menace
8. jeopardy
perilously high ... 7. Icarian (flying)
perimeter ... 5. ambit 6. border 7. outline
8. boundary 9. periphery
period ... 3. age, day, dot, end, eon,
era, eve 4. stop, term, time, year
5. cycle, epoch, limit, spell 6. degree,
moment, season 8. duration, sentence
10. conclusion 11. termination
period (pert to) ...
historical .. 4. eral 6. Eocene 7. Neocene
penitential .. 4. Lent
statutory .. 10. limitation
Tertiary .. 6. Eocene 7. Miocene, Neocene
8. Pliocene
periodic ... 4. eral 6. annual 7. etesian
8. seasonal 9. recurrent 10. rhythmical
12. intermittent
periodic (pert to) ...
sea motion .. 4. tide
wind .. 2. oe 7. chinook, etesian,
monsoon
windstorm .. 2. oe 7. tornado
9. whirlwind
periodical ... 5. paper 6. review
7. etesian, journal 8. magazine
9. recurring 11. publication
periodical cicada ... 6. locust (17 yrs)
period of ...
delay .. 10. moratorium
dryness .. 7. drought
evolution .. 6. hemera
fifty days .. 13. quinquagesima
five years .. 6. pentad
holding .. 6. tenure
instruction .. 7. session
possession .. 5. lease
probation .. 6. parole
prosperity .. 4. boom 6. golden
recovery .. 13. convalescence
14. reconstruction
sleep .. 11. hibernation
ten years .. 6. decade
time .. 3. age, day, eon 4. span
work .. 4. turn 5. shift, spell, watch
youth .. 6. nonage
peripatetic ... 7. walking 8. rambling
Peripatetic (pert to Aristotle) ... 6. school
8. disciple 10. Philosophy
peripheral ... 6. distal 7. outmost
8. external 9. outlinear 10. round about
periphery ... 3. lip, rim 4. brim
5. ambit 6. areola, border 8. confines
9. perimeter 10. borderland
13. circumference
perique ... 7. tobacco (strong) 10. otter
brown
perish ... 3. die, rot 4. fade 5. decay,
waste 8. pass away, squander 9. cease
to be, disappear 11. be destroyed

perissodactyl ... **15.** odd-numbered toes
peristyle ... **7.** columns (range of)
  8. corridor **9.** colonnade **10.** peripteral
peritoneum fold ... **7.** omentum
periwig ... **3.** wig **6.** frizzy, peruke
  9. shellfish **10.** periwinkle
periwinkle ... **4.** blue **5.** snail, vinca
  6. mussel, myrtle **9.** evergreen
perjink ... **4.** neat, nice **7.** precise
perjure ... **7.** violate **8.** forswear
perjury ... **9.** violation **12.** breech of oath
  13. false swearing
perk ... **5.** preen, prink **7.** smarten
  9. percolate **10.** perquisite
perkin ... **5.** cider
perk up ... **7.** cheer up, improve, raise
  up, refresh **10.** recuperate
permanent ... **5.** fixed **6.** innate, stable
  7. abiding, durable, lasting **8.** constant,
  enduring, inherent **9.** perpetual
  10. changeless, continuing
  12. unchangeable
permeate ... **5.** imbue **7.** pervade
  8. saturate
permission ... **5.** grace, leave **7.** consent,
  license **9.** allowance **10.** sufferance
  13. authorization
permissive ... **8.** optional **9.** allowable,
  permitted, tolerated **10.** consenting,
  permitting **13.** power of choice
permit ... **3.** let **4.** leve **5.** allow, grant,
  leave **6.** suffer **7.** consent, license,
  warrant **8.** tolerate **9.** authorize
  10. permission
permit to live ... **5.** spare **8.** reprieve
permutate ... **6.** change **9.** rearrange
  11. interchange
permutation ... **6.** barter **11.** interchange
  13. transmutation **14.** transformation
pérn ... **6.** Pernis **7.** buzzard (honey)
pernicious ... **4.** bane **5.** fatal **6.** anemia,
  deadly, malign, wicked **7.** baleful,
  baneful, harmful, hurtful, noisome,
  noxious, ruinous, vicious **10.** villainous
  11. deleterious
pernio ... **9.** chilblain
perorate ... **5.** speak (at length) **7.** declaim
  8. harangue **9.** expatiate
perpendicular ... **4.** sine **5.** erect, plumb,
  sheer, steep **7.** apothem, upright
  8. binormal, vertical **9.** rectitude
  10. standing up **11.** precipitous
perpetrate ... **6.** commit **7.** perform
  12. carry through
perpetual ... **7.** endless, eternal
  8. constant, unending **9.** continual,
  perennial, permanent, unceasing
  10. continuous **11.** everlasting
perpetually ... **9.** endlessly, eternally
  11. ceaselessly **12.** interminably
perpetuity ... **7.** annuity **8.** eternity
  11. endless time
perplex ... **3.** vex **4.** cark **5.** amaze
  6. puzzle, riddle **7.** confuse **8.** bewilder,
  entangle **9.** obfuscate **10.** complicate
perplexity ... **3.** fog **6.** tangle **7.** anxiety,
  dilemma, problem **8.** question
  9. confusion, situation **10.** complexity
  11. distraction **12.** bewilderment,
  complication
perquisite ... **3.** tip **4.** gain **6.** boodle

8. appanage, gratuity
perquod ... **7.** whereby
Perry Mason ... see *Mason, Perry*
per se ... **6.** itself **8.** directly **11.** essentially
  13. intrinsically
perse ... **4.** blue
persecute ... **5.** annoy, harry, hound
  6. harass **7.** afflict, oppress, torment
  8. hunt down **9.** martyrize
persecution ... **9.** treatment
  10. harassment, oppression
  12. mistreatment
Persephone (pert to) ...
  abductor .. **5.** Hades
  Attica, name .. **4.** Kore (Cora)
  deity of .. **11.** agriculture
  father .. **4.** Zeus
  Greek name .. **11.** Persephassa
  mother .. **7.** Demeter
  Orphic literary name .. **8.** Despoina
  queen of .. **15.** infernal regions
  Roman name .. **10.** Proserpine
  (Proserpina)
Perseus (pert to) ...
  Astron .. **13.** Constellation
  father .. **4.** Zeus
  mother .. **5.** Danae
  slayer of .. **6.** Medusa
perseverance ... **8.** patience, tenacity
  9. constancy **10.** resolution, steadiness
  11. persistence, pertinacity
  13. steadfastness
persevere ... **5.** abide **6.** endure, insist,
  keep on **7.** carry on, persist **8.** continue
Persia (Iran, Irani) ... see also *Persian*
  capital .. **6.** Tehran (Teheran)
  city .. **5.** Niriz **6.** Abadan, Shiraz, Tabriz
  7. Hamadan, Ispahan
  country (anc) .. **4.** Elam **7.** Chaldea
  gulf .. **4.** Oman **7.** Persian
  gulf port .. **7.** Bushire **9.** Mohamerah
  gulf province .. **6.** Kuwait
  gulf wind .. **6.** shamal
  lake .. **7.** Rezaieh, Urumidh (Salt)
  mountain .. **6.** Ararat, Elburz, Zagros
  9. Hindu Kush
  pert to .. **6.** Persic
  river .. **5.** Safid **9.** Euphrates
  ruins .. **10.** Persepolis (Shiraz)
Persian (pert to) ... see also *Iranian*
  blue .. **10.** regimental
  calendar reformer .. **9.** Jalalaean
  (Jalalian)
  carpet, rug .. **4.** kali **5.** Herat (Herati),
  Senna **6.** Kerman, Tabriz **11.** Baluchistan
  cushion .. **6.** musnud
  diadem .. **3.** taj
  door .. **3.** dar
  evergreen .. **4.** olax
  grass .. **6.** millet
  gum .. **10.** tragacanth
  hat .. **3.** fez **6.** turban
  idiom .. **7.** persism
  javelin .. **6.** jereed (jerid)
  rose .. **3.** gul
  rug .. see *carpet (above)*
  screen .. **6.** purdah
Persian animals, birds, fruit ...
  apple .. **6.** citron
  bird .. **4.** bulbul
  cat .. **6.** Angora

deer . . **5.** maral **6.** fallow
gazelle . . **4.** cora
lamb . . **9.** astrakhan, broadtail
lynx . . **7.** caracul
tick (venomous) . . **8.** Miana bug
Persian Myth, Religion . . .
angel . . **3.** Mah
deity . . **6.** Ormazd (Supreme)
demigod, hero . . **4.** Yima
demon . . **7.** Apaosha
fairy . . **3.** elf, fay **4.** peri
fire worshiper . . **5.** Parsi (Parsee)
god of light . . **7.** Mithras
mystic . . **4.** sufi
nymph . . **5.** houri
religion founder . . **9.** Zoroaster
religious doctrine . . **6.** Babism (Babiism)
sacred books (Zoroastrian) . . **6.** Avesta
scriptures (Muslim) . . **5.** Koran
spirit . . **7.** Ahriman
Persian people, government . . .
assembly (1906) . . **6.** Majlis (Mejlis)
caste (priestly) . . **4.** Magi **7.** Wise Men
chief . . **3.** mir **4.** Shah
chief's wife, lady . . **4.** bibi
civil officer . . **4.** khan
dynasty . . **5.** Kajar **7.** Arsacid **8.** Selencid
10. Sassanidae (Sassanid)
governor (anc) . . **6.** satrap
King . . **4.** Shah **5.** Cyrus (the Great)
6. Darius, Xerxes
language (anc) . . **4.** Zend **7.** Pahlavi
(Pahlevi)
New Year's Day . . **7.** Nowroze
people . . **4.** Leks, Lurs **5.** Arabs,
Kurds, Medes, Mukri, Perse **6.** Aryans
7. Gypsies, Hadjemi, Iranics **8.** Baluchis,
Iranians
poet . . **4.** Omar **5.** Hafiz, Saadi
ruler . . **4.** Shah **6.** atabeg (atabek), Sultan
student (Koran) . . **5.** hafiz
trader . . **4.** Sart
Wise Men . . **4.** Magi
persiflage . . . **6.** banter **8.** raillery
persimmon . . . **4.** kaki **7.** chapote
persist . . . **4.** last, urge **6.** endure **7.** prevail
9. persevere
persistent . . . **7.** durable **8.** constant,
habitual **10.** determined, inveterate
11. persevering **13.** indefatigable
persistently opposed . . . **8.** renitent
9. obstinate **12.** recalcitrant
person . . . **3.** one **4.** body, soul **5.** being,
wight **6.** figure **8.** creature **9.** character
10. individual
person (pert to) . . .
accuser, challenger . . **9.** appellant
acting for another . . **5.** proxy **9.** alternate
baptized (anc) . . **11.** illuminatus
base . . **7.** caitiff, hangdog
bringing bad luck . . **4.** jinx **5.** Jonah
bringing good luck . . **6.** mascot
canonized . . **5.** saint
careless . . **7.** trifler **11.** pococurante
charged with high mission . . **7.** apostle
charitable . . **9.** samaritan
cheerful . . **8.** optimist
clumsy . . **3.** oaf **5.** staup **6.** lummox
7. bungler
common . . **3.** lay **8.** roturier
conceited . . **4.** prig

contemptible . . **3.** cad **4.** heel, toad
7. bauchle (Scot)
crazed . . **6.** maniac **10.** monomaniac,
psychopath
credulous . . **5.** Simon
cruel . . **5.** fiend
dishonorable . . **6.** rotter
dissolute . . **4.** roué
drunken . . **4.** lush
dull . . **4.** dolt **5.** dunce, moron, stock
6. dorbel **9.** blockhead
dwarf . . **5.** shurf
educated . . **6.** pedant, pundit, savant
7. erudite, learned, student **8.** cultured,
highbrow **9.** literatus **12.** intellectual
emitting smoke . . **7.** whiffer
enterprising . . **8.** go-getter
fabulously rich . . **5.** Midas
foolish . . **3.** sop **4.** zany **5.** clown, idiot,
nutty **6.** dotard **7.** bonkers, buffoon
9. simpleton
gigantic . . **5.** giant, titan **7.** monster
gloomy . . **7.** killjoy **10.** crosspatch
good luck . . **6.** mascot
grotesque . . **9.** golliwogg
guilty . . **7.** culprit **12.** transgressor
held as pledge . . **7.** hostage
image of . . **4.** doll, idol **5.** clone **6.** poppet,
puppet
impatient . . **6.** fidget **7.** hotspur
important . . **3.** VIP **5.** mogul **7.** magnate,
notable **9.** personage
indifferent . . **5.** stoic
inexperienced . . **9.** greenhorn
insignificant . . **5.** sprat **6.** little, nobody
lazy . . **5.** drone **8.** sluggard
learned . . see *educated (above)*
left-handed . . **6.** clumsy **8.** sinister
9. portsider
loud-voiced . . **7.** stentor **8.** blowhard
low-bred . . **3.** cad **6.** vulgar
miserly . . **9.** skinflint **10.** curmudgeon
non-Jewish . . **5.** Aryan **7.** Gentile
overmodest . . **5.** prude **8.** bluenose
perfidious . . **5.** snake **7.** traitor **9.** faithless
rapacious . . **4.** wolf **5.** harpy
relaxed . . **4.** calm **8.** laid-back
representing another . . **5.** proxy **7.** stand-
in **9.** alternate
respondent to appeal . . **8.** appellee
rich . . **7.** wealthy **9.** plutocrat **10.** capitalist
11. millionaire
rude, ill-mannered . . **4.** boor **5.** yahoo
scatterbrained . . **6.** madcap
self-centered . . **6.** egoist **7.** egotist
9. extrovert, introvert
self-righteous . . **8.** pharisee
sharp-eyed . . **5.** alert, Argus
sick . . **9.** aegrotant, bedridden
skilled . . **6.** artist, master **7.** artisan
8. mechanic
staff (Mil) . . **10.** aide-de-camp
stupid . . **3.** ass **4.** dolt, gump, nerd
5. moron, stock
supercilious . . **4.** snob **9.** conceited
thankless . . **7.** ingrate
unclassified . . **11.** nondescript
unique . . **4.** oner
unknown . . **7.** inconnu **8.** inconnue
unmarried . . **6.** maiden, single
8. bachelor, celibate, spinster

untidy . . **5.** messy **6.** grungy **8.** slipshod, slovenly **9.** litterbug
valorous . . **4.** hero **8.** champion
violent-tempered . . **6.** tartar
wealthy . . **5.** nabob, pluto (comb form) **10.** capitalist **11.** millionaire
who reads, writes . . **8.** literate
witty . . **3.** wag **7.** punster **8.** comedian **10.** comedienne
worthless . . **5.** lorel, losel
writ serving . . **6.** elisor
young . . **9.** stripling **14.** whippersnapper
personage . . . **5.** image, mogul **7.** bearing, stature **8.** great man, one's body, portrait **13.** impersonation
persona grata . . . **13.** welcome person **16.** acceptable person
personal (pert to) . . .
appearance . . **8.** presence
comb form . . **4.** idio
history . . **6.** memoir
ornament . . **6.** parure
ownership, land . . **6.** estate **7.** demesne **8.** chattels, property
personality . . . **3.** ego **5.** being **6.** person **8.** identity **13.** individuality **15.** distinctiveness
persona non grata . . . **18.** unacceptable person
personate . . . **5.** enact **7.** feigned **9.** represent **10.** personated **11.** counterfeit
personification . . . **3.** Una (truth) **10.** embodiment **11.** attribution **14.** representation
person of . . .
age . . **5.** major
courage . . **7.** Spartan
eighty years . . **12.** octogenarian
encyclopedic learning . . **10.** polyhistor
fifty years . . **15.** quinquagenarian
forty years . . **14.** quadragenarian
great intellect . . **6.** genius
nervous disorders . . **8.** neurotic
ninety years . . **12.** nonagenarian
one hundred years . . **11.** centenarian
seventy years . . **14.** septuagenarian
sixty years . . **12.** sexagenarian
skill . . **6.** master, talent **7.** magnate
persons of . . .
a familiar set . . **7.** coterie
a family tree . . **6.** stirps
groups . . **4.** army, band, team **6.** chorus, troupe **7.** company **8.** assembly **9.** orchestra
organized bodies . . **5.** corps, posse
perspicacity . . . **6.** acumen, vision **8.** sagacity **9.** acuteness **11.** discernment, penetration
perspicuity . . . **8.** lucidity, sagacity **12.** translucency, transparency
perspiration . . . **5.** sudor, sweat **7.** sudoric **8.** hard work **11.** evaporation, saline fluid **13.** transpiration
persuade . . . **4.** coax, sway, urge **6.** entice, induce, reason **7.** convert, suasion **8.** convince, inveigle **9.** influence, plead with, stonewall
persuasible . . . **6.** pliant **11.** persuadable **14.** open-mindedness
persuasive . . . **8.** eloquent **9.** impelling

10. convincing, persuading
pert . . . **3.** gay **4.** bold, keen **5.** brash, sassy, saucy **6.** clever, comely, dapper, daring, lively, nimble **7.** forward **8.** handsome, skillful **9.** exquisite, officious, sprightly **11.** impertinent **12.** presumptuous
pert (girl) . . . **4.** chit, minx
pertain . . . **5.** belie **6.** belong, relate **7.** adjunct **8.** function, peculiar **9.** accessory, appendage, appertain, attribute
pertaining to . . .
act of rising . . **6.** ortive **7.** eastern
agriculture . . **7.** georgic
ancestral type . . **9.** atavistic
ancient Nile city . . **4.** Sais (Saite)
ancient Troy . . **5.** Iliac
anything remote . . **6.** forane
apostles . . **7.** Petrine
Asiatic (old) . . **8.** Chaldean
Asiatic mountain . . **6.** Altaic
Athens . . **5.** Attic
authorized doctrine . . **8.** dogmatic **10.** dogmatical
birthmark . . **6.** nevoid (naevoid)
body . . **5.** somal
body of land . . **11.** continental
book description . . **13.** bibliographic
both ears . . **8.** binaural
both sexes . . **6.** unisex **7.** epicene
breadmaking . . **6.** panary
breastbone . . **7.** sternal
bristles . . **5.** setal
bunch . . **5.** comal
canonical hours . . **7.** matinal
carving . . **6.** glypic **7.** glyptic
cheek . . **5.** malar
church, part . . **7.** apsidal
city . . **5.** civic, urban
cod family . . **6.** gadoid
coins . . **12.** numismatical
colors . . **9.** chromatic
construction . . **8.** geodesic, tectonic
cork . . **7.** suberic
cough . . **7.** tussine
court . . **5.** aulic **9.** judiciary
crown . . **7.** coronal
dance . . **6.** gestic **13.** terpsichorean
daughter . . **6.** filial
dawn . . **4.** eoan
day (ordinary) . . **6.** ferial
desert wastes . . **6.** eremic
diaphragm . . **7.** phrenic
dogma . . **9.** levitical
doves . . **9.** columbine
downward air . . **9.** katabatic
downy . . **5.** dotal
dreams . . **7.** oneiric **9.** oneirotic
ducks . . **7.** anatine
early church . . **9.** patristic
early culture . . **8.** eolithic
earth . . **4.** geal **5.** terra **7.** teluric **9.** planetary
earthquake . . **7.** seismic
east . . **4.** dawn, eoan **7.** auroral
elms . . **9.** ulmaceous
engraving . . **7.** glyptic
equal rights . . **3.** ERA **6.** libber
essence . . **5.** basic
exhaustion . . **7.** burnout **9.** tiredness

fallow deer.. **6.** damine
fashion.. **5.** modal **6.** preppy, trendy
fasting.. **8.** anorexic **9.** abstinent
fats.. **6.** adipic, sebaic **9.** cellulite
feet.. **5.** pedal
fields.. **8.** agrarian
fine arts.. **9.** aesthetic (esthetic)
fingers.. **7.** digital
first principles.. **9.** elemental
fissure.. **5.** rimal
flood.. **8.** diluvian
flowers.. **9.** floscular **10.** florescent
forehead.. **7.** metopic
frogs.. **6.** anuran, ranine
funeral music.. **10.** threnodial
funerals.. **8.** exequial
gospel.. **9.** evangelic
gulls.. **6.** larine
gums (Anat).. **8.** gingival
hair.. **5.** pilar **7.** blow-dry
hands.. **6.** chiral, manual
head.. **8.** cephalic
heaths.. **8.** ericetal
holiday.. **6.** ferial (Eccl), festal
honey.. **10.** melaginous
horse.. **6.** equine
house.. **5.** domal (Astrol)
hypothetical force.. **4.** odic
infernal regions.. **7.** avernal
ink.. **10.** atramental
insects.. **11.** entomologic
intellect.. **6.** noetic
iron.. **6.** ferric
islands.. **7.** insular
jaw.. **10.** mandibular
kidney.. **5.** renal
knots.. **5.** nodal
land.. **8.** praedial (predial)
language meaning.. **8.** semantic
laughter.. **8.** risorial
leg.. **6.** crural **7.** fibular
lips.. **6.** labial
liver.. **7.** hepatic
living organism.. **13.** parasitologic
lockjaw.. **7.** tetanic
love.. **6.** erotic **7.** amatory **8.** erotical
male.. **5.** macho, manly **7.** agnatic
marriage.. **7.** marital **8.** hymeneal
marsh.. **8.** paludine
meaning, in language.. **8.** semantic
medicine.. **6.** iatric **8.** iatrical
medulla oblongata (brain).. **6.** bulbar
memory.. **6.** mnesic **7.** mnestic
　　8. mnemonic **13.** retrospective
midday.. **8.** meridian
milk.. **7.** lactary, lacteal
mind.. **6.** mental **7.** phrenic
money matters.. **5.** T-bill **7.** bailout
　　8. economic
morning.. **5.** matin, sunup **7.** matinal
　　9. matutinal
motion.. **7.** kinetic
mouth.. **4.** oral **7.** oscular, palatal
　　8. stomatic
mustard family.. **11.** cruciferous
nephew.. **7.** nepotal
north wind.. **6.** boreal
nose.. **5.** nasal **6.** narial, rhinal
nut.. **5.** nucal
ocean.. **7.** pelagic
old age.. **6.** senile **7.** geratic **8.** gerontic

　　9. geriatric
Old World.. **13.** gerontogenous
peacock.. **8.** pavonine
people.. **4.** laic **7.** demotic
pigs.. **7.** porcine
pleasure.. **7.** hedonic
priests.. **10.** sacerdotal
prophecy.. **9.** vaticinal
public.. **7.** cameral
public prayer.. **8.** liturgic **10.** liturgical
punishment.. **5.** penal **8.** punitive
queen.. **7.** reginal
rainbow.. **6.** iridal
reason.. **6.** noetic
region without earthquakes..
　　11. peneseismic
rhubarb.. **7.** rheumic
river.. **5.** amnic
river bank.. **8.** riparian
rock.. **7.** petrean
royal court.. **5.** aulic
salvation.. **8.** soterial **9.** soterical
sarcasm.. **8.** ironical
school of philosophy.. **7.** Eleatic
sea.. **6.** marine **7.** oceanic, pelagic
　　9. thelassic
seacoast.. **8.** littoral
sense of taste.. **9.** gustatory
sepulchral mound.. **7.** tumular
shin, shinbone.. **7.** cnemial
ship's sails.. **5.** velic
singing birds.. **6.** oscine
skull.. **5.** inial
sole of foot.. **7.** plantar
spring.. **6.** vernal
stars.. **6.** astral **7.** stellar **8.** sidereal
state affairs.. **9.** pragmatic
stepmothers.. **8.** noverca
storks.. **7.** pelargic
summer.. **7.** estival (aestival)
　　8. festival
sun.. **5.** solar **6.** heliac
tail.. **6.** caudal
teaching.. **9.** pedagogic
tears.. **8.** lacrimal
tempo.. **6.** agogic
the plague.. **6.** loimic
the skin.. **5.** deric **6.** dermic
thread.. **5.** filar
tile.. **7.** tegular
time.. **7.** chronic
tin.. **7.** stranic
tissue.. **5.** telar
tongue.. **7.** glossal, lingual
tortoises.. **9.** chelonian
touch.. **7.** tactile
travel.. **6.** viatic
trees.. **8.** arboreal
verse stress.. **5.** ictic
walls.. **5.** mural **8.** parietal
wax.. **5.** ceral
weight.. **5.** baric **8.** ponderal
whales.. **5.** rotal
wife.. **7.** uxorial
wine.. **5.** vinic
wine making.. **10.** oenopoetic
wings.. **5.** alary
winter.. **6.** hiemal
womanhood.. **9.** muliebral
woods.. **6.** sylvan
wrist.. **6.** carpal

pertaining to country . . .
Asiatic . . **8.** Chaldean
Asiatic mountain . . **6.** Altaic
Athens . . **5.** Attic
Carthage . . **5.** Punic
Celts . . **4.** Erse
Cretan language . . **6.** Minoan
Dissenters meeting house . . **7.** pantile
  (from the roofing)
England . . **8.** Anglican
Ethiopian religion . . **6.** Coptic
France . . **6.** Gallic
Franks . . **5.** Salic
Gentiles . . **6.** ethnic
German State . . **8.** Bavarian
Greek epic . . **9.** Homerical
Greek philosophy . . **7.** Eleatic **8.** Platonic
Greek race (anc) . . **6.** Aeolic
Greek valley . . **6.** Nemean **8.** Argolian
Hindu books, writing . . **5.** Vedic **7.** Tantric
Hindu philosophy, inertia . . **5.** tamas
Irish . . **6.** Celtic, Gaelic
Isle of Man . . **4.** Manx
Mars . . **5.** Arean
Mediterranean . . **6.** Levant
Moses . . **6.** Mosaic
Nile city (anc) . . **4.** Sais (Saite)
Norse poem . . **5.** runic
Passover . . **7.** Paschal
Red Sea colony . . **8.** Eritrean
Rhine . . **7.** Rhenish
Scotch Highlander . . **6.** Gaelic
Spice Islands . . **7.** Molucca
Troy (anc) . . **5.** Iliac **6.** Trojan
Vulcan . . **11.** Mulcibirian
West Indies . . **9.** Antillean
pertenencia . . . **10.** concession **11.** mining
  claim
Perth . . . **6.** Atholl (Athole) **7.** Ontario
  9. Australia
pertinacious . . . **4.** firm **8.** adhering,
  resolute **9.** tenacious **10.** determined,
  inflexible, persistent, unyielding
  11. persevering
pertinacity . . . **9.** obstinacy
  11. persistency
pertinent . . . **3.** fit **6.** timely **7.** germane
  8. apposite, relevant
perturb . . . **5.** alarm **6.** excite **7.** agitate,
  derange, disturb, fluster, trouble **8.** bewilder, disorder, distress **9.** confusion
perturbation . . . **5.** alarm **7.** anxiety,
  fluster **9.** agitation, confusion
  10. excitement **11.** fearfulness
  12. bewilderment, irregularity
pertusion . . . **8.** piercing, punching
  11. perforation, punched hole
pertussis . . . **5.** cough **13.** whooping
  cough
Peru . . . see also *Peruvian*
capital . . **4.** Lima **5.** Cuzco (Inca) **14.** City
  of the Kings
hero . . **7.** Bolivar, Pizarro
lake . . **8.** Titicaca
mountain . . **5.** Andes **10.** Cordillera
port . . **6.** Callao **7.** Iquitos **8.** Mollendo
river . . **4.** Sama **5.** Santa **6.** Amazon
  7. Maranon, Ucayali **8.** Urubamba
ruins . . **4.** Inca **5.** huaco (relics)
Peruvian (pert to) . . .
animal . . **4.** paco **5.** llama **6.** alpaca

bark . . **8.** cinchona
goddess of fertility . . **4.** Mama
inn, tavern . . **5.** tambo
king (petty) . . **7.** cacique
plant . . **3.** oca
rodent . . **10.** chinchilla
tinamou . . **4.** yutu
tree . . **8.** cinchona
university . . **9.** San Marcos
volcano . . **7.** El Misti
wind (cold) . . **4.** puna
pervade . . . **4.** fill **5.** imbue **6.** extend
  8. permeate, traverse **9.** penetrate
pervading . . . **9.** prevalent, universal
perverse . . . **3.** awk **4.** awry, wogh
  5. wrong **6.** cranky, erring **7.** corrupt,
  forward, froward, wayward, willful
  (wilful) **8.** contrary, petulant **9.** obstinate
  10. ill-humored
perversion . . . **5.** error **6.** misuse
  8. apostasy **9.** sophistry **10.** corruption,
  distortion **13.** falsification
  17. misinterpretation, misrepresentation
perversion of taste . . . **7.** malacia
pervert . . . **4.** ruin **5.** upset **6.** divert,
  misuse **7.** corrupt, distort, falsify,
  heretic **8.** apostate, overturn, renegade
  9. turn aside **10.** degenerate, lead
  astray **12.** misinterpret, misrepresent
pervulgate . . . **7.** publish
Pesach, Pesah . . . **8.** Passover (Feast)
pesante . . . **5.** heavy **10.** impressive
peshkash . . . **3.** tax **7.** present, tribute
  8. offering
peskar . . . **5.** agent **7.** steward **8.** minister
  10. accountant
pesky . . . **6.** plaguy **7.** teasing **9.** harassing
  10. tormenting
pes planus . . . **8.** flatfoot **13.** talipes
  planus
pess . . . **7.** hassock (church)
pessimist . . . **5.** cynic **6.** malist **9.** defeatist,
  worrywart
pessimistic . . . **6.** gloomy **7.** cynical
  8. cowardly, hopeless **10.** despairing,
  foreboding, uncheerful
pest . . . **3.** nag **4.** bane **6.** plague
  7. ragweed **8.** epidemic, nuisance
  9. annoyance **10.** pestilence
pester . . . **3.** nag, rib **5.** annoy, tease,
  worry **6.** badger, harass, impede, infest
  7. torment **8.** entangle **9.** importune
  10. overburden
pestilence . . . **4.** bane **7.** disease, scourge
  8. epidemic **13.** bubonic plague
pestilent . . . **6.** deadly **7.** noxious
  8. annoying **9.** pestering, poisonous
  10. contagious, infectious, pernicious
  11. mischievous, troublesome
pestle . . . **4.** club **6.** muller **7.** crusher,
  pounder
pes valgus . . . **9.** bowlegged **13.** talipes
  valgus
pet . . . **4.** dear, tiff **5.** humor **6.** caress,
  coddle, cosset, dandle, fondle, pamper
  7. darling, dudgeon, indulge **8.** cade
  lamb, favorite **10.** endearment
petals (pert to) . . .
flower . . **7.** corolla
having . . **8.** petalous
orchid . . **8.** labellum

ref to . . **5.** whorl **8.** petaline, petaloid
without . . **9.** apetalous
petard . . . **9.** explosive **11.** firecracker
peteman (thieves' sl) . . . **5.** thief **7.** burglar
8. peterman **9.** cracksman, fisherman
(Hist) **10.** safeblower
Peter (pert to) . . .
Bell . . **4.** poem
Bible . . **5.** Simon (also called) **7.** epistle
(New Test)
the Great . . **4.** Czar
the Great's father . . **6.** Alexis
the Hermit . . **8.** Crusader (1st)
peter out . . . **4.** fade, fail, tire, wane
6. weaken **7.** dwindle **9.** cease to be
Peter Pan (pert to) . . .
author . . **6.** Barrie
children . . **4.** John **5.** Wendy **7.** Michael
fairy . . **10.** Tinker Bell
family . . **7.** Darling
Indian princess . . **9.** Tiger Lily
pirate . . **11.** Captain Hook
place . . **14.** Never-Never Land
petiole . . . **4.** stem **5.** stalk **8.** peduncle
9. leafstalk **10.** mesopodium
petit . . . **4.** mean **5.** petty, small **6.** little
13. insignificant
petite . . . **5.** small **6.** demure, little
petition . . . **3.** ask, beg, sue **4.** plea, pray
5. apply, plead **6.** prayer **7.** entreat,
relator, request, solicit **8.** entreaty
10. supplicate
peto . . . **5.** wahoo
petrified . . . **8.** hardened **9.** terrified
15. carved from stone
petrified body . . . **6.** fossil
petrify . . . **4.** numb **6.** deaden, harden
7. astound, stupefy **8.** paralyze
11. become stone
petroglyph . . . **11.** rock carving **15.** rock
inscription
Petrograd . . . **9.** Leningrad **12.** St
Petersburg
petroleum product . . . **6.** butane, diesel
7. naphtha, propane **8.** gasoline
petrology (science of) . . . **5.** rocks
petrosal . . . **4.** bone **5.** sinus, stony
7. petrous **8.** ganglion
petticoat . . . **4.** girl, kilt **5.** jupon,
pagne, woman **6.** kirtle **8.** basquine
9. undercoat, waistcoat **10.** fustanella,
underskirt
petticoat tails . . . **7.** teacake **9.** shortcake
pettifogger . . . **4.** tyro **5.** quack **6.** lawyer
7. shyster **8.** attorney
pettish . . . **7.** fretful, peevish **9.** irritable
pettle . . . **6.** cuddle, nestle, potter
7. cherish
petto . . . **12.** in one's breast **15.** in
contemplation
petty . . . **4.** mean, orra **5.** minor,
small **6.** paltry **7.** trivial **8.** childish,
inferior, nugatory, trifling **9.** miniscule
10. diminutive **11.** small-minded,
subordinate, unimportant **12.** narrow-
minded **13.** insignificant
14. inconsiderable
petty (pert to) . . .
captain . . **9.** centurion
fault . . **10.** peccadillo
larceny . . **10.** scrounging

mullein . . **7.** cowslip
objection . . **5.** cavil
prince . . **6.** satrap
petulance . . . **8.** ill humor, pertness
9. insolence, sauciness **10.** wantonness
11. peevishness, pettishness
petulant . . . **4.** pert **5.** cross, huffy, saucy,
testy **6.** wanton **7.** forward, fretful,
peevish, wayward, willful **8.** contrary,
immodest, insolent **9.** querulous
peu à peu . . . **9.** by degrees **14.** little by
little
pewee . . . **5.** pewit **6.** phoebe **8.** woodcock
10. flycatcher
pewit . . . **5.** pewee **7.** lapwing **12.** laughing
gull
Pfefferkuchen . . . **11.** gingerbread
Phaëthon, Class Myth (pert to) . . .
bird . . **4.** swan
car . . **3.** sun
father . . **6.** Helios
sun god . . **6.** Helios
phagomania . . . **8.** insanity **16.** insatiable
hunger
Phalacrocorax . . . **5.** coots **10.** cormorants
phalacrosis . . . **8.** alopecia, baldness
phalanger . . . **5.** tapoa **9.** marsupial
phalanx . . . **4.** bone **5.** pawns **6.** troops
7. company (Mil) **8.** infantry
phalera . . . **4.** boss **5.** cameo
phantasm . . . **5.** dream, fancy, ghost
6. idolum, spirit **7.** eidolon, fantasy,
phantom, specter (spectre) **8.** delusion,
illusion **10.** apparition
phantasy, fantasy . . . **5.** fancy, image
6. autism **8.** daydream **11.** imagination
phantom . . . **5.** fairy, ghost **7.** eidolon,
specter (spectre) **10.** simulacrum
Pharaoh (Bib) . . . **4.** faro, king
Pharaoh (pert to) . . .
ancestor . . **2.** Ra
chicken, hen . . **7.** vulture (Egypt)
fig . . **8.** sycamore
mouse . . **9.** ichneumon
phare . . . **6.** beacon, pharos **10.** lighthouse
pharisee . . . **7.** pietist **9.** hypocrite
pharmacology . . . **5.** drugs **13.** materia
medica
pharos . . . **5.** cloak **6.** beacon
10. chandelier (Eccl), lighthouse,
watchtower
phase . . . **5.** facet, stage **6.** aspect
7. caprice, chapter, horning (moon)
phases, having many . . . **11.** Hydra-
headed
phasm . . . **6.** meteor **7.** phantom
pheasant . . . **5.** cheer, monal **6.** pukras
7. kallege **8.** tragopan **12.** ruffed grouse
pheasant (pert to) . . .
brood . . **3.** nye **4.** nide (nid) **5.** flock
cuckoo . . **6.** coucal
duck . . **7.** pintail **9.** merganser
finch . . **7.** waxbill
genus . . **10.** Oreophasis
wren . . **7.** emu wren
pheasant species . . . **5.** argus, blood
6. golden, silver **7.** kallege **8.** curassow
9. Mongolian **10.** ring-necked **12.** Lady
Amherst's
phenomenal . . . **7.** unusual **8.** eventful,
sensible **9.** objective, wonderful

13. extraordinary
phenomenon . . . **4.** fact **5.** event (unusual)
  7. prodigy
phial . . . **3.** cup **4.** bowl, vial **6.** bottle,
  vessel
phiale . . . **5.** laver **6.** vessel **8.** fountain
  (Eccl)
Phi Beta Kappa (pert to) . . .
  badge . . **8.** watch key
  founding . . **21.** William and Mary College
  (1776)
  meaning . . **24.** Philosophy the guide of
  life
  society . . **11.** Greek-letter (oldest)
philabeg (filibeg) . . . **4.** kilt
Philadelphia . . .
  City of . . **13.** Brotherly Love
  fleabane . . **7.** skevish
  lawyer . . **6.** shrewd
  ref to . . **12.** Philadelphus (Ptolemy II)
  sport team . . **6.** Eagles **8.** Phillies
philander . . . **5.** flirt, lover **7.** opossum
  10. flirtation, love-making, lover of
  men
philanthropic . . . **6.** humane
  10. benevolent **12.** eleemosynary
philanthropist . . . **5.** donor **8.** altruist, do-
  gooder **9.** Robin Hood **10.** benefactor,
  benevolist, Montefiore, Rothschild
  12. humanitarian
philanthropy . . . **7.** charity **8.** good
  will **10.** almsgiving **11.** beneficence,
  benevolence (opp of misanthropy)
philatelist's concern . . . **5.** stamp
  (postage)
Philippic . . . **6.** screed, tirade **7.** oration
  8. diatribe **9.** Philippus
Philippine, Philippines . . .
  archipelago . . **4.** Sulu **5.** Malay
  bay . . **6.** Manila
  capital . . **6.** Baguio (summer), Manila
  10. Quezon City
  city . . **5.** Albay, Davao **6.** Cavite
  7. Dagupan
  district . . **7.** Lepanto
  fort . . **4.** Gota **10.** Corregidor
  island . . **4.** Cebu **5.** Leyte, Luzon, Panay,
  Samar, Ticao **6.** Negros **7.** Palawan,
  Paragua **8.** Mindanao
  mountain . . **3.** Apo, Iba **5.** Mayon
  river . . **4.** Abra, Agno **5.** Pasig
  8. Mindanao, Pampanga
  university . . **10.** Santo Tomas (1611)
  volcano . . **3.** Apo **5.** Mayon
Philippine (pert to) . . .
  animal . . **5.** civet, lemur
  ant, termite . . **4.** anay (anai)
  barracks . . **7.** cuartel
  boat, canoe, raft . . **5.** balsa, banca
  breadfruit . . **7.** camansi
  buffalo . . **7.** carabao, timarau (timerau)
  chair (on poles) . . **7.** talabon
  dagger . . **4.** itac
  drink . . **4.** beno **5.** bubud
  fabric . . **4.** pina **9.** pineapple
  fetish, idol . . **5.** anito
  food . . **3.** poi **4.** Musa, saba, taro
  hemp . . **5.** abaca **6.** Manila
  house . . **5.** bahay
  knife . . **4.** bolo
  litter, pole chair . . **7.** talabon

  lizard . . **4.** ibid (monitor)
  mango . . **5.** bauno **7.** pahutan
  market day . . **7.** tiangue
  melon . . **6.** atimon
  mudfish . . **5.** dalag
  palm . . **4.** nipa **6.** anahau (anahao)
  parrot (green) . . **5.** cagit
  reptile . . **6.** python
  rice . . **4.** paga **5.** macan
  rice field bank . . **7.** pilapil
  river . . **4.** ilog
  shrub . . **4.** alem
  sweetsop . . **4.** ates
  town . . **4.** agoa
  tree . . **3.** tui **4.** ipil (ypil) **5.** asana, ligas,
  narra, yacal **6.** molave **7.** Eugenia,
  tindalo **8.** macaasim
  turnip . . **7.** cincoma
  vehicle (public) . . **9.** carromata
  water jar . . **5.** banga
  wood . . **4.** teak **5.** ebony **6.** sandal
  8. mahogany
Philippine people (pert to) . . .
  discoverer . . **8.** Magellan (1521)
  farmer . . **3.** tao
  headman . . **4.** datu
  language . . **4.** Moro **7.** Tagalog (Tagal)
  8. Pilipino
  Muslim, Moslem . . **4.** Moro
  native worker . . **7.** polista
  Negrito . . **3.** Ati **4.** Aeta
  patriot . . **5.** Rizal
  peasant . . **3.** tao
  people . . **3.** Ati, Lao **4.** Aeta, Moro, Sulu
  5. Bikol (Chr) **7.** Tagalog, Visayan
  president . . **5.** Roxas **6.** Aquino, Marcos,
  Quezon
  priest (Moro) . . **7.** pandita
  servant . . **4.** bata **5.** alila
Philistine . . . **5.** enemy **7.** prosaic
  9. philister **10.** conformist, uncultured
  12. antagonistic **13.** prosaic person,
  unenlightened
Philistine (pert to) . . .
  anc name . . **9.** Palestine, Philistia
  assimilated by . . **7.** Semites
  city . . **4.** Gaza **5.** Ekron (Bib)
  god . . **4.** Baal **5.** Dagon
philo (comb form) . . . **6.** fond of, loving
philogeant . . . **12.** lover of earth
philogyny . . . **11.** love of women
philology . . . **11.** linguistics **14.** love of
  learning
Philomela (pert to) . . .
  father . . **7.** Pandion (King of Athens)
  sister . . **6.** Procne
  turned into . . **7.** swallow **11.** nightingale
philosopher . . .
  American . . Dewey, James (William),
  Royce **6.** Peirce **9.** Santayana
  Arab . . **8.** Averroes (Averrhoes)
  Chinese . . **6.** Lao-tzu **9.** Confucius
  Christian . . **7.** Abelard, Aquinas
  9. Augustine
  Danish . . **11.** Kierkagaard
  Dutch . . **7.** Spinoza
  English . . **4.** Mill **5.** Bacon, Locke
  6. Hobbes **7.** Bentham, Russell, Spencer
  9. Whitehead
  French . . **6.** Pascal **8.** Rousseau, Voltaire
  9. Descartes

German . . **4.** Kant **5.** Hegel **9.** Heidegger, Nietzsche **12.** Schopenhauer
Greek . . **4.** Zeno **5.** Plato **8.** Epicurus, Socrates **9.** Aristotle
Indian . . **6.** Buddha
Italian . . **5.** Bruno
Scottish . . **4.** Hume
Seven Sages (7 Wise Men of Greece) . . **4.** Bias **5.** Solon **6.** Chilon, Thales **8.** Pittacus **9.** Cleobulus **10.** Epimenides (or Periander)
Philosopher of . . .
Farney . . **8.** Voltaire
Malmesbury . . **6.** Hobbes
Sans Souci . . **17.** Frederick the Great
Syracuse . . **4.** Dion
Wimbledon . . **14.** John Horne Tooke
philosopher's school . . . **7.** Eleatic
philosophical . . . **4.** wise **7.** erudite, logical, sapient **8.** rational **9.** temperate, unruffled
philosophical being . . . **6.** entity
philosophy (pert to) . . .
choice of . . **11.** eclecticism
of law . . **13.** jurisprudence
of pantheists . . **5.** Stoic
sublimated . . **17.** Transcendentalism
theory . . **4.** yoga **9.** pantheism, Platonism, solipsism **12.** epistemology
phlegmatic . . . **4.** calm, dull, slow **5.** inert **6.** mucous, watery **7.** viscous **8.** sluggish **9.** apathetic
phlogistic . . . **5.** fiery **6.** heated **7.** burning **11.** impassioned **12.** inflammatory
Phoebad . . . **7.** seeress **9.** priestess (Delphian) **10.** prophetess
Phoebe (pert to) . . .
daughter . . **4.** Leto
epithet of . . **7.** Artemis
mother . . **4.** Gaea (earth goddess)
poetic . . **4.** moon
phoebe . . . **4.** fish **5.** craps, pewit **6.** peewee **9.** satellite (Saturn) **10.** flycatcher
Phoebus . . . **3.** Sol **6.** sun god
Phoenicia . . .
capital city . . **4.** Tyre **5.** Sidon
Colony . . **5.** Hippo **8.** Carthage
deity . . **4.** Baal
famed for . . **9.** purple dye **10.** navigation
goddess of fertility . . **6.** Baltis **7.** Astarte
god of healing . . **6.** Eshmun (Eshmoun)
king . . **6.** Agenor
region . . **5.** Syria
Phoenix . . . **4.** bird (fabled), palm **7.** capital (Ariz)
phonetic (pert to) . . .
science . . **9.** phonology
sound . . **7.** phoneme
stop . . **9.** occlusive
system . . **5.** romic
phonic . . . **6.** spoken, voiced **7.** sounded **8.** auditory **9.** accoustic, vibration
phony (comb form) . . . **5.** sound, voice
phony . . . **4.** fake **9.** contrived, simulated **11.** counterfeit
photograph . . . **4.** film **5.** image, photo **7.** picture **8.** likeness, portrait **9.** ferrotype, pictorial, portrayal **10.** centerfold, heliograph **12.** photogravure

photographic bath . . . **5.** toner **7.** reducer **9.** developer
photography, science of . . . **5.** light **6.** optics **7.** photics
photography inventors . . . **4.** Land **6.** Niepce, Talbot **8.** Daguerre
photometric unit . . . **3.** pyr, rad
phrase . . . **5.** idiom **6.** remark, saying, slogan **7.** diction, epigram, epithet, passage **8.** flattery **9.** catchword **10.** expression **11.** phraseology
phraseology . . . **5.** style **6.** jargon **7.** diction, wording **8.** parlance
phratry (Hist) . . . **4.** clan **5.** group
phrenetic . . . **3.** mad **5.** crazy **6.** madman **7.** fanatic, frantic, violent **9.** delirious **10.** passionate
phrenology, science of . . . **5.** skull **10.** craniology
Phrygia, Asia Minor . . .
cap (comical) . . **10.** liberty cap
deity . . **5.** Attis
Eccl Hist . . **9.** Montanist
founder . . **7.** Gordius (800 BC)
King . . **5.** Midas
marble (anc) . . **9.** pavonazzo (pavonazzetto)
music . . **4.** mode
river . . **7.** Meander
phylactery (Eccl) . . . **4.** case **5.** charm, chest, miter **6.** amulet, infula, record, scroll
phylarchy . . . **12.** rule by tribes
phyletic . . . **6.** racial **7.** descent, species **12.** phylogenetic
phyllophagous . . . **15.** feeding on leaves
physical . . . **6.** bodily **7.** natural, somatic **8.** material **9.** corporeal
physical force . . . **10.** attraction
physical unit . . . **3.** erg
physician . . . **5.** medic **6.** doctor, healer, intern **7.** coroner **8.** restorer
physician (pert to) . . .
ancient . . **5.** Galen
comb form . . **5.** iatro
French Nobel Prize . . **7.** Laveran
Greek (anc) . . **5.** Galen **11.** Asclepiades
quack . . **10.** medicaster
symbol . . **8.** caduceus
physicist . . . **4.** Bohr, Mach, Rabi **5.** Fermi, Pauli **6.** Dalton, Pascal, Teller **7.** Feynman, Hawking, Marconi, Maxwell **8.** Chadwick, Einstein, Sakharov **11.** Oppenheimer, Schrödinger
physiognomy . . . **3.** mug **4.** face **11.** countenance **14.** external aspect, interpretation
physique . . . **4.** body **6.** figure
physis (Gr) . . . **6.** nature
phytology, science of . . . **6.** botany, plants
piacle . . . **3.** sin **5.** crime, guilt **7.** offense **15.** sacrificial rite **17.** expiatory offering
pian . . . **5.** tumor **9.** frambesia
piano (pert to) . . .
direction . . **10.** pianissimo (softly)
duet, upper part . . **5.** primo
dumb keyboard . . **10.** digitorium
early . . **6.** spinet
Italian . . **10.** Cristofori

keyboard.. **7.** clavier **8.** pedalier
pedal.. **7.** celeste
pianolike.. **7.** celesta
player.. **7.** pianola
slang.. **11.** eighty-eight
small.. **8.** pianette
piatti... **7.** cymbals
piazza... **5.** campo, porch **6.** square
   7. gallery, portico, veranda
pic... **4.** peak **8.** picayune
picacho... **4.** hill **5.** butte
picador... **3.** wit **6.** jester **7.** debater
   8. horseman (with lance), toreador
   11. bullfighter
picaro... **5.** knave, rogue **7.** sharper
   8. vagabond **10.** picaresque
picaroon... **5.** rogue, thief **6.** pirate,
   rascal **7.** brigand, corsair **8.** prey upon
pick... **4.** cull, gaff, peck, sort **5.** elect,
   pluck, strum **6.** assort, choose, indent,
   pickax, pierce, select **7.** diamond (card),
   harvest, the best **8.** plectrum, the elite
   9. toothpick
pick (pert to)...
   flaws.. **5.** cavil
   out.. **6.** pilfer, select **7.** acquire,
   procure, specify **9.** eliminate, segregate
   11. distinguish
   pick-me-up.. **5.** tonic **6.** bracer
   9. kittiwake, stimulate **11.** restorative
   up.. **4.** tidy **6.** arrest **7.** improve
   9. stimulant **10.** recuperate
picked... **4.** trim **5.** piked, spiny **6.** choice,
   chosen, culled, dainty, peaked, spruce
   7. adorned, plucked, pointed **8.** stripped
   10. fastidious
pickerel... **4.** fish, pike **9.** Esox niger
   12. walleyed pike
picket... **3.** peg **4.** pale, post, tern
   5. fence, guard, stake **6.** bullet, fasten,
   paling, sentry, tether **7.** enclose, fortify,
   shackle **8.** sentinel **10.** go on strike
pickle... **4.** alec, peck **5.** achar, brine
   6. dawdle, nibble, piddle, pilfer, trifle
   7. chutney, vitrial
pickled... **5.** drunk **6.** soused
   9. marinated
pickled pig's feet... **5.** souse
pickle fork... **8.** runcible
pickle-herring... **7.** buffoon **11.** merry-
   andrew **12.** Pickelhering
pickpocket... **4.** wire **5.** thief **6.** bulker
picnic... **3.** fun **4.** camp, play **6.** junket,
   outing **9.** festivity
Pict (anc)... **4.** Scot **5.** Aryan **9.** aborigine
Pictland... **8.** Scotland
pictorial... **8.** painting **11.** illustrated,
   picturesque
Pict's house (Archaeol)... **8.** dwelling
   (subterranean)
picture... **3.** oil **4.** copy, draw, icon
   5. image, print, scene **6.** chromo,
   depict, pastel **7.** diorama, etching,
   portray, porture, tableau **8.** describe,
   likeness, painting, portrait **9.** engraving,
   paintings, represent, visualize
   10. photograph **11.** description
   14. representation
picture (pert to)...
   mounting, border.. **3.** mat **5.** frame
   8. kakemono, makimono (scroll)

moving.. **4.** film **5.** movie **6.** cinema
positive.. **5.** print
puzzle.. **5.** rebus
small.. **5.** cameo **9.** miniature
stand.. **5.** easel
viewer.. **11.** alethoscope, stereoscope
   12. magic lantern, stereopticon
picturesque... **5.** vivid **6.** scenic
   7. graphic **9.** pictorial
picuda... **9.** barracuda (great), picudilla
   (small)
picudo... **6.** weevil **10.** boll weevil
piddle... **3.** toy **4.** pick, play **6.** putter,
   trifle **9.** waste time
pie... **4.** food, mess **5.** chaos, patty
   6. jumble, magpie, pastry **7.** cobbler,
   dessert, measure **9.** confusion
piebald... **4.** pied **5.** mixed, pinto
   6. motley **7.** mongrel, mottled, pintado
   10. variegated **13.** heterogeneous
piece... **3.** bit **4.** join, part, role
   5. crumb, drama, piece, scrap, shred
   6. sample **7.** measure, portion, writing
   8. chessman, fragment, specimen,
   treatise
piece (pert to)...
   armor.. **5.** tasse (tace) **8.** corselet
   de résistance.. **6.** entrée **8.** main dish
   door, jamb.. **6.** lintel
   eccentric.. **3.** cam
   fastening.. **3.** gib
   fitted.. **4.** shim **5.** tenon
   flat.. **4.** slab, slat **5.** flake, strip
   meal.. **9.** by degrees, fragments
   12. piece by piece **14.** little by little
   metal.. **3.** sow
   neck.. **3.** boa **5.** rabat, scarf, stole
   8. kerchief
   of one's mind.. **6.** rebuke **7.** reproof
   13. candid opinion
   out.. **3.** eke **6.** cantle
   preventing slippage.. **5.** cleat
   short.. **4.** skit
   side.. **3.** rib **5.** stave
   split off.. **6.** sliver, splint **8.** splinter
   tapering.. **4.** gore **6.** gusset
   work (art).. **4.** pavé **6.** mosaic, niello
pieces of...
   eight.. **5.** dollar, escudo
   meat.. **5.** cabob
   silk waste.. **4.** noil
pied... **4.** foot **5.** pinto **7.** colored (2
   or more colors), dappled, piebald
   10. variegated **12.** parti-colored
pied (pert to)...
   blackbird.. **6.** thrush
   brant.. **5.** goose
   diver.. **4.** smew
   duck.. **8.** Labrador
   Friar (Eccl Hist).. **9.** mendicant
   monk.. **10.** Bernardine, Cistercian
   Piper of Hamelin.. **8.** musician **10.** rat
   charmer
   widgeon.. **8.** garganey **9.** goldeneye
Piedmont, Italy... **7.** capital (Turin)
pieplant... **7.** rhubarb
pier... **4.** anta, dock, mole, quay **5.** groin,
   wharf **6.** pillar **7.** landing **8.** buttress,
   gatepost **9.** promenade **10.** breakwater
pierce... **4.** bore, cold, gore, pain, tart
   5. enter, gride, lance, probe, spear,

spike, sting, wound **6.** riddle, tunnel
7. discern **8.** puncture **9.** penetrate,
perforate **10.** comprehend
piercing . . . **4.** keen, loud **5.** acute **6.** shrill
7. caustic, clearly, painful, piteous,
pungent, sharply, shrilly, spiking,
violent **8.** deep-felt, poignant, spearing,
stabbing **9.** searching.
Pieria, Macedonia (pert to) . . .
epithet of . . **5.** Muses
native . . **7.** Pierian
reference to . . **6.** poetry **9.** knowledge
seat of . . **5.** Muses
piet . . . **5.** ouzel **6.** magpie **7.** piebald
10. chatterbox, chattering **11.** saucy
person
Pietà (It) . . . **9.** sculpture **10.** Virgin Mary
pietose (Mus) . . . **11.** sympathetic
13. compassionate
piety . . . **4.** pity, zeal (worship) **6.** filial
8. devotion, holiness, religion
9. reverence **10.** compassion,
devoutness, sanctimony **11.** dutifulness
pig . . . **3.** car (RR), ham, hog, sow
4. boar, pork **5.** bacon, crosk, flask,
swine **6.** farrow **7.** casting, dogboat,
glutton **8.** pressman, sixpence, slattern
9. policeman **11.** stoolpigeon
pig (pert to) . . .
bed . . **3.** pen, sty **5.** reeve **6.** pigsty
female . . **3.** sow **4.** gilt
guinea . . **4.** cavy
headed . . **6.** stupid **9.** obstinate
iron . . **5.** ingot
iron, ballast (Naut) . . **9.** kentledge
iron, cast . . **9.** kentledge (Mil)
last of litter . . **4.** runt
lead, weight . . **6.** fother
litter . . **6.** farrow
piglike . . **7.** hoglike, porcine, suiform
piglike animal . . **7.** peccary **8.** babirusa
potato . . **7.** cowbane
rat . . **9.** bandicoot
skin . . **6.** saddle **8.** football
yoke . . **7.** sextant **8.** quadrant
young . . **5.** grice, shoat **6.** farrow, piglet
9. gruntling
pigdan . . . **8.** spittoon
pigeon . . . **3.** nun **4.** barb, dove, dupe,
fowl, girl, gull, ruff **5.** heart, piper,
pluck, sweet **6.** coward, fleece, pouter,
roller, turbit **7.** fantail, jacobin, pintail,
tumbler **9.** trumpeter
pigeon, pidgin (pert to) . . .
Australia . . **5.** wonga **10.** wonga-wonga
berry . . **7.** dogwood **9.** Juneberry, wild
elder
blood . . **6.** garnet
carrier . . **5.** homer **6.** homing
10. scandaroon
extinct . . **4.** dodo
food . . **7.** saltcat
genus . . **5.** Goura **7.** Columba
hawk . . **6.** falcon, merlin
house . . **7.** dovecot **9.** columbary
ref to . . **12.** peristeronic
short-beaked . . **4.** barb
wood . . **6.** cushat **8.** ringdove
young . . **5.** piper
pigment . . . **3.** red **4.** blue, gray, pink
5. black, brown, color, green, ocher

(ochre), paint, white **6.** orange, purple,
yellow **8.** colorant
pigment (pert to) . . .
arsenic, yellow . . **8.** orpiment
black . . **3.** tar **5.** sepia **7.** melanin
blue . . **5.** smalt
blue-green . . **4.** bice
brown . . **5.** sepia, umber **6.** bister (bistre),
sienna (burnt) **7.** cypress
brownish yellow . . **6.** sienna
calico yellow . . **7.** canarin (canarine)
coal tar . . **7.** aniline
cuttlefish . . **5.** sepia
madder root . . **7.** rubiate
orange red . . **7.** realgar
oxide of lead . . **8.** massicot
red . . **7.** turacin
yellow . . **5.** ocher (ochre) **7.** etiolin
pigmy . . . see *pygmy*
pignus . . . **4.** pawn **6.** pledge
pig's feet . . . **9.** pettitoes
pigtail . . . **5.** braid, queue **7.** tobacco
(rolled) **8.** rope's end (Naut)
pika . . . **6.** rodent
pike . . . **3.** ged (gedd) **4.** fish, luce, pick
6. beacon, pickax
pike (pert to) . . .
North American . . **11.** muskellunge
perch . . **6.** sauger
pikelike . . **3.** gar **4.** luce **5.** lucet **6.** robalo
8. robalito **9.** barracuda
walleyed . . **4.** doré
pikel, pikle . . . **7.** hayfork **9.** pitchfork
pikelet . . . **7.** crumpet
piker . . . **5.** thief, tramp **6.** coward
7. gambler, quitter, shirker, vagrant
8. tightwad
pilar . . . **5.** downy, hairy
pilaster . . . **4.** anta **6.** alette (part), column
Pilate (Bib) . . . **10.** procurator (Judean)
pilchard . . . **7.** sardine
pile . . . **3.** awn, mow, nap **4.** heap, load,
mole, pier, rick, shag **5.** amass, slack,
spile, stake **6.** heap up, pillar, wealth
7. fortune, store up, texture
pile (pert to) . . .
burning . . **4.** pyre
defense . . **8.** estacade
driver . . **7.** fistuca
of hay . . **3.** mow **4.** dess, rick **5.** stack
up . . **4.** heap **7.** smashup, store up
9. shipwreck **10.** exaggerate
pilfer . . . **3.** rob **4.** lift, loot **5.** filch, steal,
swipe **6.** rustle (cattle), snitch **7.** purloin
pilgrim . . . **5.** exile (Relig) **6.** palmer
8. crusader, newcomer, traveler,
wanderer, wayfarer **9.** immigrant,
sojourner **10.** tenderfoot
12. peregrinator
Pilgrim (pert to) . . .
father . . **9.** John Alden
Fathers . . **11.** Separatists (1620)
garment . . **5.** ihram (Mecca)
landing . . **12.** Plymouth Rock (1620)
Scotch . . **6.** palmer
ship . . **9.** Mayflower, Speedwell
pilgrimage to Mecca . . . **4.** hadj
Pilgrim's bottle . . . **7.** ampulla, costrel
Pilgrim's Progress . . . **8.** allegory
(Bunyan)
pill . . . **3.** rob **4.** ball, bore, pare, pell, pool

5. bolus, creek 6. bullet, pellet, pilule
8. medicine 9. cigarette 11. decorticate
pillage . . . 4. flay, loot, prey, sack
5. booty, harry, spoil, strip 6. rapine,
ravage 7. despoil, plunder, robbery
9. depredate, extortion 10. spoliation
pillar . . . 4. post, slab 5. shaft, stele
(stela), tower 6. column 7. support
8. mainstay, monument, pedestal
pillar (pert to) . . .
  airfield . . 5. pylon
  Buddhist . . 3. lat
  carved . . 9. totem pole
  little . . 8. pillaret
  of society . . 9. personage
  pillarlike . . 6. stelar
  saint . . 7. recluse, stylite
  tall, slender . . 7. obelisk
  with front figure . . 7. osiride
Pillars of Hercules site . . . 5. Abila,
Calpe 17. Strait of Gibralter ·
pillbox . . . 3. cap, hat 8. brougham,
fortress 13. fortification
pillory . . . 4. yoke 5. stock, trone
6. cangue, punish
pillow . . . 3. pad 5. block 7. cushion,
support
pillow (pert to) . . .
  case, cover . . 4. sham, slip
  long . . 7. bolster
  stuffing . . 5. kapok 8. feathers
pilose . . . 5. hairy 6. pilous
pilot . . . 4. lead 5. flyer, guide, steer
6. aviate, direct, leader 8. director,
helmsman, preacher 9. clergyman,
navigator 10. cowcatcher
pilot (pert to) . . .
  bird . . 6. plover
  expert . . 3. ace
  fish . . 6. remora 9. amberfish, whitefish
  house . . 10. wheelhouse
  jacket . . 9. pea jacket
  sky . . 8. preacher 9. clergyman
  snake . . 10. copperhead
  weed . . 9. rosinweed
  whale . . 9. blackfish
pilotless plane . . . 5. drone
Piltdown, England (pert to) . . .
  Hist yield . . 7. Dawn Man, fossils
  Prehist station . . 6. Sussex
piltock . . . 8. coalfish
pilum . . . 6. pestle 7. javelin
pilus . . . 4. hair
Pima . . . 5. Opata
pimento . . . 6. pepper 7. paprika
8. allspice, pimiento
pin . . . 3. hob, peg, pen 4. axle, bolt,
coak (coag), join 5. affix, badge,
dowel, rivet, thole 6. brooch, cotter,
fasten, secure, trifle 7. confine, enclose,
gudgeon, jewelry, spindle, stopper,
trenail 8. linchpin, ornament, transfix
10. chatelaine
pin (pert to) . . .
  axle . . 8. linchpin
  dial . . 5. style
  fish . . 11. stickleback
  game . . 7. skittle
  grass . . 9. alfilaria (forage)
  jackstraw (game) . . 8. spilikin (spillikin)
  meat fastener . . 6. skewer

quoits . . 3. hob
sailmaker's . . 3. fid
small . . 3. peg 4. lill
with looped head . . 7. eyebolt
pinafore . . . 5. apron, smock 7. tablier
8. sun dress
Pinafore . . . 5. opera (Gilbert & Sullivan)
pinag . . . 4. lake (rain season)
piñata . . . 5. globe (swinging, with gifts)
pinax . . . 4. dish 5. table 6. plaque,
scheme, tablet 7. picture 9. catalogue
pinbone . . . 7. hipbone
pince-nez . . . 7. glasses, nippers
10. eyeglasses
pincers . . . 3. tew 5. chela, tongs 6. pliers
7. forceps, pinette
pinch . . . 3. nip, rob 4. pain, raid 5. cramp,
gripe, pugil (anc), steal, stint, tweak
6. arrest, crisis, extort, scrimp, snatch,
snitch, strait, twinge 7. afflict, confine,
squeeze, urgency 8. compress, contract,
exigency, straiten
pinchbeck . . . 4. sham 5. alloy (cheap
jewelry) 8. frippery, spurious
11. counterfeit
pinched . . . 4. poor, thin 8. squeezed
10. compressed, contracted, distressed,
straitened
pinchem . . . 8. titmouse
pinda . . . 6. peanut
Pindar . . . 4. poet (lyric)
pindaric . . . 3. ode 9. irregular
12. unrestrained
pine . . . 4. flag 5. waste, yearn 6. grieve,
lament, needle, repine, sicken, weaken,
wither 8. languish 11. deteriorate
pine (pert to) . . .
  Brazil . . 6. paraná
  chemical . . 5. pinic
  exudation . . 5. resin, rosin
  family . . 3. fir 5. larch, piñon 6. spruce
  finch . . 6. siskin
  fir . . 6. balsam 12. Balm of Gilead
  fruit . . 4. cone
  genus . . 5. Pinus
  gum . . 8. sandarac
  knot . . 7. dovekie
  leaf . . 6. needle
  low-growing . . 5. piñon
  mahogany . . 6. totara
  New Zealand . . 5. kauri (kaury)
  Pacific coast . . 8. knobpine
  Philippine . . 7. Amboina 8. galagala
  screw . . 3. ara 6. pandan
  tar extract . . 6. retene
  tulip . . 10. pipsissewa
pineal . . . 5. brain, gland 8. pine cone
pineapple . . . 4. bomb, pina 5. fiber, fruit
6. ananas 8. pine cone 12. Bromeliaceae
pineapple (pert to) . . .
  cheese . . 7. Cheddar
  cloth . . 4. pina
  segment . . 3. pip
  weed . . 8. marigold
Pina Tree State . . . 5. Maine
pinguescent . . . 9. fattening
pinguid . . . 3. fat 4. oily, rich 5. fatty
8. unctuous
pinguitude . . . 7. fatness, obesity
8. oiliness 10. greasiness
pink . . . 3. cut, Red 4. deck, rose, stab

5. adorn, blink, color, coral, smart, wound **6.** flower, indent, minnow, pierce, salmon, vessel **7.** radical, serrate **8.** decorate, grayling **9.** carnation **11.** fashionable

pink (pert to) . . .
coat . . **10.** foxhunter's
eye . . **4.** duck **14.** conjunctivitis
family . . **7.** Campion **9.** Carnation **15.** Caryophyllaceae
fish . . **8.** gobylike
genus . . **6.** Silene
lady . . **3.** fly (fishing) **8.** cocktail
needle . . **9.** alfilaria
Pearl . . **6.** azalea
pill . . **7.** cure-all
root . . **8.** wormroot
pinkeen . . . **6.** minnow **19.** insignificant person
pinna . . . **3.** fin **4.** wing **7.** auricle, feather, leaflet
pinnace . . . **4.** boat **5.** woman **6.** tender (Naut) **9.** procuress **10.** prostitute
pinnacle . . . **3.** epi, tee, tor **4.** acme, apex, peak **5.** crest, crown, serac, spire **6.** finial, needle, summit
pinnate . . . **11.** featherlike
pinniped . . . **4.** seal **6.** walrus
pinochle term . . . **3.** dix **4.** meld
piñon . . . **4.** pine, seed **8.** pignolia **12.** monkey puzzle
pintado . . . **4.** cero, fish, sier (fish) **5.** pinto **6.** chintz, pigeon, sierra
pintail (pert to) . . .
duck . . **4.** smee **5.** river, ruddy
grouse . . **4.** sand **11.** sharp-tailed
pinto (horse) . . . **4.** pied **6.** calico **7.** mottled, painted, piebald, spotted
pinwing . . . **7.** penguin
pioneer . . . **4.** lead **5.** guide, miner **6.** digger, open up **7.** settler **8.** colonist, explorer **9.** excavator **10.** forerunner
Pioneer's Day . . . **4.** Utah (July 24) **5.** Idaho (June 15)
pious . . . **5.** godly, loyal **6.** devout, worthy **9.** excellent, religious **11.** reverential **13.** sanctimonious
pip . . . **3.** ace **4.** paip, peep, roup, seed, spot, trey **7.** disease **12.** officer's star
pipe . . . **2.** TD **3.** see, tee **4.** blow, clay, duct, reed, tube **5.** spout, voice **6.** convey, dudeen, hookah (hooka), outlet **7.** channel **9.** brierwood
pipe (pert to) . . .
connection . . **3.** ell, tee **5.** cross, elbow
dream . . **8.** illusion **10.** bemusement
end . . **4.** taft **6.** nozzle
line . . **9.** grapevine
Oriental . . **8.** narghile (nargile)
pastoral, shepherd's . . **3.** oat **4.** reed **7.** larigot **9.** flageolet
peace . . **7.** calumet
player . . **5.** fifer **8.** shepherd
short . . **6.** dudeen
smoke . . **5.** tewel
steam . . **5.** riser
tobacco . . **10.** meerschaum
wood . . **5.** brier (briar) **9.** brierwood
wrench . . **8.** Stillson
pipette . . . **6.** taster, tubule **7.** dripper
pipit . . . **7.** titlark

piquancy . . . **4.** zest **5.** spice **8.** pungency, raciness, tartness **11.** conciseness
piquant . . . **4.** racy, tart **5.** salty, sharp, spicy, zesty **7.** concise, cutting, pungent **11.** interesting, provocative
pique . . . **4.** dive, fret, goad **5.** anger, annoy, sting, tempt **6.** grudge, incite, nettle, offend **7.** dudgeon, offense, provoke, umbrage **8.** irritate **9.** displease **10.** irritation, resentment **11.** displeasure
pir (Muslim) . . . **4.** tomb **5.** guide, saint
pirate . . . **6.** robber **7.** corsair, mariner **8.** marauder, picaroon **9.** buccaneer **10.** freebooter **11.** appropriate
pirate (famed) . . . **4.** Kidd **6.** Morgan **7.** Lafitte **10.** Blackbeard (Capt Teach)
pirate (pert to) . . .
base, famed . . . **7.** Barbary (Coast)
bird . . **10.** jaeger gull
flag . . **10.** Jolly Roger
gallows . . **7.** yardarm
perch . . **8.** Xenarchi
ship . . **5.** rover **7.** corsair **8.** picaroon
weapon . . **4.** snee
piraya . . . **6.** caribe (fish) **7.** piranha
pirogue . . . **5.** canoe **7.** piragua
pirol . . . **6.** oriole
Pisa, Italy . . .
capital of . . **7.** Tuscany
famed for . . **9.** campanile **12.** Leaning Tower
river . . **4.** Arno
pis aller . . . **10.** last resort
piscary . . . **7.** fishery **12.** fishing place **13.** fishing rights
piscatology (science of) . . . **7.** angling, fishing **10.** halieutics
Pisces . . . **4.** fish **6.** fishes **13.** constellation
piscina . . . **4.** tank **5.** basin (Eccl) **8.** fishpond **9.** reservoir
Piscis Volans . . . **10.** flying fish **13.** constellation
Pisgah (pert to) . . .
site . . **4.** Nebo **8.** mountain (top)
view . . **12.** Land of Canaan **13.** Land of Promise
viewer . . **5.** Moses
pismire . . . **3.** ant **5.** emmet
pistachio . . . **3.** nut **5.** green
piste . . . **4.** path **5.** spoor, track, trail **10.** racecourse
pisteology, pistiology . . . **5.** faith **6.** belief
pistil . . . **5.** ovary **6.** carpel **9.** gynoecium
pistol . . . **3.** dag **7.** firearm **9.** derringer
pistol (pert to) . . .
case . . **7.** holster
lock . . **5.** rowet
slang . . **3.** gat, rod **6.** barker, cannon, heater
pistology (Theol) . . . **5.** faith
piston . . . **7.** plunger
pit . . . **4.** cave, hole, mine, pool, sump, tomb, trap, well **5.** abyss, arena, grave, sluig, snare **6.** cavity, slough **7.** alveola, cockpit, dungeon **8.** audience **9.** waterhole **10.** excavation **13.** Stock Exchange
pit (pert to) . . .
anatomy . . **5.** fossa, fovea
botany . . **7.** alveola, pitamen **8.** endocarp
bottomless . . **7.** Abaddon

fodder.. **4.** silo
Hades.. **4.** hell
Hawaiian.. **3.** imu
theater.. **7.** parquet
viper.. **9.** Viperidae **11.** rattlesnake
pitch ... **3.** key, tar **4.** camp, hurl, tilt,
tone, toss **5.** black, color, erect, fling,
heave, lurch, resin, sense, slope, throw
6. degree, encamp, plunge, settle,
topple **7.** incline **8.** flounder **9.** sales
talk
pitch (pert to) ...
high.. **6.** shrill
identity.. **6.** unison
inflammable.. **7.** piceous
mineral.. **7.** asphalt, bitumen
music.. **4.** flat **6.** accent, stress
8. paranete **9.** tonometer
pitchlike.. **7.** piceous
pitchblende ... **6.** radium **7.** uranium
pitched ball, curving away ...
8. outshoot
pitcher ... **3.** jug **4.** ewer, olla, olpe,
toby **5.** gorge **8.** cruisken (cruiskeen),
oenochoe (wine), southpaw (left-
handed)
pitcher (pert to) ...
plant, genus.. **9.** Nepenthes
10. Cephalotus, Sarracenia
plus catcher.. **7.** battery
shaped.. **9.** urceolate
shaped vessel.. **8.** aiguière
piteous ... **5.** pious **6.** devout, paltry,
tender **7.** pitiful, pitying **8.** pitiable
13. compassionate
pitfall ... **3.** pit **4.** lure, trap **5.** decoy,
snare **6.** danger **10.** difficulty
pith ... **3.** jet, nub **4.** gist, meat, pulp
6. center, kernel, marrow **7.** essence,
meaning, nucleus **9.** substance
pith helmet ... **3.** cap, hat **5.** topee (topi)
pith tree (Nile) ... **7.** ambatch (ambash)
pithy ... **4.** soft **5.** crisp, meaty, pulpy,
terse **7.** laconic **10.** meaningful
12. epigrammatic
pithy (pert to) ...
expression.. **7.** epigram
saying.. **3.** mot
sentence.. **5.** motto
pitiable ... **3.** sad **6.** woeful **7.** piteous
8. grievous, terrible **9.** miserable,
sorrowful **10.** lamentable
pitiful ... **4.** mean **6.** paltry **7.** piteous
8. pathetic, shameful **10.** despicable
12. contemptible **13.** compassionate,
tenderhearted
pitiless ... **5.** cruel **8.** ruthless **9.** merciless
10. relentless **13.** unsympathetic
pitpit ... **8.** guitguit **12.** honey creeper
Pitri, Hindu (pert to) ...
ancestor of.. **4.** gods **6.** demons **10.** four
castes
Prajapatis, one of.. **10.** progenitor
(human race)
semidivine.. **6.** father **9.** patriarch
10. forefather
pittance ... **4.** alms, dole, gift, scat
7. bequest **8.** donation **9.** allowance
11. small amount
pity ... **4.** ruth **5.** mercy, yearn **7.** remorse
8. clemency, sympathy **10.** compassion,

condolence, repentance
13. commiseration
pivot ... **3.** toe **4.** slew, slue, turn **5.** hinge
6. pintle, swivel
pivotal ... **4.** crux **5.** polar **7.** turning
pixy, pixie ... **3.** elf, imp **5.** fairy **6.** goblin,
sprite **13.** mischief-maker
Pizarro (pert to) ...
adventurer.. **7.** Spanish
conqueror of.. **4.** Peru
founder of.. **4.** Lima (capital)
placable ... **8.** peaceful **9.** agreeable,
forgiving, peaceable **10.** appeasable
placard ... **4.** bill, post **5.** edict **6.** notice,
poster **7.** affiché **9.** manifesto,
stomacher **12.** proclamation
placate ... **4.** calm **6.** pacify, soothe
7. appease **10.** conciliate **11.** tranquilize
place ... **3.** put **4.** lieu, site, spot **5.** abode,
locus, posit, situs, stead **6.** locale,
locate, region, street **7.** arrange,
demesne, deposit **8.** classify, location,
position **9.** recognize, situation
place (of) ...
amusement.. **4.** park **6.** casino, midway
bliss.. **4.** Eden **8.** paradise
confinement.. **3.** pen **4.** brig, cage,
coop, gaol, jail, stir **6.** asylum, corral,
prison **7.** dungeon **9.** calaboose
12. penitentiary
confusion.. **5.** Babel
content.. **7.** Arcadia
darkness.. **6.** Erebus
exit.. **6.** egress
honor.. **9.** right hand
origin.. **6.** cradle, source
refuge.. **3.** ark **4.** port **5.** haven
resort.. **7.** purlieu
rest.. **3.** bed, den **4.** lair, nook **5.** chair,
couch, grave, niche
sleep.. **3.** bed **4.** doss **5.** berth, couch
6. pallet **7.** hammock
suffering.. **10.** Armageddon,
Gethsemane
trial.. **5.** venue
place (pert to) ...
apart.. **6.** enisle **7.** isolate **9.** sequester
beneath.. **9.** infrapose
between.. **9.** interpose
burial.. **5.** grave **8.** catacomb, cemetery
9. graveyard **10.** necropolis
by itself.. **7.** isolate
camping.. **5.** étape
confidence in.. **7.** entrust
different.. **10.** otherwhere
for boats.. **7.** portage
for candles.. **9.** chandlery
forest (open).. **5.** glade
for keeping animals.. **3.** zoo **4.** barn
7. pasture **9.** menagerie
frequented.. **4.** dive **5.** haunt **6.** resort
from which jury is taken.. **5.** venue
hallowed.. see *sacred (below)*
hiding.. **3.** mew **4.** lair **5.** niche
high.. **7.** eminent **8.** eminence
horse training.. **4.** ring **5.** longe
in a row.. **5.** align, aline
in bondage.. **7.** enslave
in order.. **7.** arrange **11.** systematize
in statu quo.. **7.** put back, replace,
restore

interpretation on . . **8.** construe
landing . . **4.** dock, pier **5.** wharf **7.** airport
market . . **4.** mart **5.** agora **6.** rialto
meeting . . **5.** tryst
of . . **4.** lieu **5.** stead
on mound . . **3.** tee
opposite . . **6.** appose
over . . **11.** superimpose
sacred . . **4.** fane **5.** altar **6.** chapel,
   church, shrine, temple **9.** synagogue
   10. tabernacle
side-by-side . . **9.** collocate, juxtapose
sleeping . . **3.** bed **4.** bunk **5.** berth,
   couch **6.** pallet **7.** hammock
under . . **9.** infrapose
under restraint . . **6.** arrest, intern
value upon . . **5.** price **6.** assess
   8. appraise, estimate
wet . . **4.** slew **5.** marsh **6.** slough
wrestling . . **5.** arena **9.** palaestra
   (palestra)
placed . . . **3.** put **7.** located **8.** arranged,
   situated **10.** classified
placed in lodgings . . . **6.** roomed
   8. billeted
placid . . . **4.** calm **5.** quiet, suant
   6. demure, gentle, serene **8.** composed,
   peaceful **9.** agreeable, quiescent,
   unruffled **11.** undisturbed
pladaroma . . . **5.** tumor (eyelid)
plafond . . . **7.** ceiling **14.** contract bridge
plage . . . **5.** beach
plagiarism . . . **6.** piracy **8.** cribbing,
   stealing **10.** purloining **13.** appropriation
plague . . . **3.** dun, vex **4.** bane, pest, twit
   5. harry, tease, worry **6.** harass, hector,
   infest **7.** scourge, torment **8.** epidemic,
   nuisance **10.** Black Death, pestilence
   11. infestation
plaguy . . . **6.** vexing **8.** annoying
   9. difficult, harassing **10.** tormenting
   11. troublesome
plaice . . . **8.** flatfish, flounder
plaid . . . **4.** maud **6.** tartan
plain . . . **3.** lea **4.** chol, mesa, moor, wold
   5. blunt, camas, clear, frank, heath
   6. lenten **7.** artless, evident, genuine,
   legible, obvious, prairie **8.** apparent,
   distinct, explicit, ordinary **9.** downright,
   primitive, unadorned **10.** unaffected
plain (pert to) . . .
clothes . . **10.** unofficial
dealing . . **4.** open **5.** frank
knitting . . **12.** garter stitch
of Mars . . **9.** palmistry
spoken . . **15.** straightforward
Plains (pert to) . . .
Arctic . . **6.** tundra
Europe . . **6.** steppe
Florida . . **7.** savanna (savannah)
Italy . . **8.** campagna
Russia . . **6.** steppe, tundra
S African . . **6.** pampas
Sp American . . **4.** vega **5.** llano **6.** salada
   (salt-covered)
Plains Indians . . . **6.** Kiowan, Siouan
   7. Caddoan **10.** Algonquian,
   Athapascan, Uto-Aztecan
plainsman . . . **6.** cowboy **7.** llanero
   8. herdsman
Plains of Abraham . . . **10.** Quebec City

plaint . . . **6.** bewail, lament **9.** complaint
   11. lamentation
plaintiff . . . **4.** suer **6.** orator **7.** accuser
   8. claimant, libelant (libellant)
   10. complainer **11.** complainant
plaintive . . . **3.** sad **5.** cross **7.** elegiac,
   fretful, peevish, pettish, wailful, wistful
   8. mournful, petulant, repining
   9. lamenting, sorrowful **10.** melancholy
   11. complaining **12.** discontented
plait . . . **4.** fold, hair, knit, lace, plat
   5. braid, pleat, weave **6.** pleach, wimple
   9. corrugate, interlace **10.** interweave
plaited . . . **5.** Milan (straw) **6.** folded,
   kilted, sennit (palm leaves) **8.** pleached
   10. interlaced **11.** intertwined
plan . . . **3.** map, way **4.** form, idea, line,
   plat, plot **5.** chart, draft, ettle, frame,
   setup **6.** design, devise, intend, layout,
   method, scheme **7.** arrange, diagram,
   outline, pattern, project **8.** engineer,
   strategy **9.** calculate, procedure
   11. arrangement, contemplate,
   preconceive, premeditate
plan (pert to) . . .
architecture . . **5.** draft, épure
frustrator of . . **7.** marplot
preliminary . . **4.** idea **6.** map out
   8. proposal
secretly . . **4.** plot **7.** connive **8.** conspire
planate . . . **5.** plane **9.** flattened
plancher . . . **3.** bed **5.** board (occult), floor,
   plank **6.** pallet **8.** planking, platform
plancier . . . **6.** soffit **7.** cornice
plandok . . . **9.** mouse deer
plane . . . **3.** fly **4.** even, flat, ramp, scar, tool
   5. level **6.** degree, smooth **7.** jointer,
   surface **8.** airplane **10.** smoothness
plane (pert to) . . .
block . . **5.** stock
boundary . . **9.** perimeter
four-angled . . **6.** square **7.** rhombus
   8. tetragon **10.** quadrangle
handle . . **4.** tote (bench plane)
inclined . . **4.** ramp **5.** chute
iron . . **5.** blade
kind . . **3.** mig **5.** stuka **6.** router
measure . . **10.** planimeter
smoothing, chamfering . . **5.** howel
tree . . **6.** chinar (Orient) **8.** Platanus
type . . **5.** bench, block, stock **6.** trowel
   7. jointer, routing
planet . . . **4.** Mars, star **5.** Earth, Pluto,
   Venus **6.** Saturn, Uranus **7.** Jupiter,
   Mercury, Neptune **8.** wanderer
planet (pert to) . . .
astrology . . **9.** alfridary
brightest . . **5.** Venus
cone . . **8.** strobile
course . . **5.** orbit
minor . . **9.** satellite
nearest sun . . **7.** Mercury
orbit . . **7.** ellipse
red . . **4.** Mars
remotest . . **5.** Pluto (1930)
resembling . . **8.** asteroid
ringed . . **6.** Saturn
satellite . . **4.** moon
shadow . . **5.** umbra
small . . **8.** asteroid
sphere . . **6.** oblate

planet (solar system) **by size** . . . **7.** Jupiter **6.** Saturn **7.** Neptune **6.** Uranus **5.** Earth, Venus, Pluto **4.** Mars **7.** Mercury
planetarium . . . **5.** Zeiss **6.** orrery
planetary . . . **7.** earthly, erratic **9.** celestial, wandering, worldwide
planetology (study of) . . . **7.** planets **10.** satellites
plangor . . . **4.** wail **11.** lamentation
planisphere . . . **7.** sextant **9.** astrolabe
plank . . . **3.** sny **4.** deal, slab **5.** board, shole, stone **6.** timber **7.** pay down **8.** planking **10.** gravestone
plank down . . . **3.** pay **7.** advance, deposit
planner . . . **8.** designer, engineer, gardener **9.** architect, projector
plant . . . **3.** fix, sow, spy **4.** ache, bury, herb, seed, trap **5.** cache, decoy, shrub **6.** clover **7.** falsify **8.** colonize, workshop **9.** deception, detective, equipment, vegetable
plant (pert to) . . .
abnormal environs . . **4.** ecad
adjustment . . **6.** ecesis
air . . **8.** epiphyte
appendage . . **7.** stipula
biggest . . **10.** Aspidistra
body . . **6.** cormus **7.** thallus
bud . . **4.** cion **5.** scion
climbing . . **4.** vine **5.** liana
coloring matter . . **11.** chlorophyll
crossbred . . **6.** hybrid
cross-fertilization . . **9.** phytogamy
disease . . **4.** gall, rust, smut **5.** ergot **7.** blister **8.** ramentum
embryo . . **8.** plantule
enchantment-proof . . **7.** haemony (Milton's Comus)
flowerless . . **4.** fern **6.** lichen **9.** cryptogam **11.** Cryptogamia (opp of phanerogam)
growing on rock . . **6.** lichen
growing on sea bottom . . **6.** enalid
growing wild . . **9.** agrestial
history . . **12.** phytogenesis
legendary, forgetfulness . . **5.** lotus
male . . **3.** mas
mosslike . . **6.** orpine
mushroom type . . **6.** fungus
native . . **8.** indigene
orifice . . **5.** stoma
pigment lacking . . **6.** albino
poisonous . . **4.** atis **6.** datura **7.** amanita **8.** oleander
poisonous to cattle . . **4.** loco **8.** locoweed
pore . . **8.** lenticel
round-leaved . . **9.** pennywort
science of . . **6.** botany
seedless . . **6.** agamic
stem, stalk . . **4.** bine **5.** haulm **6.** caulis
tequila-yielding . . **5.** agave
tissue . . **7.** tapetum
without chlorophyll . . chlorophyll **6.** albino
without petals . . **9.** apetulous
woody . . **6.** xyloid
plant (type of) . . .
aconite . . **4.** bikh
agave, century plant . . **4.** aloe, pita **9.** amaryllis
ammoniac . . **5.** oshac

anise . . **4.** dill
aquatic . . **6.** sugamo **7.** frogbit **8.** plankton
aromatic . . **4.** mint, nard **5.** basil, tansy, thyme **8.** tarragon
arum . . **4.** sago **6.** starch **9.** arrowroot
aster family . . **5.** daisy **8.** fleabane
bitter . . **3.** rue
bitter vetch . . **3.** ers
box . . **5.** Buxus **7.** boxwood
broom . . **5.** spart **6.** Canary **7.** genista
bryophytic . . **4.** moss
burdock . . **5.** elite **8.** Xanthium
burning bush . . **5.** wahoo
butter-and-eggs . . **8.** ranstead
cactus . . **5.** dildo **6.** cereus, chaute, mescal **7.** saguaro **9.** xerophyte
century . . **4.** aloe **5.** agave **6.** maguey
dill . . **4.** anet
evergreen . . **3.** ivy **5.** holly **6.** laurel **8.** conifers **9.** mistletoe
everlasting . . **6.** orpine **11.** live-forever
furze . . **4.** ulex **5.** gorse
garlic (wild) . . **4.** moly
leguminous . . **3.** pea **4.** bean **6.** Cassia, clover, lentil
lilaceous . . **4.** aloe, iris, leek **5.** lotus, onion, tulip, yucca
linen . . **4.** flax
medicinal . . **4.** alem, aloe **5.** anise, wahoo **6.** arnica, cacoon, catnip, ipecac **7.** aconite, boneset, gentian, lobelia, rhatany **8.** camomile
pea family . . **7.** Cytisus
perennial . . **4.** Geum **5.** avens **10.** sneezewort
poisonous . . **6.** datura **8.** oleander
poisonous to cattle . . **8.** locoweed
poisonous to fowl . . **7.** henbane
prickly, thorny . . **5.** brier **6.** cactus, nettle, teasel **7.** thistle
satinpod (transparent) . . **7.** honesty
soap . . **5.** amole
tapioca . . **7.** cassava
thorny . . see *prickly* **6.** fatsia
trifoliate . . **6.** clover **8.** shamrock
plant, typical of . . .
Africa . . **5.** argel (arghel)
Alps . . **9.** edelweiss
Arabia . . **3.** kat (stimulant)
Australia . . **5.** Hakes, lilac **6.** Correa **7.** columba, fuchsia **8.** Rutaceae
China . . **5.** ramie
Egypt . . **5.** anise, cumin **7.** aniseed **8.** nepenthe
Hawaii . . **5.** olona
Japan . . **3.** tea **5.** acuba **6.** quince **7.** cydonia **8.** japonica
Japan (vine) . . **8.** Bignonia **14.** trumpet creeper
Mexico . . **4.** chia **5.** datil **6.** salvia **9.** sabadilla
Peru . . **3.** oca **7.** rhatany
Philippines . . **4.** alem (Med) **6.** agamid
Spain . . **3.** aji **6.** pepper **8.** Capsicum
Syria . . **5.** cumin
tropical vine . . **8.** redwithe **10.** tillandsia
tropics . . **4.** arum, palm, taro **5.** agave, zamia **7.** dasheen, hamelia **8.** mangrove
plantain . . . **6.** banana
plantation pines . . . **7.** pinetum

plantation trees ... **4.** holt **6.** forest
   7. nopalry (cactus), orchard
planters, Govt of ... **11.** plantocracy
plantigrade mammal ... **5.** panda
plaque ... **5.** medal, patch **6.** brooch,
   tablet **8.** ornament, platelet (Anat)
plash ... **4.** plop, pool **5.** swash **6.** puddle,
   ripple, splash
plasm ... **4.** mold **6.** matrix
plasma ... **4.** cell, whey **5.** blood (fluid)
   10. protoplasm
plaster ... **4.** teer **5.** gesso, grout, salve
   6. gypsum, parget, stucco **8.** adhesive,
   poultice **9.** inebriate
plastered ... **5.** drunk **7.** crocked, smeared
   8. mortared
plasterer ... **5.** mason
plaster of Paris ... **5.** gesso **6.** gypsum
   15. calcium sulphate
plastic ... **3.** pug **5.** gesso, vinyl **6.** slurry
   7. ductile, fictile, pliable, viscose
   8. creative **9.** compliant, formative,
   teachable **14.** impressionable
plastic, commercial ... **6.** Lucite
   7. Formica **8.** Bakelite, Vinylite
   9. Plexiglas
plasty (pert to) ...
   comb form .. **7.** molding
   eyelid .. **14.** blepharoplasty
   face lift .. **13.** rhytidoplasty
   nose .. **11.** rhinoplasty
plat ... **3.** map **4.** flat, plan, plot
   5. braid, chart, field, level, plain, plait,
   pleat **6.** flatly, scheme **7.** outline,
   plateau **8.** absolute, directly, straight
   9. tableland **10.** interweave
   15. straightforward
platanist ... **4.** fish, susu
plate ... **3.** gib **4.** disc, dish, shoe (horse)
   5. paten **6.** lamina, patera **7.** coating,
   denture, overlay **9.** bookplate,
   engraving **10.** receptacle
plate (pert to) ...
   armor .. **6.** cuisse (cuish)
   battery .. **4.** grid
   bone (Anat) .. **7.** scapula
   cooking .. **4.** grid
   culture .. **8.** bacteria
   Eccl .. **5.** paten **6.** patina
   graduated .. **4.** dial
   holder .. **8.** cassette
   horny .. **5.** scute
   horse .. **6.** plater
   insect (bony) .. **6.** scutum
   mark .. **8.** hallmark **9.** engraving
   numbered .. **4.** disc
   of glass .. **5.** slide
   perforated metal .. **3.** dod
   ship-shaped .. **3.** nef
plateau ... **4.** dish, mesa, puna **5.** plain
   6. plaque, salver **9.** tableland
platform ... **3.** map **4.** dais, deck, k'ang,
   plan **5.** arena, chart, plank, stage
   6. lissom, lyceum, podium, policy,
   pulpit, scheme **7.** estrade, outline,
   rostrum, soapbox, tribune **8.** hustings
   9. bandstand **14.** public speaking
platform (pert to) ...
   fort .. **8.** barbette
   gun .. **11.** emplacement
   mining .. **6.** sollar (soller)

nautical .. **7.** foretop, maintop
   9. gangplank
scaffold (funeral) .. **10.** catafalque
wheeled .. **5.** float
platic (Astrol) ... **8.** not exact **9.** imperfect
plating ... **5.** armor **6.** lamina **7.** shoeing
platinum wire ... **4.** oese
platitude ... **6.** cliché, old hat, truism
   7. bromide **8.** banality **9.** staleness,
   triteness **11.** commonplace
   15. commonplaceness
Plato (pert to) ...
   famed for .. **9.** Dialogues **10.** philosophy
   founder of .. **7.** Academe, academy
   name, real .. **10.** Aristocles
   pupil of .. **8.** Socrates
platoid ... **4.** flat **5.** broad
Platonic (pert to) ...
   idea .. **5.** eidos
   love .. **4.** pure **5.** ideal **6.** chaste
   8. virtuous **10.** idealistic
   11. comradeship
   philosophy .. **8.** idealism **9.** Platonism
   11. theoretical
   solids .. **10.** hexahedron, octahedron
   11. icosahedron, tetrahedron
   12. dodecahedron
platoon ... **3.** set **4.** unit **5.** squad
   7. company, coterie **11.** subdivision
platoon school ... **4.** Gary (Ind)
platter ... **4.** dish, lanx **5.** grail, plate
   6. record **9.** scutellum
platter-shaped ... **10.** scutellate
platyfish ... **8.** moonfish
platypus ... **8.** duckbill
plaudit ... **5.** cheer, éclat **6.** encore
   8. applause, approval, clapping,
   encomium **10.** plaudation
   11. acclamation, approbation
plausible ... **8.** credible, probable,
   specious **10.** applausive, believable,
   ostensible, plauditory, reasonable
   11. conceivable
plausible excuse ... **5.** alibi
play ... **3.** act, fun, toy **4.** game, jest,
   romp **5.** dally, drama, enact, feign,
   sport, wager **6.** affect, frolic **7.** disport,
   operate, pretend **9.** amusement,
   diversion, melodrama, pantomime
   10. recreation **11.** impersonate
   13. entertainment
play (pert to) ...
   exhibit a .. **5.** stage
   for time .. **5.** stall
   house .. **5.** movie **6.** cinema **7.** theater
   9. dollhouse
   musical .. **5.** opera **8.** burletta, operetta
   outline .. **8.** scenario
   part .. **4.** role **7.** prelude **8.** epilogue,
   epitasis, prologue
   pranks .. **4.** haze
   silent .. **9.** pantomime
   story .. **8.** scenario
   stupid .. **5.** boner
   the bagpipe .. **5.** skirl **6.** doodle
   the buffoon .. **5.** droll
   the coquette .. **5.** flirt
   tricks .. **4.** hoax, shab
   truant .. **5.** miche
   unskillfully .. **5.** strum
   upon words .. **3.** pun **11.** paronomasia

playa . . . **5.** beach, shore **7.** salt pan

playboy . . . **4.** fool **5.** clown, cutup
7. buffoon, reveler **8.** carouser
10. merrymaker **12.** Jack of Trumps
(Spoilfive)

player . . . **3.** dub **4.** star **5.** actor, idler,
piper **7.** gambler, trifler **8.** gamester,
musician, stroller, thespian **9.** frolicker,
performer **11.** barnstormer

player on words . . . **7.** punster

playful . . . **3.** gay **6.** lusory **7.** jocular
8. humorous, playsome, sportive
9. facetious, kittenish **11.** mischievous

playing cards . . . **4.** deck, pack **6.** tarots

playlet . . . **4.** skit **9.** short play

plaything . . . **3.** die, toy **4.** dupe **6.** bauble
7. cat's-paw

plea . . . **4.** suit **5.** claim **6.** abater, appeal,
excuse, prayer **7.** apology, defense,
pretext **8.** argument, entreaty, pretense
10. advocation, allegation **13.** nolo
contendre

plead . . . **3.** beg, sue **5.** argue **6.** adduce,
allege **7.** entreat, implore

plead (for) . . . **7.** entreat, justify, solicit
10. supplicate

pleader . . . **4.** suer **6.** lawyer **8.** advocate
9. entreater, justifier **11.** intercessor

pleading . . . **4.** oyer **8.** advocacy,
demurrer, entreaty **9.** imploring,
objection **10.** litigation **12.** intercession,
supplication

pleasant . . . **3.** fun, gay **4.** nice **5.** merry,
sweet **6.** genial **7.** affable, amusing,
leesome, winsome **8.** cheerful, friendly,
humorous, pleasing, sportive
9. agreeable, diverting, laughable,
sprightly

pleasant (pert to) . . .
manners . . **9.** amenities
sound . . **6.** dulcet **8.** euphonic
9. melodious **10.** harmonious
to peruse . . **8.** readable
weather . . **4.** fair, fine **6.** bright **8.** rainless
9. cloudless

please . . . **4.** like, suit **5.** fancy **6.** arride
7. appease, content, delight, gratify,
indulge, placate, satisfy **9.** vouchsafe

pleased . . . **4.** fain, game, glad **5.** happy
9. contented, gratified

pleasing . . . **4.** cool, lief, nice **5.** sooth
6. comely, eesome, savory **7.** amiable,
roseate, welcome **8.** pleasant
9. agreeable, desirable **10.** delectable
11. pleasureful

pleasurable . . . **7.** hedonic **8.** pleasant
10. gratifying

pleasure . . . **3.** joy **4.** gree, will, wish
5. mirth, sport **6.** choice, gaiety
7. delight, purpose **8.** gladness,
hedonism, hilarity **9.** amusement,
diversion, enjoyment, happiness,
merriment **11.** delectation
12. satisfaction **13.** gratification

pleasure (pert to) . . .
god . . **3.** Bes
ground . . **4.** park **9.** pleasance
pert to . . **7.** hedonic
philosophy . . **8.** Hedonism
seeker . . **5.** sport **7.** epicure, playboy
8. hedonist

pleat . . . **4.** fold **5.** braid, plait

pleater . . . **8.** plicator

plebeian . . . **4.** pleb (Rom) **6.** common,
vulgar **7.** ignoble, ill-bred, lowborn
8. ordinary

plebiscite . . . **4.** vote **6.** decree
10. referendum

pleck . . . **4.** plot (ground), spot **5.** speck,
stain **9.** enclosure

plectrum . . . **4.** pick **5.** uvula **6.** tongue
7. malleus **8.** plectron

pledge . . . **3.** bet, vas, vow **4.** bond,
gage, gate, oath, pawn, seal, wage
5. swear, toast, troth **6.** engage, parole,
plight **7.** chattel, earnest, promise
8. guaranty, mortgage, obligate,
security **9.** assurance **10.** collateral
11. impignorate

pledget . . . **4.** swab **8.** compress

Pleiad (pert to) . . .
Alexandria . . **10.** Seven Poets
French . . **10.** The Pléiade
lost Pleiad . . **6.** Merope **7.** Electra
philosophical (Gr) . . **12.** Seven Wise
Men

Pleiades (pert to) . . .
Seven Daughters of Atlas . . **10.** Atlantides
star . . **4.** Maia **7.** Sterope **8.** Asterope
star cluster . . **8.** in Taurus (Constellation)

plenary . . . **4.** full **5.** great **6.** entire
7. perfect **8.** absolute, complete
9. unlimited **11.** unqualified

plenipotentiary . . . **5.** envoy **8.** diplomat,
minister **10.** ambassador

plenteous . . . **6.** plenty **7.** copious, fertile,
liberal **8.** abundant, fruitful, generous
9. bounteous, bountiful, plentiful
10. productive

plentiful . . . **4.** full, rich, rife **5.** ample
6. lavish **7.** copious, fertile, liberal,
opulent, profuse **9.** abounding,
bounteous, bountiful **13.** superabundant

plentifully . . . **6.** galore **9.** abounding,
abundance

plenty . . . **4.** enow **6.** enough, galore,
uberty **8.** fullness **9.** abundance,
plenitude **10.** perfection **11.** copiousness
12. completeness, considerable
14. superabundance

plenum . . . **5.** space **8.** assembly, fullness
(of space) (opp of vacuum)

pleon . . . **6.** telson **7.** abdomen

pleonasm . . . **8.** fullness **10.** redundancy
11. diffuseness, reiteration

plethora . . . **4.** glut **6.** excess **9.** repletion
14. superabundance

plethoric . . . **6.** turgid **8.** inflated, overfull
9. bombastic **10.** overloaded

plexiform . . . **4.** rete **7.** network
11. complicated

plexus . . . **4.** rete **5.** solar **7.** network

pliable . . . **4.** limp **6.** limber, pliant,
supple **7.** plastic **8.** flexible, suitable
9. compliant, teachable

pliant . . . **7.** bending, pliable, tensile,
willowy **8.** flexible, workable, yielding
9. adaptable, compliant

plicate . . . **4.** fold **5.** pleat **6.** folded
7. plaited

plight . . . **4.** fold **5.** braid, plait **6.** status
7. embrace, promise **8.** position

9. condition, situation (bad)
11. predicament
plinth ... **4.** orlo **7.** subbase
Pliosaurus (extinct) ... **7.** reptile
plod ... **3.** dig, mog **4.** slog, toil, tore
6. drudge, trudge
plodder ... **3.** fag **4.** grub, hack **5.** slave
6. drudge
plot ... **3.** lot, map **4.** acre, area, brew,
burn, pack, plan, plat **5.** cabal, frame,
tract, trick **6.** design, scheme, scorch,
secret **7.** diagram, project **8.** conspire,
intrigue **10.** conspiracy, prearrange
11. machination
plot (of ground) ... **3.** lot **4.** acre, area,
plat **5.** grave, tract **7.** terrain
Plotinus ... **11.** philosopher (Alexandrian
School)
plotted ... **7.** charted, hatched **8.** lineated
9. conspired **10.** delineated
11. prearranged
plotter ... **5.** Haman **7.** Jacobin, planner,
schemer **8.** agitator **9.** contriver
11. conspirator
ploughshare (plowshare) **part** ... **6.** colter
(coulter)
plover ... **4.** dupe **5.** piper, sandy
7. lapwing **9.** courtesan, sandpiper,
shorebird
plover (pert to) ...
crab .. **5.** drome
crested .. **7.** lapwing
egg .. **11.** darning ball
genus .. **12.** Charadriidae
Old World .. **8.** dotterel, killdeer
page .. **6.** dunlin **9.** sandpiper
quail .. **13.** plain wanderer
ring .. **5.** pandy
plow ... **4.** rove, till **5.** break, miner,
scaut **6.** furrow, turn up **7.** break up
8. reinvest **9.** cultivate
plow (pert to) ...
fish .. **3.** ray
gang .. **6.** oxgang **7.** measure
light .. **10.** Plow Monday **13.** hoggler's
light
man .. **6.** rustic **10.** countryman,
husbandman
part .. **4.** buck, chip, hale **5.** share, slade,
stilt **6.** clevis, colter
type .. **5.** sulky **8.** mole plow
plowed land ... **5.** arada, arado
pluck ... **3.** pug, rob, tug **4.** grab, jerk,
pick, pull **5.** nerve, spunk, steal, strip,
strum **6.** avulse, divest, fleece, gather,
twitch **7.** courage, harvest, pick off,
plunder, strip of, swindle **10.** resolution,
straighten (wool)
plucky ... **4.** game **5.** brave, nervy
6. spunky, sticky **8.** adhesive, resolute,
spirited **10.** courageous
plug ... **3.** peg, tap, top **4.** blow, bung
5. horse, knock, punch, shoot, spile,
wedge **7.** commend, hydrant, stopper,
stopple, tobacco **9.** persevere, publicity,
publicize **12.** commendation
plug (pert to) ...
board .. **11.** switchboard
cannon muzzle .. **7.** tampion (tampeon,
tampoon)
dentistry .. **7.** filling

hat .. **4.** tile **5.** gibus **6.** topper
medical .. **4.** clot **6.** fibrin, tampon
7. embolus
slender .. **5.** spill
up .. **4.** calk (caulk)
plum ... **5.** drupe, money, prune **6.** Prunus
8. dividend **9.** good thing, sugarplum
plum (pert to) ...
beetle .. **8.** curculio
bitter .. **4.** sloe
California (wild) .. **5.** islay
coco .. **5.** icaco
England .. **6.** damson
Europe .. **7.** bullace
hybrid .. **7.** plumcot
India .. **7.** hog plum
Java .. **7.** jambool (jambul) **8.** jambolan
type .. **4.** gage **6.** damson **9.** greengage,
wild-goose **11.** Reine Claude
plumage ... **4.** down **6.** hackle **7.** floccus
(first down) **8.** feathers, ornament
plumb ... **4.** seal, true **5.** delve, gauge,
sound, utter **6.** adjust, fathom, sinker,
weight (lead) **7.** examine, measure,
plummet **8.** absolute, complete, vertical
9. downright **13.** perpendicular
plumbage ... **8.** leadwork
plumbog ... **9.** raspberry (dwarf)
plumcot ... **6.** hybrid **11.** plum apricot
plume ... **5.** crest, egret, preen, pride
6. plumet **7.** feather, panache
8. decorate, plumelet
plummet ... **4.** dive, drop, fall, lead, plop,
test **5.** pitch, sound, swoop **6.** fathom,
plunge, weight **9.** criterion
plump ... **3.** fat **4.** drop, dull, fall, plop,
rude, sink, tidy **5.** blunt, buxom, flock,
fubsy, obese **6.** chubby, dilate, fatten,
flatly **7.** distend **8.** blurt out, straight
9. corpulent, filled out **10.** vertically
11. well-rounded
plumpness of person ... **9.** stoutness
10. embonpoint
plunder ... **3.** rob **4.** boot, loot, pelf,
prey, raid, rape, sack **5.** booty, poach,
raven, reave, rifle, strip **6.** boodle,
fleece, maraud, profit, rapine, ravage,
spoils **7.** despoil, pillage **8.** spoliate
9. depredate
plundered ... **4.** reft **6.** looted, robbed
plunderer ... **5.** thief **6.** looter, pirate,
preyer, raider, robber **7.** spoiler, stealer
8. pillager **10.** freebooter
plunge ... **3.** bet, dip **4.** dash, dive,
fall, pool, risk, sink **5.** douse, drive,
lunge, plumb, souse **6.** gamble,
thrust **7.** baptize, immerse **8.** flounder
9. gravitate, overwhelm, speculate
plunge (into) ... **4.** clap, dive **5.** begin
7. immerge, immerse **9.** set to work,
undertake
plunger ... **5.** diver **6.** risker **7.** gambler
10. speculator
plunk ... **4.** blow, drop, pull, push, sink,
thud **5.** drive, plump, strum, throw
7. a dollar **10.** play truant
plurality ... **8.** majority **9.** multitude
11. greater part, large number
plural marriage ... **8.** polygamy
Plutarch (Gr) ... **10.** biographer
Pluto (pert to) ...

Astron.. **6**. planet (most remote)
god of.. **10**. lower world
Greek name.. **5**. Hades
kingdom.. **5**. Hades
Roman name.. **3**. Dis **5**. Orcus
wife.. **10**. Proserpina
plutocracy... **13**. rule by wealthy
 17. dominion of the rich
Plutus (pert to)...
 god of.. **6**. wealth
 son of.. **6**. lasion **7**. Demeter
pluvia... **4**. rain **9**. pluviosus
pluviometer, pluvioscope... **9**. rain
 gauge
pluvious... **5**. rainy **7**. pluvial
ply... **4**. bend, fold, mold, sail, urge
 5. exert, plait, wield **6**. employ, handle,
 lamina **8**. navigate **9**. importune,
 thickness
pneuma... **4**. soul **5**. neume **6**. breath,
 spirit **9**. breathing, life force, vital soul
pneumology (science of)... **5**. lungs
 17. respiratory organs
poach... **3**. mix, ram **4**. poke, push,
 sock, stir **5**. drive, force, shirr (egg),
 steal **6**. thrust **7**. trample **8**. encroach,
 trespass
poacher... **7**. lurcher, stalker, widgeon
Poblacht... **8**. Republic
Pocahontas (pert to)...
 father.. **8**. Powhatan (Chief)
 husband.. **9**. John Rolfe
 Indian title.. **8**. Princess
 name.. **12**. Rebecca Rolfe
 rescuer of.. **9**. John Smith (Capt)
pocket... **3**. bag, bin, cly, fob, sac
 4. poke, sack, take **5**. money, pouch,
 purse **6**. cavity, hollow **7**. conceal,
 confine, enclose **8**. envelope
pocketbook... **3**. bag, lil **5**. pouch,
 purse **6**. income, wallet **8**. notebook
 9. resources
pod... **3**. bag, kid, sac **4**. aril, boll **5**. belly,
 carob, chili, pouch, shuck **6**. legume
poem... **3**. dit, lay, ode **4**. Edda, epic,
 epos, hymn, rune, saga **5**. elegy,
 epode, idyll, psalm, verse **6**. ballad
 (ballade), jingle, rondel (roundelle),
 sonnet **7**. eclogue, erotics, rondeau
 8. limerick, rondelet **9**. dithyramb
 10. villanelle **11**. acatalectic
poem (pert to)...
 bad... **8**. doggerel
 division.. **5**. canto, epode, verse
 6. stanza **7**. refrain
 eight lines.. **7**. triolet
 foot.. **6**. iambic **7**. anapest, pyrrhic
 imitation.. **6**. parody
 Japanese.. **5**. haiku
 line.. **5**. stich **6**. octave, septet, sestet,
 tercet **7**. couplet, triplet **8**. cinquain,
 quatrain **11**. alexandrine
 meter.. **6**. iambic **8**. spondaic, trochaic
 9. dactyllic, hexameter **10**. anaepestic
 (anapestic), pentameter
 ref to.. **5**. meter, rhyme, verse
 7. cadence, helicon **8**. feminine,
 scansion **9**. masculine
 religious.. **4**. hymn **5**. psalm
 rhythmic break.. **7**. caesura
 satirical.. **3**. dit **6**. parody

poem, famed...
 Homer.. **5**. Iliad **7**. Odyssey
 Khayyám.. **8**. Rubáiyát
 Milton.. **12**. Paradise Lost
 Ovid.. **13**. Metamorphoses
 Poe.. **8**. The Raven
 Poem in Marble.. **8**. Taj Mahal
 poem of declaration.. **8**. Invictus
 Shakespeare.. **7**. Macbeth
 Spenser.. **12**. Faerie Queene
poems... **5**. poesy, sylva **6**. poetry
poet... **4**. bard **5**. odist, rimer **6**. lyrist
 7. dreamer **8**. laureate **9**. poetaster,
 rhymester, versifier
poetic word... **3**. ere, 'tis **4**. ne'er, 'twas
 5. 'twere, 'twixt
Poet Laureate (a few)... **6**. Dryden
 7. Spenser **8**. Tennyson **9**. Ben Jonson,
 Masefield **10**. Wordsworth
poetry (pert to)...
 Muse of.. **5**. Erato **6**. Thalia **8**. Calliope
 Norse god of.. **5**. Bragi
 School of (anc).. **9**. Parnassus
 type.. **4**. epic **5**. lyric **6**. ballad **8**. didactic
 9. free verse, narrative **10**. blank verse
pogoniate... **7**. bearded
pogonip... **3**. fog (Sierras)
pogonology (study of)... **6**. beards
pogrom... **8**. massacre
poi... **4**. food, taro, then (Mus)
poignant... **4**. keen **5**. acute **6**. biting,
 bitter **7**. cutting, pungent
point... **3**. aim, dot, jab, jot, neb, nib, pin
 4. apex, barb, cape, gaff, gist, node,
 peak, stop, tack **5**. focus, prong, quill,
 spike **6**. bodkin, direct, needle, period,
 summit, zenith **7**. apicula, punctum
 10. breakwater, promontory
point (pert to)...
 antler, branch.. **4**. snag
 astronomy.. **5**. apsis **6**. syzygy
 central, pivotal.. **4**. crux
 farthest from earth.. **6**. apogee
 focal.. **9**. epicenter
 geometry.. **6**. acnode **7**. crunode
 highest.. **4**. acme, apex, peak **6**. summit,
 zenith **8**. meridian, pinnacle
 lace.. **10**. petit point **11**. needlepoint
 law.. **3**. res **5**. locus
 lowest.. **5**. nadir **6**. bottom
 mathematics.. **5**. unode
 nearest earth.. **7**. perigee
 of contact.. **5**. focus
 of debate.. **5**. issue, topic
 of honor.. **7**. scruple
 of view.. **5**. angle, slant **8**. attitude
 opposite zenith.. **5**. nadir
 reference to.. **6**. apical
 salient.. **7**. feature
 starting, golf.. **3**. tee
 strong.. **5**. forte
 utmost.. **7**. extreme
 weak.. **4**. flaw **5**. fault **6**. foible
pointed... **5**. aimed, noded, piked,
 sharp, terse **6**. acuate, marked, peaked
 7. angular, concise, conical **8**. aculeate,
 piercing, poignant, spicated, stinging
 9. acuminate, pertinate, spiculate
 10. emphasized **11**. conspicuous,
 significant **12**. epigrammatic
pointed (pert to)...

architecture . . **5.** ogive **6.** Gothic
end . . **4.** cusp
fox . . **3.** red
instrument . . **3.** awl, gad **4.** prod
  6. gimlet, stylet
rod . . **4.** goad
pointer . . . **3.** arm, dog, tip **4.** sign **5.** index
  6. fescue, gnomon
pointless . . . **4.** dull **5.** blunt, inane, silly,
  vapid **6.** stupid **7.** insipid, witless
poise . . . **6.** aplomb **7.** balance, ballast
  8. carriage **9.** composure, equipoise,
  stability
poison (pert to) . . .
  arrow . . **4.** inee, upas **5.** urari **6.** curare
  (curari)
  deadly . . **4.** bane, upas **5.** arrow
  7. arsenic, cyanide, hemlock
  10. strychnine
  study of . . **10.** toxicology
poissarde . . . **8.** fishwife, low woman
poisson . . . **4.** fish
poisson bleu . . . **7.** catfish **8.** bluefish,
  grayling
poitrel . . . **5.** armor, plate **9.** stomacher
  11. breastplate
poke . . . **3.** bag, jab, jog, pry **4.** bore,
  goad, prod, root, sack **5.** grope, nudge,
  probe, purse **6.** dawdle, potter, search,
  thrust, wallet **7.** project, tobacco
poker . . . **3.** rod **6.** beadle **7.** bugbear,
  pochard **9.** hobgoblin
poker (pert to) . . .
  face . . **8.** immobile
  form of . . **4.** draw, stud
  painting . . **10.** pyrography
  picture . . **11.** pyrogravure
  stake . . **3.** pot **4.** ante **6.** roodle
poky, pokey . . . **4.** dull, mean, slow
  5. dowdy, small **6.** bonnet, narrow,
  shabby **7.** cramped, tedious
Poland . . . see also *Poland*
  ancestors . . **5.** Lakha, Slavs
  ancient name . . **7.** Polonia
  capital . . **6.** Warsaw
  city . . **4.** Lodz **6.** Gdynia, Krakow, Lublin
  river . . **7.** Dnieper, Vistula
Poland China . . . **5.** swine
polar . . . **5.** curve **6.** Arctic **7.** guiding
  8. opposite **9.** Antarctic, magnetism
Polar base (exploration) . . . **4.** Etah
Polaris . . . **5.** Alpha **9.** North Star
  11. guiding star
Polaroid inventor . . . **4.** Land
pole . . . **3.** bar, oar, pew, poy, rod, xat
  4. axle, beam, mast, prop, spar **5.** shaft,
  sprit, staff, stool, totem
pole (pert to) . . .
  bad end . . **7.** raw deal
  burn . . **7.** disease (tobacco)
  cat . . **5.** skunk, zoril **6.** ferret, musang
  7. fitchew **8.** Putorius **9.** scoundrel
  cat weed . . **12.** skunk cabbage
  electric . . **5.** anode, pitch **7.** cathode
  8. magnetic **9.** electrode
  Gaelic . . **5.** caber
  head . . **7.** tadpole
  Spanish . . **4.** pale, palo
  star . . **5.** guide **7.** polaris **8.** lodestar
  9. North Star **13.** l'Etoile du Nord
  vehicle . . **4.** cope, crab **5.** thill

well . . **5.** sweep
polemic . . . **9.** disputant **11.** contentious
  13. argumentative, controversial
polenta . . . **8.** porridge
poles of cold . . . **7.** Siberia (Verkhoyansk)
  12. Grinnell Land (Fort Conger)
police (pert to) . . .
  badge . . **6.** buzzer, shield
  club . . **8.** spontoon
  man . . **3.** cop **5.** guard **6.** bobbie, copper,
  peeler, Ranger **7.** officer, sheriff, trooper
  9. constable, detective, N W Mounted
  11. carabinière (carabineer)
  station . . **5.** thana **6.** lockup **8.** bargello
policy . . . **3.** wit **4.** plan **6.** wisdom
  8. regulate, sagacity **9.** insurance
  10. government, management,
  shrewdness **11.** contrivance
  13. judiciousness **14.** administration
policy of segregation . . . **9.** apartheid
polish . . . **3.** rub **4.** buff **5.** glaze, gloss,
  rabat, scour, shine **6.** finish, luster,
  smooth **7.** burnish, culture, furbish
  8. brighten, civilize, elegance, lapidate,
  levigate, urbanity **10.** refinement
Polish (pert to) . . .
  Bull . . **13.** Constellation
  cake . . **4.** baba
  carriage . . **7.** britska
  composer, pianist . . **6.** Chopin
  10. Paderewski
  dance . . **7.** mazurka **9.** polonaise
  11. cracovienne (krakowiak)
  nobleman . . **7.** starost
  premier . . **10.** Paderewski (pianist)
  president (1st) . . **10.** Philsudski
  scientist . . **5.** Curie (Madame)
polishing material . . . **5.** emery, rabat,
  rouge **6.** pumice **11.** rottenstone
polite . . . **4.** neat, tidy **5.** civil, suave,
  urban **6.** gentle, smooth, urbane
  7. gallant, genteel, refined **8.** polished
  9. courteous, debonaire (debonair,
  debonnaire) **10.** cultivated
  11. complaisant
politesse . . . **10.** politeness (formal)
  11. cleanliness, courtliness
  12. decorousness
politic . . . **4.** wary **7.** cunning, tactful
  8. cautious, discreet **9.** judicious,
  political, politique, provident
  10. diplomatic
political (pert to) . . .
  boss . . **7.** cacique
  district . . **4.** city, ward **5.** State **6.** canton,
  county, parish **7.** borough **10.** palatinate
  economy . . **9.** economics
  faction . . **4.** bloc, ring **5.** junta, party
  7. machine
  hanger-on . . **6.** heeler **10.** ward heeler
  influence . . **5.** lobby, rally **6.** caucus
  party (old) . . **4.** Tory, Whig **9.** Politique
politician . . . **7.** schemer **9.** intriguer,
  statesman **11.** gerrymander
  12. politicaster
politics . . . **7.** cunning **8.** scheming
  10. government, profession **15.** partisan
  rivalry **16.** political affairs
Polizei . . . **9.** the police
poll . . . **3.** cut, tax **4.** clip, head, roll,
  vote **5.** shear, skull **6.** fleece, survey

7. despoil 8. election, schedule
pollan . . . **9.** whitefish
polled . . . **5.** shorn **6.** shaved **8.** hornless
pollen . . . **4.** seed **6.** anther **8.** fine dust
  11. microspores **13.** fertilization
pollen brush (bee's) . . . **5.** scopa
pollenization . . . **5.** xenia **13.** fertilization
pollent . . . **6.** strong **8.** powerful
poller . . . **5.** voter **6.** barber **9.** plunderer
  11. extortioner, taxgatherer
pollex . . . **5.** thumb **11.** bastard wing
  (bird) **13.** dactylopodite
pollex impression . . . **10.** thumbprint
polliwog . . . **7.** tadpole
pollute . . . **4.** soil **5.** taint **6.** befoul, defile,
  ravish **7.** corrupt, debauch, profane
  9. desecrate, inebriate **11.** contaminate
pollution . . . **8.** impurity **9.** infection
  10. corruption, defilement
  13. contamination
Pollux (pert to) . . .
  brother (twin) . . **6.** Castor
  father . . **4.** Zeus
  mother . . **4.** Leda
  protector of . . **7.** sailors
  star . . **13.** Beta Geminorum
Polly's request . . . **7.** cracker
Polonius . . . **8.** courtier (Shaksp)
polony . . . **7.** sausage
poltergeist (folklore) . . . **5.** ghost **6.** spirit
poltfoot . . . **8.** clubfoot
poltroon . . . **4.** idle, lazy **6.** coward,
  craven, wretch **7.** buffoon, dastard
  8. cowardly **9.** dastardly **10.** ne'er-do-
  well, scaramouch
polverine . . . **6.** potash (of Levant)
  8. pearlash
polyandrium (Gr) . . . **8.** cemetery
polyandry . . . **8.** polygamy **14.** plural
  husbands (Tibet)
polychromatic . . . **10.** variegated
polyglot . . . **6.** jargon **9.** languages
  (confusion of) **10.** dictionary
  11. philologist **21.** Complutensian
  Polyglot (Bib)
polygon . . . **6.** isagon **7.** decagon,
  hexagon, nonagon, octagon
  8. heptagon **9.** dodecagon
polygyny . . . **8.** polygamy **11.** plural wives
polyhedron . . . **5.** solid **6.** figure
  14. trisoctahedron **17.** triakisoctahedron
polymny . . . **10.** sacred song
Polynesia . . .
  native . . **5.** Maori **6.** Kanaka **8.** Hawaiian
  10. Melanesian
  ocean . . **7.** Pacific
  origin (probable) . . **7.** Savaiki (Isl)
  South Sea Island group . . **5.** Samoa
  6. Hawaii, Tahiti **7.** Savaiki **10.** New
  Zealand
Polynesian (pert to) . . .
  butterfly . . **2.** io
  chestnut . . **4.** rata
  cloth . . **4.** tapa
  demon . . **4.** atua
  dragon . . **3.** ati
  goddess of volcanoes . . **4.** Pele
  god of forests . . **4.** Tane
  hero . . **4.** Maui
  homeland (fabled) . . **7.** Havaiki
  loincloth . . **5.** pareu

memorial . . **3.** ahu
oven . . **3.** umu
people . . **3.** Ati
social tradition . . **6.** tattoo
wages, reward . . **3.** utu
polyp . . . **5.** coral, Hydra, tumor **10.** sea
  anemone **12.** invertebrate
polyphone . . . **4.** lute
polytropic . . . **9.** versatile
pomade . . . **6.** anoint **7.** pomatum,
  unguent **8.** ointment
pome . . . **4.** pear **5.** apple, fruit **6.** quince
  11. pomegranate
pomelo . . . **8.** shaddock **10.** grapefruit
Pomerania (pert to) . . .
  animal . . **3.** dog
  capital . . **7.** Stettin
  formerly . . **5.** duchy (Prussia)
  river . . **4.** Oder
pomme de terre . . . **6.** potato
Pomona . . . **4.** city (Calif) **7.** college,
  goddess (of fruit)
pomp . . . **5.** pride, state **6.** parade
  7. cortege, display, pageant **8.** grandeur
  9. pageantry, spectacle **10.** ceremonial
  11. ostentation **12.** magnificence
pompano . . . **7.** alewife
Pompeii, Italy (pert to) . . . **10.** earthquake,
  excavation, Mt Vesuvius (site)
pompous . . . **5.** budge **6.** august,
  stilty **7.** Podsnap (Dickens), stilted
  9. bombastic, grandiose
  11. ceremonious **12.** high-sounding,
  ostentatious, stuffed shirt
Ponce de Leon (pert to) . . .
  discoverer of . . **7.** Florida **15.** Fountain
  of Youth
  famed as . . **8.** explorer
  landing site, America . . **11.** St Augustine
pond . . . **4.** pool **5.** ocean (humorous)
  6. lagoon **7.** lakelet
pond (pert to) . . .
  apple . . **9.** evergreen
  crow, hen . . **4.** coot
  dogwood . . **10.** buttonbush
  duck . . **7.** mallard
  fish . . **7.** sunfish
  frog . . **8.** ranarium
  glass . . **8.** aquarium
ponder . . . **4.** mull, muse, pore **5.** brood,
  opine, weigh **7.** perpend, reflect
  8. appraise, cogitate, consider, evaluate,
  meditate, ruminate
ponderous . . . **4.** dull, huge **5.** bulky,
  heavy **7.** weighty **8.** ungainly
  9. important, momentous
  11. elephantine
pongee . . . **4.** silk **6.** tussah **8.** shantung
poniard . . . **4.** dirk, kill **5.** sword **6.** dagger,
  pierce
ponica . . . **8.** gardener
pont . . . **5.** ferry, float **6.** bridge **7.** caisson,
  pontoon **9.** ferryboat
Pontiac . . . **4.** city (Mich) **5.** Chief (Ottawa
  Indian) **6.** Indian
pontiff . . . **4.** pope **6.** bishop **8.** pontifex
pony . . . **3.** cab, nag **4.** crib **5.** glass, horse,
  pinto **6.** bronco **7.** Express (mail, 1860),
  piebald **8.** Shetland **11.** translation
pooch . . . **3.** dog **5.** pouch
pooka . . . **6.** goblin **7.** specter

pool ... **3.** lin, pot **4.** carr, fund, game, linn, mere, pond, tank, tarn **5.** kitty, stake **6.** cartel, lagoon, league, puddle **7.** alberca, plashet **9.** billiards, reservoir, resources **10.** natatorium **11.** aggregation

pool ball ... **3.** cue **4.** spot **6.** ringer

poon tree ... **5.** domba, keena

poor ... **3.** bad **4.** mean, thin **5.** needy **6.** feeble, humble, meager, paltry, shabby, sickly **7.** hapless, unlucky **8.** indigent, inferior **9.** destitute, illogical, imperfect, infertile **10.** unskillful (unskilful) **11.** impecunious, unfavorable, unfortunate **12.** impoverished, inauspicious, insufficient **14.** unsatisfactory

poor (pert to) ...
creature .. **9.** pilgarlic
joe .. **5.** heron
John .. **3.** cod **4.** hake **8.** mean fare
man's remedy .. **8.** valerian
Richard .. **8.** Saunders (Richard)
section of city .. **4.** slum **6.** ghetto **7.** skid row **10.** shantytown
soldier .. **9.** friarbird

poorly ... **3.** ill **5.** badly **8.** abjectly, meagerly, shabbily **10.** indisposed **11.** defectively **13.** disparagingly

pop ... **4.** bang, snap, soda **5.** bulge, burst, crack **6.** bubble **7.** concert **8.** beverage

popadam ... **5.** water (fried) **10.** popper cake

popdock ... **8.** foxglove

pope ... **3.** fin **4.** ruff **6.** bishop, puffin, shrike, weevil **8.** beverage **9.** bullfinch **14.** painted bunting

Pope (pert to) ...
cathedral .. **7.** Lateran
collar .. **5.** orale
court officer .. **6.** datary
crown .. **5.** tiara **6.** triple
first .. **5.** Peter
headdress .. **5.** miter (mitre)
name .. **4.** Pius **5.** Ratti **7.** Gregory
palace .. **7.** Vatican
scarf .. **5.** fanon

Pope, Alexander (pert to) ...
essay .. **10.** Essay on Man
poem .. **13.** Rape of the Lock
satire .. **7.** Dunciad
translation .. **5.** Iliad **7.** Odyssey

popeler ... **7.** sea gull **9.** spoonbill

popinac ... **8.** huisache

popinjay ... **6.** parrot

poplar ... **5.** abele, alamo, aspen, bahan, white **10.** cottonwood **12.** balm of Gilead

poplar (pert to) ...
Arabic .. **5.** bahan, garab
balsam .. **9.** tacamahac
Fr black .. **4.** liar **10.** cottonwood
N. American .. **7.** Populus **8.** Lombardy
white .. **5.** abele, bolle

poppy ... **3.** maw **7.** Papaver (opium), ponceau **8.** foxglove

poppycock ... **3.** rot **4.** bosh **8.** nonsense

populace ... **3.** mob **4.** mass **5.** demos, plebs **6.** people **11.** inhabitants **12.** common people

popular ... **3.** lay, pop **5.** cheap, liked, usual **6.** famous, simple, vulgar **7.** crowded, demotic, secular **8.** accepted, epidemic, favorite, populous **9.** prevalent, well-known, well-liked **11.** fashionable, proletarian **12.** nontechnical

popular belief ... **4.** lore **7.** opinion **9.** tradition **12.** old wives' tale, superstition

popularity ... **4.** fame **5.** vogue **10.** reputation **15.** fashionableness

popular success ... **3.** hit

population study ... **10.** larithmics

porcelain ... **4.** frit **5.** china **6.** kaolin **7.** ramekin (mold)

porcelain (kind) ... **5.** Spode **6.** Sèvres **7.** celadon, Dresden, Limoges **8.** Haviland

porch ... **4.** door, stoa **5.** stoop **6.** harbor, loggia **7.** galilee, gallery, portico, veranda **8.** entrance **9.** colonnade

porcine animal ... **3.** hog, pig, sow **5.** shoat, swine **6.** porker **7.** peccary **8.** babirusa (babiroussa) **9.** razorback

porcupine (pert to) ...
anteater .. **7.** echidna
Canada .. **5.** urson **7.** cawquaw
disease .. **10.** ichthyosis
grass .. **5.** stipa
species .. **6.** rodent, tenrec (tendrac) **8.** hedgehog, quill pig

pore ... **3.** con **4.** duct, gaze, vent **5.** stare, stoma, study **6.** ponder **7.** eporose (without), opening, orifice, ostiole **8.** lenticel

porgy ... **4.** fish, scup **5.** bream, pargo **6.** pagrus, red tai

pork (pert to) ...
barrel .. **4.** fund (Polit) **6.** boodle
chop .. **7.** griskin
fish .. **4.** sisi

porker ... **3.** hog, pig **5.** swine, sword (obs)

porpoise ... **4.** Inia **6.** seahog **7.** dolphin, pellock **8.** cetacean, Phocaena

porr ... **4.** cram, kick, poke, push, stir **5.** poker **6.** thrust

porrect ... **6.** tender **7.** present

porridge ... **3.** pob **4.** pobs, samp **5.** atole, brose, grout, gruel **6.** cereal **7.** oatmeal, polenta, pottage **9.** stirabout

port ... **4.** gate, left, mien, wine **5.** armor, haven **6.** harbor, portal **7.** airport, bearing, opening, posture **8.** carriage, demeanor, larboard, porthole, portside **10.** deportment **11.** destruction

portable ... **6.** mobile **7.** movable

portable altar ... **10.** altar stone, superaltar (Hist)

portal ... **4.** door, gate **5.** porch **7.** gateway **8.** entrance **9.** vestibule **12.** porte-cochere

portcullis ... **3.** bar **4.** shut **5.** herse **7.** barrier, grating, lattice (Her) **13.** fortification

Porte ... **12.** Ottoman court (anc), Sublime Porte

porte-bonheur ... **5.** charm **6.** amulet

porte-cochere ... **5.** porch (carriage) **7.** gateway

portefeuille ... **9.** portfolio

portend . . . 4. bode 5. augur 7. betoken, predict, presage 8. forebode, foreshow, foretell, prophecy 9. foretoken
portent . . . 4. omen, sign 6. marvel, ostent 7. prodigy 11. forewarning
portentous . . . 4. dire 5. fatal, grave 6. solemn 7. fateful, ominous 8. sinister 9. monstrous, wonderful 10. impressive 13. extraordinary
porter . . . 3. ale 4. beer 5. hamal (hammal), stout (drink) 6. bearer 7. carrier, janitor 9. attendant 10. doorkeeper
Porter's pseudonym . . . 6. O Henry
Portia (pert to) . . .
character (Merchant of Venice) . . 7. heiress
husband . . 8. Bassanio
husband's friend . . 7. Antonio
maid . . 7. Nerissa
portico . . . 4. stoa 6. atrium, xystus (xyst) 7. pteroma, veranda 9. colonnade, peristyle, vestibule
portion . . . 3. bit, cut, dab, lot 4. dole, dose, dunt, fate, half, mete, part, some 5. piece, share, whack 6. moiety, parcel 7. section, segment 8. quantity 9. allotment, apportion, partition
portion (pert to) . . .
curve . . 3. arc 7. segment
detached . . 6. coupon
inheritance . . 7. legitim 9. dead's part
marriage . . 5. dowry
sectional . . 5. curve
widow's . . 5. dower
Portland (pert to) . . .
arrowroot, sago . . 4. arum
beds (Eng) . . 11. Upper Oolite 13. Upper Jurassic
city of . . 5. Maine 6. Oregon
stone . . 6. cement 8. concrete
vase . . 9. Barberini (Rom palace) 10. cameo glass
portmanteau . . . 3. bag 4. word (blended) 5. cloak 6. mantle, valise
portoise . . . 7. gunwale 8. portlast
Porto Rico . . . see *Puerto Rico*
portrait . . . 4. copy 5. image 7. picture 8. likeness, painting 10. similitude 11. description, portraiture 12. lifelikeness 14. representation
portrait on dollars . . .
fifty . . 5. Grant
five . . 7. Lincoln
five hundred . . 8. McKinley
five thousand . . 7. Madison
one . . 10. Washington
one hundred . . 8. Franklin
one hundred thousand . . 6. Wilson
one thousand . . 9. Cleveland
ten . . 8. Hamilton
ten thousand . . 5. Chase
twenty . . 7. Jackson
two . . 9. Jefferson
portray . . . 3. act 4. draw, form, limn 5. enact, frame, image, paint 6. depict 7. fashion, picture 8. describe 9. delineate, represent
portrayal . . . 3. act 5. drama 7. process 8. portrait 9. depiction 11. delineation, description

portreeve . . . 5. mayor 7. bailiff
Port Royal . . . 15. Cistercian abbey (Versailles)
Portugal . . . see also *Portuguese*
bridge . . 7. Salazar
capital . . 6. Lisbon
city . . 5. Braga 6. Aveiro, Guarda, Oporto 7. Granada
island . . 6. Azores 7. Madeira 8. Principe
mountain . . 15. Serra da Estrella
peninsula . . 7. Iberian
port . . 6. Aveiro
province . . 3. Goa 5. Macao, Timor 9. Cape Verde 10. Mozambique
resort . . 7. Estoril
river . . 5. Tagus (Tajo)
Portuguese (pert to) . . .
author . . 9. de Lobeira
bird, fish . . 8. man-of-war
ceremonial (Inquisition) . . 8. auto de fe
coin (gold) . . 6. escudo 7. milreis (old)
lady . . 4. dona
legislature . . 6. Cortes 12. Cortes Geraes
money of account . . 8. reis
navigator . . 6. da Gama 8. Magellan
wine . . 5. porto
Portunus (Rom Relig) . . . 10. god of gates
posada . . . 3. inn 5. hotel
Posaune . . . 8. trombone 9. organ stop
posca . . . 5. drink (Hist)
pose . . . 3. put, sit 5. model 6. baffle, puzzle, stance 7. nonplus, posture, pretend, propose 8. attitude, position, pretense, propound 9. postulate 11. affectation, impersonate
Poseidon (pert to) . . .
attributes . . 5. horse 7. dolphin, trident
cult site . . 7. Corinth
father . . 6. Cronus
god of . . 3. sea 6. waters
mother . . 4. Rhea
Roman name . . 7. Neptune
wife . . 10. Amphitrite
poser . . . 5. facer 6. puzzle 7. problem, sticker 14. attitudinarian
posh . . . 5. smart 6. spruce 7. elegant 9. luxurious
position . . . 3. job, lie 4. pose, rank, seat, site 5. coign (coigne), place, situs, stand, state 6. manner, stance, ubiety 7. opinion, posture, premise 8. attitude, location, prestige, proposal 9. viewpoint 11. affirmation, supposition
position (pert to) . . .
anchorlike . . 5. apeak
fencing . . 7. septime
finder (gun) . . 13. triangulation
golf . . 6. stance
inescapable . . 7. impasse
of affairs . . 6. status
relative . . 8. standing
secure . . 7. footing
with no responsibility . . 8. sinecure
positive . . . 4. plus, sure 5. exact 6. actual, thetic 7. certain 8. dogmatic, emphatic 9. assertive, convinced, downright 11. dictatorial
positive (pert to) . . .
charge (Elec) . . 8. positron
evidence . . 7. constat

pole .. **5.** anode
saying .. **6.** dictum
school, criminology .. **10.** Lombrosian
(by Lombroso)
positivism ... **7.** Comtism **9.** certainty,
dogmatism **10.** confidence
11. materialism
positure ... **7.** posture **11.** arrangement,
disposition **13.** configuration
posnet ... **3.** pot (3-footed) **8.** saucepan
poss ... **4.** beat, dash, push **5.** drive,
knock, pound, stamp **6.** thrust
posse ... **5.** crowd **6.** throng **7.** company
9. armed band **10.** detachment (police)
possess ... **3.** own **4.** have, know, take
5. haunt **6.** inform, occupy **7.** bewitch,
inhabit **8.** convince, demonize, persuade
possessed ... **5.** hadst, owned **6.** insane
7. haunted **8.** demoniac, obsessed
9. bewitched
possessing (pert to) ...
feeling .. **6.** souled
flavor .. **5.** sapid, tasty
land .. **5.** acred
pincer claws .. **8.** chelated
power .. **11.** plenipotent
sensation .. **8.** sentient
special ability .. **6.** gifted **8.** talented
possession ... **4.** hold **5.** asset **6.** taking,
wealth **7.** control, country, mastery
8. dominion, property **9.** obsession,
ownership **10.** equanimity
11. bewitchment
possession (pert to) ...
again .. **6.** revest
law .. **6.** seizin (seisin)
not in (possession) .. **6.** devoid
suffix .. **3.** ose
possessions ... **6.** assets, estate, wealth
7. effects **8.** property
posset ... **4.** turn **6.** curdle, pamper
8. beverage, infusion **9.** coagulate
possibility ... **4.** bare **7.** latency **9.** liability,
potential **10.** good chance, likelihood
11. contingency **13.** improbability
16. prospective value
possible ... **6.** latent, liable, likely
8. feasible **9.** plausible, potential
11. practicable
possibly ... **5.** maybe **7.** perhaps
9. perchance **11.** conceivably
post ... **3.** bet, dak (dawk), xat **4.** bitt,
fort, list, mail, trot **5.** enter, newel,
opium, place, stake, totem **6.** alette,
assign, hasten, inform, marker, office,
pillar, pledge **7.** bollard, placard,
station, upright **8.** dispatch, position
9. messenger, sternpost **12.** enter
account
post (pert to) ...
adverb .. **5.** after, later **9.** afterward
boat .. **4.** mail **5.** stage **6.** packet
boy .. **7.** courier **9.** postilion (postillion)
dance (army sl) .. **8.** struggle
goal (anc) .. **4.** meta
Indian memorial .. **3.** xat **5.** totem
meridian .. **9.** afternoon
mortem .. **7.** autopsy **8.** necropsy
10. after death
office .. **6.** correo
prefix .. **5.** after **6.** behind **10.** subsequent

stair .. **5.** newel
postage stamp paper (pert to) ...
design .. **8.** spandrel
paper .. **6.** pelure
pattern .. **6.** burele **8.** burelage
poster ... **4.** bill, card **7.** placard, sticker
8. bulletin **9.** messenger **10.** billposter
posthumous ... **5.** after **10.** after death,
post-mortem
postiche ... **9.** false hair **10.** artificial
11. counterfeit
postilion ... **5.** guide **7.** postboy
9. postrider
postimpressionist ... **6.** cubist, Derain
7. Cezanne, Matisse
postpone ... **4.** wait **5.** defer, delay, remit,
table **6.** put off, shelve **7.** adjourn,
reserve, suspend **8.** hold over, prorogue
10. pigeonhole **11.** subordinate
13. procrastinate
postponement ... **7.** remanet, respite
8. deferral, reprieve **9.** deferment
11. prorogation
postprandial ... **11.** after dinner
postulate ... **6.** assume **7.** prelude,
premise **9.** condition, predicate,
stipulate **10.** hypothesis **11.** stipulation,
supposition
posture ... **4.** pose **6.** stance **8.** attitude,
position, pretense **9.** viewpoint
11. frame of mind
pot ... **3.** jug, pan **4.** olla **5.** belly, crock,
cruse **6.** aludel, kettle, liquor, teapot
7. amphora (anc), caldron **9.** flowerpot
10. jardiniere
potash ... **6.** potass, saline **7.** potassa
8. pearlash **18.** potassium carbonate
potassium (pert to) ...
bitartrate .. **13.** cream of tartar
bromide .. **8.** sedative
carbonate .. **6.** potash
compound .. **4.** alum
dichromatic .. **6.** chrome
iodide .. **8.** medicine
nitrate .. **5.** niter **9.** saltpeter
permanganate .. **8.** oxidizer
12. disinfectant
sulphate .. **4.** alum
potate ... **9.** liquefied
potation ... **5.** draft, drink **6.** liquor
8. beverage, tippling **12.** drinking bout
potato ... **3.** oca, yam **4.** papa, spud
5. tuber
potato (pert to) ...
beetle .. **8.** hardback
bogle .. **9.** scarecrow
French .. **12.** pomme de terre
French style .. **9.** lyonnaise
genus .. **10.** Solanaceae
Indian .. **4.** yamp
moss .. **9.** pondgrass
So Am .. **7.** Uruguay
sweet .. **6.** patata
potator ... **5.** poter **7.** tippler
potboiler ... **4.** book **6.** writer **8.** painting
(for quick money) **9.** potwaller
potdar ... **7.** assayer, cashier, weigher
potence, potency ... **3.** vis **4.** élan
5. cross, power **6.** energy, gibbet
7. gallows **8.** virility **9.** authority,
influence

potent ... **4.** able **6.** cogent, mighty, strong, virile **7.** dynamic, warrant (Mil) **8.** forcible, heraldry, powerful, puissant, virulent **9.** effective, efficient **11.** efficacious, influential **13.** authoritative

potentate ... **4.** amir (ameer), emir (emeer) **5.** mogul, ruler **6.** dynast, prince **7.** emperor, monarch **8.** syzerain **9.** sovereign

potential ... **4.** mood (Gram) **5.** ergal **6.** latent, mighty **8.** possible **11.** influential, in the making, possibility, undeveloped

potentiality ... **5.** power **7.** latency **11.** possibility

poter ... **5.** toper **7.** drinker

potgun ... **5.** rumor **6.** cannon, mortar, pistol **8.** braggart

pothead ... **7.** dullard **8.** terminal (Elec) **9.** blackfish

pother ... **3.** ado, row **4.** fuss, stir **5.** worry **6.** bother, bustle, harass **7.** fluster, perplex, trouble **9.** commotion **10.** excitement, perplexity **11.** disturbance **12.** perturbation

potherb ... **4.** mint **6.** greens **7.** spinach

pothook ... **3.** rod **4.** hook (S-shaped) **5.** crook **6.** scrawl, stroke (S-like) **9.** pot lifter **10.** iron collar (penalty)

pothouse ... **3.** bar, low **6.** saloon, tavern, vulgar **7.** barroom **8.** alehouse, grogshop, mughouse **11.** public house

potiche ... **4.** vase **7.** ceramic

potion ... **4.** dose, dram, drug **5.** draft, drink **7.** draught, philter **8.** nepenthe

potlatch ... **4.** gift **5.** feast **8.** Festival

pot mender ... **6.** tinker

potomania ... **10.** dipsomania **15.** delirium tremens

potong ... **5.** crown **6.** wreath **9.** head cloth

potoroo ... **11.** rat kangaroo

potpourri ... **4.** olio, stew **6.** medley **7.** mixture, perfume **9.** anthology **11.** olla-podrida, salamagundi

potrero ... **4.** farm **7.** pasture **10.** cattle farm

pottage ... **4.** soup **6.** brewis **8.** porridge

pottah ... **5.** lease **6.** tenure **9.** title deed

potter ... **3.** pry **4.** mess, poke, push **6.** dawdle, doodle, meddle, putter, tamper, trifle **7.** saunter **8.** ceramist

potter's clay, earth ... **4.** slip **5.** argil **6.** galena, kaolin **8.** alquifou **10.** terra cotta

potter's wheel ... **4.** disk **5.** lathe, throw **6.** jigger, pallet (palet)

pottery ... **5.** Delft **6.** Samian **7.** celadon (Chin), keramos (Gr) **8.** Arretine (It), ceramics, Majolica (It) **9.** delftware (Holland), keramikos (Gr) **11.** earthenware **14.** terra sigillata (anc)

pottery (pert to) ...
black .. **6.** basalt
broken .. **5.** shard (sherd)
decorate .. **6.** stamps **9.** sigillate
decoration .. **11.** sigillation
firing box .. **6.** sagger
glasslike .. **8.** vitreous
glaze .. **6.** enamel

mineral .. **8.** feldspar
oven .. **4.** kiln
paste .. **9.** barbotine
red .. **7.** aretine

pottle ... **3.** pot **6.** basket, vessel **7.** tankard

potty ... **3.** pot **5.** crazy **7.** foolish, haughty **8.** trifling **12.** supercilious **13.** insignificant

pot-valiant ... **10.** courageous (when drunk)

pouch ... **3.** bag, pod, sac **4.** cyst, poke, sack **5.** bulge, bursa, purse **6.** gipser (Hist), pocket **7.** bladder, mailbag, silicle, sporran (sporan) **10.** pocketbook

pouch bone ... **9.** marsupial

pouched (pert to) ...
dog .. **9.** thylacine **13.** Tasmanian wolf
frog .. **9.** marsupial
gopher .. **6.** pocket
mouse .. **9.** marsupial
rat .. **8.** kangaroo
rodent *(cheek-pouched)* .. **11.** spermophile
stork .. **8.** adjutant

poultry ... **4.** fowl, hens **5.** cocks, ducks, geese **6.** capons **7.** Bantams, peahens, pigeons, turkeys **8.** chickens, peacocks, roosters, volaille **9.** cockerels, pheasants **10.** guinea fowl

poultry (breeds) ... **6.** Ancona, Bantam, Brahma **7.** Cornish, Dorking, Hamburg, Leghorn, Minorca **9.** Wyandotte **12.** Plymouth Rock **14.** Rhode Island Red

poultry (pert to) ...
disease .. **3.** pip **4.** roup, tick
dish .. **9.** galantine
farm .. **7.** hennery

pounamu ... **4.** jade **6.** weapon **8.** nephrite **10.** greenstone

pound ... **3.** hit, ram **4.** beat, ding, drum, maul, pond, quid (Brit money), tamp **5.** money, pen up, thump **6.** bruise, hammer, kennel, prison **7.** impound **9.** enclosure, pulverize

pounding instrument ... **6.** hammer, pestle

Pound of poetry ... **4.** Ezra

pounds (100) ... **6.** cental **13.** hundredweight

pour ... **4.** flow, gush, rain, teem, vent, well **5.** flood **6.** abound, effuse, stream **7.** niagara, radiate, torrent **8.** downpour **9.** discharge **11.** extravasate

pour (pert to) ...
molten glass .. **7.** dagrade
molten steel .. **4.** teem
off .. **5.** drain **6.** decant
oil upon .. **6.** anoint, pacify
out .. **11.** extravasate
sacrificial liquid .. **6.** libate

pouring hole (mold) ... **5.** sprue

pout ... **3.** bib, mop **4.** fish, moue, sulk **5.** pique **7.** catfish, eelpout, grimace **9.** sulkiness

poverty ... **4.** lack, need, want **5.** illth (opp of wealth) **6.** dearth, penury **8.** leanness, poorness, scarcity **9.** indigence, pearlweed **11.** destitution

powder ... **4.** dust, talc **5.** boral **6.** pollen,

yttria **7.** crumble **8.** cosmetic, sprinkle
9. explosive, pulverize
powder (pert to)...
antiseptic . . **6.** formin **7.** aristol
bag . . **6.** sachet
festival (Ind) . . **4.** abir (perfumed)
goa . . **7.** araroba
heater, melter . . **6.** sinter
insecticide . . **9.** hellebore
medical . . **8.** tannigen
perfumed . . **6.** empasm
polishing . . **5.** emery **7.** tripoli
smokeless . . **6.** poudre **8.** amberite
stamping . . **6.** pounce
powdered (Her) . . . **4.** semé
power . . . **3.** arm, art, can, jet, vis
  4. dint, gift, iron, sway, will **5.** force,
  magic, might, steam, vigor **6.** degree,
  energy **7.** control, faculty, magnate,
  potency **8.** capacity, efficacy, strength
  9. authority, eloquence, influence,
  magnetism, puissance **10.** efficiency,
  government **11.** mathematics (term)
power (pert to)...
creative . . **6.** Shakti
device . . **9.** telemotor
hammer . . **4.** trip
inherent . . **6.** energy
of attorney . . **5.** agent **10.** procurator
of feeling . . **7.** sensate
of mind . . **4.** wits
of resistance . . **7.** stamina
persuasive . . **8.** rhetoric **9.** political
sovereign . . **6.** throne
spiritual . . **8.** divinity
superior . . **10.** prepotency
under one's . . **10.** subjugated
unit . . **3.** erg **4.** dyne **8.** kilowatt
powerful . . . **4.** loud **5.** great **6.** cogent,
  mighty, potent, strong **7.** drastic,
  intense, leonine, skookum **8.** eloquent,
  forcible, puissant **9.** effective, effectual,
  efficient **10.** armipotent, convincing
  11. efficacious, influential
  13. authoritative
powerful force . . . **6.** libido
powerful man, businessman . . . **5.** titan
  6. tycoon **7.** magnate
powerless . . . **4.** weak **8.** impotent
pownie . . . **7.** peacock
powwow . . . **6.** frolic, priest **7.** meeting
  8. assembly, ceremony, congress,
  conjurer **9.** gathering **10.** conference,
  convention
poyou . . . **9.** armadillo
prabble . . . **7.** chatter, quarrel **8.** squabble
practic . . . **6.** artful, shrews **7.** cunning,
  skilled **9.** difficult, practical, practiced
  11. experienced
practicable, practical . . . **5.** utile
  6. usable, useful **7.** virtual, working
  8. feasible, possible, workable
  9. available, expedient, operative,
  pragmatic, realistic **11.** pragmatical,
  utilitarian
practical (pert to)...
Christianity . . **10.** New Thought
example . . **6.** praxis
joke . . **4.** hoax **5.** trick **6.** humbug
judgment . . **7.** ethical (Kant)
practically . . . **9.** virtually **11.** essentially

13. approximately
practice, practise . . . **2.** do **3.** ply,
  ure, use **4.** plot, rite **5.** drill, habit,
  train, usage **6.** action, addict, custom,
  scheme, tryout **7.** perform **8.** ceremony,
  exercise, intrigue, rehearse, training,
  vocation **9.** procedure **10.** experience,
  experiment, observance
practice (pert to)...
corrupt . . **5.** abuse
established . . **5.** canon **6.** custom
fraud . . **5.** cheat, shark **8.** trickery
specific . . **6.** praxis
voice . . **8.** intonate
witchcraft . . **3.** hex
practicer of evasions . . .
  13. tergiversator
practicer of palmistry . . .
  11. chiromancer
prad . . . **5.** horse
pragmatic . . . **7.** meddler, skilled
  8. busybody, dogmatic, meddling
  9. conceited, officious, practical
  10. systematic **11.** opinionated
pragmatical . . . **8.** dogmatic **9.** officious,
  practical **10.** meddlesome
  11. commonplace
Prague, Praha . . .
capital of . . **14.** Czechoslovakia
famed bldg . . **10.** University (1st in Cent
  Eur, 1348)
famed teachers (anc) . . **4.** Huss **6.** Jerome
founder . . **14.** Duchess Libussa (722)
prairie . . . **3.** bay **5.** llano, plain **6.** camass
  (camas, cammas), meadow, steppe
  7. quamash (camass) **9.** grassland
  10. prairillon
prairie (pert to)...
anemone, crocus . . **12.** pasque flower
antelope . . **9.** pronghorn
apple . . **9.** breadroot
artichoke . . **9.** sunflower
berry . . **9.** trompillo
chicken . . **6.** grouse
dog . . **6.** marmot
mud . . **5.** gumbo
pigeon . . **6.** plover **9.** sandpiper
rose . . **14.** Baltimore belle
schooner . . **12.** covered wagon
squirrel . . **11.** spermophile
tree (clump) . . **5.** motte
weed . . **10.** cinquefoil
wolf . . **6.** coyote
Prairie State . . . **8.** Illinois
praise . . . **4.** laud **5.** bless, extol, honor,
  kudos **6.** eulogy **7.** acclaim, applaud,
  commend, glorify, magnify, plaudit
  8. applause, encomium, eulogize,
  macarize **9.** adulation, celebrate,
  panegyric **11.** approbation
  12. commendation
praise (pert to)...
continual . . **5.** chant
high . . **5.** extol **8.** encomium
hymn of . . **8.** doxology
insincere . . **4.** bull **7.** flatter **8.** flattery
of another's blessing . . **8.** macarism
  9. Beatitude
to God . . **7.** Laus Deo
Ye The Lord . . **8.** Alleluia (Alleluiah)
  10. Hallelujah (Hallelujah)

praiseworthy ... **8.** laudable
11. commendable, meritorious
prana (Hind) ... **6.** spirit **9.** life force
10. life breath
prance ... **4.** gait **5.** caper, dance **6.** cavort, spring **7.** swagger
prank ... **3.** jig **4.** fold, joke, prat **5.** antic, caper, pleat, shine, trick **6.** frolic, prance **7.** caprice, dress up **8.** escapade **11.** monkeyshine
prankish ... **9.** facetious **10.** frolicsome
11. mischievous
prate ... **3.** gab **4.** chat, talk **6.** gossip **7.** chatter, twaddle **8.** nonsense
prattle ... **3.** gab **4.** chat, talk **5.** clack, prate **6.** babble **7.** blather **12.** impudent talk, trifling talk
prawn ... **6.** shrimp **10.** crustacean, shrimp pink
pray ... **3.** ask, beg, sue **7.** entreat, implore, request, worship **8.** devotion **10.** supplicate
praya ... **4.** bund, road **5.** beach **6.** strand
prayer ... **3.** ave **4.** bead, bene, plea, suit **5.** credo, grace, matin **6.** litany, orison, vesper **7.** request, worship **8.** petition **12.** intercession, supplication
prayer (pert to) ...
book .. **4.** ordo **6.** missal **7.** portass (portas) **8.** breviary
call (Muslim) .. **4.** azan (adan)
call tower .. **7.** minaret
cloak .. **6.** zizith (fringed) **7.** tallith
desk, ledge .. **8.** prie-dieu
evening .. **7.** complin (compline) **9.** night song
figure .. **5.** orant
incarnation .. **7.** Angelus **11.** Angelus Bell
liturgical .. **6.** litany **7.** complin
Lord's (prayer) .. **11.** Paternoster
morning .. **5.** matin
nine days' devotional .. **6.** novena
response .. **8.** antiphon
short .. **5.** grace
stick .. **4.** paho
praying ... **8.** entreaty **9.** precation **12.** supplication
praying cricket ... **6.** mantis
praying figure ... **5.** orant
preach ... **6.** exhort **7.** expound, lecture **8.** advocate, homilize **9.** discourse, sermonize
preacher ... **6.** parson, rector **7.** evangel, teacher **8.** homilist, lecturer, minister **9.** clergyman, pulpiteer
preaching ... **6.** sermon **7.** kerygma (kerugma) **10.** preachment **11.** exhortation
preaching friar ... **9.** Dominican
Preaching of Peter ... **9.** Apocrypha
preamble ... **5.** proem **7.** preface, prelude **11.** preliminary **12.** introduction
prebellum ... **7.** antewar **12.** before the war
prebend ... **7.** stipend **8.** benefice **9.** allowance
precarious ... **7.** assumed, dubious **8.** insecure, unstable **9.** hazardous, uncertain, unsettled **10.** unreliable
preceded ... **3.** led **8.** prefaced, was prior

9. anteceded, antedated **10.** introduced, went before **13.** had precedence, occurred first
precedence ... **3.** pas **4.** lead, rank **8.** priority **12.** anteposition
precedent ... **4.** sign **5.** model, usage **7.** example, leading **8.** anterior, decision, standard **10.** antecedent, forerunner **11.** going before
preceding others ... **5.** first **7.** leading, ternary (by threes) **10.** antecedent
precept ... **4.** rule, writ **5.** adage, axiom, maxim, order, sutra (sutta), torah (tora) **6.** belief **7.** command **8.** doctrine **9.** direction **11.** commandment, instruction
preceptor ... **4.** guru **5.** guide, tutor **6.** master, mentor, mullah, pundit **7.** teacher **8.** educator **10.** instructor
precinct ... **5.** ambit, space **6.** region **8.** boundary, district, environs
precious ... **4.** dear, rare **5.** great **6.** costly, valued **7.** beloved, elegant, perfect **8.** complete, esteemed, overnice, valuable **9.** downright **10.** beloved one, fastidious, particular
precious (pert to) ...
Blood (RCCh) .. **5.** Feast (July 1)
garnet .. **6.** pyrope
stone .. **3.** gem **4.** opal, ruby **5.** pearl, topaz **6.** garnet, ligure **7.** diamond, emerald, jacinth (Bib) **8.** hyacinth, sapphire
stone, sometimes .. **7.** cat's-eye **11.** alexandrite
precipice ... **4.** crag, linn, pali **5.** bluff, cliff **9.** declivity
precipitancy ... **5.** haste **8.** rashness
precipitation ... **3.** gel **4.** fall, hail, mist, rain, snow **5.** haste, sleet **8.** downpour **9.** hastening **11.** prematurity **12.** acceleration, condensation, recklessness
precipitous ... **4.** rash **5.** hasty, steep **6.** abrupt, sudden **7.** rushing (headlong) **9.** very rapid **11.** precipitate
précis ... **6.** sketch **7.** epitome, pandect, summary **8.** abstract, synopsis **9.** summarize
precise ... **4.** prim **5.** exact **7.** correct, literal, special **8.** accurate, definite, detailed, overnice **10.** meticulous, overminute, particular, scrupulous **11.** ceremonious, punctilious
preciseness ... **9.** exactness **10.** strictness **12.** definiteness **14.** fastidiousness
precision ... **6.** nicety **8.** accuracy **9.** exactness, formality **11.** preciseness **12.** definiteness
preclude ... **3.** bar **4.** omit, stop **5.** avert, debar, estop **6.** hinder, impede **7.** head off, prevent, shut out **8.** prohibit
precocious ... **7.** forward **8.** advanced **9.** premature
preconceive ... **6.** ideate, precox **7.** presume **8.** foreknow, prejudge **9.** predecide **10.** presuppose
predatory ... **7.** looting **9.** marauding, pillaging, piratical **10.** plundering, predaceous (predacious) **11.** destructive
predatory bird ... **3.** owl **4.** hawk, kite

6. falcon
predatory raid . . . 5. foray
predestine . . . 4. doom, fate 6. decree,
ordain 7. appoint 9. determine,
foretoken 10. foreordain
predetermine . . . 4. bias 7. destine
8. prejudge 9. prejudice, preordain
10. prepossess 11. premeditate
predicament . . . 3. fix 4. pass 5. state
6. plight, scrape 7. dilemma, impasse
8. quandary 9. condition, situation
predicator . . . 4. seer 5. friar 7. prophet
8. preacher 9. predicter
predict . . . 4. bode, dope, omen 7. foresee,
portend, presage 8. forecast, foretell,
prophecy 13. prognosticate
prediction . . . 6. augury 8. prophecy
9. foresight 10. foreboding
11. foretelling 15. prognostication
predilection . . . 4. bias 6. desire
8. tendency 9. prejudice 10. favoritism,
partiality, preference, propensity
11. disposition 13. preconception
14. predisposition
predominant . . . 5. chief 6. ruling
8. reigning, superior 9. hegemonic
11. controlling, influential, outstanding
predominate . . . 5. excel 7. prevail
8. dominate 10. be superior
12. preponderate
pre-eminent . . . 3. top 4. only, star
5. chief 7. palmary, ranking 8. superior
9. excellent, principal 11. outstanding
pre-emption . . . 8. monopoly, purchase
10. prior right 13. appropriation
preen . . . 3. pin, sew 4. perk 5. clasp,
dress, groom, plume, primp 6. bodkin,
brooch, stitch 9. make sleek
preface . . . 5. front, proem 6. herald,
prayer 7. prelude, problem 8. exordium,
foreword, preamble, prologue
10. paraphrase 12. introduction
prefect, praefect . . . 4. dean (Jesuit)
6. chin fu 7. monitor, officer 8. director,
minister, official 9. president
10. magistrate
prefecture . . . 7. eparchy
prefer . . . 5. elect, offer 6. choose, select
7. outrank, present, proffer, promote
9. be partial 12. give priority
preference . . . 6. choice 8. favorite,
priority 9. advantage 10. favoritism
11. alternative, prior choice
12. predilection
prefiguration . . . 4. omen 9. foretoken,
prototype 12. typification
13. preindication
prefigure . . . 7. imagine, suggest
8. foretell 10. foreshadow
prefix for . . .
about . . 3. amb 4. peri
above . . 3. epi, sur 5. hyper, super,
supra
across . . 3. dia 4. tran 5. trans
again . . 2. re
against . . 4. anti
ahead . . 3. pre
all . . 4. omni
alongside . . 3. par 4. para
an . . 2. al
apart . . 2. se 3. dia, dis

appearing to . . 5. quasi
around . . 4. peri
away . . 3. aph, apo
back . . 2. re 3. ana
backward . . 5. retro
bad . . 3. dys, mal
badly . . 3. mis
beauty . . 5. calli (kalli)
before . . 2. ob 3. pre, pro 4. ante, prae
beside . . 3. par 4. para
between . . 3. dia 4. meta 5. inter
beyond . . 4. para 5. ultra
black . . 4. atra
blood . . 4. haem, hemo
bone . . 4. oste 5. osteo
both . . 4. ambi
Chinese . . 4. Sino 5. Chino
clear . . 4. delo
dawn . . 2. eo
difficult . . 3. dys
distant . . 3. tel 4. tele
double . . 2. di
down . . 2. de 4. cata
ear . . 3. oto
earnest . . 5. serio
earth . . 3. geo
eight . . 3. oct 4. octa, octo
English . . 5. Anglo
equal . . 3. iso
equally . . 4. equi
evil . . 3. mal
far . . 3. tel 4. tele
faulty . . 3. mis
fictitious . . 6. pseudo
fire . . 3. pyr
five . . 5. penta
for . . 3. pro
former . . 2. ex
four . . 5. tetra 6. quadri
from . . 2. ab, de, ec
from away . . 3. apo
gas . . 4. aero
good . . 2. eu
half . . 4. demi, hemi, semi
hard . . 3. dys 6. stereo
ill . . 3. mal, mis
in, into . . 2. en 4. endo
iron . . 5. ferro
lizard . . 5. saura, sauro
many . . 4. mult, poly 5. multi
middle . . 4. meso 5. medio
modern . . 3. neo
mountain . . 3. oro
nail . . 4. helo
negative . . 2. il, ir, un 3. mon
new . . 3. neo
not . . 2. il, im, ir, un 3. non
numerical . . 3. uni
one . . 3. uni 4. mono
oneself . . 4. auto
out of, outer . . 2. ec, ex 3. ect, epi,
exo 4. ecto
over . . 3. epi, sur 5. super, supra
possession . . 3. ose
pray . . 3. ora
priority . . 3. pre
recent . . 3. neo
release . . 2. un
reversed . . 2. di
same, equal . . 3. iso 4. equi, homo
separation . . 2. di 3. dis

shoulder.. **6.** humero
single.. **4.** mono
son of.. **3.** Mac
ten.. **3.** dec **4.** deca
this side of.. **3.** cis
three, thrice.. **3.** ter, tri **4.** tris
through.. **3.** dia, per
to.. **2.** ap
together.. **3.** com, con, cor, syn
toward.. **2.** ob, oc
turning.. **4.** roto
twice.. **2.** bi, di
twofold.. **2.** bi, di **3.** dua
under.. **3.** sub
upon.. **2.** ep **3.** epi
upward.. **3.** ana, ano
very much.. **3.** eri
well.. **2.** eu
with.. **3.** col, com, pro, syl, syn
within.. **3.** eso **4.** endo, ento **5.** intra
without.. **2.** se **3.** ect **4.** ecto
wood.. **4.** xylo
wrong.. **3.** mis
pregnant ... **7.** fertile **8.** fruitful
  9. expecting, with child **10.** parturient
prehistoric (pert to) ...
animal.. **7.** reptile **8.** dinosaur, mastodon
  9. phytosaur
continent.. **8.** Atlantis (Atalantis)
man.. **4.** cave, Dawn **11.** lake dweller
ref to.. **9.** primitive
tool.. **6.** eolith
prejudiced ... **6.** biased **7.** partial
  8. partisan **11.** opinionated
  12. prepossessed
prejudicial ... **9.** injurious **11.** detrimental
  15. disadvantageous
prelate ... **4.** head, pope **5.** abbot, chief
  6. bishop, priest **7.** primate, red-blue
  8. minister, superior **9.** Monsignor
  (Monsignore)
prelector, praelector ... **6.** reader
  7. teacher **8.** lecturer **9.** professor
preliminary ... **5.** prior **7.** preface,
  prelude **8.** entrance, previous, proemial
  9. precedent, prefatory, threshold
  10. antecedent **11.** preparatory
  12. introduction, introductory
preliminary memo ... **8.** protocol
preliminary plan ... **4.** idea
prelude ... **5.** proem **6.** verset **7.** preface
  8. overture, ritornel (ritornelle)
premature ... **6.** infant **8.** too early,
  untimely **10.** precocious
premier ... **3.** bet (gambling) **5.** chief
  7. leading **8.** earliest **9.** principal
  13. prime minister
premiere ... **4.** show **10.** first night
  12. presentation **16.** first performance
premium ... **4.** agio **5.** bonus, prize,
  stake **6.** reward **8.** gratuity, interest
  10. recompense
premonition ... **5.** hunch **6.** notice
  7. warning **8.** forecast **10.** foreboding
  11. forewarning, information
  12. presentiment
preoccupied ... **4.** lost **6.** absent, filled
  8. absorbed, observed **9.** engrossed
  10. abstracted, pre-engaged **13.** lost
  in thought
preparation ... **8.** training **9.** equipment,

study hour **10.** groundwork **11.** making
  ready **12.** introduction
preparation (pert to) ...
of a dress.. **7.** fitting
place.. **10.** laboratory, paratorium
sugar, for candy.. **7.** fondant
without.. **5.** ad lib **9.** impromptu
prepare ... **3.** fit, fix, get **4.** cook, gird,
  make, pave, yark **5.** adapt, equip,
  ready, train **6.** adjust **7.** arrange
prepare (pert to) ...
by boiling.. **6.** decoct
for golf game.. **3.** tee
for melting glass.. **4.** frit
for publication.. **4.** edit
for seasoning.. **8.** marinate
skins.. **3.** taw
prepared ... **5.** armed, ready **7.** adapted,
  groomed, skilled, trained **8.** equipped,
  provided
prepared instruction ...
  13. propaedeutics
preponderance ... **6.** weight **8.** dominion,
  majority **9.** influence **11.** outweighing,
  superiority
prepose ... **6.** prefix **7.** preface **11.** place
  before
preposition ... **2.** at, by, ex, in, of, on,
  to, up **3.** off, out, tae **4.** into, onto,
  over, unto, upon, with
prepossession ... **4.** bent, bias
  9. obsession, prejudice **10.** preference
  11. inclination **12.** predilection
  13. appropriation, preconception
  14. predisposition
presage ... **4.** bode, omen, osse, sign
  5. token **6.** augury, betide, divine
  7. portend, predict **8.** forebode,
  foretell **11.** prediction, prognostic
  11. preindicate **13.** foreknowledge
presager ... **7.** prophet **9.** foreboder
presbytery ... **6.** church, clergy **7.** council
  8. ministry **9.** parsonage **10.** presbyters
prescribe ... **3.** set **5.** allot, guide, limit,
  order **6.** advise, bestow, direct, ordain
  7. control, dictate **9.** designate
presence ... **4.** mien, port **7.** bearing,
  posture, specter **8.** phantasm
  9. existence, proximity **10.** apparition,
  appearance, attendance **11.** personality
present ... **3.** now **4.** boon, gift, give
  5. grant, nonce, offer **6.** bestow, bounty,
  donate **7.** largess (largesse) **8.** donation,
  gratuity **9.** introduce **10.** contribute
  11. benefaction
present (pert to) ...
for acceptance.. **6.** tender
pupil to teacher.. **8.** minerval
time.. **3.** now **5.** nonce, today **7.** current
  8. juncture
to customers.. **7.** freebie, premium
  8. giveaway **9.** lagniappe (lagnappe)
to foreign ambassador.. **6.** xenium
presentation ... **4.** gift, plan **5.** debut,
  offer **7.** present **8.** bestowal, donation,
  offering **10.** appearance, exhibition
  12. introduction
presently ... **4.** anon, soon **6.** at once
  7. shortly **8.** nowadays **9.** forthwith
  10. before long **11.** immediately
preservation ... **6.** saving **9.** retention,

safeguard **10.** protection
11. maintenance, safekeeping
12. conservation, perpetuation
preservative . . . **4.** salt **5.** spice **7.** alcohol,
vinegar **10.** protective **14.** sodium
benzoate
preserve . . . **3.** can, jam, tin **4.** corn,
cure, keep, salt, save **5.** guard, jelly,
spare, store **6.** defend, pickle, retain,
secure, shield, uphold **7.** compote,
protect, sustain **8.** conserve, maintain
9. freeze-dry, safeguard
preserve (pert to) . . .
by drying . . **9.** desiccate
fruit . . **7.** compote **9.** marmalade
grape . . **5.** uvate (conserve)
in brine . . **4.** corn, cure, salt
in oil . . **8.** marinate
president . . . **4.** head **5.** ruler **8.** governor
14. chief executive
President (US) . . . **4.** Ford, Polk, Taft
5. Adams (John), Adams (John Q),
Grant, Hayes, Nixon, Tyler **6.** Arthur
(Chester), Carter, Hoover, Monroe,
Pierce, Reagan, Taylor, Truman, Wilson
7. Harding, Jackson, Johnson (Andrew),
Johnson (L B), Kennedy, Lincoln,
Madison **8.** Buchanan, Coolidge,
Fillmore, Garfield, Harrison (Benj),
Harrison (Wm Henry), McKinley,
Van Buren **9.** Cleveland, Jefferson,
Roosevelt (Theo), Roosevelt (F D)
10. Eisenhower, Washington
President (pert to) . . .
place . . **10.** Oval Office, White House
power . . **4.** veto
press . . . **3.** dun **4.** cram, iron, urge
5. crowd, force, wedge **6.** compel,
hasten, smooth, throng, thrust
7. impress, squeeze **8.** compress,
condense, insist on **9.** extractor,
importune **10.** compulsion, journalism,
newspapers **12.** conscription
press (pert to) . . .
ancient . . **6.** Aldine
bookbinder . . **7.** smasher
corrector . . **11.** proofreader
critic . . **6.** censor **8.** reviewer
ranks . . **5.** serry
pressed (pert to) . . .
amber . . **8.** amberoid
cheese . . **7.** cheddar
grapes, residue . . **4.** marc (mark)
into a mass . . **7.** kneaded
together . . **5.** dense **6.** mashed
7. compact, crowded, serried
pressing . . . **6.** urgent, urging **7.** exigent
9. insistent **10.** compelling, extraction,
motivating **11.** importunity
pressure . . . **4.** urge **5.** force **6.** compel,
stress, weight **7.** squeeze, urgency
8. exigency, instancy **9.** authority,
influence **10.** compulsion, constraint,
harassment **11.** compression
pressure (pert to) . . .
barometer . . **7.** mesobar
boiler, cooker . . **9.** autoclave
instrument (for liquids) . . **9.** manometer
10. piezometer **11.** Bourdon tube
of necessity . . **7.** urgency
resisting . . **8.** renitent

unit . . **5.** barad
prestidigitation . . . **8.** juggling
11. legerdemain **13.** sleight of hand
prestige . . . **4.** bias, face, sway **5.** clout,
éclat **6.** renown, repute **7.** sorcery
8. illusion **9.** authority, deception,
influence **10.** importance **11.** superiority
presto . . . **5.** magic **7.** command, passing,
quickly **8.** suddenly **9.** instantly
10. rapid tempo **11.** immediately
13. instantaneous
presumably . . . **7.** no doubt **8.** probably
10. ostensibly, supposedly
presume . . . **4.** dare, hope **5.** imply, judge,
think **6.** assure, impose **7.** suppose,
venture **10.** presuppose **11.** preconceive
14. take for granted
presumption . . . **4.** hope **6.** daring
7. opinion **8.** audacity **9.** arrogance,
impudence, insolence **10.** effrontery
11. implication, probability, supposition
presumptive . . . **5.** brash **7.** assumed,
Icarian **8.** arrogant, inferred, probable
10. evidential
presumptuous . . . **5.** undue **7.** forward,
haughty **8.** arrogant, insolent
9. foolhardy **11.** venturesome
pretend . . . **3.** act, aim **4.** fake, sham
5. claim, feign, feint **6.** affect,
allege, assume, pose as **7.** presume,
pretext, profess **8.** disguise, simulate
11. impersonate, make believe
pretended . . . **4.** sham **7.** alleged
8. affected, intended, proposed,
so-called **10.** ostensible
pretended omission (Rhet) . . .
9. apophasis **11.** paraleipsis (paralepsis)
pretender . . . **4.** idol, snob **5.** cowan,
quack **6.** seemer **7.** Aeolist (Eolist)
8. claimant, impostor **9.** charlatan
10. mountebank **11.** fourflusher
pretense, pretence . . . **3.** act **4.** flam,
ruse, sham, show **5.** claim, cloak,
cover, feint, horse, study **6.** excuse,
tinsel **7.** pretext **8.** artifice, stalking
10. appearance, masquerade,
subterfuge **11.** affectation, fabrication,
ostentation
pretentious . . . **4.** arty **5.** showy **6.** rococo
7. elegant, pompous **8.** affected,
boastful **9.** high-flown **12.** ostentatious
13. grandiloquent
pretentious words, use of . . .
9. bombastic **10.** lexiphanic
pretermit . . . **4.** omit **6.** pass by
7. neglect, suspend **8.** intermit, pass
over **9.** interrupt
pretext . . . **4.** flam, plea **5.** cloak, cover,
trick **6.** excuse **8.** pretense (pretence)
9. deception, semblance
pretty . . . **3.** toy **4.** cute, fair, joli, very
5. bonny (bonnie) **6.** clever, comely,
lovely, rather **7.** dollish, finical, foppish
8. handsome **9.** ingenious, tolerably
10. attractive, knickknack **11.** good-
looking, interesting **15.** pulchritudinous
prevail . . . **3.** win **5.** exist **6.** induce,
subdue **7.** succeed, triumph
8. dominate, frequent **9.** prevalent
11. predominate
prevailed . . . **3.** got, won **5.** urged

9. succeeded, triumphed
prevailing . . . **4.** rife **5.** chief, usual
6. common **7.** current, general
8. abundant, dominant **9.** prevalent
10. widespread **11.** predominant
prevail upon . . . **4.** urge **6.** induce
8. persuade
prevalent . . . **4.** rife **6.** potent **7.** current
8. dominant, powerful **9.** extensive
10. prevailing, successful, victorious,
widespread **11.** efficacious, influential
prevaricate . . . **3.** lie **5.** evade **7.** deviate,
quibble, shuffle
prevene . . . **7.** prevent **9.** forestall
10. anticipate
prevent . . . **4.** warn **5.** avert, debar,
deter, estop **7.** ward off **8.** preclude
9. forestall, frustrate **10.** circumvent
preventative, preventive . . . **8.** antidote
9. deterrent **12.** prophylactic
previous . . . **4.** past **5.** prior **6.** before,
former **7.** earlier **8.** untimely
9. foregoing, preceding, premature
11. unwarranted
previously . . . **4.** erst **6.** before **7.** earlier
8. formerly **9.** aforesaid **10.** heretofore
prey . . . **3.** rob **5.** booty, spoil **6.** quarry,
victim **7.** plunder
prey (to seize) . . . **9.** raptorial
prey upon . . . **3.** eat **4.** feed **5.** ravin
(raven) **7.** plunder, torment **9.** predacity
Priam (pert to) . . .
 daughter . . **8.** Polyxena **9.** Cassandra
 grandfather . . **4.** Ilus
 King of . . **4.** Troy
 servant . . **7.** Agelaus
 son . . **5.** Paris **6.** Hector **7.** Troilus
 wife . . **6.** Hecuba
price . . . **3.** sum **4.** cost, fare, odds,
rate **5.** offer, value, worth **6.** charge
7. expense **10.** estimation, excellence,
recompense **12.** preciousness
priceless . . . **7.** amusing **8.** precious
10. high-priced, invaluable, not salable
prick . . . **4.** goad, pain, pang **5.** sting,
wound **6.** pierce **7.** prickle, remorse
8. distress
pricked . . . **6.** dotted, pinked **7.** pointed
9. punctured
prickle . . . **4.** burr, prod, seta **5.** spike,
thorn **6.** pierce, tingle **7.** acantha
8. stinging
prickly . . . **6.** tingly **7.** pointed **8.** echinate
prickly (pert to) . . .
 flower . . **4.** burr
 pear . . **4.** tuna **5.** nopal **6.** cactus
 7. Opuntia
 plant . . **3.** ash **5.** briar, elder **6.** teasel
 7. juniper, lettuce, thistle **12.** Hercules-
 club
pride . . . **6.** vanity **7.** conceit, egotism
9. arrogance, proudness **11.** self-respect
priest . . . **3.** Eli, fra **4.** abbé, curé, lama,
père **5.** clerk, druid, padre **6.** cleric,
father **7.** prester **9.** oratorian
priest (pert to) . . .
 assistant . . **7.** acolyte
 Brit order (anc) . . **5.** Druid
 cap . . **5.** miter (mitre) **7.** biretta
 fish . . **8.** rockfish
 mantle . . **4.** cope

priest-in-the-pulpit . . **10.** cuckoopint
 relating to . . **10.** sacerdotal
 tribe (Israel) . . **4.** Levi
 vestment . . **3.** alb **5.** amice, ephod (Jew),
 stole **7.** cassock, maniple **8.** chasuble,
 surplice
priestly caste . . . **4.** Magi **7.** wise men
prig . . . **3.** beg, fog, pan **4.** buck, snob
5. dandy, filch, plead, prink, prude,
steal, thief **6.** haggle, pilfer, purist, tinker
7. bargain, entreat, pitcher **8.** pilferer
priggish, prim . . . **7.** prudish **8.** snobbish,
thievish
prim . . . **4.** fish, neat, smug **5.** primp,
smelt **6.** demure, formal **7.** precise,
prudish **8.** decorous
prima donna . . . **4.** diva **6.** singer
prima facie . . . **7.** at sight **9.** first view
10. apparently
primal . . . **5.** basic, chief, first **7.** primary
8. original **9.** elemental, primitive
primary . . . **5.** basic, color, first **6.** primal
7. initial **8.** election, primeval, pristine
9. elemental, essential, firsthand,
primitive, principal **10.** elementary
11. fundamental
primary (pert to) . . .
 armament . . **6.** cannon
 circles . . **7.** equator, horizon **8.** ecliptic,
 galactic
 colors . . **3.** red **4.** blue **6.** yellow
primate, bishop . . . **10.** Archbishop
Primates (Order of) . . . **3.** ape, man
5. lemur **6.** mammal, monkey
8. marmoset **9.** orangutan
(orangoutang)
prime . . . **4.** best, dawn **5.** first, paint
7. primary, the best **8.** original, primeval
9. primitive
prime minister . . . **7.** premier
primer . . . **5.** paint **8.** hornbook, textbook,
type size **9.** detonator **10.** battledore
primeval . . . **6.** primal **7.** primary
8. original, pristine
primeval deity . . . **5.** Titan
primitive . . . **5.** basic, first **6.** embryo,
native, quaint **7.** ancient, priscan
8. pristine **10.** aboriginal, antiquated
11. fundamental
primitive (pert to) . . .
 area . . **5.** Idaho **8.** Colorado
 art objects . . **9.** artifacts
 group . . **6.** ethnos
 self . . **2.** id **8.** instinct
primness . . . **8.** neatness, niceness
9. stiffness **11.** preciseness
primo . . . **5.** chief, first **12.** leading tenor
primordial . . . **7.** primary **8.** original
9. elemental, primitive **10.** prototypal
11. rudimentary **12.** first created
primrose (pert to) . . .
 called . . **10.** an innocent **13.** flower of
 youth
 color . . **6.** yellow **10.** snapdragon
 genus . . **7.** Primula **11.** Primulaceae
 green . . **5.** color
 League . . **13.** Conservatives (Eng)
 path . . **7.** sensual
prince . . . **4.** knez **5.** prinz **7.** dynasty,
monarch **8.** archduke **9.** potentate,
princekin, sovereign **10.** princeling

prince (pert to)...
  Albert.. **9.** frock coat
  allowance.. **8.** appenage
  petty.. **6.** satrap
princely... **5.** noble, regal, royal **6.** kingly
  10. munificent **11.** magnificent
princely Italian family... **4.** Este
Prince of...
  Afghanistan.. **4.** amir
  apostate angels.. **5.** Eblis
  Apostles.. **6.** St Paul **7.** St Peter
  darkness.. **5.** devil, Satan **7.** Ahriman
  demons.. **5.** devil **9.** Beelzebub
  destruction.. **9.** Tamerlane
  evil spirits.. **7.** Sammael
  liars.. **5.** Pinto
  Peace.. **7.** Messiah **11.** Jesus Christ
  Spanish poetry.. **4.** Vega
  the Church.. **8.** cardinal
  the ode.. **7.** Ronsard
  the sonnet.. **6.** Bellay **15.** Joachim du
    Bellay
  this world (Bib).. **5.** Satan
  Tunis.. **3.** bey
princess (pert to)...
  literally.. **5.** Sarah
  loved by Cupid.. **6.** Psyche
  loved by Zeus.. **6.** Europa
  Mohammed.. **5.** begum
  mythical.. **5.** Danae **8.** Atalanta
  royal.. **14.** eldest daughter
  Tyrian.. **4.** Dido (Elissa)
principal... **3.** top **4.** arch, head, main
  5. chief, major, prime **6.** Führer, leader,
  master, origin, source **7.** captain,
  leading, palmary, primary **8.** foremost
  9. important, organ stop, preceptor
  10. capital sum **11.** outstanding
principality... **6.** Monaco
principal meal (Rom)... **4.** cena
principle... **4.** rule **5.** axiom, canon,
  prana, tenet **6.** dictum **7.** precept,
  theorem **9.** essential **10.** foundation
principle (pert to)...
  active in tobacco.. **8.** nicotine
  distance.. **11.** perspective
  Hindu.. **5.** Sakti
  life, theosophy.. **5.** prana, tenet
  musical.. **8.** tonality
  vital.. **4.** soul **5.** anima
principles... **5.** creed **9.** generalia
  10. essentials **12.** generalities
princox, princock... **7.** coxcomb **9.** pert
  youth
prink... **4.** deck, wink **5.** adorn, preen,
  primp **6.** bedeck, glance **7.** dress up
print... **5.** stamp **7.** edition, engrave,
  impress, picture, publish **11.** indentation
printed (pert to)...
  defamation.. **5.** libel
  fabric.. **4.** silk **6.** calico **7.** percale
  sheets.. **8.** pamphlet
printer... **8.** pressman **9.** publisher
  11. typographer **12.** lithographer
printer (pert to)...
  aid.. **5.** devil **10.** apprentice
  dauber.. **5.** biron
  direction.. **4.** stet
  hand ink roller.. **6.** brayer
  ink pad.. **6.** dabber
  manuscript.. **4.** copy

mark.. **4.** dash, stet **5.** caret, serif, tilde
  8. asterisk
measure.. **2.** em, en **4.** pica
type, mixed.. **3.** pie (pi)
printing (pert to)...
  blur.. **6.** mackle, macule
  cylinder.. **6.** rounce
  error.. **7.** erratum
  form.. **3.** die
  for the blind.. **7.** braille
  mark.. **4.** dele **6.** diesis **8.** ellipsis
  measure.. **2.** em, en **5.** agate
  metal block.. **4.** quad
  press part.. **6.** platen, rounce **7.** frisket
prion... **6.** petrel **7.** sea bird
prior... **3.** ere **4.** fore, past **6.** before,
  former **8.** previous, priorate
  9. preceding **10.** antecedent
priority... **10.** precedence **11.** order of
  time
priory... **5.** abbey **8.** cloister
priscan... **9.** primitive
Priscian... **7.** grammar **10.** grammarian
Priscilla (pert to)...
  Bib.. **16.** Christian convert
  color.. **7.** fog blue
  Hist.. **7.** Puritan
  husband.. **9.** John Alden
  tale.. **24.** Courtship of Myles Standish
prism (optical device)... **5.** Porro
prismatic... **10.** iridescent, variegated
prison... **3.** jug **4.** brig, gaol, jail, keep,
  quod **5.** clink **6.** carcer **10.** guardhouse
  12. penitentiary
prison (pert to)...
  courtyard.. **4.** quad
  English (old).. **7.** Newgate **9.** Bridewell
  French.. **8.** Bastille
  guarded.. **10.** panopticon
  keeper.. **5.** guard **6.** gaoler, jailer,
    keeper, warden **7.** turnkey
  Russian.. **5.** gulag
  slang.. **3.** jug **4.** quod, rock **5.** clink,
    limbo **6.** cooler **7.** slammer **8.** big
    house, hoosegow
  spy.. **6.** canary, mouton
Prisoner of...
  Chillon.. **16.** Francois Bonivard
  Vatican.. **4.** Pope
prisoner's release... **6.** parole
pristine... **7.** primary **8.** original
  9. primitive
prittle-prattle... **7.** chatter, prattle
  8. chitchat **9.** chatterer, empty talk
privacy... **7.** privity, retreat, secrecy
  8. solitude **9.** seclusion
private... **5.** privy **6.** covert, secret
  7. one's own **8.** esoteric, eyes-
  only, hush-hush, personal, secluded,
  separate, solitary **11.** sequestered
  12. confidential **15.** uncommunicative
privateer... **4.** Kidd (Capt) **5.** caper
  6. pirate **7.** corsair, soldier (not enlisted)
  9. freelance
privately... **5.** aside **6.** secret **8.** in secret
  10. personally, unofficial **12.** unofficially
privation... **4.** loss, want **6.** misery
  7. poverty **8.** hardship **10.** divestment
  11. destitution
privilege... **3.** soc, use **5.** favor, right
  7. charter **8.** easement **9.** advantage

10. concession **12.** carte blanche
privileged . . . **6.** exempt **8.** licensed
priveleged ones . . . **5.** haves
prix . . . **5.** prize
prize . . . **3.** cup **5.** award, booty, Detur (Harvard), medal, plate, price, purse, stake, value **6.** assess, esteem, ribbon, trophy **7.** premium, respect **8.** treasure
prize fight . . . **2.** go, KO **3.** TKO **4.** bout, spar **6.** boxing **7.** contest **8.** knockout, pugilism **10.** fisticuffs
pro . . . **3.** aye, for **6.** before **8.** behalf of **9.** in front of **12.** professional
probability . . . **4.** odds **6.** chance, shoo-in (sl) **7.** vantage **9.** liability **10.** conclusion, good chance, likelihood, likeliness **11.** credibility
probe . . . **3.** dig **4.** prod, tent **5.** sound **6.** feeler, pierce, search, stylet **7.** examine, explore, feel out, inquiry **10.** instrument, scrutinize
probity . . . **6.** virtue **7.** honesty **9.** integrity, rectitude **11.** uprightness
problem . . . **3.** nut **4.** crux, knot **6.** enigma, riddle **7.** theorem **8.** question **9.** situation
pro bono publico . . . **16.** for the public good
proboscis . . . **4.** beak, nose **5.** snout, trunk
procaccia . . . **4.** cart (carrier's) **7.** carrier
procacious . . . **4.** pert **8.** insolent, petulant
procacity . . . **8.** pertness **9.** insolence, petulance
Procavis . . . **4.** cony **5.** hyrax **6.** rabbit
procedure . . . **4.** step **5.** order **6.** custom, method, policy, system **7.** process **8.** behavior **11.** continuance
proceed . . . **2.** go **4.** fare, move, pass, wend **5.** arise, issue **6.** derive **7.** emanate **8.** continue, progress **9.** originate
proceed (pert to) . . .
hastily . . **5.** speed
leisurely . . **5.** amble, mosey (mosy)
on one's way . . **4.** wend
rapidly . . **4.** zoom **6.** gallop
proceeding . . . **4.** step **5.** actum **6.** course **7.** conduct, measure, process **8.** activity, behavior **9.** procedure **11.** transaction
proceeding (pert to) . . .
by threes . . **7.** ternary
from earth . . **8.** telluric
from the sun . . **5.** polar
proceedings . . . **4.** acta **5.** trial **6.** doings **7.** affairs, lawsuit, minutes **8.** activity
proceeds . . . **4.** gain, goes **6.** income **7.** marches, profits, returns
procerity . . . **6.** height **8.** tallness
process . . . **4.** cook, writ **5.** lapse (of time), order **6.** course, notice **7.** advance, mandate, summons **8.** progress **9.** emanation, operation, outgrowth, procedure, sterilize
process (pert to) . . .
beak (small) . . **9.** rostrulum
electroplating, steeling . . **8.** acierage
fabric coloring . . **5.** batik
fish (winglike) . . **3.** fin
in organisms . . **6.** moisis
of development . . **7.** nascent

pointed . . **3.** awn
steel making . . **8.** Bessemer **11.** cementation
surveying . . **13.** triangulation
transferring pictures . . **5.** decal **12.** decalcomania
procession . . . **4.** file **5.** train **6.** parade **7.** cortege **8.** sequence **9.** formation
prochein, prochain . . . **4.** next **7.** nearest
proclaim . . . **4.** nype (sl), tout **5.** blaze, voice **6.** herald **7.** declare, enounce, presage, publish **8.** announce **10.** promulgate
proclamation . . . **4.** fiat **5.** bando, banns (bans) **6.** blaze, edict, ukase **8.** decree, notice **9.** manifesto **12.** announcement, promulgation
proclivity . . . **4.** bent **6.** desire **7.** leaning **8.** tendency **10.** propensity **11.** disposition, inclination
procrastinate . . . **5.** defer, delay, stall **7.** soldier **8.** postpone
procrastination . . . **5.** delay, stall **7.** laxness **10.** hesitation **11.** vacillation **12.** dilatoriness
procrastinator . . . **7.** delayer, trifler **8.** deferrer
procreant . . . **8.** fruitful **9.** producing **10.** generating **11.** propagative
Procrustes (Gr legend) . . . **10.** highwayman (Attica) **14.** Procrustean bed
procurator . . . **5.** agent **6.** lawyer **7.** proctor, steward
procure . . . **3.** get **4.** gain **5.** bring, fetch **6.** effect, elicit, induce, obtain **7.** acquire **8.** contrive, purchase
prod . . . **3.** egg, jab **4.** goad, poke, urge **6.** thrust
prodigal . . . **4.** cloy **6.** lavish **7.** spender **9.** plentiful **10.** squanderer **11.** extravagant, intemperate, spendthrift, squandering
prodigality . . . **5.** waste **9.** abundance **12.** extravagance, intemperance **13.** superabundant
prodigious . . . **4.** huge **5.** great **7.** amazing, immense **8.** enormous **9.** marvelous, monstrous, wonderful **10.** miraculous, portentous, tremendous **11.** astonishing **13.** extraordinary
prodigy . . . **4.** omen, sign **6.** genius, marvel, oddity, wonder **7.** miracle
prodition . . . **7.** treason **8.** betrayal
produce . . . **2.** do **4.** bear, make, show, wage **5.** carry, cause, stage, yield **6.** author, create, effect **7.** exhibit, product **8.** engender, generate, receipts **9.** originate **10.** accomplish **11.** merchandise
produce (pert to) . . .
copy of . . **4.** type
effect . . **3.** act
ideas . . **6.** ideate
noise . . **5.** sound
produced . . . **8.** extended **9.** elongated, prolonged
produced (pert to) . . .
by heat . . **7.** igneous **8.** volcanic
by kitchen gardens . . **7.** olitory **8.** potherbs

by wind . . **7.** aeolian
regularly . . **6.** staple
producer . . . **4.** doer **6.** farmer, parent
  7. creator **10.** theaterman
  12. manufacturer
producing (pert to) . . .
  cold . . **7.** algific
  fire . . **8.** sparking
  illusions . . **15.** phantasmagorial
  poison . . **6.** septic
product . . . **3.** sum **4.** crop **5.** fruit
  6. result **7.** hormone **8.** artifact, creation
  9. commodity, outgrowth
production . . . **3.** hit **4.** book, work **5.** fruit
  7. produce **8.** creation **9.** execution,
  extension **14.** accomplishment
productive . . . **4.** rich **7.** fertile, gainful
  8. creative, fruitful **9.** inventive
  10. generative
proem . . . **7.** preface, prelude **8.** foreword,
  preamble **12.** introduction
profane . . . **6.** misuse, unholy, wicked
  7. godless, impious, ungodly, worldly
  8. temporal **9.** desecrate **10.** unhallowed
  11. blasphemous, unspiritual
  12. unsanctified
profess . . . **4.** avow **5.** claim, feign
  6. affirm, allege **7.** declare
  11. acknowledge
profession . . . **5.** claim, faith, trade
  6. avowal, career, metier **7.** calling,
  pretext **8.** vocation **9.** testimony
  10. occupation **11.** affirmation
  14. acknowledgment
professional . . . **4.** paid **5.** hired **6.** expert
  7. skilled, trained **8.** finished
professional, non . . . **3.** lay **4.** laic
  7. amateur **9.** unskilled
proffer . . . **3.** bid **4.** give **5.** offer **6.** tender
proficient . . . **3.** apt **5.** adept **6.** expert,
  versed **7.** skilled **12.** accomplished
profile . . . **4.** draw, form **7.** contour,
  diagram, outline, picture **9.** biography
  14. representation
profit . . . **3.** net **4.** boot, gain, good,
  mend **5.** avail **6.** return **7.** benefit, rake-
  off, results **8.** interest **9.** advantage
  11. share of gain **12.** remuneration
profitable . . . **6.** paying, useful **7.** helpful
  8. repaying **9.** expedient, lucrative
  10. beneficial **12.** remunerative
profligate . . . **6.** wicked **7.** corrupt,
  spender, vicious **8.** depraved, prodigal,
  wasteful **9.** abandoned, dissolute,
  reprobate **10.** overthrown
  11. extravagant
profound . . . **4.** deep, wise **5.** heavy
  7. abysmal, intense, learned **8.** abstruse,
  complete, deep-felt, poignant
  9. downright, recondite, sagacious
  11. far-reaching **12.** encompassing,
  unfathomable **13.** thoroughgoing
profundity . . . **5.** depth **6.** wisdom
  8. deepness **12.** abstruseness
profuse . . . **6.** galore, lavish **7.** diffuse,
  liberal, palaver **8.** abundant, generous,
  numerous, prodigal, wasteful
  9. bountiful **10.** munificent
  11. extravagant, overflowing
profusion . . . **6.** plenty **9.** abundance
  11. diffuseness, prodigality

12. extravagance, lavish supply
progenitor . . . **4.** sire **6.** parent **8.** ancestor
  9. precursor **10.** forefather
progenitor of giants (Norse Myth) . . .
  4. Ymir **8.** rime-cold
progeny . . . **3.** son **4.** race **5.** issue
  6. family **7.** outcome **8.** children,
  daughter, outbirth **9.** offspring,
  parentage, resultant **11.** descendants
prognosis . . . **7.** outlook **8.** forecast
  9. diagnosis **10.** prediction
  14. interpretation
prognosticate . . . **4.** bode, omen
  7. betoken, predict, presage **8.** forebode,
  foreshow, foretell, prophecy
  9. foretoken
program, programme . . . **4.** bill (printed),
  card, plan **5.** edict **6.** notice, policy
  7. outline **8.** bulletin, platform,
  schedule, syllabus **9.** broadcast,
  catalogue, programma **10.** prospectus
  12. proclamation, prolegomenon
  13. advertisement
programma . . . **5.** edict **6.** decree, notice
  7. preface **12.** prolegomenon
progress . . . **4.** fare, tour, wend **5.** march
  6. course, travel **7.** advance, journey
  10. expedition **11.** progression
progress (pert to) . . .
  chart . . **5.** Gantt
  clumsily . . **8.** scramble
  intelligently . . **6.** egress **7.** telesis (telesia)
  laborious . . **4.** plod, wade
  outward . . **6.** egress
  weakly . . **6.** feebly
progressive . . . **6.** modern, onward
  7. forward, gradual, liberal
  9. advancing, improving **11.** consecutive
  12. enterprising
prohibit . . . **3.** ban, bar, bid **5.** debar,
  estop, taboo (tabu) **6.** enjoin, forbid,
  hinder **7.** prevent **9.** interdict
prohibited . . . **7.** illegal, illicit **8.** unlawful
prohibition . . . **3.** ban **7.** embargo
  8. estoppel **9.** exclusion **10.** prevention,
  temperance **11.** forbiddance
  12. interdicting
project . . . **3.** jet, jut **4.** abut, cast, idea,
  plan **5.** shoot **6.** beetle, design, device,
  scheme **7.** pattern, problem **8.** contrive,
  proposal, protrude **9.** intention
  10. conception **11.** undertaking
projectile . . . **4.** bomb **5.** shell **6.** bullet,
  rocket **7.** missile, torpedo **8.** parabola
  9. cartridge
projection . . . **3.** arm, ear, fin, jag,
  toe **4.** barb, cape, lobe, ness, prop,
  snag **5.** apsis, bulge, ledge, prong,
  redan, socle, tenon **6.** lobule, tappet
  8. headland
prolific . . . **6.** fecund **7.** fertile, teeming
  8. fruitful **9.** inventive **10.** generative
  11. propagative **12.** reproductive
prolix . . . **5.** wordy **7.** diffuse, verbose
  8. tiresome **9.** prolonged, rigmarole,
  wearisome **10.** long-winded, pleonastic,
  protracted
prolocutor . . . **6.** orator **7.** speaker,
  teacher **8.** chairman **9.** spokesman
  10. mouthpiece **11.** Lord Speaker (Eng)
prolong . . . **4.** spin **7.** draw out **8.** continue,

lengthen, postpone, protract
prolonged . . . **7.** chronic, delayed
8. extended **9.** continued, postponed
10. lengthened, protracted
promenade . . . **4.** mall, walk **6.** airing,
marina, pasear **7.** alameda, gallery
Prometheus (pert to) . . .
famed as . . **5.** Titan (a)
poem (Shelley) . . **17.** Prometheus
Unbound
tale, tragedy . . **15.** Prometheus Bound
16. Prometheus Loosed **24.** Prometheus
the Fire Bringer
prominence . . . **4.** cusp **6.** height
8. eminence, prestige, salience
9. greatness **10.** famousness,
importance **11.** distinction, obviousness,
prosiliency **12.** distinctness,
protuberance
prominent . . . **4.** high, star **5.** great
6. famous, marked **7.** obvious, salient
8. distinct, manifest **9.** important
10. celebrated, noticeable, prosilient,
protruding **11.** conspicuous, distinctive,
outstanding **13.** distinguished
promiscuous . . . **5.** mixed **8.** careless
9. haphazard, orderless
14. indiscriminate
promise . . . **3.** vow **4.** hope, oath **5.** swear
6. engage, parole, pledge, plight, votive
(by vow) **7.** betroth, predict **8.** affiance,
contract, give hope **9.** assurance, ray
of hope **11.** declaration
Promised Land . . . **6.** heaven, utopia
8. Paradise **9.** millenium, Shangri-La
11. Happy Valley **13.** Celestial City
promontory . . . **3.** tor **4.** cape, naze
(nase), ness, scaw **5.** mount, point
8. headland **10.** projection
promote . . . **4.** help **5.** exalt, nurse
6. extend, prefer **7.** actuate, advance,
dignify, elevate, finance, further,
improve **8.** increase **9.** advertise,
encourage, patronize
promoter . . . **5.** agent **6.** backer **7.** planner
8. lobbyist **9.** financier, publicist
promotion . . . **6.** brevet **7.** advance
10. preferment **11.** advertising,
furtherance, improvement
prompt . . . **3.** cue **4.** easy, hint, soon,
tell, yare (anc) **5.** alert, early, quick,
ready **6.** advise, remind **7.** animate,
suggest **8.** punctual **11.** expeditious
prompter . . . **3.** aid **4.** cuer **6.** pit man,
reader **7.** inducer, reciter **8.** reminder
promptly . . . **4.** tite (anc) **6.** at once
7. quickly **9.** willingly
promulgate . . . **7.** declare, publish
8. proclaim **9.** make known
prone . . . **3.** apt **4.** bent, flat **5.** apish
6. supine **7.** willing **8.** downward
9. prostrate, recumbent
13. ventricumbent
prone to sin . . . **8.** peccable
prong . . . **3.** nib, peg **4.** fang, fork, tine
5. spike, tooth **6.** branch
pronghorn . . . **6.** cabree (cabrie) **9.** prong
buck, springbok
prong key . . . **7.** spanner
pronoun . . . **2.** he, it, me, my, us, we, ye
3. her, him, one, she, thy, who, you

4. that, thee, them, they, thou, what,
your **5.** these, those **6.** itself, myself
7. herself, himself, oneself, ourself
8. one's self, yourself **9.** ourselves
10. themselves
pronoun (possessive) . . . **2.** my **3.** her,
his, its, our **4.** hers, mine, one's, ours,
your **5.** their, yours **6.** theirs
pronounce . . . **3.** say **5.** bless (holy),
speak, utter **6.** affirm, assert **7.** adjudge,
declare, deliver **8.** announce
9. enunciate **10.** adjudicate, articulate,
assibilate
pronouncement . . . **6.** decree **8.** judgment
9. manifesto **11.** affirmation, declaration
12. announcement
pronto . . . **5.** quick **7.** quickly **8.** promptly
11. immediately
pronunciation . . . **4.** burr **8.** orthoepy
9. utterance (clear) **11.** enunciation
pronunciation mark . . . **5.** tilde **7.** cedilla
8. dieresis
proof . . . **4.** test **5.** trial **6.** result **7.** outcome
8. evidence **9.** testimony **11.** galley
proof **12.** confirmation, verification
13. certification
proofreader's mark . . . **4.** dele, stet
5. caret, space
prop . . . **3.** beg, gib, nog **5.** brace, shore,
sprag, staff, stell **6.** shorer **7.** fulcrum,
support **9.** stanchion
propagate . . . **5.** breed **6.** extend,
spread **7.** diffuse, publish **8.** disperse,
engender, generate, increase, multiply,
transmit
propel . . . **3.** row **4.** pole, push, urge
5. drive, impel **7.** project
propeller . . . **3.** fan, gun, oar **4.** vane
5. screw **6.** driver **9.** plane part
propensity . . . **4.** bent **6.** desire **7.** leaning
8. aptitude, tendency **9.** proneness
10. proclivity **11.** disposition, inclination
proper . . . **3.** fit **4.** fine, just, meet,
prim, smug **5.** exact, right **6.** chaste,
decent, goodly, honest, kilter **7.** correct
8. decorous, inherent, orthodox,
suitable **9.** excellent, expedient
11. appropriate, grammatical,
respectable **12.** conventional
properly . . . **5.** fitly **7.** rightly, utterly
8. decently, strictly, suitably **9.** correctly
11. expediently **14.** conventionally
proper sense of worth . . . **5.** pride
property . . . **3.** res **4.** bona, gear
5. asset, goods, trait **6.** estate, nature,
realty, wealth **8.** holdings **9.** attribute,
copyright, ownership **10.** real estate
11. peculiarity, possessions
14. characteristic
property (pert to) . . .
act to regain . . **8.** replevin (repleven)
destruction of . . **8.** sabotage **9.** vandalism
landed property . . **9.** cadastral
light without heat . . **15.** phosphorescence
movable . . **4.** gear **8.** chattels
no private ownership . . **11.** aspheterism
of matter . . **7.** inertia
one's own . . **7.** alodium
right . . **4.** lien
stolen . . **4.** loot, pelf **5.** lucre, spoil
suit for recovery . . **6.** trover

transferrer . . **7.** alienor, grantor
wife to husband . . **3.** dos
woman's (Hindu) . . **9.** stridhana
(stridhan)
prophecy . . . **6.** oracle **9.** utterance
10. divination, prediction **11.** foretelling
prophesy . . . **4.** osse **5.** augur **6.** divine
7. predict, presage **8.** forecast,
foreshow, foretell **10.** vaticinate
11. preindicate **13.** prognosticate
prophet . . . **4.** seer **6.** medium, oracle
7. psychic **8.** Mohammed, preacher,
presager **9.** John Smith, predictor
10. soothsayer **11.** Joseph Smith
(Mormon)
prophet (Bib) . . . **4.** Amos **5.** Cyrus, Hosea
6. Elijah (Elias) **7.** Malachi, Obadiah
prophet, murder of . . . **8.** vaticide
prophetess . . . **5.** sibyl **7.** seeress
9. Cassandra (of evil)
prophetic, prophetical . . . **5.** vatic
6. mantic **7.** fateful, vatical **8.** oracular
9. vaticinal **10.** divinatory, presageful
11. predicative
propinquity . . . **7.** kinship **8.** nearness
9. proximity **12.** neighborhood,
relationship **13.** consanguinity
propitiate . . . **5.** atone **6.** pacify **8.** atone
for **10.** conciliate
propitiation . . . **9.** atonement, expiation
12. pacification, satisfaction
14. reconciliation
propitious . . . **4.** rosy **5.** happy, lucky
6. benign, timely **7.** helpful **9.** favorable,
opportune, promising **10.** auspicious,
benevolent, prosperous
12. advantageous, well-disposed
proponent . . . **8.** advocate **10.** propounder
proportion . . . **4.** part, rate **5.** quota, ratio,
share **6.** adjust, extent **7.** analogy,
compare, euphony, prorate **8.** equalize,
symmetry **9.** apportion
proportional . . . **4.** rate **8.** relative
10. comparable, respective
11. dimensional
proportionate . . . **5.** equal **8.** adequate,
relative **9.** analogous **10.** respective
11. comparative **13.** corresponding
proposal . . . **3.** bid **4.** plan **5.** offer
6. feeler, motion **8.** marriage **9.** intention
10. nomination, suggestion
11. proposition, supposition
propose . . . **5.** image, offer, state,
toast **6.** intend, submit **7.** purpose
8. nominate, propound **9.** postulate
proposed (pert to) . . .
for consideration . . **9.** suggested
for debate . . **6.** mooted
international language . . **2.** Ro **3.** Ido
9. Esperanto
proposition . . . **4.** plan **5.** axiom, lemma
6. porism, thesis **7.** project **8.** empirema,
proposal **9.** corollary **11.** supposition,
undertaking
proposition, proof of . . . **18.** reductio
ad absurdum
propound . . . **6.** submit **7.** propose **8.** set
forth **9.** postulate
proprietary . . . **5.** owner, title **8.** interest,
medicine (secret) **9.** ownership
10. proprietor **12.** landed estate

propriety . . . **7.** decency, decorum,
fitness **8.** standard **9.** ownership
10. convention, expedience, properness
11. correctness, suitability
12. tastefulness **13.** possessorship
propugnaculum . . . **7.** bulwark, defense
8. fortress
prorogue . . . **5.** defer **6.** extend **7.** adjourn,
prolong **8.** postpone, protract
prosaic . . . **4.** drab, dull, flat **5.** plain,
prosy **6.** prolix, stupid **7.** humdrum,
insipid, tedious **8.** ordinary, tiresome
10. unexciting **11.** commonplace
12. matter-of-fact **13.** unimaginative
proscribe . . . **3.** ban **6.** forbid, outlaw
7. condemn (to death) **8.** prohibit,
restrain **9.** interdict, ostracize
proscription . . . **5.** exile **8.** outlawry
11. prohibition **12.** interdiction
prosecute . . . **3.** sue **4.** urge **5.** chase
6. intend (law), pursue **7.** carry on,
enforce, execute
prosecutor . . . **6.** lawyer **7.** accuser,
relator **8.** attorney
proselyte . . . **3.** ger (to Judaism)
7. convert
proseuche, proseucha . . . **7.** oratory
9. synagogue **13.** place of prayer
prosody . . . **13.** versification
prospect . . . **4.** view **5.** buyer, scene, vista
6. survey **7.** explore, foresee, outlook
8. customer **9.** applicant, candidate,
foresight, intention **10.** contestant
11. probability **12.** anticipation
prosper . . . **4.** fare **5.** cheve, speed
6. thrive **7.** succeed **8.** flourish
prosperity . . . **3.** hap, ups **4.** boom, weal
6. thrift **7.** success, welfare **9.** well-being
11. good fortune
Prospero (pert to) . . .
character . . **9.** Ferdinand
daughter . . **7.** Miranda
servant . . **5.** Ariel
slave . . **7.** Caliban
The Tempest . . **11.** Duke of Milan
prosperous . . . **4.** weal **5.** lucky, palmy,
sonsy (sonsie) **7.** wealthy **8.** thriving
9. favorable, fortunate **10.** auspicious,
successful **11.** flourishing
prostitute . . . **4.** drab **5.** venal **6.** harlot
7. corrupt **8.** infamous **12.** street walker
prostrate . . . **4.** flat, raze **5.** abase, prone
6. fallen, grieve, supine **7.** exhaust
8. helpless, supinate **9.** flattened,
recumbent **10.** obsequious, submissive
prosy . . . **3.** dry **4.** dull **6.** jejune
7. prosaic, tedious **11.** commonplace
13. plain-speaking
protagonist . . . **4.** hero, lead (theater)
5. actor **6.** leader **8.** advocate,
champion, defender **9.** contender,
principal, spokesman **11.** participant
Protagoras (Gr) . . . **7.** Sophist, teacher
11. philosopher
protasis . . . **5.** maxim **9.** drama part
11. proposition **12.** introduction
protect . . . **3.** arm **4.** save **5.** guard
6. defend, insure, police, screen, sheath,
shield **7.** cherish, shelter **8.** enshield,
preserve **9.** safeguard
protected . . . **5.** armed **6.** shaded

7. aproned, guarded 8. shielded
12. invulnerable
protection . . . 3. bib, lee 4. coat, fort,
moat 5. aegis (egis), apron, armor,
guard, shade, shell, smock 6. glacis,
refuge, safety 7. defense, parapet,
shelter 8. havelock, passport, security
11. safekeeping 12. preservation
protector . . . 6. patron, regent
8. defender, guardian 10. safekeeper
protector of vineyards (Gr) . . . 7. Priapus
protégé . . . 4. ward 6. charge 9. dependent
Proteida . . . 7. Proteus 10. amphibians
11. salamanders
protein . . . 6. casein 7. albumin, mucedin,
peptone 8. globulin, lecithin, nutrient
9. protamine 11. chlorophyll
protein (pert to) . . .
blood . . 6. fibrin 8. globulin
castor oil bean . . 5. ricin (poison)
egg . . 7. albumin
milk . . 6. casein
muscles . . 8. creatine
seeds . . 7. edestin 8. aleurone, prolamin
Proteles . . . 8. aardwolf
protest . . . 4. aver, beef, deny 6. assert
7. declare 9. objection, stipulate
10. asseverate 11. expostulate
13. expostulation
protestation . . . 6. avowal (public)
7. protest 11. affirmation, obtestation
12. asseveration, supplication
Proteus (pert to) . . .
biology . . 3. olm 6. amoeba 8. bacteria
10. salamander
Gr Myth . . 6. sea god
Shakespeare . . 17. Gentleman of Verona
protocol . . . 5. rules (official) 7. compact
8. schedule 9. agreement, etiquette
10. memorandum (diplomatic)
12. original copy
protograph . . . 9. holograph
12. illustration (of species)
protoplasm . . . 5. spore 7. nucleus
9. archetype, cytoplasm 10. primordium
11. basis of life
protoplasmic (pert to) . . .
body . . 8. ectosark 9. ectoplasm,
endoplasm
cell . . 6. amoeba (ameba)
cell contents . . 9. metaplasm
substance . . 3. gel
protozoan . . . 6. amoeba (ameba),
Lobosa, phylum 11. unicellular
protract . . . 4. spin 5. defer, delay
6. extend 7. prolong, stretch 8. continue,
elongate, lengthen, postpone, protrude
9. expatiate
protrude . . . 3. jut 5. bulge 6. exsert
7. project 9. thrust out
protuberance . . . 3. jag, nub, wen 4. boss,
bump, cere, hump, knob, knot, lobe,
lump, node, snag, wart 5. bulge,
caput, inion, knurl, torus 8. eminence,
swelling 9. extrusion 10. projection
proud . . . 4. vain 5. grand, lofty, noble
6. elated, lordly 7. haughty, pleased,
stately, valiant 8. arrogant, boastful,
imposing, splendid 9. conceited,
gratified 10. impressive
11. independent, magisterial,

magnificent 12. presumptuous,
supercilious
prove . . . 3. try 4. test 5. check, nurse
6. evince, try out, verify 7. confirm,
justify, probate 8. identify, manifest
9. ascertain, establish 11. corroborate,
demonstrate
prove false . . . 6. refute
Provencal dialect . . . 9. langue d'oc
provender . . . 3. hay 4. food 5. grain
6. fodder 8. ensilage
proverb . . . 3. saw 5. adage, axiom
6. byword, enigma, saying 8. aphorism,
link verb, paroemia
proverbial . . . 10. aphoristic
11. sententious 12. epigrammatic
provide . . . 4. give 5. cater, endow, endue,
equip, stock, treat, yield 6. afford,
ration, supply 7. care for, finance
9. make ready 10. contribute
provided . . . 2. if, so 5. boden 6. sobeit
8. afforded, equipped, prepared,
supplied 11. on condition
13. conditionally
Providence founder . . . 13. Roger
Williams (1636)
provident . . . 4. wise 6. frugal, saving
7. prudent, thrifty 9. judicious
10. economical 11. precautious,
preparatory
providential . . . 5. lucky 7. prudent
9. opportune, provident 10. miraculous
11. foresighted
province . . . 4. area, beat, nome 5. arena,
range, shire, tract 6. colony, domain,
empire, eparch, region, sphere 7. circuit,
diocese, kingdom 8. district 9. territory
10. palatinate (royal) 12. jurisdiction
provincial . . . 4. rude 5. crude, local,
rural 6. narrow 7. insular, limited
8. suburban 10. restricted, uncultured
11. countrified 12. narrow-minded
15. unsophisticated
provincialism (diction) . . . 6. patois
10. patavinity
provision . . . 4. fare, food 5. board, stock,
store 6. vivres 7. proviso 9. condition
11. preparation
provisional . . . 9. makeshift, temporary,
tentative 10. promissory, substitute
11. conditional, preparatory
12. experimental 14. circumstantial
provision seller (Mil) . . . 6. sutler
proviso . . . 5. salvo 6. clause
provocative . . . 9. desirable, provoking
10. appetizing, stirring up, suggestive
11. interesting
provoke . . . 3. ire, vex 4. bate, goad,
move, rile, spur, stir 5. anger, annoy,
start 6. arouse, incite, induce, invite,
invoke, nettle, offend, stir up, summon
7. incense 8. irritate 9. challenge
10. antagonize, exasperate
provoking . . . 8. annoying, exciting
10. suggestive 11. interesting
12. antagonizing
provoking laughter . . . 7. risible
prow . . . 3. bow 4. beak, duty, good, proa,
stem 5. brave, honor, prore 6. steven
7. courage, gallant, gun deck
prowess . . . 5. valor 9. gallantry

proximal . . . **9.** immediate (opp of distal)
proximate . . . **4.** next **6.** direct **7.** closest, nearest **9.** immediate **10.** succeeding
proximity . . . **8.** nearness, nighness, relation, vicinity **9.** adjacence, closeness **11.** propinquity
proxy . . . **5.** agent, power **6.** agency, ballot, deputy **7.** proctor **9.** authority **10.** procurator, substitute
prudence . . . **6.** virtue, wisdom **7.** caution, economy **8.** sagacity **9.** foresight **11.** calculation, forethought **13.** judiciousness **14.** circumspection
prudent . . . **4.** wary, wise **5.** canny **6.** frugal **8.** cautious, discreet **9.** judicious, penny-wise, provident **10.** economical **11.** circumspect, considerate
prudish . . . **4.** prim **8.** priggish
prune . . . **3.** cut, lop **4.** clip, food, frog, plum, trim, weed **5.** dress, plume, preen, purge, shape **6.** anoint **7.** cut down, tonsure **9.** simpleton
prunelike fruit . . . **9.** myrobalan
pruning knife . . . **8.** serpette
prurient . . . **7.** itching, longing, lustful **10.** lascivious
Prussia . . .
 bay . . **4.** Kiel **6.** Danzig **10.** Pomeranian
 cathedral city . . **5.** Essen **7.** Cologne **10.** Düsseldorf
 city . . **6.** Aachen
 color . . **4.** blue **12.** gold pheasant
 Knight . . **8.** Noachite
 lagoon . . **4.** haff **12.** Frisches Haff
 lancer . . **5.** Uhlan
 land aristocracy . . **6.** Junker
 legislature . . **7.** Landtag
 mountain . . **4.** Harz
 resort . . **3.** Ems
 river . . **3.** Ems **4.** Elbe, Oder, Saar
 seaport . . **4.** Kiel **5.** Emden **7.** Stettin
 State . . **6.** German
pry . . . **4.** nose, peek **5.** lever, mouse, snoop **6.** meddle, search
prying . . . **7.** curious, peeking, peeping, peering **8.** snooping **9.** searching **10.** meddlesome **11.** inquisitive
psalm (pert to) . . .
 book . . **7.** Psalter
 Fiftieth, Vulgate . . **8.** Miserere
 Mass opening . . **7.** introit
 Ninety-fourth, Vulgate . . **6.** Venite
Psalms (Old Test) . . . **7.** Psalter
psalterium . . . **4.** lyra **6.** omasum **7.** stomach **9.** manyplies
psammite . . . **4.** rock **9.** sandstone
psephology . . . **7.** pebbles (study of)
psephomancy . . . **19.** divination by pebbles
pseudatoll . . . **9.** coral reef
pseudo . . . **4.** sham **5.** bogus, false **6.** untrue **7.** feigned **8.** spurious **9.** deceptive, imitation, pretender
pseudologist . . . **4.** liar (humorous)
pseudology . . . **5.** lying **8.** falsehood
pseudonym . . . **5.** alias **6.** anonym **7.** pen name **10.** nom de plume
pseudonym (famed) . . .
 C L Dodgson . . **12.** Lewis Carroll
 Mary Ann Evans . . **11.** George Eliot

Samuel Clemens . . **9.** Mark Twain
W S Porter . . **6.** O Henry
psychagogic . . . **9.** inspiring **10.** attractive, persuasive
psyche . . . **4.** mind, self, soul **6.** spirit
psychedelic psychologist . . . **5.** Leary
psychic . . . **6.** mental **9.** spiritual **10.** Gnosticism **11.** incorporeal **12.** spiritualist, supernatural **13.** psychological
psychic (pert to) . . .
 emanation . . **4.** aura
 devotion . . **6.** autism
 monism . . **10.** one reality
psychotic . . . **3.** mad **6.** insane **8.** neurotic **12.** psychopathic
Ptah (pert to) . . .
 Egypt Relig . . **8.** chief god (of Memphis)
 father of . . **3.** men **4.** gods
 representation . . **5.** mummy
 symbolic of . . **4.** life **8.** strength
ptarmigan . . . **4.** rype **6.** grouse
pterodactyl . . . **7.** reptile (extinct) **9.** pterosaur **11.** ornithosaur
pterography (description of) . . . **8.** feathers
pteroid . . . **8.** fernlike, winglike
pteropod . . . **6.** Clione (Arctic) **7.** mollusk
ptilosis . . . **7.** plumage **9.** madarosis **10.** loss of hair **15.** loss of eyelashes
ptisan . . . **3.** tea **5.** drink **6.** coddle **9.** decoction
Ptolemy (pert to) . . .
 author of . . **8.** Almagest
 birthplace . . **5.** Egypt (130 AD)
 famed as . . **10.** astronomer, geographer
public . . . **3.** inn **4.** open **5.** state **6.** people, vulgar **8.** communal **9.** clientele, community
public (pert to) . . .
 assembly . . **4.** Diet
 conveyance . . **3.** bus, cab, car **4.** taxi, tram **5.** train **10.** jinrikisha (jinricksha)
 display . . **10.** exhibition **13.** exhibitionism
 edict . . **3.** ban **12.** proclamation
 entertainment . . **7.** ridotto
 hangman (Eng) . . **9.** Jack Ketch
 lands . . **4.** ager (Hist) **6.** domain
 official . . **6.** notary
 position . . **8.** official
 storehouse . . **5.** étape
 walk . . **4.** mall **7.** alameda **9.** esplanade, promenade
publication . . . **4.** book **8.** pamphlet, printing **12.** notification, proclamation, promulgation
publication (pert to) . . .
 article . . **7.** feature
 condensed . . **7.** tabloid
 make-up . . **6.** format
 prelim . . **9.** prodromus
publicist . . . **5.** solon **6.** Gallup, lawyer, writer **10.** journalist, publicizer **11.** commentator
publish . . . **4.** edit, vent **5.** issue, print **6.** blazon, delate **7.** divulge **8.** proclaim **10.** promulgate **11.** disseminate
publish (pert to) . . .
 abroad . . **8.** promulge
 after death . . **10.** posthumous
 banns . . **7.** betroth **8.** marriage

far and wide.. **6.** blazon
without authority.. **6.** pirate
  10. plagiarize
publisher's description (book)...
  5. blurb **13.** advertisement
publisher's inscription (book)... **5.** facts
  8. colophon
Puccini heroine ... **4.** Mimi
pucker ... **4.** fold **5.** bulge, purse **6.** crease
  7. anxiety, fluster, wrinkle **8.** contract
puckered ... **7.** bullate **8.** wrinkled
  10. contracted
puckish ... **6.** impish **8.** Pucklike
  10. mysterious **11.** mischievous
pud ... **3.** paw **4.** hand **8.** forefoot
pudding ... **4.** duff, mush, plum, sago
  6. junket **7.** custard, dessert, tapioca
  8. roly-poly, softness, stuffing (game)
  9. Yorkshire
puddle ... **3.** mud **4.** mess, pond, pool
  5. plash, swamp **6.** muddle **7.** plashet,
  pollute
puddle duck ... **7.** mallard
puddock ... **4.** kite, toad **7.** buzzard
  9. enclosure (paddock)
pueblo ... **4.** town **7.** village
Pueblo (pert to)...
  ceremonial chamber.. **4.** kiva
  Indian (American).. **4.** Hopi, Piro, Tano,
  Zuni **5.** Acoma **7.** Keresan **12.** cliff
  dweller
  water jar.. **4.** olla
puerile ... **4.** weak **5.** young **7.** babyish,
  trivial **8.** childish, juvenile, youthful
  12. simple-minded
Puerto Rican (pert to)...
  bark, beverage.. **4.** mabi
  dove.. **4.** rola
  fish.. **4.** sama, sisi **8.** porkfish
Puerto Rico ... see also Puerto Rican
  capital.. **7.** San Juan
  city.. **5.** Ponce **7.** Arecibo
  discoverer.. **8.** Columbus
  first settlement.. **7.** Caparra
  government.. **12.** Commonwealth
  Indian name.. **9.** Borinquen
  island (off shore).. **4.** Mona **7.** Culebra
  island group.. **15.** Greater Antilles
  politically.. **12.** Commonwealth
  program (Polit).. **18.** Operation Bootstrap
  sea.. **9.** Caribbean
puff ... **4.** blow, blub, chug, flam, pant,
  pegh (Scot), pouf, waff **5.** elate **7.** efflate
puffbird ... **6.** barbet **8.** barbacou
pug ... **3.** dog, elf **4.** moth, puck, snub
  5. chaff, dwarf **6.** harlot, refuse (grain),
  sprite **8.** bargeman, mistress, pugilist
  9. footprint, hobgoblin
pugging ... **8.** grasping, thieving
pugilistic ... **6.** fistic **10.** pugnacious
pugnacious ... **9.** combative
  11. belligerent, quarrelsome
pugnacious man ... **12.** fighting cock
pug-nosed ... **5.** camus (camuse)
puisne ... **4.** puny **5.** judge, later,
  petty **6.** feeble, junior **9.** associate,
  unskilled **10.** law student, subsequent
  11. subordinate
puissance ... **5.** force, might, power
  8. strength **9.** authority
puissant ... **6.** mighty, potent **7.** mastery

8. forcible, powerful **13.** authoritative
pulchritude ... **5.** grace **6.** beauty
  10. comeliness, loveliness
pule ... **4.** peep **5.** cheep, whine **7.** ululate,
  whimper
pulicat ... **8.** bandanna (bandana)
puling ... **6.** sickly **7.** babyish, howling,
  whining **8.** childish, delicate
Pulitzer prizes ... **6.** awards
  10. journalism, literature
pull ... **2.** pu **3.** lug, tow, tug **4.** drag,
  draw, haul, yank **5.** bouse, drink,
  tweak **6.** effort, strain **7.** attract, extract
  9. influence **10.** attraction
pull (pert to)...
  apart.. **4.** rend, tear **7.** destroy
  8. demolish, enfeeble, separate
  back.. **5.** demur **6.** recoil **7.** retract
  8. withdraw
  down.. **4.** fell, raze **9.** dismantle
  off.. **3.** pug **6.** avulse, commit **8.** carry
  out **10.** accomplish
  one's leg.. **4.** hoax, joke **7.** deceive,
  flatter **8.** hoodwink **9.** make fun of
  out.. **5.** leave **6.** secede **7.** extract
  9. eradicate
  up.. **4.** stop **5.** elate **6.** aviate **7.** arraign,
  extract
pullet ... **4.** fowl **5.** child **7.** bivalve
  8. poullard
pulley (pert to)...
  groove.. **5.** gorge
  grooved.. **5.** fusee (fuzee)
  part.. **4.** arse
  wheel.. **6.** sheave (grooved)
pulp ... **3.** pap **4.** marc, mash, mass
  5. chyme **8.** magazine **10.** fleshy part
pulpit ... **4.** ambo, bema, dais, desk
  5. stage **6.** clergy **7.** rostrum **8.** platform,
  scaffold
pulpy ... **5.** mushy **7.** squashy
pulpy (pert to)...
  dregs.. **5.** magma
  fruit.. **3.** uva **4.** pome **6.** sidder (siddow)
  state.. **4.** mash, soft **6.** fleshy
pulsate ... **4.** beat, drum **5.** throb
  7. vibrate
pulsation ... **5.** ictus **6.** moving, rhythm
  7. impulse, systole **8.** acrotism (failure)
  vitality **9.** throbbing, vibrating
pulsatory ... **8.** rhythmic, systolic
  9. throbbing
pulse ... **3.** dal (split) **5.** seeds (edible),
  throb **6.** rhythm **7.** beating **8.** resonate
  9. pulsation, throbbing
pulse family ... **3.** pea **8.** Fabaceae
pulverize ... **4.** bray, mull **5.** crush,
  grind **6.** abrade, powder **7.** atomize
  8. levigate **9.** triturate **12.** disintegrate
pulverulent ... **5.** dusty **7.** crumbly
  8. powdered
puma ... **6.** cougar **7.** Quechua (Kochua)
pummel ... **4.** beat, maul **5.** thump
  6. batter, buffet, hammer, pommel,
  strike
pump ... **3.** gin, ram **4.** draw, emit, quiz
  5. eject **6.** elicit, propel **7.** extract
  10. pulsometer **11.** interrogate
pumpernickel ... **5.** bread (Westphalian)
pump handle ... **5.** sweep, swipe
pumpkin (pert to)...

head.. **4.** dolt **7.** Puritan **9.** blockhead, Roundhead
seed.. **7.** sunfish **8.** sailboat
yam.. **11.** sweet potato
pun... **4.** yoke **8.** paragram **9.** assonance, equivoque (equivoke), witticism **11.** paronomasia
punch... **3.** die **4.** blow, poke, prod, tool **5.** douse, drink, negus, paste **6.** liquor, pierce **7.** mattoir (etcher's) **8.** beverage, puncture **9.** perforate **11.** punch cattle
Punch and Judy dog... **4.** Toby
Punch Bowl... **6.** crater **9.** graveyard (Honolulu), hot spring (Yellowstone)
puncheon... **3.** die **4.** cask **5.** punch, stamp **6.** dagger
puncher... **6.** cowboy **10.** cowpuncher, perforator
punching... **8.** piercing **9.** pertusion
punctilious... **4.** nice **5.** exact **6.** formal, strict **7.** correct, precise **8.** exacting **9.** observant **10.** meticulous, scrupulous
punctuation mark... **3.** dot **4.** dash, star **5.** brace, breve, colon, comma, tilde **6.** dagger, hyphen, period, tittle, umlaut **8.** brackets, ellipsis **9.** ampersand, semicolon **10.** apostrophe, circumflex **11.** exclamation **12.** question mark
pundit... **6.** nestor, savant **7.** Brahmin, scholar, teacher **10.** learned man
pung... **4.** sled **6.** sleigh
pungent... **4.** keen, racy, sour, tart **5.** acrid, acute, sharp, smart, snell **6.** biting, bitter **7.** caustic, odorous, painful, peppery, piquant **8.** piercing, poignant, stabbing **11.** stimulating
pungent herb... **6.** Asarum
punish... **4.** fine **5.** mulct, spank, wreak **6.** amerce **7.** chasten, correct **8.** chastise, penalize **9.** castigate **10.** discipline
punishment (pert to)...
Brehon law.. **4.** eric
by torture.. **9.** strappado
church.. **15.** excommunication
condign.. **11.** retributive
law.. **5.** peine
term.. **5.** penal **7.** penalty, revenge **8.** punitive
Turk, Chin.. **9.** bastinade
Welsh law (anc).. **3.** cro **7.** galanas
punitive... **5.** penal **10.** revengeful, vindictive **11.** castigatory
Punjab, India...
capital.. **6.** Lahore (West) **8.** Amritsar (East)
language.. **7.** Panjabi
name meaning.. **10.** Five Rivers
soldier.. **4.** Sikh
summer capital.. **5.** Simla
punk... **3.** bad **5.** child **6.** amadou **7.** lighter **8.** inferior **9.** touchwood
punto... **3.** hit **5.** joint (fencing) **6.** stitch (needle)
puny... **4.** weak **5.** frail, petty **6.** little, meager, puisne, sickly **8.** delicate **14.** inconsiderable
pupa... **5.** shell **9.** chrysalis
pupil... **3.** eye, son **4.** tyro **5.** élève, youth **7.** écolier, learner, scholar **8.** disciple, neophyte

puppet... **3.** guy **4.** doll **5.** image **6.** maumet **9.** miniature, nonentity **10.** figurehead, marionette
puppeteer, famed... **4.** Sarg
puppy... **3.** dog, fop **5.** shark, whelp
purblind... **10.** dim-sighted **11.** partly blind **12.** narrow-minded, undiscerning
purchasable... **5.** venal **8.** bribable, hireling **9.** mercenary **11.** corruptible
purchase... **3.** buy, win **4.** earn, hold **5.** bribe **6.** buying, obtain **7.** acquire, bribery, procure **8.** barratry, foothold, leverage
purchaser... **5.** buyer **6.** patron, vendee **8.** customer **9.** acquéreur **13.** adjudicataire
purdah (Ind)... **4.** veil **6.** screen **7.** curtain
pure... **4.** neat, real **5.** clean, fresh, godly, sheer, utter **6.** candid, chaste, simple, vestal **7.** genuine, perfect, refined, unmixed **8.** absolute, filtered, innocent **9.** downright, faultless, inviolate, stainless, undefiled, unsullied **11.** pure-blooded, uncorrupted, unqualified **13.** unadulterated
purga (Russ)... **8.** blizzard **9.** snowstorm
purgative... **5.** jalap **6.** physic **8.** absterge **9.** catharsis, cathartic, cleansing
purgatory... **4.** hell **5.** limbo **6.** erebus **7.** torment
purified... **10.** elutriated
purified wool fat... **7.** lanolin (lanoline)
purify... **5.** clean, purge **6.** filter, refine, spurge **7.** cleanse, epurate **8.** lustrate, renovate, sanctify **9.** elutriate
purifying... **7.** smectic **8.** depurant **9.** cathartic, cleansing **10.** distilling
Purim... **7.** holiday **8.** festival (Jew) **11.** Feast of Lots
puritan... **5.** prude **7.** ascetic **9.** precisian **10.** Separatist
puritan clergyman... **10.** Cartwright
puritanical... **6.** strict **7.** ascetic **11.** strait-laced **13.** hyperorthodox
purity... **8.** chastity **9.** innocence
purl... **4.** eddy **5.** frill **6.** murmur, ripple **7.** trickle
purloin... **5.** filch, steal, swipe **6.** finger **11.** appropriate
purple... **4.** bice, lake, plum, puce **5.** lilac, mauve, pansy, regal, showy **6.** damson, orchid, ornate, Tyrian, violet **7.** Cassius, magenta, mollusk, pigment **8.** amaranth, Burgundy, imperial, mulberry **9.** brilliant, cathedral **11.** sovereignty
purple (pert to)...
bottle.. **4.** moss
cactus.. **8.** Missouri
death adder.. **10.** black snake
emperor.. **9.** butterfly
Forbidden City.. **5.** Lhasa
granadilla.. **13.** passion flower
haw.. **7.** capulin (Mex) **8.** bluewood
Heart, Order of.. **5.** medal (Mil) (est by Washington, re-est. 1932)
laurel.. **12.** rhododendron
lily.. **8.** Turk's cap
martin.. **7.** swallow
navy.. **10.** marine blue
nightshade.. **9.** trompillo

purport . . . **4.** feck, gist, mean **5.** sense, tenor **6.** allege, import, intent **7.** meaning **9.** substance

purpose . . . **3.** aim, end **4.** goal, idly, main, plan, sake **5.** avail **6.** design, intend, intent, motive **7.** meaning, resolve **8.** function **9.** determine, discourse, intention, objective, predesign

purposive . . . **5.** telic

purse . . . **3.** bag, cly **5.** pouch **6.** pucker, wallet **7.** wrinkle **8.** crumenal (obs) **10.** pocketbook **12.** porte-monnaie

purser . . . **5.** clerk (ship's) **6.** bursar **7.** boucher, cashier **9.** paymaster

purse rat . . . **12.** pocket gopher

pursue . . . **3.** run **4.** hunt, seek, tack **5.** chase, court **6.** follow **7.** carry on, proceed **9.** persecute **10.** specialize

pursuit . . . **5.** chase, quest, scent **9.** objective **10.** occupation

purvey . . . **5.** cater **6.** supply **7.** foresee, provide

purveyor of untruth (Bib) . . . **7.** Ananias

purview . . . **4.** body (statute) **5.** field (law), range, scope **7.** compass **8.** province

push . . . **2.** go **4.** bunt, butt, gang, ping, pole, prod, urge **5.** crowd, elbow, impel, nudge, press, shove **6.** attack, energy, propel, thrust **7.** importune, offensive (Mil) **10.** forge ahead, propulsion **12.** press forward

pusillanimous . . . **4.** base, weak **5.** timid **6.** craven **8.** cowardly **12.** fainthearted, mean-spirited

put . . . **3.** set **4.** butt, dupe, fool, sail **5.** place, throw **6.** impose, option, phrase, repose, rustic **7.** deposit **8.** invest in **9.** attribute

put (pert to) . . .
an end to . . **5.** quash (law)
away . . **4.** kill **5.** store **6.** murder
back . . **6.** demote **7.** replace, restore
before . . **6.** appose
down . . **6.** humble **7.** degrade, deposit, depress **8.** suppress
forth . . **5.** exert **7.** propose **9.** circulate
off . . **4.** doff, haft, sail **5.** defer, delay, evade **8.** postpone
on alert . . **5.** alarm **6.** alarum
out . . **3.** vex **4.** oust **5.** eject **9.** ostracize **10.** expatriate
over . . **4.** bilk **5.** cheat, trick **7.** deceive

put in, into . . .
action . . **6.** excite
holy place . . **8.** enshrine
motion . . **6.** arouse
opposition . . **3.** pit
order . . **4.** trim **5.** mense **6.** settle **7.** arrange **8.** organize **11.** systematize
rapture . . **8.** entrance
relation to . . **9.** correlate **10.** coordinate, co-ordinate
rhythm . . **5.** meter
scabbard . . **7.** sheathe

putrefaction . . . **3.** rot **5.** decay **13.** decomposition **14.** disintegration

puttee . . . **6.** gaiter **7.** legging

put to . . .
flight . . **4.** rout
strain . . **3.** tax
trouble . . **10.** discommode

use . . **5.** apply
wrong use . . **8.** misapply

put up . . . **3.** pay **4.** ante, hang **5.** build, offer **6.** pledge **7.** install **8.** nominate **9.** construct

put up with . . . **4.** bear **5.** stand **6.** endure, permit **7.** stomach **8.** tolerate

puzzle . . . **3.** cap **4.** crux, pose **5.** griph (griphus), poser, rebus **6.** enigma, riddle **7.** anagram, confuse, mystify, nonplus, paradox, perplex, problem **8.** entangle **9.** conundrum **10.** complicate, disconcert

puzzle (pert to) . . .
monkey . . **5.** piñon
picture . . **5.** rebus
word . . **7.** charade **9.** crossword **10.** anacrostic

puzzling . . . **6.** knotty **10.** perplexing **11.** enigmatical, paradoxical

pygarg, pygargus . . . **5.** addax **8.** sea eagle **9.** quadruped (Bib)

Pygmalion (pert to) . . .
color . . **5.** brown
endowed with life . . **7.** Galatea (statue)
king of . . **6.** Cyprus
sister . . **4.** Dido
talented as . . **8.** sculptor

pygmy, pigmy . . . **3.** elf **4.** Akka, Doko, pixy **5.** atomy, Batwa, dwarf, gnome, minim, short **6.** Abongo, Achuas **7.** manikin **9.** dandiprat

pygmy (pert to) . . .
hog . . **7.** Porcula
musk deer . . **10.** chevrotain
owl . . **8.** gnome owl
rattlesnake . . **10.** massasauga
squirrel (smallest known) . . **9.** Sciuridae

pyic . . . **8.** purulent, virulent

pyknic . . . **3.** fat **5.** round, stout

pylon . . . **4.** post **5.** tower **6.** marker **7.** gateway **14.** monumental mass

pyosis . . . **3.** pus **4.** boil **11.** suppuration

pyramid . . . **4.** cone, heap, pile, tomb **5.** tower **8.** monument **9.** speculate

pyramid (pert to) . . .
builder, largest . . **6.** Cheops (khufu)
Egypt . . **9.** The Sphinx **12.** Great Pyramid, Tomb of Cheops
group . . **5.** Gizeh **7.** Menkare **8.** Chephren **9.** Mycerinus
kidney (Anat) . . **7.** Perrein **10.** Malpighian
Mexico . . **7.** Benares
site of Cheops . . **4.** Giza (Gizeh)
texts . . **12.** inscriptions **13.** Book of the Dead
world wonder . . **12.** Great Pyramid, Tomb of Cheops

pyramidal . . . **4.** huge **7.** angular, conical **8.** enormous, imposing

pyre . . . **4.** bier, heap, pile **9.** cremation, death fire

Pyrenees (pert to) . . .
bandit . . **8.** Miquelet
mountain chain . . **11.** France-Spain
peak . . **9.** Pic d'Aneto **11.** Pic de Méthou
resort . . **3.** Pau
State . . **7.** Andorra (Fr)

pyriform . . . **10.** pear-shaped

pyrology (study of) . . . **4.** heat

pyromaniac . . . **7.** firebug **8.** arsonist

10. incendiary
pyrope . . . **3.** red **6.** garnet **7.** mineral
pyrophobia . . . **11.** dread of fire
pyrotechnics . . . **7.** oratory, science
  9. fireworks
pyrrhic . . . **4.** foot (Pros) **5.** dance
Pyrrhic victory . . . **11.** at great cost
pyrrho (comb form) . . . **3.** red **5.** tawny
Pyrrho (Gr) . . . **7.** teacher (Pyrrhonism)
pyrrhotist . . . **7.** redhead
Pyrrhulexia . . . **5.** finch **8.** grosbeak
Pythagorus (Gr) . . .
  birthplace . . **5.** Samos
  daughter . . **4.** Camo
  famed as . . **11.** philosopher
  friend . . **5.** Damon
  teacher of . . **8.** theorems **18.** influence
    of numbers
Pythian (pert to) . . .
  contests . . **6.** Delphi

Festival . . **11.** Panhellenic
patron . . **6.** Apollo
term . . **8.** ecstatic **9.** phrenetic
python . . . **3.** boa **8.** anaconda
Python (pert to) . . .
  home . . **11.** Mt Parnassus
  myth . . **14.** monster serpent
  slaver . . **6.** Apollo
  survivor of . . **10.** muddy earth (anc)
pythonic . . . **4.** huge **6.** Pythia
  (Delphi), python **8.** oracular
  9. monstrous
pythonism, art of . . . **8.** prophecy
  10. divination
pyx, pix . . . **3.** box **4.** test, veil **5.** chest
  6. coffer, vessel (Eccl) **8.** binnacle,
  ciborium **10.** tabernacle
pyxie . . . **5.** shrub **9.** evergreen
pyxis . . . **3.** box **4.** Argo (Astron), vase
  9. jewel case

Q

Q

Q . . . **5.** queue **6.** letter (17th)
QED . . . **21.** Quod Erat Demonstrandum
Q-ship (Eng) . . . **11.** mystery ship
qua, quabird . . . **10.** night heron
quachil . . . **12.** pocket gopher
quack . . . **3.** cry (duck) **5.** faker **7.** empiric
  8. impostor **9.** charlatan, pretender
  10. medicaster, mountebank
quack medicine . . . **6.** patent **7.** nostrum
quad (pert to) . . .
  printing . . **5.** crown **7.** quadrat
  school . . **4.** yard **6.** campus
  10. quadrangle
  slang (Brit) . . **5.** horse
quadra . . . **6.** fillet, listel, plinth
quadragenarian . . . **12.** forty-year-old
  (person)
Quadragesima . . . **4.** Fast, Lent **6.** Sunday
  (1st in Lent) **7.** Holy Day **9.** Forty Days
quadrangle . . . **5.** plane (four-angles)
  6. square **7.** rhombus **8.** tetragon
quadrant . . . **4.** gill **6.** fourth **7.** measure,
  quarter **8.** farthing, six hours
  10. instrument, semicircle
quadrate . . . **4.** suit **5.** adapt, agree,
  ideal **6.** square **7.** conform, perfect,
  squared **8.** balanced **10.** correspond
  13. correspondent
quadriga . . . **3.** car **7.** chariot (4-horse)
  10. four horses
quadrumane . . . **3.** ape **6.** mammal
  7. gorilla, Primate (except Man)
  10. chimpanzee **13.** feetlike hands
quadruped . . . **3.** ass, cat, cow, dog
  4. bull, calf, colt, foal, lion, mule
  5. burro, horse, jenny, panda, tiger
  6. badger, donkey, mammal **7.** bullock
  10. four-footed
quaff . . . **5.** draft, drink **6.** tipple
quag . . . **5.** quake **6.** quiver **8.** quagmire
quagga . . . **5.** zebra **7.** wild ass
quaggy . . . **5.** boggy, fenny **6.** spongy
  7. queachy **8.** yielding

quagmire . . . **3.** bay, fen **4.** lair **5.** marsh,
  swamp **6.** morass **11.** predicament
quahog . . . **4.** clam
quail . . . **3.** cow **4.** bird **5.** colin,
  cower, quake, shake **6.** blench,
  curdle, flinch, shrink, tremor, Turnix
  7. massena, tremble **8.** bobwhite,
  Coturnix **9.** coagulate, courtesan, eddish
  hen
quail (pert to) . . .
  button . . **6.** Turnix
  call . . **4.** pipe
  color . . **9.** hair brown
  flock . . **4.** bevy
  French . . **6.** caille
  hawk . . **6.** falcon
  quailhead . . **11.** lark sparrow
  snipe . . **9.** dowitcher
quaint . . . **3.** odd **4.** wise **5.** proud
  6. expert, pretty, proper **7.** curious,
  prudent, refined, strange, uncouth
  8. fanciful, peculiar
quake . . . **5.** shake **6.** quiver, shiver,
  tremor **7.** shudder, tremble, vibrate
  10. earthquake
Quaker (pert to) . . .
  bird . . **9.** albatross (sooty)
  city . . **12.** Philadelphia
  colonizer . . **4.** Penn (Wm)
  color . . **4.** drab, gray **5.** acier
  poet . . **6.** Barton **8.** Whittier
  sect . . **16.** Society of Friends
  sect founder . . **9.** George Fox
  State . . **12.** Pennsylvania
  word . . **4.** thee
qualified . . . **3.** fit **4.** able **6.** fitted
  7. adapted, capable, enabled, limited
  8. eligible, entitled, equipped, modified,
  prepared, tempered **9.** competent
  10. restrained, restricted **11.** conditional
qualify . . . **3.** fit **4.** name **5.** abate, adapt,
  be fit, equip, limit, train **6.** enable,
  modify, soften, temper **7.** assuage,

prepare **8.** diminish, mitigate, modulate, quantify, regulate, restrain, restrict

quality . . . **5.** prime, trait, value **6.** nature, pathos, strain **7.** caliber, texture **8.** accident, capacity, inferior, nobility, property **9.** attribute, character, specialty **10.** difference, excellence **14.** characteristic

quality of heredity . . . **9.** lineality

qualm . . . **4.** pall **5.** demur, doubt, spasm **6.** nausea, regret **7.** scruple **9.** faintness, misgiving **11.** compunction **12.** apprehension

quandary . . . **3.** fix **6.** pickle, plight, strait **7.** dilemma **10.** perplexity **11.** predicament

quandy . . . **9.** squaw duck

quant . . . **11.** punting pole

quantity . . . **3.** ace, any, gob, lot, sea, sum **4.** bulk, dose, drop, mass, much, raff, raft, scad, size, some **5.** batch, scads, store **6.** amount, cupful, degree, extent, hatful, number, oceans **7.** handful

quantity (pert to) . . .
fixed . . **5.** quota **8.** constant
mathematics . . **4.** surd **5.** graph **6.** scalar, vector
minute . . **4.** atom, dram, iota, mill
standard . . **4.** unit **9.** allotment
time unit . . **4.** rate

quantum . . . **4.** body **5.** share **6.** amount, energy, theory **7.** atomics, portion **8.** quantity

quap . . . **5.** heave, throb **6.** quaver **9.** palpitate

Quapaw . . . **5.** Sioux **8.** Arkansas

quarantine . . . **7.** confine, isolate **8.** pratique (marine) **9.** forty days (law), isolation, segregate **11.** confinement

quarantine flag . . . **6.** yellow **7.** warning **10.** yellow jack

quarenden . . . **5.** apple (deep red)

quarentene . . . **4.** rood **7.** furlong

quark . . . **3.** caw **5.** croak, quawk

quarl, quarle . . . **4.** sour, tile **5.** brick **6.** cundle, medusa **5.** jellyfish

quarred . . . **6.** soured **7.** curdled (beer)

quarrel . . . **3.** row **4.** spat, tiff, tile **5.** arrow, brawl, broil, cavil, flite (flyte), gnarr, scene, scrap **6.** affray, bicker, chisel, dustup, hassle **7.** diamond, wrangle **8.** argument, squabble **9.** complaint **10.** accusation, Donnybrook, free-for-all **11.** altercation **12.** disagreement **16.** misunderstanding

quarrel (pert to) . . .
hereditary . . **4.** feud **8.** vendetta
noisy . . **6.** fracas, jangle, uproar
over . . **6.** bicker **7.** contend, dispute
petty . . **4.** miff, spat, tiff

quarrelsome . . . **8.** choleric, petulant **9.** irascible, irritable, litigious **10.** discordant, pugnacious **11.** belliferent, contentious **13.** argumentative

quarry . . . **4.** delf, game, heap, mine, prey **6.** victim **8.** entrails, excavate **12.** object hunted

quart . . . **5.** gills (eight) **6.** fourth **7.** measure **8.** schooner

quarter . . . **4.** coin, side **5.** house **6.** fourth,

region **7.** measure, two bits **8.** insignia, semester **9.** direction, dismember **10.** quadrature (Astron), quadrisect

quarter (pert to) . . .
acre . . **4.** rood
animal . . **5.** horse
astronomy . . **4.** quadrature
fathom . . **6.** fourth
military . . **8.** clemency (to enemy)
music . . **4.** note **8.** crotchet
nautical . . **4.** deck, lift **6.** galley
pint . . **4.** gill
sports . . **4.** back **11.** quarterback

quartered . . . **8.** billeted **12.** quartersawed (wood)

quarters (living) . . . **4.** camp, room **5.** abode **7.** housing, lodging, shelter **8.** barracks, diggings, lodgings, lodgment **9.** dormitory

Quartodeciman . . . **10.** paschalist

quartz . . . **4.** onyx, sard **5.** flint **6.** silica **7.** mineral

quartz (pert to) . . .
banded, spotted . . **4.** onyx **5.** agate **6.** jasper **8.** sardonyx
blue-red . . **10.** bloodstone, heliotrope
brown . . **5.** smoky **9.** cairngorm
brownish-red . . **7.** sinople
chalcedony . . **4.** sard **9.** carnelian **11.** chrysoprase
flint . . **9.** hornstone **10.** touchstone
glass . . **6.** silica
green . . **5.** prase (dull) **6.** plasma (bright) **11.** chrysoprase
hard . . **5.** flint
opaque . . **6.** jasper
purple . . **8.** amethyst
red . . **4.** sard **9.** carnelian
ruby-red . . **7.** rubasse
silica . . **5.** silex
transparent . . **11.** rock crystal
violet . . **8.** amethyst
yellow . . **5.** topaz (false) **7.** citrine

quash . . . **4.** cass, void **5.** abate, annul, crush, quell, shake **6.** hush up, subdue **7.** shatter **8.** suppress **9.** overthrow **10.** extinguish

quasi . . . **4.** as if **6.** pseudo **8.** as it were, as though **9.** seemingly

Quasimodo . . . **9.** Hunchback (Notre Dame), Low Sunday (first after Easter)

quatern . . . **8.** fourfold **10.** quadrangle **12.** four quarters (having)

quaver . . . **5.** shake, trill **6.** quiver **7.** tremble, tremolo, vibrate **11.** trepidation **13.** tremulousness

quawk . . . **3.** caw **5.** heron (night) **7.** screech **8.** quagmire

quay, key . . . **4.** pier **5.** levee, wharf **7.** landing

queachy . . . **5.** boggy, bushy, fenny **6.** marshy, swampy

quean . . . **4.** girl, jade, slut **5.** vixen, wench **6.** harlot

queasy . . . **4.** sick **8.** delicate, qualmish, ticklish, troubled **9.** hazardous, ill at ease, nauseated, squeamish, uncertain, unsettled

Quebec . . .
battle site . . **15.** Plains of Abraham
capital . . **6.** Quebec (province)

city . . **6.** Verdun **8.** Montreal **11.** Three Rivers
founder . . **9.** Champlain (1608)
river . . **10.** St Lawrence
vehicle . . **7.** calèche (2-wheeled)
quebrada . . . **3.** gap **5.** brook, gorge **7.** fissure
qued, quede . . . **3.** bad **4.** evil **8.** The Devil
queen . . . **3.** ant, bee, cat **7.** empress, goddess, monarch **8.** chessman, honeybee **9.** sovereign **10.** chess piece **11.** playing card
queen (pert to) . . .
bee . . **8.** honeybee
cactus . . **7.** Mexican **10.** ornamental
conch . . **5.** shell
fern . . **5.** royal
pigeon . . **7.** crowned
Queen (pert to) . . .
Bernice's Hair (Astron) . . **13.** Coma Berenices
City of the Lakes . . **7.** Buffalo
City of the West . . **10.** Cincinnati
Mab . . **11.** Fairie Queen (Rom/Juliet)
Victoria . . **14.** Widow of Windsor (nickname by Kipling)
Queen Anne's . . .
lace . . **6.** carrot (wild)
melon . . **6.** dudaim
War . . **17.** Spanish Succession
War treaty . . **14.** Peace of Utrecht
queen of . . .
chess . . **4.** fers
fairies . . **3.** Mab **7.** Titania **8.** Gloriana
gods . . **4.** Hera (Gr), Juno (Rom)
Hearts . . **9.** Elizabeth
heaven . . **10.** Virgin Mary
Isles (Brit) . . **6.** Albion
night . . **4.** moon
Scots . . **4.** Mary
Sheba . . **6.** Balkis (Koran)
Spades (solo) . . **5.** basta
the Adriatic . . **6.** Venice
the Antilles . . **4.** Cuba
the East . . **7.** Antioch (Syria), Batavia (Java), Zenobia
the tides . . **7.** the moon
the underworld . . **3.** Hel
queen's (pert to) . . .
arm . . **6.** musket
flower . . **9.** bloodwood
hub . . **7.** tobacco
July flower . . **8.** damewort
ware . . **9.** Wedgewood
Queensland (Austral) . . .
animal . . **8.** kangaroo **9.** koala bear (teddy bear)
bean . . **8.** snuffbox
capital . . **8.** Brisbane
fire tree . . **5.** tulip
fish . . **9.** trumpeter
hemp . . **4.** sida **6.** lucern **9.** jellyleaf **11.** paddy lucern
plum . . **8.** Burdekin
tree (timber) . . **3.** box **4.** pine **5.** beech, ebony **10.** sandalwood **12.** Dundathu pine
queer . . . **3.** odd, rum **4.** sham **5.** false, funny **6.** insane, thwart **7.** strange **8.** peculiar, singular, spurious

9. eccentric, fantastic, interfere **10.** disconcert, suspicious **11.** counterfeit **12.** questionable
queer fellow . . . **4.** coot, goop **6.** galoot, geezer **9.** character
queersome . . . **3.** odd **7.** strange **8.** abnormal
Queer Street . . . **9.** imaginary
queest . . . **8.** ringdove
queet . . . **4.** coot **5.** ankle
quell . . . **3.** end **4.** calm **5.** allay, crush, quash, quiet **6.** pacify, reduce, soothe, stifle, subdue **7.** destroy, repress **8.** suppress **9.** overpower **10.** extinguish
quench . . . **4.** cool, damp, sate **5.** allay, check, slake, still **6.** stifle, subdue **7.** assuage, gratify **8.** suppress **10.** discourage, extinguish **11.** clamp down on
quenelle . . . **8.** meatball
Quercus . . . **4.** oaks
queriman . . . **4.** fish **6.** mullet
quern . . . **4.** mill (grain)
quernal . . . **5.** crown (oak leaves)
querulous . . . **7.** fretful, peevish **9.** plaintive **11.** complaining **12.** faultfinding
query . . . **5.** doubt **6.** murmur **7.** inquire, inquiry, whining **8.** question
quest . . . **3.** bay (dog's) **4.** hunt, seek **6.** desire, pursue, search **7.** inquest, request **8.** seek alms **9.** adventure **12.** solicitation
question . . . **3.** ask **4.** quiz **5.** cavil, doubt, grill, poser, query, scout, topic **6.** riddle **7.** dispute, inquire, inquiry, problem **8.** erotesis **9.** catechize (catechise) **11.** interrogate, uncertainty **12.** interpellate (formally) **13.** interrogation
question, out of the . . . **6.** absurd **7.** refused **8.** hopeless, rejected **10.** impossible, prohibited **11.** unthinkable
questionable . . . **4.** moot **7.** dubious **8.** doubtful **9.** debatable, dishonest, uncertain **10.** disputable, improbable **12.** unbelievable **13.** problematical
questioning (prolonged) . . . **11.** inquisition
question mark . . . **7.** erotema, eroteme
quet . . . **3.** auk **5.** murre **9.** guillemot
quethe . . . **3.** say **4.** call, tell, will **5.** quoth, speak **6.** clamor **8.** bequeath **9.** testament
quetzal, quezal . . . **6.** trogon **14.** national emblem (Guatemala)
Quetzalcoatl . . . **10.** god of winds (Aztec)
queue . . . **3.** cue **4.** hair, line (waiting), tail **7.** pigtail **9.** lance rest
quey . . . **6.** heifer
quia-quia . . . **9.** cigarfish
quib, quibble . . . **3.** pun **4.** carp, quip **5.** argue, cavil, cheta, evade **7.** shuffle
Quiche, Indian . . . **5.** Mayan
quick . . . **3.** apt **4.** deft, fast, yare **5.** agile, alert, brisk, fiery, fleet, hasty, rapid, ready, smart, swift **6.** lively, nimble, presto, prompt, pronto, speedy, sudden **7.** animate **9.** dexterous, impatient, impulsive, sprightly, vital

part 10. passionate 11. expeditious, hot-tempered

quicken . . . 5. hurry, rouse, speed 6. excite, hasten, incite, revive, vivify 7. animate, further, refresh, sharpen 8. energize, expedite 9. stimulate 10. accelerate 11. resuscitate 12. reinvigorate

quickly . . . 4. cito, fast, soon 5. apace 6. presto, pronto 7. briefly, hastily, rapidly 8. promptly, speedily, vigorous

quickness . . . 4. nous (humor) 5. haste 6. acumen 7. acidity, agility 8. alacrity, celerity, dispatch, pungency, rapidity 9. acuteness, briskness, fleetness, sharpness, smartness 10. expedition, promptness 13. impulsiveness

quicksand . . . 3. bog 4. syrt 6. Syrtis

quickset . . . 5. hedge 7. thicket 8. hawthorn

quicksilver . . . 5. metal 7. mercury

quid . . . 3. cud, fid 6. guinea 7. essence, tobacco 9. sovereign

quidam . . . 8. somebody 10. one unknown

quidnunc . . . 6. gossip 7. what now 11. inquisitive

quid pro quo . . . 9. tit for tat 10. equivalent, substitute 11. interchange

quiescent . . . 5. quiet, still 6. at rest, latent, silent, static 8. sleeping 10. motionless

quiet . . . 2. sh 3. pet 4. calm, ease, hush, lull, mild 5. peace, sober, still 6. gentle, hushed, modest, placid, smooth, soothe 7. halcyon, restful, silence 8. peaceful, tranquil 9. contented, peaceable, quiescent, reposeful, unruffled 10. unmolested 11. undisturbed

quietist . . . 6. mystic (Quietism)

quietive . . . 8. sedative

quietly . . . 6. calmly, gently, simply 8. modestly, silently 9. patiently, peaceably, privately 10. composedly 11. noiselessly 16. unostentatiously

quietude . . . 4. rest 5. peace 6. repose 7. silence 10. quiescence 12. tranquillity (tranquility)

quietus . . . 4. mort, obit 5. death 6. defeat 7. release 9. acquittal, deathblow, discharge (of debt)

quiff . . . 4. coif, puff 5. whiff

quilkin . . . 4. frog, toad

quill . . . 3. cop, pen 5. remex 6. bobbin 7. spindle

quilt . . . 3. pad 4. flog, gulp 5. duvet 6. caddow 7. swallow 8. coverlet 9. patchwork 11. comfortable, counterpane

quin . . . 7. scallop

quincentenary . . . 11. anniversary 13. commemoration 16. five hundred years

quindecemvir (Rom) . . . 10. custodians (Sibylline Books), fifteen men

quink . . . 5. brant, goose

quinoa . . . 6. cereal 7. pigweed

Quinquagesima Sunday . . . 10. before Lent 12. Shrove Sunday

quinque (comb form) . . . 4. five

quinsy . . . 10. sore throat 11. tonsillitis

quint . . . 3. tax (one 5th) 7. E string 8. interval, schooner (5-masted) 9. organ stop

quintal . . . 13. hundredweight

quintessence . . . 3. col 5. elite 6. elixir 7. essence, the best 10. perfection

quip . . . 3. mot 4. gibe, jest 5. sally, taunt 6. oddity 7. caprice, quibble 8. gimcrack 9. witticism 12. equivocation

quires, twenty . . . 4. ream 6. sheets (20)

quirk . . . 4. quip, turn 5. clock, shift, twist 7. caprice, evasion, quibble 8. flourish 9. deviation, mannerism, witticism 12. eccentricity

quirt . . . 4. whip 5. romal

quis . . . 8. woodcock

quisby . . . 5. idler, queer 8. bankrupt 10. down and out

quit . . . 3. rid 4. free, stop 5. cease, clear, leave, pay up, repay, yield 6. depart, resign 7. abandon, discard, forsake, release, relieve, requite 8. abdicate, liberate, renounce 9. surrender 10. relinquish 11. discontinue

quitclaim . . . 6. acquit 7. release 12. convey a claim 13. deed of release 14. relinquishment

quite . . . 3. all, yes 4. very 5. stark, truly 6. really, wholly 7. totally 8. entirely, somewhat 10. absolutely, completely, positively

quite so . . . 8. that is so, very true, very well

quite some . . . 12. considerable

quittance . . . 5. repay 6. return 7. requite 8. reprisal, requital 9. atonement, departure, repayment 10. recompense 11. acquittance

quitter . . . 5. piker 6. coward, truant 7. shirker, welsher

quiver . . . 4. case 5. quake, shake 6. quaver, sheath, shiver, tremor 7. flicker, tremble, tremolo, vibrate 11. trepidation

quiver leaf . . . 5. aspen

Quivira (pert to) . . . *famous for* . . 6. wealth *sought by* . . 8. Coronado (1541) *town site* . . 6. Kansas

Quivira, Gran . . . 12. mission ruins 16. National Monument (N Mex)

qui vive . . . 5. alert 7. excited 9. challenge 12. who goes there

quixotic . . . 7. utopian 9. visionary 10. Don Quixote (like) 11. impractical

quiz . . . 4. hoax, jest, joke, mock 5. coach 6. banter 8. ridicule 11. examination, inquisitive, interrogate, questioning

quizzical . . . 3. odd 7. amusing, teasing 9. bantering, eccentric, inquiring, perplexed

quizzing . . . 6. banter 11. questioning

quizzing glass . . . 7. monocle 8. eyeglass

quod . . . 3. jug 6. prison 8. imprison

quoddies . . . 7. herring

quod erat demonstrandum . . . 3. QED 24. which was to be demonstrated

quodlibet . . . 6. medley 8. fantasia, subtlety 13. what you please

quoit . . . 4. disc 6. discus

quoit pin . . . **3.** hob
quoits . . . **4.** game **8.** cromlech **10.** stone
  cover
quo modo . . . **5.** means **6.** manner,
  method
quondam . . . **6.** former **8.** formerly,
  sometime
quorum . . . **7.** council **8.** majority **10.** select
  body
quota . . . **4.** part **5.** share **6.** ration
  10. proportion
quotable . . . **7.** citable
quotation . . . **5.** chria, cital, motto,
  price, stock **7.** passage **8.** citation
  10. memorandum, repetition

quotation mark . . . **9.** guillemet
quote . . . **4.** cite, name **5.** price **6.** adduce,
  repeat **7.** extract **9.** quotation,
  reference
quoth . . . **4.** said **5.** spoke
quotha . . . **6.** indeed **8.** forsooth
quotidian . . . **5.** daily **8.** day by day,
  every day, ordinary **9.** recurring
  11. commonplace
quotient . . . **6.** number, result
quotity . . . **5.** group, quota **7.** integer
  10. collection
quotum . . . **5.** quota, ratio
quo vadis . . . **16.** whither goest thou
Quo Vadis tyrant . . . **4.** Nero

R

R

R . . . **3.** rho (Gr) **6.** letter (18th)
Ra, Egypt Relig (pert to) . . .
  atmosphere . . **3.** Shu
  god of . . **3.** sun
  morning sun . . **7.** Chepera, Khepera
  night sun . . **7.** Sokaris
  representation . . **3.** cat **4.** lion **5.** Bacis
    (bull) **6.** falcon **9.** solar disk
  rising sun . . **5.** Horus **9.** Marmachis
  setting sun . . **3.** Tem
  solar disk . . **4.** Aten
  son . . **6.** Khonsu
  son of . . **3.** Nut (the sky)
  wife . . **3.** Mut
raad . . . **15.** electric catfish
raad . . . **7.** council (So Afr) **9.** volksraad
raadzaal . . . **11.** council hall (So Afr)
rab . . . **5.** mixer (mortar) **6.** beater
Rab . . . **5.** title **6.** master, rabban **7.** teacher
  8. Gamaliel
rabato, rebato . . . **4.** ruff **6.** collar
  9. piccadill
rabbet . . . **4.** weld **5.** miter **6.** groove,
  recess **7.** channel **8.** dovetail
rabbi . . . **4.** lord **5.** rabat, title **6.** master
  7. teacher **9.** clergyman **11.** breastpiece
rabbi (pert to) . . .
  examiners . . **8.** sabaraim (saboraim)
  interpreters . . **7.** amoraim
  teachers . . **7.** tannaim
rabbit . . . **4.** cony (coney), hare, tyro
  5. bunny, lapin **6.** animal, novice,
  rodent **10.** cottontail **11.** Belgian hare
rabbit (pert to) . . .
  breeding ground . . **6.** warren **8.** rabbitry
  ear . . **7.** antenna **8.** toadflax
  female . . **3.** doe
  fever . . **9.** tularemia
  fiction . . **6.** Harvey
  fish . . **8.** chimaera **9.** globefish, porcupine
  foot . . **5.** charm **8.** talisman
  fur . . **4.** cony (coney) **5.** lapin
  genus . . **5.** Lepus
  male . . **4.** buck
  mouthed . . **10.** harelipped
  rat . . **9.** bandicoot
  S America . . **6.** tapeti

  shelter . . **5.** hutch
  stew . . **12.** hasenpfeffer
  tail . . **3.** fud **4.** scut
rabbitry . . . **5.** hutch **6.** warren
rabble . . . **3.** mob **4.** herd, raff, rout, skim,
  stir **5.** crowd **6.** ragtag, tumult **7.** bobtail
  8. canaille, riffraff **9.** confusion,
  rigmarole, the masses **12.** accumulation
  (chaotic)
rabble rouser . . . **6.** ragtag
Rabelais (Fr) . . . **6.** author **8.** satirist
  9. Gargantua (1st work)
rabid . . . **3.** mad **6.** raging **7.** frantic,
  furious, rampant, violent **8.** frenzied
  9. fanatical **10.** infuriated
rabies . . . **5.** lyssa **11.** hydrophobia
raccoon, ally of . . . **5.** coati, panda
race . . . **3.** cut, hie, run **4.** flow, lane, line,
  rush, slit, sort, stem **5.** breed, caste,
  flume, relay, speed **6.** course, family,
  nation, people, strain **7.** contest, regatta,
  running, scratch **10.** passageway
  11. competition, watercourse
race (pert to horses) . . .
  chariot . . **13.** Circus Maximus
  gait . . **4.** lope, pace, trot
  horse . . **4.** pony **5.** racer **6.** maiden,
    mantis, plater **8.** bangtail
  handicap . . **6.** impost
  open . . **10.** Donnybrook, free-for-all
racecourse, racetrack (pert to) . . .
  3. lap **4.** heat, oval, tout, turf **5.** track
  6. circus (anc), colors **7.** raceway,
  tipster **8.** dopester
Rachel (pert to) . . .
  daughter of . . **5.** Laban
  mother of . . **6.** Joseph **8.** Benjamin
  sister of . . **4.** Leah
  wife of . . **5.** Jacob
racing colors . . . **5.** silks
rack . . . **3.** gin **4.** gait, gear, pain, ruin
  5. agony, frame **6.** punish, strain,
  wrench **7.** agonize, support, torment,
  torture **9.** framework **10.** excruciate
rack (pert to) . . .
  barrel . . **3.** job
  comb . . **9.** toothcomb

corn.. **4.** crib
floating.. **5.** vapor
plate.. **5.** creel
skin of.. **6.** rabbit
racket ... **3.** bat, din **5.** fraud, noise,
revel **6.** bustle, clamor, crosse, outcry,
scheme **8.** vocation **9.** commotion
15. illicit business
rackety ... **5.** noisy **8.** clattery, exciting
9. turbulent **10.** boisterous
racy ... **5.** brisk, fresh, naive, smart,
spicy **6.** lively, risqué **7.** piquant,
pungent, zestful **8.** eloquent, spirited,
stirring **11.** interesting **12.** exhilarating,
full-flavored
rad ... **4.** unit **5.** eager, quick, ready
6. afraid, elated **11.** exhilarated
radar (pert to) ...
beacon.. **4.** buoy **5.** racon **6.** ramark
navigation.. **5.** navar
range (Navig).. **5.** loran **6.** shoran
sight.. **5.** scope **6.** radome, screen
7. display
signal.. **3.** pip **4.** beam, blip **5.** pulse
11. transceiver, transponder
sounding.. **5.** rawin **9.** ionosonde
television.. **7.** teleran
raddle ... **3.** rod **4.** beat, twig **5.** cheat,
color, fence, hedge **6.** branch, hurdle,
ruddle, thrash **7.** wheedle
10. interweave
radeau ... **4.** raft **5.** gloat
radial ... **3.** ray **8.** quadrant **9.** diverging
radiance ... **5.** beamy, glare, light, nitor,
sheen **6.** beauty, luster **7.** beaming,
glitter, glowing, lambent, shining
8. splendor **9.** brilliant, radiation
10. brilliancy, effulgence
12. cheerfulness
radiant ... **5.** aglow, beamy, sheen
7. beaming, glowing, lambent, shining
8. glorious **9.** beautiful, diverging,
effulgent **11.** resplendent
radiate ... **4.** beam, emit, shed **5.** gleam,
shine **7.** diffuse, diverge, emanate
9. irradiate **10.** illuminate
radiation ... **5.** alpha (particle), light, polar
(point) **10.** divergence **12.** illumination
13. radiant energy
radiation unit ... **3.** rad, rem **8.** roentgen
radical ... **3.** red **4.** atom, left, root,
surd **5.** basic, radix, ultra, vital
7. capital, drastic, extreme **8.** cardinal,
reformer **9.** extremist **10.** foundation
11. fundamental
radicated ... **6.** rooted **11.** established
radicle ... **4.** root **5.** radix **6.** etymon
7. rootlet
radio (pert to) ...
activity.. **7.** fallout **9.** radiation
antenna.. **6.** aerial
detector.. **5.** radar **11.** transceiver
frequency.. **5.** audio
interference.. **6.** static
operator.. **2.** CB **3.** ham (amateur)
11. dit-da-artist **12.** citizens' band
rays.. **5.** beams
receiver, interfering.. **7.** blooper
tube.. **4.** grid **5.** diode
radium (pert to) ...
discoverer.. **5.** Curie (1898)

emanation.. **5.** niton, radon
paint.. **8.** luminous
source of.. **7.** uranite **9.** carnotite
radius ... **4.** area, bone **5.** spoke **6.** circle,
extent **8.** diameter
radix ... **4.** root **6.** etymon, source
7. radical, radicle
raff ... **4.** heap, rake, scum **5.** sweep, trash
6. jumble, litter **7.** rubbish **8.** leavings,
riffraff
raffia ... **4.** palm **5.** fiber **6.** jupati
raffish ... **3.** low **6.** common, flashy,
frowsy **7.** unkempt **9.** worthless
12. disreputable
raffle ... **6.** chance, rabble, tangle
7. confuse, crumple, lottery, perplex,
serrate **8.** entangle, plucking, riffraff
9. stripping **10.** plundering
raft ... **3.** lot **4.** spar **5.** balsa, float **6.** rafter
7. to flock **10.** collection (large)
raft-breasted (Ornith) ... **6.** ratite
raft duck ... **5.** scoup **7.** redhead
8. bluebill
rag ... **3.** fog **4.** mist, sail **5.** cloth,
scold, shred **6.** berate, catkin, lichen,
tatter **7.** ragtime, remnant **8.** farthing
9. hoarfrost **11.** syncopation
rag (pert to) ...
bag.. **10.** depository
doll.. **3.** toy **6.** moppet, puppet
10. marionette
fish.. **10.** Icosteidae
rag picker.. **5.** tramp
weed.. **3.** Iva
wool.. **5.** mungo **6.** shoddy
ragamuffin ... **8.** titmouse **9.** ragged
boy **14.** tatterdemalion
rage ... **3.** fad **4.** fume, fury, gret, ramp,
rant, tear **5.** anger, chafe, craze,
furor (furore), storm, wrath **6.** fervor,
frenzy **7.** bluster, passion **8.** violence
9. vehemence **10.** excitement
ragged ... **5.** harsh, rough **6.** jagged,
raguly (Her), scoury, shabby, uneven
7. shreddy **9.** defective, dissonant,
irregular **10.** straggling **11.** dilapidated
raging ... **4.** grim **5.** rabid **7.** acharne
8. storming **9.** ferocious, turbulent
10. blustering, infuriated
11. overwrought
raglan ... **8.** overcoat **11.** sleeve style
Ragnarok, Norse (pert to) ...
leader.. **4.** Loki
meaning.. **16.** world destruction
repeopler of the world.. **3.** Lif
10. Lifthrasir
ragout ... **4.** beef, stew **5.** civet, salmi
6. mutton **7.** goulash, haricot
rahdar ... **14.** tollroad keeper
raid ... **4.** tata **5.** foray, seize **6.** inroad
8. invasion **9.** incursion
rail ... **3.** bar, jaw **4.** coot, jest, rant,
sora, weka **5.** cloak, crake, dress, scoff,
scold **6.** banter, revile, septum (altar)
7. courlan, garment, inveigh, limpkin,
ortolan **8.** reproach
railbird ... **9.** spectator **12.** horse watcher
railing ... **5.** fence, rails **7.** barrier, parapet
10. balustrade
raillery ... **5.** chaff, sport **6.** banter
7. asteism (Rhet) **8.** badinage, ridicule

10. persiflage
railroad (pert to) . . .
flare . . **5.** fusee
signal . . **9.** semaphore
sleeper . . **3.** tie **7.** pullman
switch . . **4.** frog
torpedo . . **9.** detonator
worker . . **6.** dinger **8.** strapper **11.** gandy
dancer
Rail Splitter . . . **14.** Abraham Lincoln
raiment . . . **4.** garb **5.** amice, dress
7. apparel, clothes, vesture **8.** clothing,
garments
rain (pert to) . . .
cloud . . **6.** nimbus
coat . . **3.** mac **4.** mino **6.** poncho **7.** slicker
10. mackintosh
comb form . . **5.** hyeto, ombro **6.** pluvio
fine . . **4.** mist **6.** serein
fowl . . **6.** cuckoo **10.** woodpecker
11. channelbill
gauge . . **8.** udometer **10.** hyetometer
glass . . **9.** barometer
icy . . **4.** hail **5.** sleet
protection . . **9.** ombrifuge
short . . **6.** shower
storm . . **5.** spate **13.** precipitation
study . . **9.** hyetology, ombrology
sudden . . **5.** plash, spate **6.** deluge
7. torrent **8.** downpour
rainbow . . . **3.** arc **4.** arch, iris, omen
rainbow (pert to) . . .
bridge (Norse Myth) . . **7.** Bifrost (to
Asgarth)
chaser . . **9.** visionary **11.** doctrinaire
flower . . **4.** iris
goddess . . **4.** Iris
term . . **6.** iridal
tree . . **5.** saman **8.** genisaro
unit . . **4.** inch
worm . . **8.** nematode **9.** earthworm
rainy . . . **3.** wet **7.** showery
rais, reis (Muslim) . . . **5.** chief, title
7. captain (ship's)
Rais . . . **10.** Mongoloids
raise . . . **3.** end **4.** grow, levy, lift, rear,
stir **5.** boost, breed, erect, exalt,
heave, hoist, rouse **6.** awaken, excite,
gather, leaven, muster, remove, uplift
7. collect, elevate, enhance, lighten,
present, produce, provoke, recruit
8. heighten, increase **9.** construct,
cultivate, promotion, propagate
10. aggrandize
raise (pert to) . . .
a nap . . **5.** tease **6.** teasel
Cain . . **3.** Ned **4.** hell **5.** cut up **7.** be
noisy **10.** vociferate
the dead . . **13.** lift the anchor
vegetables . . **12.** olericulture
raised . . . **4.** bred, hove **6.** buoyed,
enlève, hefted, lifted, reared **7.** hoisted
8. elevated, leavened, produced,
promoted
raised (pert to) . . .
spirits . . **6.** elated
to 3rd power . . **5.** cubed
troops . . **6.** levied **7.** drafted
11. conscripted
type . . **7.** braille
uproar . . **6.** rioted

with a bar . . **7.** levered
raisin . . . **4.** pasa **5.** grape, lexia
raja, rajah . . . **4.** king, rana **5.** title **6.** prince
9. dignitary
raja's consort . . . **4.** rani (ranee)
8. princess
Rajmahal hemp . . . **5.** fiber **9.** jiti fiber
Rajput . . . **5.** caste **9.** Kshatriya
rake . . . **3.** rut **4.** comb, path, raff,
roué **5.** slope, teeth, track **6.** lecher
7. debauch, seducer **8.** enfilade,
Lothario **9.** cultivate, implement,
libertine
rakehell . . . **4.** free, rake **9.** debauched,
debauchee, dissolute **10.** dissipated,
licentious, profligate
rakh . . . **3.** hay **8.** hayfield **9.** grassland
raki, rakee . . . **7.** spirits (distilled)
rale . . . **6.** rattle **8.** rhonchus **11.** morbid
sound
rallentando . . . **9.** direction (Mus)
10. ritardando, slackening
Rallidae . . . **5.** birds, coots, rails, wekas
6. crakes **10.** gallinules
rally . . . **6.** banter **7.** recover, reunite
8. assemble, recovery, ridicule
10. assemblage, call to arms
rallying cry . . . **4.** call **6.** slogan **9.** battle
cry, bugle call
ralph . . . **5.** raven
ram . . . **3.** hit, pun, tup **4.** buck, butt,
tamp **5.** Aries, crash, sheep **6.** rancid,
wether **7.** collide
Rama . . . **11.** Ramachandra (7th of fame)
19. incarnation of Vishnu
ramada . . . **5.** arbor **7.** pergola
Ramadan (Muslim) . . . **7.** fasting **10.** ninth
month (for fasting)
ramage . . . **4.** wild **5.** rough **6.** branch
(tree), unruly **7.** untamed **8.** frenzied
ramage hawk . . . **8.** brancher
ramass . . . **6.** gather **7.** collect
ramberge . . . **6.** galley (swift)
ramble . . . **3.** gad **4.** roam, rove, walk
5. jaunt, prowl, range **6.** stroll, wander
7. deviate, digress, saunter **8.** straggle
rambling . . . **7.** devious **9.** desultory,
deviation, deviative, wandering
10. circuitous, discursive, distracted
14. discursiveness
rambunctious . . . **4.** wild **6.** unruly
10. rampageous **12.** obstreperous
14. uncontrollable
ramentum . . . **5.** palea (palet) **6.** scales
8. a shaving, particle (minute)
Rameses Dynasties (pert to) . . .
famed for . . **5.** ruins **7.** papyrus
kings . . **6.** twelve
site . . **5.** Egypt
ramex . . . **6.** hernia **10.** varicocele
ram-headed goat . . . **5.** Ammon
ramie . . . **4.** hemp, rhea **5.** plant (fiber)
7. garment **9.** Boehmeria **10.** China
grass
ramification . . . **3.** arm **5.** ramus **6.** branch
8. offshoot **9.** branching **10.** divergence
12. embranchment
rammack . . . **4.** gawk, romp **5.** scamp
rammel . . . **4.** hard **6.** coarse **7.** new milk,
raw milk **9.** brushwood **11.** undergrowth
Ramona (pert to) . . .

heroine . . **9.** half-breed (Ind)
novel by . . **7.** Jackson (Helen Hunt)
shrub . . **4.** mint
ramp . . . **3.** rob **4.** rage, romp, walk
5. bound, climb, crawl, creep, storm
6. dupery, unruly **7.** incline, rampage,
swindle **8.** gradient, platform
9. helicline, impetuous **10.** cuckoopint
rampant . . . **6.** fierce, unruly, vallum (anc)
7. ramping **8.** abundant, reared up (Her)
9. exuberant, prevalent, unchecked
10. rampageous **12.** high-spirited,
unrestrained **13.** perpendicular
rampart . . . **4.** wall **5.** agger, mound, redan
6. escarp **7.** barrier, bulwark, defense,
parapet, ravelin **8.** buttress **9.** earthwork
10. embankment **13.** fortification
ram's horn (Heb) . . . **7.** shophar (shofar)
ran . . . **4.** fled, sped **6.** flowed **7.** coursed,
managed, trotted **8.** operated
ran (pert to) . . .
aground . . **8.** decamped, levanted,
stranded
away . . **4.** fled **6.** eloped **9.** absconded
out . . **5.** spilt **7.** petered, spilled
rana (Ind) . . . **5.** title **6.** prince
Rana . . . **5.** frogs **10.** amphibians (tailless)
ranarium . . . **8.** frog pond
rance . . . **4.** prop **6.** marble **7.** support
ranch . . . **4.** casa, farm **6.** estate
8. estancia, hacienda
ranchero . . . **6.** cowman **7.** vaquero
8. herdsman **9.** cattleman
rancid . . . **4.** rank **5.** musty, stale **6.** reechy
9. obnoxious, offensive **10.** unpleasant
rancor, rancour . . . **3.** ire **4.** gall **5.** spite
6. enmity, hatred, malice, rankle **7.** ill
will **9.** animosity **10.** resentment
rand . . . **4.** edge, rant **5.** ridge, storm
6. border, margin
random . . . **5.** stray **6.** casual, chance
7. aimless **8.** casually **9.** at liberty,
haphazard, orderless **10.** accidental,
fortuitous **11.** haphazardly
randy . . . **4.** wild **5.** revel, spree **6.** beggar,
coarse, frolic, virago **7.** canvass
8. carousal **9.** festivity **10.** disorderly
11. ill-mannered **12.** unmanageable
rang (pert to) . . . see also *ring*
loudly . . **7.** clanged
mournfully . . **6.** tolled **7.** knelled
slowly . . **6.** tolled
range . . . **3.** row **4.** ally, area, line, rank,
roam, size **5.** align, gamut, orbit,
scope **6.** limits, ramble, region, series,
wander **7.** arrange, compass, earshot,
habitat, pasture **8.** classify, mountain
9. cookstove
range (pert to) . . .
finder . . **9.** mekometer, telemeter
10. trekometer
man . . **5.** rider **6.** warden
of hills . . **5.** ridge
of knowledge . . **3.** ken
of stables . . **4.** mews
rangle . . . **5.** stray **6.** wander **8.** entangle,
straggle
rani, ranee (Hind) . . . **4.** wife **5.** queen
7. empress **8.** princess
rani (Romany) . . . **4.** lady, wife
Ranier, Mt . . . **10.** Washington (State)

ranine . . . **5.** frogs **7.** Raninae **8.** mink
frog
rank . . . **3.** bad, row **4.** file, foul, line, rate,
size, tier **5.** caste, class, grade, gross,
order, range **6.** degree, estate, rancid,
status, wicked **7.** arrange, glaring,
tainted **8.** absolute, abundant, classify,
eminence, flagrant, indecent, infamous,
nobility, palpable, position, prestige,
unsavory **9.** downright, formation,
luxuriant, plentiful **10.** malodorous
11. distinction
rank (pert to) . . .
and file . . **4.** army **8.** regulars
10. commonalty **11.** third estate
celestial . . **9.** hierarchy
exalted . . **8.** eminence
military (old) . . **8.** banneret
noble . . **10.** patriciate
rider . . **8.** reckless **10.** highwayman
social . . **5.** caste
rankle . . . **5.** chafe **6.** fester **7.** putrefy
8. make sore **9.** suppurate **10.** be
inflamed
rann . . . **5.** verse **6.** stanza, strain
ransack . . . **4.** rake, sack **5.** rifle **6.** search
7. plunder, rummage
ransom . . . **4.** fine **6.** redeem, rescue
7. expiate **8.** recovery
ranstead . . . **8.** toadflax (yellow)
13. butter-and-eggs
rant . . . **4.** rage, rail, rave **5.** boast **6.** steven
7. bluster, bombast, declaim **9.** gay
frolic **10.** get excited
rantipole . . . **4.** wild **6.** rakish, unruly
9. termagant
ranula . . . **4.** cyst
Ranunculaceae . . . **7.** anemone
8. aconitum, clematis, crowfoot
10. delphinium, ranunculus
rap . . . **3.** bop, hit **4.** bang, blow,
gibe, grab, knap, tirl **5.** knock, steal
6. rascal, snatch, trifle **8.** betrayal,
sentence (prison) **9.** criticism, reprimand
10. punishment **11.** skein of yarn
rapacious . . . **6.** greedy, rapine
8. grasping, ravenous **9.** devouring,
voracious **10.** avaricious, predacious
rapacity . . . **5.** greed, ravin (raven)
6. rapine **8.** appetite **9.** predacity
rapid . . . **4.** fast **5.** fleet, quick, swift
7. stretto (stretta)
rapidity . . . **5.** haste, speed **8.** celerity,
velocity **9.** fleetness, quickness
rapidly . . . **5.** amain, apace **7.** quickly,
swiftly **8.** snappily
rapids . . . **5.** rifts **6.** dalles
rapier . . . **5.** bilbo, sword **6.** verdun
7. ricasso (part)
rapine . . . **7.** pillage, plunder **8.** spoiling
10. ravishment, spoliation
rapport . . . **6.** accord **7.** empathy,
harmony, relation **9.** agreement
11. co-operation (hypnotism)
rapt . . . **8.** absorbed, ecstatic
10. enraptured, interested
11. preoccupied, transported
rapture . . . **3.** joy **4.** love **5.** bliss
6. trance **7.** delight, ecstasy **8.** rhapsody
9. transport **10.** exultation
rapturous . . . **8.** ecstatic

rara avis ... **6.** rarity **8.** rare bird
rare ... **3.** odd, raw **4.** thin **6.** scarce,
seldom, sparse **7.** notable, unusual
8. rarefied, uncommon **10.** infrequent
11. undercooked
rare (pert to) ...
  bird .. **8.** rara avis
  earth .. **6.** cerium **7.** terbium, yttrium
  metallic element .. **7.** yttrium
  object .. **5.** curio **6.** oddity **7.** antique
Rare Ben, inscription ... **15.** tomb of
Ben Jonson (Westminster Abbey)
rarebit ... **10.** cheese dish **11.** Welsh
rabbit
rarefy ... **4.** thin **6.** dilute, expand
9. attenuate
rarely ... **6.** finely, seldom **8.** not
often, scarcely **9.** extremely, unusually
11. beautifully **12.** infrequently
rarity ... **6.** oddity **7.** fewness, tenuity
8. scarcity, thinness **11.** infrequency
ras ... **4.** cape **6.** prince **11.** short-napped
13. Fascist leader
rasa ... **3.** sap (tree) **5.** fluid, taste
6. amrita, flavor **7.** essence **11.** living
water
rascal ... **3.** cad, imp **5.** knave, rogue,
scamp **6.** varlet **9.** miscreant
rascally ... **4.** mean **6.** impish **7.** knavish,
roguish **8.** scampish **11.** mischievous
rase ... **3.** cut, rub **4.** tear **5.** graze, level
6. scrape **7.** scratch
rash ... **3.** mad **4.** wild **5.** giddy, hasty,
heady, hives, scamp **6.** unwary, wanton
7. Icarian **8.** careless, eruption, heedless
9. desperate, exanthema, impetuous
10. headstrong, incautious, indiscreet
11. temerarious, thoughtless
rasher ... **5.** piece, slice **7.** portion **9.** thin
slice
rashness ... **6.** acrisy **7.** acrisia **8.** temerity
9. hastiness
rasion ... **6.** filing **7.** erasing, rasping,
shaving **8.** scraping
Rasores ... **4.** fowl **5.** birds **6.** quails
7. turkeys **8.** Columbae, Gallinae
9. pheasants **10.** partridges
rasp ... **3.** rub **4.** file **5.** belch, chafe,
erupt, grate **6.** abrade, offend, scrape
8. irritate **9.** raspberry
raspberry ... **3.** red **5.** apple, Rubus
6. raspis **7.** plumbog **8.** blackcap
rasping ... **5.** harsh **7.** chafing, grating,
raucous **8.** grinding, scraping, very
fast **9.** offensive **10.** irritating
raspings ... **6.** refuse **7.** filings, remains
rasse ... **5.** civet
rasure ... **3.** cut **5.** shave **7.** erasure,
polling, scratch, tonsure **8.** scraping
12. obliteration
rat ... **3.** rut **4.** scab, snob, wart **5.** track
6. desert, ratton, rodent **7.** scratch,
traitor **8.** deserter **9.** hairpiece,
scoundrel
rat (pert to) ...
  fish .. **8.** chimaera
  goose .. **11.** common brant
  hare .. **4.** pika
  kangaroo .. **7.** Potorus **9.** marsupial
  pineapple .. **7.** pinguin
  poison .. **8.** ratsbane

ratlike .. **4.** vole
rhyme .. **6.** jargon **13.** doggerel verse
ratafia ... **7.** biscuit (almond), curacao,
liqueur (Danzig)
ratchet ... **4.** pawl **5.** click **6.** bobbin,
detent
rate ... **4.** fare, pace **5.** price, ratio, style,
tempo, value **6.** assess, berate, charge,
reckon, regard **7.** account, deserve,
premium, reprove **8.** appraise, classify,
estimate, evaluate, interest
rate (of exchange) ... **4.** agio **5.** batta
rath (anc) ... **4.** hill, home (walled)
rath, ratha ... **3.** car **6.** temple (Seven
Pagodas, Madras) **7.** chariot
Rathaus ... **8.** town hall
rathe, rath ... **4.** soon **5.** eager, quick,
speed **7.** betimes, quickly **8.** speedily
rather ... **3.** ere, yes **6.** before **7.** earlier,
however, instead **8.** somewhat **9.** more
truly, tolerably **10.** especially, preferably
11. immediately **14.** on the other hand
ratification ... **4.** amen **5.** logic
8. sanction **9.** reasoning
11. endorsement **12.** confirmation
ratify ... **4.** amen, pass, seal **6.** enseal,
verify **7.** approve, confirm, consent,
endorse **8.** roborate, sanction
9. authorize
ratio ... **2.** pi **4.** rate, sine **5.** share
6. cosine, ration **7.** portion ⸴
10. proportion
ratiocination ... **5.** logic **7.** thought
9. reasoning
ration ... **5.** share **6.** budget **8.** relation
9. allotment, allowance, provision
11. calculation
rational ... **4.** sane, wise **5.** sober
7. logical **8.** sensible **9.** reasoning
10. reasonable **11.** philosophic
rationale ... **6.** reason **11.** explanation
12. the how and why
ratio scripta ... **13.** written reason
ratite ... (opp of carinate)**7.** Ratitae
8. unkeeled **14.** flat breastbone
ratite bird ... **3.** emu (emeu), moa
7. ostrich **9.** cassoway
ratoon ... **5.** shoot, stalk **6.** spring, sprout
rattan, ratan ... **4.** cane, palm, sega,
whip **6.** switch **7.** calamus
ratteen ... **8.** mahogany
rattle ... **3.** toy **4.** herb, rale, rick,
tirl **5.** annoy, clack **6.** assail, prison
(Nav), racket, uproar **7.** agitate,
chatter, clapper, clatter, confuse,
fluster, maracas, prattle **8.** nonsense
9. chatterer, rapid talk **10.** disconcert,
noisemaker
rattle (pert to) ...
  bones .. **8.** clappers, snappers
  9. castanets
  headed .. **8.** confused **11.** empty-headed
  13. rattlebrained
  mouse .. **3.** bat
  nut .. **10.** chinquapin
  pate .. **3.** ass
  root .. **7.** bugbane
rattlesnake ... **7.** rattler **8.** belltail,
Crotalus, pit viper **9.** Sistrurus
rattlesnake (pert to) ...
  bean .. **6.** cedron

bite . . **9.** meadow rue
fern . . **9.** chain fern, sporangia
flag (Maine) . . **13.** Don't Tread on Me (Hist)
herb . . **9.** baneberry
leaf . . **8.** plantain
pilot . . **10.** copperhead
plantain . . **6.** orchid
variety . . **3.** red **6.** banded, timber **7.** prairie **11.** diamondback
venom . . **8.** crotalus
rattletrap . . . **6.** gewgaw **7.** rickety **8.** claptrap, the mouth **10.** knickknack, ramshackle
ratton . . . **3.** rat
ratwa . . . **7.** muntjac
raucous . . . **3.** dry **4.** bray, loud **5.** harsh, noisy **6.** hoarse, raucid, rauque **8.** strident **11.** cacophonous
rauk, roke . . . **4.** poke, stir **5.** vapor **7.** scratch
raun . . . **3.** roe **4.** fish **5.** spawn
ravage . . . **4.** loot, ruin, sack **5.** havoc, spoil, waste **6.** damage, infest **7.** debauch, destroy, overrun, pillage, plunder **9.** devastate **10.** desolation **11.** despoilment, devastation, infestation
ravages of time . . . **13.** deterioration **14.** disintegration
rave . . . **4.** rage, rant **5.** crush, storm **7.** bluster, declaim, enthuse **8.** be insane, harangue
ravel . . . **4.** fray **6.** runner, slough, unwind **7.** involve, unravel, untwist, unweave **8.** entangle, separate **11.** disentangle, loose thread
ravelin . . . **7.** railing **8.** demilune, half-moon **13.** fortification
Ravel opus . . . **6.** Bolero
raven . . . **4.** bird, crow **6.** Corvus **8.** standard (vikings) **10.** raven-black **11.** Corvus corax
Raven (The) . . . **4.** poem (Edgar Allan Poe)
ravening . . . **3.** mad **5.** rabid **6.** greedy, prying **8.** desirous **9.** rapacious, turbulent
ravenous . . . **6.** greedy **8.** edacious **9.** rapacious, voracious **10.** gluttonous **11.** catawampous
ravine . . . **3.** gap **4.** dell, linn (lin), wadi (wady) **5.** chine, gorge, gulch, slade, strid **6.** arroyo, clough, gulley, nullah **8.** barranca
ravish . . . **3.** rob **4.** rape **5.** seize **7.** corrupt, debauch, delight, despoil, plunder, violate **8.** deflower, entrance **9.** enrapture, transport
raw . . . **4.** cold, sore **5.** bleak, crude, naked **6.** chilly, unripe, vulgar **7.** natural, not spun, untried **8.** immature, indecent, uncooked **9.** inclement, unskilled, windswept **10.** unprepared **11.** undeveloped, unprocessed **13.** inexperienced
rawboned . . . **4.** lank **5.** gaunt **7.** angular **8.** skeletal
rawbones . . . **5.** Death **8.** skeleton
raw-flesh-eating . . . **9.** omophagia
rawhide . . . **4.** skin (untanned), whip
rawhide whip . . . **5.** knout, quirt, thong

7. sjambok
raw sugar . . . **9.** cassonade
rax . . . **5.** reach **6.** become, strain **7.** stretch
ray . . . **4.** beam, dorn, soil, X-ray **5.** array, dress, gamma, order, skate (fish) **6.** defile, radius, stripe, vision **7.** besmear, raiment **8.** particle, radiance, stingray **11.** arrangement, irradiation
raya . . . **9.** broadbill
rayless . . . **4.** dark **5.** blind
rayon . . . **3.** ray **5.** fiber **6.** radius **14.** postal district (Switz)
raze, rase . . . **3.** cut **4.** fell, ruin **5.** erase, graze, level, shave **6.** efface, scrape **7.** destroy **8.** demolish **9.** dismantle, prostrate **10.** obliterate
razee . . . **3.** cut (Naut) **5.** prune **7.** abridge
razor (pert to) . . .
back . . **3.** hog **4.** boar **5.** ridge **10.** roustabout (circus)
bill . . **3.** auk **7.** skimmer
billed auk . . **4.** falk **5.** murre, noddy
clam . . **5.** Solen **11.** chopa blanca
grinder . . **10.** goatsucker
sharpen . . **4.** hone **5.** strop
stone . . **9.** whetstone **10.** novaculite
strap . . **5.** strop
type . . **6.** safety **7.** rattler
razz . . . **5.** chaff, tease **6.** banter, deride **8.** ridicule **9.** raspberry
razzle-dazzle . . . **5.** cinch (game), spree **6.** dazzle **7.** confuse **8.** bewilder **9.** commotion **10.** noisemaker
re . . . **4.** back (pref) **5.** about, again, anent, tone D (Mus) **8.** syllable (Mus) **10.** concerning
Re . . . **2.** Ra (Egypt) see also *Ra*
reach . . . **4.** come, gain, hawk, ryke, spar, spit **5.** equal, retch **6.** advene, arrive, attain, extend, length **7.** achieve, compass, earshot, expanse, possess, stretch **8.** distance, overtake **9.** influence **10.** understand
reach (pert to) . . .
across . . **4.** span
for applause . . **9.** captation
high point . . **9.** culminate
out . . **6.** extend **7.** stretch
under . . **7.** subtend
up . . **6.** aspire
reaction . . . **4.** kick **6.** change (Chem) **7.** tropism **8.** response **9.** influence **10.** opposition
reactionary . . . **4.** Tory **10.** malcontent **12.** conservative, recalcitrant
read . . . **3.** con **4.** pore, scan, skim, tell **5.** guess, solve **6.** advise, browse, peruse, recite, relate **7.** counsel, declare, discern, foresee, prelect (praelect), stomach **8.** decipher, describe, foretell **9.** interpret **10.** understand
readable . . . **7.** legible **12.** decipherable
reader . . . **6.** lector, lister, primer (McGuffey) **7.** browser, license, reciter, speaker, teacher **8.** anagnost (anagnostes), literate, textbook **9.** churchman, prelector (praelector) **10.** pocketbook **11.** proofreader **12.** elocutionist
readily . . . **6.** at once, easily **7.** quickly

8. probably **9.** willingly **10.** very likely
readjust . . . **7.** readapt, restore
9. rearrange **11.** reconstruct
12. rehabilitate
ready . . . **3.** apt, fit, fix **4.** bain, free,
here, ripe, yare **5.** alert, apert, eager,
handy, point, quick **6.** facile, fitted,
prompt **7.** willing **8.** cheerful, disposed,
inclined, prepared, skillful **9.** dexterous
12. unhesitating
ready acceptance . . . **11.** embracement
ready for . . . **6.** awaits **8.** liable to **10.** in
store for **11.** prepared for
ready-to-wear . . . **12.** haute couture
real . . . **4.** true, very **5.** pucka (pukka)
6. actual **7.** factual, genuine, sincere
8. absolute, existent, handmade,
tangible **9.** authentic, veritable
10. unaffected **11.** substantial
real (pert to) . . .
being . . **6.** entity
estate . . **5.** lands **6.** domain, houses,
realty **7.** demesne **8.** easement,
freehold, property **9.** tenements
13. hereditaments
map . . **4.** plot
name (backwards) . . **6.** ananym
school . . **10.** Realschule
realistic . . . **5.** vivid **8.** lifelike **9.** practical
11. descriptive
reality . . . **5.** truth **7.** realism
11. genuineness
reality, non-existent . . . **8.** nihilism
realize . . . **3.** get, win **4.** gain, know
5. sense **7.** convert **8.** conceive
10. accomplish
realm . . . **6.** domain, empire, region,
sphere **7.** country, demesne, kingdom
8. division, province **10.** department
12. jurisdiction
realm (of) . . .
darkness (Myth) . . **2.** po
Jamshid . . **6.** Persia
perfection . . **6.** Utopia
ream . . . **4.** bore, foam, scum **5.** widen
6. bundle **7.** enlarge **8.** bevel out
11. countersink **14.** enormous amount
reanimate . . . **5.** rally **6.** revive **7.** refresh
11. resuscitate **12.** reinvigorate
rear . . . **3.** aft **4.** back, grow, hind, lift,
loom, rise, rump **5.** breed, build, erect,
raise, stern, train **6.** behind, foster
7. arriere, educate, elevate, produce
8. instruct **9.** construct, establish,
posterior **10.** background
rear (pert to) . . .
admiral . . **7.** two bars (silver)
commodore, yacht club . . **7.** officer
end . . **6.** breech **7.** hind end **9.** afterpart,
posterior
horse (insect) . . **6.** mantis
most . . **4.** last
toward . . **3.** aft **5.** abalt **6.** astern
8. backward, rearward
rearing up (horse) . . . **5.** stend **6.** pesade
rearrange . . . **4.** sort **8.** readjust
10. reordinate, reorganize
reason . . . **5.** argue, cause, logic, sense,
think **6.** deduce, ground, motive, sanity
7. discuss **8.** argument, conclude,
judgment, question, solution

9. discourse, intellect **11.** explanation,
ratiocinate, rationalize **13.** justification,
understanding
reason (pert to) . . .
discursively . . **11.** ratiocinate
doctrine of, author . . **10.** Anaxagoras
higher . . **4.** mind, nous **5.** logic
Latin . . **5.** causa
ostensible . . **7.** pretext
pert to . . **6.** noetic
proof of . . **8.** argument
want of . . **7.** amentia
why . . **5.** cause **6.** motive
reasonable . . . **4.** fair, just, sane **6.** proper
7. logical **8.** rational **9.** equitable,
plausible, practical **10.** fair-minded
11. inexpensive, intelligent, justifiable
reasoning (pert to) . . .
basis of . . **7.** premise
delusive . . **7.** fallacy
exact . . **5.** logic
harmonize . . **11.** rationalize
plausible . . **8.** specious
reassure . . . **6.** assure, solace **7.** comfort,
console, hearten **8.** embolden, give
hope
reata . . . **4.** rope **5.** lasso, riata **6.** lariat
reave . . . **3.** rob **4.** rend, tear **5.** break,
burst, seize, split **7.** plunder
reb . . . **5.** rebel
rebate . . . **5.** check **6.** reduce, weaken
8. diminish, discount **9.** abatement,
deduction, remission
rebato (Hist) . . . **4.** ruff **6.** collar, rabato
9. piccadill
Rebekah (pert to) . . .
husband . . **5.** Isaac
sister . . **5.** Laban
son . . **4.** Esau **5.** Jacob
rebel . . . **3.** reb **4.** rise **6.** resist, revolt
8. renounce, turncoat **9.** insurgent
13. revolutionist
rebellion . . . **5.** Great (Eng 1642-49)
6. mutiny, revolt **8.** American (Civil
War 1861-65) **10.** resistance, revolution
12. insurrection, renunciation
rebellious . . . **8.** mutinous **9.** insurgent
10. refractory **12.** contumacious
13. insubordinate, revolutionary
rebirth . . . **7.** revival **9.** salvation
10. conversion **11.** renaissance
13. reincarnation
rebound . . . **4.** stot **5.** carom **6.** bounce,
recoil, re-echo, spring **7.** resound
8. rebounce, ricochet **11.** reverberate
rebuff . . . **4.** slap, snub **5.** chide, scold
6. defeat, lesson, recoil, refuse, reject,
resist **7.** censure, refusal (brusque),
reprove, repulse **9.** reprimand
rebuke . . . **3.** nip **4.** slap **5.** check,
chide **6.** rebuff **7.** repress, reproof,
reprove **8.** admonish, reproach, restrain
9. criticize, reprehend, reprimand
11. comeuppance
recalcitrant . . . **5.** rebel **8.** renitent
9. obstinate, recoiling, resistant
10. rebellious, refractory **11.** disobedient
12. ungovernable
recall . . . **5.** annul **6.** encore, recant,
remind, repeal, revoke, summon
7. retract **8.** remember, withdraw

9. recollect, reminisce 11. recantation
12. recollection
recant ... 6. abjure, revoke 7. disavow, retract 8. renounce, withdraw 9. repudiate 10. contradict
recapitulate ... 5. essay, sum up 6. repeat, review 7. restate 8. argument 9. reiterate, summarize
recapture ... 6. recall, regain, retake 7. recover
recede ... 3. ebb 4. wane 6. depart, retire 7. deviate, regress, retreat 8. withdraw 10. retrograde
receipt ... 5. axiom 6. acquit, answer, recipe 7. formula 12. prescription 14. acknowledgment
receipts ... 7. the take
receive ... 3. get 4. hold, take 5. admit, greet, learn, reset 6. accept, assent, derive, obtain, take in 7. acquire, contain, procure 9. apprehend
receive (pert to) ...
a confession .. 6. shrive
a reward .. 4. reap
stolen property .. 5. reset
receiver ... 5. donee, fence 7. catcher 8. believer 9. recipient, treasurer 10. receptacle
receiver (pert to) ...
fixed income .. 7. rentier
profits (law) .. 6. pernor
property in trust .. 6. bailee
stolen property .. 6. fence
recension ... 6. review 8. revising, revision 9. reviewing 11. enumeration, examination
recent ... 3. new 4. late, past 5. fresh 6. former, modern 7. current, newborn 8. neonatal, neoteric
receptacle ... 3. bag, bin, box, can, cup, pan 4. case, cask, cyst (anc), etui, pail, tank, tray, vase 5. basin, crock 6. basket, bottle, bucket, carton, holder, hopper 7. compote, hanaper, platter 8. canister, catchall 9. container 10. repository
receptacle (pert to) ...
assayer's, stonecutter's .. 7. sebilla
botany .. 5. torus
coal .. 3. bin
corporal (RCCh) .. 5. burse
grain .. 3. bin 8. elevator
holy water .. 5. stoup
vote .. 6. situla
reception ... 3. tea 5. levee, salon 6. infare, soiree 7. accueil, ovation, receipt, welcome 8. ceremony, sociable 9. admission, interview, intuition 12. housewarming 13. entertainment
reception hall, room ... 5. salon 6. atrium, parlor 9. vestibule
receptionist ... 4. host 7. hostess 8. landlord
receptive ... 6. pliant 8. sensible 9. acceptant, admissive, teachable 10. hospitable, open-minded 11. persuasible
receptor ... 5. basin 8. receiver 10. dispositor (Astron), sense organ
recess ... 3. ala, bay, pan (leaf) 4. apse, nook, rest 5. crypt, niche, pause,

sinus, space 7. adjourn, respite, retreat 9. recession, seclusion 11. indentation 12. intermission
recipe ... 5. axiom 7. formula, receipt 12. prescription
recipient ... 4. heir 5. donee 7. legatee 8. receiver
reciprocal ... 5. joint 6. mutual, shared 8. exchange 9. alternate 11. convertible, correlative, retaliatory 15. interchangeable
reciprocate ... 5. bandy 6. accord, concur 8. exchange 9. alternate, retaliate 10. correspond 11. interchange
recision ... 6. repeal 7. pruning 9. canceling (cancelling) 10. rescinding
recital ... 4. tale 5. story 6. lesson, speech 7. account, concert (exhibition) 8. musicale 9. narration, narrative, rehearsal 10. recitation, repetition 11. enumeration, reiteration
recitation ... 6. lesson, speech 7. reading 10. exhibition
recite ... 4. tell 5. quote, speak, state 6. relate, repeat 7. declaim, narrate, recount 8. rehearse, tell over 9. enumerate, pronounce 12. recapitulate
recite (pert to) ...
in monotone .. 6. intone
metrically .. 4. scan
rhetorically .. 7. declaim
to music .. 6. chant 10. cantillate
reciter ... 4. book (of extracts) 5. roter 7. relator, speaker 8. narrator
reck ... 4. care, deem, heed, mind 6. regard 7. concern 8. estimate
reckless ... 4. rash 5. perdu (perdue) 6. madcap 7. hotspur 8. careless, heedless 9. desperate, hotheaded, imprudent 10. neglectful, regardless 11. indifferent, thoughtless, unconcerned 13. inconsiderate
reckon ... 4. aret (arette), date, deem, tell 5. class, count, judge, tally, think 6. impute, number, regard, repute 7. account, compute, include, suppose 8. consider, estimate, evaluate 9. calculate, enumerate
reckoning ... 3. sum 4. bill, shot 5. score, tally 6. esteem 7. account, verdict 8. counting 9. summation 10. estimation 11. calculation
reckoning instrument ... 6. abacus 9. tabulator 10. calculator
reclaim ... 4. tame 5. renew, train 6. ransom, recall, redeem, revoke 7. convert, recover, restore 8. civilize 10. regenerate 12. rehabilitate
recline ... 3. lay, lie, sit 4. lean, loll, rest 6. repose 7. incline, lie down
reclining ... 4. flat 5. prone 6. supine 7. lolling 8. couchant, reposing 9. prostrate, recumbent
recluse ... 3. fra, nun 4. monk 6. hermit, hidden, secret, shut up 7. ascetic, eremite, retired (from world) 8. anchoret, isolated, solitary 9. anchorite 10. cloistered 11. sequestered
recognition ... 4. fame 6. recall

9. detection 10. cognizance
11. discernment 14. acknowledgment
recognize . . . 3. see 4. know 5. admit
6. detect 7. consent 8. identify,
perceive 10. appreciate, recognosce
11. acknowledge
recoil . . . 3. shy 4. funk 5. quail 6. flinch,
resile, shrink 7. rebound, retreat
8. reaction, withdraw
recollect . . . 6. recall, revive 7. think of
8. remember 10. call to mind
recollection . . . 4. mind 6. memory
9. anamnesis 11. remembrance
12. reminiscence
recommence . . . 5. renew 6. resume
8. return to 9. begin anew
recommend . . . 4. tout, urge 6. advise,
commit, denote, praise 7. commend,
consign, entrust 8. advocate
recompense . . . 3. fee, pay 4. meed
5. repay 6. reward 8. requital
9. indemnify, reimburse
10. compensate, remunerate
11. reciprocate
recompense (pert to) . . .
Brehon Law . . 4. eric
Germanic law . . 7. wergild
Scot law . . 3. cro
Welsh law . . 7. galanas
reconcile . . . 4. suit, wean 5. atone
6. adjust, pacify, settle 7. cleanse
(Eccl), conform, reunite 9. harmonize
10. conciliate, propitiate
reconciliation . . . 7. harmony, reunion
10. adjustment, conformity
12. pacification 13. reconcilement
reconciliator . . . 10. arbitrator, reconciler
13. intermediator
recondite . . . 4. dark, deep 6. hidden,
mystic, occult 7. cryptic 8. abstract,
abstruse, esoteric 9. concealed
reconnaissance . . . 6. survey 8. scouting
11. examination
reconnoiter . . . 5. scout 6. survey
reconstruct . . . 6. recast, remake
7. rebuild, remodel 9. reproduce
11. reestablish
record . . . 3. log, tab 4. disc, file, list,
memo 5. annal, diary, enter, entry,
score 6. agenda, legend, memoir,
postea 7. archive, estreat, history
8. memorial, register 9. chronicle
10. chronology, transcribe, transcript
record (pert to) . . .
criminal investigation . . 7. dossier
document . . 8. protocol
earth tremor . . 11. seismograph
formal . . 4. vita 8. register
historic . . 6. annals 7. rotulet
keeper . . 9. registrar 10. chartulary
of events . . 5. annal, fasti 7. history
official . . 5. actum
pictorial . . 5. graph
ship's voyage . . 3. log
year's . . 5. diary 8. calendar
recording terms . . . 2. LP 4. reel, tape
5. album, Dolby 6. needle, stereo, stylus
7. capstan 8. cassette 9. cartridge,
videotape
recount . . . 3. min 4. tell 5. sum up
6. reckon, relate, repeat, retail 7. narrate

8. rehearse 9. enumerate, reiterate
12. recapitulate
recoup . . . 4. gain 7. recover 8. retrieve
9. indemnity, reimburse 10. compensate
recourse . . . 3. use 5. recur 6. access,
betake, refuge, resort, return, revert
7. retreat
recover . . . 3. get 4. cure, gain, heal
5. rally, reach, upset 6. obtain, recoup,
redeem, regain, rescue, resume 7. get
well, reclaim, recruit 8. overcome,
retrieve 9. repossess 10. convalesce,
recuperate
recovery . . . 6. return 7. salvage
9. retrieval 11. reclamation, reformation,
restoration
recreant . . . 6. coward, wretch 7. dastard,
knavish 8. apostate, betrayer, cowardly,
deserter 9. reprobate 10. unfaithful
recreation . . . 4. food, game, meal,
play 5. sport 7. holiday, renewal
8. vacation 9. amusement, diversion
11. refreshment 12. reproduction
14. reconstruction
recrement . . . 5. dross 6. refuse, scoria
recruit . . . 5. raise 6. enlist, gather, muster,
novice, revive, rookie 7. recover,
refresh, restore 8. assemble, inductee,
newcomer 9. conscript, reinforce,
replenish 12. reinvigorate
rectangle . . . 10. quadrangle
13. parallelogram
rectangular . . . 6. oblong
12. quadrangular
rectify . . . 5. amend, emend, right
6. adjust, better, reform, remedy
7. correct, justify 8. emendate, regulate,
set right 10. straighten
rector . . . 5. chief 6. leader, master
(Oxford), pastor 8. director, governor
9. churchman, clergyman
10. headmaster
rectory . . . 8. benefice 9. personage
recumbent . . . 4. idle 5. lying, prone
7. leaning, resting 8. inactive, reposing
9. reclining
recuperate . . . 4. rest 6. recoup, regain
7. improve, recover, restore 9. get
better, reimburse
recur . . . 5. again 6. repeat, return
7. persist, reoccur 8. reappear
recurrent . . . 10. repetitive
recurring (pert to) . . .
continually . . 8. constant 10. habitually,
repeatedly
ninth day . . 5. nonan
seventh day . . 6. septan
third day . . 7. tertian
red . . . 4. rosy 5. color, ruddy 7. radical
8. blushing, inflamed, rutilant, sanguine
9. bloodshot 12. bloodstained
13. revolutionary
red (color) . . . 4. fire, lake, pink, puce,
rose, ruby, tile, wine 5. blood,
brick, canna, coral, flame, flesh,
henna, poppy 6. auburn, cerise,
cherry, claret, damask, maroon,
minium, raddle, salmon, titian, Turkey
7. anemone, annatto, carmine, Chinese,
crimson, lobster, magenta, nacarat,
scarlet, stammel 8. cardinal, cinnabar

9. carnation, carnelian, vermilion
red (pert to) . . .
cap (Turk) . . **8.** tarboosh
cell . . **11.** erythrocite
corpuscle . . **10.** hemoglobin (source of)
dog . . **4.** game **8.** banknote
dye . . **3.** aal, lac **4.** chay (choy) **5.** aurin
(aurine), eosin (eosine) **8.** morindin
gum . . **10.** strophulus
hair . . **6.** titian
herring . . **4.** ruse **9.** diversion
minded . . **7.** radical
planet . . **4.** Mars
race . . **7.** Indians
robbin . . **14.** scarlet tanager
truffle . . **12.** melanogaster
viper . . **10.** copperhead
Red (pert to) . . .
Book . . **7.** Austria **13.** Royal Kalendar
Crescent . . **8.** Red Cross (Turk)
Cross . . **9.** St George's (Eng)
Friar . . **13.** Knight Templar
Guard . . **4.** Army **7.** Russian
Hand . . **13.** Badge of Ulster
Horse . . **10.** Kentuckian
Planet . . **4.** Mars
Polled . . **6.** cattle (hornless)
Prince . . **7.** Russian (Frederick Charles)
Ribbon . . **14.** Order of the Bath
Rose . . **16.** House of Lancaster
Russian . . **9.** Bolshevik
Sea . . **14.** Erythraean main
Sea city . . **9.** Leningrad
Sea colony . . **7.** Eritrea
Sea gulf . . **5.** Aqaba
Square . . **6.** Moscow
The Red . . **4.** Eric (Scand)
Triangle . . **4.** YMCA (symbol)
redact . . . **4.** edit **5.** draft, frame **6.** revise
redactor . . . **6.** editor **7.** reviser
9. redacteur
reddish (pert to) . . .
blue . . **5.** smalt **9.** damascene
brown . . **3.** bay **4.** roan **5.** henna
6. auburn, russet, sorrel **8.** chestnut
dye . . **7.** annatto
yellow . . **5.** amber **6.** orange
rede . . . **6.** advice, relate **7.** counsel,
explain, predict **9.** interpret
redeem . . . **3.** pay **6.** ransom, regain,
rescue **7.** convert, fulfill, reclaim,
recover **8.** liberate **10.** repurchase,
substitute
redeemer . . . **4.** goel (Heb) **7.** saviour
(savior) **9.** deliverer, liberator
11. emancipator
Redeemer, The . . . **8.** Son of God **10.** The
Messiah, The Saviour **11.** Jesus Christ
redintegrate . . . **5.** renew, unite **7.** restore
9. reconcile **11.** re-establish
redness . . . **4.** glow **8.** blushing
10. erubescent, rubescence
redolence . . . **4.** odor **5.** aroma, scent
9. fragrance, sweetness
redolent . . . **5.** balmy **7.** odorous, scented
8. aromatic, fragrant **11.** impregnated,
reminiscent
redouble . . . **6.** re-echo, repeat **7.** reflect,
reprise (fencing) **9.** intensify
10. ingeminate, repetition
11. reduplicate

redoubt . . . **4.** fear **5.** doubt **6.** reduit
7. defense, ravelin
redound . . . **5.** surge **6.** abound, return
7. conduce, resound **8.** flow back,
overflow **10.** contribute (to)
11. reverberate
redpoll . . . **5.** finch **6.** linnet **7.** warbler
Red Polled cattle . . . **8.** hornless
redress . . . **4.** help **5.** amend, emend
6. reform, remedy **7.** correct, relieve
8. atone for, reprisal **9.** atonement
10. correction, recompense, reparation
11. reformation, restitution
reduce . . . **3.** cut **4.** bant, bate, pare,
thin **5.** abase, abate, lower, razee
6. demote, derate, humble, lessen,
subdue, weaken **7.** abridge, analyze,
cheapen, conquer, curtail, deplete,
qualify, relieve, shorten **8.** decrease,
diminish, discount, minimize, moderate
9. subjugate **10.** impoverish, slenderize
reduce in flesh . . . **8.** emaciate
reduce in rank . . . **6.** demote
reduce to . . .
ashes . . **7.** cremate
average . . **4.** mean **6.** equate
bondage . . **7.** enslave
common measure . . **12.** commensurate
half . . **9.** dimidiate
lower grade . . **6.** demote **7.** degrade
mean time . . **6.** equate
spray . . **7.** atomize
reduction . . . **6.** rebate **7.** subdual
8. decrease, demotion, discount,
lowering **9.** weakening **10.** abridgment,
cheapening, conversion, moderation
reduction (pert to) . . .
in value . . **12.** depreciation
to absurdity . . **18.** reductio ad absurdum
to common level . . **15.** standardization
to compactness . . **12.** condensation
to standard . . **15.** standardization
redundancy . . . **6.** excess **7.** profuse
8. pleonasm, verbiage **9.** prolixity,
talkative, tautology, verbosity
10. repetition **11.** periphrasis
13. diffusiveness **14.** circumlocution
redundant . . . **6.** lavish **7.** copious, diffuse,
verbose **9.** excessive, exuberant,
plethoric **10.** pleonastic **11.** overflowing,
repetitious, superfluous
13. superabundant
ree . . . **3.** dam **4.** sift, wild **5.** crazy, drunk,
river **6.** harbor, riddle **7.** channel,
fuddled **8.** coalyard **9.** enclosure,
sheepfold
re-echo . . . **7.** resound **11.** reverberate
reechy . . . **5.** fetid **6.** rancid
reed . . . **4.** stem, tube **5.** arrow, straw
6. thatch **10.** instrument
reed (pert to) . . .
bird . . **4.** wren **7.** babbler, warbler
8. bobolink
buck . . **5.** bohor, nagar **8.** antelope
bunting . . **7.** sparrow **8.** reedling
instrument . . **4.** oboe **7.** bagpipe
8. clarinet **9.** accordion, saxophone
loom . . **4.** sley
mace . . **7.** cattail, matreed
measure (Jew) . . **9.** six cubits
pipe . . **5.** kazoo **8.** mirliton

reef . . . **3.** bar, cay (cayo), key (quay) **4.** itch, lode, sail, vein **5.** islet, mange, shoal **6.** island **7.** shorten **8.** eruption
reef (pert to) . . .
coral . . **3.** key
knot . . **6.** square
mining . . **4.** lode, vein
nautical . . **5.** sails
sand . . **3.** bar
reefer . . . **5.** miner **6.** jacket, oyster **9.** cigarette **10.** midshipman
reek . . . **3.** fug, rig **4.** fume **5.** equip, exude, smell, smoke, steam **7.** malodor, seaweed **8.** fetid air, smell bad, vaporize **10.** exhalation
reel . . . **4.** eddy, pirn, rock, sail, sway, wind **5.** dance, lurch, spool, swift (yarn), swing, waver, wince **6.** tatter **7.** scrieve, stagger **8.** flounder, titubate, windlass **12.** Virginia reel
reeling . . . **5.** drunk **7.** swaying, winding **8.** rotating
reem (Bib) . . . **6.** animal (horned), wild ox **7.** unicorn
re-embody . . . **7.** combine, reshape **10.** reorganize **11.** reincarnate **13.** reincorporate
reeve . . . **3.** pen **4.** ruff **5.** strip **6.** thread **8.** official (Eng Hist) **9.** enclosure, sheepfold
refect . . . **7.** refresh, restore
refectory . . . **6.** frater (monastery) **8.** mess hall **10.** dining hall
refer . . . **4.** cite **5.** apply, recur **6.** allude, appeal, charge, impute, relate, return **7.** ascribe **9.** appertain, attribute
refer (to) . . . **4.** harp **6.** advert **7.** consult, mention
referee . . . **5.** judge **6.** umpire **7.** arbiter **8.** attorney **9.** moderator **10.** arbitrator
reference . . . **6.** regard **7.** respect **8.** allusion, relation **9.** character, relevance **10.** connection, pertinence **14.** recommendation
reference (pert to) . . .
book . . **5.** atlas **8.** handbook, syllabus **9.** thesaurus **10.** dictionary **12.** encyclopedia
referendum . . . **4.** vote **7.** mandate **8.** politics **10.** plebiscite
refine . . . **5.** smelt **6.** rarefy **7.** clarify, elevate, improve, sublime **9.** elaborate, sensitize, sublimate
refined . . . **4.** fine, nice, pure, rare **5.** urban **6.** chaste **7.** elegant, smelted **8.** cleansed, highbred, purified, well-bred **9.** clarified, courteous, perfected **10.** cultivated, fastidious, meticulous
refined spirit . . . **5.** grace **6.** elixir
refinement . . . **5.** taste **6.** polish **7.** finesse **8.** delicacy, elegance, fineness **9.** gentility **11.** cultivation, rarefaction **13.** clarification
refinery (ore) . . . **7.** smelter
refining cup . . . **5.** cupel
reflect . . . **3.** say **4.** muse, pore **5.** radar, think **6.** divert, mirror, ponder **7.** deflect **8.** cogitate, consider, meditate, ruminate, turn back **9.** reproduce **11.** reverberate
reflecting . . . **6.** musing **9.** judicious

10. reflective, ruminating, thoughtful **11.** insinuating **13.** reverberatory **15.** casting reproach
reflection . . . **4.** idea **5.** image, light **6.** musing **7.** bending, thought **8.** reaction, thinking **10.** cogitation, meditation, rumination **12.** afterthought, recollection **13.** consideration, contemplation
reflex . . . **4.** bent **6.** turned **8.** allusion, reaction, reversed **9.** duplicate, reflected **13.** introspection
reflux . . . **3.** ebb **6.** ebbing, reflow **8.** backflow, reaction **9.** refluence, returning
reform . . . **4.** mend **5.** amend, emend, renew **6.** better, remake, remass, repair **7.** convert, rebuild, reclaim, rectify, restore **9.** amendment **10.** regenerate **11.** reformation
reformation . . . **7.** rebirth **10.** conversion, emendation **12.** regeneration, reproduction **15.** re-establishment
Reformation leaders (Hist) . . . **4.** Knox **6.** Calvin, Luther, Ridley **7.** Cranmer, Latimer, Zwingli **8.** Campbell **11.** Melanchthon
reformer . . . **7.** amender, reviser **9.** reformado, reformist **10.** politician
refraction . . . **7.** rebound **9.** dioptrics **10.** deflection, dispersion **11.** anaclastics
refractor . . . **5.** prism **9.** telescope
refractory . . . **7.** restive **8.** indocile, stubborn **11.** disobedient **12.** ungovernable
refrain . . . **4.** curb, shun **5.** avoid, cease, derry, epode **6.** chorus, govern **7.** abstain, forbear **8.** response, restrain
refrain from using . . . **5.** spare **7.** boycott
refresco . . . **4.** food **5.** drink **11.** refreshment
refresh . . . **3.** air, dew **4.** cool **5.** cheer, renew, slake **6.** repose, revive **7.** freshen, relieve **8.** recreate, renovate **9.** reanimate, replenish **10.** invigorate, strengthen **11.** refreshment **12.** reinvigorate
refreshing . . . **5.** balmy **7.** bracing **8.** regaling **10.** heartening **11.** stimulating **12.** exhilarating
refrigerant . . . **3.** ice **6.** cooler **7.** ammonia, coolant, cryogen
refrigeration . . . **7.** cooling **8.** cryogeny **10.** anesthetic, cryogenics **12.** preservation
refuge . . . **3.** ark **4.** plea **5.** haven **6.** asylum, covert, excuse **7.** retreat, shelter **8.** hospital, recourse, resource **9.** sanctuary **10.** protection, safety zone
refugee . . . **5.** exile, fleer **6.** émigré **7.** escapee, evacuee **8.** fugitive, renegade
refulgence . . . **6.** luster **8.** radiance, splendor **10.** brilliancy
refund . . . **5.** repay **6.** rebate **9.** reimburse
refurbish . . . **4.** vamp **5.** renew **8.** brighten, renovate **11.** recondition
refusal . . . **3.** nay **6.** denial **9.** rejection **11.** declination
refuse . . . **3.** cot (wool), ort **4.** balk, coom (coomb), culm, deny, junk, marc, scum

5. attle, chaff, dregs, dross, repel, scrap, trash, waste, weeds **6.** debris, give up, litter, midden, naysay, reject, renege, scoria, scraps **7.** abandon, bagasse, cast off, decline, garbage, hogwash, repulse **8.** disclaim, leavings, oddments, renounce, withhold **9.** excrement, repudiate **11.** odds and ends

refuse to . . .
accept . . **6.** reject
acknowledge . . **7.** disavow **9.** repudiate
comply . . **12.** recalcitrant
proceed . . **4.** balk

refutation . . . **6.** answer **8.** disproof, elenchus, rebuttal **11.** confutation

refute . . . **4.** deny, meet **5.** rebut, refel **6.** assoil **8.** disprove, elenctic, redargue **9.** overthrow **10.** contradict

regain . . . **6.** recoup **7.** get back, recover **8.** retrieve **9.** get back to **10.** reach again

regal . . . **5.** royal **6.** groove, kingly **7.** channel, stately **8.** imperial, majestic, splendid **9.** dignified, sovereign

regale . . . **4.** dine, fete **5.** amuse, feast, treat **7.** gratify, refresh **9.** entertain **11.** refreshment

regalia . . . **6.** finery **7.** costume, emblems, symbols **8.** insignia **11.** decorations **12.** special dress **13.** paraphernalia

regard . . . **3.** air, awe **4.** care, deem, gaze, heed, hold, look, love, mind, obey (law), rate, sake, view **5.** honor, judge, think, treat **6.** aspect, behold, esteem, remark, repute **8.** attitude, consider, estimate, hold dear, listen to **9.** attention, relevance, viewpoint **10.** appearance, estimation **11.** contemplate, observation **13.** consideration

regard (pert to) . . .
for others . . **8.** altruism
for other's wish . . **9.** deference
highly . . **6.** admire **7.** lionize
with approval . . **6.** admire
with deference . . **5.** honor **7.** respect
with veneration . . **6.** revere

regardful . . . **7.** careful, mindful **8.** cautious **9.** attentive, observant **10.** altruistic, respectful, thoughtful **11.** considerate

regarding . . . **2.** re **4.** as to **5.** anent **10.** concerning, respecting

regardless . . . **6.** anyhow **8.** careless, heedless, slighted **9.** negligent **10.** neglectful **11.** inattentive, indifferent, unconcerned, unobservant **15.** notwithstanding

regards . . . **8.** respects **9.** greetings **11.** compliments

regatta cup . . . **5.** Platt **8.** Carnegie, Grimoldi

regency . . . **4.** rule **8.** dominion **10.** government

regenerate . . . **5.** shape **6.** redeem, reform, revive **7.** convert, restore **8.** re-create **9.** reproduce **11.** fashion anew

regeneration . . . **7.** renewal, revival **9.** reversion **10.** re-creation **11.** reformation **12.** reproduction **14.** divine function

regent . . . **5.** ruler **6.** deputy, ruling **7.** regnant **8.** governor

Regent diamond, 137 carats (pert to) . . .
included in . . **11.** State jewels (France)
named for . . **14.** Regent of France
placed in . . **6.** Louvre
sold (1717) to . . **4.** Pitt (Gov of Madras, Ind)

regime, regimen . . . **4.** diet, rule **6.** system **7.** therapy **10.** government, regulation **14.** administration

regiment . . . **4.** unit, wing **6.** outfit **8.** organize **11.** systematize

regiment, framework of . . . **5.** cadre

regina . . . **5.** queen

region . . . **4.** area, belt, zone **5.** clime, place, realm, space, tract **6.** sphere **7.** climate, cockpit, country, demesne, kingdom, section **8.** district, province

region (pert to) . . .
beyond Jordan . . **5.** Perea **6.** Basham
blissful . . **4.** Eden
comb form . . **5.** nesia
desert . . **3.** erg **5.** waste
indefinite . . **5.** tract
infernal . . **7.** Avernal **8.** Tartarus
meteorological . . **6.** pleion
wooded . . **4.** wold
woodless . . **5.** weald

region of . . .
contentment . . **6.** Arcady
dead (Egypt Myth) . . **6.** Amenti
fabled wealth . . **8.** Eldorado
nether darkness . . **6.** Erebus
opposite side earth . . **9.** Antipodes
Solomon's gold (Bib) . . **5.** Ophir

register . . . **3.** act **4.** list, roll **5.** annal, entry, index **6.** docket, enlist, enroll, record **7.** rotulet **8.** archives, recorder, schedule **9.** catalogue, chronicle, necrology, registrar **11.** account book, matriculate

registrar . . . **8.** recorder **9.** accounter

regius . . . **5.** royal **13.** professorship

regret . . . **3.** rue **4.** ruth **5.** grief, sorry **6.** repent, repine, sorrow **7.** deplore, remorse **9.** penitence **10.** repentance **11.** compunction **12.** self-reproach

regretful . . . **5.** sorry **8.** repining **9.** repentant

regular . . . **4.** even **5.** usual **6.** formal, normal, smooth, stated **7.** correct, orderly, typical, uniform **8.** constant, habitual, ordinary, ordinate, rhythmic, standard **9.** isometric **10.** systematic

regularity . . . **5.** order **8.** symmetry **9.** constancy **10.** smoothness, uniformity

regularly . . . **6.** always **7.** usually **8.** properly, smoothly **9.** correctly **10.** constantly, habitually **12.** methodically, periodically **13.** symmetrically

regulate . . . **3.** set **4.** rule **6.** adjust, direct, govern, manage, ordain, remedy **7.** arrange, control, dispose **8.** organize **9.** influence, methodize **11.** standardize

regulation . . . **3.** law **4.** rule **5.** bylaw, order **6.** system **7.** control, precept **9.** direction, principle

regulator . . . **7.** control **8.** governor, rheostat **9.** rheometer
Regulus . . . **4.** king, star **5.** Alpha **8.** warblers **9.** Cor Leonis (star)
rehabilitate . . . **7.** restore **9.** reeducate, reinstall
rehash . . . **7.** restate **9.** réchauffé
rehearse . . . **3.** say **4.** tell **5.** speak, sum up, train **6.** detail, recite, relate, repeat, try out **7.** mention, narrate, recount **8.** describe **9.** enumerate, reiterate **12.** recapitulate
rehoboam . . . **3.** hat **4.** bowl **6.** flagon **8.** jeroboam
Rehoboam (Bib) . . . **11.** King of Judah (1st) **12.** King of Israel (last)
reif . . . **7.** plunder, robbery
reign . . . **3.** raj **4.** rule, sway **5.** guide, realm **6.** empire **7.** kingdom, prevail **8.** dominion, flourish **11.** sovereignty **12.** supreme power
Reign of Terror (Fr Hist) . . . **7.** anarchy **9.** bloodshed, despotism **12.** confiscation
reimburse . . . **3.** pay **5.** repay **6.** refund **7.** pay back, replace **9.** indemnify **10.** recompense
Reims, Rheims (pert to) . . .
  capital (anc) . . **4.** Remi
  famed building . . **9.** Cathedral (Gothic)
  famed site . . **15.** crowning of kings (Fr)
rein . . . **4.** curb, stop **5.** check, leash **6.** direct, retard **7.** control **8.** reindeer, restrain **9.** hindrance **10.** bridle part
reina . . . **8.** rockfish
reindeer . . . **6.** tarand **7.** caribou **13.** constellation
reindeer (pert to) . . .
  age, epoch . . **11.** Paleolithic
  flower . . **9.** buttercup (white)
  genus . . **8.** Rangifer
reinforce . . . **4.** back **5.** add to, brace, reman **7.** restore, support **9.** intensify, replenish **10.** strengthen
reinforcement . . . **7.** adjunct, support **8.** addition **13.** replenishment, strengthening
reins . . . **5.** loins **7.** harness, kidneys **9.** restraint
reis . . . **6.** escudo **7.** milreis **14.** money of account
reit . . . **5.** sedge **7.** seaweed
reiterate . . . **4.** drum, harp **6.** repeat **8.** rehearse **12.** recapitulate
reject . . . **5.** repel, spurn **6.** disown, recuse (law), refuse **7.** decline, discard, dismiss **8.** athetize, disallow **9.** repudiate
rejectamenta . . . **5.** wrack **6.** refuse, reject **7.** rubbish **9.** excrement
rejection . . . **6.** heresy **7.** discard, refusal **8.** ejection **9.** exclusion, objection **11.** disapproval, repudiation
rejoice . . . **5.** cheer, elate **7.** delight, gladden **8.** jubilate
rejoinder . . . **5.** reply (law) **6.** answer, retort, return **8.** comeback
rejuvenate . . . **6.** revive **7.** restore **9.** stimulate **12.** reinvigorate
relâche . . . **10.** relaxation **12.** intermission **13.** no performance (Theat)
relapse . . . **4.** sink **5.** lapse **7.** subside

8. slip back **9.** backslide, reversion **10.** recurrence, regression **11.** falling back **12.** recidivation
relate . . . **4.** tell **5.** state **6.** assert, detail, recite, report **7.** narrate, pertain, recount **8.** describe, rehearse **9.** appertain, associate
related (pert to) . . .
  by blood . . **3.** sib **4.** akin **7.** cognate
  on father's side . . **6.** agnate **7.** cognate **8.** agnation
  on mother's side . . **5.** enate **6.** enatic **7.** cognate, enation **9.** umbilical
  story . . **7.** sidebar
  to land . . **8.** praedial (predial)
relating to . . .
  bread . . **6.** panary
  Chinese . . **7.** Sinitic
  dancing . . **6.** gestic **13.** choreographic
  fruit jelly . . **7.** pectous
  grandparents . . **4.** aval
  Hindu literature . . **5.** Vedic
  life . . **5.** vital
  morn . . **7.** matinal **8.** forenoon
  motion . . **7.** kinetic **9.** kinematic
  realities . . **7.** factual **9.** entelechy
  soft palate . . **5.** velar
  vascular fluid . . **5.** hemic
relation . . . **3.** kin **4.** mode, tale **6.** status, ubiety **7.** account, analogy, kinship, kinsman, recital, telling **8.** relative **9.** character, narration, reference, rehearsal, rishtadar (Hind law) **10.** connection **13.** consanguinity
relationship . . . **4.** outs **7.** kinship, kinsman, metochy **8.** affinity, relative **13.** consanguinity
relative . . . **3.** eme, kin, sib, son **4.** aunt **5.** niece, uncle **6.** allied, cousin, father, mother, nephew, sister **7.** brother, kindred **8.** apposite, daughter, kinsfolk **9.** pertinent **11.** comparative, correlative **13.** corresponding, proportionate
relative (pert to) . . .
  favor to . . **8.** nepotism
  rank . . **6.** degree
  to . . **7.** apropos **12.** in proportion
relax . . . **4.** ease, open, rest **5.** abate, loose, remit **6.** divert, loosen, soften, unbend **7.** detente, slacken **8.** mitigate, slow down
relaxed . . . **4.** calm, cool **6.** casual **8.** laid-back **9.** easygoing
relay . . . **3.** dak (dawk) **4.** race **5.** shift **6.** remuda **7.** relieve **8.** avantlay **10.** television (station)
release . . . **4.** drop, free, trip, undo **5.** death, let go, loose, undam, unpen, untie **6.** acquit, escape, exempt, loosen, parole, remise **7.** deliver, freedom, manumit, receipt, relieve, unleash, unloose **8.** liberate **9.** discharge **10.** liberation, relinquish **11.** acquittance, deliverance
relegate . . . **5.** exile, refer **6.** assign, banish, commit, deport, depute, remove **7.** ascribe, consign, discard, dismiss, exclude **8.** delegate
relent . . . **5.** abate, yield **6.** regret, soften, submit **7.** slacken
relentless . . . **6.** strict **9.** merciless

10. inflexible, unyielding
11. persevering, unremitting
relevant . . . **7.** germane **9.** pertinent
10. sufficient **11.** referential
reliable . . . **4.** safe, sure **5.** tried
6. stable, trusty **7.** solvent **8.** true-blue
11. trustworthy
reliance . . . **4.** hope **5.** trust **6.** belief
8. mainstay **10.** confidence, conviction,
dependence
relic . . . **5.** curio, huaca, huaco, ruins
7. antique, memento, remains
8. artifact, fragment, memorial,
souvenir, survival **9.** antiquity
relic cabinet . . . **7.** étagère, whatnot
relict . . . **5.** widow **7.** widower **8.** survivor
relied . . . **6.** banked **7.** counted, reposed,
trusted **8.** confided, depended, reckoned
relief . . . **3.** aid **4.** bote (bot), dole,
ease, fret (Arch), help **5.** spell
6. remedy, succor **7.** comfort, outline,
redress, relieve, welfare **8.** easement
10. assistance, embossment, mitigation,
substitute, sustenance **11.** alleviation,
deliverance **15.** indemnification
relieve . . . **3.** aid **4.** cure, ease, free,
help **5.** abate, allay, clear, raise, spell
6. assist, remedy, remove, succor
7. assuage, lighten, redress, refresh,
support, sustain, unloose **8.** diminish
10. substitute
religion (pert to) . . . **4.** sect **5.** creed,
deism, faith, piety, trust **6.** belief,
hermit, schism, theism, voodoo
8. monastic, theology **9.** solipsism
10. conformity, persuasion
religion, type . . . **5.** Islam **6.** Taoism
7. Jainism, Judaism **8.** Buddhism,
Hinduism **9.** Mormonism, Moslemism,
Muslimism, Shintoism **11.** Anglicanism,
Catholicism **12.** Christianity,
Confucianism **13.** Mohammedanism,
Protestantism
religious . . . **4.** holy **5.** exact, godly, pious,
rigid **6.** devout, sacred **7.** devoted,
fervent, zealous **9.** born-again,
pharasaic, spiritual **10.** devotional,
meticulous, scrupulous **11.** theological
13. conscientious
religious (pert to) . . .
assembly . . **12.** congregation
belief . . **5.** deism **6.** omnist
10. monotheism
brotherhood . . **8.** sodality **9.** ecumenism
10. fellowship **11.** ecumenicism
center . . **7.** Lambeth (Eng)
composition . . **5.** motet
cult, sect . . **5.** fakir **6.** Shaker, Shinto
7. Pietism, Sikhism **8.** cenobite
9. anchorite **11.** Hare Krishna
devotee . . **5.** fakir
devotion . . **6.** novena
division . . **6.** schism
expedition (Mil) . . **7.** crusade
fasting . . **4.** Lent **9.** Ember Days
10. Ember Weeks
festival . . **4.** mela (Ind) **5.** Purim (Jew)
image . . **4.** icon
madness, mania . . **9.** theomania
metaphysics . . **7.** gnostic
musical . . **6.** anthem

offering . . **7.** deodate **8.** oblation
Order member . . **6.** Marist **7.** Templar
poem . . **5.** psalm
psalm . . **4.** hymn, poem, song
publication (RCCh) . . **4.** ordo
relinquish . . . **3.** let **4.** cede, quit
5. forgo, leave, waive, yield **6.** desert,
desist, forego, give up, remise, resign
7. abandon, forsake, release **8.** abdicate,
renounce **9.** surrender **11.** leave behind
12. withdraw from
relinquishment . . . **9.** surrender
11. abandonment **12.** renunciation
reliquary, reliquiae (pl) . . . **3.** box **4.** arca,
tomb **5.** chest **6.** casket, chasse, shrine
8. monument
relish . . . **4.** gust, tang, zest **5.** achar,
enjoy, gusto, sauce, taste **6.** canape,
caviar, degust, flavor, liking **8.** pleasure
9. condiment, degustate, enjoyment,
flavoring, seasoning **11.** hors d'oeuvre
13. gratification
relucent . . . **5.** lucid **6.** lucent **7.** radiant,
shining **8.** lightish **9.** refulgent
reluctance . . . **8.** aversion **10.** repugnance
13. indisposition, unwillingness
14. disinclination
reluctance unit (Elec) . . . **3.** rel
reluctant . . . **5.** chary, loath **6.** averse
8. hesitant, not ready **9.** resisting,
unwilling **11.** disinclined
reluctate . . . **5.** repel **6.** oppose
9. repudiate
rely . . . **4.** hold, lean, rest **5.** count, trust
6. cleave, depend, reckon, repose
7. confide
rely on, upon . . . **4.** hope **5.** trust
6. depend, lippen **7.** believe
remain . . . **3.** lie **4.** bide, last, rest,
stay **5.** abide, tarry **6.** endure, reside
8. continue
remainder . . . **4.** rest, stub **5.** relic, stump
6. estate **7.** balance, remnant, residue,
surplus **8.** fragment, leavings, residual,
residuum
remaining . . . **4.** left, over **6.** ledger (leger)
7. durable, remnant, staying, surplus
8. residual **9.** permanent
remaining stationary . . . **6.** static
7. waiting **8.** awaiting
remains . . . **5.** ashes, ruins, stays
6. corpse, relics **7.** cadaver, fossils
9. remainder
remanent . . . **4.** left **7.** further, lasting,
remains, remnant, residue **8.** enduring,
leftover, residual **9.** permanent,
remainder **10.** additional
13. supplementary
remark . . . **3.** say, see **4.** heed, note
5. gloss, state **6.** notice, regard
7. comment, observe **8.** perceive,
point out **9.** statement **10.** annotation,
commentary, indication **11.** observation
12. interjection
remark (pert to) . . .
amusing, witty . . **3.** gag **4.** quip
clever . . **3.** mot
commonplace . . **9.** platitude
smarting . . **7.** sarcasm, stinger
upon . . **7.** explain
witless . . **5.** boner

remarkable . . . **5.** great **7.** notable,
strange, unusual **8.** uncommon
9. wonderful **10.** noteworthy, noticeable,
observable **11.** conspicuous
13. extraordinary
Rembrandt (pert to) . . .
birthplace . . **6.** Leyden (Neth)
color . . **5.** brown
famed as . . **6.** etcher (Dutch) **7.** painter
style . . **14.** Rembrandtesque
remedial . . . **6.** remedy (pert to) **7.** healing
8. curative, panacean **10.** corrective
11. therapeutic
remedy . . . **3.** aid, fix **4.** bote (bot), cure,
gain, help **5.** amend **6.** doctor, relief
8. antidote, medicine **10.** assistance,
reparation
remedy (pert to) . . .
cure-all . . **6.** elixir
mysterious (of Paracelsus) . . **7.** arcanum
quack . . **7.** nostrum
soothing . . **4.** balm **6.** balsam
universal . . **7.** panacea
remember . . . **3.** min **9.** recollect,
reminisce **10.** keep in mind
remembrance . . . **4.** fame **5.** token
6. memory, Minnie, trophy **7.** memento
8. allusion, memorial, reminder,
souvenir **12.** recollection
13. commemoration
remex . . . **12.** quill feather
remind . . . **6.** prompt, recall **8.** remember
13. call attention
reminder . . . **4.** memo, twit **7.** memento
8. souvenir **10.** memorandum
11. remembrance
reminiscence . . . **3.** act **4.** fact **5.** power
6. memory **8.** anecdote **10.** experience
11. memorabilia **12.** recollection
remise . . . **6.** giving, return **7.** release,
replace, respite **8.** granting **9.** remission,
surrender
remiss . . . **3.** lax **5.** slack **7.** lenient
8. careless, dilatory, heedless
9. negligent **10.** neglectful
11. inattentive, thoughtless
remissness . . . **7.** neglect **9.** indolence
10. negligence **12.** improvidence
remit . . . **3.** pay **5.** relax **6.** acquit, assign,
cancel, excuse, pardon, reduce, resign
7. absolve, forgive, release, restore,
suspend **8.** abrogate, liberate, mitigate,
recommit **9.** surrender
remnant . . . **3.** ash, end, ort, rag **4.** dreg,
left, rest, stub **5.** piece, relic, scrap,
shred, trace **7.** oddment, remains, yet
left **8.** fragment **9.** remainder, remaining
10. suggestion
remolade . . . **5.** sauce **8.** dressing,
ointment
remonstrate . . . **5.** plead **7.** protest
8. point out **11.** expostulate
remontant . . . **14.** flowering again
remora . . . **4.** fish, pega (pegora)
remord . . . **5.** taint **6.** ponder, rebuke
7. afflict, censure, remorse
remorse . . . **4.** pity **6.** regret, sorrow
8. distress **9.** penitence, repentent
10. compassion **11.** compunction
remorseful . . . **5.** sorry **7.** pitiful
8. contrite, merciful, penitent, pitiable

9. regretful **13.** compassionate
remorseless . . . **8.** pitiless **9.** merciless,
unpitying **10.** implacable, inflexible,
relentless, unmerciful **11.** unregretful
remote . . . **3.** far, off **5.** alien, vague
6. elenge, forane, ultima **7.** distant,
foreign **8.** abstruse, reserved, secluded,
ulterior **10.** farfetched, unsociable
11. out-of-the-way
remote control . . . **10.** pushbutton,
tele-action
remote region . . . **5.** Thule (Greenland)
remotest . . . **7.** endmost, very end
8. farthest **14.** ghost of a chance
removal . . . **8.** ejection **9.** deduction
10. divestment, evacuation, extraction
11. elimination **12.** transference
remove . . . **3.** rid **4.** dele, doff, move,
void, weed **5.** erase, evict, expel, strip
6. change, debunk, delete, depose,
divest, eloign (law) **7.** dismiss, extract,
relieve **8.** abstract, displace, evacuate,
put aside, transfer **9.** eliminate,
eradicate, translate **11.** assassinate
remove (pert to) . . .
cover . . **5.** uncap
from office . . **4.** oust **6.** depose, recall
moisture . . **3.** dry **5.** wring **9.** dehydrate
point of origin . . **6.** distal
seed from flax . . **6.** ribble
seeds . . **3.** gin, pit
stalk . . **5.** strig
to another place . . **8.** transfer **9.** translate
whole blubber . . **6.** flense
removed . . . **4.** took **5.** apart **6.** betook,
remote **7.** distant, far away **8.** reserved,
secluded **9.** separated, unrelated
10. unsociable
remover . . . **6.** porter **7.** carrier, drayman,
solvent **9.** scavenger **10.** contractor,
eradicator
remunerate . . . **3.** pay **5.** repay **6.** reward
7. requite, satisfy **9.** reimburse
10. compensate, recompense
remuneration . . . **3.** pay **6.** reward
7. payment **8.** pittance, requital
9. emolument **10.** recompense
12. compensation, satisfaction
13. reimbursement
Remus (pert to) . . .
brother . . **7.** Romulus
father . . **4.** Mars
legendary founder of . . **4.** Rome (with
brother)
slayer . . **7.** Romulus
renable . . . **4.** glib **5.** ready **6.** fluent
8. eloquent
renaissance . . . **7.** rebirth, revival
Renaissance (pert to) . . .
Archit . . **12.** Roman classic
art . . **10.** neoclassic
associated with . . **8.** Petrarch
furniture . . **6.** carved **7.** English, Flemish
Italian reference . . **12.** Resorgimento
(new arising)
lace . . **10.** Battenburg
renal . . . **6.** kidney **7.** nephric
renascence . . . **7.** rebirth, revival **14.** The
Renaissance
rencounter . . . **4.** duel **5.** clash **6.** action,
combat, flight **7.** contest, meeting

8. conflict 9. collision

rend... 3. rip 4. rive, tear 5. break, burst, sever, split, wrest 7. extract, rupture 8. fracture

render... 3. pay, put 4. give, make, melt 6. return 7. clarify, convert, deliver, execute, extract, narrate, present, requite 8. transmit 9. translate 10. understand 11. communicate

render (pert to)...
accessible.. 4. open
agreeable.. 7. dulcify
angry, choleric.. 6. enrage
conformable to Eng.. 7. Anglify
9. Anglicize
divine.. 5. deify
dull.. 8. hebetate
enduring.. 6. anneal
fat.. 3. try 6. try out
fertile.. 6. enrich
free from bacteria.. 9. sterilize
ineffective.. 4. void 5. annul
10. invalidate
intelligible.. 9. elucidate
less pliant.. 7. stiffen
muddy, turgid.. 4. roil
oblique.. 5. splay
obscure.. 6. darkle 9. obfuscate
sharp.. 9. acuminate
unconscious.. 4. stun

rendezvous... 5. tryst 6. refuge 7. meeting, retreat 11. appointment

rendition... 7. account 8. delivery 9. surrender 10. extraction 11. performance, translation 14. interpretation

renegade... 3. rat 5. rebel 7. pervert, traitor 8. apostate, deserter, fugitive, turncoat

renege... 4. deny 6. desert, revoke 7. decline 8. renounce

renew... 6. resume, revamp, revive 7. convert, refresh, restore 8. renovate 10. invigorate, regenerate 12. redintegrate

renewal... 10. conversion, renovation, resumption 11. restoration

renitent... 7. opposed 9. reluctant, resistant 12. recalcitrant

rennet... 3. lab 5. apple 6. curdle, rennin 7. extract 9. coagulate

rennin... 6. enzyme

renommé... 8. renowned 10. celebrated

Renommist... 8. braggart, renowner 9. swaggerer

renounce... 4. cede, deny 5. forgo (forego), waive 6. abjure, desert, disown, recant, reject, renege, resign 7. abandon, forsake, retract 8. abnegate, forswear, swear off 9. repudiate, surrender 10. relinquish 12. abrenunciate

renouncement... 9. rejection 10. temperance 11. abandonment, recantation

renovate... 5. renew 6. repair, resume, revive 7. restore 10. regenerate

renown... 4. fame, note 5. éclat, glory 10. reputation

renowned... 5. famed, noted 6. famous 10. celebrated 11. illustrious

13. distinguished

rent... 3. let, pay 4. dues, hire, hole, slit, tear, toll, tore, torn 5. break, cleft, lease, share, split 6. reward 7. revenue, rupture, slitted, tribute 8. tattered

rent (pert to)...
asunder.. 5. rived
harvest.. 7. onstand
in oats.. 7. avenage
paid.. 3. tac

renter... 6. lessee, lodger, tenant

renunciation... 6. denial 9. disavowal, rejection, surrender 10. abjuration, disclaimer, temperance 11. abandonment, recantation 14. relinquishment

repaid in kind... 10. retaliated

repair... 3. fix 4. darn, heal, mend 5. amend, patch, renew 6. doctor, remedy, resort 7. correct, rebuild, restore 8. atone for 9. condition 13. betake oneself

reparation... 6. amende, amends, remedy, repair, reward 7. damages, redress 8. reprisal, requital 9. atonement, indemnity 10. recompense 11. restitution 12. compensation, satisfaction

repartee... 3. wit 5. reply 6. retort 7. riposte

repast... 3. tea 4. feed, meal 5. feast, lunch, treat 6. tiffin 8. mealtime, prandial 9. collation

repatriate... 5. exile 6. banish 10. expatriate

repay... 4. meed 6. answer, avenge, refund, return 7. requite, restore 9. reimburse, retaliate 10. compensate, recompense, remunerate

repeal... 5. annul, emend, forgo (forego) 6. appeal, cancel, recall 7. abandon, abolish, rescind, retract, reverse 8. abrogate, renounce, withdraw

repeat... 4. copy, echo, rame 5. recur 7. iterate, restate 8. remember 9. duplicate, reiterate

repeat (pert to)...
mathematics.. 8. repetend
mechanically.. 6. parrot
noisily.. 3. din
performance.. 6. encore
twice (pref).. 3. bis

repeating... 4. rote 10. repetitive 11. repetitious

repel... 5. avert, check 6. offend, oppose, rebuff, refuse, reject, resist, revolt 7. disgust, repulse 9. drive back, force back

repellent... 5. harsh 6. odious 9. repulsive, resistant, revolting

repent... 3. rue 6. reform, regret 9. do penance

repentance... 4. ruth 5. shame 6. regret 9. penitence 10. contrition 11. compunction

repercussion... 4. blow 6. impact 9. afterclap, aftermath 10. reflection

repertory... 4. list 5. index, store 8. calendar, magazine, treasure 9. catalogue 10. collection, repertoire, storehouse

repetition . . . **4.** rote **5.** troll **6.** encore
8. iterance **9.** iteration **11.** reiteration
14. recapitulation
repetition (pert to) . . .
biology . . **6.** merism
music . . **5.** rondo **7.** tremolo
rhetoric . . **8.** anaphora **9.** tautology
sound . . **4.** echo
sounds (slight) . . **6.** patter
repetitive . . . **8.** habitual **9.** redundant
11. repetitious
repine . . . **4.** fret **6.** lament, regret
7. grumble **8.** complain
replace . . . **4.** stet **5.** reset, stead **6.** repone
7. restore **8.** supplant **9.** discharge,
supersede **10.** substitute
replaceable . . . **10.** expendable
replenish . . . **4.** feed, fill **5.** store **6.** refill
7. perfect, provide **8.** complete
replete . . . **3.** fat **4.** full **5.** sated
6. filled, gorged **7.** bloated **8.** abundant
9. surfeited
replevin . . . **4.** bail, writ **8.** recovery
replica . . . **3.** bis **4.** copy **6.** repeat
9. duplicate, facsimile
reply . . . **4.** echo **5.** rebut **6.** answer,
oracle, rejoin, retort **7.** defense, epistle,
respond **8.** reaction, repartee, response
9. rejoinder **11.** retaliation
report . . . **3.** cry, pop **4.** bang, note **5.** bruit,
rumor, sound, state, story **6.** delate,
recite, relate, repute **7.** account,
hearsay, recital, verdict **8.** describe
9. narration, narrative, statement
10. accounting, commentary,
responsory **11.** information, publication
report (pert to) . . .
common . . **6.** gossip
false, absurd . . **5.** rumor **6.** canard
7. slander
following lightning . . **7.** thunder
for duty . . **14.** present oneself
official . . **7.** hansard
of proceedings . . **6.** cahier
reporter . . . **3.** cub **6.** legman, pistol
7. newsman **8.** newshawk **9.** informant
12. newspaperman
reporter's rounds . . . **8.** newsbeat
reporter's sign off . . . **6.** thirty
repose . . . **3.** lie, sit **4.** ease, rely, rest
5. peace, place, sleep **7.** deposit, recline
9. quiescent, quietness **10.** quiescence,
relaxation
repository . . . **3.** ark **4.** file **5.** vault
6. chapel (RCCh), museum **8.** treasury
9. confidant, sepulcher **10.** depository,
storehouse **11.** auction room
reposoir . . . **5.** altar
repoussé . . . **7.** art work
reprehensible . . . **8.** blamable, culpable
9. accusable, obnoxious **10.** censurable,
reprovable **11.** blameworthy
reprehension . . . **5.** blame **7.** censure,
reproof **9.** reprimand **11.** reprobation
12. condemnation, denunciation
represent . . . **5.** enact **6.** denote, depict,
typify **7.** betoken, exhibit, portray,
produce **8.** describe **9.** delineate
representation . . . **3.** art **4.** copy, icon,
idea, idol, show **5.** drama **6.** avowal,
symbol **7.** picture **9.** depiction,

enactment, portrayal, spectacle
10. exhibition, profession
11. delineation, description, portraiture
12. reproduction
representation (pert to) . . .
by characters (Mus) . . **8.** notation
graphic . . **5.** chart
Medusa's head . . **9.** gorgoneum
mental . . **5.** image **7.** eidolon, phantom
of scene . . **7.** tableau
of solar system . . **6.** orrery
of star . . **7.** estoile
small . . **5.** model **9.** miniature
representative . . . **4.** heir, type **5.** agent,
envoy **6.** deputy, legate **7.** example,
tribune, typical **8.** delegate, exponent,
symbolic **9.** successor **10.** ambassador,
legislator, lieutenant, substitute
12. illustrative
repress . . . **4.** curb, rein, stop **5.** check,
crush, quell **6.** hush up, muffle, stifle
7. put down **8.** restrain, suppress
9. overpower
reprieve . . . **5.** delay **6.** pardon, relief
7. relieve, respite **8.** postpone
reprimand . . . **5.** chide, scold, slate
6. rebuke **7.** censure, reprove
reprisal . . . **7.** revenge, revenue **8.** requital
11. retaliation
reproach . . . **4.** taca, twit **5.** abuse, blame,
chide, shend, taunt **6.** accuse, revile,
vilify **7.** censure, condemn, reproof,
sarcasm, upbraid **8.** disgrace, dishonor
9. disrepute, invective **10.** accusation,
opprobrium **12.** vilification
reproach, free of . . . **9.** blameless
reprobate . . . **6.** disown, reject, wicked
7. abandon, corrupt, knavish, vicious
8. depraved, hardened, recreant
9. condemned, miscreant, reprehend,
scoundrel **10.** black sheep
12. unprincipled **13.** reprehensible
reproduce . . . **4.** copy **6.** recite, remake,
repeat **8.** multiply **9.** duplicate,
propagate
reproduction . . . **4.** copy **6.** ectype,
recall **7.** picture, replica **8.** likeness
10. repetition **11.** counterpart,
duplication **14.** representation
reproductive . . . **5.** gamic, spore
10. recreative **12.** regenerative
reproof . . . **5.** roast **6.** rebuke **7.** chiding
8. disgrace, reproach **9.** reprimand
10. admonition, censurable, refutation
11. blameworthy, confutation
12. reprehension **13.** reprehensible
reprove . . . **4.** rate **5.** blame, chide,
scold **6.** berate, rebuke **7.** censure,
correct, upbraid **8.** admonish, reproach
9. objurgate, reprehend, reprimand
reproving . . . **10.** admonitive
reptile . . . **4.** toad, worm **5.** snake,
viper **6.** dragon, iguana, lizard, turtle
7. monitor, serpent **8.** creeping, Reptilia
9. scoundrel
reptile (pert to) . . .
class . . **8.** Reptilia
crocodile . . **6.** mugger
extinct . . **9.** pterosaur **10.** diplodocus
11. pterodactyl, Pterosauria
group . . **6.** Sauria

hard-shelled.. **6.** iguana, turtle
8. terrapin, tortoise
iguanalike.. **7.** tuatara
large.. **3.** boa **9.** alligator, crocodile
10. salamander
lizard.. **3.** eft **4.** adda, newt, seps **5.** skink
(scink) **6.** Anolis, iguana, moloch
7. monitor **9.** chameleon **10.** chuckwalla
11. Gila monster
Mesozoic.. **8.** dinosaur
myth.. **6.** dragon **8.** basilisk
10. cockatrice, salamander
oldest.. **9.** sea turtle
salamander.. **3.** eft **4.** newt
scale.. **5.** scute
snake.. **3.** asp **5.** adder, cobra,
krait **6.** garter, python **8.** anaconda,
Squamata **10.** copperhead
reptilian ... **7.** saurian
Reptilian Age ... **8.** Mesozoic
Republic ... **5.** State **6.** France **7.** Andorra
(Andorre) **9.** San Marino
10. commonweal, government
12. United States
Republican Party ... **3.** GOP
7. mugwump (bolter 1884)
Republic of Plato ... **4.** Book (famed)
8. dialogue **10.** ideal State
repudiate ... **4.** deny **6.** abjure, disown,
recant, reject **7.** disavow, discard,
exclude **8.** renounce
repugnance ... **4.** hate **5.** odium **6.** nausea
7. disgust, opposed **8.** aversion,
loathing **9.** antipathy, hostility
10. abhorrence, antagonism, opposition,
reluctance **12.** disagreement
repugnant ... **6.** odious **7.** adverse,
hostile, opposed **8.** inimical **9.** offensive,
repellent, repulsive **10.** refractory
11. distasteful **12.** incompatible
14. irreconcilable
repulse ... **5.** repel **6.** denial, rebuff
7. refusal **9.** rejection
repulsive ... **4.** ugly, vile **5.** nasty
6. odious **7.** fulsome **9.** offensive,
repellent, resistant, revolting
10. disgusting, forbidding, malodorous
repurchase ... **6.** redeem
reputable ... **6.** worthy **9.** estimable,
honorable **10.** creditable **11.** respectable
reputation ... **4.** fame, name, note
5. glory, honor **9.** celebrity, notoriety
11. distinction **13.** consideration
repute ... **4.** hold, word **5.** éclat, honor
6. credit, esteem, regard, report, revere
8. prestige **9.** reputable **10.** popularity,
reputation
reputed ... **6.** deemed **7.** assumed
8. accepted, presumed, putative,
supposed **10.** understood
request ... **3.** ask, beg **4.** plea, pray, suit
6. appeal, behest, demand **7.** entreat,
solicit **8.** entreaty, petition, rogation
12. supplication
requiescat in pace ... **11.** rest in peace
requiescence ... **6.** repose
requin ... **5.** shark **8.** man-eater
require ... **3.** ask **4.** need **5.** claim, exact,
force **6.** charge, compel, demand,
enjoin, entail, oblige **8.** obligate
11. necessitate

requisition ... **5.** order **6.** demand
11. application, requirement
requital ... **7.** payment, revenge
8. reprisal **10.** recompense
11. retaliation, retribution
12. compensation
requite ... **3.** pay **5.** atone, repay
6. avenge, return, reward **7.** revenge,
satisfy **9.** retaliate **10.** compensate,
recompense **11.** interchange
reredos ... **4.** wall **6.** screen **9.** back-plate
(armor), partition
reremouse ... **3.** bat
res ... **5.** point, thing **6.** matter
rescind ... **5.** annul **6.** cancel, recall,
recant, repeal, revoke **7.** abolish
8. abrogate
rescue ... **3.** aid **4.** free, save **6.** ransom,
redeem, regain **7.** deliver, reclaim,
recover, release **8.** delivery, liberate
9. extricate **11.** deliverance
rese ... **4.** rage, rush **5.** hurry, onset,
quake, shake **7.** impulse, tremble
8. rashness
resemblance ... **6.** ringer **7.** analogy
8. affinity, likeness **9.** agreement,
semblance **10.** similarity, similitude
resembling (pert to) ...
bark.. **11.** corticiform
comb.. **8.** pectinal
goose.. **8.** anserine
gypsum.. **11.** alabastrine
horse.. **6.** equoid
man.. **7.** android
minute animals.. **11.** animalcular
rind.. **8.** cortical
salt.. **6.** haloid
seed.. **6.** ovular
snakes.. **7.** elapine **8.** viperine
star.. **7.** stellar **8.** stellate **9.** stellated
turf.. **5.** soddy
wall.. **5.** mural
resentment ... **3.** ire **5.** pique, spite
6. choler, enmity, hatred, malice, rancor
7. dudgeon, umbrage **9.** animosity,
malignity **11.** displeasure, indignation
reservation ... **5.** tract **8.** preserve
9. reticence **10.** engagement, limitation
11. withholding **13.** qualification
reserve ... **4.** bank, fund, keep, save
5. allot, spare, stock, store **6.** engage,
refuge **7.** backlog, modesty, shyness
8. coldness, distance, postpone,
withhold **9.** exception, restraint,
retention, reticence, sanctuary
10. constraint, diffidence, limitation,
substitute **11.** self-control, taciturnity
reserved ... **3.** coy **4.** cool, kept,
unco **5.** aloof, saved, staid, taken
6. modest, sedate **7.** distant **8.** reticent
15. uncommunicative
reservoir ... **4.** font, pool, sump **5.** store
6. cavity, cenote, supply **7.** piscina,
reserve **8.** fountain
reservoir of Pecquet (Anat) ... **12.** lymph
channel **13.** cisterna chyli
res gestae ... **5.** deeds, facts **8.** exploits
10. things done
resiant ... **7.** present **8.** resident
reside ... **4.** bide, live, room, stay **5.** abide,
dwell, lodge **6.** remain **7.** sojourn

8. habitate
residence . . . **4.** home, seat, stay **5.** abode
6. palace **7.** deanery **8.** domicile,
dwelling **9.** consulate, residency
10. habitation
residencia . . . **5.** court, trial
resident . . . **3.** cit **6.** intern, tenant
7. burgess, citizen **8.** diplomat, occupant
10. inhabitant
residual . . . **7.** remnant **8.** residuum
9. remainder
residue . . . **3.** ash, ort **4.** coke, dreg, marc,
rest, silt, slag **5.** ashes **6.** pomace,
relics **7.** balance, remains, remnant
8. leavings, sediment **9.** remainder
residuum . . . **7.** residue **8.** hangover,
leavings **9.** remainder
resign . . . **4.** cede, quit **5.** demit,
waive, yield **6.** give up, submit
7. abandon, consign **8.** abdicate,
renounce **9.** surrender **10.** relinquish
resignation . . . **5.** demit **8.** patience
9. demission, endurance **10.** abdication,
submission **12.** renunciation
14. relinquishment
resigned . . . **9.** contented **10.** submissive
11. acquiescent **13.** uncomplaining
resilient . . . **7.** buoyant, elastic **8.** cheerful
9. recoiling **10.** rebounding **11.** returning
to **12.** recuperative
resin . . . **3.** gum, lac **4.** aloe, tolu **5.** amber,
anime, copal, jalap, rosin **6.** dammar,
mastic
resin (pert to) . . .
  aromatic . . **4.** balm **5.** elemi, myrrh
  6. balsam **7.** acouchi, camphor, copaiba
  8. sandarac **12.** frankincense
  Bib . . **8.** bdellium
  bitter . . **8.** labdanum (ladanum)
  brown (mineral) . . **9.** elaterite
  Chian turpentine . . **3.** alk
  fossil . . **5.** amber **8.** retinite
  gum . . **5.** gugal (googul)
  hard . . **5.** rosin
  medicinal . . **7.** aroeira **9.** asafetida
  (asafoetida)
  narcotic . . **6.** charas
  pine . . **7.** galipot
  soft . . **5.** animé, copal, elemi
  translucent . . **8.** sandarac
  tropical . . **5.** copal
  varnish ingredient . . **6.** dammar
  yellowish . . **5.** amber **7.** gamboge
resinous substance . . . **3.** gum, lac
  5. copal **7.** shellac
resist . . . **4.** fend, stem **5.** rebel, repel
6. defeat, oppose **7.** prevent, ward off
8. outstand **9.** withstand **10.** counteract
resistance . . . **6.** rebuff **7.** defense
8. rheostat **9.** hostility **10.** opposition
resistance unit . . . **3.** ohm
resistant . . . **5.** tough **8.** obdurate
9. resisting **10.** unyielding
13. counteractive
resisting . . . **7.** hostile **8.** opposing
9. oppugnant, tenacious
12. antagonistic
resisting (pert to) . . .
  description . . **11.** indefinable
  power . . **4.** wiry
  pressure . . **8.** renitent

pressure bar . . **5.** strut
resolute . . . **4.** bold, firm **5.** fixed, stern
6. gritty, steady **7.** decided **8.** constant,
positive, resolved, unshaken
9. desperado, obstinate, steadfast
10. determined, inflexible, unyielding
11. perseverant, persevering
resolution . . . **4.** firm **5.** nerve **6.** motion,
steady **7.** courage, purpose, resolve,
verdict **8.** analysis, decision, resolved,
strength **9.** assurance, constancy,
fortitude **10.** conversion, conviction,
relaxation, separation **11.** persevering
12. perseverance **13.** determination,
steadfastness **15.** disentanglement
resolve . . . **4.** melt **5.** lapse (law), parse,
relax, solve **6.** assure, decide, dispel,
inform, reduce, settle **7.** analyze,
explain, purpose, unravel **8.** convince,
dissolve, separate **9.** determine,
transform **11.** disentangle
resonance . . . **8.** sonority, vibrance
10. resounding
resonant . . . **7.** echoing, ringing, vibrant
8. sonorous, sounding **10.** resounding
11. reverberant
resort . . . **3.** spa **4.** dive **5.** haunt
6. betake, casino, refuge **7.** finagle,
purlieu **8.** frequent, recourse, resource
9. expedient, fainaigue, honky-tonk
resound . . . **4.** echo, peal, ring **6.** be loud,
re-echo **8.** proclaim **11.** reverberate
resounding . . . **4.** loud **13.** reverberating
resource . . . **5.** means, skill **6.** refuge,
resort, supply **9.** expedient
10. capability **11.** contrivance
resourceful . . . **5.** sharp **9.** Daedalian,
ingenious
resources . . . **5.** funds, means, money
6. assets, supply **7.** resorts
10. expedients **12.** contrivances
respect . . . **3.** awe **4.** heed **5.** defer,
favor, honor **6.** aspect, detail, esteem,
homage, regard, repute, revere
7. concern, observe, regards **8.** attitude,
venerate **9.** attention, deference,
relevance, reverence, viewpoint
10. politeness **13.** consideration
respectable . . . **6.** decent **9.** estimable,
honorable, reputable, tolerable
11. presentable
respectful . . . **5.** civil **6.** polite **7.** careful,
duteous, heedful **8.** reverent
11. deferential
respective . . . **6.** mutual **7.** careful,
heedful, several, special **9.** attentive,
regardful **10.** particular **12.** distributive
respiration . . . **4.** rale, sigh **7.** eupnoea
9. breathing
respire . . . **7.** breathe
respite . . . **4.** rest **5.** delay, first, pause
6. breath **7.** leisure **8.** postpone, reprieve
9. extension (time) **10.** suspension
11. opportunity, short shrift
12. intermission
resplendent . . . **5.** grand **7.** aureate,
radiant, shining **8.** lustrous, splendid
9. beautiful, brilliant, refulgent
10. epiphanous **11.** illustrious
respond . . . **4.** echo **5.** react, reply
6. accord, answer, retort **8.** response

10. correspond 11. reciprocate
response . . . **4.** echo **5.** reply **6.** answer, anthem, chorus **7.** rapport, refrain **8.** antiphon (Mus), reaction
responsibility . . . **4.** care, duty, onus **6.** charge **8.** solvency **11.** reliability **14.** accountability **15.** trustworthiness
responsible . . . **6.** liable **7.** solvent **8.** amenable, reliable **10.** answerable **11.** accountable, respectable, trustworthy
responsive . . . **6.** pliant **7.** elastic **8.** reactive **9.** answering, sensitive, teachable **10.** open-minded **11.** persuasible, sympathetic
res publica . . . **5.** state **8.** republic **10.** commonweal **12.** commonwealth
rest . . . **3.** lay, set, sit **4.** base, calm, ease, lair, lean, prop, seat, slip, stay, stop **5.** cease, death, found, pause, peace, quiet, relax, renew **6.** depend, desist, ground, repose, settle **7.** balance, leisure, recline, refresh, remains, remnant, reposal, respite, silence, support, surplus **8.** at anchor, interval, lodgment, residuum **9.** cessation, quietness, remainder, stillness **10.** quiescence, remain idle **12.** intermission, peacefulness, tranquillity
rest (pert to) . . .
  assured . . **9.** be certain, believe me
  at rest . . **4.** abed, dead **6.** otiose **11.** comfortable
  day . . **7.** Sabbath
  foot . . **4.** rail **7.** hassock, ottoman
  house (Orient) . . **5.** serai
  reading . . **7.** caesura (cesura)
restaurant . . . **4.** café, deli (sl) **5.** diner **6.** eatery **7.** automat, beanery, tearoom **8.** fast-food, pizzeria, snack bar **9.** cafeteria **10.** coffee shop **11.** rathskeller **12.** luncheonette
resting . . . **4.** abed **7.** dormant **8.** drowsing **9.** quiescent
resting place . . . **4.** tomb **5.** étape, roost **6.** hearth **7.** lairage, landing, support **8.** quarters
restitution . . . **6.** return **9.** atonement, repayment **10.** recompense, reparation **12.** compensation **13.** reinstatement
restless . . . **5.** antsy, hyper, itchy **6.** roving, uneasy **7.** agitato, fidgety, fretful, unquiet, restive, wakeful **8.** agitated **9.** impatient, sleepless, unceasing, unrestful, unsettled, wandering **10.** changeable, reposeless **12.** discontented
restoration . . . **6.** repair, return **7.** renewal, revival **8.** recovery **10.** renovation, reparation **11.** improvement, restitution **14.** redintegration **15.** reestablishment
restorative . . . **6.** acopon **7.** anodyne **8.** remedial **10.** reparative
restore . . . **4.** cure, heal **5.** renew, repay **6.** redeem, refund, repone, revive **7.** rebuild, recover, replace **8.** renovate **9.** reinstate **11.** reconstruct, reestablish **12.** redintegrate, rehabilitate
restore (pert to) . . .
  after cancelling . . **4.** stet

  certainty, confidence . . **8.** reassure
  to former position . . **9.** reinstate
  to original condition . . **9.** refurbish
  to proper position . . **5.** right
restrain . . . **3.** dam **4.** bate, bind, curb, rein, stay **5.** check, cramp, deter, limit, stint **6.** arrest, bridle, fetter, halter, hinder, tether **7.** abridge, confine, control, inhibit, overawe, qualify, repress **8.** restrict, suppress, withhold **9.** constrain, detention
restraint . . . **3.** bit **4.** curb, stop **5.** check, force **7.** durance, modesty, reserve **9.** condition, hindrance, reticence **10.** abridgment, constraint, inhibition, limitation, moderation, repression, temperance **11.** confinement, deprivation, self-control **12.** tastefulness
restraint, lack of . . . **9.** looseness
restrict . . . **3.** tie **4.** bind, curb **5.** bound, cramp, limit, scant, stint **6.** censor, coerce, modify **7.** confine, qualify, repress **10.** specialize **12.** circumscribe
restricted . . . **5.** local **6.** narrow **7.** limited, topical **9.** exclusive **10.** restrained **11.** specialized
restriction . . . **5.** stint **9.** restraint **10.** limitation, narrowness, regulation, tightening **11.** reservation **12.** constriction **13.** qualification
resty . . . **5.** quiet **7.** restive **8.** sluggish
result . . . **3.** end, sum **4.** rise **5.** arise, ensue, event, fruit, issue, total **6.** accrue, answer, effect, follow, sequel, spring, upshot **7.** proceed, product **8.** solution **9.** aftermath, deduction, eventuate, terminate **10.** conclusion **11.** achievement, consequence, termination
resume . . . **5.** recur, renew **6.** reopen **7.** recover **8.** reoccupy **9.** epitomize, reiterate, summarize **10.** recommence
résumé . . . **8.** abstract **10.** compendium **11.** work history
resurrection . . . **6.** rising **7.** revival **10.** apotheosis **11.** restoration
resuscitate . . . **6.** revive **7.** restore **8.** revivify
ret . . . **3.** rot **4.** soak **5.** steep **6.** expose, impute **7.** ascribe
retable . . . **5.** ledge, shelf **6.** gradin (gradine) **8.** predella
retail . . . **4.** sale, sell **6.** repeat **8.** dispense, disperse
retain . . . **4.** hold, keep, save, stet **6.** employ **8.** maintain, preserve, remember **9.** recollect
retainer . . . **3.** fee **4.** cage **6.** menial, minion, vassal, yeoman **7.** servant **9.** attendant, bodyguard
retaining wall . . . **9.** revetment
retaliate . . . **5.** repay **6.** avenge **7.** requite **12.** make requital
retaliation . . . **6.** talion (Mosaic law, eye for eye, tooth for tooth) **7.** revenge **8.** reprisal, requital **10.** punishment **11.** comeuppance, retribution
retard . . . **4.** clog, drag, slow **5.** defer, delay, laten **6.** belate, deaden, detain, hinder, impede **8.** keep back, obstruct, postpone, slow down

retardant... **4.** clog, drag **6.** remora
8. obstacle
retardate... **6.** impede **8.** retarded
retch... **3.** gag **4.** barf (sl), hawk, spit
5. reach, vomit **6.** expand, extend,
strain **7.** stretch, upchuck
rete... **3.** net **6.** plexus **7.** network
retention... **6.** memory **7.** custody,
holding, keeping **8.** tenacity
11. maintenance, self-control
retentive... **6.** memory **7.** keeping
9. tenacious **12.** recollective
retenue... **7.** reserve **10.** discretion
11. self-control **13.** self-restraint
rethe... **5.** cruel **6.** ardent, fierce, severe
retiary... **6.** spider **7.** netlike **9.** gladiator,
retiarius
reticence... **7.** reserve, silence
9. restraint **13.** secretiveness
reticulated... **3.** web **6.** meshed, netted
7. network **12.** intercrossed
reticule... **3.** bag **4.** etui **5.** cabas (caba)
7. handbag, reticle, workbag
reticulum... **7.** network, stomach (2nd)
9. neuroglia
retinue... **4.** crew **5.** harem, suite, train
6. escort **7.** cortege, service **8.** equipage
9. entourage, retainers **10.** attendants
retire... **6.** depart, depose, pay off,
recede, vanish **7.** go to bed, retreat
8. withdraw **9.** disappear, discharge
retired... **4.** abed, left, lone, paid
7. receded **8.** departed, emeritus,
recessed, resigned, secluded, solitary,
vanished, withdrew **9.** pensioned
10. disengaged **11.** disappeared,
sequestered
retirement... **7.** deposal, payment,
privacy, retreat **8.** solitude **9.** departure,
recession, reticence **10.** withdrawal
11. resignation **13.** disemployment
retiring... **3.** shy **6.** modest **8.** reserved,
reticent **9.** diffident **10.** not forward,
retreating **11.** unobtrusive
retort... **3.** mot **4.** quip **5.** reply **6.** answer
7. riposte (ripost) **8.** repartee **9.** retaliate
11. retaliation
retract... **6.** abjure, disown, draw in,
recent, repeal **7.** disavow, rescind,
swallow **8.** take back **9.** repudiate
retraction... **6.** repeal **8.** palinode
10. revocation, withdrawal
11. recantation
retrad... **8.** backward **11.** posteriorly
retral... **8.** backward **9.** posterior
10. retrograde
retreat... **3.** den **4.** abri, lair, nest, nook,
rout **6.** asylum, recede, recoil, refuge,
retire **7.** privacy, retiral, sanctum,
shelter **8.** fallback, solitude **9.** departure,
katabasis, seclusion **10.** retirement,
withdrawal
retrench... **6.** cut off, excise, lessen,
reduce **7.** abridge, curtail, cut down
8. decrease, diminish **9.** economize,
intercept
retrenchment... **3.** cut **8.** excision
9. lessening, reduction **10.** abridgment
11. curtailment, economizing
retribution... **3.** pay **6.** return, reward
7. nemesis **8.** reprisal, requital

9. vengeance **10.** punishment
11. restitution **12.** Last Judgment
retrieve... **5.** fetch **6.** redeem, regain,
rescue, revive **8.** make good
retrograde... **4.** slow **6.** recede, retral,
revert **7.** regress **8.** backward, decadent,
rearward **10.** regressive **11.** deteriorate
12. reversionary
retroussé... **6.** pugged (nose) **8.** turned
up
retund... **4.** beat, dull **5.** blunt **6.** refute,
subdue **9.** attenuate, drive back
10. render weak
return... **5.** recur, repay, reply **6.** answer,
render, repeat, report, revert **7.** regress,
relapse, requiet, respond, restore
9. repayment **11.** restitution, retaliation
return (pert to)...
　day.. **12.** answer to writ
　evil for evil.. **7.** revenge **9.** retaliate
　tennis term.. **3.** lob
　thrust (fencing).. **7.** riposte (ripost)
　to.. **6.** resume **7.** relapse, revisit
　to first theme (Mus).. **7.** reprise
returns... **5.** gains, polls **8.** receipts
reune... **4.** join **7.** reunite **10.** reassemble
reunion... **7.** joining **8.** sociable
14. reconciliation
re-up... **8.** re-enlist
reus... **9.** defendant
Reuter's News Agency... **6.** London
reveal... **3.** bid **4.** bare, jamb, open,
tell, wray **6.** impart, unveil **7.** divulge,
exhibit, uncover **8.** disclose, discover,
evidence, indicate, manifest
11. communicate
reveal (in trust)... **7.** confide
reveal intentionally... **4.** tell **6.** betray,
expose **7.** divulge, mislead
reveille... **4.** call **5.** levet **6.** signal
(sunrise)
revel... **3.** joy **4.** orgy, riot, wake **5.** feast,
spree, watch **6.** frolic **7.** carouse, delight,
rejoice, revelry, wassail **8.** carousal,
festival **11.** celebration, merrymaking
12. conviviality
revelant... **5.** clear **8.** manifest
12. intelligible
revelation... **6.** oracle, vision **8.** The Bible
9. discovery **10.** appearance, disclosure
13. communication, manifestation
Revelation (Bib)... **10.** Apocalypse
revelry... **3.** joy **4.** evoe, orgy, riot
6. revels **8.** carnival, carousal
9. revelment, revelrout **11.** merrymaking
revenant... **5.** ghost **7.** eidolon, specter
(spectre) **9.** recurring **10.** apparition
revendicate... **7.** reclaim, recover **10.** real
action
revenge... **6.** avenge **7.** requite
8. reprisal, requital **9.** retaliate,
vengeance **10.** punishment
11. retribution
revenue... **3.** tax **5.** yield **6.** income,
profit **7.** annates
reverberate... **4.** echo, ring **5.** repel,
reply **6.** return **7.** rebound, reflect,
resound
reverberation... **4.** echo **9.** reboation
10. reflection, resounding
revere... **4.** love **5.** adore, honor

6. esteem, regard, repute **7.** respect, worship **8.** venerate
reverence ... **3.** awe **5.** dread, honor, piety **7.** respect, worship **8.** venerate **9.** adoration, deference **10.** veneration
reverent ... **5.** pious **6.** devout **7.** dutiful **10.** respectful, worshipful
reverie ... **4.** muse **5.** dream **6.** notion, trance, vision **7.** fantasy
reversal ... **6.** defeat, repeal **9.** inversion, reversion **14.** tergiversation
reverse ... **4.** back **5.** upset **6.** back up, defeat, invert, repeal, revert, revoke **7.** relapse **8.** contrary, converse, opposite, overturn **9.** transpose **10.** misfortune
reversion ... **6.** estate **7.** revival **8.** transfer **9.** inversion **10.** regression **11.** inheritance
reversion (pert to) ...
ancestral .. **7.** atavism **9.** atavistic
insurance .. **7.** annuity
land .. **7.** escheat
revert ... **5.** react, recur **6.** advert, return **7.** regress, relapse **11.** antistrophe
revest ... **4.** robe **5.** dress **6.** attire, clothe **8.** reinvest **9.** reinstate
review ... **4.** edit **6.** parade, relate, survey **8.** critique, remember **9.** criticism, criticize, re-examine **10.** certiorati, commentary, compendium, discussion, inspection, periodical, reconsider **11.** examination, reiteration **12.** recollection **15.** reconsideration
reviewer ... **6.** critic, writer **11.** commentator
revile ... **4.** rail **5.** abuse, curse **6.** berate, debase, vilify **7.** asperse **8.** reproach, ridicule
revise ... **4.** edit **5.** amend, emend **6.** redact **7.** correct, rewrite **8.** readjust
revision ... **7.** revisal **10.** correction, emendation **11.** rebeholding **13.** re-examination
revival ... **7.** rebirth, renewal **10.** quickening **11.** reanimation, renaissance, restoration **12.** resurrection
revive ... **4.** stum (wine) **5.** rally, renew, rouse **6.** come to **7.** enliven, recover, refresh, respire, restore **8.** rekindle, remember / **11.** resuscitate
revocate ... **6.** recall, revoke **7.** repress
revocation ... **6.** repeal **8.** reversal **10.** retraction, withdrawal **11.** recantation
revoke ... **5.** adeem, annul **6.** abjure, cancel, recall, recant, renege, repeal, revive **7.** abolish, retract **8.** abrogate **9.** fainaigue **11.** countermand
revolt ... **5.** rebel **6.** mutiny, offend, strike **8.** nauseate, sedition, uprising **9.** rebellion **10.** revolution **12.** insurrection
revolting ... **4.** ugly **7.** hideous **8.** shocking **9.** offensive, repellent **10.** disgusting, nauseating
revolution ... **4.** gyre, turn **5.** cycle, epoch, orbit, round **6.** revolt **7.** circuit **8.** disorder, rotation **9.** rebellion
revolutionary ... **3.** new **7.** radical **12.** catastrophic **15.** insurrectionary

Revolutionary hero ... **5.** Allen (Ethan), Gates **6.** Revere **8.** Burgoyne **10.** Cornwallis, Washington **15.** Lighthorse Harry (Gen Lee)
revolve ... **4.** pirl, roll, spin, turn **5.** recur, wheel, whirl **6.** circle, gyrate, ponder, rotate **7.** trundle **8.** meditate **9.** circulate **10.** deliberate
revolver ... **3.** gat, gun, rod **6.** pistol **7.** firearm **10.** six-shooter
revolving ... **3.** orb **4.** cowl (metal cap) **6.** rotary
revolving (pert to) ...
in thought .. **8.** perusing
light .. **10.** lighthouse
part .. **3.** cam **5.** rotor
storm .. **7.** cyclone
revue ... **6.** medley, review **9.** burlesque **13.** musical comedy
reward ... **3.** pay, utu **4.** meed **5.** award, bonus, merit, Oscar, yield **6.** hallow (to hounds) **7.** guerdon **8.** reprisal **10.** recompense, remunerate **11.** retribution **12.** compensation, remuneration
reword ... **5.** alter **7.** restate **8.** rephrase **9.** reiterate **10.** paraphrase
rex ... **4.** king
rey ... **4.** king
Reynard ... **3.** fox (epic character)
rezai ... **8.** coverlet (quilted)
rhamn ... **7.** Rhamnus **9.** buckthorn
rhapontic ... **7.** rhubarb **8.** knapweed, pieplant
rhapsodic ... **6.** poetic **8.** ecstatic
rhapsodist ... **4.** poet **8.** minstrel **9.** visionary **10.** enthusiast
rhapsody ... **6.** jumble, medley **9.** utterance (ecstatic) **10.** recitation **11.** composition
rhea ... **3.** emu (emeu) **5.** nandu **7.** ostrich
Rhea (pert to) ...
called .. **15.** Mother of the Gods
father .. **6.** Uranus
home .. **5.** Mt Ida (Crete)
mother .. **4.** Gaea
mother of .. **4.** Hera, Zeus **5.** Hades **8.** Poseidon
wife of .. **6.** Cronus
rhebok ... **5.** peele **8.** antelope
Rheims ... see *Reims*
rhema ... **4.** term, verb, word
rheophile ... **15.** living in streams
rhetoric ... **7.** diction, oratory **9.** eloquence **11.** composition
rhetorical term ... **6.** aporia, simile **10.** antithesis, oratorical **11.** catachresis
rhetoric digression ... **6.** ecbole
rheumatism root ... **7.** wild yam
rheumatism weed ... **10.** Indian hemp, pepsissewa
rhexis ... **7.** rupture
rhinal ... **5.** nasal **6.** narial
rhine ... **5.** ditch, drain **6.** runnel
Rhine (pert to) ...
breed .. **7.** rabbits
native .. **11.** Rhinelander
nymph .. **7.** Lorelei
ref to .. **7.** Rhenish
tributary .. **4.** Ruhr **6.** Neckar
wine .. **7.** Moselle

rhino . . . **4.** cash, nose (comb form) **5.** money **10.** rhinoceros
rhinoceros (pert to) . . .
Bib . . **4.** reem
bird . . **8.** hornbill **9.** beefeater
black . . **6.** borele **7.** keitlos
Malay . . **5.** abada
viper . . **5.** snake (poisonous)
rhizopod . . . **6.** amoeba **8.** Protozoa
Rhoda . . . **4.** rose
Rhode Island . . .
bay . . **12.** Narragansett
capital . . **10.** Providence
city . . **7.** Newport **9.** Pawtucket **10.** Woonsocket
famed cotton mill . . **6.** Slater
first U.S. synagogue . . **5.** Touro
founder . . **13.** Roger Williams (1636)
Rebellion . . **5.** Dorr's (1842)
resort . . **7.** Newport **11.** Block Island
river . . **9.** Pawtucket **10.** Blackstone
settlers . . **8.** Puritans
State admission . . **10.** Thirteenth
State motto . . **4.** Hope
State nickname . . **11.** Little Rhody
Rhode Island Red . . . **4.** fowl
Rhodesia . . . see *Zimbabwe*
rhododaphne . . . **8.** oleander
Rhoeadales . . . **5.** poppy **11.** Papaverales
rhomb . . . **7.** rhombus **10.** magic wheel **11.** spinning top
rhomboid . . . **13.** parallelogram
rhombus . . . **5.** rhomb **13.** parallelogram (equilateral)
Rhone tributary . . . **5.** Isere
rhubarb . . . **5.** clash, Rheum **6.** hassle **7.** citrine, dispute, yawweed **8.** argument, pieplant **9.** rhapontic **10.** discussion
Rhus . . . **5.** sumac **7.** wax tree
rhyme, rime . . . **4.** poem **6.** poetry, rhythm **7.** measure **9.** assonance
rhythm . . . **4.** beat, lilt **5.** meter, pulse, swing, tempo **6.** poetry **7.** cadence, euphony, measure, pattern **8.** movement, rhythmus, symmetry
rhythmical break . . . **7.** caesura
ria . . . **5.** creek, inlet
rial . . . **4.** coin, king **5.** great, noble, royal **6.** prince **8.** splendid **9.** excellent, stag's horn **11.** magnificent
rialto . . . **4.** mart **6.** Bridge (Venice), market **7.** theater **8.** exchange
riant . . . **3.** gay **6.** blithe, bright **7.** smiling **8.** laughing
riata . . . **4.** rope **5.** lasso **6.** lariat
rib . . . **4.** bone, meat, vein **5.** costa, ridge **6.** lierne
ribald . . . **3.** low **4.** lewd **6.** coarse, erotic, harlot, risqué, vulgar **7.** obscene **10.** scurrilous **11.** blasphemous **12.** ribble-rabble
riband . . . **6.** ribbon
ribbed . . . **3.** rep **5.** piqué **6.** corded, ridged **7.** costate
ribble-rabble . . . **6.** gabble, rabble, ribald **7.** chatter **10.** incoherent
ribbon . . . **3.** bow **4.** band, sash **5.** strip **6.** cestus, fillet, riband **10.** decoration
ribbon (pert to) . . .
badge . . **6.** cordon
band . . **5.** corse **9.** banderole
fish . . **7.** oarfish **8.** dealfish
inked . . **10.** typewriter
knot . . **7.** rosette
ribbonlike . . **8.** taenioid
snake . . **6.** garter
Society . . **7.** Ireland
worm . . **8.** tapeworm **9.** nemertine
ribwort . . . **8.** plantain
rice (pert to) . . .
bird . . **4.** rail, sora **8.** bobolink
dish . . **5.** pilaf (pilau, pilaw) **7.** risotto **8.** kedgeree **9.** jambalaya, ricetable
drink . . **5.** bubud
feeding on . . **11.** oryzivorous
field . . **5.** paddy
hen . . **9.** gallinule
inferior . . **4.** chit, pago
paste . . **3.** ame
rat . . **8.** Oryzomys
refuse . . **5.** shood (shud)
Spanish . . **5.** arroz
wild . . **4.** reed
wine . . **4.** sake
rich . . . **3.** fat **5.** opime **6.** creamy, fecund, fruity, mighty, ornate, potent **7.** copious, fertile, moneyed, opulent, wealthy **8.** abundant, affluent, colorful, powerful, resonant, valuable **9.** bountiful, expensive, luxuriant, sumptuous **10.** in the chips **13.** grandiloquent
rich (pert to) . . .
English slang . . **4.** oofy **6.** oofier
man . . **5.** Dives (Bib), Midas, nabob **7.** Croesus **9.** plutocrat **10.** capitalist **11.** millionaire
richard . . . **9.** plutocrat
riches . . . **5.** lucre, means **6.** mammon (Bib), wealth **7.** bonanza **8.** big bucks (sl), opulence **9.** affluence, megabucks (sl) **10.** prosperity
riches, demon of . . . **6.** Mammon
rick . . . **4.** heap, pile **5.** noise, scold, stack, twist **6.** pile up, rattle, sprain, wrench **7.** chatter
rickets . . . **7.** disease **8.** rachitis
rickety . . . **4.** weak **5.** crazy, shaky **6.** senile **7.** unsound **8.** unstable, unsteady **9.** tottering **10.** ramshackle
rickle . . . **4.** heap, pile, rick **5.** stack **6.** jingle, rattle
rickrack . . . **5.** braid **6.** edging **9.** insertion
ricksha, rickshaw . . . **10.** jinrikisha
ricochet . . . **5.** carom **7.** rebound **10.** bounce back
rid . . . **4.** doff, free, kill **5.** clear, empty **6.** remove, rescue **7.** deliver, destroy, discard **9.** dispose of, drive away, eliminate **11.** disencumber
riddance . . . **6.** escape **7.** discard **11.** elimination **14.** relinquishment
riddle . . . **3.** ree **4.** crux, sift **5.** rebus, sieve **6.** enigma, pierce **7.** perplex **8.** separate **9.** conundrum, perforate
ride . . . **4.** twit **5.** drive, float **6.** pester, travel **7.** be borne, journey, overlap **8.** domineer, ridicule **9.** carrousel (carousel), cavalcade, excursion **10.** forest road **12.** merry-go-round **13.** roller coaster
ride (pert to) . . .

herd.. **9.** guard over
off.. **4.** polo (term)
roughshod over.. **9.** tyrannize
shank's mare.. **4.** walk
to hog, pig.. **11.** boar hunting
to line.. **4.** herd
rident... **5.** riant **7.** smiling **8.** laughing
rider... **5.** ryder **6.** clause, knight
   7. allonge, codicil **8.** addition, horseman
   9. performer **10.** freebooter,
   highwayman **11.** endorsement,
   mosstrooper
Rider Haggard's novel... **3.** She
ridge... **3.** aas, rib **4.** hill, rand, wale,
   weal, welt **5.** arête, bulge, chine, crest
   7. wrinkle
ridge (pert to)...
   anatomy.. **4.** ruga **6.** carina
   barrier.. **5.** parma
   between furrows.. **7.** porcate **8.** porcated
   coral.. **4.** reef
   glacial.. **2.** os **5.** esker (eskar)
   military.. **6.** rideau
   mountain.. **4.** loma **5.** arête **6.** sierra
   narrow, raised.. **4.** wale
   oak.. **9.** blackjack
   raised by stroke.. **5.** wheal, whelk
   short.. **4.** kame
   sloping.. **6.** cuesta
   steep.. **7.** hogback
   stony.. **4.** rand
   zoology term.. **5.** varix
ridicule... **3.** guy, pan **4.** butt, gibe, jeer,
   mock, quiz, twit **5.** chaff, irony, sneer,
   taunt **6.** banter, deride, satire **7.** asteism,
   mockery, sarcasm **8.** derision, raillery
   9. burlesque
ridiculous... **5.** funny **6.** absurd
   7. amusing **8.** farcical **9.** grotesque,
   laughable, ludicrous **10.** impossible,
   outrageous **12.** preposterous,
   unbelievable
ridiculous failure... **6.** fiasco
riding (pert to)...
   bitts.. **11.** anchor cable
   breeches.. **8.** jodhpurs
   dress, costume.. **5.** habit
   knot.. **8.** slipknot
   rhyme.. **7.** couplet
   school.. **6.** manège
   whip.. **4.** crop **5.** quirt
rife... **7.** replete, rumored **8.** abundant
   9. abounding, plentiful, prevalent
   10. prevailing, widespread
riff... **6.** rapids, riffle, ripple **7.** midriff
   9. diaphragm **13.** improvisation
riffle... **7.** shallow, shuffle, wavelet
riffraff... **3.** mob **4.** mean **5.** offal
   6. rabble, refuse, trashy **7.** rubbish
   9. sweepings
rifle... **3.** rob **5.** reeve, steal, strip
   6. Mauser, search, snider **7.** carbine,
   despoil, firearm, pillage, plunder,
   ransack
rifle (pert to)...
   accessory.. **6.** ramrod
   ball.. **5.** Minié **6.** bullet
   bird.. **14.** bird of paradise
   bomb.. **7.** grenade
   French.. **9.** chassepot
   old form.. **4.** tige

rifler... **4.** hawk **6.** robber
rift... **3.** gap, lag **4.** rima, rive **5.** break,
   cleft, split **6.** cleave, divide **10.** falling
   out
rig... **3.** fit **4.** gear, suit **5.** dress, equip
   6. lateen **7.** bedizen, costume, rigging,
   vehicle **9.** Bermudian (Naut)
Riga (pert to)...
   balsam.. **5.** resin (Swiss pine)
   capital of.. **6.** Latvia
   native.. **4.** Lett **7.** Latvian
   rine.. **4.** hemp
rigging (ship)... **4.** gear, rope, spar
   6. tackle **9.** equipment
right... **3.** fit, pat **4.** fair, true **6.** adjust,
   dexter, proper, remedy **7.** correct,
   justice, upright **8.** becoming, suitable
   9. equitable, faultless, franchise,
   privilege, propriety **10.** put in order
   11. appropriate, prerogative
   13. justification
right (pert to)...
   angled.. **10.** orthogonal
   comb form.. **6.** dextro
   exclusive.. **6.** patent **10.** concession
   hand.. **6.** dexter
   hand page.. **5.** recto
   law.. **5.** droit
   neither right nor wrong..
      11. adiaphorous
   of belligerent (Naut).. **6.** angary
   of ownership.. **5.** title
   of procedure.. **2.** pas
   real estate.. **8.** easement
   royal.. **7.** regalia
   time.. **3.** tid
   to choice.. **6.** option
   to pasture.. **6.** eatage
   turn.. **3.** gee
righteous... **4.** holy, just **5.** godly,
   moral, pious **6.** worthy **7.** upright
   8. virtuous **9.** believers, blameless,
   equitable, guiltless
righteousness... **6.** equity, virtue
   8. holiness **9.** godliness, rectitude
   11. uprightness
rightful... **4.** just, true **5.** legal, right
   6. honest, lawful, proper **7.** fitting,
   genuine **9.** equitable **11.** appropriate
rigid... **3.** set **4.** firm, hard **5.** exact,
   stern, stiff, tense **6.** formal, narrow, not
   lax, severe, strict **7.** ascetic, austere
   8. rigorous **9.** obstinate, stringent,
   unbending **10.** inflexible, meticulous,
   unyielding
rigidity... **7.** tensity **8.** hardness, severity
   9. exactness, obstinacy, stiffness
rigol... **4.** ring **6.** circle, groove **7.** channel
Rigoletto... **5.** dance, opera (Verdi)
rigor, rigour... **4.** cold, fury **7.** cruelty
   8. asperity, rigidity, severity, violence
   9. exactness, harshness, rigidness
   10. shuddering, strictness
   13. inflexibility
rigor mortis... **10.** stiffening (death)
   12. rigor of death
rigorous... **4.** cold **5.** exact, harsh, rigid,
   stern, stiff **6.** severe, strict **7.** austere,
   drastic, violent **8.** accurate **9.** inclement,
   obstinate, puritanic **10.** inexorable,
   inflexible, relentless

rikk . . . **10.** tambourine
rile . . . **3.** vex **4.** roil **5.** anger, muddy **6.** offend **7.** agitate **8.** irritate **9.** turbidity
rill . . . **5.** brook **6.** course, runnel **7.** rillock, rivulet **9.** streamlet
rim . . . **3.** lip, web **4.** band, brim, edge, orle, tire **5.** bezel, brink, felly (felloe), verge **6.** border, flange, margin, shield **7.** enclose, horizon, rimrock **8.** boundary **9.** perimeter
rima . . . **5.** cleft **7.** fissure **8.** aperture **10.** breadfruit
rima oris . . . **16.** space between lips
rim ash . . . **9.** hackberry
rimate . . . **8.** fissured
rime . . . **4.** hoar, poem, rent **5.** chink, cleft, crack, frost, rhyme **6.** poetry **7.** fissure **8.** aperture **9.** assonance, hoarfrost **10.** ladder step
rime-cold giant (Norse) . . . **4.** Ymir (Ymer)
rimple . . . **4.** fold **6.** ripple, rumple **7.** wrinkle
rimption . . . **3.** lot **9.** abundance
Rinaldo's steed . . . **6.** Bayard
rind . . . **4.** bark, husk, peel, skin **5.** crust **6.** cortex **7.** epicarp **9.** hoarfrost
rindle . . . **5.** brook **6.** runnel **7.** rivulet
ring . . . **3.** rim, set **4.** band, halo, hoop, peal, toll **5.** arena, bague, chime, group, knell **6.** circle, clique, collar **7.** annulus, circlet, coterie, resound **8.** encircle, insignia, ornament, surround **9.** encompass **11.** association
ring (pert to) . . .
around . . **7.** environ
around the sun . . **6.** corona
barrel . . **4.** hoop
bill . . **4.** duck
bird . . **11.** reed bunting
comb form . . **4.** gyro
dove . . **6.** cushat
finger . . **5.** third
fruit jar . . **4.** lute
gem crown . . **5.** bezel
gem setting . . **6.** chaton
gun carriage . . **7.** lunette (lunet)
harness part . . **6.** terret
horse training . . **5.** longe
Latin . . **7.** annulus
leader . . **6.** rouser **9.** demagogue **12.** rabble-rouser
little . . **7.** annulet, circlet
ornament (metal) . . **3.** bee (angling)
ouzel . . **6.** thrush
rope . . **7.** grommet
sail . . **4.** hank **8.** ringtail
tail . . **3.** cat **4.** coon **5.** lemur **6.** godwit, marlin **10.** cacomistle **11.** golden eagle (young)
ringed boa . . . **5.** aboma
ringed worm . . . **7.** annelid
ringhals . . . **5.** snake (spitting)
ringing . . . **7.** clangor, orotund, pealing, tolling **8.** clanging, resonant **10.** resounding
ringle-eye . . . **7.** walleye
ringlet . . . **4.** curl, lock **5.** tress **6.** circle **7.** circlet **9.** fairy ring
ringworm . . . **5.** tinea **6.** tetter **7.** disease, serpigo **9.** millepede

rink . . . **4.** hero, race, ring **6.** circle, course **7.** warrior **8.** encircle, ice sheet (skating) **9.** encounter
rinse . . . **4.** lave, sind, wash **5.** flush **6.** sluice **7.** cleanse **8.** absterge
rinthereout, rintherout (Scot) . . . **5.** tramp **7.** vagrant **8.** vagabond
rio . . . **5.** river **6.** coffee, stream
Rio de Janeiro . . . **7.** capital (old, Braz)
Rio Grande . . . **5.** river **7.** disease (lettuce)
riot . . . **3.** din **5.** brawl, melee **6.** clamor, excess, pogrom, revolt, tumult, uproar **7.** dispute, quarrel, revelry **8.** carousal, disorder, violence **9.** commotion
riotous . . . **4.** raid **5.** aroar **6.** wanton **7.** violent **8.** dissolute, luxuriant, seditious **10.** profligate, tumultuous **12.** unrestrained
riotous jollity . . . **9.** dissolute **11.** saturnalian
rip . . . **3.** cut **4.** rend, rent, tear **5.** break, horse (old) **7.** riptide **9.** debauchee, libertine, reprobate **10.** fish basket, laceration
ripe . . . **3.** fit **5.** ready, rifle **6.** mature, mellow **7.** plunder **8.** finished, prepared, rareripe **9.** developed, full-grown, perfected **10.** consummate
ripen . . . **3.** age **5.** addle **6.** digest, mellow, nature **7.** develop, perfect, prepare **8.** complete, grow ripe
riposte, ripost . . . **5.** reply **6.** answer, retort, thrust **8.** repartee
ripping . . . **5.** bully, grand, swell **9.** admirable, hunky-dory **12.** fine and dandy
rippit . . . **9.** fist fight
ripple . . . **3.** cut, lap **4.** fret, purl, riff, tear, wave **5.** acker, eagre, graze **6.** dimple, murmur **7.** crinkle, disturb, scratch, trickle, wavelet **11.** corrugation
ripple grass plantain . . . **7.** ribwort
ris de veau . . . **10.** sweetbread
rise . . . **4.** grow, soar, well **5.** arise, begin, climb, get up, mount, raise, reach, rebel, start, surge, tower **6.** ascend, ascent, attain, be high, emerge, growth, height, revolt, spring, thrive **7.** succeed **8.** eminence, flourish, increase, levitate, reaction **9.** acclivity, ascension, beginning, elevation, originate **11.** development
rise (pert to) . . .
above . . **4.** loom **8.** surmount **11.** triumph over
again . . **7.** resurge **11.** resurrected
and fall of the sea . . **5.** scend, tidal **6.** welter
by buoyancy . . **8.** levitate
gradually . . **4.** loom
hawk's . . **6.** mounty
high . . **5.** tower
risible . . . **5.** funny **6.** absurd **9.** laughable
rising . . . **6.** ascent, ortive, revolt **7.** growing, montant, sloping, surgent **8.** elevated, emergent, gradient (by degrees), swelling **9.** acclivity, advancing, ascending, ascension
rising and falling . . . **5.** tidal **7.** surging **8.** undulant
risk . . . **4.** dare **5.** peril **6.** chance, danger,

expose, gamble, hazard, injury, plight
7. venture **8.** endanger **10.** investment
12. disadvantage
risky . . . **6.** risqué **9.** hazardous
11. venturesome
risp . . . **3.** rub **4.** file, rasp, tirl **5.** stalk
7. bulrush, scratch
risper . . . **11.** caterpillar
risqué . . . **4.** racy **5.** risky, salty **8.** off-color
9. hazardous **10.** suggestive
rissle . . . **4.** pole **5.** staff, stick
risus . . . **5.** laugh **8.** laughter
rit (rare) . . . **3.** cut, rip **4.** slit, tear **5.** split
6. pierce **7.** scratch
ritardando . . . **9.** direction, retarding
10. slackening **11.** rallentando
rite . . . **4.** cult, form **6.** ritual, sacrum
7. formula, liturgy, tonsure **8.** ceremony
9. solemnity **10.** ceremonial, initiation,
observance **12.** patriarchate
ritratto . . . **7.** picture **8.** portrait
Ritter . . . **6.** knight
ritual . . . **4.** book, code, cult, form,
rite **5.** feast, salat **6.** novena, prayer
7. liturgy **8.** ceremony **10.** ceremonial
ritus . . . **5.** usage **6.** custom
ritzy . . . **5.** smart (vulgarly), swank
6. swanky **11.** pretentious **16.** ultrafashionable
rivage . . . **4.** bank, duty **5.** coast, green,
shore
rival . . . **3.** foe, vie **4.** even, peer **5.** excel,
match **7.** compete, emulate **8.** emulator,
opponent **10.** antagonist, competitor
11. compete with
rivalry . . . **4.** feud **9.** emulation
11. competition
rive . . . **3.** rip **4.** bank, open, rent, rift, tear
5. cleft, sever, shore, split **6.** cleave
8. lacerate
rive droite . . . **9.** Right Bank (Seine)
rive gauche . . . **8.** Left Bank (Seine, Paris,
including Latin Qtr)
rivel . . . **6.** shrink **7.** shrivel, wrinkle
river . . . **2.** ea **3.** ria, rio, run **4.** ilog
5. amnis, brook, creek **6.** stream
7. rivulet, torrent **8.** riverlet **9.** streamlet
river (pert to) . . .
arm (of sea) . . **7.** estuary
bank . . **4.** ripa **5.** levee
bank, pert to . . **8.** riparian
bed . . **4.** holm **6.** alveus, bottom
7. channel
bend . . **5.** oxbow
boat . . **3.** ark
delta branch . . **5.** bayou
dog . . **10.** hellbender
dragon . . **9.** crocodile
duck . . **4.** teal
fish (spawning, from sea) . .
10. anadromous
horse . . **5.** hippo **12.** hippopotamus
inlet . . **4.** slew **5.** fiord (fjord) **6.** slough
islet . . **3.** ait **4.** holm
mouth . . **4.** lade **5.** delta **7.** estuary
mussel . . **4.** unio
Near East . . **4.** wadi (wady)
Nile measure . . **9.** Nilometer
nymph . . **4.** nais **5.** naiad
rat . . **5.** thief
ref to . . **5.** amnic

region (near) . . **8.** riverine
siren . . **7.** Lorelei
thief . . **3.** rat **6.** ackman
winding . . **3.** ess
river in . . .
Africa . . **4.** Nile, Tana **5.** Niger
Austria . . **4.** Iser **5.** Drava
Bavaria . . **4.** Eger, Isar
Belgium . . **4.** Yser
Bohemia . . **4.** Elbe, Iser
Brazil . . **3.** Rio
Bulgaria . . **5.** Mesta
China . . **3.** Wei **6.** Yellow **7.** Hwang Ho
England . . **4.** Isis **6.** Thames
France . . **5.** Seine
Germany . . **6.** Danube
Italy . . **4.** Arno **5.** Tiber
Netherlands . . **3.** Eem **4.** Maas (Meuse)
S America . . **6.** Amazon
Siberia . . **2.** Ob **4.** Lena
Switzerland . . **3.** Aar **5.** Reuss
river of . . .
Annie Laurie . . **4.** Nith
Caesar . . **7.** Rubicon
lower regions . . **4.** Styx **5.** Lethe
7. Acheron
woe . . **7.** Acheron
rixy . . . **4.** tern
road . . . **3.** via, way **4.** iter, path, raid
5. agger **7.** estrada, highway, journey,
passage **8.** pavement **9.** incursion,
roadstead **10.** expedition
road (pert to) . . .
block . . **3.** dam **4.** weir
goose . . **5.** brant
hog . . **8.** motorist **10.** monopolist
horse . . **6.** saddle (horse)
impassable . . **7.** impasse
man . . **7.** drummer, peddler **8.** salesman
9. canvasser
map . . **5.** chart, globe **9.** directory
master . . **10.** supervisor **11.** trackmaster
nautical . . **9.** roadstead
no outlet . . **8.** cul-de-sac
paving . . **6.** Tarmac **7.** ballast, macadam
runner . . **6.** cuckoo
scraper . . **4.** harl
weed . . **8.** plantain
roam . . . **2.** go **3.** err, gad **4.** rove
5. prowl, range **6.** ramble, stroll, wander
7. meander **9.** gallivant
roan . . . **5.** horse (bay, gray, chestnut)
8. antelope **9.** sheepskin, yellow-red
roanoke . . . **6.** wampum
Roanoke . . .
city . . **8.** Virginia
famed as . . **11.** First Colony (1584)
famed for . . **12.** Virginia Dare (1st white
child, 1587)
settler . . **16.** Sir Walter Raleigh **19.** Sir
Richard Grenville
roar . . . **3.** bell, blow, boom, rote (surf)
5. brool, laugh, shout **6.** bellow, steven
7. ululate **8.** cry aloud **9.** loud sound
roaring . . . **5.** aroar, great **7.** booming,
riotous **10.** disorderly
Roaring (pert to) . . .
Forties . . **8.** Broadway (NYC)
game . . **7.** curling (Scot)
Twenties . . **14.** Golden Twenties **16.** Age
of Red Hot Mamas

roast . . . **4.** beef, cook **5.** cabob, parch
6. assate, banter **7.** torrefy **8.** ridicule
9. criticize
roasting (pert to) . . .
ear . . **4.** corn
jack . . **9.** smokejack
stick . . **4.** spit
rob . . . **4.** loot, pelf **5.** pinch (sl), reave, rifle,
steal, touch **6.** pilfer, ravish, snatch,
snitch **7.** despoil, pillage, plunder
10. plagiarize
robbed . . . **5.** stole **6.** rubato (Mus)
8. snatched, snitched
robber . . . **4.** yegg **5.** crook (sl), thief
6. bandit, reaver, rifler **7.** brigand,
burglar, yeggman **8.** pillager
9. despoiler, embezzler, larcenist,
peculator **10.** depredator, highwayman,
shoplifter
robber (pert to) . . .
grave . . **5.** ghoul
high seas . . **6.** pirate **7.** corsair
9. privateer
highway . . **7.** footpad, ladrone
Indian . . **6.** dacoit
robber baron . . . **4.** Fisk **5.** Gould
robbery . . . **4.** reif **5.** theft **6.** burgle, piracy
7. larceny, pillage, plunder **8.** burglary
10. spoliation **11.** depredation
robe . . . **5.** array, cover, dress, tunic
6. invest, mantle **7.** costume, garment
8. clerical, vestment
robe (pert to) . . .
ancient Roman's . . **4.** toga
bishop's . . **6.** chimer
camel's hair . . **3.** aba
long . . **5.** talar
loose . . **5.** cymar (symar)
royal . . **6.** ermine, purple
robin . . . **4.** bird, lout, tody **6.** thrush
7. bumpkin **8.** trimming **9.** redbreast
10. toxalbumin
robin (pert to) . . .
dipper . . **14.** bufflehead duck
runaway . . **7.** dewdrop
sandpiper . . **4.** knot **5.** snipe **9.** dowitcher
songbird . . **8.** accentor
Robin Bluestring . . . **13.** Robert Walpole
robinet . . . **6.** cannon **9.** chaffinch
Robin Goodfellow . . . **4.** Puck **6.** sprite
9. hobgoblin
Robin Hood (pert to) . . .
famed as . . **6.** archer, outlaw, yeoman
followers . . **9.** Friar Tuck **10.** Little John,
Maid Marian
forest . . **8.** Sherwood (Eng)
habit . . **11.** robbing rich (for the poor)
Robinson Crusoe's man . . . **6.** Friday
roborant . . . **4.** drug **5.** tonic **6.** bracer
8. pick-me-up **9.** stimulant
roborean . . . **5.** oaken, stout **6.** strong
robot . . . **9.** automaton
Rob Roy . . . **5.** canoe **6.** outlaw (Scot)
15. Robert MacGregor
robust . . . **4.** hale **5.** hardy, lusty, rough,
sound, stout, wally **6.** hearty, sinewy,
strong, sturdy **7.** healthy **8.** muscular,
vigorous
roc . . . **4.** bird (Arabian Nights) **7.** simurgh
(simurg)
rocca . . . **4.** hold **6.** donjon **8.** fortress

rock . . . **3.** orc **4.** lull, peak, sway,
trap, tufa, tuff **5.** agate, chert, cliff,
quiet, shake, slate, stone **6.** basalt,
egeran, gneiss, refuge, schist, teeter
7. diamond, missile **8.** dolomite,
porphyry, strength **9.** whinstone
10. promontory
rock (pert to) . . .
black . . **6.** basalt
brittle . . **5.** shale
broken . . **4.** sand **5.** attle
cavity . . **5.** druse
chain . . **4.** reef
coarse . . **8.** psammite, psephite
crystal . . **6.** silica
crystalline . . **6.** gneiss, schist
decomposed . . **6.** gossan
fluid . . **4.** lava
fragments . . **5.** scree **8.** detritus, xenolith
geyser deposit . . **6.** sinter
glacial . . **7.** moraine
granitelike . . **6.** gneiss
granular . . **6.** oolite, quartz **7.** diorite
10. rockallite
gray . . **5.** slate **8.** andesite
igneous . . **4.** boss, trap **6.** basalt
7. peridot
jutting . . **3.** tor **4.** crag
nodule . . **5.** geode
pinnacle . . **4.** scar **6.** needle
porous . . **4.** tufa, tuff
rounded . . **6.** rognon
science . . **9.** petrology
Sicilian . . **6.** Scylla (opp Charybdis)
stratified . . **5.** shale
suffix . . **3.** ite, yte
volcanic . . **4.** tufa **6.** basalt, domite,
latite
rock, animal . . .
badger . . **4.** cony
cavy . . **6.** rodent
dassie . . **6.** rabbit
goat . . **4.** ibex
kangaroo . . **7.** wallaby
squirrel . . **11.** spermophile
rock, bird . . .
blackbird . . **9.** ring ouzel
dove . . **9.** guillemot **10.** rockpigeon
duck . . **9.** harlequin
goose . . **9.** kelp goose
grouse . . **9.** ptarmigan
hawk . . **6.** falcon, merlin
hopper . . **7.** penguin
lark . . **5.** pipit
pigeon . . **10.** sand grouse
sandpiper . . **5.** pipit, snipe
shrike . . **10.** rock thrush
starling . . **5.** ouzel
swallow . . **10.** rock martin
rock, fish . . .
bass . . **5.** black **7.** striped
clam . . **5.** borer
cod . . **7.** grouper
cook . . **6.** wrasse **7.** whiting
eel . . **6.** gunnel
gurnet . . **9.** fortescue
hind . . **7.** grouper (spotted)
lobster . . **8.** crayfish
salmon . . **7.** codfish **9.** amberfish
sucker . . **7.** lamprey
trout . . **9.** greenling

rock, flora . . .
bell . . **9.** columbine
brake . . **8.** polypody
candytuft . . **8.** gold-dust
cedar . . **7.** juniper
cranberry . . **8.** mountain
elm . . **11.** slippery elm
garden . . **6.** alpine
geranium . . **8.** alumroot
hair . . **6.** lichen
lily . . **9.** columbine **12.** pasqueflower
maple . . **5.** sugar
melon . . **10.** cantaloupe
shrub . . **9.** buckthorn
rocket . . . **5.** lance **6.** ascend, ascent, fire
   at **8.** aircraft, firework **9.** skyrocket,
   spaceship
rocket (famed) . . . **5.** Titan **6.** Apollo,
   Gemini, Saturn **7.** Jupiter, Mercury
   8. Redstone
Rock of Chickamauga . . . **6.** Thomas
   (Gen) (Civil War)
rocks . . . **5.** money
rocks, on the . . . **7.** aground **8.** bankrupt,
   stranded **10.** saxicoline
rocky . . . **4.** hard **5.** stony **6.** rugged
   7. sickish **8.** obdurate, unsteady
   9. unfeeling
Rocky Ford . . . **9.** muskmelon
Rocky Mountain . . .
group . . **5.** Coast **8.** Cascades **12.** Sierra
   Nevada
park . . **5.** Estes
peak . . **6.** Elbert **8.** McKinley
popular name . . **7.** Rockies
range . . **5.** Teton, Uinta
rococo . . . **6.** florid **7.** baroque, bizarre
   9. fantastic, grotesque
   13. ornamentation
rod . . . **3.** gat, gun **4.** pole, wand, whip
   5. baton, perch, power, scion, staff
   7. measure, scepter
rod (pert to) . . .
comb form . . **5.** rhabd **6.** rhabdo
fibrous . . **5.** lytta
flat . . **6.** ferula, ferule
grooved . . **4.** came (stained glass)
knitting . . **6.** needle
meat-holding . . **4.** spit
mechanical . . **6.** piston
metal . . **7.** stemmer
mixing . . **3.** rab
pointed . . **4.** goat, spit
rodlike . . **9.** vergiform
rotating . . **7.** spindle
short . . **6.** toggle
spinning . . **7.** spindle
rodd . . . **8.** crossbow, stonebow
rodent . . . **4.** cony, hare, paca, vole
   5. hutia (jutia), mouse, stoat **6.** agouti
   (agouty), beaver, gerbil, gopher
   marmot, murine **7.** lemming, leveret
   8. chipmunk, hedgehog, mongoose,
   squirrel **9.** guinea pig, porcupine
rodent (pert to) . . .
Andes . . **8.** abrocome
aquatic . . **6.** beaver **7.** muskrat
Belgian . . **8.** leporide
burrowing . . **6.** marmot **8.** sewellel
disease . . **9.** tularemia
European . . **4.** cony **5.** lerot

fur-bearing . . **6.** beaver
genus . . **3.** Mus **5.** Lepus
gnawing . . **3.** rat **4.** mole
hare . . **6.** rabbit
jumping . . **6.** jerboa
largest . . **8.** capybara (capibara)
migrating . . **7.** lemming
Mongoloid . . **3.** rat **6.** gopher **12.** pocket
   gopher
mouselike . . **4.** vole
rabbitlike . . **4.** pika
reference to . . **7.** gnawing **8.** rosorial
S American . . **4.** degu **5.** coypu **6.** agouti
   8. capybara **10.** chinchilla
spiny . . **9.** porcupine
rodeo . . . **4.** show **7.** roundup **9.** spectacle
   11. performance (public)
rodomontade . . . **4.** brag, rant **5.** boast
   7. bluster **8.** boastful, boasting,
   braggart, bragging
roe . . . **2.** ra **3.** doe **4.** deer, hind, raun
   5. coral (lobster) **8.** fish eggs
Roentgen, Röntgen (Wilhelm) . . .
famed as . . **9.** physicist
famed for . . **5.** X-rays **10.** Nobel Prize
   (1901) **12.** Roentgen rays
rogan . . . **4.** bowl (wooden) **10.** receptacle
   (maple sap)
Roger's plane (Will) . . . **9.** Winnie May
rogue . . . **3.** imp, wag **4.** kite **5.** cheat,
   knave, scamp, shark, tramp **6.** beggar,
   pirate, rascal **7.** corsair, vagrant,
   villain **8.** elephant, picaroon, vagabond
   13. mischief-maker
roguish . . . **3.** sly **4.** arch **5.** pawky
   7. knavish **8.** espiegle, rascally
   10. frolicsome, picaresque
   11. mischievous
roguishly . . . **5.** slyly **8.** impishly, trickily
   10. prankishly
roid . . . **5.** rough **6.** severe **7.** riotous
   10. frolicsome **12.** unmanageable
roil . . . **3.** vex **4.** foul, roam, romp
   5. anger, annoy, horse (Flemish),
   muddy **6.** fidget, ruffle, wander
   7. agitate, disturb **8.** irritate
roister . . . **4.** brag, rude **5.** bully **7.** bluster,
   boorish, swagger, violent **9.** gilravage
roisterer (Hist) . . . **3.** mun
roke . . . **3.** fog **4.** stir **5.** moist, smoke,
   steam, vapor **8.** moisture
roker . . . **3.** ray **8.** rockling **9.** thornback
roky . . . **4.** damp **5.** foggy, misty, smoky
   6. hoarse
role . . . **4.** duty, part **6.** office **8.** capacity,
   function **9.** character **13.** impersonation
roll . . . **3.** bun, rob **4.** coil, film, food,
   furl, list, pell, rota, sway, wind, wrap
   5. trill, troll **6.** billow, bundle, rotate,
   rumble, scroll **8.** bankroll, cylinder,
   rotation
roll (pert to) . . .
along . . **7.** trundle
back . . **6.** reduce **8.** retrench
bread . . **3.** bap
butter . . **3.** pat
cloth . . **4.** bolt
coins . . **7.** rouleau
fish . . **7.** rissole
hair . . **3.** rat **7.** chignon
military . . **5.** cadre **6.** roster

the bones.. **4.** dice **10.** shoot craps
tobacco.. **5.** cigar
to one side.. **5.** lurch
up.. **4.** furl **6.** bundle **10.** accumulate
roller... **4.** wave **5.** inker, skate, towel
  6. canary, caster, fillet, pigeon, platen
  7. bandage, rotator, sirgang **8.** cylinder
  10. Holy Roller, pulverizer
rolling (pert to)...
movement.. **6.** welter
pin.. **6.** roller **8.** cylinder
stock.. **7.** coaches, engines **8.** cabooses,
  Pullmans **9.** motor cars **11.** locomotives
stone.. **8.** wanderer
weed.. **10.** tumbleweed
rollix... **4.** play **6.** frolic **7.** rollick
romaine... **10.** cos lettuce
romal... **5.** quirt, thong
Roman... **5.** brave, Latin **6.** frugal, honest,
  simple **7.** Italian
Roman (pert to)... see also *Rome*
afterpiece (theater).. **5.** exode, farce
  8. travesty
alcove.. **8.** tablinum
apostle (Bib).. **4.** Neri
assembly.. **5.** forum **7.** comitia
augur.. **6.** auspex
awning.. **8.** velarium
barrack, hut.. **6.** canaba (cannaba)
basilica.. **7.** Lateran
booth, shelter.. **7.** taberna
bowl.. **6.** patina
boxing glove.. **6.** cestus
breastplate.. **6.** lorica
bronze.. **3.** aes
building.. **5.** aedes (worship)
case.. **5.** bulla (for amulets)
cathedral.. **7.** Lateran
chariot.. **5.** essed (esseda)
chest.. **4.** cist
circus post.. **4.** meta
circus wall.. **5.** spina
cistern.. **9.** impluvium
citadel.. **3.** arx
citizen (nonvoting).. **8.** aerarian
clan.. **4.** gens
cloak.. **5.** sagum (Mil) **6.** abolla **7.** planeta
concert hall.. **5.** odeum
court (Pope's).. **5.** Curia
cuirass.. **6.** lorica
Curia office.. **6.** datary **7.** dataria
date.. **4.** ides **5.** nones **7.** calends
dish.. **6.** patera
division (Polit).. **5.** curia
earthwork (Mil).. **5.** agger
Empire district.. **5.** Pagus
era.. **5.** Varro
farce.. **5.** exode
festival days.. **5.** feria **10.** feriae Jovi
  (festivals of Jupiter)
fish sauce.. **4.** alec **5.** garum
foot coverage, sock.. **3.** udo
galley.. **6.** bireme **7.** trireme
garment.. **4.** toga **5.** palla, stole, tunic
general's cloak.. **12.** paludamentum
  (paludament)
Govt of two men.. **10.** duumvirate
Hades.. **5.** Orcus **10.** lower world
hairpin.. **4.** acus
hall (concert).. **5.** odeum
helmet.. **5.** galea

highway.. **3.** via **4.** iter
highway, famed.. **9.** Appian Way
hills.. **7.** Viminal **8.** Aventine, Palatine,
  Quirinal **9.** Esquiline **10.** Capitoline
javelin.. **5.** pilum
land (public).. **4.** ager
language.. **5.** Latin
law.. **3.** jus **4.** cern
law, divine.. **3.** fas
market day.. **7.** nundine
marriage.. **13.** confarreation
matron's garment.. **5.** stola, stole
meal (chief).. **4.** cena (coena)
military cloak.. **5.** sagum
military machine.. **7.** terebra
military unit.. **6.** legion **7.** maniple
money.. **3.** aes
ornament (neck).. **5.** bulla
palace.. **7.** Lateran
peace.. **3.** pax
provisions (free).. **6.** annona
ram (battery).. **5.** aries
religious law.. **3.** fas
religious rite.. **5.** sacra
road.. **4.** iter **6.** Appian (paved)
robe.. **4.** toga
room.. **3.** ala **6.** atrium **8.** tablinum
seat.. **5.** sella
shelter, shop.. **7.** taberna
shield.. **6.** scutum
soldier's protection.. **7.** testudo
spirits (group).. **5.** lares (sing lar),
  manes **7.** lemures
tablet (writing).. **7.** diptych
temple.. **4.** naos **5.** cella
tent.. **7.** taberna
theater.. **5.** odeum
travesty.. **5.** exode
vase.. **7.** amphora (wine) **8.** murrhine
warship.. **6.** bireme **7.** trireme
Way (famed).. **6.** Appian
wine shop.. **7.** taberna
romance... **5.** fancy, novel, story
  7. fantasy, fiction, romanza, romaunt
  8. idealize **9.** falsehood, sentiment
  11. imagination
romance (pert to)...
language.. **6.** French **7.** Catalan, Italian,
  Spanish **9.** Provençal **10.** Portuguese
ref to.. **8.** knightly **10.** chivalrous
verse.. **7.** sestina
Roman god (of)...
chief.. **4.** Jove **7.** Jupiter
dead.. **5.** Orcus
fire.. **6.** Vulcan
Hades.. **3.** Dis **5.** Pluto **8.** Dispater
households.. **5.** Lares **7.** Penates
husbandry, animals.. **6.** Faunus
love.. **4.** Amor **5.** Cupid
mirth.. **5.** Comus
sun.. **3.** Sol
Supreme.. **4.** Jove **7.** Jupiter
two-faced.. **5.** Janus
underworld.. **3.** Dis **5.** Pluto **8.** Dispater
war.. **4.** Mars **8.** Quirinus
Roman goddess (of)...
agriculture.. **3.** Ops **5.** Ceres
beauty.. **5.** Venus
burials.. **8.** Libitina
childbirth.. **6.** Lucina
crops.. **6.** Annona

dawn.. **6.** Aurora
earth.. **6.** Tellus
fertility.. **6.** Annona
handicrafts.. **7.** Minerva
harvests.. **3.** Ops
health.. **7.** Minerva
hearth.. **5.** Vesta
horses.. **5.** Epona
love.. **5.** Venus
moon.. **4.** Luna **7.** Phoebus
mothers, nursing.. **6.** Rumina
night.. **3.** Nox
peace.. **3.** Pax **5.** Irene
religion.. **4.** Maia
strife.. **9.** Discordia
victory (war).. **6.** Vacuna
womanhood.. **4.** Juno
Romania...
capital.. **9.** Bucharest
city.. **4.** Cluj, Iasi **7.** Ploesti
mountains.. **10.** Carpathian
port.. **6.** Galati (Galatz)
privileged class.. **5.** boyar (boyard)
river.. **6.** Danube
Romanian(-born) person...
dramatist.. **7.** Ionesco
gymnast.. **8.** Comaneci (Nadia)
hero.. **7.** Michael (the Brave)
king.. **5.** Carol
president, dictator.. **9.** Ceausescu
violinist.. **6.** Enesco
writer.. **6.** Wiesel (Elie)
Roman people...
author.. **5.** Pliny, Varro
biographer.. **5.** Nepos
Bishop.. **4.** Pope
boy (free birth).. **8.** camillus
Catholic priest.. **8.** sacerdos
Catholic Society.. **6.** Jesuit
consul.. **6.** Scipio
Cupid.. **4.** Eros
deity.. **4.** faun
Diana.. **7.** Artemis
dictator.. **5.** Sulla **11.** Cincinnatus
diviner.. **5.** augur **6.** auspex
divinity (chief).. **4.** Jove
Emperor.. **4.** Nero, Otto **5.** Titus
   7. Maximus **8.** Tiberius **11.** Constantine
   12. Heliogabalus
Eros.. **5.** Cupid
farmer.. **7.** colonus
Fates.. **4.** Nona **5.** Morta **6.** Decuma
General.. **5.** Sulla, Titus **6.** Antony,
   Marius, Scipio
ghosts.. **7.** lemures
gladiator.. **7.** Samnite **9.** retiarius
gladiator trainer.. **7.** lanista
governor.. **9.** proconsul
guard.. **6.** lictor
historian.. **4.** Livy **5.** Nepos **7.** Sallust
   8. Appianus (Appian)
king (1st).. **7.** Romulus
king's adviser (Myth).. **6.** Egeria
magistrate, official.. **5.** augur **6.** aedile
   (edile), censor, consul **7.** praetor
   (pretor), tribune
maiden, betrayer to Sabrines.. **7.** Tarpeia
military officer.. **9.** proconsul
Naturalist.. **5.** Pliny
nun.. **6.** vestal
nymph (fountain).. **6.** Egeria

officer.. **6.** lictor **8.** triumvir (one of
   three)
official of public games.. **6.** aedile
   (edile) **7.** Asiarch
orator.. **5.** Pliny **6.** Cicero
palace officer.. **8.** palatine
patriot.. **4.** Cato
people (anc).. **7.** Sabines **8.** Samnites
   9. plebeians **10.** patricians
philosopher.. **4.** Cato **6.** Seneca
   7. Rosmini
physician.. **11.** Aesculapius
poet.. **4.** Ovid **5.** Lucan **6.** Horace,
   Vergil **7.** Juvenal (satirical)
politician, courtier.. **7.** Sejanus
priest.. **5.** epulo **8.** tresviri (10 in all)
   9. decemviri **10.** septemviri
priest, serving a god.. **6.** flamen
priestess.. **6.** vestal
priests of Faunus.. **7.** Luperci
race (conquered).. **6.** Sabine
saint.. **4.** Neri
scholar.. **5.** Varro
serf.. **6.** colona (fem) **7.** colonus (male)
slave (befriended lion).. **9.** Androcles
   (Androclus)
soldiers (body of).. **6.** cohort
statesman.. **4.** Cato **6.** Caesar, Cicero,
   Seneca
Tarquin rulers.. **9.** Etruscans
tenant farmer.. **7.** colonus
triumvirate, first.. **6.** Caesar, Pompey
   7. Crassus
triumvirate, second.. **6.** Antony
   7. Lepidus **8.** Octavius
troops.. **6.** alares
tyrant.. **4.** Nero
virgin.. **6.** vestal
writer (comic).. **7.** Terence
Romany, Rommany... **5.** gypsy
   10. mascot blue
Rome...
cathedral (world's largest).. **8.** St Peter's
churches.. **7.** Lateran **8.** Castello,
   Gandolfo
conqueror.. **6.** Alaric
founder (legendary).. **7.** Romulus
hills.. **5.** Seven **6.** Sabine **7.** Viminal
   8. Aventine, Palatine, Quirinal
lake.. **4.** Nemi
original city.. **12.** Roma Quadrata
palace (world's largest).. **7.** Vatican
peak (Capitoline).. **8.** Tarpeian
port (anc).. **5.** Ostia
prairie.. **8.** Campagna
river.. **5.** Tiber
seat of.. **7.** Holy See **11.** Vatican City
site, ancient.. **13.** Campus Martius
site, founding.. **12.** Palatine Hill
street (famed).. **5.** Corso
Romulus (pert to)...
brother.. **5.** Remus
city site.. **12.** Palatine Hill
father.. **4.** Mars
founder (Myth).. **4.** Rome
king (1st).. **4.** Rome
mother.. **6.** Sylvia
rescued from.. **5.** Tiber
suckled by.. **7.** she-wolf
ronde... **6.** script (heavy) **9.** round hand
rondeau... **4.** game, poem **5.** rondo

6. rondel
rondel, rondelle . . . **4.** poem **5.** tower (Fort) **8.** round gem
rondure . . . **9.** plumpness, roundness
ronier . . . **7.** palmyra
ronin . . . **6.** outlaw **7.** outcast, samurai
rood . . . **5.** cross (holy), goose **7.** measure **8.** crucifix
roodebok . . . **6.** impala **9.** duikerbok
roof . . . **3.** hip **4.** dome, eave, flat, nave, tile **5.** cover, gable, slate, spire **6.** cupola, lean-to **7.** chopper, gambrel, mansard, pitched, shingle **8.** housetop, thatched **9.** penthouse **10.** jerkinhead
roof (pert to) . . .
  boards (thin) . . **4.** sark
  brain cover . . **4.** tela **14.** telachorioidea
  frame (raised) . . **7.** coaming
  material . . **3.** tin **4.** tile **5.** paper, slate **6.** copper, shakes **7.** roofage **8.** shingles
  mouth . . **6.** palate
  ornament . . **3.** epi
  tile . . **7.** pantile
  timber . . **6.** rafter
  tin (coating) . . **5.** terne
  tool . . **3.** zax
Roof of the World, Asia . . . **6.** Pamirs (The) **9.** Bam i Dunya
rook . . . **4.** bird, crow, dupe **5.** cheat **6.** castle **7.** defraud, sharper **8.** chessman **9.** ruddy duck
rookery . . . **4.** slum **9.** confusion **13.** breeding place (rooks, herons, penguins) **14.** breeding ground (seals)
rookie, rooky . . . **6.** novice **7.** recruit **8.** beginner, newcomer
rooky . . . **4.** roky **5.** foggy
room . . . **3.** ala (anc), den **4.** aula, cell, hall, sala, seat, shed **5.** attic, lodge, place, salon, scope, space **6.** cellar, leeway, pantry, parlor, reside **7.** chamber, drawing, laundry, nursery, quarter **8.** capacity **9.** apartment, storeroom **11.** opportunity
room (pert to) . . .
  church (bishop's) . . **4.** apse
  convent . . **9.** parlatory
  dining . . **7.** cenacle, dinette **9.** refectory
  harem . . **3.** oda
  household . . **5.** ewery
  inner . . **3.** ben
  large . . **4.** aula, hall **7.** rotunda, theater **10.** auditorium
  monastery . . **4.** cell
  outer . . **3.** but
  pantry . . **6.** larder **8.** cupboard
  prayer . . **7.** oratory
  Pueblo Ind ceremonial . . **4.** kiva
  Roman . . **6.** atrium
  ship's . . **4.** brig **5.** cabin, salon
  sleeping . . **5.** lodge **6.** dormer **7.** barrack, bedroom, chamber **9.** dormitory
  tower (bell) . . **6.** belfry
roomy . . . **4.** airy **5.** ample **8.** spacious **9.** capacious, expansive **10.** commodious **11.** large-framed
roon . . . **5.** shred **6.** border **7.** darling **8.** treasure
roorback, roorbach . . . **3.** lie **6.** canard **7.** lampoon **9.** falsehood
roose . . . **5.** boast, vaunt **6.** praise

Roosevelt . . .
  president, 26th . . **8.** Theodore
  president, 32nd . . **8.** Franklin
roost . . . **3.** bed, sit **4.** jouk, pole, rest **5.** perch **6.** settle **7.** lodging, support
rooster . . . **4.** cock, male (animal) **5.** gallo **7.** percher **11.** chanticleer **12.** fighting cock
root . . . **4.** bulb, word **5.** cheer, plant, radix, tuber **6.** source **7.** radical **8.** take root **9.** establish
root (pert to) . . .
  aromatic . . **9.** sassafras
  edible . . **3.** oca, yam **4.** beet, eddo, taro **6.** carrot, potato, radish, turnip **7.** parsnip **8.** rutabaga
  food (Maori) . . **3.** roi
  medicinal . . **4.** atis **5.** jalep **6.** ipecac, senega **7.** Senegal
  out . . **4.** seek **7.** extract **9.** eliminate, eradicate
  perfume . . **5.** orris
  pungent . . **6.** ginger
  starch . . **7.** cassava
  stock . . **7.** rhizome
  stringy . . **5.** watap (watape)
  taro . . **4.** eddo
  word . . **4.** etym **6.** etymon
rooted . . . **8.** habitual **9.** implanted **10.** deep-seated **11.** established, traditional
rootlet . . . **7.** radical, rhizoid, taproot
rope . . . **3.** tew, tie, tye **4.** bind, cord, line, rood **5.** cable, cigar, lasso, longe, noose, reata, wanty **6.** fasten, halter, hawser, lariat, string, tether **7.** cordage, lanyard, measure **8.** hangman's, inveigle
rope (pert to) . . .
  boat's . . **4.** rode **6.** hawser **7.** painter
  chain . . **3.** tye **9.** stern fast
  dancer, walker . . **8.** balancer **11.** equilibrist, funambulist
  fiber . . **4.** bast, hemp, jute **5.** sisal
  flag raising . . **7.** halyard
  gun carriage . . **8.** prolonge
  guy . . **4.** stay, vang
  nautical . . **3.** tye **4.** vang, wapp **6.** parrel (parral) **7.** snotter
  of onions . . **5.** reeve
  security device . . **4.** butt **5.** cleat
  ship's . . **3.** tye **4.** stay, vang **6.** hawser, shroud **7.** painter, ratline, snotter
  splicer's tool . . **3.** fid
  straw, twisted . . **5.** sugan (soogan)
  two strand . . **7.** marline
  walker . . **11.** funambulist
ropery . . . **6.** banter **7.** roguery
roral . . . **4.** dewy, rory **5.** roric
rorqual . . . **5.** whale **7.** finback
Ros . . . **10.** Slav rulers (Russ), Varangians
rosary . . . **4.** aves **5.** beads (prayer) **7.** chaplet (of roses), garland **8.** devotion
roscoe . . . **3.** gat, gun
rose . . . **3.** cut (jewelry) **5.** color, flush, Rhoda **6.** emblem, flower, nozzle, symbol, window **7.** fixture
rose (pert to) . . .
  apple . . **4.** plum **6.** cherry **7.** jambool **8.** poma rosa
  beetle . . **6.** chafer, weevil
  City . . **8.** Portland (Oreg)

colored .. **8.** alluring **10.** auspicious, optimistic
cross .. **6.** symbol **11.** Rosicrucian **14.** cross in a circle
genus .. **4.** Rosa **6.** Acaena **8.** Rosaceae
hiller .. **7.** rosella **8.** parakeet
moss .. **9.** portulaca
of Sharon .. **6.** Althea
petal oil .. **4.** otto **5.** attar
rash .. **7.** roseola
under the rose .. **6.** secret **7.** sub rosa
wild .. **9.** eglantine
Rosetta Stone (pert to) ...
decipherer .. **11.** Champollion
famed for .. **11.** inscription **13.** hieroglyphics
site found .. **4.** Nile (1799)
type .. **11.** black basalt
roster ... **4.** list, roll, rota **5.** slate **8.** schedule
rostrum ... **4.** beak, dais, prow **5.** snout, stage **6.** pulpit **8.** platform **9.** proboscis
rosy ... **3.** red **4.** pink **7.** flushed, roseate **8.** blooming, blushing **9.** rosaceous **10.** auspicious, optimistic
rot ... **3.** die **5.** decay, spoil **6.** blight **7.** corrupt, disease, putrefy **8.** nonsense **9.** decompose **10.** degenerate **12.** putrefaction **13.** decomposition
rota ... **4.** Club (Eng), list, roll **5.** court, round (Mus) **6.** roster **15.** Sacra Romana Rota
rotate ... **4.** roll, spin, turn, whiz **5.** recur, wheel **6.** gyrate **7.** rabatte, revolve, trundle **8.** rotiform
rotation ... **4.** spin, turn **5.** round **7.** turning **8.** sequence **10.** revolution, succession
rotator ... **5.** rotor **6.** muscle **7.** whirler **9.** carrousel **12.** merry-go-round
rotche, rotch ... **5.** goose, rotge **7.** dovekie
rote ... **6.** course, custom, system **7.** by heart, routine **8.** par coeur, practice **9.** condition
roti ... **5.** roast **7.** roasted
rotor ... **5.** wheel **6.** roller, stator **7.** rotator, turbine **8.** impeller
rotten ... **3.** bad **4.** foul, punk **5.** doted, fetid **6.** putrid, wicked **7.** decayed, tainted, unsound **8.** depraved, unstable **9.** dishonest, offensive, putrefied **10.** putrescent, undermined **13.** disintegrated
Rotten Row (Hyde Park, London) ... **12.** thoroughfare (equestrian)
rottenstone ... **6.** polish **7.** tripoli
rotter ... **3.** cad **7.** bounder, shirker, slacker **10.** blackguard
rottgoose ... **5.** brant
rotund ... **3.** fat **5.** obese, plump, round, stout **6.** chubby **7.** rounded **8.** roly-poly **9.** corpulent, spherical
Rotwelsch ... **5.** argot, slang **6.** jargon **14.** secret language
roué ... **4.** rake, wolf **7.** rounder **9.** debauchee, libertine
rouge ... **5.** blush, flush **6.** polish, redden **7.** radical **8.** cosmetic
rough ... **4.** hard, rude **5.** crude, draft, harsh, raspy, rowdy, seamy, stern

6. broken, choppy, coarse, hoarse, rugged, severe, shaggy **7.** boorish, inexact, jarring, jolting, ruffled **8.** scabrous, unsmooth **9.** imperfect, turbulent **10.** incomplete, tumultuous, unfinished **11.** approximate
rough (pert to) ...
avens .. **6.** bennet (herb)
cloth .. **5.** terry
footed (bird) .. **9.** feathered
hair .. **4.** shag
hewn .. **6.** brutal **10.** unpolished **12.** uncultivated
house .. **5.** cut up **9.** rowdiness **10.** disorderly, noisy sport
jest (Mus) .. **9.** charivari
neck .. **4.** boor **5.** rowdy, tough
rider .. **9.** Roosevelt (Teddy) **10.** cavalryman
rock .. **4.** crag
shod (to ride) .. **7.** trample **8.** dominate **9.** tyrannize
rough and ...
hoarse .. **7.** raucous
lean .. **6.** craggy
ready .. **4.** rude **10.** unpolished
Ready .. **6.** Taylor (Gen Zachary)
roughen ... **4.** chap, shag **8.** asperate
roughly ... **4.** or so **6.** rudely **7.** harshly **8.** coarsely, severely, unevenly, vulgarly **9.** brusquely **10.** unsmoothly **13.** approximately
roughness ... **6.** lipper (of the sea) **8.** acrimony, asperity, pungency, unfinish **9.** gruffness, harshness, vulgarity **10.** hoarseness
roughsome ... **5.** rough **6.** rustic **7.** uncouth
roulade ... **3.** run **8.** arpeggio, division, flourish **13.** vocal flourish
roulette ... **3.** bas (bet) **4.** disk, game **5.** wheel **6.** roller **8.** wagering
rounceval ... **5.** giant, large **6.** strong, virago **9.** termagant
round ... **4.** beat, bout, rota, rung, turn **5.** cycle, orbed, rondo **6.** circle, curved, rotate, rotund, series, sphere **7.** circuit, routine **8.** circular, globular **9.** in a circle, spherical **11.** cylindrical
round (pert to) ...
bone .. **3.** hip
building .. **7.** rotunda
clam .. **6.** quahog
fish .. **9.** whitefish
head .. **5.** Swede **7.** Puritan
house .. **5.** cabin, coach **6.** lockup, prison **10.** watch house
of applause .. **7.** plaudit
regular .. **4.** beat
robin .. **6.** angler, letter **7.** pancake, request **9.** cigarfish
worm .. **4.** nema **7.** ascarid, Ascaris, eelworm
roundabout ... **5.** about, dance **6.** detour, jacket **7.** ambient, devious **8.** indirect **10.** circuitous **13.** approximately **14.** circumlocution
rounded (pert to) ...
heap of stone .. **5.** cairn
irregularly .. **7.** gibbous
leaf .. **6.** retuse

molding.. **5.** ovolo
projection.. **4.** lobe **5.** tooth
scalloped.. **7.** crenate
Round Table (pert to)...
  knight.. **7.** Galahad **8.** Lancelot
  seating.. **7.** knights (King Arthur's)
  site.. **7.** Camelot
  type.. **6.** marble
roundup... **5.** rodeo
roup... **4.** cold **6.** clamor **7.** auction
  8. shouting **10.** hoarseness
rouse... **3.** hie **4.** stir, wake **5.** alarm,
  raise, start, upset, waken **6.** awaken,
  bestir, elicit, excite, kindle **7.** disturb
  9. stimulate
rouser... **7.** stirrer **8.** surprise
  9. demagogue (demagog) **10.** instigator
roussette... **5.** shark **7.** dogfish **8.** fruit
  bat
roust... **4.** roar, stir **5.** rouse **6.** bellow,
  tumult **7.** current (tidal), roaring
  9. bellowing
roustabout... **6.** lumper **7.** laborer
  8. handy man **12.** longshoreman
rout... **3.** low, mob **4.** bray, roar
  5. crowd, snort **6.** bellow, defeat,
  rabble **7.** debacle, scatter **8.** disperse,
  stampede, vanquish **9.** agitation,
  discomfit, overpower, overthrow **11.** put
  to flight
route... **3.** way **4.** line, path **5.** march
  6. detour **7.** circuit
routh... **6.** plenty **8.** abundant
  9. abundance, plentiful
routier... **6.** robber **7.** brigand **9.** free
  lance, plunderer
routine... **3.** rut **5.** grind, habit, order,
  round, troll **6.** course, system **7.** regular
  8. everyday **9.** treadmill
rove... **3.** gad **4.** flit, part, roam **5.** range,
  stray **6.** maraud, ramble, stroll, swerve,
  wander, washer **7.** deviate **8.** straggle
rover... **5.** nomad **6.** bandit, pirate, viking
  7. corsair, pilgrim, vagrant **8.** marauder,
  wanderer
roving... **8.** errantry **9.** desultory,
  deviative **10.** discursive
row... **3.** air, oar **4.** file, fuss, live, spat,
  tier **5.** align, brawl, broil **6.** lineup,
  paddle, propel, series **7.** quarrel, ruction
  9. commotion
rowboat... **3.** cog, gig **4.** dory **5.** canoe,
  coble, skiff **6.** randan
rowdy... **5.** cutup, rough, tough
  7. boorish, ruffian **8.** larrikin, plug-ugly
  10. boisterous, disorderly
rowdy contention... **10.** donnybrook
rowel... **4.** spur **5.** wheel
rowen... **4.** crop (secondary) **5.** field
  7. stubble **9.** aftermath
rowing... **5.** sport **6.** randan **7.** regatta
  8. sculling
rox... **3.** rot **5.** decay
royal... **4.** real, rial, stag, true **5.** basil,
  noble, regal **6.** august, kingly **7.** stately
  8. imperial, majestic, princely, splendid
  9. dignified, sovereign **11.** magnificent
royal (pert to)...
  agaric.. **8.** mushroom
  bay.. **6.** laurel
  color.. **4.** blue **5.** smalt

court.. **5.** aulic **6.** ermine
crest.. **10.** fleur-de-lis (Fr)
deer's antler.. **8.** tres-tine
fur.. **6.** ermine
mace.. **7.** scepter (sceptre)
martyr.. **8.** Charles I (Eng. 1649)
maundy.. **4.** alms
officer.. **7.** naperer
rights.. **7.** regalia
rock snake.. **6.** python
stables.. **4.** mews
stars (Astrol).. **7.** Antares, Regulus
  9. Aldebaran, Fomalhaut
Royal (pert to)...
  Academy.. **4.** Arts (1768)
  Arcanum.. **7.** Society (1877)
  Canadian Mounted Police.. **8.** Mounties
  16. Northwest Mounted
  Castle.. **8.** Balmoral
  Crown.. **5.** tiara
  Highlanders.. **10.** Black Watch
  Highness.. **5.** title **6.** prince **8.** princess
  House.. **5.** Tudor **6.** Stuart, Valois
  7. Bourbon, Hanover, Windsor
  Oak (Eng Hist).. **7.** lottery **10.** Shropshire
  Psalmist.. **9.** King David
  Scot.. **16.** Lothian Regiments
royet... **4.** wild **6.** unruly **7.** romping
  11. mischievous
rub... **4.** crux, fret, wipe **6.** abrade, polish,
  scrape, smooth, stroke **7.** burnish,
  massage **8.** friction, irritate **9.** hindrance,
  triturate
rub (pert to)...
  away.. **6.** abrade
  down.. **4.** comb **5.** curry, groom
  7. massage
  elbows.. **9.** associate **10.** fraternize
  off.. **5.** erase **6.** abrade, remove
  10. obliterate
  out.. **4.** kill **5.** erase **6.** cancel,
  efface, excise **7.** expunge, wipe out
  10. obliterate
  wrong way.. **6.** ruffle **8.** irritate
  9. displease **10.** antagonize
rub-a-dub... **6.** clamor **7.** clatter, pit-a-pat,
  rat-a-tat **8.** rattatoo **9.** drumbeats
Rubáiyát (pert to)...
  author.. **11.** Omar Khayyám
  stanza form.. **8.** quatrain
  translator.. **10.** Fitzgerald (1859)
rubber... **4.** para **5.** stare **6.** eraser
  7. ebonite, elastic **8.** massager,
  sight-see **10.** caoutchouc
rubber (pert to)...
  city.. **5.** Akron
  hard.. **7.** ebonite
  India (pure).. **10.** caoutchouc
  plant.. **5.** Ficus
  ring.. **4.** lute **6.** gasket
  sap.. **5.** latex
  shoe.. **6.** galosh (galoshe)
  tree.. **3.** ule **7.** guayule
  wild.. **5.** Ceara **6.** caucho
rubbish... **4.** junk, ross **5.** attle, dross,
  stent, trash, waste **6.** debris, refuse,
  rubble, trashy **8.** nonsense, riffraff,
  trumpery **9.** worthless
rubble... **5.** brash, chalk, stone, trash
  7. rubbish **8.** nonsense **11.** foolishness
rube... **4.** dolt **6.** rustic **7.** hayseed

rubedity . . . **7.** redness **9.** ruddiness
rubella . . . **7.** measles, rubeola
rubescent . . . **3.** red **8.** flushing
9. reddening **10.** erubescent
rubiator . . . **4.** rake **5.** bully **6.** rascal
Rubicon . . . **5.** river (Caesar's) **9.** Fiumicino
(modern)
rubicund . . . **3.** red **4.** ruby **5.** ruddy
6. florid **7.** redness
rubric . . . **3.** rod **6.** paraph, ritual
8. category, red chalk **14.** title page
in red
rubrics (book of) . . . **4.** ordo
ruby (pert to) . . .
bird . . **11.** hummingbird
heraldry . . **5.** gules
stained quartz (red) . . **6.** Ancona
7. rubasse **9.** Mont Blanc
stone . . **3.** gem **5.** balas **6.** spinel
type . . **4.** size
ruck . . . **3.** rut, sit (on eggs) **4.** heap,
pile, rick **5.** cower, crowd, squat,
stack **6.** crease, crouch, furrow, horses
(race), pucker **7.** wrinkle **9.** multitude
10. generality
ruckus . . . **3.** ado, row **5.** fight **6.** rumpus,
uproar **7.** quarrel, ruction **8.** outbreak
9. commotion
rudd . . . **3.** hue **4.** carp, fish **6.** redden
7. azurine, redness **10.** complexion
rudder . . . **4.** helm **5.** guide
rudder part . . . **8.** bearding **9.** whipstaff
rude . . . **3.** raw **4.** curt **5.** rough, rowdy
6. clumsy, coarse, rugged, simple,
vulgar **7.** boorish, uncouth **8.** ignorant,
insolent **9.** barbarous, inclement,
makeshift, turbulent, unlearned,
unskilled, untrained **10.** boisterous,
unpolished **11.** impertinent, uncivilized
12. discourteous
rudeness . . . **6.** ferity **8.** curtness
9. impudence, insolence, vulgarity
11. raucousness **12.** impertinence
rudiment . . . **7.** vestige
rudimentary . . . **5.** basic **7.** initial
8. original **9.** beginning, elemental,
embryonic, vestigial **11.** undeveloped
rudimentary digit . . . **7.** dewclaw
rudiments . . . **4.** ABCs **6.** basics
rue . . . **4.** rake, Ruta **6.** grieve, regret,
repent, sorrow **7.** afflict, deplore
10. bitterness, compassion, repentance
14. disappointment
ruff . . . **3.** ree **5.** pride, reeve, ruche,
trump **6.** collar, fringe, rebato **7.** sunfish
8. drumbeat **9.** sandpiper, vainglory
ruffian . . . **4.** fish, pimp, thug **5.** rowdy,
tough **6.** brutal, cuttle, pander
8. assassin, paramour, the Devil
9. cutthroat, desperado, murderous,
vulgarian
ruffle . . . **3.** vex **4.** fret, roil **5.** anger,
annoy, frill, jabot **6.** edging, muddle,
nettle, rumple, tousle **7.** agitate, disturb,
flounce, fluster, shuffle **8.** dishevel,
disorder, drumbeat, irritate **9.** balayeuse
10. disarrange, discompose
ruffler . . . **5.** bully **7.** boaster, ruffian
8. braggart **9.** swaggerer **10.** attachment
(sewing)
rug . . . **3.** mat **4.** maud, shag **5.** Senna,

throw **6.** carpet, hooked, petate
7. Chinese, drugget, steamer **8.** coverlet,
Oriental **9.** Samarkand
ruga . . . **4.** fold **7.** wrinkle **8.** membrane
rugby . . . **5.** Fives **6.** Rugger, school (Eng)
8. football
rugby term . . . **9.** scrum half, scrummage
rugged . . . **4.** rude **5.** asper, hardy,
harsh, rough, surly **6.** craggy, fierce,
robust, seamed, shaggy, strong, sturdy
7. austere, crabbed, healthy, uncivil
8. vigorous, wrinkled **9.** irregular, not
smooth, turbulent **11.** substantial
rugged mountain crest . . . **5.** arête
ruin . . . **4.** bane, doom, fate, loss
5. blast, havoc, spoil, wrack, wreck
6. defeat **7.** debauch, destroy, subvert
8. bankrupt, demolish, downfall
9. perdition **10.** desolation, subversion
11. destruction, devastation
ruined . . . **4.** gone **7.** spoiled, wrecked
8. bankrupt, defeated **9.** destroyed
11. dilapidated **12.** irremediable
ruinous . . . **6.** deadly **7.** baneful, decayed
10. demolished, disastrous, pernicious,
submersive, tumbledown
11. destructive
ruins . . . **5.** relic, wreck **7.** remains
rukh . . . **6.** forest, jungle
rule . . . **3.** law **4.** norm, sway **5.** axiom,
canon, guide, habit, order, regle, reign
6. decree, govern, manage, method,
regime, screed **7.** counsel, measure,
precept, prevail, regency, regimen
8. dominate, persuade, standard
9. criterion, direction, influence,
principle **12.** jurisdiction
15. totalitarianism
rule by . . .
children . . **9.** paedarchy
ecclesiasts . . **9.** hierarchy
one . . **8.** monarchy
race . . **10.** ethnocracy
ten . . **8.** decarchy
the mob . . **9.** mobocracy
the people . . **9.** democracy
tribes . . **9.** phylarchy
rule out . . . **6.** cancel, excise **7.** obviate
ruler . . . **3.** min **4.** amir (ameer), czar, emir,
lord **5.** queen **6.** despot, dynast, ferule,
gerent, prince, regent, satrap, sultan,
tyrant **7.** emperor, monarch **8.** autocrat,
governor, hierarch, measurer
9. potentate
ruling . . . **3.** law **6.** decree **7.** average,
regnant, statute, verdict **8.** decision,
reigning **9.** governing, prevalent
11. predominant **12.** drawing lines
rullion . . . **4.** shoe **6.** sandal
rum . . . **3.** dye (blue), odd **4.** good **5.** queer,
tafia (taffia) **6.** liquor **8.** Demon rum
rumal . . . **6.** fabric **8.** kerchief (man's)
Rumania . . . see *Romania*
rumble . . . **4.** boom, seat (back) **5.** rumor
6. murmur, ripple, stir up **9.** complaint
11. rolling tone
rumen . . . **3.** cud **5.** tripe **6.** gullet, paunch
7. stomach (1st)
ruminant . . . **2.** ox **3.** cow, yak **4.** bull,
deer, gaur, goat, oryx, zebu **5.** bison,
camel, eland, gayal, llama, moose,

okapi, sheep, steer **6.** alpaca, nilgai, vicuna, wapiti **7.** banteng, buffalo, caribou, chamois, gemsbok, giraffe **8.** antelope, elephant, reindeer, seladang **9.** dromedary, nannygoat, pronghorn **10.** cud-chewing, hartebeest, meditative, rhinoceros, thoughtful

ruminant (pert to) . . .
  division . . **8.** Ungulata **10.** Ruminantia
  first stomach . . **5.** rumen **6.** paunch
  fourth stomach . . **8.** abomasum **9.** rennet bag
  second stomach . . **9.** reticulum
  third stomach . . **6.** omasum **9.** manyplies **10.** psalterium

ruminate . . . **4.** chew, muse **6.** ponder **7.** reflect **8.** consider, meditate

rummage . . . **4.** junk **6.** litter, search **7.** collect (by search), ransack

rumor, rumour . . . **4.** Fama, talk **5.** bruit, noise, story **6.** norate, report **7.** hearsay, tidings **11.** scuttlebutt

rump . . . **4.** bone **6.** breech, sacrum **7.** meat cut **8.** bankrupt, buttocks **9.** remainder

rumpade . . . **3.** rob **6.** hold up

rumple . . . **4.** muss **5.** touse **6.** crease, ruffle, tousle **7.** crinkle, crumple, wrinkle **8.** dishevel **10.** disarrange

rumpus . . . **3.** row **6.** fracas, hubbub, uproar **9.** commotion, confusion **11.** disturbance

rumtytoo . . . **8.** ordinary **11.** commonplace

run . . . **2.** go **3.** fly, gad, hie **4.** dart, flee, flow, lope, melt, race, scud, tend, trot **5.** blend, hurry, speed, trend **6.** charge, course, elapse, endure, extend, manage, pursue, sprint, stream **7.** average, liquefy, operate, proceed, roulade, routine, smuggle, stretch, trickle **8.** continue **9.** discharge, suppurate

run (pert to) . . .
  about . . **5.** wagon **6.** gadder **8.** roadster, runagate, vagabond
  after . . **5.** chase, fetch, toady **6.** pursue **7.** lionize
  aground . . **6.** strand **7.** founder
  along the edge . . **5.** skirt
  away . . **4.** bolt, flee **5.** elope **6.** decamp, escape **8.** stampede
  before the wind . . **4.** scud
  between ports . . **3.** ply
  down . . **3.** hit **4.** find **5.** seedy, trace **7.** run over **9.** exhausted **11.** dilapidated **12.** deteriorated
  out . . **3.** end **5.** lapse, waste **6.** elapse, emerge, escape **7.** exhaust **8.** squander
  over . . **6.** browse, exceed, ponder **7.** trample **8.** overflow **9.** reiterate
  quickly, swiftly . . **4.** dart, race, scud **5.** scoot **6.** gallop, sprint **7.** scuttle
  stocking . . **6.** ladder
  through . . **4.** stab **6.** pierce **7.** inspect, pervade **8.** rehearse, squander, transfix **11.** superabound
  up against . . **4.** find **9.** encounter, stumble on **10.** experience

runagate . . . **7.** runaway **8.** apostate, fugitive, renegade, vagabond, wanderer

rundle . . . **4.** ball, coil, rung, step **5.** round

6. circle, roller, sphere, stream

rune . . . **5.** magic **6.** secret, symbol **7.** mystery **9.** character (anc)

rung . . . **4.** step **5.** round, spoke, stair, tread **6.** degree, rundle **7.** girdled, ratline

runic . . . **5.** verse **6.** poetic **7.** writing **8.** alphabet (anc), Norsemen

runner . . . **3.** ski (skee) **4.** sled **5.** miler, racer, stolo **6.** stolon **7.** tendril **8.** operator, procurer, salesman, smuggler, sprinter **9.** messenger, solicitor

running . . . **7.** current, cursive, fleeing, flowing, melting **9.** advancing, prevalent, smuggling **10.** continuous

running knot . . . **5.** noose

running race . . . **5.** relay **6.** sprint

running toad . . . **10.** natterjack

runt . . . **3.** elf **4.** chit (letter), wrig **5.** dwarf, pygmy **6.** pigeon **10.** diminutive

runway . . . **4.** file, ramp **8.** airstrip

rupa . . . **4.** body, form (visual)

rupee . . . **4.** anna, coin **14.** money of account

rupestrian . . . **14.** composed of rock **15.** inscribed on rock

ruption . . . **7.** ruction, rupture **8.** bursting

rupture . . . **4.** rent **5.** break, burst **6.** hernia, injury, rhexis **7.** quarrel **9.** hostility **10.** disruption, falling out, separating

rural . . . **6.** rustic **7.** bucolic **8.** agrestic, pastoral **12.** agricultural

rural (pert to) . . .
  deity . . **3.** Pan **6.** Faunus
  genus . . **6.** potato
  life . . **8.** pastoral
  poem . . **7.** eclogue, georgic
  Spanish . . **9.** policeman
  term . . **8.** agrestic

Rusa . . . **4.** deer **6.** sambar

ruse . . . **4.** fall, slip, wile **5.** fraud, trick **6.** deceit **8.** artifice **9.** stratagem **10.** subterfuge

rush . . . **3.** jet **4.** dart, dash, flow, scud **5.** brook, haste, hurry, plant, press, scoot, spate, speed, surge **6.** charge, course, defeat, demand, hasten, runlet, sortie **7.** cattail, repulse **8.** outburst, reed mace, stampede **9.** attention, thronging

rush (pert to) . . .
  forth . . **5.** sally
  hour . . **4.** peak
  light . . **6.** candle, feeble
  nut . . **5.** chufa
  Scot . . **5.** sprat (herb) **6.** Juncus
  toad . . **10.** natterjack
  wheat . . **10.** couch grass

rusk . . . **5.** bread **7.** biscuit

rusma . . . **9.** quicklime **10.** depilatory

Russia . . . see also *Russian*
  Asian part . . **7.** Siberia
  capital . . **6.** Moscow **9.** Petrograd (old)
  citadel . . **7.** Kremlin
  city . . **4.** Baku, Kiev, Omsk **5.** Minsk **6.** Rostov **7.** Kharkov **8.** Smolensk **9.** Petrograd **10.** Sevastopol (Sebastopol) **11.** Vladivostok **12.** St Petersburg (Leningrad)
  coal fields . . **6.** Donets (Ukraine)

Russian / Ryukyu Islands   486

fleet base.. **10.** Sevastopol, Stalingrad
former name.. **7.** Muscovy
founder.. **4.** Ivan **15.** Ivan the Terrible
gulf.. **4.** Azov
isthmus.. **7.** Karelia
lake.. **5.** Onega **6.** Baykal **7.** Aral Sea
  10. Caspian Sea
mountains.. **4.** Ural **8.** Caucasus
peninsula.. **4.** Kola **6.** Crimea
resort.. **5.** Yalta **6.** Crimea
river.. **2.** Ob **4.** Amur, Lena, Neva,
  Ural **5.** Volga **6.** Donets **7.** Dneiper,
  Yenisei
sea.. **4.** Azov **5.** Black, White
  6. Baltic **7.** Caspian
strait.. **6.** Bering
Russian (pert to)...
antelope.. **5.** saiga
aristocratic order.. **4.** knez **5.** Boyar
assembly.. **4.** duma, rada **7.** zemstoo
association, guild.. **5.** artel
bank.. **4.** game
beer, beverage.. **5.** kvass, vodka
boat.. **6.** baidak (baydak)
braid (trim).. **8.** soutache
calendar (to 1918).. **6.** Julian
cap (peasant).. **4.** aska
carriage.. **6.** drosky, troika **9.** tarantass
  (tarantas)
cart, wagon.. **6.** telega
cathedral.. **5.** sober
cloak (fur).. **5.** shuba
council.. **4.** duma, rada **6.** soviet
dance (rustic).. **7.** ziganka
decree.. **5.** ukase
dog (wolfhound).. **6.** borzoi **7.** owtchah
dress (peasant).. **7.** sarafan
duke, prince.. **4.** knez (kniaz)
edict.. **5.** ukase
fur (lamb).. **7.** karakul (karakule)
  9. astrakhan
guild.. **5.** artel
hemp.. **4.** rine
hut.. **4.** isba
leather.. **5.** jufti (jufts) **6.** Bulgar
  8. shagreen
marsh, lagoon.. **5.** liman
massacre.. **6.** pogrom
monetary unit.. **5.** ruble (rouble)
  6. kopeck (kopek)
musical instrument.. **5.** gudok, gusla
  9. balalaika
naval academy.. **6.** Frunze
news agency.. **4.** Tass
no.. **4.** nyet
parliament.. **4.** duma
peasant.. **4.** Slav **5.** kulak **6.** muzhik
  (muzjik)
peasant village.. **3.** mir
plain (treeless).. **6.** steppe, tundra
police (secret).. **5.** Cheka
pound.. **4.** pood
prince, duke.. **4.** knez (kniaz)
ruler.. **4.** czar (tsar)
satellite.. **7.** sputnik
soup (cabbage).. **5.** stchi (shchi)
  6. borsch
stockade.. **5.** etape
synod.. **5.** sobor
tea urn.. **7.** samovar
turnip.. **8.** rutabaga

villa.. **5.** dacha
wagon (springless).. **6.** telega
wheat.. **5.** emmer
whip.. **4.** plet (plete) **5.** knout
wolfhound.. **6.** borzoi
yes.. **2.** da
Russian people...
author.. **5.** Gogol, Gorki (Gorky)
  7. Tolstoy (Tolstoi) **8.** Turgenev
  10. Dostoevski (Dostoyevsky)
  12. Solzhenitsyn
chess champ (1892).. **8.** Alekhine
composer.. **3.** Cui **7.** Borodin
  10. Rubenstein, Stravinsky
  12. Tschaikovsky **14.** Rimsky-Korsakov
conqueror.. **6.** Tatars **7.** Mongols
Cossack.. **5.** Tatar
czar.. **4.** Ivan **13.** Peter the Great
duke.. **5.** kniaz (knez, knyoz)
empress.. **7.** Czarina, Tsarina
General.. **10.** Timoshenko
grand duke.. **8.** Nicholas
language deviser.. **8.** Zamenhof
  9. Esperanto (pseudonym)
leader.. **5.** Lenin **6.** Stalin **7.** Molotov,
  Yeltsin **8.** Brezhnev **9.** Gorbachev
  10. Khrushchev
little Russian.. **7.** Russene (Ruthene)
monk.. **8.** Rasputin
people.. **4.** Lett, Slav **7.** Cossack
  8. Russniak **9.** Muscovite, Ruthenian
poet.. **7.** Pushkin, Yesenin **9.** Pasternak
premier.. **5.** Lenin **7.** Kosygin, Molotov
  8. Bulganin **10.** Khrushchev
saint.. **4.** Olga
teacher, monk.. **7.** starets
rust.. **3.** eat **5.** erode **6.** aerugo, patina
  7. erosion, oxidize **9.** corrosion
rustic... **4.** boor, carl, rube, rude
  5. churl, clown, Damon, rough, rural,
  swain, yokel **6.** coarse, simple, sturdy,
  sylvan **7.** artless, awkward, boorish,
  bucolic, Corydon, plowboy **8.** agrestic,
  pastoral **9.** agrestian **10.** clodhopper,
  countryman, unpolished
rustic (pert to)...
lover.. **5.** swain
maiden.. **9.** Thestylis
peasant.. **4.** boor
pipe.. **4.** reed
poetic.. **4.** carl
verse.. **4.** idyl (idyll)
rustle... **4.** flow **5.** steal, swish, whisk
  7. crinkle **11.** sound softly
rut... **5.** ditch, track **6.** furrow, groove,
  strake **7.** routine, wrinkle
Ruth (pert to)...
Book.. **12.** Old Testament
country.. **4.** Moab
husband.. **4.** Boaz
mother-in-law.. **5.** Naomi
ruthless... **5.** cruel **8.** pitiless **9.** merciless
  10. ironfisted
rye... **5.** bread, grain, grass **6.** cereal,
  whisky **9.** gentleman (gypsy)
rye bread... **5.** black **10.** knackebrod
  12. pumpernickel
ryot... **6.** farmer, tenant **7.** peasant
Rytina... **6.** dugong, sea cow **7.** manatee
  12. Hydrodamalis **14.** Steller's sea cow
Ryukyu Islands... **7.** Okinawa

S

S (pert to) . . .
curve . . **4.** ogee
letter . . **10.** nineteenth
shaped . . **7.** sigmate, sigmoid
suffix . . **6.** plural
Saal . . . **4.** hall, room (large)
sabalo . . . **6.** tarpon **8.** milkfish
sabana . . . **5.** plain **7.** plateau, savanna
(savannah)
sabbat . . . **8.** assembly (demons), festival
(orgies)
Sabbatarian . . . **9.** ritualist **11.** Russian
sect
Sabbath . . . **6.** Sunday **7.** holy day
sabbatical year . . . **7.** seventh **8.** vacation
14. leave of absence
sabbatism . . . **4.** rest **9.** ritualism
12. intermission (labor)
Sabbatist (pert to) . . .
devotee of . . **4.** cult (Oriental)
member . . **6.** Semite
named for . . **5.** Sabbe (goddess)
8. Sambathe
saber, sabre (pert to) . . .
bean . . **4.** jack
bill . . **6.** curlew
fish . . **7.** cutlass
knot . . **8.** military
legged (horse) . . **12.** sickle-hocked
Mohammedan . . **8.** yataghan (yatagan)
oriental . . **8.** scimiter
toothed . . **3.** cat **5.** tiger **12.** machairodont
wing . . **11.** hummingbird
sabino . . . **9.** ahuehuete, rock cedar
sabio . . . **4.** sage **6.** priest **7.** wise man
sable . . . **4.** ebon, pelt **5.** black, brush
6. mammal, marten **8.** antelope
10. mysterious, Russia iron
sabotage . . . **6.** damage, mayhem
9. undermine **11.** destruction (malicious)
Sabrina . . . **10.** river nymph **11.** River
Severn
sabuline, sabulous . . . **5.** sandy **6.** gritty
8. psammous **10.** arenaceous
sabutan . . . **5.** fibre, straw
sac . . . **3.** bag **4.** cyst, sack **5.** ascus, bursa,
pouch, purse, theca **6.** cavity, pocket,
saccus **7.** saccule, vesicle **8.** sacculus
sacalait . . . **7.** crappie **8.** warmouth
9. killifish
saccadic . . . **5.** jerky **9.** twitching **11.** eye
movement
saccharine . . . **5.** sweet **7.** honeyed
10. sweetening
saccos . . . **7.** tunicle **8.** vestment
sacerdocy . . . **10.** priesthood **13.** priestly
order
sacerdos . . . **6.** priest
sachem . . . **5.** chief (Indian) **8.** governor
(Tammany)
sachet . . . **3.** bag **5.** pouch **6.** powder
7. perfume **8.** reticule **11.** perfumed
pad
sack . . . **3.** bag **4.** loot, poke, wine **5.** ascus,
bursa, catch, pouch, purse **6.** defeat,

ravage, secure **7.** pillage, plunder
8. desolate **9.** discharge, dismissal
sack (pert to) . . .
baseball . . **3.** bag **4.** base
Bible . . **8.** mourning
but . . **4.** butt, cask **8.** trombone (anc)
cloth . . **7.** penance, sacking **15.** garb of
penitence
dress . . **4.** robe **6.** jacket, sacque
sacrament . . . **3.** act **4.** oath **5.** token
6. pledge, symbol **7.** mystery
8. ceremony, covenant, practice
9. communion, Eucharist **10.** intinction
(to administer)
Sacramento (pert to) . . .
capital, river . . **10.** California
cat . . **10.** horned pout
pike . . **9.** squawfish
salmon . . **7.** quinnat
sacrarium (anc) . . . **6.** chapel, shrine
7. oratory **8.** sacristy **9.** sanctuary,
synsacrum
sacred . . . **4.** holy **6.** divine **7.** blessed
8. hallowed, reverend **9.** dedicated,
inviolate, religious, venerable
10. inviolable, sacrosanct
11. consecrated **13.** sanctimonious
sacred (pert to) . . .
bark . . **7.** cascara **14.** cascara sagrada
bean . . **11.** Indian lotus
beetle . . **10.** scarabaeus
bird . . **4.** ibis
book . . **5.** Bible, Koran
bo tree . . **3.** fig **5.** pipal
bull . . **4.** apis, zebu
chest . . **4.** arca **9.** reliquary
comb form . . **5.** hagio, hiero
dialect (Buddh writings) . . **4.** Pali
grove . . **5.** Altis (Olympia)
image . . **4.** icon (ikon) **5.** Pietà
instrument . . **4.** Urim **7.** Thummim
malady . . **8.** epilepsy
monkey . . **6.** baboon, rhesus **8.** entellus
most . . **10.** sacrosanct
music . . **4.** hymn **5.** chant, motet
8. oratorio
river (Ind) . . **6.** Ganges (Ganga)
room . . **8.** sacristy
traffic (in sacred things) . . **6.** simony
weed . . **7.** vervain
wine vessel . . **3.** ama
writ . . **10.** Scriptures
sacrifice . . . **4.** lose, loss **5.** offer
6. give up, victim **8.** chiliomb
(1,000 oxen), hecatomb (100 oxen),
immolate, libation, oblation, offering
9. atonement, holocaust, martyrdom,
privation, surrender **11.** crucifixion,
destruction
sacrificer . . . **6.** martyr
sacrificial fire . . . **5.** ignis
sacrilege . . . **7.** robbery (church)
9. blasphemy **11.** desecration,
profanation
sacrilegious . . . **7.** impious **10.** irreverent

11. blasphemous, irreligious
sacrosanct . . . **4.** holy **6.** sacred **8.** ironical, most holy
sad . . . **3.** bad **4.** blue, dark, dire, dull **5.** dusky, sorry **6.** solemn, somber, triste, wicked **7.** doleful, pensive, unhappy **8.** dejected, downcast, grievous, pathetic, shameful, terrible **9.** cheerless, depressed, sorrowful **10.** calamitous, deplorable, depressing, melancholy **11.** distressing, unfortunate
saddle . . . **4.** meat (cut of), ride, seat **5.** cinch, ridge **6.** burden **7.** harness (part) **8.** encumber, straddle
saddle (pert to) . . .
back . . **4.** hill **5.** ridge
bag . . **7.** alforja, pannier
blanket . . **6.** corona, tilpah
boot . . **7.** gambado
cloth . . **5.** cover **7.** housing **8.** shabrack **9.** appendage **10.** horsecloth
elephant . . **6.** howdah
girth . . **5.** cinch
horse . . **5.** mount **6.** remuda **7.** palfrey
light . . **5.** pilch **7.** pillion
pack . . **7.** aparejo
part . . **6.** cantle, crutch, pommel **7.** stirrup **8.** tapadera (tapadero) **9.** saddlebow
place behind . . **5.** croup
rock . . **6.** oyster
strap . . **5.** girth **6.** latigo
saddler . . . **4.** seal **5.** horse **6.** cozier **7.** cobbler, lorimer **8.** merchant **9.** shoemaker
sadness . . . **5.** dolor **6.** pathos, sorrow **9.** dejection **10.** gloominess, melancholy **11.** unhappiness **13.** sorrowfulness
sad tree . . . **10.** hursinghar (dye yield)
safari . . . **4.** tour, trip **6.** junket **7.** caravan, journey **10.** expedition, pilgrimage
safe . . . **4.** pete (thieves' sl), sane, sure **5.** chest, vault **6.** closet, secure, unhurt **8.** cautious, cupboard, unharmed **9.** protected, strongbox **11.** trustworthy
safeblower . . . **7.** burglar, peteman **8.** peterman
safe conduct . . . **4.** pass **5.** cowle, guard **6.** convoy, escort **8.** passport **10.** precaution, protection
safecracker . . . **4.** yegg .
safekeeping . . . **4.** care **7.** custody, storage **10.** protection **12.** preservation
safety lamp (miner's) . . . **4.** Davy
safety rail . . . **9.** guardrail
saffron . . . **6.** crocus, yellow **10.** colchicine
sag . . . **4.** bend, hang, reed, rush, sink, wilt **5.** drift, droop, sedge, slump **6.** weaken **10.** depreciate
saga . . . **4.** Edda, epic, tale **5.** story, witch **6.** legend **7.** recital, sagaman **9.** narrative
Saga . . . **7.** goddess, seeress
sagacious . . . **4.** sage, wise **5.** aware, witty **6.** argute, astute, shrewd **7.** politic, sapient **9.** judicious **10.** discerning, farsighted **11.** penetrative **13.** perspicacious
sagacity . . . **3.** ken **6.** acumen, wisdom **9.** acuteness, quickness **10.** shrewdness **11.** discernment, penetration **13.** judiciousness

sage . . . **4.** mint, wise **5.** solon **6.** astute, Salvia, shrewd **7.** sapient **9.** counselor, judicious, sagebrush **10.** discerning **11.** philosopher
Sage (of) . . .
Chelsea . . **7.** Carlyle (Thomas)
Concord . . **7.** Emerson (Ralph W)
Emporia . . **5.** White (Wm Allen)
Ferney . . **8.** Voltaire
Monticello . . **9.** Jefferson (Thomas)
Pylos . . **6.** Nestor
sage (pert to) . . .
Bethlehem . . **9.** spearmint
cheese . . **7.** Cheddar
chippy . . **14.** Brewer's sparrow
cock, hen . . **6.** grouse
family . . **4.** mint
rose . . **5.** alder (yellow)
tea . . **5.** tonic
Sagebrush State . . . **6.** Nevada
sagene . . . **5.** seine **7.** measure, network
sagitta . . . **7.** otolith **8.** keystone (Arch), The Arrow
Sagittarius . . . **6.** bowman **9.** The Archer **13.** constellation
sago (pert to) . . .
palm . . **6.** gebang, gomuti
plant . . **10.** cuckoopint
product . . **6.** starch
tree . . **7.** coontie
sagoin . . . **8.** marmoset
saguaro . . . **6.** cactus, flower
saguing . . . **6.** banana
Sahara . . . **5.** cocoa (color), leste (wind) **6.** desert
sahib . . . **5.** title **6.** master **9.** gentleman
sai . . . **6.** monkey **8.** capuchin
said . . . **6.** stated **7.** uttered **9.** aforesaid **15.** before-mentioned
said to be . . . **7.** reputed, rumored **8.** reported
saiga . . . **8.** antelope
Saigon nickname . . . **14.** Paris of the East
sail . . . **3.** jib, lug **4.** luff, tack **5.** craft, float **6.** vessel, voyage **8.** navigate
sail (pert to) . . .
around . . **14.** circumnavigate
close to wind . . **4.** luff
end . . **7.** yardarm
fish . . **12.** basking shark **15.** quillback sucker
fore and aft . . **7.** spanker
foresail . . **9.** spinnaker
part . . **4.** clew, yard **5.** leech
rope . . **5.** sheet **6.** earing .
secure, lash . . **7.** trice up
strings . . **10.** reef points
type . . **3.** jib, lug, top, try **4.** main, reef, stay **6.** lateen, mizzen, square **7.** topsail **8.** mainsail, save-alls **12.** mutton-legger
sailboat . . . **4.** yawl **5.** ketch, skiff, sloop, yacht **7.** caravel (caravelle)
sailing term . . . **3.** leg, run **4.** asea, beat, jibe, scud, tack **5.** hoist (sail), point, reach **7.** gliding
sailing vessel . . . **4.** bark (barque), brig, saic, yawl **5.** sloop **7.** frigate **8.** schooner **10.** barkentine (barquentine), windjammer
sailor . . . **3.** gob, tar **4.** salt, wave **5.** middy

6. lascar, matlow 7. mariner, voyager
8. seafarer 10. bluejacket, lobscouser
(sl)
sailor (pert to) ...
associate at meals .. **8.** messmate
clothes .. **11.** bell-bottoms
kit .. **8.** ditty bag **9.** housewife
knot .. **8.** geranium
mess tub .. **3.** kid
patron saint .. **4.** Elmo
song .. **7.** chantey **9.** barcarole
Saimiri ... **4.** titi **6.** monkey **8.** squirrel
sain doux ... **4.** lard **6.** grease
saint ... **3.** Ste **5.** angel **7.** apostle, pietist
8. canonize, enshrine, sanctify **10.** holy
person **11.** godly person
Saint (pert to) ...
Anthony's fire .. **10.** erysipelas
Buddhist .. **5.** arhat
Elmo's fire (or light) .. **6.** corona, Helena
9. corposant
Esprit .. **9.** holy ghost
Francis of Assisi .. **11.** il Poverello
13. little poor man
Gaudens .. **8.** sculptor
George's flag .. **14.** national emblem
Helena's hemlock .. **7.** jellica
John Lateran .. **12.** Mother Church
John's bread .. **5.** carob **9.** algarroba
Leger (Eng) .. **9.** horse race
Luke's summer .. **12.** Indian summer
Martin .. **13.** Bishop of Tours
Martin's feast .. **9.** Martinmas
Mary-le-Bow .. **15.** Cheapside Church
(Cockney area)
Mohammedan .. **3.** pir
Patrick's breastplate .. **6.** lorica
Paul .. **12.** Saul of Tarsus
Paul's Church (London), designer ..
18. Sir Christopher Wren
Peter's dome architect ..
12. Michelangelo
Vitus' dance .. **6.** chorea
Saint, patron ...
children's .. **8.** Nicholas (Santa Claus)
desperate person's .. **4.** Jude
English .. **6.** George
French .. **5.** Denis
hospitals .. **9.** John of God **10.** Juan
Ciudad
Irish .. **7.** Patrick
Italian .. **7.** Anthony
lawyer's .. **4.** Ives
lover's .. **9.** Valentine
sailor's .. **4.** Elmo
Scottish .. **6.** Andrew
Spanish .. **5.** James
Welsh .. **5.** David
saints (pert to) ...
biography .. **9.** hagiology
11. hagiography
symbol .. **4.** halo **6.** nimbus
tomb .. **6.** shrine
worship of .. **10.** hagiolatry
sajou ... **6.** monkey **7.** sapajou
sake ... **4.** beer **6.** motive, reason
7. purpose **8.** beverage (rice)
salacious ... **4.** lewd **5.** horny (sl)
7. lustful, obscene **8.** unchaste
9. lecherous
salad plant, vegetable ... **4.** bibb **5.** cress

6. celery, endive **7.** cabbage, lettuce,
romaine **10.** watercress
salamander ... **3.** eft **4.** newt **5.** poker
6. triton **7.** axolotl, Caudata, urodela
9. fire-eater **10.** hellbender **12.** pocket
gopher
salary ... **3.** fee, pay **4.** hire, wage
5. wages **6.** reward **7.** stipend **8.** pittance
9. allowance, emolument, salt money
(anc) **10.** honorarium **12.** compensation,
remuneration
salat ... **6.** prayer (facing Mecca)
sale ... **4.** deal, vend **6.** barter, demand,
market **7.** auction, handsel (1st in
morning) **8.** contract **11.** black market
salesman ... **5.** agent **6.** vendor
7. drummer **9.** solicitor
14. representative **18.** commercial
traveler
salient ... **4.** bold **6.** trench **7.** eminent,
jetting, jumping, leaping, obvious
8. bounding, extended **9.** prominent
10. noticeable, protruding
11. conspicuous
salient angle ... **5.** arris, Doric
Salientia ... **5.** Anura, frogs, toads
8. Amphibia (tailless)
salient point ... **7.** feature (detail)
saline ... **5.** salty **6.** salina **8.** solution
10. saliferous
Salinger, J. D. (pert to) ...
character .. **6.** Phoebe **15.** Holden
Caulfield
work .. **13.** Franny and Zooey **15.** Catcher
in the Rye
saliva ... **7.** spittle **8.** digester, ptyalism
salivary gland ... **8.** racemose
sallow ... **3.** wan **4.** gray, pale **5.** muddy,
pasty **6.** pallid **9.** yellowish
sally ... **4.** jest, leap, trip **5.** issue, jaunt,
start **6.** sortie **7.** journey **8.** escapade,
outburst **9.** witticism
salmagundi ... **4.** hash, olio, stew
6. medley **7.** mixture **9.** potpourri
10. periodical (old)
salmon ... **4.** fish **5.** color **6.** orlean,
sauqui **7.** annatto, saumont
salmon (pert to) ...
adult .. **7.** gilling
after spawning .. **4.** kelt
cured .. **6.** kipper
dog .. **4.** keta
family .. **10.** Salmonidae
female .. **4.** raun **6.** baggit
genus .. **12.** Oncorhynchus
herring .. **8.** milkfish
humpbacked .. **5.** haddo, holia
kind .. **7.** quinnat
landlocked .. **7.** kokanee
male .. **3.** gib **6.** kipper
newly hatched .. **4.** pink
second year .. **6.** hepper
silver .. **4.** coho
small .. **4.** peal **6.** grilse
third year .. **4.** mort
trout .. **5.** sewen
young .. **3.** fog **4.** parr **5.** smolt **6.** grilse,
samlet **7.** essling
Salome (pert to) ...
Bib .. **6.** dancer
father .. **8.** Herodias

grandfather . . **5.** Herod
opera, by . . **7.** Strauss
salon . . . **7.** gallery **8.** New Salon (Paris), Old Salon **9.** reception **10.** assemblage, exhibition **11.** drawing room
Salon del Prado (Madrid) . . . **9.** promenade
saloon . . . **3.** bar **4.** deck **6.** tavern **7.** barroom, cantina, gallery **8.** dramshop, groggery **11.** drawing room
saloop . . . **8.** hot drink **9.** sassafras
salt . . . **3.** sal **4.** cure **5.** brine, taste **6.** flavor, halite, sailor, saline **8.** piquancy **9.** seasoning **10.** antiseptic, corrective **14.** sodium chloride
salt (pert to) . . .
acetic acid . . **7.** acetate
alkaline . . **5.** borax
astringent . . **4.** alum
block, rock . . **3.** pig
boric acid . . **6.** borate
cat . . **4.** lump **10.** pigeon food
comb form . . **4.** sali
cracker . . **7.** saltine
dish for . . **10.** saltcellar
ethereal . . **5.** ester
flat . . **5.** playa
lake . . **5.** shott (chott)
marsh, pond . . **6.** salina
native . . **6.** halite
nature of, like . . **6.** haloid
of the earth . . **7.** the best **10.** commonalty
peter, petre . . **5.** niter
rock, block . . **3.** pig
spring . . **4.** lick
tax . . **7.** gabelle
tree . . **4.** atle (atlee) **5.** cedar **7.** tamarix **8.** tamarisk
working . . **7.** halurgy
works . . **7.** saltern, saltery **9.** salthouse
saltant . . . **7.** dancing, jumping, leaping **8.** bouncing, bounding
salted . . . **5.** briny, cured **6.** corned **7.** treated **8.** brackish, hardened, seasoned **11.** experienced
salty . . . **3.** reh **5.** briny, salic, witty **6.** risqué, saline
salubrious . . . **4.** good **8.** salutary **9.** healthful, wholesome **10.** beneficial
salutary . . . **7.** healthy **8.** curative **9.** medicinal **10.** salubrious **11.** restorative
salutation . . . **2.** hi **3.** ave **4.** hail **5.** aloha, hello, howdy, skoal **6.** curtsy, homage, kowtow, Mizpah (Mizpeh), prosit, salaam (salam) **7.** Dear Sir **8.** greeting, serenade
salute . . . **4.** hail, kiss **5.** greet **6.** homage, signal **7.** address
salvage . . . **4.** save **6.** redeem, rescue **10.** redemption **11.** reclamation
salvation . . . **8.** soterial **10.** liberation, redemption **11.** deliverance, soteriology **12.** preservation
Salvation Army founder . . . **5.** Booth
salve . . . **3.** tip **4.** balm, cure **5.** allay, quiet **6.** anoint, cerate **7.** assuage, relieve **8.** flattery, medicate, ointment **9.** gloss over, lubricate, mitigator **10.** medication

salver . . . **4.** tray **9.** flatterer **11.** serving dish
salvo . . . **6.** excuse **7.** gunfire, pretext, proviso, quibble, rockets **8.** applause **9.** discharge, exception **11.** projectiles, reservation
Samaria (pert to) . . .
capital (anc) . . **6.** Israel
deity . . **6.** Nibhaz
destroyer . . **6.** Romans
founder . . **4.** Omri (925 BC)
people . . **9.** Assyrians
province of . . **9.** Palestine
rebuilder . . **5.** Herod (the Great)
Samaritan, good . . . **5.** aider **6.** helper **10.** befriender, benefactor **11.** helping hand
Sambal (Zambal) **language** . . . **4.** Tino
sambar (sambur) . . . **4.** deer, maha, rusa
same . . . **2.** id **3.** ilk, one **4.** ibid, idem, self **5.** alike, ditto **7.** cognate, identic **8.** selfsame **9.** identical **10.** equivalent
sameness . . . **6.** parity, tedium **7.** analogy, oneness **8.** identity, monotony **9.** alikeness **10.** similarity, uniformity **11.** equivalence **14.** correspondence
Samian (pert to) . . .
island . . **5.** Samos
Sage . . **10.** Pythagoras
sea . . **6.** Aegean
ware . . **8.** Arretine
samlet . . . **4.** parr **6.** salmon (young)
Samoa . . .
anthropologist who studied . . **4.** Mead
capital . . **4.** Apia
councilor . . **7.** faipule
islands . . **8.** American
islands, main . . **5.** Manua, Upolu **6.** Savaii **7.** Tutuila
natives . . **10.** Polynesian
owl (barn) . . **4.** lulu
political council . . **4.** fono
town . . **8.** Pago Pago
warrior . . **3.** toa
samovar . . . **3.** urn **6.** teapot
Samoyed, Samoyede . . . **3.** dog (Arctic) **8.** Siberian
sample . . . **4.** test **5.** model, taste **6.** swatch **7.** example, pattern **8.** specimen
sampler . . . **8.** original **9.** archetype **10.** needlework
Samson (pert to) . . .
Bib . . **5.** judge (Israelite)
death site . . **4.** Gaza (Syria)
famed as . . **9.** strong man
opera . . **16.** Samson and Delilah
tribe . . **3.** Dan
wife . . **7.** Delilah (betrayer)
Samuel . . . **4.** Book (Old Test) **5.** judge **7.** prophet
samurai . . . **6.** vassal **7.** officer
Sana native . . . **8.** Yemenite
San Andreas rift . . . **15.** earthquake fault (Calif)
San Antonio mission . . . **5.** Alamo
sanative . . . **7.** healing **8.** curative, sanatory
Sancho's master . . . **10.** Don Quixote
Sancta Sanctis . . . **20.** Holy things for the holy
sanctify . . . **5.** honor **6.** hallow

10. consecrate 11. free from sin
sanctimonious ... 4. holy 6. sacred
7. saintly 8. affected 12. hypocritical
sanction ... 4. abet, amen, fiat, okay
6. assent, permit, ratify 7. approve,
condone, endorse, support 8. approval
9. approbate, authority, authorize
11. countenance, endorsement
12. ratification 13. authorization
sanctity ... 8. holiness 9. godliness,
solemnity 10. sacredness 11. saintliness
13. inviolability
sanctuary ... 4. bema, fane, holy, naos
5. abbey, bamah, cella, haven 6. priory,
refuge, temple 7. Alsatia, convent,
retreat, shelter 8. cloister 9. monastery
10. penetralia
sanctum ... 3. den 5. study 6. adytum,
office 7. retreat
sand ... 4. grit 5. arena, nerve, pluck,
stone
sand (pert to) ...
applied to body .. 9. arenation
bog .. 4. syrt 9. quicksand
eel .. 4. grig 6. launce
flea .. 6. chigoe, red bug 7. chigger,
sandboy
fluke .. 7. sand dab 8. flounder
hill, mound .. 4. dene, dune
hog .. 7. laborer (in compressed air)
8. tunneler (tunneller)
inhabiting .. 11. arenicolous
like (sand) .. 9. arenulous 10. arenaceous
man .. 5. genie
mixture (clay) .. 4. loam 9. sandstone
pear .. 5. Pyrus
submerged bank .. 3. bar 5. hurst, shoal
sugar .. 5. niter
widgeon .. 7. gadwall
sandal ... 4. boat, shoe, sock 7. talaria
sandpiper ... 3. ree 4. knot, pume,
ruff, stib 5. stint (long-toed) 6. dunlin
8. pectoral, triddler
sandstone ... 7. sarsens 8. ganister
Sandwich Islands ... 6. Hawaii
8. Hawaiian
sandy ... 6. desert, gritty 7. arenose
8. granular, sabulous, Scotsman
9. sandpiper 10. arenaceous, ring
plover
sane ... 5. lucid, sound 7. logical
8. rational, sensible 9. practical
10. reasonable
San Francisco Mil Post ... 8. Presidio
sang ... 5. blood, sheng 7. chanted,
ginseng, Society
sang-froid ... 8. coolness 9. cold blood,
composure 11. insouciance
sanguinary ... 3. ant (slave) 4. gory
5. cruel 6. bloody, yarrow 8. sanguine
9. bloodroot, murderous
12. bloodthirsty
sanguine ... 4. warm 5. ruddy 6. ardent
7. hopeful 8. blood-red 9. confident
10. optimistic 12. bloodthirsty
sanity ... 4. wits 6. reason 8. lucidity,
saneness 9. soundness
13. wholesomeness
San Juan Hill ... 4. Cuba (Battle, 1898)
San Juan Indian ... 4. Tewa
San Kuo ... 13. Three Kingdoms (Shu,

Wei, Wu)
San Marino, Europe (pert to) ...
famed as .. 11. oldest State (Eur)
government .. 8. Republic (smallest)
mountains .. 8. Appenine
site .. 8. Mt Titano
sannup ... 6. Indian (married male) (opp
of squaw)
Sanskrit (pert to) ...
college .. 3. tol
dialect .. 4. Pali
drama .. 9. Sakuntala (Shakuntala)
epic .. 8. Ramayana
god .. 4. Kama (Cupid), Vayu (wind)
5. Indra (Great) 6. Aditya
goddess .. 3. Uma (Splendor) 4. Devi
(Mother) 5. Aditi, Gauri
human spirit .. 7. jivatma
literature .. 5. sruti (shruti)
period .. 5. Vedic
Phonet (sounds) .. 6. sandhi
poem (epic) .. 11. Race of Raghu,
Raghuvamsha
poet .. 8. Kalidasa
sacred books .. 4. Veda
soul .. 5. atman
treatise .. 9. Upanishad
Santo Domingo ... 7. capital (Dominican
Republic)
sap ... 3. gum 4. boob, dupe, fool, mine,
seve, upas 5. drain, fluid, lymph, sapor
6. juices, trench, weaken 7. essence,
schnook 8. unsettle 9. simpleton,
undermine
sapid ... 5. tasty 7. zestful 8. flavored
9. palatable, toothsome
sapient ... 4. sage, wise 6. shrewd
7. knowing 8. profound 9. sagacious
10. discerning
sapiutan ... 4. anoa 6. wild ox
sapodilla ... 5. chico 6. chicle, zapote
7. nispero 9. naseberry
sapor ... 5. savor, taste 6. flavor, relish
sapper ... 5. miner 6. digger 9. excavator
Saracen ... 4. Arab 5. nomad, pagan
6. Muslim (Moslem) 7. heathen, infidel,
ragwort 9. Moor's head (Her)
Saracen Knight ... 8. Ruggiero
Sarah (pert to) ...
bird .. 9. wake-robin
husband .. 7. Abraham
mother of .. 5. Isaac
slave of .. 5. Hagar
sarcasm ... 4. gibe 5. irony, taunt 6. satire
8. ironical, ridicule
sarcastic ... 3. dry 6. biting, ironic
7. caustic, cutting, satiric 8. ironical,
sardonic 9. malicious 10. mordacious
sarcophagic ... 10. sarcophagy 11. flesh-
eating 13. sarcophageous
sarcophagus ... 5. chest 6. coffin
9. limestone 11. Assian stone, lapis
Assius
sardine ... 4. bang 7. alewife, anchovy,
herring (young) 8. pilchard
Sardinia, Italy ...
capital .. 8. Cagliari
island .. 13. Mediterranean
sheep .. 7. mouflon (moufflon)
tower (Prehist) .. 6. nuragh
sardonic ... 3. dry 6. ironic, morose

7. cynical, satiric **8.** derisive **9.** sarcastic
11. Rabelaisian
sartor . . . **6.** tailor
sash . . . **3.** obi **4.** band, belt, benn, tobe
 6. girdle **8.** casement **10.** cummerbund
sash pulley weight . . . **5.** mouse
Saskatchewan, Canada . . .
 capital . . **6.** Regina
 city . . **8.** Moose Jaw **9.** Saskatoon
sassaby . . . **8.** antelope
sassafras (pert to) . . .
 nut . . **8.** pichurim
 oil of (part) . . **6.** safrol
 tea . . **6.** saloop
 tree . . **4.** ague
sassy . . . **4.** pert **5.** saucy **8.** impudent
Satan . . . **5.** Demon, Devil, Eblis, fiend
 6. Belial **7.** Lucifer, Scratch, Tempter
 9. archfiend **14.** Mephistopheles
 16. Prince of Darkness
Satan (pert to) . . .
 angel (bottomless pit) . . **8.** Apollyon
 associate . . **6.** Azazel **9.** Beelzebub
 before his fall . . **7.** Lucifer
 Jewish . . **8.** Asmodeus
 Scottish . . **4.** deil
 son . . **3.** Imp (jocular)
satanic . . . **5.** cruel **6.** wicked **7.** demonic
 8. devilish, infernal **10.** diabolical
satchel . . . **3.** bag **4.** case, etui, grip,
 sack **5.** cabas **6.** valise
sate . . . **4.** cloy, glut **5.** gorge **7.** gratify,
 satiate, satisfy, surfeit **8.** saturate
sated . . . **4.** full **5.** blasé **6.** gorged
satellite . . . **4.** Echo, luna, moon **5.** Atlas
 6. comsat, planet **7.** aerosat, Landsat,
 Sputnik, Telstar **8.** Explorer, follower,
 Vanguard **9.** companion, dependent
satellite of Jupiter . . . **2.** Io (1st)
 6. Europa (2nd) **8.** Callisto, Ganymede
satellite of Saturn . . . **4.** Rhea **5.** Dione,
 Mimas, Titan **6.** Phoebe, Tethys
 8. Hyperion **9.** Enceladus
satellite of Uranus . . . **5.** Ariel **6.** Oberon
 7. Titania, Umbriel
satellite's orbit . . . **4.** path
 14. geosynchronous
Sati (Egypt) . . . **5.** Queen
satiate . . . **4.** cloy, glut, sate **5.** gorge
 7. gratify, satisfy, surfeit
satin . . . **4.** silk **6.** étoile, fabric, sateen,
 satiny **9.** satinette **10.** smoothness
satire . . . **3.** wit **5.** irony, spoof **6.** parody
 7. lampoon
satiric, satirical . . . **3.** dry **6.** bitter,
 ironic **7.** abusive, caustic, cutting
 8. ironical, poignant **9.** burlesque,
 sarcastic **11.** reproachful
satisfaction . . . **3.** cro **4.** duel **6.** amends
 7. comfort, content, payment, satiety
 8. adequacy, pleasure, reprisal
 9. atonement **10.** recompense,
 reparation **11.** contentment, fulfillment
 12. compensation, propitiation,
 remuneration **15.** indemnification
satisfied . . . **5.** proud, sated **7.** content,
 pleased **8.** satiated **9.** contented,
 convinced, gratified **10.** paid in full
satisfy . . . **2.** do **3.** pay **4.** fill, sate, suit
 5. atone, solve **6.** pay off, please, supply
 7. assuage, content, fulfill, gratify,

indulge, requite, satiate **8.** atone for,
 convince
satrap (anc) . . . **5.** ruler **6.** despot, prince
 8. governor, overlord
saturate . . . **3.** ret, sop, wet **4.** fill, soak
 5. imbue, souse, steep **6.** drench,
 seethe **7.** satiate **8.** overfill, permeate
 10. impregnate
saturated . . . **4.** full **6.** soaked, sodden
Saturday . . . **6.** Samedi **9.** sabbatine
 13. Jewish Sabbath
Saturn (pert to) . . .
 Astron . . **6.** planet
 consort . . **3.** Ops
 god of . . **4.** seed
 Latin . . **8.** Saturnus
 rings . . **7.** moonlet **9.** particles
 rings, part . . **4.** ansa
 satellite . . **4.** Rhea **5.** Dione, Titan
  7. Iapetus **8.** Hyperion
 Temple treasury (State) . . **8.** aerarium
saturnalia . . . **4.** orgy **7.** debauch
 8. Festival (of Saturn) **11.** pandemonium
saturnine . . . **6.** dismal, gloomy, somber
 8. funereal
satyr . . . **4.** faun **5.** deity **7.** demigod,
 silenus **9.** butterfly, capripede,
 orangutan
sauce . . . **3.** soy **4.** alec, pulp **5.** caper,
 curry, garum, gravy, pesto **6.** gansel,
 tahini **7.** catchup (catsup), soubise,
 Tabasco, veloute **8.** amandine, dressing,
 marinara **9.** espagnole, insolence,
 seasoning **11.** beurre blanc
 12. impertinence
saucy . . . **4.** bold, pert, vain **5.** brash,
 cocky, sassy, smart **7.** forward
 8. impudent, malapert **9.** officious
 11. impertinent **13.** disrespectful
Saudi Arabia . . .
 city . . **5.** Islam
 founder . . **7.** Ibn Saud (1913)
 gulf . . **7.** Persian
 Mohammed's tomb . . **6.** Medina
 mosque . . **5.** Kaaba
 peninsula . . **7.** Arabian
 provinces . . **4.** Asir, Nejd **5.** Hejaz **6.** El
  Hasa
 sea . . **3.** Red
 sect . . **6.** Wahabi (Wahabee, Wahhabi)
sauerbraten . . . **8.** pot roast
sauger . . . **9.** pike perch
Saul (pert to) . . .
 concubine . . **6.** Rizpah
 daughter . . **6.** Michal
 father . . **4.** Kish
 herdsman . . **4.** Doeg
 of Tarsus . . **4.** Paul
 uncle . . **3.** Ner
 wife . . **7.** Ahinoam
 witch of . . **5.** Endor
Sault Ste Marie . . . **3.** Soo **6.** rapids
 9. ship canal
saumont . . . **6.** salmon
sauna . . . **4.** bath (Finnish)
saunter . . . **3.** jog, lag, mog **4.** roam,
 rove, walk **5.** range, stray **6.** dawdle,
 loiter, lounge, potter, ramble, stroll,
 wander **8.** ruminate
sauqui . . . **6.** salmon
saurian . . . **6.** lizard, Sauria **7.** reptile

9. crocodile
sausage ... **6.** banger, salami **7.** bologna, chorizo, saveloy **8.** kielbasa (kolbasi), rolliche **9.** bratwurst, pepperoni **10.** knackwurst
sausage-shaped ... **9.** allantoid **10.** botuliform
savage ... **3.** att **4.** rude, wild **5.** brute, cruel, feral, yahoo **6.** ferine, fierce, Indian **7.** brutish, howling **8.** cannibal, pitiless **9.** atrocious, barbarian, ferocious, merciless, primitive **11.** uncivilized **12.** uncultivated
savanna, savannah ... **5.** plain **9.** grassland **11.** level region
savant ... **4.** sage **6.** pundit **7.** scholar **9.** scientist **10.** classicist **12.** intellectual, man of letters
save ... **3.** but **4.** keep **5.** catch, hoard, lay by **6.** except, redeem, rescue, scrimp **7.** prevent, protect, reserve, salvage **8.** conserve **9.** economize, excepting, safeguard **10.** accumulate
savin, savine ... **5.** cedar **7.** juniper **9.** evergreen
savior, Saviour ... **8.** Redeemer **9.** deliverer, liberator **11.** emancipator, Jesus Christ
savoir-faire ... **4.** tact **5.** poise, savvy (sl) **7.** culture **9.** gentility **12.** ease of manner, mannerliness
savor, savour ... **4.** odor, zest **5.** nidor, sapor, scent, smack, smell, taste **6.** flavor, relish **9.** degustate
savory, savoury ... **5.** sapid, tasty **7.** piquant **8.** gustable **9.** agreeable **10.** appetizing, delightful
saw ... **3.** cut **4.** dict **5.** adage, maxim **6.** cliché, saying, truism **7.** noticed, proverb **9.** platitude, serration
saw (kind) ... **3.** jig, rip **4.** band, buzz, hack, whip **5.** crown, power **7.** keyhole **8.** crosscut
saw (pert to) ...
back .. **6.** sierra
bill .. **6.** motmot **9.** merganser
buck .. **8.** sawhorse **13.** ten-dollar bill
crosscut .. **5.** briar
fish .. **3.** ray
grass .. **5.** sedge
horse .. **4.** buck, rack **7.** sawbuck
log .. **5.** edger
of sawfish .. **5.** serra
surgeon's .. **6.** trepan (trephine)
teeth .. **5.** tines
two-bladed .. **6.** stadda
sawmill gate ... **4.** sash
saw-whet ... **10.** Acadian owl
saxhorn ... **4.** tuba **7.** althorn **8.** bass tuba **9.** saxcornet
saxifrage ... **6.** Seseli
Saxon (pert to) ...
color .. **5.** smalt **8.** Saxe blue **10.** Bremen blue **13.** indigo carmine
king .. **6.** Egbert **8.** Ethelred **14.** Alfred the Great
language .. **10.** Anglo-Saxon **12.** Plattdeutsch
people .. **7.** English **9.** Sassenach **10.** Anglo-Saxon **11.** Lowland Scot
serf .. **4.** esne

swineherd .. **5.** Gurth (Ivanhoe)
warrior .. **5.** thane
Saxony capital ... **7.** Dresden **10.** Wittenburg (anc)
say ... **4.** aver, cite, tell **5.** gnome, speak, state, utter **6.** affirm, answer, assert, assume, recite, remark, speech **9.** authority **11.** declaration **12.** conversation
say (pert to) ...
a blessing .. **5.** bensh
again .. **6.** repeat **7.** restate **9.** reiterate
further .. **3.** add
no (to) .. **6.** negate, refuse **8.** prohibit **10.** disapprove
one thing, mean another .. **6.** palter **7.** falsify **9.** fluctuate **10.** equivocate **12.** be capricious
uncle .. **4.** cede **9.** surrender **10.** capitulate **15.** throw in the towel
saying ... **3.** dit, mot, saw **4.** quip **5.** adage, axiom, maxim **6.** byword, enigma, phrase, remark **7.** proverb **8.** aphorism, apothegm **11.** declaration
saying, sayings (pert to) ...
collection of .. **9.** gnomology
criterion, party cry .. **10.** shibboleth
dogmatic .. **6.** dictum
religious .. **5.** logia
scab ... **3.** rat **4.** sore **5.** crust, mange **6.** rotter **7.** blemish **8.** deserter **9.** scoundrel **12.** incrustation **13.** strikebreaker
scabbard ... **6.** sheath **7.** holster, pilcher **13.** emblem of peace
scabbard fish ... **7.** cutlass **9.** frostfish
scaddle ... **5.** cruel, timid **6.** fierce **7.** nervous **8.** skittish, thievish **11.** mischievous
scads ... **4.** gobs, wads **5.** heaps, money, piles **6.** oodles **11.** great number **12.** considerable
scaffold, scaffolding ... **5.** easel, stage **7.** staging, support **8.** platform **9.** grain loft
scalawag, scallawag ... **5.** scamp **6.** rascal **7.** sculpin **10.** scapegrace
scale ... **3.** hut **4.** husk, peel, rate, shed, size **5.** climb, crust, flake, gamut **6.** ascend, degree, ladder, lamina, rustre (anc armor), series, weight **7.** compare, measure **12.** incrustation
scale (pert to) ...
botany .. **5.** palea
color .. **10.** tintometer
comb form .. **4.** cten **5.** cteno, lepis
duck .. **9.** merganser, sheldrake
fish .. **6.** ganoid **8.** scabbard
grand .. **4.** epic
music .. **3.** E la (highest note) **5.** gamut, minor **9.** chromatic, hexachord **10.** tetrachord
slide .. **7.** vernier
tail .. **6.** rodent
Zool .. **6.** scutum
scallop ... **4.** quin **5.** crena, notch **7.** mollusk **9.** serration, shellfish **12.** summer squash
scalloped ... **6.** cooked **7.** notched **8.** invected (Her) **9.** crenulate
scalpel ... **5.** knife **6.** lancet **7.** dissect

8. bistoury

scaly ... 5. flaky 6. crusty, scabby, scurfy 7. leprose 8. squamous

scamp ... 3. imp 5. cheat, knave, rogue 6. rascal, slight 7. bacalao, codfish 8. scalawag, spalpeen 9. scoundrel 15. worthless fellow

scamper ... 3. hie, run 4. dash, race, scud 5. haste 6. hasten 7. brattle 9. hasten off, skedaddle 11. hasty flight

scan ... 3. eye 6. browse, peruse 7. examine 10. scrutinize 11. contemplate 16. recite metrically

scance ... 5. blame, shine 6. glance 7. comment, glitter

scandal ... 5. odium, shame 6. gossip 7. calumny, offense, slander 8. disgrace, ignominy 10. defamation, detraction, opprobrium 11. abomination

scandalous ... 6. wicked 8. libelous, terrible 10. defamatory, slanderous 11. disgraceful, opprobrious

Scandinavia, countries ... see also *Scandinavian* 6. Norway, Sweden 7. Denmark, Iceland

Scandinavian (pert to) ...
alphabetical character . . 4. rune
ash tree . . 10. Yggdrasill
author . . 8. Andersen (Hans C)
bay . . 5. fjord
explorer . . 4. Eric
goblin, brownie . . 5. nisse 6. kobold
god . . 4. Lake, Thor
goose . . 5. nisse
hall of Odin (heroes' souls) . . 8. Valhalla
legend . . 4. Edda, saga
maiden of Odin . . 8. Valkyrie
navigator . . 4. Eric
people . . 4. Dane, Lapp 5. Swede 8. Norseman 9. Norwegian
people, type . . 8. Teutonic
pert to . . 5. runic
plateau . . 5. field
rulers . . 10. Varangians
saga narrator . . 7. sagaman
sea monster (fabled) . . 6. kraken
supernatural being (dwarf or giant) . . 5. troll

scant ... 3. few 5. chary 6. meager, narrow, scarce, slight, sparse 7. slender, sparing 12. parsimonious

scanty ... 4. rare 6. meager (meagre), narrow, scarce, sparse 7. scrimpy 12. insufficient 14. inconsiderable

scapegoat ... 4. goat (Bib) 9. sacrifice 10. substitute

scapegrace ... 5. scamp 8. scalawag (scallawag) 9. reprobate 10. profligate 12. incorrigible

scar ... 3. arr, shy 4. seam, sear 5. cliff, mound 7. blemish 8. cicatrix

scarce ... 4. rare 5. short 6. scanty 7. sparing 8. uncommon 9. deficient 10. infrequent

scarcely ... 6. barely, hardly 7. but just 12. infrequently

scarcity ... 4. lack, want 6. dearth, famine, rarity 7. paucity 8. rareness 11. infrequency 13. insufficiency

scare ... 3. cow 5. alarm, panic 7. startle, terrify 8. affright, frighten

scarecrow ... 4. ogre 5. bogle 6. effigy, goblin, malkin, shewel (sewel) 9. jackstraw 10. frightener 11. hide-and-seek

scarf ... 3. boa, tie 4. sash 5. ascot, cloud, nubia 6. tippet 7. muffler 9. rigolette 10. fascinator

scarf (pert to) ...
bird . . 9. cormorant
broad . . 5. shawl
clerical . . 5. fanon, orale, rabat, stole
feather . . 3. boa
head . . 10. fascinator
Hindu . . 4. sari
India . . 7. dopatta
Mexico . . 6. tapalo
skin . . 7. cuticle 9. epidermis

Scarlet Letter ... 5. novel (Hawthorne)

Scarlet O'Hara's home ... 4. Tara

scarp ... 5. cliff, pitch 7. descent, incline 9. declivity

scary ... 5. eerie, timid, weird 7. ghostly, uncanny 8. alarming 12. easily scared

scat ... 4. hiss 5. burst, smash 6. buffet 7. scatter

scat, scatt (Orkney Isls) ... 3. tax 7. tribute

scathe ... 4. flay, harm, hurt 6. assail, damage, injury, scorch 7. scarify 9. excoriate 10. misfortune

scatter ... 3. sow, ted 4. deal, rout 5. spray, strew 6. dispel, litter, shower, splash, spread 7. bestrew, diffuse, radiate 8. disperse, separate, squander 9. circulate, dissipate 10. disarrange, strew about

scattered ... 4. semé 5. dealt 6. sparse, strewn 8. confused, sparsile, sporadic 9. broadcast, dispersed, separated, sprinkled 10. widespread 11. distributed

scattering ... 3. few 8. Diaspora 10. dispersion, separating 13. dissemination

scatty ... 7. showery

scaup ... 4. duck 8. bluebill 9. blackhead, broadbill

scavenger ... 4. bird 8. organism 10. saprophyte 16. garbage collector

scaw ... 8. headland 10. promontory

scene ... 4. site, view 5. anger, sight, vista 6. locale 7. diorama, picture, tableau

scene (pert to) ...
behind the . . 8. secretly 9. backstage, invisible
inside . . 7. neorama
last . . 6. finale
of action . . 5. arena, stage 6. sphere
of confusion . . 5. babel
of miracle (Bib) . . 4. Cana
opera . . 5. scena
wright . . 6. artist 8. designer (scenery), stageman

scenic ... 8. dramatic 9. panoramic 11. picturesque

scenic (pert to) ...
enigma . . 7. charade
pert to . . 5. stage 7. episode, scenery
representation . . 7. diorama 13. motion picture

scent ... 4. aura, clue, nose, odor

5. aroma, flair, nairn, nidar, smell,
spoor 6. detect 7. perfume 9. fragrance
scented . . . 5. olent 6. odored
8. perfumed, smelling 11. odoriferous
scepter, sceptre . . . 3. rod 4. mace
5. baton, staff 6. emblem (royal)
8. insignia 11. sovereignty
schedule . . . 4. card, list 5. slate
7. program 8. calendar, document
9. catalogue, inventory
scheme . . . 3. aim 4. lark, plan, plot
5. cabal 6. device, devise, racket, system
7. complot, concoct, diagram, epitome,
outline, project, purpose 8. artifice,
contrive 9. boomerang 10. conspiracy,
enterprise 11. machination
schemer . . . 7. plotter 8. conniver, finagler
9. intriguer
schism . . . 4. rent, sect 5. split 6. breach
7. dissent, faction 8. division 10. falling-
out, separation
schismatic . . . 7. heretic, sectary
8. apostate 9. dissenter, sectarian
10. factionist
schist . . . 4. mica, rock 5. slate
10. hornblende
scholar . . . 6. pedant, savant 7. learner,
student 8. disciple 11. philologist
scholarly . . . 7. erudite, learned
8. academic, studious 9. philomath
10. scholastic
scholarship . . . 5. burse 8. learning
9. education, erudition, knowledge
10. foundation 11. instruction
school . . . 4. cult, sect 5. class, drill,
flock, order, teach, train 7. convent,
educate, seminar 8. instruct, seminary
9. institute
school (pert to) . . .
book . . 6. primer, reader 7. speller
English . . 4. Eton 6. Oxford 9. Cambridge
French . . 5. ecole, lycée
German . . 6. schule
head, inspector . . 9. scholarch
master . . 7. dominie 9. pedagogue
(pedagog)
ref to . . 10. scholastic
riding . . 6. manège
teacher . . 4. marm
term . . 8. semester
wrestling . . 9. gymnasium, palaestra
(palestra)
school of . . .
art . . 4. Dada
divinity . . 8. seminary
Fine Arts . . 9. Wagnerian
fishes . . 5. shoal
philosophers . . 7. Eleatic
philosophy . . 7. Gnostic
seals . . 3. pod
thieves . . 4. gang
whales . . 3. gam, pod
schooner . . . 4. boat, brig, tern 5. glass
6. vessel 7. measure, prairie (Hist)
schuit, schuyt . . . 5. sloop 6. vessel
7. eelboat
science . . . 3. art 5. ology, skill
9. knowledge 11. proficiency
science of . . .
agriculture . . 8. agronomy
better living . . 9. euthenics

better working . . 10. ergonomics
breeding . . 8. eugenics
character . . 8. ethology
children's diseases . . 10. pediatrics
(paediatrics)
controversy . . 8. polemics
creatures . . 10. entomology
dining . . 10. aristology
doctrines . . 9. esoterics
ears . . 7. otology
family symbols . . 8. heraldry
forest trees . . 7. silvics (sylvics)
good . . 6. ethics 9. euthenics
10. agathology
government . . 8. politics
happiness . . 11. eudaemonics
healing . . 9. iatrology
health . . 7. hygiene
kissing . . 13. philematology
language . . 9. philology, semantics
11. linguistics
life . . 7. biology 10. entomology
light . . 6. optics
mind . . 10. psychology
moral conduct . . 6. ethics
organism behavior . . 7. ecology
(oecology) 9. bionomics
philosophy . . 6. noesia
reality . . 10. philosophy
reasoning . . 5. logic
rocks . . 9. petrology
sea (the) . . 12. oceanography
self-defense . . 4. judo 7. jujitsu
sound . . 9. acoustics
theology interpretation . . 8. exegesis
12. hermeneutics
verse . . 7. prosody
virtue . . 8. aretaics
words . . 9. semantics
scientific . . . 5. exact 8. clinical 9. realistic,
technical 16. precise knowledge
scimitar, scimiter . . . 4. snee 5. saber
8. billhook
scintilla . . . 4. atom, iota, whit 5. spark,
trace 7. modicum
scintillate . . . 5. flash, gleam, spark 7. be
witty, glitter, twinkle 9. coruscate 10. be
eloquent
scion, cion . . . 3. son 4. slip 5. graft,
shoot 10. descendant
scold . . . 3. jaw, nag 4. carp, rail, rate
5. chide, shrew 6. berate, chider,
rebuke 7. reprove, upbraid 8. admonish
9. reprimand
scolding . . . 7. froward 8. reproach,
shrewish 10. upbraiding
12. admonishment, reprimanding
sconce . . . 3. top 4. head 5. brain,
mulct, skull 6. screen 7. bulwark,
lantern, redoubt, skelter 11. candlestick,
counterfort
scoop . . . 4. bail, beat, lade, news
5. empty, ladle, spoon 6. bucket,
hollow, shovel 8. excavate, gather in
scoop out . . . 3. dig 5. gouge 6. chisel,
hollow 7. fashion
scope . . . 4. area, room 5. ambit, arena,
range, reach 6. degree, domain
7. compass, freedom, liberty 8. latitude
9. gyroscope, intention, periscope,
telescope 10. microscope

11. stethoscope 12. kaleidoscope, spectroscope

scorch ... **4.** burn, char, sear, sere **5.** parch, singe, speed **7.** shrivel **9.** criticize

scordato ... **9.** out of tune **14.** made discordant

score ... **3.** peg, run, sum, tab **4.** debt, gain, goal, rate **5.** corge, judge, notch, scold, slash, tally **6.** berate, furrow, groove, points, reason, twenty **7.** account, arrange, scratch **8.** incision **9.** calculate, tally mark **10.** obligation **11.** arrangement, composition, orchestrate **12.** indebtedness

scoria (volcano) ... **4.** lava, slag **5.** dross **6.** refuse **7.** residue

scorn ... **4.** defy, geck, mock **5.** spurn **6.** deride, reject **7.** contemn, despise, disdain **8.** contempt, derision, disgrace **9.** contumely

scornful ... **8.** derisive, insolent **10.** disdainful **12.** contemptuous, contumelious

Scorpio (pert to) ...
constellation in .. **8.** Milky Way
genus .. **8.** Scorpius
night mansion of .. **4.** Mars
pictured as .. **8.** scorpion
star (brightest) .. **7.** Antares
zodiac sign .. **8.** eighth

scorpion ... **4.** nepa **7.** alacran, scourge (Bib) **8.** arachnid, catapult **10.** pine lizard, vinaigrier **11.** vinegarroon (vinagron) **15.** blue-tailed skink

Scot ... **3.** Mac **4.** Celt, Gael **5.** Saxon **6.** Sawney **7.** bluecap **8.** Scotsman **10.** Caledonian, Highlander

Scotland ... see also *Scottish*
capital .. **9.** Edinburgh
city .. **3.** Ayr **5.** Perth **6.** Atholl (Athole), Dundee **7.** Glasgow (largest), Renfrew **8.** Aberdeen **9.** Inverness
congress (musical) .. **3.** Mod
district .. **6.** Argyll, Atholl **10.** Midlothian
famed site .. **9.** Trossachs (Lady of the Lake) **10.** Loch Lomond **11.** Loch Katrine
firth .. **3.** Tay **4.** Loch **5.** Clyde, Forth, Moray, Tweed
islands .. **6.** Orkney **8.** Hebrides, Shetland
Latin name (anc) .. **9.** Caledonia
moors .. **10.** Lochar Moss
mountain .. **9.** Grampians
poetic name .. **6.** Scotia **9.** Caledonia
resort .. **4.** Oban
river .. **3.** Ayr, Dee, Tay **5.** Afton, Clyde, Forth, Tweed **6.** Teviot **7.** Deveron
seaport .. **5.** Leith **6.** Dundee

Scotland Yard headquarters ...
6. London **18.** Metropolitan Police

Scott, Sir Walter (pert to) ...
estate .. **10.** Abbotsford (Scot)
famed as .. **4.** poet **8.** novelist
novel .. **7.** Ivanhoe, Waverly **8.** Talisman **10.** Kenilworth **14.** Quentin Durward
poem .. **13.** Lady of the Lake

Scottish (pert to) ...
accent .. **4.** birr
alder .. **3.** arn
attendant (hunter's) .. **6.** gillie (gilly)

bagpipe music .. **7.** pibroch
beret .. **3.** tam **11.** tam-o'-shanter
bird .. **3.** gae (blue) **6.** grouse **7.** snabbie (snabby) **9.** swinepipe
blessing .. **6.** rebuke **8.** scolding
blood money .. **3.** cro **7.** galanas
blue .. **6.** homage **8.** infernal **11.** reddish-blue
bluebell .. **8.** harebell
boat .. **4.** zulu **7.** coracle, skaffie
bonnets .. **8.** mushroom
brandy .. **6.** Athole
breeches .. **5.** trews
brier, briar .. **4.** rose
broth .. **5.** brose
bull, ox .. **4.** stot
cake (tea) .. **5.** scone
cap .. **3.** tam **8.** Balmoral **9.** Glengarry **11.** tam-o'-shanter
carpet .. **13.** Kidderminster
cattle .. **8.** Aberdeen, Ayrshire
celebration .. **4.** kirn (harvest)
child .. **5.** bairn **6.** scuddy (naked)
church .. **4.** kirk
cloth .. **4.** kelt **6.** tartan
coalfish .. **7.** glashan, sillock
court officer .. **5.** macer
cup .. **4.** tass
dagger (anc) .. **4.** dirk
dagger, knife .. **8.** skean dhu
dance .. **4.** reel **5.** fling **9.** ecossaise **10.** strathspey **13.** Highland fling
devil .. **4.** deil **6.** Hornie
dirge .. **8.** coronach (as on bagpipes)
duck .. **4.** coot **6.** scoter
earth .. **4.** eard
elder .. **7.** tobacco
elm .. **7.** wych-elm
excuse .. **6.** sunyie
eye .. **2.** ee
family (same) .. **3.** ilk
festival .. **3.** Mod **7.** uphelya (Epiphany)
fish .. **4.** sile **7.** sillock **8.** spalding
fog .. **4.** haar
Gaelic .. **4.** Erse
ghost .. **6.** taisch
girl .. **4.** lass **6.** lassie, towdie **7.** winklot
goblin .. **8.** barghest
godmother .. **6.** cummer (kimmer)
grandchild .. **2.** oy (oye)
grandfather .. **8.** gudesire
hill, hillside .. **4.** brae **6.** strone
icicle .. **7.** shoggle
kilt .. **7.** filibeg
kiss (stolen) .. **8.** smoorich
lake .. **4.** loch
language .. **4.** Erse **6.** Lallan (Lalland)
liquor .. **5.** scour **6.** Athole **7.** whitter
lovage .. **10.** sea parsley
money, silver .. **6.** siller
nephew .. **6.** nepote
New Year's Day .. **7.** Cake Day **8.** hogmanay
nightingale .. **7.** warbler
ox, bullock .. **4.** nowt
plaid .. **4.** maud **6.** tartan
porridge .. **5.** brose
pouch, purse (kilt front) .. **7.** sporran
pudding .. **6.** haggis
reel (fishing) .. **4.** pirn
rod, over the door .. **10.** willow wand

sausage .. **9.** whitehass (whitehawse)
schoolmaster .. **3.** dux
shawl (plaid) .. **4.** maud
stream, brook .. **4.** sike
sweetheart .. **2.** jo
sword .. **8.** claymore
toad .. **3.** ted **4.** taed
tobacco .. **5.** elder
topaz .. **9.** cairngorm
townhall .. **8.** tolbooth (tollbooth)
uncle .. **3.** eme
village .. **3.** rew
waistcoat (under) .. **6.** fecket
whirlpool .. **7.** swilkie
whisky .. **9.** Glenlivet (Glenlivat)
   10. usquebaugh
window .. **7.** winnock
youth .. **6.** chield (chiel) **7.** callant (callan)
Scottish person (pert to) ...
   author .. **5.** Scott **9.** Stevenson (Robert
      Louis)
   biographer, famed .. **7.** Boswell
   dynasty .. **6.** Stuart
   economist .. **5.** Smith (Adam)
   engineer, inventor .. **4.** Watt
   geneticist .. **7.** Haldane
   king .. **6.** Robert (the Bruce)
   physicist .. **7.** Maxwell
   poet .. **5.** Burns
scoundrel ... **3.** cad **5.** cheat, knave,
   scamp **6.** varlet **7.** villain **8.** scalawag
   9. miscreant **10.** blackguard
   11. rapscallion
scoup ... **3.** run **4.** leap, skip **7.** scamper
scourge ... **4.** bane, flog, lash, whip
   6. punish, swinge, switch **8.** chastise
   10. affliction, infliction, punishment
Scourge of God ... **6.** Attila (King of
   Huns)
Scourge of Princes ... **7.** Aretino (It
   satirist)
scout ... **3.** spy **5.** flout, scoff **7.** lookout,
   servant **8.** emissary, watchman
   9. guillemot **11.** reconnoiter **14.** razor-
   billed auk
scow ... **4.** acon **6.** garvey **7.** lighter
scowl ... **5.** frown, lower **6.** aspect
   (gloomy), glower **7.** wrinkle (brow)
   10. sullen look
scraggly ... **5.** rough **6.** ragged
   7. unkempt **9.** irregular
scraggy ... **4.** bony **5.** rough **6.** meager,
   rugged, skinny **7.** knotted, scrawny,
   stunted
scram ... **6.** begone, benumb, decamp
   7. vamoose
scramble ... **4.** push **5.** climb, crowd,
   crush **6.** jostle, strive **7.** clamber, scatter
   8. struggle
scrap ... **3.** bit, end, ort, rag **4.** chip, junk
   5. fight, melee, piece, waste **6.** morsel,
   refuse **7.** cutting, discard, excerpt,
   extract, quarrel, remnant **8.** fragment,
   ramentum
scrape ... **3.** row, rub **4.** rake, rasp
   5. grate, graze, shave **6.** abrade, eke
   out, injure, sclaff **7.** collect, scratch
   9. economize, obeisance **10.** difficulty
   11. predicament
scraper ... **4.** harl (wool), tool **6.** barber,
   rasper **7.** abrader, fiddler, strigil

8. grattoir
scrappy ... **9.** irregular **10.** pugnacious
   11. contentious, fragmentary,
   quarrelsome
scratch ... **3.** mar, rit, rub **4.** claw, draw,
   itch, mark, rake, rist, tear **5.** erase
   6. cancel, injury, scrape **7.** blemish,
   roughen, scarify **8.** scribble, withdraw
scrawl ... **6.** doodle **7.** scratch **8.** scribble
scrawny ... **4.** lean, poor, thin **5.** spare
   6. skinny **7.** scranny **8.** rawboned
scream ... **3.** cry **4.** wail, yell **6.** shriek,
   squeal **7.** screech
screamer ... **5.** swift (bird) **7.** blunder
   8. headline
scree ... **5.** stone, talus **6.** debris, pebble
screech ... **3.** cry, say **6.** outcry, scream,
   shriek, squeal **7.** ululate
screech (pert to) ...
   hawk .. **10.** goatsucker
   martin .. **5.** swift
   owl .. **4.** barn **5.** Scops
screed ... **4.** list, rend, tear **5.** shred
   6. tirade **7.** lecture **8.** fragment
   12. dissertation
screen ... **3.** net **4.** hide, laun, mask, sift,
   sort, veil **5.** arras, blind, cloak, pavis,
   shade, sieve, spier **6.** defend, grille,
   riddle, sifter, sorter **7.** conceal, curtain,
   protect, reredos, shelter **8.** parclose
   9. partition, safeguard **10.** protection
   12. discriminate
screw ... **3.** key **4.** coil, turn **5.** horse,
   twist **6.** fasten, gimlet, rotate, spiral
   7. contort, distort, tighten, turnkey
   9. bargainer, propeller, skinflint
   10. contortion, thumbscrew
screwlike ... **6.** spiral **7.** spiroid
scribble ... **6.** doodle, scrawl **7.** scratch
   8. scrabble
scribe ... **5.** clerk **6.** author, jurist,
   lawyer, penman, writer **8.** recorder
   10. amanuensis, cuttlefish, journalist
   13. bibliographer
scriggle ... **5.** twist **6.** squirm **7.** wriggle
   8. curlicue
scrimmage ... **3.** row **5.** fight **6.** tussle
   8. football (term), practice, skirmish,
   struggle
scrimp ... **4.** save **5.** scant, stint **6.** scanty,
   scrape, sparse **7.** sparing **9.** economize
scrip ... **3.** bag **4.** list **5.** money **6.** wallet
   7. writing **8.** document, schedule
script ... **5.** ronde **6.** letter **7.** writing
   8. scenario **10.** manuscript, typescript
   11. handwriting
scriptural ... **7.** written **8.** Biblical,
   orthodox
scriptural interpreter ... **7.** exegete
scripture ... **4.** writ **5.** motto, truth
   7. passage, writing **8.** document
   10. manuscript **11.** inscription **13.** sacred
   writing
Scripture, Scriptures ... **4.** text **5.** Bible
   6. lesson **7.** Oracles, passage, Vulgate
Scripture interpretation ... **8.** exegesis
   12. hermeneutics
scrivello ... **4.** tusk (elephant's)
scrivener ... **6.** notary, scribe, writer
   8. recorder **10.** amanuensis
scroll ... **4.** list, roll **5.** draft **6.** record,

spiral, volute **7.** engross, writing
8. document, inscribe, schedule,
streamer **9.** parchment
scroll roll . . . **8.** makimono
scrub . . . **3.** mop, rub **4.** halt, mean, runt,
tree, wash **5.** abort, clean, dwarf, scour
6. cancel, drudge, paltry **7.** cleanse
8. inferior **10.** undersized
scrubby . . . **4.** base **6.** paltry, shabby,
stubby **7.** bristly, shrubby, stunted
10. underbrush **13.** insignificant
scruff . . . **4.** nape, scum, slur **5.** crust,
dross, scuff **6.** refuse **7.** surface
8. dandruff
scruple . . . **4.** coin **5.** demur, qualm
6. object, weight **9.** small part
10. hesitation **13.** unwillingness
scrupulous . . . **4.** nice **5.** exact **6.** formal,
proper, strict **8.** qualmish **10.** fastidious,
meticulous **11.** punctilious
13. conscientious
scrutinize . . . **3.** eye, pry **4.** scan **5.** probe
7. examine, inspect, observe
scud . . . **4.** dash, foam, gust, rain, sail,
skim **5.** speed **6.** clouds, shower
scuffle . . . **4.** fray **5.** melee **6.** strive,
tussle **7.** contend, contest, shamble,
shuffle **8.** struggle
sculduddery . . . **9.** grossness, obscenity
scull . . . **3.** oar **4.** gull **5.** shoal, skate
6. basket, paddle, propel **7.** rowboat
scullion . . . **4.** base **6.** menial **7.** servant
10. dishwasher, kitchenman
scullog, scullogue . . . **6.** farmer, rustic
7. laborer
sculp . . . **5.** carve **7.** engrave **8.** seal skin
9. engraving, sculpture
sculptor . . . **6.** artist, carver, imager,
molder **8.** chiseler **13.** constellation
19. Apparatus Sculptoris (constellation)
sculptor (famed) . . . **5.** Rodin **7.** Cellini,
Phidias **10.** Praxiteles **12.** Michelangelo,
Saint Gaudens
sculptor's tool . . . **6.** chisel, graver
9. ébauchoir
sculpture . . . **4.** form **5.** carve, model
6. figure, statue **9.** engraving **11.** alto-
relievo
scum . . . **4.** film, foam **5.** cover, dross,
froth, scurf, spume **6.** refuse, scoria
7. coating **8.** riffraff **10.** impurities
scup . . . **5.** bream, porgy
scurrility . . . **5.** abuse **9.** indignity,
obscenity
scurrilous . . . **3.** low **4.** vile **5.** gross
6. vulgar **7.** abusive **8.** indecent,
scurrile **9.** insulting **11.** foulmouthed,
opprobrious
scurry . . . **3.** hie **4.** dash **5.** scoot, speed
6. flurry, hasten **7.** scamper, scuttle
9. skedaddle
scurvy . . . **4.** base, mean **7.** disease
12. contemptible, discourteous
scuttle . . . **3.** hod, run **4.** dish, sink
5. haste, scoot **6.** basket, hasten, scurry,
shovel **7.** octopus, platter **8.** hatchway
10. cuttlefish
scutum . . . **5.** scute **6.** shield
13. constellation (Milky Way)
15. Scutum Sobieskii
Scylla (pert to) . . .

father . . **5.** Nisus
home . . **4.** rock (coast of Italy)
lover . . **5.** Minos
menace to . . **9.** seafarers
Myth . . **7.** monster
transformed to . . **7.** sea bird
scythe . . . **2.** sy (sye) **5.** swath
scythe handle . . . **5.** snath, snead
sea . . . **3.** Red **4.** Aral, Azov, Ross, wave
5. Black, brine, China, ocean, swell,
water **6.** aequor **7.** Caspian **8.** seashore
9. Caribbean
sea (pert to) . . .
adder . . **8.** pipefish **11.** stickleback
anemone . . **5.** polyp
Antarctic . . **4.** Ross
arm . . **4.** gulf, meer, mere **5.** bayou,
firth **7.** estuary
bird . . **3.** auk **4.** erne (ern), gull, smew,
tern **5.** booby, cahow, solan **6.** gannet,
petrel, puffin **9.** albatross **10.** shearwater
comb form . . **3.** mer
cow . . **6.** dugong, rytina (Steller's),
walrus **7.** manatee **8.** sirenian
12. hippopotamus
cucumber . . **7.** trepang
devil . . **9.** angelfish, devilfish
dog . . **4.** seal (Her) **6.** fogdog, sailor
dragon . . **8.** dragonet, sea horse
dread of . . **14.** thalassophobia
duck . . **5.** eider, scaup **6.** scoter
eagle . . **4.** erne (ern) **6.** osprey
ear . . **7.** abalone
eel . . **6.** conger
farer . . **3.** tar **6.** sailor, seaman **7.** mariner
foam . . **5.** froth **9.** sepiolite
10. meerschaum
fowl . . **3.** auk **4.** gull, tern **6.** gannet,
petrel
fox . . **5.** shark
god, deity . . **3.** Lar **5.** Aegir **6.** Triton
7. Neptune, Phorcus, Proteus
8. Poseidon
goddess . . **4.** Nina **5.** Doris **10.** Amphitrite
gull . . **3.** cob, mew **9.** kittiwake
hare . . **7.** mollusk
hen . . **4.** skua **9.** guillemot
hog . . **8.** porpoise
holly root . . **6.** eryngo (eringo)
ladder . . **6.** Jacob's
lion . . **4.** seal
mammal . . **4.** seal **5.** whale **6.** dugong
7. manatee **11.** bladdernose
mouse . . **4.** duck (harlequin) **6.** dunlin
7. annelid
nymph . . **5.** naiad, siren **6.** nereid
7. oceanid
onion . . **6.** squill
otter . . **5.** kalan
owl . . **6.** puffin **8.** lumpfish
pig . . **6.** dugong **7.** dolphin **8.** porpoise
pumpkin . . **8.** cucumber
quail . . **6.** auklet **9.** turnstone
raven . . **7.** sculpin **9.** cormorant
10. squaretail
reference to . . **5.** naval **6.** marine
7. oceanic, pelagic **8.** maritime
9. Neptunian, thalassic
robber . . **6.** jaeger, pirate **7.** corsair
9. buccaneer, privateer
serpent . . **5.** Hydra **8.** snake eel

shell.. **5.** conch
sickness.. **8.** mal de mer **9.** naupathia
spider.. **10.** spider crab
turtle.. **5.** green **9.** hawksbill
  10. loggerhead, thalassian
  11. leatherback
unicorn.. **7.** narwhal
urchin.. **5.** heart **10.** echinoderm,
  Spatangina **13.** cushionflower
wolf.. **4.** seal **6.** pirate **9.** privateer,
  submarine
sea king... **3.** Ler **5.** chief **6.** pirate,
  Viking **7.** Neptune
seal (pert to)...
bearded.. **5.** ursuk **6.** makluk
breeding ground.. **7.** rookery
eared.. **5.** otary
flock.. **3.** pod
fur (fem).. **5.** matka (matkah)
harp (male).. **7.** saddler
leather.. **3.** pin
limb.. **7.** flipper
skin.. **5.** sculp
type.. **3.** fur **7.** sea lion **8.** elephant,
  pinniped
young.. **3.** pup
sealed instrument... **6.** escrow
seam... **4.** line, load, scar **5.** joint, ridge,
  strip **6.** burden, groove, stitch, streak,
  suture **7.** crevice, stratum **9.** horseload
  10. interstice, packsaddle
seaman... **3.** gob, tar **6.** sailor, Seabee
  7. mariner
seaman's chapel... **6.** bethel, church
seamark... **6.** beacon **10.** lighthouse
seamy... **5.** rough **8.** wrinkled
  12. disreputable
séance... **7.** session, sitting **9.** treatment
séance holder... **6.** medium
sear, sere... **3.** dry **4.** burn, cook
  5. parch **6.** braise, scorch, wither
  7. dried up, shrivel **8.** deadened,
  withered **9.** cauterize **10.** threadbare
  11. deteriorate
search... **4.** comb, fish, hunt, look, seek
  5. frisk, ghoom, grope, probe, quest
  6. ferret, forage, survey **7.** inquire,
  ransack, rummage, zetetic **9.** expiscate
  10. scrutinize **11.** investigate
searchlight... **4.** beam **10.** flashlight
seashell... **4.** clam **5.** conch, snail
  7. scallop
season... **3.** age **4.** fall, salt, tide,
  time **5.** devil, inure, spice **6.** flavor,
  mature **7.** qualify **8.** accustom, preserve
  11. acclimatize
season (pert to)...
Astron.. **5.** Aries, Libra **6.** Cancer
  11. Capricornus
Eccl.. **4.** Lent **6.** Advent, Easter
  7. Trinity **8.** Epiphany **9.** Christmas
  11. Whitsuntide
Lent.. **6.** carême
Scot.. **4.** sele
yearly.. **6.** Autumn, Spring, Summer,
  Winter
seasonable... **6.** timely **7.** apropos
seasoning... **4.** sage, salt **5.** spice, thyme
  6. cloves, garlic, pepper **7.** mustard,
  paprika **8.** allspice, estragon, marjoram,
  rosemary, turmeric **9.** condiment

Seasons, goddesses of...
justice.. **4.** Dike
order (Universe).. **5.** Horae
peace.. **6.** Eirene
wise laws.. **7.** Eunomia
seat... **3.** pew **4.** root, site **5.** bench,
  chair, embed, sella, stool **6.** settee,
  settle **7.** install **9.** establish
seat (pert to)...
church.. **3.** pew **6.** sedile
of justice.. **4.** banc
of self.. **3.** ego
on elephant.. **6.** howdah
outdoor.. **6.** exedra
privileged.. **6.** curule
series (one of).. **6.** gradin (gradine)
seaweed... **4.** kelp **5.** algae, dulse, laver,
  varec, wrack **6.** Alaria **8.** agar-agar
secco... **3.** dry
secern... **7.** secrete **8.** separate
  11. distinguish **12.** discriminate
Secessionist (S Carolina)... **5.** Rhett
secluded... **5.** aloof, apart **6.** hidden,
  lonely, remote, secret **7.** private,
  retired **8.** debarred, expelled, isolated,
  recessed, retiring, screened, solitary
  9. cloistral, concealed
seclusion... **7.** privacy, retreat **8.** solitude
  9. aloofness, exclusion **10.** quarantine,
  retirement, separation
second... **3.** aid **4.** abet, back, echo,
  time **5.** jiffy, trice **6.** assist, attend,
  backer, double, moment **7.** instant,
  support, sustain **8.** inferior **9.** assistant,
  encourage, imperfect, prototype,
  reinforce **11.** corroborate, subordinate
second (pert to)...
childhood.. **6.** dotage, dotard **8.** senility
crop.. **5.** rowen
lieutenant.. **9.** shavetail
number.. **6.** addend
person.. **3.** you
rate.. **8.** inferior, mediocre
Republic.. **6.** French (1848-52)
sight.. **6.** myopia **7.** psychic **9.** intuition
  12. clairvoyance
team.. **5.** scrub **9.** Yannigans
thought.. **6.** sequel **12.** afterthought
  15. reconsideration
secondary... **4.** less **5.** minor **6.** deputy
  8. inferior, offshoot **9.** auxiliary,
  dependent, satellite **10.** contingent,
  derivative, second-rate, subsequent,
  substitute **11.** subordinate, unessential
  12. nonessential, quill feather
secondary color... **5.** green **6.** orange,
  purple
secondary school... **4.** prep **5.** lycée
  7. academy **10.** Realschule
secrecy... **4.** tile **6.** hiding **7.** mystery,
  privacy, privity **8.** velation **9.** reticence,
  seclusion **10.** confidence
  11. concealment
secret... **3.** key **4.** dern **5.** close, inner,
  privy **6.** arcane, covert, hidden, mystic,
  occult **7.** arcanum, cryptic, mystery,
  private, unknown **8.** esoteric, intimate
  (armor), reticent, secluded, skullcap
  9. concealed, recondite, secretive,
  underhand **10.** confidence, mysterious
  11. clandestine **12.** confidential

13. surreptitious

secret (pert to) . . .
agent . . **3**. spy **5**. scout **6**. espier **7**. spotter **8**. emissary **13**. undercover man
council . . **5**. by-end, junto **7**. purpose
language . . **5**. argot **7**. dialect
meeting . . **5**. tryst
movement . . **7**. stealth
name . . **9**. cryptonym
place . . **5**. cache **6**. adytum **7**. sanctum **9**. sanctuary
society . . **3**. hui (Chin) **4**. tong **7**. Camorra (It)

secretary . . . **4**. bird, desk **5**. agent **6**. scribe **7**. officer **8**. recorder **9**. confidant **10**. amanuensis, escritoire

secrete . . . **4**. bury, hide, stow **5**. exude **7**. conceal

secretion (pert to) . . .
gland . . **7**. hormone
inflammation . . **3**. pus
liver . . **4**. bile
mammal gland . . **9**. lactation
mouth . . **6**. saliva
nasal . . **10**. secernment
scale, insect . . **3**. lac
shrubs . . **4**. lerp
whale . . **9**. ambergris

secretly . . . **5**. aside, slyly **7**. sub rosa **8**. covertly **9**. not openly **13**. clandestinely

sect . . . **4**. clan, cult, part **5**. Alogi (Hist), class, group, order, party **6**. essene, school, Yezidi (Kurdish) **9**. following, Mennonite **10**. shibboleth (Bib) **12**. denomination

sectarian . . . **7**. heretic **8**. partisan **9**. dissenter, heterodox **13**. nonconformist **14**. denominational

section . . . **4**. area, part, plot **5**. panel, piece, slice, tmema, torso **6**. region **7**. portion, segment, ternion **8**. parabola, surgical **9**. paragraph, signature **11**. subdivision

secular . . . **3**. lay **4**. laic **5**. civil **6**. laical **7**. earthly, profane, worldly **8**. temporal **9**. centuried, temporary

secure . . . **3**. fix, get, pin **4**. bind, easy, fast, firm, moor, nail, safe, tape **5**. fetch, spike, trice (sail) **6**. elicit, ensure, fasten, obtain, stable **7**. acquire, assured, certain, procure, receive **8**. make fast **9**. confident, guarantee **10**. dependable **11**. undisturbed

security . . . **4**. bail, gage **5**. guard **6**. pledge, safety, vadium **7**. defense, shelter **8**. guaranty **9**. guarantee, insurance, stability **10**. protection

sedate . . . **4**. calm **5**. douce, quiet, sober, staid **6**. demure, proper, serene, solemn **7**. serious, settled **8**. composed, decorous **9**. dignified, unruffled **11**. unobtrusive **13**. contemplative, dispassionate

sedative . . . **6**. remedy **7**. anodyne, bromide, chloral, veronal **8**. atropine, barbital, lenitive, soothing **9**. calmative, mitigator, paregoric **10**. palliative, phenacetin **12**. tranquilizer (tranquillizer) **13**. phenobarbital

sedent . . . **7**. sitting (statue)

sediment . . . **4**. lees, silt **5**. dregs **7**. deposit, grounds, siltage **9**. settlings

sedition . . . **6**. revolt, strife, tumult **7**. treason **9**. commotion **10**. dissension, turbulence

seditious . . . **7**. riotous **8**. factious **9**. turbulent **11**. treasonable **15**. insurrectionary

seduce . . . **4**. lure **5**. decoy, tempt **6**. allure, enamor, entice **7**. corrupt, mislead **8**. inveigle

seducer . . . **7**. enticer, tempter **8**. Lothario **9**. debaucher

seduction . . . **5**. charm **10**. allurement, corruption, temptation **11**. debauchment

sedulous . . . **4**. busy **6**. steady **8**. diligent, untiring **9**. assiduous, laborious, unwearied **10**. persistent **11**. persevering, unremitting

see . . . **3**. spy **4**. espy, heed, know, look, scry, seat, view **5**. visit **6**. behold, descry, detect **7**. diocese, discern, witness **8**. discover, perceive **9**. apprehend, interview, visualize **10**. comprehend, understand **11**. contemplate

seed . . . **3**. egg, pip, pit, sow **4**. germ **5**. grain, ovule, plant, sperm, spore **6**. kernel, origin **7**. lineage, progeny **8**. rudiment **9**. beginning **11**. descendants

seed (pert to) . . .
apple . . **3**. pip
aromatic . . **5**. anise **7**. aniseed, caraway
coat . . **3**. pod **4**. aril, burr, husk **5**. testa **6**. carpel **8**. pericarp
container, envelope . . **3**. bur (burr), pod **6**. loment, vessel **7**. capsule
edible . . **3**. pea **4**. bean **5**. grain **6**. lentil
enclosing soft fruit . . **5**. drupe
flower . . **6**. pistil
immature . . **5**. ovule
lemon, orange, apple . . **3**. pip
licorice . . **9**. jequerity
medicinal . . **8**. flaxseed
Moringa, tropical . . **3**. ben
naked (one-seeded fruit) . . **6**. achene (akene)
oak . . **5**. acorn
one-called . . **6**. carpel
part . . **6**. tunica
poppy, opium . . **3**. maw
underground . . **6**. peanut
winged . . **6**. samara

seeds (pert to) . . .
cocoa . . **5**. cacao
feeding on . . **11**. granivorous
perfume . . **8**. abelmosk
rudiments . . **3**. ova **4**. eggs, pips, pits **6**. ovules, sperms

seedy . . . **5**. dingy, lousy, tacky **6**. shabby **7**. worn out **8**. slovenly **10**. spiritless **11**. spawn-filled **12**. bearing seeds

seek . . . **3**. beg **4**. hunt **5**. essay **6**. pursue, search **7**. explore, solicit **8**. endeavor **9**. neologize (new words) **11**. investigate

seeker . . . **6**. prober, tracer **7**. pursuer, zetetic **8**. aspirant, searcher **9**. applicant **10**. petitioner

seeker of . . .
knowledge . . **10**. philonoist

new words .. **9.** neologist
pleasure .. **7.** epicure **8.** hedonist
seem ... **4.** look **6.** appear **7.** pretend
8. resemble
seeming ... **5.** guise, quasi **8.** apparent,
illusion, illusory, pretense, specious
9. befitting
seeming contradiction ... **7.** paradox
seeming truth ... **14.** verisimilitude
seemly ... **3.** fit **4.** meet **6.** comely,
decent, proper, suited **7.** elegant, fitting
8. decorous, tasteful **9.** expedient
seep ... **4.** leak, ooze **5.** exude **6.** filter
8. transude **9.** percolate
seer, seeress ... **5.** sibyl **6.** oracle, scryer
7. Phoebad, prophet **9.** predictor,
visionary **10.** forecaster, prophetess,
soothsayer **11.** Nostradamus
14. prognosticator
seesaw ... **6.** teeter, tilter **7.** pastime
9. alternate, crossruff, fluctuate,
vacillate **11.** oscillation **12.** teeter-totter
seethe ... **4.** boil, stew, teem **5.** be hot,
steep **6.** bubble **7.** be angry
segment ... **3.** pip **4.** part **5.** tmema
6. cantle **7.** portion, section **8.** fragment
12. cross section
segment (pert to) ...
botany .. **5.** tmema **7.** lacinia
corresponding part .. **7.** isomere
curve .. **3.** arc
shaped .. **5.** toric
Zool .. **6.** somite, telson **8.** metamere,
somatome
seine ... **3.** net **5.** trawl **6.** sagene
7. dragnet, network
seism ... **10.** earthquake
seize ... **3.** bag, cly, cop, nab, net **4.** bind,
bite, grab, grip, take, trap **5.** annex,
catch, grasp, ravin, reave, usurp,
wrest **6.** arrest, clutch, collar, fasten,
ravish, snatch **7.** capture, embargo,
grapple **8.** distrain **9.** apprehend, lay
hold of **10.** confiscate, understand
11. appropriate
seizin ... **9.** occupancy **10.** possession
seizing ... **4.** cord **7.** lashing **9.** arresting,
raptorial
seizure ... **3.** fit **4.** grip, hold **5.** spasm
6. arrest, attack, frenzy, seizin
9. ownership **10.** convulsion, occupation
11. manucapture
seladang ... **4.** gaur **7.** buffalo
selah (Bib) ... **4.** sign **5.** pause
select ... **4.** cull, name, pick, take
5. elect, elite **6.** choice, choose,
picked **7.** appoint, pick out, specify
9. exclusive, segregate **10.** registrate
11. distinguish, outstanding
selection ... **5.** piece **6.** choice **7.** analect,
excerpt, passage **10.** collection
11. appointment
selective ... **5.** draft **8.** eclectic
9. exclusive **10.** particular
14. discriminative
self ... **3.** ego, own **4.** same **5.** being
6. person, psyche **7.** oneself
10. individual **11.** personality
self (pert to) ...
acting .. **9.** automatic, voluntary
assertion .. **6.** egoism, vanity

centered .. **7.** selfish **9.** egotistic
10. egocentric **11.** independent **12.** self-
absorbed
comb form .. **4.** auto
complacent .. **13.** self-satisfied
confidence .. **5.** poise **6.** aplomb
9. assurance **11.** self-reliant
contained .. **8.** reserved **10.** controlled,
sufficient (in itself) **11.** independent
15. uncommunicative
control .. **8.** stoicism **9.** restraint
10. automation, discipline, equanimity,
temperance
defense .. **6.** karate, jung fu **7.** jujitsu
determination .. **8.** autonomy
12. independence
enjoyment .. **13.** gratification
esteem .. **5.** pride **6.** vanity **7.** concept,
ego-trip
evident .. **5.** clear **9.** axiomatic
examination .. **13.** introspection,
introspective
French .. **3.** soi
love of .. **6.** egoism
ref to .. **8.** personal
reproach .. **7.** remorse
righteous .. **5.** pious **9.** Pharisaic
13. sanctimonious **14.** holier-than-thou
same .. **9.** identical
satisfied .. **4.** smug **6.** jaunty
Scottish .. **3.** sel (sell)
worship .. **8.** idolatry **9.** autolatry
selfish ... **6.** grabby (sl) **11.** egotistical,
self-seeking **12.** self-centered
sell ... **4.** vend **5.** scalp, trade **6.** barter,
market, retail **7.** auction, bargain
8. convince, exchange, persuade
9. negotiate
sell (out) ... **6.** betray, desert **8.** inform
on **9.** victimize
seller ... **6.** dealer, vender, vendor
7. peddler **8.** merchant, salesman
9. tradesman **10.** saleswoman
semantics ... **8.** meanings
11. semasiology
semblable ... **4.** like **5.** alike **7.** seeming,
similar **8.** apparent, suitable
10. ostensible, resembling
11. conformable
semblance ... **4.** copy, face, form **5.** guise,
image **6.** aspect, figure **7.** pretext,
umbrage **8.** illusion **10.** appearance,
similarity **11.** countenance,
presumption, resemblance
semeiology, semeiotics ... **5.** signs
(signaling) **11.** diagnostics
14. interpretation, symptomatology
semester ... **4.** term **6.** course, period
Seminole chief ... **7.** Osceola (1804--38)
Semitic (pert to) ...
deity .. **4.** Baal
dialect .. **4.** Geez
god (evil) .. **6.** Moloch
language .. **5.** Iraqi **6.** Syrian **7.** Arabian,
Aramaic **8.** Egyptian **11.** Palestinian
people .. **6.** Harari , Shagia (Shaikiyeh)
8. Moabites
semper eadem ... **13.** always the same
(motto of Queen Elizabeth)
semper fidelis ... **14.** always faithful
semper idem ... **13.** always the same

semper paratus ... **11.** always ready
senate ... **5.** boule **7.** council (Rom)
8. assembly **11.** legislature
18. administrative body
send ... **4.** mail, ship **5.** drive, grant,
issue, speed **6.** bestow, convey, export,
launch, propel **7.** forward **8.** dispatch,
transmit **10.** commission
send (pert to) ...
back .. **5.** remit **6.** remand, return
11. reverberate
by different person .. **5.** relay
off .. **5.** start **6.** launch **7.** impulse
8. dispatch **11.** consignment
13. demonstration
out .. **4.** emit, spew **5.** shoot
out rays .. **7.** radiate
payment .. **5.** remit
to an address .. **7.** deliver
Seneca ... **6.** Indian **9.** Iroquoian
Senegal, Africa ...
capital .. **5.** Dakar
ebony .. **9.** blackwood
gazelle .. **5.** korin
gum .. **9.** gum arabic
mahogany .. **9.** cailcedra
native .. **10.** Senegalese
senescence ... **5.** aging **10.** growing old
senicide ... **13.** killing old men (tribal)
senility ... **6.** dotage, old age **8.** caducity,
dementia **10.** feebleness
senior ... **4.** aine, dean **5.** chief, elder
7. ancient, student **8.** superior
senior member ... **5.** doyen
sensation ... **5.** sense **6.** thrill, uproar,
wonder **7.** emotion **8.** rhigosis (cold)
10. perception **12.** great success
sensational ... **5.** lurid **6.** superb
8. dramatic, exciting **9.** emotional
12. melodramatic
sense ... **4.** feel, mind, sane **5.** flair, sight,
smell **7.** feeling, meaning **8.** sapience
9. awareness, intuition, sensation,
sentience **10.** perception, understand
11. discernment, recognition
12. intelligence
senseless ... **5.** inept **6.** insane, stupid,
unwise **7.** fatuous, foolish, idiotic,
inanity **9.** illogical, inanimate, insensate,
unfeeling **10.** irrational **11.** meaningless,
purposeless, unconscious
12. unreasonable **13.** unintelligent
sense of ...
beauty .. **8.** aesthete (esthete), tasteful
9. aesthetic
dignity .. **5.** pride
distance .. **11.** telesthetic
hearing .. **8.** audition **12.** auscultation
humor .. **10.** risibility
sight .. **6.** vision
smell .. **7.** osmatic **9.** olfaction
taste .. **6.** palate
sense organ ... **3.** ear, eye **4.** nose, skin
6. tongue **8.** receptor, sensilla
senses ... **4.** wits **6.** sanity **7.** sensory
9. sensation
sensible ... **4.** sane **5.** aware, privy,
sound **7.** logical, prudent **8.** rational
9. cognizant, practical, sensitive
10. reasonable, responsive
11. intelligent, susceptible

sensitive ... **4.** nice, sore **5.** acute
6. pliant, tender, touchy **7.** sensory
8. sensible **9.** receptive **10.** responsive
11. susceptible **14.** discriminating,
impressionable
sensitivity ... **9.** emotional, hebetated
(blunted) **11.** sensibility **12.** irritability
14. discrimination
sentence ... **4.** doom **5.** maxim, motto
6. phrase, remark, saying **7.** condemn,
passage, thought, verdict **8.** decision,
judgment, proposal **9.** statement
12. condemnation
sentence (pert to) ...
balance .. **7.** parison
clause (concluding) .. **8.** apodosis
concluding .. **8.** epilogue (epilog)
construction .. **6.** syntax
difficult articulation .. **13.** tongue twister
introductory .. **8.** protasis
judicial .. **5.** futwa
pithy .. **5.** motto **8.** aphorism
punishment .. **11.** year and a day
subordinate part .. **6.** clause, phrase
sententious ... **5.** pithy, terse **7.** concise,
laconic **10.** aphoristic **13.** grandiloquent
sentient ... **4.** mind **5.** aware **7.** feeling
8. sensible **9.** conscious, sensitive
10. perceptive **13.** consciousness
sentiment ... **5.** toast **7.** emotion, feeling,
opinion **8.** attitude **10.** perception,
sentimento **11.** sensibility
14. sentimentality
sentimental ... **6.** loving **7.** maudlin,
mawkish **8.** romantic **9.** emotional
13. lackadaisical
sentimental song ... **11.** strephonade
sentinel ... **5.** guard **6.** picket, sentry
7. vedette (mounted) **8.** watchman
10. lookout man, watchtower
sepad ... **5.** think **7.** believe, suppose
sepal ... **4.** leaf **5.** petal
separate ... **4.** open, part, shed, sift, sort
5. alone, apart, sever, space **6.** cleave,
detach, divide, secern, single, sleave,
sunder, winnow **7.** disband, diverge,
diverse, divided, divorce, isolate
8. alienate, discrete, distinct, peculiar,
secluded **9.** disjoined, partition,
segregate, sequester, unrelated
10. dissociate, particular, respective
11. disembodied, unconnected
separate (pert to) ...
Chem .. **11.** fractionate
from others .. **5.** aloof **8.** isolated
metal from ore .. **5.** smelt
thread .. **6.** sleave
separation ... **6.** tmesis **7.** divorce
8. autotomy **9.** partition, secession,
seclusion **10.** alienation **11.** disjunction,
segregation **13.** sequestration
14. discontinuance, discrimination
separatist ... **7.** heretic, seceder
8. apostate **9.** dissenter **12.** secessionist
13. nonconformist
sepia ... **3.** dun, ink **5.** color **7.** pigment
10. cuttlebone, cuttlefish
sepiment ... **5.** hedge **7.** defense
9. enclosure
Sepiola ... **10.** cuttlefish
sepiolite ... **10.** meerschaum

sepoy . . . **7.** soldier **9.** policeman
seps . . . **6.** lizard **7.** serpent
sept . . . **4.** clan **5.** class, seven, tribe
   7. lineage
septic . . . **6.** morbid, pyemia (pyaemia)
   8. diseased, infected, poisoned
   9. gangrened, mortified, poisonous
   10. septicemia (blood poison)
sepulcher, sepulchre . . . **4.** bury, tomb
   5. crypt, grave, vault **6.** entomb
   9. sepulture **10.** repository
sepulchral . . . **5.** urnal **6.** gloomy, hollow
   7. charnel **8.** funereal **9.** deep-toned
sepulchral (pert to) . . .
   chest . . **4.** cist
   mound . . **7.** tumulus
   vault . . **6.** burial **8.** catacomb, monument
   9. interview
sequel . . . **5.** issue **6.** effect, series, upshot
   7. outcome **8.** follow up, sequence,
   sequitur **9.** posterity **10.** succession
sequela . . . **7.** disease (resulting)
   8. adherent **9.** inference **10.** conclusion
   11. concomitant, consequence
   15. morbid condition
sequence . . . **5.** gamut **6.** course (usual),
   series, tierce (three cards) **8.** straight
   10. succession
sequential . . . **9.** deducible, resultant
   10. continuous, succeeding
   11. consecutive
sequestered . . . **6.** lonely, secret
   7. private, recluse, retired **8.** isolated,
   secluded, solitary, withdraw
   9. concealed, separated
   12. unfrequented
sequitur . . . **9.** inference, influence, it
   follows **14.** natural sequent
sequoia, Sequoia . . . **4.** Park (Calif)
   6. Indian (famed for alphabet) **7.** big
   tree, conifer, redwood
seraglio . . . **5.** harem, serai **6.** zenana
   9. enclosure
serape . . . **5.** shawl **7.** blanket
seraph . . . **5.** angel **6.** cherub
seraphic . . . **7.** angelic, sublime
   8. cherubic **9.** unworldly
Serb . . . **4.** Slav **7.** Serbian (Servian)
Serbia, Yugoslavia . . .
   church . . **8.** Orthodox
   conqueror . . **5.** Turks
   hero . . **6.** Dushan, Nemaya (1159)
   queen . . **7.** Natalie
   Revolutionary . . **7.** Chetnik
sere . . . **4.** claw, sear, worn **5.** talon
   6. effete, yellow **8.** withered
   10. desiccated
serenade . . . **4.** sing **5.** music **8.** serenata
   9. charivari, entertain **10.** callithump
   11. celebration
serene . . . **4.** calm, cool **5.** clear, quiet
   6. placid **8.** peaceful, serenity, tranquil
   9. collected, unruffled **11.** undisturbed
   12. tranquillity (tranquility)
serenity . . . **5.** peace **6.** repose
   8. calmness, coolness **9.** composure
   10. quiescence
serf . . . **4.** esne, neif (fem), peon **5.** helot,
   slave **6.** thrall, vassal **7.** captive, villein
series . . . **3.** set **4.** nest **5.** class,
   gamut, group **8.** sequence **9.** seriation

10. succession
series, connected . . . **5.** chain, suite
   6. catena
series of . . .
   discussions . . **9.** symposium
   heroic events . . **4.** epos
   meetings . . **7.** session
   pictures . . **8.** panorama
   races . . **7.** regatta
   rings . . **4.** coil
   six . . **5.** hexad
   steps . . **5.** scale
   syllogisms . . **7.** sorites
   travels . . **7.** odyssey
serious . . . **4.** keen **5.** grave, serio (comb
   form), sober, staid **6.** demure, sedate,
   solemn **7.** capital, earnest, weighty,
   zealous **8.** resolute **9.** important
   10. thoughtful
seriousness . . . **4.** zeal **7.** gravity
   10. importance **11.** earnestness
sermon . . . **4.** talk, text **5.** psalm **6.** homily,
   lesson, preach **7.** address, lecture,
   reproof **8.** harangue **9.** discourse,
   preaching **10.** admonition
seron . . . **5.** crate **6.** hamper **7.** boxwood,
   spanner
serotine . . . **3.** bat **4.** adda **9.** late bloom
serpent . . . **3.** asp **4.** seps (anc) **5.** cobra,
   krait, racer, snake
serpent (pert to) . . .
   deity, of good . . **12.** agathodaemon
   13. agathos daemon
   fabulous . . **5.** Hydra **6.** dragon **8.** basilisk
   11. amphisbaena
   large . . **3.** boa **5.** aboma **6.** python
   8. jararaca
   monster . . **6.** ellops
   Old . . **5.** Satan
   semihuman (Hind Myth) . . **4.** Naga
   sky (Vedic Myth) . . **3.** Ahi
   worshipers (Gnostic) . . **7.** Ophites
serpentine . . . **4.** wily **5.** snaky **6.** subtle,
   zigzag **7.** sinuous, winding **8.** diabolic,
   tempting **9.** snakelike **10.** circuitous,
   meandering
serpigo . . . **8.** ringworm **11.** skin disease
serrano . . . **12.** squirrelfish
serrate . . . **7.** notched, toothed **8.** indented
   10. saw-toothed
serried . . . **5.** dense **7.** compact, concise,
   crowded
serum . . . **4.** whey **5.** blood, fluid **6.** serous
   9. antitoxin
servant . . . **3.** gyp **4.** bata, cook, maid,
   maty, mozo, serf, syce **5.** agent, boots,
   chela, nurse, slave, valet **6.** bildar,
   butler, flunky, garçon, gillie (gilly),
   menial, servus, vassal, wallah (walla)
   7. equerry (nobleman's) **8.** coistrel,
   domestic, handmaid **9.** assistant
   11. chamberlain
servant of God . . . **6.** bishop
serve . . . **2.** do **3.** act, aid **4.** deal, help,
   wait **5.** avail, cater **6.** assist, succor
   7. advance, bestead, forward, further,
   suffice, work for **8.** bear arms, fight for
   9. officiate **10.** administer, distribute
serve (pert to) . . .
   as accomplice . . **4.** abet
   as escort . . **6.** squire

food.. **4.** wait **5.** cater **7.** dish out
one's sentence.. **6.** do time
religion.. **4.** obey **7.** worship
server . . . **4.** tray **6.** player, salver
7. acolyte
Servia . . . see Serbia
service . . . **3.** aid, use **4.** help, mail,
Mass, rite **5.** favor, matin **6.** employ,
ritual **7.** benefit, nocturn, utility
8. ceremony, evensong, kindness,
ministry **9.** servitude **10.** attendance,
employment **12.** ministration
service tree . . . **4.** sorb **5.** rowan
serviette . . . **6.** napkin
servile . . . **4.** mean **6.** abject, menial,
minion **7.** fawning, slavish **8.** cringing,
faithful **9.** dependent, parasitic, truckling
10. obsequious, submissive
11. subservient, sycophantic
Servite . . . **9.** mendicant **13.** Order of
Friars (1233)
servitude . . . **7.** bondage, serfdom,
service, slavery **8.** servitus **9.** vassalage
14. apprenticeship
sesame . . . **3.** oil **4.** herb **5.** benne **7.** gingili
(seed), teel oil **8.** ajonjoli, sesamine
Sesame, Open . . . **10.** magical key
12. magic command (Arab Nights)
sess . . . **4.** heap, pile **9.** soap frame
session . . . **5.** court **6.** séance **8.** assembly
11. legislature
set . . . **3.** lay **4.** form, heal, laid, pose, post
5. brood, class, fixed, group, place,
posit, ready, staid, stand **6.** adjust,
clique, define, fasten, formal, ossify,
series, settle **7.** confirm, congeal,
coterie, station, stiffen **8.** regulate,
solidify **9.** coagulate, designate,
direction, obstinate, stabilize
10. collection, determined, solidified
11. established, prepared for
set (pert to) . . .
afloat.. **6.** launch
against.. **6.** oppose **10.** antagonize
apart.. **5.** allot, elect, taboo **6.** exempt
7. isolate, reserve, seclude **8.** allocate,
separate **9.** segregate, sequester
11. distinguish **13.** differentiate
aside.. **4.** void **5.** annul **6.** except, reject
7. abolish, discard, dismiss, earmark,
exclude **8.** overrule, postpone
at an angle.. **4.** cant
back.. **4.** loss **5.** check **6.** demote,
hinder, recess **7.** relapse **8.** restrain,
slow down
exclusive.. **5.** elect, taboo **6.** clique
fire to.. **6.** ignite, kindle **7.** emblaze,
inflame **8.** irritate
firmly.. **5.** embed, plant, posit **6.** cement,
ossify
forth.. **5.** adorn **6.** depart, expose, lay
out **7.** arrange, commend, display,
enounce, exhibit, explain, expound,
present, promote, propone, publish
8. announce, decorate, indicate,
manifest **9.** translate **10.** promulgate
11. demonstrate
free.. **6.** acquit **7.** absolve, release,
unloose **8.** liberate **10.** emancipate
11. disillusion
off.. **6.** incite, offset **7.** measure

8. beautify, detonate **9.** demarcate,
embellish **11.** distinguish
on firm basis.. **9.** establish
out.. **4.** plot **5.** allot, begin **7.** arrange
right.. **5.** teach **6.** adjust, direct, remedy
11. disillusion
up.. **3.** rig **4.** plan **5.** build, cause, erect,
exalt, hoist, print, raise **7.** elevate,
finance, install **9.** construct, establish
10. inaugurate, prearrange
set (pert to in) . . .
a groove.. **5.** dadoe
a row.. **4.** tier **5.** align, aline, range
columns.. **7.** tabular **8.** tabulate
from margin.. **6.** indent
operation.. **4.** move **5.** start **6.** launch
opposition.. **3.** pit
order.. **5.** align **6.** adjust **7.** arrange
set (pert to of) . . .
eight.. **6.** ogdoad
friends.. **7.** coterie
jeweled ornaments.. **6.** parure
laws.. **4.** code **8.** statutes
on end.. **5.** upend **10.** topsy-turvy
opinions.. **5.** credo
organ pipes.. **5.** stops
rules.. **4.** code
sheets (paper).. **5.** quire
seta . . . **4.** hair **5.** spine **7.** bristle, feather
Seth (pert to) . . .
brother.. **4.** Abel, Cain
father.. **4.** Adam
son.. **4.** Enos
wife.. **8.** Nephthys
setting . . . **5.** scene **6.** locale **8.** mounting,
planting **10.** background
settle . . . **3.** fix, pay **4.** nest, root, seat,
sink **5.** agree, clear, lodge, order, prove,
quiet, solve **6.** assign, assure, decide,
locate, pay off, purify, secure, soothe
7. arrange, clarify, confirm, mediate,
resolve **8.** colonize, ensconce, regulate
9. designate, determine, establish,
reconcile **10.** strengthen **11.** tranquilize
settled . . . **4.** paid **5.** ended, fixed
6. proved, sedate **7.** assured, decided,
located **9.** steadfast **10.** unchanging
11. established
settled in advance . . . **13.** predetermined
settled in mind . . . **10.** equanimity
settlement . . . **3.** dos **4.** camp **6.** colony,
hamlet **7.** payment **8.** fixation, sediment,
showdown **9.** community, endowment
10. adjustment **12.** colonization,
conciliation, satisfaction
13. determination, establishment
Settlement House . . . **9.** Hull House
(Chicago) **10.** University (NY)
11. Toynbee Hall (London)
settler . . . **6.** Sooner (Okla) **7.** pioneer,
planter, Puritan **8.** colonist **9.** immigrant
settlings . . . **4.** lees **5.** dregs **8.** sediment
10. settlement **12.** precipitates
seven (pert to) . . .
angles.. **8.** heptagon **9.** septangle
arts.. **5.** logic, music **7.** grammar
8. geometry, rhetoric **9.** astronomy
10. arithmetic
comb form.. **5.** hepta, septi
days and nights.. **8.** sennight
fold.. **8.** septuple

gods of happiness . . **5.** Ebisu, Hotei
6. Benten **7.** Daikoku, Jurojin
8. Bishamon **10.** Fuku-roku-ju
group . . **6.** heptad, septet **8.** septuple
12. septemvirate
Hills . . **4.** Rome
languages . . **9.** heptaglot
Latin . . **6.** septum
number . . **8.** hebdomad **9.** septenary
Old Test Books (1st seven) . .
10. Heptateuch
Seas . . **11.** world oceans
Stars . . **8.** Pleiades
tones . . **10.** heptachord, heptatonic
seventy . . . **12.** septuagenary
seventy-day period . . . **12.** septuagesima
seventy-year-old . . . **14.** septuagenarian
sever . . . **3.** cut, lop **4.** part, rend **5.** break
6. behead, cleave, detach, divide,
except, exempt **7.** disjoin **8.** accurate,
disunite, separate **9.** interpose,
segregate **10.** decapitate, disconnect,
dissociate **12.** disassociate
several . . . **4.** many **6.** divers, sundry
7. diverse, various **8.** distinct **9.** different
10. respective
severe . . . **3.** bad **4.** dure, hard, keen,
sore, tart **5.** acute, cruel, exact, grave,
harsh, rigid, snell, sober, stern **6.** biting,
bitter, chaste, sedate, simple, solemn,
strict, taxing, trying **7.** arduous, austere,
condign, drastic, extreme, intense,
painful, serious, violent **8.** accurate,
rigorous **9.** draconian, strenuous,
stringent **10.** censorious, restrained
severe critic (of Alexandria) . . .
9. Aristarch
severity . . . **5.** rigor **7.** cruelty **8.** hardness,
pungency, violence **9.** austerity,
exactness, gruffness, harshness,
solemnity, sternness, stiffness
10. bitterness, difficulty, inclemency,
simplicity, strictness **12.** rigorousness
Seville cathedral tower . . . **7.** Giralda
Seville orange . . . **9.** red-yellow **12.** bitter
orange
Sèvres blue . . . **5.** color **9.** bleu de roi,
porcelain **11.** bleu céleste
sew . . . **4.** mend **5.** baste, unite **6.** fasten,
needle, secure, stitch
sewan . . . **5.** beads, money **6.** wampum
sewing . . . **6.** sutile **8.** suturing **9.** stitching
10. needlework
sewing case . . . **4.** etui
sewing machine inventor . . . **9.** Elias
Howe
sexagenarian . . . **13.** a sixty-year-old
sexagesimal . . . **5.** sixty
sexes, common to both . . . **6.** unisex
7. epicene
sexless . . . **6.** neuter **7.** epicene
sextet, sextette . . . **6.** sestet **8.** six parts
10. group of six **13.** six-line stanza
sexton . . . **6.** beetle **7.** sacrist **9.** sacristan
12. underofficer
sextuplet . . . **7.** sestole (sestolet) **8.** six
notes
sha . . . **5.** sheep, urial (oorial)
shabbash . . . **5.** bravo **8.** well done
Shabbath . . . **7.** Sabbath (Jew)
shabbiness . . . **8.** baseness, slovenry

9. seediness
shabby . . . **4.** base, mean, worn **5.** dowdy,
faded, ratty, seedy, tacky, yucky
6. grungy, paltry, ragged, scurvy,
scuzzy, sleazy **7.** outworn, shagrag,
squalid **10.** despicable, ragamuffin,
threadbare **12.** contemptible
shack . . . **3.** coe, hut **4.** husk, plug
5. chase, hutch, tramp **6.** shanty
7. stubble **8.** vagabond **9.** hibernate
shackle . . . **3.** tie **4.** band, bind, bond,
gyve, iron, ring **5.** chain **6.** fetter,
hobble, hogtie, impede, pinion
7. manacle, trammel **8.** restrain
shackled . . . **4.** tied **5.** bound, gyved
6. curbed, ironed **7.** hobbled **8.** fettered,
hampered, hindered, manacled
10. restrained
shad . . . **4.** fish **5.** Alosa **7.** crappie,
mojarra
shade . . . **3.** hue **4.** dull, roof, tint, tone,
veil **5.** ghost, tinge, visor **6.** awning,
canopy, darken, degree, follow, nuance,
screen, shadow, shield, sprite **7.** eclipse,
foliage, parasol, protect, shelter,
umbrage **10.** overshadow, protection
11. adumbration
shade, affording . . . **9.** umbratile
shadow . . . **3.** dim, dog, spy **4.** hide,
tail **5.** cloud, image, umbra **6.** attend,
screen **7.** blacken, conceal, protect,
remains **8.** follower, hanger-on, illusion,
penumbra **9.** adumbrate, detective
10. protection
shadow fighting . . . **9.** sciamachy
shadowless . . . **6.** ascian
Shadrach (pert to) . . .
enemy . . **14.** Nebuchadnezzar
name once . . **7.** Ananias **9.** Hannaniah
one of three Hebrew youths . .
7. Meshach **8.** Abednago, Shadrach
shady . . . **4.** dark **5.** faint, fishy **6.** umbral
7. shadowy **9.** deceitful, dishonest,
underhand **10.** indistinct, unreliable
12. questionable
shaft . . . **3.** pit, rod **4.** axle, fust, mine, orlo
(part), stem, tige, tole **5.** arrow, scape,
shank, spire, stalk, thill, tower, trunk
6. column, tongue **7.** feather, missile,
obelisk **8.** monument **9.** flagstaff
shag . . . **3.** nap **4.** hair, mane, pile
5. chase, dance **6.** follow, rascal
7. tobacco **9.** cormorant, make rough
10. blackguard
shaggy . . . **5.** bushy, furry, nappy, rough
6. ragged **7.** hirsute, unkempt, villous
8. confused (of thought), uncombed
10. unpolished
shagrag . . . **6.** ragged, tagrag **7.** unkempt
8. rascally
shake . . . **3.** jar, jog, wag **4.** jolt, rock,
stir, sway, toze **5.** swing, trill **6.** dither,
dodder, quiver, shimmy, shiner,
weaken **7.** agitate, flutter, shingle,
shudder, tremble, tremolo **8.** enfeeble
10. earthquake
Shakespeare (pert to) . . .
actor . . **4.** Ward **7.** Gielgud, Olivier,
Sothern **8.** Modjeska
called . . **10.** Bard of Avon
character, female . . **6.** Juliet, Portia

7. Ophelia 9. Cleopatra
character, male . . 5. Romeo, Timon
6. Antony, Hamlet 7. Macbeth, Othello
8. Falstaff
forest . . 5. Arden
river . . 4. Avon
site . . 6. Verona 8. Elsinore
villain . . 4. Iago
wife . . 12. Anne Hathaway
shaky . . . 6. infirm, wabbly, wobbly
7. fearful, nervous, unsound 8. agitated,
unsecure 9. tottering, trembling,
uncertain, unsettled 10. precarious,
unreliable 12. questionable
shale . . . 4. rock 5. flake, scale 8. dandruff
Shalimar Gardens . . . 6. Lahore
shallow . . . 5. shoal 6. lagoon (lagune)
7. cursory, trivial 9. depthless, frivolous,
insincere 11. superficial
sham . . . 3. ape 4. fake, hoax, mock
5. dummy, false, fraud, trick 6. deceit,
humbug 7. feigned 8. pretense
9. imitation, imposture, pretended
Shamash (pert to) . . .
centers of worship . . 5. Larsa 6. Sippar
consort . . 3. Aya (Ai)
deity (Babylon) . . 6. sun god
messenger . . 6. Bunene
Sumerian equivalent . . 3. Utu (Utug)
6. Babbar
shame . . . 5. abash 7. mortify 8. disgrace,
dishonor 9. humiliate 11. abomination,
humiliation, impropriety
shameful . . . 4. mean, vile 5. gross
6. wicked 8. flagrant, improper,
indecent, infamous, terrible
9. degrading 10. outrageous,
scandalous 11. disgraceful, ignominious
12. dishonorable, disreputable,
vituperative
shameless . . . 6. arrant, brazen
8. immodest, impudent 9. audacious
10. unblushing 11. brazenfaced
shammer . . . 8. impostor
shanghai . . . 6. abduct, to drug
9. slingshot
shank . . . 3. leg 4. crus, gamb (gambe)
7. meat cut 12. travel on foot
shape . . . 4. bend, form, mold (mould),
plan 5. frame, model 6. adjust,
create, cut out, design, devise,
figure 7. arrange, conform, contour,
develop, fashion, incline 8. phantasm
10. appearance, figuration
11. arrangement
shaped like a . . .
comb . . 9. pectinate
shield . . 7. peltate, scutate
strap, thong . . 6. lorate
urn . . 9. urceolate
shapeless . . . 7. lumpish 8. deformed,
formless 9. amorphous, contorted,
distorted, unshapely
shapely . . . 3. fit 4. neat, trim 6. comely,
gainly 10. well-formed 11. symmetrical
16. well-proportioned
shapes (ornamental, garden) . . . 5. topia
7. topiary
share . . . 3. cut, lot 4. dole, part 5. enter,
quota 6. ration 7. partake, portion
8. take part 9. allowance, apportion

11. co-operative, participate
sharecropper . . . 7. metayer
shark . . . 5. fraud 6. lawyer 8. parasite,
swindler 9. trickster
shark (fish) . . . 4. gata, mako, tope
5. lamia (cub), Rhina 6. Galeos, Galeus,
requin 7. dogfish, tiburon 8. man-
eater, Mustelus, Selachii, sharklet,
Squatina 9. porbeagle 10. Carcharias,
hammerhead 11. Carcharodon,
Galeorhinus
shark-clinger . . . 4. pega 6. remora
sharp . . . 4. acid, curt, edgy, keen, tart
5. acerb, acrid, acute, alert, brisk,
crisp, edged, harsh, quick, smart,
steep, witty 6. abrupt, astute, bitter,
crafty, shrill 7. angular, caustic,
cutting, nipping, painful, pointed,
pungent, sharper 8. incisive, poignant
9. penetrant, sagacious, sarcastic,
trenchant 10. discerning, proficient
11. acrimonious, penetrating, well-
dressed
sharp (pert to) . . .
answer . . 6. retort
blow . . 4. slap
cornered . . 7. angular
edged . . 5. arris
flavor . . 4. tang
make . . 10. cacuminate
pointed . . 5. acute
saw . . 8. titmouse
Scot . . 5. snell 6. snelly
sighted . . 4. keen 6. astute 7. lyncean
sound . . 4. ping
Tuesday . . 13. Shrove Tuesday
witted . . 6. shrewd 10. discerning
11. intelligent
sharpen . . . 3. nib, ted 4. edge, hone,
whet 5. grind, point, strop 6. acuate
7. enhance, quicken 9. intensify
10. cacuminate
sharper . . . 5. cheat, knave, rogue
6. keener 8. deceiver, swindler
9. trickster
shatter . . . 5. blast, break, crash, smash,
split 8. splinter
shave . . . 3. cut 4. pare 5. cheat, strip
6. cut off 7. swindle, tonsure 9. cut
prices, thin slice
shaver . . . 3. boy, lad 4. tool 5. cheat
6. barber 8. swindler 9. youngster
11. extortioner
shavetail . . . 4. mule 6. ensign
10. lieutenant
shawl . . . 5. manta 6. serape 7. paisley
8. cashmere
Shawnee (pert to) . . .
chief . . 8. Tecumseh
Indian people . . 9. Algonquin
location (present) . . 8. Oklahoma
sheaf . . . 4. kern, omer 6. bundle 7. cluster
11. hyperpencil
shear . . . 3. cut 4. clip, snip, trim 5. sever
6. fleece, remove 7. scissor, whittle
shears . . . 5. lewis 6. forfex 8. secateur
sheatfish . . . 4. wels 7. catfish
sheath . . . 4. case 5. forel (book), glove,
ocrea, theca 6. sleeve, spathe 7. stipule
8. scabbard
sheathe . . . 4. wrap 5. cover, drape

6. encase **7.** envelop **8.** enshroud
sheave . . . **5.** wheel **6.** pulley **9.** back
water, eccentric
shebang . . . **6.** affair, boodle, outfit
7. concern **11.** contrivance
13. establishment **14.** kit and caboodle
she-cat . . . **4.** elle **9.** grimalkin
shed . . . **3.** hut **4.** abri, cote, lair, molt
5. hovel, scale, spill **6.** effuse, hangar,
lean-to, slough **7.** cottage, diffuse,
radiate, shelter
shed (light) . . . **4.** glow **7.** explain, radiate
10. illuminate
shedding . . . **7.** ecdysis (Zool), molting
sheen . . . **5.** glint, gloss, shine **6.** luster
7. glitter, shimmer **8.** splendor
9. shininess **10.** brightness
sheep . . . **3.** ewe, ram, sha, teg, tup
4. buck, lamb, Ovis, zenu **5.** bidet,
dumba, oudad **6.** argali, cosset,
gimmer, hogget, mutton, sheder,
wether **8.** ruminant, shearhog, yeanling
9. blackface
sheep (pert to) . . .
cry . . **3.** baa **5.** bleat
disease . . **3.** coe, gid, rot **4.** bane **5.** braxy
7. anthrax
faced . . **3.** shy **7.** bashful **8.** sheepish
female . . **3.** ewe, teg **6.** sheder
flock leader . . **10.** bellwether
fold . . **3.** ree **4.** cote **5.** kraal, reeve,
stell **6.** church
head . . **5.** jimmy **8.** powsowdy
headed . . **5.** silly **6.** stupid **12.** simple-
minded
kidney extract . . **5.** renes
laurel . . **6.** Kalmia
leg wool . . **4.** gare
male . . **3.** ram, tup **4.** buck **5.** heder
6. wether
owner's mark . . **4.** smit **6.** ruddle
pet . . **6.** cosset
sheeplike . . **5.** ovine **9.** tractable
skin, leather . . **4.** pelt, roan **5.** basil
7. chamois, diploma **8.** woolfell
stealing . . **7.** abigest
tick . . **3.** ked
wild . . **3.** sha **4.** Ovis **5.** urial **6.** aoudad,
argali, bharal, nayaur **7.** bighorn,
mouflon (moufflon) **9.** Thian Shan
(Marco Polo's)
sheep, breeds . . . **6.** Merino, Romney
7. Cheviot, Delaine, Dishley, Karakul,
Suffolk, Targhee **8.** Cotswold, Dartmoor
9. Kerry Hill, Leicester, Southdown,
Teeswater **10.** Corriedale, Dorset
Horn, Oxford Down, Shropshire
13. Hampshire Down
sheepish . . . **3.** shy **5.** timid **7.** bashful
9. chagrined
sheeplike . . . **5.** ovine
sheer . . . **4.** mere, pure, thin, turn **5.** brant,
steep, utter **6.** abrupt, swerve **7.** deviate,
unmixed **8.** absolute **9.** deviation,
downright, undiluted **10.** completely,
diaphonous **11.** transparent
13. perpendicular
sheet . . . **4.** leaf, rope, sail **5.** paper
6. shroud **9.** cover with, duodecimo
(12-fold), newspaper, sheathing
sheik, sheikh . . . **4.** Arab **5.** chief **6.** prince

shelf . . . **4.** berm (berme), reef, sell
5. ledge, shoal **6.** mantel **7.** stratum
8. postpone, put aside
shell . . . **3.** pod **4.** boat, bomb, husk
5. conch, crust, shard, shuck **6.** cowrie
(cowry) **7.** bombard, capsule, grenade,
missile **8.** carapace, exterior, shrapnel
9. cartridge **10.** projectile
shell (pert to) . . .
button source . . **5.** troca **6.** lorica, mucket
cone . . **7.** admiral
ear . . **7.** abalone
explosive . . **3.** dud **4.** bomb **7.** grenade
fish . . **4.** clam, pipi **6.** cockle, limpet,
mussel, oyster **7.** abalone, lobster,
mollusk, scallop **8.** barnacle **9.** trunkfish
fossil . . **8.** ammonite
game . . **10.** thimblerig **13.** sleight of
hand
marine . . **6.** cowrie (cowry)
money . . **5.** hawok, sewan, uhllo (ulo)
6. cowrie, wampum
out . . **4.** give **6.** expend, pay out
protective . . **6.** lorica
ridge . . **4.** lira **5.** varix
seaweed . . **8.** frustule
spiral . . **5.** chank, whelk **8.** caracole
trumpet (Triton's) . . **5.** conch
shelter . . . **3.** lee, pad **4.** abri, camp,
cote, digs, port, roof, shed, skug,
tent **5.** condo, cover, haven, house,
hutch, shack, shade **6.** asylum,
burrow, dugout, hangar, harbor,
refuge, screen, shield **7.** defense,
hospice, pillbox, protect, retreat
8. mantelet (mantlet), quarters, security
9. coverture, sanctuary **10.** protection
sheltered side . . . **3.** lee **4.** alee **7.** leeward
shelve . . . **5.** slope, table, waive **6.** retire
7. dismiss, incline **8.** postpone, put
aside **10.** pigeonhole
Shem (pert to) . . .
brother . . **3.** Ham
descendant . . **6.** Semite
father . . **4.** Noah
son . . **3.** Lud **4.** Aram, Elam
shenanigan . . . **7.** foolery **8.** trickery,
zaniness **9.** horseplay **10.** hanky-panky
11. monkeyshine
shend . . . **3.** mar **4.** harm, ruin **5.** spoil
6. injure, revile **7.** destroy, stupefy
8. confound, disgrace, reproach
Sheol . . . **4.** Hell **5.** Aralu, grave, Hades
6. the pit, Toppet **7.** Abaddon, Gehenna
10. underworld **11.** nether world
14. abode of the dead
shepherd . . . **5.** guide **6.** direct, escort,
feeder, herder, pastor, shadow
8. guardian, herdsman **9.** clergyman
shepherd, shepherds (pert to) . . .
band of . . **10.** pastoureau
dog . . **5.** sheep **6.** collie
flute . . **7.** musette **9.** flageolet
god . . **3.** Pan
pipe . . **3.** oat **4.** reed **7.** larigot
spider . . **13.** daddy longlegs
staff . . **4.** Kent **5.** crook
sheriff (pert to) . . .
aide . . **5.** posse
deputy . . **6.** elisor **7.** bailiff
jurisdiction . . **9.** bailiwick

sheriffdom . . **10.** shrievalty

sherry . . . **5.** jerez, Xeres **7.** oloroso
8. montilla

Shetland Island (pert to) . . .
fishing grounds (deep-sea) . . **4.** haaf
kingdom of . . **8.** Scotland
land, fee simple . . **4.** udal
promontory . . **4.** noup
Supreme Court Pres . . **4.** foud
viol . . **3.** gue

shewbread, showbread (Bib) . . . **6.** ritual
10. unleavened

shibboleth (Bib) . . . **4.** mode **5.** habit
6. saying, slogan **9.** criterion,
watchword **11.** peculiarity (speech)

shield . . . **3.** écu **4.** boss, umbo **5.** aegis
(egis), armor, cover, pavis, pelta,
scute, shade, shell, targe (anc)
6. defend, scutum, target **7.** defense,
protect, shelter **8.** insignia **9.** protector
10. escutcheon, protection

shield (pert to) . . .
Athena's . . **5.** aegis (egis)
bearer . . **8.** escudero
border . . **4.** orle **7.** bordure
emblem . . **7.** impresa
French (anc) . . **8.** rondache
heraldry . . **4.** enté **6.** points
part . . **4.** enté, orle, umbo
Roman . . **6.** scutum
sacred . . **6.** ancile (Rom)
shaped . . **7.** peltate, scutate **8.** aspidate

shift . . . **4.** eddy, fend, jibe, move,
ruse, stir, tack, veer **5.** shunt, smock,
trick **6.** baffle, change, device, rustle
7. deviate, pretext, quibble **8.** artifice,
mutation, transfer **9.** deviation,
expedient, fluctuate, vacillate
10. conversion, subterfuge
12. redistribute **13.** transposition

shifty . . . **6.** crafty, tricky **7.** devious,
evasive, furtive **9.** deceitful, makeshift
10. changeable **11.** treacherous

shill, shillaber (circus term) . . . **5.** decoy
8. employer, hanger-on **10.** accomplice

shillalagh, shillalah . . . **4.** club **6.** cudgel
7. sapling

shilly-shally . . . **8.** hesitate **9.** vacillate
10. hesitation, indecision **11.** vacillation

Shiloh . . . **4.** town (anc) **6.** Seilun (modern)
9. sanctuary (the ark) **10.** battle site
(Tenn)

shimmy . . . **5.** quake **6.** quiver **7.** chemise,
tremble, vibrate **9.** jazz dance, vibration

shin . . . **5.** climb, tibia **6.** cnemis **7.** foreleg

shindy . . . **3.** row **4.** lark, orgy, riot,
romp **5.** dance, party, revel, spree,
wince **6.** frolic, uproar **9.** wassail
8. carousal **9.** commotion, festivity
11. merrymaking

shine . . . **3.** ray **4.** beam, beek, star
5. excel, gloss, prank **6.** polish
7. furbish, glisten, glister, glitter,
radiate, splurge **8.** rutilate **9.** irradiate

shiner . . . **6.** bruise **8.** black eye
9. bootblack **10.** dollarfish

shingle . . . **4.** sign, wood **6.** hairdo
7. haircut, overlap **8.** chastise, coiffure,
detritus **9.** signboard

shining . . . **5.** aglow, lucid, nitid, shiny
6. glossy, lucent **7.** beaming, glowing,

radiant **8.** luminous, lustrous, nitidous,
rutilant, splendid **9.** refulgent
10. glistening, glittering **11.** illustrious,
irradiating, resplendent

Shinto (pert to) . . .
adherent . . **9.** Shintoist
cult . . **8.** Japanese
deity . . **8.** Hachiman
temple . . **3.** sha **5.** jinja (jinsha) **7.** yashiro
temple gateway . . **5.** torii
temple deity . . **5.** Jinja (Jinsha)

shiny . . . **5.** nitid, sleek **6.** bright
7. radiant, shining **8.** luminous, nitidous
9. unclouded

ship . . . **3.** ark **4.** lade, load, send
5. liner, tramp **6.** argosy, vessel
7. freight, steamer **9.** freighter, transport
10. watercraft

ship (pert to) . . .
abandoned . . **8.** derelict
apparatus . . **5.** crane, davit, winch
7. bollard, capstan **8.** windlass
Argonaut's . . **4.** Argo
armored . . **7.** carrack, cruiser
9. destroyer, submarine
attendant . . **7.** steward
auxiliary . . **4.** dory, life **6.** dinghy (dingy),
tender
biscuit . . **8.** hardtack **10.** pilot bread
cabin . . **6.** saloon **9.** stateroom
cargo . . **5.** oiler **6.** tanker **7.** oreboat
11. supertanker
deck . . **4.** main, poop **5.** orlop, upper
deck, cut down . . **5.** razee
deserter . . **3.** rat
duck shooting . . **4.** skag
flat bottom . . **4.** keel **5.** barge
fleet . . **6.** armada
invoice . . **8.** manifest
jail . . **4.** brig
kitchen . . **6.** galley **7.** caboose
Levantine . . **4.** saic
loader . . **9.** stevedore **12.** longshoreman
Mediterranean . . **5.** xebec **6.** galiot
(galliot) **7.** polacre
officer . . **4.** mate **6.** purser **7.** steward
9. boatswain (bosun)
one-masted . . **5.** sloop
part . . **4.** brig, keel, skeg **5.** stern, waist
6. bridge, rudder **8.** binnacle, taffrail
permit to enter . . **8.** pratique
platform (boarding) . . **9.** gangplank
privateer . . **10.** brigantine
prow . . **5.** prore (Poet)
quarters . . **5.** berth **8.** steerage
10. forecastle (fo'c's'le)
record . . **3.** log
rope . . **4.** line **6.** hawser **7.** halyard,
lanyard, painter, ratline
sailing . . **4.** bark (barque), dhow, proa,
saic **5.** ketch, sloop, xebec **6.** caique,
cutter, galley, lugger **7.** Geordie,
pinnace, polacre
side . . **3.** lee **4.** port **9.** starboard
three-oar bank . . **7.** trireme
twin-hulled . . **9.** catamaran
two-oar bank . . **6.** bireme
Venetian . . **9.** frigatoon
voyage record . . **3.** log
war . . **3.** sub **7.** cruiser, flattop
9. destroyer, submarine

11. dreadnaught
window . . **4.** port **8.** porthole
worm . . **5.** borer **6.** teredo
ship, famed . . . **4.** Nina **5.** Maine,
Pinta **6.** Bounty **7.** Monitor, Titanic
8. Clermont, Half Moon, Merrimac
9. Mayflower **10.** Golden Hind, Santa
Maria **12.** Constitution (Old Ironsides)
15. Bonhomme Richard
shipment . . . **5.** cargo **7.** carload
shippage . . . **3.** fee **4.** levy **8.** shipping
shipshape . . . **3.** nef (clock) **4.** neat, tidy,
trim **7.** orderly
shipwreck, cargo overboard . . .
6. jetsam **7.** flotsam
shire . . . **5.** horse **6.** county **8.** district,
province **11.** subdivision
shirk . . . **4.** duck, pike **5.** avoid, dodge,
evade, slink **7.** goof off **9.** fainaigue
(finagle)
shirker . . . **5.** piker **6.** truant **7.** quitter,
slacker **8.** embusqué **10.** malingerer
shirt . . . **4.** polo, sark **6.** blouse, camisa,
cilice, skivvy, T-shirt **8.** pullover
shiver . . . **5.** quake, shake **6.** be cold
7. shatter, shudder, tremble, vibrate
8. fragment **11.** trepidation
shivering . . . **4.** cold **6.** creepy **7.** nervous,
shaking **8.** fragment **9.** agitation,
twitching **10.** chilliness
shoal . . . **3.** bar **4.** bank, reef, spit **5.** crowd,
flock **6.** throng **8.** sand bank (shallow)
9. multitude
shock . . . **3.** jar **4.** blow, heap (grain),
jolt, stun **5.** appal, brunt, bushy (hair),
shake, stack, start **6.** appall, impact,
offend, stroke, trauma **7.** disgust,
horrify, startle, terrify **8.** calamity,
frighten, paralyze **9.** collision, electrify
10. concussion
shock absorber . . . **7.** cushion, snubber
shocking . . . **3.** bad **5.** awful, lurid
6. horrid **7.** ghastly, hideous **8.** horrible,
terrible **9.** appalling, frightful, offensive,
revolting, startling **10.** abominable
shoe (pert to) . . . **4.** boot, clog, geta, mule,
pump **5.** horse, moyle, sabot, scuff
6. ballet, bootee, brogan, buskin, gillie,
loafer, Oxford, patten, planch (planche),
sandal, secque **7.** chopine, rullion,
slipper, sneaker, talaria **8.** moccasin,
sabotine, solleret **10.** clodhopper
shoe (pert to) . . .
form . . **4.** last, tree
grip . . **5.** cleat
lace . . **3.** tie **5.** aglet (aiglet), lacet
6. lacing **7.** latchet **8.** bootlace
10. shoestring
maker . . **5.** sutor **7.** cobbler, Crispin
(patron saint) **8.** zapatero
part . . **3.** cap **4.** rand, vamp, welt **6.** insole
7. counter **9.** inner sole
shoebill, shoebird . . . **5.** stork
shoemaker's patron saint . . . **7.** Crispin
shogun . . . **5.** chief, title (Jap) **6.** tycoon
7. shikken
shoneen . . . **4.** snob **5.** toady
shoot . . . **3.** rod **4.** bine, dart, film, fine,
hunt, kill, plug, twig, weft **5.** bough,
craps, eject, gemma, plant, scion,
snipe, spear, sprig, throw, tuber, vimen

6. branch, sprout, stolon **7.** execute,
project **9.** discharge **10.** descendant,
photograph
shooting (pert to) . . .
fish . . **10.** archer fish
iron . . **6.** pistol **7.** firearm **8.** revolver
match . . **3.** tir **5.** skeet
objective . . **6.** target
star . . **5.** comet **6.** meteor **7.** cowslip
shop . . . **4.** mart **5.** burse, store **6.** market,
saloon **7.** atelier **8.** boutique, emporium
shopping mania . . . **9.** oniomania
shore . . . **4.** bank, prop **5.** beach,
coast, marge, playa **6.** rivage, strand
7. support **9.** foreshore, waterside
10. run aground, waterfront
shore (pert to) . . .
bird . . **3.** ree **5.** snipe **6.** avocet, curlew,
plover, wading **9.** Limicolae
inhabiting . . **8.** littoral
pine . . **4.** sand **8.** tamarack **9.** lodgepole
10. hack-me-tack
recess . . **3.** bay **4.** cove **5.** bayou, inlet
short . . . **4.** curt, rude **5.** brief, brusk,
scant, terse **6.** abrupt, scanty **7.** curtate,
friable, summary **8.** abridged, succinct
12. insufficient
short (pert to) . . .
and pointed . . **5.** terse
and stout . . **5.** dumpy **6.** stocky, stodgy
8. roly-poly, thickset
essay . . **5.** tract
legged . . **8.** breviped
letter . . **4.** chit
lived . . **9.** ephemeral
stop . . **5.** delay, pause **7.** respite
8. interval **9.** cessation
shortage . . . **4.** want **6.** ullage
10. deficiency **13.** insufficiency
shorten . . . **3.** bob, cut, lop **4.** clip, dele,
dock **5.** elide **6.** lessen, reduce, reef in
7. abridge, curtail **8.** condense, contract,
decrease, hold back **9.** decurtate
10. abbreviate
shortening a syllable . . . **7.** systole
shorthand . . . **5.** Gregg **6.** Pitman
8. Tironian (Rom) **11.** stenography
12. brachygraphy, speed writing
shortly . . . **4.** soon **6.** curtly, not
far **7.** harshly, quickly **8.** abruptly
9. presently
shortsighted . . . **4.** dull **6.** myopic, obtuse
8. purblind **11.** nearsighted
Shoshone Indian . . . **3.** Ute **4.** Hopi
5. Piute **7.** Bannock **8.** Comanche
shot . . . **4.** dram **5.** carom, speed **6.** birdie,
bullet, gamble, pellet, ruined **7.** gunfire,
missile, worn out **8.** marksman,
unnerved **9.** discharge **10.** detonation,
photograph, projectile **11.** dilapidated,
vaccination
shoulder . . . **5.** carry, shelf **6.** épaule
7. meat cut, scapula, support
8. buttress, omoplate
shoulder (pert to) . . .
armor . . **9.** épaulière
badge, ornament . . **7.** epaulet
blade . . **7.** scapula **8.** omoplate
comb form . . **3.** omo **6.** humero
inflammation . . **6.** omitis **7.** omalgia
of a road . . **4.** berm (berme)

reference.. **7.** humeral **8.** scapular
shout... **3.** cry **4.** call, hoop, hoot, root, yell **5.** cheer **7.** acclaim **8.** applause, laughter
shouting... **6.** clamor, crying **7.** calling, hooting, yelling **9.** bellowing
shove... **4.** push **5.** drive, eject, elbow **6.** propel, thrust
shovel... **4.** peel, spud **5.** scoop, skeet, spade **7.** scooper **8.** strockle **10.** antler part
show... **4.** lead **5.** movie, prove, revue, teach **6.** cinema, escort, evince, reveal **7.** betoken, display, divulge, exhibit **8.** evidence, indicate, instruct, manifest **11.** demonstrate **13.** demonstration
show (pert to)...
case (glass).. **7.** vitrine
deference.. **3.** bow **6.** salaam
disapproval.. **3.** boo **4.** hiss, pout
house.. **4.** hall **5.** odeum, opera **6.** circus **8.** coliseum, showboat
musical.. **5.** revue
off.. **6.** flaunt **10.** grandstand
of learning.. **6.** pedant
pompous.. **6.** parade **7.** display, pageant **9.** cavalcade **10.** exhibition
to a seat.. **5.** guide, usher **6.** escort **7.** conduct
up.. **6.** appear, arrive, attend, expose
shower... **4.** bath, give, rain **6.** abound **8.** sprinkle
shower of meteorites... **6.** Leonid (from Leo) **9.** Andromede
showing...
animal remains.. **6.** zootic
care.. **9.** attentive, regardful **11.** considerate
display.. **10.** exhibition **12.** presentation
envy.. **9.** invidious
first.. **8.** premiere
good judgment.. **6.** astute **8.** sensible
showy... **3.** gay **4.** arty, loud **5.** gaudy **6.** flashy, garish, sporty, tinsel **7.** pompous **8.** gorgeous, splendid, striking **9.** sumptuous **12.** ostentatious **13.** grandiloquent
shred... **3.** rag **4.** snip **5.** piece, strip **6.** sliver, tatter **7.** vestige **8.** fragment, particle
shrew... **3.** erd **4.** tana **5.** satan, scold, Sorex, vixen **6.** mammal, migale, tartar **7.** Blarina, outcast, villain **9.** scoundrel, termagant, Xanthippe
shrewd... **3.** sly **4.** cagy, foxy, sage, wily **5.** acute, canny, harsh, sharp, smart, stern **6.** artful, astute, biting, clever, crafty **7.** cunning, knowing, practic, sapient, subtile **8.** shrewish **9.** sagacious **10.** discerning **11.** penetrating, sharp-witted **13.** perspicacious
shrewdness... **6.** acumen **9.** smartness **10.** craftiness
shriek... **3.** cry, yip **4.** yell **5.** laugh **6.** holler, outcry, scream **7.** screech
shrievalty... **7.** sheriff (office of)
shrill... **4.** keen, pipy **5.** acute, clear, sharp **6.** biting, squeak **7.** screech **8.** piercing, strident **11.** high-pitched, penetrating
shrimp... **4.** pink **5.** dwarf, prawn

7. artemia **8.** crevette **10.** crustacean
shrine... **3.** box **4.** case, tomb **5.** altar, chest **6.** chapel, temple **8.** monument **9.** holy place, reliquary **10.** receptacle
shrine (pert to)...
ancient.. **4.** naos
Buddhist.. **4.** tope **5.** stupa **9.** Amaravati
India.. **6.** dagoba (dagaba) **7.** chaitya
Mecca.. **5.** Kaaba (Caaba) **11.** Great Mosque
secret, of goddesses.. **9.** anaktoron
shrink... **5.** cower, parch, quail, rivel, wince **6.** blench, cringe, flinch, huddle, recoil **7.** dwindle, shrivel **8.** contract, draw back **9.** constrict **10.** depreciate
shrinking... **3.** coy, shy **5.** timid **6.** afraid **9.** recoiling, sensitive **10.** withdrawal **11.** contraction
shrivel... **3.** age, dry **5.** parch, wizen **6.** shrink, wither **11.** deteriorate
shroud... **4.** cowl, hide, mask, veil, wrap **5.** cloak, cover, sheet **6.** clothe, screen **7.** conceal, curtain, foliage, protect **8.** cerement **9.** cerecloth **12.** graveclothes
Shrove (pert to)...
cake.. **7.** pancake
Sunday.. **13.** Quinquagesima
tide.. **9.** pre-Lenten (3 days)
Tuesday.. **9.** Mardi gras **10.** Pancake Day
shrub... **4.** bush **5.** plant (woody) **6.** frutex **8.** beverage
shrub (pert to)...
Adam's needle.. **5.** yucca **9.** lady's comb
Arabian tea, narcotic.. **3.** kat
aromatic.. **3.** tea **4.** mint, sage **5.** thyme **6.** Aralia **7.** jasmine (jasmin) **8.** lavender, rosemary
Asian.. **5.** musky **8.** abelmosk
cherry.. **6.** Prunus **7.** Cerasus **12.** laurocerasus
Chinese.. **6.** Kerria
climbing.. **5.** grape, liana, Vitis **8.** Bignonia, clematis **14.** trumpet creeper
creeping.. **5.** pyxie
dogwood.. **6.** aucuba, Cornus
evergreen.. **3.** box, yew **4.** ilex, moss, titi **5.** erica, heath, pyxie, salal, savin **6.** laurel, myrtle **7.** jasmine, juniper **8.** camellia, oleander **9.** mistletoe
flowering.. **5.** lilac **6.** azalea, laurel **7.** spiraea, syringa **10.** mignonette
fragrant.. see *aromatic (above)*
Hawaiian.. **5.** akala
Mexican.. **7.** guayule **9.** coyotillo
New Zealand.. **4.** tutu **6.** myrtle **8.** ramarama
ornamental.. **8.** hawthorn
parasitic.. **9.** mistletoe
pea.. **5.** broom
pepper.. **4.** kava **8.** kavakava
poisonous.. **4.** tutu **5.** sumac
prickly.. **5.** Rubus **6.** smilax **8.** barberry, dewberry **9.** raspberry **10.** blackberry
S America.. **5.** ceibo
tropical.. **4.** sida, titi **5.** henna **7.** lantana **8.** Oacaceae, tamarisk **10.** frangipani (frangipane)

shrunken ... **4.** lank, thin **5.** dried
  6. shrunk, wasted **8.** puckered, withered
  9. atrophied, shriveled
shudder ... **4.** grue **5.** abhor, dread,
  quake **6.** agrise, loathe, quiver, shiver,
  tremor **7.** frisson, tremble
shuffle ... **3.** mix **5.** scuff, shift **6.** huddle,
  juggle, riffle **7.** confuse, evasion,
  quibble, scuffle **10.** equivocate **12.** walk
  slovenly
shuffle off ... **5.** evade, shirk **6.** put off
  7. push off **10.** mosey along (sl)
shun ... **5.** avoid, evade, evite **6.** eschew
  10. escape from **11.** keep clear of
  12. cold shoulder
shut ... **3.** bar **4.** stop **5.** close **7.** close
  in, exclude **8.** prohibit
shut (pert to) ...
  in .. **3.** hem **5.** embar **6.** fenced,
  hemmed **7.** bottled, confine, impound,
  invalid, recluse **8.** confined, enclosed
  10. surrounded
  out .. **3.** ban, bar **6.** defeat **7.** exclude,
  lockout, occlude **8.** obstruct, preclude,
  prohibit
  up .. **3.** dam, end **4.** cage, pent
  5. close, mewed, pen in **6.** refute
  7. confine, enclose **8.** conclude,
  imprison **9.** terminate
shutter ... **3.** lid **4.** gate **5.** blind **6.** screen
  7. seclude **8.** jalousie **9.** diaphragm
shuttle ... **5.** train **6.** looper, weaver
  7. type bar **9.** alternate, vacillate
  10. oscillator **11.** money drawer
shy ... **3.** coy, mim **4.** wary **5.** aloof,
  dodge, throw, timid **6.** demure,
  modest, recoil, shrink **7.** bashful,
  evasive, fearful, quibble, rabbity
  8. hesitant, reserved, retiring, secluded,
  sheepish, skittish **9.** diffident, reluctant,
  shrinking **10.** shamefaced, unassuming
  11. distrustful, unobtrusive
Shylock (pert to) ...
  character in .. **16.** Merchant of Venice
  coin .. **5.** ducat
  daughter .. **7.** Jessica
  famed as .. **6.** usurer **11.** money lender
  12. extortionist
  friend .. **5.** Tubal
shyness ... **7.** coyness, reserve **8.** timidity
  10. diffidence **11.** bashfulness
Siam ... **8.** Thailand
Siamese (pert to) ...
  group .. **3.** Kui, Lao
  temple .. **3.** wat
  twins .. **9.** pygopagus (joined at spine)
  11. Chang and Eng
sib ... **4.** akin **6.** allied **7.** kinsman, related
  (by blood)
Siberia ... see also *Siberian*
  city .. **7.** Irkutsk **11.** Novosibirsk
  conqueror .. **9.** Timafeyev **11.** Genghis
  Khan
  government .. **7.** Russian
  gulf .. **2.** Ob (Arctic)
  Mongoloid .. **6.** Tartar
  mountains .. **4.** Ural **5.** Altai
  people .. **5.** Yakut **6.** Tartar (Tatar)
  7. Samoyed **9.** Mongolian
  plain .. **6.** steppe, tundra
  river .. **2.** Ob, Om **4.** Lena **5.** Vitim

6. Abakan **7.** Yenisei
squirrel .. **7.** miniver
storm .. **5.** buran
Siberian (pert to) ...
  antelope .. **5.** saiga
  hunters, fishers (people) .. **6.** Giliak
  (Gilyak)
  mammal .. **5.** sable
  sled dog .. **7.** Samoyed
  squirrel fur .. **7.** calaber (calabar)
  swamp .. **5.** urman
  tent .. **4.** yurt (yurta)
  windstorm .. **5.** buran (bura)
sibilate ... **4.** hiss, lisp **8.** aspirate
sibling ... **5.** child
Sibyl (Gr) ... **6.** oracle **7.** seeress
  10. prophetess **13.** fortuneteller
Sibylline Books (3) ... **7.** oracles
  16. prophetic sayings (BC)
sic ... **4.** thus
siccity ... **7.** aridity, drought, dryness
sice ... **3.** six (dice) **8.** sixpence
Sicilian Vespers (pert to) ...
  Bull (anc) .. **8.** Phalaris
  massacre of .. **6.** French (1282)
Sicily ...
  aborigines .. **6.** Sicani
  anc name .. **9.** Trinacria
  capital .. **7.** Palermo **8.** Syracuse (anc)
  composer .. **7.** Bellini
  harbor .. **7.** Palermo
  port .. **7.** Messina
  island .. **6.** Lipari (group) **11.** Pantelleria
  river .. **4.** Acis
  secret society .. **5.** Mafia
  volcano .. **4.** Etna **7.** Vulcano **9.** Stromboli
  whirlpool .. **9.** Charybdis
sick ... **3.** ill, sad, wan **4.** pale **5.** weary
  6. sickly, unwell **9.** disgusted, nauseated
  10. indisposed
sick (pert to) ...
  be .. **3.** ail
  deathly .. **5.** amort **7.** à la mort, fatally
  10. terminally
  flag .. **6.** yellow **10.** quarantine
  headache .. **8.** migraine
  of .. **7.** tired of **8.** satiated **9.** disgusted
  person .. **7.** patient **9.** aegrotant
  terms .. **3.** bay **7.** hospice **8.** syndrome
  9. infirmary **10.** dispensary **13.** intensive
  care
  worker .. **5.** nurse **11.** nursekeeper
sicken ... **4.** tire **5.** weary **6.** impair,
  weaken **7.** afflict, depress, surfeit
  8. languish **10.** impoverish
sickly ... **4.** pale, sick, weak **5.** faint
  6. ailing, feeble, infirm, weakly
  7. languid, mawkish **8.** diseased
  9. unhealthy
Siddhartha, Siddhattha ... **6.** Buddha
side ... **4.** face, team, wall **6.** behalf,
  border, region **7.** faction, lateral,
  support, surface **9.** declivity
side (pert to) ...
  board .. **5.** table **6.** buffet **8.** dressoir,
  whiskers
  by side .. **8.** parallel
  ditch .. **6.** escarp
  drum .. **5.** snare
  hog (salted) .. **6.** flitch
  kick .. **3.** pal **7.** comrade, partner

9. assistant 11. confederate
left.. 4. port 8. larboard
long.. 7. lateral, oblique, sloping
 8. indirect, slanting
meat.. 5. bacon 8. salt pork
of head.. 6. temple
of triangle.. 3. leg
on the side.. 5. apart
sheltered.. 3. lee 4. alee 8. windless
sidewalk salesman.. 8. pitchman
step.. 4. duck 5. dodge, evade, hedge
 6. astral, starry 7. quibble
view.. 7. profile
ways, wise.. 7. athwart, lateral
 9. laterally, obliquely
whiskers.. 9. sideburns 10. sideboards
windy.. 4. port 9. starboard
sidereal ... 6. astral, starry 7. stellar
 9. celestial
sidero (comb form) ... 4. iron
siderography ... 14. steel engraving
siderology (science of) ... 4. iron
sides, unequal ... 7. scalene
sidle ... 4. cant, edge, skew, tilt 7. advance
 (furtive)
siècle ... 3. age 7. century
siècle d'or ... 9. Golden Age
siege ... 7. besiege 8. assieger 9. besetting
 11. besiegement 12. wearying time
 13. beleaguerment
Siegfried (pert to) ...
hero of.. 5. opera (Wagner's)
slayer.. 5. Hagen
sword.. 7. Balmung
wife.. 9. Kriemhild
Sierra Leone ...
capital.. 8. Freetown
lingua franca.. 4. Krio
people.. 5. Mende, Temne
Sierra Nevada fog ... 7. pogonip
Sierra poet ... 13. Joaquin Miller
siesta ... 3. nap 4. lull, rest 6. cat nap,
 midday, snooze 10. forty winks
sieve ... 3. lue 4. bolt, sift, sile 5. purée
 6. bolter, filter, riddle, semmet, sifter,
 sorter, strain 7. dilluer 8. strainer
 9. segregate, separator
sievelike ... 8. cribrate
Sif (Norse), (pert to) ...
goddess of.. 4. home
wife of.. 4. Thor
sift ... 3. lue 4. bolt 5. sieve 6. dredge,
 filter, riddle, screen, sorter, winnow
 7. refiner 8. cribrate
sigh ... 3. sob 5. mourn, sithe, yearn
 6. bemoan, bewail, exhale, grieve,
 lament 7. deplore 10. lament over
 11. suspiration
sight ... 3. see 4. espy, gaze, view
 5. scene, sense 6. behold, descry,
 vision 7. discern, display 8. aperture
 10. exhibition 11. observation
sight (pert to) ...
acuteness of.. 7. oxyopia
come into.. 4. loom 5. issue
disorder.. 7. anopsia 8. paropsis
imaginary.. 6. vision
offensive.. 7. eyesore
out of.. 5. range 6. absent 8. vanished
 9. invisible 10. exorbitant
 11. disappeared

second.. 3. ESP 7. psychic
sigil ... 4. seal 5. image (magic), stamp
 8. sigillum 9. signature 11. endorsement
sigmoid ... 3. ess 5. curve 9. intestine
sign ... 3. cue, nod 4. code, hire,
 mark, neon, omen 5. token, trace
 6. emblem, engage, intone, motion,
 notice, signal, symbol 7. endorse,
 execute, insigne, portent, presage,
 symptom, vestige, warning 8. evidence,
 password 9. semaphore, subscribe,
 watchword 10. forerunner, indication,
 underwrite 11. countersign
 13. advertisement, constellation
sign (pert to) ...
astrological.. 5. Aries 6. Gemini, Pisces,
 Taurus 8. Aquarius 9. Capricorn
 11. Sagittarius
briefly.. 7. initial
by the same.. 8. likewise, moreover
 11. accordingly
diacritical.. 5. tilde 7. cedilla
language.. 11. dactylology
music.. 5. presa
off.. 8. withdraw 10. Yours truly
 11. discontinue
ref to.. 5. semic 7. semeion
representing a word.. 8. logogram
spiritual.. 9. sacrament
up.. 4. join 6. enlist 8. register
zodiac.. see *astrological (above)*
signal ... 3. cue 4. code, fire, flag,
 sign 5. alarm, flare, token 6. beacon,
 emblem, notify, wigwag 7. eminent,
 lantern, notable, warning 8. striking
 9. memorable, prominent, semaphore,
 watchword 10. lighthouse, remarkable
 11. communicate, conspicuous
 13. extraordinary
signal (pert to) ...
aviator's.. 5. roger
danger, warning.. 4. bell 5. alert, fusee
flag.. 6. ensign, wigwag
night.. 6. beacon, curlew, pharos
 10. lighthouse
preceding taps.. 6. tattoo
railroad.. 5. fusee 9. semaphore
signature ... 4. mark, sign, visa (vise)
 5. prima, sigil, stamp 6. signum
 9. autograph 11. endorsement
signed by writer ... 9. onomatous (opp
 of anonymous)
signet ... 4. mark, seal 5. sigil, stamp
 9. signature 10. impression
 11. endorsement
significance ... 6. import, moment,
 weight 7. anagoge, meaning
significant ... 4. sign 5. token 6. symbol
 7. ominous 8. sinister 9. important,
 momentous 10. expressive, indicative,
 meaningful, portentous, suggestive
 13. consequental
signification ... 6. import 7. meaning
 10. indication 11. consequence
 12. notification 13. comprehension,
 specification
signify ... 4. hint, mean, sign 5. imply,
 utter 6. denote, import, matter, signal
 7. betoken, connote, declare, specify
 8. announce, evidence, foreshow,
 indicate, intimate, manifest

11. communicate
signum . . . **4.** bell (tower), mark, sign
  5. cross **9.** signature
sika . . . **4.** deer
sike . . . **4.** rill **5.** brook, ditch, gully
  6. ravine, stream, trench
sikhara, sikhra . . . **5.** tower (pyramidal)
silage . . . **4.** feed **6.** fodder **9.** pasturage,
  provender
Silas (pert to) . . .
  Bib . . **7.** prophet **8.** Silvanus
  character . . **4.** Wegg
  companion of . . **4.** Paul (Bib)
  novel . . **11.** Silas Marner
sile . . . **3.** fry **4.** beam, drip, drop, fall,
  flow, pass, pour, sink, skim **5.** cheat,
  cover, glide, sieve, spawn **6.** betray,
  filter, strain, stream **7.** conceal, deceive,
  herring (young), subside **8.** strainer
silence . . . **3.** gag **4.** hush, kill, lull, mute,
  rest **5.** quiet, shush, still, tacet **6.** defeat,
  muffle **7.** confute, repress, secrecy
  8. oblivion, preclude, restrain, suppress
  9. eliminate, stillness **10.** silentness
  11. taciturnity **13.** noiselessness, tacit
  omission
silent . . . **3.** mum **4.** mute, tace **5.** quiet,
  still, tacet, tacit **8.** reserved, reticent,
  taciturn **9.** soundless **10.** speechless
  11. unexpressed **15.** uncommunicative
silhouette . . . **6.** shadow **7.** contour,
  outline, picture, profile **9.** delineate,
  hourglass
silica . . . **4.** opal **5.** silex
silicate . . . **4.** mica **8.** calamine, wellsite
silk (pert to) . . .
  ancient . . **6.** Mantua, sendal
  artificial . . **5.** nylon, rayon
  Assam . . **4.** eria
  black . . **5.** crape (mourning), crepe
  brown . . **4.** muga **6.** tussah
  corded . . **6.** faille **7.** Ottoman
  embroidery thread . . **5.** floss **8.** arrasene
  fiber . . **5.** floss
  gland . . **9.** serictery
  gland of . . **7.** spiders **9.** silkworms
    11. insect larva **12.** caterpillars
  gold . . **4.** tash **6.** samite **7.** brocade
  heavy . . **4.** crin
  kind of . . **5.** China, crepe, moiré, ninon,
    satin, surah, tabby, tulle **6.** pongee,
    tobine, tussah **7.** taffeta
  lining . . **8.** sarcenet (sarsenet)
  muslin . . **16.** mousseline de soie
  raw . . **8.** marabout
  rustle of . . **6.** scroop
  source . . **6.** cocoon
  thin, glossy . . **7.** alamode
  thread (for velvets) . . **4.** tram (trame)
  unspun . . **6.** sleave
  upholstery . . **7.** tabaret
  waste . . **4.** noil **6.** strass
  watered . . **5.** moiré
  yarn . . **4.** tram **7.** schappe
  yarn size . . **6.** denier
silken . . . **5.** seric, silby, sleek, suave
  6. gentle, smooth, tender **7.** elegant
  8. delicate, lustrous, silklike **9.** luxurious
  10. effeminate **12.** ingratiating
silkworm (pert to) . . .
  Assam . . **3.** eri **4.** eria

China . . **6.** pernyi **9.** Ailanthus
cocoon . . **4.** clew
disease . . **7.** pebrine
genus (moth) . . **6.** Bombyx
India . . **6.** tussah
Japan . . **7.** yamamai
silky . . . **4.** soft **5.** quiet **6.** glossy, smooth
  8. delicate **9.** sericeous **11.** filamentary
  12. ingratiating
silky fabric . . **6.** barège
sill . . . **4.** base, beam, seat, sile **5.** basis
  6. timber **9.** threshold **10.** foundation
silly . . . **3.** mad **4.** daft, fond **5.** anile, apish,
  dazed, dense, inane **6.** dottle, simple
  7. asinine, fatuous, foolish, shallow,
  trivial **9.** brainless **10.** indiscreet
  12. simple-minded
silver . . . **2.** Ag **4.** gray **5.** metal, money,
  plate, white **6.** argent **7.** bullion
  8. argentum, eloquent, metallic, sterling
silver (pert to) . . .
  alchemy . . **4.** luna **6.** occamy
  alloy . . **6.** billon
  ball . . **4.** pome
  coin . . **6.** tester
  containing . . **5.** lunar
  German . . **6.** albata
  gilded . . **7.** vermeil
  ingots . . **5.** sycee
  jackal . . **9.** silver fox
  lace (with gold) . . **5.** orris **8.** filigree
  leaf . . **4.** foil **8.** hardhack **9.** hydrangea,
    jewelweed **12.** buffalo berry
  oak . . **11.** flannelbush
  tongued . . **7.** musical **8.** eloquent
  uncoined . . **7.** bullion
silversides . . . **5.** smelt **6.** minnow
  12. silver salmon
Silver State . . . **6.** Nevada
silverware . . . **5.** vases **6.** dishes
  8. flatware **9.** ornaments, tableware
silvery . . . **7.** frosted, musical **8.** lustrous,
  metallic **9.** argentine
simian . . . **3.** ape **6.** monkey **7.** apelike
similar . . . **4.** akin, like, such **5.** alike
  7. uniform **8.** analogic **9.** analogous
  11. homogeneous
similarity . . . **7.** analogy **8.** likeness
  11. homogeneity, resemblance
  13. approximation
simile . . . **8.** allegory, metaphor
simper . . . **5.** smirk **10.** silly smile
  13. affected smile
simple . . . **4.** easy, mere **5.** naive
  6. dorian, oafish **7.** artless **8.** innocent
  9. ingenuous **10.** elementary **11.** open
  and shut **15.** unsophisticated
simpleton . . . **3.** ass, daw, oaf **4.** boob,
  dolt, dupe, fool, gaby, gawk, gump,
  simp, zang **5.** dunce, goose, idiot, ikona,
  moron, Simon, yokel, zombi **6.** dawkin,
  gander, nitwit **7.** half-wit **8.** Abderite
  9. greenhorn **10.** nincompoop
  11. Simple Simon
simplicity . . . **6.** purity **7.** modesty, naiveté
  9. clearness, ignorance, innocence,
  plainness, rusticity **10.** homeliness,
  humbleness, simpleness **11.** gullibility,
  informality **13.** ingenuousness
  14. unaffectedness
simplify . . . **7.** clarify, explain, expound

9. elucidate, interpret

simply . . . **5.** alone, truly **6.** barely, easily, merely, purely, really, solely **7.** plainly **10.** informally

simulate . . . **3.** act, ape **4.** sham **5.** feign **6.** affect, assume **7.** imitate **11.** counterfeit

simulated . . . **4.** aped, sham **5.** acted **7.** assumed, feigned, shammed **9.** pretended **10.** fictitious

simurgh, simurg (Myth) . . . **3.** roc **12.** gigantic bird

sin . . . **3.** err **4.** evil, vice **5.** crime, error, guilt, wrong **6.** felony, heresy **7.** offense **8.** iniquity, peccancy **9.** deviation **10.** immorality, wickedness **11.** misdemeanor **13.** transgression

Sinai (pert to) . . .
famed for . . **5.** Moses **15.** Ten Commandments
location . . **6.** Red Sea **11.** Gulf of Aqaba (Akaba)
mountain (Bib) . . **5.** Horeb **6.** Serbal **9.** Catharine, Umm Shomer

sinapis . . . **7.** mustard

sinawa . . . **10.** Ceylon hemp

sinay bean . . . **8.** rice bean

since . . . **2.** as **3.** ago, for **4.** ergo, gone, past, syne **5.** hence, later **7.** already, because, whereas **8.** inasmuch, until now **9.** therefore, thereupon **10.** seeing that **11.** considering **12.** subsequently

sincere . . . **4.** open, pure **5.** frank **6.** candid **7.** correct, earnest, genuine, intense, unmixed, upright, zealous **9.** authentic, unfeigned, veracious **10.** unaffected **11.** unvarnished **13.** unadulterated **15.** straightforward

sincerity . . . **4.** zeal **6.** candor **7.** honesty **10.** heartiness **11.** genuineness, sincereness

sincerity symbol . . . **8.** amethyst

sind . . . **5.** rinse **6.** drench, quench **7.** rinsing

Sind (Ind) . . .
capital . . **7.** Karachi
ibex . . **8.** wild goat
prince . . **5.** ameer

Sindbad's bird . . . **3.** roc

Sindbad the Sailor . . . **9.** character (Arabian Nights)

sindico . . . **7.** trustee **8.** assignee, receiver

sine . . . **7.** without

sinew . . . **4.** thew **5.** nerve, power **6.** muscle, string, tendon

sinewy . . . **4.** firm, wiry **5.** thewy, tough **6.** brawny, strong **7.** fibrose, stringy **8.** powerful, vigorous

sinful . . . **3.** bad **4.** evil **5.** wrong **6.** wicked **7.** vicious **10.** iniquitous **11.** unrighteous

sing . . . **3.** hum, say **4.** hymn, lilt **5.** carol, chant, croon, yodel **6.** intone, warble **7.** rejoice **8.** proclaim, vocalize **9.** celebrate

sing (pert to) . . .
exultantly . . **4.** lilt **7.** chortle **10.** cheerfully
jovially . . **5.** troll
off key . . **4.** flat
or whistle . . **7.** tweedle
shrilly . . **4.** pipe
softly . . **5.** croon

sorrowfully . . **7.** despond **8.** complain
Swisslike . . **5.** yodel
with trills . . **6.** warble **7.** roulade

singe . . . **4.** burn, sear **6.** scorch **8.** discolor

singer . . . **4.** bard, bird, diva, poet **5.** blues, siren, tenor, torch **6.** cantor, hymner **7.** caroler, crooner, warbler, yodeler **8.** minstrel, songster, vocalist **9.** chanteuse, descanter **10.** cantatrice, prima donna **11.** minnesinger

Singhalese tree . . . **4.** poon **5.** domba

singing (pert to) . . .
birds . . **6.** Oscine
canary . . **10.** white whale
fish . . **8.** toadfish
group . . **5.** choir **6.** chorus
Memnon . . **9.** Amenhotep (statue)
ref to . . **5.** melic

single . . . **3.** ace, odd, one **4.** lone, only, sole, unit **6.** simple, unique **8.** sporadic **9.** unmarried

single (pert to) . . .
algebra . . **6.** nomial
comb form . . **3.** uni
odd . . **7.** azygous
racing term . . **4.** heat
tones (one of two) . . **10.** monotonous

singleness . . . **5.** unity **8.** celibacy **9.** sincerity, unmarried

singly . . . **4.** once, only, solo **5.** alone, apart **6.** simply **8.** uniquely **9.** severally **12.** individually, particularly, single-handed

singular . . . **3.** odd **4.** each, rare, sole, unit **5.** queer **6.** unique **7.** eminent, special, strange, unusual **8.** peculiar, separate, uncommon **9.** eccentric, fantastic, whimsical **10.** individual, remarkable, unexampled **11.** exceptional **12.** unparalleled **13.** extraordinary, unprecedented **14.** characteristic

singularity . . . **6.** oddity **7.** oddness, oneness **8.** peculiar **11.** peculiarity **12.** eccentricity **13.** individuality **15.** distinctiveness

Sinic . . . **7.** Chinese, Sinitic

sinister . . . **4.** evil, grim, left **7.** adverse, corrupt, ominous **9.** dishonest, injurious, malicious, underhand **10.** disastrous, portentous **11.** unfortunate

sinistral . . . **7.** baneful **10.** left-handed **12.** illegitimate, inauspicious (opp of dextral)

sink . . . **3.** age, bog, dip, ebb, sag **4.** cave, drop, fall, mire, sump **5.** drain, droop, lapse, lower, quail **6.** cavity, deject, engulf, go down, recede, settle, sicken, weaken **7.** decline, depress, descend, despond **8.** decrease, diminish, submerge **10.** degenerate

sinuous . . . **4.** wavy **7.** winding **9.** deviating, intricate **10.** circuitous

Sioux (pert to) . . .
division . . **5.** Teton **6.** Santee
famed as . . **8.** warriors
people . . **3.** Oto (Otoe) **4.** Crow, Iowa **5.** Omaha, Osage **6.** Dakota, Plains **9.** Winnebago

sip . . . **3.** lap, sup **4.** gulp **5.** drink, quaff, taste **6.** tipple

sircar . . . **5.** ruler **6.** master **7.** servant
8. province (Mogul) **10.** government
sire . . . **5.** beget
siren . . . **5.** alarm, Circe, deity, lurer, vixen
7. charmer, enticer, foghorn, Lorelei,
mermaid **9.** bewitcher, Cleopatra,
temptress
Sirenia . . . **6.** dugong, mammal
7. manatee **14.** Steller's sea cow
siriasis . . . **9.** sunstroke
Sirius . . . **4.** star **7.** Dog Star **10.** Canis
Major, dog of Orion (Gr Myth)
sissy . . . **5.** softy **6.** prissy, sister
10. effeminate, pantywaist
11. mollycoddle
sister . . . **3.** kin, nun, sib **5.** nurse, soror
sisterhood . . . **4.** nuns **8.** sorority
Sistrurus . . . **11.** rattlesnake
sit . . . **3.** fit **4.** isle, loll, pose, rest **5.** brood,
perch, press, roost, squat **6.** repose
7. convene **8.** incubate
site . . . **4.** ruin, seat **5.** place, scene, venue
6. locale, locate **8.** location, position
site of Taj Mahal . . . **4.** Agra (Ind)
sitting . . . **4.** seat **6.** séance, sedent
7. posture, sessile, session
10. incubation **11.** convocation
situated . . . **3.** lie, set **4.** case, seat **5.** fixed
6. clutch, placed, plight **9.** ensconced,
stationed **11.** established
situated (pert to) . . .
at back . . **6.** astern **7.** postern **9.** posterior
at base . . **5.** basal
between folds . . **11.** interplical
in middle . . **6.** medial, median
on left hand . . **9.** sinistrad
on right hand . . **6.** dexter
situation . . . **3.** job **4.** case, post
5. place, situs, state **6.** office, plight
7. station **8.** locality, location, position
9. condition, placement
situation (pert to) . . .
approximate . . **11.** whereabouts
difficult . . **6.** scrape **7.** dilemma
8. quandary **9.** imbroglio
11. predicament **12.** circumstance
doomed . . **7.** rattrap
favorable . . **7.** vantage
Latin . . **5.** situs
perplexing . . **6.** strait
three choices . . **8.** trilemma
Siva, Shiva (pert to) . . .
consort . . **3.** Uma **4.** Devi
dancer . . **8.** Natajara
god, deity . . **8.** Hinduism **9.** Destroyer
title . . **8.** Mahadeva
trident . . **6.** trisul (trisula)
six (pert to) . . .
balls (Medici) . . **5.** palle
dice number . . **4.** sice
eyed . . **9.** senocular
feet of earth . . **5.** grave
fold . . **8.** sextuple
footed . . **7.** hexaped **9.** hexapodal
group . . **5.** hexad
lines . . **6.** sestet **7.** sextain
pence . . **6.** bender **7.** fiddler
pert to . . **6.** senary
pointed figure . . **4.** star
square . . **9.** hexagonal
sixty, sixties . . . **5.** cycle, saros **7.** numeral

size . . . **3.** cap **4.** area, bulk, pica,
pope, pott **5.** agate, grade **6.** adjust
7. arrange, measure, portion **8.** classify
9. magnitude **10.** gargantuan
11. measurement
sizzle . . . **3.** fry **4.** hiss **5.** speed **7.** be
angry **10.** effervesce
sjambok . . . **4.** flog, whip
skate . . . **3.** jag, ray (fish) **4.** plug, skim
5. glide, horse, scull, spree
skean . . . **4.** dirk **6.** dagger
skedaddle . . . **4.** bolt, flee, flit **6.** scurry
7. run away, scamper
skein . . . **3.** rap (120 yds), web **4.** hank,
yarn **6.** thread **7.** spireme **12.** flight
of fowl
skelder . . . **5.** cheat **7.** vagrant
9. panhandle
skeleton . . . **4.** cage **5.** bones, frame,
mummy **6.** sketch **7.** contour, diagram,
outline **8.** thinness **9.** framework
skeleton (pert to) . . .
at the feast . . **7.** kill-joy **10.** wet blanket
11. crapehanger
English dialect . . **4.** reme
framework . . **5.** cadre
in the closet . . **4.** evil **6.** secret
13. mortification
key . . **6.** master
marine animal . . **6.** sponge
polyp . . **5.** coral
skeptic, sceptic . . . **7.** doubter, infidel
8. aporetic **10.** Pyrrhonist, unbeliever
11. freethinker, irreligious, nullifidian
skeptical, sceptical . . . **8.** doubtful,
doubting **11.** incredulous, unbelieving
sketch . . . **3.** jap, jot **4.** draw, idea, limn,
plan, skit **5.** draft, trace **6.** apercu,
design **7.** diagram, drawing, outline
8. esquisse, treatise **9.** delineate
11. delineation, description
sketchy . . . **5.** rough, vague **10.** unfinished
skewer . . . **3.** pin, rod **5.** truss **6.** fasten,
pierce **9.** brochette
skid . . . **4.** clog, shoe, slip, trig **5.** brake,
check, slide **7.** travois **8.** sideslip
skiff . . . **4.** boat, skim **5.** canoe, glide,
graze **6.** caique **7.** rowboat **11.** slight
touch
skill . . . **3.** art **5.** craft, knack **6.** gifted,
talent **7.** ability, address, aptness,
cunning, finesse, mastery **8.** aptitude,
deftness, facility **9.** adeptness, dexterity,
expertise, readiness, smartness
10. adroitness, cleverness, proficient
11. proficiency
skilled . . . **5.** adept **6.** expert **7.** endowed,
trained **8.** talented **10.** conversant,
proficient
skilled (pert to) . . .
in government . . **9.** statesman
in mechanics . . **5.** sloyd
in strategy . . **7.** finesse
skillful, skilful . . . **3.** apt **4.** able, deft, fine
6. adroit, clever, crafty, daedal, expert
7. capable **8.** artistic, dextrous, tactical
9. daedalian, dexterous, ingenious
10. proficient, well-versed
12. accomplished
skim . . . **4.** flit, sail, scan, scud **5.** glide,
graze, scoon, skirr **6.** slight **8.** pass

over

skin ... **4.** bark, derm, fell, flay, hide, pare, peel, pelt, rind, scum **5.** cheat, cutis, derma, fraud, scalp **6.** fleece, lamina, scrape **7.** callous, cuticle, defraud, swindle **8.** covering, tegument **9.** epidermis **10.** integument **11.** decorticate

skin (pert to) ...
animal .. **4.** coat, hide, pelt **7.** pellage
animal's neck fold .. **6.** dewlap
beaver .. **4.** plew
comb form .. **4.** derm **5.** derma
decoration .. **6.** tattoo
destitute of .. **8.** apellous
disease .. **4.** acne **5.** hives, mange, uredo **6.** eczema, herpes, tetter **8.** ringworm **9.** urticaria
drying frame .. **5.** herse
dryness .. **7.** xerosis
fawnskin (of Dionysus) .. **6.** nebris
fold .. **5.** plica **6.** dewlap
fruit .. **7.** epicarp
gobbler's throat .. **3.** tar
layer .. **5.** cutis, derma
layer, outer .. **7.** epicarp
opening .. **4.** pore
pert to .. **6.** dermal **7.** dermoid
piece .. **5.** blype
pigment, excess .. **8.** melanism
protuberance .. **4.** mole, wart
salting bin .. **5.** kench
squirrel .. **4.** vair
tan .. **3.** taw
tanned .. **5.** suede
unsheared .. **8.** woolfell

skinflint ... **5.** cheat, miser **9.** bargainer
skink ... **4.** adda **6.** lizard
skinned ... **6.** bested **7.** euchred, fleeced
skinned (pert to) ...
dark .. **7.** melanic, swarthy
pert to .. **5.** bared **7.** denuded **8.** stripped
slang .. **7.** euchred, fleeced
thick .. **9.** pachyderm **11.** pachydermic
skinny ... **4.** lean, thin **5.** scant **6.** stingy **8.** skinlike **9.** emaciated, niggardly
skip ... **3.** dap **4.** gait, jump, leap, omit **5.** bound, caper, elide, frisk, salto, vault **6.** gambol, lackey, spring **7.** abscond **8.** ricochet
skipjack ... **3.** fop **4.** pike **5.** saury **6.** bonito **7.** bounder, parvenu, upstart **8.** bluefish, sailboat **9.** stripling (conceited) **10.** butterfish **14.** snapping beetle
skipper ... **5.** saury **6.** locust, maggot, master, serang **8.** skipjack **9.** butterfly **11.** grasshopper
ski race (obstacle) ... **6.** slalom
ski resort ... **4.** Vail **5.** Aspen
skirling ... **5.** trout **6.** salmon
skirmish ... **4.** fray **5.** brush, clash, melee **6.** combat **8.** conflict, flourish **9.** encounter **10.** velitation
skirt ... **5.** dress, evade, woman **6.** border, edging, fringe **9.** appendage, baseboard, periphery, petticoat **10.** pass around, saddle part
skirt (pert to) ...
armor .. **5.** tasse (tace) **7.** lamboys
attached to blouse .. **6.** peplum

chaser .. **9.** libertine **11.** philanderer
dance .. **6.** ballet
short .. **4.** kilt
skit ... **4.** joke, play **5.** caper **6.** parody, shower, sketch
skittish ... **3.** coy, shy **5.** jumpy **6.** fickle, frisky, tricky **7.** bashful **8.** unstable, volatile **9.** excitable **10.** capricious **13.** irresponsible
skittles ... **4.** game, play **8.** ninepins **9.** enjoyment (not all beer and skittles)
skoal ... **5.** toast **10.** salutation **11.** exclamation **14.** pledge of health
skulk ... **4.** lurk **5.** cower, dodge, hedge, sneak **8.** malinger
skull ... **4.** bean, head, mind **5.** brain **7.** cranium, harnpan **8.** brain box
skull (pert to) ...
cap .. **6.** beanie **7.** calotte **9.** zucchetto **10.** berrettino
cavity .. **5.** fossa
measure .. **11.** craniometer
monk's .. **6.** pileus
operation .. **6.** trepan
part .. **5.** inion **6.** bregma **7.** calotte, occiput
ref to .. **5.** inial **6.** cranic **7.** cranial
science of .. **10.** craniology
skull and crossbones ... **5.** death (symb) **10.** danger sign
skunk ... **5.** zoril **6.** defeat **7.** fitchew, polecat, stinker **8.** conepate (conepati), zorrillo **9.** scoundrel
sky ... **4.** blue **5.** ether, vault **6.** caelum, canopy, heaven, welkin **7.** heavens, the blue **8.** empyrean **9.** firmament **10.** blue yonder
sky (pert to) ...
color .. **4.** blue **5.** azure **7.** celeste **8.** cerulean
god .. **3.** Anu
lark .. **5.** pipit **6.** Alauda, frolic **7.** titlark
light .. **6.** window **8.** abatjour
lure .. **7.** horizon
parlor .. **5.** attic **6.** garret
pilot .. **8.** chaplain **9.** clergyman **10.** missionary
serpent .. **3.** Ahi
slab ... **3.** mud **4.** tile **5.** board, dalle, plank, slime **6.** lamina, ledger, pillar (stone), puddle **7.** portion **8.** monument **9.** flagstone
slab (pert to) ...
grave .. **5.** stele (stela)
marble .. **5.** dalle **6.** tablet
slablike .. **6.** stelar
slack ... **3.** lax **4.** lull, slow **5.** chaff, inert, let up, loose, shirk, tardy **6.** abated, remiss **7.** relaxed **8.** careless, dilatory, inactive, indolent, sluggish **9.** reluctant, secondary **10.** diminished, inadequate **11.** inattentive
slacken ... **5.** abate, delay, relax **6.** loosen, reduce, repose, retard **7.** let down, relieve **8.** hold back
slackening of strained relations ... **7.** detente (Internat)
slag ... **4.** lava **5.** dross **6.** cinder, scoria **7.** residue **9.** recrement **11.** agglomerate
slain ... **4.** dead **6.** fallen, killed **8.** murdered **12.** assassinated

slake... **4.** cool, sate **5.** abate, allay, slack **6.** quench **7.** assuage, crumble, hydrate, refresh, relieve, satisfy, slacken **8.** decrease, mitigate, moderate **10.** extinguish **12.** disintegrate

slam... **4.** bang, blow, give, shut, vole **5.** abuse, score **6.** impact **9.** criticism, criticize

slander... **5.** belie, libel, smear **6.** defame, malign, vilify **7.** asperse, blacken, distort, traduce **8.** derogate, disgrace, reproach **10.** defamation, scandalize **12.** misrepresent

slang... **4.** cant **5.** argot **6.** jargon, patois **7.** hep talk **10.** vernacular

slant... **4.** bend, cant, skew **5.** angle, bevel, slope **6.** aslant, aspect, biased, glance **7.** incline, opinion **8.** attitude, occasion **9.** obliquely, viewpoint **10.** hypotenuse **11.** inclination, opportunity

slap... **3.** hit **4.** blow, clap, cuff, snub **5.** crack, skelp, sound, twank **6.** buffet, rebuff, slight, strike **8.** chastise **12.** chastisement

slash... **3.** cut **4.** gash, lash, slit **5.** marsh, sever **6.** attack, reduce, stripe **7.** censure, scourge **8.** price cut **9.** criticize, reduction

slate... **4.** list, rock **5.** color, scold, sculp **6.** ballot, enroll, record, roster, tablet, thrash **7.** censure, roofing, writing **8.** register, schedule, slattern **9.** criticize, reprimand

slate (pert to)...
ax.. **7.** mattock
black.. **4.** gray
blue.. **9.** Swiss blue
gray.. **7.** Russian **9.** red-yellow **10.** sandy beige **13.** oriental pearl
roof.. **3.** rag
tool.. **3.** zax **7.** scantle

slater... **6.** critic **7.** hellier

slattern... **4.** slut **5.** frump, idler, mopsy **6.** sloppy **7.** trifler, trollop **8.** careless, slovenly **9.** litterbug

slaughter... **4.** kill, slay **6.** battue, murder, pogrom **7.** butcher, carnage, killing **8.** butchery, hecatomb, massacre, occision **9.** bloodshed **10.** butchering **11.** destruction

slaughterhouse... **8.** abattoir, Aceldama, butchery, matadero, shambles **9.** stockyard **12.** field of blood

Slav... **4.** Pole, Slav, Sorb, Wend **5.** Croat, Czech **6.** Slovak **7.** Russian, Serbian, Servian **8.** Bohemian, Croatian, Moravian **9.** Bulgarian

slave... **4.** boor, esne, peon, serf **5.** chela, helot, thane **6.** drudge, lascar, minion, thrall, vassal **7.** bondman, captive, chattel, enslave, odalisk, servant **8.** slave ant **9.** bondslave

slave (pert to)...
block (selling).. **7.** catasta
born.. **4.** neif
comedy (stock name).. **5.** Davus
dealer.. **5.** bichy, mango (obs)
Eleusinian (Gr Relig).. **5.** Baubo, lambe
female.. **9.** concubine, odalisque (odalisk)

free.. **5.** thane (thegn)
fugitive.. **8.** marooner
Indian.. **10.** Athapascan
The Tempest.. **7.** Caliban

slavery... **4.** bond **7.** bondage, service **8.** drudgery **9.** captivity, servitude, thralldom, vassalage **11.** enslavement **12.** enthrallment

Slave States... **5.** Texas **7.** Alabama, Florida, Georgia **8.** Arkansas, Delaware, Kentucky, Maryland, Missouri, Virginia **9.** Louisiana, Tennessee **11.** Mississippi **13.** North Carolina, South Carolina

slay... **4.** kill **5.** amuse, burke, knock, lynch, smite **6.** murder, strike **7.** butcher, destroy **9.** slaughter **10.** annihilate **11.** assassinate, destroy life, exterminate

slayer... **6.** killer **8.** criminal, murderer, regicide, vaticide **9.** matricide, patricide **10.** fratricide, sororicide

sleave... **4.** sley **5.** floss **6.** tangle **8.** separate **9.** floss silk **11.** disentangle **13.** untwisted silk

sled... **4.** luge, pung **6.** sledge, sleigh, travoy, troika **8.** toboggan

sledge... **4.** sled **6.** hammer, sleigh, strike **7.** seven-up (game), vehicle

sleep... **3.** nap, nod **4.** dorm, doss, doze, wink **5.** death, sopor **6.** drowse, snooze, somnus **7.** slumber **10.** narcolepsy, somnipathy **11.** hibernation

sleep (pert to)...
comb form.. **5.** somni
deep.. **6.** stupor **8.** lethargy **10.** narcolepsy
dreaming stage.. **3.** REM
hypnotic.. **10.** somnipathy
inducing.. **5.** dwale **6.** opiate, potion **8.** sedative **9.** soporific **10.** anesthesia, belladonna
insensible.. **4.** coma
midday.. **6.** siesta
prolonged.. **5.** sopor
upon.. **8.** consider, postpone

sleeper... **3.** tie **4.** beam **6.** rafter, rester, timber **7.** Pullman, reposer, support **8.** dormouse **9.** slumberer **10.** slow seller **11.** sleeping car

sleeping... **4.** dead **5.** inert **6.** asleep, latent **7.** dormant **8.** dormient, inactive **9.** quiescent **10.** quiescence **11.** inattentive

sleeping (pert to)...
pill.. **9.** soporific
place.. **3.** bed, cot **4.** bunk, doss **5.** berth, couch **6.** pallet **7.** cubicle **9.** dormitory
sickness.. **6.** nagana, tsetse **9.** lethargus

sleepwalking... **8.** neurosis **12.** nightwalking, somnambulism

sleepy... **4.** dull **5.** tired **6.** drowsy **8.** soporose **9.** lethargic, somnolent **11.** somniferous

sleeve... **3.** arm **5.** gigot (leg-ó-mutton) **10.** copper tube **14.** British channel

sleigh... **4.** pung **6.** cutter

sleight of hand performer... **4.** mage **8.** magician **14.** legerdemainist **15.** prestidigitator

slender... **4.** lank, lean, slim, thin **5.** gaunt, lanky, leger, reedy **6.** lissom,

narrow, svelte **7.** gracile, tenuous, trivial, willowy **9.** elongated
slender pinnacle . . . **3.** epi
sleuth . . . **6.** tracer **8.** hawkshaw **9.** detective, sleuthdog **11.** sleuthhound **12.** investigator
slice . . . **3.** cut, saw **4.** gash, slab **5.** piece, share, shave **6.** rasher, sliver, stroke **7.** portion **8.** golf term, splinter **12.** cross section
slick . . . **4.** neat, tidy **5.** alert, sleek, smart **6.** clever, smooth **8.** slippery, unctuous **9.** first-rate, lubricate **10.** glistening **12.** accomplished
slide . . . **3.** ski, skid, slip, slue **5.** chute, clasp, glide, plane (sloping), scoot, skate **6.** elapse **7.** lantern, slither **8.** toboggan **9.** avalanche **11.** deteriorate
slight . . . **3.** cut **4.** defy, rare, snub, thin **5.** faint, frail, leger, minor, oligo (comb form), scorn, small **6.** flimsy, ignore, little, meager **7.** disdain, fragile, neglect, nominal, scantly, shallow, trivial **8.** contempt, delicate **9.** disregard, indignity **10.** immaterial **11.** unimportant **13.** imperceptible, unsubstantial **14.** inconsiderable
slight (pert to) . . .
  convexity . . **6.** camber
  sound . . **4.** peep
  variation . . **6.** nuance **7.** shading
slightest . . . **5.** least **6.** barest
slightly (pert to) . . .
  damaged paper . . **6.** retree
  sour . . **8.** acescent
  tapering . . **6.** terete
slim . . . **3.** sly **4.** lean, mean, thin **5.** small, spare **6.** adroit, scanty, sparse, svelte **7.** slender, tenuous **9.** worthless
slime . . . **3.** mud **4.** ooze **5.** filth, gleet **6.** mucous
slip . . . **3.** err, pew, sin **4.** dock, fail, pier, skid, slue **5.** boner, cover, error, fault, glide, lapse, slide, strip **6.** bungle, elapse **7.** blunder, cutting, failure, faux pas, misdeed, mistake, slither **9.** youngling **10.** pillowslip **12.** undergarment **13.** transgression
slipknot . . . **5.** noose
slipper . . . **4.** mule, neap, shoe **5.** apron, moyle, Romeo **6.** pinson, sandal **7.** scuffer **8.** babouche (baboosh), covering
slippery . . . **3.** sly **4.** eely, glib **5.** slick **6.** crafty, fickle, shifty, tricky, wanton **7.** cunning, elusive, evasive **8.** unctuous, unstable **9.** deceitful, uncertain **10.** intangible, precarious, unreliable **11.** treacherous **13.** untrustworthy
slit . . . **4.** kerf **5.** cleft, slash, split **6.** furrow **7.** severed
slither . . . **5.** crawl, glide, sidle, slide
sliver . . . **3.** cut **5.** shred, slice, split **8.** fragment, splinter
sloe . . . **3.** haw **4.** plum
sloe (pert to) . . .
  berry . . **7.** juniper
  bush . . **10.** blackthorn
  color . . **9.** blue-black
  fruit (blackthorn) . . **3.** haw **4.** sloe
  gin . . **12.** sloe-flavored

slogan . . . **3.** cry **5.** motto **6.** phrase **9.** catchword, watchword **10.** shibboleth (Bib)
sloop . . . **5.** yacht **6.** cutter, schuit (schuyt) **7.** eelboat
slope . . . **3.** dip, lie **4.** bank, hade, ramp **5.** bevel, scarp, slant, talus **6.** calade, decamp, escarp, glacis **7.** terrace **9.** declivity **10.** declension **11.** inclination
sloping bank . . . **4.** brae **7.** terrace
sloth . . . **2.** ai **4.** pack (bears), pazy, unau **6.** acedia, mammal **7.** inertia **8.** idleness, slowness **9.** indolence
slothful . . . **4.** lazy **8.** inactive, indolent, sluggish
sloth monkey . . . **5.** lemur, loris
slough . . . **3.** bog **4.** husk, mire, molt, shed, skin **5.** bayou, swamp **7.** channel, discard
sloughing . . . **7.** ecdysis, molting **8.** shedding **10.** discarding
slovenly . . . **5.** dowdy, messy, tacky **6.** frowzy, sloppy, untidy **8.** careless, slattern, slipshod **9.** negligent **10.** disheveled, disorderly, slatternly
slow . . . **4.** dull, late, poky **5.** delay, inert, relax **6.** boring, hinder, retard, stupid **7.** slacken **8.** boresome, dilatory, inactive, moderate **9.** lingering **20.** inch by inch phlegmatic **13.** unprogressive
slow (pert to) . . .
  action . . **6.** dawdle **10.** deliberate
  adverb . . **10.** behindhand
  down . . **4.** idle **6.** retard **8.** wind down **10.** decelerate
  music . . **5.** largo, lento, molto, tardo **6.** adagio **7.** andante **8.** lentando **10.** lentamento
  poke . . **5.** snail **7.** dawdler
  up . . **3.** lag **6.** retard **7.** decline
  witted . . **4.** dull **6.** stupid
sludge . . . **3.** mud **4.** gunk, mire, ooze **5.** slime **8.** sediment
slug . . . **3.** hit **4.** blow, dose **5.** Arion, drink, drone, idler, Limax, space, token **6.** bullet, loiter, nugget **7.** trepang **8.** sluggard **9.** gastropod
sluggish . . . **4.** logy, slow **5.** dopey, inert **6.** drowsy, stupid, supine **7.** dronish, languid **8.** dilatory, inactive, indolent, listless, stagnant **9.** stagnancy, stupidity, torpidity
sluice . . . **4.** race **5.** flush **6.** drench, stream **7.** channel **9.** floodgate
slumber . . . **4.** doze **5.** sleep **6.** catnap, drowse, repose, snooze, somnus **14.** arms of Morpheus
slump . . . **4.** drop, fall **7.** decline, descend, dessert, sinkage **9.** fall short **10.** depreciate, depression
slur . . . **4.** blur **5.** elide **6.** defame, insult, mackle, slight, stigma **7.** calumny, traduce **8.** disgrace, innuendo, reproach, skim over **9.** aspersion, disparage **10.** calumniate, stigmatize
slush . . . **3.** mud **4.** mire, snow **5.** slime **14.** sentimentality
sly . . . **4.** arch, foxy, wary, wily, wink **5.** cagey, catty, snaky **6.** covert, crafty, feline, shrewd, sneaky, subtle **7.** cunning, furtive **8.** craftily

9. underhand **11.** mischievous, underhanded **15.** surreptitiously

smack . . . **3.** bit, bop **4.** bang, belt, buss, glow, kiss, tang **5.** clout, taste **6.** strike, vessel, wallop **8.** chastise, sailboat

smacking . . . **5.** brisk **6.** lively **7.** dashing **8.** spanking, vigorous **9.** energetic

small . . . **3.** tot, wee **4.** thin, tiny, wisp **5.** dwarf, petty **6.** humble, little, meager, minute, modest, petite **7.** faintly, trivial **8.** picayune, trifling **9.** miniature, minuscule, thumbnail **10.** diminutive, undersized **11.** unimportant **13.** insignificant **14.** contemptuously, inconsiderable

small (pert to) . . .
amount . . **3.** dab **4.** dram **5.** minim **6.** morsel **7.** modicum **8.** pittance
anvil . . **5.** teest
area . . **6.** areola (areole)
armadillo . . **4.** peba
arms . . **3.** bow **5.** rifle, sword **6.** pistol **7.** carbine, grenade
attractive . . **4.** cute **6.** dainty
bomb . . **6.** petard **7.** grenade
bottle . . **4.** vial **5.** phial
case, handbag . . **4.** etui
comb form . . **5.** lepto, micro
dab . . **3.** pat, wad **5.** chunk
deer . . **4.** fawn, napu
delicately . . **6.** mignon
distance . . **3.** hop **4.** step
drink . . **3.** nip **4.** pony, swig
drum . . **5.** bongo, tabor
field . . **5.** croft
fish . . **3.** ide
flag . . **6.** fanion
fruits . . **10.** low growing
fry . . **4.** fish, kids, tots **8.** children **10.** youngsters
insect . . **4.** flea **5.** midge
island . . **3.** ait **4.** isle
lake . . **4.** mere, pond
law . . **5.** petit
minded . . **4.** mean **5.** petty **6.** biased **10.** prejudiced, vindictive
neat . . **6.** dapper
number . . **3.** few **7.** paucity
opening . . **4.** pore **5.** stoma **7.** orifice
ox . . **4.** anoa
part . . **4.** iota **6.** detail **7.** snippet
particle . . **4.** atom, mote **8.** molecule
people . . **5.** elves **6.** common **7.** fairies, midgets, Pygmies
piece . . **3.** mot **4.** chip, tate **5.** speck **7.** driblet, morceau
post . . **9.** paper size
quantity . . **4.** drop, mite **5.** trace **7.** handful
rope (Naut) . . **7.** marline (marling)
Scot . . **3.** sma, wee
shield . . **3.** écu **9.** scutellum
stream . . **3.** run **4.** rill **6.** rillet
surface . . **5.** facet
talk . . **6.** babble **7.** prattle **8.** chitchat
task . . **5.** chore **6.** odd job
things . . **3.** fry
tower . . **6.** turret **7.** minaret
very . . **3.** wee **8.** picayune **11.** Lilliputian
world . . **9.** microcosm

smallpox . . . **7.** variola

smaragd . . . **7.** emerald

smart . . . **3.** apt **4.** chic, perk, posh, trig, trim, wise **5.** acute, alert, natty, nifty, quick, sting **6.** astute, clever, shrewd, spruce, trendy **7.** dashing, painful, pungent, stylish **8.** impudent, poignant, pricking **9.** competent, ingenious **10.** precocious **11.** fashionable, intelligent

smash . . . **4.** blow, mash, pulp, ruin **5.** break, crush, drink (spirits), stave, wreck **6.** defeat **7.** collide, debacle, destroy, failure, shatter, success **8.** accident, beverage **9.** collision, pulverize

smear . . . **3.** dab, rub **4.** daub, gaum **5.** slake, stain, sully **6.** anoint, bedaub, defame, defile, grease, malign, smirch, smudge **7.** besmear, plaster, pollute, slander **8.** besmirch

smear with . . .
egg white . . **5.** glair **8.** meringue
mud . . **5.** slime
ointment . . **6.** anoint

smell . . . **4.** odor, olid, reek **5.** aroma, fetor, scent, sense, sniff, stink **6.** detect **7.** perfume **9.** fragrance, redolence **10.** atmosphere

smell (pert to) . . .
acute . . **8.** oxyrhine
loss of sense of . . **7.** anosmia
offensive . . **3.** bad **4.** foul, olid **5.** fetor **6.** stench
sense of . . **6.** osmics **7.** osmesis **9.** olfaction

smelling salts . . . **9.** hartshorn **17.** ammonium carbonate

smelt . . . **4.** fish, fuse, melt **6.** tomcod **7.** scorify **10.** silverside

smilax . . . **8.** catbrier **10.** greenbrier

smile . . . **4.** grin **5.** laugh, smirk, sneer **6.** simper **8.** greeting

smiling . . . **5.** agrin, merry, riant **6.** rident **8.** gleaming, grinning

smirch . . . **4.** blot **5.** smear, stain, sully, taint **6.** blotch, smutch, stigma, vilify **7.** begrime, blacken, blemish, tarnish **8.** discolor **10.** blackening

smirk . . . **4.** grin, leer **6.** simper

smite . . . **4.** kill, slap **6.** lay low, strike **7.** chasten, impress, inflict, trouble **8.** chastise

smithy . . . **6.** forger, stithy **7.** farrier **8.** smithery **10.** blacksmith

smock . . . **5.** kamis, shift, tunic, woman (obs) **7.** chemise **9.** philander **11.** overgarment

smoke . . . **4.** burn, cure, floc, fume, pipe **5.** cigar, cloud, cubeb, flume, smook, vapor **6.** smudge **7.** incense, tobacco **8.** fumigate, preserve **9.** cigarette

smokestack . . . **6.** funnel **7.** chimney **8.** fumiduct

smoking apparatus (Orient) . . . **7.** tabagie **8.** narghile (nargile)

smolder, smoulder . . . **4.** burn **5.** choke, smoke **6.** smudge **7.** smother **9.** suffocate

smooth . . . **4.** comb, ease, even, iron, lene, pave **5.** bland, clear, level, plane, press, sleek, slick, suave **6.** glossy,

mangle, pacify, urbane **7.** uniform
8. hairless, unctuous **10.** facilitate,
flattering **12.** frictionless, ingratiating
smooth (pert to) . . .
breathing . . **13.** spiritus lenis
comb form . . **3.** lio
feathers, hair . . **5.** preen
hard, transparent . . **6.** glassy
phonetically . . **4.** lene
tare . . **12.** slender vetch
tongued . . **4.** glib **5.** suave
12. hypocritical
smooth and . . .
soft . . **5.** furry, silky, soapy **7.** velvety
soothing . . **5.** bland
sweet . . **11.** mellifluent
white . . **11.** alabastrine
smother . . . **4.** daub, kill **5.** befog, choke,
cover **6.** deaden, hush up, muffle, stifle,
welter **7.** overlie, smolder **8.** suppress
9. suffocate, to blanket **11.** exterminate
smudge . . . **4.** blot, smut, soil, spot
5. smear, smoke, stain **6.** smutch
7. begrime, smolder
smug . . . **4.** neat, tidy, trim **5.** smart,
suave **6.** pilfer **7.** correct **9.** confident
10. complacent **13.** self-satisfied
smuggler . . . **6.** runner **9.** rumrunner
13. contrabandist
smur . . . **4.** mist **5.** cloud, smurr **7.** drizzle
Smyrna . . . **5.** Izmir (present name)
Smyrna fig . . . **5.** eleme (elemi)
Smyrna melon . . . **6.** casaba
snack . . . **4.** nosh
snail . . . **4.** slug **5.** drone, Helix, Mitra,
whelk **6.** Nerita, Triton **7.** mollusk
9. gastropod **10.** periwinkle
snake . . . **3.** asp, ess **4.** tree, worm
5. adder, cobra, coral, racer, viper
6. garter, gopher **7.** hognose, rattler,
reptile **8.** Micrurus, moccasin
9. Heterodon **10.** bushmaster,
copperhead, sidewinder
11. cottonmouth, diamondback,
rattlesnake **12.** schaapsteker
snake (pert to) . . .
African . . **5.** mamba
bird . . **6.** darter
black . . **5.** racer
cobra . . **3.** nag (naga)
comb form . . **5.** ophio, ophis **6.** herpes
crusher . . **6.** python **8.** anaconda **14.** boa
constrictor
dance . . **4.** Hopi **6.** ophism
division (serpents) . . **7.** Ophidia
9. Serpentes
expert . . **13.** herpetologist
fear of . . **13.** herpetophobia
Florida . . **8.** moccasin
front-fanged . . **5.** cobra, mamba **6.** elapid
8. Elapine
garter . . **5.** Elaps
genus . . **7.** Ophidia
heraldic . . **5.** bisse
horned . . **8.** cerastes
India . . **5.** krait **6.** bongar
killer . . **8.** mongoose
like . . **7.** ophioid **9.** colubrine
mouth . . **6.** orchid
movement . . **4.** coil, drag, wind **5.** crawl,
sneak, twist

mythical . . **6.** Python (on Mt Parnassus)
nonpoisonous . . **4.** king **6.** garter, gopher
9. Colubrina
pert to . . **5.** ophic **7.** anguine **8.** viperine
9. colubrine, scoundrel
poisonous . . **3.** asp **5.** adder, coral
7. rattler **8.** moccasin **10.** copperhead
11. cottonmouth **13.** thanatophidia
python . . **8.** anaconda
python deity . . **5.** zombi (zombie)
reptilelike . . **9.** herpetoid
Russell's viper . . **6.** daboia, jessur
sacred . . **6.** Shesha
S America . . **5.** aboma
sand snake . . **4.** Eryx
semihuman, race of . . **4.** Naga
shaped . . **9.** anguiform
skin . . **6.** exuvia
spitting . . **9.** ringhals
snaky . . . **3.** sly **4.** wavy **7.** anguine,
sinuous, wriggly **8.** spiteful, twisting,
venomous **9.** snakelike **10.** perfidious,
serpentine **11.** treacherous
snaky sisters . . . **6.** Erinys **17.** snaky-
haired Furies
snap . . . **3.** bit **4.** bite, flip **5.** break, crack,
flick, quick, snarl, thump **6.** energy,
fasten, fillip (fingers) **7.** bargain, crackle
8. easy task, handcuff, snapshot
9. crispness, fastening, smartness
10. gingersnap, photograph, resilience
11. sharp retort
snapper . . . **4.** bean, sesi **5.** error, pargo
6. beetle, bonbon, tamure, turtle
7. cracker, grouper **8.** fastener, rosefish
9. countfish **10.** stitchwort, stringbean,
woodpecker **11.** firecracker
snappy . . . **4.** cold, fast **5.** quick **6.** lively,
sudden **7.** pungent **8.** snappish
9. crackling, energetic
snare . . . **3.** beg, gin, net, web **4.** lure,
mesh, trap **5.** benet, catch, noose, steal
6. entoil, trepan **7.** pitfall **9.** deception
snark . . . **3.** nag **5.** snort **6.** boojum
8. creature (fabled)
snarl . . . **4.** gnar, knot **5.** gnarr, growl,
scold, snare **6.** tangle **7.** confuse,
ensnare, grumble, quarrel **8.** complain,
entangle **9.** confusion **10.** complicate
12. complication
snatch . . . **4.** grab, jerk, take **5.** catch,
erept, grasp, gripe, pluck, seize, steal,
wrest **6.** clutch, kidnap, rescue **7.** seizure
sneak . . . **4.** lead (game), lurk **5.** cower,
creep, knave, slink, snoop **6.** coward,
cringe, tattle **7.** smuggle **11.** furtive
move
sneaking . . . **3.** sly **4.** mean, poor
6. craven, hidden, paltry, secret
7. furtive **8.** cowardly, stealthy
9. dastardly, niggardly, underhand
12. contemptible **13.** surreptitious
sneer . . . **4.** gibe, jeer, mock **5.** fleer,
flout, laugh, scoff, scorn
sneer, expressive . . . **8.** sardonic
snell . . . **4.** keen **5.** acute, eager, quick,
sharp, snood, swift **6.** active, biting,
severe **7.** caustic, pungent **8.** piercing
snicker . . . **5.** laugh, neigh, sneer **6.** giggle,
nicker, tittle, whinny **7.** snigger
8. laughter

sniff ... **4.** nose **5.** scent, smell, snuff **6.** detect, inhale **7.** sniffle **8.** sibilate, smell out **14.** show of contempt

snifter ... **3.** nip **4.** dram, good **5.** drink, sniff, snort **6.** snivel **9.** excellent

snip ... **3.** bit, cut **4.** clip, snap **5.** notch, piece, shred **8.** fragment, particle

snipe (pert to) ...
eel.. **6.** thread
flock.. **4.** wisp
game.. **6.** godwit
hawk.. **7.** harrier
verb.. **7.** shoot at **10.** sharpshoot

snippy ... **4.** curt, tart **5.** brief, sharp **8.** snippety, snobbish **11.** fragmentary **12.** supercilious

snirl ... **5.** gnarl, snare **6.** tangle **7.** wrinkle

snitch ... **5.** pinch, steal **6.** betray, inform, pilfer, snatch, tattle **8.** informer, particle

snob ... **4.** prig **7.** cobbler, parvenu **8.** bluenose, commoner, courtier **9.** sycophant

snobby, snobbish ... **5.** proud **6.** uppish **7.** haughty **8.** arrogant **9.** exclusive **11.** overbearing

snood ... **5.** snell **6.** fillet **7.** hairnet

snook ... **4.** fish **5.** smell **6.** robalo, search **9.** barracuda

snoop ... **3.** pry **4.** nose **5.** prowl, sneak **6.** meddle **7.** meddler **8.** busybody **10.** sneak thief

snooze ... **3.** nap **4.** doze **5.** sleep **6.** cuddle, nuzzle, siesta **7.** snoozle, snuggle

snore, snoring ... **4.** rale **5.** sleep **7.** stertor **8.** rhonchus, sibilate **10.** sibilation, stertorous **15.** hoarse breathing

snort ... **5.** drink, grunt, laugh, snore

snotty ... **5.** dirty, nasty **6.** offish, snooty **7.** high-hat **9.** offensive **12.** contemptible, supercilious

snow ... **4.** firn, neve **5.** opium **8.** narcotic **12.** interference

snow (pert to) ...
bunting.. **5.** finch **9.** snowflake
glacial.. **4.** firn, neve
grouse, quail.. **9.** ptarmigan
house.. **5.** igloo
leopard.. **5.** ounce
lily.. **6.** violet (white)
living in.. **5.** nival
mouse.. **4.** vole **7.** lemming
ref to.. **5.** nival
ridges.. **8.** sastrugi (zastrugi)
runner.. **3.** ski **4.** sled
shoe.. **3.** pac **7.** webfoot
sliding.. **9.** avalanche
slope.. **8.** glissade

snub ... **3.** cut **5.** check, quell, scold **6.** cut off, ignore, rebuff, rebuke, slight **7.** neglect, shorten **8.** restrain **9.** reprimand **10.** inhalation

snuff (pert to) ... **5.** scent, smell, sniff **6.** draw in, inhale, snoose **7.** tobacco (pulverized), umbrage **10.** extinguish, inhalation

snuff (pert to) ...
a candle.. **4.** snot
box.. **4.** mull **9.** tabatière
color.. **10.** mummy brown

type.. **6.** rappee **8.** Maccaboy **10.** Copenhagen

snug ... **4.** cozy, neat, safe, trim **5.** close, tight **6.** secure **7.** compact **8.** homelike, reticen**9.** concealed, secretive **10.** prosperous **11.** comfortable

snuggle ... **6.** cuddle, nestle

sny (shipbuilding) ... **5.** curve (of plank)

so ... **2.** as **3.** how **4.** ergo, thus, very **5.** hence **6.** if only **7.** because **8.** likewise, provided **9.** therefore **11.** accordingly, in order that **12.** consequently

so (pert to) ...
far.. **3.** yet **7.** thus far **8.** until now
Latin.. **3.** sic
so be it.. **4.** Amen
to speak.. **8.** as it were **12.** figuratively

soak ... **3.** dip, sog, sop, wet **4.** sock **5.** souse, steep **6.** drench, imbrue, strike, tipple **7.** extract, immerse **8.** drunkard, macerate, marinate, permeate, saturate **9.** percolate **10.** overcharge

soap ... **4.** sapo, suds, wash **5.** bribe **6.** lather **7.** bribery **8.** cleanser, flattery **9.** slush fund

soap (pert to) ...
box.. **4.** dais **5.** stage **8.** platform
convert to.. **8.** saponify
fish.. **10.** lizard fish
frame bar.. **4.** sess
ingredient.. **3.** lye
liniment (camphorated).. **9.** opodeldoc
making.. **14.** saponification
mottled.. **8.** Eschwege (Eschweg)
opera.. **6.** serial **9.** broadcast **13.** network serial
plant.. **5.** amole
soft.. **8.** flattery

soar ... **3.** fly **4.** flit, rise, wing **5.** float, plane **6.** ascend, aspire, be high **9.** transcend

soaring ... **6.** flight **7.** gliding, planing, winging **8.** essorant **9.** skyriding **10.** ballooning

sob ... **3.** cry **4.** bawl, weep **6.** boohoo, simper **7.** whimper **9.** shed tears

sobeit ... **4.** amen **8.** provided

sober ... **4.** calm, cool, dark, sane **5.** grave, quiet, staid **6.** gentle, sedate, solemn, somber, subdue, temper **7.** chasten, earnest, regular, serious **8.** composed, moderate, sensible **9.** abstinent, collected, dignified, temperate **10.** abstemious, thoughtful **11.** impassioned **13.** unintoxicated

sobriety ... **6.** sanity **9.** composure, restraint, soberness **10.** abstinence, moderation, temperance **11.** seriousness

sobriquet ... **5.** alias, title **6.** byname **7.** epithet **8.** cognomen, nickname **11.** appellation

soccer ... **19.** association football

soccer great ... **4.** Pele

sociable ... **5.** party **6.** affable **8.** familiar, friendly, informal **9.** reception **10.** accessible, gregarious **13.** communicative, companionable

social ... **3.** tea **5.** party **6.** smoker **9.** convivial, gathering

13. companionable
social (pert to) . . .
career . . **5.** debut
class . . **4.** clan, sept **5.** caste **6.** estate
ethics . . **6.** morals **9.** standards
    10. principles
function . . **3.** bee, tea **4.** ball **5.** party
    6. soiree **7.** reunion **9.** reception
gathering, men . . **4.** stag **6.** smoker
group . . **4.** sept **5.** tribe **6.** ethnos **8.** smart
    set **10.** upper crust **11.** cafe society
    13. kaffeeklatsch
insect . . **3.** ant, bee
outcast . . **5.** leper **6.** pariah
standing . . **6.** estate
system . . **6.** regime
socialist . . . **3.** Red **8.** Nihilist **9.** anarchist,
    communist **10.** Bolshevist
    12. collectivist
society . . . **5.** union **7.** company
    8. alliance, populace **9.** community
    10. fellowship **11.** association,
    partnership **13.** companionship,
    confederation, participation
society (pert to) . . .
bud . . **3.** deb
Chinese . . **4.** Tong
German . . **6.** Verein
high . . **5.** elite **10.** upper crust
Italian . . **5.** Mafia (Maffia)
of Friends . . **7.** Quakers
secret . . **5.** lodge, Order
Society Islands . . .
capital . . **7.** Papeete
chief island . . **6.** Tahiti
site . . **12.** South Pacific
Socrates (pert to) . . .
birthplace . . **6.** Athens
disciple of . . **5.** Plato
famed as . . **7.** teacher **11.** Grecian sage
wife . . **9.** Xanthippe (Xantippe)
sod . . . **4.** soil, turf **5.** divot, glebe, sward
    7. stratum **10.** greensward
soda . . . **3.** sal **8.** beverage **9.** saleratus,
    saltpeter
sodden . . . **5.** drunk, moist, soggy
    6. soaked, stewed, stupid **7.** drunken,
    steeped **9.** saturated **11.** intoxicated
sodium (pert to) . . .
carbonate . . **4.** soda **5.** borax, trona
    7. sal soda, saltcat
chloride . . **3.** sal, tar **4.** NaCl, salt
nitrate . . **5.** niter
salicylate . . **8.** medicine
symbol . . **2.** Na
sofa . . . **5.** couch, divan **6.** lounge, settee
    7. dos-à-dos **8.** causeuse, love seat
    9. davenport, tête-à-tête **12.** chesterfield
soft . . . **4.** easy, limp, weak **5.** bland,
    downy, mushy, pulpy **6.** dreamy,
    gentle, placid, silken, supple, tender
    7. clement, ductile, lenient, lightly,
    quietly, squashy, velvety **8.** flexible,
    gullible, merciful, tranquil **9.** temperate,
    tractable **10.** effeminate, peacefully
    11. comfortable, sentimental,
    sympathetic **13.** compassionate
soft (pert to) . . .
cancer . . **11.** encephaloma
coal . . **10.** bituminous
food . . **3.** pap

head . . **9.** simpleton
job . . **4.** snap **8.** sinecure
mass . . **4.** pulp
music . . **5.** dulce, piano
palate . . **4.** cion **5.** uvula, velum
pedal . . **3.** ban **4.** curb **6.** subdue **8.** tone
    down
soap . . **7.** blarney **8.** blandish, flattery
    9. wheedling
spoken . . **4.** mild **5.** suave
soften . . . **4.** melt, thaw **5.** allay, malax,
    relax **6.** affect, lenify, pacify, relent,
    soothe, temper, weaken **7.** appease,
    assuage, cushion, mollify, relieve
    8. emoliate, enervate, enfeeble,
    macerate, mitigate, modulate
    9. alleviate, meliorate **11.** tranquilize
soften (pert to) . . .
by kneading . . **5.** malax
by soaking . . **8.** macerate
leather . . **5.** sammy (sam)
skins . . **3.** taw
temper . . **6.** relent
softening . . . **7.** lenient **8.** emulsive
    9. relenting, relieving, tempering
    10. lightening, mitigating
softening of the brain . . . **8.** dementia
softhearted . . . **4.** kind **6.** tender
    8. merciful
softly . . . **3.** low **5.** sotto **6.** easily, gently
    10. delicately **13.** unobtrusively
soggy . . . **3.** wet **4.** damp **5.** heavy
    6. soaked, sodden, watery **9.** saturated
soil . . . **4.** clay, daub, dirt, land, loam,
    sand, spot **5.** adobe, dirty, earth,
    glebe, gumbo, humus, stain, sully
    6. bedaub, bemire, ground, region,
    smirch, vilify **7.** begrime, besmear,
    corrupt, debauch, pollute, tarnish
    8. alluvium **9.** bedraggle, bespatter
    11. contaminate **12.** fuller's earth
soil (pert to) . . .
barren . . **4.** arid, gall **8.** lifeless
goddess of . . **7.** Demeter
kind of . . **4.** clay, lair, loam, malm
    5. adobe, humus
oneself . . **4.** moil
poetic . . **5.** glebe
sojourn . . . **4.** bide, stay, stop **5.** abide
    6. reside **8.** abidance, stop over
    11. peregrinate
solace . . . **5.** allay, amuse, cheer **6.** soothe
    7. assuage, comfort, console
    9. alleviate, entertain **10.** relaxation
    11. consolation
solan . . . **5.** goose **6.** gannet
solar (pert to) . . .
deity . . **2.** Ra **3.** Shu (Su) **6.** Helios
disk . . **4.** aten
exposure . . **9.** sunstroke **10.** heatstroke
halo . . **6.** nimbus **7.** aureole **12.** vesica
    piscis
plexus . . **10.** stomach pit
system . . **6.** bodies, planet **15.** celestial
    bodies
system apparatus . . **6.** orrery
year . . **5.** epact
soldier . . . **3.** ant **5.** cadet, poilu **6.** galoot
    7. fighter, private, regular, trooper,
    veteran, warrior **8.** gendarme, servitor
    9. combatant, grenadier, musketeer

11. enlisted man
soldier (pert to) . . .
Algeria . . **6.** Zouave
cavalryman . . **6.** lancer **7.** dragoon, trooper
Croatian . . **5.** Croat
field worker . . **6.** sapper
flask . . **7.** canteen
French . . **5.** poilu
Gaelic . . **4.** Kern
girl . . **3.** WAC (Army)
Gr Myth . . **8.** Myrmidon
hireling . . **9.** mercenary
Ind (Brit) . . **5.** sepoy
Ind (Brit), with own horse . . **8.** silladar
Moroccan . . **5.** askar
of fortune . . **7.** Hessian **9.** mercenary **10.** adventurer
Prussian . . **5.** uhlan
slang . . **6.** galoot **7.** chicken **8.** shackman
soldiers, soldier's . . .
body of . . **5.** troop **6.** cohort **7.** brigade, company, platoon
captured, wounded . . **6.** losses
flask . . **7.** canteen
Maryland (Rev War) . . **10.** macaronies
overcoat . . **6.** capote
quarters . . **7.** billets **8.** barracks
Three . . **5.** tales (by Kipling)
vacation . . **4.** pass **5.** leave **8.** furlough
sole . . . **3.** one **4.** base, fish, only **5.** alone, slade **6.** entire, lonely, single, unique **8.** desolate, isolated, solitary, unshared **9.** exclusive, unmarried, unmatched **10.** underframe
sole (pert to) . . .
cookery . . **8.** Marguéry
foot . . **4.** vola **6.** planta
hand (palm) . . **4.** vola
pert to . . **7.** plantar
plow . . **5.** slade
toward the sole . . **7.** plantad
solecism . . . **5.** error **7.** blunder **9.** barbarism, deviation **11.** impropriety
solemn . . . **3.** sad **5.** grave, pious, sober **6.** august, devout, formal, gloomy, ritual, silent **7.** earnest, serious, stately, sublime **8.** funereal **9.** dignified **10.** ceremonial, devotional **11.** ceremonious, reverential **12.** awe-inspiring
solemnity . . . **4.** pomp **7.** dignity, sadness **8.** ceremony **9.** formality **10.** importance
solicit . . . **3.** ask, beg **4.** lure, seek, tout **5.** claim, court, crave, plead **6.** accost, demand, invite, obtain **7.** beseech, canvass, entreat, implore, request **8.** campaign, petition **9.** challenge, importune, panhandle, prosecute **10.** supplicate
solicitor . . . **6.** barker, lawyer **8.** attorney **9.** canvasser **10.** petitioner
solicitude . . . **4.** care, coda, heed **7.** anxiety, caution, concern **9.** attention **11.** carefulness **12.** apprehension **15.** considerateness
solid . . . **4.** cone, cube, firm, full, good, hard **5.** dense, level, sound, stiff **6.** stable, strong **7.** uniform **8.** complete, resolute, sensible, sterling **9.** estimable, unanimous **10.** dependable, inflexible

11. homogeneous, responsible, substantial, trustworthy
solid (pert to) . . .
comb form . . **6.** stereo
geometrical . . **5.** prism
seven-faced . . **11.** heptahedron
six-faced . . **4.** cube
tapering . . **4.** cone **7.** pyramid
solidarity . . . **5.** unity **10.** correality **11.** nationality **12.** completeness
solidity . . . **5.** unity **6.** volume **7.** density **8.** firmness, hardness, solvency, strength **9.** solidness, stability **11.** compactness **12.** completeness **13.** dependability **14.** substantiality
solidum . . . **4.** dado **9.** entire sum
soliloquy . . . **4.** poem **9.** discourse, monologue **16.** talking to oneself
solitaire . . . **8.** Canfield
solitary . . . **3.** one **4.** lone, only, sole **5.** alone, eremo (comb form) **6.** hermit, lonely, single **7.** recluse **8.** deserted, desolate, lonesome **10.** individual **12.** unfrequented
solitude . . . **6.** desert **7.** privacy, retreat **9.** aloneness, isolation, seclusion **10.** loneliness, wilderness
solo accompaniment . . . **9.** obbligato
Solomon (pert to) . . .
author of (reputed) . . **8.** Proverbs **9.** Canticles **12.** Ecclesiastes **15.** Wisdom of Solomon
called also . . **8.** Koheleth **11.** The Preacher
famed as . . **4.** sage **7.** wise man **12.** King of Israel
father . . **5.** David
literally . . **9.** peaceable
mother . . **9.** Bathsheba
Solomon Islands site . . . **9.** South Seas
solon . . . **4.** sage **8.** lawmaker **9.** statesman
solstice . . . **5.** limit **13.** farthest point (from equator)
solution . . . **3.** key **6.** answer **7.** solving **8.** analysis **10.** denouement, resolution **11.** explanation **15.** disentanglement
solution (pert to) . . .
alkaline . . **3.** lye
saline . . **5.** brine
strength . . **5.** titer (titre)
Somalia . . .
capital . . **9.** Mogadishu
people . . **6.** Somali **7.** Hamitic
port . . **5.** Zeila **6.** Bulhar
somber, sombre . . . **3.** sad **4.** dark **5.** grave **6.** solemn **7.** austere **9.** depressed **10.** depressing, foreboding, lackluster, melancholy **11.** dark-colored, dispiriting
some . . . **3.** any, one **5.** about **6.** plural, suffix **7.** several **10.** indefinite, more or less **13.** approximately
somebody . . . **6.** person **7.** big name **8.** luminary **9.** celebrity, personage
somersault . . . **4.** flip, leap **8.** somerset **9.** cartwheel **10.** end over end
something . . . **6.** object **8.** anything **9.** personage **12.** in some degree
something (pert to) . . .
abnormal . . **5.** freak **6.** mutant **11.** monstrosity **12.** malformation

else .. **10.** irrelevant
extra .. **5.** bonus **6.** bounty **7.** premium **9.** lagniappe
found .. **5.** cache, trove **11.** serendipity **13.** treasure-trove
frightening .. **7.** bugbear
heavy .. **4.** onus **9.** ponderant
illogical .. **7.** alogism
imagined .. **5.** story **7.** figment
inserted .. **4.** gore **5.** inset, wedge
like .. **7.** related, similar **8.** somewhat
similar .. **8.** analogue **11.** counterpart
small .. **3.** dot, jot **4.** atom, iota, whit **5.** speck **6.** sliver, tittle
soothing .. **7.** unction
superfluous .. **5.** luxus **6.** luxury
unexplained .. **5.** poser **7.** mystery
unfinished .. **4.** quab
somewhat ... **4.** part **6.** little, partly, rather **12.** in some degree
somnifacient ... **4.** drug **8.** hypnotic, sedative **9.** soporific
somniloquy ... **12.** sleep talking
somnolence ... **8.** dormancy **10.** drowsiness, sleepiness
somnus ... **5.** sleep
Somnus (pert to) ...
  brother .. **4.** Mors (Death)
  known also as .. **6.** Hypnos
  son of .. **3.** Nox (Night)
son, son of (pert to) ...
  a gun .. **5.** rogue **6.** fellow, wretch
  Anak .. **5.** giant
  a Scot .. **3.** Mac
  God .. **11.** Jesus Christ
  Heaven (China) .. **7.** Emperor
  in-law .. **5.** gener
  in Trinity .. **6.** second (person)
  Jacob .. **4.** Levi
  man .. **4.** male **6.** mortal
  Odin .. **2.** Ve
  Odysseus .. **9.** Telegonus
  Priam .. **5.** Paris
  reference to .. **3.** ben **4.** fils **5.** scion **6.** filial **9.** offspring **10.** descendant
  Seth .. **4.** Enos
  the soil .. **6.** farmer **7.** peasant
  youngest .. **5.** cadet
sonance ... **4.** tune **5.** sound **7.** sonancy
sonant ... **5.** sound, tonic, vocal **6.** voiced **8.** sounding **9.** intonated
song ... **3.** air, lay, ode **4.** aria, leed, lilt, noel, poem, tune **5.** carol, chant, ditty, melos, troll, verse **6.** ballad, melody, strain, trifle **7.** chantey (chanty), descant **8.** canticle, pittance **9.** cabaletta
song (pert to) ...
  after .. **5.** epode
  Bib .. **8.** canticle **11.** Song of Songs **13.** Song of Solomon
  boat, gondolier .. **7.** chantey (chanty)
  choral Muse .. **11.** Terpsichore
  collection .. **9.** anthology **10.** cancionero
  college .. **4.** glee
  depressing .. **5.** blues
  evening .. **6.** vesper **8.** evensong, serenade
  French .. **7.** chanson
  funeral .. **5.** dirge, elegy **6.** lament **8.** threnody **9.** epicedium
  gay .. **4.** lilt

German .. **4.** lied **9.** Kunstlied
gypsy .. **10.** zingaresca
Italian .. **7.** canzone
lament .. **8.** threnody
love .. **5.** lyric **6.** ballad **8.** madrigal, serenade
merry .. **4.** lilt
morning .. **5.** matin
mountaineer .. **5.** yodel
pert to .. **5.** melic
praise .. **5.** carol, paean (pean)
sacred .. **4.** hymn **5.** chant, motet, psalm **6.** anthem
sailor's .. **7.** chantey (chanty) **9.** barcarole
short .. **7.** arietta
simple .. **6.** ballad
words .. **6.** lyrics
songbird ... **4.** lark **5.** mavis, robin, veery **6.** canary, oriole, thrush **8.** throstle **11.** mockingbird
sonic recorder ... **9.** echograph
sonnet ... **4.** poem, song **5.** verse
sonnet (pert to) ...
  first eight lines .. **5.** octet
  last six lines .. **6.** sestet
  two quatrains .. **10.** Petrarchan
sonorous ... **4.** loud **6.** tonous **7.** ringing **8.** resonant **9.** melodious **10.** impressive, resounding
sonsy, sonsie ... **5.** buxom, happy **6.** comely **11.** good-natured
sontag ... **4.** cape **6.** jacket
soon ... **3.** ere **4.** anon **5.** early, later **6.** at once **8.** betimes, erelong, quickly, readily, shortly **8.** promptly, speedily **9.** certainly, presently **11.** immediately
Sooner State ... **8.** Oklahoma
sooner than ... **3.** ere **6.** before
soot ... **4.** smut, stup **5.** black, grime, smoke **6.** carbon, smudge **7.** residue **9.** lampblack
soothe ... **3.** pet **4.** calm, lull **5.** allay, quiet **6.** pacify, please, solace **7.** assuage, compose, mollify, relieve, satisfy **8.** mitigate, palliate **9.** alleviate **11.** tranquilize
soother ... **4.** balm **6.** luller **7.** anodyne, placebo **8.** lenitivo, pacifier, sedative **9.** flatterer
soothing ... **5.** balmy, sirup (syrup) **6.** dulcet, gentle **7.** calming **8.** lenitive, sedative **9.** appeasing, demulcent **13.** tranquilizing
soothsayer ... **4.** seer **5.** augur, vatis **6.** mantis **7.** diviner, prophet **8.** Chaldean, haruspex **9.** Cassandra **13.** praying insect **14.** prognosticator
sooty (pert to) ...
  brown .. **6.** bister **8.** teakwood
  color .. **5.** black
  mangabey .. **6.** monkey
  pert to .. **5.** albatross **10.** fuliginous
  petrel .. **7.** skimmer **10.** shearwater
sophistical ... **8.** captious **9.** deceptive, sophistic
sophistication ... **9.** sophistry **10.** corruption, experience **11.** worldliness **13.** ungullibility
soporific ... **4.** drug **6.** drowsy, opiate **7.** anodyne **8.** hypnotic, narcotic, sedative **11.** somniferous **12.** sleep

inducer, somnifacient
soprano (operatic) . . . **4.** Alda, Bori, Lind, Pons **5.** Calvé, Eames **6.** Callas, Steber
sora . . . **4.** rail **5.** crake
sorcerer . . . **4.** mage **5.** Magus **6.** wizard **7.** diviner **8.** conjurer, magician **11.** necromancer
sorceress . . . **3.** hex **5.** Circe, lamia, Medea, witch **6.** Gorgon **7.** vampire **12.** Witch of Endor
sorcery . . . **5.** magic, obeah, spell **6.** voodoo **8.** pishogue **9.** diablerie, diabolism **10.** black magic, necromancy, witchcraft
sordid . . . **3.** low **4.** base, mean, vile **5.** gross **6.** filthy, menial **7.** ignoble, servile, squalid **8.** sluttish, wretched **10.** despicable, slatternly **12.** contemptible
sore . . . **4.** pain, sair **5.** angry, vexed, wound **6.** tender **7.** painful **8.** abrasion, inflamed, offended **9.** irritated, vexatious **11.** distressing **12.** inflammation
soreness . . . **4.** ache **5.** anger **8.** vexation **10.** bitterness, tenderness **11.** painfulness **12.** irritability
sorghum . . . **4.** milo **5.** durra (dari), grain, sorgo **6.** imphee, shallu **8.** feterita
sorority . . . **4.** club **7.** society **10.** fellowship, sisterhood
sorrel . . . **3.** oca **4.** buck, herb **5.** color (horse), Rumex **7.** roselle
Sorrento, Italy (pert to) . . .
anc name . . **9.** Sorrentum
famed as . . **6.** resort
famed for . . **9.** cathedral
site . . **11.** Bay of Naples
sorrow . . . **3.** rue, woe **4.** sigh, teen, weal **5.** dolor, grief, mourn **6.** grieve, lament, misery, repent **7.** remorse, trouble **8.** calamity, distress, egrimony, mourning **9.** adversity, penitence **10.** affliction, contrition **11.** lamentation, tribulation **12.** disconsolate, wretchedness
sorrowful . . . **3.** sad **4.** blue **5.** drear, sadly **6.** dismal, dolent, dreary, rueful **7.** doleful, grieved, tearful, unhappy **8.** mournful **9.** plaintive **10.** afflictive, melancholy **11.** distressing **12.** disconsolate
sorry . . . **3.** sad **4.** hurt **5.** vexed **6.** dismal, gloomy, rueful **7.** painful, pitiful, unhappy **8.** contrite, grievous, mournful, penitent, shameful, wretched **9.** afflicted, chagrined, mortified, regretful, repentant, worthless **10.** displeased, melancholy **12.** disappointed
sort . . . **3.** ilk, way **4.** cull, kind, rank **5.** blend, class, grade, group **6.** assort, manner, nature, strain **7.** quality, species, variety **8.** classify, separate **9.** character **11.** description
sortie . . . **4.** raid **5.** foray, onset, sally **6.** attack, thrust
sottish . . . **4.** dull **6.** stupid **7.** doltish, drunken, foolish **8.** bibulous **9.** senseless
sotto (It) . . . **5.** below, under

sotto voce . . . **5.** aside **8.** secretly **9.** privately, undertone **14.** under the breath
soubrette . . . **9.** lady's maid **10.** intrigante **11.** maidservant
soudagur . . . **8.** merchant **10.** shopkeeper
soul . . . **2.** ba, ka **3.** ego, God **4.** life **5.** anima **6.** pneuma, spirit **7.** essence **8.** inspirer **9.** substance **10.** embodiment **15.** exemplification, personification
soul (pert to) . . .
beatified . . **5.** saint
destiny of . . **8.** theodicy
dwelling place . . **2.** Po **6.** heaven
Egypt . . **2.** Ba
Hindu . . **5.** atman **7.** jivatma
lost . . **9.** âme damnée, the damned
maligners . . **7.** Harpies
music . . **14.** rhythm and blues
personified . . **6.** Psyche
transmigration . . **7.** rebirth **13.** reincarnation
sound . . . **3.** bam, cry, hum **4.** beep, bong, hale, honk, rale, ring, sane, test, tone, toot **5.** drone, noise, plumb, probe, snore, valid, whole **6.** intact, jingle, report, robust, stable, sturdy **7.** feel out, perfect, resound **8.** flawless, reliable, susurrus **9.** undamaged **10.** scrutinize **11.** trustworthy
sound (pert to) . . .
addition to word end . . **8.** paragoge
atonic . . **4.** surd
dashing . . **5.** swash **6.** splash
discordant . . **6.** jangle **9.** cacophony
drum, beating . . **8.** rataplan
explosion . . **4.** boom **6.** report
fixed . . **5.** toned
harsh . . **3.** caw **4.** bray **5.** creak, twang **7.** stridor **9.** cacophony
insect's . . **5.** chirr
loud . . **4.** peal **5.** blare, clang
low . . **3.** hum **4.** moan **5.** drone
metallic . . **4.** ping, ting **5.** clank, clink, twank **8.** tinkle
pert to . . **5.** tonal **6.** sonant **10.** acoustical
prosody . . **4.** rime (rhyme)
reflected . . **4.** echo
sharp . . **3.** pop **7.** rat-a-tat, tapping
shrill . . **5.** reedy
sibilant . . **4.** hiss
similar . . **8.** assonant
small . . **4.** peep **5.** rustle
surf . . **4.** rote **5.** swish
throwing . . **8.** abat-sons
trumpet . . **7.** clarion
unit . . **7.** decibel
warning . . **5.** alarm, siren **6.** tocsin
whispering . . **8.** susurrus
with rhythm . . **5.** music
sounding . . . **5.** depth, rawin **6.** sonant **7.** ringing **8.** sonation **10.** resounding
soundness . . . **5.** truth **6.** sanity **8.** solidity, solvency, strength **9.** integrity, rectitude, stability **10.** heartiness **11.** healthiness
soup . . . **3.** fog **5.** broth, chili, purée **6.** bisque, potage, won ton **7.** borscht, chowder, pottage **8.** bouillon, consommé, gazpacho, julienne **10.** oyster stew **11.** vichyssoise **12.** mulligatawny

soupçon . . . **5.** taste **7.** portion **9.** suspicion **10.** suggestion
soup dish . . . **6.** tureen
sour . . . **3.** wry **4.** acid, tart **5.** acerb, acrid **6.** acetic, bitter, morose, off key, rancid **7.** acetose, acidify, crabbed, pungent, tainted **8.** acescent, embitter **9.** acidulous **10.** astringent, unpleasant
sour (pert to) . . .
apple . . **9.** crab apple
aspect . . **4.** dour, hard **6.** sullen
berry . . **9.** cranberry
bread . . **8.** leavened
cherry . . **7.** morello
stomach . . **4.** acor
turn sour . . **5.** prill **6.** bleeze
source . . **4.** font, germ, mine, rise, root, seed **5.** cause, fount **6.** origin, parent, quarry **8.** fountain **9.** beginning **10.** wellspring **12.** fountainhead
source (pert to) . . .
income . . **7.** revenue
insecticides . . **9.** sabadilla
iodine . . **4.** kelp
ipecac . . **4.** evea
metal . . **3.** ore **7.** bonanza
opium . . **5.** poppy
rubber . . **3.** ule
South Africa . . . see also *South African*
capital . . **8.** Cape Town, Pretoria
city . . **6.** Durban **9.** Germiston **12.** Johannesburg
division . . **5.** Natal **9.** Transvaal **14.** Cape of Good Hope **15.** Orange Free State
exports . . **4.** gold **8.** diamonds
legislature seat location . . **8.** Cape Town
people . . **5.** Boers, Zulus **6.** Bantus **7.** British **10.** Hottentots **11.** Afrikanders (Dutch)
river . . **4.** Vaal **6.** Orange
South African (pert to) . . .
antelope . . **3.** gnu **5.** eland, oribi, peele **6.** rhebok **7.** sassaby
armadillo . . **4.** para
ass (wild) . . **6.** quagga
bird . . **4.** taha
camp . . **6.** laager
Cape ash . . **9.** essenhout
cocktail . . **9.** sundowner
cony . . **3.** das
council . . **4.** Raad
dialect . . **4.** Taal **9.** Afrikaans
diamond (blue-white) . . **5.** jager
fox . . **4.** asse **5.** caama
grass hut . . **8.** rondawel (rondavel)
grassland . . **4.** veld (veldt) **8.** bushveld
mountain, hill . . **3.** kop
snake . . **8.** eggeater
tableland . . **5.** karoo
tree (dogwood) . . **7.** assagai (assegai)
village . . **5.** kraal
war . . **4.** Boer
warrior . . **4.** impi
weaverbird . . **4.** taha
whip . . **7.** sjambok
South American (pert to) . . .
animal . . **2.** ai **4.** paca **5.** llama, sloth, tapir **6.** jaguar, tapeti **7.** agouara (dog) **8.** anteater **9.** armadillo
armadillo . . **4.** apar (apara) **10.** pichiciago (burrowing)

arrow poison . . **6.** curare (curari)
balsam . . **4.** tolu
bellbird . . **8.** arapunga **9.** campanero
bird . . **4.** rara, taha **5.** agami, arara, chaja, macaw **6.** barbet **7.** oilbird, seriema, tinamou **8.** bellbird, boatbill, caracara, guacharo, puffbird
blanket . . **6.** serape
city section . . **6.** barrio
cloth . . **4.** crea
country . . **4.** Peru **5.** Chile **6.** Brazil **7.** Bolivia, Ecuador, Uruguay **8.** Paraguay, Suriname (Surinam) **9.** Argentina, Venezuela
drink . . **5.** assai
fiber . . **6.** yachan
fish . . **4.** paru **7.** piranha, scalare **8.** arapaima
Indian . . **2.** Ge (Gesan) **3.** Ona **4.** Inca **5.** Carib **6.** Tapuya
knife . . **7.** machete
leader . . **6.** Franko **7.** Pizarro
liberator . . **7.** Bolivar
mammal . . **5.** llama, tapir **6.** alpaca **8.** kinkajou **10.** chinchilla
marmoset . . **7.** tamarin
monkey . . **3.** sai **4.** saki, titi **5.** araba **8.** orabassu **9.** barrigudo
mountain range . . **5.** Andes
native . . **5.** Carib **6.** Arawak
ostrich . . **4.** rhea
palm . . **5.** assai **12.** chiquichiqui
parrot . . **5.** macaw
plains . . **6.** llanos, pampas
plainsman . . **7.** llanero
plant . . **6.** ipecac **11.** ipecacuanha
poison . . **6.** curare
river . . **3.** Apa **4.** Acre, Pará **5.** Plata **6.** Amazon, Paraná
rodent . . **5.** coypu **6.** agouti (agouty) **8.** capibara, viscacha **10.** chinchilla
snake . . **4.** lora **5.** aboma **8.** anaconda **10.** bushmaster
stork . . **7.** maguari
tinamou . . **7.** tataupa
toucan . . **7.** aracari
trumpeter . . **5.** agami
tuber . . **3.** oca
vulture . . **6.** condor
weapon . . **4.** bola
wild cat . . **4.** eyra
wind . . **7.** pampero
South Carolina . . .
capital . . **8.** Columbia
city . . **8.** Beaufort **10.** Charleston **11.** Spartanburg
monument . . **10.** Fort Sumter
mountain . . **9.** Blue Ridge, Sassafras
resort . . **11.** Myrtle Beach
State admission . . **6.** Eighth
State bird . . **4.** wren
State flower . . **9.** jessamine
State motto . . **13.** Dum Spiro, Spero (While I Breathe, I Hope)
State nickname . . **8.** Palmetto
State secession . . **5.** First (1860)
South Dakota . . .
capital . . **6.** Pierre
city . . **5.** Huron **8.** Deadwood **9.** Rapid City **10.** Sioux Falls
Indians . . **5.** Brule, Sioux

mine (US largest).. **9.** Homestake
monument.. **10.** Crazy Horse, Mt
Rushmore
mountain.. **10.** Black Hills, Harney Peak
river.. **5.** White **8.** Cheyenne, Missouri
State admission.. **8.** Fortieth (or
Thirty-ninth)
State bird.. **8.** pheasant
State flower.. **12.** pasqueflower
State motto.. **21.** Under God the People
Rule
State nickname.. **6.** Coyote **8.** Sunshine
topography.. **8.** Bad Lands **10.** Black
Hills
southeast wind... **5.** Eurus
southern... **7.** austral
Southern (pert to)...
Buddhism.. **8.** Hinayana
Cross.. **4.** Crux **12.** Stars and Bars
Crown.. **15.** Corona Australis
dish.. **3.** yam **4.** okra, pone **5.** gumbo
7. catfish, hoecake **8.** chess pie, ham
hocks **9.** cornbread **11.** hush puppies
12. chitterlings, turnip greens
shrub.. **8.** magnolia, oleander
States.. **5.** Dixie **7.** Sunbelt
southernmost city... **12.** Puerto Arenas
(Chile)
South Pole bird... **4.** skua **7.** penguin
South Pole constellation... **4.** Pavo
South Sea... **12.** Pacific Ocean
South Sea Bubble... **6.** scheme (1720)
10. stock fraud (Eng)
South Wales people... **7.** Silures
southwest wind... **4.** afer
south wind... **5.** Notus
souvenir... **5.** relic, token **6.** memory,
trophy **7.** memento **8.** keepsake,
memorial, reminder **11.** remembrance
12. recollection, remembrancer
sovereign... **5.** chief, liege, regal, ruler
6. divine, prince, ruling **7.** empress,
monarch, supreme **8.** princely, superior,
suzerain **9.** effectual, gold piece,
paramount, potentate **11.** controlling,
independent
sovereign (pert to)...
claim.. **11.** seigniorage
coin.. **4.** skiv
decree.. **5.** arrêt
pardon.. **7.** amnesty
petty.. **8.** tetrarch
power.. **6.** throne
sovereignty... **5.** realm **6.** diadem,
empery, empire **7.** dynasty, scepter
(sceptre) **8.** dominion **9.** supremacy
Soviet, Russian (pert to)...
committee.. **9.** presidium
farm.. **7.** sovkhoz (sovkhose)
government.. **9.** Communism, Sovietism
10. Bolshevism
hero.. **5.** Lenin
newspaper.. **6.** Pravda **8.** Izvestia
police, secret service.. **3.** KGB
sow... **3.** pig **4.** gilt, seed **5.** plant
7. implant, scatter **8.** disperse, squander
9. broadcast **10.** salamander
11. disseminate
sow bug... **6.** slater
sow thistle... **7.** Sonchus
soybean... **4.** Soja **8.** soya bean

soybean enzyme... **6.** urease
spa... **3.** Ems **4.** Bath **5.** Baden **6.** Bilina
(Bilin), hot tub **7.** Jacuzzi (tm)
space... **3.** gap **4.** area, rank, room,
time, void **5.** blank, inane, niche, place,
range **6.** areola, areole, degree, extent,
vacuum **7.** arrange, expanse **8.** capacity,
distance, interval **9.** concourse, elbow
room
space (pert to)...
architectural.. **6.** metope **8.** pediment
blank.. **5.** chasm **6.** hiatus, lacuna
botany (leaves).. **6.** areola
environment.. **5.** ambit **8.** ambiance
larynx.. **7.** glottis
occupied.. **6.** volume
ref to.. **5.** areal, outer **6.** cosmos, galaxy,
pulsar **7.** heavens, lacunal, spatial
8. galactic, infinity **9.** black hole, deep
space
storage.. **4.** shed **5.** attic, depot **6.** cellar,
garage **9.** storeroom, warehouse
theory.. **7.** plenism
time.. **8.** interval
travel.. **4.** NASA **7.** reentry, swingby
8. time warp
traveler.. **5.** alien **6.** cyborg **8.** aeronaut
9. astronaut, cosmonaut
vehicle.. **6.** rocket, Skylab **7.** shuttle,
sputnik
void.. **5.** chasm **7.** inanity
wall.. **5.** niche
spacious... **5.** ample, broad, roomy
9. capacious, expansive, extensive
10. commodious, far and wide,
widespread **13.** comprehensive
spadassin... **5.** bravo **7.** duelist
9. swordsman
spade... **3.** dig, loy **4.** spud, stag (3-yr
old), suit (cards) **5.** slade **6.** shovel
11. playing card
spade (pert to)...
bone.. **13.** shoulder blade
fish.. **5.** porgy **10.** paddlefish
foot.. **4.** toad
grass.. **4.** rush
Irish.. **5.** slane
money.. **7.** Chinese (early)
peat.. **5.** slade
triangular.. **5.** didle
spae... **6.** divine **8.** foretell
Spain... see also *Spanish*
cape.. **9.** Trafalgar
capital.. **6.** Madrid
city.. **4.** Irun **5.** Cadiz, Lorca **6.** Malaga
7. Cordoba, Granada, Seville **8.** Valencia
9. Barcelona
city cathedral.. **9.** Saragossa
islands.. **5.** Ceuta **6.** Canary **7.** Melilla
8. Balearic
kingdom, region.. **4.** Léon **6.** Aragon,
Basque (Provinces) **7.** Castile, Navarre
8. Asturias **9.** Catalonia
mountain.. **8.** Asturias, Pyrenees
old name.. **6.** Iberia
palace.. **8.** Escorial
plain, plateau.. **6.** Meseta
river.. **4.** Ebro, Muga **5.** Tagus
span... **3.** two **4.** arch, join, pair, team
6. bridge, extend, length, period (time)
7. breadth, measure, stretch **8.** overarch

9. encompass
spangle ... **6.** aiglet, sequin **7.** glitter, sparkle **8.** ornament, zecchino
spaniel ... **5.** trasy **6.** cocker **8.** Brittany, springer
Spanish (pert to) ...
alcazar (palace) .. **8.** Alhambra
arbor .. **6.** ramada
art museum .. **5.** Prado
battle .. **6.** Armada (1588)
bayonet .. **5.** yucca
boat .. **5.** aviso **7.** galleon (ship)
Christmas .. **7.** Navidad
cloak .. **4.** capa **5.** manta **6.** mantle **7.** zamarra (zamarro)
corral .. **5.** atajo
dance .. **5.** tango **6.** bolero, gitano **8.** fandango, flamenco, saraband
fabric .. **4.** crea (cotton) **5.** tiraz (silk)
fleet, famed .. **6.** Armada
fortress chief .. **4.** caid **7.** alcaide
friend .. **5.** amigo
fruit .. **8.** pimiento
game .. **6.** pelota **7.** jai alai
garment .. **6.** serape **8.** mantilla
gift holder .. **6.** piñata
gold .. **3.** oro **8.** El Dorado
governor .. **10.** gobernador
grass .. **5.** spart **7.** esparto
gruel .. **5.** atole
gypsy .. **7.** zincalo
holiday .. **6.** fiesta
horse .. **5.** genet **6.** jennet **7.** caballo
hotel .. **6.** posada
house .. **4.** casa **6.** casita
jar .. **4.** olla, tina **6.** tinaja
knight .. **8.** cavalier **9.** caballero
lake .. **4.** lago
language .. **6.** Basque **7.** Catalan, Spanish **8.** Galician **9.** Castilian
light opera .. **8.** zarzuela
mausoleum .. **8.** Escorial
musical instrument .. **6.** atabel, guitar **8.** castanet
plant .. **3.** aji **8.** capsicum
porridge .. **5.** atole
promenade .. **5.** paseo
raisin .. **4.** pasa
river .. **3.** ria, rio
road .. **6.** camino
room .. **4.** sala
shawl .. **5.** manta **6.** serape
sheep .. **6.** merino
sherry .. **5.** Xeres **7.** oloroso
sorcerer .. **5.** brujo
street .. **5.** calle
three .. **4.** tres
title .. **3.** don **5.** señor **6.** señora **7.** hidalgo **8.** señorita
trail .. **6.** camino
vehicle .. **7.** tartana
watch .. **5.** reloj
watchtower .. **7.** atalaya
watchword .. **6.** alerta
watercourse .. **6.** arroyo
wind .. **6.** solano
window .. **7.** ventana
witchcraft .. **8.** brujeria
year .. **3.** ano
Spanish people ...
architect .. **5.** Gaudi **11.** Churriguera

artist .. **4.** Dali, Goya, Gris, Miró **6.** Ribera **7.** Murillo **8.** Zurbarán **9.** Velázquez (Velásquez)
author .. **9.** Cervantes **11.** García Lorca, Pérez Galdos
cellist .. **6.** Casals
chaperone .. **6.** duenna
composer .. **5.** Falla
conqueror .. **6.** Cortés (Cortez) **7.** Pizarro
dictator, general .. **6.** Franco
dramatist .. **9.** Echegaray (Nobel Prize 1904)
explorer .. **6.** Balboa **11.** Ponce de León
gentleman .. **5.** señor **8.** cavalier **9.** caballero
God .. **4.** Dios
guitarist .. **7.** Segovia
herdsman .. **7.** llanero **8.** ranchero
hero .. **3.** Cid
justice of the peace .. **7.** entrada
king .. **7.** Alfonso, Charles **9.** Ferdinand
lady .. **4.** doña **6.** señora **8.** señorita
letter carrier .. **6.** correo
man .. **3.** don **6.** hombre
missionary .. **5.** Serra
monk .. **5.** padre
peasant .. **7.** paisano
people .. **7.** genta
pianist .. **6.** Iturbi
pretender to throne .. **6.** Carlos (Don)
Queen .. **8.** Isabella
singer, tenor .. **7.** Domingo (Placido)
soldier .. **8.** miquelet
soprano .. **4.** Bori (Lucrezia)
spar ... **3.** box **4.** beam, boom, gaff, mast, rung, yard **5.** sprit, steve **6.** timber **7.** dispute, quarrel, topmast, yardarm
spare ... **4.** lean, thin **5.** chary, lanky **6.** afford, exempt, frugal, meager, scanty **7.** sparing, surplus **8.** preserve **9.** duplicate, parsimony **10.** economical, occasional **11.** superfluous **12.** parsimonious
spare time ... **7.** leisure
sparing ... **5.** chary **6.** frugal, meager, saving, scanty **7.** scrimpy, thrifty **8.** merciful, reticent, stinting **9.** scrimping **12.** parsimonious
spark ... **4.** beau, fire, funk **5.** aizle, court, dandy, lover **6.** incite **7.** diamond, gallant, glitter, modicum, sparkle **8.** humorist **10.** sweetheart **11.** scintillate
sparkle ... **5.** flash, gleam, glint, shine, trace **7.** be smart, be witty, glisten, glister, glitter, radiate, reflect, spangle, twinkle **8.** be lively **9.** coruscate **10.** effervesce, illuminate **11.** scintillate **13.** scintillation
sparkling ... **4.** dewy **5.** crisp, witty **6.** bright, starry **7.** shining **8.** cheerful, eloquent, glittery, gorgeous, mousseux (wine) **9.** twinkling **10.** glittering, reflecting **12.** effervescent
sparoid fish ... **4.** scup **5.** porgy **8.** sea bream **10.** sheepshead
Sparta, Greece ... see also Spartan
capital .. **7.** Laconia (anc)
kingdom .. **12.** Peloponnesus
river .. **7.** Eurotas
spartan ... **5.** hardy, stoic **10.** courageous **13.** uncomplaining

Spartan (pert to) . . .
army division . . **4.** mora **6.** lochus
cipher writing . . **7.** scytale
class (anc) . . **8.** perioeci
commander . . **7.** lochage
dog . . **10.** bloodhound
festival . . **6.** Carnea **7.** Carneia
king . . **8.** Leonidas, Menelaus
lawgiver . . **8.** Lycurgus
magistrate . . **5.** ephor
native . . **8.** Laconian **9.** Spartiate
serf . . **5.** helot
spasmodic . . . **6.** fitful **7.** snatchy
9. excitable, irregular **10.** convulsive
12. intermittent **13.** highly wrought
spasmodic (pert to) . . .
disease . . **5.** croup **7.** tetanus
inspiration . . **8.** hiccough
twitch . . **3.** tic
spat . . . **3.** row **4.** slap, tiff **5.** spawn
6. gaiter, oyster, strike **7.** dispute,
legging, quarrel **10.** oysterseed
spate . . . **4.** gush **5.** flood **7.** freshet, torrent
9. overwhelm, rainstorm **10.** waterspout
spatial . . . **5.** areal **8.** sterical
11. dimensional
spatter . . . **3.** wet **4.** soil, spot **5.** spurt
6. dabble, splash **7.** sputter **8.** splutter,
sprinkle
spawn . . . **3.** ova, roe **4.** eggs, germ, seed
7. lay eggs **8.** generate **13.** numerous
issue
speak . . . **3.** say **4.** chat, lisp, talk, tell
5. orate, utter **6.** reveal **7.** address,
chatter, declaim, sputter **8.** converse,
proclaim **9.** discourse, pronounce
10. articulate **11.** tell in words
speak (pert to) . . .
affectedly . . **4.** mime **5.** mince
against . . **6.** oppose
boastfully . . **4.** brag **5.** vaunt **7.** enlarge
10. exaggerate
from memory . . **6.** recite
ill of . . **5.** decry **8.** backbite **9.** disparage
noisily . . **4.** rant, rime **8.** harangue
offhand . . **11.** extemporize
slowly . . **5.** drawl
softly . . **7.** whisper
under breath . . **5.** mouth **6.** mumble,
murmur, mutter **7.** grumble
speaker . . . **5.** sayer **6.** lisper, orator,
proser **8.** lecturer **9.** demagogue
10. mouthpiece, prolocutor
11. spellbinder
speaker of languages . . . **8.** linguist,
polyglot
speaking (pert to) . . .
generally . . **7.** as a rule, roughly **12.** in
the long run **13.** approximately
of . . **7.** apropos **12.** incidentally
offhand . . **13.** extemporizing
privately . . **7.** whisper **9.** in one's ear
11. into one's ear
publicly . . **7.** oratory **11.** declamation
style . . **8.** fluently
spear . . . **4.** dart, pike, stab **5.** catch, lance
6. pierce, weapon **7.** javelin, missile
9. penetrate
spear (pert to) . . .
anc Teutons . . **6.** framea (fram)
fish . . **3.** gig **4.** gaff

iron-tipped . . **7.** assagai
shaped . . **7.** hastate
three-pronged . . **7.** trident
two-pronged . . **6.** bident
spearfish . . . **6.** marlin **9.** quillback
special . . . **4.** rare **5.** extra **6.** unique
7. notable, unusual **8.** concrete,
detailed, favorite, specific, uncommon
10. individual, noteworthy, particular,
restricted **11.** distinctive, exceptional
13. extraordinary
special (pert to) . . .
ability . . **5.** forte **6.** talent **7.** charism
8. charisma
commodity . . **6.** leader **7.** feature **10.** best
seller
edition . . **5.** extra
favor . . **9.** influence, privilege
train . . **5.** flier **7.** express **10.** cannonball
specialist (pert to) . . .
atomic . . **9.** physicist
ear . . **6.** aurist **9.** otologist
eye . . **7.** oculist **15.** ophthalmologist
medical . . **6.** doctor **7.** surgeon
money . . **9.** economist
specialty . . . **5.** skill **8.** aptitude, contract
13. particularity **14.** characteristic
specie . . . **4.** cash, coin **5.** money (hard)
species . . . **4.** kind, sort, type **5.** class,
genre, genus, group **7.** general, isotope,
mankind, variety **8.** category, humanity
11. Homo sapiens **12.** nomenclature
specific . . . **5.** exact, virus **6.** remedy
7. limited, precise, special **8.** definite,
detailed, explicit, peculiar
specificity . . . **9.** haecceity
specify . . . **4.** name **5.** limit, state
6. define, detail **8.** indicate **9.** be precise,
designate, enumerate, stipulate
specimen . . . **4.** copy **5.** model, piece,
taste, token **6.** person, sample, swatch
7. example, pattern **14.** representative
specious . . . **4.** fair **5.** showy **7.** alleged
8. illusory, pleasing **9.** plausible
10. ostensible **12.** hypocritical
speck . . . **3.** bit, dot, jot, nit **4.** blot, iota,
mark, mite, mote, spot, whit **5.** fleck,
stain **7.** blemish **8.** particle **10.** sand
darter
speckled . . . **6.** menald **7.** mottled
9. sprinkled **10.** variegated
spectacle . . . **4.** show, view **5.** scene, sight
6. wonder **7.** diorama, display, pageant
8. panorama, spyglass **10.** exhibition
14. representation
spectacles . . . **7.** glasses
spectator . . . **6.** espier, viewer **7.** watcher,
witness **8.** audience, beholder, kibitzer,
looker-on, observer, onlooker
9. bystander
specter, spectre . . . **4.** bogy (bogey,
bogie) **5.** ghost, shade, spook **6.** idolum,
spirit, wraith **7.** eidolon, phantom
8. illusion, phantasm, revenant
10. apparition
spectral . . . **5.** eerie (eery) **6.** ghosty,
spooky **7.** ghostly, phantom
12. apparitional
speculate . . . **5.** guess, think **6.** gamble,
ponder, wonder **8.** consider, meditate,
ruminate, theorize **10.** deliberate,

doctrinize, philosophy 11. contemplate
speculative ... 5. risky 9. uncertain
10. thoughtful 11. inquisitive, theoretical
12. experimental 13. contemplative
speculator ... 7. lookout, scalper
8. explorer, observer, theorist
12. investigator
speculum ... 7. diopter 9. reflector
sped ... 4. hied 5. raced 6. darted,
dashed, let fly 8. galloped, hastened
10. discharged
speech ... 5. spiel 6. dilogy, orison
7. address, chatter, diction, oration
8. colloquy, harangue, language
9. elocution, utterance 12. conversation
speech (pert to) ...
abusive .. 6. tirade
blunder .. 8. improper, solecism
comb form .. 4. logo
conclusion .. 10. peroration
conversational .. 13. colloquialism
defective .. 10. disphrasia
difficulty .. 9. baryphony 10. baryphonia
famous .. 9. Philippic (Demosthenes)
goddess .. 3. Vac
hasty .. 7. stammer, stumble, stutter
impediment .. 4. lisp 8. betacism,
mytacism
intemperate .. 6. tirade
loss of .. 6. alalia 7. aphasia
movements .. 9. vocimotor
parts .. 4. verb 6. adverb 9. adjective
11. conjunction, preposition
12. interjection
pompous .. 12. magniloquent
provincial .. 6. patois 7. dialect
set speech (drama) .. 6. rhesis
term .. 6. zeugma 9. syllepsis
understatement .. 7. litotes
vitriolic .. 6. tirade
voiceless .. 7. spirate
without .. 4. mute 6. alogia
world .. 7. Volapük 9. Esperanto
speechless ... 4. dumb, mute 6. silent
7. aphasic 8. taciturn 9. voiceless
speed ... 3. fly, hie, run 4. flit, race,
zoom 5. haste, hurry, spurt 6. assist,
go fast, hasten 8. celerity, dispatch,
expedite, promptly, rapidity, velocity
9. posthaste, quickness, swiftness
10. accelerate, expedition, facilitate
12. precipitance
speedily ... 4. soon 5. apace 6. presto
7. betimes, quickly, rapidly, swiftly
8. promptly 13. expeditiously
speedy ... 4. fast 5. apace, fleet, hasty,
quick, rapid, swift 6. prompt, racing,
sudden
spell ... 4. bout, mean, snap, tell, turn
5. charm, magic, relay, shift 6. glamor,
relate, relief, trance 7. explain,
relieve, sorcery, syncope 9. take turns
11. abracadabra 12. entrancement
13. substitute for
spell (pert to) ...
binder .. 6. orator 7. charmer, spieler
bound .. 4. rapt 9. enchanted
10. astonished, interested 11. under
a spell
brief .. 4. snap
in another alphabet .. 13. transliterate

out .. 7. explain, itemize
pretended .. 11. abracadabra
under a spell .. 9. in a trance
10. hypnotized, mesmerized
with loss of letter .. 7. syncope
spend ... 3. use 4. pass 5. waste
6. employ, expend, lavish, weaken
7. consume, exhaust 8. disburse,
squander 9. dissipate, sacrifice
10. distribute
spend the summer ... 8. estivate
(aestivate)
spendthrift ... 4. daft 6. waster
7. spender, wastrel 8. prodigal
10. profligate, squanderer
Spenser, Edmund (pert to) ...
character .. 3. Una
famed as .. 4. poet
famed work .. 12. Faerie Queene
poetic stanza .. 10. Spenserian
Spenser's Ireland personified ...
5. Irene
spent ... 4. paid 5. weary 6. effete, used
up, wasted 7. worn out 8. consumed,
lavished, tired out 9. exhausted
10. squandered
speos ... 4. cave, tomb 6. grotto
sphenoid ... 11. wedge-shaped
sphere ... 3. orb 4. ball, star 5. arena,
earth, field, glove, orbit, realm,
scope 6. extent, planet 7. circuit,
heavens 8. terrible 10. atmosphere
12. jurisdiction
sphere of ...
action .. 6. domain
life .. 5. world
making .. 7. orbific
spherical (pert to) ...
aberration, free from .. 9. aplanatic
geometry .. 10. magnitudes
lune .. 7. portion
magnet .. 8. terrella (terella)
nearly .. 8. obrotund
reference to .. 6. rotund 7. globose
9. orbicular 15. celestial bodies
ungula .. 5. wedge
sphericity ... 9. globosity, rotundity,
roundness
sphinx (pert to) ...
builder (Great Sphinx) .. 6. Khafre (IV
Dynasty)
Great Sphinx site .. 4. Gaza (Egypt)
Greek myth .. 7. monster (sphinxlike)
reference to .. 9. enigmatic
11. inscrutable
Zool .. 8. hawk moth
spice ... 4. dill, herb, mace, sage 5. chili,
clove 6. cassia, nutmeg, pepper,
season, stacte 7. mustard 8. marjoram,
pungency 9. condiment, flavoring,
fragrance, seasoning
spicy ... 3. hot 4. keen, racy, sexy
5. balmy, natty, smart 6. risque
7. gingery, peppery, piquant, pungent
8. aromatic, fragrant, spirited
spider ... 3. cob, pan 5. arain 6. Epeira,
katipo, tripod, trivet 7. pokomoo, retiary,
skillet, spinner 8. arachnid, attercop,
telarian 9. tarantula 10. black widow
spider (pert to) ...
comb form .. 7. arachno

crab . . **4.** Maia (genus)
fly . . **4.** tick
genus . . **4.** Maia **6.** Aranea **7.** Agalena,
Attidae, Pholcus **9.** Drassidae
Gr Myth . . **7.** Arachne (Lydian girl)
Latin . . **6.** aranea
leaping . . **10.** saltigrade
monkey . . **6.** ateles, coaita
nest . . **5.** nidus
scorpion . . **8.** pedipalp
scorpion appendage . . **10.** pedipalpus
study of . . **10.** araneology
web (anc) . . **8.** attercop
weblike . . **9.** arachnoid
web-spinning organ . . **9.** spinneret
spieler . . . **5.** crier **6.** barker, talker
7. sharper, speaker **8.** lecturer
9. solicitor **10.** ballyhooer
spiffy . . . **4.** fine, neat **5.** smart **8.** splendid
9. excellent
spigot . . . **3.** peg, tap **5.** spile, spout
6. dossil, faucet **7.** stopper
spike . . . **3.** cob, ear **4.** brob, stab,
tine, umbo **5.** ament, piton, prong,
thorn **6.** antler, flower, pierce, spadix
7. amentum, disable, spinule, trenail
10. adulterate **12.** tenpenny nail
spikenard . . . **3.** phu (Cretan) **4.** herb,
nard **8.** ointment
spile . . . **3.** pin, rod **4.** plug, tube **5.** spill,
spout, stake **6.** Aralia, spigot
spill . . . **4.** blab, fall, shed, slop **5.** flosh,
waste **6.** let out, splash, tumble
7. divulge, scatter **8.** downpour,
overflow, overture **11.** tell secrets
spin . . . **4.** birl, fish, reel, ride, turn **5.** swirl,
twirl, twist, whirl **6.** extend, gyrate,
rotate **7.** prolong, revolve
spinach (wrinkled) . . . **5.** savoy
spinal (pert to) . . .
column . . **9.** vertebrae
cord . . **4.** alba **6.** myelon (marrow)
16. medulla oblongata
disease . . **8.** myelitis **10.** meningitis
muscle (attached) . . **5.** psoas
spindle . . . **3.** pin, rod **4.** axis, axle, hasp
5. pivot, xeres **6.** swivel **7.** capstan,
mandrel
spindle-legged . . . **4.** lean **5.** lanky
14. spindle-shanked
spindling . . . **4.** long **5.** gawky, leggy
6. skinny **7.** slender **11.** ineffectual
spine . . . **3.** awn **4.** axis, seta **5.** chine,
ridge, thorn **6.** spirit **7.** acicula,
courage, process **8.** backbone, spiculum
9. scoliosis (curvature) **12.** spinal
column
spinel . . . **5.** balas (ruby) **6.** mineral
8. spinelle
spineless . . . **4.** limp, weak **5.** frail
10. weak-willed **12.** invertebrate
spinet . . . **5.** piano **7.** giraffe **8.** virginal
10. clavichord **11.** couched harp,
harpsichord
spinnaker . . . **4.** sail
spinner . . . **3.** top **4.** liar **6.** spider, weaver
8. narrator **9.** nighthawk **10.** goatsucker
11. storyteller **12.** whippoorwill
spinning . . . **6.** rotary **7.** strobic **8.** telarian,
whirling **9.** revolving
spinning device . . . **5.** jenny **7.** distaff,

spindle **8.** throstle
spiracle . . . **4.** pore, vent **7.** orifice
8. aperture, blowhole
spiral . . . **4.** coil, curl **5.** helix **6.** galaxy,
volute **7.** helical, winding **8.** circling,
helicoid **9.** corkscrew
spire . . . **4.** coil, surl **5.** tower, twist, whorl
6. ascend, finial, summit **7.** steeple
spire finial . . . **3.** épi
spirit . . . **3.** imp, pep, vim **4.** dash,
élan, fire, life, mood, pixy, soul
5. demon, devil, fairy, genie, ghost,
heart, metal, pluck, Satan, shade,
spook, verve **6.** animus, breath, energy,
fervor, goblin, intent, morale, pneuma,
sprite **7.** bravery, courage, essence,
extract, gremlin, specter **8.** spiritus
9. animation **10.** enterprise, individual
11. real meaning **12.** cheerfulness
13. consciousness
spirit, spirit of (pert to) . . .
avarice . . **6.** Mammon
bad . . **6.** afreet **7.** Amaimon (Amaymon)
Egypt . . **2.** ba, ka **3.** akh
English folklore . . **2.** po
evil . . **4.** jinn **5.** Aecto, jinni (jinnel)
6. Azazel, Belial, Erinys **7.** Tempter
(The) **9.** Beelzebub
female . . **6.** undine **7.** banshee
good . . **8.** Eudaemon
household . . **5.** Lares **15.** Lares and
Penates
infatuation . . **3.** Ate
knights . . **8.** errantry
malignant . . **3.** Ker
mockery . . **5.** Momus
people . . **5.** ethos
refined . . **6.** elixir
tapping (theory) . . **9.** typtology
the age . . **9.** Zeitgeist
the air . . **5.** Ariel
the sea . . **5.** siren **6.** Triton **7.** mermaid,
Neptune **9.** Davy Jones
spirited . . . **3.** gay **4.** gamy, racy **5.** brisk,
eager, fiery **6.** lively, plucky, spunky
7. dashing, fervent **8.** eloquent,
generous, vigorous **9.** audacious,
energetic, spiritoso, sprightly
10. mettlesome
spiritless . . . **4.** dead, dull, meek **5.** amort,
vapid **6.** gloomy **8.** dejected, lifeless,
listless **9.** depressed, heartless
10. despondent, dispirited
spirits (pert to) . . .
Babylonian . . **5.** Igigi
dwelling . . **2.** po **5.** Hades **7.** Elysium
low . . **5.** blues, dumps, gloom
8. doldrums
of the dead . . **5.** Manes (Rom) **7.** lemures
9. chthonian (Gr)
spiritual . . . **4.** holy, pure, song **5.** pious
6. devout, divine, sacred **7.** psychic
8. churchly, internal, platonic, spectral
9. unworldly **10.** immaterial
11. disembodied, incorporeal
12. supernatural **14.** ecclesiastical,
heavenly minded
spiritual (pert to) . . .
affinity . . **8.** soul mate
apathy . . **6.** acedia
being . . **3.** ens **5.** angel **6.** seraph

darkness .. **4.** Hell **5.** tamas
director .. **9.** confessor
meaning of words .. **7.** anagoge
meeting .. **6.** séance
shrine .. **6.** adytum **7.** sanctum
spirt ... **3.** jet **4.** gush **5.** flare, spurt
6. squirt
spit ... **3.** rod **4.** rain **5.** eject, image,
stick **6.** impale, pierce, saliva, skewer,
sputum **7.** hissing, spindle, sputter
8. likeness, sprinkle, turnspit
9. exsputory **11.** expectorate
spite ... **3.** vex **4.** hate **5.** pique, shame,
venom **6.** enmity, malice, offend,
rancor, thwart **7.** dislike, ill will
8. disgrace, dishonor **9.** animosity,
cattiness, humiliate **10.** resentment
11. malevolence **12.** spitefulness
spiteful ... **4.** mean **5.** catty **7.** cattish
8. annoying, venomous **9.** malicious,
malignant **10.** irritating, vindictive
spittoon ... **6.** pigdan **8.** crachoir,
cuspidor
splash ... **3.** lap, wet **4.** spot **5.** spray,
swash **6.** blotch, flouse (floush), ripple
7. scatter, spatter, splurge **8.** cut a dash,
splatter **9.** dashingly **14.** ostentatiously
splashboard ... **4.** gate (false) **5.** plank
6. fender, screen **9.** dashboard
10. flashboard, flushboard
splay ... **3.** hem **4.** turn **5.** adorn, carve,
slant, slope **6.** clumsy, expand, spread
7. awkward, display **9.** dislocate,
displayed, expansion
spleen ... **3.** fit **4.** fire, mood, whim
5. anger, ardor, freak, gland **6.** malice,
temper **7.** impulse **8.** ill humor
10. low spirits, melancholy, resentment
11. impetuosity
spleen (pert to) ...
amarinth .. **4.** weed
excision .. **13.** splenectomize
reference to .. **6.** lienal **7.** splenic
splendid ... **4.** braw, fine **5.** grand, regal,
showy **6.** costly, superb **7.** gallant,
shining, sublime **8.** glorious, gorgeous
9. beautiful, brilliant, excellent,
sumptuous **10.** brilliance, effulgence
11. illustrious, magnificent
splendor ... **4.** gite, pomp **5.** éclat, glory
6. beauty, luster **7.** display **8.** grandeur,
radiance, richness **9.** pageantry,
showiness **10.** brilliance
12. gorgeousness, magnificence,
resplendence
splint ... **4.** scob, tace **5.** brace, plate,
strip **6.** fasten, tasset **7.** confine
splinter ... **4.** chip **5.** break, broom
6. shiver, sliver **7.** shatter **8.** fragment
9. matchwood
split ... **3.** cut, rit **4.** chap, open, rend,
rent, rive, tear **5.** break, burst, cleft,
crack, laugh, leave (sl), riven, wedge
6. bisect, cleave, cloven, depart (sl),
divide, sunder **7.** dispart, divided,
rupture, shatter **8.** separate **9.** apportion,
partition **10.** separation
split (pert to) ...
hairs .. **7.** quibble **12.** discriminate
13. differentiate
into two parts .. **5.** bifid **6.** cloven

pea .. **3.** dal **5.** dahll
the difference .. **5.** share **7.** average
10. compromise **12.** go fifty-fifty
up .. **5.** cleft **7.** disband, divorce
8. separate **9.** apportion, partition
spoil ... **3.** mar, rot **4.** loot, prey, ruin,
sack **5.** botch, decay, harry **6.** coddle,
impair, injure, pamper **7.** destroy,
estrepe, louse up (sl), pillage, plunder,
vitiate **9.** frustrate
spoilation ... **6.** rapine **7.** pillage
10. plundering, spoliation
spoiled ... **3.** bad **5.** moldy, musty
6. addled, marred, molded, preyed,
rancid, wasted **7.** botched, bungled,
decayed, tainted **8.** pampered, pillaged
9. plundered **12.** deteriorated
spoiler ... **6.** robber **7.** marplot **8.** pillager
9. despoiler, plunderer
spoils ... **4.** loot, prey, swag **5.** booty,
perks (sl) **11.** perquisites
spoilsport ... **7.** marplot **10.** wet blanket
11. party-pooper
spoke ... **3.** bar, pin, ray, rod **4.** rung,
said **5.** check, round, spake, stake
6. radius, speech **7.** uttered **9.** hindrance
10. impediment
spoke monotonously ... **6.** droned
spoken ... **4.** oral **5.** parol **9.** declaimed,
ideophone (word)
spoliation ... **6.** rapine **7.** pillage
8. ravaging **10.** spoilation
sponge ... **3.** dry, wet **4.** bath, swab
5. erase, mooch **6.** absorb, animal,
efface, eraser, extort **7.** badiaga,
cleanse, sponger, zimocca **8.** drunkard,
parasite **9.** absorbent, sycophant
10. obliterate, porousness
sponge (pert to) ...
Europe .. **7.** badiaga
fruit .. **5.** luffa (loofah)
Mediterranean .. **7.** zimocca
opening .. **7.** apopyle
orifice .. **7.** osculum
young .. **5.** ascon **6.** rhagon
sponger ... **4.** sorn **5.** leech **6.** cadger
7. moocher **8.** parasite **9.** scrounger
10. freeloader
sponsor ... **5.** angel **6.** backer, patron
7. finance **9.** financier, godparent,
guarantee, guarantor, patronize
sponsorship ... **5.** aegis (egis) **7.** subsidy
8. auspices
spontaneous ... **4.** free **6.** native
8. untaught **9.** automatic, voluntary
10. self-acting **11.** instinctive,
involuntary
spontoon ... **4.** club, pike **7.** halberd,
pantoon **9.** espantoon, truncheon
spoof ... **3.** guy **4.** fool, hoax, joke
5. trick **7.** deceive, swindle **8.** nonsense
9. deception
spook ... **5.** ghost **6.** spirit, zombie (zombi)
7. specter **8.** frighten **9.** hobgoblin
10. apparition
spooky ... **5.** eerie, weird **7.** ghostly,
haunted, uncanny **8.** spectral
spool ... **4.** reel, wind **6.** bobbin **7.** spindle
8. cylinder
spoon ... **4.** club **5.** labis, ladle **6.** shovel
7. fish for **8.** cochlear, make love,

runcible

spoonbill . . . **5.** ajaja (ayaya) **9.** sandpiper

Spoon River poet . . . **7.** Masters (E L)

spore (pert to) . . .
capsule, sac . . **5.** ascus, theca
  10. sporangium
cluster . . **5.** sorus
formation . . **6.** tetrad
fruit . . **7.** asocarp

sport . . . **3.** fun, toy **4.** game, hunt,
jest, joke, play, romp, wear **5.** dandy,
mirth **6.** banter, flaunt, frolic, gamble,
racing, skiing **7.** contest, gambler,
jesting, mockery, pastime **8.** raillery
9. amusement, bon vivant, diversion,
good loser, plaything, sportsman
10. pleasantry, recreation
13. entertainment

sport (pert to) . . .
art of (contests) . . **10.** agonistics
cheap . . **5.** piker
of kings . . **6.** racing **7.** the turf

sportive . . . **3.** gay **5.** merry **7.** jocular,
playful **8.** frolicky, playsome **9.** facetious
10. frolicsome

sports . . . **5.** Rugby, track **6.** hockey, jai
lai, soccer, squash, tennis **7.** cricket
8. baseball, football, la crosse, softball
9. athletics, palaestra **10.** acrobatics,
gymnastics **11.** racquetball

sports attendance . . . **4.** gate

sports official . . . **5.** coach, judge
6. umpire **7.** referee **8.** linesman
10. timekeeper

sporty . . . **5.** rorty, showy **6.** dressy,
flashy

spot . . . **3.** dot **4.** blet, blot, espy, flaw,
mark, site, soil **5.** fleck, place, point,
speck, stain, taint **6.** detect, locate,
macula, macule, stigma **7.** asperse,
blemish, freckle, observe, speckle,
splotch **8.** discolor, disgrace, locality,
location, position **9.** bespatter, limelight,
recognize **11.** predicament, small
amount

spot (pert to) . . .
cards . . **3.** pip
fertile . . **5.** oasis
fish . . **7.** pinfish
high . . **4.** apex **6.** climax
mineral . . **5.** macle
on the spot . . **3.** now **4.** here **7.** imperil,
present **8.** promptly
payment . . **4.** cash
secluded . . **6.** alcove
sun . . **6.** lucule **7.** granule
wood . . **3.** wem

spotless . . . **4.** pure **5.** clean **6.** chaste
8. innocent **9.** blameless, faultless,
unsullied **10.** immaculate
11. unblemished, untarnished
14. irreproachable

spotted . . . **6.** espied, marked, soiled
7. dappled, guttate (droplike), mottled,
stained, sullied **8.** speckled
9. blemished, sprinkled, tarnished
11. diversified

spouse . . . **4.** mate, wife **5.** bride
7. consort, partner **9.** companion
10. better half

spout . . . **3.** jet, jut, lip **4.** dale,

gush, pawn, rant, spew **5.** erupt,
spile, spurt **6.** pledge, recite, spigot,
squirt, trough **7.** chatter, conduit,
declaim **8.** downpour, gargoyle (carved)
9. discharge, waterfall **10.** waterspout

spouter . . . **5.** whale **6.** geyser **7.** oil well,
speaker **9.** declaimer **11.** speechifier

sprat . . . **6.** garvie **7.** herring **8.** sixpence

spray . . . **3.** jet **4.** foam **5.** stour, water
6. squirt **7.** atomize, flowers, gunfire
8. perfumer, sprinkle **9.** spindrift
10. spoondrift

spread . . . **3.** ted **4.** meal **5.** bruit, feast,
flare, strew, widen **6.** expand, extent,
sprawl, unfurl **7.** divulge, radiate, scatter
8. disperse **10.** broadcast **11.** disseminate
13. advertisement

spread (pert to) . . .
by defamation . . **5.** libel
by report . . **6.** norate
by rumor . . **5.** noise
eagle . . **8.** boastful, insignia **9.** patriotic
12. exaggeration
out . . **3.** fan **4.** open, span **5.** flare
6. deploy
over . . **5.** cover, smear
thickly . . **7.** slather
thin . . **4.** bray

spree . . . **4.** lark, orgy, romp **5.** binge,
revel **6.** bender, frolic, shindy **7.** wassail
8. carousal

sprig . . . **4.** trim, twig **5.** scion, shoot,
smart **6.** active, spruce **8.** ornament
9. youngling

sprightly . . . **3.** gay **4.** airy, pert **5.** alive,
brisk, peart **6.** blithe, lively **7.** briskly,
ghostly **8.** vigorous **10.** enlivening,
spiritedly **11.** incorporeal

spring . . . **3.** fly, hop, spa **4.** dart, font,
jump, leap, well **5.** shoot, spurt, vault,
vigor **6.** bounce, energy, geyser, origin,
season, source **9.** saltation **10.** elasticity,
resilience

spring (pert to) . . .
back . . **6.** recoil, resile **7.** rebound
of the Muses . . **7.** Pierian
ref to . . **6.** vernal
up . . **4.** grow **5.** arise, occur **6.** appear,
ascend **9.** originate

springing into being . . . **9.** renascent

springs . . . **4.** spas **5.** baths, fonts **6.** resort
(health) **7.** thermae

sprinkle . . . **3.** deg, dot, wet **4.** rain
5. bedew, spray, strew, water **6.** bedrop,
sparge, spreng **7.** baptize, scatter
9. bespatter

sprinkler . . . **11.** aspergillum (Eccl)

sprinkle with . . .
flour . . **6.** dredge
grit . . **4.** sand
heraldic . . **4.** semé
powder . . **4.** dust
water . . **3.** deg

sprint . . . **3.** run **4.** dash, race

sprite . . . **3.** elf, fay, hob, imp, nix **4.** peri
5. fairy, ghost, gnome, pixie, sylph
6. goblin, spirit **7.** brownie **9.** hobgoblin
10. apparition

sprite (pert to) . . .
fiction . . **5.** Ariel
Irish . . **10.** leprechaun

mischievous .. **4.** Puck
ref to .. **6.** elfish
sprocket ... **5.** tooth, wheel **8.** cylinder
(toothed) **10.** projection
sprout ... **3.** bud, son **4.** cion, grow
5. scion, shoot, spire, sprit **6.** branch,
ratoon, tiller **7.** burgeon, upstart
8. offshoot **9.** germinate **10.** descendant
spruce ... **4.** chic, neat, posh, smug,
tree, trig, trim **5.** adorn, natty, smart
6. dapper **7.** finical, smarten **8.** titivate
spruce (pert to) ...
beverage .. **4.** beer
black .. **7.** yew pine
fir .. **6.** Norway
genus .. **5.** Abies, Picea
Japanese .. **6.** Alcock
type .. **7.** Douglas, hemlock
white .. **8.** épinette
sprue ... **5.** dross, waste **6.** thrush
7. disease **8.** psilosis **9.** asparagus
spry ... **5.** agile, brisk, quick, smart
6. active, nimble **8.** vigorous **9.** sprightly
spud ... **5.** drill, knife, spade **6.** dagger,
paddle, potato, reamer, shovel
spume ... **4.** foam, scum **5.** froth
spunky ... **4.** game **5.** quick **6.** plucky,
touchy **8.** spirited **10.** courageous,
mettlesome **13.** quick-tempered
spur ... **3.** egg **4.** goad, move, urge
5. drive, press, ridge, rowel, spine
6. calcar, excite, griffe, incite, needle
7. provoke **8.** stimulus **9.** instigate,
stimulate **10.** incitement
spur (pert to) ...
badge .. **10.** knighthood
fowl .. **5.** quail **9.** partridge
gamecock's .. **4.** gaff **7.** gablock
mountain .. **5.** arête
pert to .. **7.** spicate
railroad .. **5.** track
wheel .. **5.** rowel
spurious ... **4.** fake, sham **5.** false
6. pseudo **7.** bastard **10.** adulterate,
apocryphal, artificial, fictitious,
fraudulent **11.** counterfeit
12. illegitimate **14.** supposititious
spurious (pert to) ...
fruit .. **10.** pseudocarp
olive .. **9.** heartwood
rainbow .. **8.** faint arc
wing .. **7.** bastard
spurn ... **4.** defy **5.** scorn **6.** reject, strike
7. contemn, disdain
spurt ... **3.** jet, jut **4.** dash, gush, spew
5. burst, spout **7.** outpour, upsurge
8. outbreak
spy ... **3.** pry, see **4.** espy, note, tout
5. scout, sneak, snoop, watch **6.** behold,
descry, detect, search **7.** examine,
snooper **8.** discover, emissary, informer,
perceive **10.** scrutinize **11.** reconnoiter
spy (pert to) ...
city .. **7.** Belgium
in clothing circles .. **4.** keek
Man of .. **14.** paleolithic man
prison .. **6.** mouton
squab ... **3.** fat **4.** fowl, sofa **5.** piper,
plump **6.** fat man, pigeon **7.** cushion
8. nestling **9.** fledgling
squabble ... **5.** brawl **6.** bicker, jangle

7. contend, quarrel, wrangle
10. disarrange (Print) **13.** collieshangie
squad ... **4.** team, unit **5.** posse
7. company
squalid ... **4.** foul, mean, poor **5.** dirty
6. filthy, sordid **7.** unclean **8.** slovenly
9. repellent, repulsive **11.** squalidness
15. poverty-stricken
squall ... **3.** cry, row **4.** blow, gale, gust,
wail, wind, yell **6.** squawk, squeal
9. commotion **11.** disturbance
squalor ... **4.** dirt, mire **5.** filth **8.** slovenry
9. dirtiness **10.** filthiness **11.** squalidness
16. unkempt condition
squamate, squamous ... **5.** scaly
6. scaled
squander ... **5.** waste **6.** lavish **7.** scatter
8. disperse, misspend **9.** dissipate,
throw away **10.** run through
squanderer ... **5.** loser **7.** wastrel
square ... **4.** even, meal **5.** bribe, plaza
6. common, honest, settle **7.** exactly,
obelisk, old fogy **8.** absolute, cube
face, directly, equalize, quadrate **9.** city
block, divergent **11.** unequivocal
13. parallelogram **14.** unsophisticate
15. straightforward
squash ... **4.** mash, pepo, pulp **5.** crush,
gourd, press **6.** cushaw, refute, simlin,
simnel, soften **7.** cymling (cymbling),
Hubbard, squeeze **8.** pattypan, suppress
9. crookneck **10.** extinguish
11. calabazilla
squat ... **3.** low **5.** dumpy, pudgy, quash,
stoop **6.** crouch, hunker, settle, stubby
7. sit down **8.** squatter, thickset
squatter ... **6.** nester (illegal) **7.** pioneer
9. sandpiper **11.** homesteader
Squatter State ... **6.** Kansas
squaw ... **6.** coween, Indian, mahala
(mahaly)
squeal ... **6.** betray, inform **7.** protest,
quarrel
squealer ... **4.** fink **6.** grouse, pigeon,
plover **7.** traitor **8.** informer
squeamish ... **4.** nice **5.** dizzy **6.** dainty,
queasy **7.** prudish **8.** overnice, qualmish
9. nauseated **10.** fastidious, scrupulous
squeeze ... **3.** hug, jam, nip **4.** cram, crux
5. crowd, crush, pinch, press, wring
6. crisis, extort **7.** embrace **8.** compress
9. constrict, influence **10.** constraint
11. compression
squeezer, fruit ... **6.** juicer, reamer
squelch ... **5.** crush, quash, quell
6. rebuke, refute, subdue **7.** repress,
silence **8.** suppress **10.** disconcert
squib ... **4.** bomb, fuse, pipe, skit, tube
6. speech, squirt **7.** explode, lampoon,
writing **9.** bespatter **10.** pasquinade
11. firecracker
squire ... **4.** beau **5.** court, lover **6.** escort
7. gallant **8.** henchman, nobleman
9. attendant, gentleman, landowner
squirm ... **5.** twist **6.** wiggle, writhe
7. wriggle
squirrel (pert to) ...
African .. **5.** xerus
American .. **5.** bunny **7.** assapan
8. chipmunk **9.** chickaree
American, flying .. **7.** assapan

Asian.. **5.** sisel **6.** suslik
Austral, flying.. **9.** phalanger
burrowing.. **6.** gopher
cage.. **9.** treadmill
color.. **4.** lead
E Ind, flying.. **6.** taguan
fish.. **7.** serrano
fur (Her).. **4.** vair
genus.. **6.** Tamias **7.** Sciurus
Java.. **8.** jelerang
like.. **8.** sciuroid
nest.. **4.** dray, drey
shrew.. **4.** tana **6.** Tupaia
skin.. **4.** vair
Spanish.. **7.** ardilla
squirrellike mammal ... **8.** banxring,
dormouse
stab ... **4.** gore, pang, pink **5.** knife, knive,
lunge, wound **6.** attack, injury, pierce,
thrust **7.** poniard, slander **8.** puncture,
stoccado
stability ... **5.** poise **7.** balance
8. firmness, strength **9.** constancy
10. permanence, stableness, steadiness
11. reliability **12.** immovability,
immutability **13.** steadfastness
stabilize ... **3.** set **5.** poise **6.** steady
7. ballast **8.** regulate
stable ... **3.** mew (Royal) **4.** barn, byre,
firm, safe **5.** fixed, solid, sound,
stall **6.** steady, strong **7.** durable,
lasting, paddock, support **8.** constant,
reliable **9.** confirmed, permanent,
steadfast **10.** stationary, unwavering
11. established, trustworthy
stableman ... **5.** groom **7.** hostler (ostler)
staccato ... **7.** détaché **8.** ricochet
12. disconnected
stack ... **4.** heap, load, pile, rick **5.** mound,
shock **6.** pile up **7.** chimney, conduit
8. quantity
stacked ... **11.** accumulated, prearranged
stacked pack, cards ... **8.** cold deck
stadium ... **5.** stage **6.** course, dromos
8. foot race (anc)
stadium race, start ... **7.** aphesis
staff ... **3.** rod **4.** club, mace, pole
5. baton, music, stave **7.** scepter,
support **8.** caduceus, insignia, pastoral
9. personnel **10.** assistants, associates
staff (pert to) ...
Bacchus.. **7.** thyrsus
bearer.. **5.** macer
magician's.. **7.** rhabdos
marshal's.. **5.** baton
member, officer.. **4.** aide **7.** attaché
mountain climbing.. **10.** alpenstock
pastoral.. **5.** pedum **7.** baculus, crosier
(crozier)
shepherd's.. **5.** crook, pedum
sovereign's.. **7.** scepter (sceptre)
stag ... **4.** colt, deer (red), hart **5.** party,
royal, spade **7.** male fox, pollard
8. gamecock, informer
stage ... **4.** dais, tier **5.** arena, phase,
scene **6.** degree **7.** display, estrade,
perform, rostrum **8.** platform, scaffold
9. dramatize, gradation **10.** proscenium,
stagecoach
stage (pert to) ...
call (trumpet).. **6.** sennet

direction.. **5.** aside, manet **6.** sennet
of disease.. **9.** catabasis
of insects.. **5.** imago, larva
part.. **5.** stair **8.** dutchman (patch)
10. proscenium
scene (side).. **8.** coulisse
scenery.. **3.** set
stagger ... **4.** reel, stot, stun, sway, walk
5. lurch **6.** excite, totter, zigzag **7.** be
drunk, tremble, vibrate **8.** astonish,
flounder, frighten, titubate, unsettle
9. alternate, fluctuate
staggering ... **5.** areel **9.** startling
10. astounding **11.** the staggers
12. unbelievable
Stagirite, The ... **9.** Aristotle
stagnant ... **4.** dull, foul **5.** inert,
stale, still **8.** inactive, sluggish,
standing **10.** motionless, not flowing
13. unprogressive
stagnate ... **3.** rot **4.** dull **5.** inert
8. stagnant, vegetate **10.** motionless
staid ... **5.** grave, sober **6.** demure, sedate,
solemn **7.** serious, settled **8.** composed,
decorous, sensible **9.** steadfast
stain ... **3.** dye **4.** blot, soil, spot, tint
5. color, paint, smear, sully **6.** infamy,
smudge, stigma **7.** blemish, corrupt,
pigment, tarnish **8.** discolor, disgrace,
dishonor, maculate **9.** pollution
10. stigmatize **11.** contaminate
13. discoloration
stained by decay ... **4.** doty
stained glass rod (lead) ... **4.** came
stair ... **4.** step **5.** riser, stage, tread
6. degree, flight (series)
staircase (pert to) ...
French.. **8.** escalier
moving.. **9.** escalator
outdoor.. **6.** perron
post.. **5.** newel
ship's.. **12.** companionway
spiral.. **8.** caracole
stairs to bath (Ind) ... **4.** ghat (ghaut)
stake ... **3.** bet, peg, pel, pin **4.** ante,
pale, pile, post, risk, spit **5.** sowel,
teest, wager **6.** chance, estate, gamble,
hazard, picket, pledge **7.** finance,
venture
stale ... **3.** old **5.** banal, fusty, trite,
vapid **6.** insipid, spoiled **9.** hackneyed,
tasteless **10.** flavorless
11. commonplace
stalemate ... **6.** corner **7.** impasse
8. cul-de-sac, deadlock **10.** blind alley,
standstill
stalk ... **4.** axis, hunt, risp, stem, walk
6. pursue, stride **7.** pedicel **8.** peduncle
11. reconnoiter
stalk (pert to) ...
cotton, sugar cane.. **6.** ratoon
dry.. **3.** hay, kex **5.** haulm (halm)
flower.. **7.** petiole
grain, grass.. **4.** culm **5.** straw **6.** ressum
strawberry.. **4.** risp
stalkless ... **7.** sessile
stall ... **3.** cot, pew **4.** crib, fail,
loge, mire, stop **5.** booth, check,
choir, stick **6.** hinder, manger, stable
7. disgust **9.** temporize **10.** dillydally
11. compartment, play for time

12. parking space **13.** procrastinate
stalwart ... **5.** brave, stout **6.** strong,
sturdy **7.** valiant **8.** partisan, resolute
9. corpulent **10.** courageous, unyielding
stamen part ... **6.** anther, pollen
8. filament
stamina ... **5.** pluck, vigor **7.** courage
8. backbone, strength **9.** endurance,
fortitude **12.** staying power
stammer ... **3.** haw, hem **4.** mant **6.** falter
7. stumble, stutter **8.** hesitate
stammering ... **8.** psellism
stamp ... **3.** die **4.** date, dink, form, mark,
seal, sign, tool **5.** brand, infix, label
6. signet **7.** engrave, impress, imprint,
postage, trading **8.** tressure (tressour)
11. endorsement **14.** characteristic
stamp (pert to) ...
border . . **8.** tressure (tressour)
collecting . . **9.** philately
collector . . **11.** philatelist
madness . . **11.** timbromania
paper . . **6.** pelure
postage . . **6.** timbre
space . . **8.** spandrel
stampede ... **3.** run **4.** rout, rush **5.** panic
6. flight **7.** debacle **11.** wild scamper
stance ... **4.** pose **7.** posture, station
8. position
stanch ... **5.** allay, check, quell **6.** steady,
strong **7.** zealous **8.** faithful **9.** steadfast
10. extinguish **11.** substantial
stanchion ... **3.** bar **4.** post, prop **5.** brace,
piton **6.** secure **7.** support, upright
stand ... **4.** bear, bier, halt, rack, stop, zarf
5. abide, arise, booth, easel, store, table
6. endure, tripod **7.** coaster, étagère,
footing, impasse, sustain, taboret
8. attitude, foothold, pedestal, position,
tolerate **9.** withstand **10.** standstill
stand (pert to) ...
against . . **6.** resist
by . . **3.** aid **6.** defend **7.** support **9.** be
present
cost of . . **5.** treat
Eccl . . **4.** ambo
for . . **6.** permit, typify **9.** represent,
symbolize
for candles . . **7.** epergne **10.** candelabra
in . . **6.** deputy **10.** substitute
it . . **4.** bear **5.** brook **6.** suffer
offish . . **4.** cold **5.** aloof **8.** reserved
10. not cordial
opposite . . **4.** face
three-legged . . **6.** teapoy, tripod, trivot
up to . . **5.** brave **6.** resist
standard ... **3.** par **4.** flag, norm **5.** grade,
model, usual **6.** ensign **7.** average,
classic, paragon, precept **8.** orthodox
9. customary, principle **13.** authoritative
standard (pert to) ...
battle . . **9.** oriflamme (oriflamb)
bearer . . **6.** leader **7.** officer **10.** politician
chem test . . **5.** titer (titre)
ensign . . **8.** gonfalon, gonfanon
flag (Rom) . . **8.** vexillum
of excellence . . **4.** idea
of intelligence . . **5.** Binet
of light . . **6.** carcel
of quantity . . **4.** unit
Ottoman Emp . . **4.** alem

standardize ... **9.** calibrate, normalize
standing ... **4.** rank **5.** fixed, state
6. at rest, status **7.** footing, settled,
station, upright **8.** duration, prestige
9. permanent **10.** durability, reputation
standing (pert to) ...
long . . **7.** durable **8.** duration
11. traditional
mode of . . **6.** stance
out . . **7.** eminent, salient
room only . . **3.** SRO
social . . **6.** estate, status **8.** prestige
upright . . **11.** orthostatic
stannum ... **2.** Sn **3.** tin
stanza ... **4.** rann, unit **5.** stave, verse
6. octave, sestet **7.** strophe, triolet
(8-lined)
stanza scheme ... **6.** ballad **10.** Gray's
Elegy, Spenserian
star ... **3.** sun **4.** hero, lead **5.** actor, shine
6. étoile **7.** destiny, fortune **8.** asterisk,
insignia, ornament **9.** emphasize,
principal **11.** hummingbird **12.** heavenly
body, luminous body
star (pert to) ... see also *Stars*
brightest . . **3.** Cor, sun **5.** Deneb **6.** Altair,
Lucida, Sirius
Bull's Eye . . **9.** Aldebaran
divination . . **9.** astrology
Dog . . **4.** Sept **6.** Sirius **8.** Canicula
12. Canis Majoris
evening . . **5.** Venus **6.** Hesper, Vesper
7. evestar **8.** Hesperus
feather . . **9.** comatulid
five-pointed . . **9.** pentagram, pentalpha
French . . **6.** étoile
gazer . . **4.** fish **10.** astronomer
giant . . **10.** Betelgeuse (Betelgeux)
group (fixed) . . **13.** constellation
guiding . . **5.** Alpha, North **7.** Polaris
8. Cynosure, loadstar, lodestar, polestar
large . . **5.** Rigel
morning . . **4.** Mars **5.** Venus **6.** Saturn
7. daystar, Jupiter, Mercury **8.** Phosphor
North . . **7.** Polaris **8.** loadstar, lodestar
of Africa . . **15.** Cullinan diamond
of Bethlehem (Bib) . . **11.** guide of Magi
of the sea . . **11.** Maris Stella (Stella
Maris)
ornament . . **4.** semé
path . . **5.** orbit
ref to . . **6.** astral, starry **7.** sideral, stellar
8. sidereal **9.** planatoid
representation . . **4.** étoile
shooting . . **5.** comet **6.** Leonid, meteor
variable . . **4.** nova **7.** cepheid, R R Lyrae
wars . . **3.** SDI
starch ... **3.** vim **4.** sago **5.** hilum,
vigor **6.** amidin, energy, farina, fecula
7. cassava **8.** glycogen **9.** arrowroot,
formality, stiffness
starchy ... **5.** stiff **6.** formal, viscid
7. amyloid, precise **9.** unbending
stare ... **4.** gape, gawk, gaze, look, ogle,
peer **5.** glare **6.** glower, goggle, wonder
starfish ... **7.** asteria **10.** echinoderm
stark ... **4.** bare, mere **5.** rigid, tense
6. barren, wholly **7.** violent **8.** absolute,
complete, entirely **9.** downright,
unadorned **10.** absolutely
starling ... **4.** myna, sali **6.** pastor

Stars (pert to) . . .
and Bars . . **15.** Confederate flag
belt, tract (luminous) . . **6.** Galaxy **8.** Milky Way
circumpolar group . . **5.** Draco **6.** Dragon
four (famed) . . **4.** Crux **13.** Southern Cross
North Pole group . . **9.** Great Bear **10.** Little Bear **11.** Septentrion
Ursa Major . . **9.** Big Dipper, Great Bear
Ursa Minor . . **10.** Little Bear **12.** Little Dipper
start . . . **4.** dart, dash, jerk, rush **5.** begin, enter, sally **6.** broach, origin, twitch **7.** get away, startle **8.** commence **9.** advantage, beginning, departure, originate **10.** inaugurate
starting point . . . **4.** text (sermon) **7.** scratch **9.** departure
startle . . . **5.** alarm, rouse, scare, shock **6.** excite, fright **8.** astonish **9.** electrify
starve . . . **3.** die **4.** kill **5.** crave **6.** famish, perish, scrimp **7.** atrophy, destroy **10.** be indigent
starved . . . **4.** thin **5.** empty **6.** frozen, hungry **8.** famished, ravenous
starwort . . . **5.** aster **9.** colicroot
stash . . . **5.** cache, plant, store **7.** lay away **8.** hide away
state . . . **3.** say **4.** aver, case, état, mode, tell **5.** utter **6.** affirm, allege, assert, plight, recite, remark, report **7.** country, declare, expound, express, narrate **8.** announce, propound **9.** condition, enunciate, postulate, pronounce, territory **10.** government, possession **11.** body politic **12.** circumstance, commonwealth
state (pert to) . . .
a fact . . **4.** aver **5.** posit **6.** avouch **7.** declare
agitated . . **9.** disturbed, perturbed
disordered . . **9.** cluttered
formally . . **8.** propound **9.** enunciate, pronounce
French . . **4.** état
hypnotic . . **6.** trance
ideal . . **6.** Utopia
office . . **8.** governor **11.** secretariat
on oath . . **6.** depose
police . . **7.** trooper
reference . . **6.** statal
secret . . **7.** arcanum
specifically . . **6.** define **7.** itemize **13.** particularize
treasury . . **4.** fisc **6.** fiscus
ultimate . . **3.** end
under foreign control . . **12.** protectorate
without proof . . **6.** allege
stately . . . **5.** grand, largo, lofty, regal, royal **6.** august, coldly, kingly **7.** haughty, queenly, togated **8.** eloquent, imperial, imposing, majestic **9.** dignified, grandiose **11.** magnificent
statement . . . **4.** bill, list **5.** audit, dixit **6.** dictum, remark, report, resumé **7.** account, invoice, premise **8.** abstract, proposal, schedule **9.** affidavit, assertion, manifesto **10.** accounting, expression, recitation **11.** declaration

12. announcement, presentation
statement (pert to) . . .
abridged . . **6.** precis, resumé **7.** summary **10.** abridgment **11.** abridgement
assumed true . . **7.** premise
contradictory . . **7.** paradox
defamatory . . **5.** libel
detailed . . **8.** schedule
dogmatic . . **6.** dictum
introductory . . **5.** proem **7.** preface, prelude **8.** foreword, prologue
legal . . **11.** declaration
mathematical . . **7.** theorem
of belief . . **5.** credo, creed
of introduction . . **8.** prologue
precise . . **8.** aphorism
self-evident . . **6.** truism
sworn . . **9.** affidavit
State nicknames . . .
Alabama . . **6.** Cotton **12.** Heart of Dixie, Yellowhammer
Alaska . . (no official)
Arizona . . **11.** Grand Canyon
Arkansas . . **17.** Land of Opportunity
California . . **6.** Golden
Colorado . . **10.** Centennial
Connecticut . . **6.** Nutmeg
Delaware . . **5.** First
Florida . . **8.** Sunshine
Georgia . . **5.** Peach
Hawaii . . **5.** Aloha
Idaho . . **3.** Gem
Illinois . . **7.** Prairie
Indiana . . **7.** Hoosier
Iowa . . **7.** Hawkeye
Kansas . . **9.** Sunflower
Kentucky . . **9.** Bluegrass
Louisiana . . **7.** Pelican
Maine . . **8.** Pine Tree
Maryland . . **4.** Free **7.** Old Line
Massachusetts . . **3.** Bay **9.** Old Colony
Michigan . . **9.** Wolverine
Minnesota . . **6.** Gopher **9.** North Star
Mississippi . . **8.** Magnolia
Missouri . . **6.** Show Me
Montana . . **8.** Treasure
Nebraska . . **4.** Beef **10.** Cornhusker
Nevada . . **6.** Silver **9.** Sagebrush
New Hampshire . . **7.** Granite
New Jersey . . **6.** Garden
New Mexico . . **17.** Land of Enchantment
New York . . **6.** Empire
North Carolina . . **7.** Tarheel **8.** Old North
North Dakota . . **5.** Sioux **11.** Flickertail
Ohio . . **7.** Buckeye
Oklahoma . . **6.** Sooner
Oregon . . **6.** Beaver
Pennsylvania . . **8.** Keystone
Rhode Island . . **11.** Little Rhody
South Carolina . . **8.** Palmetto
South Dakota . . **6.** Coyote **8.** Sunshine
Tennessee . . **9.** Volunteer
Texas . . **8.** Lone Star
Utah . . **7.** Beehive
Vermont . . **13.** Green Mountain
Virginia . . **11.** Old Dominion
Washington . . **9.** Evergreen
West Virginia . . **8.** Mountain
Wisconsin . . **6.** Badger
Wyoming . . **8.** Equality
state of . . .

dissension .. **8.** scission
disuse .. **9.** desuetude
ecstasy .. **6.** trance **7.** rapture **8.** paradise
hostility .. **6.** feudal
mind .. **4.** mood **5.** humor **6.** morale
  8. attitude
unconsciousness .. **4.** coma **5.** faint
state of being ...
a layman .. **9.** laicality
artless .. **7.** naiveté
a son .. **7.** sonship
a woman .. **10.** muliebrity
behindhand .. **9.** in arrears
beyond natural laws .. **12.** supernatural
complete .. **9.** plenitude
confined .. **10.** internment
free from error .. **9.** inerrancy
married twice, illegally .. **6.** bigamy
married twice, legally .. **6.** digamy
overfull .. **8.** plethora
passive .. **9.** stolidity
poison .. **5.** toxic **8.** toxicity
voiced .. **7.** sonancy
worse .. **8.** pejority
wrong .. **7.** errancy
static ... **5.** inert, noise **6.** stable **7.** resting
  8. electric, inactive **9.** quiescent
  10. stationary **12.** atmospherics,
  interference
station ... **4.** fire, post, rank, seat,
  stop **5.** berth, depot, place, radio,
  serai **6.** health, police **7.** calling,
  dignity **8.** location, position, prestige
  9. situation **11.** institution
stationary ... **3.** set **5.** fixed, still **6.** stable,
  static, stator **8.** immobile **9.** immovable
  10. motionless, unchanging
stationery ... **3.** pen **5.** paper **6.** pencil
  9. onionskin, papeterie **12.** writing
  páper
statue ... **4.** bust **5.** image **8.** acrolith,
  figurine, monument **9.** sculpture,
  statuette
statue (pert to) ...
at Thebes .. **6.** Memnon
gigantic .. **8.** Colossus
Guildhall (London) .. **3.** Gog **5.** Magog
holy .. **4.** icon (ikon)
male figure (support) .. **7.** telamon
part .. **5.** socle, trunk **6.** plinth
primitive .. **6.** xoanon
Pygmalion's .. **7.** Galatea
world wonder .. **6.** Helios (Rhodes)
status ... **4.** rank **5.** class, state **7.** station
  8. position, prestige, standing
status symbol ... **11.** swivel chair
statute ... **3.** act, jus, law, lex **5.** bylaw,
  canon, edict, title **6.** decree, rubric,
  treaty **8.** statutum **9.** enactment,
  ordinance **10.** regulation **11.** legislation
staunch, stanch ... **4.** firm, true
  6. hearty **7.** devoted **8.** faithful,
  resolute **9.** steadfast **10.** dependable
  11. trustworthy
stave ... **3.** bar, leg **4.** fend, pole, rung,
  slat **5.** staff, stick **6.** cudgel, lathee,
  letter, stanza **7.** baculus, support, ward
  off **8.** overcome **11.** set of verses
stave off ... **4.** fend **7.** prevent
  8. postpone
staves, bundle of ... **5.** shook

stay ... **3.** guy, leg, rib **4.** prop,
  rely, stop, wait **5.** abide, brace,
  cease, check, pause, tarry **6.** adhere,
  arrest, linger, remain, retard, status
  7. prevent, respite **8.** postpone, restrain
  9. cessation, hindrance **10.** impediment
  12. postponement
stead ... **4.** help, lieu **5.** place **6.** assist,
  behalf **7.** replace, service, support
  9. advantage, farmstead, homestead
steadfast ... **4.** firm, true **5.** fixed **6.** stable
  7. durable, staunch **8.** constant, faithful,
  reliable **9.** unwinking **10.** unchanging,
  unswerving **11.** unalterable
steadiness ... **5.** nerve **7.** balance
  9. constancy, stability **10.** uniformity
  11. reliability
steady ... **4.** firm **5.** fixed, grave, sober,
  staid **6.** stable, sturdy **7.** assured,
  equable, regular, uniform **8.** constant,
  resolute **9.** incessant, steadfast
  10. invariable, unswerving
  11. unfaltering, unmitigated
  13. uninterrupted
steal ... **3.** cly, cop, gyp, nim, rap,
  rob **4.** crib, lift, loot **5.** filch, pinch,
  poach, swipe **6.** finger, kidnap, pilfer,
  snitch **7.** purloin **8.** embezzle, peculate
  10. plagiarize **11.** appropriate
steal (pert to) ...
a march on .. **5.** evade **7.** precede
  10. anticipate **13.** gain advantage
away .. **5.** creep, slink, sneak
cattle .. **6.** rustle
feloniously .. **6.** ratten
game .. **5.** poach **8.** trespass
insane desire to .. **11.** kleptomania
nautical .. **7.** manavel
stealer ... **5.** crook, thief **6.** lifter, pirate
  7. abactor, abigens, filcher, rustler
  8. pilferer **9.** embezzler, peculator,
  purloiner **10.** pickpocket, plagiarist
  11. biblioklept **12.** kleptomaniac
stealthy ... **3.** sly **6.** artful, feline,
  secret **7.** catlike, cunning, furtive
  11. clandestine
steam ... **4.** boil, fume, heat, mist, reek
  5. force, power, smoke, stufa, vapor
  6. energy, pother (puther) **8.** vaporize
  9. evaporate
steam (pert to) ...
boat .. **5.** liner **7.** steamer **9.** steamship
  11. side-wheeler
jet of .. **5.** stufa **8.** suffione
organ .. **8.** calliope
steamboat cabin (officer's) ... **5.** texas
steamy ... **5.** misty **7.** excited **8.** vaporous
  9. steamed up
steatite ... **4.** talc **9.** soapstone
steed ... **3.** nag **5.** horse **7.** charger,
  courser, Pegasus (winged)
steel ... **5.** inure **6.** harden, smooth
  10. strengthen
steel (pert to) ...
armor plate .. **4.** tace **5.** tasse
color .. **4.** gray **9.** steel blue **12.** Prussian
  blue
conversion to .. **10.** acieration
India .. **5.** wootz **10.** wootz steel
metallurgy of .. **9.** siderurgy
process .. **8.** Bessemer **11.** cementation

type . . **6.** damask, Toledo **8.** Damascus
steep . . . **3.** ret, sop **4.** brae, buck, high, soak, stew, tall **5.** cleve (cleeve), hilly, lofty, scarp, sharp, sheer **6.** abrupt, clifty, escarp, imbrue, infuse, seethe **7.** extract, extreme **8.** elevated, headlong, macerate **9.** difficult, excessive, expensive, precipice **10.** exorbitant **11.** precipitous **13.** perpendicular
steeple . . . **5.** spire, tower **6.** flèche **7.** minaret **8.** pinnacle
steer . . . **2.** ox **3.** cow, ply, yaw **4.** helm, luff, stot **5.** guide, pilot **6.** bovina, direct, govern, manage **7.** bullock, control, operate
steer clear of . . . **4.** snub **5.** avert, avoid **9.** sidetrack, step aside **14.** be inhospitable
steer close to wind . . . **4.** luff
steeve . . . **4.** lade, pack, spar (a) **5.** store, stuff **6.** freeze
stein . . . **3.** mug **4.** Toby
stellar . . . **6.** astral, starry **7.** leading, starlit **8.** starlike, stellate **10.** theatrical
Steller's sea cow . . . **6.** Rytina
stem . . . **3.** dam **4.** axis, base, cion, corm, prow, root, stop, tige **5.** check, shaft, stalk, tuber **6.** branch, breast, oppose, scapel, stanch **7.** lineage, petiole **8.** ancestry, peduncle **9.** originate
stem (pert to) . . .
bulblike . . **4.** corm, drub
cylinder . . **5.** stele
grass . . **4.** culm
joint . . **4.** cane, node
mushroom . . **5.** stipe
plant . . **4.** bine
seedling . . **7.** tigella (tigelle) **9.** hypocotyl
strawberry . . **4.** risp
twining . . **7.** tendril
underground . . **5.** tuber
stemless herb (evergreen) . . . **5.** Galax **11.** acaulescent
stench . . . **4.** odor **5.** fetor, smell, stink
stenographer of Cicero . . . **4.** Tiro
step . . . **3.** pas, way **4.** gait, pace, rung **5.** dance, grise, phase, riser, stair, stalk, strut, tread **6.** degree, stride **7.** advance, imprint, measure, process **8.** distance, footstep **9.** footprint, gradation **10.** stepladder
step (pert to) . . .
arrangement of troops . . **7.** echelon
clumsy . . **5.** stamp
dance . . **3.** pas **6.** chassé
mincingly . . **6.** sashay
mother . . **7.** noverca
stately . . **5.** stalk
up . . **8.** approach **9.** intensify **10.** accelerate
steppe . . . **5.** plain **9.** grassland
steps (outdoor flight) . . . **6.** perron
stereotyped . . . **5.** banal, corny, trite **6.** common, old hat **9.** hackneyed **11.** cut and dried
sterile . . . **4.** arid **6.** barren **7.** useless **8.** impotent **9.** fruitless **10.** unfruitful **11.** ineffective, ineffectual **12.** unproductive
stern . . . **4.** dour, grim, hard, rear, rump

5. harsh **6.** gloomy, severe, strict, sullen, unkind **7.** austere **8.** buttocks, hind part, rigorous **9.** harshness, unfeeling **10.** strictness, unyielding **11.** hardhearted **14.** uncompromising
sternutation . . . **8.** sneezing
sternutative . . . **7.** errhine
stertorous . . . **7.** snoring **15.** hoarse breathing
stevedore . . . **5.** lader **6.** loader, stower **7.** carrier **8.** unloader **12.** longshoreman
stew . . . **3.** pot **4.** boil, cook, food, fret, fume, mess, olio, olla **5.** anger, imbue, steep, worry **6.** bustle, ragout, seethe, simmer **7.** haricot, swelter **8.** meat dish **9.** Brunswick **10.** excitement, hodgepodge **11.** predicament
steward . . . **5.** agent, reeve **6.** seaman, waiter **7.** dapifer, erenach, foreman, granger, manager, servant **8.** manciple **9.** custodian, major-domo, seneschal, treasurer **10.** magistrate **11.** chamberlain, fiscal agent
Stewart, Stuart sovereigns (last) . . . **4.** Anne **5.** Henry
stewed fruit . . . **7.** compote
stick . . . **3.** bar, bat, bow, gad, gum, rod **4.** cane, dolt, glue, mast, pogo, ship, stab, wand, wood **5.** baton, cling, fagot, paste, shaft, staff, stall, stave, stilt **6.** adhere, baffle, ballow, cleave, cohere, mallet, pierce, puzzle, thrust **7.** defraud **8.** chatwood, revolver, transfix **9.** drumstick, persevere **10.** matchstick, overcharge **13.** stick-in-the-mud
stick (pert to) . . .
bamboo . . **6.** lathee (lathi)
bundle . . **5.** fagot **6.** fasces
crooked . . **5.** caman **7.** cammock, gambrel
insects . . **5.** Emesa
mountain climbing . . **10.** alpenstock
sticker . . . **4.** burr **5.** label, poser, thorn **6.** poster, puzzle, weapon **7.** bramble **8.** adherent
sticky . . . **3.** goo **5.** gluey, humid, moist, woody **6.** clammy, slushy, viscid **7.** viscous **8.** adhesive **9.** difficult, glutinous, tenacious **10.** saccharine
stiff . . . **4.** dead, hard, hobo, limp, taut **5.** harsh, horse, idler, rigid, stark, tense **6.** corpse, formal, proper, severe, strict **7.** awkward, cadaver, starchy **8.** resolute, rigorous, starched **9.** dead-drunk, obstinate, unbending **14.** uncompromising
stiff-necked . . . **8.** stubborn **9.** ankylotic, obstinate **11.** strait-laced **12.** contumacious
stiffness . . . **8.** rigidity **9.** formality, toughness **10.** strictness **11.** starchiness
stifle . . . **3.** gag **4.** stop **5.** choke **6.** deaden, muffle, quench **7.** repress, smother **8.** strangle, throttle **9.** suffocate **10.** extinguish
stigma . . . **4.** blot, mark, scar, slur **5.** brand, odium, stain, stamp, taint **6.** defect **7.** blemish **8.** disgrace, reproach
stigmatism . . . **7.** blemish **10.** refraction

(eye)

stigmatize . . . **5.** brand **6.** defame **8.** denounce

still . . . **3.** but, mum, yet **4.** calm, even, lull, moot **5.** allay, check, inert, quiet **6.** always, hushed, pacify, silent, soothe, subdue **7.** silence, subdued **8.** inactive, restrain, suppress, tranquil, until now **9.** quiescent **10.** distillery, motionless, photograph **11.** continually **12.** nevertheless **15.** notwithstanding

still water . . . **4.** pond, pool **6.** lagoon

stilt . . . **6.** crutch **7.** yeguita (black-necked)

stilted . . . **6.** formal **7.** pompous **8.** elevated, inflated, on stilts **9.** bombastic, inelegant

stimulant . . . **3.** tea **5.** salts, tonic **6.** bracer, coffee **7.** alcohol **8.** caffeine, stimulus **9.** digitalis, sassafras **10.** adrenaline, strychnine **11.** epinephrine

stimulate . . . **3.** jog, pep **4.** goad, stir, urge, whet **5.** elate, impel, rouse, sting **6.** excite, fillip (filip), incite, spur on **7.** animate, enliven, quicken, refresh **8.** energize, motivate **9.** encourage, instigate, sensitize **10.** exhilarate, invigorate

stimulating . . . **4.** cool **7.** piquant **8.** exciting **10.** energizing, refreshing

stimulus . . . **4.** spur **5.** sting **6.** motive **7.** impetus **9.** incentive, stimulant

sting . . . **4.** bite, pain **5.** smart **6.** offend, tingle **8.** irritate

sting of conscience . . . **5.** pangs, voice **6.** qualms, twinge **11.** compunction

sting organ . . . **10.** nematocyst

stingy . . . **4.** dree, mean, near **5.** close **6.** scanty **7.** miserly, selfish **8.** covetous **9.** niggardly **10.** avaricious **11.** closefisted **12.** parsimonious

stinkbird . . . **7.** hoatzin

stint . . . **4.** duty, task **5.** limit **6.** scrimp **7.** confine **8.** be frugal, restrict **9.** be sparing

stipend . . . **3.** ann, fee, pay **5.** annat, wages **6.** salary **7.** annates, pension, subsidy **9.** allowance **12.** compensation, remuneration

stipulate . . . **5.** agree **6.** demand **7.** bargain, specify **8.** contract, indicate **9.** designate, guarantee, postulate

stipulation . . . **4.** bond **6.** clause, demand, detail **7.** compact, proviso **8.** contract, covenant **9.** agreement, condition **11.** arrangement **13.** specification

stir . . . **3.** ado, mix **4.** fuss, jail, move, poke, roil, to-do **5.** budge, churn, rally, rouse, shake, stoke, waken **6.** arouse, awaken, bestir, bustle, excite, flurry, hubbub, pother, prison, rustle, tumult **7.** agitate, animate, disturb, inflame, provoke **8.** activity, movement **9.** commotion **12.** penitentiary

stir (pert to) . . . *colors (calico)* . . **4.** teer *fire* . . **5.** stoke *together* . . **3.** mix **6.** stodge *up* . . **3.** mix **4.** rile, roil **5.** anger, awake, rouse **6.** arouse, foment, incite

stirring . . . **6.** moving **7.** rousing

8. bustling, eventful, exciting **9.** animating, inspiring **11.** stimulating

stirrup . . . **4.** ring **5.** strap **6.** saddle (part), stapes **7.** support **8.** footrest, tapadera

stitch . . . **3.** bit, hem, sew **4.** mend, pain **5.** baste, piece, ridge **6.** suture, tailor **8.** particle **9.** embroider

stitch (type) . . . **3.** hem **5.** chain, coral, cross **6.** carpet, damask, suture **7.** glover's **11.** needlepoint, over-and-over

stitchbird . . . **3.** ihi **10.** honey eater

stithy . . . **5.** anvil, forge **6.** smithy **8.** smithery

stoa . . . **7.** portico **9.** colonnade

stoat . . . **6.** ermine, weasel

stob . . . **4.** post, stab, stub **5.** stake **6.** gibbet, pierce

stoccado, stoccata . . . **4.** stab **6.** thrust (rapier)

stock . . . **4.** fund, line, race, stem **5.** breed, broth, hoard, store, trunk **6.** assets, cravat, pillar, strain, supply **7.** capital, lineage, provide, rhizome **8.** credence, original **9.** livestock, provision, replenish **10.** progenitor

stock (pert to) . . . *book* . . **6.** ledger *breeding* . . **5.** brood *certificate* . . **5.** scrip **8.** document *flower* . . **11.** gillyflower *hawk* . . **15.** peregrine falcon *in trade* . . **6.** assets, supply **11.** merchandise *market* . . **6.** Bourse **8.** Exchange **10.** Wall Street *of goods* . . **4.** line *owl* . . **8.** eagle owl *payment* . . **8.** dividend *pile* . . **7.** reserve **12.** accumulation *theater* . . **5.** plays *type* . . **6.** common **9.** preferred

stockade . . . **3.** pen **5.** étape, pound **6.** corral, kennel, laager **7.** barrier, bulwark, parapet, rampart, redoubt **8.** palisade **9.** barricade, earthwork, enclosure

stocking . . . **4.** hose, sock **6.** anklet, argyle **7.** bandage, fortune, hosiery **8.** seamless **9.** livestock **12.** bluestocking **15.** Leatherstocking (Natty Bumppo)

stocks . . . **7.** pillory, shackle **10.** securities

stoic, stoical . . . **7.** passive, Spartan **8.** enduring **9.** impassive **11.** unflinching

Stoic School founder . . . **4.** Zeno

stoker . . . **5.** firer **6.** seaman, teaser **7.** fireman, greaser **8.** trainman

stolen (pert to) . . . *goods receiver* . . **5.** fence **7.** smasher, swagman *property* . . **4.** pelf **5.** booty, spoil

stolid . . . **4.** dull, slow **5.** beefy **6.** stupid **7.** adamant, passive **9.** impassive, inanimate **11.** inexcitable, unexcitable

stoma . . . **4.** pore **5.** mouth **7.** opening, orifice

stomach . . . **3.** gut, maw **4.** craw, crop, vell **5.** belly, rumen, taste **6.** desire, endure, gaster, paunch **7.** abdomen, gizzard **8.** tolerate **10.** resentment

stomach (pert to) . . .
ache . . **5.** colic, cramp **7.** gullion
   8. rumbling **11.** borborygmus
acidity . . **4.** acor
animal . . **3.** maw
bird . . **4.** craw, crop
comb form . . **6.** gaster **7.** gastero
ref to . . **7.** gastric, pyloric
ruminant . . **5.** rumen **6.** omasum
   8. abomasum, roddikin **9.** manyplies,
   reticulum **10.** psalterium
stone . . . **3.** gem, pit **4.** kill, pelt, rock,
   seed **5.** agate, block, geode, jewel,
   lapis, shale, slate, spall **6.** attack,
   pebble **7.** diamond, peridot, sharpen
   8. monument, pavement **9.** hailstone,
   sculpture, whetstone **10.** gravestone,
   grindstone **12.** philosopher's
stone (pert to) . . .
abrasive . . **5.** emery
Age . . **8.** Eolithic **9.** Neolithic
   11. Paleolithic
alchemy . . **6.** carmot **12.** philosopher's
arch (top stone) . . **8.** keystone
Bib . . **4.** ezel
broke . . **4.** flat **8.** strapped
broken . . **6.** rubble
carved . . **5.** cameo **8.** intaglio
chisel . . **4.** celt
cutters' disease . . **9.** silicosis
   10. chalicosis
famed . . **4.** Hope, Pitt **5.** Mogul, Sancy
   6. Jonker, Orloff, Regent **7.** Blarney,
   Rosetta **8.** Cullinan, Kohinoor (Kohinur)
   9. Excelsior **10.** Great Mogul
   12. Plymouth Rock, Star of Africa
flat . . **4.** flag, slab **5.** slate
fruit . . **3.** pip **4.** paip, seed **5.** cling
   7. putamen **8.** endocarp
gem . . **4.** jade, opal, ruby, sard
   5. agate, pearl, topaz **6.** garnet, ligure,
   spinel **7.** diamond, emerald, peridot
   8. amethyst, sapphire **9.** turquoise
   11. alexandrite
gem cutting . . **6.** adamas
hammer . . **5.** kevel
hard . . **7.** adamant **9.** chatoyant (cat's-
   eye)
heap . . **5.** cairn
instrument . . **8.** lapideon
masonry . . **6.** ashlar
medical . . **4.** gall **5.** renal **7.** biliary,
   otolith **8.** calculus
oil . . **4.** hone
ornamental . . **9.** scagliola
pert to . . **7.** lithoid
pillar . . **8.** monolith
pyramid . . **6.** benben
quarry . . **6.** latomy
small . . **6.** pebble **8.** lapillus
special . . **3.** key, lap, oil, rub **4.** curb,
   flag, head, lime, lode, mile, tomb, whet
   5. birth, flint, grave, grind **6.** cobble,
   corner **8.** stepping
statue (part wood) . . **8.** acrolith
to dress . . **3.** nig
uncut . . **4.** naif
woman turned to stone by Zeus . .
   5. Niobe
stonecutter (pert to) . . .
disease of . . **9.** silicosis **10.** chalicosis

receptacle . . **7.** sebilla
tool . . **6.** eolith
type . . **6.** jadder **7.** jeweler **8.** lapidary
worker . . **5.** mason
stonecutting art . . . **10.** stereotomy
stoning, death by . . . **10.** lapidation
stony . . . **4.** cold, hard **5.** rigid, rocky
   6. rugged **7.** adamant **8.** lapidose,
   obdurate, pitiless **9.** petrified
   10. inflexible, relentless, unyielding
   15. uncompassionate
stooge . . . **4.** foil **5.** toady **6.** flunky
   7. cat's-paw **8.** henchman
stool . . . **4.** seat **5.** bench **6.** pigeon,
   tripod **7.** taboret **8.** informer
stop . . . **2.** ho **3.** bar, dam, end **4.** balk,
   foil, halt, kill, quit, stay, stem, whoa
   5. avast, block, cease, check, choke,
   close, delay **6.** arrest, desist, detain
   7. impasse, prevent, silence **8.** preclude,
   swear off **10.** standstill **11.** discontinue,
   obstruction, punctuation **12.** lower the
   boom
stop (pert to) . . .
close . . **8.** obturate
debate . . **7.** cloture
fermentation . . **4.** stum
gap . . **7.** stopper **9.** expedient, makeshift
momentarily . . **5.** pause
nautical . . **5.** avast
organ . . **5.** viola **7.** gemsbok **8.** dulsiana
seams (boat) . . **4.** calk
short . . **5.** pause **7.** respite **8.** interval
   12. intermission
unintentional . . **5.** stall
watch . . **5.** timer
with clay . . **3.** pug
stopper . . . **4.** bung, cork, plug **5.** spile
   7. bouchon
storage (pert to) . . .
bin . . **3.** mow **4.** loft, shed, silo **7.** granary
   8. elevator
fodder (in silo) . . **6.** ensile
hidden . . **5.** cache
place . . **3.** bin **4.** barn **5.** attic, depot,
   étape **6.** cellar, closet **7.** arsenal,
   granary **8.** cupboard, elevator, magazine
   10. promptuary, repository
stork . . . **4.** ibis **6.** jabiru **7.** Maguari,
   marabou **8.** adjutant
storklike . . . **8.** pelargic
storm . . . **4.** blow, fume, fury, rage,
   rain, rave, snow, wind **5.** orage
   6. attack, shower, simoom (simoon),
   tumult **7.** bluster, disturb, tempest,
   trouble **8.** calamity, eruption, outbreak,
   upheaval, violence **9.** agitation
   11. disturbance
storm (pert to) . . .
cold . . **11.** northeaster
evil storm god . . **2.** Zu **9.** blackbird
   (symb), Hlorrithi
extreme . . **4.** gale **7.** cyclone, monsoon,
   tempest, tornado **9.** hurricane
occidental . . **6.** wester
recorder (thunder) . . **11.** brontometer
sand . . **6.** tebbad
snow . . **5.** buran
stormy . . . **5.** rainy **7.** furious, riotous,
   violent **8.** agitated **9.** inclement,
   turbulent **10.** tumultuous

11. tempestuous

story . . . 3. fib, lie 4. hoax, joke, lore, saga, tale, tier, yarn 5. fable, floor 6. gossip, legend, serial 7. mystery, narrate, parable, romance 8. anecdote 9. chronicle, falsehood, tradition

story (pert to) . . .
absurd . . 4. hoax, yarn 6. canard
doleful . . 8. jeremiad
exclusive . . 4. beat, news 5. scoop
part . . 6. serial
short . . 5. conte 7. novella

storyteller . . . 4. liar 5. Aesop 6. fibber 7. relater 9. raconteur

stot . . . 2. ox 4. bull 5. steer 6. bounce 7. paunchy, stammer, stumble, stutter

stout . . . 3. fat 4. bold 5. brave, bulky, burly, hardy, obese, plump 6. fleshy, rotund, stocky, strong 7. haughty, violent 8. forcible, powerful, resolute, thickset 9. corpulent, undaunted 10. courageous, persistent

stoutness . . . 7. courage 8. strength 10. corpulence, embonpoint

stove . . . 4. etna, kiln, oven 5. grate, plate, range 6. heater 7. Coleman, furnace, smelter

stove part . . . 4. oven, pipe 6. burner 7. firebox, griddle

stow . . . 4. cram, hide, mass, pack 5. crowd, lodge, store, stuff 6. steeve 7. arrange, secrete

straddle . . . 5. salvo 6. option 7. astride 8. bestride 9. be neutral, go halfway

straggle . . . 4. rove 6. wander 7. deviate, meander

straight . . . 5. cards, erect, exact, rigid, stern 6. candid, direct, honest 7. correct, exactly, unmixed 8. directly, reliable, sequence, unbroken, vertical 9. authentic 10. horizontal, racing term 11. straightway, undeviating 13. uninterrupted 15. straightforward

straight (pert to) . . .
baseball . . 5. liner
course . . 7. beeline
edge . . 5. ruler
line . . 6. secant 8. enfilade 9. asymptote
Math . . 8. vinculum
out . . 6. candid 9. downright 11. unqualified 13. thoroughgoing 14. uncompromising
shooter . . 11. on the square
way . . 4. anon 8. directly 9. forthwith 11. immediately

straighten . . . 5. align, aline, level, order, plumb 6. tidy up 7. rectify, unravel 11. disentangle

straightforward . . . 5. frank 6. candid, direct, honest 7. sincere 8. outright 9. outspoken 10. forthright 11. undeviating

straightway . . . 4. anon 8. directly 9. downright, forthwith 10. forthright 11. immediately

strain . . . 3. sye, tax, try, tug 4. bend, dash, kind, mood, ooze, race, sort, tone, vein 5. breed, shade, stock, tense, touch 6. filter, melody, overdo, poetry, refine, sprain, streak, stress, strive 7. descent, fatigue, lineage, progeny,

stretch, tension, variety 8. ancestry, endeavor, exertion 9. constrain, overheave, percolate 10. generation

strained . . . 4. taut 5. tense 6. forced 7. intense, labored 8. wrenched 9. stretched 10. farfetched

strainer . . . 4. sile 5. sieve, tamis 6. filter, screen, sifter 8. colander, filterer 17. Hippocrates' sleeve

strait . . . 3. gut 4. neck, need 5. inlet 6. angust, narrow, strict 7. channel, limited 8. rigorous 9. difficult 10. restricted, scrupulous 11. distressful, predicament

Strait . . . 6. Bering 7. Surigao 8. Bosporus 9. Belleisle

Strait of Gibraltar . . . 17. Pillars of Hercules

Straits Settlements . . .
capital, Penang . . 10. Georgetown
capital, Singapore . . 9. Singapore
city . . 7. Malacca
peninsula . . 5. Malay
port . . 4. Prai

strand . . . 3. sea 4. bank, quay 5. beach, shore 6. maroon, thread 7. channel, current 8. filament

strange . . . 3. coy, new, odd, shy 4. rare, xeno (comb form) 5. alien, eerie, novel, queer, timid 6. exotic, quaint 7. curious, erratic, unknown, unusual 8. peculiar, singular, uncommon 9. eccentric, unrelated 10. extraneous, outlandish, tramontane, unfamiliar 12. unaccustomed, unacquainted 13. extraordinary, preternatural

stranger . . . 3. ger 5. alien, guest 7. visitor 8. intruder 9. foreigner, outlander

strangle . . . 5. choke 6. stifle 7. execute, garrote, repress, squeeze 8. suppress, throttle 9. suffocate

strap . . . 3. tie 4. belt, bind, hang, jess, rein, riem, whip 5. leash, strop, thong 6. enarme, latigo, oxreim 7. lanyard (laniard) 8. chastise

strap-shaped . . . 6. lorate 8. ligulate

strass . . . 5. glass, paste 10. silk refuse

strata . . . 6. layers 7. classes 10. formations

stratagem . . . 4. coup, ploy, ruse, trap, wile 5. trick 6. device, gambit 7. finesse 8. artifice

strategy . . . 7. tactics 8. artifice, intrigue, maneuver

stratum . . . 3. bed 4. coat 5. layer

straw . . . 4. stem 5. mulch 6. fodder, sennit, trifle 7. remains, sabutan

straw (pert to) . . .
bid . . 5. fraud 7. auction 9. worthless
coat (Jap peasant) . . 4. mino
color . . 6. flaxen
flower . . 11. everlasting
hat . . 4. baku 5. milan 6. panama
like . . 6. chaffy 11. stramineous
vote . . 5. Roper 6. Gallup

stray . . . 3. err, gad, sin 4. cavy, roam, rove, waif 5. range 6. swerve, wander 7. deviate, digress 8. aberrant, aberrate, go astray 9. wandering 10. occasional

streak . . . 3. roe 4. line, seam, vein 5. fleck, layer, stria 6. groove, strain,

strake, stripe
streaked . . . **4.** liny **6.** banded **7.** brindle, striped **8.** brindled, striated
stream . . . **3.** run **4.** burn, flow, rill, sike (syke) **5.** brook, creek, river **6.** abound, course, rillet, runlet, runnel, throng **7.** current, rivulet, torrent **9.** streamlet **11.** watercourse
stream (pert to) . . .
dry . . **6.** arroyo, spruit
gold . . **6.** placer
of consciousness . . **8.** thoughts **10.** psychology **11.** abstraction
of forgetfulness . . **5.** Lethe
underground . . **3.** aar
street . . . **4.** road **5.** calle **6.** avenue **7.** highway, roadway **8.** chaussée **9.** boulevard **12.** thoroughfare
street (pert to) . . .
car . . **4.** tram
famed . . **4.** Beal, Main, Wall **5.** Canal **6.** Beacon **7.** Downing **8.** Broadway **9.** Peachtree **12.** Threadneedle
French . . **3.** rue
narrow . . **4.** lane **5.** alley
show . . **4.** peep **5.** raree
Spanish . . **5.** calle
urchin . . **4.** Arab **5.** gamin **7.** outcast **8.** vagabond **11.** guttersnipe
Street called Straight (Bib) . . .
8. Damascus
strength . . . **3.** vis **4.** iron, thew **5.** brawn, force, might, nerve, power, rally, sinew, titer, vigor **6.** energy, health **7.** potency, stamina, sthenia, support **8.** firmness **9.** endurance, lustiness, stoutness, toughness, vehemence, willpower **10.** robustness, stronghold
strengthen . . . **4.** grow, prop **5.** brace, nerve **6.** deepen **7.** confirm, fortify, nourish, toughen **8.** increase, roborate **9.** encourage, intensify, reinforce **10.** invigorate **11.** consolidate
strengthening . . . **7.** bracing **8.** roborant **12.** invigorating, invigoration
strenuous . . . **6.** ardent, severe **7.** zealous **8.** vigorous **9.** difficult, energetic, laborious **11.** industrious
strepent . . . **4.** loud **5.** noisy
streperous . . . **4.** loud **5.** harsh **7.** noisily **9.** turbulent **10.** boisterous
strepor . . . **5.** noise
stress . . . **5.** arsis, ictus, labor **6.** accent, insist, strain, weight **7.** urgency **8.** emphasis, exigency, pressure **9.** emphasize **10.** elasticity, exaggerate **12.** exaggeration
stretcher . . . **3.** bar, lie **6.** litter, racker **9.** falsehood
stretch out . . . **6.** be long, extend **9.** expatiate
strew . . . **3.** ted **6.** spread **7.** diffuse, overlay, scatter **8.** disperse **10.** distribute **11.** disseminate
strewn . . . **4.** semé **8.** littered **9.** scattered **12.** disseminated
stria . . . **4.** line **5.** ridge, strip **6.** fillet, furrow, groove, hollow, streak, stripe **7.** channel **9.** striation
stricken . . . **7.** smitten, worn out, wounded **8.** unnerved **13.** incapacitated

strickle . . . **5.** rifle **7.** pattern **8.** template **10.** sweepboard **13.** striking board
strict . . . **4.** hard **5.** exact, harsh, rigid, stern **6.** severe **7.** ascetic, austere, precise **8.** accurate, rigorous **9.** puritanic, stringent **10.** forbidding, inexorable, inflexible, meticulous, relentless, scrupulous **11.** strait-laced, undeviating **13.** conscientious **14.** uncompromising
strict disciplinarian . . . **8.** martinet
strict discipline . . . **13.** regimentation
stricture . . . **7.** binding, censure **9.** criticism, narrowing **11.** contraction **12.** constriction
stride . . . **4.** gait, pace, step, walk **8.** bestride, progress, straddle, velocity
strident . . . **6.** shrill **7.** grating, raucous **11.** cacophonous
strife . . . **3.** war **4.** feud **5.** fight **6.** battle, combat, stasis **7.** contest, quarrel **8.** conflict, exertion, struggle **9.** logomachy **11.** altercation
strike . . . **3.** hit, pat, rap **4.** bump, bunt, slap, swat **5.** clout, labor, smite, whack **6.** attack, revolt **7.** impinge **9.** discovery
strike (pert to) . . .
a balance . . **5.** weigh **7.** average **8.** equalize **10.** compromise
against . . **7.** collide **8.** illision
and rebound . . **5.** carom (carrom) **9.** carambole
breaker . . **4.** fink, scab
dumb . . **4.** stun
heavily . . **3.** lam, ram **4.** bash, slam, slog, sock, wham **5.** punch, smite
obliquely . . **5.** carom **6.** glance
out . . **3.** fan **4.** dele **5.** elide, erase **6.** cancel, delete **9.** eliminate
to and fro . . **5.** bandy
with beak . . **4.** peck
with fist . . **5.** pound, punch
with head . . **4.** butt
with weapon . . **5.** crunt
with wonder . . **3.** awe **7.** astound
striking . . . **7.** salient **8.** dramatic, eloquent, exciting **9.** arresting, wonderful **10.** noticeable, remarkable, surprising
striking effect . . . **5.** éclat
striking part . . . **7.** clapper
string . . . **3.** ran, set **4.** bind, cord **5.** lacet, snare, twine **6.** fasten, series, thread **10.** succession
string (pert to) . . .
alphabet . . **5.** knots (for blind)
of beads . . **6.** rosary **8.** necklace
of horses . . **6.** stable
out . . **6.** line up **8.** lengthen **9.** expatiate
pottery . . **13.** Schnurkeramik (neolithic)
stringed instrument . . . **4.** harp, lute, lyre **5.** banjo, piano, recta, viola **6.** fiddle, guitar, violin, zither **7.** bandore, mandore, ukulele **8.** mandolin, psaltery **9.** mandolute **11.** harpsichord
stringed instrument bridge . . . **5.** magas
stringent . . . **4.** ropy **5.** rigid, tight **6.** cogent, severe, strict **10.** convincing **11.** acrimonious, restrictive
stringy . . . **4.** ropy **5.** gluey, tough **6.** sinewy, viscid **7.** fibrous

10. threadlike **11.** filamentous
strip . . . **4.** bare, belt, live, pare, peel, skin, slat **5.** cleat, shred, unrig **6.** denude, divest, remove, strake **7.** deprive, plunder, pull off, uncloak, uncover, undress **9.** dismantle **10.** dispossess, impoverish **11.** decorticate
strip (pert to) . . .
blubber . . **6.** flense
curved . . **5.** stave
lead (stained glass) . . **4.** came
leather . . **4.** welt **5.** thong **6.** latido **7.** belting
narrow . . **4.** lath, slat, tape, welt **5.** reeve, stave, strap
off skin . . **4.** flay
of possessions . . **4.** milk **5.** bleed, bunko (bunco), shear **6.** fleece **7.** despoil, swindle **10.** dispossess
raised . . **5.** ridge
tease dancer . . **8.** stripper **9.** ecdysiast
wood . . **5.** stave **6.** reglet, spline
stripe . . . **3.** bar, pin **4.** band, beat, line, mark, sort, type, wale, weal, welt, whip **5.** chalk, strip, vitta **6.** streak **7.** chevron **8.** insignia **9.** striation
striped (pert to) . . .
alder . . **11.** winterberry
antelope . . **5.** bongo
gillyflower . . **9.** carnation
longitudinally . . **7.** vittate
stripling . . . **3.** boy, lad **5.** youth **8.** juvenile **9.** youngster
strive . . . **3.** aim, try, tug **4.** toil **5.** labor **6.** battle, buffet, strain **7.** compete, contend, emulate **8.** endeavor, struggle
strive (pert to) . . .
for . . **3.** aim **4.** seek
to equal . . **5.** rival **6.** strain **7.** emulate
to overtake . . **5.** ensue
with . . **3.** vie **7.** compete
strobile . . . **4.** cone **8.** pine cone
strockle . . . **6.** shovel
stroke . . . **3.** fit, pat, pet, rub **4.** beat, blow, coup, flip, line, putt, shot **5.** ictus, serif, spasm, trait, whisk **6.** caress, fondle **7.** illness, solidus
stroll . . . **4.** roam, walk **5.** range, stray **6.** go slow, ramble, wander **7.** meander, saunter **8.** ambulate **9.** promenade **11.** perambulate
stroller . . . **5.** actor, tramp **6.** beggar **7.** peddler, vagrant **8.** wanderer **9.** saunterer **12.** perambulator
strolling . . . **7.** nomadic **8.** rambling **10.** meandering **13.** perambulation
strong . . . **3.** fit, hot **4.** able, firm, hale, hard, wiry **5.** fetid, hardy, lusty, solid, sound, stout, tough **6.** potent, robust, sinewy, stable, sturdy, virile **7.** healthy, intense, odorous, tainted **8.** accented, forceful, forcible, muscular, resonant, stalwart, vigorous **9.** effective, energetic **10.** outrageous, persuasive, pronounced, remarkable **11.** substantial **12.** concentrated
strong (pert to) . . .
drink . . **6.** liquor **7.** spirits **9.** distilled
flavor . . **4.** racy **5.** acrid **7.** pungent
hold . . **4.** fort **7.** citadel **8.** fastness, Fort Knox, fortress, muniment, treasury

man . . **5.** Atlas **6.** Samson (Sampson)
muscles . . **5.** brawn, thewy
music . . **4.** loud **5.** forte **7.** saccade
willed . . **8.** resolute **9.** obstinate **10.** determined
wind . . **7.** pampero
stroygood . . . **7.** wastrel **11.** spendthrift
strubbly . . . **6.** untidy **7.** unkempt
struck . . . **4.** smit **5.** smote **7.** smitten, swatted **8.** shutdown (see also *strike*)
struck (pert to) . . .
an attitude . . **5.** posed
out . . **5.** deled **6.** elided, erased, fanned **7.** deleted
with fear . . **6.** aghast **7.** alarmed
with missiles . . **6.** pelted
structure . . . **3.** dam **4.** dais, form, pier **5.** frame, house, jetty, kiosk, stage, tower **6.** bridge, make-up, pagoda **7.** edifice **8.** building, platform **9.** formation **10.** tabernacle **11.** composition **12.** constitution, construction
structure (pert to) . . .
calcareous . . **5.** coral
conical . . **7.** pyramid
crownlike . . **6.** corona
filamentous . . **4.** hair
human . . **8.** physique
monumental . . **5.** pylon
roof . . **6.** cupola, dormer
tall . . **5.** tower **7.** steeple **9.** campanile
tentlike . . **10.** tabernacle
struggle . . . **3.** tug, vie **4.** cope, wade **5.** labor **6.** effort, Peniel (Bib), strife, strike, strive, tussle **7.** contend, contest, scuffle, wrestle **8.** endeavor, flounder, scramble **10.** contention, difficulty
strumpet . . . **5.** belie **6.** harlot **8.** harridan **10.** prostitute
stub . . . **3.** end **4.** dock, tail **5.** squat, stump **6.** coupon, stocky **7.** remnant **8.** thickset **11.** counterfoil
stubble . . . **5.** beard, stump **6.** arrish **7.** bristle **8.** eelgrass
stubborn . . . **3.** set **4.** rude **5.** fixed, hardy, rough, tough **6.** coarse, mulish, sturdy **7.** restive **8.** perverse, resolute, starkish, vigorous **9.** obstinate, pigheaded **10.** determined, headstrong, inflexible, refractory, unyielding **11.** intractable **12.** recalcitrant
stuck . . . **4.** fast **7.** baffled, cohered **8.** coherent, stranded (see also *stick*)
stuck-up . . . **4.** vain **8.** arrogant **9.** conceited **10.** egocentric **12.** supercilious **13.** self-important
stud . . . **3.** dot, pin **4.** boss, knob **5.** haras **6.** enstar **7.** hobnail **8.** ornament, stallion **9.** studhorse
student . . . **4.** co-ed **5.** cadet, eleve, plebe, pupil **6.** tosher **7.** learner, scholar **8.** disciple **9.** collegian
student of . . .
behavior (human) . . **12.** psychologist
birds . . **13.** ornithologist
birds' eggs . . **8.** oologist
Eton . . **7.** Etonian
law . . **8.** stagiary
medical . . **6.** intern (interne)
military . . **5.** cadet, plebe

natural history.. **10.** naturalist
navy.. **5.** cadet **10.** midshipman
Oxford.. **8.** commoner
proverbs.. **14.** paroemiologist
punishment.. **10.** penologist
reptiles.. **13.** herpetologist
spiders.. **13.** arachnologist
students, advanced group ... **7.** seminar
13. upperclassmen
studied ... **5.** boned, pored **6.** formal
7. learned, planned, weighed
8. designed, measured, reasoned
10. well-versed **11.** intentional
12. premeditated
studio ... **4.** shop **7.** atelier, bottega
8. workshop **11.** working room
study ... **3.** con, den **4.** bone, muse,
pore, scan **5.** étude, grind, learn, weigh
7. discuss **6.** peruse, ponder **7.** analyze,
examine, pegging, reverie, science,
subject, thought **8.** endeavor, learning,
treatise **10.** discussion, inspection
11. contemplate **13.** contemplation
study of ...
animals.. **7.** zoology **9.** zoography
bees.. **8.** apiology
birds' eggs.. **6.** oology
disease.. **8.** nosology
fingerprints.. **13.** dactylography
handwriting.. **10.** graphology
insects.. **10.** entomology
man.. **12.** anthropology
mountains.. **7.** orology
old age.. **9.** nostology **10.** geriatrics
11. gerontology
population.. **10.** demography, larithmics
12. demographics
punishment.. **8.** penology
sacred images.. **9.** iconology
temples.. **7.** naology
words.. **9.** etymology **12.** lexicography
stuff ... **3.** goo, pad, ram, wad **4.** cram, fill,
stow **5.** gorge, trash **6.** fabric, matter,
potion **7.** content, element, rubbish,
satiate **8.** marinate, material, nonsense,
overfill, trumpery **9.** principle, substance
10. gluttonize
stuffiness ... **7.** prudery **8.** dullness
9. obstinacy **10.** sullenness, sultriness
11. pompousness
stuffing ... **6.** lining **7.** padding
8. contents, dressing **9.** forcemeat
stuffy ... **3.** fat **4.** dull, prim **5.** close,
stout **6.** stodgy, sullen, sultry **7.** airless,
pompous, prudish **8.** resolute
9. bombastic, obstinate **10.** old-
fogyish **11.** strait-laced **12.** conservative
13. ill-ventilated
stulm ... **4.** adit **7.** passage **8.** entrance
stumble ... **3.** err **4.** fall, trip **5.** lurch
6. boggle, bungle, chance, falter,
happen **7.** blunder, perplex, stagger,
stammer **8.** confound, flounder
stump ... **4.** butt, dare, skeg, snag,
stab, stub **5.** clump, scrab **6.** baffle,
trudge **7.** declaim, nonplus **8.** platform
9. challenge, remainder, tortillon
11. electioneer
stun ... **4.** bowl, daze **5.** amaze, daunt
6. benumb, bruise, deaden **7.** astound,
stupefy, terrify **8.** astonish, bewilder

9. overpower, overwhelm
stunning ... **8.** striking **9.** beautiful
10. astounding, stupefying, terrifying
stunt ... **4.** feat **5.** blunt, check, cramp,
crowl, dwarf, whale (2-yr) **6.** hinder
7. curtail, exploit, shorten
10. tomfoolery
stunted ... **7.** blunted, checked, dwarfed
9. curtailed, shortened
stupa ... **4.** tomb **5.** mound, tower
6. shrine **8.** monument
stupefied ... **5.** doped **6.** aghast,
sotted **7.** drugged, shocked, stunned
8. benumbed **9.** petrified
stupefy ... **4.** daze, dope, drug, numb,
pall, stun **5.** besot, blunt, shock
6. bedaze, bemuse, muddle **7.** astound,
confuse, petrify, terrify **8.** bewilder,
confound **10.** incrassate, make stupid
11. flabbergast (sl)
stupid ... **4.** clod, dull, dumb **5.** blunt,
crass, dense, inane **6.** oafish, obtuse,
simple, stolid **7.** asinine, doltish, foolish,
witless **8.** blockish, Boeotian, gullible
9. brainless, senseless **11.** heavywitted
13. unintelligent
stupid (pert to) ...
grossly .. **7.** asinine **9.** imbecilic
person .. **3.** ass, oaf **4.** clod, coot, dolt,
loon, lout, nerd **5.** goose, klutz, stirk
7. tomfool **11.** gillygaupus
render .. **8.** hebetate
stupidity ... **7.** fatuity **8.** dullness,
hebetude **11.** foolishness
12. indifference **13.** foolish remark
stupor ... **4.** coma, daze **5.** sleep, sopor
6. apathy, torpor, trance **8.** lethargy,
neurosis, numbness **9.** lassitude
15. unconsciousness
sturdy ... **4.** firm **5.** burly, hardy, lusty,
stout **6.** robust, stable, steady, strong
8. resolute, stalwart, stubborn, vigorous
10. courageous, determined, unyielding
11. substantial
sturgeon ... **6.** beluga, caviar **7.** sterlet
9. Acipenser **10.** hackleback
stutter ... **6.** falter **7.** stammer
sty ... **3.** pen **4.** boil **5.** hovel, stair,
steps, stile **6.** ladder, pimple **7.** pustule
8. swelling **9.** enclosure
style ... **3.** air, pen, way **4.** form, kind,
mode, name **5.** get-up, gusto, trend,
vogue **6.** gnomon, graver, phrase,
stylus **7.** alamode, diction, fashion
8. elegance **9.** execution **10.** appearance
12. characterize, presentation
style (pert to) ...
architecture .. **5.** Doric, Greek, Ionic,
Roman **6.** Gothic, Norman **7.** Italian
8. Colonial, Georgian **9.** Byzantine
10. Corinthian, Romanesque
11. Renaissance
painting .. **5.** genre **11.** Renaissance
type .. **5.** roman, runic **6.** italic
styled ... **5.** named **6.** called, termed,
y-clept (y-cleped) **7.** phrased
stylet ... **5.** probe **6.** trocar **7.** poniard
8. stiletto **9.** specillum
stylish ... **3.** mod **4.** chic, cool, neat, tony
5. nifty, ritzy, sharp, smart, swank **6.** chi-
chi, dressy, jaunty, modish, preppy,

snazzy, trendy **7.** alamode, voguish
11. fashionable
styptic ... **4.** alum **10.** astringent, tannic
acid **12.** constringent
Styx ferryman ... **6.** Charon
suant ... **4.** even **6.** demure, smooth,
steady **7.** equable, regular
suave ... **4.** oily, smug **5.** bland
6. urbane **7.** fulsome **8.** unctuous
9. agreeable **12.** ingratiating, mealy-
mouthed **13.** smooth-talking
suavity ... **7.** amenity **8.** civility, courtesy,
urbanity **10.** gentleness
subdue ... **3.** cow **4.** calm, tame
5. allay, crush, lower, quash, quell,
sober **6.** disarm, muffle, reduce,
soften **7.** conquer, repress, squelch
8. mitigate, overcome, suppress,
surmount, vanquish **9.** overpower,
subjugate **11.** subordinate
subdued ... **4.** meek, soft **7.** muffled,
quelled **8.** disarmed, relieved, tempered
9. conquered, toned down **10.** made
gentle, subjugated **11.** soft colored,
unperturbed
subject ... **4.** text, word **5.** cause, prone,
theme, topic **6.** matter, motive, submit,
vassal **7.** citizen, servant **8.** inferior
9. subjugate, substance **10.** predispose
11. subordinate **12.** part of speech
subjective ... **6.** mental **7.** topical
8. fanciful, illusory **9.** of the mind
10. nominative **11.** introverted
subject of ...
discourse .. **5.** theme, topic
disease .. **4.** case **7.** patient
lawsuit .. **3.** res **7.** grounds
sentence .. **4.** noun
subject to ...
abuse .. **6.** revile
analysis .. **7.** titrate
argument .. **4.** moot
change .. **7.** mutable **8.** amenable
choice .. **8.** elective
control .. **7.** rulable
death .. **6.** mortal
depression .. **5.** moody
dislike .. **8.** aversion
mistakes .. **7.** erratic
outbursts .. **9.** irritable
tension .. **8.** strained
vassalage .. **5.** feoff
sublimation ... **9.** underling
12. underscoring
sublime ... **4.** high **5.** grand, great, lofty,
noble, proud **6.** refine **7.** exalted,
haughty **8.** elevated, eloquent,
empyreal, majestic, splendid, upraised,
vaporize **9.** beautiful, expletive
11. magnanimous
Sublime Porte ... **12.** Ottoman Court
17. Turkish government
sublimity ... **4.** acme **5.** glory **6.** beauty
7. majesty **8.** grandeur **9.** greatness
10. excellence **11.** distinction
12. magnificence
submarine ... **3.** sub **4.** boat, ship
8. Nautilus, Scorpion, Thresher
11. submersible
submarine eye ... **9.** periscope
submission ... **5.** kneel **8.** fatalism,

meekness, patience, yielding
9. deference, obedience, surrender
10. compliance, confession
11. resignation **13.** nonresistance
submissive ... **4.** meek, tame **6.** humble
7. dutiful, patient **8.** obedient, resigned,
uxorious (to wife), yielding **9.** compliant
11. acquiescent, conformable
submit ... **3.** bow **4.** obey **5.** defer,
remit, stoop, yield **6.** soften, temper
7. succumb **8.** moderate **9.** acquiesce,
postulate, surrender **10.** condescend
submit to ... **4.** obey **6.** endure
11. acknowledge
subordinate ... **4.** exon **5.** minor
6. subdue **7.** servant, subject **8.** inferior,
parergon **9.** appendage, assistant,
dependent, secondary **10.** collateral,
incidental, submissive **11.** subservient
subsequent ... **5.** later **7.** ensuing
9. following, postnatal **10.** succeeding
11. consecutive
subservient ... **6.** vassal **7.** servile, subject
9. assistant, truckling **10.** obsequious,
submissive **11.** subordinate
12. instrumental
subside ... **3.** ebb **4.** bate, fall, lull, sink,
wane **5.** abate **6.** settle **7.** descend,
relapse **8.** decrease, languish
9. gravitate **11.** deteriorate
subsidiary ... **8.** inferior **9.** assistant,
auxiliary, extrinsic, tributary
10. collateral **11.** stipendiary
12. nonessential **13.** supplementary
subsist ... **2.** be **4.** live **5.** abide, exist
6. endure, remain **7.** prevail, survive
8. continue
subsist on prey ... **9.** rapacious
substance ... **3.** sum **4.** gist, meat
5. stuff **6.** import, matter, wealth
7. aliment, element, essence, meaning,
purport, summary **8.** hardness, material
9. actuality, affluence, solidness
11. consistency
substance (pert to) ...
absorbent .. **5.** fomes
aeriform .. **3.** gas **5.** argon
amorphous .. **7.** ferrite
antitoxic .. **5.** serum
aromatic .. **5.** myrrh, spice **6.** balsam
basic .. **7.** element
bitter .. **5.** aloes, aloin, linin **7.** amarine,
emetine **8.** elaterin
brittle .. **5.** glass
cleansing, purifying .. **8.** depurant
10. abstergent, clarifiant
corrosive .. **4.** acid **7.** caustic
dissolved .. **6.** solute
dissolving .. **9.** resolvent
electrical .. **3.** ion
elemental .. **5.** metal
expanding .. **8.** dilatant
fatty .. **5.** lipin, suint
ferment .. **9.** activator
flocculent .. **4.** wool
food .. **7.** protein
fruit jellying .. **6.** pectin
gelatinous .. **4.** agar
hard .. **4.** bone **5.** ivory **7.** adamant
hypnotic .. **4.** ural
inflammable .. **6.** tinder **7.** bitumen

inorganic . . **7.** mineral
ipecac root . . **7.** emetine
light . . **4.** cork
milk curdling . . **6.** rennet
moss (Ceylon) . . **4.** agar **8.** agar-agar
neutralizing . . **6.** alkali
resinous . . **3.** gum, lac **5.** copal **7.** shellac
rubberlike . . **5.** gutta
soapmaking . . **3.** lye
stabilizing . . **7.** ballast
sulphur . . **5.** hepar
tar . . **6.** cresol
unctuous . . **3.** fat, oil **7.** pinguid
vegetable . . **5.** resin, rosin
wax, waxy . . **5.** cerin **7.** suberin
　8. paraffin
whale (perfume) . . **9.** ambergris
wood ash . . **6.** potash
substantial . . . **4.** firm, real, true **5.** pucka
　(pukka), solid, stout **6.** actual, bodily,
　hearty, stable, strong, sturdy **7.** genuine
　8. abundant, tangible **9.** corporeal,
　essential, important **10.** nourishing
　12. considerable
substantiate . . . **6.** embody, verify
　7. confirm, justify **8.** underpin
　9. establish **11.** corroborate
substantive . . . **4.** firm, noun **5.** sound
　6. actual, entity **7.** pronoun **9.** essential
　11. substantial **13.** self-contained
substitute . . . **5.** proxy, vicar **6.** deputy,
　ersatz **7.** apology, replace **8.** exchange,
　nominate **9.** alternate, surrogate
　10. understudy, viceregent
　11. replacement
subterfuge . . . **4.** ruse **5.** blind, trick
　6. refuge **7.** evasion, pretext **8.** artifice,
　pretense **9.** expedient **13.** prevarication
subterranean . . . **6.** hidden, secret
　8. hypogeal, plutonic **10.** in the earth
　11. underground
subtile . . . **3.** sly **4.** rare, wily **6.** crafty,
　subtle **7.** cunning, elusive **9.** beguiling
subtle . . . **3.** sly **4.** fine, nice, rare,
　thin **6.** artful, clever, crafty, shrewd
　7. cunning, refined, subtile **8.** analytic,
　delicate **9.** beguiling, designing,
　ingenious **10.** mysterious
　14. discriminating
subtle (pert to) . . .
　emanation (invisible) . . **4.** aura
　　10. atmosphere
　sarcasm . . **5.** irony
　variation . . **6.** nuance
subtlety . . . **5.** guile **7.** cunning, finesse,
　slyness **8.** delicacy, fineness
　9. quodlibet **10.** shrewdness
subtraction, terms . . . **7.** minuend
　9. deduction **10.** difference, subtrahend
subversion . . . **4.** ruin (utter) **9.** overthrow
　10. corruption, revolution
　11. destruction
subvert . . . **4.** ruin **5.** evert, upset **6.** refute,
　uproot **7.** corrupt, destroy, pervert
　8. alienate, overturn **9.** overthrow,
　undermine
subvertive . . . **8.** eversive
subway . . . **4.** tube **5.** train **6.** tunnel
　11. underground **18.** underground
　railway
succade . . . **8.** preserve **10.** confection

succeed . . . **5.** ensue, occur **6.** attain,
　follow, thrive **7.** achieve, devolve,
　prosper, replace, triumph **8.** come next,
　flourish, supplant **10.** accomplish
succeeding . . . **4.** next **7.** ensuing, sequent
　9. following **10.** subsequent, successful
　11. in the wake of
success . . . **2.** go **3.** hit **4.** luck **5.** elate
　7. fortune, outcome **8.** accolade, smash
　hit **10.** prosperity **11.** consequence
successful . . . **5.** lucky **8.** thriving
　9. fortunate **10.** prosperous, succeeding,
　triumphant **11.** flourishing
succession . . . **3.** row, run **5.** music
　(rhythmic) **6.** series **7.** dynasty, lineage
　8. sequence **9.** posterity
succin . . . **5.** amber
succinct . . . **4.** curt **5.** brief, hasty,
　short, terse **7.** compact, concise,
　laconic, summary **10.** compressed
　11. compendious, sententious
succor, succour . . . **3.** aid **4.** abet,
　help **6.** brandy (Alpine), relief, rescue
　7. comfort, deliver, relieve, sustain
　8. befriend, mitigate **10.** assistance
succulent . . . **3.** uva **4.** lush **5.** juicy,
　pappy, tasty **6.** cactus, tender
succumb . . . **3.** die **5.** faint, yield **6.** perish,
　submit **7.** give way **8.** get tired
such (as) . . . **3.** sic **4.** like **7.** certain,
　similar **8.** analogue **9.** analogous
suction (as in clicks of Bantu) . . .
　9. implosive
Sudan, Africa . . .
　capital . . **8.** Khartoum
　desert . . **6.** Libyan, Nubian
　export . . **9.** gum arabic
　gazelle . . **4.** dama
　gum forests . . **8.** Kordofan
　lake . . **4.** Chad
　language . . **2.** Ga **6.** Arabic
　people . . **4.** Arab, Sere **5.** Fulah (Fula)
　　6. Nubian
　Plain . . **6.** Gezira
　river . . **8.** Blue Nile **9.** White Nile
　town . . **5.** Segou
sudden . . . **4.** rash **5.** hasty, swift
　6. abrupt, prompt, speedy **7.** violent
　8. headlong **9.** impetuous, impromptu,
　impulsive **10.** unexpected, unforeseen
　11. precipitate, precipitous
sudden (pert to) . . .
　all of a . . **5.** short **6.** presto **8.** suddenly
　and brilliant . . **8.** meteoric
　fear . . **13.** consternation
　sally . . **6.** sortie
　shock . . **4.** jolt
　stroke . . **4.** coup, dash
　thrust . . **3.** jab **5.** lunge
sudor . . . **5.** sweat **8.** sudation **9.** exudation
　12. perspiration
Sudra caste . . . **3.** mal (low) **5.** palli
sue . . . **3.** beg, woo **4.** plea, urge
　5. court, plead **6.** appeal, pursue
　7. entreat, request **8.** continue, petition
　9. prosecute, seek after
suet . . . **6.** tallow **8.** leaf lard
Suez Canal builder . . . **9.** de Lesseps
　(Ferdinand)
suffer . . . **3.** let **4.** bear, dree **5.** admit,
　allow **6.** endure, permit, submit

7. undergo 8. tolerate 10. experience
suffer (pert to) . . .
 distress . . 5. gripe, groan, smart 6. starve
 from heat . . 7. swelter
 remorse . . 3. rue
 ruin . . 5. wreck
sufferance . . . 4. pain 6. misery
 9. endurance, passivity 10. permission
 11. forbearance
suffering, scene of . . . 10. Gethsemane
suffice . . . 2. do 5. avail, serve 6. answer
 7. appease, content, satisfy
 11. sufficiency
sufficiency . . . 4. fill 7. ability, conceit
 8. adequacy, capacity, validity
 9. abundance 10. competency 14. self-
 confidence
sufficient . . . 3. due, fit 4. enow, full,
 good 5. ample, valid 6. enough, plenty
 7. suffice 8. adequate 9. qualified
 11. responsible 12. satisfactory
suffix, for or denoting . . .
 abounding in . . 5. ulent
 abundant . . 3. ose
 act of . . 3. ure 4. ance, tion
 advocate . . 3. ite
 alcohol . . 2. ol
 being . . 3. ure
 capable of . . 3. ile
 chemical . . 2. ac 3. ane, ene, ile, ine,
 iol, ole, ose 4. alic, idin, itol
 diminutive . . 2. el 3. cle, ole, ule 4. ette
 disease . . 4. itis
 doer . . 4. ator
 enzyme . . 3. ase
 feminine . . 3. ess
 follower . . 3. ist, ite
 full of . . 3. ose
 geological age . . 4. cene
 inflammation . . 4. itis
 inhabitants of . . 3. ese 4. ites
 jurisdiction . . 3. ric
 law . . 2. ee
 medicine . . 2. ia 3. oma 4. itis
 profession . . 3. eer
suffocate . . . 5. burke, choke 6. stifle
 7. smother 8. strangle, suppress,
 throttle 10. asphyxiate, extinguish
 12. deprive of air
suffrage . . . 4. vote 5. voice 6. assent,
 ballot, prayer 7. witness 8. petition
 9. franchise 10. assistance 11. right
 to vote 12. intercession, supplication
sugar . . . 4. cane 5. biose, bribe, candy,
 maple, money 6. doctor, season
 7. sucrose, sweeten 9. sugarcoat
 10. endearment, saccharose,
 sweetening 12. carbohydrate,
 disaccharide 14. monosaccharide
sugar (pert to) . . .
 and molasses . . 6. melada
 burnt . . 7. caramel
 chemical . . 6. acrose 7. osamine, sucrose
 8. fructose 10. saccharose
 crude . . 3. gur 5. maple 10. massecuite,
 piloncillo
 fruit, honey . . 8. levulose
 plant . . 7. sorghum
 raw . . 9. cassonade, muscovado
 sand . . 5. niter
 simple . . 6. ketose, triose 7. glucide

substitute . . 5. honey
syrup . . 7. treacle 8. molasses
tree . . 5. maple
without . . 3. sec
wood . . 6. xylose
sugar cane (pert to) . . .
 disease . . 5. sereh
 pulp, refuse . . 4. marc 7. bagasse
 stalk . . 6. ratoon
sugared . . . 5. sweet 7. honeyed
 9. sweetened 11. mellifluous,
 sugarcoated
Sugar Loaf Mt locale . . . 3. Rio
suggest . . . 4. hint, mean, move 5. imply
 6. advise, allude, prompt 7. connote,
 inspire, propose 8. indicate, intimate
 9. insinuate
suggestion . . . 4. clue, hint, idea, plan
 5. tinge, trace 6. advice, symbol
 7. soupçon 8. proposal 9. hypnotism
 10. indication, intimation 11. small
 amount, supposition
Suidae . . . 5. swine
sui generis . . . 6. unique
suit . . . 3. fit 4. plea 5. befit, cards,
 dress, habit, match, serve, tally
 6. adjust, answer, attire, become,
 prayer, wooing 7. clothes, comport,
 conform, costume, lawsuit, retinue
 8. petition, sequence 9. courtship
 10. litigation 11. accommodate
suit (pert to) . . .
 at law . . 10. litigation
 for property . . 6. trover
 maker . . 6. sartor, tailor
 starter . . 7. relator
 the occasion . . 6. timely
suitability . . . 7. fitness 9. propriety
 10. expedience, timeliness 11. eligibility
 13. qualification
suitable . . . 3. apt, due, fit, pat 4. meet
 6. proper, timely 8. adequate, apposite,
 eligible, idoneous 9. accordant,
 agreeable, competent, congruent,
 congruous, consonant, expedient
 10. compatible, consistent
 11. appropriate 12. commensurate
 13. correspondent
suitably proportioned . . .
 13. commensurable
suite . . . 3. set 5. music, staff 7. retinue
 8. sequence 9. apartment
 10. attendance, succession
 11. consequence
suitor . . . 5. swain, wooer 7. amoroso
 10. petitioner 12. party to a suit
sulk . . . 3. pet 4. mope, plow, pout
 6. furrow
sulky . . . 3. gig 4. dull, glum, plow
 5. moody, pouty, surly 6. gloomy,
 go-cart, sullen 8. carriage 9. obstinate
sullen . . . 4. dour, glum, grim, sour
 5. cross, gruff, harsh, moody, pouty,
 sulky, surly 6. crusty, gloomy, morose
 7. austere, cynical, fretful, peevish,
 pettish 8. chumpish, churlish, petulant,
 spiteful 9. obstinate, saturnine
sully . . . 4. foul 5. dirty, smear, stain,
 taint 6. defile, smirch, vilify 7. blemish,
 corrupt, debauch, disdain, pollute
 9. bespatter, denigrate 10. stigmatize

11. contaminate
sulphur (pert to) . . .
　alchemy . . **7.** chibrit
　alloy . . **6.** niello
　butterfly . . **7.** clouded **9.** cloudless
　color . . **6.** yellow
　comb form . . **5.** thion
　element . . **11.** nonmetallic
　reference to . . **7.** thionic **9.** brimstone
sultan (pert to) . . .
　decree . . **5.** irade
　fowls . . **5.** breed
　home . . **5.** serai
　Mohammedan State . . **5.** ruler **6.** prince
　　9. sovereign
　Turkish ruler . . **6.** Caliph **8.** Padishah
　　13. Grand Seignior
　wife . . **7.** sultana
sultana . . . **4.** roll (dessert), wife **5.** grape
　　8. mistress **9.** gallinule
sultry . . . **3.** hot **5.** humid, lurid **6.** torrid
　　7. dog days, sensual **10.** oppressive,
　　sweltering
sum . . . **3.** add, tot **4.** loot **5.** count,
　　gross, total, whole **6.** amount, number,
　　result **7.** summary **8.** addition, quantity
　　9. aggregate, summarize, summation
　　12. recapitulate
sum (pert to) . . .
　forfeited . . **5.** dédit
　of money . . **6.** budget
　total . . **8.** entirety
　unexpended . . **7.** savings
　up . . **3.** tot **5.** count **8.** perorate
sumac . . . **5.** Rheus **7.** dogwood
　　8. shadbush **9.** squawbush
　　13. Toxicodendron **14.** buckthorn brown
Sumatra . . .
　harbor . . **6.** Padang **9.** Palembang
　island of . . **16.** Malay Archipelago
　kingdom . . **5.** Achin, Jambi
　mountain . . **12.** Bukit Barisan
　raft (bamboo) . . **5.** rakit
　river . . **4.** Musi **5.** Jambi, Rokan **6.** Asahan
　squirrel shrew . . **4.** tana
　wildcat . . **4.** balu
sumless . . . **11.** inestimable
　　12. incalculable **13.** unaccountable
summary . . . **5.** brief, short **6.** digest,
　　prompt, resume **7.** epitome **8.** abstract
　　10. compendium **11.** abridgement,
　　enumeration, reiteration
　　14. recapitulation
summary (pert to) . . .
　book . . **5.** blurb
　concise . . **6.** précis
　of facts . . **7.** roundup
　of knowledge . . **12.** encyclopedia
　　(encyclopaedia)
　of principles . . **5.** creed
　of speech . . **5.** notes
summer . . . **3.** été **6.** season
summer (pert to) . . .
　bird . . **7.** cuckold, sparrow, tanager,
　　wryneck
　coot . . **9.** gallinule
　house . . **6.** gazebo **9.** belvedere
　lilac . . **8.** damewort
　pert to . . **7.** estival
　rash . . **11.** prickly heat
　resort . . **4.** camp

squash . . **7.** cymling, scallop **9.** crookneck
summit . . . **3.** top **4.** acme, apex, knap,
　　peak **5.** crest, crown, knoll, spire
　　6. height **7.** Everest **8.** pinnacle
　　9. fastigium **10.** perfection
　　11. culmination, mountaintop
summon . . . **4.** call, cite, page, sist
　　5. evoke **6.** call up, demand, elicit,
　　invite, muster **7.** conjure, evocate
　　8. remember **9.** conscript
sumpter . . . **4.** mule **9.** pack horse
sun . . . **3.** orb, Sol **4.** bask **6.** Helios
　　7. Phoebus **12.** heavenly body
　　13. celestial body
sun (pert to) . . .
　clock . . **6.** gnomon (part) **7.** sundial
　comb form . . **5.** helio
　crossing the equator . . **7.** equinox
　disk . . **4.** aten
　down . . **3.** eve **8.** twilight
　farthest from . . **8.** aphelion
　fish . . **4.** mola, opah **5.** bream
　god . . **2.** Ra **4.** Amen, Baal, Lier (Llew)
　　6. Apollo, Helios **7.** Khepera (Chepera),
　　Shamash, Sokaris **8.** Hyperion
　mock . . **9.** parhelion
　nearest to . . **10.** perihelion
　outer layer . . **6.** corona
　over the equator . . **7.** equinox
　path . . **4.** halo **6.** circle **8.** ecliptic
　pert to . . **5.** solar **6.** heliac **9.** heliology
　poetic . . **5.** glory, power **6.** sunset
　　7. daystar, sunrise **8.** splendor
　satellite . . **6.** planet
　spot . . **6.** facula **7.** freckle
　squall . . **9.** jellyfish
　stroke . . **8.** siriasis **9.** calenture
sundang . . . **4.** bolo **5.** knife
sunder . . . **4.** part, rend, rive **5.** sever, split
　　6. cleave, divide **7.** divorce **8.** dissever,
　　disunite, sejugate
sundry . . . **6.** divers **7.** several, various
　　8. frequent, manifold, numerous
　　9. different **10.** multiplied
　　12. multifarious **13.** miscellaneous
sunflower . . . **8.** marigold, rockrose
　　10. heliotrope
Sunflower State . . . **6.** Kansas
sunk . . . **4.** turf **7.** baffled, concave,
　　lowered **8.** dejected, overcome
　　9. depressed (see also *sink*)
sunk fence . . . **4.** ha-ha (haw-haw)
sunny . . . **4.** warm **5.** clear, merry **6.** bright,
　　sunlit **8.** cheerful **9.** sparkling, vivacious
sunrise . . . **4.** dawn
sunset . . . **3.** eve **4.** dusk **7.** evening,
　　sundown **8.** twilight
Sunset State . . . **6.** Oregon **7.** Arizona
Sunshine State . . . **9.** New Mexico
　　11. South Dakota
supawn . . . **4.** mush **12.** hasty pudding
superabundance . . . **5.** flood **6.** excess,
　　plenty **7.** surplus **8.** plethora
　　10. exuberance **11.** superfluity
superabundant . . . **4.** rank **6.** lavish
　　7. profuse **9.** excessive, exuberant,
　　luxuriant, plentiful **11.** overflowing
　　14. oversufficient
superannuate . . . **6.** retire **9.** antiquate
　　10. pension off **13.** prove obsolete
superb . . . **4.** rich **5.** grand, noble

6. lordly 7. elegant, stately 8. majestic, splendid 9. sumptuous 11. magnificent 13. extraordinary 14. superexcellent

supercilious ... 5. proud 7. haughty 8. arrogant 9. arbitrary 11. overbearing 12. contemptuous 13. hypercritical

supercilious person ... 4. snob

superficial ... 4. glib 6. slight, square 7. cursory, shallow, smatter, surface, trivial 8. apparent, external 9. frivolous, insincere

superfluity ... 6. excess, luxury, wealth 7. overset 8. frippery 10. redundancy 11. prodigality 14. superabundance

superfluous ... 4. over 5. luxus, spare 6. excess 7. surplus, useless 8. needless, wasteful 9. redundant 10. inordinate 11. extravagant 12. nonessential 13. superabundant 14. supererogatory

superhuman ... 6. divine 9. Herculean 12. supernatural 13. extraordinary

superimposed ... 4. over, upon 5. above 7. covered, layered 8. overlaid 9. overlying

superintend ... 4. boss 5. guide 6. direct, manage 7. oversee 8. overlook 9. look after, supervise 10. administer, have charge

superintendent ... 4. boss 7. curator, manager 8. director, overseer 9. inspector, straw boss 10. supervisor 11. chamberlain

superior ... 4. over, peer 5. above, chief, upper 6. higher, senior 7. exalted, mastery, ranking 8. goodness, priority 9. advantage, paramount, seniority 10. ascendancy, excellence, pre-eminent, surpassing 11. pre-eminence 12. predominancy

superlative ... 4. acme, best, peak 6. utmost 7. elative, extreme, supreme, the best 8. peerless 9. hyperbole 12. exaggeration

supernatural ... 5. eerie, magic 6. divine 10. miraculous, superhuman 13. hyperphysical, preternatural

supernatural (pert to) ...
being .. 3. God 4. atua 5. jinni (jinnee) 7. banshee (banshie), specter (spectre)
event .. 7. miracle
power .. 4. ngai 6. fetish 8. talisman 11. incantation

superscribe ... 6. direct 7. address (a letter), engrave 8. inscribe

supersede ... 4. omit 7. replace, succeed 8. displace, make void, supplant

superstition ... 6. notion, voodoo 8. folklore, idolatry 9. tradition 10. Aberglaube 12. old wives' tale

superstitious ... 6. goetic 7. magical 10. idolatrous 11. fetishistic (fetichistic)

supervene ... 5. occur 6. accrue, happen 7. be added 12. be subsequent

supervise ... 4. boss, read, scan 5. check 6. direct, govern, peruse, revise 7. inspect, oversee 11. superintend

supervisor ... 4. boss 7. foreman, proctor 9. inspector, straw boss

supine ... 5. inert, prone 6. abject, drowsy 7. servile, unalert 8. careless, inclined,

indolent, listless, sluggish 9. apathetic, lethargic, recumbent 11. inattentive, indifferent, thoughtless

supplant ... 5. upset, usurp 6. remove, uproot 7. replace 8. displace, drive out 9. eradicate, extirpate, overthrow, supersede

supple ... 3. sly 4. bent 5. agile, lithe 6. limber, nimble, pliant 7. fawning, lissome 8. flexible, yielding 9. compliant, resilient 10. obsequious, responsive 11. complaisant

supplement ... 3. add, eke 5. add to 6. sequel 7. ripieno 8. addition, appendix, complete 9. accessory 10. complement 12. nonessential 13. reinforcement

supplementary, music ... 7. ripieno

supplicate ... 3. beg 4. pray 5. crave, plead 6. appeal, obtest 7. beseech, conjure, entreat, implore, solicit 8. petition 9. importune, obsecrate

supplication ... 4. plea 6. litany, prayer 7. craving 8. entreaty, petition, rogative 11. obtestation 12. solicitation

supplies ... 6. hoards, relays, stocks, stores 8. estovers, ordnance 9. provender

supply ... 4. fund, give 5. cache, cater, hoard, relay, stock, store, yield 6. purvey, remuda 7. provide, reserve 9. provision, reservoir 10. administer, contribute

supply (pert to) ...
food .. 4. feed 5. cater 9. alimental
fuel .. 5. stoke
funds .. 5. endow
horses .. 5. relay
provisions .. 6. purvey

support ... 3. aid, arm, fid, guy, leg, peg, rib 4. abet, ally, back, base, buoy, limb, mast, prop 5. brace, cleat, shore, spile, stell, strut, tenon 6. backer, pillar, second, uphold 7. bolster, fulcrum, trestle 8. buttress, underlie 9. auxiliary, encourage, reinforce, stanchion 10. assistance, foundation 11. corroborate 12. substantiate 13. corroboration

support (pert to) ...
anatomy .. 3. rib 5. spine
cannon .. 8. trunnion
coffin .. 4. bier
mast .. 4. bibb
resilient .. 6. spring
three-legged .. 5. easel 6. tripod, trivot
upright .. 8. baluster 9. stanchion
wedge-shaped .. 5. cleat

supporters ... 6. allies, braces 7. backers, bracers, garters 10. suspenders 15. ministerialists

suppose ... 3. wis 4. deem, trow 5. allow, imply, judge, opine, think 6. assume, expect, repute 7. presume 8. conclude, consider 9. apprehend, intention 10. conjecture 11. supposition

supposed ... 8. putative

supposition ... 2. if 6. theory 7. surmise 8. supposed 9. postulate 10. assumption, conjecture, hypothesis 11. connotation, implication

suppress . . . **4.** kill, stop **5.** check, crush, elide, quash, quell **6.** hush up, muffle, retard, stifle **7.** abolish, exclude, oppress, smother **8.** hold back, prohibit, restrain, withhold **9.** interdict, overpower **10.** extinguish

suppression . . . **6.** hush up **7.** reserve **8.** hush-hush **9.** overthrow, restraint **10.** inhibition

supremacy . . . **5.** power **7.** control, mastery, primacy **8.** dominion **9.** influence **10.** ascendancy, domination, first place **11.** sovereignty **12.** championship

supreme . . . **3.** top **4.** last **5.** chief, final **6.** divine, ruling **7.** crucial, highest **8.** foremost, greatest, peerless **9.** paramount **10.** preeminent

supreme being . . . **3.** God **4.** Lord **5.** Allah, Deity, monad **6.** Brahma, Buddha **7.** Creator, Jehovah **8.** autocrat

surcease . . . **3.** end **4.** rest, stop **5.** defer, delay **6.** desist, relief **7.** respite **8.** drop work, postpone **9.** cessation

surd . . . **4.** deaf, mute **7.** aphonic, radical **9.** voiceless

sure . . . **3.** yes **4.** fast, firm, safe, true **5.** bound **6.** indeed, secure, stable, steady, strong **7.** assured, certain **8.** positive, reliable **9.** confident, steadfast, unfailing **10.** guaranteed, inevitable, infallible **11.** trustworthy **12.** indisputable **13.** incontestable **14.** unquestionable

surety . . . **4.** bail, bond, fact **6.** backer, pledge, safety **7.** sponsor **8.** security, sureness **9.** certainty **10.** confidence, engagement

surf . . . **4.** foam, rote, wave **5.** bathe, spray, surge, swell **7.** breaker

surface . . . **4.** area, face, orlo, pave, plat, skin **5.** facet, meros **6.** facing, patina **7.** outside **8.** exterior **9.** periphery

surface (pert to) . . .
artificial . . **4.** rink
front (coin) . . **7.** obverse
gem . . **5.** facet
geometric . . **6.** toroid
medical . . **7.** acrotic
toward . . **5.** ectad
under . . **6.** latent **10.** internally
water . . **4.** ryme

surfeit . . . **4.** cloy, feed, glut, jade, sate **6.** excess **7.** replete, satiate, satisfy **9.** satiation **11.** overindulge, superfluity

surge . . . **4.** eddy, flow, rush, wave **5.** swarm, swell, whirl **6.** billow, thrill **7.** estuate **9.** gurgitate **11.** rise and fall

surgeon (pert to) . . .
ancient . . **10.** chirurgeon
case (instrument) . . **6.** tweeze (tweese)
slang . . **8.** sawbones

surgery . . . **7.** aciurgy **8.** medicine **9.** operation, resection

surgery (pert to) . . .
chin . . **11.** mentoplasty
ears . . **9.** otoplasty
face lift . . **13.** rhytidoplasty **14.** blepharoplasty (eyelids)
fractures . . **10.** agmatology
mouth, lip . . **12.** cheiloplasty (chiloplasty)

nose . . **7.** nose job **11.** rhinoplasty
organ . . **10.** transplant
skin . . **12.** dermabrasion
vein . . **10.** phlebotomy
vertebra . . **11.** laminectomy

surgical (pert to) . . .
compress . . **4.** swab **5.** stupe
counterirritant . . **5.** seton
equpment . . **4.** X-ray **6.** splint **7.** CAT scan, scanner **8.** iron lung **10.** respirator, tomography, tourniquet **11.** stethoscope **12.** resuscitator
hook . . **9.** tenaculum
instrument . . **3.** saw **5.** fleam, lance, probe **6.** catlin, lancet, stylet, trepan, xyster **7.** forceps **8.** hemostat, keratome, speculum, tweezers
knife . . **7.** scalpel
puncture . . **8.** céntesis
saw . . **6.** trepan
stitch . . **5.** seton **6.** suture

Suriname (pert to) . . .
capital . . **10.** Paramaribo
former name . . **11.** Dutch Guiana
mountain . . **10.** Tumuc-Humac
toad . . **4.** pipa

surly . . . **4.** glum, grum, rude **5.** gruff **6.** abrupt, grumpy, morose, sullen **7.** crabbed **8.** arrogant, growling **10.** ill-natured **11.** intractable

surmise . . . **4.** deem **5.** fancy, guess, judge, opine, think **7.** imagine, presume **8.** mistrust **9.** suspicion **10.** assumption, conclusion, conjecture **11.** supposition

surmount . . . **3.** top **4.** pass, rise **5.** climb, excel, mount **6.** subdue **7.** conquer, surpass **8.** overcome **9.** transcend

surname . . . **6.** eponym, family, maiden **7.** agnomen **8.** cognomen **10.** patronymic **11.** appellation

surpass . . . **3.** cap, top **4.** best **5.** excel, outdo **6.** better, exceed, outvie, outwit **7.** outrank, outride **8.** go beyond, outrange, outreach, outshine, outsmart, outstrip, surmount **9.** transcend

surpassing . . . **12.** transcendent

surplice . . . **3.** fee **5.** cotta, ephod **6.** collar **7.** pelisse

surplus . . . **4.** over, rest **5.** epact **6.** excess **7.** overage, reserve **8.** overplus **9.** remaining **10.** additional, redundancy **11.** superfluous

surprise . . . **3.** awe **5.** alarm, amaze, seize, shock **6.** wonder **7.** astound, capture, perplex, startle **8.** astonish, bewilder, confound, dumfound **9.** amazement, dumbfound, overwhelm, surprisal **10.** wonderment **11.** flabbergast **12.** astonishment

surprising . . . **7.** amazing **8.** striking **9.** startling **10.** unexpected **11.** astonishing, unlooked for **13.** extraordinary

surrealism (pert to) . . .
film director . . **6.** Buñuel
founder, poet . . **6.** Breton
painter . . **4.** Dali **5.** Ernst **8.** Magritte

surrender . . . **4.** cede, give **5.** yield **6.** give up, remise, resign **7.** abandon, cession, deliver **8.** dedition, remittal **9.** extradite **10.** relinquish, submission

11. abandonment, divestiture
12. cancellation 14. relinquishment
surreptitious . . . 3. sly 6. hidden, secret
8. stealthy 9. concealed, deceitful
10. fraudulent 11. clandestine
surround . . . 4. gird, isle, wrap 5. beset,
hem in, inarm 6. circle, encase, incase,
invest 7. besiege, enclave, enclose,
envelop, environ 8. encircle, inundate,
overflow 9. encompass 12. circumscribe
14. circumnavigate
surrounding . . . 5. about, beset, midst
7. ambient, setting 9. hemming in,
perioptic 10. encircling, enveloping
11. circumpolar 12. circumjacent
survey . . . 4. plan, poll, scan 5. study,
vista 6. regard, review 7. examine,
inspect, oversee 8. traverse 9. delineate,
determine 10. scrutinize
11. examination, reconnoiter,
superintend 14. reconnaissance
surveying (pert to) . . .
instrument . . 7. alidade (alidad), transit
9. stadia rod 10. throdolite
mathematics . . 7. geodesy
process . . 13. triangulation
surveyor (pert to) . . .
helper . . 6. rodman 7. lineman, poleman
land . . 8. measurer, overseer 9. arpenteur
measure . . 5. chain
mine . . 6. dialer
survival . . . 5. relic 9. endurance, outliving
10. durability
survivor . . . 6. relict 8. outliver, remainer,
survival 11. joint tenant
susceptibility . . . 5. sense 7. emotion,
feeling, pliancy 11. sensibility
12. teachability 13. affectibility,
vulnerability 14. sentimentality
susceptible . . . 4. easy 6. liable, pliant
7. exposed, subject 8. sensible
9. receptive, sensitive, teachable
10. responsive, vulnerable
11. softhearted 13. tenderhearted
14. impressionable
suslik . . . 5. sisel 8. squirrel
11. spermophile
suspect . . . 4. fear 5. doubt, fancy,
guess 7. imagine, presume, suppose
8. distrust, mistrust 9. discredit
10. disbelieve, suspicious
suspecting . . . 4. wary 8. doubtful,
doubting 11. incredulous, mistrusting
suspend . . . 4. hang, oust, stay, stop
5. cease, debar, defer, expel, remit
6. dangle, depose, recess 7. adjourn,
pensile 8. intermit, postpone, set aside,
withhold 9. pretermit
suspended . . . 4. hung 5. inert 6. barred,
latent 7. abeyant, pendent 8. inactive
9. pendulous 11. inoperative,
interrupted
suspenders . . . 4. pegs 5. belts, hooks,
rings 6. braces, straps 7. gallows,
garters 8. galluses 9. bretelles
10. supporters 11. clothespins
suspense . . . 5. pause 7. anxiety
10. expectancy 11. uncertainty
12. apprehension, irresolution
14. indecisiveness
suspension . . . 4. stop 5. delay 7. deposal,

failure, hanging, respite 8. abeyance,
buoyancy 11. withholding
12. intermission, interruption
suspicious . . . 4. fear, hint 5. doubt,
hunch, trace 7. askance, inkling,
soupcon 8. distrust, jealousy, mistrust,
wariness 9. mere trace, misgiving
10. diffidence, intimation, skepticism,
suggestion 11. incredulity, supposition
12. apprehension
Sussex (pert to) . . .
breed (Eng) . . 4. fowl 6. cattle
kingdom (anc) . . 7. English
land measure . . 4. wist
land tract (Downs) . . 5. laine
man . . 8. Piltdown (Prehist)
spaniel . . 6. gun dog
sustain . . . 4. bear, buoy, feed, prop
5. abide, carry 6. endure, foster, keep
up, uphold 7. confirm, justify, nourish,
prolong, support, undergo 8. continue,
maintain, preserve 9. encourage,
establish 10. strengthen 11. corroborate
sustained . . . 6. tenuto, upheld
9. permanent, prolonged, supported
10. unflagging
suttee . . . 5. widow 9. cremation, sacrifice
14. self-immolation
suture . . . 5. unite 6. stitch 7. pterion
12. synarthrosis
swagger . . . 4. brag, gait, walk 5. bluff,
boast, bully, strut, swell 6. prance
7. bluster, dashing, roister, stagger,
stylish 8. domineer 11. braggadocio,
ostentation 16. ultrafashionable
swain . . . 3. boy, lad 4. beau 5. lover
6. suitor 7. admirer, gallant, peasant
8. shepherd 10. countryman
swallow . . . 3. sip 4. gulp 5. drink
6. absorb, englut, engulf, imbibe,
ingest, recant 7. consume, engorge,
retract 8. tolerate 10. bear meekly
swallow (pert to) . . .
chimney . . 5. swift
European . . 6. martin
hawk . . 4. kite
plover . . 10. pratincole
sea . . 4. tern
tail . . 4. coat 9. butterfly
the anchor . . 10. quit the sea
swamp . . . 3. bog, fen 4. mire, muck,
sink, slue, sump 5. flood, marsh
6. deluge, engulf, morass, slough
7. cienaga, pocosin 8. quagmire,
submerge 9. everglade, overwhelm
swamp (pert to) . . .
boggy . . 7. queachy 8. muskeggy
earth . . 4. muck
gas . . 6. miasma
grass . . 5. sedge
marsh . . 5. slash 8. paludine
tract . . 10. Everglades
swan . . . 3. cob, pen 4. Olor 5. swear
6. cygnet, cygnus 7. declare
9. trumpeter
swan (pert to) . . .
astronomy . . 6. Cygnus
flower . . 6. orchid
goose . . 2. Bewick's, Chinese
myth (Hind) . . 5. hansa
poem . . 12. Swan of Thames (Pope)

15. Sweet Swän of Avon (Jonson)
star (brightest). . **5.** Deneb
trumpeter. . **4.** wild
type. . **4.** mute **5.** black **8.** whooping
 11. black-necked
swap . . . **4.** beat **5.** trade **6.** barter, thrash
 8. exchange **11.** give-and-take
sward . . . **3.** sod **4.** lawn, turf **5.** grass
 10. greensward
swarm . . . **3.** fry **5.** crowd, flock, horde
 6. abound, infest, throng **7.** pervade
 9. migration, multitude **10.** congregate
 11. aggregation
swarthy . . . **3.** dun **4.** dark **5.** dusky
 8. bistered (bistred), blackish
swashbuckler . . . **5.** bravo **6.** gascon
 7. ruffian **8.** Almanzor **9.** blusterer,
 daredevil, swaggerer **10.** Drawcansir
swastika (swastica) . . . **6.** fylfot, symbol
 (since 1918) **9.** gammadion
 10. hakenkreuz
swat . . . **3.** bat, hit **5.** clout **6.** strike **7.** hit
 hard
swathe . . . **4.** band, bind, wrap **6.** enfold
 7. envelop, swaddle
sway . . . **4.** bend, bias, rock, rule, veer,
 wave **5.** lurch, power, shake, swing,
 waver, wield **6.** direct, empire, govern,
 induce, totter, waddle **7.** command,
 control, deflect, incline **8.** flounder
 9. fluctuate, influence, oscillate, vacillate
 10. ascendancy **11.** fluctuation
swayback . . . **8.** lordosis
swaying . . . **7.** pensile, sagging
 8. swinging, waddling **11.** influential,
 oscillating
swear . . . **3.** vow **4.** oath **5.** curse, vouch
 6. adjure, pledge (sacred) **7.** confirm,
 declare, promise **10.** asseverate,
 deposition **11.** bear witness
swear (pert to) . . .
at. . **5.** clash (colors), curse **8.** disagree
by. . **5.** bet on **7.** count on **8.** take oath
falsely. . **7.** perjure
off. . **4.** stop **6.** eschew, give up
 7. abandon **8.** renounce
sweat . . . **4.** work **5.** exude, grill,
 sudor **6.** drudge **7.** excrete, ferment
 8. perspire, transude **9.** exudation
 10. impatience **11.** nervousness
Sweden . . . see also *Swedish*
capital. . **9.** Stockholm
city. . **5.** Malmö **7.** Uppsala (Upsala)
 8. Göteborg
dynasty (1st). . **8.** Ynglings
gulf. . **7.** Bothnia
lake. . **6.** Vanern **7.** Vattern
mountain. . **5.** Kölen (Kjölen)
parliament. . **7.** Riksdag
peninsula. . **11.** Scandinavia
port. . **8.** Göteborg **9.** Stockholm
river. . **4.** Klar **7.** Götaalv
sea. . **6.** Baltic
university (oldest). . **7.** Uppsula (Upsala,
 1477)
Swedish (pert to) . . .
actress. . **5.** Garbo
artist. . **4.** Zorn
botanist. . **8.** Linnaeus
bread. . **10.** knäckebröd
clover. . **6.** alsike

dance. . **6.** polska
diplomat. . **12.** Hammarskjöld (Dag)
dramatist. . **10.** Strindberg
explorer. . **5.** Hedin
film director. . **7.** Bergman (Ingmar)
fir. . **10.** Scotch pine
hero (WWII). . **10.** Wallenberg
idiom. . **7.** Suecism
manual training. . **5.** sloyd (slojd)
northern inhabitants. . **5.** Lapps
novelist. . **8.** Lagerlöf (Pulitzer prize,
 1909)
opera singer. . **9.** Jenny Lind (Swedish
 Nightingale) **7.** Nilsson (Birgit)
philosopher. . **10.** Swedenborg
religion (State). . **8.** Lutheran
turnip. . **8.** rutabaga
sweep . . . **3.** oar **4.** scan **5.** clean, clear,
 cover, curve, glide, strip, surge, swish,
 trail **6.** course, vision **7.** contour
 8. traverse
sweeping . . . **8.** complete, thorough
 9. extensive **12.** all-embracing
 13. comprehensive
sweet . . . **5.** bonny, candy **10.** dolce douce
 5. fresh, spicy **6.** dulcet, gentle, sugary,
 syrupy **7.** caramel, honeyed, lovable
 8. aromatic, fragrant, luscious, pleasant,
 preserve **9.** agreeable, ambrosial,
 melodious, nectarine **10.** confection,
 saccharine **11.** mellifluous, mellisonant
sweet (pert to) . . .
and fair. . **5.** bonny
bread. . **4.** food **6.** thymus **8.** pancreas
 9. ris de veau
brier. . **4.** rose **9.** eglantine
drink. . **6.** nectar
meat. . **4.** cake **5.** candy **6.** comfit, éclair,
 pastry **7.** caramel, dessert **8.** marzipan
 10. confection
potato. . **3.** yam **6.** batata
potato, musical. . **7.** ocarina
sop. . **4.** ates, atta **6.** Annone **14.** Annona
 squamosa
sounding. . **11.** mellisonant
wine. . **4.** port **5.** Lunel
sweetheart . . . **2.** jo **3.** gra **4.** beau, lass
 5. flame, leman, lover, spark, swain
 7. darling **8.** dowsabel, honeybun
 (sl), ladylove **9.** Amaryllis, inamorata,
 valentine
swell . . . **3.** fob, nob **4.** grow, rise, surf,
 wave **5.** bulge, dandy, grand, heave,
 mound, surge **6.** billow, dilate, expand,
 growth, puff up, tiptop **7.** distend,
 inflate, stylish **8.** increase, protrude
 9. sumptuous **10.** aristocrat, prominence
 11. enlargement **12.** augmentation
swell (pert to) . . .
ocean. . **4.** surf **6.** billow, expand, roller
rolling. . **7.** seagate
slang. . **3.** nob **5.** dandy, grand
 9. first-rate
swelled (pert to) . . .
head. . **3.** ego **7.** conceit **9.** cockiness
 14. self-importance
out. . **4.** lump, node **5.** tumid **6.** bulged,
 podded, turgid **9.** grandiose
swelling . . . **4.** sore **5.** bulge, edema
 6. dropsy **9.** bombastic **10.** distention,
 increasing **12.** protuberance

swelter ... **4.** fret **5.** exude, roast, sweat **8.** perspire **10.** sultry heat
swerve ... **4.** veer **5.** dodge, sheer, shift **6.** recoil **7.** deflect, deviate **9.** deviation, turn aside
swift ... **4.** bird, fast, racy, reel **5.** alert, fleet, hasty, quick, rapid, ready **6.** lizard, prompt, speedy, sudden, winged **8.** headlong
swift (pert to) ...
  astronomer .. **5.** Lewis (Swift)
  bird .. **4.** crin **7.** chimney
  boat .. **7.** flyboat **10.** Hovercraft
  footed .. **5.** ariel (gazelle) **7.** Mercury
  satirist .. **8.** Jonathan (Swift)
swiftness ... **5.** haste, speed **8.** celerity, velocity **9.** quickness **10.** promptness
swimmer ... **5.** diver **6.** bather **7.** Cloelia (Tiber Riv), Leander (Hellespont), natator
swimming ... **5.** crawl **6.** natant **7.** vertigo **9.** dizziness, freestyle, skinny-dip **10.** sidestroke **12.** breast stroke .
swimming (pert to) ...
  birds .. **9.** natatores
  bladder .. **10.** air bladder (fish)
  pert to .. **5.** dizzy **7.** aquatic **8.** natatory
  pool .. **4.** hole, tank **10.** natatorium
  sandpiper .. **9.** phalarope
swindle ... **3.** con, gyp **4.** dupe, fake, sell **5.** bunco, cheat **6.** trepan **7.** defraud **8.** flimflam **9.** gold brick
swindler ... **3.** gyp **5.** biter, cheat, crook, knave, rogue, shark **6.** gypper **7.** sharper **9.** defrauder
swindling ... **6.** estafa
swine ... **3.** hog, pig, sow, Sus **4.** boar **7.** Anthony (smallest), peccary **8.** slattern **9.** scoundrel
swine, breed of ... **8.** Cheshire, Tamworth **9.** Berkshire, Hampshire, razorback, Yorkshire **11.** Duroc-Jersey, Poland China **12.** Chester-White
swineherd (pert to) ...
  patron saint .. **7.** Anthony
  reference to .. **7.** sybotic
swinelike ... **7.** porcine
swing ... **4.** hang, jazz, jive, lilt, sway **5.** shake, trend, waver, wield **6.** dangle, manage, rhythm, totter **7.** suspend, trapeze, vibrate **8.** pendulum, undulate **9.** fluctuate, oscillate
swingtree ... **11.** whippletree
swinish ... **5.** gross **6.** carnal, filthy, greedy **7.** beastly, porcine, sensual **8.** gluttony
swipe ... **4.** gulp **5.** draft, drink, lever, steal, swape, swath, sweep **6.** handle, pilfer, snatch **7.** purloin
swipes ... **4.** beer (Eng sl)
swirl ... **4.** curl, eddy **5.** curve, gurge, surge, twist, whirl, whorl
swirly ... **7.** knotted, tangled, twisted
Swiss (pert to) ... see also *Switzerland*
  artist .. **4.** Klee
  ax (ice) .. **6.** piolet
  bell .. **9.** alpenhorn (alphorn)
  cabin .. **6.** chalet
  composer .. **4.** Raff
  flower, emblem .. **9.** edelweiss
  herdsman .. **4.** senn

  hero .. **11.** William Tell
  language .. **6.** French, German **7.** Italian **8.** Romansch
  legislature .. **9.** Bundesrat (Bundesrath), Grosse Rat (Grossrat)
  mathematician .. **5.** Euler
  physician, alchemist .. **10.** Paracelsus
  pine .. **6.** arolla
  psychologist .. **4.** Jung
  scientist .. **6.** Haller (von)
  surgeon .. **6.** Kocher (Nobel Prize)
  theologian .. **5.** Vinet **7.** Zwingli
  warble .. **5.** yodel
  warbler .. **7.** yodeler (yodeller)
  wind .. **4.** bise
  wine .. **7.** Dezaley
switch ... **4.** lash, turn (on or off), whip **5.** shift, shunt **6.** change, divert, siding **8.** exchange, transfer
switchback (Brit) ... **13.** roller-coaster
Switzerland (pert to) ...
  ancient .. **8.** Helvetia
  canton .. **5.** Aarau
  capital .. **5.** Berne (Bern)
  city .. **5.** Basel **6.** Geneva, Zurich **7.** Locarno, Lucerne **8.** Lausanne **9.** Constance
  famed for .. **5.** banks (Finan)
  lake .. **3.** Uri **6.** Brienz, Geneva, Zurich **7.** Lucerne **8.** Maggiore **9.** Constance, Neuchâtel **10.** Stattersee
  mountain .. **4.** Alps, Jura **5.** Blanc **8.** Jungfrau **9.** Monte Rosa (peak) **10.** Matterhorn
  resort .. **7.** Urseren, Yverdon
  river .. **3.** Aar **5.** Reuss, Rhine, Rhone
  tunnel .. **5.** Cenis **7.** Gothard, Simplon **11.** Loetschberg
  university (oldest) .. **5.** Basel
  valley .. **3.** Aar
swollen ... **5.** pursy, tumid **6.** turgid **7.** bloated, bulbous, bulging, pompous **8.** enlarged, inflated, puffed up, varicose **9.** bombastic, distended, plethoric, tumescent **11.** protuberant
swoon ... **3.** fit **5.** faint, spell **7.** ecstasy, syncope **8.** languish **10.** heavy sleep
swoop ... **5.** seize, sweep **6.** attack, pounce **7.** descend
sword (pert to) ...
  ancient .. **5.** estoc **6.** glaive
  cavalry .. **5.** saber (sabre)
  curved .. **7.** cutlass, Ferrara **8.** Claymore, scimitar
  fencing .. **4.** foil, epee **6.** rapier
  fine .. **6.** Toledo **8.** Damascus
  handle .. **4.** haft, hilt
  India .. **5.** kukri
  like .. **7.** xiphoid
  Mohammedan's .. **8.** scimitar
  part .. **5.** forte, talon **6.** foible
  practice .. **5.** fence
  scabbard tip .. **7.** crampit
  Scot Highlander's .. **4.** dirk
  seaman's .. **6.** hanger
  shaped .. **6.** ensate **7.** xiphoid (xyphoid) **8.** ensiform, gladiate
  sheik's .. **4.** pata
  Siegfried's .. **4.** Gram **7.** Balmung
  Sir Bevis' .. **7.** Morglay
  Spanish .. **5.** bilbo

support.. **7.** baldric
two-handed.. **7.** espadon
type.. **4.** epee, pata **5.** blade, degen,
  estoc, gully, saber **6.** barong, creese,
  parang, rapier **7.** cutlass **9.** gladiolus
swordfish... **6.** dorado, Dorado
  (constellation), espada **7.** espadon,
  Xiphias **9.** broadbill
sword of...
Damocles.. **12.** fateful thing
God.. **6.** Khaled (Muslim hero)
mercy.. **7.** Curtana (pointless)
Sir Bevis.. **7.** Morglay (death)
St George.. **7.** Askelon
the Cid.. **6.** Colada
swordsman... **6.** fencer **7.** duelist,
  epeeist, saberer, sabreur **9.** gladiator
  11. Beau Sabreur
sworn statement... **9.** affidavit
sworn to secrecy... **5.** tiled
sybarite... **7.** epicure **10.** voluptuary
  11. luxury lover
sybil (sibil)... **4.** seer **5.** witch **7.** seeress
  10. prophetess **13.** fortuneteller
syce... **5.** groom
sycophant... **5.** toady **7.** fawning,
  spaniel **8.** hanger-on, informer, parasite
  9. charlatan, flatterer, toadeater
  10. talebearer
sycophantic... **7.** fawning, servile,
  slavish **8.** obedient, toadying
  10. obsequious **11.** bootlicking
syllable...
accented.. **5.** arsis
by syllable.. **11.** syllabation
charm.. **2.** om **6.** mantra
last.. **6.** ultima
last, omission of.. **7.** apocope
last but one.. **6.** penult
last but two.. **10.** antepenult
lengthening of.. **7.** ectasis
ref to.. **5.** affix **6.** prefix, suffix **8.** dactylic,
  syllabic
short.. **4.** mora
shortening.. **7.** systole
stress.. **5.** ictus
table.. **9.** syllabary
unaccented.. **4.** lene **6.** thesis
syllabled, three... **7.** triseme (3 moras)
  11. trisyllabic
syllabus... **6.** aperçu, digest **8.** abstract,
  synopsis **10.** compendium, conspectus
syllogism... **7.** premise, sorites
  9. deduction, reasoning **11.** epicheirema
  (epichirema) **18.** deductive reasoning
sylvan, silvan... **5.** woody **6.** groved,
  rustic, wooded **8.** forested **10.** forestlike
sylvan deity... **3.** Pan **4.** faun **5.** Satyr,
  Vidar **6.** Faunus
symbol... **2.** om **4.** icon, palm, sign,
  type **5.** badge, crest, cross, image,
  token, totem **6.** emblem, ensign, figure,
  letter, number **9.** character (graphic),
  prototype, trademark **12.** abbreviation
symbol (pert to)...
authority.. **4.** mace
bondage.. **4.** yoke
ecclesiastic.. **4.** ring
England.. **4.** lion
France.. **4.** lily
mathematics.. **7.** operand

military.. **3.** bar **4.** star **5.** eagle, wings
  6. stripe **7.** chevron, epaulet (epaulette)
  8. caduceus
peace.. **4.** dove
power.. **4.** mace
prayer figure (anc).. **5.** orant
royal.. **3.** rod **5.** crown, tiara **6.** corona
  7. scepter (sceptre)
Tammany Hall.. **5.** tiger
tribal.. **5.** totem (pole)
victory.. **4.** palm
symbol for...
arsenic.. **2.** As
calcium.. **2.** Ca
chromium.. **2.** Cr
copper.. **2.** Cu
gold.. **2.** Au
iron.. **2.** Fe
lead.. **2.** Pb
neon.. **2.** Ne
nickel.. **2.** Ni
radium.. **2.** Ra
silver.. **2.** Ag, Ar
sodium.. **2.** Na
tin.. **2.** Sn
symbolic, symbolical... **7.** typical
  9. imagerial **10.** figurative, relational
  11. allegorical, significant
  12. emblematical **14.** representative
symbolism... **7.** mystery, writing
  9. mysticism, ritualism, symbolics
  10. figuration **11.** hieroglyphy
  14. representation
symmetric, symmetrical... **7.** orderly,
  regular, spheral, uniform **8.** balanced
  10. euphonious
symmetry... **5.** order **7.** balance,
  euphony, harmony **8.** equality
  9. congruity **10.** conformity, proportion
  11. consistency
sympathetic... **4.** kind **6.** humane,
  tender **7.** empathy, pitying **8.** dewy-
  eyed **10.** responsive **13.** compassionate,
  understanding
sympathy... **4.** pity **5.** favor **7.** consent,
  harmony, support **8.** affinity, interest
  9. agreeable, agreement, tolerance
  11. sensitivity **13.** commiseration,
  understanding
sympathy, lack of... **8.** dyspathy
  9. antipathy
symphony... **6.** accord **7.** concert,
  harmony **8.** ritornel **9.** orchestra
  10. consonance **11.** composition
symposium... **4.** book, talk **7.** banquet
  8. dialogue, tippling **10.** collection,
  discussion **11.** compotation
symptom... **4.** mark, note, omen, sign
  5. alarm, token **7.** warning **10.** indication
synagogue... **6.** temple **10.** tabernacle
  12. congregation
synagogue (pert to)...
founder (anc).. **4.** Ezra
platform.. **7.** almemar
singer.. **6.** cantor, chazan (chazzan)
synchronize... **5.** agree **6.** concur
  8. coincide **9.** harmonize
  12. contemporize
syncopation... **5.** tempo **7.** ragtime,
  syncope
syncope... **5.** faint, swoon **7.** elision

8. fainting, swooning **9.** haplology
11. contraction, hyphaeresis
syndicate . . . **5.** chain (journalistic), group,
trust **6.** cartel, school **7.** combine,
council **9.** committee **10.** underworld
11. association **12.** organization
synonym . . . **7.** antonym, homonym,
metonym **8.** identity **9.** heteronym
synonymous . . . **4.** like **5.** alike **7.** similar
10. equivalent, homonymous
synopsis . . . **6.** digest, manual **7.** epitome,
summary **8.** abstract, syllabus
9. statement **10.** abridgment
(abridgement), compendium,
conspectus, tabulation
synthesis . . . **5.** logic **11.** combination,
composition **13.** incorporation
14. identification
Syracuse (pert to) . . .
ancient name . . **8.** Siracusa
city of . . **6.** Sicily
famed for . . **6.** battle (BC)
founded by . . **6.** Greeks
tyrant of . . **9.** Dionysius
Syria, Arab Republic . . . see also *Syrian*
ancient name . . **4.** Aram
capital . . **8.** Damascus
city . . **4.** Hama, Homs **6.** Aleppo, Beirut
7. Antioch, Latakia **8.** Damascus
language . . **6.** Arabic
organization, party . . **5.** Baath
river . . **6.** Barada, Jordan **7.** Orontes
9. Euphrates
Syrian (pert to) . . .
antiquarian . . **11.** Syriologist
deity . . **2.** El **4.** Baal **6.** Mammon
7. Resheph
goat . . **6.** Angora
grass . . **7.** Johnson
leader . . **5.** Assad
mallow . . **4.** okra
·people . . **7.** Ansarie (Ansarieh)
script . . **8.** Peshitta (Peshito)
10. estrangelo **11.** Syro-Chaldee
sect . . **5.** Druse
wind (hot) . . **6.** simoom (simoon)

syrinx . . . **4.** tomb **6.** larynx **7.** Panpipe
10. mouthpiece (anc lute) **13.** Arcadian
nymph
syrup, sirup . . . **4.** Karo, sapa **5.** maple
6. orgeat **7.** dhebbus, glucose, sorghum,
treacle **8.** molasses **9.** grenadine
system . . . **3.** ism, way **4.** code, plan
5. order **6.** regime, theory **8.** religion,
universe **9.** procedure **10.** hypothesis,
regularity **11.** arrangement,
orderliness
system (pert to) . . .
conduct . . **4.** code
eating . . **4.** diet **7.** dietary
geological . . **5.** Trias
management . . **6.** regime
manual training . . **5.** sloyd
mystic . . **6.** cabala
numbering . . **7.** decimal
pitch (Mus) . . **5.** neume
religious . . **4.** cult **6.** cultus
solar . . **6.** planet
weights . . **4.** long, troy **5.** cubic **6.** liquid
11. avoirdupois **12.** apothecaries
systematic . . . **4.** neat **6.** formal **7.** orderly,
regular **9.** organized, schematic
10. methodical
systematics . . . **8.** taxonomy
14. classification
systematize . . . **4.** code **6.** codify
7. arrange **8.** classify, organize,
regiment **9.** catalogue (catalog),
formulate
systematized knowledge . . . **7.** science
systole (pert to) . . .
correlative . . **8.** diastole
medical . . **11.** contraction (heart)
14. coming and going
rhyme . . **10.** shortening (syllable)
syzygy (pert to) . . .
astronomy . . **7.** appulse **11.** conjunction
Gnosticism . . **5.** aeons (pair)
rhyme . . **11.** coupled feet (group)
zoology . . **5.** union **7.** segment
szlachta . . . **8.** nobility (Poland)
szopelka . . . **4.** oboe (Russ)

T

T . . . **3.** tau (Gr) **6.** letter (20th)
taa . . . **6.** pagoda
Taal . . . **8.** language **9.** Afrikaans
taar . . . **10.** tambourine
Taaroa . . . **3.** God
tab . . . **3.** pan, tag **4.** bill, cost, flap, loop
5. aglet (aiglet), label, strip **6.** eartab,
record **7.** account, latchet, pendant
(pendent) **9.** afterpart, appendage,
reckoning **10.** accounting
tabac . . . **5.** brown, snuff **7.** tobacco
tabard . . . **4.** cape **5.** cloak **6.** chimer,
jacket, mantle
Tabard . . . **3.** Inn (Canterbury Tales)
tabatière . . . **8.** snuffbox
tabby . . . **3.** cat **4.** gown, silk **5.** dress
6. fabric, gossip **7.** old maid, taffeta

tabernacle . . . **4.** tent **5.** abode, niche
6. church, temple **7.** shelter, support
8. enshrine **9.** sanctuary **10.** habitation
table . . . **4.** fare, list, slab **5.** board, panel,
plate, stand **6.** lamina, repast, tablet,
teapoy **7.** console, plateau, weights
8. postpone, put aside, synopsis,
tabulate **9.** reference **10.** collection
14. multiplication
table (pert to) . . .
calculating . . **6.** abacus
centerpiece . . **7.** epergne
communion . . **5.** altar **8.** credence,
credenza
contents . . **5.** index
cover . . **5.** baize, tapis
dish . . **6.** tureen

land . . **4.** mesa **6.** karroo (karoo), plains **7.** plateau
linen . . **6.** napery
philosophy . . **13.** deipnosophism
salt . . **4.** NaCl
talk (versed in) . . **13.** deipnosophist
type . . **3.** tea **4.** turn **6.** coffee, gaming **7.** dinette, dresser, gate-leg, kitchen, taboret **8.** captain's, drop-leaf
tableau . . . **5.** drama, scene **7.** picture **8.** schedule **14.** representation
tablet . . . **3.** pad **4.** pill, slab **5.** facia, slate, stele **6.** troche **7.** lozenge **8.** monument, notebook
taboo, tabu . . . **3.** ban **4.** deny **5.** debar **6.** forbid **7.** embargo **8.** disallow, prohibit **9.** forbidden, interdict, proscribe **11.** prohibition **12.** interdiction
tabulate . . . **4.** list **6.** record **7.** tabular **8.** classify, schedule
tabulation . . . **7.** listing **8.** calendar, paradigm **12.** registration
taccada . . . **9.** fanflower
tacit . . . **6.** silent **7.** implied **8.** unspoken, wordless **9.** indicated, noiseless **10.** understood
taciturn . . . **6.** silent **8.** reserved, reticent **9.** saturnine
tack . . . **4.** brad, gear, jibe, join, rope, sail, trip **5.** baste, lease, route **6.** course, fasten, secure, staple, tackle **7.** clothes **9.** fastening **10.** supplement
tackle . . . **3.** cat, rig **4.** gear, tack **5.** davit, seize **6.** burton, collar, garnet **7.** cordage, grapple, harness, rigging **8.** football (term) **9.** encounter, equipment, undertake
tacky . . . **5.** crude, dowdy, seedy **6.** shabby, sticky, untidy **8.** adhesive, slovenly
tact . . . **5.** grace, poise, taste **7.** address, finesse **8.** delicacy **9.** diplomacy **10.** adroitness, cleverness, discretion **11.** discernment, savoir-faire **14.** discrimination
tadpole . . . **4.** frog, toad **8.** polliwog, porwigle **9.** youngling
tag . . . **3.** add, end, rag, tab **4.** flap, game, loop, name **5.** aglet (aiglet), label, sheep, strip **6.** fasten, follow **7.** earmark, frazzle, pendant, taglock **9.** appendage **11.** aiguillette (ornamental)
Tagalog, Tagal (pert to) . . .
child, servant . . **4.** anac, bata
deity . . **6.** Batala
game (gambling) . . **10.** panguingui
native of . . **5.** Luzon **11.** Philippines
peasant . . **3.** tao
race . . **4.** Aeta (dwarf) **7.** Malayan
Tahiti . . .
arrowroot . . **3.** pia
boat . . **4.** pahi
capital . . **7.** Papeete (of all Society Isles)
food plant . . **4.** taro
god . . **3.** oro **6.** Taaroa (Supreme)
old name . . **8.** Otaheite
robe (coronation) . . **4.** malo
woman . . **6.** wahine (vahine)
Tai, Thai people . . . **4.** Laos, Shan **7.** Siamese
tail . . . **3.** bun, cue, end **4.** arse, back,

hair, last, rear **5.** cauda, stern **6.** follow, shadow **7.** pendant **8.** entailed, streamer **9.** afterpart, appendage, extremity
tail (pert to) . . .
aircraft's . . **9.** empennage
boar's . . **6.** wreath
coin . . **5.** verso **7.** reverse
dog's . . **5.** plume, stern, twist
having a . . **7.** caudate
peacock's . . **5.** train
pert to . . **6.** caudal **9.** coccygeal
rabbit's . . **4.** scut
rudimentary . . **6.** coccyx
tailrace . . **5.** flume **7.** channel
tailing . . . **5.** chaff, waste **6.** refuse
tailless . . . **6.** tenrec (mammal) **7.** acaudal, anurous, Ranidae **8.** acaudate, ecaudate
tailor . . . **3.** cut, fit **4.** form **6.** darzee, draper, sartor **7.** fashion **8.** tailleur
tailor (pert to) . . .
goose . . **4.** iron **12.** pressing iron
made . . **6.** fitted **9.** fashioned
reference to . . **9.** sartorial
twist . . **10.** silk thread (stout)
taint . . . **3.** due, hue **5.** color, imbue, spoil, stain, sully, tinge **6.** defile, infect, poison, stigma **7.** blemish, corrupt, deprave, pollute, vitiate **8.** disgrace **9.** denigrate, infection **10.** corruption, stigmatize **11.** contaminate
tainted . . . **3.** bad **6.** soiled **7.** stained **8.** diseased **9.** corrupted
taintless . . . **4.** good **5.** clean **6.** chaste **8.** flawless, innocent
Taiwan . . .
capital . . **6.** Taipai
Taj Mahal (pert to) . . .
architecture . . **9.** Saracenic
builder . . **9.** Shah-Jahan
mausolem site . . **4.** Agra
named for . . **4.** wife
take . . . **2.** go **3.** get, win **4.** deem, doff, gain, shut **5.** atone, booty, carry, catch, seize, snare, steal, usurp **6.** accept, borrow, deduce, endure, obtain **7.** capture, conduct, control, detract, receive **8.** proceeds, receipts, subtract, tolerate **9.** apprehend **11.** appropriate   .
take (pert to) . . .
a chair . . **3.** sit
a direction . . **5.** steer
advantage of . . **5.** abuse **6.** misuse
apart . . **8.** demolish **11.** disassemble
as one's own . . **5.** adopt **6.** borrow
away . . **5.** adeem, clear, reave, steal, wrest **6.** adempt, deduct, remove **7.** deprive, detract, retract **8.** derogate, subtract, withdraw **11.** expropriate
back . . **6.** recant, repeal, return
by storm . . **5.** seize **6.** attack
by stratagem . . **4.** trap **8.** outsmart
care of . . **4.** mind **5.** guard, nurse, serve, watch **6.** beware **7.** support **10.** provide for
charge of . . **8.** attend to **9.** look after
down . . **4.** fell, raze **5.** lower, write **6.** humble, record **7.** reprove, swallow **8.** emaciate
first . . **7.** pre-empt
for granted . . **5.** infer **6.** assume, expect

7. believe, presume, suppose
in.. 3. eat, see 4. hear 5. admit, annex,
learn 6. absorb, attend 7. embrace,
include, involve, receive, shorten
9. encompass
notice.. 2. NB 3. see
off.. 5. leave 6. deduct, depart, launch,
parody, remove 8. subtract 9. imitation
on.. 4. hire 6. assume, employ, oppose
9. undertake
out.. 4. dele 5. elide 6. delete, efface
7. expunge
place of.. 8. supplant 9. supersede
the floor.. 5. speak 7. address 9. legislate
to flight.. 4. flee 7. run away, scamper
9. skedaddle
up.. 4. fill, lift 5. adopt, begin, raise
6. absorb, assume, gather, occupy
8. engage in 9. undertake
without authority.. 5. usurp
talapoin ... 6. monkey (guenon)
8. poonghie 12. Buddhist monk
talc ... 6. powder, talcum 7. agalite
8. steatite 9. soapstone
tale ... 3. lai, lay, lie 4. myth, saga, yarn
5. conte, fable, story 6. gossip, legend
7. romance 8. anecdote 9. discourse,
falsehood, narration, narrative
11. declaration 12. conversation
tale (pert to) ...
adventure.. 4. gest
bearer.. 6. gossip 7. blabber, tattler
8. informer 13. scandalmonger
chivalry.. 7. romance
doleful.. 8. jeremiad
fatality.. 5. drama 7. tragedy
symbolic.. 8. allegory
traditional.. 4. saga 8. folktale
talent ... 4. gift 5. dower, flair, forte,
money (anc), skill 6. genius 7. ability,
faculty 8. aptitude, artistry 9. attribute
11. disposition 14. accomplishment
talesman ... 5. juror 8. narrator
talisman ... 4. juju, mojo, tara 5. charm,
karma 6. amulet, fetish, grigri
(greegree), scarab 7. periapt
12. antinganting
talk ... 3. gab, gas, rap, yak, yap 4. blab,
blat, chat, chin, harp, rant, rave
5. lingo, orate, parle, prate, rumor,
speak, spiel, utter 6. babble, confab,
confer, gabble, gossip, jargon, lesson,
speech 7. address, blabber, chatter,
declaim, discuss 8. causerie, chitchat,
colloquy, converse, language, parlance
9. dalliance, discourse 11. communicate
12. conversation
talk (pert to) ...
about.. 5. rumor 6. gossip
affected, pretentious.. 4. cant, rant
ancient.. 5. parle
back.. 4. sass 6. retort 7. riposte
8. feedback, repartee
flattering.. 7. palaver
fluent.. 7. verbose, voluble
idiotically.. 6. drivel
long.. 9. gibberish, rigmarole
loud.. 5. blate
promoting.. 4. hype 8. ballyhoo
running.. 6. patter
silly.. 5. drool 6. drivel, footle 7. blather,

prattle, twaddle
slang.. 3. gab, gas 4. sass 5. spiel
slowly.. 5. drawl
small.. 3. gab 4. chat, chin 7. prattle
8. chitchat
Spanish.. 7. palabra
talkative ... 4. glib 6. fluent 7. verbose,
voluble 9. garrulous 10. loquacious
13. communicative
talker ... 6. gasser, proser, ranter
7. speaker, spieler 10. chatterbox
17. conversationalist
tall ... 4. high, long 5. lofty 6. seemly
7. procere, sky-high 8. towering
yielding 10. incredible, statuesque
11. exaggerated
tall (pert to) ...
order.. 9. falsehood 10. difficulty
person.. 10. hypermeter
structure.. 7. steeple
talk.. 4. brag 12. exaggeration
14. grandiloquence
tallest known people ... 10. Patagonian
Talleyrand's affair ... 3. XYZ
tallow source ... 4. suet
tally ... 3. run, sum, tab 4. goal,
list, mark 5. agree, check, count,
match, notch, score 6. accord, reckon,
record 7. account, compare, count
up 8. coincide, estimate 9. reckoning
10. bottom line, correspond
Talmud ... 9. Jewish law
Talmud (pert to) ...
academy.. 8. Yeshivah (Yeshiva)
commentary.. 6. Gemara
student.. 5. bahur
text.. 7. Mishnah
talon ... 3. paw 4. claw, fang, nail
6. clutch, finger, pincer
talus ... 5. ankle 8. clubfoot
tamarisk ... 4. atle (atlee) 8. salt tree
tambo ... 3. inn 6. corral, stable, tavern
10. tambourine
tambor ... 6. puffer 8. rockfish
tambour ... 4. desk, drum, lace 5. frame
6. stitch 7. drummer 8. ornament,
stockade 9. embroider
tambourine ... 4. dove, drum, taar
5. daira 7. timbrel 8. minstrel
tambourine effect (Mus) ... 7. travale
tambreet ... 3. duckbill
tamburone ... 4. drum 8. bass drum
tame ... 4. dull, meek, mild 5. inert
6. docile, gentle, humble, subdue
7. crushed, insipid, subdued 8. tone
down 9. tractable 10. cultivated
11. domesticate 12. domesticated
Tamil ... 5. Hindu 8. language (oldest
Dravidian) 9. Dravidian
tamis ... 5. sieve, tammy 8. strainer
Tammany (pert to) ...
Hall.. 14. Democratic Club
man.. 10. politician
officer.. 8. Wiskinky (Wiskinkie)
scandal.. 9. Tweed Ring
Society site.. 11. New York City (1789)
symbol.. 5. tiger
tamper with ... 4. plot 5. alter, bribe
6. meddle, monkey, scheme, tinker
7. falsify 9. influence, interfere
tampion, tampon ... 4. plug 6. tympan

7. stopper, turnpin **9.** rhynobyon
tan . . . **3.** dun, taw **4.** buff, ecru, tent,
   whip **5.** beige, brown, color, tawny
   6. rabbit, suntan, thrash **7.** sunburn
tanager . . . **4.** yeni **5.** lindo **7.** Piranga,
   redbird
tanbark . . . **3.** oak **7.** hemlock
Tancred . . . **6.** leader (1st crusade)
Tanganyika . . . see *Tanzania*
tangible . . . **4.** real **7.** tactile **8.** palpable
   9. objective, touchable **11.** perceptible,
   substantial
tangle . . . **3.** mat, mop **4.** kink, shag
   5. ravel, snare, snarl, weave **6.** entrap,
   medley, muddle, sleave, tousle
   7. ensnare, involve **8.** quandary
   9. interlock **10.** complicate, interweave
tank . . . **3.** vat **4.** lake, pond, pool
   5. basin **6.** hot tub **7.** cistern, stomach
   9. reservoir **11.** army vehicle, hard
   drinker
tanker . . . **4.** ship **5.** oiler **8.** fuel ship
tanner's bath . . **4.** bate
tanning shrub . . . **5.** alder, sumac
   (sumach)
tantalize . . . **3.** vex **5.** taunt, tease
   6. harass, plague **7.** torment
tantalum symbol . . . **2.** Ta
Tantalus (pert to) . . .
   father . . **4.** Zeus
   father of . . **5.** Niobe **6.** Pelops
   genus of . . **4.** ibis
   king (rich) . . **6.** Greece
tantamount . . . **5.** equal **9.** identical
   10. equivalent **13.** corresponding
tantara . . . **7.** fanfare **9.** tantarara
   12. trumpet blare
tantrum . . . **3.** fit **4.** rage **7.** caprice
   8. tirrivee (tirrivie) **10.** conniption
Tanzania, Africa . . .
   capital . . **11.** Dar es Salaam (Haven of
      Peace)
   famed Mt. . . **11.** Kilimanjaro
   famed plains . . **9.** Serengeti
   famed town . . **5.** Ujiji (Stanley found
      Livingstone, 1871)
   formerly . . **8.** Zanzibar **10.** Tanganyika
   language . . **7.** Swahili
   natives . . **5.** Bantu
Taoism, names . . . **6.** Kwanti, Laotze
   7. Yu Hwang
tap . . . **3.** dum, hit, hob, rap **4.** plug,
   tamp **5.** sound, spile **6.** faucet, liquor,
   siphon, spigot, strike **7.** censure,
   petcock, reprove
tape . . . **3.** gin, tie **4.** band, wick **5.** strip
   6. fillet, ribbon, secure **7.** bandage,
   measure **9.** recording
taper . . . **4.** ream, wick **5.** point, snape,
   spire **6.** candle, cierge, narrow **7.** conical
   8. decrease, diminish **9.** acuminate
   11. pyramidical
tapering (pert to) . . .
   blades . . **6.** spires
   pert to . . **6.** spired, terete **7.** conical,
      pointed **8.** fusiform **9.** narrowing
   piece . . **4.** gore **5.** miter **6.** gusset
   pillar . . **7.** obelisk
   solid . . **4.** cone
tapestry . . . **5.** arras, tapis **6.** Bayeux,
   dosser **7.** Gobelin

tapeworm . . . **6.** Taenia
tapeworm (pert to) . . .
   embryonic . . **10.** oncosphere
   like . . **8.** taenioid
   segment . . **8.** strobila
tapioca, source . . . **5.** salep **7.** cassava
   (casava)
Tapirus . . . **6.** tapirs
tapster . . . **7.** barmaid, skinker
tar . . . **3.** gob **4.** brea, pave, salt **5.** black,
   pitch **6.** cresol, maltha, sailor, seaman
   7. mariner **8.** telegram **10.** bluejacket
tarantula . . . **6.** spider **7.** mygalid **10.** wolf
   spider
tarboosh . . . **3.** fez **6.** red cap
tardy . . . **3.** lag, lax **4.** late, slow
   5. slack **6.** remiss **7.** belated, lagging,
   overdue **8.** dilatory **10.** behindhand
   11. cunctatious
tare . . . **4.** weed (Bib) **5.** vetch **8.** discount
   9. allowance, deduction
target . . . **3.** aim, tee **4.** butt, goal, goat,
   mark, prey **5.** sight **6.** object, shield,
   tassel **8.** bull's-eye, ridicule **9.** objective
tariff . . . **4.** duty, list, rate **6.** charge
   7. tribute **8.** schedule
tariffist . . . **8.** advocate **13.** protectionist
tarnish . . . **3.** dim **4.** dull, soil, spot
   5. cloud, stain, sully, taint **6.** smirch,
   stigma, vilify **7.** blemish, destroy,
   obscure **8.** besmirch, discolor **10.** lose
   luster, stigmatize
taro . . . **3.** poi **4.** eddo, food, gabi (gabe)
   5. cocco, tania (tanier) **12.** elephant's-
   ear
tarot . . . **14.** fortunetelling (cards)
tarried . . . **6.** waited **7.** dallied **8.** lingered,
   remained
tarry . . . **3.** lag **4.** bide, stay, wait
   5. abide, await, dally, delay, pause,
   stall **6.** dawdle, linger, loiter, retard
   7. outstay
tarsus . . . **5.** ankle **7.** segment
tart . . . **4.** acid, sour **5.** acrid, sharp
   6. pastry, severe **7.** caustic, pungent,
   waspish **8.** poignant, turnover
   10. astringent **11.** acrimonious
tartan . . . **4.** wool **5.** plaid **7.** pattern
   (plaid) **10.** Highlander
tartar . . . **5.** argol (argal), shrew, valet
   12. incrustation
Tartar, Tatar . . . **4.** Turk **6.** Mongol
Tartar, Tatar (pert to) . . .
   domain . . **7.** Khanate
   horseman . . **7.** Cossack
   lancer . . **5.** uhlan
   nobleman . . **5.** murza
   people . . **2.** Hu **3.** Hun **6.** Mongol
   people of . . **6.** Turkey **8.** Mongolia
   title . . **4.** Khan
tartarean . . . **5.** cruel **7.** hellish **8.** infernal
Tartarus (Myth) . . . **4.** hell **5.** Hades
   15. infernal regions (Iliad)
Tarzan (pert to) . . .
   actor . . **7.** Lincoln (Elmo) **11.** Weissmuller
   creator . . **9.** Burroughs (Edgar Rice)
   Lord . . **9.** Greystoke
   mate . . **4.** Jane
task . . . **3.** job **4.** duty, snap, test, toil
   5. chore, labor, stent, stint **6.** burden,
   dargue, impost, strain **10.** assignment,

employment **11.** undertaking
Tasmania (pert to) . . .
animal (burrowing) . . **6.** wombat
discoverer . . **6.** Tasman (1642)
marsupial . . **9.** phalanger
mountain . . **6.** Cradle **9.** Ben Lomond
strait . . **4.** Bass
taste . . . **3.** sip, sup **4.** tang **5.** flair,
sapor, savor, sense, smack, style
6. liking, palate, relish, sample
7. soupçon **8.** delicacy, elegance,
fondness, judgment **9.** gustation
10. experience **14.** discrimination
15. aesthetic liking
taste (pert to) . . .
bite . . **4.** nosh **5.** snack
decided . . **8.** fondness, penchant
French . . **7.** soupçon
fundamental . . **4.** acid, salt **5.** sweet
6. bitter
lacking . . **4.** rude **5.** bland, gross, stale
10. unpolished
ref to . . **7.** palatal **9.** gustatory
sharp . . **4.** acid, tang
tasteless . . . **4.** dull, flat **5.** vapid **6.** vulgar,
watery **7.** insipid **8.** lifeless **9.** savorless
10. inartistic
tasty . . . **5.** sapid **6.** savory **8.** saporous,
tasteful **9.** delicious, palatable,
toothsome
Tatar . . . see *Tartar*
tatouay . . . **9.** armadillo
tatter . . . **3.** rag **4.** tags, tear **5.** patch,
piece, shred **6.** ribbon
tatterdemalion . . . **5.** gamin **9.** ragpicker
10. ragamuffin
tattle . . . **4.** blab, tell **5.** prate **6.** gossip
7. chatter, divulge, prattle **8.** idle talk,
inform on
tattler . . . **6.** gossip, willet **8.** quidnunc,
redshank, telltale **10.** alarm clock,
talebearer, yellowlegs
tattoo . . . **4.** call (drum, bugle), pony,
scar **13.** entertainment
tau . . . **4.** ankh, crux, rood **5.** cross **6.** letter
(Gr) **7.** T-shaped
tau cross . . . **4.** ankh **6.** symbol **8.** crucifix,
insignia **10.** St Anthony's
taunt . . . **4.** gibe, jeer, mock, twit **5.** sneer,
tease **6.** deride **7.** provoke **8.** reproach,
ridicule **9.** aggravate
Taurus . . . **4.** bull **8.** Pleiades
13. constellation
taut . . . **4.** firm, snug, tidy **5.** tense, tight
6. severe, strict **7.** nervous **9.** distended
tautology . . . **8.** pleonasm **10.** redundancy,
repetition
tavern . . . **3.** inn, pub **5.** hotel **7.** barroom,
cabaret, Gasthof, taberna **8.** alehouse,
Gasthaus, hostelry
taw . . . **4.** game, whip **6.** marble **7.** tanning
tawdry . . . **4.** loud **5.** cheap, gaudy, showy
6. garish **7.** blatant
tawny, tawney . . . **3.** tan **5.** dusky, olive,
tenne **6.** tanned **7.** jacinth **8.** brindled
9. bullfinch
tax . . . **4.** cess, duty, geld, levy, scat
(scatt), task, toll **5.** stent **6.** assess,
burden, custom, excise, impose,
income, octroi, strain **7.** doomage,
license, tribute **8.** exaction, overtire

9. prescribe **10.** assessment
tax (pert to) . . .
ancient . . **3.** cro **4.** geld **7.** galanas
assessment . . **4.** rate **5.** ratal **7.** doomage
church . . **5.** tithe
commodity . . **6.** octroi
French history . . **6.** taille
kind . . **5.** tithe **6.** excise, surtax, taille
7. boscage **8.** auxilium, carucage
9. surcharge
liquor . . **6.** abkari (abkary)
pasturage (Shetland Isls) . . **4.** scat (scatt)
taxi . . . **3.** cab **4.** hack
tea . . . **5.** dance, party, shrub **6.** supper
8. beverage, function, sociable
9. collation, reception
tea (pert to) . . .
cake . . **5.** scone
chemical content . . **6.** tannin, theine
(thein) **8.** caffeine
Chinese . . **5.** black, hyson
Formosa . . **6.** oolong
Ind Ceylon . . **5.** pekoe
infusion . . **6.** ptisan, tisane
Labrador . . **5.** Ledum **8.** gowiddie
Paraguay . . **5.** yerba
receptacle . . **5.** caddy **8.** canister
table . . **6.** teapoy (tepoy)
type . . **3.** cha **5.** tsia **5.** Assam, black,
green, hyson, Ledum, oopak, pekoe
6. oolong **7.** cambric **8.** gowiddie
urn . . **3.** pot **7.** samovar
weak . . **7.** cambric
teach . . . **4.** show **5.** coach, drill, edify,
guide, prime, train, tutor **6.** direct,
impart, preach, school **7.** educate,
show how **8.** instruct **9.** enlighten
11. demonstrate
teacher . . . **5.** coach, guide, rabbi, tutor
6. doctor, mentor, pastor, pedant, priest,
pundit, reader, regent, rhetor, scribe
7. edifier, starets **8.** educator, preacher
9. pedagogue, preceptor **10.** instructor
teacher (pert to) . . .
Alexandrian . . **6.** Origen
Indian . . **4.** guru
Jewish . . **5.** rabbi
Mohammedan . . **3.** pir **4.** imam **6.** mullah
of the deaf . . **7.** oralist
Russian . . **7.** starets
teaching . . . **5.** moral **6.** docent **7.** precept
8. doctrine **11.** instruction
Teaching of the Twelve . . . **10.** The
Didache
team . . . **3.** two **4.** haul, join, pain, span,
yoke **5.** brood, chain, wagon **7.** vehicle
8. carriage **9.** yannigans
teamster . . . **6.** carter, driver **7.** carrier
Teapot Dome (pert to) . . .
known as . . **8.** Scandals (Teapot Dome)
leased by . . **4.** Fall (Sec'y of Interior)
lease of . . **8.** oil field
site . . **8.** Elk Hills (Wyo)
tear . . . **3.** rip **4.** rend, rent, rive **5.** revel,
sever, speed, split, spree **6.** cleave,
hasten **7.** destroy, shatter, torment
8. lacerate, separate **10.** dilacerate
tear (pert to) . . .
apart . . **7.** disjoin **8.** demolish
asunder . . **10.** dilacerate
down . . **4.** rase, raze

limb from limb . . **6.** punish **9.** dismember
to shreds . . **6.** tatter
up . . **3.** rip **6.** damage
up the roots . . **6.** arache
teardrop lace design . . . **5.** larme
tearful . . . **3.** sad **7.** maudlin, weeping
   9. lachrymal (lacrimal)
tears . . . **5.** drops (lachrymal), grief, rheum
   6. lament **9.** teardrops
tease . . . **3.** guy, nag, rag, vex **4.** twit
   5. annoy, devil, taunt **6.** bother,
   harass, heckle, needle, pester, plague
   7. provoke, torment **8.** irritate
   9. aggravate, tantalize
teaser . . . **4.** gull **6.** carder, curler, sniper,
   stoker **7.** curtain, fireman, problem
   8. pesterer, willower **9.** tormentor
   13. advertisement
technical . . . **7.** skilled, trained **8.** specific
   11. specialized **12.** professional
technocracy . . . **12.** organization **17.** rule
   by technicians
technology . . . **3.** art **7.** science
   9. technique **10.** agrotechny, virtuosity
   11. terminology **12.** nomenclature
   13. ethnotechnics
technophobe . . . **7.** Luddite
techy . . . **6.** touchy, vexing **7.** fretful,
   peevish **9.** irascible, irritable, sensitive
tedious . . . **3.** dry **4.** dull **5.** bored,
   prosy **6.** boring, prolix **7.** irksome,
   noxious **11.** displeasing, repetitious
   13. uninteresting
tedium . . . **5.** ennui **7.** boredom
   10. melancholy **11.** tediousness
teeming . . . **4.** full **6.** aswarm **7.** pouring,
   replete **8.** crowding, numerous, prolific
   9. abounding **10.** productive
   11. overflowing
teeter . . . **4.** rock **5.** waver **6.** jiggle, seesaw
   9. alternate, fluctuate, sandpiper,
   vacillate **12.** teeter-totter
teeth . . . **5.** bucks, fangs **6.** molars, tushes
   7. canines, ivories **8.** grinders, incisors
teeth (pert to) . . .
   all alike . . **7.** isodont
   cleaning . . **5.** brush, floss **10.** dentrifice,
   toothpaste
   covering . . **6.** enamel
   crustation . . **6.** tartar
   destitute of . . **5.** morné (Her) **8.** edentate
   10. edentulous
   elephant's . . **9.** scrivello **11.** scrivelloes
   false . . **8.** choppers (sl), dentures
   few . . **12.** oligodontous
   large . . **8.** megadont **9.** macrodont
   pointed . . **5.** fangs, tusks **6.** tushes
   ref to . . **4.** pulp **5.** molar **6.** dental
   7. dentine **8.** odontoid
   science . . **10.** odontology
teething . . . **6.** growth **9.** dentition,
   odontosis **10.** odontogeny
teetotaller . . . **3.** dry **7.** non-user
   9. abstainer, nephalist, Rechabite (Bib)
   11. teetotalist
teg, tag . . . **3.** doe **5.** sheep (young),
   woman **6.** fleece (sheep's)
teguexin . . . **4.** teju **6.** lizard
tegument . . . **4.** bark, coat, skin **5.** cover
   6. cortex **10.** integument
tekke . . . **3.** rug **6.** carpet **7.** convent

9. monastery
tela . . . **6.** tissue **8.** membrane
Telamon (Gr Myth, pert to) . . .
   brother . . **6.** Peleus
   companion . . **8.** Hercules
   expedition . . **8.** boar hunt **10.** Argonautic
   male figure . . **6.** column **7.** support
   son . . **4.** Ajax **6.** Teucer
telegraph (pert to) . . .
   code, inventor . . **5.** Morse (Samuel F)
   key . . **6.** tapper
   service . . **5.** cable **8.** dispatch
telephone (pert to) . . .
   inventor . . **4.** Bell (Alexander)
   term . . **3.** PBX **4.** buzz, call, dial, hold,
   horn (sl), ring, toll **5.** trunk **6.** call
   up **7.** collect, hotline **8.** exchange,
   intercom **10.** push-button, videophone
   11. switchboard **12.** speakerphone
   14. radiotelephone
telescope . . . **4.** Lick **6.** Yerkes **7.** Palomar
   8. Galilean (1609) **9.** Gregorian (Scot
   1663)
telescopic . . . **9.** farseeing
television . . . **2.** TV **3.** box, set **4.** tube
   5. telly (Brit) **8.** boob tube, idiot box
   11. small screen
television (pert to) . . .
   person . . **6.** anchor, viewer **7.** sponsor
   9. superstar **10.** newscaster
   program . . **4.** show **6.** sitcom **7.** variety
   8. newscast **9.** docudrama, soap opera
   term . . **3.** air **5.** audio, bleep, cable,
   rerun **7.** channel, minicam **8.** telecast
   10. commercial, laugh track
tell . . . **3.** say **4.** talk **5.** count, peach, utter
   6. assail, impart, inform, recite, reckon,
   relate, repeat, report, reveal **7.** divulge,
   narrate, recount **8.** acquaint, disclose,
   rehearse **9.** recognize **11.** communicate
teller . . . **6.** banker **8.** informer, narrator
   9. describer, informant
telling . . . **6.** cogent, potent **8.** forceful,
   striking **9.** affective, narration, pertinent
   11. influential, significant
telltale . . . **4.** blab, clue, hint **6.** bearer,
   device, gossip **7.** tattler **8.** informer
   9. indicator, informing **10.** indication,
   talebearer
tellurian . . . **2.** Te **7.** earthly **11.** terrestrial
   12. earth dweller
temeritous, temerarious . . . **4.** rash
   8. heedless, reckless **10.** headstrong
temerity . . . **4.** gall **5.** cheek, nerve
   8. audacity, rashness **10.** effrontery
   12. recklessness
temper . . . **4.** mood **5.** humor **6.** adjust,
   animus, anneal, attune, dander, harden,
   nature, season, soften **7.** assuage,
   mollify, tantrum **8.** hardness, mitigate,
   moderate **9.** composure **10.** equanimity,
   irritation **11.** disposition, temperament
temper (pert to) . . .
   bad . . **4.** fury, rage **5.** anger **6.** choler,
   spleen
   clay . . **6.** puddle
   even . . **4.** calm **5.** staid **6.** sedate
   in a . . **4.** huff, rage, stew **5.** tizzy
   metal . . **6.** anneal, harden **7.** toughen
temperament . . . **4.** mood **6.** crasis,
   nature **8.** artistic **11.** disposition

temperance . . . **6.** virtue **8.** calmness, sobriety **10.** abstinence, moderation **11.** self-control **13.** self-restraint **14.** abstemiousness
temperate . . . **4.** calm, cool **5.** sober **8.** moderate **10.** abstemious, restrained **14.** self-controlled
tempered . . . **5.** angry **6.** sedate **8.** annealed, disposed, moderate **9.** moderated, mollified, qualified
tempest . . . **4.** gale, wind **5.** blast, orage, storm **6.** tumult **7.** turmoil **9.** agitation, commotion, windstorm **10.** excitement **12.** thunderstorm
Tempest (pert to) . . .
  Cuban . . **6.** bayamo
  in a teapot . . **10.** triviality **12.** exaggeration
  The (character) . . **5.** Ariel (spirit) **7.** Caliban, Miranda **8.** Prospero
tempestuous . . . **5.** windy **6.** stormy **7.** excited, violent **9.** turbulent
temple . . . **4.** fane, naos **5.** cella, ratha, speos **6.** aedile, church, pagoda **7.** edifice
temple (pert to) . . .
  Anglo-Ind . . **5.** kovil (covil)
  approach . . **5.** toran (torana)
  Assyrian . . **8.** ziggurat (anc)
  Aztec temple site . . **12.** Tenochtitlan
  Chinese . . **6.** pagoda
  Hawaiian . . **5.** heiau
  Mexico . . **8.** teocalli
  Muslim . . **6.** mosque
  part . . **4.** naos **5.** cella **6.** adytum **7.** narthex, sanctum **10.** penetralia
  ref to . . **6.** hieron
  sanctuary . . **10.** penetralia
  Shinto . . **3.** Sha **5.** jinja (jinsha) **7.** yashiro
Temple Bar (London) . . . **7.** gateway
Temple Butte site . . . **11.** Grand Canyon
Temple of Heaven . . . **7.** Peiping
Temple of Onias . . . **5.** Egypt
Temple of Reason . . . **9.** Notre Dame
Temple of the Sphinx . . . **5.** Egypt
tempo . . . **4.** pace, time **5.** grave, largo, speed **6.** adagio, presto, rhythm **7.** allegro, andante **8.** moderato **11.** synchronism
temporal . . . **4.** bene, laic **5.** civil **7.** earthly, secular, worldly **9.** ephemeral, temporary **10.** transitory **11.** present time **13.** chronological
temporize . . . **5.** delay **6.** demand, parley **9.** negotiate **13.** procrastinate
tempt . . . **4.** lead, lure **5.** decoy **6.** allure, entice, induce, seduce **7.** attract **8.** persuade **9.** seduction **10.** inducement
Tempter, The . . . **5.** Devil, Satan **7.** Evil One **10.** Evil Spirit, Old Serpent **14.** Prince of Devils
temptress . . . **5.** siren **7.** Delilah (Bib), mermaid **11.** enchantress
ten (pert to) . . .
  ace . . **10.** bridge game
  Commandments . . **9.** Decalogue
  dollars . . **7.** sawbuck
  fold . . **6.** denary **7.** decuple
  footed . . **7.** decapod
  gallon hat . . **7.** Stetson **8.** sombrero
  geometric figure . . **7.** decagon
  10. decahedron
  measure . . **4.** acre, bath **6.** decare
  number . . **5.** decad **7.** several
  physics . . **3.** bel
  poetic . . **9.** decameter (decametre)
  prefix . . **4.** deca (deka)
  stringed . . **9.** decachord
  thousand . . **6.** myriad
  year period . . **6.** decade **9.** decenniad, decennium
tenable . . . **10.** defensible **12.** maintainable
tenacious . . . **5.** tough **6.** dogged, viscid **7.** viscous **8.** adhesive, cohesive, sticking, stubborn **9.** glutinous, obstinate, retentive **10.** persistent **12.** pertinacious
tenant . . . **4.** saer **5.** ceile, dreng (drengh) **6.** holder, leaser, lessee, renter, vassal **7.** cottier, dweller, villein **8.** occupant **10.** inhabitant
tenant's tribute . . . **4.** cens
tend . . . **4.** care, heed, lean, mind, wait **5.** nurse, offer, serve, watch **6.** attend, manage **7.** incline, oversee **8.** converge, minister **9.** cultivate, gravitate, look after
tendency . . . **4.** bent, bias, tide **5.** drift, drive, trend **6.** course, object **7.** bearing, leaning **8.** aptitude, relation **9.** direction, proneness **10.** proclivity, propensity **11.** disposition, inclination
tender . . . **3.** bed, pay **4.** boat, fond, gift, give, kind, soft, sore **5.** offer, young **6.** extend, gentle, humane, waiter **7.** pitiful, present, rail car **8.** delicate, merciful **9.** attendant, sensitive **10.** effeminate **11.** softhearted, sympathetic, warmhearted **12.** affectionate **13.** compassionate
tender (pert to) . . .
  animal . . **6.** cowboy, herder
  farm . . **10.** husbandman
  feeling . . **9.** sentiment
  foot . . **4.** dude **6.** novice **8.** newcomer **10.** raw recruit
  hearted . . **4.** kind **8.** merciful
  horse . . **5.** groom **6.** ostler **7.** hostler
  regard . . **4.** love **6.** tendre
  ship . . **7.** pinnace
  style . . **7.** amoroso
tenderloin . . . **4.** meat **7.** brothel **12.** city district, vice district
tenderness . . . **4.** love, pity **8.** sympathy **9.** affection **10.** compassion, gentleness
tending to . . .
  arouse . . **7.** emotive
  assist memory . . **8.** mnemonic
  check . . **10.** repressive
  clear of guilt . . **11.** exculpatory
  control . . **10.** regulating
  drive away . . **9.** repellant
  evade . . **7.** elusory
  lateness . . **7.** tardive
  separate . . **8.** divisive
  tear . . **10.** lacerative
  wear away . . **8.** abrasive
tendon . . . **4.** cord, thew **5.** sinew **8.** ligament **11.** aponeurosis
tendril . . . **4.** coil, curl **5.** shoot, sprig **6.** branch, cirrus **7.** stipule **8.** filament
tenet . . . **3.** ism **4.** rule **5.** canon, creed,

dogma, maxim **6.** belief **7.** precept
8. doctrine **9.** principle
tenne ... **5.** brown, color
Tennessee ...
  battle .. **11.** Chattanooga **14.** Above the
    Clouds
  capital .. **9.** Nashville (Athens of the
    South)
  city .. **7.** Memphis **8.** Oak Ridge
    9. Knoxville **11.** Chattanooga
  first State .. **8.** Franklin
  Mts .. **7.** Lookout **10.** Cumberland, Great
    Smoky **13.** Clingman's Dome
  museum .. **9.** Hermitage, Parthenon
    12. Atomic Energy (Oak Ridge)
    13. Ancestral Home (Pres Polk)
  park .. **6.** Shiloh
  river .. **9.** Tennessee
  State admission .. **9.** Sixteenth
  State motto .. **16.** America At Its Best
  State nickname .. **9.** Volunteer
tennis (pert to) ...
  four persons .. **7.** doubles
  player .. **6.** netman
  score .. **3.** ace **4.** love (zero) **5.** deuce
    (tie)
  series .. **3.** set
  site .. **5.** court
  stroke .. **3.** cut, lob
  term .. **3.** ace, lob, net, set **5.** serve
    6. hazard **7.** receive
  two persons .. **7.** singles
tenon ... **3.** cog **4.** tusk **5.** tooth **7.** mortise
tenor ... **4.** alto (violin), copy, mode,
  tone **5.** drift, trend **6.** course, intent,
  singer **7.** meaning, purport **8.** tenoreno
  9. male voice, procedure **10.** transcript
tense ... **4.** edgy, rapt, taut **5.** rigid, tight
  6. intent **7.** intense, nervous, stretch
  8. strained **9.** stretched **10.** breathless
tense (grammar) ... **4.** past **6.** future
  7. perfect, present **9.** preterite
  10. pluperfect **11.** past perfect,
  progressive
tensile ... **6.** pliant **7.** ductile **8.** tensible
tension ... **6.** strain, stress **7.** detente,
  nervous **9.** disaccord, stiffness
tent ... **3.** hut **4.** camp, show **5.** cover,
  lodge **6.** dossil **7.** marquee **8.** pavilion
tent (pert to) ...
  covering .. **4.** tilt
  Eskimo .. **5.** tubik (skin)
  general's .. **10.** praetorium (pretorium)
  India .. **4.** pawl
  Indian .. **5.** tepee **6.** teepee, wigwam
  occupant .. **5.** nomad **6.** camper **7.** tourist
  Russian .. **7.** kibitka
  Scottish .. **6.** pulpit
  surgical .. **6.** screen
  type .. **3.** fly, pup **4.** bell, wall **6.** Sibley
    8. pavilion
tentacle ... **4.** hair, palp **6.** feeler **7.** tendril
tentative ... **7.** feeling, testing
  9. makeshift, temporary **10.** substitute
  11. making trial, provisional
  12. experimental
tenterhooks ... **6.** strain **8.** suspense
  10. uneasiness
tenth ... **5.** decim, tithe **6.** decima **9.** organ
  stop
tenth Muse ... **6.** Sappho

Tent Maker ... **4.** Omar
tenuity ... **6.** rarity **7.** poverty **8.** delicacy,
  subtlety, thinness **9.** indigence, unreality
tenuous ... **4.** rare, thin **6.** subtle
  7. slender **8.** delicate, ethereal
  13. unsubstantial
tenure ... **4.** term **5.** lease **6.** socage
  7. holding **10.** possession
tepee, teepee ... **4.** tent **6.** wigwam
tepid ... **4.** mild, warm **8.** lukewarm
tequila ... **6.** liquor **12.** century plant
teraphim ... **5.** idols **6.** images
teras ... **7.** monster
tergiversate ... **3.** lie **5.** evade, shift
  10. apostasize, equivocate
term ... **3.** age, end, era **4.** date, name,
  time, word **5.** epoch, limit, style
  6. estate, period, tenure **7.** premise
  8. duration, semester, terminus
  12. nomenclature
term (pert to) ...
  connotation .. **6.** intent **11.** designation
  death .. **4.** doom, mort
  for years .. **10.** real estate
  glacial .. **5.** stoss
  golf .. **4.** hook **5.** bogey (bogie), divot,
    eagle, slice **6.** birdie
  grammar .. **6.** phrase, syntax
    11. phraseology
  logic .. **4.** mode **5.** major, minor
  of life .. **3.** age **5.** sands (hourglass)
  Rugby .. **5.** scrum
  sea .. **4.** ahoy **5.** avast, belay
  tennis .. **4.** love **5.** deuce, serve
termagant ... **5.** scold, shrew, vixen
  6. Amazon, virigo **7.** furious **8.** scolding
  9. turbulent **10.** boisterous, tumultuous
  11. quarrelsome
Termagant ... **5.** deity **14.** imaginary
  being
terminal ... **3.** end **4.** goal **5.** anode,
  depot, final, limit **6.** finish **7.** limital,
  station **8.** desinent, terminus, ultimate
  9. end of life, extremity **10.** concluding
  11. desinential, destination, termination
terminal (pert to) ...
  battery .. **5.** anode **7.** cathode **9.** electrode
  leaf .. **8.** apiculus
  ornament .. **6.** finial
  town (end of line) .. **8.** terminus
terminate ... **3.** end **4.** halt **5.** abort,
  cease, close, limit **6.** expire, result
  7. end with **8.** complete, conclude
termination ... **3.** end **4.** amen **5.** close,
  limit **6.** ending, result **7.** outcome
  8. terminus **9.** desinence **10.** completion,
  conclusion, expiration
termite ... **3.** ant (white) **4.** anay (anai)
  5. Isoptera (Order)
tern ... **4.** darr (black), gull **6.** Sterna
  (genus) **8.** schooner (Naut) **9.** threefold
  10. sea swallow
ternary ... **5.** three, triad **6.** tercet (Poet),
  triple **7.** ternion, trinity **9.** threefold
ternate ... **4.** tern **9.** threefold
  12. trifoliolate
terpsichore ... **5.** dance **6.** dancer
  7. dancing
Terpsichore (Myth) ... **13.** Muse of
  dancing
terra ... **5.** earth **10.** terra firma

terrace ... **4.** flaw (marble), mesa, step
7. balcony, gallery, plateau, portico
8. platform (earth) **9.** colonnade
terrain, terrane ... **4.** land **5.** tract
6. region **11.** environment
terrapin ... **4.** Emys **6.** turtle **8.** Chelonia,
Emydinae, tortoise **9.** cheloniid
terrapin, turtle (pert to) ...
color .. **9.** grapenuts
type .. **6.** potter, slider **10.** red-bellied
11. diamondback **13.** yellow-bellied
War .. **14.** Eighteen Twelve (1812)
terrene, terrestial ... **4.** land **5.** earth,
realm **6.** earthy, mortal **7.** earthly,
mundane, worldly
terrestrial planets ... **4.** Mars **5.** Venus
7. Mercury
terrible ... **3.** bad **4.** dire **5.** awful
6. tragic **7.** fearful, ghastly, hideous,
painful **8.** dreadful, horrible, terrific
9. appalling, frightful **10.** formidable,
terrifying, unpleasant
Terrible, The ... **4.** Ivan (Russ Czar)
terrier ... **3.** fox **4.** bull, Skye **5.** Cairn,
Irish, Welsh **6.** Boston **8.** Airedale,
Scottish, Sealyham **9.** Kerry blue,
schnauzer **10.** Bedlington, Clydesdale
13. Dandie Dinmont
terrific ... **5.** great **6.** superb **7.** extreme
8. dreadful, exciting, terrible
9. appalling, excessive, frightful
10. tremendous
terrify ... **3.** awe, cow **4.** stun **5.** alarm,
appal, haunt, scare, shock **6.** appall,
freeze **7.** horrify, petrify **8.** affright,
frighten
territory ... **4.** area, land **5.** banat, field
6. canton, region **7.** country **8.** district,
environs, Pashalic (Pasha's), province
10. palatinate
terror ... **3.** awe **4.** fear **5.** alarm, dread,
panic **6.** fright, horror **7.** hellion, Reign
of (Hist) **13.** consternation
terrorism ... **11.** subjugation
12. intimidation
terse ... **4.** curt, neat **5.** pithy **6.** smooth
7. compact, concise, laconic, pointed,
refined **8.** succinct **11.** sententious
12. accomplished, epigrammatic
Tertiary period ... **6.** Eocene **7.** Miocene
8. Pliocene **9.** Oligocene **12.** Age of
Mammals
tertium quid ... **12.** third someone
13. third somewhat
tertulia ... **4.** club **5.** party **7.** meeting
tessellated ... **6.** mosaic **9.** checkered
tessera ... **3.** die **4.** cube, tile **5.** token
6. marble, ticket **8.** password
11. certificate
test ... **3.** try **4.** exam, feel **5.** assay,
proof, prove, taste, tempt, trial
6. ordeal, sample **7.** examine, witness
8. evidence, standard **9.** criterion,
testimony **10.** experience, experiment
11. examination, performance
12. authenticate
test (pert to) ...
fineness .. **3.** pyx
orally .. **7.** examine
ore, value .. **5.** assay
pot .. **8.** crucible

severe .. **6.** ordeal
testa ... **7.** coating **8.** covering, tegument
testament ... **3.** New, Old **4.** will
8. covenant
testator ... **7.** legator, witness **9.** testatrix
tester ... **6.** canopy, helmet, prover,
taster **7.** assayer, candler, sampler
testify ... **4.** avow **6.** affirm, depone,
depose **7.** declare, profess, protest
8. indicate, manifest **11.** bear witness
testimonial ... **5.** token **7.** tribute, warrant
8. evidence **9.** reference **10.** compliment
11. certificate
testimony ... **7.** witness **8.** evidence
10. Scriptures **11.** affirmation,
attestation, declaration
testy, tetchy ... **6.** touchy **7.** fretful,
peevish **8.** petulant, snappish
9. irascible, obstinate **10.** headstrong
tetched in the head ... **9.** pixilated
tetrad ... **4.** four **7.** quartet (quartette),
quatern **8.** foursome **10.** quaternion
tetragon ... **4.** park **6.** square **7.** rhombus
9. courtyard **10.** quadrangle
Tetragrammaton ... **7.** Jehovah
12. Supreme Being **14.** four consonants
(unpronounced)
Teuton ... **4.** Goth **6.** German
Teutonic (pert to) ...
alphabet character .. **4.** rune
deity .. **2.** Er **3.** Tiu (Tiwaz), Tyr **4.** Frea,
Odin, Thor **5.** Aesir, Bragi, Wodin
6. Balder, Frigga **7.** Forseti **8.** Heimdall
demon .. **3.** alp
giantess .. **4.** Norn **11.** demigoddess
goddess .. **3.** Eir, Hel, Ran **4.** Norn, Urth
(Urthr), Wyrd
homicide (tribal) .. **5.** morth
land .. **4.** odal
law .. **5.** Salic
nymph (water) .. **3.** nis
race .. **5.** Goths, Jutes **6.** Franks, Saxons
7. Vandals **8.** Lombards **10.** Norwegians
13. Scandinavians
supernatural being .. **5.** troll
Teutonic goddess of ...
death .. **3.** Hel, Ran
healing .. **3.** Eir
peace .. **7.** Nerthus
Teutonic god of ...
justice .. **7.** Forseti (Forsete)
pantheon .. **5.** Aesir (group)
peace .. **6.** Balder
sea .. **5.** Aegir
skill .. **3.** Ull (Ullr)
sky .. **2.** Er **3.** Tiu (Tiwaz), Tyr
thunder .. **4.** Thor **5.** Donar
war .. **3.** Tiu (Tiwaz), Tyr
Texas ...
birthplace of Pres .. **10.** Eisenhower
capital .. **6.** Austin
cattle .. **8.** longhorn
city .. **4.** Waco **5.** Dallas, El Paso
7. Abilene, Denison, Houston
9. Arlington, Fort Worth, Galveston
10. San Antonio **13.** Corpus Christi
flags (six) .. **5.** Spain **6.** France, Mexico
8. Republic (of Texas) **11.** Confederate
12. United States
flower .. **10.** bluebonnet, yellow rose
Indian people .. **5.** Caddo

monument *(Battle)*.. **10.** San Jacinto
police.. **7.** Rangers
river.. **3.** Red **5.** Pecos **9.** Rio Grande
shrine, mission.. **5.** Alamo
State admission.. **12.** Twenty-eighth
State motto.. **5.** Tejas **10.** Friendship
State nickname.. **8.** Lone Star
text... **4.** book **5.** topic, verse **7.** passage
　8. libretto, textbook **11.** letterpress
textile screw pine... **3.** ara
textile shop... **7.** mercery
texture... **3.** web **4.** wale, warp, wooz
　5. grain, weave **6.** cobweb, fabric
　7. textile **9.** roughness, structure
　10. smoothness
Thailand (Siam), **capital**... **7.** Bangkok
Thames River town... **4.** Eton
thana... **13.** police station
thanador... **7.** officer (Hind)
thanatology doctrine... **5.** death
thane... **5.** baron (anc) **7.** servant, warrior
　9. Scots peer
thankless... **7.** ingrate **10.** ungrateful
　13. unappreciated
thanks... **5.** grace **6.** prayer **8.** gramercy
　9. gratitude **12.** appreciation
　14. acknowledgment
Thanks to God... **10.** Deo gratias
that (pert to)...
　is.. **2.** ie **5.** id est
　is to say.. **3.** viz **5.** to wit **6.** namely
　9. videlicit
　pronoun.. **3.** who **4.** what
thatch (pert to)...
　grass.. **4.** rope **6.** slough
　hair.. **3.** mop **4.** crop, mane
　palm.. **5.** Sabal **7.** Thrinax
　roofing.. **5.** reeds, straw **6.** rushes
　support.. **6.** wattle
thatcher... **7.** hellier
thaumaturgy... **5.** magic **7.** sorcery
　8. wizardry **11.** legerdemain
the (pert to)...
　end.. **5.** omega **6.** thirty
　French.. **2.** la, le **3.** les
　German.. **3.** das, der, die
　Italian.. **2.** il, la, le **4.** ella
　same.. **4.** idem **5.** ditto
　Spanish.. **2.** el, la **3.** las, los
theater, theatre... **5.** arena, drama,
　odeum, stage **6.** lyceum **8.** coliseum
　9. playhouse **12.** amphitheater
theater (pert to)...
　actress.. **7.** heroine, ingénue
　box.. **4.** loge
　curtain.. **4.** drop **6.** teaser
　district.. **6.** Rialto **8.** Broadway
　floor (lower).. **7.** parquet
　full house.. **3.** SRO
　Greek.. **5.** odeum (odeon)
　part.. **3.** box, pit **4.** loge **5.** foyer, stage
　7. balcony, gallery, parquet **8.** parterre
　9. orchestra **10.** proscenium
theatrical... **5.** showy, stagy **8.** affected,
　dramatic **10.** artificial, histrionic
　12. melodramatic
theatrical (pert to)...
　art.. **10.** histrionic
　company.. **6.** troupe
　machine.. **9.** eccyclema
　spectacle.. **5.** revue **7.** pageant

star.. **4.** hero, lead **7.** heroine
Theban (pert to)...
　bard.. **6.** Pindar
　deity.. **4.** Amen (Amon) **6.** Amen-Ra
　god.. **5.** Ammon (Zeus)
　king.. **5.** Laius **7.** Amphion, Oedipus
　8. Pentheus
　queen.. **5.** Niobe **7.** Jocasta
　soothsayer (blind).. **8.** Tiresias
　triad.. **3.** Mut **6.** Amen-Ra, Khonsu
Thebes...
　capital of.. **10.** Upper Egypt (anc)
　famed avenue.. **8.** Sphinxes
　famed for.. **5.** ruins
　location.. **4.** Nile
　ruined temple.. **5.** Ammon **6.** Karnak
　Seven against (one of).. **6.** Tydeus
theca... **3.** pod **4.** case, cell **7.** capsule
theft... **6.** holdup, piracy **7.** larceny,
　robbery **8.** burglary, stealing
　10. plagiarism **12.** embezzlement
theftlike... **7.** piratic **9.** piratical
theme... **4.** text **5.** essay, lemma, motif,
　thema, topic **6.** matter, thesis **7.** subject
　9. discourse, leitmotiv
then... **3.** poi (Mus) **4.** also, next,
　when **5.** hence **7.** besides **8.** formerly
　9. therefore **12.** subsequently
thence... **4.** away **5.** hence **9.** after that,
　elsewhere, therefore **10.** henceforth,
　thereafter
theogamy... **14.** marriage of gods
theologian... **5.** Arius (Bib) **6.** Luther
　7. Abelard, Aquinas, Erasmus
　9. Augustine
theology... **7.** irenics **8.** canonics, religion
　9. depositum **10.** doctrinism
theorem... **3.** law **4.** rule **5.** axiom,
　topic **7.** premise **9.** principle, statement
　11. proposition
theoretical... **5.** ideal **8.** academic,
　platonic **11.** conjectural, impractical,
　speculative **12.** hypothetical, not
　practical
theorize... **6.** reason **9.** postulate,
　speculate
theory... **3.** ism **4.** plan **6.** scheme
　7. formula, opinion **8.** analysis,
　doctrine **10.** hypothesis **11.** speculation,
　supposition **13.** contemplation
theory of...
　evolution.. **9.** Darwinism **10.** Lamarckism
　13. Spencerianism
　knowledge.. **12.** epistemology
　language.. **6.** bowwow **8.** ding-dong,
　pooh-pooh
　philosophy.. **13.** phenomenalism
　relativity.. **8.** Einstein
theosophist... **7.** Mahatma
theosophy... **4.** yoga **6.** cabala **7.** Nirvana
　8. kamarupa (Kama)
therapeutic... **7.** healing **8.** curative,
　remedies
therapy... **4.** cure **5.** faith **9.** dietetics,
　medicines, treatment **12.** hydrotherapy,
　therapeutics **13.** psychotherapy
there... **3.** yon **5.** ready **6.** yonder
　7. thereat, thither **11.** at that place
therefore... **2.** as, so **4.** ergo **5.** hence,
　since **6.** thence **9.** thereupon, to
　that end, wherefore **11.** accordingly

12. consequently
thermometer ... **5.** Hydra **7.** Reaumur
10. Centigrade, Fahrenheit
Thesaurus compiler ... **5.** Roget
thesis ... **5.** essay, theme, topic **6.** accent
7. premise **8.** treatise **9.** postulate
10. assumption **11.** affirmation
12. dissertation
thespian ... **3.** art **5.** actor **6.** player,
tragic **7.** actress, Thespis (founder)
8. dramatic
Thessaly, Greece ...
ancient name .. **9.** Thessalia
famed for .. **6.** horses **8.** horsemen
mountain .. **4.** Ossa **6.** Pelion
native .. **5.** Greek **10.** Thessalian
town .. **7.** Larissa
thew ... **5.** brawn, sinew **6.** manner,
muscle, virtue **8.** strength
they go out ... **6.** exeunt
thick ... **4.** burr, dull, hazy **5.** broad,
bushy, close, crass, dense, gross,
husky, plump, solid, squat **6.** coarse,
espeso, stodgy, stupid **7.** crowded,
grumous, muffled **8.** familiar, friendly,
intimate, numerous, thickset **9.** luxuriant
10. indistinct **11.** inspissated
12. impenetrable
thicken ... **3.** gel **4.** clot, curd **5.** cloud,
flock **6.** curdle, deepen, harden
7. congeal, stiffen **8.** increase, solidify
9. intensify **10.** incrassate, inspissate,
strengthen
thicket ... **4.** bosk, rone **5.** copse, grove,
hedge, shola **6.** bosket (bosquet)
7. boscage, coppice, spinney
9. brushwood, chaparral **10.** underbrush
thickheaded ... **4.** dull **5.** dense **6.** stupid
7. doltish
thickness ... **3.** ply **5.** layer **7.** density
8. diameter, intimacy **10.** opaqueness
11. consistency, measurement
thickset ... **5.** squat, stout **6.** stocky,
stodgy, stubby **14.** closely planted
thick-skinned ... **7.** callous
11. hardhearted, insensitive,
pachydermic **14.** pachydermatous
thick soup ... **5.** purée
thief ... **5.** scamp **6.** ackman, bandit,
looter, pirate, rascal, robber **7.** burglar,
filcher, rustler, stealer **8.** gangster,
larcener **9.** larcenist, scoundrel
10. freebooter, pickpocket, plagiarist
thieves (famed) ... **5.** Fagin **9.** Robin
Hood **10.** Dick Turpin, Jesse James
11. Claude Duval **12.** Jonathan Wild
13. Thief of Bagdad
thieves' Latin ... **4.** cant **5.** slang
12. secret jargon
thigh (pert to) ...
animal's .. **3.** ham **4.** hock **5.** flank
armor plate .. **6.** cuisse (cuish)
bone .. **5.** femur, ilium
ref to .. **5.** groin, meros (merus) **6.** crural
thimble ... **3.** cap **4.** ring **5.** cover, watch
thimble (pert to) ...
berry .. **9.** raspberry **10.** blackberry
eye .. **12.** chub mackerel
flower .. **8.** foxglove
rig .. **5.** cheat **7.** swindle **13.** sleight of
hand

weed .. **6.** clover
thin ... **4.** bony, lank, lean, poor, rare,
slim, weak **5.** gaunt, lanky, lathy,
reedy, sheer, spare, washy **6.** dilute,
meager, rarefy, shrill, sleazy, slinky,
sparse, watery **7.** haggard, insipid,
scraggy, scrawny, slender **8.** araneous,
rarefied **10.** attenuated, diaphanous
11. transparent
thin (pert to) ...
air .. **5.** smoke, vapor **6.** bubble
and delicate .. **8.** araneous
10. diaphanous
and haggard .. **5.** gaunt
and withered .. **7.** wizened **9.** shriveled
fabric .. **8.** gossamer
out .. **5.** peter
plate, bone .. **6.** tegmen
plate, metal .. **4.** leaf
plate, Zool .. **6.** lamina **7.** lamella
skinned .. **6.** gentle, tender, touchy
Thin Man's dog .. **4.** Asta
thine ... **4.** tuum
thing ... **3.** act, res **4.** deed, fact,
idea, unit **5.** being, event **6.** affair,
entity, gadget, object **7.** article, reality
8. anything, creature **9.** happening,
situation, something
thing (pert to) ...
added .. **6.** insert **8.** addendum
9. insertion **10.** supplement
assumed .. **7.** premise **11.** implication
complete .. **4.** unit
cursed .. **8.** anathema
done .. **5.** actum
following .. **6.** sequel
found .. **5.** trove
hard to classify .. **11.** nondescript
huge .. **7.** monster
indefinite .. **7.** so-and-so **10.** thingumbob
(thingumabob) **12.** what's-its-name
nonexisting .. **9.** nonentity
of little worth .. **6.** stiver, trifle **7.** trinket
the (thing) .. **7.** the rage
unique .. **4.** sole
things (pert to) ...
added .. **7.** addenda **11.** additaments
brought into being .. **9.** creations
found, surprise .. **11.** serendipity
intricate .. **9.** involutes
little .. **16.** inconsequentials
moving to and fro .. **7.** wigwags
of like nature .. **8.** cognates
suitable to eat .. **9.** esculents
theoretical .. **7.** noumena
to be done .. **6.** agenda
to be learned .. **7.** lessons
to follow .. **7.** sequels **8.** sequelae
to sharpen .. **10.** whetstones
widely separated .. **8.** extremes
think ... **3.** wis **4.** deem, muse, trow
5. opine **6.** reason **7.** believe, imagine,
reflect, suppose **8.** cogitate, conceive,
meditate **11.** contemplate
think (pert to) ...
better of .. **6.** repent **10.** reconsider
bring to mind .. **6.** recall **7.** imagine
10. conjecture
logically .. **6.** reason
of .. **5.** judge **6.** intend, recall **8.** consider,
remember **9.** recollect **10.** call to mind

over.. **3.** wis **4.** mull, muse **5.** brood
6. ponder **8.** meditate
up.. **6.** devise, scheme **7.** concoct
thinker, religious freedom ...
14. latitudinarian
Thin Man (pert to) ...
actor.. **3.** Loy (Myrna) **6.** Powell (William)
character.. **11.** Nick Charles, Nora
Charles
dog.. **4.** Asta
thinness ... **6.** rarity **7.** tenuity **8.** rareness
11. slenderness
third (pert to) ...
comb form.. **3.** tri **4.** trit
day (Quakers).. **7.** Tuesday
estate.. **6.** people
figure.. **7.** ferison
in number.. **8.** tertiary
music.. **6.** tierce
ordinal of.. **5.** three
person.. **6.** escort **7.** grammar
8. chaperon
power.. **4.** cube
Republic.. **6.** French (1871)
thirst ... **6.** desire, hunger **7.** craving,
dryness, longing
this ... **4.** near **9.** the nearer
Thisbe's lover (Bab) ... **7.** Paramus
thisness ... **9.** haecceity
thistle (pert to) ...
bird.. **9.** goldfinch
color.. **6.** violet (cobalt)
emblem.. **8.** Scotland
genus.. **6.** Arnica, Cosmos **7.** Carlina
star.. **7.** caltrop (caltrap)
thistledown ... **6.** pappus **12.** thistlebeard
thither ... **3.** yon **5.** hence **6.** yonder
thong ... **4.** lash, riem, whip **5.** knout,
lorum, quirt, romal, strap **6.** lorate
7. amentum, lanyard (laniard)
Thor (pert to) ...
father.. **4.** Odin
German.. **5.** Donar
god of.. **7.** thunder
other name.. **9.** Hlorrithi
stepson.. **3.** Ull (Ullr)
wife.. **3.** Sif
thorax ... **5.** chest **6.** cavity **7.** cuirass
8. pectoral **11.** breastplate
thorn ... **4.** bane **5.** briar (brier), spine
7. acantha, bramble, prickle
thorn (pert to) ...
apple.. **3.** haw **6.** Datura
back.. **3.** ray **4.** dorn **5.** skate **10.** spider
crab **11.** stickleback
bill.. **11.** hummingbird
comb form.. **5.** spini
full of.. **6.** briary
letters.. **2.** th **3.** edh
lizard.. **6.** moloch
pert to.. **6.** spinal
small.. **7.** spinule
thornless ... **5.** inerm **8.** inermous
thorny ... **5.** sharp, spiny **7.** brambly,
prickly **9.** acanthoid, bristling, difficult
thorough ... **4.** full **8.** absolute, complete
9. downright, intensive **10.** exhaustive
11. painstaking
thoroughfare ... **4.** road **6.** artery,
street **7.** highway, parkway, passage,
roadway, thruway **8.** arterial, autobahn,

highroad, pent road, turnpike, waterway
9. boulevard, concourse **10.** autostrada
thoroughgoing ... **4.** zeal **7.** extreme
9. downright **11.** painstaking
thoroughly ... **3.** all **9.** intensive, out-and-
out **11.** intensively **13.** letter-perfect
thorp, thorpe ... **4.** dorp, town **6.** hamlet
7. village
those (pert to) ...
adept at table talk.. **14.** deipnosophists
brought to terms.. **11.** transigents
in office.. **3.** ins
in the stock market.. **5.** bears, bulls
7. traders **9.** investors
of a habit.. **7.** addicts
of the same goal.. **6.** rivals
outside a profession.. **5.** laity
those who ...
read and write.. **9.** literates
ridicule.. **8.** deriders
verify.. **13.** corroborators
work together.. **13.** collaborators
thou ... **3.** tha **7.** pronoun **8.** thousand
thought ... **4.** care, heed, idea, view
5. logic **6.** deemed, opined **7.** anxiety,
opinion **9.** attention, cogitated,
reasoning **10.** cogitation, meditation,
reflection **11.** cerebration
12. deliberation, recollection
13. consideration, ratiocination
thought (pert to) ...
continuous.. **10.** meditation
deep in.. **10.** cogitabund
form.. **6.** ideate
laws of.. **7.** noetics
reader.. **11.** telepathist
thoughtful ... **4.** kind **5.** moody
7. mindful, museful, pensive, prudent,
serious **9.** attentive **10.** cogitative,
meditative, reflective, ruminative,
solicitous **11.** circumspect, considerate
13. contemplative
thoughtless ... **4.** rash **6.** stupid **7.** foolish
8. careless, heedless, reckless
9. brainless, impulsive **11.** harum-
scarum, inattentive, thought-free
12. unreflecting **13.** inconsiderate
thousand ... **3.** mil **5.** mille **7.** chiliad
10. ten hundred
Thousand and One Nights ...
13. Arabian Nights
thousand men, command of ...
11. chiliarchia
thousandth ... **9.** chiliadal **10.** millesimal
thousand years ... **7.** chiliad **9.** millenary
10. millennium
thrall ... **4.** esne, serf **5.** slave **7.** bondage,
bondman, captive, slavery **9.** thralldom
10. oppression
thrash ... **3.** lam, tan **4.** beat, cave,
drub, flog, whip **5.** flail, pound, twist
6. defeat, punish, strike, swinge, thresh
7. belabor, trounce **8.** urticate, vanquish
9. pulverize, toss about
thrashing ... **7.** beating, milling
8. drubbing, flogging, whipping
10. punishment
thread ... **4.** flax, jute, line, silk, vein, wire,
yarn **5.** fiber, floss, linen, lisle, rayon
6. cotton, dacron, sleave **8.** arrasene,
filament

thread (pert to) . . .
ancient . . **4.** byss
a needle . . **5.** reeve
ball . . **4.** clew (clue)
cell . . **5.** cnida
coiled . . **3.** cop
comb form . . **3.** nem **4.** nema **5.** nemat
    6. nemato
fish . . **7.** cutlass **9.** threadfin
    11. cobblerfish
herring . . **11.** gizzard shad
like . . **5.** filar **6.** filose
loose . . **4.** lint **7.** raveled
medical . . **5.** seton
metal . . **4.** wire
mystery lead . . **4.** clue
shoemaker's (obs) . . **6.** lingel (lingle)
silk . . **5.** floss **9.** filoselle
tangle . . **6.** sleave
tape, braid (thread) . . **5.** inkle
tester . . **9.** serimeter
weaving term . . **4.** warp, weft, woof .
    5. leash
threadbare . . . **4.** sere, worn **5.** trite
    6. shabby
threaten . . . **4.** warn **5.** curse **6.** menace
    7. portend **8.** forebode **9.** comminate
    10. intimidate **12.** anathematize
threatening . . . **4.** dark **7.** ominous
    8. imminent, lowering, menacing
three (pert to) . . .
banded armadillo . . **4.** apar **5.** apara
comb form . . **3.** ter
dimensional . . **5.** bruit, cubic
    12. stereoscopic
fold . . **4.** tern **6.** ternal, treble, triple
    7. ternate
group of . . **4.** trio **5.** triad **7.** triplet
    8. triplets
hundredth anniversary . .
    13. tercentennial
in one . . **6.** triune **7.** trinity **10.** The
    Godhead
legged stand . . **6.** teapoy, tripod, trivet
lined . . **9.** trilinear
masted vessel . . **5.** xebec **7.** frigate
    8. schooner
math term . . **2.** pi (3.1416)
prefix . . **3.** tri
R's . . **7.** reading, writing **10.** arithmetic
seeded . . **11.** trispermous
sided figure . . **6.** trigon **8.** triangle
spot . . **4.** trey
styled . . **10.** trystylous
toed sloth . . **2.** ai
Three Kingdoms (Chin) . . . **2.** Wu **3.** Shu,
    Wei
Three Kings of Cologne . . . **6.** Gaspar
    8. Melchior **9.** Balthasar **12.** Three
    Wise Men
Three Musketeers . . . **5.** Athos **6.** Aramis
    7. Porthos **9.** D'Artagnan (friend)
Three Sisters (Myth) . . . **5.** Fates **6.** Clotho
    7. Atropos **8.** Lachesis
Three Wise Men (Kings of Cologne) . . .
    6. Gaspar **8.** Melchior **9.** Balthasar
threnody . . . **5.** dirge **7.** requiem
    8. coronach
threshold . . . **3.** eve **4.** gate, sill **5.** limen
    6. portal **8.** doorsill
threw . . . see also *throw* **4.** cast **5.** flung,

slung **6.** bunged, heaved, hurled, pelted,
    tossed **7.** pitched
thrice . . . **3.** ter, tri **5.** fully **6.** highly
    10. repeatedly, three times
thrift . . . **7.** economy **8.** prudence
    9. husbandry **10.** providence
    11. thriftiness
thriftless . . . **6.** lavish **8.** prodigal, wasteful
    11. extravagant, improvident
thrifty . . . **6.** frugal, saving **7.** careful,
    prudent, sparing **9.** provident
    10. economical, forehanded, prosperous
    11. flourishing
thrill . . . **4.** tirl **6.** dindle, thrush,
    tingle, tremor **7.** delight **9.** electrify
    10. excitement
thrive . . . **4.** grow **5.** moise (Eng) **6.** batten
    7. prosper, succeed **8.** flourish, increase
throat . . . **3.** maw **4.** crop, neck **5.** gular,
    halse, mouth, voice **6.** groove,
    gullet, larynx, mutter **7.** channel,
    glottis, jugular, orifice, pharynx,
    trachea **9.** esophagus **10.** passageway
    12. constriction
throb . . . **4.** ache, beat, drum, pant **5.** pulse
    7. pulsate, vibrate **9.** palpitate
throe . . . **4.** pang **5.** agony **7.** anguish
    8. struggle
Throgmorton Street . . . **13.** Stock
    Exchange (London)
throne . . . **3.** see **4.** apse **5.** exalt
    8. enthrone **9.** royal seat
    11. sovereignty, supreme rank **12.** Chair
    of State
throng . . . **4.** crew, host, push **5.** crowd,
    horde, press, swarm **6.** bustle, stress
    7. hurried **9.** confusion, multitude
throttle . . . **5.** choke, lever, seize **6.** throat
    7. garrote **8.** strangle, suppress,
    windpipe
through . . . **2.** by **3.** dia, per **4.** into,
    thru **5.** ended **7.** perpend **8.** finished
    9. because of, by means of, completed
throughout . . . **5.** about **6.** during
    8. thorough **10.** completely, everywhere
throw . . . **3.** cob, don, lob, peg, shy
    4. bear, cast, hurl, kist, pelt, toss, yerk
    5. chuck, fling, heave, pitch, sling,
    twist, whirl **6.** baffle, strike, thwart
    7. discard, project **9.** prostrate
throw (pert to) . . .
a scare . . **7.** terrify
away . . **7.** discard **8.** handbill, squander
back . . **5.** repel **6.** reject, revert
dice (term) . . **4.** sise **7.** ambsace
in the towel . . **4.** cede, quit **9.** surrender
into confusion . . **7.** disturb, perturb,
    trouble **8.** stampede **10.** demoralize
into ecstasy . . **9.** enrapture
into shade . . **7.** eclipse
off . . **4.** cast, shed **6.** derail, reject
    7. abandon, discard
out . . **4.** emit, lade **5.** egest, eject,
    expel **6.** bounce **7.** discard, project
    9. eliminate
over . . **4.** jilt **5.** build **6.** give up, refute
    7. abandon, discard **9.** eliminate
overboard . . **8.** jettison
water upon . . **5.** douse
throwback . . . **7.** setback **9.** reversion
    10. misfortune, regression

throwing (pert to) . . .
rope . . **5.** lasso, reata, riata **6.** lariat
science . . **10.** ballistics
stick (anc) . . **6.** womera (woomera)
thrum . . . **3.** bit, hum **4.** drum, tuft **5.** strum
  6. fringe, repeat
thrush . . . **5.** brown, mavis, robin, veery
  7. disease **8.** shagbark, songbird
  9. blackbird
thrush (pert to) . . .
American . . **5.** robin, veery **12.** hermit
  thrush
European . . **5.** ouzel (ousel) **6.** missel
  7. redwing **11.** nightingale
golden . . **6.** oriole
Hawaiian . . **4.** omao
Ind . . **5.** shama
Scot . . **8.** throstle
thrust . . . **3.** dig, jab **4.** gird, poke,
  push, stab **5.** lunge **6.** extend, pierce
  7. intrude, obtrude, riposte **8.** protrude
  9. interject, interpose
thrust (pert to) . . .
aside . . **5.** shove **7.** dismiss **8.** brush
  off
down . . **7.** detrude
fencing term . . **5.** lunge **7.** allonge,
  riposte **8.** estocade
one's self in . . **5.** enter **7.** intrude
out . . **5.** eject **6.** extend **8.** protrude
thug . . . **4.** goon, yegg **6.** cuttle, gunman
  7. ruffian **8.** assassin **9.** cutthroat,
  roughneck
thumb . . . **6.** pollex, thenar
thumb (pert to) . . .
a ride . . **9.** hitchhike
bird . . **9.** goldcrest
lady's (herb) . . **9.** peachwort, persicary
mark . . **4.** soil **10.** impression
  11. fingerprint **14.** identification
nail . . **5.** small **8.** complete
over . . **4.** skim **6.** browse
part . . **6.** thenar
thump . . . **4.** bang, beat, blow, drum,
  thud, whip, yerk **5.** knock, pound
  6. hammer, pummel, strike, thrash
  8. chastise **10.** pound along
thunder . . . **4.** boom, peal, roar **5.** storm
  9. fulminate
thunder (pert to) . . .
bolt . . **5.** speed **6.** Caesar **8.** surprise
  9. lightning **11.** fulmination
fish . . **4.** raad **5.** loach **7.** catfish (electric)
god . . **4.** Thor **6.** Manito
of applause . . **5.** cheer **7.** ovation
peal . . **4.** clap **5.** crash
smitten goddess . . **6.** Semele **8.** Keraunia
thurible . . . **6.** censer
thurifer . . . **12.** censer bearer
Thursday . . . **4.** Thor **8.** fifth day **12.** god
  of thunder
thus . . . **2.** so **3.** sic **4.** ergo **5.** hence
  7. this way **9.** therefore **11.** for instance
  12. consequently
thwack . . . **3.** rap **4.** bang, blow, club
  5. crush, knock, whack **6.** defeat,
  pommel, strike, thrash **7.** belabor
thwart . . . **4.** balk, foil **5.** block, clash,
  cross, parry, spite **6.** defeat, gaffle,
  oppose, outwit **7.** oblique, prevent
  8. obstruct, stubborn **9.** frustrate,

interpose **10.** across from, disappoint
thymus . . . **5.** gland **10.** sweetbread
  (lambs, calves)
tiara . . . **5.** crown **6.** diadem **7.** coronet
  8. ornament
Tibbett opera . . . **12.** Emperor Jones
  (1932)
tibert . . . **3.** cat
Tibet, Asia . . . see also *Tibetan*
animal . . **3.** goa, sus **5.** panda
capital . . **5.** Lhasa
dialect . . **9.** Bhutanese
kingdom . . **5.** Nepal
Mts . . **8.** Himalaya **9.** Karakoram
religion . . **7.** Lamaism
river . . **5.** Hwang, Indus **7.** Yangtze
  11. Brahmaputra
ruler . . **9.** Dalai Lama
Tibetan (pert to) . . .
beer (barley) . . **5.** chang
deer . . **4.** shou
food (barley) . . **6.** tsamba
gazelle . . **3.** goa
monk, priest . . **4.** lama
ox . . **3.** yak
sheep . . **3.** sha **5.** urial **6.** bharal, nahoor,
  nayaur
wild ass . . **5.** kiang
wildcat . . **5.** manul
tibia . . . **4.** bone, shin **5.** flute **6.** cnemis
Tibur (anc) . . . **6.** Tivoli
tiburon . . . **5.** shark
Tiburtine . . . **12.** Sibyl of Tibur
tic . . . **5.** spasm **6.** twitch
tick . . . **3.** ked, tap **4.** beat, mark,
  mite, pest **5.** Argas **6.** acarid, Ixodes
  7. instant **8.** carapato, function, ticktock
  10. pajahuello (pajaroello)
ticket . . . **3.** tag **4.** note, pass, slip
  5. check, ducat, label, token **6.** ballot,
  billet, permit, record **7.** license, voucher
  8. document **11.** certificate
ticket dealer . . . **7.** scalper
tickle . . . **5.** amuse **6.** thrill, tingle
  7. delight **9.** titillate, vellicate
ticklish . . . **5.** risky **6.** fickle, queasy,
  touchy **7.** comical **8.** unstable, unsteady
  9. uncertain **10.** precarious, unreliable
tidal (pert to) . . .
creek . . **6.** estero **7.** estuary
current . . **4.** eagre **7.** tiderace
flood . . **5.** eagre
flow . . **3.** ebb **4.** bore, neap **5.** surge
tidbit, titbit . . . **5.** goody **6.** morsel
  7. saynete **8.** delicacy
tide . . . **3.** ebb, rip **4.** high, neap, time
  5. drift **6.** period, stream **7.** current
  8. low water **9.** be carried
tide (pert to) . . .
gate . . **9.** floodgate
go with . . **5.** drift, float **7.** proceed **13.** be
  fashionable
out with . . **3.** ebb **6.** recede **8.** diminish,
  fade away
over . . **6.** endure **8.** surmount **11.** live
  through
tidings . . . **4.** news, word **6.** gospel, report,
  rumors **7.** message **10.** evangelist
  11. information
tidy . . . **4.** neat, trig, trim **5.** groom, natty,
  plump **6.** spruce **7.** orderly **9.** shipshape

10. put in order 12. antimacassar, considerable

tie ... **4.** bind, bond, draw, even, knot, lash, link **5.** ascot, equal, nexus, noose, trice, truss **6.** cravat, enlace, fasten, relate, tether **7.** confine, necktie, sleeper **8.** equality, fastener, restrain, shoelace **10.** allegiance, obligation

tie (pert to) ...
off .. **5.** belay
ornament .. **3.** pin
ready-made .. **4.** teck
securely .. **7.** trammel
sports .. **8.** dead heat
uniting .. **4.** bond **5.** tache
up .. **4.** bind, wrap **5.** truss **6.** fasten **8.** restrain

tier ... **3.** row **5.** grade, layer **6.** series

Tiergarten ... **4.** park **16.** Zoological Garden

tiff ... **3.** sip **4.** huff, spat **5.** drink **7.** dudgeon, quarrel **8.** outburst **10.** fit of anger

tiffin ... **3.** tea **5.** brown, lunch **6.** repast **8.** luncheon

tiger ... **5.** bully **6.** emblem, savage **9.** swaggerer

tiger (pert to) ...
American .. **6.** jaguar
bird .. **5.** finch **8.** amadavat
family .. **3.** cat **6.** mammal **11.** Felis tigris
hunting dog .. **5.** dhole
S African .. **7.** leopard
Tasmania .. **9.** thylacine **13.** Tasmanian wolf
wolf .. **5.** hyena
young .. **3.** cub

tight ... **4.** fast, snug, taut, trim **5.** alert, close, drunk, tense **6.** narrow, stingy **7.** exactly, shapely **9.** condensed **11.** closefisted **12.** close-fitting, parsimonious

tight (pert to) ...
fisted .. **6.** stingy **12.** parsimonious
lipped .. **5.** terse **9.** secretive
wad .. **5.** miser **10.** curmudgeon

tighten ... **4.** frap, lace **5.** brace, tense **6.** fasten, tauten **7.** squeeze **9.** constrict

Tigris River city of ruins ... **7.** Nineveh (anc)

til ... **4.** tree **6.** sesame

tilde ... **4.** dash, mark, sign **6.** accent, tittle **15.** diacritical mark

tile ... **3.** red **5.** slate **6.** domino, mosaic, pament (pamment), tegula **7.** ceramic, pantile, tessera **8.** pavement

tiler ... **5.** thief **6.** slater **7.** hellier **10.** doorkeeper

till ... **3.** box **4.** farm, plow, tray, when **5.** labor, while **6.** before, casket, drawer, whilst **7.** develop **9.** cultivate

tillable ... **6.** arable

tiller ... **4.** helm **5.** stalk **6.** farmer, sprout **7.** plowman, rancher **8.** harrower **10.** cultivator, husbandman

tilt ... **3.** tip **4.** cant, heel, list **5.** joust, pitch, slant, slope **6.** career, oliver (hammer), seesaw, unload **7.** incline **8.** log house **10.** tournament **11.** altercation

timber ... **3.** log **4.** beam, tree, wood **6.** forest, lumber **7.** support **9.** underpier

timber (pert to) ...
bend .. **3.** sny
building .. **4.** sill, stud **5.** joist **6.** purlin, rafter **8.** stringer
convex .. **6.** camber
cribs (logging) .. **4.** dram
cut .. **6.** lumber **7.** fallage
decay .. **4.** doty (doaty)
end .. **5.** tenon
hard, heartwood .. **7.** duramen
Naut .. **3.** rib **4.** bitt, keel, mast, spar, wale **8.** sternson
support .. **6.** corbel
upright .. **8.** puncheon
wolf .. **4.** lobo

timbre ... **4.** tone **5.** clang, crest (Her), miter **7.** coronet **9.** resonance, tone color

timbrel ... **4.** drum **5.** tabor **7.** sistrum **10.** tambourine

time ... **3.** age, day, eon, era **4.** aeon, date, hour, term, turn, week, year **5.** clock, epoch, shift, tempo **6.** decade, minute, moment, period, season, second **7.** century **8.** duration, occasion, schedule **9.** fortnight, millenium

time (pert to) ...
accurate .. **10.** isochronon
before Christmas .. **6.** Advent
before Easter .. **4.** Lent
equal .. **10.** isochronal
geologic .. **5.** azoic
granted .. **4.** stay **5.** delay **8.** reprieve
legal .. **6.** usance **11.** year and a day
limit .. **8.** deadline
long ago .. **4.** once, yore **8.** formerly
medical .. **3.** tid **8.** ter in die (three times a day)
of vigor .. **6.** heyday
one .. **4.** once
present .. **5.** nonce **12.** contemporary
prior .. **9.** antedated **11.** retroactive
right .. **3.** tid
same .. **7.** however **9.** meanwhile **10.** concurrent **11.** synchronous **14.** simultaneously
spare .. **7.** leisure
waste .. **4.** idle, loaf **5.** dally **6.** loiter
wrong .. **11.** anachronism **13.** anachronistic

timeless ... **7.** ageless, eternal, undated **8.** dateless, unending, untimely **9.** premature **11.** everlasting **12.** interminable

timely ... **3.** apt, pat **4.** soon **5.** early **6.** prompt **9.** opportune **10.** seasonably **11.** opportunity

timepiece ... **4.** dial **5.** clock, watch **6.** gnomon **8.** egg glass, horologe **9.** clepsydra, hourglass, metronome **10.** isochronon, wristwatch **11.** chronometer

times ... **3.** ago, eld **4.** yore **5.** often **10.** frequently, yesterdays **11.** ups and downs

timid ... **3.** shy **4.** meek **5.** eerie, henny, mousy, pavid, scary **6.** afraid, trepid **7.** bashful, fearful, nervous, not bold **8.** cowardly, retiring, timorous

9. diffident, shrinking 12. fainthearted
13. pusillanimous
timocracy (pert to) . . .
defined by . . **5.** Plato
principle . . **11.** love of honor
State . . **6.** Sparta (anc)
Timon of Athens . . . **5.** Cynic (The)
  11. misanthrope
timorous . . . **5.** timid **6.** afraid **7.** bashful,
  fearful **8.** hesitant **9.** shrinking
Timothy (pert to) . . .
Bib . . **7.** convert **8.** Epistles
grass . . **3.** hay **10.** herd's grass
timpani . . . **11.** kettledrums
tin . . . **3.** can, pan **5.** money, plate
  7. element, stannum **8.** preserve **10.** not
  genuine
tin (pert to) . . .
alloy (copper) . . **6.** pewter
box . . **7.** trummel
coat with . . **5.** terne **10.** terneplate
comb form . . **6.** stanni
extract . . **8.** prillion
foil, plate . . **4.** tain
mine . . **8.** stannary
ref to . . **7.** stannic
sheet . . **6.** latten
symbol . . **2.** Sn
tinamou . . . **4.** yutu **7.** tataupa **9.** partridge
tincture . . . **4.** dash **5.** color, imbue, myrrh,
  tinge, trace **6.** iodine **7.** extract, vestige
  8. solution **9.** paregoric, suspicion
  10. extraction
tinder . . . **4.** punk **5.** spunk **6.** amadou
  9. touchwood
tine . . . **3.** nib **5.** prong, spike, tooth
tinea . . . **7.** sycosis **8.** ringworm
tinge . . . **3.** dye **4.** tint **5.** color, imbue,
  shade, stain, taint **6.** flavor **8.** coloring,
  tincture **10.** suggestion
tingle . . . **4.** ring **5.** sting **6.** dingle, thrill
  7. prickle **9.** sensation, stimulate
tinkle . . . **5.** clink **6.** dingle, tingle
tint . . . **3.** due, hue **4.** tone **5.** blush,
  color, tinge **6.** nuance
tintinnabulum . . . **4.** bell **6.** tinkle
  9. rhymester
tintype . . . **9.** ferrotype **12.** old-fashioned
tiny . . . **3.** wee **5.** small, teeny **6.** atomic,
  infant, minute, petite **9.** miniature
  10. diminutive **13.** infinitesimal
tip . . . **3.** cue, end, fee, neb, top **4.** apex,
  cant, heel, hint, lean, list, tilt **5.** crown,
  point, slant, spire, upset **6.** careen,
  inform, summit, tiptop **7.** cumshaw,
  incline **8.** bonamano, gratuity, overturn
  9. extremity, overthrow
tip (pert to) . . .
end . . **3.** neb
French . . **9.** pourboire
Italian . . **8.** bonamano
near . . **6.** apical
Near East . . **9.** baksheesh (bakshish)
scabbard . . **5.** chape **7.** crampet
  (crampette)
slender . . **6.** arista
to one side . . **4.** list, tile **5.** alist **6.** careen
up and over . . **4.** cant
tippet . . . **4.** cape, hood **5.** amice, scarf
  6. almuce **7.** muffler **8.** liripipe, palatine
  9. comforter

tipple . . . **3.** bib, nip, pot, sip **4.** suck
  5. drink, quaff **6.** fuddle, guzzle, liquor,
  tumble **7.** spirits **8.** beverage, overturn
tippler . . . **3.** sot **5.** souse, toper **7.** drinker
  9. draftsman
tipster . . . **4.** tout **8.** dopester **9.** informant,
  predictor **10.** forecaster, speculator
tipsy . . . **4.** awry **5.** drunk, shaky **6.** groggy
  7. fuddled, muddled **10.** staggering
  11. intoxicated
tiptoe . . . **5.** alert **6.** warily **7.** eagerly,
  quietly **8.** cautious, stealthy
  10. cautiously
tirade . . . **6.** screed, speech **8.** berating
  9. philippic
tire . . . **3.** fag, lag, rim **4.** bore, jade
  5. dress, weary **6.** attire **7.** exhaust,
  fatigue
tired . . . **5.** bored, jaded, spent, weary
  6. aweary
tireless . . . **8.** untiring **9.** unwearied
  10. unwearying **13.** indefatigable
tiresome . . . **3.** dry **4.** dull, tame **6.** boring,
  prolix **7.** irksome, tedious **8.** annoying
  9. fatiguing, vexatious, wearisome
  10. irritating
tissue . . . **3.** web **4.** bast, tela **5.** fiber,
  paper **6.** fabric **7.** culture **8.** meshwork
tissue (pert to) . . .
Biol . . **4.** bone **5.** nerve **6.** muscle
  8. ganglion **10.** epithelium
cell . . **8.** meristem
cellular . . **10.** epithelium
connecting . . **6.** stroma, tendon
  8. ligament
decay . . **6.** caries
fatty . . **3.** fat **4.** suet
hardening of . . **9.** sclerosis
horny . . **7.** keratin
layer . . **7.** stratum
lymphoid . . **7.** tonsils
nerve . . **8.** ganglion
ref to . . **4.** tela **5.** telar
spinal . . **4.** alba
vegetable . . **4.** bast **7.** endarch
  8. meristem
wood . . **6.** lignin, lignum
Titan . . . **4.** Rhea, Thea **5.** Coeus, Creus,
  deity, Dione, giant, Theia **6.** Phoebe,
  Tethys, Themis **7.** Cronius, Iapetus,
  Oceanus **8.** Hyperion **9.** Mnemosyne
titanic . . . **4.** huge **5.** great **7.** immense
  8. colossal, enormous, gigantic
Titan War (Thessaly) . . . **11.** Titanomachy
tithe . . . **3.** tax **4.** part **5.** teind, tenth
  11. frank pledge
titi . . . **6.** monkey **7.** sea bird **8.** ironwood
  9. buckwheat
Titian . . . **3.** red **6.** artist **7.** red hair
  9. red-haired
titillate . . . **5.** amuse **6.** thrill, tickle
  7. delight **8.** interest
titlark . . . **5.** pipit
title . . . **3.** sir **4.** dame, deed, earl, lord,
  name, sire, term, type **5.** claim, right
  6. knight, madame, squire **7.** caption,
  epithet, esquire, heading **8.** muniment
  9. designate **11.** appellation, designation
titled member, Stock Exchange . . .
  6. orchid (sl)
titmouse . . . **3.** mag, tit **4.** wren

5. Parus 6. parine, tomtit 7. jacksaw
9. mumruffin
titter ... 5. laugh, te-hee 6. giggle, tee-hee
7. snicker
tittle ... 3. dot, jot 4. iota, mark, whit
5. tilde 6. gossip, tattle 8. particle
tittle-tattle ... 6. gossip 8. idle talk
16. scandalmongering
tittupy ... 3. gay 5. shaky 6. lively
8. prancing, unsteady
titubate ... 4. reel 6. totter 7. stagger,
stammer
titular ... 7. nominal 9. incumbent (of
a title)
Tlingit ... 6. Indian (Alaska)
TNT ... 6. trotol 9. explosive
15. trinitrotoluene
to ... 2. at 4. into, till, unto 5. until
6. toward 7. as far as, thither
11. preposition
to (pert to) ...
to be .. 4. esse, être
to-do .. 3. ado 4. fuss, stir 6. bustle
9. commotion
to each his own .. 10. suum cuique
to which .. 7. whereto
to wit .. 3. viz 6. namely 8. scilicet
9. videlicet
toad ... 4. agua, Bufo, frog, pipa
6. anuran, peeper 7. crapaud
9. amphibian, Batrachia, spadefoot
10. natterjack
toad (pert to) ...
eater .. 5. toady 8. hanger-on, parasite
fish .. 6. puffer, slimer 8. frogfish
head .. 6. plover (golden)
lily .. 9. waterlily
stabber .. 9. jackknife
tree .. 4. Hyla
toadflax ... 8. flaxweed, ranstead
13. butter-and-eggs
toadstool ... 5. morel 6. fungus
8. mushroom, puffball
toady ... 4. ugly 8. parasite, truckler
9. repulsive, sycophant, toadeater
toast ... 3. tan 4. cook, leep 5. bread,
brede, brown, parch, roast, skoal
6. pledge, sippet 7. drink to 8. cinnamon
tobacco (pert to) ...
ash .. 6. dottle (dottel)
Cuban .. 4. capa 6. Vuelta (leaf)
disease .. 6. calico, mosaic 7. walloon
English .. 8. bird's-eye
epithet .. 12. Lady Nicotine
French .. 7. caporal
Greek .. 7. Knaster
hookah smoking .. 7. goracco
Indian .. 7. uppowoc
introduced by .. 7. Raleigh (Sir Walter)
Kentucky .. 9. Burley
kind .. 4. capa, shag 5. tabac 6. Burley,
Vuelta 7. caporal, henbane, Latakia,
perique, Turkish 8. Virginia 9. salvadora
paste .. 7. goracco
Persian .. 6. tumbak (tumbaki)
pipe .. 7. calumet, chibouk (chibouque)
principle (active) .. 8. nicotine
receptacle .. 4. pipe 7. humidor
S American .. 8. canaster
small cut .. 3. cud 4. plug, quid 6. dottle
(dottel) 7. carotte

Turkish .. 7. Latakia
wrapping .. 9. broadleaf
toboggan ... 4. sled 5. coast, glide
7. coaster 12. sharp decline 14. downhill
course
toby ... 3. dog (Punch's), jug, mug, rob
5. cigar 7. highway, pitcher
tocsin ... 5. alarm 9. alarm bell
13. warning signal
toe ... 3. tae, tip 5. digit 6. dactyl, hallux
7. minimus
toehold ... 7. footing 8. foothold,
purchase
toes, odd-numbered ... 13. perissodactyl
toe the line ... 4. obey
together ... 3. com, con, syn 4. mass,
with 5. union 10. conjointly
11. unanimously 12. coincidently,
concurrently, continuously
toggery ... 3. set 4. garb, togs 5. dress
7. clothes, harness 9. trappings
12. haberdashery
tolerable ... 4. so-so 8. bearable, passable
9. endurable 10. acceptable, fairly well,
sufferable 11. supportable
tolerance ... 8. patience 10. indulgence,
permission
tolerant ... 7. lenient, patient 9. indulgent
10. forbearing, permissive
tolerate ... 4. bear, bide 5. abide, allow,
brook, stand 6. endure, permit, suffer
9. put up with
toll ... 3. due, tax 4. call, duty,
peal, ring 5. knell 6. allure, charge,
custom, entice, impost, invite, strike
7. ringing 8. exaction 10. assessment
12. compensation
Tolypeutes ... 4. apar 9. armadillo
tomahawk ... 3. axe 4. kill 6. attack
7. hatchet
tomb ... 4. cist, lair 5. crypt, grave, speos,
vault 6. shrine 7. mastaba (mastabah),
orruary, tritaph 8. catacomb, cenotaph
9. mausoleum, sepulcher
tombé ... 4. drum
tomboy ... 3. meg 4. romp 5. rowdy
6. hoyden (hoiden), tomrig
tomcat ... 3. gib
tomcod ... 8. bocaccio
tome ... 4. book, opus 5. atlas 6. volume
11. papal letter, publication
tomorrow ... 5. later 6. mañana 9. the
morrow
tonant ... 7. blatant 10. thundering
tone ... 4. mode, mood, note, tang,
tune 5. pitch, reedy, sound, trend,
twang, vigor 6. accent, energy, melody,
nuance, timbre 7. cadence 8. modulate,
monotone, tonology 9. harmonize
10. inflection, intonation, modulation
tone (pert to) ...
down .. 3. dim 6. mellow, modify, soften
8. moderate
lacking .. 5. atony 6. atonal
quality, color .. 6. timbre
series .. 5. scale
single .. 8. monotone
succession .. 5. melos
thin .. 7. sfogato
vibrant .. 5. twang
toneless ... 4. weal 5. stony 6. silent

9. colorless
tonga . . . **7.** vehicle (2-wheeled)
Tonga . . . **15.** Friendly Islands
tongue . . . **3.** gab **4.** meat **5.** lingo,
   speak **6.** speech **7.** clapper, lingula
   8. language, lorriker, parlance
   9. utterance
tongue (pert to) . . .
   classical . . **5.** Greek, Latin **6.** Hebrew
   fish . . **4.** sole
   Jesus . . **7.** Aramaic
   lash . . **5.** scold **8.** scolding
   pivoted . . **4.** pawl
   reference to . . **7.** glossal, lingual
   sacred . . **4.** Pali
   shaped . . **9.** lingulate
   tied . . **4.** mute **8.** taciturn
   wagon . . **4.** neap, pole
tongueless . . . **4.** dumb, mute
   10. speechless
tonic . . . **6.** bracer, catnip, liquor **7.** bracing
   8. medicine, remedial, roborant
   9. stimulant **10.** refreshing
   11. corroborant **12.** invigorating
tonsil . . . **8.** amygdala
tonsorialist . . . **6.** barber
tonsured . . . **4.** bald **5.** shorn **6.** shaven
   7. clipped **10.** baldheaded
too . . . **3.** and **4.** also, over, very **6.** overly
   7. besides **8.** likewise **9.** extremely
   11. excessively **12.** additionally
too (pert to) . . .
   bad . . **4.** alas
   much . . **4.** trop **6.** excess **7.** nimiety
   small . . **13.** unappreciable
   soon . . **9.** premature
tool . . . **3.** axe, saw **4.** dupe, file **5.** agent
   6. device, gadget, puppet **7.** engrave,
   gimmick, utensil, utility **9.** appliance
   11. contrivance
tool (type) . . . **2.** ax (axe) **3.** adz (adze),
   awl, bit, hob, hoe, saw, sax, tap **4.** file,
   jack, pick, tong, vise **5.** brush, burin,
   drill, knife, lathe, level, plane, punch,
   razor, spade **6.** chisel, gimlet, hammer,
   lifter, peavey (peavy), pliers, reamer,
   shears, slater, slicer, square, trepan,
   wrench **7.** cleaver, mattock, mattoir,
   scalpel, spatula **11.** screwdriver
tools (pert to) . . .
   category . . **5.** power, speed **7.** cutlery,
   machine, medical **9.** precision **11.** labor-
   saving **12.** straightedge
   prehistoric . . **4.** celt **6.** eolith **9.** paleolith
   stone . . **6.** banner
   theft of . . **6.** ratten
toosh . . . **4.** gown (short), robe
   9. nightgown
toot . . . **3.** pry, spy **4.** fool, gaze, peep
   5. blare, drink, revel, shout, spree
   6. sprout **7.** whistle **8.** carousal,
   eminence, proclaim **9.** blow a horn,
   elevation
tooth . . . **3.** cog **4.** dent, fang, snag,
   tine, tusk **5.** ivory, molar, point,
   prong, taste **6.** canine, cuspid, wisdom
   7. grinder, incisor **8.** bicuspid, eyetooth
   10. projection
tooth, teeth (pert to) . . .
   ache . . **8.** dentagra **9.** dentalgia
   comb form . . **5.** denti, odont **6.** odonto

   7. odontia
   covering . . **6.** enamel
   cutting of . . **8.** teething **9.** dentition
   decay . . **6.** caries, cavity **11.** saprodontia
   destitute of . . **8.** edentate
   irregularity . . **11.** odontoloxia
   molar . . **4.** wang
   ref to . . **6.** dental **7.** odontic
   science . . **10.** odontology
   Scot . . **3.** gam
   socket . . **8.** alveolus
   toothlike . . **8.** odontoid **9.** dentiform
toothless . . . **8.** decrepid, edentate
toothsome . . . **5.** tasty **9.** delicious,
   palatable
top . . . **3.** cap, fid, lid, tip, toy **4.** acme,
   apex, pate, roof **5.** crest, criss,
   crown, excel, mensa, outdo, ridge,
   scalp **6.** finial, summit, vertex, zenith
   7. highest, supreme, surpass, topmost
   8. dominate, pinnacle, teetotum
   9. uppermost
topaz . . . **3.** gem **5.** color **7.** mineral
   11. hummingbird **13.** precious stone
tope . . . **4.** tomb, wren **5.** drink, grove,
   shark, stupa, tower **6.** guzzle, shrine
   7. dogfish
toper . . . **3.** sot **4.** tope **5.** shark **6.** barfly,
   boozer **7.** guzzler, tippler, tosspot
   8. drunkard **9.** alcoholic, inebriate
   12. bacchanalian
tophet, topheth . . . **4.** hell **5.** chaos
   8. darkness
topi, topee . . . **3.** cap, hat **8.** antelope
topiary . . . **6.** garden **9.** gardening
topic . . . **4.** plot, text **5.** theme **6.** reason,
   remedy **7.** subject **8.** argument
   11. application
topical . . . **5.** local **9.** temporary
   10. thematical
topknot . . . **5.** crest, onkos **6.** pigeon
   8. flounder **9.** headdress
topmost . . . **6.** apical **7.** highest, supreme
   8. foremost **9.** uppermost
topnotcher . . . **3.** ace **4.** hero, star
   6. tiptop **7.** supreme **9.** first-rate
   11. unsurpassed
topography . . . **7.** mapping **8.** location
   9. surveying **11.** description **15.** regional
   anatomy
topple . . . **3.** tip **4.** fall, tilt **5.** pitch,
   upset **6.** totter, tumble **8.** overturn
   9. overthrow **10.** somersault
topsail . . . **5.** raffe (raffee)
topsy-turvy . . . **8.** confused **10.** contrarily,
   disordered **11.** withershins
toque . . . **3.** hat **6.** monkey (bonnet)
   9. headdress
tor . . . **4.** crag, peak **5.** mound **8.** pinnacle
torah, tora . . . **3.** law **7.** precept **10.** Law
   of Moses, Pentateuch, revelation
torch . . . **4.** lamp **5.** blaze, flare, fusee
   (fuzee), light **7.** lighter, lucigen
   8. flambeau **10.** flashlight
torero . . . **11.** bullfighter
torment . . . **3.** rib, vex **4.** bait, pain, rack
   5. agony, devil, harry, tease, worry
   6. badger, harass, harrow, hector,
   pester, plague, stir up **7.** afflict, anguish,
   bedevil, torture **8.** distress, vexation
   9. suffering, tantalize **10.** punishment

11. persecution
torn... **4.** rent **5.** riven, split **6.** ripped
7. severed **8.** tattered **9.** alienated,
lacerated (see also *tear)*
tornado... **4.** wind **7.** cyclone, twister
8. blizzard, outburst **9.** hurricane,
whirlwind, windstorm **12.** thunderstorm
toro... **4.** bull **7.** cavalla, cowfish
torpedo... **3.** ray **4.** boat, mine **5.** shoot
6. attack, gunman **7.** explode **8.** fire
upon, firework, numbfish **9.** crampfish,
detonator, submarine
torpid... **4.** dull, numb **5.** inert **6.** stupid
7. dormant **8.** benumbed, inactive,
lifeless, listless, sluggish **9.** apathetic,
lethargic
torpor... **4.** coma **6.** acedia, apathy,
stupor **7.** languor **8.** dormancy,
lethargy **9.** inertness **10.** inactivity
12. sluggishness **13.** insensibility
torque... **5.** chain **6.** collar **7.** torsion
8. necklace, ornament
torrefy... **5.** parch, roast **6.** scorch
torrent... **5.** flood, spate **6.** stream
7. current, roaring **8.** downpour,
outburst
torrential... **12.** overwhelming
torrid... **3.** hot **4.** arid **7.** burning, parched
8. scorched, tropical **10.** oppressive,
passionate
tortilla cooking dish... **5.** comal
tortoise... **4.** emyd, Emys **6.** gopher,
turtle **7.** hicatee **8.** Chelonia, matamata
9. ellachick
tortuous... **6.** spiral **7.** devious, sinuous,
winding **8.** twisting **10.** circuitous,
roundabout **12.** labyrinthine
torture... **4.** flay, pain, rack **5.** agony,
twist **6.** impale, punish, wrench
7. crucify, distort, torment
10. punishment
tory, Tory... **6.** bandit, outlaw, Papist
8. loyalist, marauder, partisan, Royalist
11. reactionary **12.** Conservative
toss... **3.** lob **4.** cast, flip, hurl **5.** bandy,
chuck, fling, flirt, heave, pitch, throw
6. billow, thrash **7.** disturb **8.** flounder,
scramble **9.** commotion **10.** excitement
toss (pert to)...
a coin.. **4.** flip
and turn.. **6.** thrash **8.** flounder
9. vacillate
off.. **5.** drink **6.** tipple **9.** dispose of,
improvise
out.. **5.** eject **8.** trick out
together.. **8.** scramble
tosspot... **3.** sot **5.** drunk, toper **6.** flagon
8. drunkard
tossup... **6.** gamble **10.** even chance
11. uncertainty
tota... **6.** grivet, monkey
total... **3.** add, all, sum, tot **5.** gross,
utter, whole **6.** amount, entire **7.** perfect,
summary **8.** absolute, complete, entirety
9. aggregate
totally... **5.** quite **6.** wholly **8.** entirely
10. completely
totem... **4.** pole, post **6.** fetish, pillar,
symbol
totem pole... **3.** xat
toto... **3.** all **4.** baby **5.** totum

totter... **4.** reel, rock, sway **5.** pitch,
shake, waver **6.** falter, seesaw **7.** stagger
8. titubate **9.** fluctuate, vacillate
toucan... **4.** toco **7.** aracari **8.** hornbill
13. constellation (opp Southern Cross)
touch... **3.** dab, tag, tap, tig **4.** abut,
feel, meet **5.** taste, trait **6.** adjoin,
border **7.** contact **9.** acuteness
touch (pert to)...
acuteness of.. **8.** oxyaphia
bound.. **4.** abut
closely.. **7.** impinge **8.** osculate
examine.. **7.** palpate
light, lightly.. **3.** pat **5.** brush **7.** attinge,
lambent
off.. **4.** fire **6.** incite
ref to.. **7.** tactile, tactual
stone.. **8.** basanite **9.** criterion **11.** Lydian
stone
wood.. **4.** punk **6.** amadou, tinder
touching... **6.** moving **7.** contact, feeling,
tangent **8.** pathetic **9.** affecting, attingent
10. concerning **11.** interesting
touchy... **4.** sore **5.** cross, testy **7.** peevish
8. ticklish **9.** irascible, irritable, sensitive
10. precarious **13.** oversensitive
tough... **4.** hard, wiry **5.** hardy, rowdy,
stiff **6.** robust, sinewy, strong **7.** ruffian
8. adhesive, hardened, leathery,
stubborn **9.** difficult, obstinate, resistant,
tenacious **10.** unyielding
toupee... **3.** wig **6.** peruke **7.** periwig
9. false hair
tour... **4.** trip **5.** shift **6.** travel **7.** circuit,
journey **9.** barnstorm, excursion
tourmaline... **3.** gem **6.** schorl **9.** rubellite
10. indicolite
tournament... **4.** tilt **5.** games, joust, trial
6. battle **7.** contest, regatta, tourney
8. Olympics **9.** encounter **11.** Turnierfest
tourniquet... **6.** binder, garrot
7. bandage
tousle, tousel... **4.** pull, tear **6.** rumple,
tussle **8.** dishevel
tout... **3.** spy **4.** scout, watch **6.** praise
7. canvass, lookout, tipster **8.** give a
tip, informer, smuggler **9.** predictor,
solicitor
tow... **3.** tew, tug **4.** drag, draw, haul,
pull, rope **5.** chain **6.** hawser **8.** cordelle
toward... **2.** ad, at, to **4.** near **5.** anent
6. facing **7.** forward, towards, willing
8. imminent **9.** compliant, headed for
11. approaching
toward (pert to)...
blood vessels.. **5.** hemad (haemad)
center.. **5.** entad **6.** inward
direction.. **7.** leeward, seaward
8. homeward, landward, windward
9. earthward **10.** heavenward
exterior.. **5.** ectad
front.. **8.** anterior
left.. **3.** haw **5.** aport **9.** sinistrad,
sinistral
mouth.. **4.** orad
right.. **7.** dextrad **9.** dextrally
stern.. **3.** aft **5.** abaft **6.** astern
towards... **7.** ynesche
tower... **3.** tor **4.** boom, silo, soar
5. exalt, pylon, spire, stupa **6.** belfry,
height, turret, uplift **7.** bulwark, defense,

elevate, steeple, surpass **8.** domineer, fortress **9.** campanile **10.** stronghold, watchtower
tower (pert to) . . .
astrology . . **7.** mansion **14.** planetary house
bell . . **9.** campanile
chess . . **6.** castle
church . . **5.** spire **6.** belfry, cupola
glacial . . **5.** serac
India . . **5.** minar **7.** sikhara
marker . . **5.** pylon
of . . **4.** Pisa **5.** Babel, Minar **6.** Eiffel, Hunger, London **7.** silence (dakhma) **10.** Kutab Minar
Oriental . . **7.** minaret
watch . . **7.** mirador
towering . . . **4.** high, huge, tall **5.** great, lofty **6.** Alpine **7.** eminent, soaring **11.** overweening
towhee . . . **5.** finch **7.** bunting, chewink
town . . . **4.** burg, deme **6.** ciudad, hamlet, Podunk, suburb **7.** borough, commune, village **8.** boom town, township **9.** ghost town
townsman . . . **3.** cit **7.** citizen, oppidan (Eton student) **8.** resident **9.** selectman
toxic . . . **7.** noxious **8.** poisoned, venomous, virulent **9.** poisonous
toxicology (science of) . . . **7.** poisons **9.** antidotes
toxology . . . **7.** archery
toxophilite . . . **6.** archer
toy . . . **3.** pet, top **4.** doll, hoop, play, whim **5.** dally, fancy, flirt **6.** bauble, gewgaw, hoople, rattle, trifle **7.** cat's paw, trinket **8.** flirting **9.** plaything **10.** knickknack
trace . . . **4.** clew (clue), copy, find, hint, mark, nose, seek, sign **5.** refer, shade, tinge, track, trail **6.** deduce, derive, detect, follow, sketch **7.** glimpse, outline, thought, vestige **8.** evidence, traverse **9.** delineate, footprint **11.** investigate, small amount
trachea . . . **4.** duct **8.** windpipe
tracing . . . **4.** copy **6.** record **8.** ergogram **10.** cardiogram **12.** reproduction
track . . . **3.** rut, way **4.** path, rail, slot, spur, wake **5.** route, spoor, trail, tread **6.** follow, pursue **7.** nereite (worm), vestige **8.** traverse **9.** footprint, spectacle
tract . . . **4.** area, plot, zone **5.** essay, range **6.** estate, region **7.** booklet, country, expanse, leaflet, quarter, stretch **8.** brochure, district, pamphlet, treatise **9.** territory **10.** exposition **11.** subdivision **12.** dissertation
tract (pert to) . . .
arid . . **4.** dene **6.** desert
boggy, swampy . . **6.** morass **10.** Everglades
grassland . . **7.** prairie
lava . . **8.** pedregal
treeless . . **5.** llano **6.** steppe **7.** prairie
tractable . . . **4.** easy **6.** docile, gentle, pliant **7.** ductile **8.** amenable, flexible **9.** adaptable, compliant, malleable **10.** governable **11.** conformable
trade . . . **3.** buy **4.** deal, sell, swap,

wind **5.** craft **6.** barter, merger, metier **7.** bargain, calling, dealing, pursuit, traffic **8.** business, commerce, exchange, practice, purchase, vocation **10.** handicraft, occupation, profession **11.** intercourse
trade-mark, trademark . . . **4.** logo **5.** brand, label **8.** logotype
trader . . . **6.** dealer, monger, sutler **8.** merchant **9.** tradesman **10.** shopkeeper
trading association . . . **5.** hanse (hansa)
trading station (Mil) . . . **2.** PX **4.** fort, post
tradition . . . **4.** lore, myth **5.** usage **6.** custom, legend **7.** culture **8.** folklore **10.** convention (established) **12.** superstition
traditional . . . **3.** old **9.** legendary **10.** historical **12.** conventional, long-standing **15.** long-established
traditional tale . . . **4.** sage **6.** legend
traduce . . . **4.** slur **5.** abuse, belie **6.** debase, defame, malign, vilify **7.** asperse, pervert, slander **8.** disgrace **10.** calumniate
traffic . . . **3.** buy **4.** sell **5.** trade **6.** barter, simony (sacred) **8.** business, carriage, commerce, dealings **11.** familiarity, intercourse
tragedy . . . **6.** misery **8.** calamity, disaster **10.** misfortune
tragic . . . **3.** sad **4.** dire **5.** fatal **8.** dramatic, pathetic **10.** calamitous, disastrous, fatal event
tragopan . . . **8.** pheasant
trail . . . **3.** lag **4.** drag, hunt, path, slot, spur **5.** blaze, piste, route, scent, spoor, trace, track **6.** camino, follow **7.** draggle **8.** be behind, footpath **9.** lag behind
Trail (famed) . . . **6.** Mormon, Oregon **7.** Santa Fe, Spanish **8.** Chisholm, El Camino, Heritage **10.** Lewis-Clark, Wilderness **11.** Appalachian **12.** Natchez Trace, Pacific Crest
trail (pert to) . . .
blazer . . **7.** pioneer
deer . . **4.** slot
mark a . . **5.** blaze
marker . . **5.** cairn
mountain . . **4.** pass
Spanish . . **6.** camino
Trail of Tears people . . . **8.** Cherokee
train . . . **2.** el **4.** line, load, tail **5.** breed, chain, coach, drill, flier, focus, shape, suite **6.** direct, school, series **7.** caravan, cortege, educate, retinue **8.** accustom, instruct, railroad, rehearse **9.** afterpart, entourage, following **10.** attendants, conveyance, discipline, line of cars, procession **11.** progression, streamliner **13.** accommodation
trained mechanic . . . **7.** artisan
trainee . . . **6.** rookie **7.** recruit, student **8.** enrollee
traipse . . . **3.** gad **5.** trail, tramp **6.** trudge, wander **8.** gadabout
trait . . . **5.** habit, touch **6.** streak **7.** feature, quality **9.** lineament, mannerism **11.** peculiarity **13.** individuality **14.** characteristic

traitor . . . **3.** rat **8.** informer, Quisling, turncoat **10.** treasonist **13.** double-crosser, Judas Iscariot **14.** Benedict Arnold

traject . . . **3.** way **4.** sage **5.** ferry, route **6.** course **7.** passage **8.** crossing

trajectory . . . **5.** route **6.** rocket **9.** celestial **10.** fixed orbit

tram . . . **3.** car **4.** limb **5.** wagon **7.** carrier, railway, tramcar, trolley, vehicle **9.** streetcar **10.** conveyance

tramontane . . . **5.** alien **8.** polestar **9.** foreigner, North Star **11.** transalpine

tramp . . . **3.** bum **4.** hike, hobo, hoof, step, walk **5.** jaunt, nomad, tread **6.** beggar, trudge, wander **7.** sponger, traipse, trample, vagrant **8.** vagabond **9.** sundowner **10.** landlouper (landloper), pedestrian **11.** bindle stiff **12.** foot traveler

trample . . . **5.** crush, tread **6.** bruise, subdue **7.** conquer, destroy, run over **9.** press down

trance . . . **4.** coma, doze **5.** dream, spell, swoon **6.** raptus, stupor **7.** amentia, ecstasy, rapture **8.** hypnosis **9.** catalepsy, enrapture, hypnotize, spellbind

tranchant . . . **5.** sharp **7.** cutting **9.** trenchant

tranquil . . . **4.** calm, cool, easy, mild **5.** quiet, still **6.** gentle, placid, serene **7.** pacific, restful **8.** composed, peaceful **9.** quiescent **11.** undisturbed **13.** imperturbable

tranquility . . . **3.** keg **5.** peace, quiet **8.** calmness, serenity **9.** composure **10.** quiescence **12.** peacefulness

tranquilize . . . **4.** calm, lull **5.** allay, quiet, still **6.** pacify, settle, soothe **7.** appease, assuage, compose

transaction . . . **4.** deal, sale **6.** action, affair **7.** bargain **8.** business **9.** discharge, execution **10.** proceeding **11.** negotiation, performance, proposition **16.** buying and selling

transcend . . . **3.** cap **5.** excel, mount **6.** ascend, exceed **7.** surpass **8.** go beyond, outstrip, surmount

transcendent . . . **5.** above **8.** ethereal, heavenly, superior **9.** recondite **10.** superhuman, surpassing **12.** metaphysical, supernatural, transmundane **13.** extraordinary **14.** transcendental **15.** beyond knowledge

transcribe . . . **4.** copy **5.** write **6.** record **9.** reproduce, translate **10.** paraphrase

transcript . . . **4.** copy **6.** record **8.** apograph **9.** duplicate, imitation **12.** reproduction

transfer . . . **4.** cede, deed, pass, sale **5.** grant, shift **6.** assign, attorn, change, convey, depute, remove **7.** removal **8.** alienate, delivery **9.** transport **10.** conveyance, transcript

transfer (pert to) . . .
conveyance (estate) . . **5.** lease **6.** demise
crown to successor . . **6.** demise
design . . **5.** decal **12.** decalcomania
medical . . **10.** transplant

of ownership . . **6.** attorn **10.** abalienate, alienation, conveyance
of property . . **8.** disposal

transfigure . . . **5.** exalt **6.** change **7.** glorify **8.** idealize **9.** irradiate, transform, transmute **12.** metamorphose

transfix . . . **3.** pin **4.** hold **5.** spear **6.** fasten, impale, pierce **9.** hold fixed **11.** transpierce **14.** hold motionless

transform . . . **4.** turn **5.** alter **6.** change, revamp **7.** convert **9.** transmute **10.** assimilate **11.** transfigure **12.** metamorphose, transmogrify **16.** transubstantiate

transformation . . . **3.** wig **6.** change **8.** mutation **10.** conversion, false front **13.** metamorphosis, transmutation **17.** anthropomorphosis

transgress . . . **3.** err, sin **5.** cross **6.** exceed, offend, thwart **7.** disobey, infract, violate **8.** overstep, trespass **9.** break a law

transgression . . . **3.** sin **5.** crime, fault **7.** misdeed, offense **8.** trespass **9.** violation **10.** effrontery, infraction **11.** lawbreaking **12.** infringement **13.** nonconformity

transgressor . . . **6.** sinner **8.** offender **9.** wrongdoer **10.** delinquent, malefactor

transient . . . **5.** brief **6.** lodger **7.** flighty **8.** fleeting, fugitive, traveler **9.** ephemeral, migratory, momentary **10.** evanescent, short-lived, transitory

transit . . . **6.** travel **7.** passage **9.** metabasis **10.** conveyance **12.** transference

transition . . . **5.** shift **7.** passage **9.** anabolism, evolution, metabasis **10.** catabolism (katabolism), conversion, metabolism, modulation **11.** transfusion

transitory . . . **5.** brief, fleet **8.** fleeting, temporal **9.** ephemeral, temporary, transient **10.** evanescent **11.** not enduring

transitory things . . . **8.** ephemera

translate . . . **4.** read, rede **6.** decode, render **7.** convert **8.** construe, transfer **9.** interpret **10.** paraphrase

translation . . . **4.** pony, trot **7.** version **9.** rendition **10.** paraphrase **12.** transference **14.** interpretation **15.** transliteration

translucent . . . **6.** limpid **8.** luminous **11.** transparent **14.** shining through

transmit . . . **4.** send **6.** convey, render **7.** devolve, forward **8.** bequeath, hand down, transfer **11.** communicate

transmutation . . . **9.** evolution

transmute . . . **6.** change **7.** convert, resolve **8.** transform **11.** transfigure **12.** metamorphose **16.** transubstantiate

transparent . . . **4.** open **5.** clear, gauzy, lucid, sheer **6.** bright, candid, glassy, lucent **7.** crystal, pelucid, shining **8.** luminous, lustrous **9.** guileless **10.** diaphanous **11.** crystalline, perspicuous, translucent, unconcealed

transparent thing . . . **4.** mica, silk, veil **5.** beryl, water **6.** quartz, tissue **7.** crystal, diamond **8.** gossamer **9.** isinglass

transport . . . **3.** dak **4.** boat, move, raft, send, ship **5.** bring, carry, truck **6.** banish, convey, deport, vessel **7.** ecstasy, freight, passion, rapture, smuggle **8.** carriage, emigrate, entrance, palander, transfer **9.** enrapture, troopship

transpose . . . **5.** shift **6.** change, convey, invert **7.** convert, reverse **8.** transfer **9.** rearrange, translate, transmute **11.** interchange

transposition of sounds, words . . . **10.** metathesis, spoonerism

Transvaal (pert to) . . .
capital . . **8.** Pretoria
city . . **12.** Johannesburg
daisy . . **7.** gerbera
discovery . . **4.** gold, Rand (The)
famed emigration . . **9.** great trek (1836)
legislature . . **4.** raad
policeman . . **4.** zarp
settlers . . **5.** Boers
War . . **4.** Boer (1899-1902)

transverse . . . **6.** across **7.** oblique, transom **8.** diagonal **9.** crosswise **10.** crosspiece

trap . . . **3.** gin, net, pat, web **4.** cage, door, lure, rock, tipe, tree, weir **5.** catch, creel, mouth, snare **6.** ambush, corner, device, eelpot, enmesh, recess **7.** dragnet, ensnare, pitfall, springe **8.** carriage, deadfall, trapping, trickery **9.** caparison, road block, stratagem

trapper . . . **5.** lurer **6.** hunter, netter, snarer **7.** decoyer

trappings . . . **4.** gear, tack **5.** props **7.** scenery **8.** wardrobe **9.** apparatus, caparison, ornaments **10.** horse cloth **13.** paraphernalia

trash . . . **4.** bosh, dirt, junk **5.** waste **6.** debris, refuse, rubble **7.** rubbish **8.** nonsense, riffraff, trumpery **10.** balderdash

trashy . . . **5.** cheap, toshy **6.** paltry **7.** useless **8.** rubbishy **9.** worthless **11.** nonsensical

trauma . . . **5.** shock, wound **6.** injury

travail . . . **4.** pain, toil **5.** agony, labor **7.** journey, trouble **9.** suffering **11.** parturition

trave . . . **9.** crossbeam

travel . . . **2.** go **4.** fare, move, mush, post, ride, taxi, tour, trek, wend **5.** coast **6.** motion **7.** commute, journey, migrate, sojourn **8.** progress, traverse **9.** gallivant **11.** peregrinate

travel (pert to) . . .
equipment . . **7.** baggage **9.** viaticals
expense . . **8.** viaticum
group . . **7.** caravan
over obstacles . . **9.** roughshod
pert to . . **6.** viatic
place to place . . **9.** itinerate

traveler, travelers . . . **5.** farer **6.** viator **7.** caravan, tourist **8.** salesman, wayfarer **9.** journeyer

travels . . . **7.** odyssey **8.** journeys **14.** peregrinations

traverse . . . **4.** deny, pass **5.** cross **6.** refute, thwart **7.** athwart, oblique, parados **8.** navigate **10.** counteract

travesty . . . **5.** drama **6.** parody, satire **7.** lampoon **8.** disguise **9.** burlesque **10.** caricature **11.** incongruity

tray . . . **6.** salver, server **7.** ashtray, coaster

treacherous . . . **5.** false, Judas, punic, snaky **8.** disloyal, plotting, unstable **9.** deceitful, faithless, insidious **10.** perfidious, traitorous, unreliable **11.** disaffected **13.** Machiavellian (Machiavelian), untrustworthy

treachery . . . **5.** guile **6.** deceit **7.** perfidy, treason **8.** betrayal **10.** disloyalty

treacle . . . **4.** cure **6.** remedy **7.** claggum, sweeten **8.** molasses **10.** sweetening

treacle water . . . **7.** cordial

tread . . . **3.** rut **4.** gait, mark, pace, step, volt, walk **5.** crush, stair **6.** course **7.** conquer, set foot, trample **8.** footstep, shoe sole **9.** footprint

treadle . . . **5.** lever, pedal **7.** chalaza

tread underfoot . . . **5.** crush **6.** subdue **7.** oppress, run over **8.** domineer **9.** tyrannize

treason . . . **7.** perfidy **8.** betrayal, sedition **9.** treachery

treasonable, treasonous . . . **10.** perfidious, traitorous **11.** treacherous

treasure . . . **4.** fisc (fisk), fund, roon **5.** cache, chest, hoard, prize, purse, store, trove, value **6.** coffer, fiscus, riches, wealth **7.** cherish **8.** hold dear **9.** exchequer, thesaurus **10.** appreciate, depository, repository, storehouse

treasurer . . . **6.** bursar, purser **7.** cashier, curator, officer **8.** receiver **9.** paymaster **11.** chamberlain

Treasure State . . . **7.** Montana

treasure-trove . . . **5.** money (hidden) **7.** bullion **9.** discovery **14.** buried treasure

treat . . . **4.** dose **5.** Dutch, feast **6.** doctor, handle, regale, repast **7.** delight, discuss, process **8.** consider **9.** discourse, entertain, negotiate **10.** manipulate

treat (pert to) . . .
improperly . . **4.** snub **5.** flout, spite **6.** insult, misuse, offend **9.** humiliate
maliciously . . **5.** frame, spite
of morals . . **6.** ethics
royally . . **6.** regale **9.** with honor
silk (for rustle) . . **6.** scroop
snobbishly . . **7.** high hat, high-hat
surgically . . **7.** operate
tenderly . . **6.** coddle, pamper
with contempt . . **5.** flout, scorn, scout, spurn **7.** contemn
with deference . . **7.** respect

treatise . . . **5.** essay, study, tract **6.** thesis **7.** article **9.** discourse **10.** discussion **12.** dissertation

treatise on . . .
forests . . **5.** silva
fruit trees . . **6.** pomona
language . . **7.** grammar
pines . . **7.** pinetum

treatment (pert to) . . .
application (Med) . . **5.** stupe
compassionate . . **5.** mercy
harsh . . **5.** abuse **8.** misusage, severity

ill.. **5.** abuse
preparatory.. **8.** training **10.** ground
work, processing
term.. **5.** usage **8.** addition (to soil),
handling
treaty... **4.** mise, pact **6.** cartel
7. compact, entente **8.** contract
9. agreement **10.** convention
11. arrangement, negotiation
12. capitulation **13.** understanding
treaty (pert to)...
bound nations.. **6.** allies
Elm.. **12.** Philadelphia (1682)
first draft.. **8.** protocol
peace.. **5.** truce **6.** Pax Dei **9.** armistice
10. pax in bella
secret.. **13.** the Engagement (1647)
treble... **5.** three, voice **6.** latten, triple
7. soprano **9.** threefold **11.** high-pitched
treble clef... **3.** Gee **5.** G clef, staff (G
clef)
tree... **5.** plant **6.** corner, timber
7. gallows **9.** genealogy
tree (pert to)... see also *trees*
antidote for snakebite.. **6.** cedron
aromatic.. **9.** sassafras
bear.. **7.** raccoon
cactus.. **7.** saguaro
camphor.. **5.** kapur
cat.. **9.** palm civet
cobra.. **6.** mambra
cone-bearing.. **3.** fir, yew **5.** alder,
cedar, larch **7.** conifer
dwarf.. **6.** bonsai
evergreen fruit.. **5.** lemon **6.** orange
exudation.. **3.** gum, lac, sap
India.. **4.** dita **10.** devil's tree
lotus.. **4.** sadr
mineral (formed on).. **8.** dendrite
of Buddha.. **2.** bo
of chastity.. **11.** agnus castus
of life.. **10.** arbor vitae
of strength.. **3.** oak
rain.. **5.** saman (zaman) **8.** genisaro
resin.. **3.** fir **4.** pine **6.** balsam
sacred (Bib).. **7.** asherah
salt.. **4.** atle (atlee) **8.** tamarisk
snake.. **4.** gimp, lora
sprout.. **5.** copse, sprig **7.** coppice
sugar.. **5.** maple
Texas.. **5.** alamo **6.** poplar
tiger.. **7.** leopard
toad.. **4.** hyla
trunk.. **4.** bole **5.** caber, stock
umbrella.. **5.** wahoo
victor's crown.. **6.** laurel
worshiper.. **5.** dryad, nymph (wood)
trees (pert to)...
grove.. **5.** copse
plantation.. **6.** forest **7.** orchard, pinetum
poem.. **6.** Kilmer (Joyce)
ref to.. **8.** arboreal **9.** cacuminal
science.. **7.** silvics **12.** silviculture
service (rowan).. **5.** sorbs
trefoil... **6.** clover **8.** shamrock **10.** black
medic, clover leaf (Her)
tregetour (anc)... **7.** juggler **8.** magician
trek... **6.** travel **7.** journey, migrate
10. expedition
trellis... **5.** arbor **7.** lattice, pergola
8. espalier **11.** latticework

tremble... **5.** quake, shake **6.** doddle,
falter, quaver, quiver, shiver, tatter,
thrill, tremor **7.** shudder, tremolo,
twitter, vibrate **8.** be afraid **9.** be
excited, trepidate
trembling... **5.** aspen **6.** dither, trepid
7. fearful, nervous, quaking, quavery,
shaking **9.** vibrating
tremendous... **3.** big **4.** huge **5.** awful,
giant, great **6.** superb **8.** horrible,
powerful, terrific **9.** frightful,
momentous, monstrous **10.** terrifying
13. extraordinary
tremolo... **6.** quaver **10.** fluttering
tremor... **5.** palsy, quake, shake **6.** quiver,
thrill **7.** tremble **9.** vibration
tremulous... **5.** aspen, quaky, timid
7. excited, fearful, nervous, palsied,
shaking, shivery **9.** quavering, sensitive,
trembling, vibratory **11.** palpitating
trench... **3.** gaw **4.** bury, gash, leat,
moat **5.** canal, carve, ditch, drain, fosse
6. furrow, groove, gutter **7.** acequia,
intrude **8.** aqueduct, encroach, entrench,
infringe, trespass **10.** excavation
12. entrenchment
trenchant... **4.** keen **5.** acute, sharp
6. biting **7.** cutting **8.** clear-cut, incisive
11. penetrating
trencherman... **5.** eater **7.** sponger
8. gourmand **9.** chowhound
11. gormandizer
trend... **4.** tone, turn, vein **5.** drift, skirt,
swing, tenor **6.** strike **7.** deviate, revolve
8. movement, tendency **9.** direction
11. inclination
trepan... **3.** saw **4.** lure, tool **5.** snare,
trick **6.** entrap **7.** deceive, swindle
8. deceiver, trephine **9.** stratagem,
trickster
trepang... **10.** bêche-de-mer **11.** sea
cucumber **14.** sea caterpillar
trepid... **7.** quaking **8.** timorous
9. trembling
trepidation... **4.** fear **5.** alarm **6.** dismay
7. quaking **9.** agitation, confusion
10. excitement **11.** disturbance,
oscillation **12.** perturbation
13. consternation
trespass... **3.** sin **4.** tort **5.** poach
6. breach, invade, trench **7.** intrude,
offense **8.** encroach, entrench, infringe,
overstep **10.** infraction, transgress
11. misfeasance **12.** infringement
13. transgression
tress... **4.** curl, hair **5.** braid, plait
7. ringlet **10.** lock of hair
tressure... **4.** band **6.** border, fillet,
ribbon **9.** headdress
trestle... **5.** bench **7.** support, viaduct
tret... **9.** allowance
triad... **5.** chord, three, trine **7.** trinary,
trinity **9.** trivalent **12.** ternary group
trial... **2.** go **4.** bout, case, test
5. venue **6.** assize, ordeal **7.** attempt,
contest, empiric **8.** evidence, hardship
9. prolusion, trying out **10.** experiment
11. examination, tribulation
triangle... **6.** trigon **8.** virginal
13. constellation
triangle (pert to)...

connection .. **5.** delta
draw circle within .. **7.** escribe
military .. **10.** punishment
music instrument .. **10.** percussion,
triquetrum (anc)
side .. **3.** leg
three acute angles .. **6.** oxygon
two equal sides .. **9.** isosceles
unequal sides .. **7.** scalene
triangular (pert to) ...
decoration .. **8.** pediment, triqueta
muscle .. **7.** deltoid
pert to .. **10.** trilateral
piece .. **4.** gore **5.** miter, wedge **6.** gusset
sail .. **6.** lateen **9.** spinnaker
shaped .. **7.** deltoid **8.** oxygonal
tribal custom ... **7.** couvade (childbirth)
tribal symbol ... **5.** totem **9.** totem pole
tribe ... **4.** clan, kind, race, sept
5. class, group **6.** family **7.** company
11. aggregation **14.** classification
tribe (pert to) ...
birds .. **5.** flock
head of .. **5.** chief **6.** sachem **9.** patriarch
Israel .. **3.** Dan **4.** Levi **6.** Reuben
migrated .. **5.** Aryan
New Zealand .. **3.** ati
of Ben .. **5.** poets (Ben Jonson)
Tribes, Five Civilized ... **5.** Creek
7. Choctaw **8.** Cherokee, Seminole
9. Chickasaw
Tribes, Five Nations (Iroquois) ...
6. Cayuga, Mohawk, Oneida, Seneca
8. Onondaga
tribulation ... **5.** trial **6.** ordeal, sorrow
8. distress **9.** suffering
tribunal ... **3.** bar **4.** banc, seat **5.** bench,
court, curia, forum **9.** Areopagus (anc)
tributary ... **4.** fork, vein **6.** branch, feeder
8. affluent, effluent, influent **9.** auxiliary
11. subordinate **12.** contributary
tribute ... **3.** fee, pay, tax **4.** cain, duty,
levy, scat **5.** allow, grant **6.** assign,
bestow, homage, impost, praise,
rental **7.** chevage (Hist), ovation,
payment, pension, respect **8.** encomium
9. attribute, gratitude **10.** allegiance,
contribute, obligation **11.** retribution
tricar ... **8.** tricycle **10.** motorcycle (with
extra car)
trice ... **5.** jiffy **6.** moment **7.** instant
9. twinkling
trick ... **3.** fob, gag **4.** dido, dupe, feat,
flam, gull, jest, ruse, wile **5.** cheat,
child, dodge, fraud, guile, knack, prank,
shift, stunt **6.** deceit, delude **7.** deceive,
defraud, finesse, pretext **8.** artifice,
delusion, flimflam, illusion **9.** chicanery,
deception, imposture **10.** subterfuge
11. contrivance, legerdemain
trickery ... **5.** fraud, hocus **6.** deceit
7. roguery **8.** artifice, cheating, trumpery
9. chicanery, deception, duplicity
10. hanky-panky **11.** amenability,
legerdemain
trickle ... **4.** drip, drop, flow, leak **7.** distill
(distil), dribble, dripple, leakage
tricks ... **4.** shab **5.** ruses **7.** roguery
10. deceptions
trickster ... **3.** fox **5.** cheat, rogue **6.** rascal
7. slicker **8.** deceiver **12.** Artful Dodger

tricky ... **3.** sly **5.** snide **6.** artful, clever,
crafty, shrewd **7.** cunning, devious
8. rascally **9.** deceitful **13.** Machiavellian
trident ... **5.** curve, spear **6.** symbol
7. leister
tried ... **4.** true **6.** proved, tested
7. devoted **8.** faithful, reliable
11. trustworthy
tries ... **5.** tests **6.** assays **8.** attempts,
contests
trifle ... **3.** ace, bit, fig, toy **4.** doit,
fico, fool, jest **5.** dally, fable, straw
6. bauble, dabble, dawdle, doodle,
fiddle, gewgaw, palter, pewter, potter,
wanton **7.** dessert, nothing, traneen
8. flimflam, gimcrack, make love
9. bagatelle **10.** knickknack, peccadillo,
triviality **11.** small amount **12.** treat
lightly
trifler ... **7.** dallier, flaneur **8.** palterer,
putterer **10.** dilettante
trifles ... **4.** toys **6.** trivia **7.** gewgaws,
palters **8.** minutiae, trumpery
trifling ... **4.** idle, mere **5.** inane,
petty **6.** little **7.** trivial **8.** badinage,
frippery **9.** nugacious **10.** immaterial
13. insignificant
trifolium ... **6.** clover **8.** shamrock
trig ... **4.** chic, neat, prim, tidy, trim
5. natty, smart **6.** lively, spruce
7. precise **10.** methodical
trigo ... **5.** wheat
trigon ... **4.** game, harp, lyre (anc)
8. triangle
trigonometry term ... **4.** sine **6.** cosine,
secant **7.** tangent **8.** spherics
10. goniometry
trihoral ... **11.** three-hourly **15.** every
three hours
trill ... **4.** move, sing **5.** shake, twirl
6. quaver, ripple, warble **7.** mordent,
tremolo, trickle, vibrate **8.** grupetto
12. pralltriller
trillion ... **5.** trega (comb form) **14.** million
million
trim ... **3.** bob, cut, lop **4.** chic,
clip, crop, neat, perk, snod, tidy,
trig, whip **5.** adorn, natty, nifty,
panel, preen, prune, shear, shrag
6. border, dapper, defeat, punish,
reduce **7.** compact, orderly **8.** decorate,
ornament **9.** embellish, shipshape
10. decoration
trimming ... **4.** gimp, lace **5.** braid,
jabot, ruche **6.** edging, frieze, fringe,
piping **7.** falbala, ruching **8.** furbelow,
ornament **9.** chicanery, garniture
10. decoration **11.** accessories
13. passementerie
trinity ... **5.** three, triad **6.** triune
Trinity (Eccl) ... **7.** Godhead (Father,
Son, Holy Ghost) **8.** Trimurti
trinket ... **3.** toy **4.** gaud, tali (tahli)
5. bauble, jewel **6.** bangle, gewgaw,
trifle **7.** bibelot **8.** gimcrack, ornament
10. knickknack
trip ... **3.** err, run **4.** halt, skip, slip,
trap **5.** caper, dance, jaunt, speed
6. bungle, cruise, errand, flight, frolic,
voyage **7.** journey, misstep, stumble
8. obstruct **9.** excursion **10.** expedition

triple ... **3.** tri **5.** trine **6.** tercet, treble
  9. intensify, threefold **12.** three-base
  hit
triple crown ... **5.** tiara (Pope's)
triplet (one of) ... **4.** trin
tripletail ... **4.** fish, sama **9.** berrugate,
  spadefish
tripod ... **3.** cat (6-legged) **5.** easel, stand,
  three **6.** trivet
Tripoli, Libya ...
  capital of .. **12.** Tripolitania
  caravan route to .. **5.** Wadai **8.** Lake
  Chad, Timbuktu
  famed arch to .. **14.** Marcus Aurelius
  people .. **4.** Arab, Turk **6.** Berber
  ruler .. **3.** bey, dey
triptych ... **5.** volet (part) **10.** altarpiece,
  writing pad **13.** writing tablet (3-part)
trismus ... **7.** lockjaw, tetanus
  16. gnashing the teeth
trist ... see *tryst*
Tristan and Isoide ... **5.** opera (Wagner)
triste ... **3.** sad **4.** full **6.** dismal
  10. depressing
tristful ... **3.** sad **10.** melancholy
tristich group ... **10.** three lines **11.** three
  verses (stanza)
Tristram & Iseult ... **4.** poem (Arnold)
trite ... **5.** banal, corny, petty, stale,
  vapid **6.** betide, cliché, common,
  jejune **7.** bromide **9.** hackneyed, well-
  known **10.** threadbare, unoriginal
  11. commonplace, stereotyped
  13. platitudinous
triton ... **3.** eft **4.** newt **5.** shell, snail
  10. salamander
Triton (pert to) ...
  art figure .. **7.** demigod
  Gr Myth .. **10.** sea demigod
  symbol .. **7.** trumpet
triumph ... **3.** win **5.** exult, glory
  6. defeat **8.** ceremony (anc), conquest
  10. exultation **11.** achievement
trivia ... **5.** trash **7.** trifles **8.** trumpery
trivial ... **5.** banal, petty, small, trite
  6. common, paltry, slight **7.** nominal,
  piperly, shallow **8.** doggerel, ordinary,
  trifling **9.** frivolous, nugacious
  11. commonplace, unimportant
  13. insignificant
triviality ... **3.** toy **6.** bauble, gewgaw,
  trifle **8.** falderal, nugacity **9.** bagatelle,
  frivolity **10.** knickknack **14.** insignificance
troche ... **4.** pill **6.** button, rotula, tablet
  7. lozenge **8.** pastille (pastil) **9.** cough
  drop **10.** deer's tines
trochee ... **4.** foot (2-syllable) **5.** meter
  7. choreus
trod ... see *tread*
trogger ... **7.** peddler, vagrant
trogon ... **7.** quetzal
Troilus (pert to) ...
  butterfly genus .. **7.** Papilio
  legendary hero of .. **7.** Chaucer
  son of .. **5.** Priam
Trojan (pert to) ...
  astronomy .. **9.** asteroids
  epic .. **5.** Iliad **6.** Aeneid **7.** Odyssey
  expedition hero .. **4.** Ajax **8.** Achilles
  founder of .. **4.** Troy
  hero .. **5.** Paris **6.** Aeneas, Hector

  9. Palamedes
  horse .. **6.** wooden
  horse builder .. **5.** Epeus
  king .. **5.** Priam
  native .. **6.** Dardan
  soothsayer .. **7.** Helenus
  war cause .. **5.** Helen (of Troy)
  war leader .. **9.** Agamemnon
  warrior .. **6.** Agenor
troll (Myth) ... **5.** dwarf, giant, gnome
troll ... **4.** bowl, fish, roll, sing **5.** angle
  (fishing), rondo **6.** allure, entice, propel
  7. revolve, trundle **9.** circulate
trolley ... **4.** cart, tram **5.** truck **6.** barrow,
  sledge **7.** tramcar **8.** handcart
  9. streetcar
trolley, off his ... **4.** nuts **5.** balmy, batty,
  daffy, dippy, dotty, goofy **6.** cuckoo
trollop ... **5.** slump **6.** slouch **8.** slattern
trombone (pert to) ...
  ancient .. **7.** sackbut, sambuke
  instrument .. **5.** brass
  mouthpiece .. **5.** bocal
  popular size .. **5.** tenor
troop ... **4.** army, band, unit **5.** crowd
  7. company, march on, ressala
  8. quantity, soldiers **9.** go forward
  10. armed force
troop (pert to) ...
  arrangement .. **7.** echelon
  encampment .. **5.** étape
  formation .. **4.** line
  one of .. **7.** peltast **8.** chasseur
  ship .. **9.** transport
troops (pert to) ...
  assemble .. **6.** muster
  German .. **6.** Panzer
  hidden .. **6.** ambush
  Hungary .. **7.** Hussars
  mounted .. **7.** cavalry
  sally .. **6.** sortie
  term for .. **4.** army **5.** squad **6.** forces
  7. battery, militia, phalanx
  9. commandos **11.** armed forces
trophy ... **3.** cup **4.** palm **5.** award,
  medal, Oscar, prize **6.** reward **7.** laurels,
  memento **8.** memorial
tropical (pert to) ...
  animal .. **4.** eyra **5.** araba, coati, potto
  6. agouti **7.** peccary
  bird .. **3.** ani **4.** tody **5.** jalap **6.** motmot
  7. jacamar
  dolphin .. **4.** inia
  fish .. **4.** toro **6.** remora, salema
  fruit .. **3.** fig **4.** date **5.** guava, mango,
  papaw **6.** banana, papaya
  lizard .. **5.** agama
  rodent .. **6.** agouti
  tree .. **4.** coco, palm **5.** balsa, seron
  6. sapota **8.** tamarind
  vine .. **7.** cowhage, lantana **14.** trumpet
  creeper
trot ... **3.** jog, run **4.** gait, pony **5.** hurry
  7. routine **11.** translation
trotting horse ... **6.** Morgan **7.** Hackney
  12. Hambletonian
trottoir (rare) ... **8.** footpath, pavement,
  sidewalk
troubadour ... **4.** bard, poet **8.** jongleur,
  minstrel, musician **9.** trovatore
trouble ... **3.** ado, ail, irk **4.** fuss, harm,

stir **5.** annoy, grief, worry **6.** bother, effort, grieve, harass, pester, plague, sorrow **7.** agitate, anxiety, concern, disturb, perturb, torment **8.** calamity, disorder, disquiet, distress, mischief **9.** adversity, annoyance, commotion **10.** affliction, difficulty, misfortune **11.** disturbance **13.** inconvenience, interfere with

troubled . . . **6.** queasy **7.** annoyed, anxious **8.** agitated **9.** disturbed **10.** distressed

troublemaker . . . **8.** agitator, gossiper **13.** mischief-maker

troublesome . . . **5.** pesky **8.** annoying, perverse **9.** difficult, laborious, turbulent, vexatious, wearisome **10.** bothersome, burdensome, disturbing, oppressing **11.** distressing **12.** inconvenient

trough . . . **3.** bin **4.** bosh, bowl, dale, tank **5.** basin, chute, drain, toper **6.** coffin, gutter, manger, sluice, trench **7.** channel, conduit

trounce . . . **4.** beat, flog **5.** scald **6.** indict, punish, thrash **7.** censure, journey

trout . . . **4.** char, peal **7.** oquassa **9.** namaycush **11.** Dolly Varden

trout (pert to) . . .
genus . . **5.** Salmo **6.** Trutta
lake . . **9.** namaycush
Maine . . **7.** oquassa
parasite (external) . . **3.** sug
ref to . . **11.** truttaceous
type . . **3.** sea **4.** rock **5.** brook, brown, river **7.** oquassa, rainbow **8.** speckled **9.** cutthroat

trovatore . . . **10.** troubadour

trove . . . **4.** find **8.** treasure (buried) **9.** discovery **10.** thing found **13.** treasure-trove

trow . . . **4.** boat, hope **5.** barge, think, trust **6.** expect **7.** believe, suppose **9.** catamaran

trowing . . . **5.** creed **6.** belief **7.** opinion

Troy, or Ilium . . .
capital of . . **5.** Troad (anc)
defender . . **6.** Aeneas
famed for . . **5.** ruins
founder (Myth) . . **4.** Ilus (son of Tros), Tros
king . . **5.** Priam **9.** Agamemnon
king's wife . . **5.** Helen
mountain . . **3.** Ida
name, present . . **9.** Hissarlik
pert to . . **5.** Iliac **6.** Trojan
site . . **9.** Asia Minor

troy weight . . . **5.** grain, ounce, pound **11.** pennyweight

truant . . . **4.** idle **7.** shirker, trivant, vagrant **8.** absentee

truant, to play . . . **5.** miche

truce . . . **5.** pause, peace, trêve **9.** armistice, cessation **10.** brief quiet **12.** intermission

truck . . . **3.** van **4.** deal, dray, haul **5.** bogie, dance, lorry, trade **6.** barter, peddle **7.** flatcar, traffic **8.** commerce, exchange, nonsense **9.** groceries

truckle . . . **4.** fawn **5.** toady **6.** cringe, submit **7.** knuckle

truculent . . . **4.** base, mean **5.** cruel **6.** fierce, savage **8.** ruthless, scathing **9.** barbarous, ferocious **11.** destructive

trudge . . . **4.** pace, plod, slog, walk **5.** tramp **6.** go slow **7.** traipse

true . . . **2.** so **4.** fact, leal, pure, real **6.** gospel, honest, lawful **7.** certain, devoted, germane, precise, sincere, upright **8.** faithful, orthodox, reliable, straight, unerring **9.** authentic, steadfast, veracious, veritable **10.** legitimate **11.** trustworthy, unfaltering

true (pert to) . . .
blue . . **5.** loyal **8.** faithful, orthodox **10.** man of honor
copy . . **7.** estreat
not . . **5.** false **10.** figurative
poetic . . **4.** leal
skin . . **4.** derm (suff) **5.** derma
to fact . . **7.** literal
to life . . **8.** lifelike **11.** descriptive

truffle . . . **5.** fungi, tuber **8.** earthnut **10.** ascus fruit

truism . . . **5.** axiom, truth **9.** platitude **11.** commonplace

trull . . . **4.** girl, lass **5.** demon, fiend, giant, wench **7.** trollop **8.** strumpet

truly . . . **3.** yea **4.** amen **5.** sooth **6.** indeed, justly, verily **7.** exactly, rightly **8.** properly **9.** certainly **10.** accurately, positively, truthfully

trump . . . **3.** pam **4.** card, ruff (cards), suit **7.** surpass **10.** good fellow **12.** masterstroke

trumpery . . . **5.** fraud, trash **6.** deceit **7.** rubbish **8.** nonsense

trumpet . . . **4.** horn **5.** blare **6.** summon **7.** clarion **8.** proclaim **9.** organ stop **12.** elephant's cry **14.** wind instrument

trumpet (pert to) . . .
blare . . **7.** fanfare, tantara
call (stage) . . **6.** sennet
creeper . . **6.** tecoma
fish . . **7.** bellows **10.** flutemouth
lily . . **5.** calla **7.** Bermuda

trumpeter . . . **4.** bird, fish, swan **5.** agami, perch **6.** pigeon **7.** whiting **8.** musician **9.** messenger

truncheon . . . **4.** club **5.** baton, staff **6.** cudgel **8.** splinter

trunk . . . **3.** box, log **4.** body, bole, pool, soma, tank **5.** chest, stalk, torso **6.** coffer **7.** railway **8.** main stem **9.** proboscis **10.** lobster pot

trunkfish . . . **4.** toro **7.** cowfish

truss . . . **3.** tie **4.** bind, gird, pack **6.** bundle, fasten **7.** support **10.** strengthen

trust . . . **4.** hope, rely, task **5.** faith **6.** belief, commit, credit, dartle, depend, estate **7.** believe, confide, consign, custody, entrust, loyalty **8.** credence, reliance, security **9.** assurance, syndicate **10.** confidence, dependence, give credit, investment **12.** organization

trustee . . . **6.** bailee **7.** sindico **9.** fiduciary, treasurer **10.** depository **13.** administrator

trustful . . . **5.** liege **7.** reliant **8.** trusting **9.** confiding, credulous **13.** unquestioning

trustworthiness... **9**. axiopisty **12**. trustability **13**. dependability
trustworthy... **4**. safe **5**. solid **6**. honest **7**. certain **8**. reliable **9**. authentic **10**. dependable
trusty... **7**. convict **8**. faithful, prisoner **10**. dependable **11**. trustworthy
truth... **3**. tao **4**. fact, real **5**. sooth (anc) **6**. verity **7**. honesty, reality **8**. fidelity, veracity **9**. constancy, exactness, orthodoxy, sincerity **11**. correctness **14**. verisimilitude
truth (pert to)...
ancient term.. **5**. sooth **6**. certes
Chinese Philos.. **3**. tao
goddess.. **4**. Maat
personified.. **3**. Una **4**. Maat
ref to.. **6**. verily **11**. verisimilar **14**. verisimilitude
self-evident.. **5**. axiom **6**. truism
truthful... **6**. honest **7**. veridic **9**. veracious, veridical
truthfulness... **5**. truth **7**. honesty **8**. accuracy, veracity **13**. veraciousness
try... **2**. do **3**. say **4**. test **5**. annoy, assay, ettle, prove, taste, trial **6**. purify, refine, render, sample, strive **7**. attempt, contest, torment **8**. audition, endeavor, irritate **9**. prosecute, undertake **10**. experiment **11**. demonstrate, investigate
trying... **7**. irksome, painful, tasting **8**. annoying, sampling **10**. attempting **12**. exasperating **13**. experimenting
tryst... **6**. invite, market **7**. beguile, meeting **9**. agreement, betrothal **10**. engagement, rendezvous **11**. appointment **12**. meeting place
tsamba... **5**. flour **6**. barley
tsar... **4**. czar, tzar **6**. despot **8**. autocrat
tsetse, tsetse fly... **4**. kivu **8**. Glossina, parasite
tsetse fly disease... **6**. nagana **16**. sleeping sickness
T-shaped... **3**. tau
tsine... **6**. wild ox **7**. banteng
tsunami... **4**. wave (tidal)
tuatara, tuatera... **7**. reptile (iguanalike)
tub... **3**. hod, keg, kid, soe, tun, vat **4**. cask, ship, wash **5**. barge, bathe, bowie, keeve **6**. barrel, firkin, piggin, vessel **7**. bathtub, cistern, washtub **9**. container, fat person
tuba... **6**. liquor (palm) **7**. helicon, trumpet (anc) **9**. bombardon **10**. contrabass **11**. bass saxhorn **12**. mythical tree
Tubal-cain's father... **6**. Lamech
Tubal's father... **7**. Japheth
tube... **3**. cop **4**. bulb, duct, hose, pipe **5**. auget, chute, diode **6**. siphon, tunnel **7**. burette, cannula, conduit, fistula, matrass, railway, salpinx **8**. cylinder, electron, stenosis **9**. spaghetti, telescope
tuber... **3**. oca, yam **4**. beet, bulb, eddo, root, taro **5**. jalap, salep **6**. potato **12**. protuberance
tubular... **4**. pipy **5**. round **6**. tubate **8**. cannular, fistular, tubiform **11**. cylindrical

tuck... **3**. eat, nip **4**. cram, fold, poke **5**. feast, pinch, pleat, press **7**. shorten, tighten **9**. appendage
tucker... **3**. bib **4**. food, meal **5**. board **6**. ration
Tuesday (pert to)...
French.. **5**. Mardi
Norse god.. **3**. Tyr (Tiu)
Shrove.. **9**. Mardi gras
Teutonic.. **10**. Martis dies
tufa... **4**. rock, toph, tuff **5**. trass
tuft... **4**. coma, doss, hair **5**. beard, bunch, clump, crest **6**. button, goatee, pompon, tassel **7**. cluster, fetlock **8**. aigrette, feathers
tug... **3**. tow **4**. drag, draw, haul, pull, toil **5**. labor **6**. drudge, effort, strain, tussle **7**. contend, contest, wrestle **8**. struggle
tulip (pert to)...
center (World).. **7**. Holland
color.. **6**. auburn **9**. tulipwood
genus.. **6**. Tulipa
Mexican.. **6**. orchid
military slang.. **9**. explosive
tree.. **6**. timber **7**. majagua, waratah
type.. **6**. Darwin, parrot **7**. breeder, cottage
tumble... **4**. fall, flop, trip, veer **5**. pitch, spill **6**. jumble, rumple, topple, tousle, wallow **7**. stumble **8**. collapse, disorder, flounder, roll over **9**. break down, confusing **10**. handspring, somersault **11**. precipitate
tumbler... **3**. dog **4**. cart, drum **5**. glass **6**. Dunker, pigeon, vessel **7**. acrobat, gymnast, tippler, tumbrel **8**. lock part **13**. contortionist
tumbleweed... **6**. indigo **7**. bugseed, pigweed, thistle **10**. amaranthus
tumbrel, tumbril... **4**. cart **5**. wagon **8**. dumpcart **12**. cucking stool (Hist)
tumescent, tumid... **6**. turgid **7**. bloated, bulging, pompous **8**. inflated **9**. bombastic, disturbed, plethoric **11**. protuberant
tumor... **3**. wen **4**. cyst, wart **6**. cancer, goiter, growth, lipoma, struma **7**. adenoma, sarcoma **8**. ganglion, swelling **11**. excrescence **12**. protuberance
tumor, eyelid... **9**. pladaroma
tumult... **3**. din, mob **4**. fray, riot **5**. Babel, brawl, noise **6**. affray, babble, bustle, émeute, hubbub, uproar **7**. bluster, ferment, turmoil **8**. disorder, outbreak, uprising **9**. agitation, commotion, confusion **10**. excitement, turbulence **11**. disturbance
tumultuous... **4**. wild **5**. noisy, rough **7**. lawless, riotous, violent **8**. agitated, confused **9**. disturbed, turbulent **10**. boisterous, disorderly, hurly-burly
tumulus... **5**. mound, stump **6**. barrow **7**. hillock
tun... **3**. cup (anc), jar, tub, vat **4**. cask, year (Mayan, 360-day) **5**. drink **6**. guzzle, vessel **7**. measure
tuna... **5**. tunny **8**. albacore
tune... **3**. air, key **4**. aria, lilt, port, song **5**. pitch **6**. adjust, melody **7**. chorale,

harmony, sonance **9.** harmonize
10. adjustment, intonation
tune (pert to) . . .
correctly . . **3.** key
down . . **6.** reduce, soften **8.** moderate
musical instrument . . **6.** string
out of . . **9.** dissonant **11.** inaccordant
12. unconforming
tungsten . . . **7.** wolfram
Tunisia . . .
cape . . **3.** Bon
capital . . **5.** Tunis
famed ruins . . **8.** Carthage
gulf . . **5.** Gabes
oasis . . **5.** Gafsa
people . . **5.** Arabs **7.** Berbers
resort island . . **6.** Djerba
river . . **8.** Medjerda
ruler . . **3.** dey **5.** pasha
seaport . . **4.** Sfax **7.** Bizorte
tunnel . . . **4.** adit, bore, cave, tube **5.** drift
6. burrow, dig out, funnel, subway
10. excavation, smokestack
tunny . . . **4.** tuna **8.** albacore
tup . . . **3.** ram **4.** beat, butt **5.** sheep
6. mallet **7.** cuckold
turban . . . **6.** entrée, fillet, Moslem,
mundil, squash **8.** bandanna, seerband
9. headdress
turbid . . . **4.** dark, dull **5.** dense, muddy,
roily **6.** cloudy, impure, opaque
7. clouded, muddled **8.** confused,
feculent, polluted
turbot . . . **5.** brill **8.** flatfish
turbulence . . . **4.** fury **6.** tumult, uproar
7. bluster, rioting, turmoil **9.** agitation,
commotion **10.** excitement, unruliness
11. disturbance, impetuosity
14. tumultuousness
turbulent . . . **4.** loud, wild **5.** noisy, rough
6. stormy **7.** excited, furious **8.** virulent
10. tumultuous
turf . . . **3.** sod **4.** peat, slab **5.** divot, glebe,
grass, sward, track **10.** race course
turgid . . . **5.** tumid **7.** bloated, pompous,
swollen **8.** inflated **9.** bombastic,
distended, grandiose, redundant
12. magniloquent, ostentatious
13. grandiloquent
Turk . . . **5.** Tatar **6.** Tartar **7.** Osmanli,
Ottoman **9.** Kizilbash
Turkestan people . . . **5.** Uzbek (Uzbeg)
turkey . . . **4.** fowl **5.** poult **7.** bustard,
gobbler, vulture
Turkey . . . see also *Turkish*
capital . . **6.** Angora (anc), Ankara
city . . **5.** Adana, Izmir (Smyrna) **6.** Edessa,
Samsun **7.** Scutari **8.** Istanbul
(Constantinople) **10.** Adrianople
founder . . **6.** Othman
mountain . . **6.** Ararat
peninsula . . **9.** Anatolian
river . . **5.** Mesta **6.** Seyhan
Turkish (pert to) . . .
army corps . . **4.** ordu **8.** seraglio
commander, ruler . . **3.** aga (agha), bey
4. wali **5.** pasha **6.** atabeg (atabek)
court (Ottoman) . . **5.** Porte **12.** Sublime
Porte
dignitary . . **5.** pasha
dish (food) . . **5.** cabob **6.** pilaff (pilau)

drink . . **4.** boza (bozah), raki **5.** airan
6. mastic **9.** lion's milk
dynasty . . **6.** seljuk
emblem . . **8.** crescent
Empire . . **7.** Ottoman
flag . . **4.** alem, toug (former)
harem girl . . **6.** kadein (kadine)
hat, cap . . **3.** fez **6.** calpac (calpack)
hospice, inn . . **6.** imaret
infidel . . **6.** giaour
javelin . . **6.** jereed (jerid)
judge . . **4.** cadi (kadi)
minister of state . . **6.** vizier
money of account . . **5.** asper
mosque . . **4.** jami
music . . **8.** janizary
native . . **6.** Edesan (anc)
palace . . **5.** serai
pavilion . . **5.** kiosk
people . . **5.** Ersar, Tatar **7.** Bashkir,
Viddhal
pipe (long-stemmed) . . **7.** chibouk
(chibouque)
regiment . . **4.** alai
religious war . . **5.** jihad (jehad)
robe . . **6.** dolman
rug . . **5.** Melas, Tekke, Yomud, Yuruk
6. Afghan **8.** Turkoman **9.** Kurdistan
ruler . . **3.** bey, dey **4.** khan **6.** sultan
7. chambul
sailing vessel . . **4.** saic **6.** mahone
sailor . . **9.** galiongee (galionji)
soldier . . **5.** nizan, redif **6.** Arnaut
(Arnaout) **8.** Janizary **11.** bashi-bazouk
statute . . **8.** Tanzimat (1839)
sultan . . **5.** Ahmed, Selim **7.** Ilderim,
Saladin
sultan's title . . **6.** caliph (calif)
sword . . **8.** yataghan (yatagan)
tambourine . . **5.** daira
tax (from Christians) . . **6.** avania
title . . **3.** aga (agha), ali **4.** amir (ameer)
tobacco . . **7.** chibouk (chibouque), Latakia
Turkoman . . **11.** tribal group
veil (double) . . **7.** yashmak (yashmac)
vest . . **6.** jelick
whip, lash . . **7.** kurbash
turmeric . . . **3.** rea **4.** ango, herb **5.** olena
8. curcumin
turmoil . . . **3.** ado, din **5.** upset, worry
6. tumult, unrest **7.** ferment, tempest,
trouble **8.** disquiet **9.** agitation,
commotion, confusion **10.** excitement,
turbulence **12.** perturbation
turn . . . **3.** bow, lap **4.** bend, deed,
gyre, roll, slew, slue, spin, tour, veer,
vert **5.** curve, lathe, pivot, quirk,
round, shift, spell, wheel, whirl, whorl
6. abvert, change, crisis, gyrate, rotate,
swivel, zigzag **7.** deflect, deviate,
reverse, revolve **8.** aptitude, circuity,
maneuver, persuade, rotation, tendency
9. deviation, pirouette, reversion
11. convolution **12.** metamorphose
turn (pert to) . . .
about . . **9.** alternate
aside, away . . **4.** slew, slue **5.** avert,
deter, repel, shunt **6.** divert, swerve
7. deflect, deviate, digress, diverge
back . . **5.** repel **6.** coward, revert
7. evolute, head off, reflect

coat.. **7.** traitor **8.** apostate, deserter, renegade
comb form.. **5.** tropo
down.. **4.** veto **6.** refuse, reject **7.** decline
gate.. **5.** stile **9.** turnstile
inside out.. **5.** evert **6.** invert **7.** ransack
inward.. **8.** introrse **9.** introvert
left.. **3.** haw **4.** port
of duty.. **5.** spell, trick
off.. **5.** shunt **7.** dismiss, execute
10. extinguish
on axis.. **6.** obvert, rotate
one's back upon.. **4.** flee, snub **5.** avoid
6. ignore, oppose, refuse, reject
on pivot.. **6.** swivel
out.. **4.** fare, oust **5.** array, evert, expel,
track **6.** detour, output, siding **7.** dismiss
8. assemble, clearing **9.** eventuate,
gathering **10.** accomplish, extinguish
outward.. **5.** evert, splay **8.** extrorse
9. extrovert
over.. **3.** pie **4.** keel, tart **5.** sales,
shift, spill **6.** assign, pastry **7.** capsize
8. hand over, overturn
over a new leaf.. **6.** change, reform
over pages.. **4.** leaf **5.** thumb
over to others.. **4.** farm **7.** farm out
to left.. **3.** haw **4.** port
to right.. **3.** gee **9.** starboard
up.. **4.** find, keel **5.** occur **6.** appear,
arrive **7.** be found
upside down.. **4.** roll **6.** invert, whelve
7. ransack **8.** overturn
turned up (nose) ... **9.** retroussé
turning ... **6.** rotary **7.** bending, crooked,
winding **8.** rotation, twisting, whirling
9. deviating, deviation **10.** circuitous,
revolution **11.** convolution, sinistrorse
turning (pert to) ...
left to right.. **9.** dextrorse
machine.. **5.** lathe
point.. **6.** crisis **8.** decision, landmark
11. climacteric **13.** crucial period
right to left.. **11.** sinistrorse
turnip ... **4.** neep, rape, root **8.** rutabaga
turnip (pert to) ...
large.. **7.** Russian, Swedish **8.** rutabaga
shaped.. **8.** napiform
wild.. **5.** navew
Turnix ... **4.** bird (3-toed) **5.** quail
10. Hemipodius
Turpentine State ... **13.** North Carolina
turpentine tree ... **4.** pine **6.** tarata
9. terebinth
turpid ... **3.** low **4.** base, vile **8.** cowardly
turpitude ... **6.** fedity **8.** baseness,
vileness **9.** decadence, depravity
10. corruption
turquoise ... **3.** gem **4.** blue **7.** mineral,
Turkish
turret ... **4.** loom, soar **5.** tower
6. cupola (revolving), height **9.** structure
10. stronghold, watchtower
turtle (pert to) ...
edible.. **8.** terrapin
freshwater.. **4.** emyd **8.** tortoise
genus.. **4.** Emys
hawklike.. **5.** carat **9.** hawk's-bill
large.. **5.** arrau **6.** jurara, mamata
largest.. **11.** leatherback
ref to.. **9.** chelonian

sea.. **10.** thalassian
shell.. **8.** carapace
snapping.. **6.** cooter **8.** shagtail
Tuscany ...
birthplace of.. **7.** Galileo (Astronomer)
capital.. **8.** Florence
city.. **4.** Pisa **7.** Leghorn
color.. **9.** colcothar
famed tower.. **4.** Pisa (1174)
island.. **4.** Elba (1st exile, Napoleon)
native.. **6.** Tuscan
marble.. **7.** Carrara
province.. **4.** Pisa
river.. **4.** Arno **6.** Cecina **7.** Ombrone
wine.. **7.** chianti
tusk ... **4.** fang **5.** ivory, tooth **6.** canine
7. incisor **9.** scrivello (elephant's)
Tussaud, Madame's London district ...
8. Waxworks (Museum) **10.** Marylebone
tussis ... **5.** cough
tussle ... **7.** contend, contest, scuffle,
wrestle **8.** struggle
tutelage ... **7.** nurture **8.** teaching,
tutorage **9.** oversight, tutorship
11. instruction **12.** guardianship
tutelary gods (Rom) ... **5.** lares **7.** penates
tutor ... **5.** coach, teach **6.** docent, ground,
mentor, school **7.** teacher **8.** instruct
9. pedagogue (pedagog), preceptor
twaddle ... **3.** rot **6.** drivel, gabble
7. chatter, fustian, prattle **8.** claptrap,
nonsense **9.** absurdity, silly talk
10. flapdoodle **16.** trash and nonsense
twang ... **4.** tang **5.** strum **6.** accent
7. dialect **8.** pungency
tweak ... **4.** jerk, pain **5.** pinch **6.** snatch,
twitch
tweeg ... **10.** hellbender, salamander
tweezers ... **7.** pincers **10.** instrument
twelfth ... **5.** twait, uncia **8.** duodenal
9. duodenary
Twelfth Night character ... **5.** Viola
6. Olivia, Orsino **7.** Sir Toby **8.** Malvolio
12. Sir Toby Belch
Twelfthtide ... **8.** Epiphany **10.** Twelfth-
day
twelve (pert to) ...
amount.. **5.** dozen
angles.. **9.** dodecagon
prefix.. **5.** dodec **6.** dodeca
rule of.. **9.** dodecarch
series.. **8.** dodecade
Twelve, The ... **8.** Apostles
twenty (pert to) ...
Anglo-Ind.. **5.** carge, score
comb form.. **4.** icos **5.** icosa, icosi
faces.. **11.** icosahedron
pert to.. **7.** icosian **8.** vicenary
quires.. **4.** ream
symbol.. **2.** XX
years.. **9.** vicennial
twenty-fourth part (gold alloy) ...
5. carat (karat)
twibil (twibill) ... **2.** ax (axe) **6.** pickax
(pickaxe) **7.** mattock **8.** battle-ax
(battle-axe)
twice ... **2.** bi, di **6.** doubly **7.** twofold
8. two times
twig ... **4.** reis **5.** besom, birch, bough
6. branch, sallow, switch, twitch, wattle
twigs, bundle of ... **5.** fagot **6.** barsom

(sacred)
twilight ... **3.** dim **4.** blue, dusk **6.** shaded
  7. obscure **8.** foredawn, gloaming
  9. cocklight **10.** crepuscule
Twilight of the Gods ... **8.** Ragnarok
twill ... **3.** rib **5.** flute, weave **6.** fabric
  9. tricotine
twilled ... **3.** rep **5.** reedy, ridgy, sedgy,
  serge **6.** corded, fluted
twin ... **3.** two **4.** dual, mate, pair
  5. gemel, macle **6.** couple, double
  7. didymus, Siamese **8.** didymous,
  matching **9.** duplicate, identical
  11. counterpart **12.** accompanying
Twin Cities (Minn) ... **6.** St Paul
  11. Minneapolis
twine ... **4.** bend, coil, turn, wind, wrap
  5. braid, snarl, twist, weave **6.** enfold,
  enlace, tangle **7.** embrace, enclasp,
  entwine, wreathe **8.** convolve, encircle
  9. interlace **10.** intertwine, interweave
  11. intermingle
twine (pert to) ...
  color .. **4.** dune **7.** anamite
  hank of .. **3.** ran
  left to right .. **9.** dextrorse
  right to left .. **11.** sinistrorse
  Scot .. **4.** part
twinge ... **4.** ache, pain, pang **5.** pinch,
  qualm **6.** twitch
twin stars ... **6.** Castor, Pollux
twin stock ... **4.** bees **7.** beehive (two
  colonies)
twirl ... **4.** coil, eddy, gyre, spin
  5. pitch, querl, twist, whirl **6.** gyrate,
  writhe **7.** revolve **8.** flourish, rotation
  11. convolution
twist ... **3.** cue, ply **4.** coil, curl,
  slew, slub, slue, spin, turn, warp,
  wind **5.** braid, quirk, tweak, wrest
  7. contort, deflect, distort, falsify,
  meander, pervert, wreathe, wriggle
  8. convolve **9.** insinuate, interlace,
  prejudice **10.** distortion **12.** eccentricity,
  misrepresent
twisted ... **3.** wry **4.** awry, cued
  5. askew, kinky, torse, wrung **6.** warped
  7. complex, torqued, tortile, wrested,
  writhed
twisted cord ... **7.** torsade
twister ... **3.** lie **7.** cruller, tornado
  8. doughnut **9.** dust whirl **10.** sand
  column, somersault, waterspout
twit ... **4.** gibe, josh **5.** blame, taunt,
  tease, tweet **6.** banter **7.** upbraid
  8. reproach, ridicule
twitch ... **3.** nip, tic, tug **4.** hurt, jerk,
  yank **5.** pluck, shake, tweak **6.** snatch
  9. be excited, quick pull, vellicate
  11. contraction
twitter ... **5.** chirp **6.** giggle, titter
  7. chatter, tremble **9.** agitation
two (pert to) ...
  chambered .. **9.** bicameral
  colored .. **9.** dichromic
  edged .. **9.** ancipital
  faced .. **5.** false **6.** double **9.** deceitful
  11. treacherous **12.** falsehearted
  fisted .. **6.** virile
  fold .. **4.** dual, twin **6.** binary, double,
  duplex **8.** didymous

forked .. **6.** bident **9.** bifurcate
  11. dichotomous
handed .. **7.** bimanal **8.** bimanous
  10. secondhand **12.** ambidextrous
headed .. **9.** ancipital **11.** dicephalous
masted ship .. **4.** yawl, zulu
parts .. **3.** duo **4.** duad, dyad **7.** duality
poetic .. **5.** twain
prefix .. **2.** bi, di
Scot .. **3.** twa
Spanish .. **3.** dos
spot .. **5.** deuce
time .. **7.** deceive
wheeled carriage, chariot .. **3.** gig
  6. esseda **10.** jinrikisha (jinriksha)
Tyche ... **7.** Fortuna **16.** goddess of
  Fortune
tycoon ... **6.** shogun **7.** magnate
  9. financier **13.** industrialist
tylopod ... **5.** camel
tympanum ... **7.** eardrum **9.** middle ear
  10. water wheel
tympany ... **6.** tympan **7.** bombast
  9. inflation **10.** distention
typal ... **7.** typical **8.** symbolic
type ... **2.** pi **4.** font, form, kind, norm,
  sign, sort **5.** genre, genus, model,
  print, Roman, token **6.** emblem, italic,
  minion, symbol **7.** measure, pattern,
  species **8.** boldface, classify, standard
  9. archetype, character **10.** transcribe
  11. Baskerville **14.** characteristic,
  representative
type (pert to) ...
  assortment .. **4.** font, kern
  block of .. **4.** quad **7.** quadrat
  bold style .. **4.** text
  bridge .. **7.** bascule
  classic .. **5.** Roman **6.** italic **11.** black
  letter (Gothic)
  line .. **4.** slug
  measure .. **2.** em, en
  mixed .. **2.** pi
  mold .. **6.** matrix
  perfection .. **7.** paragon
  set .. **7.** compose
  setter .. **8.** linotype, monotype
  10. compositor
  size .. **4.** norm, pica, ruby **5.** agate,
  canon, pearl **6.** minion **7.** diamond
  stroke .. **5.** serif
  tray .. **6.** galley
typewriter (pert to) ...
  bar .. **6.** spacer
  cylinder .. **6.** platen, spacer
  type .. **4.** pica **5.** elite
  type of .. **6.** ticker **8.** teletype
  9. stenotype
typhoon ... **4.** wind **5.** storm **7.** cyclone
typhus fever ... **10.** tabardillo
typical ... **4.** norm **5.** typal **6.** normal
  7. regular **10.** conforming, emblematic,
  figurative **11.** precedental
  14. characteristic, representative
typify ... **6.** embody **9.** prefigure,
  represent, symbolize
Tyr (Norse) ... **3.** Tiu **6.** sky-god, war-god
tyrannical ... **5.** cruel **6.** lordly **8.** despotic
  9. imperious **10.** oppressive
  11. domineering
tyrannize ... **7.** oppress **8.** domineer

tyranny... 8. severity 9. despotism
tyrant... 4. czar, Ivan, Nero, tsar, tzar
6. despot 7. monarch
Tyre... see also Tyrian
capital of.. 9. Phoenicia (anc)
famed for.. 9. purple dye
seaport of.. 7. Lebanon
site.. 9. peninsula 13. Mediterranean
Tyrian (pert to)...
alphabet.. 7. Moabite
Cynosure.. 9. Ursa Minor
god (Teut).. 2. Er
king.. 5. Hiram
princess.. 4. Dido (Elissa)

tyro, tiro... 5. pupil 6. novice 7. amateur
8. beginner, neophyte 9. commencer,
fledgling, greenhorn 10. apprentice
11. abecedarian
Tyrol...
capital.. 9. Innsbruck
dialect.. 5. Ladin
district.. 8. Trentino
mountain.. 4. Alps 9. Dolomites
province of.. 7. Austria
river.. 4. Isar
tzar, tsar, czar... 4. king 5. ruler
6. tyrant
tzigane... 5. gypsy

U

U... 6. letter (21st)
uang... 6. beetle
uberous... 7. copious 8. abundant,
fruitful 9. plentiful
uberty... 6. plenty 12. fruitfulness
ubiety... 8. location, position, relation
9. whereness
ubiquity... 8. doctrine (Luther)
10. everywhere 12. omnipresence
U-boat... 3. sub 9. submarine
base.. 4. Kiel
Uca... 11. fiddler crab
Uchean Indian... 5. Yuchi (Uchee)
udometer... 9. rain gauge
Uffizi Gallery... 8. Florence
Uganda (pert to)...
capital.. 7. Kampala
Falls.. 4. Owen 9. Murchison
lake.. 8. Victoria
lake explorer.. 7. Stanley
mountain.. 9. Ruwenzori 18. Mountains
of the Moon
people.. 5. pygmy
ugly... 5. cross, surly 6. cranky,
homely 7. crabbed, hideous, vicious
8. gruesome, uncomely, unlovely
9. frightful, loathsome, offensive,
repulsive, unsightly 10. ill-favored, ill-
natured, unpleasant 11. ill-tempered,
quarrelsome 12. disagreeable
uhlan... 6. lancer 7. militia, soldier
10. cavalryman
uhllo... 6. wampum 8. currency (shell)
uitlander... 9. foreigner, outlander
ukase... 5. edict, order 12. proclamation
Ukraine (pert to)...
capital.. 4. Kiev 7. Kharkov
legislature.. 4. rada
official name.. 12. Ukrainian SSR
Relig.. 9. Ruthenian 13. Little Russian
scientist.. 10. Bogomolets
sea.. 5. Black
seaport.. 6. Odessa
statesman.. 7. Mazeppa
writer.. 6. Franko
ullage... 5. dregs 7. deficit, wantage
8. shortage 9. shrinkage 10. deficiency
Ulmas... 3. elm
ulna... 4. bone 5. elbow 7. cubitus

ulster... 8. overcoat
Ulster, to some... 15. Northern Ireland
ulterior... 6. future 7. further, remoter,
thither 10. additional, extraneous,
subsequent, succeeding 11. undisclosed
ultima... 4. last 5. final 8. farthest
10. most remote 12. last syllable
ultimate... 3. end 4. dire, last 5. final,
telus 6. future, latest, result 7. extreme,
maximum 8. eventful, eventual,
farthest, terminal 9. elemental
10. conclusive, end product
ultimatum... 5. offer 6. demand
13. ultimate point 14. final objective
ultimo... 3. ult 9. past month (opp of
proximo)
ultra... 6. beyond 7. extreme, radical
9. excessive, extremist, fanatical
11. extravagant 14. uncompromising
ultramarine... 11. blue pigment, lapis
lazuli 12. beyond the sea
ultramontane... 5. alien 6. beyond
9. foreigner 10. tramontane 13. beyond
the Alps, Roman Catholic
ulu (Esk)... 5. knife
ululate... 4. hoot, howl, wail, yelp
6. bellow, lament
Ulysses (pert to)...
antagonist.. 4. Irus
dog.. 5. Argos
enchantress.. 5. Circe
father.. 7. Laertes
Greek name.. 8. Odysseus
hero.. 7. Odyssey (Homer's)
literally.. 5. hater
son.. 9. Telegonus
wife.. 8. Penelope
umber... 3. raw 5. brown, burnt
6. shadow, Turkey 8. grayling, umbrette
10. brown earth
umbilicus (pert to)...
anatomy.. 5. navel
botany.. 5. hilum
geometry.. 5. focus
paleology.. 5. stick (papyrus)
zoology.. 3. pit 10. depression
umbra... 4. fish 5. ghost, shade
6. shadow 7. phantom, vestige
umbrage... 5. doubt, pique, shade, trace

6. offend, resent 7. foliage, offense, shelter 8. disfavor 9. semblance, suspicion 10. overshadow, resentment 11. displeasure

umbrella ..`. 4. gamp 5. cover, guard, shade 6. chatta, payong, pileus (of a jellyfish) 7. parasol, shelter 9. parachute, sea anchor 11. bumbershoot

umbrella tree ... 5. bendy 7. dogwood, ginseng 8. magnolia

umbrette ... 4. bird, fish 5. omber (ombre) 9. hammerkop

umpire ... 5. judge 7. arbiter, referee 8. mediator 9. moderator 10. arbitrator, negotiator

Umpqua ... 6. Indian 10. Athapascan

unable ... 6. cannot 8. helpless, impotent 9. incapable 11. incompetent, inefficient, unqualified 13. incapacitated

Una boat ... 7. catboat

unabridged ... 8. complete 11. uncondensed

unaccented ... 4. lene 6. atonic

unaccountable ... 7. lawless, strange 9. fantastic 10. mysterious 12. inexplicable, unfathomable 13. irresponsible, unpredictable

unacknowledged ... 9. anonymous, forgotten, unthanked 10. unrewarded

unadorned ... 4. bald, bare, form 5. grace, naked, stark 7. austere 13. plain-speaking

unadulterated ... 4. pure 5. naked 6. honest 7. unmixed 9. unalloyed, undiluted 11. uncorrupted

unaffected ... 4. naif, real 5. naive, plain 6. simple 7. artless, genuine, natural, sincere 8. informal 9. unaltered, untouched 12. uninfluenced 13. plain-speaking

Unalaska ... 5. Aleut 9. Eskimauan

unanimous ... 5. solid 6. agreed, mutual, united 8. agreeing 9. of one mind 10. concordant 11. consentient 12. with one voice

unanimously ... 7. una voce 12. with one voice

unapproachable ... 8. reserved 10. unsociable 12. inaccessible

unapt ... 4. dull, slow 5. inapt 8. backward 10. unskillful, unsuitable 13. inappropriate

unaroused ... 6. latent 7. dormant 8. inactive 9. unstirred

unaspirated ... 4. lene 6. smooth

unassuming ... 3. shy 6. modest 7. genuine, natural 8. informal, retiring 9. diffident 11. undeceptive 14. unostentatious

unau ... 5. sloth (2-toed)

unavailing ... 6. futile 8. gainless

unbalanced ... 6. insane, uneven, unjust 7. unequal 8. deranged, lopsided, one-sided 9. off center 10. disordered

unbecoming ... 4. rude 5. inept 8. unseemly 10. indecorous, unsuitable 12. unattractive

unbelievable ... 9. fantastic, untenable 10. incredible, unreliable 11. implausible, unthinkable

13. inconceivable

unbeliever ... 5. pagan 7. atheist, doubter, heretic, infidel, skeptic 8. agnostic

unbend ... 4. rest, thaw 5. frese, relax, yield 6. loosen 7. slacken 8. be pliant, unfasten 10. condescend, straighten

unbending ... 5. rigid, stern, stiff 8. resolute 10. inexorable, inflexible, unyielding

unbiased ... 4. fair, just 9. impartial 12. free from bias, unprejudiced

unbind ... 4. free, undo 5. loose, untie 6. loosen 7. absolve, deliver, release 8. dissolve, unfasten

unbound ... 4. free 5. loose 10. unconfined

unbounded ... 8. infinite 9. limitless, unchecked, unlimited 10. unconfined 11. measureless 12. uncontrolled, unrestrained

unbridled ... 4. free 5. loose 7. lawless, violent 10. licentious 12. uncontrolled, unrestrained

unbroken ... 4. even 5. undug, whole 6. direct, entire, intact, smooth 7. untamed 8. constant, straight, unplowed 10. continuous 13. uninterrupted

uncanny ... 5. eerie (eery), weird 6. spooky 7. ghostly, strange 8. careless 9. unnatural 10. mysterious

unceasing ... 6. eterne 7. endless, eternal 9. continual, incessant 11. everlasting

unceremonious ... 4. curt 5. blunt 6. abrupt, casual 7. offhand 8. informal 14. unconventional

uncertain ... 4. hazy 5. vague 6. chancy, fickle, fitful, shifty, unsure 7. dubious 8. doubtful, unsteady, variable 9. ambiguous, irregular, undecided 10. changeable, indefinite, irresolute, precarious 11. unequivocal 12. questionable 13. indeterminate, problematical, untrustworthy

uncertainty ... 5. doubt 6. wonder 7. dubiety 8. suspense 9. dubiosity 10. fickleness, skepticism 12. irresolution 14. precariousness

unchanging ... 7. eternal, settled, uniform 9. immutable, unvarying 10. invariable, stationary

unchaste ... 4. lewd 5. bawdy 6. impure 7. obscene 8. immodest

unchecked ... 4. free 5. loose 7. rampant 9. permanent, unbridled

unchristian ... 5. pagan 7. heathen, infidel, ungodly 9. barbarous, excessive 11. irreligious, uncivilized

uncivil ... 4. rude 6. savage 7. ill-bred 8. impolite 9. barbarous 10. indecorous, ungracious 11. ill-mannered, uncivilized 12. discourteous 13. disrespectful

uncivilized ... 4. rude, wild 5. feral 6. brutal, ferine, savage 8. barbaric 9. primitive, unrefined

uncle ... 3. eme (yeme), oom

unclean ... 4. foul, tref, vile 5. dirty 6. filthy, immund, impure 8. polluted, unchaste 11. unwholesome

Uncle Tom's Cabin (pert to) ...

author . . **5.** Stowe (Harriet Beecher)
character . . **5.** Topsy **6.** Legree **8.** Uncle
Tom **9.** Little Eva
subject . . **7.** slavery
unclose . . . **3.** ope **4.** open **6.** reveal
7. expound **8.** disclose
uncolored . . . **7.** genuine **9.** colorless
10. achromatic
uncommon . . . **3.** odd **4.** nice, rare
5. novel **6.** scarce, unique **7.** special,
strange, unusual **8.** unwonted
10. infrequent, remarkable
11. exceptional **12.** unaccustomed
13. extraordinary
uncommunicative . . . **6.** silent
8. reserved, reticent **9.** secretive
10. unsociable
uncomplaining . . . **5.** stoic **7.** stoical
uncompromising . . . **4.** firm **5.** rigid
6. strict **9.** obstinate, unbending
10. inflexible, unyielding
12. conservative, intransigent
unconcerned . . . **4.** cool, free **8.** careless
9. apathetic **10.** insouciant
11. indifferent, not involved
13. disinterested
unconditional . . . **4.** free **8.** absolute,
explicit **10.** unreserved
unconfined . . . **5.** loose **9.** boundless,
limitless, unlimited **12.** unrestrained
unconscious . . . **3.** out **6.** asleep
7. unaware **8.** heedless, ignorant,
mindless **9.** inanimate, senseless,
unfeeling **10.** abstracted, insensible
11. involuntary **12.** subconscious
unconstrained . . . **4.** easy, free **6.** candid
7. natural **8.** informal **11.** spontaneous
12. unrestrained
uncontrolled . . . **4.** free, wild **5.** loose
7. lawless **9.** impulsive, irregular,
unmanaged **10.** capricious, changeable,
licentious, ungoverned **11.** not
governed, unregulated **12.** unrestrained
unconventional . . . **4.** easy **5.** outré
6. casual **7.** devious, offbeat
8. Bohemian, informal **10.** unorthodox
13. unceremonious
uncorrupted . . . **8.** pristine
uncouth . . . **3.** odd **4.** rude **5.** crude
6. clumsy, rustic **7.** awkward, boorish,
strange **9.** inelegant, unrefined,
untrained **10.** outlandish, uncultured,
unpolished
uncover . . . **4.** bare, open **6.** detect,
divest, expose, remove, reveal, unveil
7. divulge, lay bare, take off, undrape
8. disclose, discover
uncovered . . . **4.** bald, bare, nude, open
7. exposed **8.** divested, revealed,
stripped, unveiled **9.** décolleté
10. bareheaded **11.** unprotected
unction . . . **4.** balm, rite **6.** fervor
7. lanolin, unguent **8.** flattery, function
(divine), ointment **10.** anointment
unctuous . . . **4.** oily, smug **5.** bland,
fatty, salvy, suave **6.** fervid, greasy
7. gushing, pinguid, plastic
10. flattering, oleaginous
12. hypocritical **13.** sanctimonious
uncultured . . . **7.** artless, boorish, uncouth
8. Bohemian **9.** unlearned, unrefined

10. Philistine **11.** countrified,
undeveloped
undaunted . . . **4.** bold **5.** brave **7.** Spartan,
untamed **8.** fearless, intrepid, unafraid
9. confident, dauntless **10.** courageous,
undismayed **11.** persevering,
unconquered
undecided . . . **4.** moot **7.** pending
8. doubtful, wavering **9.** uncertain,
unsettled **10.** inconstant, irresolute,
unresolved **13.** problematical
undependable . . . **6.** fickle **7.** erratic
9. uncertain **13.** irresponsible,
untrustworthy
under . . . **3.** sub **4.** alow **5.** below, least,
neath, sotto **6.** nether **7.** beneath
8. guidance **9.** lower than **10.** subjection,
underneath **11.** subordinate
undercover . . . **6.** secret **7.** furtive
11. clandestine, underground
13. surreptitious
underestimate . . . **8.** belittle, minimize
9. set too low, underrate **10.** undervalue
underfong . . . **6.** entrap **7.** ensnare,
receive, sustain **9.** undertake
10. circumvent
undergo . . . **4.** bear, dree, pass **5.** shirt
6. endure, suffer **7.** sustain
9. undermine **10.** experience
underhanded . . . **3.** sly **4.** dern, mean
5. shady **6.** covert, crafty, secret,
sneaky **8.** sneaking, unfairly **9.** deceitful,
dishonest **10.** fraudulent **11.** clandestine,
short-handed **13.** unobtrusively
15. surreptitiously
underling . . . **6.** menial, minion **7.** servant
8. inferior **11.** subordinate
underlying . . . **5.** basic **8.** cardinal
11. fundamental
undermine . . . **3.** sap **4.** ruin **5.** drain,
erode **6.** weaken **7.** subvert **8.** enfeeble,
excavate
understand . . . **3.** ken, see **4.** know
5. grasp, infer, savvy, sense **6.** follow,
reason **7.** discern, explain, realize,
signify **8.** conceive, perceive
9. apprehend, interpret **10.** comprehend
understandable . . . **5.** clear, lucid
12. intelligible
understanding . . . **5.** amity, sense
6. accord, reason, treaty **7.** compact,
concept, entente, knowing **8.** sympathy,
Verstand **9.** agreement, intellect,
knowledge, tolerance, unanimity
10. acceptance, accordance, perception
11. discernment, penetration
12. intelligence **13.** comprehension
understatement . . . **7.** litotes
understood . . . **5.** clear, known, lucid,
tacit **7.** assumed, implied, settled
8. implicit **11.** traditional
undertake . . . **3.** try **4.** dare **6.** accept,
assume, pledge **7.** attempt, promise,
reprove **8.** contract, covenant, endeavor,
engage in, set about **9.** guarantee,
underfong
undertaker . . . **5.** cerer **6.** surety
7. manager, rebuker, sponsor
8. embalmer **9.** godfather, mortician
12. entrepreneur
undertaking . . . **3.** act **4.** task **6.** cautio

7. calling, project, promise, venture
8. business 9. adventure, guarantee
10. enterprise

undertone . . . **4.** tone (low) **5.** aside
6. murmur **12.** subdued color

undertow . . . **7.** riptide

underworld . . . **3.** Dis **4.** hell **5.** Hades,
limbo, Mafia, Orcus, Sheol **6.** Erebus,
Tophet **7.** Abaddon, Xibalba **8.** Dis
pater, gangland **9.** Black Hand,
chthonian, perdition, purgatory

underwrite . . . **6.** assure, insure **7.** finance,
sponsor **8.** submit to

underwriter . . . **7.** insurer **8.** endorser
9. financier **10.** underclerk **13.** Stock
Exchange **14.** Lloyd's of London

undesirable condition . . . **6.** malady

undetermined . . . **5.** vague **7.** dubious
8. not fixed, unproved **9.** uncertain,
undecided **10.** irresolute

undeveloped . . . **5.** crude **6.** embryo,
latent **8.** immature **10.** unprepared
11. rudimentary

undignified . . . **6.** vulgar **8.** informal,
infra dig, unworthy **9.** inelegant

undine . . . **3.** nix **5.** gnome, sylph **6.** vessel
(glass) **9.** planetoid **10.** salamander

undivided . . . **3.** one **5.** total, whole
6. entire, intact, joined **7.** unitary
8. unbroken **9.** not shared
10. continuous

undo . . . **4.** open **5.** annul, loose
6. cancel, defeat, foredo, unlash,
unwrap **7.** destroy, disjoin, nullify,
release, uncover, unravel **8.** unfasten
10. disconnect, invalidate

undoing . . . **4.** ruin **6.** defeat **8.** downfall
9. annulment, overthrow
11. destruction, disassembly

undomesticated . . . **4.** wild **5.** feral
6. ferine

undone . . . **3.** raw **9.** neglected
10. defeasible

undue . . . **5.** wrong **6.** unjust **7.** extreme
8. improper, not owing **9.** excessive
10. exorbitant, immoderate, inordinate,
undeserved, unsuitable **11.** unwarranted
13. inappropriate

undulating . . . **4.** wavy **6.** waving
7. aripple, rolling **8.** rippling
11. fluctuating **16.** rising and falling

undulation . . . **4.** beat, wave **5.** heave,
surge, swell **6.** motion, waving
7. tremolo, vibrato **8.** waviness
9. pulsation **11.** convolution

undying . . . **6.** eterne **7.** ageless, endless,
eternal **8.** immortal, unending
9. deathless **11.** amaranthine
12. imperishable **14.** indestructible

unearth . . . **4.** find **5.** dig up **6.** exhume,
expose **7.** uncover **8.** disclose, discover,
disinter **12.** bring to light

unearthly . . . **5.** eerie (eery), godly, weird
7. awesome, ghostly, strange, uncanny
8. heavenly, terrific **9.** appalling,
deathlike **10.** mysterious, outlandish
12. preposterous, supernatural
13. preternatural

uneasiness . . . **5.** worry **6.** unrest
7. anxiety, malaise **8.** disquiet
10. impatience **11.** displeasure,

disquietude, disturbance
12. apprehension

uneasy . . . **5.** stiff **7.** anxious, awkward,
inquiet, restive, worried **8.** agitated,
cramping, restless **9.** difficult, impatient,
perturbed **10.** disquieted, distressed
11. constrained, troublesome

unemotional . . . **4.** cold **5.** stoic **7.** stoical
10. phlegmatic

unemployed . . . **4.** idle, lazy **6.** otiose,
unused **7.** not used **8.** inactive, leisured
11. not invested

unencumbered . . . **4.** free

unending . . . **7.** endless, eternal
8. termless, timeless **9.** boundless,
perpetual **10.** continuous
12. interminable

unequal . . . **3.** odd **4.** odds **5.** aniso
(comb form) **6.** uneven, unfair, unjust
8. variable **9.** disparate, irregular
11. fluctuating, not adequate
12. asymmetrical **16.** disproportionate

unequaled . . . **7.** supreme **8.** peerless
9. matchless, nonpareil, unmatched,
unrivaled **10.** inimitable, surpassing,
unbeatable, unexcelled **12.** unparalleled

unequivocal . . . **5.** clear, plain **6.** candid
7. sincere **8.** explicit **9.** downright
11. categorical, indubitable

unerring . . . **4.** sure, true **5.** exact **7.** certain
8. accurate, virtuous **9.** unfailing
10. infallible

unessential . . . **8.** needless **9.** extrinsic
10. irrelevant **11.** superfluous,
unimportant **13.** insignificant, void of
essence

unethical . . . **6.** amoral

uneven . . . **3.** odd **5.** erose, rough
6. rugged, unfair, unjust **7.** erratic,
unequal, varying **8.** not level **10.** ill-
matched **11.** fluctuating

unexamined . . . **7.** a priori

unexampled . . . **8.** peerless **10.** unimitated
12. unparalleled **13.** extraordinary,
unprecedented

unexpected . . . **6.** abrupt, sudden
7. unusual **9.** inopinate **10.** unforeseen
14. not anticipated

unfair . . . **4.** foul **5.** wrong **6.** biased,
uneven, unjust **8.** unseemly
9. dishonest, unethical **10.** not cricket,
unsporting **11.** inequitable, unfavorable
12. disingenuous, not equitable

unfaithful . . . **6.** betray **7.** infidel,
traitor **8.** apostate, recreant, turncoat
9. faithless **10.** inaccurate
12. nonobservant **13.** untrustworthy

unfamiliar . . . **3.** new **7.** strange, unknown
8. not known **12.** unaccustomed,
unconversant

unfasten . . . **4.** free, open, undo **5.** unbar,
unfix, unpin, untie **6.** detach, loosen,
unhook, unlock **7.** unloose **8.** unbutton
9. disengage

unfavorable . . . **3.** bad, ill **6.** averse
7. adverse, opposed **8.** contrary,
untimely **9.** repulsive **12.** inauspicious

unfeeling . . . **4.** dull **5.** cruel, stoic,
stony **6.** brutal, steely, stolid, unkind
7. callous **8.** numbness, obdurate
9. apathetic, bloodless, heartless,

inanimate, insensate 10. insensible
11. hardhearted 13. unsusceptible
16. unimpressionable
unfeigned ... 4. real 7. genuine, natural,
sincere 11. undeceptive 14. not
counterfeit 15. not hypocritical
unfermented grape juice ... 4. stum
unfertile ... 4. arid 6. barren
unfettered ... 4. free 5. broad 9. liberated,
unchained 10. unshackled
unfinished ... 5. crude, rough 7. sketchy
9. imperfect 10. incomplete
11. uncompleted
unfit ... 5. inept 6. faulty, not fit,
unable 8. disabled 9. untenable
11. handicapped, incompetent,
unqualified 12. disqualified
unfledged ... 4. eyas 5. green 6. callow
8. immature 11. undeveloped 12. not
feathered
unflinching ... 7. staunch 8. resolute,
unafraid 9. steadfast 10. unwavering,
unyielding 12. not shrinking
unfold ... 3. ope 4. open 6. evolve,
expand, flower, reveal, spread, unfurl
7. develop, display, divulge, evolute,
explain, release 8. disclose
unfortunate ... 3. ill 4. poor 6. wretch
7. hapless, unlucky 8. luckless, untimely
10. calamitous 12. inauspicious,
unsuccessful
unfounded ... 4. idle, vain 8. baseless
9. untenable 10. chimerical
11. unsupported, unwarranted
unfriendly ... 3. icy 4. cool 7. asocial,
hostile, not kind, opposed 8. inimical,
unsocial 10. unsociable 12. inhospitable
unfruitful ... 6. barren, wasted 7. sterile,
useless 9. fruitless, infertile
12. unproductive, unprofitable 13. not
productive
unfurl ... 4. expand, spread,
unfold, unroll
ungainly ... 5. gawky, lanky 6. clumsy,
gauche 7. awkward, uncouth
8. bungling 10. cumbersome,
ungraceful
ungenteel ... 6. vulgar 7. ill-bred
8. plebeian 9. inelegant 10. unmannerly
ungentle ... 4. rude 5. harsh, rough
7. ill-bred 12. discourteous
ungodly ... 6. sinful, wicked 7. impious
9. atheistic 11. unbelieving
ungovernable ... 4. wild 6. unruly
9. unbridled 10. disorderly, licentious,
rebellious, refractory 12. incorrigible,
obstreperous, recalcitrant
13. irrepressible 14. uncontrollable
unguent ... 4. balm 5. salve 6. cerate,
chrism, pomade 7. unction 8. ointment
9. lubricant, unguentum
ungula ... 4. claw, hoof, nail 6. unguis
ungulate ... 3. pig 4. deer 5. horse,
swine, tapir 6. hoofed 8. elephant,
Ungulata 10. rhinoceros 15. hoofed
quadruped
unhallowed ... 6. unholy, wicked
10. desecrated
unhappy ... 3. sad 6. dismal, woeful
8. dejected, ill-fated, wretched
9. miserable, sorrowful 10. calamitous,

displeased 11. melancholic, unfortunate
12. discontented, unsuccessful
unhealthy ... 3. ill 4. sick 6. sickly, unsafe
11. unwholesome
unhesitating ... 4. sure 5. ready
8. implicit, resolute 10. undoubting
unholy ... 6. wicked 7. impious, profane
8. shocking 10. scandalous, unhallowed
unicellular organism ... 6. amoeba
(ameba)
unicorn ... 4. reem (Bib), unie 7. monster
8. narwhale 9. monoceros, spike
team 10. pursuivant (Her), rhinoceros
(one-horned)
uniform ... 4. even 5. equal 6. livery,
outfit, simple, smooth 7. equable,
orderly, regular 8. constant, equiform
9. unvarying 10. consistent, invariable,
unchanging 11. symmetrical
uniformity ... 5. order 8. equality,
evenness, sameness, symmetry
10. compliance, conformity,
smoothness 11. consistency,
homogeneity 13. invariability
unify ... 5. merge, unite 7. combine,
make one 8. coalesce 9. integrate
11. consolidate
unimaginative ... 4. dull 7. literal, prosaic
10. unfanciful
unimpaired ... 4. free 6. entire, intact
8. unmarred 9. undamaged, unspoiled
unimpressed ... 6. unawed 7. unmoved
9. unstirred 10. unaffected, uninspired
uninformed ... 8. ignorant, nescient
9. unknowing 10. unapprized
13. unenlightened, unintelligent
uninhabited ... 5. empty 6. vacant
8. deserted, desolate, forsaken
9. abandoned, unpeopled
10. unoccupied, untenanted
uninspired ... 4. dull 6. stodgy
9. uninhaled
unintelligent ... 4. dumb 5. brute
6. stupid, unwise 7. foolish 8. ignorant
9. senseless
unintentional ... 7. unmeant 9. unwitting
10. accidental, unintended
11. inadvertent, involuntary,
unmeditated 14. unpremeditated
uninterested ... 5. bored 9. apathetic,
impartial, incurious 11. unconcerned
13. disinterested
uninteresting ... 3. dry 4. arid, drab, dull
6. boring, prolix, stupid 7. humdrum,
insipid, prosaic, tedious 8. tiresome
9. colorless 10. unexciting
union ... 3. one 4. bond 5. joint,
unity 6. accord, fusion, league,
merger 7. amalgam, entente, liaison,
oneness 8. alliance, junction, marriage
9. coalition 10. federation 11. affiliation,
association, combination, concurrence,
confederacy, conjunction
13. juxtaposition
Union (pert to) ...
ensign, British .. 12. three crosses (St
Andrew, St George, St Patrick)
General .. 7. Sherman (Civil War)
of States .. 6. Empire 12. United States
of workers .. 5. artel, guild
Union of So Africa ...

capital.. **8**. Cape Town (Legis), Pretoria
(Admin)
city.. **6**. Durban **9**. Germiston
12. Johannesburg
famed Park.. **6**. Kruger
Union of Soviet Socialist Republics ...
see also *Russia*
anc citadel.. **7**. Kremlin
capital.. **6**. Moscow
city.. **9**. Leningrad
Republics (number).. **7**. fifteen
resort.. **5**. Yalta **6**. Crimea
river.. **2**. Ob **3**. Don **4**. Lena, Neva,
Ural **5**. Volga **7**. Dnieper
sea.. **4**. Aral, Azov **5**. Black, White
6. Baltic **7**. Caspian
strait.. **6**. Bering
unique ... **3**. odd, one **4**. rare, sole
5. alone, novel **6**. single **7**. notable,
special, unusual **8**. original, peculiar,
peerless, singular **9**. matchless
12. single-valued **13**. extraordinary
unison ... **5**. union **6**. accord, assent
7. concord, harmony **9**. agreement,
unanimity **10**. concordant, consonance
unit ... **3**. ace, ane, one **4**. item, word
5. digit, group **6**. entity **7**. measure
8. syllable
unit (pert to) ...
area (land).. **3**. rod **4**. acre **7**. hectare
astronomy.. **6**. parsec
biology.. **5**. idant
electrical.. **3**. amp, mho, ohm, rel **4**. volt,
watt **5**. farad, henry, joule **6**. ampere,
proton **7**. coulomb
energy.. **3**. erg, rad **5**. ergon **6**. kilerg
7. quantum
fluidity.. **3**. rhe
force.. **4**. dyne **5**. tonal **7**. kinetic
heat.. **3**. BTU **5**. therm (therme) **7**. calorie
(calory)
induction.. **5**. henry
light.. **3**. lux, pyr, rad **5**. lumen **6**. Hefner
linear.. **3**. ell, rod **4**. foot, inch, mile,
yard **7**. furlong
magnetic.. **5**. gauss, weber **7**. maxwell,
oersted
matter.. **5**. monad
measure.. **3**. are, rod **4**. pint **5**. maund,
meter, stere
military.. **7**. brigade, platoon **8**. regiment
power.. **2**. HP **3**. bel **5**. dynam, horse
pressure.. **5**. barad, barie
reluctance.. **3**. rel
resistance.. **3**. ohm
speed.. **4**. velo
telegraphic.. **4**. baud
thermal.. **7**. calorie (calory)
velocity.. **4**. velo
volume.. **3**. ton **4**. cord, peck, pint
5. ounce, pound **6**. barrel, bushel,
gallon **8**. hogshead
weight.. **3**. ton **5**. carat (karat), ounce,
pound
wire.. **3**. mil
work.. **3**. erg **5**. ergon, joule **6**. kilerg
yarn.. **6**. denier
unite ... **3**. fay, tie, wed **4**. ally,
bind, fuse, join, knit, link, meld,
weld **5**. annex, graft, marry, merge
6. adhere, cement, concur, mingle,

solder **7**. combine, connect **8**. coalesce,
condense, converge, federate, side with
9. affiliate, associate **10**. amalgamate,
federalize **11**. consolidate, incorporate
unite (pert to) ...
by freezing.. **8**. regelate
by interweaving.. **5**. plash **6**. pleach,
splice
by joints.. **10**. articulate
closely.. **11**. concentrate
in concordance.. **9**. harmonize
timbers.. **6**. rabbet
united ... **3**. one, wed **4**. knit, tied **5**. added
6. allied, banded, joined, linked,
merged, welded **7**. cohered, grafted,
rallied, spliced **8**. cemented, clannish
9. concerted, corporate **10**. concurrent,
corporated
United Provinces ... **11**. (The)
Netherlands **13**. Dutch Republic
United States ... **9**. Etats-Unis
United States ... see also *American*
artist.. **4**. Wood **5**. Flagg, Homer,
Peale, Ryder, Sloan, Wyeth **6**. Benton,
Eakins, Hopper, O'Keefe, Stuart,
Warhol **7**. Bellows, Bingham, Cassatt
8. Rockwell, Whistler **9**. Remington
12. Grandma Moses
author.. **3**. Ade, Poe **5**. Alger, Crane,
Harte, James (Henry), Lewis (Sinclair),
Stowe, Twain (Clemens) **6**. Alcott,
Cather, Chopin, Cooper, Ferber,
Holmes, Irving, Jewett, London,
Lowell, O'Henry (Porter) **7**. Dreiser,
Ellison, Emerson, Hurston, Thoreau,
Whitman **8**. Faulkner, Melville, Whittier
9. Hawthorne, Hemingway
10. Fitzgerald, Longfellow, Tarkington
canal.. **4**. Erie **6**. Panama
capital.. see separate States
composer.. **4**. Ives, Kern **5**. Foote, Nevin
6. Berlin, Foster **7**. Copland, Rodgers
8. Gershwin **9**. Bernstein
emblem.. **5**. eagle
explorer.. **4**. Byrd, Long, Pike **5**. Boone,
Clark, Lewis, Logan, Perry
Falls.. **7**. Niagara **8**. Yosemite
9. Multnomah
Indian.. see under *Indian (Am)*
inventor.. **3**. Hoe **4**. Bell, Howe
5. Fiske, Fitch, Morse **6**. Edison, Fulton
7. Whitney
mountain.. **4**. Hood **6**. Elbert, Helena,
Shasta **7**. Rainier, Whitney **8**. Katahdin,
McKinley
naturalist.. **4**. Muir **5**. Beebe, Seton
7. Thoreau
ornithologist.. **7**. Audubon
philosopher.. **5**. James
pirate.. **4**. Kidd
poet.. **3**. Poe **4**. Nash **5**. Benét, Field,
Moore, Wylie **6**. Bryant, Holmes, Kilmer,
Lanier, Lowell, Millay **7**. Whitman
8. Whittier **10**. Longfellow
unity ... **3**. one **5**. union **6**. accord
7. concord, harmony, oneness
8. alliance **9**. agreement **10**. singleness,
uniformity **11**. conjunction, unification
12. completeness
universal ... **3**. all **5**. local, total,
usual, whole **6**. cosmic, entire, public

7. general **8.** catholic **9.** prevalent, unlimited, well-known **11.** widely known
universal (pert to) . . .
knowledge . . **9.** pantology
language . . **2.** Ro **3.** Ido **9.** Esperanto
language, written . . **10.** pasigraphy
remedy . . **7.** panacea
solvent . . **8.** alkahest
successor, heir . . **5.** heres (haeres)
universe . . . **4.** olam **5.** world **6.** cosmos, system **9.** macrocosm **10.** Great World
universe, controlling principle . . . **5.** logos
unkempt . . . **5.** messy, rough **6.** frowsy, shaggy, untidy **7.** ruffled, squalid, tousled, uncouth **9.** unrefined **10.** disarrayed, disheveled, unpolished
unkind . . . **3.** ill **5.** cruel, harsh, stern **6.** brutal, severe **8.** ungenial **9.** inclement **10.** ungracious, ungrateful **13.** unsympathetic **15.** uncompassionate
unknowable . . . **6.** mystic **8.** mystical, noumenon **9.** enigmatic **13.** indiscernible **14.** unintelligible **15.** absolute reality (Kant), ultimate reality (Spencer)
unknowable object . . . **3.** God **7.** the soul **8.** noumenon
unknown . . . **7.** inconnu, strange **8.** stranger **9.** anonymous, hereafter, incognito, unheard of **10.** unfamiliar, unrenowned **12.** incalculable
unlawful . . . **7.** bastard, illegal, illicit, lawless **9.** irregular **10.** contraband **11.** unwarranted **12.** illegitimate, unauthorized
unlearned . . . **4.** lewd **5.** gross **8.** ignorant, untaught **10.** illiterate, uneducated **11.** instinctive
unleashed . . . **4.** free **5.** loose **6.** untied **8.** released **10.** unfettered, unshackled, untethered
unleavened . . . **7.** azymous
unleavened bread . . . **4.** azym **5.** azyme **7.** matzoth
unless . . . **4.** nisi, save **6.** except **7.** without **9.** except for, excepting **10.** except that
unlettered . . . **8.** ignorant **10.** illiterate, uneducated
unlike . . . **6.** sundry, uneven **7.** dislike, diverse **9.** different, irregular **10.** dissimilar, improbable **11.** unpromising **12.** disagreeable **13.** heterogeneous
unlikelihood . . . **11.** small chance **13.** improbability
unlikeness . . . **8.** contrast **13.** dissimilarity
unlimited . . . **4.** vast **9.** boundless, unbounded, universal **10.** unconfined **11.** illimitable **12.** immeasurable, unrestricted **13.** indeterminate
unload . . . **3.** rid **4.** dump, sell **5.** empty **7.** discard, lighten **9.** disburden, discharge, liquidate
unlucky . . . **3.** bad, fey, ill **7.** infaust **8.** ill-fated, untimely **9.** ill-omened **11.** unfortunate **12.** inauspicious, not favorable
unmannerly . . . **4.** rude **7.** boorish, uncivil **8.** impolite **10.** mannerless

12. discourteous
unmelodious . . . **9.** dissonant **11.** cacophonous
unmerciful . . . **5.** cruel **6.** unkind **7.** extreme, inhuman **8.** pitiless, ruthless **9.** heartless, merciless **10.** relentless
unmistakable . . . **4.** open **5.** clear, plain **6.** patent **7.** certain, evident, obvious **8.** apparent, distinct, manifest **11.** unqualified
unmitigated . . . **4.** mere **5.** sheer **6.** arrant **8.** clear-cut, thorough **9.** downright **11.** not softened, unqualified
unmoved . . . **4.** calm, dead, firm **5.** inert **6.** serene **8.** obdurate, unshaken **9.** apathetic
unnatural . . . **5.** eerie (eery) **7.** labored, strange, uncanny **8.** abnormal, affected **9.** eccentric, irregular **10.** artificial, factitious
unnecessary . . . **4.** fuss **7.** useless **8.** needless **11.** not required, superfluous, uncalled-for **12.** nonessential
unobtrusive . . . **6.** modest **8.** retiring **11.** clandestine
unoccupied . . . **4.** idle, void **5.** empty **7.** not busy **8.** deserted **10.** unemployed, untenanted **11.** empty-headed, uninhabited
unorthodox . . . **9.** heretical **10.** fallacious, left-handed **14.** unconventional
unostentatious . . . **5.** quiet **6.** lenten, modest **10.** restrained
unparalleled . . . **5.** alone **6.** unique **8.** peerless **9.** matchless, unequaled, unmatched **10.** inimitable **13.** extraordinary
unpleasant . . . **8.** unsavory **9.** offensive **10.** not amiable, ungracious **11.** displeasing, distasteful **12.** disagreeable
unpolished . . . **5.** bruit, crude, rough **6.** coarse, rugged **7.** uncouth **8.** agrestic, unpolite **9.** inelegant **10.** agrestical **11.** countrified
unprecedented . . . **3.** new **5.** novel **10.** unexampled, unimitated **13.** extraordinary
unprejudiced . . . **4.** fair **7.** neutral **8.** unbiased **9.** impartial **10.** impersonal **13.** dispassionate
unprepared . . . **3.** raw **5.** unfit **6.** unwary **7.** unready **9.** premature, unskilled
unprepossessing . . . **4.** grim, ugly **9.** grim-faced **10.** ill-looking
unpretentious . . . **6.** humble, modest, simple **7.** natural **10.** unaffected **11.** in good taste
unprincipled . . . **7.** corrupt **9.** dishonest **10.** fraudulent, perfidious **12.** dishonorable, unscrupulous
unprofessional . . . **3.** lay **6.** laical **7.** amateur **9.** unskilled **10.** amateurish **14.** unbusinesslike
unprofitable . . . **6.** barren **7.** useless **8.** gainless **9.** fruitless **10.** unfruitful
unpropitious . . . **7.** adverse, ominous, opposed **8.** untimely **10.** disastrous **12.** inauspicious
unqualified . . . **5.** unfit **6.** unable

7. genuine, plenary 8. absolute, complete, unfitted 9. incapable 10. ineligible 11. incompetent 12. not qualified 13. unconditional

unquestionable ... 7. certain, decided, evident 8. positive 10. undeniable 11. indubitable, irrefutable 12. indisputable 13. unimpeachable

unravel ... 4. undo 5. feaze, solve 6. unfold, unlace 8. separate 9. disengage 10. disinvolve 11. disentangle

unreal ... 5. false, ideal 7. fancied 8. fanciful, illusory, spurious 9. fantastic, imaginary, visionary 10. artificial, fictitious 11. imaginative 13. unsubstantial

unreasonable ... 3. mad 6. absurd, unwise 9. excessive, fanatical, illogical, senseless 10. capricious, exorbitant, immoderate, irrational 11. extravagant, impractical 13. unjustifiable

unrecognizable ... 3. dim 5. vague 7. blurred, obscure, unclear 9. undefined 10. indistinct 14. unintelligible

unrecognized ... 6. unsung 7. unknown 13. unappreciated

unrefined ... 3. raw 4. loud, rude 5. crass, crude, gross, rough 6. coarse, common, earthy, vulgar 7. uncouth 9. inelegant 11. countrified 12. uncultivated

unrefuted ... 4. true 6. proved 8. undenied 10. unanswered

unrelaxed ... 4. taut 5. rigid, tense 7. nervous

unrelenting ... 4. grim, hard, iron 5. stern 6. severe, strict 8. rigorous 9. merciless 10. inexorable, relentless, unyielding

unreliable ... 6. fickle, unsafe 9. uncertain 10. capricious, changeable 12. undependable 13. irresponsible, untrustworthy 14. tergiversating

unremitting ... 4. busy 8. constant 9. continual, incessant, perpetual 10. continuous, persistent 11. persevering

unrequited ... 6. unpaid 9. forgotten, unthanked 10. ungrateful, unrewarded

unreserved, unreservedly ... 4. free, open 5. frank 6. openly 7. frankly 8. candidly, outright, thorough 9. outspoken 12. unrestricted

unrest ... 6. bustle 8. disquiet 9. commotion 12. restlessness

unrestrained ... 3. lax 4. free, wild 5. loose 6. candid, wanton 7. lawless, riotous 9. unbridled, unlimited 10. capricious

unrestricted ... 4. free, open 9. unlimited 11. extravagant 12. undiminished 13. communicative

unruffled ... 4. calm, cool 5. still 6. placid, poised, sedate, serene, smooth 9. quiescent, unexcited 10. unaffected 11. undisturbed

unruly ... 7. lawless 9. fractious, obstinate, turbulent 10. disorderly, licentious, refractory 11. disobedient 12. recalcitrant, ungovernable, unmanageable

unsafe ... 7. dubious, exposed, unsound 8. insecure, perilous 9. dangerous 10. unreliable 12. undependable

unsatisfactory ... 8. inferior 10. inadequate, unbearable 11. intolerable 12. insufficient, ungratiating 13. disheartening, unsupportable

unsavory ... 7. insipid 9. offensive, tasteless 10. unpleasant 11. unpalatable 12. disagreeable

unscrupulous ... 7. devious 9. dishonest 12. unparticular, unprincipled 13. untrustworthy 16. indiscriminating

unseasonable ... 8. untimely 9. premature 11. inopportune

unseemly ... 5. inapt, wrong 6. vulgar 8. improper, indecent 9. inelegant 10. indecorous, solecistic, unbecoming 11. undignified 13. ungrammatical

unseen ... 6. hidden 8. unheeded, viewless 9. invisible, unnoticed 12. undiscovered

unsettled ... 4. moot 6. fickle, queasy 8. confused, deranged, restless, unplaced, unproved, unstable 9. ambiguous, disturbed, irregular, uncertain, unquieted 10. irresolute, unoccupied, up in the air 11. unpopulated

unshorn ... 5. hairy, whole 6. shaggy

unshorn sheep (2nd year) ... 3. tag, teg

unsightly ... 4. ugly 8. uncomely, unlovely 9. inelegant, not comely 12. unattractive

unskilled ... 5. green 6. puisne 8. ignorant, malapert

unskillful ... 5. inept 7. artless, awkward 9. maladroit 12. unproficient 13. inexperienced

unsophisticated ... 4. naif, pure, soft 5. green, naive 6. simple 7. artless, genuine 8. gullible, innocent 9. ingenuous 11. uncorrupted

unsound ... 4. weak 5. crazy, dotty, risky, shaky 6. addled, fickle 8. impaired, insecure 9. defective, imperfect

unspoken ... 5. tacit 6. silent 7. implied 9. ineffable, unuttered

unstable ... 4. weak 6. fickle, fitful, labile, scanty 7. astatic, erratic, flighty, plastic 8. insecure, not solid, ticklish, unsteady 9. ephemeral, irregular, unsettled 10. inconstant, precarious, unreliable 11. fluctuating, vacillating

unsteady ... 5. dizzy, shaky 6. groggy, wobbly 7. quavery, rickety, unsound 8. titubate, unstable, wavering 9. irregular, uncertain 10. capricious, changeable, flickering, inconstant, precarious 11. fluctuating, ill-balanced, lightheaded, vacillating

unsubstantial ... 4. airy, rare, slim 5. filmy, light 6. aerial, flimsy, papery 8. illusory 9. illogical, visionary 10. immaterial, intangible, unreliable

unsuitable ... 5. inept, undue, unfit 8. untimely 10. unbecoming 11. inexpedient 13. inappropriate 14. unsatisfactory

unsullied ... 4. pure 5. clean 6. chaste

8. innocent, spotless, virginal
10. immaculate
unsure ... **4.** weak **5.** timid **6.** infirm
8. doubtful **10.** precarious **11.** vacillating
unsweetened ... **3.** dry, sec **4.** sour, tart
10. unpleasant
unsympathetic ... **6.** unkind **7.** hostile
8. pitiless **9.** heartless **10.** intolerant
11. hardhearted **12.** unresponsive
untamed ... **4.** wild **5.** feral **6.** savage
9. unsubdued **11.** uncivilized
untangle ... **4.** free **5.** loose, solve
6. sleave **9.** extricate **11.** disentangle
untenable ... **10.** incredible
11. implausible **12.** unbelievable,
unreasonable **13.** inconceivable
unthinking ... **4.** rash **7.** puerile
8. careless, heedless **9.** impetuous,
impulsive **11.** injudicious, instinctive,
involuntary, thoughtless
13. inconsiderate
untidy ... **5.** dowdy, messy **6.** frowzy,
shabby **8.** careless, frumpish, slipshod,
slovenly, unsuited, untimely
10. disheveled
untie ... **4.** free **5.** loose **6.** loosen,
unbind, unknot, unlash **8.** unfasten
9. disengage
until now ... **8.** hitherto
untiring ... **8.** sedulous, tireless
9. unwearied **10.** unflagging
13. indefatigable
untold ... **4.** vast **8.** infinite **9.** boundless,
countless **10.** uninformed, unrevealed
11. innumerable, unexpressed
12. immeasurable, incalculable,
undetermined
untouched ... **3.** new **4.** pure **6.** intact,
unused **8.** pristine, virginal
10. impenitent, unaffected
untoward ... **6.** unruly **7.** unlucky
8. perverse, stubborn, unseemly
10. indecorous, ungraceful
11. unfavorable, unfortunate
12. unpropitious
untrained ... **4.** soft, wild **5.** green
8. indocile **9.** unskilled, untutored
10. amateurish **11.** unpracticed
14. unaccomplished
untrammeled ... **4.** free **5.** loose
8. not bound **9.** unimpeded, unlimited
10. unfettered, unhampered,
unhindered
untransferable ... **11.** inalienable
untried ... **3.** new **5.** fresh, green
8. unproved **9.** unhandled
13. inexperienced
untrue ... **5.** false, wrong **8.** disloyal
9. dishonest, erroneous, incorrect, not
honest **10.** fallacious, unfaithful
untrustworthy ... **6.** tricky, unsafe
8. slippery **9.** deceitful, dishonest,
uncertain **10.** perfidious
untruth ... **3.** lie **5.** error, fable **7.** falsity
9. falsehood, treachery **10.** disloyalty
11. fabrication **13.** faithlessness
unusual ... **3.** odd **4.** rare **5.** novel, queer
6. exotic, quaint, unique **7.** strange
8. terrific, uncommon **9.** anomalous
10. infrequent, remarkable
11. exceptional **13.** extraordinary

unutterable ... **6.** sacred, secret
9. ineffable, wonderful **11.** unspeakable
13. inexpressible
unvarnished ... **5.** plain **6.** simple
7. genuine **9.** unadorned, unglossed
11. undeceptive **13.** unembellished
unvarying ... **7.** uniform **8.** constant
9. permanent **10.** monotonous
unwarranted ... **4.** idle, vain **5.** undue
7. illegal **8.** baseless **9.** excessive,
unfounded, untenable **10.** exorbitant,
unentitled **11.** unjustified
unwary ... **4.** rash **7.** unaware **8.** heedless,
off guard **9.** unguarded **10.** unwatchful
unwavering ... **4.** firm, sure **5.** solid
8. constant **9.** steadfast **10.** unweakened
11. not yielding, persevering
unwelcome ... **8.** non grata, unwanted
9. intrusive, uninvited
unwholesome ... **4.** evil, sick **6.** impure
7. corrupt, immoral, noisome, noxious
9. unhealthy **12.** insalubrious
unwieldy ... **5.** bulky **6.** clumsy
7. awkward, restive **8.** ungainly
9. ponderous **10.** cumbersome
12. unmanageable **13.** insubordinate
unwilling ... **5.** loath (loth) **6.** averse
9. reluctant **11.** disinclined, involuntary
unwilling to prosecute ... **7.** nol-pros
13. nolle prosequi
unwise ... **7.** foolish **9.** impolitic,
imprudent, senseless **10.** irrational
11. inexpedient, injudicious
unwonted ... **4.** rare **6.** unused **7.** unusual
8. uncommon **9.** not wonted
10. infrequent **12.** unaccustomed
unworldly ... **5.** eerie (eery), godly, naive,
weird **8.** heavenly **9.** spiritual, unearthly
10. immaterial **12.** supernatural
unyielding ... **3.** set **4.** firm, hard, iron
5. rigid, stern, stiff **6.** strict **7.** adamant
8. obdurate, stubborn **9.** immovable,
obstinate **10.** adamantine, determined,
inexorable, inflexible
14. uncompromising
up (pert to) ...
and coming .. **7.** go-ahead **8.** hustling
and down .. **6.** seesaw, uneven **8.** vertical
10. undulating **13.** perpendicular
in arms .. **6.** at odds **8.** prepared
9. resistant
ref to .. **10.** at the plate (game)
to .. **4.** able, till, unto **5.** until **9.** cognizant,
competent
to date .. **3.** new **6.** modern **7.** stylish
11. fashionable
upas tree, arrow poison ... **6.** antiar
upbraid ... **4.** twit **5.** blame, chide, scold,
score **6.** rebuke **7.** reprove **8.** admonish,
reproach **9.** reprimand **10.** put to shame
upheaval ... **5.** storm **6.** revolt **9.** agitation,
cataclysm, elevation **10.** convulsion
upheld ... **5.** aided **6.** backed **7.** abetted
8. defended **9.** supported, sustained
10. encouraged, maintained
uphill ... **6.** upward **7.** upgrade
9. ascending, difficult, laborious
10. slantingly
uphold ... **3.** aid **4.** abet, back, buoy
5. favor, raise **6.** defend **7.** confirm,
support, sustain **8.** maintain, preserve

9. encourage 11. corroborate, countenance, lend support
upkeep... 4. cost 6. repair 7. support 11. maintenance
upland... 4. wold 5. weald 6. coteau, inland 7. country, plateau 8. highland
uplands... 7. country 9. highlands 10. the country
uplift... 5. elate, erect, raise 7. elevate, ennoble, glorify, improve 8. upheaval 9. elevation 11. inspiration
upon... 2. on 3. sur 4. atop, onto 5. about, above 7. against 9. by means of 10. after which
upon (pert to)...
  law.. 3. sur
  prefix.. 3. epi, sur
  that.. 7. whereat 9. whereupon
  which.. 7. whereat
upper... 6. higher 8. superior
upper (pert to)...
  bed.. 4. bunk
  crust.. 7. society 11. aristocracy 13. highest circle
  end.. 3. tip 4. apex, head
  hand.. 7. mastery 8. dominion 9. advantage, influence 10. preference
  House of Congress.. 6. Senate
  shoe part.. 4. vamp
uppermost... 3. top 6. upmost 7. highest, supreme, topmost 8. farthest, foremost 9. outermost
uppish... 5. drunk, proud 6. uppity 7. haughty, peevish, stuck-up 8. arrogant, assuming, snobbish 9. high-flown
upright... 4. good, just, true 5. erect, moral, piano 6. honest, square 7. endwise, sincere 8. vertical, virtuous 9. equitable, honorable, righteous 13. perpendicular
upright (pert to)...
  chair part.. 4. slat
  comb form.. 5. ortho
  posture.. 8. orthotic 11. orthostatic
  slab.. 5. stela
  timber.. 4. jamb, stud
uprising... 4. riot 6. ascent, mutiny, revolt 7. sloping 9. acclivity, ascending, rebellion 12. insurrection
uproar... 3. din 4. riot, rout 5. noise 6. bedlam, bustle, clamor, fracas, hubbub, outcry, tumult 7. turmoil 8. outbreak 9. commotion, confusion 10. donnybrook, hurly-burly, tintamarre, turbulence 11. pandemonium 12. insurrection
upset... 3. irk 4. rile, ruin, stir 6. defeat, refute, topple 7. agitate, capsize, confuse, disturb, fluster, startle, subvert, unnerve 8. distress, overturn, startled, unnerved 9. embarrass, overthrow 10. discompose, disconcert, distressed, frustrated, overturned, refutation, revolution 11. frustration, overwrought
upshot... 3. end 5. fruit, issue 6. result, sequel 7. outcome 10. conclusion 11. consequence, eventuality, termination 12. consummation
upside down... 8. confused, disorder 9. confusion 10. resupinate, topsy-turvy

upsilon (Gr)... 5. hyoid, vowel 7. Y-shaped
upstart... 4. snob 7. bounder, parvenu 13. social climber
up-to-date... 6. modern 7. alamode, topical 8. informed 11. fashionable
upward... 2. up 3. ano (comb form) 4. over 5. above, aloft 6. onward 7. skyward 8. upstream 9. ascending
upward movement of vessels... 5. scend
uraeus (Egypt Relig)... 3. asp 6. symbol 8. symbolic
Ural... 5. river 9. mountains
Urania (pert to)...
  blue.. 12. independence
  epithet of.. 9. Aphrodite
  genus of.. 5. moths
  Gr Myth.. 4. Muse (Astron)
uranology (study of)... 7. heavens 15. celestial bodies
Uranus (pert to)...
  astronomy.. 6. planet
  daughter.. 4. Rhea
  father of.. 9. The Titans (12)
  personification of.. 6. heaven
  satellite.. 5. Ariel 6. Oberon 7. Titania, Umbriel
  son.. 6. Cronus
urare, urari... 6. curare
urban... 5. civic 6. ghetto, polite, uptown 7. oppidan, refined 8. downtown, polished 9. courteous, municipal 12. metropolitan 13. sophisticated
urbane... 5. civil, suave 6. polish, polite 7. affable 8. gracious 9. courteous 11. deferential
urbanity... 7. amenity 8. civility, courtesy 9. deference
urchin... 3. boy, elf, imp, tad 4. arab, brat 5. gamin 6. elfish 8. hedgehog 9. dandiprat, sea urchin, youngster
urge... 3. dun, egg, hie, ply, yen 4. abet, coax, goad, prod, push, spur 5. drive, egg on, impel, press 6. advise, compel, dehort, desire, exhort, fillip, hasten, incite, induce 7. animate, entreat, solicit 8. persuade 9. constrain, importune, influence, instigate 10. inducement
urgent... 3. hot 5. grave 7. clamant, exigent, instant 8. critical, pressing 9. impelling, important, insistent, necessary 11. importunate
urial... 3. sha 5. sheep 6. oorial
Uriel... 9. archangel 10. flame of God (Bib)
Urim and Thummim (Bib)... 11. instruments 12. interpreters (Mormon)
urn... 3. jar 4. ewer, urna (anc), vase 5. grave, steen 6. vessel 7. pitcher, samovar, vaselet 10. jardiniere
urn-shaped... 8. urceolus 9. urceolate
Ursa... 4. bear 9. Ursa Major (Great Bear), Ursa Minor (Little Bear)
ursal... 7. fur seal
ursuk... 11. bearded seal
Ursula... 5. Saint 7. she-bear 9. butterfly 15. British princess (legend)
urubu... 7. vulture
Uruguay...

capital.. **10**. Montevideo
city.. **4**. Melo **5**. Minar **9**. Maldonado
estuary.. **5**. Plata **12**. Rio de la Plata
lake.. **5**. Merim
river.. **7**. Uruguay
settler.. **5**. Cabot (Sebastian, 1527)
university.. **10**. Montevideo (1849)
windstorm.. **7**. pampero
urus... **2**. ox **3**. tur **7**. aurochs
usable... **3**. fit **9**. practical **10**. functional
11. serviceable, utilitarian
usage... **3**. use **4**. wont **5**. habit, ritus
6. custom, method **7**. utility **8**. behavior,
practice **9**. treatment **10**. convention
use... **3**. try **5**. apply, avail, exert, spend,
treat, wield **6**. employ, expend, occupy
7. consume, exploit, utilize **8**. function
10. manipulate **11**. consumption,
utilization
use (pert to)...
abusive language.. **4**. rail
divining rod.. **5**. dowse
frugally.. **5**. stint
pert to words.. **7**. neology, verbose
8. enallage, pleonasm **9**. verbosity
poetry.. **4**. vail
refrain from.. **7**. boycott
subterfuge.. **7**. chicane
up.. **3**. eat **7**. consume, deplete, exhaust,
fatigue
useful... **4**. good **5**. utile **7**. helpful
9. practical **10**. beneficial, commodious
11. serviceable, subservient
12. advantageous, instrumental
usefulness... **5**. avail, value **6**. profit
7. utility **13**. conduciveness
useless... **4**. idle, null, vain **6**. futile,
otiose **7**. of no use **8**. bootless,
hopeless **9**. fruitless, worthless **10**. fifth
wheel **11**. ineffectual, superfluous
12. unprofitable **13**. unserviceable
14. good for nothing
uselessness... **8**. futility **9**. inutility
10. inefficacy
usher... **4**. lead, page **5**. guide **6**. escort
7. chobdar, teacher **9**. attendant,
harbinger, precursor **10**. doorkeeper,
forerunner, inaugurate
usquebaugh... **6**. whisky **7**. cordial
ustion... **7**. burning **13**. cauterization
ustulate... **8**. scorched **10**. discolored
usual... **7**. average, typical, usitate
8. everyday, frequent **11**. status in
quo
usuer... **5**. shark **6**. loaner **7**. Shylock
11. moneylender
usurp... **4**. take **5**. seize **6**. assume
8. arrogate **11**. appropriate
Utah...
capital.. **12**. Salt Lake City
city.. **5**. Logan, Ogden, Provo
7. Bingham
dam.. **10**. Glen Canyon **12**. Flaming
Gorge
lake.. **6**. Powell **9**. Great Salt
mountain.. **5**. Uinta **7**. Wasatch **9**. King's
Peak
name desired.. **7**. Deseret
natural wonder.. **4**. Zion **5**. Bryce
13. Rainbow Bridge
settled by.. **7**. Mormons **12**. Brigham

Young **15**. Latter-day Saints
State admission.. **10**. Forty-fifth
State motto.. **8**. Industry
State nickname.. **7**. Beehive
utensil... **3**. mop, pan, pot **4**. tool
5. broom, brush **6**. device, ramrod
7. skillet, sweeper **9**. apparatus,
appliance, implement **10**. instrument
utilitarian... **5**. plain **6**. useful
8. economic **9**. practical **10**. functional
12. matter-of-fact
utility... **3**. use **4**. tool **5**. avail **6**. profit
7. benefit, service **9**. appliance,
happiness, implement **10**. usefulness
utmost... **4**. best, last **5**. final **7**. extreme,
maximum, supreme **8**. farthest, greatest
9. uttermost **11**. most distant
Utopia... **4**. Eden **6**. heaven, island
(imaginary) **7**. Erewhon **8**. paradise
9. fairyland, Shangri-La **10**. millennium
utopian... **5**. ideal **6**. Edenic **8**. Quixotic,
romantic **9**. visionary **10**. chimerical,
idealistic, millennial
utter... **3**. say **4**. emit, pass, tell,
vent **5**. issue, sheer, speak, total,
voice **6**. assert, entire, mumble,
reveal **7**. deliver, divulge, express,
extreme, publish, unusual
8. abnormal, absolute, complete, disclose,
disperse, intonate **9**. downright,
enunciate, out-and-out, pronounce
10. peremptory **11**. unqualified
13. unconditional
utter (pert to)...
harshly.. **3**. rap **4**. bray
heedlessly.. **4**. blat
in devotion.. **4**. pray
in slow tone.. **5**. drawl
musically.. **6**. warble
publicly.. **4**. tell **5**. voice **7**. enounce
softly.. **6**. murmur **7**. whisper
want.. **9**. indigency **11**. destitution
with effort.. **5**. heave
with impulse.. **9**. ejaculate
without voice.. **4**. surd **7**. spirate
utterance (pert to)...
dogmatic.. **6**. dictum
gushing.. **8**. effusion
rhythmic.. **7**. cadence
voice.. **8**. phonesis, speaking
9. phonation **12**. articulation
wise.. **6**. oracle
utterer of pithy remarks... **8**. aphorist
utterly... **5**. fully, stark **7**. totally
8. entirely **10**. absolutely, completely
17. straightforwardly
uttermost... **5**. finai **6**. utmost **7**. extreme
utu... **6**. reward **12**. compensation,
satisfaction
uva... **5**. fruit, grape
uvate... **8**. conserve (grape)
uvea... **4**. iris
uxor... **4**. wife
uxoricide... **10**. wife murder
Uz (Bib)... **8**. Job's home
Uzbekistan (pert to)...
capital.. **8**. Tashkent
city.. **9**. Samarkand
formerly part of.. **4**. USSR
people.. **5**. Uzbek **6**. Turkic
Uzziel... **5**. angel (Paradise Lost)

V

V . . . **5.** notch **6.** letter (22nd), symbol **14.** five-dollar bill

vaagmer . . . **8.** dealfish (mare of the sea)

Vac (Hind) . . . **7.** goddess (of speech)

vacant . . . **4.** free, idle, void **5.** blank, empty, inane **6.** barren, devoid **7.** leisure, vacuous **8.** unfilled **10.** disengaged, untenanted **11.** thoughtless **12.** unencumbered **14.** expressionless

vacate . . . **4.** free, quit, void **5.** annul, empty, leave **6.** depart **7.** abandon **8.** abdicate, abrogate, evacuate, withdraw

vacation . . . **4.** rest **5.** leave **6.** outing, recess, repeal **7.** nonterm, respite **8.** furlough, justitum **10.** recreation **12.** intermission **14.** leave of absence

vacation place . . . **3.** spa **4.** lake, park **5.** beach **6.** forest, resort **9.** mountains

vaccination . . . **11.** inoculation

vaccine (pert to) . . .
 discoverer . . **4.** Salk **6.** Jenner
 protection for . . **5.** virus **6.** cowpox
 term . . **5.** lymph, serum, virus

vacillate . . . **4.** sway **5.** waver **6.** dacker (daiker), seesaw, teeter, totter **7.** flutter, stagger **8.** hesitate, titubate **9.** fluctuate, oscillate **13.** procrastinate

vacillation . . . **5.** doubt **8.** wavering **9.** faltering, hesitancy **10.** fickleness, indecision, titubation **11.** oscillation, uncertainty **12.** irresolution **14.** changeableness **15.** procrastination

vacuate . . . **5.** empty **8.** evacuate

vacuous . . . **4.** dull, void **5.** blank, empty **6.** stupid **8.** unfilled **9.** senseless **11.** empty-headed, thoughtless **13.** unintelligent

vacuum . . . **3.** gap **4.** void **9.** emptiness **11.** rarefaction

vade mecum . . . **6.** manual **8.** handbook

vagabond . . . **3.** bum, vag **4.** hobo **5.** lorel, scamp, tramp **6.** beggar, picaro, rascal, rodney **7.** vagrant, wastrel **8.** Bohemian, brodyaga, wanderer **10.** ne'er-do-well

vagary . . . **4.** whim **5.** caper, fancy, jaunt, prank, trick **6.** notion, ramble **7.** caprice, whimsey (whimsy) **9.** excursion, wandering **10.** digression **13.** manifestation

vagrant . . . **3.** bum **4.** hobo **5.** rogue, tramp **6.** roving, truant **7.** nomadic, prowler, wayward **8.** brodyaga, vagabond, wanderer **9.** desultory, deviative, itinerant **10.** capricious

vague . . . **3.** dim **4.** dark, hazy **5.** loose, misty **6.** dreamy **7.** obscure, shadowy, unfixed **8.** confused, formless, nebulous, not clear **9.** ambiguous, unsettled, wandering **10.** indefinite, indistinct, intangible **13.** indeterminate

vail . . . **3.** tip **4.** doff (a hat), dole **5.** avail, bribe, yield **6.** humble, submit **7.** descend **8.** gratuity **10.** beneficial **12.** advantageous

vain . . . **4.** idle **5.** empty, proud **6.** devoid, futile, otiose, snooty **7.** foolish, trivial, useless **8.** arrogant, boastful, nugatory **9.** conceited, fruitless, worthless **10.** unavailing, unrewarded **11.** empty-headed, overweening, unimportant **12.** vainglorious

vain boasting . . . **11.** fanfaronade

vainglorious . . . **4.** vain **7.** heroics **8.** boastful **9.** gasconade

vain person . . . **3.** fop **5.** dandy **7.** coxcomb **8.** popinjay

vair . . . **3.** fur

vajra (Buddh) . . . **7.** diamond, trident (Indra's) **10.** adamantine **11.** thunderbolt

valance . . . **5.** drape **6.** border, pelmet, ruffle **7.** curtain, drapery, hanging

vale . . . **4.** dale, dell, glen **5.** earth, glade, world **6.** valley

valediction . . . **5.** adieu **7.** address **8.** farewell **11.** valedictory

valedictory . . . **7.** address, oration **10.** apopemptic **11.** leave-taking, valediction

Valentine (pert to) . . .
 romance . . **5.** Orson **8.** love song
 Saint . . **6.** martyr (Rom) **7.** holiday **8.** feast day
 State . . **7.** Arizona (adm 2/14/1912)
 sweetheart . . **11.** one's beloved

valerian . . . **4.** drug **5.** plant **7.** panacea

valet . . . **3.** man **7.** Crispin **9.** attendant, cameriere, chamberer **10.** manservant **11.** body servant **14.** valet de chambre

valetudinarian . . . **6.** infirm, shut-in, sickly, weakly **7.** invalid **11.** languishing

Valhalla (Valhall) . . . **8.** Pantheon (Bavaria) **10.** hall of Odin (Norse Myth)

valiant . . . **4.** bold, fine **5.** brave **6.** heroic, strong, sturdy **7.** doughty **8.** intrepid, stalwart, vigorous, virtuous **9.** steadfast **10.** chivalrous, courageous **11.** meritorious **12.** stouthearted

valid . . . **4.** good, just, true **5.** legal, sound **6.** cogent, lawful, proved **7.** binding, weighty **9.** authentic, effective **10.** sufficient **11.** efficacious **12.** well-grounded

validate . . . **6.** affirm, attest **7.** confirm **8.** legalize **12.** substantiate

validity . . . **5.** force **7.** cogency **9.** authority, soundness **14.** substantiality

Valjean (pert to) . . .
 discoverer . . **6.** Javert
 friend . . **6.** Marius
 hero of . . **13.** Les Miserables (Victor Hugo)
 protégé . . **7.** Cosette

valley . . . **4.** dale, dell, dene, glen, vale, wady **5.** glade, gully **6.** coulee, dingle, ravine, trough **10.** depression

valley (pert to) . . .
 anatomy . . **9.** vallecula

circular . . **6.** rincon
deep . . **6.** canyon
geology . . **5.** atrio
India . . **5.** dhoon
Jerusalem (near) . . **6.** Hinnom
 7. Gehenna, Rephaim
moon . . **5.** rille
open . . **6.** canada
where David killed Goliath . . **4.** Elah
 (Bib)
valonia oak . . . **6.** camata (fruit)
 9. evergreen
valor . . . **5.** merit, worth **6.** virtue
 7. bravery, courage, heroism, prowess
 8. boldness, chivalry **9.** gallantry
 11. distinction **12.** fearlessness
valuable . . . **4.** dear **5.** asset **6.** prized,
 useful, worthy **8.** precious **9.** estimable,
 treasured **10.** worthwhile
value . . . **3.** par, use **4.** rate **5.** price,
 prize, worth **6.** assess, esteem,
 parity, status **7.** apprize (apprise),
 cherish, compute, meaning, respect,
 utility **8.** appraise, estimate, evaluate
 9. valuation **10.** estimation, excellence,
 importance
value (pert to) . . .
equal . . **6.** parity
least possible . . **5.** plack
nominal . . **3.** par
reduction . . **12.** depreciation
valueless . . . **4.** baff **9.** worthless
 10. threepenny **14.** good-for-nothing
valve . . . **3.** tap **4.** cock, door, gate
 6. faucet, piston, spigot **7.** petcock
vamoose . . . **2.** go **4.** blow, scat **5.** leave,
 scram **6.** beat it, decamp **7.** skiddoo
 9. skedaddle
vamp . . . **4.** hose, sock **5.** flirt, patch, upper
 6. recoct, repair, seduce **7.** beguile,
 bewitch, concoct, touch up **9.** improvise,
 temptress, transform
vampire . . . **3.** bat **5.** fiend, ghost, lamia,
 witch **6.** Alukah **9.** bewitcher, sorceress,
 temptress **11.** bloodsucker, extortioner
 12. extortionist
van . . . **4.** lead, wing **5.** front, wagon
 6. shovel, summit, winnow **7.** vehicle
 9. forefront **10.** baggage car **12.** advance
 guard
vandal . . . **3.** Hun **7.** wrecker **9.** destroyer,
 mutilator, plunderer **10.** iconoclast
vandalize . . . **3.** mar **5.** wreck **6.** deface
Vandyke . . . **5.** beard, brown **6.** artist,
 collar **7.** picture
vane . . . **4.** cock **11.** weathercock,
 weathervane
vanish . . . **3.** die **4.** fade, flee, melt, pass
 6. perish **8.** evanesce **9.** cease to be,
 disappear
vanity . . . **5.** pride **6.** egoism **7.** conceit,
 egotism, falsity **8.** futility **9.** arrogance,
 emptiness, vainglory **10.** hollowness
 11. fatuousness, self-conceit
 12. boastfulness **13.** dressing table
vanity case . . . **4.** etui **6.** make-up
 7. compact **9.** cosmetics
vanquish . . . **3.** win **4.** beat, best, rout
 5. expel **6.** defeat, subdue **7.** conquer
 8. confound, overcome, suppress,
 surmount **9.** overthrow

vantage . . . **4.** gain **9.** advantage
 10. perquisite **11.** opportunity,
 superiority
vapid . . . **3.** dry **4.** dead, dull, flat
 5. inane, stale **7.** insipid, prosaic
 8. lifeless **9.** pointless, tasteless
 10. spiritless, unanimated **11.** indifferent
 13. uninteresting
vapor . . . **3.** air, fog, gas **4.** fume,
 haze, mist **5.** brume, cloud, fancy,
 humor, smoke, steam **6.** breath,
 bubble **7.** halitus **8.** humidity, illusion,
 phantasm **9.** evaporate **10.** exhalation
vaporous . . . **4.** vain **5.** foggy, misty
 6. cloudy, steamy **7.** gaseous
 8. ethereal, fanciful, fleeting
 13. unsubstantial
variable . . . **6.** fickle, fitful, mobile
 7. protean, unequal **8.** shifting, unstable,
 unsteady **10.** capricious, changeable,
 inconstant
variance . . . **3.** out **7.** dissent **9.** deviation,
 disaccord **10.** contention, difference
 11. discrepancy **12.** disagreement
varied . . . **5.** mixed **6.** daedal, motley
 7. changed, dappled, diverse, mottled,
 piebald, several, various **8.** speckled
 9. different **10.** variegated **11.** diversified
variegated . . . **5.** pinto **6.** daedal, motley,
 varied **7.** dappled, diverse, mottled,
 painted **9.** different **11.** diversified,
 many-colored
variegation . . . **7.** variety **9.** diversity
 10. multicolor
variety . . . **4.** kind, mode, sort **5.** class
 6. change **7.** species **9.** diversity,
 variation **10.** assortment, difference
 13. entertainment
variola . . . **6.** cowpox **8.** smallpox
various . . . **4.** many **6.** divers, sundry
 7. diverse, several **8.** manifold, variable
 9. different, many-sided, uncertain
 10. changeable, inconstant, variegated
 11. diversified
varnish . . . **4.** spar **5.** adorn, gloss, japan,
 paint **7.** distort, falsify, furbish, lacquer,
 pretext **8.** coat over **9.** embellish
Varuna (pert to) . . .
art consorts . . **5.** Jumna **6.** Ganges
deity . . **6.** cosmic (supreme)
god . . **3.** sea
Vedic equiv . . **13.** Avestan Ormazd
Vedic Relig . . **5.** Aditi (fem deity)
vary . . . **5.** alter, range, shift **6.** change,
 differ, modify **7.** deviate, dissent,
 diverge **8.** disagree **9.** alternate,
 diversify, fluctuate, vacillate, variegate
 13. differentiate
vas . . . **4.** duct **6.** pledge, surety, vessel
vascular (pert to) . . . **5.** hemic (haemic)
 6. vessel (blood, lymph) **7.** tubular
 9. vesicular **10.** hot-blooded
vase . . . **3.** jar, urn **4.** bowl **5.** ascus
 6. vessel **8.** ornament **10.** cassolette,
 jardiniere
vase (pert to) . . .
covered . . **7.** potiche
Etruscan . . **7.** canopic
Greek . . **5.** askos, diota **6.** deinos (dinos)
 7. amphora
Roman . . **8.** murrhine

vassal ... **3.** man **4.** esne, serf **5.** helot,
liege, slave **6.** varlet **7.** bondman,
servant, servile, subject **9.** dependent,
feudatory **11.** subordinate, subservient
12. feudal tenant
vassalage ... **5.** valor **6.** fealty **7.** courage,
enfeoff, prowess, slavery **8.** dominion
9. servitude **10.** subjection
vast ... **4.** huge **5.** broad, great, large
6. cosmic, mighty, untold **7.** immense,
mammoth **8.** colossal, enormous,
gigantic, spacious **9.** cyclopean,
extensive **11.** far-reaching
vast (pert to) ...
expanse .. **5.** ocean **6.** desert, empire,
region
numbers .. **6.** myriad
period .. **3.** eon, era **5.** cycle
space .. **5.** waste **9.** boundless,
immensity, limitless
vastness ... **6.** extent **7.** expanse
9. greatness, magnitude
vat ... **3.** bac, pit, tub, tun **4.** cask, gyle,
kier, tank **6.** barrel, vessel **7.** caldron
(cauldron), chessel, cistern, measure,
salt pit **8.** chessart
Vatican (pert to) ...
chapel .. **7.** Sistine
church .. **8.** St Peter's
city .. **10.** Papal State (Rome)
palace of .. **4.** Pope
statuary group .. **7.** Laocoon
vaticination ... **8.** prophecy **10.** prediction
11. prophesying
vault ... **3.** sky **4.** arch, dome, leap,
over, tomb **5.** bound, crypt, enbow,
groin **6.** canopy (of heaven), coffer,
curvet, grotto, welkin **10.** depository
11. testudinate
vaunt ... **4.** brag **5.** boast
Vauxhall ... **6.** resort **13.** London Quarter
(Thames) **14.** Lambeth Gardens
Veda (pert to) ...
hymns .. **8.** Sama-Veda
language .. **13.** Vedic Sanskrit
literature .. **6.** sacred (most anc)
oldest .. **7.** Rig-Veda
prose, poetry (popular) .. **11.** Atharva-
Veda
ritualistic .. **9.** Yajur-Veda
Vedic (pert to) ...
cosmic order .. **4.** Rita
dialect .. **4.** Pali
god .. **4.** Agni **5.** Dyaus **6.** Aditya, Varuna
7. Savitar
goddess .. **5.** Aditi
hymn .. **6.** mantra
language .. **4.** Pali **8.** Sanskrit
sky serpent .. **3.** Ahi
text, treatise .. **6.** shakha (sakha)
9. Upanishad
veer ... **3.** shy, yaw **4.** slue, sway, turn
5. alter, shift, sidle **6.** career, change,
swerve **7.** deviate, digress **9.** fluctuate
veery ... **6.** thrush **13.** Wilson's thrush
vegetable ... **3.** pea, yam **4.** bean,
beet, corn, leek, okra **5.** onion
6. carrot, celery, lentil, potato, radish,
squash, tomato, turnip **7.** cabbage,
lettuce, parsnip, rhubarb, shallot,
spinach (spinage) **8.** broccoli, eggplant,

rutabaga, scallion **9.** artichoke
11. cauliflower
vegetable (pert to) ...
and meat dish .. **4.** stew **6.** ragout
caterpillar .. **5.** aweto
dealer .. **8.** huckster **11.** greengrocer
12. costermonger
green .. **5.** sabzi
herb .. **7.** salsify
leafy, salad .. **5.** chard **6.** endive
7. lettuce, romaine, spinach
oil .. **7.** soybean **8.** macassar
poison .. **5.** abrin
stew .. **11.** ratatouille
sugar yielding .. **4.** beet
vegetate ... **4.** grow, rest **5.** exist
vegetation, goddess of ... **5.** Ceres
vehemence ... **3.** ire **4.** fire, fury, rage,
zeal **5.** anger, ardor **8.** violence
9. eloquence **11.** impetuosity
vehement ... **3.** hot **5.** angry, eager, fiery
6. ardent, fervid, heated **7.** animose,
furious, intense, violent, zealous
8. forceful, vigorous **9.** impetuous
10. passionate
vehicle ... **3.** ark, bus, cab, car, van, wag
4. auto, cart, dray, hack, jeep, limo (sl),
semi, shay, sled, tank **5.** buggy, coach,
lorry, moped, sulky, tonga, truck, wagon
6. go-cart, hansom, hot rod, jalopy,
landau, sleigh, travoy, troika, wheels
(sl) **7.** caleche, caravan, chariot, clunker
(sl), kibitka, minibus, omnibus, phaeton,
scooter **8.** brougham, carriage, dragster
9. buckboard, dune buggy, limousine
10. automobile, conveyance, jinrikisha
(jinriksha), motorcycle **11.** convertible
vehicle for oil colors ... **6.** megilp
(meguilp)
veil ... **3.** dim **4.** caul, film, mask **5.** cloak,
cover, orale, shade, velum, volet
6. fannel, masque, screen, shroud,
soften **7.** conceal, curtain, garment,
pretext, secrecy **8.** disguise **9.** incognito
11. superimpose
veiled ... **5.** vague **6.** masked, shaded,
velate **7.** covered **8.** shrouded
9. curtained
veiling ... **5.** tulle, voile **7.** curtain
8. covering **10.** obvelation
vein ... **3.** rib **4.** dash, hilo, lode, mood,
tang, vena, wave **5.** costa, shade,
smack, spice, tinge, touch **6.** cavity,
streak **7.** bonanza, channel, crevice,
fissure, mineral, stratum
vein (pert to) ...
arrangement .. **9.** neuration
inflammation .. **9.** phlebitis
leaf .. **3.** rib
ref to .. **5.** veiny **6.** veinal, venous
7. marbled **8.** venulose
small .. **6.** venule **7.** veinlet
stone .. **6.** gangue, matrix **9.** lodestuff
without a .. **7.** avenous
velar ... **7.** palatal, throaty **8.** gutteral
veld, veldt ... **6.** meadow **8.** bushveld
9. grassland, grassveld
velleity ... **4.** hope **6.** desire **8.** volition
9. faint hope **10.** slight wish
vellicate ... **3.** nip **5.** pinch **6.** tickle,
twitch **9.** titillate

vellum ... **9.** parchment **10.** manuscript (on parchment)
velocity ... **4.** pace **5.** speed **8.** celerity, rapidity **9.** quickness, swiftness **10.** speediness
velocity measure ... **4.** velo
velum ... **6.** palate (soft) **8.** membrane
velvet (pert to) ...
breast .. **9.** merganser
cotton .. **9.** velveteen
fabric .. **5.** panne **6.** velure
Japanese .. **6.** birodo
knife .. **6.** trevet
leaf .. **6.** mallow **7.** mullein
return .. **4.** gain **6.** profit
texture .. **4.** soft **5.** nappy **6.** smooth
venal ... **5.** hired **6.** venous **7.** corrupt, salable (saleable) **8.** hireling, vendible **9.** mercenary **11.** corruptible
vend ... **4.** hawk, sell **5.** trade **6.** market, peddle **8.** dispense **13.** publish abroad
vender, vendor ... **6.** seller **7.** alienor
vendetta ... **4.** feud **8.** bad blood
vendue ... **4.** sale **7.** auction
venerable ... **3.** old **4.** aged, hoar, sage **5.** hoary, olden, title **6.** august, sacred **7.** ancient, antique, classic, elderly, revered **9.** dignified **11.** reverential
venerate ... **4.** love **5.** adore **6.** revere **7.** worship
veneration ... **3.** awe **4.** fear **5.** dulia, piety **6.** esteem, latria **7.** respect, worship **8.** devotion **9.** adoration, reverence
Venetian (pert to) ...
barge .. **9.** bucentaur
beach, resort .. **4.** Lido
boat .. **4.** topo (toppo) **7.** gondola
bridge (famed) .. **6.** Rialto
magistrate .. **4.** doge **7.** podesta
medal (New Year's) .. **5.** osela (osella)
painter .. **6.** Titian **7.** Bellini (family), Vecchio **10.** Tintoretto
school of .. **8.** painting
song .. **9.** barcarole
window (Arch) .. **9.** Palladian
Venezuela ...
anc name .. **12.** Little Venice
capital .. **7.** Caracas
city .. **8.** LaGuaira, Valencia **9.** Maracaibo **6.** Ciudad, Guyana **13.** Ciudad Bolivar
copper center .. **4.** Aroa
Falls (world's tallest) .. **5.** Angel (found 1937)
hero, liberator .. **7.** Bolivar
lake .. **9.** Maracaibo, Tacarigua
Mt .. **5.** Andes **6.** Concha, Parima, Sierra **9.** Pacaraima
plains .. **6.** llanos
river .. **6.** Caroni **7.** Orinoco
sea .. **9.** Caribbean
snake .. **4.** lora
vengeance ... **4.** harm **7.** revenge **8.** reprisal, requital **10.** avengement, punishment **11.** retaliation, retribution
Vengeance, goddess of (Gr) ... **3.** Ara, Ate **7.** Nemesis
Vengeance, god of (Gr) ... **6.** Erinys **7.** Alastor
veni, vidi, vici ... **19.** I came, I saw, I conquered (Caesar)
venial ... **7.** trivial **9.** excusable, tolerable

10. pardonable **13.** insignificant
Venice ... see also *Venetian*
beach .. **4.** Lido
bridge .. **6.** Rialto
canal .. **5.** Grand **8.** Merceria, San Marco
capital of .. **7.** Venetia (province)
color .. **4.** blue
island .. **6.** Rialto
landmark .. **9.** Campanile **12.** Doges' Palaces **13.** Bridge of Sighs
of the North .. **9.** Stockholm
river .. **6.** Brenta
venison ... **8.** pemmican (pemican)
vennel ... **4.** lane **5.** alley, sewer **6.** gutter
venom ... **4.** gall **5.** spite, virus **6.** malice, poison **9.** animosity, malignity, virulence
venomous ... **5.** toxic **6.** deadly **7.** baneful, noxious **8.** spiteful, virulent **9.** envenomed, malicious, malignant, poisonous, rancorous
vent ... **3.** say **4.** exit, hole, slit **5.** eject, utter **6.** egress, escape, outlet **7.** air hole, fissure, opening, publish, release, ventage, volcano **8.** aperture, let loose **10.** escapement
venta ... **3.** inn
ventilate ... **3.** air, fan **5.** utter **6.** aerate **7.** discuss, publish, refresh **9.** oxygenate
ventose ... **5.** windy **9.** flatulent **12.** cupping glass
ventral ... **7.** sternal **9.** abdominal
venture ... **3.** hap, try **4.** dare, risk, wage **5.** brave, guess, stake **6.** be bold, chance, danger, gamble, hazard **7.** attempt, presume **8.** run a risk **9.** adventure, haphazard, speculate **10.** enterprise, investment **11.** speculation, undertaking
venturesome ... **4.** bold, rash **5.** brave, risky **6.** daring, heroic **8.** fearless, reckless **9.** dangerous, foolhardy, venturous **11.** adventurous, temerarious **12.** enterprising
venturous ... **4.** bold, rash **5.** hardy, risky **6.** daring **8.** fearless **9.** dangerous, hazardous **11.** temerarious, venturesome
venue ... **4.** bout, site **5.** match, onset **6.** thrust **7.** arrival, assault **9.** encounter
Venus (pert to) ...
astronomy .. **6.** planet
church .. **11.** Verticordia
goddess .. **7.** Victrix **9.** Aphrodite
goddess of (Rom) .. **6.** Beauty
son .. **5.** Cupid
sweetheart .. **6.** Adonis
zoology .. **7.** mollusk
Venus status (marble) ...
Florence .. **8.** de Medici
Louvre .. **7.** of Arles **8.** Genetrix
Melos .. **6.** de Milo
Naples .. **7.** of Capua
Rome .. **8.** Borghese **12.** of the Capitol
veracity ... **5.** truth **7.** honesty **8.** accuracy, trueness **11.** correctness **12.** truthfulness
veranda, verandah ... **4.** pyal, stoa **5.** lanai, porch, stoep **6.** loggia, piazza **7.** gallery, portico
verb (Gram) ... **5.** rhema **6.** action

verbal ... **4.** oral **5.** wordy **7.** literal, verbose **8.** verbatim **9.** talkative, vocabular
verbal noun ... **6.** gerund
verbatim ... **6.** orally **7.** literal **8.** verbally **11.** word for word
verbiage ... **4.** talk **7.** chatter, diction, fustian, wording **8.** claptrap **9.** prolixity, verbosity, wordiness **10.** redundancy
verbose ... **5.** wordy **6.** prolix **7.** diffuse **9.** redundant
verbosity ... **10.** redundancy
verboten ... **5.** taboo (tabu) **9.** forbidden **10.** prohibited
verdant ... **3.** raw **5.** color, green **6.** unripe **9.** evergreen **13.** inexperienced **15.** unsophisticated
verdelho ... **4.** wine (white)
verdict ... **4.** word **7.** finding, opinion **8.** decision, judgment **13.** consideration
verdigris ... **4.** drug **5.** green **6.** aerugo **7.** deposit (on copper)
verecund ... **6.** modest **7.** bashful
verge ... **3.** lip, rim, top **4.** edge, tend, wand **5.** brink, limit, marge, range, scope **6.** border, emblem, extend, margin **7.** incline **9.** extremity **10.** contiguous **13.** circumference
Vergil (pert to) ...
birthplace .. **6.** Mantua (It)
called .. **10.** Roman Homer
famed as .. **4.** poet
friend .. **8.** Maecenas
name (last) .. **4.** Maro
poem .. **6.** Aeneid **8.** Eclogues, Georgics
poetic form .. **4.** epic **15.** heroic hexameter (Aeneid)
verification ... **4.** oath, test **8.** averment **9.** collation **12.** confirmation **13.** ascertainment
verify ... **4.** back, test **5.** check, prove **6.** affirm, attest, second **7.** confirm, support **8.** maintain **12.** authenticate, substantiate
verily ... **3.** yea **4.** amen **5.** truly **6.** certes, indeed, in fact, really **9.** certainly **10.** positively **11.** confidently
verisimilitude ... **5.** truth **10.** likelihood **11.** probability, verisimilar
veritable ... **4.** real, true **6.** actual, gospel, honest **7.** genuine **9.** authentic
verity ... **4.** fact **5.** truth **7.** honesty, reality **8.** veracity
vermilion ... **3.** dye, red **7.** pigment, vermeil **8.** cinnabar
vermin ... **4.** lice, mice, rats **5.** filth, fleas, flies, moths, worms **7.** bedbugs, beetles, insects, spiders, weasels, weevils **8.** riffraff, termites **9.** parasites **10.** centipedes, mosquitoes **11.** cockroaches
Vermont ...
capital .. **10.** Montpelier
city .. **5.** Barre **7.** Rutland **10.** Burlington **11.** Brattleboro
first town .. **10.** Fort Dummer
hero .. **10.** Ethan Allen
historic group .. **17.** Green Mountain Boys
lake .. **9.** Champlain
mountain .. **5.** Green **7.** Taconic

9. Mansfield
museum .. **9.** Shelburne **10.** Bennington
product .. **6.** marble **10.** maple sugar
river .. **5.** Otter **11.** Connecticut
State admission .. **10.** Fourteenth
State motto .. **15.** Freedom and Unity
State nickname .. **13.** Green Mountain
vernacular ... **5.** lingo, local **6.** common, jargon, native, patois, vulgar **7.** dialect **10.** colloquial, indigenous
vernal ... **4.** mild, warm **5.** fresh **10.** springlike
verse ... **4.** epic, poem, rime **5.** canto, lyric, rhyme, stave, stich **6.** poetry, rondel, sonnet, stanza **7.** measure, strophe, triolet, trochee **8.** limerick
verse (pert to) ...
art .. **10.** orthometry
book of .. **5.** poesy **9.** anthology
devotion .. **8.** antiphon
form .. **7.** virelay **10.** villanelle
Homeric .. **4.** epic **6.** epopee
Irish .. **4.** rann
pause .. **6.** cesura **9.** diaeresis (dieresis)
romantic .. **7.** sestina
satiric .. **6.** iambic
scripture .. **4.** text
stress .. **5.** ictus
term .. **5.** ictic, meter **6.** accent, poetic, rhythm, scheme **7.** cadence **8.** eye rhyme, scansion **10.** synaeresis (syneresis) **12.** alliteration
trivial .. **6.** jingle **8.** doggerel, limerick
verse (pert to feet) ...
eight .. **9.** octameter
four .. **10.** tetrameter
one .. **9.** monometer
three .. **7.** tripody
two .. **7.** dimeter
versed ... **5.** adept **7.** erudite, learned, skilled **8.** familiar **9.** practiced **10.** acquainted, conversant, proficient
versification ... **7.** prosody **10.** orthometry
versifier ... **4.** bard, muse, poet **5.** rimer **6.** rhymer **7.** poetess **8.** ballader, eulogist **9.** poetaster, rhymester
version ... **7.** edition **9.** rendition **10.** paraphrase **11.** translation
version, Bible ... **5.** Douay, Greek, Latin **6.** Coptic, Geneva, Gothic, Italic (Itala) **7.** Aramaic, Bishops, Luther's, Revised, Targums, Vulgate **8.** Cranmer's, Georgian, Matthew's, Peshitta, Slavonic **9.** Apocrypha, King James, Serampore **10.** Pentateuch, Septuagint **11.** Alexandrian
vers libra ... **9.** free verse
verso (opp of recto) ... **7.** reverse **9.** back cover **12.** left-hand side
versus ... **3.** con **7.** against **8.** contrast, opposite **11.** alternative
vertebra, vertebrae ... **4.** axis **8.** backbone **12.** spinal column
vertebrate ... **6.** linked **8.** well-knit **9.** backboned
vertebrates (pert to) ...
division .. **6.** somite **10.** Vertebrata
feathered .. **5.** birds
group .. **4.** Aves **7.** Amniota
vertex ... **3.** top **4.** apex **6.** summit

11. culmination
vertical . . . **5.** apeak, erect, plumb, sheer
6. height **7.** upright **10.** upstanding
13. perpendicular
vertical panel . . . **5.** stile
verticil . . . **5.** whorl **6.** circle
vertigo . . . **5.** dinus **6.** megrim
9. confusion, dizziness, giddiness
11. disturbance **12.** bewilderment
verve . . . **3.** pep **4.** dash, élan **5.** vigor
6. energy, fervor, spirit **8.** vivacity
9. animation **10.** liveliness
vervet . . . **6.** monkey
very . . . **3.** eri (comb form) **4.** much,
real, très, true **5.** truly, utter **6.** actual,
in fact, really **7.** exactly, genuine
8. absolute, especial, peculiar, truthful
9. extremely, precisely, veracious,
veritable **10.** legitimate **11.** exceedingly
Very light . . . **5.** flare **6.** signal (Very
system)
vesica . . . **7.** bladder
vesicate . . . **7.** blister
vesicle . . . **3.** sac **4.** cyst **5.** bulla **6.** bubble,
cavity, vessel **7.** bladder, blemish,
blister
Vespa . . . **4.** wasp **6.** hornet
vespers . . . **6.** prayer **7.** service
8. ceremony, evensong
vessel . . . **3.** ark, can, cup, jar, jug, mug,
pod, pot, tub, urn, vas, vat **4.** boat,
bowl, dhow, drum, duct, ewer, junk,
olla, olpe, proa, said, seed, ship,
tank, vase, yawl **5.** bocal, craft, crock,
cupel, glass, gourd, jorum, ketch,
stein **6.** aftaba, aludel, ampule, barrel,
bottle, bucket, caster, cutter, dipper,
firkin, goblet, kettle, picard, retort,
trader, trough **7.** catboat, cistern,
coracle, cruiser, frigate, pitcher, psykter,
steamer, tankard, utensil **8.** aiguière,
ciborium, decanter, demijohn,
hogshead, schooner **9.** alcarraza,
catamaran, privateer, washbasin
10. receptacle **11.** earthenware
vessel (pert to) . . .
  anc . . **3.** nef **5.** yanky **6.** bireme **7.** caravel,
  galleon, trireme
  Arab . . **4.** dhow
  baptismal . . **4.** font **7.** piscina
  chemist . . **4.** etna **6.** aludel, beaker,
  retort
  Columbus . . **7.** caravel
  cooking . . **9.** autoclave
  druggist . . **4.** vial **5.** phial **8.** gallipot
  Dutch . . **4.** koff **5.** yanky **6.** galiot (galliot)
  Eccl . . **3.** ama, pyx **4.** wine **5.** amula
  7. stamnos
  Hebrides . . **7.** birlinn (birling)
  heraldry . . **7.** lymphad
  India . . **6.** shibar
  Mediterranean . . **5.** xebec **6.** settee
  (setee), tartan **7.** polacre
  merchant . . **6.** argosy **7.** baggala
  Nile houseboat . . **8.** dahabeah
  oil-burning . . **7.** cresset
  part . . **4.** deck, keel, prow, skeg **5.** brail
  8. steerage
  sacred . . **3.** ama
  Scottish . . **6.** pourie
  Thames (fishing) . . **6.** bawley

  Venice . . **9.** bucentaur
  war . . **3.** sub **5.** Maine **6.** corvet
  7. carrier, cruiser, felucca, flattop,
  Monitor **9.** submarine **11.** dreadnaught
  12. Old Ironsides
vessel (sailing) . . . **3.** hoy **4.** bark, brig,
koff, proa, saic, ship, yawl **5.** ketch,
sloop, smack, xebec
vest . . . **4.** robe **5.** endow, gilet **6.** invest,
jerkin, linder, weskit **7.** furnish, garment
9. waistcoat
vesta . . . **5.** match
Vesta (Rom) . . . **7.** goddess (Hearth)
8. asteroid
vestal . . . **4.** pure **6.** chaste **8.** virginal
vestige . . . **4.** mark, sign **5.** relic, shred,
tinge, trace, track **7.** remains **8.** footstep
9. vestigium
vestiture . . . **4.** garb **5.** dress **8.** clothing,
covering
vestment . . . **3.** alb **4.** cope, garb, gown,
hood, robe **5.** amice, cotta, dress,
ephod, miter, orale, tunic **6.** saccos,
tippet **7.** cassock, garment, maniple
8. chasuble, crucifix, dalmatic, scapular,
surplice **10.** habiliment, omophorion
vestry . . . **4.** room **5.** group (Eccl)
8. sacristy, wardrobe **10.** repository
Vesuvius (pert to) . . .
  Great Eruption (79 AD) . . **6.** buried
  city . . **7.** Pompeii **11.** Herculaneum
  mountain . . **8.** volcanic
  site . . **6.** Naples
veteran . . . **4.** long **7.** old hand, soldier
8. seasoned **9.** practiced
11. experienced
veterinarian . . . **7.** farrier, surgeon
veto . . . **6.** forbid **8.** negative, prohibit
10. disapprove **12.** interdiction
vex . . . **3.** irk **4.** cark, fret, fuss, gall,
miff, rile, roil **5.** anger, annoy, harry,
spite, tease, worry **6.** bother, harass,
nettle, plague, pother, ruffle **7.** agitate,
chagrin, despite, dispute, disturb,
pervert, provoke, torment **8.** disquiet,
irritate **9.** displease
vexation . . . **7.** anxiety, chagrin, fatigue,
trouble **8.** disquiet, irritate
9. annoyance, weariness **10.** affliction,
foreboding, harassment, irritation
11. disturbance **13.** mortification
vexatious . . . **5.** pesky **6.** thorny **7.** irksome
8. annoying **9.** disturbed, pestilent,
provoking, worrisome **10.** afflictive
11. troublesome
vexillum . . . **3.** web **4.** flag **5.** cross
6. banner, colors, ensign **7.** labarum,
pennant **8.** standard **10.** Jolly Roger
via . . . **2.** by **3.** way **4.** away, road
6. begone **7.** by way of, passage,
through
viaduct . . . **4.** span **6.** bridge **7.** trestle
vial . . . **5.** cruet, phial **6.** bottle, caster,
castor, vessel **7.** ampoule (ampul),
ampulla **9.** container
viameter . . . **7.** measure **8.** odometer
12. perambulator
viander . . . **4.** host **6.** vendor
viands . . . **4.** cate, fare, food **7.** viandry
8. victuals **10.** provisions
viaticum . . . **5.** money **8.** supplies

9. allowance, last rites **10.** provisions
14. Extreme Unction
viator ... **8.** traveler, wayfarer
vibrant ... **5.** alive **7.** pulsing, travale
   8. resonant, sonorous, vigorous
   9. energetic, thrilling, vibrating
   10. resounding
vibrate ... **4.** beat, rock, tirl, whir **5.** pulse,
   quake, swing, throb, waver **6.** dindle,
   quaver, quiver, shimmy, shiver, thrill
   7. agitate, resound, tremble **8.** brandish,
   flichter, resonate **9.** fluctuate, oscillate
vibration ... **6.** quiver, thrill, tremor
   7. flutter, pulsing **9.** resonance,
   throbbing **11.** oscillation
vibration, music ... **5.** trill **7.** sonance,
   tremolo, vibrato
vibration measure ... **9.** tonometer
vicar ... **5.** proxy **6.** curate, deputy, priest
   9. churchman, clergyman **10.** substitute,
   vicegerent
vice ... **3.** sin **4.** evil **5.** crime, fault,
   taint **6.** defect **7.** blemish, stopper
   8. iniquity **9.** depravity, in place of,
   instead of **10.** corruption, substitute,
   succeeding, wickedness, wrongdoing
   11. viciousness
viceroy ... **5.** nabob **6.** satrap **8.** governor
   9. butterfly
vicinity ... **6.** region **9.** proximity
   11. propinquity **12.** neighborhood
vicious ... **3.** bad, ill **4.** evil, foul, lewd,
   mean, ugly, vile **6.** faulty, impure,
   wicked **7.** corrupt, immoral, noxious
   8. depraved, spiteful **9.** dangerous,
   malicious, nefarious, obstinate,
   perverted **10.** iniquitous, profligate
   11. ill-tempered
vicissitude ... **6.** change **8.** mutation,
   shifting **9.** variation **10.** revolution
   11. fluctuation
victim ... **4.** dupe, gull, prey **5.** cully
   6. sucker **7.** patient **8.** sufferer
victor ... **6.** captor, master, winner
   8. unbeaten **9.** conqueror
   10. vanquisher
victor fish ... **3.** aku **6.** bonito
Victoria, victoria ... **4.** plum **5.** cross
   (Maltese) **7.** goddess **8.** asteroid,
   carriage **10.** automobile
Victorian ... **3.** era **4.** prim **6.** stuffy
   7. antique, archaic, prudish
   10. antiquated **11.** puritanical, strait-
   laced
victorious ... **7.** winning **8.** unbeaten
   9. defeating **10.** conquering, triumphant
victory ... **7.** mastery, success, triumph
   8. conquest **9.** supremacy
victory (pert to) ...
   at too great cost .. **7.** Pyrrhic
   Day .. **9.** Armistice
   goddess .. **4.** Nike
   hymn .. **9.** epinicion (epinikion)
   memorial .. **6.** trophy
   symbol .. **4.** palm
Victrola dog (symbol) ... **6.** Nipper
victuals ... **4.** food, grub **6.** viands
   8. supplies **11.** nourishment
videlicet ... **3.** viz **5.** to wit **6.** namely
   8. scilicet
vie ... **3.** bet **4.** cope, life **5.** bandy,

stake, wager **6.** endure, oppose, strive
7. compare, compete, contend, contest,
emulate **8.** struggle **9.** challenge
Vienna ...
artist .. **4.** Lieb, Pilz **6.** Makart, Zauner
   7. Kisling
boulevard (famed) .. **11.** Ringstrasse
capital of .. **7.** Austria
Ger name .. **4.** Wien
musician .. **5.** Gluck, Haydn **6.** Czerny,
   Mozart **7.** Strauss **8.** Schubert,
   Schumann **9.** Beethoven
palace .. **10.** Schönbrunn
park .. **6.** Prater
river .. **6.** Danube
Vietnam (pert to) ...
capital .. **5.** Hanoi
city .. **13.** Ho Chi Minh City (Saigon)
gulf .. **6.** Tonkin
holiday (New Year) .. **3.** Tet
historic region .. **5.** Annam **6.** Tonkin
   11. Cochin China
river .. **3.** Red **6.** Mekong
view ... **3.** aim, end, eye, ken, see **4.** look,
   scan **5.** scene, vista **6.** apercu, aspect,
   object, regard, survey **7.** examine,
   glimpse, opinion, outlook, picture
   8. attitude, judgment, panorama,
   prospect **9.** intention **10.** appearance,
   perception, scrutinize **11.** contemplate,
   expectation **13.** contemplation
vigil ... **3.** eve **4.** wake **5.** guard, watch
   6. patrol **8.** watchman **9.** keep guard
   11. wakefulness **13.** sleeplessness
vigilant ... **4.** agog, wary **5.** alert, awake,
   aware **6.** awatch **7.** wakeful **8.** cautious,
   open-eyed, watchful **9.** attentive,
   observant, sleepless **11.** circumspect
vigilantes ... **5.** posse **9.** committee
   (vigilance)
vigor, vigour ... **3.** pep, vim, vir **4.** life,
   zeal **5.** force, power, verve **6.** energy,
   health **7.** potency, stamina, sthenia
   8. strength, validity, virility **9.** animation,
   fraîcheur, vehemence **10.** liveliness
vigorous ... **4.** able, hale, racy, spry
   5. eager, frank, fresh, hardy, lusty,
   tough **6.** potent, robust, strong
   7. healthy, zealous **8.** athletic, forceful,
   spirited, vehement **9.** effective,
   energetic, sprightly, strenuous
   11. efficacious, flourishing
Viking ... **4.** Eric **5.** rover **6.** pirate
   8. Norseman, Northman, sea rover
   9. plunderer **12.** Scandinavian
vile ... **3.** bad **4.** base, evil, foul, mean
   5. cheap, lowly, nasty **6.** coarse, filthy,
   impure, odious, sinful, sordid, wicked
   7. corrupt, debased, ignoble, obscene,
   unclean, vicious **8.** depraved, infamous
   9. degrading, loathsome, nefarious,
   repulsive **10.** abominable, disgusting
   12. contaminated
vilify ... **5.** abuse, curse, libel **6.** debase,
   defame, malign, revile **7.** asperse,
   cheapen, degrade, slander, traduce
   8. belittle, disgrace, reproach, vilipend
   9. blaspheme, disparage **10.** calumniate,
   stigmatize
vilipend ... **6.** slight **7.** despise **8.** belittle
   9. disparage **10.** depreciate, slanderous

12. calumniatory
villa ... 5. aldea, dacha 9. residence, villaette 10. villanette
village ... 3. mir 4. dorp, stad 5. thorp (thorpe), tract 6. aldeia, castle, hamlet, pueblo
Village Blacksmith author ... 10. Longfellow
villain ... 4. boor, lout, ogre, serf 5. demon, heavy, knave, rogue 6. rascal 7. caitiff 9. miscreant, scoundrel
villainous ... 3. bad, low 4. base, evil, mean, vile 6. vulgar, wicked 7. boorish, knavish 8. criminal, rascally, terrible, wretched 9. dastardly 10. detestable, iniquitous 11. scoundrelly 13. objectionable
villous ... 5. nappy 6. napped, shaggy
vim ... 3. pep, zip 4. dash, élan, fire, gimp, kick 5. drive, force, verve, vigor 6. energy, esprit, spirit 8. strength
vinaigre ... 7. vinegar
vindicate ... 4. free 5. claim, clear 6. acquit, assert, avenge, defend, excuse, uphold 7. absolve, justify, support, sustain 8. maintain 9. exculpate, exonerate
vindication ... 7. defense
vindictive ... 7. hostile 8. punitive, spiteful, vengeful 10. revengeful 11. retaliatory, retributive
vine ... 3. hop, ivy 4. bine, odal 5. betel, grape, liana (liane), Vitis 7. cupseed, trailer 8. clematis, wisteria 9. grapevine 10. chilicothe 11. honeysuckle 12. morning glory
vinegar ... 4. acid, sour 6. acetum, alegar 8. vinaigre
vinegar (pert to) ...
acid .. 6. acetic
comb form .. 5. aceto
dregs .. 6. mother
eel .. 4. worm
ester .. 7. acetate
fly .. 5. fruit
preserve in .. 6. pickle 8. marinate
salt .. 7. acetate
spice .. 8. tarragon
tree .. 13. staghorn sumac
Vinegar Joe (Army) ... 9. Stillwell (Gen)
vinegarroon ... 8. scorpion, vinagron
vinegary ... 4. sour, tart 7. acetose, crabbed, pungent 9. unamiable
vineyard ... 3. cru 7. Priapus (god of) 10. plantation
vinology (science of) ... 5. vines 10. grapevines
vinous ... 4. winy 5. color
vintner ... 8. merchant (wine)
viol ... 3. gue 4. rope 5. rebec, ruana 6. vielle 7. quinton, sarinda 9. organ stop
viola ... 5. gamba 7. sarangi 9. organ stop 11. tenor violin
violate ... 5. abuse, break, wrong 6. defile, invade, ravage, ravish 7. debauch, outrage, pollute, profane 8. deflower, dishonor, mistreat 9. desecrate 10. transgress
violation ... 7. offense 10. infraction 11. anacoluthon, disturbance,

profanation 12. infringement, interruption 13. nonobservance, transgression
violence ... 5. anger, force 6. unjust 7. assault, cruelty, outrage 8. coercion 9. vehemence 10. roughhouse 11. profanation 12. infringement
violent ... 4. loud 5. acute, great, rabid, sharp, vivid 6. fierce, savage, stormy 7. extreme, furious, intense 8. coercive, vehement 9. turbulent 10. passionate 11. tempestuous
violent (pert to) ...
Norse folklore .. 8. warriors 9. beserkers
outbreak .. 4. riot 6. tumult, uproar 8. eruption
pain .. 4. pang 5. throe 6. fierce
violet (pert to) ...
color .. 5. mauve 6. purple 7. blue-red
dye .. 6. archil (orchil)
emblem of .. 7. gravity 8. chastity
genus .. 9. Violaceae
perfume .. 5. irone 6. ionone 9. orrisroot
tip .. 9. butterfly
violin (pert to) ...
ancient .. 5. rebab, rebec, rocta 12. viola de gamba
bar .. 4. fret
bass .. 11. violoncello
bow .. 5. arcus
city (famed) .. 7. Cremona (It)
make .. 5. Amati 7. Cremona 10. Guarnerius 12. Stradivarius
maker .. 5. Amati 9. Guarnieri 10. Stradivari
reference to .. 4. pins 5. belly
Scot .. 6. fiddle
small .. 3. kit
tenor .. 4. alto
violinist (famed) ... 5. Elman, Stern 7. Heifitz, Menuhin
violinist, first ... 13. concertmaster
viper ... 3. asp 5. adder, Echis, snake 6. kupper 7. serpent 8. cerastes, ophidian 9. scoundrel 10. bushmaster
vir ... 5. vigor
virage ... 5. scold, shrew, vixen, woman 7. beldame, rullion 9. termagant
Virgil ... see *Vergil*
virgin ... 3. new 4. maid, pure 6. chaste, maiden, vestal 8. spinster 9. undefiled, unsullied, untouched 13. unadulterated
virginal ... 3. new 5. piano (spinet) 6. chaste, ritual 7. natural 8. maidenly 9. unmarried, unsullied
Virginia ...
bay .. 10. Chesapeake
capital .. 8. Richmond
city .. 7. Norfolk, Roanoke 9. Arlington, Lexington, Lynchburg 11. Newport News 12. Hampton Roads
famed sites .. 8. Mt Vernon 10. Monticello 12. Williamsburg 13. Stratford Hall
first white child born .. 12. Virginia Dare
historic town .. 8. Yorktown 9. Jamestown 10. Appomattox
Indian sachem .. 8. Powhatan
mountain .. 9. Blue Ridge 11. Alleghenies
resort .. 13. Virginia Beach

river.. **4.** York **5.** James **7.** Potomac, Rapidan **12.** Rappahannock
settlement (first).. **9.** Jamestown
State admission.. **5.** Tenth
State motto.. **17.** Sic Semper Tyrannis **19.** Thus Always to Tyrants
State nickname.. **11.** Old Dominion
Virgin Islands, British...
  capital.. **8.** Road Town
  crop.. **9.** sugar cane
  group.. **7.** Leeward
  number islands.. **6.** thirty
Virgin Islands, United States...
  capital.. **8.** St Thomas **15.** Charlotte Amalia (former)
  discoverer.. **8.** Columbus (1493)
  largest.. **6.** St John **7.** St Croix **8.** St Thomas
virginity... **8.** celibacy, chastity **10.** maidenhood **12.** spinsterhood
Virgin Mary... **5.** Pietà (image) **7.** Our Lady **11.** Maris Stella, Mother of God **12.** Star of the Sea **13.** Mother of Jesus
viridity... **5.** youth **7.** verdure **9.** freshness, greenness **10.** grass color
virile... **4.** male **5.** manly **8.** forceful, powerful, vigorous **9.** masculine, masterful
virose... **5.** fetid **8.** virulent **9.** poisonous **10.** malodorous
virtu... **5.** curio **7.** antique **8.** artistry **12.** love of curios **15.** artistic quality, study of fine arts
virtual... **9.** essential, potential **10.** energizing **12.** constructive
virtually... **7.** morally **11.** potentially, practically
virtue... **5.** valor, value, worth **6.** energy, purity **7.** potency, probity **8.** chastity, efficacy, goodness, morality **9.** godliness, innocence, integrity, rectitude **11.** uprightness **13.** righteousness
virtue, logic... **8.** aretaics
virtues, cardinal... **4.** hope **5.** faith **7.** charity
virtuoso... **6.** expert **7.** scholar **11.** connoisseur, philosopher
virtuous... **4.** good, pure **5.** brave, godly, moral **6.** chaste, honest, potent **7.** upright, valiant **8.** valorous **9.** righteous **11.** efficacious
virulent... **5.** acrid, rabid **6.** deadly, potent **7.** noxious **8.** venomous **9.** animosity, malignant, poisonous **10.** infectious, resentment **11.** acrimonious
visa, visé... **7.** endorse **9.** signature **11.** certificate, endorsement (passport)
visage... **4.** face, look **5.** image **11.** countenance **14.** visible surface
vis-à-vis... **4.** seat, sofa **5.** carriage, opposite **9.** encounter **10.** face to face
viscera... **4.** guts **6.** bowels, vitals **7.** insides **8.** entrails **10.** intestines **11.** inside parts
visceral... **3.** gut **7.** enteric **10.** intestinal, splanchnic
viscid... **4.** ropy, waxy **5.** slimy **6.** sticky

7. viscous **8.** adhering, adhesive **9.** glutinous
viscosity... **8.** tenacity **10.** stickiness
viscous... **4.** ropy, sizy **5.** gluey, gummy, tarry **6.** mucous, sticky, viscid **7.** stringy **9.** glutinous **10.** stickiness
vise... **3.** jaw **4.** tool **5.** clamp, winch **6.** device **7.** squeeze
Vishnu (pert to)...
  consort.. **3.** Sri **7.** Lakshim
  deity (supreme).. **6.** bhakti **9.** preserver
  eighth.. **7.** Krishna
  epithet.. **8.** bhagavat
  seventh.. **4.** Rama
  tenth, last incarnation.. **5.** Kalki
  vehicle.. **6.** Garuda
visible... **4.** open, seen **5.** clear **6.** extant, in view **7.** evident, in sight, obvious **8.** apparent, manifest **10.** noticeable **11.** discernible, perceivable, perceptible
Visigoth king... **6.** Alaric
vision... **3.** eye **5.** dream, fancy, image, sight **6.** glance, mirage **7.** glimpse, imagine, specter **8.** eyesight **10.** apparition
vision (pert to)...
  comb form.. **4.** opto
  daylight.. **8.** photopia
  defect.. **6.** anopia, myopia
  double.. **8.** diplopia
  illusory.. **5.** image
  lacking.. **8.** purblind
  measure.. **9.** optometer
  night.. **8.** scotopia
  science of.. **5.** optic **6.** ocular **9.** binocular, monocular
visionary... **4.** aery, airy, seer, wild **5.** ideal **6.** dreamy, unreal **7.** dreamer, Laputan, utopian **8.** delusive, idealist, quixotic, romantic **9.** fantastic, imaginary **10.** chimerical, rhapsodist **11.** imaginative, impractical
visit... **3.** see, vis **4.** call, chat, go to, slum **5.** haunt **6.** attend, call on **10.** inspection, visitation **12.** conversation
visitor... **5.** guest **6.** caller **7.** company **8.** visitant
visne... **5.** venue **8.** neighbor, vicinage
vison... **4.** mink
visor, vizor... **4.** mask **6.** vizard **8.** disguise **10.** camouflage
vista... **4.** view **5.** scene, visto **7.** outlook **8.** corridor, panorama, prospect
visual... **5.** optic **6.** ocular **11.** perceptible
visualize... **7.** imagine, picture **8.** envisage, envision **9.** objectify
vital... **4.** live **5.** basic **6.** living, mortal, viable **7.** animate, exigent, needful, organic **8.** inherent, vigorous **9.** essential, important, necessary, requisite **10.** imperative **11.** fundamental **13.** indispensable
vital (pert to)...
  air.. **6.** oxygen
  force.. **6.** energy, spirit **7.** neurism **8.** bathmism, phrenism **9.** theosophy
  impulse.. **6.** libido **8.** instinct
  organs.. **6.** vitals **7.** viscera
  records.. **10.** demography, statistics
  strength.. **7.** stamina

vitality ... **3.** sap, vim **4.** life **5.** vigor **8.** strength **9.** animation, lustiness **10.** liveliness

vitals ... **7.** insides, viscera **9.** internals **11.** vital organs (heart, liver, lungs, brain)

vitamin ... **6.** biotin, niacin **7.** carotin, thiamin **10.** riboflavin **11.** lactoflavin **12.** ascorbic acid

vitellus ... **4.** yolk **7.** egg yolk

vitiate ... **5.** spoil, taint **6.** debase, impair, poison, weaken **7.** corrupt, deprave, pervert, pollute **10.** adulterate, demoralize, invalidate **11.** contaminate

vitiated ... **5.** pical **6.** wicked **7.** corrupt, debased, spoiled **9.** defective **11.** ineffective, invalidated

vitiosity ... **4.** vice **6.** defect **9.** depravity **11.** viciousness

vitium ... **5.** fault **6.** defect

vitric ... **9.** glasslike

vitrics ... **9.** glassware, glasswork

vitrify ... **5.** glaze **13.** make into glass

vitriolic ... **4.** acid **5.** sharp **6.** biting, bitter **7.** caustic **8.** scathing, virulent **11.** acrimonious

vituperate ... **5.** abuse, curse, scold **6.** berate, revile **7.** censure

vituperative ... **7.** abusive, railing **8.** reviling, scolding **10.** scurrilous **11.** maledictory, opprobrious

vivacious ... **3.** gay **4.** airy **5.** merry **6.** active, lively **8.** animated, gamesome, spirited, sportive **9.** energetic **12.** lighthearted

vivacity ... **4.** dash, élan, fire, keen, zeal, zest **5.** ardor, verve, vigor **6.** energy, gaiety (gayety) **9.** animation **10.** liveliness

Viverra ... **6.** civets **9.** civet cats

vivers ... **4.** food **8.** victuals

vix ... **8.** scarcely

vixen ... **3.** cat, fox **5.** scold, shrew, witch **6.** virago **9.** termagant **12.** female animal

viz ... **5.** to wit **6.** namely **9.** videlicet

vizard ... **4.** mask **5.** guise, visor **8.** disguise

vlei (vley) ... **5.** creek, marsh, swamp

voar ... **6.** spring (of the year)

vocabulary ... **5.** words **6.** jargon **7.** diction, lexicon **8.** glossary, wordbook **10.** dictionary

vocabulist ... **6.** writer **13.** lexicographer

vocal (pert to) ...
chink .. **7.** glottis
composition .. **4.** aria, song **5.** motet **7.** cantata
expression .. **4.** oral **9.** utterance
flourish .. **7.** roulade
handicap .. **4.** lisp **7.** stutter
sound .. **5.** vowel **6.** sonant
statue .. **6.** Memnon

vocalist ... **4.** alto **5.** basso, tenor **6.** artist, cantor, singer **7.** caroler, crooner, soprano, yodeler **8.** songster **10.** coloratura, prima donna, songstress

vocalization ... **11.** melismatics

vocalize ... **4.** sing **5.** sound, utter **6.** phrase

vocation ... **4.** call **5.** trade **6.** career

7. calling **8.** business **10.** employment, occupation, profession

vociferous ... **4.** loud **5.** noisy **7.** blatant **8.** brawling, strident **9.** clamorous, turbulent **11.** loudmouthed **12.** obstreperous

vogue ... **3.** ton **4.** mode **5.** style **6.** custom **7.** fashion **8.** practice **10.** popularity

voice ... **3.** say, vox **4.** alto, bass, tone, vote, wish **5.** rumor, tenor, utter **7.** divulge, opinion, soprano **8.** announce, falsetto **9.** utterance **10.** expression **12.** articulation

voice (pert to) ...
box .. **6.** larynx
Greek .. **9.** phthongos
handicap .. **4.** lisp **7.** stammer, stutter
loss of .. **7.** anaudia, aphonia
loud .. **12.** megalophonic
phonetics .. **9.** affricate
quality .. **6.** timbre (timber)
quiet .. **5.** sotto
raise .. **6.** insist **10.** supplicate
raise against .. **5.** decry **6.** accuse, object
singing, above natural .. **8.** falsetto
singing, natural .. **7.** dipetto
stress .. **5.** arsis
with one .. **9.** unanimous **12.** concurrently

voiced ... **6.** sonant, spoken **7.** sounded **9.** phthongal **11.** articulated

voiceless ... **4.** dumb, mute, surd **6.** atonic, silent **7.** spirate **9.** not voiced **12.** not expressed

void ... **4.** idle, lack, null, want **5.** abyss, annul, egest, empty **6.** devoid, hollow, vacant, vacuum **7.** abolish, nothing, nullify, useless **8.** evacuate **9.** destitute, emptiness **10.** unoccupied **11.** ineffectual, nonexistent

void of ...
interest .. **6.** jejune **7.** insipid
sense .. **5.** inane, silly
space .. **5.** blank **6.** vacuum

volaille ... **4.** fowl **7.** poultry

volant ... **5.** agile, light, quick **6.** flying, nimble **7.** current **8.** volatile, volitant

volatile ... **4.** airy **5.** light **6.** fickle, flying, lively, volant **7.** alcohol, ammonia, buoyant, flighty, gaseous **8.** fleeting, vaporous **9.** ephemeral, mercurial **10.** capricious, changeable, transitory **11.** vaporizable **12.** lighthearted

volatile (pert to) ...
alkali .. **7.** ammonia
flux .. **5.** smear
liquid .. **5.** ether **7.** alcohol
oil .. **7.** essence, perfume

volcanic (pert to) ...
glass .. **6.** pumice **7.** perlite **8.** obsidian
matter .. **2.** aa **4.** lava, slag, tufa **5.** trass **6.** pumice **8.** lapillus, pahoehoe
mud .. **5.** salse
orifice of gas issue .. **8.** fumarole
ref to .. **9.** excitable, explosive **11.** hot-tempered
rock .. **5.** trass **6.** dacite **8.** tephrite
saucer .. **6.** crater

volcano (pert to) ...
Africa .. **11.** Kilimanjaro
Alaska .. **6.** Katmai **8.** Wrangell

Chile .. **6.** Lascar
Ecuador .. **8.** Cotopaxi
goddess .. **4.** Pele (Hawaii)
Guatemala .. **5.** Fuego **7.** Atitlan
Hawaii .. **8.** Mauna Loa
Iceland .. **5.** Askja, Hekla
Italy .. **4.** Etna **8.** Vesuvius **9.** Stromboli
Japan .. **4.** Fuji **9.** Asamayama
Java .. **4.** Gede
Mexico .. **12.** Popocatepetl
Philippines .. **3.** Apo (Mindanao)
Sumatra .. **6.** Merapi
United States (mainland) .. **6.** Lassen,
Shasta **7.** Rainier
West Indies .. **5.** Pelée
vole ... **6.** craber, rodent **8.** water rat
10. field mouse **11.** meadow mouse
volée ... **6.** flight, volley
volery (volary) ... **6.** aviary **8.** bird cage
volition ... **4.** will **6.** choice **11.** voluntarily
13. determination
volley ... **4.** fire **5.** blast, salvo, shots
Voltaire volume ... **7.** Candide
voluble ... **4.** glib **6.** fluent **8.** rotating,
unstable **9.** garrulous, revolving,
talkative **10.** loquacious
volume ... **4.** book, bulk, mass, size, tome
6. amount **7.** compass **8.** capacity,
fullness (fulness) **9.** aggregate,
Decameron **10.** crassitude **14.** fullness
of tone
voluntary ... **4.** free **7.** prelude, willing
8. elective, intended, purposed
9. volunteer, willingly **10.** deliberate,
volitional **11.** intentional, spontaneous
13. not accidental
volunteer ... **5.** offer **6.** enlist **7.** proffer
9. be willing, voluntary **11.** be of
service
Volunteer State ... **9.** Tennessee
volute ... **4.** turn **5.** whorl **6.** cilery (cillery)
8. rolled up **10.** scroll-like
voodoo ... **5.** magic, obeah **6.** fetish
8. sorcerer
voracious ... **6.** greedy, hungry
8. edacious, esurient, ravening,
ravenous **9.** devouring, rapacious
10. gluttonous, immoderate, unsatiable
voracity ... **5.** greed **7.** edacity **8.** gluttony,
rapacity **9.** esurience
vorago ... **4.** gulf **5.** abyss
vortex ... **4.** apex, eddy **5.** whirl **7.** tornado
8. flatworm **9.** whirlpool, whirlwind
10. waterspout
votary ... **6.** zealot **7.** devotee **8.** adherent,
aesthete, follower **9.** supporter
10. enthusiast
vote ... **3.** vow **5.** elect, straw **6.** ballot,
choice, ticket **7.** declare **8.** suffrage
9. designate **10.** plebescite, referendum
vote (pert to) ...
group .. **4.** bloc
in .. **5.** elect
of assent .. **6.** placet
plump .. **14.** straight ticket
receptacle .. **6.** situla
voter ... **6.** poller **7.** elector **8.** balloter
11. constituent
voters ... **10.** electorate
votive ... **7.** devoted **11.** consecrated
vouch ... **4.** back **6.** affirm, attest,

depose **7.** confirm, declare, promise,
sponsor, support **8.** accredit **9.** assertion
11. attestation, bear witness
vouchsafe ... **4.** give **5.** deign **6.** accept,
assure, bestow, permit **7.** concede
9. guarantee **10.** condescend
voussoir ... **8.** keystone
vow ... **3.** vum **4.** oath **5.** swear,
vouch **6.** behest, devote, pledge
7. declare, promise **8.** dedicate
9. assertion **10.** consecrate,
obligation **11.** asservation
12. supplication
vowel (pert to) ...
change of .. **6.** umlaut
contradiction .. **6.** crasis **7.** digraph
9. diphthong
loss of .. **7.** aphesis
mark .. **6.** macron
point (Heb) .. **4.** sere (tsere)
separate syllables .. **9.** diaeresis (dieresis)
short .. **5.** breve
two, contracted .. **6.** crasis
two, group .. **6.** digram **7.** digraph
9. diphthong (dipthong)
unaspirated .. **4.** lene
vowels, none ... **6.** syzygy
vowels in sequence ... **8.** caesious
vox (pert to) ...
clandestina .. **7.** whisper
Dei .. **10.** Voice of God
Latin for .. **5.** voice
populi .. **16.** voice of the people
voyage ... **4.** trip **6.** cruise, travel
7. journey, passage, passing (sea)
9. excursion **10.** expedition, pilgrimage
11. undertaking
Vulcan (pert to) ...
consort .. **4.** Maia
epithet .. **8.** Mulciber
feast of .. **10.** Vulcanalia
god of .. **4.** fire
Greek .. **10.** Hephaestus
work site .. **4.** Etna
vulcanite ... **7.** ebonite
vulcanize ... **9.** rubberize
vulgar ... **3.** low **4.** lewd **5.** crude,
gross **6.** coarse, common, garish,
public, ribald **7.** boorish, general,
obscene, profane **8.** indecent, ordinary,
plebeian **9.** inelegant, offensive,
unrefined **10.** boisterous, in bad taste,
rowdydowdy
vulgarian ... **4.** snob **9.** pretender
Vulgate ... **10.** Scriptures
vulnerable ... **6.** liable **7.** exposed
8. beatable **9.** pregnable, subject
to **10.** expungable **11.** conquerable,
defenseless, susceptible
vulpine ... **4.** foxy **6.** artful, crafty,
tricky **7.** cunning, foxlike **9.** alopecoid
10. vulpecular
vult ... **4.** mien **6.** aspect **10.** expression
11. countenance
vulture (pert to) ...
African .. **8.** aasvogel
American .. **4.** aura **5.** urubu **6.** condor
13. turkey buzzard
European .. **7.** griffin **11.** lammergeier
(lammergeir)
king .. **4.** papa

large.. **6.** condor **11.** lammergeier
Mexican.. **8.** zopilote
raven.. **9.** Corvultur
Spanish.. **9.** gallinazo
term.. **5.** harpy **9.** raptorial **10.** bird of

prey, predacious
vulturous... **6.** lupine **7.** wolfish
  8. ravenous **9.** rapacious
vying... **7.** emulous **8.** rivaling
  9. competing **11.** competitive

W

W... **6.** letter (23rd) **7.** double U
WAAC... **24.** Women's Auxiliary Army
  Corps
waag... **6.** grivet, monkey
waapa... **5.** canoe
wabber... **4.** cony **5.** daman
wabble... see *wobble*
wabby... **4.** loon (red-throated)
wabe, wabi... **5.** shrub **8.** huisache
wachna... **7.** codfish
wad... **3.** pad, ram **4.** cram, lump, mass,
  plug, roll, tuft **5.** money, stuff, track
  6. bundle, pledge, wealth **7.** stopper
  8. bankroll
wadding... **4.** wads **6.** lining **7.** padding
  8. compress, stopping, stuffing
waddle... **4.** sway **5.** mince **6.** toddle,
  wabble, wamble, wobble **10.** clumsy
  gait
waddy, waddie... **3.** peg **4.** beat, club
  5. stick **6.** attack, cowboy
wade... **4.** ford, pass **5.** study **6.** attack,
  drudge, paddle, plodge **8.** struggle
wader... **4.** coot, ibis, rail **5.** crane, heron,
  snipe, stork **6.** jaçana **9.** sandpiper,
  shore bird **11.** Grallatores
wadi, wady... **5.** oasis, river **6.** ravine,
  valley **7.** channel **11.** watercourse
waeg... **9.** kittiwake
wafer... **4.** cake, disk, ring, seal, snap
  5. bread **7.** biscuit, cracker **10.** altar
  bread
waff... **3.** wag **4.** flap, wave **5.** ghost
  7. lowborn, vagrant **8.** inferior
  9. worthless **12.** disreputable
waft... **4.** gust, puff, wave **5.** carry, float,
  whiff **6.** beckon, convey, convoy, signal
  7. glimpse, pennant **9.** beckoning,
  transport
wag... **3.** wit **4.** card, wave **5.** joker,
  rogue, shake **6.** signal, waddle, wiggle
  7. farceur, vibrate **8.** humorist, jokester
  9. oscillate
wagang... **5.** death **9.** departure
  11. leave-taking
wage, wages... **3.** bet, fee, pay, utu
  4. hire, levy, pawn, risk **5.** fight, incur,
  stake, yield **6.** employ, engage, pledge,
  reward, salary **7.** attempt, contend, hire
  out, stipend, venture **9.** emolument
  10. recompense **12.** compensation,
  remuneration
wage insurance... **7.** chômage
wager... **3.** bet, bid, vie **4.** risk **5.** sport,
  stake **6.** gamble, hazard, parlay, pledge
  7. venture
waggish... **5.** droll, merry **7.** jesting,

jocular, parlous, roguish **8.** humorous,
  sportive **9.** facetious **10.** frolicsome
  11. mischievous
Wagnerian opera... **6.** Rienzi **8.** Parsifal
  9. Lohengrin **10.** Tannhauser
  15. Gotterdammerung
wagon... **3.** car, van **4.** cart, dray,
  tram, wain **5.** araba, coach, lorry,
  tonga **6.** telega **7.** caisson, chariot,
  vehicle **8.** carryall, schooner (prairie)
  12. perambulator
wagon (pert to)...
  canvas-covered.. **15.** prairie schooner
  lit.. **7.** Pullman **11.** sleeping car
  load.. **6.** fother
  maker.. **10.** wagonsmith, wainwright
  on the (wagon).. **8.** sworn off, teetotal
  part.. **4.** neap **5.** blade, thill
  police.. **3.** van **10.** Black Maria
  sideless.. **6.** rolley
wah... **5.** panda
wahine... **4.** wife **5.** woman **8.** mistress
  10. sweetheart
wahoo... **4.** bark, fish, peto **5.** shrub
  7. rock elm **8.** nonsense, tommyrot
  9. buckthorn, guarapucu **12.** umbrella
  tree
waif... **4.** Arab, flag **5.** gamin, stray
  7. vagrant, wastrel **8.** castaway,
  homeless, wanderer **9.** lost sheep
wail... **3.** cry, sob **4.** howl, moan,
  weep **5.** mourn **6.** bemoan, grieve,
  lament **7.** deplore, screech, ululate
  11. lamentation **14.** mournful outcry
wainscot... **4.** base, ceil, line **5.** panel
  6. lining **8.** paneling (panelling)
  9. partition
waist... **4.** wasp **5.** shirt **6.** basque,
  blouse, bodice, dickey, middle, taille
  7. corsage, garment **9.** garibaldi
  12. undergarment
waistcoat... **4.** vest **5.** benjy **6.** jacket,
  jerkin, weskit
wait... **4.** bide, rest, stay, stop **5.** dally,
  defer, delay, hover, serve, tarry,
  watch **6.** attend, expect, linger, remain
  7. observe **8.** hesitate, postpone
  11. expectation **12.** watchfulness
waiter... **4.** tray **6.** garçon, salver,
  server **7.** messboy, messman, servant,
  steward **8.** servitor **9.** attendant
wait on... **4.** help **5.** await, cater, serve
  6. escort **7.** toady to **9.** accompany
waive... **5.** defer, forgo (forego) **6.** desert,
  give up, reject, vacate **7.** abandon, cast
  off, forsake **8.** postpone **9.** disregard
  10. condescend, relinquish

waka ... **5.** canoe
Wakashan Indian ... **6.** Nootka
  8. Kwakiutl
wake ... **4.** call, stir **5.** rouse, track,
  vigil, waken, watch **6.** arouse, awaken,
  excite, revive **10.** death watch
wakeful ... **5.** alert **8.** restless, vigilant,
  watchful **9.** sleepless, wide-awake
Wake Island ... **6.** Ottori (Jap name)
wake-robin ... **4.** Arum **8.** Trillium
  9. Anthurium **10.** cuckoopint
  12. philodendron
wale ... **3.** rib **4.** welt **5.** ridge, wheal
  6. stripe
Wales ... see also *Welsh*
  anc .. **7.** Cambria
  city .. **7.** Rhondda, Swansea **8.** Hereford,
  Pembroke **9.** Carnarvon
  congress of literati .. **10.** eisteddfod
  deity .. **4.** Bran
  emblem (floral) .. **4.** leek
  language .. **7.** Cymraeg
  mountain .. **7.** Snowdon
  native .. **5.** Cymry (Kymry)
  patron saint .. **5.** David
  port .. **7.** Cardiff
  river .. **3.** Dee, Wye **6.** Severn
  sea .. **5.** Irish
walk ... **3.** mog, pad **4.** foot, gait,
  hike, hoof, pace, path, plod, ramp,
  step **5.** allee, amble, scuff, strut,
  tramp, tread **6.** ramble, sphere,
  stride, stroll, toddle, travel, trudge
  7. conduct, shuffle, traipse **8.** ambulate,
  behavior, frescade, province, sidewalk
  9. esplanade, promenade, wandering
  10. passageway **11.** base on balls,
  perambulate **13.** peregrination
walk (pert to) ...
  a beat .. **6.** patrol
  about .. **11.** perambulate
  clumsily .. **5.** mince **6.** lumber, totter
  health .. **14.** constitutional
  lime-bordered .. **9.** tilicetum
  proudly .. **5.** strut **6.** prance
  public .. **4.** mall **6.** arcade **7.** alameda
  9. esplanade, promenade
  wearily .. **4.** limp, plod **5.** tramp
  6. hobble, trudge
  with speed .. **10.** heel and toe
walking (pert to) ...
  about .. **7.** passant (Her) **11.** peripatetic
  bearlike .. **11.** plantigrade
  meter .. **9.** pedometer
  papers .. **7.** deposal, the sack **8.** mittimus,
  pink slip **9.** discharge, dismissal
  10. retirement
wall ... **4.** dado, dike, ha-ha, mure, pier
  5. fence, levee, panel, redan **6.** escarp,
  hinder, immure, paries, podium,
  septum, shut in **7.** barrier, defense,
  enclose, fortify, parapet, rampart
  8. espalier, palisade, restrain, stockade
  9. barricade, enclosure, encompass,
  partition, precipice, revetment
  13. fortification
wall (pert to) ...
  bracket .. **6.** corbel, sconce
  creeper .. **4.** bird
  go to the (wall) .. **4.** fail **10.** go bankrupt
  lining .. **8.** wainscot
  lizard .. **4.** newt **5.** gecko
  masonry .. **9.** revetment
  pert to .. **5.** mural **8.** parietal
  recess .. **5.** niche **6.** alcove
  Street .. **9.** Manhattan **11.** money market,
  stock market
  up .. **6.** immure
wallaby ... **8.** kangaroo, Macropus,
  wallaroo **10.** paddymelon
wallah, walla ... **5.** agent **6.** master,
  person **7.** servant
waller ... **4.** wels **9.** saltmaker, sheatfish
wallet ... **3.** bag **4.** pack, poke, sack
  5. purse **8.** billfold, knapsack
  10. pocketbook **12.** porte-monnaie
walleye ... **9.** exotropia **10.** strabismus
wallow ... **4.** fade, sail **5.** surge **6.** grovel,
  welter, wither **7.** debauch, founder,
  insipid **8.** flounder, kommetje, nauseous
  9. tasteless
Wall Street org ... **3.** SEC **4.** NYSE
  6. NASDAQ
walnut ... **6.** bannut
walrus ... **3.** pod (group) **5.** morse
  6. mammal, sea cat **8.** pinniped
  9. rosmarine (fable) **10.** pinnipedia
Waltonian ... **6.** angler **16.** disciple of
  Walton (Izaak)
wamble ... **5.** twist **6.** quiver, ramble,
  rumble, totter, writhe **7.** revolve,
  stagger, wriggle
wame ... **4.** room, womb **5.** belly
  7. stomach
wampum ... **4.** peag **5.** beads, money,
  uhllo **6.** shells **7.** jewelry, roanoke
  8. ornament **10.** wampumpeag
wan ... **3.** dim, sad **4.** ashy, dark,
  pale, sick **5.** ashen, black, dusky,
  faint, lurid **6.** dismal, gloomy, pallid,
  sickly **7.** ghastly, languid **9.** deathlike,
  sorrowful **10.** lusterless **11.** lead-colored
wand ... **3.** rod **4.** mace, pole **5.** baton,
  osier, staff, stick (magic) **6.** switch,
  wattle **7.** pointer, rhabdos (magic),
  scepter (sceptre) **8.** caduceus
  9. horsewhip
wander ... **3.** err, gad **4.** moon, rave,
  roam, rove **5.** drift, prowl, range,
  stray **6.** cruise, depart, ramble, stroll,
  travel **7.** digress, meander, saunter,
  traipse **8.** divagate, traverse **9.** circulate,
  itinerate, scamander **11.** peregrinate
wanderer ... **4.** Arab, waif **5.** gypsy,
  nomad, rover **6.** ranger, roamer, truant
  7. migrant, pilgrim, vagrant **9.** butterfly,
  itinerant, straggler **10.** covenanter
  12. peregrinator
wandering ... **5.** vague **6.** astray,
  errant, roving, vagary **8.** aberrant,
  delirium, straying **9.** delirious, deviating,
  deviation, itinerant **10.** circuitous,
  discursive, journeying **11.** noctivigant,
  perambulant **13.** peregrination
wandering (pert to) ...
  bird .. **9.** albatross
  long .. **7.** odyssey
  minstrel .. **4.** bard **10.** troubadour
  stars .. **12.** seven planets
  tattler .. **9.** shore bird
  votary .. **6.** palmer
wanderoo ... **6.** langur, monkey

W

7. macaque
wand-shaped . . . **7.** virgate
wane . . . **3.** age, ebb **4.** fail, sink, want
5. abate, peter **6.** defect, lessen, recede,
repine **7.** decline, grow dim, subside
8. decrease, diminish **10.** defervesce
13. deterioration
wanga . . . **5.** charm, spell **6.** voodoo
7. philter, sorcery
wangle . . . **4.** fake, plot **6.** adjust,
juggle, obtain, totter, wiggle **7.** finagle
(finaigue), wriggle **8.** contrive,
maneuver (manoeuvre) **9.** extricate
10. manipulate
want . . . **4.** lack, miss, need, wish **5.** crave
6. dearth, desire, hunger, penury
7. absence, craving, lacking, poverty
8. scarcity, shortage **9.** deficient,
indigence, privation **10.** inadequacy
11. destitution, requirement
want (of) . . .
appetite . . **6.** asitia
desire . . **11.** inappetence
lacking . . **4.** sans **5.** out of **7.** empty
of, scant of, short of **8.** bereft of
10. deprived of
power . . **5.** atony
sense (good) . . **5.** folly
wanting . . . **4.** void **5.** minus, needy
6. absent, bereft, devoid **7.** lacking,
missing, short of, without **9.** deficient,
destitute, imperfect
wanting (pert to) . . .
be found . . **9.** fall short **10.** be inferior
confidence . . **11.** distrustful
in energy . . **6.** atonic
in firmness . . **7.** flaccid
in intelligence . . **12.** feebleminded
wanton . . . **3.** gay **4.** lewd **5.** merry
6. frisky, harlot, unruly **7.** immoral,
lustful, wayward **8.** flagrant, insolent,
sportive, unchaste **9.** dissolute,
merciless **10.** capricious, frolicsome,
licentious **11.** extravagant
13. undisciplined
wapiti . . . **3.** elk **4.** deer, stag
war . . . **5.** fight **6.** attack, battle **8.** conflict
war (pert to) . . .
agreement . . **6.** cartel
cause of . . **10.** casus belli
club . . **4.** mace
fleet . . **6.** armada
gas . . **8.** adamsite
German . . **5.** krieg **10.** blitzkrieg
god . . **3.** Ira, Tyr **4.** Ares
goddess . . **5.** Bella **6.** Ishtar
hating . . **13.** misopolemical
hawk . . **5.** jingo **7.** bailiff
horse . . **5.** steed **7.** charger **8.** partisan
10. campaigner, politician
of words . . **9.** logomachy
religious . . **5.** jihad (jehad)
vessel, ship . . **3.** sub **7.** cruiser, frigate
8. corvette (corvet) **9.** destroyer,
submarine **11.** dreadnought
(dreadnaught)
war bird . . . **7.** aviator, tanager (scarlet)
warble . . . **4.** sing **5.** carol, trill, yodel
6. quaver **7.** twitter, vibrate
warbler . . . **4.** wren **6.** singer **8.** blackcap,
grosbeak, redstart, songster **9.** beccafico

10. bluethroat **11.** whitethroat
ward . . . **4.** jail, part, rule **5.** watch
6. govern, prison **7.** custody, keeping
8. district, garrison, guardian,
watchman **9.** dependent **10.** stronghold
12. guardianship
ward (pert to) . . .
division . . **4.** army, jail **6.** forest
8. hospital
French . . **14.** arrondissement
heeler . . **8.** henchman **10.** politician
off . . **4.** fend **5.** fence, parry, repel, stave
7. expiate, forfend, prevent
warden . . . **5.** guard, nazir **6.** dizdar
(disdar), jailer, keeper, ranger, sexton
7. alcaide (alcaid), turnkey **8.** director,
guardian, official, watchman
9. concierge, custodian **10.** gatekeeper
warder . . . **6.** warden **7.** turnkey
wardrobe . . . **4.** room **6.** closet **7.** almirah,
apparel, cabinet, clothes **8.** costumes
12. clothespress
ware . . . **4.** sage, wary, wise **5.** aware,
china, goods, spend **6.** shrewd
7. careful, heedful, pottery, prudent,
seaweed **8.** cautious, vigilant
9. cognizant, commodity, conscious,
porcelain **11.** commodities,
earthenware, merchandise
warehouse . . . **4.** silo **5.** depot, étape
6. fonduk (fondouk), godown **7.** storage
8. entrepôt
warfare . . . **7.** contest **8.** conflict, struggle
11. hostilities **12.** armed contest
wariness . . . **7.** stealth **8.** distrust
9. chariness, suspicion
warlock . . . **6.** wizard **7.** monster (Myth)
8. conjuror, magician, sorcerer
warm . . . **3.** red **4.** heat, keen, mild
5. angry, calid, eager, humid, muggy,
tepid, toast **6.** ardent, excite, genial,
hearty, heated, torrid **7.** clement,
cordial, fervent **8.** friendly, generous
10. responsive **11.** sympathetic
12. affectionate, enthusiastic **13.** near
discovery, near the object (see also
hot)
warm (pert to) . . .
bath . . **5.** therm
growing . . **9.** calescent
hearted . . **4.** kind **6.** hearty, kindly,
tender **7.** cordial **8.** friendly, generous
11. sympathetic **12.** affectionate
pert to . . **7.** thermal
praise . . **8.** encomium
room . . **10.** tepidarium
springs (Rom) . . **7.** thermae
warmblooded . . . **6.** ardent **9.** irascible
13. homoiothermic, quick-tempered
14. haematothermic (hematothermal)
warmed over . . . **5.** stale, trite
8. rehashed, reheated **9.** rechauffé,
twice-told
warmonger . . . **4.** hawk
warmth . . . **4.** élan, glow, heat, zeal
5. ardor **7.** ardency, thermal **8.** fervency
9. animation, eloquence, geniality,
vehemence **10.** enthusiasm, excitement
11. calefaction, earnestness
warn . . . **4.** flag **5.** alarm, alert **6.** advise,
exhort, inform, notify, remind, signal

7. apprise (apprize), caution, counsel, previse **8.** admonish, forebode, threaten **9.** reprehend
warning . . . **4.** bell, omen **5.** alarm, alert, radar, siren **6.** alarum, beacon, beware, caveat, signal, threat, tocsin **7.** blinker, sematic, summons **10.** admonition, admonitive **12.** caveat emptor
warp . . . **4.** bend, bias, hurl, sway, turn, woof **5.** fling, throw, twist, weave **6.** buckle, swerve **7.** contort, deflect, distort, pervert **9.** fabricate **10.** aberration, distortion **12.** misinterpret
warp (pert to) . . .
cross threads . . **4.** woof
threads . . **5.** lease **6.** stamen
yarn . . **3.** abb
warragal, warrigal . . . **5.** dingo, horse, myall
warrant . . . **4.** earn, writ **5.** order **6.** attest, ensure, permit, secure **7.** defense, justify, precept, promise, voucher **8.** document, guaranty, sanction, security **9.** authorize, guarantee, safeguard **10.** credential, instrument, protection **11.** acknowledge, certificate **13.** authorization
warranty . . . **4.** writ **5.** proof **7.** promise, warrant **8.** guaranty, sanction, security **13.** authorization
warrior . . . **4.** hero, impi **5.** brave **6.** Amazon **7.** fighter, martial, soldier **10.** halberdier
warrior (pert to) . . .
Bib . . **4.** Ehud
female . . **6.** Amazon
Indian . . **6.** sannup
Roman . . **9.** gladiator
Trojan . . **6.** Agenor, Hector
Warsaw (pert to) . . .
capital . . **6.** Poland
river . . **7.** Vistula
suburb . . **5.** Praga
wary . . **3.** shy **5.** alert, canny, chary, leery **7.** careful, guarded, prudent **8.** cautious, discreet, watchful **10.** economical **11.** circumspect
wash . . . **3.** lap, pan **4.** lave **5.** bathe, clean, elute, flush, leach, marsh, paint, purge, rinse, slosh, swash **6.** debris, drench, dry bed (river), purify, splash **7.** cleanse, immerse, launder, overlay, shampoo **8.** ablution **9.** lixiviate
wash (pert to) . . .
basin . . **4.** bowl **6.** lavabo
bear . . **7.** raccoon
dish . . **11.** pied wagtail
for gold . . **3.** pan
one's hands of . . **6.** give up, refuse **10.** relinquish
out . . **4.** fade **5.** elute, flunk **7.** failure, freshet
sale (finance) . . **10.** fictitious
washing . . . **7.** coating **8.** ablution **9.** drenching
Washington, DC (famed sites) . . .
7. Capitol (Bldg), The Mall **8.** Pentagon, Treasury **10.** Blair House, White House **11.** Mount Vernon **12.** Ford's Theater (Lincoln Museum), Supreme

Court **14.** cherry blossoms **15.** Iwo Jima Monument, Lincoln Memorial **16.** National Archives, Naval Observatory **17.** Jefferson Memorial, Library of Congress **18.** Walter Reed Hospital, Washington Monument **19.** Unknown Soldier's Tomb **22.** Smithsonian Institution **25.** Arlington National Cemetery
Washington (State of) . . .
capital . . **7.** Olympia
city . . **6.** Tacoma, Yakima **7.** Everett, Seattle, Spokane **10.** Bellingham, Walla Walla
dam . . **10.** Bonneville **11.** Grand Coulee
discoverer . . **4.** Gray **9.** Vancouver
explorer . . **5.** Clark, Lewis **6.** Wilkes **7.** Fremont
Falls . . **10.** Snoqualmie
Fort . . **5.** Lewis
lake . . **5.** Union **6.** Chelan **8.** Crescent
mountain . . **7.** Rainier **8.** Cascades, Olympics
river . . **5.** Snake, White **7.** Spokane **8.** Columbia
Sound . . **5.** Puget **7.** Rosario
State admission . . **11.** Forty-second
State motto . . **4.** Al-Ki (By and By)
State nickname . . **9.** Evergreen
wind (SW) . . **7.** chinook
wasp . . . **5.** Sphex, vespa, whamp **6.** dauber, hornet, Tiphia, vespid **8.** Vespidae **12.** Hymenopteron, yellow jacket
waspish . . . **4.** mean **5.** cross, testy **6.** cranky **7.** bearish, peevish, slender **8.** choleric, churlish, petulant, snappish, spiteful **9.** fractious, irascible, irritable **12.** cantankerous
wasp's nest . . . **8.** vespiary
wassail . . . **4.** lark, orgy, romp **5.** toast **6.** frolic, shindy **7.** carouse **8.** beverage, carousal **9.** festivity **10.** salutation **11.** celebration **12.** drinking bout
waste . . . **3.** eat **4.** idle, junk, loss, rind, ross, sack, slag, vain, wear, wild **5.** chaff, chips, dross, havoc, spill, trash **6.** barren, desert, expend, lavish, ravage, refuse **7.** atrophy, exhaust, fritter, rubbish **8.** clinkers, demolish, desolate, squander **9.** dissipate **10.** desolation, diminution **11.** destruction, devastation, dissipation, prodigality, uninhabited **12.** uncultivated, unproductive **13.** unserviceable
waste (pert to) . . .
allowance . . **4.** tret
away . . **3.** age **6.** shrink, sicken **7.** decline **8.** marasmus **11.** deteriorate
lay waste . . **4.** sack **6.** ravage **7.** destroy **8.** decimate
matter . . **3.** ort **4.** slag **5.** dross **7.** clinker
mine . . **3.** gob
silk . . **4.** knob, noil **6.** frison
time . . **4.** idle, lazy **5.** dally **6.** daddle, footle, loiter **10.** dillydally
wasted . . . **7.** haggard **8.** phthisic
wasteful . . . **6.** lavish **10.** thriftless **11.** extravagant, improvident
wasteland . . . **5.** heath, marsh, swamp

6. desert, morass 8. badlands 10. barren
land, everglades
wasting ... 5. aging 6. awaste
8. marasmic 10. enfeebling
11. consumption, devastating
13. deteriorating
wastrel ... 4. waif 5. idler 8. vagabond
10. profligate 11. spendthrift
watch ... 3. eye, spy 4. espy, heed,
mark, mind, tend, time, wake (funeral)
5. guard, vigil 6. ambush, patrol, police,
sentry 7. bivouac, lookout, observe
8. horologe, sentinel 9. ambuscade,
timepiece, vigilance 11. chronometer,
observation, wakefulness
watch (pert to) ...
chain .. 3. fob 6. Albert
face .. 5. bezel
maker .. 10. horologist
military .. 5. perdu (perdue) 6. sentry
7. vedette
stop .. 5. timer
tower .. 6. beacon 7. atalaya, mirador
10. lighthouse
word .. 6. signal 10. shibboleth (Bib)
11. countersign
works .. 10. escapement
watchful ... 3. Ira (Heb) 4. wary 5. alert,
aware 7. careful, heedful 8. cautious,
open-eyed, vigilant 9. observant,
regardful 11. circumspect
watchman ... 5. guard 6. sentry, warder
8. sentinel, watchdog 10. gatekeeper
watchword ... 4. hint, word 6. signal
8. party cry 10. intimation, shibboleth
(Bib) 11. countersign
watchworks ... 10. escapement
water ... 3. eau, ice, wet 4. aqua, rain
5. fluid, flume, spray 6. dilute, lagoon,
liquid 7. moisten 8. beverage, calendar,
irrigate, sprinkle 10. adulterate
water (pert to) ...
baptismal .. 5. laver
bath .. 7. balneum
bird .. 4. coot, loon 5. diver, ouzel
6. dipper 7. pintail, swimmer
9. merganser
bottle .. 4. olla 6. carafe
buffalo .. 2. ox 7. carabao
channel .. 5. canal, flume 6. strait
8. tailrace
chart .. 10. hydrograph
color (art) .. 9. aquarelle
comb form .. 5. hydro 6. hydato
congealed .. 3. ice 4. snow 5. glacé
6. icicle
course .. 4. clow 5. bayou, gorge, gully
6. nullah, ravine, sluice 9. watergate
cow .. 6. sea cow 7. buffalo, manatee
cure .. 10. hydropathy 12. hydrotherapy
deer .. 10. chevrotain
destitute of .. 9. anhydrous
divination by .. 10. hydromancy
eagle .. 6. osprey
element .. 6. oxygen 8. hydrogen
elephant .. 12. hippopotamus
exhibition .. 8. aquacade
fowl .. 7. pelican
gauge (rain) .. 8. udometer
goddess .. 4. Nina 7. Anahita, Anaitis
hare .. 11. swamp rabbit

heater .. 4. etna
history .. 10. hydrognosy
hog .. 8. capybara
hole .. 5. oasis 6. tinaja 7. alberca
jug .. 4. lota (lotah), olla 5. banga
6. hydria, kalpis
lava .. 12. hellgrammite
lily .. 5. lotus 6. Nuphar 7. Nelumbo
8. Nymphaea, Victoria 11. spatterdock
measure .. 10. hydrometer
meter .. 7. Venturi
mineral .. 5. Vichy 6. Shasta 7. Seltzer
monster .. 6. nicker (fabled)
nymph .. 5. naiad 6. undine 7. Oceanid
of oblivion .. 5. Lethe 12. river of Hades
opossum .. 5. yapok (yapock)
pert to .. 7. aqueous 8. hydatoid
plug .. 3. tap 4. cock, cork 6. faucet,
spigot 7. hydrant
pocket .. 6. tinaja
rat .. 4. vole 8. vagabond
reddish (with iron) .. 6. riddam
reservoir (underground) .. 6. cenote
rough .. 4. eddy 5. ocean 6. rapids
7. riptide 8. undertow
sapphire .. 6. iolite 10. saphir d'eau
scorpion .. 4. Nepa 7. Ranatra
search for .. 5. dowse
sheet of .. 5. nappe
spirit .. 3. Nix 5. Ariel, Nixie 6. kelpie,
nicker, sprite
spout .. 5. spate 8. gargoyle
sprite .. 3. Nix 5. Nixie
stratum .. 7. aquifer
study, science of .. 9. hydrology
11. hydrography
surface .. 4. ryme
swelling .. 5. edema
turkey .. 9. snakebird
vessel .. 3. jug 4. ewer, lota (lotah),
pail 5. cruse, flask 6. bottle, bucket,
tinaja 7. pitcher, stamnos 8. decanter
wheel .. 5. noria 6. sakieh (sakiyeh)
7. turbine 8. tympanum
without .. 9. anhydrous
watery ... 8. ichorous
Watling Street (London) ... 6. Galaxy
8. Milky Way 9. Roman road
wattle ... 3. rod 4. beat, flog, plat, wand
5. fence, twist, weave, withe 6. barbel,
dewlap, hurdle, lappet 8. caruncle
9. boobyalla, loose flap 10. intertwine,
interweave 11. skin process 12. native
willow
wattlebird ... 4. crow 10. honey eater
11. brush turkey
Wattle Day ... 7. holiday
wave ... 3. ola, sea, wag 4. flap, tide
5. crest, eagre, flood, ridge, surge,
swell, tilde 6. beckon, billow, comber,
flaunt, hairdo, marcel, ripple, roller,
signal 7. breaker, decuman, flutter,
tsunami, vibrate 8. brandish, coiffure,
flourish, greeting, undulate 9. fluctuate,
vibration 10. undulation
waver ... 4. reel, sway, veer 5. demur,
quake 6. falter, quiver, totter 7. flicker,
flutter, stagger, tremble, vibrate
8. hesitate 9. fluctuate, oscillate,
vacillate 12. be indecisive
wavering ... 6. fickle 8. doubtful,

unsteady 9. desultory 10. irresolute
wavy . . . 4. onde, undé (undee) 5. curly,
snaky 6. repand, undate 7. billowy,
rolling, sinuous 8. undulant
9. undulated 10. undulatory
wax . . . 4. cere, grow 6. candle, cerate,
polish 7. beeswax, cerumen 8. increase,
paraffin 9. lubricant, lubricate
12. zietrisikite (mineral)
wax (pert to) . . .
beeswax cells . . 9. honeycomb
beeswax substitute . . 7. ceresin
candle . . 6. cierge
chemical . . 9. adipocere
Chinese . . 4. pela
molded in . . 7. fictile 9. ceroplast
ref to . . 5. ceral
substance . . 5. cerin
way . . . 3. via 4. lane, mode, path, plan,
ramp, road 5. alley, habit, means, Milky,
route, track 6. avenue, course, manner,
method, street 7. highway, passage
8. causeway, distance, sidewalk
9. banquette, direction, procedure
way (pert to) . . .
astronomy . . 6. Galaxy 8. Milky Way
give . . 5. break, yield 6. weaken
7. despair 10. depreciate
god of . . 6. Hermes
in . . 7. ingress 8. entrance
in a way . . 8. as it were, somewhat
13. theoretically
inclined . . 4. ramp
out . . 4. exit 6. egress, escape
roundabout . . 6. detour
waylay . . . 3. rob 4. await, seize
6. ambush, lay for 8. surprise
9. ambuscade
wayward . . . 6. unruly 7. erratic, willful
8. perverse, stubborn, untoward
10. capricious, headstrong, refractory
11. disobedient, intractable
weak . . . 3. dim, lax, wan 4. pale,
puny, thin, worn 5. faint, frail,
washy 6. dotish, feeble, infirm, sickly,
simple, unwise, watery 7. flaccid,
foolish, fragile, insipid 8. cowardly,
decrepit, fatigued, impotent, wavering
9. enfeebled, exhausted, nerveless,
powerless 10. effeminate 11. debilitated,
ineffective 12. unconvincing
weak (pert to) . . .
fish . . 7. totuava 9. gray trout
10. squeteague
hearted . . 6. afraid 7. fearful
12. fainthearted
kneed . . 8. cowardly, yielding
10. irresolute
sister . . 6. coward 8. weakling
11. mollycoddle
weaken . . . 3. sap 4. tire 5. break 6. dilute,
impair, lessen, reduce 7. cripple,
disable, exhaust, unnerve 8. enervate
9. undermine 10. debilitate
weakness . . . 4. flaw 5. atony, fault
6. defect, foible, liking 7. failing, fatigue,
frailty 8. asthenia, debility 9. cowardice,
impotence, infirmity 10. feebleness,
infirmness 11. decrepitude
12. imperfection 13. powerlessness
weal . . . 4. mark, wale, welt 5. ridge,

wheal 6. riches, wealth 7. welfare
9. happiness, well-being
10. commonweal
wealth . . . 4. good, weal 5. money
6. assets, mammon, riches 7. capital,
fortune, welfare 8. opulence, property,
treasure 9. abundance, affluence, well-
being 10. prosperity 11. possessions
wealth (pert to) . . .
god of . . 6. Plutus
person of . . 6. monied 7. magnate,
opulent 9. plutocrat
pursuit of . . 10. plutomania
study of . . 9. economics, plutology
worship of . . 10. plutolatry
wealthy . . . 4. rich 5. ample 8. abundant,
affluent
wealthy (pert to) . . .
English slang . . 4. oofy
man . . 5. nabob 10. capitalist
rule by . . 10. plutocracy
wean . . . 6. detach 8. alienate, estrange
9. reconcile
weapon . . . 3. arm, gat, gun 4. bola, bolo,
celt, club, dart, epee, snee 5. arrow,
knife, lance, rifle, saber (sabre), spear,
sword 6. dagger, musket, pistol, poleax
(poleaxe), rapier 7. bayonet, bazooka,
carbine, gisarme, halberd, machete,
trident 8. battle-ax (battle-axe), catapult,
crossbow, revolver, stiletto, tomahawk
9. derringer, Excalibur 11. blunderbuss
wear . . . 3. use 4. bear, fray, fret,
show 5. chafe, weary 7. fatigue
12. disintegrate
wear (pert to) . . .
away . . 3. eat, end 5. erode 6. abrade
7. corrode, decline
down . . 4. tire 8. persuade 9. influence
out . . 4. tire 5. waste 7. fatigue
weariness . . . 5. ennui 6. tedium
7. boredom, fatigue 9. lassitude
wearisome . . . 4. hard 6. boring, dismal,
dreary, tiring 7. irksome, tedious
8. tiresome, toilsome 9. fatiguing,
laborious, vexatious 10. monotonous
weary . . . 3. fag, irk, sad 4. bore, jade,
pall, tire, weak 5. bored, spent, tired
6. plague 7. fatigue, languid 9. forjesket
weasel . . . 4. stot, vare 5. ratel, stoat
6. ermine, ferret
weaselike . . . 4. mink 5. otter, tayra
9. musteline, musteloid
weather (pert to) . . .
cock . . 4. vane
glass . . 9. barometer, baroscope
man . . 13. meteorologist
map . . 6. isobar
weave . . . 3. mat 4. knit, lace, reel,
spin, sway 5. plait, unite 6. devise,
wattle 7. canelle, entwine, fashion
8. contrive 9. fabricate, interlace,
interwind 10. intertwine, intertwist
11. push one's way
weaver bird . . . 4. baya, maya, taha
5. Munia
weaving (pert to) . . .
art of . . 4. loom
fabric (rich) . . 3. web 7. brocade, webbing
French . . 5. lisse 8. Jacquard
material . . 5. reeds, twigs 6. raffia

term.. **4.** beam, dent, loom, sley
7. shuttle
together.. **7.** plexure
weazen (wizen)... **6.** shrink, wither
7. shrivel
web... **3.** net, ply **4.** caul, tela,
trap, veil, warp **5.** snare **6.** tissue
7. network, texture **8.** filament,
gossamer, membrane, vexillum
12. entanglement
web (pert to)...
footed.. **7.** palmate
like.. **4.** lacy **5.** telar **7.** spidery
spinning.. **6.** telary **7.** retiary
term.. **5.** telar
toed.. **11.** totipalmate
winged.. **3.** bat
work.. **4.** maze, mesh **6.** tangle
11. Gordian knot
wed... **4.** join, mate **5.** marry, mated,
unite **6.** joined **7.** espouse, pledged,
spliced **13.** give in wedlock
wedding... **8.** ceremony, espousal,
marriage, nuptials
wedding (anniversary)...
1st.. **5.** paper
2nd.. **5.** straw
3rd.. **5.** candy
4th.. **7.** leather
5th.. **6.** wooden
7th.. **6.** floral
10th.. **3.** tin
12th.. **5.** linen
13th.. **4.** lace
15th.. **7.** crystal
20th.. **5.** china
25th.. **6.** silver
30th.. **5.** pearl
35th.. **5.** coral
40th.. **7.** emerald
45th.. **4.** ruby
50th.. **6.** golden
75th.. **7.** diamond
wedding (pert to)...
flower.. **13.** orange blossom
proclamation.. **5.** banns (bans)
snow.. **4.** rice
term.. **7.** marital, wedlock **8.** marriage,
nuptials **9.** matrimony **11.** espousement
wedge... **3.** jam **4.** club, shoe **5.** cleat,
ingot, split **6.** sector, wedgie **7.** niblick
8. triangle, voussoir **9.** machinery
wedge-shaped... **7.** cuneate **9.** cuneiform
(cuniform)
Wednesday... **5.** Woden (wise god)
9. fourth day, Woden's Day
wee... **3.** bit **4.** dock, fine, tiny **5.** small,
teeny **6.** little, minute **10.** diminutive,
teeny-weeny
weed... **3.** bur (burr), hoe, rag **4.** loco,
milk, sida, tare **5.** cigar, flesh, vetch
6. darnel, excise, Jimson, knawel,
spurge, tumble **7.** allseed, mallows,
mustard, ragweed, tobacco **8.** plantain,
purslane, toadflax **9.** cultivate,
dandelion **11.** undergrowth
weeds... **8.** garments (mourning)
week... **8.** hebdomad **9.** seven days
week (pert to)...
day.. **6.** ferial
Eccl.. **4.** Holy **7.** Passion

of Sundays.. **5.** seven **8.** hebdomad
of years.. **5.** seven
past.. **10.** yesterweek
weekly... **5.** aweek **10.** hebdomadal,
periodical **11.** publication
weeks, two... **9.** fortnight
weel... **4.** pool, trap **6.** basket **8.** fish
trap
ween... **5.** think **6.** expect **7.** believe,
imagine, suppose **8.** conceive
weep... **3.** cry, orp, sob **4.** drip, rain, wail
5. exude, mourn **7.** blubber, lapwing
9. percolate, shed tears
weeping... **6.** crying **7.** sobbing
9. festering
weeping (pert to)...
monkey.. **8.** capuchin
queen.. **5.** Niobe
tree.. **5.** cedar **6.** spruce, willow
Weeping Philosopher (anc)...
10. Heraclitus
weevil (pert to)...
cotton.. **4.** boll
malt.. **4.** boud
snout.. **8.** curculio
type (other).. **3.** pea **4.** palm, pine, rice,
seed **5.** flour
weigh... **4.** tare, test **5.** hoist, poise,
scale **6.** ponder, regard **7.** balance, be
heavy, compare, measure **8.** consider,
encumber, estimate, ruminate
9. apportion, press hard
weigh down... **4.** lade, load **6.** burden,
hamper **7.** ballast, depress, oppress
11. overbalance
weight... **4.** load, mass **5.** force,
power **6.** burden, import, moment
7. gravity, tonnage **8.** encumber,
pressure **9.** authority, heaviness,
influence **10.** importance
11. consequence **12.** significance
weight (pert to)...
allowance.. **4.** tare, tret **7.** scalage
comb form.. **4.** baro
gem.. **5.** carat (karat)
light.. **6.** suttle
system.. **3.** net **4.** troy **6.** metric
10. apothecary **11.** avoirdupois
total.. **5.** gross
weighty... **3.** fat **5.** bulky, heavy, hefty,
large, obese **6.** solemn **7.** massive,
onerous, serious **8.** forcible, powerful
9. corpulent, important, momentous,
ponderous **10.** burdensome,
cumbersome, impressive, oppressive
11. influential **13.** authoritative
weir... **3.** dam, net **4.** bank **5.** fence, levee,
seine **7.** barrier, milldam **9.** floodgate
weird... **3.** odd **4.** omen, wild **5.** eerie
(eery), queer, scary **6.** creepy, spooky
7. awesome, curious, ghostly, macabre,
strange, uncanny **8.** eldritch
9. deathlike, frightful **10.** mysterious,
prediction
Weird Sisters (Scot)... **5.** Fates
welcome... **4.** hail **5.** adopt, greet
7. acclaim, accueil **8.** grateful, greeting,
pleasing **9.** agreeable, bienvenue,
desirable **10.** acceptable, salutation
weld... **5.** unite **11.** consolidate
welfare... **4.** good, weal **5.** Salus

(goddess) **9.** good cheer **10.** prosperity
14. material plenty
welkin ... **3.** air, sky **6.** heaven
10. atmosphere
well ... **3.** fit, gay, pit **4.** gush, hale, pool
5. aweel, fount, fully **6.** easily, gusher,
hearty, justly, kindly, source **7.** cistern,
closely **8.** artesian, expertly, fountain,
friendly **10.** full degree, intimately
11. excellently **12.** satisfactory
well (pert to) ...
being .. **4.** weal **7.** comfort **8.** eucrasia
9. happiness
Bib .. **4.** Esek
born .. **5.** noble **7.** eugenic
bred .. **6.** polite **7.** genteel, refined
8. cultured, wellborn **9.** pedigreed
10. cultivated **11.** gentlemanly
12. thoroughbred
comb form .. **4.** mene
defined .. **8.** distinct **11.** distinctive
groomed .. **4.** neat **5.** sleek **6.** soigné
(soignée)
grounded .. **5.** valid **7.** logical **9.** plausible
11. established, substantial **12.** well-
informed
gushing .. **8.** artesian
heeled .. **4.** rich **5.** armed **7.** moneyed,
wealthy, well-off **8.** well-to-do
known .. **6.** famous **7.** eminent
12. acknowledged
land drain .. **4.** sump
lining .. **5.** steen
off .. **5.** lucky **10.** prosperous
oil .. **6.** gusher
pole .. **5.** sweep
prefix .. **2.** eu
timed .. **6.** timely **9.** opportune
versed .. **7.** erudite
watered .. **9.** irrigated, irriguous
welsh (welch) ... **5.** cheat **6.** not pay,
renege **7.** swindle **10.** shirk out of
Welsh (pert to) ... see also *Wales*
boat .. **7.** coracle
congress of literati .. **10.** eisteddfod
fine, for murder .. **7.** galanas
god, underworld .. **4.** Bran
instrument (reed) .. **7.** pibcorn
man .. **5.** Taffy **8.** Cambrian
onion .. **5.** cibal
population .. **6.** Cymric
rabbit .. **7.** ramekin (ramequin), rarebit
romance collection .. **10.** Mabinogion
(Mabinogi)
welt ... **4.** mark, wale **5.** ridge **6.** stripe,
thrash
welter ... **4.** reel, roll, sail, toss **6.** grovel,
tumble, wallow **7.** stagger **8.** flounder,
overturn **9.** confusion
wen ... **4.** cyst, rune **5.** tumor **7.** blemish
11. excrescence **12.** protuberance
wench ... **4.** doxy, gill, girl **5.** child,
squaw, trull, woman **6.** damsel,
maiden **7.** consort, servant **8.** strumpet
11. maidservant
wend ... **2.** go **4.** fare, pass **6.** depart,
direct, travel **7.** circuit, proceed
8. progress
went (pert to) ... see also *go*
astray .. **6.** failed **10.** miscarried
away .. **4.** left **8.** departed

before .. **3.** led **8.** preceded **9.** anteceded
swiftly .. **3.** ran **4.** sped **6.** darted
7. scooted, scudded **8.** decamped
wenzel ... **4.** jack (card game) **5.** knave
werewolf ... **6.** jaguar **8.** uturuncu,
werefolk **11.** lycanthrope
wergild ... **3.** cro **4.** eric **7.** galanas
9. Brehon Law
Wesleyan ... **9.** Methodist **14.** Wesley
follower
West African (pert to) ...
baboon .. **5.** drill **8.** mandrill
city .. **5.** Accra, Dakar
gazelle .. **4.** kudu, mohr (mhorr), oryx
lemur .. **5.** potto **8.** kinkajou
monkey .. **4.** mona **6.** guenon
native .. **7.** Ashanti (Ashantee)
people .. **5.** Igara
pepper .. **5.** cubeb
tree .. **5.** iroko, odoom
West End, London ... **7.** Mayfair
9. Belgravia **11.** fashionable
12. aristocratic
Western ... **9.** Hesperian **10.** Occidental
Westernmost US ... **9.** Aleutians **11.** Attu
Islands **12.** Cape Wrangell
West Indies ...
bird .. **4.** tody **6.** mucaro
boat .. **7.** drogher (droger)
chief .. **7.** cacique
clingfish .. **6.** testar
crop .. **5.** sugar **7.** bananas
ebony .. **9.** cocuswood
fish .. **4.** cero, paru, sesi **6.** testar
flea .. **6.** chigoe
fruit .. **5.** papaw (pawpaw)
islands .. **4.** Cuba **5.** Haiti **6.** Cayman,
Virgin **7.** Antigua, Bahamas, Leeward
8. Antilles, Windward
liquor .. **5.** mobby (mobbie), tafia (taffia)
lizard .. **6.** arbalo
magic .. **5.** obeah
music .. **7.** calypso
owl .. **6.** mucaro
resident .. **9.** Antillean
rodent .. **6.** agouti (agouty)
snuff .. **8.** Maccaboy
tea .. **8.** goatweed
tortoise .. **7.** hicatee
tree .. **4.** ausu **5.** ebony, papaw **6.** bonduc
8. bayberry **9.** sapodilla, satinwood
volcano .. **5.** Pelée
wood .. **9.** cocuswood, sapodilla
10. granadilla
Westminster clock (London) ... **6.** Big
Ben
West Pointer ... **5.** cadet, plebe
8. yearling
West Point motto ... **16.** Duty, Honor,
Country
West Virginia ...
capital .. **10.** Charleston
city .. **5.** Logan **8.** Wheeling
11. Parkersburg
crop .. **4.** coal
mountain .. **10.** Spruce Knob
11. Alleghenies
park (famed) .. **12.** Harpers Ferry
river .. **4.** Ohio **7.** Kanawha
11. Monongahela
Springs (resort) .. **8.** Berkeley **12.** White

Sulphur
State admission . . **11.** Thirty-fifth
State motto . . **19.** Montani Semper Liberi
22. Mountaineers Always Free
State nickname . . **8.** Mountain
West wind . . . **8.** Favonius, Zephyrus
wet . . . **4.** asop, damp, dank, dewy,
rain **5.** foggy, humid, leach, misty,
moist, mushy, rainy, soggy, soppy
6. dampen, drench, soaked, sodden,
watery **7.** moisten **8.** sprinkle
wet blanket . . . **7.** kill-joy **8.** deadhead
10. discourage, spoilsport
whale . . . **3.** orc **4.** cete, lash, whip
5. whack **6.** beluga, blower, thrash
7. grampus, ripsack **8.** hardhead
9. zeuglodon **13.** sulphur-bottom
whale (pert to) . . .
Arctic . . **7.** narwhal
bird . . **4.** gull **6.** petrel **9.** phalarope
blubber pot . . **6.** try-pot
blue . . **9.** Sibbaldus
bone . . **6.** baleen
carcass . . **5.** kreng
constellation . . **5.** Cetus
fat . . **7.** blubber
food . . **4.** brit
gray . . **7.** ripsack **8.** hardhead
killer . . **4.** orca
killer of . . **8.** ceticide
legendary . . **9.** Mysticeti
monster . . **4.** Cete
mustache (legend) . . **9.** Mysticeti
Order . . **7.** Cetacea
ref to . . **5.** cetic, sperm **6.** baleen
7. blubber **8.** cetacean
school of . . **3.** gam, pod
secretion (perfume) . . **9.** ambergris
small . : **7.** grampus
sperm type . . **8.** cachalot
study of . . **8.** cetology
toothed . . **10.** odontocete, zeuglodont
type . . **3.** orc **4.** blue, orca **5.** right, sperm
6. killer **7.** dolphin, rorqual **8.** cachalot,
humpback, porpoise **9.** whalebone
wax . . **10.** spermaceti
whalebone . . **6.** baleen **10.** stiffening
young . . **4.** calf **9.** shorthead
wharf . . . **4.** dock, pier, quay **5.** jetty
6. staith **7.** landing
wharf (pert to) . . .
fish . . **6.** cunner
master . . **10.** wharfinger
worker . . **9.** stevedore
whatnot . . . **5.** thing **6.** object
(nondescript) **7.** étagère **10.** miscellany
what's what . . . **4.** fact **5.** truth **7.** reality
10. what's right
what wonders has God wrought (Arabic
exclamation) . . . **9.** mashallah
whaup . . . **6.** curlew, outcry **9.** scoundrel
wheal . . . **4.** wale, weal, welt **5.** whelk
6. stripe **7.** pustule
wheat (pert to) . . .
beard . . **3.** awn
beverage . . **6.** zythem
bird . . **4.** lark **8.** wheatear **9.** chaffinch
chaff . . **4.** bran
duck . . **7.** widgeon **8.** baldpate
Europe . . **5.** emmer, spelt (speltz)
flour . . **4.** atta **5.** Hovis

hard . . **5.** durum
India . . **4.** suji **8.** semolina
storage bin . . **4.** silo **8.** elevator
wheedle . . . **4.** coax, gain **5.** tease
6. banter, cajole, entice **7.** blarney,
flatter **8.** blandish, inveigle, persuade
9. influence
wheel . . . **3.** cam, cog **4.** bike, disc, helm,
ride, roll, rota **5.** drive, pivot, rotor,
rowel, whirl **6.** caster, roller, rotate
7. bicycle, revolve, rotator, torture,
vehicle **8.** tricycle **10.** water wheel
wheel (pert to) . . .
gem-grinding . . **5.** skive
hub . . **4.** nave
man . . **5.** pilot **7.** cyclist **8.** helmsman,
pedalist **9.** bicyclist
monkey . . **3.** gin
part . . **3.** rim **5.** felly (felloe), spoke
6. hubcap
pulley . . **6.** sheave
shaped . . **8.** circular, rotiform
spoke . . **6.** radius
spur . . **5.** rowel
stopper . . **4.** grig **5.** sprag
swiveled . . **6.** caster
toothed . . **3.** cog **4.** gear **6.** pinion
turbine . . **5.** rotor
type . . **3.** cog, fly, pin **4.** cart, mill, spur
5. wagon **6.** Ferris, paddle **7.** balance,
potter's **9.** of fortune
water . . **5.** noria **6.** sakieh (sakiyeh)
wheels, logging . . . **7.** katydid
wheen . . . **3.** few **5.** group **7.** several
8. division, quantity
wheerikins . . . **10.** posteriors
wheetle . . . **5.** chirp **7.** whistle
wheeze . . . **3.** gag **4.** joke **5.** hoose (hooze)
6. cliché, saying **7.** breathe **8.** sibilate
9. witticism **10.** sibilation
whelk . . . **4.** acne **5.** snail **6.** papule,
pimple **7.** pustule
whelp . . . **3.** boy, cub, pup **5.** child, puppy,
tiger, youth **9.** give birth, youngling
when . . . **2.** as **3.** tho **5.** until **6.** though
7. how soon, whereas **8.** although,
whenever **10.** how long ago **11.** at
which time
where . . . **4.** here, spot **5.** place, there
7. whither **10.** inasmuch as **11.** at what
place, whereabouts
whereas . . . **5.** since
whereby . . . **7.** perquod
whereness . . . **6.** ubiety
whereupon . . . **4.** when **7.** on which
9. upon which **10.** after which
wherewithal . . . **5.** means, money
9. resources
whet . . . **4.** hone **5.** grind, point,
rouse **6.** excite **7.** quicken, sharpen
9. intensify, stimulate
whether . . . **2.** if **6.** either
whey . . . **4.** curd **5.** serum
whiff . . . **4.** blow, fish, gust, odor, puff,
waft **6.** breath, exhale, stanch **7.** puff
out **8.** blow away **10.** inhalation
while . . . **2.** as **3.** yet **4.** time **5.** until
7. beguile, interim, whereas **11.** space
of time
whilom . . . **4.** erst, once **5.** of old **6.** former
8. sometime **9.** erstwhile

whim ... **3.** fad, pun, toy **4.** idea
5. fancy, freak **6.** megrim, notion,
vagary **7.** boutade, caprice, whimsey
(whimsy), widgeon **8.** migraine
whimper ... **3.** cry, sob **4.** mewl, moan,
pule, weep **5.** whine **7.** sniffle
whimsey, whimsy ... **3.** wit **4.** whim
5. craze, fancy, freak **7.** caprice
whimsical ... **3.** fad, odd **4.** dish **5.** droll,
queer, witty **7.** amusing **8.** fanciful,
freakish, notional **9.** crotchety, eccentric,
fantastic, grotesque **10.** capricious
whine ... **4.** moan, pule, wail **6.** snivel
7. screech, ululate, whimper **8.** complain
12. moaning sound
whinny ... **4.** bray **5.** neigh, whine
whip ... **3.** cat, tan **4.** beat, crop,
flag, flog, goad, lace, lash, wale
5. birch, froth, quirt, seize, spank,
strap **6.** defeat, incite, punish, strike,
swinge, thrash **7.** agitate, chabouk
(chabuk), conquer, scourge **8.** emulsify,
lambaste **9.** bullwhack **10.** discipline
11. congressman
whip (pert to) ...
hand .. **8.** dominion **9.** advantage,
influence
mark .. **4.** wale, weal, welt
political .. **5.** party **11.** floor leader
riding .. **4.** crop **5.** quirt
Russian .. **4.** plet (plete) **5.** knout
sewing .. **8.** overcast
socket .. **5.** snead
whir ... **3.** fly **4.** burr, buzz, whiz **5.** hurry,
swirl, whizz **6.** hurtle **7.** revolve, vibrate
9. commotion
whirl ... **4.** eddy, reel, spin, tirl, turn
5. twirl **6.** circle, gyrate, rotate **7.** revelry,
revolve **9.** commotion, pirouette, turn
about **10.** excitement
whirlpool ... **4.** eddy **6.** gurges (Her),
vortex **7.** sea puss (sea purse)
9. maelstrom
whirlwind ... **2.** oe (Faroes) **7.** cyclone,
tornado, twister, typhoon **9.** hurricane,
maelstrom **10.** willy-willy
whisk ... **4.** tuft, whip, wist **5.** froth,
sweep, swish **6.** convey **7.** agitate
whiskers ... **4.** chin **5.** beard **8.** vibrissa
9. sideburns
whisky, whiskey ... **3.** rye **4.** corn
6. poteen, redeye **9.** moonshine
10. usquebaugh
whisky (pert to) ...
base .. **3.** rye **5.** wheat **6.** barley
drink .. **4.** soda, sour **5.** punch, smash
7. stinger
Insurrection .. **12.** Pennsylvania (1794)
Ring .. **10.** Conspiracy (1875)
term .. **6.** lively, flighty
whisper ... **3.** tip **4.** blow, buzz **5.** rumor
6. breeze, murmur **7.** divulge **14.** vox
clandestina
whist, game ... **9.** Cavendish
10. Yarborough
whistle ... **4.** hiss, pipe, sing, toot
5. alarm **6.** rustle, warble, wheeze
12. interference
whistle (pert to) ...
duck .. **9.** goldeneye
fish .. **8.** rockling

pig .. **9.** woodchuck
stop .. **12.** one-horse town
tree (for boys' whistles) .. **5.** maple
6. willow
whistling (pert to) ...
coot .. **6.** scoter
dick .. **6.** thrush
duck .. **6.** scoter **9.** goldeneye
hawk .. **5.** eagle
snipe .. **8.** woodcock
sound .. **7.** stridor
teal .. **6.** scoter **8.** tree duck
whit ... **3.** bit, jot **4.** atom, iota **5.** bodle,
speck **8.** particle
white ... **3.** wan **4.** milk, pale, snow
5. ashen, chalk, color, happy, ivory,
snowy **6.** albino, chalky, chaste, honest,
pallid **7.** ivorine, silvery **8.** innocent,
platinum **9.** alabaster, albescent,
Caucasian, favorable, fortunate,
honorable **11.** snow-covered
white (pert to) ...
admiral .. **9.** butterfly
ant .. **4.** anay (anai) **7.** termite
belly .. **6.** pigeon **7.** widgeon **14.** prairie
chicken
cat .. **7.** catfish
cell .. **9.** leucocyte
chub .. **10.** spawneater
cloud .. **6.** cirrus **7.** tendril
coal .. **10.** water power
crow .. **7.** vulture
curlew .. **4.** ibis
devil .. **7.** nailrod
elephant .. **6.** burden **8.** Oriental
ensign .. **12.** British naval
fish .. **5.** cisco **6.** atinga, beluga
8. menhaden **9.** Coregonus **10.** white
whale
grouse .. **9.** ptarmigan
growing (hoary) .. **9.** canescent
head .. **6.** pigeon **9.** blue goose **10.** surf
scoter
heat .. **5.** anger **13.** incandescence
livered .. **6.** feeble **8.** cowardly
13. pusillanimous
matter (nerve) .. **4.** alba
merganser .. **4.** smew
miller .. **11.** clothes moth
monk .. **10.** Cistercian
mule .. **3.** gin **6.** whisky (illicit)
9. moonshine
oak .. **5.** roble
of egg .. **5.** glair
partridge .. **9.** ptarmigan
person .. **9.** Caucasian
plague .. **7.** disease **8.** phthisis
11. consumption **12.** tuberculosis
plantain .. **8.** pussytoe
poplar .. **5.** aspen
pot .. **7.** pudding
pudding .. **7.** sausage **9.** whitehass
pyrite .. **9.** marcasite
shark .. **8.** man-eater
throat .. **6.** muffet (Eng) **7.** warbler
whale .. **6.** beluga
White (pert to) ...
Chapel (Jewish) .. **13.** London Quarter
Holland .. **6.** turkey
Horse .. **6.** emblem (Saxons) **7.** carving
House designer .. **5.** Hoban

Relig.. **6.** Friars **7.** Fathers, Sisters
8. Brethren
Rose (Eng).. **6.** emblem (House of York)
Sands (N Mex).. **13.** proving ground
Squadron.. **4.** Navy (US Navy 1883)
Tower.. **13.** Tower of London
whiten ... **6.** blanch, bleach **8.** etiolate
9. whitewash
whitewash ... **5.** paint **6.** defeat, whiten
7. conceal **9.** disinfect, exculpate, gloss
over
whither ... **5.** where **7.** whereto **11.** to
what place, whereabouts
whiting ... **4.** fish **5.** chalk **6.** tomcod
10. butterfish
whitish ... **4.** pale **5.** white **9.** albescent
whitlow ... **4.** herb, sore **5.** felon
6. agnail, fetlow **8.** hangnail **9.** saxifrage
10. paronychia **12.** inflammation
Whitsunday ... **9.** Pentacost
Whittington, Dick ... **9.** Lord Mayor
(London)
whittle ... **3.** cut, hew **4.** gash, hack,
pare, trim **5.** knife **6.** reduce **7.** blanket
whiz, whizz ... **3.** hum **4.** buzz, hiss,
pirr, whir, zizz **5.** whirr **6.** corker, rotate
8. sibilate **10.** speed along **12.** clever
person
who ... **3.** wer, wha **5.** which **6.** person
7. one that, pronoun
whole ... **3.** all, sum **4.** pure, sole, unit
5. gross, total, uncut, unity **6.** entire,
intact, mostly, system **7.** healthy, perfect
8. absolute, complete, entirety, totality
9. aggregate, generally, unanimous,
undivided
whole (pert to) ...
comb form.. **4.** toti, toto
footed.. **5.** frank **8.** intimate **9.** ingenuous
10. flat-footed
hearted.. **7.** devoted, earnest, sincere
8. complete **10.** unreserved
11. unmitigated
hog.. **8.** whole way **12.** all or nothing
note.. **9.** semibreve
number.. **7.** integer
skinned.. **6.** unhurt **9.** unscathed
souled.. **5.** noble **7.** devoted, sincere,
zealous **11.** noble-minded
12. wholehearted
wholesome ... **4.** sane **5.** sound **6.** hearty,
robust **7.** healthy **8.** salutary, vigorous
9. favorable, healthful **10.** beneficial,
propitious, salubrious
wholly ... **3.** all **4.** toto (comb form)
5. fully, quite **6.** solely **7.** totally
8. entirely, entirety **9.** perfectly
10. altogether, completely, thoroughly
11. exclusively
whoop ... **4.** call, hoot, urge, yell **5.** cheer,
shout **6.** halloo, hoopee **10.** enthusiasm
whooping cough ... **9.** pertussis
whoop it up ... **7.** be noisy **8.** energize
9. make merry **12.** create gaiety
whop ... **4.** bang, beat, bump, fall, flop,
whip **5.** knock **6.** strike, stroke
whopper ... **3.** lie (monstrous) **5.** story
(false)
whorl ... **4.** curl **5.** helix, spire **8.** flywheel,
verticil, volution (shell) **11.** fingerprint
wicked ... **3.** bad, ill **4.** evil, vile **6.** guilty,

sinful, unjust **7.** heinous, hellish,
profane, roguish, ungodly, vicious
8. criminal, depraved, devilish, diabolic,
flagrant **9.** abandoned, atrocious,
malicious, nefarious, perverted
10. diabolical, flagitious, iniquitous,
villainous **11.** irreligious, mischievous,
unrighteous
wickedness ... **3.** sin **4.** evil **6.** Belial
(Bib) **7.** badness **8.** baseness, iniquity
10. sinfulness **13.** maliciousness
wicked one ... **5.** Demon, Satan **7.** Evil
One **8.** The Devil
wicker (pert to) ...
basket.. **5.** cesta **6.** hamper, kipsey
7. pannier
cradle.. **8.** bassinet
material.. **5.** twigs **6.** osiers, willow,
withes
ware.. **8.** basketry, plaiting
wicket ... **4.** arch, door, gate, hoop
6. grille, window **7.** grating, guichet,
lattice **8.** loophole **12.** grated window,
ticket window
wickiup, wikiup ... **3.** hut **7.** shelter
Widal's, Widal reaction ... **16.** typhoid
fever test
widbin ... **7.** dogwood **8.** woodbine
11. honeysuckle
widdy ... **4.** rope (twig) **5.** noose, widow,
withy **6.** halter **7.** gallows **11.** gallows
bird
wide ... **5.** ample, broad, large, loose,
roomy **6.** opened **7.** liberal **8.** expanded,
spacious **9.** capacious, distended
13. comprehensive
wide-awake ... **3.** hat **4.** keen, tern
(sooty) **5.** alert **7.** knowing **8.** watchful
wide-eyed ... **4.** agog **5.** naive **6.** amazed
9. surprised
widemouthed ... **4.** loud **5.** noisy
6. greedy **7.** barking **9.** devouring
widen ... **4.** ream **6.** dilate, expand,
extend, spread **7.** amplify, broaden,
enlarge
widespread ... **4.** rife **5.** broad **7.** diffuse,
general **8.** not local, sweeping
9. dispersed, extensive, prevalent,
scattered, universal **13.** comprehensive
widgeon ... **4.** duck, smee **5.** goose
6. Mareca, zuisin **7.** poacher **8.** baldpate
9. simpleton
widow ... **6.** relict **7.** bereave, dowager,
viduate
widow (pert to) ...
bird.. **5.** finch, Vidua **6.** whidah
cremated.. **6.** suttee
fish.. **5.** viuva
monkey.. **4.** titi
suicide.. **6.** suttee
widower ... **6.** relict
widow's (pert to) ...
lock.. **8.** hairline **10.** widow's peak
mite.. **4.** coin **6.** lepton
portion.. **5.** dower
right.. **5.** terce
weeds.. **8.** mourning **9.** black veil,
widowhood
width ... **5.** girth **7.** breadth **8.** diameter,
latitude, wideness
wield ... **3.** ply, use **4.** cope, deal, rule

5. power, swing **6.** direct, employ, handle, manage **7.** control **8.** brandish **10.** manipulate
wife . . . **4.** frau, mate, rani, uxor **5.** bride, mujer **6.** matron, spouse **7.** consort **8.** gudewife (guidwife), helpmate, helpmeet **10.** better half **12.** married woman
wife (pert to) . . .
French . . **5.** femme
killing . . **9.** uxoricide
of a rajah . . **4.** Rani (Ranee)
one . . **8.** monogamy
pert to . . **7.** uxorial
slave's . . **9.** broadwife
wig . . . **4.** tête **5.** jasey **6.** peruke, toupee **7.** censure, periwig **8.** seal hood **9.** dignitary
wight . . . **3.** man **4.** loud **5.** brave, fairy, swift, witch **6.** active, nimble **7.** valiant **8.** creature, powerful **11.** living being
wigwag . . . **6.** signal **8.** to and fro **11.** oscillation
wigwam . . . **4.** tent **5.** hogan, tepee **6.** teepee
wild . . . **3.** mad **5.** feral, myall, waste, weird **6.** ferine, savage, stormy, unruly **7.** bestial, howling, riotous **8.** aberrant, desolate, dramatic, frenetic, reckless, untilled, wildwood **9.** barbarian, barbarous, ferocious, imprudent, primitive, unbridled, uncertain **10.** boisterous, chimerical, irrational, profligate, tumultuous, unexplored, wilderness **11.** harum-scarum, uncivilized, uninhabited **12.** obstreperous, uncontrolled, uncultivated **14.** uncontrollable
wild (pert to) . . .
alder . . **8.** goutweed
animal . . **3.** gnu **4.** bear, deer, lion, lynx **5.** kiang, moose, tiger **6.** dragon, onager **7.** polecat **8.** antelope **10.** wildebeest
banana . . **5.** papaw (pawpaw)
beasts . . **4.** ziim
buffalo . . **4.** arna **5.** arnee
carrot . . **8.** hilltrot
cat . . **4.** balm, eyra **6.** ocelot **7.** panther
coffee . . **9.** feverroot
crocus . . **12.** pasqueflower
fancy . . **6.** vagary
fowl . . **4.** duck **5.** goose, quail **8.** pheasant **9.** partridge
garlic . . **4.** moly
goat . . **3.** tur **4.** tahr **7.** markhor (markhoor)
gourd . . **7.** pumpkin **11.** calabazilla
growing . . **8.** agrarian
hog . . **4.** boar **9.** razorback **10.** babiroussa
hop . . **6.** bryony
horse . . **6.** tarpan
ibex . . **5.** Capra
Irishman (shrub) . . **10.** tumatakuru
jalap . . **8.** mayapple
mustard . . **8.** charlock
ox . . **3.** yak **4.** anoa
pieplant . . **7.** rhubarb
pineapple . . **7.** pinguin
plum . . **4.** sloe **5.** islay
sheep . . **3.** sha **5.** urial (oorial) **6.** argali
sweet potato . . **7.** manroot

West show . . **5.** rodeo
wildebeest . . . **3.** gnu
wilderness . . . **5.** waste, wilds **6.** forest **8.** wildwood **9.** confusion **12.** complication
wile . . . **3.** art, toy **4.** lure, ruse **5.** fraud, guile, trick **6.** deceit **7.** cunning **8.** artifice, trickery **9.** stratagem
will . . . **4.** wish **6.** behest, choice, decree, demise, desire **7.** bequest, command **8.** volition **9.** intention, testament **10.** resolution **11.** disposition, inclination **13.** determination
will (pert to) . . .
appendix . . **7.** codicil
convey . . **6.** demise **7.** bequest
having made . . **7.** testate
maker of . . **8.** testator
power . . **7.** purpose **10.** resolution **13.** determination **14.** strength of mind
proof of . . **7.** probate
to live (Buddh) . . **5.** tanha
willful, wilful . . . **3.** mad **4.** rash **5.** heady **7.** wayward **8.** perverse, stubborn **9.** impetuous, obstinate, voluntary **11.** intentional **14.** self-determined
willing . . . **4.** free **5.** prone, ready **6.** minded **8.** desirous, disposed, unforced **9.** agreeable, voluntary **10.** consenting, deliberate, ready to act, volitional **11.** intentional **12.** well-disposed
willingly . . . **4.** fain, lief **6.** freely, gladly **7.** happily, readily **10.** cheerfully **12.** with pleasure
willow . . . **3.** iva **4.** Itea **5.** osier, salix **6.** sallow, teaser
willow (pert to) . . .
basket . . **7.** prickle
genus . . **5.** Salix
green . . **6.** reseda
lark . . **12.** sedge warbler
pattern . . **7.** Nanking **11.** earthenware
twig . . **5.** withe **6.** sallow
wren . . **10.** chiffchaff
willowy . . . **5.** lithe **6.** pliant, supple, svelte **7.** slender **8.** flexible, graceful **15.** tall and graceful
Will Rogers' plane . . . **9.** Winnie May
wilsome . . . **4.** wild **6.** astray, dreary **7.** violent, willful (wilful) **8.** desolate **10.** bewildered
wilt . . . **3.** sag **4.** flag, tire **5.** droop, quail **6.** sicken, wither **8.** languish **11.** deteriorate, lose courage, make flaccid
Wilton . . . **3.** rug **6.** carpet
wily . . . **3.** sly **4.** foxy **5.** canny, smart **6.** artful, astute, crafty, shrews, subtle **7.** cunning **9.** cautelous
wimble . . . **3.** awl **4.** bore **5.** auger, brace, scoop, twist **6.** gimlet, pierce **9.** sprightly, whimsical
wimick . . . **3.** cry **7.** whimper
wimple . . . **4.** fold, veil **7.** meander **8.** covering (head)
win . . . **3.** get **4.** earn, gain **5.** to get **6.** attain, defeat, obtain, secure **7.** achieve, acquire, succeed, triumph **8.** be victor, endeavor, vanquish **9.** captivate **10.** accomplish

win (pert to) . . .
all tricks (game) . . **4**. slam
by guile . . **8**. inveigle
one's spurs . . **10**. knighthood
over . . **7**. convert **8**. convince
persuade . . **10**. conciliate
wince . . . **4**. reel **5**. start **6**. cringe, flinch,
recoil, shrink **8**. draw back, windlass
10. shrink from
wind . . . **2**. oe **3**. air **4**. bora, coil, gale,
gust, talk, turn, wrap **5**. blast, buran,
crank, trade **6**. boreal, breath, breeze,
simoom, zephyr **7**. chinook, conceit,
cyclone, deviate, etesian, meander,
monsoon, sinuate, sirocco, tempest,
tornado, typhoon **8**. convolve, williwaw
9. hurricane, idle words, windstorm
10. instrument
wind (pert to) . . .
action on land . . **8**. eolation
around . . **6**. master **8**. dominate
9. influence **13**. lead by the nose
cloud . . **4**. scud
comb form . . **5**. anemo
fall . . **7**. godsend **8**. buckshee, gratuity
flower . . **7**. anemone
gauge . . **4**. vane **10**. anemometer
god . . **4**. Adad **6**. Aeolus
god of north wind . . **6**. Boreas
god of SE wind . . **5**. Eurus
instrument . . **3**. sax **4**. fife, horn
5. flute, organ **6**. cornet **7**. bassoon,
hautboy, helicon, ocarina **8**. clarinet
9. harmonica, saxophone
in the (wind) . . **5**. drunk **7**. sailing
8. imminent **9**. happening
into a ball . . **11**. agglomerate
personified . . **6**. Caurus **7**. Caecias
8. Favonius, Zephyrus
ref to . . **7**. Aeolian (Eolian)
rose . . **5**. poppy
science . . **9**. anemology
storm . . **4**. gale **7**. cyclone, typhoon
9. hurricane
up . . **3**. end **7**. prepare **8**. complete,
conclude
yarn . . **6**. windle
wind (type) . . .
Adriatic (cold) . . **4**. bora
cold . . **4**. bise, bora, puna **7**. mistral
8. williwaw
desert . . **6**. simoom **7**. sirocco
dry . . **9**. harmattan
East . . **8**. levanter
Egypt . . **7**. khamsin (kamsin)
equator . . **5**. trade
fierce . . **4**. gale **6**. buster, squall
7. monsoon **8**. blizzard **9**. hurricane
gentle . . **4**. aura **6**. zephyr
Malta (cold) . . **7**. gregale
Mediterranean . . **6**. solano **7**. etesian
8. levanter
North . . **6**. Boreas
Northwest . . **6**. Caurus **7**. etesian
Oriental . . **7**. monsoon
Peru . . **4**. puna
S America . . **4**. puna **7**. pampero
South . . **6**. Auster
Southeast . . **5**. Eurus
Southwest . . **7**. chinook
Spain . . **6**. solano

West (personified) . . **8**. Favonius
whirl . . **2**. oe
windiness . . . **7**. conceit **12**. boastfulness
winding . . . **5**. curve, snaky **6**. spiral
7. sinuous, twining **8**. rambling,
tortuous **9**. deviative, meandrous
10. circuitous
windjammer . . . **6**. bugler, talker, vessel
(sailing) **8**. bandsman **9**. trumpeter
windlass . . . **4**. reel **5**. winch **6**. windle
7. capstan, machine (hoisting)
windle . . . **4**. reel **5**. winch **6**. basket
7. measure, redwing
window (pert to) . . .
arrangement . . **8**. fanlight **12**. fenestration
bay . . **5**. oriel
dormer, roof . . **5**. gable **7**. lucarne
8. skylight
frame . . **4**. sash
Latin . . **8**. fenestra
leading . . **4**. came
nautical . . **8**. porthole
oval . . **5**. oxeye
part . . **4**. pane, sash, sill **5**. glass
7. shutter
recess . . **6**. exedra **9**. embrasure
ship's . . **4**. port **8**. porthole
ticket . . **6**. wicket **7**. guichet
type . . **4**. port **5**. gable, oriel **7**. eucarne
8. casement, skylight
windpipe . . . **6**. gullet, throat **7**. trachea,
weasand
windrow . . . **5**. swath (swathe) **6**. furrow
Winds, Father of (Gr) . . . **8**. Astraeus
windward . . . **5**. aloof **8**. aweather
9. weatherly
Windy City . . . **7**. Chicago
wine (pert to) . . .
and honey . . **5**. clary, mulse **7**. oenomel
Baden . . **8**. Ruländer
bag . . **8**. wineskin
bibber . . **3**. sot **5**. toper **7**. tippler
8. drunkard
Bordeaux . . **6**. claret
bottle . . **6**. magnum **8**. decanter
cask . . **3**. tun
cellar . . **6**. bodega
comb form . . **4**. oeno
cruet . . **7**. burette
cup . . **3**. ama **6**. goblet **7**. chalice
divination by . . **9**. oenomancy
dry . . **3**. sec
film . . **8**. beeswing
French . . **6**. Masden, Pontac (Pontacq)
8. muscatel **9**. Hermitage
10. Montrachet **12**. Saint-Emilion,
Saint-Estèphe
glass . . **6**. rummer (Rom)
grower . . **8**. vigneron
hater of . . **11**. oenophobist
Italian . . **7**. Orvieto **8**. muscatel
kind . . **4**. port **5**. Medoc, Rhine, tinta,
Tokay **6**. canary, claret, Malaga, sherry
7. Chablis, Madeira **8**. Burgundy,
muscatel, sauterne, vermouth
9. champagne
lover of . . **11**. oenophilist
maker . . **6**. abkari (abkary)
making . . **10**. oenopoetic
merchant . . **5**. abkar
miracle scene . . **4**. Cana (Bib)

palm.. **5.** taree
Persian.. **6.** Shiraz
pitcher.. **4.** olpe **8.** oenochoe
reference to.. **5.** vinic
residue.. **4.** marc
sherry.. **5.** Xeres **7.** Catawba, Moselle, oloroso
shop·.. **3.** bar **6.** bistro, bodega
Spain.. **6.** Malaga
sparkling.. **8.** mousseux
study of.. **8.** oenology
sweet.. **5.** lunel
taster.. **10.** oenologist
Tuscan.. **7.** Chianti
white.. **6.** Malaga **8.** Riesling, sauterne, verdelho **12.** Marcobrunner
year.. **7.** vintage
wing... **3.** ala, arm, fly **6.** convey, flight, member, pinion **7.** faction **8.** addition, dispatch
wing (pert to)...
anterior.. **7.** elytron
comb form.. **7.** pterygo
false.. **5.** alula
fish.. **8.** sea robin
footed.. **6.** aliped
Greek.. **6.** pteryx
quill.. **7.** remiges
shaped.. **7.** aliform
tip.. **7.** aileron
winglike.. **4.** alar **7.** pteroid **9.** pterygoid
winged... **4.** aile (Her), fast **5.** alate, lofty, rapid, swift **7.** pennate, sublime **9.** aliferous, aligerous
winged (pert to)...
boots (of Hermes).. **7.** talaria
child.. **6.** cherub
fruit.. **6.** samara
monster.. **5.** harpy
Winged Horse (Gr Myth)... **7.** Pegasus
Winged Victory... **4.** Nike
wingless... **7.** apteral, Apteryx, exalate **8.** dealated (dealate)
wink... **3.** nap, nod **4.** hint **5.** blink, flash **6.** glance, signal, twitch **7.** flicker, instant, nictate, twinkle **9.** nictation, nictitate, twinkling **10.** palpebrate, periwinkle
winker... **3.** eye **7.** blinker, eyelash **8.** blinkard
winking... **13.** blepharospasm
winks, forty... **3.** nap **6.** catnap **10.** light sleep
winner... **3.** ace **6.** earner, reaper, victor **7.** sleeper **8.** bangster **9.** conqueror **11.** breadwinner
winning... **7.** gaining, lovable, victory, winsome **8.** alluring, charming **10.** attractive, successful, victorious **11.** acquisition, captivating
winninish, winnonish... **6.** salmon (landlocked) **10.** ouananiche
winnock... **6.** window
winnow... **3.** fan **4.** sift, stir **6.** assort, select, thresh **8.** disperse, separate **9.** eliminate
winsome... **3.** gay **5.** bonny, merry **7.** lovable, winning **8.** alluring, charming, cheerful, pleasant **10.** attractive **11.** captivating **12.** lighthearted

winter... **4.** bise, snow **5.** hiems **6.** old age, season **8.** coldness
winter (pert to)...
beer.. **6.** Schenk
berry.. **4.** Ilex **5.** holly
bloom.. **6.** azalea **10.** witch hazel
bonnet.. **4.** gull
duck.. **7.** pintail **8.** old squaw
fever.. **9.** pneumonia
god.. **5.** Hiems
lettuce.. **6.** endive
mew.. **4.** gull
pert to.. **6.** brumal, hiemal
quarters.. **10.** hibernacle **12.** hibernaculum
sleep.. **11.** hibernation
teal.. **9.** greenwing
Winter Palace (Leningrad)... **6.** museum
wipe... **3.** dry, mop, rub **5.** cheat, clean, erase **6.** cancel, remove **7.** abolish, defraud **10.** obliterate **11.** exterminate
wire... **4.** coil, cord, line, whip **5.** cable, snare **6.** thread **7.** fencing, lametta (gold), netting, reticle **8.** telegram, wirework **9.** cablegram, telegraph **10.** pickpocket **14.** knitting needle
wirepuller... **10.** influencer, machinator, politician, strategist
wiry... **4.** lean **5.** hardy, stiff, tough **6.** sinewy, strong **7.** stringy **8.** enduring, muscular
wis... **5.** think **7.** imagine, suppose
Wisconsin...
capital.. **7.** Madison
city.. **6.** Racine **7.** Kenosha, Oshkosh **8.** Green Bay **9.** Fond du Lac, Milwaukee
famed as.. **17.** America's Dairyland
first white man.. **7.** Nicolet (Jean)
lake.. **8.** Michigan, Superior **9.** Winnebago
river.. **7.** St Croix **11.** Mississippi
State admission.. **9.** Thirtieth
State motto.. **7.** Forward
State nickname.. **6.** Badger
wisdom... **5.** logos **8.** judgment, learning, sagacity, sapience **9.** erudition, knowledge **10.** discretion, profundity
wisdom god... **4.** Nebo (Nabu) **6.** Ganesa (Ganesha)
wisdom goddess... **6.** Athena **7.** Minerva (Gr)
wise... **3.** hep **4.** sage, sane, wary **5.** aware **6.** shrewd, subtle, versed **7.** erudite, knowing, learned, politic, sapient **8.** discreet, informed, profound **9.** cognizant, expedient, judicious, provident **10.** omniscient **11.** circumspect, enlightened, philosophic **13.** sophisticated
wise (pert to)...
councilor.. **6.** mentor, nestor
man.. **4.** sage **5.** solon, witan **6.** nestor, wizard **7.** Solomon
saying.. **4.** rede **5.** adage
Wise Men (three)... **6.** Gaspar **8.** Melchior **9.** Balthasar
Wise Men of Greece... **5.** Seven
Wise Men of the East... **19.** Three Kings of Cologne
wish... **4.** care, hope, will, wuss **5.** yearn **6.** aspire, desire, invoke

7. longing, request 8. optative, petition
10. aspiration 11. imprecation
wishbone... 7. furcula 8. furculum
10. fourchette 12. merry thought
wisp... 4. floc 5. brush, flock, shred
6. bundle 7. handful 8. fragment
wistful... 7. longing, pensive 8. desirous,
yearning 9. nostalgic 10. melancholy
wit... 3. pun, wag 5. humor, sense
6. acumen, esprit, satire, wisdom
7. punster 8. comedian, humorist,
repartee 9. alertness 11. philosopher,
savoir-faire 12. intelligence
13. understanding
wit (to)... 3. viz 5. truly 6. indeed,
namely, that is 8. scilicet 9. videlicet
witch... 3. hag, hex 4. baba 5. Circe,
crone, lamia, shrew, vixen 6. cummer,
Hecate (Hekate), Lilith (Lilis), wizard
7. warlock 8. old woman 9. grimalkin,
sorceress 11. witch doctor 12. ugly
old woman
witchcraft... 5. charm, magic, wanga
7. cunning, hexerei, sorcery 8. brujeria
9. sortilege, voodooism 10. bewitchery,
black magic 11. enchantment
12. invultuation
witch doctor... 3. hex 6. shaman
9. voodooist, wangateur
witchery... 5. charm, spell 7. sorcery
8. wizardry 10. allurement, necromancy
11. enchantment, fascination
with (pref)... 2. co 3. com, con, cum,
mit, syn 4. avec
with... 5. among 7. jointly 8. together
9. alongside, including 10. hand in
hand 11. association 12. concurrently
13. co-operatively
withal... 5. still 9. thereupon 10. for all
that
withdraw... 6. absent, deduct, recall,
recant, recede, remove, repeal, retire,
secede 7. abandon, detract, disavow,
forsake, refrain, regress, retract, retreat,
subside 8. alienate, evacuate, renounce
9. disengage 10. relinquish
withdrawal... 6. repeal 7. regress,
retiral, retreat 8. escapism 9. departure,
recession, seclusion 10. detachment,
extraction, retraction, separation
11. abandonment, recantation,
resignation
withdrawn... 7. ingrown 8. detached,
secluded
withe... 4. band, rope 5. snare 6. halter,
wattle, willow
wither... 3. age, die, dry 4. fade, sear,
sere, wilt 5. decay, droop, dry up,
wizen 6. blight, shrink 7. shrivel, wrinkle
8. languish 11. deteriorate
withered... 4. sere 8. shrunken
9. shriveled
withering... 7. caustic 9. shrinking
10. marcescent 12. contemptuous
13. deteriorating
withhold... 4. curb, deny 5. check
6. detain, refuse, retain 7. abstain,
prevent, refrain, repress, reserve 8. hold
back, postpone, restrain
within... 6. at home, during, inside
7. indoors 8. inside of, inwardly 9. inner

side
without... 4. sans, sine 5. minus
6. beyond, except, lack of, unless
7. lacking, not with 9. absence of,
outwardly 10. externally, out-of-doors
without (pert to)... see also *absence of*
action.. 8. deedless
animation.. 5. amort
appointment (of day).. 7. sine die
beginning, or end.. 7. eternal
cause.. 10. unprovoked
connections.. 7. tieless
delay.. 9. summarily
doubt.. 9. sine dubio
ethics.. 6. amoral
exception.. 11. universally
feet.. 4. apod 6. apodal
foliage.. 8. aphylous
friends.. 4. lorn 7. forlorn 8. forsaken
knowledge.. 8. ignorant
mate.. 3. odd
prefix.. 4. ecto
rule.. 8. anarchic
substance.. 5. inane
support.. 7. legless 9. dependent
teeth.. 8. edentate 9. toothless
this.. 7. sine hoc
warning.. 12. out of the blue
wings.. 7. apteral
withstand... 4. bear, bide, defy, last
5. abide 6. endure, oppose, resist
8. confront 10. contradict
witless... 3. mad 5. crazy, dazed
6. stupid 7. foolish, unaware 8. heedless
9. brainless, unknowing 10. indiscreet
13. unintelligent
witness... 3. eye, see 4. know 5. swear,
teste, vouch 6. attend, attest, beheld,
behold, testor 7. observe, testify
8. beholder, deponent, evidence,
observer, onlooker 9. informant,
spectator, subscribe, testimony
11. attestation
witticism... 3. mot, pun 4. jest,
joke, quip 5. droll, sally, slent
8. repartee 9. wisecrack 10. pleasantry
11. gauloiserie, witty saying
wittingly... 8. by design 9. knowingly
13. intentionally
witty... 4. wise 5. comic, droll, sharp
6. clever, facete, jocose, jocund
7. amusing, comical, jocular, knowing
8. humorous 9. facetious, whimsical
wivern, wyvern (Her)... 6. dragon
(2-legged)
wizard... 4. mage, sage 6. expert, genius,
Merlin, pellar, shaman 7. magical,
prodigy 8. conjurer, magician, sorcerer
10. Wizard of Oz 11. necromancer,
thaumaturge, witch doctor
13. thaumaturgist
Wizard of the North... 14. Sir Walter
Scott
wizen... 3. age, dry 4. thin 6. gullet,
shrink, weazen, wither 7. shrivel
8. windpipe 11. deteriorate
wlo (obs)... 3. hem 6. fringe
woad... 3. dye 4. herb 5. tinge 8. dyestuff
10. pastel blue
wobble, wabble... 4. walk 5. shake,
waver 7. stagger, tremble 8. hobbling

9. fluctuate, oscillate, vacillate
Woden, Wodan (Myth) ... **3.** god (chief)
4. Odin **9.** Wednesday (named for
Woden)
woe ... **4.** bale, bane **5.** grief **6.** misery,
sorrow **7.** anguish, trouble **8.** anathema,
calamity **10.** affliction, melancholy,
misfortune
woebegone ... **3.** sad **6.** woeful
7. unhappy **8.** dejected, desolate
10. dispirited, melancholy
woeful ... **3.** sad **6.** paltry **7.** direful,
pitiful **8.** grievous, mournful, wretched
9. afflicted, miserable, sorrowful,
woebegone **10.** deplorable
12. disconsolate
wold ... **3.** lea **4.** wood **5.** downs, plain,
weald **6.** forest, meadow **7.** low hill
wolf ... **4.** lobo **5.** lupus **6.** coyote,
mammal **7.** Isegrim **8.** werewolf
9. libertine **11.** philanderer
wolf fish ... **6.** blenny
wolfhound ... **6.** borzoi
wolflike ... **6.** lupine, thooid
wolverine ... **4.** Gulo **11.** Michigander,
Michiganite
Wolverine State ... **8.** Michigan
woman ... **4.** dame, girl, lady, rani, wife
5. adult, begum, gemme, madam,
squaw **6.** female **7.** distaff **8.** feminine,
paramour, senorita **9.** womankind
10. sweetheart
woman (pert to) ...
adviser .. **6.** Egeria (Rom Myth)
apartment of .. **3.** oda (harem)
8. thalamus
beautiful .. **4.** doll **5.** filly, pin-up, siren,
sylph, Venus **7.** charmer, Zenobia
8. Musidora
bewitching .. **4.** peri **5.** siren, vixen
7. charmer
celibate .. **7.** agapeta
chaser .. **9.** libertine **11.** philanderer
club (of women) .. **7.** sorosis **8.** sorority
comb form .. **3.** gyn
dignified, elderly .. **7.** dowager
dowdy .. **5.** frump **6.** untidy **8.** slattern
gossipy .. **3.** cat **15.** flibbertigibbet
graceful .. **5.** sylph **7.** slender
gypsy .. **5.** romni
hater .. **10.** misogynist
hatred of .. **8.** misogyny
kept .. **8.** mistress **9.** concubine
12. demimondaine
killer .. **8.** femicide
learned .. **12.** bluestocking
loose .. **4.** drab **5.** whore **6.** harlot
7. trollop **10.** prostitute **12.** streetwalker
lover of .. **11.** philogynist
modest (affectedly) .. **5.** prude
mythical (ugly) .. **6.** Gorgon
noisy .. **9.** termagant
of rank .. **4.** dame
old .. **5.** crone, frump **6.** granny **7.** carline,
dowager **8.** grandame **9.** cailleach
ruler .. **9.** matriarch
scolding .. **5.** shrew **6.** virago
socialite .. **3.** deb **6.** subdeb **9.** debutante
13. fashion leader
stately .. **4.** lady **6.** matron
suffragist .. **8.** feminist

vixenish .. **5.** shrew **6.** virago **8.** harridan
weeping .. **5.** Niobe
will maker .. **9.** testatrix
young, unmarried .. **4.** lass **6.** damsel
8. spinster **10.** demoiselle
womanhood ... **4.** Emer **10.** femininity
woman's property (free) ...
10. parapherna
wonder ... **3.** awe **6.** marvel, rarity
7. miracle, prodigy **8.** surprise
9. amazement **10.** admiration,
wonderment **12.** astonishment
wonderful ... **6.** superb, unique
7. amazing, corking, mirific, strange
8. wondrous **9.** admirable, marvelous,
mirifical **10.** remarkable, surprising
11. astonishing **13.** extraordinary
wont ... **3.** use **5.** habit, usage **6.** custom
woo ... **3.** sue **6.** invite **7.** beseech,
entreat, solicit
wood ... **4.** tree **5.** xylon **6.** lignum,
lumber, timber **8.** firewood
wood (pert to) ...
aromatic .. **5.** aloes, cedar **8.** agalloch
ash .. **6.** potash
black .. **5.** ebony
block .. **3.** nog **4.** dook
boring (of insects) .. **8.** xylotomy
bundles .. **6.** fagots
carving .. **10.** xyloglyphy
clearing .. **5.** glade
color .. **7.** biscuit
comb form .. **4.** hylo, xylo **5.** ligni, ligno,
xylon
core .. **3.** ame
curved strip .. **5.** stave
dealer .. **10.** xylopolist
deity .. **3.** Pan **4.** faun **5.** Diana, Satyr
7. Silenus **8.** Silvanus
eating .. **11.** xylophagous
goddess .. **5.** Diana
growing on .. **6.** fungus **11.** xylophilous
growth .. **7.** boscage, coppice, thicket
hard .. **3.** ash, elm **4.** rate, teak **5.** ebony,
maple **6.** walnut **8.** mahogany
inlay .. **9.** marquetry
nymph .. **4.** moth **5.** dryad
overlay .. **6.** veneer
resembling .. **6.** xyloid
stork .. **4.** ibis
strip .. **4.** lath, slat **5.** sprag, stave
6. batten
touch .. **4.** punk **5.** spunk (sponk)
9. touchwood
tough, elastic .. **3.** ash
tract .. **5.** grove **6.** forest
woodchuck ... **6.** marmot **9.** ground
hog
Woodchuck Day ... **9.** Candlemas
woodcock ... **5.** pewee **6.** peewee, shrups
10. woodpecker
wooden (pert to) ...
container .. **3.** box **4.** case **6.** barrel
horse .. **6.** Trojan
Indian .. **15.** cigar-store brave
joint .. **5.** tenon
made of .. **5.** treen
pert to .. **4.** dull **6.** clumsy, stolid, stupid
8. lifeless **14.** expressionless
pin .. **3.** fid, nog, peg **5.** dowel, spile
pole .. **4.** palo

shoe . . **5.** sabot **6.** patten
stand . . **5.** criss
tub . . **3.** soe
woodpecker . . . **4.** chab **5.** Picus **6.** yaffle,
yukkel (yuckle) **7.** flicker, wryneck
8. hickwall **9.** sapsucker **10.** carpintero,
pickerwood **11.** woodknacker
woods (pert to) . . .
inhabiting . . **7.** nemoral
lover of . . **11.** nemophilist
pert to . . **6.** sylvan (silvan) **10.** sylvestral
sacred (grove) . . **10.** Nemorensis
woodwind . . . **4.** oboe **5.** flute **7.** bassoon,
piccolo **8.** clarinet **9.** saxophone
woody . . . **6.** sylvan, xyloid **8.** ligneous
woof . . . **3.** abb **4.** weft **6.** fabric **7.** filling,
texture
wool . . . **3.** fur **4.** down, hair **5.** cloth,
llama, sheep **6.** fleece **8.** barragan
(barragon)
wool (pert to) . . .
card . . **3.** tum **4.** comb **5.** tease
clean . . **7.** garnett
cloth . . **5.** serge, tweed, yerga **6.** angora,
duffel, kersey, satara, tartan, tricot,
vicuña **7.** doeskin, flannel, ratteen
8. cashmere **10.** broadcloth
comb form . . **4.** lani
dead sheep's . . **8.** mortling
dryer . . **5.** fugal
fat . . **7.** lanolin (lanoline)
fatty substance . . **5.** suint
garment . . **6.** alpaca, linder
implement . . **6.** carder, shears, teaser
7. distaff, spindle
inferior, dirty . . **7.** cleamer
kind . . **6.** alpaca, angora, merino
8. picklock
leg . . **4.** gare
reclaimed . . **5.** mungo **6.** shoddy
reference to . . **5.** wooly **6.** lanate, lanose
10. flocculent
spun . . **4.** yarn
tuft . . **8.** floccule **9.** flocculus
undyed, natural . . **5.** beige
waste . . **3.** fud **4.** noil
yarn . . **3.** abb **7.** eis wool
wooly (woolly) . . . **5.** downy, fuzzy
6. fleecy, lanate **7.** blurred **8.** confused,
floccose, peronate
word . . . **4.** news, oath **5.** adage,
maxim, parol **6.** avowal, remark,
report **7.** command, dispute, message,
promise, tidings, vocable **8.** acrostic,
password **9.** discourse, statement
11. declaration, information
13. communication
word, words (pert to) . . .
action . . **4.** verb
battle of . . **9.** logomachy
blindness . . **6.** alexia
book . . **6.** Gradus **7.** lexicon, speller
8. glossary **9.** thesaurus **10.** dictionary
contraction . . **9.** haplology
deletion at end . . **7.** apocope
derivation . . **6.** etymon **9.** etymology
distinguishing (Bib) . . **10.** shibboleth
divine . . **5.** Logos
excessive interest . . **10.** verbomania
figurative use . . **5.** trope
figure of speech . . **7.** metonym, paronym

first on walls (Bib) . . **21.** mene, mene,
tekel, upharsin
for word . . **8.** verbatim **9.** literally
hard to pronounce . . **10.** jawbreaker
inventor of . . **6.** coiner **9.** neologist
last syllable . . **6.** ultima
last syllable but one . . **6.** penult
last syllable omitted . . **7.** apocope
law . . **7.** by parol **11.** word of mouth
letter . . **8.** logogram **9.** logogriph
11. grammalogue
longest in dictionary . .
28. antidisestablishmentarianism
loss from middle . . **7.** syncope
magical . . **6.** presto, sesame
meaning . . **9.** semantics
misuse . . **11.** catachresis, heterophemy,
malapropism
mysterious (Bib) . . **5.** selah
new . . **9.** neologism
new usage . . **7.** neology
of different name for same thing . .
9. heteronym
of honor . . **6.** parole **7.** promise
of opposite meaning . . **7.** antonym
of same derivation . . **7.** paronym
of same meaning . . **7.** synonym
of same sound . . **7.** homonym
of imitation . . **6.** echoic **9.** onomatope
12. onomatopoeia
play on . . **3.** pun
popular . . **6.** cliché **8.** buzzword
pretentious use . . **10.** lexiphanic
puzzle . . **5.** rebus **7.** anagram **8.** acrostic
9. crossword
repetition . . **5.** ploce
root . . **6.** etymon
same back to front . . **10.** palindrome
science . . **10.** lexicology
scrambled . . **7.** anagram
song hits . . **6.** lyrics
substitution . . **5.** trope **7.** metonym
theory . . **6.** bowwow **8.** pooh-pooh
The Word (Bib) . . **5.** Logos
with loss of vowel at beginning . .
7. aphasia
without vowels . . **6.** rhythm, syzygy
with vowels (all) . . **7.** eulogia, miaoued,
sequoia **12.** ambidextrous
with vowels in sequence . . **8.** caesious
wordiness . . . **8.** pleonasm, verbiage
9. prolixity, verbacity **10.** redundance
wording . . . **8.** phrasing **10.** expression
wordless . . . **5.** tacit **6.** silent
wordy . . . **6.** prolix **7.** verbose **9.** garrulous
10. long-winded **12.** long-drawn-out
work . . . **3.** gig, job, mix **4.** book,
deed, duty, make, opus, plan, task,
to-do, toil **5.** chore, ergon, labor,
solve, trade **6.** action, Arbeit, create,
effect, effort **7.** ferment, operate,
perform, product, travail **8.** business,
drudgery, endeavor, function, industry,
struggle **10.** accomplish, employment,
engagement, management, occupation,
profession **11.** achievement,
performance, undertaking
work (pert to) . . .
agreement . . **4.** code, pact **8.** contract
bag . . **7.** tote bag **8.** reticule
carelessly . . **5.** scamp

clothes .. **8.** overalls **9.** blue jeans, coveralls, dungarees
comb form .. **3.** erg **4.** ergo
divine .. **7.** miracle, theurgy **9.** occult art
hard .. **3.** peg, tew **4.** char, moil, plug, toil **5.** labor, sweat **6.** drudge **7.** travail **9.** lucubrate **18.** burn the midnight oil
hate of .. **10.** ergophobia
helper .. **3.** aid (aide) **9.** assistant, paralegal, paramedic
horse .. **4.** mule **5.** burro
hours .. **9.** flexitime (flextime)
household .. **4.** char **5.** chare
incomplete art .. **7.** ébauche
inlay .. **6.** mosaic, niello
lover of .. **9.** ergophile
measure of .. **9.** ergometer
of excellence .. **4.** opus **7.** classic
out .. **5.** solve **7.** arrange, develop **9.** calculate
over .. **6.** recast, rehash, revamp **9.** brainwash, influence
shift .. **5.** swing **9.** graveyard, moonlight
slowly .. **6.** potter, putter **7.** ca'canny
study of .. **8.** ergology
together .. **4.** team **9.** cooperate **11.** collaborate
unit of .. **3.** erg **5.** ergon, joule
up .. **4.** plan **5.** rouse **6.** excite, incite **7.** advance, agitate, develop **10.** manipulate
workable ... **6.** pliant **7.** operant **8.** feasible, operable, solvable **9.** practical **11.** practicable
worker ... **3.** CPA **5.** diver, mason, miner **6.** barman, cooper, slater, smithy, tanner, warper, wright **7.** analyst, cobbler, glazier, plumber, riveter, sandhog, servant, spinner **8.** honeybee, mechanic, strapper **9.** carpenter, clinician, machinist, stevedore **10.** accountant **11.** breadwinner
worker (pert to) ...
fellow .. **5.** buddy **8.** confrere
group .. **4.** crew, gang, team **5.** corps, staff **9.** personnel
hard .. **6.** beaver, drudge, fagger **10.** workaholic
head .. **4.** boss **7.** foreman **8.** employer, overseer **14.** superintendent
indifferent .. **4.** scab **11.** scissorbill
migrant .. **4.** hobo **6.** boomer **7.** floater, wetback
workhouse ... **6.** prison **9.** almshouse, poorhouse
workman ... **4.** peon **6.** coolie, earner **7.** artisan, laborer **8.** operator, opificer **9.** artificer, craftsman, performer
workshop ... **3.** lab **4.** mill **5.** plant **6.** studio **7.** atelier, factory **10.** laboratory **11.** ergasterion
world ... **5.** globe, realm **6.** cosmos, domain **7.** kingdom, society **8.** creation, humanity, universe **9.** multitude, the public
world (pert to) ...
external .. **6.** nonego
great .. **9.** macrocosm
lower .. **5.** Hades, Orcus
miniature .. **9.** microcosm

of fairies .. **6.** faerie (faery)
precreation .. **10.** premundane **11.** antemundane
reference to .. **7.** mundane **11.** terrestrial
worldly ... **7.** earthly, mundane, secular, terrene **11.** terrestrial **13.** materialistic, sophisticated
world's oldest city, still inhabited ... **8.** Damascus
world's speech ... **7.** Volapuk **9.** universal
worm ... **3.** ess **4.** coil, grub, wind **5.** borer, tinea **6.** blight, insect, maggot, vermin, wretch **8.** helminth **9.** trematode, vermicule **10.** Nemertinea (Nemertina)
worm (pert to) ...
Africa .. **3.** loa **6.** Guinea
aquatic, marine .. **7.** eunicid, lugworm **8.** flatworm **9.** planarian **13.** platyhelminth
arrow .. **7.** sagitta
bait .. **9.** angleworm, earthworm
bloodsucking .. **5.** leech
caddie .. **5.** cadew
cotton .. **8.** bollworm **10.** boll weevil
edible .. **6.** palolo
eye-infecting .. **3.** loa
genus .. **6.** Virmes **7.** Ascaris, Filaria **8.** Annelida **10.** Nemertinea (Nemertina)
grublike .. **5.** larva
killer .. **9.** vermicide
larva .. **4.** army, slug **5.** cadew **6.** caddis, looper **9.** wireworm **11.** caterpillar
luminous .. **8.** glowworm
marine .. **7.** eunicid
measuring .. **6.** looper **8.** inchworm
parasitic .. **7.** Ascaris, Filaria **8.** trichina, woodworm **9.** trematode **10.** Guinea worm **12.** enthelmintha
ref to .. **8.** anneloid **9.** nemertean, nemertine, nemertoid, trematoid
ring .. **5.** tinea **7.** annelid
round .. **7.** ascarid, Ascaris
segmented .. **8.** Annelida
ship .. **5.** borer **6.** teredo
silk .. **4.** eria
soft .. **4.** grub
study of .. **10.** vermeology **13.** helminthology
tape .. **6.** taenia
track .. **7.** nereite **11.** helminthite
wire .. **4.** lava **9.** millepede
worm (type) ... **3.** cut, dew, lug, pin **4.** army, boll, eria, flat, glow, inch, ring, ship, silk, slug, tape, wire, wood **5.** angle, earth, larva, leech, round, tinea **6.** marine **9.** measuring, parasitic
wormlike ... **7.** vermian **11.** helminthoid
wormy ... **6.** earthy, humble, rotten **8.** crawling **9.** groveling
worn ... **3.** old **4.** sere, used **5.** stale, trite **7.** abraded, haggard **8.** attrited, tattered, weakened **9.** exhausted, hackneyed **10.** secondhand **11.** commonplace
worn-out ... **4.** used **5.** jaded, passé, seedy, spent, trite **6.** shabby, used up **7.** haggard **8.** consumed, fatigued, impaired, tired out **9.** enfeebled, exhausted **10.** threadbare
worried ... **5.** cared, fazed **6.** stewed **7.** annoyed, anxious, fearful, fretted

8. troubled 9. perturbed
worry ... 3. nag, rux, vex 4. care, cark, faze, fret, stew 5. annoy, brood, harry 6. bother, harass, pester, plague, pother 7. anxiety, bedevil, concern, perturb, torment, trouble 8. distress 9. annoyance 10. harassment, uneasiness
worship ... 5. adore, honor, serve 6. bhakti, homage, revere 7. idolize, liturgy, respect 8. blessing, devotion, idolatry, venerate 9. adoration, deference, reverence 10. veneration
worship (pert to) ...
form of .. 6. preces, ritual 7. liturgy
house of .. 6. chapel, church, mosque, shrine 9. cathedral, synagogue 10. tabernacle
object of .. 4. icon, idol 5. totem 6. fetish
place of .. 5. altar
system of .. 4. cult 6. cultus, fetish, ritual 8. doctrine
worshiper ... 6. adorer, bhakti, votary 8. disciple, idolater 10. ignicolist 12. iconomachist
worshipful ... 6. devout 7. notable 8. esteemed 9. honorable, venerable 13. distinguished
worship of ...
a god .. 9. theolatry
angels .. 5. dulia
genii .. 10. geniolatry
god .. 6. latria (RCCh)
idols .. 8. idolatry
images .. 10. iconolatry
nature .. 11. physiolatry
one god .. 9. monolatry
snakes .. 10. ophiolatry
soul .. 7. animism
sun .. 10. heliolatry
the mob .. 9. mobolatry
worst ... 3. bad 4. beat, evil 6. defeat, wicked 7. harmful 8. inferior 10. calamitous, pernicious, unpleasant 12. disagreeable
worsted ... 4. yarn 6. crewel 7. genappe
worth ... 5. merit, price, value 6. desert, repute, riches, stiver, wealth 8. eminence, meriting, property 9. deserving 10. excellence, importance, usefulness
worthless ... 3. bad, ort 4. base, evil, mean, raca (Bib) 6. futile, nought (naught), paltry 7. fustian, useless 8. nugatory, rubbishy, unworthy 9. valueless 11. undeserving 14. good-for-nothing
worthwhile ... 6. useful 7. gainful 9. expedient, well-spent 10. invaluable, profitable
worthy ... 3. fit 7. merited 8. eligible, valuable 9. celebrity, competent, deserving, estimable, excellent, honorable, qualified, reputable 11. meritorious
worthy of ... 8. credible, meriting 9. deserving 10. entitled to
wound ... 3. cut 4. gore, harm, hurt, pain, rist, scar, sore, stab 5. sting 6. breach, damage, grieve, injury, lesion, offend, trauma 8. distress 9. detriment

wound (pert to) ...
discharge .. 5. ichor 6. sanies
dressing .. 7. bandage, pledget
mark .. 4. scab, scar, welt 7. blister
woven ... 4. spun 10. fabricated
wow ... 4. howl, rave, wail 5. whine
wrack ... 4. kelp, rack, ruin 5. tease, trash, weeds, wreck 6. refuse 7. seaweed 8. eelgrass, wreckage 9. shipwreck 11. destruction
wraith ... 4. food 5. ghost, spook 8. illusion 10. apparition 12. Doppelgänger, doubleganger
wrangle ... 4. herd, spar 5. argue, brawl 6. bicker, debate 7. contend, dispute, quarrel 8. haggling 9. altercate, bickering 11. altercation, controversy 12. disagreement
wrangler ... 6. cowboy 7. debater, student (Cambridge, Eng) 8. herdsman, opponent 9. combatant, disputant 10. antagonist
wrangling ... 11. belligerent, contentious
wrap ... 3. rug 4. cape, cere, furl, roll, wind 5. cloak, gange 6. afghan, encowl, enfold, swathe 7. blanket, conceal, package 8. covering, enshroud, enswathe, envelope 9. encompass
wrapped up ... 7. bound up, selfish 8. absorbed, included, involved 9. dependent, devoted to, engrossed 11. inseparable
wrapper ... 4. gown 5. cerer 6. fardel, kimono, tillot 7. garment, pelisse 8. envelope, peignoir
wrapping ... 6. charta 7. wrapper 8. cerement, covering 9. parchment
wrasse ... 4. fish 6. ballan, cunner, Labrus 7. seawife 11. peacock fish
wrath ... 3. ire 4. fury, grim, rage 5. anger 6. choler 7. passion 8. violence 10. turbulence 11. indignation 12. exasperation
wrathful ... 3. mad 5. angry, irate 6. ireful, raging 7. angered 8. incensed 9. indignant, malignant 10. passionate
wreak ... 4. do to 6. avenge 7. gratify, indulge, inflict 13. bring down upon
wreath ... 3. lei 4. band, orle 5. crown, torse (Her), whorl 6. anadem, circle, corona, laurel, trophy 7. coronet, festoon, garland, Iresine 8. encircle
wreathe ... 4. coil, wind 5. crown, twine, twist 7. entwine 8. decorate, encircle 9. interlace 10. twist about
wreck ... 4. raze, ruin, undo 5. crash, smash 6. jalopy 7. destroy, disable 8. accident, demolish, derelict 9. shipwreck 10. broken form 11. disassemble, The Hesperus
wreckage ... 5. ruins 6. jetsam 7. flotsam 8. driftage
wrench ... 4. jerk, pipe, pull, tear 5. twist, wrest 6. sprain, twinge 7. distort 8. crescent, distress
wrench, type of ... 3. box, pin 5. wramp 6. monkey 7. spanner 8. carriage, Stillson 9. alligator
wrest ... 4. rend, turn 5. exact, force, seize, twist, wring 6. elicit, extort, wrench 7. distort, extract, pervert,

wrestle 8. misapply
wrestle ... **3.** tug **6.** squirm, tussle
7. contend, grapple, scuffle, wriggle
8. struggle **9.** throw down **10.** twist
about **11.** come to grips
wrestling school ... **9.** palaestra
(palestra)
wretch ... **3.** dog **5.** miser, ronin
6. outlaw, pariah **7.** caitiff, cullion,
outcast **8.** derelict, sufferer **9.** miscreant
10. base person **11.** offscouring,
rapscallion **14.** good-for-nothing
16. pitiable creature
wretched ... **3.** sad **4.** base, mean
6. dismal, paltry, woeful **7.** baleful,
forlorn, squalid, unhappy, very bad
8. grievous **9.** execrable, miserable
10. despicable, distressed
12. contemptible, disreputable
wretchedness ... **6.** misery **8.** distress,
meanness, poorness **10.** paltriness
11. unhappiness **13.** penuriousness
wriggle ... **5.** twist **6.** squirm, writhe
7. meander
wriggle out of ... **4.** turn, wind **5.** dodge,
snake, twist **6.** squirm, writhe **8.** slip
away **10.** crawl out of **11.** squirm out
of **13.** find a loophole
wring ... **5.** twist, wrest **6.** extort, wrench
7. extract, torture, wrestle **8.** compress,
convolve **9.** cause pain **10.** contortion,
extraction
wrinkle ... **3.** fad **4.** fold, idea, ruga,
seam **5.** crimp, knack, ridge, rivel
6. crease, furrow, pucker, rimple, ripple,
rumple **7.** crinkle, novelty **8.** contract
9. corrugate **11.** corrugation **12.** clever
notion
wrinkled ... **4.** aged **5.** savoy **6.** rugate,
rugose, rugous **7.** creased **8.** crinkled,
crumpled, furrowed, puckered, rugulose
9. shriveled **10.** contracted, corrugated
wrinkles ... **5.** rugae
wrist ... **5.** joint **6.** carpal, carpus **8.** os
magnum **9.** capitatum
writ ... **5.** breve, tales **6.** capias, elegit,
venire **7.** process **8.** detainer, document,
mittimus, replevin, subpoena
10. certiorari, instrument **11.** fieri facias
writ (pert to) ...
common law .. **11.** fieri facias
court .. **7.** summons **8.** subpoena
execution .. **6.** elegit
jury .. **5.** tales **6.** venire
law .. **4.** capo, pone **5.** breve, error
6. capias, elegit **7.** mandate, process,
warrant **8.** citation **10.** certiorari
write ... **3.** pen **5.** draft, trace **6.** decree,
depict, draw up, enroll, indite, record,
scrive **7.** compose, scriven **8.** inscribe,
scribble **11.** communicate
write (pert to) ...
carelessly .. **6.** scrawl **8.** scrabble,
scribble
in large hand .. **7.** engross
off .. **4.** drop **6.** cancel, deduct, repeal
out .. **6.** record **8.** spill out **12.** put in
writing
poetry .. **7.** versify
up .. **6.** record, report **7.** article
9. publicize **11.** press report

writer ... **4.** hack, poet **6.** author, penman,
penner, scribe **7.** elegist, glosser,
hymnist **8.** annalist, composer, lyricist,
novelist, parodist, scriptor **9.** annotator,
columnist, scrivener **10.** chronicler,
journalist **13.** correspondent
writer's afterthoughts ... **7.** addenda
writhe ... **4.** bend, coil, curl, wind **5.** twist,
wring **6.** squirm **7.** contort, distort,
wriggle
writing ... **4.** book, poem **6.** script
7. article, epistle **8.** covenant, document,
makimono **10.** expression, penmanship,
profession **11.** chirography,
composition, handwriting, inscription,
publication
writing (pert to) ...
alternate .. **13.** boustrophedon
ancient characters .. **9.** cuneiform
ancient manuscript .. **6.** uncial
cipher .. **12.** cryptography
instrument .. **3.** pen **5.** quill **6.** stylus
italic .. **7.** cursive
mania for .. **11.** graphomania
material .. **3.** pad **5.** paper, slate **6.** tablet
9. parchment **10.** stationery
omission of a letter .. **8.** lipogram
10. lipography
pert to .. **7.** scribal
record .. **3.** log **5.** album, diary
script .. **5.** ronde
scroll .. **8.** makimono
scroll hanging .. **8.** kakemono
secret .. **4.** code **10.** cryptogram
12. cryptography
unrhymed .. **5.** prose
writings, sacred ... **5.** Bible, Koran
6. Psalms, Talmud **9.** Testament (Old,
New) **10.** Scriptures
written (pert to) ...
agreement .. **6.** cartel
characters .. **6.** script
it is .. **8.** it must be **10.** in the books,
in the cards **12.** the die is cast
law .. **10.** legislated
law, unwritten .. **6.** common
memo .. **5.** scrip
wrong ... **3.** bad, off, out, sin **4.** awry,
evil, harm, side, tort, vice **5.** amiss,
cheat, crime, false, malum, unfit
6. faulty, injure, injury, seduce, sinful,
unjust, wicked **7.** defraud, immoral,
misdeed, offense **8.** improper, iniquity,
mistaken **9.** erroneous, incorrect,
injustice, violation **10.** inaccurate,
iniquitous **11.** impropriety, inexpedient,
malfeasance, misfeasance
12. illegitimate
wrong (pert to) ...
go (wrong) .. **3.** err **4.** fail **5.** lapse
8. go astray, go to ruin **9.** backslide
10. misbelieve **11.** go to the dogs
in the .. **6.** guilty **7.** at fault, in error
8. mistaken **9.** violation
law .. **4.** tort **5.** crime, malum
name .. **8.** misnomer
nor right (neither) .. **7.** neutral
11. adiaphorous
prefix .. **3.** mis
side of .. **5.** shady
way .. **5.** amiss **6.** astray **10.** out of

place
wrongdoer... **6.** sinner **8.** criminal,
evildoer, violator **10.** malefactor,
trespasser **12.** transgressor
wroth... **3.** mad **5.** angry, irate **7.** violent
8. incensed, wrathful **9.** turbulent,
wrought up **11.** exasperated
wrought... **4.** made **6.** formed, shaped,
worked **9.** decorated, fashioned,
processed **10.** elaborated,
ornamented **11.** embroidered
12. manufactured
wrought up... **4.** agog **5.** angry, eager
7. excited **9.** disturbed, stirred up
wry... **4.** awry **6.** biased, swerve, turned
7. crooked, twisted **9.** contorted
wryneck... **4.** Jynx, weet **5.** loxia
9. snakebird **11.** torticollis
Württemberg, Germany...
capital.. **9.** Stuttgart
city.. **3.** Ulm **9.** Esslingen, Heilbronn,
Hohenheim
lake.. **9.** Constance
river.. **6.** Danube, Neckar

Wyandot... **6.** Indian (Iroquois)
Wyandotte... **4.** cave, city, fowl
Wycliff (Wyclif), **John** (pert to)...
birthplace.. **9.** Yorkshire (Eng)
disciple.. **4.** Huss
remains cast into.. **10.** Swift River
translator of.. **5.** Bible
Wyoming...
capital.. **8.** Cheyenne
city.. **4.** Cody **6.** Casper **7.** Big Horn,
Laramie **8.** Cheyenne, Sheridan
historic site.. **11.** Fort Laramie
17. Buffalo Bill Center
mountain.. **6.** Tetons **7.** Rockies
11. Gannett Peak
park.. **10.** Grand Teton **11.** Yellowstone
river.. **4.** Wind **6.** Platte **7.** Big Horn
river source.. **8.** Colorado, Columbia,
Missouri
State admission.. **11.** Forty-fourth
State bird.. **10.** meadowlark
State flower.. **16.** Indian paintbrush
State motto.. **11.** Equal Rights
Woman Suffrage.. **10.** First State

X

X... **3.** ten **5.** error **6.** letter (24th), symbol
7. unknown
xanthic... **6.** cyanic, yellow
Xanthippe, wife of... **8.** Socrates
xanthoma... **9.** xanthosis **11.** skin disease
13. yellow patches
xanthos... **6.** yellow
Xanthus (pert to)...
ancient site.. **7.** marbles (Xanthian)
placed now.. **13.** British Museum
xebec... **6.** vessel **7.** corsair
xen, xeno (comb form)... **7.** foreign
8. stranger
xenium... **4.** gift **7.** present (official)
Xenocrates (Gr)... **11.** philosopher
xenogamy... **18.** cross-fertilization
xenophobic... **9.** strangers (afraid of)
12. chauvinistic
Xenophon's historic tale... **8.** Anabasis
xenophthalmia... **11.** foreign body (eye)
14. conjunctivitis
Xenopus... **5.** toads
Xenorhynchus... **6.** storks
Xenurus... **7.** tatouay **10.** armadillos
Xeres... **5.** jerez **6.** sherry
xerophagy... **4.** Fast (Lenten)
xerotes... **7.** dryness (body)
Xerox (tm)... **4.** copy **9.** duplicate,
replicate, reproduce
Xerus... **9.** squirrels

Xerxes (pert to)...
crossing of.. **10.** Hellespont
destroyer of.. **6.** Athens (BC)
king of.. **6.** Persia
xibalba... **10.** underworld
Xinca... **6.** Indian, Jincan
Xipe, Xipe-totec... **11.** god of sowing
Xiphias... **5.** comet (sword-shaped)
6. Dorado (constellation) **9.** swordfish
xiphoid... **4.** bone **8.** ensiform
9. swordlike **12.** xiphisternum
Xiphopagus... **7.** monster (twinlike)
Xiphosura... **8.** king crab
Xiuhtocutli... **7.** fire god (Aztec)
Xmas... **9.** Christmas
X ray (pert to)...
measure.. **3.** rad **11.** quantimeter
named.. **12.** Roentgen rays
type.. **7.** CAT scan **8.** tomogram
9. myelogram **11.** arteriogram
xyloglyphy... **11.** wood carving (art)
xylography... **13.** wood engraving
xyloid... **5.** woody **8.** ligneous, woodlike
xylomancy, divination by... **4.** wood
10. wood pieces
xylophone... **5.** saron **7.** gambang,
marimba **8.** gamelang (gamelan),
gigelira, sticcado
xyrid... **4.** iris **5.** Xyris
xystus, xyst (Gr)... **16.** portico colonnade

Y

-y pl ... **3.** -ies
Y ... **4.** tube **5.** curve, track **6.** letter
(25th), prefix, suffix
yabber ... **4.** talk **6.** jabber
yabby, yabbie ... **8.** crayfish
yaboa ... **10.** night heron
yabu, yaboo ... **4.** pony
yacht ... **4.** boat, race, sail, ship
yaffle ... **6.** armful **7.** handful
10. woodpecker
yahoo ... **4.** lout, rube **5.** brute
Yahoo (pert to) ...
represented by .. **10.** Houyhnhnms
(horses of reason)
tale .. **16.** Gulliver's Travels
yakalo, yakattalo ... **8.** creature
10. crossbreed (yak, cattle)
yakka ... **4.** work **5.** labor
yaksha ... **4.** ogre **5.** demon, dryad, fairy,
gnome, jinni **6.** Kubera (Chief), spirit
7. tree-god **13.** guardian angel
Yale (pert to) ...
college .. **8.** New Haven
color .. **4.** blue **7.** Rameses
founded at .. **8.** Saybrook
founder .. **9.** Elihu Yale
graduate .. **9.** Yalensian
Yalta Conference ... **6.** Crimea (1945)
yam (pert to) ...
Fiji .. **6.** uviyam **8.** white yam
Hawaiian .. **3.** hoi
reference to .. **5.** tuber **6.** igname
Scot .. **6.** potato
tropical .. **8.** cush-cush
US .. **11.** sweet potato
yamstchik ... **7.** postboy **8.** coachman
9. postilion
yang ... **4.** good, male **6.** bright (opp of
yin)
yang-kin ... **8.** dulcimer
yank ... **4.** jerk, pull **6.** Yankee
Yankee ... **12.** New Englander
Yannigans ... **9.** scrub team (baseball)
Yao ... **6.** Indian **9.** aborigine
yap ... **3.** cur, dog, gab **4.** bark, talk, yell,
yelp **6.** jabber **7.** bumpkin, hoodlum
8. easy mark **9.** greenhorn
yapok, yapock ... **6.** monkey **7.** opossum
yapp ... **11.** bookbinding
yapster ... **3.** dog
Yaqui ... **6.** Indian
yard ... **3.** rae (sail) **4.** lawn, spar,
wand **5.** garth, stick, verge **6.** campus
7. confine, enclose, measure
9. courtyard, curtilage, enclosure,
yardstick **10.** playground
yarn ... **3.** abb, cop **4.** hank, joke, tale
5. fiber, skein, story **6.** caddis, crewel,
spinel, thread **7.** genappe **9.** falsehood
yarn (pert to) ...
clew .. **4.** ball
holder .. **3.** cop
measure .. **4.** hank, hasp **5.** skein
7. spangle
size .. **6.** denier

winder .. **10.** yarnwindle
yashiro ... **3.** sha **6.** temple (Shinto)
yashmak ... **4.** veil (double)
yati ... **7.** ascetic, devotee
yaw ... **4.** sail, tack **5.** steer, tumor
7. deviate **9.** deviation
yawl ... **4.** boat, howl, wail, yell, yowl
5. ketch **9.** jolly boat
yawn ... **3.** gap **4.** gape **5.** chasm, mouth
7. opening, stretch **8.** open wide,
oscitate **12.** seek greedily
yaws ... **9.** frambesia
yawweed ... **5.** shrub **7.** rhubarb **12.** wild
mulberry
Yazoo (pert to) ...
Fraud .. **9.** land grant (1795)
Indian .. **11.** Mississippi
river .. **11.** Mississippi
yclept, ycleped ... **5.** named **6.** called,
styled
year (pert to) ...
after year .. **10.** constantly, repeatedly
11. over and over
book .. **7.** almanac
division of .. **6.** season **8.** semester
9. trimester
Latin .. **5.** annus
of mourning .. **11.** annus luctus
of our Lord .. **10.** Anno Domini **11.** annus
Domini, year of grace
of thirteen months (384 days) ..
10. embolismic
of travel .. **10.** sabbatical, Wanderjahr
14. leave of absence
old (Zool) .. **10.** annotinous
pert to .. **5.** epact
quarter .. **5.** raith
record .. **5.** annal **8.** calendar
yearly (pert to) ...
church income .. **7.** annates
payment .. **4.** cens
recurring .. **6.** annual **7.** etesian
8. annually
yearn for ... **3.** yen **4.** ache, hope, itch,
long, pine, sigh, wish **6.** desire, hanker
yearning ... **3.** yen **4.** wish **5.** eager
7. anxious, longing **9.** hankering,
nostalgia **10.** tenderness **11.** languishing
12. homesickness
years (pert to) ...
adolescent .. **4.** teen
ago .. **4.** ages **9.** long since **10.** days
of yore, yesteryear
eight .. **9.** octennial
fifteen .. **9.** indiction
five .. **6.** pentad **7.** lustrum
hundred .. **9.** centenary **10.** centennial
ten .. **6.** decade **9.** decennary
thousand .. **7.** chiliad **10.** millennium
two .. **8.** biennial, biennium
yeast ... **4.** barm, foam, koji **5.** froth
6. leaven **7.** anamite, ferment
9. agitation
yeasty ... **5.** foamy, light, spumy **6.** frothy
8. restless **9.** frivolous, leavening

yegg... 5. thief, tramp 6. robber
7. burglar, yeggman 8. criminal
10. safeblower 11. safebreaker,
safecracker
yell... 3. cry 4. howl, roar, wail, yowl
5. cheer, shout 6. outcry, scream, shriek
yelling... 7. bawling 8. shouting, strident
9. clamorous 11. full of yells
yellow... 3. dun, sil 4. buff, cuir, deer,
ecru, flax, gull, mean, nude, yolk
5. amber, beige, color, cream, grège,
jaune, lemon, maize, ocher (ochre),
straw, taupe, topaz, twine 6. bisque,
butter, canary, Cassel, chrome, citron,
creamy, flaxen, golden, mimosa,
sallow, Seasan 7. anamite, annatto,
aureate, egg yolk, envious, etiolin,
jealous, jonquil, saffron, sulphur,
xanthic, xanthin 8. cowardly, ocherous,
primrose, recreant 9. champagne,
dandelion, flavicant, goldenrod,
jaundiced, lutescent, sunflower
10. flavescent, melancholy
11. treacherous
yellow (pert to)...
brown.. 3. dun 5. straw 6. manila
coloring.. 7. xanthic 8. xanthine
comb form.. 5. luteo
dyestuff.. 5. morin 7. annatto 8. luteolin
golden.. 2. or (Her) 4. gild, gilt
green.. 5. olive 8. tarragon
10. chartreuse, serpentine
herb.. 3. iva
jacket.. 4. wasp
medical.. 7. icterus 8. jaundice
11. xanthoderma
mustard.. 8. charlock
ocher, ochre.. 3. sil
pert to.. 7. xanthic
pigment.. 7. etiolin 8. orpiment
race.. 9. Mongolian
red.. 4. roan 5. aloma, sandy 6. bisque,
dorado, orange 7. annatto, nacarat
sensational.. 5. press 7. journal
yellow fever mosquito... 12. Aëdes
aegypti
yellowhammer... 4. yite 5. ammer, finch,
skite 6. gladdy 7. flicker 10. woodpecker
13. yellow bunting
Yellowhammer State... 7. Alabama
yellow jacket... 4. wasp 8. eucalypt
Yellowstone Park geyser... 11. Old
Faithful
yelp... 3. cry, yip 4. bark, yell 5. shout
6. outcry, shriek, squeal 7. ululate
8. complain 9. criticize
yelper... 8. redshank 10. yellowlegs
11. hunting call
yeme... 4. heed 5. guard 6. govern,
regard
Yemen (pert to)...
archeology site.. 4. Sana 5. Marib
Bib kingdom.. 5. Sheba (Saba)
capital.. 4. Sana
citadel.. 5. Damar
division of.. 6. Arabia
plateau.. 7. El Jebel
port.. 5. Mocha 7. Hodeida, Loheiya
ruler.. 4. Imam
sea.. 3. Red
yemochik... see yamstchik

yen... 4. coin, urge 5. yearn 6. desire,
hanker 7. longing
yeoman... 4. exon 5. clerk 6. butler,
seaman 8. retainer 9. assistant,
attendant 10. freeholder 11. subordinate
12. petty officer
yep... 3. yes 4. bold 5. alert, smart
6. active 8. vigorous
yerba... 4. herb, maté 5. plant
11. Paraguay tea
yes...
English.. 3. aye, yea, yep 5. uh-huh
6. assent 11. affirmation
French.. 3. oui
German.. 2. ja
Italian, Spanish.. 2. si
Russian.. 2. da
yes man... 5. toady
yesterday... 6. yester 7. the past
10. days gone by, heretofore, yesteryear
11. bygone times
yet... 3. but 5. still 6. algate 7. besides,
however 10. eventually 11. nonetheless
15. notwithstanding
yeti... 17. Abominable Snowman
yew... 5. green, Taxus 7. conifer, hemlock
9. evergreen
Yiddish... 6. Jewish 12. Judaeo-German
(Judeo-German)
yield... 3. bow, net 4. bear, bend,
cede, crop, give, lose, obey, vail
5. admit, allow, defer, grant, stoop,
waive 6. accede, afford, comply, give
up, relent, render, reward, soften,
submit 7. concede, consent, produce,
provide, requite, revenue, succumb
9. acquiesce, surrender
10. capitulate, relinquish
11. acknowledge
yielding... 4. meek, soft 6. pliant, supple
7. bearing 8. flexible 9. compliant,
deference, producing, tractable
10. compliance, manageable,
submissive
Yigdal... 4. poem (Jew Relig)
yill-caup... 6. ale cup
yin... 4. dark, evil (opp of yang)
Ymir, Ymer (pert to)...
blood of.. 3. sea
bones of.. 9. mountains
brains of.. 6. clouds
flesh of.. 5. earth
killed by.. 2. Ve 4. Odin, Vili
Norse Myth.. 3. God 13. rime-cold
giant (body-shaped world)
yodel, yodle... 4. call, sing (falsetto)
5. carol, shout 6. warble
yoga (pert to)...
follower of.. 4. yogi (yogin) 5. fakir
7. ascetic 9. occultist
objective.. 16. mental discipline
stages.. 5. jnana, karma 6. bhakti
trance.. 6. dhyana 7. dharana, samadhi
yoke... 3. two 4. join, link, pair, span,
team 5. frame, marry 6. cangue,
couple, inspan 7. bondage, enclave,
harness, oppress, pillory, shackle,
slavery 9. associate, servitude
yoked... 6. united 7. coupled 9. conjugate
yokel... 3. oaf 4. boor, clod, hick,
lout, rube 6. rustic 7. bumpkin,

hayseed, plowboy **8.** abderite (anc),
gullible **9.** simpleton **10.** countryman,
slow-witted
yokemate . . . **4.** mate **6.** fellow, spouse
7. partner **9.** companion
yolked (egg) . . . **6.** yellow **8.** lecithal,
vitellus
Yom Kippur (Jew) . . . **7.** fast day **14.** Day
of Atonement
Yom Teruah (Jew) . . . **15.** Feast of
Trumpets
Yom Tob, or Tov (Jew) . . . **8.** festival
yon, yonder . . . **4.** away **6.** beyond
7. distant, thither **11.** at a distance
yore . . . **5.** of old, olden **6.** before **9.** in
old time, long since
young . . . **3.** fry, new **4.** tyro **5.** brood,
fresh, green **6.** litter, novice, tender
7. pliable **8.** childish, immature,
juvenile, youthful **9.** offspring, succulent
13. inexperienced
young (pert to) . . .
  bear, fox . . **3.** cub
  birds . . **5.** brood
  calf (motherless) . . **5.** dogie
  hare . . **7.** leveret
  herring . . **4.** brit
  horse . . **4.** colt, foal
  oyster . . **4.** spat
  pigeon . . **5.** piper
youngling . . . **5.** youth **6.** novice
8. beginner, neophyte
youngster . . . **3.** boy, kid, lad, pup, tad
4. baby, lass, tike **5.** child, youth
6. filius, shaver, urchin **7.** Aladdin
(Arab Nights) **8.** teenager **9.** fledgling,
stripling
younker . . . **5.** child, youth **6.** knight
7. gallant **8.** nobleman **9.** stripling
youth goddess . . . **4.** Hebe
yo-yo . . . **3.** top, toy
Ypres, Belgium . . .
  famed for . . **7.** Battles (WWI)

lace . . **12.** Valenciennes
province of . . **8.** Flanders
ruins rebuilt . . **9.** Cloth Hall **15.** Gothic
Cathedral (St Martin)
ypsiliform, shape of . . . **7.** letter T (Gr)
yu (Chin) . . . **4.** jade
Yucatan, Cent America . . .
  anc domain of . . **5.** Mayas
  capital . . **6.** Mérida
  city . . **5.** Sisal
  peninsula of . . **6.** Mexico
yucca (pert to) . . .
  called . . **11.** Adam's needle
  family . . **9.** Liliaceae
  native of . . **7.** America
  species . . **9.** bear grass
  State flower of . . **9.** New Mexico
Yugoslavia . . .
  capital . . **8.** Belgrade
  former leader . . **4.** Tito (Communist)
  river . . **5.** Drava, Drina **6.** Danube
  sea . . **8.** Adriatic
yukkel . . . **7.** flicker **10.** woodpecker
Yukon . . .
  famed for . . **4.** gold (mining)
  ocean . . **6.** Arctic
  river . . **5.** Lewes, Yukon
  territory of . . **6.** Canada
  town . . **10.** Whitehorse
Yule . . . **4.** Noel **8.** Nativity (Feast of the),
yuletide **9.** Christmas **13.** Christmastide
Yule (pert to) . . .
  plant . . **5.** holly **9.** mistletoe
  good cheer . . **11.** wassail bowl
Yuma (Ariz) . . . **4.** city **9.** Talkepaia (Indian)
yun . . . **10.** Laos people (tattooed)
Yunca . . . **6.** Indian (Peru)
Yurma . . . **6.** Indian (Brazil)
Yurok . . . **6.** Indian (Calif)
yurt, yurta . . . **4.** tent (Siberia)
Yuruk . . . **10.** Turkish rug
yutu . . . **7.** tinamou
Yuzen birodo . . . **6.** velvet (designed)

Z

Z . . . **3.** end, zed, zee **5.** omega **6.** izzard,
letter (26th)
zac . . . **4.** ibex
zacate . . . **7.** herbage **9.** rice grass
Zacchaeus, Zaccheus . . . **4.** pure
8. innocent, publican (Bib)
Zachariah, Zacharias (Bib) . . .
  father . . **9.** Barachias
  father of . . **14.** John the Baptist
  literally . . **21.** Jehovah hath remembered
Zadkiel (Jew) . . . **5.** angel (of planet
Jupiter)
zaftig . . . **5.** buxom **7.** shapely
Zagreus . . . **3.** god **8.** Dionysus (identified
with)
Zaire, Africa . . .
  capital . . **8.** Kinshasa
  formerly . . **12.** Belgian Congo
  river . . **4.** Uele **5.** Kasai, Zaire (Congo)

zaman, zamang . . . **8.** rain tree
Zambia, Africa . . .
  capital . . **6.** Lusaka
  formerly . . **16.** Northern Rhodesia
  wealth . . **6.** copper (3rd largest)
Zamenhof, inventor of . . . **9.** Esperanto
zampogna . . . **7.** bagpipe, panpipe
zanja . . . **5.** canal, gully **6.** arroyo
zany . . . **3.** wag, wit **4.** dolt, fool **5.** clown,
crazy, goofy, kooky, nutty **6.** madcap,
sawney **7.** acrobat, bonkers, buffoon,
idiotic **8.** clownish **9.** simpleton
10. lieutenant, mountebank **11.** merry-
andrew
Zanzibar, Africa . . . see *Tanzania*
zap . . . **4.** slay, stun **5.** smite **6.** strike
zapatero . . . **7.** boxwood, cobbler,
dogwood
zarf . . . **9.** cup holder (Levant)

Z

zati ... **6.** monkey (bonnet)
zeal ... **5.** ardor, piety **6.** desire, fervor
   7. passion **8.** devotion **9.** eagerness
   10. enthusiasm, fanaticism
zealot ... **4.** sect **5.** bigot, freak (sl)
   6. votary **7.** devotee, faddist, fanatic,
   pietist **8.** partisan **10.** enthusiast
zealous ... **5.** eager, pious **6.** ardent,
   fervid **7.** devoted, fervent **9.** phrenetic
   11. industrious
zebra (pert to) ...
   ally .. **6.** quagga
   Burchell's .. **4.** dauw (nonstriped legs)
   hybrid .. **8.** zebrinny
   insect .. **9.** butterfly
   ref to .. **7.** zebrine, zebroid
zebrawood ... **5.** shrub **7.** araroba
   10. marblewood
zebu ... **2.** ox **5.** zebus (group) **6.** cattle
   12. Brahmany bull (sacred)
zecchino ... **6.** sequin (chequeen)
Zechariah (Bib) ... **7.** prophet **12.** King
   of Israel
zed ... **7.** letter Z (Brit)
zeekoe ... **12.** hippopotamus
zeism ... **8.** pellagra **11.** morbid state
zemi ... **4.** holy (Peru) **5.** huaca (huaco)
   6. fetish, sacred, spirit (magic)
Zemzem ... **10.** sacred well (Mecca)
Zen ... **12.** Buddhist sect
zenana ... **5.** harem, serai **7.** mission
   8. seraglio
Zenda, Prisoner of ... **9.** Ruritania
Zend-Avesta ... **10.** sacred text
   (Zoroastrian)
zenith ... **3.** top **4.** acme, apex, blue,
   peak **6.** apogee, climax, summit, vertex
   11. culmination **14.** greatest height
   (opp of nadir)
Zeno ... **5.** Stoic **11.** philosopher (Gr)
zenography, study of ... **7.** Jupiter
   (planet)
zenu ... **5.** sheep
zephyr ... **5.** shawl **6.** breath, breeze
zero ... **3.** nil **4.** hour **5.** zilch **6.** cipher,
   nought (naught) **7.** nothing, nullity
   11. temperature
zest ... **4.** tang **5.** gusto, savor **6.** flavor,
   relish **8.** membrane (fruit), piquancy,
   pungency **9.** eagerness **10.** enthusiasm
Zeus (pert to) ...
   attendant .. **4.** Nike
   consort .. **6.** Europa
   brother of .. **5.** Hades **8.** Poseidon
   deity .. **7.** supreme **12.** father of gods
   father .. **6.** Cronus
   games in his honor .. **6.** Nemean
   8. Olympian
   messenger .. **4.** Iris **6.** Hermes
   mother .. **4.** Rhea
   oracle .. **6.** Dodona
   Roman .. **7.** Jupiter
   sister .. **4.** Hera
   son .. **4.** Ares **5.** Argus **6.** Apollo, Hermes
   7. Perseus **8.** Dionysus, Hercules,
   Tantalus
   temple (Athens) .. **8.** Olympium
ziara, ziarat ... **4.** tomb (Muslim saint)
   6. shrine
zibet, zibeth ... **5.** civet
ziganka ... **5.** dance (rustic)

zigeuner ... **5.** gypsy **7.** czigany, Zincalo,
   zingaro
ziggurat ... **11.** temple tower **12.** Tower
   of Babel (Bib)
zigzag ... **5.** turns **6.** angles **7.** stagger
   8. flexuous, wavering **9.** alternate
zillion ... **4.** many **9.** countless
Zimbabwe ...
   capital .. **6.** Harare
   Falls .. **8.** Victoria
   Falls discoverer .. **11.** Livingstone (1855)
   formerly .. **8.** Rhodesia
   people .. **5.** Bantu
zinc (pert to) ...
   alloy .. **5.** bidri **7.** paktong
   alloy with copper .. **6.** oroide
   crude .. **7.** tutenag (tutenague)
   slabs .. **6.** solder **7.** spelter
   symbol .. **2.** Zn
zing ... **3.** pep, vim, zip **5.** vigor **6.** energy,
   spirit, thrill **10.** enthusiasm
zingaresca (gypsy) ... **4.** song **5.** dance
zingaro ... **5.** gypsy
Zion (pert to) ... **4.** hill (Jerusalem)
   10. Israelites **12.** chosen people
zip ... **4.** zing **5.** close, speed **6.** energy
   8. pungency **10.** sibilation
zizith ... **7.** fringes (Bib), tassels
zoanthropy ... **9.** monomania
   15. changed to animal (belief)
zobo ... **6.** hybrid **10.** zebu and yak
zodiac ... **4.** belt, zone **5.** stars **7.** circuit
zodiac signs (twelve) ... **3.** Leo **5.** Aries,
   Libra, Virgo **6.** Cancer, Gemini,
   Pisces, Taurus **7.** Scorpio **8.** Aquarius
   9. Capricorn **11.** Capricornus, Sagittarius
zoetic ... **5.** vital **6.** living **7.** organic
zombie, zombi ... **6.** corpse, voodoo
zone ... **4.** area, band, belt, isle,
   path **5.** Canal, clime, girth, tract
   6. assise, circle, course, Frigid, region,
   Torrid **7.** stratum **8.** cincture, latitude
   9. Temperate
zoo ... **9.** menagerie **10.** collection
   12. animal garden
zoo, zo (comb form) ... **6.** animal
zoologist ... **9.** biologist, scientist
zoology, science of ... **7.** animals
zoology branches ... **8.** taxonomy
   9. bionomics, phylogeny
   10. embryology, entomology
   11. herpetology, ornithology
zoom ... **4.** lens, rise **5.** climb
zoopathology, science of ... **8.** diseases
   (animal) **11.** zoonosology
zoophilist ... **11.** animal lover
zoophobia ... **13.** fear of animals
zoophyte ... **5.** coral **6.** sponge **10.** sea
   anemone
zootomy ... **13.** animal anatomy
   16. animal dissection
zootrophy ... **13.** animal rearing
zoril, zorillo ... **5.** skunk **7.** polecat
Zoroaster, Zarathustra ... **7.** Persian
   8. reformer (Relig)
Zoroastrianism (pert to) ...
   adherence to .. **5.** Parse (Parsee)
   doctrine .. **7.** dualism **11.** good and evil
   evil spirit .. **4.** deva **7.** Ahriman
   fire worshiper .. **6.** Gheber
   founder .. **9.** Zoroaster

literature .. **6.** Avesta
lord of creation .. **6.** Ormazo
religion of .. **6.** Persia (anc)
zoster ... **4.** zona **6.** girdle **8.** shingles
(Med) **12.** herpes zoster
Zouave ... **4.** Zu-Zu **8.** chasseur
11. infantryman
Zu (Bab Myth) ... **8.** storm god (evil)
9. blackbird (symbol)
Zuider Zee (pert to) ...
gulf .. **8.** North Sea
Netherlands .. **4.** dike **7.** highway
present name .. **9.** Ijsel Lake, Ijselmeer
zuisin ... **7.** widgeon
Zulu (pert to) ...
army .. **4.** impi
boy .. **6.** umfaan
conference .. **6.** indaba
marauders .. **4.** Viti
people .. **6.** Santus **7.** Kaffirs

spear .. **7.** assagai (assegai)
Zululand capital ... **6.** Eshowe
Zuñi (pert to) ...
famed for .. **19.** Seven Cities of Cibola
(Myth)
Indian .. **4.** Hopi **6.** Ashivi
kingdom of Cibola .. **16.** gold-paved
streets (Myth)
zwieback ... **4.** rusk **7.** biscuit (toasted)
Zwinger ... **6.** palace (Dresden)
zygal ... **7.** H-shaped
zygodactyl (zygodactyle) ... **8.** yoke-toed
10. paired toes
zygon ... **5.** bench **6.** thwart **9.** brain
part
zygous ... **5.** yoked **6.** paired
zymology (science of) ...
12. fermentation
zymosis ... **12.** fermentation
zythum ... **4.** beer (anc Egypt)

TABLES

BOOKS OF THE BIBLE

Old Testament Books and Abbreviations

Book, Letter Count	Abbreviation
Genesis 7	Gen
Exodus 6	Exod
Leviticus 9	Lev
Numbers 7	Num
Deuteronomy 11	Deut
Joshua 6	Josh
Judges 6	Judg
Ruth 4	Ruth
1 Samuel 6	1 Sam
2 Samuel 6	2 Sam
1 Kings 5	1 Kings
2 Kings 5	2 Kings
1 Chronicles 10	1 Chron
2 Chronicles 10	2 Chron
Ezra 4	Ezra
Nehemiah 8	Neh
Esther 6	Esther
Job 3	Job
Psalms 6	Psalms
Proverbs 8	Proverbs
Ecclesiastes 12	Eccles
Song of Solomon 13	Song of Sol
Isaiah 6	Isa
Jeremiah 8	Jer
Lamentations 12	Lam
Ezekiel 7	Ezek
Daniel 6	Dan
Hosea 5 (Osee)	Hos
Joel 4	Joel
Amos 4	Amos
Obadiah 7	Obad
Jonah 5	Joh
Micah 4	Mic
Nahum 5	Nah
Habakkuk 8	Hab
Zephaniah 9	Zeph
Haggai 6	Hag
Zechariah 9	Zech
Malachi 7	Mal

New Testament Books and Abbreviations

Book, Letter Count	Abbreviation
Matthew 7	Matt
Mark 4	Mark
Luke 4	Luke
John 4	John
Acts of the Apostles 17	Acts
Romans 6	Rom
1 Corinthians 11	1 Cor
2 Corinthians 11	2 Cor
Galatians 9	Gal
Ephesians 9	Eph
Philippians 11	Phil
Colossians 10	Col
1 Thessalonians 13	1 Thess
2 Thessalonians 13	2 Thess
1 Timothy 7	1 Tim
2 Timothy 7	2 Tim
Titus 5	Titus
Philemon 8	Philem
Hebrews 7	Heb
James 5	James
1 Peter 5	1 Pet
2 Peter 5	2 Pet
1 John 4	1 John
2 John 4	2 John
3 John 4	3 John
Jude 4	Jude
Revelation 10	(Apocalypse) Rev

Books of the Apocrypha and Abbreviations

Book, Letter Count	Abbreviation
1 Esdras 6	1 Esd
2 Esdras 6	2 Esd
Tobit 5	Tob
Judith 6	Jth
Rest of Esther 12	Rest of Esther
Wisdom of Solomon 15	Wisd of Sol
Ecclesiasticus 14	Ecclus
Baruch 6	Bar
Song of the Three Holy Children 26	Song of Three Children
Susanna 7	Sus
Bel and the Dragon 15	Bel and Dragon
Manasseh 8	Man
1 Maccabees 9	1 Macc
2 Maccabees 9	2 Macc

Books of the Bible by Letter Count

3. Job 4. Acts (of the Apostles), Amos, Ezra, Joel, John, Jude, Luke, Mark, Osee, Ruth 5. Hosea, James, Jonah, Kings, Micah, Nahum, Peter, Titus, Tobit 6. Baruch, Daniel, Esdras, Esther, Exodus, Haggai, Isaiah, Joshua, Judges, Judith, Psalms, Romans, Samuel 7. Ezekiel, Genesis, Hebrews, Malachi, Matthew, Numbers, Obadiah, Susanna, Timothy 8. Habakkuk, Jeremiah, Manasseh, Nehemiah, Philemon, Proverbs 9. Ephesians, Galatians, Leviticus, Maccabees, Zechariah, Zephaniah 10. Apocalypse, Chronicles, Colossians, Revelation 11. Corinthians, Deuteronomy, Philippians 12. Ecclesiastes, Lamentations, Rest of Esther 13. Song of Solomon, Thessalonians 14. Ecclesiasticus 15. Bel and the Dragon, Wisdom of Solomon 17. Acts of the Apostles 26. Song of the Three Holy Children

CHEMICAL ELEMENTS

Listed by atomic number, name, letter count, and symbol.

Atomic Number	Element, Letter Count	Symbol
1	hydrogen 8	H
2	helium 6	He
3	lithium 7	Li
4	beryllium 9	Be
5	boron 5	B
6	carbon 6	C
7	nitrogen 8	N
8	oxygen 6	O
9	fluorine 8	F
10	neon 4	Ne
11	sodium 6	Na
12	magnesium 9	Mg
13	aluminum 8	Al
14	silicon 7	Si
15	phosphorus 10	P
16	sulfur 6	S
17	chlorine 8	Cl
18	argon 5	Ar
19	potassium 9	K
20	calcium 7	Ca
21	scandium 8	Sc
22	titanium 8	Ti
23	vanadium 8	V
24	chromium 8	Cr
25	manganese 9	Mn
26	iron 4	Fe
27	cobalt 6	Co
28	nickel 6	Ni
29	copper 6	Cu
30	zinc 4	Zn
31	gallium 7	Ga
32	germanium 9	Ge
33	arsenic 7	As
34	selenium 8	Se
35	bromine 7	Br
36	krypton 7	Kr
37	rubidium 8	Rb
38	strontium 9	Sr
39	yttrium 7	Y
40	zirconium 9	Zr
41	niobium 7	Nb
42	molybdenum 10	Mo
43	technetium 10	Tc
44	ruthenium 9	Ru
45	rhodium 7	Rh
46	palladium 9	Pd
47	silver 6	Ag
48	cadmium 7	Cd
49	indium 6	In
50	tin 3	Sn
51	antimony 8	Sb
52	tellurium 9	Te
53	iodine 6	I
54	xenon 5	Xe
55	cesium 6	Cs
56	barium 6	Ba
57	lanthanum 9	La

Atomic Number	Element, Letter Count	Symbol
58	cerium 6	Ce
59	praseodymium 12	Pr
60	neodymium 9	Nd
61	promethium 10	Pm
62	samarium 8	Sm
63	europium 8	Eu
64	gadolinium 10	Gd
65	terbium 7	Tb
66	dysprosium 10	Dy
67	holmium 7	Ho
68	erbium 6	Er
69	thulium 7	Tm
70	ytterbium 9	Yb
71	lutetium 8	Lu
72	hafnium 7	Hf
73	tantalum 8	Ta
74	tungsten 8	W
75	rhenium 7	Re
76	osmium 6	Os
77	iridium 7	Ir
78	platinum 8	Pt
79	gold 4	Au
80	mercury 7	Hg
81	thallium 8	Tl
82	lead 4	Pb
83	bismuth 7	Bi
84	polonium 8	Po
85	astatine 8	At
86	radon 5	Rn
87	francium 8	Fr
88	radium 6	Ra
89	actinium 8	Ac
90	thorium 7	Th
91	protactinium 12	Pa
92	uranium 7	U
93	neptunium 9	Np
94	plutonium 9	Pu
95	americium 9	Am
96	curium 6	Cm
97	berkelium 9	Bk
98	californium 11	Cf
99	einsteinium 11	Es
100	fermium 7	Fm
101	mendelevium 11	Md
102	nobelium 8	No
103	lawrencium 10	Lr
104	rutherfordium 13	Rf
105	hahnium 7	Ha

Chemical Elements by Letter Count

3. tin 4. gold, iron, lead, neon, zinc 5. argon, boron, radon, xenon 6. barium, carbon, cerium, cesium, cobalt, copper, curium, erbium, helium, indium, iodine, nickel, osmium, oxygen, radium, silver, sodium, sulfur 7. arsenic, bismuth, bromine, cadmium, calcium, fermium, gallium, hafnium, hahnium, holmium, iridium, krypton, lithium, mercury, niobium, rhenium, rhodium, silicon, terbium, thorium, thulium, uranium, yttrium 8. actinium, aluminum, antimony, astatine, chlorine, chromium, europium, fluorine, francium, hydrogen, lutetium, nitrogen, nobelium, platinum, polonium, rubidium, samarium, scandium, selenium, tantalum, thallium, titanium, tungsten, vanadium 9. americium, berkelium, beryllium, germanium, lanthanum, magnesium, manganese, neodymium, neptunium, palladium, plutonium, potassium, ruthenium, strontium, tellurium, ytterbium, zirconium 10. dysprosium, gadolinium, lawrencium, molybdenum, phosphorus, promethium, technetium 11. californium, einsteinium, mendelevium 12. praseodymium, protactinium 13. rutherfordium

CHIEF JUSTICES OF THE U.S. SUPREME COURT IN CHRONOLOGICAL ORDER

Name, Letter Count	Term	Name, Letter Count	Term
Jay, John 3	1789-95	White, Edward 5	1910-21
Rutledge, John 8	1795	Taft, William 4	1921-30
Ellsworth, Oliver 9	1796-1800	Hughes, Charles 6	1930-41
Marshall, John 8	1801-35	Stone, Harlan 5	1941-46
Taney, Roger 5	1836-64	Vinson, Frederick 6	1946-53
Chase, Salmon 5	1864-73	Warren, Earl 6	1953-69
Waite, Morrison 5	1874-88	Burger, Warren 6	1969-86
Fuller, Melville 6	1888-1910	Rehnquist, William 9	1986-

Chief Justices by Letter Count

3. Jay 4. Taft 5. Chase, Stone, Taney, Waite, White 6. Burger, Fuller, Hughes, Vinson, Warren 8. Marshall, Rutledge 9. Ellsworth, Rehnquist

FAMOUS NAMES IN CROSSWORD PUZZLES

Listed alphabetically, with letter count and identification.

Aalto, Alvar 5 (Finnish architect)
Adams, John Quincy 5 (U.S. president)
Alcott, Louisa May 6 (U.S. writer)
Alexander, Grover Cleveland 9 (U.S. baseball player)
Amin, Idi 4 (Ugandan leader)
Angelico, Fra 8 (Italian painter)
Angelou, Maya 7 (U.S. poet)
Antony, Marc 6 (Roman general)
Arnaz, Desi 5 (U.S. actor & producer)
Astor, John Jacob 5 (U.S. fur trader & financier)
Attucks, Crispus 7 (American Revolution figure)
Auden, W(ystan) H(ugh) 5 (English poet)
Baer, Max 4 (U.S. boxer)
Barnes, Djuna 6 (novelist)
Beiderbecke, Bix 11(U.S. jazz musician)
Belloc, Hilaire 6 (English writer)
Ben-Gurion, David 9 (Israeli leader)
Benton, Thomas Hart 6 (U.S. painter)
Berg, Alban 4 (Austrian composer)
Bierce, Ambrose 6 (U.S. satirical writer)
Bombeck, Erma 7 (U.S. humorist)
Borges, Jorge Luis 6 (Argentine writer)
Borglum, Gutzon 7 (U. S. sculptor)
Bourke-White, Margaret 11(U.S. photographer)
Boutros-Ghali, Boutros 12 (Egyptian diplomat)
Bragg, Braxton 5 (U.S. Confederate general)
Brecht, Bertolt 6 (German dramatist)
Bryan, William Jennings 5 (U.S. politician)
Bryant, William Cullen 6 (U.S. writer)
Burne-Jones, Edward 10 (English painter)
Burroughs, Edgar Rice 9 (U.S. writer)
Cabell, James Branch 6 (U.S. novelist)
Cannon, Dyan 6 (U.S. actress)
Capote, Truman 6 (U.S. writer)
Carey, Mariah 5 (U.S. popular singer)
Caruso, Enrico 6 (Italian operatic singer)
Carver, George Washington 6 (U.S. inventor)
Casals, Pablo 6 (Spanish cellist)
Castro, Fidel 6 (Cuban leader)
Chanel, Coco 6 (French fashion designer)
Chaplin, Oona 7 (daughter of Charlie Chaplin)
Charles, Ezzard 7 (U.S. boxer)
Clemens, Samuel Langhorne 7 (U.S. writer)
Coca, Imogene 4 (U.S. comedienne)
Cooper, James Fenimore 6 (U.S. writer)
Copland, Aaron 7 (U.S. composer)
Crane, Hart 5 (U.S. poet)
Cronyn, Hume 6 (actor)
Cummings, E(dward) E(stlin) 8 (U.S. poet)

Cunningham, Merce 10 (U.S. choreographer)
Dahl, Arlene 4 (U.S. actress)
Dali, Salvador 4 (Spanish artist)
Dare, Virginia 4 (first English person born in America)
Davis, Jefferson 5 (U.S. Confederate leader)
Davis, Miles 5 (U.S. jazz musician)
de la Renta, Oscar 9 (fashion designer)
Derek, Bo 5 (U.S. actress)
Dinesen, Isak 7 (Danish writer)
Dior, Christian 4 (French fashion designer)
Doyle, Arthur Conan 5 (English writer)
Du Bois, W(illiam) E(dward) B(urghardt) 6 (U.S. writer & civil rights leader)
Dulles, John Foster 6 (U.S. diplomat)
Dunbar, Paul Laurence 6 (U.S. poet)
Duns Scotus, John 10 (Scottish theologian)
Eban, Abba 4 (Israeli leader)
Edison, Thomas Alva 6 (U.S. inventor)
Fawkes, Guy 6 (English conspirator)
Ferrari, Enzo 7 (Italian car designer & manufacturer)
Gandhi, Indira 6 (Indian leader)
Gandhi, Rajiv 6 (Indian leader)
Gardner, Erle Stanley 7 (U.S. writer)
Gerry, Elbridge 5 (U.S. jurist)
Gilman, Charlotte Perkins 6 (U.S. writer)
Hammer, Armand 6 (U.S. businessman)
Havel, Vaclav 5 (Czech writer & politician)
Helmsley, Leona 8 (U.S. businesswoman)
Hendrix, Jimi 7 (U.S. musician)
Henie, Sonja 5 (skater)
Hilton, Conrad 6 (U.S. businessman)
Holmes, Oliver Wendell 6 (U.S. jurist)
Howells, William Dean 7 (U.S. writer)
Hubbard, L. Ron 7 (U.S. writer)
Huie, William Bradford 4 (U.S. writer)
Kemal Atatürk 5 (Turkish leader)
Kent, Rockwell 4 (U.S. artist)
Keynes, John Maynard 6 (English economist)
Khrushchev, Nikita 10 (Soviet leader)
Kierkegaard, Søren 11 (Danish philosopher)
Lajoie, Nap(oleon) 6 (U.S. baseball player)
Lévi-Strauss, Claude 11 (French anthropologist)
Lewis, C(live) S(taples) 5 (English writer)
Lewis, Meade Lux 5 (U.S. jazz musician)
Lewis, Meriwether 5 (U.S. explorer)
Limbaugh, Rush 8 (U.S. radio/TV personality)
Lincoln, Elmo 7 (actor)
Mather, Cotton 6 (American clergyman & writer)

Mather, Increase 6 (American clergyman & writer)
Maupassant, Guy de 10 (French writer)
Meir, Golda 4 (Israeli leader)
Midler, Bette 6 (U.S. singer & actress)
Mies van der Rohe, Ludwig 14 (U.S. architect)
Miró, Joan 4 (Spanish artist)
Monk, Thelonious 4 (U.S. jazz musician)
Morton, Jelly Roll 6 (U.S. jazz musician)
Murphy, Audie 6 (U.S. war hero & actor)
Nasby, Petroleum V. 5 (U.S. humorist)
Negri, Pola 5 (actress)
Nin, Anaïs 3 (diarist)
O'Connor, Sandra Day 7 (U.S. jurist)
O'Neal, Shaquille 5 (U.S. basketball player)
Oates, Joyce Carol 5 (U.S. writer)
Odets, Clifford 5 (U.S. dramatist)
Olds, Ransom 4 (U.S. inventor)
Omar Khayyam 11(Persian poet)
Oswald, Lee Harvey 6 (U.S. assassin)
Ozawa, Seiji 5 (conductor)
Parrish, Maxfield 7 (U.S. artist)
Parsons, Talcott 7 (U.S. sociologist)
Pascal, Blaise 6 (French philosopher)
Peacock, Thomas Love 7 (English writer)
Pei, I. M. 3 (U.S. architect)
Piaf, Edith 4 (French singer)
Picasso, Pablo 7 (Spanish artist)
Pike, Zebulon 4 (U.S. explorer)
Plath, Sylvia 5 (U.S. poet)
Poe, Edgar Allan 3 (U.S. writer)
Pollock, Jackson 7 (U.S. artist)
Pol Pot 6 (Cambodian leader)
Pound, Ezra 5 (U.S. poet & critic)
Powell, Adam Clayton 6 (U.S. politician)
Powys, John Cowper 5 (English writer)
Presley, Elvis Aron 7 (U.S. singer & actor)
Rand, Ayn 4 (U.S. writer)
Rembrandt van Rijn 16 (Dutch artist)

Ride, Sally 4 (U.S. astronaut)
Roberts, Oral 7 (U.S. evangelist)
Rockne, Knute 6 (U.S. football coach)
Rose, Axl 4 (U.S. singer)
Rushdie, Salman 7 (writer)
Saarinen, Eero 8 (Finnish architect)
Sackville-West, Vita 13 (English writer)
Sartre, Jean-Paul 6 (French writer & philosopher)
Savalas, Telly 7 (U.S. actor)
Shelley, Percy Bysshe 7 (English poet)
Sherman, William Tecumseh 7 (U.S. Union general)
Sommer, Elke 6 (actress)
Sousa, John Philip 5 (U.S. composer)
Speaker, Tris 7 (U.S. baseball player)
Spenser, Edmund 7 (English poet)
Stanton, Elizabeth Cady 7 (U.S. reformer)
Stevenson, Robert Louis 9 (Scottish writer)
Stowe, Harriet Beecher 5 (U.S. writer)
Strachey, Lytton 8 (English writer)
Stravinsky, Igor 10 (Russian composer)
Synge, John Millington 5 (Irish dramatist)
Tharp, Twyla 5 (U.S. choreographer)
Toklas, Alice B. 6 (U.S. writer)
Torme, Mel 5 (U.S. singer)
Vaughan Williams, Ralph 15 (English composer)
Washington, Booker T. 10 (U.S. educator & reformer)
Washington, Denzel 10 (U.S. actor)
Weaver, Sigourney 6 (U.S. actress)
Webber, Andrew Lloyd 6 (English composer)
Williams, William Carlos 8 (U.S. poet)
Winfrey, Oprah 7 (U.S. TV personality)
Wodehouse, P(elham) G(renville) 9 (English writer)
Wright, Frank Lloyd 6 (U.S. architect)
Yeats, William Butler 5 (Irish writer)

NATIONS OF THE WORLD

Listed alphabetically by nation, with letter counts.

Nation	Capital	Currency
Afghanistan 11	Kabul 5	afghani 7
Albania 7	Tirana 6	lek 3
Algeria 7	Algiers 7	dinar 5
Andorra 7	Andorra la Vella 14	franc 5, peseta 6
Angola 6	Luanda 6	kwanza 6
Antigua and Barbuda 17	St. John's 7	dollar 6
Argentina 9	Buenos Aires 11	peso 4
Armenia 7	Yerevan 7	dram 4
Australia 9	Canberra 8	dollar 6
Austria 7	Vienna 6	schilling 9
Azerbaijan 10	Baku 4	manat 5
Bahamas 7	Nassau 6	dollar 6
Bahrain 7	Manama 6	dinar 5
Bangladesh 10	Dhaka 5 (Dacca)	taka 4
Barbados 8	Bridgetown 10	dollar 6
Belarus 7	Minsk 5	ruble 5
Belgium 7	Brussels 8	franc 5
Belize 6	Belmopan 8	dollar 6
Benin 5	Porto Novo 9	franc 5
Bhutan 6	Thimphu 7	ngultrum 8
Bolivia 7	La Paz 5, Sucre 5	boliviano 9
Bosnia and Herzegovina 20 (Hercegovina)	Sarajevo 8	dinar 5
Botswana 8	Gaborone 8	pula 4
Brazil 6	Brasília 8	real 4
Brunei 6	Bandar Seri Begawan 17	dollar 6
Bulgaria 8	Sofia 5	lev 3
Burkina Faso 11	Ouagadougou 11	franc 5
Burundi 7	Bujumbura 9	franc 5
Cambodia 8	Phnom Penh 9	riel 4
Cameroon 8	Yaoundé 7	franc 5
Canada 6	Ottawa 6	dollar 6
Cape Verde 9	Praia 5	escudo 6
Central African Republic 22	Bangui 6	franc 5
Chad 4	N'Djamena 8	franc 5
Chile 5	Santiago 8	peso 4
China 5	Beijing 7 (Peking, Peiping)	yuan 4
Colombia 8	Bogotá 6	peso 4
Comoros 7	Moroni 6	franc 5
Congo 5	Brazzaville 11	franc 5
Costa Rica 9	San José 7	colón 5
Croatia 7	Zagreb 6	kuna 4
Cuba 4	Havana 6	peso 4
Cyprus 6	Nicosia 7	pound 5
Czech Republic 13	Prague 6	koruna 6
Denmark 7	Copenhagen 10	krone 5
Djibouti 8	Djibouti 8	franc 5
Dominica 8	Roseau 6	dollar 6
Dominican Republic 17	Santo Domingo 12	peso 4
Ecuador 7	Quito 5	sucre 5
Egypt 5	Cairo 5	pound 5
El Salvador 10	San Salvador 11	colón 5
Equatorial Guinea 16	Malabo 6	franc 5
Eritrea 7	Asmara 6	birr 4
Estonia 7	Tallinn 7	kroon 5
Ethiopia 8	Addis Ababa 10	birr 4
Fiji 4	Suva 4	dollar 6

Nation	Capital	Currency
Finland 7	Helsinki 8	markka 6
France 6	Paris 5	franc 5
Gabon 5	Libreville 10	franc 5
Gambia 6	Banjul 6	dalasi 6
Georgia 7	Tbilisi 7	lari 4
Germany 7	Berlin 6	deutsche mark 12
Ghana 5	Accra 5	cedi 4
Greece 6	Athens 6	drachma 7
Grenada 7	St. George's 9	dollar 6
Guatemala 9	Guatemala City 13	quetzal 7
Guinea 6	Conakry 7	franc 5
Guinea-Bissau 12	Bissau 6	peso 4
Guyana 6	Georgetown 10	dollar 6
Haiti 5	Port-au-Prince 12	gourde 6
Honduras 8	Tegucigalpa 11	lempira 7
Hungary 7	Budapest 8	forint 6
Iceland 7	Reykjavik 9	króna 5
India 5	New Delhi 8	rupee 5
Indonesia 9	Jakarta 7	rupiah 6
Iran 4	Tehran 6 (Teheran)	rial 4
Iraq 4	Baghdad 7 (Bagdad)	dinar 5
Ireland 7	Dublin 6	pound 5 (punt)
Israel 6	Jerusalem 9	shekel 6
Italy 5	Rome 4	lira 4
Ivory Coast 10	Yamoussoukro 12	franc 5
Jamaica 7	Kingston 8	dollar 6
Japan 5	Tokyo 5	yen 3
Jordan 6	Amman 5	dinar 5
Kazakhstan 10	Alma-Ata 7 (Almaty)	tenge 5
Kenya 5	Nairobi 7	shilling 8
Kiribati 8	Tarawa 6	dollar 6
Korea, North 10	Pyongyang 9	won 3
Korea, South 10	Seoul 5	won 3
Kuwait 6	Kuwait 6 (Kuwait City)	dinar 5
Kyrgyzstan 10 (Kirghizstan)	Bishkek 7	som 3
Laos 4	Vientiane 9	kip 3
Latvia 6	Riga 4	lats 4
Lebanon 7	Beirut 6	pound 5
Lesotho 7	Maseru 6	loti 4
Liberia 7	Monrovia 8	dollar 6
Libya 5	Tripoli 7	dinar 5
Liechtenstein 13	Vaduz 5	franc 5
Lithuania 9	Vilnius 7	litas 5
Luxembourg 10	Luxembourg 10	franc 5
Macedonia 9	Skopje 6	denar 5
Madagascar 10	Antananarivo 12	franc 5
Malawi 6	Lilongwe 8	kwacha 6
Malaysia 8	Kuala Lumpur 11	ringgit 7
Maldives 8	Malé 4	rufiyaa 7
Mali 4	Bamako 6	franc 5
Malta 5	Valletta 8	lira 4
Marshall Islands 15	Dalap-Uliga-Darrit 16	dollar 6
Mauritania 10	Nouakchott 10	ouguiya 7
Mauritius 9	Port Louis 9	rupee 5
Mexico 6	Mexico City 10	peso 4
Micronesia 10	Palikir 7	dollar 6
Moldova 7	Kishinev 8	leu 3
Monaco 6	Monaco 6	franc 5
Mongolia 8	Ulan Bator 9	tugrik 6

Nation	Capital	Currency
Morocco 7	Rabat 5	dirham 6
Mozambique 10	Maputo 6	metical 7
Myanmar 7	Yangon 6 (Rangoon)	kyat 4
Namibia 7	Windhoek 8	dollar 6
Nauru 5	—	dollar 6
Nepal 5	Katmandu 8 (Kathmandu)	rupee 5
Netherlands 11	Amsterdam 9	guilder 7
New Zealand 10	Wellington 10	dollar 6
Nicaragua 9	Managua 7	córdoba 7
Niger 5	Niamey 6	franc 5
Nigeria 7	Abuja 5	naira 5
Norway 6	Oslo 4	krone 5
Oman 4	Muscat 6	rial 4
Pakistan 8	Islamabad 9	rupee 5
Palau 5	Koror 5	dollar 6
Panama 6	Panama City 10	balboa 6
Papua New Guinea 14	Port Moresby 11	kina 4
Paraguay 8	Asunción 8	guaraní 7
Peru 4	Lima 4	sol 3
Philippines 11	Manila 6	peso 4
Poland 6	Warsaw 6	zloty 5
Portugal 8	Lisbon 6	escudo 6
Qatar 5	Doha 4	riyal 5
Romania 7	Bucharest 9	leu 3
Russia 6	Moscow 6	ruble 5
Rwanda 6	Kigali 6	franc 5
San Marino 9	San Marino 9	lira 4
São Tomé and Príncipe 18	São Tomé 7	dobra 5
Saudi Arabia 11	Riyadh 6	riyal 5
Senegal 7	Dakar 5	franc 5
Seychelles 10	Victoria 8	rupee 5
Sierra Leone 11	Freetown 8	leone 5
Singapore 9	Singapore 9	dollar 6
Slovakia 8·	Bratislava 10	koruna 6
Slovenia 8	Ljubljana 9	tolar 5
Solomon Islands 14	Honiara 7	dollar 6
Somalia 7	Mogadishu 9	shilling 8
South Africa 11	Pretoria (administrative) 8	rand 4
Spain 5	Madrid 6	peseta 6
Sri Lanka 8	Colombo 7	rupee 5
St. Kitts and Nevis 15	Basseterre 10	dollar 6
St. Lucia 7	Castries 8	dollar 6
St. Vincent and the Grenadines 25	Kingstown 9	dollar 6
Sudan 5	Khartoum 8	pound 5
Suriname 8	Paramaribo 10	guilder 7
Swaziland 9	Mbabane 7	lilangeni 9
Sweden 6	Stockholm 9	krona 5
Switzerland 11	Bern 4	franc 5
Syria 5	Damascus 8	pound 5
Taiwan 6	Taipei 6	dollar 6
Tajikistan 10 (Tadzhikistan)	Dushanbe 8	ruble 5
Tanzania 8	Dodoma 6	shilling 8
Thailand 8	Bangkok 7	baht 4
Togo 4	Lomé 4	franc 5
Tonga 5	Nukualofa 9	pa'anga 6
Trinidad and Tobago 17	Port-of-Spain 11	dollar 6
Tunisia 7	Tunis 5	dinar 5
Turkey 6	Ankara 6	lira 4
Turkmenistan 12	Ashkhabad 9	manat 5

Nation	Capital	Currency
Tuvalu 6	Fongafale 9	dollar 6
Uganda 6	Kampala 7	shilling 8
Ukraine 7	Kiev 4	hryvnia 7
United Arab Emirates 18	Abu Dhabi 8	dirham 6
United Kingdom 13	London 6	pound 5
United States 12	Washington (DC) 10	dollar 6
Uruguay 7	Montevideo 10	peso 4
Uzbekistan 10	Tashkent 8	som 3
Vanuatu 7	Vila 4	vatu 4
Vatican City 11	—	lira 4
Venezuela 9	Caracas 7	bolívar 7
Vietnam 7	Hanoi 5	dong 4
Western Samoa 12	Apia 4	tala 4
Yemen 5	Sana 4 (Sanaa)	rial 4
Yugoslavia 10	Belgrade 8	dinar 5
Zaire 5	Kinshasa 8	zaire 5
Zambia 6	Lusaka 6	kwacha 6
Zimbabwe 8	Harare 6	dollar 6

SELECTED NOBEL PRIZE WINNERS
Listed alphabetically with letter count, prize category, and year.

Addams, Jane 6 (Peace) 1931
Agnon, Samuel 5 (Literature) 1966
Aleixandre, Vicente 10 (Literature) 1977
Alfven, Hannes 6 (Physics) 1970
Alvarez, Luis 7 (Physics) 1968
Andric, Ivo 6 (Literature) 1961
Angell, Sir Norman 6 (Peace) 1933
Appleton, Sir Edward 8 (Physics) 1947
Arafat, Yasir 6 (Peace) 1994
Arias Sánchez, Oscar 12 (Peace) 1987
Arrhenius, Svante 9 (Chemistry) 1903
Asturias, Miguel 8 (Literature) 1967
Aung San Suu Kyi 13 (Peace) 1991
Banting, Sir Frederick 7 (Physiology or
    Medicine) 1923
Bardeen, John 7 (Physics) 1956
Becker, Gary 6 (Economics) 1992
Beckett, Samuel 7 (Literature) 1969
Becquerel, Antoine Henri 9 (Physics) 1903
Begin, Menachem 5 (Peace) 1978
Bellow, Saul 6 (Literature) 1976
Benavente, Jacinto 9 (Literature) 1922
Bergson, Henri 7 (Literature) 1927
Bethe, Hans 5 (Physics) 1967
Bjornson, Bjornsterne 8 (Literature) 1903
Bloch, Felix 5 (Physics) 1952
Bohr, Niels 4 (Physics) 1922
Böll, Heinrich 4 (Literature) 1972
Borlaug, Norman 7 (Peace) 1970
Born, Max 4 (Physics) 1954
Brandt, Willy 6 (Peace) 1971
Brattain, Walter 8 (Physics) 1956
Braun, Karl (Carl) 5 (Physics) 1909
Briand, Aristide 6 (Peace) 1926
Brodsky, Joseph 7 (Literature) 1987
Buchanan, James 8 (Economics) 1986
Buchner, Eduard 7 (Chemistry) 1907
Buck, Pearl 4 (Literature) 1938
Bunche, Ralph 6 (Peace) 1950
Bunin, Ivan 5 (Literature) 1933
Butenandt, Adolf 9 (Chemistry) 1939
Butler, Nicholas Murray 6 (Peace) 1931
Camus, Albert 5 (Literature) 1957
Canetti, Elias 7 (Literature) 1981
Carducci, Giosue 8 (Literature) 1906
Carrel, Alexis 6 (Physiology or Medicine)
    1912
Cassin, René 6 (Peace) 1968
Cela, Camilo José 4 (Literature) 1989
Chadwick, Sir James 8 (Physics) 1935
Chain, Ernst 5 (Physiology or Medicine)
    1945
Chamberlain, Sir J. Austen 11 (Peace)
    1925
Chandrasekhar, Subrahmanyan 13
    (Physics) 1983
Cherenkov, Pavel 9 (Physics) 1958
Churchill, Sir Winston 9 (Literature) 1953

Compton, Arthur 7 (Physics) 1927
Corrigan, Mairead 8 (Peace) 1976
Crick, Francis 5 (Physiology or Medicine)
    1962
Cronin, James 6 (Physics) 1980
Curie, Marie 5 (Chemistry) 1911
Curie, Marie 5 (Physics) 1903
Curie, Pierre 5 (Physics) 1903
Dalai Lama 9 (Peace) 1989
Dawes, Charles 5 (Peace) 1925
de Broglie, Prince Louis-Victor 9 (Physics)
    1929
de Klerk, F.W. 7 (Peace) 1993
Delbrück, Max 8 (Physiology or Medicine)
    1969
Deledda, Grazia 7 (Literature) 1926
Dirac, Paul 5 (Physics) 1933
Eccles, Sir John 6 (Physiology or
    Medicine) 1963
Echegaray, Jose 9 (Literature) 1904
Ehrlich, Paul 7 (Physiology or Medicine)
    1908
Einstein, Albert 8 (Physics) 1921
Eliot, T.S. 5 (Literature) 1948
Elytis, Odysseus 6 (Literature) 1979
Enders, John 6 (Physiology or Medicine)
    1954
Erlanger, Joseph 8 (Physiology or
    Medicine) 1944
Esquivel, Adolfo Pérez 8 (Peace) 1980
Eucken, Rudolf 6 (Literature) 1908
Faulkner, William 8 (Literature) 1949
Fermi, Enrico 5 (Physics) 1938
Feynman, Richard 7 (Physics) 1965
Fischer, Emil 7 (Chemistry) 1902
Fischer, Ernst 7 (Chemistry) 1973
Fleming, Sir Alexander 7 (Physiology or
    Medicine) 1945
Florey, Sir Howard 6 (Physiology or
    Medicine) 1945
France, Anatole 6 (Literature) 1921
Franck, James 6 (Physics) 1925
Friedman, Milton 8 (Economics) 1976
Galsworthy, John 10 (Literature) 1932
García Márquez, Gabriel 13 (Literature)
    1982
Gell-Mann, Murray 8 (Physics) 1969
Gide, André 4 (Literature) 1947
Gjellerup, Karl 9 (Literature) 1917
Glashow, Sheldon 7 (Physics) 1979
Golding, William 7 (Literature) 1983
Golgi, Camillo 5 (Physiology or Medicine)
    1906
Gorbachev, Mikhail 9 (Peace) 1990
Gordimer, Nadine 8 (Literature) 1991
Grignard, Victor 8 (Chemistry) 1912
Haber, Fritz 5 (Chemistry) 1918
Hahn, Otto 4 (Chemistry) 1944

Hammarskjöld, Dag 12 (Peace) 1961
Hamsun, Knut 6 (Literature) 1920
Hauptmann, Gerhart 9 (Literature) 1912
Heaney, Seamus 6 (Literature) 1995
Heisenberg, Werner 10 (Physics) 1932
Hemingway, Ernest 9 (Literature) 1954
Hertz, Gustav 5 (Physics) 1925
Hesse, Hermann 5 (Literature) 1946
Heyse, Paul 5 (Literature) 1910
Hull, Cordell 4 (Peace) 1945
Jensen, Johannes 6 (Literature) 1944
Jiménez, Juan 7 (Literature) 1956
Johnson, Eyvind 7 (Literature) 1974
Joliot-Curie, Frederic 11 (Chemistry) 1935
Joliot-Curie, Irene 11 (Chemistry) 1935
Josephson, Brian 9 (Physics) 1973
Kapitsa, Pyotr 7 (Physics) 1978
Karlfeldt, Erik 9 (Literature) 1931
Kawabata, Yasunari 8 (Literature) 1968
Kellogg, Frank 7 (Peace) 1929
King, Martin Luther, Jr. 4 (Peace) 1964
Kipling, Rudyard 7 (Literature) 1907
Kissinger, Henry 9 (Peace) 1973
Koch, Robert 4 (Physiology or Medicine)
    1905
Krebs, Sir Hans 5 (Physiology or
    Medicine) 1953
Lagerkvist, Pär 10 (Literature) 1951
Lagerlöf, Selma 8 (Literature) 1909
Landsteiner, Karl 11 (Physiology or
    Medicine) 1930
Lawrence, Ernest 8 (Physics) 1939
Laxness, Halldor 7 (Literature) 1955
Le Duc Tho 8 (Peace) 1973
Leontief, Wassily 8 (Economics) 1973
Lewis, Sinclair 5 (Literature) 1930
Lorentz, Hendrik 7 (Physics) 1902
Lorenz, Konrad 6 (Physiology or Medicine)
    1973
Luthuli, Albert 7 (Peace) 1960
MacBride, Sean 8 (Peace) 1974
Maeterlinck, Maurice 11 (Literature) 1911
Mahfouz, Naguib 7 (Literature) 1988
Mandela, Nelson 7 (Peace) 1993
Mann, Thomas 4 (Literature) 1929
Marconi, Guglielmo 7 (Physics) 1909
Marshall, George 8 (Peace) 1953
Martin du Gard, Roger 12 (Literature) 1937
Martinson, Harry 9 (Literature) 1974
Mauriac, François 7 (Literature) 1952
McClintock, Barbara 10 (Physiology or
    Medicine) 1983
McMillan, Edwin 8 (Chemistry) 1951
Medawar, Peter 7 (Physiology or
    Medicine) 1960
Menchú, Rigoberta 6 (Peace) 1992
Michelson, Albert 9 (Physics) 1907
Millikan, Robert 8 (Physics) 1923
Milosz, Czeslaw 6 (Literature) 1980
Mistral, Frederic 7 (Literature) 1904

Mistral, Gabriela 7 (Literature) 1945
Mommsen, Theodor 7 (Literature) 1902
Monod, Jacques 5 (Physiology or
    Medicine) 1965
Montale, Eugenio 7 (Literature) 1975
Morrison, Toni 8 (Literature) 1993
Mössbauer, Rudolf 9 (Physics) 1961
Mother Teresa 12 (Peace) 1979
Myrdal, Alva 6 (Peace) 1982
Myrdal, Gunnar 6 (Economics) 1974
Nansen, Fridtjof 6 (Peace) 1922
Neruda, Pablo 6 (Literature) 1971
Noel-Baker, Philip 9 (Peace) 1959
O'Neill, Eugene 6 (Literature) 1936
Oe, Kenzaburo 2 (Literature) 1994
Ostwald, Wilhelm 7 (Chemistry) 1909
Pasternak, Boris 9 (Literature) 1958
Pauli, Wolfgang 5 (Physics) 1945
Pauling, Linus 7 (Chemistry) 1954
Pauling, Linus 7 (Peace) 1962
Pavlov, Ivan 6 (Physiology or Medicine)
    1904
Paz, Octavio 3 (Literature) 1990
Pearson, Lester 7 (Peace) 1957
Penzias, Arno 7 (Physics) 1978
Peres, Shimon 5 (Peace) 1994
Perse, Saint-John 5 (Literature) 1960
Pirandello, Luigi 10 (Literature) 1934
Pire, Dominique Georges 4 (Peace) 1958
Planck, Max 6 (Physics) 1918
Pontoppidan, Henrik 11 (Literature) 1917
Prudhomme, René 9 (Literature) 1901
Quasimodo, Salvatore 9 (Literature) 1959
Rabi, Isidor 4 (Physics) 1944
Rabin, Yitzhak 5 (Peace) 1994
Ramsay, Sir William 6 (Chemistry) 1904
Reymont, Wladyslaw 7 (Literature) 1924
Robles, Alfonso Garcia 6 (Peace) 1982
Roentgen (Röntgen), Wilhelm 8 (Physics)
    1901
Rolland, Romain 7 (Literature) 1915
Roosevelt, Theodore 9 (Peace) 1906
Root, Elihu 4 (Peace) 1912
Ross, Sir Ronald 4 (Physiology or
    Medicine) 1902
Rotblat, Joseph 7 (Peace) 1995
Rubbia, Carlo 6 (Physics) 1984
Russell, Bertrand 7 (Literature) 1950
Rutherford, Ernest 10 (Chemistry) 1908
Sachs, Nelly 5 (Literature) 1966
Sadat, Anwar 5 (Peace) 1978
Sakharov, Andrei 8 (Peace) 1975
Salam, Abdus 5 (Physics) 1979
Samuelson, Paul 9 (Economics) 1970
Sanger, Frederick 6 (Chemistry) 1980
Sartre, Jean-Paul 6 (Literature) 1964
Sato, Eisaku 4 (Peace) 1974
Schrödinger, Erwin 11 (Physics) 1933
Schweitzer, Albert 10 (Peace) 1952
Seaborg, Glenn 7 (Chemistry) 1951

Seferis, George 7 (Literature) 1963
Seifert, Jaroslav 7 (Literature) 1984
Shaw, George Bernard 4 (Literature) 1925
Sherrington, Sir Charles 11 (Physiology or Medicine) 1932
Shockley, William 8 (Physics) 1956
Sholokhov, Mikhail 9 (Literature) 1965
Sienkiewicz, Henryk 11 (Literature) 1905
Sillanpää, Frans 9 (Literature) 1939
Simon, Claude 5 (Literature) 1985
Singer, Isaac Bashevis 6 (Literature) 1978
Söderblom, Nathan 9 (Peace) 1930
Solzhenitsyn, Aleksandr 12 (Literature) 1970
Soyinka, Wole 7 (Literature) 1986
Spitteler, Carl 9 (Literature) 1919
Steinbeck, John 9 (Literature) 1962
Stigler, George 7 (Economics) 1982
Stresemann, Gustav 10 (Peace) 1926
Tagore, Sir Rabindranath 6 (Literature) 1913
Thomson, Sir Joseph 7 (Physics) 1906
Tinbergen, Nikolaas 9 (Physiology or Medicine) 1973
Tobin, James 5 (Economics) 1981
Tutu, Bishop Desmond 4 (Peace) 1984

Undset, Sigrid 6 (Literature) 1928
van der Waals, Johannes 11 (Physics) 1910
von Behring, Emil 10 (Physiology or Medicine) 1901
von Frisch, Karl 9 (Physiology or Medicine) 1973
von Hayek, Friedrich 8 (Economics) 1974
von Heidenstam, Verner 13 (Literature) 1916
Waksman, Selman 7 (Physiology or Medicine) 1952
Walcott, Derek 7 (Literature) 1992
Walesa, Lech 6 (Peace) 1983
Watson, James 6 (Physiology or Medicine) 1962
Weinberg, Steven 8 (Physics) 1979
White, Patrick 5 (Literature) 1973
Wiesel, Elie 6 (Peace) 1986
Wilkins, Maurice 7 (Physiology or Medicine) 1962
Williams, Betty 8 (Peace) 1976
Wilson, Robert 6 (Physics) 1978
Wilson, Woodrow 6 (Peace) 1919
Yeats, William Butler 5 (Literature) 1923
Zeeman, Pieter 6 (Physics) 1902

PULITZER PRIZE WINNERS FOR FICTION

Listed alphabetically, with letter count, year, and title of work.

Agee, James 4 (1958) *A Death in the Family*

Barnes, Margaret 6 (1931) *Years of Grace*

Bellow, Saul 6 (1976) *Humboldt's Gift*

Bromfield, Louis 9 (1927) *Early Autumn*

Buck, Pearl 4 (1932) *The Good Earth*

Butler, Robert Olen 6 (1993) *A Good Scent from a Strange Mountain*

Cather, Willa 6 (1923) *One of Ours*

Cheever, John 7 (1979) *The Stories of John Cheever*

Cozzens, James 7 (1949) *Guard of Honor*

Davis, Harold 5 (1936) *Honey in the Horn*

Drury, Allen 5 (1960) *Advise and Consent*

Faulkner, William 8 (1955) *A Fable*

Faulkner, William 8 (1963) *The Reivers*

Ferber, Edna 6 (1925) *So Big*

Flavin, Martin 6 (1944) *Journey in the Dark*

Glasgow, Ellen 7 (1942) *In This Our Life*

Grau, Shirley Ann 4 (1965) *The Keepers of the House*

Guthrie, A.B., Jr. 7 (1950) *The Way West*

Hemingway, Ernest 9 (1953) *The Old Man and the Sea*

Hersey, John 6 (1945) *A Bell for Adano*

Hijuelos, Oscar 8 (1990) *The Mambo Kings Play Songs of Love*

Johnson, Josephine 7 (1935) *Now in November*

Kantor, MacKinlay 6 (1956) *Andersonville*

Kennedy, William 7 (1984) *Ironweed*

La Farge, Oliver 7 (1930) *Laughing Boy*

Lee, Harper 3 (1961) *To Kill a Mockingbird*

Lewis, Sinclair 5 (1926) *Arrowsmith*

Lurie, Alison 5 (1985) *Foreign Affairs*

Mailer, Norman 6 (1980) *The Executioner's Song*

Malamud, Bernard 7 (1967) *The Fixer*

Marquand, John 8 (1938) *The Late George Apley*

McMurtry, Larry 8 (1986) *Lonesome Dove*

McPherson, James Alan 9 (1978) *Elbow Room*

Michener, James 8 (1948) *Tales of the South Pacific*

Miller, Caroline 6 (1934) *Lamb in His Bosom*

Mitchell, Margaret 8 (1937) *Gone with the Wind*

Momaday, N. Scott 7 (1969) *House Made of Dawn*

Morrison, Toni 8 (1988) *Beloved*

O'Connor, Edwin 7 (1962) *The Edge of Sadness*

Peterkin, Julia 8 (1929) *Scarlet Sister Mary*

Poole, Ernest 5 (1918) *His Family*

Porter, Katherine Anne 6 (1966) *The Collected Stories of Katherine Anne Porter*

Proulx, E. Annie 6 (1994) *The Shipping News*

Rawlings, Marjorie Kinnan 8 (1939) *The Yearling*

Richter, Conrad 7 (1951) *The Town*

Shaara, Michael 6 (1975) *The Killer Angels*

Shields, Carol 7 (1995) *The Stone Diaries*

Sinclair, Upton 8 (1943) *Dragon's Teeth*

Smiley, Jane 6 (1992) *A Thousand Acres*

Stafford, Jean 7 (1970) *Collected Stories*

Stegner, Wallace 7 (1972) *Angle of Repose*

Steinbeck, John 9 (1940) *The Grapes of Wrath*

Stribling, T.S. 9 (1933) *The Store*

Styron, William 6 (1968) *The Confessions of Nat Turner*

Tarkington, Booth 10 (1919) *The Magnificent Ambersons*

Tarkington, Booth 10 (1922) *Alice Adams*

Taylor, Peter 6 (1987) *A Summons to Memphis*

Taylor, Robert 6 (1959) *The Travels of Jaimie McPheeters*

Toole, John Kennedy 5 (1981) *A Confederacy of Dunces*

Tyler, Anne 5 (1989) *Breathing Lessons*

Updike, John 6 (1982) *Rabbit is Rich*

Updike, John 6 (1991) *Rabbit at Rest*

Walker, Alice 6 (1983) *The Color Purple*

Warren, Robert Penn 6 (1947) *All the King's Men*

Welty, Eudora 5 (1973) *The Optimist's Daughter*

Wharton, Edith 7 (1921) *The Age of Innocence*

Wilder, Thornton 6 (1928) *The Bridge of San Luis Rey*

Wilson, Margaret 6 (1924) *The Able McLaughlins*

Wouk, Herman 4 (1952) *The Caine Mutiny*

SHAKESPEARE'S PLAYS AND CHARACTERS

Listed by play, with characters by letter count.

Comedies

All's Well That Ends Well . . . 8. Parolles (Paroles)

As You Like It . . . 5. Arden (forest), Celia 6. Jaques 7. Orlando 8. Rosalind 10. Touchstone (fool)

The Comedy of Errors . . . 7. Ephesus (setting)

Cymbeline . . . 6. Imogen 9. Cymbeline

Love's Labour's Lost . . . 7. Navarre (setting) 10. Holofernes

Measure for Measure . . . 6. Angelo, Vienna (setting) 7. Claudio 8. Isabella

The Merchant of Venice . . . 5. Tubal 6. Portia 7. Antonio (the merchant), Jessica, Shylock (villain)

The Merry Wives of Windsor . . . 6. Pistol 7. Quickly (Mistress), Windsor (setting) 8. Falstaff (Sir John)

A Midsummer Night's Dream . . . 4. Puck (Robin Goodfellow) 6. Athens (setting), Bottom (Nick), Helena, Hermia, Oberon (Fairy King) 7. Titania (Fairy Queen) 8. Lysander 9. Demetrius

Much Ado About Nothing . . . 7. Messina (setting) 8. Beatrice, Benedick

Pericles, Prince of Tyre

The Taming of the Shrew . . . 5. Padua (setting) 9. Katherina (Kate), Petruchio

The Tempest . . . 5. Ariel (fairy) 7. Caliban (ogre), Miranda 8. Prospero

Troilus and Cressida . . . 4. Troy (setting) 7. Troilus 8. Cressida, Pandarus

Twelfth Night . . . 5. Belch (Sir Toby), Feste (fool), Viola 6. Olivia, Orsino (duke) 7. Illyria (setting) 8. Malvolio 9. Aguecheek (Sir Andrew)

The Two Gentlemen of Verona . . . 5. Julia 7. Proteus 9. Valentine

The Two Noble Kinsmen

The Winter's Tale . . . 7. Leontes, Perdita 8. Hermione 9. Autolycus (thief)

Tragedies

Antony and Cleopatra . . . 6. Antony (Mark) 7. Octavia 8. Charmian, Octavius (Caesar) 9. Cleopatra, Enobarbus 10. Mark Antony

Coriolanus . . . 8. Volumnia 10. Coriolanus

Hamlet . . . 6. Hamlet (prince) 7. Denmark (setting), Horatio, Laertes, Ophelia 8. Claudius (uncle), Elsinore (castle), Gertrude (queen), Polonius 11. Rosencrantz 12. Guildenstern

Julius Caesar . . . 6. Antony (Mark), Brutus, Portia 7. Cassius 9. Calpurnia 10. Mark Antony 12. Julius Caesar

King Lear . . . 4. Lear 5. Edgar, Regan 6. Edmund 7. Goneril 8. Cordelia

Macbeth . . . 6. Banquo, Duncan (king) 7. Macbeth, Macduff 9. Inverness (castle) 11. Lady Macbeth

Othello . . . 4. Iago (villain) 6. Cassio, Cyprus (setting), Emilia, Venice (setting) 7. Othello (the Moor) 9. Desdemona

Romeo and Juliet . . . 5. Romeo 6. Juliet, Mantua (setting), Tybalt (Juliet's cousin), Verona (setting) 7. Capulet (Juliet's family) 8. Laurence (Friar), Mercutio, Montague (Romeo's family)

Timon of Athens

Titus Andronicus

Histories

Henry IV, Parts 1, 2 . . . 3. Hal (Prince) 6. Pistol 7. Hotspur, Quickly (Mistress) 8. Falstaff (Sir John)

Henry V

Henry VI, Parts 1, 2, 3

Henry VIII

King John

Richard II

Richard III

PRESIDENTS AND FIRST LADIES OF THE UNITED STATES

Listed chronologically by term, with letter count and first names of first ladies.

Name	Term	First Lady
Washington, George 10	1789-97	Martha
Adams, John 5	1797-1801	Abigail
Jefferson, Thomas 9	1801-09	Martha
Madison, James 7	1809-17	Dorothea (Dorothy, Dolley)
Monroe, James 6	1817-25	Elizabeth (Eliza)
Adams, John Quincy 5	1825-29	Louisa
Jackson, Andrew 7	1829-37	Rachel
Van Buren, Martin 8	1837-41	Hannah
Harrison, William Henry 8	1841	Anna
Tyler, John 5	1841-45	Letitia; Julia
Polk, James Knox 4	1845-49	Sarah
Taylor, Zachary 6	1849-50	Margaret
Fillmore, Millard 8	1850-53	Abigail
Pierce, Franklin 6	1853-57	Jane
Buchanan, James 8	1857-61	—
Lincoln, Abraham 7	1861-65	Mary Todd
Johnson, Andrew 7	1865-69	Eliza
Grant, Ulysses S. 5	1869-77	Julia
Hayes, Rutherford B. 5	1877-81	Lucy
Garfield, James A. 8	1881	Lucretia
Arthur, Chester A. 6	1881-85	Ellen
Cleveland, Grover 9	1885-89	Frances
Harrison, Benjamin 8	1889-93	Caroline
Cleveland, Grover 9	1893-97	Frances
McKinley, William 8	1897-1901	Ida
Roosevelt, Theodore (Teddy) 9	1901-09	Edith
Taft, William Howard 4	1909-13	Helen
Wilson, Woodrow 6	1913-21	Ellen; Edith
Harding, Warren G. 7	1921-23	Florence
Coolidge, Calvin 8	1923-29	Grace
Hoover, Herbert 6	1929-33	Lou
Roosevelt, Franklin Delano 9	1933-45	Anna Eleanor
Truman, Harry S 6	1945-53	Bess
Eisenhower, Dwight D. 10	1953-61	Mamie
Kennedy, John Fitzgerald 7	1961-63	Jacqueline
Johnson, Lyndon Baines 7	1963-69	Claudia (Lady Bird)
Nixon, Richard Milhous 5	1969-74	Thelma (Pat)
Ford, Gerald R. 4	1974-77	Elizabeth (Betty)
Carter, Jimmy (James Earl, Jr.) 6	1977-81	Rosalynn
Reagan, Ronald 6	1981-89	Anne (Nancy)
Bush, George 4	1989-93	Barbara
Clinton, Bill (William Jefferson) 7	1993-	Hillary Rodham

Presidents of the United States by Letter Count

4. Bush, Ford, Polk, Taft. 5. Adams (John and John Quincy), Grant, Hayes, Nixon, Tyler.
6. Arthur, Carter, Hoover, Monroe, Pierce, Reagan, Taylor, Truman, Wilson. 7. Clinton,
Harding, Jackson, Johnson (Andrew and Lyndon Baines), Kennedy, Lincoln, Madison. 8.
Buchanan, Coolidge, Fillmore, Garfield, Harrison (Benjamin and William Henry),
McKinley, Van Buren. 9. Cleveland, Jefferson, Roosevelt (Franklin Delano and Theodore)
10. Eisenhower, Washington

STATES OF THE UNITED STATES

Listed alphabetically, with number counts for states and capitals.

State	Capital
Alabama 7	Montgomery 10
Alaska 6	Juneau 6
Arizona 7	Phoenix 7
Arkansas 8	Little Rock 10
California 10	Sacramento 10
Colorado 8	Denver 6
Connecticut 11	Hartford 8
Delaware 8	Dover 5
Florida 7	Tallahassee 11
Georgia 7	Atlanta 7
Hawaii 6	Honolulu 8
Idaho 5	Boise 5
Illinois 8	Springfield 11
Indiana 7	Indianapolis 12
Iowa 4	Des Moines 9
Kansas 6	Topeka 6
Kentucky 8	Frankfort 9
Louisiana 9	Baton Rouge 10
Maine 5	Augusta 7
Maryland 8	Annapolis 9
Massachusetts 13	Boston 6
Michigan 8	Lansing 7
Minnesota 9	St. Paul 6
Mississippi 11	Jackson 7
Missouri 8	Jefferson City 13
Montana 7	Helena 6
Nebraska 8	Lincoln 7
Nevada 6	Carson City 10
New Hampshire 12	Concord 7
New Jersey 9	Trenton 7
New Mexico 9	Santa Fe 7
New York 7	Albany 6
North Carolina 13	Raleigh 7
North Dakota 11	Bismarck 8
Ohio 4	Columbus 8
Oklahoma 8	Oklahoma City 12
Oregon 6	Salem 5
Pennsylvania 12	Harrisburg 10
Rhode Island 11	Providence 10
South Carolina 13	Columbia 8
South Dakota 11	Pierre 6
Tennessee 9	Nashville 9
Texas 5	Austin 6
Utah 4	Salt Lake City 12
Vermont 7	Montpelier 10
Virginia 8	Richmond 8
Washington 10	Olympia 7
West Virginia 12	Charleston 10
Wisconsin 9	Madison 7
Wyoming 7	Cheyenne 8

NOTES

Fiddle maker — Amati